THE SPORT AMERICANA ®

PRICE GUIDE

NO. 10

By
DR. JAMES BECKETT

ISBN 0-937424-39-0

About the Author

Jim Beckett, the leading authority on sport card values in the United States, maintains a wide range of activities in the world of sports. He possesses one of the finest collections of sports cards and autographs in the world, has made numerous appearances on radio and television, and has been frequently cited in many national publications. He was awarded the first "Special Achievement Award" for Contributions to the Hobby by the National Sports Collectors Convention in 1980 and the "Jock-Jasperson Award" for Hobby Dedication in 1983.

Dr. Beckett is the author of *The Sport Americana Football, Hockey, Basketball and Boxing Price Guide*, *The Official Price Guide to Football Cards*, *The Sport Americana Baseball Card Price Guide*, *The Official Price Guide to Baseball Cards*, *The Sport Americana Price Guide to Baseball Collectibles*, *The Sport Americana Baseball Memorabilia and Autograph Price Guide*, and *The Sport Americana Alphabetical Baseball Card Checklist*. In addition, he is the founder, author, and editor of *Beckett Baseball Card Monthly*, a magazine dedicated to advancing the card collecting hobby.

Jim Beckett received his Ph.D. in Statistics from Southern Methodist University in 1975. He resides in Dallas with his wife Patti and their daughters, Christina, Rebecca, and Melissa, while actively pursuing his writing and consultancy careers.

Acknowledgments

This edition of the *Price Guide* contains new sets and, of course, completely revised prices on all the cards. A great deal of hard work went into this volume, and it could not have been done without a considerable amount of help from many people. Our thanks are extended to each and every one of you.

Those who have worked closely with us on this and many other books, have again proven themselves invaluable -- Frank and Vivian Barning (*Baseball Hobby News*), Sy Berger, Cartophilium (Andrew Pywowarczuk), Mike Cramer (Pacific Trading Cards), Bill and Diane Dodge, Richard Duglin, Gervise Ford, Larry and Jeff Fritsch, Mike and Howard Gordon, John Greenwald, Wayne Grove, Bill Haber, Bill Henderson, Danny Hitt, Allan Kaye (*Baseball Card News*), Lew Lipset, Norman Liss, Major League Marketing (Dan Shedrick, Tom Day, Jack Kling), David "Otis" Miller, Dick Millerd, Brian Morris, Ralph Nozaki, Jack Pollard, Gavin Riley, Alan Rosen (Mr. Mint), John Rumierz, San Diego Sport Collectibles (Bill Goepner and Nacho Arredondo), Mike Schechter, John Spalding, Frank Steele, Murvin Sterling, Lee Temanson, Ed Twombly (New England Bullpen), and Kit Young. Finally we owe a special acknowledgment to Dennis W. Eckes, "Mr. Sport Americana." The success of the *Beckett Price Guides* has always been the result of a team effort.

Special mention goes to four people this year. Two people stood out in terms of the quantity and quality of price input provided this year. Alan Rosen (aka Mr. Mint, The Million Dollar Dealer) spent many hours thoroughly marking up a current Beckett Monthly as well as last year's annual guide. His expertise on the older and more valuable material (based on his actual buy/sell transactions) was very helpful. He has a well-deserved reputation for selling quality cards at a premium price. His reported prices to me were certainly not out of line, although even more assuredly they were not below average. On the newer material Ed Twombly of the New England Bullpen sent about three pounds worth of quality input on cards selling from 1974 to the present. I was also appreciative of the fact that Ed recognizes and points out the potential for regional bias on his prices on certain players, especially Red Sox.

Two other long-time collectors also are recognized for repeated contributions to the hobby as well as to this Price Guide. They are well-known regionally (and nationally) for their outstanding efforts as show promoters in their areas. In fact just say their first name and many collectors will know who you're talking about. They were both very unselfishly helpful on the early editions of this Guide. Looking back after ten years I just wanted to thank them for their part in the growth of the hobby and of this Price Guide. They are both fine men and outstanding collectors. Gervise Ford and Gavin Riley, still two of the best. All four of the above have my thanks as well as a lifetime subscription to *Beckett Monthly*.

Special thanks are extended to the Donruss Company, the Fleer Corporation, Major League Marketing (Score and Sportflics), and the Topps Chewing Gum Company, who have consistently provided checklists and visual materials in order that the *Price Guide* could be complete.

Many other people have provided price input, illustrative material, checklist verifications, errata, and/or background information. We should like to individually thank Abco Card Galleries, Ab D Cards (Dale Wesolewski), Jerry Adamic, Ron Adelson, A.J.'s

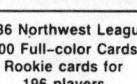
7

Sport Stop, Bob Alexander, Julie Alexander (California Card Co.), All Star Sports Collectibles, Dennis Anderson, Rick Apter, Mark Argo (Olde South Cards), Neil Armstrong (World Series Cards), B and C Collectable Cards, Derek Baker, Ball Four Cards, H.E. Barber, Ed Barry (Ed's Collectibles), Bob Bartosz, Baseball Card Shop, Bay State Cards (Lenny DeAngelico), Chris Benjamin, Carl Berg, Darrell Berger, Bernie's Bullpen, Beulah Sports, Levi Bleam, Bob Boffa, Brandon Bolest, Tim Bond (Tim's Cards & Comics), William W. Bossert, Richard Bourquin, Scott Bowers, Charles A. Brooks, Jeffrey Brown, Eric Burch, California Card Co., David Call (9th Inning Baseball Card Shop), Frank Caruso, Ira Cetron, Sandy Chan, Dwight Chapin, David Chiang, Ronald Chin, Chriss Christiansen, Dick Cianciotto, Candace Coalman, Gary L. Coburn, Barry Colla, Collection de Sport AZ, Ryan Collins, Comics Plus, Taylor Crane, James Critzer, John Curtis, Allen Custer, Dave Dame, Donna R. Davis, Richard Day, Jason DeBrower, James Dickson, Gregory S. Diehl, Ken Dinerman (California Cruizers), George Dolence, Richard Dolloff (Dolloff Coin Center), Phil Donaldson, John M. Dorsey, Kent Doss, George C. Dougherty, Ian Dubin, Richard Duglin (Baseball Cards-N-More), William Dunstone, David Ebner, Ed's Card Shop, Warren M. Eisenhardt, Bob Elliot, Doak Ewing, David and Mark Federman, David Festberg, David Footlick, Frank Fox (The Card Shop), Sharon Fraser, Steve Freeburne, Steve Freedman, Jeff Freyer, Keith Fruks, Dom Furfaro, Mike Gallela, Tony Galovich (American Card Exchange), Matt Gardner, Greg Gelet, Bob Gilbert (Brewer Sports Collectibles), Dick Goddard, Steve Gold (AU Sports), Greg Goldstein (Dragon's Den), Jeff Goldstein, Stephen Grauf, Grauer's Collectables, David Greenstein, Glen Gregson, Mike Gross, Kyle Guerry, Eric Guetschoff, Paul Hahn, Andy Hall, Charlie Hall, Hall's Nostalgia, Hershell Hanks, Lowell Harper, Duane Harris, Eric Hatch, Mark Hausner, Joel Hellman (JJ's Budget Baseball Cards), Chris Hendrickson, Joseph J. Hilton, Jimmy Hinnant, Bobby Holman, Home Plate, J.R. Sports Collectibles, David Jason, Douglas B. Jasset, Joe Jenchowski, John Moseley's Baseball Cards, Jack Johnstone, Barry Jones, Greg Jones, Stewart W. Jones, Jay Jordan, David Jurgensmeier, Jeff Kagawa, Richard Kaiman, Curtis Kaiser, Jay & Mary Kasper, Frank J. Katen, Allan Kaye, Doug Keating, Lloyd Kee, Rick Keplinger, Ken Klein, Richard Klein, David & Joe Kohler (Sportscards Plus), Ernie Kohlstruk, John Kolodziej Jr., Brian Kong, John Kubat, Thomas Kunnecke, John Kyranos, Forrest Langenfeld, Jason Lassic, Dan Lavin, Charles A. Layne, Robert Lee, Morley Leeking, Irv Lerner, David Lizotte, Paul Loach (Card & Coin Outlet), Christy Locke, Chris Lockwood, Mike London, Allie Long, Chad Long, David Lowe, Jim Macie, Mike L. Madison, Rich Maier, Alex Maki, David Manley, Paul Marchant, Jason Marion, Dr. William McAvoy, Michael McDonald (The Sports Page), Jeremy McNett, Mendal Mearkle (Chariots, Inc.), Ken Melanson, Kelly Melone, Wayne Menicucci, Blake Meyer (Lone Star Sportscards), Joe Michalowicz, Mid-Atlantic Coin Exchange, David "Otis" Miller, George J. Miller, Wayne Miller, Tom Mills, Matthew Morgan, Terry Murphy, Mark Natale, Bradley Nathan, Edward Nazzaro (The Collector), Tony Niemann (A.D.C. Sports), The Nickell's, Mike Nolde, Mike O'Brien, John Ofenloch, Keith Olbermann, Charlie Oinstein, Oldies and Goodies, Larry C. O'Malley, Ron Oser, Michael Palazzo, Bruce Parker (All-American Cards & Comics), Clay Pasternack, Bill Pekarik (Pastime Hobbies), Lucy Pelletier, Michael Perrotta, Gerald Perry, Tom Pfirrmann, Jeffrey L. Phillips, Pie-Eyes, Bob Poet, Paul Pollard, Michael L. Poynter, R & W Cards, Rick Rapa and Barry Sanders (Atlanta Sports Cards), Rick Rateike (Extra Innings, Inc.), Geoffrey Reed, Gordon Reid, Tom Reid, Troy Riggenbach, Dave Ring, Jeff Rockholt, Chris Rogers, Clifton Rouse, Henry M. Rutland, Terry Sack, Joe Sak, Jennifer Salems, Tim

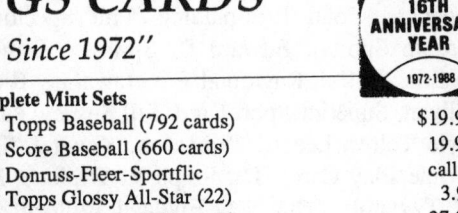

Santor (Cards & Cards), Gary Sawatzki, Robert Scagnelli, Shawn Schuetz, Jim Schuster, Brad Shaw, Gerry Shebib, Chris & Kelly Shore, David Signori, Steve Sincavage, Barry Sloate, Vince Small, Robert Smathers, Bennie K. Smith, Steven E. Smith, Matt Solomon, Walt Spader Jr., John E. Spalding, Phil Spector (Scoreboard, Inc.), Joe Spiegel (Championship Sports), Edward D. Springer, Don Steinbach, Murvin Sterling, Rick Stineman, Erik Stoffel, Raymond E. Strawn Jr., Richard E. Strobino, Richard Stroud, Barrie Sullivan, Superior Sport Card, Bill Susoev, Paul G. Sylvestro, Darius Tandon, Ian Taylor, Lyle Telfer, Lee E. Temanson, Kevin J. Terplak, Mike Tessman, Charles L. Thorpe, Triple Play Cards, Dr. Ralph R. Triplette, Robert Tse, Matthew Turner, Steve Tuttle, Ed Twombly (The New England Bullpen), Dave Van Veldhuisen, Jay Vines, Deron Wagner, Chris Waters, Bill Wesslund, Richard West, Matthew Weston, Jeff Wilhelm, David Wilkins, Jeff Williams, Keith Williams, Mark Willis, Brandon Wilson, Opry Winston, Tony Wittrien, Pete Wooten, Yesterday's Heroes, Kevin Yiee, Ted Zanidakis, and Robert Zanze.

We have appreciated all of the help we have received over the years from collectors across the country and, indeed, throughout the world. Every year we make active solicitations to individuals and groups for input to that year's edition and we are particularly appreciative of help (large and small) provided for this volume. While we receive many inquiries, comments, and questions regarding material within this book -- and, in fact, each and every one is read and digested -- time constraints prevent us from personally replying to all but a few such letters. We hope that the letters will continue, and that even though no reply is received, you will feel that you are making significant contributions to the hobby through your interest and comments.

Special thanks go the staff of *Beckett Publications* for their help on many of the little things that added up to making this book possible. Editorial Director Fred Reed was very helpful with the editing of the introductory section as well as with the supervision of the extensive support team involved in getting the book to the printer. Assistant Editor Pepper Hastings was the key person on the advertising. Both of them have my appreciation for their long hours and dedication. Lou Cather and Edna Harless Krueger cheerfully helped with the paste-up and layout even working straight through the Super Bowl. The artwork in the new Condition Guide is from the skilled hand of Jeff Amano. The overall operations of our ongoing commitment to the hobby through *Beckett Monthly* were skillfully directed by Claire Backus. Claire has been ably assisted by Mary Gregory, Julie Grove, Debbie Kingsbury, Nancy Paterson, and Ruth Price. Thanks also go to Dale Backus, Therese Bellar, Becky Forbes, Sara Jenks, Anne Lowe, and Meg Schwender for their contributions. James and Sandi Beane performed several major system programming jobs for us this year in order to help us accomplish our work faster and more accurately. The whole *Beckett Publications* team has my thanks for jobs well done. Thank you, everyone.

I am thankful that my growing family made the best of it again this year. Every year is difficult but it seems each year the situation gets a little more tolerable. Time flies, ten years ago when I started, some people thought I would be a long-term bachelor. Since getting married six and half years ago, I now remember each annual edition according to the big events that happen that particular year with my family. My family is more important to me than baseball cards; I hope your family is just as important to you too.

BILL HENDERSON'S CARDS
"King of the Commons"

"ALWAYS BUYING" Call or Write for Quote

2320 RUGER AVE. - PG10
JANESVILLE, WISCONSIN 53545
1-608-755-0922

"ALWAYS BUYING" Call or Write for Quote

HI # OR SCARCE SERIES		COMMONS EACH	EX/MT TO MINT CONDITION		GROUP LOTS FOR SALE				VG Condition		
					50 Diff.	100 Diff.	300 Asst.	500 Asst.	50	100	200 Different
1948 BOWMAN	(37-48) 15.00	10.00									
1949 BOWMAN	(145-240) 35.00-40.00	10.00	(109-144)	8.00	450.				270.		
50-51 BOWMAN	22.00	10.00	51 (2-36)	12.00	450.				270.		
1952 TOPPS	(311-407) 135.00	15.00	(2-80)	35.00	675.				405.		
1952 BOWMAN	(217-252) 15.00	10.00			450.				270.		
1953 TOPPS	(220-280) 32.00	10.00			450.				270.		
1953 BOWMAN	(129-160) 25.00	15.00	(113-128)	30.00	675.				405.		
1954 TOPPS		5.00	(51-75)	7.00	225.	440.			135.		
1954 BOWMAN		4.00	(129-224)	5.00	180.	350.			108.		
1955 TOPPS	(161-210) 10.00	5.00	(151-160)	7.50	225.	440.			135.		
1955 BOWMAN	(225-320) 8.-10. Umps	3.00	(2-96)	4.00	135.	265.	775.		80.	158.	
1956 TOPPS		3.00	(181-260)	5.00	135.	265.	775.		80.	158.	
1957 TOPPS	(265-351) 10.00	2.50	(353-407)	3.00	115.	220.	645.		70.	132.	
1958 TOPPS		1.50	(1-110)	2.00	68.	132.	385.		40.	80.	
1959 TOPPS	(507-572) 5.50	1.25	(1-110)	1.50	58.	110.	325.	530.	35.	68.	130.
1960 TOPPS	(523-572) 5.00	1.00	(441-506)	1.50	45.	88.	258.	425.	27.	53.	100.
1961 TOPPS	(523-589) 15.00	1.00	(371-522)	1.25	45.	88.	258.	425.	27.	53.	100.
1962 TOPPS	(523-590) 5.00	1.00	(371-522)	1.25	45.	88.	258.	425.	27.	53.	100.
1963 TOPPS	(447-576) 5.00	.60	(197-446)	.75	27.	53.	155.		16.	30.	
1964 TOPPS	(523-587) 2.50	.50	(371-522)	.80	23.	44.	130.	215.	14.	26.	50.
1965 TOPPS	447-522 1.00 523-598 2.50	.50	(199-446)	.75	23.	44.	130.	215.	14.	26.	50.
1966 TOPPS	(523-598) 10.00	.50	(447-522)	1.50	23.	44.	130.	215.	14.	26.	50.
1967 TOPPS	(534-609) 5.00	.50	(458-533)	1.50	23.	44.	130.	215.	14.	26.	50.
1968 TOPPS	.60	.40	(458-533)	.60	18.	35.	*100.	170.	11.	20.	38.
1969 TOPPS		.40	(219-327)	.60	18.	35.	*100.	170.	11.	20.	38.
1970 TOPPS	(634-720) 1.50	.30	(553-636)	.75	14.	26.	*78.	125.		16.	30.
1971 TOPPS	(644-752) 1.50	.30	(524-643)	.75	14.	26.	*78.	125.		16.	30.
1972 TOPPS	(657-787) 1.50	.30	(526-656)	.75	14.	26.	*78.	125.		16.	30.
1973 TOPPS	(528-660) 1.25	.25	(397-528)	.40	11.	20.	*65.	105.		20.	22.
1974 TOPPS		.25			11.	20.	*65.	*105.		12.	22.
1975 TOPPS	(8-132 .30)	.25			11.	20.	*65.	*105.		12.	22.
1976-77		.20				18.	*50.	*85.		10.	18.
1978-1980		.15				13.	*38.	*65.		8.	15.
1981 thru 1988 Topps, Fleer or Donrus		.10				8.	*22.	*35.		5.	10.
Specify Year & Company except below						Per Yr.	Per Yr.	Per Yr.			
1984-86 DONRUS		.15			7.	13.	*38.	*60.			

*These lots are all different.

Special 1 Different from each year 1949-86 from above $100.00 postpaid.
Special 100 Different from each year 1956-86 from above $1400.00 postpaid.
Special 10 Different from each year 1956-86 from above $150.00 postpaid.

All lot groups are my choice only.

All assorted lots will contain as many different as possible.
Please list alternates whenever possible.
Send your want list and I will fill them at the above price for commons. High numbers, specials, scarce series, and stars extra.

Minimum order $7.50 - Postage and handling .50 per 100 cards (minimum $1.75)

Have thousands of star and super star cards. Call or send for star list.
Also interested in purchasing your collection.
*Groups include various years of my choice.

SPECIAL IN VG CONDITION-POSTPAID

250	58-62	150.00
500	58-62	290.00
250	60-69	85.00
500	60-69	160.00
1000	60-69	310.00
250	70-79	28.00
500	70-79	55.00
1000	70-79	100.00
250	80-84	12.00
500	80-84	22.00
1000	80-84	40.00

SETS AVAILABLE
POSTAGE 2.50 PER SET

1979 Topps	$125.00
1980 Topps	125.00
1981 Topps	90.00
1982 Topps	90.00
1983 Topps	100.00
1984 Topps	90.00
1985 Topps	100.00
1986 Topps	28.00
1987 Topps	25.00
1988 Topps	20.00

Prices subject to change without notice.

ANY CARD NOT LISTED ON PRICE SHEET IS PRICED AT BECKETT-SPORTS AMERICANA PRICE GUIDE X

The Sport Americana
Price Guide
Table Of Contents

Preface

Isn't it great? Every year this book gets bigger and bigger with all the new sets coming out. But even more exciting is that every year there are more collectors, more shows, more stores, and ... more interest in the cards we love so much. This edition has been enhanced and expanded from the previous edition. The cards you collect -- who they are, what they look like, where they are from, and (most important to many of you) what their current values are -- are enumerated within. Many of the features contained in the other *Beckett Price Guides* have been incorporated into this volume since condition grading, nomenclature, and many other aspects of collecting are common to the card hobby in general. We hope you find the book both interesting and useful in your collecting pursuits.

The Beckett Guide has been successful where other attempts have failed because it is complete, current, and valid. This *Price Guide* contains not just one, but three, prices by condition for all the baseball cards in the issues listed. These account for almost all the baseball cards in existence. The prices were added to the card lists just prior to printing and reflect not the author's opinions or desires but the going retail prices for each card, based on the marketplace (sports memorabilia conventions and shows, hobby papers, current mail order catalogs, local club meetings, auction results, and other firsthand reportings of actually realized prices).

What is the BEST Price Guide available (on the market) today? Of course card sellers will prefer the Price Guide with the highest prices as the best -- while card buyers will naturally prefer the one with the lowest prices. Accuracy, however, is the true test. Use the Price Guide used by more collectors and dealers than all the others combined. Look for the Beckett name. I won't put my name on anything I won't stake my reputation on. Not the lowest and not the highest -- but the most accurate, with integrity.

To facilitate your use of this book, read the complete introductory section in the pages following before going to the pricing pages. Every collectible field has its own terminology; we've tried to capture most of these terms and definitions in our glossary. Please read carefully the section on grading and the condition of your cards as you will not be able to determine which price column is appropriate for a given card without first knowing its condition.

Welcome to the world of baseball cards.

Sincerely, Dr. James Beckett

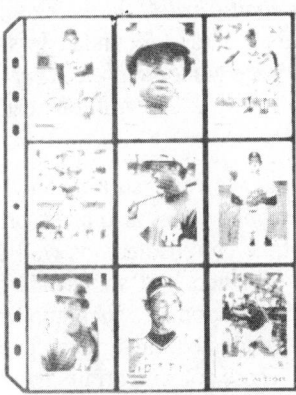

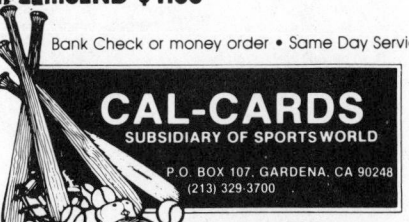

Introduction

Welcome to the exciting world of baseball card collecting, America's fastest-growing avocation. You have made a good choice in buying this book, since it will open up to you the entire panorama of this field in the simplest, most concise way.

It is estimated that nearly a quarter of a million different baseball cards have been issued during the past century. And the number of total cards put out by all manufacturers last year has been estimated at several billion with a retail value of more than $100 million. Sales of older cards by dealers may account for a like amount. With all that cardboard available in the marketplace, it should be no surprise that several million sports fans like you collect baseball cards today, and that number is growing by hundreds of thousands each year.

The growth of *Beckett Baseball Card Monthly* is another indication of this rising crescendo of popularity for baseball cards. Founded less than four years ago by Dr. James Beckett, the author of this price guide, *Beckett Monthly* has grown to the pinnacle of the baseball card hobby with nearly a half million readers anxiously awaiting each enjoyable issue.

So collecting baseball cards -- while still pursued as a hobby with youthful exuberance by kids in the neighborhood -- has also taken on the trappings of an industry, with thousands of full- and part-time card dealers, as well as vendors of supplies, clubs and conventions. In fact, each year since 1980 thousands of hobbyists have assembled for a National Sports Collectors Convention, at which hundreds of dealers have displayed their wares, seminars have been conducted, autographs penned by sports notables, and millions of cards changed hands. These colossal affairs have been staged in Los Angeles, Detroit, St. Louis, Chicago, New York, Anaheim, Arlington (TX), San Francisco, and this year in Atlantic City. So baseball card collecting is really national in scope!

This increasing interest has been reflected in card values. As more collectors compete for available supplies, card prices (especially for premium-grade cards) rise. A national publication indicated a "very strong advance" in baseball card prices during the past decade, and a quick perusal of prices in this book compared to the figures in earlier editions of this price guide will quickly confirm this. Which brings us back around again to the book you have in your hands. Many prices have literally doubled! It is the best annual guide available to this exciting world of baseball cards. Read it and use it. May your enjoyment and your card collection increase in the coming months and years.

How to Collect

Each collection is personal and reflects the individuality of its owner. There are no set rules on how to collect cards. Since card collecting is a hobby or leisure pastime, what you collect, how much you collect, and how much time and money you spend collecting are entirely up to you. The funds you have available for collecting and your own personal taste should determine how you collect. Information and ideas presented here are intended to help you get the most enjoyment from this hobby.

It is impossible to collect every card ever produced. Therefore, beginners as well as intermediate and advanced collectors usually specialize in some way. One of the reasons this hobby is popular is that individual collectors can define and tailor their collecting methods to match their own tastes. To give you some ideas of the various approaches to collecting, we will list some of the more popular areas of specialization.

Many collectors select complete sets from particular years. For example, they may concentrate on assembling complete sets from all the years since their birth or since they became avid sports fans. They may try to collect a card for every player during that specified period of time.

Many others wish to acquire only certain players. Usually such players are the superstars of the sport, but occasionally collectors will specialize in all the cards of players who attended certain colleges or came from certain towns. Some collectors are only interested in the first cards or rookie cards of certain players. A handy guide for collectors interested in pursuing the hobby this way is the recently updated *Sport Americana Alphabetical Checklist No. 3.*

Another fun way to collect cards is by team. Most fans have a favorite team, and it is natural for that loyalty to be translated into a desire for cards of the players on that favorite team. For most of the recent years, team sets (all the cards from a given team for that year) are readily available at a reasonable price. *The Sport Americana Team Baseball Card Checklist* will open up this field to the collector.

Obtaining Cards

Several avenues are open to card collectors. Cards can be purchased in the traditional way at the local candy, grocery, or drug stores, with the bubble gum or other products included. In recent years, it has also become possible to purchase complete sets of baseball cards through mail order advertisers found in traditional sports media publications, such as *The Sporting News*, *Baseball Digest*, *Street & Smith* yearbooks, and others. These sets are also advertised in the card collecting periodicals. Many collectors will begin by subscribing to at least one of the monthly hobby publications, all with good up-to-date information. In fact, subscription offers can be found in the advertising section of this book.

Most serious card collectors obtain old (and new) cards from one or more of several main sources: (1) trading or buying from other collectors or dealers; (2) responding to sale or auction ads in the monthly hobby publications; and/or (3) attending sports collectibles shows or conventions. We advise that you try all three methods since each has its own distinct advantages: (1) trading is a great way to make new friends; (2)

DEN'S COLLECTORS DEN

PLASTIC CARD PROTECTING PAGES
LARGEST SELECTION IN THE HOBBY

TRY **DEN'S** FINEST QUALITY PLASTIC SHEETS

SEND ONLY $ 1.00 for DEN'S BIG CATALOGUE CATALOGUE sent FREE with each ORDER

Featuring:
NON—MIGRATING PLASTIC IN ALL SHEETS
PLASTIC THAT DOES NOT STICK TOGETHER
STIFFNESS TO RESIST CARD CURLING
INTELLIGENT DESIGN
RESISTANCE TO CRACKING
FULL COVERAGE OF CARDS, PHOTOS, ENVELOPES

NO MIX & MATCH

STYLE	POCKETS CAPAC. CITY	RECOMMENDED FOR	PRICE EACH (DOES NOT INCLUDE P & H)			
			1•24	25•99	100•299	300•600
9 9T (TOP LOAD)	9 / 18	TOPPS (1957—PRESENT), FLEER, DONRUSS, TCMA, KELLOGG, POST CEREAL, LEAF (1960), RECENT NON-SPORTS CARDS, ALL STANDARD 2½" X 3½" CARDS	.25	.23	.21	.19
8	8 / 16	TOPPS (1952—1956), BOWMAN (1953—55)	.25	.23	.21	.19
12	12 / 24	BOWMAN (1948—50), TOPPS (1951 RED AND BLUE), RECENT TOPPS AND FLEER STICKERS	.25	.23	.21	.19
1	1 / 2	PHOTOGRAPHS (8X10)	.25	.23	.21	.19
2	2 / 4	PHOTOGRAPHS (5x7), TOPPS SUPERSTAR PHOTOS	.25	.23	.21	.19
4	4 / 8	POSTCARDS, TOPPS SUPER (1964,70,71), EXHIBITS, DONRUSS (ACTION ALL-STARS), PEREZ-STEELE HOF	.25	.23	.21	.19
18	18 / 36	T CARDS, TOPPS COINS, BAZOOKA (1963—67) INDIVIDUAL CARDS)	.35	.35	.30	.27
9G	9 / 18	GOUDEY, DIAMOND STARS, LEAF (1948)	.35	.35	.30	.27
9PB	9 / 18	PLAY BALL, BOWMAN (1951—52), DOUBLE PLAY, TOPPS MINIS, ALL GUM, INC. SPORT AND NON—SPORT	.35	.35	.30	.27
1C	1 / 2	TURKEY REDS (T3), PEPSI (1977), PRESS GUIDES, MOST WRAPPERS SPORT AND NON—SPORT	.35	.35	.30	.27
3	3 / 6	HOSTESS PANELS, HIRES, ZELLERS PANELS	.30	.25	.25	.20
6V	6 / 12	TOPPS (DOUBLE HEADERS, GREATEST MOMENTS, 1951 TEAM, CONNIE MACK, CURRENT STARS, 1965 FOOT-BALL AND HOCKEY, BUCKS, 1969—70 BASKETBALL), DADS HOCKEY, DOUBLE FOLDERS, TRIPLE FOLDERS	.35	.35	.30	.27
6D	6 / 12	RED MAN (WITH OR WITHOUT TABS), DISC, KAHN'S (1955—67)	.35	.35	.30	.27
1Y	1 / 1	YEARBOOKS, PROGRAMS, MAGAZINES, HOBBYPAPERS TABLOIDS POCKET SIZE 9"X12"	.35	.35	.30	.27
1S	1 / 2	SMALL PROGRAMS, MAGAZINE PAGES AND PHOTOS, CRACKER JACK SHEETS, POCKET SIZE 8½" X 11"	.30	.30	.25	.20
10	10 / 10	MATCHBOOK COVERS, POCKET SIZE 1 3/4" X 4 3/4"	.35	.35	.30	.27
3E	3 / 3	FIRST DAY COVERS, BASEBALL COMMEMORATIVE ENVELOPES, STANDARD SIZED ENVELOPES	.35	.35	.30	.27
3L	3 / 6	SQUIRT, PEPSI (1963), FLEER (STAMPS IN STRIPS), TOPPS (1964 AND 1969 STAMPS IN STRIPS),	.35	.35	.30	.27
6P	6 / 12	POLICE OR SAFETY CARDS (ALL SPORTS)	.25	.23	.21	.19

VISA

MasterCard

POSTAGE & HANDLING SCHEDULE
$ .01 to $ 20.00 add $ 2.00
$ 20.01 to $ 29.99 add $ 2.50
$ 30.00 to $ 49.99 add $ 3.00
$ 50.00 or more add $ 4.00

MARYLAND RESIDENTS ADD 5% SALES TAX
CANADIAN ORDERS — BOOKS ONLY
Canadian orders, orders outside the contiguous
United States, APO and FPO add 25% additional
U.S. FUNDS ONLY

MAKE CHECK OR MONEY ORDER PAYABLE TO:

DEN'S COLLECTORS DEN
Dept. BPG 10

P.O. BOX 606, LAUREL, MD 20707

DON'T SETTLE FOR LESS THAN THE BEST. BE SURE THAT THE STYLES 9,8,4,12,1 & 2 HAVE DEN'S COLLECTORS DEN EMBOSSED ON THE BORDER OF THE SHEET.

monthly hobby periodicals help you keep up with what's going on in the hobby (including when and where the conventions are happening); and (3) shows provide enjoyment and the opportunity to view millions of collectibles under one roof, in addition to meeting some of the hundreds or even thousands of other collectors with similar interests who also attend the shows.

Preserving Your Cards

Cards are fragile. They must be handled properly in order to retain their value. Careless handling can easily result in creased or bent cards. It is, however, not recommended that tweezers or tongs be used to pick up your cards since such utensils might mar or indent card surfaces and thus reduce those cards' conditions and values. In general, your cards should be handled directly as little as possible. This is sometimes easier to say than to do. Although there are still many who use custom boxes, storage trays, or even shoe boxes, plastic sheets are the preferred method of storing cards. A collection stored in plastic pages in a three-ring album allows you to view your collection at any time without the need to touch the card itself. For a large collection, some collectors may use a combination of the above methods.

When purchasing plastic sheets for your cards, be sure that you find the pocket size that fits the cards snugly. Don't put your 1951 Bowmans in a sheet designed to fit 1981 Topps. Most hobby and collectibles shops and virtually all collectors' conventions will have these plastic pages available in quantity for the various sizes offered or you can purchase them directly from the advertisers in this book.

Damp, sunny and/or hot conditions -- no, this is not a weather forecast -- are three elements to avoid in extremes if you are interested in preserving your collection. Too much (or too little) humidity can cause gradual deterioration of a card. Direct, bright sun (or fluorescent light) over time will bleach out the color of a card. Extreme heat accelerates the decomposition of the card. On the other hand, many cards have lasted more than 50 years without much scientific intervention. So be cautious, even if the above factors typically present a problem only when present in the extreme. It never hurts to be prudent.

Collecting/Investing

Collecting individual players and collecting complete sets are both popular vehicles for investment and speculation. Most investors and speculators stock up on complete sets or on quantities of players they think have good investment potential. There is obviously no guarantee in this book, or anywhere else for that matter, that cards will outperform the stock market or other investment alternatives in the future. After all, baseball cards do not pay quarterly dividends. Nevertheless, investors have noticed a favorable trend in the past performance of baseball and other sports collectibles, and certain cards and sets have outperformed just about any other investment in some years.

Some of the obvious questions are: Which cards? When to buy? When to sell? The best investment you can make is in your own education. The more you know about your collection and the hobby, the more informed the decisions you will be able to make. We're not selling investment tips. We're selling information about the current value of baseball cards. It's up to you to use that information to your best advantage.

Nomenclature

Each hobby has its own language to describe its area of interest. The nomenclature traditionally used for trading cards is derived from the *American Card Catalog*, published in 1960 by Nostalgia Press. That catalog, written by Jefferson Burdick (who is called the "Father of Card Collecting" for his pioneering work), uses letter and number designations for each separate set of cards.

The letter used in the ACC designation refers to the generic type of card. While both sport and non-sport issues are classified in the ACC, we shall confine ourselves to the sport issues. The following list defines the letters and their meanings as used by the American Card Catalog.

(none) or N - 19th Century U.S. Tobacco
B - Blankets
D - Bakery Inserts Including Bread
E - Early Candy and Gum
F - Food Inserts
H - Advertising
M - Periodicals
PC - Postcards
R - Candy and Gum Cards 1930 to Present
T - 20th Century U.S. Tobacco
UO - Gas and Oil Inserts
V - Canadian Candy
W - Exhibits, Strip Cards, Team Issues

Following the letter prefix and an optional hyphen are one-, two-, or three-digit numbers, 1-999. These typically represent the company or entity issuing the cards. In several cases, the ACC number is extended by an additional hyphen and another one- or two-digit numerical suffix. For example, the 1957 Topps regular series baseball card issue carries an ACC designation of R414-11. The "R" indicates a Candy or Gum Card produced since 1930. The "414" is the ACC designation for Topps Chewing Gum baseball card issues, and the "11" is the ACC designation for the 1957 regular issue (Topps' eleventh baseball set).

Like other traditional methods of identification, this system provides order to the process of cataloging cards; however, most serious collectors learn the ACC designation of the popular sets by repetition and familiarity, rather than by attempting to "figure out" what they might or should be.

From 1948 forward, collectors and dealers commonly refer to all sets by their year, maker, type of issue, and any other distinguishing characteristic. For example, such a characteristic could be an unusual issue or one of several regular issues put out by a specific maker in a single year. Regional issues are usually referred to by year, maker, and sometimes by title or theme of the set.

Glossary/Legend

Our glossary defines terms frequently used in the card collecting hobby. Many of these terms are also common to other types of sports memorabilia collecting. Some terms may have several meanings depending on use.

AAS - Action All Stars, a postcard-size set issued by the Donruss Company.

ACC - Acronym for *American Card Catalog*.

ALL STAR CARD - A card portraying an All Star Player of the previous year that says "All Star" on its face.

ALPH - Alphabetical.

AS - Abbreviation for All Star (card).

ATG - All Time Great card.

BLANKET - A felt square (normally 5" to 6") portraying a baseball player.

BOX - Card issued on a box or a card depicting a Boxer.

BRICK - A group of cards, usually 50 or more having common characteristics, that is intended to be bought, sold, or traded as a unit.

CABINETS - Very popular and highly valuable photographs on thick card stock produced in the 19th and early 20th century.

CHECKLIST - A list of the cards contained in a particular set. The list is always in numerical order if the cards are numbered. Some unnumbered sets are artificially numbered in alphabetical order, or by team and alphabetically within the team for convenience.

CHECKLIST CARD - A card that lists in order the cards and players in the set or series. Older checklist cards in mint condition that have not been checked off are very desirable.

CL - Abbreviation for Checklist.

COA - Abbreviation for Coach.

COIN - A small disc of metal or plastic portraying a player in its center.

COLLECTOR - A person who engages in the hobby of collecting cards primarily for his own enjoyment, with any profit motive being secondary.

COLLECTOR ISSUE - A set produced for the sake of the card itself with no product or service sponsor. It derives its name from the fact that most of these sets are produced for sale directly to the hobby market.

COMBINATION CARD - A single card depicting two or more players (but not a team card).

COMMON CARD - The typical card of any set; it has no premium value accruing from subject matter, numerical scarcity, popular demand, or anomaly.

COM - Card issued by the Post Cereal Company through their mail-in offer.

CONVENTION - A large weekend gathering of dealers and collectors at a single location for the purpose of buying, selling, and sometimes trading sports memorabilia items. Conventions are open to the public and sometimes feature celebrities, door prizes, films, contests, etc.

CONVENTION ISSUE - A set produced in conjunction with a sports collectibles convention to commemorate or promote the show.

COR - Correct or corrected card.

COUPON - See Tab.

CREASE - A wrinkle on the card, usually caused by bending the card. Creases are a common defect from careless handling.

CY - Cy Young Award.

DEALER - A person who engages in buying, selling, and trading sports collectibles or supplies. A dealer may also be a collector, but as a dealer, he anticipates a profit.

DIE-CUT - A card with part of its stock partially cut, allowing one or more parts to be folded or removed. After removal or appropriate folding, the remaining part of the card can frequently be made to stand up.

DISC - A circular-shaped card.

DISPLAY CARD - A sheet, usually containing three to nine cards, that is printed and used by the manufacturer to advertise and/or display the packages containing his products and cards. The backs of display cards are blank or contain advertisements.

DK - Diamond King (artwork produced by Perez-Steele for Donruss).

DP - Double Print (a card that was printed in double the quantity compared to the other cards in the same series).

ERA - Earned Run Average.

ERR - Error card (see also COR).

ERROR CARD - A card with erroneous information, spelling, or depiction on either side of the card. Not all errors are corrected by the producing card company.

EXHIBIT - The generic name given to thick stock, postcard-size cards with single color obverse pictures. The name is derived from the Exhibit Supply Co. of Chicago, the principal manufacturer of this type of card. These are also known as Arcade cards since they were found in many arcades.

FDP - First Draft Pick (see 1985 Topps Baseball).

FULL SHEET - A complete sheet of cards that has not been cut up into individual cards by the manufacturer. Also called an uncut sheet.

HALL OF FAMER - (HOF'er) A card that portrays a player who has been inducted into the Hall of Fame.

HIGH NUMBER - The cards in the last series of numbers in a year in which such higher-numbered cards were printed or distributed in significantly lesser amounts than the lower-numbered cards. The high-number designation refers to a scarcity of the high-numbered cards. Not all years have high numbers in terms of this definition.

HOC - House of Collectibles.

HOF - Acronym for Hall of Fame.

HOR - Horizontal pose on card as opposed to the standard vertical orientation found on most cards.

HR - Abbreviation for Home Run.

IA - In Action (type of card).

INSERT - A card of a different type, e.g., a poster, or any other sports collectible contained and sold in the same package along with a card or cards of a major set.

ISSUE - Synonymous with set, but usually used in conjunction with a manufacturer, e.g., a Topps issue.

KP - Kid Picture (a sub-series issued in the Topps Baseball sets of 1972 and 1973).

LAYERING - The separation or peeling of one or more layers of the card stock, usually at the corner of the card.

LEGITIMATE ISSUE - A set produced to promote or boost sales of a product or service, e.g., bubble gum, cereal, cigarettes, etc. Most collector issues are not legitimate issues in this sense.

LHP - Left Handed Pitcher.

LID - A circular-shaped card (possibly with tab) that forms the top of the container for the product being promoted.

LL - Living Legends (Donruss 1984) or large letters.

MAJOR SET - A set produced by a national manufacturer of cards containing a large number of cards. Usually 100 or more different cards comprise the set.

MG - Abbreviation for Manager.

MINI - A small card; specifically, a Topps baseball card of identical design but smaller dimensions than the regular Topps issue of 1975.

ML - Major League.

MVP - Most Valuable Player.

NNOF - No Name on Front (see 1949 Bowman).

NOF - Name on Front (see 1949 Bowman).

NON-SPORT CARD - A card from a set whose major theme is a subject other than a sports subject. A card of a sports figure or event that is part of a non-sport set is still a non-sport card, e.g., while the "Look 'N' See" non-sport card set contains a card of Babe Ruth, a sports figure, that card is a non-sport card.

NOTCHING - The grooving of the card, usually caused by fingernails, rubber bands, or bumping card edges against other objects.

NY - New York.

OBVERSE - The front, face, or pictured side of the card.

OLY - Olympics (see 1985 Topps Baseball; the members of the 1984 U.S. Olympic Baseball team were a featured sub-series).

OPT - Option.

P - Pitcher or Pitching pose.

P1 - First Printing.

P2 - Second Printing.

P3 - Third Printing.

PANEL - An extended card that is composed of two or more individual cards. Often the panel forms the back part of the container for the product being promoted, e.g., a Hostess panel, a Bazooka panel, an Esskay Meat panel.

PCL - Pacific Coast League.

PG - Price Guide.

PLASTIC SHEET - A clear, plastic page that is punched for insertion into a binder (with standard three-ring spacing) containing pockets for displaying cards. Many different styles of sheets exist with pockets of varying sizes to hold the many differing card formats.

PREMIUM - A card, sometimes on photographic stock, that is purchased or obtained in conjunction with/or redemption for another card or product. The premium is not packaged in the same unit as the primary item.

PUZZLE CARD - A card whose back contains a part of a picture which, when joined correctly with other puzzle cards, forms the completed picture.

PUZZLE PIECE - An die-cut piece designed to interlock with similar pieces.

RARE - A card or series of cards of very limited availability. Unfortunately, "rare" is a subjective term sometimes used indiscriminately. Rare cards are harder to obtain than scarce cards.

RB - Record Breaker card.

REGIONAL - A card issued and distributed only in a limited geographical area of the country. The producer is not a major, national producer of trading cards.

REVERSE - The back or narrative side of the card.

RHP - Right-Handed Pitcher.

ROY - Acronym for Rookie of the Year.

RR - Rated Rookies (a subset featured in the Donruss Baseball sets).

SA - Super Action or Sport Americana.

SASE - Self-Addressed, Stamped Envelope.

SB - Stolen Bases.

SCARCE - A card or series of cards of limited availability. This subjective term is sometimes used indiscriminately to promote or hype value. Scarce cards are not as difficult to obtain as rare cards.

SCR - Script name on back (see 1949 Bowman Baseball).

SEMI-HIGH - A card from the next to last series of a sequentially issued set. It has more value than an average card and generally less value than a high number. A card is not called a semi-high unless the next to last series in which it exists has an additional premium attached to it.

SERIES - The entire set of cards issued by a particular producer in a particular year, e.g., the 1971 Topps series. Also, within a particular set, series can refer to a group of (consecutively numbered) cards printed at the same time, e.g., the first series of the 1957 Topps issue (numbers 1 through 88).

SET - One each of the entire run of cards of the same type produced by a particular manufacturer during a single year. In other words, if you have a (complete) set of 1976 Topps then you have every card from number 1 up through and including number 660, i.e., all the different cards that were produced.

SKIP-NUMBERED - A set that has many unissued card numbers between the lowest number in the set and the highest number in the set, e.g., the 1948 Leaf baseball set contains 98 cards skip-numbered from number 1 to number 168. A major set in which a few numbers were not printed is not considered to be skip-numbered.

SO - Strikeouts.

SP - Single or Short Print (a card which was printed in lesser quantity compared to the other cards in the same series; see also DP and TP).

SPECIAL CARD - A card that portrays something other than a single player or team, for example, a card that portrays the previous year's statistical leaders or the results from the previous year's post-season action.

SS - Abbreviation for Shortstop.

STAMP - Adhesive-backed papers depicting a player. The stamp may be individual or in a sheet of many stamps. Moisture must be applied to the adhesive in order for the stamp to be attached to another surface.

STAR CARD - A card that portrays a player of some repute, usually determined by his ability; however, sometimes referring to sheer popularity.

STICKER - A card with a removable layer that can be affixed to (stuck onto) another surface.

STOCK - The cardboard or paper on which the card is printed.

STRIP CARDS - A sheet or strip of cards, particularly popular in the 1920s and 1930s, with the individual cards usually separated by broken or dotted lines.

SUPERSTAR CARD - A card that portrays a superstar, e.g., a Hall of Fame member or a Hall of Fame prospect.

SV - Super Veteran.

TAB - A card portion set off from the rest of the card, usually with perforations, that may be removed without damaging the central character or event depicted by the card.

TBC - Turn Back the Clock cards.

TEAM CARD - A card that depicts an entire team.

TEST SET - A set, usually containing a small number of cards, issued by a national card producer and distributed in a limited section or sections of the country. Presumably, the purpose of a test set is to test market appeal for a particular type of card.

TL - Team Leader card.

TP - Triple Print (a card that was printed in triple the quantity compared to the other cards in the same series).

TR - Trade or Traded.

TRIMMED - A card cut down from its original size. Trimmed cards are undesirable to most collectors.

VARIATION - One of two or more cards from the same series with the same number (or player with identical pose if the series is unnumbered) differing from one another by some aspect, the different feature stemming from the printing or stock of the card. This can be caused when the manufacturer of the cards notices an error in one (or more) of the cards, makes the changes, and then resumes the print run. In this case there will be two versions or variations of the same card. Sometimes one of the variations is relatively scarce.

VERT - Vertical pose on card.

WAS - Washington.

WS - World Series card.

Business of Baseball Card Collecting

Determining Value

Why are some cards more valuable than others? Obviously, the economic law of supply and demand is applicable to card collecting just as it is to any other field where a commodity is bought, sold, or traded.

Supply (the number of cards available on the market) is less than the total number of cards originally produced since attrition diminishes that original quantity. Each year a percentage of cards are typically thrown away, destroyed, or otherwise lost to collectors. This percentage is smaller today than it was in the past because more and more people have become increasingly aware of the value of their cards. For those who collect only "Mint" condition cards, the supply of older cards can be quite small indeed. Until recently, collectors were not so conscious of the need to preserve the condition of their cards. For this reason, it is difficult to know exactly how many 1953 Topps are currently available, Mint or otherwise. It is generally accepted that there are fewer 1953 Topps available than 1963, 1973, or 1983 Topps cards. If demand were equal for each of these sets, the law of supply and demand would increase the price for the least available sets. Demand, however, is not equal for all sets, so price correlations can be complicated.

The demand for a card is influenced by many factors. These include: (1) the age of the card; (2) the number of cards printed; (3) the player(s) portrayed on the card; (4) the attractiveness and popularity of the set; and perhaps most important, (5) the physical condition of the card.

In general, (1) the older the card, (2) the fewer the number of the cards printed, (3) the more famous the player, (4) the more attractive and popular the set, or (5) the better the condition of the card, the higher the value of the card will be. There are exceptions to all but one of these factors: the condition of the card. Given two cards similar in all respects except condition, the one in the best condition will always be valued higher.

While there are certain guidelines that help to establish the value of a card, the exceptions and peculiarities make any simple, direct mathematical formula to determine card values impossible.

Regional Variation

Two types of price variations exist among the sections of the country where a card is bought or sold. The first is the general price variation on all cards bought and sold in one geographical area as compared to another. Card prices are slightly higher on the East and West coasts, and slightly lower in the middle of the country. Although prices may vary from the East to the West, or from the Southwest to the Midwest, the prices listed in this guide are nonetheless presented as a consensus of all sections of this large and diverse country.

Still, prices for a particular player's cards may well be higher in his home team's area than in other regions. This exhibits the second type of regional price variation in which local players are favored over those from distant areas. For example, an Al Kaline card would be valued higher in Detroit than in Cincinnati because Kaline played in Detroit; therefore, the demand there for Al Kaline cards is higher than it is in Cincinnati.

On the other hand, a Johnny Bench card would be priced higher in Cincinnati where he played than in Detroit for similar reasons. Sometimes even common player cards command such a premium from hometown collectors.

Set Prices

A somewhat paradoxical situation exists in the price of a complete set versus the combined cost of the individual cards in the set. In nearly every case, the sum of the prices for the individual cards is higher than the cost for the complete set. This is especially prevalent in the cards of the past few years. The reasons for this apparent anomaly stem from the habits of collectors and from the carrying costs to dealers. Today each card in a set is normally produced in the same quantity as all others in its set. However, many collectors pick up only stars, superstars, and particular teams. As a result, the dealer is left with a shortage of certain player cards and an abundance of others. He therefore incurs an expense in simply "carrying" these less desirable cards in stock. On the other hand, if he sells a complete set, he gets rid of large numbers of cards at one time. For this reason, he is often willing to receive less money for a complete set. By doing this, he recovers all of his costs and also receives some profit.

The disparity between the price of the complete set and that for the sum of the individual cards has also been influenced by the fact that the major manufacturers are now pre-collating card sets. Since "pulling" individual cards from the sets of all three manufacturers involves a specific type of labor (and cost), the singles or star card market is not affected significantly by pre-collation.

Set prices also do not include rare card varieties, unless specifically stated. Of course, the prices for sets do include one example of each type for the given set, but this is the least expensive variety.

Scarce Series

Scarce series occur because cards issued before 1974 were made available to the public each year in several series of finite numbers of cards, rather than all cards of the set being available for purchase at one time. At some point during the year, usually toward the end of the baseball season, interest in current year baseball cards waned. Consequently, the manufacturers produced smaller numbers of these later series of cards. Nearly all nationwide issues from post-World War II manufacturers (1948 to 1973) exhibit these series variations. In the past Topps, for example, has issued series consisting of many different numbers of cards, including 55, 66, 80, 88, and others. Recently Topps has settled on what is now their standard sheet size of 132 cards.

While the number of cards within a given series is usually the same as the number of cards on one printed sheet, this is not always the case. For example, Bowman used 36 cards on its standard printed sheets, but in 1948 substituted 12 cards during later print runs of that year's baseball cards. Twelve of the cards from the initial sheet of 36 cards were removed and replaced by 12 different cards giving, in effect, a first series of 36 cards and a second series of 12 new cards. This replacement produced a scarcity of 24 cards -- the 12 cards removed from the original sheet and the 12 new cards added to the sheet. A full sheet of 1948 Bowman cards (second printing) shows that card numbers 37 through 48 have replaced 12 of the cards on the first printing sheet.

The Topps Gum Company has also created scarcities and/or excesses of certain cards in many of their sets. Topps, however, has most frequently gone the other direction by double printing some of the cards. Double printing causes an abundance of cards of the players who are on the same sheet more than one time. During the years from 1978 to 1981, Topps double printed 66 cards out of their large 726-card set. The Topps practice of double printing cards in earlier years is the most logical explanation for the known scarcities of particular cards in some of these Topps sets.

Grading Your Cards

Each hobby has its own grading terminology -- stamps, coins, comic books, beer cans, right down the line. Collectors of sports cards are no exception. The one invariable criterion for determining the value of a card is its condition: the better the condition of the card, the more valuable it is. However, condition grading is very subjective. Individual card dealers and collectors differ in the strictness of their grading, but the stated condition of a card should be determined without regard to whether it is being bought or sold.

The physical defects which lower the condition of a card are usually quite apparent, but each individual places his own estimation (negative value in this case) on these defects. We present the condition guide for use in determining values listed in this price guide in the hopes that excess subjectivity can be minimized.

The defects listed in the condition guide below are those either placed in the card at the time of printing -- uneven borders, focus -- or those defects that can occur to a card under normal handling -- corner sharpness, gloss, edge wear, light creases -- and finally, environmental conditions -- browning. Other defects to cards are caused by human carelessness and in all cases should be noted separately and in addition to the condition grade. Among the more common alterations are heavy creases, tape, tape stains, rubber band marks, water damage, smoke damage, trimming, paste, tears, writing, pin or tack holes, any back damage, and missing parts (tabs, tops, coupons, backgrounds).

Centering

It is important to define in words and pictures what is meant by certain frequently used hobby terms relating to grading cards. The adjacent pictures portray various stages of centering. Centering can range from well-centered to slightly off-centered to off-centered to badly off-centered to miscut.

Slightly Off-Centered: A slightly off-center card is one which upon close inspection is found to have one border bigger than the opposite border. This degree is only offensive to a purist.

Off-Centered: An off-center card has one border which is noticeably more than twice as wide as the opposite border.

Badly Off-Centered: A badly off-center card has virtually no border on one side of the card.

Miscut: A miscut card actually shows part of the adjacent card in its larger border and consequently a corresponding amount of its card is cut off.

Corner Wear

Degrees of corner wear generate several common terms used and useful to accurate grading. The wear on card corners can be expressed as fuzzy corners, corner wear or slightly rounded corners, rounded corners, badly rounded corners.

Fuzzy Corners: Fuzzy corners still come to a right angle (to a point) but the point has begun to fray slightly.

Corner Wear or Slightly Rounded Corners: The slight fraying of the corners has increased to where there is no longer a point to the corner. Nevertheless the corner is still reasonably sharp. There may be evidence of some slight loss of color in the corner also.

Rounded Corners: The corner is definitely no longer sharp but is not badly rounded.

Badly Rounded Corners: The corner is rounded to an objectionable degree. Excessive wear and rough handling are evident.

Creases

The third, and perhaps most frequent, common defect is the crease; the degree of creasing in a card is very difficult to show in a drawing or picture. On giving the specific condition of an expensive card for sale, the seller should note any creases additionally. Creases can be categorized as to severity according to the following scale.

Light Crease: A light crease is a crease which is barely noticeable on close inspection. In fact when cards are in plastic sheets or holders, a light crease may not be seen (until the card is taken out of the holder). A light crease on the front is much more serious than a light crease on the card back only.

Medium Crease: A medium crease is noticeable when held and studied at arm's length by the naked eye, but does not overly detract from the appearance of the card. It is an obvious crease, but not one that breaks the picture surface of the card.

Heavy Crease: A heavy crease is one which has torn or broken through the card's picture surface, e.g., puts a tear in the photo surface.

Alterations

Deceptive Trimming: Deceptive trimming occurs when someone alters the card in order (1) to shave off edge wear, (2) to improve the sharpness of the corners, or (3) to improve centering -- obviously their objective is to falsely increase the perceived value of the card to an unsuspecting buyer. The shrinkage is usually only evident if the trimmed card is compared to an adjacent full-sized card or if the trimmed card is itself measured.

Obvious Trimming: Obvious trimming is noticeable and unfortunate. It is usually performed by non-collectors who give no thought to the present or future value of their cards.

Deceptively Retouched Borders: This occurs when the borders (especially on those cards with dark borders) are touched up on the edges and corners with magic marker of appropriate color in order to make the card appear to be mint.

CENTERING

WELL-CENTERED

SLIGHTLY OFF-CENTERED

OFF-CENTERED

BADLY OFF-CENTERED

MISCUT

CORNER WEAR

The partial cards shown at the right have been photographed at 300%. This was done in order to magnify each card's corner wear to such a degree that differences could be shown on a printed page.

The 1962 Topps Mickey Mantle card definitely has a rounded corner. Some may say that this corner is badly rounded, but that is a judgment call.

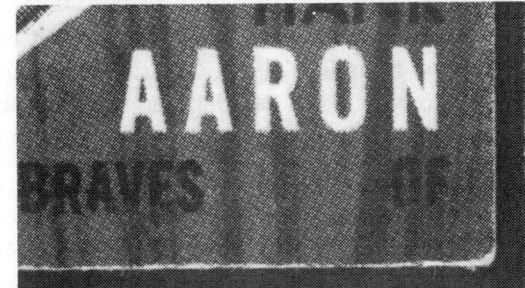

The 1962 Topps Hank Aaron card has a slightly rounded corner. Note that there is definite corner wear evident by the fraying and that there is no longer a sharp point to which the corner converges.

The 1962 Topps Gil Hodges card has corner wear; it is slightly better than the Aaron card above. Nevertheless some collectors might classify this Hodges corner as slightly rounded.

The 1962 Topps Manager's Dream card showing Mantle and Mays has slight corner wear. This is not a fuzzy corner as very slight wear is noticeable on the card's photo surface.

The 1962 Topps Don Mossi card has very slight corner wear such that it might be called a fuzzy corner. A close look at the original card shows that the corner is not perfect, but almost. However, note that corner wear is somewhat academic on this card. As you can plainly see, the heavy crease going across his name breaks through the photo surface.

Categorization of Defects

A "Very Minor Defect" would be fuzzy corners, slight off-centering, printer's lines, printer's spots, slightly out of focus, or slight loss of original gloss. A NrMT card may have one very minor defect. An Ex-MT card may have two or more very minor defects.

A "Minor Defect" would be corner wear or slight rounding, off-centering, light crease on back, wax or gum stains on reverse, loss of original gloss, writing or tape marks on back, or rubber band marks. An Excellent card may have minor defects.

A "Major Defect" would be rounded corner(s), badly off-centering, crease(s), deceptive trimming, deceptively retouched borders, pin hole, staple hole, incidental writing or tape marks on front, warping, water stains, or sun fading. A VG card may have one major defect. A Good card may have two or more major defects.

A "Catastrophic Defect" is the worst kind of defect and would include such defects as badly rounded corner(s), miscutting, heavy crease(s), obvious trimming, punch hole, tack hole, tear(s), corner missing or clipped, destructive writing on front. A Fair card may have one catastrophic defect. A Poor card has two or more catastrophic defects.

Condition Guide

MINT (M OR MT) - A card with no defects. The card has sharp corners, even borders, original gloss or shine on the surface, sharp focus of the picture, smooth edges, no signs of wear, and white borders. A mint card (that is, a card that is worth a "mint" price) does NOT have printers' lines or other printing defects or other serious quality control problems that should have been discovered by the producing card company before distribution. Note also that there is no allowance made for the age of the card.

NEAR MINT (NrMT) - A card with a very minor defect. Any of the following would be sufficient to lower the grade of a card from Mint to the Near Mint category: layering at some of the corners (fuzzy corners), a very small amount of the original gloss lost, very minor wear on the edges, slightly off-center borders, slight wear visible only on close inspection, slight off-whiteness of the borders.

EXCELLENT-MINT (EX-MT) - A card with very minor defects, but no minor defects. Two or three of the following would be sufficient to lower the grade of a card from Mint to the Excellent-Mint category: layering at some of the corners (fuzzy corners), a very small amount of the original gloss lost, minor wear on the edges, slightly off-center borders, slight wear visible only on close inspection, slight off-whiteness of the borders.

EXCELLENT (EX OR E) - A card with minor defects. Any of the following would be sufficient to lower the grade of a card from Mint to the Excellent category: slight rounding at some of the corners, a small amount of the original gloss lost, minor wear on the edges, off-center borders, wear visible only on close inspection; off-whiteness of the borders.

VERY GOOD (VG) - A card that has been handled but not abused: Some rounding at all corners, slight layering or scuffing at one or two corners, slight notching on edges, gloss lost from the surface but not scuffed, borders might be somewhat uneven but some white is visible on all borders, noticeable yellowing or browning of borders, pictures may be slightly off focus.

GOOD (G) - A well-handled card, rounding and some layering at the corners, scuffing at the corners and minor scuffing on the face, borders noticeably uneven and browning, loss of gloss on the face, notching on the edges.

FAIR (F) - Round and layering corners, brown and dirty borders, frayed edges, noticeable scuffing on the face, white not visible on one or more borders, cloudy focus.

POOR (P) - An abused card: The lowest grade of card, frequently some major physical alteration has been performed on the card, collectible only as a filler until a better-condition replacement can be obtained.

Categories between these major condition grades are frequently used, such as Very Good to Excellent (VG-E), Fair to Good (F-G), etc. Such grades indicate a card with all qualities at least in the lower of the two categories, but with several qualities in the higher of the two categories. In the case of Ex-Mt, it essentially refers to a card which is halfway between Excellent and Mint.

Unopened "Mint" cards and factory-collated sets are considered Mint in their unknown (and presumed perfect) state. However, once opened or broken out, each of these cards is graded (and valued) in its own right by taking into account any quality control defects (such as off-centering, printer's lines, machine creases, or gum stains) that may be present in spite of the fact that the card has never been handled.

Cards before 1980 which are priced in the Price Guide in a top condition of NrMT, are obviously worth an additional premium when offered in strict Mint condition. This additional premium increases relative to the age and scarcity of the card. For example, Mint cards from the late '70s may bring only a 10% premium for Mint (above NrMT), whereas high demand cards from pre-World War II vintage sets can be sold for as much as double the NrMT price when offered in strict Mint condition.

Selling Your Cards

Just about every collector sells cards or will sell cards eventually. Someday you may be interested in selling your duplicates or maybe even your whole collection. You may sell to other collectors, friends, or dealers. You may even sell cards you purchased from a certain dealer back to that same dealer. In any event, it helps to know some of the mechanics of the typical transaction between buyer and seller.

Dealers will buy cards in order to resell them to other collectors who are interested in the cards. Dealers will always pay a higher percentage for items which (in their opinion) can be resold quickly, and a much lower percentage for those items which are perceived as having low demand and hence are slow moving. In either case, dealers must buy at a price that allows for the expense of doing business and a fair margin for profit.

If you have cards for sale, the best advice we can give is that you get three offers for your cards and take the best offer, all things considered. Note, the "best" offer may not be the one for the highest amount. And remember, if a dealer really wants your cards, he won't let you get away without making his best competitive offer. Another alternative is to take your cards to a nearby convention and either auction them off in the show auction or offer them for sale to some of the dealers present.

Many people think nothing of going into a department store and paying $15 for an item of clothing for which the store paid $5. But, if you were selling your $15 card to a dealer and he offered you only $5 for it, you might think his mark-up unreasonable. To complete the analogy: most department stores (and card dealers) that pay $10 for $15 items eventually go out of business. An exception to this is when the dealer knows that a willing buyer for the merchandise you are attempting to sell is only a phone call away. Then an offer of 2/3 or maybe 70% of the book value will still allow him to make a reasonable profit due to the short time he will need to hold the merchandise. Nevertheless, most cards and collections will bring offers in the range of 25% to 50% of retail price. Material from the past five to ten years or so is very plentiful. Don't be surprised if your best offer is only 20% of the book value for these recent years.

Interesting Notes

The numerically first card of an issue is the single card most likely to obtain excessive wear. Consequently, you will typically find the price on the number one card (in Mint condition) somewhat higher than might otherwise be the case. Similarly, but to a lesser extent (because normally the less important, reverse side of the card is the one exposed), the numerically last card in an issue is also prone to abnormal wear. This extra wear and tear occurs because the first and last cards are exposed to the elements (human element included) more than any other cards. They are generally end cards in any brick formations, rubber bandings, stackings on wet surfaces, and like activities.

Sports cards have no intrinsic value. The value of a card, like the value of other collectibles, can only be determined by you and your enjoyment in viewing and possessing these cardboard swatches.

Remember, the buyer ultimately determines the price of each baseball card. You are the determining price factor because you have the ability to say "No" to the price of any card by not exchanging your hard-earned money for a given card. When the cost of a trading card exceeds the enjoyment you will receive from it, your answer should be "No." We assess and report the prices. You set them!

We are always interested in receiving the price input of collectors and dealers from around the country. We happily credit major contributors. We welcome your opinions, since your contributions assist us in ensuring a better guide each year. If you would like to join our survey list for the next editions of this book and others authored by Dr. Beckett, please send your name and address to Dr. James Beckett, 3410 MidCourt, Suite 110, Carrollton, Texas 75006.

Advertising

Within this price guide you will find advertisements for sports memorabilia material, mail order, and retail sports collectibles establishments. All advertisements were accepted in good faith based on the reputation of the advertiser; however, neither the author, the publisher, the distributors, nor the other advertisers in the price guide accept any responsibility for any particular advertiser not complying with the terms of his or her ad.

Readers should also be aware that prices in advertisements are subject to change over the annual period before a new edition of this volume is issued each spring. When replying to an advertisement late in the baseball year, the reader should take this into account, and contact the dealer by phone or in writing for up-to-date price information. Should you come into contact with any of the advertisers in this guide as a result of their advertisement herein, please mention to them this source as your contact.

Additional Reading

With the increase in popularity of the hobby in recent years, there has been a corresponding increase in available literature. Below is a list of the books and periodicals which receive our highest recommendation and which we hope will further advance your knowledge and enjoyment of our great hobby.

The Sport Americana Price Guide to Baseball Collectibles by Dr. James Beckett (First Edition, $9.95, released 1986, published by Edgewater Book Company) -- the complete guide/checklist with up to date values for box cards, coins, decals, labels, Canadian cards, stamps, stickers, pins, etc.

The Sport Americana Football, Hockey, Basketball and Boxing Card Price Guide by Dr. James Beckett (Fifth Edition, $12.95, released 1987, published by Edgewater Book Company) -- the most comprehensive price guide/checklist ever issued on football and other non-baseball sports cards. No serious hobbyist should be without it.

The Official Price Guide to Football Cards by Dr. James Beckett (Seventh Edition, $4.95, released 1987, published by The House of Collectibles) -- an abridgement of the *Sport Americana Price Guide* listed above in a convenient and economical pocket-size format providing Dr. Beckett's pricing of the major football sets since 1948.

The Sport Americana Baseball Memorabilia and Autograph Price Guide by Dr. James Beckett and Dennis W. Eckes (First Edition, $8.95, released 1982, co-published by Den's Collectors Den and Edgewater Book Company) -- the most complete book ever produced on baseball memorabilia other than baseball cards. This book presents in an illustrated, logical fashion information on baseball memorabilia and autographs which had been heretofore unavailable to the collector.

The Sport Americana Alphabetical Baseball Card Checklist by Dr. James Beckett (Third Edition, $9.95, released 1988, co-published by Den's Collectors Den and Edgewater Book Company) -- an illustrated, alphabetical listing, by the last name of the player portrayed on the card, of virtually all baseball cards (Major League and Minor League) produced up through 1988.

The Sport Americana Price Guide to the Non-Sports Cards by Christopher Benjamin and Dennis W. Eckes (Second Edition, $8.95, released 1983, co-published by Den's Collector's Den and Edgewater Book Company) -- the definitive guide to all popular non-sports American tobacco and bubble gum cards. In addition to cards, illustrations and prices for wrappers are also included. (At press time two new volumes on this series were pending.)

The Sport Americana Baseball Address List by Jack Smalling and Dennis W. Eckes (Fourth Edition, $9.95, released 1986, co-published by Den's Collector's Den and

Edgewater Book Company) -- the definitive guide for autograph hunters giving addresses and deceased information for virtually all major league baseball players past and present.

The Sport Americana Baseball Card Team Checklist by Jeff Fritsch and Dennis W. Eckes (Third Edition, $9.95, released 1987, co-published by Den's Collectors Den and Edgewater Book Company) -- includes all Topps, Bowman, Fleer, Play Ball, Goudey, and Donruss cards, with the players portrayed on the cards listed with the teams for whom they played. The book is invaluable to the collector who specializes in an individual team because it is the most complete baseball card team checklist available.

Hockey Card Checklist and Price Guide by Andrew Pywowarczuk (Seventh Edition, publisher: Cartophilium) -- contains the most complete list of hockey card checklists ever assembled including a listing of Bee Hive photos.

The Encyclopedia of Baseball Cards, Volume I: 19th Century Cards by Lew Lipset ($11.95, released 1983, published by the author) -- everything you ever wanted to know about 19th century cards.

The Encyclopedia of Baseball Cards, Volume II: Early Gum and Candy Cards by Lew Lipset ($10.95, released 1984, published by the author) -- everything you ever wanted to know about Early Candy and Gum cards.

The Encyclopedia of Baseball Cards, Volume III: 20th Century Tobacco Cards, 1909-1932 by Lew Lipset ($12.95, released 1986, published by the author) -- everything you ever wanted to know about old tobacco cards.

Beckett Baseball Card Monthly authored and edited by Dr. James Beckett -- contains the most extensive and accepted monthly price guide, feature articles, "who's hot and who's not" section, convention calendar, and numerous letters to and responses from the editor. Published 11 times annually, it is the hobby's largest paid circulation periodical.

Errata

There are thousands of names, more than 100,000 prices, and untold other words in this book. There are going to be a few typographical errors, a few misspellings, and possibly, a number or two out of place. If you catch a blooper, drop me a note directly or in care of the publisher, and we will fix it up in the next year's edition.

Prices in this Guide

Prices found in this guide reflect current retail rates just prior to the printing of this book. They do not reflect the FOR SALE prices of the author, the publisher, the distributors, the advertisers, or any card dealers associated with this guide. No one is obligated in any way to buy, sell, or trade his or her cards based on these prices. The price listings were compiled by the author from actual buy/sell transactions at sports conventions, buy/sell advertisements in the hobby papers, for sale prices from dealer catalogs and price lists, and discussions with leading hobbyists in the U.S. and Canada. All prices are in U.S. dollars.

1948 Babe Ruth Story

			NRMT	VG-E	GOOD
☐	23	Ted Lyons and .... William Bendix	30.00	15.00	3.00
☐	24	Lefty Gomez, William .... Bendix, and Bucky Harris	40.00	20.00	4.00
☐	25	Babe Ruth and .... William Bendix	75.00	37.50	7.50
☐	26	Babe Ruth and .... William Bendix	75.00	37.50	7.50
☐	27	Babe Ruth and .... Claire Trevor	75.00	37.50	7.50
☐	28	William Bendix, Babe .... Ruth, Claire Trevor	75.00	37.50	7.50

The 1948 Babe Ruth Story set of 28 black and white numbered cards (measuring 2" by 2 1/2") was issued by the Philadelphia Chewing Gum Company to commemorate the 1949 movie of the same name starring William Bendix, Claire Trevor, and Charles Bickford. Babe Ruth himself appears on several cards. The last 12 cards (17 to 28) are more difficult to obtain than other cards in the set and are more desirable in that most picture actual players as well as actors. The ACC designation is R421.

		NRMT	VG-E	GOOD
COMPLETE SET		600.00	300.00	60.00
COMMON PLAYER (1-16)		8.00	4.00	.80
COMMON PLAYER (17-28)		24.00	12.00	2.40

			NRMT	VG-E	GOOD
☐	1	The Babe Ruth Story .... In the Making	35.00	10.00	2.00
☐	2	Bat Boy Becomes .... the Babe	8.00	4.00	.80
☐	3	Claire Hodgson played ..... by Claire Trevor	8.00	4.00	.80
☐	4	Babe Ruth played by .... William Bendix; Claire Hodgson played by Claire Trevor	8.00	4.00	.80
☐	5	Brother Matthias .... played by Charles Bickford	8.00	4.00	.80
☐	6	Phil Conrad played .... by Sam Levene	8.00	4.00	.80
☐	7	Night Club Singer .... played by Gertrude Niesen	8.00	4.00	.80
☐	8	Baseball's Famous Deal ...	8.00	4.00	.80
☐	9	Babe Ruth played by .... William Bendix; Mrs.Babe Ruth played by Claire Trevor	8.00	4.00	.80
☐	10	Actors for Babe Ruth, ... Mrs. Babe Ruth, and Brother Matthias	8.00	4.00	.80
☐	11	Babe Ruth played by .... William Bendix; Miller Huggins played by Fred Lightner	8.00	4.00	.80
☐	12	Babe Ruth played by .... William Bendix; Johnny Sylvester played by George Marshall	8.00	4.00	.80
☐	13	Actors for Mr., Mrs. .... and Johnny Sylvester	8.00	4.00	.80
☐	14	When A Feller Needs .... A Friend	8.00	4.00	.80
☐	15	Dramatic Home Run	8.00	4.00	.80
☐	16	The Homer That Set .... the Record	8.00	4.00	.80
☐	17	The Slap That Started ...... Baseball's Most Famous Career	24.00	12.00	2.40
☐	18	The Babe Plays .... Santa Claus	24.00	12.00	2.40
☐	19	Actors for Ed Barrow, ... Jacob Ruppert, and Miller Huggins	24.00	12.00	2.40
☐	20	Broken Window .... Paid Off	24.00	12.00	2.40
☐	21	Regardless of the Gen-...... eration/ Babe Ruth	24.00	12.00	2.40
☐	22	Charley Grimm and	24.00	12.00	2.40

1934-36 Batter-Up

The 1934-36 Batter-Up set issued by National Chicle contains 192 blank-backed die-cut cards. Numbers 1 to 80 are 2 3/8" by 3 1/4" in size while 81 to 192 are 2 3/8" by 3". The latter are more difficult to find than the former. The pictures come in basic black and white or in tints of blue, brown, green, purple, red, or sepia. There are three combination cards (each featuring two players per card) in the high series (98, 111, and 115). The ACC designation for the set is R318. Cards with backs removed are graded fair at best.

		NRMT	VG-E	GOOD
COMPLETE SET		12000.00	4500.00	900.00
COMMON PLAYER (1-80)		24.00	12.00	2.40
COMMON PLAYER (81-192)		60.00	30.00	6.00

			NRMT	VG-E	GOOD
☐	1	Wally Berger	50.00	15.00	3.00
☐	2	Ed Brandt	24.00	12.00	2.40
☐	3	Al Lopez	50.00	25.00	5.00
☐	4	Dick Bartell	24.00	12.00	2.40
☐	5	Carl Hubbell	75.00	37.50	7.50
☐	6	Bill Terry	75.00	37.50	7.50
☐	7	Pepper Martin	30.00	15.00	3.00
☐	8	Jim Bottomley	50.00	25.00	5.00
☐	9	Tom Bridges	24.00	12.00	2.40
☐	10	Rick Ferrell	50.00	25.00	5.00
☐	11	Ray Benge	24.00	12.00	2.40
☐	12	Wes Ferrell	30.00	15.00	3.00
☐	13	Chalmer Cissell	24.00	12.00	2.40
☐	14	Pie Traynor	60.00	30.00	6.00
☐	15	Leroy Mahaffey	24.00	12.00	2.40
☐	16	Chick Hafey	50.00	25.00	5.00
☐	17	Lloyd Waner	50.00	25.00	5.00
☐	18	Jack Burns	24.00	12.00	2.40
☐	19	Buddy Myer	24.00	12.00	2.40
☐	20	Bob Johnson	27.00	13.50	2.70
☐	21	Arky Vaughan	50.00	25.00	5.00
☐	22	Red Rolfe	27.00	13.50	2.70
☐	23	Lefty Gomez	75.00	37.50	7.50
☐	24	Earl Averill	50.00	25.00	5.00
☐	25	Mickey Cochrane	75.00	37.50	7.50
☐	26	Van Lingle Mungo	24.00	12.00	2.40
☐	27	Mel Ott	90.00	45.00	9.00
☐	28	Jimmy Foxx	100.00	50.00	10.00
☐	29	Jimmy Dykes	27.00	13.50	2.70
☐	30	Bill Dickey	75.00	37.50	7.50

☐ 31	Lefty Grove	90.00	45.00	9.00
☐ 32	Joe Cronin	75.00	37.50	7.50
☐ 33	Frank Frisch	75.00	37.50	7.50
☐ 34	Al Simmons	60.00	30.00	6.00
☐ 35	Rogers Hornsby	100.00	50.00	10.00
☐ 36	Ted Lyons	50.00	25.00	5.00
☐ 37	Rabbit Maranville	50.00	25.00	5.00
☐ 38	Jimmy Wilson	24.00	12.00	2.40
☐ 39	Willie Kamm	24.00	12.00	2.40
☐ 40	Bill Hallahan	24.00	12.00	2.40
☐ 41	Gus Suhr	24.00	12.00	2.40
☐ 42	Charlie Gehringer	60.00	30.00	6.00
☐ 43	Joe Heving	24.00	12.00	2.40
☐ 44	Adam Comorosky	24.00	12.00	2.40
☐ 45	Tony Lazzeri	30.00	15.00	3.00
☐ 46	Sam Leslie	24.00	12.00	2.40
☐ 47	Bob Smith	24.00	12.00	2.40
☐ 48	Willis Hudlin	24.00	12.00	2.40
☐ 49	Carl Reynolds	24.00	12.00	2.40
☐ 50	Fred Schulte	24.00	12.00	2.40
☐ 51	Cookie Lavagetto	24.00	12.00	2.40
☐ 52	Hal Schumacher	24.00	12.00	2.40
☐ 53	Roger Cramer	27.00	13.50	2.70
☐ 54	Sylvester Johnson	24.00	12.00	2.40
☐ 55	Ollie Bejma	24.00	12.00	2.40
☐ 56	Sam Byrd	24.00	12.00	2.40
☐ 57	Hank Greenberg	90.00	45.00	9.00
☐ 58	Bill Knickerbocker	24.00	12.00	2.40
☐ 59	Bill Urbanski	24.00	12.00	2.40
☐ 60	Eddie Morgan	24.00	12.00	2.40
☐ 61	Rabbit McNair	24.00	12.00	2.40
☐ 62	Ben Chapman	24.00	12.00	2.40
☐ 63	Roy Johnson	24.00	12.00	2.40
☐ 64	Dizzy Dean	200.00	100.00	20.00
☐ 65	Zeke Bonura	24.00	12.00	2.40
☐ 66	Fred Marberry	24.00	12.00	2.40
☐ 67	Gus Mancuso	24.00	12.00	2.40
☐ 68	Joe Vosmik	24.00	12.00	2.40
☐ 69	Earl Grace	24.00	12.00	2.40
☐ 70	Tony Piet	24.00	12.00	2.40
☐ 71	Rollie Hemsley	24.00	12.00	2.40
☐ 72	Fred Fitzsimmons	24.00	12.00	2.40
☐ 73	Hack Wilson	75.00	37.50	7.50
☐ 74	Chick Fullis	24.00	12.00	2.40
☐ 75	Fred Frankhouse	24.00	12.00	2.40
☐ 76	Ethan Allen	24.00	12.00	2.40
☐ 77	Heine Manush	50.00	25.00	5.00
☐ 78	Rip Collins	24.00	12.00	2.40
☐ 79	Tony Cuccinello	24.00	12.00	2.40
☐ 80	Joe Kuhel	24.00	12.00	2.40
☐ 81	Tom Bridges	70.00	35.00	7.00
☐ 82	Clint Brown	60.00	30.00	6.00
☐ 83	Albert Blanche	60.00	30.00	6.00
☐ 84	Boze Berger	60.00	30.00	6.00
☐ 85	Goose Goslin	125.00	60.00	12.50
☐ 86	Lefty Gomez	175.00	85.00	18.00
☐ 87	Joe Glenn	60.00	30.00	6.00
☐ 88	Cy Blanton	60.00	30.00	6.00
☐ 89	Tom Carey	60.00	30.00	6.00
☐ 90	Ralph Birkofer	60.00	30.00	6.00
☐ 91	Fred Gabler	60.00	30.00	6.00
☐ 92	Dick Coffman	60.00	30.00	6.00
☐ 93	Ollie Bejma	60.00	30.00	6.00
☐ 94	Leroy Parmelee	60.00	30.00	6.00
☐ 95	Carl Reynolds	60.00	30.00	6.00
☐ 96	Ben Cantwell	60.00	30.00	6.00
☐ 97	Curtis Davis	60.00	30.00	6.00
☐ 98	Webb and Wally Moses	70.00	35.00	7.00
☐ 99	Ray Benge	60.00	30.00	6.00
☐ 100	Pie Traynor	150.00	75.00	15.00
☐ 101	Phil Cavarretta	70.00	35.00	7.00
☐ 102	Pep Young	60.00	30.00	6.00
☐ 103	Willis Hudlin	60.00	30.00	6.00
☐ 104	Mickey Haslin	60.00	30.00	6.00
☐ 105	Oswald Bluege	60.00	30.00	6.00
☐ 106	Paul Andrews	60.00	30.00	6.00
☐ 107	Ed Brandt	60.00	30.00	6.00
☐ 108	Don Taylor	60.00	30.00	6.00
☐ 109	Thornton Lee	60.00	30.00	6.00
☐ 110	Hal Schumacher	60.00	30.00	6.00
☐ 111	Hayes and Ted Lyons	100.00	50.00	10.00
☐ 112	Odell Hale	60.00	30.00	6.00
☐ 113	Earl Averill	125.00	60.00	12.50
☐ 114	Italo Chelini	60.00	30.00	6.00
☐ 115	Andrews and Bottomley	100.00	50.00	10.00
☐ 116	Bill Walker	60.00	30.00	6.00
☐ 117	Bill Dickey	200.00	100.00	20.00
☐ 118	Gerald Walker	60.00	30.00	6.00
☐ 119	Ted Lyons	125.00	60.00	12.50
☐ 120	Eldon Auker	60.00	30.00	6.00
☐ 121	Bill Hallahan	60.00	30.00	6.00
☐ 122	Fred Lindstrom	125.00	60.00	12.50
☐ 123	Oral Hildebrand	60.00	30.00	6.00
☐ 124	Luke Appling	125.00	60.00	12.50
☐ 125	Pepper Martin	80.00	40.00	8.00
☐ 126	Rick Ferrell	125.00	60.00	12.50
☐ 127	Ival Goodman	60.00	30.00	6.00
☐ 128	Joe Kuhel	60.00	30.00	6.00
☐ 129	Ernie Lombardi	125.00	60.00	12.50
☐ 130	Charlie Gehringer	175.00	85.00	18.00
☐ 131	Van Lingle Mungo	60.00	30.00	6.00
☐ 132	Larry French	60.00	30.00	6.00
☐ 133	Buddy Myer	60.00	30.00	6.00
☐ 134	Mel Harder	70.00	35.00	7.00
☐ 135	Augie Galan	60.00	30.00	6.00
☐ 136	Gabby Hartnett	125.00	60.00	12.50
☐ 137	Stan Hack	70.00	35.00	7.00
☐ 138	Billy Herman	125.00	60.00	12.50
☐ 139	Bill Jurges	60.00	30.00	6.00
☐ 140	Bill Lee	60.00	30.00	6.00
☐ 141	Zeke Bonura	60.00	30.00	6.00
☐ 142	Tony Piet	60.00	30.00	6.00
☐ 143	Paul Dean	80.00	40.00	8.00
☐ 144	Jimmy Foxx	225.00	110.00	22.00
☐ 145	Joe Medwick	150.00	75.00	15.00
☐ 146	Rip Collins	60.00	30.00	6.00
☐ 147	Mel Almada	60.00	30.00	6.00
☐ 148	Allan Cooke	60.00	30.00	6.00
☐ 149	Moe Berg	70.00	35.00	7.00
☐ 150	Dolph Camilli	60.00	30.00	6.00
☐ 151	Oscar Melillo	60.00	30.00	6.00
☐ 152	Bruce Campbell	60.00	30.00	6.00
☐ 153	Lefty Grove	200.00	100.00	20.00
☐ 154	Johnny Murphy	70.00	35.00	7.00
☐ 155	Luke Sewell	70.00	35.00	7.00
☐ 156	Leo Durocher	125.00	60.00	12.50
☐ 157	Lloyd Waner	125.00	60.00	12.50
☐ 158	Gus Bush	60.00	30.00	6.00
☐ 159	Jimmy Dykes	70.00	35.00	7.00
☐ 160	Steve O'Neill	60.00	30.00	6.00
☐ 161	General Crowder	60.00	30.00	6.00
☐ 162	Joe Cascarella	60.00	30.00	6.00
☐ 163	Daniel (Bud) Hafey	60.00	30.00	6.00
☐ 164	Gilly Campbell	60.00	30.00	6.00
☐ 165	Ray Hayworth	60.00	30.00	6.00
☐ 166	Frank Demaree	60.00	30.00	6.00
☐ 167	John Babich	60.00	30.00	6.00
☐ 168	Marvin Owen	60.00	30.00	6.00
☐ 169	Ralph Kress	60.00	30.00	6.00
☐ 170	Mule Haas	60.00	30.00	6.00
☐ 171	Frank Higgins	60.00	30.00	6.00
☐ 172	Wally Berger	60.00	30.00	6.00
☐ 173	Frank Frisch	150.00	75.00	15.00
☐ 174	Wes Ferrell	80.00	40.00	8.00
☐ 175	Pete Fox	60.00	30.00	6.00
☐ 176	John Vergez	60.00	30.00	6.00
☐ 177	Billy Rogell	60.00	30.00	6.00
☐ 178	Don Brennan	60.00	30.00	6.00
☐ 179	Jim Bottomley	125.00	60.00	12.50
☐ 180	Travis Jackson	125.00	60.00	12.50
☐ 181	Red Rolfe	90.00	45.00	9.00
☐ 182	Frank Crosetti	90.00	45.00	9.00
☐ 183	Joe Cronin	125.00	60.00	12.50
☐ 184	Schoolboy Rowe	70.00	35.00	7.00
☐ 185	Chuck Klein	125.00	60.00	12.50
☐ 186	Lon Warneke	60.00	30.00	6.00
☐ 187	Gus Suhr	60.00	30.00	6.00
☐ 188	Ben Chapman	60.00	30.00	6.00
☐ 189	Clint Brown	60.00	30.00	6.00
☐ 190	Paul Derringer	70.00	35.00	7.00
☐ 191	John Burns	60.00	30.00	6.00
☐ 192	John Broaca	80.00	30.00	6.00

1959 Bazooka

The 23 full color, unnumbered cards comprising the 1959 Bazooka set were cut from the bottom of the boxes of gum marketed nationally that year by Topps. Bazooka was the brand name which Topps had been using to sell its one cent bubblegum; this year Topps decided to distribute 25 pieces of Bazooka gum in a box. The cards themselves measure 2 13/16" by 4 15/16". Only nine cards were originally issued; 14 more were added to the set at a later date (these are marked with SP in the checklist). The latter are less plentiful and hence more valuable than the original nine. All the cards are blank backed, and the ACC designation is R414-15. The prices below are for the cards cut from the box; complete boxes intact would be worth about 50% more.

		NRMT	VG-E	GOOD
☐ 3	Wally Moon	8.00	4.00	.80
☐ 4	Hank Aaron	60.00	30.00	6.00
☐ 5	Milt Pappas	8.00	4.00	.80
☐ 6	Dick Stuart	8.00	4.00	.80
☐ 7	Bob Clemente	50.00	25.00	5.00
☐ 8	Yogi Berra	45.00	22.50	4.50
☐ 9	Ken Boyer	10.00	5.00	1.00
☐ 10	Orlando Cepeda	12.00	6.00	1.20
☐ 11	Gus Triandos	8.00	4.00	.80
☐ 12	Frank Malzone	8.00	4.00	.80
☐ 13	Willie Mays	60.00	30.00	6.00
☐ 14	Camilo Pascual	8.00	4.00	.80
☐ 15	Bob Cerv	8.00	4.00	.80
☐ 16	Vic Power	8.00	4.00	.80
☐ 17	Larry Sherry	8.00	4.00	.80
☐ 18	Al Kaline	35.00	17.50	3.50
☐ 19	Warren Spahn	30.00	15.00	3.00
☐ 20	Harmon Killebrew	30.00	15.00	3.00
☐ 21	Jackie Jensen	10.00	5.00	1.00
☐ 22	Luis Aparicio	20.00	10.00	2.00
☐ 23	Gil Hodges	24.00	12.00	2.40
☐ 24	Richie Ashburn	15.00	7.50	1.50
☐ 25	Nellie Fox	15.00	7.50	1.50
☐ 26	Robin Roberts	24.00	12.00	2.40
☐ 27	Joe Cunningham	8.00	4.00	.80
☐ 28	Early Wynn	20.00	10.00	2.00
☐ 29	Frank Robinson	30.00	15.00	3.00
☐ 30	Rocky Colavito	10.00	5.00	1.00
☐ 31	Mickey Mantle	150.00	75.00	15.00
☐ 32	Glen Hobbie	8.00	4.00	.80
☐ 33	Roy McMillan	8.00	4.00	.80
☐ 34	Harvey Kuenn	10.00	5.00	1.00
☐ 35	Johnny Antonelli	8.00	4.00	.80
☐ 36	Del Crandall	8.00	4.00	.80

1961 Bazooka

The 36 card set issued by Bazooka in 1961 follows the format established in 1960; three full color, numbered cards to each panel found on a Bazooka gum box. The individual cards measure 1 13/16" by 2 3/4" whereas the panels measure 2 3/4" by 5 1/2". The cards of 1960 and 1961 are similar in design but are easily distinguished from one another by their numbers. Complete panels of three would have a value of 30% more than the sum of the individual cards (prices) on the panel and complete boxes would command a premium of another 30% above those prices.

		NRMT	VG-E	GOOD
COMPLETE INDIV. SET		550.00	275.00	55.00
COMMON PLAYER		8.00	4.00	.80
☐ 1	Art Mahaffey	8.00	4.00	.80
☐ 2	Mickey Mantle	150.00	75.00	15.00
☐ 3	Ron Santo	10.00	5.00	1.00
☐ 4	Bud Daley	8.00	4.00	.80
☐ 5	Roger Maris	50.00	25.00	5.00
☐ 6	Eddie Yost	8.00	4.00	.80
☐ 7	Minnie Minoso	10.00	5.00	1.00
☐ 8	Dick Groat	9.00	4.50	.90
☐ 9	Frank Malzone	8.00	4.00	.80
☐ 10	Dick Donovan	8.00	4.00	.80
☐ 11	Ed Mathews	30.00	15.00	3.00
☐ 12	Jim Lemon	8.00	4.00	.80
☐ 13	Chuck Estrada	8.00	4.00	.80
☐ 14	Ken Boyer	10.00	5.00	1.00
☐ 15	Harvey Kuenn	9.00	4.50	.90
☐ 16	Ernie Broglio	8.00	4.00	.80
☐ 17	Rocky Colavito	10.00	5.00	1.00
☐ 18	Ted Kluszewski	10.00	5.00	1.00
☐ 19	Ernie Banks	35.00	17.50	3.50
☐ 20	Al Kaline	35.00	17.50	3.50
☐ 21	Ed Bailey	8.00	4.00	.80
☐ 22	Jim Perry	9.00	4.50	.90
☐ 23	Willie Mays	60.00	30.00	6.00
☐ 24	Bill Mazeroski	10.00	5.00	1.00
☐ 25	Gus Triandos	8.00	4.00	.80
☐ 26	Don Drysdale	24.00	12.00	2.40
☐ 27	Frank Herrera	8.00	4.00	.80
☐ 28	Earl Battey	8.00	4.00	.80
☐ 29	Warren Spahn	30.00	15.00	3.00
☐ 30	Gene Woodling	8.00	4.00	.80
☐ 31	Frank Robinson	30.00	15.00	3.00
☐ 32	Pete Runnels	8.00	4.00	.80

HANK AARON
OUTFIELD MILWAUKEE BRAVES

		NRMT	VG-E	GOOD
COMPLETE SET		3000.00	1200.00	250.00
COMMON PLAYER		35.00	17.50	3.50
COMMON PLAYER SP		125.00	60.00	12.50
☐ 1	Hank Aaron	250.00	125.00	25.00
☐ 2	Richie Ashburn SP	175.00	85.00	18.00
☐ 3	Ernie Banks SP	250.00	125.00	25.00
☐ 4	Ken Boyer SP	150.00	75.00	15.00
☐ 5	Orlando Cepeda	45.00	22.50	4.50
☐ 6	Bob Cerv SP	125.00	60.00	12.50
☐ 7	Rocco Colavito SP	150.00	75.00	15.00
☐ 8	Del Crandall	35.00	17.50	3.50
☐ 9	Jim Davenport	35.00	17.50	3.50
☐ 10	Don Drysdale SP	200.00	100.00	20.00
☐ 11	Nellie Fox SP	175.00	85.00	18.00
☐ 12	Jackie Jensen SP	150.00	75.00	15.00
☐ 13	Harvey Kuenn SP	150.00	75.00	15.00
☐ 14	Mickey Mantle	600.00	300.00	60.00
☐ 15	Willie Mays	250.00	125.00	25.00
☐ 16	Bill Mazeroski	45.00	22.50	4.50
☐ 17	Roy McMillan	35.00	17.50	3.50
☐ 18	Billy Pierce SP	125.00	60.00	12.50
☐ 19	Roy Sievers SP	125.00	60.00	12.50
☐ 20	Duke Snider SP	300.00	150.00	30.00
☐ 21	Gus Triandos SP	125.00	60.00	12.50
☐ 22	Bob Turley	35.00	17.50	3.50
☐ 23	Vic Wertz SP	125.00	60.00	12.50

1960 Bazooka

In 1960 Topps introduced a 36 card baseball player set in three card panels on the bottom of Bazooka gum boxes. The cards measure 1 13/16"" by 2 3/4" and the panels measure 2 3/4" by 5 1/2". The cards carried full color pictures and were numbered at the bottom underneath the team position. The checklist below contains prices for individual cards. Complete panels of three would have a value of 30% more than the sum of the individual cards (prices) on the panel and complete boxes would command a premium of another 30% above those prices.

		NRMT	VG-E	GOOD
COMPLETE INDIV.SET		600.00	300.00	60.00
COMMON PLAYER		8.00	4.00	.80
☐ 1	Ernie Banks	35.00	17.50	3.50
☐ 2	Bud Daley	8.00	4.00	.80

		NRMT	VG-E	GOOD
☐ 33	Woodie Held	8.00	4.00	.80
☐ 34	Norm Larker	8.00	4.00	.80
☐ 35	Luis Aparicio	20.00	10.00	2.00
☐ 36	Bill Tuttle	8.00	4.00	.80

1962 Bazooka

The 1962 Bazooka set of 45 full color, blank backed, unnumbered cards was issued in panels of three on Bazooka bubble gum boxes. The individual cards measure 1 13/16" by 2 3/4" whereas the panels measure 2 3/4" by 5 1/2". The cards below are numbered by panel alphabetically based on the last name of the player pictured on the far left card of the panel. The cards with SP in the checklist below are more difficult to obtain than other cards in the set as they were printed in shorter supply. Complete panels of three would have a value of 30% more than the sum of the individual cards (prices) on the panel and complete boxes would command a premium of another 30% above those prices.

		NRMT	VG-E	GOOD
COMPLETE INDIV. SET		1100.00	450.00	90.00
COMMON PLAYER		8.00	4.00	.80
☐ 1	Bob Allison SP	25.00	12.50	2.50
☐ 2	Ed Mathews SP	150.00	75.00	15.00
☐ 3	Vada Pinson SP	25.00	12.50	2.50
☐ 4	Earl Battey	8.00	4.00	.80
☐ 5	Warren Spahn	30.00	15.00	3.00
☐ 6	Lee Thomas	8.00	4.00	.80
☐ 7	Orlando Cepeda	10.00	5.00	1.00
☐ 8	Woodie Held	8.00	4.00	.80
☐ 9	Bob Aspromonte	8.00	4.00	.80
☐ 10	Dick Howser	10.00	5.00	1.00
☐ 11	Bob Clemente	50.00	25.00	5.00
☐ 12	Al Kaline	35.00	17.50	3.50
☐ 13	Joe Jay	8.00	4.00	.80
☐ 14	Roger Maris	50.00	25.00	5.00
☐ 15	Frank Howard	10.00	5.00	1.00
☐ 16	Sandy Koufax	45.00	22.50	4.50
☐ 17	Jim Gentile	8.00	4.00	.80
☐ 18	Johnny Callison	8.00	4.00	.80
☐ 19	Jim Landis	8.00	4.00	.80
☐ 20	Ken Boyer	10.00	5.00	1.00
☐ 21	Chuck Schilling	8.00	4.00	.80
☐ 22	Art Mahaffey	8.00	4.00	.80
☐ 23	Mickey Mantle	150.00	75.00	15.00
☐ 24	Dick Stuart	8.00	4.00	.80
☐ 25	Ken McBride	8.00	4.00	.80
☐ 26	Frank Robinson	30.00	15.00	3.00
☐ 27	Gil Hodges	24.00	12.00	2.40
☐ 28	Milt Pappas	8.00	4.00	.80
☐ 29	Hank Aaron	60.00	30.00	6.00
☐ 30	Luis Aparicio	20.00	10.00	2.00
☐ 31	Johnny Romano SP	25.00	12.50	2.50
☐ 32	Ernie Banks SP	175.00	85.00	18.00
☐ 33	Norm Siebern SP	25.00	12.50	2.50
☐ 34	Ron Santo	10.00	5.00	1.00
☐ 35	Norm Cash	10.00	5.00	1.00
☐ 36	Jim Piersall	10.00	5.00	1.00
☐ 37	Don Schwall	8.00	4.00	.80
☐ 38	Willie Mays	60.00	30.00	6.00
☐ 39	Norm Larker	8.00	4.00	.80
☐ 40	Bill White	9.00	4.50	.90
☐ 41	Whitey Ford	30.00	15.00	3.00
☐ 42	Rocky Colavito	10.00	5.00	1.00
☐ 43	Don Zimmer SP	25.00	12.50	2.50
☐ 44	Harmon Killebrew SP	150.00	75.00	15.00
☐ 45	Gene Woodling SP	25.00	12.50	2.50

1963 Bazooka

The 1963 Bazooka set of 36 full color, blank backed, numbered cards was issued on Bazooka bubble gum boxes. This year marked a change in format from previous Bazooka issues with a smaller sized card being issued. The individual cards measure 1 9/16" by 2 1/2" whereas the panels measure 2 1/2" by 4 11/16". The card features a white strip with the player's name printed in red and the team position printed in black on the card. The number appears in the white border at the bottom of the card. Three cards were issued per panel. Complete panels of three would have a value of 10% more than the sum of the individual cards (prices) on the panel and complete boxes would command a premium of another 30% above those prices.

		NRMT	VG-E	GOOD
COMPLETE INDIV.SET		500.00	250.00	50.00
COMMON PLAYER		5.00	2.50	.50
☐ 1	Mickey Mantle	100.00	50.00	10.00
☐ 2	Bob Rodgers	5.00	2.50	.50
☐ 3	Ernie Banks	27.00	13.50	2.70
☐ 4	Norm Siebern	5.00	2.50	.50
☐ 5	Warren Spahn	24.00	12.00	2.40
☐ 6	Bill Mazeroski	7.00	3.50	.70
☐ 7	Harmon Killebrew	24.00	12.00	2.40
☐ 8	Dick Farrell	5.00	2.50	.50
☐ 9	Hank Aaron	45.00	22.50	4.50
☐ 10	Dick Donovan	5.00	2.50	.50
☐ 11	Jim Gentile	5.00	2.50	.50
☐ 12	Willie Mays	45.00	22.50	4.50
☐ 13	Camilo Pascual	5.00	2.50	.50
☐ 14	Bob Clemente	35.00	17.50	3.50
☐ 15	Johnny Callison	5.00	2.50	.50
☐ 16	Carl Yastrzemski	60.00	30.00	6.00
☐ 17	Don Drysdale	24.00	12.00	2.40
☐ 18	Johnny Romano	5.00	2.50	.50
☐ 19	Al Jackson	5.00	2.50	.50
☐ 20	Ralph Terry	5.00	2.50	.50
☐ 21	Bill Monbouquette	5.00	2.50	.50
☐ 22	Orlando Cepeda	7.00	3.50	.70
☐ 23	Stan Musial	35.00	17.50	3.50
☐ 24	Floyd Robinson	5.00	2.50	.50
☐ 25	Chuck Hinton	5.00	2.50	.50
☐ 26	Bob Purkey	5.00	2.50	.50
☐ 27	Ken Hubbs	6.00	3.00	.60
☐ 28	Bill White	6.00	3.00	.60
☐ 29	Ray Herbert	5.00	2.50	.50
☐ 30	Brooks Robinson	30.00	15.00	3.00
☐ 31	Frank Robinson	24.00	12.00	2.40
☐ 32	Lee Thomas	5.00	2.50	.50
☐ 33	Rocky Colavito	7.00	3.50	.70
☐ 34	Al Kaline	30.00	15.00	3.00
☐ 35	Art Mahaffey	5.00	2.50	.50
☐ 36	Tommy Davis	6.00	3.00	.60

1963 Bazooka ATG

The 1963 Bazooka All Time Greats set contains 41 black and white numbered cards issued as inserts in boxes of Bazooka Bubble gum. The cards feature bust shots with gold trim and measure 1 9/16" by 2 1/2". The backs are yellow with black print containing vital information and a biography of the player. Many of the players are pictured not as they looked during their playing careers but as they looked many years after their playing days were through. The cards also exist in a scarcer variety with silver trim instead of gold; the silver trim variety cards are worth approximately double the prices listed below. Cards are numbered on the back.

		NRMT	VG-E	GOOD
	COMPLETE SET	200.00	100.00	20.00
	COMMON PLAYER	3.00	1.50	.30
☐ 1	Joe Tinker	3.00	1.50	.30
☐ 2	Harry Heilmann	3.00	1.50	.30
☐ 3	Jack Chesbro	3.00	1.50	.30
☐ 4	Christy Mathewson	8.00	4.00	.80
☐ 5	Herb Pennock	3.00	1.50	.30
☐ 6	Cy Young	5.00	2.50	.50
☐ 7	Ed Walsh	3.00	1.50	.30
☐ 8	Nap Lajoie	4.50	2.25	.45
☐ 9	Eddie Plank	3.00	1.50	.30
☐ 10	Honus Wagner	8.00	4.00	.80
☐ 11	Chief Bender	3.00	1.50	.30
☐ 12	Walter Johnson	8.00	4.00	.80
☐ 13	Mordecai Brown	3.00	1.50	.30
☐ 14	Rabbit Maranville	3.00	1.50	.30
☐ 15	Lou Gehrig	20.00	10.00	2.00
☐ 16	Ban Johnson	3.00	1.50	.30
☐ 17	Babe Ruth	30.00	15.00	3.00
☐ 18	Connie Mack	3.50	1.75	.35
☐ 19	Hank Greenberg	3.50	1.75	.35
☐ 20	John McGraw	3.50	1.75	.35
☐ 21	Al Simmons	3.00	1.50	.30
☐ 23	Jimmy Collins	3.00	1.50	.30
☐ 24	Tris Speaker	4.00	2.00	.40
☐ 25	Frank Chance	3.00	1.50	.30
☐ 26	Fred Clarke	3.00	1.50	.30
☐ 27	Wilbert Robinson	3.00	1.50	.30
☐ 28	Dazzy Vance	3.00	1.50	.30
☐ 29	Pete Alexander	3.50	1.75	.35
☐ 30	Judge Landis	3.00	1.50	.30
☐ 31	Willie Keeler	3.00	1.50	.30
☐ 32	Rogers Hornsby	5.00	2.50	.50
☐ 33	Hugh Duffy	3.00	1.50	.30
☐ 34	Mickey Cochrane	3.50	1.75	.35
☐ 35	Ty Cobb	20.00	10.00	2.00
☐ 36	Mel Ott	4.50	2.25	.45
☐ 37	Clark Griffith	3.00	1.50	.30
☐ 38	Ted Lyons	3.00	1.50	.30
☐ 39	Cap Anson	3.00	1.50	.30
☐ 40	Bill Dickey	3.50	1.75	.35
☐ 41	Eddie Collins	3.00	1.50	.30

1964 Bazooka

The 1964 Bazooka set of 36 full color, blank backed, numbered cards were issued in panels of three on the backs of Bazooka bubble gum boxes. The individual cards measure 1 9/16" by 2 1/2" whereas the panels measure 2 1/2" by 4 11/16". Many players from the 1963 set have the same numbers; however the pictures are different. Complete panels of three would have a value of 10% more than the sum of the individual cards (prices) on the panel and complete boxes would command a premium of another 30% above those prices.

		NRMT	VG-E	GOOD
	COMPLETE INDIV. SET	400.00	200.00	40.00
	COMMON PLAYER	5.00	2.50	.50
☐ 1	Mickey Mantle	100.00	50.00	10.00
☐ 2	Dick Groat	6.00	3.00	.60
☐ 3	Steve Barber	5.00	2.50	.50
☐ 4	Ken McBride	5.00	2.50	.50
☐ 5	Warren Spahn	20.00	10.00	2.00
☐ 6	Bob Friend	5.00	2.50	.50
☐ 7	Harmon Killebrew	20.00	10.00	2.00
☐ 8	Dick Farrell	5.00	2.50	.50
☐ 9	Hank Aaron	45.00	22.50	4.50
☐ 10	Rich Rollins	5.00	2.50	.50
☐ 11	Jim Gentile	5.00	2.50	.50
☐ 12	Willie Mays	45.00	22.50	4.50
☐ 13	Camilo Pascual	5.00	2.50	.50
☐ 14	Bob Clemente	35.00	17.50	3.50
☐ 15	Johnny Callison	5.00	2.50	.50
☐ 16	Carl Yastrzemski	45.00	22.50	4.50
☐ 17	Billy Williams	16.00	8.00	1.60

		NRMT	VG-E	GOOD
☐ 18	Johnny Romano	5.00	2.50	.50
☐ 19	Jim Maloney	5.00	2.50	.50
☐ 20	Norm Cash	6.00	3.00	.60
☐ 21	Willie McCovey	20.00	10.00	2.00
☐ 22	Jim Fregosi	6.00	3.00	.60
☐ 23	George Altman	5.00	2.50	.50
☐ 24	Floyd Robinson	5.00	2.50	.50
☐ 25	Chuck Hinton	5.00	2.50	.50
☐ 26	Ron Hunt	5.00	2.50	.50
☐ 27	Gary Peters	5.00	2.50	.50
☐ 28	Dick Ellsworth	5.00	2.50	.50
☐ 29	Elston Howard	7.00	3.50	.70
☐ 30	Brooks Robinson	27.00	13.50	2.70
☐ 31	Frank Robinson	20.00	10.00	2.00
☐ 32	Sandy Koufax	35.00	17.50	3.50
☐ 33	Rocky Colavito	7.00	3.50	.70
☐ 34	Al Kaline	27.00	13.50	2.70
☐ 35	Ken Boyer	6.00	3.00	.60
☐ 36	Tommy Davis	6.00	3.00	.60

1965 Bazooka

The 1965 Bazooka set of 36 full color, blank backed, numbered cards was issued in panels of three on the backs of Bazooka bubble gum boxes. The individual cards measure 1 9/16" by 2 1/2" whereas the panels measure 2 1/2" by 4 11/16". As in the previous two years some of the players have the same numbers on their cards; however all pictures are different from the previous two years. Complete panels of three would have a value of 10% more than the sum of the individual cards (prices) on the panel and complete boxes would command a premium of another 30% above those prices.

		NRMT	VG-E	GOOD
	COMPLETE INDIV. SET	350.00	175.00	35.00
	COMMON PLAYER	5.00	2.50	.50
☐ 1	Mickey Mantle	100.00	50.00	10.00
☐ 2	Larry Jackson	5.00	2.50	.50
☐ 3	Chuck Hinton	5.00	2.50	.50
☐ 4	Tony Oliva	7.00	3.50	.70
☐ 5	Dean Chance	5.00	2.50	.50
☐ 6	Jim O'Toole	5.00	2.50	.50
☐ 7	Harmon Killebrew	20.00	10.00	2.00
☐ 8	Pete Ward	5.00	2.50	.50
☐ 9	Hank Aaron	45.00	22.50	4.50
☐ 10	Dick Radatz	5.00	2.50	.50
☐ 11	Boog Powell	7.00	3.50	.70
☐ 12	Willie Mays	45.00	22.50	4.50
☐ 13	Bob Veale	5.00	2.50	.50
☐ 14	Bob Clemente	35.00	17.50	3.50
☐ 15	Johnny Callison	5.00	2.50	.50
☐ 16	Joe Torre	7.00	3.50	.70
☐ 17	Billy Williams	15.00	7.50	1.50
☐ 18	Bob Chance	5.00	2.50	.50
☐ 19	Bob Aspromonte	5.00	2.50	.50
☐ 20	Joe Christopher	5.00	2.50	.50
☐ 21	Jim Bunning	10.00	5.00	1.00
☐ 22	Jim Fregosi	6.00	3.00	.60
☐ 23	Bob Gibson	20.00	10.00	2.00
☐ 24	Juan Marichal	20.00	10.00	2.00
☐ 25	Dave Wickersham	5.00	2.50	.50
☐ 26	Ron Hunt	5.00	2.50	.50
☐ 27	Gary Peters	5.00	2.50	.50
☐ 28	Ron Santo	7.00	3.50	.70
☐ 29	Elston Howard	7.00	3.50	.70
☐ 30	Brooks Robinson	25.00	12.50	2.50
☐ 31	Frank Robinson	20.00	10.00	2.00
☐ 32	Sandy Koufax	35.00	17.50	3.50
☐ 33	Rocky Colavito	7.00	3.50	.70
☐ 34	Al Kaline	25.00	12.50	2.50
☐ 35	Ken Boyer	7.00	3.50	.70
☐ 36	Tommy Davis	6.00	3.00	.60

PICTURE GALLERY: Any set in this Price Guide not illustrated below its respective set title is pictured in the Picture Gallery section in the back of the book.

1966 Bazooka

The 1966 Bazooka set of 48 full color, blank backed, numbered cards was issued in panels of three on the backs of Bazooka bubble gum boxes. The individual cards measure 1 9/16" by 2 1/2" whereas the complete panels measure 2 1/2" by 4 11/16". The set is distinguishable from the previous years by mention of "48 card set" at the bottom of the card. Complete panels of three would have a value of 10% more than the sum of the individual cards (prices) on the panel and complete boxes would command a premium of another 30% above those prices.

		NRMT	VG-E	GOOD
COMPLETE INDIV. SET		450.00	225.00	45.00
COMMON PLAYER		5.00	2.50	.50
☐ 1	Sandy Koufax	35.00	17.50	3.50
☐ 2	Willie Horton	5.00	2.50	.50
☐ 3	Frank Howard	6.00	3.00	.60
☐ 4	Richie Allen	7.00	3.50	.70
☐ 5	Mel Stottlemyre	6.00	3.00	.60
☐ 6	Tony Conigliaro	6.00	3.00	.60
☐ 7	Mickey Mantle	100.00	50.00	10.00
☐ 8	Leon Wagner	5.00	2.50	.50
☐ 9	Ed Kranepool	5.00	2.50	.50
☐ 10	Juan Marichal	20.00	10.00	2.00
☐ 11	Harmon Killebrew	20.00	10.00	2.00
☐ 12	Johnny Callison	5.00	2.50	.50
☐ 13	Roy McMillan	5.00	2.50	.50
☐ 14	Willie McCovey	20.00	10.00	2.00
☐ 15	Rocky Colavito	7.00	3.50	.70
☐ 16	Willie Mays	45.00	22.50	4.50
☐ 17	Sam McDowell	5.00	2.50	.50
☐ 18	Vern Law	5.00	2.50	.50
☐ 19	Jim Fregosi	6.00	3.00	.60
☐ 20	Ron Fairly	5.00	2.50	.50
☐ 21	Bob Gibson	20.00	10.00	2.00
☐ 22	Carl Yastrzemski	45.00	22.50	4.50
☐ 23	Bill White	6.00	3.00	.60
☐ 24	Bob Aspromonte	5.00	2.50	.50
☐ 25	Dean Chance	5.00	2.50	.50
☐ 26	Bob Clemente	35.00	17.50	3.50
☐ 27	Tony Cloninger	5.00	2.50	.50
☐ 28	Curt Blefary	5.00	2.50	.50
☐ 29	Milt Pappas	5.00	2.50	.50
☐ 30	Hank Aaron	45.00	22.50	4.50
☐ 31	Jim Bunning	10.00	5.00	1.00
☐ 32	Frank Robinson	20.00	10.00	2.00
☐ 33	Bill Skowron	6.00	3.00	.60
☐ 34	Brooks Robinson	25.00	12.50	2.50
☐ 35	Jim Wynn	5.00	2.50	.50
☐ 36	Joe Torre	7.00	3.50	.70
☐ 37	Jim Grant	5.00	2.50	.50
☐ 38	Pete Rose	75.00	37.50	7.50
☐ 39	Ron Santo	7.00	3.50	.70
☐ 40	Tom Tresh	6.00	3.00	.60
☐ 41	Tony Oliva	7.00	3.50	.70
☐ 42	Don Drysdale	16.00	8.00	1.60
☐ 43	Pete Richert	5.00	2.50	.50
☐ 44	Bert Campaneris	6.00	3.00	.60
☐ 45	Jim Maloney	5.00	2.50	.50
☐ 46	Al Kaline	25.00	12.50	2.50
☐ 47	Eddie Fisher	5.00	2.50	.50
☐ 48	Billy Williams	15.00	7.50	1.50

1967 Bazooka

The 1967 Bazooka set of 48 full color, blank backed, numbered cards was issued in panels of three on the backs of Bazooka bubble gum boxes. The individual cards measure 1 9/16" by 2 1/2" whereas the complete panels measure 2 1/2" by 4 11/16". This set is virtually identical to the 1966 set with the exception of ten new cards as replacements for ten 1966 cards. The remaining 38 cards are identical in both pose and number. The replacement cards are listed in the checklist below with an asterisk. Complete panels of three would have a value of 10%

more than the sum of the individual cards (prices) on the panel and complete boxes would command a premium of another 30% above those prices.

		NRMT	VG-E	GOOD
COMPLETE INDIV. SET		450.00	225.00	45.00
COMMON PLAYER		5.00	2.50	.50
☐ 1	Rick Reichardt *	5.00	2.50	.50
☐ 2	Tommy Agee *	5.00	2.50	.50
☐ 3	Frank Howard *	6.00	3.00	.60
☐ 4	Richie Allen	6.00	3.00	.60
☐ 5	Mel Stottlemyre	6.00	3.00	.60
☐ 6	Tony Conigliaro	6.00	3.00	.60
☐ 7	Mickey Mantle	100.00	50.00	10.00
☐ 8	Leon Wagner	5.00	2.50	.50
☐ 9	Gary Peters *	5.00	2.50	.50
☐ 10	Juan Marichal	16.00	8.00	1.60
☐ 11	Harmon Killebrew	16.00	8.00	1.60
☐ 12	Johnny Callison	5.00	2.50	.50
☐ 13	Denny McLain *	6.00	3.00	.60
☐ 14	Willie McCovey	16.00	8.00	1.60
☐ 15	Rocky Colavito	6.00	3.00	.60
☐ 16	Willie Mays	40.00	20.00	4.00
☐ 17	Sam McDowell	5.00	2.50	.50
☐ 18	Jim Kaat *	8.00	4.00	.80
☐ 19	Jim Fregosi	6.00	3.00	.60
☐ 20	Ron Fairly	5.00	2.50	.50
☐ 21	Bob Gibson	16.00	8.00	1.60
☐ 22	Carl Yastrzemski	40.00	20.00	4.00
☐ 23	Bill White	6.00	3.00	.60
☐ 24	Bob Aspromonte	5.00	2.50	.50
☐ 25	Dean Chance	5.00	2.50	.50
☐ 26	Bob Clemente	30.00	15.00	3.00
☐ 27	Tony Cloninger	5.00	2.50	.50
☐ 28	Curt Blefary	5.00	2.50	.50
☐ 29	Phil Regan *	5.00	2.50	.50
☐ 30	Hank Aaron	40.00	20.00	4.00
☐ 31	Jim Bunning	9.00	4.50	.90
☐ 32	Frank Robinson	16.00	8.00	1.60
☐ 33	Ken Boyer *	6.00	3.00	.60
☐ 34	Brooks Robinson	21.00	10.50	2.10
☐ 35	Jim Wynn	5.00	2.50	.50
☐ 36	Joe Torre	6.00	3.00	.60
☐ 37	Tommy Davis *	5.00	2.50	.50
☐ 38	Pete Rose	75.00	37.50	7.50
☐ 39	Ron Santo	7.00	3.50	.70
☐ 40	Tom Tresh	6.00	3.00	.60
☐ 41	Tony Oliva	7.00	3.50	.70
☐ 42	Don Drysdale	16.00	8.00	1.60
☐ 43	Pete Richert	5.00	2.50	.50
☐ 44	Bert Campaneris	6.00	3.00	.60
☐ 45	Jim Maloney	5.00	2.50	.50
☐ 46	Al Kaline	21.00	10.50	2.10
☐ 47	Matty Alou *	5.00	2.50	.50
☐ 48	Billy Williams	15.00	7.50	1.50

1968 Bazooka

The 1968 Bazooka Tipps from the Topps is a set of 15 numbered boxes (measuring 5 1/2" by 6 1/4" when detached), each containing on the back panel (measuring 3" by 6 1/4") a baseball playing tip from a star, and on the side panels four mini cards, two per side, in full color, measuring 1 1/4" by 3 1/8". Although the set contains a total of 60 of these small cards, 4 are repeated; therefore there are only 56 different small cards. Some collectors cut the panels into individual cards; however most collectors retain entire panels or boxes. The prices in the checklist below therefore reflect only the values of the complete boxes.

		NRMT	VG-E	GOOD
COMPLETE BOX SET		1250.00	600.00	120.00
COMMON BOX		60.00	30.00	6.00
COMMON INDIV. PLAYER		3.00	1.50	.30
☐ 1	Maury Wills: Bunting Al Kaline/P.Casanova Clete Boyer/Tom Seaver	75.00	37.50	7.50
☐ 2	C.Yastrzemski: Batting Jim Hunter/B.Freehan Matty Alou/J.Lefebvre	150.00	75.00	15.00
☐ 3	B.Campaneris: Stealing	60.00	30.00	6.00

T.McCarver/Bob Veale
Frank Robinson/Knoop
☐ 4 Maury Wills: Sliding 60.00 30.00 6.00
Ken Holtzman/J.Azcue
T.Conigliaro/B.White
☐ 5 J.Javier: Double Play 75.00 37.50 7.50
J.Marichal/Petrocelli
J.Pepitone/Hank Aaron
☐ 6 O.Cepeda: 1st Base 150.00 75.00 15.00
R.Santo/Don Drysdale
Pete Rose/Tommy Agee
☐ 7 B.Mazeroski: 2nd Base 60.00 30.00 6.00
J.Roseboro/Jim Bunning
Frank Howard/G.Scott
☐ 8 B.Robinson: 3rd Base 75.00 37.50 7.50
T.Gonzalez/J.McGlothlin
W.Horton/H.Killebrew
☐ 9 Jim Fregosi: Shortstop 60.00 30.00 6.00
Max Alvis/Bob Gibson
Tony Oliva/V.Pinson
☐ 10 Joe Torre: Catching 60.00 30.00 6.00
Dean Chance/F.Jenkins
T.Davis/Rick Monday
☐ 11 Jim Lonborg: Pitching 200.00 100.00 20.00
Joel Horlen/Jim Wynn
C.Flood/Mickey Mantle
☐ 12 Mike McCormick: 75.00 37.50 7.50
Fielding Pitcher
D.Mincher/Tony Perez
R.Clemente/Al Downing
☐ 13 F.Crosetti: Coaching 60.00 30.00 6.00
Rod Carew/Don Wilson
R.Swoboda/W.McCovey
☐ 14 Willie Mays: Outfield 100.00 50.00 10.00
R.Allen/Gary Peters
B.Williams/R.Staub
☐ 15 L.Brock: Base Running 200.00 100.00 20.00
Tommy Agee/Pete Rose
R.Santo/Don Drysdale

1969-70 Bazooka

The 1969-1970 Bazooka Baseball Extra News set contains 12 complete panels, each comprising a large action shot of a significant event in baseball history and four small cards, comparable to those in the Tipps from the Topps set of 1968, of Hall of Fame baseball players. Although some collectors cut the panels into individual cards (measuring 3" by 6 1/4" or 1 1/4" by 3 1/8"), most collectors retain the entire panel, or box (measuring 5 1/2" by 6 1/4"). The prices in the checklist below reflect the value for the entire panel, or box, as these cards are more widely seen and collected as complete panels or boxes.

	NRMT	VG-E	GOOD
COMPLETE PANEL SET	100.00	50.00	10.00
COMMON PANEL	6.50	3.25	.65
COMMON INDIV. PLAYER	.50	.25	.05

☐ 1 No-Hit Duel by .... 9.00 4.50 .90
Toney and Vaughn:
Ty Cobb
Willie Keeler
Mordecai Brown
Eddie Plank
☐ 2 Alexander Conquers .... 6.50 3.25 .65
Yankees:
Al Simmons
Ban Johnson
Walter Johnson
Rogers Hornsby
☐ 3 Yanks' Lazzeri Sets .... 6.50 3.25 .65
AL Record:
Christy Mathewson
Chief Bender
Grover Alexander
Cy Young
☐ 4 Homerun Almost Hit 10.00 5.00 1.00
Out of Stadium:
Lou Gehrig
Hugh Duffy
Tris Speaker
Joe Tinker
☐ 5 Four Consecutive 20.00 10.00 2.00
Homers by Lou:

John McGraw
Frank Chance
Babe Ruth
Mickey Cochrane
☐ 6 No-Hit Game by .... 6.50 3.25 .65
Walter Johnson:
Cy Young
Walter Johnson
Johnny Evers
John McGraw
☐ 7 Twelve RBIs by 12.00 6.00 1.20
Bottomley:
Johnny Evers
Eddie Collins
Lou Gehrig
Ty Cobb
☐ 8 Ty Ties Record: 10.00 5.00 1.00
Honus Wagner
Mickey Cochrane
Eddie Collins
Mel Ott
☐ 9 Babe Ruth Hits Three 12.00 6.00 1.20
Homers in Game:
Cap Anson
Tris Speaker
Jack Chesbro
Al Simmons
☐ 10 Calls Shot in 12.00 6.00 1.20
Series Game:
Rabbit Maranville
Ed Walsh
Nap Lajoie
Connie Mack
☐ 11 Ruth's 60th Homer 12.00 6.00 1.20
Sets New Record:
Joe Tinker
Nap Lajoie
Mel Ott
Frank Chance
☐ 12 Double Shutout by .... 6.50 3.25 .65
Ed Reulbach:
Rogers Hornsby
Rabbit Maranville
Christy Mathewson
Honus Wagner

1971 Bazooka

The 1971 Bazooka set of 36 full color, unnumbered cards was issued in 12 panels of three cards each on the backs of boxes containing one cent Bazooka bubble gum. Individual cards measure 2" by 2 5/8" whereas the panels measure 2 5/8" by 5 5/16". The panels are numbered in the checklist alphabetically by the player's last name on the left most card of the panel. Complete panels of three would have a value of 10% more than the sum of the individual cards (prices) on the panel and complete boxes would command a premium of another 30% above those prices.

	NRMT	VG-E	GOOD
COMPLETE INDIV.SET	150.00	75.00	15.00
COMMON PLAYER	1.50	.75	.15

☐ 1 Tommie Agee .... 1.50 .75 .15
☐ 2 Harmon Killebrew .... 6.00 3.00 .60
☐ 3 Reggie Jackson 18.00 9.00 1.80
☐ 4 Bert Campaneris .... 1.50 .75 .15
☐ 5 Pete Rose 30.00 15.00 3.00
☐ 6 Orlando Cepeda .... 2.50 1.25 .25
☐ 7 Rico Carty .... 1.50 .75 .15
☐ 8 Johnny Bench 18.00 9.00 1.80
☐ 9 Tommy Harper .... 1.50 .75 .15
☐ 10 Bill Freehan .... 1.50 .75 .15
☐ 11 Roberto Clemente 18.00 9.00 1.80
☐ 12 Claude Osteen .... 1.50 .75 .15
☐ 13 Jim Fregosi .... 2.00 1.00 .20
☐ 14 Billy Williams .... 8.00 4.00 .80
☐ 15 Dave McNally .... 2.00 1.00 .20
☐ 16 Randy Hundley .... 1.50 .75 .15
☐ 17 Willie Mays 18.00 9.00 1.80
☐ 18 Jim Hunter .... 8.00 4.00 .80
☐ 19 Juan Marichal .... 9.00 4.50 .90
☐ 20 Frank Howard .... 2.00 1.00 .20
☐ 21 Bill Melton .... 1.50 .75 .15

☐ 22	Willie McCovey	10.00	5.00	1.00
☐ 23	Carl Yastrzemski	20.00	10.00	2.00
☐ 24	Clyde Wright	1.50	.75	.15
☐ 25	Jim Merritt	1.50	.75	.15
☐ 26	Luis Aparicio	8.00	4.00	.80
☐ 27	Bobby Murcer	2.00	1.00	.20
☐ 28	Rico Petrocelli	1.50	.75	.15
☐ 29	Sam McDowell	1.50	.75	.15
☐ 30	Clarence Gaston	1.50	.75	.15
☐ 31	Brooks Robinson	14.00	7.00	1.40
☐ 32	Hank Aaron	18.00	9.00	1.80
☐ 33	Larry Dierker	1.50	.75	.15
☐ 34	Rusty Staub	2.00	1.00	.20
☐ 35	Bob Gibson	9.00	4.50	.90
☐ 36	Amos Otis	2.00	1.00	.20

1958 Bell Brand

The 1958 Bell Brand Potato Chips set of 10 unnumbered cards features members of the Los Angeles Dodgers exclusively. Each card has a 1/4" dark green border, and the Gino Cimoli, Johnny Podres, and Duke Snider cards are more difficult to find; they are marked with an asterisk in the checklist below. The cards measure 3" by 4". This set marks the first year for the Dodgers in Los Angeles and includes a Campanella card despite the fact that he never played for the team in California. The ACC designation is F339-1.

		NRMT	VG-E	GOOD
COMPLETE SET		750.00	375.00	75.00
COMMON PLAYER (1-10)		30.00	15.00	3.00
☐ 1	Roy Campanella	100.00	50.00	10.00
☐ 2	Gino Cimoli *	125.00	60.00	12.50
☐ 3	Don Drysdale	65.00	32.50	6.50
☐ 4	Jim Gilliam	35.00	17.50	3.50
☐ 5	Gil Hodges	55.00	27.50	5.50
☐ 6	Sandy Koufax	80.00	40.00	8.00
☐ 7	Johnny Podres *	125.00	60.00	12.50
☐ 8	Pee Wee Reese	65.00	32.50	6.50
☐ 9	Duke Snider *	200.00	100.00	20.00
☐ 10	Don Zimmer	30.00	15.00	3.00

1960 Bell Brand

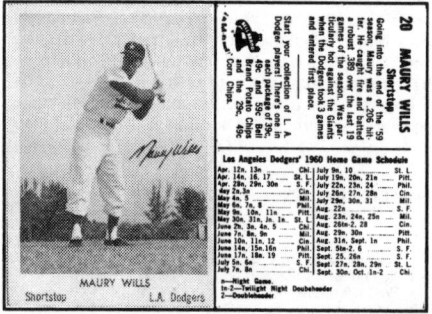

The 1960 Bell Brand Potato Chips set of 20 full color, numbered cards features Los Angeles Dodgers only. Because these cards, measuring 2 1/2" by 3 1/2", were issued in packages of potato chips, many cards suffered from stains. Clem Labine, Johnny Klippstein, and Walter Alston are somewhat more difficult to obtain than other cards in the set; they are marked with an asterisk in the checklist below. The ACC designation is F339- 2.

	NRMT	VG-E	GOOD
COMPLETE SET	400.00	200.00	40.00

COMMON PLAYER (1-20)	15.00	7.50	1.50
☐ 1 Norm Larker	15.00	7.50	1.50
☐ 2 Duke Snider	45.00	22.50	4.50
☐ 3 Danny McDevitt	15.00	7.50	1.50
☐ 4 Jim Gilliam	18.00	9.00	1.80
☐ 5 Rip Repulski	15.00	7.50	1.50
☐ 6 Clem Labine *	75.00	37.50	7.50
☐ 7 John Roseboro	15.00	7.50	1.50
☐ 8 Carl Furillo	18.00	9.00	1.80
☐ 9 Sandy Koufax	45.00	22.50	4.50
☐ 10 Joe Pignatano	15.00	7.50	1.50
☐ 11 Chuck Essegian	15.00	7.50	1.50
☐ 12 John Klippstein *	90.00	45.00	9.00
☐ 13 Ed Roebuck	15.00	7.50	1.50
☐ 14 Don Demeter	15.00	7.50	1.50
☐ 15 Roger Craig	18.00	9.00	1.80
☐ 16 Stan Williams	15.00	7.50	1.50
☐ 17 Don Zimmer	15.00	7.50	1.50
☐ 18 Walt Alston *	90.00	45.00	9.00
☐ 19 Johnny Podres	18.00	9.00	1.80
☐ 20 Maury Wills	25.00	12.50	2.50

1961 Bell Brand

The 1961 Bell Brand Potato Chips set of 20 full color cards features Los Angeles Dodger players only and is numbered by the uniform numbers of the players. The cards are slightly smaller (2 7/16" by 3 1/2") than the 1960 Bell Brand cards and are on thinner paper stock. The ACC designation is F339-3.

		NRMT	VG-E	GOOD
COMPLETE SET		300.00	120.00	25.00
COMMON PLAYER (1-51)		10.00	5.00	1.00
☐ 3	Willie Davis	12.00	6.00	1.20
☐ 4	Duke Snider	36.00	15.00	3.00
☐ 5	Norm Larker	10.00	5.00	1.00
☐ 8	John Roseboro	10.00	5.00	1.00
☐ 9	Wally Moon	10.00	5.00	1.00
☐ 11	Bob Lillis	10.00	5.00	1.00
☐ 12	Tom Davis	12.00	6.00	1.20
☐ 14	Gil Hodges	20.00	10.00	2.00
☐ 16	Don Demeter	10.00	5.00	1.00
☐ 19	Jim Gilliam	12.00	6.00	1.20
☐ 22	John Podres	12.00	6.00	1.20
☐ 24	Walt Alston MG	20.00	10.00	2.00
☐ 30	Maury Wills	18.00	9.00	1.80
☐ 32	Sandy Koufax	36.00	18.00	3.60
☐ 34	Norm Sherry	10.00	5.00	1.00
☐ 37	Ed Roebuck	10.00	5.00	1.00
☐ 38	Roger Craig	12.00	6.00	1.20
☐ 40	Stan Williams	10.00	5.00	1.00
☐ 43	Charlie Neal	10.00	5.00	1.00
☐ 51	Larry Sherry	10.00	5.00	1.00

1962 Bell Brand

The 1962 Bell Brand Potato Chips set of 20 full color cards features Los Angeles Dodger players only and is numbered by the uniform numbers of the players. These cards were printed on a high quality glossy

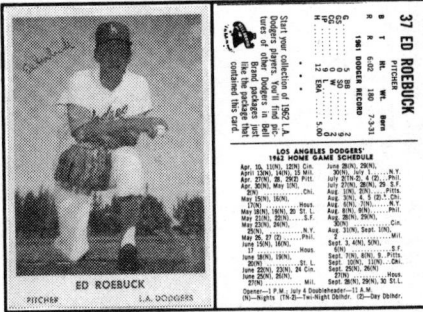

ED ROEBUCK   PISTCHER   L.A. DODGERS

paper, much better than the previous two years, virtually eliminating the grease stains. This set is distinguished by a 1962 Home schedule on the backs of the cards. The cards measure 2 7/16" by 3 1/2", the same size as the year before. The ACC designation is F339-4.

	NRMT	VG-E	GOOD
COMPLETE SET	250.00	125.00	25.00
COMMON PLAYER (1-56)	10.00	5.00	1.00

		NRMT	VG-E	GOOD
☐	3 Willie Davis	12.00	6.00	1.20
☐	4 Duke Snider	35.00	17.50	3.50
☐	6 Ron Fairly	10.00	5.00	1.00
☐	8 John Roseboro	10.00	5.00	1.00
☐	9 Wally Moon	10.00	5.00	1.00
☐	12 Tom Davis	12.00	6.00	1.20
☐	16 Ron Perranoski	10.00	5.00	1.00
☐	19 Jim Gilliam	12.00	6.00	1.20
☐	20 Daryl Spencer	10.00	5.00	1.00
☐	22 John Podres	12.00	6.00	1.20
☐	24 Walt Alston MG	20.00	10.00	2.00
☐	25 Frank Howard	12.00	6.00	1.20
☐	30 Maury Wills	18.00	9.00	1.80
☐	32 Sandy Koufax	35.00	17.50	3.50
☐	34 Norm Sherry	10.00	5.00	1.00
☐	37 Ed Roebuck	10.00	5.00	1.00
☐	40 Stan Williams	10.00	5.00	1.00
☐	51 Larry Sherry	10.00	5.00	1.00
☐	53 Don Drysdale	24.00	12.00	2.40
☐	56 Lee Walls	10.00	5.00	1.00

1951 Berk Ross

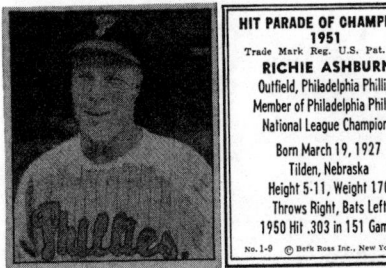

HIT PARADE OF CHAMPIONS
1951
Trade Mark Reg. U.S. Pat. Off.
RICHIE ASHBURN
Outfield, Philadelphia Phillies
Member of Philadelphia Phillies
National League Champions

Born March 19, 1927
Tilden, Nebraska
Height 5-11, Weight 170
Throws Right, Bats Left
1950 Hit .303 in 151 Games

No. 1-9   © Berk Ross Inc., New York, N.Y.

The 1951 Berk Ross set consists of 72 cards (each measuring 2 1/16" by 2 1/2") with tinted photographs, divided evenly into four series (designated in the checklist as A, B, C and D). The cards were marketed in boxes containing two card panels, without gum, and the set includes stars of other sports as well as baseball players. Intact panels are worth 20% more than the sum of the individual cards. The ACC designation is W532-1. In every series the first ten cards are baseball players; the set has a heavy emphasis on Yankees and Phillies players as they were in the World Series the year before.

	NRMT	VG-E	GOOD
COMPLETE SET	300.00	150.00	30.00
COMMON BASEBALL	4.50	2.25	.45
COMMON FOOTBALL	3.50	1.75	.35
COMMON OTHERS	2.50	1.25	.25

		NRMT	VG-E	GOOD
☐	A1 Al Rosen	6.00	3.00	.60
☐	A2 Bob Lemon	10.00	5.00	1.00
☐	A3 Phil Rizzuto	12.00	6.00	1.20
☐	A4 Hank Bauer	6.00	3.00	.60
☐	A5 Billy Johnson	4.50	2.25	.45
☐	A6 Jerry Coleman	4.50	2.25	.45
☐	A7 Johnny Mize	10.00	5.00	1.00
☐	A8 Dom DiMaggio	7.50	3.75	.75
☐	A9 Richie Ashburn	7.50	3.75	.75
☐	A10 Del Ennis	4.50	2.25	.45
☐	A11 Bob Cousy	6.00	3.00	.60
☐	A12 Dick Schnittker	2.50	1.25	.25
☐	A13 Ezzard Charles	3.50	1.75	.35
☐	A14 Leon Hart	3.50	1.75	.35
☐	A15 James Martin	3.50	1.75	.35
☐	A16 Ben Hogan	3.50	1.75	.35
☐	A17 Bill Durnan	3.50	1.75	.35
☐	A18 Bill Quackenbush	2.50	1.25	.25
☐	B1 Stan Musial	35.00	17.50	3.50
☐	B2 Warren Spahn	12.00	6.00	1.20
☐	B3 Tom Henrich	6.00	3.00	.60
☐	B4 Yogi Berra	20.00	10.00	2.00
☐	B5 Joe DiMaggio	65.00	32.50	6.50
☐	B6 Bobby Brown	6.00	3.00	.60
☐	B7 Granny Hamner	4.50	2.25	.45
☐	B8 Willie Jones	4.50	2.25	.45
☐	B9 Stan Lopata	4.50	2.25	.45
☐	B10 Mike Goliat	4.50	2.25	.45
☐	B11 Sherman White	3.50	1.75	.35
☐	B12 Joe Maxim	2.50	1.25	.25
☐	B13 Ray Robinson	4.50	2.25	.45
☐	B14 Doak Walker	6.00	3.00	.60
☐	B15 Emil Sitko	2.50	1.25	.25
☐	B16 Jack Stewart	2.50	1.25	.25
☐	B17 Dick Button	2.50	1.25	.25
☐	B18 Melvin Patton	2.50	1.25	.25
☐	C1 Ralph Kiner	10.00	5.00	1.00
☐	C2 Bill Goodman	4.50	2.25	.45
☐	C3 Allie Reynolds	6.00	3.00	.60
☐	C4 Vic Raschi	6.00	3.00	.60
☐	C5 Joe Page	4.50	2.25	.45
☐	C6 Eddie Lopat	6.00	3.00	.60
☐	C7 Andy Seminick	4.50	2.25	.45
☐	C8 Dick Sisler	4.50	2.25	.45
☐	C9 Eddie Waitkus	4.50	2.25	.45
☐	C10 Ken Heintzelman	4.50	2.25	.45
☐	C11 Paul Unruh	2.50	1.25	.25
☐	C12 Jake LaMotta	3.50	1.75	.35
☐	C13 Ike Williams	2.50	1.25	.25
☐	C14 Wade Walker	2.50	1.25	.25
☐	C15 Rodney Franz	2.50	1.25	.25
☐	C16 Sid Abel	3.50	1.75	.35
☐	C17 Claire Sherman	2.50	1.25	.25
☐	C18 Jesse Owens	4.50	2.25	.45
☐	D1 Gene Woodling	4.50	2.25	.45
☐	D2 Cliff Mapes	4.50	2.25	.45
☐	D3 Fred Sontort	4.50	2.25	.45
☐	D4 Tommy Byrne	4.50	2.25	.45
☐	D5 Whitey Ford	12.00	6.00	1.20
☐	D6 Jim Konstanty	4.50	2.25	.45
☐	D7 Russ Meyer	4.50	2.25	.45
☐	D8 Robin Roberts	10.00	5.00	1.00
☐	D9 Curt Simmons	4.50	2.25	.45
☐	D10 Sam Jethroe	4.50	2.25	.45
☐	D11 Bill Sharman	3.50	1.75	.35
☐	D12 Sandy Saddler	2.50	1.25	.25
☐	D13 Margaret DuPont	2.50	1.25	.25
☐	D14 Arnold Galiffa	3.50	1.75	.35
☐	D15 Charlie Justice	4.50	2.25	.45
☐	D16 Glen Cunningham	2.50	1.25	.25
☐	D17 Gregory Rice	2.50	1.25	.25
☐	D18 Harrison Dillard	2.50	1.25	.25

1952 Berk Ross

The 1952 Berk Ross set of 72 unnumbered, tinted photocards, each measuring 2" by 3", seems to have been patterned after the highly successful 1951 Bowman set. The reverses of Ewell Blackwell and Nellie Fox are transposed while Phil Rizzuto comes

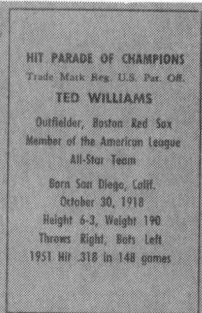

HIT PARADE OF CHAMPIONS
Trade Mark Reg. U.S. Pat. Off.

TED WILLIAMS

Outfielder, Boston Red Sox
Member of the American League
All-Star Team

Born San Diego, Calif.
October 30, 1918
Height 6-3, Weight 190
Throws Right, Bats Left
1951 Hit .318 in 148 games

with two different poses. There is a card of Joe DiMaggio even though he retired after the 1951 season. The ACC designation for this set is W532-2, and the cards have been assigned numbers in the alphabetical checklist below.

	NRMT	VG-E	GOOD
COMPLETE SET	2400.00	900.00	175.00
COMMON PLAYER (1-72)	9.00	4.50	.90

		NRMT	VG-E	GOOD
☐	1 Richie Ashburn	16.00	8.00	1.60
☐	2 Hank Bauer	13.50	6.50	1.25
☐	3 Yogi Berra	65.00	32.50	6.50
☐	4 Ewell Blackwell	12.00	6.00	1.20
	(photo actually Nellie Fox)			
☐	5 Bobby Brown	12.00	6.00	1.20
☐	6 Jim Busby	9.00	4.50	.90
☐	7 Roy Campanella	100.00	50.00	10.00
☐	8 Chico Carrasquel	9.00	4.50	.90
☐	9 Jerry Coleman	10.00	5.00	1.00
☐	10 Joe Collins	9.00	4.50	.90
☐	11 Alvin Dark	12.00	6.00	1.20
☐	12 Dom DiMaggio	13.50	6.50	1.25
☐	13 Joe DiMaggio	450.00	225.00	45.00
☐	14 Larry Doby	12.00	6.00	1.20
☐	15 Bobby Doerr	25.00	12.50	2.50
☐	16 Bob Elliott	9.00	4.50	.90
☐	17 Del Ennis	9.00	4.50	.90
☐	18 Ferris Fain	9.00	4.50	.90
☐	19 Bob Feller	50.00	25.00	5.00
☐	20 Nellie Fox	13.50	6.50	1.25
	(photo actually Ewell Blackwell)			
☐	21 Ned Garver	9.00	4.50	.90
☐	22 Clint Hartung	9.00	4.50	.90
☐	23 Jim Hearn	9.00	4.50	.90
☐	24 Gil Hodges	35.00	17.50	3.50
☐	25 Monte Irvin	25.00	12.50	2.50
☐	26 Larry Jansen	9.00	4.50	.90
☐	27 Sheldon Jones	9.00	4.50	.90
☐	28 George Kell	25.00	12.50	2.50
☐	29 Monte Kennedy	9.00	4.50	.90
☐	30 Ralph Kiner	25.00	12.50	2.50
☐	31 Dave Koslo	9.00	4.50	.90
☐	32 Bob Kuzava	9.00	4.50	.90
☐	33 Bob Lemon	25.00	12.50	2.50
☐	34 Whitey Lockman	9.00	4.50	.90
☐	35 Ed Lopat	13.50	6.50	1.25
☐	36 Sal Maglie	12.00	6.00	1.20
☐	37 Mickey Mantle	800.00	325.00	60.00
☐	38 Billy Martin	25.00	12.50	2.50
☐	39 Willie Mays	250.00	125.00	25.00
☐	40 Gil McDougald	13.50	6.50	1.25
☐	41 Minnie Minoso	13.50	6.50	1.25
☐	42 Johnny Mize	25.00	12.50	2.50
☐	43 Tom Morgan	9.00	4.50	.90
☐	44 Don Mueller	9.00	4.50	.90
☐	45 Stan Musial	150.00	75.00	15.00
☐	46 Don Newcombe	13.50	6.50	1.25
☐	47 Ray Noble	9.00	4.50	.90
☐	48 Joe Ostrowski	9.00	4.50	.90
☐	49 Mel Parnell	9.00	4.50	.90
☐	50 Vic Raschi	12.00	6.00	1.20
☐	51 Pee Wee Reese	40.00	20.00	4.00
☐	52 Allie Reynolds	15.00	7.50	1.50
☐	53 Bill Rigney	9.00	4.50	.90
☐	54A Phil Rizzuto (bunting)	40.00	20.00	4.00
☐	54B Phil Rizzuto (swinging)	40.00	20.00	4.00
☐	55 Robin Roberts	25.00	12.50	2.50

☐	56 Eddie Robinson	9.00	4.50	.90
☐	57 Jackie Robinson	150.00	75.00	15.00
☐	58 Preacher Roe	13.50	6.50	1.25
☐	59 Johnny Sain	13.50	6.50	1.25
☐	60 Red Schoendienst	12.00	6.00	1.20
☐	61 Duke Snider	100.00	50.00	10.00
☐	62 George Spencer	9.00	4.50	.90
☐	63 Eddie Stanky	9.00	4.50	.90
☐	64 Hank Thompson	9.00	4.50	.90
☐	65 Bobby Thomson	12.00	6.00	1.20
☐	66 Vic Wertz	9.00	4.50	.90
☐	67 Wally Westlake	9.00	4.50	.90
☐	68 Wes Westrum	9.00	4.50	.90
☐	69 Ted Williams	250.00	125.00	25.00
☐	70 Gene Woodling	9.00	4.50	.90
☐	71 Gus Zernial	9.00	4.50	.90

1986 Big League Chew

This 12-card set was produced by Big League Chew and was inserted in with their packages of chewing gum, which were shaped and styled after a pouch of chewing tobacco. The cards were found one per pouch of shredded chewing gum or were available through a mail-in offer of two coupons and 2.00 for a complete set. The players featured are members of the 500 career home run club. The backs are printed in blue ink on white card stock. The cards are standard size, 2 1/2" by 3 1/2" and are subtitled "Home Run Legends." The front of each card shows a year inside a small flag; the year is the year that player passed 500 homers.

	MINT	EXC	G-VG
COMPLETE SET	4.00	2.00	.40
COMMON PLAYER	.30	.15	.03

		MINT	EXC	G-VG
☐	1 Hank Aaron	.50	.25	.05
☐	2 Babe Ruth	.75	.35	.07
☐	3 Willie Mays	.50	.25	.05
☐	4 Frank Robinson	.30	.15	.03
☐	5 Harmon Killebrew	.30	.15	.03
☐	6 Mickey Mantle	.75	.35	.07
☐	7 Jimmie Foxx	.30	.15	.03
☐	8 Ted Williams	.50	.25	.05
☐	9 Ernie Banks	.40	.20	.04
☐	10 Eddie Mathews	.30	.15	.03
☐	11 Mel Ott	.30	.15	.03
☐	12 500 HR Members	.30	.15	.03

1987 Boardwalk and Baseball

This 33-card set was produced by Topps for distribution by the new "Boardwalk and Baseball" Theme Park located near Orlando, Florida. The cards are standard size, 2 1/2" by 3 1/2", and come in a custom blue collector box. The full-color fronts are surrounded by a pink and black frame border. The card backs are printed in pink and black on white

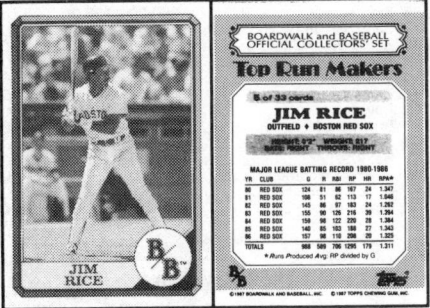

card stock. The set is subtitled "Top Run Makers." Hence no pitchers are included in the set. The checklist for the set is given on the back panel of the box.

		MINT	EXC	G-VG
COMPLETE SET (33)		4.00	2.00	.40
COMMON PLAYER (1-33)		.10	.05	.01
☐ 1	Mike Schmidt	.40	.20	.04
☐ 2	Eddie Murray	.30	.15	.03
☐ 3	Dale Murphy	.40	.20	.04
☐ 4	Dave Winfield	.25	.12	.02
☐ 5	Jim Rice	.25	.12	.02
☐ 6	Cecil Cooper	.10	.05	.01
☐ 7	Dwight Evans	.15	.07	.01
☐ 8	Rickey Henderson	.30	.15	.03
☐ 9	Robin Yount	.25	.12	.02
☐ 10	Andre Dawson	.25	.12	.02
☐ 11	Gary Carter	.25	.12	.02
☐ 12	Keith Hernandez	.20	.10	.02
☐ 13	George Brett	.35	.17	.03
☐ 14	Bill Buckner	.10	.05	.01
☐ 15	Tony Armas	.10	.05	.01
☐ 16	Harold Baines	.15	.07	.01
☐ 17	Don Baylor	.10	.05	.01
☐ 18	Steve Garvey	.25	.12	.02
☐ 19	Lance Parrish	.15	.07	.01
☐ 20	Dave Parker	.15	.07	.01
☐ 21	Buddy Bell	.15	.07	.01
☐ 22	Cal Ripken	.30	.15	.03
☐ 23	Bob Horner	.15	.07	.01
☐ 24	Tim Raines	.30	.15	.03
☐ 25	Jack Clark	.20	.10	.02
☐ 26	Leon Durham	.10	.05	.01
☐ 27	Pedro Guerrero	.20	.10	.02
☐ 28	Kent Hrbek	.15	.07	.01
☐ 29	Kirk Gibson	.20	.10	.02
☐ 30	Ryne Sandberg	.25	.12	.02
☐ 31	Wade Boggs	.50	.25	.05
☐ 32	Don Mattingly	.75	.35	.07
☐ 33	Darryl Strawberry	.40	.20	.04

1987 Bohemian Padres

The Bohemian Hearth Bread Company issued this 22-card set of San Diego Padres. The cards measure 2 1/2" by 3 1/2" and feature a distinctive yellow

border on the front of the cards. Card backs provide career year-by-year statistics.

		MINT	EXC	G-VG
COMPLETE SET		20.00	10.00	2.00
COMMON PLAYER		.50	.25	.05
☐ 1	Garry Templeton	.75	.35	.07
☐ 4	Joe Cora	.75	.35	.07
☐ 5	Randy Ready	.75	.35	.07
☐ 6	Steve Garvey	3.00	1.50	.30
☐ 7	Kevin Mitchell	1.00	.50	.10
☐ 8	John Kruk	2.00	1.00	.20
☐ 9	Benito Santiago	4.00	2.00	.40
☐ 10	Larry Bowa MG	1.00	.50	.10
☐ 11	Tim Flannery	.50	.25	.05
☐ 14	Carmelo Martinez	.75	.35	.07
☐ 16	Marvell Wynne	.50	.25	.05
☐ 19	Tony Gwynn	6.00	3.00	.60
☐ 21	James Steels	.50	.25	.05
☐ 22	Stan Jefferson	.75	.35	.07
☐ 30	Eric Show	.75	.35	.07
☐ 31	Ed Whitson	.50	.25	.05
☐ 34	Storm Davis	.50	.25	.05
☐ 37	Craig Lefferts	.50	.25	.05
☐ 40	Andy Hawkins	.50	.25	.05
☐ 41	Lance McCullers	.75	.35	.07
☐ 43	Dave Dravecky	.75	.35	.07
☐ 54	Rich Gossage	1.00	.50	.10

1947 Bond Bread

The 1947 Bond Bread Jackie Robinson set features 13 unnumbered cards of Jackie in different action or portrait poses; each card measures 2 1/4" by 3 1/2". Card number 7, which is the only card in the set to contain a facsimile autograph, was apparently issued in greater quantity than other cards in the set. Several of the cards have a horizontal format; these are marked in the checklist below by HOR. The ACC designation is D302.

		NRMT	VG-E	GOOD
COMPLETE SET		3500.00	1400.00	250.00
COMMON PLAYER (1-13)		300.00	150.00	30.00
☐ 1	Sliding into base, cap, ump in photo, HOR	300.00	150.00	30.00
☐ 2	Running down 3rd base line	300.00	150.00	30.00
☐ 3	Batting, bat behind head, facing camera	300.00	150.00	30.00
☐ 4	Moving towards second, throw almost to glove, HOR	300.00	150.00	30.00
☐ 5	Taking throw at first, HOR	300.00	150.00	30.00
☐ 6	Jumping high in the air for ball	300.00	150.00	30.00
☐ 7	Profile with glove in front of head (facsimile autograph)	175.00	85.00	18.00

☐ 8	Leaping over 2nd base ..... ready to throw	300.00	150.00	30.00
☐ 9	Portrait, holding .... glove over head	300.00	150.00	30.00
☐ 10	Portrait, holding .... bat perpendicular to body	300.00	150.00	30.00
☐ 11	Reaching for throw, ... glove near ankle	300.00	150.00	30.00
☐ 12	Leaping for throw, ... no scoreboard in background	300.00	150.00	30.00
☐ 13	Portrait, holding .... bat parallel to body	300.00	150.00	30.00

☐ 35	Snuffy Stirnweiss	9.00	4.50	.90
☐ 36	Stan Musial	250.00	125.00	25.00
☐ 37	Clint Hartung	18.00	9.00	1.80
☐ 38	Red Schoendienst	25.00	12.50	2.50
☐ 39	Augie Galan	18.00	9.00	1.80
☐ 40	Marty Marion	25.00	12.50	2.50
☐ 41	Rex Barney	18.00	9.00	1.80
☐ 42	Ray Poat	18.00	9.00	1.80
☐ 43	Bruce Edwards	18.00	9.00	1.80
☐ 44	Johnny Wyrostek	18.00	9.00	1.80
☐ 45	Hank Sauer	21.00	10.50	2.10
☐ 46	Herman Wehmeier	18.00	9.00	1.80
☐ 47	Bobby Thomson	25.00	12.50	2.50
☐ 48	Dave Koslo	35.00	9.00	2.00

1948 Bowman

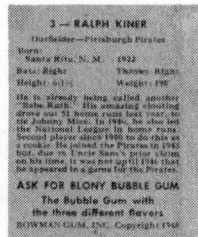

The 48-card Bowman set of 1948 was the first major set of the post-war period. Each 2 1/16" by 2 1/2" card had a black and white photo of a current player, with his biographical information printed in black ink on a gray back. Due to the printing process and the 36-card sheet size upon which Bowman was then printing, the 12 cards marked with an SP in the checklist are scarcer numerically, as they were removed from the printing sheet in order to make room for the 12 high numbers (37-48). Many cards are found with over-printed, transposed, or blank backs.

	NRMT	VG-E	GOOD
COMPLETE SET	1450.00	600.00	120.00
COMMON PLAYER (1-36)	9.00	4.50	.90
COMMON PLAYER (37-48)	18.00	9.00	1.80
COMMON PLAYER SP	27.00	13.50	2.70

☐ 1	Bob Elliott	40.00	8.00	2.00
☐ 2	Ewell Blackwell	18.00	9.00	1.80
☐ 3	Ralph Kiner	50.00	25.00	5.00
☐ 4	Johnny Mize	35.00	17.50	3.50
☐ 5	Bob Feller	60.00	30.00	6.00
☐ 6	Yogi Berra	175.00	85.00	18.00
☐ 7	Peter Reiser SP	35.00	17.50	3.50
☐ 8	Phil Rizzuto SP	125.00	60.00	12.50
☐ 9	Walker Cooper	9.00	4.50	.90
☐ 10	Buddy Rosar	9.00	4.50	.90
☐ 11	Johnny Lindell	9.00	4.50	.90
☐ 12	Johnny Sain	24.00	12.00	2.40
☐ 13	Willard Marshall SP	27.00	13.50	2.70
☐ 14	Allie Reynolds	24.00	12.00	2.40
☐ 15	Eddie Joost	9.00	4.50	.90
☐ 16	Jack Lohrke SP	27.00	13.50	2.70
☐ 17	Enos Slaughter	35.00	17.50	3.50
☐ 18	Warren Spahn	75.00	37.50	7.50
☐ 19	Tommy Henrich	15.00	7.50	1.50
☐ 20	Buddy Kerr SP	27.00	13.50	2.70
☐ 21	Ferris Fain	15.00	7.50	1.50
☐ 22	Floyd Bevens SP	27.00	13.50	2.70
☐ 23	Larry Jansen	9.00	4.50	.90
☐ 24	Dutch Leonard SP	27.00	13.50	2.70
☐ 25	Barney McCosky	9.00	4.50	.90
☐ 26	Frank Shea SP	27.00	13.50	2.70
☐ 27	Sid Gordon	9.00	4.50	.90
☐ 28	Emil Verban SP	27.00	13.50	2.70
☐ 29	Joe Page SP	27.00	13.50	2.70
☐ 30	Whitey Lockman SP	27.00	13.50	2.70
☐ 31	Bill McCahan	9.00	4.50	.90
☐ 32	Bill Rigney	9.00	4.50	.90
☐ 33	Bill Johnson	9.00	4.50	.90
☐ 34	Sheldon Jones SP	27.00	13.50	2.70

1949 Bowman

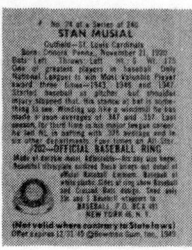

The cards in this 240-card set measure 2 1/16" by 2 1/2". In 1949 Bowman took an intermediate step between black and white and full color with this set of tinted photos on colored backgrounds. Collectors should note the series price variations which reflect some inconsistencies in the printing process. There are four major varieties in name printing which are noted in the checklist below: NOF: name on front; NNOF: no name on front; PR: printed name on back; and SCR: script name on back. These variations resulted when Bowman used twelve of the lower numbers to fill out the last press sheet of 36 cards adding to numbers 217-240.

	NRMT	VG-E	GOOD
COMPLETE SET	9500.00	3750.00	750.00
COMMON CARD 1-3/5-36/73 ..	10.00	5.00	1.00
COMMON CARD (37-72)	11.00	5.50	1.10
COMMON CARD (4/74-108)	9.00	4.50	.90
COMMON CARD (109-144)	8.00	4.00	.80
COMMON CARD (145-180)	45.00	22.50	4.50
COMMON CARD (181-216)	40.00	20.00	4.00
COMMON CARD (217-240)	40.00	20.00	4.00

☐ 1	Vern Bickford	40.00	8.00	2.00
☐ 2	Whitey Lockman	10.00	5.00	1.00
☐ 3	Bob Porterfield	10.00	5.00	1.00
☐ 4A	Jerry Priddy NNOF	12.00	6.00	1.20
☐ 4B	Jerry Priddy NOF	30.00	15.00	3.00
☐ 5	Hank Sauer	12.00	6.00	1.20
☐ 6	Phil Cavarretta	12.00	6.00	1.20
☐ 7	Joe Dobson	10.00	5.00	1.00
☐ 8	Murray Dickson	10.00	5.00	1.00
☐ 9	Ferris Fain	12.00	6.00	1.20
☐ 10	Ted Gray	10.00	5.00	1.00
☐ 11	Lou Boudreau	30.00	15.00	3.00
☐ 12	Cass Michaels	10.00	5.00	1.00
☐ 13	Bob Chesnes	10.00	5.00	1.00
☐ 14	Curt Simmons	15.00	7.50	1.50
☐ 15	Ned Garver	10.00	5.00	1.00
☐ 16	Al Kozar	10.00	5.00	1.00
☐ 17	Earl Torgeson	10.00	5.00	1.00
☐ 18	Bobby Thomson	15.00	7.50	1.50
☐ 19	Bobby Brown	15.00	7.50	1.50
☐ 20	Gene Hermanski	10.00	5.00	1.00
☐ 21	Frank Baumholtz	10.00	5.00	1.00
☐ 22	Peanuts Lowrey	10.00	5.00	1.00
☐ 23	Bobby Doerr	30.00	15.00	3.00
☐ 24	Stan Musial	200.00	100.00	20.00
☐ 25	Carl Scheib	10.00	5.00	1.00
☐ 26	George Kell	30.00	15.00	3.00
☐ 27	Bob Feller	60.00	30.00	6.00
☐ 28	Don Kolloway	10.00	5.00	1.00
☐ 29	Ralph Kiner	30.00	15.00	3.00

☐ 30	Andy Seminick	10.00	5.00	1.00
☐ 31	Dick Kokos	10.00	5.00	1.00
☐ 32	Eddie Yost	10.00	5.00	1.00
☐ 33	Warren Spahn	50.00	25.00	5.00
☐ 34	Dave Koslo	10.00	5.00	1.00
☐ 35	Vic Raschi	15.00	7.50	1.50
☐ 36	Pee Wee Reese	50.00	25.00	5.00
☐ 37	John Wyrostek	11.00	5.50	1.10
☐ 38	Emil Verban	11.00	5.50	1.10
☐ 39	Billy Goodman	12.50	6.25	1.25
☐ 40	Red Munger	11.00	5.50	1.10
☐ 41	Lou Brissie	11.00	5.50	1.10
☐ 42	Hoot Evers	11.00	5.50	1.10
☐ 43	Dale Mitchell	12.50	6.25	1.25
☐ 44	Dave Philley	11.00	5.50	1.10
☐ 45	Wally Westlake	11.00	5.50	1.10
☐ 46	Robin Roberts	75.00	37.50	7.50
☐ 47	Johnny Sain	14.00	7.00	1.40
☐ 48	Willard Marshall	11.00	5.50	1.10
☐ 49	Frank Shea	11.00	5.50	1.10
☐ 50	Jackie Robinson	300.00	150.00	30.00
☐ 51	Herman Wehmeier	11.00	5.50	1.10
☐ 52	Johnny Schmitz	11.00	5.50	1.10
☐ 53	Jack Kramer	11.00	5.50	1.10
☐ 54	Marty Marion	14.00	7.00	1.40
☐ 55	Eddie Joost	11.00	5.50	1.10
☐ 56	Pat Mullin	11.00	5.50	1.10
☐ 57	Gene Bearden	12.50	6.25	1.25
☐ 58	Bob Elliott	12.50	6.25	1.25
☐ 59	Jack Lohrke	11.00	5.50	1.10
☐ 60	Yogi Berra	125.00	60.00	12.50
☐ 61	Rex Barney	11.00	5.50	1.10
☐ 62	Grady Hatton	11.00	5.50	1.10
☐ 63	Andy Pafko	11.00	5.50	1.10
☐ 64	Dom DiMaggio	14.00	7.00	1.40
☐ 65	Enos Slaughter	30.00	15.00	3.00
☐ 66	Elmer Valo	11.00	5.50	1.10
☐ 67	Alvin Dark	14.00	7.00	1.40
☐ 68	Sheldon Jones	11.00	5.50	1.10
☐ 69	Tommy Henrich	14.00	7.00	1.40
☐ 70	Carl Furillo	25.00	12.50	2.50
☐ 71	Vern Stephens	12.50	6.25	1.25
☐ 72	Tommy Holmes	12.50	6.25	1.25
☐ 73	Billy Cox	14.00	7.00	1.40
☐ 74	Tom McBride	9.00	4.50	.90
☐ 75	Eddie Mayo	9.00	4.50	.90
☐ 76	Bill Nicholson	9.00	4.50	.90
☐ 77	Ernie Bonham	9.00	4.50	.90
☐ 78A	Sam Zoldak NNOF	12.00	6.00	1.20
☐ 78B	Sam Zoldak NOF	30.00	15.00	3.00
☐ 79	Ron Northey	9.00	4.50	.90
☐ 80	Bill McCahan	9.00	4.50	.90
☐ 81	Virgil Stallcup	9.00	4.50	.90
☐ 82	Joe Page	14.00	7.00	1.40
☐ 83A	Bob Scheffing NNOF	12.00	6.00	1.20
☐ 83B	Bob Scheffing NOF	30.00	15.00	3.00
☐ 84	Roy Campanella	200.00	100.00	20.00
☐ 85A	Johnny Mize NNOF	30.00	15.00	3.00
☐ 85B	Johnny Mize NOF	75.00	37.50	7.50
☐ 86	Johnny Pesky	10.00	5.00	1.00
☐ 87	Randy Gumpert	9.00	4.50	.90
☐ 88A	Bill Salkeld NNOF	12.00	6.00	1.20
☐ 88B	Bill Salkeld NOF	30.00	15.00	3.00
☐ 89	Mizell Platt	9.00	4.50	.90
☐ 90	Gil Coan	9.00	4.50	.90
☐ 91	Dick Wakefield	9.00	4.50	.90
☐ 92	Willie Jones	9.00	4.50	.90
☐ 93	Ed Stevens	9.00	4.50	.90
☐ 94	Mickey Vernon	14.00	7.00	1.40
☐ 95	Howie Pollet	9.00	4.50	.90
☐ 96	Taft Wright	9.00	4.50	.90
☐ 97	Danny Litwhiler	9.00	4.50	.90
☐ 98A	Phil Rizzuto NNOF	35.00	17.50	3.50
☐ 98B	Phil Rizzuto NOF	90.00	45.00	9.00
☐ 99	Frank Gustine	9.00	4.50	.90
☐ 100	Gil Hodges	75.00	37.50	7.50
☐ 101	Sid Gordon	9.00	4.50	.90
☐ 102	Stan Spence	9.00	4.50	.90
☐ 103	Joe Tipton	9.00	4.50	.90
☐ 104	Ed Stanky	12.50	6.25	1.25
☐ 105	Bill Kennedy	9.00	4.50	.90
☐ 106	Jake Early	9.00	4.50	.90
☐ 107	Eddie Lake	9.00	4.50	.90
☐ 108	Ken Heintzelman	9.00	4.50	.90
☐ 109A	Ed Fitzgerald SCR	10.00	5.00	1.00
☐ 109B	Ed Fitzgerald PR	25.00	12.50	2.50
☐ 110	Early Wynn	50.00	25.00	5.00
☐ 111	Red Schoendienst	14.00	7.00	1.40
☐ 112	Sam Chapman	8.00	4.00	.80
☐ 113	Ray LaManno	8.00	4.00	.80
☐ 114	Allie Reynolds	14.00	7.00	1.40
☐ 115	Dutch Leonard	8.00	4.00	.80
☐ 116	Joe Hatton	8.00	4.00	.80
☐ 117	Walker Cooper	8.00	4.00	.80
☐ 118	Sam Mele	8.00	4.00	.80
☐ 119	Floyd Baker	8.00	4.00	.80
☐ 120	Cliff Fannin	8.00	4.00	.80
☐ 121	Mark Christman	8.00	4.00	.80
☐ 122	George Vico	8.00	4.00	.80
☐ 123	Johnny Blatnick	8.00	4.00	.80
☐ 124A	Danny Murtaugh SCR	10.00	5.00	1.00
☐ 124B	Danny Murtaugh PR	25.00	12.50	2.50
☐ 125	Ken Keltner	8.00	4.00	.80
☐ 126A	Al Brazle SCR	10.00	5.00	1.00
☐ 126B	Al Brazle PR	25.00	12.50	2.50
☐ 127A	Hank Majeski SCR	10.00	5.00	1.00
☐ 127B	Hank Majeski PR	25.00	12.50	2.50
☐ 128	Johnny VanderMeer	12.50	6.25	1.25
☐ 129	Bill Johnson	8.00	4.00	.80
☐ 130	Harry Walker	9.00	4.50	.90
☐ 131	Paul Lehner	8.00	4.00	.80
☐ 132A	Al Evans SCR	10.00	5.00	1.00
☐ 132B	Al Evans PR	25.00	12.50	2.50
☐ 133	Aaron Robinson	8.00	4.00	.80
☐ 134	Hank Borowy	8.00	4.00	.80
☐ 135	Stan Rojek	8.00	4.00	.80
☐ 136	Hank Edwards	8.00	4.00	.80
☐ 137	Ted Wilks	8.00	4.00	.80
☐ 138	Buddy Rosar	8.00	4.00	.80
☐ 139	Hank Arft	8.00	4.00	.80
☐ 140	Ray Scarborough	8.00	4.00	.80
☐ 141	Ulysses Lupien	8.00	4.00	.80
☐ 142	Eddie Waitkus	8.00	4.00	.80
☐ 143A	Bob Dillinger SCR	10.00	5.00	1.00
☐ 143B	Bob Dillinger PR	25.00	12.50	2.50
☐ 144	Mickey Haefner	8.00	4.00	.80
☐ 145	Sylvester Donnelly	45.00	22.50	4.50
☐ 146	Mike McCormick	45.00	22.50	4.50
☐ 147	Bert Singleton	45.00	22.50	4.50
☐ 148	Bob Swift	45.00	22.50	4.50
☐ 149	Roy Partee	45.00	22.50	4.50
☐ 150	Allie Clark	45.00	22.50	4.50
☐ 151	Mickey Harris	45.00	22.50	4.50
☐ 152	Clarence Maddern	45.00	22.50	4.50
☐ 153	Phil Masi	45.00	22.50	4.50
☐ 154	Clint Hartung	45.00	22.50	4.50
☐ 155	Mickey Guerra	45.00	22.50	4.50
☐ 156	Al Zarilla	45.00	22.50	4.50
☐ 157	Walt Masterson	45.00	22.50	4.50
☐ 158	Harry Brecheen	50.00	25.00	5.00
☐ 159	Glen Moulder	45.00	22.50	4.50
☐ 160	Jim Blackburn	45.00	22.50	4.50
☐ 161	Jocko Thompson	45.00	22.50	4.50
☐ 162	Preacher Roe	75.00	37.50	7.50
☐ 163	Clyde McCullough	45.00	22.50	4.50
☐ 164	Vic Wertz	50.00	25.00	5.00
☐ 165	Snuffy Stirnweiss	50.00	25.00	5.00
☐ 166	Mike Tresh	45.00	22.50	4.50
☐ 167	Babe Martin	45.00	22.50	4.50
☐ 168	Doyle Lade	45.00	22.50	4.50
☐ 169	Jeff Heath	45.00	22.50	4.50
☐ 170	Bill Rigney	50.00	25.00	5.00
☐ 171	Dick Fowler	45.00	22.50	4.50
☐ 172	Eddie Pellagrini	45.00	22.50	4.50
☐ 173	Eddie Stewart	45.00	22.50	4.50
☐ 174	Terry Moore	60.00	30.00	6.00
☐ 175	Luke Appling	75.00	37.50	7.50
☐ 176	Ken Raffensberger	45.00	22.50	4.50
☐ 177	Stan Lopata	45.00	22.50	4.50
☐ 178	Tom Brown	45.00	22.50	4.50
☐ 179	Hugh Casey	50.00	25.00	5.00
☐ 180	Connie Berry	45.00	22.50	4.50
☐ 181	Gus Niarhos	40.00	20.00	4.00
☐ 182	Hall Peck	40.00	20.00	4.00
☐ 183	Lou Stringer	40.00	20.00	4.00
☐ 184	Bob Chipman	40.00	20.00	4.00
☐ 185	Pete Reiser	50.00	25.00	5.00
☐ 186	Buddy Kerr	40.00	20.00	4.00
☐ 187	Phil Marchildon	40.00	20.00	4.00
☐ 188	Karl Drews	40.00	20.00	4.00
☐ 189	Earl Wooten	40.00	20.00	4.00
☐ 190	Jim Hearn	40.00	20.00	4.00
☐ 191	Joe Haynes	40.00	20.00	4.00
☐ 192	Harry Gumbert	40.00	20.00	4.00
☐ 193	Ken Trinkle	40.00	20.00	4.00
☐ 194	Ralph Branca	60.00	30.00	6.00
☐ 195	Eddie Bockman	40.00	20.00	4.00
☐ 196	Fred Hutchinson	50.00	25.00	5.00
☐ 197	Johnny Lindell	40.00	20.00	4.00
☐ 198	Steve Gromek	40.00	20.00	4.00
☐ 199	Tex Hughson	40.00	20.00	4.00
☐ 200	Jess Dobernic	40.00	20.00	4.00
☐ 201	Sibby Sisti	40.00	20.00	4.00
☐ 202	Larry Jansen	40.00	20.00	4.00
☐ 203	Barney McCosky	40.00	20.00	4.00
☐ 204	Bob Savage	40.00	20.00	4.00
☐ 205	Dick Sisler	40.00	20.00	4.00
☐ 206	Bruce Edwards	40.00	20.00	4.00
☐ 207	Johnny Hopp	45.00	22.50	4.50
☐ 208	Dizzy Trout	45.00	22.50	4.50

		NRMT	VG-E	GOOD
☐ 209	Charlie Keller	60.00	30.00	6.00
☐ 210	Joe Gordon	60.00	30.00	6.00
☐ 211	Boo Ferriss	40.00	20.00	4.00
☐ 212	Ralph Hamner	40.00	20.00	4.00
☐ 213	Red Barrett	40.00	20.00	4.00
☐ 214	Richie Ashburn	175.00	85.00	18.00
☐ 215	Kirby Higbe	40.00	20.00	4.00
☐ 216	Schoolboy Rowe	50.00	25.00	5.00
☐ 217	Marino Pieretti	40.00	20.00	4.00
☐ 218	Dick Kryhoski	40.00	20.00	4.00
☐ 219	Virgil"Fire" Trucks	45.00	22.50	4.50
☐ 220	Johnny McCarthy	40.00	20.00	4.00
☐ 221	Bob Muncrief	40.00	20.00	4.00
☐ 222	Alex Kellner	40.00	20.00	4.00
☐ 223	Bobby Hofman	40.00	20.00	4.00
☐ 224	Satchell Paige	900.00	450.00	90.00
☐ 225	Gerry Coleman	60.00	30.00	6.00
☐ 226	Duke Snider	600.00	300.00	60.00
☐ 227	Fritz Ostermueller	40.00	20.00	4.00
☐ 228	Jackie Mayo	40.00	20.00	4.00
☐ 229	Ed Lopat	75.00	37.50	7.50
☐ 230	Augie Galan	40.00	20.00	4.00
☐ 231	Earl Johnson	40.00	20.00	4.00
☐ 232	George McQuinn	40.00	20.00	4.00
☐ 233	Larry Doby	75.00	37.50	7.50
☐ 234	Rip Sewell	40.00	20.00	4.00
☐ 235	Jim Russell	40.00	20.00	4.00
☐ 236	Fred Sanford	40.00	20.00	4.00
☐ 237	Monte Kennedy	40.00	20.00	4.00
☐ 238	Bob Lemon	150.00	75.00	15.00
☐ 239	Frank McCormick	45.00	22.50	4.50
☐ 240	Babe Young (photo actually Bobby Young)	75.00	20.00	4.00

1950 Bowman

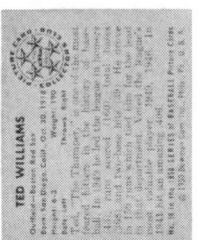

The cards in this 252-card set measure 2 1/16" by 2 1/2". This set, marketed in 1950 by Bowman, represented a major improvement in terms of quality over their previous efforts. Each card was a beautifully colored line drawing developed from a simple photograph. The first 72 cards are the scarcest in the set while the final 72 cards may be found with or without the copyright line. This was the only Bowman sports set to carry the famous "5-Star" logo.

		NRMT	VG-E	GOOD
COMPLETE SET		5600.00	1800.00	300.00
COMMON PLAYER (1-72)		25.00	12.50	2.50
COMMON PLAYER (73-252)		9.00	4.50	.90
☐ 1	Mel Parnell	120.00	15.00	3.00
☐ 2	Vern Stephens	27.00	13.50	2.70
☐ 3	Dom DiMaggio	30.00	15.00	3.00
☐ 4	Gus Zernial	30.00	15.00	3.00
☐ 5	Bob Kuzava	25.00	12.50	2.50
☐ 6	Bob Feller	90.00	45.00	9.00
☐ 7	Jim Hegan	27.00	13.50	2.70
☐ 8	George Kell	40.00	20.00	4.00
☐ 9	Vic Wertz	27.00	13.50	2.70
☐ 10	Tommy Henrich	30.00	15.00	3.00
☐ 11	Phil Rizzuto	70.00	35.00	7.00
☐ 12	Joe Page	30.00	15.00	3.00
☐ 13	Ferris Fain	27.00	13.50	2.70
☐ 14	Alex Kellner	25.00	12.50	2.50
☐ 15	Al Kozar	25.00	12.50	2.50
☐ 16	Roy Sievers	30.00	15.00	3.00
☐ 17	Sid Hudson	25.00	12.50	2.50
☐ 18	Eddie Robinson	25.00	12.50	2.50
☐ 19	Warren Spahn	70.00	35.00	7.00

		NRMT	VG-E	GOOD
☐ 20	Bob Elliott	27.00	13.50	2.70
☐ 21	Pee Wee Reese	70.00	35.00	7.00
☐ 22	Jackie Robinson	350.00	175.00	35.00
☐ 23	Don Newcombe	40.00	20.00	4.00
☐ 24	Johnny Schmitz	25.00	12.50	2.50
☐ 25	Hank Sauer	27.00	13.50	2.70
☐ 26	Grady Hatton	25.00	12.50	2.50
☐ 27	Herman Wehmeier	25.00	12.50	2.50
☐ 28	Bobby Thomson	30.00	15.00	3.00
☐ 29	Eddie Stanky	27.00	13.50	2.70
☐ 30	Eddie Waitkus	25.00	12.50	2.50
☐ 31	Del Ennis	27.00	13.50	2.70
☐ 32	Robin Roberts	50.00	25.00	5.00
☐ 33	Ralph Kiner	40.00	20.00	4.00
☐ 34	Murry Dickson	25.00	12.50	2.50
☐ 35	Enos Slaughter	40.00	20.00	4.00
☐ 36	Eddie Kazak	25.00	12.50	2.50
☐ 37	Luke Appling	35.00	17.50	3.50
☐ 38	Bill Wight	25.00	12.50	2.50
☐ 39	Larry Doby	32.00	16.00	3.20
☐ 40	Bob Lemon	40.00	20.00	4.00
☐ 41	Hoot Evers	25.00	12.50	2.50
☐ 42	Art Houtteman	25.00	12.50	2.50
☐ 43	Bobby Doerr	40.00	20.00	4.00
☐ 44	Joe Dobson	25.00	12.50	2.50
☐ 45	Al Zarilla	25.00	12.50	2.50
☐ 46	Yogi Berra	175.00	85.00	18.00
☐ 47	Jerry Coleman	30.00	15.00	3.00
☐ 48	Lou Brissie	25.00	12.50	2.50
☐ 49	Elmer Valo	25.00	12.50	2.50
☐ 50	Dick Kokos	25.00	12.50	2.50
☐ 51	Ned Garver	25.00	12.50	2.50
☐ 52	Sam Mele	25.00	12.50	2.50
☐ 53	Clyde Vollmer	25.00	12.50	2.50
☐ 54	Gil Coan	25.00	12.50	2.50
☐ 55	Buddy Kerr	25.00	12.50	2.50
☐ 56	Del Crandall	30.00	15.00	3.00
☐ 57	Vern Bickford	25.00	12.50	2.50
☐ 58	Carl Furillo	35.00	17.50	3.50
☐ 59	Ralph Branca	30.00	15.00	3.00
☐ 60	Andy Pafko	27.00	13.50	2.70
☐ 61	Bob Rush	25.00	12.50	2.50
☐ 62	Ted Kluszewski	35.00	17.50	3.50
☐ 63	Ewell Blackwell	27.00	13.50	2.70
☐ 64	Al Dark	30.00	15.00	3.00
☐ 65	Dave Koslo	25.00	12.50	2.50
☐ 66	Larry Jansen	25.00	12.50	2.50
☐ 67	Willie Jones	25.00	12.50	2.50
☐ 68	Curt Simmons	27.00	13.50	2.70
☐ 69	Wally Westlake	25.00	12.50	2.50
☐ 70	Bob Chesnes	25.00	12.50	2.50
☐ 71	Red Schoendienst	30.00	15.00	3.00
☐ 72	Howie Pollet	25.00	12.50	2.50
☐ 73	Willard Marshall	9.00	4.50	.90
☐ 74	Johnny Antonelli	12.00	6.00	1.20
☐ 75	Roy Campanella	150.00	75.00	15.00
☐ 76	Rex Barney	9.00	4.50	.90
☐ 77	Duke Snider	120.00	60.00	12.00
☐ 78	Mickey Owen	9.00	4.50	.90
☐ 79	Johnny VanderMeer	10.00	5.00	1.00
☐ 80	Howard Fox	9.00	4.50	.90
☐ 81	Ron Northey	9.00	4.50	.90
☐ 82	Whitey Lockman	9.00	4.50	.90
☐ 83	Sheldon Jones	9.00	4.50	.90
☐ 84	Richie Ashburn	22.00	11.00	2.20
☐ 85	Ken Heintzelman	9.00	4.50	.90
☐ 86	Stan Rojek	9.00	4.50	.90
☐ 87	Bill Werle	9.00	4.50	.90
☐ 88	Marty Marion	12.00	6.00	1.20
☐ 89	Red Munger	9.00	4.50	.90
☐ 90	Harry Brecheen	9.00	4.50	.90
☐ 91	Cass Michaels	9.00	4.50	.90
☐ 92	Hank Majeski	9.00	4.50	.90
☐ 93	Gene Bearden	9.00	4.50	.90
☐ 94	Lou Boudreau	25.00	12.50	2.50
☐ 95	Aaron Robinson	9.00	4.50	.90
☐ 96	Virgil Trucks	9.00	4.50	.90
☐ 97	Maurice McDermott	9.00	4.50	.90
☐ 98	Ted Williams	350.00	175.00	35.00
☐ 99	Billy Goodman	10.00	5.00	1.00
☐ 100	Vic Raschi	14.00	7.00	1.40
☐ 101	Bobby Brown	14.00	7.00	1.40
☐ 102	Billy Johnson	9.00	4.50	.90
☐ 103	Eddie Joost	9.00	4.50	.90
☐ 104	Sam Chapman	9.00	4.50	.90
☐ 105	Bob Dillinger	9.00	4.50	.90
☐ 106	Cliff Fannin	9.00	4.50	.90
☐ 107	Sam Dente	9.00	4.50	.90
☐ 108	Ray Scarborough	9.00	4.50	.90
☐ 109	Sid Gordon	9.00	4.50	.90
☐ 110	Tommy Holmes	10.00	5.00	1.00
☐ 111	Walker Cooper	9.00	4.50	.90
☐ 112	Gil Hodges	40.00	20.00	4.00
☐ 113	Gene Hermanski	9.00	4.50	.90
☐ 114	Wayne Terwilliger	9.00	4.50	.90

☐ 115	Roy Smalley	9.00	4.50	.90
☐ 116	Virgil Stallcup	9.00	4.50	.90
☐ 117	Bill Rigney	9.00	4.50	.90
☐ 118	Clint Hartung	9.00	4.50	.90
☐ 119	Dick Sisler	9.00	4.50	.90
☐ 120	John Thompson	9.00	4.50	.90
☐ 121	Andy Seminick	9.00	4.50	.90
☐ 122	Johnny Hopp	10.00	5.00	1.00
☐ 123	Dino Restelli	9.00	4.50	.90
☐ 124	Clyde McCullough	9.00	4.50	.90
☐ 125	Del Rice	9.00	4.50	.90
☐ 126	Al Brazle	9.00	4.50	.90
☐ 127	Dave Philley	9.00	4.50	.90
☐ 128	Phil Masi	9.00	4.50	.90
☐ 129	Joe Gordon	10.00	5.00	1.00
☐ 130	Dale Mitchell	10.00	5.00	1.00
☐ 131	Steve Gromek	9.00	4.50	.90
☐ 132	James "Mickey" Vernon	10.00	5.00	1.00
☐ 133	Don Kolloway	9.00	4.50	.90
☐ 134	Paul Trout	9.00	4.50	.90
☐ 135	Pat Mullin	9.00	4.50	.90
☐ 136	Warren Rosar	9.00	4.50	.90
☐ 137	Johnny Pesky	10.00	5.00	1.00
☐ 138	Allie Reynolds	12.00	6.00	1.20
☐ 139	Johnny Mize	35.00	17.50	3.50
☐ 140	Pete Suder	9.00	4.50	.90
☐ 141	Joe Coleman	9.00	4.50	.90
☐ 142	Sherman Lollar	10.00	5.00	1.00
☐ 143	Eddie Stewart	9.00	4.50	.90
☐ 144	Al Evans	9.00	4.50	.90
☐ 145	Jack Graham	9.00	4.50	.90
☐ 146	Floyd Baker	9.00	4.50	.90
☐ 147	Mike Garcia	10.00	5.00	1.00
☐ 148	Early Wynn	30.00	15.00	3.00
☐ 149	Bob Swift	9.00	4.50	.90
☐ 150	George Vico	9.00	4.50	.90
☐ 151	Fred Hutchinson	10.00	5.00	1.00
☐ 152	Ellis Kinder	9.00	4.50	.90
☐ 153	Walt Masterson	9.00	4.50	.90
☐ 154	Gus Niarhos	9.00	4.50	.90
☐ 155	Frank Shea	9.00	4.50	.90
☐ 156	Fred Sanford	9.00	4.50	.90
☐ 157	Mike Guerra	9.00	4.50	.90
☐ 158	Paul Lehner	9.00	4.50	.90
☐ 159	Joe Tipton	9.00	4.50	.90
☐ 160	Mickey Harris	9.00	4.50	.90
☐ 161	Sherry Robertson	9.00	4.50	.90
☐ 162	Eddie Yost	9.00	4.50	.90
☐ 163	Earl Torgeson	9.00	4.50	.90
☐ 164	Sibby Sisti	9.00	4.50	.90
☐ 165	Bruce Edwards	9.00	4.50	.90
☐ 166	Joe Hatton	9.00	4.50	.90
☐ 167	Preacher Roe	14.00	7.00	1.40
☐ 168	Bob Scheffing	9.00	4.50	.90
☐ 169	Hank Edwards	9.00	4.50	.90
☐ 170	Dutch Leonard	9.00	4.50	.90
☐ 171	Harry Gumbert	9.00	4.50	.90
☐ 172	Peanuts Lowrey	9.00	4.50	.90
☐ 173	Lloyd Merriman	9.00	4.50	.90
☐ 174	Hank Thompson	10.00	5.00	1.00
☐ 175	Monte Kennedy	9.00	4.50	.90
☐ 176	Sylvester Donnelly	9.00	4.50	.90
☐ 177	Hank Borowy	9.00	4.50	.90
☐ 178	Eddie Fitzgerald	9.00	4.50	.90
☐ 179	Chuck Diering	9.00	4.50	.90
☐ 180	Harry Walker	10.00	5.00	1.00
☐ 181	Marino Pieretti	9.00	4.50	.90
☐ 182	Sam Zoldak	9.00	4.50	.90
☐ 183	Mickey Haefner	9.00	4.50	.90
☐ 184	Randy Gumpert	9.00	4.50	.90
☐ 185	Howie Judson	10.00	5.00	1.00
☐ 186	Ken Keltner	9.00	4.50	.90
☐ 187	Lou Stringer	9.00	4.50	.90
☐ 188	Earl Johnson	9.00	4.50	.90
☐ 189	Owen Friend	9.00	4.50	.90
☐ 190	Ken Wood	9.00	4.50	.90
☐ 191	Dick Starr	9.00	4.50	.90
☐ 192	Bob Chipman	9.00	4.50	.90
☐ 193	Pete Reiser	10.00	5.00	1.00
☐ 194	Billy Cox	10.00	5.00	1.00
☐ 195	Phil Cavarretta	10.00	5.00	1.00
☐ 196	Doyle Lade	9.00	4.50	.90
☐ 197	Johnny Wyrostek	9.00	4.50	.90
☐ 198	Danny Litwhiler	9.00	4.50	.90
☐ 199	Jack Kramer	9.00	4.50	.90
☐ 200	Kirby Higbe	9.00	4.50	.90
☐ 201	Pete Castiglione	9.00	4.50	.90
☐ 202	Cliff Chambers	9.00	4.50	.90
☐ 203	Danny Murtaugh	10.00	5.00	1.00
☐ 204	Granny Hamner	9.00	4.50	.90
☐ 205	Mike Goliat	9.00	4.50	.90
☐ 206	Stan Lopata	9.00	4.50	.90
☐ 207	Max Lanier	10.00	5.00	1.00
☐ 208	Jim Hearn	9.00	4.50	.90
☐ 209	Johnny Lindell	9.00	4.50	.90

☐ 210	Ted Gray	9.00	4.50	.90
☐ 211	Charley Keller	10.00	5.00	1.00
☐ 212	Gerry Priddy	9.00	4.50	.90
☐ 213	Carl Scheib	9.00	4.50	.90
☐ 214	Dick Fowler	9.00	4.50	.90
☐ 215	Ed Lopat	14.00	7.00	1.40
☐ 216	Bob Porterfield	9.00	4.50	.90
☐ 217	Casey Stengel MG	65.00	32.50	6.50
☐ 218	Cliff Mapes	9.00	4.50	.90
☐ 219	Hank Bauer	25.00	12.50	2.50
☐ 220	Leo Durocher MG	25.00	12.50	2.50
☐ 221	Don Mueller	12.00	6.00	1.20
☐ 222	Bobby Morgan	9.00	4.50	.90
☐ 223	Jim Russell	9.00	4.50	.90
☐ 224	Jack Banta	9.00	4.50	.90
☐ 225	Eddie Sawyer MG	10.00	5.00	1.00
☐ 226	Jim Konstanty	12.00	6.00	1.20
☐ 227	Bob Miller	9.00	4.50	.90
☐ 228	Bill Nicholson	9.00	4.50	.90
☐ 229	Frank Frisch	25.00	12.50	2.50
☐ 230	Bill Serena	9.00	4.50	.90
☐ 231	Preston Ward	9.00	4.50	.90
☐ 232	Al Rosen	25.00	12.50	2.50
☐ 233	Allie Clark	9.00	4.50	.90
☐ 234	Bobby Shantz	12.00	6.00	1.20
☐ 235	Harold Gilbert	9.00	4.50	.90
☐ 236	Bob Cain	9.00	4.50	.90
☐ 237	Bill Salkeld	9.00	4.50	.90
☐ 238	Vernal Jones	9.00	4.50	.90
☐ 239	Bill Howerton	9.00	4.50	.90
☐ 240	Eddie Lake	9.00	4.50	.90
☐ 241	Neil Berry	9.00	4.50	.90
☐ 242	Dick Kryhoski	9.00	4.50	.90
☐ 243	Johnny Groth	9.00	4.50	.90
☐ 244	Dale Coogan	9.00	4.50	.90
☐ 245	Al Papai	9.00	4.50	.90
☐ 246	Walt Dropo	12.00	6.00	1.20
☐ 247	Irv Noren	10.00	5.00	1.00
☐ 248	Sam Jethroe	10.00	5.00	1.00
☐ 249	Snuffy Stirnweiss	10.00	5.00	1.00
☐ 250	Ray Coleman	9.00	4.50	.90
☐ 251	John Moss	9.00	4.50	.90
☐ 252	Billy DeMars	35.00	5.00	1.00

1951 Bowman

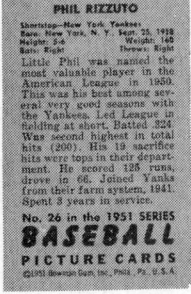

The cards in this 324-card set measure 2 1/16" by 3 1/8". Many of the obverses of the cards appearing in the 1951 Bowman set are enlargements of those appearing in the previous year. The high number series (253-324) is highly valued and contains the true "Rookie" cards of Mickey Mantle and Willie Mays. Card number 195 depicts Paul Richards in caricature. George Kell's card (#46) incorrectly lists him as being in the "1941" Bowman series. Player names are found printed in a panel on the front of the card. These cards were supposedly also sold in sheets in variety stores in the Philadelphia area.

	NRMT	VG-E	GOOD
COMPLETE SET	12000.00	4500.00	900.00
COMMON PLAYER (1-36)	12.00	6.00	1.20
COMMON PLAYER (37-72)	10.00	5.00	1.00
COMMON PLAYER (73-252)	8.00	4.00	.80
COMMON PLAYER (253-324)	30.00	15.00	3.00
☐ 1 Whitey Ford	400.00	50.00	10.00
☐ 2 Yogi Berra	200.00	100.00	20.00

☐	3	Robin Roberts	40.00	20.00	4.00
☐	4	Del Ennis	13.50	6.50	1.25
☐	5	Dale Mitchell	13.50	6.50	1.25
☐	6	Don Newcombe	18.00	9.00	1.80
☐	7	Gil Hodges	40.00	20.00	4.00
☐	8	Paul Lehner	12.00	6.00	1.20
☐	9	Sam Chapman	12.00	6.00	1.20
☐	10	Red Schoendienst	16.00	8.00	1.60
☐	11	Red Munger	12.00	6.00	1.20
☐	12	Hank Majeski	12.00	6.00	1.20
☐	13	Eddie Stanky	13.50	6.50	1.25
☐	14	Al Dark	15.00	7.50	1.50
☐	15	Johnny Pesky	13.50	6.50	1.25
☐	16	Maurice McDermott	12.00	6.00	1.20
☐	17	Pete Castiglione	12.00	6.00	1.20
☐	18	Gil Coan	12.00	6.00	1.20
☐	19	Sid Gordon	12.00	6.00	1.20
☐	20	Del Crandell	13.50	6.50	1.25
		(sic, Crandall)			
☐	21	Snuffy Stirnweiss	12.00	6.00	1.20
☐	22	Hank Sauer	13.50	6.50	1.25
☐	23	Hoot Evers	12.00	6.00	1.20
☐	24	Ewell Blackwell	13.50	6.50	1.25
☐	25	Vic Raschi	16.00	8.00	1.60
☐	26	Phil Rizzuto	35.00	17.50	3.50
☐	27	Jim Konstanty	13.50	6.50	1.25
☐	28	Eddie Waitkus	12.00	6.00	1.20
☐	29	Allie Clark	12.00	6.00	1.20
☐	30	Bob Feller	55.00	27.50	5.50
☐	31	Roy Campanella	100.00	50.00	10.00
☐	32	Duke Snider	90.00	45.00	9.00
☐	33	Bob Hooper	12.00	6.00	1.20
☐	34	Marty Marion	15.00	7.50	1.50
☐	35	Al Zarilla	12.00	6.00	1.20
☐	36	Joe Dobson	12.00	6.00	1.20
☐	37	Whitey Lockman	10.00	5.00	1.00
☐	38	Al Evans	10.00	5.00	1.00
☐	39	Ray Scarborough	10.00	5.00	1.00
☐	40	Gus Bell	12.00	6.00	1.20
☐	41	Eddie Yost	10.00	5.00	1.00
☐	42	Vern Bickford	10.00	5.00	1.00
☐	43	Billy DeMars	10.00	5.00	1.00
☐	44	Roy Smalley	10.00	5.00	1.00
☐	45	Art Houtteman	10.00	5.00	1.00
☐	46	George Kell 1941	35.00	17.50	3.50
☐	47	Grady Hatton	10.00	5.00	1.00
☐	48	Ken Raffensberger	10.00	5.00	1.00
☐	49	Jerry Coleman	11.00	5.50	1.10
☐	50	Johnny Mize	35.00	17.50	3.50
☐	51	Andy Seminick	10.00	5.00	1.00
☐	52	Dick Sisler	10.00	5.00	1.00
☐	53	Bob Lemon	30.00	15.00	3.00
☐	54	Ray Boone	11.00	5.50	1.10
☐	55	Gene Hermanski	10.00	5.00	1.00
☐	56	Ralph Branca	12.00	6.00	1.20
☐	57	Alex Kellner	10.00	5.00	1.00
☐	58	Enos Slaughter	30.00	15.00	3.00
☐	59	Randy Gumpert	10.00	5.00	1.00
☐	60	Chico Carrasquel	10.00	5.00	1.00
☐	61	Jim Hearn	10.00	5.00	1.00
☐	62	Lou Boudreau	27.00	13.50	2.70
☐	63	Bob Dillinger	10.00	5.00	1.00
☐	64	Bill Werle	10.00	5.00	1.00
☐	65	Mickey Vernon	11.00	5.50	1.10
☐	66	Bob Elliott	11.00	5.50	1.10
☐	67	Roy Sievers	11.00	5.50	1.10
☐	68	Dick Kokos	10.00	5.00	1.00
☐	69	Johnny Schmitz	10.00	5.00	1.00
☐	70	Ron Northey	10.00	5.00	1.00
☐	71	Jerry Priddy	10.00	5.00	1.00
☐	72	Lloyd Merriman	10.00	5.00	1.00
☐	73	Tommy Byrne	9.00	4.50	.90
☐	74	Billy Johnson	9.00	4.50	.90
☐	75	Russ Meyer	8.00	4.00	.80
☐	76	Stan Lopata	8.00	4.00	.80
☐	77	Mike Goliat	8.00	4.00	.80
☐	78	Early Wynn	30.00	15.00	3.00
☐	79	Jim Hegan	9.00	4.50	.90
☐	80	Pee Wee Reese	45.00	22.50	4.50
☐	81	Carl Furillo	15.00	7.50	1.50
☐	82	Joe Tipton	8.00	4.00	.80
☐	83	Carl Scheib	8.00	4.00	.80
☐	84	Barney McCosky	8.00	4.00	.80
☐	85	Eddie Kazak	8.00	4.00	.80
☐	86	Harry Brecheen	9.00	4.50	.90
☐	87	Floyd Baker	8.00	4.00	.80
☐	88	Eddie Robinson	8.00	4.00	.80
☐	89	Hank Thompson	9.00	4.50	.90
☐	90	Dave Koslo	8.00	4.00	.80
☐	91	Clyde Vollmer	8.00	4.00	.80
☐	92	Vern Stephens	9.00	4.50	.90
☐	93	Danny O'Connell	8.00	4.00	.80
☐	94	Clyde McCullough	8.00	4.00	.80
☐	95	Sherry Robertson	8.00	4.00	.80
☐	96	Sandy Consuegra	8.00	4.00	.80
☐	97	Bob Kuzava	8.00	4.00	.80
☐	98	Willard Marshall	8.00	4.00	.80
☐	99	Earl Torgeson	8.00	4.00	.80
☐	100	Sherm Lollar	9.00	4.50	.90
☐	101	Owen Friend	8.00	4.00	.80
☐	102	Dutch Leonard	8.00	4.00	.80
☐	103	Andy Pafko	9.00	4.50	.90
☐	104	Virgil Trucks	9.00	4.50	.90
☐	105	Don Kolloway	8.00	4.00	.80
☐	106	Pat Mullin	8.00	4.00	.80
☐	107	Johnny Wyrostek	8.00	4.00	.80
☐	108	Virgil Stallcup	8.00	4.00	.80
☐	109	Allie Reynolds	15.00	7.50	1.50
☐	110	Bobby Brown	12.00	6.00	1.20
☐	111	Curt Simmons	10.00	5.00	1.00
☐	112	Willie Jones	8.00	4.00	.80
☐	113	Bill Nicholson	8.00	4.00	.80
☐	114	Sam Zoldak	8.00	4.00	.80
☐	115	Steve Gromek	8.00	4.00	.80
☐	116	Bruce Edwards	8.00	4.00	.80
☐	117	Eddie Miksis	8.00	4.00	.80
☐	118	Preacher Roe	12.50	6.25	1.25
☐	119	Eddie Joost	8.00	4.00	.80
☐	120	Joe Coleman	8.00	4.00	.80
☐	121	Gerry Staley	8.00	4.00	.80
☐	122	Joe Garagiola	40.00	20.00	4.00
☐	123	Howie Judson	8.00	4.00	.80
☐	124	Gus Niarhos	8.00	4.00	.80
☐	125	Bill Rigney	8.00	4.00	.80
☐	126	Bobby Thomson	12.50	6.25	1.25
☐	127	Sal Maglie	15.00	7.50	1.50
☐	128	Ellis Kinder	8.00	4.00	.80
☐	129	Matt Batts	8.00	4.00	.80
☐	130	Tom Saffell	8.00	4.00	.80
☐	131	Cliff Chambers	8.00	4.00	.80
☐	132	Cass Michaels	8.00	4.00	.80
☐	133	Sam Dente	8.00	4.00	.80
☐	134	Warren Spahn	40.00	20.00	4.00
☐	135	Walker Cooper	8.00	4.00	.80
☐	136	Ray Coleman	8.00	4.00	.80
☐	137	Dick Starr	8.00	4.00	.80
☐	138	Phil Cavarretta	9.00	4.50	.90
☐	139	Doyle Lade	8.00	4.00	.80
☐	140	Eddie Lake	8.00	4.00	.80
☐	141	Fred Hutchinson	9.00	4.50	.90
☐	142	Aaron Robinson	8.00	4.00	.80
☐	143	Ted Kluszewski	14.00	7.00	1.40
☐	144	Herman Wehmeier	8.00	4.00	.80
☐	145	Fred Sanford	8.00	4.00	.80
☐	146	Johnny Hopp	9.00	4.50	.90
☐	147	Ken Heintzelman	8.00	4.00	.80
☐	148	Granny Hamner	8.00	4.00	.80
☐	149	Bubba Church	8.00	4.00	.80
☐	150	Mike Garcia	9.00	4.50	.90
☐	151	Larry Doby	12.50	6.25	1.25
☐	152	Cal Abrams	8.00	4.00	.80
☐	153	Rex Barney	8.00	4.00	.80
☐	154	Pete Suder	8.00	4.00	.80
☐	155	Lou Brissie	8.00	4.00	.80
☐	156	Del Rice	8.00	4.00	.80
☐	157	Al Brazle	8.00	4.00	.80
☐	158	Chuck Diering	8.00	4.00	.80
☐	159	Eddie Stewart	8.00	4.00	.80
☐	160	Phil Masi	8.00	4.00	.80
☐	161	Wes Westrum	8.00	4.00	.80
☐	162	Larry Jansen	8.00	4.00	.80
☐	163	Monte Kennedy	8.00	4.00	.80
☐	164	Bill Wight	8.00	4.00	.80
☐	165	Ted Williams	300.00	150.00	30.00
☐	166	Stan Rojek	8.00	4.00	.80
☐	167	Murry Dickson	8.00	4.00	.80
☐	168	Sam Mele	8.00	4.00	.80
☐	169	Sid Hudson	8.00	4.00	.80
☐	170	Sibby Sisti	8.00	4.00	.80
☐	171	Buddy Kerr	8.00	4.00	.80
☐	172	Ned Garver	8.00	4.00	.80
☐	173	Hank Arft	8.00	4.00	.80
☐	174	Mickey Owen	8.00	4.00	.80
☐	175	Wayne Terwilliger	8.00	4.00	.80
☐	176	Vic Wertz	9.00	4.50	.90
☐	177	Charlie Keller	9.00	4.50	.90
☐	178	Ted Gray	8.00	4.00	.80
☐	179	Danny Litwhiler	8.00	4.00	.80
☐	180	Howie Fox	8.00	4.00	.80
☐	181	Casey Stengel MG	55.00	27.50	5.50
☐	182	Tom Ferrick	8.00	4.00	.80
☐	183	Hank Bauer	14.00	7.00	1.40
☐	184	Eddie Sawyer MG	9.00	4.50	.90
☐	185	Jimmy Bloodworth	8.00	4.00	.80
☐	186	Richie Ashburn	17.00	8.50	1.70
☐	187	Al Rosen	12.00	6.00	1.20
☐	188	Bobby Avila	9.00	4.50	.90
☐	189	Erv Palica	8.00	4.00	.80
☐	190	Joe Hatton	8.00	4.00	.80
☐	191	Billy Hitchcock	8.00	4.00	.80

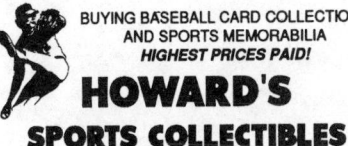

☐ 192	Hank Wyse	8.00	4.00	.80
☐ 193	Ted Wilks	8.00	4.00	.80
☐ 194	Peanuts Lowrey	8.00	4.00	.80
☐ 195	Paul Richards	12.00	6.00	1.20
	(caricature)			
☐ 196	Billy Pierce	14.00	7.00	1.40
☐ 197	Bob Cain	8.00	4.00	.80
☐ 198	Monte Irvin	35.00	17.50	3.50
☐ 199	Sheldon Jones	8.00	4.00	.80
☐ 200	Jack Kramer	8.00	4.00	.80
☐ 201	Steve O'Neill	8.00	4.00	.80
☐ 202	Mike Guerra	8.00	4.00	.80
☐ 203	Vernon Law	11.00	5.50	1.10
☐ 204	Vic Lombardi	8.00	4.00	.80
☐ 205	Mickey Grasso	8.00	4.00	.80
☐ 206	Conrado Marrero	8.00	4.00	.80
☐ 207	Billy Southworth	8.00	4.00	.80
☐ 208	Blix Donnelly	8.00	4.00	.80
☐ 209	Ken Wood	8.00	4.00	.80
☐ 210	Les Moss	8.00	4.00	.80
☐ 211	Hal Jeffcoat	8.00	4.00	.80
☐ 212	Bob Rush	8.00	4.00	.80
☐ 213	Neil Berry	8.00	4.00	.80
☐ 214	Bob Swift	8.00	4.00	.80
☐ 215	Ken Peterson	8.00	4.00	.80
☐ 216	Connie Ryan	8.00	4.00	.80
☐ 217	Joe Page	11.00	5.50	1.10
☐ 218	Ed Lopat	14.00	7.00	1.40
☐ 219	Gene Woodling	13.00	6.50	1.30
☐ 220	Bob Miller	8.00	4.00	.80
☐ 221	Dick Whitman	8.00	4.00	.80
☐ 222	Thurman Tucker	8.00	4.00	.80
☐ 223	Johnny VanderMeer	11.00	5.50	1.10
☐ 224	Billy Cox	9.00	4.50	.90
☐ 225	Dan Bankhead	8.00	4.00	.80
☐ 226	Jimmy Dykes	9.00	4.50	.90
☐ 227	Bobby Schantz	11.00	5.50	1.10
	(sic, Shantz)			
☐ 228	Cloyd Boyer	9.00	4.50	.90
☐ 229	Bill Howerton	8.00	4.00	.80
☐ 230	Max Lanier	9.00	4.50	.90
☐ 231	Luis Aloma	8.00	4.00	.80
☐ 232	Nelson Fox	35.00	17.50	3.50
☐ 233	Leo Durocher MG	25.00	12.50	2.50
☐ 234	Clint Hartung	8.00	4.00	.80
☐ 235	Jack Lohrke	8.00	4.00	.80
☐ 236	Warren Rosar	8.00	4.00	.80
☐ 237	Billy Goodman	9.00	4.50	.90
☐ 238	Peter Reiser	10.00	5.00	1.00
☐ 239	Bill MacDonald	8.00	4.00	.80
☐ 240	Joe Haynes	8.00	4.00	.80
☐ 241	Irv Noren	8.00	4.00	.80
☐ 242	Sam Jethroe	8.00	4.00	.80
☐ 243	Johnny Antonelli	9.00	4.50	.90
☐ 244	Cliff Fannin	8.00	4.00	.80
☐ 245	John Berardino	9.00	4.50	.90
☐ 246	Bill Serena	8.00	4.00	.80
☐ 247	Bob Ramazotti	8.00	4.00	.80
☐ 248	Johnny Klippstein	8.00	4.00	.80
☐ 249	Johnny Groth	8.00	4.00	.80
☐ 250	Hank Borowy	8.00	4.00	.80
☐ 251	Willard Ramsdell	8.00	4.00	.80
☐ 252	Dixie Howell	8.00	4.00	.80
☐ 253	Mickey Mantle	5500.00	1800.00	300.00
☐ 254	Jackie Jensen	60.00	30.00	6.00
☐ 255	Milo Candini	30.00	15.00	3.00
☐ 256	Ken Sylvestri	30.00	15.00	3.00
☐ 257	Birdie Tebbetts	35.00	17.50	3.50
☐ 258	Luke Easter	35.00	17.50	3.50
☐ 259	Chuck Dressen MG	35.00	17.50	3.50
☐ 260	Carl Erskine	45.00	22.50	4.50
☐ 261	Wally Moses	35.00	17.50	3.50
☐ 262	Gus Zernial	35.00	17.50	3.50
☐ 263	Howie Pollet	30.00	15.00	3.00
☐ 264	Don Richmond	30.00	15.00	3.00
☐ 265	Steve Bilko	30.00	15.00	3.00
☐ 266	Harry Dorish	30.00	15.00	3.00
☐ 267	Ken Holcomb	30.00	15.00	3.00
☐ 268	Don Mueller	35.00	17.50	3.50
☐ 269	Ray Noble	30.00	15.00	3.00
☐ 270	Willard Nixon	30.00	15.00	3.00
☐ 271	Tommy Wright	30.00	15.00	3.00
☐ 272	Billy Meyer MG	30.00	15.00	3.00
☐ 273	Danny Murtaugh	35.00	17.50	3.50
☐ 274	George Metkovich	30.00	15.00	3.00
☐ 275	Bucky Harris MG	40.00	20.00	4.00
☐ 276	Frank Quinn	30.00	15.00	3.00
☐ 277	Roy Hartsfield	30.00	15.00	3.00
☐ 278	Norman Roy	30.00	15.00	3.00
☐ 279	Jim Delsing	30.00	15.00	3.00
☐ 280	Frank Overmire	30.00	15.00	3.00
☐ 281	Al Widmar	30.00	15.00	3.00
☐ 282	Frank Frisch	45.00	22.50	4.50
☐ 283	Walt Dubiel	30.00	15.00	3.00
☐ 284	Gene Bearden	30.00	15.00	3.00

☐ 285	Johnny Lipon	30.00	15.00	3.00
☐ 286	Bob Usher	30.00	15.00	3.00
☐ 287	Jim Blackburn	30.00	15.00	3.00
☐ 288	Bobby Adams	30.00	15.00	3.00
☐ 289	Cliff Mapes	30.00	15.00	3.00
☐ 290	Bill Dickey	100.00	50.00	10.00
☐ 291	Tommy Henrich	45.00	22.50	4.50
☐ 292	Eddie Pellegrini	30.00	15.00	3.00
☐ 293	Ken Johnson	30.00	15.00	3.00
☐ 294	Jocko Thompson	30.00	15.00	3.00
☐ 295	Al Lopez MG	45.00	22.50	4.50
☐ 296	Bob Kennedy	35.00	17.50	3.50
☐ 297	Dave Philley	30.00	15.00	3.00
☐ 298	Joe Astroth	30.00	15.00	3.00
☐ 299	Clyde King	30.00	15.00	3.00
☐ 300	Hal Rice	30.00	15.00	3.00
☐ 301	Tommy Glaviano	30.00	15.00	3.00
☐ 302	Jim Busby	30.00	15.00	3.00
☐ 303	Marv Rotblatt	30.00	15.00	3.00
☐ 304	Al Gettell	30.00	15.00	3.00
☐ 305	Willie Mays	1200.00	500.00	90.00
☐ 306	Jim Piersall	45.00	22.50	4.50
☐ 307	Walt Masterson	30.00	15.00	3.00
☐ 308	Ted Beard	30.00	15.00	3.00
☐ 309	Mel Queen	30.00	15.00	3.00
☐ 310	Erv Dusak	30.00	15.00	3.00
☐ 311	Mickey Harris	30.00	15.00	3.00
☐ 312	Gene Mauch	40.00	20.00	4.00
☐ 313	Ray Mueller	30.00	15.00	3.00
☐ 314	Johnny Sain	35.00	17.50	3.50
☐ 315	Zack Taylor	30.00	15.00	3.00
☐ 316	Duane Pillette	30.00	15.00	3.00
☐ 317	Smokey Burgess	35.00	17.50	3.50
☐ 318	Warren Hacker	30.00	15.00	3.00
☐ 319	Red Rolfe	35.00	17.50	3.50
☐ 320	Hal White	30.00	15.00	3.00
☐ 321	Earl Johnson	30.00	15.00	3.00
☐ 322	Luke Sewell	35.00	17.50	3.50
☐ 323	Joe Adcock	40.00	20.00	4.00
☐ 324	Johnny Pramesa	60.00	15.00	3.00

1952 Bowman

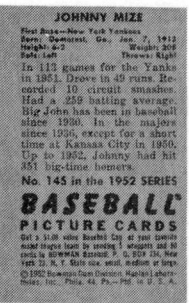

The cards in this 252-card set measure 2 1/16" by 3 1/8". While the Bowman set of 1952 retained the card size introduced in 1951, it employed a modification of color tones from the two preceding years. The cards also appeared with a facsimile autograph on the front and, for the first time since 1949, premium advertising on the back. The 1952 set was sold in sheets as well as in gum packs. Artwork for 15 cards that were never issued was recently discovered.

	NRMT	VG-E	GOOD
COMPLETE SET	6000.00	2000.00	400.00
COMMON PLAYER (1-36)	11.00	5.50	1.10
COMMON PLAYER (37-144)	9.00	4.50	.90
COMMON PLAYER (145-180)	8.00	4.00	.80
COMMON PLAYER (181-216)	7.00	3.50	.70
COMMON PLAYER (217-252)	16.00	8.00	1.60

☐ 1	Yogi Berra	250.00	60.00	10.00
☐ 2	Bobby Thomson	16.00	8.00	1.60
☐ 3	Fred Hutchinson	13.50	6.50	1.25
☐ 4	Robin Roberts	30.00	15.00	3.00
☐ 5	Minnie Minoso	25.00	12.50	2.50
☐ 6	Virgil Stallcup	11.00	5.50	1.10

☐	7	Mike Garcia	13.50	6.50	1.25
☐	8	Pee Wee Reese	45.00	22.50	4.50
☐	9	Vern Stephens	13.50	6.50	1.25
☐	10	Bob Hooper	11.00	5.50	1.10
☐	11	Ralph Kiner	30.00	15.00	3.00
☐	12	Max Surkont	11.00	5.50	1.10
☐	13	Cliff Mapes	11.00	5.50	1.10
☐	14	Cliff Chambers	11.00	5.50	1.10
☐	15	Sam Mele	11.00	5.50	1.10
☐	16	Turk Lown	11.00	5.50	1.10
☐	17	Ed Lopat	18.00	9.00	1.80
☐	18	Don Mueller	13.50	6.50	1.25
☐	19	Bob Cain	11.00	5.50	1.10
☐	20	Willie Jones	11.00	5.50	1.10
☐	21	Nelson Fox	18.00	9.00	1.80
☐	22	Willard Ramsdell	11.00	5.50	1.10
☐	23	Bob Lemon	27.00	13.50	2.70
☐	24	Carl Furillo	16.00	8.00	1.60
☐	25	Mickey McDermott	11.00	5.50	1.10
☐	26	Eddie Joost	11.00	5.50	1.10
☐	27	Joe Garagiola	30.00	15.00	3.00
☐	28	Ray Hartsfield	11.00	5.50	1.10
☐	29	Ned Garver	11.00	5.50	1.10
☐	30	Red Schoendienst	15.00	7.50	1.50
☐	31	Eddie Yost	11.00	5.50	1.10
☐	32	Eddie Miksis	11.00	5.50	1.10
☐	33	Gil McDougald	30.00	15.00	3.00
☐	34	Alvin Dark	13.50	6.50	1.25
☐	35	Granny Hamner	11.00	5.50	1.10
☐	36	Cass Michaels	11.00	5.50	1.10
☐	37	Vic Raschi	12.00	6.00	1.20
☐	38	Whitey Lockman	10.00	5.00	1.00
☐	39	Vic Wertz	10.00	5.00	1.00
☐	40	Bubba Church	9.00	4.50	.90
☐	41	Chico Carrasquel	9.00	4.50	.90
☐	42	Johnny Wyrostek	9.00	4.50	.90
☐	43	Bob Feller	55.00	27.50	5.50
☐	44	Roy Campanella	90.00	45.00	9.00
☐	45	Johnny Pesky	9.00	4.50	.90
☐	46	Carl Scheib	9.00	4.50	.90
☐	47	Pete Castiglione	9.00	4.50	.90
☐	48	Vern Bickford	9.00	4.50	.90
☐	49	Jim Hearn	9.00	4.50	.90
☐	50	Gerry Staley	9.00	4.50	.90
☐	51	Gil Coan	9.00	4.50	.90
☐	52	Phil Rizzuto	40.00	20.00	4.00
☐	53	Richie Ashburn	16.00	8.00	1.60
☐	54	Billy Pierce	10.00	5.00	1.00
☐	55	Ken Raffensberger	9.00	4.50	.90
☐	56	Clyde King	9.00	4.50	.90
☐	57	Clyde Vollmer	9.00	4.50	.90
☐	58	Hank Majeski	9.00	4.50	.90
☐	59	Murry Dickson	9.00	4.50	.90
☐	60	Sid Gordon	9.00	4.50	.90
☐	61	Tommy Byrne	9.00	4.50	.90
☐	62	Joe Presko	9.00	4.50	.90
☐	63	Irv Noren	9.00	4.50	.90
☐	64	Roy Smalley	9.00	4.50	.90
☐	65	Hank Bauer	12.00	6.00	1.20
☐	66	Sal Maglie	11.00	5.50	1.10
☐	67	Johnny Groth	9.00	4.50	.90
☐	68	Jim Busby	9.00	4.50	.90
☐	69	Joe Adcock	10.00	5.00	1.00
☐	70	Carl Erskine	12.00	6.00	1.20
☐	71	Vernon Law	10.00	5.00	1.00
☐	72	Earl Torgeson	9.00	4.50	.90
☐	73	Gerry Coleman	10.00	5.00	1.00
☐	74	Wes Westrum	9.00	4.50	.90
☐	75	George Kell	27.00	13.50	2.70
☐	76	Del Ennis	10.00	5.00	1.00
☐	77	Eddie Robinson	9.00	4.50	.90
☐	78	Lloyd Merriman	9.00	4.50	.90
☐	79	Lou Brissie	9.00	4.50	.90
☐	80	Gil Hodges	35.00	17.50	3.50
☐	81	Billy Goodman	10.00	5.00	1.00
☐	82	Gus Zernial	10.00	5.00	1.00
☐	83	Howie Pollet	9.00	4.50	.90
☐	84	Sam Jethroe	9.00	4.50	.90
☐	85	Marty Marion	11.00	5.50	1.10
☐	86	Cal Abrams	9.00	4.50	.90
☐	87	Mickey Vernon	10.00	5.00	1.00
☐	88	Bruce Edwards	9.00	4.50	.90
☐	89	Billy Hitchcock	9.00	4.50	.90
☐	90	Larry Jansen	9.00	4.50	.90
☐	91	Don Kolloway	9.00	4.50	.90
☐	92	Eddie Waitkus	9.00	4.50	.90
☐	93	Paul Richards	10.00	5.00	1.00
☐	94	Luke Sewell	9.00	4.50	.90
☐	95	Luke Easter	10.00	5.00	1.00
☐	96	Ralph Branca	11.00	5.50	1.10
☐	97	Willard Marshall	9.00	4.50	.90
☐	98	Jimmy Dykes	9.00	4.50	.90
☐	99	Clyde McCullough	9.00	4.50	.90
☐	100	Sibby Sisti	9.00	4.50	.90
☐	101	Mickey Mantle	1000.00	400.00	80.00
☐	102	Peanuts Lowrey	9.00	4.50	.90
☐	103	Joe Haynes	9.00	4.50	.90
☐	104	Hal Jeffcoat	9.00	4.50	.90
☐	105	Bobby Brown	11.00	5.50	1.10
☐	106	Randy Gumpert	9.00	4.50	.90
☐	107	Del Rice	9.00	4.50	.90
☐	108	George Metkovich	9.00	4.50	.90
☐	109	Tom Morgan	9.00	4.50	.90
☐	110	Max Lanier	9.00	4.50	.90
☐	111	Hoot Evers	9.00	4.50	.90
☐	112	Smokey Burgess	10.00	5.00	1.00
☐	113	Al Zarilla	9.00	4.50	.90
☐	114	Frank Hiller	9.00	4.50	.90
☐	115	Larry Doby	11.00	5.50	1.10
☐	116	Duke Snider	75.00	37.50	7.50
☐	117	Bill Wight	9.00	4.50	.90
☐	118	Ray Murray	9.00	4.50	.90
☐	119	Bill Howerton	9.00	4.50	.90
☐	120	Chet Nichols	9.00	4.50	.90
☐	121	Al Corwin	9.00	4.50	.90
☐	122	Billy Johnson	9.00	4.50	.90
☐	123	Sid Hudson	9.00	4.50	.90
☐	124	Birdie Tebbetts	9.00	4.50	.90
☐	125	Howie Fox	9.00	4.50	.90
☐	126	Phil Cavarretta	10.00	5.00	1.00
☐	127	Dick Sisler	9.00	4.50	.90
☐	128	Don Newcombe	12.00	6.00	1.20
☐	129	Gus Niarhos	9.00	4.50	.90
☐	130	Allie Clark	9.00	4.50	.90
☐	131	Bob Swift	9.00	4.50	.90
☐	132	Dave Cole	9.00	4.50	.90
☐	133	Dick Kryhoski	9.00	4.50	.90
☐	134	Al Brazle	9.00	4.50	.90
☐	135	Mickey Harris	9.00	4.50	.90
☐	136	Gene Hermanski	9.00	4.50	.90
☐	137	Stan Rojek	9.00	4.50	.90
☐	138	Ted Wilks	9.00	4.50	.90
☐	139	Jerry Priddy	9.00	4.50	.90
☐	140	Ray Scarborough	9.00	4.50	.90
☐	141	Hank Edwards	9.00	4.50	.90
☐	142	Early Wynn	27.00	13.50	2.70
☐	143	Sandy Consuegra	9.00	4.50	.90
☐	144	Joe Hatton	9.00	4.50	.90
☐	145	Johnny Mize	35.00	17.50	3.50
☐	146	Leo Durocher MG	20.00	10.00	2.00
☐	147	Marlin Stuart	8.50	4.25	.85
☐	148	Ken Heintzelman	8.50	4.25	.85
☐	149	Howie Judson	8.50	4.25	.85
☐	150	Herman Wehmeier	8.50	4.25	.85
☐	151	Al Rosen	12.00	6.00	1.20
☐	152	Billy Cox	10.00	5.00	1.00
☐	153	Fred Hatfield	8.50	4.25	.85
☐	154	Ferris Fain	10.00	5.00	1.00
☐	155	Billy Meyer	8.50	4.25	.85
☐	156	Warren Spahn	40.00	20.00	4.00
☐	157	Jim Delsing	8.50	4.25	.85
☐	158	Bucky Harris MG	20.00	10.00	2.00
☐	159	Dutch Leonard	8.50	4.25	.85
☐	160	Eddie Stanky	11.00	5.50	1.10
☐	161	Jackie Jensen	14.00	7.00	1.40
☐	162	Monte Irvin	25.00	12.50	2.50
☐	163	Johnny Lipon	8.50	4.25	.85
☐	164	Connie Ryan	8.50	4.25	.85
☐	165	Saul Rogovin	8.50	4.25	.85
☐	166	Bobby Adams	8.50	4.25	.85
☐	167	Bobby Avila	10.00	5.00	1.00
☐	168	Preacher Roe	12.00	6.00	1.20
☐	169	Walt Dropo	10.00	5.00	1.00
☐	170	Joe Astroth	8.50	4.25	.85
☐	171	Mel Queen	8.50	4.25	.85
☐	172	Ebba St.Claire	8.50	4.25	.85
☐	173	Gene Bearden	8.50	4.25	.85
☐	174	Mickey Grasso	8.50	4.25	.85
☐	175	Ransom Jackson	8.50	4.25	.85
☐	176	Harry Brecheen	8.50	4.25	.85
☐	177	Gene Woodling	12.00	6.00	1.20
☐	178	Dave Williams	10.00	5.00	1.00
☐	179	Pete Suder	8.50	4.25	.85
☐	180	Eddie Fitzgerald	8.50	4.25	.85
☐	181	Joe Collins	8.50	4.25	.85
☐	182	Dave Koslo	7.00	3.50	.70
☐	183	Pat Mullin	7.00	3.50	.70
☐	184	Curt Simmons	8.00	4.00	.80
☐	185	Eddie Stewart	7.00	3.50	.70
☐	186	Frank Smith	7.00	3.50	.70
☐	187	Jim Hegan	8.00	4.00	.80
☐	188	Charlie Dressen MG	9.00	4.50	.90
☐	189	Jim Piersall	11.00	5.50	1.10
☐	190	Dick Fowler	7.00	3.50	.70
☐	191	Bob Friend	11.00	5.50	1.10
☐	192	John Cusick	7.00	3.50	.70
☐	193	Bobby Young	7.00	3.50	.70
☐	194	Bob Porterfield	7.00	3.50	.70
☐	195	Frank Baumholtz	7.00	3.50	.70
☐	196	Stan Musial	250.00	125.00	25.00

☐ 197 Charlie Silvera	7.00	3.50	.70
☐ 198 Chuck Diering	7.00	3.50	.70
☐ 199 Ted Gray	7.00	3.50	.70
☐ 200 Ken Silvestri	7.00	3.50	.70
☐ 201 Ray Coleman	7.00	3.50	.70
☐ 202 Harry Perkowski	7.00	3.50	.70
☐ 203 Steve Gromek	7.00	3.50	.70
☐ 204 Andy Pafko	7.00	3.50	.70
☐ 205 Walt Masterson	7.00	3.50	.70
☐ 206 Elmer Valo	7.00	3.50	.70
☐ 207 George Strickland	7.00	3.50	.70
☐ 208 Walker Cooper	7.00	3.50	.70
☐ 209 Dick Littlefield	7.00	3.50	.70
☐ 210 Archie Wilson	7.00	3.50	.70
☐ 211 Paul Minner	7.00	3.50	.70
☐ 212 Solly Hemus	7.00	3.50	.70
☐ 213 Monte Kennedy	7.00	3.50	.70
☐ 214 Ray Boone	7.00	3.50	.70
☐ 215 Sheldon Jones	7.00	3.50	.70
☐ 216 Matt Batts	7.00	3.50	.70
☐ 217 Casey Stengel	75.00	37.50	7.50
☐ 218 Willie Mays	600.00	300.00	60.00
☐ 219 Neil Berry	16.00	8.00	1.60
☐ 220 Russ Meyer	16.00	8.00	1.60
☐ 221 Lou Kretlow	16.00	8.00	1.60
☐ 222 Dixie Howell	16.00	8.00	1.60
☐ 223 Harry Simpson	16.00	8.00	1.60
☐ 224 Johnny Schmitz	16.00	8.00	1.60
☐ 225 Del Wilber	16.00	8.00	1.60
☐ 226 Alex Kellner	16.00	8.00	1.60
☐ 227 Clyde Sukeforth	16.00	8.00	1.60
☐ 228 Bob Chipman	16.00	8.00	1.60
☐ 229 Hank Arft	16.00	8.00	1.60
☐ 230 Frank Shea	16.00	8.00	1.60
☐ 231 Dee Fondy	16.00	8.00	1.60
☐ 232 Enos Slaughter	50.00	25.00	5.00
☐ 233 Bob Kuzava	16.00	8.00	1.60
☐ 234 Fred Fitzsimmons	16.00	8.00	1.60
☐ 235 Steve Souchock	16.00	8.00	1.60
☐ 236 Tommy Brown	16.00	8.00	1.60
☐ 237 Sherman Lollar	18.00	9.00	1.80
☐ 238 Roy McMillan	18.00	9.00	1.80
☐ 239 Dale Mitchell	18.00	9.00	1.80
☐ 240 Billy Loes	25.00	12.50	2.50
☐ 241 Mel Parnell	18.00	9.00	1.80
☐ 242 Everett Kell	16.00	8.00	1.60
☐ 243 Red Munger	16.00	8.00	1.60
☐ 244 Lew Burdette	40.00	20.00	4.00
☐ 245 George Schmees	16.00	8.00	1.60
☐ 246 Jerry Snyder	16.00	8.00	1.60
☐ 247 John Pramesa	16.00	8.00	1.60
☐ 248 Bill Werle	16.00	8.00	1.60
☐ 249 Hank Thompson	18.00	9.00	1.80
☐ 250 Ivan Delock	16.00	8.00	1.60
☐ 251 Jack Lohrke	16.00	8.00	1.60
☐ 252 Frank Crosetti	75.00	15.00	3.00

1953 Bowman Color

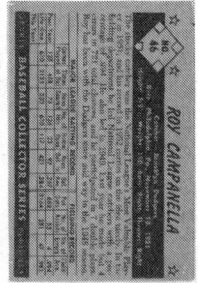

The cards in this 160-card set measure 2 1/2" by 3 3/4". The 1953 Bowman Color set, considered by many to be the best looking set of the modern era, contains Kodachrome photographs with no names or facsimile autographs on the face. Numbers 113 to 160 are somewhat more difficult to obtain. There are two cards of Al Corwin (126 and 149). Card number 159 is actually a picture of Floyd Baker.

	NRMT	VG-E	GOOD
COMPLETE SET	6750.00	2500.00	500.00

COMMON PLAYER (1-96)	15.00	7.50	1.50
COMMON PLAYER (97-112)	18.00	9.00	1.80
COMMON PLAYER (113-128)	32.00	16.00	3.20
COMMON PLAYER (129-160)	25.00	12.50	2.50

☐	1 Dave Williams	50.00	10.00	2.00
☐	2 Vic Wertz	15.00	7.50	1.50
☐	3 Sam Jethroe	15.00	7.50	1.50
☐	4 Art Houtteman	15.00	7.50	1.50
☐	5 Sid Gordon	15.00	7.50	1.50
☐	6 Joe Ginsberg	15.00	7.50	1.50
☐	7 Harry Chiti	15.00	7.50	1.50
☐	8 Al Rosen	20.00	10.00	2.00
☐	9 Phil Rizzuto	60.00	30.00	6.00
☐	10 Richie Ashburn	25.00	12.50	2.50
☐	11 Bobby Shantz	18.00	9.00	1.80
☐	12 Carl Erskine	20.00	10.00	2.00
☐	13 Gus Zernial	15.00	7.50	1.50
☐	14 Billy Loes	18.00	9.00	1.80
☐	15 Jim Busby	15.00	7.50	1.50
☐	16 Bob Friend	18.00	9.00	1.80
☐	17 Jerry Staley	15.00	7.50	1.50
☐	18 Nelson Fox	25.00	12.50	2.50
☐	19 Alvin Dark	18.00	9.00	1.80
☐	20 Don Lenhardt	15.00	7.50	1.50
☐	21 Joe Garagiola	35.00	17.50	3.50
☐	22 Bob Porterfield	15.00	7.50	1.50
☐	23 Herman Wehmeier	15.00	7.50	1.50
☐	24 Jackie Jensen	20.00	10.00	2.00
☐	25 Hoot Evers	15.00	7.50	1.50
☐	26 Roy McMillan	15.00	7.50	1.50
☐	27 Vic Raschi	20.00	10.00	2.00
☐	28 Smokey Burgess	18.00	9.00	1.80
☐	29 Bobby Avila	18.00	9.00	1.80
☐	30 Phil Cavarretta	18.00	9.00	1.80
☐	31 Jimmy Dykes	15.00	7.50	1.50
☐	32 Stan Musial	250.00	125.00	25.00
☐	33 Pee Wee Reese HOR	100.00	50.00	10.00
☐	34 Gil Coan	15.00	7.50	1.50
☐	35 Maurice McDermott	15.00	7.50	1.50
☐	36 Minnie Minoso	20.00	10.00	2.00
☐	37 Jim Wilson	15.00	7.50	1.50
☐	38 Harry Byrd	15.00	7.50	1.50
☐	39 Paul Richards MG	15.00	7.50	1.50
☐	40 Larry Doby	18.00	9.00	1.80
☐	41 Sammy White	15.00	7.50	1.50
☐	42 Tommy Brown	15.00	7.50	1.50
☐	43 Mike Garcia	18.00	9.00	1.80
☐	44 Berra/Bauer/Mantle	250.00	125.00	25.00
☐	45 Walt Dropo	15.00	7.50	1.50
☐	46 Roy Campanella	150.00	75.00	15.00
☐	47 Ned Garver	15.00	7.50	1.50
☐	48 Hank Sauer	18.00	9.00	1.80
☐	49 Eddie Stanky	18.00	9.00	1.80
☐	50 Lou Kretlow	15.00	7.50	1.50
☐	51 Monte Irvin	30.00	15.00	3.00
☐	52 Marty Marion	18.00	9.00	1.80
☐	53 Del Rice	15.00	7.50	1.50
☐	54 Chico Carrasquel	15.00	7.50	1.50
☐	55 Leo Durocher MG	22.00	11.00	2.20
☐	56 Bob Cain	15.00	7.50	1.50
☐	57 Lou Boudreau MG	27.00	13.50	2.70
☐	58 Willard Marshall	15.00	7.50	1.50
☐	59 Mickey Mantle	900.00	450.00	90.00
☐	60 Granny Hamner	15.00	7.50	1.50
☐	61 George Kell	30.00	15.00	3.00
☐	62 Ted Kluszewski	22.00	11.00	2.20
☐	63 Gil McDougald	22.00	11.00	2.20
☐	64 Curt Simmons	18.00	9.00	1.80
☐	65 Robin Roberts	35.00	17.50	3.50
☐	66 Mel Parnell	18.00	9.00	1.80
☐	67 Mel Clark	15.00	7.50	1.50
☐	68 Allie Reynolds	22.00	11.00	2.20
☐	69 Charley Grimm MG	18.00	9.00	1.80
☐	70 Clint Courtney	15.00	7.50	1.50
☐	71 Paul Minner	15.00	7.50	1.50
☐	72 Ted Gray	15.00	7.50	1.50
☐	73 Billy Pierce	18.00	9.00	1.80
☐	74 Don Mueller	15.00	7.50	1.50
☐	75 Saul Rogovin	15.00	7.50	1.50
☐	76 Jim Hearn	15.00	7.50	1.50
☐	77 Mickey Grasso	15.00	7.50	1.50
☐	78 Carl Furillo	22.00	11.00	2.20
☐	79 Ray Boone	18.00	9.00	1.80
☐	80 Ralph Kiner	30.00	15.00	3.00
☐	81 Enos Slaughter	30.00	15.00	3.00
☐	82 Joe Astroth	15.00	7.50	1.50
☐	83 Jack Daniels	15.00	7.50	1.50
☐	84 Hank Bauer	20.00	10.00	2.00
☐	85 Solly Hemus	15.00	7.50	1.50
☐	86 Harry Simpson	15.00	7.50	1.50
☐	87 Harry Perkowski	15.00	7.50	1.50
☐	88 Joe Dobson	15.00	7.50	1.50
☐	89 Sandy Consuegra	15.00	7.50	1.50

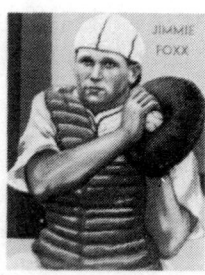

			NRMT	VG-E	GOOD
☐	90	Joe Nuxhall	18.00	9.00	1.80
☐	91	Steve Souchock	15.00	7.50	1.50
☐	92	Gil Hodges	50.00	25.00	5.00
☐	93	Phil Rizzuto and Billy Martin	90.00	45.00	9.00
☐	94	Bob Addis	15.00	7.50	1.50
☐	95	Wally Moses	15.00	7.50	1.50
☐	96	Sal Maglie	20.00	10.00	2.00
☐	97	Ed Mathews	65.00	32.50	6.50
☐	98	Hector Rodriguez	18.00	9.00	1.80
☐	99	Warren Spahn	65.00	32.50	6.50
☐	100	Bill Wight	18.00	9.00	1.80
☐	101	Red Schoendienst	20.00	10.00	2.00
☐	102	Jim Hegan	18.00	9.00	1.80
☐	103	Del Ennis	18.00	9.00	1.80
☐	104	Luke Easter	18.00	9.00	1.80
☐	105	Eddie Joost	18.00	9.00	1.80
☐	106	Ken Raffensberger	18.00	9.00	1.80
☐	107	Alex Kellner	18.00	9.00	1.80
☐	108	Bobby Adams	18.00	9.00	1.80
☐	109	Ken Wood	18.00	9.00	1.80
☐	110	Bob Rush	18.00	9.00	1.80
☐	111	Jim Dyck	18.00	9.00	1.80
☐	112	Toby Atwell	18.00	9.00	1.80
☐	113	Karl Drews	32.00	16.00	3.20
☐	114	Bob Feller	150.00	75.00	15.00
☐	115	Cloyd Boyer	32.00	16.00	3.20
☐	116	Eddie Yost	32.00	16.00	3.20
☐	117	Duke Snider	400.00	200.00	40.00
☐	118	Billy Martin	150.00	75.00	15.00
☐	119	Dale Mitchell	35.00	17.50	3.50
☐	120	Marlin Stuart	32.00	16.00	3.20
☐	121	Yogi Berra	350.00	175.00	35.00
☐	122	Bill Serena	32.00	16.00	3.20
☐	123	Johnny Lipon	32.00	16.00	3.20
☐	124	Charlie Dressen MG	45.00	22.50	4.50
☐	125	Fred Hatfield	32.00	16.00	3.20
☐	126	Al Corwin	32.00	16.00	3.20
☐	127	Dick Kryhoski	32.00	16.00	3.20
☐	128	Whitey Lockman	35.00	17.50	3.50
☐	129	Russ Meyer	25.00	12.50	2.50
☐	130	Cass Michaels	25.00	12.50	2.50
☐	131	Connie Ryan	25.00	12.50	2.50
☐	132	Fred Hutchinson	30.00	15.00	3.00
☐	133	Willie Jones	25.00	12.50	2.50
☐	134	Johnny Pesky	30.00	15.00	3.00
☐	135	Bobby Morgan	25.00	12.50	2.50
☐	136	Jim Brideweser	25.00	12.50	2.50
☐	137	Sam Dente	25.00	12.50	2.50
☐	138	Bubba Church	25.00	12.50	2.50
☐	139	Pete Runnels	30.00	15.00	3.00
☐	140	Al Brazle	25.00	12.50	2.50
☐	141	Frank Shea	25.00	12.50	2.50
☐	142	Larry Miggins	25.00	12.50	2.50
☐	143	Al Lopez MG	45.00	22.50	4.50
☐	144	Warren Hacker	25.00	12.50	2.50
☐	145	George Shuba	30.00	15.00	3.00
☐	146	Early Wynn	80.00	40.00	8.00
☐	147	Clem Koshorek	25.00	12.50	2.50
☐	148	Billy Goodman	30.00	15.00	3.00
☐	149	Al Corwin	25.00	12.50	2.50
☐	150	Carl Scheib	25.00	12.50	2.50
☐	151	Joe Adcock	35.00	17.50	3.50
☐	152	Clyde Vollmer	25.00	12.50	2.50
☐	153	Whitey Ford	250.00	125.00	25.00
☐	154	Turk Lown	25.00	12.50	2.50
☐	155	Allie Clark	25.00	12.50	2.50
☐	156	Max Surkont	25.00	12.50	2.50
☐	157	Sherman Lollar	30.00	15.00	3.00
☐	158	Howard Fox	25.00	12.50	2.50
☐	159	Mickey Vernon (photo actually Floyd Baker)	30.00	15.00	3.00
☐	160	Cal Abrams	40.00	15.00	3.00

1953 Bowman BW

The cards in this 64-card set measure 2 1/2" by 3 3/4". Some collectors believe that the high cost of producing the 1953 color series forced Bowman to issue this set in black and white, since the two sets are identical in design except for the element of color. This set was also produced in fewer numbers than its color counterpart, and is popular among collectors for the challenge involved in completing it.

			NRMT	VG-E	GOOD
	COMPLETE SET		1800.00	600.00	120.00
	COMMON PLAYER (1-64)		20.00	10.00	2.00
☐	1	Gus Bell	75.00	15.00	3.00
☐	2	Willard Nixon	20.00	10.00	2.00
☐	3	Bill Rigney	20.00	10.00	2.00
☐	4	Pat Mullin	20.00	10.00	2.00
☐	5	Dee Fondy	20.00	10.00	2.00
☐	6	Ray Murray	20.00	10.00	2.00
☐	7	Andy Seminick	20.00	10.00	2.00
☐	8	Pete Suder	20.00	10.00	2.00
☐	9	Walt Masterson	20.00	10.00	2.00
☐	10	Dick Sisler	20.00	10.00	2.00
☐	11	Dick Gernert	20.00	10.00	2.00
☐	12	Randy Jackson	20.00	10.00	2.00
☐	13	Joe Tipton	20.00	10.00	2.00
☐	14	Bill Nicholson	20.00	10.00	2.00
☐	15	Johnny Mize	85.00	42.50	8.50
☐	16	Stu Miller	25.00	12.50	2.50
☐	17	Virgil Trucks	25.00	12.50	2.50
☐	18	Billy Hoeft	25.00	12.50	2.50
☐	19	Paul LaPalme	20.00	10.00	2.00
☐	20	Eddie Robinson	20.00	10.00	2.00
☐	21	Clarence Podbielan	20.00	10.00	2.00
☐	22	Matt Batts	20.00	10.00	2.00
☐	23	Wilmer Mizell	25.00	12.50	2.50
☐	24	Del Wilber	20.00	10.00	2.00
☐	25	Johnny Sain	40.00	20.00	4.00
☐	26	Preacher Roe	40.00	20.00	4.00
☐	27	Bob Lemon	75.00	37.50	7.50
☐	28	Hoyt Wilhelm	75.00	37.50	7.50
☐	29	Sid Hudson	20.00	10.00	2.00
☐	30	Walker Cooper	20.00	10.00	2.00
☐	31	Gene Woodling	30.00	15.00	3.00
☐	32	Rocky Bridges	20.00	10.00	2.00
☐	33	Bob Kuzava	20.00	10.00	2.00
☐	34	Ebba St.Claire	20.00	10.00	2.00
☐	35	Johnny Wyrostek	20.00	10.00	2.00
☐	36	Jim Piersall	30.00	15.00	3.00
☐	37	Hal Jeffcoat	20.00	10.00	2.00
☐	38	Dave Cole	20.00	10.00	2.00
☐	39	Casey Stengel	225.00	110.00	22.00
☐	40	Larry Jansen	20.00	10.00	2.00
☐	41	Bob Ramazotti	20.00	10.00	2.00
☐	42	Howie Judson	20.00	10.00	2.00
☐	43	Hal Bevan	20.00	10.00	2.00
☐	44	Jim Delsing	20.00	10.00	2.00
☐	45	Irv Noren	20.00	10.00	2.00
☐	46	Bucky Harris	35.00	17.50	3.50
☐	47	Jack Lohrke	20.00	10.00	2.00
☐	48	Steve Ridzik	20.00	10.00	2.00
☐	49	Floyd Baker	20.00	10.00	2.00
☐	50	Dutch Leonard	20.00	10.00	2.00
☐	51	Lou Burdette	30.00	15.00	3.00
☐	52	Ralph Branca	25.00	12.50	2.50
☐	53	Morris Martin	20.00	10.00	2.00
☐	54	Bill Miller	20.00	10.00	2.00
☐	55	Don Johnson	20.00	10.00	2.00
☐	56	Roy Smalley	20.00	10.00	2.00
☐	57	Andy Pafko	20.00	10.00	2.00
☐	58	Jim Konstanty	25.00	12.50	2.50
☐	59	Duane Pillette	20.00	10.00	2.00
☐	60	Billy Cox	25.00	12.50	2.50
☐	61	Tom Gorman	20.00	10.00	2.00
☐	62	Keith Thomas	20.00	10.00	2.00
☐	63	Steve Gromek	20.00	10.00	2.00
☐	64	Andy Hansen	30.00	10.00	2.00

1954 Bowman

The cards in this 224-card set measure 2 1/2" by 3 3/4". A contractual problem apparently resulted in the deletion of the number 66 Ted Williams card from this Bowman set, thereby creating a scarcity which is highly valued among collectors. The set price below does NOT include number 66 Williams. Many errors in players' statistics exist (and some were corrected) while a few players' names were printed on the front, instead of appearing as a facsimile autograph.

	NRMT	VG-E	GOOD
COMPLETE SET	2500.00	900.00	150.00
COMMON PLAYER (1-128)	4.00	2.00	.40
COMMON PLAYER (129-224)	5.00	2.50	.50

			NRMT	VG-E	GOOD
☐	1	Phil Rizzuto	100.00	20.00	4.00
☐	2	Jackie Jensen	6.00	3.00	.60
☐	3	Marion Fricano	4.00	2.00	.40
☐	4	Bob Hooper	4.00	2.00	.40
☐	5	Bill Hunter	4.00	2.00	.40
☐	6	Nelson Fox	8.00	4.00	.80
☐	7	Walt Dropo	4.00	2.00	.40
☐	8	Jim Busby	4.00	2.00	.40
☐	9	Davey Williams	4.00	2.00	.40
☐	10	Carl Erskine	6.00	3.00	.60
☐	11	Sid Gordon	4.00	2.00	.40
☐	12	Roy McMillan	4.00	2.00	.40
☐	13	Paul Minner	4.00	2.00	.40
☐	14	Gerry Staley	4.00	2.00	.40
☐	15	Richie Ashburn	9.00	4.50	.90
☐	16	Jim Wilson	4.00	2.00	.40
☐	17	Tom Gorman	4.00	2.00	.40
☐	18	Hoot Evers	4.00	2.00	.40
☐	19	Bobby Shantz	5.00	2.50	.50
☐	20	Art Houtteman	4.00	2.00	.40
☐	21	Vic Wertz	5.00	2.50	.50
☐	22	Sam Mele	4.00	2.00	.40
☐	23	Harvey Kuenn	11.00	5.50	1.10
☐	24	Bob Porterfield	4.00	2.00	.40
☐	25	Wes Westrum	4.00	2.00	.40
☐	26	Billy Cox	5.00	2.50	.50
☐	27	Dick Cole	4.00	2.00	.40
☐	28	Jim Greengrass	4.00	2.00	.40
☐	29	Johnny Klippstein	4.00	2.00	.40
☐	30	Del Rice	4.00	2.00	.40
☐	31	Smoky Burgess	5.00	2.50	.50
☐	32	Del Crandall	5.00	2.50	.50
☐	33A	Vic Raschi	6.00	3.00	.60
		(no mention of			
		trade on back)			
☐	33B	Vic Raschi	15.00	7.50	1.50
		(traded to St.Louis)			
☐	34	Sammy White	4.00	2.00	.40
☐	35	Eddie Joost	4.00	2.00	.40
☐	36	George Strickland	4.00	2.00	.40
☐	37	Dick Kokos	4.00	2.00	.40
☐	38	Minnie Minoso	7.00	3.50	.70
☐	39	Ned Garver	4.00	2.00	.40
☐	40	Gil Coan	4.00	2.00	.40
☐	41	Alvin Dark	5.00	2.50	.50
☐	42	Billy Loes	5.00	2.50	.50
☐	43	Bob Friend	5.00	2.50	.50
☐	44	Harry Perkowski	4.00	2.00	.40
☐	45	Ralph Kiner	20.00	10.00	2.00
☐	46	Rip Repulski	4.00	2.00	.40
☐	47	Granny Hamner	4.00	2.00	.40
☐	48	Jack Dittmer	4.00	2.00	.40
☐	49	Harry Byrd	4.00	2.00	.40
☐	50	George Kell	17.00	8.50	1.70
☐	51	Alex Kellner	4.00	2.00	.40
☐	52	Joe Ginsberg	4.00	2.00	.40
☐	53	Don Lenhardt	4.00	2.00	.40
☐	54	Chico Carrasquel	4.00	2.00	.40
☐	55	Jim Delsing	4.00	2.00	.40
☐	56	Maurice McDermott	4.00	2.00	.40
☐	57	Hoyt Wilhelm	17.00	8.50	1.70
☐	58	Pee Wee Reese	25.00	12.50	2.50
☐	59	Bob Schultz	4.00	2.00	.40
☐	60	Fred Baczewski	4.00	2.00	.40
☐	61	Eddie Miksis	4.00	2.00	.40
☐	62	Enos Slaughter	17.00	8.50	1.70
☐	63	Earl Torgeson	4.00	2.00	.40
☐	64	Eddie Mathews	22.00	11.00	2.20
☐	65	Mickey Mantle	500.00	250.00	50.00
☐	66A	Jim Piersall	100.00	50.00	10.00
☐	66B	Ted Williams	1500.00	500.00	100.00
☐	67	Carl Scheib	4.00	2.00	.40
☐	68	Bobby Avila	4.00	2.00	.40
☐	69	Clint Courtney	4.00	2.00	.40
☐	70	Willard Marshall	4.00	2.00	.40
☐	71	Ted Gray	4.00	2.00	.40
☐	72	Eddie Yost	4.00	2.00	.40
☐	73	Don Mueller	5.00	2.50	.50
☐	74	Jim Gilliam	7.00	3.50	.70
☐	75	Max Surkont	4.00	2.00	.40
☐	76	Joe Nuxhall	5.00	2.50	.50
☐	77	Bob Rush	4.00	2.00	.40
☐	78	Sal Yvars	4.00	2.00	.40
☐	79	Curt Simmons	5.00	2.50	.50
☐	80	Johnny Logan	5.00	2.50	.50
☐	81	Jerry Coleman	5.00	2.50	.50
☐	82	Billy Goodman	5.00	2.50	.50
☐	83	Ray Murray	4.00	2.00	.40
☐	84	Larry Doby	6.50	3.25	.65
☐	85	Jim Dyck	4.00	2.00	.40
☐	86	Harry Dorish	4.00	2.00	.40
☐	87	Don Lund	4.00	2.00	.40
☐	88	Tom Umphlett	4.00	2.00	.40
☐	89	Willie Mays	200.00	100.00	20.00
☐	90	Roy Campanella	75.00	37.50	7.50
☐	91	Cal Abrams	4.00	2.00	.40
☐	92	Ken Raffensberger	4.00	2.00	.40
☐	93	Bill Serena	4.00	2.00	.40
☐	94	Solly Hemus	4.00	2.00	.40
☐	95	Robin Roberts	17.00	8.50	1.70
☐	96	Joe Adcock	5.00	2.50	.50
☐	97	Gil McDougald	7.00	3.50	.70
☐	98	Ellis Kinder	4.00	2.00	.40
☐	99	Pete Suder	4.00	2.00	.40
☐	100	Mike Garcia	5.00	2.50	.50
☐	101	Don Larsen	9.00	4.50	.90
☐	102	Billy Pierce	5.00	2.50	.50
☐	103	Steve Souchock	4.00	2.00	.40
☐	104	Frank Shea	4.00	2.00	.40
☐	105	Sal Maglie	6.00	3.00	.60
☐	106	Clem Labine	5.00	2.50	.50
☐	107	Paul LaPalme	4.00	2.00	.40
☐	108	Bobby Adams	4.00	2.00	.40
☐	109	Roy Smalley	4.00	2.00	.40
☐	110	Red Schoendienst	6.50	3.25	.65
☐	111	Murry Dickson	4.00	2.00	.40
☐	112	Andy Pafko	4.00	2.00	.40
☐	113	Allie Reynolds	7.50	3.75	.75
☐	114	Willard Nixon	4.00	2.00	.40
☐	115	Don Bollweg	4.00	2.00	.40
☐	116	Luke Easter	4.00	2.00	.40
☐	117	Dick Kryhoski	4.00	2.00	.40
☐	118	Bob Boyd	4.00	2.00	.40
☐	119	Fred Hatfield	4.00	2.00	.40
☐	120	Mel Hoderlein	4.00	2.00	.40
☐	121	Ray Katt	4.00	2.00	.40
☐	122	Carl Furillo	7.50	3.75	.75
☐	123	Toby Atwell	4.00	2.00	.40
☐	124	Gus Bell	4.00	2.00	.40
☐	125	Warren Hacker	4.00	2.00	.40
☐	126	Cliff Chambers	4.00	2.00	.40
☐	127	Del Ennis	5.00	2.50	.50
☐	128	Ebba St.Claire	4.00	2.00	.40
☐	129	Hank Bauer	7.50	3.75	.75
☐	130	Milt Bolling	5.00	2.50	.50
☐	131	Joe Astroth	5.00	2.50	.50
☐	132	Bob Feller	35.00	17.50	3.50
☐	133	Duane Pillette	5.00	2.50	.50
☐	134	Luis Aloma	5.00	2.50	.50
☐	135	Johnny Pesky	6.00	3.00	.60
☐	136	Clyde Vollmer	5.00	2.50	.50
☐	137	Al Corwin	5.00	2.50	.50
☐	138	Gil Hodges	27.00	13.50	2.70
☐	139	Preston Ward	5.00	2.50	.50
☐	140	Saul Rogovin	5.00	2.50	.50

☐ 141	Joe Garagiola	21.00	10.50	2.10
☐ 142	Al Brazle	5.00	2.50	.50
☐ 143	Willie Jones	5.00	2.50	.50
☐ 144	Ernie Johnson	5.00	2.50	.50
☐ 145	Billy Martin	25.00	12.50	2.50
☐ 146	Dick Gernert	5.00	2.50	.50
☐ 147	Joe DeMaestri	5.00	2.50	.50
☐ 148	Dale Mitchell	6.00	3.00	.60
☐ 149	Bob Young	5.00	2.50	.50
☐ 150	Cass Michaels	5.00	2.50	.50
☐ 151	Pat Mullin	5.00	2.50	.50
☐ 152	Mickey Vernon	6.00	3.00	.60
☐ 153	Whitey Lockman	6.00	3.00	.60
☐ 154	Don Newcombe	8.00	4.00	.80
☐ 155	Frank Thomas	6.00	3.00	.60
☐ 156	Rocky Bridges	5.00	2.50	.50
☐ 157	Turk Lown	5.00	2.50	.50
☐ 158	Stu Miller	5.00	2.50	.50
☐ 159	Johnny Lindell	5.00	2.50	.50
☐ 160	Danny O'Connell	5.00	2.50	.50
☐ 161	Yogi Berra	75.00	37.50	7.50
☐ 162	Ted Lepcio	5.00	2.50	.50
☐ 163A	Dave Philley (no mention of trade on back)	6.00	3.00	.60
☐ 163B	Dave Philley (traded to Cleveland)	15.00	7.50	1.50
☐ 164	Early Wynn	20.00	10.00	2.00
☐ 165	Johnny Groth	5.00	2.50	.50
☐ 166	Sandy Consuegra	5.00	2.50	.50
☐ 167	Billy Hoeft	5.00	2.50	.50
☐ 168	Ed Fitzgerald	5.00	2.50	.50
☐ 169	Larry Jansen	5.00	2.50	.50
☐ 170	Duke Snider	75.00	37.50	7.50
☐ 171	Carlos Bernier	5.00	2.50	.50
☐ 172	Andy Seminick	5.00	2.50	.50
☐ 173	Dee Fondy	5.00	2.50	.50
☐ 174	Pete Castiglione	5.00	2.50	.50
☐ 175	Mel Clark	5.00	2.50	.50
☐ 176	Vern Bickford	5.00	2.50	.50
☐ 177	Whitey Ford	40.00	20.00	4.00
☐ 178	Del Wilber	5.00	2.50	.50
☐ 179	Morris Martin	5.00	2.50	.50
☐ 180	Joe Tipton	5.00	2.50	.50
☐ 181	Les Moss	5.00	2.50	.50
☐ 182	Sherman Lollar	6.00	3.00	.60
☐ 183	Matt Batts	5.00	2.50	.50
☐ 184	Mickey Grasso	5.00	2.50	.50
☐ 185	Daryl Spencer	5.00	2.50	.50
☐ 186	Russ Meyer	5.00	2.50	.50
☐ 187	Vernon Law	6.00	3.00	.60
☐ 188	Frank Smith	5.00	2.50	.50
☐ 189	Randy Jackson	5.00	2.50	.50
☐ 190	Joe Presko	5.00	2.50	.50
☐ 191	Karl Drews	5.00	2.50	.50
☐ 192	Lou Burdette	7.00	3.50	.70
☐ 193	Eddie Robinson	6.00	3.00	.60
☐ 194	Sid Hudson	5.00	2.50	.50
☐ 195	Bob Cain	5.00	2.50	.50
☐ 196	Bob Lemon	20.00	10.00	2.00
☐ 197	Lou Kretlow	5.00	2.50	.50
☐ 198	Virgil Trucks	6.00	3.00	.60
☐ 199	Steve Gromek	5.00	2.50	.50
☐ 200	Conrado Marrero	5.00	2.50	.50
☐ 201	Bobby Thomson	7.00	3.50	.70
☐ 202	George Shuba	6.00	3.00	.60
☐ 203	Vic Janowicz	6.00	3.00	.60
☐ 204	Jackie Collum	5.00	2.50	.50
☐ 205	Hal Jeffcoat	5.00	2.50	.50
☐ 206	Steve Bilko	5.00	2.50	.50
☐ 207	Stan Lopata	5.00	2.50	.50
☐ 208	Johnny Antonelli	6.00	3.00	.60
☐ 209	Gene Woodling	7.00	3.50	.70
☐ 210	Jim Piersall	7.00	3.50	.70
☐ 211	Al Robertson	5.00	2.50	.50
☐ 212	Owen Friend	5.00	2.50	.50
☐ 213	Dick Littlefield	5.00	2.50	.50
☐ 214	Ferris Fain	6.00	3.00	.60
☐ 215	Johnny Bucha	5.00	2.50	.50
☐ 216	Jerry Snyder	5.00	2.50	.50
☐ 217	Henry Thompson	6.00	3.00	.60
☐ 218	Preacher Roe	7.00	3.50	.70
☐ 219	Hal Rice	5.00	2.50	.50
☐ 220	Hobie Landrith	5.00	2.50	.50
☐ 221	Frank Baumholtz	5.00	2.50	.50
☐ 222	Memo Luna	5.00	2.50	.50
☐ 223	Steve Ridzik	5.00	2.50	.50
☐ 224	Bill Bruton	15.00	3.00	.60

1955 Bowman

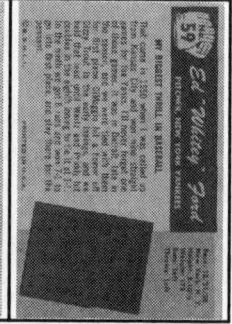

The cards in this 320-card set measure 2 1/2" by 3 3/4". The Bowman set of 1955 is known as the "TV set" because each player photograph is cleverly shown within a television set design. The set contains umpire cards, some transposed pictures (e.g., Johnsons and Bollings), an incorrect spelling for Harvey Kuenn, and a traded line for Palica (all of which are noted in the checklist below). Some three-card advertising strips exist.

		NRMT	VG-E	GOOD
COMPLETE SET		3000.00	1000.00	200.00
COMMON PLAYER (1-96)		4.00	2.00	.40
COMMON PLAYER (97-224)		3.00	1.50	.30
COMMON PLAYER (225-320)		9.00	4.50	.90
COMMON UMPIRES (225-320)		12.00	6.00	1.20
☐	1 Hoyt Wilhelm	60.00	7.50	1.50
☐	2 Alvin Dark	5.00	2.50	.50
☐	3 Joe Coleman	4.00	2.00	.40
☐	4 Eddie Waitkus	4.00	2.00	.40
☐	5 Jim Robertson	4.00	2.00	.40
☐	6 Pete Suder	4.00	2.00	.40
☐	7 Gene Baker	4.00	2.00	.40
☐	8 Warren Hacker	4.00	2.00	.40
☐	9 Gil McDougald	6.50	3.25	.65
☐	10 Phil Rizzuto	27.00	13.50	2.70
☐	11 Billy Bruton	5.00	2.50	.50
☐	12 Andy Pafko	4.00	2.00	.40
☐	13 Clyde Vollmer	4.00	2.00	.40
☐	14 Gus Keriazakos	4.00	2.00	.40
☐	15 Frank Sullivan	4.00	2.00	.40
☐	16 Jim Piersall	6.00	3.00	.60
☐	17 Del Ennis	5.00	2.50	.50
☐	18 Stan Lopata	4.00	2.00	.40
☐	19 Bobby Avila	4.00	2.00	.40
☐	20 Al Smith	4.00	2.00	.40
☐	21 Don Hoak	5.00	2.50	.50
☐	22 Roy Campanella	50.00	25.00	5.00
☐	23 Al Kaline	45.00	22.50	4.50
☐	24 Al Aber	4.00	2.00	.40
☐	25 Minnie Minoso	6.00	3.00	.60
☐	26 Virgil Trucks	5.00	2.50	.50
☐	27 Preston Ward	4.00	2.00	.40
☐	28 Dick Cole	4.00	2.00	.40
☐	29 Red Schoendienst	6.00	3.00	.60
☐	30 Bill Sarni	4.00	2.00	.40
☐	31 Johnny Temple	5.00	2.50	.50
☐	32 Wally Post	5.00	2.50	.50
☐	33 Nelson Fox	7.50	3.75	.75
☐	34 Clint Courtney	4.00	2.00	.40
☐	35 Bill Tuttle	4.00	2.00	.40
☐	36 Wayne Belardi	4.00	2.00	.40
☐	37 Pee Wee Reese	27.00	13.50	2.70
☐	38 Early Wynn	17.00	8.50	1.70
☐	39 Bob Darnell	4.00	2.00	.40
☐	40 Vic Wertz	5.00	2.50	.50
☐	41 Mel Clark	4.00	2.00	.40
☐	42 Bob Greenwood	4.00	2.00	.40
☐	43 Bob Buhl	4.00	2.00	.40
☐	44 Danny O'Connell	4.00	2.00	.40
☐	45 Tom Umphlett	4.00	2.00	.40
☐	46 Mickey Vernon	5.00	2.50	.50
☐	47 Sammy White	4.00	2.00	.40
☐	48A Milt Bolling ERR (name on back is	5.00	2.50	.50

Frank Bolling)

☐ 48B	Milt Bolling COR	15.00	7.50	1.50
☐ 49	Jim Greengrass	4.00	2.00	.40
☐ 50	Hobie Landrith	4.00	2.00	.40
☐ 51	Elvin Tappe	4.00	2.00	.40
☐ 52	Hal Rice	4.00	2.00	.40
☐ 53	Alex Kellner	4.00	2.00	.40
☐ 54	Don Bollweg	4.00	2.00	.40
☐ 55	Cal Abrams	4.00	2.00	.40
☐ 56	Billy Cox	5.00	2.50	.50
☐ 57	Bob Friend	5.00	2.50	.50
☐ 58	Frank Thomas	5.00	2.50	.50
☐ 59	Whitey Ford	27.00	13.50	2.70
☐ 60	Enos Slaughter	17.00	8.50	1.70
☐ 61	Paul LaPalme	4.00	2.00	.40
☐ 62	Royce Lint	4.00	2.00	.40
☐ 63	Irv Noren	5.00	2.50	.50
☐ 64	Curt Simmons	5.00	2.50	.50
☐ 65	Don Zimmer	6.50	3.25	.65
☐ 66	George Shuba	5.00	2.50	.50
☐ 67	Don Larsen	6.50	3.25	.65
☐ 68	Elston Howard	15.00	7.50	1.50
☐ 69	Bill Hunter	4.00	2.00	.40
☐ 70	Lou Burdette	5.00	2.50	.50
☐ 71	Dave Jolly	4.00	2.00	.40
☐ 72	Chet Nichols	4.00	2.00	.40
☐ 73	Eddie Yost	4.00	2.00	.40
☐ 74	Jerry Snyder	4.00	2.00	.40
☐ 75	Brooks Lawrence	4.00	2.00	.40
☐ 76	Tom Poholsky	4.00	2.00	.40
☐ 77	Jim McDonald	4.00	2.00	.40
☐ 78	Gil Coan	4.00	2.00	.40
☐ 79	Willie Miranda	4.00	2.00	.40
☐ 80	Lou Limmer	4.00	2.00	.40
☐ 81	Bob Morgan	4.00	2.00	.40
☐ 82	Lee Walls	4.00	2.00	.40
☐ 83	Max Surkont	4.00	2.00	.40
☐ 84	George Freese	4.00	2.00	.40
☐ 85	Cass Michaels	4.00	2.00	.40
☐ 86	Ted Gray	4.00	2.00	.40
☐ 87	Randy Jackson	4.00	2.00	.40
☐ 88	Steve Bilko	4.00	2.00	.40
☐ 89	Lou Boudreau MG	17.00	8.50	1.70
☐ 90	Art Dittmar	4.00	2.00	.40
☐ 91	Dick Marlowe	4.00	2.00	.40
☐ 92	George Zuverink	4.00	2.00	.40
☐ 93	Andy Seminick	4.00	2.00	.40
☐ 94	Hank Thompson	5.00	2.50	.50
☐ 95	Sal Maglie	6.00	3.00	.60
☐ 96	Ray Narleski	4.00	2.00	.40
☐ 97	Johnny Podres	6.50	3.25	.65
☐ 98	Jim Gilliam	6.50	3.25	.65
☐ 99	Jerry Coleman	5.00	2.50	.50
☐ 100	Tom Morgan	4.00	2.00	.40
☐ 101A	Don Johnson ERR	4.00	2.00	.40
	(photo actually			
	Ernie Johnson)			
☐ 101B	Don Johnson COR	10.00	5.00	1.00
☐ 102	Bobby Thomson	5.00	2.50	.50
☐ 103	Eddie Mathews	18.00	9.00	1.80
☐ 104	Bob Porterfield	3.00	1.50	.30
☐ 105	Johnny Schmitz	3.00	1.50	.30
☐ 106	Del Rice	3.00	1.50	.30
☐ 107	Solly Hemus	3.00	1.50	.30
☐ 108	Lou Kretlow	3.00	1.50	.30
☐ 109	Vern Stephens	3.00	1.50	.30
☐ 110	Bob Miller	3.00	1.50	.30
☐ 111	Steve Ridzik	3.00	1.50	.30
☐ 112	Granny Hamner	3.00	1.50	.30
☐ 113	Bob Hall	3.00	1.50	.30
☐ 114	Vic Janowicz	3.00	1.50	.30
☐ 115	Roger Bowman	3.00	1.50	.30
☐ 116	Sandy Consuegra	3.00	1.50	.30
☐ 117	Johnny Groth	3.00	1.50	.30
☐ 118	Bobby Adams	3.00	1.50	.30
☐ 119	Joe Astroth	3.00	1.50	.30
☐ 120	Ed Burtschy	3.00	1.50	.30
☐ 121	Rufus Crawford	3.00	1.50	.30
☐ 122	Al Corwin	3.00	1.50	.30
☐ 123	Marv Grissom	3.00	1.50	.30
☐ 124	Johnny Antonelli	4.00	2.00	.40
☐ 125	Paul Giel	3.00	1.50	.30
☐ 126	Billy Goodman	3.00	1.50	.30
☐ 127	Hank Majeski	3.00	1.50	.30
☐ 128	Mike Garcia	4.00	2.00	.40
☐ 129	Hal Naragon	3.00	1.50	.30
☐ 130	Richie Ashburn	8.00	4.00	.80
☐ 131	Willard Marshall	3.00	1.50	.30
☐ 132A	Harvey Kueen ERR	6.00	3.00	.60
	(sic, Kuenn)			
☐ 132B	Harvey Kuenn COR	15.00	7.50	1.50
☐ 133	Charles King	3.00	1.50	.30
☐ 134	Bob Feller	35.00	17.50	3.50
☐ 135	Lloyd Merriman	3.00	1.50	.30
☐ 136	Rocky Bridges	3.00	1.50	.30
☐ 137	Bob Talbot	3.00	1.50	.30
☐ 138	Davey Williams	4.00	2.00	.40
☐ 139	Shantz Brothers	4.00	2.00	.40
	Wilmer and Bobby			
☐ 140	Bobby Shantz	4.00	2.00	.40
☐ 141	Wes Westrum	3.00	1.50	.30
☐ 142	Rudy Regalado	3.00	1.50	.30
☐ 143	Don Newcombe	6.50	3.25	.65
☐ 144	Art Houtteman	3.00	1.50	.30
☐ 145	Bob Nieman	3.00	1.50	.30
☐ 146	Don Liddle	3.00	1.50	.30
☐ 147	Sam Mele	3.00	1.50	.30
☐ 148	Bob Chakales	3.00	1.50	.30
☐ 149	Cloyd Boyer	3.00	1.50	.30
☐ 150	Bill Klaus	3.00	1.50	.30
☐ 151	Jim Brideweser	3.00	1.50	.30
☐ 152	Johnny Klippstein	3.00	1.50	.30
☐ 153	Eddie Robinson	3.00	1.50	.30
☐ 154	Frank Lary	4.00	2.00	.40
☐ 155	Gerry Staley	3.00	1.50	.30
☐ 156	Jim Hughes	3.00	1.50	.30
☐ 157A	Ernie Johnson ERR	4.00	2.00	.40
	(photo actually			
	Don Johnson)			
☐ 157B	Ernie Johnson COR	10.00	5.00	1.00
☐ 158	Gil Hodges	20.00	10.00	2.00
☐ 159	Harry Byrd	3.00	1.50	.30
☐ 160	Bill Skowron	7.00	3.50	.70
☐ 161	Matt Batts	3.00	1.50	.30
☐ 162	Charlie Maxwell	3.00	1.50	.30
☐ 163	Sid Gordon	3.00	1.50	.30
☐ 164	Toby Atwell	3.00	1.50	.30
☐ 165	Maurice McDermott	3.00	1.50	.30
☐ 166	Jim Busby	3.00	1.50	.30
☐ 167	Bob Grim	4.00	2.00	.40
☐ 168	Yogi Berra	45.00	22.50	4.50
☐ 169	Carl Furillo	7.00	3.50	.70
☐ 170	Carl Erskine	6.00	3.00	.60
☐ 171	Robin Roberts	16.00	8.00	1.60
☐ 172	Willie Jones	3.00	1.50	.30
☐ 173	Chico Carrasquel	3.00	1.50	.30
☐ 174	Sherman Lollar	4.00	2.00	.40
☐ 175	Wilmer Shantz	3.00	1.50	.30
☐ 176	Joe DeMaestri	3.00	1.50	.30
☐ 177	Willard Nixon	3.00	1.50	.30
☐ 178	Tom Brewer	3.00	1.50	.30
☐ 179	Hank Aaron	100.00	50.00	10.00
☐ 180	Johnny Logan	4.00	2.00	.40
☐ 181	Eddie Miksis	3.00	1.50	.30
☐ 182	Bob Rush	3.00	1.50	.30
☐ 183	Ray Katt	3.00	1.50	.30
☐ 184	Willie Mays	100.00	50.00	10.00
☐ 185	Vic Raschi	5.00	2.50	.50
☐ 186	Alex Grammas	3.00	1.50	.30
☐ 187	Fred Hatfield	3.00	1.50	.30
☐ 188	Ned Garver	3.00	1.50	.30
☐ 189	Jack Collum	3.00	1.50	.30
☐ 190	Fred Baczewski	3.00	1.50	.30
☐ 191	Bob Lemon	16.00	8.00	1.60
☐ 192	George Strickland	3.00	1.50	.30
☐ 193	Howie Judson	3.00	1.50	.30
☐ 194	Joe Nuxhall	4.00	2.00	.40
☐ 195A	Erv Palica	4.00	2.00	.40
	(without trade)			
☐ 195B	Erv Palica	14.00	7.00	1.40
	(with trade)			
☐ 196	Russ Meyer	3.00	1.50	.30
☐ 197	Ralph Kiner	17.00	8.50	1.70
☐ 198	Dave Pope	3.00	1.50	.30
☐ 199	Vernon Law	4.00	2.00	.40
☐ 200	Dick Littlefield	3.00	1.50	.30
☐ 201	Allie Reynolds	7.00	3.50	.70
☐ 202	Mickey Mantle	350.00	175.00	35.00
☐ 203	Steve Gromek	3.00	1.50	.30
☐ 204A	Frank Bolling ERR	4.00	2.00	.40
	(name on back is			
	Milt Bolling)			
☐ 204B	Frank Bolling COR	10.00	5.00	1.00
☐ 205	Rip Repulski	3.00	1.50	.30
☐ 206	Ralph Beard	3.00	1.50	.30
☐ 207	Frank Shea	3.00	1.50	.30
☐ 208	Eddy Fitzgerald	3.00	1.50	.30
☐ 209	Smokey Burgess	4.00	2.00	.40
☐ 210	Earl Torgeson	3.00	1.50	.30
☐ 211	Sonny Dixon	3.00	1.50	.30
☐ 212	Jack Dittmer	3.00	1.50	.30
☐ 213	George Kell	16.00	8.00	1.60
☐ 214	Billy Pierce	4.00	2.00	.40
☐ 215	Bob Kuzava	3.00	1.50	.30
☐ 216	Preacher Roe	4.50	2.25	.45
☐ 217	Del Crandall	4.00	2.00	.40
☐ 218	Joe Adcock	4.00	2.00	.40
☐ 219	Whitey Lockman	3.00	1.50	.30
☐ 220	Jim Hearn	3.00	1.50	.30
☐ 221	Hector Brown	3.00	1.50	.30

☐ 222	Russ Kemmerer	3.00	1.50	.30
☐ 223	Hal Jeffcoat	3.00	1.50	.30
☐ 224	Dee Fondy	3.00	1.50	.30
☐ 225	Paul Richards	10.00	5.00	1.00
☐ 226	W. McKinley UMP	12.00	6.00	1.20
☐ 227	Frank Baumholtz	9.00	4.50	.90
☐ 228	John Phillips	9.00	4.50	.90
☐ 229	Jim Brosnan	11.00	5.50	1.10
☐ 230	Al Brazle	9.00	4.50	.90
☐ 231	Jim Konstanty	10.00	5.00	1.00
☐ 232	Birdie Tebbetts	10.00	5.00	1.00
☐ 233	Bill Serena	9.00	4.50	.90
☐ 234	Dick Bartell	9.00	4.50	.90
☐ 235	J. Paparella UMP	12.00	6.00	1.20
☐ 236	Murry Dickson	9.00	4.50	.90
☐ 237	Johnny Wyrostek	9.00	4.50	.90
☐ 238	Eddie Stanky	11.00	5.50	1.10
☐ 239	Edwin Rommel UMP	12.00	6.00	1.20
☐ 240	Billy Loes	10.00	5.00	1.00
☐ 241	Johnny Pesky	10.00	5.00	1.00
☐ 242	Ernie Banks	175.00	85.00	18.00
☐ 243	Gus Bell	10.00	5.00	1.00
☐ 244	Duane Pillette	9.00	4.50	.90
☐ 245	Bill Miller	9.00	4.50	.90
☐ 246	Hank Bauer	18.00	9.00	1.80
☐ 247	Dutch Leonard	9.00	4.50	.90
☐ 248	Harry Dorish	9.00	4.50	.90
☐ 249	Billy Gardner	12.00	6.00	1.20
☐ 250	Larry Napp UMP	12.00	6.00	1.20
☐ 251	Stan Jok	9.00	4.50	.90
☐ 252	Roy Smalley	9.00	4.50	.90
☐ 253	Jim Wilson	9.00	4.50	.90
☐ 254	Bennett Flowers	9.00	4.50	.90
☐ 255	Pete Runnels	10.00	5.00	1.00
☐ 256	Owen Friend	9.00	4.50	.90
☐ 257	Tom Alston	9.00	4.50	.90
☐ 258	John Stevens UMP	12.00	6.00	1.20
☐ 259	Don Mossi	11.00	5.50	1.10
☐ 260	Edwin Hurley UMP	12.00	6.00	1.20
☐ 261	Walt Moryn	9.00	4.50	.90
☐ 262	Jim Lemon	10.00	5.00	1.00
☐ 263	Eddie Joost	9.00	4.50	.90
☐ 264	Bill Henry	9.00	4.50	.90
☐ 265	Albert Barlick UMP	12.00	6.00	1.20
☐ 266	Mike Fornieles	9.00	4.50	.90
☐ 267	Jim Honochick UMP	30.00	15.00	3.00
☐ 268	Roy Lee Hawes	9.00	4.50	.90
☐ 269	Joe Amalfitano	9.00	4.50	.90
☐ 270	Chico Fernandez	9.00	4.50	.90
☐ 271	Bob Hooper	9.00	4.50	.90
☐ 272	John Flaherty UMP	12.00	6.00	1.20
☐ 273	Bubba Church	9.00	4.50	.90
☐ 274	Jim Delsing	9.00	4.50	.90
☐ 275	William Grieve UMP	12.00	6.00	1.20
☐ 276	Ike Delock	9.00	4.50	.90
☐ 277	Ed Runge UMP	12.00	6.00	1.20
☐ 278	Charles Neal	12.00	6.00	1.20
☐ 279	Hank Soar UMP	12.00	6.00	1.20
☐ 280	Clyde McCullough	9.00	4.50	.90
☐ 281	Charles Berry UMP	12.00	6.00	1.20
☐ 282	Phil Cavarretta	10.00	5.00	1.00
☐ 283	Nestor Chylak UMP	12.00	6.00	1.20
☐ 284	Bill Jackowski UMP	12.00	6.00	1.20
☐ 285	Walt Dropo	10.00	5.00	1.00
☐ 286	Frank Secory UMP	12.00	6.00	1.20
☐ 287	Ron Mrozinski	9.00	4.50	.90
☐ 288	Dick Smith	9.00	4.50	.90
☐ 289	Arthur Gore UMP	12.00	6.00	1.20
☐ 290	Hershell Freeman	9.00	4.50	.90
☐ 291	Frank Dascoli UMP	12.00	6.00	1.20
☐ 292	Marv Blaylock	9.00	4.50	.90
☐ 293	Thomas Gorman UMP	12.00	5.00	1.20
☐ 294	Wally Moses	10.00	5.00	1.00
☐ 295	Lee Ballanfant UMP	12.00	6.00	1.20
☐ 296	Bill Virdon	22.00	11.00	2.20
☐ 297	Dusty Boggess UMP	12.00	6.00	1.20
☐ 298	Charlie Grimm	10.00	5.00	1.00
☐ 299	Lon Warneke UMP	12.00	6.00	1.20
☐ 300	Tommy Byrne	10.00	5.00	1.00
☐ 301	William Engeln UMP	12.00	6.00	1.20
☐ 302	Frank Malzone	15.00	7.50	1.50
☐ 303	Jocko Conlan UMP	35.00	17.50	3.50
☐ 304	Harry Chiti	9.00	4.50	.90
☐ 305	Frank Umont UMP	12.00	6.00	1.20
☐ 306	Bob Cerv	12.00	6.00	1.20
☐ 307	Babe Pinelli UMP	14.00	7.00	1.40
☐ 308	Al Lopez MG	30.00	15.00	3.00
☐ 309	Hal Dixon UMP	12.00	6.00	1.20
☐ 310	Ken Lehman	9.00	4.50	.90
☐ 311	Lawrence Goetz UMP	12.00	6.00	1.20
☐ 312	Bill Wight	9.00	4.50	.90
☐ 313	Augie Donatelli UMP	17.00	8.50	1.70
☐ 314	Dale Mitchell	10.00	5.00	1.00
☐ 315	Cal Hubbard UMP	35.00	17.50	3.50
☐ 316	Marion Fricano	9.00	4.50	.90
☐ 317	William Summers UMP	12.00	6.00	1.20
☐ 318	Sid Hudson	9.00	4.50	.90
☐ 319	Albert Schroll	9.00	4.50	.90
☐ 320	George Susce Jr.	18.00	5.00	1.00

1953-54 Briggs

GIL HODGES

The cards in this 37 card set measure 2 1/4" by 3 1/2". The 1953-54 Briggs Hot Dog set of color cards contains 25 Senators and 12 known players from the Dodgers, Yankees, and Giants. They were issued in two card panels in the Washington, D.C. area as part of the hot dog package itself. The cards are unnumbered and are printed on waxed cardboard, and the style of the Senator cards differs from that of the Ney York players. The latter appear in poses which also exist in the Dan Dee and Stahl Meyer card sets. The ACC designation is F154. In the checklist below the Washington players are numbered 1-25 alphabetically by name and the New York players are numbered 26-37 similarly.

		NRMT	VG-E	GOOD
	COMPLETE SET	6000.00	2500.00	500.00
	COMMON PLAYERS	100.00	50.00	10.00
☐ 1	Jim Busby	100.00	50.00	10.00
☐ 2	Tommy Byrne	100.00	50.00	10.00
☐ 3	Sonny Dixon	100.00	50.00	10.00
☐ 4	Ed Fitzgerald	100.00	50.00	10.00
☐ 5	Mickey Grasso	100.00	50.00	10.00
☐ 6	Mel Hoderlein	100.00	50.00	10.00
☐ 7	Jackie Jensen	150.00	75.00	15.00
☐ 8	Connie Marrero	100.00	50.00	10.00
☐ 9	Carmen Mauro	100.00	50.00	10.00
☐ 10	Walt Masterson	100.00	50.00	10.00
☐ 11	Mickey McDermott	100.00	50.00	10.00
☐ 12	Bob Oldis	100.00	50.00	10.00
☐ 13	Bob Porterfield	100.00	50.00	10.00
☐ 14	Pete Runnels	125.00	60.00	12.50
☐ 15	Johnny Schmitz	100.00	50.00	10.00
☐ 16	Angel Scull	100.00	50.00	10.00
☐ 17	Spec Shea	100.00	50.00	10.00
☐ 18	Chuck Stobbs	100.00	50.00	10.00
☐ 19	Wayne Terwilliger	100.00	50.00	10.00
☐ 20	Joe Tipton	100.00	50.00	10.00
☐ 21	Tom Umphlett	100.00	50.00	10.00
☐ 22	Mickey Vernon	125.00	60.00	12.50
☐ 23	Clyde Vollmer	100.00	50.00	10.00
☐ 24	Gene Werbil	100.00	50.00	10.00
☐ 25	Eddie Yost	100.00	50.00	10.00
☐ 26	Hank Bauer	150.00	75.00	15.00
☐ 27	Carl Erskine	150.00	75.00	15.00
☐ 28	Gil Hodges	250.00	125.00	25.00
☐ 29	Monte Irvin	200.00	100.00	20.00
☐ 30	Whitey Lockman	100.00	50.00	10.00
☐ 31	Mickey Mantle	1800.00	750.00	150.00
☐ 32	Willie Mays	850.00	425.00	85.00
☐ 33	Gil McDougald	150.00	75.00	15.00
☐ 34	Don Mueller	100.00	50.00	10.00
☐ 35	Don Newcombe	150.00	75.00	15.00
☐ 36	Phil Rizzuto	200.00	100.00	20.00
☐ 37	Duke Snider	450.00	225.00	45.00

1977 Burger King Yankees

The cards in this 24 card set measure 2 1/2" by 3 1/2". The cards in this set marked with an asterisk have different poses than those cards in the regular 1977 Topps set. The checklist card is unnumbered and the Piniella card was issued subsequent to the original printing.

		NRMT	VG-E	GOOD
COMPLETE SET		32.00	16.00	3.20
COMMON PLAYER (1-23)		.30	.15	.03
☐ 1	Yankees Team	.75	.35	.07
	Billy Martin MG			
☐ 2	Thurman Munson *	3.50	1.75	.35
☐ 3	Fran Healy	.30	.15	.03
☐ 4	Jim Hunter	1.75	.85	.17
☐ 5	Ed Figueroa	.30	.15	.03
☐ 6	Don Gullett *	.40	.20	.04
☐ 7	Mike Torrez *	.40	.20	.04
☐ 8	Ken Holtzman	.30	.15	.03
☐ 9	Dick Tidrow	.30	.15	.03
☐ 10	Sparky Lyle	.50	.25	.05
☐ 11	Ron Guidry	1.75	.85	.17
☐ 12	Chris Chambliss	.40	.20	.04
☐ 13	Willie Randolph *	.75	.35	.07
☐ 14	Bucky Dent *	.50	.25	.05
☐ 15	Graig Nettles *	1.25	.60	.12
☐ 16	Fred Stanley	.30	.15	.03
☐ 17	Reggie Jackson	3.50	1.75	.35
☐ 18	Mickey Rivers	.40	.20	.04
☐ 19	Roy White	.30	.15	.03
☐ 20	Jim Wynn	.30	.15	.03
☐ 21	Paul Blair *	.40	.20	.04
☐ 22	Carlos May *	.30	.15	.03
☐ 23	Lou Piniella	18.00	9.00	1.80
☐ xx	Checklist card	.15	.02	.00
	(unnumbered)			

1978 Burger King Astros

The cards in this 23 card set measure 2 1/2" by 3 1/2". Released in local Houston Burger King outlets during the 1978 season, this Houston Astros series contains the standard 22 numbered player cards and one unnumbered checklist. The player poses found to differ from the regular Topps issue are marked with asterisks.

		NRMT	VG-E	GOOD
COMPLETE SET		10.00	5.00	1.00
COMMON PLAYER (1-23)		.30	.15	.03
☐ 1	Bill Virdon MG	.75	.35	.07
☐ 2	Joe Ferguson	.30	.15	.03
☐ 3	Ed Herrmann	.30	.15	.03
☐ 4	J.R. Richard	1.00	.50	.10
☐ 5	Joe Niekro	1.00	.50	.10
☐ 6	Floyd Bannister	1.00	.50	.10
☐ 7	Joaquin Andujar	1.00	.50	.10

		NRMT	VG-E	GOOD
☐ 8	Ken Forsch	.40	.20	.04
☐ 9	Mark Lemongello	.30	.15	.03
☐ 10	Joe Sambito	.40	.20	.04
☐ 11	Gene Pentz	.30	.15	.03
☐ 12	Bob Watson	.50	.25	.05
☐ 13	Julio Gonzales	.30	.15	.03
☐ 14	Enos Cabell	.30	.15	.03
☐ 15	Roger Metzger	.30	.15	.03
☐ 16	Art Howe	.30	.15	.03
☐ 17	Jose Cruz	.90	.45	.09
☐ 18	Cesar Cedeno	.75	.35	.07
☐ 19	Terry Puhl	.40	.20	.04
☐ 20	Wilbur Howard	.30	.15	.03
☐ 21	Dave Bergman *	.40	.20	.04
☐ 22	Jesus Alou *	.40	.20	.04
☐ 23	Checklist card	.05	.01	.00
	(unnumbered)			

1978 Burger King Rangers

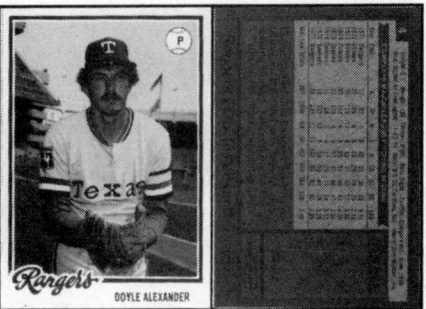

The cards in this 23 card set measure 2 1/2" by 3 1/2". This set of 22 numbered player cards (featuring the Texas Rangers) and one unnumbered checklist was issued regionally by Burger King in 1978. Astericks denote poses different from those found in the regular Topps cards of this year.

		NRMT	VG-E	GOOD
COMPLETE SET		10.00	5.00	1.00
COMMON PLAYER (1-23)		.30	.15	.03
☐ 1	Billy Hunter MG	.30	.15	.03
☐ 2	Jim Sundberg	.50	.25	.05
☐ 3	John Ellis	.30	.15	.03
☐ 4	Doyle Alexander	.60	.30	.06
☐ 5	Jon Matlack *	.60	.30	.06
☐ 6	Dock Ellis	.30	.15	.03
☐ 7	Doc Medich	.30	.15	.03
☐ 8	Fergie Jenkins *	1.50	.75	.15
☐ 9	Len Barker	.30	.15	.03
☐ 10	Reggie Cleveland *	.30	.15	.03
☐ 11	Mike Hargrove	.50	.25	.05
☐ 12	Bump Wills	.30	.15	.03
☐ 13	Toby Harrah	.75	.35	.07
☐ 14	Bert Campaneris	.50	.25	.05
☐ 15	Sandy Alomar	.30	.15	.03
☐ 16	Kurt Bevacqua	.30	.15	.03
☐ 17	Al Oliver *	1.00	.50	.10

		NRMT	VG-E	GOOD
☐ 18	Juan Beniquez	.50	.25	.05
☐ 19	Claudell Washington	.75	.35	.07
☐ 20	Richie Zisk	.50	.25	.05
☐ 21	John Lowenstein *	.30	.15	.03
☐ 22	Bobby Thompson *	.30	.15	.03
☐ 23	Checklist card	.05	.01	.00
	(unnumbered)			

1978 Burger King Tigers

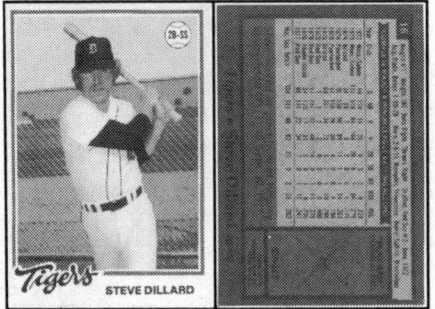

The cards in this 23 card set measure 2 1/2" by 3 1/2". Twenty-three color cards, 22 players and one numbered checklist, comprise the 1978 Burger King Tigers set issued in the Detroit area. The cards marked with an asterisk contain photos different from those appearing on the Topps regular issue cards of that year.

		NRMT	VG-E	GOOD
COMPLETE SET	....	30.00	15.00	3.00
COMMON PLAYER (1-23)	....	.30	.15	.03
☐ 1	Ralph Houk MG	.40	.20	.04
☐ 2	Milt May	.30	.15	.03
☐ 3	John Wockenfuss	.30	.15	.03
☐ 4	Mark Fidrych	.75	.35	.07
☐ 5	Dave Rozema	.30	.15	.03
☐ 6	Jack Billingham *	.30	.15	.03
☐ 7	Jim Slaton *	.30	.15	.03
☐ 8	Jack Morris *	8.00	4.00	.80
☐ 9	John Hiller	.50	.25	.05
☐ 10	Steve Foucault	.30	.15	.03
☐ 11	Milt Wilcox	.30	.15	.03
☐ 12	Jason Thompson	.60	.30	.06
☐ 13	Lou Whitaker *	6.00	3.00	.60
☐ 14	Aurelio Rodriguez	.30	.15	.03
☐ 15	Alan Trammell *	10.00	5.00	1.00
☐ 16	Steve Dillard *	.30	.15	.03
☐ 17	Phil Mankowski	.30	.15	.03
☐ 18	Steve Kemp	.60	.30	.06
☐ 19	Ron LeFlore	.40	.20	.04
☐ 20	Tim Corcoran	.30	.15	.03
☐ 21	Mickey Stanley	.40	.20	.04
☐ 22	Rusty Staub	.75	.35	.07
☐ 23	Checklist card	.05	.01	.00
	(unnumbered)			

1978 Burger King Yankees

The cards in this 23 card set measure 2 1/2" by 3 1/2". These cards were distributed in packs of three players plus a checklist at Burger King's New York area outlets. Cards with an asterisk have different poses than those in the Topps regular issue.

		NRMT	VG-E	GOOD
COMPLETE SET	....	8.00	4.00	.80
COMMON PLAYER (1-23)	....	.15	.07	.01
☐ 1	Billy Martin MG	.40	.20	.04
☐ 2	Thurman Munson	2.25	1.10	.22
☐ 3	Cliff Johnson	.15	.07	.01

CLIFF JOHNSON

		NRMT	VG-E	GOOD
☐ 4	Ron Guidry	1.50	.75	.15
☐ 5	Ed Figueroa	.15	.07	.01
☐ 6	Dick Tidrow	.15	.07	.01
☐ 7	Jim Hunter	1.50	.75	.15
☐ 8	Don Gullett	.15	.07	.01
☐ 9	Sparky Lyle	.35	.17	.03
☐ 10	Rich Gossage *	.90	.45	.09
☐ 11	Rawly Eastwick *	.15	.07	.01
☐ 12	Chris Chambliss	.20	.10	.02
☐ 13	Willie Randolph	.40	.20	.04
☐ 14	Graig Nettles	.75	.35	.07
☐ 15	Bucky Dent	.20	.10	.02
☐ 16	Jim Spencer *	.15	.07	.01
☐ 17	Fred Stanley	.15	.07	.01
☐ 18	Lou Piniella	.35	.17	.03
☐ 19	Roy White	.20	.10	.02
☐ 20	Mickey Rivers	.20	.10	.02
☐ 21	Reggie Jackson	2.25	1.10	.22
☐ 22	Paul Blair	.15	.07	.01
☐ 23	Checklist card	.05	.01	.00
	(unnumbered)			

1979 Burger King Phillies

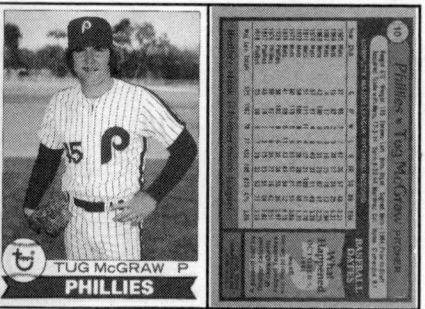

TUG McGRAW P
PHILLIES

The cards in this 23 card set measure 2 1/2" by 3 1/2". The 1979 Burger King Phillies set follows the regular format of 22 player cards and one unnumbered checklist card. The asterisk indicates where the pose differs from the Topps card of that year.

		NRMT	VG-E	GOOD
COMPLETE SET	....	5.00	2.50	.50
COMMON PLAYER (1-23)	....	.10	.05	.01
☐ 1	Danny Ozark MG *	.10	.05	.01
☐ 2	Bob Boone	.25	.12	.02
☐ 3	Tim McCarver	.25	.12	.02
☐ 4	Steve Carlton	1.50	.75	.15
☐ 5	Larry Christenson	.10	.05	.01
☐ 6	Dick Ruthven	.10	.05	.01
☐ 7	Ron Reed	.10	.05	.01
☐ 8	Randy Lerch	.10	.05	.01
☐ 9	Warren Brusstar	.10	.05	.01
☐ 10	Tug McGraw	.25	.12	.02
☐ 11	Nino Espinosa *	.10	.05	.01
☐ 12	Doug Bird *	.10	.05	.01
☐ 13	Pete Rose *	2.50	1.25	.25

□ 14 Manny Trillo *	.15	.07	.01
□ 15 Larry Bowa	.35	.17	.03
□ 16 Mike Schmidt	1.75	.85	.17
□ 17 Pete Mackanin *	.10	.05	.01
□ 18 Jose Cardenal	.10	.05	.01
□ 19 Greg Luzinski	.35	.17	.03
□ 20 Garry Maddox	.15	.07	.01
□ 21 Bake McBride	.10	.05	.01
□ 22 Greg Gross *	.10	.05	.01
□ 23 Checklist card	.05	.01	.00
(unnumbered)			

1979 Burger King Yankees

The cards in this 23 card set measure 2 1/2" X 3 1/2". There are 22 numbered cards and one unnumbered checklist in the 1979 Burger King Yankee set. The poses of Guidry, Tiant, John and Beniquez, each marked with an asterisk below, are different from their poses appearing in the regular Topps issue. The team card has a picture of Lemon rather than Martin.

		NRMT	VG-E	GOOD
COMPLETE SET		5.00	2.50	.50
COMMON PLAYER (1-23)		.10	.05	.01
□	1 Yankees Team: Bob Lemon MG *	.30	.15	.03
□	2 Thurman Munson	1.50	.75	.15
□	3 Cliff Johnson	.10	.05	.01
□	4 Ron Guidry *	1.00	.50	.10
□	5 Jay Johnstone	.20	.10	.02
□	6 Jim Hunter	1.00	.50	.10
□	7 Jim Beattie	.10	.05	.01
□	8 Luis Tiant *	.25	.12	.02
□	9 Tommy John *	.50	.25	.05
□	10 Rich Gossage	.60	.30	.06
□	11 Ed Figueroa	.10	.05	.01
□	12 Chris Chambliss	.15	.07	.01
□	13 Willie Randolph	.30	.15	.03
□	14 Bucky Dent	.15	.07	.01
□	15 Graig Nettles	.50	.25	.05
□	16 Fred Stanley	.10	.05	.01
□	17 Jim Spencer	.10	.05	.01
□	18 Lou Piniella	.30	.15	.03
□	19 Roy White	.15	.07	.01
□	20 Mickey Rivers	.15	.07	.01
□	21 Reggie Jackson	1.75	.85	.17
□	22 Juan Beniquez *	.20	.10	.02
□	23 Checklist card	.05	.01	.00
	(unnumbered)			

1980 Burger King Phillies

The cards in this 23 card set measure 2 1/2" by 3 1/2". The 1980 edition of Burger King Phillies follows the established pattern of 22 numbered player cards and one unnumbered checklist. Cards marked with astericks contain poses different from those found in the regular 1980 Topps cards. This was the first

Burger King set to carry the Burger King logo and hence does not generate the same confusion that the three previous years do for collectors trying to distinguish Burger King cards from the very similar Topps cards of the same years.

		MINT	EXC	G-VG
COMPLETE SET		4.50	2.25	.45
COMMON PLAYER (1-23)		.10	.05	.01
□	1 Dallas Green MG *	.20	.10	.02
□	2 Bob Boone	.20	.10	.02
□	3 Keith Moreland *	.80	.40	.08
□	4 Pete Rose	2.50	1.25	.25
□	5 Manny Trillo	.15	.07	.01
□	6 Mike Schmidt	1.75	.85	.17
□	7 Larry Bowa	.35	.17	.03
□	8 John Vukovich *	.10	.05	.01
□	9 Bake McBride	.10	.05	.01
□	10 Garry Maddox	.15	.07	.01
□	11 Greg Luzinski	.25	.12	.02
□	12 Greg Gross	.10	.05	.01
□	13 Del Unser	.10	.05	.01
□	14 Lonnie Smith *	.15	.07	.01
□	15 Steve Carlton	1.25	.60	.12
□	16 Larry Christenson	.10	.05	.01
□	17 Nino Espinosa	.10	.05	.01
□	18 Randy Lerch	.10	.05	.01
□	19 Dick Ruthven	.10	.05	.01
□	20 Tug McGraw	.25	.12	.02
□	21 Ron Reed	.10	.05	.01
□	22 Kevin Saucier *	.10	.05	.01
□	23 Checklist card	.05	.01	.00
	(unnumbered)			

1980 Burger King Pitch/Hit/Run

The cards in this 34 card set measure 2 1/2" by 3 1/2". The "Pitch, Hit, and Run" set was a promotion introduced by Burger King in 1980. The cards carry a Burger King logo on the front and those marked by an asterisk in the checklist contain a different photo from that found in the regularly issued Topps series. Cards 1-11 are pitchers, 12-22 are hitters, and 23-33 are speedsters. Within each subgroup, the players are numbered corresponding to the alphabetical order of their names. The unnumbered checklist card was triple printed and is the least valuable card in the set.

		MINT	EXC	G-VG
COMPLETE SET		10.00	5.00	1.00
COMMON PLAYER (1-34)		.10	.05	.01
☐ 1	Vida Blue *	.15	.07	.01
☐ 2	Steve Carlton *	1.00	.50	.10
☐ 3	Rollie Fingers	.30	.15	.03
☐ 4	Ron Guidry *	.40	.20	.04
☐ 5	Jerry Koosman *	.15	.07	.01
☐ 6	Phil Niekro	.50	.25	.05
☐ 7	Jim Palmer *	.75	.35	.07
☐ 8	J.R. Richard	.10	.05	.01
☐ 9	Nolan Ryan *	1.00	.50	.10
☐ 10	Tom Seaver *	1.00	.50	.10
☐ 11	Bruce Sutter	.20	.10	.02
☐ 12	Don Baylor	.15	.07	.01
☐ 13	George Brett	1.00	.50	.10
☐ 14	Rod Carew	.75	.35	.07
☐ 15	George Foster	.15	.07	.01
☐ 16	Keith Hernandez *	.75	.35	.07
☐ 17	Reggie Jackson *	1.25	.60	.12
☐ 18	Fred Lynn *	.25	.12	.02
☐ 19	Dave Parker	.30	.15	.03
☐ 20	Jim Rice	.75	.35	.07
☐ 21	Pete Rose	2.00	1.00	.20
☐ 22	Dave Winfield *	1.00	.50	.10
☐ 23	Bobby Bonds *	.15	.07	.01
☐ 24	Enos Cabell	.10	.05	.01
☐ 25	Cesar Cedeno	.15	.07	.01
☐ 26	Julio Cruz	.10	.05	.01
☐ 27	Ron LeFlore *	.10	.05	.01
☐ 28	Dave Lopes *	.15	.07	.01
☐ 29	Omar Moreno *	.10	.05	.01
☐ 30	Joe Morgan *	.75	.35	.07
☐ 31	Bill North	.10	.05	.01
☐ 32	Frank Taveras	.10	.05	.01
☐ 33	Willie Wilson	.25	.12	.02
☐ 34	Unnumbered Checklist	.05	.01	.00

1982 Burger King Indians

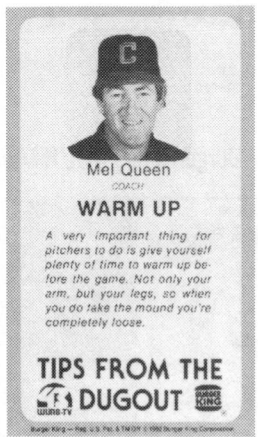

Mel Queen
COACH

WARM UP

A very important thing for pitchers to do is give yourself plenty of time to warm up before the game. Not only your arm, but your legs, so when you do take the mound you're completely loose.

TIPS FROM THE DUGOUT

The cards in this 12 card set measure 3" by 5". Tips From The Dugout is the series title of this set issued on a one card per week basis by the Burger King chain in the Cleveland area. Each card contains a black and white photo of manager Dave Garcia or coaches Goryl, McCraw, Queen and Sommers, under whom appears a paragraph explaining some aspect of inside baseball. The photo and "Tip" are set upon a large yellow area surrounded by green borders. The cards are not numbered and are blank-backed. The logos of Burger King and WUAB-TV appear at the base of the card.

		MINT	EXC	G-VG
COMPLETE SET		4.00	2.00	.40
COMMON PLAYER		.40	.20	.04
☐ 1	Dave Garcia: Be in the Game	.40	.20	.04
☐ 2	Dave Garcia: Sportsmanship	.40	.20	.04
☐ 3	Johnny Goryl: Rounding Bases	.40	.20	.04
☐ 4	Johnny Goryl: 3B Running	.40	.20	.04
☐ 5	Tom McCraw: Follow Thru	.40	.20	.04
☐ 6	Tom McCraw: Selecting a Bat	.40	.20	.04
☐ 7	Tom McCraw: Watch the Ball	.40	.20	.04
☐ 8	Mel Queen: Master One Pitch	.40	.20	.04
☐ 9	Mel Queen: Warm Up	.40	.20	.04
☐ 10	Dennis Sommers: Protect Fingers	.40	.20	.04
☐ 11	Dennis Sommers: Tagging 1st Base	.40	.20	.04
☐ 12	Dennis Sommers	.40	.20	.04

1986 Burger King All Pro

This 20 card set was distributed in Burger King restaurants across the country. They were produced as panels of three where the middle card was actually a special discount coupon card. The folded panel was given with the purchase of a Whopper. Each individual card measures 2 1/2" by 3 1/2". The team logos have been airbrushed from the pictures. The cards are numbered on the front at the top.

		MINT	EXC	G-VG
COMPLETE SET		6.00	3.00	.60
COMMON PLAYER		.20	.10	.02
☐ 1	Tony Pena	.20	.10	.02
☐ 2	Dave Winfield	.40	.20	.04
☐ 3	Fernando Valenzuela	.40	.20	.04
☐ 4	Pete Rose	.80	.40	.08
☐ 5	Mike Schmidt	.60	.30	.06
☐ 6	Steve Carlton	.40	.20	.04
☐ 7	Glenn Wilson	.20	.10	.02
☐ 8	Jim Rice	.40	.20	.04
☐ 9	Wade Boggs	.80	.40	.08
☐ 10	Juan Samuel	.30	.15	.03
☐ 11	Dale Murphy	.60	.30	.06
☐ 12	Reggie Jackson	.60	.30	.06
☐ 13	Kirk Gibson	.40	.20	.04
☐ 14	Eddie Murray	.50	.25	.05
☐ 15	Cal Ripken	.50	.25	.05
☐ 16	Willie McGee	.30	.15	.03
☐ 17	Dwight Gooden	.60	.30	.06
☐ 18	Steve Garvey	.50	.25	.05
☐ 19	Don Mattingly	1.00	.50	.10
☐ 20	George Brett	.60	.30	.06

1987 Burger King All-Pro

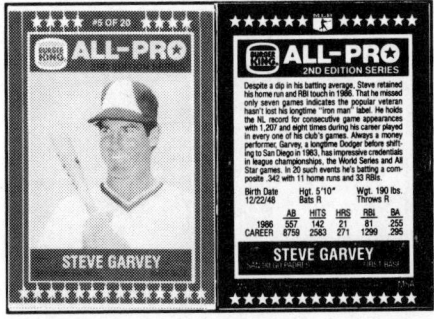

This 20-card set consists of 10 panels of two cards each joined together along with a promotional coupon. Individual cards measure 2 1/2" by 3 1/2" whereas the panels measure 3 1/2" by 7 5/8". MSA (Mike Schechter Associates produced the cards for Burger King; there are no Major League logos on the cards. The cards are numbered on the front.

	MINT	EXC	G-VG
COMPLETE SET	5.00	2.50	.50
COMMON PLAYER	.20	.10	.02

☐ 1	Wade Boggs	.75	.35	.07
☐ 2	Gary Carter	.40	.20	.04
☐ 3	Will Clark	.60	.30	.06
☐ 4	Roger Clemens	.60	.30	.06
☐ 5	Steve Garvey	.40	.20	.04
☐ 6	Ron Darling	.30	.15	.03
☐ 7	Pedro Guerrero	.30	.15	.03
☐ 8	Von Hayes	.30	.15	.03
☐ 9	Rickey Henderson	.50	.25	.05
☐ 10	Keith Hernandez	.40	.20	.04
☐ 11	Wally Joyner	.60	.30	.06
☐ 12	Mike Krukow	.20	.10	.02
☐ 13	Don Mattingly	.90	.45	.09
☐ 14	Ozzie Smith	.30	.15	.03
☐ 15	Tony Pena	.20	.10	.02
☐ 16	Jim Rice	.30	.15	.03
☐ 17	Mike Schmidt	.60	.30	.06
☐ 18	Ryne Sandberg	.40	.20	.04
☐ 19	Darryl Strawberry	.50	.25	.05
☐ 20	Fernando Valenzuela	.30	.15	.03

1933 Butter Cream R306

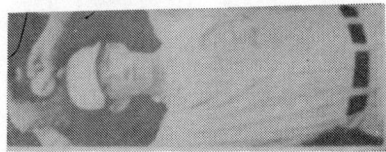

The small, elongated (measuring 1 1/4" by 3 1/2") cards of this 29 card set are unnumbered and contain many cut-down, blurry black and white photos. The producer's name is sometimes printed on the reverse. Despite their limitations, Butter Cream cards are highly prized by collectors, and carry the ACC designation R306. The cards have been alphabetized and numbered for reference in the checklist below.

	NRMT	VG-E	GOOD
COMPLETE SET	7500.00	3000.00	600.00
COMMON PLAYER (1-29)	200.00	100.00	20.00

☐ 1	Earl Averill	300.00	150.00	30.00
☐ 2	Ed Brandt	200.00	100.00	20.00
☐ 3	Guy T. Bush	200.00	100.00	20.00
☐ 4	Gordon Cochrane	350.00	175.00	35.00
☐ 5	Joe Cronin	350.00	175.00	35.00
☐ 6	George Earnshaw	200.00	100.00	20.00
☐ 7	Wesley Ferrell	200.00	100.00	20.00
☐ 8	Jimmy E. Foxx	500.00	250.00	50.00
☐ 9	Frank C. Frisch	350.00	175.00	35.00
☐ 10	Charles M. Gelbert	200.00	100.00	20.00
☐ 11	Lefty Grove	400.00	200.00	40.00
☐ 12	Leo Hartnett	300.00	150.00	30.00
☐ 13	Babe Herman	300.00	150.00	30.00
☐ 14	Charles Klein	350.00	175.00	35.00
☐ 15	Ray Kremer	200.00	100.00	20.00
☐ 16	Fred C. Lindstrom	300.00	150.00	30.00
☐ 17	Ted A. Lyons	300.00	150.00	30.00
☐ 18	Pepper Martin	250.00	125.00	25.00
☐ 19	Robert O'Farrell	200.00	100.00	20.00
☐ 20	Ed A. Rommell	200.00	100.00	20.00
☐ 21	Charles Root	200.00	100.00	20.00
☐ 22	Harold Ruel	200.00	100.00	20.00
☐ 23	Al Simmons	300.00	150.00	30.00
☐ 24	Bill N. Terry	350.00	175.00	35.00
☐ 25	George Uhle	200.00	100.00	20.00
☐ 26	Lloyd J. Waner	300.00	150.00	30.00
☐ 27	Paul C. Waner	300.00	150.00	30.00
☐ 28	Hack Wilson	350.00	175.00	35.00
☐ 29	Glenn Wright	200.00	100.00	20.00

1950-56 Callahan HOF

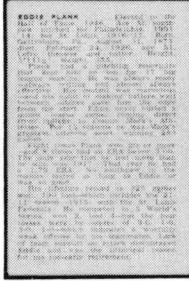

The cards in this 82 card set measure 1 3/4" by 2 1/2". The 1950-56 Callahan Hall of Fame set was issued over a number of years at the Baseball Hall of Fame museum in Cooperstown, New York. New cards were added to the set each year when new members were inducted into the Hall of Fame. The cards with (2) in the checklist exist in two different biographies. The year of each card's first inclusion in the set is also given in parentheses; those not listed parenthetically below were issued in 1950 as well as in all the succeeding years and are hence the most common. Naturally the supply of cards is directly related to how many years a player was included in the set; cards that were not issued until 1955 are much scarcer than those printed all the years between 1950 and 1956. The ACC designation is W576. One frequently finds "complete" sets in the original box; take care to investigate the year of issue, the set may be complete in the sense of all the cards issued up to a certain year, but not all 82 cards below. For example, a "complete" 1950 set would obviously not include any of the cards marked below with ('52), ('54), or ('55) as none of those cards existed in 1950 since those respective players had not yet been inducted. The complete set price below refers to a set including all 82 cards below with variations. Since the cards are unnumbered, they are numbered below for reference alphabetically by player's name.

	NRMT	VG-E	GOOD
COMPLETE SET	300.00	150.00	30.00
COMMON PLAYER ('50)	1.00	.50	.10
COMMON PLAYER ('52)	2.50	1.25	.25

COMMON PLAYER ('54)	3.50	1.75	.35
COMMON PLAYER ('55)	5.00	2.50	.50

☐	1 Grover Alexander	2.00	1.00	.20
☐	2 Cap Anson	1.50	.75	.15
☐	3 Frank Baker ('55)	5.00	2.50	.50
☐	4 Edward Barrow ('54)	3.50	1.75	.35
☐	5 Chief Bender(2)('54)	3.50	1.75	.35
☐	6 Roger Bresnahan	1.00	.50	.10
☐	7 Dan Brouthers	1.00	.50	.10
☐	8 Mordecai Brown	1.00	.50	.10
☐	9 Morgan Bulkeley	1.00	.50	.10
☐	10 Jesse Burkett	1.00	.50	.10
☐	11 Alexander Cartwright	1.00	.50	.10
☐	12 Henry Chadwick	1.00	.50	.10
☐	13 Frank Chance	1.00	.50	.10
☐	14 Happy Chandler ('52)	20.00	10.00	2.00
☐	15 Jack Chesbro	1.00	.50	.10
☐	16 Fred Clarke	1.00	.50	.10
☐	17 Ty Cobb	20.00	10.00	2.00
☐	18A Mickey Cochran ERR	10.00	5.00	1.00
	(sic, Cochrane)			
☐	18B Mickey Cochrane COR ...	2.00	1.00	.20
☐	19 Eddie Collins (2)	1.50	.75	.15
☐	20 Jimmie Collins	1.00	.50	.10
☐	21 Charles Comiskey	1.00	.50	.10
☐	22 Tom Connolly ('54)	3.50	1.75	.35
☐	23 Candy Cummings	1.00	.50	.10
☐	24 Dizzy Dean ('54)	12.00	6.00	1.20
☐	25 Ed Delahanty	1.00	.50	.10
☐	26 Bill Dickey ('54)(2)	7.50	3.75	.75
☐	27 Joe DiMaggio ('55)	45.00	22.50	4.50
☐	28 Hugh Duffy	1.00	.50	.10
☐	29 Johnny Evers	1.00	.50	.10
☐	30 Buck Ewing	1.00	.50	.10
☐	31 Jimmie Foxx	4.00	2.00	.40
☐	32 Frank Frisch	1.50	.75	.15
☐	33 Lou Gehrig	20.00	10.00	2.00
☐	34 Charles Gehringer	1.50	.75	.15
☐	35 Clark Griffith	1.00	.50	.10
☐	36 Lefty Grove	2.00	1.00	.20
☐	37 Gabby Hartnett ('55)	5.00	2.50	.50
☐	38 Harry Heilmann ('52)	2.50	1.25	.25
☐	39 Rogers Hornsby	3.50	1.75	.35
☐	40 Carl Hubbell	1.50	.75	.15
☐	41 Hughey Jennings	1.00	.50	.10
☐	42 Ban Johnson	1.00	.50	.10
☐	43 Walter Johnson	6.00	3.00	.60
☐	44 Willie Keeler	1.00	.50	.10
☐	45 Mike Kelly	1.50	.75	.15
☐	46 Bill Klem ('54)	3.50	1.75	.35
☐	47 Napoleon Lajoie	1.50	.75	.15
☐	48 Kenesaw Landis	1.00	.50	.10
☐	49 Ted Lyons ('55)	5.00	2.50	.50
☐	50 Connie Mack	1.00	.50	.10
☐	51 Walter Maranville('54)	3.50	1.75	.35
☐	52 Christy Mathewson	6.00	3.00	.60
☐	53 Tommy McCarthy	1.00	.50	.10
☐	54 Joe McGinnity	1.00	.50	.10
☐	55 John McGraw	1.00	.50	.10
☐	56 Charles Nicholls	1.00	.50	.10
☐	57 Jim O'Rourke	1.00	.50	.10
☐	58 Mel Ott	2.00	1.00	.20
☐	59 Herb Pennock	1.00	.50	.10
☐	60 Eddie Plank	1.00	.50	.10
☐	61 Charles Radbourne	1.00	.50	.10
☐	62 Wilbert Robinson	1.00	.50	.10
☐	63 Babe Ruth	45.00	22.50	4.50
☐	64 Ray Schalk ('55)	5.00	2.50	.50
☐	65 Al Simmons ('54)	3.50	1.75	.35
☐	66 George Sisler (2)	1.50	.75	.15
☐	67 A.G. Spalding	1.00	.50	.10
☐	68 Tris Speaker	3.00	1.50	.30
☐	69 Bill Terry ('54)	5.00	2.50	.50
☐	70 Joe Tinker	1.00	.50	.10
☐	71 Pie Traynor	1.50	.75	.15
☐	72 Dazzy Vance ('55)	5.00	2.50	.50
☐	73 Rube Waddell	1.00	.50	.10
☐	74 Hans Wagner	5.00	2.50	.50
☐	75 Bobby Wallace ('54)	5.00	2.50	.50
☐	76 Ed Walsh	1.00	.50	.10
☐	77 Paul Waner ('52)	4.00	2.00	.40
☐	78 George Wright	1.00	.50	.10
☐	79 Harry Wright ('54)	3.50	1.75	.35
☐	80 Cy Young	3.00	1.50	.30
☐	81 Museum Interior	3.50	1.75	.35
	('54) (2)			
☐	82 Museum Exterior	3.50	1.75	.35
	('54) (2)			

1985 CIGNA Phillies

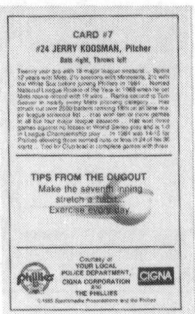

This colorful 16 card set (measuring 2 5/8" by 4 1/8") features the Philadelphia Phillies and was also sponsored by CIGNA Corporation. Cards are numbered on the back and contain a safety tip as such the set is frequently categorized and referenced as a safety set. Cards are also numbered by uniform number on the front.

		MINT	EXC	G-VG
COMPLETE SET		4.50	2.25	.45
COMMON PLAYER		.20	.10	.02

☐	1 Juan Samuel	.60	.30	.06
☐	2 Von Hayes	.60	.30	.06
☐	3 Ozzie Virgil	.30	.15	.03
☐	4 Mike Schmidt	1.25	.60	.12
☐	5 Greg Gross	.20	.10	.02
☐	6 Tim Corcoran	.20	.10	.02
☐	7 Jerry Koosman	.30	.15	.03
☐	8 Jeff Stone	.25	.12	.02
☐	9 Glenn Wilson	.50	.25	.05
☐	10 Steve Jeltz	.20	.10	.02
☐	11 Garry Maddox	.20	.10	.02
☐	12 Steve Carlton	.75	.35	.07
☐	13 John Denny	.25	.12	.02
☐	14 Kevin Gross	.20	.10	.02
☐	15 Shane Rawley	.40	.20	.04
☐	16 Charlie Hudson	.20	.10	.02

1986 CIGNA Phillies

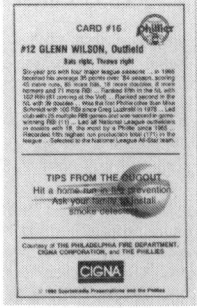

This 16 card set was sponsored by CIGNA Corp. and was given away by the Philadelphia area Fire Departments. Cards measure 2 3/4" by 4 1/8" and feature full color fronts. The card backs are printed in maroon and black on white card stock. Although the uniform numbers are given on the front of the card, the cards are numbered on the back in the order listed below.

		MINT	EXC	G-VG
COMPLETE SET		4.00	2.00	.40
COMMON PLAYER		.20	.10	.02
☐ 1	Juan Samuel	.60	.30	.06
☐ 2	Don Carman	.30	.15	.03
☐ 3	Von Hayes	.60	.30	.06
☐ 4	Kent Tekulve	.30	.15	.03
☐ 5	Greg Gross	.20	.10	.02
☐ 6	Shane Rawley	.40	.20	.04
☐ 7	Darren Daulton	.30	.15	.03
☐ 8	Kevin Gross	.20	.10	.02
☐ 9	Steve Jeltz	.20	.10	.02
☐ 10	Mike Schmidt	1.00	.50	.10
☐ 11	Steve Bedrosian	.50	.25	.05
☐ 12	Gary Redus	.30	.15	.03
☐ 13	Charles Hudson	.20	.10	.02
☐ 14	John Russell	.20	.10	.02
☐ 15	Fred Toliver	.20	.10	.02
☐ 16	Glenn Wilson	.40	.20	.04

☐ 27	Rocky Colavito	.10	.05	.01
☐ 28	Tony Perez	.10	.05	.01
☐ 29	Gil Hodges	.10	.05	.01
☐ 30	Ralph Kiner	.10	.05	.01
☐ 31	Joe DiMaggio	.00	.00	.00
	(not included in set)			
☐ 32	Johnny Mize	.15	.07	.01
☐ 33	Yogi Berra	.20	.10	.02
☐ 34	Lee May	.10	.05	.01

1987 Classic Game

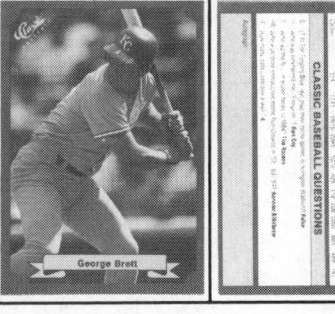

This 100-card set was actually distributed as part of a trivia board game. The card backs contain several trivia questions (and answers) which are used to play the game. A dark green border frames the full color photo. The games were produced by Game Time, Ltd. and were available in toy stores as well as from card dealers.

1985 Circle K

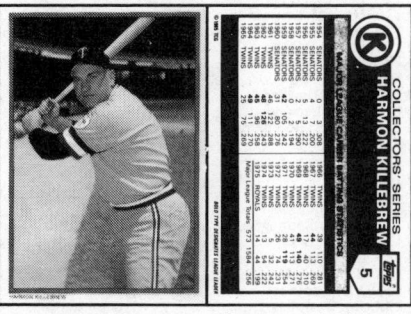

The cards in this 33 card set measure 2 1/2" by 3 1/2" and were issued with accompanying box. In 1985, Topps produced this set for Circle K; cards were printed in Ireland. Cards are numbered on the back according to each player's rank on the all-time career Home Run list. The backs are printed in blue and red on white card stock. The card fronts are glossy and each player is named in the lower left corner. Most of the obverses are in color, although the older vintage players are pictured in black and white. Joe DiMaggio was not included in the set.

		MINT	EXC	G-VG
COMPLETE SET		3.50	1.75	.35
COMMON PLAYER		.10	.05	.01
☐ 1	Hank Aaron	.35	.17	.03
☐ 2	Babe Ruth	.70	.35	.07
☐ 3	Willie Mays	.35	.17	.03
☐ 4	Frank Robinson	.15	.07	.01
☐ 5	Harmon Killebrew	.15	.07	.01
☐ 6	Mickey Mantle	.70	.35	.07
☐ 7	Jimmie Foxx	.15	.07	.01
☐ 8	Willie McCovey	.20	.10	.02
☐ 9	Ted Williams	.35	.17	.03
☐ 10	Ernie Banks	.20	.10	.02
☐ 11	Eddie Mathews	.15	.07	.01
☐ 12	Mel Ott	.20	.10	.02
☐ 13	Reggie Jackson	.35	.17	.03
☐ 14	Lou Gehrig	.35	.17	.03
☐ 15	Stan Musial	.25	.12	.02
☐ 16	Willie Stargell	.20	.10	.02
☐ 17	Carl Yastrzemski	.35	.17	.03
☐ 18	Billy Williams	.15	.07	.01
☐ 19	Mike Schmidt	.35	.17	.03
☐ 20	Duke Snider	.30	.15	.03
☐ 21	Al Kaline	.20	.10	.02
☐ 22	Johnny Bench	.20	.10	.02
☐ 23	Frank Howard	.10	.05	.01
☐ 24	Orlando Cepeda	.10	.05	.01
☐ 25	Norm Cash	.10	.05	.01
☐ 26	Dave Kingman	.10	.05	.01

		MINT	EXC	G-VG
COMPLETE SET (100)		20.00	10.00	2.00
COMMON PLAYER (1-100)		.10	.05	.01
☐ 1	Pete Rose	1.00	.50	.10
☐ 2	Len Dykstra	.15	.07	.01
☐ 3	Darryl Strawberry	.50	.25	.05
☐ 4	Keith Hernandez	.25	.12	.02
☐ 5	Gary Carter	.30	.15	.03
☐ 6	Wally Joyner	1.00	.50	.10
☐ 7	Andres Thomas	.15	.07	.01
☐ 8	Pat Dodson	.10	.05	.01
☐ 9	Kirk Gibson	.20	.10	.02
☐ 10	Don Mattingly	1.25	.60	.12
☐ 11	Dave Winfield	.25	.12	.02
☐ 12	Rickey Henderson	.30	.15	.03
☐ 13	Dan Pasqua	.15	.07	.01
☐ 14	Don Baylor	.15	.07	.01
☐ 15	Bo Jackson	1.00	.50	.10
☐ 16	Pete Incaviglia	.75	.35	.07
☐ 17	Kevin Bass	.10	.05	.01
☐ 18	Barry Larkin	.20	.10	.02
☐ 19	Dave Magadan	.20	.10	.02
☐ 20	Steve Sax	.15	.07	.01
☐ 21	Eric Davis	1.25	.60	.12
☐ 22	Mike Pagliarulo	.15	.07	.01
☐ 23	Fred Lynn	.15	.07	.01
☐ 24	Reggie Jackson	.50	.25	.05
☐ 25	Larry Parrish	.15	.07	.01
☐ 26	Tony Gwynn	.65	.30	.06
☐ 27	Steve Garvey	.40	.20	.04
☐ 28	Glenn Davis	.20	.10	.02
☐ 29	Tim Raines	.35	.17	.03
☐ 30	Vince Coleman	.35	.17	.03
☐ 31	Willie McGee	.20	.10	.02
☐ 32	Ozzie Smith	.20	.10	.02
☐ 33	Dave Parker	.20	.10	.02
☐ 34	Tony Pena	.15	.07	.01
☐ 35	Ryne Sandberg	.30	.15	.03
☐ 36	Brett Butler	.15	.07	.01
☐ 37	Dale Murphy	.60	.30	.06
☐ 38	Bob Horner	.15	.07	.01
☐ 39	Pedro Guerrero	.20	.10	.02
☐ 40	Brook Jacoby	.15	.07	.01
☐ 41	Carlton Fisk	.15	.07	.01
☐ 42	Harold Baines	.15	.07	.01
☐ 43	Rob Deer	.15	.07	.01
☐ 44	Robin Yount	.25	.12	.02
☐ 45	Paul Molitor	.20	.10	.02

☐	46	Jose Canseco	1.00	.50	.10
☐	47	George Brett	.50	.25	.05
☐	48	Jim Presley	.20	.10	.02
☐	49	Rich Gedman	.10	.05	.01
☐	50	Larry Parrish	.10	.05	.01
☐	51	Eddie Murray	.35	.17	.03
☐	52	Cal Ripken	.35	.17	.03
☐	53	Kent Hrbek	.20	.10	.02
☐	54	Gary Gaetti	.20	.10	.02
☐	55	Kirby Puckett	.50	.25	.05
☐	56	George Bell	.30	.15	.03
☐	57	Tony Fernandez	.20	.10	.02
☐	58	Jesse Barfield	.25	.12	.02
☐	59	Jim Rice	.25	.12	.02
☐	60	Wade Boggs	1.00	.50	.10
☐	61	Marty Barrett	.10	.05	.01
☐	62	Mike Schmidt	.60	.30	.06
☐	63	Von Hayes	.15	.07	.01
☐	64	Jeff Leonard	.15	.07	.01
☐	65	Chris Brown	.15	.07	.01
☐	66	Dave Smith	.10	.05	.01
☐	67	Mike Krukow	.10	.05	.01
☐	68	Ron Guidry	.20	.10	.02
☐	69	Rob Woodward	.10	.05	.01
☐	70	Rob Murphy	.15	.07	.01
☐	71	Andrew Galarraga	.25	.12	.02
☐	72	Dwight Gooden	.60	.30	.06
☐	73	Bob Ojeda	.15	.07	.01
☐	74	Sid Fernandez	.20	.10	.02
☐	75	Jesse Orosco	.10	.05	.01
☐	76	Roger McDowell	.15	.07	.01
☐	77	John Tudor	.20	.10	.02
		(misspelled Tutor)			
☐	78	Tom Browning	.10	.05	.01
☐	79	Rick Aguilera	.15	.07	.01
☐	80	Lance McCullers	.10	.05	.01
☐	81	Mike Scott	.25	.12	.02
☐	82	Nolan Ryan	.35	.17	.03
☐	83	Bruce Hurst	.15	.07	.01
☐	84	Roger Clemens	.60	.30	.06
☐	85	Oil Can Boyd	.10	.05	.01
☐	86	Dave Righetti	.20	.10	.02
☐	87	Dennis Rasmussen	.10	.05	.01
☐	88	Bret Saberhagen	.25	.12	.02
☐	89	Mark Langston	.20	.10	.02
☐	90	Jack Morris	.20	.10	.02
☐	91	Fernando Valenzuela	.25	.12	.02
☐	92	Orel Hershiser	.20	.10	.02
☐	93	Rick Honeycutt	.10	.05	.01
☐	94	Jeff Reardon	.15	.07	.01
☐	95	John Habyan	.10	.05	.01
☐	96	Goose Gossage	.20	.10	.02
☐	97	Todd Worrell	.25	.12	.02
☐	98	Floyd Youmans	.15	.07	.01
☐	99	Don Aase	.10	.05	.01
☐	100	John Franco	.15	.07	.01

1987 Classic Travel Update

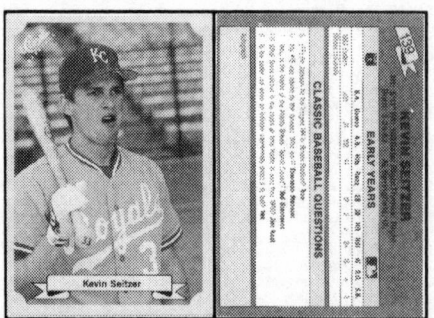

This 50-card set was actually distributed as part of an update to a trivia board game, but (unlike the original Classic game) was sold without the game. The set is sometimes referred to as the "Travel Edition" of the game. The card backs contain several trivia questions (and answers) which are used to play the game. A yellow border frames the full color photo. The games were produced by Game Time, Ltd. and were available in toy stores as well as from

card dealers. Cards are numbered beginning with 101 as they are an extension of the original set.

		MINT	EXC	G-VG
COMPLETE SET		8.00	4.00	.80
COMMON PLAYER		.10	.05	MINT
COMPLETE SET		8.00	4.00	.80
COMMON PLAYER		.10	.05	.01

☐	101	Mike Schmidt	.40	.20	.04
☐	102	Eric Davis	1.00	.50	.10
☐	103	Pete Rose	.50	.25	.05
☐	104	Don Mattingly	1.25	.60	.12
☐	105	Wade Boggs	1.00	.50	.10
☐	106	Dale Murphy	.25	.12	.02
☐	107	Glenn Davis	.15	.07	.01
☐	108	Wally Joyner	.75	.35	.07
☐	109	Bo Jackson	.50	.25	.05
☐	110	Cory Snyder	.30	.15	.03
☐	111	Jim Lindeman	.10	.05	.01
☐	112	Kirby Puckett	.35	.17	.03
☐	113	Barry Bonds	.15	.07	.01
☐	114	Roger Clemens	.40	.20	.04
☐	115	Oddibe McDowell	.10	.05	.01
☐	116	Bret Saberhagen	.20	.10	.02
☐	117	Joe Magrane	.15	.07	.01
☐	118	Scott Fletcher	.10	.05	.01
☐	119	Mark McLemore	.10	.05	.01
☐	120	Who Me (Joe Niekro)	.10	.05	.01
☐	121	Mark McGwire	1.00	.50	.10
☐	122	Darryl Strawberry	.50	.25	.05
☐	123	Mike Scott	.15	.07	.01
☐	124	Andre Dawson	.20	.10	.02
☐	125	Jose Canseco	.75	.35	.07
☐	126	Kevin McReynolds	.15	.07	.01
☐	127	Joe Carter	.20	.10	.02
☐	128	Casey Candaele	.10	.05	.01
☐	129	Matt Nokes	1.00	.50	.10
☐	130	Kal Daniels	.50	.25	.05
☐	131	Pete Incaviglia	.25	.12	.02
☐	132	Benito Santiago	1.00	.50	.10
☐	133	Barry Larkin	.20	.10	.02
☐	134	Gary Pettis	.10	.05	.01
☐	135	B.J. Surhoff	.25	.12	.02
☐	136	Juan Nieves	.10	.05	.01
☐	137	Jim Deshaies	.10	.05	.01
☐	138	Pete O'Brien	.15	.07	.01
☐	139	Kevin Seitzer	1.25	.60	.12
☐	140	Devon White	.25	.12	.02
☐	141	Rob Deer	.15	.07	.01
☐	142	Kurt Stillwell	.15	.07	.01
☐	143	Edwin Correa	.10	.05	.01
☐	144	Dion James	.10	.05	.01
☐	145	Danny Tartabull	.25	.12	.02
☐	146	Jerry Browne	.10	.05	.01
☐	147	Ted Higuera	.15	.07	.01
☐	148	Jack Clark	.20	.10	.02
☐	149	Ruben Sierra	.40	.20	.04
☐	150	McGwire/Eric Davis	.75	.35	.07

1981 Coke

The cards in this 132 card set measure 2 1/2" by 3 1/2". In 1981, Topps produced 11 sets of 12 cards each for the Coca-Cola Company. Each set features 11 star players for a particular team plus an advertising card with the team name on the front. Although the cards are numbered in the upper right corner of the back from 1 to 11, they are re-numbered below within team, i.e., Boston Red Sox (1-12), Chicago Cubs (13-24), Chicago White Sox (25-36), Cincinnati Reds (37-48), Detroit Tigers (49-60), Houston Astros (61-72), Kansas City Royals (73-84), New York Mets (85-96), Philadelphia Phillies (97-108), Pittsburgh Pirates (109-120), and St. Louis Cardinals (121-132). Within each team the player actually numbered #1 (on the card back) is the first player below and the player numbered #11 is the last in that team's list. These player cards are quite similar to the 1981 Topps issue but feature a Coca-Cola logo on both the front and the back. The advertising card for each team features, on its back, an offer for obtaining an uncut sheet of 1981 Topps cards. These promotional cards were actually issued by Coke in only a few of the cities, and most of these cards have reached collectors hands through dealers who have purchased the cards through suppliers.

	MINT	EXC	G-VG
COMPLETE SET	15.00	7.50	1.50
COMMON PLAYER	.05	.02	.00
COMMON CHECKLIST	.03	.01	.00

		MINT	EXC	G-VG
☐	1 Tom Burgmeier	.05	.02	.00
☐	2 Dennis Eckersley	.15	.07	.01
☐	3 Dwight Evans	.40	.20	.04
☐	4 Bob Stanley	.10	.05	.01
☐	5 Glenn Hoffman	.05	.02	.00
☐	6 Carney Lansford	.30	.15	.03
☐	7 Frank Tanana	.10	.05	.01
☐	8 Tony Perez	.25	.12	.02
☐	9 Jim Rice	1.00	.50	.10
☐	10 Dave Stapleton	.10	.05	.01
☐	11 Carl Yastrzemski	1.50	.75	.15
☐	12 Red Sox Checklist (unnumbered)	.03	.01	.00
☐	13 Tim Blackwell	.05	.02	.00
☐	14 Bill Buckner	.20	.10	.02
☐	15 Ivan DeJesus	.05	.02	.00
☐	16 Leon Durham	.35	.17	.03
☐	17 Steve Henderson	.05	.02	.00
☐	18 Mike Krukow	.15	.07	.01
☐	19 Ken Reitz	.05	.02	.00
☐	20 Rick Reuschel	.15	.07	.01
☐	21 Scot Thompson	.05	.02	.00
☐	22 Dick Tidrow	.05	.02	.00
☐	23 Mike Tyson	.05	.02	.00
☐	24 Cubs Checklist (unnumbered)	.03	.01	.00
☐	25 Britt Burns	.25	.12	.02
☐	26 Todd Cruz	.05	.02	.00
☐	27 Rich Dotson	.35	.17	.03
☐	28 Jim Essian	.05	.02	.00
☐	29 Ed Farmer	.05	.02	.00
☐	30 Lamar Johnson	.05	.02	.00
☐	31 Ron LeFlore	.10	.05	.01
☐	32 Chet Lemon	.15	.07	.01
☐	33 Bob Molinaro	.05	.02	.00
☐	34 Jim Morrison	.05	.02	.00
☐	35 Wayne Nordhagen	.05	.02	.00
☐	36 White Sox Checklist (unnumbered)	.03	.01	.00
☐	37 Johnny Bench	1.00	.50	.10
☐	38 Dave Collins	.10	.05	.01
☐	39 Dave Concepcion	.20	.10	.02
☐	40 Dan Driessen	.05	.02	.00
☐	41 George Foster	.30	.15	.03
☐	42 Ken Griffey	.10	.05	.01
☐	43 Tom Hume	.05	.02	.00
☐	44 Ray Knight	.25	.12	.02
☐	45 Ron Oester	.10	.05	.01
☐	46 Tom Seaver	1.00	.50	.10
☐	47 Mario Soto	.15	.07	.01
☐	48 Reds Checklist (unnumbered)	.03	.01	.00
☐	49 Champ Summers	.05	.02	.00
☐	50 Al Cowens	.05	.02	.00
☐	51 Rich Hebner	.05	.02	.00
☐	52 Steve Kemp	.10	.05	.01
☐	53 Aurelio Lopez	.05	.02	.00
☐	54 Jack Morris	.75	.35	.07
☐	55 Lance Parrish	.75	.35	.07
☐	56 Johnny Wockenfuss	.05	.02	.00
☐	57 Alan Trammell	.90	.45	.09
☐	58 Lou Whitaker	.60	.30	.06
☐	59 Kirk Gibson	1.25	.60	.12
☐	60 Tigers Checklist (unnumbered)	.03	.01	.00
☐	61 Alan Ashby	.05	.02	.00
☐	62 Cesar Cedeno	.10	.05	.01
☐	63 Jose Cruz	.20	.10	.02
☐	64 Art Howe	.05	.02	.00
☐	65 Rafael Landestoy	.05	.02	.00
☐	66 Joe Niekro	.20	.10	.02
☐	67 Terry Puhl	.10	.05	.01
☐	68 J.R. Richard	.20	.10	.02
☐	69 Nolan Ryan	1.00	.50	.10
☐	70 Joe Sambito	.10	.05	.01
☐	71 Don Sutton	.75	.35	.07
☐	72 Astros Checklist (unnumbered)	.03	.01	.00
☐	73 Willie Aikens	.10	.05	.01
☐	74 George Brett	1.25	.60	.12
☐	75 Larry Gura	.10	.05	.01
☐	76 Dennis Leonard	.10	.05	.01
☐	77 Hal McRae	.10	.05	.01
☐	78 Amos Otis	.10	.05	.01
☐	79 Dan Quisenberry	.25	.12	.02
☐	80 U.L. Washington	.05	.02	.00
☐	81 John Wathan	.10	.05	.01
☐	82 Frank White	.20	.10	.02
☐	83 Willie Wilson	.25	.12	.02
☐	84 Royals Checklist (unnumbered)	.03	.01	.00
☐	85 Neil Allen	.10	.05	.01
☐	86 Doug Flynn	.05	.02	.00
☐	87 Dave Kingman	.25	.12	.02
☐	88 Randy Jones	.05	.02	.00
☐	89 Pat Zachry	.05	.02	.00
☐	90 Lee Mazzilli	.10	.05	.01
☐	91 Rusty Staub	.15	.07	.01
☐	92 Craig Swan	.05	.02	.00
☐	93 Frank Taveras	.05	.02	.00
☐	94 Alex Trevino	.05	.02	.00
☐	95 Joel Youngblood	.05	.02	.00
☐	96 Mets Checklist (unnumbered)	.03	.01	.00
☐	97 Bob Boone	.15	.07	.01
☐	98 Larry Bowa	.25	.12	.02
☐	99 Steve Carlton	1.00	.50	.10
☐	100 Greg Luzinski	.20	.10	.02
☐	101 Garry Maddox	.10	.05	.01
☐	102 Bake McBride	.05	.02	.00
☐	103 Tug McGraw	.15	.07	.01
☐	104 Pete Rose	1.75	.85	.17
☐	105 Mike Schmidt	1.25	.60	.12
☐	106 Lonnie Smith	.10	.05	.01
☐	107 Manny Trillo	.05	.02	.00
☐	108 Phillies Checklist (unnumbered)	.03	.01	.00
☐	109 Jim Bibby	.05	.02	.00
☐	110 John Candelaria	.10	.05	.01
☐	111 Mike Easler	.10	.05	.01
☐	112 Tim Foli	.05	.02	.00
☐	113 Phil Garner	.10	.05	.01
☐	114 Bill Madlock	.25	.12	.02
☐	115 Omar Moreno	.05	.02	.00
☐	116 Ed Ott	.05	.02	.00
☐	117 Dave Parker	.60	.30	.06
☐	118 Willie Stargell	.90	.45	.09
☐	119 Kent Tekulve	.10	.05	.01
☐	120 Pirates Checklist (unnumbered)	.03	.01	.00
☐	121 Bob Forsch	.10	.05	.01
☐	122 George Hendrick	.10	.05	.01
☐	123 Keith Hernandez	.75	.35	.07
☐	124 Tom Herr	.15	.07	.01
☐	125 Sixto Lezcano	.05	.02	.00
☐	126 Ken Oberkfell	.05	.02	.00
☐	127 Darrell Porter	.10	.05	.01
☐	128 Tony Scott	.05	.02	.00
☐	129 Lary Sorensen	.05	.02	.00
☐	130 Bruce Sutter	.25	.12	.02
☐	131 Garry Templeton	.10	.05	.01
☐	132 Cardinals Checklist (unnumbered)	.03	.01	.00

1982 Coke Red Sox

The cards in this 22 card set measure 2 1/2" by 3 1/2". This set of Boston Red Sox ballplayers was issued locally in the Boston area as a joint promotion by Brigham's Ice Cream Stores and Coca-Cola. The pictures are identical to those in the Topps regular

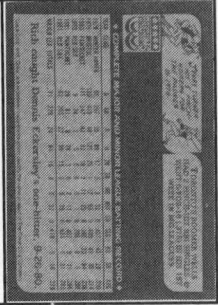

RED SOX
CATCHER **RICH GEDMAN**

1982 issue, except that the colors are brighter and the Brigham and Coke logos appear inside the frame line. The reverses are done in red, black and gray, in contrast to the Topps set, and the number appears to the right of the position listing. The cards were initally distributed in three-card cello packs with an ice cream or Coca-Cola purchase but later became available as sets within the hobby. The unnumbered title or advertising card carries a premium offer on the reverse.

		MINT	EXC	G-VG
COMPLETE SET		4.00	2.00	.40
COMMON PLAYER		.05	.02	.00
☐ 1	Gary Allenson	.05	.02	.00
☐ 2	Tom Burgmeier	.05	.02	.00
☐ 3	Mark Clear	.05	.02	.00
☐ 4	Steve Crawford	.05	.02	.00
☐ 5	Dennis Eckersley	.15	.07	.01
☐ 6	Dwight Evans	.75	.35	.07
☐ 7	Rich Gedman	.75	.35	.07
☐ 8	Garry Hancock	.05	.02	.00
☐ 9	Glen Hoffman	.05	.02	.00
☐ 10	Carney Lansford	.25	.12	.02
☐ 11	Rick Miller	.05	.02	.00
☐ 12	Reid Nichols	.05	.02	.00
☐ 13	Bob Ojeda	.25	.12	.02
☐ 14	Tony Perez	.35	.17	.03
☐ 15	Chuck Rainey	.05	.02	.00
☐ 16	Jerry Remy	.05	.02	.00
☐ 17	Jim Rice	1.00	.50	.10
☐ 18	Bob Stanley	.15	.07	.01
☐ 19	Dave Stapleton	.05	.02	.00
☐ 20	Mike Torrez	.10	.05	.01
☐ 21	John Tudor	.35	.17	.03
☐ 22	Carl Yastrzemski	1.50	.75	.15
☐ 23	Title Card (unnumbered)	.03	.01	.00

1982 Coke Reds

PITCHER **GREG HARRIS**

The cards in this 22 card set measure 2 1/2" by 3 1/2". The 1982 Coca-Cola Cincinnati Reds set, issued in conjunction with Topps, contains 22 cards of current Reds players. Although the cards of 15

players feature the exact photo used in the Topps' regular issue, the Coke photos have better coloration and appear sharper than their Topps counterparts. Six players, Cedeno, Harris, Hurdle, Kern, Krenchicki, and Trevino are new to the Redleg uniform via trades, while Joel Householder had formerly appeared on the Reds' 1982 Topps "Future Stars" card. The cards are numbered 1 to 22 on the red and gray reverse, and the Coke logo appears on both sides of the card. There is an unnumbered title card which contains a premium offer on the reverse.

		MINT	EXC	G-VG
COMPLETE SET		4.00	2.00	.40
COMMON PLAYER		.05	.02	.00
☐ 1	Johnny Bench	1.25	.60	.12
☐ 2	Bruce Berenyi	.05	.02	.00
☐ 3	Larry Biittner	.05	.02	.00
☐ 4	Cesar Cedeno	.10	.05	.01
☐ 5	Dave Concepcion	.20	.10	.02
☐ 6	Dan Driessen	.10	.05	.01
☐ 7	Greg Harris	.15	.07	.01
☐ 8	Paul Householder	.05	.02	.00
☐ 9	Tom Hume	.05	.02	.00
☐ 10	Clint Hurdle	.05	.02	.00
☐ 11	Jim Kern	.05	.02	.00
☐ 12	Wayne Krenchicki	.05	.02	.00
☐ 13	Rafael Landestoy	.05	.02	.00
☐ 14	Charlie Leibrandt	.25	.12	.02
☐ 15	Mike O'Berry	.05	.02	.00
☐ 16	Ron Oester	.10	.05	.01
☐ 17	Frank Pastore	.05	.02	.00
☐ 18	Joe Price	.05	.02	.00
☐ 19	Tom Seaver	1.25	.60	.12
☐ 20	Mario Soto	.25	.12	.02
☐ 21	Alex Trevino	.05	.02	.00
☐ 22	Mike Vail	.05	.02	.00
☐ 23	Title Card (unnumbered)	.03	.01	.00

1985 Coke White Sox

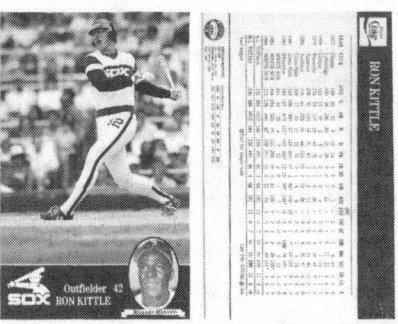

Outfielder 42
SOX RON KITTLE

This 30-card set features present and past Chicago White Sox players and personnel. Cards measure 2 5/8" by 4 1/8" and feature a red band at the bottom of the card. Within the red band are the White Sox logo, the player's name, position, uniform number, and a small oval portrait of an all-time White Sox Great at a similar position. the cards were available two at a time at Tuesday night White Sox home games or as a complete set through membership in the Coca-Cola White Sox Fan Club. The cards below are numbered by uniform number; the last three cards are unnumbered.

		MINT	EXC	G-VG
COMPLETE SET		10.00	5.00	1.00
COMMON PLAYER		.25	.12	.02
☐ 0	Oscar Gamble Zeke Bonura	.25	.12	.02
☐ 1	Scott Fletcher	.60	.30	.06

Luke Appling
| ☐ 3 Harold Baines | .75 | .35 | .07 |

Bill Melton
| ☐ 5 Luis Salazar | .25 | .12 | .02 |

Chico Carrasquel
| ☐ 7 Marc Hill | .25 | .12 | .02 |

Sherm Lollar
| ☐ 8 Daryl Boston | .25 | .12 | .02 |

Jim Landis
| ☐ 10 Tony LaRussa | .35 | .17 | .03 |

Al Lopez
| ☐ 12 Julio Cruz | .35 | .17 | .03 |

Nellie Fox
| ☐ 13 Ozzie Guillen | .90 | .45 | .09 |

Luis Aparicio
| ☐ 17 Jerry Hairston | .25 | .12 | .02 |

Smoky Burgess
| ☐ 20 Joe DeSa | .25 | .12 | .02 |

Carlos May
| ☐ 22 Joel Skinner | .25 | .12 | .02 |

J.C. Martin
| ☐ 23 Rudy Law | .25 | .12 | .02 |

Bill Skowron
| ☐ 24 Floyd Bannister | .50 | .25 | .05 |

Red Faber
| ☐ 29 Greg Walker | .75 | .35 | .07 |

Dick Allen
| ☐ 30 Gene Nelson | .35 | .17 | .03 |

Early Wynn
| ☐ 32 Tim Hulett | .25 | .12 | .02 |

Pete Ward
| ☐ 34 Richard Dotson | .50 | .25 | .05 |

Ed Walsh
| ☐ 37 Dan Spillner | .25 | .12 | .02 |

Thornton Lee
| ☐ 40 Britt Burns | .35 | .17 | .03 |

Gary Peters
| ☐ 41 Tom Seaver | 1.25 | .60 | .12 |

Ted Lyons
| ☐ 40 Ron Kittle | .50 | .25 | .05 |

Minnie Minoso
| ☐ 43 Bob James | .50 | .25 | .05 |

Hoyt Wilhelm
| ☐ 44 Tom Paciorek | .35 | .17 | .03 |

Eddie Collins
| ☐ 46 Tim Lollar | .25 | .12 | .02 |

Billy Pierce
| ☐ 50 Juan Agosto | .25 | .12 | .02 |

Wilbur Wood
| ☐ 72 Carlton Fisk | .60 | .30 | .06 |

Ray Schalk
| ☐ xx Comiskey Park | .25 | .12 | .02 |
(unnumbered)
| ☐ xx Nancy Faust | .25 | .12 | .02 |
(park organist)
(unnumbered)
| ☐ xx Ribbie and Roobarb | .25 | .12 | .02 |
(unnumbered)

1986 Coke White Sox

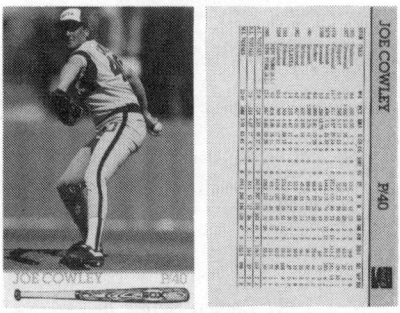

This colorful 30-card set features a borderless photo on top of a blue-on-white name, position, and uniform number. Card backs provide complete major and minor season-by-season career statistical information. Since the cards are unnumbered, they are numbered below according to uniform number. The cards measure approximately 2 5/8" by 4". The five unnumbered non-player cards are listed at the end of the checklist below.

	MINT	EXC	G-VG
COMPLETE SET	9.00	4.50	.90
COMMON PLAYER	.20	.10	.02

☐ 1 Wayne Tolleson	.30	.15	.03
☐ 3 Harold Baines	1.00	.50	.10
☐ 7 Marc Hill	.20	.10	.02
☐ 8 Daryl Boston	.30	.15	.03
☐ 12 Julio Cruz	.20	.10	.02
☐ 13 Ozzie Guillen	.50	.25	.05
☐ 17 Jerry Hairston	.20	.10	.02
☐ 19 Floyd Bannister	.40	.20	.04
☐ 20 Reid Nichols	.20	.10	.02
☐ 22 Joel Skinner	.30	.15	.03
☐ 24 Dave Schmidt	.30	.15	.03
☐ 26 Bobby Bonilla	.50	.25	.05
☐ 29 Greg Walker	.60	.30	.06
☐ 30 Gene Nelson	.20	.10	.02
☐ 32 Tim Hulett	.20	.10	.02
☐ 33 Neil Allen	.30	.15	.03
☐ 34 Richard Dotson	.40	.20	.04
☐ 40 Joe Cowley	.30	.15	.03
☐ 41 Tom Seaver	1.00	.50	.10
☐ 42 Ron Kittle	.40	.20	.04
☐ 43 Bob James	.20	.10	.02
☐ 44 John Cangelosi	.40	.20	.04
☐ 50 Juan Agosto	.20	.10	.02
☐ 52 Joel Davis	.30	.15	.03
☐ 72 Carlton Fisk	.60	.30	.06
☐ xx Nancy Faust ORG	.20	.10	.02
(unnumbered)			
☐ xx Ken"Hawk" Harrelson	.30	.15	.03
(unnumbered)			
☐ xx Tony LaRussa MG	.20	.10	.02
(unnumbered)			
☐ xx Minnie Minoso CO	.20	.10	.02
(unnumbered)			
☐ xx Ribbie and Roobarb	.20	.10	.02
(unnumbered)			

1987 Coke Tigers

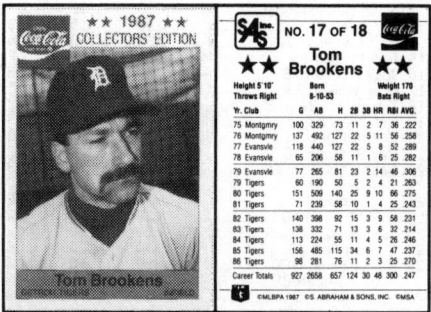

Coca-Cola in collaboration with S. Abraham and Sons issued a set of 18 cards featuring the Detroit Tigers. The cards are numbered on the back. The cards are distinguished by the bright yellow border framing the full-color picture of the player on the front. The cards were issued in panels of four: three player cards and a team logo card. The cards measure the standard 2 1/2" by 3 1/2" and were produced by MSA, Mike Schechter Associates.

	MINT	EXC	G-VG
COMPLETE SET	4.50	2.25	.45
COMMON PLAYER	.20	.10	.02

☐ 1 Kirk Gibson	.50	.25	.05
☐ 2 Larry Herndon	.30	.15	.03
☐ 3 Walt Terrell	.30	.15	.03
☐ 4 Alan Trammell	.75	.35	.07
☐ 5 Frank Tanana	.30	.15	.03
☐ 6 Pat Sheridan	.20	.10	.02
☐ 7 Jack Morris	.50	.25	.05
☐ 8 Mike Heath	.20	.10	.02

			MINT	EXC	G-VG
☐	9	Dave Bergman	.20	.10	.02
☐	10	Chet Lemon	.30	.15	.03
☐	11	Dwight Lowry	.20	.10	.02
☐	12	Dan Petry	.30	.15	.03
☐	13	Darrell Evans	.40	.20	.04
☐	14	Darnell Coles	.20	.10	.02
☐	15	Willie Hernandez	.30	.15	.03
☐	16	Lou Whitaker	.40	.20	.04
☐	17	Tom Brookens	.20	.10	.02
☐	18	John Grubb	.20	.10	.02

1987 Coke White Sox

This colorful 30-card set features a card front with a blue-bordered photo and name, position, and uniform number. Card backs provide complete major and minor season-by-season career statistical information. Since the cards are unnumbered, they are numbered below in uniform number order. The cards measure approximately 2 5/8" by 4". The three unnumbered non-player cards are listed at the end. The card set, sponsored by Coca-Cola, is an exclusive for fan club members who join (for 10.00) in 1987.

			MINT	EXC	G-VG
	COMPLETE SET (30)		7.00	3.50	.70
	COMMON PLAYER		.20	.10	.02
☐	1	Jerry Royster 1	.20	.10	.02
☐	2	Harold Baines 3	.50	.25	.05
☐	3	Ron Karkovice 5	.20	.10	.02
☐	4	Daryl Boston 8	.30	.15	.03
☐	5	Fred Manrique 10	.30	.15	.03
☐	6	Steve Lyons 12	.20	.10	.02
☐	7	Ozzie Guillen 13	.40	.20	.04
☐	8	Russ Morman 14	.20	.10	.02
☐	9	Donnie Hill 15	.20	.10	.02
☐	10	Jim Fregosi MG 16	.30	.15	.03
☐	11	Jerry Hairston 17	.20	.10	.02
☐	12	Floyd Bannister 19	.30	.15	.03
☐	13	Gary Redus 21	.30	.15	.03
☐	14	Ivan Calderon 22	.60	.30	.06
☐	15	Ron Hassey 25	.20	.10	.02
☐	16	Jose DeLeon 26	.30	.15	.03
☐	17	Greg Walker 29	.50	.25	.05
☐	18	Tim Hulett 32	.20	.10	.02
☐	19	Neil Allen 33	.30	.15	.03
☐	20	Richard Dotson 34	.30	.15	.03
☐	21	Ray Searage 36	.20	.10	.02
☐	22	Bobby Thigpen 37	.30	.15	.03
☐	23	Jim Winn 40	.20	.10	.02
☐	24	Bob James 43	.20	.10	.02
☐	25	Joel McKeon 50	.20	.10	.02
☐	26	Joel Davis 52	.20	.10	.02
☐	27	Carlton Fisk 72	.40	.20	.04
☐	28	Nancy Faust ORG (unnumbered)	.20	.10	.02
☐	29	Minnie Minoso (unnumbered)	.30	.15	.03
☐	30	Robbie and Roobarb (unnumbered)	.20	.10	.02

1986 Conlon Series I

This 60-card set was produced from the black and white photos in the Charles Martin Conlon collection. Each set comes with a special card which contains the number of that set out of the 12,000 sets which were produced. The cards measure 2 1/2" by 3 1/2" and are printed in sepia tones.

			MINT	EXC	G-VG
	COMPLETE SET		12.00	6.00	1.20
	COMMON PLAYER		.20	.10	.02
☐	1	Henry Louis Gehrig	.60	.30	.06
☐	2	Tyrus Raymond Cobb	.60	.30	.06
☐	3	Grover C. Alexander	.30	.15	.03

☐	4	Walter Perry Johnson	.45	.22	.04
☐	5	William Joseph Klem	.20	.10	.02
☐	6	Tyrus Raymond Cobb	.60	.30	.06
☐	7	Gordon S. Cochrane	.30	.15	.03
☐	8	Paul Glee Waner	.20	.10	.02
☐	9	Joseph Edward Cronin	.20	.10	.02
☐	10	Jay Hanna Dean	.45	.22	.04
☐	11	Leo Ernest Durocher	.30	.15	.03
☐	12	James Emory Foxx	.30	.15	.03
☐	13	George Herman Ruth	.75	.35	.07
☐	14	Miguel Angel Gonzalez Frank Francis Frisch Clyde Ellsworth Wares	.20	.10	.02
☐	15	Carl Owen Hubbell	.30	.15	.03
☐	16	Miller James Huggins	.20	.10	.02
☐	17	Henry Louis Gehrig	.60	.30	.06
☐	18	Connie McGillicuddy	.30	.15	.03
☐	19	Henry Emmett Manush	.20	.10	.02
☐	20	George Herman Ruth	.75	.35	.07
☐	22	John L.R. Martin	.20	.10	.02
☐	23	Christopher Mathewson	.45	.22	.04
☐	24	Tyrus Raymond Cobb	.60	.30	.06
☐	25	Stanley R. Harris	.20	.10	.02
☐	26	Waite Charles Hoyt	.20	.10	.02
☐	27	Richard W. Marquard	.20	.10	.02
☐	28	Joseph V. McCarthy	.20	.10	.02
☐	29	John Joseph McGraw	.20	.10	.02
☐	30	Tristram Speaker	.30	.15	.03
☐	31	William Harold Terry	.30	.15	.03
☐	32	Christopher Mathewson	.45	.22	.04
☐	33	Charles D. Stengel	.45	.22	.04
☐	34	Robert William Meusel	.20	.10	.02
☐	35	George Edward Waddell	.20	.10	.02
☐	36	Melvin Thomas Ott	.30	.15	.03
☐	37	Roger T. Peckinpaugh	.20	.10	.02
☐	38	Harold Joseph Traynor	.20	.10	.02
☐	39	Charles Albert Bender	.20	.10	.02
☐	40	John Wesley Coombs	.20	.10	.02
☐	41	Tyrus Raymond Cobb	.60	.30	.06
☐	42	Harry Edwin Heilmann	.20	.10	.02
☐	43	Charles L. Gehringer	.30	.15	.03
☐	44	Rogers Hornsby	.45	.22	.04
☐	45	Vernon Gomez	.45	.22	.04
☐	46	Christopher Mathewson	.45	.22	.04
☐	47	Robert Moses Grove	.45	.22	.04
☐	48	George Herman Ruth	.75	.35	.07
☐	49	Frederick C. Merkle	.20	.10	.02
☐	50	George Herman Ruth	.75	.35	.07
☐	51	Herbert J. Pennock	.20	.10	.02
☐	52	Henry Louis Gehrig	.60	.30	.06
☐	53	Fred Clifford Clarke	.20	.10	.02
☐	54	George Herman Ruth	.75	.35	.07
☐	55	John Peter Wagner	.45	.22	.04
☐	56	Lewis Robert Wilson	.30	.15	.03
☐	57	Henry Louis Gehrig	.60	.30	.06
☐	58	Lloyd James Waner	.20	.10	.02
☐	59	Charles Martin Conlon	.20	.10	.02
☐	60	Conlon and Margie	.20	.10	.02
☐	xx	Set Number Card (unnumbered)	.20	.10	.02

1987 Conlon Series II

The second series of 60 Charles Martin Conlon photo cards was produced by World Wide Sports in conjunction with The Sporting News. The cards are standard size, 2 1/2" by 3 1/2" and are in a sepia tone. Supposedly 12,000 sets were produced. The

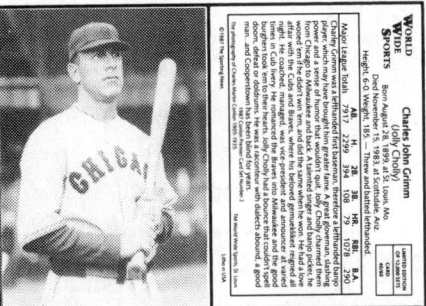

photos were selected and background information
written by Paul MacFarlane of The Sporting News.

		MINT	EXC	G-VG
	COMPLETE SET	10.00	5.00	1.00
	COMMON PLAYER	.20	.10	.02
☐ 1	Henry Gehrig	.60	.30	.06
☐ 2	Vernon Gomez	.45	.22	.04
☐ 3	Christopher Mathewson ...	.45	.22	.04
☐ 4	Grover Alexander	.30	.15	.03
☐ 5	Tyrus Cobb	.60	.30	.06
☐ 6	Walter Johnson	.45	.22	.04
☐ 7	Charles Adams	.20	.10	.02
☐ 8	Nicholas Altrock	.20	.10	.02
☐ 9	Al Schacht	.20	.10	.02
☐ 10	Hugh Critz	.20	.10	.02
☐ 11	Henry Cullop	.20	.10	.02
☐ 12	Jacob Daubert	.20	.10	.02
☐ 13	William Donovan	.20	.10	.02
☐ 14	Charles Hafey	.20	.10	.02
☐ 15	William Hallahan	.20	.10	.02
☐ 16	Fred Haney	.20	.10	.02
☐ 17	Charles Hartnett	.20	.10	.02
☐ 18	Walter Henline	.20	.10	.02
☐ 19	Edwin Rommel	.20	.10	.02
☐ 20	Ralph Pinelli	.20	.10	.02
☐ 21	Robert Meusel	.20	.10	.02
☐ 22	Emil Meusel	.20	.10	.02
☐ 23	Smead Jolley	.20	.10	.02
☐ 24	Isaac Boone	.20	.10	.02
☐ 25	Earl Webb	.20	.10	.02
☐ 26	Charles Comiskey	.30	.15	.03
☐ 27	Edward Collins	.30	.15	.03
☐ 28	George Weaver	.20	.10	.02
☐ 29	Edward Cicotte	.20	.10	.02
☐ 30	Samuel Crawford	.20	.10	.02
☐ 31	Charles Dressen	.20	.10	.02
☐ 32	Arthur Fletcher	.20	.10	.02
☐ 33	Hugh Duffy	.30	.15	.03
☐ 34	Ira Flagstead	.20	.10	.02
☐ 35	Harry Hooper	.20	.10	.02
☐ 36	George Lewis	.20	.10	.02
☐ 37	James Dykes	.20	.10	.02
☐ 38	Leon Goslin	.20	.10	.02
☐ 39	Henry Gowdy	.20	.10	.02
☐ 40	Charles Grimm	.20	.10	.02
☐ 41	Mark Koenig	.20	.10	.02
☐ 42	James Hogan	.20	.10	.02
☐ 43	William Jacobson	.20	.10	.02
☐ 44	Fielder Jones	.20	.10	.02
☐ 45	George Kelly	.20	.10	.02
☐ 46	Adolpho Luque	.20	.10	.02
☐ 47	Walter Maranville	.20	.10	.02
☐ 48	Carl Mays	.20	.10	.02
☐ 49	Edward Plank	.30	.15	.03
☐ 50	Hubert Pruett	.20	.10	.02
☐ 51	John Quinn	.20	.10	.02
☐ 52	Charles Rhem	.20	.10	.02
☐ 53	Amos Rusie	.30	.15	.03
☐ 54	Edd Roush	.20	.10	.02
☐ 55	Raymond Schalk	.20	.10	.02
☐ 56	Ernest Shore	.20	.10	.02
☐ 57	Joe Wood	.20	.10	.02
☐ 58	George Sisler	.30	.15	.03
☐ 59	James Thorpe	.45	.22	.04
☐ 60	Earl Whitehill	.20	.10	.02

1914 Cracker Jack

The cards in this 144 card set measure 2 1/4" by
3". This "Series of colored pictures of Famous Ball
Players and Managers" was issued in packages of
Cracker Jack in 1914. The cards have tinted photos
set against red backgrounds and many are found
with caramel stains. The set also contains Federal
League players. The company claims to have printed
15 million cards. The 1914 series can be
distinguished from the 1915 issue by the advertising
found on the back of the cards. The ACC catalog
number is E145-1.

		NRMT	VG-E	GOOD
	COMPLETE SET	13500.00	5000.00	1000.00
	COMMON PLAYER (1-144)	55.00	27.50	5.50
☐ 1	Otto Knabe	75.00	37.50	7.50
☐ 2	Frank Baker	125.00	60.00	12.50
☐ 3	Joe Tinker	125.00	60.00	12.50
☐ 4	Larry Doyle	55.00	27.50	5.50
☐ 5	Ward Miller	55.00	27.50	5.50
☐ 6	Eddie Plank	150.00	75.00	15.00
	(Phila. AL)			
☐ 7	Eddie Collins	150.00	75.00	15.00
	(Phila. AL)			
☐ 8	Rube Oldring	55.00	27.50	5.50
☐ 9	Artie Hoffman	55.00	27.50	5.50
☐ 10	John McInnis	65.00	32.50	6.50
☐ 11	George Stovall	55.00	27.50	5.50
☐ 12	Connie Mack	200.00	100.00	20.00
☐ 13	Art Wilson	55.00	27.50	5.50
☐ 14	Sam Crawford	125.00	60.00	12.50
☐ 15	Reb Russell	55.00	27.50	5.50
☐ 16	Howie Camnitz	55.00	27.50	5.50
☐ 17	Roger Bresnahan	125.00	60.00	12.50
	(Catcher)			
☐ 18	Johnny Evers	125.00	60.00	12.50
☐ 19	Chief Bender	150.00	75.00	15.00
	(Phila. AL)			
☐ 20	Cy Falkenberg	55.00	27.50	5.50
☐ 21	Heine Zimmerman	55.00	27.50	5.50
☐ 22	Joe Wood	75.00	37.50	7.50
☐ 23	Charles Comiskey	150.00	75.00	15.00
☐ 24	George Mullen	55.00	27.50	5.50
☐ 25	Michael Simon	55.00	27.50	5.50
☐ 26	James Scott	55.00	27.50	5.50
☐ 27	Bill Carrigan	55.00	27.50	5.50
☐ 28	Jack Barry	55.00	27.50	5.50
☐ 29	Vean Gregg (Cleve)	55.00	27.50	5.50
☐ 30	Ty Cobb	1800.00	750.00	150.00
☐ 31	Heine Wagner	55.00	27.50	5.50
☐ 32	Mordecai Brown	125.00	60.00	12.50
☐ 33	Amos Strunk	55.00	27.50	5.50
☐ 34	Ira Thomas	55.00	27.50	5.50
☐ 35	Harry Hooper	125.00	60.00	12.50
☐ 36	Ed Walsh	125.00	60.00	12.50
☐ 37	Grover Alexander	250.00	125.00	25.00
☐ 38	Red Dooin (Phila. NL)	65.00	32.50	6.50
☐ 39	Chick Gandil	55.00	27.50	5.50
☐ 40	Jimmy Austin	65.00	32.50	6.50
	(St.L. AL)			
☐ 41	Tommy Leach	55.00	27.50	5.50
☐ 42	Al Bridwell	55.00	27.50	5.50
☐ 43	Rube Marquard (NY NL)	160.00	75.00	15.00
☐ 44	Charles Tesreau	55.00	27.50	5.50
☐ 45	Fred Luderus	55.00	27.50	5.50
☐ 46	Bob Groom	55.00	27.50	5.50
☐ 47	Josh Devore	65.00	32.50	6.50

(Phila. NL)

☐ 48	Harry Lord	125.00	60.00	12.50
☐ 49	John Miller	55.00	27.50	5.50
☐ 50	John Hummell	55.00	27.50	5.50
☐ 51	Nap Rucker	55.00	27.50	5.50
☐ 52	Zach Wheat	125.00	60.00	12.50
☐ 53	Otto Miller	55.00	27.50	5.50
☐ 54	Marty O'Toole	55.00	27.50	5.50
☐ 55	Dick Hoblitzel(Cinc.)	65.00	32.50	6.50
☐ 56	Clyde Milan	55.00	27.50	5.50
☐ 57	Walter Johnson	600.00	300.00	60.00
☐ 58	Wally Schang	55.00	27.50	5.50
☐ 59	Harry Gessler	55.00	27.50	5.50
☐ 60	Rollie Zeider	125.00	60.00	12.50
☐ 61	Ray Schalk	125.00	60.00	12.50
☐ 62	Jay Cashion	125.00	60.00	12.50
☐ 63	Babe Adams	55.00	27.50	5.50
☐ 64	Jimmy Archer	55.00	27.50	5.50
☐ 65	Tris Speaker	300.00	150.00	30.00
☐ 66	Napoleon Lajoie	350.00	175.00	35.00
	(Cleve.)			
☐ 67	Otis Crandall	55.00	27.50	5.50
☐ 68	Honus Wagner	500.00	250.00	50.00
☐ 69	John McGraw	175.00	85.00	18.00
☐ 70	Fred Clarke	125.00	60.00	12.50
☐ 71	Chief Meyers	55.00	27.50	5.50
☐ 72	John Boehling	55.00	27.50	5.50
☐ 73	Max Carey	125.00	60.00	12.50
☐ 74	Frank Owens	55.00	27.50	5.50
☐ 75	Miller Huggins	125.00	60.00	12.50
☐ 76	Claude Hendrix	55.00	27.50	5.50
☐ 77	Hugh Jennings	125.00	60.00	12.50
☐ 78	Fred Merkle	65.00	32.50	6.50
☐ 79	Ping Bodie	55.00	27.50	5.50
☐ 80	Ed Ruelbach	55.00	27.50	5.50
☐ 81	J.C. Delehanty	55.00	27.50	5.50
☐ 82	Gavvy Cravath	65.00	32.50	6.50
☐ 83	Russ Ford	55.00	27.50	5.50
☐ 84	E.E. Knetzer	55.00	27.50	5.50
☐ 85	Buck Herzog	55.00	27.50	5.50
☐ 86	Burt Shotten	55.00	27.50	5.50
☐ 87	Forrest Cady	55.00	27.50	5.50
☐ 88	Christy Mathewson	600.00	300.00	60.00
	(Pitching)			
☐ 89	Lawrence Cheney	55.00	27.50	5.50
☐ 90	Frank Smith	55.00	27.50	5.50
☐ 91	Roger Peckinpaugh	65.00	32.50	6.50
☐ 92	Al Demaree (N.Y. NL)	65.00	32.50	6.50
☐ 93	Derrill Pratt	125.00	60.00	12.50
	(Throwing)			
☐ 94	Eddie Cicotte	65.00	32.50	6.50
☐ 95	Ray Keating	55.00	27.50	5.50
☐ 96	Beals Becker	55.00	27.50	5.50
☐ 97	John (Rube) Benton	55.00	27.50	5.50
☐ 98	Frank LaPorte	55.00	27.50	5.50
☐ 99	Frank Chance	450.00	225.00	45.00
☐ 100	Thomas Seaton	55.00	27.50	5.50
☐ 101	Frank Schulte	55.00	27.50	5.50
☐ 102	Ray Fisher	55.00	27.50	5.50
☐ 103	Joe Jackson	1200.00	500.00	100.00
☐ 104	Vic Saier	55.00	27.50	5.50
☐ 105	James Lavender	55.00	27.50	5.50
☐ 106	Joe Birmingham	55.00	27.50	5.50
☐ 107	Tom Downey	55.00	27.50	5.50
☐ 108	Sherwood Magee	65.00	32.50	6.50
	(Phila. NL)			
☐ 109	Fred Blanding	55.00	27.50	5.50
☐ 110	Bob Bescher	55.00	27.50	5.50
☐ 111	Jim Callahan	125.00	60.00	12.50
☐ 112	Ed Sweeney	55.00	27.50	5.50
☐ 113	George Suggs	55.00	27.50	5.50
☐ 114	Geo. J. Moriarty	55.00	27.50	5.50
☐ 115	Addison Brennan	55.00	27.50	5.50
☐ 116	Rollie Zeider	55.00	27.50	5.50
☐ 117	Ted Easterly	55.00	27.50	5.50
☐ 118	Ed Konetchy (Pitts.)	65.00	32.50	6.50
☐ 119	George Perring	55.00	27.50	5.50
☐ 120	Mike Doolan	55.00	27.50	5.50
☐ 121	Perdue (Boston NL)	65.00	32.50	6.50
☐ 122	Owen Bush	55.00	27.50	5.50
☐ 123	Slim Sallee	55.00	27.50	5.50
☐ 124	Earl Moore	55.00	27.50	5.50
☐ 125	Bert Niehoff	55.00	27.50	5.50
☐ 126	Walter Blair	55.00	27.50	5.50
☐ 127	Butch Schmidt	55.00	27.50	5.50
☐ 128	Steve Evans	55.00	27.50	5.50
☐ 129	Ray Caldwell	55.00	27.50	5.50
☐ 130	Ivy Wingo	55.00	27.50	5.50
☐ 131	George Baumgardner	55.00	27.50	5.50
☐ 132	Les Nunamaker	55.00	27.50	5.50
☐ 133	Branch Rickey	150.00	75.00	15.00
☐ 134	Armando Marsans	65.00	32.50	6.50
	(Cincinnati)			
☐ 135	Bill Killefer	55.00	27.50	5.50
☐ 136	Rabbit Maranville	125.00	60.00	12.50
☐ 137	William Rariden	55.00	27.50	5.50
☐ 138	Hank Gowdy	65.00	32.50	6.50
☐ 139	Rebel Oakes	55.00	27.50	5.50
☐ 140	Danny Murphy	55.00	27.50	5.50
☐ 141	Cy Barger	55.00	27.50	5.50
☐ 142	Eugene Packard	55.00	27.50	5.50
☐ 143	Jake Daubert	65.00	32.50	6.50
☐ 144	James C. Walsh	75.00	37.50	7.50

1915 Cracker Jack

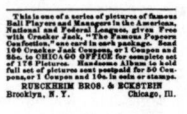

106
Joseph Birmingham, manager of the Cleveland American League team, was born in Elmira, N. Y., August 6, 1884. He played on local nines in 1901 and with the Mercersburg, Pa., Preparatory School team during 1902 and 1903. In 1906 he played baseball professionally with the A. J. G. Club of the New York State League, and was secured by Cleveland in August of the same year.

This is one of a series of pictures of famous Ball Players and Managers in the American, National and Federal Leagues, given Free with Cracker Jack, "The Famous Popcorn Confection," and card in each package. Send 100 Cracker Jack Coupons, or 1 Coupon and 25c, to CHICAGO OFFICE for complete set of 176 Pictures. Handsome Album to hold full set of pictures sent postpaid for 50 Coupons, or 1 Coupon and 10c. In safe at Chicago.

RUECKHEIM BROS. & ECKSTEIN
Brooklyn, N. Y.   Chicago, Ill.

BIRMINGHAM, Cleveland - Americans

The cards in this 176 card set measure 2 1/4" by 3". When turned over in a lateral motion, a 1915 "series of 176" Cracker Jack card shows the back printing upside-down. Cards were available in boxes of Cracker Jack or from the company for "100 Cracker Jack coupons, or one coupon and 25 cents." An album was available for "50 coupons or one coupon and 10 cents." The set essentially duplicates E145-1 (1914 Cracker Jack) except for some additional cards and new poses. Players in the Federal League are indicated by FED in the checklist below. The ACC designation is E145-2.

		NRMT	VG-E	GOOD
COMPLETE SET		11500.00	4000.00	900.00
COMMON PLAYER (1-144)		40.00	20.00	4.00
COMMON PLAYER (145-176)		50.00	25.00	5.00
☐ 1	Otto Knabe	60.00	30.00	6.00
☐ 2	Frank Baker	110.00	55.00	11.00
☐ 3	Joe Tinker	110.00	55.00	11.00
☐ 4	Larry Doyle	40.00	20.00	4.00
☐ 5	Ward Miller	40.00	20.00	4.00
☐ 6	Eddie Plank	135.00	65.00	13.50
	(St.L. FED)			
☐ 7	Eddie Collins	135.00	65.00	13.50
	(Chicago AL)			
☐ 8	Rube Oldring	40.00	20.00	4.00
☐ 9	Artie Hoffman	40.00	20.00	4.00
☐ 10	John McInnis	50.00	25.00	5.00
☐ 11	George Stovall	40.00	20.00	4.00
☐ 12	Connie Mack	175.00	85.00	18.00
☐ 13	Art Wilson	40.00	20.00	4.00
☐ 14	Sam Crawford	110.00	55.00	11.00
☐ 15	Reb Russell	40.00	20.00	4.00
☐ 16	Howie Camnitz	40.00	20.00	4.00
☐ 17	Roger Bresnahan	110.00	55.00	11.00
☐ 18	Johnny Evers	110.00	55.00	11.00
☐ 19	Chief Bender	135.00	65.00	13.50
	(Baltimore FED)			
☐ 20	Cy Falkenberg	40.00	20.00	4.00
☐ 21	Heine Zimmerman	40.00	20.00	4.00
☐ 22	Joe Wood	60.00	30.00	6.00
☐ 23	Charles Comiskey	135.00	65.00	13.50
☐ 24	George Mullen	40.00	20.00	4.00
☐ 25	Michael Simon	40.00	20.00	4.00
☐ 26	James Scott	40.00	20.00	4.00
☐ 27	Bill Carrigan	40.00	20.00	4.00
☐ 28	Jack Barry	40.00	20.00	4.00
☐ 29	Vean Gregg	50.00	25.00	5.00
	(Boston AL)			
☐ 30	Ty Cobb	1500.00	600.00	120.00
☐ 31	Heine Wagner	40.00	20.00	4.00
☐ 32	Mordecai Brown	110.00	55.00	11.00
☐ 33	Amos Strunk	40.00	20.00	4.00
☐ 34	Ira Thomas	40.00	20.00	4.00
☐ 35	Harry Hooper	110.00	55.00	11.00

☐ 36	Ed Walsh	110.00	55.00	11.00
☐ 37	Grover C. Alexander	200.00	100.00	20.00
☐ 38	Red Dooin (Cinc.)	50.00	25.00	5.00
☐ 39	Chick Gandil	40.00	20.00	4.00
☐ 40	Jimmy Austin	50.00	25.00	5.00
	(Pitts. FED)			
☐ 41	Tommy Leach	40.00	20.00	4.00
☐ 42	Al Bridwell	40.00	20.00	4.00
☐ 43	Rube Marquard	135.00	65.00	13.50
	(Brooklyn FED)			
☐ 44	Charles Tesreau	40.00	20.00	4.00
☐ 45	Fred Luderus	40.00	20.00	4.00
☐ 46	Bob Groom	40.00	20.00	4.00
☐ 47	Josh Devore	50.00	25.00	5.00
	(Boston NL)			
☐ 48	Steve O'Neill	50.00	25.00	5.00
☐ 49	John Miller	40.00	20.00	4.00
☐ 50	John Hummell	40.00	20.00	4.00
☐ 51	Nap Rucker	40.00	20.00	4.00
☐ 52	Zach Wheat	110.00	55.00	11.00
☐ 53	Otto Miller	40.00	20.00	4.00
☐ 54	Marty O'Toole	40.00	20.00	4.00
☐ 55	Dick Hoblitzel	50.00	25.00	5.00
	(Boston AL)			
☐ 56	Clyde Milan	40.00	20.00	4.00
☐ 57	Walter Johnson	500.00	250.00	50.00
☐ 58	Wally Schang	40.00	20.00	4.00
☐ 59	Harry Gessler	40.00	20.00	4.00
☐ 60	Oscar Dugey	50.00	25.00	5.00
☐ 61	Ray Schalk	110.00	55.00	11.00
☐ 62	Willie Mitchell	50.00	25.00	5.00
☐ 63	Babe Adams	40.00	20.00	4.00
☐ 64	Jimmy Archer	40.00	20.00	4.00
☐ 65	Tris Speaker	250.00	125.00	25.00
☐ 66	Napoleon Lajoie	300.00	150.00	30.00
	(Phila. AL)			
☐ 67	Otis Crandall	40.00	20.00	4.00
☐ 68	Honus Wagner	450.00	225.00	45.00
☐ 69	John McGraw	135.00	65.00	13.50
☐ 70	Fred Clarke	110.00	55.00	11.00
☐ 71	Chief Meyers	40.00	20.00	4.00
☐ 72	John Boehling	40.00	20.00	4.00
☐ 73	Max Carey	110.00	55.00	11.00
☐ 74	Frank Owens	40.00	20.00	4.00
☐ 75	Miller Huggins	110.00	55.00	11.00
☐ 76	Claude Hendrix	40.00	20.00	4.00
☐ 77	Hugh Jennings	110.00	55.00	11.00
☐ 78	Fred Merkle	50.00	25.00	5.00
☐ 79	Ping Bodie	40.00	20.00	4.00
☐ 80	Ed Ruelbach	40.00	20.00	4.00
☐ 81	J.C. Delehanty	40.00	20.00	4.00
☐ 82	Gavvy Cravath	50.00	25.00	5.00
☐ 83	Russ Ford	40.00	20.00	4.00
☐ 84	E.E. Knetzer	40.00	20.00	4.00
☐ 85	Buck Herzog	40.00	20.00	4.00
☐ 86	Burt Shotten	40.00	20.00	4.00
☐ 87	Forrest Cady	40.00	20.00	4.00
☐ 88	Christy Mathewson	500.00	250.00	50.00
	(Portrait)			
☐ 89	Lawrence Cheney	40.00	20.00	4.00
☐ 90	Frank Smith	40.00	20.00	4.00
☐ 91	Roger Peckinpaugh	50.00	25.00	5.00
☐ 92	Al Demaree	50.00	25.00	5.00
	(Phila. NL)			
☐ 93	Derrill Pratt	50.00	25.00	5.00
	(Portrait)			
☐ 94	Eddie Cicotte	50.00	25.00	5.00
☐ 95	Ray Keating	40.00	20.00	4.00
☐ 96	Beals Becker	40.00	20.00	4.00
☐ 97	John (Rube) Benton	40.00	20.00	4.00
☐ 98	Frank LaPorte	40.00	20.00	4.00
☐ 99	Hal Chase	135.00	65.00	13.50
☐ 100	Thomas Seaton	40.00	20.00	4.00
☐ 101	Frank Schulte	40.00	20.00	4.00
☐ 102	Ray Fisher	40.00	20.00	4.00
☐ 103	Joe Jackson	1000.00	400.00	80.00
☐ 104	Vic Saier	40.00	20.00	4.00
☐ 105	James Lavender	40.00	20.00	4.00
☐ 106	Joe Birmingham	40.00	20.00	4.00
☐ 107	Thomas Downey	40.00	20.00	4.00
☐ 108	Sherwood Magee	50.00	25.00	5.00
	(Boston NL)			
☐ 109	Fred Blanding	40.00	20.00	4.00
☐ 110	Bob Bescher	40.00	20.00	4.00
☐ 111	Herbie Moran	50.00	25.00	5.00
☐ 112	Ed Sweeney	40.00	20.00	4.00
☐ 113	George Suggs	40.00	20.00	4.00
☐ 114	Geo. J. Moriarty	40.00	20.00	4.00
☐ 115	Addison Brennan	40.00	20.00	4.00
☐ 116	Rollie Zeider	40.00	20.00	4.00
☐ 117	Ted Easterly	40.00	20.00	4.00
☐ 118	Ed Konetchy	50.00	25.00	5.00
	(Pitts. FED)			
☐ 119	George Perring	40.00	20.00	4.00
☐ 120	Mike Doolan	40.00	20.00	4.00

☐ 121	Perdue (St.L. NL)	50.00	25.00	5.00
☐ 122	Owen Bush	40.00	20.00	4.00
☐ 123	Slim Sallee	40.00	20.00	4.00
☐ 124	Earl Moore	40.00	20.00	4.00
☐ 125	Bert Niehoff	50.00	25.00	5.00
	(Phila. NL)			
☐ 126	Walter Blair	40.00	20.00	4.00
☐ 127	Butch Schmidt	40.00	20.00	4.00
☐ 128	Steve Evans	40.00	20.00	4.00
☐ 129	Ray Caldwell	40.00	20.00	4.00
☐ 130	Ivy Wingo	40.00	20.00	4.00
☐ 131	Geo. Baumgardner	40.00	20.00	4.00
☐ 132	Les Nunamaker	40.00	20.00	4.00
☐ 133	Branch Rickey	135.00	65.00	13.50
☐ 134	Armando Marsans	50.00	25.00	5.00
	(St.L. FED)			
☐ 135	William Killefer	40.00	20.00	4.00
☐ 136	Rabbit Maranville	110.00	55.00	11.00
☐ 137	William Rariden	40.00	20.00	4.00
☐ 138	Hank Gowdy	50.00	25.00	5.00
☐ 139	Rebel Oakes	40.00	20.00	4.00
☐ 140	Danny Murphy	40.00	20.00	4.00
☐ 141	Cy Barger	40.00	20.00	4.00
☐ 142	Eugene Packard	40.00	20.00	4.00
☐ 143	Jake Daubert	50.00	25.00	5.00
☐ 144	James C. Walsh	40.00	20.00	4.00
☐ 145	Ted Cather	50.00	25.00	5.00
☐ 146	George Tyler	50.00	25.00	5.00
☐ 147	Lee Magee	50.00	25.00	5.00
☐ 148	Owen Wilson	50.00	25.00	5.00
☐ 149	Hal Janvrin	50.00	25.00	5.00
☐ 150	Doc Johnston	50.00	25.00	5.00
☐ 151	George Whitted	50.00	25.00	5.00
☐ 152	George McQuillen	50.00	25.00	5.00
☐ 153	Bill James	50.00	25.00	5.00
☐ 154	Dick Rudolph	50.00	25.00	5.00
☐ 155	Joe Connolly	50.00	25.00	5.00
☐ 156	Jean Dubuc	50.00	25.00	5.00
☐ 157	George Kaiserling	50.00	25.00	5.00
☐ 158	Fritz Maisel	50.00	25.00	5.00
☐ 159	Heinie Groh	60.00	30.00	6.00
☐ 160	Benny Kauff	50.00	25.00	5.00
☐ 161	Ed Rousch	135.00	65.00	13.50
☐ 162	George Stallings	50.00	25.00	5.00
☐ 163	Bert Whaling	50.00	25.00	5.00
☐ 164	Bob Shawkey	60.00	30.00	6.00
☐ 165	Eddie Murphy	50.00	25.00	5.00
☐ 166	Joe Bush	50.00	25.00	5.00
☐ 167	Clark Griffith	135.00	65.00	13.50
☐ 168	Vin Campbell	50.00	25.00	5.00
☐ 169	Raymond Collins	50.00	25.00	5.00
☐ 170	Hans Lobert	50.00	25.00	5.00
☐ 171	Earl Hamilton	50.00	25.00	5.00
☐ 172	Erskine Mayer	50.00	25.00	5.00
☐ 173	Tilly Walker	50.00	25.00	5.00
☐ 174	Robert Veach	50.00	25.00	5.00
☐ 175	Joseph Benz	50.00	25.00	5.00
☐ 176	Jim Vaughn	75.00	37.50	7.50

1982 Cracker Jack

The cards in this 16 card set measure 2 1/2" by 3 1/2"; cards came in two sheets of 8 cards, plus an advertising card with a title in the center, which measured 7 1/2" by 10 1/2". Cracker Jack reentered the baseball card market for the first time since 1915 to promote the first "Old Timers Baseball Classic" held July 19, 1982. The color player photos have a Cracker Jack border and have either green (NL) or red (AL) frame lines and name panels. The Cracker Jack logo appears on both sides of each card, with AL players numbered 1-8 and NL players numbered 9-16. Of the 16 ballplayers pictured, five did not appear at the game. At first, the two sheets were available only through the mail but are now commonly found in hobby circles. The set was prepared for Cracker Jack by Topps. The prices below reflect individual card prices; the price for complete panels would be about 20' more than the sum of the card prices for those players on the panel.

	MINT	EXC	G-VG
COMPLETE SET	6.00	3.00	.60
COMMON PLAYER	.15	.07	.01

		MINT	EXC	G-VG
☐ 1	Larry Doby	.15	.07	.01
☐ 2	Bob Feller	.60	.30	.06
☐ 3	Whitey Ford	.60	.30	.06
☐ 4	Al Kaline	.60	.30	.06
☐ 5	Harmon Killebrew	.35	.17	.03
☐ 6	Mickey Mantle	2.00	1.00	.20
☐ 7	Tony Oliva	.15	.07	.01
☐ 8	Brooks Robinson	.60	.30	.06
☐ 9	Hank Aaron	.80	.40	.08
☐ 10	Ernie Banks	.50	.25	.05
☐ 11	Ralph Kiner	.30	.15	.03
☐ 12	Ed Mathews	.30	.15	.03
☐ 13	Willie Mays	.80	.40	.08
☐ 14	Robin Roberts	.30	.15	.03
☐ 15	Duke Snider	.60	.30	.06
☐ 16	Warren Spahn	.50	.25	.05

1980-83 Cramer Legends

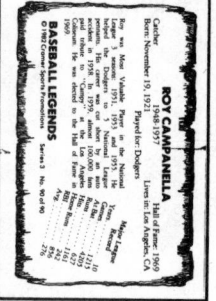

This 124-card set is actually four 30-card subsets plus a four-card wax box bottom panel. The set was distributed by series over several years beginning in 1980 with the first 30 cards. The set was produced by Pacific Trading Cards and is frequently referred to as Cramer Legends for the founder of Pacific Trading cards, Mike Cramer. Cards are standard size, 2 1/2" by 3 1/2" and are golden-toned. Even though the wax box cards are numbered from 121-124 and called "series 5", the set is considered complete without them.

	MINT	EXC	G-VG
COMPLETE SET (120)	12.00	6.00	1.20
COMMON PLAYER	.10	.05	.01

		MINT	EXC	G-VG
☐ 1	Babe Ruth	.60	.30	.06
☐ 2	Heinie Manush	.10	.05	.01
☐ 3	Rabbit Maranville	.10	.05	.01
☐ 4	Earl Averill	.10	.05	.01
☐ 5	Joe DiMaggio	.40	.20	.04
☐ 6	Mickey Mantle	.60	.30	.06
☐ 7	Hank Aaron	.25	.12	.02
☐ 8	Stan Musial	.20	.10	.02
☐ 9	Bill Terry	.10	.05	.01
☐ 10	Sandy Koufax	.20	.10	.02
☐ 11	Ernie Lombardi	.10	.05	.01

		MINT	EXC	G-VG
☐ 12	Dizzy Dean	.20	.10	.02
☐ 13	Lou Gehrig	.40	.20	.04
☐ 14	Walter Alston	.10	.05	.01
☐ 15	Jackie Robinson	.20	.10	.02
☐ 16	Jimmie Foxx	.10	.05	.01
☐ 17	Billy Southworth	.10	.05	.01
☐ 18	Honus Wagner	.20	.10	.02
☐ 19	Duke Snider	.20	.10	.02
☐ 20	Rogers Hornsby	.20	.10	.02
☐ 21	Paul Waner	.10	.05	.01
☐ 22	Luke Appling	.10	.05	.01
☐ 23	Billy Herman	.10	.05	.01
☐ 24	Lloyd Waner	.10	.05	.01
☐ 25	Fred Hutchinson	.10	.05	.01
☐ 26	Eddie Collins	.10	.05	.01
☐ 27	Lefty Grove	.20	.10	.02
☐ 28	Chuck Connors	.20	.10	.02
☐ 29	Lefty O'Doul	.10	.05	.01
☐ 30	Hank Greenberg	.10	.05	.01
☐ 31	Ty Cobb	.40	.20	.04
☐ 32	Enos Slaughter	.10	.05	.01
☐ 33	Ernie Banks	.10	.05	.01
☐ 34	Christy Mathewson	.10	.05	.01
☐ 35	Mel Ott	.10	.05	.01
☐ 36	Pie Traynor	.10	.05	.01
☐ 37	Clark Griffith	.10	.05	.01
☐ 38	Mickey Cochrane	.10	.05	.01
☐ 39	Joe Cronin	.10	.05	.01
☐ 40	Leo Durocher	.10	.05	.01
☐ 41	Home Run Baker	.10	.05	.01
☐ 42	Joe Tinker	.10	.05	.01
☐ 43	John McGraw	.10	.05	.01
☐ 44	Bill Dickey	.10	.05	.01
☐ 45	Walter Johnson	.20	.10	.02
☐ 46	Frankie Frisch	.10	.05	.01
☐ 47	Casey Stengel	.20	.10	.02
☐ 48	Willie Mays	.25	.12	.02
☐ 49	Johnny Mize	.10	.05	.01
☐ 50	Roberto Clemente	.20	.10	.02
☐ 51	Burleigh Grimes	.10	.05	.01
☐ 52	Pee Wee Reese	.10	.05	.01
☐ 53	Bob Feller	.20	.10	.02
☐ 54	Brooks Robinson	.20	.10	.02
☐ 55	Sam Crawford	.10	.05	.01
☐ 56	Robin Roberts	.10	.05	.01
☐ 57	Warren Spahn	.20	.10	.02
☐ 58	Joe McCarthy	.10	.05	.01
☐ 59	Jocko Conlan	.10	.05	.01
☐ 60	Satchel Paige	.20	.10	.02
☐ 61	Ted Williams	.25	.12	.02
☐ 62	George Kelly	.10	.05	.01
☐ 63	Gil Hodges	.10	.05	.01
☐ 64	Jim Bottomley	.10	.05	.01
☐ 65	Al Kaline	.20	.10	.02
☐ 66	Harvey Kuenn	.10	.05	.01
☐ 67	Yogi Berra	.20	.10	.02
☐ 68	Nellie Fox	.10	.05	.01
☐ 69	Harmon Killebrew	.10	.05	.01
☐ 70	Ed Roush	.10	.05	.01
☐ 71	Mordecai Brown	.10	.05	.01
☐ 72	Gabby Hartnett	.10	.05	.01
☐ 73	Early Wynn	.10	.05	.01
☐ 74	Nap Lajoie	.10	.05	.01
☐ 75	Charlie Grimm	.10	.05	.01
☐ 76	Joe Garagiola	.20	.10	.02
☐ 77	Ted Lyons	.10	.05	.01
☐ 78	Mickey Vernon	.10	.05	.01
☐ 79	Lou Boudreau	.10	.05	.01
☐ 80	Al Dark	.10	.05	.01
☐ 81	Ralph Kiner	.10	.05	.01
☐ 82	Phil Rizzuto	.10	.05	.01
☐ 83	Stan Hack	.10	.05	.01
☐ 84	Frank Chance	.10	.05	.01
☐ 85	Ray Schalk	.10	.05	.01
☐ 86	Bill McKechnie	.10	.05	.01
☐ 87	Travis Jackson	.10	.05	.01
☐ 88	Pete Reiser	.10	.05	.01
☐ 89	Carl Hubbell	.10	.05	.01
☐ 90	Roy Campanella	.20	.10	.02
☐ 91	Cy Young	.10	.05	.01
☐ 92	Kiki Cuyler	.10	.05	.01
☐ 93	Chief Bender	.10	.05	.01
☐ 94	Richie Ashburn	.10	.05	.01
☐ 95	Riggs Stephenson	.10	.05	.01
☐ 96	Minnie Minoso	.10	.05	.01
☐ 97	Hack Wilson	.10	.05	.01
☐ 98	Al Lopez	.10	.05	.01
☐ 99	Willie Keeler	.10	.05	.01
☐ 100	Fred Lindstrom	.10	.05	.01
☐ 101	Roger Maris	.20	.10	.02
☐ 102	Roger Bresnahan	.10	.05	.01
☐ 103	Monty Stratton	.10	.05	.01
☐ 104	Goose Goslin	.10	.05	.01
☐ 105	Earl Combs	.10	.05	.01
☐ 106	Pepper Martin	.10	.05	.01

☐ 107	Joe Jackson	.20	.10	.02
☐ 108	George Sisler	.10	.05	.01
☐ 109	Red Ruffing	.10	.05	.01
☐ 110	Johnny Vander Meer	.10	.05	.01
☐ 111	Herb Pennock	.10	.05	.01
☐ 112	Chuck Klein	.10	.05	.01
☐ 113	Paul Derringer	.10	.05	.01
☐ 114	Addie Joss	.10	.05	.01
☐ 115	Bobby Thomson	.10	.05	.01
☐ 116	Chick Hafey	.10	.05	.01
☐ 117	Lefty Gomez	.10	.05	.01
☐ 118	George Kell	.10	.05	.01
☐ 119	Al Simmons	.10	.05	.01
☐ 120	Bob Lemon	.10	.05	.01
☐ 121	Hoyt Wilhelm (wax box card)	.20	.10	.02
☐ 122	Arky Vaughan (wax box card)	.20	.10	.02
☐ 123	Frank Robinson (wax box card)	.20	.10	.02
☐ 124	Grover Alexander (wax box card)	.20	.10	.02

☐ 48	Dickie Noles	.20	.10	.02
☐ xx	Team Picture (unnumbered)	.40	.20	.04
☐ xx	Coaches Card (unnumbered)	.30	.15	.03

1983 Cubs Thorn Apple Valley

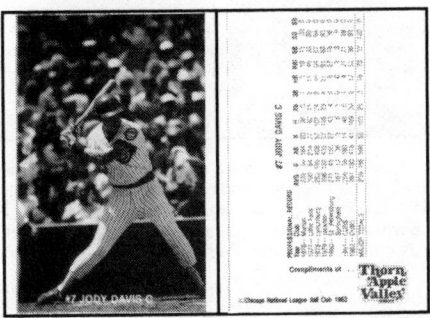

This set of 28 Chicago Cubs features full-color action photos on the front and was sponsored by Thorn Apple Valley. The cards measure 2 1/4" by 3 1/2". The backs provide year-by-year statistics. The cards are unnumbered except for uniform number; they are listed below by uniform with the special cards listed at the end.

		MINT	EXC	G-VG
	COMPLETE SET	9.00	4.50	.90
	COMMON PLAYER	.25	.12	.02
☐ 1	Larry Bowa	.45	.22	.04
☐ 6	Keith Moreland	.45	.22	.04
☐ 7	Jody Davis	.60	.30	.06
☐ 10	Leon Durham	.60	.30	.06
☐ 11	Ron Cey	.45	.22	.04
☐ 16	Steve Lake	.25	.12	.02
☐ 20	Thad Bosley	.25	.12	.02
☐ 21	Jay Johnstone	.35	.17	.03
☐ 22	Bill Buckner	.45	.22	.04
☐ 23	Ryne Sandberg	2.50	1.25	.25
☐ 24	Jerry Morales	.25	.12	.02
☐ 25	Gary Woods	.25	.12	.02
☐ 27	Mel Hall	.60	.30	.06
☐ 29	Tom Veryzer	.25	.12	.02
☐ 30	Chuck Rainey	.25	.12	.02
☐ 31	Fergie Jenkins	.60	.30	.06
☐ 32	Craig Lefferts	.35	.17	.03
☐ 33	Joe Carter	1.50	.75	.15
☐ 34	Steve Trout	.35	.17	.03
☐ 36	Mike Proly	.25	.12	.02
☐ 39	Bill Campbell	.25	.12	.02
☐ 41	Warren Brusstar	.25	.12	.02
☐ 44	Dick Ruthven	.25	.12	.02
☐ 46	Lee Smith	.45	.22	.04
☐ 48	Dickie Noles	.25	.12	.02
☐ 26	Manager/Coaches Lee Elia MG Ruben Amaro Billy Connors Duffy Dyer Fred Koenig John Vukovich (unnumbered)	.25	.12	.02
☐ 27	Team Photo (unnumbered)	.25	.12	.02

1982 Cubs Red Lobster

The cards in this 28 card set measure 2 1/4" by 3 1/2". This set of Chicago Cubs players was co-produced by the Cubs and Chicago-area Red Lobster restaurants and was introduced as a promotional giveaway on August 20, 1982, at Wrigley Field. The cards contain borderless color photos of 25 players, manager Lee Elia, the coaching staff, and a team picture. A facsimile autograph appears on the front, and the cards run in sequence by uniform number. While the coaches have a short biographical sketch on back, the player cards simply list the individual's professional record.

		MINT	EXC	G-VG
	COMPLETE SET	10.00	5.00	1.00
	COMMON PLAYER	.20	.10	.02
☐ 1	Larry Bowa	.50	.25	.05
☐ 4	Lee Elia MG	.20	.10	.02
☐ 6	Keith Moreland	.50	.25	.05
☐ 7	Jody Davis	.60	.30	.06
☐ 10	Leon Durham	.60	.30	.06
☐ 15	Junior Kennedy	.20	.10	.02
☐ 17	Bump Wills	.20	.10	.02
☐ 18	Scot Thompson	.20	.10	.02
☐ 21	Jay Johnstone	.30	.15	.03
☐ 22	Bill Buckner	.50	.25	.05
☐ 23	Ryne Sandberg	4.00	2.00	.40
☐ 24	Jerry Morales	.20	.10	.02
☐ 25	Gary Woods	.20	.10	.02
☐ 28	Steve Henderson	.20	.10	.02
☐ 29	Bob Molinaro	.20	.10	.02
☐ 31	Fergie Jenkins	.75	.35	.07
☐ 33	Al Ripley	.20	.10	.02
☐ 34	Randy Martz	.20	.10	.02
☐ 36	Mike Proly	.20	.10	.02
☐ 37	Ken Kravec	.20	.10	.02
☐ 38	Willie Hernandez	.60	.30	.06
☐ 39	Bill Campbell	.20	.10	.02
☐ 41	Dick Tidrow	.20	.10	.02
☐ 46	Lee Smith	.75	.35	.07
☐ 47	Doug Bird	.20	.10	.02

1984 Cubs Seven-Up

This 28-card set was sponsored by 7-Up. The cards are in full color and measure 2 1/4" by 3 1/2". The card backs are printed in black on white card stock. This set is tougher to find than the other similar Cubs

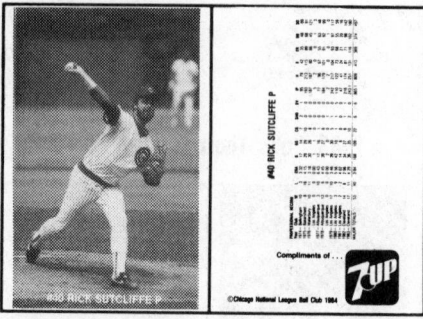

sets since the Cubs were more successful (on the field) in 1984 winning their division, that is, virtually all of the cards printed were distributed during the "Baseball Card Day" promotion (August 12th) which was much better attended that year.

		MINT	EXC	G-VG
COMPLETE SET		12.00	6.00	1.20
COMMON PLAYER		.40	.20	.04
☐ 1	Larry Bowa	.75	.35	.07
☐ 6	Keith Moreland	.60	.30	.06
☐ 7	Jody Davis	.75	.35	.07
☐ 10	Leon Durham	.60	.30	.06
☐ 11	Ron Cey	.60	.30	.06
☐ 15	Ron Hassey	.40	.20	.04
☐ 18	Richie Hebner	.40	.20	.04
☐ 19	Dave Owen	.40	.20	.04
☐ 20	Bob Dernier	.50	.25	.05
☐ 21	Jay Johnstone	.60	.30	.06
☐ 23	Ryne Sandberg	2.50	1.25	.25
☐ 24	Scott Sanderson	.50	.25	.05
☐ 25	Gary Woods	.40	.20	.04
☐ 27	Thad Bosley	.40	.20	.04
☐ 28	Henry Cotto	.40	.20	.04
☐ 34	Steve Trout	.50	.25	.05
☐ 36	Gary Matthews	.50	.25	.05
☐ 39	George Frazier	.40	.20	.04
☐ 40	Rick Sutcliffe	.75	.35	.07
☐ 41	Warren Brusstar	.40	.20	.04
☐ 42	Rich Bordi	.40	.20	.04
☐ 43	Dennis Eckersley	.50	.25	.05
☐ 44	Dick Ruthven	.40	.20	.04
☐ 46	Lee Smith	.60	.30	.06
☐ 47	Rick Reuschel	.60	.30	.06
☐ 49	Tim Stoddard	.40	.20	.04
☐ xx	Coaches (unnumbered)	.40	.20	.04
☐ xx	Jim Frey MG (unnumbered)	.40	.20	.04

1985 Cubs Seven-Up Cubs

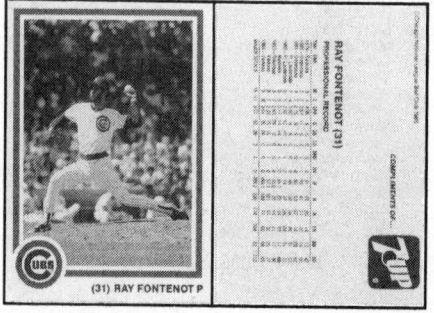

(31) RAY FONTENOT P

This 28-card set was distributed on August 14th at Wrigley Field for the game against the Expos. The cards measure 2 1/2" by 3 1/2" and were distributed wrapped in cellophane. The cards are unnumbered except for uniform number. The card backs are printed in black on white with a 7-Up logo in the upper right hand corner.

		MINT	EXC	G-VG
COMPLETE SET		6.00	3.00	.60
COMMON PLAYER		.15	.07	.01
☐ 1	Larry Bowa	.35	.17	.03
☐ 6	Keith Moreland	.35	.17	.03
☐ 7	Jody Davis	.45	.22	.04
☐ 10	Leon Durham	.35	.17	.03
☐ 11	Ron Cey	.25	.12	.02
☐ 15	Davey Lopes	.25	.12	.02
☐ 16	Steve Lake	.15	.07	.01
☐ 18	Rich Hebner	.15	.07	.01
☐ 20	Bob Dernier	.25	.12	.02
☐ 21	Scott Sanderson	.15	.07	.01
☐ 22	Billy Hatcher	.35	.17	.03
☐ 23	Ryne Sandberg	1.75	.85	.17
☐ 24	Brian Dayett	.15	.07	.01
☐ 25	Gary Woods	.15	.07	.01
☐ 27	Thad Bosley	.15	.07	.01
☐ 28	Chris Speier	.15	.07	.01
☐ 31	Ray Fontenot	.15	.07	.01
☐ 34	Steve Trout	.25	.12	.02
☐ 36	Gary Matthews	.25	.12	.02
☐ 39	George Frazier	.15	.07	.01
☐ 40	Rick Sutcliffe	.50	.25	.05
☐ 41	Warren Brusstar	.15	.07	.01
☐ 42	Lary Sorensen	.15	.07	.01
☐ 43	Dennis Eckersley	.25	.12	.02
☐ 44	Dick Ruthven	.15	.07	.01
☐ 46	Lee Smith	.35	.17	.03
☐ xx	Jim Frey MG (unnumbered)	.15	.07	.01
☐ xx	Cubs Coaching Staff Ruben Amaro Billy Connors Johnny Oates John Vukovich Don Zimmer (unnumbered)	.15	.07	.01

1986 Cubs Gatorade

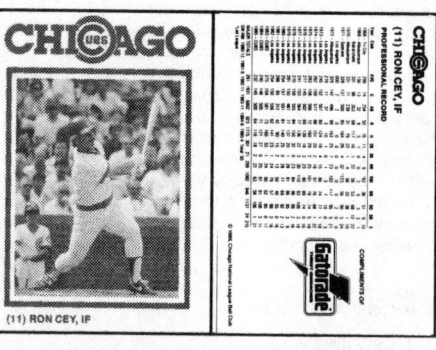

(11) RON CEY, IF

This 28 card set was given out at Wrigley Field on the Cubs' special "baseball card" promotion held July 17th for the game against the Giants. The set was sponsored by Gatorade. The cards are unnumbered except for uniform number. Card backs feature blue print on white card stock. The cards measure 2 7/8" by 4 1/4" and are in full color.

		MINT	EXC	G-VG
COMPLETE SET		6.00	3.00	.60
COMMON PLAYER		.10	.05	.01
☐ 4	Gene Michael MG	.15	.07	.01
☐ 6	Keith Moreland	.30	.15	.03
☐ 7	Jody Davis	.50	.25	.05
☐ 10	Leon Durham	.30	.15	.03
☐ 11	Ron Cey	.30	.15	.03
☐ 12	Shawon Dunston	.50	.25	.05
☐ 15	Davey Lopes	.20	.10	.02
☐ 16	Terry Francona	.10	.05	.01
☐ 18	Steve Christmas	.20	.10	.02

☐ 19	Manny Trillo	.15	.07	.01
☐ 20	Bob Dernier	.15	.07	.01
☐ 21	Scott Sanderson	.10	.05	.01
☐ 22	Jerry Mumphrey	.15	.07	.01
☐ 23	Ryne Sandberg	1.50	.75	.15
☐ 27	Thad Bosley	.10	.05	.01
☐ 28	Chris Speier	.15	.07	.01
☐ 29	Steve Lake	.10	.05	.01
☐ 31	Ray Fontenot	.10	.05	.01
☐ 34	Steve Trout	.15	.07	.01
☐ 36	Gary Matthews	.20	.10	.02
☐ 39	George Frazier	.10	.05	.01
☐ 40	Rick Sutcliffe	.40	.20	.04
☐ 43	Dennis Eckersley	.15	.07	.01
☐ 46	Lee Smith	.25	.12	.02
☐ 48	Jay Baller	.10	.05	.01
☐ 49	Jamie Moyer	.20	.10	.02
☐ 50	Guy Hoffman	.10	.05	.01
☐ xx	Coaches Card .... (unnumbered)	.10	.05	.01

1987 Cubs David Berg

(46) LEE SMITH RHP

This 28-card set was given out at Wrigley Field on the Cubs' special "baseball card" promotion held July 29th. The set was sponsored by David Berg Pure Beef Hot Dogs. The cards are unnumbered except for uniform number. Card backs feature red and blue print on white card stock. The cards measure 2 7/8" by 4 1/4" and are in full color.

		MINT	EXC	G-VG
COMPLETE SET		5.00	2.50	.50
COMMON PLAYER		.15	.07	.01
☐ 1	Dave Martinez	.25	.12	.02
☐ 4	Gene Michael MG	.15	.07	.01
☐ 6	Keith Moreland	.25	.12	.02
☐ 7	Jody Davis	.35	.17	.03
☐ 8	Andre Dawson	.75	.35	.07
☐ 10	Leon Durham	.25	.12	.02
☐ 11	Jim Sundberg	.15	.07	.01
☐ 12	Shawon Dunston	.25	.12	.02
☐ 19	Manny Trillo	.15	.07	.01
☐ 20	Bob Dernier	.15	.07	.01
☐ 21	Scott Sanderson	.15	.07	.01
☐ 22	Jerry Mumphrey	.15	.07	.01
☐ 23	Ryne Sandberg	.75	.35	.07
☐ 24	Brian Dayett	.15	.07	.01
☐ 29	Chico Walker	.25	.12	.02
☐ 31	Greg Maddux	.15	.07	.01
☐ 33	Frank DiPino	.15	.07	.01
☐ 34	Steve Trout	.15	.07	.01
☐ 36	Gary Matthews	.25	.12	.02
☐ 37	Ed Lynch	.15	.07	.01
☐ 39	Ron Davis	.15	.07	.01
☐ 40	Rick Sutcliffe	.35	.17	.03
☐ 46	Lee Smith	.25	.12	.02
☐ 47	Dickie Noles	.15	.07	.01
☐ 49	Jamie Moyer	.15	.07	.01
☐ xx	Coaching Staff	.15	.07	.01

1954 Dan Dee

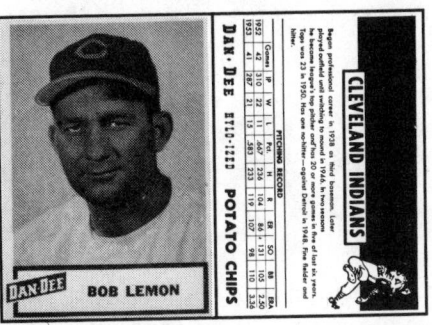

BOB LEMON

The cards in this 29 card set measure 2 1/2" by 3 5/8". Most of the cards marketed by Dan Dee in bags of potato chips in 1954 depict players from the Indians or Pirates. The pictures used for Yankee players were also employed in the Briggs and Stahl-Meyer sets. Dan Dee cards have a waxed surface, but are commonly found with product stains. Smith and Cooper are the known scarcities. The ACC designation is F342.

		NRMT	VG-E	GOOD
COMPLETE SET		2800.00	1200.00	250.00
COMMON PLAYER (1-29)		40.00	20.00	4.00
☐ 1	Bobby Avila	40.00	20.00	4.00
☐ 2	Hank Bauer	50.00	25.00	5.00
☐ 3	Walker Cooper	250.00	125.00	25.00
☐ 4	Larry Doby	50.00	25.00	5.00
☐ 5	Luke Easter	40.00	20.00	4.00
☐ 6	Bob Feller	150.00	75.00	15.00
☐ 7	Bob Friend	60.00	30.00	6.00
☐ 8	Mike Garcia	40.00	20.00	4.00
☐ 9	Sid Gordon	40.00	20.00	4.00
☐ 10	Jim Hegan	40.00	20.00	4.00
☐ 11	Gil Hodges	100.00	50.00	10.00
☐ 12	Art Houtteman	40.00	20.00	4.00
☐ 13	Monte Irvin	75.00	37.50	7.50
☐ 14	Paul LaPalme	50.00	25.00	5.00
☐ 15	Bob Lemon	75.00	37.50	7.50
☐ 16	Al Lopez	75.00	37.50	7.50
☐ 17	Mickey Mantle	700.00	350.00	70.00
☐ 18	Dale Mitchell	40.00	20.00	4.00
☐ 19	Phil Rizzuto	100.00	50.00	10.00
☐ 20	Curt Roberts	50.00	25.00	5.00
☐ 21	Al Rosen	50.00	25.00	5.00
☐ 22	Red Schoendienst	50.00	25.00	5.00
☐ 23	Paul Smith	350.00	175.00	35.00
☐ 24	Duke Snider	150.00	75.00	15.00
☐ 25	George Strickland	40.00	20.00	4.00
☐ 26	Max Surkont	50.00	25.00	5.00
☐ 27	Frank Thomas	100.00	50.00	10.00
☐ 28	Wally Westlake	40.00	20.00	4.00
☐ 29	Early Wynn	75.00	37.50	7.50

1933 Delong

The cards in this 24 card set measures 2" by 3". The 1933 Delong Gum set of 24 multi-colored cards was, along with the 1933 Goudey Big League series, one of the first baseball card sets issued with chewing gum. It was the only card set issued by this company. The reverse text was written by Austen Lake, who also wrote the sports tips found on the Diamond Stars series which began in 1934, leading to speculation that Delong was bought out by National Chicle. The ACC designation is R333.

	NRMT	VG-E	GOOD
COMPLETE SET	6000.00	2000.00	400.00

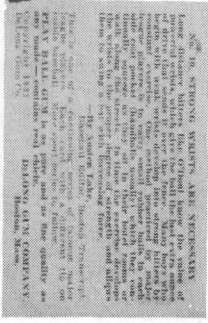

FRANK J. (LEFTY) O'DOUL
BROOKLYN DODGERS

COMMON PLAYER (1-24) 125.00   60.00   12.50

		NRMT	VG-E	GOOD
☐	1 Marty McManus	125.00	60.00	12.50
☐	2 Al Simmons	200.00	100.00	20.00
☐	3 Oscar Melillo	125.00	60.00	12.50
☐	4 William Terry	250.00	125.00	25.00
☐	5 Charlie Gehringer	250.00	125.00	25.00
☐	6 Mickey Cochrane	250.00	125.00	25.00
☐	7 Lou Gehrig	1750.00	750.00	150.00
☐	8 Kiki Cuyler	200.00	100.00	20.00
☐	9 Bill Urbanski	125.00	60.00	12.50
☐	10 Lefty O'Doul	150.00	75.00	15.00
☐	11 Fred Lindstrom	200.00	100.00	20.00
☐	12 Pie Traynor	225.00	110.00	22.00
☐	13 Rabbit Maranville	200.00	100.00	20.00
☐	14 Lefty Gomez	250.00	125.00	25.00
☐	15 Riggs Stephenson	125.00	60.00	12.50
☐	16 Lon Warneke	125.00	60.00	12.50
☐	17 Pepper Martin	150.00	75.00	15.00
☐	18 Jim Dykes	125.00	60.00	12.50
☐	19 Chick Hafey	200.00	100.00	20.00
☐	20 Joe Vosmik	125.00	60.00	12.50
☐	21 Jimmie Foxx	450.00	225.00	45.00
☐	22 Chuck Klein	225.00	110.00	22.00
☐	23 Lefty Grove	300.00	150.00	30.00
☐	24 Goose Goslin	200.00	100.00	20.00

1934-36 Diamond Stars

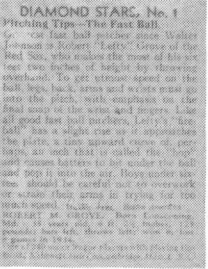

"LEFTY" GROVE

The cards in this 108 card set measure 2 3/8" by 2 7/8". The Diamond Stars set produced by National Chicle from 1934-36 is also commonly known as R327 (ACC). The year of production can be determined by the statistics contained on the back of the card. There are at least 168 possible front/back combinations counting blue (B) and green (G) backs over all three years. The last twelve cards are repeat players and are quite scarce. A blank backed proof sheet of 12 additional cards was recently discovered and has been reproduced from this original artwork and assigned numbers and text by Sport Americana. The checklist below lists the year(s) and back color(s) for the cards. Cards 32 through 72 were issued only in 1935 with green ink on back. Cards 73 through 84 were issued three ways: 35B, 35G, and 36B. Card numbers 85 through

108 were issued only in 1936 with blue ink on back. The complete set price below refers to the set of 108, one of each number.

		NRMT	VG-E	GOOD
	COMPLETE SET	6500.00	2000.00	400.00
	COMMON PLAYER (1-31)	25.00	12.50	2.50
	COMMON PLAYER (32-72)	30.00	15.00	3.00
	COMMON PLAYER (73-84)	35.00	17.50	3.50
	COMMON PLAYER (85-96)	50.00	25.00	5.00
	COMMON PLAYER (97-108)	150.00	75.00	15.00
☐	1 Lefty Grove .... (34G, 35G)	300.00	50.00	10.00
☐	2A Al Simmons .... (34G, 35G) (Sox on uniform)	60.00	30.00	6.00
☐	2B Al Simmons .... (36B) (No name on uniform)	90.00	45.00	9.00
☐	3 Rabbit Maranville .... (34G, 35G)	45.00	22.50	4.50
☐	4 Buddy Myer .... (34G, 35G, 36B)	25.00	12.50	2.50
☐	5 Tommy Bridges .... (34G, 35G, 36B)	30.00	15.00	3.00
☐	6 Max Bishop .... (34G, 35G)	25.00	12.50	2.50
☐	7 Lew Fonseca .... (34G, 35G)	25.00	12.50	2.50
☐	8 Joe Vosmik .... (34G, 35G, 36B)	25.00	12.50	2.50
☐	9 Mickey Cochrane .... (34G, 35G, 36B)	60.00	30.00	6.00
☐	10A Leroy Mahaffey .... (34G, 35G) (A's on uniform)	25.00	12.50	2.50
☐	10B Leroy Mahaffey .... (36B) (No name on uniform)	40.00	20.00	4.00
☐	11 Bill Dickey .... (34G, 35G)	90.00	45.00	9.00
☐	12 F. Walker 34G, 35G, 36B)	25.00	12.50	2.50
☐	13 George Blaeholder .... (34G, 35G)	25.00	12.50	2.50
☐	14 Bill Terry .... (34G, 35G)	60.00	30.00	6.00
☐	15 Dick Bartell .... (34G, 35G)	25.00	12.50	2.50
☐	16 Lloyd Waner .... (34G, 35G, 36B)	45.00	22.50	4.50
☐	17 Frank Frisch .... (34G, 35G)	60.00	30.00	6.00
☐	18 Chick Hafey .... (34G, 35G)	45.00	22.50	4.50
☐	19 Van Lingle Mungo .... (34G, 35G)	25.00	12.50	2.50
☐	20 Frank Hogan .... (34G, 35G)	25.00	12.50	2.50
☐	21 Johnny Vergez .... (34G, 35G)	25.00	12.50	2.50
☐	22 J. Wilson .... (34G, 35G, 36B)	25.00	12.50	2.50
☐	23 Bill Hallahan .... (34G, 35G)	25.00	12.50	2.50
☐	24 Earl Adams .... (34G, 35G)	25.00	12.50	2.50
☐	25 Wally Berger .... (35G)	30.00	15.00	3.00
☐	26 Pepper Martin 35G, 36B)	30.00	15.00	3.00
☐	27 Pie Traynor (35G)	75.00	37.50	7.50
☐	28 Al Lopez (35G)	60.00	30.00	6.00
☐	29 Red Rolfe (35G)	30.00	15.00	3.00
☐	30A Heine Manush .... (35G) (W on sleeve)	60.00	30.00	6.00
☐	30B Heine Manush .... (36B) (No W on sleeve)	90.00	45.00	9.00
☐	31 Kiki Cuyler .... (35G, 36B)	45.00	22.50	4.50
☐	32 Sam Rice	50.00	25.00	5.00
☐	33 Schoolboy Rowe	35.00	17.50	3.50
☐	34 Stan Hack	35.00	17.50	3.50
☐	35 Earl Averill	50.00	25.00	5.00
☐	36A "Earnie" Lombardi .... (sic, Ernie)	75.00	37.50	7.50
☐	36B "Ernie" Lombardi	60.00	30.00	6.00
☐	37 Billy Urbanski	30.00	15.00	3.00
☐	38 Ben Chapman	30.00	15.00	3.00
☐	39 Carl Hubbell	60.00	30.00	6.00
☐	40 Blondy Ryan	30.00	15.00	3.00

☐ 41	Harvey Hendrick	30.00	15.00	3.00
☐ 42	Jimmy Dykes	30.00	15.00	3.00
☐ 43	Ted Lyons	50.00	25.00	5.00
☐ 44	Rogers Hornsby	150.00	75.00	15.00
☐ 45	Jo Jo White	30.00	15.00	3.00
☐ 46	Red Lucas	30.00	15.00	3.00
☐ 47	Bob Bolton	30.00	15.00	3.00
☐ 48	Rick Ferrell	50.00	25.00	5.00
☐ 49	Buck Jordan	30.00	15.00	3.00
☐ 50	Mel Ott	90.00	45.00	9.00
☐ 51	Burgess Whitehead	30.00	15.00	3.00
☐ 52	Tuck Stainback	30.00	15.00	3.00
☐ 53	Oscar Melillo	30.00	15.00	3.00
☐ 54A	"Hank" Greenburg (sic, Greenberg)	125.00	60.00	12.50
☐ 54B	"Hank" Greenberg	100.00	50.00	10.00
☐ 55	Tony Cuccinello	30.00	15.00	3.00
☐ 56	Gus Suhr	30.00	15.00	3.00
☐ 57	Cy Blanton	30.00	15.00	3.00
☐ 58	Glenn Myatt	30.00	15.00	3.00
☐ 59	Jim Bottomley	60.00	30.00	6.00
☐ 60	Red Ruffing	60.00	30.00	6.00
☐ 61	Bill Werber	30.00	15.00	3.00
☐ 62	Fred Frankhouse	30.00	15.00	3.00
☐ 63	Travis Jackson	60.00	30.00	6.00
☐ 64	Jimmy Foxx	150.00	75.00	15.00
☐ 65	Zeke Bonura	30.00	15.00	3.00
☐ 66	Ducky Medwick	60.00	30.00	6.00
☐ 67	Marvin Owen	30.00	15.00	3.00
☐ 68	Sam Leslie	30.00	15.00	3.00
☐ 69	Earl Grace	30.00	15.00	3.00
☐ 70	Hal Trosky	30.00	15.00	3.00
☐ 71	Ossie Bluege	30.00	15.00	3.00
☐ 72	Tony Piet	30.00	15.00	3.00
☐ 73	Fritz Ostermueller	35.00	17.50	3.50
☐ 74	Tony Lazzeri	55.00	27.50	5.50
☐ 75	Jack Burns	35.00	17.50	3.50
☐ 76	Billy Rogell	35.00	17.50	3.50
☐ 77	Charlie Gehringer	75.00	37.50	7.50
☐ 78	Joe Kuhel	35.00	17.50	3.50
☐ 79	Willis Hudlin	35.00	17.50	3.50
☐ 80	Lou Chiozza	35.00	17.50	3.50
☐ 81	Bill Delancey	35.00	17.50	3.50
☐ 82A	Johnny Babich (Dodgers on uniform)	40.00	20.00	4.00
☐ 82B	Johnny Babich (No name on uniform)	40.00	20.00	4.00
☐ 83	Paul Waner	60.00	30.00	6.00
☐ 84	Sam Byrd	35.00	17.50	3.50
☐ 85	Moose Solters	50.00	25.00	5.00
☐ 86	Frank Crosetti	70.00	35.00	7.00
☐ 87	Steve O'Neill	50.00	25.00	5.00
☐ 88	George Selkirk	60.00	30.00	6.00
☐ 89	Joe Stripp	50.00	25.00	5.00
☐ 90	Ray Hayworth	50.00	25.00	5.00
☐ 91	Bucky Harris	80.00	40.00	8.00
☐ 92	Ethan Allen	50.00	25.00	5.00
☐ 93	General Crowder	50.00	25.00	5.00
☐ 94	Wes Ferrell	60.00	30.00	6.00
☐ 95	Luke Appling	90.00	45.00	9.00
☐ 96	Lew Riggs	50.00	25.00	5.00
☐ 97	Al Lopez	250.00	125.00	25.00
☐ 98	Schoolboy Rowe	175.00	85.00	18.00
☐ 99	Pie Traynor	300.00	150.00	30.00
☐ 100	Earl Averill	250.00	125.00	25.00
☐ 101	Dick Bartell	150.00	75.00	15.00
☐ 102	Van Lingle Mungo	150.00	75.00	15.00
☐ 103	Bill Dickey	350.00	175.00	35.00
☐ 104	Red Rolfe	150.00	75.00	15.00
☐ 105	Ernie Lombardi	250.00	125.00	25.00
☐ 106	Red Lucas	150.00	75.00	15.00
☐ 107	Stan Hack	150.00	75.00	15.00
☐ 108	Wally Berger	200.00	100.00	20.00

1981 Donruss

The cards in this 605-card set measure 2 1/2" by 3 1/2". In 1981 Donruss launched itself into the baseball card market with a set containing 600 numbered cards and five unnumbered checklists. Even though the five checklist cards are unnumbered they are numbered below (601-605) for convenience in reference. The cards are printed on thin stock and more than one pose exists for several popular players. The numerous errors of the first print run were later corrected by the company. These are marked P1 and P2 in the checklist below.

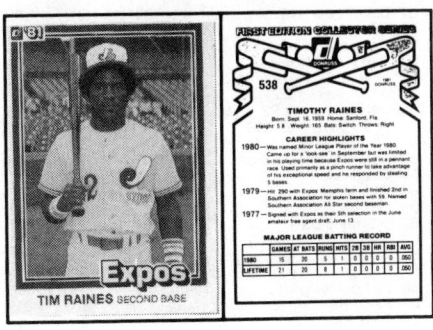

		MINT	EXC	G-VG
COMPLETE SET (P1)		27.00	13.50	2.70
COMPLETE SET (P2)		22.00	11.00	2.20
COMMON PLAYER (1-605)		.03	.01	.00
☐ 1	Ozzie Smith	.40	.10	.02
☐ 2	Rollie Fingers	.30	.15	.03
☐ 3	Rick Wise	.06	.03	.00
☐ 4	Gene Richards	.03	.01	.00
☐ 5	Alan Trammell	.35	.17	.03
☐ 6	Tom Brookens	.03	.01	.00
☐ 7A	Duffy Dyer P1 1980 batting average has decimal point	.10	.05	.01
☐ 7B	Duffy Dyer P2 1980 batting average has no decimal point	.06	.03	.00
☐ 8	Mark Fidrych	.10	.05	.01
☐ 9	Dave Rozema	.03	.01	.00
☐ 10	Ricky Peters	.03	.01	.00
☐ 11	Mike Schmidt	1.00	.50	.10
☐ 12	Willie Stargell	.30	.15	.03
☐ 13	Tim Foli	.03	.01	.00
☐ 14	Manny Sanguillen	.06	.03	.00
☐ 15	Grant Jackson	.03	.01	.00
☐ 16	Eddie Solomon	.03	.01	.00
☐ 17	Omar Moreno	.03	.01	.00
☐ 18	Joe Morgan	.30	.15	.03
☐ 19	Rafael Landestoy	.03	.01	.00
☐ 20	Bruce Bochy	.03	.01	.00
☐ 21	Joe Sambito	.06	.03	.00
☐ 22	Manny Trillo	.06	.03	.00
☐ 23A	Dave Smith P1 Line box around stats is not complete	.35	.17	.03
☐ 23B	Dave Smith P2 Box totally encloses stats at top	.35	.17	.03
☐ 24	Terry Puhl	.06	.03	.00
☐ 25	Bump Wills	.03	.01	.00
☐ 26A	John Ellis P1 ERR Photo on front shows Danny Walton	.60	.30	.06
☐ 26B	John Ellis P2 COR	.10	.05	.01
☐ 27	Jim Kern	.03	.01	.00
☐ 28	Richie Zisk	.06	.03	.00
☐ 29	John Mayberry	.06	.03	.00
☐ 30	Bob Davis	.03	.01	.00
☐ 31	Jackson Todd	.03	.01	.00
☐ 32	Al Woods	.03	.01	.00
☐ 33	Steve Carlton	.60	.30	.06
☐ 34	Lee Mazzilli	.06	.03	.00
☐ 35	John Stearns	.03	.01	.00
☐ 36	Roy Lee Jackson	.06	.03	.00
☐ 37	Mike Scott	.50	.25	.05
☐ 38	Lamar Johnson	.03	.01	.00
☐ 39	Kevin Bell	.03	.01	.00
☐ 40	Ed Farmer	.03	.01	.00
☐ 41	Ross Baumgarten	.03	.01	.00
☐ 42	Leo Sutherland	.03	.01	.00
☐ 43	Dan Meyer	.03	.01	.00
☐ 44	Ron Reed	.03	.01	.00
☐ 45	Mario Mendoza	.03	.01	.00
☐ 46	Rick Honeycutt	.06	.03	.00
☐ 47	Glenn Abbott	.03	.01	.00
☐ 48	Leon Roberts	.03	.01	.00
☐ 49	Rod Carew	.60	.30	.06
☐ 50	Bert Campaneris	.06	.03	.00
☐ 51A	Tom Donahue P1 ERR Name on front misspelled Donahue	.15	.07	.01
☐ 51B	Tom Donohue P2 COR	.10	.05	.01

☐ 52	Dave Frost	.03	.01	.00
☐ 53	Ed Halicki	.03	.01	.00
☐ 54	Dan Ford	.06	.03	.00
☐ 55	Garry Maddox	.06	.03	.00
☐ 56A	Steve Garvey P1 "Surpassed 25 HR"	1.00	.50	.10
☐ 56B	Steve Garvey P2 "Surpassed 21 HR"	.60	.30	.06
☐ 57	Bill Russell	.06	.03	.00
☐ 58	Don Sutton	.30	.15	.03
☐ 59	Reggie Smith	.10	.05	.01
☐ 60	Rick Monday	.06	.03	.00
☐ 61	Ray Knight	.10	.05	.01
☐ 62	Johnny Bench	.50	.25	.05
☐ 63	Mario Soto	.10	.05	.01
☐ 64	Doug Bair	.03	.01	.00
☐ 65	George Foster	.20	.10	.02
☐ 66	Jeff Burroughs	.06	.03	.00
☐ 67	Keith Hernandez	.35	.17	.03
☐ 68	Tom Herr	.10	.05	.01
☐ 69	Bob Forsch	.06	.03	.00
☐ 70	John Fulgham	.03	.01	.00
☐ 71A	Bobby Bonds P1 ERR 986 lifetime HR	.30	.15	.03
☐ 71B	Bobby Bonds P2 COR 326 lifetime HR	.10	.05	.01
☐ 72A	Rennie Stennett P1 "breaking broke leg"	.10	.05	.01
☐ 72B	Rennie Stennett P2 Word "broke" deleted	.06	.03	.00
☐ 73	Joe Strain	.03	.01	.00
☐ 74	Ed Whitson	.06	.03	.00
☐ 75	Tom Griffin	.03	.01	.00
☐ 76	Billy North	.03	.01	.00
☐ 77	Gene Garber	.03	.01	.00
☐ 78	Mike Hargrove	.06	.03	.00
☐ 79	Dave Rosello	.03	.01	.00
☐ 80	Ron Hassey	.03	.01	.00
☐ 81	Sid Monge	.03	.01	.00
☐ 82A	Joe Charboneau P1 '78 highlights, "For some reason"	.15	.07	.01
☐ 82B	Joe Charboneau P2 phrase "For some reason" deleted	.10	.05	.01
☐ 83	Cecil Cooper	.15	.07	.01
☐ 84	Sal Bando	.06	.03	.00
☐ 85	Moose Haas	.06	.03	.00
☐ 86	Mike Caldwell	.06	.03	.00
☐ 87A	Larry Hisle P1 '77 highlights, line ends with "28 RBI"	.15	.07	.01
☐ 87B	Larry Hisle P2 correct line "28 HR"	.10	.05	.01
☐ 88	Luis Gomez	.03	.01	.00
☐ 89	Larry Parrish	.10	.05	.01
☐ 90	Gary Carter	.60	.30	.06
☐ 91	Bill Gullickson	.35	.17	.03
☐ 92	Fred Norman	.03	.01	.00
☐ 93	Tommy Hutton	.03	.01	.00
☐ 94	Carl Yastrzemski	.80	.40	.08
☐ 95	Glenn Hoffman	.06	.03	.00
☐ 96	Dennis Eckersley	.06	.03	.00
☐ 97A	Tom Burgmeier P1 ERR Throws: Right	.10	.05	.01
☐ 97B	Tom Burgmeier P2 COR Throws: Left	.06	.03	.00
☐ 98	Win Remmerswaal	.03	.01	.00
☐ 99	Bob Horner	.25	.12	.02
☐ 100	George Brett	.80	.40	.08
☐ 101	Dave Chalk	.03	.01	.00
☐ 102	Dennis Leonard	.06	.03	.00
☐ 103	Renie Martin	.03	.01	.00
☐ 104	Amos Otis	.10	.05	.01
☐ 105	Graig Nettles	.15	.07	.01
☐ 106	Eric Soderholm	.03	.01	.00
☐ 107	Tommy John	.20	.10	.02
☐ 108	Tom Underwood	.03	.01	.00
☐ 109	Lou Piniella	.10	.05	.01
☐ 110	Mickey Klutts	.03	.01	.00
☐ 111	Bobby Murcer	.10	.05	.01
☐ 112	Eddie Murray	.80	.40	.08
☐ 113	Rick Dempsey	.06	.03	.00
☐ 114	Scott McGregor	.06	.03	.00
☐ 115	Ken Singleton	.10	.05	.01
☐ 116	Gary Roenicke	.06	.03	.00
☐ 117	Dave Revering	.03	.01	.00
☐ 118	Mike Norris	.03	.01	.00
☐ 119	Rickey Henderson	1.00	.50	.10
☐ 120	Mike Heath	.03	.01	.00
☐ 121	Dave Cash	.03	.01	.00
☐ 122	Randy Jones	.06	.03	.00
☐ 123	Eric Rasmussen	.03	.01	.00
☐ 124	Jerry Mumphrey	.06	.03	.00
☐ 125	Richie Hebner	.03	.01	.00
☐ 126	Mark Wagner	.03	.01	.00
☐ 127	Jack Morris	.30	.15	.03
☐ 128	Dan Petry	.15	.07	.01
☐ 129	Bruce Robbins	.03	.01	.00
☐ 130	Champ Summers	.03	.01	.00
☐ 131A	Pete Rose P1 last line ends with "see card 251"	1.75	.85	.17
☐ 131B	Pete Rose P2 last line corrected "see card 371"	1.25	.60	.12
☐ 132	Willie Stargell	.30	.15	.03
☐ 133	Ed Ott	.03	.01	.00
☐ 134	Jim Bibby	.03	.01	.00
☐ 135	Bert Blyleven	.15	.07	.01
☐ 136	Dave Parker	.30	.15	.03
☐ 137	Bill Robinson	.06	.03	.00
☐ 138	Enos Cabell	.03	.01	.00
☐ 139	Dave Bergman	.03	.01	.00
☐ 140	J.R. Richard	.10	.05	.01
☐ 141	Ken Forsch	.06	.03	.00
☐ 142	Larry Bowa	.15	.07	.01
☐ 143	Frank LaCorte (photo actually Randy Niemann)	.03	.01	.00
☐ 144	Dennis Walling	.03	.01	.00
☐ 145	Buddy Bell	.15	.07	.01
☐ 146	Ferguson Jenkins	.18	.09	.01
☐ 147	Danny Darwin	.06	.03	.00
☐ 148	John Grubb	.03	.01	.00
☐ 149	Alfredo Griffin	.10	.05	.01
☐ 150	Jerry Garvin	.03	.01	.00
☐ 151	Paul Mirabella	.03	.01	.00
☐ 152	Rick Bosetti	.03	.01	.00
☐ 153	Dick Ruthven	.03	.01	.00
☐ 154	Frank Taveras	.03	.01	.00
☐ 155	Craig Swan	.03	.01	.00
☐ 156	Jeff Reardon	.65	.30	.06
☐ 157	Steve Henderson	.03	.01	.00
☐ 158	Jim Morrison	.03	.01	.00
☐ 159	Glenn Borgmann	.03	.01	.00
☐ 160	LaMarr Hoyt	.30	.15	.03
☐ 161	Rich Wortham	.03	.01	.00
☐ 162	Thad Bosley	.03	.01	.00
☐ 163	Julio Cruz	.03	.01	.00
☐ 164A	Del Unser P1 no "3B" heading	.10	.05	.01
☐ 164B	Del Unser P2 Batting record on back corrected ("3B")	.06	.03	.00
☐ 165	Jim Anderson	.03	.01	.00
☐ 166	Jim Beattie	.03	.01	.00
☐ 167	Shane Rawley	.10	.05	.01
☐ 168	Joe Simpson	.03	.01	.00
☐ 169	Rod Carew	.60	.30	.06
☐ 170	Fred Patek	.03	.01	.00
☐ 171	Frank Tanana	.06	.03	.00
☐ 172	Alfredo Martinez	.03	.01	.00
☐ 173	Chris Knapp	.03	.01	.00
☐ 174	Joe Rudi	.06	.03	.00
☐ 175	Greg Luzinski	.15	.07	.01
☐ 176	Steve Garvey	.60	.30	.06
☐ 177	Joe Ferguson	.03	.01	.00
☐ 178	Bob Welch	.10	.05	.01
☐ 179	Dusty Baker	.10	.05	.01
☐ 180	Rudy Law	.03	.01	.00
☐ 181	Dave Concepcion	.15	.07	.01
☐ 182	Johnny Bench	.55	.27	.05
☐ 183	Mike LaCoss	.03	.01	.00
☐ 184	Ken Griffey	.10	.05	.01
☐ 185	Dave Collins	.06	.03	.00
☐ 186	Brian Asselstine	.03	.01	.00
☐ 187	Garry Templeton	.10	.05	.01
☐ 188	Mike Phillips	.03	.01	.00
☐ 189	Pete Vuckovich	.06	.03	.00
☐ 190	John Urrea	.03	.01	.00
☐ 191	Tony Scott	.03	.01	.00
☐ 192	Darrell Evans	.15	.07	.01
☐ 193	Milt May	.03	.01	.00
☐ 194	Bob Knepper	.10	.05	.01
☐ 195	Randy Moffitt	.03	.01	.00
☐ 196	Larry Herndon	.06	.03	.00
☐ 197	Rick Camp	.03	.01	.00
☐ 198	Andre Thornton	.10	.05	.01
☐ 199	Tom Veryzer	.03	.01	.00
☐ 200	Gary Alexander	.03	.01	.00
☐ 201	Rick Waits	.03	.01	.00
☐ 202	Rick Manning	.03	.01	.00
☐ 203	Paul Molitor	.20	.10	.02
☐ 204	Jim Gantner	.03	.01	.00
☐ 205	Paul Mitchell	.03	.01	.00
☐ 206	Reggie Cleveland	.03	.01	.00
☐ 207	Sixto Lezcano	.03	.01	.00
☐ 208	Bruce Benedict	.03	.01	.00
☐ 209	Rodney Scott	.03	.01	.00

☐ 210	John Tamargo	.03	.01	.00
☐ 211	Bill Lee	.06	.03	.00
☐ 212	Andre Dawson	.35	.17	.03
☐ 213	Rowland Office	.03	.01	.00
☐ 214	Carl Yastrzemski	.80	.40	.08
☐ 215	Jerry Remy	.03	.01	.00
☐ 216	Mike Torrez	.06	.03	.00
☐ 217	Skip Lockwood	.03	.01	.00
☐ 218	Fred Lynn	.20	.10	.02
☐ 219	Chris Chambliss	.06	.03	.00
☐ 220	Willie Aikens	.06	.03	.00
☐ 221	John Wathan	.06	.03	.00
☐ 222	Dan Quisenberry	.20	.10	.02
☐ 223	Willie Wilson	.15	.07	.01
☐ 224	Clint Hurdle	.03	.01	.00
☐ 225	Bob Watson	.06	.03	.00
☐ 226	Jim Spencer	.03	.01	.00
☐ 227	Ron Guidry	.25	.12	.02
☐ 228	Reggie Jackson	.80	.40	.08
☐ 229	Oscar Gamble	.06	.03	.00
☐ 230	Jeff Cox	.03	.01	.00
☐ 231	Luis Tiant	.10	.05	.01
☐ 232	Rich Dauer	.03	.01	.00
☐ 233	Dan Graham	.03	.01	.00
☐ 234	Mike Flanagan	.10	.05	.01
☐ 235	John Lowenstein	.03	.01	.00
☐ 236	Benny Ayala	.03	.01	.00
☐ 237	Wayne Gross	.03	.01	.00
☐ 238	Rick Langford	.03	.01	.00
☐ 239	Tony Armas	.10	.05	.01
☐ 240A	Bob Lacy P1 ERR Name misspelled Bob "Lacy"	.30	.15	.03
☐ 240B	Bob Lacey P2 COR	.10	.05	.01
☐ 241	Gene Tenace	.03	.01	.00
☐ 242	Bob Shirley	.03	.01	.00
☐ 243	Gary Lucas	.10	.05	.01
☐ 244	Jerry Turner	.03	.01	.00
☐ 245	John Wockenfuss	.03	.01	.00
☐ 246	Stan Papi	.03	.01	.00
☐ 247	Milt Wilcox	.03	.01	.00
☐ 248	Dan Schatzeder	.03	.01	.00
☐ 249	Steve Kemp	.10	.05	.01
☐ 250	Jim Lentine	.03	.01	.00
☐ 251	Pete Rose	1.25	.60	.12
☐ 252	Bill Madlock	.18	.09	.01
☐ 253	Dale Berra	.06	.03	.00
☐ 254	Kent Tekulve	.06	.03	.00
☐ 255	Enrique Romo	.03	.01	.00
☐ 256	Mike Easler	.06	.03	.00
☐ 257	Chuck Tanner MG	.06	.03	.00
☐ 258	Art Howe	.03	.01	.00
☐ 259	Alan Ashby	.03	.01	.00
☐ 260	Nolan Ryan	.50	.25	.05
☐ 261A	Vern Ruhle P1 ERR Photo on front actually Ken Forsch	.60	.30	.06
☐ 261B	Vern Ruhle P2 COR	.10	.05	.01
☐ 262	Bob Boone	.10	.05	.01
☐ 263	Cesar Cedeno	.10	.05	.01
☐ 264	Jeff Leonard	.20	.10	.02
☐ 265	Pat Putnam	.03	.01	.00
☐ 266	Jon Matlack	.06	.03	.00
☐ 267	Dave Rajsich	.03	.01	.00
☐ 268	Bill Sample	.03	.01	.00
☐ 269	Damaso Garcia	.30	.15	.03
☐ 270	Tom Buskey	.03	.01	.00
☐ 271	Joey McLaughlin	.03	.01	.00
☐ 272	Barry Bonnell	.03	.01	.00
☐ 273	Tug McGraw	.10	.05	.01
☐ 274	Mike Jorgensen	.03	.01	.00
☐ 275	Pat Zachry	.03	.01	.00
☐ 276	Neil Allen	.06	.03	.00
☐ 277	Joel Youngblood	.03	.01	.00
☐ 278	Greg Pryor	.03	.01	.00
☐ 279	Britt Burns	.25	.12	.02
☐ 280	Rich Dotson	.50	.25	.05
☐ 281	Chet Lemon	.10	.05	.01
☐ 282	Rusty Kuntz	.03	.01	.00
☐ 283	Ted Cox	.03	.01	.00
☐ 284	Sparky Lyle	.10	.05	.01
☐ 285	Larry Cox	.03	.01	.00
☐ 286	Floyd Bannister	.06	.03	.00
☐ 287	Byron McLaughlin	.03	.01	.00
☐ 288	Rodney Craig	.03	.01	.00
☐ 289	Bobby Grich	.10	.05	.01
☐ 290	Dickie Thon	.10	.05	.01
☐ 291	Mark Clear	.06	.03	.00
☐ 292	Dave Lemanczyk	.03	.01	.00
☐ 293	Jason Thompson	.06	.03	.00
☐ 294	Rick Miller	.03	.01	.00
☐ 295	Lonnie Smith	.06	.03	.00
☐ 296	Ron Cey	.15	.07	.01
☐ 297	Steve Yeager	.03	.01	.00
☐ 298	Bobby Castillo	.03	.01	.00
☐ 299	Manny Mota	.06	.03	.00
☐ 300	Jay Johnstone	.06	.03	.00
☐ 301	Dan Driessen	.06	.03	.00
☐ 302	Joe Nolan	.03	.01	.00
☐ 303	Paul Householder	.06	.03	.00
☐ 304	Harry Spilman	.03	.01	.00
☐ 305	Cesar Geronimo	.03	.01	.00
☐ 306A	Gary Mathews P1 ERR . Name misspelled	.30	.15	.03
☐ 306B	Gary Matthews P2 COR	.10	.05	.01
☐ 307	Ken Reitz	.03	.01	.00
☐ 308	Ted Simmons	.15	.07	.01
☐ 309	John Littlefield	.06	.03	.00
☐ 310	George Frazier	.03	.01	.00
☐ 311	Dane Iorg	.03	.01	.00
☐ 312	Mike Ivie	.03	.01	.00
☐ 313	Dennis Littlejohn	.03	.01	.00
☐ 314	Gary Lavelle	.03	.01	.00
☐ 315	Jack Clark	.25	.12	.02
☐ 316	Jim Wohlford	.03	.01	.00
☐ 317	Rick Matula	.03	.01	.00
☐ 318	Toby Harrah	.06	.03	.00
☐ 319A	Dwane Kuiper P1 ERR . Name misspelled	.15	.07	.01
☐ 319B	Duane Kuiper P2 COR .	.10	.05	.01
☐ 320	Len Barker	.06	.03	.00
☐ 321	Victor Cruz	.03	.01	.00
☐ 322	Dell Alston	.03	.01	.00
☐ 323	Robin Yount	.40	.20	.04
☐ 324	Charlie Moore	.03	.01	.00
☐ 325	Lary Sorensen	.03	.01	.00
☐ 326A	Gorman Thomas P1 .... 2nd line on back: "30 HR mark 4th"	.30	.15	.03
☐ 326B	Gorman Thomas P2 ..... "30 HR mark 3rd"	.10	.05	.01
☐ 327	Bob Rodgers MG	.06	.03	.00
☐ 328	Phil Niekro	.25	.12	.02
☐ 329	Chris Speier	.06	.03	.00
☐ 330A	Steve Rodgers P1 ERR Name misspelled	.30	.15	.03
☐ 330B	Steve Rogers P2 COR ..	.10	.05	.01
☐ 331	Woodie Fryman	.03	.01	.00
☐ 332	Warren Cromartie	.03	.01	.00
☐ 333	Jerry White	.03	.01	.00
☐ 334	Tony Perez	.15	.07	.01
☐ 335	Carlton Fisk	.15	.07	.01
☐ 336	Dick Drago	.03	.01	.00
☐ 337	Steve Renko	.03	.01	.00
☐ 338	Jim Rice	.50	.25	.05
☐ 339	Jerry Royster	.03	.01	.00
☐ 340	Frank White	.10	.05	.01
☐ 341	Jamie Quirk	.03	.01	.00
☐ 342A	Paul Spittorff P1 ERR ... Name misspelled	.15	.07	.01
☐ 342B	Paul Splittorff P2 COR	.10	.05	.01
☐ 343	Marty Pattin	.03	.01	.00
☐ 344	Pete LaCock	.03	.01	.00
☐ 345	Willie Randolph	.10	.05	.01
☐ 346	Rick Cerone	.06	.03	.00
☐ 347	Rich Gossage	.15	.07	.01
☐ 348	Reggie Jackson	.75	.35	.07
☐ 349	Ruppert Jones	.03	.01	.00
☐ 350	Dave McKay	.03	.01	.00
☐ 351	Yogi Berra CO	.18	.09	.01
☐ 352	Doug DeCinces	.10	.05	.01
☐ 353	Jim Palmer	.35	.17	.03
☐ 354	Tippy Martinez	.06	.03	.00
☐ 355	Al Bumbry	.03	.01	.00
☐ 356	Earl Weaver MG	.10	.05	.01
☐ 357A	Bob Picciolo P1 ERR .... Name misspelled	.15	.07	.01
☐ 357B	Rob Picciolo P2 COR ...	.06	.03	.00
☐ 358	Matt Keough	.03	.01	.00
☐ 359	Dwayne Murphy	.06	.03	.00
☐ 360	Brian Kingman	.03	.01	.00
☐ 361	Bill Fahey	.03	.01	.00
☐ 362	Steve Mura	.03	.01	.00
☐ 363	Dennis Kinney	.03	.01	.00
☐ 364	Dave Winfield	.50	.25	.05
☐ 365	Lou Whitaker	.25	.12	.02
☐ 366	Lance Parrish	.35	.17	.03
☐ 367	Tim Corcoran	.03	.01	.00
☐ 368	Pat Underwood	.03	.01	.00
☐ 369	Al Cowens	.06	.03	.00
☐ 370	Sparky Anderson MG	.06	.03	.00
☐ 371	Pete Rose	1.25	.60	.12
☐ 372	Phil Garner	.03	.01	.00
☐ 373	Steve Nicosia	.03	.01	.00
☐ 374	John Candelaria	.10	.05	.01
☐ 375	Don Robinson	.06	.03	.00
☐ 376	Lee Lacy	.06	.03	.00
☐ 377	John Milner	.03	.01	.00

☐ 378	Craig Reynolds	.03	.01	.00
☐ 379A	Luis Pujois P1 ERR Name misspelled	.15	.07	.01
☐ 379B	Luis Pujols P2 COR	.06	.03	.00
☐ 380	Joe Niekro	.10	.05	.01
☐ 381	Joaquin Andujar	.15	.07	.01
☐ 382	Keith Moreland	.45	.22	.04
☐ 383	Jose Cruz	.15	.07	.01
☐ 384	Bill Virdon MG	.06	.03	.00
☐ 385	Jim Sundberg	.06	.03	.00
☐ 386	Doc Medich	.03	.01	.00
☐ 387	Al Oliver	.15	.07	.01
☐ 388	Jim Norris	.03	.01	.00
☐ 389	Bob Bailor	.03	.01	.00
☐ 390	Ernie Whitt	.03	.01	.00
☐ 391	Otto Velez	.03	.01	.00
☐ 392	Roy Howell	.03	.01	.00
☐ 393	Bob Walk	.06	.03	.00
☐ 394	Doug Flynn	.03	.01	.00
☐ 395	Pete Falcone	.03	.01	.00
☐ 396	Tom Hausman	.03	.01	.00
☐ 397	Elliott Maddox	.03	.01	.00
☐ 398	Mike Squires	.03	.01	.00
☐ 399	Marvis Foley	.03	.01	.00
☐ 400	Steve Trout	.06	.03	.00
☐ 401	Wayne Nordhagen	.03	.01	.00
☐ 402	Tony LaRussa MG	.06	.03	.00
☐ 403	Bruce Bochte	.06	.03	.00
☐ 404	Bake McBride	.06	.03	.00
☐ 405	Jerry Narron	.03	.01	.00
☐ 406	Rob Dressler	.03	.01	.00
☐ 407	Dave Heaverlo	.03	.01	.00
☐ 408	Tom Paciorek	.03	.01	.00
☐ 409	Carney Lansford	.15	.07	.01
☐ 410	Brian Downing	.06	.03	.00
☐ 411	Don Aase	.06	.03	.00
☐ 412	Jim Barr	.03	.01	.00
☐ 413	Don Baylor	.15	.07	.01
☐ 414	Jim Fregosi	.06	.03	.00
☐ 415	Dallas Green MG	.06	.03	.00
☐ 416	Dave Lopes	.10	.05	.01
☐ 417	Jerry Reuss	.06	.03	.00
☐ 418	Rick Sutcliffe	.25	.12	.02
☐ 419	Derrel Thomas	.03	.01	.00
☐ 420	Tommy Lasorda MG	.10	.05	.01
☐ 421	Charles Leibrandt	.45	.22	.04
☐ 422	Tom Seaver	.50	.25	.05
☐ 423	Ron Oester	.06	.03	.00
☐ 424	Junior Kennedy	.03	.01	.00
☐ 425	Tom Seaver	.50	.25	.05
☐ 426	Bobby Cox MG	.03	.01	.00
☐ 427	Leon Durham	.70	.35	.07
☐ 428	Terry Kennedy	.10	.05	.01
☐ 429	Silvio Martinez	.03	.01	.00
☐ 430	George Hendrick	.10	.05	.01
☐ 431	Red Schoendienst MG	.06	.03	.00
☐ 432	Johnnie LeMaster	.03	.01	.00
☐ 433	Vida Blue	.10	.05	.01
☐ 434	John Montefusco	.06	.03	.00
☐ 435	Terry Whitfield	.03	.01	.00
☐ 436	Dave Bristol MG	.03	.01	.00
☐ 437	Dale Murphy	1.25	.60	.12
☐ 438	Jerry Dybzinski	.03	.01	.00
☐ 439	Jorge Orta	.03	.01	.00
☐ 440	Wayne Garland	.03	.01	.00
☐ 441	Miguel Dilone	.03	.01	.00
☐ 442	Dave Garcia MG	.03	.01	.00
☐ 443	Don Money	.06	.03	.00
☐ 444A	Buck Martinez P1 ERR (reverse negative)	.15	.07	.01
☐ 444B	Buck Martinez P2 COR	.10	.04	.01
☐ 445	Jerry Augustine	.03	.01	.00
☐ 446	Ben Oglivie	.06	.03	.00
☐ 447	Jim Slaton	.06	.03	.00
☐ 448	Doyle Alexander	.06	.03	.00
☐ 449	Tony Bernazard	.06	.03	.00
☐ 450	Scott Sanderson	.06	.03	.00
☐ 451	Dave Palmer	.06	.03	.00
☐ 452	Stan Bahnsen	.03	.01	.00
☐ 453	Dick Williams MG	.06	.03	.00
☐ 454	Rick Burleson	.06	.03	.00
☐ 455	Gary Allenson	.03	.01	.00
☐ 456	Bob Stanley	.06	.03	.00
☐ 457A	John Tudor P1 ERR lifetime W-L "9.7"	1.25	.60	.12
☐ 457B	John Tudor P2 COR corrected "9-7"	1.00	.50	.10
☐ 458	Dwight Evans	.25	.12	.02
☐ 459	Glenn Hubbard	.06	.03	.00
☐ 460	U.L. Washington	.03	.01	.00
☐ 461	Larry Gura	.06	.03	.00
☐ 462	Rich Gale	.03	.01	.00
☐ 463	Hal McRae	.06	.03	.00
☐ 464	Jim Frey MG	.06	.03	.00
☐ 465	Bucky Dent	.10	.05	.01
☐ 466	Dennis Werth	.03	.01	.00
☐ 467	Ron Davis	.03	.01	.00
☐ 468	Reggie Jackson	.75	.35	.07
☐ 469	Bobby Brown	.03	.01	.00
☐ 470	Mike Davis	.45	.22	.04
☐ 471	Gaylord Perry	.30	.15	.03
☐ 472	Mark Belanger	.06	.03	.00
☐ 473	Jim Palmer	.35	.17	.03
☐ 474	Sammy Stewart	.03	.01	.00
☐ 475	Tim Stoddard	.03	.01	.00
☐ 476	Steve Stone	.06	.03	.00
☐ 477	Jeff Newman	.03	.01	.00
☐ 478	Steve McCatty	.03	.01	.00
☐ 479	Billy Martin MG	.15	.07	.01
☐ 480	Mitchell Page	.03	.01	.00
☐ 481	Cy Young Winner 1980 Steve Carlton	.30	.15	.03
☐ 482	Bill Buckner	.15	.07	.01
☐ 483A	Ivan DeJesus P1 ERR lifetime hits "702"	.10	.05	.01
☐ 483B	Ivan DeJesus P2 COR lifetime hits "642"	.06	.03	.00
☐ 484	Cliff Johnson	.03	.01	.00
☐ 485	Lenny Randle	.03	.01	.00
☐ 486	Larry Milbourne	.03	.01	.00
☐ 487	Roy Smalley	.06	.03	.00
☐ 488	John Castino	.06	.03	.00
☐ 489	Ron Jackson	.03	.01	.00
☐ 490A	Dave Roberts P1 Career Highlights: "Showed pop in"	.10	.05	.01
☐ 490B	Dave Roberts P2 "Declared himself"	.06	.03	.00
☐ 491	MVP: George Brett	.50	.25	.05
☐ 492	Mike Cubbage	.03	.01	.00
☐ 493	Rob Wilfong	.03	.01	.00
☐ 494	Danny Goodwin	.03	.01	.00
☐ 495	Jose Morales	.03	.01	.00
☐ 496	Mickey Rivers	.06	.03	.00
☐ 497	Mike Edwards	.03	.01	.00
☐ 498	Mike Sadek	.03	.01	.00
☐ 499	Lenn Sakata	.03	.01	.00
☐ 500	Gene Michael MG	.06	.03	.00
☐ 501	Dave Roberts	.03	.01	.00
☐ 502	Steve Dillard	.03	.01	.00
☐ 503	Jim Essian	.03	.01	.00
☐ 504	Rance Mulliniks	.03	.01	.00
☐ 505	Darrell Porter	.06	.03	.00
☐ 506	Joe Torre MG	.10	.05	.01
☐ 507	Terry Crowley	.03	.01	.00
☐ 508	Bill Travers	.03	.01	.00
☐ 509	Nelson Norman	.03	.01	.00
☐ 510	Bob McClure	.03	.01	.00
☐ 511	Steve Howe	.20	.10	.02
☐ 512	Dave Rader	.03	.01	.00
☐ 513	Mick Kelleher	.03	.01	.00
☐ 514	Kiko Garcia	.03	.01	.00
☐ 515	Larry Biittner	.03	.01	.00
☐ 516A	Willie Norwood P1 Career Highlights "Spent most of"	.10	.05	.01
☐ 516B	Willie Norwood P2 "Traded to Seattle"	.06	.03	.00
☐ 517	Bo Diaz	.10	.05	.01
☐ 518	Juan Beniquez	.06	.03	.00
☐ 519	Scot Thompson	.03	.01	.00
☐ 520	Jim Tracy	.03	.01	.00
☐ 521	Carlos Lezcano	.03	.01	.00
☐ 522	Joe Amalfitano MG	.03	.01	.00
☐ 523	Preston Hanna	.03	.01	.00
☐ 524A	Ray Burris P1 Career Highlights: "Went on ..."	.10	.05	.01
☐ 524B	Ray Burris P2 "Drafted by ..."	.06	.03	.00
☐ 525	Broderick Perkins	.03	.01	.00
☐ 526	Mickey Hatcher	.06	.03	.00
☐ 527	John Goryl MG	.03	.01	.00
☐ 528	Dick Davis	.03	.01	.00
☐ 529	Butch Wynegar	.06	.03	.00
☐ 530	Sal Butera	.03	.01	.00
☐ 531	Jerry Koosman	.10	.05	.01
☐ 532A	Geoff Zahn P1 Career Highlights: "Was 2nd in"	.10	.05	.01
☐ 532B	Geoff Zahn P2 "Signed a 3 year"	.06	.03	.00
☐ 533	Dennis Martinez	.06	.03	.00
☐ 534	Gary Thomasson	.03	.01	.00
☐ 535	Steve Macko	.03	.01	.00
☐ 536	Jim Kaat	.15	.07	.01
☐ 537	Best Hitters George Brett Rod Carew	1.00	.50	.10
☐ 538	Tim Raines	5.00	2.50	.50

☐ 539	Keith Smith	.03	.01	.00
☐ 540	Ken Macha	.03	.01	.00
☐ 541	Burt Hooton	.06	.03	.00
☐ 542	Butch Hobson	.03	.01	.00
☐ 543	Bill Stein	.03	.01	.00
☐ 544	Dave Stapleton	.06	.03	.00
☐ 545	Bob Pate	.03	.01	.00
☐ 546	Doug Corbett	.10	.05	.01
☐ 547	Darrell Jackson	.03	.01	.00
☐ 548	Pete Redfern	.03	.01	.00
☐ 549	Roger Erickson	.03	.01	.00
☐ 550	Al Hrabosky	.06	.03	.00
☐ 551	Dick Tidrow	.03	.01	.00
☐ 552	Dave Ford	.03	.01	.00
☐ 553	Dave Kingman	.15	.07	.01
☐ 554A	Mike Vail P1	.10	.05	.01
	Career Highlights:			
	"After two ..."			
☐ 554B	Mike Vail P2	.06	.03	.00
	"Traded to ..."			
☐ 555A	Jerry Martin P1	.10	.05	.01
	Career Highlights:			
	"Overcame a ..."			
☐ 555B	Jerry Martin P2	.06	.03	.00
	"Traded to ..."			
☐ 556A	Jesus Figueroa P1	.10	.05	.01
	Career Highlights:			
	"Had an ..."			
☐ 556B	Jesus Figueroa P2	.06	.03	.00
	"Traded to ..."			
☐ 557	Don Stanhouse	.03	.01	.00
☐ 558	Barry Foote	.03	.01	.00
☐ 559	Tim Blackwell	.03	.01	.00
☐ 560	Bruce Sutter	.18	.09	.01
☐ 561	Rick Reuschel	.10	.05	.01
☐ 562	Lynn McGlothen	.03	.01	.00
☐ 563A	Bob Owchinko P1	.10	.05	.01
	Career Highlights:			
	"Traded to ..."			
☐ 563B	Bob Owchinko P2	.06	.03	.00
	"Involved in a ..."			
☐ 564	John Verhoeven	.03	.01	.00
☐ 565	Ken Landreaux	.06	.03	.00
☐ 566A	Glen Adams P1 ERR	.15	.07	.01
	Name misspelled			
☐ 566B	Glenn Adams P2 COR ..	.06	.03	.00
☐ 567	Hosken Powell	.03	.01	.00
☐ 568	Dick Noles	.03	.01	.00
☐ 569	Danny Ainge	.25	.12	.02
☐ 570	Bobby Mattick MG	.03	.01	.00
☐ 571	Joe Lefebvre	.06	.03	.00
☐ 572	Bobby Clark	.03	.01	.00
☐ 573	Dennis Lamp	.03	.01	.00
☐ 574	Randy Lerch	.03	.01	.00
☐ 575	Mookie Wilson	.35	.17	.03
☐ 576	Ron LeFlore	.06	.03	.00
☐ 577	Jim Dwyer	.03	.01	.00
☐ 578	Bill Castro	.03	.01	.00
☐ 579	Greg Minton	.03	.01	.00
☐ 580	Mark Littell	.03	.01	.00
☐ 581	Andy Hassler	.03	.01	.00
☐ 582	Dave Stieb	.25	.12	.02
☐ 583	Ken Oberkfell	.06	.03	.00
☐ 584	Larry Bradford	.03	.01	.00
☐ 585	Fred Stanley	.03	.01	.00
☐ 586	Bill Caudill	.06	.03	.00
☐ 587	Doug Capilla	.03	.01	.00
☐ 588	George Riley	.03	.01	.00
☐ 589	Willie Hernandez	.15	.07	.01
☐ 590	MVP: Mike Schmidt	.45	.22	.04
☐ 591	Cy Young Winner 1980: .	.06	.03	.00
	Steve Stone			
☐ 592	Rick Sofield	.03	.01	.00
☐ 593	Bombo Rivera	.03	.01	.00
☐ 594	Gary Ward	.10	.05	.01
☐ 595A	Dave Edwards P1	.10	.05	.01
	Career Highlights:			
	"Sidelined the"			
☐ 595B	Dave Edwards P2	.06	.03	.00
	"Traded to ..."			
☐ 596	Mike Proly	.03	.01	.00
☐ 597	Tommy Boggs	.03	.01	.00
☐ 598	Greg Gross	.03	.01	.00
☐ 599	Elias Sosa	.03	.01	.00
☐ 600	Pat Kelly	.03	.01	.00
☐ 601A	Checklist 1 P1 ERR	.10	.01	.00
	unnumbered			
	(51 Donahue)			
☐ 601B	Checklist 1 P2 COR	.75	.07	.01
	unnumbered			
	(51 Donohue)			
☐ 602	Checklist 2	.10	.01	.00
☐ 603A	Checklist 3 P1 ERR	.10	.01	.00
	unnumbered			

	(306 Mathews)			
☐ 603B	Checklist 3 P2 COR	.10	.01	.00
	unnumbered			
	(306 Matthews)			
☐ 604A	Checklist 4 P1 ERR	.10	.01	.00
	unnumbered			
	(379 Pujois)			
☐ 604B	Checklist 4 P2 COR	.10	.01	.00
	unnumbered			
	(379 Pujols)			
☐ 605A	Checklist 5 P1 ERR	.10	.01	.00
	unnumbered			
	(566 Glen Adams)			
☐ 605B	Checklist 5 P2 COR	.10	.01	.00
	unnumbered			
	(566 Glenn Adams)			

1982 Donruss

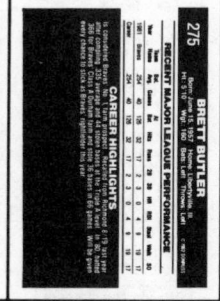

The 1982 Donruss set contains 653 numbered cards and the seven unnumbered checklists; each card measures 2 1/2" by 3 1/2". The first 26 cards of this set are entitled Donruss Diamond Kings (DK) and feature the artwork of Dick Perez of Perez-Steele Galleries. The set was marketed with puzzle pieces rather than with bubble gum. There are 63 pieces to the puzzle, which when put together make a collage of Babe Ruth entitled "Hall of Fame Diamond King." The card stock in this year's Donruss cards is considerably thicker than that of the 1981 cards. The seven unnumbered checklist cards are arbitrarily assigned numbers 654 through 660 and are listed at the end of the list below.

		MINT	EXC	G-VG
COMPLETE SET		26.00	13.00	2.60
COMMON PLAYER (1-660)		.03	.01	.00

☐	1	Pete Rose DK	1.50	.75	.15
☐	2	Gary Carter DK	.55	.27	.05
☐	3	Steve Garvey DK	.55	.27	.05
☐	4	Vida Blue DK	.10	.05	.01
☐	5A	Alan Trammel DK ERR .	.90	.45	.09
		(name misspelled)			
☐	5B	Alan Trammell DK	.40	.20	.04
		COR			
☐	6	Len Barker DK	.08	.04	.01
☐	7	Dwight Evans DK	.20	.10	.02
☐	8	Rod Carew DK	.50	.25	.05
☐	9	George Hendrick DK	.10	.05	.01
☐	10	Phil Niekro DK	.30	.15	.03
☐	11	Richie Zisk DK	.08	.04	.01
☐	12	Dave Parker DK	.30	.15	.03
☐	13	Nolan Ryan DK	.50	.25	.05
☐	14	Ivan DeJesus DK	.08	.04	.01
☐	15	George Brett DK	.75	.35	.07
☐	16	Tom Seaver DK	.50	.25	.05
☐	17	Dave Kingman DK	.12	.06	.01
☐	18	Dave Winfield DK	.45	.22	.04
☐	19	Mike Norris DK	.08	.04	.01
☐	20	Carlton Fisk DK	.20	.10	.02
☐	21	Ozzie Smith DK	.20	.10	.02
☐	22	Roy Smalley DK	.08	.04	.01
☐	23	Buddy Bell DK	.10	.05	.01
☐	24	Ken Singleton DK	.10	.05	.01
☐	25	John Mayberry DK	.08	.04	.01

☐ 26	Gorman Thomas DK	.10	.05	.01
☐ 27	Earl Weaver MG	.08	.04	.01
☐ 28	Rollie Fingers	.20	.10	.02
☐ 29	Sparky Anderson MG	.08	.04	.01
☐ 30	Dennis Eckersley	.06	.03	.00
☐ 31	Dave Winfield	.45	.22	.04
☐ 32	Burt Hooton	.03	.01	.00
☐ 33	Rick Waits	.03	.01	.00
☐ 34	George Brett	.65	.30	.06
☐ 35	Steve McCatty	.03	.01	.00
☐ 36	Steve Rogers	.06	.03	.00
☐ 37	Bill Stein	.03	.01	.00
☐ 38	Steve Renko	.03	.01	.00
☐ 39	Mike Squires	.03	.01	.00
☐ 40	George Hendrick	.06	.03	.00
☐ 41	Bob Knepper	.10	.05	.01
☐ 42	Steve Carlton	.50	.25	.05
☐ 43	Larry Biittner	.03	.01	.00
☐ 44	Chris Welsh	.06	.03	.00
☐ 45	Steve Nicosia	.03	.01	.00
☐ 46	Jack Clark	.25	.12	.02
☐ 47	Chris Chambliss	.06	.03	.00
☐ 48	Ivan DeJesus	.03	.01	.00
☐ 49	Lee Mazzilli	.06	.03	.00
☐ 50	Julio Cruz	.03	.01	.00
☐ 51	Pete Redfern	.03	.01	.00
☐ 52	Dave Stieb	.20	.10	.02
☐ 53	Doug Corbett	.03	.01	.00
☐ 54	Jorge Bell	6.50	3.25	.65
☐ 55	Joe Simpson	.03	.01	.00
☐ 56	Rusty Staub	.12	.06	.01
☐ 57	Hector Cruz	.03	.01	.00
☐ 58	Claudell Washington	.08	.04	.01
☐ 59	Enrique Romo	.03	.01	.00
☐ 60	Gary Lavelle	.06	.03	.00
☐ 61	Tim Flannery	.03	.01	.00
☐ 62	Joe Nolan	.03	.01	.00
☐ 63	Larry Bowa	.15	.07	.01
☐ 64	Sixto Lezcano	.03	.01	.00
☐ 65	Joe Sambito	.06	.03	.00
☐ 66	Bruce Kison	.03	.01	.00
☐ 67	Wayne Nordhagen	.03	.01	.00
☐ 68	Woodie Fryman	.03	.01	.00
☐ 69	Billy Sample	.03	.01	.00
☐ 70	Amos Otis	.10	.05	.01
☐ 71	Matt Keough	.03	.01	.00
☐ 72	Toby Harrah	.06	.03	.00
☐ 73	Dave Righetti	1.50	.75	.15
☐ 74	Carl Yastrzemski	.75	.35	.07
☐ 75	Bob Welch	.10	.05	.01
☐ 76A	Alan Trammel ERR (name misspelled)	.80	.40	.08
☐ 76B	Alan Trammell CORR	.30	.15	.03
☐ 77	Rick Dempsey	.06	.03	.00
☐ 78	Paul Molitor	.20	.10	.02
☐ 79	Dennis Martinez	.06	.03	.00
☐ 80	Jim Slaton	.03	.01	.00
☐ 81	Champ Summers	.03	.01	.00
☐ 82	Carney Lansford	.12	.06	.01
☐ 83	Barry Foote	.03	.01	.00
☐ 84	Steve Garvey	.50	.25	.05
☐ 85	Rick Manning	.03	.01	.00
☐ 86	John Wathan	.06	.03	.00
☐ 87	Brian Kingman	.03	.01	.00
☐ 88	Andre Dawson	.35	.17	.03
☐ 89	Jim Kern	.03	.01	.00
☐ 90	Bobby Grich	.08	.04	.01
☐ 91	Bob Forsch	.06	.03	.00
☐ 92	Art Howe	.03	.01	.00
☐ 93	Marty Bystrom	.03	.01	.00
☐ 94	Ozzie Smith	.25	.12	.02
☐ 95	Dave Parker	.25	.12	.02
☐ 96	Doyle Alexander	.06	.03	.00
☐ 97	Al Hrabosky	.06	.03	.00
☐ 98	Frank Taveras	.03	.01	.00
☐ 99	Tim Blackwell	.03	.01	.00
☐ 100	Floyd Bannister	.08	.04	.01
☐ 101	Alfredo Griffin	.08	.04	.01
☐ 102	Dave Engle	.03	.01	.00
☐ 103	Mario Soto	.08	.04	.01
☐ 104	Ross Baumgarten	.03	.01	.00
☐ 105	Ken Singleton	.10	.05	.01
☐ 106	Ted Simmons	.15	.07	.01
☐ 107	Jack Morris	.25	.12	.02
☐ 108	Bob Watson	.06	.03	.00
☐ 109	Dwight Evans	.18	.09	.01
☐ 110	Tom Lasorda MG	.10	.05	.01
☐ 111	Bert Blyleven	.15	.07	.01
☐ 112	Dan Quisenberry	.18	.09	.01
☐ 113	Rickey Henderson	.65	.30	.06
☐ 114	Gary Carter	.50	.25	.05
☐ 115	Brian Downing	.06	.03	.00
☐ 116	Al Oliver	.12	.06	.01
☐ 117	LaMarr Hoyt	.10	.05	.01
☐ 118	Cesar Cedeno	.08	.04	.01
☐ 119	Keith Moreland	.10	.05	.01
☐ 120	Bob Shirley	.03	.01	.00
☐ 121	Terry Kennedy	.08	.04	.01
☐ 122	Frank Pastore	.03	.01	.00
☐ 123	Gene Garber	.03	.01	.00
☐ 124	Tony Pena	.35	.17	.03
☐ 125	Allen Ripley	.03	.01	.00
☐ 126	Randy Martz	.03	.01	.00
☐ 127	Richie Zisk	.06	.03	.00
☐ 128	Mike Scott	.35	.17	.03
☐ 129	Lloyd Moseby	.20	.10	.02
☐ 130	Rob Wilfong	.03	.01	.00
☐ 131	Tim Stoddard	.03	.01	.00
☐ 132	Gorman Thomas	.12	.06	.01
☐ 133	Dan Petry	.15	.07	.01
☐ 134	Bob Stanley	.06	.03	.00
☐ 135	Lou Piniella	.10	.05	.01
☐ 136	Pedro Guerrero	.40	.20	.04
☐ 137	Len Barker	.06	.03	.00
☐ 138	Rich Gale	.03	.01	.00
☐ 139	Wayne Gross	.03	.01	.00
☐ 140	Tim Wallach	1.50	.75	.15
☐ 141	Gene Mauch MG	.06	.03	.00
☐ 142	Doc Medich	.03	.01	.00
☐ 143	Tony Bernazard	.06	.03	.00
☐ 144	Bill Virdon MG	.06	.03	.00
☐ 145	John Littlefield	.03	.01	.00
☐ 146	Dave Bergman	.03	.01	.00
☐ 147	Dick Davis	.03	.01	.00
☐ 148	Tom Seaver	.40	.20	.04
☐ 149	Matt Sinatro	.03	.01	.00
☐ 150	Chuck Tanner MG	.06	.03	.00
☐ 151	Leon Durham	.20	.10	.02
☐ 152	Gene Tenace	.06	.03	.00
☐ 153	Al Bumbry	.03	.01	.00
☐ 154	Mark Brouhard	.03	.01	.00
☐ 155	Rick Peters	.03	.01	.00
☐ 156	Jerry Remy	.03	.01	.00
☐ 157	Rick Reuschel	.10	.05	.01
☐ 158	Steve Howe	.06	.03	.00
☐ 159	Alan Bannister	.03	.01	.00
☐ 160	U.L. Washington	.03	.01	.00
☐ 161	Rick Langford	.03	.01	.00
☐ 162	Bill Gullickson	.08	.04	.01
☐ 163	Mark Wagner	.03	.01	.00
☐ 164	Geoff Zahn	.03	.01	.00
☐ 165	Ron LeFlore	.06	.03	.00
☐ 166	Dane Iorg	.03	.01	.00
☐ 167	Joe Niekro	.10	.05	.01
☐ 168	Pete Rose	1.25	.60	.12
☐ 169	Dave Collins	.06	.03	.00
☐ 170	Rick Wise	.06	.03	.00
☐ 171	Jim Bibby	.06	.03	.00
☐ 172	Larry Herndon	.06	.03	.00
☐ 173	Bob Horner	.25	.12	.02
☐ 174	Steve Dillard	.03	.01	.00
☐ 175	Mookie Wilson	.10	.05	.01
☐ 176	Dan Meyer	.03	.01	.00
☐ 177	Fernando Arroyo	.03	.01	.00
☐ 178	Jackson Todd	.03	.01	.00
☐ 179	Darrell Jackson	.03	.01	.00
☐ 180	Al Woods	.03	.01	.00
☐ 181	Jim Anderson	.03	.01	.00
☐ 182	Dave Kingman	.15	.07	.01
☐ 183	Steve Henderson	.03	.01	.00
☐ 184	Brian Asselstine	.03	.01	.00
☐ 185	Rod Scurry	.03	.01	.00
☐ 186	Fred Breining	.06	.03	.00
☐ 187	Danny Boone	.03	.01	.00
☐ 188	Junior Kennedy	.03	.01	.00
☐ 189	Sparky Lyle	.12	.06	.01
☐ 190	Whitey Herzog MG	.06	.03	.00
☐ 191	Dave Smith	.08	.04	.01
☐ 192	Ed Ott	.03	.01	.00
☐ 193	Greg Luzinski	.12	.06	.01
☐ 194	Bill Lee	.06	.03	.00
☐ 195	Don Zimmer MG	.06	.03	.00
☐ 196	Hal McRae	.06	.03	.00
☐ 197	Mike Norris	.06	.03	.00
☐ 198	Duane Kuiper	.03	.01	.00
☐ 199	Rick Cerone	.03	.01	.00
☐ 200	Jim Rice	.40	.20	.04
☐ 201	Steve Yeager	.03	.01	.00
☐ 202	Tom Brookens	.03	.01	.00
☐ 203	Jose Morales	.03	.01	.00
☐ 204	Roy Howell	.03	.01	.00
☐ 205	Tippy Martinez	.03	.01	.00
☐ 206	Moose Haas	.06	.03	.00
☐ 207	Al Cowens	.06	.03	.00
☐ 208	Dave Stapleton	.03	.01	.00
☐ 209	Bucky Dent	.08	.04	.01
☐ 210	Ron Cey	.12	.06	.01
☐ 211	Jorge Orta	.03	.01	.00
☐ 212	Jamie Quirk	.03	.01	.00
☐ 213	Jeff Jones	.03	.01	.00

☐ 214	Tim Raines	.90	.45	.09
☐ 215	Jon Matlack	.06	.03	.00
☐ 216	Rod Carew	.50	.25	.05
☐ 217	Jim Kaat	.15	.07	.01
☐ 218	Joe Pittman	.03	.01	.00
☐ 219	Larry Christenson	.03	.01	.00
☐ 220	Juan Bonilla	.06	.03	.00
☐ 221	Mike Easler	.06	.03	.00
☐ 222	Vida Blue	.10	.05	.01
☐ 223	Rick Camp	.03	.01	.00
☐ 224	Mike Jorgensen	.03	.01	.00
☐ 225	Jody Davis	.65	.30	.06
☐ 226	Mike Parrott	.03	.01	.00
☐ 227	Jim Clancy	.06	.03	.00
☐ 228	Hosken Powell	.03	.01	.00
☐ 229	Tom Hume	.03	.01	.00
☐ 230	Britt Burns	.08	.04	.01
☐ 231	Jim Palmer	.30	.15	.03
☐ 232	Bob Rodgers MG	.06	.03	.00
☐ 233	Milt Wilcox	.03	.01	.00
☐ 234	Dave Revering	.03	.01	.00
☐ 235	Mike Torrez	.06	.03	.00
☐ 236	Robert Castillo	.03	.01	.00
☐ 237	Von Hayes	1.00	.50	.10
☐ 238	Renie Martin	.03	.01	.00
☐ 239	Dwayne Murphy	.06	.03	.00
☐ 240	Rodney Scott	.03	.01	.00
☐ 241	Fred Patek	.03	.01	.00
☐ 242	Mickey Rivers	.06	.03	.00
☐ 243	Steve Trout	.06	.03	.00
☐ 244	Jose Cruz	.12	.06	.01
☐ 245	Manny Trillo	.06	.03	.00
☐ 246	Lary Sorensen	.03	.01	.00
☐ 247	Dave Edwards	.03	.01	.00
☐ 248	Dan Driessen	.06	.03	.00
☐ 249	Tommy Boggs	.03	.01	.00
☐ 250	Dale Berra	.06	.03	.00
☐ 251	Ed Whitson	.06	.03	.00
☐ 252	Lee Smith	.65	.30	.06
☐ 253	Tom Paciorek	.03	.01	.00
☐ 254	Pat Zachry	.03	.01	.00
☐ 255	Luis Leal	.03	.01	.00
☐ 256	John Castino	.03	.01	.00
☐ 257	Rich Dauer	.03	.01	.00
☐ 258	Cecil Cooper	.15	.07	.01
☐ 259	Dave Rozema	.03	.01	.00
☐ 260	John Tudor	.20	.10	.02
☐ 261	Jerry Mumphrey	.06	.03	.00
☐ 262	Jay Johnstone	.06	.03	.00
☐ 263	Bo Diaz	.08	.04	.01
☐ 264	Dennis Leonard	.06	.03	.00
☐ 265	Jim Spencer	.03	.01	.00
☐ 266	John Milner	.03	.01	.00
☐ 267	Don Aase	.06	.03	.00
☐ 268	Jim Sundberg	.06	.03	.00
☐ 269	Lamar Johnson	.03	.01	.00
☐ 270	Frank LaCorte	.03	.01	.00
☐ 271	Barry Evans	.03	.01	.00
☐ 272	Enos Cabell	.03	.01	.00
☐ 273	Del Unser	.03	.01	.00
☐ 274	George Foster	.15	.07	.01
☐ 275	Brett Butler	.60	.30	.06
☐ 276	Lee Lacy	.06	.03	.00
☐ 277	Ken Reitz	.03	.01	.00
☐ 278	Keith Hernandez	.30	.15	.03
☐ 279	Doug DeCinces	.10	.05	.01
☐ 280	Charlie Moore	.03	.01	.00
☐ 281	Lance Parrish	.25	.12	.02
☐ 282	Ralph Houk MG	.06	.03	.00
☐ 283	Rich Gossage	.20	.10	.02
☐ 284	Jerry Reuss	.06	.03	.00
☐ 285	Mike Stanton	.03	.01	.00
☐ 286	Frank White	.08	.04	.01
☐ 287	Bob Owchinko	.03	.01	.00
☐ 288	Scott Sanderson	.06	.03	.00
☐ 289	Bump Wills	.03	.01	.00
☐ 290	Dave Frost	.03	.01	.00
☐ 291	Chet Lemon	.06	.03	.00
☐ 292	Tito Landrum	.03	.01	.00
☐ 293	Vern Ruhle	.03	.01	.00
☐ 294	Mike Schmidt	.65	.30	.06
☐ 295	Sam Mejias	.03	.01	.00
☐ 296	Gary Lucas	.03	.01	.00
☐ 297	John Candelaria	.08	.04	.01
☐ 298	Jerry Martin	.03	.01	.00
☐ 299	Dale Murphy	.90	.45	.09
☐ 300	Mike Lum	.03	.01	.00
☐ 301	Tom Hausman	.03	.01	.00
☐ 302	Glenn Abbott	.03	.01	.00
☐ 303	Roger Erickson	.03	.01	.00
☐ 304	Otto Velez	.03	.01	.00
☐ 305	Danny Goodwin	.03	.01	.00
☐ 306	John Mayberry	.06	.03	.00
☐ 307	Lenny Randle	.03	.01	.00
☐ 308	Bob Bailor	.03	.01	.00
☐ 309	Jerry Morales	.03	.01	.00
☐ 310	Rufino Linares	.03	.01	.00
☐ 311	Kent Tekulve	.06	.03	.00
☐ 312	Joe Morgan	.25	.12	.02
☐ 313	John Urrea	.03	.01	.00
☐ 314	Paul Householder	.03	.01	.00
☐ 315	Garry Maddox	.06	.03	.00
☐ 316	Mike Ramsey	.03	.01	.00
☐ 317	Alan Ashby	.03	.01	.00
☐ 318	Bob Clark	.03	.01	.00
☐ 319	Tony LaRussa MG	.06	.03	.00
☐ 320	Charlie Lea	.06	.03	.00
☐ 321	Danny Darwin	.06	.03	.00
☐ 322	Cesar Geronimo	.03	.01	.00
☐ 323	Tom Underwood	.03	.01	.00
☐ 324	Andre Thornton	.08	.04	.01
☐ 325	Rudy May	.03	.01	.00
☐ 326	Frank Tanana	.06	.03	.00
☐ 327	Davey Lopes	.08	.04	.01
☐ 328	Richie Hebner	.03	.01	.00
☐ 329	Mike Flanagan	.08	.04	.01
☐ 330	Mike Caldwell	.06	.03	.00
☐ 331	Scott McGregor	.08	.04	.01
☐ 332	Jerry Augustine	.03	.01	.00
☐ 333	Stan Papi	.03	.01	.00
☐ 334	Rick Miller	.03	.01	.00
☐ 335	Graig Nettles	.15	.07	.01
☐ 336	Dusty Baker	.08	.04	.01
☐ 337	Dave Garcia MG	.03	.01	.00
☐ 338	Larry Gura	.06	.03	.00
☐ 339	Cliff Johnson	.03	.01	.00
☐ 340	Warren Cromartie	.03	.01	.00
☐ 341	Steve Comer	.03	.01	.00
☐ 342	Rick Burleson	.06	.03	.00
☐ 343	John Martin	.03	.01	.00
☐ 344	Craig Reynolds	.03	.01	.00
☐ 345	Mike Proly	.03	.01	.00
☐ 346	Ruppert Jones	.03	.01	.00
☐ 347	Omar Moreno	.03	.01	.00
☐ 348	Greg Minton	.06	.03	.00
☐ 349	Rick Mahler	.20	.10	.02
☐ 350	Alex Trevino	.03	.01	.00
☐ 351	Mike Krukow	.08	.04	.01
☐ 352A	Shane Rawley ERR (photo actually Jim Anderson)	.75	.35	.07
☐ 352B	Shane Rawley COR	.15	.07	.01
☐ 353	Garth Iorg	.03	.01	.00
☐ 354	Pete Mackanin	.03	.01	.00
☐ 355	Paul Moskau	.03	.01	.00
☐ 356	Richard Dotson	.10	.05	.01
☐ 357	Steve Stone	.06	.03	.00
☐ 358	Larry Hisle	.06	.03	.00
☐ 359	Aurelio Lopez	.03	.01	.00
☐ 360	Oscar Gamble	.06	.03	.00
☐ 361	Tom Burgmeier	.03	.01	.00
☐ 362	Terry Forster	.08	.04	.01
☐ 363	Joe Charboneau	.06	.03	.00
☐ 364	Ken Brett	.03	.01	.00
☐ 365	Tony Armas	.10	.05	.01
☐ 366	Chris Speier	.06	.03	.00
☐ 367	Fred Lynn	.20	.10	.02
☐ 368	Buddy Bell	.15	.07	.01
☐ 369	Jim Essian	.03	.01	.00
☐ 370	Terry Puhl	.06	.03	.00
☐ 371	Greg Gross	.03	.01	.00
☐ 372	Bruce Sutter	.20	.10	.02
☐ 373	Joe Lefebvre	.03	.01	.00
☐ 374	Ray Knight	.08	.04	.01
☐ 375	Bruce Benedict	.03	.01	.00
☐ 376	Tim Foli	.03	.01	.00
☐ 377	Al Holland	.06	.03	.00
☐ 378	Ken Kravec	.03	.01	.00
☐ 379	Jeff Burroughs	.06	.03	.00
☐ 380	Pete Falcone	.03	.01	.00
☐ 381	Ernie Whitt	.06	.03	.00
☐ 382	Brad Havens	.06	.03	.00
☐ 383	Terry Crowley	.03	.01	.00
☐ 384	Don Money	.06	.03	.00
☐ 385	Dan Schatzeder	.03	.01	.00
☐ 386	Gary Allenson	.03	.01	.00
☐ 387	Yogi Berra MG	.15	.07	.01
☐ 388	Ken Landreaux	.06	.03	.00
☐ 389	Mike Hargrove	.06	.03	.00
☐ 390	Darryl Motley	.12	.06	.01
☐ 391	Dave McKay	.03	.01	.00
☐ 392	Stan Bahnsen	.03	.01	.00
☐ 393	Ken Forsch	.03	.01	.00
☐ 394	Mario Mendoza	.03	.01	.00
☐ 395	Jim Morrison	.03	.01	.00
☐ 396	Mike Ivie	.03	.01	.00
☐ 397	Broderick Perkins	.03	.01	.00
☐ 398	Darrell Evans	.15	.07	.01
☐ 399	Ron Reed	.03	.01	.00
☐ 400	Johnny Bench	.45	.22	.04

☐ 401	Steve Bedrosian	1.25	.60	.12
☐ 402	Bill Robinson	.03	.01	.00
☐ 403	Bill Buckner	.12	.06	.01
☐ 404	Ken Oberkfell	.03	.01	.00
☐ 405	Cal Ripken Jr.	7.50	3.75	.75
☐ 406	Jim Gantner	.03	.01	.00
☐ 407	Kirk Gibson	.50	.25	.05
☐ 408	Tony Perez	.15	.07	.01
☐ 409	Tommy John	.18	.09	.01
☐ 410	Dave Stewart	.60	.30	.06
☐ 411	Dan Spillner	.03	.01	.00
☐ 412	Willie Aikens	.06	.03	.00
☐ 413	Mike Heath	.03	.01	.00
☐ 414	Ray Burris	.03	.01	.00
☐ 415	Leon Roberts	.03	.01	.00
☐ 416	Mike Witt	1.00	.50	.10
☐ 417	Bob Molinaro	.03	.01	.00
☐ 418	Steve Braun	.03	.01	.00
☐ 419	Nolan Ryan	.45	.22	.04
☐ 420	Tug McGraw	.10	.05	.01
☐ 421	Dave Concepcion	.12	.06	.01
☐ 422A	Juan Eichelberger ERR (photo actually Gary Lucas)	.65	.30	.06
☐ 422B	Juan Eichelberger COR	.08	.04	.01
☐ 423	Rick Rhoden	.10	.05	.01
☐ 424	Frank Robinson MG	.15	.07	.01
☐ 425	Eddie Miller	.03	.01	.00
☐ 426	Bill Caudill	.06	.03	.00
☐ 427	Doug Flynn	.03	.01	.00
☐ 428	Larry Andersen	.03	.01	.00
☐ 429	Al Williams	.03	.01	.00
☐ 430	Jerry Garvin	.03	.01	.00
☐ 431	Glenn Adams	.03	.01	.00
☐ 432	Barry Bonnell	.03	.01	.00
☐ 433	Jerry Narron	.03	.01	.00
☐ 434	John Stearns	.03	.01	.00
☐ 435	Mike Tyson	.03	.01	.00
☐ 436	Glenn Hubbard	.03	.01	.00
☐ 437	Eddie Solomon	.03	.01	.00
☐ 438	Jeff Leonard	.12	.06	.01
☐ 439	Randy Bass	.03	.01	.00
☐ 440	Mike LaCoss	.03	.01	.00
☐ 441	Gary Matthews	.08	.04	.01
☐ 442	Mark Littell	.03	.01	.00
☐ 443	Don Sutton	.25	.12	.02
☐ 444	John Harris	.03	.01	.00
☐ 445	Vada Pinson CO	.08	.04	.01
☐ 446	Elias Sosa	.03	.01	.00
☐ 447	Charlie Hough	.10	.05	.01
☐ 448	Willie Wilson	.15	.07	.01
☐ 449	Fred Stanley	.03	.01	.00
☐ 450	Tom Veryzer	.03	.01	.00
☐ 451	Ron Davis	.03	.01	.00
☐ 452	Mark Clear	.03	.01	.00
☐ 453	Bill Russell	.06	.03	.00
☐ 454	Lou Whitaker	.15	.07	.01
☐ 455	Dan Graham	.03	.01	.00
☐ 456	Reggie Cleveland	.03	.01	.00
☐ 457	Sammy Stewart	.03	.01	.00
☐ 458	Pete Vuckovich	.10	.05	.01
☐ 459	John Wockenfuss	.03	.01	.00
☐ 460	Glenn Hoffman	.03	.01	.00
☐ 461	Willie Randolph	.10	.05	.01
☐ 462	Fernando Valenzuela	.60	.30	.06
☐ 463	Ron Hassey	.03	.01	.00
☐ 464	Paul Splittorff	.06	.03	.00
☐ 465	Rob Picciolo	.03	.01	.00
☐ 466	Larry Parrish	.08	.04	.01
☐ 467	Johnny Grubb	.03	.01	.00
☐ 468	Dan Ford	.03	.01	.00
☐ 469	Silvio Martinez	.03	.01	.00
☐ 470	Kiko Garcia	.03	.01	.00
☐ 471	Bob Boone	.08	.04	.01
☐ 472	Luis Salazar	.03	.01	.00
☐ 473	Randy Niemann	.03	.01	.00
☐ 474	Tom Griffin	.03	.01	.00
☐ 475	Phil Niekro	.25	.12	.02
☐ 476	Hubie Brooks	.20	.10	.02
☐ 477	Dick Tidrow	.03	.01	.00
☐ 478	Jim Beattie	.03	.01	.00
☐ 479	Damaso Garcia	.08	.04	.01
☐ 480	Mickey Hatcher	.06	.03	.00
☐ 481	Joe Price	.03	.01	.00
☐ 482	Ed Farmer	.03	.01	.00
☐ 483	Eddie Murray	.65	.30	.06
☐ 484	Ben Oglivie	.06	.03	.00
☐ 485	Kevin Saucier	.03	.01	.00
☐ 486	Bobby Murcer	.10	.05	.01
☐ 487	Bill Campbell	.03	.01	.00
☐ 488	Reggie Smith	.10	.05	.01
☐ 489	Wayne Garland	.03	.01	.00
☐ 490	Jim Wright	.03	.01	.00
☐ 491	Billy Martin MG	.15	.07	.01
☐ 492	Jim Fanning MG	.03	.01	.00
☐ 493	Don Baylor	.15	.07	.01
☐ 494	Rick Honeycutt	.06	.03	.00
☐ 495	Carlton Fisk	.18	.09	.01
☐ 496	Denny Walling	.03	.01	.00
☐ 497	Bake McBride	.03	.01	.00
☐ 498	Darrell Porter	.06	.03	.00
☐ 499	Gene Richards	.03	.01	.00
☐ 500	Ron Oester	.06	.03	.00
☐ 501	Ken Dayley	.30	.15	.03
☐ 502	Jason Thompson	.06	.03	.00
☐ 503	Milt May	.03	.01	.00
☐ 504	Doug Bird	.03	.01	.00
☐ 505	Bruce Bochte	.03	.01	.00
☐ 506	Neil Allen	.06	.03	.00
☐ 507	Joey McLaughlin	.03	.01	.00
☐ 508	Butch Wynegar	.03	.01	.00
☐ 509	Gary Roenicke	.06	.03	.00
☐ 510	Robin Yount	.50	.25	.05
☐ 511	Dave Tobik	.03	.01	.00
☐ 512	Rich Gedman	.60	.30	.06
☐ 513	Gene Nelson	.10	.05	.01
☐ 514	Rick Monday	.06	.03	.00
☐ 515	Miguel Dilone	.03	.01	.00
☐ 516	Clint Hurdle	.03	.01	.00
☐ 517	Jeff Newman	.03	.01	.00
☐ 518	Grant Jackson	.03	.01	.00
☐ 519	Andy Hassler	.03	.01	.00
☐ 520	Pat Putnam	.03	.01	.00
☐ 521	Greg Pryor	.03	.01	.00
☐ 522	Tony Scott	.03	.01	.00
☐ 523	Steve Mura	.03	.01	.00
☐ 524	Johnnie LeMaster	.03	.01	.00
☐ 525	Dick Ruthven	.03	.01	.00
☐ 526	John McNamara MG	.03	.01	.00
☐ 527	Larry McWilliams	.03	.01	.00
☐ 528	Johnny Ray	.75	.35	.07
☐ 529	Pat Tabler	.75	.35	.07
☐ 530	Tom Herr	.10	.05	.01
☐ 531A	San Diego Chicken (with TM)	1.00	.50	.10
☐ 531B	San Diego Chicken (without TM)	.75	.35	.07
☐ 532	Sal Butera	.03	.01	.00
☐ 533	Mike Griffin	.03	.01	.00
☐ 534	Kelvin Moore	.03	.01	.00
☐ 535	Reggie Jackson	.55	.27	.05
☐ 536	Ed Romero	.03	.01	.00
☐ 537	Derrel Thomas	.03	.01	.00
☐ 538	Mike O'Berry	.03	.01	.00
☐ 539	Jack O'Connor	.03	.01	.00
☐ 540	Bob Ojeda	.60	.30	.06
☐ 541	Roy Lee Jackson	.03	.01	.00
☐ 542	Lynn Jones	.03	.01	.00
☐ 543	Gaylord Perry	.25	.12	.02
☐ 544A	Phil Garner ERR (reverse negative)	.75	.35	.07
☐ 544B	Phil Garner COR	.10	.05	.01
☐ 545	Garry Templeton	.08	.04	.01
☐ 546	Rafael Ramirez	.03	.01	.00
☐ 547	Jeff Reardon	.15	.07	.01
☐ 548	Ron Guidry	.20	.10	.02
☐ 549	Tim Laudner	.30	.15	.03
☐ 550	John Henry Johnson	.03	.01	.00
☐ 551	Chris Bando	.03	.01	.00
☐ 552	Bobby Brown	.03	.01	.00
☐ 553	Larry Bradford	.03	.01	.00
☐ 554	Scott Fletcher	.50	.25	.05
☐ 555	Jerry Royster	.03	.01	.00
☐ 556	Shooty Babitt (spelled Babbitt on front)	.03	.01	.00
☐ 557	Kent Hrbek	2.50	1.25	.25
☐ 558	Yankee Winners Ron Guidry Tommy John	.15	.07	.01
☐ 559	Mark Bomback	.03	.01	.00
☐ 560	Julio Valdez	.03	.01	.00
☐ 561	Buck Martinez	.03	.01	.00
☐ 562	Mike Marshall (Dodger hitter)	1.25	.60	.12
☐ 563	Rennie Stennett	.03	.01	.00
☐ 564	Steve Crawford	.06	.03	.00
☐ 565	Bob Babcock	.03	.01	.00
☐ 566	Johnny Podres CO	.06	.03	.00
☐ 567	Paul Serna	.03	.01	.00
☐ 568	Harold Baines	.45	.22	.04
☐ 569	Dave LaRoche	.03	.01	.00
☐ 570	Lee May	.06	.03	.00
☐ 571	Gary Ward	.06	.03	.00
☐ 572	John Denny	.08	.04	.01
☐ 573	Roy Smalley	.06	.03	.00
☐ 574	Bob Brenly	.40	.20	.04
☐ 575	Bronx Bombers Reggie Jackson	.40	.20	.04

	Dave Winfield			
☐ 576	Luis Pujols	.03	.01	.00
☐ 577	Butch Hobson	.03	.01	.00
☐ 578	Harvey Kuenn MG	.06	.03	.00
☐ 579	Cal Ripken Sr. CO	.10	.05	.01
☐ 580	Juan Berenguer	.06	.03	.00
☐ 581	Benny Ayala	.03	.01	.00
☐ 582	Vance Law	.03	.01	.00
☐ 583	Rick Leach	.06	.03	.00
☐ 584	George Frazier	.03	.01	.00
☐ 585	Phillies Finest	.75	.35	.07
	Pete Rose			
	Mike Schmidt			
☐ 586	Joe Rudi	.06	.03	.00
☐ 587	Juan Beniquez	.06	.03	.00
☐ 588	Luis DeLeon	.10	.05	.01
☐ 589	Craig Swan	.03	.01	.00
☐ 590	Dave Chalk	.03	.01	.00
☐ 591	Billy Gardner	.03	.01	.00
☐ 592	Sal Bando	.06	.03	.00
☐ 593	Bert Campaneris	.08	.04	.01
☐ 594	Steve Kemp	.08	.04	.01
☐ 595A	Randy Lerch ERR	.65	.30	.06
	(Braves)			
☐ 595B	Randy Lerch COR	.08	.04	.01
	(Brewers)			
☐ 596	Bryan Clark	.03	.01	.00
☐ 597	David Ford	.03	.01	.00
☐ 598	Mike Scioscia	.08	.04	.01
☐ 599	John Lowenstein	.03	.01	.00
☐ 600	Rene Lachemann MG	.03	.01	.00
☐ 601	Mick Kelleher	.03	.01	.00
☐ 602	Ron Jackson	.03	.01	.00
☐ 603	Jerry Koosman	.08	.04	.01
☐ 604	Dave Goltz	.03	.01	.00
☐ 605	Ellis Valentine	.03	.01	.00
☐ 606	Lonnie Smith	.08	.04	.01
☐ 607	Joaquin Andujar	.12	.06	.01
☐ 608	Garry Hancock	.03	.01	.00
☐ 609	Jerry Turner	.03	.01	.00
☐ 610	Bob Bonner	.03	.01	.00
☐ 611	Jim Dwyer	.03	.01	.00
☐ 612	Terry Bulling	.03	.01	.00
☐ 613	Joel Youngblood	.03	.01	.00
☐ 614	Larry Milbourne	.03	.01	.00
☐ 615	Gene Roof	.08	.04	.01
	(name on front			
	is Phil Roof)			
☐ 616	Keith Drumwright	.03	.01	.00
☐ 617	Dave Rosello	.03	.01	.00
☐ 618	Rickey Keeton	.03	.01	.00
☐ 619	Dennis Lamp	.03	.01	.00
☐ 620	Sid Monge	.03	.01	.00
☐ 621	Jerry White	.03	.01	.00
☐ 622	Luis Aguayo	.03	.01	.00
☐ 623	Jamie Easterly	.03	.01	.00
☐ 624	Steve Sax	1.25	.60	.12
☐ 625	Dave Roberts	.03	.01	.00
☐ 626	Rick Bosetti	.03	.01	.00
☐ 627	Terry Francona	.20	.10	.02
☐ 628	Pride of Reds	.35	.17	.03
	Tom Seaver			
	Johnny Bench			
☐ 629	Paul Mirabella	.03	.01	.00
☐ 630	Rance Mulliniks	.03	.01	.00
☐ 631	Kevin Hickey	.06	.03	.00
☐ 632	Reid Nichols	.03	.01	.00
☐ 633	Dave Geisel	.03	.01	.00
☐ 634	Ken Griffey	.08	.04	.01
☐ 635	Bob Lemon MG	.12	.06	.01
☐ 636	Orlando Sanchez	.03	.01	.00
☐ 637	Bill Almon	.03	.01	.00
☐ 638	Danny Ainge	.10	.05	.01
☐ 639	Willie Stargell	.30	.15	.03
☐ 640	Bob Sykes	.03	.01	.00
☐ 641	Ed Lynch	.10	.05	.01
☐ 642	John Ellis	.03	.01	.00
☐ 643	Ferguson Jenkins	.15	.07	.01
☐ 644	Lenn Sakata	.03	.01	.00
☐ 645	Julio Gonzalez	.03	.01	.00
☐ 646	Jesse Orosco	.15	.07	.01
☐ 647	Jerry Dybzinski	.03	.01	.00
☐ 648	Tommy Davis	.08	.04	.01
☐ 649	Ron Gardenhire	.08	.04	.01
☐ 650	Felipe Alou	.06	.03	.00
☐ 651	Harvey Haddix	.06	.03	.00
☐ 652	Willie Upshaw	.08	.04	.01
☐ 653	Bill Madlock	.15	.07	.01
☐ 654A	DK Checklist	.25	.03	.00
	(unnumbered)			
	(with Trammel)			
☐ 654B	DK Checklist	.12	.02	.00
	(unnumbered)			
	(with Trammell)			
☐ 655	Checklist 1	.08	.01	.00

	(unnumbered)			
☐ 656	Checklist 2	.08	.01	.00
	(unnumbered)			
☐ 657	Checklist 3	.08	.01	.00
	(unnumbered)			
☐ 658	Checklist 4	.08	.01	.00
	(unnumbered)			
☐ 659	Checklist 5	.08	.01	.00
	(unnumbered)			
☐ 660	Checklist 6	.08	.01	.00
	(unnumbered)			

1983 Donruss

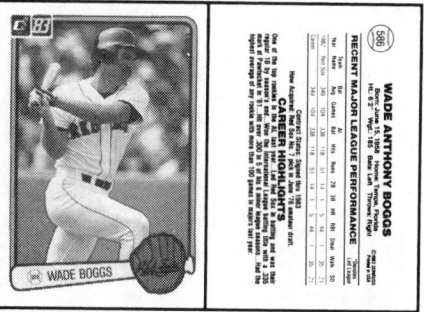

The cards in this 660-card set measure 2 1/2" by 3 1/2". The 1983 Donruss baseball set, issued with a 63-piece Diamond King puzzle, again leads off with a 26-card Diamond Kings (DK) series. Of the remaining 634 cards, two are combination cards, one portrays the San Diego Chicken, one shows the completed Ty Cobb puzzle, and seven are unnumbered checklist cards. The seven unnumbered checklist cards are arbitrarily assigned numbers 654 through 660 and are listed at the end of the list below. The Donruss logo and the year of issue are shown in the upper left corner of the obverse. The card backs have black print on yellow and white and are numbered on a small ball design. The complete set price below includes only the more common of each variation pair.

		MINT	EXC	G-VG
COMPLETE SET (660)		36.00	18.00	3.60
COMMON PLAYER (1-660)		.03	.01	.00
☐ 1	Fernando Valenzuela DK		.15	.03
☐ 2	Rollie Fingers DK	.25	.12	.02
☐ 3	Reggie Jackson DK	.50	.25	.05
☐ 4	Jim Palmer DK	.35	.17	.03
☐ 5	Jack Morris DK	.30	.15	.03
☐ 6	George Foster DK	.15	.07	.01
☐ 7	Jim Sundberg DK	.08	.04	.01
☐ 8	Willie Stargell DK	.30	.15	.03
☐ 9	Dave Stieb DK	.20	.10	.02
☐ 10	Joe Niekro DK	.10	.05	.01
☐ 11	Rickey Henderson DK	.55	.27	.05
☐ 12	Dale Murphy DK	.80	.40	.08
☐ 13	Toby Harrah DK	.08	.04	.01
☐ 14	Bill Buckner DK	.10	.05	.01
☐ 15	Willie Wilson DK	.15	.07	.01
☐ 16	Steve Carlton DK	.40	.20	.04
☐ 17	Ron Guidry DK	.25	.12	.02
☐ 18	Steve Rogers DK	.08	.04	.01
☐ 19	Kent Hrbek DK	.40	.20	.04
☐ 20	Keith Hernandez DK	.30	.15	.03
☐ 21	Floyd Bannister DK	.08	.04	.01
☐ 22	Johnny Bench DK	.40	.20	.04
☐ 23	Britt Burns DK	.08	.04	.01
☐ 24	Joe Morgan DK	.25	.12	.02
☐ 25	Carl Yastrzemski DK	.80	.40	.08
☐ 26	Terry Kennedy DK	.08	.04	.01
☐ 27	Gary Roenicke	.06	.03	.00
☐ 28	Dwight Bernard	.03	.01	.00
☐ 29	Pat Underwood	.03	.01	.00
☐ 30	Gary Allenson	.03	.01	.00
☐ 31	Ron Guidry	.20	.10	.02

☐ 32	Burt Hooton	.03	.01	.00
☐ 33	Chris Bando	.03	.01	.00
☐ 34	Vida Blue	.08	.04	.01
☐ 35	Rickey Henderson	.50	.25	.05
☐ 36	Ray Burris	.03	.01	.00
☐ 37	John Butcher	.03	.01	.00
☐ 38	Don Aase	.06	.03	.00
☐ 39	Jerry Koosman	.08	.04	.01
☐ 40	Bruce Sutter	.15	.07	.01
☐ 41	Jose Cruz	.10	.05	.01
☐ 42	Pete Rose	1.00	.50	.10
☐ 43	Cesar Cedeno	.08	.04	.01
☐ 44	Floyd Chiffer	.06	.03	.00
☐ 45	Larry McWilliams	.03	.01	.00
☐ 46	Alan Fowlkes	.03	.01	.00
☐ 47	Dale Murphy	.75	.35	.07
☐ 48	Doug Bird	.03	.01	.00
☐ 49	Hubie Brooks	.10	.05	.01
☐ 50	Floyd Bannister	.08	.04	.01
☐ 51	Jack O'Connor	.03	.01	.00
☐ 52	Steve Senteney	.03	.01	.00
☐ 53	Gary Gaetti	1.75	.85	.17
☐ 54	Damaso Garcia	.08	.04	.01
☐ 55	Gene Nelson	.03	.01	.00
☐ 56	Mookie Wilson	.08	.04	.01
☐ 57	Allen Ripley	.03	.01	.00
☐ 58	Bob Horner	.20	.10	.02
☐ 59	Tony Pena	.15	.07	.01
☐ 60	Gary Lavelle	.06	.03	.00
☐ 61	Tim Lollar	.03	.01	.00
☐ 62	Frank Pastore	.03	.01	.00
☐ 63	Garry Maddox	.06	.03	.00
☐ 64	Bob Forsch	.06	.03	.00
☐ 65	Harry Spilman	.03	.01	.00
☐ 66	Geoff Zahn	.03	.01	.00
☐ 67	Salome Barojas	.03	.01	.00
☐ 68	David Palmer	.06	.03	.00
☐ 69	Charlie Hough	.08	.04	.01
☐ 70	Dan Quisenberry	.18	.09	.01
☐ 71	Tony Armas	.10	.05	.01
☐ 72	Rick Sutcliffe	.18	.09	.01
☐ 73	Steve Balboni	.08	.04	.01
☐ 74	Jerry Remy	.03	.01	.00
☐ 75	Mike Scioscia	.06	.03	.00
☐ 76	John Wockenfuss	.03	.01	.00
☐ 77	Jim Palmer	.30	.15	.03
☐ 78	Rollie Fingers	.20	.10	.02
☐ 79	Joe Nolan	.03	.01	.00
☐ 80	Pete Vuckovich	.06	.03	.00
☐ 81	Rick Leach	.03	.01	.00
☐ 82	Rick Miller	.03	.01	.00
☐ 83	Graig Nettles	.15	.07	.01
☐ 84	Ron Cey	.10	.05	.01
☐ 85	Miguel Dilone	.03	.01	.00
☐ 86	John Wathan	.06	.03	.00
☐ 87	Kelvin Moore	.03	.01	.00
☐ 88A	Byrn Smith ERR (sic, Bryn)	.15	.07	.01
☐ 88B	Bryn Smith COR	.75	.35	.07
☐ 89	Dave Hostetler	.06	.03	.00
☐ 90	Rod Carew	.40	.20	.04
☐ 91	Lonnie Smith	.08	.04	.01
☐ 92	Bob Knepper	.08	.04	.01
☐ 93	Marty Bystrom	.03	.01	.00
☐ 94	Chris Welsh	.03	.01	.00
☐ 95	Jason Thompson	.06	.03	.00
☐ 96	Tom O'Malley	.06	.03	.00
☐ 97	Phil Niekro	.20	.10	.02
☐ 98	Neil Allen	.06	.03	.00
☐ 99	Bill Buckner	.10	.05	.01
☐ 100	Ed VandeBerg	.06	.03	.00
☐ 101	Jim Clancy	.06	.03	.00
☐ 102	Robert Castillo	.03	.01	.00
☐ 103	Bruce Berenyi	.03	.01	.00
☐ 104	Carlton Fisk	.15	.07	.01
☐ 105	Mike Flanagan	.08	.04	.01
☐ 106	Cecil Cooper	.15	.07	.01
☐ 107	Jack Morris	.20	.10	.02
☐ 108	Mike Morgan	.03	.01	.00
☐ 109	Luis Aponte	.06	.03	.00
☐ 110	Pedro Guerrero	.35	.17	.03
☐ 111	Len Barker	.06	.03	.00
☐ 112	Willie Wilson	.15	.07	.01
☐ 113	Dave Beard	.03	.01	.00
☐ 114	Mike Gates	.03	.01	.00
☐ 115	Reggie Jackson	.45	.22	.04
☐ 116	George Wright	.06	.03	.00
☐ 117	Vance Law	.03	.01	.00
☐ 118	Nolan Ryan	.40	.20	.04
☐ 119	Mike Krukow	.08	.04	.01
☐ 120	Ozzie Smith	.25	.12	.02
☐ 121	Broderick Perkins	.03	.01	.00
☐ 122	Tom Seaver	.40	.20	.04
☐ 123	Chris Chambliss	.06	.03	.00
☐ 124	Chuck Tanner MG	.03	.01	.00
☐ 125	Johnnie LeMaster	.03	.01	.00
☐ 126	Mel Hall	.75	.35	.07
☐ 127	Bruce Bochte	.06	.03	.00
☐ 128	Charlie Puleo	.03	.01	.00
☐ 129	Luis Leal	.03	.01	.00
☐ 130	John Pacella	.03	.01	.00
☐ 131	Glenn Gulliver	.03	.01	.00
☐ 132	Don Money	.03	.01	.00
☐ 133	Dave Rozema	.03	.01	.00
☐ 134	Bruce Hurst	.15	.07	.01
☐ 135	Rudy May	.03	.01	.00
☐ 136	Tom Lasorda MG	.06	.03	.00
☐ 137	Dan Spillner (photo actually Ed Whitson)	.08	.04	.01
☐ 138	Jerry Martin	.03	.01	.00
☐ 139	Mike Norris	.06	.03	.00
☐ 140	Al Oliver	.12	.06	.01
☐ 141	Daryl Sconiers	.03	.01	.00
☐ 142	Lamar Johnson	.03	.01	.00
☐ 143	Harold Baines	.25	.12	.02
☐ 144	Alan Ashby	.03	.01	.00
☐ 145	Garry Templeton	.08	.04	.01
☐ 146	Al Holland	.06	.03	.00
☐ 147	Bo Diaz	.08	.04	.01
☐ 148	Dave Concepcion	.10	.05	.01
☐ 149	Rick Camp	.03	.01	.00
☐ 150	Jim Morrison	.03	.01	.00
☐ 151	Randy Martz	.03	.01	.00
☐ 152	Keith Hernandez	.30	.15	.03
☐ 153	John Lowenstein	.03	.01	.00
☐ 154	Mike Caldwell	.06	.03	.00
☐ 155	Milt Wilcox	.03	.01	.00
☐ 156	Rich Gedman	.12	.06	.01
☐ 157	Rich Gossage	.18	.09	.01
☐ 158	Jerry Reuss	.06	.03	.00
☐ 159	Ron Hassey	.03	.01	.00
☐ 160	Larry Gura	.06	.03	.00
☐ 161	Dwayne Murphy	.06	.03	.00
☐ 162	Woodie Fryman	.03	.01	.00
☐ 163	Steve Comer	.03	.01	.00
☐ 164	Ken Forsch	.03	.01	.00
☐ 165	Dennis Lamp	.03	.01	.00
☐ 166	David Green	.06	.03	.00
☐ 167	Terry Puhl	.06	.03	.00
☐ 168	Mike Schmidt	.50	.25	.05
☐ 169	Eddie Milner	.20	.10	.02
☐ 170	John Curtis	.03	.01	.00
☐ 171	Don Robinson	.03	.01	.00
☐ 172	Rich Gale	.03	.01	.00
☐ 173	Steve Bedrosian	.25	.12	.02
☐ 174	Willie Hernandez	.15	.07	.01
☐ 175	Ron Gardenhire	.03	.01	.00
☐ 176	Jim Beattie	.03	.01	.00
☐ 177	Tim Laudner	.06	.03	.00
☐ 178	Buck Martinez	.03	.01	.00
☐ 179	Kent Hrbek	.35	.17	.03
☐ 180	Alfredo Griffin	.08	.04	.01
☐ 181	Larry Andersen	.03	.01	.00
☐ 182	Pete Falcone	.03	.01	.00
☐ 183	Jody Davis	.15	.07	.01
☐ 184	Glenn Hubbard	.03	.01	.00
☐ 185	Dale Berra	.06	.03	.00
☐ 186	Greg Minton	.06	.03	.00
☐ 187	Gary Lucas	.03	.01	.00
☐ 188	Dave Van Gorder	.03	.01	.00
☐ 189	Bob Dernier	.06	.03	.00
☐ 190	Willie McGee	1.75	.85	.17
☐ 191	Dickie Thon	.06	.03	.00
☐ 192	Bob Boone	.08	.04	.01
☐ 193	Britt Burns	.06	.03	.00
☐ 194	Jeff Reardon	.12	.06	.01
☐ 195	Jon Matlack	.06	.03	.00
☐ 196	Don Slaught	.25	.12	.02
☐ 197	Fred Stanley	.03	.01	.00
☐ 198	Rick Manning	.03	.01	.00
☐ 199	Dave Righetti	.20	.10	.02
☐ 200	Dave Stapleton	.03	.01	.00
☐ 201	Steve Yeager	.03	.01	.00
☐ 202	Enos Cabell	.03	.01	.00
☐ 203	Sammy Stewart	.03	.01	.00
☐ 204	Moose Haas	.03	.01	.00
☐ 205	Lenn Sakata	.03	.01	.00
☐ 206	Charlie Moore	.03	.01	.00
☐ 207	Alan Trammell	.25	.12	.02
☐ 208	Jim Rice	.35	.17	.03
☐ 209	Roy Smalley	.06	.03	.00
☐ 210	Bill Russell	.06	.03	.00
☐ 211	Andre Thornton	.08	.04	.01
☐ 212	Willie Aikens	.06	.03	.00
☐ 213	Dave McKay	.03	.01	.00
☐ 214	Tim Blackwell	.03	.01	.00
☐ 215	Buddy Bell	.10	.05	.01
☐ 216	Doug DeCinces	.10	.05	.01
☐ 217	Tom Herr	.08	.04	.01

☐ 218	Frank LaCorte	.03	.01	.00
☐ 219	Steve Carlton	.35	.17	.03
☐ 220	Terry Kennedy	.08	.04	.01
☐ 221	Mike Easler	.06	.03	.00
☐ 222	Jack Clark	.25	.12	.02
☐ 223	Gene Garber	.06	.03	.00
☐ 224	Scott Holman	.06	.03	.00
☐ 225	Mike Proly	.03	.01	.00
☐ 226	Terry Bulling	.03	.01	.00
☐ 227	Jerry Garvin	.03	.01	.00
☐ 228	Ron Davis	.03	.01	.00
☐ 229	Tom Hume	.03	.01	.00
☐ 230	Marc Hill	.03	.01	.00
☐ 231	Dennis Martinez	.06	.03	.00
☐ 232	Jim Gantner	.03	.01	.00
☐ 233	Larry Pashnick	.03	.01	.00
☐ 234	Dave Collins	.06	.03	.00
☐ 235	Tom Burgmeier	.03	.01	.00
☐ 236	Ken Landreaux	.06	.03	.00
☐ 237	John Denny	.10	.05	.01
☐ 238	Hal McRae	.06	.03	.00
☐ 239	Matt Keough	.03	.01	.00
☐ 240	Doug Flynn	.03	.01	.00
☐ 241	Fred Lynn	.20	.10	.02
☐ 242	Billy Sample	.03	.01	.00
☐ 243	Tom Paciorek	.03	.01	.00
☐ 244	Joe Sambito	.06	.03	.00
☐ 245	Sid Monge	.03	.01	.00
☐ 246	Ken Oberkfell	.03	.01	.00
☐ 247	Joe Pittman (photo actually Juan Eichelberger)	.10	.05	.01
☐ 248	Mario Soto	.08	.04	.01
☐ 249	Claudell Washington	.08	.04	.01
☐ 250	Rick Rhoden	.08	.04	.01
☐ 251	Darrell Evans	.12	.06	.01
☐ 252	Steve Henderson	.03	.01	.00
☐ 253	Manny Castillo	.03	.01	.00
☐ 254	Craig Swan	.03	.01	.00
☐ 255	Joey McLaughlin	.03	.01	.00
☐ 256	Pete Redfern	.03	.01	.00
☐ 257	Ken Singleton	.08	.04	.01
☐ 258	Robin Yount	.30	.15	.03
☐ 259	Elias Sosa	.03	.01	.00
☐ 260	Bob Ojeda	.10	.05	.01
☐ 261	Bobby Murcer	.08	.04	.01
☐ 262	Candy Maldonado	.75	.35	.07
☐ 263	Rick Waits	.03	.01	.00
☐ 264	Greg Pryor	.03	.01	.00
☐ 265	Bob Owchinko	.03	.01	.00
☐ 266	Chris Speier	.06	.03	.00
☐ 267	Bruce Kison	.03	.01	.00
☐ 268	Mark Wagner	.03	.01	.00
☐ 269	Steve Kemp	.08	.04	.01
☐ 270	Phil Garner	.06	.03	.00
☐ 271	Gene Richards	.03	.01	.00
☐ 272	Renie Martin	.03	.01	.00
☐ 273	Dave Roberts	.03	.01	.00
☐ 274	Dan Driessen	.06	.03	.00
☐ 275	Rufino Linares	.03	.01	.00
☐ 276	Lee Lacy	.06	.03	.00
☐ 277	Ryne Sandberg	4.00	2.00	.40
☐ 278	Darrell Porter	.06	.03	.00
☐ 279	Cal Ripken	1.00	.50	.10
☐ 280	Jamie Easterly	.03	.01	.00
☐ 281	Bill Fahey	.03	.01	.00
☐ 282	Glenn Hoffman	.03	.01	.00
☐ 283	Willie Randolph	.08	.04	.01
☐ 284	Fernando Valenzuela	.35	.17	.03
☐ 285	Alan Bannister	.03	.01	.00
☐ 286	Paul Splittorff	.06	.03	.00
☐ 287	Joe Rudi	.06	.03	.00
☐ 288	Bill Gullickson	.06	.03	.00
☐ 289	Danny Darwin	.06	.03	.00
☐ 290	Andy Hassler	.03	.01	.00
☐ 291	Ernesto Escarrega	.03	.01	.00
☐ 292	Steve Mura	.03	.01	.00
☐ 293	Tony Scott	.03	.01	.00
☐ 294	Manny Trillo	.06	.03	.00
☐ 295	Greg Harris	.06	.03	.00
☐ 296	Luis DeLeon	.03	.01	.00
☐ 297	Kent Tekulve	.08	.04	.01
☐ 298	Atlee Hammaker	.08	.04	.01
☐ 299	Bruce Benedict	.03	.01	.00
☐ 300	Fergie Jenkins	.12	.06	.01
☐ 301	Dave Kingman	.12	.06	.01
☐ 302	Bill Caudill	.06	.03	.00
☐ 303	John Castino	.03	.01	.00
☐ 304	Ernie Whitt	.06	.03	.00
☐ 305	Randy Johnson	.06	.03	.00
☐ 306	Garth Iorg	.03	.01	.00
☐ 307	Gaylord Perry	.20	.10	.02
☐ 308	Ed Lynch	.03	.01	.00
☐ 309	Keith Moreland	.08	.04	.01
☐ 310	Rafael Ramirez	.03	.01	.00
☐ 311	Bill Madlock	.15	.07	.01
☐ 312	Milt May	.03	.01	.00
☐ 313	John Montefusco	.06	.03	.00
☐ 314	Wayne Krenchicki	.03	.01	.00
☐ 315	George Vukovich	.03	.01	.00
☐ 316	Joaquin Andujar	.10	.05	.01
☐ 317	Craig Reynolds	.03	.01	.00
☐ 318	Rick Burleson	.06	.03	.00
☐ 319	Richard Dotson	.08	.04	.01
☐ 320	Steve Rogers	.06	.03	.00
☐ 321	Dave Schmidt	.15	.07	.01
☐ 322	Bud Black	.30	.15	.03
☐ 323	Jeff Burroughs	.06	.03	.00
☐ 324	Von Hayes	.25	.12	.02
☐ 325	Butch Wynegar	.06	.03	.00
☐ 326	Carl Yastrzemski	.60	.30	.06
☐ 327	Ron Roenicke	.03	.01	.00
☐ 328	Howard Johnson	2.50	1.25	.25
☐ 329	Rick Dempsey	.06	.03	.00
☐ 330A	Jim Slaton (bio printed black on white)	.08	.04	.01
☐ 330B	Jim Slaton (bio printed black on yellow)	.08	.04	.01
☐ 331	Benny Ayala	.03	.01	.00
☐ 332	Ted Simmons	.12	.06	.01
☐ 333	Lou Whitaker	.15	.07	.01
☐ 334	Chuck Rainey	.03	.01	.00
☐ 335	Lou Piniella	.10	.05	.01
☐ 336	Steve Sax	.18	.09	.01
☐ 337	Toby Harrah	.06	.03	.00
☐ 338	George Brett	.60	.30	.06
☐ 339	Davey Lopes	.08	.04	.01
☐ 340	Gary Carter	.40	.20	.04
☐ 341	John Grubb	.03	.01	.00
☐ 342	Tim Foli	.03	.01	.00
☐ 343	Jim Kaat	.10	.05	.01
☐ 344	Mike LaCoss	.03	.01	.00
☐ 345	Larry Christenson	.03	.01	.00
☐ 346	Juan Bonilla	.03	.01	.00
☐ 347	Omar Moreno	.03	.01	.00
☐ 348	Chili Davis	.30	.15	.03
☐ 349	Tommy Boggs	.03	.01	.00
☐ 350	Rusty Staub	.10	.05	.01
☐ 351	Bump Wills	.03	.01	.00
☐ 352	Rick Sweet	.03	.01	.00
☐ 353	Jim Gott	.10	.05	.01
☐ 354	Terry Felton	.03	.01	.00
☐ 355	Jim Kern	.03	.01	.00
☐ 356	Bill Almon	.03	.01	.00
☐ 357	Tippy Martinez	.03	.01	.00
☐ 358	Roy Howell	.03	.01	.00
☐ 359	Dan Petry	.12	.06	.01
☐ 360	Jerry Mumphrey	.06	.03	.00
☐ 361	Mark Clear	.06	.03	.00
☐ 362	Mike Marshall	.25	.12	.02
☐ 363	Lary Sorenson	.03	.01	.00
☐ 364	Amos Otis	.08	.04	.01
☐ 365	Rick Langford	.03	.01	.00
☐ 366	Brad Mills	.03	.01	.00
☐ 367	Brian Downing	.06	.03	.00
☐ 368	Mike Richardt	.03	.01	.00
☐ 369	Aurelio Rodriguez	.03	.01	.00
☐ 370	Dave Smith	.08	.04	.01
☐ 371	Tug McGraw	.10	.05	.01
☐ 372	Doug Bair	.03	.01	.00
☐ 373	Ruppert Jones	.03	.01	.00
☐ 374	Alex Trevino	.03	.01	.00
☐ 375	Ken Dayley	.06	.03	.00
☐ 376	Rod Scurry	.03	.01	.00
☐ 377	Bob Brenly	.08	.04	.01
☐ 378	Scot Thompson	.03	.01	.00
☐ 379	Julio Cruz	.03	.01	.00
☐ 380	John Stearns	.03	.01	.00
☐ 381	Dale Murray	.03	.01	.00
☐ 382	Frank Viola	1.50	.75	.15
☐ 383	Al Bumbry	.03	.01	.00
☐ 384	Ben Oglivie	.06	.03	.00
☐ 385	Dave Tobik	.03	.01	.00
☐ 386	Bob Stanley	.06	.03	.00
☐ 387	Andre Robertson	.03	.01	.00
☐ 388	Jorge Orta	.03	.01	.00
☐ 389	Ed Whitson	.06	.03	.00
☐ 390	Don Hood	.03	.01	.00
☐ 391	Tom Underwood	.03	.01	.00
☐ 392	Tim Wallach	.25	.12	.02
☐ 393	Steve Renko	.03	.01	.00
☐ 394	Mickey Rivers	.06	.03	.00
☐ 395	Greg Luzinski	.10	.05	.01
☐ 396	Art Howe	.03	.01	.00
☐ 397	Alan Wiggins	.25	.12	.02
☐ 398	Jim Barr	.03	.01	.00
☐ 399	Ivan DeJesus	.03	.01	.00
☐ 400	Tom Lawless	.08	.04	.01

☐ 401	Bob Walk	.03	.01	.00
☐ 402	Jimmy Smith	.03	.01	.00
☐ 403	Lee Smith	.12	.06	.01
☐ 404	George Hendrick	.08	.04	.01
☐ 405	Eddie Murray	.50	.25	.05
☐ 406	Marshall Edwards	.03	.01	.00
☐ 407	Lance Parrish	.25	.12	.02
☐ 408	Carney Lansford	.10	.05	.01
☐ 409	Dave Winfield	.35	.17	.03
☐ 410	Bob Welch	.08	.04	.01
☐ 411	Larry Milbourne	.03	.01	.00
☐ 412	Dennis Leonard	.06	.03	.00
☐ 413	Dan Meyer	.03	.01	.00
☐ 414	Charlie Lea	.06	.03	.00
☐ 415	Rick Honeycutt	.06	.03	.00
☐ 416	Mike Witt	.25	.12	.02
☐ 417	Steve Trout	.06	.03	.00
☐ 418	Glenn Brummer	.03	.01	.00
☐ 419	Denny Walling	.03	.01	.00
☐ 420	Gary Matthews	.08	.04	.01
☐ 421	Charlie Leibrandt	.08	.04	.01
	(Liebrandt on			
	front of card)			
☐ 422	Juan Eichelberger	.06	.03	.00
	(photo actually			
	Joe Pittman)			
☐ 423	Matt Guante	.08	.04	.01
☐ 424	Bill Laskey	.08	.04	.01
☐ 425	Jerry Royster	.03	.01	.00
☐ 426	Dickie Noles	.03	.01	.00
☐ 427	George Foster	.15	.07	.01
☐ 428	Mike Moore	.25	.12	.02
☐ 429	Gary Ward	.06	.03	.00
☐ 430	Barry Bonnell	.03	.01	.00
☐ 431	Ron Washington	.03	.01	.00
☐ 432	Rance Mulliniks	.03	.01	.00
☐ 433	Mike Stanton	.03	.01	.00
☐ 434	Jesse Orosco	.10	.05	.01
☐ 435	Larry Bowa	.12	.06	.01
☐ 436	Biff Pocoroba	.03	.01	.00
☐ 437	Johnny Ray	.15	.07	.01
☐ 438	Joe Morgan	.25	.12	.02
☐ 439	Eric Show	.15	.07	.01
☐ 440	Larry Biittner	.03	.01	.00
☐ 441	Greg Gross	.03	.01	.00
☐ 442	Gene Tenace	.06	.03	.00
☐ 443	Danny Heep	.03	.01	.00
☐ 444	Bobby Clark	.03	.01	.00
☐ 445	Kevin Hickey	.03	.01	.00
☐ 446	Scott Sanderson	.06	.03	.00
☐ 447	Frank Tanana	.08	.04	.01
☐ 448	Cesar Geronimo	.03	.01	.00
☐ 449	Jimmy Sexton	.03	.01	.00
☐ 450	Mike Hargrove	.06	.03	.00
☐ 451	Doyle Alexander	.06	.03	.00
☐ 452	Dwight Evans	.18	.09	.01
☐ 453	Terry Forster	.08	.04	.01
☐ 454	Tom Brookens	.03	.01	.00
☐ 455	Rich Dauer	.03	.01	.00
☐ 456	Rob Picciolo	.03	.01	.00
☐ 457	Terry Crowley	.03	.01	.00
☐ 458	Ned Yost	.03	.01	.00
☐ 459	Kirk Gibson	.30	.15	.03
☐ 460	Reid Nichols	.03	.01	.00
☐ 461	Oscar Gamble	.06	.03	.00
☐ 462	Dusty Baker	.08	.04	.01
☐ 463	Jack Perconte	.03	.01	.00
☐ 464	Frank White	.08	.04	.01
☐ 465	Mickey Klutts	.03	.01	.00
☐ 466	Warren Cromartie	.03	.01	.00
☐ 467	Larry Parrish	.08	.04	.01
☐ 468	Bobby Grich	.08	.04	.01
☐ 469	Dane Iorg	.03	.01	.00
☐ 470	Joe Niekro	.10	.05	.01
☐ 471	Ed Farmer	.03	.01	.00
☐ 472	Tim Flannery	.03	.01	.00
☐ 473	Dave Parker	.25	.12	.02
☐ 474	Jeff Leonard	.12	.06	.01
☐ 475	Al Hrabosky	.06	.03	.00
☐ 476	Ron Hodges	.03	.01	.00
☐ 477	Leon Durham	.10	.05	.01
☐ 478	Jim Essian	.03	.01	.00
☐ 479	Roy Lee Jackson	.03	.01	.00
☐ 480	Brad Havens	.03	.01	.00
☐ 481	Joe Price	.03	.01	.00
☐ 482	Tony Bernazard	.06	.03	.00
☐ 483	Scott McGregor	.08	.04	.01
☐ 484	Paul Molitor	.18	.09	.01
☐ 485	Mike Ivie	.03	.01	.00
☐ 486	Ken Griffey	.08	.04	.01
☐ 487	Dennis Eckersley	.06	.03	.00
☐ 488	Steve Garvey	.40	.20	.04
☐ 489	Mike Fischlin	.03	.01	.00
☐ 490	U.L. Washington	.03	.01	.00
☐ 491	Steve McCatty	.03	.01	.00
☐ 492	Roy Johnson	.03	.01	.00
☐ 493	Don Baylor	.12	.06	.01
☐ 494	Bobby Johnson	.03	.01	.00
☐ 495	Mike Squires	.03	.01	.00
☐ 496	Bert Roberge	.03	.01	.00
☐ 497	Dick Ruthven	.03	.01	.00
☐ 498	Tito Landrum	.03	.01	.00
☐ 499	Sixto Lezcano	.03	.01	.00
☐ 500	Johnny Bench	.35	.17	.03
☐ 501	Larry Whisenton	.03	.01	.00
☐ 502	Manny Sarmiento	.03	.01	.00
☐ 503	Fred Breining	.03	.01	.00
☐ 504	Bill Campbell	.03	.01	.00
☐ 505	Todd Cruz	.03	.01	.00
☐ 506	Bob Bailor	.03	.01	.00
☐ 507	Dave Stieb	.18	.09	.01
☐ 508	Al Williams	.03	.01	.00
☐ 509	Dan Ford	.03	.01	.00
☐ 510	Gorman Thomas	.10	.05	.01
☐ 511	Chet Lemon	.06	.03	.00
☐ 512	Mike Torrez	.06	.03	.00
☐ 513	Shane Rawley	.06	.03	.00
☐ 514	Mark Belanger	.06	.03	.00
☐ 515	Rodney Craig	.03	.01	.00
☐ 516	Onix Concepcion	.03	.01	.00
☐ 517	Mike Heath	.03	.01	.00
☐ 518	Andre Dawson	.35	.17	.03
☐ 519	Luis Sanchez	.03	.01	.00
☐ 520	Terry Bogener	.03	.01	.00
☐ 521	Rudy Law	.03	.01	.00
☐ 522	Ray Knight	.08	.04	.01
☐ 523	Joe Lefebvre	.03	.01	.00
☐ 524	Jim Wohlford	.03	.01	.00
☐ 525	Julio Franco	1.25	.60	.12
☐ 526	Ron Oester	.06	.03	.00
☐ 527	Rick Mahler	.06	.03	.00
☐ 528	Steve Nicosia	.03	.01	.00
☐ 529	Junior Kennedy	.03	.01	.00
☐ 530A	Whitey Herzog MG	.10	.05	.01
	(bio printed			
	black on white)			
☐ 530B	Whitey Herzog MG	.10	.05	.01
	(bio printed			
	black on yellow)			
☐ 531A	Don Sutton	.35	.17	.03
	(blue border			
	on photo)			
☐ 531B	Don Sutton	.35	.17	.03
	(green border			
	on photo)			
☐ 532	Mark Brouhard	.03	.01	.00
☐ 533A	Sparky Anderson MG	.10	.05	.01
	(bio printed			
	black on white)			
☐ 533B	Sparky Anderson MG	.10	.05	.01
	(bio printed			
	black on yellow)			
☐ 534	Roger LaFrancois	.03	.01	.00
☐ 535	George Frazier	.03	.01	.00
☐ 536	Tom Niedenfuer	.08	.04	.01
☐ 537	Ed Glynn	.03	.01	.00
☐ 538	Lee May	.06	.03	.00
☐ 539	Bob Kearney	.06	.03	.00
☐ 540	Tim Raines	.40	.20	.04
☐ 541	Paul Mirabella	.03	.01	.00
☐ 542	Luis Tiant	.10	.05	.01
☐ 543	Ron LeFlore	.06	.03	.00
☐ 544	Dave LaPoint	.15	.07	.01
☐ 545	Randy Moffitt	.03	.01	.00
☐ 546	Luis Aguayo	.03	.01	.00
☐ 547	Brad Lesley	.06	.03	.00
☐ 548	Luis Salazar	.03	.01	.00
☐ 549	John Candelaria	.08	.04	.01
☐ 550	Dave Bergman	.03	.01	.00
☐ 551	Bob Watson	.06	.03	.00
☐ 552	Pat Tabler	.15	.07	.01
☐ 553	Brent Gaff	.03	.01	.00
☐ 554	Al Cowens	.03	.01	.00
☐ 555	Tom Brunansky	.30	.15	.03
☐ 556	Lloyd Moseby	.15	.07	.01
☐ 557A	Pascual Perez ERR	2.00	1.00	.20
	(Twins in glove)			
☐ 557B	Pascual Perez COR	.10	.05	.01
	(Braves in glove)			
☐ 558	Willie Upshaw	.08	.04	.01
☐ 559	Richie Zisk	.06	.03	.00
☐ 560	Pat Zachry	.03	.01	.00
☐ 561	Jay Johnstone	.06	.03	.00
☐ 562	Carlos Diaz	.08	.04	.01
☐ 563	John Tudor	.15	.07	.01
☐ 564	Frank Robinson MG	.15	.07	.01
☐ 565	Dave Edwards	.03	.01	.00
☐ 566	Paul Householder	.03	.01	.00
☐ 567	Ron Reed	.03	.01	.00
☐ 568	Mike Ramsey	.03	.01	.00

☐ 569	Kiko Garcia	.03	.01	.00
☐ 570	Tommy John	.15	.07	.01
☐ 571	Tony LaRussa MG	.06	.03	.00
☐ 572	Joel Youngblood	.03	.01	.00
☐ 573	Wayne Tolleson	.25	.12	.02
☐ 574	Keith Creel	.03	.01	.00
☐ 575	Billy Martin MG	.15	.07	.01
☐ 576	Jerry Dybzinski	.03	.01	.00
☐ 577	Rick Cerone	.06	.03	.00
☐ 578	Tony Perez	.15	.07	.01
☐ 579	Greg Brock	.45	.22	.04
☐ 580	Glen Wilson	.60	.30	.06
☐ 581	Tim Stoddard	.03	.01	.00
☐ 582	Bob McClure	.03	.01	.00
☐ 583	Jim Dwyer	.03	.01	.00
☐ 584	Ed Romero	.03	.01	.00
☐ 585	Larry Herndon	.03	.01	.00
☐ 586	Wade Boggs	16.00	8.00	1.60
☐ 587	Jay Howell	.06	.03	.00
☐ 588	Dave Stewart	.10	.05	.01
☐ 589	Bert Blyleven	.15	.07	.01
☐ 590	Dick Howser MG	.08	.04	.01
☐ 591	Wayne Gross	.03	.01	.00
☐ 592	Terry Francona	.06	.03	.00
☐ 593	Don Werner	.03	.01	.00
☐ 594	Bill Stein	.03	.01	.00
☐ 595	Jesse Barfield	.75	.35	.07
☐ 596	Bobby Molinaro	.03	.01	.00
☐ 597	Mike Vail	.03	.01	.00
☐ 598	Tony Gwynn	8.00	4.00	.80
☐ 599	Gary Rajsich	.06	.03	.00
☐ 600	Jerry Ujdur	.03	.01	.00
☐ 601	Cliff Johnson	.03	.01	.00
☐ 602	Jerry White	.03	.01	.00
☐ 603	Bryan Clark	.03	.01	.00
☐ 604	Joe Ferguson	.03	.01	.00
☐ 605	Guy Sularz	.03	.01	.00
☐ 606A	Ozzie Virgil (green border on photo)	.10	.05	.01
☐ 606B	Ozzie Virgil (orange border on photo)	.10	.05	.01
☐ 607	Terry Harper	.03	.01	.00
☐ 608	Harvey Kuenn MG	.06	.03	.00
☐ 609	Jim Sundberg	.06	.03	.00
☐ 610	Willie Stargell	.25	.12	.02
☐ 611	Reggie Smith	.08	.04	.01
☐ 612	Rob Wilfong	.03	.01	.00
☐ 613	The Niekro Brothers Joe Niekro Phil Niekro	.12	.06	.01
☐ 614	Lee Elia MG	.03	.01	.00
☐ 615	Mickey Hatcher	.03	.01	.00
☐ 616	Jerry Hairston	.03	.01	.00
☐ 617	John Martin	.03	.01	.00
☐ 618	Wally Backman	.20	.10	.02
☐ 619	Storm Davis	.25	.12	.02
☐ 620	Alan Knicely	.03	.01	.00
☐ 621	John Stuper	.06	.03	.00
☐ 622	Matt Sinatro	.03	.01	.00
☐ 623	Gene Petralli	.06	.03	.00
☐ 624	Duane Walker	.06	.03	.00
☐ 625	Dick Williams MG	.03	.01	.00
☐ 626	Pat Corrales MG	.03	.01	.00
☐ 627	Vern Ruhle	.03	.01	.00
☐ 628	Joe Torre MG	.08	.04	.01
☐ 629	Anthony Johnson	.06	.03	.00
☐ 630	Steve Howe	.06	.03	.00
☐ 631	Gary Woods	.03	.01	.00
☐ 632	LaMarr Hoyt	.08	.04	.01
☐ 633	Steve Swisher	.03	.01	.00
☐ 634	Terry Leach	.20	.10	.02
☐ 635	Jeff Newman	.03	.01	.00
☐ 636	Brett Butler	.12	.06	.01
☐ 637	Gary Gray	.03	.01	.00
☐ 638	Lee Mazzilli	.06	.03	.00
☐ 639A	Ron Jackson ERR (A's in glove)	10.00	5.00	1.00
☐ 639B	Ron Jackson COR (Angels in glove, red border on photo)	.15	.07	.01
☐ 639C	Ron Jackson COR (Angels in glove, green border on photo)	.50	.25	.05
☐ 640	Juan Beniquez	.06	.03	.00
☐ 641	Dave Rucker	.03	.01	.00
☐ 642	Luis Pujols	.03	.01	.00
☐ 643	Rick Monday	.06	.03	.00
☐ 644	Hosken Powell	.03	.01	.00
☐ 645	The Chicken	.25	.12	.02
☐ 646	Dave Engle	.03	.01	.00
☐ 647	Dick Davis	.03	.01	.00

☐ 648	Frank Robinson Vida Blue Joe Morgan	.12	.06	.01
☐ 649	Al Chambers	.06	.03	.00
☐ 650	Jesus Vega	.06	.03	.00
☐ 651	Jeff Jones	.03	.01	.00
☐ 652	Marvis Foley	.03	.01	.00
☐ 653	Ty Cobb Puzzle Card	.06	.03	.00
☐ 654A	Dick Perez/Diamond King Checklist (unnumbered) (word "checklist" omitted from back)	.15	.02	.00
☐ 654B	Dick Perez/Diamond King Checklist (unnumbered) (word "checklist" is on back)	.15	.02	.00
☐ 655	Checklist 1 (unnumbered)	.07	.01	.00
☐ 656	Checklist 2 (unnumbered)	.07	.01	.00
☐ 657	Checklist 3 (unnumbered)	.07	.01	.00
☐ 658	Checklist 4 (unnumbered)	.07	.01	.00
☐ 659	Checklist 5 (unnumbered)	.07	.01	.00
☐ 660	Checklist 6 (unnumbered)	.07	.01	.00

1983 Donruss Action All-Stars

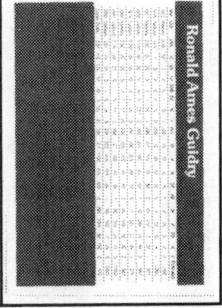

The cards in this 60-card set measure 3 1/2" by 5". The 1983 Action All Stars series depicts 60 major leagers in a distinctive new style. Each card contains a large close-up on the left and an action photo on the right. Team affiliations appear as part of the background design, and the cards have cranberry color borders. The backs contain the card number, the player's major league line record, and biographical material. A 63-piece Mickey Mantle puzzle (three pieces on one card per pack) was marketed as an insert premium.

		MINT	EXC	G-VG
	COMPLETE SET	6.00	3.00	.60
	COMMON PLAYER	.05	.02	.00
☐	1 Eddie Murray	.40	.20	.04
☐	2 Dwight Evans	.15	.07	.01
☐	3 Reggie Jackson	.50	.25	.05
☐	4 Greg Luzinski	.10	.05	.01
☐	5 Larry Herndon	.05	.02	.00
☐	6 Al Oliver	.10	.05	.01
☐	7 Bill Buckner	.10	.05	.01
☐	8 Jason Thompson	.05	.02	.00
☐	9 Andre Dawson	.30	.15	.03
☐	10 Greg Minton	.05	.02	.00
☐	11 Terry Kennedy	.05	.02	.00
☐	12 Phil Niekro	.20	.10	.02
☐	13 Willie Wilson	.15	.07	.01
☐	14 Johnny Bench	.30	.15	.03
☐	15 Ron Guidry	.15	.07	.01
☐	16 Hal McRae	.05	.02	.00
☐	17 Damaso Garcia	.05	.02	.00
☐	18 Gary Ward	.05	.02	.00

			MINT	EXC	G-VG
☐	19	Cecil Cooper	.10	.05	.01
☐	20	Keith Hernandez	.25	.12	.02
☐	21	Ron Cey	.05	.02	.00
☐	22	Rickey Henderson	.40	.20	.04
☐	23	Nolan Ryan	.35	.17	.03
☐	24	Steve Carlton	.30	.15	.03
☐	25	John Stearns	.05	.02	.00
☐	26	Jim Sundberg	.05	.02	.00
☐	27	Joaquin Andujar	.05	.02	.00
☐	28	Gaylord Perry	.20	.10	.02
☐	29	Jack Clark	.20	.10	.02
☐	30	Bill Madlock	.10	.05	.01
☐	31	Pete Rose	.60	.30	.06
☐	32	Mookie Wilson	.05	.02	.00
☐	33	Rollie Fingers	.15	.07	.01
☐	34	Lonnie Smith	.05	.02	.00
☐	35	Tony Pena	.10	.05	.01
☐	36	Dave Winfield	.25	.12	.02
☐	37	Tim Lollar	.05	.02	.00
☐	38	Rod Carew	.30	.15	.03
☐	39	Toby Harrah	.05	.02	.00
☐	40	Buddy Bell	.05	.02	.00
☐	41	Bruce Sutter	.10	.05	.01
☐	42	George Brett	.50	.25	.05
☐	43	Carlton Fisk	.10	.05	.01
☐	44	Carl Yastrzemski	.50	.25	.05
☐	45	Dale Murphy	.50	.25	.05
☐	46	Bob Horner	.15	.07	.01
☐	47	Dave Concepcion	.10	.05	.01
☐	48	Dave Stieb	.15	.07	.01
☐	49	Kent Hrbek	.20	.10	.02
☐	50	Lance Parrish	.20	.10	.02
☐	51	Joe Niekro	.10	.05	.01
☐	52	Cal Ripken	.40	.20	.04
☐	53	Fernando Valenzuela	.30	.15	.03
☐	54	Richie Zisk	.05	.02	.00
☐	55	Leon Durham	.05	.02	.00
☐	56	Robin Yount	.30	.15	.03
☐	57	Mike Schmidt	.50	.25	.05
☐	58	Gary Carter	.45	.22	.04
☐	59	Fred Lynn	.15	.07	.01
☐	60	Checklist card	.10	.01	.00

☐	6	Jackie Robinson	.15	.07	.01
☐	7	Mickey Mantle	.50	.25	.05
☐	8	Luke Appling	.05	.02	.00
☐	9	Ted Williams	.15	.07	.01
☐	10	Johnny Mize	.05	.02	.00
☐	11	Satchel Paige	.05	.02	.00
☐	12	Lou Boudreau	.05	.02	.00
☐	13	Jimmie Foxx	.10	.05	.01
☐	14	Duke Snider	.15	.07	.01
☐	15	Monte Irvin	.05	.02	.00
☐	16	Hank Greenberg	.05	.02	.00
☐	17	Roberto Clemente	.15	.07	.01
☐	18	Al Kaline	.15	.07	.01
☐	19	Frank Robinson	.10	.05	.01
☐	20	Joe Cronin	.05	.02	.00
☐	21	Burleigh Grimes	.05	.02	.00
☐	22	The Waner Brothers	.05	.02	.00
		Paul Waner			
		Lloyd Waner			
☐	23	Grover Alexander	.05	.02	.00
☐	24	Yogi Berra	.15	.07	.01
☐	25	Cool Papa Bell	.05	.02	.00
☐	26	Bill Dickey	.05	.02	.00
☐	27	Cy Young	.10	.05	.01
☐	28	Charlie Gehringer	.05	.02	.00
☐	29	Dizzy Dean	.15	.07	.01
☐	30	Bob Lemon	.05	.02	.00
☐	31	Red Ruffing	.05	.02	.00
☐	32	Stan Musial	.15	.07	.01
☐	33	Carl Hubbell	.10	.05	.01
☐	34	Hank Aaron	.15	.07	.01
☐	35	John McGraw	.05	.02	.00
☐	36	Bob Feller	.15	.07	.01
☐	37	Casey Stengel	.10	.05	.01
☐	38	Ralph Kiner	.10	.05	.01
☐	39	Roy Campanella	.15	.07	.01
☐	40	Mel Ott	.10	.05	.01
☐	41	Robin Roberts	.10	.05	.01
☐	42	Early Wynn	.05	.02	.00
☐	43	Mantle Puzzle card	.05	.02	.00
☐	44	Checklist card	.05	.01	.00

1983 Donruss HOF Heroes

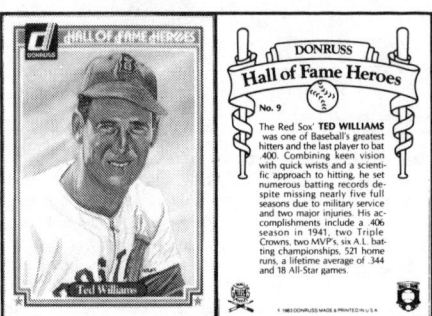

The cards in this 44-card set measure 2 1/2" by 3 1/2". Although it was issued with the same Mantle puzzle as the Action All Stars set, the Donruss Hall of Fame Heroes set is completely different in content and design. Of the 44 cards in the set, 42 are Dick Perez artwork portraying Hall of Fame members, while one card depicts the completed Mantle puzzle and the last card is a checklist. The red, white, and blue backs contain the card number and a short player biography. The cards were packaged 8 cards plus one puzzle card (3 pieces) for 30 cents in the summer of 1983.

		MINT	EXC	G-VG
COMPLETE SET		4.00	2.00	.40
COMMON PLAYER		.05	.02	.00
☐	1 Ty Cobb	.40	.20	.04
☐	2 Walter Johnson	.15	.07	.01
☐	3 Christy Mathewson	.15	.07	.01
☐	4 Josh Gibson	.15	.07	.01
☐	5 Honus Wagner	.15	.07	.01

1984 Donruss

The 1984 Donruss set contains a total of 660 cards, each measuring 2 1/2" by 3 1/2"; however, only 658 are numbered. The first 26 cards in the set are again Diamond Kings (DK) although the drawings this year were styled differently and are easily differentiated from other DK issues. A new feature, Rated Rookies (RR), was introduced with this set with Bill Madden's 20 selections comprising numbers 27 through 46. Two "Living Legend" cards designated A (featuring Gaylord Perry and Rollie Fingers) and B (featuring Johnny Bench and Carl Yastrzemski) were issued as bonus cards in wax packs, but were not issued in the vending sets sold to hobby dealers. The seven unnumbered checklist cards are arbitrarily assigned numbers 652 through 658 and are listed at the end of the list below. The designs on the fronts of the Donruss cards changed considerably from the past two years. The backs contain statistics and are printed in green and black ink. The cards were distributed with a 63-piece puzzle of Duke Snider.

		MINT	EXC	G-VG
	COMPLETE SET (658)	225.00	110.00	22.00
	COMMON PLAYER (1-660)	.09	.04	.01
☐ 1A	Robin Yount DK ERR (Perez Steel)	.75	.15	.03
☐ 1B	Robin Yount DK COR	1.50	.30	.06
☐ 2A	Dave Concepcion DK ERR (Perez Steel)	.15	.07	.01
☐ 2B	Dave Concepcion DK COR	.30	.15	.03
☐ 3A	Dwayne Murphy DK ERR (Perez Steel)	.15	.07	.01
☐ 3B	Dwayne Murphy DK COR	.30	.15	.03
☐ 4A	John Castino DK ERR (Perez Steel)	.15	.07	.01
☐ 4B	John Castino DK COR	.30	.15	.03
☐ 5A	Leon Durham DK ERR (Perez Steel)	.15	.07	.01
☐ 5B	Leon Durham DK COR	.30	.15	.03
☐ 6A	Rusty Staub DK ERR (Perez Steel)	.15	.07	.01
☐ 6B	Rusty Staub DK COR	.30	.15	.03
☐ 7A	Jack Clark DK ERR (Perez Steel)	.40	.20	.04
☐ 7B	Jack Clark DK COR	.80	.40	.08
☐ 8A	Dave Dravecky DK ERR (Perez Steel)	.15	.07	.01
☐ 8B	Dave Dravecky DK COR	.30	.15	.03
☐ 9A	Al Oliver DK ERR (Perez Steel)	.15	.07	.01
☐ 9B	Al Oliver DK COR	.30	.15	.03
☐ 10A	Dave Righetti DK ERR (Perez Steel)	.25	.12	.02
☐ 10B	Dave Righetti DK COR	.50	.25	.05
☐ 11A	Hal McRae DK ERR (Perez Steel)	.15	.07	.01
☐ 11B	Hal McRae DK COR	.30	.15	.03
☐ 12A	Ray Knight DK ERR (Perez Steel)	.15	.07	.01
☐ 12B	Ray Knight DK COR	.30	.15	.03
☐ 13A	Bruce Sutter DK ERR (Perez Steel)	.15	.07	.01
☐ 13B	Bruce Sutter DK COR	.30	.15	.03
☐ 14A	Bob Horner DK ERR (Perez Steel)	.25	.12	.02
☐ 14B	Bob Horner DK COR	.50	.25	.05
☐ 15A	Lance Parrish DK ERR (Perez Steel)	.30	.15	.03
☐ 15B	Lance Parrish DK COR	.60	.30	.06
☐ 16A	Matt Young DK ERR (Perez Steel)	.15	.07	.01
☐ 16B	Matt Young DK COR	.30	.15	.03
☐ 17A	Fred Lynn DK ERR (Perez Steel)	.20	.10	.02
☐ 17B	Fred Lynn DK COR	.40	.20	.04
☐ 18A	Ron Kittle DK ERR (Perez Steel)	.20	.10	.02
☐ 18B	Ron Kittle DK COR	.40	.20	.04
☐ 19A	Jim Clancy DK ERR (Perez Steel)	.15	.07	.01
☐ 19B	Jim Clancy DK COR	.30	.15	.03
☐ 20A	Bill Madlock DK ERR (Perez Steel)	.15	.07	.01
☐ 20B	Bill Madlock DK COR	.30	.15	.03
☐ 21A	Larry Parrish DK ERR (Perez Steel)	.15	.07	.01
☐ 21B	Larry Parrish DK COR	.30	.15	.03
☐ 22A	Eddie Murray DK ERR (Perez Steel)	1.00	.50	.10
☐ 22B	Eddie Murray DK COR	2.00	1.00	.20
☐ 23A	Mike Schmidt DK ERR (Perez Steel)	1.25	.60	.12
☐ 23B	Mike Schmidt DK COR	2.50	1.25	.25
☐ 24A	Pedro Guerrero DK ERR (Perez Steel)	.35	.17	.03
☐ 24B	Pedro Guerrero DK COR	.70	.35	.07
☐ 25A	Andre Thornton DK ERR (Perez Steel)	.15	.07	.01
☐ 25B	Andre Thornton DK COR	.30	.15	.03
☐ 26A	Wade Boggs DK ERR (Perez Steel)	3.00	1.50	.30
☐ 26B	Wade Boggs DK COR	6.00	3.00	.60
☐ 27	Joel Skinner RR	.25	.12	.02
☐ 28	Tommy Dunbar RR	.15	.07	.01
☐ 29A	Mike Stenhouse RR ERR (no back number)	.25	.12	.02

		MINT	EXC	G-VG
☐ 29B	Mike Stenhouse RR COR (number on back)	2.00	1.00	.20
☐ 30A	Ron Darling RR ERR (no number on back)	6.00	3.00	.60
☐ 30B	Ron Darling RR COR	10.00	5.00	1.00
☐ 31	Dion James RR	1.50	.75	.15
☐ 32	Tony Fernandez RR	7.50	3.75	.75
☐ 33	Angel Salazar RR	.15	.07	.01
☐ 34	Kevin McReynolds RR	7.50	3.75	.75
☐ 35	Dick Schofield RR	.75	.35	.07
☐ 36	Brad Komminsk RR	.25	.12	.02
☐ 37	Tim Teufel RR	.60	.30	.06
☐ 38	Doug Frobel RR	.15	.07	.01
☐ 39	Greg Gagne RR	.60	.30	.06
☐ 40	Mike Fuentes RR	.15	.07	.01
☐ 41	Joe Carter RR	9.00	4.50	.90
☐ 42	Mike Brown RR (Angels OF)	.25	.12	.02
☐ 43	Mike Jeffcoat RR	.15	.07	.01
☐ 44	Sid Fernandez RR	6.00	3.00	.60
☐ 45	Brian Dayett RR	.25	.12	.02
☐ 46	Chris Smith RR	.15	.07	.01
☐ 47	Eddie Murray	1.00	.50	.10
☐ 48	Robin Yount	.60	.30	.06
☐ 49	Lance Parrish	.35	.17	.03
☐ 50	Jim Rice	.60	.30	.06
☐ 51	Dave Winfield	.60	.30	.06
☐ 52	Fernando Valenzuela	.50	.25	.05
☐ 53	George Brett	1.00	.50	.10
☐ 54	Rickey Henderson	1.00	.50	.10
☐ 55	Gary Carter	.65	.30	.06
☐ 56	Buddy Bell	.15	.07	.01
☐ 57	Reggie Jackson	1.00	.50	.10
☐ 58	Harold Baines	.25	.12	.02
☐ 59	Ozzie Smith	.35	.17	.03
☐ 60	Nolan Ryan	.70	.35	.07
☐ 61	Pete Rose	2.50	1.25	.25
☐ 62	Ron Oester	.09	.04	.01
☐ 63	Steve Garvey	.70	.35	.07
☐ 64	Jason Thompson	.15	.07	.01
☐ 65	Jack Clark	.35	.17	.03
☐ 66	Dale Murphy	1.50	.75	.15
☐ 67	Leon Durham	.20	.10	.02
☐ 68	Darryl Strawberry	16.00	8.00	1.60
☐ 69	Richie Zisk	.09	.04	.01
☐ 70	Kent Hrbek	.45	.22	.04
☐ 71	Dave Stieb	.25	.12	.02
☐ 72	Ken Schrom	.15	.07	.01
☐ 73	George Bell	1.50	.75	.15
☐ 74	John Moses	.15	.07	.01
☐ 75	Ed Lynch	.09	.04	.01
☐ 76	Chuck Rainey	.09	.04	.01
☐ 77	Biff Pocoroba	.09	.04	.01
☐ 78	Cecilio Guante	.09	.04	.01
☐ 79	Jim Barr	.09	.04	.01
☐ 80	Kurt Bevacqua	.09	.04	.01
☐ 81	Tom Foley	.09	.04	.01
☐ 82	Joe Lefebvre	.09	.04	.01
☐ 83	Andy Van Slyke	1.50	.75	.15
☐ 84	Bob Lillis MG	.09	.04	.01
☐ 85	Rick Adams	.09	.04	.01
☐ 86	Jerry Hairston	.09	.04	.01
☐ 87	Bob James	.20	.10	.02
☐ 88	Joe Altobelli MG	.09	.04	.01
☐ 89	Ed Romero	.09	.04	.01
☐ 90	John Grubb	.09	.04	.01
☐ 91	John Henry Johnson	.09	.04	.01
☐ 92	Juan Espino	.09	.04	.01
☐ 93	Candy Maldonado	.30	.15	.03
☐ 94	Andre Thornton	.15	.07	.01
☐ 95	Onix Concepcion	.09	.04	.01
☐ 96	Donnie Hill (listed as P, should be 2B)	.15	.07	.01
☐ 97	Andre Dawson (wrong middle name, should be Nolan)	.45	.22	.04
☐ 98	Frank Tanana	.15	.07	.01
☐ 99	Curt Wilkerson	.15	.07	.01
☐ 100	Larry Gura	.15	.07	.01
☐ 101	Dwayne Murphy	.15	.07	.01
☐ 102	Tom Brennan	.09	.04	.01
☐ 103	Dave Righetti	.30	.15	.03
☐ 104	Steve Sax	.25	.12	.02
☐ 105	Dan Petry	.20	.10	.02
☐ 106	Cal Ripken	1.00	.50	.10
☐ 107	Paul Molitor	.25	.12	.02
☐ 108	Fred Lynn	.25	.12	.02
☐ 109	Neil Allen	.15	.07	.01
☐ 110	Joe Niekro	.15	.07	.01
☐ 111	Steve Carlton	.60	.30	.06
☐ 112	Terry Kennedy	.15	.07	.01
☐ 113	Bill Madlock	.20	.10	.02
☐ 114	Chili Davis	.20	.10	.02

☐ 115	Jim Gantner	.09	.04	.01	☐ 210	Al Bumbry	.09	.04	.01
☐ 116	Tom Seaver	.60	.30	.06	☐ 211	Mark Brouhard	.09	.04	.01
☐ 117	Bill Buckner	.20	.10	.02	☐ 212	Howard Bailey	.09	.04	.01
☐ 118	Bill Caudill	.09	.04	.01	☐ 213	Bruce Hurst	.20	.10	.02
☐ 119	Jim Clancy	.09	.04	.01	☐ 214	Bob Shirley	.09	.04	.01
☐ 120	John Castino	.09	.04	.01	☐ 215	Pat Zachry	.09	.04	.01
☐ 121	Dave Concepcion	.15	.07	.01	☐ 216	Julio Franco	.25	.12	.02
☐ 122	Greg Luzinski	.20	.10	.02	☐ 217	Mike Armstrong	.09	.04	.01
☐ 123	Mike Boddicker	.20	.10	.02	☐ 218	Dave Beard	.09	.04	.01
☐ 124	Pete Ladd	.09	.04	.01	☐ 219	Steve Rogers	.15	.07	.01
☐ 125	Juan Berenguer	.09	.04	.01	☐ 220	John Butcher	.09	.04	.01
☐ 126	John Montefusco	.09	.04	.01	☐ 221	Mike Smithson	.15	.07	.01
☐ 127	Ed Jurak	.09	.04	.01	☐ 222	Frank White	.15	.07	.01
☐ 128	Tom Niedenfuer	.15	.07	.01	☐ 223	Mike Heath	.09	.04	.01
☐ 129	Bert Blyleven	.20	.10	.02	☐ 224	Chris Bando	.09	.04	.01
☐ 130	Bud Black	.09	.04	.01	☐ 225	Roy Smalley	.09	.04	.01
☐ 131	Gorman Heimueller	.09	.04	.01	☐ 226	Dusty Baker	.15	.07	.01
☐ 132	Dan Schatzeder	.09	.04	.01	☐ 227	Lou Whitaker	.25	.12	.02
☐ 133	Ron Jackson	.09	.04	.01	☐ 228	John Lowenstein	.09	.04	.01
☐ 134	Tom Henke	1.00	.50	.10	☐ 229	Ben Oglivie	.15	.07	.01
☐ 135	Kevin Hickey	.09	.04	.01	☐ 230	Doug DeCinces	.15	.07	.01
☐ 136	Mike Scott	.40	.20	.04	☐ 231	Lonnie Smith	.15	.07	.01
☐ 137	Bo Diaz	.15	.07	.01	☐ 232	Ray Knight	.15	.07	.01
☐ 138	Glenn Brummer	.09	.04	.01	☐ 233	Gary Matthews	.15	.07	.01
☐ 139	Sid Monge	.09	.04	.01	☐ 234	Juan Bonilla	.09	.04	.01
☐ 140	Rich Gale	.09	.04	.01	☐ 235	Rod Scurry	.09	.04	.01
☐ 141	Brett Butler	.20	.10	.02	☐ 236	Atlee Hammaker	.15	.07	.01
☐ 142	Brian Harper	.09	.04	.01	☐ 237	Mike Caldwell	.09	.04	.01
☐ 143	John Rabb	.09	.04	.01	☐ 238	Keith Hernandez	.35	.17	.03
☐ 144	Gary Woods	.09	.04	.01	☐ 239	Larry Bowa	.15	.07	.01
☐ 145	Pat Putnam	.09	.04	.01	☐ 240	Tony Bernazard	.09	.04	.01
☐ 146	Jim Acker	.20	.10	.02	☐ 241	Damaso Garcia	.09	.04	.01
☐ 147	Mickey Hatcher	.09	.04	.01	☐ 242	Tom Brunansky	.25	.12	.02
☐ 148	Todd Cruz	.09	.04	.01	☐ 243	Dan Driessen	.09	.04	.01
☐ 149	Tom Tellmann	.09	.04	.01	☐ 244	Ron Kittle	.25	.12	.02
☐ 150	John Wockenfuss	.09	.04	.01	☐ 245	Tim Stoddard	.09	.04	.01
☐ 151	Wade Boggs	10.00	5.00	1.00	☐ 246	Bob L. Gibson	.09	.04	.01
☐ 152	Don Baylor	.15	.07	.01		(Brewers Pitcher)			
☐ 153	Bob Welch	.15	.07	.01	☐ 247	Marty Castillo	.09	.04	.01
☐ 154	Alan Bannister	.09	.04	.01	☐ 248	Don Mattingly	75.00	37.50	7.50
☐ 155	Willie Aikens	.09	.04	.01		("traiing" on back)			
☐ 156	Jeff Burroughs	.09	.04	.01	☐ 249	Jeff Newman	.09	.04	.01
☐ 157	Bryan Little	.09	.04	.01	☐ 250	Alejandro Pena	.30	.15	.03
☐ 158	Bob Boone	.15	.07	.01	☐ 251	Toby Harrah	.15	.07	.01
☐ 159	Dave Hostetler	.09	.04	.01	☐ 252	Cesar Geronimo	.09	.04	.01
☐ 160	Jerry Dybzinski	.09	.04	.01	☐ 253	Tom Underwood	.09	.04	.01
☐ 161	Mike Madden	.15	.07	.01	☐ 254	Doug Flynn	.09	.04	.01
☐ 162	Luis DeLeon	.09	.04	.01	☐ 255	Andy Hassler	.09	.04	.01
☐ 163	Willie Hernandez	.30	.15	.03	☐ 256	Odell Jones	.09	.04	.01
☐ 164	Frank Pastore	.09	.04	.01	☐ 257	Rudy Law	.09	.04	.01
☐ 165	Rick Camp	.09	.04	.01	☐ 258	Harry Spilman	.09	.04	.01
☐ 166	Lee Mazzilli	.15	.07	.01	☐ 259	Marty Bystrom	.09	.04	.01
☐ 167	Scot Thompson	.09	.04	.01	☐ 260	Dave Rucker	.09	.04	.01
☐ 168	Bob Forsch	.15	.07	.01	☐ 261	Ruppert Jones	.09	.04	.01
☐ 169	Mike Flanagan	.15	.07	.01	☐ 262	Jeff R. Jones	.09	.04	.01
☐ 170	Rick Manning	.09	.04	.01		(Reds OF)			
☐ 171	Chet Lemon	.15	.07	.01	☐ 263	Gerald Perry	.60	.30	.06
☐ 172	Jerry Remy	.09	.04	.01	☐ 264	Gene Tenace	.09	.04	.01
☐ 173	Ron Guidry	.25	.12	.02	☐ 265	Brad Wellman	.09	.04	.01
☐ 174	Pedro Guerrero	.40	.20	.04	☐ 266	Dickie Noles	.09	.04	.01
☐ 175	Willie Wilson	.25	.12	.02	☐ 267	Jamie Allen	.09	.04	.01
☐ 176	Carney Lansford	.20	.10	.02	☐ 268	Jim Gott	.15	.07	.01
☐ 177	Al Oliver	.20	.10	.02	☐ 269	Ron Davis	.09	.04	.01
☐ 178	Jim Sundberg	.09	.04	.01	☐ 270	Benny Ayala	.09	.04	.01
☐ 179	Bobby Grich	.15	.07	.01	☐ 271	Ned Yost	.09	.04	.01
☐ 180	Rich Dotson	.15	.07	.01	☐ 272	Dave Rozema	.09	.04	.01
☐ 181	Joaquin Andujar	.15	.07	.01	☐ 273	Dave Stapleton	.09	.04	.01
☐ 182	Jose Cruz	.15	.07	.01	☐ 274	Lou Piniella	.15	.07	.01
☐ 183	Mike Schmidt	1.25	.60	.12	☐ 275	Jose Morales	.09	.04	.01
☐ 184	Gary Redus	.45	.22	.04	☐ 276	Brod Perkins	.09	.04	.01
☐ 185	Garry Templeton	.15	.07	.01	☐ 277	Butch Davis	.15	.07	.01
☐ 186	Tony Pena	.20	.10	.02	☐ 278	Tony Phillips	.15	.07	.01
☐ 187	Greg Minton	.09	.04	.01	☐ 279	Jeff Reardon	.20	.10	.02
☐ 188	Phil Niekro	.35	.17	.03	☐ 280	Ken Forsch	.09	.04	.01
☐ 189	Ferguson Jenkins	.20	.10	.02	☐ 281	Pete O'Brien	2.00	1.00	.20
☐ 190	Mookie Wilson	.15	.07	.01	☐ 282	Tom Paciorek	.09	.04	.01
☐ 191	Jim Beattie	.09	.04	.01	☐ 283	Frank LaCorte	.09	.04	.01
☐ 192	Gary Ward	.15	.07	.01	☐ 284	Tim Lollar	.09	.04	.01
☐ 193	Jesse Barfield	.50	.25	.05	☐ 285	Greg Gross	.09	.04	.01
☐ 194	Pete Filson	.09	.04	.01	☐ 286	Alex Trevino	.09	.04	.01
☐ 195	Roy Lee Jackson	.09	.04	.01	☐ 287	Gene Garber	.09	.04	.01
☐ 196	Rick Sweet	.09	.04	.01	☐ 288	Dave Parker	.30	.15	.03
☐ 197	Jesse Orosco	.15	.07	.01	☐ 289	Lee Smith	.20	.10	.02
☐ 198	Steve Lake	.09	.04	.01	☐ 290	Dave LaPoint	.09	.04	.01
☐ 199	Ken Dayley	.15	.07	.01	☐ 291	John Shelby	.35	.17	.03
☐ 200	Manny Sarmiento	.09	.04	.01	☐ 292	Charlie Moore	.09	.04	.01
☐ 201	Mark Davis	.09	.04	.01	☐ 293	Alan Trammell	.45	.22	.04
☐ 202	Tim Flannery	.09	.04	.01	☐ 294	Tony Armas	.15	.07	.01
☐ 203	Bill Scherrer	.15	.07	.01	☐ 295	Shane Rawley	.15	.07	.01
☐ 204	Al Holland	.09	.04	.01	☐ 296	Greg Brock	.15	.07	.01
☐ 205	Dave Von Ohlen	.09	.04	.01	☐ 297	Hal McRae	.15	.07	.01
☐ 206	Mike LaCoss	.09	.04	.01	☐ 298	Mike Davis	.15	.07	.01
☐ 207	Juan Beniquez	.09	.04	.01	☐ 299	Tim Raines	.60	.30	.06
☐ 208	Juan Agosto	.09	.04	.01	☐ 300	Bucky Dent	.15	.07	.01
☐ 209	Bobby Ramos	.09	.04	.01	☐ 301	Tommy John	.25	.12	.02

302	Carlton Fisk	.20	.10	.02
303	Darrell Porter	.09	.04	.01
304	Dickie Thon	.15	.07	.01
305	Garry Maddox	.09	.04	.01
306	Cesar Cedeno	.15	.07	.01
307	Gary Lucas	.09	.04	.01
308	Johnny Ray	.25	.12	.02
309	Andy McGaffigan	.09	.04	.01
310	Claudell Washington	.15	.07	.01
311	Ryne Sandberg	2.00	1.00	.20
312	George Foster	.25	.12	.02
313	Spike Owen	.30	.15	.03
314	Gary Gaetti	.50	.25	.05
315	Willie Upshaw	.15	.07	.01
316	Al Williams	.09	.04	.01
317	Jorge Orta	.09	.04	.01
318	Orlando Mercado	.09	.04	.01
319	Junior Ortiz	.09	.04	.01
320	Mike Proly	.09	.04	.01
321	Randy Johnson	.09	.04	.01
322	Jim Morrison	.09	.04	.01
323	Max Venable	.09	.04	.01
324	Tony Gwynn	3.00	1.50	.30
325	Duane Walker	.09	.04	.01
326	Ozzie Virgil	.09	.04	.01
327	Jeff Lahti	.09	.04	.01
328	Bill Dawley	.15	.07	.01
329	Rob Wilfong	.09	.04	.01
330	Marc Hill	.09	.04	.01
331	Ray Burris	.09	.04	.01
332	Allan Ramirez	.09	.04	.01
333	Chuck Porter	.09	.04	.01
334	Wayne Krenchicki	.09	.04	.01
335	Gary Allenson	.09	.04	.01
336	Bobby Meacham	.20	.10	.02
337	Joe Beckwith	.09	.04	.01
338	Rick Sutcliffe	.20	.10	.02
339	Mark Huismann	.15	.07	.01
340	Tim Conroy	.15	.07	.01
341	Scott Sanderson	.09	.04	.01
342	Larry Biittner	.09	.04	.01
343	Dave Stewart	.15	.07	.01
344	Darryl Motley	.09	.04	.01
345	Chris Codiroli	.15	.07	.01
346	Rich Behenna	.09	.04	.01
347	Andre Robertson	.09	.04	.01
348	Mike Marshall	.20	.10	.02
349	Larry Herndon	.09	.04	.01
350	Rich Dauer	.09	.04	.01
351	Cecil Cooper	.15	.07	.01
352	Rod Carew	.60	.30	.06
353	Willie McGee	.40	.20	.04
354	Phil Garner	.09	.04	.01
355	Joe Morgan	.35	.17	.03
356	Luis Salazar	.09	.04	.01
357	John Candelaria	.15	.07	.01
358	Bill Laskey	.09	.04	.01
359	Bob McClure	.09	.04	.01
360	Dave Kingman	.20	.10	.02
361	Ron Cey	.15	.07	.01
362	Matt Young	.20	.10	.02
363	Lloyd Moseby	.20	.10	.02
364	Frank Viola	.40	.20	.04
365	Eddie Milner	.15	.07	.01
366	Floyd Bannister	.15	.07	.01
367	Dan Ford	.09	.04	.01
368	Moose Haas	.09	.04	.01
369	Doug Bair	.09	.04	.01
370	Ray Fontenot	.15	.07	.01
371	Luis Aponte	.09	.04	.01
372	Jack Fimple	.09	.04	.01
373	Neal Heaton	.25	.12	.02
374	Greg Pryor	.09	.04	.01
375	Wayne Gross	.09	.04	.01
376	Charlie Lea	.09	.04	.01
377	Steve Lubratich	.09	.04	.01
378	Jon Matlack	.15	.07	.01
379	Julio Cruz	.09	.04	.01
380	John Mizerock	.09	.04	.01
381	Kevin Gross	.25	.12	.02
382	Mike Ramsey	.09	.04	.01
383	Doug Gwosdz	.09	.04	.01
384	Kelly Paris	.15	.07	.01
385	Pete Falcone	.09	.04	.01
386	Milt May	.09	.04	.01
387	Fred Breining	.09	.04	.01
388	Craig Lefferts	.15	.07	.01
389	Steve Henderson	.09	.04	.01
390	Randy Moffitt	.09	.04	.01
391	Ron Washington	.09	.04	.01
392	Gary Roenicke	.09	.04	.01
393	Tom Candiotti	.25	.12	.02
394	Larry Pashnick	.09	.04	.01
395	Dwight Evans	.25	.12	.02
396	Goose Gossage	.20	.10	.02
397	Derrel Thomas	.09	.04	.01
398	Juan Eichelberger	.09	.04	.01
399	Leon Roberts	.09	.04	.01
400	Davey Lopes	.15	.07	.01
401	Bill Gullickson	.15	.07	.01
402	Geoff Zahn	.09	.04	.01
403	Billy Sample	.09	.04	.01
404	Mike Squires	.09	.04	.01
405	Craig Reynolds	.09	.04	.01
406	Eric Show	.09	.04	.01
407	John Denny	.15	.07	.01
408	Dann Bilardello	.09	.04	.01
409	Bruce Benedict	.09	.04	.01
410	Kent Tekulve	.15	.07	.01
411	Mel Hall	.15	.07	.01
412	John Stuper	.09	.04	.01
413	Rick Dempsey	.15	.07	.01
414	Don Sutton	.35	.17	.03
415	Jack Morris	.30	.15	.03
416	John Tudor	.25	.12	.02
417	Willie Randolph	.15	.07	.01
418	Jerry Reuss	.15	.07	.01
419	Don Slaught	.15	.07	.01
420	Steve McCatty	.09	.04	.01
421	Tim Wallach	.25	.12	.02
422	Larry Parrish	.15	.07	.01
423	Brian Downing	.15	.07	.01
424	Britt Burns	.15	.07	.01
425	David Green	.15	.07	.01
426	Jerry Mumphrey	.09	.04	.01
427	Ivan DeJesus	.09	.04	.01
428	Mario Soto	.15	.07	.01
429	Gene Richards	.09	.04	.01
430	Dale Berra	.09	.04	.01
431	Darrell Evans	.20	.10	.02
432	Glenn Hubbard	.09	.04	.01
433	Jody Davis	.20	.10	.02
434	Danny Heep	.09	.04	.01
435	Ed Nunez	.25	.12	.02
436	Bobby Castillo	.09	.04	.01
437	Ernie Whitt	.09	.04	.01
438	Scott Ullger	.09	.04	.01
439	Doyle Alexander	.15	.07	.01
440	Domingo Ramos	.09	.04	.01
441	Craig Swan	.09	.04	.01
442	Warren Brusstar	.09	.04	.01
443	Len Barker	.09	.04	.01
444	Mike Easler	.15	.07	.01
445	Renie Martin	.09	.04	.01
446	Dennis Rasmussen	.45	.22	.04
447	Ted Power	.20	.10	.02
448	Charlie Hudson	.30	.15	.03
449	Danny Cox	1.25	.60	.12
450	Kevin Bass	.30	.15	.03
451	Daryl Sconiers	.09	.04	.01
452	Scott Fletcher	.15	.07	.01
453	Bryn Smith	.15	.07	.01
454	Jim Dwyer	.09	.04	.01
455	Rob Picciolo	.09	.04	.01
456	Enos Cabell	.09	.04	.01
457	Dennis Boyd	1.00	.50	.10
458	Butch Wynegar	.09	.04	.01
459	Burt Hooton	.09	.04	.01
460	Ron Hassey	.09	.04	.01
461	Danny Jackson	.65	.30	.06
462	Bob Kearney	.09	.04	.01
463	Terry Francona	.15	.07	.01
464	Wayne Tolleson	.09	.04	.01
465	Mickey Rivers	.15	.07	.01
466	John Wathan	.15	.07	.01
467	Bill Almon	.09	.04	.01
468	George Vukovich	.09	.04	.01
469	Steve Kemp	.15	.07	.01
470	Ken Landreaux	.09	.04	.01
471	Milt Wilcox	.09	.04	.01
472	Tippy Martinez	.09	.04	.01
473	Ted Simmons	.15	.07	.01
474	Tim Foli	.09	.04	.01
475	George Hendrick	.15	.07	.01
476	Terry Puhl	.15	.07	.01
477	Von Hayes	.25	.12	.02
478	Bobby Brown	.09	.04	.01
479	Lee Lacy	.15	.07	.01
480	Joel Youngblood	.09	.04	.01
481	Jim Slaton	.09	.04	.01
482	Mike Fitzgerald	.15	.07	.01
483	Keith Moreland	.15	.07	.01
484	Ron Roenicke	.09	.04	.01
485	Luis Leal	.09	.04	.01
486	Bryan Oelkers	.09	.04	.01
487	Bruce Berenyi	.09	.04	.01
488	LaMarr Hoyt	.15	.07	.01
489	Joe Nolan	.09	.04	.01
490	Marshall Edwards	.09	.04	.01
491	Mike Laga	.15	.07	.01

☐ 492	Rick Cerone	.09	.04	.01
☐ 493	Rick Miller	.15	.07	.01
	(listed as Mike			
	on card front)			
☐ 494	Rick Honeycutt	.15	.07	.01
☐ 495	Mike Hargrove	.15	.07	.01
☐ 496	Joe Simpson	.09	.04	.01
☐ 497	Keith Atherton	.09	.04	.01
☐ 498	Chris Welsh	.09	.04	.01
☐ 499	Bruce Kison	.09	.04	.01
☐ 500	Bobby Johnson	.09	.04	.01
☐ 501	Jerry Koosman	.15	.07	.01
☐ 502	Frank DiPino	.09	.04	.01
☐ 503	Tony Perez	.20	.10	.02
☐ 504	Ken Oberkfell	.09	.04	.01
☐ 505	Mark Thurmond	.20	.10	.02
☐ 506	Joe Price	.09	.04	.01
☐ 507	Pascual Perez	.09	.04	.01
☐ 508	Marvell Wynne	.15	.07	.01
☐ 509	Mike Krukow	.15	.07	.01
☐ 510	Dick Ruthven	.09	.04	.01
☐ 511	Al Cowens	.09	.04	.01
☐ 512	Cliff Johnson	.09	.04	.01
☐ 513	Randy Bush	.09	.04	.01
☐ 514	Sammy Stewart	.09	.04	.01
☐ 515	Bill Schroeder	.20	.10	.02
☐ 516	Aurelio Lopez	.09	.04	.01
☐ 517	Mike Brown	.15	.07	.01
	(Red Sox pitcher)			
☐ 518	Graig Nettles	.20	.10	.02
☐ 519	Dave Sax	.09	.04	.01
☐ 520	Gerry Willard	.15	.07	.01
☐ 521	Paul Splittorff	.15	.07	.01
☐ 522	Tom Burgmeier	.09	.04	.01
☐ 523	Chris Speier	.09	.04	.01
☐ 524	Bobby Clark	.09	.04	.01
☐ 525	George Wright	.09	.04	.01
☐ 526	Dennis Lamp	.09	.04	.01
☐ 527	Tony Scott	.09	.04	.01
☐ 528	Ed Whitson	.15	.07	.01
☐ 529	Ron Reed	.09	.04	.01
☐ 530	Charlie Puleo	.09	.04	.01
☐ 531	Jerry Royster	.09	.04	.01
☐ 532	Don Robinson	.09	.04	.01
☐ 533	Steve Trout	.15	.07	.01
☐ 534	Bruce Sutter	.25	.12	.02
☐ 535	Bob Horner	.25	.12	.02
☐ 536	Pat Tabler	.20	.10	.02
☐ 537	Chris Chambliss	.15	.07	.01
☐ 538	Bob Ojeda	.20	.10	.02
☐ 539	Alan Ashby	.09	.04	.01
☐ 540	Jay Johnstone	.15	.07	.01
☐ 541	Bob Dernier	.15	.07	.01
☐ 542	Brook Jacoby	2.50	1.25	.25
☐ 543	U.L. Washington	.09	.04	.01
☐ 544	Danny Darwin	.09	.04	.01
☐ 545	Kiko Garcia	.09	.04	.01
☐ 546	Vance Law	.09	.04	.01
☐ 547	Tug McGraw	.20	.10	.02
☐ 548	Dave Smith	.15	.07	.01
☐ 549	Len Matuszek	.09	.04	.01
☐ 550	Tom Hume	.09	.04	.01
☐ 551	Dave Dravecky	.20	.10	.02
☐ 552	Rick Rhoden	.15	.07	.01
☐ 553	Duane Kuiper	.09	.04	.01
☐ 554	Rusty Staub	.20	.10	.02
☐ 555	Bill Campbell	.09	.04	.01
☐ 556	Mike Torrez	.09	.04	.01
☐ 557	Dave Henderson	.09	.04	.01
☐ 558	Len Whitehouse	.09	.04	.01
☐ 559	Barry Bonnell	.09	.04	.01
☐ 560	Rick Lysander	.09	.04	.01
☐ 561	Garth Iorg	.09	.04	.01
☐ 562	Bryan Clark	.09	.04	.01
☐ 563	Brian Giles	.09	.04	.01
☐ 564	Vern Ruhle	.09	.04	.01
☐ 565	Steve Bedrosian	.30	.15	.03
☐ 566	Larry McWilliams	.09	.04	.01
☐ 567	Jeff Leonard	.25	.12	.02
☐ 568	Alan Wiggins	.15	.07	.01
☐ 569	Jeff Russell	.15	.07	.01
☐ 570	Salome Barojas	.09	.04	.01
☐ 571	Dane Iorg	.09	.04	.01
☐ 572	Bob Knepper	.15	.07	.01
☐ 573	Gary Lavelle	.09	.04	.01
☐ 574	Gorman Thomas	.15	.07	.01
☐ 575	Manny Trillo	.09	.04	.01
☐ 576	Jim Palmer	.40	.20	.04
☐ 577	Dale Murray	.09	.04	.01
☐ 578	Tom Brookens	.09	.04	.01
☐ 579	Rich Gedman	.20	.10	.02
☐ 580	Bill Doran	1.50	.75	.15
☐ 581	Steve Yeager	.09	.04	.01
☐ 582	Dan Spillner	.09	.04	.01
☐ 583	Dan Quisenberry	.20	.10	.02

☐ 584	Rance Mulliniks	.09	.04	.01
☐ 585	Storm Davis	.15	.07	.01
☐ 586	Dave Schmidt	.15	.07	.01
☐ 587	Bill Russell	.15	.07	.01
☐ 588	Pat Sheridan	.25	.12	.02
☐ 589	Rafael Ramirez	.15	.07	.01
	ERR (A's on front)			
☐ 590	Bud Anderson	.09	.04	.01
☐ 591	George Frazier	.09	.04	.01
☐ 592	Lee Tunnell	.20	.10	.02
☐ 593	Kirk Gibson	.35	.17	.03
☐ 594	Scott McGregor	.15	.07	.01
☐ 595	Bob Bailor	.09	.04	.01
☐ 596	Tommy Herr	.15	.07	.01
☐ 597	Luis Sanchez	.09	.04	.01
☐ 598	Dave Engle	.09	.04	.01
☐ 599	Craig McMurtry	.15	.07	.01
☐ 600	Carlos Diaz	.09	.04	.01
☐ 601	Tom O'Malley	.09	.04	.01
☐ 602	Nick Esasky	.45	.22	.04
☐ 603	Ron Hodges	.09	.04	.01
☐ 604	Ed VandeBerg	.09	.04	.01
☐ 605	Alfredo Griffin	.15	.07	.01
☐ 606	Glenn Hoffman	.09	.04	.01
☐ 607	Hubie Brooks	.20	.10	.02
☐ 608	Richard Barnes	.09	.04	.01
☐ 609	Greg Walker	1.00	.50	.10
☐ 610	Ken Singleton	.15	.07	.01
☐ 611	Mark Clear	.09	.04	.01
☐ 612	Buck Martinez	.09	.04	.01
☐ 613	Ken Griffey	.15	.07	.01
☐ 614	Reid Nichols	.09	.04	.01
☐ 615	Doug Sisk	.15	.07	.01
☐ 616	Bob Brenly	.15	.07	.01
☐ 617	Joey McLaughlin	.09	.04	.01
☐ 618	Glenn Wilson	.25	.12	.02
☐ 619	Bob Stoddard	.09	.04	.01
☐ 620	Lenn Sakata	.09	.04	.01
☐ 621	Mike Young	.75	.35	.07
☐ 622	John Stefero	.15	.07	.01
☐ 623	Carmelo Martinez	.35	.17	.03
☐ 624	Dave Bergman	.09	.04	.01
☐ 625	Runnin' Reds	.20	.10	.02
	(sic, Redbirds)			
	David Green			
	Willie McGee			
	Lonnie Smith			
	Ozzie Smith			
☐ 626	Rudy May	.09	.04	.01
☐ 627	Matt Keough	.09	.04	.01
☐ 628	Jose DeLeon	.30	.15	.03
☐ 629	Jim Essian	.09	.04	.01
☐ 630	Darnell Coles	.60	.30	.06
☐ 631	Mike Warren	.15	.07	.01
☐ 632	Del Crandall MG	.09	.04	.01
☐ 633	Dennis Martinez	.15	.07	.01
☐ 634	Mike Moore	.15	.07	.01
☐ 635	Lary Sorensen	.09	.04	.01
☐ 636	Rick Nelson	.15	.07	.01
☐ 637	Omar Moreno	.09	.04	.01
☐ 638	Charlie Hough	.15	.07	.01
☐ 639	Dennis Eckersley	.15	.07	.01
☐ 640	Walt Terrell	.45	.22	.04
☐ 641	Denny Walling	.09	.04	.01
☐ 642	Dave Anderson	.15	.07	.01
☐ 643	Jose Oquendo	.30	.15	.03
☐ 644	Bob Stanley	.15	.07	.01
☐ 645	Dave Geisel	.09	.04	.01
☐ 646	Scott Garrelts	.60	.30	.06
☐ 647	Gary Pettis	.60	.30	.06
☐ 648	Duke Snider	.15	.07	.01
	Puzzle Card			
☐ 649	Johnnie LeMaster	.09	.04	.01
☐ 650	Dave Collins	.15	.07	.01
☐ 651	The Chicken	.25	.12	.02
☐ 652	DK Checklist	.10	.01	.00
	(unnumbered)			
☐ 653	Checklist 1-130	.08	.01	.00
	(unnumbered)			
☐ 654	Checklist 131-234	.08	.01	.00
	(unnumbered)			
☐ 655	Checklist 235-338	.08	.01	.00
	(unnumbered)			
☐ 656	Checklist 339-442	.08	.01	.00
	(unnumbered)			
☐ 657	Checklist 443-546	.08	.01	.00
	(unnumbered)			
☐ 658	Checklist 547-651	.08	.01	.00
	(unnumbered)			
☐ A	Living Legends A	2.50	1.25	.25
	Gaylord Perry			
	Rollie Fingers			
☐ B	Living Legends B	4.00	2.00	.40
	Carl Yastrzemski			
	Johnny Bench			

1984 Donruss Action All-Stars

		50	Eddie Murray	.45	.22	.04
☐	51	Ron Guidry	.20	.10	.02
☐	52	Jim Rice	.30	.15	.03
☐	53	Tom Seaver	.35	.17	.03
☐	54	Pete Rose	.75	.35	.07
☐	55	George Brett	.50	.25	.05
☐	56	Dan Quisenberry	.15	.07	.01
☐	57	Mike Schmidt	.50	.25	.05
☐	58	Ted Simmons	.10	.05	.01
☐	59	Dave Righetti	.20	.10	.02
☐	60	Checklist card	.10	.01	.00

1984 Donruss Champions

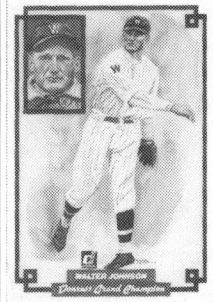
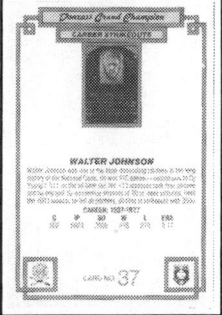

The cards in this 60-card set measure 3 1/2" by 5". For the second year in a row, Donruss issued a postcard-size card set. The set was distributed with a 63-piece Ted Williams puzzle. Unlike last year, when the fronts of the cards contained both an action and a portrait shot of the player, the fronts of this year's cards contain only an action photo. On the backs, the top section contains the card number and a full-color portrait of the player pictured on the front. The bottom half features the player's career statistics.

	MINT	EXC	G-VG
COMPLETE SET	6.00	3.00	.60
COMMON PLAYER	.05	.02	.00

			MINT	EXC	G-VG
☐	1	Gary Lavelle	.05	.02	.00
☐	2	Willie McGee	.15	.07	.01
☐	3	Tony Pena	.10	.05	.01
☐	4	Lou Whitaker	.15	.07	.01
☐	5	Robin Yount	.25	.12	.02
☐	6	Doug DeCinces	.05	.02	.00
☐	7	John Castino	.05	.02	.00
☐	8	Terry Kennedy	.05	.02	.00
☐	9	Rickey Henderson	.40	.20	.04
☐	10	Bob Horner	.20	.10	.02
☐	11	Harold Baines	.15	.07	.01
☐	12	Buddy Bell	.05	.02	.00
☐	13	Fernando Valenzuela	.30	.15	.03
☐	14	Nolan Ryan	.35	.17	.03
☐	15	Andre Thornton	.05	.02	.00
☐	16	Gary Redus	.05	.02	.00
☐	17	Pedro Guerrero	.25	.12	.02
☐	18	Andre Dawson	.30	.15	.03
☐	19	Dave Stieb	.10	.05	.01
☐	20	Cal Ripken	.40	.20	.04
☐	21	Ken Griffey	.05	.02	.00
☐	22	Wade Boggs	1.00	.50	.10
☐	23	Keith Hernandez	.25	.12	.02
☐	24	Steve Carlton	.35	.17	.03
☐	25	Hal McRae	.05	.02	.00
☐	26	John Lowenstein	.05	.02	.00
☐	27	Fred Lynn	.15	.07	.01
☐	28	Bill Buckner	.10	.05	.01
☐	29	Chris Chambliss	.05	.02	.00
☐	30	Richie Zisk	.05	.02	.00
☐	31	Jack Clark	.20	.10	.02
☐	32	George Hendrick	.05	.02	.00
☐	33	Bill Madlock	.10	.05	.01
☐	34	Lance Parrish	.20	.10	.02
☐	35	Paul Molitor	.20	.10	.02
☐	36	Reggie Jackson	.50	.25	.05
☐	37	Kent Hrbek	.20	.10	.02
☐	38	Steve Garvey	.40	.20	.04
☐	39	Carney Lansford	.10	.05	.01
☐	40	Dale Murphy	.60	.30	.06
☐	41	Greg Luzinski	.10	.05	.01
☐	42	Larry Parrish	.05	.02	.00
☐	43	Ryne Sandberg	.50	.25	.05
☐	44	Dickie Thon	.05	.02	.00
☐	45	Bert Blyleven	.10	.05	.01
☐	46	Ron Oester	.05	.02	.00
☐	47	Dusty Baker	.05	.02	.00
☐	48	Steve Rogers	.05	.02	.00
☐	49	Jim Clancy	.05	.02	.00

The cards in this 60-card set measure 3 1/2" by 5". The 1984 Donruss Champions set is a hybrid photo/artwork issue. Grand Champions, listed GC in the checklist below, feature the artwork of Dick Perez of Perez-Steele Galleries. Current players in the set feature photographs. The theme of this postcard-size set features a Grand Champion and those current players that are directly behind him in a baseball statistical category, for example, Season Home Runs (1-7), Career Home Runs (8-13), Season Batting Average (14-19), Career Batting Average (20-25), Career Hits (26-30), Career Victories (31-36), Career Strikeouts (37-42), Most Valuable Players (43-49), World Series stars (50-54), and All-Star heroes (55-59). The cards were issued in cello packs with pieces of the Duke Snider puzzle.

	MINT	EXC	G-VG
COMPLETE SET	6.00	3.00	.60
COMMON PLAYER	.05	.02	.00

			MINT	EXC	G-VG
☐	1	Babe Ruth GC	.60	.30	.06
☐	2	George Foster	.10	.05	.01
☐	3	Dave Kingman	.10	.05	.01
☐	4	Jim Rice	.30	.15	.03
☐	5	Gorman Thomas	.05	.02	.00
☐	6	Ben Oglivie	.05	.02	.00
☐	7	Jeff Burroughs	.05	.02	.00
☐	8	Hank Aaron GC	.30	.15	.03
☐	9	Reggie Jackson	.40	.20	.04
☐	10	Carl Yastrzemski	.40	.20	.04
☐	11	Mike Schmidt	.40	.20	.04
☐	12	Graig Nettles	.10	.05	.01
☐	13	Greg Luzinski	.05	.02	.00
☐	14	Ted Williams GC	.35	.17	.03
☐	15	George Brett	.40	.20	.04
☐	16	Wade Boggs	.75	.35	.07
☐	17	Hal McRae	.05	.02	.00
☐	18	Bill Buckner	.10	.05	.01
☐	19	Eddie Murray	.35	.17	.03
☐	20	Rogers Hornsby GC	.10	.05	.01
☐	21	Rod Carew	.30	.15	.03
☐	22	Bill Madlock	.10	.05	.01
☐	23	Lonnie Smith	.05	.02	.00
☐	24	Cecil Cooper	.10	.05	.01
☐	25	Ken Griffey	.05	.02	.00
☐	26	Ty Cobb GC	.40	.20	.04
☐	27	Pete Rose	.60	.30	.06
☐	28	Rusty Staub	.05	.02	.00
☐	29	Tony Perez	.15	.07	.01
☐	30	Al Oliver	.10	.05	.01

			MINT	EXC	G-VG
☐	31	Cy Young GC	.10	.05	.01
☐	32	Gaylord Perry	.15	.07	.01
☐	33	Ferguson Jenkins	.10	.05	.01
☐	34	Phil Niekro	.20	.10	.02
☐	35	Jim Palmer	.25	.12	.02
☐	36	Tommy John	.10	.05	.01
☐	37	Walter Johnson GC	.15	.07	.01
☐	38	Steve Carlton	.30	.15	.03
☐	39	Nolan Ryan	.35	.17	.03
☐	40	Tom Seaver	.35	.17	.03
☐	41	Don Sutton	.15	.07	.01
☐	42	Bert Blyleven	.10	.05	.01
☐	43	Frank Robinson GC	.15	.07	.01
☐	44	Joe Morgan	.15	.07	.01
☐	45	Rollie Fingers	.15	.07	.01
☐	46	Keith Hernandez	.25	.12	.02
☐	47	Robin Yount	.25	.12	.02
☐	48	Cal Ripken	.30	.15	.03
☐	49	Dale Murphy	.50	.25	.05
☐	50	Mickey Mantle GC	.60	.30	.06
☐	51	Johnny Bench	.35	.17	.03
☐	52	Carlton Fisk	.10	.05	.01
☐	53	Tug McGraw	.05	.02	.00
☐	54	Paul Molitor	.15	.07	.01
☐	55	Carl Hubbell GC	.10	.05	.01
☐	56	Steve Garvey	.30	.15	.03
☐	57	Dave Parker	.20	.10	.02
☐	58	Gary Carter	.30	.15	.03
☐	59	Fred Lynn	.15	.07	.01
☐	60	Checklist card	.10	.01	.00

1985 Donruss

The cards in this 660-card set measure 2 1/2" by 3 1/2". The 1985 Donruss regular issue cards have fronts that feature jet black borders on which orange lines have been placed. The fronts contain the standard team logo, player's name, position, and Donruss logo. The cards were distributed with puzzle pieces from a Dick Perez rendition of Lou Gehrig. The first 26 cards of the set feature Diamond Kings (DK), for the fourth year in a row; the artwork on the Diamond Kings was again produced by the Perez-Steele Galleries. Cards 27-46 feature Rated Rookies (RR). The unnumbered checklist cards are arbitrarily numbered below as numbers 654 through 660.

			MINT	EXC	G-VG
		COMPLETE SET	125.00	60.00	12.50
		COMMON PLAYER	.06	.03	.00
☐	1	Ryne Sandberg DK	.50	.25	.05
☐	2	Doug DeCinces DK	.10	.05	.01
☐	3	Richard Dotson DK	.10	.05	.01
☐	4	Bert Blyleven DK	.15	.07	.01
☐	5	Lou Whitaker DK	.20	.10	.02
☐	6	Dan Quisenberry DK	.15	.07	.01
☐	7	Don Mattingly DK	6.00	3.00	.60
☐	8	Carney Lansford DK	.10	.05	.01
☐	9	Frank Tanana DK	.10	.05	.01
☐	10	Willie Upshaw DK	.10	.05	.01
☐	11	Claudell Washington DK	.10	.05	.01
☐	12	Mike Marshall DK	.15	.07	.01
☐	13	Joaquin Andujar DK	.10	.05	.01
☐	14	Cal Ripken DK	.50	.25	.05
☐	15	Jim Rice DK	.35	.17	.03
☐	16	Don Sutton DK	.25	.12	.02

			MINT	EXC	G-VG
☐	17	Frank Viola DK	.20	.10	.02
☐	18	Alvin Davis DK	.45	.22	.04
☐	19	Mario Soto DK	.10	.05	.01
☐	20	Jose Cruz DK	.10	.05	.01
☐	21	Charlie Lea DK	.10	.05	.01
☐	22	Jesse Orosco DK	.10	.05	.01
☐	23	Juan Samuel DK	.35	.17	.03
☐	24	Tony Pena DK	.15	.07	.01
☐	25	Tony Gwynn DK	.75	.35	.07
☐	26	Bob Brenly DK	.10	.05	.01
☐	27	Danny Tartabull RR	7.00	3.50	.70
☐	28	Mike Bielecki RR	.15	.07	.01
☐	29	Steve Lyons RR	.15	.07	.01
☐	30	Jeff Reed RR	.10	.05	.01
☐	31	Tony Brewer RR	.10	.05	.01
☐	32	John Morris RR	.20	.10	.02
☐	33	Daryl Boston RR	.40	.20	.04
☐	34	Alfonso Pulido RR	.10	.05	.01
☐	35	Steve Kiefer RR	.20	.10	.02
☐	36	Larry Sheets RR	2.00	1.00	.20
☐	37	Scott Bradley RR	.35	.17	.03
☐	38	Calvin Schiraldi RR	.40	.20	.04
☐	39	Shawon Dunston RR	1.25	.60	.12
☐	40	Charlie Mitchell RR	.10	.05	.01
☐	41	Billy Hatcher RR	1.25	.60	.12
☐	42	Russ Stephans RR	.10	.05	.01
☐	43	Alejandro Sanchez RR	.10	.05	.01
☐	44	Steve Jeltz RR	.15	.07	.01
☐	45	Jim Traber RR	.60	.30	.06
☐	46	Doug Loman RR	.20	.10	.02
☐	47	Eddie Murray	.50	.25	.05
☐	48	Robin Yount	.30	.15	.03
☐	49	Lance Parrish	.25	.12	.02
☐	50	Jim Rice	.35	.17	.03
☐	51	Dave Winfield	.35	.17	.03
☐	52	Fernando Valenzuela	.30	.15	.03
☐	53	George Brett	.55	.27	.05
☐	54	Dave Kingman	.15	.07	.01
☐	55	Gary Carter	.35	.17	.03
☐	56	Buddy Bell	.15	.07	.01
☐	57	Reggie Jackson	.45	.22	.04
☐	58	Harold Baines	.25	.12	.02
☐	59	Ozzie Smith	.25	.12	.02
☐	60	Nolan Ryan	.40	.20	.04
☐	61	Mike Schmidt	.75	.35	.07
☐	62	Dave Parker	.20	.10	.02
☐	63	Tony Gwynn	.75	.35	.07
☐	64	Tony Pena	.15	.07	.01
☐	65	Jack Clark	.25	.12	.02
☐	66	Dale Murphy	.75	.35	.07
☐	67	Ryne Sandberg	.50	.25	.05
☐	68	Keith Hernandez	.30	.15	.03
☐	69	Alvin Davis	1.75	.85	.17
☐	70	Kent Hrbek	.35	.17	.03
☐	71	Willie Upshaw	.10	.05	.01
☐	72	Dave Engle	.06	.03	.00
☐	73	Alfredo Griffin	.10	.05	.01
☐	74A	Jack Perconte (Career Highlights four lines)	.15	.07	.01
☐	74B	Jack Perconte (Career Highlights three lines)	.15	.07	.01
☐	75	Jesse Orosco	.10	.05	.01
☐	76	Jody Davis	.15	.07	.01
☐	77	Bob Horner	.20	.10	.02
☐	78	Larry McWilliams	.06	.03	.00
☐	79	Joel Youngblood	.06	.03	.00
☐	80	Alan Wiggins	.10	.05	.01
☐	81	Ron Oester	.06	.03	.00
☐	82	Ozzie Virgil	.06	.03	.00
☐	83	Ricky Horton	.25	.12	.02
☐	84	Bill Doran	.15	.07	.01
☐	85	Rod Carew	.40	.20	.04
☐	86	LaMarr Hoyt	.10	.05	.01
☐	87	Tim Wallach	.15	.07	.01
☐	88	Mike Flanagan	.10	.05	.01
☐	89	Jim Sundberg	.06	.03	.00
☐	90	Chet Lemon	.10	.05	.01
☐	91	Bob Stanley	.06	.03	.00
☐	92	Willie Randolph	.10	.05	.01
☐	93	Bill Russell	.06	.03	.00
☐	94	Julio Franco	.15	.07	.01
☐	95	Dan Quisenberry	.15	.07	.01
☐	96	Bill Caudill	.06	.03	.00
☐	97	Bill Gullickson	.10	.05	.01
☐	98	Danny Darwin	.06	.03	.00
☐	99	Curtis Wilkerson	.06	.03	.00
☐	100	Bud Black	.06	.03	.00
☐	101	Tony Phillips	.06	.03	.00
☐	102	Tony Bernazard	.06	.03	.00
☐	103	Jay Howell	.06	.03	.00
☐	104	Burt Hooton	.06	.03	.00
☐	105	Milt Wilcox	.06	.03	.00
☐	106	Rich Dauer	.06	.03	.00

☐ 107	Don Sutton	.20	.10	.02
☐ 108	Mike Witt	.15	.07	.01
☐ 109	Bruce Sutter	.15	.07	.01
☐ 110	Enos Cabell	.06	.03	.00
☐ 111	John Denny	.10	.05	.01
☐ 112	Dave Dravecky	.10	.05	.01
☐ 113	Marvell Wynne	.06	.03	.00
☐ 114	Johnnie LeMaster	.06	.03	.00
☐ 115	Chuck Porter	.06	.03	.00
☐ 116	John Gibbons	.10	.05	.01
☐ 117	Keith Moreland	.10	.05	.01
☐ 118	Darnell Coles	.10	.05	.01
☐ 119	Dennis Lamp	.06	.03	.00
☐ 120	Ron Davis	.06	.03	.00
☐ 121	Nick Esasky	.10	.05	.01
☐ 122	Vance Law	.06	.03	.00
☐ 123	Gary Roenicke	.06	.03	.00
☐ 124	Bill Schroeder	.06	.03	.00
☐ 125	Dave Rozema	.06	.03	.00
☐ 126	Bobby Meacham	.06	.03	.00
☐ 127	Marty Barrett	.25	.12	.02
☐ 128	R.J. Reynolds	.35	.17	.03
☐ 129	Ernie Camacho	.06	.03	.00
	(photo actually			
	Rich Thompson)			
☐ 130	Jorge Orta	.06	.03	.00
☐ 131	Lary Sorensen	.06	.03	.00
☐ 132	Terry Francona	.06	.03	.00
☐ 133	Fred Lynn	.15	.07	.01
☐ 134	Bob Jones	.06	.03	.00
☐ 135	Jerry Hairston	.06	.03	.00
☐ 136	Kevin Bass	.15	.07	.01
☐ 137	Garry Maddox	.06	.03	.00
☐ 138	Dave LaPoint	.06	.03	.00
☐ 139	Kevin McReynolds	.55	.27	.05
☐ 140	Wayne Krenchicki	.06	.03	.00
☐ 141	Rafael Ramirez	.06	.03	.00
☐ 142	Rod Scurry	.06	.03	.00
☐ 143	Greg Minton	.06	.03	.00
☐ 144	Tim Stoddard	.06	.03	.00
☐ 145	Steve Henderson	.06	.03	.00
☐ 146	George Bell	.65	.30	.06
☐ 147	Dave Meier	.15	.07	.01
☐ 148	Sammy Stewart	.06	.03	.00
☐ 149	Mark Brouhard	.06	.03	.00
☐ 150	Larry Herndon	.06	.03	.00
☐ 151	Oil Can Boyd	.15	.07	.01
☐ 152	Brian Dayett	.06	.03	.00
☐ 153	Tom Niedenfuer	.10	.05	.01
☐ 154	Brook Jacoby	.15	.07	.01
☐ 155	Onix Concepcion	.06	.03	.00
☐ 156	Tim Conroy	.06	.03	.00
☐ 157	Joe Hesketh	.20	.10	.02
☐ 158	Brian Downing	.10	.05	.01
☐ 159	Tommy Dunbar	.06	.03	.00
☐ 160	Marc Hill	.06	.03	.00
☐ 161	Phil Garner	.06	.03	.00
☐ 162	Jerry Davis	.10	.05	.01
☐ 163	Bill Campbell	.06	.03	.00
☐ 164	John Franco	.45	.22	.04
☐ 165	Len Barker	.06	.03	.00
☐ 166	Benny Distefano	.10	.05	.01
☐ 167	George Frazier	.06	.03	.00
☐ 168	Tito Landrum	.06	.03	.00
☐ 169	Cal Ripken	.45	.22	.04
☐ 170	Cecil Cooper	.15	.07	.01
☐ 171	Alan Trammell	.25	.12	.02
☐ 172	Wade Boggs	5.50	2.75	.55
☐ 173	Don Baylor	.15	.07	.01
☐ 174	Pedro Guerrero	.30	.15	.03
☐ 175	Frank White	.10	.05	.01
☐ 176	Rickey Henderson	.50	.25	.05
☐ 177	Charlie Lea	.06	.03	.00
☐ 178	Pete O'Brien	.15	.07	.01
☐ 179	Doug DeCinces	.10	.05	.01
☐ 180	Ron Kittle	.20	.10	.02
☐ 181	George Hendrick	.10	.05	.01
☐ 182	Joe Niekro	.10	.05	.01
☐ 183	Juan Samuel	1.25	.60	.12
☐ 184	Mario Soto	.10	.05	.01
☐ 185	Goose Gossage	.15	.07	.01
☐ 186	Johnny Ray	.15	.07	.01
☐ 187	Bob Brenly	.10	.05	.01
☐ 188	Craig McMurtry	.06	.03	.00
☐ 189	Leon Durham	.15	.07	.01
☐ 190	Dwight Gooden	10.00	5.00	1.00
☐ 191	Barry Bonnell	.06	.03	.00
☐ 192	Tim Teufel	.10	.05	.01
☐ 193	Dave Stieb	.15	.07	.01
☐ 194	Mickey Hatcher	.06	.03	.00
☐ 195	Jesse Barfield	.25	.12	.02
☐ 196	Al Cowens	.06	.03	.00
☐ 197	Hubie Brooks	.15	.07	.01
☐ 198	Steve Trout	.10	.05	.01
☐ 199	Glenn Hubbard	.06	.03	.00
☐ 200	Bill Madlock	.15	.07	.01
☐ 201	Jeff Robinson	.40	.20	.04
	(Giants pitcher)			
☐ 202	Eric Show	.06	.03	.00
☐ 203	Dave Concepcion	.10	.05	.01
☐ 204	Ivan DeJesus	.06	.03	.00
☐ 205	Neil Allen	.10	.05	.01
☐ 206	Jerry Mumphrey	.06	.03	.00
☐ 207	Mike Brown	.06	.03	.00
	(Angels OF)			
☐ 208	Carlton Fisk	.15	.07	.01
☐ 209	Bryn Smith	.06	.03	.00
☐ 210	Tippy Martinez	.06	.03	.00
☐ 211	Dion James	.15	.07	.01
☐ 212	Willie Hernandez	.15	.07	.01
☐ 213	Mike Easler	.10	.05	.01
☐ 214	Ron Guidry	.20	.10	.02
☐ 215	Rick Honeycutt	.06	.03	.00
☐ 216	Brett Butler	.10	.05	.01
☐ 217	Larry Gura	.06	.03	.00
☐ 218	Ray Burris	.06	.03	.00
☐ 219	Steve Rogers	.06	.03	.00
☐ 220	Frank Tanana	.10	.05	.01
☐ 221	Ned Yost	.06	.03	.00
☐ 222	Bret Saberhagen	6.00	3.00	.60
☐ 223	Mike Davis	.10	.05	.01
☐ 224	Bert Blyleven	.15	.07	.01
☐ 225	Steve Kemp	.10	.05	.01
☐ 226	Jerry Reuss	.15	.05	.01
☐ 227	Darrell Evans	.15	.07	.01
☐ 228	Wayne Gross	.06	.03	.00
☐ 229	Jim Gantner	.06	.03	.00
☐ 230	Bob Boone	.10	.05	.01
☐ 231	Lonnie Smith	.10	.05	.01
☐ 232	Frank DiPino	.06	.03	.00
☐ 233	Jerry Koosman	.10	.05	.01
☐ 234	Graig Nettles	.15	.07	.01
☐ 235	John Tudor	.15	.07	.01
☐ 236	John Rabb	.06	.03	.00
☐ 237	Rick Manning	.06	.03	.00
☐ 238	Mike Fitzgerald	.06	.03	.00
☐ 239	Gary Matthews	.10	.05	.01
☐ 240	Jim Presley	2.00	1.00	.20
☐ 241	Dave Collins	.06	.03	.00
☐ 242	Gary Gaetti	.30	.15	.03
☐ 243	Dann Bilardello	.06	.03	.00
☐ 244	Rudy Law	.06	.03	.00
☐ 245	John Lowenstein	.06	.03	.00
☐ 246	Tom Tellman	.06	.03	.00
☐ 247	Howard Johnson	.75	.35	.07
☐ 248	Ray Fontenot	.06	.03	.00
☐ 249	Tony Armas	.10	.05	.01
☐ 250	Candy Maldonado	.15	.07	.01
☐ 251	Mike Jeffcoat	.06	.03	.00
☐ 252	Dane Iorg	.06	.03	.00
☐ 253	Bruce Bochte	.06	.03	.00
☐ 254	Pete Rose	1.50	.75	.15
☐ 255	Don Aase	.10	.05	.01
☐ 256	George Wright	.06	.03	.00
☐ 257	Britt Burns	.10	.05	.01
☐ 258	Mike Scott	.30	.15	.03
☐ 259	Len Matuszek	.06	.03	.00
☐ 260	Dave Rucker	.06	.03	.00
☐ 261	Craig Lefferts	.06	.03	.00
☐ 262	Jay Tibbs	.25	.12	.02
☐ 263	Bruce Benedict	.06	.03	.00
☐ 264	Don Robinson	.06	.03	.00
☐ 265	Gary Lavelle	.06	.03	.00
☐ 266	Scott Sanderson	.06	.03	.00
☐ 267	Matt Young	.06	.03	.00
☐ 268	Ernie Whitt	.06	.03	.00
☐ 269	Houston Jimenez	.06	.03	.00
☐ 270	Ken Dixon	.25	.12	.02
☐ 271	Peter Ladd	.06	.03	.00
☐ 272	Juan Berenguer	.06	.03	.00
☐ 273	Roger Clemens	14.00	7.00	1.40
☐ 274	Rick Cerone	.06	.03	.00
☐ 275	Dave Anderson	.06	.03	.00
☐ 276	George Vukovich	.06	.03	.00
☐ 277	Greg Pryor	.06	.03	.00
☐ 278	Mike Warren	.06	.03	.00
☐ 279	Bob James	.06	.03	.00
☐ 280	Bobby Grich	.10	.05	.01
☐ 281	Mike Mason	.10	.05	.01
☐ 282	Ron Reed	.06	.03	.00
☐ 283	Alan Ashby	.06	.03	.00
☐ 284	Mark Thurmond	.06	.03	.00
☐ 285	Joe Lefebvre	.06	.03	.00
☐ 286	Ted Power	.10	.05	.01
☐ 287	Chris Chambliss	.10	.05	.01
☐ 288	Lee Tunnell	.06	.03	.00
☐ 289	Rich Bordi	.06	.03	.00
☐ 290	Glenn Brummer	.06	.03	.00
☐ 291	Mike Boddicker	.15	.07	.01
☐ 292	Rollie Fingers	.18	.09	.01

☐ 293	Lou Whitaker	.18	.09	.01
☐ 294	Dwight Evans	.18	.09	.01
☐ 295	Don Mattingly	18.00	9.00	1.80
☐ 296	Mike Marshall	.15	.07	.01
☐ 297	Willie Wilson	.15	.07	.01
☐ 298	Mike Heath	.06	.03	.00
☐ 299	Tim Raines	.40	.20	.04
☐ 300	Larry Parrish	.10	.05	.01
☐ 301	Geoff Zahn	.06	.03	.00
☐ 302	Rich Dotson	.10	.05	.01
☐ 303	David Green	.06	.03	.00
☐ 304	Jose Cruz	.10	.05	.01
☐ 305	Steve Carlton	.40	.20	.04
☐ 306	Gary Redus	.06	.03	.00
☐ 307	Steve Garvey	.40	.20	.04
☐ 308	Jose DeLeon	.06	.03	.00
☐ 309	Randy Lerch	.06	.03	.00
☐ 310	Claudell Washington	.10	.05	.01
☐ 311	Lee Smith	.10	.05	.01
☐ 312	Darryl Strawberry	2.50	1.25	.25
☐ 313	Jim Beattie	.06	.03	.00
☐ 314	John Butcher	.06	.03	.00
☐ 315	Damaso Garcia	.10	.05	.01
☐ 316	Mike Smithson	.06	.03	.00
☐ 317	Luis Leal	.06	.03	.00
☐ 318	Ken Phelps	.25	.12	.02
☐ 319	Wally Backman	.10	.05	.01
☐ 320	Ron Cey	.10	.05	.01
☐ 321	Brad Komminsk	.10	.05	.01
☐ 322	Jason Thompson	.06	.03	.00
☐ 323	Frank Williams	.15	.07	.01
☐ 324	Tim Lollar	.06	.03	.00
☐ 325	Eric Davis	30.00	15.00	3.00
☐ 326	Von Hayes	.15	.07	.01
☐ 327	Andy Van Slyke	.15	.07	.01
☐ 328	Craig Reynolds	.06	.03	.00
☐ 329	Dick Schofield	.10	.05	.01
☐ 330	Scott Fletcher	.10	.05	.01
☐ 331	Jeff Reardon	.15	.07	.01
☐ 332	Rick Dempsey	.10	.05	.01
☐ 333	Ben Oglivie	.10	.05	.01
☐ 334	Dan Petry	.15	.07	.01
☐ 335	Jackie Gutierrez	.10	.05	.01
☐ 336	Dave Righetti	.18	.09	.01
☐ 337	Alejandro Pena	.10	.05	.01
☐ 338	Mel Hall	.10	.05	.01
☐ 339	Pat Sheridan	.06	.03	.00
☐ 340	Keith Atherton	.06	.03	.00
☐ 341	David Palmer	.06	.03	.00
☐ 342	Gary Ward	.10	.05	.01
☐ 343	Dave Stewart	.15	.07	.01
☐ 344	Mark Gubicza	.35	.17	.03
☐ 345	Carney Lansford	.10	.05	.01
☐ 346	Jerry Willard	.06	.03	.00
☐ 347	Ken Griffey	.10	.05	.01
☐ 348	Franklin Stubbs	.65	.30	.06
☐ 349	Aurelio Lopez	.06	.03	.00
☐ 350	Al Bumbry	.06	.03	.00
☐ 351	Charlie Moore	.06	.03	.00
☐ 352	Luis Sanchez	.06	.03	.00
☐ 353	Darrell Porter	.06	.03	.00
☐ 354	Bill Dawley	.06	.03	.00
☐ 355	Charles Hudson	.06	.03	.00
☐ 356	Garry Templeton	.10	.05	.01
☐ 357	Cecilio Guante	.06	.03	.00
☐ 358	Jeff Leonard	.15	.07	.01
☐ 359	Paul Molitor	.20	.10	.02
☐ 360	Ron Gardenhire	.06	.03	.00
☐ 361	Larry Bowa	.10	.05	.01
☐ 362	Bob Kearney	.06	.03	.00
☐ 363	Garth Iorg	.06	.03	.00
☐ 364	Tom Brunansky	.20	.10	.02
☐ 365	Brad Gulden	.06	.03	.00
☐ 366	Greg Walker	.15	.07	.01
☐ 367	Mike Young	.15	.07	.01
☐ 368	Rick Waits	.06	.03	.00
☐ 369	Doug Bair	.06	.03	.00
☐ 370	Bob Shirley	.06	.03	.00
☐ 371	Bob Ojeda	.10	.05	.01
☐ 372	Bob Welch	.10	.05	.01
☐ 373	Neal Heaton	.06	.03	.00
☐ 374	Danny Jackson	.10	.05	.01
☐ 375	Donnie Hill	.06	.03	.00
☐ 376	Mike Stenhouse	.06	.03	.00
☐ 377	Bruce Kison	.06	.03	.00
☐ 378	Wayne Tolleson	.06	.03	.00
☐ 379	Floyd Bannister	.10	.05	.01
☐ 380	Vern Ruhle	.06	.03	.00
☐ 381	Tim Corcoran	.06	.03	.00
☐ 382	Kurt Kepshire	.10	.05	.01
☐ 383	Bobby Brown	.06	.03	.00
☐ 384	Dave Van Gorder	.06	.03	.00
☐ 385	Rick Mahler	.06	.03	.00
☐ 386	Lee Mazzilli	.06	.03	.00
☐ 387	Bill Laskey	.06	.03	.00
☐ 388	Thad Bosley	.06	.03	.00
☐ 389	Al Chambers	.06	.03	.00
☐ 390	Tony Fernandez	.25	.12	.02
☐ 391	Ron Washington	.06	.03	.00
☐ 392	Bill Swaggerty	.10	.05	.01
☐ 393	Bob L. Gibson	.06	.03	.00
☐ 394	Marty Castillo	.06	.03	.00
☐ 395	Steve Crawford	.06	.03	.00
☐ 396	Clay Christiansen	.10	.05	.01
☐ 397	Bob Bailor	.06	.03	.00
☐ 398	Mike Hargrove	.06	.03	.00
☐ 399	Charlie Leibrandt	.10	.05	.01
☐ 400	Tom Burgmeier	.06	.03	.00
☐ 401	Razor Shines	.10	.05	.01
☐ 402	Rob Wilfong	.06	.03	.00
☐ 403	Tom Henke	.20	.10	.02
☐ 404	Al Jones	.10	.05	.01
☐ 405	Mike LaCoss	.06	.03	.00
☐ 406	Luis DeLeon	.06	.03	.00
☐ 407	Greg Gross	.06	.03	.00
☐ 408	Tom Hume	.06	.03	.00
☐ 409	Rick Camp	.06	.03	.00
☐ 410	Milt May	.06	.03	.00
☐ 411	Henry Cotto	.15	.07	.01
☐ 412	David Von Ohlen	.06	.03	.00
☐ 413	Scott McGregor	.10	.05	.01
☐ 414	Ted Simmons	.10	.05	.01
☐ 415	Jack Morris	.20	.10	.02
☐ 416	Bill Buckner	.10	.05	.01
☐ 417	Butch Wynegar	.06	.03	.00
☐ 418	Steve Sax	.15	.07	.01
☐ 419	Steve Balboni	.06	.03	.00
☐ 420	Dwayne Murphy	.06	.03	.00
☐ 421	Andre Dawson	.30	.15	.03
☐ 422	Charlie Hough	.10	.05	.01
☐ 423	Tommy John	.15	.07	.01
☐ 424A	Tom Seaver ERR (photo actually Floyd Bannister)	1.00	.50	.10
☐ 424B	Tom Seaver COR	5.00	2.50	.50
☐ 425	Tommy Herr	.10	.05	.01
☐ 426	Terry Puhl	.06	.03	.00
☐ 427	Al Holland	.06	.03	.00
☐ 428	Eddie Milner	.06	.03	.00
☐ 429	Terry Kennedy	.10	.05	.01
☐ 430	John Candelaria	.10	.05	.01
☐ 431	Manny Trillo	.06	.03	.00
☐ 432	Ken Oberkfell	.06	.03	.00
☐ 433	Rick Sutcliffe	.20	.10	.02
☐ 434	Ron Darling	.90	.45	.09
☐ 435	Spike Owen	.06	.03	.00
☐ 436	Frank Viola	.15	.07	.01
☐ 437	Lloyd Moseby	.15	.07	.01
☐ 438	Kirby Puckett	11.00	5.50	1.10
☐ 439	Jim Clancy	.06	.03	.00
☐ 440	Mike Moore	.06	.03	.00
☐ 441	Doug Sisk	.06	.03	.00
☐ 442	Dennis Eckersley	.10	.05	.01
☐ 443	Gerald Perry	.10	.05	.01
☐ 444	Dale Berra	.06	.03	.00
☐ 445	Dusty Baker	.10	.05	.01
☐ 446	Ed Whitson	.06	.03	.00
☐ 447	Cesar Cedeno	.10	.05	.01
☐ 448	Rick Schu	.25	.12	.02
☐ 449	Joaquin Andujar	.15	.07	.01
☐ 450	Mark Bailey	.15	.07	.01
☐ 451	Ron Romanick	.15	.07	.01
☐ 452	Julio Cruz	.06	.03	.00
☐ 453	Miguel Dilone	.06	.03	.00
☐ 454	Storm Davis	.10	.05	.01
☐ 455	Jaime Cocanower	.10	.05	.01
☐ 456	Barbaro Garbey	.10	.05	.01
☐ 457	Rich Gedman	.10	.05	.01
☐ 458	Phil Niekro	.20	.10	.02
☐ 459	Mike Scioscia	.06	.03	.00
☐ 460	Pat Tabler	.15	.07	.01
☐ 461	Darryl Motley	.06	.03	.00
☐ 462	Chris Codiroli	.06	.03	.00
☐ 463	Doug Flynn	.06	.03	.00
☐ 464	Billy Sample	.06	.03	.00
☐ 465	Mickey Rivers	.06	.03	.00
☐ 466	John Wathan	.10	.05	.01
☐ 467	Bill Krueger	.06	.03	.00
☐ 468	Andre Thornton	.10	.05	.01
☐ 469	Rex Hudler	.10	.05	.01
☐ 470	Sid Bream	.35	.17	.03
☐ 471	Kirk Gibson	.25	.12	.02
☐ 472	John Shelby	.06	.03	.00
☐ 473	Moose Haas	.06	.03	.00
☐ 474	Doug Corbett	.06	.03	.00
☐ 475	Willie McGee	.35	.17	.03
☐ 476	Bob Knepper	.10	.05	.01
☐ 477	Kevin Gross	.06	.03	.00
☐ 478	Carmelo Martinez	.10	.05	.01
☐ 479	Kent Tekulve	.10	.05	.01

☐ 480	Chili Davis	.10	.05	.01
☐ 481	Bobby Clark	.06	.03	.00
☐ 482	Mookie Wilson	.10	.05	.01
☐ 483	Dave Owen	.10	.05	.01
☐ 484	Ed Nunez	.06	.03	.00
☐ 485	Rance Mulliniks	.06	.03	.00
☐ 486	Ken Schrom	.06	.03	.00
☐ 487	Jeff Russell	.06	.03	.00
☐ 488	Tom Paciorek	.06	.03	.00
☐ 489	Dan Ford	.06	.03	.00
☐ 490	Mike Caldwell	.06	.03	.00
☐ 491	Scottie Earl	.10	.05	.01
☐ 492	Jose Rijo	.30	.15	.03
☐ 493	Bruce Hurst	.10	.05	.01
☐ 494	Ken Landreaux	.06	.03	.00
☐ 495	Mike Fischlin	.06	.03	.00
☐ 496	Don Slaught	.06	.03	.00
☐ 497	Steve McCatty	.06	.03	.00
☐ 498	Gary Lucas	.06	.03	.00
☐ 499	Gary Pettis	.10	.05	.01
☐ 500	Marvis Foley	.06	.03	.00
☐ 501	Mike Squires	.06	.03	.00
☐ 502	Jim Pankovitz	.10	.05	.01
☐ 503	Luis Aguayo	.06	.03	.00
☐ 504	Ralph Citarella	.10	.05	.01
☐ 505	Bruce Bochy	.06	.03	.00
☐ 506	Bob Owchinko	.06	.03	.00
☐ 507	Pascual Perez	.06	.03	.00
☐ 508	Lee Lacy	.06	.03	.00
☐ 509	Atlee Hammaker	.06	.03	.00
☐ 510	Bob Dernier	.06	.03	.00
☐ 511	Ed VandeBerg	.06	.03	.00
☐ 512	Cliff Johnson	.06	.03	.00
☐ 513	Len Whitehouse	.06	.03	.00
☐ 514	Dennis Martinez	.10	.05	.01
☐ 515	Ed Romero	.06	.03	.00
☐ 516	Rusty Kuntz	.06	.03	.00
☐ 517	Rick Miller	.06	.03	.00
☐ 518	Dennis Rasmussen	.10	.05	.01
☐ 519	Steve Yeager	.06	.03	.00
☐ 520	Chris Bando	.06	.03	.00
☐ 521	U.L. Washington	.06	.03	.00
☐ 522	Curt Young	.55	.27	.05
☐ 523	Angel Salazar	.06	.03	.00
☐ 524	Curt Kaufman	.10	.05	.01
☐ 525	Odell Jones	.06	.03	.00
☐ 526	Juan Agosto	.06	.03	.00
☐ 527	Denny Walling	.06	.03	.00
☐ 528	Andy Hawkins	.06	.03	.00
☐ 529	Sixto Lezcano	.06	.03	.00
☐ 530	Skeeter Barnes	.06	.03	.00
☐ 531	Randy Johnson	.06	.03	.00
☐ 532	Jim Morrison	.06	.03	.00
☐ 533	Warren Brusstar	.06	.03	.00
☐ 534A	Jeff Pendleton ERR (wrong first name)	1.00	.50	.10
☐ 534B	Terry Pendleton COR	2.50	1.25	.25
☐ 535	Vic Rodriguez	.10	.05	.01
☐ 536	Bob McClure	.06	.03	.00
☐ 537	Dave Bergman	.06	.03	.00
☐ 538	Mark Clear	.06	.03	.00
☐ 539	Mike Pagliarulo	2.25	1.10	.22
☐ 540	Terry Whitfield	.06	.03	.00
☐ 541	Joe Beckwith	.06	.03	.00
☐ 542	Jeff Burroughs	.10	.05	.01
☐ 543	Dan Schatzeder	.06	.03	.00
☐ 544	Donnie Scott	.06	.03	.00
☐ 545	Jim Slaton	.06	.03	.00
☐ 546	Greg Luzinski	.15	.07	.01
☐ 547	Mark Salas	.20	.10	.02
☐ 548	Dave Smith	.10	.05	.01
☐ 549	John Wockenfuss	.06	.03	.00
☐ 550	Frank Pastore	.06	.03	.00
☐ 551	Tim Flannery	.06	.03	.00
☐ 552	Rick Rhoden	.10	.05	.01
☐ 553	Mark Davis	.06	.03	.00
☐ 554	Jeff Dedmon	.10	.05	.01
☐ 555	Gary Woods	.06	.03	.00
☐ 556	Danny Heep	.06	.03	.00
☐ 557	Mark Langston	1.75	.85	.17
☐ 558	Darrell Brown	.06	.03	.00
☐ 559	Jimmy Key	1.75	.85	.17
☐ 560	Rick Lysander	.06	.03	.00
☐ 561	Doyle Alexander	.10	.05	.01
☐ 562	Mike Stanton	.06	.03	.00
☐ 563	Sid Fernandez	.75	.35	.07
☐ 564	Richie Hebner	.06	.03	.00
☐ 565	Alex Trevino	.06	.03	.00
☐ 566	Brian Harper	.06	.03	.00
☐ 567	Dan Gladden	.35	.17	.03
☐ 568	Luis Salazar	.06	.03	.00
☐ 569	Tom Foley	.06	.03	.00
☐ 570	Larry Andersen	.06	.03	.00
☐ 571	Danny Cox	.15	.07	.01
☐ 572	Joe Sambito	.06	.03	.00
☐ 573	Juan Beniquez	.06	.03	.00
☐ 574	Joel Skinner	.06	.03	.00
☐ 575	Randy St.Claire	.10	.05	.01
☐ 576	Floyd Rayford	.06	.03	.00
☐ 577	Roy Howell	.06	.03	.00
☐ 578	John Grubb	.06	.03	.00
☐ 579	Ed Jurak	.06	.03	.00
☐ 580	John Montefusco	.06	.03	.00
☐ 581	Orel Hershiser	2.50	1.25	.25
☐ 582	Tom Waddell	.10	.05	.01
☐ 583	Mark Huismann	.06	.03	.00
☐ 584	Joe Morgan	.20	.10	.02
☐ 585	Jim Wohlford	.06	.03	.00
☐ 586	Dave Schmidt	.10	.05	.01
☐ 587	Jeff Kunkel	.10	.05	.01
☐ 588	Hal McRae	.10	.05	.01
☐ 589	Bill Almon	.06	.03	.00
☐ 590	Carmen Castillo	.06	.03	.00
☐ 591	Omar Moreno	.06	.03	.00
☐ 592	Ken Howell	.25	.12	.02
☐ 593	Tom Brookens	.06	.03	.00
☐ 594	Joe Nolan	.06	.03	.00
☐ 595	Willie Lozado	.10	.05	.01
☐ 596	Tom Nieto	.10	.05	.01
☐ 597	Walt Terrell	.10	.05	.01
☐ 598	Al Oliver	.10	.05	.01
☐ 599	Shane Rawley	.10	.05	.01
☐ 600	Denny Gonzalez	.10	.05	.01
☐ 601	Mark Grant	.10	.05	.01
☐ 602	Mike Armstrong	.06	.03	.00
☐ 603	George Foster	.15	.07	.01
☐ 604	Davey Lopes	.10	.05	.01
☐ 605	Salome Barojas	.06	.03	.00
☐ 606	Roy Lee Jackson	.06	.03	.00
☐ 607	Pete Filson	.06	.03	.00
☐ 608	Duane Walker	.06	.03	.00
☐ 609	Glenn Wilson	.10	.05	.01
☐ 610	Rafael Santana	.15	.07	.01
☐ 611	Roy Smith	.10	.05	.01
☐ 612	Ruppert Jones	.06	.03	.00
☐ 613	Joe Cowley	.06	.03	.00
☐ 614	Al Nipper (photo actually Mike Brown)	.25	.12	.02
☐ 615	Gene Nelson	.06	.03	.00
☐ 616	Joe Carter	1.00	.50	.10
☐ 617	Ray Knight	.10	.05	.01
☐ 618	Chuck Rainey	.06	.03	.00
☐ 619	Dan Driessen	.06	.03	.00
☐ 620	Daryl Sconiers	.06	.03	.00
☐ 621	Bill Stein	.06	.03	.00
☐ 622	Roy Smalley	.06	.03	.00
☐ 623	Ed Lynch	.06	.03	.00
☐ 624	Jeff Stone	.30	.15	.03
☐ 625	Bruce Berenyi	.06	.03	.00
☐ 626	Kelvin Chapman	.10	.05	.01
☐ 627	Joe Price	.06	.03	.00
☐ 628	Steve Bedrosian	.15	.07	.01
☐ 629	Vic Mata	.15	.07	.01
☐ 630	Mike Krukow	.10	.05	.01
☐ 631	Phil Bradley	1.50	.75	.15
☐ 632	Jim Gott	.06	.03	.00
☐ 633	Randy Bush	.06	.03	.00
☐ 634	Tom Browning	.50	.25	.05
☐ 635	Lou Gehrig Puzzle Card	.10	.05	.01
☐ 636	Reid Nichols	.06	.03	.00
☐ 637	Dan Pasqua	1.25	.60	.12
☐ 638	German Rivera	.10	.05	.01
☐ 639	Don Schulze	.10	.05	.01
☐ 640A	Mike Jones (Career Highlights, five lines)	.15	.07	.01
☐ 640B	Mike Jones (Career Highlights, four lines)	.15	.07	.01
☐ 641	Pete Rose	1.00	.50	.10
☐ 642	Wade Rowdon	.20	.10	.02
☐ 643	Jerry Narron	.06	.03	.00
☐ 644	Darrell Miller	.20	.10	.02
☐ 645	Tim Hulett	.20	.10	.02
☐ 646	Andy McGaffigan	.06	.03	.00
☐ 647	Kurt Bevacqua	.06	.03	.00
☐ 648	John Russell	.20	.10	.02
☐ 649	Ron Robinson	.20	.10	.02
☐ 650	Donnie Moore	.10	.05	.01
☐ 651A	Two for the Title Dave Winfield Don Mattingly (yellow letters)	3.50	1.75	.35
☐ 651B	Two for the Title Dave Winfield Don Mattingly (white letters)	5.00	2.50	.50
☐ 652	Tim Laudner	.10	.05	.01

		MINT	EXC	G-VG
☐ 653	Steve Farr	.10	.05	.01
☐ 654	DK Checklist 1-26	.09	.01	.00
	(unnumbered)			
☐ 655	Checklist 27-130	.07	.01	.00
	(unnumbered)			
☐ 656	Checklist 131-234	.07	.01	.00
	(unnumbered)			
☐ 657	Checklist 235-338	.07	.01	.00
	(unnumbered)			
☐ 658	Checklist 339-442	.07	.01	.00
	(unnumbered)			
☐ 659	Checklist 443-546	.07	.01	.00
	(unnumbered)			
☐ 660	Checklist 547-653	.07	.01	.00
	(unnumbered)			

1985 Donruss Wax Box Cards

The boxes in which the wax packs (of the 1985 Donruss regular issue baseball cards) were contained feature four baseball cards, with backs. The complete set price of the regular issue set does not include these cards; they are considered a separate set. The cards measure the standard 2 1/2" by 3 1/2" and are styled the same as the regular Donruss cards. The cards are numbered but with the prefix PC before the number. The value of the panel uncut is slightly greater, perhaps by 25% greater, than the value of the individual cards cut up carefully.

		MINT	EXC	G-VG
	COMPLETE SET	4.50	2.25	.45
	COMMON PLAYER	.10	.05	.01
☐ PC1	Dwight Gooden	4.00	2.00	.40
☐ PC2	Ryne Sandberg	.50	.25	.05
☐ PC3	Ron Kittle	.20	.10	.02
☐ PUZ	Lou Gehrig	.10	.05	.01
	Puzzle Card			

1985 Donruss Super DK's

The cards in this 28-card set measure 4 15/16 by 6 3/4". The 1985 Donruss Diamond Kings Supers set contains enlarged cards of the first 26 cards of the Donruss regular set of this year. In addition, the Diamond Kings checklist card, a card of artist Dick Perez, and a Lou Gehrig puzzle card are included in the set. The set was the brain-child of the Perez-Steele Galleries and could be obtained via a write-in offer on the wrappers of the Donruss regular cards of this year. The Gehrig puzzle card is actually a 12-piece jigsaw puzzle. The back of the checklist card is blank; however, the Dick Perez card back gives a short history of Dick Perez and the Perez-Steele Galleries. The offer for obtaining this set was detailed

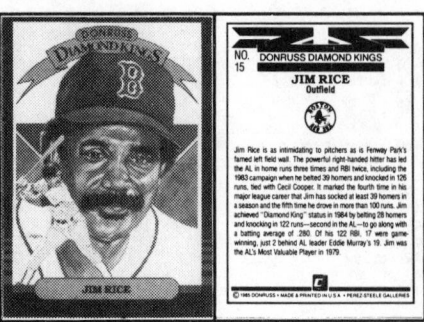

on the wax pack wrappers; three wrappers plus 9.00 was required for this mail-in offer.

		MINT	EXC	G-VG
	COMPLETE SET (28)	10.00	5.00	1.00
	COMMON PLAYER (1-26)	.20	.10	.02
☐ 1	Ryne Sandberg	.80	.40	.08
☐ 2	Doug DeCinces	.20	.10	.02
☐ 3	Richard Dotson	.20	.10	.02
☐ 4	Bert Blyleven	.30	.15	.03
☐ 5	Lou Whitaker	.30	.15	.03
☐ 6	Dan Quisenberry	.30	.15	.03
☐ 7	Don Mattingly	4.00	2.00	.40
☐ 8	Carney Lansford	.30	.15	.03
☐ 9	Frank Tanana	.20	.10	.02
☐ 10	Willie Upshaw	.20	.10	.02
☐ 11	Claudell Washington	.20	.10	.02
☐ 12	Mike Marshall	.25	.12	.02
☐ 13	Joaquin Andujar	.20	.10	.02
☐ 14	Cal Ripken	1.25	.60	.12
☐ 15	Jim Rice	.70	.35	.07
☐ 16	Don Sutton	.50	.25	.05
☐ 17	Frank Viola	.50	.25	.05
☐ 18	Alvin Davis	.60	.30	.06
☐ 19	Mario Soto	.20	.10	.02
☐ 20	Jose Cruz	.20	.10	.02
☐ 21	Charlie Lea	.20	.10	.02
☐ 22	Jesse Orosco	.20	.10	.02
☐ 23	Juan Samuel	.50	.25	.05
☐ 24	Tony Pena	.30	.15	.03
☐ 25	Tony Gwynn	1.25	.60	.12
☐ 26	Bob Brenly	.20	.10	.02
☐ 27	Checklist card	.10	.01	.00
	(unnumbered)			
☐ 28	Dick Perez (unnumbered)	.10	.05	.01
	(History of DK's)			

1985 Donruss Action All-Stars

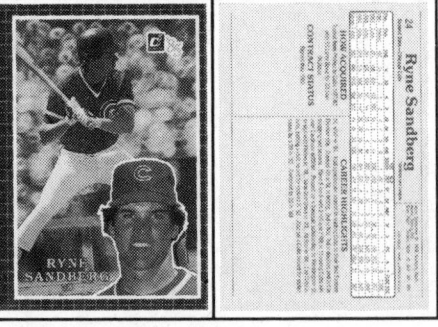

The cards in this 60-card set measure 3 1/2" by 5". For the third year in a row, Donruss issued a set of Action All-Stars. This set features action photos on the obverse which also contains a portrait inset of the player. The backs, unlike the year before, do not contain a full color picture of the player but list, if space is available, full statistical data, biographical data, career highlights, and acquisition and contract status. The cards were issued with a Lou Gehrig puzzle card.

	MINT	EXC	G-VG
COMPLETE SET	6.00	3.00	.60
COMMON PLAYER	.05	.02	.00

		MINT	EXC	G-VG
☐	1 Tim Raines	.35	.17	.03
☐	2 Jim Gantner	.05	.02	.00
☐	3 Mario Soto	.05	.02	.00
☐	4 Spike Owen	.05	.02	.00
☐	5 Lloyd Moseby	.10	.05	.01
☐	6 Damaso Garcia	.05	.02	.00
☐	7 Cal Ripken	.35	.17	.03
☐	8 Dan Quisenberry	.15	.07	.01
☐	9 Eddie Murray	.40	.20	.04
☐	10 Tony Pena	.10	.05	.01
☐	11 Buddy Bell	.10	.05	.01
☐	12 Dave Winfield	.25	.12	.02
☐	13 Ron Kittle	.20	.10	.02
☐	14 Rich Gossage	.10	.05	.01
☐	15 Dwight Evans	.15	.07	.01
☐	16 Alvin Davis	.15	.07	.01
☐	17 Mike Schmidt	.50	.25	.05
☐	18 Pascual Perez	.05	.02	.00
☐	19 Tony Gwynn	.40	.20	.04
☐	20 Nolan Ryan	.40	.20	.04
☐	21 Robin Yount	.25	.12	.02
☐	22 Mike Marshall	.15	.07	.01
☐	23 Brett Butler	.10	.05	.01
☐	24 Ryne Sandberg	.30	.15	.03
☐	25 Dale Murphy	.60	.30	.06
☐	26 George Brett	.50	.25	.05
☐	27 Jim Rice	.30	.15	.03
☐	28 Ozzie Smith	.20	.10	.02
☐	29 Larry Parrish	.05	.02	.00
☐	30 Jack Clark	.20	.10	.02
☐	31 Manny Trillo	.05	.02	.00
☐	32 Dave Kingman	.10	.05	.01
☐	33 Geoff Zahn	.05	.02	.00
☐	34 Pedro Guerrero	.20	.10	.02
☐	35 Dave Parker	.20	.10	.02
☐	36 Rollie Fingers	.15	.07	.01
☐	37 Fernando Valenzuela	.25	.12	.02
☐	38 Wade Boggs	.80	.40	.08
☐	39 Reggie Jackson	.60	.30	.06
☐	40 Kent Hrbek	.25	.12	.02
☐	41 Keith Hernandez	.25	.12	.02
☐	42 Lou Whitaker	.15	.07	.01
☐	43 Tom Herr	.05	.02	.00
☐	44 Alan Trammell	.20	.10	.02
☐	45 Butch Wynegar	.05	.02	.00
☐	46 Leon Durham	.05	.02	.00
☐	47 Dwight Gooden	1.00	.50	.10
☐	48 Don Mattingly	1.50	.75	.15
☐	49 Phil Niekro	.20	.10	.02
☐	50 Johnny Ray	.10	.05	.01
☐	51 Doug DeCinces	.10	.05	.01
☐	52 Willie Upshaw	.05	.02	.00
☐	53 Lance Parrish	.15	.07	.01
☐	54 Jody Davis	.05	.02	.00
☐	55 Steve Carlton	.30	.15	.03
☐	56 Juan Samuel	.20	.10	.02
☐	57 Gary Carter	.30	.15	.03
☐	58 Harold Baines	.15	.07	.01
☐	59 Eric Show	.05	.02	.00
☐	60 Checklist Card	.10	.01	.00

1985 Donruss Highlights

This 56-card set features the players and pitchers of the month for each league as well as a number of highlight cards commemorating the 1985 season. The Donruss Company dedicated the last two cards to their own selections for Rookies of the Year (ROY). This set proved to be more popular than the Donruss Company had predicted, as their first and only print run was exhausted before card dealers' initial orders were filled.

	MINT	EXC	G-VG
COMPLETE SET	18.00	9.00	1.80
COMMON PLAYER	.10	.05	.01

		MINT	EXC	G-VG
☐	1 Tom Seaver: Sets	.45	.22	.04

Dale Murphy

National League Player of the Month
April

Before the '85 National League season was even one month old, fans were fitting Dale Murphy for a place in the record books alongside Hack Wilson who, in '30 set National League records of 56 homers and 190 RBI. The reason for such lofty comparisons was obvious. Murphy tied a major league record for most RBI in one month with 29 in April of '85. In addition, the Atlanta Braves perennial All-Star centerfielder and two-time winner of the Most Valuable Player Award, hit nine homers, including 8 doubles, 62 total bases and 17 runs scored in just 19 games. Along with his offensive stats, Murphy kept his consecutive games playing streak going through 515 entering May.

NO. 5

© 1985 LEAF-DONRUSS   MADE & PRINTED IN U.S.A.

		MINT	EXC	G-VG
	Opening Day Record			
☐	2 Rollie Fingers:	.20	.10	.02
	Sets AL Save Mark			
☐	3 Mike Davis:	.10	.05	.01
	AL Player April			
☐	4 Charlie Leibrandt:	.10	.05	.01
	AL Pitcher April			
☐	5 Dale Murphy:	.90	.45	.09
	NL Player April			
☐	6 Fernando Valenzuela:	.45	.22	.04
	NL Pitcher April			
☐	7 Larry Bowa:	.15	.07	.01
	NL Shortstop Record			
☐	8 Dave Concepcion: Joins	.10	.05	.01
	Reds' 2000th Hit Club			
☐	9 Tony Perez:	.20	.10	.02
	Eldest Grand Slammer			
☐	10 Pete Rose:	1.75	.85	.17
	NL Career Run Leader			
☐	11 George Brett:	.90	.45	.09
	AL Player May			
☐	12 Dave Stieb:	.20	.10	.02
	AL Pitcher May			
☐	13 Dave Parker:	.25	.12	.02
	NL Player May			
☐	14 Andy Hawkins:	.10	.05	.01
	NL Pitcher May			
☐	15 Andy Hawkins: Records	.10	.05	.01
	11th Straight Win			
☐	16 Von Hayes: Two	.20	.10	.02
	Homers in First Inning			
☐	17 Rickey Henderson:	.90	.45	.09
	AL Player June			
☐	18 Jay Howell:	.10	.05	.01
	AL Pitcher June			
☐	19 Pedro Guerrero:	.30	.15	.03
	NL Player June			
☐	20 John Tudor:	.20	.10	.02
	NL Pitcher June			
☐	21 Hernandez/Carter:	.45	.22	.04
	Marathon Game			
	Iron Men			
☐	22 Nolan Ryan:	.60	.30	.06
	Records 4000th K			
☐	23 LaMarr Hoyt:	.10	.05	.01
	All-Star Game MVP			
☐	24 Oddibe McDowell: 1st	.60	.30	.06
	Ranger to Hit for Cycle			
☐	25 George Brett:	.90	.45	.09
	AL Player July			
☐	26 Bret Saberhagen:	.75	.35	.07
	AL Pitcher July			
☐	27 Keith Hernandez:	.35	.17	.03
	NL Player July			
☐	28 Fernando Valenzuela:	.35	.17	.03
	NL Pitcher July			
☐	29 McGee/Coleman: Record	1.25	.50	.12
	Setting Base Stealers			
☐	30 Tom Seaver: Notches	.45	.22	.04
	300th Career Win			
☐	31 Rod Carew: Strokes	.45	.22	.04
	3000th Hit			
☐	32 Dwight Gooden:	1.50	.75	.15
	Establishes Met Record			
☐	33 Dwight Gooden:	1.50	.75	.15
	Achieves Strikeout			
	Milestone			
☐	34 Eddie Murray:	.75	.35	.07
	Explodes for 9 RBI			
☐	35 Don Baylor:	.20	.10	.02
	AL Career HBP Leader			
☐	36 Don Mattingly:	3.00	1.50	.30
	AL Player August			
☐	37 Dave Righetti:	.20	.10	.02
	AL Pitcher August			

		MINT	EXC	G-VG
☐ 38	Willie McGee: NL Player August	.35	.17	.03
☐ 39	Shane Rawley: NL Pitcher August	.10	.05	.01
☐ 40	Pete Rose: Ty-Breaking Hit	1.75	.85	.17
☐ 41	Andre Dawson: Hits 3 HR's Drives in 8 Runs	.35	.17	.03
☐ 42	Rickey Henderson: Sets Yankee Theft Mark	.90	.45	.09
☐ 43	Tom Browning: 20 Wins ... in Rookie Season	.20	.10	.02
☐ 44	Don Mattingly: Yankee Milestone for Hits	3.00	1.50	.30
☐ 45	Don Mattingly: AL Player September	3.00	1.50	.30
☐ 46	Charlie Leibrandt: AL Pitcher September	.10	.05	.01
☐ 47	Gary Carter: NL Player September	.45	.22	.04
☐ 48	Dwight Gooden: NL Pitcher for September	1.50	.75	.15
☐ 49	Wade Boggs: Major League Record Setter	2.25	1.10	.22
☐ 50	Phil Niekro: Hurls Shutout for 300th Win	.30	.15	.03
☐ 51	Darrell Evans: Venerable HR King	.15	.07	.01
☐ 52	Willie McGee: NL Switch-Hitting Record	.30	.15	.03
☐ 53	Dave Winfield: Equals DiMaggio Feat	.45	.22	.04
☐ 54	Vince Coleman: Donruss NL ROY	2.50	1.25	.25
☐ 55	Ozzie Guillen: Donruss AL ROY	.50	.25	.05
☐ 56	Checklist card (unnumbered)	.10	.01	.00

1986 Donruss

The cards in this 660-card set measure 2 1/2" by 3 1/2". The 1986 Donruss regular issue cards have fronts that feature blue borders. The fronts contain the standard team logo, player's name, position, and Donruss logo. The cards were distributed with puzzle pieces from a Dick Perez rendition of Hank Aaron. The first 26 cards of the set are Diamond Kings (DK), for the fifth year in a row; the artwork on the Diamond Kings was again produced by the Perez-Steele Galleries. Cards 27-46 again feature Rated Rookies (RR); Danny Tartabull is included in this subset for the second year in a row. The unnumbered checklist cards are arbitrarily numbered below as numbers 654 through 660.

	MINT	EXC	G-VG
COMPLETE SET	60.00	30.00	6.00
COMMON PLAYER	.04	.02	.00

☐ 1 Kirk Gibson DK	.30	.07	.01
☐ 2 Goose Gossage DK	.18	.09	.01
☐ 3 Willie McGee DK	.25	.12	.02
☐ 4 George Bell DK	.35	.17	.03
☐ 5 Tony Armas DK	.10	.05	.01
☐ 6 Chili Davis DK	.10	.05	.01

☐ 7 Cecil Cooper DK	.12	.06	.01
☐ 8 Mike Boddicker DK	.10	.05	.01
☐ 9 Davey Lopes DK	.10	.05	.01
☐ 10 Bill Doran DK	.10	.05	.01
☐ 11 Bret Saberhagen DK	.45	.22	.04
☐ 12 Brett Butler DK	.10	.05	.01
☐ 13 Harold Baines DK	.20	.10	.02
☐ 14 Mike Davis DK	.10	.05	.01
☐ 15 Tony Perez DK	.12	.06	.01
☐ 16 Willie Randolph DK	.10	.05	.01
☐ 17 Bob Boone DK	.10	.05	.01
☐ 18 Orel Hershiser DK	.30	.15	.03
☐ 19 Johnny Ray DK	.12	.06	.01
☐ 20 Gary Ward DK	.10	.05	.01
☐ 21 Rick Mahler DK	.10	.05	.01
☐ 22 Phil Bradley DK	.25	.12	.02
☐ 23 Jerry Koosman DK	.10	.05	.01
☐ 24 Tom Brunansky DK	.15	.07	.01
☐ 25 Andre Dawson DK	.30	.15	.03
☐ 26 Dwight Gooden DK	.90	.45	.09
☐ 27 Kal Daniels RR	6.00	3.00	.60
☐ 28 Fred McGriff RR	1.25	.60	.12
☐ 29 Cory Snyder RR	3.00	1.50	.30
☐ 30 Jose Guzman RR	.25	.12	.02
☐ 31 Ty Gainey RR	.20	.10	.02
☐ 32 Johnny Abrego RR	.10	.05	.01
☐ 33A Andres Galarraga RR (no accent)	2.00	1.00	.20
☐ 33B Andre's Galarraga RR (accent over e)	3.00	1.50	.30
☐ 34 Dave Shipanoff RR	.15	.07	.01
☐ 35 Mark McLemore RR	.15	.07	.01
☐ 36 Marty Clary RR	.10	.05	.01
☐ 37 Paul O'Neill RR	.25	.12	.02
☐ 38 Danny Tartabull RR	1.00	.50	.10
☐ 39 Jose Canseco RR	11.00	5.50	1.10
☐ 40 Juan Nieves RR	.50	.25	.05
☐ 41 Lance McCullers RR	.30	.15	.03
☐ 42 Rick Surhoff RR	.10	.05	.01
☐ 43 Todd Worrell RR	1.25	.60	.12
☐ 44 Bob Kipper RR	.20	.10	.02
☐ 45 John Habyan RR	.15	.07	.01
☐ 46 Mike Woodard RR	.10	.05	.01
☐ 47 Mike Boddicker	.10	.05	.01
☐ 48 Robin Yount	.30	.15	.03
☐ 49 Lou Whitaker	.15	.07	.01
☐ 50 Oil Can Boyd	.10	.05	.01
☐ 51 Rickey Henderson	.35	.17	.03
☐ 52 Mike Marshall	.12	.06	.01
☐ 53 George Brett	.45	.22	.04
☐ 54 Dave Kingman	.12	.06	.01
☐ 55 Hubie Brooks	.10	.05	.01
☐ 56 Oddibe McDowell	.45	.22	.04
☐ 57 Doug DeCinces	.07	.03	.01
☐ 58 Britt Burns	.07	.03	.01
☐ 59 Ozzie Smith	.20	.10	.02
☐ 60 Jose Cruz	.10	.05	.01
☐ 61 Mike Schmidt	.50	.25	.05
☐ 62 Pete Rose	.75	.35	.07
☐ 63 Steve Garvey	.35	.17	.03
☐ 64 Tony Pena	.10	.05	.01
☐ 65 Chili Davis	.10	.05	.01
☐ 66 Dale Murphy	.50	.25	.05
☐ 67 Ryne Sandberg	.30	.15	.03
☐ 68 Gary Carter	.30	.15	.03
☐ 69 Alvin Davis	.15	.07	.01
☐ 70 Kent Hrbek	.15	.07	.01
☐ 71 George Bell	.35	.17	.03
☐ 72 Kirby Puckett	2.00	1.00	.20
☐ 73 Lloyd Moseby	.12	.06	.01
☐ 74 Bob Kearney	.04	.02	.00
☐ 75 Dwight Gooden	2.00	1.00	.20
☐ 76 Gary Matthews	.07	.03	.01
☐ 77 Rick Mahler	.04	.02	.00
☐ 78 Benny Distefano	.04	.02	.00
☐ 79 Jeff Leonard	.12	.06	.01
☐ 80 Kevin McReynolds	.25	.12	.02
☐ 81 Ron Oester	.04	.02	.00
☐ 82 John Russell	.04	.02	.00
☐ 83 Tommy Herr	.10	.05	.01
☐ 84 Jerry Mumphrey	.04	.02	.00
☐ 85 Ron Romanick	.04	.02	.00
☐ 86 Daryl Boston	.07	.03	.01
☐ 87 Andre Dawson	.30	.15	.03
☐ 88 Eddie Murray	.40	.20	.04
☐ 89 Dion James	.07	.03	.01
☐ 90 Chet Lemon	.07	.03	.01
☐ 91 Bob Stanley	.07	.03	.01
☐ 92 Willie Randolph	.07	.03	.01
☐ 93 Mike Scioscia	.04	.02	.00
☐ 94 Tom Waddell	.04	.02	.00
☐ 95 Danny Jackson	.07	.03	.01
☐ 96 Mike Davis	.07	.03	.01
☐ 97 Mike Fitzgerald	.04	.02	.00
☐ 98 Gary Ward	.07	.03	.01

☐ 99	Pete O'Brien	.10	.05	.01
☐ 100	Bret Saberhagen	.65	.30	.06
☐ 101	Alfredo Griffin	.07	.03	.01
☐ 102	Brett Butler	.07	.03	.01
☐ 103	Ron Guidry	.15	.07	.01
☐ 104	Jerry Reuss	.07	.03	.01
☐ 105	Jack Morris	.18	.09	.01
☐ 106	Rick Dempsey	.07	.03	.01
☐ 107	Ray Burris	.04	.02	.00
☐ 108	Brian Downing	.07	.03	.01
☐ 109	Willie McGee	.18	.09	.01
☐ 110	Bill Doran	.10	.05	.01
☐ 111	Kent Tekulve	.07	.03	.01
☐ 112	Tony Gwynn	.65	.30	.06
☐ 113	Marvell Wynne	.04	.02	.00
☐ 114	David Green	.04	.02	.00
☐ 115	Jim Gantner	.04	.02	.00
☐ 116	George Foster	.12	.06	.01
☐ 117	Steve Trout	.04	.02	.00
☐ 118	Mark Langston	.15	.07	.01
☐ 119	Tony Fernandez	.15	.07	.01
☐ 120	John Butcher	.04	.02	.00
☐ 121	Ron Robinson	.04	.02	.00
☐ 122	Dan Spillner	.04	.02	.00
☐ 123	Mike Young	.10	.05	.01
☐ 124	Paul Molitor	.15	.07	.01
☐ 125	Kirk Gibson	.18	.09	.01
☐ 126	Ken Griffey	.07	.03	.01
☐ 127	Tony Armas	.07	.03	.01
☐ 128	Mariano Duncan	.25	.12	.02
☐ 129	Pat Tabler	.10	.05	.01
☐ 130	Frank White	.07	.03	.01
☐ 131	Carney Lansford	.10	.05	.01
☐ 132	Vance Law	.04	.02	.00
☐ 133	Dick Schofield	.07	.03	.01
☐ 134	Wayne Tolleson	.04	.02	.00
☐ 135	Greg Walker	.10	.05	.00
☐ 136	Denny Walling	.04	.02	.00
☐ 137	Ozzie Virgil	.04	.02	.00
☐ 138	Ricky Horton	.04	.02	.00
☐ 139	LaMarr Hoyt	.07	.03	.01
☐ 140	Wayne Krenchicki	.04	.02	.00
☐ 141	Glenn Hubbard	.04	.02	.00
☐ 142	Cecilio Guante	.04	.02	.00
☐ 143	Mike Krukow	.07	.03	.01
☐ 144	Lee Smith	.10	.05	.01
☐ 145	Edwin Nunez	.07	.03	.01
☐ 146	Dave Stieb	.15	.07	.01
☐ 147	Mike Smithson	.04	.02	.00
☐ 148	Ken Dixon	.04	.02	.00
☐ 149	Danny Darwin	.04	.02	.00
☐ 150	Chris Pittaro	.04	.02	.00
☐ 151	Bill Buckner	.07	.03	.01
☐ 152	Mike Pagliarulo	.20	.10	.02
☐ 153	Bill Russell	.04	.02	.00
☐ 154	Brook Jacoby	.12	.06	.01
☐ 155	Pat Sheridan	.04	.02	.00
☐ 156	Mike Gallego	.07	.03	.01
☐ 157	Jim Wohlford	.04	.02	.00
☐ 158	Gary Pettis	.07	.03	.01
☐ 159	Toby Harrah	.04	.02	.00
☐ 160	Richard Dotson	.07	.03	.01
☐ 161	Bob Knepper	.07	.03	.01
☐ 162	Dave Dravecky	.07	.03	.01
☐ 163	Greg Gross	.04	.02	.00
☐ 164	Eric Davis	5.00	2.50	.50
☐ 165	Gerald Perry	.07	.03	.01
☐ 166	Rick Rhoden	.07	.03	.01
☐ 167	Keith Moreland	.07	.03	.01
☐ 168	Jack Clark	.20	.10	.02
☐ 169	Storm Davis	.07	.03	.01
☐ 170	Cecil Cooper	.12	.06	.01
☐ 171	Alan Trammell	.25	.12	.02
☐ 172	Roger Clemens	4.00	2.00	.40
☐ 173	Don Mattingly	6.50	3.25	.65
☐ 174	Pedro Guerrero	.25	.12	.02
☐ 175	Willie Wilson	.15	.07	.01
☐ 176	Dwayne Murphy	.07	.03	.01
☐ 177	Tim Raines	.30	.15	.03
☐ 178	Larry Parrish	.07	.03	.01
☐ 179	Mike Witt	.12	.06	.01
☐ 180	Harold Baines	.18	.09	.01
☐ 181	Vince Coleman	2.50	1.25	.25
	(BA 2.67 on back)			
☐ 182	Jeff Heathcock	.07	.03	.01
☐ 183	Steve Carlton	.30	.15	.03
☐ 184	Mario Soto	.07	.03	.01
☐ 185	Goose Gossage	.15	.07	.01
☐ 186	Johnny Ray	.10	.05	.01
☐ 187	Dan Gladden	.07	.03	.01
☐ 188	Bob Horner	.18	.09	.01
☐ 189	Rick Sutcliffe	.15	.07	.01
☐ 190	Keith Hernandez	.25	.12	.02
☐ 191	Phil Bradley	.18	.09	.01
☐ 192	Tom Brunansky	.15	.07	.01
☐ 193	Jesse Barfield	.30	.15	.03
☐ 194	Frank Viola	.15	.07	.01
☐ 195	Willie Upshaw	.07	.03	.01
☐ 196	Jim Beattie	.04	.02	.00
☐ 197	Darryl Strawberry	.65	.30	.06
☐ 198	Ron Cey	.10	.05	.01
☐ 199	Steve Bedrosian	.15	.07	.01
☐ 200	Steve Kemp	.07	.03	.01
☐ 201	Manny Trillo	.04	.02	.00
☐ 202	Garry Templeton	.07	.03	.01
☐ 203	Dave Parker	.18	.09	.01
☐ 204	John Denny	.07	.03	.01
☐ 205	Terry Pendleton	.10	.05	.01
☐ 206	Terry Puhl	.07	.03	.01
☐ 207	Bobby Grich	.07	.03	.01
☐ 208	Ozzie Guillen	.45	.22	.04
☐ 209	Jeff Reardon	.12	.06	.01
☐ 210	Cal Ripken	.40	.20	.04
☐ 211	Bill Schroeder	.04	.02	.00
☐ 212	Dan Petry	.10	.05	.01
☐ 213	Jim Rice	.25	.12	.02
☐ 214	Dave Righetti	.15	.07	.01
☐ 215	Fernando Valenzuela	.25	.12	.02
☐ 216	Julio Franco	.12	.06	.01
☐ 217	Darryl Motley	.04	.02	.00
☐ 218	Dave Collins	.04	.02	.00
☐ 219	Tim Wallach	.12	.06	.01
☐ 220	George Wright	.04	.02	.00
☐ 221	Tommy Dunbar	.04	.02	.00
☐ 222	Steve Balboni	.04	.02	.00
☐ 223	Jay Howell	.04	.02	.00
☐ 224	Joe Carter	.30	.15	.03
☐ 225	Ed Whitson	.04	.02	.00
☐ 226	Orel Hershiser	.35	.17	.03
☐ 227	Willie Hernandez	.12	.06	.01
☐ 228	Lee Lacy	.04	.02	.00
☐ 229	Rollie Fingers	.15	.07	.01
☐ 230	Bob Boone	.07	.03	.01
☐ 231	Joaquin Andujar	.10	.05	.01
☐ 232	Craig Reynolds	.04	.02	.00
☐ 233	Shane Rawley	.07	.03	.01
☐ 234	Eric Show	.04	.02	.00
☐ 235	Jose DeLeon	.04	.02	.00
☐ 236	Jose Uribe	.25	.12	.02
☐ 237	Moose Haas	.04	.02	.00
☐ 238	Wally Backman	.07	.03	.01
☐ 239	Dennis Eckersley	.07	.03	.01
☐ 240	Mike Moore	.07	.03	.01
☐ 241	Damaso Garcia	.07	.03	.01
☐ 242	Tim Teufel	.07	.03	.01
☐ 243	Dave Concepcion	.07	.03	.01
☐ 244	Floyd Bannister	.07	.03	.01
☐ 245	Fred Lynn	.15	.07	.01
☐ 246	Charlie Moore	.04	.02	.00
☐ 247	Walt Terrell	.04	.02	.00
☐ 248	Dave Winfield	.25	.12	.02
☐ 249	Dwight Evans	.15	.07	.01
☐ 250	Dennis Powell	.15	.07	.01
☐ 251	Andre Thornton	.07	.03	.01
☐ 252	Onix Concepcion	.04	.02	.00
☐ 253	Mike Heath	.04	.02	.00
☐ 254A	David Palmer ERR (position 2B)	.10	.05	.01
☐ 254B	David Palmer COR (position P)	.60	.30	.06
☐ 255	Donnie Moore	.07	.03	.01
☐ 256	Curtis Wilkerson	.04	.02	.00
☐ 257	Julio Cruz	.04	.02	.00
☐ 258	Nolan Ryan	.30	.15	.03
☐ 259	Jeff Stone	.07	.03	.01
☐ 260	John Tudor	.12	.06	.01
☐ 261	Mark Thurmond	.07	.03	.01
☐ 262	Jay Tibbs	.04	.02	.00
☐ 263	Rafael Ramirez	.04	.02	.00
☐ 264	Larry McWilliams	.04	.02	.00
☐ 265	Mark Davis	.04	.02	.00
☐ 266	Bob Dernier	.04	.02	.00
☐ 267	Matt Young	.04	.02	.00
☐ 268	Jim Clancy	.04	.02	.00
☐ 269	Mickey Hatcher	.04	.02	.00
☐ 270	Sammy Stewart	.04	.02	.00
☐ 271	Bob L. Gibson	.10	.05	.01
☐ 272	Nelson Simmons	.10	.05	.01
☐ 273	Rich Gedman	.07	.03	.01
☐ 274	Butch Wynegar	.07	.03	.01
☐ 275	Ken Howell	.07	.03	.01
☐ 276	Mel Hall	.10	.05	.01
☐ 277	Jim Sundberg	.07	.03	.01
☐ 278	Chris Codiroli	.04	.02	.00
☐ 279	Herman Winningham	.15	.07	.01
☐ 280	Rod Carew	.30	.15	.03
☐ 281	Don Slaught	.04	.02	.00
☐ 282	Scott Fletcher	.07	.03	.01
☐ 283	Bill Dawley	.04	.02	.00
☐ 284	Andy Hawkins	.07	.03	.01

☐ 285 Glenn Wilson	.10	.05	.01
☐ 286 Nick Esasky	.07	.03	.01
☐ 287 Claudell Washington	.07	.03	.01
☐ 288 Lee Mazzilli	.04	.02	.00
☐ 289 Jody Davis	.10	.05	.01
☐ 290 Darrell Porter	.04	.02	.00
☐ 291 Scott McGregor	.07	.03	.01
☐ 292 Ted Simmons	.10	.05	.01
☐ 293 Aurelio Lopez	.04	.02	.00
☐ 294 Marty Barrett	.12	.06	.01
☐ 295 Dale Berra	.04	.02	.00
☐ 296 Greg Brock	.07	.03	.01
☐ 297 Charlie Leibrandt	.07	.03	.01
☐ 298 Bill Krueger	.04	.02	.00
☐ 299 Bryn Smith	.07	.03	.01
☐ 300 Burt Hooton	.04	.02	.00
☐ 301 Stu Cliburn	.10	.05	.01
☐ 302 Luis Salazar	.04	.02	.00
☐ 303 Ken Dayley	.04	.02	.00
☐ 304 Frank DiPino	.04	.02	.00
☐ 305 Von Hayes	.12	.06	.01
☐ 306 Gary Redus	.07	.03	.01
☐ 307 Craig Lefferts	.04	.02	.00
☐ 308 Sammy Khalifa	.10	.05	.01
☐ 309 Scott Garrelts	.07	.03	.01
☐ 310 Rick Cerone	.04	.02	.00
☐ 311 Shawon Dunston	.10	.05	.01
☐ 312 Howard Johnson	.25	.12	.02
☐ 313 Jim Presley	.35	.17	.03
☐ 314 Gary Gaetti	.15	.07	.01
☐ 315 Luis Leal	.04	.02	.00
☐ 316 Mark Salas	.07	.03	.01
☐ 317 Bill Caudill	.04	.02	.00
☐ 318 Dave Henderson	.04	.02	.00
☐ 319 Rafael Santana	.04	.02	.00
☐ 320 Leon Durham	.10	.05	.01
☐ 321 Bruce Sutter	.12	.06	.01
☐ 322 Jason Thompson	.07	.03	.01
☐ 323 Bob Brenly	.07	.03	.01
☐ 324 Carmelo Martinez	.07	.03	.01
☐ 325 Eddie Milner	.07	.03	.01
☐ 326 Juan Samuel	.15	.07	.01
☐ 327 Tom Nieto	.04	.02	.00
☐ 328 Dave Smith	.07	.03	.01
☐ 329 Urbano Lugo	.07	.03	.01
☐ 330 Joel Skinner	.07	.03	.01
☐ 331 Bill Gullickson	.07	.03	.01
☐ 332 Floyd Rayford	.04	.02	.00
☐ 333 Ben Oglivie	.07	.03	.01
☐ 334 Lance Parrish	.18	.09	.01
☐ 335 Jackie Gutierrez	.04	.02	.00
☐ 336 Dennis Rasmussen	.07	.03	.01
☐ 337 Terry Whitfield	.04	.02	.00
☐ 338 Neal Heaton	.04	.02	.00
☐ 339 Jorge Orta	.04	.02	.00
☐ 340 Donnie Hill	.04	.02	.00
☐ 341 Joe Hesketh	.07	.03	.01
☐ 342 Charlie Hough	.07	.03	.01
☐ 343 Dave Rozema	.04	.02	.00
☐ 344 Greg Pryor	.04	.02	.00
☐ 345 Mickey Tettleton	.10	.05	.01
☐ 346 George Vukovich	.04	.02	.00
☐ 347 Don Baylor	.10	.05	.01
☐ 348 Carlos Diaz	.04	.02	.00
☐ 349 Barbaro Garbey	.04	.02	.00
☐ 350 Larry Sheets	.15	.07	.01
☐ 351 Ted Higuera	1.50	.75	.15
☐ 352 Juan Beniquez	.07	.03	.01
☐ 353 Bob Forsch	.07	.03	.01
☐ 354 Mark Bailey	.04	.02	.00
☐ 355 Larry Andersen	.04	.02	.00
☐ 356 Terry Kennedy	.07	.03	.01
☐ 357 Don Robinson	.04	.02	.00
☐ 358 Jim Gott	.04	.02	.00
☐ 359 Earnie Riles	.25	.12	.02
☐ 360 John Christensen	.07	.03	.01
☐ 361 Ray Fontenot	.04	.02	.00
☐ 362 Spike Owen	.04	.02	.00
☐ 363 Jim Acker	.04	.02	.00
☐ 364 Ron Davis	.10	.05	.01
☐ 365 Tom Hume	.04	.02	.00
☐ 366 Carlton Fisk	.15	.07	.01
☐ 367 Nate Snell	.07	.03	.01
☐ 368 Rick Manning	.04	.02	.00
☐ 369 Darrell Evans	.12	.06	.01
☐ 370 Ron Hassey	.04	.02	.00
☐ 371 Wade Boggs	2.50	1.25	.25
☐ 372 Rick Honeycutt	.07	.03	.01
☐ 373 Chris Bando	.04	.02	.00
☐ 374 Bud Black	.04	.02	.00
☐ 375 Steve Henderson	.04	.02	.00
☐ 376 Charlie Lea	.04	.02	.00
☐ 377 Reggie Jackson	.40	.20	.04
☐ 378 Dave Schmidt	.07	.03	.01
☐ 379 Bob James	.04	.02	.00
☐ 380 Glenn Davis	1.50	.75	.15
☐ 381 Tim Corcoran	.04	.02	.00
☐ 382 Danny Cox	.12	.06	.01
☐ 383 Tim Flannery	.04	.02	.00
☐ 384 Tom Browning	.12	.06	.01
☐ 385 Rick Camp	.04	.02	.00
☐ 386 Jim Morrison	.04	.02	.00
☐ 387 Dave LaPoint	.04	.02	.00
☐ 388 Davey Lopes	.07	.03	.01
☐ 389 Al Cowens	.04	.02	.00
☐ 390 Doyle Alexander	.07	.03	.01
☐ 391 Tim Laudner	.07	.03	.01
☐ 392 Don Aase	.07	.03	.01
☐ 393 Jaime Cocanower	.04	.02	.00
☐ 394 Randy O'Neal	.07	.03	.01
☐ 395 Mike Easler	.07	.03	.01
☐ 396 Scott Bradley	.07	.03	.01
☐ 397 Tom Niedenfuer	.07	.03	.01
☐ 398 Jerry Willard	.04	.02	.00
☐ 399 Lonnie Smith	.07	.03	.01
☐ 400 Bruce Bochte	.04	.02	.00
☐ 401 Terry Francona	.04	.02	.00
☐ 402 Jim Slaton	.04	.02	.00
☐ 403 Bill Stein	.04	.02	.00
☐ 404 Tim Hulett	.04	.02	.00
☐ 405 Alan Ashby	.04	.02	.00
☐ 406 Tim Stoddard	.04	.02	.00
☐ 407 Garry Maddox	.04	.02	.00
☐ 408 Ted Power	.07	.03	.01
☐ 409 Len Barker	.04	.02	.00
☐ 410 Denny Gonzalez	.04	.02	.00
☐ 411 George Frazier	.04	.02	.00
☐ 412 Andy Van Slyke	.10	.05	.01
☐ 413 Jim Dwyer	.04	.02	.00
☐ 414 Paul Householder	.04	.02	.00
☐ 415 Alejandro Sanchez	.04	.02	.00
☐ 416 Steve Crawford	.04	.02	.00
☐ 417 Dan Pasqua	.15	.07	.01
☐ 418 Enos Cabell	.04	.02	.00
☐ 419 Mike Jones	.04	.02	.00
☐ 420 Steve Kiefer	.07	.03	.01
☐ 421 Tim Burke	.30	.15	.03
☐ 422 Mike Mason	.04	.02	.00
☐ 423 Ruppert Jones	.04	.02	.00
☐ 424 Jerry Hairston	.04	.02	.00
☐ 425 Tito Landrum	.04	.02	.00
☐ 426 Jeff Calhoun	.07	.03	.01
☐ 427 Don Carman	.25	.12	.02
☐ 428 Tony Perez	.12	.06	.01
☐ 429 Jerry Davis	.04	.02	.00
☐ 430 Bob Walk	.04	.02	.00
☐ 431 Brad Wellman	.04	.02	.00
☐ 432 Terry Forster	.07	.03	.01
☐ 433 Billy Hatcher	.12	.06	.01
☐ 434 Clint Hurdle	.04	.02	.00
☐ 435 Ivan Calderon	1.25	.60	.12
☐ 436 Pete Filson	.04	.02	.00
☐ 437 Tom Henke	.15	.07	.01
☐ 438 Dave Engle	.04	.02	.00
☐ 439 Tom Filer	.07	.03	.01
☐ 440 Gorman Thomas	.10	.05	.01
☐ 441 Rick Aguilera	.35	.17	.03
☐ 442 Scott Sanderson	.04	.02	.00
☐ 443 Jeff Dedmon	.04	.02	.00
☐ 444 Joe Orsulak	.15	.07	.01
☐ 445 Atlee Hammaker	.04	.02	.00
☐ 446 Jerry Royster	.04	.02	.00
☐ 447 Buddy Bell	.10	.05	.01
☐ 448 Dave Rucker	.04	.02	.00
☐ 449 Ivan DeJesus	.04	.02	.00
☐ 450 Jim Pankovits	.04	.02	.00
☐ 451 Jerry Narron	.04	.02	.00
☐ 452 Bryan Little	.04	.02	.00
☐ 453 Gary Lucas	.04	.02	.00
☐ 454 Dennis Martinez	.07	.03	.01
☐ 455 Ed Romero	.04	.02	.00
☐ 456 Bob Melvin	.15	.07	.01
☐ 457 Glenn Hoffman	.04	.02	.00
☐ 458 Bob Shirley	.04	.02	.00
☐ 459 Bob Welch	.07	.03	.01
☐ 460 Carmen Castillo	.04	.02	.00
☐ 461 Dave Leiper	.07	.03	.00
☐ 462 Tim Birtsas	.15	.07	.01
☐ 463 Randy St.Claire	.04	.02	.00
☐ 464 Chris Welsh	.04	.02	.00
☐ 465 Greg Harris	.04	.02	.00
☐ 466 Lynn Jones	.04	.02	.00
☐ 467 Dusty Baker	.07	.03	.01
☐ 468 Roy Smith	.04	.02	.00
☐ 469 Andre Robertson	.04	.02	.00
☐ 470 Ken Landreaux	.04	.02	.00
☐ 471 Dave Bergman	.04	.02	.00
☐ 472 Gary Roenicke	.04	.02	.00
☐ 473 Pete Vuckovich	.07	.03	.01
☐ 474 Kirk McCaskill	.45	.22	.04

☐ 475 Jeff Lahti	.04	.02	.00
☐ 476 Mike Scott	.35	.17	.03
☐ 477 Darren Daulton	.25	.12	.02
☐ 478 Graig Nettles	.12	.06	.01
☐ 479 Bill Almon	.04	.02	.00
☐ 480 Greg Minton	.04	.02	.00
☐ 481 Randy Ready	.07	.03	.01
☐ 482 Lenny Dykstra	1.25	.60	.12
☐ 483 Thad Bosley	.04	.02	.00
☐ 484 Harold Reynolds	.45	.22	.04
☐ 485 Al Oliver	.10	.05	.01
☐ 486 Roy Smalley	.04	.02	.00
☐ 487 John Franco	.10	.05	.01
☐ 488 Juan Agosto	.04	.02	.00
☐ 489 Al Pardo	.07	.03	.01
☐ 490 Bill Wegman	.15	.07	.01
☐ 491 Frank Tanana	.07	.03	.01
☐ 492 Brian Fisher	.30	.15	.03
☐ 493 Mark Clear	.04	.02	.00
☐ 494 Len Matuszek	.04	.02	.00
☐ 495 Ramon Romero	.07	.03	.01
☐ 496 John Wathan	.07	.03	.01
☐ 497 Rob Picciolo	.04	.02	.00
☐ 498 U.L. Washington	.04	.02	.00
☐ 499 John Candelaria	.07	.03	.01
☐ 500 Duane Walker	.04	.02	.00
☐ 501 Gene Nelson	.04	.02	.00
☐ 502 John Mizerock	.04	.02	.00
☐ 503 Luis Aguayo	.04	.02	.00
☐ 504 Kurt Kepshire	.15	.07	.01
☐ 505 Ed Wojna	.04	.02	.00
☐ 506 Joe Price	.04	.02	.00
☐ 507 Milt Thompson	.60	.30	.06
☐ 508 Junior Ortiz	.04	.02	.00
☐ 509 Vida Blue	.07	.03	.01
☐ 510 Steve Engel	.07	.03	.01
☐ 511 Karl Best	.07	.03	.01
☐ 512 Cecil Fielder	.30	.15	.03
☐ 513 Frank Eufemia	.10	.05	.01
☐ 514 Tippy Martinez	.04	.02	.00
☐ 515 Billy Robidoux	.20	.10	.02
☐ 516 Bill Scherrer	.04	.02	.00
☐ 517 Bruce Hurst	.10	.05	.01
☐ 518 Rich Bordi	.04	.02	.00
☐ 519 Steve Yeager	.04	.02	.00
☐ 520 Tony Bernazard	.04	.02	.00
☐ 521 Hal McRae	.07	.03	.01
☐ 522 Jose Rijo	.07	.03	.01
☐ 523 Mitch Webster	.60	.30	.06
☐ 524 Jack Howell	.45	.22	.04
☐ 525 Alan Bannister	.04	.02	.00
☐ 526 Ron Kittle	.10	.05	.01
☐ 527 Phil Garner	.04	.02	.00
☐ 528 Kurt Bevacqua	.04	.02	.00
☐ 529 Kevin Gross	.04	.02	.00
☐ 530 Bo Diaz	.07	.03	.01
☐ 531 Ken Oberkfell	.04	.02	.00
☐ 532 Rick Reuschel	.07	.03	.01
☐ 533 Ron Meridith	.10	.05	.01
☐ 534 Steve Braun	.04	.02	.00
☐ 535 Wayne Gross	.04	.02	.00
☐ 536 Ray Searage	.04	.02	.00
☐ 537 Tom Brookens	.04	.02	.00
☐ 538 Al Nipper	.04	.02	.00
☐ 539 Billy Sample	.04	.02	.00
☐ 540 Steve Sax	.12	.06	.01
☐ 541 Dan Quisenberry	.12	.06	.01
☐ 542 Tony Phillips	.04	.02	.00
☐ 543 Floyd Youmans	.60	.30	.06
☐ 544 Steve Buechele	.25	.12	.02
☐ 545 Craig Gerber	.07	.03	.01
☐ 546 Joe DeSa	.04	.02	.00
☐ 547 Brian Harper	.04	.02	.00
☐ 548 Kevin Bass	.10	.05	.01
☐ 549 Tom Foley	.04	.02	.00
☐ 550 Dave Van Gorder	.04	.02	.00
☐ 551 Bruce Bochy	.04	.02	.00
☐ 552 R.J. Reynolds	.07	.03	.01
☐ 553 Chris Brown	.75	.35	.07
☐ 554 Bruce Benedict	.04	.02	.00
☐ 555 Warren Brusstar	.04	.02	.00
☐ 556 Danny Heep	.04	.02	.00
☐ 557 Darnell Coles	.07	.03	.01
☐ 558 Greg Gagne	.07	.03	.01
☐ 559 Ernie Whitt	.04	.02	.00
☐ 560 Ron Washington	.04	.02	.00
☐ 561 Jimmy Key	.15	.07	.01
☐ 562 Billy Swift	.10	.05	.01
☐ 563 Ron Darling	.30	.15	.03
☐ 564 Dick Ruthven	.04	.02	.00
☐ 565 Zane Smith	.25	.12	.02
☐ 566 Sid Bream	.07	.03	.01
☐ 567A Joel Youngblood ERR (position P)	.10	.05	.01
☐ 567B Joel Youngblood COR	.60	.30	.06
(position IF)			
☐ 568 Mario Ramirez	.04	.02	.00
☐ 569 Tom Runnels	.07	.03	.01
☐ 570 Rick Schu	.07	.03	.01
☐ 571 Bill Campbell	.04	.02	.00
☐ 572 Dickie Thon	.04	.02	.00
☐ 573 Al Holland	.04	.02	.00
☐ 574 Reid Nichols	.04	.02	.00
☐ 575 Bert Roberge	.04	.02	.00
☐ 576 Mike Flanagan	.07	.03	.01
☐ 577 Tim Leary	.04	.02	.00
☐ 578 Mike Laga	.07	.03	.01
☐ 579 Steve Lyons	.04	.02	.00
☐ 580 Phil Niekro	.15	.07	.01
☐ 581 Gilberto Reyes	.15	.07	.01
☐ 582 Jamie Easterly	.04	.02	.00
☐ 583 Mark Gubicza	.07	.03	.01
☐ 584 Stan Javier	.20	.10	.02
☐ 585 Bill Laskey	.04	.02	.00
☐ 586 Jeff Russell	.04	.02	.00
☐ 587 Dickie Noles	.04	.02	.00
☐ 588 Steve Farr	.04	.02	.00
☐ 589 Steve Ontiveros	.15	.07	.01
☐ 590 Mike Hargrove	.04	.02	.00
☐ 591 Marty Bystrom	.04	.02	.00
☐ 592 Franklin Stubbs	.10	.05	.01
☐ 593 Larry Herndon	.04	.02	.00
☐ 594 Bill Swaggerty	.04	.02	.00
☐ 595 Carlos Ponce	.07	.03	.01
☐ 596 Pat Perry	.12	.06	.01
☐ 597 Ray Knight	.07	.03	.01
☐ 598 Steve Lombardozzi	.25	.12	.02
☐ 599 Brad Havens	.04	.02	.00
☐ 600 Pat Clements	.15	.07	.01
☐ 601 Joe Niekro	.10	.05	.01
☐ 602 Hank Aaron Puzzle Card	.10	.05	.01
☐ 603 Dwayne Henry	.10	.05	.01
☐ 604 Mookie Wilson	.07	.03	.01
☐ 605 Buddy Biancalana	.04	.02	.00
☐ 606 Rance Mulliniks	.04	.02	.00
☐ 607 Alan Wiggins	.04	.02	.00
☐ 608 Joe Cowley	.04	.02	.00
☐ 609A Tom Seaver (green borders on name)	.40	.20	.04
☐ 609B Tom Seaver (yellow borders on name)	1.25	.60	.12
☐ 610 Neil Allen	.04	.02	.00
☐ 611 Don Sutton	.20	.10	.02
☐ 612 Fred Toliver	.15	.07	.01
☐ 613 Jay Baller	.10	.05	.01
☐ 614 Marc Sullivan	.07	.03	.01
☐ 615 John Grubb	.04	.02	.00
☐ 616 Bruce Kison	.04	.02	.00
☐ 617 Bill Madlock	.10	.05	.01
☐ 618 Chris Chambliss	.07	.03	.01
☐ 619 Dave Stewart	.10	.05	.01
☐ 620 Tim Lollar	.04	.02	.00
☐ 621 Gary Lavelle	.04	.02	.00
☐ 622 Charlie Hudson	.04	.02	.00
☐ 623 Joel Davis	.20	.10	.02
☐ 624 Joe Johnson	.20	.10	.02
☐ 625 Sid Fernandez	.20	.10	.02
☐ 626 Dennis Lamp	.04	.02	.00
☐ 627 Terry Harper	.04	.02	.00
☐ 628 Jack Lazorko	.04	.02	.00
☐ 629 Roger McDowell	.65	.30	.06
☐ 630 Mark Funderburk	.15	.07	.01
☐ 631 Ed Lynch	.04	.02	.00
☐ 632 Rudy Law	.04	.02	.00
☐ 633 Roger Mason	.15	.07	.01
☐ 634 Mike Felder	.20	.10	.02
☐ 635 Ken Schrom	.04	.02	.00
☐ 636 Bob Ojeda	.07	.03	.01
☐ 637 Ed VandeBerg	.04	.02	.00
☐ 638 Bobby Meacham	.04	.02	.00
☐ 639 Cliff Johnson	.04	.02	.00
☐ 640 Garth Iorg	.04	.02	.00
☐ 641 Dan Driessen	.04	.02	.00
☐ 642 Mike Brown OF	.04	.02	.00
☐ 643 John Shelby	.35	.17	.03
☐ 644 Pete Rose (Ty-Breaking)			
☐ 645 The Knuckle Brothers Phil Niekro Joe Niekro	.10	.05	.01
☐ 646 Jesse Orosco	.07	.03	.01
☐ 647 Billy Beane	.20	.10	.02
☐ 648 Cesar Cedeno	.07	.03	.01
☐ 649 Bert Blyleven	.10	.05	.01
☐ 650 Max Venable	.04	.02	.00
☐ 651 Fleet Feet Vince Coleman	.30	.15	.03

Willie McGee

☐ 652	Calvin Schiraldi	....	.10	.05	.01
☐ 653	King of Kings	....	.65	.30	.06
	(Pete Rose)				
☐ 654	CL: Diamond Kings	....	.08	.01	.00
	(unnumbered)				
☐ 655A	CL 1: 27-130	....	.10	.01	.00
	(unnumbered)				
	(45 Beane ERR)				
☐ 655B	CL 1: 27-130	....	.50	.05	.01
	(unnumbered)				
	(45 Habyan COR)				
☐ 656	CL 2: 131-234	....	.06	.01	.00
	(unnumbered)				
☐ 657	CL 3: 235-338	....	.06	.01	.00
	(unnumbered)				
☐ 658	CL 4: 339-442	....	.06	.01	.00
	(unnumbered)				
☐ 659	CL 5: 443-546	....	.06	.01	.00
	(unnumbered)				
☐ 660	CL 6: 547-653	....	.06	.01	.00
	(unnumbered)				

1986 Donruss Wax Box Cards

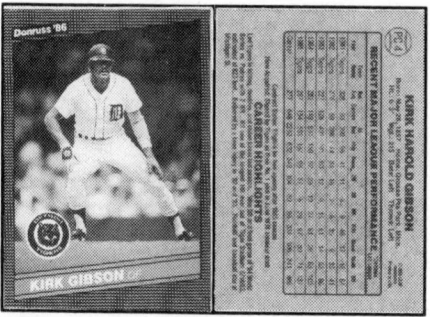

The cards in this 4-card set measure the standard 2 1/2" by 3 1/2". Cards have essentially the same design as the 1986 Donruss regular issue set. The cards were printed on the bottoms of the regular issue wax pack boxes. The four cards (PC4 to PC6 plus a Hank Aaron puzzle card) are considered a separate set in their own right and are not typically included in a complete set of the regular issue 1986 Donruss cards. The value of the panel uncut is slightly greater, perhaps by 25% greater, than the value of the individual cards cut up carefully.

	MINT	EXC	G-VG
COMPLETE SET	.60	.30	.06
COMMON PLAYERS	.10	.05	.01

☐ PC4	Kirk Gibson	....	.35	.17	.03
☐ PC5	Willie Hernandez	....	.15	.07	.01
☐ PC6	Doug DeCinces	....	.10	.05	.01
☐ PUZ	Hank Aaron	....	.10	.05	.01
	Puzzle Card				

1986 Donruss All-Stars

The cards in this 60-card set measure 3 1/2" by 5". Players featured were involved in the 1985 All-Star game played in Minnesota. Cards are very similar in design to the 1986 Donruss regular issue set. The backs give each player's All-Star game statistics and have an orange-yellow border.

	MINT	EXC	G-VG
COMPLETE SET	6.00	3.00	.60
COMMON PLAYERS	.05	.02	.00

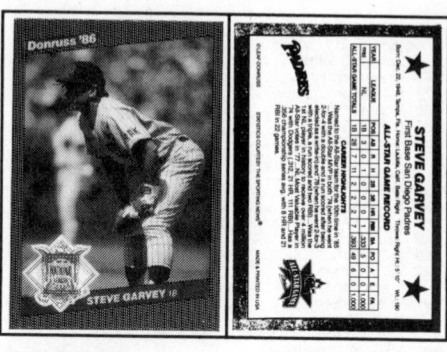

☐ 1	Tony Gwynn	....	.35	.17	.03
☐ 2	Tommy Herr	....	.05	.02	.00
☐ 3	Steve Garvey	....	.30	.15	.03
☐ 4	Dale Murphy	....	.50	.25	.05
☐ 5	Darryl Strawberry	....	.45	.22	.04
☐ 6	Graig Nettles	....	.10	.05	.01
☐ 7	Terry Kennedy	....	.05	.02	.00
☐ 8	Ozzie Smith	....	.20	.10	.02
☐ 9	LaMarr Hoyt	....	.05	.02	.00
☐ 10	Rickey Henderson	....	.40	.20	.04
☐ 11	Lou Whitaker	....	.10	.05	.01
☐ 12	George Brett	....	.40	.20	.04
☐ 13	Eddie Murray	....	.35	.17	.03
☐ 14	Cal Ripken	....	.30	.15	.03
☐ 15	Dave Winfield	....	.25	.12	.02
☐ 16	Jim Rice	....	.25	.12	.02
☐ 17	Carlton Fisk	....	.10	.05	.01
☐ 18	Jack Morris	....	.15	.07	.01
☐ 19	Jose Cruz	....	.05	.02	.00
☐ 20	Tim Raines	....	.25	.12	.02
☐ 21	Nolan Ryan	....	.35	.17	.03
☐ 22	Tony Pena	....	.10	.05	.01
☐ 23	Jack Clark	....	.20	.10	.02
☐ 24	Dave Parker	....	.15	.07	.01
☐ 25	Tim Wallach	....	.10	.05	.01
☐ 26	Ozzie Virgil	....	.05	.02	.00
☐ 27	Fernando Valenzuela	....	.25	.12	.02
☐ 28	Dwight Gooden	....	.80	.40	.08
☐ 29	Glenn Wilson	....	.10	.05	.01
☐ 30	Garry Templeton	....	.05	.02	.00
☐ 31	Goose Gossage	....	.10	.05	.01
☐ 32	Ryne Sandberg	....	.30	.15	.03
☐ 33	Jeff Reardon	....	.10	.05	.01
☐ 34	Pete Rose	....	.90	.45	.09
☐ 35	Scott Garrelts	....	.05	.02	.00
☐ 36	Willie McGee	....	.15	.07	.01
☐ 37	Ron Darling	....	.20	.10	.02
☐ 38	Dick Williams MG	....	.05	.02	.00
☐ 39	Paul Molitor	....	.20	.10	.02
☐ 40	Damaso Garcia	....	.05	.02	.00
☐ 41	Phil Bradley	....	.15	.07	.01
☐ 42	Dan Petry	....	.10	.05	.01
☐ 43	Willie Hernandez	....	.10	.05	.01
☐ 44	Tom Brunansky	....	.15	.07	.01
☐ 45	Alan Trammell	....	.20	.10	.02
☐ 46	Donnie Moore	....	.05	.02	.00
☐ 47	Wade Boggs	....	.90	.45	.09
☐ 48	Ernie Whitt	....	.05	.02	.00
☐ 49	Harold Baines	....	.15	.07	.01
☐ 50	Don Mattingly	....	1.50	.75	.15
☐ 51	Gary Ward	....	.05	.02	.00
☐ 52	Bert Blyleven	....	.10	.05	.01
☐ 53	Jimmy Key	....	.15	.07	.01
☐ 54	Cecil Cooper	....	.10	.05	.01
☐ 55	Dave Stieb	....	.10	.05	.01
☐ 56	Rich Gedman	....	.05	.02	.00
☐ 57	Jay Howell	....	.05	.02	.00
☐ 58	Sparky Anderson MG	....	.05	.02	.00
☐ 59	Minneapolis Metrodome	...	.05	.02	.00
☐ 60	Checklist card	....	.05	.01	.00
	(unnumbered)				

1986 Donruss All-Star Box

The cards in this 4-card set measure the standard 2 1/2" by 3 1/2" in spite of the fact that they form the bottom of the wax pack box for the larger Donruss All-Star cards. These box cards have

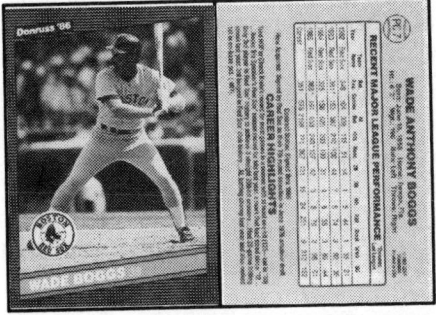

essentially the same design as the 1986 Donruss regular issue set. The cards were printed on the bottoms of the Donruss All-Star (3 1/2" by 5") wax pack boxes. The four cards (PC7 to PC9 plus a Hank Aaron puzzle card) are considered a separate set in their own right and are not typically included in a complete set of the regular issue 1986 Donruss All-Star (or regular) cards. The value of the panel uncut is slightly greater, perhaps by 25% greater, than the value of the individual cards cut up carefully.

	MINT	EXC	G-VG
COMPLETE SET	2.00	1.00	.20
COMMON PLAYERS	.10	.05	.01
☐ PC7 Wade Boggs	1.75	.85	.17
☐ PC8 Lee Smith	.15	.07	.01
☐ PC9 Cecil Cooper	.15	.07	.01
☐ PUZ Hank Aaron	.10	.05	.01
Puzzle Card			

1986 Donruss Pop-Ups

This set is the companion of the 1986 Donruss All-Star (60) set; as such it features the first 18 cards of that set (the All-Star starting line-ups) in a pop-up, die-cut type of card. These cards (measuring 2 1/2" by 5") can be "popped up" to feature a standing card showing the player in action in front of the Metrodome ballpark background. Although this set is unnumbered it is numbered in the same order as its companion set, presumably according to the respective batting orders of the starting line-ups. The first nine numbers below are National Leaguers and the last nine are American Leaguers. See also the

Donruss All-Star checklist card which contains a checklist for the Pop-Ups as well.

		MINT	EXC	G-VG
COMPLETE SET		4.00	2.00	.40
COMMON PLAYERS (1-18)		.10	.05	.01
☐ 1	Tony Gwynn	.40	.20	.04
☐ 2	Tommy Herr	.10	.05	.01
☐ 3	Steve Garvey	.50	.25	.05
☐ 4	Dale Murphy	.70	.35	.07
☐ 5	Darryl Strawberry	.60	.30	.06
☐ 6	Graig Nettles	.15	.07	.01
☐ 7	Terry Kennedy	.10	.05	.01
☐ 8	Ozzie Smith	.20	.10	.02
☐ 9	LaMarr Hoyt	.10	.05	.01
☐ 10	Rickey Henderson	.60	.30	.06
☐ 11	Lou Whitaker	.20	.10	.02
☐ 12	George Brett	.60	.30	.06
☐ 13	Eddie Murray	.50	.25	.05
☐ 14	Cal Ripken	.50	.25	.05
☐ 15	Dave Winfield	.40	.20	.04
☐ 16	Jim Rice	.35	.17	.03
☐ 17	Carlton Fisk	.20	.10	.02
☐ 18	Jack Morris	.25	.12	.02

1986 Donruss Super DK's

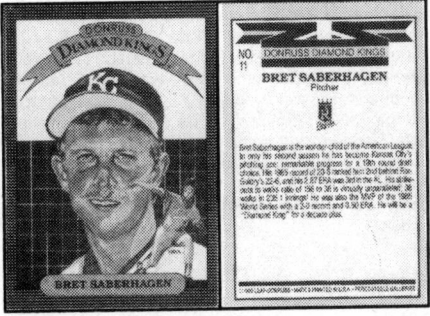

This 29-card set of large Diamond Kings features the full-color artwork of Dick Perez. The set could be obtained from Perez-Steele Galleries by sending three Donruss wrappers and 9.00. The cards measure 4 7/8" by 6 13/16" and are identical in design to the Diamond King cards in the Donruss regular issue.

		MINT	EXC	G-VG
COMPLETE SET		9.00	4.50	.90
COMMON PLAYER (1-26)		.20	.10	.02
☐ 1	Kirk Gibson	.40	.20	.04
☐ 2	Goose Gossage	.30	.15	.03
☐ 3	Willie McGee	.30	.15	.03
☐ 4	George Bell	.40	.20	.04
☐ 5	Tony Armas	.20	.10	.02
☐ 6	Chili Davis	.20	.10	.02
☐ 7	Cecil Cooper	.30	.15	.03
☐ 8	Mike Boddicker	.30	.15	.03
☐ 9	Davey Lopes	.20	.10	.02
☐ 10	Bill Doran	.30	.15	.03
☐ 11	Bret Saberhagen	.50	.25	.05
☐ 12	Brett Butler	.30	.15	.03
☐ 13	Harold Baines	.40	.20	.04
☐ 14	Mike Davis	.20	.10	.02
☐ 15	Tony Perez	.40	.20	.04
☐ 16	Willie Randolph	.30	.15	.03
☐ 17	Bob Boone	.30	.15	.03
☐ 18	Orel Hershiser	.40	.20	.04
☐ 19	Johnny Ray	.30	.15	.03
☐ 20	Gary Ward	.20	.10	.02
☐ 21	Rick Mahler	.20	.10	.02
☐ 22	Phil Bradley	.40	.20	.04
☐ 23	Jerry Koosman	.30	.15	.03
☐ 24	Tom Brunansky	.40	.20	.04
☐ 25	Andre Dawson	.60	.30	.06
☐ 26	Dwight Gooden	1.00	.50	.10
☐ 27	Pete Rose	1.25	.60	.12
	King of Kings			

		MINT	EXC	G-VG
☐ 28	Checklist card	.10	.01	.00
	(unnumbered)			
☐ 29	Aaron Puzzle	.20	.10	.02
	(unnumbered)			

1986 Donruss Rookies

The 1986 Donruss "The Rookies" set features 56 cards plus a 15-piece puzzle of Hank Aaron. Cards are in full color and are standard size, 2 1/2" by 3 1/2". The set was distributed in a small green box with gold lettering. Although the set was wrapped in cellophane, the top card was #1 Joyner resulting in a percentage of (Joyner) cards arriving in less than perfect condition. Card fronts are similar in design to the 1986 Donruss regular issue except for the presence of "The Rookies" logo in the lower left corner and a bluish green border instead of a blue border.

		MINT	EXC	G-VG
	COMPLETE SET	18.00	9.00	1.80
	COMMON PLAYER	.07	.03	.01
☐ 1	Wally Joyner	6.00	1.50	.30
☐ 2	Tracy Jones	.75	.35	.07
☐ 3	Allan Anderson	.20	.10	.02
☐ 4	Ed Correa	.30	.15	.03
☐ 5	Reggie Williams	.20	.10	.02
☐ 6	Charlie Kerfeld	.20	.10	.02
☐ 7	Andres Galarraga	.75	.35	.07
☐ 8	Bob Tewksbury	.25	.12	.02
☐ 9	Al Newman	.20	.10	.02
☐ 10	Andres Thomas	.20	.10	.02
☐ 11	Barry Bonds	1.00	.50	.10
☐ 12	Juan Nieves	.20	.10	.02
☐ 13	Mark Eichhorn	.30	.15	.03
☐ 14	Dan Plesac	.35	.17	.03
☐ 15	Cory Snyder	1.75	.85	.17
☐ 16	Kelly Gruber	.10	.05	.01
☐ 17	Kevin Mitchell	.50	.25	.05
☐ 18	Steve Lombardozzi	.10	.05	.01
☐ 19	Mitch Williams	.25	.12	.02
☐ 20	John Cerutti	.25	.12	.02
☐ 21	Todd Worrell	.60	.30	.06
☐ 22	Jose Canseco	4.00	2.00	.40
☐ 23	Pete Incaviglia	2.00	1.00	.20
☐ 24	Jose Guzman	.10	.05	.01
☐ 25	Scott Bailes	.20	.10	.02
☐ 26	Greg Mathews	.40	.20	.04
☐ 27	Eric King	.30	.15	.03
☐ 28	Paul Assenmacher	.20	.10	.02
☐ 29	Jeff Sellers	.20	.10	.02
☐ 30	Bobby Bonilla	.40	.20	.04
☐ 31	Doug Drabek	.35	.17	.03
☐ 32	Will Clark	3.00	1.50	.30
☐ 33	Leon"Bip" Roberts	.15	.07	.01
☐ 34	Jim Deshaies	.45	.22	.04
☐ 35	Mike Lavalliere	.20	.10	.02
☐ 36	Scott Bankhead	.25	.12	.02
☐ 37	Dale Sveum	.75	.35	.07
☐ 38	Bo Jackson	2.50	1.25	.25
☐ 39	Rob Thompson	.45	.22	.04
☐ 40	Eric Plunk	.20	.10	.02
☐ 41	Bill Bathe	.15	.07	.01
☐ 42	John Kruk	1.50	.75	.15
☐ 43	Andy Allanson	.20	.10	.02

		MINT	EXC	G-VG
☐ 44	Mark Portugal	.20	.10	.02
☐ 45	Danny Tartabull	1.00	.50	.10
☐ 46	Bob Kipper	.07	.03	.01
☐ 47	Gene Walter	.20	.10	.02
☐ 48	Rey Quinones	.30	.15	.03
☐ 49	Bobby Witt	.40	.20	.04
☐ 50	Bill Mooneyham	.15	.07	.01
☐ 51	John Cangelosi	.30	.15	.03
☐ 52	Ruben Sierra	3.00	1.50	.30
☐ 53	Rob Woodward	.15	.07	.01
☐ 54	Ed Hearn	.20	.10	.02
☐ 55	Joel McKeon	.20	.10	.02
☐ 56	Checklist card	.15	.02	.00

1986 Donruss Highlights

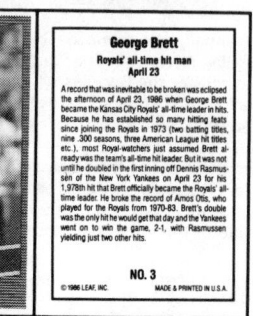

Donruss' second edition of Highlights was released late in 1986. The cards are standard size measuring 2 1/2" by 3 1/2" and are glossy in appearance. Cards commemorate events during the 1986 season, as well as players and pitchers of the month from each league. The set was distributed in its own red, white, blue, and gold box along with a small Hank Aaron puzzle. Card fronts are similar to the regular 1986 Donruss issue except that the Highlights logo is positioned in the lower left- hand corner and the borders are in gold instead of blue. The backs are printed in black and gold on white card stock.

		MINT	EXC	G-VG
	COMPLETE SET	7.00	3.50	.70
	COMMON PLAYER	.06	.03	.00
☐ 1	Will Clark	.40	.10	.02
	Homers in			
	First At-Bat			
☐ 2	Jose Rijo	.06	.03	.00
	Oakland Milestone			
	for Strikeouts			
☐ 3	George Brett	.35	.17	.03
	Royals'			
	All-Time Hit Man			
☐ 4	Mike Schmidt	.45	.22	.04
	Phillies			
	RBI Leader			
☐ 5	Roger Clemens	.40	.20	.04
	KKKKKKKKKK			
	KKKKKKKKKK			
☐ 6	Roger Clemens	.40	.20	.04
	AL Pitcher April			
☐ 7	Kirby Puckett	.35	.17	.03
	AL Player April			
☐ 8	Dwight Gooden	.45	.22	.04
	NL Pitcher April			
☐ 9	Johnny Ray	.06	.03	.00
	NL Player April			
☐ 10	Reggie Jackson	.45	.22	.04
	Eclipses			
	Mantle HR Record			
☐ 11	Wade Boggs	.70	.35	.07
	First Five Hit			
	Game of Career			
☐ 12	Don Aase	.06	.03	.00
	AL Pitcher May			
☐ 13	Wade Boggs	.70	.35	.07
	AL Player May			
☐ 14	Jeff Reardon	.10	.05	.01

NL Pitcher May			
☐ 15 Hubie Brooks	.10	.05	.01
NL Player May			
☐ 16 Don Sutton	.15	.07	.01
Notches 300th			
☐ 17 Roger Clemens	.40	.20	.04
Starts 14-0			
☐ 18 Roger Clemens	.40	.20	.04
AL Pitcher June			
☐ 19 Kent Hrbek	.15	.07	.01
AL Player June			
☐ 20 Rick Rhoden	.06	.03	.00
NL Pitcher June			
☐ 21 Kevin Bass	.10	.05	.01
NL Player June			
☐ 22 Bob Horner	.15	.07	.01
Blasts four			
HRs in one Game			
☐ 23 Wally Joyner	.85	.40	.08
Starting			
All-Star Rookie			
☐ 24 Darryl Strawberry	.45	.22	.04
Starts third			
Straight All-Star Game			
☐ 25 Fernando Valenzuela	.25	.12	.02
Ties All-Star Game			
Record			
☐ 26 Roger Clemens	.40	.20	.04
All-Star Game MVP			
☐ 27 Jack Morris	.15	.07	.01
AL Pitcher July			
☐ 28 Scott Fletcher	.06	.03	.00
AL Player July			
☐ 29 Todd Worrell	.20	.10	.02
NL Pitcher July			
☐ 30 Eric Davis	.75	.35	.07
NL Player July			
☐ 31 Bert Blyleven	.10	.05	.01
Records			
3000th Strikeout			
☐ 32 Bobby Doerr	.15	.07	.01
'86 HOF Inductee			
☐ 33 Ernie Lombardi	.15	.07	.01
'86 HOF Inductee			
☐ 34 Willie McCovey	.20	.10	.02
'86 HOF Inductee			
☐ 35 Steve Carlton	.25	.12	.02
Notches 4000th K			
☐ 36 Mike Schmidt	.45	.22	.04
Surpasses			
DiMaggio Record			
☐ 37 Juan Samuel	.10	.05	.01
Records 3rd			
"Quadruple Double"			
☐ 38 Mike Witt	.10	.05	.01
AL Pitcher August			
☐ 39 Doug DeCinces	.06	.03	.00
AL Player August			
☐ 40 Bill Gullickson	.06	.03	.00
NL Pitcher August			
☐ 41 Dale Murphy	.45	.22	.04
NL Player August			
☐ 42 Joe Carter	.20	.10	.02
Sets Tribe			
Offensive Record			
☐ 43 Bo Jackson	.70	.35	.07
Longest HR in			
Royals Stadium			
☐ 44 Joe Cowley	.06	.03	.00
Majors 1st No-			
Hitter in 2 Years			
☐ 45 Jim Deshaies	.10	.05	.01
Sets ML			
Strikeout Record			
☐ 46 Mike Scott	.20	.10	.02
No Hitter			
Clinches Division			
☐ 47 Bruce Hurst	.10	.05	.01
AL Pitcher September			
☐ 48 Don Mattingly	1.00	.50	.10
AL Player September			
☐ 49 Mike Krukow	.10	.05	.01
NL Pitcher September			
☐ 50 Steve Sax	.15	.07	.01
NL Player September			
☐ 51 John Cangelosi	.15	.07	.01
AL Rookie			
Steals Record			
☐ 52 Dave Righetti	.15	.07	.01
ML Save Mark			
☐ 53 Don Mattingly	1.00	.50	.10
Yankee Record for			
Hits and Doubles			
☐ 54 Todd Worrell	.30	.15	.03
Donruss NL ROY			

☐ 55 Jose Canseco	1.00	.50	.10
Donruss AL ROY			
☐ 56 Checklist card	.10	.01	.00

1987 Donruss

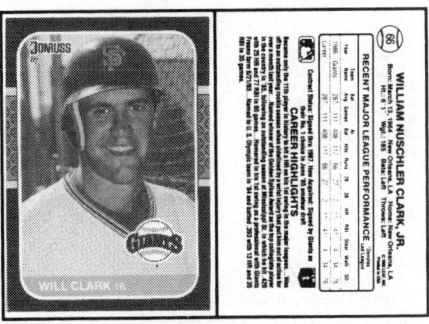

This 660-card set was distributed along with a puzzle of Roberto Clemente. The checklist cards are numbered throughout the set as multiples of 100. The wax pack boxes again contain a separate four cards printed on the bottom of the box. Cards measure 2 1/2" by 3 1/2" and feature a black and gold border on the front; the backs are also done in black and gold on white card stock. The popular Diamond King subset returns for the sixth consecutive year. Some of the Diamond King (1-26) selections are repeats from prior years; Perez-Steele Galleries has indicated that a five-year rotation will be maintained in order to avoid depleting the pool of available worthy "kings" on some of the teams. Three of the Diamond Kings have a variation (on the reverse) where the yellow strip behind the words "Donruss Diamond Kings" is not printed and hence the background is white.

		MINT	EXC	G-VG
COMPLETE SET		33.00	15.00	3.00
COMMON PLAYER		.03	.01	.00
☐	1 Wally Joyner DK	1.50	.30	.06
☐	2 Roger Clemens DK	.60	.30	.06
☐	3 Dale Murphy DK	.45	.22	.04
☐	4 Darryl Strawberry DK	.45	.22	.04
☐	5 Ozzie Smith DK	.15	.07	.01
☐	6 Jose Canseco DK	.75	.35	.07
☐	7 Charlie Hough DK	.10	.05	.01
☐	8 Brook Jacoby DK	.10	.05	.01
☐	9 Fred Lynn DK	.15	.07	.01
☐	10 Rick Rhoden DK	.10	.05	.01
☐	11 Chris Brown DK	.15	.07	.01
☐	12 Von Hayes DK	.12	.06	.01
☐	13 Jack Morris DK	.15	.07	.01
☐	14A Kevin McReynolds DK ..	.75	.35	.07
	(yellow strip			
	missing on back)			
☐	14B Kevin McReynolds DK ..	.30	.15	.03
☐	15 George Brett DK	.40	.20	.04
☐	16 Ted Higuera DK	.25	.12	.02
☐	17 Hubie Brooks DK	.10	.05	.01
☐	18 Mike Scott DK	.25	.12	.02
☐	19 Kirby Puckett DK	.40	.20	.04
☐	20 Dave Winfield DK	.30	.15	.03
☐	21 Lloyd Moseby DK	.12	.06	.01
☐	22A Eric Davis DK	3.00	1.50	.30
	(yellow strip			
	missing on back)			
☐	22B Eric Davis DK	1.00	.50	.10
☐	23 Jim Presley DK	.25	.12	.02
☐	24 Keith Moreland DK	.10	.05	.01
☐	25A Greg Walker DK	.50	.25	.05
	(yellow strip			
	missing on back)			
☐	25B Greg Walker DK	.15	.07	.01
☐	26 Steve Sax DK	.15	.07	.01
☐	27 DK Checklist 1-26	.10	.01	.00

28	B.J. Surhoff RR	1.25	.60	.12
29	Randy Myers RR	.35	.17	.03
30	Ken Gerhart RR	.30	.15	.03
31	Benito Santiago RR	2.25	1.10	.22
32	Greg Swindell RR	.50	.25	.05
33	Mike Birkbeck RR	.15	.07	.01
34	Terry Steinbach RR	.60	.30	.06
35	Bo Jackson RR	1.50	.75	.15
36	Greg Maddux RR	.15	.07	.01
37	Jim Lindeman RR	.50	.25	.05
38	Devon White RR	1.75	.85	.17
39	Eric Bell RR	.20	.10	.02
40	Will Fraser RR	.20	.10	.02
41	Jerry Browne RR	.20	.10	.02
42	Chris James RR	1.00	.50	.10
43	Rafael Palmeiro RR	.65	.30	.06
44	Pat Dodson RR	.25	.12	.02
45	Duane Ward RR	.15	.07	.01
46	Mark McGwire RR	7.50	3.75	.75
47	Bruce Fields RR	.10	.05	.01
	(photo actually Bruce Fields)			
48	Eddie Murray	.30	.15	.03
49	Ted Higuera	.20	.10	.02
50	Kirk Gibson	.20	.10	.02
51	Oil Can Boyd	.06	.03	.00
52	Don Mattingly	2.50	1.25	.25
53	Pedro Guerrero	.20	.10	.02
54	George Brett	.35	.17	.03
55	Jose Rijo	.06	.03	.00
56	Tim Raines	.25	.12	.02
57	Ed Correa	.25	.12	.02
58	Mike Witt	.12	.06	.01
59	Greg Walker	.10	.05	.01
60	Ozzie Smith	.20	.10	.02
61	Glenn Davis	.25	.12	.02
62	Glenn Wilson	.10	.05	.01
63	Tom Browning	.06	.03	.00
64	Tony Gwynn	.40	.20	.04
65	R.J. Reynolds	.06	.03	.00
66	Will Clark	1.75	.85	.17
67	Ozzie Virgil	.03	.01	.00
68	Rick Sutcliffe	.12	.06	.01
69	Gary Carter	.30	.15	.03
70	Mike Moore	.03	.01	.00
71	Bert Blyleven	.10	.05	.01
72	Tony Fernandez	.18	.09	.01
73	Kent Hrbek	.18	.09	.01
74	Lloyd Moseby	.10	.05	.01
75	Alvin Davis	.12	.06	.01
76	Keith Hernandez	.25	.12	.02
77	Ryne Sandberg	.30	.15	.03
78	Dale Murphy	.45	.22	.04
79	Sid Bream	.06	.03	.00
80	Chris Brown	.12	.06	.01
81	Steve Garvey	.30	.15	.03
82	Mario Soto	.06	.03	.00
83	Shane Rawley	.06	.03	.00
84	Willie McGee	.15	.07	.01
85	Jose Cruz	.10	.05	.01
86	Brian Downing	.06	.03	.00
87	Ozzie Guillen	.10	.05	.01
88	Hubie Brooks	.10	.05	.01
89	Cal Ripken	.30	.15	.03
90	Juan Nieves	.06	.03	.00
91	Lance Parrish	.15	.07	.01
92	Jim Rice	.25	.12	.02
93	Ron Guidry	.15	.07	.01
94	Fernando Valenzuela	.25	.12	.02
95	Andy Allanson	.12	.06	.01
96	Willie Wilson	.12	.06	.01
97	Jose Canseco	2.00	1.00	.20
98	Jeff Reardon	.10	.05	.01
99	Bobby Witt	.30	.15	.03
100	Checklist	.06	.01	.00
101	Jose Guzman	.06	.03	.00
102	Steve Balboni	.03	.01	.00
103	Tony Phillips	.03	.01	.00
104	Brook Jacoby	.10	.05	.01
105	Dave Winfield	.30	.15	.03
106	Orel Hershiser	.15	.07	.01
107	Lou Whitaker	.15	.07	.01
108	Fred Lynn	.15	.07	.01
109	Bill Wegman	.03	.01	.00
110	Donnie Moore	.03	.01	.00
111	Jack Clark	.18	.09	.01
112	Bob Knepper	.06	.03	.00
113	Von Hayes	.10	.05	.01
114	Leon "Bip" Roberts	.10	.05	.01
115	Tony Pena	.10	.05	.01
116	Scott Garrelts	.06	.03	.00
117	Paul Molitor	.12	.06	.01
118	Darryl Strawberry	.45	.22	.04
119	Shawon Dunston	.10	.05	.01
120	Jim Presley	.18	.09	.01
121	Jesse Barfield	.18	.09	.01
122	Gary Gaetti	.15	.07	.01
123	Kurt Stillwell	.30	.15	.03
124	Joel Davis	.03	.01	.00
125	Mike Boddicker	.06	.03	.00
126	Robin Yount	.30	.15	.03
127	Alan Trammell	.20	.10	.02
128	Dave Righetti	.15	.07	.01
129	Dwight Evans	.12	.06	.01
130	Mike Scioscia	.03	.01	.00
131	Julio Franco	.10	.05	.01
132	Bret Saberhagen	.35	.17	.03
133	Mike Davis	.06	.03	.00
134	Joe Hesketh	.06	.03	.00
135	Wally Joyner	2.50	1.25	.25
136	Don Slaught	.03	.01	.00
137	Daryl Boston	.03	.01	.00
138	Nolan Ryan	.30	.15	.03
139	Mike Schmidt	.40	.20	.04
140	Tommy Herr	.06	.03	.00
141	Garry Templeton	.06	.03	.00
142	Kal Daniels	1.00	.50	.10
143	Billy Sample	.03	.01	.00
144	Johnny Ray	.10	.05	.01
145	Rob Thompson	.30	.15	.03
146	Bob Dernier	.03	.01	.00
147	Danny Tartabull	.35	.17	.03
148	Ernie Whitt	.03	.01	.00
149	Kirby Puckett	.45	.22	.04
150	Mike Young	.06	.03	.00
151	Ernest Riles	.06	.03	.00
152	Frank Tanana	.06	.03	.00
153	Rich Gedman	.06	.03	.00
154	Willie Randolph	.06	.03	.00
155	Bill Madlock	.10	.05	.01
156	Joe Carter	.18	.09	.01
157	Danny Jackson	.06	.03	.00
158	Carney Lansford	.10	.05	.01
159	Bryn Smith	.06	.03	.00
160	Gary Pettis	.06	.03	.00
161	Oddibe McDowell	.18	.09	.01
162	John Cangelosi	.15	.07	.01
163	Mike Scott	.25	.12	.02
164	Eric Show	.03	.01	.00
165	Juan Samuel	.15	.07	.01
166	Nick Esasky	.03	.01	.00
167	Zane Smith	.06	.03	.00
168	Mike Brown	.03	.01	.00
	(Pirates OF)			
169	Keith Moreland	.06	.03	.00
170	John Tudor	.10	.05	.01
171	Ken Dixon	.03	.01	.00
172	Jim Gantner	.03	.01	.00
173	Jack Morris	.15	.07	.01
174	Bruce Hurst	.10	.05	.01
175	Dennis Rasmussen	.06	.03	.00
176	Mike Marshall	.10	.05	.01
177	Dan Quisenberry	.12	.06	.01
178	Eric Plunk	.10	.05	.01
179	Tim Wallach	.10	.05	.01
180	Steve Buechele	.03	.01	.00
181	Don Sutton	.15	.07	.01
182	Dave Schmidt	.06	.03	.00
183	Terry Pendleton	.06	.03	.00
184	Jim Deshaies	.25	.12	.02
185	Steve Bedrosian	.15	.07	.01
186	Pete Rose	.60	.30	.06
187	Dave Dravecky	.06	.03	.00
188	Rick Reuschel	.06	.03	.00
189	Dan Gladden	.06	.03	.00
190	Rick Mahler	.03	.01	.00
191	Thad Bosley	.03	.01	.00
192	Ron Darling	.20	.10	.02
193	Matt Young	.03	.01	.00
194	Tom Brunansky	.12	.06	.01
195	Dave Stieb	.12	.06	.01
196	Frank Viola	.12	.06	.01
197	Tom Henke	.10	.05	.01
198	Karl Best	.03	.01	.00
199	Dwight Gooden	.80	.40	.08
200	Checklist	.06	.01	.00
201	Steve Trout	.06	.03	.00
202	Rafael Ramirez	.03	.01	.00
203	Bob Walk	.03	.01	.00
204	Roger Mason	.06	.03	.00
205	Terry Kennedy	.06	.03	.00
206	Ron Oester	.03	.01	.00
207	John Russell	.03	.01	.00
208	Greg Mathews	.25	.12	.02
209	Charlie Kerfeld	.06	.03	.00
210	Reggie Jackson	.40	.20	.04
211	Floyd Bannister	.06	.03	.00
212	Vance Law	.03	.01	.00
213	Rich Bordi	.03	.01	.00
214	Dan Plesac	.35	.17	.03

☐ 215 Dave Collins	.03	.01	.00
☐ 216 Bob Stanley	.03	.01	.00
☐ 217 Joe Niekro	.10	.05	.01
☐ 218 Tom Niedenfuer	.06	.03	.00
☐ 219 Brett Butler	.10	.05	.01
☐ 220 Charlie Leibrandt	.06	.03	.00
☐ 221 Steve Ontiveros	.03	.01	.00
☐ 222 Tim Burke	.03	.01	.00
☐ 223 Curtis Wilkerson	.03	.01	.00
☐ 224 Pete Incaviglia	1.50	.75	.15
☐ 225 Lonnie Smith	.06	.03	.00
☐ 226 Chris Codiroli	.03	.01	.00
☐ 227 Scott Bailes	.20	.10	.02
☐ 228 Rickey Henderson	.35	.17	.03
☐ 229 Ken Howell	.03	.01	.00
☐ 230 Darnell Coles	.06	.03	.00
☐ 231 Don Aase	.03	.01	.00
☐ 232 Tim Leary	.03	.01	.00
☐ 233 Bob Boone	.06	.03	.00
☐ 234 Ricky Horton	.03	.01	.00
☐ 235 Mark Bailey	.03	.01	.00
☐ 236 Kevin Gross	.03	.01	.00
☐ 237 Lance McCullers	.06	.03	.00
☐ 238 Cecilio Guante	.03	.01	.00
☐ 239 Bob Melvin	.03	.01	.00
☐ 240 Billy Jo Robidoux	.06	.03	.00
☐ 241 Roger McDowell	.10	.05	.01
☐ 242 Leon Durham	.10	.05	.01
☐ 243 Ed Nunez	.03	.01	.00
☐ 244 Jimmy Key	.12	.06	.01
☐ 245 Mike Smithson	.03	.01	.00
☐ 246 Bo Diaz	.06	.03	.00
☐ 247 Carlton Fisk	.10	.05	.01
☐ 248 Larry Sheets	.12	.06	.01
☐ 249 Juan Castillo	.03	.01	.00
☐ 250 Eric King	.20	.10	.02
☐ 251 Doug Drabek	.25	.12	.02
☐ 252 Wade Boggs	1.50	.75	.15
☐ 253 Mariano Duncan	.06	.03	.00
☐ 254 Pat Tabler	.10	.05	.01
☐ 255 Frank White	.06	.03	.00
☐ 256 Alfredo Griffin	.06	.03	.00
☐ 257 Floyd Youmans	.10	.05	.01
☐ 258 Rob Wilfong	.03	.01	.00
☐ 259 Pete O'Brien	.10	.05	.01
☐ 260 Tim Hulett	.03	.01	.00
☐ 261 Dickie Thon	.03	.01	.00
☐ 262 Darren Daulton	.03	.01	.00
☐ 263 Vince Coleman	.45	.22	.04
☐ 264 Andy Hawkins	.03	.01	.00
☐ 265 Eric Davis	1.75	.85	.17
☐ 266 Andres Thomas	.20	.10	.02
☐ 267 Mike Diaz	.20	.10	.02
☐ 268 Chili Davis	.08	.04	.01
☐ 269 Jody Davis	.08	.04	.01
☐ 270 Phil Bradley	.12	.06	.01
☐ 271 George Bell	.30	.15	.03
☐ 272 Keith Atherton	.03	.01	.00
☐ 273 Storm Davis	.06	.03	.00
☐ 274 Rob Deer	.15	.07	.01
☐ 275 Walt Terrell	.03	.01	.00
☐ 276 Roger Clemens	1.50	.75	.15
☐ 277 Mike Easler	.06	.03	.00
☐ 278 Steve Sax	.12	.06	.01
☐ 279 Andre Thornton	.06	.03	.00
☐ 280 Jim Sundberg	.03	.01	.00
☐ 281 Bill Bathe	.10	.05	.01
☐ 282 Jay Tibbs	.03	.01	.00
☐ 283 Dick Schofield	.03	.01	.00
☐ 284 Mike Mason	.03	.01	.00
☐ 285 Jerry Hairston	.03	.01	.00
☐ 286 Bill Doran	.08	.04	.01
☐ 287 Tim Flannery	.03	.01	.00
☐ 288 Gary Redus	.06	.03	.00
☐ 289 John Franco	.08	.04	.01
☐ 290 Paul Assenmacher	.10	.05	.01
☐ 291 Joe Orsulak	.03	.01	.00
☐ 292 Lee Smith	.08	.04	.01
☐ 293 Mike Laga	.03	.01	.00
☐ 294 Rick Dempsey	.06	.03	.00
☐ 295 Mike Felder	.06	.03	.00
☐ 296 Tom Brookens	.03	.01	.00
☐ 297 Al Nipper	.03	.01	.00
☐ 298 Mike Pagliarulo	.12	.06	.01
☐ 299 Franklin Stubbs	.08	.04	.01
☐ 300 Checklist	.06	.01	.00
☐ 301 Steve Farr	.03	.01	.00
☐ 302 Bill Mooneyham	.08	.04	.01
☐ 303 Andres Galarraga	.25	.12	.02
☐ 304 Scott Fletcher	.06	.03	.00
☐ 305 Jack Howell	.06	.03	.00
☐ 306 Russ Morman	.15	.07	.01
☐ 307 Todd Worrell	.25	.12	.02
☐ 308 Dave Smith	.06	.03	.00
☐ 309 Jeff Stone	.06	.03	.00

☐ 310 Ron Robinson	.03	.01	.00
☐ 311 Bruce Bochy	.03	.01	.00
☐ 312 Jim Winn	.03	.01	.00
☐ 313 Mark Davis	.03	.01	.00
☐ 314 Jeff Dedmon	.03	.01	.00
☐ 315 Jamie Moyer	.12	.06	.01
☐ 316 Wally Backman	.06	.03	.00
☐ 317 Ken Phelps	.06	.03	.00
☐ 318 Steve Lombardozzi	.06	.03	.00
☐ 319 Rance Mulliniks	.03	.01	.00
☐ 320 Tim Laudner	.06	.03	.00
☐ 321 Mark Eichhorn	.25	.12	.02
☐ 322 Lee Guetterman	.25	.12	.02
☐ 323 Sid Fernandez	.18	.09	.01
☐ 324 Jerry Mumphrey	.03	.01	.00
☐ 325 David Palmer	.03	.01	.00
☐ 326 Bill Almon	.03	.01	.00
☐ 327 Candy Maldonado	.10	.05	.01
☐ 328 John Kruk	.75	.35	.07
☐ 329 John Denny	.06	.03	.00
☐ 330 Milt Thompson	.10	.05	.01
☐ 331 Mike Lavalliere	.15	.07	.01
☐ 332 Alan Ashby	.03	.01	.00
☐ 333 Doug Corbett	.03	.01	.00
☐ 334 Ron Karkovice	.08	.04	.01
☐ 335 Mitch Webster	.08	.04	.01
☐ 336 Lee Lacy	.03	.01	.00
☐ 337 Glenn Braggs	.55	.27	.05
☐ 338 Dwight Lowry	.15	.07	.01
☐ 339 Don Baylor	.10	.05	.01
☐ 340 Brian Fisher	.06	.03	.00
☐ 341 Reggie Williams	.20	.10	.02
☐ 342 Tom Candiotti	.06	.03	.00
☐ 343 Rudy Law	.03	.01	.00
☐ 344 Curt Young	.06	.03	.00
☐ 345 Mike Fitzgerald	.03	.01	.00
☐ 346 Ruben Sierra	1.75	.85	.17
☐ 347 Mitch Williams	.20	.10	.02
☐ 348 Jorge Orta	.03	.01	.00
☐ 349 Mickey Tettleton	.03	.01	.00
☐ 350 Ernie Camacho	.03	.01	.00
☐ 351 Ron Kittle	.08	.04	.01
☐ 352 Ken Landreaux	.03	.01	.00
☐ 353 Chet Lemon	.03	.01	.00
☐ 354 John Shelby	.03	.01	.00
☐ 355 Mark Clear	.03	.01	.00
☐ 356 Doug DeCinces	.06	.03	.00
☐ 357 Ken Dayley	.03	.01	.00
☐ 358 Phil Garner	.03	.01	.00
☐ 359 Steve Jeltz	.03	.01	.00
☐ 360 Ed Whitson	.03	.01	.00
☐ 361 Barry Bonds	.45	.22	.04
☐ 362 Vida Blue	.06	.03	.00
☐ 363 Cecil Cooper	.08	.04	.01
☐ 364 Bob Ojeda	.08	.04	.01
☐ 365 Dennis Eckersley	.06	.03	.00
☐ 366 Mike Morgan	.03	.01	.00
☐ 367 Willie Upshaw	.06	.03	.00
☐ 368 Allan Anderson	.12	.06	.01
☐ 369 Bill Gullickson	.06	.03	.00
☐ 370 Bobby Thigpen	.20	.10	.02
☐ 371 Juan Beniquez	.03	.01	.00
☐ 372 Charlie Moore	.03	.01	.00
☐ 373 Dan Petry	.08	.04	.01
☐ 374 Rod Scurry	.03	.01	.00
☐ 375 Tom Seaver	.30	.15	.03
☐ 376 Ed VandeBerg	.03	.01	.00
☐ 377 Tony Bernazard	.03	.01	.00
☐ 378 Greg Pryor	.03	.01	.00
☐ 379 Dwayne Murphy	.03	.01	.00
☐ 380 Andy McGaffigan	.03	.01	.00
☐ 381 Kirk McCaskill	.06	.03	.00
☐ 382 Greg Harris	.03	.01	.00
☐ 383 Rich Dotson	.06	.03	.00
☐ 384 Craig Reynolds	.03	.01	.00
☐ 385 Greg Gross	.03	.01	.00
☐ 386 Tito Landrum	.03	.01	.00
☐ 387 Craig Lefferts	.03	.01	.00
☐ 388 Dave Parker	.15	.07	.01
☐ 389 Bob Horner	.15	.07	.01
☐ 390 Pat Clements	.06	.03	.00
☐ 391 Jeff Leonard	.10	.05	.01
☐ 392 Chris Speier	.03	.01	.00
☐ 393 John Moses	.06	.03	.00
☐ 394 Garth Iorg	.03	.01	.00
☐ 395 Greg Gagne	.08	.04	.01
☐ 396 Nate Snell	.03	.01	.00
☐ 397 Bryan Clutterbuck	.08	.04	.01
☐ 398 Darrell Evans	.10	.05	.01
☐ 399 Steve Crawford	.03	.01	.00
☐ 400 Checklist	.06	.01	.00
☐ 401 Phil Lombardi	.20	.10	.02
☐ 402 Rick Honeycutt	.03	.01	.00
☐ 403 Ken Schrom	.03	.01	.00
☐ 404 Bud Black	.03	.01	.00

□	Name				□	Name			
405	Donnie Hill	.03	.01	.00	500	Checklist	.06	.01	.00
406	Wayne Krenchicki	.03	.01	.00	501	Chris Bando	.03	.01	.00
407	Chuck Finley	.08	.04	.01	502	Dave Cone	.25	.12	.02
408	Toby Harrah	.03	.01	.00	503	Jay Howell	.03	.01	.00
409	Steve Lyons	.03	.01	.00	504	Tom Foley	.03	.01	.00
410	Kevin Bass	.08	.04	.01	505	Ray Chadwick	.08	.04	.01
411	Marvell Wynne	.03	.01	.00	506	Mike Loynd	.20	.10	.02
412	Ron Roenicke	.03	.01	.00	507	Neil Allen	.03	.01	.00
413	Tracy Jones	.50	.25	.05	508	Danny Darwin	.03	.01	.00
414	Gene Garber	.03	.01	.00	509	Rick Schu	.03	.01	.00
415	Mike Bielecki	.03	.01	.00	510	Jose Oquendo	.06	.03	.00
416	Frank DiPino	.03	.01	.00	511	Gene Walter	.06	.03	.00
417	Andy Van Slyke	.08	.04	.01	512	Terry McGriff	.20	.10	.02
418	Jim Dwyer	.03	.01	.00	513	Ken Griffey	.06	.03	.00
419	Ben Oglivie	.06	.03	.00	514	Benny Distefano	.03	.01	.00
420	Dave Bergman	.03	.01	.00	515	Terry Mulholland	.10	.05	.01
421	Joe Sambito	.03	.01	.00	516	Ed Lynch	.03	.01	.00
422	Bob Tewksbury	.20	.10	.02	517	Bill Swift	.03	.01	.00
423	Len Matuszek	.03	.01	.00	518	Manny Lee	.06	.03	.00
424	Mike Kingery	.15	.07	.01	519	Andre David	.03	.01	.00
425	Dave Kingman	.10	.05	.01	520	Scott McGregor	.06	.03	.00
426	Al Newman	.10	.05	.01	521	Rick Manning	.03	.01	.00
427	Gary Ward	.06	.03	.00	522	Willie Hernandez	.08	.04	.01
428	Ruppert Jones	.03	.01	.00	523	Marty Barrett	.10	.05	.01
429	Harold Baines	.15	.07	.01	524	Wayne Tolleson	.03	.01	.00
430	Pat Perry	.03	.01	.00	525	Jose Gonzalez	.25	.12	.02
431	Terry Puhl	.03	.01	.00	526	Cory Snyder	.75	.35	.07
432	Don Carman	.03	.01	.00	527	Buddy Biancalana	.03	.01	.00
433	Eddie Milner	.03	.01	.00	528	Moose Haas	.03	.01	.00
434	LaMarr Hoyt	.06	.03	.00	529	Wilfredo Tejada	.08	.04	.01
435	Rick Rhoden	.06	.03	.00	530	Stu Cliburn	.03	.01	.00
436	Jose Uribe	.03	.01	.00	531	Dale Mohorcic	.25	.12	.02
437	Ken Oberkfell	.03	.01	.00	532	Ron Hassey	.03	.01	.00
438	Ron Davis	.03	.01	.00	533	Ty Gainey	.03	.01	.00
439	Jesse Orosco	.06	.03	.00	534	Jerry Royster	.03	.01	.00
440	Scott Bradley	.06	.03	.00	535	Mike Maddux	.10	.05	.01
441	Randy Bush	.03	.01	.00	536	Ted Power	.06	.03	.00
442	John Cerutti	.20	.10	.02	537	Ted Simmons	.10	.05	.01
443	Roy Smalley	.03	.01	.00	538	Rafael Belliard	.10	.05	.01
444	Kelly Gruber	.03	.01	.00	539	Chico Walker	.12	.06	.01
445	Bob Kearney	.03	.01	.00	540	Bob Forsch	.06	.03	.00
446	Ed Hearn	.08	.04	.01	541	John Stefero	.03	.01	.00
447	Scott Sanderson	.03	.01	.00	542	Dale Sveum	.50	.25	.05
448	Bruce Benedict	.03	.01	.00	543	Mark Thurmond	.03	.01	.00
449	Junior Ortiz	.03	.01	.00	544	Jeff Sellers	.10	.05	.01
450	Mike Aldrete	.45	.22	.04	545	Joel Skinner	.06	.03	.00
451	Kevin McReynolds	.20	.10	.02	546	Alex Trevino	.03	.01	.00
452	Rob Murphy	.20	.10	.02	547	Randy Kutcher	.10	.05	.01
453	Kent Tekulve	.06	.03	.00	548	Joaquin Andujar	.08	.04	.01
454	Curt Ford	.15	.07	.01	549	Casey Candaele	.20	.10	.02
455	Davey Lopes	.06	.03	.00	550	Jeff Russell	.03	.01	.00
456	Bobby Grich	.06	.03	.00	551	John Candelaria	.06	.03	.00
457	Jose DeLeon	.03	.01	.00	552	Joe Cowley	.03	.01	.00
458	Andre Dawson	.20	.10	.02	553	Danny Cox	.08	.04	.01
459	Mike Flanagan	.06	.03	.00	554	Denny Walling	.03	.01	.00
460	Joey Meyer	.35	.17	.03	555	Bruce Ruffin	.25	.12	.02
461	Chuck Cary	.20	.10	.02	556	Buddy Bell	.10	.05	.01
462	Bill Buckner	.08	.04	.01	557	Jimmy Jones	.20	.10	.02
463	Bob Shirley	.03	.01	.00	558	Bobby Bonilla	.35	.17	.03
464	Jeff Hamilton	.20	.10	.02	559	Jeff Robinson	.03	.01	.00
465	Phil Niekro	.15	.07	.01		(Giants pitcher)			
466	Mark Gubicza	.06	.03	.00	560	Ed Olwine	.08	.04	.01
467	Jerry Willard	.03	.01	.00	561	Glenallen Hill	.20	.10	.02
468	Bob Sebra	.15	.07	.01	562	Lee Mazzilli	.03	.01	.00
469	Larry Parrish	.06	.03	.00	563	Mike Brown	.03	.01	.00
470	Charlie Hough	.06	.03	.00		(pitcher)			
471	Hal McRae	.06	.03	.00	564	George Frazier	.03	.01	.00
472	Dave Leiper	.06	.03	.00	565	Mike Sharperson	.10	.05	.01
473	Mel Hall	.06	.03	.00	566	Mark Portugal	.10	.05	.01
474	Dan Pasqua	.10	.05	.01	567	Rick Leach	.03	.01	.00
475	Bob Welch	.06	.03	.00	568	Mark Langston	.10	.05	.01
476	Johnny Grubb	.03	.01	.00	569	Rafael Santana	.03	.01	.00
477	Jim Traber	.06	.03	.00	570	Manny Trillo	.03	.01	.00
478	Chris Bosio	.20	.10	.02	571	Cliff Speck	.08	.04	.01
479	Mark McLemore	.03	.01	.00	572	Bob Kipper	.03	.01	.00
480	John Morris	.03	.01	.00	573	Kelly Downs	.25	.12	.02
481	Billy Hatcher	.10	.05	.01	574	Randy Asadoor	.10	.05	.01
482	Dan Schatzeder	.03	.01	.00	575	Dave Magadan	.85	.40	.08
483	Rich Gossage	.12	.06	.01	576	Marvin Freeman	.25	.12	.02
484	Jim Morrison	.03	.01	.00	577	Jeff Lahti	.03	.01	.00
485	Bob Brenly	.06	.03	.00	578	Jeff Calhoun	.06	.03	.00
486	Bill Schroeder	.03	.01	.00	579	Gus Polidor	.06	.03	.00
487	Mookie Wilson	.06	.03	.00	580	Gene Nelson	.03	.01	.00
488	Dave Martinez	.30	.15	.03	581	Tim Teufel	.06	.03	.00
489	Harold Reynolds	.06	.03	.00	582	Odell Jones	.03	.01	.00
490	Jeff Hearron	.10	.05	.01	583	Mark Ryal	.10	.05	.01
491	Mickey Hatcher	.03	.01	.00	584	Randy O'Neal	.03	.01	.00
492	Barry Larkin	.80	.40	.08	585	Mike Greenwell	2.00	1.00	.20
493	Bob James	.03	.01	.00	586	Ray Knight	.06	.03	.00
494	John Habyan	.03	.01	.00	587	Ralph Bryant	.20	.10	.02
495	Jim Adduci	.15	.07	.01	588	Carmen Castillo	.03	.01	.00
496	Mike Heath	.03	.01	.00	589	Ed Wojna	.03	.01	.00
497	Tim Stoddard	.03	.01	.00	590	Stan Javier	.03	.01	.00
498	Tony Armas	.06	.03	.00	591	Jeff Musselman	.25	.12	.02
499	Dennis Powell	.06	.03	.00	592	Mike Stanley	.40	.20	.04

☐ 593	Darrell Porter	.03	.01	.00
☐ 594	Drew Hall	.15	.07	.01
☐ 595	Rob Nelson	.20	.10	.02
☐ 596	Bryan Oelkers	.03	.01	.00
☐ 597	Scott Nielsen	.15	.07	.01
☐ 598	Brian Holton	.10	.05	.01
☐ 599	Kevin Mitchell	.30	.15	.03
☐ 600	Checklist	.06	.01	.00
☐ 601	Jackie Gutierrez	.03	.01	.00
☐ 602	Barry Jones	.15	.07	.01
☐ 603	Jerry Narron	.03	.01	.00
☐ 604	Steve Lake	.03	.01	.00
☐ 605	Jim Pankovits	.03	.01	.00
☐ 606	Ed Romero	.03	.01	.00
☐ 607	Dave LaPoint	.03	.01	.00
☐ 608	Don Robinson	.03	.01	.00
☐ 609	Mike Krukow	.06	.03	.00
☐ 610	Dave Valle	.03	.01	.00
☐ 611	Len Dykstra	.15	.07	.01
☐ 612	Roberto Clemente Puzzle Card	.06	.03	.00
☐ 613	Mike Trujillo	.06	.03	.00
☐ 614	Damaso Garcia	.06	.03	.00
☐ 615	Neal Heaton	.03	.01	.00
☐ 616	Juan Berenguer	.03	.01	.00
☐ 617	Steve Carlton	.25	.12	.02
☐ 618	Gary Lucas	.03	.01	.00
☐ 619	Geno Petralli	.03	.01	.00
☐ 620	Rick Aguilera	.06	.03	.00
☐ 621	Fred McGriff	.25	.12	.02
☐ 622	Dave Henderson	.03	.01	.00
☐ 623	Dave Clark	.30	.15	.03
☐ 624	Angel Salazar	.03	.01	.00
☐ 625	Randy Hunt	.03	.01	.00
☐ 626	John Gibbons	.03	.01	.00
☐ 627	Kevin Brown	.15	.07	.01
☐ 628	Bill Dawley	.03	.01	.00
☐ 629	Aurelio Lopez	.03	.01	.00
☐ 630	Charlie Hudson	.03	.01	.00
☐ 631	Ray Soff	.08	.04	.01
☐ 632	Ray Hayward	.10	.05	.01
☐ 633	Spike Owen	.03	.01	.00
☐ 634	Glenn Hubbard	.03	.01	.00
☐ 635	Kevin Elster	.30	.15	.03
☐ 636	Mike LaCoss	.03	.01	.00
☐ 637	Dwayne Henry	.03	.01	.00
☐ 638	Rey Quinones	.25	.12	.02
☐ 639	Jim Clancy	.03	.01	.00
☐ 640	Larry Andersen	.03	.01	.00
☐ 641	Calvin Schiraldi	.08	.04	.01
☐ 642	Stan Jefferson	.30	.15	.03
☐ 643	Marc Sullivan	.03	.01	.00
☐ 644	Mark Grant	.03	.01	.00
☐ 645	Cliff Johnson	.03	.01	.00
☐ 646	Howard Johnson	.15	.07	.01
☐ 647	Dave Sax	.03	.01	.00
☐ 648	Dave Stewart	.08	.04	.01
☐ 649	Danny Heep	.03	.01	.00
☐ 650	Joe Johnson	.03	.01	.00
☐ 651	Bob Brower	.20	.10	.02
☐ 652	Rob Woodward	.06	.03	.00
☐ 653	John Mizerock	.03	.01	.00
☐ 654	Tim Pyznarski	.15	.07	.01
☐ 655	Luis Aquino	.08	.04	.01
☐ 656	Mickey Brantley	.10	.05	.01
☐ 657	Doyle Alexander	.06	.03	.00
☐ 658	Sammy Stewart	.03	.01	.00
☐ 659	Jim Acker	.03	.01	.00
☐ 660	Pete Ladd	.03	.01	.00

1987 Donruss Wax Box Cards

The cards in this 4-card set measure the standard 2 1/2" by 3 1/2". Cards have essentially the same design as the 1987 Donruss regular issue set. The cards were printed on the bottoms of the regular issue wax pack boxes. The four cards (PC10 to PC12 plus a Roberto Clemente puzzle card) are considered a separate set in their own right and are not typically included in a complete set of the regular issue 1987 Donruss cards. The value of the panel uncut is slightly greater, perhaps by 25% greater, than the value of the individual cards cut up carefully.

	MINT	EXC	G-VG
COMPLETE SET	1.25	.60	.12
COMMON PLAYERS	.10	.05	.01

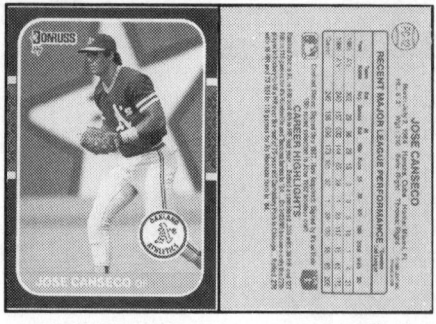

☐ PC10	Dale Murphy	.50	.25	.05
☐ PC11	Jeff Reardon	.15	.07	.01
☐ PC12	Jose Canseco	1.00	.50	.10
☐ PUZ	Roberto Clemente (Puzzle Card)	.10	.05	.01

1987 Donruss Super DK's

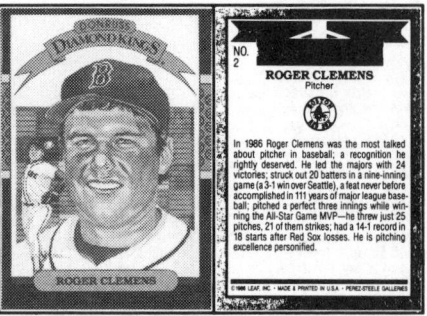

This 28-card set was available through a mail-in offer detailed on the wax packs. The set was sent in return for 8.00 and three wrappers plus 1.50 postage and handling. The set features the popular Diamond King subseries in large (approximately 4 7/8" by 6 13/16") form. Dick Perez of Perez-Steele Galleries did another outstanding job on the artwork. The cards are essentially a large version of the Donruss regular issue Diamond Kings.

		MINT	EXC	G-VG
COMPLETE SET		10.00	5.00	1.00
COMMON PLAYER (1-26)		.15	.07	.01
☐ 1	Wally Joyner	1.50	.75	.15
☐ 2	Roger Clemens	1.25	.60	.12
☐ 3	Dale Murphy	.75	.35	.07
☐ 4	Darryl Strawberry	.75	.35	.07
☐ 5	Ozzie Smith	.35	.17	.03
☐ 6	Jose Canseco	1.25	.60	.12
☐ 7	Charlie Hough	.15	.07	.01
☐ 8	Brook Jacoby	.20	.10	.02
☐ 9	Fred Lynn	.25	.12	.02
☐ 10	Rick Rhoden	.15	.07	.01
☐ 11	Chris Brown	.25	.12	.02
☐ 12	Von Hayes	.30	.15	.03
☐ 13	Jack Morris	.25	.12	.02
☐ 14	Kevin McReynolds	.30	.15	.03
☐ 15	George Brett	.65	.30	.06
☐ 16	Ted Higuera	.35	.17	.03
☐ 17	Hubie Brooks	.25	.12	.02
☐ 18	Mike Scott	.35	.17	.03
☐ 19	Kirby Puckett	.75	.35	.07
☐ 20	Dave Winfield	.50	.25	.05
☐ 21	Lloyd Moseby	.25	.12	.02
☐ 22	Eric Davis	1.50	.75	.15
☐ 23	Jim Presley	.35	.17	.03
☐ 24	Keith Moreland	.15	.07	.01

		MINT	EXC	G-VG
☐ 25	Greg Walker	.20	.10	.02
☐ 26	Steve Sax	.25	.12	.02
☐ 27	DK Checklist 1-26	.10	.01	.00
☐ 28	Roberto Clemente Large Puzzle (unnumbered)	.15	.07	.01

1987 Donruss All-Stars

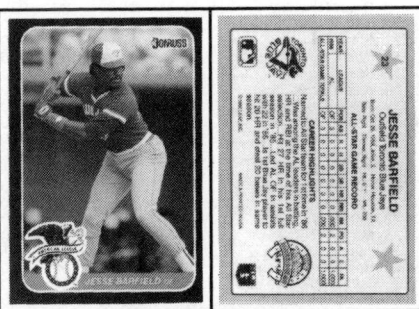

This 60-card set features cards measuring 3 1/2" by 5". Card fronts are in full color with a black border. The card backs are printed in black and blue on white card stock. Cards are numbered on the back. Card backs feature statistical information about the player's performance in past All-Star games. The set was distributed in packs which also contained a Pop-Up.

		MINT	EXC	G-VG
	COMPLETE SET	6.00	3.00	.60
	COMMON PLAYER	.05	.02	.00
☐ 1	Wally Joyner	.75	.35	.07
☐ 2	Dave Winfield	.25	.12	.02
☐ 3	Lou Whitaker	.15	.07	.01
☐ 4	Kirby Puckett	.45	.22	.04
☐ 5	Cal Ripken	.35	.17	.03
☐ 6	Rickey Henderson	.45	.22	.04
☐ 7	Wade Boggs	.85	.40	.08
☐ 8	Roger Clemens	.75	.35	.07
☐ 9	Lance Parrish	.15	.07	.01
☐ 10	Dick Howser MG	.05	.02	.00
☐ 11	Keith Hernandez	.25	.12	.02
☐ 12	Darryl Strawberry	.45	.22	.04
☐ 13	Ryne Sandberg	.35	.17	.03
☐ 14	Dale Murphy	.45	.22	.04
☐ 15	Ozzie Smith	.25	.12	.02
☐ 16	Tony Gwynn	.45	.22	.04
☐ 17	Mike Schmidt	.45	.22	.04
☐ 18	Dwight Gooden	.65	.30	.06
☐ 19	Gary Carter	.35	.17	.03
☐ 20	Whitey Herzog MG	.05	.02	.00
☐ 21	Jose Canseco	.75	.35	.07
☐ 22	John Franco	.10	.05	.01
☐ 23	Jesse Barfield	.15	.07	.01
☐ 24	Rick Rhoden	.10	.05	.01
☐ 25	Harold Baines	.15	.07	.01
☐ 26	Sid Fernandez	.15	.07	.01
☐ 27	George Brett	.45	.22	.04
☐ 28	Steve Sax	.15	.07	.01
☐ 29	Jim Presley	.15	.07	.01
☐ 30	Dave Smith	.05	.02	.00
☐ 31	Eddie Murray	.35	.17	.03
☐ 32	Mike Scott	.25	.12	.02
☐ 33	Don Mattingly	1.00	.50	.10
☐ 34	Dave Parker	.25	.12	.02
☐ 35	Tony Fernandez	.20	.10	.02
☐ 36	Tim Raines	.35	.17	.03
☐ 37	Brook Jacoby	.15	.07	.01
☐ 38	Chili Davis	.10	.05	.01
☐ 39	Rich Gedman	.05	.02	.00
☐ 40	Kevin Bass	.10	.05	.01
☐ 41	Frank White	.10	.05	.01
☐ 42	Glenn Davis	.25	.12	.02
☐ 43	Willie Hernandez	.10	.05	.01
☐ 44	Chris Brown	.15	.07	.01
☐ 45	Jim Rice	.25	.12	.02
☐ 46	Tony Pena	.10	.05	.01
☐ 47	Don Aase	.05	.02	.00

☐ 48	Hubie Brooks	.10	.05	.01
☐ 49	Charlie Hough	.05	.02	.00
☐ 50	Jody Davis	.10	.05	.01
☐ 51	Mike Witt	.10	.05	.01
☐ 52	Jeff Reardon	.10	.05	.01
☐ 53	Ken Schrom	.05	.02	.00
☐ 54	Fernando Valenzuela	.25	.12	.02
☐ 55	Dave Righetti	.20	.10	.02
☐ 56	Shane Rawley	.10	.05	.01
☐ 57	Ted Higuera	.20	.10	.02
☐ 58	Mike Krukow	.05	.02	.00
☐ 59	Lloyd Moseby	.10	.05	.01
☐ 60	Checklist Card	.10	.01	.00

1987 Donruss All-Star Box

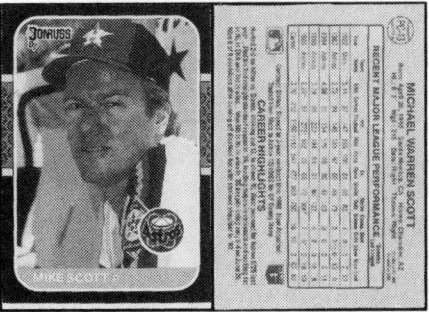

The cards in this 4-card set measure the standard 2 1/2" by 3 1/2" in spite of the fact that they form the bottom of the wax pack box for the larger Donruss All-Star cards. These box cards have essentially the same design as the 1987 Donruss regular issue set. The cards were printed on the bottoms of the Donruss All-Star (3 1/2" by 5") wax pack boxes. The four cards (PC13 to PC15 plus a Roberto Clemente puzzle card) are considered a separate set in their own right and are not typically included in a complete set of the 1987 Donruss All-Star (or regular) cards. The value of the panel uncut is slightly greater, perhaps by 25% greater, than the value of the individual cards cut up carefully.

		MINT	EXC	G-VG
	COMPLETE SET	1.00	.50	.10
	COMMON PLAYERS	.10	.05	.01
☐ PC13	Mike Scott	.35	.17	.03
☐ PC14	Roger Clemens	.75	.35	.07
☐ PC15	Mike Krukow	.15	.07	.01
☐ PUZ	Roberto Clemente Puzzle Card	.10	.05	.01

1987 Donruss Pop-Ups

This 20-card set features "fold-out" cards measuring 2 1/2" by 5". Card fronts are in full color. Cards are unnumbered but are listed in the same order as the Donruss All-Stars on the All-Star checklist card. Card backs present essentially no information about the player. The set was distributed in packs which also contained All-Star cards (3 1/2" by 5").

		MINT	EXC	G-VG
	COMPLETE SET	4.00	2.00	.40
	COMMON PLAYER (1-20)	.10	.05	.01
☐ 1	Wally Joyner	.75	.35	.07
☐ 2	Dave Winfield	.25	.12	.02
☐ 3	Lou Whitaker	.15	.07	.01
☐ 4	Kirby Puckett	.45	.22	.04

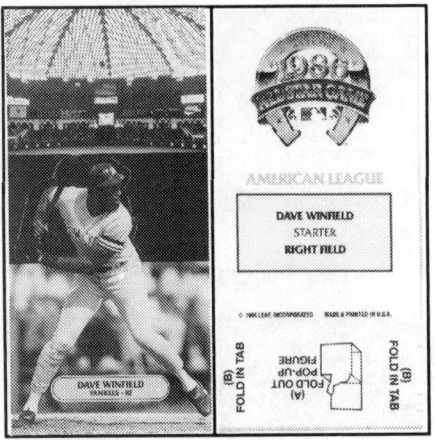

☐	5	Cal Ripken	.35	.17	.03
☐	6	Rickey Henderson	.45	.22	.04
☐	7	Wade Boggs	.85	.40	.08
☐	8	Roger Clemens	.75	.35	.07
☐	9	Lance Parrish	.20	.10	.02
☐	10	Dick Howser MG	.10	.05	.01
☐	11	Keith Hernandez	.25	.12	.02
☐	12	Darryl Strawberry	.45	.22	.04
☐	13	Ryne Sandberg	.35	.17	.03
☐	14	Dale Murphy	.25	.12	.02
☐	15	Ozzie Smith	.45	.22	.04
☐	16	Tony Gwynn	.45	.22	.04
☐	17	Mike Schmidt	.45	.22	.04
☐	18	Dwight Gooden	.65	.30	.06
☐	19	Gary Carter	.35	.17	.03
☐	20	Whitey Herzog MG	.10	.05	.01

1987 Donruss Opening Day

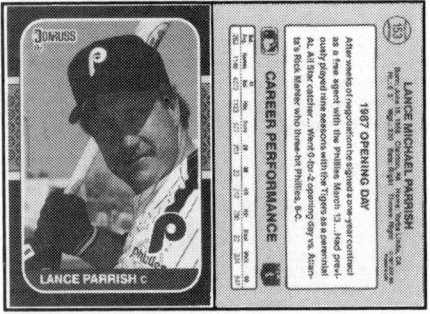

This innovative set of 272 cards features a card for each of the players in the starting line-ups of all the teams on Opening Day 1987. Cards are the standard size, 2 1/2" by 3 1/2" and are packaged as a complete set in a specially designed box. Cards are very similar in design to the 1987 regular Donruss issue except that these "OD" cards have a maroon border instead of a black border. The set features the first card in a Major League uniform of Joey Cora, Mark Davidson, Donnell Nixon, Bob Patterson, and Alonzo Powell. Teams in the same city share a checklist card. A 15-piece puzzle of Roberto Clemente is also included with every complete set. The error on Bobby Bonds was corrected very early in the press run, supposedly less than one percent of the sets have the error.

	MINT	EXC	G-VG
COMPLETE SET (272)	24.00	12.00	2.40

COMMON PLAYER (1-248)		.05	.02	.00
COMMON LOGO (249-272)		.05	.02	.00

☐	1	Doug DeCinces	.05	.02	.00
☐	2	Mike Witt	.10	.05	.01
☐	3	George Hendrick	.05	.02	.00
☐	4	Dick Schofield	.05	.02	.00
☐	5	Devon White	1.00	.50	.10
☐	6	Butch Wynegar	.05	.02	.00
☐	7	Wally Joyner	1.50	.75	.15
☐	8	Mark McLemore	.10	.05	.01
☐	9	Brian Downing	.05	.02	.00
☐	10	Gary Pettis	.05	.02	.00
☐	11	Bill Doran	.10	.05	.01
☐	12	Phil Garner	.05	.02	.00
☐	13	Jose Cruz	.10	.05	.01
☐	14	Kevin Bass	.10	.05	.01
☐	15	Mike Scott	.25	.12	.02
☐	16	Glenn Davis	.15	.07	.01
☐	17	Alan Ashby	.05	.02	.00
☐	18	Billy Hatcher	.15	.07	.01
☐	19	Craig Reynolds	.05	.02	.00
☐	20	Carney Lansford	.10	.05	.01
☐	21	Mike Davis	.10	.05	.01
☐	22	Reggie Jackson	.35	.17	.03
☐	23	Mickey Tettleton	.05	.02	.00
☐	24	Jose Canseco	1.50	.75	.15
☐	25	Rob Nelson	.10	.05	.01
☐	26	Tony Phillips	.05	.02	.00
☐	27	Dwayne Murphy	.05	.02	.00
☐	28	Alfredo Griffin	.05	.02	.00
☐	29	Curt Young	.10	.05	.01
☐	30	Willie Upshaw	.10	.05	.01
☐	31	Mike Sharperson	.10	.05	.01
☐	32	Rance Mulliniks	.05	.02	.00
☐	33	Ernie Whitt	.05	.02	.00
☐	34	Jesse Barfield	.25	.12	.02
☐	35	Tony Fernandez	.20	.10	.02
☐	36	Lloyd Moseby	.15	.07	.01
☐	37	Jimmy Key	.15	.07	.01
☐	38	Fred McGriff	.25	.12	.02
☐	39	George Bell	.35	.17	.03
☐	40	Dale Murphy	.40	.20	.04
☐	41	Rick Mahler	.05	.02	.00
☐	42	Ken Griffey	.05	.02	.00
☐	43	Andres Thomas	.05	.02	.00
☐	44	Dion James	.10	.05	.01
☐	45	Ozzie Virgil	.05	.02	.00
☐	46	Ken Oberkfell	.05	.02	.00
☐	47	Gary Roenicke	.05	.02	.00
☐	48	Glenn Hubbard	.05	.02	.00
☐	49	Bill Schroeder	.05	.02	.00
☐	50	Greg Brock	.05	.02	.00
☐	51	Billy Jo Robidoux	.05	.02	.00
☐	52	Glenn Braggs	.25	.12	.02
☐	53	Jim Gantner	.05	.02	.00
☐	54	Paul Molitor	.20	.10	.02
☐	55	Dale Sveum	.15	.07	.01
☐	56	Ted Higuera	.15	.07	.01
☐	57	Rob Deer	.15	.07	.01
☐	58	Robin Yount	.25	.12	.02
☐	59	Jim Lindeman	.15	.07	.01
☐	60	Vince Coleman	.35	.17	.03
☐	61	Tommy Herr	.10	.05	.01
☐	62	Terry Pendleton	.10	.05	.01
☐	63	John Tudor	.15	.07	.01
☐	64	Tony Pena	.10	.05	.01
☐	65	Ozzie Smith	.25	.12	.02
☐	66	Tito Landrum	.05	.02	.00
☐	67	Jack Clark	.25	.12	.02
☐	68	Bob Dernier	.05	.02	.00
☐	69	Rick Sutcliffe	.15	.07	.01
☐	70	Andre Dawson	.35	.17	.03
☐	71	Keith Moreland	.05	.02	.00
☐	72	Jody Davis	.10	.05	.01
☐	73	Brian Dayett	.05	.02	.00
☐	74	Leon Durham	.10	.05	.01
☐	75	Ryne Sandberg	.25	.12	.02
☐	76	Shawon Dunston	.10	.05	.01
☐	77	Mike Marshall	.15	.07	.01
☐	78	Bill Madlock	.10	.05	.01
☐	79	Orel Hershiser	.20	.10	.02
☐	80	Mike Ramsey	.10	.05	.01
☐	81	Ken Landreaux	.05	.02	.00
☐	82	Mike Scioscia	.05	.02	.00
☐	83	Franklin Stubbs	.05	.02	.00
☐	84	Mariano Duncan	.05	.02	.00
☐	85	Steve Sax	.15	.07	.01
☐	86	Mitch Webster	.05	.02	.00
☐	87	Reid Nichols	.05	.02	.00
☐	88	Tim Wallach	.15	.07	.01
☐	89	Floyd Youmans	.10	.05	.01
☐	90	Andres Galarraga	.25	.12	.02
☐	91	Hubie Brooks	.10	.05	.01

☐ 92	Jeff Reed	.05	.02	.00
☐ 93	Alonzo Powell	.15	.07	.01
☐ 94	Vance Law	.05	.02	.00
☐ 95	Bob Brenly	.10	.05	.01
☐ 96	Will Clark	1.00	.50	.10
☐ 97	Chili Davis	.10	.05	.01
☐ 98	Mike Krukow	.05	.02	.00
☐ 99	Jose Uribe	.05	.02	.00
☐ 100	Chris Brown	.20	.10	.02
☐ 101	Rob Thompson	.15	.07	.01
☐ 102	Candy Maldonado	.15	.07	.01
☐ 103	Jeff Leonard	.15	.07	.01
☐ 104	Tom Candiotti	.05	.02	.00
☐ 105	Chris Bando	.05	.02	.00
☐ 106	Cory Snyder	.60	.30	.06
☐ 107	Pat Tabler	.10	.05	.01
☐ 108	Andre Thornton	.05	.02	.00
☐ 109	Joe Carter	.20	.10	.02
☐ 110	Tony Bernazard	.05	.02	.00
☐ 111	Julio Franco	.10	.05	.01
☐ 112	Brook Jacoby	.10	.05	.01
☐ 113	Brett Butler	.10	.05	.01
☐ 114	Donnell Nixon	.10	.05	.01
☐ 115	Alvin Davis	.15	.07	.01
☐ 116	Mark Langston	.20	.10	.02
☐ 117	Harold Reynolds	.15	.07	.01
☐ 118	Ken Phelps	.05	.02	.00
☐ 119	Mike Kingery	.05	.02	.00
☐ 120	Dave Valle	.05	.02	.00
☐ 121	Rey Quinones	.10	.05	.01
☐ 122	Phil Bradley	.15	.07	.01
☐ 123	Jim Presley	.15	.07	.01
☐ 124	Keith Hernandez	.30	.15	.03
☐ 125	Kevin McReynolds	.20	.10	.02
☐ 126	Rafael Santana	.05	.02	.00
☐ 127	Bob Ojeda	.10	.05	.01
☐ 128	Darryl Strawberry	.60	.30	.06
☐ 129	Mookie Wilson	.05	.02	.00
☐ 130	Gary Carter	.30	.15	.03
☐ 131	Tim Teufel	.05	.02	.00
☐ 132	Howard Johnson	.20	.10	.02
☐ 133	Cal Ripken	.35	.17	.03
☐ 134	Rick Burleson	.05	.02	.00
☐ 135	Fred Lynn	.15	.07	.01
☐ 136	Eddie Murray	.25	.12	.02
☐ 137	Ray Knight	.10	.05	.01
☐ 138	Alan Wiggins	.05	.02	.00
☐ 139	John Shelby	.05	.02	.00
☐ 140	Mike Boddicker	.10	.05	.01
☐ 141	Ken Gerhart	.10	.05	.01
☐ 142	Terry Kennedy	.10	.05	.01
☐ 143	Steve Garvey	.35	.17	.03
☐ 144	Marvell Wynne	.05	.02	.00
☐ 145	Kevin Mitchell	.15	.07	.01
☐ 146	Tony Gwynn	.60	.30	.06
☐ 147	Joey Cora	.15	.07	.01
☐ 148	Benito Santiago	1.25	.60	.12
☐ 149	Eric Show	.05	.02	.00
☐ 150	Garry Templeton	.10	.05	.01
☐ 151	Carmelo Martinez	.05	.02	.00
☐ 152	Von Hayes	.15	.07	.01
☐ 153	Lance Parrish	.15	.07	.01
☐ 154	Milt Thompson	.10	.05	.01
☐ 155	Mike Easler	.05	.02	.00
☐ 156	Juan Samuel	.20	.10	.02
☐ 157	Steve Jeltz	.05	.02	.00
☐ 158	Glenn Wilson	.10	.05	.01
☐ 159	Shane Rawley	.10	.05	.01
☐ 160	Mike Schmidt	.35	.17	.03
☐ 161	Andy Van Slyke	.15	.07	.01
☐ 162	Johnny Ray	.15	.07	.01
☐ 163A	Barry Bonds ERR (photo actually Johnny Ray)	25.00	5.00	1.00
☐ 163B	Barry Bonds COR	.50	.25	.05
☐ 164	Junior Ortiz	.05	.02	.00
☐ 165	Rafael Belliard	.05	.02	.00
☐ 166	Bob Patterson	.15	.07	.01
☐ 167	Bobby Bonilla	.15	.07	.01
☐ 168	Sid Bream	.10	.05	.01
☐ 169	Jim Morrison	.05	.02	.00
☐ 170	Jerry Browne	.10	.05	.01
☐ 171	Scott Fletcher	.05	.02	.00
☐ 172	Ruben Sierra	1.00	.50	.10
☐ 173	Larry Parrish	.10	.05	.01
☐ 174	Pete O'Brien	.10	.05	.01
☐ 175	Pete Incaviglia	.50	.25	.05
☐ 176	Don Slaught	.05	.02	.00
☐ 177	Oddibe McDowell	.10	.05	.01
☐ 178	Charlie Hough	.10	.05	.01
☐ 179	Steve Buechele	.05	.02	.00
☐ 180	Bob Stanley	.05	.02	.00
☐ 181	Wade Boggs	1.00	.50	.10
☐ 182	Jim Rice	.25	.12	.02
☐ 183	Bill Buckner	.10	.05	.01
☐ 184	Dwight Evans	.20	.10	.02
☐ 185	Spike Owen	.05	.02	.00
☐ 186	Don Baylor	.10	.05	.01
☐ 187	Marc Sullivan	.05	.02	.00
☐ 188	Marty Barrett	.10	.05	.01
☐ 189	Dave Henderson	.05	.02	.00
☐ 190	Bo Diaz	.10	.05	.01
☐ 191	Barry Larkin	.25	.12	.02
☐ 192	Kal Daniels	.60	.30	.06
☐ 193	Terry Francona	.05	.02	.00
☐ 194	Tom Browning	.10	.05	.01
☐ 195	Ron Oester	.05	.02	.00
☐ 196	Buddy Bell	.10	.05	.01
☐ 197	Eric Davis	1.00	.50	.10
☐ 198	Dave Parker	.20	.10	.02
☐ 199	Steve Balboni	.05	.02	.00
☐ 200	Danny Tartabull	.25	.12	.02
☐ 201	Ed Hearn	.05	.02	.00
☐ 202	Buddy Biancalana	.05	.02	.00
☐ 203	Danny Jackson	.10	.05	.01
☐ 204	Frank White	.10	.05	.01
☐ 205	Bo Jackson	.60	.30	.06
☐ 206	George Brett	.40	.20	.04
☐ 207	Kevin Seitzer	3.00	1.50	.30
☐ 208	Willie Wilson	.15	.07	.01
☐ 209	Orlando Mercado	.05	.02	.00
☐ 210	Darrell Evans	.15	.07	.01
☐ 211	Larry Herndon	.05	.02	.00
☐ 212	Jack Morris	.20	.10	.02
☐ 213	Chet Lemon	.10	.05	.01
☐ 214	Mike Heath	.05	.02	.00
☐ 215	Darnell Coles	.05	.02	.00
☐ 216	Alan Trammell	.25	.12	.02
☐ 217	Terry Harper	.05	.02	.00
☐ 218	Lou Whitaker	.15	.07	.01
☐ 219	Gary Gaetti	.20	.10	.02
☐ 220	Tom Nieto	.05	.02	.00
☐ 221	Kirby Puckett	.50	.25	.05
☐ 222	Tom Brunansky	.10	.05	.01
☐ 223	Greg Gagne	.05	.02	.00
☐ 224	Dan Gladden	.05	.02	.00
☐ 225	Mark Davidson	.15	.07	.01
☐ 226	Bert Blyleven	.10	.05	.01
☐ 227	Steve Lombardozzi	.05	.02	.00
☐ 228	Kent Hrbek	.25	.12	.02
☐ 229	Gary Redus	.05	.02	.00
☐ 230	Ivan Calderon	.15	.07	.01
☐ 231	Tim Hulett	.05	.02	.00
☐ 232	Carlton Fisk	.20	.10	.02
☐ 233	Greg Walker	.15	.07	.01
☐ 234	Ron Karkovice	.05	.02	.00
☐ 235	Ozzie Guillen	.15	.07	.01
☐ 236	Harold Baines	.20	.10	.02
☐ 237	Donnie Hill	.05	.02	.00
☐ 238	Rich Dotson	.10	.05	.01
☐ 239	Mike Pagliarulo	.15	.07	.01
☐ 240	Joel Skinner	.05	.02	.00
☐ 241	Don Mattingly	2.00	1.00	.20
☐ 242	Gary Ward	.05	.02	.00
☐ 243	Dave Winfield	.30	.15	.03
☐ 244	Dan Pasqua	.10	.05	.01
☐ 245	Wayne Tolleson	.05	.02	.00
☐ 246	Willie Randolph	.10	.05	.01
☐ 247	Dennis Rasmussen	.05	.02	.00
☐ 248	Rickey Henderson	.40	.20	.04
☐ 249	Angels Logo	.05	.02	.00
☐ 250	Astros Logo	.05	.02	.00
☐ 251	A's Logo	.05	.02	.00
☐ 252	Blue Jays Logo	.05	.02	.00
☐ 253	Braves Logo	.05	.02	.00
☐ 254	Brewers Logo	.05	.02	.00
☐ 255	Cardinals Logo	.05	.02	.00
☐ 256	Dodgers Logo	.05	.02	.00
☐ 257	Expos Logo	.05	.02	.00
☐ 258	Giants Logo	.05	.02	.00
☐ 259	Indians Logo	.05	.02	.00
☐ 260	Mariners Logo	.05	.02	.00
☐ 261	Orioles Logo	.05	.02	.00
☐ 262	Padres Logo	.05	.02	.00
☐ 263	Phillies Logo	.05	.02	.00
☐ 264	Pirates Logo	.05	.02	.00
☐ 265	Rangers Logo	.05	.02	.00
☐ 266	Red Sox Logo	.05	.02	.00
☐ 267	Reds Logo	.05	.02	.00
☐ 268	Royals Logo	.05	.02	.00
☐ 269	Tigers Logo	.05	.02	.00
☐ 270	Twins Logo	.05	.02	.00
☐ 271	Chicago Logos	.05	.02	.00
☐ 272	New York Logos	.05	.02	.00

1987 Donruss Rookies

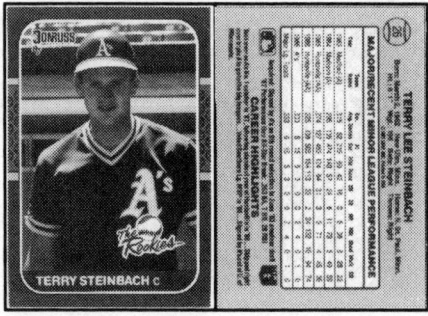

The 1987 Donruss "The Rookies" set features 56 cards plus a 15-piece puzzle of Roberto Clemente. Cards are in full color and are standard size, 2 1/2" by 3 1/2". The set was distributed in a small green and black box with gold lettering. Card fronts are similar in design to the 1987 Donruss regular issue except for the presence of "The Rookies" logo in the lower left corner and a green border instead of a black border.

	MINT	EXC	G-VG
COMPLETE SET	12.50	6.25	1.25
COMMON PLAYER	.06	.03	.00
☐ 1 Mark McGwire	3.00	1.00	.20
☐ 2 Eric Bell	.06	.03	.00
☐ 3 Mark Williamson	.20	.10	.02
☐ 4 Mike Greenwell	.75	.35	.07
☐ 5 Ellis Burks	1.25	.60	.12
☐ 6 DeWayne Buice	.20	.10	.02
☐ 7 Mark McLemore	.06	.03	.00
☐ 8 Devon White	.60	.30	.06
☐ 9 Willie Fraser	.06	.03	.00
☐ 10 Len Lancaster	.20	.10	.02
☐ 11 Ken Williams	.35	.17	.03
☐ 12 Matt Nokes	2.00	1.00	.20
☐ 13 Jeff Robinson	.30	.15	.03
(Tigers pitcher)			
☐ 14 Bo Jackson	.60	.30	.06
☐ 15 Kevin Seitzer	2.50	1.25	.25
☐ 16 Billy Ripken	.50	.25	.05
☐ 17 B.J. Surhoff	.40	.20	.04
☐ 18 Chuck Crim	.20	.10	.02
☐ 19 Mike Birkbeck	.06	.03	.00
☐ 20 Chris Bosio	.06	.03	.00
☐ 21 Les Straker	.20	.10	.02
☐ 22 Mark Davidson	.20	.10	.02
☐ 23 Gene Larkin	.25	.12	.02
☐ 24 Ken Gerhart	.10	.05	.01
☐ 25 Luis Polonia	.25	.12	.02
☐ 26 Terry Steinbach	.25	.12	.02
☐ 27 Mickey Brantley	.20	.10	.02
☐ 28 Mike Stanley	.15	.07	.01
☐ 29 Jerry Browne	.10	.05	.01
☐ 30 Todd Benzinger	.45	.22	.04
☐ 31 Fred McGriff	.25	.12	.02
☐ 32 Mike Henneman	.25	.12	.02
☐ 33 Casey Candaele	.10	.05	.01
☐ 34 Dave Magadan	.40	.20	.04
☐ 35 David Cone	.15	.07	.01
☐ 36 Mike Jackson	.15	.07	.01
☐ 37 John Mitchell	.20	.10	.02
☐ 38 Mike Dunne	.60	.30	.06
☐ 39 John Smiley	.30	.15	.03
☐ 40 Joe Magrane	.50	.25	.05
☐ 41 Jim Lindeman	.30	.15	.03
☐ 42 Shane Mack	.50	.25	.05
☐ 43 Stanley Jefferson	.15	.07	.01
☐ 44 Benito Santiago	1.00	.50	.10
☐ 45 Matt Williams	.40	.20	.04
☐ 46 Dave Meads	.15	.07	.01
☐ 47 Rafael Palmeiro	.25	.12	.02
☐ 48 Bill Long	.20	.10	.02
☐ 49 Bob Brower	.10	.05	.01
☐ 50 James Steels	.20	.10	.02
☐ 51 Paul Noce	.15	.07	.01
☐ 52 Greg Maddux	.10	.05	.01
☐ 53 Jeff Musselman	.10	.05	.01
☐ 54 Brian Holton	.06	.03	.00
☐ 55 Chuck Jackson	.15	.07	.01
☐ 56 Checklist Card	.10	.01	.00

1987 Donruss Highlights

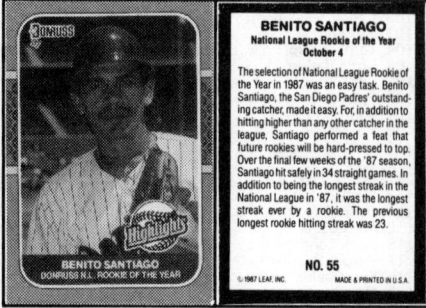

Donruss' third edition of Highlights was released late in 1987. The cards are standard size measuring 2 1/2" by 3 1/2" and are glossy in appearance. Cards commemorate events during the 1987 season, as well as players and pitchers of the month from each league. The set was distributed in its own red, black, blue, and gold box along with a small Roberto Clemente puzzle. Card fronts are similar to the regular 1987 Donruss issue except that the Highlights logo is positioned in the lower right- hand corner and the borders are in blue instead of black. The backs are printed in black and gold on white card stock.

	MINT	EXC	G-VG
COMPLETE SET (56)	7.50	3.75	.75
COMMON PLAYER (1-56)	.06	.03	.00
☐ 1 Juan Nieves	.10	.05	.01
First No-Hitter			
☐ 2 Mike Schmidt	.35	.17	.03
Hits 500th Homer			
☐ 3 Eric Davis	.50	.25	.05
NL Player April			
☐ 4 Sid Fernandez	.15	.07	.01
NL Pitcher April			
☐ 5 Brian Downing	.06	.03	.00
AL Player April			
☐ 6 Bret Saberhagen	.20	.10	.02
AL Pitcher April			
☐ 7 Tim Raines	.20	.10	.02
Free Agent Returns			
☐ 8 Eric Davis	.50	.25	.05
NL Player May			
☐ 9 Steve Bedrosian	.10	.05	.01
NL Pitcher May			
☐ 10 Larry Parrish	.06	.03	.00
AL Player May			
☐ 11 Jim Clancy	.06	.03	.00
AL Pitcher May			
☐ 12 Tony Gwynn	.25	.12	.02
NL Player June			
ERR (over "20" hits)			
☐ 13 Orel Hershiser	.20	.10	.02
NL Pitcher June			
☐ 14 Wade Boggs	.60	.30	.06
AL Player June			
☐ 15 Steve Ontiveros	.06	.03	.00
AL Pitcher June			
☐ 16 Tim Raines	.20	.10	.02
All Star Game Hero			
☐ 17 Don Mattingly	.75	.35	.07
Consecutive Game			
Homerun Streak			
☐ 18 Ray Dandridge	.15	.07	.01
1987 HOF Inductee			
☐ 19 Jim "Catfish" Hunter	.15	.07	.01
1987 HOF Inductee			
☐ 20 Billy Williams	.15	.07	.01
1987 HOF Inductee			
☐ 21 Bo Diaz	.06	.03	.00

		NL Player July			
☐	22	Floyd Youmans	.06	.03	.00
		NL Pitcher July			
☐	23	Don Mattingly	.75	.35	.07
		AL Player July			
☐	24	Frank Viola	.15	.07	.01
		AL Pitcher July			
☐	25	Bobby Witt	.15	.07	.01
		Strikes Out Four Batters in One Inning			
☐	26	Kevin Seitzer	.75	.35	.07
		Ties AL 9-Inning Game Hit Mark			
☐	27	Mark McGwire	.75	.35	.07
		Sets Rookie HR Record			
☐	28	Andre Dawson	.25	.12	.02
		Sets Cubs' 1st Year Homer Mark			
☐	29	Paul Molitor	.15	.07	.01
		Hits in 39 Straight Games			
☐	30	Kirby Puckett	.30	.15	.03
		Record Weekend			
☐	31	Andre Dawson	.25	.12	.02
		NL Player August			
☐	32	Doug Drabek	.10	.05	.01
		NL Pitcher August			
☐	33	Dwight Evans	.10	.05	.01
		AL Player August			
☐	34	Mark Langston	.10	.05	.01
		AL Pitcher August			
☐	35	Wally Joyner	.35	.17	.03
		100 RBI in 1st Two Major League Seasons			
☐	36	Vince Coleman	.25	.12	.02
		100 SB in 1st Three Major League Seasons			
☐	37	Eddie Murray	.25	.12	.02
		Orioles' All Time Homer King			
☐	38	Cal Ripken	.25	.12	.02
		Ends Consecutive Innings Streak			
☐	39	Blue Jays	.06	.03	.00
		Hit Record 10 Homers In One Game (McGriff/Ducey/Whitt)			
☐	40	McGwire/Canseco	.75	.35	.07
		Equal A's RBI Marks			
☐	41	Bob Boone	.06	.03	.00
		Sets All-Time Catching Record			
☐	42	Darryl Strawberry	.35	.17	.03
		Sets Mets' One-Season Home Run Mark			
☐	43	Howard Johnson	.20	.10	.02
		NL's All-Time Switchhit HR King			
☐	44	Wade Boggs	.60	.30	.06
		Five Straight 200 Hit Seasons			
☐	45	Benito Santiago	.75	.35	.07
		Eclipses Rookie Game Hitting Streak			
☐	46	Mark McGwire	.75	.35	.07
		Eclipses Jackson's A's HR Record			
☐	47	Kevin Seitzer	.75	.35	.07
		13th Rookie to Collect 200 Hits			
☐	48	Don Mattingly	.75	.35	.07
		Sets Slam Record			
☐	49	Darryl Strawberry	.35	.17	.03
		NL Player September			
☐	50	Pascual Perez	.06	.03	.00
		NL Pitcher September			
☐	51	Alan Trammell	.20	.10	.02
		AL Player September			
☐	52	Doyle Alexander	.06	.03	.00
		AL Pitcher September			
☐	53	Nolan Ryan	.25	.12	.02
		Strikeout King Again			
☐	54	Mark McGwire	.75	.35	.07
		Donruss AL ROY			
☐	55	Benito Santiago	.75	.35	.07
		Donruss NL ROY			
☐	56	Checklist Card	.10	.01	.00

1988 Donruss

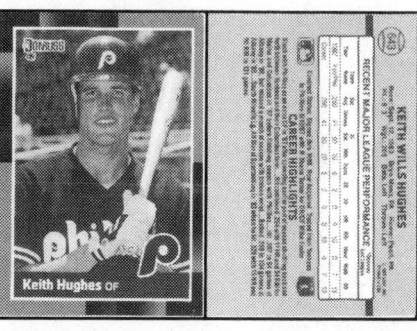

Keith Hughes OF

This 660-card set was distributed along with a puzzle of Stan Musial. The six regular checklist cards are numbered throughout the set as multiples of 100. Cards measure 2 1/2" by 3 1/2" and feature a distinctive black and blue border on the front. The popular Diamond King subset returns for the seventh consecutive year. Rated Rookies are featured again as cards 28-47.

			MINT	EXC	G-VG
		COMPLETE SET (660)	27.00	13.50	2.70
		COMMON PLAYER (1-660)	.03	.01	.00
☐	1	Mark McGwire DK	1.00	.50	.10
☐	2	Tim Raines DK	.25	.12	.02
☐	3	Benito Santiago DK	.50	.25	.05
☐	4	Alan Trammell DK	.20	.10	.02
☐	5	Danny Tartabull DK	.20	.10	.02
☐	6	Ron Darling DK	.20	.10	.02
☐	7	Paul Molitor DK	.20	.10	.02
☐	8	Devon White DK	.25	.12	.02
☐	9	Andre Dawson DK	.25	.12	.02
☐	10	Julio Franco DK	.10	.05	.01
☐	11	Scott Fletcher DK	.10	.05	.01
☐	12	Tony Fernandez DK	.20	.10	.02
☐	13	Shane Rawley DK	.10	.05	.01
☐	14	Kal Daniels DK	.25	.12	.02
☐	15	Jack Clark DK	.25	.12	.02
☐	16	Dwight Evans DK	.15	.07	.01
☐	17	Tommy John DK	.15	.07	.01
☐	18	Andy Van Slyke DK	.15	.07	.01
☐	19	Gary Gaetti DK	.20	.10	.02
☐	20	Mark Langston DK	.15	.07	.01
☐	21	Will Clark DK	.35	.17	.03
☐	22	Glenn Hubbard DK	.10	.05	.01
☐	23	Billy Hatcher DK	.15	.07	.01
☐	24	Bob Welch DK	.10	.05	.01
☐	25	Ivan Calderon DK	.20	.10	.02
☐	26	Cal Ripken Jr. DK	.30	.15	.03
☐	27	DK Checklist 1-26	.06	.01	.00
☐	28	Mackey Sasser	.25	.12	.02
☐	29	Jeff Treadway	.40	.20	.04
☐	30	Mike Campbell	.20	.10	.02
☐	31	Lance Johnson	.30	.15	.03
☐	32	Nelson Liriano	.30	.15	.03
☐	33	Shawn Abner	.40	.20	.04
☐	34	Roberto Alomar	.30	.15	.03
☐	35	Shawn Hillegas	.25	.12	.02
☐	36	Joey Meyer	.15	.07	.01
☐	37	Kevin Elster	.15	.07	.01
☐	38	Jose Lind	.30	.15	.03
☐	39	Kirt Manwaring	.30	.15	.03
☐	40	Mark Grace	.45	.22	.04
☐	41	Jody Reed	.30	.15	.03
☐	42	John Farrell	.25	.12	.02
☐	43	Al Leiter	.30	.15	.03
☐	44	Gary Thurman	.40	.20	.04
☐	45	Vincente Palacios	.20	.10	.02
☐	46	Eddie Williams	.30	.15	.03
☐	47	Jack McDowell	.40	.20	.04
☐	48	Ken Dixon	.03	.01	.00
☐	49	Mike Birkbeck	.03	.01	.00
☐	50	Eric King	.03	.01	.00
☐	51	Roger Clemens	.50	.25	.05
☐	52	Pat Clements	.03	.01	.00
☐	53	Fernando Valenzuela	.20	.10	.02
☐	54	Mark Gubicza	.03	.01	.00
☐	55	Jay Howell	.03	.01	.00

☐ 56	Floyd Youmans	.06	.03	.00
☐ 57	Ed Correa	.06	.03	.00
☐ 58	DeWayne Buice	.15	.07	.01
☐ 59	Jose DeLeon	.03	.01	.00
☐ 60	Danny Cox	.10	.05	.01
☐ 61	Nolan Ryan	.30	.15	.03
☐ 62	Steve Bedrosian	.10	.05	.01
☐ 63	Tom Browning	.06	.03	.00
☐ 64	Mark Davis	.03	.01	.00
☐ 65	R.J. Reynolds	.06	.03	.00
☐ 66	Kevin Mitchell	.10	.05	.01
☐ 67	Ken Oberkfell	.03	.01	.00
☐ 68	Rick Sutcliffe	.12	.06	.01
☐ 69	Dwight Gooden	.40	.20	.04
☐ 70	Scott Bankhead	.10	.05	.01
☐ 71	Bert Blyleven	.10	.05	.01
☐ 72	Jimmy Key	.10	.05	.01
☐ 73	Les Straker	.20	.10	.02
☐ 74	Jim Clancy	.03	.01	.00
☐ 75	Mike Moore	.03	.01	.00
☐ 76	Ron Darling	.15	.07	.01
☐ 77	Ed Lynch	.03	.01	.00
☐ 78	Dale Murphy	.35	.17	.03
☐ 79	Doug Drabek	.06	.03	.00
☐ 80	Scott Garrelts	.06	.03	.00
☐ 81	Ed Whitson	.03	.01	.00
☐ 82	Rob Murphy	.06	.03	.00
☐ 83	Shane Rawley	.06	.03	.00
☐ 84	Greg Mathews	.10	.05	.01
☐ 85	Jim Deshaies	.10	.05	.01
☐ 86	Mike Witt	.10	.05	.01
☐ 87	Donnie Hill	.03	.01	.00
☐ 88	Jeff Reed	.03	.01	.00
☐ 89	Mike Boddicker	.06	.03	.00
☐ 90	Ted Higuera	.15	.07	.01
☐ 91	Walt Terrell	.06	.03	.00
☐ 92	Bob Stanley	.06	.03	.00
☐ 93	Dave Righetti	.12	.06	.01
☐ 94	Orel Hershiser	.15	.07	.01
☐ 95	Chris Bando	.03	.01	.00
☐ 96	Bret Saberhagen	.15	.07	.01
☐ 97	Curt Young	.06	.03	.00
☐ 98	Tim Burke	.06	.03	.00
☐ 99	Charlie Hough	.06	.03	.00
☐ 100	Checklist	.06	.01	.00
☐ 101	Bobby Witt	.06	.03	.00
☐ 102	George Brett	.30	.15	.03
☐ 103	Mickey Tettleton	.03	.01	.00
☐ 104	Scott Bailes	.03	.01	.00
☐ 105	Mike Pagliarulo	.10	.05	.01
☐ 106	Mike Scioscia	.03	.01	.00
☐ 107	Tom Brookens	.03	.01	.00
☐ 108	Ray Knight	.06	.03	.00
☐ 109	Dan Plesac	.06	.03	.00
☐ 110	Wally Joyner	.60	.30	.06
☐ 111	Bob Forsch	.03	.01	.00
☐ 112	Mike Scott	.20	.10	.02
☐ 113	Kevin Gross	.03	.01	.00
☐ 114	Benito Santiago	.60	.30	.06
☐ 115	Bob Kipper	.03	.01	.00
☐ 116	Mike Krukow	.06	.03	.00
☐ 117	Chris Bosio	.06	.03	.00
☐ 118	Sid Fernandez	.10	.05	.01
☐ 119	Jody Davis	.06	.03	.00
☐ 120	Mike Morgan	.03	.01	.00
☐ 121	Mark Eichhorn	.06	.03	.00
☐ 122	Jeff Reardon	.10	.05	.01
☐ 123	John Franco	.10	.05	.01
☐ 124	Richard Dotson	.06	.03	.00
☐ 125	Eric Bell	.06	.03	.00
☐ 126	Juan Nieves	.06	.03	.00
☐ 127	Jack Morris	.15	.07	.01
☐ 128	Rick Rhoden	.06	.03	.00
☐ 129	Rich Gedman	.06	.03	.00
☐ 130	Ken Howell	.03	.01	.00
☐ 131	Brook Jacoby	.10	.05	.01
☐ 132	Danny Jackson	.06	.03	.00
☐ 133	Gene Nelson	.03	.01	.00
☐ 134	Neal Heaton	.03	.01	.00
☐ 135	Willie Fraser	.06	.03	.00
☐ 136	Jose Guzman	.03	.01	.00
☐ 137	Ozzie Guillen	.06	.03	.00
☐ 138	Bob Knepper	.06	.03	.00
☐ 139	Mike Jackson	.15	.07	.01
☐ 140	Joe Magrane	.35	.17	.03
☐ 141	Jimmy Jones	.06	.03	.00
☐ 142	Ted Power	.03	.01	.00
☐ 143	Ozzie Virgil	.03	.01	.00
☐ 144	Felix Fermin	.12	.06	.01
☐ 145	Kelly Downs	.06	.03	.00
☐ 146	Shawon Dunston	.06	.03	.00
☐ 147	Scott Bradley	.06	.03	.00
☐ 148	Dave Stieb	.10	.05	.01
☐ 149	Frank Viola	.12	.06	.01
☐ 150	Terry Kennedy	.06	.03	.00
☐ 151	Bill Wegman	.03	.01	.00
☐ 152	Matt Nokes	1.25	.60	.12
☐ 153	Wade Boggs	1.00	.50	.10
☐ 154	Wayne Tolleson	.03	.01	.00
☐ 155	Mariano Duncan	.06	.03	.00
☐ 156	Julio Franco	.10	.05	.01
☐ 157	Charlie Leibrandt	.06	.03	.00
☐ 158	Terry Steinbach	.20	.10	.02
☐ 159	Mike Fitzgerald	.03	.01	.00
☐ 160	Jack Lazorko	.03	.01	.00
☐ 161	Mitch Williams	.03	.01	.00
☐ 162	Greg Walker	.10	.05	.01
☐ 163	Alan Ashby	.03	.01	.00
☐ 164	Tony Gwynn	.30	.15	.03
☐ 165	Bruce Ruffin	.06	.03	.00
☐ 166	Ron Robinson	.03	.01	.00
☐ 167	Zane Smith	.06	.03	.00
☐ 168	Junior Ortiz	.03	.01	.00
☐ 169	Jamie Moyer	.03	.01	.00
☐ 170	Tony Pena	.10	.05	.01
☐ 171	Cal Ripken	.25	.12	.02
☐ 172	B.J. Surhoff	.20	.10	.02
☐ 173	Lou Whitaker	.12	.06	.01
☐ 174	Ellis Burks	1.00	.50	.10
☐ 175	Ron Guidry	.12	.06	.01
☐ 176	Steve Sax	.10	.05	.01
☐ 177	Danny Tartabull	.20	.10	.02
☐ 178	Carney Lansford	.06	.03	.00
☐ 179	Casey Candaele	.06	.03	.00
☐ 180	Scott Fletcher	.06	.03	.00
☐ 181	Mark McLemore	.03	.01	.00
☐ 182	Ivan Calderon	.10	.05	.01
☐ 183	Jack Clark	.20	.10	.02
☐ 184	Glenn Davis	.15	.07	.01
☐ 185	Luis Aguayo	.03	.01	.00
☐ 186	Bo Diaz	.06	.03	.00
☐ 187	Stan Jefferson	.06	.03	.00
☐ 188	Sid Bream	.06	.03	.00
☐ 189	Bob Brenly	.06	.03	.00
☐ 190	Dion James	.06	.03	.00
☐ 191	Leon Durham	.06	.03	.00
☐ 192	Jesse Orosco	.06	.03	.00
☐ 193	Alvin Davis	.10	.05	.01
☐ 194	Gary Gaetti	.12	.06	.01
☐ 195	Fred McGriff	.12	.06	.01
☐ 196	Steve Lombardozzi	.03	.01	.00
☐ 197	Rance Mulliniks	.03	.01	.00
☐ 198	Rey Quinones	.03	.01	.00
☐ 199	Gary Carter	.25	.12	.02
☐ 200	Checklist	.06	.01	.00
☐ 201	Keith Moreland	.06	.03	.00
☐ 202	Ken Griffey	.06	.03	.00
☐ 203	Tommy Gregg	.15	.07	.01
☐ 204	Will Clark	.40	.20	.04
☐ 205	John Kruk	.20	.10	.02
☐ 206	Buddy Bell	.10	.05	.01
☐ 207	Von Hayes	.10	.05	.01
☐ 208	Tommy Herr	.06	.03	.00
☐ 209	Craig Reynolds	.03	.01	.00
☐ 210	Gary Pettis	.06	.03	.00
☐ 211	Harold Baines	.10	.05	.01
☐ 212	Vance Law	.03	.01	.00
☐ 213	Ken Gerhart	.06	.03	.00
☐ 214	Jim Gantner	.03	.01	.00
☐ 215	Chet Lemon	.06	.03	.00
☐ 216	Dwight Evans	.12	.06	.01
☐ 217	Don Mattingly	1.50	.75	.15
☐ 218	Franklin Stubbs	.06	.03	.00
☐ 219	Pat Tabler	.06	.03	.00
☐ 220	Bo Jackson	.40	.20	.04
☐ 221	Tony Phillips	.03	.01	.00
☐ 222	Tim Wallach	.08	.04	.01
☐ 223	Ruben Sierra	.30	.15	.03
☐ 224	Steve Buechele	.03	.01	.00
☐ 225	Frank White	.06	.03	.00
☐ 226	Alfredo Griffin	.06	.03	.00
☐ 227	Greg Swindell	.10	.05	.01
☐ 228	Willie Randolph	.06	.03	.00
☐ 229	Mike Marshall	.10	.05	.01
☐ 230	Alan Trammell	.15	.07	.01
☐ 231	Eddie Murray	.25	.12	.02
☐ 232	Dale Sveum	.08	.04	.01
☐ 233	Dick Schofield	.03	.01	.00
☐ 234	Jose Oquendo	.03	.01	.00
☐ 235	Bill Doran	.08	.04	.01
☐ 236	Milt Thompson	.08	.04	.01
☐ 237	Marvell Wynne	.03	.01	.00
☐ 238	Bobby Bonilla	.06	.03	.00
☐ 239	Chris Speier	.03	.01	.00
☐ 240	Glenn Braggs	.10	.05	.01
☐ 241	Wally Backman	.03	.01	.00
☐ 242	Ryne Sandberg	.25	.12	.02
☐ 243	Phil Bradley	.10	.05	.01
☐ 244	Kelly Gruber	.03	.01	.00
☐ 245	Tom Brunansky	.10	.05	.01

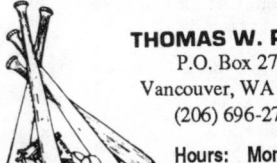

☐ 246	Ron Oester	.03	.01	.00	☐ 340	Claudell Washington	.06	.03	.00
☐ 247	Bobby Thigpen	.03	.01	.00	☐ 341	Jose Gonzalez	.06	.03	.00
☐ 248	Fred Lynn	.12	.06	.01	☐ 342	Mel Hall	.06	.03	.00
☐ 249	Paul Molitor	.15	.07	.01	☐ 343	Jim Eisenreich	.10	.05	.01
☐ 250	Darrell Evans	.08	.04	.01	☐ 344	Tony Bernazard	.03	.01	.00
☐ 251	Gary Ward	.06	.03	.00	☐ 345	Tim Raines	.25	.12	.02
☐ 252	Bruce Hurst	.08	.04	.01	☐ 346	Bob Brower	.03	.01	.00
☐ 253	Bob Welch	.06	.03	.00	☐ 347	Larry Parrish	.06	.03	.00
☐ 254	Joe Carter	.12	.06	.01	☐ 348	Thad Bosley	.03	.01	.00
☐ 255	Willie Wilson	.08	.04	.01	☐ 349	Dennis Eckersley	.06	.03	.00
☐ 256	Mark McGwire	1.25	.60	.12	☐ 350	Cory Snyder	.25	.12	.02
☐ 257	Mitch Webster	.06	.03	.00	☐ 351	Rick Cerone	.03	.01	.00
☐ 258	Brian Downing	.06	.03	.00	☐ 352	John Shelby	.03	.01	.00
☐ 259	Mike Stanley	.10	.05	.01	☐ 353	Larry Herndon	.03	.01	.00
☐ 260	Carlton Fisk	.10	.05	.01	☐ 354	John Habyan	.03	.01	.00
☐ 261	Billy Hatcher	.08	.04	.01	☐ 355	Chuck Crim	.12	.06	.01
☐ 262	Glenn Wilson	.08	.04	.01	☐ 356	Gus Polidor	.03	.01	.00
☐ 263	Ozzie Smith	.15	.07	.01	☐ 357	Ken Dayley	.03	.01	.00
☐ 264	Randy Ready	.06	.03	.00	☐ 358	Danny Darwin	.03	.01	.00
☐ 265	Kurt Stillwell	.06	.03	.00	☐ 359	Lance Parrish	.12	.06	.01
☐ 266	David Palmer	.03	.01	.00	☐ 360	James Steels	.12	.06	.01
☐ 267	Mike Diaz	.03	.01	.00	☐ 361	Al Pedrique	.20	.10	.02
☐ 268	Rob Thompson	.06	.03	.00	☐ 362	Mike Aldrete	.10	.05	.01
☐ 269	Andre Dawson	.20	.10	.02	☐ 363	Juan Castillo	.03	.01	.00
☐ 270	Lee Guetterman	.06	.03	.00	☐ 364	Len Dykstra	.10	.05	.01
☐ 271	Willie Upshaw	.06	.03	.00	☐ 365	Luis Quinones	.08	.04	.01
☐ 272	Randy Bush	.03	.01	.00	☐ 366	Jim Presley	.10	.05	.01
☐ 273	Larry Sheets	.10	.05	.01	☐ 367	Lloyd Moseby	.10	.05	.01
☐ 274	Rob Deer	.10	.05	.01	☐ 368	Kirby Puckett	.35	.17	.03
☐ 275	Kirk Gibson	.15	.07	.01	☐ 369	Eric Davis	1.00	.50	.10
☐ 276	Marty Barrett	.08	.04	.01	☐ 370	Gary Redus	.06	.03	.00
☐ 277	Rickey Henderson	.30	.15	.03	☐ 371	Dave Schmidt	.06	.03	.00
☐ 278	Pedro Guerrero	.20	.10	.02	☐ 372	Mark Clear	.03	.01	.00
☐ 279	Brett Butler	.08	.04	.01	☐ 373	Dave Bergman	.03	.01	.00
☐ 280	Kevin Seitzer	1.25	.60	.12	☐ 374	Charles Hudson	.03	.01	.00
☐ 281	Mike Davis	.06	.03	.00	☐ 375	Calvin Schiraldi	.06	.03	.00
☐ 282	Andres Galarraga	.15	.07	.01	☐ 376	Alex Trevino	.03	.01	.00
☐ 283	Devon White	.25	.12	.02	☐ 377	Tom Candiotti	.03	.01	.00
☐ 284	Pete O'Brien	.10	.05	.01	☐ 378	Steve Farr	.03	.01	.00
☐ 285	Jerry Hairston	.03	.01	.00	☐ 379	Mike Gallego	.03	.01	.00
☐ 286	Kevin Bass	.08	.04	.01	☐ 380	Andy McGaffigan	.03	.01	.00
☐ 287	Carmelo Martinez	.06	.03	.00	☐ 381	Kirk McCaskill	.06	.03	.00
☐ 288	Juan Samuel	.12	.06	.01	☐ 382	Oddibe McDowell	.10	.05	.01
☐ 289	Kal Daniels	.25	.12	.02	☐ 383	Floyd Bannister	.06	.03	.00
☐ 290	Albert Hall	.03	.01	.00	☐ 384	Denny Walling	.03	.01	.00
☐ 291	Andy Van Slyke	.10	.05	.01	☐ 385	Don Carman	.03	.01	.00
☐ 292	Lee Smith	.10	.05	.01	☐ 386	Todd Worrell	.12	.06	.01
☐ 293	Vince Coleman	.25	.12	.02	☐ 387	Eric Show	.03	.01	.00
☐ 294	Tom Niedenfuer	.06	.03	.00	☐ 388	Dave Parker	.12	.06	.01
☐ 295	Robin Yount	.20	.10	.02	☐ 389	Rick Mahler	.03	.01	.00
☐ 296	Jeff Robinson	.06	.03	.00	☐ 390	Mike Dunne	.30	.15	.03
	(Pirates pitcher)				☐ 391	Candy Maldonado	.10	.05	.01
☐ 297	Todd Benzinger	.45	.22	.04	☐ 392	Bob Dernier	.03	.01	.00
☐ 298	Dave Winfield	.25	.12	.02	☐ 393	Dave Valle	.03	.01	.00
☐ 299	Mickey Hatcher	.03	.01	.00	☐ 394	Ernie Whitt	.03	.01	.00
☐ 300	Checklist	.06	.01	.00	☐ 395	Juan Berenguer	.03	.01	.00
☐ 301	Bud Black	.03	.01	.00	☐ 396	Mike Young	.06	.03	.00
☐ 302	Jose Canseco	.60	.30	.06	☐ 397	Mike Felder	.03	.01	.00
☐ 303	Tom Foley	.03	.01	.00	☐ 398	Willie Hernandez	.08	.04	.01
☐ 304	Pete Incaviglia	.25	.12	.02	☐ 399	Jim Rice	.25	.12	.02
☐ 305	Bob Boone	.06	.03	.00	☐ 400	Checklist	.06	.01	.00
☐ 306	Bill Long	.15	.07	.01	☐ 401	Tommy John	.10	.05	.01
☐ 307	Willie McGee	.15	.07	.01	☐ 402	Brian Holton	.03	.01	.00
☐ 308	Ken Caminiti	.35	.17	.03	☐ 403	Carmen Castillo	.03	.01	.00
☐ 309	Darren Daulton	.03	.01	.00	☐ 404	Jamie Quirk	.03	.01	.00
☐ 310	Tracy Jones	.10	.05	.01	☐ 405	Dwayne Murphy	.06	.03	.00
☐ 311	Greg Booker	.03	.01	.00	☐ 406	Jeff Parrett	.20	.10	.02
☐ 312	Mike LaValliere	.03	.01	.00	☐ 407	Don Sutton	.12	.06	.01
☐ 313	Chili Davis	.08	.04	.01	☐ 408	Jerry Browne	.03	.01	.00
☐ 314	Glenn Hubbard	.03	.01	.00	☐ 409	Jim Winn	.03	.01	.00
☐ 315	Paul Noce	.15	.07	.01	☐ 410	Dave Smith	.06	.03	.00
☐ 316	Keith Hernandez	.20	.10	.02	☐ 411	Shane Mack	.20	.10	.02
☐ 317	Mark Langston	.10	.05	.01	☐ 412	Greg Gross	.03	.01	.00
☐ 318	Keith Atherton	.03	.01	.00	☐ 413	Nick Esasky	.06	.03	.00
☐ 319	Tony Fernandez	.12	.06	.01	☐ 414	Damaso Garcia	.03	.01	.00
☐ 320	Kent Hrbek	.12	.06	.01	☐ 415	Brian Fisher	.06	.03	.00
☐ 321	John Cerutti	.03	.01	.00	☐ 416	Brian Dayett	.03	.01	.00
☐ 322	Mike Kingery	.03	.01	.00	☐ 417	Curt Ford	.06	.03	.00
☐ 323	Dave Magadan	.15	.07	.01	☐ 418	Mark Williamson	.15	.07	.01
☐ 324	Rafael Palmeiro	.10	.05	.01	☐ 419	Bill Schroeder	.06	.03	.00
☐ 325	Jeff Dedmon	.03	.01	.00	☐ 420	Mike Henneman	.25	.12	.02
☐ 326	Barry Bonds	.12	.06	.01	☐ 421	John Marzano	.35	.17	.03
☐ 327	Jeffrey Leonard	.08	.04	.01	☐ 422	Ron Kittle	.10	.05	.01
☐ 328	Tim Flannery	.03	.01	.00	☐ 423	Matt Young	.03	.01	.00
☐ 329	Dave Concepcion	.08	.04	.01	☐ 424	Steve Balboni	.03	.01	.00
☐ 330	Mike Schmidt	.30	.15	.03	☐ 425	Luis Polonia	.30	.15	.03
☐ 331	Bill Dawley	.03	.01	.00	☐ 426	Randy St.Claire	.06	.03	.00
☐ 332	Larry Andersen	.03	.01	.00	☐ 427	Greg Harris	.03	.01	.00
☐ 333	Jack Howell	.06	.03	.00	☐ 428	Johnny Ray	.08	.04	.01
☐ 334	Ken Williams	.35	.17	.03	☐ 429	Ray Searage	.03	.01	.00
☐ 335	Bryn Smith	.03	.01	.00	☐ 430	Ricky Horton	.03	.01	.00
☐ 336	Billy Ripken	.35	.17	.03	☐ 431	Gerald Young	.35	.17	.03
☐ 337	Greg Brock	.06	.03	.00	☐ 432	Rick Schu	.03	.01	.00
☐ 338	Mike Heath	.03	.01	.00	☐ 433	Paul O'Neill	.06	.03	.00
☐ 339	Mike Greenwell	.40	.20	.04	☐ 434	Rich Gossage	.10	.05	.01

☐ 435	John Cangelosi	.03	.01	.00
☐ 436	Mike LaCoss	.03	.01	.00
☐ 437	Gerald Perry	.06	.03	.00
☐ 438	Dave Martinez	.06	.03	.00
☐ 439	Darryl Strawberry	.30	.15	.03
☐ 440	John Moses	.03	.01	.00
☐ 441	Greg Gagne	.06	.03	.00
☐ 442	Jesse Barfield	.15	.07	.01
☐ 443	George Frazier	.03	.01	.00
☐ 444	Garth Iorg	.03	.01	.00
☐ 445	Ed Nunez	.03	.01	.00
☐ 446	Rick Aguilera	.06	.03	.00
☐ 447	Jerry Mumphrey	.03	.01	.00
☐ 448	Rafael Ramirez	.03	.01	.00
☐ 449	John Smiley	.20	.10	.02
☐ 450	Atlee Hammaker	.06	.03	.00
☐ 451	Lance McCullers	.06	.03	.00
☐ 452	Guy Hoffman	.03	.01	.00
☐ 453	Chris James	.10	.05	.01
☐ 454	Terry Leach	.08	.04	.01
☐ 455	Dave Meads	.12	.06	.01
☐ 456	Bill Buckner	.08	.04	.01
☐ 457	John Pawlowski	.15	.07	.01
☐ 458	Bob Sebra	.03	.01	.00
☐ 459	Jim Dwyer	.03	.01	.00
☐ 460	Jay Aldrich	.15	.07	.01
☐ 461	Frank Tanana	.06	.03	.00
☐ 462	Oil Can Boyd	.06	.03	.00
☐ 463	Dan Pasqua	.08	.04	.01
☐ 464	Tim Crews	.20	.10	.02
☐ 465	Andy Allanson	.06	.03	.00
☐ 466	Bill Pecota	.20	.10	.02
☐ 467	Steve Ontiveros	.03	.01	.00
☐ 468	Hubie Brooks	.06	.03	.00
☐ 469	Paul Kilgus	.15	.07	.01
☐ 470	Dale Mohorcic	.06	.03	.00
☐ 471	Dan Quisenberry	.12	.06	.01
☐ 472	Dave Stewart	.10	.05	.01
☐ 473	Dave Clark	.08	.04	.01
☐ 474	Joel Skinner	.03	.01	.00
☐ 475	Dave Anderson	.03	.01	.00
☐ 476	Dan Petry	.06	.03	.00
☐ 477	Carl Nichols	.15	.07	.01
☐ 478	Ernest Riles	.03	.01	.00
☐ 479	George Hendrick	.06	.03	.00
☐ 480	John Morris	.03	.01	.00
☐ 481	Manny Hernandez	.15	.07	.01
☐ 482	Jeff Stone	.06	.03	.00
☐ 483	Chris Brown	.10	.05	.01
☐ 484	Mike Bielecki	.03	.01	.00
☐ 485	Dave Dravecky	.06	.03	.00
☐ 486	Rick Manning	.03	.01	.00
☐ 487	Bill Almon	.03	.01	.00
☐ 488	Jim Sundberg	.03	.01	.00
☐ 489	Ken Phelps	.06	.03	.00
☐ 490	Tom Henke	.08	.04	.01
☐ 491	Dan Gladden	.06	.03	.00
☐ 492	Barry Larkin	.12	.06	.01
☐ 493	Fred Manrique	.20	.10	.02
☐ 494	Mike Griffin	.03	.01	.00
☐ 495	Mark Knudson	.15	.07	.01
☐ 496	Bill Madlock	.08	.04	.01
☐ 497	Tim Stoddard	.03	.01	.00
☐ 498	Sam Horn	1.25	.60	.12
☐ 499	Tracy Woodson	.25	.12	.02
☐ 500	Checklist	.06	.01	.00
☐ 501	Ken Schrom	.03	.01	.00
☐ 502	Angel Salazar	.03	.01	.00
☐ 503	Eric Plunk	.06	.03	.00
☐ 504	Joe Hesketh	.06	.03	.00
☐ 505	Greg Minton	.03	.01	.00
☐ 506	Geno Petralli	.03	.01	.00
☐ 507	Bob James	.03	.01	.00
☐ 508	Robbie Wine	.20	.10	.02
☐ 509	Jeff Calhoun	.03	.01	.00
☐ 510	Steve Lake	.03	.01	.00
☐ 511	Mark Grant	.03	.01	.00
☐ 512	Frank Williams	.03	.01	.00
☐ 513	Jeff Blauser	.25	.12	.02
☐ 514	Bob Walk	.03	.01	.00
☐ 515	Craig Lefferts	.03	.01	.00
☐ 516	Manny Trillo	.03	.01	.00
☐ 517	Jerry Reed	.03	.01	.00
☐ 518	Rick Leach	.03	.01	.00
☐ 519	Mark Davidson	.15	.07	.01
☐ 520	Jeff Ballard	.20	.10	.02
☐ 521	Dave Stapleton	.08	.04	.01
☐ 522	Pat Sheridan	.03	.01	.00
☐ 523	Al Nipper	.03	.01	.00
☐ 524	Steve Trout	.03	.01	.00
☐ 525	Jeff Hamilton	.06	.03	.00
☐ 526	Tommy Hinzo	.20	.10	.02
☐ 527	Lonnie Smith	.06	.03	.00
☐ 528	Greg Cadaret	.15	.07	.01
☐ 529	Bob McClure	.06	.03	.00

	("Rob" on front)			
☐ 530	Chuck Finley	.03	.01	.00
☐ 531	Jeff Russell	.03	.01	.00
☐ 532	Steve Lyons	.03	.01	.00
☐ 533	Terry Puhl	.03	.01	.00
☐ 534	Eric Nolte	.15	.07	.01
☐ 535	Kent Tekulve	.06	.03	.00
☐ 536	Pat Pacillo	.10	.05	.01
☐ 537	Charlie Puleo	.03	.01	.00
☐ 538	Tom Prince	.20	.10	.02
☐ 539	Greg Maddux	.03	.01	.00
☐ 540	Jim Lindeman	.08	.04	.01
☐ 541	Pete Stanicek	.30	.15	.03
☐ 542	Steve Kiefer	.08	.04	.01
☐ 543	Jim Morrison	.03	.01	.00
☐ 544	Spike Owen	.03	.01	.00
☐ 545	Jay Buhner	.35	.17	.03
☐ 546	Mike Devereaux	.30	.15	.03
☐ 547	Jerry Don Gleaton	.03	.01	.00
☐ 548	Jose Rijo	.06	.03	.00
☐ 549	Dennis Martinez	.06	.03	.00
☐ 550	Mike Loynd	.03	.01	.00
☐ 551	Darrell Miller	.03	.01	.00
☐ 552	Dave LaPoint	.03	.01	.00
☐ 553	John Tudor	.10	.05	.01
☐ 554	Rocky Childress	.15	.07	.01
☐ 555	Wally Ritchie	.15	.07	.01
☐ 556	Terry McGriff	.06	.03	.00
☐ 557	Dave Leiper	.03	.01	.00
☐ 558	Jeff Robinson	.20	.10	.02
	(Tigers pitcher)			
☐ 559	Jose Uribe	.03	.01	.00
☐ 560	Ted Simmons	.08	.04	.01
☐ 561	Lester Lancaster	.15	.07	.01
☐ 562	Keith Miller	.25	.12	.02
☐ 563	Harold Reynolds	.06	.03	.00
☐ 564	Gene Larkin	.25	.12	.02
☐ 565	Cecil Fielder	.06	.03	.00
☐ 566	Roy Smalley	.03	.01	.00
☐ 567	Duane Ward	.03	.01	.00
☐ 568	Bill Wilkinson	.15	.07	.01
☐ 569	Howard Johnson	.10	.05	.01
☐ 570	Frank DiPino	.03	.01	.00
☐ 571	Pete Smith	.15	.07	.01
☐ 572	Darnell Coles	.03	.01	.00
☐ 573	Don Robinson	.03	.01	.00
☐ 574	Rob Nelson	.06	.03	.00
☐ 575	Dennis Rasmussen	.06	.03	.00
☐ 576	Steve Jeltz	.03	.01	.00
☐ 577	Tom Pagnozzi	.15	.07	.01
☐ 578	Ty Gainey	.03	.01	.00
☐ 579	Gary Lucas	.03	.01	.00
☐ 580	Ron Hassey	.03	.01	.00
☐ 581	Herm Winningham	.03	.01	.00
☐ 582	Rene Gonzales	.15	.07	.01
☐ 583	Brad Komminsk	.06	.03	.00
☐ 584	Doyle Alexander	.06	.03	.00
☐ 585	Jeff Sellers	.03	.01	.00
☐ 586	Bill Gullickson	.06	.03	.00
☐ 587	Tim Belcher	.10	.05	.01
☐ 588	Doug Jones	.15	.07	.01
☐ 589	Melido Perez	.15	.07	.01
☐ 590	Rick Honeycutt	.03	.01	.00
☐ 591	Pascual Perez	.03	.01	.00
☐ 592	Curt Wilkerson	.03	.01	.00
☐ 593	Steve Howe	.03	.01	.00
☐ 594	John Davis	.20	.10	.02
☐ 595	Storm Davis	.06	.03	.00
☐ 596	Sammy Stewart	.03	.01	.00
☐ 597	Neil Allen	.06	.03	.00
☐ 598	Alejandro Pena	.06	.03	.00
☐ 599	Mark Thurmond	.03	.01	.00
☐ 600	Checklist	.06	.01	.00
☐ 601	Jose Mesa	.15	.07	.01
☐ 602	Don August	.12	.06	.01
☐ 603	Terry Leach	.06	.03	.00
☐ 604	Tom Newell	.15	.07	.01
☐ 605	Randall Byers	.20	.10	.02
☐ 606	Jim Gott	.03	.01	.00
☐ 607	Harry Spilman	.03	.01	.00
☐ 608	John Candelaria	.06	.03	.00
☐ 609	Mike Brumley	.15	.07	.01
☐ 610	Mickey Brantley	.10	.05	.01
☐ 611	Jose Nunez	.15	.07	.01
☐ 612	Tom Nieto	.03	.01	.00
☐ 613	Rick Reuschel	.06	.03	.00
☐ 614	Lee Mazzilli	.06	.03	.00
☐ 615	Scott Lusader	.20	.10	.02
☐ 616	Bobby Meacham	.03	.01	.00
☐ 617	Kevin McReynolds	.12	.06	.01
☐ 618	Gene Garber	.03	.01	.00
☐ 619	Barry Lyons	.20	.10	.02
☐ 620	Randy Myers	.10	.05	.01
☐ 621	Donnie Moore	.06	.03	.00
☐ 622	Domingo Ramos	.03	.01	.00

☐ 623	Ed Romero	.03	.01	.00
☐ 624	Greg Myers	.20	.10	.02
☐ 625	Ripken Family	.10	.05	.01
☐ 626	Pat Perry	.03	.01	.00
☐ 627	Andres Thomas	.03	.01	.00
☐ 628	Matt Williams	.35	.17	.03
☐ 629	Dave Hengel	.20	.10	.02
☐ 630	Jeff Musselman	.03	.01	.00
☐ 631	Tim Laudner	.03	.01	.00
☐ 632	Bob Ojeda	.06	.03	.00
☐ 633	Rafael Santana	.03	.01	.00
☐ 634	Wes Gardner	.20	.10	.02
☐ 635	Roberto Kelly	.35	.17	.03
☐ 636	Mike Flanagan	.06	.03	.00
☐ 637	Jay Bell	.35	.17	.03
☐ 638	Bob Melvin	.03	.01	.00
☐ 639	Damon Berryhill	.20	.10	.02
☐ 640	David Wells	.20	.10	.02
☐ 641	Puzzle Card	.06	.03	.00
	(Stan Musial)			
☐ 642	Doug Sisk	.03	.01	.00
☐ 643	Keith Hughes	.30	.15	.03
☐ 644	Tom Glavine	.20	.10	.02
☐ 645	Al Newman	.03	.01	.00
☐ 646	Scott Sanderson	.03	.01	.00
☐ 647	Scott Terry	.08	.04	.01
☐ 648	Tim Teufel	.06	.03	.00
☐ 649	Garry Templeton	.06	.03	.00
☐ 650	Manny Lee	.03	.01	.00
☐ 651	Roger McDowell	.08	.04	.01
☐ 652	Mookie Wilson	.08	.04	.01
☐ 653	David Cone	.08	.04	.01
☐ 654	Ron Gant	.20	.10	.02
☐ 655	Joe Price	.03	.01	.00
☐ 656	George Bell	.20	.10	.02
☐ 657	Gregg Jefferies	1.25	.60	.12
☐ 658	Todd Stottlemyre	.30	.15	.03
☐ 659	Geronimo Berroa	.25	.12	.02
☐ 660	Jerry Royster	.03	.01	.00

1988 Donruss Bonus Cards

This 26-card set was distributed along with the regular 1988 Donruss issue as random inserts with the rack and wax packs. These bonus cards are numbered with the prefix BC for bonus cards and were supposedly produced in the same quantities as the other 660 regular issue cards. The 'most valuable" player was selected from each of the 26 teams. Cards measure 2 1/2" by 3 1/2" and feature the same distinctive black and blue border on the front as the regular issue. The cards are distinguished by the MVP logo in the upper left corner of the obverse.

		MINT	EXC	G-VG
COMPLETE SET (660)		12.00	6.00	1.20
COMMON PLAYER (1-660)		.10	.05	.01
☐ BC1	Cal Ripken	.35	.17	.03
☐ BC2	Eric Davis	1.00	.50	.10
☐ BC3	Paul Molitor	.20	.10	.02
☐ BC4	Mike Schmidt	.50	.25	.05
☐ BC5	Ivan Calderon	.15	.07	.01
☐ BC6	Tony Gwynn	.40	.20	.04
☐ BC7	Wade Boggs	1.00	.50	.10
☐ BC8	Andy Van Slyke	.10	.05	.01

☐ BC9	Joe Carter	.20	.10	.02
☐ BC10	Andre Dawson	.30	.15	.03
☐ BC11	Alan Trammell	.30	.15	.03
☐ BC12	Mike Scott	.30	.15	.03
☐ BC13	Wally Joyner	.75	.35	.07
☐ BC14	Dale Murphy	.50	.25	.05
☐ BC15	Kirby Puckett	.50	.25	.05
☐ BC16	Pedro Guerrero	.25	.12	.02
☐ BC17	Kevin Seitzer	1.00	.50	.10
☐ BC18	Tim Raines	.35	.17	.03
☐ BC19	George Bell	.30	.15	.03
☐ BC20	Darryl Strawberry	.60	.30	.06
☐ BC21	Don Mattingly	1.50	.75	.15
☐ BC22	Ozzie Smith	.25	.12	.02
☐ BC23	Mark McGwire	1.00	.50	.10
☐ BC24	Will Clark	.45	.22	.04
☐ BC25	Alvin Davis	.10	.05	.01
☐ BC26	Ruben Sierra	.30	.15	.03

1988 Donruss Super DK's

This 26-player card set was available through a mail-in offer detailed on the wax packs. The set was sent in return for 8.00 and three wrappers plus 1.50 postage and handling. The set features the popular Diamond King subseries in large (approximately 4 7/8" by 6 13/16") form. Dick Perez of Perez-Steele Galleries did another outstanding job on the artwork. The cards are essentially a large version of the Donruss regular issue Diamond Kings.

		MINT	EXC	G-VG
COMPLETE SET		10.00	5.00	1.00
COMMON PLAYER (1-26)		.15	.07	.01
☐ 1	Mark McGwire DK	2.00	1.00	.20
☐ 2	Tim Raines DK	.60	.30	.06
☐ 3	Benito Santiago DK	1.00	.50	.10
☐ 4	Alan Trammell DK	.40	.20	.04
☐ 5	Danny Tartabull DK	.40	.20	.04
☐ 6	Ron Darling DK	.30	.15	.03
☐ 7	Paul Molitor DK	.35	.17	.03
☐ 8	Devon White DK	.50	.25	.05
☐ 9	Andre Dawson DK	.50	.25	.05
☐ 10	Julio Franco DK	.15	.07	.01
☐ 11	Scott Fletcher DK	.15	.07	.01
☐ 12	Tony Fernandez DK	.35	.17	.03
☐ 13	Shane Rawley DK	.15	.07	.01
☐ 14	Kal Daniels DK	.50	.25	.05
☐ 15	Jack Clark DK	.50	.25	.05
☐ 16	Dwight Evans DK	.25	.12	.02
☐ 17	Tommy John DK	.25	.12	.02
☐ 18	Andy Van Slyke DK	.25	.12	.02
☐ 19	Gary Gaetti DK	.35	.17	.03
☐ 20	Mark Langston DK	.25	.12	.02
☐ 21	Will Clark DK	.75	.35	.07
☐ 22	Glenn Hubbard DK	.15	.07	.01
☐ 23	Billy Hatcher DK	.25	.12	.02
☐ 24	Bob Welch DK	.15	.07	.01
☐ 25	Ivan Calderon DK	.30	.15	.03
☐ 26	Cal Ripken Jr. DK	.60	.30	.06

PLEASE NOTE: Prices and availability of merchandise offered for sale by our advertisers may change during the year.

		MINT	EXC	G-VG
☐ 55	Juan Samuel	.15	.07	.01
☐ 56	Orel Hershiser	.15	.07	.01
☐ 57	Tim Raines	.25	.12	.02
☐ 58	Sid Fernandez	.15	.07	.01
☐ 59	Tim Wallach	.10	.05	.01
☐ 60	Lee Smith	.10	.05	.01
☐ 61	Steve Bedrosian	.10	.05	.01
☐ 62	Tim Raines	.25	.12	.02
☐ 63	Ozzie Smith	.20	.10	.02
☐ 64	NL Checklist	.10	.05	.01

1988 Donruss All-Stars

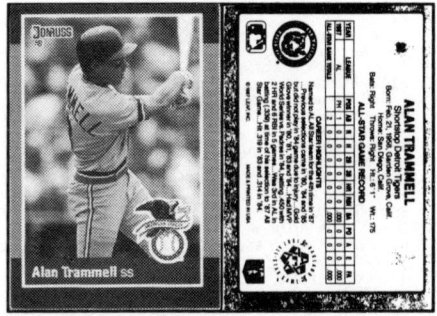

This 64-card set features cards measuring standard size, 2 1/2" by 3 1/2". Card fronts are in full color with a solid blue and black border. The card backs are printed in black and blue on white card stock. Cards are numbered on the back inside a blue star in the upper right hand corner. Card backs feature statistical information about the player's performance in past All-Star games. The set was distributed in packs which also contained a Pop-Up.

		MINT	EXC	G-VG
	COMPLETE SET	7.50	3.00	.60
	COMMON PLAYER	.10	.05	.01
☐ 1	Don Mattingly	.75	.35	.07
☐ 2	Dave Winfield	.25	.12	.02
☐ 3	Willie Randolph	.10	.05	.01
☐ 4	Rickey Henderson	.30	.15	.03
☐ 5	Cal Ripken	.25	.12	.02
☐ 6	George Bell	.20	.10	.02
☐ 7	Wade Boggs	.60	.30	.06
☐ 8	Bret Saberhagen	.20	.10	.02
☐ 9	Terry Kennedy	.10	.05	.01
☐ 10	John McNamara MG	.10	.05	.01
☐ 11	Jay Howell	.10	.05	.01
☐ 12	Harold Baines	.10	.05	.01
☐ 13	Harold Reynolds	.10	.05	.01
☐ 14	Bruce Hurst	.10	.05	.01
☐ 15	Kirby Puckett	.30	.15	.03
☐ 16	Matt Nokes	.30	.15	.03
☐ 17	Pat Tabler	.10	.05	.01
☐ 18	Dan Plesac	.10	.05	.01
☐ 19	Mark McGwire	.75	.35	.07
☐ 20	Mike Witt	.10	.05	.01
☐ 21	Larry Parrish	.10	.05	.01
☐ 22	Alan Trammell	.20	.10	.02
☐ 23	Dwight Evans	.10	.05	.01
☐ 24	Jack Morris	.15	.07	.01
☐ 25	Tony Fernandez	.15	.07	.01
☐ 26	Mark Langston	.10	.05	.01
☐ 27	Kevin Seitzer	.60	.30	.06
☐ 28	Tom Henke	.10	.05	.01
☐ 29	Dave Righetti	.15	.07	.01
☐ 30	Oakland Stadium	.10	.05	.01
☐ 31	Wade Boggs	.60	.30	.06
☐ 32	AL Checklist	.10	.05	.01
☐ 33	Jack Clark	.25	.12	.02
☐ 34	Darryl Strawberry	.30	.15	.03
☐ 35	Ryne Sandberg	.25	.12	.02
☐ 36	Andre Dawson	.25	.12	.02
☐ 37	Ozzie Smith	.20	.10	.02
☐ 38	Eric Davis	.75	.35	.07
☐ 39	Mike Schmidt	.40	.20	.04
☐ 40	Mike Scott	.20	.10	.02
☐ 41	Gary Carter	.25	.12	.02
☐ 42	Davey Johnson MG	.10	.05	.01
☐ 43	Rick Sutcliffe	.10	.05	.01
☐ 44	Willie McGee	.15	.07	.01
☐ 45	Hubie Brooks	.10	.05	.01
☐ 46	Dale Murphy	.40	.20	.04
☐ 47	Bo Diaz	.10	.05	.01
☐ 48	Pedro Guerrero	.20	.10	.02
☐ 49	Keith Hernandez	.20	.10	.02
☐ 50	Ozzie Virgil	.10	.05	.01
☐ 51	Tony Gwynn	.35	.17	.03
☐ 52	Rick Reuschel	.10	.05	.01
☐ 53	John Franco	.10	.05	.01
☐ 54	Jeffrey Leonard	.10	.05	.01

1988 Donruss Pop-Ups

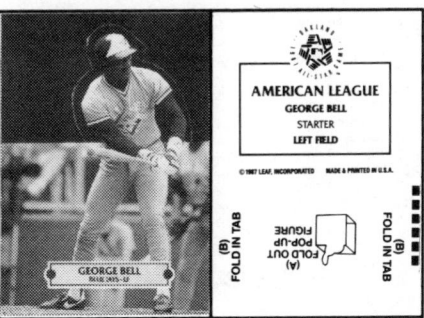

This 20-card set features "fold-out" cards measuring standard size, 2 1/2" by 3 1/2". Card fronts are in full color. Cards are unnumbered but are listed in the same order as the Donruss All-Stars on the All-Star checklist card. Card backs present essentially no information about the player. The set was distributed in packs which also contained All-Star cards. In order to remain in mint condition, the cards should not be popped up.

		MINT	EXC	G-VG
	COMPLETE SET	5.00	2.50	.50
	COMMON PLAYER	.10	.05	.01
☐ 1	Don Mattingly	1.00	.50	.10
☐ 2	Dave Winfield	.30	.15	.03
☐ 3	Willie Randolph	.10	.05	.01
☐ 4	Rickey Henderson	.35	.17	.03
☐ 5	Cal Ripken	.30	.15	.03
☐ 6	George Bell	.20	.10	.02
☐ 7	Wade Boggs	.75	.35	.07
☐ 8	Bret Saberhagen	.20	.10	.02
☐ 9	Terry Kennedy	.10	.05	.01
☐ 10	John McNamara MG	.10	.05	.01
☐ 11	Jack Clark	.25	.12	.02
☐ 12	Darryl Strawberry	.35	.17	.03
☐ 13	Ryne Sandberg	.25	.12	.02
☐ 14	Andre Dawson	.25	.12	.02
☐ 15	Ozzie Smith	.20	.10	.02
☐ 16	Eric Davis	1.00	.50	.10
☐ 17	Mike Schmidt	.50	.25	.05
☐ 18	Mike Scott	.20	.10	.02
☐ 19	Gary Carter	.25	.12	.02
☐ 20	Davey Johnson MG	.10	.05	.01

1986 Dorman's Cheese

This 20-card set was issued in panels of two cards. The individual cards measure 1 1/2" by 2" whereas the panels measure 3" by 2". Team logos have been removed from the photos as these cards were not licensed by Major League Baseball (team owners). The backs contain a minimum of information.

	MINT	EXC	G-VG
COMPLETE SET	18.00	9.00	1.80
COMMON PLAYER	.75	.35	.07

		MINT	EXC	G-VG
☐ 1	George Brett	1.25	.60	.12
☐ 2	Jack Morris	.75	.35	.07
☐ 3	Gary Carter	1.00	.50	.10
☐ 4	Cal Ripken	1.00	.50	.10
☐ 5	Dwight Gooden	1.25	.60	.12
☐ 6	Kent Hrbek	.75	.35	.07
☐ 7	Rickey Henderson	1.25	.60	.12
☐ 8	Mike Schmidt	1.25	.60	.12
☐ 9	Keith Hernandez	1.00	.50	.10
☐ 10	Dale Murphy	1.25	.60	.12
☐ 11	Reggie Jackson	1.00	.50	.10
☐ 12	Eddie Murray	1.00	.50	.10
☐ 13	Don Mattingly	3.00	1.50	.30
☐ 14	Ryne Sandberg	1.00	.50	.10
☐ 15	Willie McGee	.75	.35	.07
☐ 16	Robin Yount	1.00	.50	.10
☐ 17	Rick Sutcliffe	.75	.35	.07
☐ 18	Wade Boggs	2.00	1.00	.20
☐ 19	Dave Winfield	1.00	.50	.10
☐ 20	Jim Rice	1.00	.50	.10

1941 Double Play

HAROLD REESE   KIRBY HIGBE
BROOKLYN DODGERS, Shortstop.   BROOKLYN DODGERS, Pitcher.
Born July 23, 1919. Bats right.   Born April 8, 1915. Bats right.
Throws right. Height 5 ft. 10 in.   Throws right. Height 5 ft. 11 in.
Weight 160 lbs. Batted .272.   Weight 188 lbs. Won 14, Lost 19.
No. 23 Double Play   No. 24 Double Play

The cards in this 75-card set measure 2 1/2" by 3 1/8". The 1941 Double Play set, listed as R330 in the American Card Catalog, was a blank-backed issue distributed by Gum Products. It consists of 75 numbered cards (two consecutive numbers per card), each depicting two players in sepia tone photographs. Cards 81-100 contain action poses, and the last 50 numbers of the set are slightly harder to find. Cards that have been cut in half to form "singles" have a greatly reduced value.

	NRMT	VG-E	GOOD
COMPLETE SET	2000.00	850.00	150.00
COMMON PAIRS (1-100)	15.00	7.50	1.50
COMMON PAIRS (101-150)	18.00	9.00	1.80

		NRMT	VG-E	GOOD
☐ 1	Larry French and 2 Vance Page	15.00	7.50	1.50
☐ 3	Billy Herman and 4 Stan Hack	21.00	10.50	2.10
☐ 5	Lonnie Frey and 6 Johnny VanderMeer	18.00	9.00	1.80
☐ 7	Paul Derringer and 8 Bucky Walters	18.00	9.00	1.80
☐ 9	Frank McCormick and 10 Bill Werber	15.00	7.50	1.50
☐ 11	Jimmy Ripple and 12 Ernie Lombardi	21.00	10.50	2.10
☐ 13	Alex Kampouris and 14 Whitlow Wyatt	15.00	7.50	1.50
☐ 15	Mickey Owen and 16 Paul Waner	21.00	10.50	2.10
☐ 17	Cookie Lavagetto and 18 Pete Reiser	18.00	9.00	1.80
☐ 19	James Wasdell and 20 Dolf Camilli	15.00	7.50	1.50
☐ 21	Dixie Walker and 22 Joe Medwick	21.00	10.50	2.10

		NRMT	VG-E	GOOD
☐ 23	Pee Wee Reese and 24 Kirby Higbe	60.00	30.00	6.00
☐ 25	Harry Danning and 26 Cliff Melton	15.00	7.50	1.50
☐ 27	Harry Gumbert and 28 Burgess Whitehead	15.00	7.50	1.50
☐ 29	Joe Orengo and 30 Joe Moore	15.00	7.50	1.50
☐ 31	Mel Ott and 32 Norman Young	40.00	20.00	4.00
☐ 33	Lee Handley and 34 Arky Vaughan	21.00	10.50	2.10
☐ 35	Bob Klinger and 36 Stanley Brown	15.00	7.50	1.50
☐ 37	Terry Moore and 38 Gus Mancuso	15.00	7.50	1.50
☐ 39	Johnny Mize and 40 Enos Slaughter	60.00	30.00	6.00
☐ 41	Johnny Cooney and 42 Sibby Sisti	15.00	7.50	1.50
☐ 43	Max West and 44 Carvel Rowell	15.00	7.50	1.50
☐ 45	Danny Litwhiler and 46 Merrill May	15.00	7.50	1.50
☐ 47	Frank Hayes and 48 Al Brancato	15.00	7.50	1.50
☐ 49	Bob Johnson and 50 Bill Nagel	15.00	7.50	1.50
☐ 51	Buck Newsom and 52 Hank Greenberg	30.00	15.00	3.00
☐ 53	Barney McCosky and 54 Charlie Gehringer	30.00	15.00	3.00
☐ 55	Mike Higgins and 56 Dick Bartell	15.00	7.50	1.50
☐ 57	Ted Williams and 58 Jim Tabor	150.00	75.00	15.00
☐ 59	Joe Cronin and 60 Jimmie Foxx	90.00	45.00	9.00
☐ 61	Lefty Gomez and 62 Phil Rizzuto	100.00	50.00	10.00
☐ 63	Joe DiMaggio and 64 Charlie Keller	250.00	125.00	25.00
☐ 65	Red Rolfe and 66 Bill Dickey	50.00	25.00	5.00
☐ 67	Joe Gordon and 68 Red Ruffing	40.00	20.00	4.00
☐ 69	Mike Tresh and 70 Luke Appling	21.00	10.50	2.10
☐ 71	Moose Solters and 72 Johnny Rigney	15.00	7.50	1.50
☐ 73	Buddy Myer and 74 Ben Chapman	15.00	7.50	1.50
☐ 75	Cecil Travis and 76 George Case	15.00	7.50	1.50
☐ 77	Joe Krakauskas and 78 Bob Feller	50.00	25.00	5.00
☐ 79	Ken Keltner and 80 Hal Trosky	15.00	7.50	1.50
☐ 81	Ted Williams and 82 Joe Cronin	200.00	100.00	20.00
☐ 83	Joe Gordon and 84 Charlie Keller	21.00	10.50	2.10
☐ 85	Hank Greenberg and 86 Red Ruffing	80.00	40.00	8.00
☐ 87	Hal Trosky and 88 George Case	15.00	7.50	1.50
☐ 89	Mel Ott and 90 Burgess Whitehead	40.00	20.00	4.00
☐ 91	Harry Danning and 92 Harry Gumbert	15.00	7.50	1.50
☐ 93	Norman Young and 94 Cliff Melton	15.00	7.50	1.50
☐ 95	Jimmy Ripple and 96 Bucky Walters	15.00	7.50	1.50
☐ 97	Stanley Jack and 98 Bob Klinger	15.00	7.50	1.50
☐ 99	Johnny Mize and 100 Dan Litwhiler	25.00	12.50	2.50
☐ 101	Dom Dallesandro and 102 Augie Galan	18.00	9.00	1.80
☐ 103	Bill Lee and 104 Phil Cavarretta	18.00	9.00	1.80
☐ 105	Lefty Grove and 106 Bobby Doerr	80.00	40.00	8.00
☐ 107	Frank Pytlak and 108 Dom DiMaggio	21.00	10.50	2.10
☐ 109	Jerry Priddy and 110 Johnny Murphy	18.00	9.00	1.80
☐ 111	Tommy Henrich and 112 Marius Russo	21.00	10.50	2.10
☐ 113	Frank Crosetti and 114 John Sturm	21.00	10.50	2.10
☐ 115	Ival Goodman and 116 Myron McCormick	18.00	9.00	1.80
☐ 117	Eddie Joost and	18.00	9.00	1.80

		118 Ernie Koy			
☐	119	Lloyd Waner and	24.00	12.00	2.40
		120 Hank Majeski			
☐	121	Buddy Hassett and	18.00	9.00	1.80
		122 Eugene Moore			
☐	123	Nick Etten and	18.00	9.00	1.80
		124 John Rizzo			
☐	125	Sam Chapman and	18.00	9.00	1.80
		126 Wally Moses			
☐	127	Johnny Babich and	18.00	9.00	1.80
		128 Dick Siebert			
☐	129	Nelson Potter and	18.00	9.00	1.80
		130 Benny McCoy			
☐	131	Clarence Campbell and ..	30.00	15.00	3.00
		132 Lou Boudreau			
☐	133	Rollie Hemsley and	18.00	9.00	1.80
		134 Mel Harder			
☐	135	Gerald Walker and	18.00	9.00	1.80
		136 Joe Heving			
☐	137	Johnny Rucker and	18.00	9.00	1.80
		138 Ace Adams			
☐	139	Morris Arnovich and	40.00	20.00	4.00
		140 Carl Hubbell			
☐	141	Lew Riggs and	30.00	15.00	3.00
		142 Leo Durocher			
☐	143	Fred Fitzsimmons and	18.00	9.00	1.80
		144 Joe Vosmik			
☐	145	Frank Crespi and	18.00	9.00	1.80
		146 Jim Brown			
☐	147	Don Heffner and	18.00	9.00	1.80
		148 Harland Clift			
☐	149	Debs Garms and	18.00	9.00	1.80
		150 Elbert Fletcher			

☐	28	Allie Reynolds	50.00	25.00	5.00
☐	29	Ray Scarborough	35.00	17.50	3.50
☐	30	Birdie Tebbetts	35.00	17.50	3.50
☐	31	Maurice McDermott	35.00	17.50	3.50
☐	32	Johnny Pesky	35.00	17.50	3.50
☐	33	Dom DiMaggio	50.00	25.00	5.00
☐	34	Vern Stephens	35.00	17.50	3.50
☐	35	Bob Elliott	35.00	17.50	3.50
☐	36	Enos Slaughter	125.00	60.00	12.50

1981 Drake's

The cards in this 33 card set measure 2 1/2" by 3 1/2". The 1981 Drake's Bakeries set contains National and American League stars. Produced in conjunction with Topps and released to the public in Drake's Cakes, this set features red frames for American League players and blue frames for National League players. A Drake's Cakes logo with the words "Big Hitters" appears on the lower front of each card. The backs are quite similar to the 1981 Topps backs but contain the Drake's logo, a different card number, and a short paragraph entitled "What Makes a Big Hitter?" at the top of the card.

1950 Drake's

 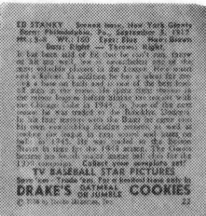

The cards in this 36-card set measure 2 1/2" by 2 1/2". The 1950 Drake's Cookies set contains numbered black and white cards. The players are pictured inside a simulated television screen and the caption "TV Baseball Series" appears on the cards. The ACC designation is D358.

			NRMT	VG-E	GOOD
		COMPLETE SET	2000.00	900.00	150.00
		COMMON PLAYER (1-36)	35.00	17.50	3.50
☐	1	Preacher Roe	50.00	25.00	5.00
☐	2	Clint Hartung	35.00	17.50	3.50
☐	3	Earl Torgeson	35.00	17.50	3.50
☐	4	Lou Brissie	35.00	17.50	3.50
☐	5	Duke Snider	200.00	100.00	20.00
☐	6	Roy Campanella	250.00	125.00	25.00
☐	7	Sheldon Jones	35.00	17.50	3.50
☐	8	Whitey Lockman	35.00	17.50	3.50
☐	9	Bobby Thomson	45.00	22.50	4.50
☐	10	Dick Sisler	35.00	17.50	3.50
☐	11	Gil Hodges	100.00	50.00	10.00
☐	12	Eddie Waitkus	35.00	17.50	3.50
☐	13	Bobby Kerr	35.00	17.50	3.50
☐	14	Warren Spahn	125.00	60.00	12.50
☐	15	Buddy Kerr	35.00	17.50	3.50
☐	16	Sid Gordon	35.00	17.50	3.50
☐	17	Willard Marshall	35.00	17.50	3.50
☐	18	Carl Furillo	50.00	25.00	5.00
☐	19	Pee Wee Reese	125.00	60.00	12.50
☐	20	Alvin Dark	45.00	22.50	4.50
☐	21	Del Ennis	35.00	17.50	3.50
☐	22	Ed Stanky	35.00	17.50	3.50
☐	23	Tom Henrich	45.00	22.50	4.50
☐	24	Yogi Berra	200.00	100.00	20.00
☐	25	Phil Rizzuto	125.00	60.00	12.50
☐	26	Jerry Coleman	35.00	17.50	3.50
☐	27	Joe Page	35.00	17.50	3.50

			MINT	EXC	G-VG
		COMPLETE SET	5.50	2.75	.55
		COMMON PLAYER	.05	.02	.00
☐	1	Carl Yastrzemski	.70	.35	.07
☐	2	Rod Carew	.50	.25	.05
☐	3	Pete Rose	1.00	.50	.10
☐	4	Dave Parker	.25	.12	.02
☐	5	George Brett	.75	.35	.07
☐	6	Eddie Murray	.70	.35	.07
☐	7	Mike Schmidt	.75	.35	.07
☐	8	Jim Rice	.35	.17	.03
☐	9	Fred Lynn	.20	.10	.02
☐	10	Reggie Jackson	.75	.35	.07
☐	11	Steve Garvey	.55	.27	.05
☐	12	Ken Singleton	.05	.02	.00
☐	13	Bill Buckner	.05	.02	.00
☐	14	Dave Winfield	.35	.17	.03
☐	15	Jack Clark	.25	.12	.02
☐	16	Cecil Cooper	.10	.05	.01
☐	17	Bob Horner	.25	.12	.02
☐	18	George Foster	.10	.05	.01
☐	19	Dave Kingman	.10	.05	.01
☐	20	Cesar Cedeno	.05	.02	.00
☐	21	Joe Charboneau	.05	.02	.00
☐	22	George Hendrick	.05	.02	.00
☐	23	Gary Carter	.45	.22	.04
☐	24	Al Oliver	.10	.05	.01
☐	25	Bruce Bochte	.05	.02	.00
☐	26	Jerry Mumphrey	.05	.02	.00
☐	27	Steve Kemp	.05	.02	.00
☐	28	Bob Watson	.05	.02	.00
☐	29	John Castino	.05	.02	.00
☐	30	Tony Armas	.10	.05	.01
☐	31	John Mayberry	.05	.02	.00
☐	32	Carlton Fisk	.15	.07	.01
☐	33	Lee Mazzilli	.05	.02	.00

1982 Drake's

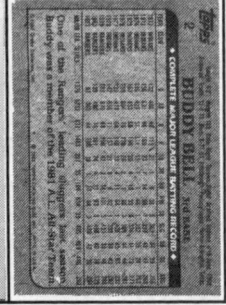

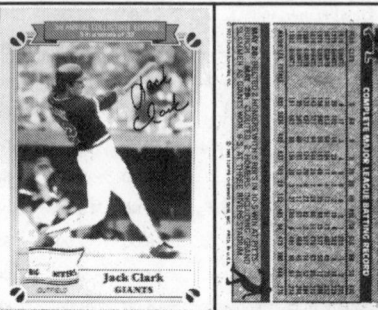

The cards in this 33 card set measure 2 1/2" by 3 1/2". The 1982 Drake's Big Hitters series cards each has the title "2nd Annual Collectors' Edition" in a ribbon design at the top of the picture area. Each color player photo has "photo mount" designs in the corners, red for the AL and green for the NL. The reverses are green and blue, the same as the regular 1982 Topps format, and the photos are larger than those of the previous year. Of the 33 hitters featured, 19 represent the National League. There are 21 returnees from the 1981 set and only one photo, that of Kennedy, is the same as that appearing in the regular Topps issue. The Drake's logo appears centered in the bottom border on the obverse.

		MINT	EXC	G-VG
	COMPLETE SET	5.50	2.75	.55
	COMMON PLAYER	.05	.02	.00
☐	1 Tony Armas	.10	.05	.01
☐	2 Buddy Bell	.10	.05	.01
☐	3 Johnny Bench	.40	.20	.04
☐	4 George Brett	.75	.35	.07
☐	5 Bill Buckner	.05	.02	.00
☐	6 Rod Carew	.45	.22	.04
☐	7 Gary Carter	.45	.22	.04
☐	8 Jack Clark	.25	.12	.02
☐	9 Cecil Cooper	.10	.05	.01
☐	10 Jose Cruz	.05	.02	.00
☐	11 Dwight Evans	.15	.07	.01
☐	12 Carlton Fisk	.15	.07	.01
☐	13 George Foster	.10	.05	.01
☐	14 Steve Garvey	.45	.22	.04
☐	15 Kirk Gibson	.35	.17	.03
☐	16 Mike Hargrove	.05	.02	.00
☐	17 George Hendrick	.05	.02	.00
☐	18 Bob Horner	.20	.10	.02
☐	19 Reggie Jackson	.75	.35	.07
☐	20 Terry Kennedy	.05	.02	.00
☐	21 Dave Kingman	.10	.05	.01
☐	22 Greg Luzinski	.10	.05	.01
☐	23 Bill Madlock	.10	.05	.01
☐	24 John Mayberry	.05	.02	.00
☐	25 Eddie Murray	.65	.30	.06
☐	26 Graig Nettles	.15	.07	.01
☐	27 Jim Rice	.30	.15	.03
☐	28 Pete Rose	.90	.45	.09
☐	29 Mike Schmidt	.75	.35	.07
☐	30 Ken Singleton	.05	.02	.00
☐	31 Dave Winfield	.35	.17	.03
☐	32 Butch Wynegar	.05	.02	.00
☐	33 Richie Zisk	.05	.02	.00

1983 Drake's

The cards in this 33 card series measure 2 1/2" by 3 1/2". For the third year in a row, Drake's Cakes, in conjunction with Topps, issued a set entitled Big Hitters. The fronts appear very similar to those of the previous two years with slight variations on the

framelines and player identification sections. The backs are the same as the Topps backs of this year except for the card number and the Drake's logo.

		MINT	EXC	G-VG
	COMPLETE SET	5.50	2.75	.55
	COMMON PLAYER	.05	.02	.00
☐	1 Don Baylor	.10	.05	.01
☐	2 Bill Buckner	.10	.05	.01
☐	3 Rod Carew	.45	.22	.04
☐	4 Gary Carter	.45	.22	.04
☐	5 Jack Clark	.25	.12	.02
☐	6 Cecil Cooper	.10	.05	.01
☐	7 Dwight Evans	.15	.07	.01
☐	8 George Foster	.10	.05	.01
☐	9 Pedro Guerrero	.35	.17	.03
☐	10 George Hendrick	.05	.02	.00
☐	11 Bob Horner	.25	.12	.02
☐	12 Reggie Jackson	.70	.35	.07
☐	13 Steve Kemp	.05	.02	.00
☐	14 Dave Kingman	.10	.05	.01
☐	15 Bill Madlock	.10	.05	.01
☐	16 Gary Matthews	.05	.02	.00
☐	17 Hal McRae	.05	.02	.00
☐	18 Dale Murphy	.75	.35	.07
☐	19 Eddie Murray	.65	.30	.06
☐	20 Ben Oglivie	.05	.02	.00
☐	21 Al Oliver	.10	.05	.01
☐	22 Jim Rice	.30	.15	.03
☐	23 Cal Ripken	.45	.22	.04
☐	24 Pete Rose	.90	.45	.09
☐	25 Mike Schmidt	.75	.35	.07
☐	26 Ken Singleton	.05	.02	.00
☐	27 Gorman Thomas	.05	.02	.00
☐	28 Jason Thompson	.05	.02	.00
☐	29 Mookie Wilson	.05	.02	.00
☐	30 Willie Wilson	.10	.05	.01
☐	31 Dave Winfield	.35	.17	.03
☐	32 Carl Yastrzemski	.70	.35	.07
☐	33 Robin Yount	.35	.17	.03

1984 Drake's

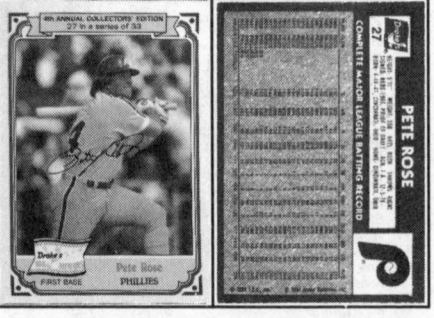

The cards in this 33 card set measure 2 1/2" by 3 1/2". The Fourth Annual Collectors Edition of baseball cards produced by Drake's Cakes in conjunction with Topps continued this now annual set entitled Big Hitters. As in previous years, the front contains a frameline in which the title of the set, the Drake's logo, and the player's name, his team, and position appear. The cards all feature the player in a batting action pose. While the cards fronts are different from the Topps fronts of this year, the backs differ only in the card number and the use of the Drake's logo instead of the Topps logo.

	MINT	EXC	G-VG
COMPLETE SET	5.50	2.75	.55
COMMON PLAYER	.05	.02	.00

			MINT	EXC	G-VG
☐	1	Don Baylor	.10	.05	.01
☐	2	Wade Boggs	.90	.45	.09
☐	3	George Brett	.75	.35	.07
☐	4	Bill Buckner	.05	.02	.00
☐	5	Rod Carew	.45	.22	.04
☐	6	Gary Carter	.45	.22	.04
☐	7	Ron Cey	.05	.02	.00
☐	8	Cecil Cooper	.10	.05	.01
☐	9	Andre Dawson	.30	.15	.03
☐	10	Steve Garvey	.45	.22	.04
☐	11	Pedro Guerrero	.30	.15	.03
☐	12	George Hendrick	.05	.02	.00
☐	13	Keith Hernandez	.30	.15	.03
☐	14	Bob Horner	.20	.10	.02
☐	15	Reggie Jackson	.70	.35	.07
☐	16	Steve Kemp	.05	.02	.00
☐	17	Ron Kittle	.10	.05	.01
☐	18	Greg Luzinski	.10	.05	.01
☐	19	Fred Lynn	.15	.07	.01
☐	20	Bill Madlock	.10	.05	.01
☐	21	Gary Matthews	.05	.02	.00
☐	22	Dale Murphy	.75	.35	.07
☐	23	Eddie Murray	.60	.30	.06
☐	24	Al Oliver	.10	.05	.01
☐	25	Jim Rice	.30	.15	.03
☐	26	Cal Ripken	.45	.22	.04
☐	27	Pete Rose	.90	.45	.09
☐	28	Mike Schmidt	.75	.35	.07
☐	29	Darryl Strawberry	1.00	.50	.10
☐	30	Alan Trammell	.20	.10	.02
☐	31	Mookie Wilson	.05	.02	.00
☐	32	Dave Winfield	.35	.17	.03
☐	33	Robin Yount	.30	.15	.03

			MINT	EXC	G-VG
☐	1	Tony Armas	.10	.05	.01
☐	2	Harold Baines	.15	.07	.01
☐	3	Don Baylor	.10	.05	.01
☐	4	George Brett	.75	.35	.07
☐	5	Gary Carter	.50	.25	.05
☐	6	Ron Cey	.05	.02	.00
☐	7	Jose Cruz	.05	.02	.00
☐	8	Alvin Davis	.15	.07	.01
☐	9	Chili Davis	.05	.02	.00
☐	10	Dwight Evans	.15	.07	.01
☐	11	Steve Garvey	.40	.20	.04
☐	12	Kirk Gibson	.25	.12	.02
☐	13	Pedro Guerrero	.25	.12	.02
☐	14	Tony Gwynn	.45	.22	.04
☐	15	Keith Hernandez	.25	.12	.02
☐	16	Kent Hrbek	.20	.10	.02
☐	17	Reggie Jackson	.70	.35	.07
☐	18	Gary Matthews	.05	.02	.00
☐	19	Don Mattingly	1.50	.75	.15
☐	20	Dale Murphy	.75	.35	.07
☐	21	Eddie Murray	.60	.30	.06
☐	22	Dave Parker	.25	.12	.02
☐	23	Lance Parrish	.20	.10	.02
☐	24	Tim Raines	.35	.17	.03
☐	25	Jim Rice	.30	.15	.03
☐	26	Cal Ripken	.45	.22	.04
☐	27	Juan Samuel	.20	.10	.02
☐	28	Ryne Sandberg	.30	.15	.03
☐	29	Mike Schmidt	.60	.30	.06
☐	30	Darryl Strawberry	.70	.35	.07
☐	31	Alan Trammell	.25	.12	.02
☐	32	Dave Winfield	.30	.15	.03
☐	33	Robin Yount	.30	.15	.03
☐	34	Mike Boddicker	.05	.02	.00
☐	35	Steve Carlton	.30	.15	.03
☐	36	Dwight Gooden	.90	.45	.09
☐	37	Willie Hernandez	.10	.05	.01
☐	38	Mark Langston	.15	.07	.01
☐	39	Dan Quisenberry	.10	.05	.01
☐	40	Dave Righetti	.20	.10	.02
☐	41	Tom Seaver	.35	.17	.03
☐	42	Bob Stanley	.05	.02	.00
☐	43	Rick Sutcliffe	.15	.07	.01
☐	44	Bruce Sutter	.10	.05	.01

1985 Drake's

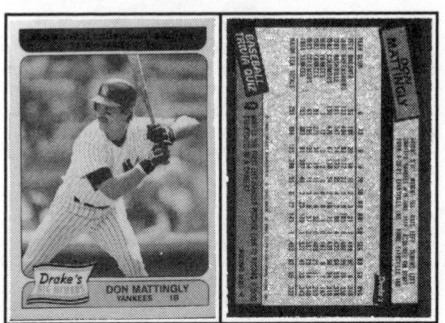

The cards in this 44 card set measure 2 1/2" by 3 1/2". The Fifth Annual Collectors Edition of baseball cards produced by Drake's Cakes in conjunction with Topps continued this apparently annual set with a new twist, for the first time, 11 pitchers were included. The "Big Hitters" are numbered 1-33 and the pitchers are numbered 34-44; each subgroup is ordered alphabetically. The cards are numbered in the upper right corner of the backs of the cards. The complete set could be obtained directly from the company by sending 2.95 with four proofs of purchase.

	MINT	EXC	G-VG
COMPLETE SET	9.00	4.50	.90
COMMON PLAYER	.05	.02	.00

1986 Drake's

This set of 37 cards was distributed as back panels of various Drake's snack products. Each individual card measures 2 1/2" by 3 1/2". Each specially marked package features two, three, or four cards on the back. The set is easily recognized by the Drake's logo and "6th Annual Collector's Edition" at the top of the obverse. Cards are numbered on the front and the back. Cards below are coded based on the product upon which they appeared, for example, Apple Pies (AP), Cherry Pies (CP), Chocolate Donut Delites (CDD), Coffee Cake Jr. (CCJ), Creme Shortcakes (CS), Devil Dogs (DD), Fudge Brownies (FUD), Funny Bones (FB), Peanut Butter Squares (PBS), Powdered Sugar Donut Delites (PSDD), Ring Ding Jr. (RDJ), Sunny Doodles (SD), Swiss Rolls (SR), Yankee Doodles (YD), and Yodels (Y). The last nine cards are pitchers.

		MINT	EXC	G-VG
COMPLETE SET		27.00	13.50	2.70
COMMON PLAYER (1-37)		.30	.15	.03
☐ 1	Gary Carter Y	.80	.40	.08
☐ 2	Dwight Evans Y	.40	.20	.04
☐ 3	Reggie Jackson SR	1.00	.50	.10
☐ 4	Dave Parker SR	.40	.20	.04
☐ 5	Rickey Henderson FB	1.00	.50	.10
☐ 6	Pedro Guerrero FB	.50	.25	.05
☐ 7	Don Mattingly YD	3.00	1.50	.30
☐ 8	Mike Marshall YD	.40	.20	.04
☐ 9	Keith Moreland YD	.30	.15	.03
☐ 10	Keith Hernandez CS	.60	.30	.06
☐ 11	Cal Ripken CS	.80	.40	.08
☐ 12	Dale Murphy RDJ	1.25	.60	.12
☐ 13	Jim Rice RDJ	.60	.30	.06
☐ 14	George Brett CCJ	.80	.40	.08
☐ 15	Tim Raines CCJ	.60	.30	.06
☐ 16	Darryl Strawberry DD	1.25	.60	.12
☐ 17	Bill Buckner DD	.30	.15	.03
☐ 18	Dave Winfield AP	.50	.25	.05
☐ 19	Ryne Sandberg AP	.50	.25	.05
☐ 20	Steve Balboni AP	.30	.15	.03
☐ 21	Tom Herr AP	.30	.15	.03
☐ 22	Pete Rose CP	1.50	.75	.15
☐ 23	Willie McGee CP	.50	.25	.05
☐ 24	Harold Baines CP	.40	.20	.04
☐ 25	Eddie Murray CP	.80	.40	.08
☐ 26	Mike Schmidt SD/FUD	1.25	.60	.12
☐ 27	Wade Boggs SD/FUD	2.00	1.00	.20
☐ 28	Kirk Gibson SD/FUD	.50	.25	.05
☐ 29	Bret Saberhagen PBS	.50	.25	.05
☐ 30	John Tudor PBS	.40	.20	.04
☐ 31	Orel Hershiser PBS	.40	.20	.04
☐ 32	Ron Guidry CDD	.50	.25	.05
☐ 33	Nolan Ryan CDD	.80	.40	.08
☐ 34	Dave Stieb CDD	.40	.20	.04
☐ 35	Dwight Gooden SDD	1.00	.50	.10
☐ 36	Fernando Valenzuela SDD	.50	.25	.05
☐ 37	Tom Browning SDD	.30	.15	.03

☐ 11	Tony Gwynn	1.00	.50	.10
☐ 12	Rickey Henderson	.75	.35	.07
☐ 13	Dale Murphy	1.00	.50	.10
☐ 14	George Brett	1.00	.50	.10
☐ 15	Jim Rice	.60	.30	.06
☐ 16	Wade Boggs	2.00	1.00	.20
☐ 17	Kevin Bass	.30	.15	.03
☐ 18	Dave Parker	.40	.20	.04
☐ 19	Kirby Puckett	.75	.35	.07
☐ 20	Gary Carter	.60	.30	.06
☐ 21	Ryne Sandberg	.60	.30	.06
☐ 22	Harold Baines	.40	.20	.04
☐ 23	Mike Schmidt	1.00	.50	.10
☐ 24	Eddie Murray	.75	.35	.07
☐ 25	Steve Sax	.40	.20	.04
☐ 26	Dwight Gooden	.75	.35	.07
☐ 27	Jack Morris	.40	.20	.04
☐ 28	Ron Darling	.40	.20	.04
☐ 29	Fernando Valenzuela	.50	.25	.05
☐ 30	John Tudor	.40	.20	.04
☐ 31	Roger Clemens	.75	.35	.07
☐ 32	Nolan Ryan	.75	.35	.07
☐ 33	Mike Scott	.50	.25	.05

1966 East Hills Pirates

BOB VEALE   (Pitcher)   #39

The 1966 East Hills Pirates set consists of 25 large (3 1/4" by 4 1/4"), full color photos of Pittsburgh Pirate ballplayers. These blank-backed cards are numbered in the lower right corner according to the uniform number of the individual depicted. The set was distributed by various stores located in the East Hills Shopping Center. The ACC catalog number is F405.

		NRMT	VG-E	GOOD
COMPLETE SET		22.00	11.00	2.20
COMMON PLAYER (1-45)		.35	.17	.03
☐ 3	Harry Walker MG	.50	.25	.05
☐ 7	Bob Bailey	.35	.17	.03
☐ 8	Willie Stargell	5.00	2.50	.50
☐ 9	Bill Mazeroski	1.50	.75	.15
☐ 10	Jim Pagliaroni	.35	.17	.03
☐ 11	Jose Pagan	.35	.17	.03
☐ 12	Jerry May	.35	.17	.03
☐ 14	Gene Alley	.50	.25	.05
☐ 15	Manny Mota	.65	.30	.06
☐ 16	Andy Rodgers	.35	.17	.03
☐ 17	Donn Clendenon	.50	.25	.05
☐ 18	Matty Alou	.65	.30	.06
☐ 19	Pete Mikkelsen	.35	.17	.03
☐ 20	Jesse Gonder	.35	.17	.03
☐ 21	Bob Clemente	9.00	4.50	.90
☐ 22	Woody Fryman	.35	.17	.03
☐ 24	Jerry Lynch	.35	.17	.03
☐ 25	Tommie Sisk	.35	.17	.03
☐ 26	Roy Face	1.00	.50	.10
☐ 28	Steve Blass	.50	.25	.05
☐ 32	Vernon Law	1.00	.50	.10
☐ 34	Al McBean	.35	.17	.03
☐ 39	Bob Veale	.50	.25	.05
☐ 43	Don Cardwell	.35	.17	.03
☐ 45	Gene Michael	.50	.25	.05

1987 Drake's

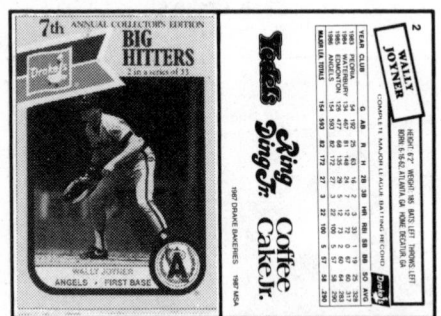

This 33-card set features 25 top hitters and eight top pitchers. Cards were printed in groups of two, three, or four on the backs of Drake's bakery products. Individual cards measure 2 1/2" by 3 1/2" and tout the 7th annual edition. Card backs feature year-by-year season statistics. The cards are numbered such that the pitchers are listed numerically last.

		MINT	EXC	G-VG
COMPLETE SET		24.00	12.00	2.40
COMMON PLAYER		.30	.15	.03
☐ 1	Darryl Strawberry	1.00	.50	.10
☐ 2	Wally Joyner	1.00	.50	.10
☐ 3	Von Hayes	.30	.15	.03
☐ 4	Jose Canseco	1.00	.50	.10
☐ 5	Dave Winfield	.60	.30	.06
☐ 6	Cal Ripken	.75	.35	.07
☐ 7	Keith Moreland	.30	.15	.03
☐ 8	Don Mattingly	3.00	1.50	.30
☐ 9	Willie McGee	.40	.20	.04
☐ 10	Keith Hernandez	.60	.30	.06

1954 Esskay

ROBERT L. TURLEY, Pitcher
Born Sept. 19, 1930
Hometown, Troy, Illinois
Throws Right — Bats Right

The cards in this 36 card set measure 2 1/4" by 3 1/2". The 1954 Esskay Meats set contains color, unnumbered cards featuring Baltimore Orioles only. The cards were issued in panels of two on boxes of Esskay hot dogs; consequently, many have grease stains on the cards and are quite difficult to obtain in mint condition. The 1954 Esskay set can be distinguished from the 1955 Esskay set supposedly by the white or off-white (the 1955 set) backs of the cards. The backs of the 1954 cards are also supposedly "waxed" to a greater degree than the 1955 cards. The ACC designation is F181-1. Since the cards are unnumbered, they are ordered below in alphabetical order for convenience.

		NRMT	VG-E	GOOD
COMPLETE SET		3000.00	1300.00	250.00
COMMON PLAYER (1-36)		80.00	40.00	8.00
☐ 1	Cal Abrams	80.00	40.00	8.00
☐ 2	Neil Berry	80.00	40.00	8.00
☐ 3	Michael Blyzka	80.00	40.00	8.00
☐ 4	Harry Brecheen	100.00	50.00	10.00
☐ 5	Gil Coan	80.00	40.00	8.00
☐ 6	Joe Coleman	80.00	40.00	8.00
☐ 7	Clint Courtney	100.00	50.00	10.00
☐ 8	Charles E. Diering	80.00	40.00	8.00
☐ 9	Jimmie Dykes	100.00	50.00	10.00
☐ 10	Frank Fanovich	80.00	40.00	8.00
☐ 11	Howard Fox	80.00	40.00	8.00
☐ 12	Jim Fridley	80.00	40.00	8.00
☐ 13	Chico Garcia	80.00	40.00	8.00
☐ 14	Jehosie Heard	80.00	40.00	8.00
☐ 15	Darrell Johnson	100.00	50.00	10.00
☐ 16	Robert D. Kennedy	100.00	50.00	10.00
☐ 17	Dick Kokos	80.00	40.00	8.00
☐ 18	Dave Koslo	80.00	40.00	8.00
☐ 19	Lou Kretlow	80.00	40.00	8.00
☐ 20	Richard D. Kryhoski	80.00	40.00	8.00
☐ 21	Robert Kuzava	80.00	40.00	8.00
☐ 22	Don Larsen	175.00	85.00	18.00
☐ 23	Don Lenhardt	80.00	40.00	8.00
☐ 24	Dick Littlefield	80.00	40.00	8.00
☐ 25	Sam Mele	80.00	40.00	8.00
☐ 26	John Lester Moss	80.00	40.00	8.00
☐ 27	Ray L. Murray	80.00	40.00	8.00
☐ 28	Bobo Newsom	110.00	55.00	11.00
☐ 29	Tom Oliver	80.00	40.00	8.00
☐ 30	Duane Pillette	80.00	40.00	8.00
☐ 31	Francis M. Skaff	80.00	40.00	8.00
☐ 32	Marlin Stuart	80.00	40.00	8.00
☐ 33	Robert L. Turley	175.00	85.00	18.00
☐ 34	Eddie Waitkus	80.00	40.00	8.00
☐ 35	Vic Wertz	110.00	55.00	11.00
☐ 36	Robert G. Young	80.00	40.00	8.00

1955 Esskay

ROBERT L. KUZAVA, Pitcher
Born May 28, 1923
Hometown, Wyandotte, Mich.
Throws Left — Bats Right

Collect and Save ESSKAY Trading Cards.
Dealer or write to address in coupon

The cards in this 27 card set measure 2 1/4" by 3 1/2". The 1955 Esskay Meats set was issued in panels of two on boxes of Esskay hot dogs. This set of full color, blank back, unnumbered cards features Baltimore Orioles only. Many of the players in the 1954 Esskay set were also issued in this set. The ACC designation is F181-2. Since the cards are unnumbered, they are ordered below in alphabetical order for convenience. The 1955 set is supposedly somewhat more difficult to find than the 1954 set.

		NRMT	VG-E	GOOD
COMPLETE SET		2700.00	1250.00	250.00
COMMON PLAYER (1-27)		100.00	50.00	10.00
☐ 1	Cal Abrams	100.00	50.00	10.00
☐ 2	Robert Alexander	100.00	50.00	10.00
☐ 3	Harry Brecheen	120.00	60.00	12.00
☐ 4	Harry Byrd	100.00	50.00	10.00
☐ 5	Gil Coan	100.00	50.00	10.00
☐ 6	Joe Coleman	100.00	50.00	10.00
☐ 7	William Cox	120.00	60.00	12.00
☐ 8	Charles E. Diering	100.00	50.00	10.00
☐ 9	Walter Evers	120.00	60.00	12.00
☐ 10	Don Johnson	100.00	50.00	10.00
☐ 11	Robert D. Kennedy	120.00	60.00	12.00
☐ 12	Lou Kretlow	100.00	50.00	10.00
☐ 13	Robert Kuzava	100.00	50.00	10.00
☐ 14	Fred Marsh	100.00	50.00	10.00
☐ 15	Charles Maxwell	120.00	60.00	12.00
☐ 16	Jim McDonald	100.00	50.00	10.00
☐ 17	Bill Miller	100.00	50.00	10.00
☐ 18	Willie Miranda	120.00	60.00	12.00
☐ 19	Raymond L. Moore	100.00	50.00	10.00
☐ 20	John Lester Moss	100.00	50.00	10.00
☐ 21	Bobo Newsom	120.00	60.00	12.00
☐ 22	Duane Pillette	100.00	50.00	10.00
☐ 23	Harold W. Smith	120.00	60.00	12.00
☐ 24	Gus Triandos	120.00	60.00	12.00
☐ 25	Eddie Waitkus	100.00	50.00	10.00
☐ 26	Gene Woodling	150.00	75.00	15.00
☐ 27	Robert G. Young	100.00	50.00	10.00

1959 Fleer

The cards in this 80-card set measure 2 1/2" by 3 1/2". The 1959 Fleer set, designated as R418-1 in the ACC, portrays the life of Ted Williams. The wording of the wrapper, "Baseball's Greatest Series," has led to speculation that Fleer contemplated similar sets honoring other baseball immortals, but chose to develop instead the format of the 1960 and 1961 issues. Card number 68, which was withdrawn early in production, is considered scarce and has even been counterfeited; the fake has

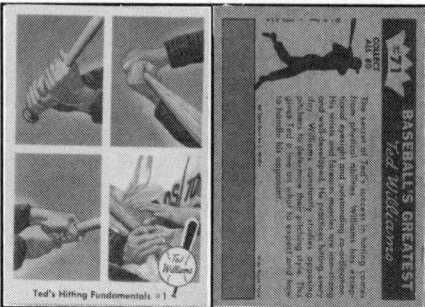

Ted's Hitting Fundamentals #1

a rosy coloration and a cross-hatch pattern visible over the picture area.

		NRMT	VG-E	GOOD
	COMPLETE SET	250.00	125.00	25.00
	COMMON CARDS	1.25	.60	.12
☐ 1	The Early Years	6.00	1.00	.20
☐ 2	Ted's Idol Babe Ruth	4.00	2.00	.40
☐ 3	Practice Makes Perfect	1.25	.60	.12
☐ 4	Learns Fine Points	1.25	.60	.12
☐ 5	Ted's Fame Spreads	1.25	.60	.12
☐ 6	Ted Turns Pro	1.25	.60	.12
☐ 7	From Mound to Plate	1.25	.60	.12
☐ 8	1937 First Full Season	1.25	.60	.12
☐ 9	First Step to Majors	1.25	.60	.12
☐ 10	Gunning as Pasttime	1.25	.60	.12
☐ 11	First Spring Training (with Jimmie Foxx)	2.00	1.00	.20
☐ 12	Burning Up Minors	1.25	.60	.12
☐ 13	1939 Shows Will Stay	1.25	.60	.12
☐ 14	Outstanding Rookie '39	1.25	.60	.12
☐ 15	Licks Sophomore Jinx	1.25	.60	.12
☐ 16	1941 Greatest Year	1.25	.60	.12
☐ 17	How Ted Hit .400	1.25	.60	.12
☐ 18	1941 All Star Hero	1.25	.60	.12
☐ 19	Ted Wins Triple Crown	1.25	.60	.12
☐ 20	On to Naval Training	1.25	.60	.12
☐ 21	Honors for Williams	1.25	.60	.12
☐ 22	1944 Ted Solos	1.25	.60	.12
☐ 23	Williams Wins Wings	1.25	.60	.12
☐ 24	1945 Sharpshooter	1.25	.60	.12
☐ 25	1945 Ted Discharged	1.25	.60	.12
☐ 26	Off to Flying Start	1.25	.60	.12
☐ 27	7/9/46 One Man Show	1.25	.60	.12
☐ 28	The Williams Shift	1.25	.60	.12
☐ 29	Ted Hits for Cycle	1.25	.60	.12
☐ 30	Beating Williams Shift	1.25	.60	.12
☐ 31	Sox Lose Series	1.25	.60	.12
☐ 32	Most Valuable Player	1.25	.60	.12
☐ 33	Another Triple Crown	1.25	.60	.12
☐ 34	Runs Scored Record	1.25	.60	.12
☐ 35	Sox Miss Pennant	1.25	.60	.12
☐ 36	Banner Year for Ted	1.25	.60	.12
☐ 37	1949 Sox Miss Again	1.25	.60	.12
☐ 38	1949 Power Rampage	1.25	.60	.12
☐ 39	1950 Great Start	1.25	.60	.12
☐ 40	Ted Crashes into Wall	1.25	.60	.12
☐ 41	1950 Ted Recovers	1.25	.60	.12
☐ 42	Slowed by Injury	1.25	.60	.12
☐ 43	Double Play Lead	1.25	.60	.12
☐ 44	Back to Marines	1.25	.60	.12
☐ 45	Farewell to Baseball	1.25	.60	.12
☐ 46	Ready for Combat	1.25	.60	.12
☐ 47	Ted Crash Lands Jet	1.25	.60	.12
☐ 48	1953 Ted Returns	1.25	.60	.12
☐ 49	Smash Return	1.25	.60	.12
☐ 50	1954 Spring Injury	1.25	.60	.12
☐ 51	Ted is Patched Up	1.25	.60	.12
☐ 52	1954 Ted's Comeback	1.25	.60	.12
☐ 53	Comeback is Success	1.25	.60	.12
☐ 54	Ted Hooks Big One	1.25	.60	.12
☐ 55	Retirement "No Go"	1.25	.60	.12
☐ 56	2000th Hit	1.25	.60	.12
☐ 57	400th Homer	1.25	.60	.12
☐ 58	Williams Hits .388	1.25	.60	.12
☐ 59	Hot September for Ted	1.25	.60	.12
☐ 60	More Records for Ted	1.25	.60	.12
☐ 61	1957 Outfielder Ted	1.25	.60	.12
☐ 62	1958 6th Batting Title	1.25	.60	.12
☐ 63	Ted's All-Star Record	1.25	.60	.12
☐ 64	Daughter and Daddy	1.25	.60	.12
☐ 65	1958 August 30	1.25	.60	.12
☐ 66	1958 Powerhouse	1.25	.60	.12

☐ 67	Two Famous Fishermen	2.00	1.00	.20
☐ 68	Ted Signs for 1959	150.00	75.00	15.00
☐ 69	A Future Ted Williams	1.25	.60	.12
☐ 70	Williams and Thorpe	2.00	1.00	.20
☐ 71	Hitting Fund. 1	1.25	.60	.12
☐ 72	Hitting Fund. 2	1.25	.60	.12
☐ 73	Hitting Fund. 3	1.25	.60	.12
☐ 74	Here's How	1.25	.60	.12
☐ 75	Williams' Value to Sox	1.25	.60	.12
☐ 76	On Base Record	1.25	.60	.12
☐ 77	Ted Relaxes	1.25	.60	.12
☐ 78	Honors for Williams	1.25	.60	.12
☐ 79	Where Ted Stands	1.25	.60	.12
☐ 80	Ted's Goals for 1959	2.50	.60	.10

1960 Fleer

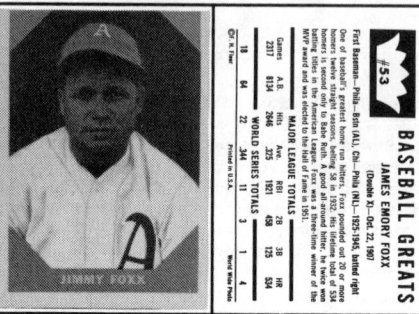

The cards in this 79-card set measure 2 1/2" by 3 1/2". The cards from the 1960 Fleer series of Baseball Greats are sometimes mistaken for 1930s cards by collectors not familiar with this set. The cards each contain a tinted photo of a baseball immortal, and were issued in one series. There are no known scarcities, although a number 80 card (Pepper Martin reverse with either a Tinker, Collins, or Grove obverse) exists (this is not considered part of the set). The catalog designation for 1960 Fleer is R418-2.

		NRMT	VG-E	GOOD
	COMPLETE SET (79)	150.00	75.00	15.00
	COMMON PLAYER (1-79)	1.00	.50	.10
☐ 1	Napoleon Lajoie	6.00	1.00	.20
☐ 2	Christy Mathewson	3.00	1.50	.30
☐ 3	George H. Ruth	18.00	9.00	1.80
☐ 4	Carl Hubbell	1.50	.75	.15
☐ 5	Grover Alexander	2.00	1.00	.20
☐ 6	Walter P. Johnson	3.50	1.75	.35
☐ 7	Charles A. Bender	1.00	.50	.10
☐ 8	Roger P. Bresnahan	1.00	.50	.10
☐ 9	Mordecai P. Brown	1.00	.50	.10
☐ 10	Tristram Speaker	1.50	.75	.15
☐ 11	Joseph (Arky) Vaughan	1.00	.50	.10
☐ 12	Zachariah Wheat	1.00	.50	.10
☐ 13	George Sisler	1.00	.50	.10
☐ 14	Connie Mack	1.50	.75	.15
☐ 15	Clark C. Griffith	1.00	.50	.10
☐ 16	Louis Boudreau	1.50	.75	.15
☐ 17	Ernest Lombardi	1.00	.50	.10
☐ 18	Henry Manush	1.00	.50	.10
☐ 19	Martin Marion	1.00	.50	.10
☐ 20	Edward Collins	1.00	.50	.10
☐ 21	James Maranville	1.00	.50	.10
☐ 22	Joseph Medwick	1.00	.50	.10
☐ 23	Edward Barrow	1.00	.50	.10
☐ 24	Gordon Cochrane	1.50	.75	.15
☐ 25	James J. Collins	1.00	.50	.10
☐ 26	Robert Feller	4.00	2.00	.40
☐ 27	Lucius Appling	1.50	.75	.15
☐ 28	Lou Gehrig	9.00	4.50	.90
☐ 29	Charles Hartnett	1.00	.50	.10
☐ 30	Charles Klein	1.00	.50	.10
☐ 31	Anthony Lazzeri	1.00	.50	.10
☐ 32	Aloysius Simmons	1.00	.50	.10
☐ 33	Wilbert Robinson	1.00	.50	.10
☐ 34	Edgar Rice	1.00	.50	.10

		NRMT	VG-E	GOOD
☐ 35	Herbert Pennock	1.00	.50	.10
☐ 36	Melvin Ott	1.50	.75	.15
☐ 37	Frank O'Doul	1.00	.50	.10
☐ 38	John Mize	2.00	1.00	.20
☐ 39	Edmund Miller	1.00	.50	.10
☐ 40	Joseph Tinker	1.00	.50	.10
☐ 41	John Baker	1.00	.50	.10
☐ 42	Tyrus Cobb	9.00	4.50	.90
☐ 43	Paul Derringer	1.00	.50	.10
☐ 44	Adrian Anson	1.00	.50	.10
☐ 45	James Bottomley	1.00	.50	.10
☐ 46	Edward S. Plank	1.00	.50	.10
☐ 47	Denton (Cy) Young	2.50	1.25	.25
☐ 48	Hack Wilson	1.50	.75	.15
☐ 49	Edward Walsh	1.00	.50	.10
☐ 50	Frank Chance	1.00	.50	.10
☐ 51	Arthur Vance	1.00	.50	.10
☐ 52	William Terry	1.50	.75	.15
☐ 53	James Foxx	2.50	1.25	.25
☐ 54	Vernon Gomez	1.50	.75	.15
☐ 55	Branch Rickey	1.00	.50	.10
☐ 56	Raymond Schalk	1.00	.50	.10
☐ 57	John Evers	1.00	.50	.10
☐ 58	Charles Gehringer	1.50	.75	.15
☐ 59	Burleigh Grimes	1.00	.50	.10
☐ 60	Robert (Lefty) Grove	2.00	1.00	.20
☐ 61	George Waddell	1.00	.50	.10
☐ 62	John (Honus) Wagner	3.50	1.75	.35
☐ 63	Charles (Red) Ruffing	1.00	.50	.10
☐ 64	Kenesaw M. Landis	1.00	.50	.10
☐ 65	Harry Heilmann	1.00	.50	.10
☐ 66	John McGraw	1.50	.75	.15
☐ 67	Hugh Jennings	1.00	.50	.10
☐ 68	Harold Newhouser	1.00	.50	.10
☐ 69	Waite Hoyt	1.00	.50	.10
☐ 70	Louis (Bobo) Newsom	1.00	.50	.10
☐ 71	Howard (Earl) Averill	1.00	.50	.10
☐ 72	Theodore Williams	10.00	5.00	1.00
☐ 73	Warren Giles	1.00	.50	.10
☐ 74	Ford Frick	1.00	.50	.10
☐ 75	Hazen (Kiki) Cuyler	1.00	.50	.10
☐ 76	Paul Waner	1.00	.50	.10
☐ 77	Harold Pie) Traynor	1.00	.50	.10
☐ 78	Lloyd Waner	1.00	.50	.10
☐ 79	Ralph Kiner	2.00	1.00	.20
☐ 80	Pepper Martin *	100.00	50.00	10.00
	(Collins, Tinker, or Grove pictured)			

1961 Fleer

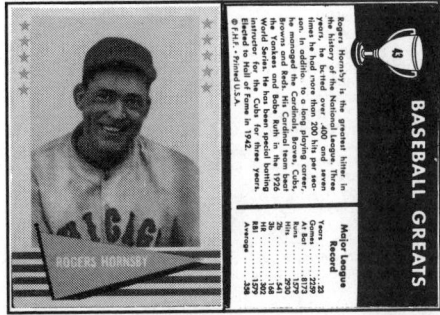

The cards in this 154-card set measure 2 1/2" by 3 1/2". In 1961, Fleer continued its Baseball Greats format by issuing this series of cards. The set was released in two distinct series, 1-88 and 89-154 (of which the last is more difficult to obtain). The players within each series are conveniently numbered in alphabetical order. It appears that this set continued to be issued the following year by Fleer. The catalog number is F418-3.

		NRMT	VG-E	GOOD
	COMPLETE SET	325.00	150.00	30.00
	COMMON PLAYER (1-88)	1.00	.50	.10
	COMMON PLAYER (89-154)	2.25	1.10	.22
☐ 1	Baker/Cobb/Wheat	9.00	1.00	.20
	(checklist back)			

☐ 2	Grover C. Alexander	1.50	.75	.15
☐ 3	Nick Altrock	1.00	.50	.10
☐ 4	Cap Anson	1.00	.50	.10
☐ 5	Earl Averill	1.00	.50	.10
☐ 6	Frank Baker	1.00	.50	.10
☐ 7	Dave Bancroft	1.00	.50	.10
☐ 8	Chief Bender	1.00	.50	.10
☐ 9	Jim Bottomley	1.00	.50	.10
☐ 10	Roger Bresnahan	1.00	.50	.10
☐ 11	Mordecai Brown	1.00	.50	.10
☐ 12	Max Carey	1.00	.50	.10
☐ 13	Jack Chesbro	1.00	.50	.10
☐ 14	Ty Cobb	9.00	4.50	.90
☐ 15	Mickey Cochrane	1.00	.50	.10
☐ 16	Eddie Collins	1.00	.50	.10
☐ 17	Earle Combs	1.00	.50	.10
☐ 18	Charles Comiskey	1.00	.50	.10
☐ 19	Kiki Cuyler	1.00	.50	.10
☐ 20	Paul Derringer	1.00	.50	.10
☐ 21	Howard Ehmke	1.00	.50	.10
☐ 22	W. Evans	1.00	.50	.10
☐ 23	Johnny Evers	1.00	.50	.10
☐ 24	Urban Faber	1.00	.50	.10
☐ 25	Bob Feller	4.00	2.00	.40
☐ 26	Wes Ferrell	1.00	.50	.10
☐ 27	Lew Fonseca	1.00	.50	.10
☐ 28	Jimmy Foxx	2.00	1.00	.20
☐ 29	Ford Frick	1.00	.50	.10
☐ 30	Frank Frisch	1.50	.75	.15
☐ 31	Lou Gehrig	9.00	4.50	.90
☐ 32	Charlie Gehringer	1.50	.75	.15
☐ 33	Warren Giles	1.00	.50	.10
☐ 34	Lefty Gomez	1.50	.75	.15
☐ 35	Goose Goslin	1.00	.50	.10
☐ 36	Clark Griffith	1.00	.50	.10
☐ 37	Burleigh Grimes	1.00	.50	.10
☐ 38	Lefty Grove	2.00	1.00	.20
☐ 39	Chick Hafey	1.00	.50	.10
☐ 40	Jesse Haines	1.00	.50	.10
☐ 41	Gabby Hartnett	1.00	.50	.10
☐ 42	Harry Heilmann	1.00	.50	.10
☐ 43	Rogers Hornsby	2.50	1.25	.25
☐ 44	Waite Hoyt	1.00	.50	.10
☐ 45	Carl Hubbell	1.50	.75	.15
☐ 46	Miller Huggins	1.00	.50	.10
☐ 47	Hugh Jennings	1.00	.50	.10
☐ 48	Ban Johnson	1.00	.50	.10
☐ 49	Walter Johnson	3.50	1.75	.35
☐ 50	Ralph Kiner	2.00	1.00	.20
☐ 51	Chuck Klein	1.00	.50	.10
☐ 52	Johnny Kling	1.00	.50	.10
☐ 53	K.M. Landis	1.00	.50	.10
☐ 54	Tony Lazzeri	1.00	.50	.10
☐ 55	Ernie Lombardi	1.00	.50	.10
☐ 56	Dolf Luque	1.00	.50	.10
☐ 57	Heine Manush	1.00	.50	.10
☐ 58	Marty Marion	1.00	.50	.10
☐ 59	Christy Mathewson	3.00	1.50	.30
☐ 60	John McGraw	1.50	.75	.15
☐ 61	Joe Medwick	1.00	.50	.10
☐ 62	E. (Bing) Miller	1.00	.50	.10
☐ 63	Johnny Mize	2.00	1.00	.20
☐ 64	John Mostil	1.00	.50	.10
☐ 65	Art Nehf	1.00	.50	.10
☐ 66	Hal Newhouser	1.00	.50	.10
☐ 67	D. (Bobo) Newsom	1.00	.50	.10
☐ 68	Mel Ott	1.50	.75	.15
☐ 69	Allie Reynolds	1.00	.50	.10
☐ 70	Sam Rice	1.00	.50	.10
☐ 71	Eppa Rixey	1.00	.50	.10
☐ 72	Edd Roush	1.00	.50	.10
☐ 73	Schoolboy Rowe	1.00	.50	.10
☐ 74	Red Ruffing	1.00	.50	.10
☐ 75	Babe Ruth	18.00	9.00	1.80
☐ 76	Joe Sewell	1.00	.50	.10
☐ 77	Al Simmons	1.00	.50	.10
☐ 78	George Sisler	1.00	.50	.10
☐ 79	Tris Speaker	1.50	.75	.15
☐ 80	Fred Toney	1.00	.50	.10
☐ 81	Dazzy Vance	1.00	.50	.10
☐ 82	Jim Vaughn	1.00	.50	.10
☐ 83	Ed Walsh	1.00	.50	.10
☐ 84	Lloyd Waner	1.00	.50	.10
☐ 85	Paul Waner	1.00	.50	.10
☐ 86	Zack Wheat	1.00	.50	.10
☐ 87	Hack Wilson	1.50	.75	.15
☐ 88	Jimmy Wilson	1.00	.50	.10
☐ 89	Sisler and Traynor	9.00	1.50	.30
	(checklist back)			
☐ 90	Babe Adams	2.25	1.10	.22
☐ 91	Dale Alexander	2.25	1.10	.22
☐ 92	Jim Bagby	2.25	1.10	.22
☐ 93	Ossie Bluege	2.25	1.10	.22
☐ 94	Lou Boudreau	4.00	2.00	.40
☐ 95	Tom Bridges	2.25	1.10	.22

			NRMT	VG-E	GOOD
☐ 96	Donie Bush	2.25	1.10	.22
☐ 97	Dolph Camilli	2.25	1.10	.22
☐ 98	Frank Chance	3.00	1.50	.30
☐ 99	Jimmy Collins	3.00	1.50	.30
☐ 100	Stan Coveleskie	3.00	1.50	.30
☐ 101	Hugh Critz	2.25	1.10	.22
☐ 102	Alvin Crowder	2.25	1.10	.22
☐ 103	Joe Dugan	2.25	1.10	.22
☐ 104	Bibb Falk	2.25	1.10	.22
☐ 105	Rick Ferrell	3.00	1.50	.30
☐ 106	Art Fletcher	2.25	1.10	.22
☐ 107	Dennis Galehouse	2.25	1.10	.22
☐ 108	Chick Galloway	2.25	1.10	.22
☐ 109	Mule Haas	2.25	1.10	.22
☐ 110	Stan Hack	2.25	1.10	.22
☐ 111	Bump Hadley	2.25	1.10	.22
☐ 112	Billy B. Hamilton	3.00	1.50	.30
☐ 113	Joe Hauser	2.25	1.10	.22
☐ 114	Babe Herman	2.25	1.10	.22
☐ 115	Travis Jackson	3.50	1.75	.35
☐ 116	Eddie Joost	2.25	1.10	.22
☐ 117	Addie Joss	3.50	1.75	.35
☐ 118	Joe Judge	2.25	1.10	.22
☐ 119	Joe Kuhel	2.25	1.10	.22
☐ 120	Napoleon Lajoie	6.00	3.00	.60
☐ 121	Dutch Leonard	2.25	1.10	.22
☐ 122	Ted Lyons	3.00	1.50	.30
☐ 123	Connie Mack	6.00	3.00	.60
☐ 124	Rabbit Maranville	3.00	1.50	.30
☐ 125	Fred Marberry	2.25	1.10	.22
☐ 126	Joe McGinnity	4.00	2.00	.40
☐ 127	Oscar Melillo	2.25	1.10	.22
☐ 128	Ray Mueller	2.25	1.10	.22
☐ 129	Kid Nichols	3.50	1.75	.35
☐ 130	Lefty O'Doul	2.25	1.10	.22
☐ 131	Bob O'Farrell	2.25	1.10	.22
☐ 132	Roger Peckinpaugh	2.25	1.10	.22
☐ 133	Herb Pennock	3.00	1.50	.30
☐ 134	George Pipgras	2.25	1.10	.22
☐ 135	Eddie Plank	3.50	1.75	.35
☐ 136	Ray Schalk	3.00	1.50	.30
☐ 137	Hal Schumacher	2.25	1.10	.22
☐ 138	Luke Sewell	2.25	1.10	.22
☐ 139	Bob Shawkey	2.25	1.10	.22
☐ 140	Riggs Stephenson	2.25	1.10	.22
☐ 141	Billy Sullivan	2.25	1.10	.22
☐ 142	Bill Terry	5.00	2.50	.50
☐ 143	Joe Tinker	3.00	1.50	.30
☐ 144	Pie Traynor	4.00	2.00	.40
☐ 145	Hal Trosky	2.25	1.10	.22
☐ 146	George Uhle	2.25	1.10	.22
☐ 147	Johnny VanderMeer	3.00	1.50	.30
☐ 148	Arky Vaughan	3.00	1.50	.30
☐ 149	Rube Waddell	3.00	1.50	.30
☐ 150	Honus Wagner	9.00	4.50	.90
☐ 151	Dixie Walker	2.25	1.10	.22
☐ 152	Ted Williams	16.00	8.00	1.60
☐ 153	Cy Young	7.50	3.75	.75
☐ 154	Ross Young	5.00	1.50	.30

1963 Fleer

BROOKS ROBINSON
Baltimore Orioles—3rd Base

The cards in this 66-card set measure 2 1/2" by 3 1/2". The Fleer set of current baseball players was marketed in 1963 in a gum card-style waxed wrapper package which contained a cherry cookie instead of gum. The cards were printed in sheets of 66 with the scarce card of Adcock apparently being replaced by the unnumbered checklist card for the final press

run. The complete set price includes the checklist card. The catalog designation is R418-4.

		NRMT	VG-E	GOOD
COMPLETE SET		350.00	150.00	30.00
COMMON PLAYER (1-66)		1.25	.60	.12
☐ 1	Steve Barber	2.50	.60	.10
☐ 2	Ron Hansen	1.25	.60	.12
☐ 3	Milt Pappas	1.50	.75	.15
☐ 4	Brooks Robinson	12.00	6.00	1.20
☐ 5	Willie Mays	27.00	13.50	2.70
☐ 6	Lou Clinton	1.25	.60	.12
☐ 7	Bill Monbouquette	1.25	.60	.12
☐ 8	Carl Yastrzemski	27.00	13.50	2.70
☐ 9	Ray Herbert	1.25	.60	.12
☐ 10	Jim Landis	1.25	.60	.12
☐ 11	Dick Donovan	1.25	.60	.12
☐ 12	Tito Francona	1.25	.60	.12
☐ 13	Jerry Kindall	1.25	.60	.12
☐ 14	Frank Lary	1.25	.60	.12
☐ 15	Dick Howser	2.50	1.25	.25
☐ 16	Jerry Lumpe	1.25	.60	.12
☐ 17	Norm Siebern	1.25	.60	.12
☐ 18	Don Lee	1.25	.60	.12
☐ 19	Albie Pearson	1.25	.60	.12
☐ 20	Bob Rodgers	1.50	.75	.15
☐ 21	Leon Wagner	1.25	.60	.12
☐ 22	Jim Kaat	3.00	1.50	.30
☐ 23	Vic Power	1.25	.60	.12
☐ 24	Rich Rollins	1.25	.60	.12
☐ 25	Bobby Richardson	3.00	1.50	.30
☐ 26	Ralph Terry	2.00	1.00	.20
☐ 27	Tom Cheney	1.25	.60	.12
☐ 28	Chuck Cottier	1.25	.60	.12
☐ 29	Jim Piersall	2.00	1.00	.20
☐ 30	Dave Stenhouse	1.25	.60	.12
☐ 31	Glen Hobbie	1.25	.60	.12
☐ 32	Ron Santo	2.00	1.00	.20
☐ 33	Gene Freese	1.25	.60	.12
☐ 34	Vada Pinson	2.00	1.00	.20
☐ 35	Bob Purkey	1.25	.60	.12
☐ 36	Joe Amalfitano	1.25	.60	.12
☐ 37	Bob Aspromonte	1.25	.60	.12
☐ 38	Dick Farrell	1.25	.60	.12
☐ 39	Al Spangler	1.25	.60	.12
☐ 40	Tommy Davis	1.75	.85	.17
☐ 41	Don Drysdale	7.50	3.75	.75
☐ 42	Sandy Koufax	20.00	10.00	2.00
☐ 43	Maury Wills	15.00	7.50	1.50
☐ 44	Frank Bolling	1.25	.60	.12
☐ 45	Warren Spahn	8.50	4.25	.85
☐ 46	Joe Adcock SP	60.00	30.00	6.00
☐ 47	Roger Craig	2.00	1.00	.20
☐ 48	Al Jackson	1.50	.75	.15
☐ 49	Rod Kanehl	1.25	.60	.12
☐ 50	Ruben Amaro	1.25	.60	.12
☐ 51	John Callison	1.50	.75	.15
☐ 52	Clay Dalrymple	1.25	.60	.12
☐ 53	Don Demeter	1.25	.60	.12
☐ 54	Art Mahaffey	1.25	.60	.12
☐ 55	Smokey Burgess	1.50	.75	.15
☐ 56	Roberto Clemente	24.00	12.00	2.40
☐ 57	Roy Face	1.75	.85	.17
☐ 58	Vernon Law	1.50	.75	.15
☐ 59	Bill Mazeroski	2.00	1.00	.20
☐ 60	Ken Boyer	2.00	1.00	.20
☐ 61	Bob Gibson	8.00	4.00	.80
☐ 62	Gene Oliver	1.25	.60	.12
☐ 63	Bill White	1.75	.85	.17
☐ 64	Orlando Cepeda	3.00	1.50	.30
☐ 65	Jim Davenport	1.50	.75	.15
☐ 66	Bill O'Dell	1.50	.75	.15
☐ 67	Checklist card (unnumbered)	100.00	15.00	3.00

1968 Fleer World Series

This set of 64 cards was apparently a limited test issue for the World Series set concept that was mass marketed by Fleer two and three years later. The cards are slightly oversized, 2 3/4" by 3 1/2" and are black and white on the front and red and white on the back. All the years are represented except for 1904 when no World Series was played. In the list below, the winning series team is listed first.

			NRMT	VG-E	GOOD
COMPLETE SET			30.00	12.50	2.50
COMMON PLAYER			.50	.25	.05

□	1	1903 Red Sox/Pirates	.50	.25	.05
□	2	1905 Giants/A's	.60	.30	.06
		(Christy Mathewson)			
□	3	1906 White Sox/Cubs	.50	.25	.05
□	4	1907 Cubs/Tigers	.50	.25	.05
□	5	1908 Cubs/Tigers	.60	.30	.06
		(Tinker/Evers/Chance)			
□	6	1909 Pirates/Tigers	.75	.35	.07
		(Wagner/Cobb)			
□	7	1910 A's/Cubs	.50	.25	.05
□	8	1911 A's/Giants	.50	.25	.05
		(John McGraw)			
□	9	1912 Red Sox/Giants	.50	.25	.05
□	10	1913 A's/Giants	.50	.25	.05
□	11	1914 Braves/A's	.50	.25	.05
□	12	1915 Red Sox/Phillies	.75	.35	.07
		(Babe Ruth)			
□	13	1916 Red Sox/Dodgers ...	.75	.35	.07
		(Babe Ruth)			
□	14	1917 White Sox/Giants ...	.50	.25	.05
□	15	1918 Red Sox/Cubs	.50	.25	.05
□	16	1919 Reds/White Sox	.50	.25	.05
□	17	1920 Indians/Dodgers	.50	.25	.05
□	18	1921 Giants/Yankees	.50	.25	.05
		(Waite Hoyt)			
□	19	1922 Yankees/Giants	.50	.25	.05
		(Frisch/Groh)			
□	20	1923 Yankees/Giants	.75	.35	.07
		(Babe Ruth)			
□	21	1924 Senators/Giants	.50	.25	.05
□	22	1925 Pirates/Senators	.60	.30	.06
		(Walter Johnson)			
□	23	1926 Cardinals/Yankees .	.50	.25	.05
		(Alexander/Lazzeri)			
□	24	1927 Yankees/Pirates	.50	.25	.05
□	25	1928 Yankees/Cardinals .	.75	.35	.07
		(Ruth/Gehrig)			
□	26	1929 A's/Cubs	.50	.25	.05
□	27	1930 A's/Cardinals	.50	.25	.05
□	28	1931 Cardinals/A's	.50	.25	.05
		(Pepper Martin)			
□	29	1932 Yankees/Cubs	.75	.35	.07
		(Babe Ruth)			
□	30	1933 Giants/Senators	.60	.30	.06
		(Mel Ott)			
□	31	1934 Cardinals/Tigers	.60	.30	.06
		(Dizzy/Paul Dean)			
□	32	1935 Tigers/Cubs	.50	.25	.05
□	33	1936 Yankees/Giants	.50	.25	.05
□	34	1937 Yankees/Giants	.50	.25	.05
		(Carl Hubbell)			
□	35	1938 Yankees/Cubs	.50	.25	.05
□	36	1939 Yankees/Reds	.75	.35	.07
		(Joe DiMaggio)			
□	37	1940 Reds/Tigers	.50	.25	.05
□	38	1941 Yankees/Dodgers ...	.50	.25	.05
		(Mickey Owen)			
□	39	1942 Cardinals/Yankees .	.50	.25	.05
□	40	1943 Yankees/Cardinals .	.50	.25	.05
		(Joe McCarthy)			
□	41	1944 Cardinals/Browns ...	.50	.25	.05
□	42	1945 Tigers/Cubs	.50	.25	.05
		(Hank Greenberg)			
□	43	1946 Cardinals/Red Sox .	.50	.25	.05
		(Enos Slaughter)			
□	44	1947 Yankees/Dodgers ...	.50	.25	.05
		(Al Gionfriddo)			
□	45	1948 Indians/Braves	.60	.30	.06

		(Bob Feller)			
□	46	1949 Yankees/Dodgers ...	.50	.25	.05
		(Reynolds/Roe)			
□	47	1950 Yankees/Phillies	.50	.25	.05
□	48	1951 Yankees/Giants	.50	.25	.05
□	49	1952 Yankees/Dodgers ...	.60	.30	.06
		(Mize/Snider)			
□	50	1953 Yankees/Dodgers ...	.60	.30	.06
		(Casey Stengel)			
□	51	1954 Giants/Indians	.50	.25	.05
		(Dusty Rhodes)			
□	52	1955 Dodgers/Yankees ...	.50	.25	.05
		(Johnny Podres)			
□	53	1956 Yankees/Dodgers ...	.60	.30	.06
		(Don Larsen)			
□	54	1957 Braves/Yankees	.50	.25	.05
		(Lew Burdette)			
□	55	1958 Yankees/Braves	.50	.25	.05
		(Hank Bauer)			
□	56	1959 Dodgers/White Sox .	.50	.25	.05
		(Larry Sherry)			
□	57	1960 Pirates/Yankees	.50	.25	.05
□	58	1961 Yankees/Reds	.50	.25	.05
		(Whitey Ford)			
□	59	1962 Yankees/Giants	.50	.25	.05
□	60	1963 Dodgers/Yankees ...	.60	.30	.06
		(Sandy Koufax)			
□	61	1964 Cardinals/Yankees .	.75	.35	.07
		(Mickey Mantle)			
□	62	1965 Dodgers/Twins	.50	.25	.05
□	63	1966 Orioles/Dodgers	.50	.25	.05
□	64	1967 Cardinals/Red Sox .	.60	.30	.06
		(Bob Gibson)			

1970 Fleer World Series

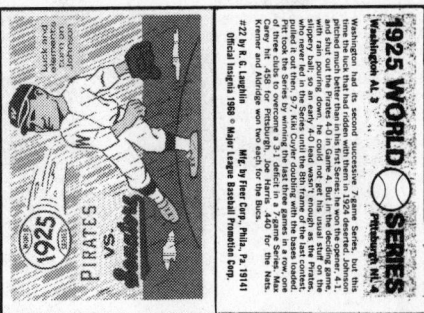

This set of 66 cards was distributed by Fleer. The cards are standard size, 2 1/2" by 3 1/2" and are in crude color on the front with light blue printing on white card stock on the back. All the years are represented except for 1904 when no World Series was played. In the list below, the winning series team is listed first. The year of the Series on the obverse is inside a white baseball.

			NRMT	VG-E	GOOD
COMPLETE SET			15.00	7.50	1.50
COMMON PLAYER			.25	.12	.02

□	1	1903 Red Sox/Pirates	.25	.12	.02
□	2	1905 Giants/A's	.35	.17	.03
		(Christy Mathewson)			
□	3	1906 White Sox/Cubs	.25	.12	.02
□	4	1907 Cubs/Tigers	.25	.12	.02
□	5	1908 Cubs/Tigers	.35	.17	.03
		(Tinker/Evers/Chance)			
□	6	1909 Pirates/Tigers	.35	.17	.03
		(Wagner/Cobb)			
□	7	1910 A's/Cubs	.25	.12	.02
		(Bender/Coombs)			
□	8	1911 A's/Giants	.25	.12	.02
		(John McGraw)			
□	9	1912 Red Sox/Giants	.25	.12	.02
□	10	1913 A's/Giants	.25	.12	.02
□	11	1914 Braves/A's	.25	.12	.02
□	12	1915 Red Sox/Phillies	.60	.30	.06
		(Babe Ruth)			
□	13	1916 Red Sox/Dodgers ...	.60	.30	.06

(Babe Ruth)

☐ 14	1917 White Sox/Giants ...		.25	.12	.02
☐ 15	1918 Red Sox/Cubs		.25	.12	.02
☐ 16	1919 Reds/White Sox		.25	.12	.02
☐ 17	1920 Indians/Dodgers		.25	.12	.02
	(Stan Coveleski)				
☐ 18	1921 Giants/Yankees		.25	.12	.02
	(Commissioner Landis)				
☐ 19	1922 Giants/Yankees		.25	.12	.02
☐ 20	1923 Yankees/Giants		.60	.30	.06
	(Babe Ruth)				
☐ 21	1924 Senators/Giants		.25	.12	.02
	(John McGraw)				
☐ 22	1925 Pirates/Senators		.35	.17	.03
	(Walter Johnson)				
☐ 23	1926 Cardinals/Yankees .		.25	.12	.02
	(Alexander/Lazzeri)				
☐ 24	1927 Yankees/Pirates		.25	.12	.02
☐ 25	1928 Yankees/Cardinals .		.60	.30	.06
	(Ruth/Gehrig)				
☐ 26	1929 A's/Cubs		.25	.12	.02
☐ 27	1930 A's/Cardinals		.25	.12	.02
☐ 28	1931 Cardinals/A's		.25	.12	.02
	(Pepper Martin)				
☐ 29	1932 Yankees/Cubs		.60	.30	.06
	(Ruth/Gehrig)				
☐ 30	1933 Giants/Senators		.35	.17	.03
	(Mel Ott)				
☐ 31	1934 Cardinals/Tigers		.25	.12	.02
☐ 32	1935 Tigers/Cubs		.35	.17	.03
	(Gehringer/Bridges)				
☐ 33	1936 Yankees/Giants		.25	.12	.02
☐ 34	1937 Yankees/Giants		.25	.12	.02
	(Carl Hubbell)				
☐ 35	1938 Yankees/Cubs		.45	.22	.04
	(Lou Gehrig)				
☐ 36	1939 Yankees/Reds		.25	.12	.02
☐ 37	1940 Reds/Tigers		.25	.12	.02
☐ 38	1941 Yankees/Dodgers ...		.25	.12	.02
☐ 39	1942 Cardinals/Yankees .		.25	.12	.02
☐ 40	1943 Yankees/Cardinals .		.25	.12	.02
☐ 41	1944 Cardinals/Browns ..		.25	.12	.02
☐ 42	1945 Tigers/Cubs		.25	.12	.02
	(Hank Greenberg)				
☐ 43	1946 Cardinals/Red Sox .		.25	.12	.02
	(Enos Slaughter)				
☐ 44	1947 Yankees/Dodgers ...		.25	.12	.02
	(Al Gionfriddo)				
☐ 45	1948 Indians/Braves		.25	.12	.02
☐ 46	1949 Yankees/Dodgers ...		.25	.12	.02
	(Reynolds/Roe)				
☐ 47	1950 Yankees/Phillies		.25	.12	.02
☐ 48	1951 Yankees/Giants		.25	.12	.02
☐ 49	1952 Yankees/Dodgers ...		.35	.17	.03
	(Mize/Snider)				
☐ 50	1953 Yankees/Dodgers ...		.25	.12	.02
	(Carl Erskine)				
☐ 51	1954 Giants/Indians		.25	.12	.02
	(Johnny Antonelli)				
☐ 52	1955 Dodgers/Yankees ...		.25	.12	.02
	(Johnny Podres)				
☐ 53	1956 Yankees/Dodgers ...		.25	.12	.02
☐ 54	1957 Braves/Yankees		.25	.12	.02
	(Lew Burdette)				
☐ 55	1958 Yankees/Braves		.25	.12	.02
	(Bob Turley)				
☐ 56	1959 Dodgers/White Sox		.25	.12	.02
	(Chuck Essegian)				
☐ 57	1960 Pirates/Yankees		.25	.12	.02
☐ 58	1961 Yankees/Reds		.25	.12	.02
	(Whitey Ford)				
☐ 59	1962 Yankees/Giants		.25	.12	.02
☐ 60	1963 Dodgers/Yankees ...		.25	.12	.02
	(Moose Skowron)				
☐ 61	1964 Cardinals/Yankees .		.25	.12	.02
	(Bobby Richardson)				
☐ 62	1965 Dodgers/Twins		.25	.12	.02
☐ 63	1966 Orioles/Dodgers		.25	.12	.02
☐ 64	1967 Cardinals/Red Sox .		.25	.12	.02
☐ 65	1968 Tigers/Cardinals		.25	.12	.02
☐ 66	1969 Mets/Orioles		.35	.17	.03

1971 Fleer World Series

This set of 68 cards was distributed by Fleer. The cards are standard size, 2 1/2" by 3 1/2" and are in crude color on the front with brown printing on white card stock on the back. All the years are represented in this set as 1904 when no World Series

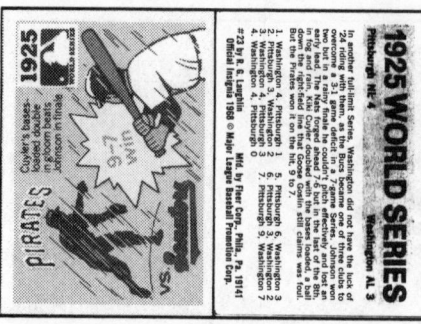

was played is represented by a card explaining why there was no World Series that year. In the list below, the winning series team is listed first. The year of the Series on the obverse is inside a white square over the official World Series logo.

			NRMT	VG-E	GOOD
COMPLETE SET			15.00	7.50	1.50
COMMON PLAYER			.25	.12	.02

☐ 1	1903 Red Sox/Pirates		.35	.17	.03
	(Cy Young)				
☐ 2	1904 NO Series		.35	.17	.03
	(John McGraw)				
☐ 3	1905 Giants/A's		.35	.17	.03
	(Matty/Bender/McGinnity)				
☐ 4	1906 White Sox/Cubs		.25	.12	.02
☐ 5	1907 Cubs/Tigers		.25	.12	.02
☐ 6	1908 Cubs/Tigers		.45	.22	.04
	(Ty Cobb)				
☐ 7	1909 Pirates/Tigers		.25	.12	.02
☐ 8	1910 A's/Cubs		.25	.12	.02
	(Eddie Collins)				
☐ 9	1911 A's/Giants		.25	.12	.02
	(Home Run Baker)				
☐ 10	1912 Red Sox/Giants		.25	.12	.02
☐ 11	1913 A's/Giants		.35	.17	.03
	(Christy Mathewson)				
☐ 12	1914 Braves/A's		.25	.12	.02
☐ 13	1915 Red Sox/Phillies		.25	.12	.02
	(Grover Alexander)				
☐ 14	1916 Red Sox/Dodgers ...		.25	.12	.02
☐ 15	1917 White Sox/Giants ...		.25	.12	.02
	(Red Faber)				
☐ 16	1918 Red Sox/Cubs		.60	.30	.06
	(Babe Ruth)				
☐ 17	1919 Reds/White Sox		.25	.12	.02
☐ 18	1920 Indians/Dodgers		.25	.12	.02
☐ 19	1921 Giants/Yankees		.25	.12	.02
	(Waite Hoyt)				
☐ 20	1922 Giants/Yankees		.25	.12	.02
☐ 21	1923 Yankees/Giants		.25	.12	.02
	(Herb Pennock)				
☐ 22	1924 Senators/Giants		.35	.17	.03
	(Walter Johnson)				
☐ 23	1925 Pirates/Senators		.35	.17	.03
	(Cuyler/W.Johnson)				
☐ 24	1926 Cardinals/Yankees .		.35	.17	.03
	(Rogers Hornsby)				
☐ 25	1927 Yankees/Pirates		.25	.12	.02
☐ 26	1928 Yankees/Cardinals .		.45	.22	.04
	(Lou Gehrig)				
☐ 27	1929 A's/Cubs		.25	.12	.02
☐ 28	1930 A's/Cardinals		.35	.17	.03
	(Jimmie Foxx)				
☐ 29	1931 Cardinals/A's		.25	.12	.02
	(Pepper Martin)				
☐ 30	1932 Yankees/Cubs		.60	.30	.06
	(Babe Ruth)				
☐ 31	1933 Giants/Senators		.25	.12	.02
	(Carl Hubbell)				
☐ 32	1934 Cardinals/Tigers		.25	.12	.02
☐ 33	1935 Tigers/Cubs		.35	.17	.03
	(Mickey Cochrane)				
☐ 34	1936 Yankees/Giants		.25	.12	.02
	(Red Rolfe)				
☐ 35	1937 Yankees/Giants		.25	.12	.02
	(Tony Lazzeri)				
☐ 36	1938 Yankees/Cubs		.25	.12	.02
☐ 37	1939 Yankees/Reds		.25	.12	.02
☐ 38	1940 Reds/Tigers		.25	.12	.02
☐ 39	1941 Yankees/Dodgers ...		.25	.12	.02
☐ 40	1942 Cardinals/Yankees .		.25	.12	.02

☐ 41	1943 Yankees/Cardinals .	.25	.12	.02		
☐ 42	1944 Cardinals/Browns ...	.25	.12	.02		
☐ 43	1945 Tigers/Cubs	.25	.12	.02		
	(Hank Greenberg)					
☐ 44	1946 Cardinals/Red Sox .	.25	.12	.02		
	(Enos Slaughter)					
☐ 45	1947 Yankees/Dodgers ...	.25	.12	.02		
☐ 46	1948 Indians/Braves	.25	.12	.02		
☐ 47	1949 Yankees/Dodgers ...	.25	.12	.02		
	(Preacher Roe)					
☐ 48	1950 Yankees/Phillies	.25	.12	.02		
	(Allie Reynolds)					
☐ 49	1951 Yankees/Giants	.25	.12	.02		
	(Ed Lopat)					
☐ 50	1952 Yankees/Dodgers ...	.35	.17	.03		
	(Johnny Mize)					
☐ 51	1953 Yankees/Dodgers ...	.25	.12	.02		
☐ 52	1954 Giants/Indians	.25	.12	.02		
☐ 53	1955 Dodgers/Yankees ...	.35	.17	.03		
	(Duke Snider)					
☐ 54	1956 Yankees/Dodgers ...	.25	.12	.02		
☐ 55	1957 Braves/Yankees	.25	.12	.02		
☐ 56	1958 Yankees/Braves	.25	.12	.02		
	(Hank Bauer)					
☐ 57	1959 Dodgers/White Sox	.35	.17	.03		
	(Duke Snider)					
☐ 58	1960 Pirates/Yankees	.25	.12	.02		
☐ 59	1961 Yankees/Reds	.25	.12	.02		
	(Whitey Ford)					
☐ 60	1962 Yankees/Giants	.25	.12	.02		
☐ 61	1963 Dodgers/Yankees ...	.25	.12	.02		
☐ 62	1964 Cardinals/Yankees .	.25	.12	.02		
☐ 63	1965 Dodgers/Twins	.25	.12	.02		
☐ 64	1966 Orioles/Dodgers	.25	.12	.02		
☐ 65	1967 Cardinals/Red Sox .	.25	.12	.02		
☐ 65	1968 Tigers/Cardinals	.25	.12	.02		
☐ 66	1969 Mets/Orioles	.35	.17	.03		
☐ 68	1970 Orioles/Reds	.35	.17	.03		

☐ 15	John McGraw	.45	.22	.04
☐ 16	Home Run Baker	.45	.22	.04
☐ 17	Johnny Evers	.45	.22	.04
☐ 18	Nap Lajoie	.45	.22	.04
☐ 19	Cy Young	.45	.22	.04
☐ 20	Eddie Collins	.45	.22	.04
☐ 21	John Glasscock	.35	.17	.03
☐ 22	Hal Chase	.35	.17	.03
☐ 23	Mordecai Brown	.45	.22	.04
☐ 24	Jake Daubert	.35	.17	.03
☐ 25	Mike Donlin	.35	.17	.03
☐ 26	John Clarkson	.45	.22	.04
☐ 27	Buck Herzog	.35	.17	.03
☐ 28	Art Nehf	.35	.17	.03

1981 Fleer

The cards in this 660-card set measure 2 1/2" by 3 1/2". This issue of cards marks Fleer's first entry into the current player baseball card market since 1963. Players from the same team are conveniently grouped together by number in the set. The teams are ordered (by 1980 standings) as follows: Philadelphia (1-27), Kansas City (28-50), Houston (51-78), New York Yankees (79-109), Los Angeles (110-141), Montreal (142-168), Baltimore (169-195), Cincinnati (196-220), Boston (221-241), Atlanta (242-267), California (268-290), Chicago Cubs (291-315), New York Mets (316-338), Chicago White Sox (339-350 and 352-359), Pittsburgh (360-386), Cleveland (387-408), Toronto (409-431), San Francisco (432-458), Detroit (459-483), San Diego (484-506), Milwaukee (507-527), St. Louis (528-550), Minnesota (551-571), Oakland (351 and 572-594), Seattle (595-616), and Texas (617- 637). Cards 638-660 feature specials and checklists. There were three distinct printings: the two following the primary run were designed to correct numerous errors. The variations caused by these multiple printings are noted in the checklist below (P1, P2, or P3).

1975 Fleer Pioneers

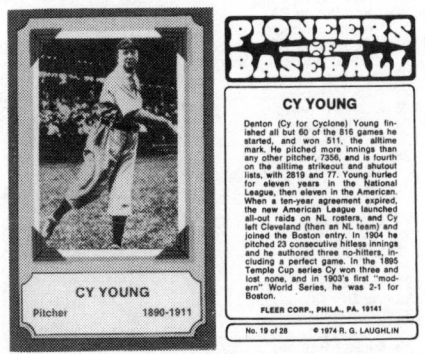

This 28-card set of brown and white sepia-toned photos of old timers is subtitled "Pioneers of Baseball. The artwork was done by R.G. Laughlin. The cards measure 2 1/2" by 4". The card backs are a narrative about the particular player. The cards are numbered on the back at the bottom.

	NRMT	VG-E	GOOD
COMPLETE SET	9.00	4.50	.90
COMMON PLAYER	.35	.17	.03

☐ 1	Cap Anson	.75	.20	.04
☐ 2	Harry Wright	.45	.22	.04
☐ 3	Buck Ewing	.45	.22	.04
☐ 4	A.G. Spalding	.45	.22	.04
☐ 5	Old Hoss Radbourn	.45	.22	.04
☐ 6	Dan Brouthers	.45	.22	.04
☐ 7	Roger Bresnahan	.45	.22	.04
☐ 8	Mike Kelly	.45	.22	.04
☐ 9	Ned Hanlon	.35	.17	.03
☐ 10	Ed Delahanty	.45	.22	.04
☐ 11	Pud Galvin	.45	.22	.04
☐ 12	Amos Rusie	.45	.22	.04
☐ 13	Tommy McCarthy	.45	.22	.04
☐ 14	Ty Cobb	.75	.35	.07

	MINT	EXC	G-VG
COMPLETE SET (P1)	30.00	15.00	3.00
COMPLETE SET (P2)	22.00	11.00	2.20
COMPLETE SET (P3)	23.00	11.50	2.30
COMMON PLAYER (1-660)	.03	.01	.00

☐	1	Pete Rose	2.00	.50	.10
☐	2	Larry Bowa	.15	.07	.01
☐	3	Manny Trillo	.06	.03	.00
☐	4	Bob Boone	.06	.03	.00
☐	5	Mike Schmidt	.80	.40	.08
		See 640A			
☐	6A	Steve Carlton P1	.65	.30	.06
		Pitcher of Year			
		See also 660A			
		Back "1066 Cardinals"			
☐	6B	Steve Carlton P2	.65	.30	.06
		Pitcher of Year			
		Back "1066 Cardinals"			
☐	6C	Steve Carlton P3	1.75	.85	.17
		"1966 Cardinals"			

☐	7	Tug McGraw	.10	.05	.01
		See 657A			
☐	8	Larry Christenson	.03	.01	.00
☐	9	Bake McBride	.06	.03	.00
☐	10	Greg Luzinski	.10	.05	.01
☐	11	Ron Reed	.03	.01	.00
☐	12	Dickie Noles	.03	.01	.00
☐	13	Keith Moreland	.45	.22	.04
☐	14	Bob Walk	.06	.03	.00
☐	15	Lonnie Smith	.08	.04	.01
☐	16	Dick Ruthven	.03	.01	.00
☐	17	Sparky Lyle	.10	.05	.01
☐	18	Greg Gross	.03	.01	.00
☐	19	Garry Maddox	.06	.03	.00
☐	20	Nino Espinosa	.03	.01	.00
☐	21	George Vukovich	.03	.01	.00
☐	22	John Vukovich	.03	.01	.00
☐	23	Ramon Aviles	.03	.01	.00
☐	24A	Ken Saucier P1	.06	.03	.00
		Name on front "Ken"			
☐	24B	Ken Saucier P2	.06	.03	.00
		Name on front "Ken"			
☐	24C	Kevin Saucier P3	.35	.17	.03
		Name on front "Kevin"			
☐	25	Randy Lerch	.03	.01	.00
☐	26	Del Unser	.03	.01	.00
☐	27	Tim McCarver	.10	.05	.01
☐	28	George Brett	.85	.40	.08
		See 655A			
☐	29	Willie Wilson	.15	.07	.01
		See 653A			
☐	30	Paul Splittorff	.06	.03	.00
☐	31	Dan Quisenberry	.18	.09	.01
☐	32A	Amos Otis P1	.12	.06	.01
		Batting Pose			
		"Outfield"			
		(32 on back)			
☐	32B	Amos Otis P2	.12	.06	.01
		"Series Starter"			
		(483 on back)			
☐	33	Steve Busby	.06	.03	.00
☐	34	U.L. Washington	.03	.01	.00
☐	35	Dave Chalk	.03	.01	.00
☐	36	Darrell Porter	.06	.03	.00
☐	37	Marty Pattin	.03	.01	.00
☐	38	Larry Gura	.06	.03	.00
☐	39	Renie Martin	.03	.01	.00
☐	40	Rich Gale	.03	.01	.00
☐	41A	Hal McRae P1	.50	.25	.05
		"Royals" on front			
		in black letters			
☐	41B	Hal McRae P2	.10	.05	.01
		"Royals" on front			
		in blue letters			
☐	42	Dennis Leonard	.06	.03	.00
☐	43	Willie Aikens	.06	.03	.00
☐	44	Frank White	.10	.05	.01
☐	45	Clint Hurdle	.03	.01	.00
☐	46	John Wathan	.06	.03	.00
☐	47	Pete LaCock	.03	.01	.00
☐	48	Rance Mulliniks	.03	.01	.00
☐	49	Jeff Twitty	.03	.01	.00
☐	50	Jamie Quirk	.03	.01	.00
☐	51	Art Howe	.03	.01	.00
☐	52	Ken Forsch	.06	.03	.00
☐	53	Vern Ruhle	.03	.01	.00
☐	54	Joe Niekro	.10	.05	.01
☐	55	Frank LaCorte	.03	.01	.00
☐	56	J.R. Richard	.10	.05	.01
☐	57	Nolan Ryan	.50	.25	.05
☐	58	Enos Cabell	.03	.01	.00
☐	59	Cesar Cedeno	.10	.05	.01
☐	60	Jose Cruz	.15	.07	.01
☐	61	Bill Virdon MG	.06	.03	.00
☐	62	Terry Puhl	.06	.03	.00
☐	63	Joaquin Andujar	.12	.06	.01
☐	64	Alan Ashby	.03	.01	.00
☐	65	Joe Sambito	.06	.03	.00
☐	66	Denny Walling	.03	.01	.00
☐	67	Jeff Leonard	.20	.10	.02
☐	68	Luis Pujols	.03	.01	.00
☐	69	Bruce Bochy	.03	.01	.00
☐	70	Rafael Landestoy	.03	.01	.00
☐	71	Dave Smith	.35	.17	.03
☐	72	Danny Heep	.25	.12	.02
☐	73	Julio Gonzalez	.03	.01	.00
☐	74	Craig Reynolds	.03	.01	.00
☐	75	Gary Woods	.03	.01	.00
☐	76	Dave Bergman	.03	.01	.00
☐	77	Randy Niemann	.03	.01	.00
☐	78	Joe Morgan	.30	.15	.03
☐	79	Reggie Jackson	.75	.35	.07
		See 650A			
☐	80	Bucky Dent	.10	.05	.01
☐	81	Tommy John	.15	.07	.01
☐	82	Luis Tiant	.10	.05	.01
☐	83	Rick Cerone	.06	.03	.00
☐	84	Dick Howser MG	.10	.05	.01
☐	85	Lou Piniella	.10	.05	.01
☐	86	Ron Davis	.03	.01	.00
☐	87A	Craig Nettles P1	12.00	6.00	1.20
		ERR (Name on back			
		misspelled "Craig")			
☐	87B	Graig Nettles P2 COR	.30	.15	.03
		"Graig"			
☐	88	Ron Guidry	.25	.12	.02
☐	89	Rich Gossage	.20	.10	.02
☐	90	Rudy May	.03	.01	.00
☐	91	Gaylord Perry	.25	.12	.02
☐	92	Eric Soderholm	.03	.01	.00
☐	93	Bob Watson	.06	.03	.00
☐	94	Bobby Murcer	.10	.05	.01
☐	95	Bobby Brown	.03	.01	.00
☐	96	Jim Spencer	.03	.01	.00
☐	97	Tom Underwood	.03	.01	.00
☐	98	Oscar Gamble	.06	.03	.00
☐	99	Johnny Oates	.03	.01	.00
☐	100	Fred Stanley	.03	.01	.00
☐	101	Ruppert Jones	.03	.01	.00
☐	102	Dennis Werth	.03	.01	.00
☐	103	Joe Lefebvre	.06	.03	.00
☐	104	Brian Doyle	.06	.03	.00
☐	105	Aurelio Rodriguez	.03	.01	.00
☐	106	Doug Bird	.03	.01	.00
☐	107	Mike Griffin	.03	.01	.00
☐	108	Tim Lollar	.06	.03	.00
☐	109	Willie Randolph	.10	.05	.01
☐	110	Steve Garvey	.50	.25	.05
☐	111	Reggie Smith	.10	.05	.01
☐	112	Don Sutton	.25	.12	.02
☐	113	Burt Hooton	.03	.01	.00
☐	114A	Dave Lopes P1	.50	.25	.05
		small hand on back			
☐	114B	Dave Lopes P2	.10	.05	.01
		no hand			
☐	115	Dusty Baker	.08	.04	.01
☐	116	Tom Lasorda MG	.08	.04	.01
☐	117	Bill Russell	.06	.03	.00
☐	118	Jerry Reuss	.06	.03	.00
☐	119	Terry Forster	.06	.03	.00
☐	120A	Bob Welch P1	.20	.10	.02
		Name on back Bob			
☐	120B	Bob Welch P2	.20	.10	.02
		Name on back Robert			
☐	121	Don Stanhouse	.03	.01	.00
☐	122	Rick Monday	.06	.03	.00
☐	123	Derrel Thomas	.03	.01	.00
☐	124	Joe Ferguson	.03	.01	.00
☐	125	Rick Sutcliffe	.25	.12	.02
☐	126A	Ron Cey P1	.50	.25	.05
		small hand on back			
☐	126B	Ron Cey P2	.15	.07	.01
		no hand			
☐	127	Dave Goltz	.03	.01	.00
☐	128	Jay Johnstone	.06	.03	.00
☐	129	Steve Yeager	.03	.01	.00
☐	130	Gary Weiss	.03	.01	.00
☐	131	Mike Scioscia	.40	.20	.04
☐	132	Vic Davalillo	.03	.01	.00
☐	133	Doug Rau	.03	.01	.00
☐	134	Pepe Frias	.03	.01	.00
☐	135	Mickey Hatcher	.06	.03	.00
☐	136	Steve Howe	.20	.10	.02
☐	137	Robert Castillo	.03	.01	.00
☐	138	Gary Thomasson	.03	.01	.00
☐	139	Rudy Law	.03	.01	.00
☐	140	Fernand Valenzuela	5.00	2.50	.50
		(sic, Fernando)			
☐	141	Manny Mota	.06	.03	.00
☐	142	Gary Carter	.50	.25	.05
☐	143	Steve Rogers	.08	.04	.01
☐	144	Warren Cromartie	.03	.01	.00
☐	145	Andre Dawson	.35	.17	.03
☐	146	Larry Parrish	.10	.05	.01
☐	147	Rowland Office	.03	.01	.00
☐	148	Ellis Valentine	.03	.01	.00
☐	149	Dick Williams MG	.06	.03	.00
☐	150	Bill Gullickson	.35	.17	.03
☐	151	Elias Sosa	.03	.01	.00
☐	152	John Tamargo	.03	.01	.00
☐	153	Chris Speier	.03	.01	.00
☐	154	Ron LeFlore	.06	.03	.00
☐	155	Rodney Scott	.03	.01	.00
☐	156	Stan Bahnsen	.03	.01	.00
☐	157	Bill Lee	.06	.03	.00
☐	158	Fred Norman	.03	.01	.00
☐	159	Woodie Fryman	.03	.01	.00
☐	160	Dave Palmer	.06	.03	.00
☐	161	Jerry White	.03	.01	.00
☐	162	Roberto Ramos	.03	.01	.00

☐ 163	John D'Acquisto	.03	.01	.00
☐ 164	Tommy Hutton	.03	.01	.00
☐ 165	Charlie Lea	.20	.10	.02
☐ 166	Scott Sanderson	.06	.03	.00
☐ 167	Ken Macha	.03	.01	.00
☐ 168	Tony Bernazard	.06	.03	.00
☐ 169	Jim Palmer	.35	.17	.03
☐ 170	Steve Stone	.06	.03	.00
☐ 171	Mike Flanagan	.10	.05	.01
☐ 172	Al Bumbry	.03	.01	.00
☐ 173	Doug DeCinces	.10	.05	.01
☐ 174	Scott McGregor	.06	.03	.00
☐ 175	Mark Belanger	.06	.03	.00
☐ 176	Tim Stoddard	.03	.01	.00
☐ 177A	Rick Dempsey P1 small hand on front	.50	.25	.05
☐ 177B	Rick Dempsey P2 no hand	.10	.05	.01
☐ 178	Earl Weaver MG	.08	.04	.01
☐ 179	Tippy Martinez	.06	.03	.00
☐ 180	Dennis Martinez	.06	.03	.00
☐ 181	Sammy Stewart	.03	.01	.00
☐ 182	Rich Dauer	.03	.01	.00
☐ 183	Lee May	.06	.03	.00
☐ 184	Eddie Murray	.75	.35	.07
☐ 185	Benny Ayala	.03	.01	.00
☐ 186	John Lowenstein	.03	.01	.00
☐ 187	Gary Roenicke	.06	.03	.00
☐ 188	Ken Singleton	.10	.05	.01
☐ 189	Dan Graham	.03	.01	.00
☐ 190	Terry Crowley	.03	.01	.00
☐ 191	Kiko Garcia	.03	.01	.00
☐ 192	Dave Ford	.03	.01	.00
☐ 193	Mark Corey	.03	.01	.00
☐ 194	Lenn Sakata	.03	.01	.00
☐ 195	Doug DeCinces	.10	.05	.01
☐ 196	Johnny Bench	.50	.25	.05
☐ 197	Dave Concepcion	.12	.06	.01
☐ 198	Ray Knight	.10	.05	.01
☐ 199	Ken Griffey	.08	.04	.01
☐ 200	Tom Seaver	.50	.25	.05
☐ 201	Dave Collins	.06	.03	.00
☐ 202A	George Foster P1 Slugger number on back 216	.20	.10	.02
☐ 202B	George Foster P2 Slugger number on back 202	.20	.10	.02
☐ 203	Junior Kennedy	.03	.01	.00
☐ 204	Frank Pastore	.03	.01	.00
☐ 205	Dan Driessen	.06	.03	.00
☐ 206	Hector Cruz	.03	.01	.00
☐ 207	Paul Moskau	.03	.01	.00
☐ 208	Charlie Leibrandt	.40	.20	.04
☐ 209	Harry Spilman	.03	.01	.00
☐ 210	Joe Price	.06	.03	.00
☐ 211	Tom Hume	.03	.01	.00
☐ 212	Joe Nolan	.03	.01	.00
☐ 213	Doug Bair	.03	.01	.00
☐ 214	Mario Soto	.10	.05	.01
☐ 215A	Bill Bonham P1 small hand on back	.50	.25	.05
☐ 215B	Bill Bonham P2 no hand	.06	.03	.00
☐ 216	George Foster See 202	.20	.10	.02
☐ 217	Paul Householder	.08	.04	.01
☐ 218	Ron Oester	.06	.03	.00
☐ 219	Sam Mejias	.03	.01	.00
☐ 220	Sheldon Burnside	.03	.01	.00
☐ 221	Carl Yastrzemski	.80	.40	.08
☐ 222	Jim Rice	.45	.22	.04
☐ 223	Fred Lynn	.20	.10	.02
☐ 224	Carlton Fisk	.18	.09	.01
☐ 225	Rick Burleson	.06	.03	.00
☐ 226	Dennis Eckersley	.06	.03	.00
☐ 227	Butch Hobson	.03	.01	.00
☐ 228	Tom Burgmeier	.03	.01	.00
☐ 229	Garry Hancock	.03	.01	.00
☐ 230	Don Zimmer MG	.06	.03	.00
☐ 231	Steve Renko	.03	.01	.00
☐ 232	Dwight Evans	.20	.10	.02
☐ 233	Mike Torrez	.06	.03	.00
☐ 234	Bob Stanley	.06	.03	.00
☐ 235	Jim Dwyer	.03	.01	.00
☐ 236	Dave Stapleton	.06	.03	.00
☐ 237	Glen Hoffman	.06	.03	.00
☐ 238	Jerry Remy	.03	.01	.00
☐ 239	Dick Drago	.03	.01	.00
☐ 240	Bill Campbell	.03	.01	.00
☐ 241	Tony Perez	.15	.07	.01
☐ 242	Phil Niekro	.25	.12	.02
☐ 243	Dale Murphy	1.25	.60	.12
☐ 244	Bob Horner	.25	.12	.02
☐ 245	Jeff Burroughs	.06	.03	.00
☐ 246	Rick Camp	.03	.01	.00
☐ 247	Bob Cox MG	.03	.01	.00
☐ 248	Bruce Benedict	.03	.01	.00
☐ 249	Gene Garber	.03	.01	.00
☐ 250	Jerry Royster	.03	.01	.00
☐ 251A	Gary Matthews P1 small hand on back	.50	.25	.05
☐ 251B	Gary Matthews P2 no hand	.10	.05	.01
☐ 252	Chris Chambliss	.06	.03	.00
☐ 253	Luis Gomez	.03	.01	.00
☐ 254	Bill Nahorodny	.03	.01	.00
☐ 255	Doyle Alexander	.06	.03	.00
☐ 256	Brian Asselstine	.03	.01	.00
☐ 257	Biff Pocoroba	.03	.01	.00
☐ 258	Mike Lum	.03	.01	.00
☐ 259	Charlie Spikes	.03	.01	.00
☐ 260	Glenn Hubbard	.06	.03	.00
☐ 261	Tommy Boggs	.03	.01	.00
☐ 262	Al Hrabosky	.06	.03	.00
☐ 263	Rick Matula	.03	.01	.00
☐ 264	Preston Hanna	.03	.01	.00
☐ 265	Larry Bradford	.03	.01	.00
☐ 266	Rafael Ramirez	.25	.12	.02
☐ 267	Larry McWilliams	.06	.03	.00
☐ 268	Rod Carew	.50	.25	.05
☐ 269	Bobby Grich	.10	.05	.01
☐ 270	Carney Lansford	.15	.07	.01
☐ 271	Don Baylor	.18	.09	.01
☐ 272	Joe Rudi	.06	.03	.00
☐ 273	Dan Ford	.03	.01	.00
☐ 274	Jim Fregosi	.08	.04	.01
☐ 275	Dave Frost	.03	.01	.00
☐ 276	Frank Tanana	.06	.03	.00
☐ 277	Dickie Thon	.08	.04	.01
☐ 278	Jason Thompson	.06	.03	.00
☐ 279	Rick Miller	.03	.01	.00
☐ 280	Bert Campaneris	.08	.04	.01
☐ 281	Tom Donohue	.03	.01	.00
☐ 282	Brian Downing	.06	.03	.00
☐ 283	Fred Patek	.03	.01	.00
☐ 284	Bruce Kison	.03	.01	.00
☐ 285	Dave LaRoche	.03	.01	.00
☐ 286	Don Aase	.06	.03	.00
☐ 287	Jim Barr	.03	.01	.00
☐ 288	Alfredo Martinez	.03	.01	.00
☐ 289	Larry Harlow	.03	.01	.00
☐ 290	Andy Hassler	.03	.01	.00
☐ 291	Dave Kingman	.15	.07	.01
☐ 292	Bill Buckner	.12	.06	.01
☐ 293	Rick Reuschel	.10	.05	.01
☐ 294	Bruce Sutter	.18	.09	.01
☐ 295	Jerry Martin	.03	.01	.00
☐ 296	Scot Thompson	.03	.01	.00
☐ 297	Ivan DeJesus	.03	.01	.00
☐ 298	Steve Dillard	.03	.01	.00
☐ 299	Dick Tidrow	.03	.01	.00
☐ 300	Randy Martz	.03	.01	.00
☐ 301	Lenny Randle	.03	.01	.00
☐ 302	Lynn McGlothen	.03	.01	.00
☐ 303	Cliff Johnson	.03	.01	.00
☐ 304	Tim Blackwell	.03	.01	.00
☐ 305	Dennis Lamp	.03	.01	.00
☐ 306	Bill Caudill	.06	.03	.00
☐ 307	Carlos Lezcano	.03	.01	.00
☐ 308	Jim Tracy	.03	.01	.00
☐ 309	Doug Capilla	.03	.01	.00
☐ 310	Willie Hernandez	.15	.07	.01
☐ 311	Mike Vail	.03	.01	.00
☐ 312	Mike Krukow	.10	.05	.01
☐ 313	Barry Foote	.03	.01	.00
☐ 314	Larry Biittner	.03	.01	.00
☐ 315	Mike Tyson	.03	.01	.00
☐ 316	Lee Mazzilli	.06	.03	.00
☐ 317	John Stearns	.03	.01	.00
☐ 318	Alex Trevino	.03	.01	.00
☐ 319	Craig Swan	.03	.01	.00
☐ 320	Frank Taveras	.03	.01	.00
☐ 321	Steve Henderson	.03	.01	.00
☐ 322	Neil Allen	.06	.03	.00
☐ 323	Mark Bomback	.03	.01	.00
☐ 324	Mike Jorgensen	.03	.01	.00
☐ 325	Joe Torre MG	.10	.05	.01
☐ 326	Elliott Maddox	.03	.01	.00
☐ 327	Pete Falcone	.03	.01	.00
☐ 328	Ray Burris	.03	.01	.00
☐ 329	Claudell Washington	.06	.03	.00
☐ 330	Doug Flynn	.03	.01	.00
☐ 331	Joel Youngblood	.03	.01	.00
☐ 332	Bill Almon	.03	.01	.00
☐ 333	Tom Hausman	.03	.01	.00
☐ 334	Pat Zachry	.03	.01	.00
☐ 335	Jeff Reardon	.60	.30	.06
☐ 336	Wally Backman	.50	.25	.05
☐ 337	Dan Norman	.03	.01	.00

☐ 338 Jerry Morales	.03	.01	.00
☐ 339 Ed Farmer	.03	.01	.00
☐ 340 Bob Molinaro	.03	.01	.00
☐ 341 Todd Cruz	.03	.01	.00
☐ 342A Britt Burns P1	.50	.25	.05
small hand on front			
☐ 342B Britt Burns P2	.25	.12	.02
no hand			
☐ 343 Kevin Bell	.03	.01	.00
☐ 344 Tony LaRussa MG	.06	.03	.00
☐ 345 Steve Trout	.06	.03	.00
☐ 346 Harold Baines	1.75	.85	.17
☐ 347 Richard Wortham	.03	.01	.00
☐ 348 Wayne Nordhagen	.03	.01	.00
☐ 349 Mike Squires	.03	.01	.00
☐ 350 Lamar Johnson	.03	.01	.00
☐ 351 Rickey Henderson	1.00	.50	.10
☐ 352 Francisco Barrios	.03	.01	.00
☐ 353 Thad Bosley	.03	.01	.00
☐ 354 Chet Lemon	.06	.03	.00
☐ 355 Bruce Kimm	.03	.01	.00
☐ 356 Richard Dotson	.45	.22	.04
☐ 357 Jim Morrison	.03	.01	.00
☐ 358 Mike Proly	.03	.01	.00
☐ 359 Greg Pryor	.03	.01	.00
☐ 360 Dave Parker	.30	.15	.03
☐ 361 Omar Moreno	.03	.01	.00
☐ 362A Kent Tekulve P1	.15	.07	.01
Back "1071 Waterbury"			
and "1078 Pirates"			
☐ 362B Kent Tekulve P2	.10	.05	.01
"1971 Waterbury" and			
"1978 Pirates"			
☐ 363 Willie Stargell	.30	.15	.03
☐ 364 Phil Garner	.06	.03	.00
☐ 365 Ed Ott	.03	.01	.00
☐ 366 Don Robinson	.06	.03	.00
☐ 367 Chuck Tanner MG	.06	.03	.00
☐ 368 Jim Rooker	.03	.01	.00
☐ 369 Dale Berra	.06	.03	.00
☐ 370 Jim Bibby	.03	.01	.00
☐ 371 Steve Nicosia	.03	.01	.00
☐ 372 Mike Easler	.06	.03	.00
☐ 373 Bill Robinson	.06	.03	.00
☐ 374 Lee Lacy	.06	.03	.00
☐ 375 John Candelaria	.10	.05	.01
☐ 376 Manny Sanguillen	.06	.03	.00
☐ 377 Rick Rhoden	.10	.05	.01
☐ 378 Grant Jackson	.03	.01	.00
☐ 379 Tim Foli	.03	.01	.00
☐ 380 Rod Scurry	.10	.05	.01
☐ 381 Bill Madlock	.15	.07	.01
☐ 382A Kurt Bevacqua P1 ERR		.10	.02
P on cap backwards			
☐ 382B Kurt Bevacqua P2	.06	.03	.00
COR			
☐ 383 Bert Blyleven	.15	.07	.01
☐ 384 Eddie Solomon	.03	.01	.00
☐ 385 Enrique Romo	.03	.01	.00
☐ 386 John Milner	.03	.01	.00
☐ 387 Mike Hargrove	.06	.03	.00
☐ 388 Jorge Orta	.03	.01	.00
☐ 389 Toby Harrah	.06	.03	.00
☐ 390 Tom Veryzer	.03	.01	.00
☐ 391 Miguel Dilone	.03	.01	.00
☐ 392 Dan Spillner	.03	.01	.00
☐ 393 Jack Brohamer	.03	.01	.00
☐ 394 Wayne Garland	.03	.01	.00
☐ 395 Sid Monge	.03	.01	.00
☐ 396 Rick Waits	.03	.01	.00
☐ 397 Joe Charboneau	.10	.05	.01
☐ 398 Gary Alexander	.03	.01	.00
☐ 399 Jerry Dybzinski	.03	.01	.00
☐ 400 Mike Stanton	.03	.01	.00
☐ 401 Mike Paxton	.03	.01	.00
☐ 402 Gary Gray	.06	.03	.00
☐ 403 Rick Manning	.03	.01	.00
☐ 404 Bo Diaz	.10	.05	.01
☐ 405 Ron Hassey	.03	.01	.00
☐ 406 Ross Grimsley	.03	.01	.00
☐ 407 Victor Cruz	.03	.01	.00
☐ 408 Len Barker	.06	.03	.00
☐ 409 Bob Bailor	.03	.01	.00
☐ 410 Otto Velez	.03	.01	.00
☐ 411 Ernie Whitt	.06	.03	.00
☐ 412 Jim Clancy	.06	.03	.00
☐ 413 Barry Bonnell	.03	.01	.00
☐ 414 Dave Stieb	.25	.12	.02
☐ 415 Damaso Garcia	.30	.15	.03
☐ 416 John Mayberry	.06	.03	.00
☐ 417 Roy Howell	.03	.01	.00
☐ 418 Dan Ainge	.25	.12	.02
☐ 419A Jesse Jefferson P1	.06	.03	.00
Back says Pirates			
☐ 419B Jesse Jefferson P2	.06	.03	.00

Back says Pirates			
☐ 419C Jesse Jefferson P3	.35	.17	.03
Back says Blue Jays			
☐ 420 Joey McLaughlin	.03	.01	.00
☐ 421 Lloyd Moseby	1.25	.60	.12
☐ 422 Al Woods	.03	.01	.00
☐ 423 Garth Iorg	.03	.01	.00
☐ 424 Doug Ault	.03	.01	.00
☐ 425 Ken Schrom	.20	.10	.02
☐ 426 Mike Willis	.03	.01	.00
☐ 427 Steve Braun	.03	.01	.00
☐ 428 Bob Davis	.03	.01	.00
☐ 429 Jerry Garvin	.03	.01	.00
☐ 430 Alfredo Griffin	.10	.05	.01
☐ 431 Bob Mattick MG	.03	.01	.00
☐ 432 Vida Blue	.10	.05	.01
☐ 433 Jack Clark	.25	.12	.02
☐ 434 Willie McCovey	.30	.15	.03
☐ 435 Mike Ivie	.03	.01	.00
☐ 436A Darrel Evans P1 ERR	.40	.20	.04
Name on front "Darrel"			
☐ 436B Darrell Evans P2	.15	.07	.01
Name on front "Darrell"			
☐ 437 Terry Whitfield	.03	.01	.00
☐ 438 Rennie Stennett	.03	.01	.00
☐ 439 John Montefusco	.06	.03	.00
☐ 440 Jim Wohlford	.03	.01	.00
☐ 441 Bill North	.03	.01	.00
☐ 442 Milt May	.03	.01	.00
☐ 443 Max Venable	.03	.01	.00
☐ 444 Ed Whitson	.06	.03	.00
☐ 445 Al Holland	.15	.07	.01
☐ 446 Randy Moffitt	.03	.01	.00
☐ 447 Bob Knepper	.12	.06	.01
☐ 448 Gary Lavelle	.06	.03	.00
☐ 449 Greg Minton	.06	.03	.00
☐ 450 Johnnie LeMaster	.03	.01	.00
☐ 451 Larry Herndon	.06	.03	.00
☐ 452 Rich Murray	.03	.01	.00
☐ 453 Joe Pettini	.03	.01	.00
☐ 454 Allen Ripley	.03	.01	.00
☐ 455 Dennis Littlejohn	.03	.01	.00
☐ 456 Tom Griffin	.03	.01	.00
☐ 457 Alan Hargesheimer	.03	.01	.00
☐ 458 Joe Strain	.03	.01	.00
☐ 459 Steve Kemp	.08	.04	.01
☐ 460 Sparky Anderson MG	.08	.04	.01
☐ 461 Alan Trammell	.30	.15	.03
☐ 462 Mark Fidrych	.10	.05	.01
☐ 463 Lou Whitaker	.20	.10	.02
☐ 464 Dave Rozema	.03	.01	.00
☐ 465 Milt Wilcox	.03	.01	.00
☐ 466 Champ Summers	.03	.01	.00
☐ 467 Lance Parrish	.30	.15	.03
☐ 468 Dan Petry	.12	.06	.01
☐ 469 Pat Underwood	.03	.01	.00
☐ 470 Rick Peters	.03	.01	.00
☐ 471 Al Cowens	.03	.01	.00
☐ 472 John Wockenfuss	.03	.01	.00
☐ 473 Tom Brookens	.03	.01	.00
☐ 474 Richie Hebner	.03	.01	.00
☐ 475 Jack Morris	.35	.17	.03
☐ 476 Jim Lentine	.03	.01	.00
☐ 477 Bruce Robbins	.03	.01	.00
☐ 478 Mark Wagner	.03	.01	.00
☐ 479 Tim Corcoran	.03	.01	.00
☐ 480A Stan Papi P1	.15	.07	.01
Front as Pitcher			
☐ 480B Stan Papi P2	.10	.05	.01
Front as Shortstop			
☐ 481 Kirk Gibson	2.00	1.00	.20
☐ 482 Dan Schatzeder	.03	.01	.00
☐ 483A Amos Otis P1	.12	.06	.01
See card 32			
☐ 483B Amos Otis P2	.12	.06	.01
See card 32			
☐ 484 Dave Winfield	.45	.22	.04
☐ 485 Rollie Fingers	.30	.15	.03
☐ 486 Gene Richards	.03	.01	.00
☐ 487 Randy Jones	.06	.03	.00
☐ 488 Ozzie Smith	.25	.12	.02
☐ 489 Gene Tenace	.03	.01	.00
☐ 490 Bill Fahey	.03	.01	.00
☐ 491 John Curtis	.03	.01	.00
☐ 492 Dave Cash	.03	.01	.00
☐ 493A Tim Flannery P1	.15	.07	.01
Batting right			
☐ 493B Tim Flannery P2	.08	.04	.01
Batting left			
☐ 494 Jerry Mumphrey	.06	.03	.00
☐ 495 Bob Shirley	.03	.01	.00
☐ 496 Steve Mura	.03	.01	.00
☐ 497 Eric Rasmussen	.03	.01	.00
☐ 498 Broderick Perkins	.03	.01	.00
☐ 499 Barry Evans	.03	.01	.00

☐ 500	Chuck Baker	.03	.01	.00
☐ 501	Luis Salazar	.06	.03	.00
☐ 502	Gary Lucas	.10	.05	.01
☐ 503	Mike Armstrong	.10	.05	.01
☐ 504	Jerry Turner	.03	.01	.00
☐ 505	Dennis Kinney	.03	.01	.00
☐ 506	Willie Montanez	.03	.01	.00
☐ 507	Gorman Thomas	.10	.05	.01
☐ 508	Ben Oglivie	.08	.04	.01
☐ 509	Larry Hisle	.06	.03	.00
☐ 510	Sal Bando	.08	.04	.01
☐ 511	Robin Yount	.40	.20	.04
☐ 512	Mike Caldwell	.06	.03	.00
☐ 513	Sixto Lezcano	.03	.01	.00
☐ 514A	Bill Travers P1 ERR	.20	.10	.02
	"Jerry Augustine"			
	with Augustine back			
☐ 514B	Bill Travers P2 COR	.10	.05	.01
☐ 515	Paul Molitor	.20	.10	.02
☐ 516	Moose Haas	.06	.03	.00
☐ 517	Bill Castro	.03	.01	.00
☐ 518	Jim Slaton	.06	.03	.00
☐ 519	Lary Sorensen	.03	.01	.00
☐ 520	Bob McClure	.03	.01	.00
☐ 521	Charlie Moore	.03	.01	.00
☐ 522	Jim Gantner	.03	.01	.00
☐ 523	Reggie Cleveland	.03	.01	.00
☐ 524	Don Money	.03	.01	.00
☐ 525	Bill Travers	.03	.01	.00
☐ 526	Buck Martinez	.03	.01	.00
☐ 527	Dick Davis	.03	.01	.00
☐ 528	Ted Simmons	.15	.07	.01
☐ 529	Garry Templeton	.10	.05	.01
☐ 530	Ken Reitz	.03	.01	.00
☐ 531	Tony Scott	.03	.01	.00
☐ 532	Ken Oberkfell	.06	.03	.00
☐ 533	Bob Sykes	.03	.01	.00
☐ 534	Keith Smith	.03	.01	.00
☐ 535	John Littlefield	.03	.01	.00
☐ 536	Jim Kaat	.15	.07	.01
☐ 537	Bob Forsch	.06	.03	.00
☐ 538	Mike Phillips	.03	.01	.00
☐ 539	Terry Landrum	.08	.04	.01
☐ 540	Leon Durham	.60	.30	.06
☐ 541	Terry Kennedy	.10	.05	.01
☐ 542	George Hendrick	.08	.04	.01
☐ 543	Dane Iorg	.03	.01	.00
☐ 544	Mark Littell	.03	.01	.00
☐ 545	Keith Hernandez	.30	.15	.03
☐ 546	Silvio Martinez	.03	.01	.00
☐ 547A	Don Hood P1 ERR	.20	.10	.02
	"Pete Vuckovich"			
	with Vuckovich back			
☐ 547B	Don Hood P2 COR	.10	.05	.01
☐ 548	Bobby Bonds	.10	.05	.01
☐ 549	Mike Ramsey	.03	.01	.00
☐ 550	Tom Herr	.12	.06	.01
☐ 551	Roy Smalley	.06	.03	.00
☐ 552	Jerry Koosman	.08	.04	.01
☐ 553	Ken Landreaux	.06	.03	.00
☐ 554	John Castino	.06	.03	.00
☐ 555	Doug Corbett	.08	.04	.01
☐ 556	Bombo Rivera	.03	.01	.00
☐ 557	Ron Jackson	.03	.01	.00
☐ 558	Butch Wynegar	.06	.03	.00
☐ 559	Hosken Powell	.03	.01	.00
☐ 560	Pete Redfern	.03	.01	.00
☐ 561	Roger Erickson	.03	.01	.00
☐ 562	Glenn Adams	.03	.01	.00
☐ 563	Rick Sofield	.03	.01	.00
☐ 564	Geoff Zahn	.03	.01	.00
☐ 565	Pete Mackanin	.03	.01	.00
☐ 566	Mike Cubbage	.03	.01	.00
☐ 567	Darrell Jackson	.03	.01	.00
☐ 568	Dave Edwards	.03	.01	.00
☐ 569	Rob Wilfong	.03	.01	.00
☐ 570	Sal Butera	.03	.01	.00
☐ 571	Jose Morales	.03	.01	.00
☐ 572	Rick Langford	.03	.01	.00
☐ 573	Mike Norris	.06	.03	.00
☐ 574	Rickey Henderson	1.00	.50	.10
☐ 575	Tony Armas	.10	.05	.01
☐ 576	Dave Revering	.03	.01	.00
☐ 577	Jeff Newman	.03	.01	.00
☐ 578	Bob Lacey	.03	.01	.00
☐ 579	Brian Kingman	.03	.01	.00
☐ 580	Mitchell Page	.03	.01	.00
☐ 581	Billy Martin MG	.12	.06	.01
☐ 582	Rob Picciolo	.03	.01	.00
☐ 583	Mike Heath	.03	.01	.00
☐ 584	Mickey Klutts	.03	.01	.00
☐ 585	Orlando Gonzalez	.03	.01	.00
☐ 586	Mike Davis	.45	.22	.04
☐ 587	Wayne Gross	.03	.01	.00
☐ 588	Matt Keough	.03	.01	.00

☐ 589	Steve McCatty	.03	.01	.00
☐ 590	Dwayne Murphy	.06	.03	.00
☐ 591	Mario Guerrero	.03	.01	.00
☐ 592	Dave McKay	.03	.01	.00
☐ 593	Jim Essian	.03	.01	.00
☐ 594	Dave Heaverlo	.03	.01	.00
☐ 595	Maury Wills MG	.08	.04	.01
☐ 596	Juan Beniquez	.06	.03	.00
☐ 597	Rodney Craig	.03	.01	.00
☐ 598	Jim Anderson	.03	.01	.00
☐ 599	Floyd Bannister	.08	.04	.01
☐ 600	Bruce Bochte	.06	.03	.00
☐ 601	Julio Cruz	.06	.03	.00
☐ 602	Ted Cox	.03	.01	.00
☐ 603	Dan Meyer	.03	.01	.00
☐ 604	Larry Cox	.03	.01	.00
☐ 605	Bill Stein	.03	.01	.00
☐ 606	Steve Garvey	.50	.25	.05
☐ 607	Dave Roberts	.03	.01	.00
☐ 608	Leon Roberts	.03	.01	.00
☐ 609	Reggie Walton	.03	.01	.00
☐ 610	Dave Edler	.03	.01	.00
☐ 611	Larry Milbourne	.03	.01	.00
☐ 612	Kim Allen	.03	.01	.00
☐ 613	Mario Mendoza	.03	.01	.00
☐ 614	Tom Paciorek	.03	.01	.00
☐ 615	Glenn Abbott	.03	.01	.00
☐ 616	Joe Simpson	.03	.01	.00
☐ 617	Mickey Rivers	.06	.03	.00
☐ 618	Jim Kern	.03	.01	.00
☐ 619	Jim Sundberg	.06	.03	.00
☐ 620	Richie Zisk	.06	.03	.00
☐ 621	Jon Matlack	.06	.03	.00
☐ 622	Ferguson Jenkins	.15	.07	.01
☐ 623	Pat Corrales MG	.06	.03	.00
☐ 624	Ed Figueroa	.03	.01	.00
☐ 625	Buddy Bell	.15	.07	.01
☐ 626	Al Oliver	.12	.06	.01
☐ 627	Doc Medich	.03	.01	.00
☐ 628	Bump Wills	.03	.01	.00
☐ 629	Rusty Staub	.10	.05	.01
☐ 630	Pat Putnam	.03	.01	.00
☐ 631	John Grubb	.03	.01	.00
☐ 632	Danny Darwin	.06	.03	.00
☐ 633	Ken Clay	.03	.01	.00
☐ 634	Jim Norris	.03	.01	.00
☐ 635	John Butcher	.12	.06	.01
☐ 636	Dave Roberts	.03	.01	.00
☐ 637	Billy Sample	.03	.01	.00
☐ 638	Carl Yastrzemski	.80	.40	.08
☐ 639	Cecil Cooper	.15	.07	.01
☐ 640A	Mike Schmidt P1	1.00	.50	.10
	(Portrait)			
	"Third Base"			
	(number on back 5)			
☐ 640B	Mike Schmidt P2	1.00	.50	.10
	"1980 Home Run King"			
	(640 on back)			
☐ 641A	CL: Phils/Royals P1	.10	.01	.00
	41 is Hal McRae			
☐ 641B	CL: Phils/Royals P2	.10	.01	.00
	41 is Hal McRae,			
	Double Threat			
☐ 642	CL: Astros/Yankees	.08	.01	.00
☐ 643	CL: Expos/Dodgers	.08	.01	.00
☐ 644A	CL: Reds/Orioles P1	.10	.01	.00
	202 is George Foster			
☐ 644B	CL: Reds/Orioles P2	.10	.01	.00
	202 is Foster Slugger			
☐ 645A	Rose/Bowa/Schmidt	2.00	1.00	.20
	Triple Threat P1			
	(No number on back)			
☐ 645B	Rose/Bowa/Schmidt	1.00	.50	.10
	Triple Threat P2			
	(Back numbered 645)			
☐ 646	CL: Braves/Red Sox	.08	.01	.00
☐ 647	CL: Cubs/Angels	.08	.01	.00
☐ 648	CL: Mets/White Sox	.08	.01	.00
☐ 649	CL: Indians/Pirates	.08	.01	.00
☐ 650A	Reggie Jackson	1.00	.50	.10
	Mr. Baseball P1			
	Number on back 79			
☐ 650B	Reggie Jackson	.75	.35	.07
	Mr. Baseball P2			
	Number on back 650			
☐ 651	CL: Giants/Blue Jays	.08	.01	.00
☐ 652A	CL: Tigers/Padres P1	.10	.01	.00
	483 is listed			
☐ 652B	CL: Tigers/Padres P2	.10	.01	.00
	483 is deleted			
☐ 653A	Willie Wilson P1	.15	.07	.01
	Most Hits Most Runs			
	Number on back 29			
☐ 653B	Willie Wilson P2	.15	.07	.01
	Most Hits Most Runs			

		MINT	EXC	G-VG
☐ 654A	CL: Brewers/Cards P1	.10	.01	.00
	Number on back 653			
	514 Jerry Augustine			
	547 Pete Vuckovich			
☐ 654B	CL: Brewers/Cards P2	.10	.01	.00
	514 Billy Travers			
	547 Don Hood			
☐ 655A	George Brett P1	1.25	.60	.12
	.390 Average			
	Number on back 28			
☐ 655B	George Brett P2	.75	.35	.07
	.390 Average			
	Number on back 655			
☐ 656	CL: Twins/Oakland A's ..	.08	.01	.00
☐ 657A	Tug McGraw P1	.10	.05	.01
	Game Saver			
	Number on back 7			
☐ 657B	Tug McGraw P2	.10	.05	.01
	Game Saver			
	Number on back 657			
☐ 658	CL: Rangers/Mariners ...	.08	.01	.00
☐ 659A	Checklist P1	.10	.01	.00
	of Special Cards			
	Last lines on front			
	Wilson Most Hits			
☐ 659B	Checklist P2	.10	.01	.00
	of Special Cards			
	Last lines on front			
	Otis Series Starter			
☐ 660A	Steve Carlton P1	.65	.30	.06
	Golden Arm			
	Back "1066 Cardinals"			
	Number on back 6			
☐ 660B	Steve Carlton P2	.65	.30	.06
	Golden Arm			
	Number on back 660			
	Back "1066 Cardinals"			
☐ 660C	Steve Carlton P3	2.00	1.00	.20
	Golden Arm			
	"1966 Cardinals"			

1981 Fleer Stickers Cards

The stickers in this 128 sticker set measure 2 1/2" by 3 1/2". The 1981 Fleer Baseball Star Stickers consist of numbered cards with peelable, full color sticker fronts and three unnumbered checklist. The backs of the numbered player cards are the same as the 1981 Fleer regular issue cards except for the numbers, while the checklist cards (cards 126-128 below) have sticker fronts of Jackson (1-42), Brett (43-83) and Schmidt (84- 125).

		MINT	EXC	G-VG
COMPLETE SET		45.00	22.50	4.50
COMMON PLAYER (1-128)		.20	.10	.02
☐ 1	Steve Garvey	2.00	1.00	.20
☐ 2	Ron LeFlore	.20	.10	.02
☐ 3	Ron Cey	.30	.15	.03
☐ 4	Dave Revering	.20	.10	.02
☐ 5	Tony Armas	.30	.15	.03
☐ 6	Mike Norris	.20	.10	.02
☐ 7	Steve Kemp	.30	.15	.03
☐ 8	Bruce Bochte	.20	.10	.02
☐ 9	Mike Schmidt	3.00	1.50	.30
☐ 10	Scott McGregor	.30	.15	.03
☐ 11	Buddy Bell	.40	.20	.04

☐ 12	Carney Lansford	.40	.20	.04
☐ 13	Carl Yastrzemski	2.50	1.25	.25
☐ 14	Ben Oglivie	.20	.10	.02
☐ 15	Willie Stargell	1.25	.60	.12
☐ 16	Cecil Cooper	.40	.20	.04
☐ 17	Gene Richards	.20	.10	.02
☐ 18	Jim Kern	.20	.10	.02
☐ 19	Jerry Koosman	.30	.15	.03
☐ 20	Larry Bowa	.40	.20	.04
☐ 21	Kent Tekulve	.20	.10	.02
☐ 22	Dan Driessen	.20	.10	.02
☐ 23	Phil Niekro	.80	.40	.08
☐ 24	Dan Quisenberry	.50	.25	.05
☐ 25	Dave Winfield	1.75	.85	.17
☐ 26	Dave Parker	.80	.40	.08
☐ 27	Rick Langford	.20	.10	.02
☐ 28	Amos Otis	.30	.15	.03
☐ 29	Bill Buckner	.30	.15	.03
☐ 30	Al Bumbry	.20	.10	.02
☐ 31	Bake McBride	.20	.10	.02
☐ 32	Mickey Rivers	.20	.10	.02
☐ 33	Rick Burleson	.30	.15	.03
☐ 34	Dennis Eckersley	.30	.15	.03
☐ 35	Cesar Cedeno	.30	.15	.03
☐ 36	Enos Cabell	.20	.10	.02
☐ 37	Johnny Bench	2.00	1.00	.20
☐ 38	Robin Yount	2.00	1.00	.20
☐ 39	Mark Belanger	.20	.10	.02
☐ 40	Rod Carew	1.75	.85	.17
☐ 41	George Foster	.80	.40	.08
☐ 42	Lee Mazzilli	.20	.10	.02
☐ 43	Triple Threat:	2.00	1.00	.20
	Pete Rose			
	Larry Bowa			
	Mike Schmidt			
☐ 44	J.R. Richard	.30	.15	.03
☐ 45	Lou Piniella	.30	.15	.03
☐ 46	Ken Landreaux	.20	.10	.02
☐ 47	Rollie Fingers	.60	.30	.06
☐ 48	Joaquin Andujar	.30	.15	.03
☐ 49	Tom Seaver	2.00	1.00	.20
☐ 50	Bobby Grich	.30	.15	.03
☐ 51	Jon Matlack	.20	.10	.02
☐ 52	Jack Clark	.80	.40	.08
☐ 53	Jim Rice	1.50	.75	.15
☐ 54	Rickey Henderson	2.00	1.00	.20
☐ 55	Roy Smalley	.20	.10	.02
☐ 56	Mike Flanagan	.30	.15	.03
☐ 57	Steve Rogers	.20	.10	.02
☐ 58	Carlton Fisk	.50	.25	.05
☐ 59	Don Sutton	.75	.35	.07
☐ 60	Ken Griffey	.30	.15	.03
☐ 61	Burt Hooton	.20	.10	.02
☐ 62	Dusty Baker	.30	.15	.03
☐ 63	Vida Blue	.30	.15	.03
☐ 64	Al Oliver	.40	.20	.04
☐ 65	Jim Bibby	.20	.10	.02
☐ 66	Tony Perez	.75	.35	.07
☐ 67	Davy Lopes	.30	.15	.03
☐ 68	Bill Russell	.20	.10	.02
☐ 69	Larry Parrish	.30	.15	.03
☐ 70	Garry Maddox	.20	.10	.02
☐ 71	Phil Garner	.20	.10	.02
☐ 72	Graig Nettles	.50	.25	.05
☐ 73	Gary Carter	2.00	1.00	.20
☐ 74	Pete Rose	5.00	2.50	.50
☐ 75	Greg Luzinski	.40	.20	.04
☐ 76	Ron Guidry	.60	.30	.06
☐ 77	Gorman Thomas	.30	.15	.03
☐ 78	Jose Cruz	.30	.15	.03
☐ 79	Bob Boone	.30	.15	.03
☐ 80	Bruce Sutter	.40	.20	.04
☐ 81	Chris Chambliss	.30	.15	.03
☐ 82	Paul Molitor	.75	.35	.07
☐ 83	Tug McGraw	.30	.15	.03
☐ 84	Ferguson Jenkins	.50	.25	.05
☐ 85	Steve Carlton	1.75	.85	.17
☐ 86	Miguel Dilone	.20	.10	.02
☐ 87	Reggie Smith	.30	.15	.03
☐ 88	Rick Cerone	.20	.10	.02
☐ 89	Alan Trammell	1.00	.50	.10
☐ 90	Doug DeCinces	.30	.15	.03
☐ 91	Sparky Lyle	.30	.15	.03
☐ 92	Warren Cromartie	.20	.10	.02
☐ 93	Rick Reuschel	.30	.15	.03
☐ 94	Larry Hisle	.20	.10	.02
☐ 95	Paul Splittorff	.30	.15	.03
☐ 96	Manny Trillo	.20	.10	.02
☐ 97	Frank White	.30	.15	.03
☐ 98	Fred Lynn	.60	.30	.06
☐ 99	Bob Horner	.60	.30	.06
☐ 100	Omar Moreno	.20	.10	.02
☐ 101	Dave Concepcion	.30	.15	.03
☐ 102	Larry Gura	.30	.15	.03
☐ 103	Ken Singleton	.30	.15	.03

			MINT	EXC	G-VG
☐	104	Steve Stone	.20	.10	.02
☐	105	Richie Zisk	.20	.10	.02
☐	106	Willie Wilson	.40	.20	.04
☐	107	Willie Randolph	.40	.20	.04
☐	108	Nolan Ryan	2.00	1.00	.20
☐	109	Joe Morgan	1.00	.50	.10
☐	110	Bucky Dent	.30	.15	.03
☐	111	Dave Kingman	.40	.20	.04
☐	112	John Castino	.20	.10	.02
☐	113	Joe Rudi	.20	.10	.02
☐	114	Ed Farmer	.20	.10	.02
☐	115	Reggie Jackson	2.50	1.25	.25
☐	116	George Brett	2.50	1.25	.25
☐	117	Eddie Murray	2.50	1.25	.25
☐	118	Rich Gossage	.60	.30	.06
☐	119	Dale Murphy	3.00	1.50	.30
☐	120	Ted Simmons	.30	.15	.03
☐	121	Tommy John	.60	.30	.06
☐	122	Don Baylor	.50	.25	.05
☐	123	Andre Dawson	1.50	.75	.15
☐	124	Jim Palmer	1.25	.60	.12
☐	125	Garry Templeton	.30	.15	.03
☐	126	CL 1: Reggie Jackson	1.25	.60	.12
☐	127	CL 2: George Brett	1.25	.60	.12
☐	128	CL 3: Mike Schmidt	1.25	.60	.12

1982 Fleer

Rod Carew
ANGELS • FIRST BASE

The cards in this 660-card set measure 2 1/2" by 3 1/2". The 1982 Fleer set is again ordered by teams; in fact the players within each team are listed in alphabetical order. The teams are ordered (by 1981 standings) as follows: Los Angeles (1- 29), New York Yankees (30-56), Cincinnati (57-84), Oakland (85-109), St. Louis (110-132), Milwaukee (133-156), Baltimore (157- 182), Montreal (183-211), Houston (212-237), Philadelphia (238- 262), Detroit (263-286), Boston (287-312), Texas (313-334), Chicago White Sox (335-358), Cleveland (359-382), San Francisco (383-403), Kansas City (404-427), Atlanta (428-449), California (450-474), Pittsburgh (475-501), Seattle (502-519), New York Mets (520-544), Minnesota (545-565), San Diego (566-585), Chicago Cubs (586-607), and Toronto (608-627). Cards numbered 628 through 646 are special cards highlighting some of the stars and leaders of the 1981 season. The last 14 cards in the set (647-660) are checklist cards. The backs feature player statistics and a full color team logo in the upper right-hand corner of each card.

	MINT	EXC	G-VG
COMPLETE SET	25.00	12.50	2.50
COMMON PLAYER (1-660)	.03	.01	.00

☐	1	Dusty Baker	.12	.03	.01
☐	2	Robert Castillo	.03	.01	.00
☐	3	Ron Cey	.10	.05	.01
☐	4	Terry Forster	.06	.03	.00
☐	5	Steve Garvey	.45	.22	.04
☐	6	Dave Goltz	.03	.01	.00
☐	7	Pedro Guerrero	.35	.17	.03
☐	8	Burt Hooton	.03	.01	.00
☐	9	Steve Howe	.06	.03	.00

☐	10	Jay Johnstone	.06	.03	.00
☐	11	Ken Landreaux	.06	.03	.00
☐	12	Davey Lopes	.08	.04	.01
☐	13	Mike Marshall	1.25	.60	.12
☐	14	Bobby Mitchell	.06	.03	.00
☐	15	Rick Monday	.06	.03	.00
☐	16	Tom Niedenfuer	.30	.15	.03
☐	17	Ted Power	.30	.15	.03
☐	18	Jerry Reuss	.06	.03	.00
☐	19	Ron Roenicke	.06	.03	.00
☐	20	Bill Russell	.06	.03	.00
☐	21	Steve Sax	1.25	.60	.12
☐	22	Mike Scioscia	.06	.03	.00
☐	23	Reggie Smith	.08	.04	.01
☐	24	Dave Stewart	.50	.25	.05
☐	25	Rick Sutcliffe	.20	.10	.02
☐	26	Derrel Thomas	.03	.01	.00
☐	27	Fernando Valenzuela	.50	.25	.05
☐	28	Bob Welch	.10	.05	.01
☐	29	Steve Yeager	.03	.01	.00
☐	30	Bobby Brown	.03	.01	.00
☐	31	Rick Cerone	.03	.01	.00
☐	32	Ron Davis	.03	.01	.00
☐	33	Bucky Dent	.08	.04	.01
☐	34	Barry Foote	.03	.01	.00
☐	35	George Frazier	.03	.01	.00
☐	36	Oscar Gamble	.06	.03	.00
☐	37	Rich Gossage	.20	.10	.02
☐	38	Ron Guidry	.20	.10	.02
☐	39	Reggie Jackson	.50	.25	.05
☐	40	Tommy John	.15	.07	.01
☐	41	Rudy May	.03	.01	.00
☐	42	Larry Milbourne	.03	.01	.00
☐	43	Jerry Mumphrey	.06	.03	.00
☐	44	Bobby Murcer	.10	.05	.01
☐	45	Gene Nelson	.20	.10	.02
☐	46	Graig Nettles	.15	.07	.01
☐	47	Johnny Oates	.03	.01	.00
☐	48	Lou Piniella	.10	.05	.01
☐	49	Willie Randolph	.08	.04	.01
☐	50	Rick Reuschel	.08	.04	.01
☐	51	Dave Revering	.03	.01	.00
☐	52	Dave Righetti	1.50	.75	.15
☐	53	Aurelio Rodriguez	.03	.01	.00
☐	54	Bob Watson	.06	.03	.00
☐	55	Dennis Werth	.03	.01	.00
☐	56	Dave Winfield	.45	.22	.04
☐	57	Johnny Bench	.45	.22	.04
☐	58	Bruce Berenyi	.03	.01	.00
☐	59	Larry Biittner	.03	.01	.00
☐	60	Scott Brown	.03	.01	.00
☐	61	Dave Collins	.06	.03	.00
☐	62	Geoff Combe	.03	.01	.00
☐	63	Dave Concepcion	.10	.05	.01
☐	64	Dan Driessen	.06	.03	.00
☐	65	Joe Edelen	.03	.01	.00
☐	66	George Foster	.15	.07	.01
☐	67	Ken Griffey	.08	.04	.01
☐	68	Paul Householder	.03	.01	.00
☐	69	Tom Hume	.03	.01	.00
☐	70	Junior Kennedy	.03	.01	.00
☐	71	Ray Knight	.10	.05	.01
☐	72	Mike LaCoss	.03	.01	.00
☐	73	Rafael Landestoy	.03	.01	.00
☐	74	Charlie Leibrandt	.08	.04	.01
☐	75	Sam Mejias	.03	.01	.00
☐	76	Paul Moskau	.03	.01	.00
☐	77	Joe Nolan	.03	.01	.00
☐	78	Mike O'Berry	.03	.01	.00
☐	79	Ron Oester	.06	.03	.00
☐	80	Frank Pastore	.03	.01	.00
☐	81	Joe Price	.03	.01	.00
☐	82	Tom Seaver	.40	.20	.04
☐	83	Mario Soto	.08	.04	.01
☐	84	Mike Vail	.03	.01	.00
☐	85	Tony Armas	.10	.05	.01
☐	86	Shooty Babitt	.03	.01	.00
☐	87	Dave Beard	.03	.01	.00
☐	88	Rick Bosetti	.03	.01	.00
☐	89	Keith Drumright	.03	.01	.00
☐	90	Wayne Gross	.03	.01	.00
☐	91	Mike Heath	.03	.01	.00
☐	92	Rickey Henderson	.50	.25	.05
☐	93	Cliff Johnson	.03	.01	.00
☐	94	Jeff Jones	.03	.01	.00
☐	95	Matt Keough	.03	.01	.00
☐	96	Brian Kingman	.03	.01	.00
☐	97	Mickey Klutts	.03	.01	.00
☐	98	Rick Langford	.03	.01	.00
☐	99	Steve McCatty	.03	.01	.00
☐	100	Dave McKay	.03	.01	.00
☐	101	Dwayne Murphy	.06	.03	.00
☐	102	Jeff Newman	.03	.01	.00
☐	103	Mike Norris	.06	.03	.00
☐	104	Bob Owchinko	.03	.01	.00

☐ 105	Mitchell Page	.03	.01	.00
☐ 106	Rob Picciolo	.03	.01	.00
☐ 107	Jim Spencer	.03	.01	.00
☐ 108	Fred Stanley	.03	.01	.00
☐ 109	Tom Underwood	.03	.01	.00
☐ 110	Joaquin Andujar	.12	.06	.01
☐ 111	Steve Braun	.03	.01	.00
☐ 112	Bob Forsch	.06	.03	.00
☐ 113	George Hendrick	.08	.04	.01
☐ 114	Keith Hernandez	.30	.15	.03
☐ 115	Tom Herr	.08	.04	.01
☐ 116	Dane Iorg	.03	.01	.00
☐ 117	Jim Kaat	.15	.07	.01
☐ 118	Tito Landrum	.03	.01	.00
☐ 119	Sixto Lezcano	.03	.01	.00
☐ 120	Mark Littell	.03	.01	.00
☐ 121	John Martin	.03	.01	.00
☐ 122	Silvio Martinez	.03	.01	.00
☐ 123	Ken Oberkfell	.03	.01	.00
☐ 124	Darrell Porter	.06	.03	.00
☐ 125	Mike Ramsey	.03	.01	.00
☐ 126	Orlando Sanchez	.03	.01	.00
☐ 127	Bob Shirley	.03	.01	.00
☐ 128	Lary Sorensen	.03	.01	.00
☐ 129	Bruce Sutter	.18	.09	.01
☐ 130	Bob Sykes	.03	.01	.00
☐ 131	Garry Templeton	.08	.04	.01
☐ 132	Gene Tenace	.06	.03	.00
☐ 133	Jerry Augustine	.03	.01	.00
☐ 134	Sal Bando	.06	.03	.00
☐ 135	Mark Brouhard	.03	.01	.00
☐ 136	Mike Caldwell	.06	.03	.00
☐ 137	Reggie Cleveland	.03	.01	.00
☐ 138	Cecil Cooper	.15	.07	.01
☐ 139	Jamie Easterly	.03	.01	.00
☐ 140	Marshall Edwards	.03	.01	.00
☐ 141	Rollie Fingers	.20	.10	.02
☐ 142	Jim Gantner	.03	.01	.00
☐ 143	Moose Haas	.06	.03	.00
☐ 144	Larry Hisle	.06	.03	.00
☐ 145	Roy Howell	.03	.01	.00
☐ 146	Rickey Keeton	.03	.01	.00
☐ 147	Randy Lerch	.03	.01	.00
☐ 148	Paul Molitor	.20	.10	.02
☐ 149	Don Money	.03	.01	.00
☐ 150	Charlie Moore	.03	.01	.00
☐ 151	Ben Oglivie	.06	.03	.00
☐ 152	Ted Simmons	.12	.06	.01
☐ 153	Jim Slaton	.06	.03	.00
☐ 154	Gorman Thomas	.10	.05	.01
☐ 155	Robin Yount	.50	.25	.05
☐ 156	Pete Vuckovich	.10	.05	.01
☐ 157	Benny Ayala	.03	.01	.00
☐ 158	Mark Belanger	.06	.03	.00
☐ 159	Al Bumbry	.03	.01	.00
☐ 160	Terry Crowley	.03	.01	.00
☐ 161	Rich Dauer	.03	.01	.00
☐ 162	Doug DeCinces	.10	.05	.01
☐ 163	Rick Dempsey	.06	.03	.00
☐ 164	Jim Dwyer	.03	.01	.00
☐ 165	Mike Flanagan	.08	.04	.01
☐ 166	Dave Ford	.03	.01	.00
☐ 167	Dan Graham	.03	.01	.00
☐ 168	Wayne Krenchicki	.03	.01	.00
☐ 169	John Lowenstein	.03	.01	.00
☐ 170	Dennis Martinez	.06	.03	.00
☐ 171	Tippy Martinez	.03	.01	.00
☐ 172	Scott McGregor	.08	.04	.01
☐ 173	Jose Morales	.03	.01	.00
☐ 174	Eddie Murray	.60	.30	.06
☐ 175	Jim Palmer	.30	.15	.03
☐ 176	Cal Ripken	7.50	3.75	.75
☐ 177	Gary Roenicke	.06	.03	.00
☐ 178	Lenn Sakata	.03	.01	.00
☐ 179	Ken Singleton	.10	.05	.01
☐ 180	Sammy Stewart	.03	.01	.00
☐ 181	Tim Stoddard	.03	.01	.00
☐ 182	Steve Stone	.06	.03	.00
☐ 183	Stan Bahnsen	.03	.01	.00
☐ 184	Ray Burris	.03	.01	.00
☐ 185	Gary Carter	.50	.25	.05
☐ 186	Warren Cromartie	.03	.01	.00
☐ 187	Andre Dawson	.35	.17	.03
☐ 188	Terry Francona	.20	.10	.02
☐ 189	Woodie Fryman	.03	.01	.00
☐ 190	Bill Gullickson	.06	.03	.00
☐ 191	Grant Jackson	.03	.01	.00
☐ 192	Wallace Johnson	.06	.03	.00
☐ 193	Charlie Lea	.06	.03	.00
☐ 194	Bill Lee	.06	.03	.00
☐ 195	Jerry Manuel	.03	.01	.00
☐ 196	Brad Mills	.06	.03	.00
☐ 197	John Milner	.03	.01	.00
☐ 198	Rowland Office	.03	.01	.00
☐ 199	David Palmer	.06	.03	.00
☐ 200	Larry Parrish	.08	.04	.01
☐ 201	Mike Phillips	.03	.01	.00
☐ 202	Tim Raines	.90	.45	.09
☐ 203	Bobby Ramos	.03	.01	.00
☐ 204	Jeff Reardon	.20	.10	.02
☐ 205	Steve Rogers	.08	.04	.01
☐ 206	Scott Sanderson	.06	.03	.00
☐ 207	Rodney Scott (photo actually Tim Raines)	.15	.07	.01
☐ 208	Elias Sosa	.03	.01	.00
☐ 209	Chris Speier	.03	.01	.00
☐ 210	Tim Wallach	1.50	.75	.15
☐ 211	Jerry White	.03	.01	.00
☐ 212	Alan Ashby	.03	.01	.00
☐ 213	Cesar Cedeno	.08	.04	.01
☐ 214	Jose Cruz	.12	.06	.01
☐ 215	Kiko Garcia	.03	.01	.00
☐ 216	Phil Garner	.06	.03	.00
☐ 217	Danny Heep	.03	.01	.00
☐ 218	Art Howe	.03	.01	.00
☐ 219	Bob Knepper	.10	.05	.01
☐ 220	Frank LaCorte	.03	.01	.00
☐ 221	Joe Niekro	.10	.05	.01
☐ 222	Joe Pittman	.03	.01	.00
☐ 223	Terry Puhl	.06	.03	.00
☐ 224	Luis Pujols	.03	.01	.00
☐ 225	Craig Reynolds	.03	.01	.00
☐ 226	J.R. Richard	.10	.05	.01
☐ 227	Dave Roberts	.03	.01	.00
☐ 228	Vern Ruhle	.03	.01	.00
☐ 229	Nolan Ryan	.50	.25	.05
☐ 230	Joe Sambito	.06	.03	.00
☐ 231	Tony Scott	.03	.01	.00
☐ 232	Dave Smith	.08	.04	.01
☐ 233	Harry Spilman	.03	.01	.00
☐ 234	Don Sutton	.30	.15	.03
☐ 235	Dickie Thon	.08	.04	.01
☐ 236	Denny Walling	.03	.01	.00
☐ 237	Gary Woods	.03	.01	.00
☐ 238	Luis Aguayo	.03	.01	.00
☐ 239	Ramon Aviles	.03	.01	.00
☐ 240	Bob Boone	.08	.04	.01
☐ 241	Larry Bowa	.15	.07	.01
☐ 242	Warren Brusstar	.03	.01	.00
☐ 243	Steve Carlton	.50	.25	.05
☐ 244	Larry Christenson	.03	.01	.00
☐ 245	Dick Davis	.03	.01	.00
☐ 246	Greg Gross	.03	.01	.00
☐ 247	Sparky Lyle	.12	.06	.01
☐ 248	Garry Maddox	.06	.03	.00
☐ 249	Gary Matthews	.08	.04	.01
☐ 250	Bake McBride	.06	.03	.00
☐ 251	Tug McGraw	.10	.05	.01
☐ 252	Keith Moreland	.10	.05	.01
☐ 253	Dickie Noles	.03	.01	.00
☐ 254	Mike Proly	.03	.01	.00
☐ 255	Ron Reed	.03	.01	.00
☐ 256	Pete Rose	1.25	.60	.12
☐ 257	Dick Ruthven	.03	.01	.00
☐ 258	Mike Schmidt	.75	.35	.07
☐ 259	Lonnie Smith	.08	.04	.01
☐ 260	Manny Trillo	.06	.03	.00
☐ 261	Del Unser	.03	.01	.00
☐ 262	George Vukovich	.03	.01	.00
☐ 263	Tom Brookens	.03	.01	.00
☐ 264	George Cappuzzello	.03	.01	.00
☐ 265	Marty Castillo	.06	.03	.00
☐ 266	Al Cowens	.03	.01	.00
☐ 267	Kirk Gibson	.40	.20	.04
☐ 268	Richie Hebner	.03	.01	.00
☐ 269	Ron Jackson	.03	.01	.00
☐ 270	Lynn Jones	.03	.01	.00
☐ 271	Steve Kemp	.08	.04	.01
☐ 272	Rick Leach	.06	.03	.00
☐ 273	Aurelio Lopez	.03	.01	.00
☐ 274	Jack Morris	.30	.15	.03
☐ 275	Kevin Saucier	.03	.01	.00
☐ 276	Lance Parrish	.30	.15	.03
☐ 277	Rick Peters	.03	.01	.00
☐ 278	Dan Petry	.10	.05	.01
☐ 279	David Rozema	.03	.01	.00
☐ 280	Stan Papi	.03	.01	.00
☐ 281	Dan Schatzeder	.03	.01	.00
☐ 282	Champ Summers	.03	.01	.00
☐ 283	Alan Trammell	.30	.15	.03
☐ 284	Lou Whitaker	.18	.09	.01
☐ 285	Milt Wilcox	.03	.01	.00
☐ 286	John Wockenfuss	.03	.01	.00
☐ 287	Gary Allenson	.03	.01	.00
☐ 288	Tom Burgmeier	.03	.01	.00
☐ 289	Bill Campbell	.03	.01	.00
☐ 290	Mark Clear	.03	.01	.00
☐ 291	Steve Crawford	.06	.03	.00
☐ 292	Dennis Eckersley	.06	.03	.00

☐ 293	Dwight Evans	.18	.09	.01	☐ 388	Darrell Evans	.15	.07	.01
☐ 294	Rich Gedman	.55	.27	.05	☐ 389	Tom Griffin	.03	.01	.00
☐ 295	Garry Hancock	.03	.01	.00	☐ 390	Larry Herndon	.06	.03	.00
☐ 296	Glenn Hoffman	.03	.01	.00	☐ 391	Al Holland	.06	.03	.00
☐ 297	Bruce Hurst	.30	.15	.03	☐ 392	Gary Lavelle	.06	.03	.00
☐ 298	Carney Lansford	.12	.06	.01	☐ 393	Johnnie LeMaster	.03	.01	.00
☐ 299	Rick Miller	.03	.01	.00	☐ 394	Jerry Martin	.03	.01	.00
☐ 300	Reid Nichols	.03	.01	.00	☐ 395	Milt May	.03	.01	.00
☐ 301	Bob Ojeda	.55	.27	.05	☐ 396	Greg Minton	.06	.03	.00
☐ 302	Tony Perez	.15	.07	.01	☐ 397	Joe Morgan	.25	.12	.02
☐ 303	Chuck Rainey	.03	.01	.00	☐ 398	Joe Pettini	.03	.01	.00
☐ 304	Jerry Remy	.03	.01	.00	☐ 399	Alan Ripley	.03	.01	.00
☐ 305	Jim Rice	.45	.22	.04	☐ 400	Billy Smith	.03	.01	.00
☐ 306	Joe Rudi	.06	.03	.00	☐ 401	Rennie Stennett	.03	.01	.00
☐ 307	Bob Stanley	.06	.03	.00	☐ 402	Ed Whitson	.06	.03	.00
☐ 308	Dave Stapleton	.03	.01	.00	☐ 403	Jim Wohlford	.03	.01	.00
☐ 309	Frank Tanana	.06	.03	.00	☐ 404	Willie Aikens	.06	.03	.00
☐ 310	Mike Torrez	.06	.03	.00	☐ 405	George Brett	.70	.35	.07
☐ 311	John Tudor	.20	.10	.02	☐ 406	Ken Brett	.03	.01	.00
☐ 312	Carl Yastrzemski	.75	.35	.07	☐ 407	Dave Chalk	.03	.01	.00
☐ 313	Buddy Bell	.15	.07	.01	☐ 408	Rich Gale	.03	.01	.00
☐ 314	Steve Comer	.03	.01	.00	☐ 409	Cesar Geronimo	.03	.01	.00
☐ 315	Danny Darwin	.06	.03	.00	☐ 410	Larry Gura	.06	.03	.00
☐ 316	John Ellis	.03	.01	.00	☐ 411	Clint Hurdle	.03	.01	.00
☐ 317	John Grubb	.03	.01	.00	☐ 412	Mike Jones	.03	.01	.00
☐ 318	Rick Honeycutt	.06	.03	.00	☐ 413	Dennis Leonard	.06	.03	.00
☐ 319	Charlie Hough	.08	.04	.01	☐ 414	Renie Martin	.03	.01	.00
☐ 320	Ferguson Jenkins	.15	.07	.01	☐ 415	Lee May	.06	.03	.00
☐ 321	John Henry Johnson	.03	.01	.00	☐ 416	Hal McRae	.06	.03	.00
☐ 322	Jim Kern	.03	.01	.00	☐ 417	Darryl Motley	.10	.05	.01
☐ 323	Jon Matlack	.06	.03	.00	☐ 418	Rance Mulliniks	.03	.01	.00
☐ 324	Doc Medich	.03	.01	.00	☐ 419	Amos Otis	.08	.04	.01
☐ 325	Mario Mendoza	.03	.01	.00	☐ 420	Ken Phelps	.60	.30	.06
☐ 326	Al Oliver	.12	.06	.01	☐ 421	Jamie Quirk	.03	.01	.00
☐ 327	Pat Putnam	.03	.01	.00	☐ 422	Dan Quisenberry	.18	.09	.01
☐ 328	Mickey Rivers	.06	.03	.00	☐ 423	Paul Splittorff	.06	.03	.00
☐ 329	Leon Roberts	.03	.01	.00	☐ 424	U.L. Washington	.03	.01	.00
☐ 330	Billy Sample	.03	.01	.00	☐ 425	John Wathan	.06	.03	.00
☐ 331	Bill Stein	.03	.01	.00	☐ 426	Frank White	.08	.04	.01
☐ 332	Jim Sundberg	.06	.03	.00	☐ 427	Willie Wilson	.15	.07	.01
☐ 333	Mark Wagner	.03	.01	.00	☐ 428	Brian Asselstine	.03	.01	.00
☐ 334	Bump Wills	.03	.01	.00	☐ 429	Bruce Benedict	.03	.01	.00
☐ 335	Bill Almon	.03	.01	.00	☐ 430	Tommy Boggs	.03	.01	.00
☐ 336	Harold Baines	.35	.17	.03	☐ 431	Larry Bradford	.03	.01	.00
☐ 337	Ross Baumgarten	.03	.01	.00	☐ 432	Rick Camp	.03	.01	.00
☐ 338	Tony Bernazard	.06	.03	.00	☐ 433	Chris Chambliss	.06	.03	.00
☐ 339	Britt Burns	.08	.04	.01	☐ 434	Gene Garber	.06	.03	.00
☐ 340	Richard Dotson	.10	.05	.01	☐ 435	Preston Hanna	.03	.01	.00
☐ 341	Jim Essian	.03	.01	.00	☐ 436	Bob Horner	.25	.12	.02
☐ 342	Ed Farmer	.03	.01	.00	☐ 437	Glenn Hubbard	.03	.01	.00
☐ 343	Carlton Fisk	.18	.09	.01	☐ 438A	All Hrabosky	15.00	7.50	1.50
☐ 344	Kevin Hickey	.06	.03	.00		(height 5'1")			
☐ 345	LaMarr Hoyt	.08	.04	.01	☐ 438B	Al Hrabosky	1.00	.50	.10
☐ 346	Lamar Johnson	.03	.01	.00		(height 5'1")			
☐ 347	Jerry Koosman	.08	.04	.01	☐ 438C	Al Hrabosky	.10	.05	.01
☐ 348	Rusty Kuntz	.03	.01	.00		(height 5'10")			
☐ 349	Dennis Lamp	.03	.01	.00	☐ 439	Rufino Linares	.05	.02	.00
☐ 350	Ron LeFlore	.06	.03	.00	☐ 440	Rick Mahler	.20	.10	.02
☐ 351	Chet Lemon	.08	.04	.01	☐ 441	Ed Miller	.03	.01	.00
☐ 352	Greg Luzinski	.12	.06	.01	☐ 442	John Montefusco	.06	.03	.00
☐ 353	Bob Molinaro	.03	.01	.00	☐ 443	Dale Murphy	.90	.45	.09
☐ 354	Jim Morrison	.03	.01	.00	☐ 444	Phil Niekro	.25	.12	.02
☐ 355	Wayne Nordhagen	.03	.01	.00	☐ 445	Gaylord Perry	.25	.12	.02
☐ 356	Greg Pryor	.03	.01	.00	☐ 446	Biff Pocoroba	.03	.01	.00
☐ 357	Mike Squires	.03	.01	.00	☐ 447	Rafael Ramirez	.06	.03	.00
☐ 358	Steve Trout	.06	.03	.00	☐ 448	Jerry Royster	.03	.01	.00
☐ 359	Alan Bannister	.03	.01	.00	☐ 449	Claudell Washington	.08	.04	.01
☐ 360	Len Barker	.06	.03	.00	☐ 450	Don Aase	.06	.03	.00
☐ 361	Bert Blyleven	.12	.06	.01	☐ 451	Don Baylor	.15	.07	.01
☐ 362	Joe Charboneau	.06	.03	.00	☐ 452	Juan Beniquez	.06	.03	.00
☐ 363	John Denny	.08	.04	.01	☐ 453	Rick Burleson	.06	.03	.00
☐ 364	Bo Diaz	.08	.04	.01	☐ 454	Bert Campaneris	.08	.04	.01
☐ 365	Miguel Dilone	.03	.01	.00	☐ 455	Rod Carew	.50	.25	.05
☐ 366	Jerry Dybzinski	.03	.01	.00	☐ 456	Bob Clark	.03	.01	.00
☐ 367	Wayne Garland	.03	.01	.00	☐ 457	Brian Downing	.06	.03	.00
☐ 368	Mike Hargrove	.06	.03	.00	☐ 458	Dan Ford	.03	.01	.00
☐ 369	Toby Harrah	.06	.03	.00	☐ 459	Ken Forsch	.03	.01	.00
☐ 370	Ron Hassey	.03	.01	.00	☐ 460A	Dave Frost (5 mm space before ERA)	.40	.20	.04
☐ 371	Von Hayes	1.00	.50	.10	☐ 460B	Dave Frost (1 mm space)	.05	.02	.00
☐ 372	Pat Kelly	.03	.01	.00	☐ 461	Bobby Grich	.08	.04	.01
☐ 373	Duane Kuiper	.03	.01	.00	☐ 462	Larry Harlow	.03	.01	.00
☐ 374	Rick Manning	.03	.01	.00	☐ 463	John Harris	.03	.01	.00
☐ 375	Sid Monge	.03	.01	.00	☐ 464	Andy Hassler	.03	.01	.00
☐ 376	Jorge Orta	.03	.01	.00	☐ 465	Butch Hobson	.03	.01	.00
☐ 377	Dave Rosello	.03	.01	.00	☐ 466	Jesse Jefferson	.03	.01	.00
☐ 378	Dan Spillner	.03	.01	.00	☐ 467	Bruce Kison	.03	.01	.00
☐ 379	Mike Stanton	.03	.01	.00	☐ 468	Fred Lynn	.20	.10	.02
☐ 380	Andre Thornton	.08	.04	.01	☐ 469	Angel Moreno	.03	.01	.00
☐ 381	Tom Veryzer	.03	.01	.00	☐ 470	Ed Ott	.03	.01	.00
☐ 382	Rick Waits	.03	.01	.00	☐ 471	Fred Patek	.03	.01	.00
☐ 383	Doyle Alexander	.06	.03	.00	☐ 472	Steve Renko	.03	.01	.00
☐ 384	Vida Blue	.08	.04	.01	☐ 473	Mike Witt	1.00	.50	.10
☐ 385	Fred Breining	.06	.03	.00	☐ 474	Geoff Zahn	.03	.01	.00
☐ 386	Enos Cabell	.03	.01	.00					
☐ 387	Jack Clark	.25	.12	.02					

☐ 475	Gary Alexander	.03	.01	.00
☐ 476	Dale Berra	.06	.03	.00
☐ 477	Kurt Bevacqua	.03	.01	.00
☐ 478	Jim Bibby	.06	.03	.00
☐ 479	John Candelaria	.08	.04	.01
☐ 480	Victor Cruz	.03	.01	.00
☐ 481	Mike Easler	.06	.03	.00
☐ 482	Tim Foli	.03	.01	.00
☐ 483	Lee Lacy	.06	.03	.00
☐ 484	Vance Law	.03	.01	.00
☐ 485	Bill Madlock	.12	.06	.01
☐ 486	Willie Montanez	.03	.01	.00
☐ 487	Omar Moreno	.03	.01	.00
☐ 488	Steve Nicosia	.03	.01	.00
☐ 489	Dave Parker	.25	.12	.02
☐ 490	Tony Pena	.15	.07	.01
☐ 491	Pascual Perez	.06	.03	.00
☐ 492	Johnny Ray	.75	.35	.07
☐ 493	Rick Rhoden	.08	.04	.01
☐ 494	Bill Robinson	.06	.03	.00
☐ 495	Don Robinson	.06	.03	.00
☐ 496	Enrique Romo	.03	.01	.00
☐ 497	Rod Scurry	.03	.01	.00
☐ 498	Eddie Solomon	.03	.01	.00
☐ 499	Willie Stargell	.25	.12	.02
☐ 500	Kent Tekulve	.08	.04	.01
☐ 501	Jason Thompson	.06	.03	.00
☐ 502	Glenn Abbott	.03	.01	.00
☐ 503	Jim Anderson	.03	.01	.00
☐ 504	Floyd Bannister	.08	.04	.01
☐ 505	Bruce Bochte	.06	.03	.00
☐ 506	Jeff Burroughs	.06	.03	.00
☐ 507	Bryan Clark	.03	.01	.00
☐ 508	Ken Clay	.03	.01	.00
☐ 509	Julio Cruz	.03	.01	.00
☐ 510	Dick Drago	.03	.01	.00
☐ 511	Gary Gray	.03	.01	.00
☐ 512	Dan Meyer	.03	.01	.00
☐ 513	Jerry Narron	.03	.01	.00
☐ 514	Tom Paciorek	.03	.01	.00
☐ 515	Casey Parsons	.03	.01	.00
☐ 516	Lenny Randle	.03	.01	.00
☐ 517	Shane Rawley	.10	.05	.01
☐ 518	Joe Simpson	.03	.01	.00
☐ 519	Richie Zisk	.06	.03	.00
☐ 520	Neil Allen	.06	.03	.00
☐ 521	Bob Bailor	.03	.01	.00
☐ 522	Hubie Brooks	.20	.10	.02
☐ 523	Mike Cubbage	.03	.01	.00
☐ 524	Pete Falcone	.03	.01	.00
☐ 525	Doug Flynn	.03	.01	.00
☐ 526	Tom Hausman	.03	.01	.00
☐ 527	Ron Hodges	.03	.01	.00
☐ 528	Randy Jones	.06	.03	.00
☐ 529	Mike Jorgensen	.03	.01	.00
☐ 530	Dave Kingman	.15	.07	.01
☐ 531	Ed Lynch	.10	.05	.01
☐ 532	Mike Marshall (screwball pitcher)	.06	.03	.00
☐ 533	Lee Mazzilli	.06	.03	.00
☐ 534	Dyar Miller	.03	.01	.00
☐ 535	Mike Scott	.30	.15	.03
☐ 536	Rusty Staub	.10	.05	.01
☐ 537	John Stearns	.03	.01	.00
☐ 538	Craig Swan	.03	.01	.00
☐ 539	Frank Taveras	.03	.01	.00
☐ 540	Alex Trevino	.03	.01	.00
☐ 541	Ellis Valentine	.03	.01	.00
☐ 542	Mookie Wilson	.08	.04	.01
☐ 543	Joel Youngblood	.03	.01	.00
☐ 544	Pat Zachry	.03	.01	.00
☐ 545	Glenn Adams	.03	.01	.00
☐ 546	Fernando Arroyo	.03	.01	.00
☐ 547	John Verhoeven	.03	.01	.00
☐ 548	Sal Butera	.03	.01	.00
☐ 549	John Castino	.03	.01	.00
☐ 550	Don Cooper	.03	.01	.00
☐ 551	Doug Corbett	.03	.01	.00
☐ 552	Dave Engle	.03	.01	.00
☐ 553	Roger Erickson	.03	.01	.00
☐ 554	Danny Goodwin	.03	.01	.00
☐ 555A	Darrell Jackson (black hat)	1.00	.50	.10
☐ 555B	Darrell Jackson (red hat)	.08	.04	.01
☐ 556	Pete Mackanin	.03	.01	.00
☐ 557	Jack O'Connor	.03	.01	.00
☐ 558	Hosken Powell	.03	.01	.00
☐ 559	Pete Redfern	.03	.01	.00
☐ 560	Roy Smalley	.06	.03	.00
☐ 561	Chuck Baker	.03	.01	.00
☐ 562	Gary Ward	.06	.03	.00
☐ 563	Rob Wilfong	.03	.01	.00
☐ 564	Al Williams	.03	.01	.00
☐ 565	Butch Wynegar	.06	.03	.00
☐ 566	Randy Bass	.03	.01	.00
☐ 567	Juan Bonilla	.03	.01	.00
☐ 568	Danny Boone	.03	.01	.00
☐ 569	John Curtis	.03	.01	.00
☐ 570	Juan Eichelberger	.03	.01	.00
☐ 571	Barry Evans	.03	.01	.00
☐ 572	Tim Flannery	.03	.01	.00
☐ 573	Ruppert Jones	.03	.01	.00
☐ 574	Terry Kennedy	.08	.04	.01
☐ 575	Joe Lefebvre	.03	.01	.00
☐ 576A	John Littlefield ERR (left handed)	65.00	32.50	6.50
☐ 576B	John Littlefield COR (right handed)	.08	.04	.01
☐ 577	Gary Lucas	.03	.01	.00
☐ 578	Steve Mura	.03	.01	.00
☐ 579	Broderick Perkins	.03	.01	.00
☐ 580	Gene Richards	.03	.01	.00
☐ 581	Luis Salazar	.03	.01	.00
☐ 582	Ozzie Smith	.25	.12	.02
☐ 583	John Urrea	.03	.01	.00
☐ 584	Chris Welsh	.06	.03	.00
☐ 585	Rick Wise	.06	.03	.00
☐ 586	Doug Bird	.03	.01	.00
☐ 587	Tim Blackwell	.03	.01	.00
☐ 588	Bobby Bonds	.08	.04	.01
☐ 589	Bill Buckner	.12	.06	.01
☐ 590	Bill Caudill	.06	.03	.00
☐ 591	Hector Cruz	.03	.01	.00
☐ 592	Jody Davis	.50	.25	.05
☐ 593	Ivan DeJesus	.03	.01	.00
☐ 594	Steve Dillard	.03	.01	.00
☐ 595	Leon Durham	.15	.07	.01
☐ 596	Rawly Eastwick	.03	.01	.00
☐ 597	Steve Henderson	.03	.01	.00
☐ 598	Mike Krukow	.08	.04	.01
☐ 599	Mike Lum	.03	.01	.00
☐ 600	Randy Martz	.03	.01	.00
☐ 601	Jerry Morales	.03	.01	.00
☐ 602	Ken Reitz	.03	.01	.00
☐ 603A	Lee Smith ERR (Cubs logo reversed)	1.00	.50	.10
☐ 603B	Lee Smith COR	.70	.35	.07
☐ 604	Dick Tidrow	.03	.01	.00
☐ 605	Jim Tracy	.03	.01	.00
☐ 606	Mike Tyson	.03	.01	.00
☐ 607	Ty Waller	.06	.03	.00
☐ 608	Danny Ainge	.10	.05	.01
☐ 609	Jorge Bell	6.50	3.25	.65
☐ 610	Mark Bomback	.03	.01	.00
☐ 611	Barry Bonnell	.03	.01	.00
☐ 612	Jim Clancy	.06	.03	.00
☐ 613	Damaso Garcia	.08	.04	.01
☐ 614	Jerry Garvin	.03	.01	.00
☐ 615	Alfredo Griffin	.08	.04	.01
☐ 616	Garth Iorg	.03	.01	.00
☐ 617	Luis Leal	.03	.01	.00
☐ 618	Ken Macha	.03	.01	.00
☐ 619	John Mayberry	.06	.03	.00
☐ 620	Joey McLaughlin	.03	.01	.00
☐ 621	Lloyd Moseby	.15	.07	.01
☐ 622	Dave Stieb	.15	.07	.01
☐ 623	Jackson Todd	.03	.01	.00
☐ 624	Willie Upshaw	.08	.04	.01
☐ 625	Otto Velez	.03	.01	.00
☐ 626	Ernie Whitt	.06	.03	.00
☐ 627	Al Woods	.03	.01	.00
☐ 628	All Star Game Cleveland, Ohio	.06	.03	.00
☐ 629	All Star Infielders Frank White and Bucky Dent	.06	.03	.00
☐ 630	Big Red Machine Dan Driessen Dave Concepcion George Foster	.08	.04	.01
☐ 631	Bruce Sutter Top NL Relief Pitcher	.10	.05	.01
☐ 632	"Steve and Carlton" Steve Carlton and Carlton Fisk	.20	.10	.02
☐ 633	Carl Yastrzemski 3000th Game	.30	.15	.03
☐ 634	Dynamic Duo Johnny Bench and Tom Seaver	.25	.12	.02
☐ 635	West Meets East Fernando Valenzuela and Gary Carter	.25	.12	.02
☐ 636A	Fernando Valenzuela: NL SO King ("he" NL)	.45	.22	.04
☐ 636B	Fernando Valenzuela: NL SO King ("the" NL)	.25	.12	.02
☐ 637	Mike Schmidt Home Run King	.35	.17	.03

☐ 638	NL All Stars Gary Carter and Dave Parker	.20	.10	.02
☐ 639	Perfect Game Len Barker and Bo Diaz (catcher actually Ron Hassey)	.08	.04	.01
☐ 640	Pete and Re-Pete Pete Rose and Son	1.25	.60	.12
☐ 641	Phillies Finest Lonnie Smith Mike Schmidt Steve Carlton	.30	.15	.03
☐ 642	Red Sox Reunion Fred Lynn and Dwight Evans	.08	.04	.01
☐ 643	Rickey Henderson Most Hits and Runs	.30	.15	.03
☐ 644	Rollie Fingers Most Saves AL	.10	.05	.01
☐ 645	Tom Seaver Most 1981 Wins	.20	.10	.02
☐ 646A	Yankee Powerhouse Reggie Jackson and Dave Winfield (comma on back after outfielder)	.75	.35	.07
☐ 646B	Yankee Powerhouse Reggie Jackson and Dave Winfield (no comma)	.40	.20	.04
☐ 647	CL: Yankees/Dodgers	.08	.01	.00
☐ 648	CL: A's/Reds	.07	.01	.00
☐ 649	CL: Cards/Brewers	.07	.01	.00
☐ 650	CL: Expos/Orioles	.07	.01	.00
☐ 651	CL: Astros/Phillies	.07	.01	.00
☐ 652	CL: Tigers/Red Sox	.07	.01	.00
☐ 653	CL: Rangers/White Sox	.07	.01	.00
☐ 654	CL: Giants/Indians	.07	.01	.00
☐ 655	CL: Royals/Braves	.07	.01	.00
☐ 656	CL: Angels/Pirates	.07	.01	.00
☐ 657	CL: Mariners/Mets	.07	.01	.00
☐ 658	CL: Padres/Twins	.07	.01	.00
☐ 659	CL: Blue Jays/Cubs	.07	.01	.00
☐ 660	Specials Checklist	.10	.01	.00

1983 Fleer

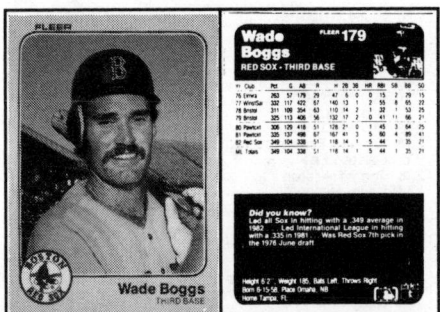

Wade Boggs
THIRD BASE

The cards in this 660-card set measure 2 1/2" by 3 1/2". In 1983, for the third straight year, Fleer has produced a baseball series numbering 660 cards. Of these, 1-628 are player cards, 629-646 are special cards, and 647-660 are checklist cards. The player cards are again ordered alphabetically within team. The team order relates back to each team's on-field performance during the previous year, i.e., World Champion Cardinals (1-25), AL Champion Brewers (26-51), Baltimore (52-75), California (76-103), Kansas City (104-128), Atlanta (129-152), Philadelphia (153-176), Boston (177-200), Los Angeles (201-227), Chicago White Sox (228-251), San Francisco (252-276), Montreal (277-301), Pittsburgh (302-326), Detroit (327-351), San Diego (352-375), New York Yankees (376-399), Cleveland

(400-423), Toronto (424-444), Houston (445-469), Seattle (470-489), Chicago Cubs (490-512), Oakland (513-535), New York Mets (536-561), Texas (562-583), Cincinnati (584-606), and Minnesota (607-628). The front of each card has a colorful team logo at bottom left and the player's name and position at lower right. The reverses are done in shades of brown on white. The cards are numbered on the back next to a small black and white photo of the player.

		MINT	EXC	G-VG
COMPLETE SET		36.00	18.00	3.60
COMMON PLAYER (1-660)		.03	.01	.00
☐ 1	Joaquin Andujar	.15	.04	.01
☐ 2	Doug Bair	.03	.01	.00
☐ 3	Steve Braun	.03	.01	.00
☐ 4	Glenn Brummer	.03	.01	.00
☐ 5	Bob Forsch	.06	.03	.00
☐ 6	David Green	.06	.03	.00
☐ 7	George Hendrick	.06	.03	.00
☐ 8	Keith Hernandez	.30	.15	.03
☐ 9	Tom Herr	.08	.04	.01
☐ 10	Dane Iorg	.03	.01	.00
☐ 11	Jim Kaat	.12	.06	.01
☐ 12	Jeff Lahti	.06	.03	.00
☐ 13	Tito Landrum	.03	.01	.00
☐ 14	Dave LaPoint	.15	.07	.01
☐ 15	Willie McGee	2.00	1.00	.20
☐ 16	Steve Mura	.03	.01	.00
☐ 17	Ken Oberkfell	.03	.01	.00
☐ 18	Darrell Porter	.06	.03	.00
☐ 19	Mike Ramsey	.03	.01	.00
☐ 20	Gene Roof	.06	.03	.00
☐ 21	Lonnie Smith	.08	.04	.01
☐ 22	Ozzie Smith	.25	.12	.02
☐ 23	John Stuper	.06	.03	.00
☐ 24	Bruce Sutter	.15	.07	.01
☐ 25	Gene Tenace	.06	.03	.00
☐ 26	Jerry Augustine	.03	.01	.00
☐ 27	Dwight Bernard	.03	.01	.00
☐ 28	Mark Brouhard	.03	.01	.00
☐ 29	Mike Caldwell	.06	.03	.00
☐ 30	Cecil Cooper	.15	.07	.01
☐ 31	Jamie Easterly	.03	.01	.00
☐ 32	Marshall Edwards	.03	.01	.00
☐ 33	Rollie Fingers	.18	.09	.01
☐ 34	Jim Gantner	.03	.01	.00
☐ 35	Moose Haas	.03	.01	.00
☐ 36	Roy Howell	.03	.01	.00
☐ 37	Peter Ladd	.03	.01	.00
☐ 38	Bob McClure	.03	.01	.00
☐ 39	Doc Medich	.03	.01	.00
☐ 40	Paul Molitor	.18	.09	.01
☐ 41	Don Money	.03	.01	.00
☐ 42	Charlie Moore	.03	.01	.00
☐ 43	Ben Oglivie	.06	.03	.00
☐ 44	Ed Romero	.03	.01	.00
☐ 45	Ted Simmons	.12	.06	.01
☐ 46	Jim Slaton	.03	.01	.00
☐ 47	Don Sutton	.25	.12	.02
☐ 48	Gorman Thomas	.10	.05	.01
☐ 49	Pete Vuckovich	.06	.03	.00
☐ 50	Ned Yost	.03	.01	.00
☐ 51	Robin Yount	.30	.15	.03
☐ 52	Benny Ayala	.03	.01	.00
☐ 53	Bob Bonner	.03	.01	.00
☐ 54	Al Bumbry	.03	.01	.00
☐ 55	Terry Crowley	.03	.01	.00
☐ 56	Storm Davis	.25	.12	.02
☐ 57	Rich Dauer	.03	.01	.00
☐ 58	Rick Dempsey (posing batting lefty)	.06	.03	.00
☐ 59	Jim Dwyer	.03	.01	.00
☐ 60	Mike Flanagan	.08	.04	.01
☐ 61	Dan Ford	.03	.01	.00
☐ 62	Glenn Gulliver	.03	.01	.00
☐ 63	John Lowenstein	.03	.01	.00
☐ 64	Dennis Martinez	.06	.03	.00
☐ 65	Tippy Martinez	.03	.01	.00
☐ 66	Scott McGregor	.08	.04	.01
☐ 67	Eddie Murray	.55	.27	.05
☐ 68	Joe Nolan	.03	.01	.00
☐ 69	Jim Palmer	.30	.15	.03
☐ 70	Cal Ripken Jr.	1.00	.50	.10
☐ 71	Gary Roenicke	.06	.03	.00
☐ 72	Lenn Sakata	.03	.01	.00
☐ 73	Ken Singleton	.08	.04	.01
☐ 74	Sammy Stewart	.03	.01	.00
☐ 75	Tim Stoddard	.03	.01	.00
☐ 76	Don Aase	.06	.03	.00
☐ 77	Don Baylor	.12	.06	.01

☐ 78	Juan Beniquez	.06	.03	.00	☐ 173	Mike Schmidt	.55	.27	.05
☐ 79	Bob Boone	.08	.04	.01	☐ 174	Manny Trillo	.06	.03	.00
☐ 80	Rick Burleson	.06	.03	.00	☐ 175	Ozzie Virgil	.06	.03	.00
☐ 81	Rod Carew	.40	.20	.04	☐ 176	George Vuckovich	.03	.01	.00
☐ 82	Bobby Clark	.03	.01	.00	☐ 177	Gary Allenson	.03	.01	.00
☐ 83	Doug Corbett	.03	.01	.00	☐ 178	Luis Aponte	.06	.03	.00
☐ 84	John Curtis	.03	.01	.00	☐ 179	Wade Boggs	16.00	8.00	1.60
☐ 85	Doug DeCinces	.10	.05	.01	☐ 180	Tom Burgmeier	.03	.01	.00
☐ 86	Brian Downing	.06	.03	.00	☐ 181	Mark Clear	.03	.01	.00
☐ 87	Joe Ferguson	.03	.01	.00	☐ 182	Dennis Eckersley	.06	.03	.00
☐ 88	Tim Foli	.03	.01	.00	☐ 183	Dwight Evans	.15	.07	.01
☐ 89	Ken Forsch	.03	.01	.00	☐ 184	Rich Gedman	.10	.05	.01
☐ 90	Dave Goltz	.03	.01	.00	☐ 185	Glenn Hoffman	.03	.01	.00
☐ 91	Bobby Grich	.08	.04	.01	☐ 186	Bruce Hurst	.12	.06	.01
☐ 92	Andy Hassler	.03	.01	.00	☐ 187	Carney Lansford	.10	.05	.01
☐ 93	Reggie Jackson	.45	.22	.04	☐ 188	Rick Miller	.03	.01	.00
☐ 94	Ron Jackson	.03	.01	.00	☐ 189	Reid Nichols	.03	.01	.00
☐ 95	Tommy John	.15	.07	.01	☐ 190	Bob Ojeda	.10	.05	.01
☐ 96	Bruce Kison	.03	.01	.00	☐ 191	Tony Perez	.15	.07	.01
☐ 97	Fred Lynn	.18	.09	.01	☐ 192	Chuck Rainey	.03	.01	.00
☐ 98	Ed Ott	.03	.01	.00	☐ 193	Jerry Remy	.03	.01	.00
☐ 99	Steve Renko	.03	.01	.00	☐ 194	Jim Rice	.30	.15	.03
☐ 100	Luis Sanchez	.03	.01	.00	☐ 195	Bob Stanley	.06	.03	.00
☐ 101	Rob Wilfong	.03	.01	.00	☐ 196	Dave Stapleton	.03	.01	.00
☐ 102	Mike Witt	.25	.12	.02	☐ 197	Mike Torrez	.06	.03	.00
☐ 103	Geoff Zahn	.03	.01	.00	☐ 198	John Tudor	.15	.07	.01
☐ 104	Willie Aikens	.03	.01	.00	☐ 199	Julio Valdez	.03	.01	.00
☐ 105	Mike Armstrong	.03	.01	.00	☐ 200	Carl Yastrzemski	.65	.30	.06
☐ 106	Vida Blue	.08	.04	.01	☐ 201	Dusty Baker	.08	.04	.01
☐ 107	Bud Black	.25	.12	.02	☐ 202	Joe Beckwith	.03	.01	.00
☐ 108	George Brett	.60	.30	.06	☐ 203	Greg Brock	.45	.22	.04
☐ 109	Bill Castro	.03	.01	.00	☐ 204	Ron Cey	.10	.05	.01
☐ 110	Onix Concepcion	.03	.01	.00	☐ 205	Terry Forster	.08	.04	.01
☐ 111	Dave Frost	.03	.01	.00	☐ 206	Steve Garvey	.40	.20	.04
☐ 112	Cesar Geronimo	.03	.01	.00	☐ 207	Pedro Guerrero	.35	.17	.03
☐ 113	Larry Gura	.06	.03	.00	☐ 208	Burt Hooton	.03	.01	.00
☐ 114	Steve Hammond	.03	.01	.00	☐ 209	Steve Howe	.06	.03	.00
☐ 115	Don Hood	.03	.01	.00	☐ 210	Ken Landreaux	.06	.03	.00
☐ 116	Dennis Leonard	.06	.03	.00	☐ 211	Mike Marshall	.20	.10	.02
☐ 117	Jerry Martin	.03	.01	.00	☐ 212	Candy Maldonado	.75	.35	.07
☐ 118	Lee May	.06	.03	.00	☐ 213	Rick Monday	.06	.03	.00
☐ 119	Hal McRae	.06	.03	.00	☐ 214	Tom Niedenfuer	.08	.04	.01
☐ 120	Amos Otis	.08	.04	.01	☐ 215	Jorge Orta	.03	.01	.00
☐ 121	Greg Pryor	.03	.01	.00	☐ 216	Jerry Reuss	.06	.03	.00
☐ 122	Dan Quisenberry	.15	.07	.01	☐ 217	Ron Roenicke	.03	.01	.00
☐ 123	Don Slaught	.25	.12	.02	☐ 218	Vicente Romo	.03	.01	.00
☐ 124	Paul Splittorff	.06	.03	.00	☐ 219	Bill Russell	.06	.03	.00
☐ 125	U.L. Washington	.03	.01	.00	☐ 220	Steve Sax	.18	.09	.01
☐ 126	John Wathan	.06	.03	.00	☐ 221	Mike Scioscia	.06	.03	.00
☐ 127	Frank White	.08	.04	.01	☐ 222	Dave Stewart	.10	.05	.01
☐ 128	Willie Wilson	.15	.07	.01	☐ 223	Derrel Thomas	.03	.01	.00
☐ 129	Steve Bedrosian	.40	.20	.04	☐ 224	Fernando Valenzuela	.35	.17	.03
☐ 130	Bruce Benedict	.03	.01	.00	☐ 225	Bob Welch	.08	.04	.01
☐ 131	Tommy Boggs	.03	.01	.00	☐ 226	Ricky Wright	.06	.03	.00
☐ 132	Brett Butler	.10	.05	.01	☐ 227	Steve Yeager	.03	.01	.00
☐ 133	Rick Camp	.03	.01	.00	☐ 228	Bill Almon	.03	.01	.00
☐ 134	Chris Chambliss	.06	.03	.00	☐ 229	Harold Baines	.25	.12	.02
☐ 135	Ken Dayley	.06	.03	.00	☐ 230	Salome Barojas	.03	.01	.00
☐ 136	Gene Garber	.06	.03	.00	☐ 231	Tony Bernazard	.06	.03	.00
☐ 137	Terry Harper	.03	.01	.00	☐ 232	Britt Burns	.08	.04	.01
☐ 138	Bob Horner	.20	.10	.02	☐ 233	Richard Dotson	.08	.04	.01
☐ 139	Glenn Hubbard	.03	.01	.00	☐ 234	Ernesto Escarrega	.03	.01	.00
☐ 140	Rufino Linares	.03	.01	.00	☐ 235	Carlton Fisk	.15	.07	.01
☐ 141	Rick Mahler	.06	.03	.00	☐ 236	Jerry Hairston	.03	.01	.00
☐ 142	Dale Murphy	.80	.40	.08	☐ 237	Kevin Hickey	.03	.01	.00
☐ 143	Phil Niekro	.20	.10	.02	☐ 238	LaMarr Hoyt	.08	.04	.01
☐ 144	Pascual Perez	.06	.03	.00	☐ 239	Steve Kemp	.08	.04	.01
☐ 145	Biff Pocoroba	.03	.01	.00	☐ 240	Jim Kern	.03	.01	.00
☐ 146	Rafael Ramirez	.03	.01	.00	☐ 241	Ron Kittle	.60	.30	.06
☐ 147	Jerry Royster	.03	.01	.00	☐ 242	Jerry Koosman	.08	.04	.01
☐ 148	Ken Smith	.03	.01	.00	☐ 243	Dennis Lamp	.03	.01	.00
☐ 149	Bob Walk	.03	.01	.00	☐ 244	Rudy Law	.03	.01	.00
☐ 150	Claudell Washington	.08	.04	.01	☐ 245	Vance Law	.03	.01	.00
☐ 151	Bob Watson	.06	.03	.00	☐ 246	Ron LeFlore	.06	.03	.00
☐ 152	Larry Whisenton	.03	.01	.00	☐ 247	Greg Luzinski	.10	.05	.01
☐ 153	Porfirio Altamirano	.03	.01	.00	☐ 248	Tom Paciorek	.03	.01	.00
☐ 154	Marty Bystrom	.03	.01	.00	☐ 249	Aurelio Rodriguez	.03	.01	.00
☐ 155	Steve Carlton	.35	.17	.03	☐ 250	Mike Squires	.03	.01	.00
☐ 156	Larry Christenson	.03	.01	.00	☐ 251	Steve Trout	.06	.03	.00
☐ 157	Ivan DeJesus	.03	.01	.00	☐ 252	Jim Barr	.03	.01	.00
☐ 158	John Denny	.10	.05	.01	☐ 253	Dave Bergman	.03	.01	.00
☐ 159	Bob Dernier	.06	.03	.00	☐ 254	Fred Breining	.03	.01	.00
☐ 160	Bo Diaz	.08	.04	.01	☐ 255	Bob Brenly	.08	.04	.01
☐ 161	Ed Farmer	.03	.01	.00	☐ 256	Jack Clark	.25	.12	.02
☐ 162	Greg Gross	.03	.01	.00	☐ 257	Chili Davis	.15	.07	.01
☐ 163	Mike Krukow	.08	.04	.01	☐ 258	Darrell Evans	.12	.06	.01
☐ 164	Garry Maddox	.06	.03	.00	☐ 259	Alan Fowlkes	.03	.01	.00
☐ 165	Gary Matthews	.08	.04	.01	☐ 260	Rich Gale	.03	.01	.00
☐ 166	Tug McGraw	.10	.05	.01	☐ 261	Atlee Hammaker	.06	.03	.00
☐ 167	Bob Molinaro	.03	.01	.00	☐ 262	Al Holland	.06	.03	.00
☐ 168	Sid Monge	.03	.01	.00	☐ 263	Duane Kuiper	.03	.01	.00
☐ 169	Ron Reed	.03	.01	.00	☐ 264	Bill Laskey	.08	.04	.01
☐ 170	Bill Robinson	.03	.01	.00	☐ 265	Gary Lavelle	.06	.03	.00
☐ 171	Pete Rose	1.00	.50	.10	☐ 266	Johnnie LeMaster	.03	.01	.00
☐ 172	Dick Ruthven	.03	.01	.00	☐ 267	Renie Martin	.03	.01	.00

☐ 268	Milt May	.03	.01	.00
☐ 269	Greg Minton	.06	.03	.00
☐ 270	Joe Morgan	.20	.10	.02
☐ 271	Tom O'Malley	.06	.03	.00
☐ 272	Reggie Smith	.08	.04	.01
☐ 273	Guy Sularz	.03	.01	.00
☐ 274	Champ Summers	.03	.01	.00
☐ 275	Max Venable	.03	.01	.00
☐ 276	Jim Wohlford	.03	.01	.00
☐ 277	Ray Burris	.03	.01	.00
☐ 278	Gary Carter	.40	.20	.04
☐ 279	Warren Cromartie	.03	.01	.00
☐ 280	Andre Dawson	.35	.17	.03
☐ 281	Terry Francona	.06	.03	.00
☐ 282	Doug Flynn	.03	.01	.00
☐ 283	Woody Fryman	.03	.01	.00
☐ 284	Bill Gullickson	.08	.04	.01
☐ 285	Wallace Johnson	.06	.03	.00
☐ 286	Charlie Lea	.06	.03	.00
☐ 287	Randy Lerch	.03	.01	.00
☐ 288	Brad Mills	.03	.01	.00
☐ 289	Dan Norman	.03	.01	.00
☐ 290	Al Oliver	.10	.05	.01
☐ 291	David Palmer	.06	.03	.00
☐ 292	Tim Raines	.40	.20	.04
☐ 293	Jeff Reardon	.12	.06	.01
☐ 294	Steve Rogers	.08	.04	.01
☐ 295	Scott Sanderson	.06	.03	.00
☐ 296	Dan Schatzeder	.03	.01	.00
☐ 297	Bryn Smith	.08	.04	.01
☐ 298	Chris Speier	.06	.03	.00
☐ 299	Tim Wallach	.25	.12	.02
☐ 300	Jerry White	.03	.01	.00
☐ 301	Joel Youngblood	.03	.01	.00
☐ 302	Ross Baumgarten	.03	.01	.00
☐ 303	Dale Berra	.06	.03	.00
☐ 304	John Candelaria	.08	.04	.01
☐ 305	Dick Davis	.03	.01	.00
☐ 306	Mike Easler	.06	.03	.00
☐ 307	Richie Hebner	.03	.01	.00
☐ 308	Lee Lacy	.06	.03	.00
☐ 309	Bill Madlock	.12	.06	.01
☐ 310	Larry McWilliams	.03	.01	.00
☐ 311	John Milner	.03	.01	.00
☐ 312	Omar Moreno	.03	.01	.00
☐ 313	Jim Morrison	.03	.01	.00
☐ 314	Steve Nicosia	.03	.01	.00
☐ 315	Dave Parker	.20	.10	.02
☐ 316	Tony Pena	.15	.07	.01
☐ 317	Johnny Ray	.15	.07	.01
☐ 318	Rick Rhoden	.08	.04	.01
☐ 319	Don Robinson	.03	.01	.00
☐ 320	Enrique Romo	.03	.01	.00
☐ 321	Manny Sarmiento	.03	.01	.00
☐ 322	Rod Scurry	.03	.01	.00
☐ 323	Jim Smith	.03	.01	.00
☐ 324	Willie Stargell	.25	.12	.02
☐ 325	Jason Thompson	.06	.03	.00
☐ 326	Kent Tekulve	.08	.04	.01
☐ 327	Tom Brookens	.03	.01	.00
☐ 328	Enos Cabell	.03	.01	.00
☐ 329	Kirk Gibson	.30	.15	.03
☐ 330	Larry Herndon	.06	.03	.00
☐ 331	Mike Ivie	.03	.01	.00
☐ 332	Howard Johnson	2.50	1.25	.25
☐ 333	Lynn Jones	.03	.01	.00
☐ 334	Rick Leach	.03	.01	.00
☐ 335	Chet Lemon	.06	.03	.00
☐ 336	Jack Morris	.20	.10	.02
☐ 337	Lance Parrish	.25	.12	.02
☐ 338	Larry Pashnick	.03	.01	.00
☐ 339	Dan Petry	.10	.05	.01
☐ 340	Dave Rozema	.03	.01	.00
☐ 341	Dave Rucker	.03	.01	.00
☐ 342	Elias Sosa	.03	.01	.00
☐ 343	Dave Tobik	.03	.01	.00
☐ 344	Alan Trammell	.30	.15	.03
☐ 345	Jerry Turner	.03	.01	.00
☐ 346	Jerry Ujdur	.03	.01	.00
☐ 347	Pat Underwood	.03	.01	.00
☐ 348	Lou Whitaker	.15	.07	.01
☐ 349	Milt Wilcox	.03	.01	.00
☐ 350	Glenn Wilson	.60	.30	.06
☐ 351	John Wockenfuss	.03	.01	.00
☐ 352	Kurt Bevacqua	.03	.01	.00
☐ 353	Juan Bonilla	.03	.01	.00
☐ 354	Floyd Chiffer	.03	.01	.00
☐ 355	Luis DeLeon	.03	.01	.00
☐ 356	Dave Dravecky	.55	.27	.05
☐ 357	Dave Edwards	.03	.01	.00
☐ 358	Juan Eichelberger	.03	.01	.00
☐ 359	Tim Flannery	.03	.01	.00
☐ 360	Tony Gwynn	8.00	4.00	.80
☐ 361	Ruppert Jones	.03	.01	.00
☐ 362	Terry Kennedy	.08	.04	.01
☐ 363	Joe Lefebvre	.03	.01	.00
☐ 364	Sixto Lezcano	.03	.01	.00
☐ 365	Tim Lollar	.03	.01	.00
☐ 366	Gary Lucas	.03	.01	.00
☐ 367	John Montefusco	.06	.03	.00
☐ 368	Broderick Perkins	.03	.01	.00
☐ 369	Joe Pittman	.03	.01	.00
☐ 370	Gene Richards	.03	.01	.00
☐ 371	Luis Salazar	.03	.01	.00
☐ 372	Eric Show	.15	.07	.01
☐ 373	Garry Templeton	.08	.04	.01
☐ 374	Chris Welsh	.03	.01	.00
☐ 375	Alan Wiggins	.20	.10	.02
☐ 376	Rick Cerone	.06	.03	.00
☐ 377	Dave Collins	.06	.03	.00
☐ 378	Roger Erickson	.03	.01	.00
☐ 379	George Frazier	.03	.01	.00
☐ 380	Oscar Gamble	.06	.03	.00
☐ 381	Goose Gossage	.18	.09	.01
☐ 382	Ken Griffey	.08	.04	.01
☐ 383	Ron Guidry	.20	.10	.02
☐ 384	Dave LaRoche	.03	.01	.00
☐ 385	Rudy May	.03	.01	.00
☐ 386	John Mayberry	.06	.03	.00
☐ 387	Lee Mazzilli	.06	.03	.00
☐ 388	Mike Morgan	.03	.01	.00
☐ 389	Jerry Mumphrey	.06	.03	.00
☐ 390	Bobby Murcer	.10	.05	.01
☐ 391	Graig Nettles	.15	.07	.01
☐ 392	Lou Piniella	.10	.05	.01
☐ 393	Willie Randolph	.08	.04	.01
☐ 394	Shane Rawley	.08	.04	.01
☐ 395	Dave Righetti	.25	.12	.02
☐ 396	Andre Robertson	.03	.01	.00
☐ 397	Roy Smalley	.06	.03	.00
☐ 398	Dave Winfield	.35	.17	.03
☐ 399	Butch Wynegar	.06	.03	.00
☐ 400	Chris Bando	.03	.01	.00
☐ 401	Alan Bannister	.03	.01	.00
☐ 402	Len Barker	.06	.03	.00
☐ 403	Tom Brennan	.03	.01	.00
☐ 404	Carmelo Castillo	.06	.03	.00
☐ 405	Miguel Dilone	.03	.01	.00
☐ 406	Jerry Dybzinski	.03	.01	.00
☐ 407	Mike Fischlin	.03	.01	.00
☐ 408	Ed Glynn (photo actually Bud Anderson)	.06	.03	.00
☐ 409	Mike Hargrove	.06	.03	.00
☐ 410	Toby Harrah	.06	.03	.00
☐ 411	Ron Hassey	.03	.01	.00
☐ 412	Von Hayes	.20	.10	.02
☐ 413	Rick Manning	.03	.01	.00
☐ 414	Bake McBride	.06	.03	.00
☐ 415	Larry Milbourne	.03	.01	.00
☐ 416	Bill Nahorodny	.03	.01	.00
☐ 417	Jack Perconte	.03	.01	.00
☐ 418	Lary Sorensen	.03	.01	.00
☐ 419	Dan Spillner	.03	.01	.00
☐ 420	Rick Sutcliffe	.15	.07	.01
☐ 421	Andre Thornton	.08	.04	.01
☐ 422	Rick Waits	.03	.01	.00
☐ 423	Eddie Whitson	.06	.03	.00
☐ 424	Jesse Barfield	.75	.35	.07
☐ 425	Barry Bonnell	.03	.01	.00
☐ 426	Jim Clancy	.06	.03	.00
☐ 427	Damaso Garcia	.06	.03	.00
☐ 428	Jerry Garvin	.03	.01	.00
☐ 429	Alfredo Griffin	.08	.04	.01
☐ 430	Garth Iorg	.03	.01	.00
☐ 431	Roy Lee Jackson	.03	.01	.00
☐ 432	Luis Leal	.03	.01	.00
☐ 433	Buck Martinez	.03	.01	.00
☐ 434	Joey McLaughlin	.03	.01	.00
☐ 435	Lloyd Moseby	.15	.07	.01
☐ 436	Rance Mulliniks	.03	.01	.00
☐ 437	Dale Murray	.03	.01	.00
☐ 438	Wayne Nordhagen	.03	.01	.00
☐ 439	Gene Petralli	.06	.03	.00
☐ 440	Hosken Powell	.03	.01	.00
☐ 441	Dave Stieb	.15	.07	.01
☐ 442	Willie Upshaw	.08	.04	.01
☐ 443	Ernie Whitt	.06	.03	.00
☐ 444	Al Woods	.03	.01	.00
☐ 445	Alan Ashby	.06	.03	.00
☐ 446	Jose Cruz	.10	.05	.01
☐ 447	Kiko Garcia	.03	.01	.00
☐ 448	Phil Garner	.06	.03	.00
☐ 449	Danny Heep	.03	.01	.00
☐ 450	Art Howe	.03	.01	.00
☐ 451	Bob Knepper	.08	.04	.01
☐ 452	Alan Knicely	.03	.01	.00
☐ 453	Ray Knight	.10	.05	.01
☐ 454	Frank LaCorte	.03	.01	.00
☐ 455	Mike LaCoss	.03	.01	.00

☐ 456 Randy Moffitt	.03	.01	.00
☐ 457 Joe Niekro	.10	.05	.01
☐ 458 Terry Puhl	.06	.03	.00
☐ 459 Luis Pujols	.03	.01	.00
☐ 460 Craig Reynolds	.03	.01	.00
☐ 461 Bert Roberge	.03	.01	.00
☐ 462 Vern Ruhle	.03	.01	.00
☐ 463 Nolan Ryan	.35	.17	.03
☐ 464 Joe Sambito	.06	.03	.00
☐ 465 Tony Scott	.03	.01	.00
☐ 466 Dave Smith	.08	.04	.01
☐ 467 Harry Spilman	.03	.01	.00
☐ 468 Dickie Thon	.06	.03	.00
☐ 469 Denny Walling	.03	.01	.00
☐ 470 Larry Andersen	.03	.01	.00
☐ 471 Floyd Bannister	.08	.04	.01
☐ 472 Jim Beattie	.03	.01	.00
☐ 473 Bruce Bochte	.03	.01	.00
☐ 474 Manny Castillo	.03	.01	.00
☐ 475 Bill Caudill	.06	.03	.00
☐ 476 Bryan Clark	.03	.01	.00
☐ 477 Al Cowens	.06	.03	.00
☐ 478 Julio Cruz	.03	.01	.00
☐ 479 Todd Cruz	.03	.01	.00
☐ 480 Gary Gray	.03	.01	.00
☐ 481 Dave Henderson	.06	.03	.00
☐ 482 Mike Moore	.25	.12	.02
☐ 483 Gaylord Perry	.20	.10	.02
☐ 484 Dave Revering	.03	.01	.00
☐ 485 Joe Simpson	.03	.01	.00
☐ 486 Mike Stanton	.03	.01	.00
☐ 487 Rick Sweet	.03	.01	.00
☐ 488 Ed VandeBerg	.06	.03	.00
☐ 489 Richie Zisk	.06	.03	.00
☐ 490 Doug Bird	.03	.01	.00
☐ 491 Larry Bowa	.12	.06	.01
☐ 492 Bill Buckner	.10	.05	.01
☐ 493 Bill Campbell	.03	.01	.00
☐ 494 Jody Davis	.15	.07	.01
☐ 495 Leon Durham	.12	.06	.01
☐ 496 Steve Henderson	.03	.01	.00
☐ 497 Willie Hernandez	.12	.06	.01
☐ 498 Ferguson Jenkins	.15	.07	.01
☐ 499 Jay Johnstone	.06	.03	.00
☐ 500 Junior Kennedy	.03	.01	.00
☐ 501 Randy Martz	.03	.01	.00
☐ 502 Jerry Morales	.03	.01	.00
☐ 503 Keith Moreland	.08	.04	.01
☐ 504 Dickie Noles	.03	.01	.00
☐ 505 Mike Proly	.03	.01	.00
☐ 506 Allen Ripley	.03	.01	.00
☐ 507 Ryne Sandberg	4.00	2.00	.40
☐ 508 Lee Smith	.12	.06	.01
☐ 509 Pat Tabler	.25	.12	.02
☐ 510 Dick Tidrow	.03	.01	.00
☐ 511 Bump Wills	.03	.01	.00
☐ 512 Gary Woods	.03	.01	.00
☐ 513 Tony Armas	.10	.05	.01
☐ 514 Dave Beard	.03	.01	.00
☐ 515 Jeff Burroughs	.06	.03	.00
☐ 516 John D'Acquisto	.03	.01	.00
☐ 517 Wayne Gross	.03	.01	.00
☐ 518 Mike Heath	.03	.01	.00
☐ 519 Rickey Henderson	.60	.30	.06
☐ 520 Cliff Johnson	.03	.01	.00
☐ 521 Matt Keough	.03	.01	.00
☐ 522 Brian Kingman	.03	.01	.00
☐ 523 Rick Langford	.03	.01	.00
☐ 524 Davey Lopes	.08	.04	.01
☐ 525 Steve McCatty	.03	.01	.00
☐ 526 Dave McKay	.03	.01	.00
☐ 527 Dan Meyer	.03	.01	.00
☐ 528 Dwayne Murphy	.06	.03	.00
☐ 529 Jeff Newman	.03	.01	.00
☐ 530 Mike Norris	.06	.03	.00
☐ 531 Bob Owchinko	.03	.01	.00
☐ 532 Joe Rudi	.06	.03	.00
☐ 533 Jimmy Sexton	.03	.01	.00
☐ 534 Fred Stanley	.03	.01	.00
☐ 535 Tom Underwood	.03	.01	.00
☐ 536 Neil Allen	.06	.03	.00
☐ 537 Wally Backman	.08	.04	.01
☐ 538 Bob Bailor	.03	.01	.00
☐ 539 Hubie Brooks	.12	.06	.01
☐ 540 Carlos Diaz	.08	.04	.01
☐ 541 Pete Falcone	.03	.01	.00
☐ 542 George Foster	.15	.07	.01
☐ 543 Ron Gardenhire	.03	.01	.00
☐ 544 Brian Giles	.03	.01	.00
☐ 545 Ron Hodges	.03	.01	.00
☐ 546 Randy Jones	.06	.03	.00
☐ 547 Mike Jorgensen	.03	.01	.00
☐ 548 Dave Kingman	.12	.06	.01
☐ 549 Ed Lynch	.03	.01	.00
☐ 550 Jesse Orosco	.08	.04	.01
☐ 551 Rick Ownbey	.06	.03	.00
☐ 552 Charlie Puleo	.03	.01	.00
☐ 553 Gary Rajsich	.03	.01	.00
☐ 554 Mike Scott	.30	.15	.03
☐ 555 Rusty Staub	.10	.05	.01
☐ 556 John Stearns	.03	.01	.00
☐ 557 Craig Swan	.03	.01	.00
☐ 558 Ellis Valentine	.03	.01	.00
☐ 559 Tom Veryzer	.03	.01	.00
☐ 560 Mookie Wilson	.08	.04	.01
☐ 561 Pat Zachry	.03	.01	.00
☐ 562 Buddy Bell	.10	.05	.01
☐ 563 John Butcher	.03	.01	.00
☐ 564 Steve Comer	.03	.01	.00
☐ 565 Danny Darwin	.06	.03	.00
☐ 566 Bucky Dent	.08	.04	.01
☐ 567 John Grubb	.03	.01	.00
☐ 568 Rick Honeycutt	.06	.03	.00
☐ 569 Dave Hostetler	.06	.03	.00
☐ 570 Charlie Hough	.08	.04	.01
☐ 571 Lamar Johnson	.03	.01	.00
☐ 572 Jon Matlack	.06	.03	.00
☐ 573 Paul Mirabella	.03	.01	.00
☐ 574 Larry Parrish	.08	.04	.01
☐ 575 Mike Richardt	.03	.01	.00
☐ 576 Mickey Rivers	.06	.03	.00
☐ 577 Billy Sample	.03	.01	.00
☐ 578 Dave Schmidt	.15	.07	.01
☐ 579 Bill Stein	.03	.01	.00
☐ 580 Jim Sundberg	.06	.03	.00
☐ 581 Frank Tanana	.08	.04	.01
☐ 582 Mark Wagner	.03	.01	.00
☐ 583 George Wright	.06	.03	.00
☐ 584 Johnny Bench	.35	.17	.03
☐ 585 Bruce Berenyi	.03	.01	.00
☐ 586 Larry Biittner	.03	.01	.00
☐ 587 Cesar Cedeno	.08	.04	.01
☐ 588 Dave Concepcion	.10	.05	.01
☐ 589 Dan Driessen	.06	.03	.00
☐ 590 Greg Harris	.06	.03	.00
☐ 591 Ben Hayes	.03	.01	.00
☐ 592 Paul Householder	.03	.01	.00
☐ 593 Tom Hume	.03	.01	.00
☐ 594 Wayne Krenchicki	.03	.01	.00
☐ 595 Rafael Landestoy	.03	.01	.00
☐ 596 Charlie Leibrandt	.08	.04	.01
☐ 597 Eddie Milner	.15	.07	.01
☐ 598 Ron Oester	.06	.03	.00
☐ 599 Frank Pastore	.03	.01	.00
☐ 600 Joe Price	.03	.01	.00
☐ 601 Tom Seaver	.35	.17	.03
☐ 602 Bob Shirley	.03	.01	.00
☐ 603 Mario Soto	.08	.04	.01
☐ 604 Alex Trevino	.03	.01	.00
☐ 605 Mike Vail	.03	.01	.00
☐ 606 Duane Walker	.06	.03	.00
☐ 607 Tom Brunansky	.20	.10	.02
☐ 608 Bobby Castillo	.03	.01	.00
☐ 609 John Castino	.03	.01	.00
☐ 610 Ron Davis	.03	.01	.00
☐ 611 Lenny Faedo	.03	.01	.00
☐ 612 Terry Felton	.03	.01	.00
☐ 613 Gary Gaetti	1.75	.85	.17
☐ 614 Mickey Hatcher	.03	.01	.00
☐ 615 Brad Havens	.03	.01	.00
☐ 616 Kent Hrbek	.75	.35	.07
☐ 617 Randy Johnson	.03	.01	.00
☐ 618 Tim Laudner	.10	.05	.01
☐ 619 Jeff Little	.03	.01	.00
☐ 620 Bobby Mitchell	.03	.01	.00
☐ 621 Jack O'Connor	.03	.01	.00
☐ 622 John Pacella	.03	.01	.00
☐ 623 Pete Redfern	.03	.01	.00
☐ 624 Jesus Vega	.03	.01	.00
☐ 625 Frank Viola	1.50	.75	.15
☐ 626 Ron Washington	.03	.01	.00
☐ 627 Gary Ward	.06	.03	.00
☐ 628 Al Williams	.03	.01	.00
☐ 629 Red Sox All-Stars	.18	.09	.01
Carl Yastrzemski			
Dennis Eckersley			
Mark Clear			
☐ 630 "300 Career Wins"	.10	.05	.01
Gaylord Perry and			
Terry Bulling 5/6/82			
☐ 631 Pride of Venezuela	.06	.03	.00
Dave Concepcion and			
Manny Trillo			
☐ 632 All-Star Infielders	.15	.07	.01
Robin Yount and			
Buddy Bell			
☐ 633 Mr.Vet and Mr.Rookie	.20	.10	.02
Dave Winfield and			
Kent Hrbek			
☐ 634 Fountain of Youth	.60	.30	.06

	Willie Stargell and Pete Rose			
☐ 635	Big Chiefs	.06	.03	.00
	Toby Harrah and Andre Thornton			
☐ 636	Smith Brothers	.08	.04	.01
	Ozzie and Lonnie			
☐ 637	Base Stealers' Threat	.12	.06	.01
	Bo Diaz and Gary Carter			
☐ 638	All-Star Catchers	.15	.07	.01
	Carlton Fisk and Gary Carter			
☐ 639	The Silver Shoe	.30	.15	.03
	Rickey Henderson			
☐ 640	Home Run Threats	.18	.09	.01
	Ben Oglivie and Reggie Jackson			
☐ 641	Two Teams Same Day	.06	.03	.00
	Joel Youngblood August 4, 1982			
☐ 642	Last Perfect Game	.06	.03	.00
	Ron Hassey and Len Barker			
☐ 643	Black and Blue	.06	.03	.00
	Bud Black			
☐ 644	Black and Blue	.06	.03	.00
	Vida Blue			
☐ 645	Speed and Power	.30	.15	.03
	Reggie Jackson			
☐ 646	Speed and Power	.30	.15	.03
	Rickey Henderson			
☐ 647	CL: Cards/Brewers	.07	.01	.00
☐ 648	CL: Orioles/Angels	.07	.01	.00
☐ 649	CL: Royals/Braves	.07	.01	.00
☐ 650	CL: Phillies/Red Sox	.07	.01	.00
☐ 651	CL: Dodgers/White Sox	.07	.01	.00
☐ 652	CL: Giants/Expos	.07	.01	.00
☐ 653	CL: Pirates/Tigers	.07	.01	.00
☐ 654	CL: Padres/Yankees	.07	.01	.00
☐ 655	CL: Indians/Blue Jays	.07	.01	.00
☐ 656	CL: Astros/Mariners	.07	.01	.00
☐ 657	CL: Cubs/A's	.07	.01	.00
☐ 658	CL: Mets/Rangers	.07	.01	.00
☐ 659	CL: Reds/Twins	.07	.01	.00
☐ 660	CL: Specials/Teams	.09	.01	.00

1984 Fleer

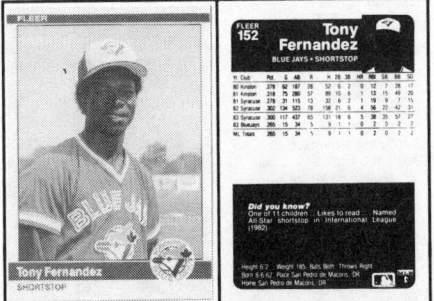

The cards in this 660-card set measure 2 1/2" by 3 1/2". The 1984 Fleer card set featured fronts with full-color team logos along with the player's name and position and the Fleer identification. The set features many imaginative photos, several multi-player cards, and many more action shots than the 1983 card set. The backs are quite similar to the 1983 backs except that blue rather than brown ink is used. The player cards are alphabetized within team and the teams are ordered by their 1983 season finish and won-lost record, e.g., Baltimore (1-23), Philadelphia (24-49), Chicago White Sox (50-73), Detroit (74-95), Los Angeles (96-118), New York Yankees (119-144), Toronto (145- 169), Atlanta (170-193), Milwaukee (194-219), Houston (220-244), Pittsburgh (245-269), Montreal (270-293),

San Diego (294-317), St. Louis (318-340), Kansas City (341-364), San Francisco (365- 387), Boston (388-412), Texas (413-435), Oakland (436-461), Cincinnati (462-485), Chicago (486-507), California (508-532), Cleveland (533-555), Minnesota (556-579), New York Mets (580- 603), and Seattle (604-625). Specials (626-646) and checklist cards (647-660) make up the end of the set.

		MINT	EXC	G-VG
COMPLETE SET		85.00	42.50	8.50
COMMON PLAYER (1-660)		.05	.02	.00
☐ 1	Mike Boddicker	.20	.05	.01
☐ 2	Al Bumbry	.05	.02	.00
☐ 3	Todd Cruz	.05	.02	.00
☐ 4	Rich Dauer	.05	.02	.00
☐ 5	Storm Davis	.10	.05	.01
☐ 6	Rick Dempsey	.10	.05	.01
☐ 7	Jim Dwyer	.05	.02	.00
☐ 8	Mike Flanagan	.10	.05	.01
☐ 9	Dan Ford	.05	.02	.00
☐ 10	John Lowenstein	.05	.02	.00
☐ 11	Dennis Martinez	.10	.05	.01
☐ 12	Tippy Martinez	.05	.02	.00
☐ 13	Scott McGregor	.10	.05	.01
☐ 14	Eddie Murray	.60	.30	.06
☐ 15	Joe Nolan	.05	.02	.00
☐ 16	Jim Palmer	.30	.15	.03
☐ 17	Cal Ripken	.75	.35	.07
☐ 18	Gary Roenicke	.05	.02	.00
☐ 19	Lenn Sakata	.05	.02	.00
☐ 20	John Shelby	.30	.15	.03
☐ 21	Ken Singleton	.10	.05	.01
☐ 22	Sammy Stewart	.05	.02	.00
☐ 23	Tim Stoddard	.05	.02	.00
☐ 24	Marty Bystrom	.05	.02	.00
☐ 25	Steve Carlton	.40	.20	.04
☐ 26	Ivan DeJesus	.05	.02	.00
☐ 27	John Denny	.10	.05	.01
☐ 28	Bob Dernier	.05	.02	.00
☐ 29	Bo Diaz	.10	.05	.01
☐ 30	Kiko Garcia	.05	.02	.00
☐ 31	Greg Gross	.05	.02	.00
☐ 32	Kevin Gross	.25	.12	.02
☐ 33	Von Hayes	.15	.07	.01
☐ 34	Willie Hernandez	.20	.10	.02
☐ 35	Al Holland	.05	.02	.00
☐ 36	Charles Hudson	.25	.12	.02
☐ 37	Joe Lefebvre	.05	.02	.00
☐ 38	Sixto Lezcano	.05	.02	.00
☐ 39	Garry Maddox	.05	.02	.00
☐ 40	Gary Matthews	.10	.05	.01
☐ 41	Len Matuszek	.05	.02	.00
☐ 42	Tug McGraw	.10	.05	.01
☐ 43	Joe Morgan	.20	.10	.02
☐ 44	Tony Perez	.15	.07	.01
☐ 45	Ron Reed	.05	.02	.00
☐ 46	Pete Rose	1.00	.50	.10
☐ 47	Juan Samuel	4.50	2.25	.45
☐ 48	Mike Schmidt	.60	.30	.06
☐ 49	Ozzie Virgil	.05	.02	.00
☐ 50	Juan Agosto	.05	.02	.00
☐ 51	Harold Baines	.20	.10	.02
☐ 52	Floyd Bannister	.10	.05	.01
☐ 53	Salome Barojas	.05	.02	.00
☐ 54	Britt Burns	.10	.05	.01
☐ 55	Julio Cruz	.05	.02	.00
☐ 56	Richard Dotson	.10	.05	.01
☐ 57	Jerry Dybzinski	.05	.02	.00
☐ 58	Carlton Fisk	.15	.07	.01
☐ 59	Scott Fletcher	.20	.10	.02
☐ 60	Jerry Hairston	.05	.02	.00
☐ 61	Kevin Hickey	.05	.02	.00
☐ 62	Marc Hill	.05	.02	.00
☐ 63	LaMarr Hoyt	.10	.05	.01
☐ 64	Ron Kittle	.20	.10	.02
☐ 65	Jerry Koosman	.10	.05	.01
☐ 66	Dennis Lamp	.05	.02	.00
☐ 67	Rudy Law	.05	.02	.00
☐ 68	Vance Law	.05	.02	.00
☐ 69	Greg Luzinski	.10	.05	.01
☐ 70	Tom Paciorek	.05	.02	.00
☐ 71	Mike Squires	.05	.02	.00
☐ 72	Dick Tidrow	.05	.02	.00
☐ 73	Greg Walker	.65	.30	.06
☐ 74	Glenn Abbott	.05	.02	.00
☐ 75	Howard Bailey	.05	.02	.00
☐ 76	Doug Bair	.05	.02	.00
☐ 77	Juan Berenguer	.05	.02	.00
☐ 78	Tom Brookens	.05	.02	.00
☐ 79	Enos Cabell	.05	.02	.00

Tony Fernandez — 152 — BLUE JAYS • SHORTSTOP

☐ 80	Kirk Gibson	.25	.12	.02	☐ 175	Chris Chambliss	.10	.05	.01
☐ 81	John Grubb	.05	.02	.00	☐ 176	Ken Dayley	.10	.05	.01
☐ 82	Larry Herndon	.05	.02	.00	☐ 177	Pete Falcone	.05	.02	.00
☐ 83	Wayne Krenchicki	.05	.02	.00	☐ 178	Terry Forster	.10	.05	.01
☐ 84	Rick Leach	.05	.02	.00	☐ 179	Gene Garber	.05	.02	.00
☐ 85	Chet Lemon	.10	.05	.01	☐ 180	Terry Harper	.05	.02	.00
☐ 86	Aurelio Lopez	.05	.02	.00	☐ 181	Bob Horner	.20	.10	.02
☐ 87	Jack Morris	.25	.12	.02	☐ 182	Glenn Hubbard	.05	.02	.00
☐ 88	Lance Parrish	.25	.12	.02	☐ 183	Randy Johnson	.05	.02	.00
☐ 89	Dan Petry	.10	.05	.01	☐ 184	Craig McMurtry	.10	.05	.01
☐ 90	Dave Rozema	.05	.02	.00	☐ 185	Donnie Moore	.10	.05	.01
☐ 91	Alan Trammell	.30	.15	.03	☐ 186	Dale Murphy	.75	.35	.07
☐ 92	Lou Whitaker	.15	.07	.01	☐ 187	Phil Niekro	.20	.10	.02
☐ 93	Milt Wilcox	.05	.02	.00	☐ 188	Pascual Perez	.05	.02	.00
☐ 94	Glenn Wilson	.15	.07	.01	☐ 189	Biff Pocoroba	.05	.02	.00
☐ 95	John Wockenfuss	.05	.02	.00	☐ 190	Rafael Ramirez	.05	.02	.00
☐ 96	Dusty Baker	.10	.05	.01	☐ 191	Jerry Royster	.05	.02	.00
☐ 97	Joe Beckwith	.05	.02	.00	☐ 192	Claudell Washington	.10	.05	.01
☐ 98	Greg Brock	.10	.05	.01	☐ 193	Bob Watson	.05	.02	.00
☐ 99	Jack Fimple	.05	.02	.00	☐ 194	Jerry Augustine	.05	.02	.00
☐ 100	Pedro Guerrero	.30	.15	.03	☐ 195	Mark Brouhard	.05	.02	.00
☐ 101	Rick Honeycutt	.10	.05	.01	☐ 196	Mike Caldwell	.05	.02	.00
☐ 102	Burt Hooton	.05	.02	.00	☐ 197	Tom Candiotti	.25	.12	.02
☐ 103	Steve Howe	.05	.02	.00	☐ 198	Cecil Cooper	.15	.07	.01
☐ 104	Ken Landreaux	.05	.02	.00	☐ 199	Rollie Fingers	.20	.10	.02
☐ 105	Mike Marshall	.20	.10	.02	☐ 200	Jim Gantner	.05	.02	.00
☐ 106	Rick Monday	.10	.05	.01	☐ 201	Bob L. Gibson	.10	.05	.01
☐ 107	Jose Morales	.05	.02	.00	☐ 202	Moose Haas	.05	.02	.00
☐ 108	Tom Niedenfuer	.10	.05	.01	☐ 203	Roy Howell	.05	.02	.00
☐ 109	Alejandro Pena	.25	.12	.02	☐ 204	Pete Ladd	.05	.02	.00
☐ 110	Jerry Reuss	.10	.05	.01	☐ 205	Rick Manning	.05	.02	.00
☐ 111	Bill Russell	.05	.02	.00	☐ 206	Bob McClure	.05	.02	.00
☐ 112	Steve Sax	.15	.07	.01	☐ 207	Paul Molitor	.20	.10	.02
☐ 113	Mike Scioscia	.05	.02	.00	☐ 208	Don Money	.05	.02	.00
☐ 114	Derrel Thomas	.05	.02	.00	☐ 209	Charlie Moore	.05	.02	.00
☐ 115	Fernando Valenzuela	.35	.17	.03	☐ 210	Ben Oglivie	.10	.05	.01
☐ 116	Bob Welch	.10	.05	.01	☐ 211	Chuck Porter	.05	.02	.00
☐ 117	Steve Yeager	.05	.02	.00	☐ 212	Ed Romero	.05	.02	.00
☐ 118	Pat Zachry	.05	.02	.00	☐ 213	Ted Simmons	.15	.07	.01
☐ 119	Don Baylor	.15	.07	.01	☐ 214	Jim Slaton	.05	.02	.00
☐ 120	Bert Campaneris	.10	.05	.01	☐ 215	Don Sutton	.20	.10	.02
☐ 121	Rick Cerone	.05	.02	.00	☐ 216	Tom Tellmann	.05	.02	.00
☐ 122	Ray Fontenot	.10	.05	.01	☐ 217	Pete Vuckovich	.10	.05	.01
☐ 123	George Frazier	.05	.02	.00	☐ 218	Ned Yost	.05	.02	.00
☐ 124	Oscar Gamble	.05	.02	.00	☐ 219	Robin Yount	.30	.15	.03
☐ 125	Goose Gossage	.20	.10	.02	☐ 220	Alan Ashby	.05	.02	.00
☐ 126	Ken Griffey	.10	.05	.01	☐ 221	Kevin Bass	.20	.10	.02
☐ 127	Ron Guidry	.20	.10	.02	☐ 222	Jose Cruz	.10	.05	.01
☐ 128	Jay Howell	.10	.05	.01	☐ 223	Bill Dawley	.15	.07	.01
☐ 129	Steve Kemp	.10	.05	.01	☐ 224	Frank DiPino	.05	.02	.00
☐ 130	Matt Keough	.05	.02	.00	☐ 225	Bill Doran	.80	.40	.08
☐ 131	Don Mattingly	33.00	11.00	2.00	☐ 226	Phil Garner	.05	.02	.00
☐ 132	John Montefusco	.05	.02	.00	☐ 227	Art Howe	.05	.02	.00
☐ 133	Omar Moreno	.05	.02	.00	☐ 228	Bob Knepper	.10	.05	.01
☐ 134	Dale Murray	.05	.02	.00	☐ 229	Ray Knight	.10	.05	.01
☐ 135	Graig Nettles	.15	.07	.01	☐ 230	Frank LaCorte	.05	.02	.00
☐ 136	Lou Piniella	.10	.05	.01	☐ 231	Mike LaCoss	.05	.02	.00
☐ 137	Willie Randolph	.10	.05	.01	☐ 232	Mike Madden	.10	.05	.01
☐ 138	Shane Rawley	.10	.05	.01	☐ 233	Jerry Mumphrey	.05	.02	.00
☐ 139	Dave Righetti	.20	.10	.02	☐ 234	Joe Niekro	.10	.05	.01
☐ 140	Andre Robertson	.05	.02	.00	☐ 235	Terry Puhl	.10	.05	.01
☐ 141	Bob Shirley	.05	.02	.00	☐ 236	Luis Pujols	.05	.02	.00
☐ 142	Roy Smalley	.05	.02	.00	☐ 237	Craig Reynolds	.05	.02	.00
☐ 143	Dave Winfield	.35	.17	.03	☐ 238	Vern Ruhle	.05	.02	.00
☐ 144	Butch Wynegar	.05	.02	.00	☐ 239	Nolan Ryan	.35	.17	.03
☐ 145	Jim Acker	.15	.07	.01	☐ 240	Mike Scott	.30	.15	.03
☐ 146	Doyle Alexander	.10	.05	.01	☐ 241	Tony Scott	.05	.02	.00
☐ 147	Jesse Barfield	.35	.17	.03	☐ 242	Dave Smith	.10	.05	.01
☐ 148	Jorge Bell	1.00	.50	.10	☐ 243	Dickie Thon	.10	.05	.01
☐ 149	Barry Bonnell	.05	.02	.00	☐ 244	Denny Walling	.05	.02	.00
☐ 150	Jim Clancy	.05	.02	.00	☐ 245	Dale Berra	.05	.02	.00
☐ 151	Dave Collins	.05	.02	.00	☐ 246	Jim Bibby	.05	.02	.00
☐ 152	Tony Fernandez	4.50	2.25	.45	☐ 247	John Candelaria	.10	.05	.01
☐ 153	Damaso Garcia	.10	.05	.01	☐ 248	Jose DeLeon	.25	.12	.02
☐ 154	Dave Geisel	.05	.02	.00	☐ 249	Mike Easler	.10	.05	.01
☐ 155	Jim Gott	.05	.02	.00	☐ 250	Cecilio Guante	.05	.02	.00
☐ 156	Alfredo Griffin	.10	.05	.01	☐ 251	Richie Hebner	.05	.02	.00
☐ 157	Garth Iorg	.05	.02	.00	☐ 252	Lee Lacy	.05	.02	.00
☐ 158	Roy Lee Jackson	.05	.02	.00	☐ 253	Bill Madlock	.15	.07	.01
☐ 159	Cliff Johnson	.05	.02	.00	☐ 254	Milt May	.05	.02	.00
☐ 160	Luis Leal	.05	.02	.00	☐ 255	Lee Mazzilli	.05	.02	.00
☐ 161	Buck Martinez	.05	.02	.00	☐ 256	Larry McWilliams	.05	.02	.00
☐ 162	Joey McLaughlin	.05	.02	.00	☐ 257	Jim Morrison	.05	.02	.00
☐ 163	Randy Moffitt	.05	.02	.00	☐ 258	Dave Parker	.20	.10	.02
☐ 164	Lloyd Moseby	.15	.07	.01	☐ 259	Tony Pena	.15	.07	.01
☐ 165	Rance Mulliniks	.05	.02	.00	☐ 260	Johnny Ray	.15	.07	.01
☐ 166	Jorge Orta	.05	.02	.00	☐ 261	Rick Rhoden	.10	.05	.01
☐ 167	Dave Stieb	.15	.07	.01	☐ 262	Don Robinson	.05	.02	.00
☐ 168	Willie Upshaw	.10	.05	.01	☐ 263	Manny Sarmiento	.05	.02	.00
☐ 169	Ernie Whitt	.05	.02	.00	☐ 264	Rod Scurry	.05	.02	.00
☐ 170	Len Barker	.05	.02	.00	☐ 265	Kent Tekulve	.10	.05	.01
☐ 171	Steve Bedrosian	.20	.10	.02	☐ 266	Gene Tenace	.05	.02	.00
☐ 172	Bruce Benedict	.05	.02	.00	☐ 267	Jason Thompson	.05	.02	.00
☐ 173	Brett Butler	.15	.07	.01	☐ 268	Lee Tunnell	.20	.10	.02
☐ 174	Rick Camp	.05	.02	.00	☐ 269	Marvell Wynne	.10	.05	.01

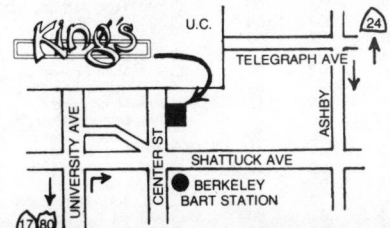

☐ 270 Ray Burris	.05	.02	.00
☐ 271 Gary Carter	.35	.17	.03
☐ 272 Warren Cromartie	.05	.02	.00
☐ 273 Andre Dawson	.30	.15	.03
☐ 274 Doug Flynn	.05	.02	.00
☐ 275 Terry Francona	.05	.02	.00
☐ 276 Bill Gullickson	.10	.05	.01
☐ 277 Bob James	.20	.10	.02
☐ 278 Charlie Lea	.05	.02	.00
☐ 279 Bryan Little	.05	.02	.00
☐ 280 Al Oliver	.10	.05	.01
☐ 281 Tim Raines	.40	.20	.04
☐ 282 Bobby Ramos	.05	.02	.00
☐ 283 Jeff Reardon	.15	.07	.01
☐ 284 Steve Rogers	.10	.05	.01
☐ 285 Scott Sanderson	.05	.02	.00
☐ 286 Dan Schatzeder	.05	.02	.00
☐ 287 Bryn Smith	.05	.02	.00
☐ 288 Chris Speier	.05	.02	.00
☐ 289 Manny Trillo	.05	.02	.00
☐ 290 Mike Vail	.05	.02	.00
☐ 291 Tim Wallach	.15	.07	.01
☐ 292 Chris Welsh	.05	.02	.00
☐ 293 Jim Wohlford	.05	.02	.00
☐ 294 Kurt Bevacqua	.05	.02	.00
☐ 295 Juan Bonilla	.05	.02	.00
☐ 296 Bobby Brown	.05	.02	.00
☐ 297 Luis DeLeon	.05	.02	.00
☐ 298 Dave Dravecky	.15	.07	.01
☐ 299 Tim Flannery	.05	.02	.00
☐ 300 Steve Garvey	.40	.20	.04
☐ 301 Tony Gwynn	1.50	.75	.15
☐ 302 Andy Hawkins	.20	.10	.02
☐ 303 Ruppert Jones	.05	.02	.00
☐ 304 Terry Kennedy	.10	.05	.01
☐ 305 Tim Lollar	.05	.02	.00
☐ 306 Gary Lucas	.05	.02	.00
☐ 307 Kevin McReynolds	4.00	2.00	.40
☐ 308 Sid Monge	.05	.02	.00
☐ 309 Mario Ramirez	.05	.02	.00
☐ 310 Gene Richards	.05	.02	.00
☐ 311 Luis Salazar	.05	.02	.00
☐ 312 Eric Show	.05	.02	.00
☐ 313 Elias Sosa	.05	.02	.00
☐ 314 Garry Templeton	.10	.05	.01
☐ 315 Mark Thurmond	.20	.10	.02
☐ 316 Ed Whitson	.05	.02	.00
☐ 317 Alan Wiggins	.10	.05	.01
☐ 318 Neil Allen	.10	.05	.01
☐ 319 Joaquin Andujar	.15	.07	.01
☐ 320 Steve Braun	.05	.02	.00
☐ 321 Glenn Brummer	.05	.02	.00
☐ 322 Bob Forsch	.10	.05	.01
☐ 323 David Green	.05	.02	.00
☐ 324 George Hendrick	.10	.05	.01
☐ 325 Tom Herr	.10	.05	.01
☐ 326 Dane Iorg	.05	.02	.00
☐ 327 Jeff Lahti	.05	.02	.00
☐ 328 Dave LaPoint	.05	.02	.00
☐ 329 Willie McGee	.30	.15	.03
☐ 330 Ken Oberkfell	.05	.02	.00
☐ 331 Darrell Porter	.05	.02	.00
☐ 332 Jamie Quirk	.05	.02	.00
☐ 333 Mike Ramsey	.05	.02	.00
☐ 334 Floyd Rayford	.05	.02	.00
☐ 335 Lonnie Smith	.10	.05	.01
☐ 336 Ozzie Smith	.25	.12	.02
☐ 337 John Stuper	.05	.02	.00
☐ 338 Bruce Sutter	.15	.07	.01
☐ 339 Andy Van Slyke	.90	.45	.09
☐ 340 Dave Von Ohlen	.05	.02	.00
☐ 341 Willie Aikens	.05	.02	.00
☐ 342 Mike Armstrong	.05	.02	.00
☐ 343 Bud Black	.05	.02	.00
☐ 344 George Brett	.50	.25	.05
☐ 345 Onix Concepcion	.05	.02	.00
☐ 346 Keith Creel	.05	.02	.00
☐ 347 Larry Gura	.05	.02	.00
☐ 348 Don Hood	.05	.02	.00
☐ 349 Dennis Leonard	.10	.05	.01
☐ 350 Hal McRae	.10	.05	.01
☐ 351 Amos Otis	.10	.05	.01
☐ 352 Gaylord Perry	.20	.10	.02
☐ 353 Greg Pryor	.05	.02	.00
☐ 354 Dan Quisenberry	.15	.07	.01
☐ 355 Steve Renko	.05	.02	.00
☐ 356 Leon Roberts	.05	.02	.00
☐ 357 Pat Sheridan	.20	.10	.02
☐ 358 Joe Simpson	.05	.02	.00
☐ 359 Don Slaught	.10	.05	.01
☐ 360 Paul Splittorff	.10	.05	.01
☐ 361 U.L. Washington	.05	.02	.00
☐ 362 John Wathan	.10	.05	.01
☐ 363 Frank White	.10	.05	.01
☐ 364 Willie Wilson	.15	.07	.01

☐ 365 Jim Barr	.05	.02	.00
☐ 366 Dave Bergman	.05	.02	.00
☐ 367 Fred Breining	.05	.02	.00
☐ 368 Bob Brenly	.10	.05	.01
☐ 369 Jack Clark	.25	.12	.02
☐ 370 Chili Davis	.15	.07	.01
☐ 371 Mark Davis	.05	.02	.00
☐ 372 Darrell Evans	.15	.07	.01
☐ 373 Atlee Hammaker	.10	.05	.01
☐ 374 Mike Krukow	.10	.05	.01
☐ 375 Duane Kuiper	.05	.02	.00
☐ 376 Bill Laskey	.05	.02	.00
☐ 377 Gary Lavelle	.05	.02	.00
☐ 378 Johnnie LeMaster	.05	.02	.00
☐ 379 Jeff Leonard	.15	.07	.01
☐ 380 Randy Lerch	.05	.02	.00
☐ 381 Renie Martin	.05	.02	.00
☐ 382 Andy McGaffigan	.05	.02	.00
☐ 383 Greg Minton	.05	.02	.00
☐ 384 Tom O'Malley	.05	.02	.00
☐ 385 Max Venable	.05	.02	.00
☐ 386 Brad Wellman	.05	.02	.00
☐ 387 Joel Youngblood	.05	.02	.00
☐ 388 Gary Allenson	.05	.02	.00
☐ 389 Luis Aponte	.05	.02	.00
☐ 390 Tony Armas	.10	.05	.01
☐ 391 Doug Bird	.05	.02	.00
☐ 392 Wade Boggs	6.00	3.00	.60
☐ 393 Dennis Boyd	.45	.22	.04
☐ 394 Mike Brown	.10	.05	.01
(Red Sox pitcher)			
☐ 395 Mark Clear	.05	.02	.00
☐ 396 Dennis Eckersley	.10	.05	.01
☐ 397 Dwight Evans	.20	.10	.02
☐ 398 Rich Gedman	.15	.07	.01
☐ 399 Glenn Hoffman	.05	.02	.00
☐ 400 Bruce Hurst	.15	.07	.01
☐ 401 John Henry Johnson	.05	.02	.00
☐ 402 Ed Jurak	.05	.02	.00
☐ 403 Rick Miller	.05	.02	.00
☐ 404 Jeff Newman	.05	.02	.00
☐ 405 Reid Nichols	.05	.02	.00
☐ 406 Bob Ojeda	.10	.05	.01
☐ 407 Jerry Remy	.05	.02	.00
☐ 408 Jim Rice	.35	.17	.03
☐ 409 Bob Stanley	.05	.02	.00
☐ 410 Dave Stapleton	.05	.02	.00
☐ 411 John Tudor	.20	.10	.02
☐ 412 Carl Yastrzemski	.60	.30	.06
☐ 413 Buddy Bell	.15	.07	.01
☐ 414 Larry Biittner	.05	.02	.00
☐ 415 John Butcher	.05	.02	.00
☐ 416 Danny Darwin	.05	.02	.00
☐ 417 Bucky Dent	.10	.05	.01
☐ 418 Dave Hostetler	.05	.02	.00
☐ 419 Charlie Hough	.10	.05	.01
☐ 420 Bobby Johnson	.05	.02	.00
☐ 421 Odell Jones	.05	.02	.00
☐ 422 Jon Matlack	.10	.05	.01
☐ 423 Pete O'Brien	1.00	.50	.10
☐ 424 Larry Parrish	.10	.05	.01
☐ 425 Mickey Rivers	.10	.05	.01
☐ 426 Billy Sample	.05	.02	.00
☐ 427 Dave Schmidt	.10	.05	.01
☐ 428 Mike Smithson	.10	.05	.01
☐ 429 Bill Stein	.05	.02	.00
☐ 430 Dave Stewart	.15	.07	.01
☐ 431 Jim Sundberg	.10	.05	.01
☐ 432 Frank Tanana	.10	.05	.01
☐ 433 Dave Tobik	.05	.02	.00
☐ 434 Wayne Tolleson	.10	.05	.01
☐ 435 George Wright	.05	.02	.00
☐ 436 Bill Almon	.05	.02	.00
☐ 437 Keith Atherton	.05	.02	.00
☐ 438 Dave Beard	.05	.02	.00
☐ 439 Tom Burgmeier	.05	.02	.00
☐ 440 Jeff Burroughs	.10	.05	.01
☐ 441 Chris Codiroli	.10	.05	.01
☐ 442 Tim Conroy	.10	.05	.01
☐ 443 Mike Davis	.10	.05	.01
☐ 444 Wayne Gross	.05	.02	.00
☐ 445 Garry Hancock	.05	.02	.00
☐ 446 Mike Heath	.05	.02	.00
☐ 447 Rickey Henderson	.50	.25	.05
☐ 448 Donnie Hill	.10	.05	.01
☐ 449 Bob Kearney	.05	.02	.00
☐ 450 Bill Krueger	.10	.05	.01
☐ 451 Rick Langford	.05	.02	.00
☐ 452 Carney Lansford	.10	.05	.01
☐ 453 Davey Lopes	.10	.05	.01
☐ 454 Steve McCatty	.05	.02	.00
☐ 455 Dan Meyer	.05	.02	.00
☐ 456 Dwayne Murphy	.10	.05	.01
☐ 457 Mike Norris	.05	.02	.00
☐ 458 Ricky Peters	.05	.02	.00

☐ 459 Tony Phillips	.10	.05	.01
☐ 460 Tom Underwood	.05	.02	.00
☐ 461 Mike Warren	.10	.05	.01
☐ 462 Johnny Bench	.40	.20	.04
☐ 463 Bruce Berenyi	.05	.02	.00
☐ 464 Dann Bilardello	.05	.02	.00
☐ 465 Cesar Cedeno	.10	.05	.01
☐ 466 Dave Concepcion	.10	.05	.01
☐ 467 Dan Driessen	.05	.02	.00
☐ 468 Nick Esasky	.35	.17	.03
☐ 469 Rich Gale	.05	.02	.00
☐ 470 Ben Hayes	.05	.02	.00
☐ 471 Paul Householder	.05	.02	.00
☐ 472 Tom Hume	.05	.02	.00
☐ 473 Alan Knicely	.05	.02	.00
☐ 474 Eddie Milner	.05	.02	.00
☐ 475 Ron Oester	.05	.02	.00
☐ 476 Kelly Paris	.10	.05	.01
☐ 477 Frank Pastore	.05	.02	.00
☐ 478 Ted Power	.10	.05	.01
☐ 479 Joe Price	.05	.02	.00
☐ 480 Charlie Puleo	.05	.02	.00
☐ 481 Gary Redus	.25	.12	.02
☐ 482 Bill Scherrer	.10	.05	.01
☐ 483 Mario Soto	.10	.05	.01
☐ 484 Alex Trevino	.05	.02	.00
☐ 485 Duane Walker	.05	.02	.00
☐ 486 Larry Bowa	.10	.05	.01
☐ 487 Warren Brusstar	.05	.02	.00
☐ 488 Bill Buckner	.10	.05	.01
☐ 489 Bill Campbell	.05	.02	.00
☐ 490 Ron Cey	.10	.05	.01
☐ 491 Jody Davis	.10	.05	.01
☐ 492 Leon Durham	.10	.05	.01
☐ 493 Mel Hall	.15	.07	.01
☐ 494 Ferguson Jenkins	.15	.07	.01
☐ 495 Jay Johnstone	.10	.05	.01
☐ 496 Craig Lefferts	.10	.05	.01
☐ 497 Carmelo Martinez	.25	.12	.02
☐ 498 Jerry Morales	.05	.02	.00
☐ 499 Keith Moreland	.10	.05	.01
☐ 500 Dickie Noles	.05	.02	.00
☐ 501 Mike Proly	.05	.02	.00
☐ 502 Chuck Rainey	.05	.02	.00
☐ 503 Dick Ruthven	.05	.02	.00
☐ 504 Ryne Sandberg	1.00	.50	.10
☐ 505 Lee Smith	.15	.07	.01
☐ 506 Steve Trout	.10	.05	.01
☐ 507 Gary Woods	.05	.02	.00
☐ 508 Juan Beniquez	.05	.02	.00
☐ 509 Bob Boone	.10	.05	.01
☐ 510 Rick Burleson	.10	.05	.01
☐ 511 Rod Carew	.45	.22	.04
☐ 512 Bobby Clark	.05	.02	.00
☐ 513 John Curtis	.05	.02	.00
☐ 514 Doug DeCinces	.10	.05	.01
☐ 515 Brian Downing	.10	.05	.01
☐ 516 Tim Foli	.05	.02	.00
☐ 517 Ken Forsch	.05	.02	.00
☐ 518 Bobby Grich	.10	.05	.01
☐ 519 Andy Hassler	.05	.02	.00
☐ 520 Reggie Jackson	.50	.25	.05
☐ 521 Ron Jackson	.05	.02	.00
☐ 522 Tommy John	.15	.07	.01
☐ 523 Bruce Kison	.05	.02	.00
☐ 524 Steve Lubratich	.05	.02	.00
☐ 525 Fred Lynn	.15	.07	.01
☐ 526 Gary Pettis	.35	.17	.03
☐ 527 Luis Sanchez	.05	.02	.00
☐ 528 Daryl Sconiers	.05	.02	.00
☐ 529 Ellis Valentine	.05	.02	.00
☐ 530 Rob Wilfong	.05	.02	.00
☐ 531 Mike Witt	.20	.10	.02
☐ 532 Geoff Zahn	.05	.02	.00
☐ 533 Bud Anderson	.05	.02	.00
☐ 534 Chris Bando	.05	.02	.00
☐ 535 Alan Bannister	.05	.02	.00
☐ 536 Bert Blyleven	.15	.07	.01
☐ 537 Tom Brennan	.05	.02	.00
☐ 538 Jamie Easterly	.05	.02	.00
☐ 539 Juan Eichelberger	.05	.02	.00
☐ 540 Jim Essian	.05	.02	.00
☐ 541 Mike Fischlin	.05	.02	.00
☐ 542 Julio Franco	.25	.12	.02
☐ 543 Mike Hargrove	.05	.02	.00
☐ 544 Toby Harrah	.05	.02	.00
☐ 545 Ron Hassey	.05	.02	.00
☐ 546 Neal Heaton	.25	.12	.02
☐ 547 Bake McBride	.05	.02	.00
☐ 548 Broderick Perkins	.05	.02	.00
☐ 549 Lary Sorensen	.05	.02	.00
☐ 550 Dan Spillner	.05	.02	.00
☐ 551 Rick Sutcliffe	.20	.10	.02
☐ 552 Pat Tabler	.15	.07	.01
☐ 553 Gorman Thomas	.10	.05	.01

☐ 554 Andre Thornton	.10	.05	.01
☐ 555 George Vukovich	.05	.02	.00
☐ 556 Darrell Brown	.05	.02	.00
☐ 557 Tom Brunansky	.20	.10	.02
☐ 558 Randy Bush	.05	.02	.00
☐ 559 Bobby Castillo	.05	.02	.00
☐ 560 John Castino	.05	.02	.00
☐ 561 Ron Davis	.05	.02	.00
☐ 562 Dave Engle	.05	.02	.00
☐ 563 Lenny Faedo	.05	.02	.00
☐ 564 Pete Filson	.05	.02	.00
☐ 565 Gary Gaetti	.40	.20	.04
☐ 566 Mickey Hatcher	.05	.02	.00
☐ 567 Kent Hrbek	.35	.17	.03
☐ 568 Rusty Kuntz	.05	.02	.00
☐ 569 Tim Laudner	.10	.05	.01
☐ 570 Rick Lysander	.05	.02	.00
☐ 571 Bobby Mitchell	.05	.02	.00
☐ 572 Ken Schrom	.10	.05	.01
☐ 573 Ray Smith	.05	.02	.00
☐ 574 Tim Teufel	.35	.17	.03
☐ 575 Frank Viola	.25	.12	.02
☐ 576 Gary Ward	.10	.05	.01
☐ 577 Ron Washington	.05	.02	.00
☐ 578 Len Whitehouse	.05	.02	.00
☐ 579 Al Williams	.05	.02	.00
☐ 580 Bob Bailor	.05	.02	.00
☐ 581 Mark Bradley	.10	.05	.01
☐ 582 Hubie Brooks	.15	.07	.01
☐ 583 Carlos Diaz	.05	.02	.00
☐ 584 George Foster	.15	.07	.01
☐ 585 Brian Giles	.05	.02	.00
☐ 586 Danny Heep	.05	.02	.00
☐ 587 Keith Hernandez	.30	.15	.03
☐ 588 Ron Hodges	.05	.02	.00
☐ 589 Scott Holman	.05	.02	.00
☐ 590 Dave Kingman	.15	.07	.01
☐ 591 Ed Lynch	.05	.02	.00
☐ 592 Jose Oquendo	.25	.12	.02
☐ 593 Jesse Orosco	.10	.05	.01
☐ 594 Junior Ortiz	.05	.02	.00
☐ 595 Tom Seaver	.35	.17	.03
☐ 596 Doug Sisk	.10	.05	.01
☐ 597 Rusty Staub	.10	.05	.01
☐ 598 John Stearns	.05	.02	.00
☐ 599 Darryl Strawberry	10.00	5.00	1.00
☐ 600 Craig Swan	.05	.02	.00
☐ 601 Walt Terrell	.35	.17	.03
☐ 602 Mike Torrez	.05	.02	.00
☐ 603 Mookie Wilson	.10	.05	.01
☐ 604 Jamie Allen	.10	.05	.01
☐ 605 Jim Beattie	.05	.02	.00
☐ 606 Tony Bernazard	.05	.02	.00
☐ 607 Manny Castillo	.05	.02	.00
☐ 608 Bill Caudill	.05	.02	.00
☐ 609 Bryan Clark	.05	.02	.00
☐ 610 Al Cowens	.05	.02	.00
☐ 611 Dave Henderson	.10	.05	.01
☐ 612 Steve Henderson	.05	.02	.00
☐ 613 Orlando Mercado	.05	.02	.00
☐ 614 Mike Moore	.10	.05	.01
☐ 615 Ricky Nelson	.15	.07	.01
(Jamie Nelson's stats on back)			
☐ 616 Spike Owen	.20	.10	.02
☐ 617 Pat Putnam	.05	.02	.00
☐ 618 Ron Roenicke	.05	.02	.00
☐ 619 Mike Stanton	.05	.02	.00
☐ 620 Bob Stoddard	.05	.02	.00
☐ 621 Rick Sweet	.05	.02	.00
☐ 622 Roy Thomas	.05	.02	.00
☐ 623 Ed VandeBerg	.05	.02	.00
☐ 624 Matt Young	.20	.10	.02
☐ 625 Richie Zisk	.05	.02	.00
☐ 626 Fred Lynn 1982 AS Game RB	.15	.07	.01
☐ 627 Manny Trillo 1983 AS Game RB	.10	.05	.01
☐ 628 Steve Garvey NL Iron Man	.20	.10	.02
☐ 629 Rod Carew AL Batting Runner-Up	.20	.10	.02
☐ 630 Wade Boggs AL Batting Champion	.50	.25	.05
☐ 631 Tim Raines: Letting Go of the Raines	.20	.10	.02
☐ 632 Al Oliver Double Trouble	.10	.05	.01
☐ 633 Steve Sax AS Second Base	.10	.05	.01
☐ 634 Dickie Thon AS Shortstop	.10	.05	.01
☐ 635 Ace Firemen Dan Quisenberry and Tippy Martinez	.10	.05	.01

☐ 636	Reds Reunited	.40	.20	.04
	Joe Morgan			
	Pete Rose			
	Tony Perez			
☐ 637	Backstop Stars	.10	.05	.01
	Lance Parrish			
	Bob Boone			
☐ 638	Geo.Brett and G.Perry ...	.25	.12	.02
	Pine Tar 7/24/83			
☐ 639	1983 No Hitters	.10	.05	.01
	Dave Righetti			
	Mike Warren			
	Bob Forsch			
☐ 640	Bench and Yaz	.25	.12	.02
	Retiring Superstars			
☐ 641	Gaylord Perry	.10	.05	.01
	Going Out In Style			
☐ 642	Steve Carlton	.20	.10	.02
	300 Club and			
	Strikeout Record			
☐ 643	Altobelli and Owens	.10	.05	.01
	WS Managers			
☐ 644	Rick Dempsey	.10	.05	.01
	World Series MVP			
☐ 645	Mike Boddicker	.10	.05	.01
	WS Rookie Winner			
☐ 646	Scott McGregor	.10	.05	.01
	WS Clincher			
☐ 647	CL: Orioles/Royals	.08	.01	.00
☐ 648	CL: Phillies/Giants	.07	.01	.00
☐ 649	CL: White Sox/Red Sox .	.07	.01	.00
☐ 650	CL: Tigers/Rangers	.07	.01	.00
☐ 651	CL: Dodgers/A's	.07	.01	.00
☐ 652	CL: Yankees/Reds	.07	.01	.00
☐ 653	CL: Blue Jays/Cubs	.07	.01	.00
☐ 654	CL: Braves/Angels	.07	.01	.00
☐ 655	CL: Brewers/Indians	.07	.01	.00
☐ 656	CL: Astros/Twins	.07	.01	.00
☐ 657	CL: Pirates/Mets	.07	.01	.00
☐ 658	CL: Expos/Mariners	.07	.01	.00
☐ 659	CL: Padres/Specials	.07	.01	.00
☐ 660	CL: Cardinals/Teams	.08	.01	.00

1984 Fleer Update

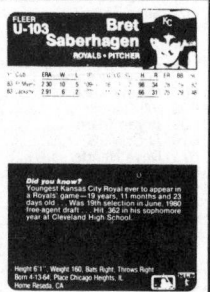

The cards in this 132-card set measure 2 1/2" by 3 1/2". For the first time, the Fleer Gum Company issued a traded, extended, or update set. The purpose of the set was the same as the traded sets issued by Topps over the past four years, i.e., to portray players with their proper team for the current year and to portray rookies who were not in their regular issue. Like the Topps Traded sets of the past four years, the Fleer Update sets were distributed through hobby channels only. The set was quite popular with collectors, and apparently, the print run was relatively short, as the set was quickly in short supply and exhibited a rapid and dramatic price increase. The cards are numbered on the back with a U prefix; the order corresponds to the alphabetical order of the subjects' names.

	MINT	EXC	G-VG
COMPLETE SET	250.00	125.00	25.00
COMMON PLAYER	.20	.10	.02

☐	1U	Willie Aikens	.30	.10	.02
☐	2U	Luis Aponte	.20	.10	.02
☐	3U	Mark Bailey	.30	.15	.03
☐	4U	Bob Bailor	.20	.10	.02
☐	5U	Dusty Baker	.30	.15	.03
☐	6U	Steve Balboni	.30	.15	.03
☐	7U	Alan Bannister	.20	.10	.02
☐	8U	Marty Barrett	3.50	1.75	.35
☐	9U	Dave Beard	.20	.10	.02
☐	10U	Joe Beckwith	.20	.10	.02
☐	11U	Dave Bergman	.20	.10	.02
☐	12U	Tony Bernazard	.30	.15	.03
☐	13U	Bruce Bochte	.30	.15	.03
☐	14U	Barry Bonnell	.20	.10	.02
☐	15U	Phil Bradley	6.00	3.00	.60
☐	16U	Fred Breining	.20	.10	.02
☐	17U	Mike Brown	.30	.15	.03
		(Angels OF)			
☐	18U	Bill Buckner	.40	.20	.04
☐	19U	Ray Burris	.20	.10	.02
☐	20U	John Butcher	.20	.10	.02
☐	21U	Brett Butler	.40	.20	.04
☐	22U	Enos Cabell	.20	.10	.02
☐	23U	Bill Campbell	.20	.10	.02
☐	24U	Bill Caudill	.20	.10	.02
☐	25U	Bobby Clark	.20	.10	.02
☐	26U	Bryan Clark	.20	.10	.02
☐	27U	Roger Clemens	80.00	40.00	8.00
☐	28U	Jaime Cocanower	.30	.15	.03
☐	29U	Ron Darling	10.00	5.00	1.00
☐	30U	Alvin Davis	6.00	3.00	.60
☐	31U	Bob Dernier	.30	.15	.03
☐	32U	Carlos Diaz	.20	.10	.02
☐	33U	Mike Easler	.30	.15	.03
☐	34U	Dennis Eckersley	.30	.15	.03
☐	35U	Jim Essian	.20	.10	.02
☐	36U	Darrell Evans	.40	.20	.04
☐	37U	Mike Fitzgerald	.30	.15	.03
☐	38U	Tim Foli	.20	.10	.02
☐	39U	John Franco	2.50	1.25	.25
☐	40U	George Frazier	.20	.10	.02
☐	41U	Rich Gale	.20	.10	.02
☐	42U	Barbaro Garbey	.30	.15	.03
☐	43U	Dwight Gooden	60.00	30.00	6.00
☐	44U	Goose Gossage	.75	.35	.07
☐	45U	Wayne Gross	.20	.10	.02
☐	46U	Mark Gubicza	1.00	.50	.10
☐	47U	Jackie Gutierrez	.30	.15	.03
☐	48U	Toby Harrah	.20	.10	.02
☐	49U	Ron Hassey	.20	.10	.02
☐	50U	Richie Hebner	.20	.10	.02
☐	51U	Willie Hernandez	.75	.35	.07
☐	52U	Ed Hodge	.20	.10	.02
☐	53U	Ricky Horton	.75	.35	.07
☐	54U	Art Howe	.20	.10	.02
☐	55U	Dane Iorg	.20	.10	.02
☐	56U	Brook Jacoby	3.50	1.75	.35
☐	57U	Dion James	1.00	.50	.10
☐	58U	Mike Jeffcoat	.30	.15	.03
☐	59U	Ruppert Jones	.20	.10	.02
☐	60U	Bob Kearney	.20	.10	.02
☐	61U	Jimmy Key	7.50	3.75	.75
☐	62U	Dave Kingman	.50	.25	.05
☐	63U	Brad Komminsk	.50	.25	.05
☐	64U	Jerry Koosman	.40	.20	.04
☐	65U	Wayne Krenchicki	.20	.10	.02
☐	66U	Rusty Kuntz	.20	.10	.02
☐	67U	Frank LaCorte	.20	.10	.02
☐	68U	Dennis Lamp	.20	.10	.02
☐	69U	Tito Landrum	.20	.10	.02
☐	70U	Mark Langston	7.50	3.75	.75
☐	71U	Rick Leach	.20	.10	.02
☐	72U	Craig Lefferts	.20	.10	.02
☐	73U	Gary Lucas	.20	.10	.02
☐	74U	Jerry Martin	.20	.10	.02
☐	75U	Carmelo Martinez	.30	.15	.03
☐	76U	Mike Mason	.40	.20	.04
☐	77U	Gary Matthews	.30	.15	.03
☐	78U	Andy McGaffigan	.20	.10	.02
☐	79U	Joey McLaughlin	.20	.10	.02
☐	80U	Joe Morgan	2.50	1.25	.25
☐	81U	Darryl Motley	.30	.15	.03
☐	82U	Graig Nettles	1.00	.50	.10
☐	83U	Phil Niekro	2.50	1.25	.25
☐	84U	Ken Oberkfell	.20	.10	.02
☐	85U	Al Oliver	.40	.20	.04
☐	86U	Jorge Orta	.20	.10	.02
☐	87U	Amos Otis	.30	.15	.03
☐	88U	Bob Owchinko	.20	.10	.02
☐	89U	Dave Parker	1.50	.75	.15
☐	90U	Jack Perconte	.20	.10	.02
☐	91U	Tony Perez	1.00	.50	.10
☐	92U	Gerald Perry	.75	.35	.07
☐	93U	Kirby Puckett	65.00	32.50	6.50
☐	94U	Shane Rawley	.40	.20	.04

☐ 95U	Floyd Rayford	.20	.10	.02
☐ 96U	Ron Reed	.20	.10	.02
☐ 97U	R.J. Reynolds	1.50	.75	.15
☐ 98U	Gene Richards	.20	.10	.02
☐ 99U	Jose Rijo	1.00	.50	.10
☐ 100U	Jeff Robinson	.50	.25	.05
	(Giants pitcher)			
☐ 101U	Ron Romanick	.40	.20	.04
☐ 102U	Pete Rose	25.00	12.50	2.50
☐ 103U	Bret Saberhagen	25.00	12.50	2.50
☐ 104U	Scott Sanderson	.30	.15	.03
☐ 105U	Dick Schofield	.75	.35	.07
☐ 106U	Tom Seaver	9.00	4.50	.90
☐ 107U	Jim Slaton	.20	.10	.02
☐ 108U	Mike Smithson	.20	.10	.02
☐ 109U	Lary Sorensen	.20	.10	.02
☐ 110U	Tim Stoddard	.20	.10	.02
☐ 111U	Jeff Stone	.75	.35	.07
☐ 112U	Champ Summers	.20	.10	.02
☐ 113U	Jim Sundberg	.30	.15	.03
☐ 114U	Rick Sutcliffe	.75	.35	.07
☐ 115U	Craig Swan	.20	.10	.02
☐ 116U	Derrel Thomas	.20	.10	.02
☐ 117U	Gorman Thomas	.30	.15	.03
☐ 118U	Alex Trevino	.20	.10	.02
☐ 119U	Manny Trillo	.30	.15	.03
☐ 120U	John Tudor	.50	.25	.05
☐ 121U	Tom Underwood	.20	.10	.02
☐ 122U	Mike Vail	.20	.10	.02
☐ 123U	Tom Waddell	.30	.15	.03
☐ 124U	Gary Ward	.30	.15	.03
☐ 125U	Terry Whitfield	.20	.10	.02
☐ 126U	Curtis Wilkerson	.30	.15	.03
☐ 127U	Frank Williams	.40	.20	.04
☐ 128U	Glenn Wilson	.40	.20	.04
☐ 129U	John Wockenfuss	.20	.10	.02
☐ 130U	Ned Yost	.20	.10	.02
☐ 131U	Mike Young	1.00	.50	.10
☐ 132U	Checklist: 1-132	.20	.02	.00

1985 Fleer

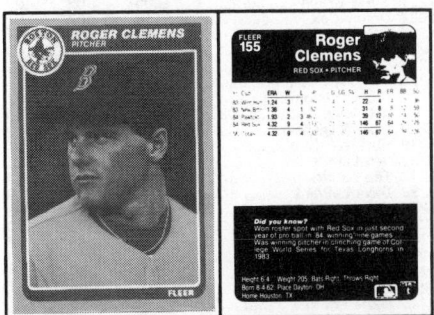

The cards in this 660-card set measure 2 1/2" by 3 1/2". The 1985 Fleer set features fronts which contain the team logo along with the player's name and position. The borders enclosing the photo are color-coded to correspond to the player's team. In each case, the color is one of the standard colors of that team, e.g., orange for Baltimore, red for St. Louis, etc. The backs feature the same name, number, and statistics format that Fleer has been using over the past few years. The cards are ordered alphabetically within team. The teams are ordered based on their respective performance during the prior year, e.g., World Champion Detroit Tigers (1-25), NL Champion San Diego (26- 48), Chicago Cubs (49-71), New York Mets (72-95), Toronto (96- 119), New York Yankees (120-147), Boston (148-169), Baltimore (170-195), Kansas City (196-218), St. Louis (219-243), Philadelphia (244-269), Minnesota (270-292), California (293- 317), Atlanta (318-342), Houston (343-365), Los Angeles (366- 391), Montreal (392-413), Oakland (414-436), Cleveland (437-460), Pittsburgh (461-481), Seattle (482-505),

Chicago White Sox (506- 530), Cincinnati (531-554), Texas (555-575), Milwaukee (576-601), and San Francisco (602-625). Specials (626-643), Rookie pairs (644-653), and checklist cards (654-660) complete the set. The black and white photo on the reverse is included for the third straight year.

		MINT	EXC	G-VG
COMPLETE SET		80.00	40.00	8.00
COMMON PLAYER (1-660)		.05	.02	.00
☐ 1	Doug Bair	.10	.03	.01
☐ 2	Juan Berenguer	.05	.02	.00
☐ 3	Dave Bergman	.05	.02	.00
☐ 4	Tom Brookens	.05	.02	.00
☐ 5	Marty Castillo	.05	.02	.00
☐ 6	Darrell Evans	.15	.07	.01
☐ 7	Barbaro Garbey	.10	.05	.01
☐ 8	Kirk Gibson	.25	.12	.02
☐ 9	John Grubb	.05	.02	.00
☐ 10	Willie Hernandez	.15	.07	.01
☐ 11	Larry Herndon	.05	.02	.00
☐ 12	Howard Johnson	.50	.25	.05
☐ 13	Ruppert Jones	.05	.02	.00
☐ 14	Rusty Kuntz	.05	.02	.00
☐ 15	Chet Lemon	.05	.02	.00
☐ 16	Aurelio Lopez	.05	.02	.00
☐ 17	Sid Monge	.05	.02	.00
☐ 18	Jack Morris	.20	.10	.02
☐ 19	Lance Parrish	.25	.12	.02
☐ 20	Dan Petry	.10	.05	.01
☐ 21	Dave Rozema	.05	.02	.00
☐ 22	Bill Scherrer	.05	.02	.00
☐ 23	Alan Trammell	.25	.12	.02
☐ 24	Lou Whitaker	.15	.07	.01
☐ 25	Milt Wilcox	.05	.02	.00
☐ 26	Kurt Bevacqua	.05	.02	.00
☐ 27	Greg Booker	.05	.02	.00
☐ 28	Bobby Brown	.05	.02	.00
☐ 29	Luis DeLeon	.05	.02	.00
☐ 30	Dave Dravecky	.10	.05	.00
☐ 31	Tim Flannery	.05	.02	.00
☐ 32	Steve Garvey	.35	.17	.03
☐ 33	Goose Gossage	.15	.07	.01
☐ 34	Tony Gwynn	.75	.35	.07
☐ 35	Greg Harris	.05	.02	.00
☐ 36	Andy Hawkins	.05	.02	.00
☐ 37	Terry Kennedy	.10	.05	.01
☐ 38	Craig Lefferts	.05	.02	.00
☐ 39	Tim Lollar	.05	.02	.00
☐ 40	Carmelo Martinez	.10	.05	.01
☐ 41	Kevin McReynolds	.45	.22	.04
☐ 42	Graig Nettles	.15	.07	.01
☐ 43	Luis Salazar	.05	.02	.00
☐ 44	Eric Show	.05	.02	.00
☐ 45	Garry Templeton	.10	.05	.01
☐ 46	Mark Thurmond	.05	.02	.00
☐ 47	Ed Whitson	.05	.02	.00
☐ 48	Alan Wiggins	.10	.05	.01
☐ 49	Rich Bordi	.05	.02	.00
☐ 50	Larry Bowa	.10	.05	.01
☐ 51	Warren Brusstar	.05	.02	.00
☐ 52	Ron Cey	.10	.05	.01
☐ 53	Henry Cotto	.10	.05	.01
☐ 54	Jody Davis	.10	.05	.01
☐ 55	Bob Dernier	.05	.02	.00
☐ 56	Leon Durham	.10	.05	.01
☐ 57	Dennis Eckersley	.10	.05	.01
☐ 58	George Frazier	.05	.02	.00
☐ 59	Richie Hebner	.05	.02	.00
☐ 60	Dave Lopes	.10	.05	.01
☐ 61	Gary Matthews	.10	.05	.01
☐ 62	Keith Moreland	.10	.05	.01
☐ 63	Rick Reuschel	.10	.05	.01
☐ 64	Dick Ruthven	.05	.02	.00
☐ 65	Ryne Sandberg	.45	.22	.04
☐ 66	Scott Sanderson	.05	.02	.00
☐ 67	Lee Smith	.10	.05	.01
☐ 68	Tim Stoddard	.05	.02	.00
☐ 69	Rick Sutcliffe	.15	.07	.01
☐ 70	Steve Trout	.10	.05	.01
☐ 71	Gary Woods	.05	.02	.00
☐ 72	Wally Backman	.10	.05	.01
☐ 73	Bruce Berenyi	.05	.02	.00
☐ 74	Hubie Brooks	.10	.05	.01
☐ 75	Kelvin Chapman	.10	.05	.01
☐ 76	Ron Darling	1.00	.50	.10
☐ 77	Sid Fernandez	1.00	.50	.10
☐ 78	Mike Fitzgerald	.05	.02	.00
☐ 79	George Foster	.15	.07	.01
☐ 80	Brent Gaff	.05	.02	.00
☐ 81	Ron Gardenhire	.05	.02	.00
☐ 82	Dwight Gooden	7.50	3.75	.75

☐ 83	Tom Gorman	.05	.02	.00	☐ 177	Mike Flanagan	.10	.05	.01
☐ 84	Danny Heep	.05	.02	.00	☐ 178	Dan Ford	.05	.02	.00
☐ 85	Keith Hernandez	.30	.15	.03	☐ 179	Wayne Gross	.05	.02	.00
☐ 86	Ray Knight	.10	.05	.01	☐ 180	John Lowenstein	.05	.02	.00
☐ 87	Ed Lynch	.05	.02	.00	☐ 181	Dennis Martinez	.10	.05	.01
☐ 88	Jose Oquendo	.10	.05	.01	☐ 182	Tippy Martinez	.05	.02	.00
☐ 89	Jesse Orosco	.10	.05	.01	☐ 183	Scott McGregor	.10	.05	.01
☐ 90	Rafael Santana	.20	.10	.02	☐ 184	Eddie Murray	.45	.22	.04
☐ 91	Doug Sisk	.05	.02	.00	☐ 185	Joe Nolan	.05	.02	.00
☐ 92	Rusty Staub	.10	.05	.01	☐ 186	Floyd Rayford	.05	.02	.00
☐ 93	Darryl Strawberry	2.50	1.25	.25	☐ 187	Cal Ripken	.45	.22	.04
☐ 94	Walt Terrell	.10	.05	.01	☐ 188	Gary Roenicke	.05	.02	.00
☐ 95	Mookie Wilson	.10	.05	.01	☐ 189	Lenn Sakata	.05	.02	.00
☐ 96	Jim Acker	.05	.02	.00	☐ 190	John Shelby	.05	.02	.00
☐ 97	Willie Aikens	.05	.02	.00	☐ 191	Ken Singleton	.10	.05	.01
☐ 98	Doyle Alexander	.10	.05	.01	☐ 192	Sammy Stewart	.05	.02	.00
☐ 99	Jesse Barfield	.30	.15	.03	☐ 193	Bill Swaggerty	.10	.05	.01
☐ 100	George Bell	.45	.22	.04	☐ 194	Tom Underwood	.05	.02	.00
☐ 101	Jim Clancy	.05	.02	.00	☐ 195	Mike Young	.15	.07	.01
☐ 102	Dave Collins	.05	.02	.00	☐ 196	Steve Balboni	.05	.02	.00
☐ 103	Tony Fernandez	.25	.12	.02	☐ 197	Joe Beckwith	.05	.02	.00
☐ 104	Damaso Garcia	.10	.05	.01	☐ 198	Bud Black	.05	.02	.00
☐ 105	Jim Gott	.05	.02	.00	☐ 199	George Brett	.45	.22	.04
☐ 106	Alfredo Griffin	.10	.05	.01	☐ 200	Onix Concepcion	.05	.02	.00
☐ 107	Garth Iorg	.05	.02	.00	☐ 201	Mark Gubicza	.25	.12	.02
☐ 108	Roy Lee Jackson	.05	.02	.00	☐ 202	Larry Gura	.05	.02	.00
☐ 109	Cliff Johnson	.05	.02	.00	☐ 203	Mark Huismann	.05	.02	.00
☐ 110	Jimmy Key	1.25	.60	.12	☐ 204	Dane Iorg	.05	.02	.00
☐ 111	Dennis Lamp	.05	.02	.00	☐ 205	Danny Jackson	.10	.05	.01
☐ 112	Rick Leach	.05	.02	.00	☐ 206	Charlie Leibrandt	.10	.05	.01
☐ 113	Luis Leal	.05	.02	.00	☐ 207	Hal McRae	.10	.05	.01
☐ 114	Buck Martinez	.05	.02	.00	☐ 208	Darryl Motley	.05	.02	.00
☐ 115	Lloyd Moseby	.15	.07	.01	☐ 209	Jorge Orta	.05	.02	.00
☐ 116	Rance Mulliniks	.05	.02	.00	☐ 210	Greg Pryor	.05	.02	.00
☐ 117	Dave Stieb	.15	.07	.01	☐ 211	Dan Quisenberry	.15	.07	.01
☐ 118	Willie Upshaw	.10	.05	.01	☐ 212	Bret Saberhagen	1.00	.50	.10
☐ 119	Ernie Whitt	.05	.02	.00	☐ 213	Pat Sheridan	.05	.02	.00
☐ 120	Mike Armstrong	.05	.02	.00	☐ 214	Don Slaught	.05	.02	.00
☐ 121	Don Baylor	.15	.07	.01	☐ 215	U.L. Washington	.05	.02	.00
☐ 122	Marty Bystrom	.05	.02	.00	☐ 216	John Wathan	.10	.05	.01
☐ 123	Rick Cerone	.05	.02	.00	☐ 217	Frank White	.10	.05	.01
☐ 124	Joe Cowley	.05	.02	.00	☐ 218	Willie Wilson	.15	.07	.01
☐ 125	Brian Dayett	.05	.02	.00	☐ 219	Neil Allen	.05	.02	.00
☐ 126	Tim Foli	.05	.02	.00	☐ 220	Joaquin Andujar	.10	.05	.01
☐ 127	Ray Fontenot	.05	.02	.00	☐ 221	Steve Braun	.05	.02	.00
☐ 128	Ken Griffey	.10	.05	.01	☐ 222	Danny Cox	.15	.07	.01
☐ 129	Ron Guidry	.15	.07	.01	☐ 223	Bob Forsch	.10	.05	.01
☐ 130	Toby Harrah	.05	.02	.00	☐ 224	David Green	.05	.02	.00
☐ 131	Jay Howell	.05	.02	.00	☐ 225	George Hendrick	.10	.05	.01
☐ 132	Steve Kemp	.10	.05	.01	☐ 226	Tom Herr	.10	.05	.01
☐ 133	Don Mattingly	12.50	6.25	1.25	☐ 227	Ricky Horton	.25	.12	.02
☐ 134	Bobby Meacham	.05	.02	.00	☐ 228	Art Howe	.05	.02	.00
☐ 135	John Montefusco	.05	.02	.00	☐ 229	Mike Jorgensen	.05	.02	.00
☐ 136	Omar Moreno	.05	.02	.00	☐ 230	Kurt Kepshire	.10	.05	.01
☐ 137	Dale Murray	.05	.02	.00	☐ 231	Jeff Lahti	.05	.02	.00
☐ 138	Phil Niekro	.20	.10	.02	☐ 232	Tito Landrum	.05	.02	.00
☐ 139	Mike Pagliarulo	1.50	.75	.15	☐ 233	Dave LaPoint	.05	.02	.00
☐ 140	Willie Randolph	.10	.05	.01	☐ 234	Willie McGee	.30	.15	.03
☐ 141	Dennis Rasmussen	.15	.07	.01	☐ 235	Tom Nieto	.05	.02	.00
☐ 142	Dave Righetti	.20	.10	.02	☐ 236	Terry Pendleton	.75	.35	.07
☐ 143	Jose Rijo	.30	.15	.03	☐ 237	Darrell Porter	.05	.02	.00
☐ 144	Andre Robertson	.05	.02	.00	☐ 238	Dave Rucker	.05	.02	.00
☐ 145	Bob Shirley	.05	.02	.00	☐ 239	Lonnie Smith	.10	.05	.01
☐ 146	Dave Winfield	.35	.17	.03	☐ 240	Ozzie Smith	.25	.12	.02
☐ 147	Butch Wynegar	.05	.02	.00	☐ 241	Bruce Sutter	.15	.07	.01
☐ 148	Gary Allenson	.05	.02	.00	☐ 242	Andy Van Slyke	.15	.07	.01
☐ 149	Tony Armas	.10	.05	.01	☐ 243	Dave Von Ohlen	.05	.02	.00
☐ 150	Marty Barrett	.15	.07	.01	☐ 244	Larry Andersen	.05	.02	.00
☐ 151	Wade Boggs	3.00	1.50	.30	☐ 245	Bill Campbell	.05	.02	.00
☐ 152	Dennis Boyd	.15	.07	.01	☐ 246	Steve Carlton	.35	.17	.03
☐ 153	Bill Buckner	.10	.05	.01	☐ 247	Tim Corcoran	.05	.02	.00
☐ 154	Mark Clear	.05	.02	.00	☐ 248	Ivan DeJesus	.05	.02	.00
☐ 155	Roger Clemens	10.00	5.00	1.00	☐ 249	John Denny	.10	.05	.01
☐ 156	Steve Crawford	.05	.02	.00	☐ 250	Bo Diaz	.10	.05	.01
☐ 157	Mike Easler	.10	.05	.01	☐ 251	Greg Gross	.05	.02	.00
☐ 158	Dwight Evans	.15	.07	.01	☐ 252	Kevin Gross	.05	.02	.00
☐ 159	Rich Gedman	.10	.05	.01	☐ 253	Von Hayes	.15	.07	.01
☐ 160	Jackie Gutierrez	.20	.10	.02	☐ 254	Al Holland	.05	.02	.00
	(W.Boggs on deck)				☐ 255	Charles Hudson	.05	.02	.00
☐ 161	Bruce Hurst	.10	.05	.01	☐ 256	Jerry Koosman	.10	.05	.01
☐ 162	John Henry Johnson	.05	.02	.00	☐ 257	Joe Lefebvre	.05	.02	.00
☐ 163	Rick Miller	.05	.02	.00	☐ 258	Sixto Lezcano	.05	.02	.00
☐ 164	Reid Nichols	.05	.02	.00	☐ 259	Garry Maddox	.05	.02	.00
☐ 165	Al Nipper	.25	.12	.02	☐ 260	Len Matuszek	.05	.02	.00
☐ 166	Bob Ojeda	.10	.05	.01	☐ 261	Tug McGraw	.10	.05	.01
☐ 167	Jerry Remy	.05	.02	.00	☐ 262	Al Oliver	.10	.05	.01
☐ 168	Jim Rice	.35	.17	.03	☐ 263	Shane Rawley	.10	.05	.01
☐ 169	Bob Stanley	.05	.02	.00	☐ 264	Juan Samuel	.40	.20	.04
☐ 170	Mike Boddicker	.10	.05	.01	☐ 265	Mike Schmidt	.50	.25	.05
☐ 171	Al Bumbry	.05	.02	.00	☐ 266	Jeff Stone	.25	.12	.02
☐ 172	Todd Cruz	.05	.02	.00	☐ 267	Ozzie Virgil	.05	.02	.00
☐ 173	Rich Dauer	.05	.02	.00	☐ 268	Glenn Wilson	.10	.05	.01
☐ 174	Storm Davis	.10	.05	.01	☐ 269	John Wockenfuss	.05	.02	.00
☐ 175	Rick Dempsey	.05	.02	.00	☐ 270	Darrell Brown	.05	.02	.00
☐ 176	Jim Dwyer	.05	.02	.00	☐ 271	Tom Brunansky	.15	.07	.01

☐ 272	Randy Bush	.05	.02	.00	☐ 366	Dave Anderson	.05	.02	.00
☐ 273	John Butcher	.05	.02	.00	☐ 367	Bob Bailor	.05	.02	.00
☐ 274	Bobby Castillo	.05	.02	.00	☐ 368	Greg Brock	.10	.05	.01
☐ 275	Ron Davis	.05	.02	.00	☐ 369	Carlos Diaz	.05	.02	.00
☐ 276	Dave Engle	.05	.02	.00	☐ 370	Pedro Guerrero	.25	.12	.02
☐ 277	Pete Filson	.05	.02	.00	☐ 371	Orel Hershiser	2.00	1.00	.20
☐ 278	Gary Gaetti	.25	.12	.02	☐ 372	Rick Honeycutt	.05	.02	.00
☐ 279	Mickey Hatcher	.05	.02	.00	☐ 373	Burt Hooton	.05	.02	.00
☐ 280	Ed Hodge	.05	.02	.00	☐ 374	Ken Howell	.20	.10	.02
☐ 281	Kent Hrbek	.30	.15	.03	☐ 375	Ken Landreaux	.05	.02	.00
☐ 282	Houston Jimenez	.05	.02	.00	☐ 376	Candy Maldonado	.15	.07	.01
☐ 283	Tim Laudner	.10	.05	.01	☐ 377	Mike Marshall	.15	.07	.01
☐ 284	Rick Lysander	.05	.02	.00	☐ 378	Tom Niedenfuer	.10	.05	.01
☐ 285	Dave Meier	.10	.05	.01	☐ 379	Alejandro Pena	.10	.05	.01
☐ 286	Kirby Puckett	10.00	5.00	1.00	☐ 380	Jerry Reuss	.10	.05	.01
☐ 287	Pat Putnam	.05	.02	.00	☐ 381	R.J. Reynolds	.35	.17	.03
☐ 288	Ken Schrom	.05	.02	.00	☐ 382	German Rivera	.10	.05	.01
☐ 289	Mike Smithson	.05	.02	.00	☐ 383	Bill Russell	.05	.02	.00
☐ 290	Tim Teufel	.05	.02	.00	☐ 384	Steve Sax	.20	.10	.02
☐ 291	Frank Viola	.15	.07	.01	☐ 385	Mike Scioscia	.05	.02	.00
☐ 292	Ron Washington	.05	.02	.00	☐ 386	Franklin Stubbs	.45	.22	.04
☐ 293	Don Aase	.05	.02	.00	☐ 387	Fernando Valenzuela	.35	.17	.03
☐ 294	Juan Beniquez	.05	.02	.00	☐ 388	Bob Welch	.10	.05	.01
☐ 295	Bob Boone	.10	.05	.01	☐ 389	Terry Whitfield	.05	.02	.00
☐ 296	Mike Brown	.05	.02	.00	☐ 390	Steve Yeager	.05	.02	.00
	(Angels OF)				☐ 391	Pat Zachry	.05	.02	.00
☐ 297	Rod Carew	.35	.17	.03	☐ 392	Fred Breining	.05	.02	.00
☐ 298	Doug Corbett	.05	.02	.00	☐ 393	Gary Carter	.35	.17	.03
☐ 299	Doug DeCinces	.10	.05	.01	☐ 394	Andre Dawson	.30	.15	.03
☐ 300	Brian Downing	.10	.05	.01	☐ 395	Miguel Dilone	.05	.02	.00
☐ 301	Ken Forsch	.05	.02	.00	☐ 396	Dan Driessen	.05	.02	.00
☐ 302	Bobby Grich	.10	.05	.01	☐ 397	Doug Flynn	.05	.02	.00
☐ 303	Reggie Jackson	.40	.20	.04	☐ 398	Terry Francona	.05	.02	.00
☐ 304	Tommy John	.15	.07	.01	☐ 399	Bill Gullickson	.10	.05	.01
☐ 305	Curt Kaufman	.10	.05	.01	☐ 400	Bob James	.05	.02	.00
☐ 306	Bruce Kison	.05	.02	.00	☐ 401	Charlie Lea	.05	.02	.00
☐ 307	Fred Lynn	.15	.07	.01	☐ 402	Bryan Little	.05	.02	.00
☐ 308	Gary Pettis	.10	.05	.01	☐ 403	Gary Lucas	.05	.02	.00
☐ 309	Ron Romanick	.10	.05	.01	☐ 404	David Palmer	.05	.02	.00
☐ 310	Luis Sanchez	.05	.02	.00	☐ 405	Tim Raines	.35	.17	.03
☐ 311	Dick Schofield	.10	.05	.01	☐ 406	Mike Ramsey	.05	.02	.00
☐ 312	Daryl Sconiers	.05	.02	.00	☐ 407	Jeff Reardon	.15	.07	.01
☐ 313	Jim Slaton	.05	.02	.00	☐ 408	Steve Rogers	.10	.05	.01
☐ 314	Derrel Thomas	.05	.02	.00	☐ 409	Dan Schatzeder	.05	.02	.00
☐ 315	Rob Wilfong	.05	.02	.00	☐ 410	Bryn Smith	.05	.02	.00
☐ 316	Mike Witt	.15	.07	.01	☐ 411	Mike Stenhouse	.05	.02	.00
☐ 317	Geoff Zahn	.05	.02	.00	☐ 412	Tim Wallach	.15	.07	.01
☐ 318	Len Barker	.05	.02	.00	☐ 413	Jim Wohlford	.05	.02	.00
☐ 319	Steve Bedrosian	.15	.07	.01	☐ 414	Bill Almon	.05	.02	.00
☐ 320	Bruce Benedict	.05	.02	.00	☐ 415	Keith Atherton	.05	.02	.00
☐ 321	Rick Camp	.05	.02	.00	☐ 416	Bruce Bochte	.05	.02	.00
☐ 322	Chris Chambliss	.10	.05	.01	☐ 417	Tom Burgmeier	.05	.02	.00
☐ 323	Jeff Dedmon	.10	.05	.01	☐ 418	Ray Burris	.05	.02	.00
☐ 324	Terry Forster	.10	.05	.01	☐ 419	Bill Caudill	.05	.02	.00
☐ 325	Gene Garber	.05	.02	.00	☐ 420	Chris Codiroli	.05	.02	.00
☐ 326	Albert Hall	.10	.05	.01	☐ 421	Tim Conroy	.05	.02	.00
☐ 327	Terry Harper	.05	.02	.00	☐ 422	Mike Heath	.05	.02	.00
☐ 328	Bob Horner	.20	.10	.02	☐ 423	Jim Essian	.05	.02	.00
☐ 329	Glenn Hubbard	.05	.02	.00	☐ 424	Mike Heath	.05	.02	.00
☐ 330	Randy Johnson	.05	.02	.00	☐ 425	Rickey Henderson	.45	.22	.04
☐ 331	Brad Komminsk	.10	.05	.01	☐ 426	Donnie Hill	.05	.02	.00
☐ 332	Rick Mahler	.05	.02	.00	☐ 427	Dave Kingman	.10	.05	.01
☐ 333	Craig McMurtry	.05	.02	.00	☐ 428	Bill Krueger	.05	.02	.00
☐ 334	Donnie Moore	.05	.02	.00	☐ 429	Carney Lansford	.10	.05	.01
☐ 335	Dale Murphy	.60	.30	.06	☐ 430	Steve McCatty	.05	.02	.00
☐ 336	Ken Oberkfell	.05	.02	.00	☐ 431	Joe Morgan	.15	.07	.01
☐ 337	Pascual Perez	.05	.02	.00	☐ 432	Dwayne Murphy	.05	.02	.00
☐ 338	Gerald Perry	.15	.07	.01	☐ 433	Tony Phillips	.05	.02	.00
☐ 339	Rafael Ramirez	.05	.02	.00	☐ 434	Lary Sorensen	.05	.02	.00
☐ 340	Jerry Royster	.05	.02	.00	☐ 435	Mike Warren	.05	.02	.00
☐ 341	Alex Trevino	.05	.02	.00	☐ 436	Curt Young	.45	.22	.04
☐ 342	Claudell Washington	.10	.05	.01	☐ 437	Luis Aponte	.05	.02	.00
☐ 343	Alan Ashby	.05	.02	.00	☐ 438	Chris Bando	.05	.02	.00
☐ 344	Mark Bailey	.10	.05	.01	☐ 439	Tony Bernazard	.05	.02	.00
☐ 345	Kevin Bass	.15	.07	.01	☐ 440	Bert Blyleven	.10	.05	.01
☐ 346	Enos Cabell	.05	.02	.00	☐ 441	Brett Butler	.10	.05	.01
☐ 347	Jose Cruz	.10	.05	.01	☐ 442	Ernie Camacho	.05	.02	.00
☐ 348	Bill Dawley	.05	.02	.00	☐ 443	Joe Carter	1.25	.60	.12
☐ 349	Frank DiPino	.05	.02	.00	☐ 444	Carmelo Castillo	.05	.02	.00
☐ 350	Bill Doran	.15	.07	.01	☐ 445	Jamie Easterly	.05	.02	.00
☐ 351	Phil Garner	.05	.02	.00	☐ 446	Steve Farr	.15	.07	.01
☐ 352	Bob Knepper	.10	.05	.01	☐ 447	Mike Fischlin	.05	.02	.00
☐ 353	Mike LaCoss	.05	.02	.00	☐ 448	Julio Franco	.15	.07	.01
☐ 354	Jerry Mumphrey	.05	.02	.00	☐ 449	Mel Hall	.10	.05	.01
☐ 355	Joe Niekro	.10	.05	.01	☐ 450	Mike Hargrove	.05	.02	.00
☐ 356	Terry Puhl	.05	.02	.00	☐ 451	Neal Heaton	.05	.02	.00
☐ 357	Craig Reynolds	.05	.02	.00	☐ 452	Brook Jacoby	.15	.07	.01
☐ 358	Vern Ruhle	.05	.02	.00	☐ 453	Mike Jeffcoat	.05	.02	.00
☐ 359	Nolan Ryan	.35	.17	.03	☐ 454	Don Schulze	.10	.05	.01
☐ 360	Joe Sambito	.05	.02	.00	☐ 455	Roy Smith	.05	.02	.00
☐ 361	Mike Scott	.30	.15	.03	☐ 456	Pat Tabler	.15	.07	.01
☐ 362	Dave Smith	.10	.05	.01	☐ 457	Andre Thornton	.10	.05	.01
☐ 363	Julio Solano	.10	.05	.01	☐ 458	George Vukovich	.05	.02	.00
☐ 364	Dickie Thon	.05	.02	.00	☐ 459	Tom Waddell	.10	.05	.01
☐ 365	Denny Walling	.05	.02	.00	☐ 460	Jerry Willard	.05	.02	.00

☐ 461	Dale Berra	.05	.02	.00
☐ 462	John Candelaria	.10	.05	.01
☐ 463	Jose DeLeon	.05	.02	.00
☐ 464	Doug Frobel	.05	.02	.00
☐ 465	Cecilio Guante	.05	.02	.00
☐ 466	Brian Harper	.05	.02	.00
☐ 467	Lee Lacy	.05	.02	.00
☐ 468	Bill Madlock	.12	.06	.01
☐ 469	Lee Mazzilli	.05	.02	.00
☐ 470	Larry McWilliams	.05	.02	.00
☐ 471	Jim Morrison	.05	.02	.00
☐ 472	Tony Pena	.15	.07	.01
☐ 473	Johnny Ray	.10	.05	.01
☐ 474	Rick Rhoden	.10	.05	.01
☐ 475	Don Robinson	.05	.02	.00
☐ 476	Rod Scurry	.05	.02	.00
☐ 477	Kent Tekulve	.10	.05	.01
☐ 478	Jason Thompson	.05	.02	.00
☐ 479	John Tudor	.15	.07	.01
☐ 480	Lee Tunnell	.05	.02	.00
☐ 481	Marvell Wynne	.05	.02	.00
☐ 482	Salome Barojas	.05	.02	.00
☐ 483	Dave Beard	.05	.02	.00
☐ 484	Jim Beattie	.05	.02	.00
☐ 485	Barry Bonnell	.05	.02	.00
☐ 486	Phil Bradley	1.25	.60	.12
☐ 487	Al Cowens	.05	.02	.00
☐ 488	Alvin Davis	1.25	.60	.12
☐ 489	Dave Henderson	.10	.05	.01
☐ 490	Steve Henderson	.05	.02	.00
☐ 491	Bob Kearney	.05	.02	.00
☐ 492	Mark Langston	1.25	.60	.12
☐ 493	Larry Milbourne	.05	.02	.00
☐ 494	Paul Mirabella	.05	.02	.00
☐ 495	Mike Moore	.10	.05	.01
☐ 496	Edwin Nunez	.05	.02	.00
☐ 497	Spike Owen	.05	.02	.00
☐ 498	Jack Perconte	.05	.02	.00
☐ 499	Ken Phelps	.05	.02	.00
☐ 500	Jim Presley	1.50	.75	.15
☐ 501	Mike Stanton	.05	.02	.00
☐ 502	Bob Stoddard	.05	.02	.00
☐ 503	Gorman Thomas	.10	.05	.01
☐ 504	Ed VandeBerg	.05	.02	.00
☐ 505	Matt Young	.05	.02	.00
☐ 506	Juan Agosto	.05	.02	.00
☐ 507	Harold Baines	.20	.10	.02
☐ 508	Floyd Bannister	.10	.05	.01
☐ 509	Britt Burns	.10	.05	.01
☐ 510	Julio Cruz	.05	.02	.00
☐ 511	Richard Dotson	.10	.05	.01
☐ 512	Jerry Dybzinski	.05	.02	.00
☐ 513	Carlton Fisk	.15	.07	.01
☐ 514	Scott Fletcher	.10	.05	.01
☐ 515	Jerry Hairston	.05	.02	.00
☐ 516	Marc Hill	.05	.02	.00
☐ 517	LaMarr Hoyt	.10	.05	.01
☐ 518	Ron Kittle	.15	.07	.01
☐ 519	Rudy Law	.05	.02	.00
☐ 520	Vance Law	.05	.02	.00
☐ 521	Greg Luzinski	.10	.05	.01
☐ 522	Gene Nelson	.05	.02	.00
☐ 523	Tom Paciorek	.05	.02	.00
☐ 524	Ron Reed	.05	.02	.00
☐ 525	Bert Roberge	.05	.02	.00
☐ 526	Tom Seaver	.30	.15	.03
☐ 527	Roy Smalley	.05	.02	.00
☐ 528	Dan Spillner	.05	.02	.00
☐ 529	Mike Squires	.05	.02	.00
☐ 530	Greg Walker	.15	.07	.01
☐ 531	Cesar Cedeno	.10	.05	.01
☐ 532	Dave Concepcion	.10	.05	.01
☐ 533	Eric Davis	20.00	10.00	2.00
☐ 534	Nick Esasky	.10	.05	.01
☐ 535	Tom Foley	.05	.02	.00
☐ 536	John Franco	.50	.25	.05
☐ 537	Brad Gulden	.05	.02	.00
☐ 538	Tom Hume	.05	.02	.00
☐ 539	Wayne Krenchicki	.05	.02	.00
☐ 540	Andy McGaffigan	.05	.02	.00
☐ 541	Eddie Milner	.05	.02	.00
☐ 542	Ron Oester	.05	.02	.00
☐ 543	Bob Owchinko	.05	.02	.00
☐ 544	Dave Parker	.18	.09	.01
☐ 545	Frank Pastore	.05	.02	.00
☐ 546	Tony Perez	.15	.07	.01
☐ 547	Ted Power	.10	.05	.01
☐ 548	Joe Price	.05	.02	.00
☐ 549	Gary Redus	.10	.05	.01
☐ 550	Pete Rose	.90	.45	.09
☐ 551	Jeff Russell	.05	.02	.00
☐ 552	Mario Soto	.10	.05	.01
☐ 553	Jay Tibbs	.25	.12	.02
☐ 554	Duane Walker	.05	.02	.00
☐ 555	Alan Bannister	.05	.02	.00
☐ 556	Buddy Bell	.15	.07	.01
☐ 557	Danny Darwin	.05	.02	.00
☐ 558	Charlie Hough	.10	.05	.01
☐ 559	Bobby Jones	.05	.02	.00
☐ 560	Odell Jones	.05	.02	.00
☐ 561	Jeff Kunkel	.10	.05	.01
☐ 562	Mike Mason	.10	.05	.01
☐ 563	Pete O'Brien	.15	.07	.01
☐ 564	Larry Parrish	.10	.05	.01
☐ 565	Mickey Rivers	.10	.05	.01
☐ 566	Billy Sample	.05	.02	.00
☐ 567	Dave Schmidt	.10	.05	.01
☐ 568	Donnie Scott	.05	.02	.00
☐ 569	Dave Stewart	.15	.07	.01
☐ 570	Frank Tanana	.10	.05	.01
☐ 571	Wayne Tolleson	.05	.02	.00
☐ 572	Gary Ward	.10	.05	.01
☐ 573	Curtis Wilkerson	.05	.02	.00
☐ 574	George Wright	.05	.02	.00
☐ 575	Ned Yost	.05	.02	.00
☐ 576	Mark Brouhard	.05	.02	.00
☐ 577	Mike Caldwell	.05	.02	.00
☐ 578	Bobby Clark	.05	.02	.00
☐ 579	Jaime Cocanower	.05	.02	.00
☐ 580	Cecil Cooper	.15	.07	.01
☐ 581	Rollie Fingers	.15	.07	.01
☐ 582	Jim Gantner	.05	.02	.00
☐ 583	Moose Haas	.05	.02	.00
☐ 584	Dion James	.20	.10	.02
☐ 585	Pete Ladd	.05	.02	.00
☐ 586	Rick Manning	.05	.02	.00
☐ 587	Bob McClure	.05	.02	.00
☐ 588	Paul Molitor	.20	.10	.02
☐ 589	Charlie Moore	.05	.02	.00
☐ 590	Ben Oglivie	.10	.05	.01
☐ 591	Chuck Porter	.05	.02	.00
☐ 592	Randy Ready	.25	.12	.02
☐ 593	Ed Romero	.05	.02	.00
☐ 594	Bill Schroeder	.05	.02	.00
☐ 595	Ray Searage	.05	.02	.00
☐ 596	Ted Simmons	.10	.05	.01
☐ 597	Jim Sundberg	.05	.02	.00
☐ 598	Don Sutton	.20	.10	.02
☐ 599	Tom Tellmann	.05	.02	.00
☐ 600	Rick Waits	.05	.02	.00
☐ 601	Robin Yount	.30	.15	.03
☐ 602	Dusty Baker	.10	.05	.01
☐ 603	Bob Brenly	.10	.05	.01
☐ 604	Jack Clark	.20	.10	.02
☐ 605	Chili Davis	.10	.05	.01
☐ 606	Mark Davis	.05	.02	.00
☐ 607	Dan Gladden	.35	.17	.03
☐ 608	Atlee Hammaker	.05	.02	.00
☐ 609	Mike Krukow	.10	.05	.01
☐ 610	Duane Kuiper	.05	.02	.00
☐ 611	Bob Lacey	.05	.02	.00
☐ 612	Bill Laskey	.05	.02	.00
☐ 613	Gary Lavelle	.05	.02	.00
☐ 614	Johnnie LeMaster	.05	.02	.00
☐ 615	Jeff Leonard	.15	.07	.01
☐ 616	Randy Lerch	.05	.02	.00
☐ 617	Greg Minton	.05	.02	.00
☐ 618	Steve Nicosia	.05	.02	.00
☐ 619	Gene Richards	.05	.02	.00
☐ 620	Jeff Robinson	.40	.20	.04
	(Giants pitcher)			
☐ 621	Scot Thompson	.05	.02	.00
☐ 622	Manny Trillo	.05	.02	.00
☐ 623	Brad Wellman	.05	.02	.00
☐ 624	Frank Williams	.20	.10	.02
☐ 625	Joel Youngblood	.05	.02	.00
☐ 626	Cal Ripken IA	.25	.12	.02
☐ 627	Mike Schmidt IA	.30	.15	.03
☐ 628	Giving The Signs	.05	.02	.00
	Sparky Anderson			
☐ 629	AL Pitcher's Nightmare	.25	.12	.02
	Dave Winfield			
	Rickey Henderson			
☐ 630	NL Pitcher's Nightmare	.25	.12	.02
	Mike Schmidt			
	Ryne Sandberg			
☐ 631	NL All-Stars	.25	.12	.02
	Darryl Strawberry			
	Gary Carter			
	Steve Garvey			
	Ozzie Smith			
☐ 632	A-S Winning Battery	.10	.05	.01
	Gary Carter			
	Charlie Lea			
☐ 633	NL Pennant Clinchers	.12	.06	.01
	Steve Garvey			
	Goose Gossage			
☐ 634	NL Rookie Phenoms	.90	.45	.09
	Dwight Gooden			
	Juan Samuel			

		MINT	EXC	G-VG
☐ 635	Toronto's Big Guns .... Willie Upshaw	.10	.05	.01
☐ 636	Toronto's Big Guns .... Lloyd Moseby	.10	.05	.01
☐ 637	HOLLAND: Al Holland	.05	.02	.00
☐ 638	TUNNELL: Lee Tunnell ...	.05	.02	.00
☐ 639	500th Homer .... Reggie Jackson	.30	.15	.03
☐ 640	4000th Hit .... Pete Rose	.45	.22	.04
☐ 641	Father and Son .... Cal Ripken Jr. and Sr.	.20	.10	.02
☐ 642	Cubs: Division Champs ...	.05	.02	.00
☐ 643	Two Perfect Games and One No-Hitter: Mike Witt David Palmer Jack Morris	.10	.05	.01
☐ 644	Willie Lozado and .... Vic Mata	.15	.07	.01
☐ 645	Kelly Gruber and .... Randy O'Neal	.25	.12	.02
☐ 646	Jose Roman and .... Joel Skinner	.15	.07	.01
☐ 647	Steve Kiefer and .... Danny Tartabull	5.00	2.50	.50
☐ 648	Rob Deer and .... Alejandro Sanchez	2.00	1.00	.20
☐ 649	Bill Hatcher and .... Shawon Dunston	1.50	.75	.15
☐ 650	Ron Robinson and .... Mike Bielecki	.20	.10	.02
☐ 651	Zane Smith and .... Paul Zuvella	.75	.35	.07
☐ 652	Joe Hesketh and .... Glenn Davis	4.50	2.25	.45
☐ 653	John Russell and .... Steve Jeltz	.20	.10	.02
☐ 654	CL: Tigers/Padres .... and Cubs/Mets	.07	.01	.00
☐ 655	CL: Blue Jays/Yankees .. and Red Sox/Orioles	.07	.01	.00
☐ 656	CL: Royals/Cardinals ..... and Phillies/Twins	.07	.01	.00
☐ 657	CL: Angels/Braves .... and Astros/Dodgers	.07	.01	.00
☐ 658	CL: Expos/A's .... and Indians/Pirates	.07	.01	.00
☐ 659	CL: Mariners/White Sox ... and Reds/Rangers	.07	.01	.00
☐ 660	CL: Brewers/Giants .... and Special Cards	.10	.05	.00

		MINT	EXC	G-VG
☐ 1	Buddy Bell	.05	.02	.00
☐ 2	Bert Blyleven	.05	.02	.00
☐ 3	Wade Boggs	.75	.35	.07
☐ 4	George Brett	.50	.25	.05
☐ 5	Rod Carew	.35	.17	.03
☐ 6	Steve Carlton	.30	.15	.03
☐ 7	Alvin Davis	.15	.07	.01
☐ 8	Andre Dawson	.25	.12	.02
☐ 9	Steve Garvey	.30	.15	.03
☐ 10	Goose Gossage	.10	.05	.01
☐ 11	Tony Gwynn	.40	.20	.04
☐ 12	Keith Hernandez	.25	.12	.02
☐ 13	Kent Hrbek	.25	.12	.02
☐ 14	Reggie Jackson	.50	.25	.05
☐ 15	Dave Kingman	.10	.05	.01
☐ 16	Ron Kittle	.10	.05	.01
☐ 17	Mark Langston	.10	.05	.01
☐ 18	Jeff Leonard	.10	.05	.01
☐ 19	Bill Madlock	.10	.05	.01
☐ 20	Don Mattingly	1.25	.60	.12
☐ 21	Jack Morris	.15	.07	.01
☐ 22	Dale Murphy	.60	.30	.06
☐ 23	Eddie Murray	.40	.20	.04
☐ 24	Tony Pena	.10	.05	.01
☐ 25	Dan Quisenberry	.10	.05	.01
☐ 26	Tim Raines	.30	.15	.03
☐ 27	Jim Rice	.25	.12	.02
☐ 28	Cal Ripken	.35	.17	.03
☐ 29	Pete Rose	.75	.35	.07
☐ 30	Nolan Ryan	.35	.17	.03
☐ 31	Ryne Sandberg	.30	.15	.03
☐ 32	Steve Sax	.10	.05	.01
☐ 33	Mike Schmidt	.50	.25	.05
☐ 34	Tom Seaver	.35	.17	.03
☐ 35	Ozzie Smith	.20	.10	.02
☐ 36	Mario Soto	.05	.02	.00
☐ 37	Dave Stieb	.10	.05	.01
☐ 38	Darryl Strawberry	.50	.25	.05
☐ 39	Rick Sutcliffe	.10	.05	.01
☐ 40	Alan Trammell	.20	.10	.02
☐ 41	Willie Upshaw	.05	.02	.00
☐ 42	Fernando Valenzuela	.25	.12	.02
☐ 43	Dave Winfield	.25	.12	.02
☐ 44	Robin Yount	.25	.12	.02

1985 Fleer Update

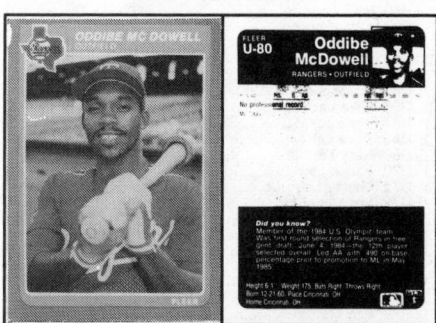

This 132-card set was issued late in the collecting year and features new players and players on new teams compared to the 1985 Fleer regular issue cards. Cards measure 2 1/2" by 3 1/2" and were distributed together as a complete set within a special box. The cards are numbered with a U prefix and are ordered alphabetically by the player's name.

		MINT	EXC	G-VG
COMPLETE SET		16.00	8.00	1.60
COMMON PLAYER (1-132)	....	.06	.03	.00
☐ U1	Don Aase	.15	.07	.01
☐ U2	Bill Almon	.06	.03	.00
☐ U3	Dusty Baker	.10	.05	.01
☐ U4	Dale Berra	.10	.05	.01
☐ U5	Karl Best	.15	.07	.01
☐ U6	Tim Birtsas	.30	.15	.03
☐ U7	Vida Blue	.15	.07	.01
☐ U8	Rich Bordi	.06	.03	.00
☐ U9	Daryl Boston	.20	.10	.02
☐ U10	Hubie Brooks	.20	.10	.02

1985 Fleer Limited Edition

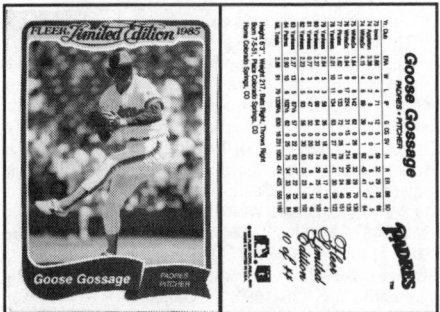

This 44-card set features standard size cards (2 1/2" by 3 1/2") which were distributed in a colorful box as a complete set. The back of the box gives a complete checklist of the cards in the set. The cards are ordered alphabetically by the player's name. Backs of the cards are yellow and white whereas the fronts show a picture of the player inside a red banner-type border.

		MINT	EXC	G-VG
COMPLETE SET		4.50	2.25	.45
COMMON PLAYER (1-44)	....	.05	.02	.00

☐ U11	Chris Brown	1.25	.60	.12
☐ U12	Tom Browning	.35	.17	.03
☐ U13	Al Bumbry	.06	.03	.00
☐ U14	Tim Burke	.35	.17	.03
☐ U15	Ray Burris	.06	.03	.00
☐ U16	Jeff Burroughs	.06	.03	.00
☐ U17	Ivan Calderon	1.25	.60	.12
☐ U18	Jeff Calhoun	.15	.07	.01
☐ U19	Bill Campbell	.06	.03	.00
☐ U20	Don Carman	.30	.15	.03
☐ U21	Gary Carter	.75	.35	.07
☐ U22	Bobby Castillo	.06	.03	.00
☐ U23	Bill Caudill	.10	.05	.01
☐ U24	Rick Cerone	.06	.03	.00
☐ U25	Jack Clark	.50	.25	.05
☐ U26	Pat Clements	.25	.12	.02
☐ U27	Stewart Cliburn	.15	.07	.01
☐ U28	Vince Coleman	4.50	2.25	.45
☐ U29	Dave Collins	.10	.05	.01
☐ U30	Fritz Connally	.15	.07	.01
☐ U31	Henry Cotto	.06	.03	.00
☐ U32	Danny Darwin	.10	.05	.01
☐ U33	Darren Daulton	.25	.12	.02
☐ U34	Jerry Davis	.15	.07	.01
☐ U35	Brian Dayett	.10	.05	.01
☐ U36	Ken Dixon	.25	.12	.02
☐ U37	Tommy Dunbar	.10	.05	.01
☐ U38	Mariano Duncan	.35	.17	.03
☐ U39	Bob Fallon	.10	.05	.01
☐ U40	Brian Fisher	.35	.17	.03
☐ U41	Mike Fitzgerald	.06	.03	.00
☐ U42	Ray Fontenot	.06	.03	.00
☐ U43	Greg Gagne	.50	.25	.05
☐ U44	Oscar Gamble	.10	.05	.01
☐ U45	Jim Gott	.06	.03	.00
☐ U46	David Green	.06	.03	.00
☐ U47	Alfredo Griffin	.10	.05	.01
☐ U48	Ozzie Guillen	.85	.40	.08
☐ U49	Toby Harrah	.10	.05	.01
☐ U50	Ron Hassey	.06	.03	.00
☐ U51	Rickey Henderson	1.00	.50	.10
☐ U52	Steve Henderson	.06	.03	.00
☐ U53	George Hendrick	.10	.05	.01
☐ U54	Teddy Higuera	2.50	1.25	.25
☐ U55	Al Holland	.10	.05	.01
☐ U56	Burt Hooton	.06	.03	.00
☐ U57	Jay Howell	.10	.05	.01
☐ U58	LaMarr Hoyt	.10	.05	.01
☐ U59	Tim Hulett	.15	.07	.01
☐ U60	Bob James	.10	.05	.01
☐ U61	Cliff Johnson	.06	.03	.00
☐ U62	Howard Johnson	1.00	.50	.10
☐ U63	Ruppert Jones	.10	.05	.01
☐ U64	Steve Kemp	.10	.05	.01
☐ U65	Bruce Kison	.06	.03	.00
☐ U66	Mike LaCoss	.06	.03	.00
☐ U67	Lee Lacy	.10	.05	.01
☐ U68	Dave LaPoint	.06	.03	.00
☐ U69	Gary Lavelle	.06	.03	.00
☐ U70	Vance Law	.06	.03	.00
☐ U71	Manny Lee	.15	.07	.01
☐ U72	Sixto Lezcano	.06	.03	.00
☐ U73	Tim Lollar	.06	.03	.00
☐ U74	Urbano Lugo	.10	.05	.01
☐ U75	Fred Lynn	.25	.12	.02
☐ U76	Steve Lyons	.15	.07	.01
☐ U77	Mickey Mahler	.06	.03	.00
☐ U78	Ron Mathis	.15	.07	.01
☐ U79	Len Matuszek	.10	.05	.01
☐ U80	Oddibe McDowell (part of bio actually Roger's)	1.00	.50	.10
☐ U81	Roger McDowell (part of bio actually Oddibe's)	1.00	.50	.10
☐ U82	Donnie Moore	.10	.05	.01
☐ U83	Ron Musselman	.10	.05	.01
☐ U84	Al Oliver	.20	.10	.02
☐ U85	Joe Orsulak	.20	.10	.02
☐ U86	Dan Pasqua	.75	.35	.07
☐ U87	Chris Pittaro	.15	.07	.01
☐ U88	Rick Reuschel	.15	.07	.01
☐ U89	Earnie Riles	.35	.17	.03
☐ U90	Jerry Royster	.06	.03	.00
☐ U91	Dave Rozema	.06	.03	.00
☐ U92	Dave Rucker	.06	.03	.00
☐ U93	Vern Ruhle	.06	.03	.00
☐ U94	Mark Salas	.25	.12	.02
☐ U95	Luis Salazar	.06	.03	.00
☐ U96	Joe Sambito	.10	.05	.01
☐ U97	Billy Sample	.06	.03	.00
☐ U98	Alex Sanchez	.10	.05	.01
☐ U99	Calvin Schiraldi	.25	.12	.02
☐ U100	Rick Schu	.25	.12	.02
☐ U101	Larry Sheets	1.00	.50	.10

☐ U102	Ron Shephard	.10	.05	.01
☐ U103	Nelson Simmons	.15	.07	.01
☐ U104	Don Slaught	.10	.05	.01
☐ U105	Roy Smalley	.10	.05	.01
☐ U106	Lonnie Smith	.10	.05	.01
☐ U107	Nate Snell	.15	.07	.01
☐ U108	Lary Sorensen	.06	.03	.00
☐ U109	Chris Speier	.06	.03	.00
☐ U110	Mike Stenhouse	.10	.05	.01
☐ U111	Tim Stoddard	.06	.03	.00
☐ U112	John Stuper	.06	.03	.00
☐ U113	Jim Sundberg	.10	.05	.01
☐ U114	Bruce Sutter	.25	.12	.02
☐ U115	Don Sutton	.50	.25	.05
☐ U116	Bruce Tanner	.15	.07	.01
☐ U117	Kent Tekulve	.10	.05	.01
☐ U118	Walt Terrell	.10	.05	.01
☐ U119	Mickey Tettleton	.10	.05	.01
☐ U120	Rich Thompson	.10	.05	.01
☐ U121	Louis Thornton	.10	.05	.01
☐ U122	Alex Trevino	.06	.03	.00
☐ U123	John Tudor	.20	.10	.02
☐ U124	Jose Uribe	.25	.12	.02
☐ U125	Dave Valle	.10	.05	.01
☐ U126	Dave Von Ohlen	.06	.03	.00
☐ U127	Curt Wardle	.10	.05	.01
☐ U128	U.L. Washington	.06	.03	.00
☐ U129	Ed Whitson	.10	.05	.01
☐ U130	Herm Winningham	.20	.10	.02
☐ U131	Rich Yett	.10	.05	.01
☐ U132	Checklist U1-U132	.06	.01	.00

1986 Fleer

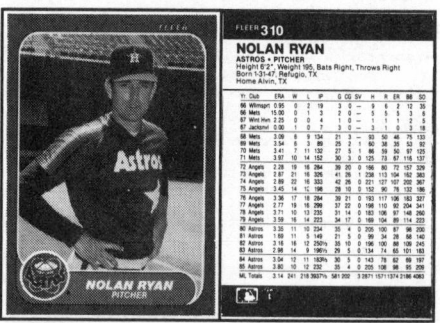

The cards in this 660-card set measure 2 1/2" by 3 1/2". The 1986 Fleer set features fronts which contain the team logo along with the player's name and position. The player cards are alphabetized within team and the teams are ordered by their 1985 season finish and won-lost record, e.g., Kansas City (1-25), St. Louis (26-49), Toronto (50-73), New York Mets (74-97), New York Yankees (98-122), Los Angeles (123-147), California (148- 171), Cincinnati (172-196), Chicago White Sox (197-220), Detroit (221-243), Montreal (244-267), Baltimore (268-291), Houston (292- 314), San Diego (315-338), Boston (339-360), Chicago Cubs (361- 385), Minnesota (386-409), Oakland (410-432), Philadelphia (433- 457), Seattle (458-481), Milwaukee (482-506), Atlanta (507-532), San Francisco (533-555), Texas (556-578), Cleveland (579-601), and Pittsburgh (602-625). Specials (626-643), Rookie pairs (644- 653), and checklist cards (654-660) complete the set. The border enclosing the photo is dark blue. The backs feature the same name, number, and statistics format that Fleer has been using over the past few years. The Dennis and Tippy Martinez cards were apparently switched in the set numbering as their adjacent numbers (279 and 280) were reversed on the Orioles checklist card.

		MINT	EXC	G-VG
	COMPLETE SET	36.00	18.00	3.60
	COMMON PLAYER	.04	.02	.00
☐	1 Steve Balboni	.10	.02	.01
☐	2 Joe Beckwith	.04	.02	.00
☐	3 Buddy Biancalana	.04	.02	.00
☐	4 Bud Black	.04	.02	.00
☐	5 George Brett	.40	.20	.04
☐	6 Onix Concepcion	.04	.02	.00
☐	7 Steve Farr	.04	.02	.00
☐	8 Mark Gubicza	.07	.03	.01
☐	9 Dane Iorg	.04	.02	.00
☐	10 Danny Jackson	.07	.03	.01
☐	11 Lynn Jones	.04	.02	.00
☐	12 Mike Jones	.04	.02	.00
☐	13 Charlie Leibrandt	.07	.03	.01
☐	14 Hal McRae	.07	.03	.01
☐	15 Omar Moreno	.04	.02	.00
☐	16 Darryl Motley	.04	.02	.00
☐	17 Jorge Orta	.04	.02	.00
☐	18 Dan Quisenberry	.15	.07	.01
☐	19 Bret Saberhagen	.55	.27	.05
☐	20 Pat Sheridan	.04	.02	.00
☐	21 Lonnie Smith	.07	.03	.01
☐	22 Jim Sundberg	.07	.03	.01
☐	23 John Wathan	.07	.03	.01
☐	24 Frank White	.07	.03	.01
☐	25 Willie Wilson	.15	.07	.01
☐	26 Joaquin Andujar	.10	.05	.01
☐	27 Steve Braun	.04	.02	.00
☐	28 Bill Campbell	.04	.02	.00
☐	29 Cesar Cedeno	.07	.03	.01
☐	30 Jack Clark	.20	.10	.02
☐	31 Vince Coleman	1.75	.85	.17
☐	32 Danny Cox	.12	.06	.01
☐	33 Ken Dayley	.04	.02	.00
☐	34 Ivan DeJesus	.04	.02	.00
☐	35 Bob Forsch	.07	.03	.01
☐	36 Brian Harper	.04	.02	.00
☐	37 Tom Herr	.10	.05	.01
☐	38 Ricky Horton	.07	.03	.01
☐	39 Kurt Kepshire	.04	.02	.00
☐	40 Jeff Lahti	.04	.02	.00
☐	41 Tito Landrum	.04	.02	.00
☐	42 Willie McGee	.15	.07	.01
☐	43 Tom Nieto	.04	.02	.00
☐	44 Terry Pendleton	.10	.05	.01
☐	45 Darrell Porter	.04	.02	.00
☐	46 Ozzie Smith	.20	.10	.02
☐	47 John Tudor	.12	.06	.01
☐	48 Andy Van Slyke	.10	.05	.01
☐	49 Todd Worrell	1.00	.50	.10
☐	50 Jim Acker	.04	.02	.00
☐	51 Doyle Alexander	.07	.03	.01
☐	52 Jesse Barfield	.25	.12	.02
☐	53 George Bell	.35	.17	.03
☐	54 Jeff Burroughs	.07	.03	.01
☐	55 Bill Caudill	.04	.02	.00
☐	56 Jim Clancy	.04	.02	.00
☐	57 Tony Fernandez	.15	.07	.01
☐	58 Tom Filer	.07	.03	.01
☐	59 Damaso Garcia	.07	.03	.01
☐	60 Tom Henke	.12	.06	.01
☐	61 Garth Iorg	.04	.02	.00
☐	62 Cliff Johnson	.04	.02	.00
☐	63 Jimmy Key	.15	.07	.01
☐	64 Dennis Lamp	.04	.02	.00
☐	65 Gary Lavelle	.04	.02	.00
☐	66 Buck Martinez	.04	.02	.00
☐	67 Lloyd Moseby	.12	.06	.01
☐	68 Rance Mulliniks	.04	.02	.00
☐	69 Al Oliver	.10	.05	.01
☐	70 Dave Stieb	.12	.06	.01
☐	71 Louis Thornton	.10	.05	.01
☐	72 Willie Upshaw	.07	.03	.01
☐	73 Ernie Whitt	.04	.02	.00
☐	74 Rick Aguilera	.35	.17	.03
☐	75 Wally Backman	.07	.03	.01
☐	76 Gary Carter	.30	.15	.03
☐	77 Ron Darling	.25	.12	.02
☐	78 Len Dykstra	.85	.40	.08
☐	79 Sid Fernandez	.18	.09	.01
☐	80 George Foster	.12	.06	.01
☐	81 Dwight Gooden	1.50	.75	.15
☐	82 Tom Gorman	.04	.02	.00
☐	83 Danny Heep	.04	.02	.00
☐	84 Keith Hernandez	.25	.12	.02
☐	85 Howard Johnson	.20	.10	.02
☐	86 Ray Knight	.07	.03	.01
☐	87 Terry Leach	.07	.03	.01
☐	88 Ed Lynch	.04	.02	.00
☐	89 Roger McDowell	.45	.22	.04
☐	90 Jesse Orosco	.07	.03	.01
☐	91 Tom Paciorek	.04	.02	.01
☐	92 Ronn Reynolds	.07	.03	.01
☐	93 Rafael Santana	.04	.02	.00
☐	94 Doug Sisk	.04	.02	.00
☐	95 Rusty Staub	.10	.05	.01
☐	96 Darryl Strawberry	.55	.27	.05
☐	97 Mookie Wilson	.07	.03	.01
☐	98 Neil Allen	.07	.03	.01
☐	99 Don Baylor	.10	.05	.01
☐	100 Dale Berra	.04	.02	.00
☐	101 Rich Bordi	.04	.02	.00
☐	102 Marty Bystrom	.04	.02	.00
☐	103 Joe Cowley	.04	.02	.00
☐	104 Brian Fisher	.25	.12	.02
☐	105 Ken Griffey	.07	.03	.01
☐	106 Ron Guidry	.15	.07	.01
☐	107 Ron Hassey	.04	.02	.00
☐	108 Rickey Henderson	.40	.20	.04
☐	109 Don Mattingly	4.00	2.00	.40
☐	110 Bobby Meacham	.04	.02	.00
☐	111 John Montefusco	.07	.03	.01
☐	112 Phil Niekro	.15	.07	.01
☐	113 Mike Pagliarulo	.20	.10	.02
☐	114 Dan Pasqua	.20	.10	.02
☐	115 Willie Randolph	.07	.03	.01
☐	116 Dave Righetti	.15	.07	.01
☐	117 Andre Robertson	.04	.02	.00
☐	118 Billy Sample	.04	.02	.00
☐	119 Bob Shirley	.04	.02	.00
☐	120 Ed Whitson	.04	.02	.00
☐	121 Dave Winfield	.30	.15	.03
☐	122 Butch Wynegar	.04	.02	.00
☐	123 Dave Anderson	.04	.02	.00
☐	124 Bob Bailor	.04	.02	.00
☐	125 Greg Brock	.07	.03	.01
☐	126 Enos Cabell	.04	.02	.00
☐	127 Bobby Castillo	.04	.02	.00
☐	128 Carlos Diaz	.04	.02	.00
☐	129 Mariano Duncan	.25	.12	.02
☐	130 Pedro Guerrero	.25	.12	.02
☐	131 Orel Hershiser	.35	.17	.03
☐	132 Rick Honeycutt	.04	.02	.00
☐	133 Ken Howell	.04	.02	.00
☐	134 Ken Landreaux	.04	.02	.00
☐	135 Bill Madlock	.10	.05	.01
☐	136 Candy Maldonado	.10	.05	.01
☐	137 Mike Marshall	.12	.06	.01
☐	138 Len Matuszek	.04	.02	.00
☐	139 Tom Niedenfuer	.07	.03	.01
☐	140 Alejandro Pena	.07	.03	.01
☐	141 Jerry Reuss	.07	.03	.01
☐	142 Bill Russell	.04	.02	.00
☐	143 Steve Sax	.12	.06	.01
☐	144 Mike Scioscia	.04	.02	.00
☐	145 Fernando Valenzuela	.30	.15	.03
☐	146 Bob Welch	.07	.03	.01
☐	147 Terry Whitfield	.04	.02	.00
☐	148 Juan Beniquez	.07	.03	.01
☐	149 Bob Boone	.07	.03	.01
☐	150 John Candelaria	.07	.03	.01
☐	151 Rod Carew	.30	.15	.03
☐	152 Stewart Cliburn	.10	.05	.01
☐	153 Doug DeCinces	.07	.03	.01
☐	154 Brian Downing	.07	.03	.01
☐	155 Ken Forsch	.04	.02	.00
☐	156 Craig Gerber	.07	.03	.01
☐	157 Bobby Grich	.07	.03	.01
☐	158 George Hendrick	.07	.03	.01
☐	159 Al Holland	.04	.02	.00
☐	160 Reggie Jackson	.35	.17	.03
☐	161 Ruppert Jones	.04	.02	.00
☐	162 Urbano Lugo	.07	.03	.01
☐	163 Kirk McCaskill	.35	.17	.03
☐	164 Donnie Moore	.07	.03	.01
☐	165 Gary Pettis	.07	.03	.01
☐	166 Ron Romanick	.04	.02	.00
☐	167 Dick Schofield	.07	.03	.01
☐	168 Daryl Sconiers	.04	.02	.00
☐	169 Jim Slaton	.04	.02	.00
☐	170 Don Sutton	.15	.07	.01
☐	171 Mike Witt	.12	.06	.01
☐	172 Buddy Bell	.10	.05	.01
☐	173 Tom Browning	.10	.05	.01
☐	174 Dave Concepcion	.07	.03	.01
☐	175 Eric Davis	4.00	2.00	.40
☐	176 Bo Diaz	.07	.03	.01
☐	177 Nick Esasky	.07	.03	.01
☐	178 John Franco	.10	.05	.01
☐	179 Tom Hume	.04	.02	.00
☐	180 Wayne Krenchicki	.04	.02	.00
☐	181 Andy McGaffigan	.04	.02	.00
☐	182 Eddie Milner	.04	.02	.00
☐	183 Ron Oester	.04	.02	.00
☐	184 Dave Parker	.15	.07	.01

☐ 185	Frank Pastore	.04	.02	.00
☐ 186	Tony Perez	.10	.05	.01
☐ 187	Ted Power	.07	.03	.01
☐ 188	Joe Price	.04	.02	.00
☐ 189	Gary Redus	.07	.03	.01
☐ 190	Ron Robinson	.04	.02	.00
☐ 191	Pete Rose	.65	.30	.06
☐ 192	Mario Soto	.07	.03	.01
☐ 193	John Stuper	.04	.02	.00
☐ 194	Jay Tibbs	.04	.02	.00
☐ 195	Dave Van Gorder	.04	.02	.00
☐ 196	Max Venable	.04	.02	.00
☐ 197	Juan Agosto	.04	.02	.00
☐ 198	Harold Baines	.15	.07	.01
☐ 199	Floyd Bannister	.07	.03	.01
☐ 200	Britt Burns	.07	.03	.01
☐ 201	Julio Cruz	.04	.02	.00
☐ 202	Joel Davis	.20	.10	.02
☐ 203	Richard Dotson	.07	.03	.01
☐ 204	Carlton Fisk	.15	.07	.01
☐ 205	Scott Fletcher	.07	.03	.01
☐ 206	Ozzie Guillen	.40	.20	.04
☐ 207	Jerry Hairston	.04	.02	.00
☐ 208	Tim Hulett	.04	.02	.00
☐ 209	Bob James	.04	.02	.00
☐ 210	Ron Kittle	.12	.06	.01
☐ 211	Rudy Law	.04	.02	.00
☐ 212	Bryan Little	.04	.02	.00
☐ 213	Gene Nelson	.04	.02	.00
☐ 214	Reid Nichols	.04	.02	.00
☐ 215	Luis Salazar	.04	.02	.00
☐ 216	Tom Seaver	.25	.12	.02
☐ 217	Dan Spillner	.04	.02	.00
☐ 218	Bruce Tanner	.10	.05	.01
☐ 219	Greg Walker	.10	.05	.01
☐ 220	Dave Wehrmeister	.04	.02	.00
☐ 221	Juan Berenguer	.04	.02	.00
☐ 222	Dave Bergman	.04	.02	.00
☐ 223	Tom Brookens	.04	.02	.00
☐ 224	Darrell Evans	.10	.05	.01
☐ 225	Barbaro Garbey	.04	.02	.00
☐ 226	Kirk Gibson	.18	.09	.01
☐ 227	John Grubb	.04	.02	.00
☐ 228	Willie Hernandez	.12	.06	.01
☐ 229	Larry Herndon	.04	.02	.00
☐ 230	Chet Lemon	.07	.03	.01
☐ 231	Aurelio Lopez	.04	.02	.00
☐ 232	Jack Morris	.18	.09	.01
☐ 233	Randy O'Neal	.04	.02	.00
☐ 234	Lance Parrish	.18	.09	.01
☐ 235	Dan Petry	.10	.05	.01
☐ 236	Alex Sanchez	.04	.02	.00
☐ 237	Bill Scherrer	.04	.02	.00
☐ 238	Nelson Simmons	.10	.05	.01
☐ 239	Frank Tanana	.07	.03	.01
☐ 240	Walt Terrell	.07	.03	.01
☐ 241	Alan Trammell	.25	.12	.02
☐ 242	Lou Whitaker	.15	.07	.01
☐ 243	Milt Wilcox	.04	.02	.00
☐ 244	Hubie Brooks	.10	.05	.01
☐ 245	Tim Burke	.25	.12	.02
☐ 246	Andre Dawson	.30	.15	.03
☐ 247	Mike Fitzgerald	.04	.02	.00
☐ 248	Terry Francona	.04	.02	.00
☐ 249	Bill Gullickson	.07	.03	.01
☐ 250	Joe Hesketh	.07	.03	.01
☐ 251	Bill Laskey	.04	.02	.00
☐ 252	Vance Law	.04	.02	.00
☐ 253	Charlie Lea	.04	.02	.00
☐ 254	Gary Lucas	.04	.02	.00
☐ 255	David Palmer	.04	.02	.00
☐ 256	Tim Raines	.30	.15	.03
☐ 257	Jeff Reardon	.12	.06	.01
☐ 258	Bert Roberge	.04	.02	.00
☐ 259	Dan Schatzeder	.04	.02	.00
☐ 260	Bryn Smith	.07	.03	.01
☐ 261	Randy St.Claire	.04	.02	.00
☐ 262	Scot Thompson	.04	.02	.00
☐ 263	Tim Wallach	.15	.07	.01
☐ 264	U.L. Washington	.04	.02	.00
☐ 265	Mitch Webster	.45	.22	.04
☐ 266	Herm Winningham	.15	.07	.01
☐ 267	Floyd Youmans	.55	.27	.05
☐ 268	Don Aase	.07	.03	.01
☐ 269	Mike Boddicker	.10	.05	.01
☐ 270	Rich Dauer	.04	.02	.00
☐ 271	Storm Davis	.07	.03	.01
☐ 272	Rick Dempsey	.07	.03	.01
☐ 273	Ken Dixon	.04	.02	.00
☐ 274	Jim Dwyer	.04	.02	.00
☐ 275	Mike Flanagan	.07	.03	.01
☐ 276	Wayne Gross	.04	.02	.00
☐ 277	Lee Lacy	.07	.03	.01
☐ 278	Fred Lynn	.15	.07	.01
☐ 279	Tippy Martinez	.04	.02	.00
☐ 280	Dennis Martinez	.07	.03	.01
☐ 281	Scott McGregor	.07	.03	.01
☐ 282	Eddie Murray	.35	.17	.03
☐ 283	Floyd Rayford	.04	.02	.00
☐ 284	Cal Ripken	.35	.17	.03
☐ 285	Gary Roenicke	.04	.02	.00
☐ 286	Larry Sheets	.45	.22	.04
☐ 287	John Shelby	.04	.02	.00
☐ 288	Nate Snell	.10	.05	.01
☐ 289	Sammy Stewart	.04	.02	.00
☐ 290	Alan Wiggins	.04	.02	.00
☐ 291	Mike Young	.10	.05	.01
☐ 292	Alan Ashby	.04	.02	.00
☐ 293	Mark Bailey	.04	.02	.00
☐ 294	Kevin Bass	.10	.05	.01
☐ 295	Jeff Calhoun	.07	.03	.01
☐ 296	Jose Cruz	.10	.05	.01
☐ 297	Glenn Davis	.55	.27	.05
☐ 298	Bill Dawley	.04	.02	.00
☐ 299	Frank DiPino	.04	.02	.00
☐ 300	Bill Doran	.10	.05	.01
☐ 301	Phil Garner	.04	.02	.00
☐ 302	Jeff Heathcock	.07	.03	.01
☐ 303	Charlie Kerfeld	.20	.10	.02
☐ 304	Bob Knepper	.07	.03	.01
☐ 305	Ron Mathis	.10	.05	.01
☐ 306	Jerry Mumphrey	.04	.02	.00
☐ 307	Jim Pankovits	.04	.02	.00
☐ 308	Terry Puhl	.04	.02	.00
☐ 309	Craig Reynolds	.04	.02	.00
☐ 310	Nolan Ryan	.30	.15	.03
☐ 311	Mike Scott	.30	.15	.03
☐ 312	Dave Smith	.07	.03	.01
☐ 313	Dickie Thon	.04	.02	.00
☐ 314	Denny Walling	.04	.02	.00
☐ 315	Kurt Bevacqua	.04	.02	.00
☐ 316	Al Bumbry	.04	.02	.00
☐ 317	Jerry Davis	.04	.02	.00
☐ 318	Luis DeLeon	.04	.02	.00
☐ 319	Dave Dravecky	.07	.03	.01
☐ 320	Tim Flannery	.04	.02	.00
☐ 321	Steve Garvey	.35	.17	.03
☐ 322	Goose Gossage	.15	.07	.01
☐ 323	Tony Gwynn	.45	.22	.04
☐ 324	Andy Hawkins	.04	.02	.00
☐ 325	LaMarr Hoyt	.07	.03	.01
☐ 326	Roy Lee Jackson	.04	.02	.00
☐ 327	Terry Kennedy	.07	.03	.01
☐ 328	Craig Lefferts	.04	.02	.00
☐ 329	Carmelo Martinez	.07	.03	.01
☐ 330	Lance McCullers	.25	.12	.02
☐ 331	Kevin McReynolds	.15	.07	.01
☐ 332	Graig Nettles	.12	.06	.01
☐ 333	Jerry Royster	.04	.02	.00
☐ 334	Eric Show	.04	.02	.00
☐ 335	Tim Stoddard	.04	.02	.00
☐ 336	Garry Templeton	.07	.03	.01
☐ 337	Mark Thurmond	.04	.02	.00
☐ 338	Ed Wojna	.15	.07	.01
☐ 339	Tony Armas	.10	.05	.01
☐ 340	Marty Barrett	.12	.06	.01
☐ 341	Wade Boggs	2.25	1.10	.22
☐ 342	Dennis Boyd	.10	.05	.01
☐ 343	Bill Buckner	.10	.05	.01
☐ 344	Mark Clear	.04	.02	.00
☐ 345	Roger Clemens	2.50	1.25	.25
☐ 346	Steve Crawford	.04	.02	.00
☐ 347	Mike Easler	.07	.03	.01
☐ 348	Dwight Evans	.15	.07	.01
☐ 349	Rich Gedman	.10	.05	.01
☐ 350	Jackie Gutierrez	.04	.02	.00
☐ 351	Glenn Hoffman	.04	.02	.00
☐ 352	Bruce Hurst	.10	.05	.01
☐ 353	Bruce Kison	.04	.02	.00
☐ 354	Tim Lollar	.04	.02	.00
☐ 355	Steve Lyons	.04	.02	.00
☐ 356	Al Nipper	.04	.02	.00
☐ 357	Bob Ojeda	.07	.03	.01
☐ 358	Jim Rice	.30	.15	.03
☐ 359	Bob Stanley	.07	.03	.01
☐ 360	Mike Trujillo	.07	.03	.01
☐ 361	Thad Bosley	.04	.02	.00
☐ 362	Warren Brusstar	.04	.02	.00
☐ 363	Ron Cey	.10	.05	.01
☐ 364	Jody Davis	.10	.05	.01
☐ 365	Bob Dernier	.04	.02	.00
☐ 366	Shawon Dunston	.10	.05	.01
☐ 367	Leon Durham	.10	.05	.01
☐ 368	Dennis Eckersley	.07	.03	.01
☐ 369	Ray Fontenot	.04	.02	.00
☐ 370	George Frazier	.04	.02	.00
☐ 371	Bill Hatcher	.20	.10	.02
☐ 372	Dave Lopes	.07	.03	.01
☐ 373	Gary Matthews	.07	.03	.01
☐ 374	Ron Meredith	.07	.03	.01

☐ 375	Keith Moreland	.07	.03	.01	☐ 470	Edwin Nunez	.04	.02	.00
☐ 376	Reggie Patterson	.04	.02	.00	☐ 471	Spike Owen	.04	.02	.00
☐ 377	Dick Ruthven	.04	.02	.00	☐ 472	Jack Perconte	.04	.02	.00
☐ 378	Ryne Sandberg	.30	.15	.03	☐ 473	Jim Presley	.30	.15	.03
☐ 379	Scott Sanderson	.04	.02	.00	☐ 474	Donnie Scott	.04	.02	.00
☐ 380	Lee Smith	.10	.05	.01	☐ 475	Bill Swift	.10	.05	.01
☐ 381	Lary Sorensen	.04	.02	.00	☐ 476	Danny Tartabull	.55	.27	.05
☐ 382	Chris Speier	.04	.02	.00	☐ 477	Gorman Thomas	.10	.05	.01
☐ 383	Rick Sutcliffe	.15	.07	.01	☐ 478	Roy Thomas	.04	.02	.00
☐ 384	Steve Trout	.07	.03	.01	☐ 479	Ed VandeBerg	.04	.02	.00
☐ 385	Gary Woods	.04	.02	.00	☐ 480	Frank Wills	.10	.05	.01
☐ 386	Bert Blyleven	.10	.05	.01	☐ 481	Matt Young	.04	.02	.00
☐ 387	Tom Brunansky	.15	.07	.01	☐ 482	Ray Burris	.04	.02	.00
☐ 388	Randy Bush	.04	.02	.00	☐ 483	Jaime Cocanower	.04	.02	.00
☐ 389	John Butcher	.04	.02	.00	☐ 484	Cecil Cooper	.12	.06	.01
☐ 390	Ron Davis	.04	.02	.00	☐ 485	Danny Darwin	.07	.03	.01
☐ 391	Dave Engle	.04	.02	.00	☐ 486	Rollie Fingers	.15	.07	.01
☐ 392	Frank Eufemia	.07	.03	.01	☐ 487	Jim Gantner	.04	.02	.00
☐ 393	Pete Filson	.04	.02	.00	☐ 488	Bob L. Gibson	.04	.02	.00
☐ 394	Gary Gaetti	.15	.07	.01	☐ 489	Moose Haas	.04	.02	.00
☐ 395	Greg Gagne	.10	.05	.01	☐ 490	Teddy Higuera	1.00	.50	.10
☐ 396	Mickey Hatcher	.04	.02	.00	☐ 491	Paul Householder	.04	.02	.00
☐ 397	Kent Hrbek	.18	.09	.01	☐ 492	Pete Ladd	.04	.02	.00
☐ 398	Tim Laudner	.07	.03	.01	☐ 493	Rick Manning	.04	.02	.00
☐ 399	Rick Lysander	.04	.02	.00	☐ 494	Bob McClure	.04	.02	.00
☐ 400	Dave Meier	.04	.02	.00	☐ 495	Paul Molitor	.18	.09	.01
☐ 401	Kirby Puckett	1.50	.75	.15	☐ 496	Charlie Moore	.04	.02	.00
☐ 402	Mark Salas	.07	.03	.01	☐ 497	Ben Oglivie	.07	.03	.01
☐ 403	Ken Schrom	.04	.02	.00	☐ 498	Randy Ready	.07	.03	.01
☐ 404	Roy Smalley	.04	.02	.00	☐ 499	Earnie Riles	.25	.12	.02
☐ 405	Mike Smithson	.04	.02	.00	☐ 500	Ed Romero	.04	.02	.00
☐ 406	Mike Stenhouse	.07	.03	.01	☐ 501	Bill Schroeder	.04	.02	.00
☐ 407	Tim Teufel	.07	.03	.01	☐ 502	Ray Searage	.04	.02	.00
☐ 408	Frank Viola	.15	.07	.01	☐ 503	Ted Simmons	.10	.05	.01
☐ 409	Ron Washington	.04	.02	.00	☐ 504	Pete Vuckovich	.07	.03	.01
☐ 410	Keith Atherton	.04	.02	.00	☐ 505	Rick Waits	.04	.02	.00
☐ 411	Dusty Baker	.07	.03	.01	☐ 506	Robin Yount	.25	.12	.02
☐ 412	Tim Birtsas	.20	.10	.02	☐ 507	Len Barker	.04	.02	.00
☐ 413	Bruce Bochte	.04	.02	.00	☐ 508	Steve Bedrosian	.15	.07	.01
☐ 414	Chris Codiroli	.04	.02	.00	☐ 509	Bruce Benedict	.04	.02	.00
☐ 415	Dave Collins	.04	.02	.00	☐ 510	Rick Camp	.04	.02	.00
☐ 416	Mike Davis	.07	.03	.01	☐ 511	Rick Cerone	.04	.02	.00
☐ 417	Alfredo Griffin	.07	.03	.01	☐ 512	Chris Chambliss	.07	.03	.01
☐ 418	Mike Heath	.04	.02	.00	☐ 513	Jeff Dedmon	.04	.02	.00
☐ 419	Steve Henderson	.04	.02	.00	☐ 514	Terry Forster	.07	.03	.01
☐ 420	Donnie Hill	.04	.02	.00	☐ 515	Gene Garber	.04	.02	.00
☐ 421	Jay Howell	.04	.02	.00	☐ 516	Terry Harper	.04	.02	.00
☐ 422	Tommy John	.12	.06	.01	☐ 517	Bob Horner	.18	.09	.01
☐ 423	Dave Kingman	.12	.06	.01	☐ 518	Glenn Hubbard	.04	.02	.00
☐ 424	Bill Krueger	.04	.02	.00	☐ 519	Joe Johnson	.20	.10	.02
☐ 425	Rick Langford	.04	.02	.00	☐ 520	Brad Komminsk	.07	.03	.01
☐ 426	Carney Lansford	.10	.05	.01	☐ 521	Rick Mahler	.04	.02	.00
☐ 427	Steve McCatty	.04	.02	.00	☐ 522	Dale Murphy	.50	.25	.05
☐ 428	Dwayne Murphy	.07	.03	.01	☐ 523	Ken Oberkfell	.04	.02	.00
☐ 429	Steve Ontiveros	.20	.10	.02	☐ 524	Pascual Perez	.04	.02	.00
☐ 430	Tony Phillips	.04	.02	.00	☐ 525	Gerald Perry	.07	.03	.01
☐ 431	Jose Rijo	.07	.03	.01	☐ 526	Rafael Ramirez	.04	.02	.00
☐ 432	Mickey Tettleton	.10	.05	.01	☐ 527	Steve Shields	.07	.03	.01
☐ 433	Luis Aguayo	.04	.02	.00	☐ 528	Zane Smith	.12	.06	.01
☐ 434	Larry Andersen	.04	.02	.00	☐ 529	Bruce Sutter	.15	.07	.01
☐ 435	Steve Carlton	.25	.12	.02	☐ 530	Milt Thompson	.50	.25	.05
☐ 436	Don Carman	.20	.10	.02	☐ 531	Claudell Washington	.07	.03	.01
☐ 437	Tim Corcoran	.04	.02	.00	☐ 532	Paul Zuvella	.07	.03	.01
☐ 438	Darren Daulton	.20	.10	.02	☐ 533	Vida Blue	.07	.03	.01
☐ 439	John Denny	.07	.03	.01	☐ 534	Bob Brenly	.07	.03	.01
☐ 440	Tom Foley	.04	.02	.00	☐ 535	Chris Brown	.65	.30	.06
☐ 441	Greg Gross	.04	.02	.00	☐ 536	Chili Davis	.10	.05	.01
☐ 442	Kevin Gross	.04	.02	.00	☐ 537	Mark Davis	.04	.02	.00
☐ 443	Von Hayes	.12	.06	.01	☐ 538	Rob Deer	.25	.12	.02
☐ 444	Charles Hudson	.04	.02	.00	☐ 539	Dan Driessen	.04	.02	.00
☐ 445	Garry Maddox	.04	.02	.00	☐ 540	Scott Garrelts	.07	.03	.01
☐ 446	Shane Rawley	.07	.03	.01	☐ 541	Dan Gladden	.07	.03	.01
☐ 447	Dave Rucker	.04	.02	.00	☐ 542	Jim Gott	.04	.02	.00
☐ 448	John Russell	.04	.02	.00	☐ 543	David Green	.04	.02	.00
☐ 449	Juan Samuel	.15	.07	.01	☐ 544	Atlee Hammaker	.04	.02	.00
☐ 450	Mike Schmidt	.45	.22	.04	☐ 545	Mike Jeffcoat	.04	.02	.00
☐ 451	Rick Schu	.07	.03	.01	☐ 546	Mike Krukow	.07	.03	.01
☐ 452	Dave Shipanoff	.15	.07	.01	☐ 547	Dave LaPoint	.04	.02	.00
☐ 453	Dave Stewart	.10	.05	.01	☐ 548	Jeff Leonard	.10	.05	.01
☐ 454	Jeff Stone	.07	.03	.01	☐ 549	Greg Minton	.04	.02	.00
☐ 455	Kent Tekulve	.07	.03	.01	☐ 550	Alex Trevino	.04	.02	.00
☐ 456	Ozzie Virgil	.10	.05	.01	☐ 551	Manny Trillo	.04	.02	.00
☐ 457	Glenn Wilson	.04	.02	.00	☐ 552	Jose Uribe	.25	.12	.02
☐ 458	Jim Beattie	.07	.03	.01	☐ 553	Brad Wellman	.04	.02	.00
☐ 459	Karl Best	.04	.02	.00	☐ 554	Frank Williams	.04	.02	.00
☐ 460	Barry Bonnell	.20	.10	.02	☐ 555	Joel Youngblood	.04	.02	.00
☐ 461	Phil Bradley	1.00	.50	.10	☐ 556	Alan Bannister	.04	.02	.00
☐ 462	Ivan Calderon	.04	.02	.00	☐ 557	Glenn Brummer	.04	.02	.00
☐ 463	Al Cowens	.20	.10	.02	☐ 558	Steve Buechele	.25	.12	.02
☐ 464	Alvin Davis	.04	.02	.00	☐ 559	Jose Guzman	.25	.12	.02
☐ 465	Dave Henderson	.20	.10	.02	☐ 560	Toby Harrah	.04	.02	.00
☐ 466	Bob Kearney	.04	.02	.00	☐ 561	Greg Harris	.04	.02	.00
☐ 467	Mark Langston	.04	.02	.00	☐ 562	Dwayne Henry	.10	.05	.01
☐ 468	Bob Long	.04	.02	.00	☐ 563	Burt Hooton	.04	.02	.00
☐ 469	Mike Moore	.07	.03	.01	☐ 564	Charlie Hough	.07	.03	.01

☐ 565 Mike Mason	.04	.02	.00
☐ 566 Oddibe McDowell	.30	.15	.03
☐ 567 Dickie Noles	.04	.02	.00
☐ 568 Pete O'Brien	.15	.07	.01
☐ 569 Larry Parrish	.07	.03	.01
☐ 570 Dave Rozema	.04	.02	.00
☐ 571 Dave Schmidt	.07	.03	.01
☐ 572 Don Slaught	.04	.02	.00
☐ 573 Wayne Tolleson	.04	.02	.00
☐ 574 Duane Walker	.04	.02	.00
☐ 575 Gary Ward	.07	.03	.01
☐ 576 Chris Welsh	.04	.02	.00
☐ 577 Curtis Wilkerson	.04	.02	.00
☐ 578 George Wright	.04	.02	.00
☐ 579 Chris Bando	.04	.02	.00
☐ 580 Tony Bernazard	.04	.02	.00
☐ 581 Brett Butler	.07	.03	.01
☐ 582 Ernie Camacho	.04	.02	.00
☐ 583 Joe Carter	.30	.15	.03
☐ 584 Carmen Castillo	.04	.02	.00
☐ 585 Jamie Easterly	.04	.02	.00
☐ 586 Julio Franco	.10	.05	.01
☐ 587 Mel Hall	.07	.03	.01
☐ 588 Mike Hargrove	.04	.02	.00
☐ 589 Neal Heaton	.04	.02	.00
☐ 590 Brook Jacoby	.15	.07	.01
☐ 591 Otis Nixon	.15	.07	.01
☐ 592 Jerry Reed	.07	.03	.01
☐ 593 Vern Ruhle	.04	.02	.00
☐ 594 Pat Tabler	.10	.05	.01
☐ 595 Rich Thompson	.07	.03	.01
☐ 596 Andre Thornton	.07	.03	.01
☐ 597 Dave Von Ohlen	.04	.02	.00
☐ 598 George Vukovich	.04	.02	.00
☐ 599 Tom Waddell	.04	.02	.00
☐ 600 Curt Wardle	.07	.03	.01
☐ 601 Jerry Willard	.04	.02	.00
☐ 602 Bill Almon	.04	.02	.00
☐ 603 Mike Bielecki	.07	.03	.01
☐ 604 Sid Bream	.07	.03	.01
☐ 605 Mike Brown OF	.04	.02	.00
☐ 606 Pat Clements	.20	.10	.02
☐ 607 Jose DeLeon	.04	.02	.00
☐ 608 Denny Gonzalez	.04	.02	.00
☐ 609 Cecilio Guante	.04	.02	.00
☐ 610 Steve Kemp	.07	.03	.01
☐ 611 Sam Khalifa	.10	.05	.01
☐ 612 Lee Mazzilli	.04	.02	.00
☐ 613 Larry McWilliams	.04	.02	.00
☐ 614 Jim Morrison	.04	.02	.00
☐ 615 Joe Orsulak	.15	.07	.01
☐ 616 Tony Pena	.12	.06	.01
☐ 617 Johnny Ray	.10	.05	.01
☐ 618 Rick Reuschel	.07	.03	.01
☐ 619 R.J. Reynolds	.07	.03	.01
☐ 620 Rick Rhoden	.07	.03	.01
☐ 621 Don Robinson	.04	.02	.00
☐ 622 Jason Thompson	.07	.03	.01
☐ 623 Lee Tunnell	.04	.02	.00
☐ 624 Jim Winn	.04	.02	.00
☐ 625 Marvell Wynne	.04	.02	.00
☐ 626 Dwight Gooden IA	.40	.20	.04
☐ 627 Don Mattingly IA	1.50	.75	.15
☐ 628 4192 (Pete Rose)	.40	.20	.04
☐ 629 3000 Career Hits ... Rod Carew	.20	.10	.02
☐ 630 300 Career Wins ... Tom Seaver Phil Niekro	.15	.07	.01
☐ 631 Ouch (Don Baylor)	.07	.03	.01
☐ 632 Instant Offense ... Darryl Strawberry Tim Raines	.25	.12	.02
☐ 633 Shortstops Supreme ... Cal Ripken Alan Trammell	.15	.07	.01
☐ 634 Boggs and "Hero" ... Wade Boggs George Brett	.50	.25	.05
☐ 635 Braves Dynamic Duo ... Bob Horner Dale Murphy	.25	.12	.02
☐ 636 Cardinal Ignitors ... Willie McGee Vince Coleman	.30	.15	.03
☐ 637 Terror on Basepaths ... Vince Coleman	.30	.15	.03
☐ 638 Charlie Hustle / Dr.K ... Pete Rose Dwight Gooden	.75	.35	.07
☐ 639 1984 and 1985 AL Batting Champs Wade Boggs Don Mattingly	1.75	.85	.17
☐ 640 NL West Sluggers ... Dale Murphy Steve Garvey Dave Parker	.20	.10	.02
☐ 641 Staff Aces ... Fernando Valenzuela Dwight Gooden	.30	.15	.03
☐ 642 Blue Jay Stoppers ... Jimmy Key Dave Stieb	.07	.03	.01
☐ 643 AL All-Star Backstops ... Carlton Fisk Rich Gedman	.07	.03	.01
☐ 644 Gene Walter and ... Benito Santiago	8.00	4.00	.80
☐ 645 Mike Woodard and ... Collin Ward	.15	.07	.01
☐ 646 Kal Daniels and ... Paul O'Neill	4.00	2.00	.40
☐ 647 Andres Galarraga and ... Fred Toliver	1.50	.75	.15
☐ 648 Bob Kipper and ... Curt Ford	.30	.15	.03
☐ 649 Jose Canseco and ... Eric Plunk	8.00	4.00	.80
☐ 650 Mark McLemore and ... Gus Polidor	.15	.07	.01
☐ 651 Rob Woodward and ... Mickey Brantley	.40	.20	.04
☐ 652 Billy Jo Robidoux and ... Mark Funderburk	.20	.10	.02
☐ 653 Cecil Fielder and ... Cory Snyder	3.00	1.50	.30
☐ 654 CL: Royals/Cardinals ... Blue Jays/Mets	.07	.01	.00
☐ 655 CL: Yankees/Dodgers ... Angels/Reds	.07	.01	.00
☐ 656 CL: White Sox/Tigers ... Expos/Orioles (279 Dennis, 280 Tippy)	.07	.01	.00
☐ 657 CL: Astros/Padres ... Red Sox/Cubs	.07	.01	.00
☐ 658 CL: Twins/A's ... Phillies/Mariners	.07	.01	.00
☐ 659 CL: Brewers/Braves ... Giants/Rangers	.07	.01	.00
☐ 660 CL: Indians/Pirates ... Special Cards	.07	.01	.00

1986 Fleer Wax Box Cards

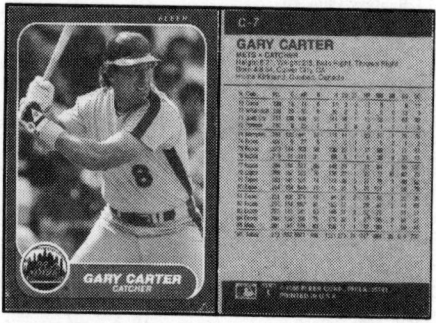

The cards in this 8-card set measure the standard 2 1/2" by 3 1/2" and were found on the bottom of the Fleer regular issue wax pack and cello pack boxes as four-card panel. Cards have essentially the same design as the 1986 Fleer regular issue set. These 8 cards (C1 to C8) are considered a separate set in their own right and are not typically included in a complete set of the regular issue 1986 Fleer cards. The value of the panel uncut is slightly greater, perhaps by 25% greater, than the value of the individual cards cut up carefully.

	MINT	EXC	G-VG
COMPLETE SET	2.00	1.00	.20
COMMON PLAYERS	.10	.05	.01

☐	C1 Royals Logo	.10	.05	.01
☐	C2 George Brett	.50	.25	.05
☐	C3 Ozzie Guillen	.20	.10	.02
☐	C4 Dale Murphy	.75	.35	.07
☐	C5 Cardinals Logo	.10	.05	.01
☐	C6 Tom Browning	.15	.07	.01
☐	C7 Gary Carter	.30	.15	.03
☐	C8 Carlton Fisk	.15	.07	.01

1986 Fleer All-Star Inserts

Fleer selected a 12-card (Major League) All-Star team to be included as inserts in their 39 cent wax packs and 59 cent cello packs. However not all wax packs contain the insert. Cards measure 2 1/2" by 3 1/2" and feature attractive red backgrounds (American Leaguers) and blue backgrounds (National Leaguers). The 12 selections cover each position, left and right-handed starting pitchers, a reliever, and a designated hitter.

		MINT	EXC	G-VG
	COMPLETE SET	15.00	7.50	1.50
	COMMON PLAYER	.15	.07	.01
☐	1 Don Mattingly First Base	7.50	3.75	.75
☐	2 Tom Herr Second Base	.15	.07	.01
☐	3 George Brett Third Base	1.00	.50	.10
☐	4 Gary Carter Catcher	.75	.35	.07
☐	5 Cal Ripken Shortstop	.80	.40	.08
☐	6 Dave Parker Outfield	.30	.15	.03
☐	7 Rickey Henderson Outfield	1.25	.60	.12
☐	8 Pedro Guerrero Outfield	.30	.15	.03
☐	9 Dan Quisenberry Relief Pitcher	.20	.10	.02
☐	10 Dwight Gooden Right-Hand Pitcher	2.50	1.25	.25
☐	11 Gorman Thomas Designated Hitter	.15	.07	.01
☐	12 John Tudor Left-Hand Pitcher	.20	.10	.02

1986 Fleer Future HOF

These attractive cards were issued as inserts with the Fleer three-packs. They are the same size as the regular issue (2 1/2" by 3 1/2") and feature players that Fleer predicts will be "Future Hall of Famers." The card backs describe career highlights, records, and honors won by the player. The cards are numbered on the back; Pete Rose is given the honor

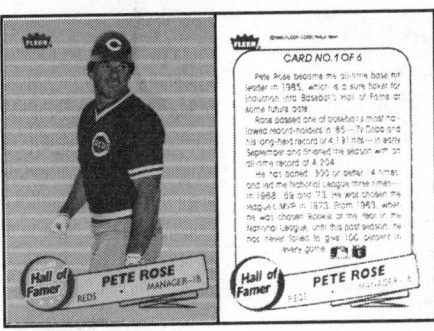

of being card #1.

		MINT	EXC	G-VG
	COMPLETE SET	6.00	3.00	.60
	COMMON PLAYER (1-6)	.90	.45	.09
☐	1 Pete Rose	2.50	1.25	.25
☐	2 Steve Carlton	.90	.45	.09
☐	3 Tom Seaver	1.00	.50	.10
☐	4 Rod Carew	.90	.45	.09
☐	5 Nolan Ryan	1.00	.50	.10
☐	6 Reggie Jackson	1.25	.60	.12

1986 Fleer League Leaders

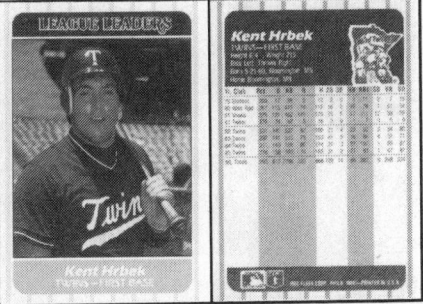

This 44-card set is also sometimes referred to as the Walgreen's set. Although the set was distributed through Walgreen's, there is no mention on the cards or box of that fact. The cards are easily recognizable by the fact that they contain the phrase "Fleer League Leaders" at the top of the obverse. Both sides of the cards are designed with a blue stripe on white pattern. The checklist for the set is given on the outside of the red, white, blue, and gold box in which the set was packaged. Cards are numbered on the back and measure the standard 2 1/2" by 3 1/2".

		MINT	EXC	G-VG
	COMPLETE SET	5.00	2.50	.50
	COMMON PLAYER	.10	.05	.01
☐	1 Wade Boggs	.60	.30	.06
☐	2 George Brett	.40	.20	.04
☐	3 Jose Canseco	.75	.35	.07
☐	4 Rod Carew	.30	.15	.03
☐	5 Gary Carter	.30	.15	.03
☐	6 Jack Clark	.20	.10	.02
☐	7 Vince Coleman	.50	.25	.05
☐	8 Jose Cruz	.10	.05	.01
☐	9 Alvin Davis	.15	.07	.01
☐	10 Mariano Duncan	.10	.05	.01
☐	11 Leon Durham	.10	.05	.01
☐	12 Carlton Fisk	.15	.07	.01
☐	13 Julio Franco	.10	.05	.01
☐	14 Scott Garrelts	.10	.05	.01

☐ 15	Steve Garvey	.35	.17	.03
☐ 16	Dwight Gooden	.50	.25	.05
☐ 17	Ozzie Guillen	.20	.10	.02
☐ 18	Willie Hernandez	.10	.05	.01
☐ 19	Bob Horner	.20	.10	.02
☐ 20	Kent Hrbek	.20	.10	.02
☐ 21	Charlie Leibrandt	.10	.05	.01
☐ 22	Don Mattingly	.85	.40	.08
☐ 23	Oddibe McDowell	.20	.10	.02
☐ 24	Willie McGee	.20	.10	.02
☐ 25	Keith Moreland	.10	.05	.01
☐ 26	Lloyd Moseby	.10	.05	.01
☐ 27	Dale Murphy	.50	.25	.05
☐ 28	Phil Niekro	.20	.10	.02
☐ 29	Joe Orsulak	.10	.05	.01
☐ 30	Dave Parker	.20	.10	.02
☐ 31	Lance Parrish	.20	.10	.02
☐ 32	Kirby Puckett	.35	.17	.03
☐ 33	Tim Raines	.35	.17	.03
☐ 34	Earnie Riles	.15	.07	.01
☐ 35	Cal Ripken	.35	.17	.03
☐ 36	Pete Rose	.60	.30	.06
☐ 37	Bret Saberhagen	.30	.15	.03
☐ 38	Juan Samuel	.15	.07	.01
☐ 39	Ryne Sandberg	.30	.15	.03
☐ 40	Tom Seaver	.30	.15	.03
☐ 41	Lee Smith	.10	.05	.01
☐ 42	Ozzie Smith	.25	.12	.02
☐ 43	Dave Stieb	.15	.07	.01
☐ 44	Robin Yount	.30	.15	.03

☐ 25	LaMarr Hoyt	.10	.05	.01
☐ 26	Reggie Jackson	.50	.25	.05
☐ 27	Don Mattingly	.85	.40	.08
☐ 28	Oddibe McDowell	.15	.07	.01
☐ 29	Willie McGee	.20	.10	.02
☐ 30	Paul Molitor	.20	.10	.02
☐ 31	Dale Murphy	.50	.25	.05
☐ 32	Eddie Murray	.35	.17	.03
☐ 33	Dave Parker	.20	.10	.02
☐ 34	Tony Pena	.15	.07	.01
☐ 35	Jeff Reardon	.15	.07	.01
☐ 36	Cal Ripken	.35	.17	.03
☐ 37	Pete Rose	.60	.30	.06
☐ 38	Bret Saberhagen	.30	.15	.03
☐ 39	Juan Samuel	.15	.07	.01
☐ 40	Ryne Sandberg	.30	.15	.03
☐ 41	Mike Schmidt	.50	.25	.05
☐ 42	Lee Smith	.10	.05	.01
☐ 43	Don Sutton	.25	.12	.02
☐ 44	Lou Whitaker	.15	.07	.01

1986 Fleer Mini

The Fleer "Classic Miniatures" set consists of 120 small cards with all new pictures of the players as compared to the 1986 Fleer regular issue. The cards are only 1 13/16" by 2 9/16", making them one of the smallest (in size) produced in recent memory. Card backs provide career year-by-year statistics. The complete set was distributed in a red, white, and silver box along with 18 logo stickers. The card numbering is done in team order as is the usual Fleer style.

1986 Fleer Limited Edition

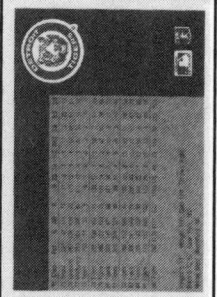

The 44-card boxed set was produced by Fleer for McCrory's. The cards are standard size 2 1/2" by 3 1/2" and have green and yellow borders. Card backs are printed in red and black on white card stock. Cards are numbered on the back; the back of the original box gives a complete checklist of the players in the set. The set box also contains six logo stickers.

		MINT	EXC	G-VG
COMPLETE SET		4.50	2.25	.45
COMMON PLAYER		.10	.05	.01

☐	1	Doyle Alexander	.15	.07	.01
☐	2	Joaquin Andujar	.15	.07	.01
☐	3	Harold Baines	.20	.10	.02
☐	4	Wade Boggs	.65	.30	.06
☐	5	Phil Bradley	.20	.10	.02
☐	6	George Brett	.40	.20	.04
☐	7	Hubie Brooks	.15	.07	.01
☐	8	Chris Brown	.20	.10	.02
☐	9	Tom Brunansky	.20	.10	.02
☐	10	Gary Carter	.35	.17	.03
☐	11	Vince Coleman	.40	.20	.04
☐	12	Cecil Cooper	.15	.07	.01
☐	13	Jose Cruz	.10	.05	.01
☐	14	Mike Davis	.10	.05	.01
☐	15	Carlton Fisk	.15	.07	.01
☐	16	Julio Franco	.10	.05	.01
☐	17	Damaso Garcia	.10	.05	.01
☐	18	Rich Gedman	.10	.05	.01
☐	19	Kirk Gibson	.25	.12	.02
☐	20	Dwight Gooden	.50	.25	.05
☐	21	Pedro Guerrero	.25	.12	.02
☐	22	Tony Gwynn	.40	.20	.04
☐	23	Rickey Henderson	.50	.25	.05
☐	24	Orel Hershiser	.20	.10	.02

		MINT	EXC	G-VG
COMPLETE SET		11.00	5.50	1.10
COMMON PLAYER		.05	.02	.00

☐	1	George Brett	.30	.15	.03
☐	2	Dan Quisenberry	.10	.05	.01
☐	3	Bret Saberhagen	.20	.10	.02
☐	4	Lonnie Smith	.05	.02	.00
☐	5	Willie Wilson	.10	.05	.01
☐	6	Jack Clark	.20	.10	.02
☐	7	Vince Coleman	.30	.15	.03
☐	8	Tom Herr	.05	.02	.00
☐	9	Willie McGee	.15	.07	.01
☐	10	Ozzie Smith	.20	.10	.02
☐	11	John Tudor	.10	.05	.01
☐	12	Jesse Barfield	.15	.07	.01
☐	13	George Bell	.25	.12	.02
☐	14	Tony Fernandez	.15	.07	.01
☐	15	Damaso Garcia	.05	.02	.00
☐	16	Dave Stieb	.10	.05	.01
☐	17	Gary Carter	.25	.12	.02
☐	18	Ron Darling	.15	.07	.01
☐	19A	Dwight Gooden (R on Mets logo)	1.00	.50	.10
☐	19B	Dwight Gooden (no R on Mets logo)	1.50	.75	.15
☐	20	Keith Hernandez	.20	.10	.02
☐	21	Darryl Strawberry	.35	.17	.03
☐	22	Ron Guidry	.15	.07	.01
☐	23	Rickey Henderson	.25	.12	.02
☐	24	Don Mattingly	2.00	1.00	.20
☐	25	Dave Righetti	.20	.10	.02
☐	26	Dave Winfield	.20	.10	.02
☐	27	Mariano Duncan	.10	.05	.01

☐ 28	Pedro Guerrero	.15	.07	.01
☐ 29	Bill Madlock	.10	.05	.01
☐ 30	Mike Marshall	.10	.05	.01
☐ 31	Fernando Valenzuela	.20	.10	.02
☐ 32	Reggie Jackson	.25	.12	.02
☐ 33	Gary Pettis	.05	.02	.00
☐ 34	Ron Romanick	.05	.02	.00
☐ 35	Don Sutton	.15	.07	.01
☐ 36	Mike Witt	.10	.05	.01
☐ 37	Buddy Bell	.10	.05	.01
☐ 38	Tom Browning	.05	.02	.00
☐ 39	Dave Parker	.15	.07	.01
☐ 40	Pete Rose	.65	.30	.06
☐ 41	Mario Soto	.05	.02	.00
☐ 42	Harold Baines	.10	.05	.01
☐ 43	Carlton Fisk	.10	.05	.01
☐ 44	Ozzie Guillen	.10	.05	.01
☐ 45	Ron Kittle	.10	.05	.01
☐ 46	Tom Seaver	.20	.10	.02
☐ 47	Kirk Gibson	.15	.07	.01
☐ 48	Jack Morris	.15	.07	.01
☐ 49	Lance Parrish	.10	.05	.01
☐ 50	Alan Trammell	.15	.07	.01
☐ 51	Lou Whitaker	.10	.05	.01
☐ 52	Hubie Brooks	.10	.05	.01
☐ 53	Andre Dawson	.25	.12	.02
☐ 54	Tim Raines	.25	.12	.02
☐ 55	Bryn Smith	.05	.02	.00
☐ 56	Tim Wallach	.10	.05	.01
☐ 57	Mike Boddicker	.10	.05	.01
☐ 58	Eddie Murray	.25	.12	.02
☐ 59	Cal Ripken	.25	.12	.02
☐ 60	John Shelby	.05	.02	.00
☐ 61	Mike Young	.05	.02	.00
☐ 62	Jose Cruz	.10	.05	.01
☐ 63	Glenn Davis	.20	.10	.02
☐ 64	Phil Garner	.05	.02	.00
☐ 65	Nolan Ryan	.25	.12	.02
☐ 66	Mike Scott	.20	.10	.02
☐ 67	Steve Garvey	.20	.10	.02
☐ 68	Goose Gossage	.10	.05	.01
☐ 69	Tony Gwynn	.30	.15	.03
☐ 70	Andy Hawkins	.05	.02	.00
☐ 71	Garry Templeton	.05	.02	.00
☐ 72	Wade Boggs	.75	.35	.07
☐ 73	Roger Clemens	.75	.35	.07
☐ 74	Dwight Evans	.15	.07	.01
☐ 75	Rich Gedman	.05	.02	.00
☐ 76	Jim Rice	.20	.10	.02
☐ 77	Shawon Dunston	.10	.05	.01
☐ 78	Leon Durham	.10	.05	.01
☐ 79	Keith Moreland	.05	.02	.00
☐ 80	Ryne Sandberg	.20	.10	.02
☐ 81	Rick Sutcliffe	.10	.05	.01
☐ 82	Bert Blyleven	.10	.05	.01
☐ 83	Tom Brunansky	.15	.07	.01
☐ 84	Kent Hrbek	.15	.07	.01
☐ 85	Kirby Puckett	.30	.15	.03
☐ 86	Bruce Bochte	.05	.02	.00
☐ 87	Jose Canseco	1.25	.60	.12
☐ 88	Mike Davis	.05	.02	.00
☐ 89	Jay Howell	.05	.02	.00
☐ 90	Dwayne Murphy	.05	.02	.00
☐ 91	Steve Carlton	.20	.10	.02
☐ 92	Von Hayes	.10	.05	.01
☐ 93	Juan Samuel	.15	.07	.01
☐ 94	Mike Schmidt	.35	.17	.03
☐ 95	Glenn Wilson	.10	.05	.01
☐ 96	Phil Bradley	.15	.07	.01
☐ 97	Alvin Davis	.15	.07	.01
☐ 98	Jim Presley	.15	.07	.01
☐ 99	Danny Tartabull	.25	.12	.02
☐ 100	Cecil Cooper	.10	.05	.01
☐ 101	Paul Molitor	.15	.07	.01
☐ 102	Ernie Riles	.10	.05	.01
☐ 103	Robin Yount	.20	.10	.02
☐ 104	Bob Horner	.15	.07	.01
☐ 105	Dale Murphy	.35	.17	.03
☐ 106	Bruce Sutter	.10	.05	.01
☐ 107	Claudell Washington	.05	.02	.00
☐ 108	Chris Brown	.15	.07	.01
☐ 109	Chili Davis	.05	.02	.00
☐ 110	Scott Garrelts	.05	.02	.00
☐ 111	Oddibe McDowell	.10	.05	.01
☐ 112	Pete O'Brien	.10	.05	.01
☐ 113	Gary Ward	.05	.02	.00
☐ 114	Brett Butler	.10	.05	.01
☐ 115	Julio Franco	.10	.05	.01
☐ 116	Brook Jacoby	.10	.05	.01
☐ 117	Mike Brown OF	.05	.02	.00
☐ 118	Joe Orsulak	.10	.05	.01
☐ 119	Tony Pena	.10	.05	.01
☐ 120	R.J. Reynolds	.10	.05	.01

1986 Fleer Sluggers/Pitchers

Fleer produced this 44-card boxed set although it was primarily distributed by Kress, McCrory, Newberry, T.G.Y., and other similar stores. The set features 22 sluggers and 22 pitchers and is subtitled "Baseball's Best". Cards are standard- size, 2 1/2" by 3 1/2", and were packaged in a red, white, blue, and yellow custom box along with six logo stickers. The set checklist is given on the back of the box.

			MINT	EXC	G-VG
	COMPLETE SET		5.00	2.50	.50
	COMMON PLAYER		.10	.05	.01
☐ 1	Bert Blyleven		.15	.07	.01
☐ 2	Wade Boggs		.60	.30	.06
☐ 3	George Brett		.40	.20	.04
☐ 4	Tom Browning		.10	.05	.01
☐ 5	Jose Canseco		1.00	.50	.10
☐ 6	Will Clark		.50	.25	.05
☐ 7	Roger Clemens		.60	.30	.06
☐ 8	Alvin Davis		.15	.07	.01
☐ 9	Julio Franco		.15	.07	.01
☐ 10	Kirk Gibson		.20	.10	.02
☐ 11	Dwight Gooden		.50	.25	.05
☐ 12	Goose Gossage		.15	.07	.01
☐ 13	Pedro Guerrero		.20	.10	.02
☐ 14	Ron Guidry		.20	.10	.02
☐ 15	Tony Gwynn		.35	.17	.03
☐ 16	Orel Hershiser		.20	.10	.02
☐ 17	Kent Hrbek		.20	.10	.02
☐ 18	Reggie Jackson		.40	.20	.04
☐ 19	Wally Joyner		1.50	.75	.15
☐ 20	Charlie Leibrandt		.10	.05	.01
☐ 21	Don Mattingly		1.00	.50	.10
☐ 22	Willie McGee		.20	.10	.02
☐ 23	Jack Morris		.20	.10	.02
☐ 24	Dale Murphy		.50	.25	.05
☐ 25	Eddie Murray		.30	.15	.03
☐ 26	Jeff Reardon		.15	.07	.01
☐ 27	Rick Reuschel		.10	.05	.01
☐ 28	Cal Ripken		.30	.15	.03
☐ 29	Pete Rose		.60	.30	.06
☐ 30	Nolan Ryan		.35	.17	.03
☐ 31	Bret Saberhagen		.25	.12	.02
☐ 32	Ryne Sandberg		.25	.12	.02
☐ 33	Mike Schmidt		.50	.25	.05
☐ 34	Tom Seaver		.30	.15	.03
☐ 35	Bryn Smith		.10	.05	.01
☐ 36	Mario Soto		.10	.05	.01
☐ 37	Dave Stieb		.15	.07	.01
☐ 38	Darryl Strawberry		.50	.25	.05
☐ 39	Rick Sutcliffe		.15	.07	.01
☐ 40	John Tudor		.15	.07	.01
☐ 41	Fernando Valenzuela		.30	.15	.03
☐ 42	Bobby Witt		.25	.12	.02
☐ 43	Mike Witt		.15	.07	.01
☐ 44	Robin Yount		.30	.15	.03

CHECK GLOSSARY: If you're not sure about a term or an abbreviation in this book, we've provided help. Just check our glossary and legend sections in the introductory material at the front of the book.

1986 Fleer Slug/Pitch Box Cards

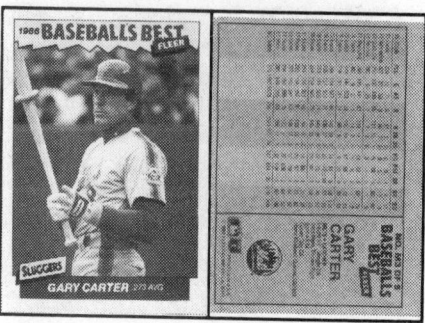

The cards in this 6-card set each measure the standard 2 1/2" by 3 1/2". Cards have essentially the same design as the 1986 Fleer Sluggers vs. Pitchers set of Baseball's Best. The cards were printed on the bottom of the counter display box which held 24 small boxed sets; hence theoretically these box cards are 1/24 as plentiful as the regular boxed set cards. These 6 cards, numbered M1 to M5 with one blank-back (unnumbered) card, are considered a separate set in their own right and are not typically included in a complete set of the 1986 Fleer Sluggers vs. Pitchers set of 44. The value of the panels uncut is slightly greater, perhaps by 25% greater, than the value of the individual cards cut up carefully.

	MINT	EXC	G-VG
COMPLETE SET	2.50	1.25	.25
COMMON PLAYERS	.10	.05	.01

		MINT	EXC	G-VG
☐	M1 Harold Baines	.25	.12	.02
☐	M2 Steve Carlton	.75	.35	.07
☐	M3 Gary Carter	.60	.30	.06
☐	M4 Vince Coleman	.75	.35	.07
☐	M5 Kirby Puckett	.75	.35	.07
☐	xx Team Logo	.10	.05	.01
	(unnumbered, blank back)			

1986 Fleer Sticker Cards

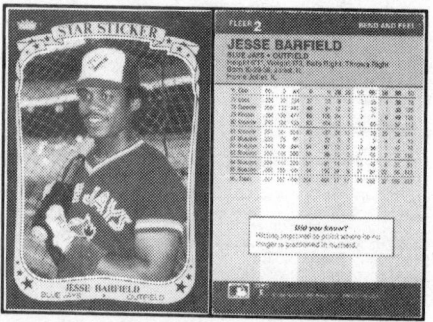

The stickers in this 132-sticker card set are standard card size, 2 1/2" by 3 1/2". The card photo on the front is surrounded by a yellow border and a cranberry frame. The backs are printed in blue and black on white card stock. The backs contain year by year statistical information. They are numbered on the back in the upper left hand corner.

		MINT	EXC	G-VG
	COMPLETE SET (1-132)	24.00	12.00	2.40
	COMMON PLAYER	.05	.02	.00
☐	1 Harold Baines	.15	.07	.01
☐	2 Jesse Barfield	.25	.12	.02
☐	3 Don Baylor	.15	.07	.01
☐	4 Juan Beniquez	.05	.02	.00
☐	5 Tim Birtsas	.10	.05	.01
☐	6 Bert Blyleven	.15	.07	.01
☐	7 Bruce Bochte	.05	.02	.00
☐	8 Wade Boggs	1.50	.75	.15
☐	9 Dennis Boyd	.10	.05	.01
☐	10 Phil Bradley	.20	.10	.02
☐	11 George Brett	.75	.35	.07
☐	12 Hubie Brooks	.10	.05	.01
☐	13 Chris Brown	.50	.25	.05
☐	14 Tom Browning	.15	.07	.01
☐	15 Tom Brunansky	.15	.07	.01
☐	16 Bill Buckner	.10	.05	.01
☐	17 Britt Burns	.05	.02	.00
☐	18 Brett Butler	.10	.05	.01
☐	19 Jose Canseco	3.00	1.50	.30
☐	20 Rod Carew	.35	.17	.03
☐	21 Steve Carlton	.35	.17	.03
☐	22 Don Carman	.15	.07	.01
☐	23 Gary Carter	.50	.25	.05
☐	24 Jack Clark	.35	.17	.03
☐	25 Vince Coleman	1.50	.75	.15
☐	26 Cecil Cooper	.10	.05	.01
☐	27 Jose Cruz	.10	.05	.01
☐	28 Ron Darling	.25	.12	.02
☐	29 Alvin Davis	.20	.10	.02
☐	30 Jody Davis	.10	.05	.01
☐	31 Mike Davis	.10	.05	.01
☐	32 Andre Dawson	.35	.17	.03
☐	33 Mariano Duncan	.20	.10	.02
☐	34 Shawon Dunston	.10	.05	.01
☐	35 Leon Durham	.10	.05	.01
☐	36 Darrell Evans	.10	.05	.01
☐	37 Tony Fernandez	.15	.07	.01
☐	38 Carlton Fisk	.20	.10	.02
☐	39 John Franco	.10	.05	.01
☐	40 Julio Franco	.10	.05	.01
☐	41 Damaso Garcia	.10	.05	.01
☐	42 Scott Garrelts	.10	.05	.01
☐	43 Steve Garvey	.50	.25	.05
☐	44 Rich Gedman	.10	.05	.01
☐	45 Kirk Gibson	.25	.12	.02
☐	46 Dwight Gooden	1.50	.75	.15
☐	47 Pedro Guerrero	.25	.12	.02
☐	48 Ron Guidry	.20	.10	.02
☐	49 Ozzie Guillen	.20	.10	.02
☐	50 Tony Gwynn	.45	.22	.04
☐	51 Andy Hawkins	.05	.02	.00
☐	52 Von Hayes	.10	.05	.01
☐	53 Rickey Henderson	.75	.35	.07
☐	54 Tom Henke	.10	.05	.01
☐	55 Keith Hernandez	.30	.15	.03
☐	56 Willie Hernandez	.10	.05	.01
☐	57 Tommy Herr	.10	.05	.01
☐	58 Orel Hershiser	.35	.17	.03
☐	59 Teddy Higuera	.50	.25	.05
☐	60 Bob Horner	.25	.12	.02
☐	61 Charlie Hough	.10	.05	.01
☐	62 Jay Howell	.05	.02	.00
☐	63 LaMarr Hoyt	.10	.05	.01
☐	64 Kent Hrbek	.25	.12	.02
☐	65 Reggie Jackson	.50	.25	.05
☐	66 Bob James	.05	.02	.00
☐	67 Dave Kingman	.10	.05	.01
☐	68 Ron Kittle	.10	.05	.01
☐	69 Charlie Leibrandt	.10	.05	.01
☐	70 Fred Lynn	.15	.07	.01
☐	71 Mike Marshall	.15	.07	.01
☐	72 Don Mattingly	2.50	1.25	.25
☐	73 Oddibe McDowell	.30	.15	.03
☐	74 Willie McGee	.25	.12	.02
☐	75 Scott McGregor	.10	.05	.01
☐	76 Paul Molitor	.25	.12	.02
☐	77 Charlie Moore	.05	.02	.00
☐	78 Keith Moreland	.10	.05	.01
☐	79 Jack Morris	.15	.07	.01
☐	80 Dale Murphy	1.00	.50	.10
☐	81 Eddie Murray	.75	.35	.07
☐	82 Phil Niekro	.25	.12	.02
☐	83 Joe Orsulak	.10	.05	.01
☐	84 Dave Parker	.25	.12	.02
☐	85 Lance Parrish	.20	.10	.02
☐	86 Larry Parrish	.10	.05	.01
☐	87 Tony Pena	.15	.07	.01
☐	88 Gary Pettis	.10	.05	.01
☐	89 Jim Presley	.30	.15	.03

☐ 90	Kirby Puckett	.75	.35	.07
☐ 91	Dan Quisenberry	.15	.07	.01
☐ 92	Tim Raines	.30	.15	.03
☐ 93	Johnny Ray	.10	.05	.01
☐ 94	Jeff Reardon	.15	.07	.01
☐ 95	Rick Reuschel	.10	.05	.01
☐ 96	Jim Rice	.25	.12	.02
☐ 97	Dave Righetti	.20	.10	.02
☐ 98	Earnie Riles	.20	.10	.02
☐ 99	Cal Ripken	.50	.25	.05
☐ 100	Ron Romanick	.05	.02	.00
☐ 101	Pete Rose	1.25	.60	.12
☐ 102	Nolan Ryan	.60	.30	.06
☐ 103	Bret Saberhagen	.50	.25	.05
☐ 104	Mark Salas	.10	.05	.01
☐ 105	Juan Samuel	.20	.10	.02
☐ 106	Ryne Sandberg	.50	.25	.05
☐ 107	Mike Schmidt	.60	.30	.06
☐ 108	Mike Scott	.20	.10	.02
☐ 109	Tom Seaver	.35	.17	.03
☐ 110	Bryn Smith	.10	.05	.01
☐ 111	Dave Smith	.10	.05	.01
☐ 112	Lonnie Smith	.10	.05	.01
☐ 113	Ozzie Smith	.30	.15	.03
☐ 114	Mario Soto	.10	.05	.01
☐ 115	Dave Stieb	.15	.07	.01
☐ 116	Darryl Strawberry	.75	.35	.07
☐ 117	Bruce Sutter	.15	.07	.01
☐ 118	Garry Templeton	.10	.07	.01
☐ 119	Gorman Thomas	.15	.07	.01
☐ 120	Andre Thornton	.10	.05	.01
☐ 121	Alan Trammell	.30	.15	.03
☐ 122	John Tudor	.15	.07	.01
☐ 123	Fernando Valenzuela	.25	.12	.02
☐ 124	Frank Viola	.20	.10	.02
☐ 125	Gary Ward	.05	.02	.00
☐ 126	Lou Whitaker	.20	.10	.02
☐ 127	Frank White	.10	.05	.01
☐ 128	Glenn Wilson	.10	.05	.01
☐ 129	Willie Wilson	.20	.10	.02
☐ 130	Dave Winfield	.35	.17	.03
☐ 131	Robin Yount	.35	.17	.03
☐ 132	Checklist Card	1.50	.75	.15
	Dwight Gooden			
	Dale Murphy			

1986 Fleer Sticker Wax Box

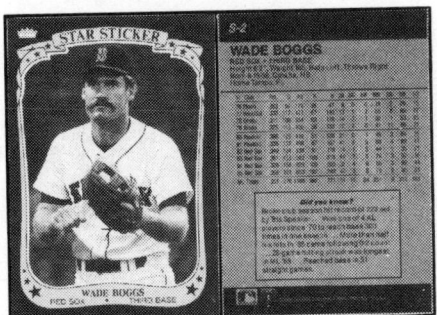

The bottoms of the Star Sticker wax boxes contained a set of four cards done in a similar format to the stickers; these cards (they are not stickers but truly cards) are numbered with the prefix S and are considered a separate set. Each individual card measures 2 1/2" by 3 1/2". The value of the panel uncut is slightly greater, perhaps by 25% greater, than the value of the individual cards cut up carefully.

		MINT	EXC	G-VG
COMPLETE SET (8)		1.50	.75	.15
COMMON PLAYER (1-8)		.10	.05	.01
☐ S1	Team Logo	.10	.05	.01
	(checklist back)			
☐ S2	Wade Boggs	1.00	.50	.10
☐ S3	Steve Garvey	.50	.25	.05
☐ S4	Dave Winfield	.50	.25	.05

1986 Fleer Update

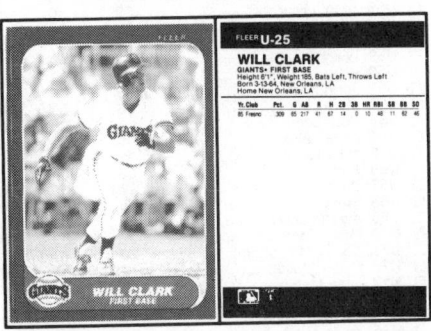

This 132-card set was distributed by Fleer to dealers as a complete set within a custom box. In addition to the complete set of 132 cards, the box also contains 25 Team Logo Stickers. The card fronts look very similar to the 1986 Fleer regular issue. The cards are numbered (with a U prefix) alphabetically according to player's last name. Cards measure the standard size, 2 1/2" by 3 1/2".

		MINT	EXC	G-VG
COMPLETE SET		16.00	8.00	1.60
COMMON PLAYER		.06	.03	.00
☐ U1	Mike Aldrete	.60	.30	.06
☐ U2	Andy Allanson	.20	.10	.02
☐ U3	Neil Allen	.06	.03	.00
☐ U4	Joaquin Andujar	.10	.05	.01
☐ U5	Paul Assenmacher	.20	.10	.02
☐ U6	Scott Bailes	.20	.10	.02
☐ U7	Jay Baller	.10	.05	.01
☐ U8	Scott Bankhead	.15	.07	.01
☐ U9	Bill Bathe	.10	.05	.01
☐ U10	Don Baylor	.10	.05	.01
☐ U11	Billy Beane	.15	.07	.01
☐ U12	Steve Bedrosian	.15	.07	.01
☐ U13	Juan Beniquez	.06	.03	.00
☐ U14	Barry Bonds	.80	.40	.08
☐ U15	Bobby Bonilla	.40	.20	.04
	(wrong birthday)			
☐ U16	Rich Bordi	.06	.03	.00
☐ U17	Bill Campbell	.06	.03	.00
☐ U18	Tom Candiotti	.10	.05	.01
☐ U19	John Cangelosi	.25	.12	.02
☐ U20	Jose Canseco	3.00	1.50	.30
	(headings on back			
	for a pitcher)			
☐ U21	Chuck Cary	.20	.10	.02
☐ U22	Juan Castillo	.15	.07	.01
☐ U23	Rick Cerone	.06	.03	.00
☐ U24	John Cerutti	.25	.12	.02
☐ U25	Will Clark	3.00	1.50	.30
☐ U26	Mark Clear	.06	.03	.00
☐ U27	Darnell Coles	.15	.07	.01
☐ U28	Dave Collins	.06	.03	.00
☐ U29	Tim Conroy	.06	.03	.00
☐ U30	Ed Correa	.25	.12	.02
☐ U31	Joe Cowley	.06	.03	.00
☐ U32	Bill Dawley	.06	.03	.00
☐ U33	Rob Deer	.30	.15	.03
☐ U34	John Denny	.10	.05	.01
☐ U35	Jim Deshaies	.40	.20	.04
☐ U36	Doug Drabek	.30	.15	.03
☐ U37	Mike Easler	.10	.05	.01
☐ U38	Mark Eichhorn	.30	.15	.03
☐ U39	Dave Engle	.06	.03	.00
☐ U40	Mike Fischlin	.06	.03	.00
☐ U41	Scott Fletcher	.10	.05	.01
☐ U42	Terry Forster	.10	.05	.01
☐ U43	Terry Francona	.06	.03	.00
☐ U44	Andres Galarraga	.75	.35	.07
☐ U45	Lee Guetterman	.30	.15	.03
☐ U46	Bill Gullickson	.10	.05	.01
☐ U47	Jackie Gutierrez	.06	.03	.00
☐ U48	Moose Haas	.06	.03	.00
☐ U49	Billy Hatcher	.25	.12	.02
☐ U50	Mike Heath	.06	.03	.00
☐ U51	Guy Hoffman	.06	.03	.00
☐ U52	Tom Hume	.06	.03	.00

☐ U53	Pete Incaviglia	2.00	1.00	.20
☐ U54	Dane Iorg	.06	.03	.00
☐ U55	Chris James	1.25	.60	.12
☐ U56	Stan Javier	.20	.10	.02
☐ U57	Tommy John	.15	.07	.01
☐ U58	Tracy Jones	.75	.35	.07
☐ U59	Wally Joyner	4.00	2.00	.40
☐ U60	Wayne Krenchicki	.06	.03	.00
☐ U61	John Kruk	1.25	.60	.12
☐ U62	Mike LaCoss	.06	.03	.00
☐ U63	Pete Ladd	.06	.03	.00
☐ U64	Dave LaPoint	.06	.03	.00
☐ U65	Mike LaValliere	.25	.12	.02
☐ U66	Rudy Law	.06	.03	.00
☐ U67	Dennis Leonard	.10	.05	.01
☐ U68	Steve Lombardozzi	.25	.12	.02
☐ U69	Aurelio Lopez	.06	.03	.00
☐ U70	Mickey Mahler	.06	.03	.00
☐ U71	Candy Maldonado	.20	.10	.02
☐ U72	Roger Mason	.15	.07	.01
☐ U73	Greg Mathews	.30	.15	.03
☐ U74	Andy McGaffigan	.06	.03	.00
☐ U75	Joel McKeon	.20	.10	.02
☐ U76	Kevin Mitchell	.50	.25	.05
☐ U77	Bill Mooneyham	.15	.07	.01
☐ U78	Omar Moreno	.06	.03	.00
☐ U79	Jerry Mumphrey	.06	.03	.00
☐ U80	Al Newman	.15	.07	.01
☐ U81	Phil Niekro	.25	.12	.02
☐ U82	Randy Niemann	.06	.03	.00
☐ U83	Juan Nieves	.30	.15	.03
☐ U84	Bob Ojeda	.15	.07	.01
☐ U85	Rick Ownbey	.06	.03	.00
☐ U86	Tom Paciorek	.06	.03	.00
☐ U87	David Palmer	.06	.03	.00
☐ U88	Jeff Parrett	.25	.12	.02
☐ U89	Pat Perry	.20	.10	.02
☐ U90	Dan Plesac	.35	.17	.03
☐ U91	Darrell Porter	.06	.03	.00
☐ U92	Luis Quinones	.15	.07	.01
☐ U93	Rey Quinones	.30	.15	.03
☐ U94	Gary Redus	.10	.05	.01
☐ U95	Jeff Reed	.15	.07	.01
☐ U96	Bip Roberts	.15	.07	.01
☐ U97	Billy Joe Robidoux	.10	.05	.01
☐ U98	Gary Roenicke	.06	.03	.00
☐ U99	Ron Roenicke	.06	.03	.00
☐ U100	Angel Salazar	.06	.03	.00
☐ U101	Joe Sambito	.06	.03	.00
☐ U102	Billy Sample	.06	.03	.00
☐ U103	Dave Schmidt	.10	.05	.01
☐ U104	Ken Schrom	.10	.05	.01
☐ U105	Ruben Sierra	2.50	1.25	.25
☐ U106	Ted Simmons	.15	.07	.01
☐ U107	Sammy Stewart	.06	.03	.00
☐ U108	Kurt Stillwell	.45	.22	.04
☐ U109	Dale Sveum	.75	.35	.07
☐ U110	Tim Teufel	.10	.05	.01
☐ U111	Bob Tewksbury	.25	.12	.02
☐ U112	Andres Thomas	.20	.10	.02
☐ U113	Jason Thompson	.06	.03	.00
☐ U114	Milt Thompson	.20	.10	.02
☐ U115	Rob Thompson	.35	.17	.03
☐ U116	Jay Tibbs	.06	.03	.00
☐ U117	Fred Toliver	.10	.05	.01
☐ U118	Wayne Tolleson	.06	.03	.00
☐ U119	Alex Trevino	.06	.03	.00
☐ U120	Manny Trillo	.06	.03	.00
☐ U121	Ed VandeBerg	.06	.03	.00
☐ U122	Ozzie Virgil	.06	.03	.00
☐ U123	Tony Walker	.20	.10	.02
☐ U124	Gene Walter	.10	.05	.01
☐ U125	Duane Ward	.20	.10	.02
☐ U126	Jerry Willard	.06	.03	.00
☐ U127	Mitch Williams	.25	.12	.02
☐ U128	Reggie Williams	.20	.10	.02
☐ U129	Bobby Witt	.35	.17	.03
☐ U130	Marvell Wynne	.06	.03	.00
☐ U131	Steve Yeager	.06	.03	.00
☐ U132	Checklist Card	.10	.01	.00

1987 Fleer

This 660-card set features a distinctive blue border which fades to white on the card fronts. The backs are printed in blue, red, and pink on white card stock. The bottom of the card back shows an innovative graph of the player's ability, e.g., "He's got the stuff"

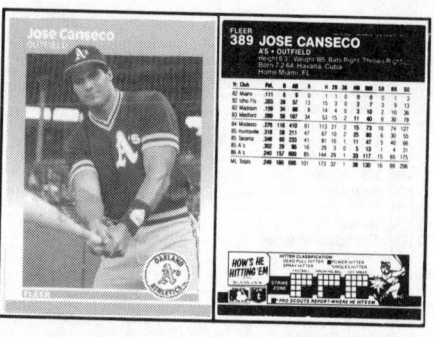

for pitchers and "How he's hitting 'em," for hitters. Cards are numbered on the back and are again the standard 2 1/2" by 3 1/2". Cards are again organized numerically by teams, i.e., World Champion Mets (1-25), Boston Red Sox (26-48), Houston Astros (49-72), California Angels (73- 95), New York Yankees (96-120), Texas Rangers (121-143), Detroit Tigers (144-168), Philadelphia Phillies (169-192), Cincinnati Reds (193-218), Toronto Blue Jays (219-240), Cleveland Indians (241-263), San Francisco Giants (264-288), St. Louis Cardinals (289-312), Montreal Expos (313-337), Milwaukee Brewers (338-361), Kansas City Royals (362-384), Oakland A's (385-410), Los Angeles Dodgers (436-460), Baltimore Orioles (461-483), Chicago White Sox (484-508), Atlanta Braves (509-532), Minnesota Twins (533-554), Chicago Cubs (555-578), Seattle Mariners (579-600), and Pittsburgh Pirates (601-624). The last 36 cards in the set consist of Specials (625-643), Rookie Pairs (644-653), and checklists (654-660).

		MINT	EXC	G-VG
COMPLETE SET		42.00	18.00	3.50
COMMON PLAYER		.04	.02	.00
☐ 1	Rick Aguilera	.10	.03	.01
☐ 2	Richard Anderson	.15	.07	.01
☐ 3	Wally Backman	.07	.03	.01
☐ 4	Gary Carter	.30	.15	.03
☐ 5	Ron Darling	.20	.10	.02
☐ 6	Len Dykstra	.15	.07	.01
☐ 7	Kevin Elster	.30	.15	.03
☐ 8	Sid Fernandez	.18	.09	.01
☐ 9	Dwight Gooden	.80	.40	.08
☐ 10	Ed Hearn	.10	.05	.01
☐ 11	Danny Heep	.04	.02	.00
☐ 12	Keith Hernandez	.25	.12	.02
☐ 13	Howard Johnson	.15	.07	.01
☐ 14	Ray Knight	.07	.03	.01
☐ 15	Lee Mazzilli	.04	.02	.00
☐ 16	Roger McDowell	.10	.05	.01
☐ 17	Kevin Mitchell	.30	.15	.03
☐ 18	Randy Niemann	.04	.02	.00
☐ 19	Bob Ojeda	.07	.03	.01
☐ 20	Jesse Orosco	.07	.03	.01
☐ 21	Rafael Santana	.04	.02	.00
☐ 22	Doug Sisk	.04	.02	.00
☐ 23	Darryl Strawberry	.40	.20	.04
☐ 24	Tim Teufel	.04	.02	.00
☐ 25	Mookie Wilson	.07	.03	.01
☐ 26	Tony Armas	.07	.03	.01
☐ 27	Marty Barrett	.10	.05	.01
☐ 28	Don Baylor	.10	.05	.01
☐ 29	Wade Boggs	1.50	.75	.15
☐ 30	Oil Can Boyd	.07	.03	.01
☐ 31	Bill Buckner	.07	.03	.01
☐ 32	Roger Clemens	1.25	.60	.12
☐ 33	Steve Crawford	.04	.02	.00
☐ 34	Dwight Evans	.12	.06	.01
☐ 35	Rich Gedman	.07	.03	.01
☐ 36	Dave Henderson	.04	.02	.00
☐ 37	Bruce Hurst	.10	.05	.01
☐ 38	Tim Lollar	.04	.02	.00
☐ 39	Al Nipper	.04	.02	.00
☐ 40	Spike Owen	.04	.02	.00
☐ 41	Jim Rice	.25	.12	.02
☐ 42	Ed Romero	.04	.02	.00

☐ 43	Joe Sambito	.04	.02	.00
☐ 44	Calvin Schiraldi	.07	.03	.01
☐ 45	Tom Seaver	.30	.15	.03
☐ 46	Jeff Sellers	.10	.05	.01
☐ 47	Bob Stanley	.04	.02	.00
☐ 48	Sammy Stewart	.04	.02	.00
☐ 49	Larry Andersen	.04	.02	.00
☐ 50	Alan Ashby	.04	.02	.00
☐ 51	Kevin Bass	.10	.05	.01
☐ 52	Jeff Calhoun	.04	.02	.00
☐ 53	Jose Cruz	.10	.05	.01
☐ 54	Danny Darwin	.04	.02	.00
☐ 55	Glenn Davis	.25	.12	.02
☐ 56	Jim Deshaies	.30	.15	.03
☐ 57	Bill Doran	.10	.05	.01
☐ 58	Phil Garner	.04	.02	.00
☐ 59	Billy Hatcher	.10	.05	.01
☐ 60	Charlie Kerfeld	.07	.03	.01
☐ 61	Bob Knepper	.07	.03	.01
☐ 62	Dave Lopes	.07	.03	.01
☐ 63	Aurelio Lopez	.04	.02	.00
☐ 64	Jim Pankovits	.04	.02	.00
☐ 65	Terry Puhl	.04	.02	.00
☐ 66	Craig Reynolds	.04	.02	.00
☐ 67	Nolan Ryan	.30	.15	.03
☐ 68	Mike Scott	.25	.12	.02
☐ 69	Dave Smith	.07	.03	.01
☐ 70	Dickie Thon	.04	.02	.00
☐ 71	Tony Walker	.15	.07	.01
☐ 72	Denny Walling	.04	.02	.00
☐ 73	Bob Boone	.07	.03	.01
☐ 74	Rick Burleson	.07	.03	.01
☐ 75	John Candelaria	.07	.03	.01
☐ 76	Doug Corbett	.04	.02	.00
☐ 77	Doug DeCinces	.07	.03	.01
☐ 78	Brian Downing	.07	.03	.01
☐ 79	Chuck Finley	.10	.05	.01
☐ 80	Terry Forster	.07	.03	.01
☐ 81	Bob Grich	.07	.03	.01
☐ 82	George Hendrick	.07	.03	.01
☐ 83	Jack Howell	.07	.03	.01
☐ 84	Reggie Jackson	.30	.15	.03
☐ 85	Ruppert Jones	.04	.02	.00
☐ 86	Wally Joyner	2.50	1.25	.25
☐ 87	Gary Lucas	.04	.02	.00
☐ 88	Kirk McCaskill	.07	.03	.01
☐ 89	Donnie Moore	.04	.02	.00
☐ 90	Gary Pettis	.07	.03	.01
☐ 91	Vern Ruhle	.04	.02	.00
☐ 92	Dick Schofield	.04	.02	.00
☐ 93	Don Sutton	.12	.06	.01
☐ 94	Rob Wilfong	.04	.02	.00
☐ 95	Mike Witt	.10	.05	.01
☐ 96	Doug Drabek	.30	.15	.03
☐ 97	Mike Easler	.07	.03	.01
☐ 98	Mike Fischlin	.04	.02	.00
☐ 99	Brian Fisher	.07	.03	.01
☐ 100	Ron Guidry	.15	.07	.01
☐ 101	Rickey Henderson	.30	.15	.03
☐ 102	Tommy John	.12	.06	.01
☐ 103	Ron Kittle	.10	.05	.01
☐ 104	Don Mattingly	3.00	1.50	.30
☐ 105	Bobby Meacham	.04	.02	.00
☐ 106	Joe Niekro	.10	.05	.01
☐ 107	Mike Pagliarulo	.12	.06	.01
☐ 108	Dan Pasqua	.10	.05	.01
☐ 109	Willie Randolph	.07	.03	.01
☐ 110	Dennis Rasmussen	.07	.03	.01
☐ 111	Dave Righetti	.15	.07	.01
☐ 112	Gary Roenicke	.04	.02	.00
☐ 113	Rod Scurry	.04	.02	.00
☐ 114	Bob Shirley	.04	.02	.00
☐ 115	Joel Skinner	.04	.02	.00
☐ 116	Tim Stoddard	.04	.02	.00
☐ 117	Bob Tewksbury	.20	.10	.02
☐ 118	Wayne Tolleson	.04	.02	.00
☐ 119	Claudell Washington	.07	.03	.01
☐ 120	Dave Winfield	.25	.12	.02
☐ 121	Steve Buechele	.04	.02	.00
☐ 122	Ed Correa	.25	.12	.02
☐ 123	Scott Fletcher	.07	.03	.01
☐ 124	Jose Guzman	.07	.03	.01
☐ 125	Toby Harrah	.04	.02	.00
☐ 126	Greg Harris	.04	.02	.00
☐ 127	Charlie Hough	.07	.03	.01
☐ 128	Pete Incaviglia	1.25	.60	.12
☐ 129	Mike Mason	.04	.02	.00
☐ 130	Oddibe McDowell	.20	.10	.02
☐ 131	Dave Mohorcic	.25	.12	.02
☐ 132	Pete O'Brien	.10	.05	.01
☐ 133	Tom Paciorek	.04	.02	.00
☐ 134	Larry Parrish	.07	.03	.01
☐ 135	Geno Petralli	.04	.02	.00
☐ 136	Darrell Porter	.04	.02	.00
☐ 137	Jeff Russell	.04	.02	.00
☐ 138	Ruben Sierra	1.50	.75	.15
☐ 139	Don Slaught	.04	.02	.00
☐ 140	Gary Ward	.07	.03	.01
☐ 141	Curtis Wilkerson	.04	.02	.00
☐ 142	Mitch Williams	.20	.10	.02
☐ 143	Bobby Witt	.30	.15	.03
☐ 144	Dave Bergman	.04	.02	.00
☐ 145	Tom Brookens	.04	.02	.00
☐ 146	Bill Campbell	.04	.02	.00
☐ 147	Chuck Cary	.20	.10	.02
☐ 148	Darnell Coles	.07	.03	.01
☐ 149	Dave Collins	.04	.02	.00
☐ 150	Darrell Evans	.10	.05	.01
☐ 151	Kirk Gibson	.20	.10	.02
☐ 152	John Grubb	.04	.02	.00
☐ 153	Willie Hernandez	.10	.05	.01
☐ 154	Larry Herndon	.04	.02	.00
☐ 155	Eric King	.20	.10	.02
☐ 156	Chet Lemon	.04	.02	.00
☐ 157	Dwight Lowry	.15	.07	.01
☐ 158	Jack Morris	.15	.07	.01
☐ 159	Randy O'Neal	.04	.02	.00
☐ 160	Lance Parrish	.15	.07	.01
☐ 161	Dan Petry	.10	.05	.01
☐ 162	Pat Sheridan	.04	.02	.00
☐ 163	Jim Slaton	.04	.02	.00
☐ 164	Frank Tanana	.07	.03	.01
☐ 165	Walt Terrell	.04	.02	.00
☐ 166	Mark Thurmond	.04	.02	.00
☐ 167	Alan Trammell	.18	.09	.01
☐ 168	Lou Whitaker	.12	.06	.01
☐ 169	Luis Aguayo	.04	.02	.00
☐ 170	Steve Bedrosian	.15	.07	.01
☐ 171	Don Carman	.04	.02	.00
☐ 172	Darren Daulton	.04	.02	.00
☐ 173	Greg Gross	.04	.02	.00
☐ 174	Kevin Gross	.04	.02	.00
☐ 175	Von Hayes	.10	.05	.01
☐ 176	Charles Hudson	.04	.02	.00
☐ 177	Tom Hume	.04	.02	.00
☐ 178	Steve Jeltz	.04	.02	.00
☐ 179	Mike Maddux	.10	.05	.01
☐ 180	Shane Rawley	.07	.03	.01
☐ 181	Gary Redus	.04	.02	.00
☐ 182	Ron Roenicke	.04	.02	.00
☐ 183	Bruce Ruffin	.25	.12	.02
☐ 184	John Russell	.04	.02	.00
☐ 185	Juan Samuel	.15	.07	.01
☐ 186	Dan Schatzeder	.04	.02	.00
☐ 187	Mike Schmidt	.35	.17	.03
☐ 188	Rick Schu	.04	.02	.00
☐ 189	Jeff Stone	.07	.03	.01
☐ 190	Kent Tekulve	.07	.03	.01
☐ 191	Milt Thompson	.10	.05	.01
☐ 192	Glenn Wilson	.10	.05	.01
☐ 193	Buddy Bell	.10	.05	.01
☐ 194	Tom Browning	.07	.03	.01
☐ 195	Sal Butera	.04	.02	.00
☐ 196	Dave Concepcion	.07	.03	.01
☐ 197	Kal Daniels	.90	.45	.09
☐ 198	Eric Davis	2.00	1.00	.20
☐ 199	John Denny	.07	.03	.01
☐ 200	Bo Diaz	.07	.03	.01
☐ 201	Nick Esasky	.10	.05	.01
☐ 202	John Franco	.10	.05	.01
☐ 203	Bill Gullickson	.07	.03	.01
☐ 204	Barry Larkin	.85	.40	.08
☐ 205	Eddie Milner	.04	.02	.00
☐ 206	Rob Murphy	.20	.10	.02
☐ 207	Ron Oester	.04	.02	.00
☐ 208	Dave Parker	.15	.07	.01
☐ 209	Tony Perez	.10	.05	.01
☐ 210	Ted Power	.07	.03	.01
☐ 211	Joe Price	.04	.02	.00
☐ 212	Ron Robinson	.04	.02	.00
☐ 213	Pete Rose	.50	.25	.05
☐ 214	Mario Soto	.07	.03	.01
☐ 215	Kurt Stillwell	.35	.17	.03
☐ 216	Max Venable	.04	.02	.00
☐ 217	Chris Welsh	.04	.02	.00
☐ 218	Carl Willis	.10	.05	.01
☐ 219	Jesse Barfield	.20	.10	.02
☐ 220	George Bell	.30	.15	.03
☐ 221	Bill Caudill	.04	.02	.00
☐ 222	John Cerutti	.20	.10	.02
☐ 223	Jim Clancy	.04	.02	.00
☐ 224	Mark Eichhorn	.20	.10	.02
☐ 225	Tony Fernandez	.15	.07	.01
☐ 226	Damaso Garcia	.07	.03	.01
☐ 227	Kelly Gruber ERR (wrong birth year)	.04	.02	.00
☐ 228	Tom Henke	.10	.05	.01
☐ 229	Garth Iorg	.04	.02	.00
☐ 230	Joe Johnson	.04	.02	.00
☐ 231	Cliff Johnson	.04	.02	.00

☐ 232 Jimmy Key	.12	.06	.01
☐ 233 Dennis Lamp	.04	.02	.00
☐ 234 Rick Leach	.04	.02	.00
☐ 235 Buck Martinez	.04	.02	.00
☐ 236 Lloyd Moseby	.10	.05	.01
☐ 237 Rance Mulliniks	.04	.02	.00
☐ 238 Dave Stieb	.10	.05	.01
☐ 239 Willie Upshaw	.07	.03	.01
☐ 240 Ernie Whitt	.04	.02	.00
☐ 241 Andy Allanson	.12	.06	.01
☐ 242 Scott Bailes	.15	.07	.01
☐ 243 Chris Bando	.04	.02	.00
☐ 244 Tony Bernazard	.04	.02	.00
☐ 245 John Butcher	.04	.02	.00
☐ 246 Brett Butler	.07	.03	.01
☐ 247 Ernie Camacho	.04	.02	.00
☐ 248 Tom Candiotti	.04	.02	.00
☐ 249 Joe Carter	.18	.09	.01
☐ 250 Carmen Castillo	.04	.02	.00
☐ 251 Julio Franco	.10	.05	.01
☐ 252 Mel Hall	.07	.03	.01
☐ 253 Brook Jacoby	.10	.05	.01
☐ 254 Phil Niekro	.15	.07	.01
☐ 255 Otis Nixon	.12	.06	.01
☐ 256 Dickie Noles	.04	.02	.00
☐ 257 Bryan Oelkers	.07	.03	.01
☐ 258 Ken Schrom	.04	.02	.00
☐ 259 Don Schulze	.04	.02	.00
☐ 260 Cory Snyder	.80	.40	.08
☐ 261 Pat Tabler	.10	.05	.01
☐ 262 Andre Thornton	.07	.03	.01
☐ 263 Rich Yett	.04	.02	.00
☐ 264 Mike Aldrete	.45	.22	.04
☐ 265 Juan Berenguer	.07	.03	.01
☐ 266 Vida Blue	.07	.03	.01
☐ 267 Bob Brenly	.07	.03	.01
☐ 268 Chris Brown	.15	.07	.01
☐ 269 Will Clark	1.75	.85	.17
☐ 270 Chili Davis	.10	.05	.01
☐ 271 Mark Davis	.04	.02	.00
☐ 272 Kelly Downs	.25	.12	.02
☐ 273 Scott Garrelts	.07	.03	.01
☐ 274 Dan Gladden	.07	.03	.01
☐ 275 Mike Krukow	.07	.03	.01
☐ 276 Randy Kutcher	.12	.06	.01
☐ 277 Mike LaCoss	.04	.02	.00
☐ 278 Jeff Leonard	.10	.05	.01
☐ 279 Candy Maldonado	.10	.05	.01
☐ 280 Roger Mason	.04	.02	.00
☐ 281 Bob Melvin	.04	.02	.00
☐ 282 Greg Minton	.04	.02	.00
☐ 283 Jeff Robinson	.07	.03	.01
(Giants pitcher)			
☐ 284 Harry Spilman	.04	.02	.00
☐ 285 Robby Thompson	.30	.15	.03
☐ 286 Jose Uribe	.04	.02	.00
☐ 287 Frank Williams	.04	.02	.00
☐ 288 Joel Youngblood	.04	.02	.00
☐ 289 Jack Clark	.20	.10	.02
☐ 290 Vince Coleman	.45	.22	.04
☐ 291 Tim Conroy	.04	.02	.00
☐ 292 Danny Cox	.10	.05	.01
☐ 293 Ken Dayley	.04	.02	.00
☐ 294 Curt Ford	.07	.03	.01
☐ 295 Bob Forsch	.07	.03	.01
☐ 296 Tom Herr	.07	.03	.01
☐ 297 Ricky Horton	.04	.02	.00
☐ 298 Clint Hurdle	.04	.02	.00
☐ 299 Jeff Lahti	.04	.02	.00
☐ 300 Steve Lake	.04	.02	.00
☐ 301 Tito Landrum	.04	.02	.00
☐ 302 Mike LaValliere	.20	.10	.02
☐ 303 Greg Mathews	.25	.12	.02
☐ 304 Willie McGee	.15	.07	.01
☐ 305 Jose Oquendo	.07	.03	.01
☐ 306 Terry Pendleton	.07	.03	.01
☐ 307 Pat Perry	.07	.03	.01
☐ 308 Ozzie Smith	.15	.07	.01
☐ 309 Ray Soff	.08	.04	.01
☐ 310 John Tudor	.10	.05	.01
☐ 311 Andy Van Slyke	.10	.05	.01
ERR (Bats R, Throws L)			
☐ 312 Todd Worrell	.25	.12	.02
☐ 313 Dann Bilardello	.04	.02	.00
☐ 314 Hubie Brooks	.10	.05	.01
☐ 315 Tim Burke	.07	.03	.01
☐ 316 Andre Dawson	.25	.12	.02
☐ 317 Mike Fitzgerald	.04	.02	.00
☐ 318 Tom Foley	.04	.02	.00
☐ 319 Andres Galarraga	.25	.12	.02
☐ 320 Joe Hesketh	.07	.03	.01
☐ 321 Wallace Johnson	.04	.02	.00
☐ 322 Wayne Krenchicki	.04	.02	.00
☐ 323 Vance Law	.04	.02	.00
☐ 324 Dennis Martinez	.07	.03	.01
☐ 325 Bob McClure	.04	.02	.00
☐ 326 Andy McGaffigan	.04	.02	.00
☐ 327 Al Newman	.10	.05	.01
☐ 328 Tim Raines	.30	.15	.03
☐ 329 Jeff Reardon	.10	.05	.01
☐ 330 Luis Rivera	.10	.05	.01
☐ 331 Bob Sebra	.15	.07	.01
☐ 332 Bryn Smith	.07	.03	.01
☐ 333 Jay Tibbs	.04	.02	.00
☐ 334 Tim Wallach	.10	.05	.01
☐ 335 Mitch Webster	.07	.03	.01
☐ 336 Jim Wohlford	.04	.02	.00
☐ 337 Floyd Youmans	.10	.05	.01
☐ 338 Chris Bosio	.20	.10	.02
☐ 339 Glenn Braggs	.50	.25	.05
☐ 340 Rick Cerone	.04	.02	.00
☐ 341 Mark Clear	.04	.02	.00
☐ 342 Bryan Clutterbuck	.10	.05	.01
☐ 343 Cecil Cooper	.10	.05	.01
☐ 344 Rob Deer	.15	.07	.01
☐ 345 Jim Gantner	.04	.02	.00
☐ 346 Ted Higuera	.20	.10	.02
☐ 347 John H. Johnson	.04	.02	.00
☐ 348 Tim Leary	.04	.02	.00
☐ 349 Rick Manning	.04	.02	.00
☐ 350 Paul Molitor	.12	.06	.01
☐ 351 Charlie Moore	.04	.02	.00
☐ 352 Juan Nieves	.15	.07	.01
☐ 353 Ben Oglivie	.07	.03	.01
☐ 354 Dan Plesac	.30	.15	.03
☐ 355 Ernest Riles	.07	.03	.01
☐ 356 Billy Jo Robidoux	.07	.03	.01
☐ 357 Bill Schroeder	.04	.02	.00
☐ 358 Dale Sveum	.50	.25	.05
☐ 359 Gorman Thomas	.10	.05	.01
☐ 360 Bill Wegman	.07	.03	.01
☐ 361 Robin Yount	.25	.12	.02
☐ 362 Steve Balboni	.04	.02	.00
☐ 363 Scott Bankhead	.10	.05	.01
☐ 364 Buddy Biancalana	.04	.02	.00
☐ 365 Bud Black	.04	.02	.00
☐ 366 George Brett	.35	.17	.03
☐ 367 Steve Farr	.04	.02	.00
☐ 368 Mark Gubicza	.07	.03	.01
☐ 369 Bo Jackson	1.25	.60	.12
☐ 370 Danny Jackson	.07	.03	.01
☐ 371 Mike Kingery	.20	.10	.02
☐ 372 Rudy Law	.04	.02	.00
☐ 373 Charlie Leibrandt	.07	.03	.01
☐ 374 Dennis Leonard	.07	.03	.01
☐ 375 Hal McRae	.07	.03	.01
☐ 376 Jorge Orta	.04	.02	.00
☐ 377 Jamie Quirk	.04	.02	.00
☐ 378 Dan Quisenberry	.12	.06	.01
☐ 379 Bret Saberhagen	.25	.12	.02
☐ 380 Angel Salazar	.04	.02	.00
☐ 381 Lonnie Smith	.07	.03	.01
☐ 382 Jim Sundberg	.04	.02	.00
☐ 383 Frank White	.07	.03	.01
☐ 384 Willie Wilson	.12	.06	.01
☐ 385 Joaquin Andujar	.07	.03	.01
☐ 386 Doug Bair	.04	.02	.00
☐ 387 Dusty Baker	.07	.03	.01
☐ 388 Bruce Bochte	.04	.02	.00
☐ 389 Jose Canseco	2.00	1.00	.20
☐ 390 Chris Codiroli	.04	.02	.00
☐ 391 Mike Davis	.07	.03	.01
☐ 392 Alfredo Griffin	.07	.03	.01
☐ 393 Moose Haas	.04	.02	.00
☐ 394 Donnie Hill	.04	.02	.00
☐ 395 Jay Howell	.04	.02	.00
☐ 396 Dave Kingman	.10	.05	.01
☐ 397 Carney Lansford	.10	.05	.01
☐ 398 Dave Leiper	.10	.05	.01
☐ 399 Bill Mooneyham	.10	.05	.01
☐ 400 Dwayne Murphy	.04	.02	.00
☐ 401 Steve Ontiveros	.04	.02	.00
☐ 402 Tony Phillips	.04	.02	.00
☐ 403 Eric Plunk	.04	.02	.00
☐ 404 Jose Rijo	.07	.03	.01
☐ 405 Terry Steinbach	.50	.25	.05
☐ 406 Dave Stewart	.10	.05	.01
☐ 407 Mickey Tettleton	.04	.02	.00
☐ 408 Dave Von Ohlen	.04	.02	.00
☐ 409 Jerry Willard	.04	.02	.00
☐ 410 Curt Young	.07	.03	.01
☐ 411 Bruce Bochy	.04	.02	.00
☐ 412 Dave Dravecky	.07	.03	.01
☐ 413 Tim Flannery	.04	.02	.00
☐ 414 Steve Garvey	.30	.15	.03
☐ 415 Goose Gossage	.12	.06	.01
☐ 416 Tony Gwynn	.45	.22	.04
☐ 417 Andy Hawkins	.04	.02	.00
☐ 418 LaMarr Hoyt	.07	.03	.01
☐ 419 Terry Kennedy	.07	.03	.01

☐ 420	John Kruk	.85	.40	.08
☐ 421	Dave LaPoint	.04	.02	.00
☐ 422	Craig Lefferts	.04	.02	.00
☐ 423	Carmelo Martinez	.04	.02	.00
☐ 424	Lance McCullers	.04	.02	.00
☐ 425	Kevin McReynolds	.20	.10	.02
☐ 426	Graig Nettles	.12	.06	.01
☐ 427	Bip Roberts	.10	.05	.01
☐ 428	Jerry Royster	.04	.02	.00
☐ 429	Benito Santiago	1.00	.50	.10
☐ 430	Eric Show	.04	.02	.00
☐ 431	Bob Stoddard	.04	.02	.00
☐ 432	Garry Templeton	.07	.03	.01
☐ 433	Gene Walter	.04	.02	.00
☐ 434	Ed Whitson	.04	.02	.00
☐ 435	Marvell Wynne	.04	.02	.00
☐ 436	Dave Anderson	.04	.02	.00
☐ 437	Greg Brock	.07	.03	.01
☐ 438	Enos Cabell	.04	.02	.00
☐ 439	Mariano Duncan	.07	.03	.01
☐ 440	Pedro Guerrero	.20	.10	.02
☐ 441	Orel Hershiser	.15	.07	.01
☐ 442	Rick Honeycutt	.04	.02	.00
☐ 443	Ken Howell	.04	.02	.00
☐ 444	Ken Landreaux	.04	.02	.00
☐ 445	Bill Madlock	.10	.05	.01
☐ 446	Mike Marshall	.12	.06	.01
☐ 447	Len Matuszek	.04	.02	.00
☐ 448	Tom Niedenfuer	.07	.03	.01
☐ 449	Alejandro Pena	.07	.03	.01
☐ 450	Dennis Powell	.07	.03	.01
☐ 451	Jerry Reuss	.07	.03	.01
☐ 452	Bill Russell	.04	.02	.00
☐ 453	Steve Sax	.12	.06	.01
☐ 454	Mike Scioscia	.04	.02	.00
☐ 455	Franklin Stubbs	.07	.03	.01
☐ 456	Alex Trevino	.04	.02	.00
☐ 457	Fernando Valenzuela	.25	.12	.02
☐ 458	Ed VandeBerg	.04	.02	.00
☐ 459	Bob Welch	.07	.03	.01
☐ 460	Reggie Williams	.15	.07	.01
☐ 461	Don Aase	.04	.02	.00
☐ 462	Juan Beniquez	.04	.02	.00
☐ 463	Mike Boddicker	.07	.03	.01
☐ 464	Juan Bonilla	.04	.02	.00
☐ 465	Rich Bordi	.04	.02	.00
☐ 466	Storm Davis	.07	.03	.01
☐ 467	Rick Dempsey	.04	.02	.00
☐ 468	Ken Dixon	.04	.02	.00
☐ 469	Jim Dwyer	.04	.02	.00
☐ 470	Mike Flanagan	.07	.03	.01
☐ 471	Jackie Gutierrez	.04	.02	.00
☐ 472	Brad Havens	.04	.02	.00
☐ 473	Lee Lacy	.04	.02	.00
☐ 474	Fred Lynn	.15	.07	.01
☐ 475	Scott McGregor	.07	.03	.01
☐ 476	Eddie Murray	.25	.12	.02
☐ 477	Tom O'Malley	.04	.02	.00
☐ 478	Cal Ripken Jr.	.25	.12	.02
☐ 479	Larry Sheets	.10	.05	.01
☐ 480	John Shelby	.04	.02	.00
☐ 481	Nate Snell	.04	.02	.00
☐ 482	Jim Traber	.10	.05	.01
☐ 483	Mike Young	.07	.03	.01
☐ 484	Neil Allen	.07	.03	.01
☐ 485	Harold Baines	.15	.07	.01
☐ 486	Floyd Bannister	.07	.03	.01
☐ 487	Daryl Boston	.04	.02	.00
☐ 488	Ivan Calderon	.20	.10	.02
☐ 489	John Cangelosi	.20	.10	.02
☐ 490	Steve Carlton	.25	.12	.02
☐ 491	Joe Cowley	.04	.02	.00
☐ 492	Julio Cruz	.04	.02	.00
☐ 493	Bill Dawley	.04	.02	.00
☐ 494	Jose DeLeon	.04	.02	.00
☐ 495	Richard Dotson	.07	.03	.01
☐ 496	Carlton Fisk	.12	.06	.01
☐ 497	Ozzie Guillen	.10	.05	.01
☐ 498	Jerry Hairston	.04	.02	.00
☐ 499	Ron Hassey	.04	.02	.00
☐ 500	Tim Hulett	.04	.02	.00
☐ 501	Bob James	.04	.02	.00
☐ 502	Steve Lyons	.04	.02	.00
☐ 503	Joel McKeon	.15	.07	.01
☐ 504	Gene Nelson	.04	.02	.00
☐ 505	Dave Schmidt	.07	.03	.01
☐ 506	Ray Searage	.04	.02	.00
☐ 507	Bobby Thigpen	.20	.10	.02
☐ 508	Greg Walker	.10	.05	.01
☐ 509	Jim Acker	.04	.02	.00
☐ 510	Doyle Alexander	.07	.03	.01
☐ 511	Paul Assenmacher	.10	.05	.01
☐ 512	Bruce Benedict	.04	.02	.00
☐ 513	Chris Chambliss	.07	.03	.01
☐ 514	Jeff Dedmon	.04	.02	.00
☐ 515	Gene Garber	.04	.02	.00
☐ 516	Ken Griffey	.07	.03	.01
☐ 517	Terry Harper	.04	.02	.00
☐ 518	Bob Horner	.15	.07	.01
☐ 519	Glenn Hubbard	.04	.02	.00
☐ 520	Rick Mahler	.04	.02	.00
☐ 521	Omar Moreno	.04	.02	.00
☐ 522	Dale Murphy	.50	.25	.05
☐ 523	Ken Oberkfell	.04	.02	.00
☐ 524	Ed Olwine	.10	.05	.01
☐ 525	David Palmer	.04	.02	.00
☐ 526	Rafael Ramirez	.04	.02	.00
☐ 527	Billy Sample	.04	.02	.00
☐ 528	Ted Simmons	.07	.03	.01
☐ 529	Zane Smith	.10	.05	.01
☐ 530	Bruce Sutter	.12	.06	.01
☐ 531	Andres Thomas	.20	.10	.02
☐ 532	Ozzie Virgil	.04	.02	.00
☐ 533	Allan Anderson	.12	.06	.01
☐ 534	Keith Atherton	.04	.02	.00
☐ 535	Billy Beane	.07	.03	.01
☐ 536	Bert Blyleven	.10	.05	.01
☐ 537	Tom Brunansky	.12	.06	.01
☐ 538	Randy Bush	.04	.02	.00
☐ 539	George Frazier	.04	.02	.00
☐ 540	Gary Gaetti	.15	.07	.01
☐ 541	Greg Gagne	.07	.03	.01
☐ 542	Mickey Hatcher	.04	.02	.00
☐ 543	Neal Heaton	.04	.02	.00
☐ 544	Kent Hrbek	.15	.07	.01
☐ 545	Roy Lee Jackson	.04	.02	.00
☐ 546	Tim Laudner	.07	.03	.01
☐ 547	Steve Lombardozzi	.07	.03	.01
☐ 548	Mark Portugal	.10	.05	.01
☐ 549	Kirby Puckett	.45	.22	.04
☐ 550	Jeff Reed	.07	.03	.01
☐ 551	Mark Salas	.04	.02	.00
☐ 552	Roy Smalley	.04	.02	.00
☐ 553	Mike Smithson	.04	.02	.00
☐ 554	Frank Viola	.12	.06	.01
☐ 555	Thad Bosley	.04	.02	.00
☐ 556	Ron Cey	.07	.03	.01
☐ 557	Jody Davis	.10	.05	.01
☐ 558	Ron Davis	.04	.02	.00
☐ 559	Bob Dernier	.04	.02	.00
☐ 560	Frank DiPino	.04	.02	.00
☐ 561	Shawon Dunston	.10	.05	.01
☐ 562	Leon Durham	.10	.05	.01
☐ 563	Dennis Eckersley	.07	.03	.01
☐ 564	Terry Francona	.04	.02	.00
☐ 565	Dave Gumpert	.04	.02	.00
☐ 566	Guy Hoffman	.04	.02	.00
☐ 567	Ed Lynch	.04	.02	.00
☐ 568	Gary Matthews	.07	.03	.01
☐ 569	Keith Moreland	.07	.03	.01
☐ 570	Jamie Moyer	.15	.07	.01
☐ 571	Jerry Mumphrey	.04	.02	.00
☐ 572	Ryne Sandberg	.25	.12	.02
☐ 573	Scott Sanderson	.04	.02	.00
☐ 574	Lee Smith	.07	.03	.01
☐ 575	Chris Speier	.04	.02	.00
☐ 576	Rick Sutcliffe	.10	.05	.01
☐ 577	Manny Trillo	.04	.02	.00
☐ 578	Steve Trout	.07	.03	.01
☐ 579	Karl Best	.04	.02	.00
☐ 580	Scott Bradley	.07	.03	.01
☐ 581	Phil Bradley	.15	.07	.01
☐ 582	Mickey Brantley	.10	.05	.01
☐ 583	Mike Brown (Mariners pitcher)	.04	.02	.00
☐ 584	Alvin Davis	.12	.06	.01
☐ 585	Lee Guetterman	.25	.12	.02
☐ 586	Mark Huismann	.07	.03	.01
☐ 587	Bob Kearney	.04	.02	.00
☐ 588	Pete Ladd	.04	.02	.00
☐ 589	Mark Langston	.12	.06	.01
☐ 590	Mike Moore	.07	.03	.01
☐ 591	Mike Morgan	.04	.02	.00
☐ 592	John Moses	.07	.03	.01
☐ 593	Ken Phelps	.07	.03	.01
☐ 594	Jim Presley	.20	.10	.02
☐ 595	Rey Quinones ERR (Quinonez on front)	.30	.15	.03
☐ 596	Harold Reynolds	.07	.03	.01
☐ 597	Billy Swift	.04	.02	.00
☐ 598	Danny Tartabull	.35	.17	.03
☐ 599	Steve Yeager	.04	.02	.00
☐ 600	Matt Young	.04	.02	.00
☐ 601	Bill Almon	.04	.02	.00
☐ 602	Rafael Belliard	.10	.05	.01
☐ 603	Mike Bielecki	.04	.02	.00
☐ 604	Barry Bonds	.45	.22	.04
☐ 605	Bobby Bonilla	.35	.17	.03
☐ 606	Sid Bream	.07	.03	.01
☐ 607	Mike Brown	.04	.02	.00

(Pirates OF)

☐ 608	Pat Clements	.04	.02	.00
☐ 609	Mike Diaz	.25	.12	.02
☐ 610	Cecilio Guante	.04	.02	.00
☐ 611	Barry Jones	.15	.07	.01
☐ 612	Bob Kipper	.04	.02	.00
☐ 613	Larry McWilliams	.04	.02	.00
☐ 614	Jim Morrison	.04	.02	.00
☐ 615	Joe Orsulak	.04	.02	.00
☐ 616	Junior Ortiz	.04	.02	.00
☐ 617	Tony Pena	.10	.05	.01
☐ 618	Johnny Ray	.10	.05	.01
☐ 619	Rick Reuschel	.07	.03	.01
☐ 620	R.J. Reynolds	.07	.03	.01
☐ 621	Rick Rhoden	.07	.03	.01
☐ 622	Don Robinson	.04	.02	.00
☐ 623	Bob Walk	.04	.02	.00
☐ 624	Jim Winn	.04	.02	.00
☐ 625	Youthful Power	.50	.25	.05
	Pete Incaviglia			
	Jose Canseco			
☐ 626	300 Game Winners	.10	.05	.01
	Don Sutton			
	Phil Niekro			
☐ 627	AL Firemen	.07	.03	.01
	Dave Righetti			
	Don Aase			
☐ 628	Rookie All-Stars	1.25	.60	.12
	Wally Joyner			
	Jose Canseco			
☐ 629	Magic Mets	.50	.25	.05
	Gary Carter			
	Sid Fernandez			
	Dwight Gooden			
	Keith Hernandez			
	Darryl Strawberry			
☐ 630	NL Best Righties	.07	.03	.01
	Mike Scott			
	Mike Krukow			
☐ 631	Sensational Southpaws ..	.10	.05	.01
	Fernando Valenzuela			
	John Franco			
☐ 632	Count'Em	.10	.05	.01
	Bob Horner			
☐ 633	AL Pitcher's Nightmare ..	.40	.20	.04
	Jose Canseco			
	Jim Rice			
	Kirby Puckett			
☐ 634	All-Star Battery	.30	.15	.03
	Gary Carter			
	Roger Clemens			
☐ 635	4000 Strikeouts	.15	.07	.01
	Steve Carlton			
☐ 636	Big Bats at First	.15	.07	.01
	Glenn Davis			
	Eddie Murray			
☐ 637	On Base	.35	.17	.03
	Wade Boggs			
	Keith Hernandez			
☐ 638	Sluggers Left Side	1.00	.50	.10
	Don Mattingly			
	Darryl Strawberry			
☐ 639	Former MVP's	.15	.07	.01
	Dave Parker			
	Ryne Sandberg			
☐ 640	Dr. K , Super K	.75	.35	.07
	Dwight Gooden			
	Roger Clemens			
☐ 641	AL West Stoppers	.07	.03	.01
	Mike Witt			
	Charlie Hough			
☐ 642	Doubles and Triples	.10	.05	.01
	Juan Samuel			
	Tim Raines			
☐ 643	Outfielders with Punch ...	.10	.05	.01
	Harold Baines			
	Jesse Barfield			
☐ 644	Dave Clark and	.65	.30	.06
	Greg Swindell			
☐ 645	Ron Karkovice and	.20	.10	.02
	Russ Morman			
☐ 646	Devon White and	1.75	.85	.17
	Willie Fraser			
☐ 647	Mike Stanley and	.45	.22	.04
	Jerry Browne			
☐ 648	Dave Magadan and	.85	.40	.08
	Phil Lombardi			
☐ 649	Jose Gonzalez and	.30	.15	.03
	Ralph Bryant			
☐ 650	Jimmy Jones and	.30	.15	.03
	Randy Asadoor			
☐ 651	Tracy Jones and	.60	.30	.06
	Marvin Freeman			
☐ 652	John Stefero and	9.00	4.50	.90
	Kevin Seitzer			

☐ 653	Rob Nelson and .... Steve Fireovid	.20	.10	.02
☐ 654	CL: Mets/Red Sox Astros/Angels	.06	.01	.00
☐ 655	CL: Yankees/Rangers .... Tigers/Phillies	.06	.01	.00
☐ 656	CL: Reds/Blue Jays Indians/Giants ERR (230/231 wrong)	.06	.01	.00
☐ 657	CL: Cardinals/Expos ...... Brewers/Royals	.06	.01	.00
☐ 658	CL: A's/Padres Dodgers/Orioles	.06	.01	.00
☐ 659	CL: White Sox/Braves .... Twins/Cubs	.06	.01	.00
☐ 660	CL: Mariners/Pirates ..... Special Cards ERR (580/581 wrong)	.06	.01	.00

1987 Fleer Wax Box Cards

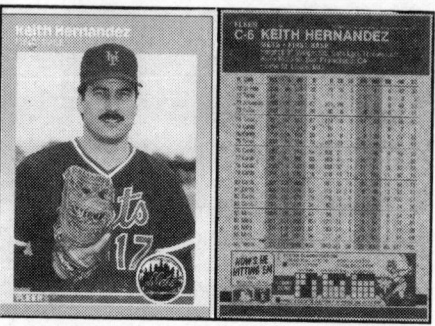

The cards in this 16-card set measure the standard 2 1/2" by 3 1/2". Cards have essentially the same design as the 1987 Fleer regular issue set. The cards were printed on the bottoms of the regular issue wax pack boxes. These 16 cards (C1 to C16) are considered a separate set in their own right and are not typically included in a complete set of the regular issue 1987 Fleer cards. The value of the panel uncut is slightly greater, perhaps by 25% greater, than the value of the individual cards cut up carefully.

		MINT	EXC	G-VG
	COMPLETE SET	5.00	2.50	.50
	COMMON PLAYERS	.10	.05	.01
☐ C1	Mets Logo	.10	.05	.01
☐ C2	Jesse Barfield	.25	.12	.02
☐ C3	George Brett	.50	.25	.05
☐ C4	Dwight Gooden	.75	.35	.07
☐ C5	Boston Logo	.10	.05	.01
☐ C6	Keith Hernandez	.25	.12	.02
☐ C7	Wally Joyner	1.00	.50	.10
☐ C8	Dale Murphy	.60	.30	.06
☐ C9	Astros Logo	.10	.05	.01
☐ C10	Dave Parker	.20	.10	.02
☐ C11	Kirby Puckett	.45	.22	.04
☐ C12	Dave Righetti	.25	.12	.02
☐ C13	Angels Logo	.10	.05	.01
☐ C14	Ryne Sandberg	.30	.15	.03
☐ C15	Mike Schmidt	.50	.25	.05
☐ C16	Robin Yount	.30	.15	.03

1987 Fleer All-Star Inserts

This 12-card set was distributed as an insert in packs of the Fleer regular issue. The cards are 2 1/2" by 3 1/2" and designed with a color player photo superimposed on a gray or black background with yellow stars. The player's name, team, and position are printed in orange on black or gray at the bottom

		MINT	EXC	G-VG
☐ 2	Jose Canseco	1.50	.75	.15
☐ 3	Dwight Gooden	1.50	.75	.15
☐ 4	Rickey Henderson	1.00	.50	.10
☐ 5	Keith Hernandez	.60	.30	.06
☐ 6	Jim Rice	.60	.30	.06

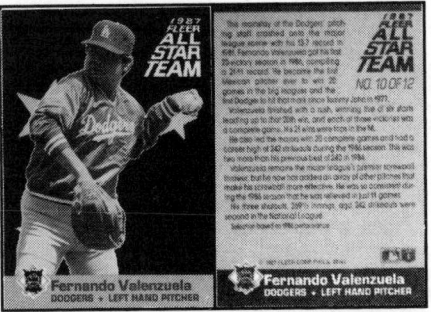

of the obverse. The card backs are done predominantly in gray, red, and black. Cards are numbered on the back in the upper right hand corner.

	MINT	EXC	G-VG
COMPLETE SET	12.00	6.00	1.20
COMMON PLAYER	.15	.07	.01

		MINT	EXC	G-VG
☐ 1	Don Mattingly First Base	5.00	2.50	.50
☐ 2	Gary Carter Catcher	1.00	.50	.10
☐ 3	Tony Fernandez Shortstop	.45	.22	.04
☐ 4	Steve Sax Second Base	.25	.12	.02
☐ 5	Kirby Puckett Outfield	1.25	.60	.12
☐ 6	Mike Schmidt Third Base	1.25	.60	.12
☐ 7	Mike Easler Designated Hitter	.15	.07	.01
☐ 8	Todd Worrell Relief Pitcher	.45	.22	.04
☐ 9	George Bell Outfield	.60	.30	.06
☐ 10	Fernando Valenzuela Left Hand Starter	.60	.30	.06
☐ 11	Roger Clemens Right Hand Starter	1.25	.60	.12
☐ 12	Tim Raines Outfield	.75	.35	.07

1987 Fleer Headliners

This six-card set was distributed as a special insert in rack packs. The obverse features the player photo against a beige background with irregular red stripes. Cards are 2 1/2" by 3 1/2". The cards are numbered on the back.

	MINT	EXC	G-VG
COMPLETE SET	5.00	2.50	.50
COMMON PLAYER	.60	.30	.06

	MINT	EXC	G-VG
☐ 1 Wade Boggs	2.50	1.25	.25

1987 Fleer Sticker Cards

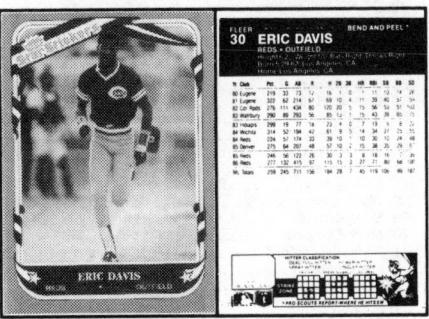

These Star Stickers were distributed as a separate issue by Fleer with five star stickers and a logo sticker in each wax pack. The 132-card (sticker) set features 2 1/2" by 3 1/2" full color fronts and even statistics on the sticker back, which is an indication that the Fleer Company understands that these stickers are rarely used as stickers but more like traditional cards. The card fronts are surrounded by a green border and the backs are printed in green and yellow on white card stock.

	MINT	EXC	G-VG
COMPLETE SET (132)	21.00	10.50	2.10
COMMON PLAYER (1-132)	.05	.02	.00

		MINT	EXC	G-VG
☐ 1	Don Aase	.05	.02	.00
☐ 2	Harold Baines	.15	.07	.01
☐ 3	Floyd Bannister	.10	.05	.01
☐ 4	Jesse Barfield	.20	.10	.02
☐ 5	Marty Barrett	.10	.05	.01
☐ 6	Kevin Bass	.10	.05	.01
☐ 7	Don Baylor	.10	.05	.01
☐ 8	Steve Bedrosian	.15	.07	.01
☐ 9	George Bell	.25	.12	.02
☐ 10	Bert Blyleven	.10	.05	.01
☐ 11	Mike Boddicker	.10	.05	.01
☐ 12	Wade Boggs	1.50	.75	.15
☐ 13	Phil Bradley	.20	.10	.02
☐ 14	Sid Bream	.10	.05	.01
☐ 15	George Brett	.50	.25	.05
☐ 16	Hubie Brooks	.10	.05	.01
☐ 17	Tom Brunansky	.15	.07	.01
☐ 18	Tom Candiotti	.05	.02	.00
☐ 19	Jose Canseco	1.00	.50	.10
☐ 20	Gary Carter	.35	.17	.03
☐ 21	Joe Carter	.20	.10	.02
☐ 22	Will Clark	1.00	.50	.10
☐ 23	Mark Clear	.05	.02	.00
☐ 24	Roger Clemens	.75	.35	.07
☐ 25	Vince Coleman	.45	.22	.04
☐ 26	Jose Cruz	.10	.05	.01
☐ 27	Ron Darling	.15	.07	.01
☐ 28	Alvin Davis	.10	.05	.01
☐ 29	Chili Davis	.10	.05	.01
☐ 30	Eric Davis	1.50	.75	.15
☐ 31	Glenn Davis	.20	.10	.02
☐ 32	Mike Davis	.10	.05	.01
☐ 33	Andre Dawson	.45	.22	.04
☐ 34	Doug DeCinces	.10	.05	.01
☐ 35	Brian Downing	.05	.02	.00
☐ 36	Shawon Dunston	.10	.05	.01
☐ 37	Mark Eichhorn	.10	.05	.01
☐ 38	Dwight Evans	.20	.10	.02
☐ 39	Tony Fernandez	.15	.07	.01
☐ 40	Bob Forsch	.05	.02	.00
☐ 41	John Franco	.10	.05	.01
☐ 42	Julio Franco	.10	.05	.01
☐ 43	Gary Gaetti	.20	.10	.02
☐ 44	Gene Garber	.05	.02	.00
☐ 45	Scott Garrelts	.05	.02	.00

☐	46 Steve Garvey	.45	.22	.04
☐	47 Kirk Gibson	.25	.12	.02
☐	48 Dwight Gooden	.75	.35	.07
☐	49 Ken Griffey	.10	.05	.01
☐	50 Ozzie Guillen	.15	.07	.01
☐	51 Bill Gullickson	.10	.05	.01
☐	52 Tony Gwynn	.50	.25	.05
☐	53 Mel Hall	.10	.05	.01
☐	54 Greg Harris	.05	.02	.00
☐	55 Von Hayes	.10	.05	.01
☐	56 Rickey Henderson	.50	.25	.05
☐	57 Tom Henke	.10	.05	.01
☐	58 Keith Hernandez	.25	.12	.02
☐	59 Willie Hernandez	.10	.05	.01
☐	60 Ted Higuera	.25	.12	.02
☐	61 Bob Horner	.20	.10	.02
☐	62 Charlie Hough	.10	.05	.01
☐	63 Jay Howell	.05	.02	.00
☐	64 Kent Hrbek	.20	.10	.02
☐	65 Bruce Hurst	.10	.05	.01
☐	66 Pete Incaviglia	.30	.15	.03
☐	67 Bob James	.10	.05	.01
☐	68 Wally Joyner	1.00	.50	.10
☐	69 Mike Krukow	.10	.05	.01
☐	70 Mark Langston	.15	.07	.01
☐	71 Carney Lansford	.10	.05	.01
☐	72 Fred Lynn	.15	.07	.01
☐	73 Bill Madlock	.10	.05	.01
☐	74 Don Mattingly	2.50	1.25	.25
☐	75 Kirk McCaskill	.10	.05	.01
☐	76 Lance McCullers	.10	.05	.01
☐	77 Oddibe McDowell	.20	.10	.02
☐	78 Paul Molitor	.25	.12	.02
☐	79 Keith Moreland	.10	.05	.01
☐	80 Jack Morris	.20	.10	.02
☐	81 Jim Morrison	.05	.02	.00
☐	82 Jerry Mumphrey	.05	.02	.00
☐	83 Dale Murphy	.65	.30	.06
☐	84 Eddie Murray	.45	.22	.04
☐	85 Ben Oglivie	.10	.05	.01
☐	86 Bob Ojeda	.10	.05	.01
☐	87 Jesse Orosco	.05	.02	.00
☐	88 Dave Parker	.20	.10	.02
☐	89 Larry Parrish	.10	.05	.01
☐	90 Tony Pena	.10	.05	.01
☐	91 Jim Presley	.20	.10	.02
☐	92 Kirby Puckett	.60	.30	.06
☐	93 Dan Quisenberry	.15	.07	.01
☐	94 Tim Raines	.35	.17	.03
☐	95 Dennis Rasmussen	.05	.02	.00
☐	96 Shane Rawley	.10	.05	.01
☐	97 Johnny Ray	.10	.05	.01
☐	98 Jeff Reardon	.15	.07	.01
☐	99 Jim Rice	.30	.15	.03
☐	100 Dave Righetti	.20	.10	.02
☐	101 Cal Ripken Jr	.45	.22	.04
☐	102 Pete Rose	.75	.35	.07
☐	103 Nolan Ryan	.50	.25	.05
☐	104 Juan Samuel	.20	.10	.02
☐	105 Ryne Sandberg	.30	.15	.03
☐	106 Steve Sax	.15	.07	.01
☐	107 Mike Schmidt	.60	.30	.06
☐	108 Mike Scott	.25	.12	.02
☐	109 Dave Smith	.10	.05	.01
☐	110 Lee Smith	.10	.05	.01
☐	111 Lonnie Smith	.10	.05	.01
☐	112 Ozzie Smith	.25	.12	.02
☐	113 Cory Snyder	.50	.25	.05
☐	114 Darryl Strawberry	.50	.25	.05
☐	115 Don Sutton	.30	.15	.03
☐	116 Kent Tekulve	.05	.02	.00
☐	117 Andres Thomas	.10	.05	.01
☐	118 Alan Trammell	.30	.15	.03
☐	119 John Tudor	.15	.07	.01
☐	120 Fernando Valenzuela	.25	.12	.02
☐	121 Bob Welch	.10	.05	.01
☐	122 Lou Whitaker	.20	.10	.02
☐	123 Frank White	.10	.05	.01
☐	124 Reggie Williams	.10	.05	.01
☐	125 Willie Wilson	.10	.05	.01
☐	126 Dave Winfield	.25	.12	.02
☐	127 Mike Witt	.10	.05	.01
☐	128 Todd Worrell	.25	.12	.02
☐	129 Curt Young	.10	.05	.01
☐	130 Robin Yount	.30	.15	.03
☐	131 Checklist Jose Canseco Don Mattingly	1.25	.60	.12
☐	132 Checklist Bo Jackson Eric Davis	1.00	.50	.10

1987 Fleer Sticker Wax Box

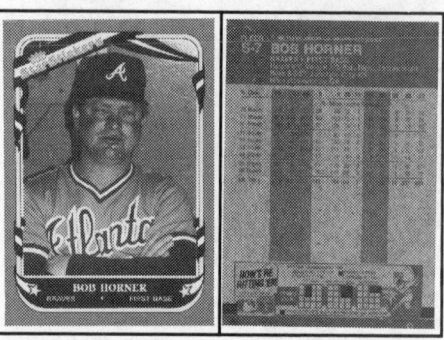

The bottoms of the Star Sticker wax boxes contained two different sets of four cards done in a similar format to the stickers (they are not stickers but truly cards) are numbered with the prefix S and are considered a separate set. The value of the panels uncut is slightly greater, perhaps by 25% greater, than the value of the individual cards cut up carefully.

		MINT	EXC	G-VG
COMPLETE SET (8)		2.50	1.25	.25
COMMON PLAYER (1-8)		.10	.05	.01

			MINT	EXC	G-VG
☐	S1	Detroit Logo	.10	.05	.01
☐	S2	Wade Boggs	.75	.35	.07
☐	S3	Bert Blyleven	.20	.10	.02
☐	S4	Jose Cruz	.20	.10	.02
☐	S5	Glenn Davis	.20	.10	.02
☐	S6	Phillies Logo	.10	.05	.01
☐	S7	Bob Horner	.30	.15	.03
☐	S8	Don Mattingly	1.50	.75	.15

1987 Fleer Award Winners

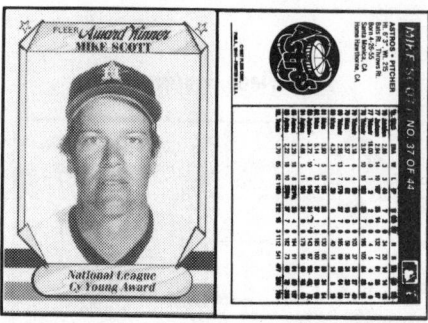

This small set of 44 cards was produced for 7-Eleven stores by Fleer. The cards measure the standard 2 1/2" by 3 1/2" and feature full color fronts and yellow, white, and black backs. The card fronts are distinguished by their yellow frame around the player's full-color photo. The box for the cards describes the set as the "1987 Limited Edition Baseball's Award Winners." The checklist for the set is given on the back of the set box.

		MINT	EXC	G-VG
COMPLETE SET (44)		4.00	2.00	.40
COMMON PLAYER (1-44)		.10	.05	.01

			MINT	EXC	G-VG
☐	1	Marty Barrett	.10	.05	.01
☐	2	George Bell	.20	.10	.02
☐	3	Bert Blyleven	.15	.07	.01

		MINT	EXC	G-VG
☐ 4	Bob Boone	.10	.05	.01
☐ 5	John Candelaria	.10	.05	.01
☐ 6	Jose Canseco	.50	.25	.05
☐ 7	Gary Carter	.25	.12	.02
☐ 8	Joe Carter	.20	.10	.02
☐ 9	Roger Clemens	.50	.25	.05
☐ 10	Cecil Cooper	.10	.05	.01
☐ 11	Eric Davis	.65	.30	.06
☐ 12	Tony Fernandez	.15	.07	.01
☐ 13	Scott Fletcher	.10	.05	.01
☐ 14	Bob Forsch	.10	.05	.01
☐ 15	Dwight Gooden	.45	.22	.04
☐ 16	Ron Guidry	.15	.07	.01
☐ 17	Ozzie Guillen	.15	.07	.01
☐ 18	Bill Gullickson	.10	.05	.01
☐ 19	Tony Gwynn	.40	.20	.04
☐ 20	Bob Knepper	.10	.05	.01
☐ 21	Ray Knight	.15	.07	.01
☐ 22	Mark Langston	.15	.07	.01
☐ 23	Candy Maldonado	.15	.07	.01
☐ 24	Don Mattingly	.75	.35	.07
☐ 25	Roger McDowell	.15	.07	.01
☐ 26	Dale Murphy	.45	.22	.04
☐ 27	Dave Parker	.20	.10	.02
☐ 28	Lance Parrish	.15	.07	.01
☐ 29	Gary Pettis	.15	.07	.01
☐ 30	Kirby Puckett	.40	.20	.04
☐ 31	Johnny Ray	.15	.07	.01
☐ 32	Dave Righetti	.20	.10	.02
☐ 33	Cal Ripken	.35	.17	.03
☐ 34	Bret Saberhagen	.25	.12	.02
☐ 35	Ryne Sandberg	.35	.17	.03
☐ 36	Mike Schmidt	.45	.22	.04
☐ 37	Mike Scott	.20	.10	.02
☐ 38	Ozzie Smith	.20	.10	.02
☐ 39	Robbie Thompson	.15	.07	.01
☐ 40	Fernando Valenzuela	.20	.10	.02
☐ 41	Mitch Webster ER (Mike on front)	.20	.10	.02
☐ 42	Frank White	.10	.05	.01
☐ 43	Mike Witt	.15	.07	.01
☐ 44	Todd Worrell	.25	.12	.02

		MINT	EXC	G-VG
☐ 13	Alvin Davis	.15	.07	.01
☐ 14	Eric Davis	.65	.30	.06
☐ 15	Rob Deer	.15	.07	.01
☐ 16	Brian Downing	.10	.05	.01
☐ 17	Gene Garber	.10	.05	.01
☐ 18	Steve Garvey	.30	.15	.03
☐ 19	Dwight Gooden	.45	.22	.04
☐ 20	Mark Gubicza	.10	.05	.01
☐ 21	Mel Hall	.15	.07	.01
☐ 22	Terry Harper	.10	.05	.01
☐ 23	Von Hayes	.15	.07	.01
☐ 24	Rickey Henderson	.40	.20	.04
☐ 25	Tom Henke	.15	.07	.01
☐ 26	Willie Hernandez	.15	.07	.01
☐ 27	Ted Higuera	.25	.12	.02
☐ 28	Rick Honeycutt	.10	.05	.01
☐ 29	Kent Hrbek	.20	.10	.02
☐ 30	Wally Joyner	.50	.25	.05
☐ 31	Charlie Kerfeld	.15	.07	.01
☐ 32	Fred Lynn	.15	.07	.01
☐ 33	Don Mattingly	.75	.35	.07
☐ 34	Tim Raines	.35	.17	.03
☐ 35	Dennis Rasmussen	.10	.05	.01
☐ 36	Johnny Ray	.15	.07	.01
☐ 37	Jim Rice	.25	.12	.02
☐ 38	Pete Rose	.65	.30	.06
☐ 39	Lee Smith	.15	.07	.01
☐ 40	Cory Snyder	.35	.17	.03
☐ 41	Darryl Strawberry	.50	.25	.05
☐ 42	Kent Tekulve	.10	.05	.01
☐ 43	Willie Wilson	.15	.07	.01
☐ 44	Bobby Witt	.15	.07	.01

1987 Fleer Game Winners

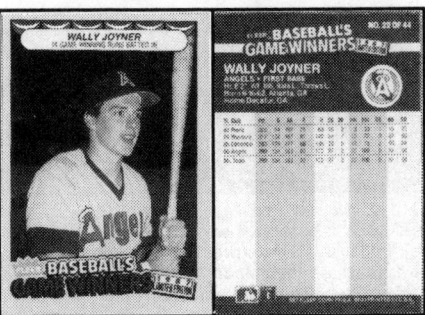

This small 44-card boxed set was produced by Fleer for distribution by several store chains, including Bi-Mart, Pay'n'Save, Mott's, M.E.Moses, and Winn's. The cards measure the standard 2 1/2" by 3 1/2" and feature full color fronts. The set is titled "Baseball's Game Winners. Each individual boxed set includes the 44 cards and 6 logo stickers. The checklist for the set is found on the back panel of the box.

		MINT	EXC	G-VG
COMPLETE SET (44)		4.00	2.00	.40
COMMON PLAYER (1-44)		.10	.05	.01
☐ 1	Harold Baines	.15	.07	.01
☐ 2	Don Baylor	.15	.07	.01
☐ 3	George Bell	.30	.15	.03
☐ 4	Tony Bernazard	.10	.05	.01
☐ 5	Wade Boggs	.65	.30	.06
☐ 6	George Brett	.50	.25	.05
☐ 7	Hubie Brooks	.15	.07	.01
☐ 8	Jose Canseco	.50	.25	.05
☐ 9	Gary Carter	.35	.17	.03
☐ 10	Roger Clemens	.50	.25	.05
☐ 11	Eric Davis	.65	.30	.06
☐ 12	Glenn Davis	.20	.10	.02
☐ 13	Shawon Dunston	.15	.07	.01
☐ 14	Mark Eichhorn	.15	.07	.01
☐ 15	Gary Gaetti	.20	.10	.02
☐ 16	Steve Garvey	.30	.15	.03
☐ 17	Kirk Gibson	.20	.10	.02
☐ 18	Dwight Gooden	.45	.22	.04
☐ 19	Von Hayes	.15	.07	.01

1987 Fleer Exciting Stars

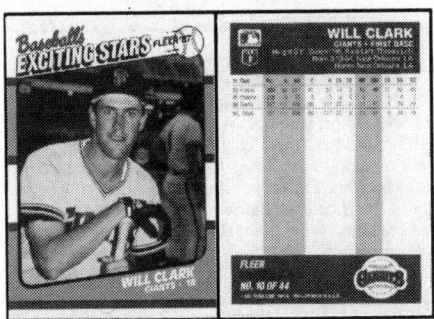

This small 44-card boxed set was produced by Fleer for distribution by the Cumberland Farm stores. The cards measure the standard 2 1/2" by 3 1/2" and feature full color fronts. The set is titled "Baseball's Exciting Stars. Each individual boxed set includes the 44 cards and 6 logo stickers. The checklist for the set is found on the back panel of the box.

		MINT	EXC	G-VG
COMPLETE SET (44)		4.00	2.00	.40
COMMON PLAYER (1-44)		.10	.05	.01
☐ 1	Don Aase	.10	.05	.01
☐ 2	Rick Aguilera	.15	.07	.01
☐ 3	Jesse Barfield	.20	.10	.02
☐ 4	Wade Boggs	.65	.30	.06
☐ 5	Dennis "Oil Can" Boyd	.15	.07	.01
☐ 6	Sid Bream	.10	.05	.01
☐ 7	Jose Canseco	.50	.25	.05
☐ 8	Steve Carlton	.30	.15	.03
☐ 9	Gary Carter	.35	.17	.03
☐ 10	Will Clark	.50	.25	.05
☐ 11	Roger Clemens	.50	.25	.05
☐ 12	Danny Cox	.15	.07	.01

		MINT	EXC	G-VG
☐ 20	Willie Hernandez	.15	.07	.01
☐ 21	Ted Higuera	.25	.12	.02
☐ 22	Wally Joyner	.50	.25	.05
☐ 23	Bob Knepper	.10	.05	.01
☐ 24	Mike Krukow	.10	.05	.01
☐ 25	Jeff Leonard	.15	.07	.01
☐ 26	Don Mattingly	.75	.35	.07
☐ 27	Kirk McCaskill	.15	.07	.01
☐ 28	Kevin McReynolds	.15	.07	.01
☐ 29	Jim Morrison	.10	.05	.01
☐ 30	Dale Murphy	.50	.25	.05
☐ 31	Pete O'Brien	.15	.07	.01
☐ 32	Bob Ojeda	.15	.07	.01
☐ 33	Larry Parrish	.10	.05	.01
☐ 34	Ken Phelps	.10	.05	.01
☐ 35	Dennis Rasmussen	.10	.05	.01
☐ 36	Ernest Riles	.15	.07	.01
☐ 37	Cal Ripken	.35	.17	.03
☐ 38	Ron Robinson	.10	.05	.01
☐ 39	Steve Sax	.15	.07	.01
☐ 40	Mike Schmidt	.50	.25	.05
☐ 41	John Tudor	.15	.07	.01
☐ 42	Fernando Valenzuela	.25	.12	.02
☐ 43	Mike Witt	.15	.07	.01
☐ 44	Curt Young	.15	.07	.01

		MINT	EXC	G-VG
☐ 23	Bob Horner	.20	.10	.02
☐ 24	Pete Incaviglia	.25	.12	.02
☐ 25	Wally Joyner	.50	.25	.05
☐ 26	Mark Langston	.15	.07	.01
☐ 27	Don Mattingly ERR	1.00	.50	.10
	(Pirates logo			
	on back)			
☐ 28	Dale Murphy	.50	.25	.05
☐ 29	Kirk McCaskill	.15	.07	.01
☐ 30	Willie McGee	.20	.10	.02
☐ 31	Dave Righetti	.20	.10	.02
☐ 32	Pete Rose	.60	.30	.06
☐ 33	Bruce Ruffin	.15	.07	.01
☐ 34	Steve Sax	.15	.07	.01
☐ 35	Mike Schmidt	.50	.25	.05
☐ 36	Larry Sheets	.20	.10	.02
☐ 37	Eric Show	.10	.05	.01
☐ 38	Dave Smith	.15	.07	.01
☐ 39	Cory Snyder	.35	.17	.03
☐ 40	Frank Tanana	.15	.07	.01
☐ 41	Alan Trammell	.25	.12	.02
☐ 42	Reggie Williams	.10	.05	.01
☐ 43	Mookie Wilson	.10	.05	.01
☐ 44	Todd Worrell	.25	.12	.02

1987 Fleer Hottest Stars

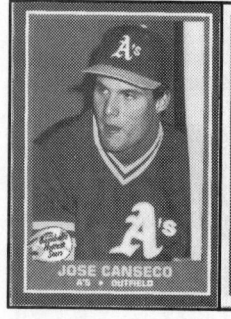
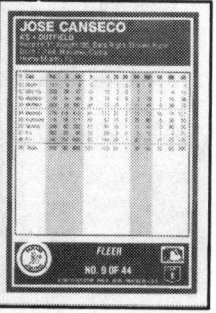

This 44-card boxed set was produced by Fleer for distribution by Revco stores all over the country. The cards measure the standard 2 1/2" by 3 1/2" and feature full color fronts and red, white, and black backs. The card fronts are easily distinguished by their solid red outside borders and and white and blue inner borders framing the player's picture. The box for the cards proclaims "1987 Limited Edition Baseball's Hottest Stars" and is styled in the same manner and color scheme as the cards themselves. The checklist for the set is given on the back of the set box.

		MINT	EXC	G-VG
COMPLETE SET (44)		4.00	2.00	.40
COMMON PLAYER (1-44)		.10	.05	.01
☐ 1	Joaquin Andujar	.10	.05	.01
☐ 2	Harold Baines	.15	.07	.01
☐ 3	Kevin Bass	.15	.07	.01
☐ 4	Don Baylor	.15	.07	.01
☐ 5	Barry Bonds	.25	.12	.02
☐ 6	George Brett	.50	.25	.05
☐ 7	Tom Brunansky	.20	.10	.02
☐ 8	Brett Butler	.15	.07	.01
☐ 9	Jose Canseco	.50	.25	.05
☐ 10	Roger Clemens	.50	.25	.05
☐ 11	Ron Darling	.20	.10	.02
☐ 12	Eric Davis	.65	.30	.06
☐ 13	Andre Dawson	.30	.15	.03
☐ 14	Doug DeCinces	.15	.07	.01
☐ 15	Leon Durham	.15	.07	.01
☐ 16	Mark Eichhorn	.15	.07	.01
☐ 17	Scott Garrelts	.10	.05	.01
☐ 18	Dwight Gooden	.45	.22	.04
☐ 19	Dave Henderson	.10	.05	.01
☐ 20	Rickey Henderson	.40	.20	.04
☐ 21	Keith Hernandez	.30	.15	.03
☐ 22	Ted Higuera	.25	.12	.02

1987 Fleer League Leaders

This small set of 44 cards was produced for Walgreens by Fleer. The cards measure the standard 2 1/2" by 3 1/2" and feature full color fronts and red, white, and blue backs. The card fronts are easily distinguished by their light blue vertical stripes over a white background. The box for the cards proclaims a "Walgreens Exclusive" and is styled in the same manner and color scheme as the cards themselves. The checklist for the set is given on the back of the set box.

		MINT	EXC	G-VG
COMPLETE SET (44)		4.00	2.00	.40
COMMON PLAYER (1-44)		.10	.05	.01
☐ 1	Jesse Barfield	.25	.12	.02
☐ 2	Mike Boddicker	.15	.07	.01
☐ 3	Wade Boggs	.65	.30	.06
☐ 4	Phil Bradley	.20	.10	.02
☐ 5	George Brett	.50	.25	.05
☐ 6	Hubie Brooks	.15	.07	.01
☐ 7	Chris Brown	.15	.07	.01
☐ 8	Jose Canseco	.50	.25	.05
☐ 9	Joe Carter	.20	.10	.02
☐ 10	Roger Clemens	.50	.25	.05
☐ 11	Vince Coleman	.40	.20	.04
☐ 12	Joe Cowley	.10	.05	.01
☐ 13	Kal Daniels	.40	.20	.04
☐ 14	Glenn Davis	.20	.10	.02
☐ 15	Jody Davis	.15	.07	.01
☐ 16	Darrell Evans	.15	.07	.01
☐ 17	Dwight Evans	.20	.10	.02
☐ 18	John Franco	.15	.07	.01
☐ 19	Julio Franco	.15	.07	.01
☐ 20	Dwight Gooden	.45	.22	.04
☐ 21	Goose Gossage	.15	.07	.01
☐ 22	Tom Herr	.10	.05	.01
☐ 23	Ted Higuera	.25	.12	.02
☐ 24	Bob Horner	.20	.10	.02
☐ 25	Pete Incaviglia	.25	.12	.02
☐ 26	Wally Joyner	.50	.25	.05

		MINT	EXC	G-VG
☐ 27	Dave Kingman	.15	.07	.01
☐ 28	Don Mattingly	.75	.35	.07
☐ 29	Willie McGee	.20	.10	.02
☐ 30	Donnie Moore	.10	.05	.01
☐ 31	Keith Moreland	.15	.07	.01
☐ 32	Eddie Murray	.35	.17	.03
☐ 33	Mike Pagliarulo	.15	.07	.01
☐ 34	Larry Parrish	.10	.05	.01
☐ 35	Tony Pena	.15	.07	.01
☐ 36	Kirby Puckett	.40	.20	.04
☐ 37	Pete Rose	.50	.25	.05
☐ 38	Juan Samuel	.20	.10	.02
☐ 39	Ryne Sandberg	.30	.15	.03
☐ 40	Mike Schmidt	.50	.25	.05
☐ 41	Darryl Strawberry	.50	.25	.05
☐ 42	Greg Walker	.15	.07	.01
☐ 43	Bob Welch	.10	.05	.01
☐ 44	Todd Worrell	.25	.12	.02

☐ 33	Dan Quisenberry	.15	.07	.01
☐ 34	Tim Raines	.35	.17	.03
☐ 35	Willie Randolph	.15	.07	.01
☐ 36	Cal Ripken	.35	.17	.03
☐ 37	Pete Rose	.50	.25	.05
☐ 38	Nolan Ryan	.35	.17	.03
☐ 39	Juan Samuel	.20	.10	.02
☐ 40	Mike Schmidt	.50	.25	.05
☐ 41	Ozzie Smith	.20	.10	.02
☐ 42	Andres Thomas	.10	.05	.01
☐ 43	Fernando Valenzuela	.25	.12	.02
☐ 44	Mike Witt	.15	.07	.01

1987 Fleer Limited Edition

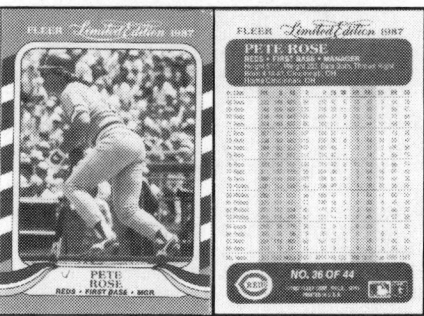

This 44-card boxed set was produced by Fleer for distribution by McCrory's and is sometimes referred to as the McCrory's set. The numerical checklist on the back of the box shows that the set is numbered alphabetically. The cards measure 2 1/2" by 3 1/2".

1987 Fleer Limited All-Stars

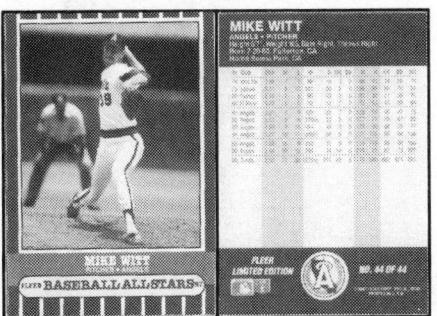

This small set of 44 cards was produced for Ben Franklin stores by Fleer. The cards measure the standard 2 1/2" by 3 1/2" and feature full color fronts and red, white, and blue backs. The card fronts are easily distinguished by their white vertical stripes over a bright red background. The box for the cards proclaims "Limited Edition Baseball All-Stars" and is styled in the same manner and color scheme as the cards themselves. The checklist for the set is given on the back of the set box.

		MINT	EXC	G-VG
COMPLETE SET (44)		4.00	2.00	.40
COMMON PLAYER (1-44)		.10	.05	.01
☐ 1	Harold Baines	.15	.07	.01
☐ 2	Jesse Barfield	.25	.12	.02
☐ 3	Wade Boggs	.65	.30	.06
☐ 4	Dennis "Oil Can" Boyd	.15	.07	.01
☐ 5	Scott Bradley	.10	.05	.01
☐ 6	Jose Canseco	.50	.25	.05
☐ 7	Gary Carter	.30	.15	.03
☐ 8	Joe Carter	.25	.12	.02
☐ 9	Mark Clear	.10	.05	.01
☐ 10	Roger Clemens	.50	.25	.05
☐ 11	Jose Cruz	.15	.07	.01
☐ 12	Chili Davis	.15	.07	.01
☐ 13	Jody Davis	.15	.07	.01
☐ 14	Rob Deer	.15	.07	.01
☐ 15	Brian Downing	.10	.05	.01
☐ 16	Sid Fernandez	.15	.07	.01
☐ 17	John Franco	.15	.07	.01
☐ 18	Andres Galarraga	.30	.15	.03
☐ 19	Dwight Gooden	.45	.22	.04
☐ 20	Tony Gwynn	.50	.25	.05
☐ 21	Charlie Hough	.15	.07	.01
☐ 22	Bruce Hurst	.15	.07	.01
☐ 23	Wally Joyner	.50	.25	.05
☐ 24	Carney Lansford	.15	.07	.01
☐ 25	Fred Lynn	.15	.07	.01
☐ 26	Don Mattingly	.75	.35	.07
☐ 27	Willie McGee	.20	.10	.02
☐ 28	Jack Morris	.20	.10	.02
☐ 29	Dale Murphy	.50	.25	.05
☐ 30	Bob Ojeda	.10	.05	.01
☐ 31	Tony Pena	.15	.07	.01
☐ 32	Kirby Puckett	.40	.20	.04

		MINT	EXC	G-VG
COMPLETE SET		4.50	2.25	.45
COMMON PLAYER		.05	.02	.00
☐ 1	Floyd Bannister	.05	.02	.00
☐ 2	Marty Barrett	.10	.05	.01
☐ 3	Steve Bedrosian	.15	.07	.01
☐ 4	George Bell	.25	.12	.02
☐ 5	George Brett	.35	.17	.03
☐ 6	Jose Canseco	.60	.30	.06
☐ 7	Joe Carter	.15	.07	.01
☐ 8	Will Clark	.35	.17	.03
☐ 9	Roger Clemens	.60	.30	.06
☐ 10	Vince Coleman	.35	.17	.03
☐ 11	Glenn Davis	.20	.10	.02
☐ 12	Mike Davis	.05	.02	.00
☐ 13	Len Dykstra	.10	.05	.01
☐ 14	John Franco	.10	.05	.01
☐ 15	Julio Franco	.10	.05	.01
☐ 16	Steve Garvey	.35	.17	.03
☐ 17	Kirk Gibson	.25	.12	.02
☐ 18	Dwight Gooden	.50	.25	.05
☐ 19	Tony Gwynn	.40	.20	.04
☐ 20	Keith Hernandez	.25	.12	.02
☐ 21	Teddy Higuera	.20	.10	.02
☐ 22	Kent Hrbek	.15	.07	.01
☐ 23	Wally Joyner	.60	.30	.06
☐ 24	Mike Krukow	.05	.02	.00
☐ 25	Mike Marshall	.10	.05	.01
☐ 26	Don Mattingly	.75	.35	.07
☐ 27	Oddibe McDowell	.10	.05	.01
☐ 28	Jack Morris	.15	.07	.01
☐ 29	Lloyd Moseby	.05	.02	.00
☐ 30	Dale Murphy	.45	.22	.04
☐ 31	Eddie Murray	.30	.15	.03
☐ 32	Tony Pena	.10	.05	.01
☐ 33	Jim Presley	.15	.07	.01
☐ 34	Jeff Reardon	.10	.05	.01
☐ 35	Jim Rice	.25	.12	.02
☐ 36	Pete Rose	.60	.30	.06
☐ 37	Mike Schmidt	.35	.17	.03
☐ 38	Mike Scott	.20	.10	.02
☐ 39	Lee Smith	.05	.02	.00
☐ 40	Lonnie Smith	.05	.02	.00
☐ 41	Gary Ward	.05	.02	.00
☐ 42	Dave Winfield	.25	.12	.02
☐ 43	Todd Worrell	.15	.07	.01
☐ 44	Robin Yount	.25	.12	.02

1987 Fleer Limited Box Cards

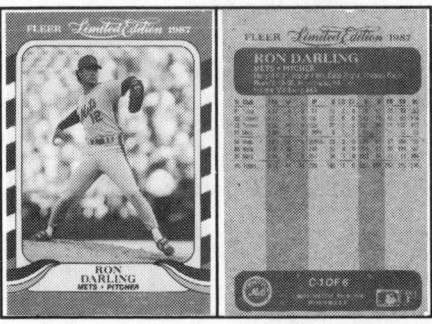

The cards in this 6-card set each measure the standard 2 1/2" by 3 1/2". Cards have essentially the same design as the 1987 Fleer Limited Edition cards which were distributed by McCrory's. The cards were printed on the bottom of the counter display box which held 24 small boxed sets; hence theoretically these box cards are 1/24 as plentiful as the regular boxed set cards. These 6 cards, numbered C1 to C6, are considered a separate set in their own right and are not typically included in a complete set of the 1987 Fleer Limited Edition set of 44. The value of the panels uncut is slightly greater, perhaps by 25% greater, than the value of the individual cards cut up carefully.

	MINT	EXC	G-VG
COMPLETE SET	1.50	.75	.15
COMMON PLAYERS	.10	.05	.01

		MINT	EXC	G-VG
☐	C1 Ron Darling	.30	.15	.03
☐	C2 Bill Buckner	.20	.10	.02
☐	C3 John Candelaria	.20	.10	.02
☐	C4 Jack Clark	.50	.25	.05
☐	C5 Bret Saberhagen	.50	.25	.05
☐	C6 Team Logo	.10	.05	.01
	(checklist back)			

1987 Fleer Mini

The 1987 Fleer "Classic Miniatures" set consists of 120 small cards with all new pictures of the players as compared to the 1987 Fleer regular issue. The cards are only 1 13/16" by 2 9/16", making them one of the smallest cards available. Card backs provide career year-by-year statistics. The complete set was distributed in a blue, red, white, and silver box along with 18 logo stickers. The card numbering is by alphabetical order.

		MINT	EXC	G-VG
	COMPLETE SET (120)	10.00	5.00	1.00
	COMMON PLAYER (1-120)	.05	.02	.00
☐	1 Don Aase	.05	.02	.00
☐	2 Joaquin Andujar	.05	.02	.00
☐	3 Harold Baines	.10	.05	.01
☐	4 Jesse Barfield	.15	.07	.01
☐	5 Kevin Bass	.05	.02	.00
☐	6 Don Baylor	.10	.05	.01
☐	7 George Bell	.20	.10	.02
☐	8 Tony Bernazard	.05	.02	.00
☐	9 Bert Blyleven	.10	.05	.01
☐	10 Wade Boggs	.75	.35	.07
☐	11 Phil Bradley	.15	.07	.01
☐	12 Sid Bream	.05	.02	.00
☐	13 George Brett	.35	.17	.03
☐	14 Hubie Brooks	.10	.05	.01
☐	15 Chris Brown	.10	.05	.01
☐	16 Tom Candiotti	.05	.02	.00
☐	17 Jose Canseco	.50	.25	.05
☐	18 Gary Carter	.25	.12	.02
☐	19 Joe Carter	.15	.07	.01
☐	20 Roger Clemens	.50	.25	.05
☐	21 Vince Coleman	.25	.12	.02
☐	22 Cecil Cooper	.10	.05	.01
☐	23 Ron Darling	.15	.07	.01
☐	24 Alvin Davis	.10	.05	.01
☐	25 Chili Davis	.10	.05	.01
☐	26 Eric Davis	.75	.35	.07
☐	27 Glenn Davis	.15	.07	.01
☐	28 Mike Davis	.10	.05	.01
☐	29 Doug DeCinces	.10	.05	.01
☐	30 Rob Deer	.10	.05	.01
☐	31 Jim Deshaies	.10	.05	.01
☐	32 Bo Diaz	.05	.02	.00
☐	33 Richard Dotson	.10	.05	.01
☐	34 Brian Downing	.05	.02	.00
☐	35 Shawon Dunston	.10	.05	.01
☐	36 Mark Eichhorn	.10	.05	.01
☐	37 Dwight Evans	.10	.05	.01
☐	38 Tony Fernandez	.10	.05	.01
☐	39 Julio Franco	.10	.05	.01
☐	40 Gary Gaetti	.15	.07	.01
☐	41 Andres Galarraga	.25	.12	.02
☐	42 Scott Garrelts	.05	.02	.00
☐	43 Steve Garvey	.25	.12	.02
☐	44 Kirk Gibson	.15	.07	.01
☐	45 Dwight Gooden	.45	.22	.04
☐	46 Ken Griffey	.05	.02	.00
☐	47 Mark Gubicza	.05	.02	.00
☐	48 Ozzie Guillen	.10	.05	.01
☐	49 Bill Gullickson	.05	.02	.00
☐	50 Tony Gwynn	.45	.22	.04
☐	51 Von Hayes	.10	.05	.01
☐	52 Rickey Henderson	.35	.17	.03
☐	53 Keith Hernandez	.25	.12	.02
☐	54 Willie Hernandez	.10	.05	.01
☐	55 Ted Higuera	.15	.07	.01
☐	56 Charlie Hough	.05	.02	.00
☐	57 Kent Hrbek	.10	.05	.01
☐	58 Pete Incaviglia	.20	.10	.02
☐	59 Wally Joyner	.60	.30	.06
☐	60 Bob Knepper	.05	.02	.00
☐	61 Mike Krukow	.05	.02	.00
☐	62 Mark Langston	.10	.05	.01
☐	63 Carney Lansford	.10	.05	.01
☐	64 Jim Lindeman	.10	.05	.01
☐	65 Bill Madlock	.10	.05	.01
☐	66 Don Mattingly	1.25	.60	.12
☐	67 Kirk McCaskill	.05	.02	.00
☐	68 Lance McCullers	.05	.02	.00
☐	69 Keith Moreland	.05	.02	.00
☐	70 Jack Morris	.15	.07	.01
☐	71 Jim Morrison	.05	.02	.00
☐	72 Lloyd Moseby	.10	.05	.01
☐	73 Jerry Mumphrey	.05	.02	.00
☐	74 Dale Murphy	.50	.25	.05
☐	75 Eddie Murray	.40	.20	.04
☐	76 Pete O'Brien	.10	.05	.01
☐	77 Bob Ojeda	.10	.05	.01
☐	78 Jesse Orosco	.05	.02	.00
☐	79 Dan Pasqua	.10	.05	.01
☐	80 Dave Parker	.15	.07	.01
☐	81 Larry Parrish	.05	.02	.00
☐	82 Jim Presley	.15	.07	.01
☐	83 Kirby Puckett	.45	.22	.04
☐	84 Dan Quisenberry	.15	.07	.01
☐	85 Tim Raines	.35	.17	.03
☐	86 Dennis Rasmussen	.05	.02	.00
☐	87 Johnny Ray	.10	.05	.01
☐	88 Jeff Reardon	.10	.05	.01
☐	89 Jim Rice	.25	.12	.02

		MINT	EXC	G-VG
☐ 90	Dave Righetti	.15	.07	.01
☐ 91	Earnest Riles	.05	.02	.00
☐ 92	Cal Ripken	.35	.17	.03
☐ 93	Ron Robinson	.05	.02	.00
☐ 94	Juan Samuel	.15	.07	.01
☐ 95	Ryne Sandberg	.25	.12	.02
☐ 96	Steve Sax	.10	.05	.01
☐ 97	Mike Schmidt	.50	.25	.05
☐ 98	Ken Schrom	.05	.02	.00
☐ 99	Mike Scott	.25	.12	.02
☐ 100	Ruben Sierra	.50	.25	.05
☐ 101	Lee Smith	.10	.05	.01
☐ 102	Ozzie Smith	.15	.07	.01
☐ 103	Cory Snyder	.25	.12	.02
☐ 104	Kent Tekulve	.05	.02	.00
☐ 105	Andres Thomas	.05	.02	.00
☐ 106	Rob Thompson	.10	.05	.01
☐ 107	Alan Trammell	.20	.10	.02
☐ 108	John Tudor	.10	.05	.01
☐ 109	Fernando Valenzuela	.20	.10	.02
☐ 110	Greg Walker	.10	.05	.01
☐ 111	Mitch Webster	.05	.02	.00
☐ 112	Lou Whitaker	.10	.05	.01
☐ 113	Frank White	.05	.02	.00
☐ 114	Reggie Williams	.05	.02	.00
☐ 115	Glenn Wilson	.10	.05	.01
☐ 116	Willie Wilson	.10	.05	.01
☐ 117	Dave Winfield	.25	.12	.02
☐ 118	Mike Witt	.10	.05	.01
☐ 119	Todd Worrell	.20	.10	.02
☐ 120	Floyd Youmans	.10	.05	.01

		MINT	EXC	G-VG
☐ 24	Eddie Murray	.35	.17	.03
☐ 25	Phil Niekro	.15	.07	.01
☐ 26	Ben Oglivie	.05	.02	.00
☐ 27	Jesse Orosco	.05	.02	.00
☐ 28	Joe Orsulak	.05	.02	.00
☐ 29	Larry Parrish	.05	.02	.00
☐ 30	Tim Raines	.30	.15	.03
☐ 31	Shane Rawley	.05	.02	.00
☐ 32	Dave Righetti	.15	.07	.01
☐ 33	Pete Rose	.60	.30	.06
☐ 34	Steve Sax	.10	.05	.01
☐ 35	Mike Schmidt	.35	.17	.03
☐ 36	Mike Scott	.20	.10	.02
☐ 37	Don Sutton	.20	.10	.02
☐ 38	Alan Trammell	.20	.10	.02
☐ 39	John Tudor	.10	.05	.01
☐ 40	Gary Ward	.05	.02	.00
☐ 41	Lou Whitaker	.10	.05	.01
☐ 42	Willie Wilson	.10	.05	.01
☐ 43	Todd Worrell	.15	.07	.01
☐ 44	Floyd Youmans	.10	.05	.01

1987 Fleer Sluggers/Pitchers

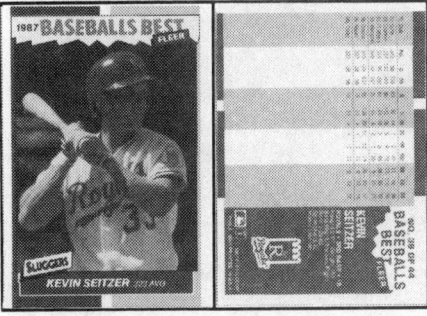

Fleer produced this 44-card boxed set although it was primarily distributed by McCrory, McLellan, Newberry, H.L.Green, T.G.Y., and other similar stores. The set features 28 sluggers and 16 pitchers and is subtitled "Baseball's Best". Cards are standard-size, 2 1/2" by 3 1/2", and were packaged in a red, white, blue, and yellow custom box along with six logo stickers. The set checklist is given on the back of the box. The checklist on the back of the set box misspells McGwire as McGuire.

		MINT	EXC	G-VG
COMPLETE SET		4.00	2.00	.40
COMMON PLAYER		.10	.05	.01
☐ 1	Kevin Bass	.15	.07	.01
☐ 2	Jesse Barfield	.20	.10	.02
☐ 3	George Bell	.30	.15	.03
☐ 4	Wade Boggs	.65	.30	.06
☐ 5	Sid Bream	.10	.05	.01
☐ 6	George Brett	.40	.20	.04
☐ 7	Ivan Calderon	.30	.15	.03
☐ 8	Jose Canseco	.50	.25	.05
☐ 9	Jack Clark	.25	.12	.02
☐ 10	Roger Clemens	.50	.25	.05
☐ 11	Eric Davis	.65	.30	.06
☐ 12	Andre Dawson	.30	.15	.03
☐ 13	Sid Fernandez	.15	.07	.01
☐ 14	John Franco	.15	.07	.01
☐ 15	Dwight Gooden	.40	.20	.04
☐ 16	Pedro Guerrero	.20	.10	.02
☐ 17	Tony Gwynn	.40	.20	.04
☐ 18	Rickey Henderson	.40	.20	.04
☐ 19	Tom Henke	.15	.07	.01
☐ 20	Ted Higuera	.25	.12	.02
☐ 21	Pete Incaviglia	.25	.12	.02
☐ 22	Wally Joyner	.50	.25	.05
☐ 23	Jeff Leonard	.15	.07	.01
☐ 24	Joe Magrane	.20	.10	.02
☐ 25	Don Mattingly	.75	.35	.07
☐ 26	Mark McGwire	1.00	.50	.10
☐ 27	Jack Morris	.20	.10	.02
☐ 28	Dale Murphy	.45	.22	.04
☐ 29	Dave Parker	.20	.10	.02

1987 Fleer Record Setters

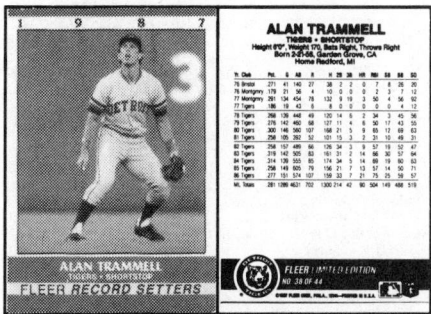

This 44-card boxed set was produced by Fleer for distribution by Eckerd's Drug Stores and is sometimes referred to as the Eckerd's set. Six team logo stickers are included in the box with the complete set. The numerical checklist on the back of the box shows that the set is numbered alphabetically. The cards measure 2 1/2" by 3 1/2".

		MINT	EXC	G-VG
COMPLETE SET		4.50	2.25	.45
COMMON PLAYER		.05	.02	.00
☐ 1	George Brett	.35	.17	.03
☐ 2	Chris Brown	.15	.07	.01
☐ 3	Jose Canseco	.60	.30	.06
☐ 4	Roger Clemens	.60	.30	.06
☐ 5	Alvin Davis	.15	.07	.01
☐ 6	Shawon Dunston	.10	.05	.01
☐ 7	Tony Fernandez	.15	.07	.01
☐ 8	Carlton Fisk	.10	.05	.01
☐ 9	Gary Gaetti	.15	.07	.01
☐ 10	Gene Garber	.05	.02	.00
☐ 11	Rich Gedman	.05	.02	.00
☐ 12	Dwight Gooden	.50	.25	.05
☐ 13	Ozzie Guillen	.10	.05	.01
☐ 14	Bill Gullickson	.05	.02	.00
☐ 15	Billy Hatcher	.10	.05	.01
☐ 16	Orel Hershiser	.15	.07	.01
☐ 17	Wally Joyner	.60	.30	.06
☐ 18	Ray Knight	.10	.05	.01
☐ 19	Craig Lefferts	.05	.02	.00
☐ 20	Don Mattingly	.75	.35	.07
☐ 21	Kevin Mitchell	.10	.05	.01
☐ 22	Lloyd Moseby	.05	.02	.00
☐ 23	Dale Murphy	.45	.22	.04

			MINT	EXC	G-VG
☐ 30	Ken Phelps		.10	.05	.01
☐ 31	Kirby Puckett		.35	.17	.03
☐ 32	Tim Raines		.30	.15	.03
☐ 33	Jeff Reardon		.15	.07	.01
☐ 34	Dave Righetti		.20	.10	.02
☐ 35	Cal Ripken		.30	.15	.03
☐ 36	Bret Saberhagen		.25	.12	.02
☐ 37	Mike Schmidt		.45	.22	.04
☐ 38	Mike Scott		.25	.12	.02
☐ 39	Kevin Seitzer		1.00	.50	.10
☐ 40	Darryl Strawberry		.50	.25	.05
☐ 41	Rick Sutcliffe		.15	.07	.01
☐ 42	Pat Tabler		.15	.07	.01
☐ 43	Fernando Valenzuela		.25	.12	.02
☐ 44	Mike Witt		.15	.07	.01

1987 Fleer Slug/Pitch Box Cards

The cards in this 6-card set each measure the standard 2 1/2" by 3 1/2". Cards have essentially the same design as the 1987 Fleer Sluggers vs. Pitchers set of Baseball's Best. The cards were printed on the bottom of the counter display box which held 24 small boxed sets; hence theoretically these box cards are 1/24 as plentiful as the regular boxed set cards. These 6 cards, numbered M1 to M5 with one blank-back (unnumbered) card, are considered a separate set in their own right and are not typically included in a complete set of the 1987 Fleer Sluggers vs. Pitchers set of 44. The value of the panels uncut is slightly greater, perhaps by 25% greater, than the value of the individual cards cut up carefully.

		MINT	EXC	G-VG
COMPLETE SET		2.00	1.00	.20
COMMON PLAYERS		.10	.05	.01
☐ M1	Steve Bedrosian	.30	.15	.03
☐ M2	Will Clark	.75	.35	.07
☐ M3	Vince Coleman	.50	.25	.05
☐ M4	Bo Jackson	.50	.25	.05
☐ M5	Cory Snyder	.50	.25	.05
☐ xx	Team Logo	.10	.05	.01
	(unnumbered, blank back)			

1987 Fleer Update

This 132-card set was distributed by Fleer to dealers as a complete set within a custom box. In addition to the complete set of 132 cards, the box also contains 25 Team Logo stickers. The card fronts look very similar to the 1987 Fleer regular issue. The cards are numbered (with a U prefix) alphabetically according to player's last name. Cards measure the standard size, 2 1/2" by 3 1/2".

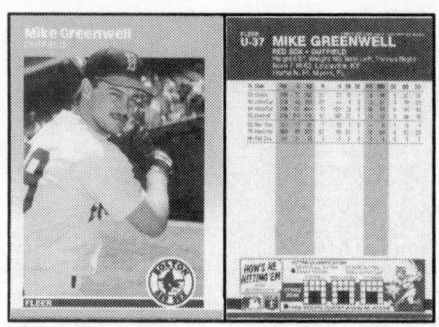

			MINT	EXC	G-VG
COMPLETE SET (132)			11.00	5.50	1.10
COMMON PLAYER (1-132)			.06	.03	.00
☐	U1	Scott Bankhead	.10	.05	.01
☐	U2	Eric Bell	.10	.05	.01
☐	U3	Juan Beniquez	.06	.03	.00
☐	U4	Juan Berenguer	.06	.03	.00
☐	U5	Mike Birkbeck	.10	.05	.01
☐	U6	Randy Bockus	.20	.10	.02
☐	U7	Greg Booker	.06	.03	.00
☐	U8	Thad Bosley	.06	.03	.00
☐	U9	Greg Brock	.10	.05	.01
☐	U10	Bob Brower	.15	.07	.01
☐	U11	Chris Brown	.20	.10	.02
☐	U12	Jerry Browne	.10	.05	.01
☐	U13	Ralph Bryant	.10	.05	.01
☐	U14	DeWayne Buice	.20	.10	.02
☐	U15	Ellis Burks	1.25	.60	.12
☐	U16	Casey Candaele	.20	.10	.02
☐	U17	Steve Carlton	.25	.12	.02
☐	U18	Juan Castillo	.06	.03	.00
☐	U19	Chuck Crim	.10	.05	.01
☐	U20	Mark Davidson	.20	.10	.02
☐	U21	Mark Davis	.06	.03	.00
☐	U22	Storm Davis	.10	.05	.01
☐	U23	Bill Dawley	.06	.03	.00
☐	U24	Andre Dawson	.35	.17	.03
☐	U25	Brian Dayett	.06	.03	.00
☐	U26	Rick Dempsey	.06	.03	.00
☐	U27	Ken Dowell	.20	.10	.02
☐	U28	Dave Dravecky	.10	.05	.01
☐	U29	Mike Dunne	.60	.30	.06
☐	U30	Dennis Eckersley	.10	.05	.01
☐	U31	Cecil Fielder	.10	.05	.01
☐	U32	Brian Fisher	.10	.05	.01
☐	U33	Willie Fraser	.10	.05	.01
☐	U34	Ken Gerhart	.25	.12	.02
☐	U35	Jim Gott	.06	.03	.00
☐	U36	Dan Gladden	.10	.05	.01
☐	U37	Mike Greenwell	1.00	.50	.10
☐	U38	Cecelio Guante	.06	.03	.00
☐	U39	Albert Hall	.06	.03	.00
☐	U40	Atlee Hammaker	.06	.03	.00
☐	U41	Mickey Hatcher	.06	.03	.00
☐	U42	Mike Heath	.06	.03	.00
☐	U43	Neal Heaton	.06	.03	.00
☐	U44	Mike Henneman	.30	.15	.03
☐	U45	Guy Hoffman	.10	.05	.01
☐	U46	Charles Hudson	.06	.03	.00
☐	U47	Chuck Jackson	.15	.07	.01
☐	U48	Mike Jackson	.15	.07	.01
☐	U49	Reggie Jackson	.40	.20	.04
☐	U50	Chris James	.40	.20	.04
☐	U51	Dion James	.15	.07	.01
☐	U52	Stan Javier	.10	.05	.01
☐	U53	Stan Jefferson	.25	.12	.02
☐	U54	Jimmy Jones	.15	.07	.01
☐	U55	Tracy Jones	.30	.15	.03
☐	U56	Terry Kennedy	.10	.05	.01
☐	U57	Mike Kingery	.10	.05	.01
☐	U58	Ray Knight	.10	.05	.01
☐	U59	Gene Larkin	.25	.12	.02
☐	U60	Mike LaValliere	.10	.05	.01
☐	U61	Jack Lazorko	.10	.05	.01
☐	U62	Terry Leach	.15	.07	.01
☐	U63	Rick Leach	.06	.03	.00
☐	U64	Craig Lefferts	.06	.03	.00
☐	U65	Jim Lindeman	.30	.15	.03
☐	U66	Bill Long	.20	.10	.02
☐	U67	Mike Loynd	.20	.10	.02
☐	U68	Greg Maddux	.20	.10	.02

☐	U69	Bill Madlock	.15	.07	.01
☐	U70	Dave Magadan	.50	.25	.05
☐	U71	Joe Magrane	.60	.30	.06
☐	U72	Fred Manrique	.25	.12	.02
☐	U73	Mike Mason	.06	.03	.00
☐	U74	Lloyd McClendon	.20	.10	.02
☐	U75	Fred McGriff	.50	.25	.05
☐	U76	Mark McGwire	3.50	1.75	.35
☐	U77	Mark McLemore	.10	.05	.01
☐	U78	Kevin McReynolds	.20	.10	.02
☐	U79	Dave Meads	.15	.07	.01
☐	U80	Greg Minton	.06	.03	.00
☐	U81	John Mitchell	.20	.10	.02
☐	U82	Kevin Mitchell	.15	.07	.01
☐	U83	John Morris	.06	.03	.00
☐	U84	Jeff Musselman	.30	.15	.03
☐	U85	Randy Myers	.30	.15	.03
☐	U86	Gene Nelson	.06	.03	.00
☐	U87	Joe Niekro	.15	.07	.01
☐	U88	Tom Nieto	.06	.03	.00
☐	U89	Reid Nichols	.06	.03	.00
☐	U90	Matt Nokes	2.00	1.00	.20
☐	U91	Dickie Noles	.06	.03	.00
☐	U92	Edwin Nunez	.06	.03	.00
☐	U93	Jose Nunez	.15	.07	.01
☐	U94	Paul O'Neill	.10	.05	.01
☐	U95	Jim Paciorek	.15	.07	.01
☐	U96	Lance Parrish	.15	.07	.01
☐	U97	Bill Pecota	.25	.12	.02
☐	U98	Tony Pena	.15	.07	.01
☐	U99	Luis Polonia	.30	.15	.03
☐	U100	Randy Ready	.10	.05	.01
☐	U101	Jeff Reardon	.20	.10	.02
☐	U102	Gary Redus	.10	.05	.01
☐	U103	Rick Rhoden	.15	.07	.01
☐	U104	Wally Ritchie	.15	.07	.01
☐	U105	Jeff Robinson	.30	.15	.03
		(wrong Jeff's			
		stats on back)			
☐	U106	Mark Salas	.10	.05	.01
☐	U107	Dave Schmidt	.10	.05	.01
☐	U108	Kevin Seitzer ERR	2.00	1.00	.20
		(wrong birth year)			
☐	U109	John Shelby	.06	.03	.00
☐	U110	John Smiley	.30	.15	.03
☐	U111	Lary Sorensen	.06	.03	.00
☐	U112	Chris Speier	.06	.03	.00
☐	U113	Randy St.Claire	.06	.03	.00
☐	U114	Jim Sundberg	.06	.03	.00
☐	U115	B.J. Surhoff	.80	.40	.08
☐	U116	Greg Swindell	.30	.15	.03
☐	U117	Danny Tartabull	.40	.20	.04
☐	U118	Dorn Taylor	.15	.07	.01
☐	U119	Lee Tunnell	.06	.03	.00
☐	U120	Ed VandeBerg	.06	.03	.00
☐	U121	Andy Van Slyke	.20	.10	.02
☐	U122	Gary Ward	.10	.05	.01
☐	U123	Devon White	.80	.40	.08
☐	U124	Alan Wiggins	.10	.05	.01
☐	U125	Bill Wilkinson	.10	.05	.01
☐	U126	Jim Winn	.06	.03	.00
☐	U127	Frank Williams	.06	.03	.00
☐	U128	Kenny Williams	.40	.20	.04
☐	U129	Matt Williams	.40	.20	.04
☐	U130	Herm Willingham	.10	.05	.01
☐	U131	Matt Young	.10	.05	.01
☐	U132	Checklist	.10	.01	.00

1987 Fleer World Series

This 12-card set of 2 1/2" by 3 1/2" cards features highlights of the previous year's World Series between the Mets and the Red Sox. The sets were packaged as a complete set insert with the collated sets (of the 1987 Fleer regular issue) which were sold by Fleer directly to hobby card dealers; they were not available in the general retail candy store outlets.

		MINT	EXC	G-VG
COMPLETE SET (12)		4.00	2.00	.40
COMMON PLAYER (1-12)		.25	.12	.02
☐ 1	Bruce Hurst	.35	.17	.03
	Left Hand Finesse			
	Beats Mets			
☐ 2	Keith Hernandez and	.60	.30	.06
	Wade Boggs			
☐ 3	Roger Clemens HOR	.75	.35	.07

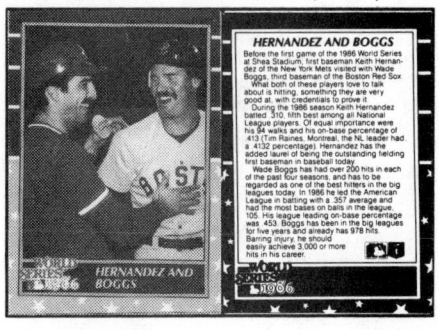

☐ 4	Clutch Hitting	.45	.22	.04
	(Gary Carter)			
☐ 5	Ron Darling	.35	.17	.03
	Picks Up Slack			
☐ 6	Marty Barrett	.35	.17	.03
	.433 Series BA			
☐ 7	Dwight Gooden	.60	.30	.06
☐ 8	Strategy at Work	.25	.12	.02
	(Mets Conference)			
☐ 9	Dewey Evans	.35	.17	.03
	(Congratulated by			
	Rich Gedman)			
☐ 10	One Strike From	.25	.12	.02
	Boston Victory			
	(Dave Henderson)			
☐ 11	Series Home Run Duo	.35	.17	.03
	(Ray Knight and			
	Darryl Strawberry)			
☐ 12	Ray Knight	.35	.17	.03
	(Series MVP)			

1988 Fleer

This 660-card set features a distinctive white background with red and blue diagonal stripes across the card. The backs are printed in gray and red on white card stock. The bottom of the card back shows an innovative breakdown of the player's demonstrated ability with respect to day, night, home, and road games. Cards are numbered on the back and are again the standard 2 1/2" by 3 1/2". Cards are again organized numerically by teams, i.e., World Champion Twins (1-25), St. Louis Cardinals (26-50), Detroit Tigers (51-75), San Francisco Giants (76-101), Toronto Blue Jays (102-126), New York Mets (127-154), Milwaukee Brewers (155-178), Montreal Expos (179-201), New York Yankees (202-226), Cincinnati Reds (227-250), Kansas City Royals (251- 274), Oakland A's (275-296), Philadelphia Phillies (297-320), Pittsburgh Pirates (321-342), Boston Red Sox (343-367), Seattle Mariners (368-390), Chicago White Sox (391-413), Chicago Cubs (414-436), Houston Astros (437-460), Texas

Rangers (461-483), California Angels (484-507), Los Angeles Dodgers (508-530), Atlanta Braves (531-552), Baltimore Orioles (553-575), San Diego Padres (576-599), and Cleveland Indians (600-621). The last 39 cards in the set consist of Specials (622-640), Rookie Pairs (641-653), and checklists (654-660).

		MINT	EXC	G-VG
	COMPLETE SET (660)	27.00	13.50	2.70
	COMMON PLAYER (1-660)	.03	.01	.00
☐ 1	Keith Atherton	.03	.01	.00
☐ 2	Don Baylor	.08	.04	.01
☐ 3	Juan Berenguer	.06	.03	.00
☐ 4	Bert Blyleven	.10	.05	.01
☐ 5	Tom Brunansky	.10	.05	.01
☐ 6	Randy Bush	.03	.01	.00
☐ 7	Steve Carlton	.20	.10	.02
☐ 8	Mark Davidson	.15	.07	.01
☐ 9	George Frazier	.03	.01	.00
☐ 10	Gary Gaetti	.12	.06	.01
☐ 11	Greg Gagne	.06	.03	.00
☐ 12	Dan Gladden	.06	.03	.00
☐ 13	Kent Hrbek	.12	.06	.01
☐ 14	Gene Larkin	.25	.12	.02
☐ 15	Tim Laudner	.03	.01	.00
☐ 16	Steve Lombardozzi	.03	.01	.00
☐ 17	Al Newman	.03	.01	.00
☐ 18	Joe Niekro	.08	.04	.01
☐ 19	Kirby Puckett	.35	.17	.03
☐ 20	Jeff Reardon	.08	.04	.01
☐ 21	Dan Schatzader	.06	.03	.00
	(sic, Schatzeder)			
☐ 22	Roy Smalley	.03	.01	.00
☐ 23	Mike Smithson	.03	.01	.00
☐ 24	Les Straker	.15	.07	.01
☐ 25	Frank Viola	.10	.05	.01
☐ 26	Jack Clark	.25	.12	.02
☐ 27	Vince Coleman	.25	.12	.02
☐ 28	Danny Cox	.08	.04	.01
☐ 29	Bill Dawley	.03	.01	.00
☐ 30	Ken Dayley	.03	.01	.00
☐ 31	Doug DeCinces	.06	.03	.00
☐ 32	Curt Ford	.06	.03	.00
☐ 33	Bob Forsch	.03	.01	.00
☐ 34	David Green	.03	.01	.00
☐ 35	Tom Herr	.06	.03	.00
☐ 36	Ricky Horton	.03	.01	.00
☐ 37	Lance Johnson	.30	.15	.03
☐ 38	Steve Lake	.03	.01	.00
☐ 39	Jim Lindeman	.15	.07	.01
☐ 40	Joe Magrane	.35	.17	.03
☐ 41	Greg Mathews	.06	.03	.00
☐ 42	Willie McGee	.15	.07	.01
☐ 43	John Morris	.06	.03	.00
☐ 44	Jose Oquendo	.03	.01	.00
☐ 45	Tony Pena	.08	.04	.01
☐ 46	Terry Pendleton	.06	.03	.00
☐ 47	Ozzie Smith	.12	.06	.01
☐ 48	John Tudor	.10	.05	.01
☐ 49	Lee Tunnell	.03	.01	.00
☐ 50	Todd Worrell	.12	.06	.01
☐ 51	Doyle Alexander	.06	.03	.00
☐ 52	Dave Bergman	.03	.01	.00
☐ 53	Tom Brookens	.03	.01	.00
☐ 54	Darrell Evans	.08	.04	.01
☐ 55	Kirk Gibson	.15	.07	.01
☐ 56	Mike Heath	.03	.01	.00
☐ 57	Mike Henneman	.25	.12	.02
☐ 58	Willie Hernandez	.08	.04	.01
☐ 59	Larry Herndon	.03	.01	.00
☐ 60	Eric King	.03	.01	.00
☐ 61	Chet Lemon	.06	.03	.00
☐ 62	Scott Lusader	.20	.10	.02
☐ 63	Bill Madlock	.08	.04	.01
☐ 64	Jack Morris	.15	.07	.01
☐ 65	Jim Morrison	.03	.01	.00
☐ 66	Matt Nokes	1.25	.60	.12
☐ 67	Dan Petry	.06	.03	.00
☐ 68	Jeff Robinson	.20	.10	.02
☐ 69	Pat Sheridan	.03	.01	.00
☐ 70	Nate Snell	.03	.01	.00
☐ 71	Frank Tanana	.06	.03	.00
☐ 72	Walt Terrell	.06	.03	.00
☐ 73	Mark Thurmond	.03	.01	.00
☐ 74	Alan Trammell	.20	.10	.02
☐ 75	Lou Whitaker	.12	.06	.01
☐ 76	Mike Aldrete	.10	.05	.01
☐ 77	Bob Brenly	.06	.03	.00
☐ 78	Will Clark	.45	.22	.04
☐ 79	Chili Davis	.08	.04	.01
☐ 80	Kelly Downs	.06	.03	.00
☐ 81	Dave Dravecky	.06	.03	.00
☐ 82	Scott Garrelts	.06	.03	.00
☐ 83	Atlee Hammaker	.06	.03	.00
☐ 84	Dave Henderson	.03	.01	.00
☐ 85	Mike Krukow	.06	.03	.00
☐ 86	Mike LaCoss	.03	.01	.00
☐ 87	Craig Lefferts	.03	.01	.00
☐ 88	Jeff Leonard	.08	.04	.01
☐ 89	Candy Maldonado	.10	.05	.01
☐ 90	Bob Melvin	.03	.01	.00
☐ 91	Ed Milner	.03	.01	.00
☐ 92	Kevin Mitchell	.08	.04	.01
☐ 93	Jon Perlman	.15	.07	.01
☐ 94	Rick Reuschel	.06	.03	.00
☐ 95	Don Robinson	.03	.01	.00
☐ 96	Chris Speier	.03	.01	.00
☐ 97	Harry Spilman	.03	.01	.00
☐ 98	Robbie Thompson	.08	.04	.01
☐ 99	Jose Uribe	.03	.01	.00
☐ 100	Mark Wasinger	.15	.07	.01
☐ 101	Matt Williams	.35	.17	.03
☐ 102	Jesse Barfield	.15	.07	.01
☐ 103	George Bell	.25	.12	.02
☐ 104	Juan Beniquez	.06	.03	.00
☐ 105	John Cerutti	.03	.01	.00
☐ 106	Jim Clancy	.03	.01	.00
☐ 107	Rob Ducey	.25	.12	.02
☐ 108	Mark Eichhorn	.06	.03	.00
☐ 109	Tony Fernandez	.12	.06	.01
☐ 110	Cecil Fielder	.06	.03	.00
☐ 111	Kelly Gruber	.03	.01	.00
☐ 112	Tom Henke	.08	.04	.01
☐ 113	Garth Iorq	.06	.03	.00
	(sic, Iorg)			
☐ 114	Jimmy Key	.10	.05	.01
☐ 115	Rick Leach	.03	.01	.00
☐ 116	Manny Lee	.10	.05	.01
☐ 117	Nelson Liriano	.25	.12	.02
☐ 118	Fred McGriff	.20	.10	.02
☐ 119	Lloyd Moseby	.10	.05	.01
☐ 120	Rance Mulliniks	.03	.01	.00
☐ 121	Jeff Musselman	.10	.05	.01
☐ 122	Jose Nunez	.15	.07	.01
☐ 123	Dave Stieb	.08	.04	.01
☐ 124	Willie Upshaw	.06	.03	.00
☐ 125	Duane Ward	.08	.04	.01
☐ 126	Ernie Whitt	.03	.01	.00
☐ 127	Rick Aguilera	.06	.03	.00
☐ 128	Wally Backman	.06	.03	.00
☐ 129	Mark Carreon	.25	.12	.02
☐ 130	Gary Carter	.25	.12	.02
☐ 131	David Cone	.20	.10	.02
☐ 132	Ron Darling	.15	.07	.01
☐ 133	Len Dykstra	.10	.05	.01
☐ 134	Sid Fernandez	.10	.05	.01
☐ 135	Dwight Gooden	.50	.25	.05
☐ 136	Keith Hernandez	.25	.12	.02
☐ 137	Gregg Jefferies	1.25	.60	.12
☐ 138	Howard Johnson	.10	.05	.01
☐ 139	Terry Leach	.06	.03	.00
☐ 140	Barry Lyons	.15	.07	.01
☐ 141	Dave Magadan	.15	.07	.01
☐ 142	Roger McDowell	.08	.04	.01
☐ 143	Kevin McReynolds	.12	.06	.01
☐ 144	Keith Miller	.30	.15	.03
☐ 145	John Mitchell	.20	.10	.02
☐ 146	Randy Myers	.15	.07	.01
☐ 147	Bob Ojeda	.06	.03	.00
☐ 148	Jesse Orosco	.06	.03	.00
☐ 149	Rafael Santana	.03	.01	.00
☐ 150	Doug Sisk	.03	.01	.00
☐ 151	Darryl Strawberry	.35	.17	.03
☐ 152	Tim Teufel	.06	.03	.00
☐ 153	Gene Walter	.03	.01	.00
☐ 154	Mookie Wilson	.06	.03	.00
☐ 155	Jay Aldrich	.15	.07	.01
☐ 156	Chris Bosio	.06	.03	.00
☐ 157	Glenn Braggs	.10	.05	.01
☐ 158	Greg Brock	.06	.03	.00
☐ 159	Juan Castillo	.08	.04	.01
☐ 160	Mark Clear	.03	.01	.00
☐ 161	Cecil Cooper	.08	.04	.01
☐ 162	Chuck Crim	.12	.06	.01
☐ 163	Rob Deer	.08	.04	.01
☐ 164	Mike Felder	.03	.01	.00
☐ 165	Jim Gantner	.03	.01	.00
☐ 166	Ted Higuera	.12	.06	.01
☐ 167	Steve Kiefer	.08	.04	.01
☐ 168	Rick Manning	.03	.01	.00
☐ 169	Paul Molitor	.15	.07	.01
☐ 170	Juan Nieves	.06	.03	.00
☐ 171	Dan Plesac	.06	.03	.00
☐ 172	Earnest Riles	.03	.01	.00
☐ 173	Bill Schroeder	.03	.01	.00
☐ 174	Steve Stanicek	.35	.17	.03
☐ 175	B.J. Surhoff	.25	.12	.02

☐ 176 Dale Sveum	.08	.04	.01	☐ 271 Danny Tartabull	.20	.10	.02
☐ 177 Bill Wegman	.03	.01	.00	☐ 272 Gary Thurman	.35	.17	.03
☐ 178 Robin Yount	.25	.12	.02	☐ 273 Frank White	.06	.03	.00
☐ 179 Hubie Brooks	.06	.03	.00	☐ 274 Willie Wilson	.08	.04	.01
☐ 180 Tim Burke	.06	.03	.00	☐ 275 Tony Bernazard	.03	.01	.00
☐ 181 Casey Candaele	.06	.03	.00	☐ 276 Jose Canseco	.60	.30	.06
☐ 182 Mike Fitzgerald	.03	.01	.00	☐ 277 Mike Davis	.06	.03	.00
☐ 183 Tom Foley	.03	.01	.00	☐ 278 Storm Davis	.06	.03	.00
☐ 184 Andres Galarraga	.15	.07	.01	☐ 279 Dennis Eckersley	.06	.03	.00
☐ 185 Neal Heaton	.03	.01	.00	☐ 280 Alfredo Griffin	.06	.03	.00
☐ 186 Wallace Johnson	.03	.01	.00	☐ 281 Rick Honeycutt	.03	.01	.00
☐ 187 Vance Law	.03	.01	.00	☐ 282 Jay Howell	.03	.01	.00
☐ 188 Dennis Martinez	.06	.03	.00	☐ 283 Reggie Jackson	.30	.15	.03
☐ 189 Bob McClure	.03	.01	.00	☐ 284 Dennis Lamp	.03	.01	.00
☐ 190 Andy McGaffigan	.03	.01	.00	☐ 285 Carney Lansford	.08	.04	.01
☐ 191 Reid Nichols	.03	.01	.00	☐ 286 Mark McGwire	1.50	.75	.15
☐ 192 Pascual Perez	.03	.01	.00	☐ 287 Dwayne Murphy	.06	.03	.00
☐ 193 Tim Raines	.25	.12	.02	☐ 288 Gene Nelson	.03	.01	.00
☐ 194 Jeff Reed	.03	.01	.00	☐ 289 Steve Ontiveros	.03	.01	.00
☐ 195 Bob Sebra	.03	.01	.00	☐ 290 Tony Phillips	.03	.01	.00
☐ 196 Bryn Smith	.03	.01	.00	☐ 291 Eric Plunk	.06	.03	.00
☐ 197 Randy St.Claire	.03	.01	.00	☐ 292 Luis Polonia	.30	.15	.03
☐ 198 Tim Wallach	.08	.04	.01	☐ 293 Rick Rodriguez	.15	.07	.01
☐ 199 Mitch Webster	.06	.03	.00	☐ 294 Terry Steinbach	.10	.05	.01
☐ 200 Herm Winningham	.03	.01	.00	☐ 295 Dave Stewart	.08	.04	.01
☐ 201 Floyd Youmans	.06	.03	.00	☐ 296 Curt Young	.06	.03	.00
☐ 202 Brad Arnsberg	.20	.10	.02	☐ 297 Luis Aguayo	.03	.01	.00
☐ 203 Rick Cerone	.03	.01	.00	☐ 298 Steve Bedrosian	.10	.05	.01
☐ 204 Pat Clements	.03	.01	.00	☐ 299 Jeff Calhoun	.03	.01	.00
☐ 205 Henry Cotto	.03	.01	.00	☐ 300 Don Carman	.03	.01	.00
☐ 206 Mike Easler	.03	.01	.00	☐ 301 Todd Frohwirth	.15	.07	.01
☐ 207 Ron Guidry	.10	.05	.01	☐ 302 Greg Gross	.03	.01	.00
☐ 208 Bill Gullickson	.06	.03	.00	☐ 303 Kevin Gross	.03	.01	.00
☐ 209 Rickey Henderson	.25	.12	.02	☐ 304 Von Hayes	.10	.05	.01
☐ 210 Charles Hudson	.03	.01	.00	☐ 305 Keith Hughes	.30	.15	.03
☐ 211 Tommy John	.10	.05	.01	☐ 306 Mike Jackson	.12	.06	.01
☐ 212 Roberto Kelly	.35	.17	.03	☐ 307 Chris James	.15	.07	.01
☐ 213 Ron Kittle	.08	.04	.01	☐ 308 Steve Jeltz	.03	.01	.00
☐ 214 Don Mattingly	1.50	.75	.15	☐ 309 Mike Maddux	.03	.01	.00
☐ 215 Bobby Meacham	.03	.01	.00	☐ 310 Lance Parrish	.12	.06	.01
☐ 216 Mike Pagliarulo	.08	.04	.01	☐ 311 Shane Rawley	.06	.03	.00
☐ 217 Dan Pasqua	.08	.04	.01	☐ 312 Wally Ritchie	.15	.07	.01
☐ 218 Willie Randolph	.08	.04	.01	☐ 313 Bruce Ruffin	.03	.01	.00
☐ 219 Rick Rhoden	.06	.03	.00	☐ 314 Juan Samuel	.12	.06	.01
☐ 220 Dave Righetti	.12	.06	.01	☐ 315 Mike Schmidt	.30	.15	.03
☐ 221 Jerry Royster	.03	.01	.00	☐ 316 Rick Schu	.03	.01	.00
☐ 222 Tim Stoddard	.03	.01	.00	☐ 317 Jeff Stone	.06	.03	.00
☐ 223 Wayne Tolleson	.03	.01	.00	☐ 318 Kent Tekulve	.06	.03	.00
☐ 224 Gary Ward	.06	.03	.00	☐ 319 Milt Thompson	.06	.03	.00
☐ 225 Claudell Washington	.06	.03	.00	☐ 320 Glenn Wilson	.06	.03	.00
☐ 226 Dave Winfield	.25	.12	.02	☐ 321 Rafael Belliard	.03	.01	.00
☐ 227 Buddy Bell	.08	.04	.01	☐ 322 Barry Bonds	.15	.07	.01
☐ 228 Tom Browning	.06	.03	.00	☐ 323 Bobby Bonilla	.08	.04	.01
☐ 229 Dave Concepcion	.08	.04	.01	☐ 324 Sid Bream	.06	.03	.00
☐ 230 Kal Daniels	.25	.12	.02	☐ 325 John Cangelosi	.03	.01	.00
☐ 231 Eric Davis	1.00	.50	.10	☐ 326 Mike Diaz	.03	.01	.00
☐ 232 Bo Diaz	.06	.03	.00	☐ 327 Doug Drabek	.06	.03	.00
☐ 233 Nick Esasky	.06	.03	.00	☐ 328 Mike Dunne	.30	.15	.03
☐ 234 John Franco	.08	.04	.01	☐ 329 Brian Fisher	.06	.03	.00
☐ 235 Guy Hoffman	.03	.01	.00	☐ 330 Brett Gideon	.20	.10	.02
☐ 236 Tom Hume	.03	.01	.00	☐ 331 Terry Harper	.03	.01	.00
☐ 237 Tracy Jones	.08	.04	.01	☐ 332 Bob Kipper	.03	.01	.00
☐ 238 Bill Landrum	.15	.07	.01	☐ 333 Mike LaValliere	.03	.01	.00
☐ 239 Barry Larkin	.12	.06	.01	☐ 334 Jose Lind	.30	.15	.03
☐ 240 Terry McGriff	.12	.06	.01	☐ 335 Junior Ortiz	.03	.01	.00
☐ 241 Rob Murphy	.06	.03	.00	☐ 336 Vincent Palacios	.20	.10	.02
☐ 242 Ron Oester	.03	.01	.00	☐ 337 Bob Patterson	.20	.10	.02
☐ 243 Dave Parker	.15	.07	.01	☐ 338 Al Pedrique	.20	.10	.02
☐ 244 Pat Perry	.03	.01	.00	☐ 339 R.J. Reynolds	.06	.03	.00
☐ 245 Ted Power	.03	.01	.00	☐ 340 John Smiley	.20	.10	.02
☐ 246 Dennis Rasmussen	.03	.01	.00	☐ 341 Andy Van Slyke	.10	.05	.01
☐ 247 Ron Robinson	.03	.01	.00	☐ 342 Bob Walk	.03	.01	.00
☐ 248 Kurt Stillwell	.06	.03	.00	☐ 343 Marty Barrett	.08	.04	.01
☐ 249 Jeff Treadway	.40	.20	.04	☐ 344 Todd Benzinger	.45	.22	.04
☐ 250 Frank Williams	.03	.01	.00	☐ 345 Wade Boggs	1.00	.50	.10
☐ 251 Steve Balboni	.03	.01	.00	☐ 346 Tom Bolton	.15	.07	.01
☐ 252 Bud Black	.03	.01	.00	☐ 347 Oil Can Boyd	.06	.03	.00
☐ 253 Thad Bosley	.03	.01	.00	☐ 348 Ellis Burks	1.00	.50	.10
☐ 254 George Brett	.30	.15	.03	☐ 349 Roger Clemens	.60	.30	.06
☐ 255 John Davis	.20	.10	.02	☐ 350 Steve Crawford	.30	.15	.03
☐ 256 Steve Farr	.03	.01	.00	☐ 351 Dwight Evans	.10	.05	.01
☐ 257 Gene Garber	.03	.01	.00	☐ 352 Wes Gardner	.15	.07	.01
☐ 258 Jerry Don Gleaton	.03	.01	.00	☐ 353 Rich Gedman	.06	.03	.00
☐ 259 Mark Gubicza	.06	.03	.00	☐ 354 Mike Greenwell	.75	.35	.07
☐ 260 Bo Jackson	.35	.17	.03	☐ 355 Sam Horn	1.25	.60	.12
☐ 261 Danny Jackson	.06	.03	.00	☐ 356 Bruce Hurst	.08	.04	.01
☐ 262 Ross Jones	.15	.07	.01	☐ 357 John Marzano	.35	.17	.03
☐ 263 Charlie Leibrandt	.06	.03	.00	☐ 358 Al Nipper	.03	.01	.00
☐ 264 Bill Pecota	.20	.10	.02	☐ 359 Spike Owen	.03	.01	.00
☐ 265 Melido Perez	.15	.07	.01	☐ 360 Jody Reed	.30	.15	.03
☐ 266 Jamie Quirk	.03	.01	.00	☐ 361 Jim Rice	.20	.10	.02
☐ 267 Dan Quisenberry	.10	.05	.01	☐ 362 Ed Romero	.03	.01	.00
☐ 268 Bret Saberhagen	.20	.10	.02	☐ 363 Kevin Romine	.15	.07	.01
☐ 269 Angel Salazar	.03	.01	.00	☐ 364 Joe Sambito	.03	.01	.00
☐ 270 Kevin Seitzer	.80	.40	.08	☐ 365 Calvin Schiraldi	.06	.03	.00

☐ 366 Jeff Sellers	.03	.01	.00
☐ 367 Bob Stanley	.06	.03	.00
☐ 368 Scott Bankhead	.06	.03	.00
☐ 369 Phil Bradley	.10	.05	.01
☐ 370 Scott Bradley	.06	.03	.00
☐ 371 Mickey Brantley	.08	.04	.01
☐ 372 Mike Campbell	.20	.10	.02
☐ 373 Alvin Davis	.10	.05	.01
☐ 374 Lee Guetterman	.06	.03	.00
☐ 375 Dave Hengel	.25	.12	.02
☐ 376 Mike Kingery	.03	.01	.00
☐ 377 Mark Langston	.10	.05	.01
☐ 378 Edgar Martinez	.15	.07	.01
☐ 379 Mike Moore	.03	.01	.00
☐ 380 Mike Morgan	.03	.01	.00
☐ 381 John Moses	.03	.01	.00
☐ 382 Donnell Nixon	.15	.07	.01
☐ 383 Edwin Nunez	.03	.01	.00
☐ 384 Ken Phelps	.06	.03	.00
☐ 385 Jim Presley	.10	.05	.01
☐ 386 Rey Quinones	.06	.03	.00
☐ 387 Jerry Reed	.03	.01	.00
☐ 388 Harold Reynolds	.06	.03	.00
☐ 389 Dave Valle	.08	.04	.01
☐ 390 Bill Wilkinson	.15	.07	.01
☐ 391 Harold Baines	.12	.06	.01
☐ 392 Floyd Bannister	.06	.03	.00
☐ 393 Daryl Boston	.03	.01	.00
☐ 394 Ivan Calderon	.12	.06	.01
☐ 395 Jose DeLeon	.03	.01	.00
☐ 396 Richard Dotson	.06	.03	.00
☐ 397 Carlton Fisk	.10	.05	.01
☐ 398 Ozzie Guillen	.06	.03	.00
☐ 399 Ron Hassey	.03	.01	.00
☐ 400 Donnie Hill	.03	.01	.00
☐ 401 Bob James	.03	.01	.00
☐ 402 Dave LaPoint	.03	.01	.00
☐ 403 Bill Lindsey	.15	.07	.01
☐ 404 Bill Long	.15	.07	.01
☐ 405 Steve Lyons	.03	.01	.00
☐ 406 Fred Manrique	.15	.07	.01
☐ 407 Jack McDowell	.35	.17	.03
☐ 408 Gary Redus	.06	.03	.00
☐ 409 Ray Searage	.03	.01	.00
☐ 410 Bobby Thigpen	.03	.01	.00
☐ 411 Greg Walker	.08	.04	.01
☐ 412 Kenny Williams	.35	.17	.03
☐ 413 Jim Winn	.03	.01	.00
☐ 414 Jody Davis	.08	.04	.01
☐ 415 Andre Dawson	.25	.12	.02
☐ 416 Brian Dayett	.03	.01	.00
☐ 417 Bob Dernier	.03	.01	.00
☐ 418 Frank DiPino	.03	.01	.00
☐ 419 Shawon Dunston	.06	.03	.00
☐ 420 Leon Durham	.08	.04	.01
☐ 421 Les Lancaster	.15	.07	.01
☐ 422 Ed Lynch	.03	.01	.00
☐ 423 Greg Maddux	.10	.05	.01
☐ 424 Dave Martinez	.10	.05	.01
☐ 425 Keith Moreland	.10	.05	.01
(photo actually			
Jody Davis)			
☐ 426 Jamie Moyer	.03	.01	.00
☐ 427 Jerry Mumphrey	.03	.01	.00
☐ 428 Paul Noce	.15	.07	.01
☐ 429 Rafael Palmeiro	.20	.10	.02
☐ 430 Wade Rowdon	.10	.05	.01
☐ 431 Ryne Sandberg	.20	.10	.02
☐ 432 Scott Sanderson	.03	.01	.00
☐ 433 Lee Smith	.08	.04	.01
☐ 434 Jim Sundberg	.06	.03	.00
☐ 435 Rick Sutcliffe	.10	.05	.01
☐ 436 Manny Trillo	.03	.01	.00
☐ 437 Juan Agosto	.03	.01	.00
☐ 438 Larry Andersen	.03	.01	.00
☐ 439 Alan Ashby	.03	.01	.00
☐ 440 Kevin Bass	.08	.04	.01
☐ 441 Ken Caminiti	.35	.17	.03
☐ 442 Rocky Childress	.15	.07	.01
☐ 443 Jose Cruz	.06	.03	.00
☐ 444 Danny Darwin	.06	.03	.00
☐ 445 Glenn Davis	.15	.07	.01
☐ 446 Jim Deshaies	.06	.03	.00
☐ 447 Bill Doran	.08	.04	.01
☐ 448 Ty Gainey	.08	.04	.01
☐ 449 Billy Hatcher	.08	.04	.01
☐ 450 Jeff Heathcock	.03	.01	.00
☐ 451 Bob Knepper	.06	.03	.00
☐ 452 Rob Mallicoat	.15	.07	.01
☐ 453 Dave Meads	.12	.06	.01
☐ 454 Craig Reynolds	.03	.01	.00
☐ 455 Nolan Ryan	.25	.12	.02
☐ 456 Mike Scott	.15	.07	.01
☐ 457 Dave Smith	.06	.03	.00
☐ 458 Denny Walling	.03	.01	.00

☐ 459 Robbie Wine	.20	.10	.02
☐ 460 Gerald Young	.30	.15	.03
☐ 461 Bob Brower	.12	.06	.01
☐ 462A Jerry Browne ERR	5.00	.75	.15
(photo actually			
Bob Brower)			
☐ 462B Jerry Browne COR	.15	.07	.01
☐ 463 Steve Buechele	.03	.01	.00
☐ 464 Edwin Correa	.06	.03	.00
☐ 465 Cecil Espy	.15	.07	.01
☐ 466 Scott Fletcher	.06	.03	.00
☐ 467 Jose Guzman	.03	.01	.00
☐ 468 Greg Harris	.03	.01	.00
☐ 469 Charlie Hough	.06	.03	.00
☐ 470 Pete Incaviglia	.20	.10	.02
☐ 471 Paul Kilgus	.15	.07	.01
☐ 472 Mike Loynd	.03	.01	.00
☐ 473 Oddibe McDowell	.10	.05	.01
☐ 474 Dale Mohorcic	.06	.03	.00
☐ 475 Pete O'Brien	.10	.05	.01
☐ 476 Larry Parrish	.06	.03	.00
☐ 477 Geno Petralli	.03	.01	.00
☐ 478 Jeff Russell	.03	.01	.00
☐ 479 Ruben Sierra	.30	.15	.03
☐ 480 Mike Stanley	.06	.03	.00
☐ 481 Curtis Wilkerson	.03	.01	.00
☐ 482 Mitch Williams	.03	.01	.00
☐ 483 Bobby Witt	.06	.03	.00
☐ 484 Tony Armas	.06	.03	.00
☐ 485 Bob Boone	.06	.03	.00
☐ 486 Bill Buckner	.06	.03	.00
☐ 487 DeWayne Buice	.20	.10	.02
☐ 488 Brian Downing	.06	.03	.00
☐ 489 Chuck Finley	.03	.01	.00
☐ 490 Willie Fraser	.03	.01	.00
☐ 491 Jack Howell	.06	.03	.00
☐ 492 Ruppert Jones	.03	.01	.00
☐ 493 Wally Joyner	.60	.30	.06
☐ 494 Jack Lazorko	.08	.04	.01
☐ 495 Gary Lucas	.03	.01	.00
☐ 496 Kirk McCaskill	.06	.03	.00
☐ 497 Mark McLemore	.03	.01	.00
☐ 498 Darrell Miller	.06	.03	.00
☐ 499 Greg Minton	.03	.01	.00
☐ 500 Donnie Moore	.06	.03	.00
☐ 501 Gus Polidor	.03	.01	.00
☐ 502 Johnny Ray	.08	.04	.01
☐ 503 Mark Ryal	.08	.04	.01
☐ 504 Dick Schofield	.03	.01	.00
☐ 505 Don Sutton	.12	.06	.01
☐ 506 Devon White	.20	.10	.02
☐ 507 Mike Witt	.10	.05	.01
☐ 508 Dave Anderson	.03	.01	.00
☐ 509 Tim Belcher	.10	.05	.01
☐ 510 Ralph Bryant	.06	.03	.00
☐ 511 Tim Crews	.15	.07	.01
☐ 512 Mike Devereaux	.30	.15	.03
☐ 513 Mariano Duncan	.03	.01	.00
☐ 514 Pedro Guerrero	.20	.10	.02
☐ 515 Jeff Hamilton	.10	.05	.01
☐ 516 Mickey Hatcher	.03	.01	.00
☐ 517 Brad Havens	.03	.01	.00
☐ 518 Orel Hershiser	.15	.07	.01
☐ 519 Shawn Hillegas	.25	.12	.02
☐ 520 Ken Howell	.03	.01	.00
☐ 521 Tim Leary	.03	.01	.00
☐ 522 Mike Marshall	.10	.05	.01
☐ 523 Steve Sax	.10	.05	.01
☐ 524 Mike Scioscia	.03	.01	.00
☐ 525 Mike Sharperson	.08	.04	.01
☐ 526 John Shelby	.03	.01	.00
☐ 527 Franklin Stubbs	.06	.03	.00
☐ 528 Fernando Valenzuela	.20	.10	.02
☐ 529 Bob Welch	.06	.03	.00
☐ 530 Matt Young	.03	.01	.00
☐ 531 Jim Acker	.03	.01	.00
☐ 532 Paul Assenmacher	.03	.01	.00
☐ 533 Jeff Blauser	.25	.12	.02
☐ 534 Joe Boever	.15	.07	.01
☐ 535 Martin Clary	.08	.04	.01
☐ 536 Kevin Coffman	.15	.07	.01
☐ 537 Jeff Dedmon	.03	.01	.00
☐ 538 Ronnie Gant	.20	.10	.02
☐ 539 Tom Glavine	.20	.10	.02
☐ 540 Ken Griffey	.06	.03	.00
☐ 541 Albert Hall	.03	.01	.00
☐ 542 Glenn Hubbard	.03	.01	.00
☐ 543 Dion James	.06	.03	.00
☐ 544 Dale Murphy	.35	.17	.03
☐ 545 Ken Oberkfell	.03	.01	.00
☐ 546 David Palmer	.03	.01	.00
☐ 547 Gerald Perry	.06	.03	.00
☐ 548 Charlie Puleo	.03	.01	.00
☐ 549 Ted Simmons	.08	.04	.01
☐ 550 Zane Smith	.08	.04	.01

☐ 551	Andres Thomas	.03	.01	.00
☐ 552	Ozzie Virgil	.03	.01	.00
☐ 553	Don Aase	.06	.03	.00
☐ 554	Jeff Ballard	.15	.07	.01
☐ 555	Eric Bell	.08	.04	.01
☐ 556	Mike Boddicker	.06	.03	.00
☐ 557	Ken Dixon	.03	.01	.00
☐ 558	Jim Dwyer	.03	.01	.00
☐ 559	Ken Gerhart	.10	.05	.01
☐ 560	Rene Gonzales	.15	.07	.01
☐ 561	Mike Griffin	.03	.01	.00
☐ 562	John Habyan	.08	.04	.01
☐ 563	Terry Kennedy	.06	.03	.00
☐ 564	Ray Knight	.06	.03	.00
☐ 565	Lee Lacy	.06	.03	.00
☐ 566	Fred Lynn	.12	.06	.01
☐ 567	Eddie Murray	.25	.12	.02
☐ 568	Tom Niedenfuer	.06	.03	.00
☐ 569	Bill Ripken	.35	.17	.03
☐ 570	Cal Ripken Jr.	.25	.12	.02
☐ 571	Dave Schmidt	.06	.03	.00
☐ 572	Larry Sheets	.10	.05	.01
☐ 573	Pete Stanicek	.30	.15	.03
☐ 574	Mark Williamson	.15	.07	.01
☐ 575	Mike Young	.06	.03	.00
☐ 576	Shawn Abner	.30	.15	.03
☐ 577	Greg Booker	.03	.01	.00
☐ 578	Chris Brown	.10	.05	.01
☐ 579	Keith Comstock	.20	.10	.02
☐ 580	Joey Cora	.15	.07	.01
☐ 581	Mark Davis	.03	.01	.00
☐ 582	Tim Flannery	.03	.01	.00
☐ 583	Goose Gossage	.10	.05	.01
☐ 584	Mark Grant	.08	.04	.01
☐ 585	Tony Gwynn	.35	.17	.03
☐ 586	Andy Hawkins	.03	.01	.00
☐ 587	Stan Jefferson	.15	.07	.01
☐ 588	Jimmy Jones	.06	.03	.00
☐ 589	John Kruk	.20	.10	.02
☐ 590	Shane Mack	.35	.17	.03
☐ 591	Carmelo Martinez	.03	.01	.00
☐ 592	Lance McCullers	.03	.01	.00
☐ 593	Eric Nolte	.15	.07	.01
☐ 594	Randy Ready	.03	.01	.00
☐ 595	Luis Salazar	.03	.01	.00
☐ 596	Benito Santiago	.60	.30	.06
☐ 597	Eric Show	.03	.01	.00
☐ 598	Garry Templeton	.06	.03	.00
☐ 599	Ed Whitson	.03	.01	.00
☐ 600	Scott Bailes	.03	.01	.00
☐ 601	Chris Bando	.03	.01	.00
☐ 602	Jay Bell	.30	.15	.03
☐ 603	Brett Butler	.08	.04	.01
☐ 604	Tom Candiotti	.03	.01	.00
☐ 605	Joe Carter	.12	.06	.01
☐ 606	Carmen Castillo	.03	.01	.00
☐ 607	Brian Dorsett	.15	.07	.01
☐ 608	John Farrell	.25	.12	.02
☐ 609	Julio Franco	.08	.04	.01
☐ 610	Mel Hall	.06	.03	.00
☐ 611	Tommy Hinzo	.20	.10	.02
☐ 612	Brook Jacoby	.10	.05	.01
☐ 613	Doug Jones	.15	.07	.01
☐ 614	Ken Schrom	.03	.01	.00
☐ 615	Cory Snyder	.25	.12	.02
☐ 616	Sammy Stewart	.03	.01	.00
☐ 617	Greg Swindell	.10	.05	.01
☐ 618	Pat Tabler	.08	.04	.01
☐ 619	Ed VandeBerg	.03	.01	.00
☐ 620	Eddie Williams	.30	.15	.03
☐ 621	Rich Yett	.03	.01	.00
☐ 622	Slugging Sophomores Wally Joyner Cory Snyder	.40	.20	.04
☐ 623	Dominican Dynamite George Bell Pedro Guerrero	.10	.05	.01
☐ 624	Oakland's Power Team Mark McGwire Jose Canseco	.50	.25	.05
☐ 625	Classic Relief Dave Righetti Dan Plesac	.10	.05	.01
☐ 626	All Star Righties Bret Saberhagen Mike Witt1 Jack Morris	.10	.05	.01
☐ 627	Game Closers John Franco Steve Bedrosian	.08	.04	.01
☐ 628	Masters/Double Play Ozzie Smith Ryne Sandberg	.10	.05	.01
☐ 629	Rookie Record Setter Mark McGwire	.50	.25	.05

☐ 630	Changing the Guard Mike Greenwell Ellis Burks Todd Benzinger	.40	.20	.04
☐ 631	NL Batting Champs Tony Gwynn Tim Raines	.20	.10	.02
☐ 632	Pitching Magic Mike Scott Orel Hershiser	.12	.06	.01
☐ 633	Big Bats at First Pat Tabler Mark McGwire	.35	.17	.03
☐ 634	Hitting King/Thief Tony Gwynn Vince Coleman	.15	.07	.01
☐ 635	Slugging Shortstops Tony Fernandez Cal Ripken Alan Trammell	.15	.07	.01
☐ 636	Tried/True Sluggers Mike Schmidt Gary Carter	.15	.07	.01
☐ 637	Crunch Time Darryl Strawberry Eric Davis	.30	.15	.03
☐ 638	AL All-Stars Matt Nokes Kirby Puckett	.30	.15	.03
☐ 639	NL All-Stars Keith Hernandez Dale Murphy	.15	.07	.01
☐ 640	The O's Brothers Billy Ripken Cal Ripken	.10	.05	.01
☐ 641	Mark Grace and Darrin Jackson	.50	.25	.05
☐ 642	Damon Berryhill and Jeff Montgomery	.30	.15	.03
☐ 643	Felix Fermin and Jesse Reid	.20	.10	.02
☐ 644	Greg Myers and Greg Tabor	.30	.15	.03
☐ 645	Joey Meyer and Jim Eppard	.30	.15	.03
☐ 646	Adam Peterson and Randy Velarde	.30	.15	.03
☐ 647	Peter Smith and Chris Gwynn	.50	.25	.05
☐ 648	Tom Newell and Greg Jelks	.30	.15	.03
☐ 649	Mario Diaz and Clay Parker	.30	.15	.03
☐ 650	Jack Savage and Todd Simmons	.30	.15	.03
☐ 651	John Burkett and Kirt Manwaring	.35	.17	.03
☐ 652	Dave Otto and Walt Weiss	.35	.17	.03
☐ 653	Jeff King and Randell Byers	.30	.15	.03
☐ 654	CL: Twins/Cards Tigers/Giants	.06	.01	.00
☐ 655	CL: Blue Jays/Mets Brewers/Expos	.06	.01	.00
☐ 656	CL: Yankees/Reds Royals/A's	.06	.01	.00
☐ 657	CL: Phillies/Pirates Red Sox/Mariners	.06	.01	.00
☐ 658	CL: White Sox/Cubs Astros/Rangers	.06	.01	.00
☐ 659	CL: Angels/Dodgers Braves/Orioles	.06	.01	.00
☐ 660	CL: Padres/Indians Rookies/Specials	.06	.01	.00

1988 Fleer Wax Box Cards

The cards in this 16-card set measure the standard 2 1/2" by 3 1/2". Cards have essentially the same design as the 1988 Fleer regular issue set. The cards were printed on the bottoms of the regular issue wax pack boxes. These 16 cards (C1 to C16) are considered a separate set in their own right and are not typically included in a complete set of the regular issue 1988 Fleer cards. The value of the panel uncut is slightly greater, perhaps by 25% greater, than the

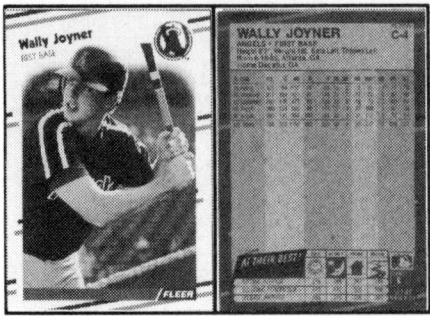

value of the individual cards cut up carefully.

	MINT	EXC	G-VG
COMPLETE SET	3.00	1.50	.30
COMMON PLAYERS	.10	.05	.01
☐ C1 Cardinals Logo	.10	.05	.01
☐ C2 Dwight Evans	.15	.07	.01
☐ C3 Andres Galarraga	.15	.07	.01
☐ C4 Wally Joyner	.50	.25	.05
☐ C5 Twins Logo	.10	.05	.01
☐ C6 Dale Murphy	.35	.17	.03
☐ C7 Kirby Puckett	.30	.15	.03
☐ C8 Shane Rawley	.15	.07	.01
☐ C9 Giants Logo	.10	.05	.01
☐ C10 Ryne Sandberg	.25	.12	.02
☐ C11 Mike Schmidt	.40	.20	.04
☐ C12 Kevin Seitzer	.75	.35	.07
☐ C13 Tigers Logo	.10	.05	.01
☐ C14 Dave Stewart	.15	.07	.01
☐ C15 Tim Wallach	.15	.07	.01
☐ C16 Todd Worrell	.20	.10	.02

1988 Fleer All-Star Inserts

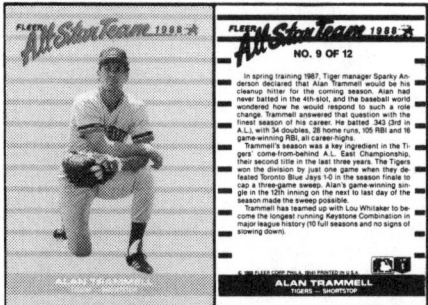

The cards in this 12-card set measure the standard 2 1/2" by 3 1/2". These cards were inserted (randomly) in wax and cello packs of the 1988 Fleer regular issue set. The cards show the player silhouetted against a light green background with dark green stripes. The player's name, team, and position are printed in yellow at the bottom of the obverse. The card backs are done predominantly in green, white, and black. Cards are numbered on the back. These 12 cards are considered a separate set in their own right and are not typically included in a complete set of the regular issue 1988 Fleer cards. The players are the "best" at each position, three pitchers, eight position players, and a designated hitter.

	MINT	EXC	G-VG
COMPLETE SET	10.00	5.00	1.00
COMMON PLAYERS	.25	.12	.02

☐ 1	Matt Nokes	1.25	.60	.12
	Catcher			
☐ 2	Tom Henke	.25	.12	.02
	Relief Pitcher			
☐ 3	Ted Higuera	.45	.22	.04
	Left Hand Pitcher			
☐ 4	Roger Clemens	1.50	.75	.15
	Right Hand Pitcher			
☐ 5	George Bell	.60	.30	.06
	Outfielder			
☐ 6	Andre Dawson	.60	.30	.06
	Outfielder			
☐ 7	Eric Davis	2.00	1.00	.20
	Outfielder			
☐ 8	Wade Boggs	2.00	1.00	.20
	Third Baseman			
☐ 9	Alan Trammell	.60	.30	.06
	Shortstop			
☐ 10	Juan Samuel	.35	.17	.03
	Second Baseman			
☐ 11	Jack Clark	.60	.30	.06
	First Baseman			
☐ 12	Paul Molitor	.45	.22	.04
	Designated Hitter			

1988 Fleer Headliners

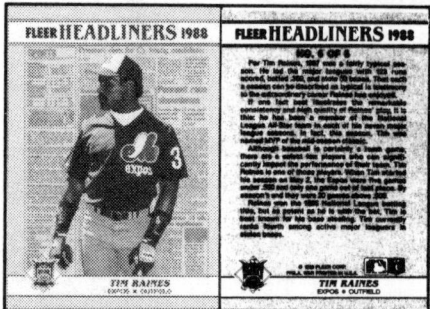

This six-card set was distributed as a special insert in rack packs. The obverse features the player photo superimposed on a gray newsprint background. Cards are 2 1/2" by 3 1/2". The cards are printed in red, black, and white on the back describing why that particular player made headlines the previous season. The cards are numbered on the back.

	MINT	EXC	G-VG
COMPLETE SET	5.00	2.50	.50
COMMON PLAYER	.60	.30	.06
☐ 1 Don Mattingly	2.50	1.25	.25
☐ 2 Mark McGwire	1.50	.75	.15
☐ 3 Jack Morris	.60	.30	.06
☐ 4 Darryl Strawberry	1.00	.50	.10
☐ 5 Dwight Gooden	1.00	.50	.10
☐ 6 Tim Raines	.80	.40	.08

1928 Fro Joy

The cards in this 6-card set measure 2 1/16" by 4". The Fro Joy set of 1928 was designed to exploit the advertising potential of the mighty Babe Ruth. Six black and white cards explained specific baseball techniques while the reverse advertising extolled the virtues of Fro Joy ice cream and ice cream cones.

	NRMT	VG-E	GOOD
COMPLETE SET	750.00	375.00	75.00
COMMON PLAYER (1-6)	100.00	50.00	10.00
☐ 1 George Herman	150.00	75.00	15.00
(Babe) Ruth			
☐ 2 Look Out,	100.00	50.00	10.00

Boys—Girls:

Fro-joy Ice Cream, in Fro-joy Cones, builds bone and strength. Eat one every day.

Chock-full of

"YOUTH UNITS"

PICTURE NO. 1

This is the first in a series of six pictures of "Babe" Ruth being given free with Fro-joy Cone Work, August 6th-11th, 1928. The complete set can be secured for a large reproduction of "Babe" Ruth's autographed photo. Ask your dealer for a FREE circular giving full details.

George Herman ("Babe") Ruth

			MINT	EXC	G-VG
		Mr. Pitcher			
☐	3	Bang; The Babe Lines one out	100.00	50.00	10.00
☐	4	When the Babe Comes Out	100.00	50.00	10.00
☐	5	Babe Ruth's Grip	100.00	50.00	10.00
☐	6	Ruth is a Crack Fielder	100.00	50.00	10.00

1983 Gardner's Brewers

The cards in this 22-card set measure 2 1/2" by 3 1/2". The 1983 Gardner's Brewers set features Milwaukee Brewer players and manager Harvey Kuenn. Topps printed the set for the Madison (Wisconsin) bakery, hence, the backs are identical to the 1983 Topps backs except for the card number. The fronts of the cards, however, feature all new photos and include the Gardner's logo and the Brewers' logo. Many of the cards are grease laden, as they were issued with packages of bread and hamburger and hot- dog buns.

			MINT	EXC	G-VG
		COMPLETE SET	20.00	10.00	2.00
		COMMON PLAYER	.40	.20	.04
☐	1	Harvey Kuenn MG	1.00	.50	.10
☐	2	Dwight Bernard	.40	.20	.04
☐	3	Mark Brouhard	.40	.20	.04
☐	4	Mike Caldwell	.60	.30	.06
☐	5	Cecil Cooper	1.50	.75	.15
☐	6	Marshall Edwards	.40	.20	.04
☐	7	Rollie Fingers	3.00	1.50	.30
☐	8	Jim Gantner	.60	.30	.06
☐	9	Moose Haas	.60	.30	.06
☐	10	Bob McClure	.40	.20	.04
☐	11	Paul Molitor	3.00	1.50	.30
☐	12	Don Money	.60	.30	.06
☐	13	Charlie Moore	.60	.30	.06
☐	14	Ben Oglivie	.60	.30	.06
☐	15	Ed Romero	.40	.20	.04

			MINT	EXC	G-VG
☐	16	Ted Simmons	1.50	.75	.15
☐	17	Jim Slaton	.60	.30	.06
☐	18	Don Sutton	3.00	1.50	.30
☐	19	Gorman Thomas	1.00	.50	.10
☐	20	Pete Vuckovich	.60	.30	.06
☐	21	Ned Yost	.40	.20	.04
☐	22	Robin Yount	5.00	2.50	.50

1984 Gardner's Brewers

The cards in this 22 card set measure 2 1/2" by 3 1/2". For the second year in a row, the Gardner Bakery Company issued a set of cards available in packages of Gardner Bakery products. The set was manufactured by Topps, and the backs of the cards are identical to the Topps cards of this year except for the numbers. The Gardner logo appears on the fronts of the cards with the player's name, position abbreviation, the name Brewers, and the words 1984 Series II.

			MINT	EXC	G-VG
		COMPLETE SET (22)	10.00	5.00	1.00
		COMMON PLAYER	.30	.15	.03
☐	1	Rene Lachemann MG	.40	.20	.04
☐	2	Mark Brouhard	.30	.15	.03
☐	3	Mike Caldwell	.40	.20	.04
☐	4	Bobby Clark	.30	.15	.03
☐	5	Cecil Cooper	.90	.45	.09
☐	6	Rollie Fingers	1.75	.85	.17
☐	7	Jim Gantner	.50	.25	.05
☐	8	Moose Haas	.40	.20	.04
☐	9	Roy Howell	.30	.15	.03
☐	10	Pete Ladd	.30	.15	.03
☐	11	Rick Manning	.30	.15	.03
☐	12	Bob McClure	.30	.15	.03
☐	13	Paul Molitor	1.75	.85	.17
☐	14	Charlie Moore	.40	.20	.04
☐	15	Ben Oglivie	.50	.25	.05
☐	16	Ed Romero	.30	.15	.03
☐	17	Ted Simmons	.90	.45	.09
☐	18	Jim Sundberg	.40	.20	.04
☐	19	Don Sutton	1.75	.85	.17
☐	20	Tom Tellman	.30	.15	.03
☐	21	Pete Vuckovich	.50	.25	.05
☐	22	Robin Yount	3.00	1.50	.30

1985 Gardner's Brewers

The cards in this 22 card set measure 2 1/2" by 3 1/2". For the third year in a row, the Gardner Bakery Company issued a set of cards available in packages of Gardner Bakery products. The set was manufactured by Topps, and the backs of the cards are identical to the Topps cards of this year except for the card numbers and copyright information. The Gardner logo appears on the fronts of the cards with the player's name, position abbreviation, and the name Brewers.

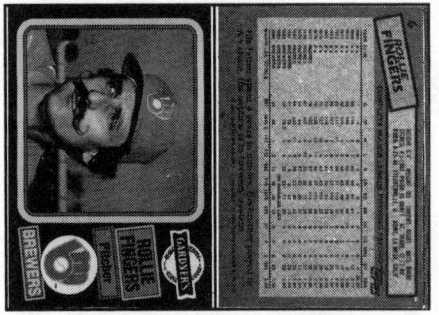

	MINT	EXC	G-VG
COMPLETE SET	9.00	4.50	.90
COMMON PLAYER	.30	.15	.03

		MINT	EXC	G-VG
☐	1 George Bamberger MG	.40	.20	.04
☐	2 Mark Brouhard	.30	.15	.03
☐	3 Bobby Clark	.30	.15	.03
☐	4 Jaime Cocanower	.30	.15	.03
☐	5 Cecil Cooper	.90	.45	.09
☐	6 Rollie Fingers	1.75	.85	.17
☐	7 Jim Gantner	.40	.20	.04
☐	8 Moose Haas	.40	.20	.04
☐	9 Dion James	.50	.25	.05
☐	10 Pete Ladd	.30	.15	.03
☐	11 Rick Manning	.30	.15	.03
☐	12 Bob McClure	.30	.15	.03
☐	13 Paul Molitor	1.75	.85	.17
☐	14 Charlie Moore	.40	.20	.04
☐	15 Ben Oglivie	.40	.20	.04
☐	16 Chuck Porter	.30	.15	.03
☐	17 Ed Romero	.30	.15	.03
☐	18 Bill Schroeder	.40	.20	.04
☐	19 Ted Simmons	.90	.45	.09
☐	20 Tom Tellman	.30	.15	.03
☐	21 Pete Vuckovich	.40	.20	.04
☐	22 Robin Yount	3.00	1.50	.30

1987 Gatorade Indians

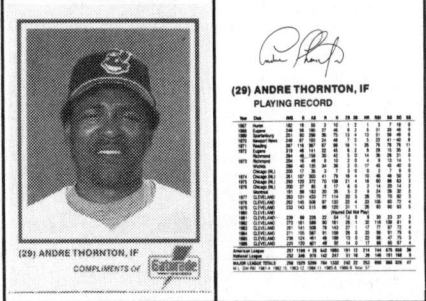

Gatorade sponsored this perforated set of 30 full-color cards of the Cleveland Indians. The cards measure 2 1/8" by 3" (or 3 1/8") and feature the Gatorade logo prominently on the fronts of the cards. The cards were distributed as a tri-folded sheet (each part approximately 9 5/8" by 11 3/16") on April 25th at the stadium during the game against the Yankees. The large team photo is approximately 11 3/16" by 9 5/8". Card backs for the individual players contain year-by-year stats for that player.

	MINT	EXC	G-VG
COMPLETE SET (30)	5.00	2.50	.50
COMMON PLAYER	.15	.07	.01

		MINT	EXC	G-VG
☐	2 Brett Butler	.25	.12	.02

☐	4 Tony Bernazard	.15	.07	.01
☐	6 Andy Allanson	.15	.07	.01
☐	7 Pat Corrales MG	.15	.07	.01
☐	8 Carmen Castillo	.15	.07	.01
☐	10 Pat Tabler	.25	.12	.02
☐	11 Jamie Easterly	.15	.07	.01
☐	12 Dave Clark	.25	.12	.02
☐	13 Ernie Camacho	.15	.07	.01
☐	14 Julio Franco	.25	.12	.02
☐	17 Junior Noboa	.15	.07	.01
☐	18 Ken Schrom	.15	.07	.01
☐	20 Otis Nixon	.15	.07	.01
☐	21 Greg Swindell	.25	.12	.02
☐	22 Frank Wills	.15	.07	.01
☐	23 Chris Bando	.15	.07	.01
☐	24 Rick Dempsey	.15	.07	.01
☐	26 Brook Jacoby	.35	.17	.03
☐	27 Mel Hall	.25	.12	.02
☐	28 Cory Snyder	.50	.25	.05
☐	29 Andre Thornton	.25	.12	.02
☐	30 Joe Carter	.35	.17	.03
☐	35 Phil Niekro	.35	.17	.03
☐	36 Ed VandeBerg	.15	.07	.01
☐	42 Rich Yett	.15	.07	.01
☐	43 Scott Bailes	.15	.07	.01
☐	46 Doug Jones	.15	.07	.01
☐	49 Tom Candiotti	.15	.07	.01
☐	54 Tom Waddell	.15	.07	.01
☐	xx Indians MG/Coaches	.15	.07	.01
	Bobby Bonds 25			
	Johnny Goryl 45			
	Pat Corrales MG 7			
	Doc Edwards 32			
	Jack Aker 1			
☐	xx Team Photo	.15	.07	.01
	(large size)			

1953 Glendale

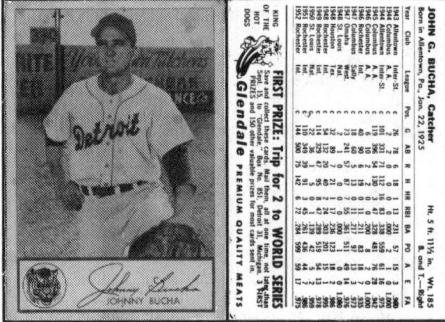

The cards in this 28 card set measure 2 5/8" by 3 3/4". The 1953 Glendale Meats set of full-color, unnumbered cards features Detroit Tiger ballplayers exclusively and was distributed one per package of Glendale Meats in the Detroit area. The back contains the complete major and minor league record through the 1952 season. The scarcer cards of the set command higher prices, with the Houtteman card being the most difficult to find. There is an album associated with the set (which also is quite scarce now). The ACC designation for this scarce regional set is F151. Since the cards are unnumbered, they are ordered below alphabetically.

	NRMT	VG-E	GOOD
COMPLETE SET	4200.00	1800.00	300.00
COMMON PLAYER (1-28)	100.00	50.00	10.00

		NRMT	VG-E	GOOD
☐	1 Matt Batts	100.00	50.00	10.00
☐	2 Johnny Bucha	100.00	50.00	10.00
☐	3 Frank Carswell	100.00	50.00	10.00
☐	4 Jim Delsing	100.00	50.00	10.00
☐	5 Walt Dropo	100.00	50.00	10.00
☐	6 Hal Erickson	100.00	50.00	10.00
☐	7 Paul Foytack	100.00	50.00	10.00
☐	8 Owen Friend	100.00	50.00	10.00
☐	9 Ned Garver	100.00	50.00	10.00
☐	10 Joe Ginsberg	300.00	150.00	30.00

		NRMT	VG-E	GOOD
☐ 11	Ted Gray	100.00	50.00	10.00
☐ 12	Fred Hatfield	100.00	50.00	10.00
☐ 13	Ray Herbert	100.00	50.00	10.00
☐ 14	Bill Hitchcock	100.00	50.00	10.00
☐ 15	Bill Hoeft	200.00	100.00	20.00
☐ 16	Art Houtteman	1800.00	750.00	150.00
☐ 17	Milt Jordan	150.00	75.00	15.00
☐ 18	Harvey Kuenn	200.00	100.00	20.00
☐ 19	Don Lund	100.00	50.00	10.00
☐ 20	Dave Madison	100.00	50.00	10.00
☐ 21	Dick Marlowe	100.00	50.00	10.00
☐ 22	Pat Mullin	100.00	50.00	10.00
☐ 23	Bob Nieman	100.00	50.00	10.00
☐ 24	Johnny Pesky	100.00	50.00	10.00
☐ 25	Jerry Priddy	100.00	50.00	10.00
☐ 26	Steve Souchock	100.00	50.00	10.00
☐ 27	Russ Sullivan	100.00	50.00	10.00
☐ 28	Bill Wight	150.00	75.00	15.00

1961 Golden Press

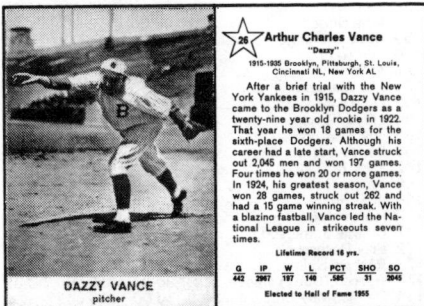

DAZZY VANCE
pitcher

The cards in this 33 card set measure 2 1/2" by 3 1/2". The 1961 Golden Press set of full color cards features members of Baseball's Hall of Fame. The cards came in a booklet with perforations for punching the cards out of the book. The catalog designation is W524. The price for the full book intact is 25% higher than the complete set price listed.

		NRMT	VG-E	GOOD
	COMPLETE SET	45.00	22.50	4.50
	COMMON PLAYER (1-33)	.50	.25	.05
☐ 1	Mel Ott	1.50	.75	.15
☐ 2	Grover C. Alexander	1.50	.75	.15
☐ 3	Babe Ruth	9.00	4.50	.90
☐ 4	Hank Greenberg	.75	.35	.07
☐ 5	Bill Terry	.75	.35	.07
☐ 6	Carl Hubbell	.75	.35	.07
☐ 7	Rogers Hornsby	2.00	1.00	.20
☐ 8	Dizzy Dean	3.50	1.75	.35
☐ 9	Joe DiMaggio	6.00	3.00	.60
☐ 10	Charlie Gehringer	.75	.35	.07
☐ 11	Gabby Hartnett	.50	.25	.05
☐ 12	Mickey Cochrane	.75	.35	.07
☐ 13	George Sisler	.65	.30	.06
☐ 14	Joe Cronin	.65	.30	.06
☐ 15	Pie Traynor	.65	.30	.06
☐ 16	Lou Gehrig	6.00	3.00	.60
☐ 17	Lefty Grove	1.25	.60	.12
☐ 18	Chief Bender	.50	.25	.05
☐ 19	Frankie Frisch	.65	.30	.06
☐ 20	Al Simmons	.50	.25	.05
☐ 21	Home Run Baker	.50	.25	.05
☐ 22	Jimmy Foxx	1.50	.75	.15
☐ 23	John McGraw	.75	.35	.07
☐ 24	Christy Mathewson	2.50	1.25	.25
☐ 25	Ty Cobb	6.00	3.00	.60
☐ 26	Dazzy Vance	.50	.25	.05
☐ 27	Bill Dickey	.75	.35	.07
☐ 28	Eddie Collins	.50	.25	.05
☐ 29	Walter Johnson	2.50	1.25	.25
☐ 30	Tris Speaker	1.25	.60	.12
☐ 31	Nap Lajoie	1.25	.60	.12
☐ 32	Honus Wagner	2.50	1.25	.25
☐ 33	Cy Young	1.50	.75	.15

1933 Goudey

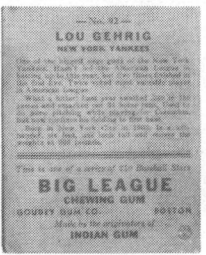

The cards in this 240 card set measure 2 3/8" by 2 7/8". The 1933 Goudey set, designated R319 by the ACC, was that company's first baseball issue. The four Babe Ruth and two Lou Gehrig cards in the set are extremely popular with collectors. Card number 106, Napoleon Lajoie, was not printed in 1933, and was circulated to a limited number of collectors in 1934 upon request (it was printed along with the 1934 Goudey cards). An album was offered to house the 1933 set. Several minor leaguers are depicted. Card number 1 (Bengough) is very rarely found in mint condition; in fact, as a general rule all the first series cards are more difficult to find in Mint condition. Players with more than one card are also sometimes differentiated below by their pose: BAT (Batting), FIELD (Fielding), PIT (Pitching), THROW (Throwing). One of the Babe Ruth cards was double printed (DP) apparently in place of the Lajoie and hence is easier to obtain than the others. Due to the scarcity of the Lajoie card, the set is considered complete at 239 cards and is priced as such below.

		NRMT	VG-E	GOOD
	COMPLETE SET (239)	18000.00	6000.00	1200.00
	COMMON PLAYER (1-40)	40.00	20.00	4.00
	COMMON PLAYER (41-44)	30.00	15.00	3.00
	COMMON PLAYER (45-52)	40.00	20.00	4.00
	COMMON PLAYER (53-240)	30.00	15.00	3.00
☐ 1	Benny Bengough	500.00	30.00	6.00
☐ 2	Dazzy Vance	80.00	40.00	8.00
☐ 3	Hugh Critz	40.00	20.00	4.00
☐ 4	Heine Schuble	40.00	20.00	4.00
☐ 5	Babe Herman	50.00	25.00	5.00
☐ 6	Jimmy Dykes	50.00	25.00	5.00
☐ 7	Ted Lyons	80.00	40.00	8.00
☐ 8	Roy Johnson	40.00	20.00	4.00
☐ 9	Dave Harris	40.00	20.00	4.00
☐ 10	Glenn Myatt	40.00	20.00	4.00
☐ 11	Billy Rogell	40.00	20.00	4.00
☐ 12	George Pipgras	40.00	20.00	4.00
☐ 13	Lafayette Thompson	40.00	20.00	4.00
☐ 14	Henry Johnson	40.00	20.00	4.00
☐ 15	Victor Sorrell	40.00	20.00	4.00
☐ 16	George Blaeholder	40.00	20.00	4.00
☐ 17	Watson Clark	40.00	20.00	4.00
☐ 18	Muddy Ruel	40.00	20.00	4.00
☐ 19	Bill Dickey	160.00	80.00	16.00
☐ 20	Bill Terry THROW	100.00	50.00	10.00
☐ 21	Phil Collins	40.00	20.00	4.00
☐ 22	Pie Traynor	100.00	50.00	10.00
☐ 23	Kiki Cuyler	80.00	40.00	8.00
☐ 24	Horace Ford	40.00	20.00	4.00
☐ 25	Paul Waner	80.00	40.00	8.00
☐ 26	Chalmer Cissell	40.00	20.00	4.00
☐ 27	George Connally	40.00	20.00	4.00
☐ 28	Dick Bartell	40.00	20.00	4.00
☐ 29	Jimmy Foxx	160.00	80.00	16.00
☐ 30	Frank Hogan	40.00	20.00	4.00
☐ 31	Tony Lazzeri	60.00	30.00	6.00
☐ 32	Bud Clancy	40.00	20.00	4.00
☐ 33	Ralph Kress	40.00	20.00	4.00
☐ 34	Bob O'Farrell	40.00	20.00	4.00
☐ 35	Al Simmons	100.00	50.00	10.00
☐ 36	Tommy Thevenow	40.00	20.00	4.00
☐ 37	Jimmy Wilson	40.00	20.00	4.00
☐ 38	Fred Bickell	40.00	20.00	4.00

☐ 39	Mark Koenig	40.00	20.00	4.00	
☐ 40	Taylor Douthit	40.00	20.00	4.00	
☐ 41	Gus Mancuso	30.00	15.00	3.00	
☐ 42	Eddie Collins	70.00	35.00	7.00	
☐ 43	Lew Fonseca	30.00	15.00	3.00	
☐ 44	Jim Bottomley	60.00	30.00	6.00	
☐ 45	Larry Benton	40.00	20.00	4.00	
☐ 46	Ethan Allen	40.00	20.00	4.00	
☐ 47	Heine Manush BAT	80.00	40.00	8.00	
☐ 48	Marty McManus	40.00	20.00	4.00	
☐ 49	Frank Frisch	100.00	50.00	10.00	
☐ 50	Ed Brandt	40.00	20.00	4.00	
☐ 51	Charlie Grimm	50.00	25.00	5.00	
☐ 52	Andy Cohen	40.00	20.00	4.00	
☐ 53	Babe Ruth	2200.00	850.00	150.00	
☐ 54	Ray Kremer	30.00	15.00	3.00	
☐ 55	Pat Malone	30.00	15.00	3.00	
☐ 56	Charlie Ruffing	70.00	35.00	7.00	
☐ 57	Earl Clark	30.00	15.00	3.00	
☐ 58	Lefty O'Doul	40.00	20.00	4.00	
☐ 59	Bing Miller	30.00	15.00	3.00	
☐ 60	Waite Hoyt	60.00	30.00	6.00	
☐ 61	Max Bishop	30.00	15.00	3.00	
☐ 62	Pepper Martin	40.00	20.00	4.00	
☐ 63	Joe Cronin BAT	70.00	35.00	7.00	
☐ 64	Burleigh Grimes	60.00	30.00	6.00	
☐ 65	Milt Gaston	30.00	15.00	3.00	
☐ 66	George Grantham	30.00	15.00	3.00	
☐ 67	Guy Bush	30.00	15.00	3.00	
☐ 68	Horace Lisenbee	30.00	15.00	3.00	
☐ 69	Randy Moore	30.00	15.00	3.00	
☐ 70	Floyd (Pete) Scott	30.00	15.00	3.00	
☐ 71	Robert J. Burke	30.00	15.00	3.00	
☐ 72	Owen Carroll	30.00	15.00	3.00	
☐ 73	Jess Haines	60.00	30.00	6.00	
☐ 74	Eppa Rixey	60.00	30.00	6.00	
☐ 75	Willie Kamm	30.00	15.00	3.00	
☐ 76	Mickey Cochrane	80.00	40.00	8.00	
☐ 77	Adam Comorosky	30.00	15.00	3.00	
☐ 78	Jack Quinn	30.00	15.00	3.00	
☐ 79	Red Faber	60.00	30.00	6.00	
☐ 80	Clyde Manion	30.00	15.00	3.00	
☐ 81	Sam Jones	30.00	15.00	3.00	
☐ 82	Dibrell Williams	30.00	15.00	3.00	
☐ 83	Pete Jablonowski	30.00	15.00	3.00	
☐ 84	Glenn Spencer	30.00	15.00	3.00	
☐ 85	Heine Sand	30.00	15.00	3.00	
☐ 86	Phil Todt	30.00	15.00	3.00	
☐ 87	Frank O'Rourke	30.00	15.00	3.00	
☐ 88	Russell Rollings	30.00	15.00	3.00	
☐ 89	Tris Speaker	160.00	80.00	16.00	
☐ 90	Jess Petty	30.00	15.00	3.00	
☐ 91	Tom Zachary	30.00	15.00	3.00	
☐ 92	Lou Gehrig	900.00	450.00	90.00	
☐ 93	John Welch	30.00	15.00	3.00	
☐ 94	Bill Walker	30.00	15.00	3.00	
☐ 95	Alvin Crowder	30.00	15.00	3.00	
☐ 96	Willis Hudlin	30.00	15.00	3.00	
☐ 97	Joe Morrissey	30.00	15.00	3.00	
☐ 98	Walter Berger	30.00	15.00	3.00	
☐ 99	Tony Cuccinello	30.00	15.00	3.00	
☐ 100	George Uhle	30.00	15.00	3.00	
☐ 101	Richard Coffman	30.00	15.00	3.00	
☐ 102	Travis Jackson	60.00	30.00	6.00	
☐ 103	Earl Combs	60.00	30.00	6.00	
☐ 104	Fred Marberry	30.00	15.00	3.00	
☐ 105	Bernie Friberg	30.00	15.00	3.00	
☐ 106	Napoleon Lajoie	9000.00	3600.00	750.00	
	(not issued until 1934)				
☐ 107	Heine Manush	70.00	35.00	7.00	
☐ 108	Joe Kuhel	30.00	15.00	3.00	
☐ 109	Joe Cronin	70.00	35.00	7.00	
☐ 110	Goose Goslin	60.00	30.00	6.00	
☐ 111	Monte Weaver	30.00	15.00	3.00	
☐ 112	Fred Schulte	30.00	15.00	3.00	
☐ 113	Oswald Bluege	30.00	15.00	3.00	
☐ 114	Luke Sewell	30.00	15.00	3.00	
☐ 115	Cliff Heathcote	30.00	15.00	3.00	
☐ 116	Eddie Morgan	30.00	15.00	3.00	
☐ 117	Rabbit Maranville	60.00	30.00	6.00	
☐ 118	Val Picinich	30.00	15.00	3.00	
☐ 119	Rogers Hornsby FIELD	160.00	80.00	16.00	
☐ 120	Carl Reynolds	30.00	15.00	3.00	
☐ 121	Walter Stewart	30.00	15.00	3.00	
☐ 122	Alvin Crowder	30.00	15.00	3.00	
☐ 123	Jack Russell	30.00	15.00	3.00	
☐ 124	Earl Whitehill	30.00	15.00	3.00	
☐ 125	Bill Terry	100.00	50.00	10.00	
☐ 126	Joe Moore	30.00	15.00	3.00	
☐ 127	Mel Ott	125.00	60.00	12.50	
☐ 128	Chuck Klein	80.00	40.00	8.00	
☐ 129	Hal Schumacher PIT	30.00	15.00	3.00	
☐ 130	Fred Fitzsimmons	30.00	15.00	3.00	
☐ 131	Fred Frankhouse	30.00	15.00	3.00	
☐ 132	Jim Elliott	30.00	15.00	3.00	
☐ 133	Fred Lindstrom	60.00	30.00	6.00	
☐ 134	Sam Rice	60.00	30.00	6.00	
☐ 135	Woody English	30.00	15.00	3.00	
☐ 136	Flint Rhem	30.00	15.00	3.00	
☐ 137	Fred (Red) Lucas	30.00	15.00	3.00	
☐ 138	Herb Pennock	60.00	30.00	6.00	
☐ 139	Ben Cantwell	30.00	15.00	3.00	
☐ 140	Bump Hadley	30.00	15.00	3.00	
☐ 141	Ray Benge	30.00	15.00	3.00	
☐ 142	Paul Richards	30.00	15.00	3.00	
☐ 143	Glenn Wright	30.00	15.00	3.00	
☐ 144	Babe Ruth BAT DP	1800.00	750.00	150.00	
☐ 145	George Walberg	30.00	15.00	3.00	
☐ 146	Walter Stewart PIT	30.00	15.00	3.00	
☐ 147	Leo Durocher	60.00	30.00	6.00	
☐ 148	Eddie Farrell	30.00	15.00	3.00	
☐ 149	Babe Ruth	2200.00	850.00	150.00	
☐ 150	Ray Kolp	30.00	15.00	3.00	
☐ 151	Jake Flowers	30.00	15.00	3.00	
☐ 152	Zack Taylor	30.00	15.00	3.00	
☐ 153	Buddy Myer	30.00	15.00	3.00	
☐ 154	Jimmy Foxx	160.00	80.00	16.00	
☐ 155	Joe Judge	30.00	15.00	3.00	
☐ 156	Danny MacFayden	30.00	15.00	3.00	
☐ 157	Sam Byrd	30.00	15.00	3.00	
☐ 158	Moe Berg	40.00	20.00	4.00	
☐ 159	Oswald Bluege	30.00	15.00	3.00	
☐ 160	Lou Gehrig	900.00	450.00	90.00	
☐ 161	Al Spohrer	30.00	15.00	3.00	
☐ 162	Leo Mangum	30.00	15.00	3.00	
☐ 163	Luke Sewell	30.00	15.00	3.00	
☐ 164	Lloyd Waner	60.00	30.00	6.00	
☐ 165	Joe Sewell	60.00	30.00	6.00	
☐ 166	Sam West	30.00	15.00	3.00	
☐ 167	Jack Russell	30.00	15.00	3.00	
☐ 168	Goose Goslin	60.00	30.00	6.00	
☐ 169	Al Thomas	30.00	15.00	3.00	
☐ 170	Harry McCurdy	30.00	15.00	3.00	
☐ 171	Charlie Jamieson	30.00	15.00	3.00	
☐ 172	Billy Hargrave	30.00	15.00	3.00	
☐ 173	Roscoe Holm	30.00	15.00	3.00	
☐ 174	Warren (Curly) Ogden	30.00	15.00	3.00	
☐ 175	Dan Howley	30.00	15.00	3.00	
☐ 176	John Ogden	30.00	15.00	3.00	
☐ 177	Walter French	30.00	15.00	3.00	
☐ 178	Jackie Warner	30.00	15.00	3.00	
☐ 179	Fred Leach	30.00	15.00	3.00	
☐ 180	Eddie Moore	30.00	15.00	3.00	
☐ 181	Babe Ruth	2200.00	850.00	150.00	
☐ 182	Andy High	30.00	15.00	3.00	
☐ 183	George Walberg	30.00	15.00	3.00	
☐ 184	Charley Berry	30.00	15.00	3.00	
☐ 185	Bob Smith	30.00	15.00	3.00	
☐ 186	John Schulte	30.00	15.00	3.00	
☐ 187	Heine Manush	60.00	30.00	6.00	
☐ 188	Rogers Hornsby	160.00	80.00	16.00	
☐ 189	Joe Cronin	40.00	20.00	4.00	
☐ 190	Fred Schulte	30.00	15.00	3.00	
☐ 191	Ben Chapman	30.00	15.00	3.00	
☐ 192	Walter Brown	30.00	15.00	3.00	
☐ 193	Lynford Lary	30.00	15.00	3.00	
☐ 194	Earl Averill	60.00	30.00	6.00	
☐ 195	Evar Swanson	30.00	15.00	3.00	
☐ 196	Leroy Mahaffey	30.00	15.00	3.00	
☐ 197	Rick Ferrell	60.00	30.00	6.00	
☐ 198	Jack Burns	30.00	15.00	3.00	
☐ 199	Tom Bridges	30.00	15.00	3.00	
☐ 200	Bill Hallahan	30.00	15.00	3.00	
☐ 201	Ernie Orsatti	30.00	15.00	3.00	
☐ 202	Gabby Hartnett	60.00	30.00	6.00	
☐ 203	Lon Warneke	30.00	15.00	3.00	
☐ 204	Riggs Stephenson	40.00	20.00	4.00	
☐ 205	Heine Meine	30.00	15.00	3.00	
☐ 206	Gus Suhr	30.00	15.00	3.00	
☐ 207	Mel Ott BAT	125.00	60.00	12.50	
☐ 208	Bernie James	30.00	15.00	3.00	
☐ 209	Adolfo Luque	30.00	15.00	3.00	
☐ 210	Virgil Davis	30.00	15.00	3.00	
☐ 211	Hack Wilson	100.00	50.00	10.00	
☐ 212	Billy Urbanski	30.00	15.00	3.00	
☐ 213	Earl Adams	30.00	15.00	3.00	
☐ 214	John Kerr	30.00	15.00	3.00	
☐ 215	Russ Van Atta	30.00	15.00	3.00	
☐ 216	Vernon Gomez	150.00	75.00	15.00	
☐ 217	Frank Crosetti	60.00	30.00	6.00	
☐ 218	Wes Ferrell	40.00	20.00	4.00	
☐ 219	Mule Haas	30.00	15.00	3.00	
☐ 220	Lefty Grove	200.00	100.00	20.00	
☐ 221	Dale Alexander	30.00	15.00	3.00	
☐ 222	Charley Gehringer	100.00	50.00	10.00	
☐ 223	Dizzy Dean	350.00	175.00	35.00	
☐ 224	Frank Demaree	30.00	15.00	3.00	
☐ 225	Bill Jurges	30.00	15.00	3.00	
☐ 226	Charley Root	30.00	15.00	3.00	

		NRMT	VG-E	GOOD
☐ 227	Billy Herman	60.00	30.00	6.00
☐ 228	Tony Piet	30.00	15.00	3.00
☐ 229	Floyd (Arky) Vaughan	60.00	30.00	6.00
☐ 230	Carl Hubbell PIT	100.00	50.00	10.00
☐ 231	Joe Moore FIELD	30.00	15.00	3.00
☐ 232	Lefty O'Doul	40.00	20.00	4.00
☐ 233	Johnny Vergez	30.00	15.00	3.00
☐ 234	Carl Hubbell	100.00	50.00	10.00
☐ 235	Fred Fitzsimmons	40.00	20.00	4.00
☐ 236	George Davis	30.00	15.00	3.00
☐ 237	Gus Mancuso	30.00	15.00	3.00
☐ 238	Hugh Critz	30.00	15.00	3.00
☐ 239	Leroy Parmelee	30.00	15.00	3.00
☐ 240	Hal Schumacher	60.00	15.00	3.00

1934 Goudey

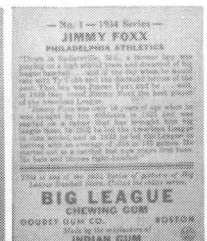

The cards in this 96 card set measure 2 3/8" by 2 7/8". The 1934 Goudey set of color cards carries the ACC catalog number R320. Cards 1-48 are considered to be the easiest to find (although card number 1, Foxx, is very scarce in mint condition) while 73-96 are much more difficult to find. Cards of this 1934 Goudey series are slightly less abundant than cards of the 1933 Goudey set. Of the 96 cards, 84 contain a "Lou Gehrig Says" line on the front in a blue design, while 12 of the high series contain a "Chuck Klein Says" line in a red design. These Chuck Klein cards are indicated in the checklist below by CK and are in fact the 12 National Leaguers in the high series.

	NRMT	VG-E	GOOD
COMPLETE SET	9000.00	3000.00	600.00
COMMON PLAYER (1-48)	30.00	15.00	3.00
COMMON PLAYER (49-72)	40.00	20.00	4.00
COMMON PLAYER (73-96)	125.00	60.00	12.50

☐ 1	Jimmy Foxx	350.00	75.00	15.00
☐ 2	Mickey Cochrane	80.00	40.00	8.00
☐ 3	Charlie Grimm	40.00	20.00	4.00
☐ 4	Woody English	30.00	15.00	3.00
☐ 5	Ed Brandt	30.00	15.00	3.00
☐ 6	Dizzy Dean	350.00	175.00	35.00
☐ 7	Leo Durocher	50.00	25.00	5.00
☐ 8	Tony Piet	30.00	15.00	3.00
☐ 9	Ben Chapman	30.00	15.00	3.00
☐ 10	Chuck Klein	60.00	30.00	6.00
☐ 11	Paul Waner	60.00	30.00	6.00
☐ 12	Carl Hubbell	80.00	40.00	8.00
☐ 13	Frank Frisch	80.00	40.00	8.00
☐ 14	Willie Kamm	30.00	15.00	3.00
☐ 15	Alvin Crowder	30.00	15.00	3.00
☐ 16	Joe Kuhel	30.00	15.00	3.00
☐ 17	Hugh Critz	30.00	15.00	3.00
☐ 18	Heinie Manush	60.00	30.00	6.00
☐ 19	Lefty Grove	125.00	60.00	12.50
☐ 20	Frank Hogan	30.00	15.00	3.00
☐ 21	Bill Terry	80.00	40.00	8.00
☐ 22	Arky Vaughan	60.00	30.00	6.00
☐ 23	Charlie Gehringer	80.00	40.00	8.00
☐ 24	Ray Benge	30.00	15.00	3.00
☐ 25	Roger Cramer	30.00	15.00	3.00
☐ 26	Gerald Walker	30.00	15.00	3.00
☐ 27	Luke Appling	60.00	30.00	6.00
☐ 28	Ed Coleman	30.00	15.00	3.00
☐ 29	Larry French	30.00	15.00	3.00
☐ 30	Julius Solters	30.00	15.00	3.00
☐ 31	Buck Jordan	30.00	15.00	3.00
☐ 32	Blondy Ryan	30.00	15.00	3.00

☐ 33	Frank Hurst	30.00	15.00	3.00
☐ 34	Chick Hafey	60.00	30.00	6.00
☐ 35	Ernie Lombardi	60.00	30.00	6.00
☐ 36	Walter Betts	30.00	15.00	3.00
☐ 37	Lou Gehrig	1350.00	600.00	120.00
☐ 38	Oral Hildebrand	30.00	15.00	3.00
☐ 39	Fred Walker	30.00	15.00	3.00
☐ 40	John Stone	30.00	15.00	3.00
☐ 41	George Earnshaw	30.00	15.00	3.00
☐ 42	John Allen	30.00	15.00	3.00
☐ 43	Dick Porter	30.00	15.00	3.00
☐ 44	Tom Bridges	30.00	15.00	3.00
☐ 45	Oscar Melillo	30.00	15.00	3.00
☐ 46	Joe Stripp	30.00	15.00	3.00
☐ 47	John Frederick	30.00	15.00	3.00
☐ 48	Tex Carleton	30.00	15.00	3.00
☐ 49	Sam Leslie	40.00	20.00	4.00
☐ 50	Walter Beck	40.00	20.00	4.00
☐ 51	Rip Collins	40.00	20.00	4.00
☐ 52	Herman Bell	40.00	20.00	4.00
☐ 53	George Watkins	40.00	20.00	4.00
☐ 54	Wesley Schulmerich	40.00	20.00	4.00
☐ 55	Ed Holley	40.00	20.00	4.00
☐ 56	Mark Koenig	40.00	20.00	4.00
☐ 57	Bill Swift	40.00	20.00	4.00
☐ 58	Earl Grace	40.00	20.00	4.00
☐ 59	Joe Mowry	40.00	20.00	4.00
☐ 60	Lynn Nelson	40.00	20.00	4.00
☐ 61	Lou Gehrig	1500.00	600.00	120.00
☐ 62	Hank Greenberg	125.00	60.00	12.50
☐ 63	Minter Hayes	40.00	20.00	4.00
☐ 64	Frank Grube	40.00	20.00	4.00
☐ 65	Cliff Bolton	40.00	20.00	4.00
☐ 66	Mel Harder	50.00	25.00	5.00
☐ 67	Bob Weiland	40.00	20.00	4.00
☐ 68	Bob Johnson	50.00	25.00	5.00
☐ 69	John Marcum	40.00	20.00	4.00
☐ 70	Pete Fox	40.00	20.00	4.00
☐ 71	Lyle Tinning	40.00	20.00	4.00
☐ 72	Arndt Jorgens	40.00	20.00	4.00
☐ 73	Ed Wells	125.00	60.00	12.50
☐ 74	Bob Boken	125.00	60.00	12.50
☐ 75	Bill Werber	125.00	60.00	12.50
☐ 76	Hal Trosky	125.00	60.00	12.50
☐ 77	Joe Vosmik	125.00	60.00	12.50
☐ 78	Pinky Higgins	125.00	60.00	12.50
☐ 79	Ed Durham	125.00	60.00	12.50
☐ 80	Marty McManus CK	125.00	60.00	12.50
☐ 81	Bob Brown CK	125.00	60.00	12.50
☐ 82	Bill Hallahan CK	125.00	60.00	12.50
☐ 83	Jim Mooney CK	125.00	60.00	12.50
☐ 84	Paul Derringer CK	150.00	75.00	15.00
☐ 85	Adam Comorosky CK	125.00	60.00	12.50
☐ 86	Lloyd Johnson CK	125.00	60.00	12.50
☐ 87	George Darrow CK	125.00	60.00	12.50
☐ 88	Homer Peel CK	125.00	60.00	12.50
☐ 89	Linus Frey CK	125.00	60.00	12.50
☐ 90	Ki-Ki Cuyler CK	250.00	125.00	25.00
☐ 91	Dolph Camilli CK	125.00	60.00	12.50
☐ 92	Steve Larkin	125.00	60.00	12.50
☐ 93	Fred Ostermueller	125.00	60.00	12.50
☐ 94	Red Rolfe	150.00	75.00	15.00
☐ 95	Myril Hoag	125.00	60.00	12.50
☐ 96	James DeShong	150.00	60.00	12.00

1935 Goudey

The cards in this 36 card set (the number of different front pictures) measure 2 3/8" by 2 7/8". The 1935 Goudey set is sometimes called the Goudey Puzzle Set, the Goudey 4 in 1's, or R321 (ACC). There are 36 different card fronts but 114 different front/back combinations. The card number in the checklist refers to the back puzzle number, as the backs can be arranged to form a puzzle picturing a player or team. To avoid the confusion caused by two different fronts having the same back number, the rarer cards have been arbitrarily given a "1" prefix. The scarcer puzzle cards are hence all listed at the numerical end of the list below, i.e. rare puzzle 1 is listed as number 11, rare puzzle 2 is listed as 12, etc. The BLUE in the checklist refers to a card with a blue border, as most cards have a red border. The set price below includes only the 36 different fronts, making no distinction as to which backs are present. The following is the list of the puzzle back pictures: 1) Detroit Tigers; 2) Chuck Klein; 3) Frankie Frisch; 4) Mickey Cochrane; 5) Joe Cronin; 6) Jimmy Foxx; 7) Al Simmons; 8) Cleveland Indians; and 9) Washington Senators.

	NRMT	VG-E	GOOD
COMPLETE SET (36)	2800.00	1200.00	250.00
COMMON CARDS (1-9)	25.00	12.50	2.50
COMMON CARDS (11-17)	35.00	17.50	3.50

☐ 1A F.Frisch/Dizzy Dean Orsatti/Carleton	75.00	37.50	7.50
☐ 1B Mahaffey/Jimmie Foxx Williams/Higgins	50.00	25.00	5.00
☐ 1C Heine Manush/Lary Weaver/Hadley	35.00	17.50	3.50
☐ 1D Cochrane/C.Gehringer Bridges/Rogell	50.00	25.00	5.00
☐ 1E Paul Waner/Bush W.Hoyt/Lloyd Waner	50.00	25.00	5.00
☐ 1F B.Grimes/Chuck Klein K.Cuyler/English	50.00	25.00	5.00
☐ 1G Leslie/Frey Joe Stripp/Clark	25.00	12.50	2.50
☐ 1H Piet/Comorosky Bottomley/Adams	35.00	17.50	3.50
☐ 1I Earnshaw/Dykes Luke Sewell/Appling	35.00	17.50	3.50
☐ 1J Babe Ruth/McManus Brandt/Maranville	450.00	225.00	45.00
☐ 1K Bill Terry/Schumacher Mancuso/Jackson	50.00	25.00	5.00
☐ 1L Kamm/Hildebrand Averill/Trosky	35.00	17.50	3.50
☐ 2A F.Frisch/Dizzy Dean Orsatti/Carleton	75.00	37.50	7.50
☐ 2B Mahaffey/Jimmie Foxx Williams/Higgins	50.00	25.00	5.00
☐ 2C Heine Manush/Lary Weaver/Hadley	35.00	17.50	3.50
☐ 2D Cochrane/C.Gehringer Bridges/Rogell	50.00	25.00	5.00
☐ 2E Kamm/Hildebrand Earl Averill/Trosky	35.00	17.50	3.50
☐ 2F Earnshaw/Dykes Luke Sewell/Appling	35.00	17.50	3.50
☐ 3A Babe Ruth/McManus Brandt/Maranville	450.00	225.00	45.00
☐ 3B Bill Terry/Schumacher Mancuso/T.Jackson	50.00	25.00	5.00
☐ 3C Paul Waner/Bush W.Hoyt/Lloyd Waner	50.00	25.00	5.00
☐ 3D B.Grimes/Chuck Klein K.Cuyler/English	50.00	25.00	5.00
☐ 3E Leslie/Frey Joe Stripp/Clark	25.00	12.50	2.50
☐ 3F Piet/Comorosky Jim Bottomley/Adams	35.00	17.50	3.50
☐ 4A Critz/D.Bartell BLUE Mel Ott/Mancuso	50.00	25.00	5.00
☐ 4B Pie Traynor/Lucas BLUE . Tom Thevenow/Wright	35.00	17.50	3.50
☐ 4C Berry/Burke BLUE Kress/Dazzy Vance	35.00	17.50	3.50
☐ 4D R.Ruffing/Malone BLUE .. Lazzeri/Bill Dickey	75.00	37.50	7.50
☐ 4E Moore/Hogan BLUE Frankhouse/Brandt	25.00	12.50	2.50
☐ 4F Martin/O'Farrell BLUE Byrd/MacFayden	25.00	12.50	2.50
☐ 5A Ruel/Al Simmons Kamm/M.Cochrane	50.00	25.00	5.00
☐ 5B Willis Hudlin/Myatt Comorosky/Bottomley	35.00	17.50	3.50
☐ 5C Paul Waner/Bush W.Hoyt/Lloyd Waner	50.00	25.00	5.00

☐ 5D West/Oscar Melillo Blaeholder/Coffman	25.00	12.50	2.50
☐ 5E Leslie/Frey Joe Stripp/Clark	25.00	12.50	2.50
☐ 5F Schuble/Marberry Goose Goslin/Crowder	35.00	17.50	3.50
☐ 6A Ruel/Al Simmons Kamm/M.Cochrane	50.00	25.00	5.00
☐ 6B Willis Hudlin/Myatt Comorosky/Bottomley	35.00	17.50	3.50
☐ 6C Wilson/Allen Jonnard/Brickell	25.00	12.50	2.50
☐ 6D West/Oscar Melillo Blaeholder/Coffman	25.00	12.50	2.50
☐ 6E Joe Cronin/Reynolds Bishop/Cissell	35.00	17.50	3.50
☐ 6F Schuble/Marberry Goose Goslin/Crowder	35.00	17.50	3.50
☐ 7A Critz/Bartell BLUE Mel Ott/Mancuso	50.00	25.00	5.00
☐ 7B Pie Traynor/Lucas BLUE . Tom Thevenow/Wright	35.00	17.50	3.50
☐ 7C Berry/Burke BLUE Kress/Dazzy Vance	35.00	17.50	3.50
☐ 7D R.Ruffing/Malone BLUE .. Lazzeri/Bill Dickey	75.00	37.50	7.50
☐ 7E Moore/Hogan BLUE Frankhouse/Brandt	25.00	12.50	2.50
☐ 7F Martin/O'Farrell BLUE Byrd/MacFayden	25.00	12.50	2.50
☐ 8A M.Koenig/Fitzsimmons Benge/Zachary	25.00	12.50	2.50
☐ 8B Hayes/Ted Lyons Haas/Zeke Bonura	35.00	17.50	3.50
☐ 8C Burns/Rollie Hemsley Grube/Weiland	25.00	12.50	2.50
☐ 8D Campbell/Meyers Goodman/Kampouris	25.00	12.50	2.50
☐ 8E DeShong/Allen Red Rolfe/Walker	25.00	12.50	2.50
☐ 8F P.Fox/Hank Greenberg Walker/Rowe	35.00	17.50	3.50
☐ 8G Werber/Rick Ferrell W.Ferrell/Ostermueller	35.00	17.50	3.50
☐ 8H Joe Kuhel/Whitehill Meyer/Stone	25.00	12.50	2.50
☐ 8I J.Vosmik/Knickerbocker .. Mel Harder/Stewart	25.00	12.50	2.50
☐ 8J Johnson/Coleman Marcum/Cramer	25.00	12.50	2.50
☐ 8K Herman/Suhr Padden/Blanton	25.00	12.50	2.50
☐ 8L Spohrer/Rhem Cantwell/Benton	25.00	12.50	2.50
☐ 8M M.Koenig/Fitzsimmons ... Benge/Zachary	25.00	12.50	2.50
☐ 9B Hayes/Ted Lyons Haas/Zeke Bonura	35.00	17.50	3.50
☐ 9C Burns/Rollie Hemsley Grube/Weiland	25.00	12.50	2.50
☐ 9D Campbell/Meyers Goodman/Kampouris	25.00	12.50	2.50
☐ 9E DeShong/Allen Red Rolfe/Walker	25.00	12.50	2.50
☐ 9F P.Fox/Hank Greenberg Walker/Rowe	35.00	17.50	3.50
☐ 9G Werber/Rick Ferrell W.Ferrell/Ostermueller	35.00	17.50	3.50
☐ 9H Joe Kuhel/Whitehill Meyer/Stone	25.00	12.50	2.50
☐ 9I J.Vosmik/Knickerbocker .. Mel Harder/Stewart	25.00	12.50	2.50
☐ 9J Johnson/Coleman Marcum/Cramer	25.00	12.50	2.50
☐ 9K Herman/Suhr Padden/Blanton	25.00	12.50	2.50
☐ 9L Spohrer/Rhem Cantwell/Benton	25.00	12.50	2.50
☐ 11E Wilson/Allen Jonnard/Brickell	35.00	17.50	3.50
☐ 11F West/Melillo Blaeholder/Coffman	35.00	17.50	3.50
☐ 11G Joe Cronin/Reynolds Bishop/Cissel	50.00	25.00	5.00
☐ 11H Schuble/Marberry Goose Goslin/Crowder	50.00	25.00	5.00
☐ 11J Ruel/Al Simmons Kamm/M.Cochrane	75.00	37.50	7.50
☐ 11K Hudlin/Myatt Comorosky/Bottomley	50.00	25.00	5.00
☐ 12A Critz/Bartell BLUE Mel Ott/Mancuso	60.00	30.00	6.00
☐ 12B P.Traynor/Lucas BLUE .. Thevenow/Wright	50.00	25.00	5.00
☐ 12C Berry/Burke BLUE	50.00	25.00	5.00

		NRMT	VG-E	GOOD
	Kress/D.Vance			
☐ 12D	R.Ruffing/Malone BLUE .	100.00	50.00	10.00
	Lazzeri/Bill Dickey			
☐ 12E	Moore/Hogan BLUE	35.00	17.50	3.50
	Frankhouse/Brandt			
☐ 12F	Martin/O'Farrell BLUE ...	35.00	17.50	3.50
	Byrd/MacFayden			
☐ 13A	Ruel/Al Simmons	75.00	37.50	7.50
	Kamm/M.Cochrane			
☐ 13B	Hudlin/Myatt	50.00	25.00	5.00
	Comorosky/Bottomley			
☐ 13C	Wilson/Allen	35.00	17.50	3.50
	Jonnard/Brickell			
☐ 13D	West/Oscar Melillo	35.00	17.50	3.50
	Blaeholder/Coffman			
☐ 13E	Joe Cronin/Reynolds	50.00	25.00	5.00
	Bishop/Cissell			
☐ 13F	Schuble/Marberry	50.00	25.00	5.00
	Goose Goslin/Crowder			
☐ 14A	Babe Ruth/McManus	650.00	325.00	65.00
	Brandt/Maranville			
☐ 14B	Bill Terry/Schumacher ..	75.00	37.50	7.50
	Mancuso/Jackson			
☐ 14C	Paul Waner/Bush	75.00	37.50	7.50
	W.Hoyt/Lloyd Waner			
☐ 14D	B.Grimes/Chuck Klein ...	75.00	37.50	7.50
	K.Cuyler/English			
☐ 14E	Leslie/Frey	35.00	17.50	3.50
	Joe Stripp/Clark			
☐ 14F	Piet/Comorosky	50.00	25.00	5.00
	Jim Bottomley/Adams			
☐ 15A	Babe Ruth/McManus	650.00	325.00	65.00
	Brandt/Maranville			
☐ 15B	Bill Terry/Schumacher ..	75.00	37.50	7.50
	Mancuso/T.Jackson			
☐ 15C	Wilson/Allen	35.00	17.50	3.50
	Jonnard/Brickell			
☐ 15D	B.Grimes/Chuck Klein ...	75.00	37.50	7.50
	K.Cuyler/English			
☐ 15E	Joe Cronin/Reynolds	50.00	25.00	5.00
	Bishop/Cissell			
☐ 15F	Piet/Comorosky	50.00	25.00	5.00
	Jim Bottomley/Adams			
☐ 16A	F.Frisch/Dizzy Dean	100.00	50.00	10.00
	E.Orsatti/Carleton			
☐ 16B	Mahaffey/Jimmie Foxx ..	75.00	37.50	7.50
	Williams/Higgins			
☐ 16C	Heine Manush/Lary	50.00	25.00	5.00
	Weaver/Hadley			
☐ 16D	Cochrane/C.Gehringer ..	75.00	37.50	7.50
	Tom Bridges/Rogell			
☐ 16E	Kamm/Hildebrand	50.00	25.00	5.00
	Earl Averill/Trosky			
☐ 16F	G.Earnshaw/Dykes	50.00	25.00	5.00
	Luke Sewell/Appling			
☐ 17A	F.Frisch/Dizzy Dean	100.00	50.00	10.00
	E.Orsatti/Carleton			
☐ 17B	Mahaffey/Jimmie Foxx ..	75.00	37.50	7.50
	Williams/Higgins			
☐ 17C	Heine Manush/Lary	50.00	25.00	5.00
	Weaver/Hadley			
☐ 17D	Cochrane/C.Gehringer ..	75.00	37.50	7.50
	Tom Bridges/Rogell			
☐ 17E	Kamm/Hildebrand	50.00	25.00	5.00
	Earl Averill/Trosky			
☐ 17F	G.Earnshaw/Dykes	50.00	25.00	5.00
	Luke Sewell/Appling			

1936 Goudey

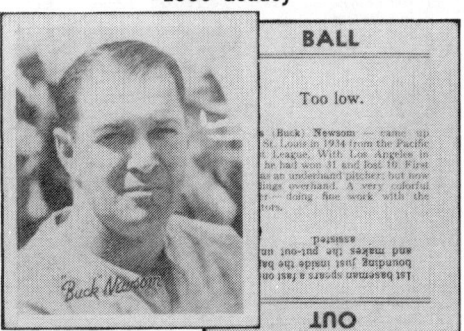

BALL

Too low.

(Buck) Newsom — came up
from St. Louis in 1934 from the Pacific
League. With Los Angeles in
1933 he had won 31 and lost 19. First
class as an underhand pitcher, but now
slings overhand. A very colorful
player — doing fine work with the
Tigers.

"Buck" Newsom

1st baseman spears a fast one
bounds just inside first base
and makes the put-out un-
assisted.

OUT

The cards in this 25 card black and white set measure
2 3/8" by 2 7/8". In contrast to the color artwork
of its previous sets, the 1936 Goudey set contained
a simple black and white player photograph. A
facsimile autograph appeared within the picture
area. Each card was issued with a number of different
"game situation" backs, and there may be as many
as 200 different front/back combinations. The ACC
designation is R322.

		NRMT	VG-E	GOOD
COMPLETE SET		1000.00	375.00	75.00
COMMON PLAYER (1-25)		25.00	12.50	2.50
☐ 1	Wally Berger	25.00	12.50	2.50
☐ 2	Zeke Bonura	25.00	12.50	2.50
☐ 3	Stan Bordagaray	25.00	12.50	2.50
☐ 4	Bill Brubaker	25.00	12.50	2.50
☐ 5	Dolph Camilli	25.00	12.50	2.50
☐ 6	Clyde Castleman	25.00	12.50	2.50
☐ 7	Mickey Cochrane	100.00	50.00	10.00
☐ 8	Joe Coscarart	25.00	12.50	2.50
☐ 9	Frank Crosetti	40.00	20.00	4.00
☐ 10	Kiki Cuyler	60.00	30.00	6.00
☐ 11	Paul Derringer	30.00	15.00	3.00
☐ 12	Jimmy Dykes	30.00	15.00	3.00
☐ 13	Rick Ferrell	60.00	30.00	6.00
☐ 14	Lefty Gomez	100.00	50.00	10.00
☐ 15	Hank Greenberg	100.00	50.00	10.00
☐ 16	Bucky Harris	50.00	25.00	5.00
☐ 17	Rollie Hemsley	25.00	12.50	2.50
☐ 18	Pinky Higgins	25.00	12.50	2.50
☐ 19	Oral Hildbrand	25.00	12.50	2.50
☐ 20	Chuck Klein	60.00	30.00	6.00
☐ 21	Pepper Martin	35.00	17.50	3.50
☐ 22	Bobo Newsom	30.00	15.00	3.00
☐ 23	Joe Vosmik	25.00	12.50	2.50
☐ 24	Paul Waner	60.00	30.00	6.00
☐ 25	Bill Werber	25.00	12.50	2.50

1938 Goudey Heads Up

 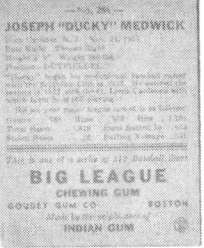

The cards in this 48 card set measure 2 3/8" by 2
7/8". The 1938 Goudey set is commonly referred to
as the Heads-Up set, or R323 (ACC). These very
popular but difficult to obtain cards came in two
series of the same 24 players. The first series,
numbers 241-264, is distinguished from the second
series, numbers 265-288, in that the second
contains etched cartoons and comments
surrounding the player picture. Although the set
starts with number 241, it is not a continuation of the
1933 Goudey set, but a separate set in its own right.

		NRMT	VG-E	GOOD
COMPLETE SET		7000.00	2800.00	500.00
COMMON PLAYER (241-264)	....	50.00	25.00	5.00
COMMON PLAYER (265-288)	....	65.00	32.50	6.50
☐ 241	Charlie Gehringer	200.00	100.00	20.00
☐ 242	Pete Fox	50.00	25.00	5.00
☐ 243	Joe Kuhel	50.00	25.00	5.00
☐ 244	Frank Demaree	50.00	25.00	5.00
☐ 245	Frank Pytlak	50.00	25.00	5.00
☐ 246	Ernie Lombardi	100.00	50.00	10.00
☐ 247	Joe Vosmik	50.00	25.00	5.00
☐ 248	Dick Bartell	50.00	25.00	5.00
☐ 249	Jimmie Foxx	250.00	125.00	25.00
☐ 250	Joe DiMaggio	1000.00	400.00	80.00
☐ 251	Bump Hadley	50.00	25.00	5.00
☐ 252	Zeke Bonura	50.00	25.00	5.00
☐ 253	Hank Greenberg	200.00	100.00	20.00

☐ 254	Van Lingle Mungo	50.00	25.00	5.00
☐ 255	Moose Solters	50.00	25.00	5.00
☐ 256	Vernon Kennedy	50.00	25.00	5.00
☐ 257	Al Lopez	100.00	50.00	10.00
☐ 258	Bobby Doerr	150.00	75.00	15.00
☐ 259	Billy Werber	50.00	25.00	5.00
☐ 260	Rudy York	50.00	25.00	5.00
☐ 261	Rip Radcliff	50.00	25.00	5.00
☐ 262	Joe Medwick	150.00	75.00	15.00
☐ 263	Marvin Owen	50.00	25.00	5.00
☐ 264	Bob Feller	350.00	175.00	35.00
☐ 265	Charlie Gehringer	250.00	125.00	25.00
☐ 266	Pete Fox	65.00	32.50	6.50
☐ 267	Joe Kuhel	65.00	32.50	6.50
☐ 268	Frank Demaree	65.00	32.50	6.50
☐ 269	Frank Pytlak	65.00	32.50	6.50
☐ 270	Ernie Lombardi	125.00	60.00	12.50
☐ 271	Joe Vosmik	65.00	32.50	6.50
☐ 272	Dick Bartell	65.00	32.50	6.50
☐ 273	Jimmie Foxx	300.00	150.00	30.00
☐ 274	Joe DiMaggio	1250.00	500.00	100.00
☐ 275	Bump Hadley	65.00	32.50	6.50
☐ 276	Zeke Bonura	65.00	32.50	6.50
☐ 277	Hank Greenberg	250.00	125.00	25.00
☐ 278	Van Lingle Mungo	65.00	32.50	6.50
☐ 279	Moose Solters	65.00	32.50	6.50
☐ 280	Vernon Kennedy	65.00	32.50	6.50
☐ 281	Al Lopez	125.00	60.00	12.50
☐ 282	Bobby Doerr	175.00	85.00	18.00
☐ 283	Billy Werber	65.00	32.50	6.50
☐ 284	Rudy York	65.00	32.50	6.50
☐ 285	Rip Radcliff	65.00	32.50	6.50
☐ 286	Joe Medwick	175.00	85.00	18.00
☐ 287	Marvin Owen	65.00	32.50	6.50
☐ 288	Bob Feller	400.00	200.00	40.00

☐ 12	Fritz Ostermueller	25.00	12.50	2.50
☐ 13	Frank Hayes	25.00	12.50	2.50
☐ 14	John Kramer	25.00	12.50	2.50
☐ 15	Dario Lodigiani	25.00	12.50	2.50
☐ 16	George Case	25.00	12.50	2.50
☐ 17	Vito Tamulis	25.00	12.50	2.50
☐ 18	Whitlow Wyatt	25.00	12.50	2.50
☐ 19	Bill Posedel	25.00	12.50	2.50
☐ 20	Carl Hubbell	100.00	50.00	10.00
☐ 21	Harold Warstler	125.00	60.00	12.50
☐ 22	Joe Sullivan	250.00	125.00	25.00
☐ 23	Norman Young	175.00	85.00	18.00
☐ 24	Stanley Andrews	225.00	110.00	22.00
☐ 25	Morris Arnovich	150.00	75.00	15.00
☐ 26	Elbert Fletcher	25.00	12.50	2.50
☐ 27	Bill Crough	60.00	30.00	6.00
☐ 28	Al Todd	25.00	12.50	2.50
☐ 29	Debs Garms	50.00	25.00	5.00
☐ 30	Jim Tobin	25.00	12.50	2.50
☐ 31	Chester Ross	25.00	12.50	2.50
☐ 32	George Coffman	40.00	20.00	4.00
☐ 33	Mel Ott	125.00	60.00	12.50

Robert Gould W605

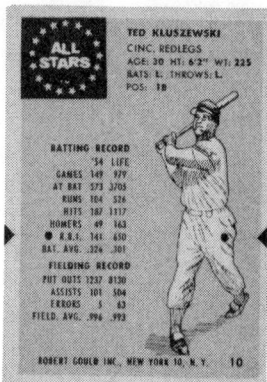

The cards in this 28 card set measure 2 1/2" by 3 1/2". The 1955 Robert F. Gould set of black and white on green cards were toy store cardboard holders for small plastic statues. The statues were attached to the card by a rubber band through two holes on the side of the card. The ACC designation is W605. The cards are numbered in the bottom right corner of the obverse and are blank-backed.

		NRMT	VG-E	GOOD
COMPLETE SET		1000.00	450.00	90.00
COMMON PLAYER		20.00	10.00	2.00
☐ 1	Willie Mays	250.00	125.00	25.00
☐ 2	Gus Zernial	20.00	10.00	2.00
☐ 3	Red Schoendienst	30.00	15.00	3.00
☐ 4	Chico Carrasquel	20.00	10.00	2.00
☐ 5	Jim Hegan	20.00	10.00	2.00
☐ 6	Curt Simmons	25.00	12.50	2.50
☐ 7	Bob Porterfield	20.00	10.00	2.00
☐ 8	Jim Busby	20.00	10.00	2.00
☐ 9	Don Mueller	20.00	10.00	2.00
☐ 10	Ted Kluszewski	35.00	17.50	3.50
☐ 11	Ray Boone	20.00	10.00	2.00
☐ 12	Smokey Burgess	25.00	12.50	2.50
☐ 13	Bob Rush	20.00	10.00	2.00
☐ 14	Early Wynn	65.00	32.50	6.50
☐ 15	Bill Bruton	20.00	10.00	2.00
☐ 16	Gus Bell	20.00	10.00	2.00
☐ 17	Jim Finigan	20.00	10.00	2.00
☐ 18	Granny Hamner	20.00	10.00	2.00
☐ 19	Hank Thompson	20.00	10.00	2.00
☐ 20	Joe Coleman	20.00	10.00	2.00
☐ 21	Don Newcombe	35.00	17.50	3.50
☐ 22	Richie Ashburn	50.00	25.00	5.00
☐ 23	Bobby Thomson	30.00	15.00	3.00
☐ 24	Sid Gordon	20.00	10.00	2.00
☐ 25	Gerry Coleman	25.00	12.50	2.50
☐ 26	Ernie Banks	125.00	60.00	12.50

1941 Goudey

The cards in this 33 card set measure 2 3/8" by 2 7/8". The 1941 Series of blank backed baseball cards was the last baseball issue marketed by Goudey before the war closed the door on that company for good. Each black and white player photo comes with four color backgrounds (blue, green, red, or yellow). Cards without numbers are probably miscut. Cards 21-25 are especially scarce in relation to the rest of the set. In fact the eight hardest to find cards in the set are, in order, 22, 24, 23, 25, 21, 27, 29, and 32. The ACC catalog number is R324.

		NRMT	VG-E	GOOD
COMPLETE SET		2000.00	850.00	150.00
COMMON PLAYER (1-33)		25.00	12.50	2.50
☐ 1	Hugh Mulcahy	25.00	12.50	2.50
☐ 2	Harland Clift	25.00	12.50	2.50
☐ 3	Louis Chiozza	25.00	12.50	2.50
☐ 4	Warren Rosar	25.00	12.50	2.50
☐ 5	George McQuinn	25.00	12.50	2.50
☐ 6	George Dickman	25.00	12.50	2.50
☐ 7	Wayne Ambler	25.00	12.50	2.50
☐ 8	Bob Muncrief	25.00	12.50	2.50
☐ 9	Bill Dietrich	25.00	12.50	2.50
☐ 10	Taft Wright	25.00	12.50	2.50
☐ 11	Don Heffner	25.00	12.50	2.50

		MINT	EXC	G-VG
☐ 27	Billy Pierce	30.00	15.00	3.00
☐ 28	Mel Parnell	25.00	12.50	2.50

1981 Granny Goose

Rickey Henley Henderson
35 Outfield
Height: 5'10"
Weight: 198
Bats: Right
Throws: Left

In 1980 Rickey became the first American Leaguer and the 3rd in baseball history to steal 100 bases in a season. Rickey was 2nd in the league in walks with 117, and led the A's with 179 hits.

© 1981 East West Promotions, Inc.

This set is the hardest to obtain of the three years Granny Goose issued cards of the Oakland A's. The Revering card was supposedly destroyed by the printer soon after he was traded away and hence is in shorter supply than the other 14 cards in the set. Wayne Gross is also supposedly available in lesser quantity compared to the other players. Cards are standard size (2 1/2" by 3 1/2") and were issued in bags of potato chips. Cards are numbered on the front and back by the player's uniform number.

		MINT	EXC	G-VG
	COMPLETE SET	70.00	35.00	7.00
	COMMON PLAYER	1.00	.50	.10
☐ 1	Billy Martin MG	5.00	2.50	.50
☐ 2	Mike Heath	1.00	.50	.10
☐ 5	Jeff Newman	1.00	.50	.10
☐ 6	Mitchell Page	1.00	.50	.10
☐ 8	Rob Picciolo	1.00	.50	.10
☐ 10	Wayne Gross	6.00	3.00	.60
☐ 13	Dave Revering SP	35.00	17.50	3.50
☐ 17	Mike Norris	1.00	.50	.10
☐ 20	Tony Armas	3.00	1.50	.30
☐ 21	Dwayne Murphy	3.00	1.50	.30
☐ 22	Rick Langford	1.50	.75	.15
☐ 27	Matt Keough	1.00	.50	.10
☐ 35	Rickey Henderson	20.00	10.00	2.00
☐ 39	Dave McKay	1.00	.50	.10
☐ 54	Steve McCatty	1.00	.50	.10

1982 Granny Goose

The cards in this 15 card set measure 2 1/2" by 3 1/2". Granny Goose Foods, Inc., a California based company, repeated its successful promotional idea of 1981 by issuing a new set of Oakland A's baseball cards for 1982. Each color player picture is surrounded by white borders and has trim and lettering done in Oakland's green and yellow colors. The cards are numbered according to the uniform number of the player, and the backs carry vital statistics done in black print on a white background. The cards were distributed in packages of potato chips and were also handed out on Fan Appreciation Day at the stadium. Although Picciolo was traded, his card was not withdrawn (as was Revering last year) and, therefore, its value is no greater than other cards in the set.

	MINT	EXC	G-VG
COMPLETE SET	12.50	6.25	1.25

Rickey Henley Henderson
35 Outfield
Height: 5'10"
Weight: 198
Bats: Right
Throws: Left

Rickey was named to the Sporting News All Star team in 1981. He led the A.L. in hits (135), runs (89) and stolen bases (56). He was fourth in the League in batting at .319 and was a Gold Glove recipient.

© 1982 Granny Goose Foods, Inc.

		MINT	EXC	G-VG
	COMMON PLAYER	.40	.20	.04
☐ 1	Tony Armas	.90	.45	.09
☐ 2	Wayne Gross	.40	.20	.04
☐ 3	Mike Heath	.40	.20	.04
☐ 4	Rickey Henderson	6.50	3.25	.65
☐ 5	Cliff Johnson	.40	.20	.04
☐ 6	Matt Keough	.40	.20	.04
☐ 7	Rick Langford	.40	.20	.04
☐ 8	Davey Lopes	.75	.35	.07
☐ 9	Billy Martin MG	1.50	.75	.15
☐ 10	Steve McCatty	.40	.20	.04
☐ 11	Dwayne Murphy	.90	.45	.09
☐ 12	Jeff Newman	.40	.20	.04
☐ 13	Mike Norris	.40	.20	.04
☐ 14	Rob Picciolo	.40	.20	.04
☐ 15	Fred Stanley	.40	.20	.04

1983 Granny Goose

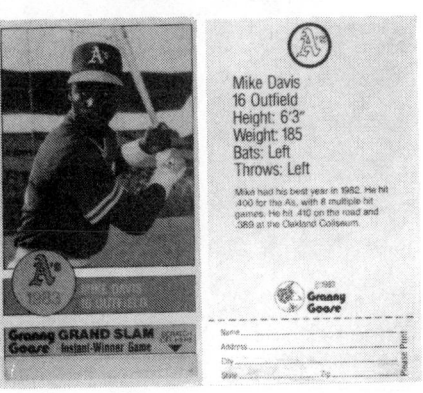

Mike Davis
16 Outfield
Height: 6'3"
Weight: 185
Bats: Left
Throws: Left

Mike had his best year in 1982. He hit .400 for the A's, with 8 multiple hit games. He hit .410 on the road and .389 at the Oakland Coliseum.

© 1983 Granny Goose

The cards in this 15 card set measure 2 1/2" by 4 1/4". The 1983 Granny Goose Potato Chips set again features Oakland A's players. The cards that were issued in bags of potato chips have a tear off coupon on the bottom with a scratch off section featuring prizes. In addition to their release in bags of potato chips, the Granny Goose cards were also given away to fans attending the Oakland game of July 3, 1983. These give away cards did not contain the coupon on the bottom. Prices listed below are for cards without the detachable tabs that came on the bottom of the cards; cards with tabs intact are valued 50% higher than the prices below.

		MINT	EXC	G-VG
	COMPLETE SET	9.00	4.50	.90
	COMMON PLAYER	.40	.20	.04
☐ 2	Mike Heath	.40	.20	.04

☐ 4	Carney Lansford	1.00	.50	.10
☐ 10	Wayne Gross	.40	.20	.04
☐ 14	Steve Boros MG	.40	.20	.04
☐ 15	Davey Lopes	.75	.35	.07
☐ 16	Mike Davis	.90	.45	.09
☐ 17	Mike Norris	.50	.25	.05
☐ 21	Dwayne Murphy	.90	.45	.09
☐ 22	Rick Langford	.40	.20	.04
☐ 27	Matt Keough	.40	.20	.04
☐ 31	Tom Underwood	.40	.20	.04
☐ 33	Dave Beard	.40	.20	.04
☐ 35	Rickey Henderson	5.00	2.50	.50
☐ 39	Tom Burgmeier	.40	.20	.04
☐ 54	Steve McCatty	.40	.20	.04

1958 Hires

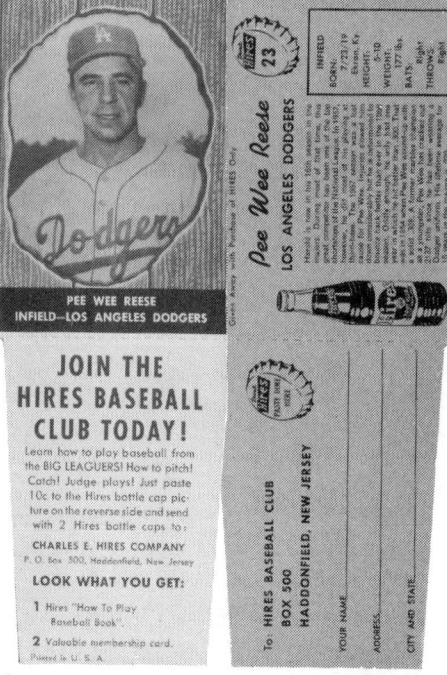

**PEE WEE REESE
INFIELD—LOS ANGELES DODGERS**

**JOIN THE
HIRES BASEBALL
CLUB TODAY!**

Learn how to play baseball from
the BIG LEAGUERS! How to pitch!
Catch! Judge plays! Just paste
10c to the Hires bottle cap picture on the reverse side and send
with 2 Hires bottle caps to:

CHARLES E. HIRES COMPANY
P. O. Box 500, Haddonfield, New Jersey

LOOK WHAT YOU GET:

1 Hires "How To Play
Baseball Book".

2 Valuable membership card.

Printed In U. S. A.

The cards in this 66 card set measure 2 5/16" by
3 1/2" or 2 5/16" by 7" with tabs. The 1958 Hires
Root Beer set of numbered, colored cards was issued
with detachable coupons as inserts with Hires Root
Beer cartons. Cards with the coupon still intact are
worth double the prices listed below. The card front
picture is surrounded by a wood grain effect which
makes it look like the player is seen through a knot
hole. The numbering of this set is rather strange in
that it begins with 10 and skips 69.

		NRMT	VG-E	GOOD
COMPLETE SET		900.00	450.00	90.00
COMMON PLAYER (10-76)		7.50	3.75	.75
☐ 10	Richie Ashburn	25.00	12.50	2.50
☐ 11	Chico Carrasquel	7.50	3.75	.75
☐ 12	Dave Philley	7.50	3.75	.75
☐ 13	Don Newcombe	12.00	6.00	1.20
☐ 14	Wally Post	7.50	3.75	.75
☐ 15	Rip Repulski	7.50	3.75	.75
☐ 16	Chico Fernandez	7.50	3.75	.75
☐ 17	Larry Doby	12.00	6.00	1.20
☐ 18	Hector Brown	7.50	3.75	.75
☐ 19	Danny O'Connell	7.50	3.75	.75
☐ 20	Granny Hamner	7.50	3.75	.75
☐ 21	Dick Groat	10.00	5.00	1.00
☐ 22	Ray Narleski	7.50	3.75	.75

☐ 23	Pee Wee Reese	40.00	20.00	4.00
☐ 24	Bob Friend	9.00	4.50	.90
☐ 25	Willie Mays	150.00	75.00	15.00
☐ 26	Bob Nieman	7.50	3.75	.75
☐ 27	Frank Thomas	9.00	4.50	.90
☐ 28	Curt Simmons	9.00	4.50	.90
☐ 29	Stan Lopata	7.50	3.75	.75
☐ 30	Bob Skinner	7.50	3.75	.75
☐ 31	Ron Kline	7.50	3.75	.75
☐ 32	Willie Miranda	7.50	3.75	.75
☐ 33	Bobby Avila	7.50	3.75	.75
☐ 34	Clem Labine	9.00	4.50	.90
☐ 35	Ray Jablonski	7.50	3.75	.75
☐ 36	Bill Mazeroski	12.00	6.00	1.20
☐ 37	Billy Gardner	7.50	3.75	.75
☐ 38	Pete Runnels	9.00	4.50	.90
☐ 39	Jack Sanford	7.50	3.75	.75
☐ 40	Dave Sisler	7.50	3.75	.75
☐ 41	Don Zimmer	10.00	5.00	1.00
☐ 42	Johnny Podres	10.00	5.00	1.00
☐ 43	Dick Farrell	7.50	3.75	.75
☐ 44	Hank Aaron	150.00	75.00	15.00
☐ 45	Bill Virdon	10.00	5.00	1.00
☐ 46	Bobby Thomson	10.00	5.00	1.00
☐ 47	Willard Nixon	7.50	3.75	.75
☐ 48	Billy Loes	7.50	3.75	.75
☐ 49	Hank Sauer	9.00	4.50	.90
☐ 50	Johnny Antonelli	9.00	4.50	.90
☐ 51	Daryl Spencer	7.50	3.75	.75
☐ 52	Ken Lehman	7.50	3.75	.75
☐ 53	Sammy White	7.50	3.75	.75
☐ 54	Charley Neal	9.00	4.50	.90
☐ 55	Don Drysdale	30.00	15.00	3.00
☐ 56	Jackie Jensen	10.00	5.00	1.00
☐ 57	Ray Katt	7.50	3.75	.75
☐ 58	Frank Sullivan	7.50	3.75	.75
☐ 59	Roy Face	9.00	4.50	.90
☐ 60	Willie Jones	7.50	3.75	.75
☐ 61	Duke Snider	75.00	37.50	7.50
☐ 62	Whitey Lockman	9.00	4.50	.90
☐ 63	Gino Cimoli	7.50	3.75	.75
☐ 64	Marv Grissom	7.50	3.75	.75
☐ 65	Gene Baker	7.50	3.75	.75
☐ 66	George Zuverink	7.50	3.75	.75
☐ 67	Ted Kluszewski	12.00	6.00	1.20
☐ 68	Jim Busby	7.50	3.75	.75
☐ 69	Not Issued	0.00	.00	.00
☐ 70	Curt Barclay	7.50	3.75	.75
☐ 71	Hank Foiles	7.50	3.75	.75
☐ 72	Gene Stephens	7.50	3.75	.75
☐ 73	Al Worthington	7.50	3.75	.75
☐ 74	Al Walker	7.50	3.75	.75
☐ 75	Bob Boyd	7.50	3.75	.75
☐ 76	Al Pilarcik	7.50	3.75	.75

1958 Hires Test

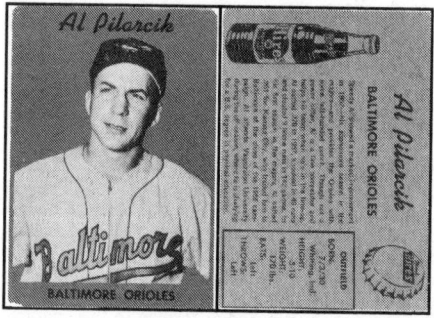

The cards in this 8-card test set measure 2 5/16"
by 3 1/2" or 2 5/16" by 7" with tabs. The 1958 Hires
Root Beer test set features unnumbered, color
cards. The card front photos are shown on a yellow
or orange back ground instead of the wood grain
background used in the Hires regular set. The cards
contain a detachable coupon just as the regular Hires
issue does. Cards were test marketed on a very
limited basis in a few cities. Cards with the coupon
still intact are worth double the prices in the checklist

below. The checklist below is ordered alphabetically.

		NRMT	VG-E	GOOD
COMPLETE SET		750.00	375.00	75.00
COMMON PLAYER (1-8)		75.00	37.50	7.50
☐ 1	Johnny Antonelli	90.00	45.00	9.00
☐ 2	Jim Busby	75.00	37.50	7.50
☐ 3	Chico Fernandez	75.00	37.50	7.50
☐ 4	Bob Friend	90.00	45.00	9.00
☐ 5	Vern Law	90.00	45.00	9.00
☐ 6	Stan Lopata	75.00	37.50	7.50
☐ 7	Willie Mays	300.00	150.00	30.00
☐ 8	Al Pilarcik	75.00	37.50	7.50

1959 Home Run Derby

MICKEY MANTLE
NEW YORK YANKEES

This 20-card set was produced in 1959 by American Motors to publicize a TV program. The cards are black and white and blank backed. The cards measure approximately 3 1/8" by 5 1/4". The cards are unnumbered and are ordered alphabetically below for convenience.

		NRMT	VG-E	GOOD
COMPLETE SET (20)		2700.00	1200.00	250.00
COMMON PLAYER (1-20)		50.00	25.00	5.00
☐ 1	Hank Aaron	300.00	125.00	25.00
☐ 2	Bob Allison	50.00	25.00	5.00
☐ 3	Ernie Banks	150.00	75.00	15.00
☐ 4	Ken Boyer	75.00	37.50	7.50
☐ 5	Bob Cerv	50.00	25.00	5.00
☐ 6	Rocky Colavito	75.00	37.50	7.50
☐ 7	Gil Hodges	100.00	50.00	12.50
☐ 8	Jackie Jensen	75.00	37.50	7.50
☐ 9	Al Kaline	175.00	85.00	18.00
☐ 10	Harmon Killebrew	150.00	75.00	15.00
☐ 11	Jim Lemon	50.00	25.00	5.00
☐ 12	Mickey Mantle	750.00	300.00	60.00
☐ 13	Ed Mathews	150.00	75.00	15.00
☐ 14	Willie Mays	300.00	125.00	25.00
☐ 15	Wally Post	50.00	25.00	5.00
☐ 16	Frank Robinson	150.00	75.00	15.00
☐ 17	Mark Scott	50.00	25.00	5.00
	(TV show host)			
☐ 18	Duke Snider	225.00	100.00	20.00
☐ 19	Dick Stuart	50.00	25.00	5.00
☐ 20	Gus Triandos	50.00	25.00	5.00

1947 Homogenized Bond

The cards in this 48-card set measure 2 1/4" by 3 1/2". The 1947 W571/D305 Homogenized Bread are sets of unnumbered cards containing 44 baseball players and four boxers. The W571 set exists in two styles. Style one is identical to the D305 set except for the back printing while style two has perforated edges and movie stars depicted on the backs. The second style of W571 cards contains only 13 cards. The four boxers in the checklist below are indicated by BOX. The checklist below is ordered alphabetically.

		NRMT	VG-E	GOOD
COMPLETE SET		350.00	175.00	35.00
COMMON PLAYER (1-48)		4.50	2.25	.45
COMMON BOXER		2.25	1.10	.22
☐ 1	Rex Barney	4.50	2.25	.45
☐ 2	Larry Berra	20.00	10.00	2.00
☐ 3	Ewell Blackwell	4.50	2.25	.45
☐ 4	Lou Boudreau	9.00	4.50	.90
☐ 5	Ralph Branca	6.00	3.00	.60
☐ 6	Harry Brecheen	4.50	2.25	.45
☐ 7	Primo Carnera BOX	2.25	1.10	.22
☐ 8	Marcel Cerdan BOX	2.25	1.10	.22
☐ 9	Dom DiMaggio	6.00	3.00	.60
☐ 10	Joe DiMaggio	60.00	30.00	6.00
☐ 11	Bobbie Doerr	9.00	4.50	.90
☐ 12	Bruce Edwards	4.50	2.25	.45
☐ 13	Bob Elliott	6.00	3.00	.60
☐ 14	Del Ennis	6.00	3.00	.60
☐ 15	Bob Feller	20.00	10.00	2.00
☐ 16	Carl Furillo	7.50	3.75	.75
☐ 17	Joe Gordon	6.00	3.00	.60
☐ 18	Sid Gordon	4.50	2.25	.45
☐ 19	Joe Hatten	4.50	2.25	.45
☐ 20	Gil Hodges	15.00	7.50	1.50
☐ 21	Tommy Holmes	6.00	3.00	.60
☐ 22	Larry Jansen	4.50	2.25	.45
☐ 23	Sheldon Jones	4.50	2.25	.45
☐ 24	Edwin Joost	4.50	2.25	.45
☐ 25	Charlie Keller	6.00	3.00	.60
☐ 26	Ken Keltner	4.50	2.25	.45
☐ 27	Buddy Kerr	4.50	2.25	.45
☐ 28	Ralph Kiner	12.00	6.00	1.20
☐ 29	Jake LaMotta BOX	4.50	2.25	.45
☐ 30	John Lindell	4.50	2.25	.45
☐ 31	Whitey Lockman	4.00	2.00	.40
☐ 32	Joe Louis BOX	7.50	3.75	.75
☐ 33	Willard Marshall	4.50	2.25	.45
☐ 34	Johnny Mize	12.00	6.00	1.20
☐ 35	Stan Musial	30.00	15.00	3.00
☐ 36	Andy Pafko	4.50	2.25	.45
☐ 37	Johnny Pesky	4.50	2.25	.45
☐ 38	Pee Wee Reese	20.00	10.00	2.00
☐ 39	Phil Rizzuto	15.00	7.50	1.50
☐ 40	Aaron Robinson	4.50	2.25	.45
☐ 41	Jackie Robinson	30.00	15.00	3.00
☐ 42	John Sain	7.50	3.75	.75
☐ 43	Enos Slaughter	10.00	5.00	1.00
☐ 44	Vern Stephens	6.00	3.00	.60
☐ 45	George Tebbetts	4.50	2.25	.45
☐ 46	Bobby Thomson	6.00	3.00	.60

		NRMT	VG-E	GOOD
☐ 47	Johnny VanderMeer	6.00	3.00	.60
☐ 48	Ted Williams	40.00	20.00	4.00

1975 Hostess

The cards in this 150-card set measure 2 1/4" by 3 1/4" individually or 3 1/4" by 7 1/4" as panels of three. The 1975 Hostess set was issued in panels of three cards each on the backs of family sized packages of Hostess cakes. Card number 125, Bill Madlock, was listed correctly as an infielder and incorrectly as a pitcher. Number 11, Burt Hooton, and number 89, Doug Rader, are spelled two different ways. Some panels are more scarce than others as they were issued only on the backs of less popular Hostess products. These scarcer panels are shown with asterisks in the checklist. Although complete panel prices are not explicitly listed, they would generally have a value 25% greater than the sum of the values of the individual players on that panel.

		NRMT	VG-E	GOOD
COMPLETE INDIV.SET		135.00	65.00	13.50
COMMON PLAYER		.30	.15	.03

			NRMT	VG-E	GOOD
☐	1	Bob Tolan	.30	.15	.03
☐	2	Cookie Rojas	.30	.15	.03
☐	3	Darrell Evans	.60	.30	.06
☐	4	Sal Bando	.40	.20	.04
☐	5	Joe Morgan	2.00	1.00	.20
☐	6	Mickey Lolich	.50	.25	.05
☐	7	Don Sutton	2.00	1.00	.20
☐	8	Bill Melton	.30	.15	.03
☐	9	Tim Foli	.30	.15	.03
☐	10	Joe LaHoud	.30	.15	.03
☐	11A	Bert Hooten (sic)	1.00	.50	.10
☐	11B	Burt Hooton	1.00	.50	.10
☐	12	Paul Blair	.30	.15	.03
☐	13	Jim Barr	.30	.15	.03
☐	14	Toby Harrah	.40	.20	.04
☐	15	John Milner	.30	.15	.03
☐	16	Ken Holtzman	.40	.20	.04
☐	17	Cesar Cedeno	.40	.20	.04
☐	18	Dwight Evans	.75	.35	.07
☐	19	Willie McCovey	2.50	1.25	.25
☐	20	Tony Oliva	.60	.30	.06
☐	21	Manny Sanguillen	.40	.20	.04
☐	22	Mickey Rivers	.40	.20	.04
☐	23	Lou Brock	2.50	1.25	.25
☐	24	Graig Nettles	1.50	.75	.15
		(Craig on front)			
☐	25	Jim Wynn	.40	.20	.04
☐	26	George Scott	.30	.15	.03
☐	27	Greg Luzinski	.50	.25	.05
☐	28	Bert Campaneris	.40	.20	.04
☐	29	Pete Rose	10.00	5.00	1.00
☐	30	Buddy Bell	.50	.25	.05
☐	31	Gary Matthews	.40	.20	.04
☐	32	Freddie Patek	.30	.15	.03

			NRMT	VG-E	GOOD
☐	33	Mike Lum	.30	.15	.03
☐	34	Ellie Rodriguez	.30	.15	.03
☐	35	Milt May	.50	.25	.05
		(photo actually Lee May)			
☐	36	Willie Horton	.40	.20	.04
☐	37	Dave Winfield	3.00	1.50	.30
☐	38	Tom Grieve	.40	.20	.04
☐	39	Barry Foote	.30	.15	.03
☐	40	Joe Rudi	.40	.20	.04
☐	41	Bake McBride	.30	.15	.03
☐	42	Mike Cuellar	.40	.20	.04
☐	43	Garry Maddox	.40	.20	.04
☐	44	Carlos May	.30	.15	.03
☐	45	Bud Harrelson	.30	.15	.03
☐	46	Dave Chalk	.30	.15	.03
☐	47	Dave Concepcion	.50	.25	.05
☐	48	Carl Yastrzemski	6.00	3.00	.60
☐	49	Steve Garvey	4.00	2.00	.40
☐	50	Amos Otis	.40	.20	.04
☐	51	Rick Reuschel	.50	.25	.05
☐	52	Rollie Fingers	1.00	.50	.10
☐	53	Bob Watson	.40	.20	.04
☐	54	John Ellis	.30	.15	.03
☐	55	Bob Bailey	.30	.15	.03
☐	56	Rod Carew	4.00	2.00	.40
☐	57	Rich Hebner	.30	.15	.03
☐	58	Nolan Ryan	4.50	2.25	.45
☐	59	Reggie Smith	.50	.25	.05
☐	60	Joe Coleman	.30	.15	.03
☐	61	Ron Cey	.50	.25	.05
☐	62	Darrell Porter	.40	.20	.04
☐	63	Steve Carlton	4.00	2.00	.40
☐	64	Gene Tenace	.30	.15	.03
☐	65	Jose Cardenal	.30	.15	.03
☐	66	Bill Lee	.40	.20	.04
☐	67	Dave Lopes	.40	.20	.04
☐	68	Wilbur Wood	.40	.20	.04
☐	69	Steve Renko	.30	.15	.03
☐	70	Joe Torre	.50	.25	.05
☐	71	Ted Sizemore	.30	.15	.03
☐	72	Bobby Grich	.40	.20	.04
☐	73	Chris Speier	.30	.15	.03
☐	74	Bert Blyleven	.60	.30	.06
☐	75	Tom Seaver	4.00	2.00	.40
☐	76	Nate Colbert	.30	.15	.03
☐	77	Don Kessinger	.40	.20	.04
☐	78	George Medich	.30	.15	.03
☐	79	Andy Messersmith *	.50	.25	.05
☐	80	Robin Yount *	7.50	3.75	.75
☐	81	Al Oliver *	1.00	.50	.10
☐	82	Bill Singer *	.40	.20	.04
☐	83	Johnny Bench *	4.00	2.00	.40
☐	84	Gaylord Perry *	2.00	1.00	.20
☐	85	Dave Kingman *	1.00	.50	.10
☐	86	Ed Herrmann *	.40	.20	.04
☐	87	Ralph Garr *	.40	.20	.04
☐	88	Reggie Jackson *	6.00	3.00	.60
☐	89A	Doug Radar ERR * (sic, Rader)	1.00	.50	.10
☐	89B	Doug Rader COR *	2.00	1.00	.20
☐	90	Elliott Maddox *	.40	.20	.04
☐	91	Bill Russell *	.50	.25	.05
☐	92	John Mayberry *	.40	.20	.04
☐	93	Dave Cash *	.40	.20	.04
☐	94	Jeff Burroughs *	.40	.20	.04
☐	95	Ted Simmons *	.90	.45	.09
☐	96	Joe Decker *	.40	.20	.04
☐	97	Bill Buckner *	.90	.45	.09
☐	98	Bobby Darwin *	.40	.20	.04
☐	99	Phil Niekro *	2.50	1.25	.25
☐	100	Jim Sundberg *	.40	.20	.04
☐	101	Greg Gross	.30	.15	.03
☐	102	Luis Tiant	.50	.25	.05
☐	103	Glenn Beckert	.30	.15	.03
☐	104	Hal McRae	.40	.20	.04
☐	105	Mike Jorgensen	.30	.15	.03
☐	106	Mike Hargrove	.40	.20	.04
☐	107	Don Gullett	.40	.20	.04
☐	108	Tito Fuentes	.30	.15	.03
☐	109	John Grubb	.30	.15	.03
☐	110	Jim Kaat	.75	.35	.07
☐	111	Felix Millan	.30	.15	.03
☐	112	Don Money	.30	.15	.03
☐	113	Rick Monday	.40	.20	.04
☐	114	Dick Bosman	.30	.15	.03
☐	115	Roger Metzger	.30	.15	.03
☐	116	Fergie Jenkins	.75	.35	.07
☐	117	Dusty Baker	.50	.25	.05
☐	118	Billy Champion *	.40	.20	.04
☐	119	Bob Gibson *	3.00	1.50	.30
☐	120	Bill Freehan *	.50	.25	.05
☐	121	Cesar Geronimo	.30	.15	.03
☐	122	Jorge Orta	.30	.15	.03
☐	123	Cleon Jones	.30	.15	.03

☐ 124	Steve Busby	.40	.20	.04
☐ 125A	Bill Madlock ERR (pitcher)	1.50	.75	.15
☐ 125B	Bill Madlock COR (infielder)	1.50	.75	.15
☐ 126	Jim Palmer	2.50	1.25	.25
☐ 127	Tony Perez	.75	.35	.07
☐ 128	Larry Hisle	.40	.20	.04
☐ 129	Rusty Staub	.50	.25	.05
☐ 130	Hank Aaron *	6.50	3.25	.65
☐ 131	Rennie Stennett *	.40	.20	.04
☐ 132	Rico Petrocelli *	.50	.25	.05
☐ 133	Mike Schmidt	5.50	2.75	.55
☐ 134	Sparky Lyle	.50	.25	.05
☐ 135	Willie Stargell	2.50	1.25	.25
☐ 136	Ken Henderson	.30	.15	.03
☐ 137	Willie Montanez	.30	.15	.03
☐ 138	Thurman Munson	3.50	1.75	.35
☐ 139	Richie Zisk	.40	.20	.04
☐ 140	George Hendrick	.40	.20	.04
☐ 141	Bobby Murcer	.50	.25	.05
☐ 142	Lee May	.40	.20	.04
☐ 143	Carlton Fisk	.75	.35	.07
☐ 144	Brooks Robinson	3.00	1.50	.30
☐ 145	Bobby Bonds	.50	.25	.05
☐ 146	Gary Sutherland	.30	.15	.03
☐ 147	Oscar Gamble	.30	.15	.03
☐ 148	Jim Hunter	2.00	1.00	.20
☐ 149	Tug McGraw	.50	.25	.05
☐ 150	Dave McNally	.40	.20	.04

1975 Hostess Twinkie

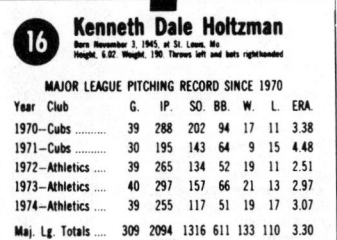

16	Kenneth Dale Holtzman
	Born November 3, 1945, at St. Louis, Mo. Height, 6.02. Weight, 190. Throws left and bats righthanded

MAJOR LEAGUE PITCHING RECORD SINCE 1970

Year	Club	G.	IP.	SO.	BB.	W.	L.	ERA.
1970	Cubs	39	288	202	94	17	11	3.38
1971	Cubs	30	195	143	64	9	15	4.48
1972	Athletics	39	265	134	52	19	11	2.51
1973	Athletics	40	297	157	66	21	13	2.97
1974	Athletics	39	255	117	51	19	17	3.07
Maj. Lg. Totals		309	2094	1316	611	133	110	3.30

The cards in this 60-card set measure 2 1/4" by 3 1/4". The 1975 Hostess Twinkie set was issued on a limited basis in the far western part of the country. The set contains the same numbers as the regular set to number 36; however, the set is skip numbered after number 36. The cards were issued as the backs for 25-cent Twinkies packs. The fronts are indistinguishable from the regular Hostess cards; however the card backs are different in that the Twinkie cards have a thick black bar in the middle of the reverse.

		NRMT	VG-E	GOOD
COMPLETE SET		75.00	37.50	7.50
COMMON PLAYER		.60	.30	.06
☐ 1	Bob Tolan	.60	.30	.06
☐ 2	Cookie Rojas	.60	.30	.06
☐ 3	Darrell Evans	1.00	.50	.10
☐ 4	Sal Bando	.75	.35	.07
☐ 5	Joe Morgan	2.50	1.25	.25
☐ 6	Mickey Lolich	.90	.45	.09
☐ 7	Don Sutton	2.00	1.00	.20
☐ 8	Bill Melton	.60	.30	.06
☐ 9	Tim Foli	.60	.30	.06
☐ 10	Joe LaHoud	.60	.30	.06
☐ 11	Bert Hooten (sic)	1.00	.50	.10
☐ 12	Paul Blair	.60	.30	.06
☐ 13	Jim Barr	.60	.30	.06
☐ 14	Toby Harrah	.75	.35	.07
☐ 15	John Milner	.60	.30	.06
☐ 16	Ken Holtzman	.75	.35	.07
☐ 17	Cesar Cedeno	.75	.35	.07
☐ 18	Dwight Evans	1.25	.60	.12
☐ 19	Willie McCovey	3.00	1.50	.30
☐ 20	Tony Oliva	1.00	.50	.10
☐ 21	Manny Sanguillen	.75	.35	.07
☐ 22	Mickey Rivers	.75	.35	.07

☐ 23	Lou Brock	3.00	1.50	.30
☐ 24	Graig Nettles (Craig on front)	1.50	.75	.15
☐ 25	Jim Wynn	.75	.35	.07
☐ 26	George Scott	.60	.30	.06
☐ 27	Greg Luzinski	.90	.45	.09
☐ 28	Bert Campaneris	.75	.35	.07
☐ 29	Pete Rose	10.00	5.00	1.00
☐ 30	Buddy Bell	.90	.45	.09
☐ 31	Gary Matthews	.75	.35	.07
☐ 32	Freddie Patek	.60	.30	.06
☐ 33	Mike Lum	.60	.30	.06
☐ 34	Ellie Rodriguez	.60	.30	.06
☐ 35	Milt May (Lee May picture)	.90	.45	.09
☐ 36	Willie Horton	.75	.35	.07
☐ 40	Joe Rudi	.75	.35	.07
☐ 43	Garry Maddox	.75	.35	.07
☐ 46	Dave Chalk	.60	.30	.06
☐ 49	Steve Garvey	4.50	2.25	.45
☐ 52	Rollie Fingers	1.50	.75	.15
☐ 58	Nolan Ryan	5.00	2.50	.50
☐ 61	Ron Cey	.90	.45	.09
☐ 64	Gene Tenace	.60	.30	.06
☐ 65	Jose Cardenal	.60	.30	.06
☐ 67	Dave Lopes	.75	.35	.07
☐ 68	Wilbur Wood	.75	.35	.07
☐ 73	Chris Speier	.60	.30	.06
☐ 77	Don Kessinger	.75	.35	.07
☐ 79	Andy Messersmith	.75	.35	.07
☐ 80	Robin Yount	8.00	4.00	.80
☐ 82	Bill Singer	.60	.30	.06
☐ 103	Glenn Beckert	.60	.30	.06
☐ 110	Jim Kaat	1.00	.50	.10
☐ 112	Don Money	.60	.30	.06
☐ 113	Rick Monday	.75	.35	.07
☐ 122	Jorge Orta	.60	.30	.06
☐ 125	Bill Madlock	1.25	.60	.12
☐ 130	Hank Aaron	7.50	3.75	.75
☐ 136	Ken Henderson	.60	.30	.06

1976 Hostess

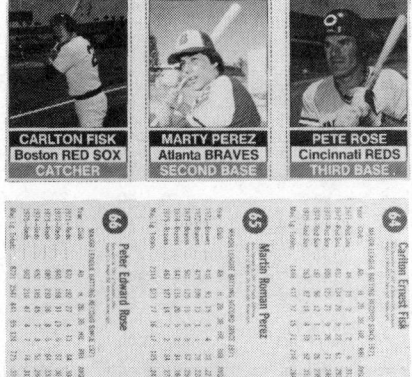

CARLTON FISK	MARTY PEREZ	PETE ROSE
Boston RED SOX	Atlanta BRAVES	Cincinnati REDS
CATCHER	SECOND BASE	THIRD BASE

The cards in this 150-card set measure 2 1/4" by 3 1/4" individually or 3 1/4" by 7 1/4" as panels of three. The 1976 Hostess set contains color, numbered cards issued in panels of three cards each on family sized packages of Hostess cakes. Scarcer panels (those only found on less popular Hostess products) are listed in the checklist below with asterisks. Complete panels of three have a value 25% more than the sum of the individual cards on the panel. Nine additional numbers (151- 159) were apparently planned but never actually issued. These exist as proof cards and are quite scarce, e.g., 151 Ferguson Jenkins, 152 Mike Cuellar, 153 Tom Murphy, 154 Al Cowens, 155 Barry Foote, 156 Steve Carlton, 157 Richie Zisk, 158 Ken Holtzman, and 159 Cliff Johnson.

		NRMT	VG-E	GOOD
	COMPLETE INDIV.SET(150)	135.00	65.00	13.50
	COMMON PLAYER (1-150)	.30	.15	.03

		NRMT	VG-E	GOOD
☐	1 Fred Lynn	1.25	.60	.12
☐	2 Joe Morgan	2.00	1.00	.20
☐	3 Phil Niekro	2.00	1.00	.20
☐	4 Gaylord Perry	1.50	.75	.15
☐	5 Bob Watson	.40	.20	.04
☐	6 Bill Freehan	.50	.25	.05
☐	7 Lou Brock	2.50	1.25	.25
☐	8 Al Fitzmorris	.30	.15	.03
☐	9 Rennie Stennett	.30	.15	.03
☐	10 Tony Oliva	.60	.30	.06
☐	11 Robin Yount	3.50	1.75	.35
☐	12 Rick Manning	.30	.15	.03
☐	13 Bobby Grich	.40	.20	.04
☐	14 Terry Forster	.40	.20	.04
☐	15 Dave Kingman	.60	.30	.06
☐	16 Thurman Munson	3.50	1.75	.35
☐	17 Rick Reuschel	.50	.25	.05
☐	18 Bobby Bonds	.50	.25	.05
☐	19 Steve Garvey	4.00	2.00	.40
☐	20 Vida Blue	.40	.20	.04
☐	21 Dave Rader	.30	.15	.03
☐	22 Johnny Bench	3.50	1.75	.35
☐	23 Luis Tiant	.50	.25	.05
☐	24 Darrell Evans	.60	.30	.06
☐	25 Larry Dierker	.30	.15	.03
☐	26 Willie Horton	.40	.20	.04
☐	27 John Ellis	.30	.15	.03
☐	28 Al Cowens	.40	.20	.04
☐	29 Jerry Reuss	.40	.20	.04
☐	30 Reggie Smith	.50	.25	.05
☐	31 Bobby Darwin *	.40	.20	.04
☐	32 Fritz Peterson *	.40	.20	.04
☐	33 Rod Carew *	4.00	2.00	.40
☐	34 Carlos May *	.40	.20	.04
☐	35 Tom Seaver *	4.50	2.25	.45
☐	36 Brooks Robinson *	4.00	2.00	.40
☐	37 Jose Cardenal	.30	.15	.03
☐	38 Ron Blomberg	.30	.15	.03
☐	39 Leroy Stanton	.30	.15	.03
☐	40 Dave Cash	.30	.15	.03
☐	41 John Montefusco	.40	.20	.04
☐	42 Bob Tolan	.30	.15	.03
☐	43 Carl Morton	.30	.15	.03
☐	44 Rick Burleson	.40	.20	.04
☐	45 Don Gullett	.40	.20	.04
☐	46 Vern Ruhle	.30	.15	.03
☐	47 Cesar Cedeno	.40	.20	.04
☐	48 Toby Harrah	.40	.20	.04
☐	49 Willie Stargell	2.50	1.25	.25
☐	50 Al Hrabosky	.40	.20	.04
☐	51 Amos Otis	.40	.20	.04
☐	52 Bud Harrelson	.30	.15	.03
☐	53 Jim Hughes	.30	.15	.03
☐	54 George Scott	.30	.15	.03
☐	55 Mike Vail *	.40	.20	.04
☐	56 Jim Palmer *	3.00	1.50	.30
☐	57 Jorge Orta *	.40	.20	.04
☐	58 Chris Chambliss *	.50	.25	.05
☐	59 Dave Chalk *	.40	.20	.04
☐	60 Ray Burris *	.40	.20	.04
☐	61 Bert Campaneris *	.50	.25	.05
☐	62 Gary Carter *	5.50	2.75	.55
☐	63 Ron Cey *	.75	.35	.07
☐	64 Carlton Fisk *	1.00	.50	.10
☐	65 Marty Perez *	.40	.20	.04
☐	66 Pete Rose *	10.00	5.00	1.00
☐	67 Roger Metzger *	.40	.20	.04
☐	68 Jim Sundberg *	.40	.20	.04
☐	69 Ron LeFlore *	.40	.20	.04
☐	70 Ted Sizemore *	.40	.20	.04
☐	71 Steve Busby *	.50	.25	.05
☐	72 Manny Sanguillen *	.50	.25	.05
☐	73 Larry Hisle *	.40	.20	.04
☐	74 Pete Broberg *	.40	.20	.04
☐	75 Boog Powell *	.75	.35	.07
☐	76 Ken Singleton *	.75	.35	.07
☐	77 Rich Gossage *	1.50	.75	.15
☐	78 Jerry Grote *	.40	.20	.04
☐	79 Nolan Ryan *	5.00	2.50	.50
☐	80 Rick Monday *	.50	.25	.05
☐	81 Graig Nettles *	.75	.35	.07
☐	82 Chris Speier *	.30	.15	.03
☐	83 Dave Winfield *	3.00	1.50	.30
☐	84 Mike Schmidt *	5.50	2.75	.55
☐	85 Buzz Capra *	.30	.15	.03
☐	86 Tony Perez *	.75	.35	.07
☐	87 Dwight Evans *	.75	.35	.07
☐	88 Mike Hargrove *	.30	.15	.03
☐	89 Joe Coleman *	.30	.15	.03

☐	90 Greg Gross	.30	.15	.03
☐	91 John Mayberry	.40	.20	.04
☐	92 John Candelaria	.50	.25	.05
☐	93 Bake McBride	.30	.15	.03
☐	94 Hank Aaron	5.50	2.75	.55
☐	95 Buddy Bell	.50	.25	.05
☐	96 Steve Braun	.30	.15	.03
☐	97 Jon Matlack	.40	.20	.04
☐	98 Lee May	.40	.20	.04
☐	99 Wilbur Wood	.40	.20	.04
☐	100 Bill Madlock	.75	.35	.07
☐	101 Frank Tanana	.40	.20	.04
☐	102 Mickey Rivers	.40	.20	.04
☐	103 Mike Ivie	.30	.15	.03
☐	104 Rollie Fingers	1.00	.50	.10
☐	105 Dave Lopes	.40	.20	.04
☐	106 George Foster	.90	.45	.09
☐	107 Denny Doyle	.30	.15	.03
☐	108 Earl Williams	.30	.15	.03
☐	109 Tom Veryzer	.30	.15	.03
☐	110 J.R. Richard	.40	.20	.04
☐	111 Jeff Burroughs	.30	.15	.03
☐	112 Al Oliver	.75	.35	.07
☐	113 Ted Simmons	.75	.35	.07
☐	114 George Brett	6.50	3.25	.65
☐	115 Frank Duffy	.30	.15	.03
☐	116 Bert Blyleven	.50	.25	.05
☐	117 Darrell Porter	.30	.15	.03
☐	118 Don Baylor	.50	.25	.05
☐	119 Bucky Dent	.50	.25	.05
☐	120 Felix Millan	.30	.15	.03
☐	121 Mike Cuellar	.40	.20	.04
☐	122 Gene Tenace	.30	.15	.03
☐	123 Bobby Murcer	.50	.25	.05
☐	124 Willie McCovey	2.00	1.00	.20
☐	125 Greg Luzinski	.50	.25	.05
☐	126 Larry Parrish	.60	.30	.06
☐	127 Jim Rice	4.00	2.00	.40
☐	128 Dave Concepcion	.50	.25	.05
☐	129 Jim Wynn	.40	.20	.04
☐	130 Tom Grieve	.40	.20	.04
☐	131 Mike Cosgrove	.30	.15	.03
☐	132 Dan Meyer	.30	.15	.03
☐	133 Dave Parker	2.00	1.00	.20
☐	134 Don Kessinger	.40	.20	.04
☐	135 Hal McRae	.40	.20	.04
☐	136 Don Money	.30	.15	.03
☐	137 Dennis Eckersley	.40	.20	.04
☐	138 Fergie Jenkins	.60	.30	.06
☐	139 Mike Torrez	.40	.20	.04
☐	140 Jerry Morales	.30	.15	.03
☐	141 Jim Hunter	2.00	1.00	.20
☐	142 Gary Matthews	.40	.20	.04
☐	143 Randy Jones	.40	.20	.04
☐	144 Mike Jorgensen	.30	.15	.03
☐	145 Larry Bowa	.50	.25	.05
☐	146 Reggie Jackson	4.50	2.25	.45
☐	147 Steve Yeager	.30	.15	.03
☐	148 Dave May	.30	.15	.03
☐	149 Carl Yastrzemski	5.00	2.50	.50
☐	150 Cesar Geronimo	.30	.15	.03

1976 Hostess Twinkie

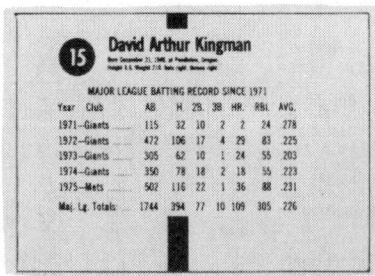

The cards in this 60-card set measure 2 1/4" by 3 1/4". The 1976 Hostess Twinkies set contains the first 60 cards of the 1976 Hostess set. These cards were issued as backs on 25- cent Twinkie packages as in the 1975 Twinkies set. The fronts are indistinguishable from the regular Hostess cards; however the card backs are different in that the

Twinkie cards have a thick black bar in the middle of the reverse.

		NRMT	VG-E	GOOD
COMPLETE SET		75.00	37.50	7.50
COMMON PLAYER		.60	.30	.06

☐	1	Fred Lynn	1.25	.60	.12
☐	2	Joe Morgan	2.50	1.25	.25
☐	3	Phil Niekro	2.00	1.00	.20
☐	4	Gaylord Perry	1.50	.75	.15
☐	5	Bob Watson	.75	.35	.07
☐	6	Bill Freehan	.75	.35	.07
☐	7	Lou Brock	3.00	1.50	.30
☐	8	Al Fitzmorris	.60	.30	.06
☐	9	Rennie Stennett	.60	.30	.06
☐	10	Tony Oliva	1.00	.50	.10
☐	11	Robin Yount	3.50	1.75	.35
☐	12	Rick Manning	.60	.30	.06
☐	13	Bobby Grich	.75	.35	.07
☐	14	Terry Forster	.75	.35	.07
☐	15	Dave Kingman	.90	.45	.09
☐	16	Thurman Munson	3.50	1.75	.35
☐	17	Rick Reuschel	.90	.45	.09
☐	18	Bobby Bonds	.90	.45	.09
☐	19	Steve Garvey	4.50	2.25	.45
☐	20	Vida Blue	.75	.35	.07
☐	21	Dave Rader	.60	.30	.06
☐	22	Johnny Bench	3.50	1.75	.35
☐	23	Luis Tiant	.90	.45	.09
☐	24	Darrell Evans	1.00	.50	.10
☐	25	Larry Dierker	.60	.30	.06
☐	26	Willie Horton	.75	.35	.07
☐	27	John Ellis	.60	.30	.06
☐	28	Al Cowens	.75	.35	.07
☐	29	Jerry Reuss	.75	.35	.07
☐	30	Reggie Smith	.90	.45	.09
☐	31	Bobby Darwin	.60	.30	.06
☐	32	Fritz Peterson	.60	.30	.06
☐	33	Rod Carew	4.50	2.25	.45
☐	34	Carlos May	.60	.30	.06
☐	35	Tom Seaver	4.50	2.25	.45
☐	36	Brooks Robinson	4.00	2.00	.40
☐	37	Jose Cardenal	.60	.30	.06
☐	38	Ron Blomberg	.60	.30	.06
☐	39	Leroy Stanton	.60	.30	.06
☐	40	Dave Cash	.60	.30	.06
☐	41	John Montefusco	.75	.35	.07
☐	42	Bob Tolan	.60	.30	.06
☐	43	Carl Morton	.60	.30	.06
☐	44	Rick Burleson	.75	.35	.07
☐	45	Don Gullett	.75	.35	.07
☐	46	Vern Ruhle	.60	.30	.06
☐	47	Cesar Cedeno	.75	.35	.07
☐	48	Toby Harrah	.75	.35	.07
☐	49	Willie Stargell	2.50	1.25	.25
☐	50	Al Hrabosky	.75	.35	.07
☐	51	Amos Otis	.75	.35	.07
☐	52	Bud Harrelson	.60	.30	.06
☐	53	Jim Hughes	.60	.30	.06
☐	54	George Scott	.60	.30	.06
☐	55	Mike Vail	.60	.30	.06
☐	56	Jim Palmer	3.00	1.50	.30
☐	57	Jorge Orta	.60	.30	.06
☐	58	Chris Chambliss	.75	.35	.07
☐	59	Dave Chalk	.60	.30	.06
☐	60	Ray Burris	.60	.30	.06

1977 Hostess

The cards in this 150-card set measure 2 1/4" by 3 1/4" individually or 3 1/4" by 7 1/4" as panels of three. The 1977 Hostess set contains color, numbered cards issued in panels of three cards each with Hostess family sized caked products. Scarcer panels are listed in the checklist below with asterisks. Although complete panel prices are not explicitly listed below, they would generally have a value 25% greater than the sum of the individual players on the panel.

		NRMT	VG-E	GOOD
COMPLETE INDIV. SET		135.00	65.00	13.50
COMMON PLAYER		.30	.15	.03

☐	1	Jim Palmer	2.50	1.25	.25

BILL STEIN — Seattle MARINERS — SECOND BASE

ROLLIE FINGERS — San Diego PADRES — PITCHER

BRIAN DOWNING — Chicago WHITE SOX — CATCHER

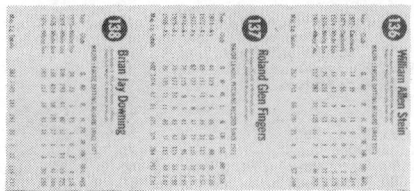

☐	2	Joe Morgan	2.00	1.00	.20
☐	3	Reggie Jackson	4.50	2.25	.45
☐	4	Carl Yastrzemski	5.50	2.75	.55
☐	5	Thurman Munson	3.50	1.75	.35
☐	6	Johnny Bench	3.50	1.75	.35
☐	7	Tom Seaver	3.50	1.75	.35
☐	8	Pete Rose	8.50	4.25	.85
☐	9	Rod Carew	3.50	1.75	.35
☐	10	Luis Tiant	.50	.25	.05
☐	11	Phil Garner	.30	.15	.03
☐	12	Sixto Lezcano	.30	.15	.03
☐	13	Mike Torrez	.30	.15	.03
☐	14	Dave Lopes	.40	.20	.04
☐	15	Doug DeCinces	.50	.25	.05
☐	16	Jim Spencer	.30	.15	.03
☐	17	Hal McRae	.40	.20	.04
☐	18	Mike Hargrove	.30	.15	.03
☐	19	Willie Montanez *	.40	.20	.04
☐	20	Roger Metzger *	.40	.20	.04
☐	21	Dwight Evans *	1.50	.75	.15
☐	22	Steve Rogers *	.75	.35	.07
☐	23	Jim Rice *	4.00	2.00	.40
☐	24	Pete Falcone *	.40	.20	.04
☐	25	Greg Luzinski *	.90	.45	.09
☐	26	Randy Jones *	.50	.25	.05
☐	27	Willie Stargell *	3.00	1.50	.30
☐	28	John Hiller *	.40	.20	.04
☐	29	Bobby Murcer *	.50	.25	.05
☐	30	Rick Monday *	.50	.25	.05
☐	31	John Montefusco *	.40	.20	.04
☐	32	Lou Brock *	3.00	1.50	.30
☐	33	Bill North *	.40	.20	.04
☐	34	Robin Yount *	3.00	1.50	.30
☐	35	Steve Garvey *	5.00	2.50	.50
☐	36	George Brett *	6.50	3.25	.65
☐	37	Toby Harrah *	.50	.25	.05
☐	38	Jerry Royster *	.40	.20	.04
☐	39	Bob Watson *	.40	.20	.04
☐	40	George Foster	.90	.45	.09
☐	41	Gary Carter	3.50	1.75	.35
☐	42	John Denny	.40	.20	.04
☐	43	Mike Schmidt	4.50	2.25	.45
☐	44	Dave Winfield	3.00	1.50	.30
☐	45	Al Oliver	.75	.35	.07
☐	46	Mark Fidrych	.50	.25	.05
☐	47	Larry Herndon	.30	.15	.03
☐	48	Dave Goltz	.30	.15	.03
☐	49	Jerry Morales	.30	.15	.03
☐	50	Ron LeFlore	.40	.20	.04
☐	51	Fred Lynn	1.25	.60	.12
☐	52	Vida Blue	.40	.20	.04
☐	53	Rick Manning	.30	.15	.03
☐	54	Bill Buckner	.50	.25	.05
☐	55	Lee May	.40	.20	.04
☐	56	John Mayberry	.40	.20	.04
☐	57	Darrell Chaney	.30	.15	.03
☐	58	Cesar Cedeno	.40	.20	.04
☐	59	Ken Griffey	.40	.20	.04
☐	60	Dave Kingman	.60	.30	.06
☐	61	Ted Simmons	.75	.35	.07
☐	62	Larry Bowa	.60	.30	.06
☐	63	Frank Tanana	.40	.20	.04
☐	64	Jason Thompson	.40	.20	.04
☐	65	Ken Brett	.30	.15	.03
☐	66	Roy Smalley	.40	.20	.04
☐	67	Ray Burris	.30	.15	.03
☐	68	Rick Burleson	.40	.20	.04
☐	69	Buddy Bell	.50	.25	.05
☐	70	Don Sutton	2.00	1.00	.20

☐ 71	Mark Belanger	.40	.20	.04
☐ 72	Dennis Leonard	.40	.20	.04
☐ 73	Gaylord Perry	1.50	.75	.15
☐ 74	Dick Ruthven	.30	.15	.03
☐ 75	Jose Cruz	.50	.25	.05
☐ 76	Cesar Geronimo	.30	.15	.03
☐ 77	Jerry Koosman	.50	.25	.05
☐ 78	Garry Templeton	.90	.45	.09
☐ 79	Jim Hunter	2.00	1.00	.20
☐ 80	John Candelaria	.50	.25	.05
☐ 81	Nolan Ryan	4.00	2.00	.40
☐ 82	Rusty Staub	.60	.30	.06
☐ 83	Jim Barr	.30	.15	.03
☐ 84	Butch Wynegar	.40	.20	.04
☐ 85	Jose Cardenal	.30	.15	.03
☐ 86	Claudell Washington	.50	.25	.05
☐ 87	Bill Travers	.30	.15	.03
☐ 88	Rick Waits	.30	.15	.03
☐ 89	Ron Cey	.50	.25	.05
☐ 90	Al Bumbry	.30	.15	.03
☐ 91	Bucky Dent	.50	.25	.05
☐ 92	Amos Otis	.40	.20	.04
☐ 93	Tom Grieve	.40	.20	.04
☐ 94	Enos Cabell	.30	.15	.03
☐ 95	Dave Concepcion	.50	.25	.05
☐ 96	Felix Millan	.30	.15	.03
☐ 97	Bake McBride	.30	.15	.03
☐ 98	Chris Chambliss	.40	.20	.04
☐ 99	Butch Metzger	.30	.15	.03
☐ 100	Rennie Stennett	.30	.15	.03
☐ 101	Dave Roberts	.30	.15	.03
☐ 102	Lyman Bostock	.40	.20	.04
☐ 103	Rick Reuschel	.50	.25	.05
☐ 104	Carlton Fisk	.75	.35	.07
☐ 105	Jim Slaton	.30	.15	.03
☐ 106	Dennis Eckersley	.40	.20	.04
☐ 107	Ken Singleton	.50	.25	.05
☐ 108	Ralph Garr	.30	.15	.03
☐ 109	Freddie Patek *	.40	.20	.04
☐ 110	Jim Sundberg *	.40	.20	.04
☐ 111	Phil Niekro *	2.00	1.00	.20
☐ 112	J.R. Richard *	.50	.25	.05
☐ 113	Gary Nolan *	.40	.20	.04
☐ 114	Jon Matlack *	.50	.25	.05
☐ 115	Keith Hernandez *	3.50	1.75	.35
☐ 116	Graig Nettles *	1.00	.50	.10
☐ 117	Steve Carlton *	3.50	1.75	.35
☐ 118	Bill Madlock *	1.50	.75	.15
☐ 119	Jerry Reuss *	.50	.25	.05
☐ 120	Aurelio Rodriguez *	.40	.20	.04
☐ 121	Dan Ford *	.40	.20	.04
☐ 122	Ray Fosse *	.40	.20	.04
☐ 123	George Hendrick *	.50	.25	.05
☐ 124	Alan Ashby	.30	.15	.03
☐ 125	Joe Lis	.30	.15	.03
☐ 126	Sal Bando	.40	.20	.04
☐ 127	Richie Zisk	.40	.20	.04
☐ 128	Rich Gossage	.75	.35	.07
☐ 129	Don Baylor	.50	.25	.05
☐ 130	Dave McKay	.30	.15	.03
☐ 131	Bob Grich	.40	.20	.04
☐ 132	Dave Pagan	.30	.15	.03
☐ 133	Dave Cash	.30	.15	.03
☐ 123	Steve Braun	.30	.15	.03
☐ 135	Dan Meyer	.30	.15	.03
☐ 136	Bill Stein	.30	.15	.03
☐ 137	Rollie Fingers	1.25	.60	.12
☐ 138	Brian Downing	.50	.25	.05
☐ 139	Bill Singer	.30	.15	.03
☐ 140	Doyle Alexander	.50	.25	.05
☐ 141	Gene Tenace	.30	.15	.03
☐ 142	Gary Matthews	.40	.20	.04
☐ 143	Don Gullett	.40	.20	.04
☐ 144	Wayne Garland	.30	.15	.03
☐ 145	Pete Broberg	.30	.15	.03
☐ 146	Joe Rudi	.40	.20	.04
☐ 147	Glenn Abbott	.30	.15	.03
☐ 148	George Scott	.30	.15	.03
☐ 149	Bert Campaneris	.40	.20	.04
☐ 150	Andy Messersmith	.40	.20	.04

1978 Hostess

The cards in this 150-card set measure 2 1/4" by 3 1/4" individually or 3 1/4" by 7 1/4" as panels of three. The 1978 Hostess set contains full color, numbered cards issued in panels of three cards each on family packages of Hostess cake products.

TOMMY JOHN LOS ANGELES DODGERS — **GREG LUZINSKI** PHILADELPHIA PHILLIES — **ENOS CABELL** HOUSTON ASTROS

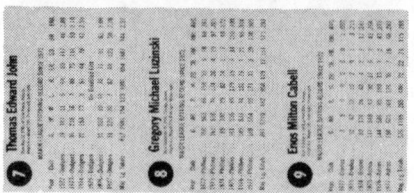

Scarcer panels are listed in the checklist with asterisks. The 1978 Hostess panels are considered by some collectors to be somewhat more difficult to obtain than Hostess panels of other years. Although complete panel prices are not explicitly listed below, they would generally have a value 25% greater than the sum of the individual players on the panel.

		NRMT	VG-E	GOOD
COMPLETE INDIV. SET		135.00	65.00	13.50
COMMON PLAYER		.30	.15	.03
☐ 1	Butch Hobson	.30	.15	.03
☐ 2	George Foster	.90	.45	.09
☐ 3	Bob Forsch	.40	.20	.04
☐ 4	Tony Perez	.75	.35	.07
☐ 5	Bruce Sutter	.90	.45	.09
☐ 6	Hal McRae	.40	.20	.04
☐ 7	Tommy John	.90	.45	.09
☐ 8	Greg Luzinski	.50	.25	.05
☐ 9	Enos Cabell	.30	.15	.03
☐ 10	Doug DeCinces	.50	.25	.05
☐ 11	Willie Stargell	2.00	1.00	.20
☐ 12	Ed Halicki	.30	.15	.03
☐ 13	Larry Hisle	.40	.20	.04
☐ 14	Jim Slaton	.30	.15	.03
☐ 15	Buddy Bell	.50	.25	.05
☐ 16	Earl Williams	.30	.15	.03
☐ 17	Glenn Abbott	.30	.15	.03
☐ 18	Dan Ford	.30	.15	.03
☐ 19	Gary Matthews	.40	.20	.04
☐ 20	Eric Soderholm	.30	.15	.03
☐ 21	Bump Wills	.30	.15	.03
☐ 22	Keith Hernandez	2.50	1.25	.25
☐ 23	Dave Cash	.30	.15	.03
☐ 24	George Scott	.30	.15	.03
☐ 25	Ron Guidry	1.50	.75	.15
☐ 26	Dave Kingman	.60	.30	.06
☐ 27	George Brett	5.00	2.50	.50
☐ 28	Bob Watson *	.40	.20	.04
☐ 29	Bob Boone *	.60	.30	.06
☐ 30	Reggie Smith *	.60	.30	.06
☐ 31	Eddie Murray *	10.00	5.00	1.00
☐ 32	Gary Lavelle *	.40	.20	.04
☐ 33	Rennie Stennett *	.40	.20	.04
☐ 34	Duane Kuiper *	.40	.20	.04
☐ 35	Sixto Lezcano *	.40	.20	.04
☐ 36	Dave Rozema *	.40	.20	.04
☐ 37	Butch Wynegar *	.50	.25	.05
☐ 38	Mitchell Page *	.40	.20	.04
☐ 39	Bill Stein *	.40	.20	.04
☐ 40	Elliott Maddox	.30	.15	.03
☐ 41	Mike Hargrove	.40	.20	.04
☐ 42	Bobby Bonds	.50	.25	.05
☐ 43	Garry Templeton	.50	.25	.05
☐ 44	Johnny Bench	3.50	1.75	.35
☐ 45	Jim Rice	3.50	1.75	.35
☐ 46	Bill Buckner	.50	.25	.05
☐ 47	Reggie Jackson	4.00	2.00	.40
☐ 48	Freddie Patek	.30	.15	.03
☐ 49	Steve Carlton	3.50	1.75	.35
☐ 50	Cesar Cedeno	.40	.20	.04
☐ 51	Steve Yeager	.30	.15	.03
☐ 52	Phil Garner	.30	.15	.03
☐ 53	Lee May	.40	.20	.04
☐ 54	Darrell Evans	.60	.30	.06
☐ 55	Steve Kemp	.40	.20	.04

			NRMT	VG-E	GOOD
☐	56	Dusty Baker	.40	.20	.04
☐	57	Ray Fosse	.30	.15	.03
☐	58	Manny Sanguillen	.40	.20	.04
☐	59	Tom Johnson	.30	.15	.03
☐	60	Lee Stanton	.30	.15	.03
☐	61	Jeff Burroughs	.40	.20	.04
☐	62	Bobby Grich	.40	.20	.04
☐	63	Dave Winfield	3.00	1.50	.30
☐	64	Dan Driessen	.40	.20	.04
☐	65	Ted Simmons	.75	.35	.07
☐	66	Jerry Remy	.30	.15	.03
☐	67	Al Cowens	.40	.20	.04
☐	68	Sparky Lyle	.60	.30	.06
☐	69	Manny Trillo	.40	.20	.04
☐	70	Don Sutton	2.00	1.00	.20
☐	71	Larry Bowa	.60	.30	.06
☐	72	Jose Cruz	.50	.25	.05
☐	73	Willie McCovey	2.00	1.00	.20
☐	74	Bert Blyleven	.60	.30	.06
☐	75	Ken Singleton	.50	.25	.05
☐	76	Bill North	.30	.15	.03
☐	77	Jason Thompson	.40	.20	.04
☐	78	Dennis Eckersley	.40	.20	.04
☐	79	Jim Sundberg	.40	.20	.04
☐	80	Jerry Koosman	.50	.25	.05
☐	81	Bruce Bochte	.30	.15	.03
☐	82	George Hendrick	.40	.20	.04
☐	83	Nolan Ryan	3.50	1.75	.35
☐	84	Roy Howell	.30	.15	.03
☐	85	Roger Metzger	.30	.15	.03
☐	86	Doc Medich	.30	.15	.03
☐	87	Joe Morgan	2.00	1.00	.20
☐	88	Dennis Leonard	.40	.20	.04
☐	89	Willie Randolph	.60	.30	.06
☐	90	Bobby Murcer	.50	.25	.05
☐	91	Rick Manning	.30	.15	.03
☐	92	J.R. Richard	.40	.20	.04
☐	93	Ron Cey	.50	.25	.05
☐	94	Sal Bando	.40	.20	.04
☐	95	Ron LeFlore	.40	.20	.04
☐	96	Dave Goltz	.30	.15	.03
☐	97	Dan Meyer	.30	.15	.03
☐	98	Chris Chambliss	.40	.20	.04
☐	99	Biff Pocoroba	.30	.15	.03
☐	100	Oscar Gamble	.40	.20	.04
☐	101	Frank Tanana	.40	.20	.04
☐	102	Len Randle	.30	.15	.03
☐	103	Tommy Hutton	.30	.15	.03
☐	104	John Candelaria	.50	.25	.05
☐	105	George Orta	.30	.15	.03
☐	106	Ken Reitz	.30	.15	.03
☐	107	Bill Campbell	.30	.15	.03
☐	108	Dave Concepcion	.50	.25	.05
☐	109	Joe Ferguson	.30	.15	.03
☐	110	Mickey Rivers	.40	.20	.04
☐	111	Paul Splittorff	.40	.20	.04
☐	112	Dave Lopes	.50	.25	.05
☐	113	Mike Schmidt	5.00	2.50	.50
☐	114	Joe Rudi	.40	.20	.04
☐	115	Milt May	.30	.15	.03
☐	116	Jim Palmer	2.00	1.00	.20
☐	117	Bill Madlock	1.00	.50	.10
☐	118	Roy Smalley	.40	.20	.04
☐	119	Cecil Cooper	.90	.45	.09
☐	120	Rick Langford	.30	.15	.03
☐	121	Ruppert Jones	.40	.20	.04
☐	122	Phil Niekro	1.50	.75	.15
☐	123	Toby Harrah	.40	.20	.04
☐	124	Chet Lemon	.40	.20	.04
☐	125	Gene Tenace	.30	.15	.03
☐	126	Steve Henderson	.30	.15	.03
☐	127	Mike Torrez	.30	.15	.03
☐	128	Pete Rose	8.50	4.25	.85
☐	129	John Denny	.40	.20	.04
☐	130	Darrell Porter	.40	.20	.04
☐	131	Rick Reuschel	.50	.25	.05
☐	132	Graig Nettles	.75	.35	.07
☐	133	Garry Maddox	.40	.20	.04
☐	134	Mike Flanagan	.40	.20	.04
☐	135	Dave Parker	2.00	1.00	.20
☐	136	Terry Whitfield	.30	.15	.03
☐	137	Wayne Garland	.30	.15	.03
☐	138	Robin Yount	3.00	1.50	.30
☐	139	Gaylord Perry	1.50	.75	.15
☐	140	Rod Carew	3.50	1.75	.35
☐	141	Greg Gross	.30	.15	.03
☐	142	Barry Bonnell	.30	.15	.03
☐	143	Willie Montanez	.30	.15	.03
☐	144	Rollie Fingers	1.25	.60	.12
☐	145	Lyman Bostock	.40	.20	.04
☐	146	Gary Carter	3.50	1.75	.35
☐	147	Ron Blomberg	.30	.15	.03
☐	148	Bob Bailor	.30	.15	.03
☐	149	Tom Seaver	3.50	1.75	.35
☐	150	Thurman Munson	3.00	1.50	.30

1979 Hostess

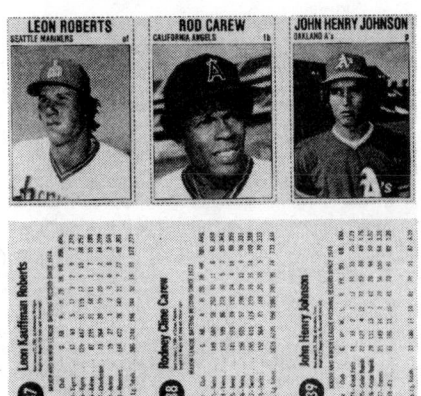

The cards in this 150-card set measure 3 1/4" by 7 1/4" as panels of three. The 1979 Hostess set contains full color, numbered cards issued in panels of three cards each on the backs of family sized Hostess cake products. Scarcer panels are listed in the checklist below with asterisks. Although complete panel prices are not explicitly listed below they would generally have a value 25% greater than the sum of the individual players on the panel.

			NRMT	VG-E	GOOD
	COMPLETE INDIV. SET		135.00	65.00	13.50
	COMMON PLAYER		.30	.15	.03
☐	1	John Denny	.40	.20	.04
☐	2	Jim Rice	3.50	1.75	.35
☐	3	Doug Bair	.30	.15	.03
☐	4	Darrell Porter	.40	.20	.04
☐	5	Ross Grimsley	.30	.15	.03
☐	6	Bobby Murcer	.50	.25	.05
☐	7	Lee Mazzilli	.30	.15	.03
☐	8	Steve Garvey	3.50	1.75	.35
☐	9	Mike Schmidt	4.50	2.25	.45
☐	10	Terry Whitfield	.30	.15	.03
☐	11	Jim Palmer	2.50	1.25	.25
☐	12	Omar Moreno	.30	.15	.03
☐	13	Duane Kuiper	.30	.15	.03
☐	14	Mike Caldwell	.40	.20	.04
☐	15	Steve Kemp	.40	.20	.04
☐	16	Dave Goltz	.30	.15	.03
☐	17	Mitchell Page	.30	.15	.03
☐	18	Bill Stein	.30	.15	.03
☐	19	Gene Tenace	.40	.20	.04
☐	20	Jeff Burroughs	.40	.20	.04
☐	21	Francisco Barrios	.30	.15	.03
☐	22	Mike Torrez	.30	.15	.03
☐	23	Ken Reitz	.30	.15	.03
☐	24	Gary Carter	3.50	1.75	.35
☐	25	Al Hrabosky	.40	.20	.04
☐	26	Thurman Munson	3.00	1.50	.30
☐	27	Bill Buckner	.50	.25	.05
☐	28	Ron Cey *	.60	.30	.06
☐	29	J.R. Richard *	.50	.25	.05
☐	30	Greg Luzinski *	.90	.45	.09
☐	31	Ed Ott *	.40	.20	.04
☐	32	Dennis Martinez *	.50	.25	.05
☐	33	Darrell Evans *	.75	.35	.07
☐	34	Ron LeFlore	.40	.20	.04
☐	35	Rick Waits	.30	.15	.03
☐	36	Cecil Cooper	.75	.35	.07
☐	37	Leon Roberts	.30	.15	.03
☐	38	Rod Carew	3.00	1.50	.30
☐	39	John Henry Johnson	.30	.15	.03
☐	40	Chet Lemon	.40	.20	.04
☐	41	Craig Swan	.30	.15	.03
☐	42	Gary Matthews	.40	.20	.04
☐	43	Lamar Johnson	.30	.15	.03
☐	44	Ted Simmons	.75	.35	.07
☐	45	Ken Griffey	.40	.20	.04

☐ 46	Fred Patek	.30	.15	.03
☐ 47	Frank Tanana	.40	.20	.04
☐ 48	Goose Gossage	.90	.45	.09
☐ 49	Burt Hooton	.30	.15	.03
☐ 50	Ellis Valentine	.30	.15	.03
☐ 51	Ken Forsch	.30	.15	.03
☐ 52	Bob Knepper	.50	.25	.05
☐ 53	Dave Parker	2.00	1.00	.20
☐ 54	Doug DeCinces	.50	.25	.05
☐ 55	Robin Yount	3.00	1.50	.30
☐ 56	Rusty Staub	.50	.25	.05
☐ 57	Gary Alexander	.30	.15	.03
☐ 58	Julio Cruz	.30	.15	.03
☐ 59	Matt Keough	.30	.15	.03
☐ 60	Roy Smalley	.30	.15	.03
☐ 61	Joe Morgan	2.00	1.00	.20
☐ 62	Phil Niekro	2.00	1.00	.20
☐ 63	Don Baylor	.50	.25	.05
☐ 64	Dwight Evans	.75	.35	.07
☐ 65	Tom Seaver	3.00	1.50	.30
☐ 66	George Hendrick	.40	.20	.04
☐ 67	Rick Reuschel	.50	.25	.05
☐ 68	George Brett	5.00	2.50	.50
☐ 69	Lou Piniella	.50	.25	.05
☐ 70	Enos Cabell	.30	.15	.03
☐ 71	Steve Carlton	3.00	1.50	.30
☐ 72	Reggie Smith	.50	.25	.05
☐ 73	Rick Dempsey *	.50	.25	.05
☐ 74	Vida Blue *	.50	.25	.05
☐ 75	Phil Garner *	.40	.20	.04
☐ 76	Rick Manning *	.40	.20	.04
☐ 77	Mark Fidrych *	.50	.25	.05
☐ 78	Mario Guerrero *	.40	.20	.04
☐ 79	Bob Stinson *	.40	.20	.04
☐ 80	Al Oliver *	.90	.45	.09
☐ 81	Doug Flynn *	.40	.20	.04
☐ 82	John Mayberry	.40	.20	.04
☐ 83	Gaylord Perry	1.50	.75	.15
☐ 84	Joe Rudi	.40	.20	.04
☐ 85	Dave Concepcion	.50	.25	.05
☐ 86	John Candelaria	.40	.20	.04
☐ 87	Pete Vuckovich	.40	.20	.04
☐ 88	Ivan DeJesus	.30	.15	.03
☐ 89	Ron Guidry	1.50	.75	.15
☐ 90	Hal McRae	.40	.20	.04
☐ 91	Cesar Cedeno	.40	.20	.04
☐ 92	Don Sutton	2.00	1.00	.20
☐ 93	Andre Thornton	.40	.20	.04
☐ 94	Roger Erickson	.30	.15	.03
☐ 95	Larry Hisle	.40	.20	.04
☐ 96	Jason Thompson	.40	.20	.04
☐ 97	Jim Sundberg	.40	.20	.04
☐ 98	Bob Horner	2.50	1.25	.25
☐ 99	Ruppert Jones	.40	.20	.04
☐ 100	Willie Montanez	.30	.15	.03
☐ 101	Nolan Ryan	3.00	1.50	.30
☐ 102	Ozzie Smith	3.00	1.50	.30
☐ 103	Eric Soderholm	.30	.15	.03
☐ 104	Willie Stargell	2.00	1.00	.20
☐ 105A	Bob Bailor ERR	.50	.25	.05
	(reverse negative)			
☐ 105B	Bob Bailor COR	.75	.35	.07
☐ 106	Carlton Fisk	.90	.45	.09
☐ 107	George Foster	.90	.45	.09
☐ 108	Keith Hernandez	2.50	1.25	.25
☐ 109	Dennis Leonard	.40	.20	.04
☐ 110	Graig Nettles	.75	.35	.07
☐ 111	Jose Cruz	.50	.25	.05
☐ 112	Bobby Grich	.40	.20	.04
☐ 113	Bob Boone	.50	.25	.05
☐ 114	Dave Lopes	.40	.20	.04
☐ 115	Eddie Murray	4.50	2.25	.45
☐ 116	Jack Clark	2.50	1.25	.25
☐ 117	Lou Whitaker	1.50	.75	.15
☐ 118	Miguel Dilone	.30	.15	.03
☐ 119	Sal Bando	.40	.20	.04
☐ 120	Reggie Jackson	4.00	2.00	.40
☐ 121	Dale Murphy	8.50	4.25	.85
☐ 122	Jon Matlack	.40	.20	.04
☐ 123	Bruce Bochte	.30	.15	.03
☐ 124	John Stearns	.30	.15	.03
☐ 125	Dave Winfield	3.00	1.50	.30
☐ 126	Jorge Orta	.30	.15	.03
☐ 127	Garry Templeton	.40	.20	.04
☐ 128	Johnny Bench	3.00	1.50	.30
☐ 129	Butch Hobson	.30	.15	.03
☐ 130	Bruce Sutter	1.00	.50	.10
☐ 131	Bucky Dent	.40	.20	.04
☐ 132	Amos Otis	.40	.20	.04
☐ 133	Bert Blyleven	.50	.25	.05
☐ 134	Larry Bowa	.50	.25	.05
☐ 135	Ken Singleton	.50	.25	.05
☐ 136	Sixto Lezcano	.30	.15	.03
☐ 137	Roy Howell	.30	.15	.03
☐ 138	Bill Madlock	.90	.45	.09
☐ 139	Dave Revering	.30	.15	.03
☐ 140	Richie Zisk	.40	.20	.04
☐ 141	Butch Wynegar	.40	.20	.04
☐ 142	Alan Ashby	.30	.15	.03
☐ 143	Sparky Lyle	.50	.25	.05
☐ 144	Pete Rose	8.50	4.25	.85
☐ 145	Dennis Eckersley	.40	.20	.04
☐ 146	Dave Kingman	.60	.30	.06
☐ 147	Buddy Bell	.50	.25	.05
☐ 148	Mike Hargrove	.40	.20	.04
☐ 149	Jerry Koosman	.50	.25	.05
☐ 150	Toby Harrah	.40	.20	.04

1985 Hostess Braves

The cards in this 22-card set measure 2 1/2" by 3 1/2" and feature players of the Atlanta Braves. Cards were produced by Topps for Hostess (Continental Baking Co.) and are quite attractive. The card backs are similar in design to the 1985 Topps regular issue; however all photos are different from those that Topps used as these were apparently taken during Spring Training. Cards were available in boxes of Hostess products in packs of four (three players and a contest card).

		MINT	EXC	G-VG
COMPLETE SET		7.50	3.75	.75
COMMON PLAYER (1-22)		.25	.12	.02
☐ 1	Eddie Haas MG	.25	.12	.02
☐ 2	Len Barker	.25	.12	.02
☐ 3	Steve Bedrosian	.60	.30	.06
☐ 4	Bruce Benedict	.25	.12	.02
☐ 5	Rick Camp	.25	.12	.02
☐ 6	Rick Cerone	.25	.12	.02
☐ 7	Chris Chambliss	.35	.17	.03
☐ 8	Terry Forster	.50	.25	.05
☐ 9	Gene Garber	.25	.12	.02
☐ 10	Albert Hall	.25	.12	.02
☐ 11	Bob Horner	.90	.45	.09
☐ 12	Glenn Hubbard	.35	.17	.03
☐ 13	Brad Komminsk	.35	.17	.03
☐ 14	Rick Mahler	.35	.17	.03
☐ 15	Craig McMurtry	.25	.12	.02
☐ 16	Dale Murphy	3.50	1.75	.35
☐ 17	Ken Oberkfell	.25	.12	.02
☐ 18	Pascual Perez	.25	.12	.02
☐ 19	Gerald Perry	.35	.17	.03
☐ 20	Rafael Ramirez	.25	.12	.02
☐ 21	Bruce Sutter	.60	.30	.06
☐ 22	Claudell Washington	.50	.25	.05

1953 Hunter's Wieners

The cards in this 26 card set measure 2 1/4" by 3 1/2". The 1953 Hunter's Wieners set of full color, blank backed unnumbered cards feature St. Louis Cardinal players only. The cards have red borders and were issued in panels of two on hot dog packages. The ACC designation is F153-1. The list below is numbered according to alphabetical order.

	NRMT	VG-E	GOOD
COMPLETE SET	2250.00	900.00	180.00
COMMON PLAYER (1-26)	60.00	30.00	6.00

			NRMT	VG-E	GOOD
☐	1	Steve Bilko	60.00	30.00	6.00
☐	2	Alpha Brazle	60.00	30.00	6.00
☐	3	Cloyd Boyer	75.00	37.50	7.50
☐	4	Cliff Chambers	60.00	30.00	6.00
☐	5	Mike Clark	60.00	30.00	6.00
☐	6	Jack Crimian	60.00	30.00	6.00
☐	7	Les Fusselman	60.00	30.00	6.00
☐	8	Harvey Haddix	90.00	45.00	9.00
☐	9	Solly Hemus	60.00	30.00	6.00
☐	10	Ray Jablonski	60.00	30.00	6.00
☐	11	Will Johnson	60.00	30.00	6.00
☐	12	Harry Lowrey	60.00	30.00	6.00
☐	13	Larry Miggins	60.00	30.00	6.00
☐	14	Stuart Miller	60.00	30.00	6.00
☐	15	Wilmer Mizell	60.00	30.00	6.00
☐	16	Stan Musial	750.00	375.00	75.00
☐	17	Joe Presko	60.00	30.00	6.00
☐	18	Del Rice	60.00	30.00	6.00
☐	19	Hal Rice	60.00	30.00	6.00
☐	20	Willard Schmidt	60.00	30.00	6.00
☐	21	Al Schoendienst	125.00	60.00	12.50
☐	22	Dick Sisler	60.00	30.00	6.00
☐	23	Enos Slaughter	175.00	85.00	18.00
☐	24	Gerry Staley	60.00	30.00	6.00
☐	25	Ed Stanky	90.00	45.00	9.00
☐	26	John Yuhas	60.00	30.00	6.00

1954 Hunter's Wieners

The cards in this 30 card set measure 2 1/4" by 3 1/2". The 1954 Hunter's Wieners set of full color, blank backed, unnumbered cards features St. Louis Cardinals only. They were issued in pairs on the backs of hot dog packages as in 1953; however one of the cards is a statistical record of the player's career. The poses are very similar to those used in the 1953 set; however, there are captions which read "What's My Name" and "What's My Record." The ACC designation is F153-2.

			NRMT	VG-E	GOOD
		COMPLETE SET	3000.00	1200.00	250.00
		COMMON PLAYER (1-30)	90.00	45.00	9.00
☐	1	Tom Alston	90.00	45.00	9.00
☐	2	Steve Bilko	90.00	45.00	9.00
☐	3	Alpha Brazle	90.00	45.00	9.00
☐	4	Tom Burgess	90.00	45.00	9.00
☐	5	Cot Deal	90.00	45.00	9.00
☐	6	Alex Grammas	90.00	45.00	9.00
☐	7	Harvey Haddix	120.00	60.00	12.00
☐	8	Solly Hemus	90.00	45.00	9.00
☐	9	Ray Jablonski	90.00	45.00	9.00
☐	10	Royce Lint	90.00	45.00	9.00
☐	11	Harry Lowrey	90.00	45.00	9.00
☐	12	Memo Luna	90.00	45.00	9.00
☐	13	Stu Miller	120.00	60.00	12.00
☐	14	Stan Musial	1000.00	400.00	80.00
☐	15	Tom Poholsky	90.00	45.00	9.00
☐	16	Bill Posedel	90.00	45.00	9.00
☐	17	Joe Presko	90.00	45.00	9.00
☐	18	Vic Raschi	150.00	75.00	15.00
☐	19	Dick Rand	90.00	45.00	9.00
☐	20	Rip Repulski	90.00	45.00	9.00
☐	21	Del Rice	90.00	45.00	9.00
☐	22	John Riddle	90.00	45.00	9.00
☐	23	Mike Ryba	90.00	45.00	9.00
☐	24	Al Schoendienst	150.00	75.00	15.00
☐	25	Dick Schofield	120.00	60.00	12.00
☐	26	Enos Slaughter	225.00	110.00	22.00
☐	27	Gerry Staley	90.00	45.00	9.00
☐	28	Ed Stanky	120.00	60.00	12.00
☐	29	Ed Yuhas	90.00	45.00	9.00
☐	30	Sal Yvars	90.00	45.00	9.00

1955 Hunter's Wieners

The cards in this 30 card set measure 2" by 4 3/4". The 1955 Hunter's Wieners set of full color, blank back, unnumbered cards features St. Louis Cardinals only. This year presented a different format from the previous two years in that there are two pictures on the front of each card, one full figure shot and a close up bust shot. The card was actually the side panel of the hot dog package rather than the back as in the previous two years. The ACC designation of this scarce regional issue is F153- 3.

			NRMT	VG-E	GOOD
		COMPLETE SET	3500.00	1500.00	300.00
		COMMON PLAYER (1-30)	110.00	55.00	11.00
☐	1	Tom Alston	110.00	55.00	11.00
☐	2	Ken Boyer	200.00	100.00	20.00
☐	3	Harry Elliott	110.00	55.00	11.00
☐	4	Jack Faszholz	110.00	55.00	11.00
☐	5	Joe Frazier	110.00	55.00	11.00
☐	6	Alex Grammas	110.00	55.00	11.00
☐	7	Harvey Haddix	135.00	65.00	13.50
☐	8	Solly Hemus	110.00	55.00	11.00
☐	9	Larry Jackson	110.00	55.00	11.00
☐	10	Tony Jacobs	110.00	55.00	11.00
☐	11	Gordon Jones	110.00	55.00	11.00
☐	12	Paul LaPalme	110.00	55.00	11.00
☐	13	Brooks Lawrence	110.00	55.00	11.00
☐	14	Wally Moon	135.00	65.00	13.50
☐	15	Stan Musial	1250.00	500.00	100.00
☐	16	Tom Poholsky	110.00	55.00	11.00
☐	17	Bill Posedel	110.00	55.00	11.00
☐	18	Vic Raschi	160.00	80.00	16.00
☐	19	Rip Repulski	110.00	55.00	11.00
☐	20	Del Rice	110.00	55.00	11.00
☐	21	John Riddle	110.00	55.00	11.00
☐	22	Bill Sarni	110.00	55.00	11.00
☐	23	Al Schoendienst	160.00	80.00	16.00
☐	24	Dick Schofield	135.00	65.00	13.50
☐	25	Frank Smith	110.00	55.00	11.00
☐	26	Ed Stanky	135.00	65.00	13.50
☐	27	Bob Tiefenauer	110.00	55.00	11.00
☐	28	Bill Virdon	160.00	80.00	16.00
☐	29	Fred Walker	110.00	55.00	11.00
☐	30	Floyd Woolridge	110.00	55.00	11.00

1962 Jello

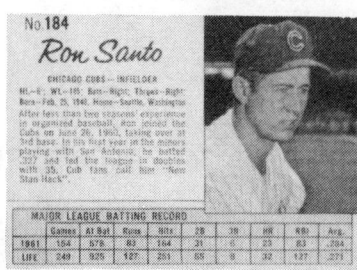

The cards in this 200 card (only 197 were ever issued) set measure 2 1/2" by 3 3/8". The 1962 Jello set has the same checklist as the Post Cereal set of the same year, but is considered by some to be a test issue. The cards are grouped numerically by team, for example, New York Yankees (1-13), Detroit (14-26), Baltimore (27-36), Cleveland (37-45), Chicago White Sox (46-55), Boston (56-64), Washington (65-73), Los Angeles Angels (74-82), Minnesota (83-91), Kansas City (92-100), Los Angeles Dodgers (101-115), Cincinnati (116-130), San Francisco (131-144), Milwaukee (145-157), St. Louis (158-168), Pittsburgh (169-181), Chicago

Cubs (182-191), and Philadelphia (192-200). Although the players and numbers are identical in both sets, the Jello series has its own list of scarce and difficult cards. Numbers 29, 82 and 176 were never issued. A Jello card is easily distinguished from its counterpart in Post by the absence of the Post logo. The catalog designation is F229-1.

		NRMT	VG-E	GOOD
COMPLETE SET		3000.00	1200.00	250.00
COMMON PLAYER (1-200)		4.00	2.00	.40

	#	Player	NRMT	VG-E	GOOD
☐	1	Bill Skowron	15.00	7.50	1.50
☐	2	Bobby Richardson	15.00	7.50	1.50
☐	3	Cletis Boyer	6.00	3.00	.60
☐	4	Tony Kubek	10.00	5.00	1.00
☐	5	Mickey Mantle	500.00	250.00	50.00
☐	6	Roger Maris	100.00	50.00	10.00
☐	7	Yogi Berra	60.00	30.00	6.00
☐	8	Elston Howard	6.00	3.00	.60
☐	9	Whitey Ford	40.00	20.00	4.00
☐	10	Ralph Terry	5.00	2.50	.50
☐	11	John Blanchard	5.00	2.50	.50
☐	12	Luis Arroyo	5.00	2.50	.50
☐	13	Bill Stafford	10.00	5.00	1.00
☐	14	Norm Cash	5.00	2.50	.50
☐	15	Jake Wood	4.00	2.00	.40
☐	16	Steve Boros	4.00	2.00	.40
☐	17	Chico Fernandez	4.00	2.00	.40
☐	18	Bill Bruton	4.00	2.00	.40
☐	19	Ken Aspromonte	4.00	2.00	.40
☐	20	Al Kaline	30.00	15.00	3.00
☐	21	Dick Brown	4.00	2.00	.40
☐	22	Frank Lary	5.00	2.50	.50
☐	23	Don Mossi	5.00	2.50	.50
☐	24	Phil Regan	4.00	2.00	.40
☐	25	Charley Maxwell	4.00	2.00	.40
☐	26	Jim Bunning	15.00	7.50	1.50
☐	27	Jim Gentile	5.00	2.50	.50
☐	28	Marv Breeding	5.00	2.50	.50
☐	29	Not issued	0.00	.00	.00
☐	30	Ron Hansen	5.00	2.50	.50
☐	31	Jackie Brandt	15.00	7.50	1.50
☐	32	Dick Williams	5.00	2.50	.50
☐	33	Gus Triandos	5.00	2.50	.50
☐	34	Milt Pappas	5.00	2.50	.50
☐	35	Hoyt Wilhelm	25.00	12.50	2.50
☐	36	Chuck Estrada	5.00	2.50	.50
☐	37	Vic Power	4.00	2.00	.40
☐	38	Johnny Temple	4.00	2.00	.40
☐	39	Bubba Phillips	15.00	7.50	1.50
☐	40	Tito Francona	5.00	2.50	.50
☐	41	Willie Kirkland	4.00	2.00	.40
☐	42	John Romano	4.00	2.00	.40
☐	43	Jim Perry	5.00	2.50	.50
☐	44	Woodie Held	4.00	2.00	.40
☐	45	Chuck Essegian	4.00	2.00	.40
☐	46	Roy Sievers	5.00	2.50	.50
☐	47	Nellie Fox	10.00	5.00	1.00
☐	48	Al Smith	4.00	2.00	.40
☐	49	Luis Aparicio	20.00	10.00	2.00
☐	50	Jim Landis	4.00	2.00	.40
☐	51	Minnie Minoso	6.00	3.00	.60
☐	52	Andy Carey	15.00	7.50	1.50
☐	53	Sherman Lollar	4.00	2.00	.40
☐	54	Bill Pierce	5.00	2.50	.50
☐	55	Early Wynn	15.00	7.50	1.50
☐	56	Chuck Schilling	15.00	7.50	1.50
☐	57	Pete Runnels	6.00	3.00	.60
☐	58	Frank Malzone	6.00	3.00	.60
☐	59	Don Buddin	7.00	3.50	.70
☐	60	Gary Geiger	15.00	7.50	1.50
☐	61	Carl Yastrzemski	200.00	100.00	20.00
☐	62	Jackie Jensen	15.00	7.50	1.50
☐	63	Jim Pagliaroni	15.00	7.50	1.50
☐	64	Don Schwall	6.00	3.00	.60
☐	65	Dale Long	6.00	3.00	.60
☐	66	Chuck Cottier	6.00	3.00	.60
☐	67	Billy Klaus	15.00	7.50	1.50
☐	68	Coot Veal	6.00	3.00	.60
☐	69	Marty Keough	25.00	12.50	2.50
☐	70	Willie Tasby	25.00	12.50	2.50
☐	71	Gene Woodling	6.00	3.00	.60
☐	72	Gene Green	25.00	12.50	2.50
☐	73	Dick Donovan	6.00	3.00	.60
☐	74	Steve Bilko	6.00	3.00	.60
☐	75	Rocky Bridges	15.00	7.50	1.50
☐	76	Eddie Yost	10.00	5.00	1.00
☐	77	Leon Wagner	8.00	4.00	.80
☐	78	Albie Pearson	6.00	3.00	.60
☐	79	Ken Hunt	8.00	4.00	.80
☐	80	Earl Averill	25.00	12.50	2.50
☐	81	Ryne Duren	6.00	3.00	.60
☐	82	Not issued	0.00	.00	.00
☐	83	Bob Allison	4.00	2.00	.40
☐	84	Billy Martin	10.00	5.00	1.00
☐	85	Harmon Killebrew	25.00	12.50	2.50
☐	86	Zoilo Versalles	5.00	2.50	.50
☐	87	Lenny Green	20.00	10.00	2.00
☐	88	Bill Tuttle	5.00	2.50	.50
☐	89	Jim Lemon	4.00	2.00	.40
☐	90	Earl Battey	15.00	7.50	1.50
☐	91	Camilo Pascual	5.00	2.50	.50
☐	92	Norm Sieburn	6.00	3.00	.60
☐	93	Jerry Lumpe	6.00	3.00	.60
☐	94	Dick Howser	8.00	4.00	.80
☐	95	Gene Stephens	25.00	12.50	2.50
☐	96	Leo Posada	8.00	4.00	.80
☐	97	Joe Pignatano	6.00	3.00	.60
☐	98	Jim Archer	6.00	3.00	.60
☐	99	Haywood Sullivan	15.00	7.50	1.50
☐	100	Art Ditmar	6.00	3.00	.60
☐	101	Gil Hodges	25.00	12.50	2.50
☐	102	Charlie Neal	6.00	3.00	.60
☐	103	Daryl Spencer	6.00	3.00	.60
☐	104	Maury Wills	15.00	7.50	1.50
☐	105	Tommy Davis	8.00	4.00	.80
☐	106	Willie Davis	8.00	4.00	.80
☐	107	John Roseboro	25.00	12.50	2.50
☐	108	John Podres	8.00	4.00	.80
☐	109	Sandy Koufax	60.00	30.00	6.00
☐	110	Don Drysdale	30.00	15.00	3.00
☐	111	Larry Sherry	15.00	7.50	1.50
☐	112	Jim Gilliam	15.00	7.50	1.50
☐	113	Norm Larker	30.00	15.00	3.00
☐	114	Duke Snider	50.00	25.00	5.00
☐	115	Stan Williams	15.00	7.50	1.50
☐	116	Gordy Coleman	50.00	25.00	5.00
☐	117	Don Blasingame	15.00	7.50	1.50
☐	118	Gene Freese	30.00	15.00	3.00
☐	119	Ed Kasko	30.00	15.00	3.00
☐	120	Gus Bell	15.00	7.50	1.50
☐	121	Vada Pinson	8.00	4.00	.80
☐	122	Frank Robinson	20.00	10.00	2.00
☐	123	Bob Purkey	6.00	3.00	.60
☐	124	Joey Jay	6.00	3.00	.60
☐	125	Jim Brosnan	6.00	3.00	.60
☐	126	Jim O'Toole	6.00	3.00	.60
☐	127	Jerry Lynch	6.00	3.00	.60
☐	128	Wally Post	6.00	3.00	.60
☐	129	Ken Hunt	6.00	3.00	.60
☐	130	Jerry Zimmerman	6.00	3.00	.60
☐	131	Willie McCovey	30.00	15.00	3.00
☐	132	Jose Pagan	15.00	7.50	1.50
☐	133	Felipe Alou	7.00	3.50	.70
☐	134	Jim Davenport	8.00	4.00	.80
☐	135	Harvey Kuenn	8.00	4.00	.80
☐	136	Orlando Cepeda	15.00	7.50	1.50
☐	137	Ed Bailey	7.00	3.50	.70
☐	138	Sam Jones	7.00	3.50	.70
☐	139	Mike McCormick	7.00	3.50	.70
☐	140	Juan Marichal	40.00	20.00	4.00
☐	141	Jack Sanford	6.00	3.00	.60
☐	142	Willie Mays	125.00	60.00	12.50
☐	143	Stu Miller	50.00	25.00	5.00
☐	144	Joe Amalfitano	6.00	3.00	.60
☐	145	Joe Adcock	5.00	2.50	.50
☐	146	Frank Bolling	5.00	2.50	.50
☐	147	Ed Mathews	25.00	12.50	2.50
☐	148	Roy McMillan	4.00	2.00	.40
☐	149	Hank Aaron	125.00	60.00	12.50
☐	150	Gino Cimoli	15.00	7.50	1.50
☐	151	Frank Thomas	5.00	2.50	.50
☐	152	Joe Torre	7.00	3.50	.70
☐	153	Lew Burdette	7.00	3.50	.70
☐	154	Bob Buhl	4.00	2.00	.40
☐	155	Carlton Willey	4.00	2.00	.40
☐	156	Lee Maye	15.00	7.50	1.50
☐	157	Al Spangler	25.00	12.50	2.50
☐	158	Bill White	30.00	15.00	3.00
☐	159	Ken Boyer	10.00	5.00	1.00
☐	160	Joe Cunningham	6.00	3.00	.60
☐	161	Carl Warwick	7.00	3.50	.70
☐	162	Carl Sawatski	5.00	2.50	.50
☐	163	Lindy McDaniel	5.00	2.50	.50
☐	164	Ernie Broglio	7.00	3.50	.70
☐	165	Larry Jackson	5.00	2.50	.50
☐	166	Curt Flood	15.00	7.50	1.50
☐	167	Curt Simmons	20.00	10.00	2.00
☐	168	Alex Grammas	15.00	7.50	1.50
☐	169	Dick Stuart	5.00	2.50	.50
☐	170	Bill Mazeroski	15.00	7.50	1.50
☐	171	Don Hoak	7.00	3.50	.70
☐	172	Dick Groat	8.00	4.00	.80
☐	173	Roberto Clemente	125.00	60.00	12.50
☐	174	Bob Skinner	15.00	7.50	1.50
☐	175	Bill Virdon	20.00	10.00	2.00
☐	176	Not issued	0.00	.00	.00

		NRMT	VG-E	GOOD
☐ 177	Elroy Face	7.00	3.50	.70
☐ 178	Bob Friend	5.00	2.50	.50
☐ 179	Vernon Law	15.00	7.50	1.50
☐ 180	Harvey Haddix	20.00	10.00	2.00
☐ 181	Hal Smith	15.00	7.50	1.50
☐ 182	Ed Bouchee	15.00	7.50	1.50
☐ 183	Don Zimmer	6.00	3.00	.60
☐ 184	Ron Santo	6.00	3.00	.60
☐ 185	Andre Rodgers	4.00	2.00	.40
☐ 186	Richie Ashburn	10.00	5.00	1.00
☐ 187	George Altman	4.00	2.00	.40
☐ 188	Ernie Banks	15.00	7.50	1.50
☐ 189	Sam Taylor	5.00	2.50	.50
☐ 190	Don Elston	4.00	2.00	.40
☐ 191	Jerry Kindall	12.00	6.00	1.20
☐ 192	Pancho Herrera	4.00	2.00	.40
☐ 193	Tony Taylor	4.00	2.00	.40
☐ 194	Ruben Amaro	12.00	6.00	1.20
☐ 195	Don Demeter	4.00	2.00	.40
☐ 196	Bobby Gene Smith	4.00	2.00	.40
☐ 197	Clay Dalrymple	4.00	2.00	.40
☐ 198	Robin Roberts	15.00	7.50	1.50
☐ 199	Art Mahaffey	4.00	2.00	.40
☐ 200	John Buzhardt	4.00	2.00	.40

1963 Jello

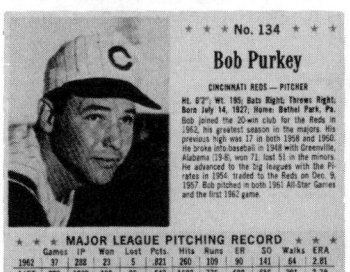

The cards in this 200 card set measure 2 1/2" by 3 3/8". The 1963 Jello set contains the same players and numbers as the Post Cereal set of the same year. The players are grouped by team with American Leaguers comprising 1-100 and National Leaguers 101-200. The ordering of teams is as follows: Minnesota (1-11), New York Yankees, Los Angeles Angels (24-34), Chicago White Sox (35-45), Detroit (46-56), Baltimore (57-66), Cleveland (67-76), Boston (77-84), Kansas City (85-92), Washington (93- 100), San Francisco (101-112), Los Angeles Dodgers (113-124), Cincinnati (125-136), Pittsburgh (137-147), Milwaukee (148-157), St. Louis (158-168), Chicago Cubs (169-176), Philadelphia (177-184), Houston (185-192), and New York Mets (193-200). As in 1962, the Jello series has its own list of scarcities (many resulting from an unpopular package size) and these are marked with an asterisk in the checklist. Since the Post Cereal logo was removed from the 1963 cereal set, Jello cards are primarily distinguishable by (1) smaller card size and (2) smaller print. The catalog designation is F229-2.

	NRMT	VG-E	GOOD
COMPLETE SET	2000.00	900.00	175.00
COMMON PLAYER (1-200)	1.50	.75	.15

		NRMT	VG-E	GOOD
☐ 1	Vic Power	1.50	.75	.15
☐ 2	Bernie Allen *	15.00	7.50	1.50
☐ 3	Zoilo Versalles *	20.00	10.00	2.00
☐ 4	Rich Rollins	1.50	.75	.15
☐ 5	Harmon Killebrew	8.00	4.00	.80
☐ 6	Lenny Green *	20.00	10.00	2.00
☐ 7	Bob Allison	2.00	1.00	.20
☐ 8	Earl Battey *	12.00	6.00	1.20
☐ 9	Camilo Pascual	1.50	.75	.15
☐ 10	Jim Kaat *	40.00	20.00	4.00
☐ 11	Jack Kralick	1.50	.75	.15
☐ 12	Bill Skowron *	15.00	7.50	1.50

		NRMT	VG-E	GOOD
☐ 13	Bobby Richardson	1.50	.75	.15
☐ 14	Cletis Boyer	2.00	1.00	.20
☐ 15	Mickey Mantle	200.00	100.00	20.00
☐ 16	Roger Maris	50.00	25.00	5.00
☐ 17	Yogi Berra	20.00	10.00	2.00
☐ 18	Elston Howard *	30.00	15.00	3.00
☐ 19	Whitey Ford	10.00	5.00	1.00
☐ 20	Ralph Terry	1.50	.75	.15
☐ 21	John Blanchard *	12.00	6.00	1.20
☐ 22	Bill Stafford *	20.00	10.00	2.00
☐ 23	Tom Tresh	2.00	1.00	.20
☐ 24	Steve Bilko	1.50	.75	.15
☐ 25	Bill Moran	1.50	.75	.15
☐ 26	Joe Koppe	1.50	.75	.15
☐ 27	Felix Torres	1.50	.75	.15
☐ 28	Leon Wagner	1.50	.75	.15
☐ 29	Albie Pearson	1.50	.75	.15
☐ 30	Lee Thomas	1.50	.75	.15
☐ 31	Bob Rodgers *	20.00	10.00	2.00
☐ 32	Dean Chance	2.00	1.00	.20
☐ 33	Ken McBride *	20.00	10.00	2.00
☐ 34	George Thomas *	20.00	10.00	2.00
☐ 35	Joe Cunningham *	20.00	10.00	2.00
☐ 36	Nelson Fox	3.00	1.50	.30
☐ 37	Luis Aparicio	4.00	2.00	.40
☐ 38	Al Smith	1.50	.75	.15
☐ 39	Floyd Robinson	1.50	.75	.15
☐ 40	Jim Landis	1.50	.75	.15
☐ 41	Charlie Maxwell	1.50	.75	.15
☐ 42	Sherman Lollar	2.00	1.00	.20
☐ 43	Early Wynn	4.00	2.00	.40
☐ 44	Juan Pizarro *	15.00	7.50	1.50
☐ 45	Ray Herbert *	20.00	10.00	2.00
☐ 46	Norm Cash	1.50	.75	.15
☐ 47	Steve Boros	25.00	12.50	2.50
☐ 48	Dick McAuliffe	1.50	.75	.15
☐ 49	Bill Bruton *	15.00	7.50	1.50
☐ 50	Rocky Colavito	2.00	1.00	.20
☐ 51	Al Kaline	12.00	6.00	1.20
☐ 52	Dick Brown *	20.00	10.00	2.00
☐ 53	Jim Bunning	3.00	1.50	.30
☐ 54	Hank Aguirre	1.50	.75	.15
☐ 55	Frank Lary *	20.00	10.00	2.00
☐ 56	Don Mossi *	20.00	10.00	2.00
☐ 57	Jim Gentile	2.00	1.00	.20
☐ 58	Jackie Brandt	1.50	.75	.15
☐ 59	Brooks Robinson	12.00	6.00	1.20
☐ 60	Ron Hansen	1.50	.75	.15
☐ 61	Jerry Adair *	40.00	20.00	4.00
☐ 62	John"Boog" Powell	2.00	1.00	.20
☐ 63	Russ Snyder *	20.00	10.00	2.00
☐ 64	Steve Barber	1.50	.75	.15
☐ 65	Milt Pappas *	15.00	7.50	1.50
☐ 66	Robin Roberts	5.00	2.50	.50
☐ 67	Tito Francona	1.50	.75	.15
☐ 68	Jerry Kindall *	20.00	10.00	2.00
☐ 69	Woody Held	1.50	.75	.15
☐ 70	Bubba Phillips	1.50	.75	.15
☐ 71	Chuck Essegian	1.50	.75	.15
☐ 72	Willie Kirkland *	20.00	10.00	2.00
☐ 73	Al Luplow	1.50	.75	.15
☐ 74	Ty Cline *	40.00	20.00	4.00
☐ 75	Dick Donovan	1.50	.75	.15
☐ 76	John Romano	1.50	.75	.15
☐ 77	Pete Runnels	2.00	1.00	.20
☐ 78	Ed Bressoud *	15.00	7.50	1.50
☐ 79	Frank Malzone	2.00	1.00	.20
☐ 80	Carl Yastrzemski	60.00	30.00	6.00
☐ 81	Gary Geiger	1.50	.75	.15
☐ 82	Lou Clinton *	15.00	7.50	1.50
☐ 83	Earl Wilson	1.50	.75	.15
☐ 84	Bill Monbouquette	1.50	.75	.15
☐ 85	Norm Sieburn	1.50	.75	.15
☐ 86	Jerry Lumpe	1.50	.75	.15
☐ 87	Manny Jimenez	1.50	.75	.15
☐ 88	Gino Cimoli	1.50	.75	.15
☐ 89	Ed Charles *	40.00	20.00	4.00
☐ 90	Ed Rakow	1.50	.75	.15
☐ 91	Bobby Del Greco *	40.00	20.00	4.00
☐ 92	Haywood Sullivan *	20.00	10.00	2.00
☐ 93	Chuck Hinton	1.50	.75	.15
☐ 94	Ken Retzer *	20.00	10.00	2.00
☐ 95	Harry Bright *	20.00	10.00	2.00
☐ 96	Bob Johnson	1.50	.75	.15
☐ 97	Dave Stenhouse *	15.00	7.50	1.50
☐ 98	Chuck Cottier	1.50	.75	.15
☐ 99	Tom Cheney	1.50	.75	.15
☐ 100	Claude Osteen *	25.00	12.50	2.50
☐ 101	Orlando Cepeda	3.00	1.50	.30
☐ 102	Chuck Hiller *	15.00	7.50	1.50
☐ 103	Jose Pagan *	15.00	7.50	1.50
☐ 104	Jim Davenport	2.00	1.00	.20
☐ 105	Harvey Kuenn	2.00	1.00	.20
☐ 106	Willie Mays	60.00	30.00	6.00
☐ 107	Felipe Alou	2.00	1.00	.20

☐ 108 Tom Haller	2.00	1.00	.20
☐ 109 Juan Marichal	5.00	2.50	.50
☐ 110 Jack Sanford	1.50	.75	.15
☐ 111 Bill O'Dell	1.50	.75	.15
☐ 112 Willie McCovey *	100.00	50.00	10.00
☐ 113 Lee Walls *	15.00	7.50	1.50
☐ 114 Jim Gilliam *	15.00	7.50	1.50
☐ 115 Maury Wills	3.00	1.50	.30
☐ 116 Ron Fairly	1.50	.75	.15
☐ 117 Tommy Davis	2.00	1.00	.20
☐ 118 Duke Snider	8.00	4.00	.80
☐ 119 Willie Davis	1.50	.75	.15
☐ 120 John Roseboro	1.50	.75	.15
☐ 121 Sandy Koufax	20.00	10.00	2.00
☐ 122 Stan Williams *	20.00	10.00	2.00
☐ 123 Don Drysdale	5.00	2.50	.50
☐ 124 Daryl Spencer	1.50	.75	.15
☐ 125 Gordy Coleman	1.50	.75	.15
☐ 126 Don Blasingame *	20.00	10.00	2.00
☐ 127 Leo Cardenas	1.50	.75	.15
☐ 128 Eddie Kasko *	15.00	7.50	1.50
☐ 129 Jerry Lynch	1.50	.75	.15
☐ 130 Vada Pinson	2.00	1.00	.20
☐ 131 Frank Robinson	6.00	3.00	.60
☐ 132 John Edwards *	20.00	10.00	2.00
☐ 133 Joey Jay	1.50	.75	.15
☐ 134 Bob Purkey	1.50	.75	.15
☐ 135 Marty Keough *	40.00	20.00	4.00
☐ 136 Jim O'Toole *	20.00	10.00	2.00
☐ 137 Dick Stuart	1.50	.75	.15
☐ 138 Bill Mazeroski	2.00	1.00	.20
☐ 139 Dick Groat	2.00	1.00	.20
☐ 140 Don Hoak	1.50	.75	.15
☐ 141 Bob Skinner	1.50	.75	.15
☐ 142 Bill Virdon	2.00	1.00	.20
☐ 143 Roberto Clemente	50.00	25.00	5.00
☐ 144 Smokey Burgess	1.50	.75	.15
☐ 145 Bob Friend	2.00	1.00	.20
☐ 146 Al McBean *	20.00	10.00	2.00
☐ 147 Elroy Face	2.00	1.00	.20
☐ 148 Joe Adcock	2.00	1.00	.20
☐ 149 Frank Bolling	1.50	.75	.15
☐ 150 Roy McMillan	1.50	.75	.15
☐ 151 Eddie Mathews	10.00	5.00	1.00
☐ 152 Hank Aaron	60.00	30.00	6.00
☐ 153 Del Crandall *	20.00	10.00	2.00
☐ 154 Bob Shaw	1.50	.75	.15
☐ 155 Lew Burdette	2.00	1.00	.20
☐ 156 Joe Torre *	25.00	12.50	2.50
☐ 157 Tony Cloninger *	25.00	12.50	2.50
☐ 158 Bill White	2.00	1.00	.20
☐ 159 Julian Javier *	20.00	10.00	2.00
☐ 160 Ken Boyer	1.50	.75	.15
☐ 161 Julio Gotay *	20.00	10.00	2.00
☐ 162 Curt Flood	2.00	1.00	.20
☐ 163 Charlie James *	40.00	20.00	4.00
☐ 164 Gene Oliver *	20.00	10.00	2.00
☐ 165 Ernie Broglio	1.50	.75	.15
☐ 166 Bob Gibson *	60.00	30.00	6.00
☐ 167 Lindy McDaniel *	15.00	7.50	1.50
☐ 168 Ray Washburn	1.50	.75	.15
☐ 169 Ernie Banks	10.00	5.00	1.00
☐ 170 Ron Santo	2.00	1.00	.20
☐ 171 George Altman	1.50	.75	.15
☐ 172 Billy Williams *	50.00	25.00	5.00
☐ 173 Andre Rodgers *	20.00	10.00	2.00
☐ 174 Ken Hubbs	2.00	1.00	.20
☐ 175 Don Landrum *	20.00	10.00	2.00
☐ 176 Dick Bertell *	20.00	10.00	2.00
☐ 177 Roy Sievers	2.00	1.00	.20
☐ 178 Tony Taylor *	20.00	10.00	2.00
☐ 179 John Callison	1.50	.75	.15
☐ 180 Don Demeter	1.50	.75	.15
☐ 181 Tony Gonzalez *	20.00	10.00	2.00
☐ 182 Wes Covington *	20.00	10.00	2.00
☐ 183 Art Mahaffey	1.50	.75	.15
☐ 184 Clay Dalrymple	1.50	.75	.15
☐ 185 Al Spangler	1.50	.75	.15
☐ 186 Roman Mejias	1.50	.75	.15
☐ 187 Bob Aspromonte *	25.00	12.50	2.50
☐ 188 Norm Larker	1.50	.75	.15
☐ 189 Johnny Temple	1.50	.75	.15
☐ 190 Carl Warwick *	20.00	10.00	2.00
☐ 191 Bob Lillis *	15.00	7.50	1.50
☐ 192 Dick Farrell *	30.00	15.00	3.00
☐ 193 Gil Hodges	6.00	3.00	.60
☐ 194 Marv Throneberry	2.00	1.00	.20
☐ 195 Charlie Neal *	20.00	10.00	2.00
☐ 196 Frank Thomas	2.00	1.00	.20
☐ 197 Richie Ashburn	3.00	1.50	.30
☐ 198 Felix Mantilla *	15.00	7.50	1.50
☐ 199 Rod Kanehl *	15.00	7.50	1.50
☐ 200 Roger Craig *	25.00	12.50	2.50

1953 Johnston Cookies

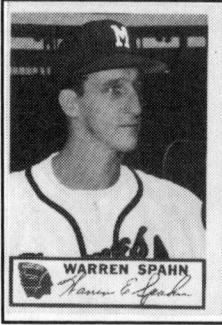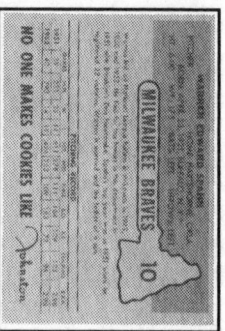

The cards in this 25 card set measure 2 9/16" by 3 5/8". The 1953 Johnston's Cookies set of numbered cards features Milwaukee Braves players only. This set is the most plentiful of the three Johnston's Cookies sets and no known scarcities exist. The ACC designation is D356-1.

	NRMT	VG-E	GOOD
COMPLETE SET	150.00	75.00	15.00
COMMON PLAYER (1-25)	5.00	2.50	.50

		NRMT	VG-E	GOOD
☐ 1	Charlie Grimm MG	6.00	3.00	.60
☐ 2	John Antonelli	6.00	3.00	.60
☐ 3	Vern Bickford	5.00	2.50	.50
☐ 4	Bob Buhl	5.00	2.50	.50
☐ 5	Lew Burdette	10.00	5.00	1.00
☐ 6	Dave Cole	5.00	2.50	.50
☐ 7	Ernie Johnson	5.00	2.50	.50
☐ 8	Dave Jolly	5.00	2.50	.50
☐ 9	Don Liddle	5.00	2.50	.50
☐ 10	Warren Spahn	30.00	15.00	3.00
☐ 11	Max Surkont	5.00	2.50	.50
☐ 12	Jim Wilson	5.00	2.50	.50
☐ 13	Sibbi Sisti	5.00	2.50	.50
☐ 14	Walker Cooper	5.00	2.50	.50
☐ 15	Del Crandall	6.00	3.00	.60
☐ 16	Ebba St.Claire	5.00	2.50	.50
☐ 17	Joe Adcock	6.00	3.00	.60
☐ 18	George Crowe	5.00	2.50	.50
☐ 19	Jack Dittmer	5.00	2.50	.50
☐ 20	Johnny Logan	6.00	3.00	.60
☐ 21	Ed Mathews	30.00	15.00	3.00
☐ 22	Bill Bruton	6.00	3.00	.60
☐ 23	Sid Gordon	5.00	2.50	.50
☐ 24	Andy Pafko	6.00	3.00	.60
☐ 25	Jim Pendleton	5.00	2.50	.50

1954 Johnston Cookies

The cards in this 35 card set measure 2" by 3 7/8". The 1954 Johnston's Cookies set of color cards of Milwaukee Braves are numbered according to the player's uniform number, except for the non-players, Lacks and Taylor, who are found at the end of the set. The Bobby Thomson card was withdrawn early in the year after his injury and is scarce. The ACC catalog number for this set is D356-2.

	NRMT	VG-E	GOOD
COMPLETE SET	500.00	250.00	50.00
COMMON PLAYER (1-50)	7.00	3.50	.70

		NRMT	VG-E	GOOD
☐ 1	Del Crandall	9.00	4.50	.90
☐ 3	Jim Pendleton	7.00	3.50	.70
☐ 4	Danny O'Connell	7.00	3.50	.70
☐ 5	Hank Aaron	175.00	85.00	18.00
☐ 6	Jack Dittmer	7.00	3.50	.70
☐ 9	Joe Adcock	9.00	4.50	.90
☐ 10	Bob Buhl	7.00	3.50	.70
☐ 11	Phil Paine	7.00	3.50	.70
☐ 12	Ben Johnson	7.00	3.50	.70

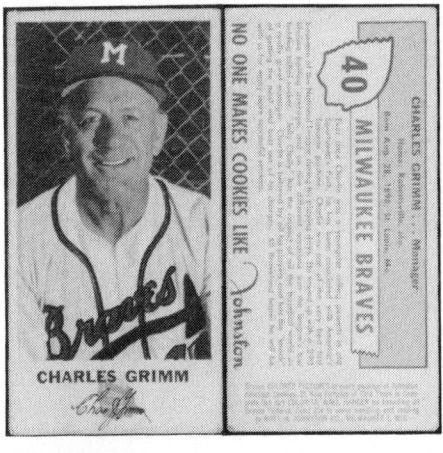

		NRMT	VG-E	GOOD
	COMPLETE SET	600.00	300.00	60.00
	COMMON PLAYER (1-51)	12.00	6.00	1.20
☐ 1	Del Crandall P1	15.00	7.50	1.50
☐ 3	Jim Pendleton P3	12.00	6.00	1.20
☐ 4	Danny O'Connell P3	12.00	6.00	1.20
☐ 6	Jack Dittmer P6	12.00	6.00	1.20
☐ 9	Joe Adcock P2	15.00	7.50	1.50
☐ 10	Bob Buhl P6	12.00	6.00	1.20
☐ 11	Phil Paine P5	12.00	6.00	1.20
☐ 12	Ray Crone P5	12.00	6.00	1.20
☐ 15	Charlie Gorin P1	12.00	6.00	1.20
☐ 16	Dave Jolly P4	12.00	6.00	1.20
☐ 17	Chet Nichols P2	12.00	6.00	1.20
☐ 18	Chuck Tanner P5	18.00	9.00	1.80
☐ 19	Jim Wilson P6	12.00	6.00	1.20
☐ 20	Dave Koslo P4	12.00	6.00	1.20
☐ 21	Warren Spahn P3	50.00	25.00	5.00
☐ 22	Gene Conley P3	12.00	6.00	1.20
☐ 23	Johnny Logan P4	15.00	7.50	1.50
☐ 24	Charlie White P2	12.00	6.00	1.20
☐ 28	Johnny Cooney P4	12.00	6.00	1.20
☐ 30	Roy Smalley P3	12.00	6.00	1.20
☐ 31	Bucky Walters P6	15.00	7.50	1.50
☐ 32	Ernie Johnson P5	12.00	6.00	1.20
☐ 33	Lew Burdette P1	25.00	12.50	2.50
☐ 34	Bobby Thomson P6	18.00	9.00	1.80
☐ 35	Bob Keely P1	12.00	6.00	1.20
☐ 38	Bill Bruton P4	15.00	7.50	1.50
☐ 39	George Crowe P3	12.00	6.00	1.20
☐ 40	Charlie Grimm MG P6	15.00	7.50	1.50
☐ 41	Eddie Mathews P5	50.00	25.00	5.00
☐ 44	Hank Aaron P1	200.00	100.00	20.00
☐ 47	Joey Jay P2	12.00	6.00	1.20
☐ 48	Andy Pafko P2 P4	12.00	6.00	1.20
☐ 49	Dr. Charles Leaks P2	12.00	6.00	1.20
	(unnumbered)			
☐ 50	Duffy Lewis P5	12.00	6.00	1.20
	(unnumbered)			
☐ 51	Joe Taylor P3	12.00	6.00	1.20
	(unnumbered)			

printed on thinner cardboard. Each player in the checklist has been marked to show on which panel or strip he appeared (Pafko appears twice). A complete panel of six cards is worth 25% more than the sum of the individual players. The ACC designation is D356-3.

☐ 13	Sibbi Sisti	7.00	3.50	.70
☐ 15	Charles Gorin	7.00	3.50	.70
☐ 16	Chet Nichols	7.00	3.50	.70
☐ 17	Dave Jolly	7.00	3.50	.70
☐ 19	Jim Wilson	7.00	3.50	.70
☐ 20	Ray Crone	7.00	3.50	.70
☐ 21	Warren Spahn	35.00	17.50	3.50
☐ 22	Gene Conley	7.00	3.50	.70
☐ 23	Johnny Logan	9.00	4.50	.90
☐ 24	Charlie White	7.00	3.50	.70
☐ 27	George Metkovich	7.00	3.50	.70
☐ 28	Johnny Cooney	7.00	3.50	.70
☐ 29	Paul Burris	7.00	3.50	.70
☐ 31	Bucky Walters	9.00	4.50	.90
☐ 32	Ernie Johnson	7.00	3.50	.70
☐ 33	Lou Burdette	15.00	7.50	1.50
☐ 34	Bob Thomson	150.00	75.00	15.00
☐ 35	Bob Keely	7.00	3.50	.70
☐ 38	Bill Bruton	9.00	4.50	.90
☐ 40	Charlie Grimm MG	9.00	4.50	.90
☐ 41	Eddie Mathews	35.00	17.50	3.50
☐ 42	Sam Calderone	7.00	3.50	.70
☐ 47	Joey Jay	7.00	3.50	.70
☐ 48	Andy Pafko	7.00	3.50	.70
☐ 49	Dr. Charles Lacks	7.00	3.50	.70
	(unnumbered)			
☐ 50	Joseph F. Taylor	7.00	3.50	.70
	(unnumbered)			

1955 Johnston Cookies

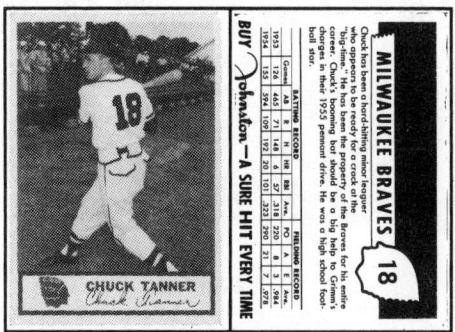

The cards in this 35 card set measure 2 3/4" by 4". This set of Milwaukee Braves issued in 1955 by Johnston Cookies are numbered by the uniform number of the player depicted, except for non-players Lacks, Lewis and Taylor. The cards were issued in strips of six which accounts for the rouletted edges found on single cards. They are larger in size than the two previous sets but are

1955 Kahn's

Compliments of Kahn's Wieners
"THE WIENER THE WORLD AWAITED"

The cards in this 6 card set measure 3 1/4" by 4". The 1955 Kahn's Wieners set received very limited distribution. The cards were supposedly given away at an amusement park. The set portrays the players in street clothes rather than in uniform and hence are sometimes referred to as "street clothes" Kahn's. All Kahn's sets from 1955 through 1963 are black and white and contain a 1/2" tab. Cards with the tab still intact are worth approximately 50% more than cards without the tab. Cards feature a facsimile autograph of the player on the front. Cards are blank-backed. Cincinnati Redlegs players only are featured.

	NRMT	VG-E	GOOD
COMPLETE SET	2100.00	900.00	180.00
COMMON PLAYER (1-6)	300.00	150.00	30.00
☐ 1 Gus Bell	600.00	300.00	60.00
☐ 2 Ted Kluszewski	400.00	200.00	40.00
☐ 3 Roy McMillan	300.00	150.00	30.00
☐ 4 Joe Nuxhall	300.00	150.00	30.00
☐ 5 Wally Post	300.00	150.00	30.00
☐ 6 Johnny Temple	300.00	150.00	30.00

1956 Kahn's

Compliments of Kahn's Wieners
"THE WIENER THE WORLD AWAITED"

The cards in this 15 card set measure 3 1/4" by 4". The 1956 Kahn's set was the first set to be issued with Kahn's meat products. The cards are blank backed. The set is distinguished by the old style, short sleeve shirts on the players and the existence of backgounds (Kahn's cards of later years utilize a blank background). Cards which have the tab still intact are worth approximately 50% more than cards without the tab. Cincinnati Redlegs players only are featured.

	NRMT	VG-E	GOOD
COMPLETE SET	900.00	450.00	90.00
COMMON PLAYER (1-15)	50.00	25.00	5.00
☐ 1 Ed Bailey	50.00	25.00	5.00
☐ 2 Gus Bell	60.00	30.00	6.00
☐ 3 Joe Black	60.00	30.00	6.00
☐ 4 Smoky Burgess	60.00	30.00	6.00
☐ 5 Art Fowler	50.00	25.00	5.00
☐ 6 Hershel Freeman	50.00	25.00	5.00
☐ 7 Ray Jablonski	50.00	25.00	5.00
☐ 8 John Klippstein	50.00	25.00	5.00
☐ 9 Ted Kluszewski	90.00	45.00	9.00
☐ 10 Brooks Lawrence	50.00	25.00	5.00
☐ 11 Roy McMillan	50.00	25.00	5.00
☐ 12 Joe Nuxhall	60.00	30.00	6.00
☐ 13 Wally Post	50.00	25.00	5.00
☐ 14 Frank Robinson	180.00	90.00	18.00
☐ 15 Johnny Temple	50.00	25.00	5.00

YOU CAN HELP: Your input is solicited for future editions of this guide. Write the author at 3410 MidCourt, Suite 110, Carrollton, TX 75006.

1957 Kahn's

Compliments of Kahn's Wieners
"THE WIENER THE WORLD AWAITED"

The cards in this 29 card set measure 3 1/4" by 4". The 1957 Kahn's Wieners set contains black and white, blank backed, unnumbered cards. The set features the Cincinnati Redlegs and Pittsburgh Pirates only. The cards feature a light background. Each card features a facsimile autograph of the player on the front. The Groat card exists with a "Richard Groat" autograph and also exists with the printed name "Dick Groat" on the card. The ACC designation is D155-3.

	NRMT	VG-E	GOOD
COMPLETE SET	1600.00	700.00	140.00
COMMON PLAYER	40.00	20.00	4.00
☐ 1 Tom Acker	40.00	20.00	4.00
☐ 2 Ed Bailey	40.00	20.00	4.00
☐ 3 Gus Bell	50.00	25.00	5.00
☐ 4 Smoky Burgess	50.00	25.00	5.00
☐ 5 Robert Clemente	350.00	175.00	35.00
☐ 6 George Crowe	40.00	20.00	4.00
☐ 7 Elroy Face	60.00	30.00	6.00
☐ 8 Hershel Freeman	40.00	20.00	4.00
☐ 9 Bob Friend	50.00	25.00	5.00
☐ 10 Dick Groat	75.00	37.50	7.50
☐ 11 Richard Groat	150.00	75.00	15.00
☐ 12 Don Gross	40.00	20.00	4.00
☐ 13 Warren Hacker	40.00	20.00	4.00
☐ 14 Don Hoak	40.00	20.00	4.00
☐ 15 Hal Jeffcoat	40.00	20.00	4.00
☐ 16 Ron Kline	40.00	20.00	4.00
☐ 17 John Klippstein	40.00	20.00	4.00
☐ 18 Ted Kluszewski	75.00	37.50	7.50
☐ 19 Brooks Lawrence	40.00	20.00	4.00
☐ 20 Dale Long	40.00	20.00	4.00
☐ 21 Bill Mazeroski	90.00	45.00	9.00
☐ 22 Roy McMillan	40.00	20.00	4.00
☐ 23 Joe Nuxhall	50.00	25.00	5.00
☐ 24 Wally Post	40.00	20.00	4.00
☐ 25 Frank Robinson	150.00	75.00	15.00
☐ 26 John Temple	40.00	20.00	4.00
☐ 27 Frank Thomas	50.00	25.00	5.00
☐ 28 Bob Thurman	40.00	20.00	4.00
☐ 29 Lee Walls	40.00	20.00	4.00

1958 Kahn's

The cards in this 29 card set measure 3 1/4" by 4". The 1958 Kahn's Wieners set of unnumbered, black and white cards features Cincinnati Redlegs, Philadelphia Phillies, and Pittsburgh Pirates. The backs present a story for each player entitled "My Greatest Thrill in Baseball". A method of distinguishing 1958 Kahn's from 1959 Kahn's is that the word Wieners is found on the front of the 1958

Compliments of Kahn's Wieners
"THE WIENER THE WORLD AWAITED"

Compliments of Kahn's
"THE WIENER THE WORLD AWAITED"

but not on the front of the 1959 cards. Cards of Wally Post, Charlie Rabe, and Frank Thomas are somewhat more difficult to find and are marked with an asterisk in the checklist below.

	NRMT	VG-E	GOOD
COMPLETE SET	2200.00	900.00	180.00
COMMON PLAYER (1-29)	40.00	20.00	4.00
☐ 1 Ed Bailey	40.00	20.00	4.00
☐ 2 Gene Baker	40.00	20.00	4.00
☐ 3 Gus Bell	50.00	25.00	5.00
☐ 4 Smoky Burgess	50.00	25.00	5.00
☐ 5 Roberto Clemente	350.00	175.00	35.00
☐ 6 George Crowe	40.00	20.00	4.00
☐ 7 Elroy Face	60.00	30.00	6.00
☐ 8 Hank Foiles	40.00	20.00	4.00
☐ 9 Dee Fondy	40.00	20.00	4.00
☐ 10 Bob Friend	50.00	25.00	5.00
☐ 11 Dick Groat	60.00	30.00	6.00
☐ 12 Harvey Haddix	50.00	25.00	5.00
☐ 13 Don Hoak	40.00	20.00	4.00
☐ 14 Hal Jeffcoat	40.00	20.00	4.00
☐ 15 Ron Kline	40.00	20.00	4.00
☐ 16 Ted Kluszewski	75.00	37.50	7.50
☐ 17 Vernon Law	50.00	25.00	5.00
☐ 18 Brooks Lawrence	40.00	20.00	4.00
☐ 19 Bill Mazeroski	75.00	37.50	7.50
☐ 20 Roy McMillan	40.00	20.00	4.00
☐ 21 Joe Nuxhall	50.00	25.00	5.00
☐ 22 Wally Post *	250.00	125.00	25.00
☐ 23 John Powers	40.00	20.00	4.00
☐ 24 Bob Purkey	40.00	20.00	4.00
☐ 25 Charlie Rabe *	250.00	125.00	25.00
☐ 26 Frank Robinson	150.00	75.00	15.00
☐ 27 Bob Skinner	40.00	20.00	4.00
☐ 28 Johnny Temple	40.00	20.00	4.00
☐ 29 Frank Thomas *	250.00	125.00	25.00

1959 Kahn's

The cards in this 38 card set measure 3 1/4" by 4". The 1959 Kahn's set features Cincinnati, Cleveland, and Pittsburgh players. The backs feature stories entitled "The Toughest Play I have to Make," or "The Toughest Batter I Have To Face." The Brodowski card is very scarce while Haddix, Held and McLish are considered quite difficult to obtain; these scarcities are the asterisked cards in the checklist below.

	NRMT	VG-E	GOOD
COMPLETE SET	2500.00	1000.00	200.00
COMMON PLAYER (1-38)	30.00	15.00	3.00
☐ 1 Ed Bailey	30.00	15.00	3.00
☐ 2 Gary Bell	30.00	15.00	3.00
☐ 3 Gus Bell	35.00	17.50	3.50
☐ 4 Dick Brodowski *	350.00	175.00	35.00
☐ 5 Smoky Burgess	35.00	17.50	3.50
☐ 6 Roberto Clemente	300.00	150.00	30.00
☐ 7 Rocky Colavito	65.00	32.50	6.50
☐ 8 Elroy Face	45.00	22.50	4.50
☐ 9 Bob Friend	35.00	17.50	3.50
☐ 10 Joe Gordon	35.00	17.50	3.50
☐ 11 Jim Grant	30.00	15.00	3.00
☐ 12 Dick Groat	45.00	22.50	4.50
☐ 13 Harvey Haddix * (blank back)	250.00	125.00	25.00
☐ 14 Woodie Held *	250.00	125.00	25.00
☐ 15 Don Hoak	30.00	15.00	3.00
☐ 16 Ron Kline	30.00	15.00	3.00
☐ 17 Ted Kluszewski	60.00	30.00	6.00
☐ 18 Vernon Law	35.00	17.50	3.50
☐ 19 Jerry Lynch	30.00	15.00	3.00
☐ 20 Billy Martin	75.00	37.50	7.50
☐ 21 Bill Mazeroski	60.00	30.00	6.00
☐ 22 Cal McLish *	250.00	125.00	25.00
☐ 23 Roy McMillan	30.00	15.00	3.00
☐ 24 Minnie Minoso	45.00	22.50	4.50
☐ 25 Russ Nixon	30.00	15.00	3.00
☐ 26 Joe Nuxhall	35.00	17.50	3.50
☐ 27 Jim Perry	35.00	17.50	3.50
☐ 28 Vada Pinson	45.00	22.50	4.50
☐ 29 Vic Power	30.00	15.00	3.00
☐ 30 Bob Purkey	30.00	15.00	3.00
☐ 31 Frank Robinson	125.00	60.00	12.50
☐ 32 Herb Score	45.00	22.50	4.50
☐ 33 Bob Skinner	30.00	15.00	3.00
☐ 34 George Strickland	30.00	15.00	3.00
☐ 35 Dick Stuart	35.00	17.50	3.50
☐ 36 Johnny Temple	30.00	15.00	3.00
☐ 37 Frank Thomas	35.00	17.50	3.50
☐ 38 George Witt	30.00	15.00	3.00

1960 Kahn's

The cards in this 42 card set measure 3 1/4" by 4". The 1960 Kahn's set features players of the Chicago Cubs, Chicago White Sox, Cincinnati Redlegs, Cleveland Indians, Pittsburgh Pirates, and St. Louis Cardinals. The backs give vital player information and records through the 1959 season. Kline appears with either St. Louis or Pittsburgh. The Harvey Kuenn card (asterisked below) appears with a blank back, and is scarce.

	NRMT	VG-E	GOOD
COMPLETE SET	1250.00	500.00	100.00
COMMON PLAYER (1-42)	18.00	9.00	1.80
☐ 1 Ed Bailey	18.00	9.00	1.80
☐ 2 Gary Bell	18.00	9.00	1.80
☐ 3 Gus Bell	21.00	10.50	2.10

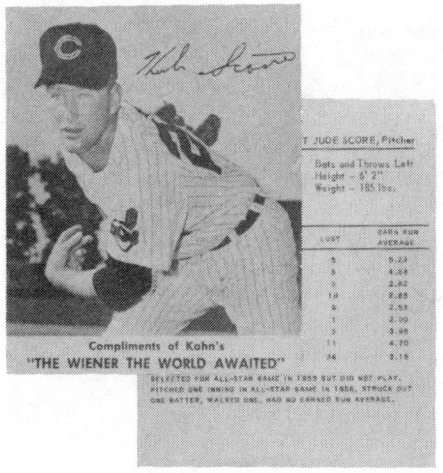

T JUDE SCORE, Pitcher

Bats and Throws Left
Height – 6' 2"
Weight – 185 lbs.

Compliments of Kahn's
"THE WIENER THE WORLD AWAITED"

SELECTED FOR ALL-STAR GAME IN 1955 BUT DID NOT PLAY.
PITCHED ONE INNING IN ALL-STAR GAME IN 1956, STRUCK OUT
ONE BATTER, WALKED ONE, HAD NO EARNED RUN AVERAGE.

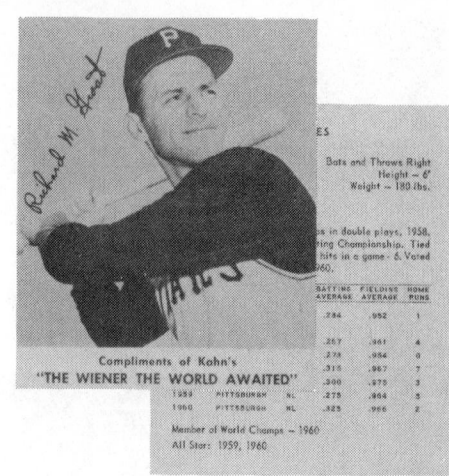

ES

Bats and Throws Right
Height – 6'
Weight – 180 lbs.

Compliments of Kahn's
"THE WIENER THE WORLD AWAITED"

Member of World Champs – 1960
All Star: 1959, 1960

☐ 4	Smoky Burgess	21.00	10.50	2.10
☐ 5	Gino Cimoli	18.00	9.00	1.80
☐ 6	Roberto Clemente	200.00	100.00	20.00
☐ 7	Roy Face	24.00	12.00	2.40
☐ 8	Tito Francona	18.00	9.00	1.80
☐ 9	Bob Friend	21.00	10.50	2.10
☐ 10	Jim Grant	18.00	9.00	1.80
☐ 11	Dick Groat	24.00	12.00	2.40
☐ 12	Harvey Haddix	21.00	10.50	2.10
☐ 13	Woodie Held	18.00	9.00	1.80
☐ 14	Bill Henry	18.00	9.00	1.80
☐ 15	Don Hoak	18.00	9.00	1.80
☐ 16	Jay Hook	18.00	9.00	1.80
☐ 17	Eddie Kasko	18.00	9.00	1.80
☐ 18A	Ron Kline (Pittsburgh)	40.00	20.00	4.00
☐ 18B	Ron Kline (St. Louis)	40.00	20.00	4.00
☐ 19	Ted Kluszewski	40.00	20.00	4.00
☐ 20	Harvey Kuenn (blank back)	200.00	100.00	20.00
☐ 21	Vernon Law	21.00	10.50	2.10
☐ 22	Brooks Lawrence	18.00	9.00	1.80
☐ 23	Jerry Lynch	18.00	9.00	1.80
☐ 24	Billy Martin	40.00	20.00	4.00
☐ 25	Bill Mazeroski	30.00	15.00	3.00
☐ 26	Cal McLish	18.00	9.00	1.80
☐ 27	Roy McMillan	18.00	9.00	1.80
☐ 28	Don Newcombe	24.00	12.00	2.40
☐ 29	Russ Nixon	18.00	9.00	1.80
☐ 30	Joe Nuxhall	21.00	10.50	2.10
☐ 31	Jim O'Toole	18.00	9.00	1.80
☐ 32	Jim Perry	21.00	10.50	2.10
☐ 33	Vada Pinson	24.00	12.00	2.40
☐ 34	Vic Power	18.00	9.00	1.80
☐ 35	Bob Purkey	18.00	9.00	1.80
☐ 36	Frank Robinson	90.00	45.00	9.00
☐ 37	Herb Score	24.00	12.00	2.40
☐ 38	Bob Skinner	18.00	9.00	1.80
☐ 39	Dick Stuart	21.00	10.50	2.10
☐ 40	Johnny Temple	18.00	9.00	1.80
☐ 41	Frank Thomas	21.00	10.50	2.10
☐ 42	Lee Walls	18.00	9.00	1.80

1961 Kahn's

The cards in this 43 card set measure 3 1/4" by 4".
The 1961 Kahn's Wieners set of black and white,
unnumbered cards features players from Cincinnati,
Cleveland, and Pittsburgh. This year was the first
year Kahn's made complete sets available to the
public; hence they are more available, especially in
the better condition grades, than the Kahn's of the
previous years. The backs give vital player
information and year by year career statistics
through 1960. The ACC designation is F155-7.

		NRMT	VG-E	GOOD
COMPLETE SET		500.00	250.00	50.00
COMMON PLAYER (1-43)		10.00	5.00	1.00
☐ 1	John Antonelli	11.00	5.50	1.10
☐ 2	Ed Bailey	10.00	5.00	1.00
☐ 3	Gary Bell	10.00	5.00	1.00
☐ 4	Gus Bell	10.00	5.00	1.00
☐ 5	Jim Brosnan	11.00	5.50	1.10
☐ 6	Smoky Burgess	11.00	5.50	1.10
☐ 7	Gino Cimoli	10.00	5.00	1.00
☐ 8	Roberto Clemente	150.00	75.00	15.00
☐ 9	Gordie Coleman	10.00	5.00	1.00
☐ 10	Jimmy Dykes	11.00	5.50	1.10
☐ 11	Roy Face	12.00	6.00	1.20
☐ 12	Tito Francona	10.00	5.00	1.00
☐ 13	Gene Freese	10.00	5.00	1.00
☐ 14	Bob Friend	11.00	5.50	1.10
☐ 15	Jim Grant	10.00	5.00	1.00
☐ 16	Dick Groat	15.00	7.50	1.50
☐ 17	Harvey Haddix	11.00	5.50	1.10
☐ 18	Woodie Held	10.00	5.00	1.00
☐ 19	Don Hoak	10.00	5.00	1.00
☐ 20	Jay Hook	10.00	5.00	1.00
☐ 21	Joey Jay	10.00	5.00	1.00
☐ 22	Eddie Kasko	10.00	5.00	1.00
☐ 23	Willie Kirkland	10.00	5.00	1.00
☐ 24	Vernon Law	11.00	5.50	1.10
☐ 25	Jerry Lynch	10.00	5.00	1.00
☐ 26	Jim Maloney	11.00	5.50	1.10
☐ 27	Bill Mazeroski	18.00	9.00	1.80
☐ 28	Wilmer Mizell	10.00	5.00	1.00
☐ 29	Rocky Nelson	10.00	5.00	1.00
☐ 30	Jim O'Toole	11.00	5.50	1.10
☐ 31	Jim Perry	11.00	5.50	1.10
☐ 32	Bubba Phillips	10.00	5.00	1.00
☐ 33	Vada Pinson	15.00	7.50	1.50
☐ 34	Wally Post	10.00	5.00	1.00
☐ 35	Vic Power	10.00	5.00	1.00
☐ 36	Bob Purkey	10.00	5.00	1.00
☐ 37	Frank Robinson	60.00	30.00	6.00
☐ 38	John Romano	10.00	5.00	1.00
☐ 39	Dick Schofield	10.00	5.00	1.00
☐ 40	Bob Skinner	10.00	5.00	1.00
☐ 41	Hal Smith	10.00	5.00	1.00
☐ 42	Dick Stuart	11.00	5.50	1.10
☐ 43	Johnny Temple	10.00	5.00	1.00

1962 Kahn's

The cards in this 38 card set measure 3 1/4" by 4".
The 1962 Kahn's Wieners set of black and white,
unnumbered cards features Cincinnati, Cleveland,
Minnesota, and Pittsburgh players. Card numbers 1
Bell, 33 Power, and 34 Purkey exist in two different
forms; these variations are listed in the checklist

Compliments of Kahn's
"THE WIENER THE WORLD AWAITED"

1962 Kahn's Atlanta

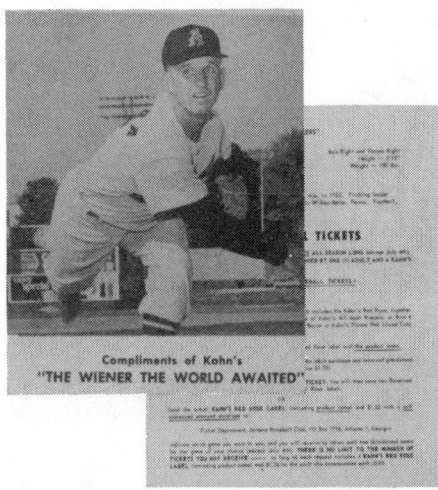

Compliments of Kahn's
"THE WIENER THE WORLD AWAITED"

below. The backs of the cards contain career information. The ACC designation is F155-8. The set price below includes the set with all variation cards.

	NRMT	VG-E	GOOD
COMPLETE SET	850.00	425.00	85.00
COMMON PLAYER	8.00	4.00	.80
☐ 1A Gary Bell (with fat man)	90.00	45.00	9.00
☐ 1B Gary Bell (no fat man)	30.00	15.00	3.00
☐ 2 Jim Brosnan	9.00	4.50	.90
☐ 3 Smoky Burgess	9.00	4.50	.90
☐ 4 Chico Cardenas	8.00	4.00	.80
☐ 5 Roberto Clemente	125.00	60.00	12.50
☐ 6 Ty Cline	8.00	4.00	.80
☐ 7 Gordon Coleman	8.00	4.00	.80
☐ 8 Dick Donovan	10.00	5.00	1.00
☐ 9 John Edwards	8.00	4.00	.80
☐ 10 Tito Francona	8.00	4.00	.80
☐ 11 Gene Freese	8.00	4.00	.80
☐ 12 Bob Friend	9.00	4.50	.90
☐ 13 Joe Gibbon	90.00	45.00	9.00
☐ 14 Jim Grant	8.00	4.00	.80
☐ 15 Dick Groat	12.00	6.00	1.20
☐ 16 Harvey Haddix	9.00	4.50	.90
☐ 17 Woodie Held	8.00	4.00	.80
☐ 18 Bill Henry	8.00	4.00	.80
☐ 19 Don Hoak	8.00	4.00	.80
☐ 20 Ken Hunt	8.00	4.00	.80
☐ 21 Joey Jay	8.00	4.00	.80
☐ 22 Eddie Kasko	8.00	4.00	.80
☐ 23 Willie Kirkland	8.00	4.00	.80
☐ 24 Barry Latman	8.00	4.00	.80
☐ 25 Jerry Lynch	8.00	4.00	.80
☐ 26 Jim Maloney	9.00	4.50	.90
☐ 27 Bill Mazeroski	15.00	7.50	1.50
☐ 28 Jim O'Toole	8.00	4.00	.80
☐ 29 Jim Perry	9.00	4.50	.90
☐ 30 Bubba Phillips	8.00	4.00	.80
☐ 31 Vada Pinson	12.00	6.00	1.20
☐ 32 Wally Post	8.00	4.00	.80
☐ 33A Vic Power (Indians)	30.00	15.00	3.00
☐ 33B Vic Power (Twins)	90.00	45.00	9.00
☐ 34A Bob Purkey (with autograph)	30.00	15.00	3.00
☐ 34B Bob Purkey (no autograph)	90.00	45.00	9.00
☐ 35 Frank Robinson	50.00	25.00	5.00
☐ 36 John Romano	8.00	4.00	.80
☐ 37 Dick Stuart	9.00	4.50	.90
☐ 38 Bill Virdon	12.00	6.00	1.20

SOMETHING MISSING? Many additional baseball collectibles are listed and priced in the newly released Price Guide to Baseball collectibles published in the same format as this book. See ordering details herein.

The cards in this 24 card set measure 3 1/4" by 4". The 1962 Kahn's Wieners Atlanta set features unnumbered, black and white cards of the Atlanta Crackers of the International League. The backs contain player statistical information as well as instructions on how to obtain free tickets. The ACC designation is F155-9.

	NRMT	VG-E	GOOD
COMPLETE SET	250.00	125.00	25.00
COMMON PLAYER	10.00	5.00	1.00
☐ 1 Jim Beauchamp	12.00	6.00	1.20
☐ 2 Gerry Buchek	10.00	5.00	1.00
☐ 3 Bob Burda	10.00	5.00	1.00
☐ 4 Dick Dietz	12.00	6.00	1.20
☐ 5 Bob Duliba	10.00	5.00	1.00
☐ 6 Harry Fanok	10.00	5.00	1.00
☐ 7 Phil Gagliano	12.00	6.00	1.20
☐ 8 John Glenn	10.00	5.00	1.00
☐ 9 Leroy Gregory	10.00	5.00	1.00
☐ 10 Dick Hughes	10.00	5.00	1.00
☐ 11 Johnny Kucks	12.00	6.00	1.20
☐ 12 Johnny Lewis	10.00	5.00	1.00
☐ 13 Tim McCarver	30.00	15.00	3.00
☐ 14 Bob Milliken	10.00	5.00	1.00
☐ 15 Joe Morgan	10.00	5.00	1.00
☐ 16 Ron Plaza	10.00	5.00	1.00
☐ 17 Bob Sadowski	10.00	5.00	1.00
☐ 18 Jim Saul	10.00	5.00	1.00
☐ 19 Willard Schmidt	10.00	5.00	1.00
☐ 20 Joe Schultz	10.00	5.00	1.00
☐ 21 Mike Shannon	20.00	10.00	2.00
☐ 22 Paul Toth	10.00	5.00	1.00
☐ 23 Lou Vickery	10.00	5.00	1.00
☐ 24 Fred Whitfield	10.00	5.00	1.00

1963 Kahn's

The cards in this 30 card set measure 3 1/4" by 4". The 1963 Kahn's Wieners set of black and white, unnumbered cards features players from Cincinnati, Cleveland, St. Louis, Pittsburgh and the New York Yankees. The cards feature a white border around the picture of the players. The backs contain career information. The ACC designation is F155-10.

	NRMT	VG-E	GOOD
COMPLETE SET	400.00	200.00	40.00
COMMON PLAYER	8.00	4.00	.80
☐ 1 Bob Bailey	8.00	4.00	.80

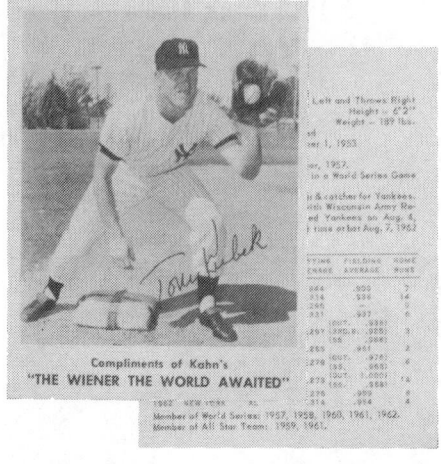

Compliments of Kahn's
"THE WIENER THE WORLD AWAITED"

			NRMT	VG-E	GOOD
		COMPLETE SET	600.00	300.00	60.00
		COMMON PLAYER (1-31)	8.00	4.00	.80
☐	1	Max Alvis	8.00	4.00	.80
☐	2	Bob Bailey	8.00	4.00	.80
☐	3	Chico Cardenas	8.00	4.00	.80
☐	4	Roberto Clemente	125.00	60.00	12.50
☐	5	Donn Clendenon	9.00	4.50	.90
☐	6	Vic Davalillo	9.00	4.50	.90
☐	7	Dick Donovan	8.00	4.00	.80
☐	8	John Edwards	8.00	4.00	.80
☐	9	Bob Friend	9.00	4.50	.90
☐	10	Jim Grant	8.00	4.00	.80
☐	11	Tommy Harper	9.00	4.50	.90
☐	12	Woodie Held	8.00	4.00	.80
☐	13	Joey Jay	8.00	4.00	.80
☐	14	Jack Kralick	8.00	4.00	.80
☐	15	Jerry Lynch	8.00	4.00	.80
☐	16	Jim Maloney	9.00	4.50	.90
☐	17	Bill Mazeroski	15.00	7.50	1.50
☐	18	Alvin McBean	8.00	4.00	.80
☐	19	Joe Nuxhall	9.00	4.50	.90
☐	20	Jim Pagliaroni	8.00	4.00	.80
☐	21	Vada Pinson	12.00	6.00	1.20
☐	22	Bob Purkey	8.00	4.00	.80
☐	23	Pedro Ramos	8.00	4.00	.80
☐	24	Frank Robinson	50.00	25.00	5.00
☐	25	John Romano	8.00	4.00	.80
☐	26	Pete Rose	300.00	150.00	30.00
☐	27	John Tsitouris	8.00	4.00	.80
☐	28	Bob Veale	9.00	4.50	.90
☐	29	Bill Virdon	12.00	6.00	1.20
☐	30	Leon Wagner	8.00	4.00	.80
☐	31	Fred Whitfield	8.00	4.00	.80

			NRMT	VG-E	GOOD
☐	2	Don Blasingame	8.00	4.00	.80
☐	3	Clete Boyer	10.00	5.00	1.00
☐	4	Smoky Burgess	9.00	4.50	.90
☐	5	Chico Cardenas	8.00	4.00	.80
☐	6	Roberto Clemente	125.00	60.00	12.50
☐	7	Donn Clendenon	9.00	4.50	.90
☐	8	Gordon Coleman	8.00	4.00	.80
☐	9	John Edwards	8.00	4.00	.80
☐	10	Gene Freese	8.00	4.00	.80
☐	11	Bob Friend	9.00	4.50	.90
☐	12	Joe Gibbon	8.00	4.00	.80
☐	13	Dick Groat	12.00	6.00	1.20
☐	14	Harvey Haddix	10.00	5.00	1.00
☐	15	Elston Howard	15.00	7.50	1.50
☐	16	Joey Jay	8.00	4.00	.80
☐	17	Eddie Kasko	8.00	4.00	.80
☐	18	Tony Kubek	15.00	7.50	1.50
☐	19	Jerry Lynch	8.00	4.00	.80
☐	20	Jim Maloney	9.00	4.50	.90
☐	21	Bill Mazeroski	15.00	7.50	1.50
☐	22	Joe Nuxhall	9.00	4.50	.90
☐	23	Jim O'Toole	8.00	4.00	.80
☐	24	Vada Pinson	12.00	6.00	1.20
☐	25	Bob Purkey	8.00	4.00	.80
☐	26	Bobby Richardson	15.00	7.50	1.50
☐	27	Frank Robinson	50.00	25.00	5.00
☐	28	Bill Stafford	8.00	4.00	.80
☐	29	Ralph Terry	10.00	5.00	1.00
☐	30	Bill Virdon	12.00	6.00	1.20

1964 Kahn's

Compliments of Kahn's
"THE WIENER THE WORLD AWAITED"

The cards in this 31 card set measure 3" by 3 1/2". The 1964 Kahn's set marks the beginning of the full color cards and the elimination of the tabs which existed on previous Kahn's cards. The set of unnumbered cards contains player information through the 1963 season on the backs. The set features Cincinnati, Cleveland and Pittsburgh players.

1965 Kahn's

 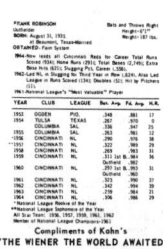

Compliments of Kahn's
"THE WIENER THE WORLD AWAITED"

The cards in this 45 card set measure 3" by 3 1/2". The 1965 Kahn's set contains full color, unnumbered cards. The set features Cincinnati, Cleveland, Pittsburgh, and Milwaukee players. Backs contain statistical information through the 1964 season.

			NRMT	VG-E	GOOD
		COMPLETE SET	600.00	300.00	60.00
		COMMON PLAYER (1-45)	8.00	4.00	.80
☐	1	Henry Aaron	100.00	50.00	10.00
☐	2	Max Alvis	8.00	4.00	.80
☐	3	Joe Azcue	8.00	4.00	.80
☐	4	Bob Bailey	8.00	4.00	.80
☐	5	Frank Bolling	8.00	4.00	.80
☐	6	Chico Cardenas	8.00	4.00	.80
☐	7	Rico Carty	12.00	6.00	1.20
☐	8	Donn Clendenon	9.00	4.50	.90
☐	9	Tony Cloninger	8.00	4.00	.80
☐	10	Gordon Coleman	8.00	4.00	.80
☐	11	Vic Davalillo	8.00	4.00	.80
☐	12	John Edwards	8.00	4.00	.80
☐	13	Sammy Ellis	8.00	4.00	.80
☐	14	Bob Friend	9.00	4.50	.90
☐	15	Tommy Harper	9.00	4.50	.90
☐	16	Chuck Hinton	8.00	4.00	.80
☐	17	Dick Howser	12.00	6.00	1.20
☐	18	Joey Jay	8.00	4.00	.80
☐	19	Deron Johnson	9.00	4.50	.90
☐	20	Jack Kralick	8.00	4.00	.80
☐	21	Denver LeMaster	8.00	4.00	.80
☐	22	Jerry Lynch	8.00	4.00	.80
☐	23	Jim Maloney	9.00	4.50	.90
☐	24	Lee Maye	8.00	4.00	.80
☐	25	Bill Mazeroski	15.00	7.50	1.50
☐	26	Alvin McBean	8.00	4.00	.80

		NRMT	VG-E	GOOD
☐ 27	Bill McCool	8.00	4.00	.80
☐ 28	Sam McDowell	10.00	5.00	1.00
☐ 29	Don McMahon	8.00	4.00	.80
☐ 30	Denis Menke	8.00	4.00	.80
☐ 31	Joe Nuxhall	9.00	4.50	.90
☐ 32	Gene Oliver	8.00	4.00	.80
☐ 33	Jim O'Toole	8.00	4.00	.80
☐ 34	Jim Pagliaroni	8.00	4.00	.80
☐ 35	Vada Pinson	12.00	6.00	1.20
☐ 36	Frank Robinson	45.00	22.50	4.50
☐ 37	Pete Rose	200.00	100.00	20.00
☐ 38	Willie Stargell	75.00	37.50	7.50
☐ 39	Ralph Terry	10.00	5.00	1.00
☐ 40	Luis Tiant	12.00	6.00	1.20
☐ 41	Joe Torre	15.00	7.50	1.50
☐ 42	John Tsitouris	8.00	4.00	.80
☐ 43	Bob Veale	9.00	4.50	.90
☐ 44	Bill Virdon	12.00	6.00	1.20
☐ 45	Leon Wagner	8.00	4.00	.80

1966 Kahn's

The cards in this 32 card set measure 2 13/16" by 4". 1966 Kahn's full color, unnumbered set features players from Atlanta, Cincinnati, Cleveland, and Pittsburgh. The set is identified by yellow and white vertical stripes and the name Kahn's written in red across a red rose at the top. The cards contain a 1 5/16" ad in the form of a tab. Cards with the ad (tab) are worth twice as much as cards without the ad, i.e., double the prices below.

		NRMT	VG-E	GOOD
COMPLETE SET		350.00	175.00	35.00
COMMON PLAYER (1-32)		5.00	2.50	.50
☐ 1	Henry Aaron (portrait, no wind-breaker under jersey	60.00	30.00	6.00
☐ 2	Felipe Alou: Braves (full pose, batting screen in background)	6.00	3.00	.60
☐ 3	Max Alvis: Indians (kneeling, full pose, with bat, no patch on jersey)	5.00	2.50	.50
☐ 4	Bob Bailey	5.00	2.50	.50
☐ 5	Wade Blasingame	5.00	2.50	.50
☐ 6	Frank Bolling	5.00	2.50	.50
☐ 7	Chico Cardenas: Reds (fielding, feet at base)	5.00	2.50	.50
☐ 8	Roberto Clemente	60.00	30.00	6.00
☐ 9	Tony Cloninger: Braves (pitching, foulpole in background)	5.00	2.50	.50
☐ 10	Vic Davalillo	5.00	2.50	.50
☐ 11	John Edwards: Reds (catching)	5.00	2.50	.50
☐ 12	Sam Ellis: Reds (white hat)	5.00	2.50	.50
☐ 13	Pedro Gonzalez	5.00	2.50	.50

		NRMT	VG-E	GOOD
☐ 14	Tommy Harper: Reds (arm cocked)	6.00	3.00	.60
☐ 15	Deron Johnson: Reds (batting with batting cage in background)	5.00	2.50	.50
☐ 16	Mack Jones	5.00	2.50	.50
☐ 17	Denver Lemaster	5.00	2.50	.50
☐ 18	Jim Maloney: Reds (pitching, white hat)	6.00	3.00	.60
☐ 19	Bill Mazeroski: Pirates (throwing)	9.00	4.50	.90
☐ 20	Bill McCool: Reds (white hat)	5.00	2.50	.50
☐ 21	Sam McDowell: Indians (kneeling)	6.00	3.00	.60
☐ 22	Denis Menke: Braves (white windbreaker under jersey)	5.00	2.50	.50
☐ 23	Joe Nuxhall	6.00	3.00	.60
☐ 24	Jim Pagliaroni: Pirates (catching)	5.00	2.50	.50
☐ 25	Milt Pappas	6.00	3.00	.60
☐ 26	Vada Pinson: Reds (fielding, ball on ground)	9.00	4.50	.90
☐ 27	Pete Rose: Reds (with glove)	100.00	50.00	10.00
☐ 28	Sonny Siebert: Indians (pitching, signature at feet)	5.00	2.50	.50
☐ 29	Willie Stargell: Pirates (batting, clouds in sky)	40.00	20.00	4.00
☐ 30	Joe Torre: Braves (catching with hand on mask)	10.00	5.00	1.00
☐ 31	Bob Veale: Pirates (hands at knee with glasses)	6.00	3.00	.60
☐ 32	Fred Whitfield	5.00	2.50	.50

1967 Kahn's

The cards in this 41 card set measure 2 13/16" by 4". The 1967 Kahn's set of full color, unnumbered cards is almost identical in style to the 1966 issue. Different meat products had different background colors (yellow and white stripes, red and white stripes, etc.). The set features players from Atlanta, Cincinnati, Cleveland, New York Mets and Pittsburgh. Cards with the ads (see 1966 set) are worth twice as much as cards without the ad, i.e., double the prices below.

		NRMT	VG-E	GOOD
COMPLETE SET		400.00	200.00	40.00
COMMON PLAYER (1-41)		5.00	2.50	.50
☐ 1	Henry Aaron: Braves (swinging pose, batting glove, ball, and hat on ground)	60.00	30.00	6.00
☐ 2	Gene Alley: Pirates	6.00	3.00	.60

(portrait)

☐ 3	Felipe Alou: Braves .... (full pose, bat on shoulder)	6.00	3.00	.60
☐ 4	Matty Alou: Pirates .... (portrait with bat, "Matio Rojas Alou")	6.00	3.00	.60
☐ 5	Max Alvis: Indians .... (fielding, hands on knees)	5.00	2.50	.50
☐ 6	Ken Boyer	9.00	4.50	.90
☐ 7	Chico Cardenas: Reds ...... (fielding, hand on knee)	5.00	2.50	.50
☐ 8	Rico Carty	7.00	3.50	.70
☐ 9	Tony Cloninger: Braves .... (pitching, no foul-pole in background)	5.00	2.50	.50
☐ 10	Tommy Davis	7.00	3.50	.70
☐ 11	John Edwards: Reds .... (kneeling with bat)	5.00	2.50	.50
☐ 12	Sam Ellis: Reds .... (all red hat)	5.00	2.50	.50
☐ 13	Jack Fisher	5.00	2.50	.50
☐ 14	Steve Hargan: Indians ...... (pitching, no clouds, blue sky)	5.00	2.50	.50
☐ 15	Tommy Harper: Reds .... (fielding, glove on ground)	6.00	3.00	.60
☐ 16	Tommy Helms	6.00	3.00	.60
☐ 17	Deron Johnson: Reds .... (batting, blue sky)	6.00	3.00	.60
☐ 18	Ken Johnson	5.00	2.50	.50
☐ 19	Cleon Jones	5.00	2.50	.50
☐ 20	Ed Kranepool	6.00	3.00	.60
☐ 21	Jim Maloney: Reds .... (pitching, red hat, follow thru delivery)	6.00	3.00	.60
☐ 22	Lee May: Reds .... (hands on knee)	6.00	3.00	.60
☐ 23	Bill Mazeroski: .... Pirates (portrait)	9.00	4.50	.90
☐ 24	Bill McCool: Reds (red ..... hat, left hand out)	5.00	2.50	.50
☐ 25	Sam McDowell: Indians .... (pitching, left hand under glove)	6.00	3.00	.60
☐ 26	Denis Menke: Braves .... (blue sleeves)	5.00	2.50	.50
☐ 27	Jim Pagliaroni: .... Pirates (catching, no chest protector)	5.00	2.50	.50
☐ 28	Don Pavletich	5.00	2.50	.50
☐ 29	Tony Perez: Reds .... (throwing)	15.00	7.50	1.50
☐ 30	Vada Pinson: Reds .... (ready to throw)	9.00	4.50	.90
☐ 31	Dennis Ribant	5.00	2.50	.50
☐ 32	Pete Rose: Reds .... (batting)	100.00	50.00	10.00
☐ 33	Art Shamsky: Reds	5.00	2.50	.50
☐ 34	Bob Shaw	5.00	2.50	.50
☐ 35	Sonny Siebert: .... Indians (pitching, signature at knees)	5.00	2.50	.50
☐ 36	Willie Stargell: .... Pirates (batting, no clouds)	40.00	20.00	4.00
☐ 37	Joe Torre: Braves .... (catching, mask on ground)	10.00	5.00	1.00
☐ 38	Bob Veale: Pirates .... (portrait, hands not shown)	6.00	3.00	.60
☐ 39	Leon Wagner: Indians .... (fielding)	5.00	2.50	.50
☐ 40	Fred Whitfield	5.00	2.50	.50
☐ 41	Woody Woodward	5.00	2.50	.50

1968 Kahn's

The cards in this 50-card set contain two different sizes. The smaller of the two sizes, which contains 12 cards, is 2 13/16" by 3 1/4" with the ad tab and 2 13/16" by 1 7/8" without the ad tab. The larger size, which contains 38 cards, measures 2 13/16" by 3 7/8" with the ad tab and 2 13/16" by 2 11/16"

JOHN BENCH

without the ad tab. The 1968 Kahn's set of full color, blank backed, unnumbered cards features players from Atlanta, Chicago Cubs, Chicago White Sox, Cincinnati, Cleveland, Detroit, New York Mets, and Pittsburgh. In the set of 12, listed with the letter A in the checklist, Maloney exists with either yellow or yellow and green stripes at the top of the card. The large set of 38, listed with a letter B in the checklist, contains five cards which exist in two variations. The variations in this large set have either yellow or red stripes at the top of the cards, with Maloney being an exception. Maloney has either a yellow stripe or a Blue Mountain ad at the top. Cards with the ad tabs (see other Kahn's sets) are worth twice as much as cards without the ad, i.e., double the prices below.

		NRMT	VG-E	GOOD
COMPLETE SET	....	500.00	250.00	50.00
COMMON PLAYER	....	5.00	2.50	.50
☐ A1	Hank Aaron	60.00	30.00	6.00
☐ A2	Gene Alley	6.00	3.00	.60
☐ A3	Max Alvis	5.00	2.50	.50
☐ A4	Clete Boyer	6.00	3.00	.60
☐ A5	Chico Cardenas	5.00	2.50	.50
☐ A6	Bill Freehan	7.00	3.50	.70
☐ A7	Jim Maloney (2)	6.00	3.00	.60
☐ A8	Lee May	6.00	3.00	.60
☐ A9	Bill Mazeroski	9.00	4.50	.90
☐ A10	Vada Pinson	9.00	4.50	.90
☐ A11	Joe Torre	10.00	5.00	1.00
☐ A12	Bob Veale	6.00	3.00	.60
☐ B1	Hank Aaron: Braves .... (full pose, batting bat cocked)	60.00	30.00	6.00
☐ B2	Tommy Agee	5.00	2.50	.50
☐ B3	Gene Alley: Pirates .... (fielding, full pose)	6.00	3.00	.60
☐ B4	Felipe Alou (full .... pose, batting, swinging, player in background)	6.00	3.00	.60
☐ B5	Matty Alou: Pirates .... (portrait with bat, "Matio Alou" (2)	6.00	3.00	.60
☐ B6	Max Alvis (fielding, ... glove on ground)	5.00	2.50	.50
☐ B7	Gerry Arrigo: Reds .... (pitching, follow thru delivery)	5.00	2.50	.50
☐ B8	John Bench	200.00	100.00	20.00
☐ B9	Clete Boyer	6.00	3.00	.60
☐ B10	Larry Brown	5.00	2.50	.50
☐ B11	Leo Cardenas: Reds .... (leaping in the air)	5.00	2.50	.50
☐ B12	Bill Freehan	6.00	3.00	.60
☐ B13	Steve Hargan: .... Indians (pitching, clouds in background)	5.00	2.50	.50
☐ B14	Joel Horlen: White .... Sox (portrait)	5.00	2.50	.50
☐ B15	Tony Horton: Indians ..... (portrait, signed Anthony)	6.00	3.00	.60
☐ B16	Willie Horton	6.00	3.00	.60

		NRMT	VG-E	GOOD
☐ B17	Ferguson Jenkins	15.00	7.50	1.50
☐ B18	Deron Johnson: .... Braves	5.00	2.50	.50
☐ B19	Mack Jones: Reds	5.00	2.50	.50
☐ B20	Bob Lee	5.00	2.50	.50
☐ B21	Jim Maloney: Reds .... (red hat, pitching hands up) (2)	6.00	3.00	.60
☐ B22	Lee May: Reds .... (batting)	6.00	3.00	.60
☐ B23	Bill Mazeroski: .... Pirates (fielding, hands in front of body)	9.00	4.50	.90
☐ B24	Dick McAuliffe	5.00	2.50	.50
☐ B25	Bill McCool (red hat, left hand down)	5.00	2.50	.50
☐ B26	Sam McDowell: .... Indians (pitching, left hand over glove (2)	6.00	3.00	.60
☐ B27	Tony Perez (fielding .... ball in glove) (2)	15.00	7.50	1.50
☐ B28	Gary Peters: White .... Sox (portrait)	5.00	2.50	.50
☐ B29	Vada Pinson: Reds .... (batting)	9.00	4.50	.90
☐ B30	Chico Ruiz	5.00	2.50	.50
☐ B31	Ron Santo: Cubs .... (batting, follow thru (2)	9.00	4.50	.90
☐ B32	Art Shamsky: Mets	5.00	2.50	.50
☐ B33	Luis Tiant: Indians .... (hands over head)	7.00	3.50	.70
☐ B34	Joe Torre: Braves .... (batting)	10.00	5.00	1.00
☐ B35	Bob Veale: Pirates .... (hands chest high)	6.00	3.00	.60
☐ B36	Leon Wagner: Indians .... (batting)	5.00	2.50	.50
☐ B37	Billy Williams: Cubs .... (bat behind back)	30.00	15.00	3.00
☐ B38	Earl Wilson	5.00	2.50	.50

1969 Kahn's

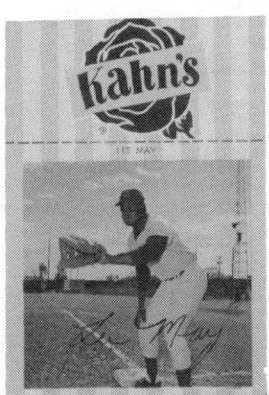

The cards in this 25 card set contain two different sizes. The three small cards (see 1968 description) measure 2 13/16" by 3 1/4" and the 22 large cards (see 1968 description) measure 2 13/16" by 3 15/16". The 1969 Kahn's Wieners set of full color, unnumbered cards features players from Atlanta, Chicago Cubs, Chicago White Sox, Cincinnati, Cleveland, Pittsburgh, and St. Louis. The small cards have the letter A in the checklist while the large cards have the letter B in the checklist. Four of the larger cards exist in two variations (red or yellow color stripes at the top of the card). These variations are identified in the checklist below. Cards with the ad tabs (see other Kahn's sets) are worth twice as much

as cards without the ad, i.e., double the prices below.

		NRMT	VG-E	GOOD
COMPLETE SET	....	250.00	125.00	25.00
COMMON PLAYER	....	5.00	2.50	.50
☐ A1	Hank Aaron (portrait)	60.00	30.00	6.00
☐ A2	Jim Maloney (pitch- ...... ing, hands at side)	6.00	3.00	.60
☐ A3	Tony Perez (glove on)	12.00	6.00	1.20
☐ B1	Hank Aaron	60.00	30.00	6.00
☐ B2	Matty Alou (batting)	6.00	3.00	.60
☐ B3	Max Alvis ('69 patch)	5.00	2.50	.50
☐ B4	Gerry Arrigo (leg up)	5.00	2.50	.50
☐ B5	Steve Blass	6.00	3.00	.60
☐ B6	Clay Carroll	5.00	2.50	.50
☐ B7	Tony Cloninger: Reds	5.00	2.50	.50
☐ B8	George Culver	5.00	2.50	.50
☐ B9	Joel Horlen .... (pitching)	5.00	2.50	.50
☐ B10	Tony Horton (batting)	6.00	3.00	.60
☐ B11	Alex Johnson	5.00	2.50	.50
☐ B12	Jim Maloney	6.00	3.00	.60
☐ B13	Lee May (foot on .... bag) (2)	6.00	3.00	.60
☐ B14	Bill Mazeroski .... (hands on knees) (2)	9.00	4.50	.90
☐ B15	Sam McDowell .... (leg up) (2)	6.00	3.00	.60
☐ B16	Tony Perez	12.00	6.00	1.20
☐ B17	Gary Peters .... (pitching)	5.00	2.50	.50
☐ B18	Ron Santo .... (emblem) (2)	9.00	4.50	.90
☐ B19	Luis Tiant (glove .... at knee)	7.00	3.50	.70
☐ B20	Joe Torre: Cardinals	10.00	5.00	1.00
☐ B21	Bob Veale (hands at ...... knees, no glasses)	6.00	3.00	.60
☐ B22	Billy Williams (bat .... behind head)	30.00	15.00	3.00

1987 Kahn's Weiners Reds

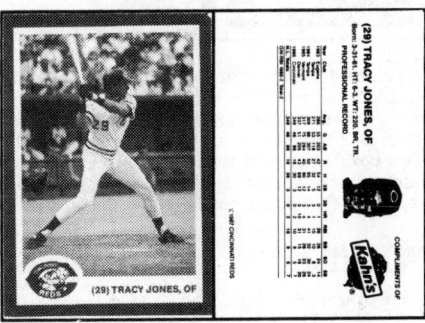

(29) TRACY JONES, OF

These 30-card sets were issued to the first 20,000 fans at the August 2nd game between the Reds and the San Francisco Giants. Cards are standard size, 2 1/2" by 3 1/2". The cards are unnumbered except for uniform number and feature full-color photos on the front.

		MINT	EXC	G-VG
COMPLETE SET	....	15.00	7.50	1.50
COMMON PLAYER	....	.40	.20	.04
☐ 6	Bo Diaz	.60	.30	.06
☐ 10	Terry Francona	.50	.25	.05
☐ 11	Kurt Stillwell	.60	.30	.06
☐ 12	Nick Esasky	.50	.25	.05
☐ 13	Dave Concepcion	.60	.30	.06
☐ 15	Barry Larkin	.75	.35	.07
☐ 16	Ron Oester	.40	.20	.04
☐ 21	Paul O'Neill	.50	.25	.05
☐ 23	Lloyd McClendon	.40	.20	.04
☐ 25	Buddy Bell	.60	.30	.06
☐ 28	Kal Daniels	1.50	.75	.15
☐ 29	Tracy Jones	.75	.35	.07
☐ 30	Guy Hoffman	.40	.20	.04
☐ 31	John Franco	.60	.30	.06

		MINT	EXC	G-VG
☐ 32	Tom Browning	.50	.25	.05
☐ 33	Ron Robinson	.50	.25	.05
☐ 34	Bill Gullickson	.50	.25	.05
☐ 35	Pat Pacillo	.50	.25	.05
☐ 39	Dave Parker	.75	.35	.07
☐ 43	Bill Landrum	.40	.20	.04
☐ 44	Eric Davis	4.00	2.00	.40
☐ 46	Rob Murphy	.50	.25	.05
☐ 47	Frank Williams	.50	.25	.05
☐ 48	Ted Power	.40	.20	.04
☐ xx	Pete Rose MG	1.50	.75	.15
☐ xx	Coaches Card	.50	.25	.05
	Scott Breeden			
	Billy DeMars			
	Tommy Helms			
	Bruce Kimm			
	Jim Lett			
	Tony Perez			
☐ xx	Ad Card	.40	.20	.04
	Save 25 cents			
	on Corn Dogs			
☐ xx	Ad Card	.40	.20	.04
	Save 30 cents			
	on Smokeys			

1986 Kay-Bee Young Stars

This 33-card, standard-sized (2 1/2" by 3 1/2") set was produced by Topps, although manufactured in Northern Ireland. This boxed set retailed in Kay-Bee stores for 1.99; the checklist was listed on the back of the box. The set is subtitled "Young Superstars of Baseball" and does indeed feature many young players. The cards are numbered on the back.

		MINT	EXC	G-VG
	COMPLETE SET	4.50	2.25	.45
	COMMON PLAYER	.10	.05	.01
☐ 1	Rick Aguilera	.15	.07	.01
☐ 2	Chris Brown	.25	.12	.02
☐ 3	Tom Browning	.10	.05	.01
☐ 4	Tom Brunansky	.15	.07	.01
☐ 5	Vince Coleman	.35	.17	.03
☐ 6	Ron Darling	.25	.12	.02
☐ 7	Alvin Davis	.20	.10	.02
☐ 8	Mariano Duncan	.10	.05	.01
☐ 9	Shawon Dunston	.15	.07	.01
☐ 10	Sid Fernandez	.20	.10	.02
☐ 11	Tony Fernandez	.20	.10	.02
☐ 12	Brian Fisher	.15	.07	.01
☐ 13	John Franco	.15	.07	.01
☐ 14	Julio Franco	.15	.07	.01
☐ 16	Dwight Gooden	.75	.35	.07
☐ 16	Ozzie Guillen	.15	.07	.01
☐ 17	Tony Gwynn	.45	.22	.04
☐ 18	Jimmy Key	.20	.10	.02
☐ 19	Don Mattingly	1.00	.50	.10
☐ 20	Oddibe McDowell	.15	.07	.01
☐ 21	Roger McDowell	.15	.07	.01
☐ 22	Dan Pasqua	.15	.07	.01
☐ 23	Terry Pendleton	.10	.05	.01
☐ 24	Jim Presley	.20	.10	.02
☐ 25	Kirby Puckett	.45	.22	.04
☐ 26	Earnie Riles	.10	.05	.01
☐ 27	Bret Saberhagen	.25	.12	.02
☐ 28	Mark Salas	.10	.05	.01
☐ 29	Juan Samuel	.20	.10	.02
☐ 30	Jeff Stone	.10	.05	.01

		MINT	EXC	G-VG
☐ 31	Darryl Strawberry	.50	.25	.05
☐ 32	Andy Van Slyke	.15	.07	.01
☐ 33	Frank Viola	.15	.07	.01

1987 Kay-Bee Superstars

This small 33-card boxed set was produced by Topps for Kay-Bee Toy Stores. The set is subtitled "Super Stars of Baseball" and measures the standard 2 1/2" by 3 1/2" with full-color fronts. The card backs are printed in blue and black on white card stock. The checklist for the set is printed on the back panel of the yellow box.

		MINT	EXC	G-VG
	COMPLETE SET (33)	4.00	2.00	.40
	COMMON PLAYER (1-33)	.10	.05	.01
☐ 1	Harold Baines	.15	.07	.01
☐ 2	Jesse Barfield	.20	.10	.02
☐ 3	Don Baylor	.15	.07	.01
☐ 4	Wade Boggs	.60	.30	.06
☐ 5	George Brett	.45	.22	.04
☐ 6	Hubie Brooks	.10	.05	.01
☐ 7	Jose Canseco	.50	.25	.05
☐ 8	Gary Carter	.30	.15	.03
☐ 9	Joe Carter	.20	.10	.02
☐ 10	Roger Clemens	.50	.25	.05
☐ 11	Vince Coleman	.35	.17	.03
☐ 12	Glenn Davis	.20	.10	.02
☐ 13	Dwight Gooden	.40	.20	.04
☐ 14	Pedro Guerrero	.20	.10	.02
☐ 15	Tony Gwynn	.40	.20	.04
☐ 16	Rickey Henderson	.35	.17	.03
☐ 17	Keith Hernandez	.25	.12	.02
☐ 18	Wally Joyner	.50	.25	.05
☐ 19	Don Mattingly	.75	.35	.07
☐ 20	Jack Morris	.20	.10	.02
☐ 21	Dale Murphy	.45	.22	.04
☐ 22	Eddie Murray	.35	.17	.03
☐ 23	Dave Parker	.20	.10	.02
☐ 24	Kirby Puckett	.35	.17	.03
☐ 25	Tim Raines	.30	.15	.03
☐ 26	Jim Rice	.25	.12	.02
☐ 27	Dave Righetti	.20	.10	.02
☐ 28	Ryne Sandberg	.25	.12	.02
☐ 29	Mike Schmidt	.40	.20	.04
☐ 30	Mike Scott	.20	.10	.02
☐ 31	Darryl Strawberry	.40	.20	.04
☐ 32	Fernando Valenzuela	.25	.12	.02
☐ 33	Dave Winfield	.25	.12	.02

1970 Kellogg's

The cards in this 75-card set measure 2 1/4" by 3 1/2". The 1970 Kellogg's set was Kellogg's first venture into the baseball card producing field. The design incorporates a brilliant color photo of the player set against an indistinct background, which is then covered with a layer of plastic to simulate a 3-D look. Cards 16-30 seem to be in shorter supply than the other cards in the set.

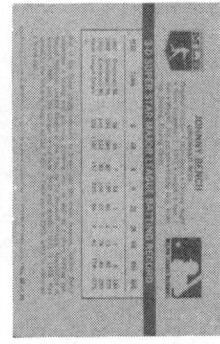

		NRMT	VG-E	GOOD
	COMPLETE SET	75.00	37.50	7.50
	COMMON PLAYER (1-15)	.60	.30	.06
	COMMON PLAYER (16-30)	.75	.35	.07
	COMMON PLAYER (31-75)	.60	.30	.06
☐ 1	Ed Kranepool	.75	.35	.07
☐ 2	Pete Rose	12.50	6.25	1.25
☐ 3	Cleon Jones	.60	.30	.06
☐ 4	Willie McCovey	3.00	1.50	.30
☐ 5	Mel Stottlemyre	.75	.35	.07
☐ 6	Frank Howard	.75	.35	.07
☐ 7	Tom Seaver	5.00	2.50	.50
☐ 8	Don Sutton	2.00	1.00	.20
☐ 9	Jim Wynn	.75	.35	.07
☐ 10	Jim Maloney	.75	.35	.07
☐ 11	Tommie Agee	.60	.30	.06
☐ 12	Willie Mays	7.50	3.75	.75
☐ 13	Juan Marichal	3.00	1.50	.30
☐ 14	Dave McNally	.75	.35	.07
☐ 15	Frank Robinson	3.50	1.75	.35
☐ 16	Carlos May	.75	.35	.07
☐ 17	Bill Singer	.75	.35	.07
☐ 18	Rick Reichardt	.75	.35	.07
☐ 19	Boog Powell	1.00	.50	.10
☐ 20	Gaylord Perry	3.00	1.50	.30
☐ 21	Brooks Robinson	5.00	2.50	.50
☐ 22	Luis Aparicio	3.50	1.75	.35
☐ 23	Joel Horlen	.75	.35	.07
☐ 24	Mike Epstein	.75	.35	.07
☐ 25	Tom Haller	.75	.35	.07
☐ 26	Willie Crawford	.75	.35	.07
☐ 27	Roberto Clemente	7.50	3.75	.75
☐ 28	Matty Alou	.75	.35	.07
☐ 29	Willie Stargell	4.00	2.00	.40
☐ 30	Tim Cullen	.75	.35	.07
☐ 31	Randy Hundley	.60	.30	.06
☐ 32	Reggie Jackson	6.00	3.00	.60
☐ 33	Rich Allen	.75	.35	.07
☐ 34	Tim McCarver	.75	.35	.07
☐ 35	Ray Culp	.50	.25	.05
☐ 36	Jim Fregosi	.75	.35	.07
☐ 37	Billy Williams	3.00	1.50	.30
☐ 38	Johnny Odom	.60	.30	.06
☐ 39	Bert Campaneris	.75	.35	.07
☐ 40	Ernie Banks	4.00	2.00	.40
☐ 41	Chris Short	.60	.30	.06
☐ 42	Ron Santo	.90	.45	.09
☐ 43	Glenn Beckert	.60	.30	.06
☐ 44	Lou Brock	3.50	1.75	.35
☐ 45	Larry Hisle	.75	.35	.07
☐ 46	Reggie Smith	.75	.35	.07
☐ 47	Rod Carew	3.50	1.75	.35
☐ 48	Curt Flood	.75	.35	.07
☐ 49	Jim Lonborg	.75	.35	.07
☐ 50	Sam McDowell	.75	.35	.07
☐ 51	Sal Bando	.75	.35	.07
☐ 52	Al Kaline	4.00	2.00	.40
☐ 53	Gary Nolan	.60	.30	.06
☐ 54	Rico Petrocelli	.60	.30	.06
☐ 55	Ollie Brown	.60	.30	.06
☐ 56	Luis Tiant	.75	.35	.07
☐ 57	Bill Freehan	.75	.35	.07
☐ 58	Johnny Bench	4.50	2.25	.45
☐ 59	Joe Pepitone	.75	.35	.07
☐ 60	Bobby Murcer	.90	.45	.09
☐ 61	Harmon Killebrew	3.00	1.50	.30
☐ 62	Don Wilson	.60	.30	.06
☐ 63	Tony Oliva	.90	.45	.09
☐ 64	Jim Perry	.75	.35	.07

☐ 65	Mickey Lolich	.90	.45	.09
☐ 66	Jose Laboy	.60	.30	.06
☐ 67	Dean Chance	.60	.30	.06
☐ 68	Bud Harrelson	.60	.30	.06
☐ 69	Willie Horton	.75	.35	.07
☐ 70	Wally Bunker	.60	.30	.06
☐ 71	Bob Gibson	3.00	1.50	.30
☐ 72	Joe Morgan	3.00	1.50	.30
☐ 73	Denny McLain	.90	.45	.09
☐ 74	Tommy Harper	.60	.30	.06
☐ 75	Don Mincher	.60	.30	.06

1971 Kellogg's

The cards in this 75-card set measure 2 1/4" by 3 1/2". The 1971 set of 3-D cards marketed by the Kellogg Company is the scarcest of all that company's issues. It was distributed as single cards, one in each package of cereal, without the usual complete set mail-in offer. In addition, card dealers were unable to obtain this set in quantity, as they have in other years. All the cards are available with and without the copyright notice on the back; the version without carries a slight premium for most numbers. Prices listed below are for the more common variety with copyright.

		NRMT	VG-E	GOOD
	COMPLETE SET	600.00	300.00	60.00
	COMMON PLAYER (1-75)	5.00	2.50	.50
☐ 1	Wayne Simpson	5.00	2.50	.50
☐ 2	Tom Seaver	25.00	12.50	2.50
☐ 3	Jim Perry	6.00	3.00	.60
☐ 4	Bob Robertson	5.00	2.50	.50
☐ 5	Roberto Clemente	30.00	15.00	3.00
☐ 6	Gaylord Perry	12.00	6.00	1.20
☐ 7	Felipe Alou	6.00	3.00	.60
☐ 8	Denis Menke	5.00	2.50	.50
☐ 9	Don Kessinger	5.00	2.50	.50
☐ 10	Willie Mays	30.00	15.00	3.00
☐ 11	Jim Hickman	5.00	2.50	.50
☐ 12	Tony Oliva	7.50	3.75	.75
☐ 13	Manny Sanguillen	6.00	3.00	.60
☐ 14	Frank Howard	6.00	3.00	.60
☐ 15	Frank Robinson	15.00	7.50	1.50
☐ 16	Willie Davis	6.00	3.00	.60
☐ 17	Lou Brock	18.00	9.00	1.80
☐ 18	Cesar Tovar	5.00	2.50	.50
☐ 19	Luis Aparicio	12.00	6.00	1.20
☐ 20	Boog Powell	7.50	3.75	.75
☐ 21	Dick Selma	5.00	2.50	.50
☐ 22	Danny Walton	5.00	2.50	.50
☐ 23	Carl Morton	5.00	2.50	.50
☐ 24	Sonny Siebert	5.00	2.50	.50
☐ 25	Jim Merritt	5.00	2.50	.50
☐ 26	Jose Cardenal	5.00	2.50	.50
☐ 27	Don Mincher	5.00	2.50	.50
☐ 28	Clyde Wright	5.00	2.50	.50
☐ 29	Les Cain	5.00	2.50	.50
☐ 30	Danny Cater	5.00	2.50	.50
☐ 31	Don Sutton	12.00	6.00	1.20
☐ 32	Chuck Dobson	5.00	2.50	.50
☐ 33	Willie McCovey	15.00	7.50	1.50
☐ 34	Mike Epstein	5.00	2.50	.50

			NRMT	VG-E	GOOD
☐ 35	Paul Blair		5.00	2.50	.50
☐ 36	Gary Nolan		5.00	2.50	.50
☐ 37	Sam McDowell		6.00	3.00	.60
☐ 38	Amos Otis		6.00	3.00	.60
☐ 39	Ray Fosse		5.00	2.50	.50
☐ 40	Mel Stottlemyre		6.00	3.00	.60
☐ 41	Clarence Gaston		5.00	2.50	.50
☐ 42	Dick Dietz		5.00	2.50	.50
☐ 43	Roy White		6.00	3.00	.60
☐ 44	Al Kaline		18.00	9.00	1.80
☐ 45	Carlos May		5.00	2.50	.50
☐ 46	Tommie Agee		5.00	2.50	.50
☐ 47	Tommy Harper		5.00	2.50	.50
☐ 48	Larry Dierker		5.00	2.50	.50
☐ 49	Mike Cuellar		6.00	3.00	.60
☐ 50	Ernie Banks		18.00	9.00	1.80
☐ 51	Bob Gibson		15.00	7.50	1.50
☐ 52	Reggie Smith		6.00	3.00	.60
☐ 53	Matty Alou		6.00	3.00	.60
☐ 54	Alex Johnson		5.00	2.50	.50
☐ 55	Harmon Killebrew		15.00	7.50	1.50
☐ 56	Bill Grabarkewitz		5.00	2.50	.50
☐ 57	Richie Allen		7.50	3.75	.75
☐ 58	Tony Perez		10.00	5.00	1.00
☐ 59	Dave McNally		6.00	3.00	.60
☐ 60	Jim Palmer		15.00	7.50	1.50
☐ 61	Billy Williams		15.00	7.50	1.50
☐ 62	Joe Torre		7.50	3.75	.75
☐ 63	Jim Northrup		5.00	2.50	.50
☐ 64	Jim Fregosi		6.00	3.00	.60
☐ 65	Pete Rose		60.00	30.00	6.00
☐ 66	Bud Harrelson		5.00	2.50	.50
☐ 67	Tony Taylor		5.00	2.50	.50
☐ 68	Willie Stargell		18.00	9.00	1.80
☐ 69	Tony Horton		6.00	3.00	.60
☐ 70	Claude Osteen		5.00	2.50	.50
☐ 71	Glenn Beckert		5.00	2.50	.50
☐ 72	Nate Colbert		5.00	2.50	.50
☐ 73	Rick Monday		6.00	3.00	.60
☐ 74	Tommy John		10.00	5.00	1.00
☐ 75	Chris Short		5.00	2.50	.50

			NRMT	VG-E	GOOD
☐ 12	Bill Melton		.40	.20	.04
☐ 13	Jim Palmer		2.50	1.25	.25
☐ 14	Doug Rader		.50	.25	.05
☐ 15	Dave Roberts		.40	.20	.04
☐ 16	Bobby Murcer		.60	.30	.06
☐ 17	Wes Parker		.50	.25	.05
☐ 18	Joe Coleman		.40	.20	.04
☐ 19	Manny Sanguillen		.50	.25	.05
☐ 20	Reggie Jackson		5.00	2.50	.50
☐ 21	Ralph Garr		.40	.20	.04
☐ 22	Jim Hunter		2.00	1.00	.20
☐ 23	Rick Wise		.40	.20	.04
☐ 24	Glenn Beckert		.40	.20	.04
☐ 25	Tony Oliva		.75	.35	.07
☐ 26	Bob Gibson		2.50	1.25	.25
☐ 27	Mike Cuellar		.50	.25	.05
☐ 28	Chris Speier		.40	.20	.04
☐ 29	Dave McNally		.50	.25	.05
☐ 30	Leo Cardenas		.40	.20	.04
☐ 31	Bill Freehan		.50	.25	.05
☐ 32	Bud Harrelson		.40	.20	.04
☐ 33	Sam McDowell		.50	.25	.05
☐ 34	Claude Osteen		.50	.25	.05
☐ 35	Reggie Smith		.50	.25	.05
☐ 36	Sonny Siebert		.40	.20	.04
☐ 37	Lee May		.50	.25	.05
☐ 38	Mickey Lolich		.60	.30	.06
☐ 39	Cookie Rojas		.40	.20	.04
☐ 40	Dick Drago		.40	.20	.04
☐ 41	Nate Colbert		.40	.20	.04
☐ 42	Andy Messersmith		.50	.25	.05
☐ 43	Dave Johnson		.60	.30	.06
☐ 44	Steve Blass		.40	.20	.04
☐ 45	Bob Robertson		.40	.20	.04
☐ 46	Billy Williams		2.50	1.25	.25
☐ 47	Juan Marichal		2.50	1.25	.25
☐ 48	Lou Brock		3.00	1.50	.30
☐ 49	Roberto Clemente		6.00	3.00	.60
☐ 50	Mel Stottlemyre		.50	.25	.05
☐ 51	Don Wilson		.40	.20	.04
☐ 52	Sal Bando		.50	.25	.05
☐ 53	Willie Stargell		3.00	1.50	.30
☐ 54	Willie Mays		7.50	3.75	.75

1972 Kellogg's

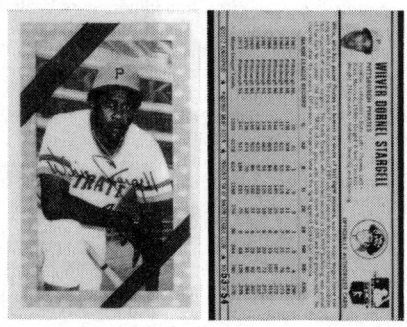

The cards in this 54-card set measure 2 1/8" by 3 1/4". The dimensions of the cards in the 1972 Kellogg's set were reduced in comparison to those of the 1971 series. In addition, the length of the set was set at 54 cards rather than the 75 of the previous year. The cards of this Kellogg's set are characterized by the diagonal bands found on the obverse.

			NRMT	VG-E	GOOD
	COMPLETE SET		45.00	22.50	4.50
	COMMON PLAYER (1-54)		.40	.20	.04
☐	1	Tom Seaver	5.00	2.50	.50
☐	2	Amos Otis	.60	.30	.06
☐	3	Willie Davis	.50	.25	.05
☐	4	Wilbur Wood	.50	.25	.05
☐	5	Bill Parsons	.40	.20	.04
☐	6	Pete Rose	12.50	6.25	1.25
☐	7	Willie McCovey	3.00	1.50	.30
☐	8	Ferguson Jenkins	.75	.35	.07
☐	9	Vida Blue	.50	.25	.05
☐	10	Joe Torre	.75	.35	.07
☐	11	Merv Rettenmund	.40	.20	.04

1972 Kellogg's ATG

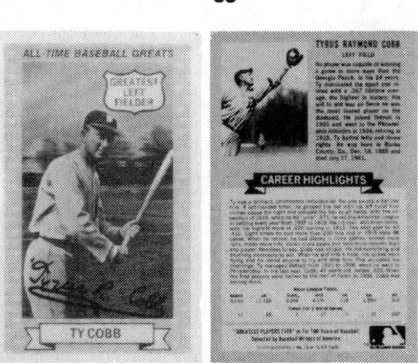

The cards in this 15-card set measure 2 1/4" by 3 1/2". The 1972 All-Time Greats 3-D set was issued with Kellogg's Danish Go Rounds. The set is a reissue of a 1970 set issued by Rold Gold Pretzels to commemorate baseball's first 100 years. The set contains two different cards of Babe Ruth.

			NRMT	VG-E	GOOD
	COMPLETE SET		12.00	6.00	1.20
	COMMON PLAYER (1-15)		.40	.20	.04
☐	1	Walter Johnson	1.00	.50	.10
☐	2	Rogers Hornsby	.60	.30	.06
☐	3	John McGraw	.40	.20	.04
☐	4	Mickey Cochrane	.50	.25	.05
☐	5	George Sisler	.50	.25	.05
☐	6	Babe Ruth	2.50	1.25	.25
☐	7	Lefty Grove	.60	.30	.06
☐	8	Pie Traynor	.40	.20	.04
☐	9	Honus Wagner	1.00	.50	.10
☐	10	Eddie Collins	.40	.20	.04

		NRMT	VG-E	GOOD
□ 11	Tris Speaker	.60	.30	.06
□ 12	Cy Young	.60	.30	.06
□ 13	Lou Gehrig	1.50	.75	.15
□ 14	Babe Ruth	2.50	1.25	.25
□ 15	Ty Cobb	1.50	.75	.15

1973 Kellogg's 2D

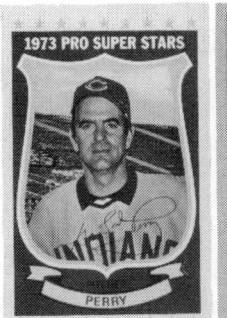
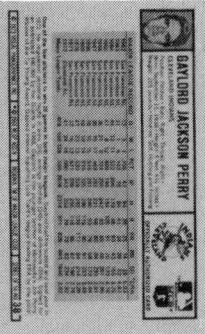

The cards in this 54-card set measure 2 1/4" by 3 1/2". The 1973 Kellogg's set is the only non 3-D set produced by the Kellogg Company. Apparently Kellogg's decided to have the cards produced through Visual Panographics rather than by Xograph as in the other years. The complete set could be obtained from the company through a box-top redemption procedure. The card size is slightly larger than the previous year.

		NRMT	VG-E	GOOD
	COMPLETE SET	40.00	20.00	4.00
	COMMON PLAYER (1-54)	.40	.20	.04
□ 1	Amos Otis	.60	.30	.06
□ 2	Ellie Rodriguez	.40	.20	.04
□ 3	Mickey Lolich	.60	.30	.06
□ 4	Tony Oliva	.60	.30	.06
□ 5	Don Sutton	1.75	.85	.17
□ 6	Pete Rose	10.00	5.00	1.00
□ 7	Steve Carlton	3.50	1.75	.35
□ 8	Bobby Bonds	.60	.30	.06
□ 9	Wilbur Wood	.50	.25	.05
□ 10	Billy Williams	2.50	1.25	.25
□ 11	Steve Blass	.40	.20	.04
□ 12	Jon Matlack	.50	.25	.05
□ 13	Cesar Cedeno	.50	.25	.05
□ 14	Bob Gibson	2.50	1.25	.25
□ 15	Sparky Lyle	.60	.30	.06
□ 16	Nolan Ryan	3.50	1.75	.35
□ 17	Jim Palmer	2.50	1.25	.25
□ 18	Ray Fosse	.40	.20	.04
□ 19	Bobby Murcer	.60	.30	.06
□ 20	Jim Hunter	2.00	1.00	.20
□ 21	Tom McCraw	.40	.20	.04
□ 22	Reggie Jackson	4.50	2.25	.45
□ 23	Bill Stoneman	.40	.20	.04
□ 24	Lou Piniella	.60	.30	.06
□ 25	Willie Stargell	3.50	1.75	.35
□ 26	Dick Allen	.60	.30	.06
□ 27	Carlton Fisk	1.25	.60	.12
□ 28	Ferguson Jenkins	.75	.35	.07
□ 29	Phil Niekro	2.00	1.00	.20
□ 30	Gary Nolan	.40	.20	.04
□ 31	Joe Torre	.60	.30	.06
□ 32	Bobby Tolan	.40	.20	.04
□ 33	Nate Colbert	.40	.20	.04
□ 34	Joe Morgan	2.50	1.25	.25
□ 35	Bert Blyleven	.60	.30	.06
□ 36	Joe Rudi	.50	.25	.05
□ 37	Ralph Garr	.40	.20	.04
□ 38	Gaylord Perry	1.50	.75	.15
□ 39	Bobby Grich	.50	.25	.05
□ 40	Lou Brock	2.50	1.25	.25
□ 41	Pete Broberg	.40	.20	.04
□ 42	Manny Sanguillen	.50	.25	.05
□ 43	Willie Davis	.50	.25	.05
□ 44	Dave Kingman	.75	.35	.07

		NRMT	VG-E	GOOD
□ 45	Carlos May	.40	.20	.04
□ 46	Tom Seaver	3.50	1.75	.35
□ 47	Mike Cuellar	.50	.25	.05
□ 48	Joe Coleman	.40	.20	.04
□ 49	Claude Osteen	.50	.25	.05
□ 50	Steve Kline	.40	.20	.04
□ 51	Rod Carew	3.50	1.75	.35
□ 52	Al Kaline	3.00	1.50	.30
□ 53	Larry Dierker	.40	.20	.04
□ 54	Ron Santo	.60	.30	.06

1974 Kellogg's

The cards in this 54-card set measure 2 1/8" by 3 1/4". In 1974 the Kellogg's set returned to its 3-D format; it also returned to the smaller-size card. Complete sets could be obtained from the company through a box-top offer.

		NRMT	VG-E	GOOD
	COMPLETE SET	40.00	20.00	4.00
	COMMON PLAYER (1-54)	.30	.15	.03
□ 1	Bob Gibson	2.50	1.25	.25
□ 2	Rick Monday	.40	.20	.04
□ 3	Joe Coleman	.30	.15	.03
□ 4	Bert Campaneris	.40	.20	.04
□ 5	Carlton Fisk	.90	.45	.09
□ 6	Jim Palmer	2.50	1.25	.25
□ 7	Ron Santo	.50	.25	.05
□ 8	Nolan Ryan	3.50	1.75	.35
□ 9	Greg Luzinski	.60	.30	.06
□ 10	Buddy Bell	.60	.30	.06
□ 11	Bob Watson	.40	.20	.04
□ 12	Bill Singer	.30	.15	.03
□ 13	Dave May	.30	.15	.03
□ 14	Jim Brewer	.30	.15	.03
□ 15	Manny Sanguillen	.40	.20	.04
□ 16	Jeff Burroughs	.40	.20	.04
□ 17	Amos Otis	.40	.20	.04
□ 18	Ed Goodson	.30	.15	.03
□ 19	Nate Colbert	.30	.15	.03
□ 20	Reggie Jackson	4.50	2.25	.45
□ 21	Ted Simmons	.75	.35	.07
□ 22	Bobby Murcer	.50	.25	.05
□ 23	Willie Horton	.40	.20	.04
□ 24	Orlando Cepeda	.75	.35	.07
□ 25	Ron Hunt	.30	.15	.03
□ 26	Wayne Twitchell	.30	.15	.03
□ 27	Ron Fairly	.30	.15	.03
□ 28	Johnny Bench	3.50	1.75	.35
□ 29	John Mayberry	.30	.15	.03
□ 30	Rod Carew	3.50	1.75	.35
□ 31	Ken Holtzman	.40	.20	.04
□ 32	Billy Williams	2.00	1.00	.20
□ 33	Dick Allen	.60	.30	.06
□ 34	Wilbur Wood	.40	.20	.04
□ 35	Danny Thompson	.30	.15	.03
□ 36	Joe Morgan	2.00	1.00	.20
□ 37	Willie Stargell	2.50	1.25	.25
□ 38	Pete Rose	10.00	5.00	1.00
□ 39	Bobby Bonds	.50	.25	.05
□ 40	Chris Speier	.30	.15	.03
□ 41	Sparky Lyle	.50	.25	.05
□ 42	Cookie Rojas	.30	.15	.03
□ 43	Tommy Davis	.40	.20	.04
□ 44	Jim Hunter	1.75	.85	.17
□ 45	Willie Davis	.40	.20	.04
□ 46	Bert Blyleven	.50	.25	.05

☐ 47	Pat Kelly	.30	.15	.03
☐ 48	Ken Singleton	.40	.20	.04
☐ 49	Manny Mota	.40	.20	.04
☐ 50	Dave Johnson	.50	.25	.05
☐ 51	Sal Bando	.40	.20	.04
☐ 52	Tom Seaver	3.50	1.75	.35
☐ 53	Felix Millan	.30	.15	.03
☐ 54	Ron Blomberg	.30	.15	.03

☐ 47	Sparky Lyle	.90	.45	.09
☐ 48	Dave Cash	.60	.30	.06
☐ 49	Luis Tiant	.90	.45	.09
☐ 50	Cesar Geronimo	.60	.30	.06
☐ 51	Carl Yastrzemski	10.00	5.00	1.00
☐ 52	Ken Brett	.60	.30	.06
☐ 53	Hal McRae	.75	.35	.07
☐ 54	Reggie Jackson	8.00	4.00	.80
☐ 55	Rollie Fingers	2.50	1.25	.25
☐ 56	Mike Schmidt	10.00	5.00	1.00
☐ 57	Richie Hebner	.60	.30	.06

1975 Kellogg's

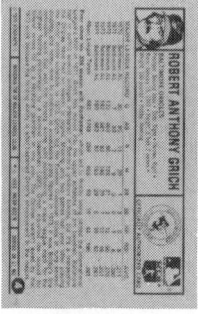

The cards in this 57-card set measure 2 1/8" by 3 1/4". The 1975 Kellogg's 3-D set could be obtained card by card in cereal boxes or as a set from a box-top offer from the company. Card number 44 Jim Hunter exists with the A's emblem or the Yankee's emblem on the back of the card.

		NRMT	VG-E	GOOD
COMPLETE SET		100.00	50.00	10.00
COMMON PLAYER (1-57)		.60	.30	.06
☐ 1	Roy White	.75	.35	.07
☐ 2	Ross Grimsley	.60	.30	.06
☐ 3	Reggie Smith	.75	.35	.07
☐ 4	Bob Grich	.75	.35	.07
☐ 5	Greg Gross	.60	.30	.06
☐ 6	Bob Watson	.75	.35	.07
☐ 7	Johnny Bench	6.00	3.00	.60
☐ 8	Jeff Burroughs	.75	.35	.07
☐ 9	Elliott Maddox	.60	.30	.06
☐ 10	Jon Matlack	.75	.35	.07
☐ 11	Pete Rose	16.00	8.00	1.60
☐ 12	Lee Stanton	.60	.30	.06
☐ 13	Bake McBride	.60	.30	.06
☐ 14	Jorge Orta	.60	.30	.06
☐ 15	Al Oliver	1.25	.60	.12
☐ 16	John Briggs	.60	.30	.06
☐ 17	Steve Garvey	6.00	3.00	.60
☐ 18	Brooks Robinson	5.00	2.50	.50
☐ 19	John Hiller	.75	.35	.07
☐ 20	Lynn McGlothen	.60	.30	.06
☐ 21	Cleon Jones	.60	.30	.06
☐ 22	Fergie Jenkins	1.25	.60	.12
☐ 23	Bill North	.60	.30	.06
☐ 24	Steve Busby	.75	.35	.07
☐ 25	Richie Zisk	.75	.35	.07
☐ 26	Nolan Ryan	6.00	3.00	.60
☐ 27	Joe Morgan	3.50	1.75	.35
☐ 28	Joe Rudi	.75	.35	.07
☐ 29	Jose Cardenal	.60	.30	.06
☐ 30	Andy Messersmith	.75	.35	.07
☐ 31	Willie Montanez	.60	.30	.06
☐ 32	Bill Buckner	1.00	.50	.10
☐ 33	Rod Carew	6.00	3.00	.60
☐ 34	Lou Piniella	.90	.45	.09
☐ 35	Ralph Garr	.75	.35	.07
☐ 36	Mike Marshall	.75	.35	.07
☐ 37	Garry Maddox	.75	.35	.07
☐ 38	Dwight Evans	1.50	.75	.15
☐ 39	Lou Brock	5.00	2.50	.50
☐ 40	Ken Singleton	.90	.45	.09
☐ 41	Steve Braun	.60	.30	.06
☐ 42	Rich Allen	1.00	.50	.10
☐ 43	John Grubb	.60	.30	.06
☐ 44	Jim Hunter (2)	4.00	2.00	.40
☐ 45	Gaylord Perry	2.50	1.25	.25
☐ 46	George Hendrick	.90	.45	.09

1976 Kellogg's

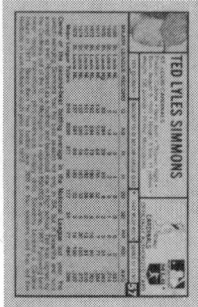

The cards in this 57-card set measure 2 1/8" by 3 1/4". The 1976 Kellogg's 3-D set could be obtained card by card in cereal boxes or as a set from the company for box-tops. Card number 6, that of Clay Carroll, exists with both a Reds or White Sox emblem on the back. Cards 1-3 (marked in the checklist below with SP) were apparently printed apart from the other 54 and are in shorter supply.

		NRMT	VG-E	GOOD
COMPLETE SET		50.00	25.00	5.00
COMMON PLAYER (1-3) SP		6.00	3.00	.60
COMMON PLAYER (4-57)		.30	.15	.03
☐ 1	Steve Hargan SP	6.00	3.00	.60
☐ 2	Claudell Washington SP	6.00	3.00	.60
☐ 3	Don Gullett SP	6.00	3.00	.60
☐ 4	Randy Jones	.40	.20	.04
☐ 5	Jim Hunter	2.00	1.00	.20
☐ 6	Clay Carroll (2)	.60	.30	.06
☐ 7	Joe Rudi	.40	.20	.04
☐ 8	Reggie Jackson	4.50	2.25	.45
☐ 9	Felix Millan	.30	.15	.03
☐ 10	Jim Rice	3.00	1.50	.30
☐ 11	Bert Blyleven	.50	.25	.05
☐ 12	Ken Singleton	.40	.20	.04
☐ 13	Don Sutton	1.50	.75	.15
☐ 14	Joe Morgan	2.50	1.25	.25
☐ 15	Dave Parker	1.50	.75	.15
☐ 16	Dave Cash	.30	.15	.03
☐ 17	Ron LeFlore	.40	.20	.04
☐ 18	Greg Luzinski	.60	.30	.06
☐ 19	Dennis Eckersley	.40	.20	.04
☐ 20	Bill Madlock	.90	.45	.09
☐ 21	George Scott	.30	.15	.03
☐ 22	Willie Stargell	2.50	1.25	.25
☐ 23	Al Hrabosky	.40	.20	.04
☐ 24	Carl Yastrzemski	4.50	2.25	.45
☐ 25	Jim Kaat	.75	.35	.07
☐ 26	Marty Perez	.30	.15	.03
☐ 27	Bob Watson	.30	.15	.03
☐ 28	Eric Soderholm	.30	.15	.03
☐ 29	Bill Lee	.30	.15	.03
☐ 30	Frank Tanana	.40	.20	.04
☐ 31	Fred Lynn	1.50	.75	.15
☐ 32	Tom Seaver	3.50	1.75	.35
☐ 33	Steve Busby	.40	.20	.04
☐ 34	Gary Carter	4.00	2.00	.40
☐ 35	Rick Wise	.30	.15	.03
☐ 36	Johnny Bench	3.00	1.50	.30
☐ 37	Jim Palmer	2.00	1.00	.20
☐ 38	Bobby Murcer	.50	.25	.05
☐ 39	Von Joshua	.30	.15	.03
☐ 40	Lou Brock	2.50	1.25	.25

		NRMT	VG-E	GOOD
☐ 41	Mickey Rivers (2)	.40	.20	.04
☐ 42	Manny Sanguillen	.40	.20	.04
☐ 43	Jerry Reuss	.40	.20	.04
☐ 44	Ken Griffey	.40	.20	.04
☐ 45	Jorge Orta	.30	.15	.03
☐ 46	John Mayberry	.30	.15	.03
☐ 47	Vida Blue (2)	.40	.20	.04
☐ 48	Rod Carew	3.00	1.50	.30
☐ 49	Jon Matlack	.40	.20	.04
☐ 50	Boog Powell	.50	.25	.05
☐ 51	Mike Hargrove	.40	.20	.04
☐ 52	Paul Lindblad	.30	.15	.03
☐ 53	Thurman Munson	3.00	1.50	.30
☐ 54	Steve Garvey	3.50	1.75	.35
☐ 55	Pete Rose	10.00	5.00	1.00
☐ 56	Greg Gross	.30	.15	.03
☐ 57	Ted Simmons	.75	.35	.07

		NRMT	VG-E	GOOD
☐ 36	Fred Patek	.25	.12	.02
☐ 37	Garry Maddox	.25	.12	.02
☐ 38	Ken Reitz	.25	.12	.02
☐ 39	Bobby Grich	.35	.17	.03
☐ 40	Cesar Geronimo	.25	.12	.02
☐ 41	Jim Lonborg	.35	.17	.03
☐ 42	Ed Figueroa	.25	.12	.02
☐ 43	Bill Madlock	.75	.35	.07
☐ 44	Jerry Remy	.25	.12	.02
☐ 45	Frank Tanana	.35	.17	.03
☐ 46	Al Oliver	.75	.35	.07
☐ 47	Charlie Hough	.35	.17	.03
☐ 48	Lou Piniella	.50	.25	.05
☐ 49	Ken Griffey	.35	.17	.03
☐ 50	Jose Cruz	.50	.25	.05
☐ 51	Rollie Fingers	1.00	.50	.10
☐ 52	Chris Chambliss	.35	.17	.03
☐ 53	Rod Carew	3.00	1.50	.30
☐ 54	Andy Messersmith	.35	.17	.03
☐ 55	Mickey Rivers	.35	.17	.03
☐ 56	Butch Wynegar	.35	.17	.03
☐ 57	Steve Carlton	3.00	1.50	.30

1977 Kellogg's

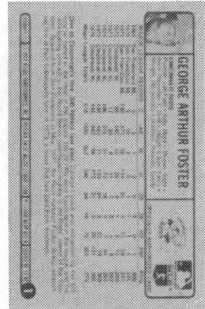

The cards in this 57-card set measure 2 1/8" by 3 1/4". The 1977 Kellogg's series of 3-D baseball player cards could be obtained card by card from cereal boxes or by sending in box-tops and money. Each player's picture appears in miniature form on the reverse, an idea begun in 1971 and replaced in subsequent years by the use of a picture of the Kellogg's mascot.

		NRMT	VG-E	GOOD
COMPLETE SET		35.00	17.50	3.50
COMMON PLAYER (1-57)		.25	.12	.02
☐ 1	George Foster	.90	.45	.09
☐ 2	Bert Campaneris	.30	.15	.03
☐ 3	Fergie Jenkins	.60	.30	.06
☐ 4	Dock Ellis	.25	.12	.02
☐ 5	John Montefusco	.25	.12	.02
☐ 6	George Brett	6.00	3.00	.60
☐ 7	John Candelaria	.35	.17	.03
☐ 8	Fred Norman	.25	.12	.02
☐ 9	Bill Travers	.25	.12	.02
☐ 10	Hal McRae	.35	.17	.03
☐ 11	Doug Rau	.25	.12	.02
☐ 12	Greg Luzinski	.50	.25	.05
☐ 13	Ralph Garr	.30	.15	.03
☐ 14	Steve Garvey	3.50	1.75	.35
☐ 15	Rick Manning	.25	.12	.02
☐ 16	Lyman Bostock	.35	.17	.03
☐ 17	Randy Jones	.25	.12	.02
☐ 18	Ron Cey	.50	.25	.05
☐ 19	Dave Parker	1.00	.50	.10
☐ 20	Pete Rose	8.00	4.00	.80
☐ 21	Wayne Garland	.25	.12	.02
☐ 22	Bill North	.25	.12	.02
☐ 23	Thurman Munson	2.50	1.25	.25
☐ 24	Tom Poquette	.25	.12	.02
☐ 25	Ron LeFlore	.25	.12	.02
☐ 26	Mark Fidrych	.35	.17	.03
☐ 27	Sixto Lezcano	.25	.12	.02
☐ 28	Dave Winfield	2.50	1.25	.25
☐ 29	Jerry Koosman	.35	.17	.03
☐ 30	Mike Hargrove	.25	.12	.02
☐ 31	Willie Montanez	.25	.12	.02
☐ 32	Don Stanhouse	.25	.12	.02
☐ 33	Jay Johnstone	.35	.17	.03
☐ 34	Bake McBride	.25	.12	.02
☐ 35	Dave Kingman	.60	.30	.06

1978 Kellogg's

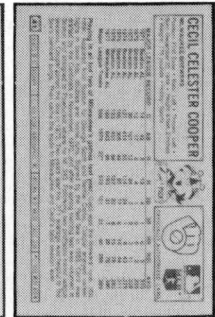

The cards in this 57-card set measure 2 1/8" by 3 1/4". This 1978 3-D Kellogg's series marks the first year in which Tony the Tiger appears on the reverse of each card next to the team and MLB logos. Once again the set could be obtained as individually wrapped cards in cereal boxes or as a set via a mail-in offer.

		NRMT	VG-E	GOOD
COMPLETE SET		30.00	15.00	3.00
COMMON PLAYER (1-57)		.20	.10	.02
☐ 1	Steve Carlton	2.50	1.25	.25
☐ 2	Bucky Dent	.30	.15	.03
☐ 3	Mike Schmidt	4.00	2.00	.40
☐ 4	Ken Griffey	.30	.15	.03
☐ 5	Al Cowens	.20	.10	.02
☐ 6	George Brett	4.00	2.00	.40
☐ 7	Lou Brock	2.00	1.00	.20
☐ 8	Rich Gossage	.75	.35	.07
☐ 9	Tom Johnson	.20	.10	.02
☐ 10	George Foster	.75	.35	.07
☐ 11	Dave Winfield	2.50	1.25	.25
☐ 12	Dan Meyer	.20	.10	.02
☐ 13	Chris Chambliss	.30	.15	.03
☐ 14	Paul Dade	.20	.10	.02
☐ 15	Jeff Burroughs	.20	.10	.02
☐ 16	Jose Cruz	.40	.20	.04
☐ 17	Mickey Rivers	.30	.15	.03
☐ 18	John Candelaria	.30	.15	.03
☐ 19	Ellis Valentine	.20	.10	.02
☐ 20	Hal McRae	.30	.15	.03
☐ 21	Dave Rozema	.20	.10	.02
☐ 22	Lenny Randle	.20	.10	.02
☐ 23	Willie McCovey	2.00	1.00	.20
☐ 24	Ron Cey	.50	.25	.05
☐ 25	Eddie Murray	8.00	4.00	.80
☐ 26	Larry Bowa	.40	.20	.04
☐ 27	Tom Seaver	3.00	1.50	.30
☐ 28	Garry Maddox	.30	.15	.03
☐ 29	Rod Carew	2.50	1.25	.25
☐ 30	Thurman Munson	2.50	1.25	.25
☐ 31	Gary Templeton	.40	.20	.04

		NRMT	VG-E	GOOD
☐ 32	Eric Soderholm	.20	.10	.02
☐ 33	Greg Luzinski	.40	.20	.04
☐ 34	Reggie Smith	.30	.15	.03
☐ 35	Dave Goltz	.20	.10	.02
☐ 36	Tommy John	.60	.30	.06
☐ 37	Ralph Garr	.20	.10	.02
☐ 38	Alan Bannister	.20	.10	.02
☐ 39	Bob Bailor	.20	.10	.02
☐ 40	Reggie Jackson	3.50	1.75	.35
☐ 41	Cecil Cooper	.50	.25	.05
☐ 42	Burt Hooton	.20	.10	.02
☐ 43	Sparky Lyle	.40	.20	.04
☐ 44	Steve Ontiveros	.20	.10	.02
☐ 45	Rick Reuschel	.30	.15	.03
☐ 46	Lyman Bostock	.30	.15	.03
☐ 47	Mitchell Page	.20	.10	.02
☐ 48	Bruce Sutter	.75	.35	.07
☐ 49	Jim Rice	2.50	1.25	.25
☐ 50	Ken Forsch	.20	.10	.02
☐ 51	Nolan Ryan	2.50	1.25	.25
☐ 52	Dave Parker	1.50	.75	.15
☐ 53	Bert Blyleven	.40	.20	.04
☐ 54	Frank Tanana	.30	.15	.03
☐ 55	Ken Singleton	.40	.20	.04
☐ 56	Mike Hargrove	.30	.15	.03
☐ 57	Don Sutton	1.50	.75	.15

☐ 28	Phil Niekro	1.25	.60	.12
☐ 29	Tom Seaver	2.50	1.25	.25
☐ 30	Fred Lynn	.75	.35	.07
☐ 31	Bill Bonham	.15	.07	.01
☐ 32	George Foster	.60	.30	.06
☐ 33	Terry Puhl	.20	.10	.02
☐ 34	John Candelaria	.20	.10	.02
☐ 35	Bob Knepper	.25	.12	.02
☐ 36	Fred Patek	.15	.07	.01
☐ 37	Chris Chambliss	.20	.10	.02
☐ 38	Bob Forsch	.20	.10	.02
☐ 39	Ken Griffey	.25	.12	.02
☐ 40	Jack Clark	1.50	.75	.15
☐ 41	Dwight Evans	.75	.35	.07
☐ 42	Lee Mazzilli	.20	.10	.02
☐ 43	Mario Guerrero	.15	.07	.01
☐ 44	Larry Bowa	.35	.17	.03
☐ 45	Carl Yastrzemski	3.50	1.75	.35
☐ 46	Reggie Jackson	3.00	1.50	.30
☐ 47	Rick Reuschel	.25	.12	.02
☐ 48	Mike Flanagan	.25	.12	.02
☐ 49	Gaylord Perry	1.25	.60	.12
☐ 50	George Brett	3.50	1.75	.35
☐ 51	Craig Reynolds	.15	.07	.01
☐ 52	Dave Lopes	.25	.12	.02
☐ 53	Bill Almon	.15	.07	.01
☐ 54	Roy Howell	.15	.07	.01
☐ 55	Frank Tanana	.20	.10	.02
☐ 56	Doug Rau	.15	.07	.01
☐ 57	Rick Monday	.20	.10	.02
☐ 58	Jon Matlack	.20	.10	.02
☐ 59	Ron Jackson	.15	.07	.01
☐ 60	Jim Sundberg	.20	.10	.02

1979 Kellogg's

 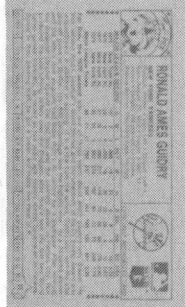

The cards in this 60-card set measure 1 15/16" by 3 1/4". The 1979 edition of Kellogg's 3-D baseball cards have a 3/16" reduced width from the previous year; a nicely designed curved panel above the picture gives this set a distinctive appearance. The set contains the largest number of cards issued in a Kellogg's set since the 1971 series.

		NRMT	VG-E	GOOD
COMPLETE SET		21.00	10.50	2.10
COMMON PLAYER (1-60)		.15	.07	.01
☐ 1	Bruce Sutter	.60	.30	.06
☐ 2	Ted Simmons	.40	.20	.04
☐ 3	Ross Grimsley	.15	.07	.01
☐ 4	Wayne Nordhagen	.15	.07	.01
☐ 5	Jim Palmer	1.50	.75	.15
☐ 6	John Henry Johnson	.15	.07	.01
☐ 7	Jason Thompson	.15	.07	.01
☐ 8	Pat Zachry	.15	.07	.01
☐ 9	Dennis Eckersley	.20	.10	.02
☐ 10	Paul Splittorff	.20	.10	.02
☐ 11	Ron Guidry	1.25	.60	.12
☐ 12	Jeff Burroughs	.15	.07	.01
☐ 13	Rod Carew	2.50	1.25	.25
☐ 14	Buddy Bell	.30	.15	.03
☐ 15	Jim Rice	2.50	1.25	.25
☐ 16	Garry Maddox	.20	.10	.02
☐ 17	Willie McCovey	1.50	.75	.15
☐ 18	Steve Carlton	2.50	1.25	.25
☐ 19	J.R. Richard	.25	.12	.02
☐ 20	Paul Molitor	1.00	.50	.10
☐ 21	Dave Parker	1.00	.50	.10
☐ 22	Pete Rose	6.00	3.00	.60
☐ 23	Vida Blue	.25	.12	.02
☐ 24	Richie Zisk	.15	.07	.01
☐ 25	Darrell Porter	.15	.07	.01
☐ 26	Dan Driessen	.15	.07	.01
☐ 27	Geoff Zahn	.15	.07	.01

1980 Kellogg's

 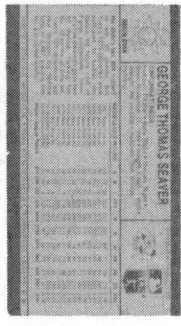

The cards in this 60-card set measure 1 7/8" by 3 1/4". The 1980 Kellogg's 3-D set is quite similar to, but smaller (narrower) than, the other recent Kellogg's issues. Sets could be obtained card by card from cereal boxes or as a set from a box-top offer from the company.

		MINT	EXC	G-VG
COMPLETE SET		18.00	9.00	1.80
COMMON PLAYER (1-60)		.15	.07	.01
☐ 1	Ross Grimsley	.15	.07	.01
☐ 2	Mike Schmidt	3.00	1.50	.30
☐ 3	Mike Flanagan	.25	.12	.02
☐ 4	Ron Guidry	.75	.35	.07
☐ 5	Bert Blyleven	.35	.17	.03
☐ 6	Dave Kingman	.35	.17	.03
☐ 7	Jeff Newman	.15	.07	.01
☐ 8	Steve Rogers	.25	.12	.02
☐ 9	George Brett	3.00	1.50	.30
☐ 10	Bruce Sutter	.60	.30	.06
☐ 11	Gorman Thomas	.25	.12	.02
☐ 12	Darrell Porter	.15	.07	.01
☐ 13	Roy Smalley	.15	.07	.01
☐ 14	Steve Carlton	2.00	1.00	.20
☐ 15	Jim Palmer	1.50	.75	.15
☐ 16	Bob Bailor	.15	.07	.01
☐ 17	Jason Thompson	.15	.07	.01
☐ 18	Graig Nettles	.35	.17	.03
☐ 19	Ron Cey	.35	.17	.03
☐ 20	Nolan Ryan	2.00	1.00	.20
☐ 21	Ellis Valentine	.15	.07	.01

		MINT	EXC	G-VG
☐ 22	Larry Hisle	.15	.07	.01
☐ 23	Dave Parker	.75	.35	.07
☐ 24	Eddie Murray	2.50	1.25	.25
☐ 25	Willie Stargell	1.50	.75	.15
☐ 26	Reggie Jackson	2.50	1.25	.25
☐ 27	Carl Yastrzemski	2.50	1.25	.25
☐ 28	Andre Thornton	.25	.12	.02
☐ 29	Dave Lopes	.25	.12	.02
☐ 30	Ken Singleton	.35	.17	.03
☐ 31	Steve Garvey	2.00	1.00	.20
☐ 32	Dave Winfield	2.00	1.00	.20
☐ 33	Steve Kemp	.25	.12	.02
☐ 34	Claudell Washington	.25	.12	.02
☐ 35	Pete Rose	5.00	2.50	.50
☐ 36	Cesar Cedeno	.25	.12	.02
☐ 37	John Stearns	.15	.07	.01
☐ 38	Lee Mazzilli	.15	.07	.01
☐ 39	Larry Bowa	.35	.17	.03
☐ 40	Fred Lynn	.60	.30	.06
☐ 41	Carlton Fisk	.60	.30	.06
☐ 42	Vida Blue	.25	.12	.02
☐ 43	Keith Hernandez	1.50	.75	.15
☐ 44	Jim Rice	1.50	.75	.15
☐ 45	Ted Simmons	.35	.17	.03
☐ 46	Chet Lemon	.25	.12	.02
☐ 47	Ferguson Jenkins	.50	.25	.05
☐ 48	Gary Matthews	.25	.12	.02
☐ 49	Tom Seaver	2.00	1.00	.20
☐ 50	George Foster	.60	.30	.06
☐ 51	Phil Niekro	1.00	.50	.10
☐ 52	Johnny Bench	2.00	1.00	.20
☐ 53	Buddy Bell	.35	.17	.03
☐ 54	Lance Parrish	1.00	.50	.10
☐ 55	Joaquin Andujar	.25	.12	.02
☐ 56	Don Baylor	.35	.17	.03
☐ 57	Jack Clark	1.00	.50	.10
☐ 58	J.R. Richard	.25	.12	.02
☐ 59	Bruce Bochte	.15	.07	.01
☐ 60	Rod Carew	2.00	1.00	.20

1981 Kellogg's

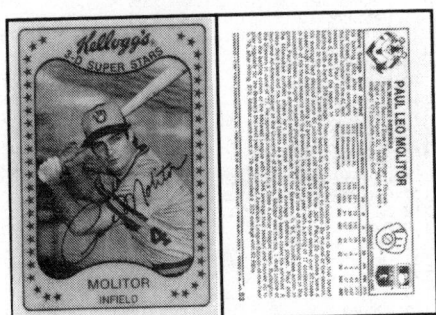

The cards in this 66-card set measure 2 1/2" by 3 1/2". The 1981 Kellogg's set witnessed an increase in both the size of the card and the size of the set. For the first time, cards were not packed in cereal sizes but available only by mail- in procedure. The offer for the card set was advertised on boxes of Kellogg's Corn Flakes. The cards were printed on a different stock than in previous years, presumably to prevent the cracking problem which has plagued all Kellogg's 3-D issues. At the end of the promotion, the remainder of the sets not distributed (to cereal-eaters), were "sold" into the organized hobby, thus creating a situation where the set is relatively plentiful compared to other years of Kellogg's.

	MINT	EXC	G-VG
COMPLETE SET	6.00	3.00	.60
COMMON PLAYER	.06	.03	.00

☐ 1	George Foster	.15	.07	.01
☐ 2	Jim Palmer	.30	.15	.03
☐ 3	Reggie Jackson	.75	.35	.07
☐ 4	Al Oliver	.10	.05	.01
☐ 5	Mike Schmidt	.90	.45	.09

☐ 6	Nolan Ryan	.40	.20	.04
☐ 7	Bucky Dent	.10	.05	.01
☐ 8	George Brett	.90	.45	.09
☐ 9	Jim Rice	.35	.17	.03
☐ 10	Steve Garvey	.45	.22	.04
☐ 11	Willie Stargell	.45	.22	.04
☐ 12	Phil Niekro	.25	.12	.02
☐ 13	Dave Parker	.25	.12	.02
☐ 14	Cesar Cedeno	.10	.05	.01
☐ 15	Don Baylor	.10	.05	.01
☐ 16	J.R. Richard	.06	.03	.00
☐ 17	Tony Perez	.10	.05	.01
☐ 18	Eddie Murray	.75	.35	.07
☐ 19	Chet Lemon	.06	.03	.00
☐ 20	Ben Oglivie	.06	.03	.00
☐ 21	Dave Winfield	.40	.20	.04
☐ 22	Joe Morgan	.25	.12	.02
☐ 23	Vida Blue	.06	.03	.00
☐ 24	Willie Wilson	.10	.05	.01
☐ 25	Steve Henderson	.06	.03	.00
☐ 26	Rod Carew	.40	.20	.04
☐ 27	Garry Templeton	.06	.03	.00
☐ 28	Dave Concepcion	.10	.05	.01
☐ 29	Dave Lopes	.06	.03	.00
☐ 30	Ken Landreaux	.06	.03	.00
☐ 31	Keith Hernandez	.35	.17	.03
☐ 32	Cecil Cooper	.10	.05	.01
☐ 33	Rickey Henderson	.50	.25	.05
☐ 34	Frank White	.06	.03	.00
☐ 35	George Hendrick	.06	.03	.00
☐ 36	Reggie Smith	.06	.03	.00
☐ 37	Tug McGraw	.10	.05	.01
☐ 38	Tom Seaver	.45	.22	.04
☐ 39	Ken Singleton	.10	.05	.01
☐ 40	Fred Lynn	.15	.07	.01
☐ 41	Rich Gossage	.10	.05	.01
☐ 42	Terry Puhl	.06	.03	.00
☐ 43	Larry Bowa	.15	.07	.01
☐ 44	Phil Garner	.06	.03	.00
☐ 45	Ron Guidry	.20	.10	.02
☐ 46	Lee Mazzilli	.06	.03	.00
☐ 47	Dave Kingman	.10	.05	.01
☐ 48	Carl Yastrzemski	.90	.45	.09
☐ 49	Rick Burleson	.06	.03	.00
☐ 50	Steve Carlton	.40	.20	.04
☐ 51	Alan Trammell	.30	.15	.03
☐ 52	Tommy John	.15	.07	.01
☐ 53	Paul Molitor	.25	.12	.02
☐ 54	Joe Charbonneau	.06	.03	.00
☐ 55	Rick Langford	.06	.03	.00
☐ 56	Bruce Sutter	.10	.05	.01
☐ 57	Robin Yount	.25	.12	.02
☐ 58	Steve Stone	.06	.03	.00
☐ 59	Larry Gura	.06	.03	.00
☐ 60	Mike Flanagan	.06	.03	.00
☐ 61	Bob Horner	.25	.12	.02
☐ 62	Bruce Bochte	.06	.03	.00
☐ 63	Pete Rose	1.00	.50	.10
☐ 64	Buddy Bell	.10	.05	.01
☐ 65	Johnny Bench	.40	.20	.04
☐ 66	Mike Hargrove	.06	.03	.00

1982 Kellogg's

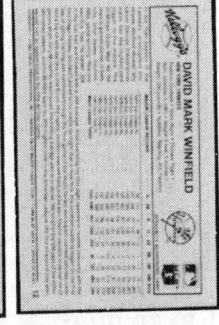

The cards in this 64-card set measure 2 1/8" by 3 1/4". The 1982 version of 3-D cards prepared for the Kellogg Company by Visual Panographics, Inc., is not only smaller in physical dimensions from the 1981

series (which was standard card size at 2 1/2" by 3 1/2") but is also two cards shorter in length (64 in '82 and 66 in '81). In addition, while retaining the policy of not inserting single cards into cereal packages and offering the sets through box-top mail-ins only, the Kellogg Company accepted box tops from four types of cereals, as opposed to only one type the previous year. Each card features a color 3-D ballplayer picture with a vertical line of white stars on each side set upon a blue background. The player's name and the word Kellogg's are printed in red on the obverse, and the card number is found on the bottom right of the reverse.

		MINT	EXC	G-VG
	COMPLETE SET	11.00	5.50	1.10
	COMMON PLAYER	.06	.03	.00
☐ 1	Richie Zisk	.06	.03	.00
☐ 2	Bill Buckner	.10	.05	.01
☐ 3	George Brett	.90	.45	.09
☐ 4	Rickey Henderson	.60	.30	.06
☐ 5	Jack Morris	.15	.07	.01
☐ 6	Ozzie Smith	.25	.12	.02
☐ 7	Rollie Fingers	.15	.07	.01
☐ 8	Tom Seaver	.50	.25	.05
☐ 9	Fernando Valuenzuela	.45	.22	.04
☐ 10	Hubie Brooks	.10	.05	.01
☐ 11	Nolan Ryan	.50	.25	.05
☐ 12	Dave Winfield	.35	.17	.03
☐ 13	Bob Horner	.20	.10	.02
☐ 14	Reggie Jackson	.65	.30	.06
☐ 15	Burt Hooton	.06	.03	.00
☐ 16	Mike Schmidt	.90	.45	.09
☐ 17	Bruce Sutter	.15	.07	.01
☐ 18	Pete Rose	1.00	.50	.10
☐ 19	Dave Kingman	.10	.05	.01
☐ 20	Neil Allen	.06	.03	.00
☐ 21	Don Sutton	.30	.15	.03
☐ 22	Dave Concepcion	.10	.05	.01
☐ 23	Keith Hernandez	.30	.15	.03
☐ 24	Gary Carter	.45	.22	.04
☐ 25	Carlton Fisk	.20	.10	.02
☐ 26	Ron Guidry	.20	.10	.02
☐ 27	Steve Carlton	.35	.17	.03
☐ 28	Robin Yount	.35	.17	.03
☐ 29	John Castino	.06	.03	.00
☐ 30	Johnny Bench	.40	.20	.04
☐ 31	Bob Knepper	.10	.05	.01
☐ 32	Rich Gossage	.15	.07	.01
☐ 33	Buddy Bell	.10	.05	.01
☐ 34	Art Howe	.06	.03	.00
☐ 35	Tony Armas	.10	.05	.01
☐ 36	Phil Niekro	.25	.12	.02
☐ 37	Len Barker	.06	.03	.00
☐ 38	Bob Grich	.10	.05	.01
☐ 39	Steve Kemp	.06	.03	.00
☐ 40	Kirk Gibson	.30	.15	.03
☐ 41	Carney Lansford	.10	.05	.01
☐ 42	Jim Palmer	.30	.15	.03
☐ 43	Carl Yastrzemski	.65	.30	.06
☐ 44	Rick Burleson	.06	.03	.00
☐ 45	Dwight Evans	.15	.07	.01
☐ 46	Ron Cey	.10	.05	.01
☐ 47	Steve Garvey	.45	.22	.04
☐ 48	Dave Parker	.20	.10	.02
☐ 49	Mike Easler	.06	.03	.00
☐ 50	Dusty Baker	.06	.03	.00
☐ 51	Rod Carew	.40	.20	.04
☐ 52	Chris Chambliss	.06	.03	.00
☐ 53	Tim Raines	.45	.22	.04
☐ 54	Chet Lemon	.06	.03	.00
☐ 55	Bill Madlock	.15	.07	.01
☐ 56	George Foster	.15	.07	.01
☐ 57	Dwayne Murphy	.06	.03	.00
☐ 58	Ken Singleton	.10	.05	.01
☐ 59	Mike Norris	.06	.03	.00
☐ 60	Cecil Cooper	.10	.05	.01
☐ 61	Al Oliver	.15	.07	.01
☐ 62	Willie Wilson	.10	.05	.01
☐ 63	Vida Blue	.06	.03	.00
☐ 64	Eddie Murray	.75	.35	.07

1983 Kellogg's

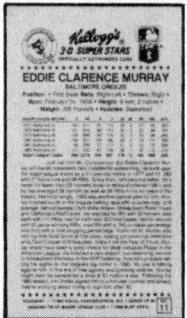

The cards in this 60-card set measure 1 7/8" by 3 1/4". For the 14th year in a row, the Kellogg Company issued a card set of Major League players. The set of 3-D cards contains the photo, player's autograph, Kellogg's logo, and name and position of the player on the front of the card. The backs feature the player's team logo, career statistics, player biography, and a narrative on the player's career.

		MINT	EXC	G-VG
	COMPLETE SET	11.00	5.50	1.10
	COMMON PLAYER	.06	.03	.00
☐ 1	Rod Carew	.45	.22	.04
☐ 2	Rollie Fingers	.20	.10	.02
☐ 3	Reggie Jackson	.65	.30	.06
☐ 4	George Brett	.85	.40	.08
☐ 5	Hal McRae	.06	.03	.00
☐ 6	Pete Rose	1.00	.50	.10
☐ 7	Fernando Valenzuela	.35	.17	.03
☐ 8	Rickey Henderson	.65	.30	.06
☐ 9	Carl Yastrzemski	.65	.30	.06
☐ 10	Rich Gossage	.15	.07	.01
☐ 11	Eddie Murray	.65	.30	.06
☐ 12	Buddy Bell	.10	.05	.01
☐ 13	Jim Rice	.40	.20	.04
☐ 14	Robin Yount	.35	.17	.03
☐ 15	Dave Winfield	.35	.17	.03
☐ 16	Harold Baines	.20	.10	.02
☐ 17	Garry Templeton	.06	.03	.00
☐ 18	Bill Madlock	.10	.05	.01
☐ 19	Pete Vuckovich	.06	.03	.00
☐ 20	Pedro Guerrero	.25	.12	.02
☐ 21	Ozzie Smith	.25	.12	.02
☐ 22	George Foster	.10	.05	.01
☐ 23	Willie Wilson	.10	.05	.01
☐ 24	Johnny Ray	.10	.05	.01
☐ 25	George Hendrick	.06	.03	.00
☐ 26	Andre Thornton	.06	.03	.00
☐ 27	Leon Durham	.10	.05	.01
☐ 28	Cecil Cooper	.10	.05	.01
☐ 29	Don Baylor	.10	.05	.01
☐ 30	Lonnie Smith	.06	.03	.00
☐ 31	Nolan Ryan	.45	.22	.04
☐ 32	Dan Quisenberry	.10	.05	.01
☐ 33	Len Barker	.06	.03	.00
☐ 34	Neil Allen	.06	.03	.00
☐ 35	Jack Morris	.20	.10	.02
☐ 36	Dave Stieb	.10	.05	.01
☐ 37	Bruce Sutter	.10	.05	.01
☐ 38	Jim Sundberg	.06	.03	.00
☐ 39	Jim Palmer	.30	.15	.03
☐ 40	Lance Parrish	.20	.10	.02
☐ 41	Floyd Bannister	.06	.03	.00
☐ 42	Larry Gura	.06	.03	.00
☐ 43	Britt Burns	.06	.03	.00
☐ 44	Toby Harrah	.06	.03	.00
☐ 45	Steve Carlton	.35	.17	.03
☐ 46	Greg Minton	.06	.03	.00
☐ 47	Gorman Thomas	.10	.05	.01
☐ 48	Jack Clark	.25	.12	.02
☐ 49	Keith Hernandez	.30	.15	.03
☐ 50	Greg Luzinski	.10	.05	.01
☐ 51	Fred Lynn	.15	.07	.01
☐ 52	Dale Murphy	.85	.40	.08
☐ 53	Kent Hrbek	.35	.17	.03
☐ 54	Bob Horner	.20	.10	.02

		MINT	EXC	G-VG
☐ 55	Gary Carter	.45	.22	.04
☐ 56	Carlton Fisk	.15	.07	.01
☐ 57	Dave Concepcion	.10	.05	.01
☐ 58	Mike Schmidt	.85	.40	.08
☐ 59	Bill Buckner	.10	.05	.01
☐ 60	Bob Grich	.10	.05	.01

☐ 31	Rod Carew: 77AL	.04	.02	.00
☐ 32	George Foster: 77NL	.02	.01	.00
☐ 33	Jim Rice: 78AL	.02	.01	.00
☐ 34	Dave Parker: 78NL	.02	.01	.00
☐ 35	Don Baylor: 79AL	.01	.00	.00
☐ 36	Keith Hernandez: 79NL	.02	.01	.00
☐ 37	Willie Stargell: 79NL	.03	.01	.00
☐ 38	George Brett: 80AL	.05	.02	.00
☐ 39	Mike Schmidt: 80NL	.06	.03	.00
☐ 40	Rollie Fingers: 81AL	.02	.01	.00
☐ 41	Mike Schmidt: 81NL	.06	.03	.00
☐ 42	'68 HL: Don Drysdale (scoreless innings)	.02	.01	.00
☐ 43	'74 HL: Hank Aaron (home run record)	.06	.03	.00
☐ 44	'81 HL: Pete Rose (NL most hits)	.12	.06	.01

1982 K-Mart

 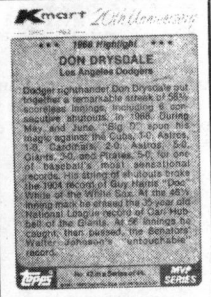

The cards in this 44-card set measure 2 1/2" by 3 1/2". This set was produced by Topps for K Mart's 20th Anniversary Celebration. The set features Topps cards of National and American League MVP's from 1962 through 1981. The backs highlight individual MVP winning performances. The dual National League MVP winners of 1979 and special cards commemorating the accomplishments of Drysdale (scoreless consecutive innings pitched streak), Aaron (home run record), and Rose (National League most hits lifetime record) round out the set. The 1975 Fred Lynn card is an original construction from the multi-player "Rookie Outfielders" card of Lynn of 1975. The Maury Wills card #2, similarly, was created after the fact as Maury was not originally included in the 1962 Topps set. The set was "Mass" produced for K-Mart distribution as a complete set in a box. Some collectors consider this to be one of the most plentiful sets ever produced.

		MINT	EXC	G-VG
COMPLETE SET		.75	.35	.07
COMMON PLAYER		.01	.00	.00
☐ 1	Mickey Mantle: 62AL	.15	.07	.01
☐ 2	Maury Wills: 62NL	.02	.01	.00
☐ 3	Elston Howard: 63AL	.01	.00	.00
☐ 4	Sandy Koufax: 63NL	.04	.02	.00
☐ 5	Brooks Robinson: 64AL	.04	.02	.00
☐ 6	Ken Boyer: 64NL	.01	.00	.00
☐ 7	Zoilo Versalles: 65AL	.01	.00	.00
☐ 8	Willie Mays: 65NL	.06	.03	.00
☐ 9	Frank Robinson: 66AL	.03	.01	.00
☐ 10	Bob Clemente: 66NL	.05	.02	.00
☐ 11	Carl Yastrzemski: 67AL	.06	.03	.00
☐ 12	Orlando Cepeda: 67NL	.01	.00	.00
☐ 13	Denny McLain: 68AL	.01	.00	.00
☐ 14	Bob Gibson: 68NL	.03	.01	.00
☐ 15	Harmon Killebrew: 69AL	.02	.01	.00
☐ 16	Willie McCovey: 69NL	.03	.01	.00
☐ 17	Boog Powell: 70AL	.01	.00	.00
☐ 18	Johnny Bench: 70NL	.04	.02	.00
☐ 19	Vida Blue: 71AL	.01	.00	.00
☐ 20	Joe Torre: 71NL	.01	.00	.00
☐ 21	Rich Allen: 72AL	.01	.00	.00
☐ 22	Johnny Bench: 72NL	.04	.02	.00
☐ 23	Reggie Jackson: 73AL	.05	.02	.00
☐ 24	Pete Rose: 73NL	.10	.05	.01
☐ 25	Jeff Burroughs: 74AL	.01	.00	.00
☐ 26	Steve Garvey: 74NL	.04	.02	.00
☐ 27	Fred Lynn: 75AL	.02	.01	.00
☐ 28	Joe Morgan: 75NL	.02	.01	.00
☐ 29	Thurman Munson: 76AL	.04	.02	.00
☐ 30	Joe Morgan: 76NL	.02	.01	.00

1987 K-Mart

Topps produced this 33-card boxed set for K-Mart. The set celebrates K-Mart's 25th anniversary and is subtitled, "Stars of the Decades." Card fronts feature a color photo of the player oriented diagonally. Cards measure 2 1/2" by 3 1/2" and are numbered on the back. Card backs provide statistics for the player's best decade.

		MINT	EXC	G-VG
COMPLETE SET		4.00	2.00	.40
COMMON PLAYER		.10	.05	.01
☐ 1	Hank Aaron	.25	.12	.02
☐ 2	Roberto Clemente	.20	.10	.02
☐ 3	Bob Gibson	.10	.05	.01
☐ 4	Harmon Killebrew	.10	.05	.01
☐ 5	Mickey Mantle	.60	.30	.06
☐ 6	Juan Marichal	.10	.05	.01
☐ 7	Roger Maris	.20	.10	.02
☐ 8	Willie Mays	.25	.12	.02
☐ 9	Brooks Robinson	.15	.07	.01
☐ 10	Frank Robinson	.10	.05	.01
☐ 11	Carl Yastrzemski	.25	.12	.02
☐ 12	Johnny Bench	.15	.07	.01
☐ 13	Lou Brock	.15	.07	.01
☐ 14	Rod Carew	.15	.07	.01
☐ 15	Steve Carlton	.25	.12	.02
☐ 16	Reggie Jackson	.25	.12	.02
☐ 17	Jim Palmer	.10	.05	.01
☐ 18	Jim Rice	.15	.07	.01
☐ 19	Pete Rose	.50	.25	.05
☐ 20	Nolan Ryan	.25	.12	.02
☐ 21	Tom Seaver	.25	.12	.02
☐ 22	Willie Stargell	.15	.07	.01
☐ 23	Wade Boggs	.50	.25	.05
☐ 24	George Brett	.25	.12	.02
☐ 25	Gary Carter	.15	.07	.01
☐ 26	Dwight Gooden	.40	.20	.04
☐ 27	Rickey Henderson	.25	.12	.02
☐ 28	Don Mattingly	.60	.30	.06
☐ 29	Dale Murphy	.30	.15	.03
☐ 30	Eddie Murray	.25	.12	.02
☐ 31	Mike Schmidt	.25	.12	.02
☐ 32	Darryl Strawberry	.25	.12	.02
☐ 33	Fernando Valenzuela	.15	.07	.01

1960 Lake to Lake

The cards in this 28 card set measure 2 1/2" by 3 1/4". The 1960 Lake to Lake set of unnumbered, blue tinted cards features Milwaukee Braves players only. For some reason, this set of Braves does not include Eddie Mathews. The cards were issued on milk cartons by Lake to Lake Dairy. Most cards have staple holes in the upper right corner. The backs are in red and give details and prizes associated with the card promotion. Cards with staple holes can be considered very good to excellent at best. The ACC designation is F102-1.

	NRMT	VG-E	GOOD
COMPLETE SET	500.00	250.00	50.00
COMMON PLAYER (1-28)	8.00	4.00	.80

		NRMT	VG-E	GOOD
☐	1 Hank Aaron	175.00	85.00	18.00
☐	2 Joe Adcock	10.00	5.00	1.00
☐	3 Ray Boone	90.00	45.00	9.00
☐	4 Bill Bruton	175.00	85.00	18.00
☐	5 Bob Buhl	8.00	4.00	.80
☐	6 Lew Burdette	12.00	6.00	1.20
☐	7 Chuck Cottier	8.00	4.00	.80
☐	8 Wes Covington	8.00	4.00	.80
☐	9 Del Crandall	10.00	5.00	1.00
☐	10 Chuck Dressen	8.00	4.00	.80
☐	11 Bob Giggie	8.00	4.00	.80
☐	12 Joey Jay	8.00	4.00	.80
☐	13 Johnny Logan	10.00	5.00	1.00
☐	14 Felix Mantilla	8.00	4.00	.80
☐	15 Lee Maye	8.00	4.00	.80
☐	16 Don McMahon	8.00	4.00	.80
☐	17 George Myatt	8.00	4.00	.80
☐	18 Andy Pafko	8.00	4.00	.80
☐	19 Juan Pizarro	8.00	4.00	.80
☐	20 Mel Roach	8.00	4.00	.80
☐	21 Bob Rush	8.00	4.00	.80
☐	22 Bob Scheffing	8.00	4.00	.80
☐	23 Red Schoendienst	12.00	6.00	1.20
☐	24 Warren Spahn	35.00	17.50	3.50
☐	25 Al Spangler	8.00	4.00	.80
☐	26 Frank Torre	8.00	4.00	.80
☐	27 Carlton Willey	8.00	4.00	.80
☐	28 Whit Wyatt	8.00	4.00	.80

1948-49 Leaf

The cards in this 98 card set measure 2 3/8" by 2 7/8". The 1948-49 Leaf set was the first post-war baseball series issued in color. This effort was not entirely successful due to a lack of refinement which resulted in many color variations and cards out of register. In addition, the set was skip numbered from 1-168, with 49 of the 98 cards printed in limited quantities (marked with an asterisk in the checklist). Cards 102 and 136 have variations, and cards are sometimes found with overprinted or incorrect backs.

	NRMT	VG-E	GOOD
COMPLETE SET	13500.00	5000.00	900.00
COMMON NUMBERS	13.50	6.50	1.25
COMMON * NUMBERS	175.00	85.00	18.00

		NRMT	VG-E	GOOD
☐	1 Joe DiMaggio	600.00	200.00	40.00
☐	3 Babe Ruth	800.00	400.00	80.00
☐	4 Stan Musial	175.00	85.00	18.00
☐	5 Virgil Trucks *	175.00	85.00	18.00
☐	8 Satchel Paige *	1000.00	400.00	80.00
☐	10 Dizzy Trout	13.50	6.50	1.25
☐	11 Phil Rizzuto	60.00	30.00	6.00
☐	13 Cass Michaels *	175.00	85.00	18.00
☐	14 Billy Johnson	13.50	6.50	1.25
☐	17 Frank Overmire	13.50	6.50	1.25
☐	19 Johnny Wyrostek *	175.00	85.00	18.00
☐	20 Hank Sauer *	175.00	85.00	18.00
☐	22 Al Evans	13.50	6.50	1.25
☐	26 Sam Chapman	13.50	6.50	1.25
☐	27 Mickey Harris	13.50	6.50	1.25
☐	28 Jim Hegan	13.50	6.50	1.25
☐	29 Elmer Valo	13.50	6.50	1.25
☐	30 Billy Goodman *	175.00	85.00	18.00
☐	31 Lou Brissie	13.50	6.50	1.25
☐	32 Warren Spahn	75.00	37.50	7.50
☐	33 Peanuts Lowrey *	175.00	85.00	18.00
☐	36 Al Zarilla *	175.00	85.00	18.00
☐	38 Ted Kluszewski	21.00	10.50	2.10
☐	39 Ewell Blackwell	13.50	6.50	1.25
☐	42 Kent Peterson	13.50	6.50	1.25
☐	43 Ed Stevens *	175.00	85.00	18.00
☐	45 Ken Keltner *	175.00	85.00	18.00
☐	46 Johnny Mize	50.00	25.00	5.00
☐	47 George Vico	13.50	6.50	1.25
☐	48 Johnny Schmitz *	175.00	85.00	18.00
☐	49 Del Ennis	13.50	6.50	1.25
☐	50 Dick Wakefield	13.50	6.50	1.25
☐	51 Al Dark *	225.00	110.00	22.00
☐	53 Johnny VanDerMeer	18.00	9.00	1.80
☐	54 Bobby Adams *	175.00	85.00	18.00
☐	55 Tommy Henrich *	200.00	100.00	20.00
☐	56 Larry Jansen	13.50	6.50	1.25
☐	57 Bob McCall	13.50	6.50	1.25
☐	59 Luke Appling	30.00	15.00	3.00
☐	61 Jake Early	13.50	6.50	1.25
☐	62 Eddie Joost *	175.00	85.00	18.00
☐	63 Barney McCosky *	175.00	85.00	18.00
☐	65 Robert Elliott (misspelled Elliot on card front)	18.00	9.00	1.80
☐	66 Orval Grove *	175.00	85.00	18.00
☐	68 Eddie Miller *	175.00	85.00	18.00
☐	70 Honus Wagner	135.00	65.00	13.50
☐	72 Hank Edwards	13.50	6.50	1.25
☐	73 Pat Seerey	13.50	6.50	1.25
☐	75 Dom DiMaggio *	225.00	110.00	22.00
☐	76 Ted Williams	250.00	125.00	25.00
☐	77 Roy Smalley	13.50	6.50	1.25
☐	78 Hoot Evers *	175.00	85.00	18.00
☐	79 Jackie Robinson	200.00	100.00	20.00
☐	81 Whitey Kurowski *	175.00	85.00	18.00
☐	82 Johnny Lindell	13.50	6.50	1.25
☐	83 Bobby Doerr	60.00	30.00	6.00
☐	84 Sid Hudson	13.50	6.50	1.25
☐	85 Dave Philley *	175.00	85.00	18.00
☐	86 Ralph Weigel	13.50	6.50	1.25
☐	88 Frank Gustine *	175.00	85.00	18.00
☐	91 Ralph Kiner	50.00	25.00	5.00
☐	93 Bob Feller *	650.00	325.00	65.00
☐	95 George Stirnweiss	13.50	6.50	1.25
☐	97 Marty Marion	18.00	9.00	1.80

		NRMT	VG-E	GOOD
☐ 98	Hal Newhouser *	225.00	110.00	22.00
☐ 102A	Gene Hermansk (sic)	135.00	65.00	13.50
☐ 102B	Gene Hermanski	13.50	6.50	1.25
☐ 104	Eddie Stewart *	175.00	85.00	18.00
☐ 106	Lou Boudreau	50.00	25.00	5.00
☐ 108	Matt Batts *	175.00	85.00	18.00
☐ 111	Jerry Priddy	13.50	6.50	1.25
☐ 113	Dutch Leonard *	175.00	85.00	18.00
☐ 117	Joe Gordon	18.00	9.00	1.80
☐ 120	George Kell *	350.00	175.00	35.00
☐ 121	Johnny Pesky *	200.00	100.00	20.00
☐ 123	Cliff Fannin *	175.00	85.00	18.00
☐ 125	Andy Pafko	13.50	6.50	1.25
☐ 127	Enos Slaughter *	350.00	175.00	35.00
☐ 128	Buddy Rosar	13.50	6.50	1.25
☐ 129	Kirby Higbe *	175.00	85.00	18.00
☐ 131	Sid Gordon *	175.00	85.00	18.00
☐ 133	Tommy Holmes *	200.00	100.00	20.00
☐ 136A	Cliff Aberson (full sleeve)	13.50	6.50	1.25
☐ 136B	Cliff Aberson (short sleeve)	60.00	30.00	6.00
☐ 137	Harry Walker *	175.00	85.00	18.00
☐ 138	Larry Doby *	225.00	110.00	22.00
☐ 139	Johnny Hopp	13.50	6.50	1.25
☐ 142	Danny Murtaugh *	200.00	100.00	20.00
☐ 143	Dick Sisler *	175.00	85.00	18.00
☐ 144	Bob Dillinger *	175.00	85.00	18.00
☐ 146	Pete Reiser *	200.00	100.00	20.00
☐ 149	Hank Majeski *	175.00	85.00	18.00
☐ 153	Floyd Baker *	175.00	85.00	18.00
☐ 158	Harry Brecheen *	175.00	85.00	18.00
☐ 159	Mizell Platt	13.50	6.50	1.25
☐ 160	Bob Scheffing *	175.00	85.00	18.00
☐ 161	Vern Stephens *	200.00	100.00	20.00
☐ 163	Fred Hutchinson *	225.00	110.00	22.00
☐ 165	Dale Mitchell *	200.00	100.00	20.00
☐ 168	Phil Cavarretta *	200.00	100.00	20.00

1960 Leaf

The cards in this 144 card set measure 2 1/2" by 3 1/2". The 1960 Leaf set was issued in a regular gum package style but with a marble instead of gum. The series was a joint production by Sports Novelties, Inc., and Leaf, two Chicago-based companies. Cards 73-144 are more difficult to find than the lower numbers. Photo variations exist (probably proof cards) for the seven cards listed with an asterisk and there is a well-known error card, number 25 showing Brooks Lawrence (in a Reds uniform) with Jim Grant's name on front, and Grant's biography and record on back. The corrected version with Grant's photo is the more difficult variety.

	NRMT	VG-E	GOOD
COMPLETE SET	850.00	425.00	85.00
COMMON PLAYER (1-72)	1.00	.50	.10
COMMON PLAYER (73-144)	10.00	5.00	1.00

☐ 1	Luis Aparicio *	5.00	1.50	.30
☐ 2	Woodson Held	1.00	.50	.10
☐ 3	Frank Lary	1.00	.50	.10
☐ 4	Camilo Pascual	1.00	.50	.10
☐ 5	Juan Herrera	1.00	.50	.10

☐ 6	Felipe Alou	1.25	.60	.12
☐ 7	Benjamin Daniels	1.00	.50	.10
☐ 8	Roger Craig	2.00	1.00	.20
☐ 9	Edward Kasko	1.00	.50	.10
☐ 10	Robert Anton Grim	1.25	.60	.12
☐ 11	James Busby	1.00	.50	.10
☐ 12	Kenton Boyer	2.50	1.25	.25
☐ 13	Robert Boyd	1.00	.50	.10
☐ 14	Samuel Jones	1.00	.50	.10
☐ 15	Lawence Jackson	1.00	.50	.10
☐ 16	Elroy Face	1.50	.75	.15
☐ 17	Walter Moryn *	1.00	.50	.10
☐ 18	James Gilliam	2.50	1.25	.25
☐ 19	Donald Newcombe	1.50	.75	.15
☐ 20	Glen Hobbie	1.00	.50	.10
☐ 21	Pedro Ramos	1.00	.50	.10
☐ 22	Rinold Duren	1.50	.75	.15
☐ 23	Joseph Jay *	1.00	.50	.10
☐ 24	Louis Berberet	1.00	.50	.10
☐ 25A	Jim Grant COR	15.00	7.50	1.50
☐ 25B	Jim Grant ERR (photo actually Brooks Lawrence)	10.00	5.00	1.00
☐ 26	Thomas Borland	1.00	.50	.10
☐ 27	Brooks Robinson	12.00	6.00	1.20
☐ 28	Jerry Adair	1.00	.50	.10
☐ 29	Ronald Jackson	1.00	.50	.10
☐ 30	George Strickland	1.00	.50	.10
☐ 31	Everett Rocky Bridges	1.00	.50	.10
☐ 32	William Tuttle	1.00	.50	.10
☐ 33	Kenneth Hunt	1.00	.50	.10
☐ 34	Harold Griggs	1.00	.50	.10
☐ 35	James Coates *	1.00	.50	.10
☐ 36	Brooks Lawrence	1.00	.50	.10
☐ 37	Edwin (Duke) Snider	15.00	7.50	1.50
☐ 38	Albert Spangler	1.00	.50	.10
☐ 39	James Owens	1.00	.50	.10
☐ 40	William Virdon	1.50	.75	.15
☐ 41	Ernest Broglio	1.00	.50	.10
☐ 42	Andre Rodgers	1.00	.50	.10
☐ 43	Julio Becquer	1.00	.50	.10
☐ 44	Antonio(Tony) Taylor	1.00	.50	.10
☐ 45	Gerald Lynch	1.00	.50	.10
☐ 46	Cletis Boyer	1.50	.75	.15
☐ 47	Jerry Lumpe	1.00	.50	.10
☐ 48	Charles Maxwell	1.00	.50	.10
☐ 49	James Perry	1.50	.75	.15
☐ 50	Daniel McDevitt	1.00	.50	.10
☐ 51	Juan Pizarro	1.00	.50	.10
☐ 52	Dallas Green	1.50	.75	.15
☐ 53	Robert Friend	1.25	.60	.12
☐ 54	Jack Sanford	1.00	.50	.10
☐ 55	Manuel (Jim) Rivera	1.00	.50	.10
☐ 56	Theodore Wills	1.00	.50	.10
☐ 57	Milton Pappas	1.25	.60	.12
☐ 58	Harold Smith *	1.00	.50	.10
☐ 59	Roberto Avila	1.00	.50	.10
☐ 60	Clement Labine	1.25	.60	.12
☐ 61	Norman Rehm *	1.00	.50	.10
☐ 62	John Gabler	1.00	.50	.10
☐ 63	John Tsitouris	1.00	.50	.10
☐ 64	David Sisler	1.00	.50	.10
☐ 65	Victor Power	1.00	.50	.10
☐ 66	Earl Battey	1.00	.50	.10
☐ 67	Robert Purkey	1.00	.50	.10
☐ 68	Myron(Moe) Drabowsky	1.00	.50	.10
☐ 69	James (Hoyt) Wilhelm	5.00	2.50	.50
☐ 70	Humberto Robinson	1.00	.50	.10
☐ 71	Dorrel(Whitey) Herzog	2.00	1.00	.20
☐ 72	Richard Donovan *	1.00	.50	.10
☐ 73	Gordon Jones	10.00	5.00	1.00
☐ 74	Joe Hicks	10.00	5.00	1.00
☐ 75	Ray Culp	10.00	5.00	1.00
☐ 76	Dick Drott	10.00	5.00	1.00
☐ 77	Bob Duliba	10.00	5.00	1.00
☐ 78	Art Ditmar	10.00	5.00	1.00
☐ 79	Steve Korcheck	10.00	5.00	1.00
☐ 80	Henry Mason	10.00	5.00	1.00
☐ 81	Harry Simpson	10.00	5.00	1.00
☐ 82	Gene Green	10.00	5.00	1.00
☐ 83	Bob Shaw	10.00	5.00	1.00
☐ 84	Howard Reed	10.00	5.00	1.00
☐ 85	Dick Stigman	10.00	5.00	1.00
☐ 86	Rip Repulski	10.00	5.00	1.00
☐ 87	Seth Morehead	10.00	5.00	1.00
☐ 88	Camilo Carreon	10.00	5.00	1.00
☐ 89	John Blanchard	12.00	6.00	1.20
☐ 90	Billy Hoeft	10.00	5.00	1.00
☐ 91	Fred Hopke	10.00	5.00	1.00
☐ 92	Joe Martin	10.00	5.00	1.00
☐ 93	Wally Shannon	10.00	5.00	1.00
☐ 94	Two Hal Smith's Hal R. Smith Hal W. Smith	15.00	7.50	1.50
☐ 95	Al Schroll	10.00	5.00	1.00

			NRMT	VG-E	GOOD
☐	96	John Kucks	12.00	6.00	1.20
☐	97	Tom Morgan	10.00	5.00	1.00
☐	98	Willie Jones	10.00	5.00	1.00
☐	99	Marshall Renfroe	10.00	5.00	1.00
☐	100	Willie Tasby	10.00	5.00	1.00
☐	101	Irv Noren	10.00	5.00	1.00
☐	102	Russ Snyder	10.00	5.00	1.00
☐	103	Bob Turley	15.00	7.50	1.50
☐	104	Jim Woods	10.00	5.00	1.00
☐	105	Ronnie Kline	10.00	5.00	1.00
☐	106	Steve Bilko	10.00	5.00	1.00
☐	107	Elmer Valo	10.00	5.00	1.00
☐	108	Tom McAvoy	10.00	5.00	1.00
☐	109	Stan Williams	12.00	6.00	1.20
☐	110	Earl Averill Jr.	10.00	5.00	1.00
☐	111	Lee Walls	10.00	5.00	1.00
☐	112	Paul Richards MG	12.00	6.00	1.20
☐	113	Ed Sadowski	10.00	5.00	1.00
☐	114	Stover McIlwain	10.00	5.00	1.00
☐	115	Chuck Tanner (photo actually Ken Kuhn)	15.00	7.50	1.50
☐	116	Lou Klimchock	10.00	5.00	1.00
☐	117	Neil Chrisley	10.00	5.00	1.00
☐	118	John Callison	12.00	6.00	1.20
☐	119	Hal Smith	10.00	5.00	1.00
☐	120	Carl Sawatski	10.00	5.00	1.00
☐	121	Frank Leja	10.00	5.00	1.00
☐	122	Earl Torgeson	10.00	5.00	1.00
☐	123	Art Schult	10.00	5.00	1.00
☐	124	Jim Brosnan	12.00	6.00	1.20
☐	125	George Anderson	18.00	9.00	1.80
☐	126	Joe Pignatano	10.00	5.00	1.00
☐	127	Rocky Nelson	10.00	5.00	1.00
☐	128	Orlando Cepeda	25.00	12.50	2.50
☐	129	Daryl Spencer	10.00	5.00	1.00
☐	130	Ralph Lumenti	10.00	5.00	1.00
☐	131	Sam Taylor	10.00	5.00	1.00
☐	132	Harry Brecheen	10.00	5.00	1.00
☐	133	Johnny Groth	10.00	5.00	1.00
☐	134	Wayne Terwilliger	10.00	5.00	1.00
☐	135	Kent Hadley	10.00	5.00	1.00
☐	136	Faye Throneberry	10.00	5.00	1.00
☐	137	Jack Meyer	10.00	5.00	1.00
☐	138	Chuck Cottier	10.00	5.00	1.00
☐	139	Joe DeMaestri	10.00	5.00	1.00
☐	140	Gene Freese	10.00	5.00	1.00
☐	141	Curt Flood	15.00	7.50	1.50
☐	142	Gino Cimoli	10.00	5.00	1.00
☐	143	Clay Dalrymple	10.00	5.00	1.00
☐	144	Jim Bunning	30.00	10.00	2.00

1960 MacGregor Staff

This 25-card set represents members of the MacGregor Sporting Goods Advisory Staff. Since the cards are unnumbered they ordered below in alphabetical order. The cards are blank backed and measure approximately 3 3/4" by 5". The photos are in black and white. The catalog designation for the set is H825-1. Cards have a facsimile autograph in white lettering on the front.

			NRMT	VG-E	GOOD
	COMPLETE SET		350.00	150.00	25.00
	COMMON PLAYER		6.00	2.50	.50
☐	1	Hank Aaron	75.00	37.50	7.50
☐	2	Richie Ashburn	12.00	6.00	1.20
☐	3	Gus Bell	6.00	2.50	.50
☐	4	Lou Berberet	6.00	2.50	.50
☐	5	Jerry Casale	6.00	2.50	.50
☐	6	Del Crandall	6.50	3.00	.60
☐	7	Art Ditmar	6.00	2.50	.50
☐	8	Gene Freese	6.00	2.50	.50
☐	9	James Gilliam	8.50	4.00	.80
☐	10	Ted Kluszewski	10.00	5.00	1.00
☐	11	Jim Landis	6.00	2.50	.50
☐	12	Al Lopez	10.00	5.00	1.00
☐	13	Willie Mays	75.00	37.50	7.50
☐	14	Bill Mazeroski	8.50	4.00	.80
☐	15	Mike McCormick	6.50	3.00	.60
☐	16	Gil McDougald	10.00	5.00	1.00
☐	17	Russ Nixon	6.00	2.50	.50
☐	18	Bill Rigney	6.00	2.50	.50
☐	19	Robin Roberts	20.00	10.00	2.00
☐	20	Frank Robinson	35.00	17.50	3.50
☐	21	John Roseboro	6.00	2.50	.50
☐	22	Red Schoendienst	8.50	4.00	.80
☐	23	Bill Skowron	12.00	6.00	1.20
☐	24	Daryl Spencer	6.00	2.50	.50
☐	25	Johnny Temple	6.00	2.50	.50

1965 MacGregor Staff

TONY OLIVA

MEMBER OF THE *MacGregor* / BRUNSWICK ADVISORY STAFF

This 10-card set represents members of the MacGregor Sporting Goods Advisory Staff. Since the cards are unnumbered they ordered below in alphabetical order. The cards are blank backed and measure approximately 3 9/16" by 5 1/8". The photos are in black and white. The catalog designation for the set is H825-2.

			NRMT	VG-E	GOOD
	COMPLETE SET		150.00	75.00	15.00
	COMMON PLAYER		5.00	2.50	.50
☐	1	Roberto Clemente	60.00	25.00	5.00
☐	2	Al Downing	6.00	3.00	.60
☐	3	Johnny Edwards	5.00	2.50	.50
☐	4	Ron Hansen	5.00	2.50	.50
☐	5	Deron Johnson	6.00	3.00	.60
☐	6	Willie Mays	75.00	37.50	7.50
☐	7	Tony Oliva	12.00	6.00	1.20
☐	8	Claude Osteen	6.00	3.00	.60
☐	9	Bobby Richardson	12.00	6.00	1.20
☐	10	Zoilo Versalles	5.00	2.50	.50

PICTURE GALLERY: Any set in this Price Guide not illustrated below its respective set title is pictured in the Picture Gallery section in the back of the book.

1984 Mets Fan Club

The cards in this 8-player set measure 2 1/2" by 3 1/2". The sheets were produced by Topps for the New York Mets and feature only Mets. The full sheet measures 7 1/2" by 10 1/2". Cards are together on the sheet but are perforated for those collectors who want to separate the individual player cards. The middle (ninth) card is a Mets Fan club membership card which details various promotional days at Shea Stadium on the back. The cards are numbered on the back and printed in orange and blue.

		MINT	EXC	G-VG
	COMPLETE SET	15.00	7.50	1.50
	COMMON PLAYER	.50	.25	.05
☐ 1	Dave Johnson MG	.75	.35	.07
☐ 2	Ron Darling	1.25	.60	.12
☐ 3	George Foster	1.25	.60	.12
☐ 4	Keith Hernandez	2.50	1.25	.25
☐ 5	Jesse Orosco	.50	.25	.05
☐ 6	Rusty Staub	1.25	.60	.12
☐ 7	Darryl Strawberry	9.00	4.50	.90
☐ 8	Mookie Wilson	.75	.35	.07

1985 Mets Fan Club

The cards in this 8-player set measure 2 1/2" by 3 1/2". The sheets were produced by Topps for the New York Mets and feature only Mets. The full sheet measures 7 1/2" by 10 1/2". Cards are together on the sheet but are perforated for those collectors who want to separate the individual player cards. The middle (ninth) card is a Mets Fan club membership card. The set was available as a membership premium for joining the Junior Mets Fan Club for 4.00.

		MINT	EXC	G-VG
	COMPLETE SET	20.00	10.00	2.00
	COMMON PLAYER	.50	.25	.05
☐ 1	Wally Backman	.75	.35	.07
☐ 2	Bruce Berenyi	.50	.25	.05
☐ 3	Gary Carter	2.50	1.25	.25
☐ 4	George Foster	1.25	.60	.12
☐ 5	Dwight Gooden	10.00	5.00	1.00
☐ 6	Keith Hernandez	2.50	1.25	.25
☐ 7	Doug Sisk	.50	.25	.05
☐ 8	Darryl Strawberry	5.00	2.50	.50

1986 Mets Fan Club

The cards in this 8-player set measure 2 1/2" by 3 1/2". The sheets were produced by Topps for the New York Mets and feature only Mets. The full sheet measures 7 1/2" by 10 1/2". Cards are together on the sheet but are perforated for those collectors who want to separate the individual player cards. The middle (ninth) card is a Mets Fan club membership card. The set was available as a membership premium for joining the Junior Mets Fan Club for 5.00.

		MINT	EXC	G-VG
	COMPLETE SET	15.00	7.50	1.50
	COMMON PLAYER	.50	.25	.05
☐ 1	Wally Backman	.75	.35	.07
☐ 2	Gary Carter	2.50	1.25	.25
☐ 3	Ron Darling	1.25	.60	.12
☐ 4	Dwight Gooden	5.00	2.50	.50
☐ 5	Keith Hernandez	2.50	1.25	.25
☐ 6	Howard Johnson	1.50	.75	.15
☐ 7	Roger McDowell	1.00	.50	.10
☐ 8	Darryl Strawberry	5.00	2.50	.50

1987 Mets Fan Club

The cards in this 8-player set measure 2 1/2" by 3 1/2". The sheets were produced by Topps for the New York Mets and feature only Mets. The full sheet measures 7 1/2" by 10 1/2". Cards are together on the sheet but are perforated for those collectors who want to separate the individual player cards. The cards have an outer orange border. The set was available as a membership premium for joining the Junior Mets Fan Club for 6.00. The set and club were also sponsored by Farmland Dairies Milk. The cards are unnumbered on the back although they do contain the player's uniform number on the front.

		MINT	EXC	G-VG
	COMPLETE SET	10.00	5.00	1.00
	COMMON PLAYER	.50	.25	.05
☐ 1	Gary Carter 8	2.50	1.25	.25
☐ 2	Ron Darling 12	1.25	.60	.12
☐ 3	Lenny Dykstra 4	1.00	.50	.10
☐ 4	Roger McDowell 42	1.00	.50	.10
☐ 5	Kevin McReynolds 22	1.50	.75	.15
☐ 6	Bob Ojeda 19	1.00	.50	.10
☐ 7	Darryl Strawberry 18	5.00	2.50	.50
☐ 8	Mookie Wilson 1	.75	.35	.07
☐ 9	Mets Team Card (1986 World Champs)	.50	.25	.05

1933 Geo. C. Miller

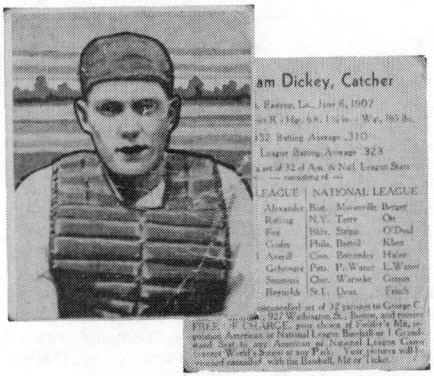

The cards in this 32 card set measure 2 1/2" by 3". This set of soft tone color baseball cards issued in 1933 by the George C. Miller Company consists of 16 players from each league. The bottom portion of the reverse contained a premium offer and many cards are found with this section cut off. Cards without the coupon are considered fair to good condition at best. The Andrews card (with coupon intact) is considered scarce in relation to all other common players. The ACC catalog number is R300.

		NRMT	VG-E	GOOD
	COMPLETE SET	11000.00	5000.00	900.00
	COMMON PLAYER (1-32)	250.00	125.00	25.00
☐ 1	Dale Alexander	250.00	125.00	25.00
☐ 2	Ivy Andrews	1500.00	500.00	100.00

☐ 3	Earl Averill	350.00	175.00	35.00
☐ 4	Dick Bartell	250.00	125.00	25.00
☐ 5	Wally Berger	250.00	125.00	25.00
☐ 6	Jim Bottomley	350.00	175.00	35.00
☐ 7	Joe Cronin	400.00	200.00	40.00
☐ 8	Dizzy Dean	750.00	375.00	75.00
☐ 9	Bill Dickey	500.00	250.00	50.00
☐ 10	Jimmy Dykes	250.00	125.00	25.00
☐ 11	Wes Ferrell	250.00	125.00	25.00
☐ 12	Jimmy Foxx	500.00	250.00	50.00
☐ 13	Frank Frisch	450.00	225.00	45.00
☐ 14	Charlie Gehringer	450.00	225.00	45.00
☐ 15	Goose Goslin	350.00	175.00	35.00
☐ 16	Charlie Grimm	250.00	125.00	25.00
☐ 17	Lefty Grove	450.00	225.00	45.00
☐ 18	Chick Hafey	350.00	175.00	35.00
☐ 19	Ray Hayworth	250.00	125.00	25.00
☐ 20	Chuck Klein	400.00	200.00	40.00
☐ 21	Rabbit Maranville	350.00	175.00	35.00
☐ 22	Oscar Melillo	250.00	125.00	25.00
☐ 23	Lefty O'Doul	250.00	125.00	25.00
☐ 24	Mel Ott	450.00	225.00	45.00
☐ 25	Carl Reynolds	250.00	125.00	25.00
☐ 26	Red Ruffing	350.00	175.00	35.00
☐ 27	Al Simmons	350.00	175.00	35.00
☐ 28	Joe Stripp	250.00	125.00	25.00
☐ 29	Bill Terry	400.00	200.00	40.00
☐ 30	Lloyd Waner	350.00	175.00	35.00
☐ 31	Paul Waner	350.00	175.00	35.00
☐ 32	Lon Warneke	250.00	125.00	25.00

☐ 15	Ron Kittle	.15	.07	.01
☐ 16	Bill Madlock	.15	.07	.01
☐ 17	Dale Murphy	.75	.35	.07
☐ 18	Al Oliver	.15	.07	.01
☐ 19	Darrell Porter	.15	.07	.01
☐ 20	Cal Ripken	.65	.30	.06
☐ 21	Pete Rose	1.00	.50	.10
☐ 22	Steve Sax	.25	.12	.02
☐ 23	Mike Schmidt	.75	.35	.07
☐ 24	Ted Simmons	.15	.07	.01
☐ 25	Ozzie Smith	.35	.17	.03
☐ 26	Dave Stieb	.15	.07	.01
☐ 27	Fernando Valenzuela	.35	.17	.03
☐ 28	Lou Whitaker	.25	.12	.02
☐ 29	Dave Winfield	.35	.17	.03
☐ 30	Robin Yount	.35	.17	.03

1987 MnM's Star Lineup

The Mars Candy Company is the sponsor of this 24-card set of cards. The cards were printed in perforated pairs. The pairs measure 5" by 3 1/2" whereas the individual cards measure the standard 2 1/2" by 3 1/2". The players are shown without team logos. The cards were designed and produced by MSA, Mike Schechter Associates. The cards are numbered on the front and back. The backs show statistics for every year since 1980 even if the player was not even playing during those earlier years. The values below are for individual players; panels intact would be valued at 25% more than the sum of the two individual players.

		MINT	EXC	G-VG
	COMPLETE SET	18.00	9.00	1.80
	COMMON PLAYER	.50	.25	.05
☐ 1	Wally Joyner	1.50	.75	.15
☐ 2	Tony Pena	.50	.25	.05
☐ 3	Mike Schmidt	1.00	.50	.10
☐ 4	Ryne Sandberg	1.00	.50	.10
☐ 5	Wade Boggs	2.00	1.00	.20
☐ 6	Jack Morris	.75	.35	.07
☐ 7	Roger Clemens	1.25	.60	.12
☐ 8	Harold Baines	.75	.35	.07
☐ 9	Dale Murphy	1.00	.50	.10
☐ 10	Jose Canseco	1.00	.50	.10
☐ 11	Don Mattingly	3.00	1.50	.30
☐ 12	Gary Carter	1.00	.50	.10
☐ 13	Cal Ripken Jr.	1.00	.50	.10
☐ 14	George Brett	1.00	.50	.10
☐ 15	Kirby Puckett	1.00	.50	.10
☐ 16	Joe Carter	.75	.35	.07
☐ 17	Mike Witt	.60	.30	.06
☐ 18	Mike Scott	.75	.35	.07
☐ 19	Fernando Valenzuela	.75	.35	.07
☐ 20	Steve Garvey	1.00	.50	.10
☐ 21	Steve Sax	.60	.30	.06
☐ 22	Nolan Ryan	1.00	.50	.10
☐ 23	Tony Gwynn	1.00	.50	.10
☐ 24	Ozzie Smith	.75	.35	.07

1984 Milton Bradley

The cards in this 30 card set measure 2 1/2" by 3 1/2". This set of full color cards was produced by Topps for the Milton Bradley Co. The set was included in a board game entitled Championship Baseball. The fronts feature portraits of the players and the name, Championship Baseball, by Milton Bradley. The backs feature the Topps logo, statistics for the past year (pitchers' cards have career statistics), and dice rolls which are part of the board game. Pitcher cards have no dice roll charts. There are 15 players from each league. These unnumbered cards are listed below in alphabetical order. The cap logos and uniforms have been air-brushed to remove all team references.

		MINT	EXC	G-VG
	COMPLETE SET	8.00	4.00	.80
	COMMON PLAYER	.15	.07	.01
☐ 1	Wade Boggs	1.00	.50	.10
☐ 2	George Brett	.75	.35	.07
☐ 3	Rod Carew	.35	.17	.03
☐ 4	Steve Carlton	.35	.17	.03
☐ 5	Gary Carter	.35	.17	.03
☐ 6	Dave Concepcion	.15	.07	.01
☐ 7	Cecil Cooper	.15	.07	.01
☐ 8	Andre Dawson	.35	.17	.03
☐ 9	Carlton Fisk	.15	.07	.01
☐ 10	Steve Garvey	.35	.17	.03
☐ 11	Pedro Guerrero	.25	.12	.02
☐ 12	Ron Guidry	.25	.12	.02
☐ 13	Rickey Henderson	.65	.30	.06
☐ 14	Reggie Jackson	.65	.30	.06

1959 Morrell

The cards in this 12 card set measure 2 1/2" by 3 1/2". The 1959 Morrell Meats set of full color, unnumbered cards features Los Angeles Dodger players only. The photos used are the same as those selected for the Dodger team issue postcards in 1959. The Morrell Meats logo is on the backs of the cards. The Clem Labine card actually features a picture of Stan Williams and the Norm Larker card actually features a picture of Joe Pignatano. The ACC designation is F172-1.

	NRMT	VG-E	GOOD
COMPLETE SET	800.00	400.00	80.00
COMMON PLAYER (1-12)	50.00	25.00	5.00
☐ 1 Don Drysdale	100.00	50.00	10.00
☐ 2 Carl Furillo	60.00	30.00	6.00
☐ 3 Jim Gilliam	60.00	30.00	6.00
☐ 4 Gil Hodges	100.00	50.00	10.00
☐ 5 Sandy Koufax	150.00	75.00	15.00
☐ 6 Clem Labine (photo actually Stan Williams)	50.00	25.00	5.00
☐ 7 Norm Larker (photo actually Joe Pignatano)	50.00	25.00	5.00
☐ 8 Charlie Neal	50.00	25.00	5.00
☐ 9 Johnny Podres	60.00	30.00	6.00
☐10 John Roseboro	50.00	25.00	5.00
☐11 Duke Snider	150.00	75.00	15.00
☐12 Don Zimmer	60.00	30.00	6.00

1960 Morrell

The cards in this 12 card set measure 2 1/2" by 3 1/2". The 1960 Morrell Meats set of full color, unnumbered cards is similar in format to the 1959 Morrell set but can be distinguished from the 1959 set by a red heart which appears in the Morrell logo on the back. The photos used are the same as those selected for the Dodger team issue postcards in 1960. The Furillo, Hodges, and Snider cards received limited distribution and are hence more scarce. The ACC designation is F172-2. The cards were printed in Japan.

	NRMT	VG-E	GOOD
COMPLETE SET	500.00	250.00	50.00
COMMON PLAYER (1-12)	15.00	7.50	1.50
☐ 1 Walt Alston MG	25.00	12.50	2.50
☐ 2 Roger Craig	20.00	10.00	2.00
☐ 3 Don Drysdale	40.00	20.00	4.00
☐ 4 Carl Furillo SP	75.00	37.50	7.50
☐ 5 Gil Hodges SP	125.00	60.00	12.50
☐ 6 Sandy Koufax	75.00	37.50	7.50
☐ 7 Wally Moon	15.00	7.50	1.50
☐ 8 Charlie Neal	15.00	7.50	1.50
☐ 9 Johnny Podres	20.00	10.00	2.00
☐10 John Roseboro	15.00	7.50	1.50
☐11 Larry Sherry	15.00	7.50	1.50
☐12 Duke Snider SP	150.00	75.00	15.00

1961 Morrell

The cards in this 6 card set measure 2 1/2" by 3 1/2". The 1961 Morrell Meats set of full color, unnumbered cards features Los Angeles Dodger players only and contains statistical information on the backs of the cards in brown print. The ACC designation is F172-3.

	NRMT	VG-E	GOOD
COMPLETE SET	150.00	75.00	15.00
COMMON PLAYER (1-6)	15.00	7.50	1.50
☐1 Tommy Davis	20.00	10.00	2.00
☐2 Don Drysdale	40.00	20.00	4.00
☐3 Frank Howard	20.00	10.00	2.00
☐4 Sandy Koufax	75.00	37.50	7.50
☐5 Norm Larker	15.00	7.50	1.50
☐6 Maury Wills	30.00	15.00	3.00

1983 Mother's Giants

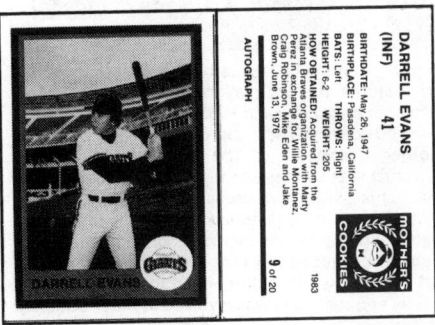

The cards in this 20-card set measure 2 1/2" by 3 1/2". For the first time in 30 years, Mother's Cookies issued a baseball card set. The full color set, produced by hobbyist Barry Colla, features San Francisco Giants players only. Fifteen cards were issued at the Astros vs. Giants game of August 7, 1983. Five of the cards were redeemable by sending in a coupon. The five additional cards received from redemption of the coupon were not guaranteed to be the five needed to complete the set. The fronts feature the player's photo, his name, and the Giants' logo, while the backs feature player biographies and the Mother's Cookies logo. The backs also contain a space in which to obtain the player's autograph.

	MINT	EXC	G-VG
COMPLETE SET	14.00	7.00	1.40
COMMON PLAYER	.50	.25	.05
☐ 1 Frank Robinson MG	1.50	.75	.15
☐ 2 Jack Clark	2.50	1.25	.25
☐ 3 Chili Davis	1.50	.75	.15
☐ 4 Johnnie LeMaster	.50	.25	.05
☐ 5 Greg Minton	.50	.25	.05
☐ 6 Bob Brenly	.75	.35	.07
☐ 7 Fred Breining	.50	.25	.05
☐ 8 Jeff Leonard	1.00	.50	.10
☐ 9 Darrell Evans	1.25	.60	.12
☐10 Tom O'Malley	.50	.25	.05
☐11 Duane Kuiper	.50	.25	.05
☐12 Mike Krukow	.75	.35	.07
☐13 Atlee Hammaker	.60	.30	.06
☐14 Gary Lavelle	.60	.30	.06
☐15 Bill Laskey	.50	.25	.05
☐16 Max Venable	.50	.25	.05
☐17 Joel Youngblood	.50	.25	.05
☐18 Dave Bergman	.50	.25	.05
☐19 Mike Vail	.50	.25	.05
☐20 Andy McGaffigan	.50	.25	.05

1984 Mother's A's

The cards in this 28 card set measure 2 1/2" by 3 1/2". In 1984, the Los Angeles based Mother's Cookies Co. issued five sets of cards featuring

players from major league teams. The Oakland A's set features current players depicted by photos. Similar to their 1952 and 1953 issues, the cards have rounded corners. The backs of the cards contain the Mother's Cookies logo. The cards were distributed in partial sets to fans at the respective stadiums of the teams involved. Whereas 20 cards were given to each patron, a redemption card, redeemable for eight more cards was included. Unfortunately, the eight cards received by redeeming the coupon were not necessarily the eight needed to complete a set. Hobbyist Barry Colla was involved in the production of these sets.

		MINT	EXC	G-VG
	COMPLETE SET	12.50	6.25	1.25
	COMMON PLAYER	.40	.20	.04
☐ 1	Steve Boros MG	.40	.20	.04
☐ 2	Rickey Henderson	3.00	1.50	.30
☐ 3	Joe Morgan	1.50	.75	.15
☐ 4	Dwayne Murphy	.60	.30	.06
☐ 5	Mike Davis	.60	.30	.06
☐ 6	Bruce Bochte	.40	.20	.04
☐ 7	Carney Lansford	.75	.35	.07
☐ 8	Steve McCatty	.40	.20	.04
☐ 9	Mike Heath	.40	.20	.04
☐ 10	Chris Codiroli	.40	.20	.04
☐ 11	Bill Almon	.40	.20	.04
☐ 12	Bill Caudill	.50	.25	.05
☐ 13	Donnie Hill	.40	.20	.04
☐ 14	Lary Sorensen	.40	.20	.04
☐ 15	Dave Kingman	.75	.35	.07
☐ 16	Garry Hancock	.40	.20	.04
☐ 17	Jeff Burroughs	.50	.25	.05
☐ 18	Tom Burgmeier	.40	.20	.04
☐ 19	Jim Essian	.40	.20	.04
☐ 20	Mike Warren	.40	.20	.04
☐ 21	Davey Lopes	.50	.25	.05
☐ 22	Ray Burris	.40	.20	.04
☐ 23	Tony Phillips	.40	.20	.04
☐ 24	Tim Conroy	.40	.20	.04
☐ 25	Jeff Bettendorf	.40	.20	.04
☐ 26	Keith Atherton	.40	.20	.04
☐ 27	A's Coaches	.40	.20	.04
☐ 28	A's Checklist	.40	.04	.00

1984 Mother's Astros

The cards in this 28 card set measure 2 1/2" by 3 1/2". In 1984, the Los Angeles based Mother's Cookies Co. issued five sets of cards featuring players from major league teams. The Houston Astros set features current players depicted by photos. Similar to their 1952 and 1953 issues, the cards have rounded corners. The backs of the cards contain the Mother's Cookies logo. The cards were distributed in partial sets to fans at the respective stadiums of the teams involved. Whereas 20 cards were given to each patron, a redemption card, redeemable for eight more cards was included.

Unfortunately, the eight cards received by redeeming the coupon were not necessarily the eight needed to complete a set. Hobbyist Barry Colla was involved in the production of these sets.

		MINT	EXC	G-VG
	COMPLETE SET	11.00	5.50	1.10
	COMMON PLAYER	.30	.15	.03
☐ 1	Nolan Ryan	3.00	1.50	.30
☐ 2	Joe Niekro	.75	.35	.07
☐ 3	Alan Ashby	.30	.15	.03
☐ 4	Bill Doran	1.00	.50	.10
☐ 5	Phil Garner	.40	.20	.04
☐ 6	Ray Knight	.50	.25	.05
☐ 7	Dickie Thon	.40	.20	.04
☐ 8	Jose Cruz	.60	.30	.06
☐ 9	Jerry Mumphrey	.40	.20	.04
☐ 10	Terry Puhl	.40	.20	.04
☐ 11	Enos Cabell	.30	.15	.03
☐ 12	Harry Spilman	.30	.15	.03
☐ 13	Dave Smith	.40	.20	.04
☐ 14	Mike Scott	1.25	.60	.12
☐ 15	Bob Lillis MG	.30	.15	.03
☐ 16	Bob Knepper	.50	.25	.05
☐ 17	Frank DiPino	.40	.20	.04
☐ 18	Tom Wieghaus	.30	.15	.03
☐ 19	Denny Walling	.30	.15	.03
☐ 20	Tony Scott	.30	.15	.03
☐ 21	Alan Bannister	.30	.15	.03
☐ 22	Bill Dawley	.30	.15	.03
☐ 23	Vern Ruhle	.30	.15	.03
☐ 24	Mike LaCoss	.30	.15	.03
☐ 25	Mike Madden	.30	.15	.03
☐ 26	Craig Reynolds	.40	.20	.04
☐ 27	Astros' Coaches	.30	.15	.03
☐ 28	Astros' Checklist	.30	.03	.00

1984 Mother's Giants

The cards in this 28 card set measure 2 1/2" by 3 1/2". In 1984, the Los Angeles based Mother's Cookies Co. issued five sets of cards featuring players from major league teams. The San Francisco Giants set features previous Giant All-Star selections depicted by drawings. Similar to their 1952 and 1953 issues, the cards have rounded corners. The backs of the cards contain the Mother's Cookies logo. The cards were distributed in partial sets to fans at the respective stadiums of the teams involved. Whereas 20 cards were given to each patron, a redemption card, redeemable for eight more cards was included. Unfortunately, the eight cards received by redeeming the coupon were not necessarily the eight needed to complete a set. Hobbyist Barry Colla was involved in the production of these sets.

	MINT	EXC	G-VG
COMPLETE SET	13.00	6.50	1.30
COMMON PLAYER	.40	.20	.04
☐ 1 Willie Mays	2.50	1.25	.25
☐ 2 Willie McCovey	1.75	.85	.17
☐ 3 Juan Marichal	1.50	.75	.15
☐ 4 Gaylord Perry	1.25	.60	.12
☐ 5 Tom Haller	.40	.20	.04
☐ 6 Jim Davenport	.50	.25	.05
☐ 7 Jack Clark	1.25	.60	.12
☐ 8 Greg Minton	.40	.20	.04
☐ 9 Atlee Hammaker	.50	.25	.05
☐ 10 Gary Lavelle	.40	.20	.04
☐ 11 Orlando Cepeda	.90	.45	.09
☐ 12 Bobby Bonds	.60	.30	.06
☐ 13 John Antonelli	.40	.20	.04
☐ 14 Bob Schmidt	.40	.20	.04
(photo actually			
Wes Westrum)			
☐ 15 Sam Jones	.40	.20	.04
☐ 16 Mike McCormick	.40	.20	.04
☐ 17 Ed Bailey	.40	.20	.04
☐ 18 Stu Miller	.40	.20	.04
☐ 19 Felipe Alou	.50	.25	.05
☐ 20 Jim Ray Hart	.40	.20	.04
☐ 21 Dick Dietz	.40	.20	.04
☐ 22 Chris Speier	.40	.20	.04
☐ 23 Bobby Murcer	.60	.30	.06
☐ 24 John Montefusco	.40	.20	.04
☐ 25 Vida Blue	.50	.25	.05
☐ 26 Ed Whitson	.40	.20	.04
☐ 27 Darrell Evans	.75	.35	.07
☐ 28 Checklist	.40	.04	.00

1984 Mother's Mariners

The cards in this 28 card set measure 2 1/2" by 3 1/2". In 1984, The Los Angeles-based Mother's Cookies Co. issued five sets of cards featuring players from major league teams. The Seattle Mariners set features current players depicted by photos. Similar to their 1952 and 1953 issues, the cards have rounded corners. The backs of the cards contain the Mother's Cookies logo. The cards were distributed in partial sets to fans at the respective stadiums of the teams involved. Whereas 20 cards were given to each patron, a redemption card, redeemable for eight more cards was included. Unfortunately, the eight cards received by redeeming the coupon were not necessarily the eight needed to complete a set. Hobbyist Barry Colla was involved in the production of these sets.

	MINT	EXC	G-VG
COMPLETE SET	12.50	6.25	1.25
COMMON PLAYER	.40	.20	.04
☐ 1 Del Crandall MG	.50	.25	.05
☐ 2 Barry Bonnell	.40	.20	.04
☐ 3 Dave Henderson	.50	.25	.05
☐ 4 Bob Kearney	.40	.20	.04
☐ 5 Mike Moore	.50	.25	.05
☐ 6 Spike Owen	.40	.20	.04
☐ 7 Gorman Thomas	.60	.30	.06
☐ 8 Ed VandeBerg	.40	.20	.04
☐ 9 Matt Young	.50	.25	.05
☐ 10 Larry Milbourne	.40	.20	.04
☐ 11 Dave Beard	.40	.20	.04
☐ 12 Jim Beattie	.40	.20	.04
☐ 13 Mark Langston	1.25	.60	.12
☐ 14 Orlando Mercado	.40	.20	.04
☐ 15 Jack Perconte	.40	.20	.04
☐ 16 Pat Putnam	.40	.20	.04
☐ 17 Paul Mirabella	.40	.20	.04
☐ 18 Domingo Ramos	.40	.20	.04
☐ 19 Al Cowens	.50	.25	.05
☐ 20 Mike Stanton	.40	.20	.04
☐ 21 Steve Henderson	.40	.20	.04
☐ 22 Bob Stoddard	.40	.20	.04
☐ 23 Alvin Davis	1.75	.85	.17
☐ 24 Phil Bradley	1.75	.85	.17
☐ 25 Roy Thomas	.40	.20	.04
☐ 26 Darnell Coles	.60	.30	.06
☐ 27 Mariners' Coaches	.40	.20	.04
☐ 28 Mariners' Checklist	.40	.04	.00

1984 Mother's Padres

The cards in this 28 card set measure 2 1/2" by 3 1/2". In 1984, the Los Angeles based Mother's Cookies Co. issued five sets of cards featuring players from major league teams. The San Diego Padres set features current players depicted by photos. Similar to their 1952 and 1953 issues, the cards have rounded corners. The backs of the cards contain the Mother's Cookies logo. The cards were distributed in partial sets to fans at the respective stadiums of the teams involved. Whereas 20 cards were given to each patron, a redemption card, redeemable for eight more cards was included. Unfortunately, the eight cards received by redeeming the coupon were not necessarily the eight needed to complete a set. Hobbyist Barry Colla was involved in the production of these sets.

	MINT	EXC	G-VG
COMPLETE SET	15.00	7.50	1.50
COMMON PLAYER	.50	.25	.05
☐ 1 Dick Williams MG	.60	.30	.06
☐ 2 Rich Gossage	1.00	.50	.10
☐ 3 Tim Lollar	.50	.25	.05
☐ 4 Eric Show	.50	.25	.05
☐ 5 Terry Kennedy	.60	.30	.06
☐ 6 Kurt Bevacqua	.50	.25	.05
☐ 7 Steve Garvey	2.00	1.00	.20

☐ 8	Garry Templeton	.60	.30	.06
☐ 9	Tony Gwynn	3.00	1.50	.30
☐ 10	Alan Wiggins	.60	.30	.06
☐ 11	Dave Dravecky	.75	.35	.07
☐ 12	Tim Flannery	.50	.25	.05
☐ 13	Kevin McReynolds	1.50	.75	.15
☐ 14	Bobby Brown	.50	.25	.05
☐ 15	Ed Whitson	.50	.25	.05
☐ 16	Doug Gwosdz	.50	.25	.05
☐ 17	Luis DeLeon	.50	.25	.05
☐ 18	Andy Hawkins	.50	.25	.05
☐ 19	Craig Lefferts	.50	.25	.05
☐ 20	Carmelo Martinez	.60	.30	.06
☐ 21	Sid Monge	.50	.25	.05
☐ 22	Graig Nettles	.75	.35	.07
☐ 23	Mario Ramirez	.50	.25	.05
☐ 24	Luis Salazar	.50	.25	.05
☐ 25	Champ Summers	.50	.25	.05
☐ 26	Mark Thurmond	.50	.25	.05
☐ 27	Padres' Coaches	.50	.25	.05
☐ 28	Padres' Checklist	.50	.05	.01

1985 Mother's A's

The cards in this 28 card set measure 2 1/2" by 3 1/2". In 1985, the Los Angeles based Mother's Cookies Co. again issued five sets of cards featuring players from major league teams. The Oakland A's set features current players depicted by photos on cards with rounded corners. The backs of the cards contain the Mother's Cookies logo. Cards were passed out at the stadium on July 6.

		MINT	EXC	G-VG
COMPLETE SET		9.00	4.50	.90
COMMON PLAYER		.30	.15	.03
☐ 1	Jackie Moore MG	.30	.15	.03
☐ 2	Dave Kingman	.60	.30	.06
☐ 3	Don Sutton	1.25	.60	.12
☐ 4	Mike Heath	.30	.15	.03
☐ 5	Alfredo Griffin	.60	.30	.06
☐ 6	Dwayne Murphy	.50	.25	.05
☐ 7	Mike Davis	.60	.30	.06
☐ 8	Carney Lansford	.60	.30	.06
☐ 9	Chris Codiroli	.30	.15	.03
☐ 10	Bruce Bochte	.30	.15	.03
☐ 11	Mickey Tettleton	.30	.15	.03
☐ 12	Donnie Hill	.30	.15	.03
☐ 13	Rob Picciolo	.30	.15	.03
☐ 14	Dave Collins	.40	.20	.04
☐ 15	Dusty Baker	.40	.20	.04
☐ 16	Tim Conroy	.30	.15	.03
☐ 17	Keith Atherton	.30	.15	.03
☐ 18	Jay Howell	.40	.20	.04
☐ 19	Mike Warren	.30	.15	.03
☐ 20	Steve McCatty	.30	.15	.03
☐ 21	Bill Krueger	.30	.15	.03
☐ 22	Curt Young	.50	.25	.05
☐ 23	Dan Meyer	.30	.15	.03
☐ 24	Mike Gallego	.30	.15	.03
☐ 25	Jeff Kaiser	.30	.15	.03
☐ 26	Steve Henderson	.30	.15	.03
☐ 27	A's Coaches	.30	.15	.03
☐ 28	A's Checklist	.30	.03	.00

1985 Mother's Astros

The cards in this 28 card set measure 2 1/2" by 3 1/2". In 1985, the Los Angeles-based Mother's Cookies Co. again issued five sets of cards featuring players from major league teams. The Houston Astros set features current players depicted by photos on cards with rounded corners. The backs of the cards contain the Mother's Cookies logo. Cards were passed out at the stadium on July 13. The checklist card features the Astros logo on the obverse.

		MINT	EXC	G-VG
COMPLETE SET		9.00	4.50	.90
COMMON PLAYER		.30	.15	.03
☐ 1	Bob Lillis MG	.30	.15	.03
☐ 2	Nolan Ryan	2.00	1.00	.20
☐ 3	Phil Garner	.40	.20	.04
☐ 4	Jose Cruz	.60	.30	.06
☐ 5	Denny Walling	.30	.15	.03
☐ 6	Joe Niekro	.75	.35	.07
☐ 7	Terry Puhl	.40	.20	.04
☐ 8	Bill Doran	.75	.35	.07
☐ 9	Dickie Thon	.40	.20	.04
☐ 10	Enos Cabell	.30	.15	.03
☐ 11	Frank DiPino	.30	.15	.03
☐ 12	Julio Solano	.30	.15	.03
☐ 13	Alan Ashby	.30	.15	.03
☐ 14	Craig Reynolds	.30	.15	.03
☐ 15	Jerry Mumphrey	.30	.15	.03
☐ 16	Bill Dawley	.30	.15	.03
☐ 17	Mark Bailey	.30	.15	.03
☐ 18	Mike Scott	1.25	.60	.12
☐ 19	Harry Spilman	.30	.15	.03
☐ 20	Bob Knepper	.50	.25	.05
☐ 21	Dave Smith	.50	.25	.05
☐ 22	Kevin Bass	.75	.35	.07
☐ 23	Tim Tolman	.30	.15	.03
☐ 24	Jeff Calhoun	.30	.15	.03
☐ 25	Jim Pankovits	.30	.15	.03
☐ 26	Ron Mathis	.30	.15	.03
☐ 27	Astros' Coaches	.30	.15	.03
☐ 28	Astros' Checklist	.30	.03	.00

1985 Mother's Giants

The cards in this 28 card set measure 2 1/2" by 3 1/2". In 1985, the Los Angeles based Mother's Cookies Co. again issued five sets of cards featuring players from major league teams. The San Francisco Giants set features current players depicted by photos on cards with rounded corners. The backs of the cards contain the Mother's Cookies logo. Cards were passed out at the stadium on June 30.

		MINT	EXC	G-VG
COMPLETE SET		9.00	4.50	.90
COMMON PLAYER		.30	.15	.03
☐ 1	Jim Davenport MG	.30	.15	.03

			MINT	EXC	G-VG
☐	2	Chili Davis	.75	.35	.07
☐	3	Dan Gladden	.60	.30	.06
☐	4	Jeff Leonard	.75	.35	.07
☐	5	Manny Trillo	.30	.15	.03
☐	6	Atlee Hammaker	.30	.15	.03
☐	7	Bob Brenly	.50	.25	.05
☐	8	Greg Minton	.30	.15	.03
☐	9	Bill Laskey	.30	.15	.03
☐	10	Vida Blue	.40	.20	.04
☐	11	Mike Krukow	.50	.25	.05
☐	12	Frank Williams	.30	.15	.03
☐	13	Jose Uribe	.40	.20	.04
☐	14	Johnnie LeMaster	.30	.15	.03
☐	15	Scot Thompson	.30	.15	.03
☐	16	Dave LaPoint	.30	.15	.03
☐	17	David Green	.30	.15	.03
☐	18	Chris Brown	.90	.45	.09
☐	19	Joel Youngblood	.30	.15	.03
☐	20	Mark Davis	.40	.20	.04
☐	21	Jim Gott	.30	.15	.03
☐	22	Doug Gwosdz	.30	.15	.03
☐	23	Scott Garrelts	.50	.25	.05
☐	24	Gary Rajsich	.30	.15	.03
☐	25	Rob Deer	.75	.35	.07
☐	26	Brad Wellman	.30	.15	.03
☐	27	Giants' Coaches	.30	.15	.03
☐	28	Giants' Checklist	.30	.03	.00

1985 Mother's Mariners

The cards in this 28 card set measure 2 1/2" by 3 1/2". In 1985, the Los Angeles based Mother's Cookies Co. again issued five sets of cards featuring players from major league teams. The Seattle Mariners set features current players depicted by photos on cards with rounded corners. The backs of the cards contain the Mother's Cookies logo. Cards were passed out at the stadium on August 10.

			MINT	EXC	G-VG
		COMPLETE SET	11.00	5.50	1.10
		COMMON PLAYER	.30	.15	.03
☐	1	Chuck Cottier MG	.30	.15	.03
☐	2	Alvin Davis	1.25	.60	.12
☐	3	Mark Langston	1.00	.50	.10
☐	4	Dave Henderson	.40	.20	.04
☐	5	Ed VandeBerg	.30	.15	.03

☐	6	Al Cowens	.30	.15	.03
☐	7	Spike Owen	.40	.20	.04
☐	8	Mike Moore	.40	.20	.04
☐	9	Gorman Thomas	.50	.25	.05
☐	10	Barry Bonnell	.30	.15	.03
☐	11	Jack Perconte	.30	.15	.03
☐	12	Domingo Ramos	.30	.15	.03
☐	13	Bob Kearney	.30	.15	.03
☐	14	Matt Young	.40	.20	.04
☐	15	Jim Beattie	.30	.15	.03
☐	16	Mike Stanton	.30	.15	.03
☐	17	David Valle	.30	.15	.03
☐	18	Ken Phelps	.50	.25	.05
☐	19	Salome Barojas	.30	.15	.03
☐	20	Jim Presley	1.75	.85	.17
☐	21	Phil Bradley	1.25	.60	.12
☐	22	Dave Geisel	.30	.15	.03
☐	23	Harold Reynolds	.75	.35	.07
☐	24	Ed Nunez	.40	.20	.04
☐	25	Mike Morgan	.30	.15	.03
☐	26	Ivan Calderon	1.00	.50	.10
☐	27	Mariners Coaches	.30	.15	.03
☐	28	Checklist	.30	.03	.00

1985 Mother's Padres

The cards in this 28 card set measure 2 1/2" by 3 1/2". In 1985, the Los Angeles based Mother's Cookies Co. again issued five sets of cards featuring players from major league teams. The San Diego Padres set features current players depicted by photos on cards with rounded corners. The backs of the cards contain the Mother's Cookies logo. Cards were passed out at the stadium on August 11.

			MINT	EXC	G-VG
		COMPLETE SET	11.00	5.50	1.10
		COMMON PLAYER	.30	.15	.03
☐	1	Dick Williams MG	.40	.20	.04
☐	2	Tony Gwynn	2.00	1.00	.20
☐	3	Kevin McReynolds	1.00	.50	.10
☐	4	Graig Nettles	.75	.35	.07
☐	5	Rich Gossage	.75	.35	.07
☐	6	Steve Garvey	1.50	.75	.15
☐	7	Garry Templeton	.40	.20	.04
☐	8	Dave Dravecky	.50	.25	.05
☐	9	Eric Show	.30	.15	.03
☐	10	Terry Kennedy	.40	.20	.04
☐	11	Luis DeLeon	.30	.15	.03
☐	12	Bruce Bochy	.30	.15	.03
☐	13	Andy Hawkins	.30	.15	.03
☐	14	Kurt Bevacqua	.30	.15	.03
☐	15	Craig Lefferts	.30	.15	.03
☐	16	Mario Ramirez	.30	.15	.03
☐	17	LaMarr Hoyt	.40	.20	.04
☐	18	Jerry Royster	.30	.15	.03
☐	19	Tim Stoddard	.30	.15	.03
☐	20	Tim Flannery	.30	.15	.03
☐	21	Mark Thurmond	.30	.15	.03
☐	22	Greg Booker	.30	.15	.03
☐	23	Bobby Brown	.30	.15	.03
☐	24	Carmelo Martinez	.40	.20	.04
☐	25	Al Bumbry	.30	.15	.03
☐	26	Jerry Davis	.30	.15	.03
☐	27	Padres' Coaches	.30	.15	.03
☐	28	Padres' Checklist	.30	.03	.00

1986 Mother's A's

This set consists of 28 full-color, rounded-corner cards each measuring 2 1/2" by 3 1/2". Starter sets (only 20 cards but also including a certificate for eight more cards) were given out at the ballpark and collectors were encouraged to trade to fill in the rest of their set. The cards were originally given away on July 20th at Oakland Coliseum.

	MINT	EXC	G-VG
COMPLETE SET	13.50	6.00	1.00
COMMON PLAYER	.30	.15	.03
☐ 1 Jackie Moore MG	.30	.15	.03
☐ 2 Dave Kingman	.60	.30	.06
☐ 3 Dusty Baker	.40	.20	.04
☐ 4 Joaquin Andujar	.50	.25	.05
☐ 5 Alfredo Griffin	.50	.25	.05
☐ 6 Dwayne Murphy	.50	.25	.05
☐ 7 Mike Davis	.50	.25	.05
☐ 8 Carney Lansford	.50	.25	.05
☐ 9 Jose Canseco	6.50	3.25	.65
☐ 10 Bruce Bochte	.30	.15	.03
☐ 11 Mickey Tettleton	.30	.15	.03
☐ 12 Donnie Hill	.30	.15	.03
☐ 13 Jose Rijo	.40	.20	.04
☐ 14 Rick Langford	.30	.15	.03
☐ 15 Chris Codiroli	.30	.15	.03
☐ 16 Moose Haas	.30	.15	.03
☐ 17 Keith Atherton	.30	.15	.03
☐ 18 Jay Howell	.40	.20	.04
☐ 19 Tony Phillips	.30	.15	.03
☐ 20 Steve Henderson	.30	.15	.03
☐ 21 Bill Krueger	.30	.15	.03
☐ 22 Steve Ontiveros	.30	.15	.03
☐ 23 Bill Bathe	.40	.20	.04
☐ 24 Ricky Peters	.30	.15	.03
☐ 25 Tim Birtsas	.40	.20	.04
☐ 26 A's Trainers and Equipment Mgrs	.30	.15	.03
☐ 27 A's Coaches	.30	.15	.03
☐ 28 Checklist card	.30	.03	.00

1986 Mother's Astros

This set consists of 28 full-color, rounded-corner cards each measuring 2 1/2" by 3 1/2". Starter sets (only 20 cards but also including a certificate for eight more cards) were given out at the ballpark and collectors were encouraged to trade to fill in the rest of their set. Cards were originally given out at the Astrodome on July 10th. Since the 1986 All-Star Game was held in Houston, the set features Astro All-Stars since 1962 as painted by artist Richard Wallich.

	MINT	EXC	G-VG
COMPLETE SET	8.00	4.00	.80
COMMON PLAYER	.30	.15	.03
☐ 1 Dick Farrell	.30	.15	.03
☐ 2 Hal Woodeshick	.30	.15	.03
☐ 3 Joe Morgan	1.00	.50	.10

☐ 4 Claude Raymond	.30	.15	.03
☐ 5 Mike Cuellar	.40	.20	.04
☐ 6 Rusty Staub	.50	.25	.05
☐ 7 Jimmy Wynn	.40	.20	.04
☐ 8 Larry Dierker	.40	.20	.04
☐ 9 Denis Menke	.30	.15	.03
☐ 10 Don Wilson	.30	.15	.03
☐ 11 Cesar Cedeno	.40	.20	.04
☐ 12 Lee May	.40	.20	.04
☐ 13 Bob Watson	.40	.20	.04
☐ 14 Ken Forsch	.30	.15	.03
☐ 15 Joaquin Andujar	.40	.20	.04
☐ 16 Terry Puhl	.40	.20	.04
☐ 17 Joe Niekro	.50	.25	.05
☐ 18 Craig Reynolds	.30	.15	.03
☐ 19 Joe Sambito	.30	.15	.03
☐ 20 Jose Cruz	.50	.25	.05
☐ 21 J.R. Richard	.50	.25	.05
☐ 22 Bob Knepper	.40	.20	.04
☐ 23 Nolan Ryan	1.50	.75	.15
☐ 24 Ray Knight	.40	.20	.04
☐ 25 Bill Dawley	.30	.15	.03
☐ 26 Dickie Thon	.30	.15	.03
☐ 27 Jerry Mumphrey	.30	.15	.03
☐ 28 Checklist card	.30	.03	.00

1986 Mother's Giants

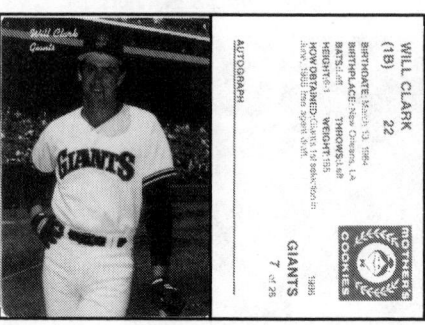

This set consists of 28 full-color, rounded-corner cards each measuring 2 1/2" by 3 1/2". Starter sets (only 20 cards but also including a certificate for eight more cards) were given out at the ballpark and collectors were encouraged to trade to fill in the rest of their set. Cards were originally given out at Candlestick Park on July 13th.

	MINT	EXC	G-VG
COMPLETE SET	9.00	4.50	.90
COMMON PLAYER	.30	.15	.03
☐ 1 Roger Craig MG	.50	.25	.05
☐ 2 Chili Davis	.60	.30	.06
☐ 3 Dan Gladden	.40	.20	.04
☐ 4 Jeff Leonard	.60	.30	.06
☐ 5 Bob Brenly	.40	.20	.04
☐ 6 Atlee Hammaker	.40	.20	.04
☐ 7 Will Clark	2.50	1.25	.25
☐ 8 Greg Minton	.30	.15	.03

			MINT	EXC	G-VG
☐	9	Candy Maldonado	.60	.30	.06
☐	10	Vida Blue	.40	.20	.04
☐	11	Mike Krukow	.50	.25	.05
☐	12	Bob Melvin	.40	.20	.04
☐	13	Jose Uribe	.40	.20	.04
☐	14	Dan Driessen	.30	.15	.03
☐	15	Jeff Robinson	.40	.20	.04
☐	16	Rob Thompson	.60	.30	.06
☐	17	Mike LaCoss	.30	.15	.03
☐	18	Chris Brown	.60	.30	.06
☐	19	Scott Garrelts	.50	.25	.05
☐	20	Mark Davis	.40	.20	.04
☐	21	Jim Gott	.30	.15	.03
☐	22	Brad Wellman	.30	.15	.03
☐	23	Roger Mason	.40	.20	.04
☐	24	Bill Laskey	.30	.15	.03
☐	25	Brad Gulden	.30	.15	.03
☐	26	Joel Youngblood	.30	.15	.03
☐	27	Juan Berenguer	.40	.20	.04
☐	28	Checklist card	.30	.03	.00

1986 Mother's Mariners

This set consists of 28 full-color, rounded-corner cards each measuring 2 1/2" by 3 1/2". Starter sets (only 20 cards but also including a certificate for eight more cards) were given out at the ballpark and collectors were encouraged to trade to fill in the rest of their set. Cards were originally given out on July 27th at the Seattle Kingdome.

			MINT	EXC	G-VG
		COMPLETE SET	9.00	4.50	.90
		COMMON PLAYER	.30	.15	.03
☐	1	Dick Williams MG	.40	.20	.04
☐	2	Alvin Davis	.75	.35	.07
☐	3	Mark Langston	.75	.35	.07
☐	4	Dave Henderson	.40	.20	.04
☐	5	Steve Yeager	.30	.15	.03
☐	6	Al Cowens	.30	.15	.03
☐	7	Jim Presley	.90	.45	.09
☐	8	Phil Bradley	.75	.35	.07
☐	9	Gorman Thomas	.50	.25	.05
☐	10	Barry Bonnell	.30	.15	.03
☐	11	Milt Wilcox	.30	.15	.03
☐	12	Domingo Ramos	.30	.15	.03
☐	13	Paul Mirabella	.30	.15	.03
☐	14	Matt Young	.30	.15	.03
☐	15	Ivan Calderon	.75	.35	.07
☐	16	Bill Swift	.30	.15	.03
☐	17	Pete Ladd	.30	.15	.03
☐	18	Ken Phelps	.50	.25	.05
☐	19	Karl Best	.30	.15	.03
☐	20	Spike Owen	.40	.20	.04
☐	21	Mike Moore	.40	.20	.04
☐	22	Danny Tartabull	1.25	.60	.12
☐	23	Bob Kearney	.30	.15	.03
☐	24	Edwin Nunez	.30	.15	.03
☐	25	Mike Morgan	.30	.15	.03
☐	26	Roy Thomas	.30	.15	.03
☐	27	Jim Beattie	.30	.15	.03
☐	28	Checklist card	.30	.03	.00

1987 Mother's Cookies A's

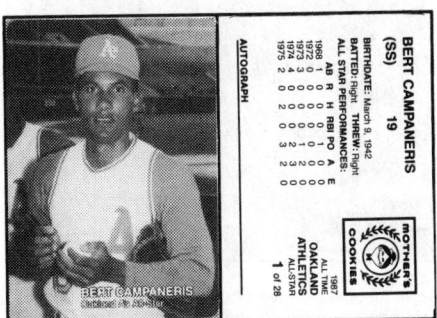

This set consists of 28 full-color, rounded-corner cards each measuring 2 1/2" by 3 1/2". Starter sets (only 20 cards but also including a certificate for eight more cards) were given out at the ballpark and collectors were encouraged to trade to fill in the rest of their set. The cards were originally given away on July 5th at Oakland Coliseum during a game against the Boston Red Sox. This set is actually an All-Time All-Star set including every A's All-Star player since 1968 (when the franchise moved to Oakland). The vintage photos (each shot during the year of All-Star appearance) were taken from the collection of Doug McWilliams. The sets were supposedly given out free to the first 25,000 paid admissions at the game.

			MINT	EXC	G-VG
		COMPLETE SET (28)	10.00	5.00	1.00
		COMMON PLAYER (1-28)	.30	.15	.03
☐	1	Bert Campaneris	.30	.15	.03
☐	2	Rick Monday	.30	.15	.03
☐	3	John Odom	.30	.15	.03
☐	4	Sal Bando	.40	.20	.04
☐	5	Reggie Jackson	1.50	.75	.15
☐	6	Jim Hunter	1.00	.50	.10
☐	7	Vida Blue	.40	.20	.04
☐	8	Dave Duncan	.30	.15	.03
☐	9	Joe Rudi	.40	.20	.04
☐	10	Rollie Fingers	.75	.35	.07
☐	11	Ken Holtzman	.30	.15	.03
☐	12	Dick Williams	.40	.20	.04
☐	13	Alvin Dark	.40	.20	.04
☐	14	Gene Tenace	.30	.15	.03
☐	15	Claudell Washington	.40	.20	.04
☐	16	Phil Garner	.30	.15	.03
☐	17	Wayne Gross	.30	.15	.03
☐	18	Matt Keough	.30	.15	.03
☐	19	Jeff Newman	.30	.15	.03
☐	20	Rickey Henderson	1.50	.75	.15
☐	21	Tony Armas	.40	.20	.04
☐	22	Mike Norris	.30	.15	.03
☐	23	Billy Martin	.50	.25	.05
☐	24	Bill Caudill	.40	.20	.04
☐	25	Jay Howell	.40	.20	.04
☐	26	Jose Canseco	1.50	.75	.15
☐	27	Jose and Reggie	1.00	.50	.10
☐	28	Checklist Card	.30	.03	.00

1987 Mother's Cookies Astros

This set consists of 28 full-color, rounded-corner cards each measuring 2 1/2" by 3 1/2". Starter sets (only 20 cards but also including a certificate for eight more cards) were given out at the ballpark and collectors were encouraged to trade to fill in the rest of their set. Cards were originally given out at the Astrodome on July 17th during a game against the Phillies. Photos were taken by Barry Colla. The sets

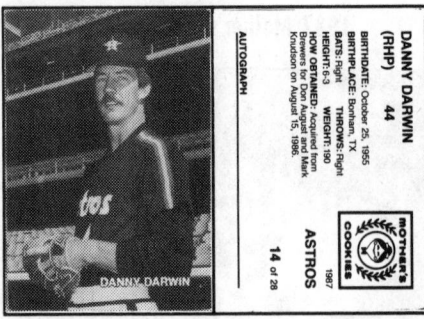

DANNY DARWIN DANNY DARWIN (RHP) 44 AUTOGRAPH BIRTHDATE: October 25, 1955 BIRTHPLACE: Bonham, TX. BATS: Right THROWS: Right HEIGHT: 6-3 WEIGHT: 190 HOW OBTAINED: Acquired from Brewers for Don August and Mark Knudson on August 15, 1986. ASTROS 14 of 28 1987

were supposedly given out free to the first 25,000 paid admissions at the game.

		MINT	EXC	G-VG
COMPLETE SET		9.00	4.50	.90
COMMON PLAYER		.30	.15	.03
☐ 1	Hal Lanier MG	.40	.20	.04
☐ 2	Mike Scott	1.00	.50	.10
☐ 3	Jose Cruz	.60	.30	.06
☐ 4	Bill Doran	.75	.35	.07
☐ 5	Bob Knepper	.40	.20	.04
☐ 6	Phil Garner	.40	.20	.04
☐ 7	Terry Puhl	.40	.20	.04
☐ 8	Nolan Ryan	2.00	1.00	.20
☐ 9	Kevin Bass	.50	.25	.05
☐ 10	Glenn Davis	.75	.35	.07
☐ 11	Alan Ashby	.40	.20	.04
☐ 12	Charlie Kerfeld	.40	.20	.04
☐ 13	Denny Walling	.30	.15	.03
☐ 14	Danny Darwin	.40	.20	.04
☐ 15	Mark Bailey	.30	.15	.03
☐ 16	Davey Lopes	.40	.20	.04
☐ 17	Dave Meads	.30	.15	.03
☐ 18	Aurelio Lopez	.30	.15	.03
☐ 19	Craig Reynolds	.30	.15	.03
☐ 20	Dave Smith	.40	.20	.04
☐ 21	Larry Andersen	.30	.15	.03
☐ 22	Jim Pankovits	.30	.15	.03
☐ 23	Jim Deshaies	.50	.25	.05
☐ 24	Bert Pena	.30	.15	.03
☐ 25	Dickie Thon	.40	.20	.04
☐ 26	Billy Hatcher	.75	.35	.07
☐ 27	Astros' Coaches	.30	.15	.03
☐ 28	Checklist	.30	.03	.00

1987 Mother's Cookies Dodgers

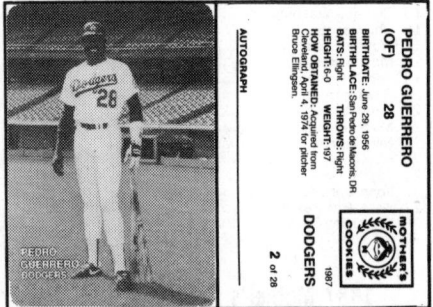

PEDRO GUERRERO PEDRO GUERRERO (OF) 28 AUTOGRAPH BIRTHDATE: June 29, 1956 BIRTHPLACE: San Pedro de Macoris, DR BATS: Right THROWS: Right HEIGHT: 6-0 WEIGHT: 197 HOW OBTAINED: Acquired from Cleveland, April 4, 1974 for pitcher Bruce Ellingsen. DODGERS 2 of 28 1987

This set consists of 28 full-color, rounded-corner cards each measuring 2 1/2" by 3 1/2". Starter sets (only 20 cards but also including a certificate for eight more cards) were given out at the ballpark and collectors were encouraged to trade to fill in the rest of their set. Cards were originally given out at Dodger Stadium on August 9th. Photos were taken by Barry Colla. The sets were supposedly given out free to all game attendees 14 years of age and under.

		MINT	EXC	G-VG
COMPLETE SET		9.00	4.50	.90
COMMON PLAYER		.30	.15	.03
☐ 1	Tom Lasorda MG	.50	.25	.05
☐ 2	Pedro Guerrero	1.00	.50	.10
☐ 3	Steve Sax	.60	.30	.06
☐ 4	Fernando Valenzuela	1.00	.50	.10
☐ 5	Mike Marshall	.60	.30	.06
☐ 6	Orel Hershiser	.75	.35	.07
☐ 7	Mariano Duncan	.40	.20	.04
☐ 8	Bill Madlock	.50	.25	.05
☐ 9	Bob Welch	.50	.25	.05
☐ 10	Mike Scioscia	.40	.20	.04
☐ 11	Mike Ramsey	.40	.20	.04
☐ 12	Matt Young	.30	.15	.03
☐ 13	Franklin Stubbs	.40	.20	.04
☐ 14	Tom Niedenfuer	.40	.20	.04
☐ 15	Reggie Williams	.40	.20	.04
☐ 16	Rick Honeycutt	.30	.15	.03
☐ 17	Dave Anderson	.30	.15	.03
☐ 18	Alejandro Pena	.30	.15	.03
☐ 19	Ken Howell	.30	.15	.03
☐ 20	Len Matuszek	.30	.15	.03
☐ 21	Tim Leary	.30	.15	.03
☐ 22	Tracy Woodson	.40	.20	.04
☐ 23	Alex Trevino	.30	.15	.03
☐ 24	Ken Landreaux	.30	.15	.03
☐ 25	Mickey Hatcher	.30	.15	.03
☐ 26	Brian Holton	.30	.15	.03
☐ 27	Dodgers' Coaches	.30	.15	.03
☐ 28	Checklist	.30	.03	.00

1987 Mother's Cookies Giants

ROBBY THOMPSON ROBBY THOMPSON (2B) 6 AUTOGRAPH BIRTHDATE: May 10, 1962 BIRTHPLACE: West Palm Beach, FL. BATS: Right THROWS: Right HEIGHT: 5-11 WEIGHT: 170 HOW OBTAINED: no selection in June, 1983 free agent draft, secondary phase. GIANTS 10 of 28 1987

This set consists of 28 full-color, rounded-corner cards each measuring 2 1/2" by 3 1/2". Starter sets (only 20 cards but also including a certificate for eight more cards) were given out at the ballpark and collectors were encouraged to fill in the rest of their set. Cards were originally given out at Candlestick Park on June 27th during a game against the Astros. Photos were taken by Dennis Desprois. The sets were supposedly given out free to the first 25,000 paid admissions at the game.

		MINT	EXC	G-VG
COMPLETE SET (28)		9.00	4.50	.90
COMMON PLAYER (1-28)		.30	.15	.03
☐ 1	Roger Craig MG	.50	.25	.05
☐ 2	Will Clark	1.25	.60	.12
☐ 3	Chili Davis	.50	.25	.05
☐ 4	Bob Brenly	.40	.20	.04
☐ 5	Chris Brown	.60	.30	.06
☐ 6	Mike Krukow	.40	.20	.04
☐ 7	Candy Maldonado	.75	.35	.07
☐ 8	Jeffrey Leonard	.75	.35	.07
☐ 9	Greg Minton	.30	.15	.03
☐ 10	Robby Thompson	.50	.25	.05
☐ 11	Scott Garrelts	.40	.20	.04
☐ 12	Bob Melvin	.30	.15	.03
☐ 13	Jose Uribe	.40	.20	.04
☐ 14	Mark Davis	.30	.15	.03
☐ 15	Eddie Milner	.30	.15	.03

☐ 16	Harry Spilman	.30	.15	.03
☐ 17	Kelly Downs	.40	.20	.04
☐ 18	Chris Speier	.40	.20	.04
☐ 19	Jim Gott	.30	.15	.03
☐ 20	Joel Youngblood	.30	.15	.03
☐ 21	Mike LaCoss	.30	.15	.03
☐ 22	Matt Williams	.50	.25	.05
☐ 23	Roger Mason	.30	.15	.03
☐ 24	Mike Aldrete	.75	.35	.07
☐ 25	Jeff Robinson	.50	.25	.05
☐ 26	Mark Grant	.30	.15	.03
☐ 27	Giants' Coaches	.30	.15	.03
☐ 28	Checklist Card	.30	.03	.00

1987 Mother's Cookies Mariners

This set consists of 28 full-color, rounded- corner cards each measuring 2 1/2" by 3 1/2". Starter sets (only 20 cards but also including a certificate for eight more cards) were given out at the ballpark and collectors were encouraged to trade to fill in the rest of their set. Cards were originally given out on August 9th at the Seattle Kingdome. Photos were taken by Barry Colla. The sets were supposedly given out free to the first 20,000 paid admissions at the game.

		MINT	EXC	G-VG
COMPLETE SET		9.00	4.50	.90
COMMON PLAYER		.30	.15	.03
☐ 1	Dick Williams MG	.40	.20	.04
☐ 2	Alvin Davis	.60	.30	.06
☐ 3	Mike Moore	.40	.20	.04
☐ 4	Jim Presley	.75	.35	.07
☐ 5	Mark Langston	.75	.35	.07
☐ 6	Phil Bradley	.60	.30	.06
☐ 7	Ken Phelps	.40	.20	.04
☐ 8	Mike Morgan	.30	.15	.03
☐ 9	David Valle	.30	.15	.03
☐ 10	Harold Reynolds	.50	.25	.05
☐ 11	Edwin Nunez	.40	.20	.04
☐ 12	Bob Kearney	.30	.15	.03
☐ 13	Scott Bankhead	.40	.20	.04
☐ 14	Scott Bradley	.40	.20	.04
☐ 15	Mickey Brantley	.50	.25	.05
☐ 16	Mark Huismann	.40	.20	.04
☐ 17	Mike Kingery	.40	.20	.04
☐ 18	John Moses	.30	.15	.03
☐ 19	Donell Nixon	.40	.20	.04
☐ 20	Rey Quinones	.40	.20	.04
☐ 21	Domingo Ramos	.30	.15	.03
☐ 22	Jerry Reed	.30	.15	.03
☐ 23	Rich Renteria	.30	.15	.03
☐ 24	Rich Monteleone	.30	.15	.03
☐ 25	Mike Trujillo	.30	.15	.03
☐ 26	Bill Wilkinson	.30	.15	.03
☐ 27	John Christensen	.30	.15	.03
☐ 28	Checklist Card	.30	.03	.00

> **FAMILY FUN:** Have fun with all members of your family. Take them along to a sports collectibles convention in your area.

1987 Mother's Cookies McGwire

This set consists of 4 full-color, rounded-corner cards each measuring 2 1/2" by 3 1/2" and showing a different pose of A's slugging rookie Mark McGwire. Cards were originally given out at the national Card Collectors Convention in San Francisco. Later they were available through a mail-in offer involving collectors sending in two proofs-of-purchase from any Mother's Cookies products to get one free card. Photos were taken by Doug McWilliams. The cards are numbered on the back.

		MINT	EXC	G-VG
COMPLETE SET (4)		15.00	7.50	1.50
COMMON PLAYER (1-4)		4.00	2.00	.40
☐ 1	Mark McGwire .... close-up shot, head and shoulders	4.00	2.00	.40
☐ 2	Mark McGwire .... waist up, holding bat	5.00	2.50	.50
☐ 3	Mark McGwire .... batting stance, ready to swing	5.00	2.50	.50
☐ 4	Mark McGwire .... home run swing, follow through	6.00	3.00	.60

1987 Mother's Cookies Rangers

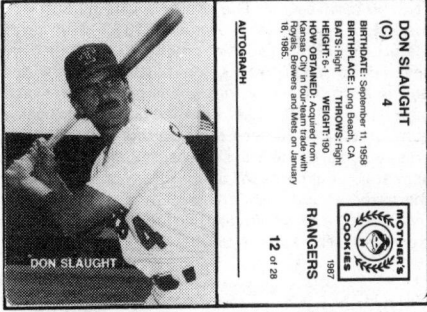

This set consists of 28 full-color, rounded- corner cards each measuring 2 1/2" by 3 1/2". Starter sets (only 20 cards but also including a certificate for eight more cards) were given out at the ballpark and collectors were encouraged to trade to fill in the rest of their set. Cards were originally given out on July 17th during the game against the Yankees. Photos were taken by Barry Colla. The sets were supposedly given out free to the first 25,000 paid admissions at the game.

		MINT	EXC	G-VG
COMPLETE SET		9.00	4.50	.90
COMMON PLAYER		.30	.15	.03
☐ 1	Bobby Valentine MG	.50	.25	.05
☐ 2	Pete Incaviglia	.75	.35	.07
☐ 3	Charlie Hough	.50	.25	.05
☐ 4	Oddibe McDowell	.50	.25	.05
☐ 5	Larry Parrish	.50	.25	.05
☐ 6	Scott Fletcher	.50	.25	.05
☐ 7	Steve Buechele	.30	.15	.03
☐ 8	Tom Paciorek	.30	.15	.03
☐ 9	Pete O'Brien	.60	.30	.06
☐ 10	Darrell Porter	.40	.20	.04
☐ 11	Greg Harris	.30	.15	.03
☐ 12	Don Slaught	.40	.20	.04
☐ 13	Ruben Sierra	1.25	.60	.12
☐ 14	Curtis Wilkerson	.30	.15	.03
☐ 15	Dale Mohorcic	.50	.25	.05
☐ 16	Ron Meredith	.30	.15	.03
☐ 17	Mitch Williams	.40	.20	.04
☐ 18	Bob Brower	.40	.20	.04
☐ 19	Edwin Correa	.40	.20	.04
☐ 20	Geno Petralli	.30	.15	.03
☐ 21	Mike Loynd	.40	.20	.04
☐ 22	Jerry Browne	.30	.15	.03
☐ 23	Jose Guzman	.40	.20	.04
☐ 24	Jeff Kunkel	.30	.15	.03
☐ 25	Bobby Witt	.50	.25	.05
☐ 26	Jeff Russell	.30	.15	.03
☐ 27	Ranger's Trainers	.30	.15	.03
☐ 28	Checklist Card	.30	.03	.00

N28 Allen and Ginter

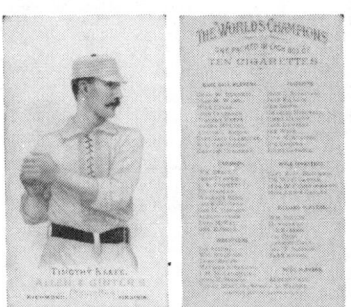

This 50-card set of The World's Champions was marketed by Allen and Ginter in 1887. The cards feature color lithographs of champion athletes from seven categories of sport, with baseball, rowing and boxing each having 10 individuals portrayed. Cards numbered 1 to 10 depict baseball players and cards numbered 11 to 20 depict popular boxers of the era. This set is called the first series although no such title appears on the cards. All 50 cards are checklisted on the reverse, and they are unnumbered. An album (ACC: A16) and an advertising banner (ACC: G20) were also issued in conjunction with this set.

		NRMT	VG-E	GOOD
COMPLETE SET		2800.00	1200.00	250.00
COMMON BASEBALL (1-10)		125.00	60.00	12.50
COMMON BOXERS (11-20)		25.00	12.50	2.50
COMMON OTHERS (21-50)		10.00	5.00	1.00
☐ 1	Adrian C. Anson	600.00	300.00	60.00
☐ 2	Chas. W. Bennett	125.00	60.00	12.50
☐ 3	R.L. Caruthers	125.00	60.00	12.50
☐ 4	John Clarkson	250.00	125.00	25.00
☐ 5	Charles Comiskey	300.00	150.00	30.00
☐ 6	Capt. Jack Glasscock	125.00	60.00	12.50
☐ 7	Timothy Keefe	250.00	125.00	25.00
☐ 8	Mike Kelly	350.00	175.00	35.00
☐ 9	Joseph Mulvey	125.00	60.00	12.50
☐ 10	John M. Ward	300.00	150.00	30.00
☐ 11	Jimmy Carney	25.00	12.50	2.50

☐ 12	Jimmy Carroll	25.00	12.50	2.50
☐ 13	Jack Dempsey	45.00	22.50	4.50
☐ 14	Jake Kilrain	25.00	12.50	2.50
☐ 15	Joe Lannon	25.00	12.50	2.50
☐ 16	Jack McAuliffe	25.00	12.50	2.50
☐ 17	Charlie Mitchell	25.00	12.50	2.50
☐ 18	Jem Smith	25.00	12.50	2.50
☐ 19	John L. Sullivan	75.00	37.50	7.50
☐ 20	Ike Weir	25.00	12.50	2.50
☐ 21	Wm. Beach	10.00	5.00	1.00
☐ 22	Geo. Bubear	10.00	5.00	1.00
☐ 23	Jacob Gaudaur	10.00	5.00	1.00
☐ 24	Albert Hamm	10.00	5.00	1.00
☐ 25	Ed. Hanlan	10.00	5.00	1.00
☐ 26	Geo. H. Hosmer	10.00	5.00	1.00
☐ 27	John McKay	10.00	5.00	1.00
☐ 28	Wallace Ross	10.00	5.00	1.00
☐ 29	John Teemer	10.00	5.00	1.00
☐ 30	E.A. Trickett	10.00	5.00	1.00
☐ 31	Joe Acton	10.00	5.00	1.00
☐ 32	Theo. Bauer	10.00	5.00	1.00
☐ 33	Young Bibby (Geo. Mehling)	10.00	5.00	1.00
☐ 34	J.F. McLaughlin	10.00	5.00	1.00
☐ 35	John McMahon	10.00	5.00	1.00
☐ 36	Wm. Muldoon	10.00	5.00	1.00
☐ 37	Matsada Sorakichi	10.00	5.00	1.00
☐ 38	Capt. A.H. Bogardus	10.00	5.00	1.00
☐ 39	Dr. W.F. Carver	10.00	5.00	1.00
☐ 40	Hon. W.F. Cody (Buffalo Bill)	50.00	25.00	5.00
☐ 41	Miss Annie Oakley	30.00	15.00	3.00
☐ 42	Yank Adams	10.00	5.00	1.00
☐ 43	Maurice Daly	10.00	5.00	1.00
☐ 44	Jos. Dion	10.00	5.00	1.00
☐ 45	J. Schaefer	10.00	5.00	1.00
☐ 46	Wm. Sexton	10.00	5.00	1.00
☐ 47	Geo. F. Slosson	10.00	5.00	1.00
☐ 48	M. Vignaux	10.00	5.00	1.00
☐ 49	Albert Frey	10.00	5.00	1.00
☐ 50	J.L. Malone	10.00	5.00	1.00

N29 Allen and Ginter

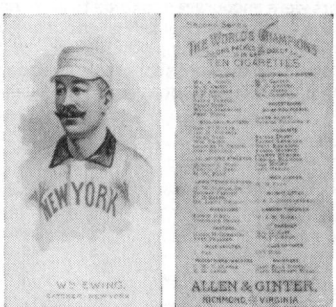

The second series of The World's Champions was probably issued in 1888. Like the first series, the cards are backlisted and unnumbered. However, there are 17 distinct categories of sports represented in this set, with only six baseball players portrayed (as opposed to 10 in the first series). Each card has a color lithograph of the individual set against a white background. An album (ACC: A17) and an advertising banner (ACC: G21) were issued in conjunction with the set. The numbering below is alphabetical within sport, e.g., baseball players (1-6), boxers (7-14), and other sports (15-50).

		NRMT	VG-E	GOOD
COMPLETE SET		2350.00	1000.00	200.00
COMMON BASEBALL (1-6)		300.00	150.00	30.00
COMMON BOXERS (7-14)		30.00	15.00	3.00
COMMON OTHERS (15-50)		12.50	6.25	1.25
☐ 1	Wm. Ewing	600.00	300.00	60.00
☐ 2	Jas. H. Fogarty	300.00	150.00	30.00
☐ 3	Charles H. Getzin	300.00	150.00	30.00
☐ 4	Geo. F. Miller	300.00	150.00	30.00
☐ 5	John Morrell	300.00	150.00	30.00

				NRMT	VG-E	GOOD
☐	6	James Ryan		300.00	150.00	30.00
☐	7	Patsey Duffy		30.00	15.00	3.00
☐	8	Billy Edwards		30.00	15.00	3.00
☐	9	Jack Havlin		30.00	15.00	3.00
☐	10	Patsey Kerrigan		30.00	15.00	3.00
☐	11	Geo. La Blance		30.00	15.00	3.00
☐	12	Jack McGee		30.00	15.00	3.00
☐	13	Frank Murphy		30.00	15.00	3.00
☐	14	Johnny Murphy		30.00	15.00	3.00
☐	15	Capt. J.C. Daly		12.50	6.25	1.25
☐	16	M.W. Ford		12.50	6.25	1.25
☐	17	Duncan C. Ross		12.50	6.25	1.25
☐	18	W.E. Crist		12.50	6.25	1.25
☐	19	H.G. Crocken		12.50	6.25	1.25
☐	20	Willie Harradon		12.50	6.25	1.25
☐	21	F.F. Ives		12.50	6.25	1.25
☐	22	Wm. A. Rowe		12.50	6.25	1.25
☐	23	Percy Stone		12.50	6.25	1.25
☐	24	Ralph Temple		12.50	6.25	1.25
☐	25	Fred Wood		12.50	6.25	1.25
☐	26	Dr. James Dwight		12.50	6.25	1.25
☐	27	Thomas Pettit		12.50	6.25	1.25
☐	28	R.D. Sears		12.50	6.25	1.25
☐	29	H.W. Slocum Jr.		12.50	6.25	1.25
☐	30	Theobaud Bauer		12.50	6.25	1.25
☐	31	Edwin Bibby		12.50	6.25	1.25
☐	32	Hugh McCormack		12.50	6.25	1.25
☐	33	Axel Paulsen		12.50	6.25	1.25
☐	34	T. Ray		12.50	6.25	1.25
☐	35	C.W.V. Clarke		12.50	6.25	1.25
☐	36	E.D. Lange		12.50	6.25	1.25
☐	37	E.C. Carter		12.50	6.25	1.25
☐	38	Wm. Cummings		12.50	6.25	1.25
☐	39	W.G. George		12.50	6.25	1.25
☐	40	L.E. Myers		12.50	6.25	1.25
☐	41	James Albert		12.50	6.25	1.25
☐	42	Patrick Fitzgerald		12.50	6.25	1.25
☐	43	W.B. Page		12.50	6.25	1.25
☐	44	C.A.J. Queckberner		12.50	6.25	1.25
☐	45	W.J.M. Barry		12.50	6.25	1.25
☐	46	Wm. G. East		12.50	6.25	1.25
☐	47	Wm. O'Connor		12.50	6.25	1.25
☐	48	Gus Hill		12.50	6.25	1.25
☐	49	Capt. Paul Boyton		12.50	6.25	1.25
☐	50	Capt. Matthew Webb		12.50	6.25	1.25

N43 Allen and Ginter

The primary designs of this 50 card set are identical to those of N29, but these are placed on a much larger card with extraneous background detail. The set was produced in 1888 by Allen and Ginter as inserts for a larger tobacco package than those in which sets N28 and N29 were marketed. Cards of this set, which is backlisted, are considered to be much scarcer than their counterparts in N29.

			NRMT	VG-E	GOOD
COMPLETE SET			3200.00	1200.00	250.00
COMMON BASEBALL (1-6)			400.00	200.00	40.00
COMMON BOXERS (7-14)			35.00	17.50	3.50
COMMON OTHERS (15-50)			15.00	7.50	1.50

				NRMT	VG-E	GOOD
☐	1	William Ewing		700.00	350.00	70.00
☐	2	Jas. J. Fogarty		400.00	200.00	40.00
☐	3	Charles Getzein		400.00	200.00	40.00
☐	4	Geo. F. Miller		400.00	200.00	40.00
☐	5	John Morrell		400.00	200.00	40.00
☐	6	James Ryan		400.00	200.00	40.00
☐	7	Patsey Duffy		35.00	17.50	3.50
☐	8	Billy Edwards		35.00	17.50	3.50
☐	9	Jack Havlin		35.00	17.50	3.50
☐	10	Patsey Kerrigan		35.00	17.50	3.50
☐	11	George LaBlanche		35.00	17.50	3.50
☐	12	Jack McGee		35.00	17.50	3.50
☐	13	Frank Murphy		35.00	17.50	3.50
☐	14	Johnny Murphy		35.00	17.50	3.50
☐	15	James Albert		15.00	7.50	1.50
☐	16	W.J.M. Barry		15.00	7.50	1.50
☐	17	Theobaud Bauer		15.00	7.50	1.50
☐	18	Edwin Bibby		15.00	7.50	1.50
☐	19	Capt. Paul Boyton		15.00	7.50	1.50
☐	20	E.C. Carter		15.00	7.50	1.50
☐	21	C.W.V. Clarke		15.00	7.50	1.50
☐	22	W.E. Crist		15.00	7.50	1.50
☐	23	H.G. Crocker		15.00	7.50	1.50
☐	24	Wm. Cummings		15.00	7.50	1.50
☐	25	Capt. J.C. Daly		15.00	7.50	1.50

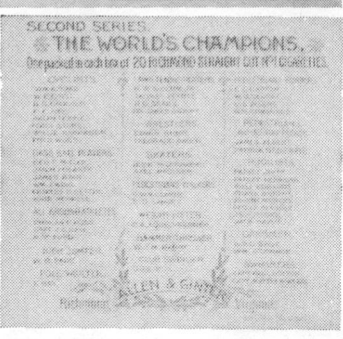

				NRMT	VG-E	GOOD
☐	26	Dr. James Dwight		15.00	7.50	1.50
☐	27	Wm. G. East		15.00	7.50	1.50
☐	28	Patrick Fitzgerald		15.00	7.50	1.50
☐	29	M.W. Ford		15.00	7.50	1.50
☐	30	W.G. George		15.00	7.50	1.50
☐	31	Willie Harradon		15.00	7.50	1.50
☐	32	Gus Hill		15.00	7.50	1.50
☐	33	F.F. Ives		15.00	7.50	1.50
☐	34	E.D. Lange		15.00	7.50	1.50
☐	35	Hugh McCormack		15.00	7.50	1.50
☐	36	L.E. Myers		15.00	7.50	1.50
☐	37	Wm. O'Connor		15.00	7.50	1.50
☐	38	W.B. Page		15.00	7.50	1.50
☐	39	Axel. Paulsen		15.00	7.50	1.50
☐	40	Thomas Pettitt		15.00	7.50	1.50
☐	41	C.A.J. Queckberner		15.00	7.50	1.50
☐	42	T. Ray		15.00	7.50	1.50
☐	43	Duncan C. Ross		15.00	7.50	1.50
☐	44	Wm. A. Rowe		15.00	7.50	1.50
☐	45	R.D. Sears		15.00	7.50	1.50
☐	46	H.W. Slocum Jr.		15.00	7.50	1.50
☐	47	Percy Stone		15.00	7.50	1.50
☐	48	Ralph Temple		15.00	7.50	1.50
☐	49	Capt. Matthew Webb		15.00	7.50	1.50
☐	50	Fred Wood		15.00	7.50	1.50

N162 Goodwin

This 50 card set issued by Goodwin was one of the major competitors to the N28 and N29 sets marketed by Allen and Ginter. It contains individuals representing 18 sports, with eight baseball players pictured. Each color card is backlisted and bears advertising for "Old Judge" and "Gypsy Queen" cigarettes on the front. The set was released to the public in 1888 and an album (ACC: A36) is associated with it as a premium issue.

			NRMT	VG-E	GOOD
COMPLETE SET			3300.00	1350.00	250.00
COMMON BASEBALL (1-8)			200.00	100.00	20.00
COMMON BOXER			25.00	12.50	2.50
COMMON OTHERS			10.00	5.00	1.00

				NRMT	VG-E	GOOD
☐	1	Andrews: Phila.		200.00	100.00	20.00
☐	2	Anson: Chicago		900.00	450.00	90.00

☐	3	Brouthers: Detroit	500.00	250.00	50.00
☐	4	Caruthers: Brooklyn	200.00	100.00	20.00
☐	5	Dunlap: Detroit	200.00	100.00	20.00
☐	6	Glasscock: Indianapolis	200.00	100.00	20.00
☐	7	Keefe: New York	500.00	250.00	50.00
☐	8	Kelly: Boston	600.00	300.00	60.00
☐	9	Acton (Wrestler)	10.00	5.00	1.00
☐	10	Albert (Pedestrian)	10.00	5.00	1.00
☐	11	Beach (Oarsman)	10.00	5.00	1.00
☐	12	Beecher (Football)	60.00	30.00	6.00
☐	13	Beeckman (Lawn Tennis)	10.00	5.00	1.00
☐	14	Bogardus (Marksman)	10.00	5.00	1.00
☐	15	Buffalo Bill (Wild West Hunter)	40.00	20.00	4.00
☐	16	Daly (Billiards)	10.00	5.00	1.00
☐	17	Dempsey (Pugilist)	60.00	30.00	6.00
☐	18	D'oro (Pool)	10.00	5.00	1.00
☐	19	Dwight (Lawn Tennis)	15.00	7.50	1.50
☐	20	Fitzgerald (Pedestrian)	10.00	5.00	1.00
☐	21	Garrison (Jockey)	10.00	5.00	1.00
☐	22	Gaudaur (Oarsman)	10.00	5.00	1.00
☐	23	Hanlan (Oarsman)	10.00	5.00	1.00
☐	24	Kilrain (Pugilist)	25.00	12.50	2.50
☐	25	MacKenzie (Chess)	10.00	5.00	1.00
☐	26	McLaughlin (Jockey)	10.00	5.00	1.00
☐	27	Mitchell (Pugilist)	25.00	12.50	2.50
☐	28	Muldoon (Wrestler)	10.00	5.00	1.00
☐	29	Murphy (Jockey)	10.00	5.00	1.00
☐	30	Myers (Runner)	10.00	5.00	1.00
☐	31	Page (High Jumper)	10.00	5.00	1.00
☐	32	Prince (Bicyclist)	10.00	5.00	1.00
☐	33	Ross (Broadswordsman)	10.00	5.00	1.00
☐	34	Rowe (Bicyclist)	10.00	5.00	1.00
☐	35	Rowell (Pedestrian)	10.00	5.00	1.00
☐	36	Schaefer (Billiards)	10.00	5.00	1.00
☐	37	Sears (Lawn Tennis)	10.00	5.00	1.00
☐	38	Sexton (Billiards)	10.00	5.00	1.00
☐	39	Slosson (Billiards)	10.00	5.00	1.00
☐	40	Smith (Pugilist)	25.00	12.50	2.50
☐	41	Steinitz (Chess)	10.00	5.00	1.00
☐	42	Stevens (Bicyclist)	10.00	5.00	1.00
☐	43	Sullivan (Pugilist)	75.00	37.50	7.50
☐	44	Taylor (Lawn Tennis)	10.00	5.00	1.00
☐	45	Teemer (Oarsman)	10.00	5.00	1.00
☐	46	Vignaux (Billiards)	10.00	5.00	1.00
☐	47	Voss (Strongest Man in the World)	10.00	5.00	1.00
☐	48	Wood (Bicyclist)	10.00	5.00	1.00
☐	49	Wood (Jockey)	10.00	5.00	1.00
☐	50	Zukertort (Chess)	10.00	5.00	1.00

N172 Old Judge

The Goodwin Company's baseball series depicts hundreds of ballplayers from more than 40 major and minor league teams as well as boxers and wrestlers. The cards (approximately 1 1/2" by 2 1/2") are actually photographs from the Hall studio in New York which were pasted onto thick cardboard. The pictures are sepia in color with either a white or pink cast, and the cards are blank backed. They are found either numbered or unnumbered, with or without a copyright date, and with hand printed or machine printed names. All known cards have the name "Goodwin Co., New York" at the base.

The cards were marketed during the period 1887-1890 in packs of "Old Judge" and "Gypsy Queen" cigarettes (cards marked with the latter brand are worth double the values listed below). They have been listed alphabetically and assigned numbers in the checklist below for simplicity's sake; the various poses known for some players also have not been listed for the same reason. Some of the players are pictured in horizontal (HOR) poses. In all, more than 2300 different Goodwin cards are known to collectors, with more being discovered every year. Cards from the "Spotted Tie" sub-series are denoted in the checklist below by SPOT.

		NRMT	VG-E	GOOD
COMPLETE SET		50000.	20000.	4000.
COMMON PLAYER		50.00	25.00	5.00
COMMON PLAYER (DOUBLE)		80.00	40.00	8.00
COMMON BROWNS CHAMP		100.00	50.00	10.00
COMMON PLAYER (PCL)		150.00	75.00	15.00
COMMON SPOTTED TIE		225.00	110.00	22.00

			NRMT	VG-E	GOOD
☐	1	Gus Albert: Cleveland-Milwaukee	50.00	25.00	5.00
☐	2	Charles Alcott: St. Louis Whites-Mansfield	50.00	25.00	5.00
☐	3	Alexander: Des Moines	50.00	25.00	5.00
☐	4	Myron Allen: K.C.	50.00	25.00	5.00
☐	5	Bob Allen: Pitts.-Phila. N.L.	50.00	25.00	5.00
☐	6	Uncle Bill Alvord: Toledo-Des Moines	50.00	25.00	5.00
☐	7	Varney Anderson: St.Paul	50.00	25.00	5.00
☐	8	Ed Andrews: Phila.	50.00	25.00	5.00
☐	9	Andrews and Hoover: Philadelphia	80.00	40.00	8.00
☐	10	Wally Andrews: Omaha	50.00	25.00	5.00
☐	11	Bill Annis: Omaha-Worchester	50.00	25.00	5.00
☐	12	Cap Anson: Chicago	600.00	300.00	60.00
☐	13	Old Hoss Ardner: Kansas City-St. Joe	50.00	25.00	5.00
☐	14	Tug Arundel: Indianapolis-Whites	50.00	25.00	5.00
☐	15	Bakley: Jersey-Cleve.	50.00	25.00	5.00
☐	16	Clarence Baldwin: Cincinnati	50.00	25.00	5.00
☐	17	Mark (Fido) Baldwin:	50.00	25.00	5.00

	Chicago-Columbus			
☐ 18	Lady Baldwin:	50.00	25.00	5.00
	Detroit			
☐ 19	James Banning: Wash. ...	50.00	25.00	5.00
☐ 20	Samuel Barkley:	50.00	25.00	5.00
	Pittsburgh-K.C.			
☐ 21	John Barnes:	50.00	25.00	5.00
	Mgr. St. Paul			
☐ 22	Bald Billy Barnie:	80.00	40.00	8.00
	Mgr. Baltimore			
☐ 23	Charles Bassett:	50.00	25.00	5.00
	Indianapolis-N.Y.			
☐ 24	Charles Bastian:	50.00	25.00	5.00
	Phila.-Chicago			
☐ 25	Bastian and Shriver:	80.00	40.00	8.00
	Philadelphia			
☐ 26	Ollie Beard: Cinc.	50.00	25.00	5.00
☐ 27	Ebenezer Beatin:	50.00	25.00	5.00
	Cleve.			
☐ 28	Jake Beckley:	225.00	110.00	22.00
	"Eagle Eye"			
	Whites-Pittsburgh			
☐ 29	Stephen Behel SPOT	225.00	110.00	22.00
☐ 30	Charles Bennett:	50.00	25.00	5.00
	Detroit-Boston			
☐ 31	Louis Bierbauer: A's	50.00	25.00	5.00
☐ 32	Bierbauer and Gamble ...	80.00	40.00	8.00
	Athletics			
☐ 33	Bill Bishop:	50.00	25.00	5.00
	Pittsburgh-Syracuse			
☐ 34	William Blair:	50.00	25.00	5.00
	A's-Hamiltons			
☐ 35	Ned Bligh: Columbus	50.00	25.00	5.00
☐ 36	Bogart: Indianapolis	50.00	25.00	5.00
☐ 37	Boyce: Washington	50.00	25.00	5.00
☐ 38	Jake Boyd: Maroons	50.00	25.00	5.00
☐ 39	Honest John Boyle:	50.00	25.00	5.00
	St. Louis-Chicago			
☐ 40	Handsome Henry Boyle .	50.00	25.00	5.00
	Indianapolis-N.Y.			
☐ 41	Nick Bradley:	50.00	25.00	5.00
	K.C.- Worchester			
☐ 42	George(Grin) Bradley	50.00	25.00	5.00
	Sioux City			
☐ 43	Stephen Brady SPOT	225.00	110.00	22.00
☐ 44	Breckinridge:	150.00	75.00	15.00
	Sacramento PCL			
☐ 45	Jim Brennan:	50.00	25.00	5.00
	Kansas City- A's			
☐ 46	Timothy Brosnan:	50.00	25.00	5.00
	Minn.-Sioux City			
☐ 47	Cal Broughton:	50.00	25.00	5.00
	Detroit-Boston			
☐ 48	Big Dan Brouthers:	225.00	110.00	22.00
	Detroit-Boston			
☐ 49	Thomas Brown:	50.00	25.00	5.00
	Pittsburgh-Boston			
☐ 50	Brown:	50.00	25.00	5.00
	California-N.Y.			
☐ 51	Pete Browning:	100.00	50.00	10.00
	"Gladiator"			
	Louisville			
☐ 52	Charles Brynan:	50.00	25.00	5.00
	Chicago-Des Moines			
☐ 53	Al Buckenberger:	50.00	25.00	5.00
	Mgr. Columbus			
☐ 54	Dick Buckley:	50.00	25.00	5.00
	Indianapolis-N.Y.			
☐ 55	Charles Buffington:	50.00	25.00	5.00
	Philadelphia			
☐ 56	Ernest Burch:	50.00	25.00	5.00
	Brooklyn-Whites			
☐ 57	Bill Burdick:	50.00	25.00	5.00
	Omaha-Indianapolis			
☐ 58	Black Jack Burdock:	50.00	25.00	5.00
	Boston-Brooklyn			
☐ 59	Robert Burks:	50.00	25.00	5.00
	Sioux City			
☐ 60	George(Watch) Burnham	80.00	40.00	8.00
	Mgr. Indianapolis			
☐ 61	Burns: Omaha	50.00	25.00	5.00
☐ 62	Jimmy Burns: K.C.	50.00	25.00	5.00
☐ 63	Tommy (Oyster) Burns ..	50.00	25.00	5.00
	Baltimore-Brooklyn			
☐ 64	Thomas E. Burns:	50.00	25.00	5.00
	Chicago			
☐ 65A	Doc Bushong: Brook. ...	50.00	25.00	5.00
☐ 65B	Doc Bushong:	100.00	50.00	10.00
	Browns Champ			
☐ 66	Patsy Cahill: Ind.	50.00	25.00	5.00
☐ 67	Count Campau:	50.00	25.00	5.00
	Kansas City-Detroit			
☐ 69	Bart Cantz:	50.00	25.00	5.00
	Whites-Baltimore			
☐ 70	Handsome Jack Carney .	50.00	25.00	5.00
	Washington			
☐ 71	Hick Carpenter	50.00	25.00	5.00
	Cincinnati			
☐ 72	Cliff Carroll: Wash.	50.00	25.00	5.00
☐ 73	Scrappy Carroll:	50.00	25.00	5.00
	St.Paul-Chicago			
☐ 74	Frederick Carroll:	50.00	25.00	5.00
	Pitts.			
☐ 75	Jumbo Cartwright:	50.00	25.00	5.00
	Kansas City-St. Joe			
☐ 76A	Bob Caruthers:	80.00	40.00	8.00
	"Parisian"			
	Brooklyn			
☐ 76B	Bob Caruthers:	150.00	75.00	15.00
	"Parisian"			
	Browns Champs			
☐ 77	Daniel Casey: Phila.	50.00	25.00	5.00
☐ 78	Icebox Chamberlain:	50.00	25.00	5.00
	St. Louis			
☐ 79	Cupid Childs:	50.00	25.00	5.00
	Phila.-Syracuse			
☐ 80	Bob Clark:	50.00	25.00	5.00
	Washington			
☐ 81	Owen Clark:	50.00	25.00	5.00
	Washington			
☐ 82	Clarke and Hughes:	80.00	40.00	8.00
	Brooklyn HOR			
☐ 83	William(Dad) Clarke:	50.00	25.00	5.00
	Chicago-Omaha			
☐ 84	John Clarkson:	225.00	110.00	22.00
	Chicago-Boston			
☐ 85	Jack Clements:	50.00	25.00	5.00
	Philadelphia			
☐ 86	Elmer Cleveland:	50.00	25.00	5.00
	Omaha-New York			
☐ 87	Monk Cline:	50.00	25.00	5.00
	K.C.-Sioux City			
☐ 88	Cody: Des Moines	50.00	25.00	5.00
☐ 89	John Coleman:	50.00	25.00	5.00
	Pittsburgh - A's			
☐ 90	Bill Collins:	50.00	25.00	5.00
	New York-Newark			
☐ 91	Hub Collins:	50.00	25.00	5.00
	Louisville-Brooklyn			
☐ 92A	Charles Comiskey:	275.00	135.00	27.00
	Browns Champs			
☐ 92B	Commy Comiskey:	225.00	110.00	22.00
	St. Louis-Chicago			
☐ 93	Pete Connell:	50.00	25.00	5.00
	Des Moines			
☐ 94A	Roger Connor:	225.00	110.00	22.00
	All-Star			
☐ 94B	Roger Connor:	225.00	110.00	22.00
	New York			
☐ 95	Richard Conway:	50.00	25.00	5.00
	Boston-Worchester			
☐ 96	Peter Conway:	50.00	25.00	5.00
	Det.-Pitts.-Ind.			
☐ 97	James Conway: K.C.	50.00	25.00	5.00
☐ 98	Paul Cook:	50.00	25.00	5.00
	Louisville			
☐ 99	Jimmy Cooney:	50.00	25.00	5.00
	Omaha-Chicago			
☐ 100	Larry Corcoran:	50.00	25.00	5.00
	Indianapolis-London			
☐ 101	Pop Corkhill:	50.00	25.00	5.00
	Cincinnnati-Brooklyn			
☐ 102	Roscoe Coughlin:	50.00	25.00	5.00
	Maroons-Chicago			
☐ 103	Cannon Ball Crane:	50.00	25.00	5.00
	New York			
☐ 104	Samuel Crane: Wash.	50.00	25.00	5.00
☐ 105	Jack Crogan: Maroons ...	50.00	25.00	5.00
☐ 106	John Crooks:	50.00	25.00	5.00
	Whites-Omaha			
☐ 107	Lave Cross:	35.00	17.50	3.50
	Louisville-A's-Phila.			
☐ 108	Bill Crossley: Milw.	50.00	25.00	5.00
☐ 109A	Joe Crotty SPOT	225.00	110.00	22.00
☐ 109B	Joe Crotty:	50.00	25.00	5.00
	Sioux City			
☐ 110	Billy Crowell:	50.00	25.00	5.00
	Cleveland-St. Joe			
☐ 111	Jim Cudworth:	50.00	25.00	5.00
	St. Louis-Worchester			
☐ 112	Bert Cunningham:	50.00	25.00	5.00
	Baltimore-Phila.			
☐ 113	Tacks Curtis:	50.00	25.00	5.00
	St. Joe			
☐ 114	Ed Cushman SPOT	225.00	110.00	22.00
☐ 115	Tony Cusick: Mil.	50.00	25.00	5.00
☐ 116	Dailey: Oakland PCL	150.00	75.00	15.00
☐ 117	Edward Dailey:	50.00	25.00	5.00
	Phil.-Wash.-Columbus			

☐ 118	Bill Daley: Boston	50.00	25.00	5.00
☐ 119	Con Daley:	50.00	25.00	5.00
	Boston-Indianapolis			
☐ 120	Abner Dalrymple:	50.00	25.00	5.00
	Pittsburgh-Denver			
☐ 121	Tom Daly:	50.00	25.00	5.00
	Chicago-Wash.-Cleve.			
☐ 122	James Daly: Minn.	50.00	25.00	5.00
☐ 123	Law Daniels: K.C.	50.00	25.00	5.00
☐ 124	Dell Darling:	50.00	25.00	5.00
	Chicago			
☐ 125	Wm. Darnbrough:	50.00	25.00	5.00
	Denver			
☐ 126	D. Davin: Milwaukee	50.00	25.00	5.00
☐ 127	Jumbo Davis: K.C.	50.00	25.00	5.00
☐ 128	Pat Dealey: Wash.	50.00	25.00	5.00
☐ 129	Thomas Deasley:	50.00	25.00	5.00
	New York-Washington			
☐ 130	Edward Decker: Phil.	50.00	25.00	5.00
☐ 131	Big Ed Delahanty:	300.00	150.00	30.00
	Philadelphia			
☐ 132	Jeremiah Denny:	50.00	25.00	5.00
	Indianapolis-New York			
☐ 133	James Devlin: St.L.	50.00	25.00	5.00
☐ 134	Thomas Dolan:	50.00	25.00	5.00
	Whites-			
	St. Louis-Denver			
☐ 135	Jack Donahue:	150.00	75.00	15.00
	San Francisco PCL			
☐ 136A	James Donahue SPOT .	225.00	110.00	22.00
☐ 136B	James Donahue: K.C.	50.00	25.00	5.00
☐ 137	James Donnelly:	50.00	25.00	5.00
	Washington			
☐ 138	Dooley: Oakland PCL	150.00	75.00	15.00
☐ 139	J. Doran: Omaha	50.00	25.00	5.00
☐ 140	Michael Dorgan: N.Y.	50.00	25.00	5.00
☐ 141	Doyle: San Fran. PCL	150.00	75.00	15.00
☐ 142	Homerun Duffe: St.L.	50.00	25.00	5.00
☐ 143	Hugh Duffy: Chicago	225.00	110.00	22.00
☐ 144	Dan Dugdale:	50.00	25.00	5.00
	Maroons-Minneapolis			
☐ 145	Dugrahm: Maroons	50.00	25.00	5.00
☐ 146	Duck Duke: Minn.	50.00	25.00	5.00
☐ 147	Sure Shot Dunlap:	50.00	25.00	5.00
	Pittsburgh			
☐ 148	J. Dunn: Maroons	50.00	25.00	5.00
☐ 149	Jesse(Cyclone)Duryea ...	50.00	25.00	5.00
	St. Paul-Cinc.			
☐ 150	John Dwyer:	50.00	25.00	5.00
	Chicago-Maroons			
☐ 151	Billy Earle:	50.00	25.00	5.00
	Cincinnati-St.Paul			
☐ 152	Buck Ebright: Wash.	50.00	25.00	5.00
☐ 153	Red Ehret:	50.00	25.00	5.00
	Louisville			
☐ 154	R. Emmerke:	50.00	25.00	5.00
	Des Moines			
☐ 155	Dude Esterbrook:	50.00	25.00	5.00
	Louisville-Ind.-			
	New York-All Star			
☐ 156	Henry Esterday:	50.00	25.00	5.00
	K.C.-Columbus			
☐ 157	Long John Ewing:	50.00	25.00	5.00
	Louisville-A's			
☐ 158	Buck Ewing: New York ...	225.00	110.00	22.00
☐ 159	Ewing and Mascot:	150.00	75.00	15.00
	New York			
☐ 160	Jay Faatz: Cleveland	50.00	25.00	5.00
☐ 161	Clinkgers Fagan:	50.00	25.00	5.00
	Kansas City-Denver			
☐ 162	William Farmer:	50.00	25.00	5.00
	Pittsburgh-St. Paul			
☐ 163	Sidney Farrar:	50.00	25.00	5.00
	Philadelphia			
☐ 164	John(Moose) Farrell:	50.00	25.00	5.00
	Wash.-Baltimore			
☐ 165	Charles(Duke)Farrell	50.00	25.00	5.00
	Chicago			
☐ 166	Frank Fennelly:	50.00	25.00	5.00
	Cincinnati-A's			
☐ 167	Chas. Ferguson:	50.00	25.00	5.00
	Phila.			
☐ 168	Colonel Ferson:	50.00	25.00	5.00
	Washington			
☐ 169	Wallace Fessenden:	80.00	40.00	8.00
	Umpire National			
☐ 170	Jocko Fields: Pitts.	50.00	25.00	5.00
☐ 171	Fischer: Maroons	50.00	25.00	5.00
☐ 172	Thomas Flanigan:	50.00	25.00	5.00
	Cleve.-Sioux City			
☐ 173	Silver Flint:	50.00	25.00	5.00
	Chicago			
☐ 174	Thomas Flood:	50.00	25.00	5.00
	St. Joe			
☐ 175	Flynn: Omaha	50.00	25.00	5.00

☐ 176	James Fogarty:	50.00	25.00	5.00
	Philadelphia			
☐ 177	Frank(Monkey)Foreman .	50.00	25.00	5.00
	Baltimore-Cinc.			
☐ 178	Thomas Forster:	50.00	25.00	5.00
	Milwaukee-Hartford			
☐ 179A	Elmer E. Foster	225.00	110.00	22.00
	SPOT			
☐ 179B	Elmer Foster:	50.00	25.00	5.00
	New York-Chicago			
☐ 180	F.W. Foster SPOT	225.00	110.00	22.00
	T.W. Forster (sic)			
☐ 181A	Scissors Foutz:	100.00	50.00	10.00
	Browns Champ			
☐ 181B	Scissors Foutz:	50.00	25.00	5.00
	Brooklyn			
☐ 182	Julie Freeman:	50.00	25.00	5.00
	St.L.-Milwaukee			
☐ 183	Will Fry: St. Joe	50.00	25.00	5.00
☐ 184	Fudger: Oakland PCL	150.00	75.00	15.00
☐ 185	William Fuller:	50.00	25.00	5.00
	Milwaukee			
☐ 186	Shorty Fuller:	50.00	25.00	5.00
	St.Louis			
☐ 187	Christopher Fullmer:	50.00	25.00	5.00
	Baltimore			
☐ 188	Fullmer and Tucker:	80.00	40.00	8.00
	Baltimore HOR			
☐ 189	Honest John Gaffney:	80.00	40.00	8.00
	Mgr. Washington			
☐ 190	Pud Galvin: Pitts.	225.00	110.00	22.00
☐ 191	Robert Gamble: A's	50.00	25.00	5.00
☐ 192	Charles Ganzel:	50.00	25.00	5.00
	Detroit-Boston			
☐ 193	Frank (Gid) Gardner:	50.00	25.00	5.00
	Phila.-Washington			
☐ 194	Gardner and Murray:	80.00	40.00	8.00
	Washington HOR			
☐ 195	Ed Gastfield: Omaha	50.00	25.00	5.00
☐ 196	Hank Gastreich:	50.00	25.00	5.00
	Columbus			
☐ 197	Emil Geiss: Chicago	50.00	25.00	5.00
☐ 198	Frenchy Genins:	50.00	25.00	5.00
	Sioux City			
☐ 199	William George: N.Y.	50.00	25.00	5.00
☐ 200	Move Up Joe Gerhardt ..	50.00	25.00	5.00
	All Star-Jersey City			
☐ 201	Pretzels Getzein:	50.00	25.00	5.00
	Detroit-Ind.			
☐ 202	Robert Gilks: Cleve.	50.00	25.00	5.00
☐ 203	Pete Gillespie: N.Y.	50.00	25.00	5.00
☐ 204	Barney Gilligan :	50.00	25.00	5.00
	Washington-Detroit			
☐ 205	Frank Gilmore: Wash.	50.00	25.00	5.00
☐ 206	Lee Gisbon: A's	50.00	25.00	5.00
☐ 207	Pebbly Jack Glasscock ...	80.00	40.00	8.00
	Indianapolis-N.Y.			
☐ 208	Kid Gleason: Phila.	50.00	25.00	5.00
☐ 209A	Brother Bill Gleason	50.00	25.00	5.00
	A's-Louisville			
☐ 209B	William Bill Gleason	100.00	50.00	10.00
	Browns Champs			
☐ 210	Mouse Glenn:	50.00	25.00	5.00
	Sioux City			
☐ 211	Walt Goldsby: Balt.	50.00	25.00	5.00
☐ 212	Michael Goodfellow:	50.00	25.00	5.00
	Cleveland-Detroit			
☐ 213	George Pianolegs Gore ..	50.00	25.00	5.00
	New York			
☐ 214	Frank Graves: Minn.	50.00	25.00	5.00
☐ 215	William Greenwood:	50.00	25.00	5.00
	Baltimore-Columbus			
☐ 216	Michael Greer:	50.00	25.00	5.00
	Cleveland-Brooklyn			
☐ 217	Mike Griffin:	50.00	25.00	5.00
	Baltimore-Phila NL			
☐ 218	Clark Griffith: Milw.	250.00	125.00	25.00
☐ 219	Henry Gruber: Cleve.	50.00	25.00	5.00
☐ 220	Addison Gumbert:	50.00	25.00	5.00
	Chicago-Boston			
☐ 221	Thomas Gunning:	50.00	25.00	5.00
	Philadelphia-A's			
☐ 222	Joseph Gunson: K.C.	50.00	25.00	5.00
☐ 223	George Haddock:	50.00	25.00	5.00
	Washington			
☐ 224	William Hafner: K.C.	50.00	25.00	5.00
☐ 225	Willie Hahm:	50.00	25.00	5.00
	Chicago Mascot			
☐ 226	William Hallman:	50.00	25.00	5.00
	Philadelphia			
☐ 227	Charlie Hallstrom:	50.00	25.00	5.00
	Minn.			
☐ 228	Billy Hamilton:	250.00	125.00	25.00
	Kansas City-Phila.			
☐ 229	Hamm and Williamson: ...	80.00	40.00	8.00

230B	Frank Hankinson: Kansas City	50.00	25.00	5.00
231	Ned Hanlon: Det.-Boston-Pitts.	80.00	40.00	8.00
232	William Hanrahan: Maroons-Minn.	50.00	25.00	5.00
233	Hapeman: Sacramento PCL	150.00	75.00	15.00
234	Pa Harkins: Brooklyn-Baltimore	50.00	25.00	5.00
235	William Hart: Cinc.-Des Moines	50.00	25.00	5.00
236	Wm. Hasamdear: K.C.	50.00	25.00	5.00
237	Colonel Hatfield: New York	50.00	25.00	5.00
238	Egyptian Healey: Wash.-Indianapolis	50.00	25.00	5.00
239	J.C. Healy: Omaha-Denver	50.00	25.00	5.00
240	Guy Hecker: Louisville	50.00	25.00	5.00
241	Tony Hellman: Sioux City	50.00	25.00	5.00
242	Hardie Henderson: Brook.-Pitts.-Balt.	50.00	25.00	5.00
243	Henderson and Greer: Brooklyn	80.00	40.00	8.00
244	Moxie Hengle: Maroons-Minneapolis	50.00	25.00	5.00
245	John Henry: Phila.	50.00	25.00	5.00
246	Edward Herr: Whites-Milwaukee	50.00	25.00	5.00
247	Hunkey Hines: Whites	50.00	25.00	5.00
248	Paul Hines: Wash.-Indianapolis	50.00	25.00	5.00
249	Texas Wonder Hoffman: Denver	50.00	25.00	5.00
250	Eddie Hogan: Cleve.	50.00	25.00	5.00
251A	William Holbert SPOT	225.00	110.00	22.00
251B	William Holbert: Brooklyn-Mets-Jersey City	50.00	25.00	5.00
252	James(Bugs) Holliday: Des Moines-Cinc.	50.00	25.00	5.00
253	Charles Hoover: Maroons-Chi.-K.C.	50.00	25.00	5.00
254	Buster Hoover: Phila.-Toronto	50.00	25.00	5.00
255	Jack Horner: Milwaukee-New Haven	50.00	25.00	5.00
256	Horner and Warner: Milwaukee	80.00	40.00	8.00
257	Michael Horning: Boston-Balt.-N.Y.	50.00	25.00	5.00
258	Pete Hotaling: Cleveland	50.00	25.00	5.00
259	William Howes: Minn..-St. Paul	50.00	25.00	5.00
260	Dummy Hoy: Washington	100.00	50.00	10.00
261A	Nat Hudson: Browns Champ	100.00	50.00	10.00
261B	Nat Hudson: St. Louis	50.00	25.00	5.00
262	Mickey Hughes: Brk.	50.00	25.00	5.00
263	Hungler: Sioux City	50.00	25.00	5.00
264	Wild Bill Hutchinson: Chicago	50.00	25.00	5.00
265	John Irwin: Wash.-Wilkes Barre	50.00	25.00	5.00
266	Cutrate Irwin: Phila.-Boston-Wash.	50.00	25.00	5.00
267	A.C. Jantzen: Minn.	50.00	25.00	5.00
268	Frederick Jevne: Minn.-St. Paul	50.00	25.00	5.00
269	John Johnson: K.C.-Columbus	50.00	25.00	5.00
270	Richard Johnston: Boston	50.00	25.00	5.00
271	Jordan: Minneapolis	50.00	25.00	5.00
272	Heinie Kappell: Columbus-Cincinnati	50.00	25.00	5.00
273	Keas: Milwaukee	50.00	25.00	5.00
274	Sir Timothy Keefe: New York	225.00	110.00	22.00
275	Keefe and Richardson Stealing 2nd Base New York HOR	150.00	75.00	15.00
276	George Keefe: Wash.	50.00	25.00	5.00
277	James Keenan: Cinc.	50.00	25.00	5.00
278	Mike (King) Kelly "10,000" Chic-Boston	350.00	175.00	35.00
279	Honest John Kelly: Mgr. Louisville	80.00	40.00	8.00
280	Kelly: (Umpire) Western Association	80.00	40.00	8.00
281	Charles Kelly: Philadelphia	50.00	25.00	5.00
282	Kelly and Powell: Umpire and Manager Sioux City	80.00	40.00	8.00
283A	Rudolph Kemmler: Browns Champ	100.00	50.00	10.00
283B	Rudolph Kemmler: St. Paul	50.00	25.00	5.00
284	Theodore Kennedy: Des Moines-Omaha	50.00	25.00	5.00
285	J.J. Kenyon: Whites-Des Moines	50.00	25.00	5.00
286	John Kerins: Louisville	50.00	25.00	5.00
287	Matthew Kilroy: Baltimore-Boston	50.00	25.00	5.00
288	Charles King: St.L.-Chi.	50.00	25.00	5.00
289	Aug. Kloff: Minn.-St.Joe	50.00	25.00	5.00
290	William Klusman: Milwaukee-Denver	50.00	25.00	5.00
291	Phillip Knell: St. Joe-Phila.	50.00	25.00	5.00
292	Fred Knouf: St. Louis	50.00	25.00	5.00
293	Charles Kremmeyer: Sacramento PCL	150.00	75.00	15.00
294	William Krieg: Wash.-St. Joe-Minn.	50.00	25.00	5.00
295	Krieg and Kloff: Minneapolis	80.00	40.00	8.00
296	Gus Krock: Chicago	50.00	25.00	5.00
297	Willie Kuehne: Pittsburgh	50.00	25.00	5.00
298	Frederick Lange: Maroons	50.00	25.00	5.00
299	Ted Larkin: A's	50.00	25.00	5.00
300A	Arlie Latham: Browns Champ	100.00	50.00	10.00
300B	Arlie Latham: St. Louis-Chicago	80.00	40.00	8.00
301	John Lauer: Pittsburgh	50.00	25.00	5.00
302	Lawless: Columbus	50.00	25.00	5.00
303	John Leighton: Omaha	50.00	25.00	5.00
304	Levy: San Fran. PCL	150.00	75.00	15.00
305	Tom Loftus MG: Whites-Cleveland	50.00	25.00	5.00
306	Lohbeck: Cleveland	50.00	25.00	5.00
308	Danny Long: Oak. PCL	150.00	75.00	15.00
309	Tom Lovett: Omaha-Brooklyn	50.00	25.00	5.00
310	Bobby (Link) Lowe: Milwaukee	100.00	50.00	10.00
311A	Jack Lynch SPOT	225.00	110.00	22.00
311B	John Lynch: All Stars	50.00	25.00	5.00
312	Dennis Lyons: A's	50.00	25.00	5.00
313	Harry Lyons: St. L.	50.00	25.00	5.00
314	Connie Mack: Wash.	450.00	225.00	45.00
315	Joe (Reddie) Mack: Louisville	50.00	25.00	5.00
316	James (Little Mack) Macullar: Des Moines-Milwaukee	50.00	25.00	5.00
317	Kid Madden: Boston	50.00	25.00	5.00
318	Daniel Mahoney: St. Joe	50.00	25.00	5.00
319	Willard(Grasshopper) Maines: St. Paul	50.00	25.00	5.00
320	Fred Mann: St.Louis-Hartford	50.00	25.00	5.00
321	Jimmy Manning: K.C.	50.00	25.00	5.00
322	Charles(Lefty) Marr: Col.-Cinc.	50.00	25.00	5.00
323	Mascot (Willie Breslin): New York	80.00	40.00	8.00
324	Samuel Maskery: Milwaukee-Des Moines	50.00	25.00	5.00
325	Bobby Mathews: A's	50.00	25.00	5.00
326	Michael Mattimore: New York-A's	50.00	25.00	5.00
327	Albert Maul: Pitts.	50.00	25.00	5.00
328A	Albert Mays SPOT	225.00	110.00	22.00
328B	Albert Mays: Columbus	50.00	25.00	5.00
329	James McAleer: Cleveland	50.00	25.00	5.00
330	Thomas McCarthy: Phila.-St. Louis	225.00	110.00	22.00

☐ 331	John McCarthy: K.C.	50.00	25.00	5.00
☐ 332	James McCauley: .... Maroons-Phila.	50.00	25.00	5.00
☐ 333	William McClellan: .... Brooklyn-Denver	50.00	25.00	5.00
☐ 334	John McCormack: .... Whites	50.00	25.00	5.00
☐ 335	Big Jim McCormick: .... Chicago-Pittsburgh	50.00	25.00	5.00
☐ 336	McCreachery: .... Mgr. Indianapolis	80.00	40.00	8.00
☐ 337	Thomas McCullum· .... Minneapolis	50.00	25.00	5.00
☐ 338	James(Chippy)McGarr: .. St. Louis-K.C.	50.00	25.00	5.00
☐ 339	Jack McGeachy: Ind.	50.00	25.00	5.00
☐ 340	John McGlone: .... Cleveland-Detroit	50.00	25.00	5.00
☐ 341	James(Deacon)McGuire . Phila.-Toronto	50.00	25.00	5.00
☐ 342	Bill (Gunner) .... McGunnigle: Mgr. Brooklyn	80.00	40.00	8.00
☐ 343	Ed McKean: Cleveland ...	50.00	25.00	5.00
☐ 344	Alex McKinnon: .... Pittsburgh	50.00	25.00	5.00
☐ 345	Thomas McLaughlin .... SPOT	225.00	110.00	22.00
☐ 346	John (Bid) McPhee: .... Cincinnati	50.00	25.00	5.00
☐ 347	James McQuaid: .... Denver	50.00	25.00	5.00
☐ 348	John McQuaid: .... Umpire Amer. Assoc.	80.00	40.00	8.00
☐ 349	Jame McTamany: .... Brook.-Col.-K.C.	50.00	25.00	5.00
☐ 350	George McVey: .... Mil.-Denver-St. Joe	50.00	25.00	5.00
☐ 351	Meegan: San Fran. PCL ..	150.00	75.00	15.00
☐ 352	John Messitt: Omaha	50.00	25.00	5.00
☐ 353	George(Doggie)Miller ..... Pittsburgh	50.00	25.00	5.00
☐ 354	Joseph Miller: .... Omaha-Minneapolis	50.00	25.00	5.00
☐ 355	Jocko Milligan: .... St. Louis-Phila.	50.00	25.00	5.00
☐ 356	E.L. Mills: .... Milwaukee	50.00	25.00	5.00
☐ 357	Minnehan: .... Minneapolis	50.00	25.00	5.00
☐ 358	Samuel Moffet: Ind.	50.00	25.00	5.00
☐ 359	Honest Morrill: .... Boston-Washington	50.00	25.00	5.00
☐ 360	Ed(Cannonball)Morris ..... Pittsburgh	50.00	25.00	5.00
☐ 361	Morrisey: St. Paul	50.00	25.00	5.00
☐ 362	Tony(Count) Mullane: ..... Cincinnati	50.00	25.00	5.00
☐ 363	Joseph Mulvey: .... Philadelphia	50.00	25.00	5.00
☐ 364	P.L. Murphy: St. Paul	50.00	25.00	5.00
☐ 365	P.J. Murphy: New York ..	50.00	25.00	5.00
☐ 366	Miah Murray: Wash.	50.00	25.00	5.00
☐ 367	James (Truthful) .... Mutrie: Mgr. N.Y.	50.00	25.00	5.00
☐ 368	George Myers: .... Indianapolis-Phila.	50.00	25.00	5.00
☐ 369	Al (Cod) Myers: .... Washington	50.00	25.00	5.00
☐ 370	Thomas Nagle: .... Omaha-Chi.	50.00	25.00	5.00
☐ 371	Billy Nash: Boston	50.00	25.00	5.00
☐ 372	Jack (Candy) Nelson: ..... SPOT	225.00	110.00	22.00
☐ 373	Kid Nichols: Omaha	300.00	150.00	30.00
☐ 374	Samuel Nichols: .... Pittsburgh	50.00	25.00	5.00
☐ 375	J.W. Nicholson .... Maroons-Minn.	50.00	25.00	5.00
☐ 376	Tom(Parson)Nicholson ... Whites-Cleveland	50.00	25.00	5.00
☐ 377A	Nicholls Nicol .... Browns Champ	100.00	50.00	10.00
☐ 377B	Hugh Nicol: Cinc.	50.00	25.00	5.00
☐ 378	Nicol and Reilly: .... Cincinnati	80.00	40.00	8.00
☐ 379	Frederick Nyce .... Whites-Burlington	50.00	25.00	5.00
☐ 380	Doc Oberlander .... Cleveland-Syracuse	50.00	25.00	5.00
☐ 381	Jack O'Brien .... Brooklyn-Baltimore	50.00	25.00	5.00
☐ 382	William O'Brien: .... Washington	50.00	25.00	5.00
☐ 383	O'Brien and Irwin:	80.00	40.00	8.00
☐ 384	Darby O'Brien: .... Brooklyn	50.00	25.00	5.00
☐ 385	John O'Brien: Cleve.	50.00	25.00	5.00
☐ 386	P.J. O'Connell: .... Omaha-Des Moines	50.00	25.00	5.00
☐ 387	John O'Connor: .... Cincinnati-Columbus	50.00	25.00	5.00
☐ 388	Hank O'Day: .... Washington-New York	50.00	25.00	5.00
☐ 389A	James O'Neil: .... St. Louis-Chicago	50.00	25.00	5.00
☐ 389B	James O'Neil: .... Browns Champs	100.00	50.00	10.00
☐ 390	O'Neill: Oakland PCL	150.00	75.00	15.00
☐ 391	Orator O'Rourke: .... New York	225.00	110.00	22.00
☐ 392	Thomas O'Rourke: .... Boston-Jersey City	50.00	25.00	5.00
☐ 393A	David Orr SPOT	225.00	110.00	22.00
☐ 393B	David Orr: All Star- ...... Brooklyn-Columbus	50.00	25.00	5.00
☐ 394	Parsons: Minneapolis	50.00	25.00	5.00
☐ 395	Owen Patton: .... Minn.-Des Moines	50.00	25.00	5.00
☐ 396	James Peeples: .... Brooklyn-Columbus	50.00	25.00	5.00
☐ 397	Peeples and Henderson . Brooklyn	80.00	40.00	8.00
☐ 398	Hip Perrier: .... San Francisco PCL	150.00	75.00	15.00
☐ 399	Patrick Pettee: .... Milwaukee-London	50.00	25.00	5.00
☐ 400	Pettee and Lowe: .... Milwaukee	80.00	40.00	8.00
☐ 401	Bob Pettit: Chicago	50.00	25.00	5.00
☐ 402	Dandelion Pfeffer: .... Chi.	50.00	25.00	5.00
☐ 403	Dick Phelan: .... Des Moines	50.00	25.00	5.00
☐ 404	William Phillips: .... Brooklyn-Kansas City	50.00	25.00	5.00
☐ 405	Horace Phillips: .... Pittsburgh	50.00	25.00	5.00
☐ 406	John Pickett: .... St. Paul-K.C.-Phila.	50.00	25.00	5.00
☐ 407	George Pinkney: .... Brooklyn	50.00	25.00	5.00
☐ 408	Thomas Poorman: .... A's-Milwaukee	50.00	25.00	5.00
☐ 409	Henry Porter: .... Brooklyn-Kansas City	50.00	25.00	5.00
☐ 410	James Powell: .... Sioux City	50.00	25.00	5.00
☐ 411	Tom Powers: .... San Francisco PCL	150.00	75.00	15.00
☐ 412	Bill Blonie Purcell: .... Baltimore-A's	50.00	25.00	5.00
☐ 413	Thomas Quinn: .... Baltimore	50.00	25.00	5.00
☐ 414	Joseph Quinn: .... Des Moines-Boston	50.00	25.00	5.00
☐ 415	Old Hoss Radbourne: ..... Boston	225.00	110.00	22.00
☐ 416	Shorty Radford: .... Brooklyn-Cleveland	50.00	25.00	5.00
☐ 417	Tom Ramsey: .... Louisville	50.00	25.00	5.00
☐ 418	Rehse: Minneapolis	50.00	25.00	5.00
☐ 419	Long John Reilly: .... Cincinnati	50.00	25.00	5.00
☐ 420	Charles Reilly: .... (Princeton) St.Paul	50.00	25.00	5.00
☐ 421	Charles Reynolds: .... Kansas City	50.00	25.00	5.00
☐ 422	Hardie Richardson .... Detroit-Boston	50.00	25.00	5.00
☐ 423	Danny Richardson: .... New York	50.00	25.00	5.00
☐ 424	Frank Ringo: .... St. Paul	50.00	25.00	5.00
☐ 425	Charles Ripslager .... SPOT	225.00	110.00	22.00
☐ 426	John Roach: New York ...	50.00	25.00	5.00
☐ 427	Wilbert Robinson .... (Uncle Robbie): A's	250.00	125.00	25.00
☐ 428	M.C. Robinson: Minn.	50.00	25.00	5.00
☐ 429A	Yank Robinson: .... St. Louis	50.00	25.00	5.00
☐ 429B	Wm.(Yank) Robinson: .. Browns Champs	100.00	50.00	10.00
☐ 430	George Rooks: .... Maroons-Detroit	50.00	25.00	5.00
☐ 431	James(Chief) Roseman .. SPOT	225.00	110.00	22.00

432	Davis Rowe: Mgr. K.C.-Denver	50.00	25.00	5.00
433	Jack Rowe: Detroit-Pittsburgh	50.00	25.00	5.00
434	Amos (Hoosier Thunderbolt) Rusie: Ind.-New York	350.00	175.00	35.00
435	James Ryan: Chicago	50.00	25.00	5.00
436	Henry Sage: Des Moines-Toledo	50.00	25.00	5.00
437	Sage and Van Dyke: Des Moines-Toledo	80.00	40.00	8.00
438	Frank Salee Omaha-Boston	50.00	25.00	5.00
439	Sanders: Omaha	50.00	25.00	5.00
440	Al (Ben) Sanders: Philadelphia	50.00	25.00	5.00
441	Frank Scheibeck: Detroit	50.00	25.00	5.00
442	Albert Schellhase: St. Joseph	50.00	25.00	5.00
443	William Schenkle: Milwaukee	50.00	25.00	5.00
444	Bill Schildknecht: Des Moines-Milwaukee	50.00	25.00	5.00
445	Gus "Pink Whiskers" Schmelz Mgr. Cincinnati	50.00	25.00	5.00
446	R. F. Schoch: Wash.	50.00	25.00	5.00
447	Lewis(Jumbo)Schoeneck Maroons-Indianapolis	50.00	25.00	5.00
448	Pop Schriver: Phila.	50.00	25.00	5.00
449	John Seery: Ind.	50.00	25.00	5.00
450	William Serad Cincinnati-Toronto	50.00	25.00	5.00
451	Edward Seward: A's	50.00	25.00	5.00
452	George(Orator)Shafer Des Moines	50.00	25.00	5.00
453	Frank Shafer: St. Paul	50.00	25.00	5.00
454	Daniel Shannon: Omaha-L'ville-Phila.	50.00	25.00	5.00
455	William Sharsig: Mgr. Athletics	80.00	40.00	8.00
456	Samuel Shaw: Baltimore-Newark	50.00	25.00	5.00
457	John Shaw: Minneapolis	50.00	25.00	5.00
458	William Shindle: Baltimore-Phila.	50.00	25.00	5.00
459	George Shock: Wash.	50.00	25.00	5.00
460	Otto Shomberg: Ind.	50.00	25.00	5.00
461	Lev Shreve: Ind.	50.00	25.00	5.00
462	Ed (Baldy) Silch: Brooklyn-Denver	50.00	25.00	5.00
463	Michael Slattery: New York	50.00	25.00	5.00
464	Sam(Skyrocket)Smith: Louisville	50.00	25.00	5.00
465	John "Phenomenal" Smith: Balt.-A's	80.00	40.00	8.00
466	Elmer Smith: Cincinnati	50.00	25.00	5.00
467	Fred (Sam) Smith: Des Moines	50.00	25.00	5.00
468	George(Germany)Smith Brooklyn	50.00	25.00	5.00
469	Pop Smith: Pitt.-Bos.-Phila.	50.00	25.00	5.00
470	Nick Smith: St. Joe	50.00	25.00	5.00
471	Pop Snyder: Cleve.	50.00	25.00	5.00
472	P.T. Somers: St. Louis	50.00	25.00	5.00
473	Joe Sommer: Balt.	50.00	25.00	5.00
474	Pete Sommers: Chicago-New York	50.00	25.00	5.00
475	William Sowders: Boston-Pittsburgh	50.00	25.00	5.00
476	John Sowders: St. Paul-Kansas City	50.00	25.00	5.00
477	Charles Sprague: Maroons-Chi.-Cleve.	50.00	25.00	5.00
478	Edward Sproat: Whites	50.00	25.00	5.00
479	Harry Staley: Whites-Pittsburgh	50.00	25.00	5.00
480	Daniel Stearns: Des Moines-K.C.	50.00	25.00	5.00
481	Billy "Cannonball" Stemmyer: Boston-Cleveland	50.00	25.00	5.00
482	Stengel: Columbus	50.00	25.00	5.00
483	B.F. Stephens: Milw.	50.00	25.00	5.00
484	John C. Sterling: Minneapolis	50.00	25.00	5.00
485	Stockwell: S.F. PCL	150.00	75.00	15.00
486	Harry Stovey: A's-Boston	150.00	75.00	15.00
487	C. Scott Stratton: Louisville	50.00	25.00	5.00
488	Joseph Straus: Omaha-Milwaukee	50.00	25.00	5.00
489	John (Cub) Stricker: Cleveland	50.00	25.00	5.00
490	J.O. Struck: Milw.	50.00	25.00	5.00
491	Marty Sullivan: Chicago-Ind.	50.00	25.00	5.00
492	Michael Sullivan: A's	50.00	25.00	5.00
493	Billy Sunday: Chicago-Pittsburgh	225.00	110.00	22.00
494	Sy Sutcliffe: Cleve.	50.00	25.00	5.00
495	Ezra Sutton: Boston-Milwaukee	50.00	25.00	5.00
496	Ed Cyrus Swartwood: Brook.-D.Moines-Ham.	50.00	25.00	5.00
497	Parke Swartzel: K.C.	50.00	25.00	5.00
498	Peter Sweeney: Wash.	50.00	25.00	5.00
499	Sylvester: Sacra. PCL	150.00	75.00	15.00
500	Ed (Dimples) Tate: Boston-Baltimore	50.00	25.00	5.00
501	Patsy Tebeau: Chi.-Cleve.-Minn.	50.00	25.00	5.00
502	John Tener: Chicago	80.00	40.00	8.00
503	Bill (Adonis) Terry: Brooklyn	50.00	25.00	5.00
504	Big Sam Thompson: Detroit-Philadelphia	225.00	110.00	22.00
505	Silent Mike Tiernan: New York	50.00	25.00	5.00
506	Ledell Titcomb: N.Y.	50.00	25.00	5.00
507	Phillip Tomney: Louisville	50.00	25.00	5.00
508	Stephen Toole: Brooklyn-K.C.-Rochester	50.00	25.00	5.00
509	George Townsend: A's	50.00	25.00	5.00
510	William Traffley: Des Moines	50.00	25.00	5.00
511	George Treadway: St. Paul-Denver	50.00	25.00	5.00
512	Samuel Trott: Baltimore-Newark	50.00	25.00	5.00
513	Trott and Burns: Baltimore HOR	80.00	40.00	8.00
514	Tom(Foghorn) Tucker: Baltimore	50.00	25.00	5.00
515	William Tuckerman: St. Paul	50.00	25.00	5.00
516	Turner: Minneapolis	50.00	25.00	5.00
517	Lawrence Twitchell: Detroit-Cleveland	50.00	25.00	5.00
518	James Tyng: Phila.	50.00	25.00	5.00
519	William Van Dyke: Des Moines-Toledo	50.00	25.00	5.00
520	George Rip VanHaltren Chicago	50.00	25.00	5.00
521	Harry(Farmer)Vaughn: Louisville-New York	50.00	25.00	5.00
522	Peek-a-Boo Veach: St. Paul	50.00	25.00	5.00
523	Veach: Sacra. PCL	150.00	75.00	15.00
524	Leon Viau: Cincinnati	50.00	25.00	5.00
525	John Vinton: Minneapolis	50.00	25.00	5.00
526	Joseph Visner: Brooklyn	50.00	25.00	5.00
527	Christian VonDer Ahe Owner Browns Champs	175.00	85.00	18.00
528	Joseph Walsh: Omaha	50.00	25.00	5.00
529	John (Monte) Ward: New York	225.00	110.00	22.00
530	E.H. Warner: Milwaukee	50.00	25.00	5.00
531	William Watkins: Mgr. Detroit-Kansas City	80.00	40.00	8.00
532	Bill(Farmer) Weaver: Louisville	50.00	25.00	5.00
533	Charles Weber: Sioux City	50.00	25.00	5.00
535	William Weidner: Columbus	50.00	25.00	5.00
536A	Curtis Welch: Browns Champ	100.00	50.00	10.00
536B	Curtis Welch: A's	50.00	25.00	5.00
537	Welch and Gleason: Athletics	80.00	40.00	8.00
538	Smilin'Mickey Welch: All Star-New York	225.00	110.00	22.00

☐ 539	Jake Wells: K.C.	50.00	25.00	5.00
☐ 540	Frank Wells: .... Des Moines-Mil.	80.00	40.00	8.00
☐ 541	Joseph Werrick: .... Louisville-St. Paul	50.00	25.00	5.00
☐ 542	Milton (Buck) West: .... Minneapolis	50.00	25.00	5.00
☐ 543	Gus "Cannonball" .... Weyhing: A's	50.00	25.00	5.00
☐ 544	John Weyhing: .... Athletics-Columbus	50.00	25.00	5.00
☐ 545	Bobby Wheelock: .... Boston-Detroit	50.00	25.00	5.00
☐ 546	Whitacre: A's	50.00	25.00	5.00
☐ 547	Pat Whitaker: Balt.	50.00	25.00	5.00
☐ 548	Deacon White: .... Detroit-Pittsburgh	50.00	25.00	5.00
☐ 549	William White: .... Louisville	50.00	25.00	5.00
☐ 550	Jim "Grasshopper" .... Whitney: Wash.-Indianapolis	50.00	25.00	5.00
☐ 551	Arthur Whitney: .... Pittsburgh-New York	50.00	25.00	5.00
☐ 552	G.Whitney: .... St. Joseph	50.00	25.00	5.00
☐ 553	James Williams: .... Mgr. Cleveland	80.00	40.00	8.00
☐ 554	Ned Williamson: Chi.	80.00	40.00	8.00
☐ 555	Williamson and Mascot ...	80.00	40.00	8.00
☐ 556	C.H. Willis: Omaha	50.00	25.00	5.00
☐ 557	Walt Wilmot: .... Washington-Chicago	50.00	25.00	5.00
☐ 558	George Winkleman: .... Minneapolis-Hartford	50.00	25.00	5.00
☐ 559	Samuel Wise: .... Boston-Washington	50.00	25.00	5.00
☐ 560	William(Chicken)Wolf ...... Louisville	50.00	25.00	5.00
☐ 561	George (Dandy) Wood: .... Philadelphia	50.00	25.00	5.00
☐ 562	Peter Wood: Phila.	50.00	25.00	5.00
☐ 563	Harry Wright: .... Mgr. Philadelphia	450.00	225.00	45.00
☐ 564	Charles(Chief)Zimmer .... Cleveland	50.00	25.00	5.00
☐ 565	Frank Zinn: .... Athletics	50.00	25.00	5.00

☐ 2	Marve Beardsley	10.00	5.00	1.00
☐ 3	Chas. P. Blatt	10.00	5.00	1.00
☐ 4	Blondin	10.00	5.00	1.00
☐ 5	Paul Boynton	10.00	5.00	1.00
☐ 6	E.A.(Ernie) Burch BB	300.00	150.00	30.00
☐ 7	Patsy Cardiff	10.00	5.00	1.00
☐ 8	Phillip Casey	10.00	5.00	1.00
☐ 9	J.C. Cockburn	10.00	5.00	1.00
☐ 10	Dell Darling BB	300.00	150.00	30.00
☐ 11	Jack Dempsey BOX	50.00	25.00	5.00
☐ 12	Della Ferrell	10.00	5.00	1.00
☐ 13	Clarence Freeman	10.00	5.00	1.00
☐ 14	Louis George	10.00	5.00	1.00
☐ 15	W.G. George	10.00	5.00	1.00
☐ 16	George W. Hamilton	10.00	5.00	1.00
☐ 17	Edward Hanlan	10.00	5.00	1.00
☐ 18	C.H. Heins	10.00	5.00	1.00
☐ 19	Hardie Henderson BB	300.00	150.00	30.00
☐ 20	Thomas H. Hume	10.00	5.00	1.00
☐ 21	J.H. Jordon	10.00	5.00	1.00
☐ 22	Johnny Kane	10.00	5.00	1.00
☐ 23	James McLaughlin	10.00	5.00	1.00
☐ 24	John McPherson	10.00	5.00	1.00
☐ 25	Joseph Morsler	10.00	5.00	1.00
☐ 26	William Muldoon	10.00	5.00	1.00
☐ 27	S. Muller	10.00	5.00	1.00
☐ 28	Isaac Murphy	10.00	5.00	1.00
☐ 29	John Murphy	10.00	5.00	1.00
☐ 30	L.E. Myers	10.00	5.00	1.00
☐ 31	Annie Oakley	25.00	12.50	2.50
☐ 32	Daniel O'Leary	10.00	5.00	1.00
☐ 33	James O'Neil BB	325.00	160.00	32.00
☐ 34	Wm. Byrd Page	10.00	5.00	1.00
☐ 35	Axel Paulsen	10.00	5.00	1.00
☐ 36	Master Ray Perry	10.00	5.00	1.00
☐ 37	Duncan C. Ross	10.00	5.00	1.00
☐ 38	W.A. Rowe	10.00	5.00	1.00
☐ 39	Jacob Schaefer	10.00	5.00	1.00
☐ 40	M. Schloss	10.00	5.00	1.00
☐ 41	Jem Smith	10.00	5.00	1.00
☐ 42	Lillian Smith	10.00	5.00	1.00
☐ 43	Hattie Stewart	10.00	5.00	1.00
☐ 44	John L. Sullivan BOX	60.00	30.00	6.00
☐ 45	Arthur Wallace	10.00	5.00	1.00
☐ 46	Tommy Warren BOX	25.00	12.50	2.50
☐ 47	Ada Webb	10.00	5.00	1.00
☐ 48	John Wessels	10.00	5.00	1.00
☐ 49	Clarence Whistler	10.00	5.00	1.00
☐ 50	Charles Wood	10.00	5.00	1.00

N184 Kimball's

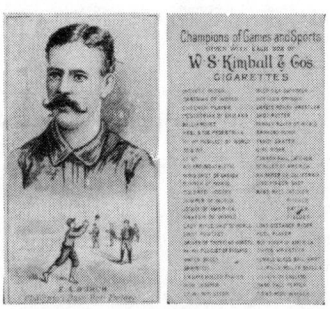

This set of 50 color pictures of contemporary athletes was Kimball's answer to the sets produced by Allen , Ginter (N28 and N29) and Goodwin (N162). Issued in 1888, the cards are backlisted but are not numbered. The cards are listed below in alphabetical order without regard to sport. There are four baseball players in the set. An album (ACC: A42) was offered as a premium in exchange for coupons found in the tobacco packages. The baseball players are noted in the checklist below by BB after their name.

	NRMT	VG-E	GOOD
COMPLETE SET	1650.00	750.00	150.00
COMMON BASEBALL	300.00	150.00	30.00
COMMON BOXER	25.00	12.50	2.50
COMMON OTHERS	10.00	5.00	1.00
☐ 1 Wm. Beach	10.00	5.00	1.00

N284 Buchner

The baseball players found in this Buchner set are a part of a larger group of cards portraying policemen, jockeys and actors, all of which were issued with the tobacco brand "Gold Coin." Nine players from eight teams, plus four Brooklyn players, are all portrayed in identical poses according to position. St. Louis has 14 players depicted in poses which are not repeated. There are 53 additional cards which vary according to pose, team change, spelling, etc. In all, there are 118 individuals portrayed on 143 cards. The set was issued circa 1887. The cards are numbered below in alphabetical order within team with teams themselves listed in alphabetical order: Baltimore (1-

4), Boston (5-13), Brooklyn (14-17), Chicago (18-26), Detroit (27-35), Indianapolis (36-47), LaCrosse (48-51), Milwaukee (52-55), New York Mets (56-63), New York (64-73), Philadelphia (74-83), Pittsburg (84-92), St. Louis (93-106), and Washington (107-117).

		NRMT	VG-E	GOOD
	COMPLETE SET	9000.00	4000.00	800.00
	COMMON PLAYERS	50.00	25.00	5.00
☐	1 Burns: Baltimore	50.00	25.00	5.00
☐	2 Fulmer: Baltimore	50.00	25.00	5.00
☐	3 Kilroy: Baltimore	50.00	25.00	5.00
☐	4 Purcell: Baltimore	50.00	25.00	5.00
☐	5 John Burdock: Boston	50.00	25.00	5.00
☐	6 Bill Daley: Boston	50.00	25.00	5.00
☐	7 Joe Hornung: Boston	50.00	25.00	5.00
☐	8 Johnston: Boston	50.00	25.00	5.00
☐	9A King Kelly: Boston (right field)	150.00	75.00	15.00
☐	9B King Kelly: Boston (catcher)	180.00	90.00	18.00
☐	10 Morrill (2): Boston	50.00	25.00	5.00
☐	11 Hoss Radbourn (2): Boston	125.00	60.00	12.50
☐	12 Sutton: Boston	50.00	25.00	5.00
☐	13 Wise: Boston	50.00	25.00	5.00
☐	14 McClellan: Brooklyn	50.00	25.00	5.00
☐	15 Peoples: Brooklyn	50.00	25.00	5.00
☐	16 Phillips: Brooklyn	50.00	25.00	5.00
☐	17 Porter: Brooklyn	50.00	25.00	5.00
☐	18 Adrian Anson (2): Chicago	250.00	125.00	25.00
☐	19 Burns: Chicago	50.00	25.00	5.00
☐	20 John Clarkson (2): Chicago	125.00	60.00	12.50
☐	21 Silver Flint: Chicago	50.00	25.00	5.00
☐	22 Pfeffer: Chicago	50.00	25.00	5.00
☐	23 Ryan: Chicago	50.00	25.00	5.00
☐	24 Billy Sullivan: Chicago	80.00	40.00	8.00
☐	25 Billy Sunday: Chicago	100.00	50.00	10.00
☐	26A Williamson: Chicago (shortstop)	50.00	25.00	5.00
☐	26B Williamson: Chicago (second base)	50.00	25.00	5.00
☐	27 Bennett: Detroit	50.00	25.00	5.00
☐	28A Dan Brouthers: Detroit (fielding)	125.00	60.00	12.50
☐	28B Dan Brouthers: Detroit (batting)	125.00	60.00	12.50
☐	29 Dunlap: Detroit	50.00	25.00	5.00
☐	30 Getzein: Detroit	50.00	25.00	5.00
☐	31 Hanlon: Detroit	50.00	25.00	5.00
☐	32 Manning: Detroit	50.00	25.00	5.00
☐	33 Richardson (2): Detroit	50.00	25.00	5.00
☐	34 Sam Thompson (2): Detroit	125.00	60.00	12.50
☐	35 White: Detroit	50.00	25.00	5.00
☐	36 Arundel: Indianapolis	50.00	25.00	5.00
☐	37 Bassett: Indianapolis	50.00	25.00	5.00
☐	38 Boyle: Indianapolis	50.00	25.00	5.00
☐	39 Cahill: Indianapolis	50.00	25.00	5.00
☐	40 Denny (2): Indianapolis	50.00	25.00	5.00
☐	41 Jack Glasscock (2): Indianapolis	50.00	25.00	5.00
☐	42 Healy: Indianapolis	50.00	25.00	5.00
☐	43 Meyers: Indianapolis	50.00	25.00	5.00
☐	44 McGeachy: Indianapolis	50.00	25.00	5.00
☐	45 Polhemus: Indianapolis	50.00	25.00	5.00
☐	46 Seery (2): Indianapolis	50.00	25.00	5.00
☐	47 Shomberg: Indianapolis	50.00	25.00	5.00
☐	48 Corbett: Lacrosse	50.00	25.00	5.00
☐	49 Crowley: Lacrosse	50.00	25.00	5.00
☐	50 Kennedy: Lacrosse	50.00	25.00	5.00
☐	51 Rooks: Lacrosse	50.00	25.00	5.00
☐	52 Forster: Milwaukee	50.00	25.00	5.00
☐	53 Hart: Milwaukee	50.00	25.00	5.00
☐	54 Morrissy: Milwaukee	50.00	25.00	5.00
☐	55 Strauss: Milwaukee	50.00	25.00	5.00
☐	56 Cushman: NY Mets	50.00	25.00	5.00
☐	57 Jim Donahue: NY Mets	50.00	25.00	5.00
☐	58 Esterbrooke (sic): NY Mets	50.00	25.00	5.00
☐	59 Joe Gerhardt: NY Mets	50.00	25.00	5.00
☐	60 Frank Hankinson: NY Mets	50.00	25.00	5.00
☐	61 Jack Nelson: NY Mets	50.00	25.00	5.00
☐	62 Dave Orr: NY Mets	50.00	25.00	5.00
☐	63 James Rosemann: NY Mets	50.00	25.00	5.00
☐	64 Roger Connor (2): New York	125.00	60.00	12.50
☐	65 Deasley: New York	50.00	25.00	5.00
☐	66A Mike Dorgan: New York (fielding)	50.00	25.00	5.00
☐	66B Mike Dorgan: New York (batting)	50.00	25.00	5.00
☐	67 Buck Ewing (2): New York	125.00	60.00	12.50
☐	68A Pete Gillespie: New York (fielding)	50.00	25.00	5.00
☐	68B Pete Gillespie: New York (batting)	50.00	25.00	5.00
☐	69 George Gore: New York	50.00	25.00	5.00
☐	70 Tim Keefe (2): New York	125.00	60.00	12.50
☐	71 Jim O'Rourke: New York	125.00	60.00	12.50
☐	73 John M. Ward (3): New York	125.00	60.00	12.50
☐	74 Andrews (2): Philadelphia	50.00	25.00	5.00
☐	75 Bastian: Philadelphia	50.00	25.00	5.00
☐	76 Dan Casey: Philadelphia	50.00	25.00	5.00
☐	77 Clements: Philadelphia	50.00	25.00	5.00
☐	78 Sid Farrar: Philadelphia	50.00	25.00	5.00
☐	79 Ferguson: Philadelphia	50.00	25.00	5.00
☐	80 Fogerty: Philadelphia	50.00	25.00	5.00
☐	81 Irwin: Philadelphia	50.00	25.00	5.00
☐	82 Mulvey (2): Philadelphia	50.00	25.00	5.00
☐	83A Pete Wood: Philadelphia (fielding)	50.00	25.00	5.00
☐	83B Pete Wood: Philadelphia (stealing)	50.00	25.00	5.00
☐	84 Barkley: Pittsburg	50.00	25.00	5.00
☐	85 Beecher: Pittsburg	50.00	25.00	5.00
☐	86 Brown: Pittsburg	50.00	25.00	5.00
☐	87 Carroll: Pittsburg	50.00	25.00	5.00
☐	88 Coleman: Pittsburg	50.00	25.00	5.00
☐	89 McCormick: Pittsburg	50.00	25.00	5.00
☐	90 Miller: Pittsburg	50.00	25.00	5.00
☐	91 Smith: Pittsburg	50.00	25.00	5.00
☐	92 Whitney: Pittsburg	50.00	25.00	5.00
☐	93 Barkley: St. Louis	80.00	40.00	8.00
☐	94 Bushong: St. Louis	80.00	40.00	8.00
☐	95 Bob Carruthers (sic): St. Louis	125.00	60.00	12.50
☐	96 Charles Comiskey: St. Louis	175.00	85.00	18.00
☐	97 Dave Foutz: St. Louis	80.00	40.00	8.00
☐	98 William Gleason: St. Louis	80.00	40.00	8.00
☐	99 Arlie Latham: St. Louis	80.00	40.00	8.00
☐	100 McGinnis: St. Louis	80.00	40.00	8.00
☐	101 Hugh Nicol: St. Louis	80.00	40.00	8.00
☐	102 James O'Neil: St. Louis	80.00	40.00	8.00
☐	103 Robinson: St. Louis	80.00	40.00	8.00
☐	104 Sullivan: St. Louis	80.00	40.00	8.00
☐	105 Chris Von Der Ahe: St. Louis	150.00	75.00	15.00
☐	106 Curt Welch: St. Louis	80.00	40.00	8.00
☐	107 Carroll: Washington	50.00	25.00	5.00
☐	108 Craig: Washington	50.00	25.00	5.00
☐	109 Crane: Washington	50.00	25.00	5.00
☐	110 Dailey: Washington	50.00	25.00	5.00
☐	111 Donnelly: Washington	50.00	25.00	5.00
☐	112 Farrell (2): Washington	50.00	25.00	5.00
☐	113 Gilligan: Washington	50.00	25.00	5.00
☐	114A Hines: Washington (fielding)	50.00	25.00	5.00
☐	114B Hines: Washington (batting)	50.00	25.00	5.00
☐	115 Myers: Washington	50.00	25.00	5.00
☐	116 O'Brien: Washington	50.00	25.00	5.00
☐	117 Whitney: Washington	50.00	25.00	5.00

NEED HELP: Special terms and abbreviations are listed in glossary.

N300 Mayo

The Mayo Tobacco Works of Richmond, Va., issssued this set of 48 ballplayers about 1895. The cards contain sepia portraits although some pictures appear to be black and white. There are 40 different individuals known in the set; cards 1 to 28 appear in uniform, while the last twelve (29-40) appear in street clothes. Eight of the former also appear with variations in uniform. The player's name appears within the picture area and a ''Mayo's Cut Plug'' ad is printed in a panel at the base of the card.

	NRMT	VG-E	GOOD
COMPLETE SET	7250.00	3000.00	600.00
COMMON PLAYERS	125.00	60.00	12.50
☐ 1 Cap Anson: Chicago	750.00	375.00	75.00
☐ 2 Bannon RF: Boston	125.00	60.00	12.50
☐ 3A Dan Brouthers 1B: Baltimore	300.00	150.00	30.00
☐ 3B Dan Brouthers 1B: Louisville	350.00	175.00	35.00
☐ 4 John Clarkson P: St. Louis	250.00	125.00	25.00
☐ 5 T.W. Corcoran SS: Brooklyn	125.00	60.00	12.50
☐ 6 Cross 2B: Philadelphia	125.00	60.00	12.50
☐ 7 Hugh Duffy CF: Boston	300.00	150.00	30.00
☐ 8A Buck Ewing RF: Cincinnati	350.00	175.00	35.00
☐ 8B Buck Ewing RF: Cleveland	350.00	175.00	35.00
☐ 9 Dave Foutz 1B: Brooklyn	125.00	60.00	12.50
☐ 10 Ganzel C: Boston	125.00	60.00	12.50
☐ 11A Glasscock SS: Pittsburgh	150.00	75.00	15.00
☐ 11B Glasscock SS: Louisville	150.00	75.00	15.00
☐ 12 Griffin CF: Brooklyn	125.00	60.00	12.50
☐ 13A Haddock P: Philadelphia	125.00	60.00	12.50
☐ 13B Haddock P: no team	125.00	60.00	12.50
☐ 14 Joyce CF: Brooklyn	125.00	60.00	12.50
☐ 15 Wm. Kennedy P: Brooklyn	125.00	60.00	12.50
☐ 16A Tom F. Kinslow C: Pitts.	125.00	60.00	12.50
☐ 16B Tom F. Kinslow C: no team	125.00	60.00	12.50
☐ 17 Arlie Latham 3B: Cincinnati	125.00	60.00	12.50
☐ 18 Long SS: Boston	125.00	60.00	12.50
☐ 19 Lovett P: Boston	125.00	60.00	12.50
☐ 20 Lowe 2B: Boston	150.00	75.00	15.00
☐ 21 McCarthy LF: Boston	250.00	125.00	25.00
☐ 22 Murphy SS: New York	125.00	60.00	12.50
☐ 23 Billy Nash 3B: Boston	125.00	60.00	12.50
☐ 24 Nicols P: Boston	125.00	60.00	12.50
☐ 25A Pfeffer 2B: Louisville	125.00	60.00	12.50
☐ 25B Pfeffer (retired)	125.00	60.00	12.50
☐ 26A Amos Rusie P: New York	400.00	200.00	40.00
☐ 26B Amos Russie (sic) P:	350.00	175.00	35.00

	New York			
☐ 27 Tucker 1B: Boston	125.00	60.00	12.50
☐ 28A John Ward 2B: New York	300.00	150.00	30.00
☐ 28B John Ward (retired)	350.00	175.00	35.00
☐ 29 Chas. S. Abbey CF: Washington	125.00	60.00	12.50
☐ 30 E.W. Cartwright FB: Washington	150.00	75.00	15.00
☐ 31 W. F. Dahlen SS: Chicago	150.00	75.00	15.00
☐ 32 T.P. Daly SB: Brooklyn	125.00	60.00	12.50
☐ 33 E.J. Delehanty LF: Phila.	400.00	200.00	40.00
☐ 34 W.W. Hallman SB: Phila.	125.00	60.00	12.50
☐ 35 W.R. Hamilton CF: Phila.	300.00	150.00	30.00
☐ 36 W. Robinson C: Baltimore	300.00	150.00	30.00
☐ 37 James Ryan RF: Chicago	125.00	60.00	12.50
☐ 38 Wm. Shindle TB: Brooklyn	125.00	60.00	12.50
☐ 39 Geo. J. Smith SS: Cinc.	125.00	60.00	12.50
☐ 40 Otis H. Stockdale P: Washington	125.00	60.00	12.50

1969 Nabisco Team Flakes

The cards in this 24 card set measure either 1 15/16" by 3" or 1 3/4" by 2 15/16" depending on the amount of yellow border area provided between the "cut lines." The 1969 Nabisco Team Flakes set of full color, blank-backed and unnumbered cards was issued on the backs of Team Flakes cereal boxes. The cards are numbered in the checklist below in alphabetical order. There were three different panels or box backs containing eight cards each. The cards have yellow borders and are devoid of team insignias. The catalog designation is F275-34.

	NRMT	VG-E	GOOD
COMPLETE SET	300.00	150.00	30.00
COMMON PLAYER (1-24)	4.00	2.00	.40
☐ 1 Hank Aaron	36.00	18.00	3.60
☐ 2 Richie Allen	5.00	2.50	.50
☐ 3 Lou Brock	24.00	12.00	2.40
☐ 4 Paul Casanova	4.00	2.00	.40
☐ 5 Roberto Clemente	33.00	15.00	3.00
☐ 6 Al Ferrara	4.00	2.00	.40
☐ 7 Bill Freehan	5.00	2.50	.50
☐ 8 Jim Fregosi	5.00	2.50	.50
☐ 9 Bob Gibson	18.00	9.00	1.80
☐ 10 Tony Horton	5.00	2.50	.50
☐ 11 Tommy John	8.00	4.00	.80
☐ 12 Al Kaline	24.00	12.00	2.40
☐ 13 Jim Lonborg	5.00	2.50	.50
☐ 14 Juan Marichal	18.00	9.00	1.80
☐ 15 Willie Mays	36.00	18.00	3.60
☐ 16 Rick Monday	4.00	2.00	.40
☐ 17 Tony Oliva	8.00	4.00	.80
☐ 18 Brooks Robinson	24.00	12.00	2.40

☐ 19 Frank Robinson	21.00	10.50	2.10
☐ 20 Pete Rose	60.00	30.00	6.00
☐ 21 Ron Santo	5.00	2.50	.50
☐ 22 Tom Seaver	30.00	15.00	3.00
☐ 23 Rusty Staub	6.00	3.00	.60
☐ 24 Mel Stottlemyre	5.00	2.50	.50

1986 National Photo Royals

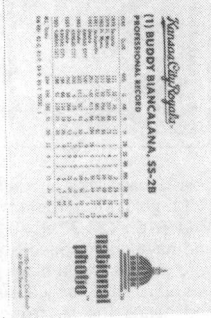

(1) BUDDY BIANCALANA, SS-2B

The set contains 24 cards which are numbered only by uniform number except for the checklist card and discount card, which entitles the bearer to a 40% discount at National Photo. Cards measure 2 7/8" by 4 1/4". Cards were distributed at the stadium on August 14th. The set was supposedly later available for 3.00 directly from the Royals.

	MINT	EXC	G-VG
COMPLETE SET	10.00	5.00	1.00
COMMON PLAYER	.30	.15	.03
☐ 1 Buddy Biancalana	.30	.15	.03
☐ 3 Jorge Orta	.30	.15	.03
☐ 4 Greg Pryor	.30	.15	.03
☐ 5 George Brett	2.00	1.00	.20
☐ 6 Willie Wilson	.60	.30	.06
☐ 8 Jim Sundberg	.30	.15	.03
☐ 10 Dick Howser MG	.50	.25	.05
☐ 11 Hal McRae	.40	.20	.04
☐ 20 Frank White	.50	.25	.05
☐ 21 Lonnie Smith	.40	.20	.04
☐ 22 Dennis Leonard	.40	.20	.04
☐ 23 Mark Gubicza	.40	.20	.04
☐ 24 Darryl Motley	.30	.15	.03
☐ 25 Danny Jackson	.40	.20	.04
☐ 26 Steve Farr	.30	.15	.03
☐ 29 Dan Quisenberry	.50	.25	.05
☐ 31 Bret Saberhagen	.75	.35	.07
☐ 35 Lynn Jones	.30	.15	.03
☐ 37 Charlie Leibrandt	.50	.25	.05
☐ 38 Mark Huismann	.30	.15	.03
☐ 40 Buddy Black	.40	.20	.04
☐ 45 Steve Balboni	.40	.20	.04
☐ xx Discount card (unnumbered)	.30	.15	.03
☐ xx Checklist card (unnumbered)	.30	.15	.03

1984 Nestle Dream Team

The cards in this 22-card set measure 2 1/2" by 3 1/2". In conjunction with Topps, the Nestle Company issued this set entitled the Dream Team. The fronts have the Nestle trademark in the upper frameline, and the backs are identical to the Topps cards of this year except for the number and the Nestle's logo. Cards 1-11 feature stars of the American League while cards 12-22 show National League stars. Each league's "Dream team" consists of eight position players and three pitchers. The

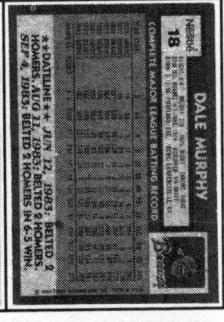

cards were included with the Nestle chocolate bars as a pack of four (three player cards and a checklist header card). This set should not be confused with the Nestle 792 card (same player-number correspondence as 1984 Topps 792) set.

	MINT	EXC	G-VG
COMPLETE SET	14.00	7.00	1.40
COMMON PLAYER	.35	.17	.03
☐ 1 Eddie Murray	1.50	.75	.15
☐ 2 Lou Whitaker	.50	.25	.05
☐ 3 George Brett	1.75	.85	.17
☐ 4 Cal Ripken	1.50	.75	.15
☐ 5 Jim Rice	.90	.45	.09
☐ 6 Dave Winfield	.90	.45	.09
☐ 7 Lloyd Moseby	.35	.17	.03
☐ 8 Lance Parrish	.60	.30	.06
☐ 9 LaMarr Hoyt	.35	.17	.03
☐ 10 Ron Guidry	.60	.30	.06
☐ 11 Dan Quisenberry	.50	.25	.05
☐ 12 Steve Garvey	1.25	.60	.12
☐ 13 Johnny Ray	.35	.17	.03
☐ 14 Mike Schmidt	1.75	.85	.17
☐ 15 Ozzie Smith	.75	.35	.07
☐ 16 Andre Dawson	.75	.35	.07
☐ 17 Tim Raines	.75	.35	.07
☐ 18 Dale Murphy	1.75	.85	.17
☐ 19 Tony Pena	.35	.17	.03
☐ 20 John Denny	.35	.17	.03
☐ 21 Steve Carlton	.90	.45	.09
☐ 22 Al Holland	.35	.17	.03
☐ 23 Checklist card (unnumbered)	.35	.03	.00

1984 Nestle 792

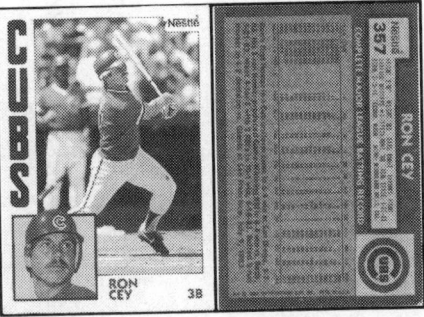

The cards in this 792-card set measure 2 1/2" by 3 1/2" and are extremely similar to the 1984 Topps regular issue (except for the Nestle logo instead of Topps logo on the front). In conjunction with Topps, the Nestle Company issued this set as six sheets available as a premium. The set was (as detailed on the back of the checklist card for the Nestle Dream Team cards) originally available from the Nestle Company in full sheets of 132 cards, 24" by 48", for

4.95 plus five Nestle candy wrappers per sheet. The backs are virtually identical to the Topps cards of this year, i.e., same player-number correspondence. These sheets have been cut up into individual cards and are available from a few dealers around the country. This is one of the few instances in this hobby where the complete uncut sheet is worth considerably less than the sum of the individual cards due to the expense required in having the sheet cut professionally (and precisely) into individual cards. Supposedly less than 5000 sets were printed. Since the checklist is exactly the same as that of the 1984 Topps, these Nestle cards are generally priced as a multiple of the corresponding Topps card. The list below shows only the exceptions; cards (above common card price) not listed below are priced at six times the corresponding 1984 Topps price.

		MINT	EXC	G-VG
COMPLETE SET		425.00	175.00	35.00
COMMON PLAYER		.25	.12	.02
☐ 1	HL: Steve Carlton	2.25	.50	.10
☐ 2	HL: Rickey Henderson ...	2.50	1.25	.25
☐ 4	HL: Nolan Ryan, etc. ...	2.00	1.00	.20
☐ 6	HL: John Bench, etc. ...	2.50	1.25	.25
☐ 8	Don Mattingly	150.00	75.00	15.00
☐ 10	Robin Yount	3.50	1.75	.35
☐ 30	Wade Boggs	30.00	15.00	3.00
☐ 65	Kirk Gibson	2.50	1.25	.25
☐ 100	Reggie Jackson	7.50	3.75	.75
☐ 120	Keith Hernandez	3.00	1.50	.30
☐ 130	Ozzie Smith	2.00	1.00	.20
☐ 150	Dale Murphy	10.00	5.00	1.00
☐ 182	Darryl Strawberry	35.00	17.50	3.50
☐ 195	Jack Morris	2.00	1.00	.20
☐ 200	Andre Dawson	3.00	1.50	.30
☐ 210	Joe Morgan	2.00	1.00	.20
☐ 220	Fernando Valenzuela	3.50	1.75	.35
☐ 230	Rickey Henderson	7.50	3.75	.75
☐ 240	Eddie Murray	6.00	3.00	.60
☐ 251	Tony Gwynn	10.00	5.00	1.00
☐ 278	Jorge Bell	7.50	3.75	.75
☐ 300	Pete Rose	20.00	10.00	2.00
☐ 345	Kent Hrbek	3.00	1.50	.30
☐ 370	Tim Raines	4.00	2.00	.40
☐ 380	Steve Garvey	6.00	3.00	.60
☐ 388	Mike Schmidt AS	3.00	1.50	.30
☐ 390	Tim Raines AS	2.00	1.00	.20
☐ 391	Dale Murphy AS	3.00	1.50	.30
☐ 392	Andre Dawson AS	2.00	1.00	.20
☐ 393	Gary Carter AS	2.00	1.00	.20
☐ 395	Steve Carlton AS	2.00	1.00	.20
☐ 397	Eddie Murray AS	3.00	1.50	.30
☐ 399	George Brett AS	2.00	1.00	.20
☐ 400	Cal Ripken AS	3.00	1.50	.30
☐ 401	Jim Rice AS	2.00	1.00	.20
☐ 402	Dave Winfield AS	2.00	1.00	.20
☐ 415	Tommy John	1.50	.75	.15
☐ 434	Harold Baines	2.00	1.00	.20
☐ 447	Tom Brunansky	2.00	1.00	.20
☐ 450	Gary Carter	4.50	2.25	.45
☐ 460	Dave Winfield	4.50	2.25	.45
☐ 470	Nolan Ryan	6.00	3.00	.60
☐ 488	Jesse Barfield	3.00	1.50	.30
☐ 490	Cal Ripken	7.50	3.75	.75
☐ 495	Rollie Fingers	2.00	1.00	.20
☐ 500	George Brett	7.50	3.75	.75
☐ 510	Alan Trammell	3.00	1.50	.30
☐ 550	Jim Rice	4.00	2.00	.40
☐ 559	Mike Scott	2.00	1.00	.20
☐ 560	Carlton Fisk	1.50	.75	.15
☐ 596	Ryne Sandberg	10.00	5.00	1.00
☐ 600	Rod Carew	4.50	2.25	.45
☐ 635	Dave Righetti	2.00	1.00	.20
☐ 650	Phil Niekro	2.50	1.25	.25
☐ 670	Rich Gossage	1.50	.75	.15
☐ 680	Fred Lynn	2.00	1.00	.20
☐ 690	Jack Clark	2.50	1.25	.25
☐ 700	Mike Schmidt	7.50	3.75	.75
☐ 740	Tom Seaver	6.00	3.00	.60
☐ 750	Jim Palmer	3.50	1.75	.35
☐ 760	Bob Horner	2.50	1.25	.25
☐ 775	Dave Parker	2.00	1.00	.20
☐ 780	Steve Carlton	4.50	2.25	.45

1987 Nestle Dream Team

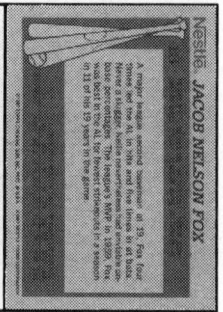

This 33-card set is, in a sense, three sets: Golden Era (1-11 gold), AL Modern Era (12-22 red), and NL Modern Era (23-33 blue). Cards are 2 1/2" by 3 1/2" and have color coded borders by era. The first 11 card photos are in black and white. The Nestle set was apparently not licensed by Major league Baseball and hence the team logos are not shown in the photos. Six-packs of certain Nestle candy bars contained three cards; cards were also available through a send-in offer.

		MINT	EXC	G-VG
COMPLETE SET		6.00	3.00	.60
COMMON PLAYER		.15	.07	.01
☐ 1	Lou Gehrig	.45	.22	.04
☐ 2	Rogers Hornsby	.25	.12	.02
☐ 3	Pie Traynor	.15	.07	.01
☐ 4	Honus Wagner	.25	.12	.02
☐ 5	Babe Ruth	.75	.35	.07
☐ 6	Tris Speaker	.25	.12	.02
☐ 7	Ty Cobb	.45	.22	.04
☐ 8	Mickey Cochrane	.25	.12	.02
☐ 9	Walter Johnson	.35	.17	.03
☐ 10	Carl Hubbell	.25	.12	.02
☐ 11	Jimmy Foxx	.25	.12	.02
☐ 12	Rod Carew	.25	.12	.02
☐ 13	Nellie Fox	.15	.07	.01
☐ 14	Brooks Robinson	.25	.12	.02
☐ 15	Luis Aparicio	.15	.07	.01
☐ 16	Frank Robinson	.25	.12	.02
☐ 17	Mickey Mantle	.75	.35	.07
☐ 18	Ted Williams	.45	.22	.04
☐ 19	Yogi Berra	.35	.17	.03
☐ 20	Bob Feller	.35	.17	.03
☐ 21	Whitey Ford	.35	.17	.03
☐ 22	Harmon Killebrew	.25	.12	.02
☐ 23	Stan Musial	.35	.17	.03
☐ 24	Jackie Robinson	.45	.22	.04
☐ 25	Eddie Mathews	.25	.12	.02
☐ 26	Ernie Banks	.25	.12	.02
☐ 27	Roberto Clemente	.35	.17	.03
☐ 28	Willie Mays	.45	.22	.04
☐ 29	Hank Aaron	.45	.22	.04
☐ 30	Johnny Bench	.35	.17	.03
☐ 31	Bob Gibson	.25	.12	.02
☐ 32	Warren Spahn	.25	.12	.02
☐ 33	Duke Snider	.35	.17	.03

1954 N.Y. Journal American

The cards in this 59 card set measure 2" by 4". The 1954 New York Journal American set contains black and white, unnumbered cards issued in conjunction with the newspaper. News stands were given boxes of cards to be distributed with purchases and each card had a serial number for redemption in the contest. The set spotlights New York teams only and carries game schedules on the reverse. The cards have been assigned numbers in the listing below

		NRMT	VG-E	GOOD
☐ 56	Allie Reynolds	12.00	6.00	1.20
☐ 57	Phil Rizzuto	25.00	12.50	2.50
☐ 58	Eddie Robinson	6.00	3.00	.60
☐ 59	Gene Woodling	7.50	3.75	.75

1960 Nu-Card Hi-Lites

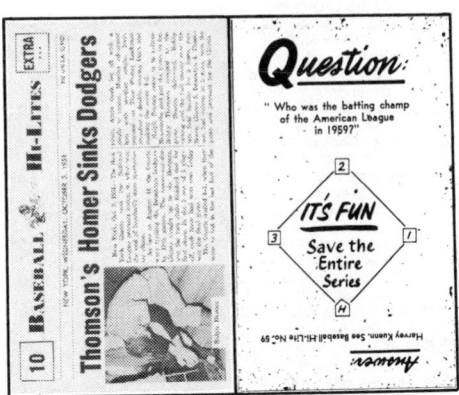

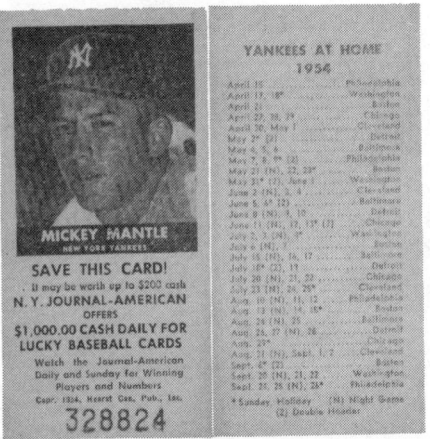

alphabetically within team so that Brooklyn Dodgers are 1-19, New York Giants are 20-39, and New York Yankees are 40-59. There is speculation that a 20th Dodger card may exist. The ACC designation for this set is M127.

	NRMT	VG-E	GOOD
COMPLETE SET	1000.00	400.00	80.00
COMMON PLAYER	6.00	3.00	.60

		NRMT	VG-E	GOOD
☐ 1	Joe Black	7.50	3.75	.75
☐ 2	Roy Campanella	60.00	30.00	6.00
☐ 3	Billy Cox	7.50	3.75	.75
☐ 4	Carl Erskine	10.00	5.00	1.00
☐ 5	Carl Furillo	12.00	6.00	1.20
☐ 6	Junior Gilliam	12.00	6.00	1.20
☐ 7	Gil Hodges	25.00	12.50	2.50
☐ 8	Jim Hughes	6.00	3.00	.60
☐ 9	Clem Labine	7.50	3.75	.75
☐ 10	Billy Loes	6.00	3.00	.60
☐ 11	Russ Meyer	6.00	3.00	.60
☐ 12	Don Newcombe	12.00	6.00	1.20
☐ 13	Ervin Palica	20.00	10.00	2.00
☐ 14	Pee Wee Reese	40.00	20.00	4.00
☐ 15	Jackie Robinson	90.00	45.00	9.00
☐ 16	Preacher Roe	12.00	6.00	1.20
☐ 17	George Shuba	6.00	3.00	.60
☐ 18	Duke Snider	75.00	37.50	7.50
☐ 19	Dick Williams	7.50	3.75	.75
☐ 20	John Antonelli	7.50	3.75	.75
☐ 21	Alvin Dark	9.00	4.50	.90
☐ 22	Marv Grissom	6.00	3.00	.60
☐ 23	Ruben Gomez	6.00	3.00	.60
☐ 24	Jim Hearn	6.00	3.00	.60
☐ 25	Bobby Hofman	6.00	3.00	.60
☐ 26	Monte Irvin	20.00	10.00	2.00
☐ 27	Larry Jansen	6.00	3.00	.60
☐ 28	Ray Katt	6.00	3.00	.60
☐ 29	Don Liddle	6.00	3.00	.60
☐ 30	Whitey Lockman	7.50	3.75	.75
☐ 31	Sal Maglie	12.00	6.00	1.20
☐ 32	Willie Mays	125.00	60.00	12.50
☐ 33	Don Mueller	7.50	3.75	.75
☐ 34	Dusty Rhodes	7.50	3.75	.75
☐ 35	Hank Thompson	7.50	3.75	.75
☐ 36	Wes Westrum	6.00	3.00	.60
☐ 37	Hoyt Wilhelm	25.00	12.50	2.50
☐ 38	Davey Williams	7.50	3.75	.75
☐ 39	Al Worthington	6.00	3.00	.60
☐ 40	Hank Bauer	12.00	6.00	1.20
☐ 41	Yogi Berra	60.00	30.00	6.00
☐ 42	Harry Byrd	6.00	3.00	.60
☐ 43	Andy Carey	6.00	3.00	.60
☐ 44	Jerry Coleman	7.50	3.75	.75
☐ 45	Joe Collins	6.00	3.00	.60
☐ 46	Whitey Ford	35.00	17.50	3.50
☐ 47	Steve Kraly	6.00	3.00	.60
☐ 48	Bob Kuzava	6.00	3.00	.60
☐ 49	Frank Leja	6.00	3.00	.60
☐ 50	Ed Lopat	12.00	6.00	1.20
☐ 51	Mickey Mantle	300.00	150.00	30.00
☐ 52	Gil McDougald	12.00	6.00	1.20
☐ 53	Bill Miller	6.00	3.00	.60
☐ 54	Tom Morgan	6.00	3.00	.60
☐ 55	Irv Noren	6.00	3.00	.60

The cards in this 72 card set measure 3 1/4" by 5 3/8". In 1960, the Nu-Card Company introduced its Baseball Hi-Lites set of newspaper style cards. Each card singled out an individual baseball achievement with a picture and story. The reverses contain a baseball quiz. Cards 1-18 are more valuable if found printed totally in black on the front; these are copyrighted CVC as opposed to the NCI designation found on the red and black printed fronts.

	NRMT	VG-E	GOOD
COMPLETE SET	125.00	60.00	12.50
COMMON PLAYER (1-72)	1.00	.50	.10

		NRMT	VG-E	GOOD
☐ 1	Babe Hits 3 Homers In A Series Game	6.50	3.25	.65
☐ 2	Podres Pitching Wins Series	1.00	.50	.10
☐ 3	Bevans Pitches No Hitter, Almost	1.00	.50	.10
☐ 4	Box Score Devised By Reporter	1.00	.50	.10
☐ 5	VanderMeer Pitches Two No Hitters	1.25	.60	.12
☐ 6	Indians Take Bums	1.00	.50	.10
☐ 7	DiMag Comes Thru	6.00	3.00	.60
☐ 8	Mathewson Pitches Three WS Shutouts	1.50	.75	.15
☐ 9	Haddix Pitches 12 Perfect Innings	1.25	.60	.12
☐ 10	Thomson's Homer Sinks Dodgers	2.00	1.00	.20
☐ 11	Hubbell Strikes Out Five A.L. Stars	1.25	.60	.12
☐ 12	Pickoff Ends Series	1.00	.50	.10
☐ 13	Cards Take Series From Yanks	1.00	.50	.10
☐ 14	Dizzy And Daffy Dean Win Series	3.00	1.50	.30
☐ 15	Owen Drops 3rd Strike	1.00	.50	.10
☐ 16	Ruth Calls Shot	6.50	3.25	.65
☐ 17	Merkle Pulls Boner	1.00	.50	.10
☐ 18	Larsen Hurls Perfect World Series Game	2.00	1.00	.20
☐ 19	Bean Ball Ends Career of Mickey Cochrane	1.25	.60	.12
☐ 20	Banks Belts 47 Homers Earns MVP	2.50	1.25	.25
☐ 21	Stan Musial Hits Five Homers in One Day	3.50	1.75	.35
☐ 22	Mickey Mantle Hits Longest Homer	9.00	4.50	.90
☐ 23	Sievers Captures Home Run Title	1.00	.50	.10
☐ 24	Gehrig 2130 Consecutive Game Record Ends	5.00	2.50	.50
☐ 25	Red Schoendienst Key	1.00	.50	.10

	Player Braves Pennant			
☐ 26	Midget Pinch-Hits	2.50	1.25	.25
	For St. Louis			
☐ 27	Willie Mays Makes	4.50	2.25	.45
	Greatest Catch			
☐ 28	Homer by Yogi Berra	3.00	1.50	.30
	Puts Yanks In 1st			
☐ 29	Campy NL MVP	4.00	2.00	.40
☐ 30	Bob Turley Hurls Yanks	1.00	.50	.10
	To WS Champions			
☐ 31	Dodgers Take Series	1.00	.50	.10
	From Sox in Six			
☐ 32	Furillo Hero as Dodgers ...	1.00	.50	.10
	Beat Chicago in 3rd			
	World Series Game			
☐ 33	Adcock Gets 4 Homers	1.00	.50	.10
	And A Double			
☐ 34	Dickey Chosen All-	1.50	.75	.15
	Star Catcher			
☐ 35	Burdette Beats Yanks	1.25	.60	.12
	In Three WS Games			
☐ 36	Umpires Clear	1.00	.50	.10
	White Sox Bench			
☐ 37	Reese Honored As	2.50	1.25	.25
	Greatest Dodger SS			
☐ 38	Joe DiMaggio Hits	6.00	3.00	.60
	In 56 Straight			
☐ 39	Ted Williams Hits	4.50	2.25	.45
	.406 For Season			
☐ 40	Walter Johnson	2.50	1.25	.25
	Pitches 56 Straight			
☐ 41	Hodges Hits 4 Home	1.50	.75	.15
	Runs In Nite Game			
☐ 42	Greenberg Returns to	1.50	.75	.15
	Tigers From Army			
☐ 43	Ty Cobb Named Best	6.50	3.25	.65
	Player Of All Time			
☐ 44	Robin Roberts Wins	1.50	.75	.15
	28 Games			
☐ 45	Rizzuto's Two Runs	1.50	.75	.15
	Save 1st Place			
☐ 46	Tigers Beat Out	1.00	.50	.10
	Senators For Pennant			
☐ 47	Babe Ruth Hits	6.50	3.25	.65
	60th Home Run			
☐ 48	Cy Young Honored	2.00	1.00	.20
☐ 49	Killebrew Starts	2.50	1.25	.25
	Spring Training			
☐ 50	Mantle Hits Longest	9.00	4.50	.90
	Homer at Stadium			
☐ 51	Braves Take Pennant	1.00	.50	.10
☐ 52	Ted Williams Hero	4.00	2.00	.40
	Of All-Star Game			
☐ 53	Robinson Saves Dodgers ..	4.00	2.00	.40
	For Play-off Series			
☐ 54	Snodgrass Muffs Fly	1.00	.50	.10
☐ 55	Snider Belts 2 Homers	3.00	1.50	.30
	Ties Homer Record			
☐ 56	Giants Win 26 Straight	1.00	.50	.10
☐ 57	Ted Kluszewski Stars	1.25	.60	.12
	In 1st Series Win			
☐ 58	Ott Walks 5 Times	1.50	.75	.15
	In Single Game			
☐ 59	Harvey Kuenn Takes	1.00	.50	.10
	A.L. Batting Title			
☐ 60	Bob Feller Hurls 3rd	3.00	1.50	.30
	No-Hitter of Career			
☐ 61	Yanks Champs Again	1.25	.60	.12
☐ 62	Aaron's Bat Beats	4.00	2.00	.40
	Yankees In Series			
☐ 63	Warren Spahn Beats	2.00	1.00	.20
	Yanks in W.S.			
☐ 64	Ump's Wrong Call Helps ...	1.00	.50	.10
	Dodgers Beat Yanks			
☐ 65	Kaline Hits 3 Homers	2.50	1.25	.25
	Two In Same Inning			
☐ 66	Bob Allison Named AL	1.00	.50	.10
	Rookie of the Year			
☐ 67	McCovey Blasts Way	2.50	1.25	.25
	Into Giant Lineup			
☐ 68	Colavito Hits Four	1.25	.60	.12
	Homers in One Game			
☐ 69	Erskine Sets Strike Out	1.00	.50	.10
	Record in World Series			
☐ 70	Sal Maglie Pitches	1.25	.60	.12
	No-Hit Game			
☐ 71	Early Wynn Victory	1.50	.75	.15
	Crushes Yanks			
☐ 72	Nellie Fox AL MVP	1.50	.75	.15

1961 Nu-Card Scoops

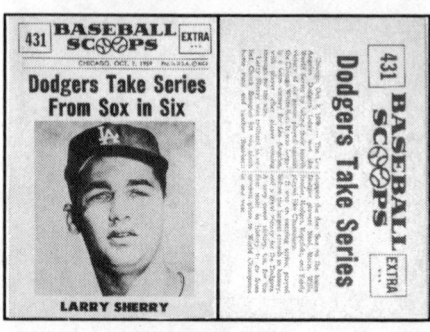

The cards in this 80 card set measure 2 1/2" by 3 1/2". This series depicts great moments in the history of individual ballplayers. Each card is designed as a miniature newspaper front-page, complete with data and picture. Both the number (401-480) and title are printed in red on the obverse, and the story is found on the back. An album was issued to hold the set. The set has apparently been reprinted, which has served to suppress the demand for the originals as well as the reprints.

		NRMT	VG-E	GOOD
COMPLETE SET		75.00	37.50	7.50
COMMON PLAYER (401-480)		.40	.20	.04
☐ 401	Jim Gentile	.40	.20	.04
☐ 402	Warren Spahn	1.50	.75	.15
	(No-hitter)			
☐ 403	Bill Mazeroski	.60	.30	.06
☐ 404	Willie Mays:	3.50	1.75	.35
	(three triples)			
☐ 405	Woodie Held	.40	.20	.04
☐ 406	Vern Law	.40	.20	.04
☐ 407	Pete Runnels	.40	.20	.04
☐ 408	Lew Burdette	.50	.25	.05
	(No-hitter)			
☐ 409	Dick Stuart	.40	.20	.04
☐ 410	Don Cardwell	.40	.20	.04
☐ 411	Camilo Pascual	.40	.20	.04
☐ 412	Ed Mathews	1.50	.75	.15
☐ 413	Dick Groat	.60	.30	.06
☐ 414	Gene Autry	1.50	.75	.15
☐ 415	Bobby Richardson	.60	.30	.06
☐ 416	Roger Maris	3.50	1.75	.35
☐ 417	Fred Merkle	.40	.20	.04
☐ 418	Don Larsen	.50	.25	.05
☐ 419	Mickey Cochrane	.75	.35	.07
☐ 420	Ernie Banks	2.00	1.00	.20
☐ 421	Stan Musial	3.00	1.50	.30
☐ 422	Mickey Mantle	7.50	3.75	.75
	(longest homer)			
☐ 423	Roy Sievers	.40	.20	.04
☐ 424	Lou Gehrig	4.00	2.00	.40
☐ 425	Red Schoendienst	.50	.25	.05
☐ 426	Eddie Gaedel	1.50	.75	.15
☐ 427	Willie Mays	3.50	1.75	.35
	(greatest catch)			
☐ 428	Jackie Robinson	3.50	1.75	.35
☐ 429	Roy Campanella	3.50	1.75	.35
☐ 430	Bob Turley	.40	.20	.04
☐ 431	Larry Sherry	.40	.20	.04
☐ 432	Carl Furillo	.50	.25	.05
☐ 433	Joe Adcock	.50	.25	.05
☐ 434	Bill Dickey	.75	.35	.07
☐ 435	Burdette 3 wins	.50	.25	.05
☐ 436	Umpire Clears Bench	.40	.20	.04
☐ 437	Pee Wee Reese	2.00	1.00	.20
☐ 438	Joe DiMaggio	5.00	2.50	.50
	(56 Game Hit Streak)			
☐ 439	Ted Williams	4.00	2.00	.40
	Hits .406			
☐ 440	Walter Johnson	2.00	1.00	.20
☐ 441	Gil Hodges	1.50	.75	.15
☐ 442	Hank Greenberg	1.00	.50	.10
☐ 443	Ty Cobb	5.00	2.50	.50
☐ 444	Robin Roberts	1.50	.75	.15
☐ 445	Phil Rizzuto	1.50	.75	.15

☐ 446	Hal Newhouser	.60	.30	.06
☐ 447	Babe Ruth 60th Homer	6.00	3.00	.60
☐ 448	Cy Young	1.50	.75	.15
☐ 449	Harmon Killebrew	2.00	1.00	.20
☐ 450	Mickey Mantle	7.50	3.75	.75
	(longest homer)			
☐ 451	Braves Take Pennant	.40	.20	.04
☐ 452	Ted Williams	4.00	2.00	.40
	(All-Star Hero)			
☐ 453	Yogi Berra	3.00	1.50	.30
☐ 454	Fred Snodgrass	.40	.20	.04
☐ 455	Ruth 3 Homers	6.00	3.00	.60
☐ 456	Giants 26 Game Streak	.40	.20	.04
☐ 457	Ted Kluszewski	.50	.25	.05
☐ 458	Mel Ott	1.00	.50	.10
☐ 459	Harvey Kuenn	.60	.30	.06
☐ 460	Bob Feller	2.50	1.25	.25
☐ 461	Casey Stengel	1.50	.75	.15
☐ 462	Hank Aaron	3.50	1.75	.35
☐ 463	Spahn Beats Yanks	1.00	.50	.10
☐ 464	Ump's Wrong Call	.40	.20	.04
☐ 465	Al Kaline	2.00	1.00	.20
☐ 466	Bob Allison	.40	.20	.04
☐ 467	Joe DiMaggio	5.00	2.50	.50
	(Four Homers)			
☐ 468	Rocky Colavito	.60	.30	.06
☐ 469	Carl Erskine	.50	.25	.05
☐ 470	Sal Maglie	.50	.25	.05
☐ 471	Early Wynn	1.25	.60	.12
☐ 472	Nellie Fox	.75	.35	.07
☐ 473	Marty Marion	.60	.30	.06
☐ 474	Johnny Podres	.50	.25	.05
☐ 475	Mickey Owen	.40	.20	.04
☐ 476	Dean Brothers	2.00	1.00	.20
	(Dizzy and Daffy)			
☐ 477	Christy Mathewson	2.00	1.00	.20
☐ 478	Harvey Haddix	.40	.20	.04
☐ 479	Carl Hubbell	.75	.35	.07
☐ 480	Bobby Thomson	.60	.30	.06

1952 Num Num

The cards in this 20 card set measure 3 1/2" by 4 1/2". The 1952 Num Num Potato Chips issue features black and white, numbered cards of the Cleveland Indians. Cards came with and without coupons (tabs). The cards were issued without coupons directly by the Cleveland baseball club. When the complete set was obtained the tabs were cut off and exchanged for an autographed baseball. Card Number 16, Kennedy, is rather scarce. Cards with the tabs still intact are worth approximately 25% more than the values listed below. The ACC designation is F337- 2.

		NRMT	VG-E	GOOD
	COMPLETE SET	600.00	300.00	60.00
	COMMON PLAYER (1-20)	16.00	8.00	1.60
☐ 1	Lou Brissie	16.00	8.00	1.60
☐ 2	Jim Hegan	18.00	9.00	1.80
☐ 3	Birdie Tebbetts	16.00	8.00	1.60
☐ 4	Bob Lemon	40.00	20.00	4.00
☐ 5	Bob Feller	60.00	30.00	6.00
☐ 6	Early Wynn	40.00	20.00	4.00
☐ 7	Mike Garcia	20.00	10.00	2.00
☐ 8	Steve Gromek	16.00	8.00	1.60
☐ 9	Bob Chakales	16.00	8.00	1.60
☐ 10	Al Rosen	30.00	15.00	3.00
☐ 11	Dick Rozek	16.00	8.00	1.60
☐ 12	Luke Easter	16.00	8.00	1.60
☐ 13	Ray Boone	18.00	9.00	1.80
☐ 14	Bobby Avila	18.00	9.00	1.80
☐ 15	Dale Mitchell	20.00	10.00	2.00
☐ 16	Bob Kennedy	250.00	125.00	25.00
☐ 17	Harry Simpson	16.00	8.00	1.60
☐ 18	Larry Doby	30.00	15.00	3.00
☐ 19	Sam Jones	18.00	9.00	1.80
☐ 20	Al Lopez MG	40.00	20.00	4.00

1986 Oh Henry Indians

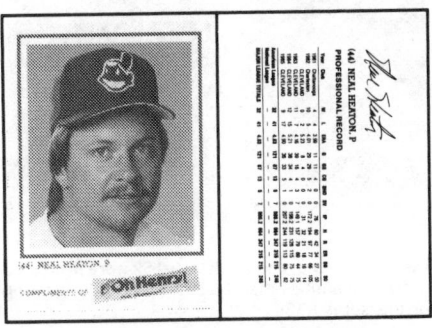

This 30-card set features Cleveland Indians and was distributed at the stadium to fans in attendance on Baseball Card Day. The cards were printed in one folded sheet which was perforated for easy separation into individual cards. The cards have white borders with a blue frame around each photo. The card backs include detailed career year-by-year statistics. The individual cards measure 2 1/4" by 3 1/8" and have full-color fronts.

		MINT	EXC	G-VG
	COMPLETE SET	7.00	3.50	.70
	COMMON PLAYER	.20	.10	.02
☐ 2	Brett Butler	.40	.20	.04
☐ 4	Tony Bernazard	.30	.15	.03
☐ 6	Andy Allanson	.30	.15	.03
☐ 7	Pat Corrales MG	.20	.10	.02
☐ 8	Carmen Castillo	.20	.10	.02
☐ 10	Pat Tabler	.50	.25	.05
☐ 13	Ernie Camacho	.30	.15	.03
☐ 14	Julio Franco	.50	.25	.05
☐ 15	Dan Rohn	.30	.15	.03
☐ 18	Ken Schrom	.30	.15	.03
☐ 20	Otis Nixon	.30	.15	.03
☐ 22	Fran Mullins	.20	.10	.02
☐ 23	Chris Bando	.20	.10	.02
☐ 24	Ed Williams	.50	.25	.05
☐ 26	Brook Jacoby	.50	.25	.05
☐ 27	Mel Hall	.40	.20	.04
☐ 29	Andre Thornton	.30	.15	.03
☐ 30	Joe Carter	.75	.35	.07
☐ 35	Phil Niekro	.75	.35	.07
☐ 36	Jamie Easterly	.20	.10	.02
☐ 37	Don Schulze	.20	.10	.02
☐ 42	Rick Yett	.20	.10	.02
☐ 43	Scott Bailes	.20	.10	.02
☐ 44	Neal Heaton	.20	.10	.02
☐ 46	Jim Kern	.20	.10	.02
☐ 48	Dickie Noles	.20	.10	.02
☐ 49	Tom Candiotti	.20	.10	.02
☐ 53	Reggie Ritter	.20	.10	.02
☐ 54	Tom Waddell	.20	.10	.02
☐ xx	Coaching Staff	.20	.10	.02
	Jack Aker			
	Bobby Bonds			
	Doc Edwards			
	John Goryl			

1939 Playball

The cards in this 162 card set measure 2 1/2" by 3 1/8". Gum Incorporated introduced a brief (war-shortened) but innovative era of baseball card production with its set of 1939. The combination of actual player photos (black and white), large card size, and extensive biography proved extremely popular. Player names are found either entirely capitalized or with initial caps only, and a "sample card" overprint is not uncommon. Card number 126

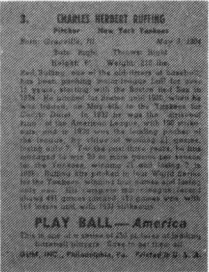

was never issued, and cards 116-162 were produced in lesser quantities than 1-115. The ACC designation for this set is R334.

	NRMT	VG-E	GOOD
COMPLETE SET	5000.00	1800.00	350.00
COMMON PLAYER (1-115)	7.00	3.50	.70
COMMON PLAYER (116-162)	50.00	25.00	5.00

		NRMT	VG-E	GOOD
☐	1 Jake Powell	50.00	5.00	1.00
☐	2 Lee Grissom	7.00	3.50	.70
☐	3 Red Ruffing	40.00	20.00	4.00
☐	4 Eldon Auker	7.00	3.50	.70
☐	5 Luke Sewell	9.00	4.50	.90
☐	6 Leo Durocher	30.00	15.00	3.00
☐	7 Bobby Doerr	35.00	17.50	3.50
☐	8 Henry Pippen	7.00	3.50	.70
☐	9 James Tobin	7.00	3.50	.70
☐	10 James DeShong	7.00	3.50	.70
☐	11 Johnny Rizzo	7.00	3.50	.70
☐	12 Hershel Martin	7.00	3.50	.70
☐	13 Luke Hamlin	7.00	3.50	.70
☐	14 Jim Tabor	7.00	3.50	.70
☐	15 Paul Derringer	9.00	4.50	.90
☐	16 John Peacock	7.00	3.50	.70
☐	17 Emerson Dickman	7.00	3.50	.70
☐	18 Harry Danning	7.00	3.50	.70
☐	19 Paul Dean	12.00	6.00	1.20
☐	20 Joe Heving	7.00	3.50	.70
☐	21 Dutch Leonard	9.00	4.50	.90
☐	22 Bucky Walters	9.00	4.50	.90
☐	23 Burgess Whitehead	7.00	3.50	.70
☐	24 Richard Coffman	7.00	3.50	.70
☐	25 George Selkirk	9.00	4.50	.90
☐	26 Joe DiMaggio	650.00	325.00	65.00
☐	27 Fred Ostermueller	7.00	3.50	.70
☐	28 Sylvester Johnson	7.00	3.50	.70
☐	29 John (Jack) Wilson	7.00	3.50	.70
☐	30 Bill Dickey	80.00	40.00	8.00
☐	31 Sam West	7.00	3.50	.70
☐	32 Bob Seeds	7.00	3.50	.70
☐	33 Del Young	7.00	3.50	.70
☐	34 Frank Demaree	7.00	3.50	.70
☐	35 Bill Jurges	7.00	3.50	.70
☐	36 Frank McCormick	9.00	4.50	.90
☐	37 Virgil Davis	7.00	3.50	.70
☐	38 Billy Myers	7.00	3.50	.70
☐	39 Rick Ferrell	35.00	17.50	3.50
☐	40 James Bagby Jr.	7.00	3.50	.70
☐	41 Lon Warneke	7.00	3.50	.70
☐	42 Arndt Jorgens	7.00	3.50	.70
☐	43 Melo Almada	7.00	3.50	.70
☐	44 Don Heffner	7.00	3.50	.70
☐	45 Merrill May	7.00	3.50	.70
☐	46 Morris Arnovich	7.00	3.50	.70
☐	47 Buddy Lewis	7.00	3.50	.70
☐	48 Lefty Gomez	60.00	30.00	6.00
☐	49 Eddie Miller	7.00	3.50	.70
☐	50 Charlie Gehringer	60.00	30.00	6.00
☐	51 Mel Ott	80.00	40.00	8.00
☐	52 Tommy Henrich	15.00	7.50	1.50
☐	53 Carl Hubbell	60.00	30.00	6.00
☐	54 Harry Gumpert	7.00	3.50	.70
☐	55 Arky Vaughan	35.00	17.50	3.50
☐	56 Hank Greenberg	80.00	40.00	8.00
☐	57 Buddy Hassett	7.00	3.50	.70
☐	58 Lou Chiozza	7.00	3.50	.70
☐	59 Ken Chase	7.00	3.50	.70
☐	60 Schoolboy Rowe	9.00	4.50	.90
☐	61 Tony Cuccinello	7.00	3.50	.70
☐	62 Tom Carey	7.00	3.50	.70
☐	63 Emmett Mueller	7.00	3.50	.70
☐	64 Wally Moses	9.00	4.50	.90
☐	65 Harry Craft	7.00	3.50	.70
☐	66 Jimmy Ripple	7.00	3.50	.70
☐	67 Ed Joost	7.00	3.50	.70
☐	68 Fred Sington	7.00	3.50	.70
☐	69 Elbie Fletcher	7.00	3.50	.70
☐	70 Fred Frankhouse	7.00	3.50	.70
☐	71 Monte Pearson	7.00	3.50	.70
☐	72 Debs Garms	7.00	3.50	.70
☐	73 Hal Schumacher	7.00	3.50	.70
☐	74 Cookie Lavagetto	9.00	4.50	.90
☐	75 Stan Bordagaray	7.00	3.50	.70
☐	76 Goody Rosen	7.00	3.50	.70
☐	77 Lew Riggs	7.00	3.50	.70
☐	78 Julius Solters	7.00	3.50	.70
☐	79 Jo Jo Moore	7.00	3.50	.70
☐	80 Pete Fox	7.00	3.50	.70
☐	81 Babe Dahlgren	9.00	4.50	.90
☐	82 Chuck Klein	50.00	25.00	5.00
☐	83 Gus Suhr	7.00	3.50	.70
☐	84 Skeeter Newsom	7.00	3.50	.70
☐	85 Johnny Cooney	7.00	3.50	.70
☐	86 Dolph Camilli	7.00	3.50	.70
☐	87 Milburn Schoffner	7.00	3.50	.70
☐	88 Charlie Keller	15.00	7.50	1.50
☐	89 Lloyd Waner	35.00	17.50	3.50
☐	90 Robert Klinger	7.00	3.50	.70
☐	91 John Knott	7.00	3.50	.70
☐	92 Ted Williams	450.00	225.00	45.00
☐	93 Charles Gelbert	7.00	3.50	.70
☐	94 Heinie Manush	35.00	17.50	3.50
☐	95 Whit Wyatt	9.00	4.50	.90
☐	96 Babe Phelps	7.00	3.50	.70
☐	97 Bob Johnson	9.00	4.50	.90
☐	98 Pinky Whitney	7.00	3.50	.70
☐	99 Wally Berger	9.00	4.50	.90
☐	100 Charles Myer	7.00	3.50	.70
☐	101 Roger Cramer	9.00	4.50	.90
☐	102 Lem Young	7.00	3.50	.70
☐	103 Moe Berg	9.00	4.50	.90
☐	104 Tom Bridges	9.00	4.50	.90
☐	105 Rabbit McNair	7.00	3.50	.70
☐	106 Dolly Stark	9.00	4.50	.90
☐	107 Joe Vosmik	7.00	3.50	.70
☐	108 Frank Hayes	7.00	3.50	.70
☐	109 Myril Hoag	7.00	3.50	.70
☐	110 Fred Fitzsimmons	7.00	3.50	.70
☐	111 Van Lingle Mungo	9.00	4.50	.90
☐	112 Paul Waner	40.00	20.00	4.00
☐	113 Al Schacht	9.00	4.50	.90
☐	114 Cecil Travis	7.00	3.50	.70
☐	115 Ralph Kress	7.00	3.50	.70
☐	116 Gene Desautels	50.00	25.00	5.00
☐	117 Wayne Ambler	50.00	25.00	5.00
☐	118 Lynn Nelson	50.00	25.00	5.00
☐	119 Will Hershberger	50.00	25.00	5.00
☐	120 Rabbit Warstler	50.00	25.00	5.00
☐	121 Bill Posedel	50.00	25.00	5.00
☐	122 George McQuinn	50.00	25.00	5.00
☐	123 Ray T. Davis	50.00	25.00	5.00
☐	124 Walter Brown	50.00	25.00	5.00
☐	125 Cliff Melton	50.00	25.00	5.00
☐	126 Not issued	0.00	.00	.00
☐	127 Gil Brack	50.00	25.00	5.00
☐	128 Joe Bowman	50.00	25.00	5.00
☐	129 Bill Swift	50.00	25.00	5.00
☐	130 Bill Brubaker	50.00	25.00	5.00
☐	131 Mort Cooper	50.00	25.00	5.00
☐	132 Jim Brown	50.00	25.00	5.00
☐	133 Lynn Myers	50.00	25.00	5.00
☐	134 Tot Presnell	50.00	25.00	5.00
☐	135 Mickey Owen	50.00	25.00	5.00
☐	136 Roy Bell	50.00	25.00	5.00
☐	137 Pete Appleton	50.00	25.00	5.00
☐	138 George Case	50.00	25.00	5.00
☐	139 Vito Tamulis	50.00	25.00	5.00
☐	140 Ray Hayworth	50.00	25.00	5.00
☐	141 Pete Coscarart	50.00	25.00	5.00
☐	142 Ira Hutchinson	50.00	25.00	5.00
☐	143 Earl Averill	150.00	75.00	15.00
☐	144 Zeke Bonura	50.00	25.00	5.00
☐	145 Hugh Mulcahy	50.00	25.00	5.00
☐	146 Tom Sunkel	50.00	25.00	5.00
☐	147 George Coffman	50.00	25.00	5.00
☐	148 Bill Trotter	50.00	25.00	5.00
☐	149 Max West	50.00	25.00	5.00
☐	150 James Walkup	50.00	25.00	5.00
☐	151 Hugh Casey	50.00	25.00	5.00
☐	152 Roy Weatherly	50.00	25.00	5.00
☐	153 Paul Trout	50.00	25.00	5.00
☐	154 Johnny Hudson	50.00	25.00	5.00
☐	155 Jimmy Outlaw	50.00	25.00	5.00
☐	156 Ray Berres	50.00	25.00	5.00
☐	157 Don Padgett	50.00	25.00	5.00
☐	158 Bud Thomas	50.00	25.00	5.00
☐	159 Red Evans	50.00	25.00	5.00
☐	160 Gene Moore	50.00	25.00	5.00
☐	161 Lonnie Frey	50.00	25.00	5.00
☐	162 Whitey Moore	75.00	25.00	5.00

1940 Playball

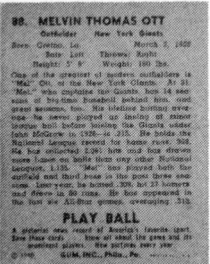

The cards in this 240 card series measure 2 1/2" by 3 1/8". Gum Inc. improved upon its 1939 design by enclosing the 1940 black and white player photo with a frame line and printing the player's name in a panel below the picture (often using a nickname). The set included many Hall of Famers and Old Timers. Cards 181-240 are scarcer than cards 1-180. The backs contain an extensive biography and a dated copyright line. The ACC catalog number is R335.

	NRMT	VG-E	GOOD
COMPLETE SET	8000.00	2700.00	500.00
COMMON PLAYER (1-120)	9.00	4.50	.90
COMMON PLAYER (121-180)	10.00	5.00	1.00
COMMON PLAYER (181-240)	30.00	15.00	3.00

		NRMT	VG-E	GOOD
☐	1 Joe DiMaggio	1000.00	300.00	60.00
☐	2 Art Jorgens	9.00	4.50	.90
☐	3 Babe Dahlgren	11.00	5.50	1.10
☐	4 Tommy Henrich	15.00	7.50	1.50
☐	5 Monte Pearson	9.00	4.50	.90
☐	6 Lefty Gomez	65.00	32.50	6.50
☐	7 Bill Dickey	90.00	45.00	9.00
☐	8 George Selkirk	11.00	5.50	1.10
☐	9 Charlie Keller	15.00	7.50	1.50
☐	10 Red Ruffing	45.00	22.50	4.50
☐	11 Jake Powell	9.00	4.50	.90
☐	12 Johnny Schulte	9.00	4.50	.90
☐	13 Jack Knott	9.00	4.50	.90
☐	14 Rabbit McNair	9.00	4.50	.90
☐	15 George Case	9.00	4.50	.90
☐	16 Cecil Travis	9.00	4.50	.90
☐	17 Buddy Myer	9.00	4.50	.90
☐	18 Charlie Gelbert	9.00	4.50	.90
☐	19 Ken Chase	9.00	4.50	.90
☐	20 Buddy Lewis	9.00	4.50	.90
☐	21 Rick Ferrell	35.00	17.50	3.50
☐	22 Sammy West	9.00	4.50	.90
☐	23 Dutch Leonard	11.00	5.50	1.10
☐	24 Frank Hayes	9.00	4.50	.90
☐	25 Bob Johnson	11.00	5.50	1.10
☐	26 Wally Moses	9.00	4.50	.90
☐	27 Ted Williams	450.00	225.00	45.00
☐	28 Gene Desautels	9.00	4.50	.90
☐	29 Doc Cramer	11.00	5.50	1.10
☐	30 Moe Berg	11.00	5.50	1.10
☐	31 Jack Wilson	9.00	4.50	.90
☐	32 Jim Bagby	9.00	4.50	.90
☐	33 Fritz Ostermueller	9.00	4.50	.90
☐	34 John Peacock	9.00	4.50	.90
☐	35 Joe Heving	9.00	4.50	.90
☐	36 Jim Tabor	9.00	4.50	.90
☐	37 Emerson Dickman	9.00	4.50	.90
☐	38 Bobby Doerr	35.00	17.50	3.50
☐	39 Tom Carey	9.00	4.50	.90
☐	40 Hank Greenberg	90.00	45.00	9.00
☐	41 Charley Gehringer	65.00	32.50	6.50
☐	42 Bud Thomas	9.00	4.50	.90
☐	43 Pete Fox	9.00	4.50	.90
☐	44 Dizzy Trout	11.00	5.50	1.10
☐	45 Red Kress	9.00	4.50	.90
☐	46 Earl Averill	45.00	22.50	4.50
☐	47 Ol' Os Vitt	9.00	4.50	.90
☐	48 Luke Sewell	11.00	5.50	1.10
☐	49 Stormy Weatherly	9.00	4.50	.90
☐	50 Hal Trosky	11.00	5.50	1.10
☐	51 Don Heffner	9.00	4.50	.90
☐	52 Myril Hoag	9.00	4.50	.90
☐	53 Mac McQuinn	9.00	4.50	.90
☐	54 Bill Trotter	9.00	4.50	.90
☐	55 Slick Coffman	9.00	4.50	.90
☐	56 Eddie Miller	9.00	4.50	.90
☐	57 Max West	9.00	4.50	.90
☐	58 Bill Posedel	9.00	4.50	.90
☐	59 Rabbit Warstler	9.00	4.50	.90
☐	60 John Cooney	9.00	4.50	.90
☐	61 Tony Cuccinello	9.00	4.50	.90
☐	62 Buddy Hassett	9.00	4.50	.90
☐	63 Pete Coscarart	9.00	4.50	.90
☐	64 Van Lingle Mungo	11.00	5.50	1.10
☐	65 Fitz Fitzsimmons	9.00	4.50	.90
☐	66 Babe Phelps	9.00	4.50	.90
☐	67 Whit Wyatt	11.00	5.50	1.10
☐	68 Dolph Camilli	9.00	4.50	.90
☐	69 Cookie Lavagetto	11.00	5.50	1.10
☐	70 Hot Potato Hamlin	9.00	4.50	.90
☐	71 Mel Almada	9.00	4.50	.90
☐	72 Chuck Dressen	11.00	5.50	1.10
☐	73 Bucky Walters	11.00	5.50	1.10
☐	74 Duke Derringer	11.00	5.50	1.10
☐	75 Buck McCormick	11.00	5.50	1.10
☐	76 Lonny Frey	9.00	4.50	.90
☐	77 Bill Hershberger	9.00	4.50	.90
☐	78 Lew Riggs	9.00	4.50	.90
☐	79 Harry Wildfire Craft	9.00	4.50	.90
☐	80 Billy Myers	9.00	4.50	.90
☐	81 Wally Berger	11.00	5.50	1.10
☐	82 Hank Gowdy	9.00	4.50	.90
☐	83 Cliff Melton	9.00	4.50	.90
☐	84 Jo Jo Moore	9.00	4.50	.90
☐	85 Hal Schumacher	9.00	4.50	.90
☐	86 Harry Gumbert	9.00	4.50	.90
☐	87 Carl Hubbell	65.00	32.50	6.50
☐	88 Mel Ott	90.00	45.00	9.00
☐	89 Bill Jurges	9.00	4.50	.90
☐	90 Frank Demaree	9.00	4.50	.90
☐	91 Suitcase Seeds	9.00	4.50	.90
☐	92 Whitey Whitehead	9.00	4.50	.90
☐	93 Harry Danning	9.00	4.50	.90
☐	94 Gus Suhr	9.00	4.50	.90
☐	95 Mul Mulcahy	9.00	4.50	.90
☐	96 Heinie Mueller	9.00	4.50	.90
☐	97 Morry Arnovich	9.00	4.50	.90
☐	98 Pinky May	9.00	4.50	.90
☐	99 Syl Johnson	9.00	4.50	.90
☐	100 Hersh Martin	9.00	4.50	.90
☐	101 Del Young	9.00	4.50	.90
☐	102 Chuck Klein	50.00	25.00	5.00
☐	103 Elbie Fletcher	9.00	4.50	.90
☐	104 Big Poison Waner	40.00	20.00	4.00
☐	105 Little Poison Waner	35.00	17.50	3.50
☐	106 Pep Young	9.00	4.50	.90
☐	107 Arky Vaughan	35.00	17.50	3.50
☐	108 Johnny Rizzo	9.00	4.50	.90
☐	109 Don Padgett	9.00	4.50	.90
☐	110 Tom Sunkell	9.00	4.50	.90
☐	111 Mickey Owen	11.00	5.50	1.10
☐	112 Jimmy Brown	9.00	4.50	.90
☐	113 Mort Cooper	11.00	5.50	1.10
☐	114 Lon Warneke	9.00	4.50	.90
☐	115 Mike Gonzales	9.00	4.50	.90
☐	116 Al Schacht	11.00	5.50	1.10
☐	117 Dolly Stark	11.00	5.50	1.10
☐	118 Schoolboy Hoyt	40.00	20.00	4.00
☐	119 Ol Pete Alexander	65.00	32.50	6.50
☐	120 Walter Johnson	125.00	60.00	12.50
☐	121 Atley Donald	10.00	5.00	1.00
☐	122 Sandy Sundra	10.00	5.00	1.00
☐	123 Hildy Hildebrand	10.00	5.00	1.00
☐	124 Colonel Earle Combs	45.00	22.50	4.50
☐	125 Art Fletcher	10.00	5.00	1.00
☐	126 Jake Solters	10.00	5.00	1.00
☐	127 Muddy Ruel	10.00	5.00	1.00
☐	128 Pete Appleton	10.00	5.00	1.00
☐	129 Bucky Harris	30.00	15.00	3.00
☐	130 Deerfoot Milan	10.00	5.00	1.00
☐	131 Zeke Bonura	10.00	5.00	1.00
☐	132 Connie Mack	65.00	32.50	6.50
☐	133 Jimmie Foxx	125.00	60.00	12.50
☐	134 Joe Cronin	65.00	32.50	6.50
☐	135 Line Drive Nelson	10.00	5.00	1.00
☐	136 Cotton Pippen	10.00	5.00	1.00
☐	137 Bing Miller	10.00	5.00	1.00
☐	138 Beau Bell	10.00	5.00	1.00
☐	139 Elden Auker	10.00	5.00	1.00
☐	140 Dick Coffman	10.00	5.00	1.00
☐	141 Casey Stengel	90.00	45.00	9.00
☐	142 Highpockets Kelly	40.00	20.00	4.00
☐	143 Gene Moore	10.00	5.00	1.00
☐	144 Joe Vosmik	10.00	5.00	1.00
☐	145 Vito Tamulis	10.00	5.00	1.00

☐ 146	Tot Pressnell	10.00	5.00	1.00
☐ 147	Johnny Hudson	10.00	5.00	1.00
☐ 148	Hugh Casey	10.00	5.00	1.00
☐ 149	Pinky Shoffner	10.00	5.00	1.00
☐ 150	Whitey Moore	10.00	5.00	1.00
☐ 151	Edwin Joost	10.00	5.00	1.00
☐ 152	Jimmy Wilson	10.00	5.00	1.00
☐ 153	Bill McKechnie	35.00	17.50	3.50
☐ 154	Jumbo Brown	10.00	5.00	1.00
☐ 155	Ray Hayworth	10.00	5.00	1.00
☐ 156	Daffy Dean	15.00	7.50	1.50
☐ 157	Lou Chiozza	10.00	5.00	1.00
☐ 158	Travis Jackson	35.00	17.50	3.50
☐ 159	Pancho Snyder	10.00	5.00	1.00
☐ 160	Hans Lobert	10.00	5.00	1.00
☐ 161	Debs Garms	10.00	5.00	1.00
☐ 162	Joe Bowman	10.00	5.00	1.00
☐ 163	Spud Davis	10.00	5.00	1.00
☐ 164	Ray Berres	10.00	5.00	1.00
☐ 165	Bob Klinger	10.00	5.00	1.00
☐ 166	Bill Brubaker	10.00	5.00	1.00
☐ 167	Frankie Frisch	60.00	30.00	6.00
☐ 168	Honus Wagner	125.00	60.00	12.50
☐ 169	Gabby Street	10.00	5.00	1.00
☐ 170	Tris Speaker	90.00	45.00	9.00
☐ 171	Harry Heilmann	60.00	30.00	6.00
☐ 172	Chief Bender	45.00	22.50	4.50
☐ 173	Larry Lajoie	90.00	45.00	9.00
☐ 174	Johnny Evers	50.00	25.00	5.00
☐ 175	Christy Mathewson	125.00	60.00	12.50
☐ 176	Heinie Manush	35.00	17.50	3.50
☐ 177	Homerun Baker	45.00	22.50	4.50
☐ 178	Max Carey	45.00	22.50	4.50
☐ 179	George Sisler	65.00	32.50	6.50
☐ 180	Mickey Cochrane	90.00	45.00	9.00
☐ 181	Spud Chandler	40.00	20.00	4.00
☐ 182	Knick Knickerbocker	30.00	15.00	3.00
☐ 183	Marvin Breuer	30.00	15.00	3.00
☐ 184	Mule Haas	30.00	15.00	3.00
☐ 185	Joe Kuhel	30.00	15.00	3.00
☐ 186	Taft Wright	30.00	15.00	3.00
☐ 187	Jimmy Dykes	35.00	17.50	3.50
☐ 188	Joe Krakauskas	30.00	15.00	3.00
☐ 189	Jim Bloodworth	30.00	15.00	3.00
☐ 190	Charley Berry	30.00	15.00	3.00
☐ 191	John Babich	30.00	15.00	3.00
☐ 192	Dick Siebert	30.00	15.00	3.00
☐ 193	Chubby Dean	30.00	15.00	3.00
☐ 194	Sam Chapman	30.00	15.00	3.00
☐ 195	Dee Miles	30.00	15.00	3.00
☐ 196	Noony Nonnenkamp	30.00	15.00	3.00
☐ 197	Lou Finney	30.00	15.00	3.00
☐ 198	Denny Galehouse	30.00	15.00	3.00
☐ 199	Pinky Higgins	30.00	15.00	3.00
☐ 200	Soup Campbell	30.00	15.00	3.00
☐ 201	Barney McCosky	30.00	15.00	3.00
☐ 202	Al Milnar	30.00	15.00	3.00
☐ 203	Bad News Hale	30.00	15.00	3.00
☐ 204	Harry Eisenstat	30.00	15.00	3.00
☐ 205	Rollie Hemsley	30.00	15.00	3.00
☐ 206	Chet Laabs	30.00	15.00	3.00
☐ 207	Gus Mancuso	30.00	15.00	3.00
☐ 208	Lee Gamble	30.00	15.00	3.00
☐ 209	Hy Vandenberg	30.00	15.00	3.00
☐ 210	Bill Lohrman	30.00	15.00	3.00
☐ 211	Pop Joiner	30.00	15.00	3.00
☐ 212	Babe Young	30.00	15.00	3.00
☐ 213	John Rucker	30.00	15.00	3.00
☐ 214	Ken O'Dea	30.00	15.00	3.00
☐ 215	Johnnie McCarthy	30.00	15.00	3.00
☐ 216	Joe Marty	30.00	15.00	3.00
☐ 217	Walter Beck	30.00	15.00	3.00
☐ 218	Wally Millies	30.00	15.00	3.00
☐ 219	Russ Bauers	30.00	15.00	3.00
☐ 220	Mace Brown	30.00	15.00	3.00
☐ 221	Lee Handley	30.00	15.00	3.00
☐ 222	Max Butcher	30.00	15.00	3.00
☐ 223	Hugh Jennings	65.00	32.50	6.50
☐ 224	Pie Traynor	100.00	50.00	10.00
☐ 225	Shoeless Joe Jackson	450.00	225.00	45.00
☐ 226	Harry Hooper	75.00	37.50	7.50
☐ 227	Pop Haines	65.00	32.50	6.50
☐ 228	Charley Grimm	40.00	20.00	4.00
☐ 229	Buck Herzog	30.00	15.00	3.00
☐ 230	Red Faber	65.00	32.50	6.50
☐ 231	Dolf Luque	30.00	15.00	3.00
☐ 232	Goose Goslin	65.00	32.50	6.50
☐ 233	Moose Earnshaw	35.00	17.50	3.50
☐ 234	Frank (Husk) Chance	75.00	37.50	7.50
☐ 235	John J. McGraw	100.00	50.00	10.00
☐ 236	Jim Bottomley	65.00	32.50	6.50
☐ 237	Wee Willie Keeler	75.00	37.50	7.50
☐ 238	Tony Lazzeri	40.00	20.00	4.00
☐ 239	George Uhle	30.00	15.00	3.00
☐ 240	Bill Atwood	50.00	15.00	3.00

1941 Playball

The cards in this 72 card set measure 2 1/2" by 3 1/8". Many of the cards in the 1941 Play Ball series are simply color versions of pictures appearing in the 1940 set. This was the only color baseball card set produced by Gum, Inc., and it carries the ACC designation R336. Card numbers 49-72 are slightly more difficult to obtain as they were not issued until 1942. In 1942, numbers 1-48 were also reissued but without the copyright date. The cards were also printed on paper without a cardboard backing; these are generally encountered in sheets or strips.

		NRMT	VG-E	GOOD
	COMPLETE SET	4800.00	1800.00	350.00
	COMMON PLAYER (1-48)	18.00	9.00	1.80
	COMMON PLAYER (49-72)	27.00	13.50	2.70
☐ 1	Eddie Miller	60.00	10.00	2.00
☐ 2	Max West	18.00	9.00	1.80
☐ 3	Bucky Walters	21.00	10.50	2.10
☐ 4	Paul Derringer	21.00	10.50	2.10
☐ 5	Buck McCormick	21.00	10.50	2.10
☐ 6	Carl Hubbell	90.00	45.00	9.00
☐ 7	Harry Danning	18.00	9.00	1.80
☐ 8	Mel Ott	100.00	50.00	10.00
☐ 9	Pinky May	18.00	9.00	1.80
☐ 10	Arky Vaughan	45.00	22.50	4.50
☐ 11	Debs Garms	18.00	9.00	1.80
☐ 12	Jimmy Brown	18.00	9.00	1.80
☐ 13	Jimmy Foxx	150.00	75.00	15.00
☐ 14	Ted Williams	500.00	250.00	50.00
☐ 15	Joe Cronin	65.00	32.50	6.50
☐ 16	Hal Trosky	18.00	9.00	1.80
☐ 17	Roy Weatherly	18.00	9.00	1.80
☐ 18	Hank Greenberg	100.00	50.00	10.00
☐ 19	Charlie Gehringer	90.00	45.00	9.00
☐ 20	Red Ruffing	65.00	32.50	6.50
☐ 21	Charlie Keller	21.00	10.50	2.10
☐ 22	Indian Bob Johnson	21.00	10.50	2.10
☐ 23	George McQuinn	18.00	9.00	1.80
☐ 24	Dutch Leonard	21.00	10.50	2.10
☐ 25	Gene Moore	18.00	9.00	1.80
☐ 26	Harry Gumpert	18.00	9.00	1.80
☐ 27	Babe Young	18.00	9.00	1.80
☐ 28	Joe Marty	18.00	9.00	1.80
☐ 29	Jack Wilson	18.00	9.00	1.80
☐ 30	Lou Finney	18.00	9.00	1.80
☐ 31	Joe Kuhel	18.00	9.00	1.80
☐ 32	Taft Wright	18.00	9.00	1.80
☐ 33	Al Milnar	18.00	9.00	1.80
☐ 34	Rollie Hemsley	18.00	9.00	1.80
☐ 35	Pinky Higgins	18.00	9.00	1.80
☐ 36	Barney McCosky	18.00	9.00	1.80
☐ 37	Bruce Campbell	18.00	9.00	1.80
☐ 38	Atley Donald	18.00	9.00	1.80
☐ 39	Tom Henrich	24.00	12.00	2.40
☐ 40	John Babich	18.00	9.00	1.80
☐ 41	Frank "Blimp" Hayes	18.00	9.00	1.80
☐ 42	Wally Moses	18.00	9.00	1.80
☐ 43	Al Brancato	18.00	9.00	1.80
☐ 44	Sam Chapman	18.00	9.00	1.80
☐ 45	Eldon Auker	18.00	9.00	1.80
☐ 46	Sid Hudson	18.00	9.00	1.80
☐ 47	Buddy Lewis	18.00	9.00	1.80
☐ 48	Cecil Travis	18.00	9.00	1.80
☐ 49	Babe Dahlgren	27.00	13.50	2.70

☐ 50	Johnny Cooney	27.00	13.50	2.70
☐ 51	Dolph Camilli	27.00	13.50	2.70
☐ 52	Kirby Higbe	27.00	13.50	2.70
☐ 53	Luke Hamlin	27.00	13.50	2.70
☐ 54	Pee Wee Reese	250.00	125.00	25.00
☐ 55	Whit Wyatt	27.00	13.50	2.70
☐ 56	Johnny VanderMeer	35.00	17.50	3.50
☐ 57	Moe Arnovich	27.00	13.50	2.70
☐ 58	Frank Demaree	27.00	13.50	2.70
☐ 59	Bill Jurges	27.00	13.50	2.70
☐ 60	Chuck Klein	75.00	37.50	7.50
☐ 61	Vince DiMaggio	90.00	45.00	9.00
☐ 62	Elbie Fletcher	27.00	13.50	2.70
☐ 63	Dom DiMaggio	75.00	37.50	7.50
☐ 64	Bobby Doerr	75.00	37.50	7.50
☐ 65	Tommy Bridges	30.00	15.00	3.00
☐ 66	Harland Clift	27.00	13.50	2.70
☐ 67	Walt Judnich	27.00	13.50	2.70
☐ 68	John Knott	27.00	13.50	2.70
☐ 69	George Case	27.00	13.50	2.70
☐ 70	Bill Dickey	200.00	100.00	20.00
☐ 71	Joe DiMaggio	1000.00	400.00	80.00
☐ 72	Lefty Gomez	200.00	50.00	10.00

☐ xx Coaching Staff	.25	.12	.02
Bobby Bonds			
John Goryl			
Don McMahon			
Ed Napolean			
Dennis Sommers			

1979 Police Giants

Tips from the Giants

Line Drive
A ball hit on a direct line, as opposed to a fly ball or pop fly.

If you see a crime occuring or if someone bothers you make a line drive for the police and report it.

#39 Bob Knepper
Pitcher

KNBR 68

Presented as a community service by the San Francisco Giants, KNBR, and the San Francisco Police Department.

1985 Polaroid Indians

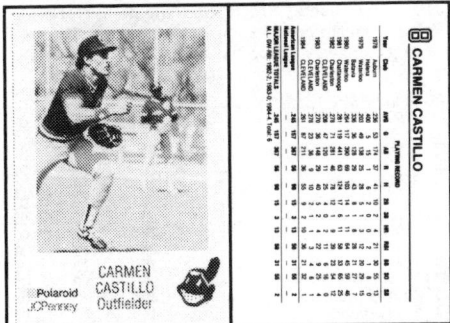

Polaroid
JCPenney

CARMEN
CASTILLO
Outfielder

This 32-card set features cards (each measuring 2 13/16" by 4 1/8") of the Cleveland Indians. The cards are unnumbered except for uniform number, as they are listed below. The set was also sponsored by J.C. Penney and was distributed at the stadium to fans in attendance on Baseball Card Day.

		MINT	EXC	G-VG
	COMPLETE SET	9.00	4.50	.90
	COMMON PLAYER	.25	.12	.02
☐ 2	Brett Butler	.45	.22	.04
☐ 4	Tony Bernazard	.35	.17	.03
☐ 8	Carmen Castillo	.25	.12	.02
☐ 10	Pat Tabler	.45	.22	.04
☐ 12	Benny Ayala	.25	.12	.02
☐ 13	Ernie Camacho	.35	.17	.03
☐ 14	Julio Franco	.35	.17	.03
☐ 16	Jerry Willard	.25	.12	.02
☐ 18	Pat Corrales MG	.25	.12	.02
☐ 20	Otis Nixon	.35	.17	.03
☐ 21	Mike Hargrove	.35	.17	.03
☐ 22	Mike Fischlin	.25	.12	.02
☐ 23	Chris Bando	.25	.12	.02
☐ 24	George Vukovich	.25	.12	.02
☐ 26	Brook Jacoby	.45	.22	.04
☐ 27	Mel Hall	.45	.22	.04
☐ 28	Bert Blyleven	.45	.22	.04
☐ 29	Andre Thornton	.35	.17	.03
☐ 30	Joe Carter	.75	.35	.07
☐ 32	Rick Behenna	.25	.12	.02
☐ 33	Roy Smith	.25	.12	.02
☐ 35	Jerry Reed	.25	.12	.02
☐ 36	Jamie Easterly	.25	.12	.02
☐ 38	Dave Von Ohlen	.25	.12	.02
☐ 41	Rich Thompson	.25	.12	.02
☐ 43	Bryan Clark	.25	.12	.02
☐ 44	Neal Heaton	.35	.17	.03
☐ 48	Vern Ruhle	.25	.12	.02
☐ 49	Jeff Barkley	.25	.12	.02
☐ 50	Ramon Romero	.25	.12	.02
☐ 54	Tom Waddell	.25	.12	.02

The cards in this 30 card set measure 2 5/8" by 4 1/8". The 1979 Police Giants set features cards numbered by the player's uniform number. This full color set features the player's photo, the Giants' logo, and the player's name, number and position on the front of the cards. A facsimile autograph in an attractive blue ink is also contained on the front. The backs, printed in orange and black, feature Tips from the Giants, the Giants' and sponsoring radio station, KNBR, logos and a line listing the Giants, KNBR, and the San Francisco Police Department as sponsors of the set. The 15 cards which are shown with an asterisk below were available only from the Police. The other 15 cards were given away at the ballpark on June 17, 1979.

		NRMT	VG-E	GOOD
	COMPLETE SET	15.00	7.50	1.50
	COMMON PLAYER	.30	.15	.03
☐ 1	Dave Bristol MG	.30	.15	.03
☐ 2	Marc Hill	.30	.15	.03
☐ 3	Mike Sadek *	.40	.20	.04
☐ 5	Tom Haller	.30	.15	.03
☐ 6	Joe Altobelli CO *	.40	.20	.04
☐ 8	Larry Shepard CO *	.40	.20	.04
☐ 9	Heity Cruz	.30	.15	.03
☐ 10	Johnnie LeMaster	.30	.15	.03
☐ 12	Jim Davenport	.50	.25	.05
☐ 14	Vida Blue	.50	.25	.05
☐ 15	Mike Ivie	.30	.15	.03
☐ 16	Roger Metzger	.30	.15	.03
☐ 17	Randy Moffitt	.30	.15	.03
☐ 18	Bill Madlock	1.00	.50	.10
☐ 21	Rob Andrews *	.40	.20	.04
☐ 22	Jack Clark *	2.50	1.25	.25
☐ 25	Dave Roberts	.30	.15	.03
☐ 26	John Montefusco	.40	.20	.04
☐ 28	Ed Halicki *	.40	.20	.04
☐ 30	John Tamargo	.30	.15	.03
☐ 31	Larry Herndon	.40	.20	.04
☐ 36	Bill North *	.40	.20	.04
☐ 39	Bob Knepper *	.80	.40	.08
☐ 40	John Curtis *	.40	.20	.04
☐ 41	Darrell Evans *	1.25	.60	.12
☐ 43	Tom Griffin *	.40	.20	.04
☐ 44	Willie McCovey *	3.00	1.50	.30
☐ 45	Terry Whitfield *	.40	.20	.04
☐ 46	Gary Lavelle *	.40	.20	.04
☐ 49	Max Venable *	.40	.20	.04

1980 Police Dodgers

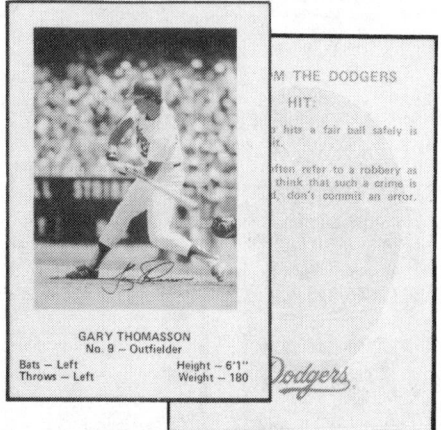

GARY THOMASSON
No. 9 — Outfielder

Bats — Left Height — 6'1"
Throws — Left Weight — 180

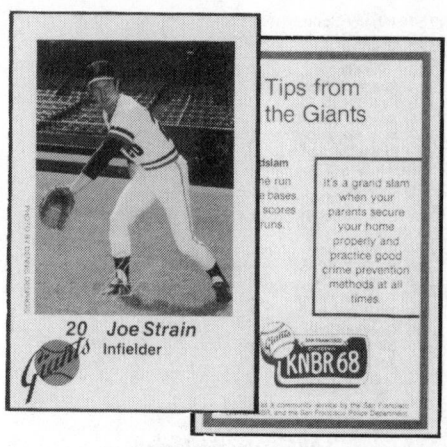

Tips from
the Giants

20 Joe Strain
Infielder

KNBR 68

The cards in this 30 card set measure 2 13/16" by 4 1/8". The full color 1980 Police Los Angeles Dodgers set features the player's name, uniform number, position, and biographical data on the fronts in addition to the photo. The backs feature Tips from the Dodgers, the LAPD logo, and the Dodgers' logo. The cards are listed below according to uniform number.

		MINT	EXC	G-VG
COMPLETE SET		8.00	4.00	.80
COMMON PLAYER		.25	.12	.02
☐ 5	Johnny Oates	.25	.12	.02
☐ 6	Steve Garvey	1.25	.60	.12
☐ 7	Steve Yeager	.25	.12	.02
☐ 8	Reggie Smith	.35	.17	.03
☐ 9	Gary Thomasson	.25	.12	.02
☐ 10	Ron Cey	.45	.22	.04
☐ 12	Dusty Baker	.35	.17	.03
☐ 13	Joe Ferguson	.25	.12	.02
☐ 15	Davey Lopes	.35	.17	.03
☐ 16	Rick Monday	.35	.17	.03
☐ 18	Bill Russell	.35	.17	.03
☐ 20	Don Sutton	.85	.40	.08
☐ 21	Jay Johnstone	.35	.17	.03
☐ 23	Teddy Martinez	.25	.12	.02
☐ 27	Joe Beckwith	.25	.12	.02
☐ 28	Pedro Guerrero	1.25	.60	.12
☐ 29	Don Stanhouse	.25	.12	.02
☐ 30	Derrel Thomas	.25	.12	.02
☐ 31	Doug Rau	.25	.12	.02
☐ 34	Ken Brett	.25	.12	.02
☐ 35	Bob Welch	.45	.22	.04
☐ 37	Robert Castillo	.25	.12	.02
☐ 38	Dave Goltz	.25	.12	.02
☐ 41	Jerry Reuss	.35	.17	.03
☐ 43	Rick Sutcliffe	.75	.35	.07
☐ 44	Mickey Hatcher	.25	.12	.02
☐ 46	Burt Hooton	.25	.12	.02
☐ 49	Charlie Hough	.45	.22	.04
☐ xx	Team Card (unnumbered)	.25	.12	.02

1980 Police Giants

The cards in this 31 card set measure 2 5/8" by 4 1/8". The 1980 Police San Francisco Giants set features cards numbered by the player's uniform number. This full color set features the player's photo, the Giants' logo, and the player's name, number and position on the front of the cards. A facsimile autograph in an attractive blue ink is also contained on the front. The backs, printed in orange and black, feature Tips from the Giants, the Giants'

and sponsoring radio station, KNBR, logos and a line listing the Giants, KNBR, and the San Francisco Police Department as sponsors of the set. The sets were given away at the ballpark on May 31, 1980.

		MINT	EXC	G-VG
COMPLETE SET		10.00	5.00	1.00
COMMON PLAYER		.25	.12	.02
☐ 1	Dave Bristol MG	.25	.12	.02
☐ 2	Marc Hill	.25	.12	.02
☐ 3	Mike Sadek	.25	.12	.02
☐ 5	Jim Lefebvre	.25	.12	.02
☐ 6	Rennie Stennett	.25	.12	.02
☐ 7	Milt May	.25	.12	.02
☐ 8	Vern Benson CO	.25	.12	.02
☐ 9	Jim Wohlford	.25	.12	.02
☐ 10	Johnnie LeMaster	.25	.12	.02
☐ 12	Jim Davenport	.45	.22	.04
☐ 14	Vida Blue	.45	.22	.04
☐ 15	Mike Ivie	.25	.12	.02
☐ 16	Roger Metzger	.25	.12	.02
☐ 17	Randy Moffitt	.25	.12	.02
☐ 19	Al Holland	.35	.17	.03
☐ 20	Joe Strain	.25	.12	.02
☐ 22	Jack Clark	2.00	1.00	.20
☐ 26	John Montefusco	.35	.17	.03
☐ 28	Ed Halicki	.25	.12	.02
☐ 31	Larry Herndon	.35	.17	.03
☐ 32	Ed Whitson	.35	.17	.03
☐ 36	Bill North	.25	.12	.02
☐ 38	Greg Minton	.35	.17	.03
☐ 39	Bob Knepper	.45	.22	.04
☐ 41	Darrell Evans	1.00	.50	.10
☐ 42	John Van Ornum	.25	.12	.02
☐ 43	Tom Griffin	.25	.12	.02
☐ 44	Willie McCovey	2.00	1.00	.20
☐ 45	Terry Whitfield	.25	.12	.02
☐ 46	Gary Lavelle	.35	.17	.03
☐ 47	Don McMahon CO	.25	.12	.02

1981 Police Braves

The cards in this 27 card set measure 2 5/8" by 4 1/8". This first Atlanta Police set features full color cards sponsored by the Braves, the Atlanta Police Department, Coca-Cola and Hostess. The cards are numbered by uniform number, which is contained on the front along with an Atlanta Police Athletic League logo, a black and white Braves logo, and a green bow in the upper right corner of the frameline. The backs feature brief player biographies, logos of Coke and Hostess, and Tips from the Braves. It is reported that 33,000 of these sets were printed. The Terry Harper card is supposed to be more difficult to obtain than other cards in the set.

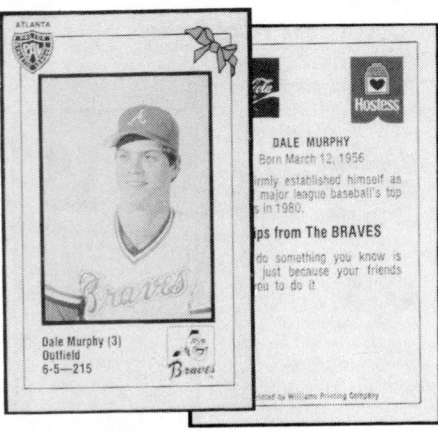

DALE MURPHY
Born March 12, 1956

...rmly established himself as
... major league baseball's top
...s in 1980.

...ps from The BRAVES

...do something you know is
... just because your friends
...ou to do it.

Dale Murphy (3)
Outfield
6-5—215

		MINT	EXC	G-VG
	COMPLETE SET	12.00	6.00	1.20
	COMMON PLAYER	.30	.15	.03
☐ 1	Jerry Royster	.30	.15	.03
☐ 3	Dale Murphy	3.50	1.75	.35
☐ 4	Biff Pocoroba	.30	.15	.03
☐ 5	Bob Horner	1.25	.60	.12
☐ 6	Bobby Cox MG	.30	.15	.03
☐ 9	Luis Gomez	.30	.15	.03
☐ 10	Chris Chambliss	.40	.20	.04
☐ 15	Bill Nahorodny	.30	.15	.03
☐ 16	Rafael Ramirez	.40	.20	.04
☐ 17	Glenn Hubbard	.40	.20	.04
☐ 18	Claudell Washington	.50	.25	.05
☐ 19	Terry Harper	.75	.35	.07
☐ 20	Bruce Benedict	.30	.15	.03
☐ 24	John Montefusco	.40	.20	.04
☐ 25	Rufino Linares	.30	.15	.03
☐ 26	Gene Garber	.40	.20	.04
☐ 30	Brian Asselstine	.30	.15	.03
☐ 34	Larry Bradford	.30	.15	.03
☐ 35	Phil Niekro	1.75	.85	.17
☐ 37	Rick Camp	.30	.15	.03
☐ 39	Al Hrabosky	.50	.25	.05
☐ 40	Tommy Boggs	.30	.15	.03
☐ 42	Rick Mahler	.40	.20	.04
☐ 44	Hank Aaron CO	2.50	1.25	.25
☐ 45	Ed Miller	.30	.15	.03
☐ 46	Gaylord Perry	1.50	.75	.15
☐ 49	Preston Hanna	.30	.15	.03

1981 Police Dodgers

KEN LANDREAUX
No. 44 — Outfield
LAPD SALUTES THE 1981
Dodgers.

The cards in this 32 card set measure 2 13/16" by 4 1/8". The full color set of 1981 Los Angeles Dodgers features the player's name, number, position and a line stating that the LAPD salutes the

1981 Dodgers, in addition to the player's photo. The backs feature the LAPD logo and short narratives, attributable to the player on the front of the card, revealing police associated tips. The cards of Ken Landreaux and Dave Stewart are reported to be more difficult to obtain than other cards in this set due to the fact that they are replacements for Stanhouse (released 4/17/81) and Hatcher (traded for Landreaux 3/30/81). The complete set price below refers to all 32 cards, i.e., including the variations.

		MINT	EXC	G-VG
	COMPLETE SET (32)	10.00	5.00	1.00
	COMMON PLAYER	.25	.12	.02
☐ 2	Tom Lasorda MG	.45	.22	.04
☐ 3	Rudy Law	.25	.12	.02
☐ 6	Steve Garvey	1.25	.60	.12
☐ 7	Steve Yeager	.25	.12	.02
☐ 8	Reggie Smith	.35	.17	.03
☐ 10	Ron Cey	.45	.22	.04
☐ 12	Dusty Baker	.35	.17	.03
☐ 13	Joe Ferguson	.25	.12	.02
☐ 14	Mike Scioscia	.25	.12	.02
☐ 15	Davey Lopes	.35	.17	.03
☐ 16	Rick Monday	.35	.17	.03
☐ 18	Bill Russell	.35	.17	.03
☐ 21	Jay Johnstone	.35	.17	.03
☐ 26	Don Stanhouse	.50	.25	.05
☐ 27	Joe Beckwith	.25	.12	.02
☐ 28	Pedro Guerrero	1.00	.50	.10
☐ 30	Derrel Thomas	.25	.12	.02
☐ 34	Fernando Valenzuela	2.50	1.25	.25
☐ 35	Bob Welch	.45	.22	.04
☐ 36	Pepe Frias	.25	.12	.02
☐ 37	Robert Castillo	.25	.12	.02
☐ 38	Dave Goltz	.25	.12	.02
☐ 41	Jerry Reuss	.35	.17	.03
☐ 43	Rick Sutcliffe	.75	.35	.07
☐ 44A	Mickey Hatcher	.50	.25	.05
☐ 44B	Ken Landreaux	1.25	.60	.12
☐ 46	Burt Hooton	.25	.12	.02
☐ 48	Dave Stewart	1.50	.75	.15
☐ 51	Terry Forster	.35	.17	.03
☐ 57	Steve Howe	.35	.17	.03
☐ xx	Team Photo (Checklist) (unnumbered)	.25	.12	.02
☐ xx	Coaching Staff (unnumbered)	.25	.12	.02

1981 Police Mariners

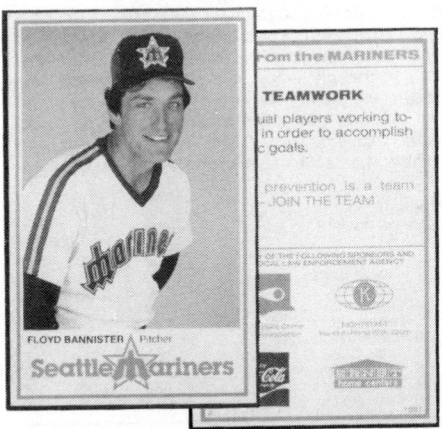

FLOYD BANNISTER Pitcher

The cards in this 16 card set measure 2 5/8" by 4 1/8". The full color Seattle Mariners Police set of this year was sponsored by the Washington State Crime Prevention Association, the Kiwanis Club, Coca-Cola and Ernst Home Centers. The fronts feature the player's name, his position, and the Seattle Mariners name in addition to the player's photo. The backs, in red and blue, feature Tips from the Mariners and the logos of the four sponsors of the set. The cards are numbered in the lower left corners of the backs.

		MINT	EXC	G-VG
COMPLETE SET		5.00	2.50	.50
COMMON PLAYER		.30	.15	.03
☐ 1	Jeff Burroughs	.40	.20	.04
☐ 2	Floyd Bannister	.50	.25	.05
☐ 3	Glenn Abbott	.30	.15	.03
☐ 4	Jim Anderson	.30	.15	.03
☐ 5	Danny Meyer	.30	.15	.03
☐ 6	Julio Cruz	.40	.20	.04
☐ 7	Dave Edler	.30	.15	.03
☐ 8	Kenny Clay	.30	.15	.03
☐ 9	Lenny Randle	.30	.15	.03
☐ 10	Mike Parrott	.30	.15	.03
☐ 11	Tom Paciorek	.40	.20	.04
☐ 12	Jerry Narron	.30	.15	.03
☐ 13	Richie Zisk	.40	.20	.04
☐ 14	Maury Wills MG	.75	.35	.07
☐ 15	Joe Simpson	.30	.15	.03
☐ 16	Shane Rawley	.60	.30	.06

1981 Police Royals

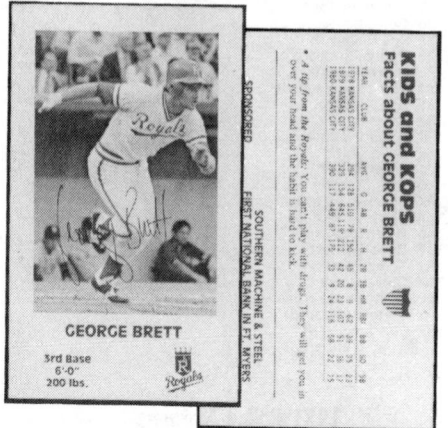

GEORGE BRETT
3rd Base
6'0"
200 lbs.

The cards in this 10-card set measure 2 1/2" by 4 1/8". The 1981 Police Kansas City Royals set features full color cards of Royals players. The fronts feature the player's name, position, height and weight, and the Royals' logo in addition to the photo and facsimile autograph of the player. The backs feature player statistics, Tips from the Royals, and identification of the sponsoring organizations.

		MINT	EXC	G-VG
COMPLETE SET		30.00	15.00	3.00
COMMON PLAYER		2.00	1.00	.20
☐ 1	Willie Aikens	2.00	1.00	.20
☐ 2	George Brett	12.50	6.25	1.25
☐ 3	Rich Gale	2.00	1.00	.20
☐ 4	Clint Hurdle	2.00	1.00	.20
☐ 5	Dennis Leonard	2.50	1.25	.25
☐ 6	Hal McRae	2.50	1.25	.25
☐ 7	Amos Otis	2.50	1.25	.25
☐ 8	U.L. Washington	2.00	1.00	.20
☐ 9	Frank White	3.50	1.75	.35
☐ 10	Willie Wilson	4.50	2.25	.45

1982 Police Braves

Phil Niekro (35)
Pitcher

The cards in this 30 card set measure 2 5/8" by 4 1/8". The Atlanta Police Department followed up on their successful 1981 safety set by publishing a new Braves set for 1982. Featured in excellent color photos are manager Joe Torre, 24 players, and 5 coaches. The cards are numbered, by uniform number, on the front only, while the backs contain a short biography of the individual and a Tips from the Braves section. The logos for the Atlanta PAL and the Braves appear on the front; those of Coca-Cola and Hostess are found on the back. A line commemorating Atlanta's record-shattering, season-beginning win streak is located in the upper right corner on every card obverse. The player list on the reverse of the Torre card is a roster list and not a checklist for the set. There were 8,000 sets reportedly printed. The Bob Watson card is supposedly more difficult to obtain than others in this set.

		MINT	EXC	G-VG
COMPLETE SET		20.00	10.00	2.00
COMMON PLAYER		.35	.17	.03
☐ 1	Jerry Royster	.35	.17	.03
☐ 3	Dale Murphy	6.00	3.00	.60
☐ 4	Biff Pocoroba	.35	.17	.03
☐ 5	Bob Horner	1.50	.75	.15
☐ 6	Randy Johnson	.35	.17	.03
☐ 8	Bob Watson	1.50	.75	.15
☐ 9	Joe Torre MG	.75	.35	.07
☐ 10	Chris Chambliss	.50	.25	.05
☐ 15	Claudell Washington	.50	.25	.05
☐ 16	Rafael Ramirez	.35	.17	.03
☐ 17	Glenn Hubbard	.35	.17	.03
☐ 20	Bruce Benedict	.35	.17	.03
☐ 22	Brett Butler	1.00	.50	.10
☐ 23	Tommy Aaron CO	.35	.17	.03
☐ 25	Rufino Linares	.35	.17	.03
☐ 26	Gene Garber	.50	.25	.05
☐ 27	Larry McWilliams	.35	.17	.03
☐ 28	Larry Whisenton	.35	.17	.03
☐ 32	Steve Bedrosian	1.00	.50	.10
☐ 35	Phil Niekro	2.50	1.25	.25
☐ 37	Rick Camp	.35	.17	.03
☐ 38	Joe Cowley	.35	.17	.03
☐ 39	Al Hrabosky	.50	.25	.05
☐ 42	Rick Mahler	.35	.17	.03
☐ 43	Bob Walk	.35	.17	.03
☐ 45	Bob Gibson CO	1.50	.75	.15
☐ 49	Preston Hanna	.35	.17	.03
☐ 52	Joe Pignatano CO	.35	.17	.03
☐ 53	Dal Maxvill CO	.35	.17	.03
☐ 54	Rube Walker CO	.35	.17	.03

			MINT	EXC	G-VG
☐ xx	Brewer Coaches		.25	.12	.02
	(unnumbered)				

1982 Police Brewers

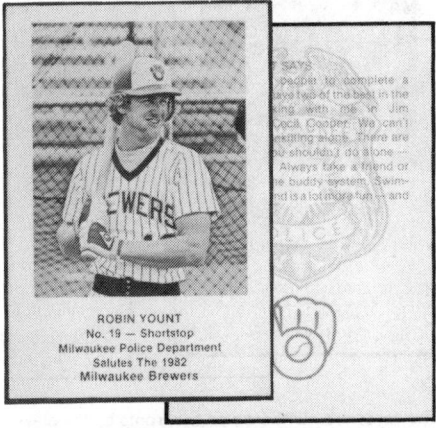

ROBIN YOUNT
No. 19 — Shortstop
Milwaukee Police Department
Salutes The 1982
Milwaukee Brewers

The cards in this 30 card set measure 2 13/16" by 4 1/8". The 1982 series of 30 Milwaukee Brewers baseball cards is noted for its excellent color photographs set upon a simple white background. The set was initially distributed at the stadium on May 5th, but was also handed out by several local police departments, and credit lines for the Wisconsin State Fair Park Police (no shield design on reverse), Milwaukee, Brookfield, and Wauwatosa PD's have already been found. The reverses feature advice concerning safety measures, social situations, and crime prevention (Romero card in both Spanish and English). The team card carries a checklist which lists the Brewer's coaches separately although they all appear on a single card; VP/GM Harry Dalton is not mentioned on this list but is included in the set. The prices below are for the basic set without regard to the Police Department listed on the backs. Cards from the more obscure corners and small towns of Wisconsin (where fewer cards were produced) will be valued higher.

			MINT	EXC	G-VG
	COMPLETE SET		9.00	4.50	.90
	COMMON PLAYER		.25	.12	.02
☐ 4	Paul Molitor		1.00	.50	.10
☐ 5	Ned Yost		.25	.12	.02
☐ 7	Don Money		.35	.17	.03
☐ 9	Larry Hisle		.35	.17	.03
☐ 10	Bob McClure		.25	.12	.02
☐ 11	Ed Romero		.25	.12	.02
☐ 13	Roy Howell		.25	.12	.02
☐ 15	Cecil Cooper		.50	.25	.05
☐ 17	Jim Gantner		.35	.17	.03
☐ 19	Robin Yount		1.50	.75	.15
☐ 20	Gorman Thomas		.50	.25	.05
☐ 22	Charlie Moore		.25	.12	.02
☐ 23	Ted Simmons		.50	.25	.05
☐ 24	Ben Oglivie		.35	.17	.03
☐ 26	Kevin Bass		.50	.25	.05
☐ 28	Jamie Easterly		.25	.12	.02
☐ 29	Mark Brouhard		.25	.12	.02
☐ 30	Moose Haas		.35	.17	.03
☐ 34	Rollie Fingers		.75	.35	.07
☐ 35	Randy Lerch		.25	.12	.02
☐ 41	Jim Slaton		.35	.17	.03
☐ 45	Doug Jones		.25	.12	.02
☐ 46	Jerry Augustine		.25	.12	.02
☐ 47	Dwight Bernard		.25	.12	.02
☐ 48	Mike Caldwell		.35	.17	.03
☐ 50	Pete Vuckovich		.35	.17	.03
☐ xx	Team Card		.25	.12	.02
	(unnumbered)				
☐ xx	Harry Dalton GM		.25	.12	.02
	(unnumbered)				
☐ xx	Buck Rodgers MG		.25	.12	.02
	(unnumbered)				

1982 Police Dodgers

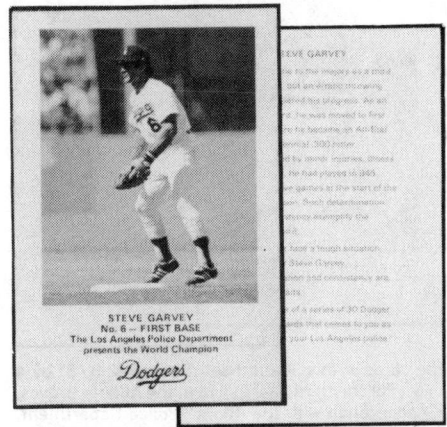

STEVE GARVEY
No. 6 — FIRST BASE
The Los Angeles Police Department
presents the World Champion
Dodgers

The cards in this 30 card set measure 2 13/16" by 4 1/8". The 1982 Los Angeles Dodgers police set depicts the players and events of the 1981 season. There is a World Series trophy card, three cards commemorating the Division, League, and World Series wins, one manager card, and 25 player cards. The obverses have brilliant color photos set on white, and the player cards are numbered according to the uniform number of the individual. The reverses contain biographical material, information about stadium events, and a safety feature emphasizing "the team that wouldn't quit."

			MINT	EXC	G-VG
	COMPLETE SET		6.00	3.00	.60
	COMMON PLAYER		.15	.07	.01
☐ 2	Tom Lasorda MG		.25	.12	.02
☐ 6	Steve Garvey		1.00	.50	.10
☐ 7	Steve Yeager		.15	.07	.01
☐ 8	Mark Belanger		.25	.12	.02
☐ 10	Ron Cey		.35	.17	.03
☐ 12	Dusty Baker		.25	.12	.02
☐ 14	Mike Scioscia		.15	.07	.01
☐ 16	Rick Monday		.25	.12	.02
☐ 18	Bill Russell		.25	.12	.02
☐ 21	Jay Johnstone		.25	.12	.02
☐ 26	Alejandro Pena		.35	.17	.03
☐ 28	Pedro Guerrero		1.00	.50	.10
☐ 30	Derrel Thomas		.15	.07	.01
☐ 31	Jorge Orta		.15	.07	.01
☐ 34	Fernando Valenzuela		1.00	.50	.10
☐ 35	Bob Welch		.35	.17	.03
☐ 38	Dave Goltz		.15	.07	.01
☐ 40	Ron Roenicke		.15	.07	.01
☐ 41	Jerry Reuss		.25	.12	.02
☐ 44	Ken Landreaux		.15	.07	.01
☐ 46	Burt Hooton		.15	.07	.01
☐ 48	Dave Stewart		.35	.17	.03
☐ 49	Tom Niedenfuer		.25	.12	.02
☐ 51	Terry Forster		.35	.17	.03
☐ 52	Steve Sax		.75	.35	.07
☐ 57	Steve Howe		.25	.12	.02
☐ xx	World Series Trophy		.15	.07	.01
	(checklist back)				
	(unnumbered)				
☐ xx	World Series		.15	.07	.01
	Commemorative				
	(unnumbered)				
☐ xx	NL Champions		.15	.07	.01
	(unnumbered)				
☐ xx	Division Champs		.15	.07	.01
	(unnumbered)				

1983 Police Braves

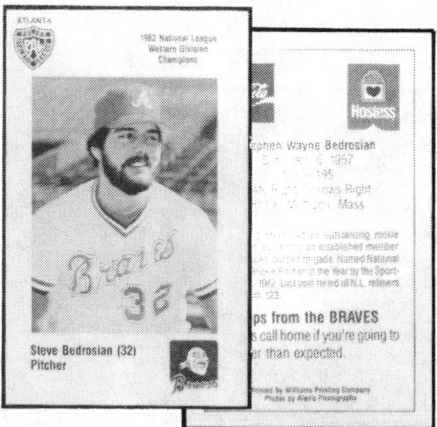

Steve Bedrosian (32)
Pitcher

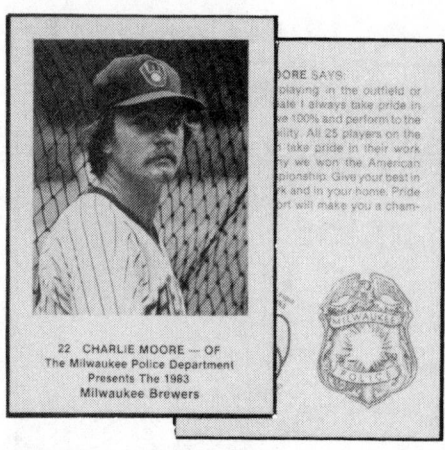

22 CHARLIE MOORE — OF
The Milwaukee Police Department
Presents The 1963
Milwaukee Brewers

The cards in this 30-card set measure 2 5/8" by 4 1/8". For the third year in a row, the Atlanta Braves, in cooperation with the Atlanta Police Department, Coca-Cola, and Hostess, issued a full color safety set. The set features Joe Torre, five coaches, and 24 of the Atlanta Braves. Numbered only by uniform number, the statement that the Braves were the 1982 National League Western Division Champions is included on the fronts along with the Braves and Police Athletic biographies, a short narrative on the player, Tips from the Braves, and the Coke and Hostess logos.

The cards are numbered on the fronts by the player uniform number and contain the line, "The Milwaukee Police Department Presents the 1983 Milwaukee Braves." The backs contain a brief narrative attributable to the player on the front, the Milwaukee Police logo, and a Milwaukee Brewers logo stating that they were the 1982 American League Champions. In all, 28 variations of these Police sets have been found to date. Prices below are for the basic set without regard to the Police Department listed on the backs of the cards; cards from the more obscure corners and small towns of Wisconsin (whose cards were produced in lesser quantities) will be valued higher.

		MINT	EXC	G-VG
COMPLETE SET		14.00	7.00	1.40
COMMON PLAYER		.35	.17	.03
☐ 1	Jerry Royster	.35	.17	.03
☐ 3	Dale Murphy	4.00	2.00	.40
☐ 4	Biff Pocoroba	.35	.17	.03
☐ 5	Bob Horner	1.25	.60	.12
☐ 6	Randy Johnson	.35	.17	.03
☐ 8	Bob Watson	.50	.25	.05
☐ 9	Joe Torre MG	.60	.30	.06
☐ 10	Chris Chambliss	.50	.25	.05
☐ 11	Ken Smith	.35	.17	.03
☐ 15	Claudell Washington	.50	.25	.05
☐ 16	Rafael Ramirez	.35	.17	.03
☐ 17	Glenn Hubbard	.35	.17	.03
☐ 19	Terry Harper	.35	.17	.03
☐ 20	Bruce Benedict	.35	.17	.03
☐ 22	Brett Butler	.75	.35	.07
☐ 24	Larry Owen	.35	.17	.03
☐ 26	Gene Garber	.35	.17	.03
☐ 27	Pascual Perez	.35	.17	.03
☐ 29	Craig McMurtry	.35	.17	.03
☐ 32	Steve Bedrosian	.75	.35	.07
☐ 33	Pete Falcone	.35	.17	.03
☐ 35	Phil Niekro	1.50	.75	.15
☐ 36	Sonny Jackson CO	.35	.17	.03
☐ 37	Rick Camp	.35	.17	.03
☐ 45	Bob Gibson CO	1.50	.75	.15
☐ 49	Rick Behenna	.35	.17	.03
☐ 51	Terry Forster	.50	.25	.05
☐ 52	Joe Pignatano CO	.35	.17	.03
☐ 53	Dal Maxvill CO	.35	.17	.03
☐ 54	Rube Walker CO	.35	.17	.03

1983 Police Brewers

The cards in this 30 card set measure 2 13/16" by 4 1/8". The 1983 Police Milwaukee Brewers set contains full color cards issued by the Milwaukee Police Department in conjunction with the Brewers.

		MINT	EXC	G-VG
COMPLETE SET		7.00	3.50	.70
COMMON PLAYER		.20	.10	.02
☐ xx	Dave Garcia CO	.20	.10	.02
☐ 4	Paul Molitor	.75	.35	.07
☐ 5	Ned Yost	.20	.10	.02
☐ 7	Don Money	.25	.12	.02
☐ 8	Rob Picciolo	.20	.10	.02
☐ 10	Bob McClure	.20	.10	.02
☐ 11	Ed Romero	.20	.10	.02
☐ 12	Larry Haney CO	.20	.10	.02
☐ 13	Roy Howell	.20	.10	.02
☐ 15	Cecil Cooper	.50	.25	.05
☐ 16	Marshall Edwards	.20	.10	.02
☐ 17	Jim Gantner	.30	.15	.03
☐ 18	Ron Hansen CO	.20	.10	.02
☐ 19	Robin Yount	1.00	.50	.10
☐ 20	Gorman Thomas	.40	.20	.04
☐ 21	Don Sutton	.75	.35	.07
☐ 22	Charlie Moore	.25	.12	.02
☐ 23	Ted Simmons	.50	.25	.05
☐ 24	Ben Oglivie	.30	.15	.03
☐ 26	Bob Skube	.20	.10	.02
☐ 27	Pete Ladd	.20	.10	.02
☐ 28	Jamie Easterly	.20	.10	.02
☐ 30	Moose Haas	.30	.15	.03
☐ 32	Harvey Kuenn MG	.40	.20	.04
☐ 34	Rollie Fingers	.75	.35	.07
☐ 40	Bob L. Gibson	.20	.10	.02
☐ 41	Jim Slaton	.20	.10	.02
☐ 42	Tom Tellmann	.20	.10	.02
☐ 45	Pat Dobson CO	.30	.15	.03
☐ 46	Jerry Augustine	.20	.10	.02
☐ 48	Mike Caldwell	.30	.15	.03
☐ 50	Pete Vuckovich	.30	.15	.03
☐ xx	Team Photo	.20	.10	.02
	(Checklist back) (unnumbered)			

1983 Police Dodgers

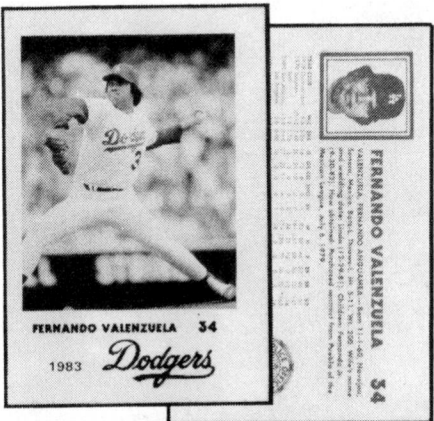

The cards in this 30 card set measure 2 13/16" by 4 1/8". The full color Police Los Angeles Dodgers set of 1983 features the player's name and uniform number on the front along with the Dodger's logo, the year, and the player's photo. The backs feature a small insert portrait picture of the player, player biographies, and career statistics. The logo of the Los Angeles Police Department, the sponsor of the set, is found on the backs of the cards.

	MINT	EXC	G-VG
COMPLETE SET	5.00	2.50	.50
COMMON PLAYER	.15	.07	.01
☐ 2 Tom Lasorda MG	.20	.10	.02
☐ 3 Steve Sax	.50	.25	.05
☐ 5 Mike Marshall	.60	.30	.06
☐ 7 Steve Yeager	.15	.07	.01
☐ 12 Dusty Baker	.25	.12	.02
☐ 14 Mike Scioscia	.15	.07	.01
☐ 16 Rick Monday	.25	.12	.02
☐ 17 Greg Brock	.35	.17	.03
☐ 18 Bill Russell	.25	.12	.02
☐ 20 Candy Maldonado	.30	.15	.03
☐ 21 Ricky Wright	.15	.07	.01
☐ 22 Mark Bradley	.15	.07	.01
☐ 23 Dave Sax	.15	.07	.01
☐ 26 Alejandro Pena	.25	.12	.02
☐ 27 Joe Beckwith	.15	.07	.01
☐ 28 Pedro Guerrero	.75	.35	.07
☐ 30 Derrel Thomas	.15	.07	.01
☐ 34 Fernando Valenzuela	.75	.35	.07
☐ 35 Bob Welch	.25	.12	.02
☐ 38 Pat Zachry	.15	.07	.01
☐ 40 Ron Roenicke	.15	.07	.01
☐ 41 Jerry Reuss	.25	.12	.02
☐ 43 Jose Morales	.15	.07	.01
☐ 44 Ken Landreaux	.15	.07	.01
☐ 46 Burt Hooton	.15	.07	.01
☐ 47 Larry White	.15	.07	.01
☐ 48 Dave Stewart	.25	.12	.02
☐ 49 Tom Niedenfuer	.25	.12	.02
☐ 57 Steve Howe	.25	.12	.02
☐ xx Coaching Staff (unnumbered)	.15	.07	.01

1983 Police Royals

The cards in this 10 card set measure 2 1/2" by 4 1/8". The 1983 Police Kansas City Royals set features full color cards of Royals players. The fronts feature the player's name, height and weight, and the Royals' logo in addition to the player's photo and a facsimile autograph. The backs feature Kids and Cops Facts about the players, Tips from the Royals,

and identification of the sponsors of the set. The cards are unnumbered.

	MINT	EXC	G-VG
COMPLETE SET	25.00	12.50	2.50
COMMON PLAYER	1.50	.75	.15
☐ 1 Willie Aikens	1.50	.75	.15
☐ 2 George Brett	10.00	5.00	1.00
☐ 3 Dennis Leonard	2.00	1.00	.20
☐ 4 Hal McRae	2.00	1.00	.20
☐ 5 Amos Otis	2.00	1.00	.20
☐ 6 Dan Quisenberry	3.00	1.50	.30
☐ 7 U.L. Washington	1.50	.75	.15
☐ 8 John Wathan	2.00	1.00	.20
☐ 9 Frank White	3.00	1.50	.30
☐ 10 Willie Wilson	3.50	1.75	.35

1984 Police Braves

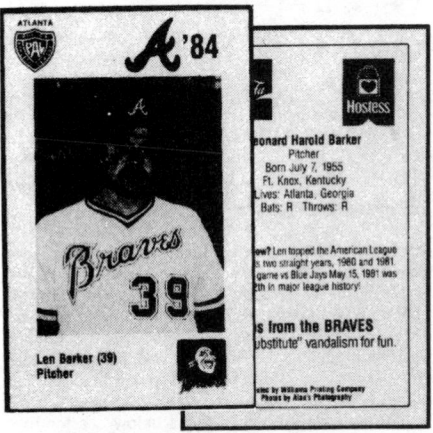

The cards in this 30 card set measure 2 5/8" by 4 1/8". For the fourth straight year, the Atlanta Police Department issued a full color set of Atlanta Braves. The cards were given out two per week by Atlanta police officers. In addition to the police department, the set was sponsored by Coke and Hostess. The backs of the cards of Perez and Ramirez are in Spanish. The Joe Torre card contains the checklist.

	MINT	EXC	G-VG
COMPLETE SET	12.00	6.00	1.20
COMMON PLAYER	.35	.17	.03
☐ 1 Jerry Royster	.35	.17	.03
☐ 3 Dale Murphy	4.00	2.00	.40

			MINT	EXC	G-VG
☐	5	Bob Horner	1.25	.60	.12
☐	6	Randy Johnson	.35	.17	.03
☐	8	Bob Watson	.50	.25	.05
☐	9	Joe Torre MG	.60	.30	.06
		(checklist back)			
☐	10	Chris Chambliss	.50	.25	.05
☐	11	Mike Jorgensen	.35	.17	.03
☐	15	Claudell Washington	.50	.25	.05
☐	16	Rafael Ramirez	.35	.17	.03
☐	17	Glenn Hubbard	.35	.17	.03
☐	19	Terry Harper	.35	.17	.03
☐	20	Bruce Benedict	.35	.17	.03
☐	25	Alex Trevino	.35	.17	.03
☐	26	Gene Garber	.35	.17	.03
☐	27	Pascual Perez	.35	.17	.03
☐	28	Gerald Perry	.50	.25	.05
☐	29	Craig McMurtry	.35	.17	.03
☐	31	Donnie Moore	.50	.25	.05
☐	32	Steve Bedrosian	.75	.35	.07
☐	33	Pete Falcone	.35	.17	.03
☐	37	Rick Camp	.35	.17	.03
☐	39	Len Barker	.35	.17	.03
☐	42	Rick Mahler	.35	.17	.03
☐	45	Bob Gibson CO	1.25	.60	.12
☐	51	Terry Forster	.50	.25	.05
☐	52	Joe Pignatano CO	.35	.17	.03
☐	53	Dal Maxvill CO	.35	.17	.03
☐	54	Rube Walker CO	.35	.17	.03
☐	55	Luke Appling CO	.60	.30	.06

			MINT	EXC	G-VG
☐	15	Cecil Cooper	.50	.25	.05
☐	17	Jim Gantner	.25	.12	.02
☐	19	Robin Yount	.75	.35	.07
☐	20	Don Sutton	.60	.30	.06
☐	21	Bill Schroeder	.25	.12	.02
☐	22	Charlie Moore	.15	.07	.01
☐	23	Ted Simmons	.35	.17	.03
☐	24	Ben Oglivie	.25	.12	.02
☐	25	Bob Clark	.15	.07	.01
☐	27	Pete Ladd	.15	.07	.01
☐	28	Rick Manning	.15	.07	.01
☐	29	Mark Brouhard	.15	.07	.01
☐	30	Moose Haas	.15	.07	.01
☐	34	Rollie Fingers	.60	.30	.06
☐	42	Tom Tellmann	.15	.07	.01
☐	43	Chuck Porter	.15	.07	.01
☐	46	Jerry Augustine	.15	.07	.01
☐	47	Jaime Cocanower	.15	.07	.01
☐	48	Mike Caldwell	.25	.12	.02
☐	50	Pete Vuckovich	.25	.12	.02
☐	xx	Coaches Card	.15	.07	.01
		(unnumbered)			
☐	xx	Team Photo	.15	.07	.01
		(Checklist back)			
		(unnumbered)			

1984 Police Brewers

The cards in this 30-card set measure 2 13/16" by 4 1/8". Again this year, the police departments in and around Milwaukee issued sets of the Milwaukee Brewers. Although each set contained the same players and numbers, the individual police departments placed their own name on the fronts of cards to show that they were the particular jurisdiction issuing the set. The backs contain the Brewers logo, a safety tip, and in some cases, a badge of the jurisdiction. To date, 59 variations of this set have been found. Prices below are for the basic set without regard to the Police Department issuing the cards; cards from the more obscure corners and small towns of Wisconsin will be valued higher. Cards are numbered by uniform number.

			MINT	EXC	G-VG
COMPLETE SET			5.00	2.50	.50
COMMON PLAYER			.15	.07	.01
☐	2	Randy Ready	.25	.12	.02
☐	4	Paul Molitor	.60	.30	.06
☐	8	Jim Sundberg	.25	.12	.02
☐	9	Rene Lachemann MG	.15	.07	.01
☐	10	Bob McClure	.15	.07	.01
☐	11	Ed Romero	.15	.07	.01
☐	13	Roy Howell	.15	.07	.01
☐	14	Dion James	.35	.17	.03

1984 Police Dodgers

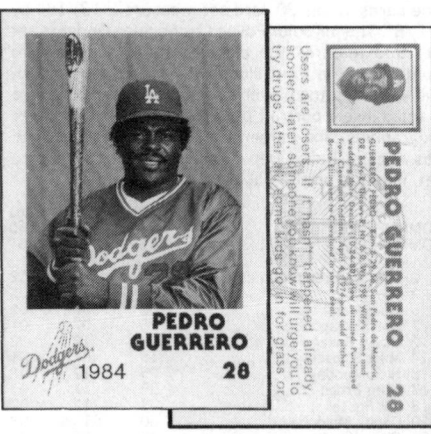

The cards in this 30 card set measure 2 13/16" by 4 1/8". For the fifth straight year, the Los Angeles Police Department sponsored a set of Dodger baseball cards. The set is numbered by player uniform number, which is featured on both the fronts and backs of the cards. The Dodgers' logo appears on the front, and the LAPD logo is superimposed on the backs of the cards. The backs are printed in Dodger blue ink and contain a small photo of the player on the front. Player biographical data and "Dare to Say No" antidrug information are featured on the back.

			MINT	EXC	G-VG
COMPLETE SET			5.00	2.50	.50
COMMON PLAYER			.15	.07	.01
☐	2	Tom Lasorda MG	.25	.12	.02
☐	3	Steve Sax	.50	.25	.05
☐	5	Mike Marshall	.60	.30	.06
☐	7	Steve Yeager	.15	.07	.01
☐	9	Greg Brock	.25	.12	.02
☐	10	Dave Anderson	.15	.07	.01
☐	14	Mike Scioscia	.15	.07	.01
☐	16	Rick Monday	.25	.12	.02
☐	17	Rafael Landestoy	.15	.07	.01
☐	18	Bill Russell	.25	.12	.02
☐	20	Candy Maldonado	.35	.17	.03
☐	21	Bob Bailor	.15	.07	.01
☐	25	German Rivera	.15	.07	.01
☐	26	Alejandro Pena	.25	.12	.02
☐	27	Carlos Diaz	.15	.07	.01
☐	28	Pedro Guerrero	.75	.35	.07

		MINT	EXC	G-VG
☐ 31	Jack Fimple	.15	.07	.01
☐ 34	Fernando Valenzuela	.75	.35	.07
☐ 35	Bob Welch	.25	.12	.02
☐ 38	Pat Zachry	.15	.07	.01
☐ 40	Rick Honeycutt	.25	.12	.02
☐ 41	Jerry Reuss	.25	.12	.02
☐ 43	Jose Morales	.15	.07	.01
☐ 44	Ken Landreaux	.15	.07	.01
☐ 45	Terry Whitfield	.15	.07	.01
☐ 46	Burt Hooton	.15	.07	.01
☐ 49	Tom Niedenfuer	.25	.12	.02
☐ 55	Orel Hershiser	.75	.35	.07
☐ 56	Richard Rodas	.15	.07	.01
☐ xx	Coaching Staff (unnumbered)	.15	.07	.01

1985 Police Braves

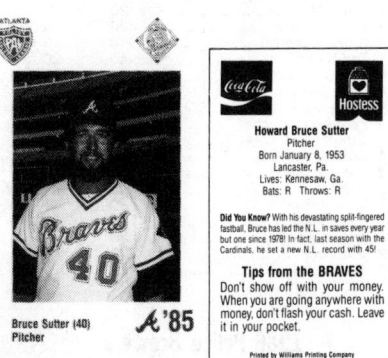

Howard Bruce Sutter
Pitcher
Born January 8, 1953
Lancaster, Pa.
Lives: Kennesaw, Ga.
Bats: R   Throws: R

Did You Know? With his devastating split-fingered fastball, Bruce has led the N.L. in saves every year but one since 1978! In fact, last season with the Cardinals, he set a new N.L. record with 45!

Tips from the BRAVES
Don't show off with your money. When you are going anywhere with money, don't flash your cash. Leave it in your pocket.

Printed by Williams Printing Company
Photos by Alan's Photography

Bruce Sutter (40)
Pitcher
A '85

The cards in this 30 card set measure 2 5/8" by 4 1/8". For the fifth straight year, the Atlanta Police Department issued a full color set of Atlanta Braves. The set was also sponsored by Coca Cola and Hostess. In the upper right of the obverse is a logo commemorating the 20th anniversary of the Braves in Atlanta. Cards are numbered by uniform number. Cards feature a safety tip on the back. Each card except for Manager Haas has an interesting "Did You Know" fact about the player.

		MINT	EXC	G-VG
COMPLETE SET		12.00	6.00	1.20
COMMON PLAYER		.30	.15	.03
☐ 2	Albert Hall	.40	.20	.04
☐ 3	Dale Murphy	3.50	1.75	.35
☐ 5	Rick Cerone	.30	.15	.03
☐ 7	Bobby Wine CO	.30	.15	.03
☐ 10	Chris Chambliss	.40	.20	.04
☐ 11	Bob Horner	1.25	.60	.12
☐ 12	Paul Runge	.40	.20	.04
☐ 15	Claudell Washington	.50	.25	.05
☐ 16	Rafael Ramirez	.30	.15	.03
☐ 17	Glenn Hubbard	.30	.15	.03
☐ 18	Paul Zuvella	.30	.15	.03
☐ 19	Terry Harper	.30	.15	.03
☐ 20	Bruce Benedict	.30	.15	.03
☐ 22	Eddie Haas MG	.30	.15	.03
☐ 24	Ken Oberkfell	.30	.15	.03
☐ 26	Gene Garber	.40	.20	.04
☐ 27	Pascual Perez	.30	.15	.03
☐ 28	Gerald Perry	.40	.20	.04
☐ 29	Craig McMurtry	.30	.15	.03
☐ 32	Steve Bedrosian	.60	.30	.06
☐ 33	Johnny Sain CO	.50	.25	.05
☐ 34	Zane Smith	.75	.35	.07
☐ 36	Brad Komminsk	.40	.20	.04
☐ 37	Rick Camp	.30	.15	.03
☐ 39	Len Barker	.30	.15	.03
☐ 40	Bruce Sutter	.60	.30	.06
☐ 42	Rick Mahler	.30	.15	.03
☐ 51	Terry Forster	.50	.25	.05
☐ 52	Leo Mazzone CO	.30	.15	.03
☐ 53	Bobby Dews CO	.30	.15	.03

1985 Police Brewers

y Burris says:
ur advance scouts are very important
s. They check out opposing teams
re we play them and give us tips on
to play individual ballplayers. They act
ur eyes and ears. You, too, can be a
ut for the police in your neighborhood.
and your friends can prevent crime by
g the eyes and ears of your local
ce. Call them immediately to report
thing unusual or suspicious that you

ch the Friday **Milwaukee Journal**
rts Weekend Section for the 2 players
ured on next week's baseball cards. You
d win free tickets to a Brewer game!

48   **Ray Burris**   P
The Chilton Police Department and
The Chilton Local Merchants, Service Clubs
and Financial Institutions
present the 1985
Milwaukee Brewers

The cards in this 30 card set measure 2 3/4" by 4 1/8". Again this year, the police departments in and around Milwaukee issued sets of the Milwaukee Brewers. The backs contain the Brewers logo, a safety tip, and in some cases, a badge of the jurisdiction. Prices below are for the basic set without regard to the Police Department issuing the cards; cards from the more obscure corners and small towns of Wisconsin (smaller production) will be valued higher. Cards are numbered by uniform number.

		MINT	EXC	G-VG
COMPLETE SET		5.00	2.50	.50
COMMON PLAYER		.15	.07	.01
☐ 2	Randy Ready	.25	.12	.02
☐ 4	Paul Molitor	.60	.30	.06
☐ 5	Doug Loman	.25	.12	.02
☐ 7	Paul Householder	.15	.07	.01
☐ 10	Bob McClure	.15	.07	.01
☐ 11	Ed Romero	.15	.07	.01
☐ 14	Dion James	.35	.17	.03
☐ 15	Cecil Cooper	.45	.22	.04
☐ 17	Jim Gantner	.25	.12	.02
☐ 18	Danny Darwin	.15	.07	.01
☐ 19	Robin Yount	.75	.35	.07
☐ 21	Bill Schroeder	.25	.12	.02
☐ 22	Charlie Moore	.15	.07	.01
☐ 23	Ted Simmons	.35	.17	.03
☐ 24	Ben Oglivie	.25	.12	.02
☐ 26	Brian Giles	.15	.07	.01
☐ 27	Pete Ladd	.15	.07	.01
☐ 28	Rick Manning	.15	.07	.01
☐ 29	Mark Brouhard	.15	.07	.01
☐ 30	Moose Haas	.15	.07	.01
☐ 31	George Bamberger MG	.15	.07	.01
☐ 34	Rollie Fingers	.60	.30	.06
☐ 40	Bob L. Gibson	.15	.07	.01
☐ 41	Ray Searage	.15	.07	.01
☐ 47	Jaime Cocanower	.15	.07	.01
☐ 48	Ray Burris	.15	.07	.01
☐ 49	Ted Higuera	.75	.35	.07
☐ 50	Pete Vuckovich	.25	.12	.02
☐ xx	Team Roster (unnumbered)	.15	.07	.01
☐ xx	Coaches (unnumbered)	.15	.07	.01
☐ xx	Newspaper Carrier (unnumbered)	.15	.07	.01

1986 Police Astros

This 26-card safety set was also sponsored by Kool-Aid. The backs contain a biographical paragraph above a "Tip from the Dugout". The front features a full-color photo of the player, his name, and

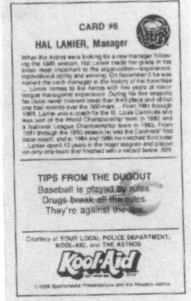

Departments in the Atlanta area. Cards are numbered below by uniform number.

	MINT	EXC	G-VG
COMPLETE SET	10.00	5.00	1.00
COMMON PLAYER	.20	.10	.02

		MINT	EXC	G-VG
☐ 2	Russ Nixon COA	.20	.10	.02
☐ 3	Dale Murphy	2.50	1.25	.25
☐ 4	Bob Skinner COA	.30	.15	.03
☐ 5	Billy Sample	.20	.10	.02
☐ 7	Chuck Tanner MG	.30	.15	.03
☐ 8	Willie Stargell COA	1.00	.50	.10
☐ 9	Ozzie Virgil	.30	.15	.03
☐ 10	Chris Chambliss	.30	.15	.03
☐ 11	Bob Horner	.75	.35	.07
☐ 14	Andres Thomas	.50	.25	.05
☐ 15	Claudell Washington	.30	.15	.03
☐ 16	Rafael Ramirez	.20	.10	.02
☐ 17	Glenn Hubbard	.20	.10	.02
☐ 18	Omar Moreno	.20	.10	.02
☐ 19	Terry Harper	.20	.10	.02
☐ 20	Bruce Benedict	.20	.10	.02
☐ 23	Ted Simmons	.40	.20	.04
☐ 24	Ken Oberkfell	.20	.10	.02
☐ 26	Gene Garber	.30	.15	.03
☐ 29	Craig McMurtry	.20	.10	.02
☐ 30	Paul Assenmacher	.20	.10	.02
☐ 33	Johnny Sain COA	.30	.15	.03
☐ 34	Zane Smith	.50	.25	.05
☐ 38	Joe Johnson	.30	.15	.03
☐ 40	Bruce Sutter	.40	.20	.04
☐ 42	Rick Mahler	.30	.15	.03
☐ 46	David Palmer	.30	.15	.03
☐ 48	Duane Ward	.30	.15	.03
☐ 49	Jeff Dedmon	.20	.10	.02
☐ 52	Al Monchak COA	.20	.10	.02

uniform number. The cards are numbered on the back and measure 2 5/8" by 4 1/8". The backs are printed in orange and blue on white card stock. Sets were distributed at the Astrodome on June 14th as well as given away throughout the summer by the Houston Police.

	MINT	EXC	G-VG
COMPLETE SET	5.00	2.50	.50
COMMON PLAYER	.10	.05	.01

		MINT	EXC	G-VG
☐ 1	Jim Pankovits	.10	.05	.01
☐ 2	Nolan Ryan	1.00	.50	.10
☐ 3	Mike Scott	.65	.30	.06
☐ 4	Kevin Bass	.50	.25	.05
☐ 5	Bill Doran	.50	.25	.05
☐ 6	Hal Lanier MG	.20	.10	.02
☐ 7	Denny Walling	.10	.05	.01
☐ 8	Alan Ashby	.10	.05	.01
☐ 9	Phil Garner	.15	.07	.01
☐ 10	Charlie Kerfeld	.20	.10	.02
☐ 11	Dave Smith	.25	.12	.02
☐ 12	Jose Cruz	.50	.25	.05
☐ 13	Craig Reynolds	.10	.05	.01
☐ 14	Mark Bailey	.10	.05	.01
☐ 15	Bob Knepper	.25	.12	.02
☐ 16	Julio Solano	.10	.05	.01
☐ 17	Dickie Thon	.15	.07	.01
☐ 18	Mike Madden	.10	.05	.01
☐ 19	Jeff Calhoun	.15	.07	.01
☐ 20	Tony Walker	.15	.07	.01
☐ 21	Terry Puhl	.15	.07	.01
☐ 22	Glenn Davis	.75	.35	.07
☐ 23	Billy Hatcher	.25	.12	.02
☐ 24	Jim Deshaies	.30	.15	.03
☐ 25	Frank DiPino	.15	.07	.01
☐ 26	Coaching Staff	.10	.05	.01

1986 Police Brewers

This 32-card safety set was also sponsored by WTMJ Radio and Kinney Shoes. The backs contain the usual biographical info and safety tip. The front features a full-color photo of the player, his name, position, and uniform number. The cards measure 2 5/8" by 4 1/8". Cards were freely distributed throughout the summer by the Police Departments in the Milwaukee area. Cards are numbered below by uniform number.

	MINT	EXC	G-VG
COMPLETE SET	6.00	3.00	.60
COMMON PLAYER	.10	.05	.01

		MINT	EXC	G-VG
☐ 1	Ernest Riles	.30	.15	.03
☐ 2	Randy Ready	.20	.10	.02
☐ 3	Juan Castillo	.15	.07	.01
☐ 4	Paul Molitor	.60	.30	.06
☐ 7	Paul Householder	.10	.05	.01
☐ 8	Andy Etchebarren COA	.10	.05	.01
☐ 10	Bob McClure	.15	.07	.01
☐ 11	Rick Cerone	.15	.07	.01
☐ 12	Larry Haney COA	.10	.05	.01
☐ 13	Billy Jo Robidoux	.20	.10	.02
☐ 15	Cecil Cooper	.40	.20	.04
☐ 16	Mike Felder	.25	.12	.02
☐ 17	Jim Gantner	.15	.07	.01
☐ 18	Danny Darwin	.15	.07	.01

1986 Police Braves

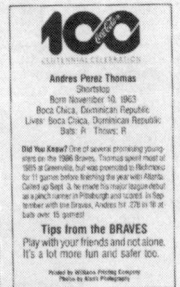

This 30 card safety set was also sponsored by Coca-Cola. The backs contain the usual biographical info and safety tip. The front features a full-color photo of the player, his name, and uniform number. The cards measure 2 5/8" by 4 1/8". Cards were freely distributed throughout the summer by the Police

☐ 19	Robin Yount	1.00	.50	.10
☐ 20	Juan Nieves	.25	.12	.02
☐ 21	Bill Schroeder	.15	.07	.01
☐ 22	Charlie Moore	.10	.05	.01
☐ 24	Ben Oglivie	.20	.10	.02
☐ 25	Mark Clear	.15	.07	.01
☐ 28	Rick Manning	.10	.05	.01
☐ 31	George Bamberger MG	.20	.10	.02
☐ 33	Frank Howard COA	.20	.10	.02
☐ 35	Tony Muser COA	.10	.05	.01
☐ 37	Dan Plesac	.30	.15	.03
☐ 38	Herm Starrette COA	.10	.05	.01
☐ 39	Tim Leary	.10	.05	.01
☐ 42	Tom Trebelhorn COA	.25	.12	.02
☐ 45	Rob Deer	.50	.25	.05
☐ 46	Bill Wegman	.20	.10	.02
☐ 47	Jaime Cocanower	.10	.05	.01
☐ 49	Teddy Higuera	.75	.35	.07

1986 Police Dodgers

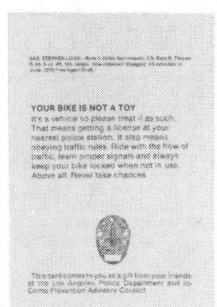

STEVE SAX 3

This 30-card set features full-color cards each measuring 2 13/16" by 4 1/8". The cards are unnumbered except for uniform numbers. The backs give a safety tip as well as a short capsule biography. The sets were given away at Dodger Stadium on May 18th.

		MINT	EXC	G-VG
COMPLETE SET		5.00	2.50	.50
COMMON PLAYER		.10	.05	.01
☐ 2	Tom Lasorda MG	.25	.12	.02
☐ 3	Steve Sax	.50	.25	.05
☐ 5	Mike Marshall	.50	.25	.05
☐ 9	Greg Brock	.20	.10	.02
☐ 10	Dave Anderson	.10	.05	.01
☐ 12	Bill Madlock	.25	.12	.02
☐ 14	Mike Scioscia	.15	.07	.01
☐ 17	Len Matuszek	.10	.05	.01
☐ 18	Bill Russell	.20	.10	.02
☐ 22	Franklin Stubbs	.25	.12	.02
☐ 23	Enos Cabell	.10	.05	.01
☐ 25	Mariano Duncan	.20	.10	.02
☐ 26	Alejandro Pena	.15	.07	.01
☐ 27	Carlos Diaz	.10	.05	.01
☐ 28	Pedro Guerrero	.75	.35	.07
☐ 29	Alex Trevino	.10	.05	.01
☐ 31	Ed VandeBerg	.10	.05	.01
☐ 34	Fernando Valenzuela	.75	.35	.07
☐ 35	Bob Welch	.25	.12	.02
☐ 40	Rick Honeycutt	.15	.07	.01
☐ 41	Jerry Reuss	.15	.07	.01
☐ 43	Ken Howell	.10	.05	.01
☐ 44	Ken Landreaux	.10	.05	.01
☐ 45	Terry Whitfield	.10	.05	.01
☐ 48	Dennis Powell	.15	.07	.01
☐ 49	Tom Niedenfuer	.20	.10	.02
☐ 51	Reggie Williams	.20	.10	.02
☐ 55	Orel Hershiser	.35	.17	.03
☐ xx	Coaching Staff	.10	.05	.01
	(unnumbered)			
	Don McMahon			
	Mark Cresse			
	Ben Hines			
	Ron Perranoski			
	Monty Basgall			
	Manny Mota			
	Joe Amalfitano			

☐ xx	Team Photo	.10	.05	.01
	(unnumbered)			
	(checklist back)			

1987 Police Astros

This 26-card safety set was also sponsored by the Astros, Deer Park Hospital, and Sports Media Presentations. The backs contain a biographical paragraph above a "Tip from the Dugout". The front features a full-color photo of the player, his name, position, and uniform number. The cards are numbered on the back and measure 2 5/8" by 4 1/8". The first twelve cards were distributed at the Astrodome on July 14th and the rest were given away later in the summer by the Deer Park Hospital.

		MINT	EXC	G-VG
COMPLETE SET		5.00	2.50	.50
COMMON PLAYER		.15	.07	.01
☐ 1	Larry Andersen	.15	.07	.01
☐ 2	Mark Bailey	.15	.07	.01
☐ 3	Jose Cruz	.35	.17	.03
☐ 4	Danny Darwin	.25	.12	.02
☐ 5	Bill Doran	.50	.25	.05
☐ 6	Billy Hatcher	.50	.25	.05
☐ 7	Hal Lanier MG	.25	.12	.02
☐ 8	Davey Lopes	.25	.12	.02
☐ 9	Dave Meads	.15	.07	.01
☐ 10	Craig Reynolds	.15	.07	.01
☐ 11	Mike Scott	.75	.35	.07
☐ 12	Denny Walling	.15	.07	.01
☐ 13	Aurelio Lopez	.15	.07	.01
☐ 14	Dickie Thon	.25	.12	.02
☐ 15	Terry Puhl	.25	.12	.02
☐ 16	Nolan Ryan	1.00	.50	.10
☐ 17	Dave Smith	.25	.12	.02
☐ 18	Julio Solano	.15	.07	.01
☐ 19	Jim Deshaies	.25	.12	.02
☐ 20	Bob Knepper	.25	.12	.02
☐ 21	Alan Ashby	.25	.12	.02
☐ 22	Kevin Bass	.35	.17	.03
☐ 23	Glenn Davis	.50	.25	.05
☐ 24	Phil Garner	.25	.12	.02
☐ 25	Jim Pankovits	.15	.07	.01
☐ 26	Coaching Staff	.15	.07	.01

1987 Police Brewers

This 30-card safety set was also sponsored by WTMJ Radio and Kinney Shoes. The backs contain the usual biographical info and safety tip. The front features a full-color photo of the player, his name, position, and uniform number. The cards measure 2 5/8" by 4 1/8". Cards were freely distributed throughout the summer by the Police Departments in the Milwaukee

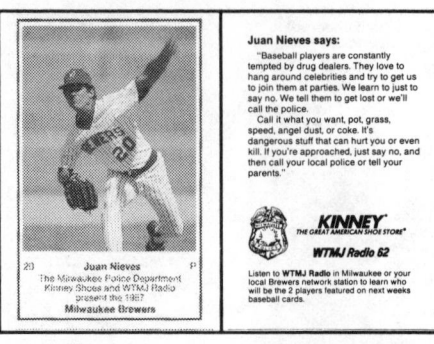

Juan Nieves says:

"Baseball players are constantly tempted by drug dealers. They love to hang around celebrities and try to get us to join them at parties. We learn to just to say no. We tell them to get lost or we'll call the police.

Call it what you want, pot, grass, speed, angel dust, or coke. It's dangerous stuff that can hurt you or even kill. If you're approached, just say no, and then call your local police or tell your parents."

KINNEY
THE GREAT AMERICAN SHOE STORE®

WTMJ Radio 62

Listen to WTMJ Radio in Milwaukee or your local Brewers network station to learn who will be the 2 players featured on next weeks baseball cards.

20   Juan Nieves   P
The Milwaukee Police Department
Kinney Shoes and WTMJ Radio
present the 1987
Milwaukee Brewers

area and throughout other parts of Wisconsin. Cards are numbered below by uniform number.

		MINT	EXC	G-VG
COMPLETE SET		5.00	2.50	.50
COMMON PLAYER		.15	.07	.01
☐ 1	Ernest Riles	.25	.12	.02
☐ 2	Edgar Diaz	.25	.12	.02
☐ 3	Juan Castillo	.15	.07	.01
☐ 4	Paul Molitor	.75	.35	.07
☐ 5	B.J. Surhoff	.75	.35	.07
☐ 7	Dale Sveum	.50	.25	.05
☐ 9	Greg Brock	.25	.12	.02
☐ 13	Billy Jo Robidoux	.25	.12	.02
☐ 14	Jim Paciorek	.15	.07	.01
☐ 15	Cecil Cooper	.35	.17	.03
☐ 16	Mike Felder	.15	.07	.01
☐ 17	Jim Gantner	.25	.12	.02
☐ 19	Robin Yount	1.00	.50	.10
☐ 20	Juan Nieves	.35	.17	.03
☐ 21	Bill Schroeder	.25	.12	.02
☐ 25	Mark Clear	.15	.07	.01
☐ 26	Glenn Braggs	.50	.25	.05
☐ 28	Rick Manning	.15	.07	.01
☐ 29	Chris Bosio	.25	.12	.02
☐ 32	Chuck Crim	.15	.07	.01
☐ 34	Mark Ciardi	.15	.07	.01
☐ 37	Dan Plesac	.35	.17	.03
☐ 38	John Henry Johnson	.15	.07	.01
☐ 40	Mike Birkbeck	.15	.07	.01
☐ 42	Tom Trebelhorn MG	.25	.12	.02
☐ 45	Rob Deer	.35	.17	.03
☐ 46	Bill Wegman	.15	.07	.01
☐ 49	Teddy Higuera	.50	.25	.05
☐ xx	Coaching Staff	.15	.07	.01
☐ xx	Brewers Team	.15	.07	.01
	(Checklist on back)			

1987 Police Dodgers

OREL HERSHISER   55

This 30-card set features full-color cards each measuring 2 13/16" by 4 1/8". The cards are unnumbered except for uniform numbers. The backs give a safety tip as well as a short capsule biography. Cards were given away at Dodger Stadium on April

24th and later during the summer by LAPD officers at a rate of two cards per week.

		MINT	EXC	G-VG
COMPLETE SET		5.00	2.50	.50
COMMON PLAYER		.15	.07	.01
☐ 1	Tom Lasorda 2	.35	.17	.03
☐ 2	Steve Sax 3	.50	.25	.05
☐ 3	Mike Marshall 5	.50	.25	.05
☐ 4	Dave Anderson 10	.15	.07	.01
☐ 5	Bill Madlock 12	.25	.12	.02
☐ 6	Mike Scioscia 14	.25	.12	.02
☐ 7	Gilberto Reyes 15	.15	.07	.01
☐ 8	Len Matuszek 17	.15	.07	.01
☐ 9	Reggie Williams 21	.25	.12	.02
☐ 10	Franklin Stubbs 22	.25	.12	.02
☐ 11	Tim Leary 23	.15	.07	.01
☐ 12	Mariano Duncan 25	.25	.12	.02
☐ 13	Alejandro Pena 26	.15	.07	.01
☐ 14	Pedro Guerrero 28	.75	.35	.07
☐ 15	Alex Trevino 29	.15	.07	.01
☐ 16	Jeff Hamilton 33	.25	.12	.02
☐ 17	Fernando Valenzuela 34	.75	.35	.07
☐ 18	Bob Welch 35	.35	.17	.03
☐ 19	Matt Young 36	.15	.07	.01
☐ 20	Rick Honeycutt 40	.15	.07	.01
☐ 21	Jerry Reuss 41	.25	.12	.02
☐ 22	Ken Howell 43	.15	.07	.01
☐ 23	Ken Landreaux 44	.15	.07	.01
☐ 24	Ralph Bryant 46	.25	.12	.02
☐ 25	Jose Gonzalez 47	.25	.12	.02
☐ 26	Tom Niedenfuer 49	.25	.12	.02
☐ 27	Brian Holton 51	.15	.07	.01
☐ 28	Orel Hershiser 55	.50	.25	.05
☐ 29	Coaching Staff	.15	.07	.01
☐ 30	Dodgers Stadium	.15	.07	.01
	(25th Anniversary)			

1960 Post Cereal

These large cards measure 7" by 8 3/4". The 1960 Post Cereal Sports Stars set contains nine cards depicting current baseball, football and basketball players. Each card comprised the entire back of a Grape Nuts Box and is blank backed. The color player photos are set on a colored background surrounded by a wooden frame design, and they are unnumbered (assigned numbers below for reference). The catalog designation is F278-26.

		NRMT	VG-E	GOOD
COMPLETE SET		2100.00	900.00	180.00
COMMON PLAYER (1-9)		90.00	45.00	9.00
☐ 1	Bob Cousy (basketball)	90.00	45.00	9.00
☐ 2	Don Drysdale (baseball)	200.00	100.00	20.00
☐ 3	Frank Gifford (football)	200.00	100.00	20.00
☐ 4	Al Kaline (baseball)	250.00	125.00	25.00
☐ 5	Harmon Killebrew (baseball)	200.00	100.00	20.00
☐ 6	Ed Mathews (baseball)	200.00	100.00	20.00
☐ 7	Mickey Mantle (baseball)	1000.00	400.00	80.00
☐ 8	Bob Pettit (basketball)	90.00	45.00	9.00
☐ 9	John Unitas (football)	200.00	100.00	20.00

1961 Post Cereal

The cards in this 200 card set measure 2 1/2" by 3 1/2". The 1961 Post set was this company's first major set. The cards were available on thick cardbox stock, singly or in various panel sizes from cereal

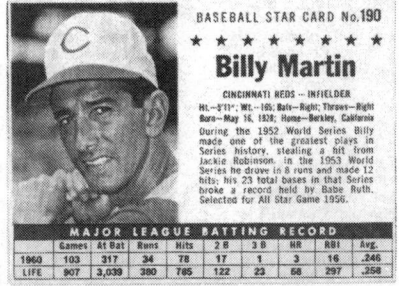

BASEBALL STAR CARD No.190

★ ★ ★ ★ ★ ★ ★ ★ ★
Billy Martin

CINCINNATI REDS — INFIELDER

Ht.—5'11"; Wt.—165; Bats—Right; Throws—Right
Born—May 16, 1928; Home—Berkley, California

During the 1952 World Series Billy made one of the greatest plays in Series history, stealing a hit from Jackie Robinson. In the 1953 World Series he drove in 8 runs and made 12 hits; his 23 total bases in that Series broke a record held by Babe Ruth. Selected for All Star Game 1956.

MAJOR LEAGUE BATTING RECORD									
	Games	At Bat	Runs	Hits	2 B	3 B	HR	RBI	Avg.
1960	103	317	34	78	17	1	3	16	.246
LIFE	907	3,039	380	765	122	23	58	297	.258

boxes (BOX), or in team sheets, printed on thinner cardboard stock, directly from the Post Cereal Company (COM). Many variations exist and are noted in the checklist below. There are many cards which were produced in lesser quantities; the prices below reflect the relative scarcity of the cards. Cards 10, 23, 70, 73, 94, 113, 135, 163, and 183 are examples of cards printed in limited quantities and hence commanding premium prices. The cards are numbered essentially in team groups, i.e., New York Yankees (1-18), Chicago White Sox (19-34), Detroit (35-46), Boston (47-56), Cleveland (57-67), Baltimore (68-80), Kansas City (81-90), Minnesota (91-100), Milwaukee (101-114), Philadelphia (115-124), Pittsburgh (125- 140), San Francisco (141-155), Los Angeles Dodgers (156-170), St. Louis (171-180), Cincinnati (181-190), and Chicago Cubs (191-200). The catalog number is F278-33. The complete set prices refer to both ways of collecting the set, all variations (357) or one of each player (200).

	NRMT	VG-E	GOOD
COMPLETE SET (357)	1500.00	600.00	120.00
COMPLETE SET (200)	1000.00	400.00	80.00
COMMON PLAYER (1-200)	1.00	.50	.10

		NRMT	VG-E	GOOD
☐	1A Yogi Berra COM	12.50	6.25	1.25
☐	1B Yogi Berra BOX	15.00	7.50	1.50
☐	2A Elston Howard COM	1.50	.75	.15
☐	2B Elston Howard BOX	2.50	1.25	.25
☐	3A Bill Skowron COM	1.50	.75	.15
☐	3B Bill Skowron BOX	1.50	.75	.15
☐	4A Mickey Mantle COM	60.00	30.00	6.00
☐	4B Mickey Mantle BOX	60.00	30.00	6.00
☐	5 Bob Turley COM only	10.00	5.00	1.00
☐	6A Whitey Ford COM	6.00	3.00	.60
☐	6B Whitey Ford BOX	6.00	3.00	.60
☐	7A Roger Maris COM	10.00	5.00	1.00
☐	7B Roger Maris BOX	10.00	5.00	1.00
☐	8A B.Richardson COM	1.50	.75	.15
☐	8B B.Richardson BOX	1.50	.75	.15
☐	9A Tony Kubek COM	1.50	.75	.15
☐	9B Tony Kubek BOX	1.50	.75	.15
☐	10 G.McDougald BOX only	25.00	12.50	2.50
☐	11 Cletis Boyer BOX only	1.00	.50	.10
☐	12A Hector Lopes COM	1.00	.50	.10
☐	12B Hector Lopes BOX	1.00	.50	.10
☐	13 Bob Cerv BOX only	1.00	.50	.10
☐	14 Ryne Duren BOX only	1.00	.50	.10
☐	15 Bobby Shantz BOX only	1.00	.50	.10
☐	16 Art Ditmar BOX only	1.00	.50	.10
☐	17 Jim Coates BOX only	1.00	.50	.10
☐	18 J.Blanchard BOX only	1.00	.50	.10
☐	19A Luis Aparicio COM	3.50	1.75	.35
☐	19B Luis Aparicio BOX	3.50	1.75	.35
☐	20A Nelson Fox COM	2.50	1.25	.25
☐	20B Nelson Fox BOX	2.50	1.25	.25
☐	21A Bill Pierce COM	2.50	1.25	.25
☐	21B Bill Pierce BOX	5.00	2.50	.50
☐	22A Early Wynn COM	5.00	2.50	.50
☐	22B Early Wynn BOX	10.00	5.00	1.00
☐	23 Bob Shaw BOX only	65.00	32.50	6.50
☐	24A Al Smith COM	1.00	.50	.10
☐	24B Al Smith BOX	2.50	1.25	.25
☐	25A Minnie Minoso COM	1.50	.75	.15
☐	25B Minnie Minoso BOX	2.00	1.00	.20
☐	26A Roy Sievers COM	1.00	.50	.10
☐	26B Roy Sievers BOX	1.00	.50	.10

		NRMT	VG-E	GOOD
☐	27A Jim Landis COM	1.00	.50	.10
☐	27B Jim Landis BOX	2.00	1.00	.20
☐	28A Sherm Lollar COM	1.00	.50	.10
☐	28B Sherm Lollar BOX	2.00	1.00	.20
☐	29 Gerry Staley BOX only	1.00	.50	.10
☐	30A Gene Freese COM (Reds)	4.00	2.00	.40
☐	30B Gene Freese BOX (White Sox)	1.00	.50	.10
☐	31 Ted Kluszewski BOX only	1.00	.50	.10
☐	32 Turk Lown BOX only	1.00	.50	.10
☐	33A Jim Rivera COM	1.00	.50	.10
☐	33B Jim Rivera BOX	1.00	.50	.10
☐	34 F.Baumann BOX only	1.00	.50	.10
☐	35A Al Kaline COM	8.00	4.00	.80
☐	35B Al Kaline BOX	12.00	6.00	1.20
☐	36A Rocky Colavito COM	3.00	1.50	.30
☐	36B Rocky Colavito BOX	4.00	2.00	.40
☐	37A C.Maxwell COM	1.00	.50	.10
☐	37B C.Maxwell BOX	2.50	1.25	.25
☐	38A Frank Lary COM	1.00	.50	.10
☐	38B Frank Lary BOX	1.00	.50	.10
☐	39A Jim Bunning COM	2.00	1.00	.20
☐	39B Jim Bunning BOX	2.00	1.00	.20
☐	40A Norm Cash COM	1.00	.50	.10
☐	40B Norm Cash BOX	1.00	.50	.10
☐	41B Frank Bolling COM (Braves)	3.00	1.50	.30
☐	41A Frank Bolling BOX (Tigers)	5.00	2.50	.50
☐	42A Don Mossi COM	1.00	.50	.10
☐	42B Don Mossi BOX	1.00	.50	.10
☐	43A Lou Berberet COM	1.00	.50	.10
☐	43B Lou Berberet BOX	1.00	.50	.10
☐	44 Dave Sisler BOX only	1.00	.50	.10
☐	45 Ed Yost BOX only	1.00	.50	.10
☐	46 Pete Burnside BOX only	1.00	.50	.10
☐	47A Pete Runnels COM	1.50	.75	.15
☐	47B Pete Runnels BOX	3.00	1.50	.30
☐	48A Frank Malzone COM	1.00	.50	.10
☐	48B Frank Malzone BOX	1.00	.50	.10
☐	49A Vic Wertz COM	3.00	1.50	.30
☐	49B Vic Wertz BOX	4.00	2.00	.40
☐	50A Tom Brewer COM	1.00	.50	.10
☐	50B Tom Brewer BOX	2.00	1.00	.20
☐	51A Willie Tasby COM (Sold to Wash.)	5.00	2.50	.50
☐	51B Willie Tasby BOX (no sale mention)	1.00	.50	.10
☐	52A Russ Nixon COM	1.00	.50	.10
☐	52B Russ Nixon BOX	2.00	1.00	.20
☐	53A Don Buddin COM	1.00	.50	.10
☐	53B Don Buddin BOX	1.00	.50	.10
☐	54A B.Monbouquette COM	1.00	.50	.10
☐	54B B.Monbouquette BOX	1.00	.50	.10
☐	55A Frank Sullivan COM (Phillies)	5.00	2.50	.50
☐	55B Frank Sullivan BOX (Red Sox)	1.00	.50	.10
☐	56A H.Sullivan COM	1.00	.50	.10
☐	56B H.Sullivan BOX	1.00	.50	.10
☐	57A Harvey Kuenn COM (Giants)	4.00	2.00	.40
☐	57B Harvey Kuenn BOX (Indians)	3.00	1.50	.30
☐	58A Gary Bell COM	2.00	1.00	.20
☐	58B Gary Bell BOX	4.00	2.00	.40
☐	59A Jim Perry COM	1.00	.50	.10
☐	59B Jim Perry BOX	1.00	.50	.10
☐	60A Jim Grant COM	2.00	1.00	.20
☐	60B Jim Grant BOX	3.00	1.50	.30
☐	61A Johnny Temple COM	1.00	.50	.10
☐	61B Johnny Temple BOX	1.00	.50	.10
☐	62A Paul Foytack COM	1.00	.50	.10
☐	62B Paul Foytack BOX	1.00	.50	.10
☐	63A Vic Power COM	1.00	.50	.10
☐	63B Vic Power BOX	1.00	.50	.10
☐	64A Tito Francona COM	1.00	.50	.10
☐	64B Tito Francona BOX	1.00	.50	.10
☐	65A Ken Aspromonte COM (Sold to L.A.)	5.00	2.50	.50
☐	65B Ken Aspromonte BOX (no sale mention)	5.00	2.50	.50
☐	66 Bob Wilson BOX only	1.00	.50	.10
☐	67A John Romano COM	1.00	.50	.10
☐	67B John Romano BOX	1.00	.50	.10
☐	68A Jim Gentile COM	1.00	.50	.10
☐	68B Jim Gentile BOX	2.00	1.00	.20
☐	69A Gus Triandos COM	1.00	.50	.10
☐	69B Gus Triandos BOX	3.00	1.50	.30
☐	70 G.Woodling BOX only	25.00	12.50	2.50
☐	71A Milt Pappas COM	1.00	.50	.10

71B Milt Pappas BOX	3.00	1.50	.30
72A Ron Hansen COM	1.00	.50	.10
72B Ron Hansen BOX	2.00	1.00	.20
73 Chuck Estrada COM only	65.00	32.50	6.50
74A Steve Barber COM	1.00	.50	.10
74B Steve Barber BOX	2.00	1.00	.20
75A B.Robinson COM	8.00	4.00	.80
75B B.Robinson BOX	12.00	6.00	1.20
76A Jackie Brandt COM	1.00	.50	.10
76B Jackie Brandt BOX	1.00	.50	.10
77A Marv Breeding COM	1.00	.50	.10
77B Marv Breeding BOX	1.00	.50	.10
78 Hal Brown BOX only	1.00	.50	.10
79 Billy Klaus BOX only	1.00	.50	.10
80A Hoyt Wilhelm COM	5.00	2.50	.50
80B Hoyt Wilhelm BOX	4.00	2.00	.40
81A Jerry Lumpe COM	3.00	1.50	.30
81B Jerry Lumpe BOX	4.00	2.00	.40
82A Norm Siebern COM	1.00	.50	.10
82B Norm Siebern BOX	1.00	.50	.10
83A Bud Daley COM	3.00	1.50	.30
83B Bud Daley BOX	2.00	1.00	.20
84A Bill Tuttle COM	1.00	.50	.10
84B Bill Tuttle BOX	2.00	1.00	.20
85A M.Throneberry COM	2.00	1.00	.20
85B M.Throneberry BOX	2.00	1.00	.20
86A Dick Williams COM	1.00	.50	.10
86B Dick Williams BOX	1.00	.50	.10
87A Ray Herbert COM	1.00	.50	.10
87B Ray Herbert BOX	1.00	.50	.10
88A Whitey Herzog COM	1.00	.50	.10
88B Whitey Herzog BOX	1.00	.50	.10
89A Ken Hamlin COM (Sold to L.A.)	10.00	5.00	1.00
89B Ken Hamlin BOX (no sale mention)	1.00	.50	.10
90A Hank Bauer COM	1.00	.50	.10
90B Hank Bauer BOX	1.00	.50	.10
91A Bob Allison COM (Minnesota)	4.00	2.00	.40
91B Bob Allison BOX (Minneapolis)	4.00	2.00	.40
92A Harmon Killebrew (Minnesota) COM	10.00	5.00	1.00
92B Harmon Killebrew (Minneapolis) BOX	15.00	7.50	1.50
93A Jim Lemon COM (Minnesota)	15.00	7.50	1.50
93B Jim Lemon BOX (Minneapolis)	30.00	15.00	3.00
94A Chuck Stobbs (Minnesota) COM only	100.00	50.00	10.00
95A Reno Bertoia COM (Minnesota)	4.00	2.00	.40
95B Reno Bertoia BOX (Minneapolis)	1.00	.50	.10
96A Billy Gardner COM (Minnesota)	4.00	2.00	.40
96B Billy Gardner BOX (Minnesota)	1.00	.50	.10
97A Earl Battey COM (Minnesota)	4.00	2.00	.40
97B Earl Battey BOX (Minnesota)	1.00	.50	.10
98A Pedro Ramos COM (Minnesota)	4.00	2.00	.40
98B Pedro Ramos BOX (Minneapolis)	1.00	.50	.10
99A Camilo Pascual COM (Minnesota)	4.00	2.00	.40
99B Camilo Pascual BOX (Minnesota)	1.00	.50	.10
100A Billy Consolo COM (Minnesota)	4.00	2.00	.40
100B Billy Consolo BOX (Minneapolis)	1.00	.50	.10
101A Warren Spahn COM	8.00	4.00	.80
101B Warren Spahn BOX	12.00	6.00	1.20
102A Lew Burdette COM	1.50	.75	.15
102B Lew Burdette BOX	1.50	.75	.15
103A Bob Buhl COM	1.00	.50	.10
103B Bob Buhl BOX	1.00	.50	.10
104A Joe Adcock COM	2.00	1.00	.20
104B Joe Adcock BOX	3.00	1.50	.30
105A John Logan COM	2.00	1.00	.20
105B John Logan BOX	3.00	1.50	.30
106 Ed Mathews COM only	20.00	10.00	2.00
107A Hank Aaron COM	15.00	7.50	1.50
107B Hank Aaron BOX	15.00	7.50	1.50
108A Wes Covington COM	1.00	.50	.10
108B Wes Covington BOX	1.00	.50	.10
109A Bill Bruton COM (Tigers)	3.00	1.50	.30
109B Bill Bruton BOX (Braves)	4.00	2.00	.40
110A Del Crandall COM	1.00	.50	.10
110B Del Crandall BOX	3.00	1.50	.30
111 Red Schoendienst BOX only	1.00	.50	.10
112 Juan Pizarro BOX only	1.00	.50	.10
113 Chuck Cottier BOX only	7.50	3.75	.75
114 Al Spangler BOX only	1.00	.50	.10
115A Dick Farrell COM	3.00	1.50	.30
115B Dick Farrell BOX	4.00	2.00	.40
116A Jim Owens COM	3.00	1.50	.30
116B Jim Owens BOX	4.00	2.00	.40
117A Robin Roberts COM	5.00	2.50	.50
117B Robin Roberts BOX	4.00	2.00	.40
118A Tony Taylor COM	1.00	.50	.10
118B Tony Taylor BOX	1.00	.50	.10
119A Lee Walls COM	1.00	.50	.10
119B Lee Walls BOX	1.00	.50	.10
120A Tony Curry COM	1.00	.50	.10
120B Tony Curry BOX	1.00	.50	.10
121A Pancho Herrera COM	1.00	.50	.10
121B Pancho Herrera BOX	1.00	.50	.10
122A Ken Walters COM	1.00	.50	.10
122B Ken Walters BOX	1.00	.50	.10
123A John Callison COM	1.00	.50	.10
123B John Callison BOX	1.00	.50	.10
124A Gene Conley COM (Red Sox)	7.50	3.75	.75
124B Gene Conley BOX (Phillies)	1.00	.50	.10
125A Bob Friend COM	1.50	.75	.15
125B Bob Friend BOX	3.00	1.50	.30
126A Vernon Law COM	1.50	.75	.15
126B Vernon Law BOX	3.00	1.50	.30
127A Dick Stuart COM	1.00	.50	.10
127B Dick Stuart BOX	1.00	.50	.10
128A Bill Mazeroski COM	1.50	.75	.15
128B Bill Mazeroski BOX	1.00	.50	.10
129A Dick Groat COM	1.50	.75	.15
129B Dick Groat BOX	2.00	1.00	.20
130A Don Hoak COM	1.00	.50	.10
130B Don Hoak BOX	1.00	.50	.10
131A Bob Skinner COM	1.00	.50	.10
131B Bob Skinner BOX	1.00	.50	.10
132A Bob Clemente COM	15.00	7.50	1.50
132B Bob Clemente BOX	20.00	10.00	2.00
133 Roy Face BOX only	2.50	1.25	.25
134 H.Haddix BOX only	1.00	.50	.10
135 Bill Virdon BOX only	25.00	12.50	2.50
136A Gino Cimoli COM	1.00	.50	.10
136B Gino Cimoli BOX	1.00	.50	.10
137 Rocky Nelson BOX only	1.00	.50	.10
138A Smoky Burgess COM	1.00	.50	.10
138B Smoky Burgess BOX	1.00	.50	.10
139 Hal Smith BOX only	1.00	.50	.10
140 Wilmer Mizell BOX only	1.00	.50	.10
141A M.McCormick COM	1.00	.50	.10
141B M.McCormick BOX	1.00	.50	.10
142A John Antonelli COM (Cleveland)	4.00	2.00	.40
142B John Antonelli BOX (San Francisco)	3.00	1.50	.30
143A Sam Jones COM	2.00	1.00	.20
143B Sam Jones BOX	4.00	2.00	.40
144A Orlando Cepeda COM	4.00	2.00	.40
144B Orlando Cepeda BOX	5.00	2.50	.50
145A Willie Mays COM	15.00	7.50	1.50
145B Willie Mays BOX	15.00	7.50	1.50
146A Willie Kirkland (Cleve.) COM	3.00	1.50	.30
146B Willie Kirkland (San Fran.) BOX	3.00	1.50	.30
147A Willie McCovey COM	6.00	3.00	.60
147B Willie McCovey BOX	4.00	2.00	.40
148A Don Blasingame COM	1.00	.50	.10
148B Don Blasingame BOX	1.00	.50	.10
149A Jim Davenport COM	1.00	.50	.10
149B Jim Davenport BOX	1.00	.50	.10
150A Hobie Landrith COM	1.00	.50	.10
150B Hobie Landrith BOX	1.00	.50	.10
151 Bob Schmidt BOX only	1.00	.50	.10
152A Ed Bressoud COM	1.00	.50	.10
152B Ed Bressoud BOX	1.00	.50	.10
153A Andre Rodgers (no trade mention) BOX only	8.00	4.00	.80
153B Andre Rodgers (Traded to Milw.) BOX only	2.00	1.00	.20
154 Jack Sanford	1.00	.50	.10

BOX only
☐ 155	Billy O'Dell	1.00	.50	.10

BOX only
☐ 156A	Norm Larker COM	2.00	1.00	.20
☐ 156B	Norm Larker BOX	2.00	1.00	.20
☐ 157A	Charlie Neal COM	1.00	.50	.10
☐ 157B	Charlie Neal BOX	1.00	.50	.10
☐ 158A	Jim Gilliam COM	2.00	1.00	.20
☐ 158B	Jim Gilliam BOX	3.00	1.50	.30
☐ 159A	Wally Moon COM	1.00	.50	.10
☐ 159B	Wally Moon BOX	1.00	.50	.10
☐ 160A	Don Drysdale COM	5.00	2.50	.50
☐ 160B	Don Drysdale BOX	5.00	2.50	.50
☐ 161A	Larry Sherry COM	1.00	.50	.10
☐ 161B	Larry Sherry BOX	1.00	.50	.10
☐ 162	Stan Williams	4.00	2.00	.40

BOX only
☐ 163	Mel Roach BOX only	45.00	22.50	4.50
☐ 164A	Maury Wills COM	3.00	1.50	.30
☐ 164B	Maury Wills BOX	3.00	1.50	.30
☐ 165	Tommy Davis BOX only	1.00	.50	.10
☐ 166A	John Roseboro COM	1.00	.50	.10
☐ 166B	John Roseboro BOX	1.00	.50	.10
☐ 167A	Duke Snider COM	6.00	3.00	.60
☐ 167B	Duke Snider BOX	3.00	1.50	.30
☐ 168A	Gil Hodges COM	5.00	2.50	.50
☐ 168B	Gil Hodges BOX	3.00	1.50	.30
☐ 169	John Podres BOX only	1.00	.50	.10
☐ 170	Ed Roebuck BOX only	1.00	.50	.10
☐ 171A	Ken Boyer COM	5.00	2.50	.50
☐ 171B	Ken Boyer BOX	6.00	3.00	.60
☐ 172A	J.Cunningham COM	1.50	.75	.15
☐ 172B	J.Cunningham BOX	2.00	1.00	.20
☐ 173A	Daryl Spencer COM	1.00	.50	.10
☐ 173B	Daryl Spencer BOX	1.00	.50	.10
☐ 174A	Larry Jackson COM	1.50	.75	.15
☐ 174B	Larry Jackson BOX	2.00	1.00	.20
☐ 175A	Lindy McDaniel COM	1.00	.50	.10
☐ 175B	Lindy McDaniel BOX	1.00	.50	.10
☐ 176A	Bill White COM	1.50	.75	.15
☐ 176B	Bill White BOX	1.00	.50	.10
☐ 177A	Alex Grammas COM	1.00	.50	.10
☐ 177B	Alex Grammas BOX	1.00	.50	.10
☐ 178A	Curt Flood COM	1.50	.75	.15
☐ 178B	Curt Flood BOX	1.00	.50	.10
☐ 179A	Ernie Broglio COM	1.00	.50	.10
☐ 179B	Ernie Broglio BOX	1.00	.50	.10
☐ 180A	Hal Smith COM	1.00	.50	.10
☐ 180B	Hal Smith BOX	1.00	.50	.10
☐ 181A	Vada Pinson COM	1.50	.75	.15
☐ 181B	Vada Pinson BOX	1.00	.50	.10
☐ 182A	Frank Robinson COM	20.00	10.00	2.00
☐ 182B	Frank Robinson BOX	15.00	7.50	1.50
☐ 183	Roy McMillan	45.00	22.50	4.50

BOX only
☐ 184A	Bob Purkey COM	1.00	.50	.10
☐ 184B	Bob Purkey BOX	1.00	.50	.10
☐ 185A	Ed Kasko COM	1.00	.50	.10
☐ 185B	Ed Kasko BOX	1.00	.50	.10
☐ 186A	Gus Bell COM	1.50	.75	.15
☐ 186B	Gus Bell BOX	2.00	1.00	.20
☐ 187A	Jerry Lynch COM	1.00	.50	.10
☐ 187B	Jerry Lynch BOX	1.00	.50	.10
☐ 188A	Ed Bailey COM	1.00	.50	.10
☐ 188B	Ed Bailey BOX	1.00	.50	.10
☐ 189A	Jim O'Toole COM	1.00	.50	.10
☐ 189B	Jim O'Toole BOX	1.00	.50	.10
☐ 190A	Billy Martin COM	4.00	2.00	.40

(Sold to Milw.)
☐ 190B	Billy Martin BOX	1.50	.75	.15

(no sale mention)
☐ 191A	Ernie Banks COM	6.00	3.00	.60
☐ 191B	Ernie Banks BOX	10.00	5.00	1.00
☐ 192A	Richie Ashburn COM	2.00	1.00	.20
☐ 192B	Richie Ashburn BOX	1.50	.75	.15
☐ 193A	Frank Thomas COM	6.00	3.00	.60
☐ 193B	Frank Thomas BOX	20.00	10.00	2.00
☐ 194A	Don Cardwell COM	1.50	.75	.15
☐ 194B	Don Cardwell BOX	2.00	1.00	.20
☐ 195A	George Altman COM	1.00	.50	.10
☐ 195B	George Altman BOX	1.00	.50	.10
☐ 196A	Ron Santo COM	1.50	.75	.15
☐ 196B	Ron Santo BOX	1.00	.50	.10
☐ 197A	Glen Hobbie COM	1.00	.50	.10
☐ 197B	Glen Hobbie BOX	1.00	.50	.10
☐ 198A	Sam Taylor COM	1.00	.50	.10
☐ 198B	Sam Taylor BOX	1.00	.50	.10
☐ 199A	Jerry Kindall COM	1.00	.50	.10
☐ 199B	Jerry Kindall BOX	1.00	.50	.10
☐ 200A	Don Elston COM	1.00	.50	.10
☐ 200B	Don Elston BOX	1.00	.50	.10

1962 Post Cereal

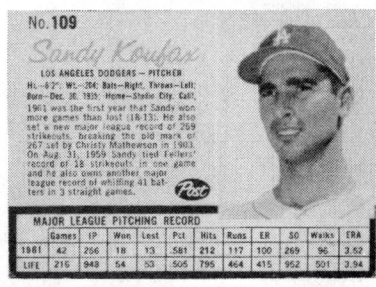

The cards in this 200 card series measure 2 1/2" by 3 1/2". The 1962 Post set is the easiest of the Post sets to complete. The cards are grouped numerically by team, for example, New York Yankees (1-13), Detroit (14-26), Baltimore (27-36), Cleveland (37-45), Chicago White Sox (46-55), Boston (56-64), Washington (65-73), Los Angeles Angels (74-82), Minnesota (83- 91), Kansas City (92-100), Los Angeles Dodgers (101-115), Cincinnati (116-130), San Francisco (131-144), Milwaukee (145- 157), St. Louis (158-168), Pittsburgh (169-181), Chicago Cubs (182-191), and Philadelphia (192-200). Cards 5B and 6B were printed on thin stock in a two card panel and distributed in a magazine promotion. The scarce cards are 55, 92, 101, 116, 121, and 140. The checklist for this set is the same as that of 1962 Jello and 1962 Post Canadian, but those sets are considered separate issues. The catalog number for this set is F278-37.

			NRMT	VG-E	GOOD
	COMPLETE SET		900.00	425.00	85.00
	COMMON PLAYER (1-200)		.80	.40	.08
☐	1	Bill Skowron	1.00	.50	.10
☐	2	Bobby Richardson	1.50	.75	.15
☐	3	Cletis Boyer	1.00	.50	.10
☐	4	Tony Kubek	1.25	.60	.12
☐	5A	Mickey Mantle	50.00	25.00	5.00
☐	5B	Mickey Mantle AD	50.00	25.00	5.00
☐	6A	Roger Maris	10.00	5.00	1.00
☐	6B	Roger Maris AD	10.00	5.00	1.00
☐	7	Yogi Berra	8.00	4.00	.80
☐	8	Elston Howard	1.50	.75	.15
☐	9	Whitey Ford	5.00	2.50	.50
☐	10	Ralph Terry	1.50	.75	.15
☐	11	John Blanchard	.80	.40	.08
☐	12	Luis Arroyo	1.50	.75	.15
☐	13	Bill Stafford	.80	.40	.08
☐	14	Norm Cash	1.00	.50	.10
☐	15	Jake Wood	.80	.40	.08
☐	16	Steve Boros	.80	.40	.08
☐	17	Chico Fernandez	.80	.40	.08
☐	18	Bill Bruton	.80	.40	.08
☐	19	Rocky Colavito	1.50	.75	.15
☐	20	Al Kaline	6.00	3.00	.60
☐	21	Dick Brown	.80	.40	.08
☐	22	Frank Lary	1.00	.50	.10
☐	23	Don Mossi	1.50	.75	.15
☐	24	Phil Regan	.80	.40	.08
☐	25	Charley Maxwell	.80	.40	.08
☐	26	Jim Bunning	3.00	1.50	.30
☐	27A	Jim Gentile	1.50	.75	.15

Home: Baltimore
☐	27B	Jim Gentile	9.00	4.50	.90

Home: San Lorenzo
☐	28	Marv Breeding	.80	.40	.08
☐	29	Brooks Robinson	8.00	4.00	.80
☐	30	Ron Hansen	.80	.40	.08
☐	31	Jackie Brandt	.80	.40	.08
☐	32	Dick Williams	1.00	.50	.10
☐	33	Gus Triandos	.80	.40	.08
☐	34	Milt Pappas	1.00	.50	.10
☐	35	Hoyt Wilhelm	5.00	2.50	.50
☐	36	Chuck Estrada	3.00	1.50	.30
☐	37	Vic Power	.80	.40	.08

☐ 38	Johnny Temple	.80	.40	.08
☐ 39	Bubba Phillips	.80	.40	.08
☐ 40	Tito Francona	.80	.40	.08
☐ 41	Willie Kirkland	.80	.40	.08
☐ 42	John Romano	.80	.40	.08
☐ 43	Jim Perry	1.00	.50	.10
☐ 44	Woodie Held	.80	.40	.08
☐ 45	Chuck Essegian	.80	.40	.08
☐ 46	Roy Sievers	.80	.40	.08
☐ 47	Nellie Fox	2.00	1.00	.20
☐ 48	Al Smith	.80	.40	.08
☐ 49	Luis Aparicio	2.50	1.25	.25
☐ 50	Jim Landis	.80	.40	.08
☐ 51	Minnie Minoso	1.50	.75	.15
☐ 52	Andy Carey	.80	.40	.08
☐ 53	Sherman Lollar	1.00	.50	.10
☐ 54	Bill Pierce	1.00	.50	.10
☐ 55	Early Wynn	20.00	10.00	2.00
☐ 56	Chuck Schilling	.80	.40	.08
☐ 57	Pete Runnels	1.00	.50	.10
☐ 58	Frank Malzone	1.00	.50	.10
☐ 59	Don Buddin	.80	.40	.08
☐ 60	Gary Geiger	1.00	.50	.10
☐ 61	Carl Yastrzemski	25.00	12.50	2.50
☐ 62	Jackie Jensen	1.00	.50	.10
☐ 63	Jim Pagliaroni	.80	.40	.08
☐ 64	Don Schwall	.80	.40	.08
☐ 65	Dale Long	.80	.40	.08
☐ 66	Chuck Cottier	.80	.40	.08
☐ 67	Billy Klaus	.80	.40	.08
☐ 68	Coot Veal	.80	.40	.08
☐ 69	Marty Keough	25.00	12.50	2.50
☐ 70	Willie Tasby	.80	.40	.08
☐ 71	Gene Woodling	.80	.40	.08
☐ 72	Gene Green	1.50	.75	.15
☐ 73	Dick Donovan	.80	.40	.08
☐ 74	Steve Bilko	.80	.40	.08
☐ 75	Rocky Bridges	.80	.40	.08
☐ 76	Eddie Yost	.80	.40	.08
☐ 77	Leon Wagner	.80	.40	.08
☐ 78	Albie Pearson	.80	.40	.08
☐ 79	Ken Hunt	.80	.40	.08
☐ 80	Earl Averill Jr.	.80	.40	.08
☐ 81	Ryne Duren	.80	.40	.08
☐ 82	Ted Kluszewski	2.00	1.00	.20
☐ 83	Bob Allison	12.00	6.00	1.20
☐ 84	Billy Martin	2.00	1.00	.20
☐ 85	Harmon Killebrew	4.00	2.00	.40
☐ 86	Zoilo Versalles	.80	.40	.08
☐ 87	Lenny Green	.80	.40	.08
☐ 88	Bill Tuttle	.80	.40	.08
☐ 89	Jim Lemon	1.00	.50	.10
☐ 90	Earl Battey	.80	.40	.08
☐ 91	Camilo Pascual	.80	.40	.08
☐ 92	Norm Sieburn	35.00	17.50	3.50
☐ 93	Jerry Lumpe	.80	.40	.08
☐ 94	Dick Howser	1.25	.60	.12
☐ 95A	Gene Stephens	1.50	.75	.15
	Born: Jan. 5			
☐ 95B	Gene Stephens	9.00	4.50	.90
	Born: Jan. 20			
☐ 96	Leo Posada	.80	.40	.08
☐ 97	Joe Pignatano	.80	.40	.08
☐ 98	Jim Archer	.80	.40	.08
☐ 99	Haywood Sullivan	.80	.40	.08
☐ 100	Art Ditmar	.80	.40	.08
☐ 101	Gil Hodges	45.00	22.50	4.50
☐ 102	Charlie Neal	.80	.40	.08
☐ 103	Daryl Spencer	15.00	7.50	1.50
☐ 104	Maury Wills	2.50	1.25	.25
☐ 105	Tommy Davis	1.00	.50	.10
☐ 106	Willie Davis	1.00	.50	.10
☐ 107	John Roseboro	.80	.40	.08
☐ 108	John Podres	1.50	.75	.15
☐ 109A	Sandy Koufax	12.00	6.00	1.20
☐ 109B	Sandy Koufax	30.00	15.00	3.00
	(with blue lines)			
☐ 110	Don Drysdale	6.00	3.00	.60
☐ 111	Larry Sherry	2.50	1.25	.25
☐ 112	Jim Gilliam	1.50	.75	.15
☐ 113	Norm Larker	25.00	12.50	2.50
☐ 114	Duke Snider	4.00	2.00	.40
☐ 115	Stan Williams	.80	.40	.08
☐ 116	Gordy Coleman	50.00	25.00	5.00
☐ 117	Don Blasingame	.80	.40	.08
☐ 118	Gene Freese	.80	.40	.08
☐ 119	Ed Kasko	.80	.40	.08
☐ 120	Gus Bell	1.00	.50	.10
☐ 121	Vada Pinson	1.50	.75	.15
☐ 122	Frank Robinson	15.00	7.50	1.50
☐ 123	Bob Purkey	.80	.40	.08
☐ 124A	Joey Jay	1.00	.50	.10
☐ 124B	Joey Jay	10.00	5.00	1.00
	(with blue lines)			
☐ 125	Jim Brosnan	20.00	10.00	2.00

☐ 126	Jim O'Toole	.80	.40	.08
☐ 127	Jerry Lynch	35.00	17.50	3.50
☐ 128	Wally Post	.80	.40	.08
☐ 129	Ken Hunt	.80	.40	.08
☐ 130	Jerry Zimmerman	.80	.40	.08
☐ 131	Willie McCovey	45.00	22.50	4.50
☐ 132	Jose Pagan	.80	.40	.08
☐ 133	Felipe Alou	.80	.40	.08
☐ 134	Jim Davenport	.80	.40	.08
☐ 135	Harvey Kuenn	1.00	.50	.10
☐ 136	Orlando Cepeda	2.50	1.25	.25
☐ 137	Ed Bailey	.80	.40	.08
☐ 138	Sam Jones	.80	.40	.08
☐ 139	Mike McCormick	1.00	.50	.10
☐ 140	Juan Marichal	50.00	25.00	5.00
☐ 141	Jack Sanford	.80	.40	.08
☐ 142	Willie Mays	20.00	10.00	2.00
☐ 143	Stu Miller	3.00	1.50	.30
☐ 144	Joe Amalfitano	10.00	5.00	1.00
☐ 145A	Joe Adcock	1.00	.50	.10
☐ 145B	Joe Adock (sic) ERR	30.00	15.00	3.00
☐ 146	Frank Bolling	.80	.40	.08
☐ 147	Ed Mathews	4.00	2.00	.40
☐ 148	Roy McMillan	.80	.40	.08
☐ 149	Hank Aaron	20.00	10.00	2.00
☐ 150	Gino Cimoli	.80	.40	.08
☐ 151	Frank Thomas	1.00	.50	.10
☐ 152	Joe Torre	1.25	.60	.12
☐ 153	Lew Burdette	1.25	.60	.12
☐ 154	Bob Buhl	.80	.40	.08
☐ 155	Carlton Willey	.80	.40	.08
☐ 156	Lee Maye	.80	.40	.08
☐ 157	Al Spangler	.80	.40	.08
☐ 158	Bill White	25.00	12.50	2.50
☐ 159	Ken Boyer	2.00	1.00	.20
☐ 160	Joe Cunningham	.80	.40	.08
☐ 161	Carl Warwick	.80	.40	.08
☐ 162	Carl Sawatski	.80	.40	.08
☐ 163	Lindy McDaniel	.80	.40	.08
☐ 164	Ernie Broglio	.80	.40	.08
☐ 165	Larry Jackson	.80	.40	.08
☐ 166	Curt Flood	1.25	.60	.12
☐ 167	Curt Simmons	1.00	.50	.10
☐ 168	Alex Grammas	.80	.40	.08
☐ 169	Dick Stuart	1.00	.50	.10
☐ 170	Bill Mazeroski	1.25	.60	.12
☐ 171	Don Hoak	.80	.40	.08
☐ 172	Dick Groat	1.25	.60	.12
☐ 173A	Roberto Clemente	15.00	7.50	1.50
☐ 173B	Roberto Clemente	40.00	20.00	4.00
	(with blue lines)			
☐ 174	Bob Skinner	.80	.40	.08
☐ 175	Bill Virdon	1.00	.50	.10
☐ 176	Smoky Burgess	1.00	.50	.10
☐ 177	Elroy Face	1.25	.60	.12
☐ 178	Bob Friend	1.00	.50	.10
☐ 179	Vernon Law	1.00	.50	.10
☐ 180	Harvey Haddix	1.00	.50	.10
☐ 181	Hal Smith	.80	.40	.08
☐ 182	Ed Bouchee	.80	.40	.08
☐ 183	Don Zimmer	1.00	.50	.10
☐ 184	Ron Santo	1.25	.60	.12
☐ 185	Andre Rodgers	.80	.40	.08
☐ 186	Richie Ashburn	1.50	.75	.15
☐ 187	George Altman	.80	.40	.08
☐ 188	Ernie Banks	6.00	3.00	.60
☐ 189	Sam Taylor	2.50	1.25	.25
☐ 190	Don Elston	.80	.40	.08
☐ 191	Jerry Kindall	.80	.40	.08
☐ 192	Pancho Herrera	.80	.40	.08
☐ 193	Tony Taylor	.80	.40	.08
☐ 194	Ruben Amaro	.80	.40	.08
☐ 195	Don Demeter	.80	.40	.08
☐ 196	Bobby Gene Smith	.80	.40	.08
☐ 197	Clay Dalrymple	.80	.40	.08
☐ 198	Robin Roberts	4.00	2.00	.40
☐ 199	Art Mahaffey	.80	.40	.08
☐ 200	John Buzhardt	.80	.40	.08

1963 Post Cereal

The cards in this 200 card set measure 2 1/2" by 3 1/2". The players are grouped by team with American Leaguers comprising 1-100 and National Leaguers 101-200. The ordering of teams is as follows: Minnesota (1-11), New York Yankees, Los Angeles Angels (24-34), Chicago White Sox (35-45), Detroit (46- 56), Baltimore (57-66), Cleveland (67-

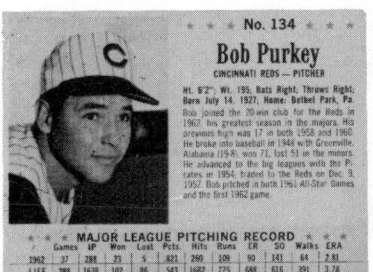

★ ★ ★ No. 134 ★ ★ ★
Bob Purkey
CINCINNATI REDS — PITCHER

Ht. 6'2", Wt. 195, Bats Right, Throws Right, Born July 14, 1927, Home: Bethel Park, Pa.
Bob joined the 20-win club for the Reds in 1962, his greatest season in the majors. His previous high was 17 in both 1958 and 1960. He broke into baseball in 1948 with Greenville, Alabama (19-8); won 71, lost 51 in the minors. He advanced to the big leagues with the Pirates in 1954, traded to the Reds on Dec. 9, 1957. Bob pitched in both 1961 All-Star Games and the first 1962 game.

★ ★ ★ MAJOR LEAGUE PITCHING RECORD ★ ★ ★

	Games	IP	Won	Lost	Pcts.	Hits	Runs	ER	SO	Walks	ERA
1962	37	288	23	5	.821	290	109	90	141	64	2.81
LIFE	285	1638	102	86	.543	1682	775	688	616	391	3.78

76), Boston (77-84), Kansas City (85-92), Washington (93-100), San Francisco (101-112), Los Angeles Dodgers (113-124), Cincinnati (125-136), Pittsburgh (137- 147), Milwaukee (148-157), St. Louis (158-168), Chicago Cubs (169-176), Philadelphia (177-184), Houston (185-192), and New York Mets (193-200). In contrast to the 1962 issue, the 1963 Post baseball card series is very difficult to complete. There are many card scarcities reflected in the price list below. Cards of the Post set are easily confused with those of the 1963 Jello set, which are 1/4" narrower (a difference which is often eliminated by bad cutting). The catalog designation is F278- 38.

	NRMT	VG-E	GOOD
COMPLETE SET	2500.00	1000.00	200.00
COMMON PLAYER (1-200)	1.25	.60	.12

		NRMT	VG-E	GOOD
☐	1 Vic Power	1.25	.60	.12
☐	2 Bernie Allen	1.25	.60	.12
☐	3 Zoilo Versalles	2.50	1.25	.25
☐	4 Rich Rollins	1.25	.60	.12
☐	5 Harmon Killebrew	10.00	5.00	1.00
☐	6 Lenny Green	30.00	15.00	3.00
☐	7 Bob Allison	1.25	.60	.12
☐	8 Earl Battey	2.50	1.25	.25
☐	9 Camilo Pascual	1.25	.60	.12
☐	10 Jim Kaat	2.50	1.25	.25
☐	11 Jack Kralick	1.25	.60	.12
☐	12 Bill Skowron	1.50	.75	.15
☐	13 Bobby Richardson	1.50	.75	.15
☐	14 Cletis Boyer	1.50	.75	.15
☐	15 Mickey Mantle	250.00	125.00	25.00
☐	16 Roger Maris	125.00	60.00	12.50
☐	17 Yogi Berra	9.00	4.50	.90
☐	18 Elston Howard	1.50	.75	.15
☐	19 Whitey Ford	6.00	3.00	.60
☐	20 Ralph Terry	1.50	.75	.15
☐	21 John Blanchard	1.25	.60	.12
☐	22 Bill Stafford	1.25	.60	.12
☐	23 Tom Tresh	1.50	.75	.15
☐	24 Steve Bilko	2.50	1.25	.25
☐	25 Bill Moran	1.25	.60	.12
☐	26A Joe Koppe	1.50	.75	.15
	BA: .277			
☐	26B Joe Koppe	7.50	3.75	.75
	BA: .227			
☐	27 Felix Torres	1.25	.60	.12
☐	28A Leon Wagner	1.50	.75	.15
	BA: .278			
☐	28B Leon Wagner	7.50	3.75	.75
	BA: .272			
☐	29 Albie Pearson	1.25	.60	.12
☐	30 Lee Thomas	50.00	25.00	5.00
	(photo actually George Thomas)			
☐	31 Bob Rodgers	1.25	.60	.12
☐	32 Dean Chance	1.25	.60	.12
☐	33 Ken McBride	1.25	.60	.12
☐	34 George Thomas	1.25	.60	.12
	(photo actually Lee Thomas)			
☐	35 Joe Cunningham	1.25	.60	.12
☐	36 Nelson Fox	2.00	1.00	.20
☐	37 Luis Aparicio	3.00	1.50	.30
☐	38 Al Smith	20.00	10.00	2.00
☐	39 Floyd Robinson	60.00	30.00	6.00
☐	40 Jim Landis	1.25	.60	.12
☐	41 Charlie Maxwell	1.25	.60	.12
☐	42 Sherman Lollar	1.25	.60	.12
☐	43 Early Wynn	3.50	1.75	.35

		NRMT	VG-E	GOOD
☐	44 Juan Pizarro	1.25	.60	.12
☐	45 Ray Herbert	1.25	.60	.12
☐	46 Norm Cash	1.50	.75	.15
☐	47 Steve Boros	1.25	.60	.12
☐	48 Dick McAuliffe	15.00	7.50	1.50
☐	49 Bill Bruton	2.50	1.25	.25
☐	50 Rocky Colavito	2.00	1.00	.20
☐	51 Al Kaline	9.00	4.50	.90
☐	52 Dick Brown	1.25	.60	.12
☐	53 Jim Bunning	80.00	40.00	8.00
☐	54 Hank Aguirre	1.25	.60	.12
☐	55 Frank Lary	1.25	.60	.12
☐	56 Don Mossi	1.25	.60	.12
☐	57 Jim Gentile	1.25	.60	.12
☐	58 Jackie Brandt	1.25	.60	.12
☐	59 Brooks Robinson	8.00	4.00	.80
☐	60 Ron Hansen	2.50	1.25	.25
☐	61 Jerry Adair	125.00	60.00	12.50
☐	62 John (Boog) Powell	2.00	1.00	.20
☐	63 Russ Snyder	1.25	.60	.12
☐	64 Steve Barber	1.25	.60	.12
☐	65 Milt Pappas	1.50	.75	.15
☐	66 Robin Roberts	3.50	1.75	.35
☐	67 Tito Francona	1.25	.60	.12
☐	68 Jerry Kindall	1.25	.60	.12
☐	69 Woody Held	1.25	.60	.12
☐	70 Bubba Phillips	10.00	5.00	1.00
☐	71 Chuck Essegian	1.25	.60	.12
☐	72 Willie Kirkland	1.25	.60	.12
☐	73 Al Luplow	1.25	.60	.12
☐	74 Ty Cline	1.25	.60	.12
☐	75 Dick Donovan	1.25	.60	.12
☐	76 John Romano	1.25	.60	.12
☐	77 Pete Runnels	1.25	.60	.12
☐	78 Ed Bressoud	1.25	.60	.12
☐	79 Frank Malzone	1.25	.60	.12
☐	80 Carl Yastrzemski	225.00	110.00	22.00
☐	81 Gary Geiger	1.25	.60	.12
☐	82 Lou Clinton	1.25	.60	.12
☐	83 Earl Wilson	1.25	.60	.12
☐	84 Bill Monbouquette	1.25	.60	.12
☐	85 Norm Sieburn	1.25	.60	.12
☐	86 Jerry Lumpe	60.00	30.00	6.00
☐	87 Manny Jimenez	60.00	30.00	6.00
☐	88 Gino Cimoli	1.25	.60	.12
☐	89 Ed Charles	1.25	.60	.12
☐	90 Ed Rakow	1.25	.60	.12
☐	91 Bob Del Greco	1.25	.60	.12
☐	92 Haywood Sullivan	1.25	.60	.12
☐	93 Chuck Hinton	1.25	.60	.12
☐	94 Ken Retzer	1.25	.60	.12
☐	95 Harry Bright	1.25	.60	.12
☐	96 Bob Johnson	1.25	.60	.12
☐	97 Dave Stenhouse	10.00	5.00	1.00
☐	98 Chuck Cottier	15.00	7.50	1.50
☐	99 Tom Cheney	1.25	.60	.12
☐	100 Claude Osteen	10.00	5.00	1.00
☐	101 Orlando Cepeda	2.50	1.25	.25
☐	102 Charley Hiller	1.25	.60	.12
☐	103 Jose Pagan	1.25	.60	.12
☐	104 Jim Davenport	1.25	.60	.12
☐	105 Harvey Kuenn	2.50	1.25	.25
☐	106 Willie Mays	25.00	12.50	2.50
☐	107 Felipe Alou	1.25	.60	.12
☐	108 Tom Haller	60.00	30.00	6.00
☐	109 Juan Marichal	4.00	2.00	.40
☐	110 Jack Sanford	1.25	.60	.12
☐	111 Bill O'Dell	1.25	.60	.12
☐	112 Willie McCovey	4.00	2.00	.40
☐	113 Lee Walls	1.25	.60	.12
☐	114 Jim Gilliam	1.50	.75	.15
☐	115 Maury Wills	2.00	1.00	.20
☐	116 Ron Fairly	1.25	.60	.12
☐	117 Tommy Davis	2.50	1.25	.25
☐	118 Duke Snider	4.00	2.00	.40
☐	119 Willie Davis	125.00	60.00	12.50
☐	120 John Roseboro	1.25	.60	.12
☐	121 Sandy Koufax	15.00	7.50	1.50
☐	122 Stan Williams	1.25	.60	.12
☐	123 Don Drysdale	4.00	2.00	.40
☐	124 Daryl Spencer	1.25	.60	.12
☐	125 Gordy Coleman	1.25	.60	.12
☐	126 Don Blasingame	1.25	.60	.12
☐	127 Leo Cardenas	1.25	.60	.12
☐	128 Eddie Kasko	125.00	60.00	12.50
☐	129 Jerry Lynch	10.00	5.00	1.00
☐	130 Vada Pinson	1.50	.75	.15
☐	131A Frank Robinson	6.00	3.00	.60
	(no stripes)			
☐	131B Frank Robinson	10.00	5.00	1.00
	(stripes on hat)			
☐	132 John Edwards	1.25	.60	.12
☐	133 Joey Jay	1.25	.60	.12
☐	134 Bob Purkey	1.25	.60	.12
☐	135 Marty Keough	15.00	7.50	1.50

☐ 136	Jim O'Toole	1.25	.60	.12
☐ 137	Dick Stuart	1.25	.60	.12
☐ 138	Bill Mazeroski	1.50	.75	.15
☐ 139	Dick Groat	1.50	.75	.15
☐ 140	Don Hoak	20.00	10.00	2.00
☐ 141	Bob Skinner	10.00	5.00	1.00
☐ 142	Bill Virdon	1.50	.75	.15
☐ 143	Roberto Clemente	15.00	7.50	1.50
☐ 144	Smoky Burgess	1.50	.75	.15
☐ 145	Bob Friend	1.25	.60	.12
☐ 146	Al McBean	1.25	.60	.12
☐ 147	Elroy Face	1.50	.75	.15
☐ 148	Joe Adcock	1.50	.75	.15
☐ 149	Frank Bolling	1.25	.60	.12
☐ 150	Roy McMillan	1.25	.60	.12
☐ 151	Eddie Mathews	7.50	3.75	.75
☐ 152	Hank Aaron	75.00	37.50	7.50
☐ 153	Del Crandall	25.00	12.50	2.50
☐ 154A	Bob Shaw COR	1.50	.75	.15
☐ 154B	Bob Shaw ERR	10.00	5.00	1.00
	(two "in 1959" in			
	same sentence)			
☐ 155	Lew Burdette	1.50	.75	.15
☐ 156	Joe Torre	2.00	1.00	.20
☐ 157	Tony Cloninger	1.25	.60	.12
☐ 158	Bill White	1.50	.75	.15
☐ 159	Julian Javier	1.25	.60	.12
☐ 160	Ken Boyer	2.00	1.00	.20
☐ 161	Julio Gotay	1.25	.60	.12
☐ 162	Curt Flood	75.00	37.50	7.50
☐ 163	Charlie James	2.50	1.25	.25
☐ 164	Gene Oliver	1.25	.60	.12
☐ 165	Ernie Broglio	1.25	.60	.12
☐ 166	Bob Gibson	4.00	2.00	.40
☐ 167A	Lindy McDaniel	4.00	2.00	.40
	(no asterisk)			
☐ 167B	Lindy McDaniel	4.00	2.00	.40
	(asterisk traded line)			
☐ 168	Ray Washburn	1.25	.60	.12
☐ 169	Ernie Banks	5.00	2.50	.50
☐ 170	Ron Santo	1.50	.75	.15
☐ 171	George Altman	1.25	.60	.12
☐ 172	Billy Williams	90.00	45.00	9.00
☐ 173	Andre Rodgers	6.00	3.00	.60
☐ 174	Ken Hubbs	15.00	7.50	1.50
☐ 175	Don Landrum	1.25	.60	.12
☐ 176	Dick Bertell	12.00	6.00	1.20
☐ 177	Roy Sievers	1.25	.60	.12
☐ 178	Tony Taylor	1.25	.60	.12
☐ 179	John Callison	1.25	.60	.12
☐ 180	Don Demeter	1.25	.60	.12
☐ 181	Tony Gonzalez	8.00	4.00	.80
☐ 182	Wes Covington	15.00	7.50	1.50
☐ 183	Art Mahaffey	1.25	.60	.12
☐ 184	Clay Dalrymple	1.25	.60	.12
☐ 185	Al Spangler	2.50	1.25	.25
☐ 186	Roman Mejias	1.25	.60	.12
☐ 187	Bob Aspromonte	250.00	125.00	25.00
☐ 188	Norm Larker	25.00	12.50	2.50
☐ 189	Johnny Temple	1.25	.60	.12
☐ 190	Carl Warwick	1.25	.60	.12
☐ 191	Bob Lillis	1.25	.60	.12
☐ 192	Dick Farrell	1.25	.60	.12
☐ 193	Gil Hodges	3.50	1.75	.35
☐ 194	Marv Throneberry	1.25	.60	.12
☐ 195	Charlie Neal	6.00	3.00	.60
☐ 196	Frank Thomas	125.00	60.00	12.50
☐ 197	Richie Ashburn	15.00	7.50	1.50
☐ 198	Felix Mantilla	1.25	.60	.12
☐ 199	Rod Kanehl	12.00	6.00	1.20
☐ 200	Roger Craig	2.00	1.00	.20

1986 Quaker Granola

This set of 33 cards was available in packages of Quaker Oats Chewy Granola, three player cards plus a complete set offer card in each package. The set was also available through a mail-in offer where anyone sending in four UPC seals from Chewy Granola (before 12/31/86) would receive a complete set. The cards were produced by Topps for Quaker Oats and are 2 1/2" by 3 1/2". Card backs are printed in red and blue on gray card stock. The cards are numbered on the front and the back.

	MINT	EXC	G-VG
COMPLETE SET	6.00	3.00	.60

COMMON PLAYER		.10	.05	.01
☐ 1	Willie McGee	.20	.10	.02
☐ 2	Dwight Gooden	.50	.25	.05
☐ 3	Vince Coleman	.35	.17	.03
☐ 4	Gary Carter	.30	.15	.03
☐ 5	Jack Clark	.20	.10	.02
☐ 6	Steve Garvey	.30	.15	.03
☐ 7	Tony Gwynn	.40	.20	.04
☐ 8	Dale Murphy	.50	.25	.05
☐ 9	Dave Parker	.20	.10	.02
☐ 10	Tim Raines	.35	.17	.03
☐ 11	Pete Rose	.60	.30	.06
☐ 12	Nolan Ryan	.40	.20	.04
☐ 13	Ryne Sandberg	.25	.12	.02
☐ 14	Mike Schmidt	.50	.25	.05
☐ 15	Ozzie Smith	.25	.12	.02
☐ 16	Darryl Strawberry	.50	.25	.05
☐ 17	Fernando Valenzuela	.25	.12	.02
☐ 18	Don Mattingly	1.00	.50	.10
☐ 19	Bret Saberhagen	.30	.15	.03
☐ 20	Ozzie Guillen	.15	.07	.01
☐ 21	Bert Blyleven	.15	.07	.01
☐ 22	Wade Boggs	.75	.35	.07
☐ 23	George Brett	.50	.25	.05
☐ 24	Darrell Evans	.15	.07	.01
☐ 25	Rickey Henderson	.50	.25	.05
☐ 26	Reggie Jackson	.50	.25	.05
☐ 27	Eddie Murray	.35	.17	.03
☐ 28	Phil Niekro	.20	.10	.02
☐ 29	Dan Quisenberry	.15	.07	.01
☐ 30	Jim Rice	.30	.15	.03
☐ 31	Cal Ripken	.35	.17	.03
☐ 32	Tom Seaver	.30	.15	.03
☐ 33	Dave Winfield	.30	.15	.03
☐ 34	Offer Card for	.03	.01	.00
	the complete set			
	(unnumbered)			

1984 Ralston Purina

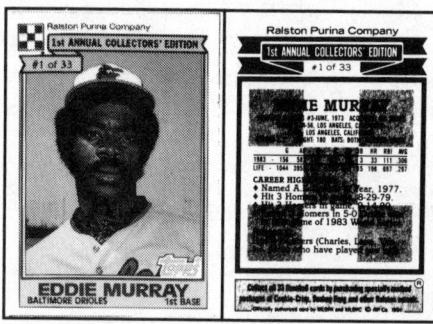

The cards in this 33 card set measure 2 1/2" by 3 1/2". In 1984 the Ralston Purina Company issued what it has entitled "The First Annual Collectors Edition of Baseball Cards." The cards feature portrait photos of the players rather than batting action shots. The Topps logo appears along with the Ralston logo on the front of the card. The backs are completely different from the Topps cards of this year; in fact, they contain neither a Topps logo nor a Topps copyright. Large quantities of these cards were obtained by card dealers for direct distribution into the organized hobby, hence the relatively low price of the set.

	MINT	EXC	G-VG
COMPLETE SET	3.00	1.50	.30
COMMON PLAYER	.05	.02	.00
□ 1 Eddie Murray	.25	.12	.02
□ 2 Ozzie Smith	.15	.07	.01
□ 3 Ted Simmons	.05	.02	.00
□ 4 Pete Rose	.50	.25	.05
□ 5 Greg Luzinski	.05	.02	.00
□ 6 Andre Dawson	.20	.10	.02
□ 7 Dave Winfield	.15	.07	.01
□ 8 Tom Seaver	.25	.12	.02
□ 9 Jim Rice	.15	.07	.01
□ 10 Fernando Valenzuela	.15	.07	.01
□ 11 Wade Boggs	.50	.25	.05
□ 12 Dale Murphy	.40	.20	.04
□ 13 George Brett	.35	.17	.03
□ 14 Nolan Ryan	.25	.12	.02
□ 15 Rickey Henderson	.35	.17	.03
□ 16 Steve Carlton	.20	.10	.02
□ 17 Rod Carew	.25	.12	.02
□ 18 Steve Garvey	.25	.12	.02
□ 19 Reggie Jackson	.35	.17	.03
□ 20 Dave Concepcion	.05	.02	.00
□ 21 Robin Yount	.20	.10	.02
□ 22 Mike Schmidt	.40	.20	.04
□ 23 Jim Palmer	.20	.10	.02
□ 24 Bruce Sutter	.10	.05	.01
□ 25 Dan Quisenberry	.10	.05	.01
□ 26 Bill Madlock	.10	.05	.01
□ 27 Cecil Cooper	.05	.02	.00
□ 28 Gary Carter	.25	.12	.02
□ 29 Fred Lynn	.10	.05	.01
□ 30 Pedro Guerrero	.15	.07	.01
□ 31 Ron Guidry	.10	.05	.01
□ 32 Keith Hernandez	.20	.10	.02
□ 33 Carlton Fisk	.10	.05	.01

1987 Ralston Purina

The Ralston Purina Company issued a set of 15 cards picturing players without their respective team logos. The cards were distributed as inserts inside packages of certain flavors of Ralston Purina's breakfast cereals. The cards measure 2 1/2" by 3 1/2" and are in full-color on the front. The cards are numbered on the back in the lower right hand corner; the player's uniform number is prominently displayed on the front.

	MINT	EXC	G-VG
COMPLETE SET	6.00	3.00	.60
COMMON PLAYER	.35	.17	.03
□ 1 Nolan Ryan	.60	.30	.06
□ 2 Steve Garvey	.50	.25	.05
□ 3 Wade Boggs	1.00	.50	.10
□ 4 Dave Winfield	.50	.25	.05
□ 5 Don Mattingly	2.00	1.00	.20

	MINT	EXC	G-VG
□ 6 Don Sutton	.35	.17	.03
□ 7 Dave Parker	.35	.17	.03
□ 8 Eddie Murray	.60	.30	.06
□ 9 Gary Carter	.45	.22	.04
□ 10 Roger Clemens	.75	.35	.07
□ 11 Fernando Valenzuela	.45	.22	.04
□ 12 Cal Ripken	.60	.30	.06
□ 13 Ozzie Smith	.35	.17	.03
□ 14 Mike Schmidt	.60	.30	.06
□ 15 Ryne Sandberg	.35	.17	.03

1983 Rangers Affiliated Food

The cards in this 28 card set measure 2 3/8" by 3 1/2". The Affiliated Food Stores chain of Arlington, Texas, produced this set of Texas Rangers late during the 1983 baseball season. Complete sets were given to children 13 and under at the September 3, 1983, Rangers game. The cards are numbered by uniform number and feature the player's name, card number, and the words "1983 Rangers" on the bottom front. The backs contain biographical data, career totals, a small black and white insert picture of the player, and the Affiliated Food Stores' logo. The coaches card is unnumbered.

	MINT	EXC	G-VG
COMPLETE SET	5.00	2.50	.50
COMMON PLAYER	.15	.07	.01
□ 1 Bill Stein	.15	.07	.01
□ 2 Mike Richardt	.15	.07	.01
□ 3 Wayne Tolleson	.25	.12	.02
□ 5 Billy Sample	.15	.07	.01
□ 6 Bobby Jones	.15	.07	.01
□ 7 Bucky Dent	.35	.17	.03
□ 8 Bobby Johnson	.15	.07	.01
□ 9 Pete O'Brien	.75	.35	.07
□ 10 Jim Sundberg	.25	.12	.02
□ 11 Doug Rader MG	.25	.12	.02
□ 12 Dave Hostetler	.15	.07	.01
□ 14 Larry Biittner	.15	.07	.01
□ 15 Larry Parrish	.35	.17	.03
□ 17 Mickey Rivers	.25	.12	.02
□ 21 Odell Jones	.15	.07	.01
□ 24 Dave Schmidt	.25	.12	.02
□ 25 Buddy Bell	.50	.25	.05
□ 26 George Wright	.15	.07	.01
□ 28 Frank Tanana	.25	.12	.02
□ 29 John Butcher	.15	.07	.01
□ 32 John Matlack	.25	.12	.02
□ 40 Rick Honeycutt	.25	.12	.02
□ 41 Dave Tobik	.15	.07	.01
□ 44 Danny Darwin	.25	.12	.02
□ 46 Jim Anderson	.15	.07	.01
□ 48 Mike Smithson	.15	.07	.01
□ 49 Charlie Hough	.35	.17	.03
□ xx Rangers Coaches:	.15	.07	.01

(unnumbered)
Wayne Terwilliger 42
Merv Rettenmund 22
Dick Such 52
Glenn Ezell 18
Rich Donnelly 37

1984 Rangers Jarvis Press

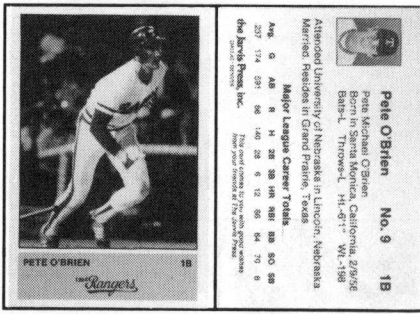

The cards in this 30 card set measure 2 1/2" by 3 1/2". The Jarvis Press of Dallas issued this full-color regional set of Texas Rangers. Cards are numbered on the front by the players uniform number. The cards were issued on an uncut sheet. Twenty-seven player cards, a manager card, a trainer card (unnumbered) and a coaches card (unnumbered) comprise this set. The backs are black and white and contain biographical information, statistics, and an additional photo of the player.

		MINT	EXC	G-VG
COMPLETE SET		5.00	2.50	.50
COMMON PLAYER		.15	.07	.01
☐ 1	Bill Stein	.15	.07	.01
☐ 2	Alan Bannister	.15	.07	.01
☐ 3	Wayne Tolleson	.25	.12	.02
☐ 5	Billy Sample	.15	.07	.01
☐ 6	Bobby Jones	.15	.07	.01
☐ 7	Ned Yost	.15	.07	.01
☐ 9	Pete O'Brien	.50	.25	.05
☐ 11	Doug Rader MG	.25	.12	.02
☐ 13	Tommy Dunbar	.25	.12	.02
☐ 14	Jim Anderson	.15	.07	.01
☐ 15	Larry Parrish	.35	.17	.03
☐ 16	Mike Mason	.25	.12	.02
☐ 17	Mickey Rivers	.25	.12	.02
☐ 19	Curtis Wilkerson	.25	.12	.02
☐ 20	Jeff Kunkel	.25	.12	.02
☐ 21	Odell Jones	.15	.07	.01
☐ 24	Dave Schmidt	.25	.12	.02
☐ 25	Buddy Bell	.50	.25	.05
☐ 26	George Wright	.15	.07	.01
☐ 28	Frank Tanana	.25	.12	.02
☐ 30	Marv Foley	.15	.07	.01
☐ 31	Dave Stewart	.35	.17	.03
☐ 32	Gary Ward	.25	.12	.02
☐ 36	Dickie Noles	.15	.07	.01
☐ 43	Donnie Scott	.15	.07	.01
☐ 44	Danny Darwin	.25	.12	.02
☐ 49	Charlie Hough	.35	.17	.03
☐ 53	Joey McLaughlin	.15	.07	.01
☐ xx	Bill Ziegler (Trainer) (unnumbered)	.15	.07	.01
☐ xx	Rangers Coaches: (unnumbered) Merv Rettenmund 22 Rich Donnelly 37 Glenn Ezell 18 Dick Such 52 Wayne Terwilliger 42	.15	.07	.01

1985 Rangers Performance

The cards in this 28 card set measure 2 3/8" by 3 1/2". Performance Printing sponsored this full-color regional set of Texas Rangers. Cards are numbered on the back by the players uniform number. The cards were also issued on an uncut sheet. Twenty-five player cards, a manager card, a trainer card

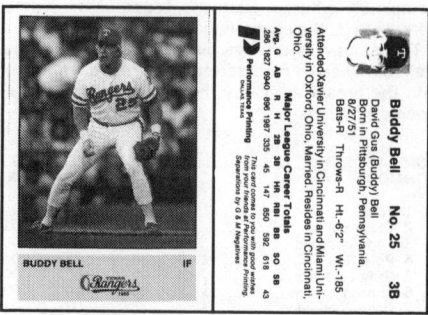

(unnumbered) and a coaches card (unnumbered) comprise this set. The backs are black and white and contain biographical information, statistics, and an additional photo of the player.

		MINT	EXC	G-VG
COMPLETE SET		5.00	2.50	.50
COMMON PLAYER		.15	.07	.01
☐ 0	Oddibe McDowell	.60	.30	.06
☐ 1	Bill Stein	.15	.07	.01
☐ 2	Bobby Valentine MG	.35	.17	.03
☐ 3	Wayne Tolleson	.15	.07	.01
☐ 4	Don Slaught	.25	.12	.02
☐ 5	Alan Bannister	.15	.07	.01
☐ 6	Bobby Jones	.15	.07	.01
☐ 7	Glenn Brummer	.15	.07	.01
☐ 8	Luis Pujols	.15	.07	.01
☐ 9	Pete O'Brien	.50	.25	.05
☐ 11	Toby Harrah	.25	.12	.02
☐ 13	Tommy Dunbar	.15	.07	.01
☐ 15	Larry Parrish	.35	.17	.03
☐ 16	Mike Mason	.15	.07	.01
☐ 19	Curtis Wilkerson	.15	.07	.01
☐ 24	Dave Schmidt	.25	.12	.02
☐ 25	Buddy Bell	.50	.25	.05
☐ 27	Greg Harris	.25	.12	.02
☐ 30	Dave Rozema	.15	.07	.01
☐ 32	Gary Ward	.25	.12	.02
☐ 36	Dickie Noles	.15	.07	.01
☐ 41	Chris Welsh	.15	.07	.01
☐ 44	Cliff Johnson	.15	.07	.01
☐ 46	Burt Hooton	.15	.07	.01
☐ 48	Dave Stewart	.35	.17	.03
☐ 49	Charlie Hough	.35	.17	.03
☐ xx	Trainers: Bill Ziegler Danny Wheat (unnumbered)	.15	.07	.01
☐ xx	Rangers Coaches: (unnumbered) Art Howe 10 Rich Donnelly 37 Glenn Ezell 18 Tom House 35 Wayne Terwilliger 42	.15	.07	.01

1986 Rangers Performance

Performance Printing of Dallas produced a 28 card set of Texas Rangers which were given out at the stadium on August 23rd. Cards measure 2 3/8" by 3 1/2" and are in full color. The cards are unnumbered except for uniform number which is given on the card back. Card backs feature black printing on white card stock with a small picture of the player's head in the upper left corner. The set seems to be more desirable than the previous Ranger sets due to the Rangers' 1986 success which was directly related to their outstanding rookie crop.

		MINT	EXC	G-VG
COMPLETE SET		7.00	3.50	.70
COMMON PLAYER		.10	.05	.01
☐ 0	Oddibe McDowell	.50	.25	.05

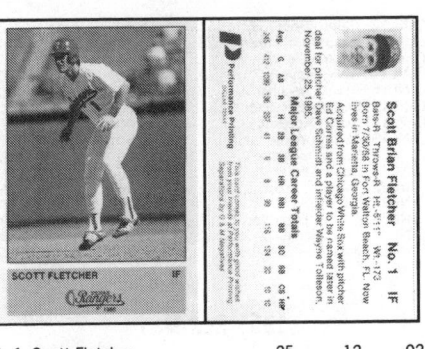

| | | | Avg | G | AB | R | H | 2B | 3B | HR | RBI | SB | BB | SO |

Scott Brian Fletcher No. 1 1F
Bats-R Throws-R Ht.-5'11" Wt.-173
Born 7/30/68 in Fort Walton Beach, FL. Now
lives in Marietta, Georgia.
Acquired from Chicago White Sox with pitcher
Ed Correa and shortstop Dave Schmidt and infielder Wayne Tolleson,
shortened in the deal for pitcher Dave Schmidt and infielder Wayne Tolleson. Now
November 25, 1985.

Major League Career Totals

(Performance Printing logo)

□	1	Scott Fletcher	.25	.12	.02
□	2	Bobby Valentine MG	.25	.12	.02
□	3	Ruben Sierra	1.25	.60	.12
□	4	Don Slaught	.15	.07	.01
□	9	Pete O'Brien	.50	.25	.05
□	11	Toby Harrah	.20	.10	.02
□	12	Geno Petralli	.10	.05	.01
□	15	Larry Parrish	.25	.12	.02
□	16	Mike Mason	.10	.05	.01
□	17	Darrell Porter	.10	.05	.01
□	18	Edwin Correa	.50	.25	.05
□	19	Curtis Wilkerson	.10	.05	.01
□	22	Steve Buechele	.20	.10	.02
□	23	Jose Guzman	.35	.17	.03
□	24	Ricky Wright	.10	.05	.01
□	27	Greg Harris	.15	.07	.01
□	28	Mitch Williams	.30	.15	.03
□	29	Pete Incaviglia	1.25	.60	.12
□	32	Gary Ward	.20	.10	.02
□	34	Dale Mohorcic	.30	.15	.03
□	40	Jeff Russell	.10	.05	.01
□	44	Tom Paciorek	.10	.05	.01
□	46	Mike Loynd	.30	.15	.03
□	48	Bobby Witt	.50	.25	.05
□	49	Charlie Hough	.25	.12	.02
□	xx	Coaching Staff:	.10	.05	.01

(unnumbered)
Art Howe 10
Joe Ferguson 13
Tim Foli 14
Tom Robson 31
Tom House 35

| □ | xx | Trainers: | .10 | .05 | .01 |

(unnumbered)
Bill Zeigler
Danny Wheat

1955 Rawlings Stan Musial

This six card set was actually the side panels of the
box containing a Rawlings baseball glove. Rawlings
Sporting Goods was headquartered in St. Louis. The
cards are numbered and come in two sizes. Cards
1-4 are larger, 2 5/8" by 3 3/4" whereas numbers
1A and 2A are smaller, 2 1/8" by 3 1/8". The cards
are blank backed and have a black and white picture
on a light blue background.

		NRMT	VG-E	GOOD
COMPLETE SET (6)		600.00	300.00	60.00
COMMON PLAYER		100.00	50.00	10.00
□ 1	Stan Musial	150.00	75.00	15.00
	(portrait)			
□ 2	Stan Musial	150.00	75.00	15.00
	(kneeling)			
□ 3	Stan Musial	150.00	75.00	15.00
	(swinging HOR)			
□ 4	Stan Musial	150.00	75.00	15.00
	(batting stance)			
□ 1A	Stan Musial	100.00	50.00	10.00
	(portrait with hand and bat visible)			
□ 2A	Stan Musial	100.00	50.00	10.00
	(portrait, same picture as #1)			

1954 Red Heart

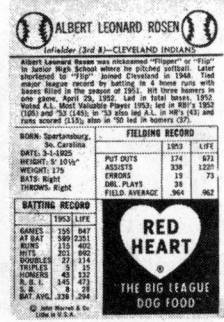

The cards in this 33 card set measure 2 5/8" by 3
3/4". The 1954 Red Heart baseball series was
marketed by Red Heart dog food, which, incidentally,
was a subsidiary of Morrell Meats. The set consists
of three series of eleven unnumbered cards each of
which could be ordered from the company via an
offer (two can labels plus ten cents for each series)
on the can label. Each series has a specific color
background (red, green or blue) behind the color
player photo. Cards with red backgrounds are
considered scarcer and are marked with an asterisk
in the checklist (which has been alphabetized and
numbered for reference). The ACC designation is
F156.

		NRMT	VG-E	GOOD
COMPLETE SET		1000.00	425.00	85.00
COMMON PLAYER (1-33)		15.00	7.50	1.50
□ 1	Richie Ashburn *	35.00	17.50	3.50
□ 2	Frank Baumholtz *	18.00	9.00	1.80
□ 3	Gus Bell	15.00	7.50	1.50
□ 4	Billy Cox	15.00	7.50	1.50
□ 5	Alvin Dark	18.00	9.00	1.80
□ 6	Carl Erskine *	21.00	10.50	2.10
□ 7	Ferris Fain	15.00	7.50	1.50
□ 8	Dee Fondy	15.00	7.50	1.50
□ 9	Nelson Fox	24.00	12.00	2.40
□ 10	Jim Gilliam	18.00	9.00	1.80
□ 11	Jim Hegan *	18.00	9.00	1.80
□ 12	George Kell	30.00	15.00	3.00
□ 13	Ralph Kiner *	35.00	17.50	3.50
□ 14	Ted Kluszewski *	24.00	12.00	2.40
□ 15	Harvey Kuenn *	18.00	9.00	1.80
□ 16	Bob Lemon *	35.00	17.50	3.50
□ 17	Sherman Lollar	15.00	7.50	1.50
□ 18	Mickey Mantle	350.00	175.00	35.00
□ 19	Billy Martin	30.00	15.00	3.00
□ 20	Gil McDougald *	21.00	10.50	2.10
□ 21	Roy McMillan	15.00	7.50	1.50
□ 22	Minnie Minoso	18.00	9.00	1.80
□ 23	Stan Musial *	175.00	85.00	18.00

		NRMT	VG-E	GOOD
☐ 24	Billy Pierce	18.00	9.00	1.80
☐ 25	Al Rosen *	24.00	12.00	2.40
☐ 26	Hank Sauer	15.00	7.50	1.50
☐ 27	Red Schoendienst *	21.00	10.50	2.10
☐ 28	Enos Slaughter	35.00	17.50	3.50
☐ 29	Duke Snider	60.00	30.00	6.00
☐ 30	Warren Spahn	35.00	17.50	3.50
☐ 31	Sammy White	15.00	7.50	1.50
☐ 32	Eddie Yost	15.00	7.50	1.50
☐ 33	Gus Zernial	15.00	7.50	1.50

1952 Red Man

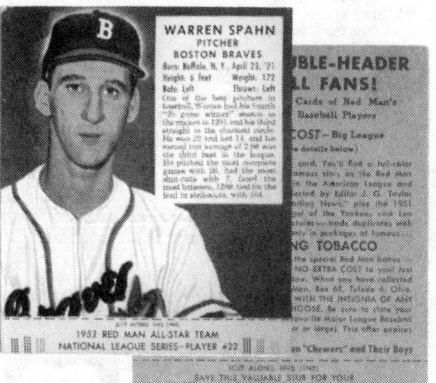

The cards in this 52 card set measure 3 1/2" by 4" (or 3 1/2" by 3 5/8" without the tab). This Red Man issue was the first nationally available tobacco issue since the T cards of the teens early in this century. This 52 card set contains 26 top players from each league. Cards that have the tab (coupon) attached are generally worth double the price of cards with the tab removed. Card numbers are located on the tabs. The prices listed below refer to cards without tabs.

		NRMT	VG-E	GOOD
COMPLETE SET		500.00	200.00	40.00
COMMON PLAYER		4.50	2.25	.45
☐ AL1	Casey Stengel MG	18.00	9.00	1.80
☐ AL2	Roberto Avila	4.50	2.25	.45
☐ AL3	Yogi Berra	25.00	12.50	2.50
☐ AL4	Gil Coan	4.50	2.25	.45
☐ AL5	Dom DiMaggio	7.50	3.75	.75
☐ AL6	Larry Doby	6.00	3.00	.60
☐ AL7	Ferris Fain	4.50	2.25	.45
☐ AL8	Bob Feller	25.00	12.50	2.50
☐ AL9	Nelson Fox	9.00	4.50	.90
☐ AL10	Johnny Groth	4.50	2.25	.45
☐ AL11	Jim Hegan	4.50	2.25	.45
☐ AL12	Eddie Joost	4.50	2.25	.45
☐ AL13	George Kell	15.00	7.50	1.50
☐ AL14	Gil McDougald	7.50	3.75	.75
☐ AL15	Minnie Minoso	7.50	3.75	.75
☐ AL16	Billy Pierce	6.00	3.00	.60
☐ AL17	Bob Porterfield	4.50	2.25	.45
☐ AL18	Erdie Robinson	4.50	2.25	.45
☐ AL19	Saul Rogovin	4.50	2.25	.45
☐ AL20	Bobby Shantz	6.00	3.00	.60
☐ AL21	Vern Stephens	4.50	2.25	.45
☐ AL22	Vic Wertz	4.50	2.25	.45
☐ AL23	Ted Williams	75.00	37.50	7.50
☐ AL24	Early Wynn	15.00	7.50	1.50
☐ AL25	Eddie Yost	4.50	2.25	.45
☐ AL26	Gus Zernial	4.50	2.25	.45
☐ NL1	Leo Durocher MG	12.50	6.25	1.25
☐ NL2	Richie Ashburn	10.00	5.00	1.00
☐ NL3	Ewell Blackwell	6.00	3.00	.60
☐ NL4	Cliff Chambers	4.50	2.25	.45
☐ NL5	Murray Dickson	4.50	2.25	.45
☐ NL6	Sid Gordon	4.50	2.25	.45
☐ NL7	Granny Hamner	4.50	2.25	.45
☐ NL8	Jim Hearn	4.50	2.25	.45
☐ NL9	Monte Irvin	15.00	7.50	1.50
☐ NL10	Larry Jansen	4.50	2.25	.45
☐ NL11	Willie Jones	4.50	2.25	.45

		NRMT	VG-E	GOOD
☐ NL12	Ralph Kiner	15.00	7.50	1.50
☐ NL13	Whitey Lockman	4.50	2.25	.45
☐ NL14	Sal Maglie	7.50	3.75	.75
☐ NL15	Willie Mays	50.00	25.00	5.00
☐ NL16	Stan Musial	50.00	25.00	5.00
☐ NL17	Pee Wee Reese	20.00	10.00	2.00
☐ NL18	Robin Roberts	15.00	7.50	1.50
☐ NL19	Al Schoendienst	7.50	3.75	.75
☐ NL20	Enos Slaughter	15.00	7.50	1.50
☐ NL21	Duke Snider	35.00	17.50	3.50
☐ NL22	Warren Spahn	15.00	7.50	1.50
☐ NL23	Ed Stanky	6.00	3.00	.60
☐ NL24	Bobby Thomson	7.50	3.75	.75
☐ NL25	Earl Torgeson	4.50	2.25	.45
☐ NL26	Wes Westrum	4.50	2.25	.45

1953 Red Man

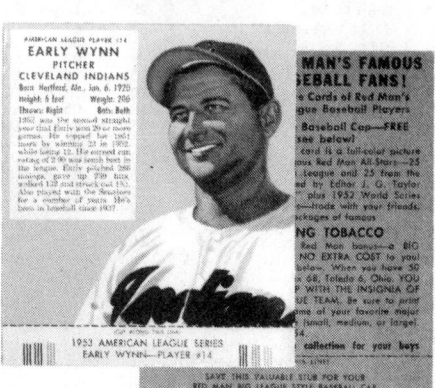

The cards in this 52 card set measure 3 1/2" by 4" (or 3 1/2" by 3 5/8" without the tab). The 1953 Red Man set contains 26 National League stars and 26 American League stars. Card numbers are located both on the write-up of the player and on the tab. Cards that have the tab (coupon) attached are generally worth double the price of cards with the tab removed. The prices listed below refer to cards without tabs.

		NRMT	VG-E	GOOD
COMPLETE SET		450.00	175.00	37.00
COMMON PLAYER		4.50	2.25	.45
☐ AL1	Casey Stengel MG	18.00	9.00	1.80
☐ AL2	Hank Bauer	7.50	3.75	.75
☐ AL3	Yogi Berra	25.00	12.50	2.50
☐ AL4	Walt Dropo	4.50	2.25	.45
☐ AL5	Nelson Fox	9.00	4.50	.90
☐ AL6	Jackie Jensen	7.50	3.75	.75
☐ AL7	Eddie Joost	4.50	2.25	.45
☐ AL8	George Kell	15.00	7.50	1.50
☐ AL9	Dale Mitchell	4.50	2.25	.45
☐ AL10	Phil Rizzuto	15.00	7.50	1.50
☐ AL11	Eddie Robinson	4.50	2.25	.45
☐ AL12	Gene Woodling	6.00	3.00	.60
☐ AL13	Gus Zernial	4.50	2.25	.45
☐ AL14	Early Wynn	15.00	7.50	1.50
☐ AL15	Joe Dobson	4.50	2.25	.45
☐ AL16	Billy Pierce	6.00	3.00	.60
☐ AL17	Bob Lemon	15.00	7.50	1.50
☐ AL18	Johnny Mize	15.00	7.50	1.50
☐ AL19	Bob Porterfield	4.50	2.25	.45
☐ AL20	Bobby Shantz	6.00	3.00	.60
☐ AL21	Mickey Vernon	6.00	3.00	.60
☐ AL22	Dom DiMaggio	7.50	3.75	.75
☐ AL23	Gil McDougald	7.50	3.75	.75
☐ AL24	Al Rosen	7.50	3.75	.75
☐ AL25	Mel Parnell	6.00	3.00	.60
☐ AL26	Bobby Avila	4.50	2.25	.45
☐ NL1	Charlie Dressen MG	6.00	3.00	.60
☐ NL2	Bobby Adams	4.50	2.25	.45
☐ NL3	Richie Ashburn	10.00	5.00	1.00
☐ NL4	Joe Black	6.00	3.00	.60
☐ NL5	Roy Campanella	35.00	17.50	3.50
☐ NL6	Ted Kluszewski	7.50	3.75	.75

☐ NL7	Whitey Lockman	4.50	2.25	.45
☐ NL8	Sal Maglie	7.50	3.75	.75
☐ NL9	Andy Pafko	4.50	2.25	.45
☐ NL10	Pee Wee Reese	20.00	10.00	2.00
☐ NL11	Robin Roberts	15.00	7.50	1.50
☐ NL12	Al Schoendienst	7.50	3.75	.75
☐ NL13	Enos Slaughter	15.00	7.50	1.50
☐ NL14	Duke Snider	35.00	17.50	3.50
☐ NL15	Ralph Kiner	15.00	7.50	1.50
☐ NL16	Hank Sauer	4.50	2.25	.45
☐ NL17	Del Ennis	4.50	2.25	.45
☐ NL18	Granny Hamner	4.50	2.25	.45
☐ NL19	Warren Spahn	15.00	7.50	1.50
☐ NL20	Wes Westrum	4.50	2.25	.45
☐ NL21	Hoyt Wilhelm	15.00	7.50	1.50
☐ NL22	Murray Dickson	4.50	2.25	.45
☐ NL23	Warren Hacker	4.50	2.25	.45
☐ NL24	Gerry Staley	4.50	2.25	.45
☐ NL25	Bobby Thomson	7.50	3.75	.75
☐ NL26	Stan Musial	50.00	25.00	5.00

1954 Red Man

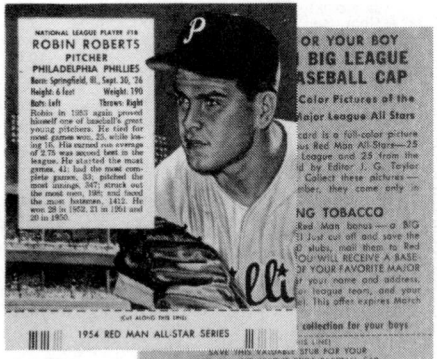

The cards in this 50 card set measure 3 1/2" by 4" (or 3 1/2" by 3 5/8" without the tab). The 1954 Red Man set witnessed a reduction to 25 players from each league. George Kell, Sam Mele, and Dave Philley are known to exist with two different teams. Card number 19 of the National League exists as Enos Slaughter and as Gus Bell. Card numbers are on the write-ups of the players. Cards that have the tab (coupon) attached are generally worth double the price of cards with the tab removed. The prices listed below refer to cards without tabs. The complete set price below refers to all 54 cards including the four variations.

	NRMT	VG-E	GOOD
COMPLETE SET (54)	500.00	200.00	40.00
COMMON PLAYERS	4.50	2.25	.45
☐ AL1 Bobby Avila	4.50	2.25	.45
☐ AL2 Jim Busby	4.50	2.25	.45
☐ AL3 Nelson Fox	9.00	4.50	.90
☐ AL4A George Kell	15.00	7.50	1.50
(Boston)			
☐ AL4B George Kell	30.00	15.00	3.00
(Chicago)			
☐ AL5 Sherman Lollar	4.50	2.25	.45
☐ AL6A Sam Mele	10.00	5.00	1.00
(Baltimore)			
☐ AL6B Sam Mele	20.00	10.00	2.00
(Chicago)			
☐ AL7 Minnie Minoso	7.50	3.75	.75
☐ AL8 Mel Parnell	6.00	3.00	.60
☐ AL9A Dave Philley	10.00	5.00	1.00
(Cleveland)			
☐ AL9B Dave Philley	20.00	10.00	2.00
(Philadelphia)			
☐ AL10 Billy Pierce	6.00	3.00	.60
☐ AL11 Jim Piersall	7.50	3.75	.75
☐ AL12 Al Rosen	7.50	3.75	.75

☐ AL13	Mickey Vernon	6.00	3.00	.60
☐ AL14	Sammy White	4.50	2.25	.45
☐ AL15	Gene Woodling	6.00	3.00	.60
☐ AL16	Whitey Ford	20.00	10.00	2.00
☐ AL17	Phil Rizzuto	15.00	7.50	1.50
☐ AL18	Bob Porterfield	4.50	2.25	.45
☐ AL19	Chico Carrasquel	4.50	2.25	.45
☐ AL20	Yogi Berra	25.00	12.50	2.50
☐ AL21	Bob Lemon	15.00	7.50	1.50
☐ AL22	Ferris Fain	4.50	2.25	.45
☐ AL23	Hank Bauer	7.50	3.75	.75
☐ AL24	Jim Delsing	4.50	2.25	.45
☐ AL25	Gil McDougald	7.50	3.75	.75
☐ NL1	Richie Ashburn	10.00	5.00	1.00
☐ NL2	Billy Cox	4.50	2.25	.45
☐ NL3	Del Crandall	4.50	2.25	.45
☐ NL4	Carl Erskine	6.00	3.00	.60
☐ NL5	Monte Irvin	15.00	7.50	1.50
☐ NL6	Ted Kluszewski	7.50	3.75	.75
☐ NL7	Don Mueller	4.50	2.25	.45
☐ NL8	Andy Pafko	4.50	2.25	.45
☐ NL9	Del Rice	4.50	2.25	.45
☐ NL10	Al Schoendienst	7.50	3.75	.75
☐ NL11	Warren Spahn	15.00	7.50	1.50
☐ NL12	Curt Simmons	6.00	3.00	.60
☐ NL13	Roy Campanella	35.00	17.50	3.50
☐ NL14	Jim Gilliam	7.50	3.75	.75
☐ NL15	Pee Wee Reese	20.00	10.00	2.00
☐ NL16	Duke Snider	35.00	17.50	3.50
☐ NL17	Rip Repulski	4.50	2.25	.45
☐ NL18	Robin Roberts	15.00	7.50	1.50
☐ NL19A	Enos Slaughter	30.00	15.00	3.00
☐ NL19B	Gus Bell	25.00	12.50	2.50
☐ NL20	Johnny Logan	4.50	2.25	.45
☐ NL21	John Antonelli	6.00	3.00	.60
☐ NL22	Gil Hodges	18.00	9.00	1.80
☐ NL23	Eddie Mathews	15.00	7.50	1.50
☐ NL24	Lew Burdette	6.00	3.00	.60
☐ NL25	Willie Mays	50.00	25.00	5.00

1955 Red Man

The cards in this 50 card set measure 3 1/2" by 4" (or 3 1/2" by 3 5/8" without the tab). The 1955 Red Man set contains 25 players from each league. Card numbers are on the write-ups of the players. Cards that have the tab (coupon) attached are generally worth double the price of cards with the tab removed. The prices listed below refer to cards without tabs.

	NRMT	VG-E	GOOD
COMPLETE SET	400.00	175.00	37.00
COMMON PLAYER	4.50	2.25	.45
☐ AL1 Ray Boone	4.50	2.25	.45
☐ AL2 Jim Busby	4.50	2.25	.45
☐ AL3 Whitey Ford	20.00	10.00	2.00
☐ AL4 Nelson Fox	9.00	4.50	.90
☐ AL5 Bob Grim	4.50	2.25	.45
☐ AL6 Jack Harshman	4.50	2.25	.45
☐ AL7 Jim Hegan	4.50	2.25	.45
☐ AL8 Bob Lemon	15.00	7.50	1.50
☐ AL9 Irv Noren	4.50	2.25	.45

			NRMT	VG-E	GOOD
☐	AL10	Bob Porterfield	4.50	2.25	.45
☐	AL11	Al Rosen	7.50	3.75	.75
☐	AL12	Mickey Vernon	6.00	3.00	.60
☐	AL13	Vic Wertz	4.50	2.25	.45
☐	AL14	Early Wynn	15.00	7.50	1.50
☐	AL15	Bobby Avila	4.50	2.25	.45
☐	AL16	Yogi Berra	25.00	12.50	2.50
☐	AL17	Joe Coleman	4.50	2.25	.45
☐	AL18	Larry Doby	6.00	3.00	.60
☐	AL19	Jackie Jensen	6.00	3.00	.60
☐	AL20	Pete Runnels	4.50	2.25	.45
☐	AL21	Jim Piersall	7.50	3.75	.75
☐	AL22	Hank Bauer	7.50	3.75	.75
☐	AL23	Chico Carrasquel	4.50	2.25	.45
☐	AL24	Minnie Minoso	7.50	3.75	.75
☐	AL25	Sandy Consuegra	4.50	2.25	.45
☐	NL1	Richie Ashburn	10.00	5.00	1.00
☐	NL2	Del Crandall	4.50	2.25	.45
☐	NL3	Gil Hodges	18.00	9.00	1.80
☐	NL4	Brooks Lawrence	4.50	2.25	.45
☐	NL5	Johnny Logan	4.50	2.25	.45
☐	NL6	Sal Maglie	7.50	3.75	.75
☐	NL7	Willie Mays	50.00	25.00	5.00
☐	NL8	Don Mueller	4.50	2.25	.45
☐	NL9	Bill Sarni	4.50	2.25	.45
☐	NL10	Warren Spahn	15.00	7.50	1.50
☐	NL11	Hank Thompson	4.50	2.25	.45
☐	NL12	Hoyt Wilhelm	15.00	7.50	1.50
☐	NL13	John Antonelli	6.00	3.00	.60
☐	NL14	Carl Erskine	6.00	3.00	.60
☐	NL15	Granny Hamner	4.50	2.25	.45
☐	NL16	Ted Kluszewski	7.50	3.75	.75
☐	NL17	Pee Wee Reese	20.00	10.00	2.00
☐	NL18	Al Schoendienst	7.50	3.75	.75
☐	NL19	Duke Snider	35.00	17.50	3.50
☐	NL20	Frank Thomas	4.50	2.25	.45
☐	NL21	Ray Jablonski	4.50	2.25	.45
☐	NL22	Dusty Rhodes	4.50	2.25	.45
☐	NL23	Gus Bell	4.50	2.25	.45
☐	NL24	Curt Simmons	4.50	2.25	.45
☐	NL25	Marv Grissom	4.50	2.25	.45

1955 Rodeo Meats

Hector Lopez

The cards in this 47 card set measure 2 1/2" by 3 1/2". The 1955 Rodeo Meats set contains unnumbered, color cards of the first Kansas City A's team. There are many background color variations noted in the checklist, and the card reverses carry a scrapbook offer. The Grimes and Kryhoski cards listed in the scrapbook album were apparently never issued. The ACC catalog number is F152-1. The cards have been arranged in alphabetical order and assigned numbers for reference.

			NRMT	VG-E	GOOD
	COMPLETE SET		3000.00	1200.00	250.00
	COMMON PLAYER (1-47)		50.00	25.00	5.00
☐	1	Joe Astroth	50.00	25.00	5.00
☐	2	Harold Bevan	75.00	37.50	7.50
☐	3	Charles Bishop	75.00	37.50	7.50
☐	4	Don Bollweg	75.00	37.50	7.50
☐	5	Lou Boudreau	150.00	75.00	15.00
☐	6	Cloyd Boyer (salmon)	50.00	25.00	5.00
☐	7	Cloyd Boyer (light blue)	75.00	37.50	7.50
☐	8	Ed Burtschy	125.00	60.00	12.50

			NRMT	VG-E	GOOD
☐	9	Art Ceccarelli	75.00	37.50	7.50
☐	10	Joe DeMaestri (yellow)	50.00	25.00	5.00
☐	11	Joe DeMaestri (green)	50.00	25.00	5.00
☐	12	Art Ditmar	50.00	25.00	5.00
☐	13	John Dixon	75.00	37.50	7.50
☐	14	Jim Finigan	50.00	25.00	5.00
☐	15	Marion Fricano	75.00	37.50	7.50
☐	16	Tom Gorman	50.00	25.00	5.00
☐	17	John Gray	75.00	37.50	7.50
☐	18	Ray Herbert	50.00	25.00	5.00
☐	19	Forest Jacobs	125.00	60.00	12.50
☐	20	Alex Kellner	50.00	25.00	5.00
☐	21	Harry Kraft	50.00	25.00	5.00
☐	22	Jack Littrell	50.00	25.00	5.00
☐	23	Hector Lopez	50.00	25.00	5.00
☐	24	Oscar Melillo	50.00	25.00	5.00
☐	25	Arnold Portocarrero (purple)	75.00	37.50	7.50
☐	26	Arnold Portocarrero (gray)	50.00	25.00	5.00
☐	27	Vic Power (yellow)	50.00	25.00	5.00
☐	28	Vic Power (pink)	75.00	37.50	7.50
☐	29	Vic Raschi	75.00	37.50	7.50
☐	30	Bill Renna (lavender)	50.00	25.00	5.00
☐	31	Bill Renna (dark pink)	75.00	37.50	7.50
☐	32	Al Robertson	75.00	37.50	7.50
☐	33	Johnny Sain	100.00	50.00	10.00
☐	34	Bobby Shantz	100.00	50.00	10.00
☐	35	Bobby Schantz (misspelling)	125.00	60.00	12.50
☐	36	Wilmer Shantz (orange)	50.00	25.00	5.00
☐	37	Wilmer Shantz (lavender)	50.00	25.00	5.00
☐	38	Harry Simpson	50.00	25.00	5.00
☐	39	Enos Slaughter	175.00	85.00	18.00
☐	40	Lou Sleator	50.00	25.00	5.00
☐	41	George Susce	75.00	37.50	7.50
☐	42	Bob Trice	75.00	37.50	7.50
☐	43	Elmer Valo (yellow)	75.00	37.50	7.50
☐	44	Elmer Valo (green sky)	50.00	25.00	5.00
☐	45	Bill Wilson (yellow)	75.00	37.50	7.50
☐	46	Bill Wilson (lavender sky)	50.00	25.00	5.00
☐	47	Gus Zernial	50.00	25.00	5.00

1956 Rodeo Meats

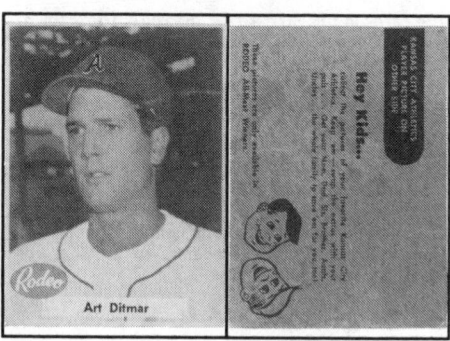

Art Ditmar

The cards in this 13 card set measure 2 1/2" by 3 1/2". The unnumbered, color cards of the 1956 Rodeo baseball series are easily distinguished from their 1955 counterparts by the absence of the scrapbook offer on the reverse. They were available only in packages of Rodeo All-Meat Wieners. The ACC designation is F152-2, and the cards have been assigned numbers in alphabetical order in the checklist below.

			NRMT	VG-E	GOOD
	COMPLETE SET		750.00	375.00	75.00
	COMMON PLAYER (1-12)		50.00	25.00	5.00
☐	1	Joe Astroth	50.00	25.00	5.00
☐	2	Lou Boudreau	150.00	75.00	15.00
☐	3	Joe DeMaestri	50.00	25.00	5.00
☐	4	Art Ditmar	50.00	25.00	5.00
☐	5	Jim Finigan	50.00	25.00	5.00

		NRMT	VG-E	GOOD
☐ 6	Hector Lopez	50.00	25.00	5.00
☐ 7	Vic Power	50.00	25.00	5.00
☐ 8	Bobby Shantz	100.00	50.00	10.00
☐ 9	Harry Simpson	50.00	25.00	5.00
☐ 10	Enos Slaughter	175.00	85.00	18.00
☐ 11	Elmer Valo	50.00	25.00	5.00
☐ 12	Gus Zernial	50.00	25.00	5.00

1958 S.F. Call-Bulletin

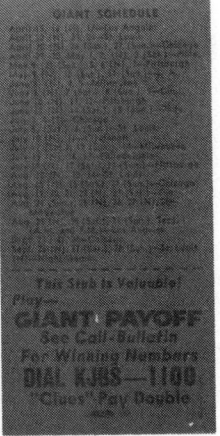

The cards in this 25 card set measure 2" by 4". The 1958 San Francisco Call-Bulletin set of unnumbered cards features black print on orange paper. These cards were given away as inserts in the San Francisco Call-Bulletin newspaper. The backs of the cards list the Giants home schedule and a radio station ad. The cards are entitled "Giant Payoff" and feature San Francisco Giant players only. The bottom part of the card (tab) could be detached as a ticket stub; hence, cards with the tab intact are worth approximately 50% more than the prices listed below. The ACC designation is M126. The Tom Bowers card was issued in very short supply; also Bressoud, Jablonski, and Kirkland are somewhat tougher to find than the others. All of these tougher cards are asterisked in the checklist below.

		NRMT	VG-E	GOOD
COMPLETE SET		700.00	325.00	65.00
COMMON PLAYER (1-25)		10.00	5.00	1.00
☐ 1	John Antonelli	12.50	6.25	1.25
☐ 2	Curt Barclay	10.00	5.00	1.00
☐ 3	Tom Bowers *	200.00	100.00	20.00
☐ 4	Ed Bressoud *	40.00	20.00	4.00
☐ 5	Orlando Cepeda	50.00	25.00	5.00
☐ 6	Ray Crone	10.00	5.00	1.00
☐ 7	Jim Davenport	12.50	6.25	1.25
☐ 8	Paul Giel	10.00	5.00	1.00
☐ 9	Ruben Gomez	10.00	5.00	1.00
☐ 10	Marv Grissom	10.00	5.00	1.00
☐ 11	Ray Jablonski *	20.00	10.00	2.00
☐ 12	Willie Kirkland *	50.00	25.00	5.00
☐ 13	Whitey Lockman	10.00	5.00	1.00
☐ 14	Willie Mays	200.00	100.00	20.00
☐ 15	Mike McCormick	12.50	6.25	1.25
☐ 16	Stu Miller	10.00	5.00	1.00
☐ 17	Ray Monzant	10.00	5.00	1.00
☐ 18	Danny O'Connell	10.00	5.00	1.00
☐ 19	Bill Rigney	12.50	6.25	1.25
☐ 20	Hank Sauer	12.50	6.25	1.25
☐ 21	Bob Schmidt	10.00	5.00	1.00
☐ 22	Daryl Spencer	10.00	5.00	1.00
☐ 23	Valmy Thomas	10.00	5.00	1.00
☐ 24	Bobby Thomson	16.00	8.00	1.60
☐ 25	Al Worthington	10.00	5.00	1.00

1988 Score

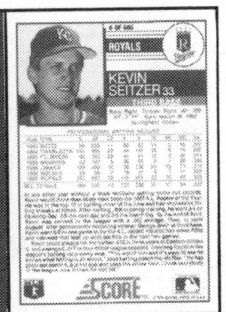

This 660-card set was distributed by Major League Marketing. Cards measure 2 1/2" by 3 1/2" and feature six distinctive border colors on the front. Highlights (652-660) and Rookie Prospects (623-647) are included in the set. Reggie Jackson's career is honored with a 5-card subset on cards 500- 504. The set is distinguished by the fact that each card back shows a full-color picture of the player.

		MINT	EXC	G-VG
COMPLETE SET		20.00	10.00	2.00
COMMON PLAYER		.03	.01	.00
☐ 1	Don Mattingly	1.25	.50	.10
☐ 2	Wade Boggs	.75	.35	.07
☐ 3	Tim Raines	.25	.12	.02
☐ 4	Andre Dawson	.25	.12	.02
☐ 5	Mark McGwire	1.00	.50	.10
☐ 6	Kevin Seitzer	1.25	.60	.12
☐ 7	Wally Joyner	.50	.25	.05
☐ 8	Jesse Barfield	.15	.07	.01
☐ 9	Pedro Guerrero	.20	.10	.02
☐ 10	Eric Davis	.75	.35	.07
☐ 11	George Brett	.30	.15	.03
☐ 12	Ozzie Smith	.12	.06	.01
☐ 13	Rickey Henderson	.25	.12	.02
☐ 14	Jim Rice	.20	.10	.02
☐ 15	Matt Nokes	1.25	.60	.12
☐ 16	Mike Schmidt	.30	.15	.03
☐ 17	Dave Parker	.15	.07	.01
☐ 18	Eddie Murray	.25	.12	.02
☐ 19	Andres Galarraga	.15	.07	.01
☐ 20	Tony Fernandez	.12	.06	.01
☐ 21	Kevin McReynolds	.15	.07	.01
☐ 22	B.J. Surhoff	.20	.10	.02
☐ 23	Pat Tabler	.08	.04	.01
☐ 24	Kirby Puckett	.30	.15	.03
☐ 25	Benny Santiago	.60	.30	.06
☐ 26	Ryne Sandberg	.20	.10	.02
☐ 27	Kelly Downs	.06	.03	.00
☐ 28	Jose Cruz	.08	.04	.01
☐ 29	Pete O'Brien	.10	.05	.01
☐ 30	Mark Langston	.10	.05	.01
☐ 31	Lee Smith	.10	.05	.01
☐ 32	Juan Samuel	.15	.07	.01
☐ 33	Kevin Bass	.08	.04	.01
☐ 34	R.J. Reynolds	.06	.03	.00
☐ 35	Steve Sax	.10	.05	.01
☐ 36	John Kruk	.20	.10	.02
☐ 37	Alan Trammell	.20	.10	.02
☐ 38	Chris Bosio	.06	.03	.00
☐ 39	Brook Jacoby	.10	.05	.01
☐ 40	Willie McGee	.15	.07	.01
☐ 41	Dave Magadan	.15	.07	.01
☐ 42	Fred Lynn	.12	.06	.01
☐ 43	Kent Hrbek	.12	.06	.01
☐ 44	Brian Downing	.06	.03	.00
☐ 45	Jose Canseco	.45	.22	.04
☐ 46	Jim Presley	.10	.05	.01
☐ 47	Mike Stanley	.15	.07	.01
☐ 48	Tony Pena	.08	.04	.01
☐ 49	David Cone	.12	.06	.01
☐ 50	Rick Sutcliffe	.10	.05	.01
☐ 51	Doug Drabek	.06	.03	.00
☐ 52	Bill Doran	.08	.04	.01
☐ 53	Mike Scioscia	.03	.01	.00
☐ 54	Candy Maldonado	.10	.05	.01
☐ 55	Dave Winfield	.25	.12	.02

☐ 56 Lou Whitaker	.12	.06	.01
☐ 57 Tom Henke	.08	.04	.01
☐ 58 Ken Gerhart	.08	.04	.01
☐ 59 Glenn Braggs	.10	.05	.01
☐ 60 Julio Franco	.08	.04	.01
☐ 61 Charlie Leibrandt	.06	.03	.00
☐ 62 Gary Gaetti	.12	.06	.01
☐ 63 Bob Boone	.06	.03	.00
☐ 64 Luis Polonia	.30	.15	.03
☐ 65 Dwight Evans	.12	.06	.01
☐ 66 Phil Bradley	.10	.05	.01
☐ 67 Mike Boddicker	.06	.03	.00
☐ 68 Vince Coleman	.25	.12	.02
☐ 69 Howard Johnson	.10	.05	.01
☐ 70 Tim Wallach	.08	.04	.01
☐ 71 Keith Moreland	.06	.03	.00
☐ 72 Barry Larkin	.12	.06	.01
☐ 73 Alan Ashby	.03	.01	.00
☐ 74 Rick Rhoden	.06	.03	.00
☐ 75 Darrell Evans	.08	.04	.01
☐ 76 Dave Stieb	.10	.05	.01
☐ 77 Dan Plesac	.08	.04	.01
☐ 78 Jack Clark	.20	.10	.02
☐ 79 Frank White	.06	.03	.00
☐ 80 Joe Carter	.12	.06	.01
☐ 81 Mike Witt	.10	.05	.01
☐ 82 Terry Steinbach	.25	.12	.02
☐ 83 Alvin Davis	.10	.05	.01
☐ 84 Tom Herr	.06	.03	.00
☐ 85 Vance Law	.03	.01	.00
☐ 86 Kal Daniels	.25	.12	.02
☐ 87 Rick Honeycutt	.03	.01	.00
☐ 88 Alfredo Griffin	.06	.03	.00
☐ 89 Bret Saberhagen	.20	.10	.02
☐ 90 Bert Blyleven	.10	.05	.01
☐ 91 Jeff Reardon	.08	.04	.01
☐ 92 Cory Snyder	.25	.12	.02
☐ 93 Greg Walker	.08	.04	.01
☐ 94 Joe Magrane	.35	.17	.03
☐ 95 Rob Deer	.08	.04	.01
☐ 96 Ray Knight	.06	.03	.00
☐ 97 Casey Candaele	.06	.03	.00
☐ 98 John Cerutti	.03	.01	.00
☐ 99 Eric Bell	.08	.04	.01
☐ 100 Will Clark	.35	.17	.03
☐ 101 Buddy Bell	.08	.04	.01
☐ 102 Willie Wilson	.10	.05	.01
☐ 103 Dave Schmidt	.06	.03	.00
☐ 104 Dennis Eckersley	.06	.03	.00
☐ 105 Don Sutton	.12	.06	.01
☐ 106 Danny Tartabull	.20	.10	.02
☐ 107 Fred McGriff	.25	.12	.02
☐ 108 Les Straker	.15	.07	.01
☐ 109 Lloyd Moseby	.10	.05	.01
☐ 110 Roger Clemens	.50	.25	.05
☐ 111 Glenn Hubbard	.03	.01	.00
☐ 112 Ken Williams	.35	.17	.03
☐ 113 Ruben Sierra	.30	.15	.03
☐ 114 Stan Jefferson	.15	.07	.01
☐ 115 Milt Thompson	.06	.03	.00
☐ 116 Bobby Bonilla	.08	.04	.01
☐ 117 Wayne Tolleson	.03	.01	.00
☐ 118 Matt Williams	.35	.17	.03
☐ 119 Chet Lemon	.06	.03	.00
☐ 120 Dale Sveum	.08	.04	.01
☐ 121 Dennis Boyd	.06	.03	.00
☐ 122 Brett Butler	.08	.04	.01
☐ 123 Terry Kennedy	.06	.03	.00
☐ 124 Jack Howell	.06	.03	.00
☐ 125 Curt Young	.06	.03	.00
☐ 126 Dale Valle	.08	.04	.01
☐ 127 Curt Wilkerson	.03	.01	.00
☐ 128 Tim Teufel	.06	.03	.00
☐ 129 Ozzie Virgil	.03	.01	.00
☐ 130 Brian Fisher	.06	.03	.00
☐ 131 Lance Parrish	.10	.05	.01
☐ 132 Tom Browning	.06	.03	.00
☐ 133 Larry Andersen	.03	.01	.00
☐ 134 Bob Brenly	.08	.04	.01
("Brenley" on front)			
☐ 135 Mike Marshall	.10	.05	.01
☐ 136 Gerald Perry	.06	.03	.00
☐ 137 Bobby Meacham	.03	.01	.00
☐ 138 Larry Herndon	.03	.01	.00
☐ 139 Fred Manrique	.15	.07	.01
☐ 140 Charlie Hough	.06	.03	.00
☐ 141 Ron Darling	.12	.06	.01
☐ 142 Herm Winningham	.03	.01	.00
☐ 143 Mike Diaz	.03	.01	.00
☐ 144 Mike Jackson	.12	.06	.01
☐ 145 Denny Walling	.03	.01	.00
☐ 146 Rob Thompson	.06	.03	.00
☐ 147 Franklin Stubbs	.06	.03	.00
☐ 148 Albert Hall	.03	.01	.00
☐ 149 Bobby Witt	.06	.03	.00

☐ 150 Lance McCullers	.06	.03	.00
☐ 151 Scott Bradley	.06	.03	.00
☐ 152 Mark McLemore	.08	.04	.01
☐ 153 Tim Laudner	.03	.01	.00
☐ 154 Greg Swindell	.08	.04	.01
☐ 155 Marty Barrett	.08	.04	.01
☐ 156 Mike Heath	.03	.01	.00
☐ 157 Gary Ward	.06	.03	.00
☐ 158 Lee Mazzilli	.08	.04	.01
("Mazilli" on front)			
☐ 159 Tom Foley	.03	.01	.00
☐ 160 Robin Yount	.20	.10	.02
☐ 161 Steve Bedrosian	.10	.05	.01
☐ 162 Bob Walk	.03	.01	.00
☐ 163 Nick Esasky	.06	.03	.00
☐ 164 Ken Caminiti	.35	.17	.03
☐ 165 Jose Uribe	.03	.01	.00
☐ 166 Dave Anderson	.03	.01	.00
☐ 167 Ed Whitson	.03	.01	.00
☐ 168 Ernie Whitt	.03	.01	.00
☐ 169 Cecil Cooper	.08	.04	.01
☐ 170 Mike Pagliarulo	.08	.04	.01
☐ 171 Pat Sheridan	.03	.01	.00
☐ 172 Chris Bando	.03	.01	.00
☐ 173 Lee Lacy	.03	.01	.00
☐ 174 Steve Lombardozzi	.03	.01	.00
☐ 175 Mike Greenwell	.50	.25	.05
☐ 176 Greg Minton	.03	.01	.00
☐ 177 Moose Haas	.03	.01	.00
☐ 178 Mike Kingery	.03	.01	.00
☐ 179 Greg Harris	.03	.01	.00
☐ 180 Bo Jackson	.35	.17	.03
☐ 181 Carmelo Martinez	.03	.01	.00
☐ 182 Alex Trevino	.03	.01	.00
☐ 183 Ron Oester	.03	.01	.00
☐ 184 Danny Darwin	.06	.03	.00
☐ 185 Mike Krukow	.06	.03	.00
☐ 186 Rafael Palmeiro	.20	.10	.02
☐ 187 Tim Burke	.06	.03	.00
☐ 188 Roger McDowell	.08	.04	.01
☐ 189 Garry Templeton	.06	.03	.00
☐ 190 Terry Pendleton	.06	.03	.00
☐ 191 Larry Parrish	.06	.03	.00
☐ 192 Rey Quinones	.06	.03	.00
☐ 193 Joaquin Andujar	.08	.04	.01
☐ 194 Tom Brunansky	.10	.05	.01
☐ 195 Donnie Moore	.03	.01	.00
☐ 196 Dan Pasqua	.08	.04	.01
☐ 197 Jim Gantner	.03	.01	.00
☐ 198 Mark Eichhorn	.06	.03	.00
☐ 199 John Grubb	.03	.01	.00
☐ 200 Bill Ripken	.30	.15	.03
☐ 201 Sam Horn	1.00	.50	.10
☐ 202 Todd Worrell	.12	.06	.01
☐ 203 Terry Leach	.06	.03	.00
☐ 204 Garth Iorg	.03	.01	.00
☐ 205 Brian Dayett	.03	.01	.00
☐ 206 Bo Diaz	.06	.03	.00
☐ 207 Craig Reynolds	.03	.01	.00
☐ 208 Brian Holton	.12	.06	.01
☐ 209 Marvell Wynne	.08	.04	.01
("Marvelle" on front)			
☐ 210 Dave Concepcion	.08	.04	.01
☐ 211 Mike Davis	.06	.03	.00
☐ 212 Devon White	.20	.10	.02
☐ 213 Mickey Brantley	.08	.04	.01
☐ 214 Greg Gagne	.06	.03	.00
☐ 215 Oddibe McDowell	.10	.05	.01
☐ 216 Jimmy Key	.08	.04	.01
☐ 217 Dave Bergman	.03	.01	.00
☐ 218 Calvin Schiraldi	.06	.03	.00
☐ 219 Larry Sheets	.10	.05	.01
☐ 220 Mike Easler	.06	.03	.00
☐ 221 Kurt Stillwell	.06	.03	.00
☐ 222 Chuck Jackson	.15	.07	.01
☐ 223 Dave Martinez	.10	.05	.01
☐ 224 Tim Leary	.03	.01	.00
☐ 225 Steve Garvey	.25	.12	.02
☐ 226 Greg Mathews	.06	.03	.00
☐ 227 Doug Sisk	.03	.01	.00
☐ 228 Dave Henderson	.03	.01	.00
☐ 229 Jimmy Dwyer	.03	.01	.00
☐ 230 Larry Owen	.03	.01	.00
☐ 231 Andre Thornton	.06	.03	.00
☐ 232 Mark Salas	.03	.01	.00
☐ 233 Tom Brookens	.03	.01	.00
☐ 234 Greg Brock	.06	.03	.00
☐ 235 Rance Mulliniks	.03	.01	.00
☐ 236 Bob Brower	.10	.05	.01
☐ 237 Joe Niekro	.08	.04	.01
☐ 238 Scott Bankhead	.06	.03	.00
☐ 239 Doug DeCinces	.06	.03	.00
☐ 240 Tommy John	.10	.05	.01
☐ 241 Rich Gedman	.06	.03	.00
☐ 242 Ted Power	.03	.01	.00

☐ 243	Dave Meads	.10	.05	.01	☐ 338	Eric Show	.03	.01	.00
☐ 244	Jim Sundberg	.06	.03	.00	☐ 339	Mitch Williams	.03	.01	.00
☐ 245	Ken Oberkfell	.03	.01	.00	☐ 340	Paul Molitor	.12	.06	.01
☐ 246	Jimmy Jones	.10	.05	.01	☐ 341	Gus Polidor	.08	.04	.01
☐ 247	Ken Landreaux	.03	.01	.00	☐ 342	Steve Trout	.03	.01	.00
☐ 248	Jose Oquendo	.03	.01	.00	☐ 343	Jerry Don Gleaton	.03	.01	.00
☐ 249	John Mitchell	.20	.10	.02	☐ 344	Bob Knepper	.06	.03	.00
☐ 250	Don Baylor	.08	.04	.01	☐ 345	Mitch Webster	.06	.03	.00
☐ 251	Scott Fletcher	.06	.03	.00	☐ 346	John Morris	.06	.03	.00
☐ 252	Al Newman	.03	.01	.00	☐ 347	Andy Hawkins	.03	.01	.00
☐ 253	Carney Lansford	.08	.04	.01	☐ 348	Dave Leiper	.03	.01	.00
☐ 254	Johnny Ray	.08	.04	.01	☐ 349	Ernest Riles	.03	.01	.00
☐ 255	Gary Pettis	.03	.01	.00	☐ 350	Dwight Gooden	.40	.20	.04
☐ 256	Ken Phelps	.06	.03	.00	☐ 351	Dave Righetti	.12	.06	.01
☐ 257	Tim Stoddard	.03	.01	.00	☐ 352	Pat Dodson	.10	.05	.01
☐ 258	Rick Leach	.03	.01	.00	☐ 353	John Habyan	.08	.04	.01
☐ 259	Ed Romero	.03	.01	.00	☐ 354	Jim Deshaies	.06	.03	.00
☐ 260	Sid Bream	.06	.03	.00	☐ 355	Butch Wynegar	.03	.01	.00
☐ 261	Tom Niedenfuer	.06	.03	.00	☐ 356	Bryn Smith	.03	.01	.00
☐ 262	Rick Dempsey	.06	.03	.00	☐ 357	Matt Young	.03	.01	.00
☐ 263	Lonnie Smith	.06	.03	.00	☐ 358	Tom Pagnozzi	.20	.10	.02
☐ 264	Bob Forsch	.03	.01	.00	☐ 359	Floyd Rayford	.03	.01	.00
☐ 265	Barry Bonds	.12	.06	.01	☐ 360	Darryl Strawberry	.35	.17	.03
☐ 266	Willie Randolph	.08	.04	.01	☐ 361	Sal Butera	.03	.01	.00
☐ 267	Mike Ramsey	.15	.07	.01	☐ 362	Domingo Ramos	.03	.01	.00
☐ 268	Don Slaught	.03	.01	.00	☐ 363	Chris Brown	.10	.05	.01
☐ 269	Mickey Tettleton	.03	.01	.00	☐ 364	Jose Gonzalez	.10	.05	.01
☐ 270	Jerry Reuss	.06	.03	.00	☐ 365	Dave Smith	.06	.03	.00
☐ 271	Marc Sullivan	.03	.01	.00	☐ 366	Andy McGaffigan	.03	.01	.00
☐ 272	Jim Morrison	.03	.01	.00	☐ 367	Stan Javier	.03	.01	.00
☐ 273	Steve Balboni	.03	.01	.00	☐ 368	Henry Cotto	.03	.01	.00
☐ 274	Dick Schofield	.03	.01	.00	☐ 369	Mike Birkbeck	.08	.04	.01
☐ 275	John Tudor	.10	.05	.01	☐ 370	Len Dykstra	.10	.05	.01
☐ 276	Gene Larkin	.20	.10	.02	☐ 371	Dave Collins	.03	.01	.00
☐ 277	Harold Reynolds	.06	.03	.00	☐ 372	Spike Owen	.03	.01	.00
☐ 278	Jerry Browne	.03	.01	.00	☐ 373	Geno Petralli	.03	.01	.00
☐ 279	Willie Upshaw	.06	.03	.00	☐ 374	Ron Karkovice	.03	.01	.00
☐ 280	Ted Higuera	.12	.06	.01	☐ 375	Shane Rawley	.06	.03	.00
☐ 281	Terry McGriff	.10	.05	.01	☐ 376	DeWayne Buice	.15	.07	.01
☐ 282	Terry Puhl	.03	.01	.00	☐ 377	Bill Pecota	.20	.10	.02
☐ 283	Mark Wasinger	.15	.07	.01	☐ 378	Leon Durham	.08	.04	.01
☐ 284	Luis Salazar	.03	.01	.00	☐ 379	Ed Olwine	.03	.01	.00
☐ 285	Ted Simmons	.08	.04	.01	☐ 380	Bruce Hurst	.08	.04	.01
☐ 286	John Shelby	.03	.01	.00	☐ 381	Bob McClure	.03	.01	.00
☐ 287	John Smiley	.20	.10	.02	☐ 382	Mark Thurmond	.03	.01	.00
☐ 288	Curt Ford	.06	.03	.00	☐ 383	Buddy Biancalana	.03	.01	.00
☐ 289	Steve Crawford	.03	.01	.00	☐ 384	Tim Conroy	.03	.01	.00
☐ 290	Dan Quisenberry	.10	.05	.01	☐ 385	Tony Gwynn	.30	.15	.03
☐ 291	Alan Wiggins	.03	.01	.00	☐ 386	Greg Gross	.03	.01	.00
☐ 292	Randy Bush	.03	.01	.00	☐ 387	Barry Lyons	.20	.10	.02
☐ 293	John Candelaria	.06	.03	.00	☐ 388	Mike Felder	.03	.01	.00
☐ 294	Tony Phillips	.03	.01	.00	☐ 389	Pat Clements	.03	.01	.00
☐ 295	Mike Morgan	.03	.01	.00	☐ 390	Ken Griffey	.06	.03	.00
☐ 296	Bill Wegman	.03	.01	.00	☐ 391	Mark Davis	.03	.01	.00
☐ 297	Terry Francona	.03	.01	.00	☐ 392	Jose Rijo	.06	.03	.00
☐ 298	Mickey Hatcher	.03	.01	.00	☐ 393	Mike Young	.06	.03	.00
☐ 299	Andres Thomas	.03	.01	.00	☐ 394	Willie Fraser	.08	.04	.01
☐ 300	Bob Stanley	.06	.03	.00	☐ 395	Dion James	.06	.03	.00
☐ 301	Alfredo Pedrique	.15	.07	.01	☐ 396	Steve Shields	.06	.03	.00
☐ 302	Jim Lindeman	.15	.07	.01	☐ 397	Randy St.Claire	.03	.01	.00
☐ 303	Wally Backman	.06	.03	.00	☐ 398	Danny Jackson	.06	.03	.00
☐ 304	Paul O'Neill	.10	.05	.01	☐ 399	Cecil Fielder	.06	.03	.00
☐ 305	Hubie Brooks	.08	.04	.01	☐ 400	Keith Hernandez	.20	.10	.02
☐ 306	Steve Buechele	.03	.01	.00	☐ 401	Don Carman	.03	.01	.00
☐ 307	Bobby Thigpen	.03	.01	.00	☐ 402	Chuck Crim	.10	.05	.01
☐ 308	George Hendrick	.06	.03	.00	☐ 403	Rob Woodward	.03	.01	.00
☐ 309	John Moses	.03	.01	.00	☐ 404	Junior Ortiz	.03	.01	.00
☐ 310	Ron Guidry	.10	.05	.01	☐ 405	Glenn Wilson	.06	.03	.00
☐ 311	Bill Schroeder	.03	.01	.00	☐ 406	Ken Howell	.03	.01	.00
☐ 312	Jose Nunez	.15	.07	.01	☐ 407	Jeff Kunkel	.03	.01	.00
☐ 313	Bud Black	.03	.01	.00	☐ 408	Jeff Reed	.03	.01	.00
☐ 314	Joe Sambito	.03	.01	.00	☐ 409	Chris James	.10	.05	.01
☐ 315	Scott McGregor	.06	.03	.00	☐ 410	Zane Smith	.08	.04	.01
☐ 316	Rafael Santana	.03	.01	.00	☐ 411	Ken Dixon	.03	.01	.00
☐ 317	Frank Williams	.03	.01	.00	☐ 412	Ricky Horton	.03	.01	.00
☐ 318	Mike Fitzgerald	.03	.01	.00	☐ 413	Frank DiPino	.03	.01	.00
☐ 319	Rick Mahler	.03	.01	.00	☐ 414	Shane Mack	.15	.07	.01
☐ 320	Jim Gott	.03	.01	.00	☐ 415	Danny Cox	.08	.04	.01
☐ 321	Mariano Duncan	.03	.01	.00	☐ 416	Andy Van Slyke	.10	.05	.01
☐ 322	Jose Guzman	.03	.01	.00	☐ 417	Danny Heep	.03	.01	.00
☐ 323	Lee Guetterman	.06	.03	.00	☐ 418	John Cangelosi	.03	.01	.00
☐ 324	Dan Gladden	.06	.03	.00	☐ 419	John Christensen	.03	.01	.00
☐ 325	Gary Carter	.25	.12	.02	☐ 420	Joey Cora	.15	.07	.01
☐ 326	Tracy Jones	.10	.05	.01	☐ 421	Mike Lavalliere	.03	.01	.00
☐ 327	Floyd Youmans	.06	.03	.00	☐ 422	Kelly Gruber	.03	.01	.00
☐ 328	Bill Dawley	.03	.01	.00	☐ 423	Bruce Benedict	.03	.01	.00
☐ 329	Paul Noce	.15	.07	.01	☐ 424	Len Matuszek	.03	.01	.00
☐ 330	Angel Salazar	.03	.01	.00	☐ 425	Kent Tekulve	.06	.03	.00
☐ 331	Goose Gossage	.10	.05	.01	☐ 426	Rafael Ramirez	.03	.01	.00
☐ 332	George Frazier	.03	.01	.00	☐ 427	Mike Flanagan	.06	.03	.00
☐ 333	Ruppert Jones	.03	.01	.00	☐ 428	Mike Gallego	.03	.01	.00
☐ 334	Billy Jo Robidoux	.06	.03	.00	☐ 429	Juan Castillo	.08	.04	.01
☐ 335	Mike Scott	.15	.07	.01	☐ 430	Neal Heaton	.03	.01	.00
☐ 336	Randy Myers	.10	.05	.01	☐ 431	Phil Garner	.03	.01	.00
☐ 337	Bob Sebra	.03	.01	.00	☐ 432	Mike Dunne	.25	.12	.02

☐ 433	Wallace Johnson	.03	.01	.00
☐ 434	Jack O'Connor	.03	.01	.00
☐ 435	Steve Jeltz	.03	.01	.00
☐ 436	Donnell Nixon	.15	.07	.01
☐ 437	Jack Lazorko	.03	.01	.00
☐ 438	Keith Comstock	.15	.07	.01
☐ 439	Jeff Robinson (Pirates pitcher)	.06	.03	.00
☐ 440	Graig Nettles	.10	.05	.01
☐ 441	Mel Hall	.06	.03	.00
☐ 442	Gerald Young	.30	.15	.03
☐ 443	Gary Redus	.06	.03	.00
☐ 444	Charlie Moore	.03	.01	.00
☐ 445	Bill Madlock	.08	.04	.01
☐ 446	Mark Clear	.03	.01	.00
☐ 447	Greg Booker	.03	.01	.00
☐ 448	Rick Schu	.03	.01	.00
☐ 449	Ron Kittle	.08	.04	.01
☐ 450	Dale Murphy	.30	.15	.03
☐ 451	Bob Dernier	.03	.01	.00
☐ 452	Dale Mohorcic	.06	.03	.00
☐ 453	Rafael Belliard	.03	.01	.00
☐ 454	Charlie Puleo	.03	.01	.00
☐ 455	Dwayne Murphy	.06	.03	.00
☐ 456	Jim Eisenreich	.06	.03	.00
☐ 457	David Palmer	.03	.01	.00
☐ 458	Dave Stewart	.08	.04	.01
☐ 459	Pasqual Perez	.03	.01	.00
☐ 460	Glenn Davis	.12	.06	.01
☐ 461	Dan Petry	.06	.03	.00
☐ 462	Jim Winn	.03	.01	.00
☐ 463	Darrell Miller	.06	.03	.00
☐ 464	Mike Moore	.03	.01	.00
☐ 465	Mike LaCoss	.03	.01	.00
☐ 466	Steve Farr	.03	.01	.00
☐ 467	Jerry Mumphrey	.03	.01	.00
☐ 468	Kevin Gross	.03	.01	.00
☐ 469	Bruce Bochy	.03	.01	.00
☐ 470	Orel Hershiser	.12	.06	.01
☐ 471	Eric King	.03	.01	.00
☐ 472	Ellis Burks	1.00	.50	.10
☐ 473	Darren Daulton	.03	.01	.00
☐ 474	Mookie Wilson	.06	.03	.00
☐ 475	Frank Viola	.10	.05	.01
☐ 476	Ron Robinson	.03	.01	.00
☐ 477	Bob Melvin	.03	.01	.00
☐ 478	Jeff Musselman	.10	.05	.01
☐ 479	Charlie Kerfeld	.03	.01	.00
☐ 480	Richard Dotson	.06	.03	.00
☐ 481	Kevin Mitchell	.08	.04	.01
☐ 482	Gary Roenicke	.03	.01	.00
☐ 483	Tim Flannery	.03	.01	.00
☐ 484	Rich Yett	.03	.01	.00
☐ 485	Pete Incaviglia	.20	.10	.02
☐ 486	Rick Cerone	.03	.01	.00
☐ 487	Tony Armas	.06	.03	.00
☐ 488	Jerry Reed	.06	.03	.00
☐ 489	Davey Lopes	.06	.03	.00
☐ 490	Frank Tanana	.06	.03	.00
☐ 491	Mike Loynd	.08	.04	.01
☐ 492	Bruce Ruffin	.03	.01	.00
☐ 493	Chris Speier	.03	.01	.00
☐ 494	Tom Hume	.03	.01	.00
☐ 495	Jesse Orosco	.06	.03	.00
☐ 496	Robbie Wine	.20	.10	.02
☐ 497	Jeff Montgomery	.20	.10	.02
☐ 498	Jeff Dedmon	.03	.01	.00
☐ 499	Luis Aguayo	.03	.01	.00
☐ 500	Reggie Jackson (Oakland A's)	.20	.10	.02
☐ 501	Reggie Jackson (Baltimore Orioles)	.20	.10	.02
☐ 502	Reggie Jackson (New York Yankees)	.20	.10	.02
☐ 503	Reggie Jackson (California Angels)	.15	.07	.01
☐ 504	Reggie Jackson (Oakland A's)	.15	.07	.01
☐ 505	Billy Hatcher	.08	.04	.01
☐ 506	Ed Lynch	.03	.01	.00
☐ 507	Willie Hernandez	.08	.04	.01
☐ 508	Jose DeLeon	.03	.01	.00
☐ 509	Joel Youngblood	.03	.01	.00
☐ 510	Bob Welch	.06	.03	.00
☐ 511	Steve Ontiveros	.03	.01	.00
☐ 512	Randy Ready	.03	.01	.00
☐ 513	Juan Nieves	.06	.03	.00
☐ 514	Jeff Russell	.03	.01	.00
☐ 515	Von Hayes	.08	.04	.01
☐ 516	Mark Gubicza	.06	.03	.00
☐ 517	Ken Dayley	.03	.01	.00
☐ 518	Don Aase	.03	.01	.00
☐ 519	Rick Reuschel	.06	.03	.00
☐ 520	Mike Henneman	.20	.10	.02
☐ 521	Rick Aguilera	.06	.03	.00
☐ 522	Jay Howell	.03	.01	.00
☐ 523	Ed Correa	.06	.03	.00
☐ 524	Manny Trillo	.03	.01	.00
☐ 525	Kirk Gibson	.15	.07	.01
☐ 526	Wally Ritchie	.15	.07	.01
☐ 527	Al Nipper	.03	.01	.00
☐ 528	Atlee Hammaker	.06	.03	.00
☐ 529	Shawon Dunston	.06	.03	.00
☐ 530	Jim Clancy	.03	.01	.00
☐ 531	Tom Paciorek	.03	.01	.00
☐ 532	Joel Skinner	.03	.01	.00
☐ 533	Scott Garrelts	.06	.03	.00
☐ 534	Tom O'Malley	.03	.01	.00
☐ 535	John Franco	.08	.04	.01
☐ 536	Paul Kilgus	.12	.06	.01
☐ 537	Darrell Porter	.03	.01	.00
☐ 538	Walt Terrell	.06	.03	.00
☐ 539	Bill Long	.15	.07	.01
☐ 540	George Bell	.20	.10	.02
☐ 541	Jeff Sellers	.03	.01	.00
☐ 542	Joe Boever	.15	.07	.01
☐ 543	Steve Howe	.03	.01	.00
☐ 544	Scott Sanderson	.03	.01	.00
☐ 545	Jack Morris	.15	.07	.01
☐ 546	Todd Benzinger	.30	.15	.03
☐ 547	Steve Henderson	.03	.01	.00
☐ 548	Eddie Milner	.03	.01	.00
☐ 549	Jeff Robinson (Tigers pitcher)	.20	.10	.02
☐ 550	Cal Ripken	.20	.10	.02
☐ 551	Jody Davis	.08	.04	.01
☐ 552	Kirk McCaskill	.06	.03	.00
☐ 553	Craig Lefferts	.03	.01	.00
☐ 554	Darnell Coles	.03	.01	.00
☐ 555	Phil Niekro	.12	.06	.01
☐ 556	Mike Aldrete	.10	.05	.01
☐ 557	Pat Perry	.03	.01	.00
☐ 558	Juan Agosto	.03	.01	.00
☐ 559	Rob Murphy	.06	.03	.00
☐ 560	Dennis Rasmussen	.06	.03	.00
☐ 561	Manny Lee	.03	.01	.00
☐ 562	Jeff Blauser	.25	.12	.02
☐ 563	Bob Ojeda	.06	.03	.00
☐ 564	Dave Dravecky	.06	.03	.00
☐ 565	Gene Garber	.03	.01	.00
☐ 566	Ron Roenicke	.03	.01	.00
☐ 567	Tommy Hinzo	.20	.10	.02
☐ 568	Eric Nolte	.15	.07	.01
☐ 569	Ed Hearn	.03	.01	.00
☐ 570	Mark Davidson	.15	.07	.01
☐ 571	Jim Walewander	.20	.10	.02
☐ 572	Donnie Hill	.03	.01	.00
☐ 573	Jamie Moyer	.03	.01	.00
☐ 574	Ken Schrom	.03	.01	.00
☐ 575	Nolan Ryan	.25	.12	.02
☐ 576	Jim Acker	.03	.01	.00
☐ 577	Jamie Quirk	.03	.01	.00
☐ 578	Jay Aldrich	.15	.07	.01
☐ 579	Claudell Washington	.06	.03	.00
☐ 580	Jeff Leonard	.08	.04	.01
☐ 581	Carmen Castillo	.03	.01	.00
☐ 582	Darryl Boston	.03	.01	.00
☐ 583	Jeff DeWillis	.15	.07	.01
☐ 584	John Marzano	.30	.15	.03
☐ 585	Bill Gullickson	.06	.03	.00
☐ 586	Andy Allanson	.03	.01	.00
☐ 587	Lee Tunnell	.03	.01	.00
☐ 588	Gene Nelson	.03	.01	.00
☐ 589	Dave LaPoint	.03	.01	.00
☐ 590	Harold Baines	.10	.05	.01
☐ 591	Bill Buckner	.08	.04	.01
☐ 592	Carlton Fisk	.10	.05	.01
☐ 593	Rick Manning	.03	.01	.00
☐ 594	Doug Jones	.15	.07	.01
☐ 595	Tom Candiotti	.03	.01	.00
☐ 596	Steve Lake	.03	.01	.00
☐ 597	Jose Lind	.25	.12	.02
☐ 598	Ross Jones	.15	.07	.01
☐ 599	Gary Matthews	.06	.03	.00
☐ 600	Fernando Valenzuela	.20	.10	.02
☐ 601	Dennis Martinez	.06	.03	.00
☐ 602	Les Lancaster	.15	.07	.01
☐ 603	Ozzie Guillen	.06	.03	.00
☐ 604	Tony Bernazard	.03	.01	.00
☐ 605	Chili Davis	.08	.04	.01
☐ 606	Roy Smalley	.03	.01	.00
☐ 607	Ivan Calderon	.10	.05	.01
☐ 608	Jay Tibbs	.03	.01	.00
☐ 609	Guy Hoffman	.03	.01	.00
☐ 610	Doyle Alexander	.06	.03	.00
☐ 611	Mike Bielecki	.03	.01	.00
☐ 612	Shawn Hillegas	.20	.10	.02
☐ 613	Keith Atherton	.03	.01	.00
☐ 614	Eric Plunk	.06	.03	.00
☐ 615	Sid Fernandez	.10	.05	.01

☐ 616	Dennis Lamp	.03	.01	.00
☐ 617	Dave Engle	.03	.01	.00
☐ 618	Harry Spilman	.03	.01	.00
☐ 619	Don Robinson	.03	.01	.00
☐ 620	John Farrell	.20	.10	.02
☐ 621	Nelson Liriano	.20	.10	.02
☐ 622	Floyd Bannister	.06	.03	.00
☐ 623	Randy Milligan	.35	.17	.03
☐ 624	Kevin Elster	.20	.10	.02
☐ 625	Jody Reed	.25	.12	.02
☐ 626	Shawn Abner	.30	.15	.03
☐ 627	Kurt Manwaring	.25	.12	.02
☐ 628	Pete Stanicek	.25	.12	.02
☐ 629	Rob Ducey	.25	.12	.02
☐ 630	Steve Kiefer	.10	.05	.01
☐ 631	Gary Thurman	.35	.17	.03
☐ 632	Darrel Akerfelds	.20	.10	.02
☐ 633	Dave Clark	.15	.07	.01
☐ 634	Roberto Kelly	.30	.15	.03
☐ 635	Keith Hughes	.30	.15	.03
☐ 636	John Davis	.20	.10	.02
☐ 637	Mike Devereaux	.30	.15	.03
☐ 638	Tom Glavine	.20	.10	.02
☐ 639	Keith Miller	.30	.15	.03
☐ 640	Chris Gwynn	.40	.20	.04
☐ 641	Tim Crews	.20	.10	.02
☐ 642	Mackey Sasser	.25	.12	.02
☐ 643	Vincente Palacios	.20	.10	.02
☐ 644	Kevin Romine	.15	.07	.01
☐ 645	Gregg Jefferies	1.00	.50	.10
☐ 646	Jeff Treadway	.35	.17	.03
☐ 647	Ronnie Gant	.20	.10	.02
☐ 648	Mark McGwire and Matt Nokes (Rookie Sluggers)	.50	.25	.05
☐ 649	Eric Davis and Tim Raines (Speed and Power)	.30	.15	.03
☐ 650	Don Mattingly and Jack Clark	.50	.25	.05
☐ 651	Tony Fernandez, Alan Trammell, and Cal Ripken	.12	.06	.01
☐ 652	Vince Coleman HL 100 Stolen Bases	.15	.07	.01
☐ 653	Kirby Puckett HL 10 Hits in a Row	.15	.07	.01
☐ 654	Benito Santiago HL Hitting Streak	.20	.10	.02
☐ 655	Juan Nieves HL No Hitter	.06	.03	.00
☐ 656	Steve Bedrosian HL Saves Record	.08	.04	.01
☐ 657	Mike Schmidt HL 500 Homers	.20	.10	.02
☐ 658	Don Mattingly HL Home Run Streak	.45	.22	.04
☐ 659	Mark McGwire HL Rookie Home Run Record	.40	.20	.04
☐ 660	Paul Molitor HL Hitting Streak	.10	.05	.01

1985 7-Eleven Twins

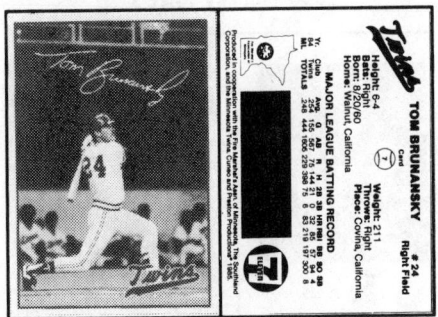

This 13-card set of Minnesota Twins was produced and distributed by the Twins in conjunction with the 7-Eleven stores and the Fire Marshall's Association. The cards measure approximately 2 1/2" by 3 1/2"

and are in full color. Supposedly 20,000 sets of cards were distributed during the promotion which began on June 2nd and lasted throughout the month of July. The card backs have some statistics and a fire safety tip.

		MINT	EXC	G-VG
COMPLETE SET		6.00	3.00	.60
COMMON PLAYER		.25	.12	.02
☐ 1	Kirby Puckett	1.50	.75	.15
☐ 2	Frank Viola	.75	.35	.07
☐ 3	Mickey Hatcher	.25	.12	.02
☐ 4	Kent Hrbek	.75	.35	.07
☐ 5	John Butcher	.25	.12	.02
☐ 6	Roy Smalley	.35	.17	.03
☐ 7	Tom Brunansky	.50	.25	.05
☐ 8	Ron Davis	.25	.12	.02
☐ 9	Gary Gaetti	.75	.35	.07
☐ 10	Tim Teufel	.35	.17	.03
☐ 11	Mike Smithson	.25	.12	.02
☐ 12	Tim Laudner	.35	.17	.03
☐ xx	Checklist Card	.25	.02	.00

1984 Smokey Angels

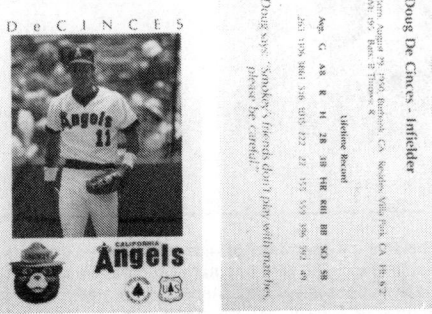

The cards in this 32 card set measure 2 1/2" by 3 3/4" and feature the California Angels in full color. Sets were given out to persons 15 and under attending the June 16th game against the Indians. Unlike the Padres set of this year, Smokey the Bear is not featured on these cards. The player's photo, the Angels' logo, and the Smokey the Bear logo appear on the front, in addition to the California Department of Forestry and the U.S. Forest Service logos. The abbreviated backs contain short biographical data, career statistics, and an anti-wildfire hint from the player on the front. Since the cards are unnumbered, they are ordered and numbered below alphabetically by the player's name.

		MINT	EXC	G-VG
COMPLETE SET (32)		8.00	4.00	.80
COMMON PLAYER		.20	.10	.02
☐ 1	Don Aase	.30	.15	.03
☐ 2	Juan Beniquez	.30	.15	.03
☐ 3	Bob Boone	.30	.15	.03
☐ 4	Rick Burleson	.30	.15	.03
☐ 5	Rod Carew	1.00	.50	.10
☐ 6	John Curtis	.20	.10	.02
☐ 7	Doug DeCinces	.40	.20	.04
☐ 8	Brian Downing	.30	.15	.03
☐ 9	Ken Forsch	.20	.10	.02
☐ 10	Bobby Grich	.40	.20	.04
☐ 11	Reggie Jackson	1.50	.75	.15
☐ 12	Ron Jackson	.20	.10	.02
☐ 13	Tommy John	.60	.30	.06
☐ 14	Curt Kaufman	.20	.10	.02
☐ 15	Bruce Kison	.20	.10	.02

		MINT	EXC	G-VG
☐ 16	Frank LaCorte	.20	.10	.02
☐ 17	Logo Card (Forestry Dept.)	.20	.10	.02
☐ 18	Fred Lynn	.50	.25	.05
☐ 19	John McNamara MG	.20	.10	.02
☐ 20	Jerry Narron	.20	.10	.02
☐ 21	Gary Pettis	.40	.20	.04
☐ 22	Rob Picciolo	.20	.10	.02
☐ 23	Ron Romanick	.20	.10	.02
☐ 24	Luis Sanchez	.20	.10	.02
☐ 25	Dick Schofield	.30	.15	.03
☐ 26	Daryl Sconiers	.20	.10	.02
☐ 27	Jim Slaton	.20	.10	.02
☐ 28	Smokey the Bear	.20	.10	.02
☐ 29	Ellis Valentine	.20	.10	.02
☐ 30	Rob Wilfong	.20	.10	.02
☐ 31	Mike Witt	.60	.30	.06
☐ 32	Geoff Zahn	.30	.15	.03

1984 Smokey Dodgers

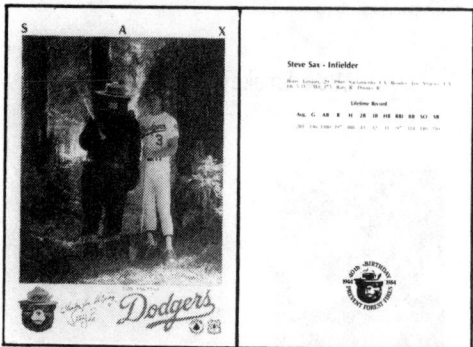

This four card set was not widely distributed and has not proven to be very popular with collectors. Cards were supposedly distributed by fire agencies in Southern California at fairs, mall displays, and special events. Cards are approximately 5" by 7" and feature a color picture of Smokey the Bear with a Dodger. The cards were printed on relatively thin card stock; printing on the back is black on white.

		MINT	EXC	G-VG
	COMPLETE SET	7.00	3.50	.70
	COMMON PLAYER	.50	.25	.05
☐ 1	Ken Landreaux with Smokey	1.75	.85	.17
☐ 2	Tom Niedenfuer with Smokey	1.75	.85	.17
☐ 3	Steve Sax with Smokey	3.50	1.75	.35
☐ 4	Smokey the Bear (batting pose)	.50	.25	.05

1984 Smokey Padres

The cards in this 29 card set measure 2 1/2" by 3 3/4". This unnumbered, full color set features the Fire Prevention Bear and a Padres player, coach, manager, or associate on each card. The set was given out at the ballpark at the May 14th game against the Expos. Logos of the California Department of Forestry and the U.S. Forest Service appear in conjunction with a Smokey the Bear logo on the obverse. The set commemorates the 40th birthday of Smokey the Bear. The backs contain short biographical data, statistics and a fire prevention hint from the player pictured on the front.

		MINT	EXC	G-VG
	COMPLETE SET	9.00	4.50	.90
	COMMON PLAYER	.25	.12	.02
☐ 1	Kurt Bevacqua	.25	.12	.02
☐ 2	Bobby Brown	.25	.12	.02
☐ 3	Dave Campbell (Broadcast Team)	.25	.12	.02
☐ 4	The Chicken (Mascot)	.35	.17	.03
☐ 5	Jerry Coleman (Broadcast Team)	.25	.12	.02
☐ 6	Luis DeLeon	.25	.12	.02
☐ 7	Dave Dravecky	.35	.17	.03
☐ 8	Harry Dunlop CO	.25	.12	.02
☐ 9	Tim Flannery	.25	.12	.02
☐ 10	Steve Garvey	1.25	.60	.12
☐ 11	Doug Gwosdz	.25	.12	.02
☐ 12	Tony Gwynn	1.50	.75	.15
☐ 13	Harold (Doug) Harvey (ex-UMP)	.25	.12	.02
☐ 14	Terry Kennedy	.35	.17	.03
☐ 15	Jack Krol COACH	.25	.12	.02
☐ 16	Tim Lollar	.25	.12	.02
☐ 17	Jack McKeon (VP for Baseball Operations)	.25	.12	.02
☐ 18	Kevin McReynolds	.75	.35	.07
☐ 19	Sid Monge	.25	.12	.02
☐ 20	Luis Salazar	.25	.12	.02
☐ 21	Norm Sherry CO	.25	.12	.02
☐ 22	Eric Show	.35	.17	.03
☐ 23	Smokey the Bear	.25	.12	.02
☐ 24	Garry Templeton	.35	.17	.03
☐ 25	Mark Thurmond	.35	.17	.03
☐ 26	Ozzie Virgil CO	.25	.12	.02
☐ 27	Ed Whitson	.35	.17	.03
☐ 28	Alan Wiggins	.35	.17	.03
☐ 29	Dick Williams MG	.35	.17	.03

1985 Smokey Angels

The cards in this 24 card set measure 4 1/4" by 6" and feature the California Angels in full color. The player's photo, the Angels' logo, and the Smokey the Bear logo appear on the front, in addition to the

California Department of Forestry and the U.S. Forest Service logos. The abbreviated backs contain short biographical data and an anti-wildfire hint.

		MINT	EXC	G-VG
COMPLETE SET		6.00	3.00	.60
COMMON PLAYER		.20	.10	.02
☐ 1	Mike Witt	.60	.30	.06
☐ 2	Reggie Jackson	1.25	.60	.12
☐ 3	Bob Boone	.40	.20	.04
☐ 4	Mike Brown	.20	.10	.02
☐ 5	Rod Carew	1.00	.50	.10
☐ 6	Doug DeCinces	.40	.20	.04
☐ 7	Brian Downing	.30	.15	.03
☐ 8	Ken Forsch	.20	.10	.02
☐ 9	Gary Pettis	.30	.15	.03
☐ 10	Jerry Narron	.20	.10	.02
☐ 11	Ron Romanick	.20	.10	.02
☐ 12	Bobby Grich	.30	.15	.03
☐ 13	Dick Schofield	.30	.15	.03
☐ 14	Juan Beniquez	.20	.10	.02
☐ 15	Geoff Zahn	.20	.10	.02
☐ 16	Luis Sanchez	.20	.10	.02
☐ 17	Jim Slaton	.20	.10	.02
☐ 18	Doug Corbett	.20	.10	.02
☐ 19	Ruppert Jones	.20	.10	.02
☐ 20	Rob Wilfong	.20	.10	.02
☐ 21	Donnie Moore	.30	.15	.03
☐ 22	Pat Clements	.20	.10	.02
☐ 23	Tommy John	.50	.25	.05
☐ 24	Gene Mauch MG	.20	.10	.02

1986 Smokey Angels

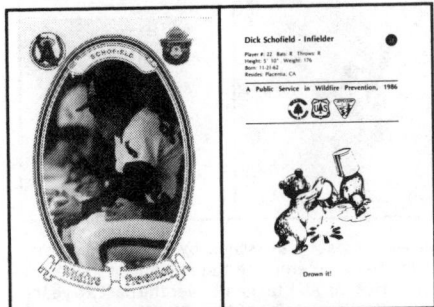

The Forestry Service (in conjunction with the California Angels) produced this large, attractive 24 card set. The cards feature Smokey the Bear pictured in the upper right corner of the card. The card backs give a fire safety tip. The set was given out free at Anaheim Stadium on August 9th. The cards measure 4 1/4" by 6" and are subtitled "Wildfire Prevention" on the front.

		MINT	EXC	G-VG
COMPLETE SET		7.00	3.50	.70
COMMON PLAYER		.20	.10	.02
☐ 1	Mike Witt	.50	.25	.05
☐ 2	Reggie Jackson	.90	.45	.09
☐ 3	Bob Boone	.30	.15	.03
☐ 4	Don Sutton	.60	.30	.06
☐ 5	Kirk McCaskill	.30	.15	.03
☐ 6	Doug DeCinces	.40	.20	.04
☐ 7	Brian Downing	.30	.15	.03
☐ 8	Doug Corbett	.20	.10	.02
☐ 9	Gary Pettis	.30	.15	.03
☐ 10	Jerry Narron	.20	.10	.02
☐ 11	Ron Romanick	.20	.10	.02
☐ 12	Bobby Grich	.30	.15	.03
☐ 13	Dick Schofield	.30	.15	.03
☐ 14	George Hendrick	.30	.15	.03
☐ 15	Rick Burleson	.30	.15	.03
☐ 16	John Candelaria	.30	.15	.03
☐ 17	Jim Slaton	.30	.15	.03
☐ 18	Darrell Miller	.20	.10	.02
☐ 19	Ruppert Jones	.20	.10	.02
☐ 20	Rob Wilfong	.20	.10	.02

☐ 21	Donnie Moore	.30	.15	.03
☐ 22	Wally Joyner	1.50	.75	.15
☐ 23	Terry Forster	.30	.15	.03
☐ 24	Gene Mauch MG	.30	.15	.03

1987 Smokey AL

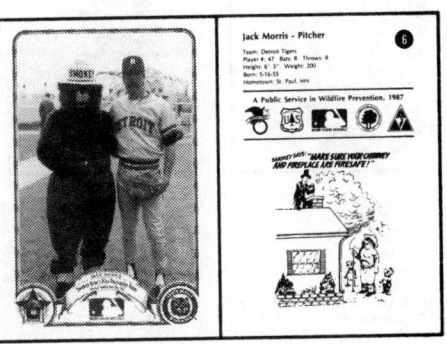

The U.S. Forestry Service (in conjunction with Major League Baseball) produced this large, attractive 14 player card set to commemorate the 43rd birthday of Smokey. The cards feature Smokey the Bear pictured on every card with the player. The card backs give a fire safety tip. The cards measure 4" by 6" and are subtitled "National Smokey Bear Day 1987" on the front. The cards were printed on an uncut (but perforated) sheet that measured 18" by 24".

		MINT	EXC	G-VG
COMPLETE SET (16)		5.00	2.50	.50
COMMON PLAYER		.25	.12	.02
☐ 1	Jose Canseco	1.00	.50	.10
☐ 2	Dennis Oil Can Boyd	.25	.12	.02
☐ 3	John Candelaria	.25	.12	.02
☐ 4	Harold Baines	.35	.17	.03
☐ 5	Joe Carter	.45	.22	.04
☐ 6	Jack Morris	.45	.22	.04
☐ 7	Buddy Biancalana	.25	.12	.02
☐ 8	Kirby Puckett	.75	.35	.07
☐ 9	Mike Pagliarulo	.35	.17	.03
☐ 10	Larry Sheets	.35	.17	.03
☐ 11	Mike Moore	.25	.12	.02
☐ 12	Charlie Hough	.35	.17	.03
☐ 13	National Smokey Bear Day 1987	.25	.12	.02
☐ 14	Tom Henke	.35	.17	.03
☐ 15	Jim Gantner	.25	.12	.02
☐ 16	American League Smokey Bear Day 1987	.25	.12	.02

1987 Smokey Angels

The U.S. Forestry Service (in conjunction with the California Angels) produced this large, attractive 24 card set to commemorate the 43rd birthday of Smokey. The cards feature Smokey the Bear pictured at the bottom of every card. The card backs give a cartoon fire safety tip. The cards measure 4" by 6" and are subtitled "Wildfire Prevention" on the front.

		MINT	EXC	G-VG
COMPLETE SET		7.00	3.50	.70
COMMON PLAYER		.25	.12	.02
☐ 1	John Candelaria	.35	.17	.03
☐ 2	Don Sutton	.75	.35	.07
☐ 3	Mike Witt	.60	.30	.06

				MINT	EXC	G-VG
☐	4	Gary Lucas		.25	.12	.02
☐	5	Kirk McCaskill		.35	.17	.03
☐	6	Chuck Finley		.25	.12	.02
☐	7	Willie Fraser		.25	.12	.02
☐	8	Donnie Moore		.35	.17	.03
☐	9	Urbano Lugo		.25	.12	.02
☐	10	Butch Wynegar		.35	.17	.03
☐	11	Darrell Miller		.25	.12	.02
☐	12	Wally Joyner		1.50	.75	.15
☐	13	Mark McLemore		.25	.12	.02
☐	14	Mark Ryal		.25	.12	.02
☐	15	Dick Schofield		.35	.17	.03
☐	16	Jack Howell		.35	.17	.03
☐	17	Doug DeCinces		.35	.17	.03
☐	18	Gus Polidor		.25	.12	.02
☐	19	Brian Downing		.35	.17	.03
☐	20	Gary Pettis		.35	.17	.03
☐	21	Ruppert Jones		.25	.12	.02
☐	22	George Hendrick		.35	.17	.03
☐	23	Devon White		1.00	.50	.10
☐	24	Checklist Card		.25	.02	.00

1987 Smokey Cardinals

The U.S. Forestry Service (in conjunction with the St. Louis Cardinals) produced this large, attractive 25-card set to commemorate the 43rd birthday of Smokey. The cards feature Smokey the Bear pictured in the top right corner of every card. The card backs give a cartoon fire safety tip. The cards measure 4" by 6" and are subtitled "Wildfire Prevention" on the front. Sets were supposedly available from the Cardinals team for 3.50 postpaid. Also a limited number of 8 1/2" by 12" full-color team photos were available from the team to those who sent in a large SASE. The large team photo is not considered part of the complete set.

			MINT	EXC	G-VG
COMPLETE SET			7.00	3.00	.50
COMMON PLAYER			.25	.12	.02
☐	1	Ray Soff	.25	.12	.02
☐	2	Todd Worrell	.60	.30	.06

				MINT	EXC	G-VG
☐	3	John Tudor		.45	.22	.04
☐	4	Pat Perry		.35	.17	.03
☐	5	Rick Horton		.25	.12	.02
☐	6	Dan Cox		.35	.17	.03
☐	7	Bob Forsch		.35	.17	.03
☐	8	Greg Matthews		.35	.17	.03
☐	9	Bill Dawley		.25	.12	.02
☐	10	Steve Lake		.25	.12	.02
☐	11	Tony Pena		.35	.17	.03
☐	12	Tom Pagnozzi		.25	.12	.02
☐	13	Jack Clark		.75	.35	.07
☐	14	Jim Lindeman		.45	.22	.04
☐	15	Mike Laga		.25	.12	.02
☐	16	Terry Pendleton		.45	.22	.04
☐	17	Ozzie Smith		.75	.35	.07
☐	18	Jose Oquendo		.35	.17	.03
☐	19	Tom Lawless		.25	.12	.02
☐	20	Tom Herr		.35	.17	.03
☐	21	Curt Ford		.25	.12	.02
☐	22	Willie McGee		.60	.30	.06
☐	23	Tito Landrum		.25	.12	.02
☐	24	Vince Coleman		.75	.35	.07
☐	25	Whitey Herzog MG		.35	.17	.03
☐	xx	Team Photo (large)		.90	.45	.09

1987 Smokey Dodger All-Stars

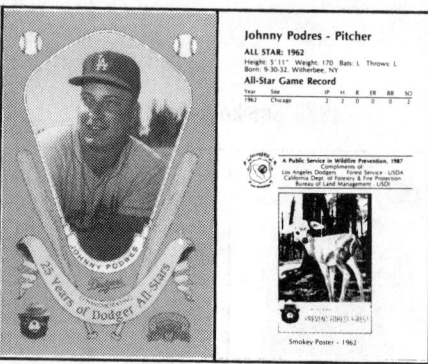

Smokey Poster - 1962

This 40-card set was issued by the U.S. Forestry Service to commemorate the Los Angeles Dodgers selected for the All-Star game over the past 25 years. The cards measure 2 1/2" by 3 3/4" and have full-color fronts.

			MINT	EXC	G-VG
COMPLETE SET			7.00	3.50	.70
COMMON PLAYER			.15	.07	.01
☐	1	Walt Alston	.35	.17	.03
☐	2	Dusty Baker	.25	.12	.02
☐	3	Jim Brewer	.15	.07	.01
☐	4	Ron Cey	.25	.12	.02
☐	5	Tommy Davis	.25	.12	.02
☐	6	Willie Davis	.25	.12	.02
☐	7	Don Drysdale	.75	.35	.07
☐	8	Steve Garvey	.75	.35	.07
☐	9	Bill Grabarkewitz	.15	.07	.01
☐	10	Pedro Guerrero	.75	.35	.07
☐	11	Tom Haller	.15	.07	.01
☐	12	Orel Hershiser	.35	.17	.03
☐	13	Burt Hooton	.15	.07	.01
☐	14	Steve Howe	.25	.12	.02
☐	15	Tommy John	.35	.17	.03
☐	16	Sandy Koufax	.75	.35	.07
☐	17	Tom Lasorda	.45	.22	.04
☐	18	Jim Lefebvre	.15	.07	.01
☐	19	Davey Lopes	.25	.12	.02
☐	20	Mike Marshall (pitcher)	.35	.17	.03
☐	21	Mike Marshall (outfielder)	.50	.25	.05
☐	22	Andy Messersmith	.25	.12	.02
☐	23	Rick Monday	.25	.12	.02
☐	24	Manny Mota	.25	.12	.02
☐	25	Claude Osteen	.25	.12	.02
☐	26	Johnny Podres	.25	.12	.02
☐	27	Phil Regan	.15	.07	.01
☐	28	Jerry Reuss	.25	.12	.02

☐ 29	Rick Rhoden	.25	.12	.02
☐ 30	John Roseboro	.15	.07	.01
☐ 31	Bill Russell	.25	.12	.02
☐ 32	Steve Sax	.35	.17	.03
☐ 33	Bill Singer	.15	.07	.01
☐ 34	Reggie Smith	.25	.12	.02
☐ 35	Don Sutton	.50	.25	.05
☐ 36	Fernando Valenzuela	.50	.25	.05
☐ 37	Bob Welch	.25	.12	.02
☐ 38	Maury Wills	.35	.17	.03
☐ 39	Jim Wynn	.25	.12	.02
☐ 40	Checklist Card	.15	.02	.00

1987 Smokey National League

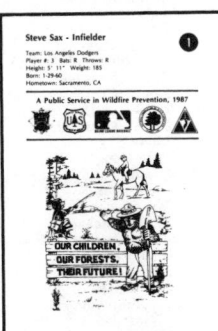

Steve Sax - Infielder ❶

Team: Los Angeles Dodgers
Player #: 3 Bats: R Throws: R
Height: 5' 11" Weight: 185
Born: 1-29-60
Hometown: Sacramento, CA

A Public Service in Wildfire Prevention, 1987

OUR CHILDREN,
OUR FORESTS,
THEIR FUTURE!

The U.S. Forestry Service (in conjunction with Major League Baseball) produced this large, attractive 14 player card set to commemorate the 43rd birthday of Smokey. The cards feature Smokey the Bear pictured on every card with the player. The card backs give a fire safety tip. The cards measure 4" by 6" and are subtitled "National Smokey Bear Day 1987" on the front.

		MINT	EXC	G-VG
	COMPLETE SET	5.00	2.50	.50
	COMMON PLAYER	.25	.12	.02
☐ 1	Steve Sax	.35	.17	.03
☐ 2	Dale Murphy	1.50	.75	.15
☐ 3	Jody Davis	.35	.17	.03
☐ 4	Bill Gullickson	.25	.12	.02
☐ 5	Mike Scott	.60	.30	.06
☐ 6	Roger McDowell	.35	.17	.03
☐ 7	Steve Bedrosian	.60	.30	.06
☐ 8	Johnny Ray	.35	.17	.03
☐ 9	Ozzie Smith	.60	.30	.06
☐ 10	Steve Garvey	.75	.35	.07
☐ 11	National Smokey Bear Day	.25	.12	.02
☐ 12	Mike Krukow	.25	.12	.02
☐ 13	Smokey the Bear	.25	.12	.02
☐ 14	Mike Fitzgerald	.25	.12	.02
☐ 15	National League Logo	.25	.12	.02

1933 Sport Kings

The cards in this 48-card set measure 2 3/8" by 2 7/8". The 1933 Sport Kings set, issued by the Goudey Gum Company, contains cards for the most famous athletic heroes of the times. No less than 18 different sports are represented in the set. The baseball cards of Cobb, Hubbell, and Ruth, and the football cards of Rockne and Thorpe command premium prices. The ACC designation for this set is R338.

	NRMT	VG-E	GOOD
COMPLETE SET	4500.00	1800.00	350.00

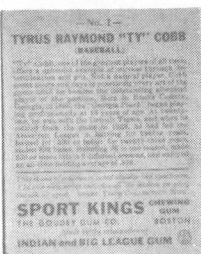

SPORT KINGS GUM

TY COBB

No. 1
TYRUS RAYMOND "TY" COBB
(BASEBALL)

SPORT KINGS
THE GOUDEY GUM CO.   BOSTON
INDIAN and BIG LEAGUE GUM

	COMMON PLAYER (1-24)	18.00	9.00	1.80
	COMMON PLAYER (25-36)	27.00	13.50	2.70
	COMMON PLAYER (37-48)	40.00	20.00	4.00
☐ 1	Ty Cobb: baseball	750.00	200.00	40.00
☐ 2	Babe Ruth: baseball	1000.00	400.00	80.00
☐ 3	Nat Holman: basketball	30.00	15.00	3.00
☐ 4	Red Grange: football	150.00	75.00	15.00
☐ 5	Ed Wachter: basketball	30.00	15.00	3.00
☐ 6	Jim Thorpe: football	175.00	85.00	18.00
☐ 7	B. Walthour, Sr.: cycling	18.00	9.00	1.80
☐ 8	Walter Hagen: golf	30.00	15.00	3.00
☐ 9	Ed Blood: skiing	18.00	9.00	1.80
☐ 10	Anton Lekang: skiing	18.00	9.00	1.80
☐ 11	C. Jewtraw: ice skating	18.00	9.00	1.80
☐ 12	Bobby McLean: ice skating	18.00	9.00	1.80
☐ 13	Laverne Fator: jockey	18.00	9.00	1.80
☐ 14	Jim Londos: wrestling	18.00	9.00	1.80
☐ 15	Reggie McNamara: bicycling	18.00	9.00	1.80
☐ 16	Bill Tilden: tennis	30.00	15.00	3.00
☐ 17	Jack Dempsey: boxing	90.00	45.00	9.00
☐ 18	Gene Tunney: boxing	75.00	37.50	7.50
☐ 19	Eddie Shore: hockey	75.00	37.50	7.50
☐ 20	Duke Kahanamoku: swimming	30.00	15.00	3.00
☐ 21	John Weissmuller: swimming	175.00	85.00	18.00
☐ 22	Gene Sarazen: golf	30.00	15.00	3.00
☐ 23	Vincent Richards: tennis	18.00	9.00	1.80
☐ 24	Howie Morenz: hockey	90.00	45.00	9.00
☐ 25	Ralph Snoddy: speedboat	27.00	13.50	2.70
☐ 26	James R. Wedell: aviator	27.00	13.50	2.70
☐ 27	Col. R. Turner: aviator	27.00	13.50	2.70
☐ 28	James Doolittle: aviator	30.00	15.00	3.00
☐ 29	Ace Bailey: hockey	75.00	37.50	7.50
☐ 30	Ching Johnson: hockey	75.00	37.50	7.50
☐ 31	B. Walthour, Jr.: cycling	27.00	13.50	2.70
☐ 32	Joe Lopchick: basketball	65.00	32.50	6.50
☐ 33	Eddie Burke: basketball	45.00	22.50	4.50
☐ 34	Irving Jaffee: ice skating	28.00	14.00	2.80
☐ 35	Knute Rockne: football	350.00	175.00	35.00
☐ 36	Willie Hoppe: billiards	27.00	13.50	2.70
☐ 37	Helene Madison: swimming	40.00	20.00	4.00
☐ 38	Bobby Jones: golf	60.00	30.00	6.00
☐ 39	Jack Westrope: jockey	40.00	20.00	4.00
☐ 40	Don George: wrestling	40.00	20.00	4.00
☐ 41	Jim Browning: wrestling	40.00	20.00	4.00
☐ 42	Carl Hubbell: baseball	175.00	85.00	18.00
☐ 43	Primo Carnera: boxing	60.00	30.00	6.00
☐ 44	Max Baer: boxing	60.00	30.00	6.00
☐ 45	Babe Didrickson: track	200.00	100.00	20.00
☐ 46	Ellsworth Vines: tennis	40.00	20.00	4.00
☐ 47	J.H. Stevens: bob-sled	40.00	20.00	4.00
☐ 48	L. Seppala: dog-sled	90.00	25.00	5.00

1986 Sportflics

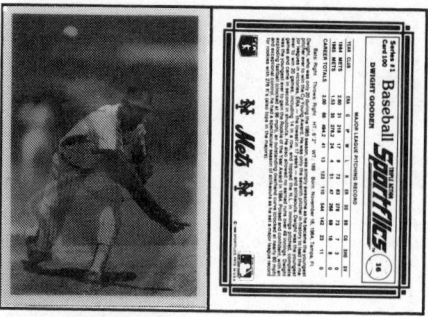

This 200-card set was marketed with 133 small trivia cards. This inaugural set for Sportflics was well-received by the public. Sportflics was distributed by Major League Marketing; the company is also affiliated with Wrigley and Amurol. The set features 139 single player "magic motion" cards (which can be tilted to show three different pictures of the same player), 50 "Tri-Stars" (which show three different players), 10 "Big Six" cards (which show six players who share similar achievements), and one World Champs card featuring 12 members of the victorious Kansas City Royals. All cards measure 2 1/2" by 3 1/2".

		MINT	EXC	G-VG
	COMPLETE SET	36.00	18.00	3.60
	COMMON PLAYER	.15	.07	.01
☐	1 George Brett	1.25	.60	.12
☐	2 Don Mattingly	4.50	2.25	.45
☐	3 Wade Boggs	2.50	1.25	.25
☐	4 Eddie Murray	.90	.45	.09
☐	5 Dale Murphy	1.25	.60	.12
☐	6 Rickey Henderson	1.00	.50	.10
☐	7 Harold Baines	.40	.20	.04
☐	8 Cal Ripken	1.00	.50	.10
☐	9 Orel Hershiser	.50	.25	.05
☐	10 Bret Saberhagen	.65	.30	.06
☐	11 Tim Raines	.60	.30	.06
☐	12 Fernando Valenzuela	.50	.25	.05
☐	13 Tony Gwynn	1.00	.50	.10
☐	14 Pedro Guerrero	.40	.20	.04
☐	15 Keith Hernandez	.40	.20	.04
☐	16 Ernie Riles	.30	.15	.03
☐	17 Jim Rice	.50	.25	.05
☐	18 Ron Guidry	.40	.20	.04
☐	19 Willie McGee	.50	.25	.05
☐	20 Ryne Sandberg	1.00	.50	.10
☐	21 Kirk Gibson	.50	.25	.05
☐	22 Ozzie Guillen	.60	.30	.06
☐	23 Dave Parker	.40	.20	.04
☐	24 Vince Coleman	2.00	1.00	.20
☐	25 Tom Seaver	.75	.35	.07
☐	26 Brett Butler	.20	.10	.02
☐	27 Steve Carlton	.60	.30	.06
☐	28 Gary Carter	.65	.30	.06
☐	29 Cecil Cooper	.30	.15	.03
☐	30 Jose Cruz	.20	.10	.02
☐	31 Alvin Davis	.25	.12	.02
☐	32 Dwight Evans	.30	.15	.03
☐	33 Julio Franco	.20	.10	.02
☐	34 Damaso Garcia	.15	.07	.01
☐	35 Steve Garvey	1.00	.50	.10
☐	36 Kent Hrbek	.40	.20	.04
☐	37 Reggie Jackson	1.00	.50	.10
☐	38 Fred Lynn	.35	.17	.03
☐	39 Paul Molitor	.35	.17	.03
☐	40 Jim Presley	.40	.20	.04
☐	41 Dave Righetti	.35	.17	.03
☐	42 Robin Yount	.50	.25	.05
☐	43 Nolan Ryan	.75	.35	.07
☐	44 Mike Schmidt	1.25	.60	.12
☐	45 Lee Smith	.25	.12	.02
☐	46 Rick Sutcliffe	.25	.12	.02
☐	47 Bruce Sutter	.30	.15	.03
☐	48 Lou Whitaker	.35	.17	.03
☐	49 Dave Winfield	.65	.30	.06
☐	50 Pete Rose	2.00	1.00	.20
☐	51 NL MVPs Ryne Sandberg Steve Garvey Pete Rose	.90	.45	.09
☐	52 Slugging Stars George Brett Harold Baines Jim Rice	.60	.30	.06
☐	53 No-Hitters Phil Niekro Jerry Reuss Mike Witt	.25	.12	.02
☐	54 Big Hitters Don Mattingly Cal Ripken Robin Yount	1.00	.50	.10
☐	55 Bullpen Aces Dan Quisenberry Goose Gossage Lee Smith	.25	.12	.02
☐	56 Rookies of The Year Darryl Strawberry Steve Sax Pete Rose	.90	.45	.09
☐	57 AL MVP's Cal Ripken Don Baylor Reggie Jackson	.60	.30	.06
☐	58 Repeat Batting Champs Dave Parker Bill Madlock Pete Rose	.90	.45	.09
☐	59 Cy Young Winners LaMarr Hoyt Mike Flanagan Ron Guidry	.25	.12	.02
☐	60 Double Award Winners Fernando Valenzuela Rick Sutcliffe Tom Seaver	.30	.15	.03
☐	61 Home Run Champs Reggie Jackson Jim Rice Tony Armas	.70	.35	.07
☐	62 NL MVP's Keith Hernandez Dale Murphy Mike Schmidt	.90	.45	.09
☐	63 AL MVP's Robin Yount George Brett Fred Lynn	.60	.30	.06
☐	64 Comeback Players Bert Blyleven Jerry Koosman John Denny	.20	.10	.02
☐	65 Cy Young Relievers Willie Hernandez Rollie Fingers Bruce Sutter	.20	.10	.02
☐	66 Rookies of The Year Bob Horner Andre Dawson Gary Matthews	.25	.12	.02
☐	67 Rookies of THe Year Ron Kittle Carlton Fisk Tom Seaver	.35	.17	.03
☐	68 Home Run Champs Mike Schmidt George Foster Dave Kingman	.35	.17	.03
☐	69 Double Award Winners Cal Ripken Rod Carew Pete Rose	.90	.45	.09
☐	70 Cy Young Winners Rick Sutcliffe Steve Carlton Tom Seaver	.40	.20	.04
☐	71 Top Sluggers Reggie Jackson Fred Lynn Robin Yount	.40	.20	.04
☐	72 Rookies of The Year Dave Righetti Fernando Valenzuela Rick Sutcliffe	.35	.17	.03
☐	73 Rookies of The Year Fred Lynn Eddie Murray	.70	.35	.07

	Cal Ripken			
☐ 74	Rookies of The Year	.30	.15	.03
	Alvin Davis			
	Lou Whitaker			
	Rod Carew			
☐ 75	Batting Champs	1.50	.75	.15
	Don Mattingly			
	Wade Boggs			
	Carney Lansford			
☐ 76	Jesse Barfield	.50	.25	.05
☐ 77	Phil Bradley	.40	.20	.04
☐ 78	Chris Brown	.60	.30	.06
☐ 79	Tom Browning	.30	.15	.03
☐ 80	Tom Brunansky	.30	.15	.03
☐ 81	Bill Buckner	.20	.10	.02
☐ 82	Chili Davis	.20	.10	.02
☐ 83	Mike Davis	.20	.10	.02
☐ 84	Rich Gedman	.25	.12	.02
☐ 85	Willie Hernandez	.25	.12	.02
☐ 86	Ron Kittle	.25	.12	.02
☐ 87	Lee Lacy	.15	.07	.01
☐ 88	Bill Madlock	.20	.10	.02
☐ 89	Mike Marshall	.25	.12	.02
☐ 90	Keith Moreland	.15	.07	.01
☐ 91	Graig Nettles	.25	.12	.02
☐ 92	Lance Parrish	.30	.15	.03
☐ 93	Kirby Puckett	1.00	.50	.10
☐ 94	Juan Samuel	.35	.17	.03
☐ 95	Steve Sax	.25	.12	.02
☐ 96	Dave Stieb	.25	.12	.02
☐ 97	Darryl Strawberry	1.25	.60	.12
☐ 98	Willie Upshaw	.15	.07	.01
☐ 99	Frank Viola	.25	.12	.02
☐ 100	Dwight Gooden	1.50	.75	.15
☐ 101	Joaquin Andujar	.25	.12	.02
☐ 102	George Bell	.60	.30	.06
☐ 103	Bert Blyleven	.25	.12	.02
☐ 104	Mike Boddicker	.20	.10	.02
☐ 105	Britt Burns	.15	.07	.01
☐ 106	Rod Carew	.75	.35	.07
☐ 107	Jack Clark	.40	.20	.04
☐ 108	Danny Cox	.25	.12	.02
☐ 109	Ron Darling	.45	.22	.04
☐ 110	Andre Dawson	.60	.30	.06
☐ 111	Leon Durham	.20	.10	.02
☐ 112	Tony Fernandez	.40	.20	.04
☐ 113	Tommy Herr	.15	.07	.01
☐ 114	Teddy Higuera	.60	.30	.06
☐ 115	Bob Horner	.35	.17	.03
☐ 116	Dave Kingman	.25	.12	.02
☐ 117	Jack Morris	.35	.17	.03
☐ 118	Dan Quisenberry	.25	.12	.02
☐ 119	Jeff Reardon	.25	.12	.02
☐ 120	Bryn Smith	.15	.07	.01
☐ 121	Ozzie Smith	.35	.17	.03
☐ 122	John Tudor	.25	.12	.02
☐ 123	Tim Wallach	.25	.12	.02
☐ 124	Willie Wilson	.25	.12	.02
☐ 125	Carlton Fisk	.30	.15	.03
☐ 126	RBI Sluggers	.30	.15	.03
	Gary Carter			
	Al Oliver			
	George Foster			
☐ 127	Run Scorers	.60	.30	.06
	Tim Raines			
	Ryne Sandberg			
	Keith Hernandez			
☐ 128	Run Scorers	.50	.25	.05
	Paul Molitor			
	Cal Ripken			
	Willie Wilson			
☐ 129	No-Hitters	.20	.10	.02
	John Candelaria			
	Dennis Eckersley			
	Bob Forsch			
☐ 130	World Series MVP's	.70	.35	.07
	Pete Rose			
	Ron Cey			
	Rollie Fingers			
☐ 131	All-Star Game MVPs	.20	.10	.02
	Dave Concepcion			
	George Foster			
	Bill Madlock			
☐ 132	Cy Young Winners	.25	.12	.02
	John Denny			
	Fernando Valenzuela			
	Vida Blue			
☐ 133	Comeback Players	.20	.10	.02
	Rich Dotson			
	Joaquin Andujar			
	Doyle Alexander			
☐ 134	Big Winners	.40	.20	.04
	Rick Sutcliffe			
	Tom Seaver			
	John Denny			
☐ 135	Veteran Pitchers	.50	.25	.05
	Tom Seaver			
	Phil Niekro			
	Don Sutton			
☐ 136	Rookies of The Year	1.25	.60	.12
	Dwight Gooden			
	Vince Coleman			
	Alfredo Griffin			
☐ 137	All-Star Game MVPs	.45	.22	.04
	Gary Carter			
	Fred Lynn			
	Steve Garvey			
☐ 138	Veteran Hitters	.70	.35	.07
	Tony Perez			
	Rusty Staub			
	Pete Rose			
☐ 139	Power Hitters	.60	.30	.06
	Mike Schmidt			
	Jim Rice			
	George Foster			
☐ 140	Batting Champs	.35	.17	.03
	Tony Gwynn			
	Al Oliver			
	Bill Buckner			
☐ 141	No-Hitters	.40	.20	.04
	Nolan Ryan			
	Jack Morris			
	Dave Righetti			
☐ 142	No-Hitters	.35	.17	.03
	Tom Seaver			
	Bert Blyleven			
	Vida Blue			
☐ 143	Strikeout Kings	1.25	.60	.12
	Nolan Ryan			
	Fernando Valenzuela			
	Dwight Gooden			
☐ 144	Base Stealers	.40	.20	.04
	Tim Raines			
	Willie Wilson			
	Davey Lopes			
☐ 145	RBI Sluggers	.40	.20	.04
	Tony Armas			
	Cecil Cooper			
	Eddie Murray			
☐ 146	AL MVP's	.45	.22	.04
	Rod Carew			
	Jim Rice			
	Rollie Fingers			
☐ 147	World Series MVP's	.40	.20	.04
	Alan Trammell			
	Rick Dempsey			
	Reggie Jackson			
☐ 148	World Series MVP's	.45	.22	.04
	Darrell Porter			
	Pedro Guerrero			
	Mike Schmidt			
☐ 149	ERA Leaders	.20	.10	.02
	Mike Boddicker			
	Rick Sutcliffe			
	Ron Guidry			
☐ 150	Comeback Players	.40	.20	.04
	Reggie Jackson			
	Dave Kingman			
	Fred Lynn			
☐ 151	Buddy Bell	.20	.10	.02
☐ 152	Dennis Boyd	.20	.10	.02
☐ 153	Dave Concepcion	.20	.10	.02
☐ 154	Brian Downing	.15	.07	.01
☐ 155	Shawon Dunston	.25	.12	.02
☐ 156	John Franco	.30	.15	.03
☐ 157	Scott Garrelts	.20	.10	.02
☐ 158	Bob James	.15	.07	.01
☐ 159	Charlie Leibrandt	.20	.10	.02
☐ 160	Oddibe McDowell	.60	.30	.06
☐ 161	Roger McDowell	.60	.30	.06
☐ 162	Mike Moore	.20	.10	.02
☐ 163	Phil Niekro	.50	.25	.05
☐ 164	Al Oliver	.25	.12	.02
☐ 165	Tony Pena	.25	.12	.02
☐ 166	Ted Power	.20	.10	.02
☐ 167	Mike Scioscia	.15	.07	.01
☐ 168	Mario Soto	.20	.10	.02
☐ 169	Bob Stanley	.20	.10	.02
☐ 170	Gary Templeton	.20	.10	.02
☐ 171	Andre Thornton	.20	.10	.02
☐ 172	Alan Trammell	.50	.25	.05
☐ 173	Doug DeCinces	.25	.12	.02
☐ 174	Greg Walker	.25	.12	.02
☐ 175	Don Sutton	.45	.22	.04
☐ 176	1985 Award Winners	1.25	.60	.12
	Ozzie Guillen			
	Bret Saberhagen			
	Don Mattingly			
	Vince Coleman			
	Dwight Gooden			

		MINT	EXC	G-VG
☐ 177	1985 Hot Rookies	.80	.40	.08
	Stew Cliburn			
	Brian Fisher			
	Joe Hesketh			
	Joe Orsulak			
	Mark Salas			
	Larry Sheets			
☐ 178	1986 Rookies To Watch .	5.00	2.50	.50
	Jose Canseco			
	Mark Funderburk			
	Mike Greenwell			
	Steve Lombardozzi			
	Billy Joe Robidoux			
	Dan Tartabull			
☐ 179	1985 Gold Glovers	.90	.45	.09
	George Brett			
	Ron Guidry			
	Keith Hernandez			
	Don Mattingly			
	Willie McGee			
	Dale Murphy			
☐ 180	Active Lifetime .300	.90	.45	.09
	Wade Boggs			
	George Brett			
	Rod Carew			
	Cecil Cooper			
	Don Mattingly			
	Willie Wilson			
☐ 181	Active Lifetime .300	.90	.45	.09
	Tony Gwynn			
	Bill Madlock			
	Pedro Guerrero			
	Dave Parker			
	Pete Rose			
	Keith Hernandez			
☐ 182	1985 Milestones	.90	.45	.09
	Rod Carew			
	Phil Niekro			
	Pete Rose			
	Nolan Ryan			
	Tom Seaver			
	Matt Tallman (fan)			
☐ 183	1985 Triple Crown	.90	.45	.09
	Wade Boggs			
	Darrell Evans			
	Don Mattingly			
	Willie McGee			
	Dale Murphy			
	Dave Parker			
☐ 184	1985 Highlights	1.25	.60	.12
	Wade Boggs			
	Dwight Gooden			
	Rickey Henderson			
	Don Mattingly			
	Willie McGee			
	John Tudor			
☐ 185	1985 20 Game Winners .	.90	.45	.09
	Dwight Gooden			
	Ron Guidry			
	John Tudor			
	Joaquin Andujar			
	Bret Saberhagen			
	Tom Browning			
☐ 186	World Series Champs	.50	.25	.05
	L. Smith, Dane Iorg			
	W. Wilson, Leibrandt			
	G. Brett, Saberhagen			
	D. Motley, Quisenberry			
	D. Jackson, Sundberg			
	S. Balboni, F. White			
☐ 187	Hubie Brooks	.25	.12	.02
☐ 188	Glenn Davis	.60	.30	.06
☐ 189	Darrell Evans	.25	.12	.02
☐ 190	Rich Gossage	.30	.15	.03
☐ 191	Andy Hawkins	.15	.07	.01
☐ 192	Jay Howell	.15	.07	.01
☐ 193	LaMarr Hoyt	.20	.10	.02
☐ 194	Davey Lopes	.15	.07	.01
☐ 195	Mike Scott	.50	.25	.05
☐ 196	Ted Simmons	.20	.10	.02
☐ 197	Gary Ward	.15	.07	.01
☐ 198	Bob Welch	.20	.10	.02
☐ 199	Mike Young	.20	.10	.02
☐ 200	Buddy Biancalana	.15	.07	.01

1986 Sportflics Decade Greats

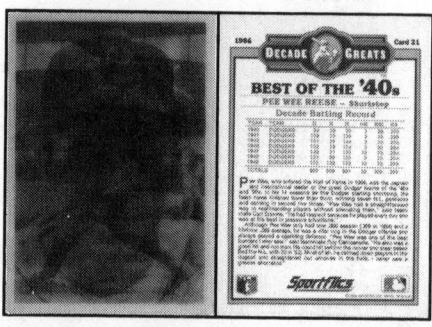

This set of 75 three-phase "animated" cards was produced by Sportflics and manufactured by Opti-Graphics of Arlington, Texas. Cards are standard size, 2 1/2" by 3 1/2", and feature both sepia (players of the '30s and '40s) and full color cards. The concept of the set was that the best players at each position for each decade (from the '30s to the '80s) were chosen. The bios were written by Les Woodcock. Also included with the set in the specially designed collector box are 51 trivia cards with historical questions about the six decades of All-Star games.

		MINT	EXC	G-VG
	COMPLETE SET	15.00	7.50	1.50
	COMMON PLAYER (1-75)	.15	.07	.01
☐ 1	Babe Ruth	2.50	1.25	.25
☐ 2	Jimmie Foxx	.35	.17	.03
☐ 3	Lefty Grove	.35	.17	.03
☐ 4	Hank Greenberg	.35	.17	.03
☐ 5	Al Simmons	.25	.12	.02
☐ 6	Carl Hubbell	.25	.12	.02
☐ 7	Joe Cronin	.25	.12	.02
☐ 8	Mel Ott	.25	.12	.02
☐ 9	Lefty Gomez	.25	.12	.02
☐ 10	Lou Gehrig	1.00	.50	.10
	(Best '30s Player)			
☐ 11	Pie Traynor	.25	.12	.02
☐ 12	Charlie Gehringer	.25	.12	.02
☐ 13	Best '30s Catchers	.25	.12	.02
	Bill Dickey			
	Mickey Cochrane			
	Gabby Hartnett			
☐ 14	Best '30s Pitchers	.35	.17	.03
	Dizzy Dean			
	Red Ruffing			
	Paul Derringer			
☐ 15	Best '30s Outfielders	.25	.12	.02
	Paul Waner			
	Joe Medwick			
	Earl Averill			
☐ 16	Bob Feller	.75	.35	.07
☐ 17	Lou Boudreau	.25	.12	.02
☐ 18	Enos Slaughter	.25	.12	.02
☐ 19	Hal Newhouser	.15	.07	.01
☐ 20	Joe DiMaggio	1.25	.60	.12
☐ 21	Pee Wee Reese	.45	.22	.04
☐ 22	Phil Rizzuto	.35	.17	.03
☐ 23	Ernie Lombardi	.25	.12	.02
☐ 24	Best '40s Infielders	.25	.12	.02
	Johnny Mize			
	Joe Gordon			
	George Kell			
☐ 25	Ted Williams	1.00	.50	.10
	(Best '40s Player)			
☐ 26	Mickey Mantle	2.50	1.25	.25
☐ 27	Warren Spahn	.35	.17	.03
☐ 28	Jackie Robinson	.75	.35	.07
☐ 29	Ernie Banks	.35	.17	.03
☐ 30	Stan Musial	.60	.30	.06
	(Best '50s Player)			
☐ 31	Yogi Berra	.60	.30	.06
☐ 32	Duke Snider	.75	.35	.07
☐ 33	Roy Campanella	.75	.35	.07
☐ 34	Eddie Mathews	.35	.17	.03
☐ 35	Ralph Kiner	.25	.12	.02

☐ 36 Early Wynn	.25	.12	.02
☐ 37 Double Play Duo	.25	.12	.02
Nellie Fox			
Luis Aparicio			
☐ 38 Best '50s First Base	.25	.12	.02
Gil Hodges			
Ted Kluszewski			
Mickey Vernon			
☐ 39 Best '50s Pitchers	.25	.12	.02
Bob Lemon			
Don Newcombe			
Robin Roberts			
☐ 40 Henry Aaron	1.00	.50	.10
☐ 41 Frank Robinson	.35	.17	.03
☐ 42 Bob Gibson	.35	.17	.03
☐ 43 Roberto Clemente	1.00	.50	.10
☐ 44 Whitey Ford	.50	.25	.05
☐ 45 Brooks Robinson	.50	.25	.05
☐ 46 Juan Marichal	.35	.17	.03
☐ 47 Carl Yastrzemski	1.00	.50	.10
☐ 48 Best '60s First Base	.35	.17	.03
Willie McCovey			
Harmon Killebrew			
Orlando Cepeda			
☐ 49 Best '60s Catchers	.15	.07	.01
Joe Torre			
Elston Howard			
Bill Freehan			
☐ 50 Willie Mays	1.00	.50	.10
(Best '50s Player)			
☐ 51 Best '60s Outfielders	.25	.12	.02
Al Kaline			
Tony Oliva			
Billy Williams			
☐ 52 Tom Seaver	.75	.35	.07
☐ 53 Reggie Jackson	1.00	.50	.10
☐ 54 Steve Carlton	.75	.35	.07
☐ 55 Mike Schmidt	1.00	.50	.10
☐ 56 Joe Morgan	.35	.17	.03
☐ 57 Jim Rice	.35	.17	.03
☐ 58 Jim Palmer	.35	.17	.03
☐ 59 Lou Brock	.45	.22	.04
☐ 60 Pete Rose	1.50	.75	.15
(Best '70s Player)			
☐ 61 Steve Garvey	.75	.35	.07
☐ 62 Best '70s Catchers	.25	.12	.02
Thurman Munson			
Carlton Fisk			
Ted Simmons			
☐ 63 Best '70s Pitchers	.25	.12	.02
Vida Blue			
Catfish Hunter			
Nolan Ryan			
☐ 64 George Brett	1.00	.50	.10
☐ 65 Don Mattingly	2.00	1.00	.20
☐ 66 Fernando Valenzuela	.35	.17	.03
☐ 67 Dale Murphy	1.00	.50	.10
☐ 68 Wade Boggs	1.25	.60	.12
☐ 69 Rickey Henderson	1.00	.50	.10
☐ 70 Eddie Murray	.75	.35	.07
(Best '80s Player)			
☐ 71 Ron Guidry	.25	.12	.02
☐ 72 Best '80s Catchers	.25	.12	.02
Gary Carter			
Lance Parrish			
Tony Pena			
☐ 73 Best '80s Infielders	.25	.12	.02
Cal Ripken			
Lou Whitaker			
Robin Yount			
☐ 74 Best '80s Outfielders	.25	.12	.02
Pedro Guerrero			
Tim Raines			
Dave Winfield			
☐ 75 Dwight Gooden	1.00	.50	.10

1986 Sportflics Rookies

This set of 50 three-phase "animated" cards features top rookies of 1986 as well as a few outstanding rookies from the past. These "Magic Motion" cards are standard size 2 1/2" by 3 1/2" and feature a distinctive light blue border on the front of the card. Cards were distributed in a light blue box, which also contained 34 trivia cards each measuring 1 3/4" by 2". There are 47 single player cards along with two Tri-Stars and one Big Six.

		MINT	EXC	G-VG
COMPLETE SET (50)		15.00	7.50	1.50
COMMON PLAYER (1-50)		.10	.05	.01
☐ 1 John Kruk		.75	.35	.07
☐ 2 Edwin Correa		.25	.12	.02
☐ 3 Pete Incaviglia		1.25	.60	.12
☐ 4 Dale Sveum		.35	.17	.03
☐ 5 Juan Nieves		.35	.17	.03
☐ 6 Will Clark		2.00	1.00	.20
☐ 7 Wally Joyner		3.00	1.50	.30
☐ 8 Lance McCullers		.20	.10	.02
☐ 9 Scott Bailes		.20	.10	.02
☐ 10 Dan Plesac		.20	.10	.02
☐ 11 Jose Canseco		2.50	1.25	.25
☐ 12 Bobby Witt		.35	.17	.03
☐ 13 Barry Bonds		.75	.35	.07
☐ 14 Andres Thomas		.20	.10	.02
☐ 15 Jim Deshaies		.30	.15	.03
☐ 16 Ruben Sierra		1.75	.85	.17
☐ 17 Steve Lombardozzi		.10	.05	.01
☐ 18 Cory Snyder		1.25	.60	.12
☐ 19 Reggie Williams		.20	.10	.02
☐ 20 Mitch Williams		.20	.10	.02
☐ 21 Glenn Braggs		.45	.22	.04
☐ 22 Danny Tartabull		.75	.35	.07
☐ 23 Charlie Kerfeld		.20	.10	.02
☐ 24 Paul Assenmacher		.15	.07	.01
☐ 25 Robby Thompson		.35	.17	.03
☐ 26 Bobby Bonilla		.35	.17	.03
☐ 27 Andres Galarraga		.75	.35	.07
☐ 28 Billy Jo Robidoux		.15	.07	.01
☐ 29 Bruce Ruffin		.25	.12	.02
☐ 30 Greg Swindell		.45	.22	.04
☐ 31 John Cangelosi		.20	.10	.02
☐ 32 Jim Traber		.15	.07	.01
☐ 33 Russ Morman		.20	.10	.02
☐ 34 Barry Larkin		.75	.35	.07
☐ 35 Todd Worrell		.75	.35	.07
☐ 36 John Cerutti		.25	.12	.02
☐ 37 Mike Kingery		.15	.07	.01
☐ 38 Mark Eichhorn		.30	.15	.03
☐ 39 Scott Bankhead		.15	.07	.01
☐ 40 Bo Jackson		1.00	.50	.10
☐ 41 Greg Mathews		.30	.15	.03
☐ 42 Eric King		.25	.12	.02
☐ 43 Kal Daniels		1.25	.60	.12
☐ 44 Calvin Schiraldi		.15	.07	.01
☐ 45 Mickey Brantley		.30	.15	.03
☐ 46 Tri-Stars		.60	.30	.06
Willie Mays				
Pete Rose				
Fred Lynn				
☐ 47 Tri-Stars		.60	.30	.06
Tom Seaver				
Fern. Valenzuela				
Dwight Gooden				
☐ 48 Big Six		.60	.30	.06
Eddie Murray				
Lou Whitaker				
Dave Righetti				
Steve Sax				
Cal Ripken Jr.				
Darryl Strawberry				
☐ 49 Kevin Mitchell		.40	.20	.04
☐ 50 Mike Diaz		.30	.15	.03

1987 Sportflics

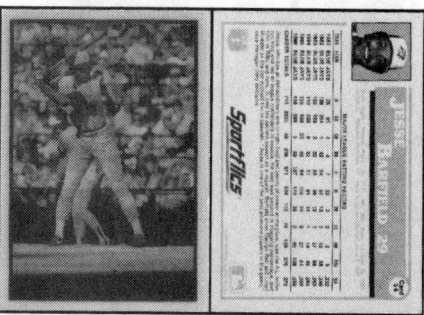

This 200-card set was produced by Sportflics and again features three sequence action pictures on each card. Cards measure 2 1/2" by 3 1/2" and are in full color. Also included with the cards were 136 small team logo and trivia cards. There are 165 individual players, 20 Tri-Stars (the top three players in each league at each position), and 15 other miscellaneous multi-player cards. The cards feature a red border on the front. A full-color face shot of the player is printed on the back of the card. Cards are numbered on the back in the upper right corner. The cards in the factory collated sets are copyrighted 1986, while the cards in the wax packs are copyrighted 1987.

	MINT	EXC	G-VG
COMPLETE SET	35.00	17.50	3.50
COMMON PLAYER	.15	.07	.01

		MINT	EXC	G-VG
☐ 1	Don Mattingly	3.50	1.75	.35
☐ 2	Wade Boggs	2.00	1.00	.20
☐ 3	Dale Murphy	1.00	.50	.10
☐ 4	Rickey Henderson	.75	.35	.07
☐ 5	George Brett	.75	.35	.07
☐ 6	Eddie Murray	.75	.35	.07
☐ 7	Kirby Puckett	.75	.35	.07
☐ 8	Ryne Sandberg	.50	.25	.05
☐ 9	Cal Ripken	.50	.25	.05
☐ 10	Roger Clemens	1.25	.60	.12
☐ 11	Ted Higuera	.35	.17	.03
☐ 12	Steve Sax	.25	.12	.02
☐ 13	Chris Brown	.25	.12	.02
☐ 14	Jesse Barfield	.35	.17	.03
☐ 15	Kent Hrbek	.30	.15	.03
☐ 16	Robin Yount	.40	.20	.04
☐ 17	Glenn Davis	.40	.20	.04
☐ 18	Hubie Brooks	.25	.12	.02
☐ 19	Mike Scott	.35	.17	.03
☐ 20	Darryl Strawberry	.75	.35	.07
☐ 21	Alvin Davis	.25	.12	.02
☐ 22	Eric Davis	1.50	.75	.15
☐ 23	Danny Tartabull	.50	.25	.05
☐ 24A	Cory Snyder ERR '86 ... (photo on back is Pat Tabler)	3.00	1.50	.30
☐ 24B	Cory Snyder COR '87 ...	1.50	.75	.15
☐ 25	Pete Rose	1.25	.60	.12
☐ 26	Wally Joyner	2.00	1.00	.20
☐ 27	Pedro Guerrero	.30	.15	.03
☐ 28	Tom Seaver	.65	.30	.06
☐ 29	Bob Knepper	.20	.10	.02
☐ 30	Mike Schmidt	1.00	.50	.10
☐ 31	Tony Gwynn	.80	.40	.08
☐ 32	Don Slaught	.15	.07	.01
☐ 33	Todd Worrell	.35	.17	.03
☐ 34	Tim Raines	.40	.20	.04
☐ 35	Dave Parker	.30	.15	.03
☐ 36	Bob Ojeda	.20	.10	.02
☐ 37	Pete Incaviglia	.90	.45	.09
☐ 38	Bruce Hurst	.25	.12	.02
☐ 39	Bobby Witt	.35	.17	.03
☐ 40	Steve Garvey	.65	.30	.06
☐ 41	Dave Winfield	.50	.25	.05
☐ 42	Jose Cruz	.20	.10	.02
☐ 43	Orel Hershiser	.25	.12	.02
☐ 44	Reggie Jackson	1.00	.50	.10
☐ 45	Chili Davis	.20	.10	.02
☐ 46	Robby Thompson	.30	.15	.03
☐ 47	Dennis Boyd	.20	.10	.02
☐ 48	Kirk Gibson	.35	.17	.03
☐ 49	Fred Lynn	.25	.12	.02
☐ 50	Gary Carter	.60	.30	.06
☐ 51	George Bell	.50	.25	.05
☐ 52	Pete O'Brien	.25	.12	.02
☐ 53	Ron Darling	.35	.17	.03
☐ 54	Paul Molitor	.30	.15	.03
☐ 55	Mike Pagliarulo	.25	.12	.02
☐ 56	Mike Boddicker	.20	.10	.02
☐ 57	Dave Righetti	.30	.15	.03
☐ 58	Len Dykstra	.25	.12	.02
☐ 59	Mike Witt	.25	.12	.02
☐ 60	Tony Bernazard	.15	.07	.01
☐ 61	John Kruk	.45	.22	.04
☐ 62	Mike Krukow	.20	.10	.02
☐ 63	Sid Fernandez	.35	.17	.03
☐ 64	Gary Gaetti	.35	.17	.03
☐ 65	Vince Coleman	.60	.30	.06
☐ 66	Pat Tabler	.30	.15	.03
☐ 67	Mike Scioscia	.15	.07	.01
☐ 68	Scott Garrelts	.15	.07	.01
☐ 69	Brett Butler	.25	.12	.02
☐ 70	Bill Buckner	.20	.10	.02
☐ 71A	Dennis Rasmussen ERR '86 copyright (photo on back is John Montefusco)	1.00	.50	.10
☐ 71B	Dennis Rasmussen COR '87 copyright (photo with mustache)	.50	.25	.05
☐ 72	Tim Wallach	.30	.15	.03
☐ 73	Bob Horner	.30	.15	.03
☐ 74	Willie McGee	.30	.15	.03
☐ 75	Tri-Stars Don Mattingly Wally Joyner Eddie Murray	1.50	.75	.15
☐ 76	Jesse Orosco	.15	.07	.01
☐ 77	Tri-Stars Todd Worrell Jeff Reardon Lee Smith	.25	.12	.02
☐ 78	Candy Maldonado	.30	.15	.03
☐ 79	Tri-Stars Ozzie Smith Hubie Brooks Shawon Dunston	.25	.12	.02
☐ 80	Tri-Stars George Bell Jose Canseco Jim Rice	.90	.45	.09
☐ 81	Bert Blyleven	.25	.12	.02
☐ 82	Mike Marshall	.25	.12	.02
☐ 83	Ron Guidry	.25	.12	.02
☐ 84	Julio Franco	.20	.10	.02
☐ 85	Willie Wilson	.25	.12	.02
☐ 86	Lee Lacy	.15	.07	.01
☐ 87	Jack Morris	.30	.15	.03
☐ 88	Ray Knight	.25	.12	.02
☐ 89	Phil Bradley	.30	.15	.03
☐ 90	Jose Canseco	2.00	1.00	.20
☐ 91	Gary Ward	.15	.07	.01
☐ 92	Mike Easler	.15	.07	.01
☐ 93	Tony Pena	.25	.12	.02
☐ 94	Dave Smith	.20	.10	.02
☐ 95	Will Clark	1.25	.60	.12
☐ 96	Lloyd Moseby	.20	.10	.02
☐ 97	Jim Rice	.50	.25	.05
☐ 98	Shawon Dunston	.25	.12	.02
☐ 99	Don Sutton	.35	.17	.03
☐ 100	Dwight Gooden	.85	.40	.08
☐ 101	Lance Parrish	.30	.15	.03
☐ 102	Mark Langston	.30	.15	.03
☐ 103	Floyd Youmans	.20	.10	.02
☐ 104	Lee Smith	.25	.12	.02
☐ 105	Willie Hernandez	.25	.12	.02
☐ 106	Doug DeCinces	.20	.10	.02
☐ 107	Ken Schrom	.15	.07	.01
☐ 108	Don Carman	.15	.07	.01
☐ 109	Brook Jacoby	.25	.12	.02
☐ 110	Steve Bedrosian	.30	.15	.03
☐ 111	Tri-Stars Roger Clemens Jack Morris Ted Higuera	.65	.30	.06
☐ 112	Tri-Stars Marty Barrett Tony Bernazard Lou Whitaker	.20	.10	.02
☐ 113	Tri-Stars Cal Ripken Scott Fletcher	.35	.17	.03

Tony Fernandez
☐ 114 Tri-Stars .... 1.00 .50 .10
Wade Boggs
George Brett
Gary Gaetti
☐ 115 Tri-Stars .... .50 .25 .05
Mike Schmidt
Chris Brown
Tim Wallach
☐ 116 Tri-Stars .... .30 .15 .03
Ryne Sandberg
Johnny Ray
Bill Doran
☐ 117 Tri-Stars .... .35 .17 .03
Dave Parker
Tony Gwynn
Kevin Bass
☐ 118 Big Six Rookies .... 3.00 1.50 .30
Ty Gainey
Terry Steinbach
David Clark
Pat Dodson
Phil Lombardi
Benito Santiago
☐ 119 Hi-Lite Tri-Stars .... .50 .25 .05
Dave Righetti
Fernando Valenzuela
Mike Scott
☐ 120 Tri-Stars .... .75 .35 .07
Fernando Valenzuela
Mike Scott
Dwight Gooden
☐ 121 Johnny Ray .... .20 .10 .02
☐ 122 Keith Moreland .... .20 .10 .02
☐ 123 Juan Samuel .... .30 .15 .03
☐ 124 Wally Backman .... .20 .10 .02
☐ 125 Nolan Ryan .... .75 .35 .07
☐ 126 Greg Harris .... .15 .07 .01
☐ 127 Kirk McCaskill .... .20 .10 .02
☐ 128 Dwight Evans .... .30 .15 .03
☐ 129 Rick Rhoden .... .20 .10 .02
☐ 130 Bill Madlock .... .25 .12 .02
☐ 131 Oddibe McDowell .... .30 .15 .03
☐ 132 Darrell Evans .... .25 .12 .02
☐ 133 Keith Hernandez .... .35 .17 .03
☐ 134 Tom Brunansky .... .25 .12 .02
☐ 135 Kevin McReynolds .... .35 .17 .03
☐ 136 Scott Fletcher .... .15 .07 .01
☐ 137 Lou Whitaker .... .25 .12 .02
☐ 138 Carney Lansford .... .20 .10 .02
☐ 139 Andre Dawson .... .35 .17 .03
☐ 140 Carlton Fisk .... .25 .12 .02
☐ 141 Buddy Bell .... .20 .10 .02
☐ 142 Ozzie Smith .... .35 .17 .03
☐ 143 Dan Pasqua .... .25 .12 .02
☐ 144 Kevin Mitchell .... .30 .15 .03
☐ 145 Bret Saberhagen .... .35 .17 .03
☐ 146 Charlie Kerfeld .... .20 .10 .02
☐ 147 Phil Niekro .... .35 .17 .03
☐ 148 John Candelaria .... .20 .10 .02
☐ 149 Rich Gedman .... .20 .10 .02
☐ 150 Fernando Valenzuela ...... .45 .22 .04
☐ 151 Tri-Stars .... .35 .17 .03
Gary Carter
Mike Scioscia
Tony Pena
☐ 152 Tri-Stars .... .65 .30 .06
Tim Raines
Jose Cruz
Vince Coleman
☐ 153 Tri-Stars .... .35 .17 .03
Jesse Barfield
Harold Baines
Dave Winfield
☐ 154 Tri-Stars .... .25 .12 .02
Lance Parrish
Don Slaught
Rich Gedman
☐ 155 Tri-Stars .... .80 .40 .08
Dale Murphy
Kevin McReynolds
Eric Davis
☐ 156 Hi-Lite Tri-Stars .... .50 .25 .05
Don Sutton
Mike Schmidt
Jim Deshaies
☐ 157 Speedburners .... .45 .22 .04
Rickey Henderson
John Cangelosi
Gary Pettis
☐ 158 Big Six Rookies .... 3.00 1.50 .30
Randy Asadoor
Casey Candaele
Kevin Seitzer
Rafael Palmeiro

Tim Pyznarski
Dave Cochrane
☐ 159 Big Six .... 2.50 1.25 .25
Don Mattingly
Rickey Henderson
Roger Clemens
Dale Murphy
Eddie Murray
Dwight Gooden
☐ 160 Roger McDowell .... .25 .12 .02
☐ 161 Brian Downing .... .15 .07 .01
☐ 162 Bill Doran .... .25 .12 .02
☐ 163 Don Baylor .... .25 .12 .02
☐ 164 Alfredo Griffin .... .20 .10 .02
☐ 165 Don Aase .... .15 .07 .01
☐ 166 Glenn Wilson .... .25 .12 .02
☐ 167 Dan Quisenberry .... .20 .10 .02
☐ 168 Frank White .... .20 .10 .02
☐ 169 Cecil Cooper .... .20 .10 .02
☐ 170 Jody Davis .... .25 .12 .02
☐ 171 Harold Baines .... .30 .15 .03
☐ 172 Rob Deer .... .30 .15 .03
☐ 173 John Tudor .... .25 .12 .02
☐ 174 Larry Parrish .... .20 .10 .02
☐ 175 Kevin Bass .... .25 .12 .02
☐ 176 Joe Carter .... .40 .20 .04
☐ 177 Mitch Webster .... .25 .12 .02
☐ 178 Dave Kingman .... .30 .15 .03
☐ 179 Jim Presley .... .40 .20 .04
☐ 180 Mel Hall .... .25 .12 .02
☐ 181 Shane Rawley .... .20 .10 .02
☐ 182 Marty Barrett .... .30 .15 .03
☐ 183 Damaso Garcia .... .15 .07 .01
☐ 184 Bobby Grich .... .20 .10 .02
☐ 185 Leon Durham .... .20 .10 .02
☐ 186 Ozzie Guillen .... .20 .10 .02
☐ 187 Tony Fernandez .... .30 .15 .03
☐ 188 Alan Trammell .... .35 .17 .03
☐ 189 Jim Clancy .... .15 .07 .01
☐ 190 Bo Jackson .... 1.50 .75 .15
☐ 191 Bob Forsch .... .15 .07 .01
☐ 192 John Franco .... .25 .12 .02
☐ 193 Von Hayes .... .30 .15 .03
☐ 194 Tri-Stars .... .25 .12 .02
Don Aase
Dave Righetti
Mark Eichhorn
☐ 195 Tri-Stars .... .50 .25 .05
Keith Hernandez
Will Clark
Glenn Davis
☐ 196 Hi-Lite Tri-Stars .... .60 .30 .06
Roger Clemens
Joe Cowley
Bob Horner
☐ 197 Big Six .... 1.00 .50 .10
George Brett
Hubie Brooks
Tony Gwynn
Ryne Sandberg
Tim Raines
Wade Boggs
☐ 198 Tri-Stars .... .50 .25 .05
Kirby Puckett
Rickey Henderson
Fred Lynn
☐ 199 Speedburners .... 1.00 .50 .10
Tim Raines
Vince Coleman
Eric Davis
☐ 200 Steve Carlton .... .40 .20 .04

1987 Sportflics Dealer Panels

These "Magic Motion" card panels of four were issued only to dealers who were ordering other Sportflics product in quantity. If cut into individual cards, the interior white borders will be slightly narrower than the regular issue Sportflics since the panels of four measure a shade under 4 7/8" by 6 7/8". The cards have a 1986 copyright on the back same as the factory collated sets. Other than the slight difference in size, these cards are essentially styled the same as the regular issue of 1987 Sportflics. This set of sixteen top players was accompanied by the inclusion of four smaller panels

COMMON PLAYER .... .40 .20 .04

☐	1	Texas Rangers	.40	.20	.04
☐	2	New York Mets	.50	.25	.05
☐	3	Cleveland Indians	.40	.20	.04
☐	4	Cincinnati Reds	.50	.25	.05
☐	5	Toronto Blue Jays	.40	.20	.04
☐	6	Philadelphia Phillies	.40	.20	.04
☐	7	New York Yankees	.50	.25	.05
☐	8	Houston Astros	.40	.20	.04
☐	9	Boston Red Sox	.50	.25	.05
☐	10	San Francisco Giants	.40	.20	.04
☐	11	California Angels	.40	.20	.04
☐	12	St. Louis Cardinals	.50	.25	.05
☐	13	Kansas City Royals	.50	.25	.05
☐	14	Los Angeles Dodgers	.50	.25	.05
☐	15	Detroit Tigers	.50	.25	.05
☐	16	San Diego Padres	.40	.20	.04
☐	17	Minnesota Twins	.50	.25	.05
☐	18	Pittsburgh Pirates	.40	.20	.04
☐	19	Milwaukee Brewers	.40	.20	.04
☐	20	Montreal Expos	.40	.20	.04
☐	21	Baltimore Orioles	.50	.25	.05
☐	22	Chicago Cubs	.40	.20	.04
☐	23	Oakland Athletics	.50	.25	.05
☐	24	Atlanta Braves	.40	.20	.04
☐	25	Seattle Mariners	.40	.20	.04
☐	26	Chicago White Sox	.40	.20	.04

of four team logo/team fact cards. The 16 small team cards correspond directly to the 16 players in the sets. The checklist below prices the panels and gives the card number for each player, which is the same as the player's card number in the Sportflics regular set.

	MINT	EXC	G-VG
COMPLETE SET	15.00	7.50	1.50
COMMON PANEL	4.00	2.00	.40

		MINT	EXC	G-VG
☐ 1	Don Mattingly 1 .... Roger Clemens 10 Mike Schmidt 30 Tim Raines 34	6.00	3.00	.60
☐ 2	Wade Boggs 2 .... Eddie Murray 6 Wally Joyner 26 Fern.Valenzuela 150	5.00	2.50	.50
☐ 3	Dale Murphy 3 .... Tony Gwynn 31 Jim Rice 97 Keith Hernandez 133	4.00	2.00	.40
☐ 4	Rickey Henderson 4 .... George Brett 5 Cal Ripken 9 Dwight Gooden 100	4.00	2.00	.40

1987 Sportflics Team Preview

This 26-card set features a card for each Major League team. Each card shows 12 different players on that team via four "Magic Motion" trios. The cards are numbered on the backs. The narrative on the back gives Outlook, Newcomers to Watch, and Summary for each team. The list of players appearing on the front is given at the bottom of the reverse of each card. Cards are standard size, 2 1/2" by 3 1/2". The was distributed as a complete set in its own box along with 26 team logo trivia cards measuring 1 3/4" by 2".

	MINT	EXC	G-VG
COMPLETE SET	7.00	3.50	.70

1987 Sportflics Rookie Packs

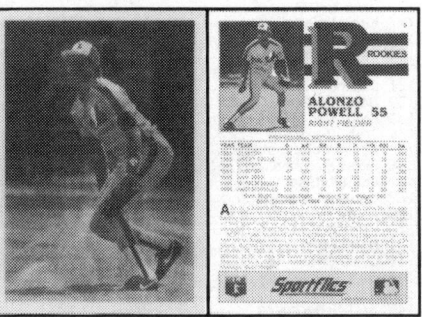

This two pack set consists of 10 "rookie" players and 2 trivia cards. Each of the two different packs had half the set and the outside of the wrapper told which cards were inside. The cards are all 2 1/2" by 3 1/2". The set includes the first major league baseball cards ever of Alonzo Powell, John Smiley, and Brick Smith. Dealers received one rookie pack with every Team Preview set they ordered. The card backs also feature a full-color small photo of the player.

	MINT	EXC	G-VG
COMPLETE SET	7.00	3.50	.70
COMMON PLAYER	.50	.25	.05

		MINT	EXC	G-VG
☐ 1	Terry Steinbach .... (pack two)	1.00	.50	.10
☐ 2	Rafael Palmeiro .... (pack one)	.75	.35	.07
☐ 3	Dave Magadan .... (pack two)	.75	.35	.07
☐ 4	Marvin Freeman .... (pack one)	.50	.25	.05
☐ 5	Brick Smith .... (pack two)	.50	.25	.05
☐ 6	B.J. Surhoff .... (pack one)	.75	.35	.07
☐ 7	John Smiley .... (pack one)	.75	.35	.07
☐ 8	Alonzo Powell .... (pack one)	.50	.25	.05
☐ 9	Benny Santiago .... (pack one)	2.50	1.25	.25
☐ 10	Devon White .... (pack one)	1.50	.75	.15

1987 Sportflics Rookies I

These "Magic Motion" cards were issued as a series of 25 cards packaged in its own complete set box along with 17 trivia cards. Cards are 2 1/2" by 3 1/2." The three front photos show the player in two action poses and one portrait pose. The card backs also provide a full-color photo (1 3/8" by 2 1/4") of the player as well as the usual statistics and biographical notes. The front photos are framed by a wide, round-cornered, red border and have the player's name and uniform number at the bottom.

	MINT	EXC	G-VG
COMPLETE SET (25)	10.00	5.00	1.00
COMMON PLAYER (1-25)	.20	.10	.02

		MINT	EXC	G-VG
☐	1 Eric Bell	.20	.10	.02
☐	2 Chris Bosio	.20	.10	.02
☐	3 Bob Brower	.20	.10	.02
☐	4 Jerry Browne	.20	.10	.02
☐	5 Ellis Burks	.90	.45	.09
☐	6 Casey Candaele	.20	.10	.02
☐	7 Ken Gerhart	.20	.10	.02
☐	8 Mike Greenwell	.90	.45	.09
☐	9 Stan Jefferson	.30	.15	.03
☐	10 Dave Magadan	.60	.30	.06
☐	11 Joe Magrane	.50	.25	.05
☐	12 Fred McGriff	.30	.15	.03
☐	13 Mark McGwire	2.00	1.00	.20
☐	14 Mark McLemore	.20	.10	.02
☐	15 Jeff Musselman	.20	.10	.02
☐	16 Matt Nokes	.90	.45	.09
☐	17 Paul O'Neill	.30	.15	.03
☐	18 Luis Polonia	.30	.15	.03
☐	19 Benny Santiago	1.00	.50	.10
☐	20 Kevin Seitzer	1.50	.75	.15
☐	21 John Smiley	.30	.15	.03
☐	22 Terry Steinbach	.60	.30	.06
☐	23 B.J. Surhoff	.60	.30	.06
☐	24 Devon White	.90	.45	.09
☐	25 Matt Williams	.40	.20	.04

		MINT	EXC	G-VG
☐	26 DeWayne Buice	.30	.15	.03
☐	27 Willie Fraser	.20	.10	.02
☐	28 Billy Ripken	.50	.25	.05
☐	29 Mike Henneman	.30	.15	.03
☐	30 Shawn Hillegas	.20	.10	.02
☐	31 Shane Mack	.30	.15	.03
☐	32 Rafael Palmeiro	.50	.25	.05
☐	33 Mike Jackson	.20	.10	.02
☐	34 Gene Larkin	.30	.15	.03
☐	35 Jimmy Jones	.20	.10	.02
☐	36 Gerald Young	.50	.25	.05
☐	37 Ken Caminiti	.50	.25	.05
☐	38 Sam Horn	1.00	.50	.10
☐	39 David Cone	.30	.15	.03
☐	40 Mike Dunne	.60	.30	.06
☐	41 Ken Williams	.50	.25	.05
☐	42 John Morris	.20	.10	.02
☐	43 Jim Lindeman	.30	.15	.03
☐	44 Todd Benzinger	.50	.25	.05
☐	45 Mike Stanley	.40	.20	.04
☐	46 Les Straker	.30	.15	.03
☐	47 Jeff Robinson	.20	.10	.02
☐	48 Jeff Blauser	.30	.15	.03
☐	49 John Marzano	.50	.25	.05
☐	50 Keith Miller	.30	.15	.03

1988 Sportflics

This 225-card set was produced by Sportflics and again features three sequence action pictures on each card. Cards measure 2 1/2" by 3 1/2" and are in full color. There are 219 individual players, 3 Highlights trios, and 3 Rookie Prospect trio cards. The cards feature a red border on the front. A full-color action picture of the player is printed on the back of the card. Cards are numbered on the back in the lower right corner.

	MINT	EXC	G-VG
COMPLETE SET	35.00	17.50	3.50
COMMON PLAYER	.15	.07	.01

		MINT	EXC	G-VG
☐	1 Don Mattingly	3.00	1.50	.30
☐	2 Tim Raines	.50	.25	.05
☐	3 Andre Dawson	.50	.25	.05
☐	4 George Bell	.40	.20	.04
☐	5 Joe Carter	.30	.15	.03

1987 Sportflics Rookies II

These "Magic Motion" cards were issued as a series of 25 cards packaged in its own complete set box along with 17 trivia cards. Cards are 2 1/2" by 3 1/2." In this second set the card numbering begins with number 26. The three front photos show the player in two action poses and one portrait pose. The card backs also provide a full-color photo (1 3/8" by 2 1/4") of the player as well as the usual statistics and biographical notes. The front photos are framed by a wide, round-cornered, red border and have the player's name and uniform number at the bottom.

	MINT	EXC	G-VG
COMPLETE SET (25)	8.00	4.00	.80
COMMON PLAYER (26-50)	.20	.10	.02

☐ 6	Matt Nokes	1.00	.50	.10	☐ 101	Dave Parker	.30	.15	.03
☐ 7	Dave Winfield	.40	.20	.04	☐ 102	Glenn Davis	.25	.12	.02
☐ 8	Kirby Puckett	.65	.30	.06	☐ 103	Greg Walker	.25	.12	.02
☐ 9	Will Clark	.65	.30	.06	☐ 104	Rick Rhoden	.25	.12	.02
☐ 10	Eric Davis	1.00	.50	.10	☐ 105	Mitch Webster	.15	.07	.01
☐ 11	Rickey Henderson	.65	.30	.06	☐ 106	Lenny Dykstra	.25	.12	.02
☐ 12	Ryne Sandberg	.40	.20	.04	☐ 107	Gene Larkin	.25	.12	.02
☐ 13	Jesse Barfield	.30	.15	.03	☐ 108	Floyd Youmans	.15	.07	.01
☐ 14	Ozzie Guillen	.25	.12	.02	☐ 109	Andy Van Slyke	.25	.12	.02
☐ 15	Bret Saberhagen	.30	.15	.03	☐ 110	Mike Scioscia	.15	.07	.01
☐ 16	Tony Gwynn	.60	.30	.06	☐ 111	Kirk Gibson	.35	.17	.03
☐ 17	Kevin Seitzer	1.25	.60	.12	☐ 112	Kal Daniels	.50	.25	.05
☐ 18	Jack Clark	.35	.17	.03	☐ 113	Ruben Sierra	.60	.30	.06
☐ 19	Danny Tartabull	.40	.20	.04	☐ 114	Sam Horn	.90	.45	.09
☐ 20	Ted Higuera	.30	.15	.03	☐ 115	Ray Knight	.25	.12	.02
☐ 21	Charlie Leibrandt	.15	.07	.01	☐ 116	Jimmy Key	.25	.12	.02
☐ 22	Benny Santiago	.75	.35	.07	☐ 117	Bo Diaz	.15	.07	.01
☐ 23	Fred Lynn	.25	.12	.02	☐ 118	Mike Greenwell	.60	.30	.06
☐ 24	Rob Thompson	.15	.07	.01	☐ 119	Barry Bonds	.45	.22	.04
☐ 25	Alan Trammell	.40	.20	.04	☐ 120	Reggie Jackson	.45	.22	.04
☐ 26	Tony Fernandez	.30	.15	.03	☐ 121	Mike Pagliarulo	.25	.12	.02
☐ 27	Rick Sutcliffe	.30	.15	.03	☐ 122	Tommy John	.25	.12	.02
☐ 28	Gary Carter	.40	.20	.04	☐ 123	Bill Madlock	.25	.12	.02
☐ 29	Cory Snyder	.45	.22	.04	☐ 124	Ken Caminiti	.45	.22	.04
☐ 30	Lou Whitaker	.25	.12	.02	☐ 125	Gary Ward	.15	.07	.01
☐ 31	Keith Hernandez	.35	.17	.03	☐ 126	Candy Maldonado	.25	.12	.02
☐ 32	Mike Witt	.25	.12	.02	☐ 127	Harold Reynolds	.15	.07	.01
☐ 33	Harold Baines	.25	.12	.02	☐ 128	Joe Magrane	.45	.22	.04
☐ 34	Robin Yount	.45	.22	.04	☐ 129	Mike Henneman	.35	.17	.03
☐ 35	Mike Schmidt	.65	.30	.06	☐ 130	Jim Gantner	.15	.07	.01
☐ 36	Dion James	.15	.07	.01	☐ 131	Bobby Bonilla	.25	.12	.02
☐ 37	Tom Candiotti	.15	.07	.01	☐ 132	John Farrell	.35	.17	.03
☐ 38	Tracy Jones	.25	.12	.02	☐ 133	Frank Tanana	.15	.07	.01
☐ 39	Nolan Ryan	.60	.30	.06	☐ 134	Zane Smith	.25	.12	.02
☐ 40	Fernando Valenzuela	.45	.22	.04	☐ 135	Dave Righetti	.30	.15	.03
☐ 41	Vance Law	.15	.07	.01	☐ 136	Rick Reuschel	.25	.12	.02
☐ 42	Roger McDowell	.25	.12	.02	☐ 137	Dwight Evans	.30	.15	.03
☐ 43	Carlton Fisk	.30	.15	.03	☐ 138	Howard Johnson	.35	.17	.03
☐ 44	Scott Garrelts	.15	.07	.01	☐ 139	Terry Leach	.25	.12	.02
☐ 45	Lee Guetterman	.15	.07	.01	☐ 140	Casey Candaele	.25	.12	.02
☐ 46	Mark Langston	.30	.15	.03	☐ 141	Tom Herr	.25	.12	.02
☐ 47	Willie Randolph	.25	.12	.02	☐ 142	Tony Pena	.25	.12	.02
☐ 48	Bill Doran	.25	.12	.02	☐ 143	Lance Parrish	.35	.17	.03
☐ 49	Larry Parrish	.15	.07	.01	☐ 144	Ellis Burks	1.00	.50	.10
☐ 50	Wade Boggs	1.25	.60	.12	☐ 145	Pete O'Brien	.25	.12	.02
☐ 51	Shane Rawley	.15	.07	.01	☐ 146	Mike Boddicker	.25	.12	.02
☐ 52	Alvin Davis	.25	.12	.02	☐ 147	Buddy Bell	.25	.12	.02
☐ 53	Jeff Reardon	.25	.12	.02	☐ 148	Bo Jackson	.50	.25	.05
☐ 54	Jim Presley	.25	.12	.02	☐ 149	Frank White	.25	.12	.02
☐ 55	Kevin Bass	.25	.12	.02	☐ 150	George Brett	.60	.30	.06
☐ 56	Kevin McReynolds	.25	.12	.02	☐ 151	Tim Wallach	.25	.12	.02
☐ 57	B.J. Surhoff	.30	.15	.03	☐ 152	Cal Ripken Jr.	.45	.22	.04
☐ 58	Julio Franco	.25	.12	.02	☐ 153	Brett Butler	.25	.12	.02
☐ 59	Eddie Murray	.60	.30	.06	☐ 154	Gary Gaetti	.35	.17	.03
☐ 60	Jody Davis	.15	.07	.01	☐ 155	Darryl Strawberry	.65	.30	.06
☐ 61	Todd Worrell	.25	.12	.02	☐ 156	Alredo Griffin	.25	.12	.02
☐ 62	Von Hayes	.25	.12	.02	☐ 157	Marty Barrett	.25	.12	.02
☐ 63	Billy Hatcher	.25	.12	.02	☐ 158	Jim Rice	.35	.17	.03
☐ 64	John Kruk	.35	.17	.03	☐ 159	Terry Pendleton	.25	.12	.02
☐ 65	Tom Henke	.25	.12	.02	☐ 160	Orel Hershiser	.25	.12	.02
☐ 66	Mike Scott	.35	.17	.03	☐ 161	Larry Sheets	.25	.12	.02
☐ 67	Vince Coleman	.45	.22	.04	☐ 162	Dave Stewart	.25	.12	.02
☐ 68	Ozzie Smith	.35	.17	.03	☐ 163	Shawon Dunston	.25	.12	.02
☐ 69	Ken Williams	.35	.17	.03	☐ 164	Keith Moreland	.15	.07	.01
☐ 70	Steve Bedrosian	.25	.12	.02	☐ 165	Ken Oberkfell	.15	.07	.01
☐ 71	Luis Polonia	.35	.17	.03	☐ 166	Ivan Calderon	.30	.15	.03
☐ 72	Brook Jacoby	.25	.12	.02	☐ 167	Bob Welch	.25	.12	.02
☐ 73	Ron Darling	.30	.15	.03	☐ 168	Fred McGriff	.35	.17	.03
☐ 74	Lloyd Moseby	.25	.12	.02	☐ 169	Pete Incaviglia	.45	.22	.04
☐ 75	Wally Joyner	.75	.35	.07	☐ 170	Dale Murphy	.65	.30	.06
☐ 76	Dan Quisenberry	.25	.12	.02	☐ 171	Mike Dunne	.45	.22	.04
☐ 77	Scott Fletcher	.15	.07	.01	☐ 172	Chili Davis	.25	.12	.02
☐ 78	Kirk McCaskill	.15	.07	.01	☐ 173	Milt Thompson	.25	.12	.02
☐ 79	Paul Molitor	.30	.15	.03	☐ 174	Terry Steinbach	.35	.17	.03
☐ 80	Mike Aldrete	.25	.12	.02	☐ 175	Oddibe McDowell	.25	.12	.02
☐ 81	Neal Heaton	.15	.07	.01	☐ 176	Jack Morris	.30	.15	.03
☐ 82	Jeffrey Leonard	.25	.12	.02	☐ 177	Sid Fernandez	.25	.12	.02
☐ 83	Dave Magadan	.25	.12	.02	☐ 178	Ken Griffey	.25	.12	.02
☐ 84	Danny Cox	.25	.12	.02	☐ 179	Lee Smith	.25	.12	.02
☐ 85	Lance McCullers	.15	.07	.01	☐ 180	Highlights 1987	.35	.17	.03
☐ 86	Jay Howell	.15	.07	.01		Kirby Puckett			
☐ 87	Charlie Hough	.15	.07	.01		Juan Nieves			
☐ 88	Gene Garber	.15	.07	.01		Mike Schmidt			
☐ 89	Jesse Orosco	.15	.07	.01	☐ 181	Brian Downing	.15	.07	.01
☐ 90	Don Robinson	.15	.07	.01	☐ 182	Andres Galarraga	.30	.15	.03
☐ 91	Willie McGee	.30	.15	.03	☐ 183	Rob Deer	.25	.12	.02
☐ 92	Bert Blyleven	.25	.12	.02	☐ 184	Greg Brock	.15	.07	.01
☐ 93	Phil Bradley	.25	.12	.02	☐ 185	Doug DeCinces	.15	.07	.01
☐ 94	Terry Kennedy	.15	.07	.01	☐ 186	Johnny Ray	.15	.07	.01
☐ 95	Kent Hrbek	.30	.15	.03	☐ 187	Hubie Brooks	.15	.07	.01
☐ 96	Juan Samuel	.30	.15	.03	☐ 188	Darrell Evans	.25	.12	.02
☐ 97	Pedro Guerrero	.35	.17	.03	☐ 189	Mel Hall	.25	.12	.02
☐ 98	Sid Bream	.15	.07	.01	☐ 190	Jim Deshaies	.15	.07	.01
☐ 99	Devon White	.40	.20	.04	☐ 191	Dan Plesac	.25	.12	.02
☐ 100	Mark McGwire	1.00	.50	.10	☐ 192	Willie Wilson	.25	.12	.02

		MINT	EXC	G-VG
☐ 193	Mike LaValliere	.15	.07	.01
☐ 194	Tom Brunansky	.25	.12	.02
☐ 195	John Franco	.25	.12	.02
☐ 196	Frank Viola	.30	.15	.03
☐ 197	Bruce Hurst	.25	.12	.02
☐ 198	John Tudor	.25	.12	.02
☐ 199	Bob Forsch	.15	.07	.01
☐ 200	Dwight Gooden	.75	.35	.07
☐ 201	Jose Canseco	.75	.35	.07
☐ 202	Carney Lansford	.25	.12	.02
☐ 203	Kelly Downs	.15	.07	.01
☐ 204	Glenn Wilson	.25	.12	.02
☐ 205	Pat Tabler	.25	.12	.02
☐ 206	Mike Davis	.15	.07	.01
☐ 207	Roger Clemens	.75	.35	.07
☐ 208	Dave Smith	.25	.12	.02
☐ 209	Curt Young	.25	.12	.02
☐ 210	Mark Eichhorn	.25	.12	.02
☐ 211	Juan Nieves	.25	.12	.02
☐ 212	Bob Boone	.15	.07	.01
☐ 213	Don Sutton	.35	.17	.03
☐ 214	Willie Upshaw	.15	.07	.01
☐ 215	Jim Clancy	.15	.07	.01
☐ 216	Bill Ripken	.35	.17	.03
☐ 217	Ozzie Virgil	.15	.07	.01
☐ 218	Dave Concepcion	.25	.12	.02
☐ 219	Alan Ashby	.15	.07	.01
☐ 220	Mike Marshall	.25	.12	.02
☐ 221	Highlights 1987 Mark McGwire Paul Molitor Vince Coleman	.75	.35	.07
☐ 222	Highlights 1987 Benito Santiago Steve Bedrosian Don Mattingly	.75	.35	.07
☐ 223	Rookie Prospects Shawn Abner Jay Buhner Gary Thurman	1.00	.50	.10
☐ 224	Rookie Prospects Tim Crews Vincente Palacios John Davis	.60	.30	.06
☐ 225	Rookie Prospects Jody Reed Jeff Treadway Keith Miller	.80	.40	.08

		MINT	EXC	G-VG
	COMMON PANEL	.40	.20	.04
	COMMON PLAYER (1-11) DP	.20	.10	.02
	COMMON PLAYER (12-33)	.20	.10	.02
☐ 1	George Brett DP	.60	.30	.06
☐ 2	George Foster DP	.20	.10	.02
☐ 3	Ben Oglivie DP	.20	.10	.02
☐ 4	Steve Garvey DP	.60	.30	.06
☐ 5	Reggie Jackson DP	.75	.35	.07
☐ 6	Bill Buckner DP	.20	.10	.02
☐ 7	Jim Rice DP	.30	.15	.03
☐ 8	Mike Schmidt DP	.60	.30	.06
☐ 9	Rod Carew DP	.50	.25	.05
☐ 10	Dave Parker DP	.20	.10	.02
☐ 11	Pete Rose DP	1.00	.50	.10
☐ 12	Garry Templeton	.20	.10	.02
☐ 13	Rick Burleson	.20	.10	.02
☐ 14	Dave Kingman	.20	.10	.02
☐ 15	Eddie Murray	2.00	1.00	.20
☐ 16	Don Sutton	.60	.30	.06
☐ 17	Dusty Baker	.20	.10	.02
☐ 18	Jack Clark	.50	.25	.05
☐ 19	Dave Winfield	1.00	.50	.10
☐ 20	Johnny Bench	.80	.40	.08
☐ 21	Lee Mazzilli	.20	.10	.02
☐ 22	Al Oliver	.30	.15	.03
☐ 23	Jerry Mumphrey	.20	.10	.02
☐ 24	Tony Armas	.30	.15	.03
☐ 25	Fred Lynn	.40	.20	.04
☐ 26	Ron LeFlore	.40	.20	.04
☐ 27	Steve Kemp	.50	.25	.05
☐ 28	Rickey Henderson	2.00	1.00	.20
☐ 29	John Castino	.20	.10	.02
☐ 30	Cecil Cooper	.30	.15	.03
☐ 31	Bruce Bochte	.20	.10	.02
☐ 32	Joe Charboneau	.20	.10	.02
☐ 33	Chet Lemon	.20	.10	.02

1982 Squirt

The cards in this 22 card set measure 2 1/2" by 3 1/2". Although the 1982 "Exclusive Limited Edition" was prepared for Squirt by Topps, the format and pictures are completely different from the regular Topps cards of this year. Each color picture is obliquely cut and the word Squirt is printed in red in the top left corner. The cards are numbered 1 through 22 and the reverses are yellow and black on white. The cards were issued on four types of panels: (1) yellow attachment card at top with picture card in center and scratch-off game at bottom; (2) yellow attachment card at top with scratch-off game in center and picture card at bottom; (3) white attachment card at top with "Collect all 22" panel in center and picture card at bottom; (4) two card panel with attachment card at top. The two card panels have parallel cards; that is, numbers 1 and 12 together, numbers 2 and 13 together, etc. Two card panels have a value equal to the sum of the individual cards on the panel.

	MINT	EXC	G-VG
COMPLETE SET	5.00	2.50	.50
COMMON PLAYER	.15	.07	.01

1981 Squirt

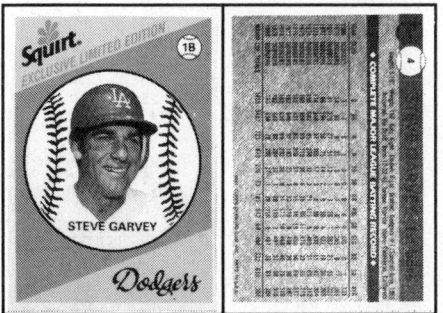

The cards in this 22 panel set consist of 33 different individual cards, each measuring 2 1/2" by 3 1/2" while the panels measure 2 1/2" by 10 1/2" as the 1981 Squirt cards were issued individually as well as in two card panels. Cards numbered 1-11 appear twice, whereas cards 12-33 appear only once in the 22 panel set. The pattern for pairings was 1/12 and 1/23, 2/13 and 2/24, 3/14 and 3/25, and so forth on up to 11/22 and 11/33. Two card panels have a value equal to the sum of the individual cards on the panel. Supposedly panels 4/15, 5/27, and 6/28 are more difficult to find than the others.

	MINT	EXC	G-VG
COMPLETE PANEL SET	15.00	7.50	1.50
COMPLETE IND. SET	9.00	4.50	.90

			NRMT	VG-E	GOOD
☐	1	Cecil Cooper	.20	.10	.02
☐	2	Jerry Remy	.15	.07	.01
☐	3	George Brett	.75	.35	.07
☐	4	Alan Trammell	.35	.17	.03
☐	5	Reggie Jackson	.75	.35	.07
☐	6	Kirk Gibson	.35	.17	.03
☐	7	Dave Winfield	.45	.22	.04
☐	8	Carlton Fisk	.25	.12	.02
☐	9	Ron Guidry	.25	.12	.02
☐	10	Dennis Leonard	.15	.07	.01
☐	11	Rollie Fingers	.25	.12	.02
☐	12	Pete Rose	1.00	.50	.10
☐	13	Phil Garner	.15	.07	.01
☐	14	Mike Schmidt	.75	.35	.07
☐	15	Dave Concepcion	.15	.07	.01
☐	16	George Hendrick	.15	.07	.01
☐	17	Andre Dawson	.35	.17	.03
☐	18	George Foster	.25	.12	.02
☐	19	Gary Carter	.45	.22	.04
☐	20	Fernando Valenzuela	.35	.17	.03
☐	21	Tom Seaver	.50	.25	.05
☐	22	Bruce Sutter	.25	.12	.02

1976 SSPC

The cards in this 630 card set measure 2 1/2" by 3 1/2". The 1976 "Pure Card" set issued by TCMA derives its name from the lack of borders, logos, signatures, etc., which often clutter up the picture areas of some baseball sets. It differs from other sets produced by this company in that it cannot be re-issued due to an agreement entered into by the manufacturer. Thus, while not technically a legitimate issue, it is significant because it cannot be reprinted, unlike other collector issues. There are no scarcities known. The cards are numbered in team groups, i.e., Atlanta (1-21), Cincinnati (22-46), Houston (47- 65), Los Angeles (66-91), San Francisco (92-113), San Diego (114- 133), Chicago White Sox (134-158), Kansas City (159-195), California (186-204), Minnesota (205-225), Milwaukee (226-251), Texas (252-273), St. Louis (274-300), Chicago Cubs (301-321), Montreal (322-351), Detroit (352-373), Baltimore (374-401), Boston (402-424), New York Yankees (425-455), Philadelphia (456- 477), Oakland (478-503), Cleveland (504-532), New York Mets (533- 560), and Pittsburgh (561-586). The rest of the numbers are filled in with checklists (589-595), miscellaneous players, and a heavy dose of coaches.

	NRMT	VG-E	GOOD
COMPLETE SET	60.00	30.00	6.00
COMMON PLAYER (1-630)	.10	.05	.01

☐	1	Buzz Capra	.15	.05	.01
☐	2	Tom House	.15	.07	.01
☐	3	Max Leon	.10	.05	.01
☐	4	Carl Morton	.10	.05	.01
☐	5	Phil Niekro	2.00	1.00	.20
☐	6	Mike Thompson	.10	.05	.01
☐	7	Elias Sosa	.10	.05	.01

☐	8	Larvell Blanks	.10	.05	.01
☐	9	Darrell Evans	.40	.20	.04
☐	10	Rod Gilbreath	.10	.05	.01
☐	11	Mike Lum	.10	.05	.01
☐	12	Craig Robinson	.10	.05	.01
☐	13	Earl Williams	.10	.05	.01
☐	14	Vic Correll	.10	.05	.01
☐	15	Biff Pocoroba	.10	.05	.01
☐	16	Dusty Baker	.25	.12	.02
☐	17	Ralph Garr	.15	.07	.01
☐	18	Cito Gaston	.10	.05	.01
☐	19	Dave May	.10	.05	.01
☐	20	Rowland Office	.10	.05	.01
☐	21	Bob Beall	.10	.05	.01
☐	22	Sparky Anderson MG	.25	.12	.02
☐	23	Jack Billingham	.10	.05	.01
☐	24	Pedro Borbon	.10	.05	.01
☐	25	Clay Carroll	.10	.05	.01
☐	26	Pat Darcy	.10	.05	.01
☐	27	Don Gullett	.15	.07	.01
☐	28	Clay Kirby	.10	.05	.01
☐	29	Gary Nolan	.10	.05	.01
☐	30	Fred Norman	.10	.05	.01
☐	31	Johnny Bench	4.00	2.00	.40
☐	32	Bill Plummer	.10	.05	.01
☐	33	Darrel Chaney	.10	.05	.01
☐	34	Dave Concepcion	.25	.12	.02
☐	35	Terry Crowley	.10	.05	.01
☐	36	Dan Driessen	.15	.07	.01
☐	37	Doug Flynn	.10	.05	.01
☐	38	Joe Morgan	2.00	1.00	.20
☐	39	Tony Perez	.75	.35	.07
☐	40	Ken Griffey	.25	.12	.02
☐	41	Pete Rose	10.00	5.00	1.00
☐	42	Ed Armbrister	.10	.05	.01
☐	43	John Vukovich	.10	.05	.01
☐	44	George Foster	.90	.45	.09
☐	45	Cesar Geronimo	.10	.05	.01
☐	46	Merv Rettenmund	.10	.05	.01
☐	47	Jim Crawford	.10	.05	.01
☐	48	Ken Forsch	.10	.05	.01
☐	49	Doug Konieczny	.10	.05	.01
☐	50	Joe Niekro	.35	.17	.03
☐	51	Cliff Johnson	.10	.05	.01
☐	52	Skip Jutze	.10	.05	.01
☐	53	Milt May	.10	.05	.01
☐	54	Rob Andrews	.10	.05	.01
☐	55	Ken Boswell	.10	.05	.01
☐	56	Tommy Helms	.10	.05	.01
☐	57	Roger Metzger	.10	.05	.01
☐	58	Larry Milbourne	.10	.05	.01
☐	59	Doug Rader	.15	.07	.01
☐	60	Bob Watson	.15	.07	.01
☐	61	Enos Cabell	.10	.05	.01
☐	62	Jose Cruz	.40	.20	.04
☐	63	Cesar Cedeno	.25	.12	.02
☐	64	Greg Gross	.10	.05	.01
☐	65	Wilbur Howard	.10	.05	.01
☐	66	Al Downing	.10	.05	.01
☐	67	Burt Hooton	.10	.05	.01
☐	68	Charlie Hough	.25	.12	.02
☐	69	Tommy John	.75	.35	.07
☐	70	Andy Messersmith	.15	.07	.01
☐	71	Doug Rau	.10	.05	.01
☐	72	Rick Rhoden	.25	.12	.02
☐	73	Don Sutton	1.25	.60	.12
☐	74	Rick Auerbach	.10	.05	.01
☐	75	Ron Cey	.50	.25	.05
☐	76	Ivan DeJesus	.10	.05	.01
☐	77	Steve Garvey	4.00	2.00	.40
☐	78	Lee Lacy	.15	.07	.01
☐	79	Dave Lopes	.25	.12	.02
☐	80	Ken McMullen	.10	.05	.01
☐	81	Joe Ferguson	.10	.05	.01
☐	82	Paul Powell	.10	.05	.01
☐	83	Steve Yeager	.10	.05	.01
☐	84	Willie Crawford	.10	.05	.01
☐	85	Henry Cruz	.10	.05	.01
☐	86	Charlie Manuel	.10	.05	.01
☐	87	Manny Mota	.15	.07	.01
☐	88	Tom Paciorek	.10	.05	.01
☐	89	Jim Wynn	.15	.07	.01
☐	90	Walt Alston MG	.60	.30	.06
☐	91	Bill Buckner	.50	.25	.05
☐	92	Jim Barr	.10	.05	.01
☐	93	Mike Caldwell	.15	.07	.01
☐	94	John D'Acquisto	.10	.05	.01
☐	95	Dave Heaverlo	.10	.05	.01
☐	96	Gary Lavelle	.10	.05	.01
☐	97	John Montefusco	.15	.07	.01
☐	98	Charlie Williams	.10	.05	.01
☐	99	Chris Arnold	.10	.05	.01
☐	100	Marc Hill	.10	.05	.01
☐	101	Dave Rader	.10	.05	.01
☐	102	Bruce Miller	.10	.05	.01

☐ 103	Willie Montanez	.10	.05	.01
☐ 104	Steve Ontiveros	.10	.05	.01
☐ 105	Chris Speier	.10	.05	.01
☐ 106	Derrel Thomas	.10	.05	.01
☐ 107	Gary Thomasson	.10	.05	.01
☐ 108	Glenn Adams	.10	.05	.01
☐ 109	Von Joshua	.10	.05	.01
☐ 110	Gary Matthews	.20	.10	.02
☐ 111	Bobby Murcer	.40	.20	.04
☐ 112	Horace Speed	.10	.05	.01
☐ 113	Wes Westrum MG	.10	.05	.01
☐ 114	Rich Folkers	.10	.05	.01
☐ 115	Alan Foster	.10	.05	.01
☐ 116	Dave Freisleben	.10	.05	.01
☐ 117	Dan Frisella	.10	.05	.01
☐ 118	Randy Jones	.20	.10	.02
☐ 119	Dan Spillner	.10	.05	.01
☐ 120	Larry Hardy	.10	.05	.01
☐ 121	Randy Hundley	.10	.05	.01
☐ 122	Fred Kendall	.10	.05	.01
☐ 123	John McNamara MG	.15	.07	.01
☐ 124	Tito Fuentes	.10	.05	.01
☐ 125	Enzo Hernandez	.10	.05	.01
☐ 126	Steve Huntz	.10	.05	.01
☐ 127	Mike Ivie	.10	.05	.01
☐ 128	Hector Torres	.10	.05	.01
☐ 129	Ted Kubiak	.10	.05	.01
☐ 130	John Grubb	.10	.05	.01
☐ 131	John Scott	.10	.05	.01
☐ 132	Bob Tolan	.10	.05	.01
☐ 133	Dave Winfield	3.50	1.75	.35
☐ 134	Bill Gogolewski	.10	.05	.01
☐ 135	Dan Osborn	.10	.05	.01
☐ 136	Jim Kaat	.60	.30	.06
☐ 137	Claude Osteen	.15	.07	.01
☐ 138	Cecil Upshaw	.10	.05	.01
☐ 139	Wilbur Wood	.15	.07	.01
☐ 140	Lloyd Allen	.10	.05	.01
☐ 141	Brian Downing	.25	.12	.02
☐ 142	Jim Essian	.10	.05	.01
☐ 143	Bucky Dent	.25	.12	.02
☐ 144	Jorge Orta	.10	.05	.01
☐ 145	Lee Richard	.10	.05	.01
☐ 146	Bill Stein	.10	.05	.01
☐ 147	Ken Henderson	.10	.05	.01
☐ 148	Carlos May	.10	.05	.01
☐ 149	Nyls Nyman	.10	.05	.01
☐ 150	Bob Coluccio	.10	.05	.01
☐ 151	Chuck Tanner MG	.15	.07	.01
☐ 152	Pat Kelly	.10	.05	.01
☐ 153	Jerry Hairston	.10	.05	.01
☐ 154	Pete Varney	.10	.05	.01
☐ 155	Bill Melton	.10	.05	.01
☐ 156	Rich Gossage	.90	.45	.09
☐ 157	Terry Forster	.25	.12	.02
☐ 158	Rich Hinton	.10	.05	.01
☐ 159	Nelson Briles	.15	.07	.01
☐ 160	Al Fitzmorris	.10	.05	.01
☐ 161	Steve Mingori	.10	.05	.01
☐ 162	Marty Pattin	.10	.05	.01
☐ 163	Paul Splittorff	.15	.07	.01
☐ 164	Dennis Leonard	.20	.10	.02
☐ 165	Buck Martinez	.10	.05	.01
☐ 166	Bob Stinson	.10	.05	.01
☐ 167	George Brett	7.00	3.50	.70
☐ 168	Harmon Killebrew	2.50	1.25	.25
☐ 169	John Mayberry	.15	.07	.01
☐ 170	Fred Patek	.10	.05	.01
☐ 171	Cookie Rojas	.10	.05	.01
☐ 172	Rodney Scott	.10	.05	.01
☐ 173	Tony Solaita	.10	.05	.01
☐ 174	Frank White	.30	.15	.03
☐ 175	Al Cowens	.15	.07	.01
☐ 176	Hal McRae	.20	.10	.02
☐ 177	Amos Otis	.25	.12	.02
☐ 178	Vada Pinson	.35	.17	.03
☐ 179	Jim Wohlford	.10	.05	.01
☐ 180	Doug Bird	.10	.05	.01
☐ 181	Mark Littell	.10	.05	.01
☐ 182	Bob McClure	.10	.05	.01
☐ 183	Steve Busby	.15	.07	.01
☐ 184	Fran Healy	.10	.05	.01
☐ 185	Whitey Herzog MG	.20	.10	.02
☐ 186	Andy Hassler	.10	.05	.01
☐ 187	Nolan Ryan	4.00	2.00	.40
☐ 188	Bill Singer	.10	.05	.01
☐ 189	Frank Tanana	.15	.07	.01
☐ 190	Ed Figueroa	.10	.05	.01
☐ 191	Dave Collins	.15	.07	.01
☐ 192	Dick Williams	.15	.07	.01
☐ 193	Ellie Rodriguez	.10	.05	.01
☐ 194	Dave Chalk	.10	.05	.01
☐ 195	Winston Llenas	.10	.05	.01
☐ 196	Rudy Meoli	.10	.05	.01
☐ 197	Orlando Ramirez	.10	.05	.01
☐ 198	Jerry Remy	.10	.05	.01
☐ 199	Billy Smith	.10	.05	.01
☐ 200	Bruce Bochte	.15	.07	.01
☐ 201	Joe Lahoud	.10	.05	.01
☐ 202	Morris Nettles	.10	.05	.01
☐ 203	Mickey Rivers	.25	.12	.02
☐ 204	Leroy Stanton	.10	.05	.01
☐ 205	Vic Albury	.10	.05	.01
☐ 206	Tom Burgmeier	.10	.05	.01
☐ 207	Bill Butler	.10	.05	.01
☐ 208	Bill Campbell	.10	.05	.01
☐ 209	Ray Corbin	.10	.05	.01
☐ 210	Joe Decker	.10	.05	.01
☐ 211	Jim Hughes	.10	.05	.01
☐ 212	Ed Bane (photo actually Mike Pazik)	.10	.05	.01
☐ 213	Glenn Borgman	.10	.05	.01
☐ 214	Rod Carew	4.00	2.00	.40
☐ 215	Steve Brye	.10	.05	.01
☐ 216	Dan Ford	.10	.05	.01
☐ 217	Tony Oliva	.75	.35	.07
☐ 218	Dave Goltz	.10	.05	.01
☐ 219	Bert Blyleven	.45	.22	.04
☐ 220	Larry Hisle	.15	.07	.01
☐ 221	Steve Braun	.10	.05	.01
☐ 222	Jerry Terrell	.10	.05	.01
☐ 223	Eric Soderholm	.10	.05	.01
☐ 224	Phil Roof	.10	.05	.01
☐ 225	Danny Thompson	.10	.05	.01
☐ 226	Jim Colborn	.10	.05	.01
☐ 227	Tom Murphy	.10	.05	.01
☐ 228	Ed Rodriquez	.10	.05	.01
☐ 229	Jim Slaton	.10	.05	.01
☐ 230	Ed Sprague	.10	.05	.01
☐ 231	Charlie Moore	.10	.05	.01
☐ 232	Darrell Porter	.15	.07	.01
☐ 233	Kurt Bevacqua	.10	.05	.01
☐ 234	Pedro Garcia	.10	.05	.01
☐ 235	Mike Hegan	.10	.05	.01
☐ 236	Don Money	.10	.05	.01
☐ 237	George Scott	.10	.05	.01
☐ 238	Robin Yount	3.00	1.50	.30
☐ 239	Hank Aaron	6.00	3.00	.60
☐ 240	Rob Ellis	.10	.05	.01
☐ 241	Sixto Lezcano	.15	.07	.01
☐ 242	Bob Mitchell	.10	.05	.01
☐ 243	Gorman Thomas	.35	.17	.03
☐ 244	Bill Travers	.10	.05	.01
☐ 245	Pete Broberg	.10	.05	.01
☐ 246	Bill Sharp	.10	.05	.01
☐ 247	Bobby Darwin	.10	.05	.01
☐ 248	Rick Austin (photo actually Larry Anderson)	.10	.05	.01
☐ 249	Larry Anderson (photo actually Rick Austin)	.10	.05	.01
☐ 250	Tom Bianco	.10	.05	.01
☐ 251	L. Currence	.10	.05	.01
☐ 252	Steve Foucault	.10	.05	.01
☐ 253	Bill Hands	.10	.05	.01
☐ 254	Steve Hargan	.10	.05	.01
☐ 255	Fergie Jenkins	.60	.30	.06
☐ 256	Bob Sheldon	.10	.05	.01
☐ 257	Jim Umbarger	.10	.05	.01
☐ 258	Clyde Wright	.10	.05	.01
☐ 259	Bill Fahey	.10	.05	.01
☐ 260	Jim Sundberg	.15	.07	.01
☐ 261	Leo Cardenas	.10	.05	.01
☐ 262	Jim Fregosi	.20	.10	.02
☐ 263	Mike Hargrove	.15	.07	.01
☐ 264	Toby Harrah	.20	.10	.02
☐ 265	Roy Howell	.10	.05	.01
☐ 266	Lenny Randle	.10	.05	.01
☐ 267	Roy Smalley	.20	.10	.02
☐ 268	Jim Spencer	.10	.05	.01
☐ 269	Jeff Burroughs	.15	.07	.01
☐ 270	Tom Grieve	.15	.07	.01
☐ 271	Joe Lovitto	.10	.05	.01
☐ 272	Frank Lucchesi MG	.10	.05	.01
☐ 273	Dave Nelson	.10	.05	.01
☐ 274	Ted Simmons	.60	.30	.06
☐ 275	Lou Brock	3.00	1.50	.30
☐ 276	Ron Fairly	.15	.07	.01
☐ 277	Bake McBride	.15	.07	.01
☐ 278	Reggie Smith	.25	.12	.02
☐ 279	Willie Davis	.15	.07	.01
☐ 280	Ken Reitz	.10	.05	.01
☐ 281	Buddy Bradford	.10	.05	.01
☐ 282	Luis Melendez	.10	.05	.01
☐ 283	Mike Tyson	.10	.05	.01
☐ 284	Ted Sizemore	.10	.05	.01
☐ 285	Mario Guerrero	.10	.05	.01
☐ 286	Larry Lintz	.10	.05	.01

☐ 287	Ken Rudolph	.10	.05	.01
☐ 288	Dick Billings	.10	.05	.01
☐ 289	Jerry Mumphrey	.10	.05	.01
☐ 290	Mike Wallace	.10	.05	.01
☐ 291	Al Hrabosky	.15	.07	.01
☐ 292	Ken Reynolds	.10	.05	.01
☐ 293	Mike Garman	.10	.05	.01
☐ 294	Bob Forsch	.15	.07	.01
☐ 295	John Denny	.20	.10	.02
☐ 296	Harry Rasmussen	.10	.05	.01
☐ 297	Lynn McGlothen	.10	.05	.01
☐ 298	Mike Barlow	.10	.05	.01
☐ 299	Greg Terlecky	.10	.05	.01
☐ 300	Red Schoendienst MG	.15	.07	.01
☐ 301	Rick Reuschel	.25	.12	.02
☐ 302	Steve Stone	.20	.10	.02
☐ 303	Bill Bonham	.10	.05	.01
☐ 304	Oscar Zamora	.10	.05	.01
☐ 305	Ken Frailing	.10	.05	.01
☐ 306	Milt Wilcox	.10	.05	.01
☐ 307	Darold Knowles	.10	.05	.01
☐ 308	Jim Marshall	.10	.05	.01
☐ 309	Bill Madlock	.90	.45	.09
☐ 310	Jose Cardenal	.10	.05	.01
☐ 311	Rick Monday	.15	.07	.01
☐ 312	Jerry Morales	.10	.05	.01
☐ 313	Tim Hosley	.10	.05	.01
☐ 314	Gene Hiser	.10	.05	.01
☐ 315	Don Kessinger	.15	.07	.01
☐ 316	Manny Trillo	.15	.07	.01
☐ 317	Pete LaCock	.10	.05	.01
☐ 318	George Mitterwald	.10	.05	.01
☐ 319	Steve Swisher	.10	.05	.01
☐ 320	Rob Sperring	.10	.05	.01
☐ 321	Vic Harris	.10	.05	.01
☐ 322	Ron Dunn	.10	.05	.01
☐ 323	Jose Morales	.10	.05	.01
☐ 324	Pete Mackanin	.10	.05	.01
☐ 325	Jim Cox	.10	.05	.01
☐ 326	Larry Parrish	.40	.20	.04
☐ 327	Mike Jorgensen	.10	.05	.01
☐ 328	Tim Foli	.10	.05	.01
☐ 329	Hal Breeden	.10	.05	.01
☐ 330	Nate Colbert	.10	.05	.01
☐ 331	Pepe Frias	.10	.05	.01
☐ 332	Pat Scanlon	.10	.05	.01
☐ 333	Bob Bailey	.10	.05	.01
☐ 334	Gary Carter	4.50	2.25	.45
☐ 335	Pepe Mangual	.10	.05	.01
☐ 336	Larry Biittner	.10	.05	.01
☐ 337	Jim Lyttle	.10	.05	.01
☐ 338	Gary Roenicke	.15	.07	.01
☐ 339	Tony Scott	.10	.05	.01
☐ 340	Jerry White	.10	.05	.01
☐ 341	Jim Dwyer	.10	.05	.01
☐ 342	Ellis Valentine	.10	.05	.01
☐ 343	Fred Scherman	.10	.05	.01
☐ 344	Dennis Blair	.10	.05	.01
☐ 345	Woodie Fryman	.10	.05	.01
☐ 346	Chuck Taylor	.10	.05	.01
☐ 347	Dan Warthen	.10	.05	.01
☐ 348	Dan Carrithers	.10	.05	.01
☐ 349	Steve Rogers	.20	.10	.02
☐ 350	Dale Murray	.10	.05	.01
☐ 351	Duke Snider	2.00	1.00	.20
☐ 352	Ralph Houk MG	.15	.07	.01
☐ 353	John Hiller	.15	.07	.01
☐ 354	Mickey Lolich	.30	.15	.03
☐ 355	Dave Lemanczyk	.10	.05	.01
☐ 356	Lerrin LaGrow	.10	.05	.01
☐ 357	Fred Arroyo	.10	.05	.01
☐ 358	Joe Coleman	.10	.05	.01
☐ 359	Ben Oglivie	.20	.10	.02
☐ 360	Willie Horton	.15	.07	.01
☐ 361	John Knox	.10	.05	.01
☐ 362	Leon Roberts	.10	.05	.01
☐ 363	Ron LeFlore	.15	.07	.01
☐ 364	G. Sutherland	.10	.05	.01
☐ 365	Dan Meyer	.10	.05	.01
☐ 366	Aurelio Rodriguez	.10	.05	.01
☐ 367	Tom Veryzer	.10	.05	.01
☐ 368	Jack Pierce	.10	.05	.01
☐ 369	Gene Michael	.15	.07	.01
☐ 370	Billy Baldwin	.10	.05	.01
☐ 371	Gates Brown	.15	.07	.01
☐ 372	Mickey Stanley	.15	.07	.01
☐ 373	Terry Humphrey	.10	.05	.01
☐ 374	Doyle Alexander	.20	.10	.02
☐ 375	Mike Cuellar	.15	.07	.01
☐ 376	Wayne Garland	.10	.05	.01
☐ 377	Ross Grimsley	.10	.05	.01
☐ 378	Grant Jackson	.10	.05	.01
☐ 379	Dyar Miller	.10	.05	.01
☐ 380	Jim Palmer	3.00	1.50	.30
☐ 381	Mike Torrez	.15	.07	.01
☐ 382	Mike Willis	.10	.05	.01
☐ 383	Dave Duncan	.10	.05	.01
☐ 384	Ellie Hendricks	.10	.05	.01
☐ 385	Jim Hutto	.10	.05	.01
☐ 386	Bob Bailor	.10	.05	.01
☐ 387	Doug DeCinces	.40	.20	.04
☐ 388	Bob Grich	.30	.15	.03
☐ 389	Lee May	.20	.10	.02
☐ 390	Tony Muser	.10	.05	.01
☐ 391	Tim Nordbrook	.10	.05	.01
☐ 392	Brooks Robinson	3.50	1.75	.35
☐ 393	Royle Stillman	.10	.05	.01
☐ 394	Don Baylor	.40	.20	.04
☐ 395	Paul Blair	.15	.07	.01
☐ 396	Al Bumbry	.10	.05	.01
☐ 397	Larry Harlow	.10	.05	.01
☐ 398	Tommy Davis	.20	.10	.02
☐ 399	Jim Northrup	.15	.07	.01
☐ 400	Ken Singleton	.35	.17	.03
☐ 401	Tom Shopay	.10	.05	.01
☐ 402	Fred Lynn	1.25	.60	.12
☐ 403	Carlton Fisk	1.00	.50	.10
☐ 404	Cecil Cooper	.60	.30	.06
☐ 405	Jim Rice	3.00	1.50	.30
☐ 406	Juan Beniquez	.15	.07	.01
☐ 407	Denny Doyle	.10	.05	.01
☐ 408	Dwight Evans	.90	.45	.09
☐ 409	Carl Yastrzemski	7.00	3.50	.70
☐ 410	Rick Burleson	.15	.07	.01
☐ 411	Bernie Carbo	.10	.05	.01
☐ 412	Doug Griffin	.10	.05	.01
☐ 413	Rico Petrocelli	.15	.07	.01
☐ 414	Bob Montgomery	.10	.05	.01
☐ 415	Tim Blackwell	.10	.05	.01
☐ 416	Rick Miller	.10	.05	.01
☐ 417	Darrell Johnson	.10	.05	.01
☐ 418	Jim Burton	.10	.05	.01
☐ 419	Jim Willoughby	.10	.05	.01
☐ 420	Rogelio Moret	.10	.05	.01
☐ 421	Bill Lee	.15	.07	.01
☐ 422	Dick Drago	.10	.05	.01
☐ 423	Diego Segui	.10	.05	.01
☐ 424	Luis Tiant	.30	.15	.03
☐ 425	Jim Hunter	2.00	1.00	.20
☐ 426	Rick Sawyer	.10	.05	.01
☐ 427	Rudy May	.10	.05	.01
☐ 428	Dick Tidrow	.10	.05	.01
☐ 429	Sparky Lyle	.30	.15	.03
☐ 430	Doc Medich	.10	.05	.01
☐ 431	Pat Dobson	.15	.07	.01
☐ 432	Dave Pagan	.10	.05	.01
☐ 433	Thurman Munson	3.00	1.50	.30
☐ 434	Chris Chambliss	.15	.07	.01
☐ 435	Roy White	.15	.07	.01
☐ 436	Walt Williams	.10	.05	.01
☐ 437	Graig Nettles	.75	.35	.07
☐ 438	Rick Dempsey	.15	.07	.01
☐ 439	Bobby Bonds	.30	.15	.03
☐ 440	Ed Herrmann	.10	.05	.01
☐ 441	Sandy Alomar	.10	.05	.01
☐ 442	Fred Stanley	.10	.05	.01
☐ 443	Terry Whitfield	.10	.05	.01
☐ 444	Rich Bladt	.10	.05	.01
☐ 445	Lou Piniella	.30	.15	.03
☐ 446	Rich Coggins	.10	.05	.01
☐ 447	Ed Brinkman	.10	.05	.01
☐ 448	Jim Mason	.10	.05	.01
☐ 449	Larry Murray	.10	.05	.01
☐ 450	Ron Blomberg	.10	.05	.01
☐ 451	Elliott Maddox	.10	.05	.01
☐ 452	Kerry Dineen	.10	.05	.01
☐ 453	Billy Martin MG	.60	.30	.06
☐ 454	Dave Bergman	.10	.05	.01
☐ 455	Otto Velez	.10	.05	.01
☐ 456	Joe Hoerner	.10	.05	.01
☐ 457	Tug McGraw	.35	.17	.03
☐ 458	Gene Garber	.15	.07	.01
☐ 459	Steve Carlton	3.00	1.50	.30
☐ 460	Larry Christenson	.10	.05	.01
☐ 461	Tom Underwood	.10	.05	.01
☐ 462	Jim Lonborg	.15	.07	.01
☐ 463	Jay Johnstone	.15	.07	.01
☐ 464	Larry Bowa	.35	.17	.03
☐ 465	Dave Cash	.10	.05	.01
☐ 466	Ollie Brown	.10	.05	.01
☐ 467	Greg Luzinski	.30	.15	.03
☐ 468	Johnny Oates	.10	.05	.01
☐ 469	Mike Anderson	.10	.05	.01
☐ 470	Mike Schmidt	6.50	3.25	.65
☐ 471	Bob Boone	.20	.10	.02
☐ 472	Tom Hutton	.10	.05	.01
☐ 473	Rich Allen	.40	.20	.04
☐ 474	Tony Taylor	.10	.05	.01
☐ 475	Jerry Martin	.10	.05	.01
☐ 476	Danny Ozark MG	.10	.05	.01

☐ 477	Dick Ruthven	.10	.05	.01
☐ 478	Jim Todd	.10	.05	.01
☐ 479	Paul Lindblad	.10	.05	.01
☐ 480	Rollie Fingers	1.25	.60	.12
☐ 481	Vida Blue	.25	.12	.02
☐ 482	Ken Holtzman	.15	.07	.01
☐ 483	Dick Bosman	.10	.05	.01
☐ 484	Sonny Siebert	.10	.05	.01
☐ 485	Glenn Abbott	.10	.05	.01
☐ 486	Stan Bahnsen	.10	.05	.01
☐ 487	Mike Norris	.15	.07	.01
☐ 488	Alvin Dark MG	.15	.07	.01
☐ 489	Claudell Washington	.25	.12	.02
☐ 490	Joe Rudi	.15	.07	.01
☐ 491	Bill North	.10	.05	.01
☐ 492	Bert Campaneris	.20	.10	.02
☐ 493	Gene Tenace	.15	.07	.01
☐ 494	Reggie Jackson	5.50	2.75	.55
☐ 495	Phil Garner	.15	.07	.01
☐ 496	Billy Williams	2.00	1.00	.20
☐ 497	Sal Bando	.20	.10	.02
☐ 498	Jim Holt	.10	.05	.01
☐ 499	Ted Martinez	.10	.05	.01
☐ 500	Ray Fosse	.10	.05	.01
☐ 501	Matt Alexander	.10	.05	.01
☐ 502	Larry Haney	.10	.05	.01
☐ 503	Angel Mangual	.10	.05	.01
☐ 504	Fred Beene	.10	.05	.01
☐ 505	Tom Buskey	.10	.05	.01
☐ 506	Dennis Eckersley	.20	.10	.02
☐ 507	Roric Harrison	.10	.05	.01
☐ 508	Don Hood	.10	.05	.01
☐ 509	Jim Kern	.10	.05	.01
☐ 510	Dave LaRoche	.10	.05	.01
☐ 511	Fritz Peterson	.10	.05	.01
☐ 512	Jim Strickland	.10	.05	.01
☐ 513	Rick Waits	.10	.05	.01
☐ 514	Alan Ashby	.10	.05	.01
☐ 515	John Ellis	.10	.05	.01
☐ 516	Rick Cerone	.10	.05	.01
☐ 517	Buddy Bell	.40	.20	.04
☐ 518	Jack Brohamer	.10	.05	.01
☐ 519	Rico Carty	.15	.07	.01
☐ 520	Ed Crosby	.10	.05	.01
☐ 521	Frank Duffy	.10	.05	.01
☐ 522	Duane Kuiper (photo actually Rick Manning)	.10	.05	.01
☐ 523	Joe Lis	.10	.05	.01
☐ 524	Boog Powell	.60	.30	.06
☐ 525	Frank Robinson	2.00	1.00	.20
☐ 526	Oscar Gamble	.15	.07	.01
☐ 527	George Hendrick	.15	.07	.01
☐ 528	John Lowenstein	.10	.05	.01
☐ 529	Rick Manning (photo actually Duane Kuiper)	.10	.05	.01
☐ 530	Tommy Smith	.10	.05	.01
☐ 531	Charlie Spikes	.10	.05	.01
☐ 532	Steve Kline	.10	.05	.01
☐ 533	Ed Kranepool	.15	.07	.01
☐ 534	Mike Vail	.10	.05	.01
☐ 535	Del Unser	.10	.05	.01
☐ 536	Felix Millan	.10	.05	.01
☐ 537	Rusty Staub	.35	.17	.03
☐ 538	Jesus Alou	.10	.05	.01
☐ 539	Wayne Garrett	.10	.05	.01
☐ 540	Mike Phillips	.10	.05	.01
☐ 541	Joe Torre	.40	.20	.04
☐ 542	Dave Kingman	.75	.35	.07
☐ 543	Gene Clines	.10	.05	.01
☐ 544	Jack Heidemann	.10	.05	.01
☐ 545	Bud Harrelson	.15	.07	.01
☐ 546	John Stearns	.15	.07	.01
☐ 547	John Milner	.10	.05	.01
☐ 548	Bob Apodaca	.10	.05	.01
☐ 549	Skip Lockwood	.10	.05	.01
☐ 550	Ken Sanders	.10	.05	.01
☐ 551	Tom Seaver	4.00	2.00	.40
☐ 552	Rick Baldwin	.10	.05	.01
☐ 553	Hank Webb	.10	.05	.01
☐ 554	Jon Matlack	.15	.07	.01
☐ 555	Randy Tate	.10	.05	.01
☐ 556	Tom Hall	.10	.05	.01
☐ 557	George Stone	.10	.05	.01
☐ 558	Craig Swan	.15	.07	.01
☐ 559	Jerry Cram	.10	.05	.01
☐ 560	Roy Staiger	.10	.05	.01
☐ 561	Kent Tekulve	.20	.10	.02
☐ 562	Jerry Reuss	.15	.07	.01
☐ 563	John Candelaria	.25	.12	.02
☐ 564	Larry Demery	.10	.05	.01
☐ 565	Dave Giusti	.15	.07	.01
☐ 566	Jim Rooker	.10	.05	.01
☐ 567	Ramon Hernandez	.10	.05	.01

☐ 568	Bruce Kison	.15	.07	.01
☐ 569	Ken Brett	.10	.05	.01
☐ 570	Bob Moose	.15	.07	.01
☐ 571	Manny Sanguillen	.20	.10	.02
☐ 572	Dave Parker	2.00	1.00	.20
☐ 573	Willie Stargell	3.00	1.50	.30
☐ 574	Richie Zisk	.15	.07	.01
☐ 575	Rennie Stennett	.10	.05	.01
☐ 576	Al Oliver	.90	.45	.09
☐ 577	Bill Robinson	.15	.07	.01
☐ 578	Bob Robertson	.10	.05	.01
☐ 579	Rich Hebner	.10	.05	.01
☐ 580	Ed Kirkpatrick	.10	.05	.01
☐ 581	Duffy Dyer	.10	.05	.01
☐ 582	Craig Reynolds	.10	.05	.01
☐ 583	Frank Taveras	.10	.05	.01
☐ 584	Willie Randolph	.75	.35	.07
☐ 585	Art Howe	.10	.05	.01
☐ 586	Dan Murtaugh MG	.10	.05	.01
☐ 587	Rick McKinney	.10	.05	.01
☐ 588	Ed Goodson	.10	.05	.01
☐ 589	Checklist 1 George Brett Al Cowens	1.00	.50	.10
☐ 590	Checklist 2 Keith Hernandez Lou Brock	1.00	.50	.10
☐ 591	Checklist 3 Jerry Koosman Duke Snider	.50	.25	.05
☐ 592	Checklist 4 Maury Wills John Knox	.25	.12	.02
☐ 593	Checklist 5 Jim Hunter Nolan Ryan	1.25	.60	.12
☐ 594	Checklist 6 Ralph Branca Carl Erskine Pee Wee Reese	.30	.15	.03
☐ 595	Checklist 7 Willie Mays Herb Score	.75	.35	.07
☐ 596	Larry Cox	.10	.05	.01
☐ 597	Gene Mauch MG	.15	.07	.01
☐ 598	Whitey Wietelmann	.10	.05	.01
☐ 599	Wayne Simpson	.10	.05	.01
☐ 600	Mel Thomason	.10	.05	.01
☐ 601	Ike Hampton	.10	.05	.01
☐ 602	Ken Crosby	.10	.05	.01
☐ 603	Ralph Rowe	.10	.05	.01
☐ 604	Jim Tyrone	.10	.05	.01
☐ 605	Mick Kelleher	.10	.05	.01
☐ 606	Mario Mendoza	.10	.05	.01
☐ 607	Mike Rogodzinski	.10	.05	.01
☐ 608	Bob Gallagher	.10	.05	.01
☐ 609	Jerry Koosman	.20	.10	.02
☐ 610	Joe Frazier	.10	.05	.01
☐ 611	Karl Kuehl	.10	.05	.01
☐ 612	Frank LaCorte	.10	.05	.01
☐ 613	Ray Bare	.10	.05	.01
☐ 614	Billy Muffett	.10	.05	.01
☐ 615	Bill Laxton	.10	.05	.01
☐ 616	Willie Mays	5.00	2.50	.50
☐ 617	Phil Cavarretta COA	.15	.07	.01
☐ 618	Ted Kluszewski COA	.25	.12	.02
☐ 619	Elston Howard COA	.35	.17	.03
☐ 620	Alex Grammas COA	.10	.05	.01
☐ 621	Mickey Vernon COA	.15	.07	.01
☐ 622	Dick Sisler COA	.10	.05	.01
☐ 623	Harvey Haddix COA	.15	.07	.01
☐ 624	Bobby Winkles COA	.10	.05	.01
☐ 625	John Pesky COA	.10	.05	.01
☐ 626	Jim Davenport COA	.15	.07	.01
☐ 627	Dave Tomlin	.10	.05	.01
☐ 628	Roger Craig COA	.25	.12	.02
☐ 629	Joe Amalfitano COA	.10	.05	.01
☐ 630	Jim Reese COA	.15	.07	.01

1953 Stahl Meyer

The cards in this 9 card set measure 3 1/4" by 4 1/2". The 1953 Stahl Meyer set of full color, unnumbered cards includes three players from each of the three New York teams. The cards have white borders. The Lockman card is the most plentiful of any card in the set. Some batting and fielding statistics and short biography are included on the back. The cards are ordered in the checklist below by alphabetical order without regard to team affiliation.

	NRMT	VG-E	GOOD
COMPLETE SET	2700.00	1200.00	250.00
COMMON PLAYER (1-9)	100.00	50.00	10.00
☐1 Hank Bauer	125.00	60.00	12.50
☐2 Roy Campanella	450.00	225.00	45.00
☐3 Gil Hodges	225.00	110.00	22.00
☐4 Monte Irvin	175.00	85.00	18.00
☐5 Whitey Lockman	100.00	50.00	10.00
☐6 Mickey Mantle	1500.00	600.00	120.00
☐7 Phil Rizzuto	225.00	110.00	22.00
☐8 Duke Snider	450.00	225.00	45.00
☐9 Bobby Thomson	125.00	60.00	12.50

1954 Stahl Meyer

The cards in this 12 card set measure 3 1/4" by 4 1/2". The 1954 Stahl Meyer set of full color, unnumbered cards includes four players from each of the three New York teams. The cards have yellow borders and the backs, oriented horizontally, include an ad for a baseball kit and the player's statistics. No player biography is included on the back. The cards are ordered in the checklist below by alphabetical order without regard to team affiliation.

	NRMT	VG-E	GOOD
COMPLETE SET	4000.00	1800.00	350.00
COMMON PLAYER (1-12)	125.00	60.00	12.50
☐ 1 Hank Bauer	150.00	75.00	15.00
☐ 2 Carl Erskine	150.00	75.00	15.00
☐ 3 Gil Hodges	250.00	125.00	25.00
☐ 4 Monte Irvin	200.00	100.00	20.00
☐ 5 Whitey Lockman	125.00	60.00	12.50
☐ 6 Mickey Mantle	1750.00	750.00	150.00
☐ 7 Willie Mays	900.00	450.00	90.00
☐ 8 Gil McDougald	150.00	75.00	15.00
☐ 9 Don Mueller	125.00	60.00	12.50
☐10 Don Newcombe	150.00	75.00	15.00
☐11 Phil Rizzuto	250.00	125.00	25.00
☐12 Duke Snider	450.00	225.00	45.00

1955 Stahl Meyer

The cards in this 12 card set measure 3 1/4" by 4 1/2". The 1955 Stahl Meyer set of full color, unnumbered cards contains four players each from the three New York teams. As in the 1954 set, the cards have yellow borders; however, the back of the cards contain a sketch of Mickey Mantle with an ad for a baseball cap or a pennant. The cards are ordered in the checklist below by alphabetical order without regard to team affiliation.

	NRMT	VG-E	GOOD
COMPLETE SET	3000.00	1200.00	250.00
COMMON PLAYER (1-12)	125.00	60.00	12.50
☐ 1 Hank Bauer	150.00	75.00	15.00
☐ 2 Carl Erskine	150.00	75.00	15.00
☐ 3 Gil Hodges	250.00	125.00	25.00
☐ 4 Monte Irvin	200.00	100.00	20.00
☐ 5 Whitey Lockman	125.00	60.00	12.50
☐ 6 Mickey Mantle	1750.00	750.00	150.00
☐ 7 Gil McDougald	150.00	75.00	15.00
☐ 8 Don Mueller	125.00	60.00	12.50
☐ 9 Don Newcombe	150.00	75.00	15.00
☐10 Dusty Rhodes	125.00	60.00	12.50
☐11 Phil Rizzuto	250.00	125.00	25.00
☐12 Duke Snider	450.00	225.00	45.00

1962 Sugardale

The cards in this 22 card set measure 3 3/4" by 5 1/8". The 1962 Sugardale Meats set of black and white, numbered and lettered cards features the Cleveland Indians and the Pittsburgh Pirates. The Indians are numbered while the Pirates are lettered. The backs, in red print, give player tips. The Bob Nieman card was just recently discovered and is quite scarce. The catalog designation is F174-1.

	NRMT	VG-E	GOOD
COMPLETE SET	1100.00	450.00	90.00
COMMON PLAYER (1-19)	40.00	20.00	4.00
COMMON PLAYER (A-D)	50.00	25.00	5.00
☐ 1 Barry Latman	40.00	20.00	4.00
☐ 2 Gary Bell	40.00	20.00	4.00
☐ 3 Dick Donovan	40.00	20.00	4.00
☐ 4 Frank Funk	40.00	20.00	4.00
☐ 5 Jim Perry	50.00	25.00	5.00
☐ 6 not issued	0.00	.00	.00
☐ 7 John Romano	40.00	20.00	4.00
☐ 8 Ty Cline	40.00	20.00	4.00
☐ 9 Tito Francona	40.00	20.00	4.00
☐10 Bob Nieman	200.00	100.00	20.00
☐11 Willie Kirkland	40.00	20.00	4.00
☐12 Woody Held	40.00	20.00	4.00
☐13 Jerry Kindall	40.00	20.00	4.00
☐14 Bubba Phillips	40.00	20.00	4.00
☐15 Mel Harder	40.00	20.00	4.00
☐16 Salty Parker	40.00	20.00	4.00
☐17 Ray Katt	40.00	20.00	4.00
☐18 Mel McGaha	40.00	20.00	4.00
☐19 Pedro Ramos	40.00	20.00	4.00
☐ A Dick Groat	75.00	37.50	7.50
☐ B Robert Clemente	400.00	200.00	40.00
☐ C Don Hoak	50.00	25.00	5.00
☐ D Dick Stuart	60.00	30.00	6.00

1963 Sugardale

The cards in this 31 card set measure 3 3/4" by 5 1/8". The 1963 Sugardale Meats set of 31 black and white, numbered cards features the Cleveland Indians and Pittsburgh Pirates. The backs are printed in red and give player tips. The 1963 Sugardale set can be distinguished from the 1962 Sugardale set by examining the biographies on the card for mention of the 1962 season. The Perry and Skinner cards were withdrawn after June trades and are difficult to obtain.

	NRMT	VG-E	GOOD
COMPLETE SET	1100.00	450.00	90.00
COMMON PLAYER (1-33)	40.00	20.00	4.00
COMMON PLAYER (34-38)	50.00	25.00	5.00
☐ 1 Barry Latman	40.00	20.00	4.00
☐ 2 Gary Bell	40.00	20.00	4.00
☐ 3 Dick Donovan	40.00	20.00	4.00
☐ 4 Joe Adcock	50.00	25.00	5.00
☐ 5 Jim Perry	150.00	75.00	15.00
☐ 6 Not issued	0.00	.00	.00
☐ 7 John Romano	40.00	20.00	4.00
☐ 8 Mike de la Hoz	40.00	20.00	4.00
☐ 9 Tito Francona	40.00	20.00	4.00
☐10 Gene Green	40.00	20.00	4.00
☐11 Willie Kirkland	40.00	20.00	4.00
☐12 Woody Held	40.00	20.00	4.00
☐13 Jerry Kindall	40.00	20.00	4.00
☐14 Max Alvis	40.00	20.00	4.00
☐15 Mel Harder	40.00	20.00	4.00
☐16 George Strickland	40.00	20.00	4.00
☐17 Elmer Valo	40.00	20.00	4.00
☐18 Birdie Tebbetts	40.00	20.00	4.00
☐19 Pedro Ramos	40.00	20.00	4.00
☐20 Al Luplow	40.00	20.00	4.00
☐21 Not issued	0.00	.00	.00
☐22 Not issued	0.00	.00	.00
☐23 Jim Grant	40.00	20.00	4.00

		NRMT	VG-E	GOOD
☐ 24	Victor Davalillo	40.00	20.00	4.00
☐ 25	Jerry Walker	40.00	20.00	4.00
☐ 26	Sam McDowell	50.00	25.00	5.00
☐ 27	Fred Whitfield	40.00	20.00	4.00
☐ 28	Jack Kralick	40.00	20.00	4.00
☐ 29	Not issued	0.00	.00	.00
☐ 30	Not issued	0.00	.00	.00
☐ 31	Not issued	0.00	.00	.00
☐ 32	Not issued	0.00	.00	.00
☐ 33	Bob Allen	40.00	20.00	4.00
☐ 34	Don Cardwell	50.00	25.00	5.00
☐ 35	Bob Skinner	150.00	75.00	15.00
☐ 36	Don Schwall	50.00	25.00	5.00
☐ 37	Jim Pagliaroni	50.00	25.00	5.00
☐ 38	Dick Schofield	50.00	25.00	5.00

	Single Wins 1935 W.S.			
☐ 14	Great Slugging: Lou	90.00	45.00	9.00
	Gehrig's Four Homers			
☐ 15	Four Men To Stop Him:	25.00	12.50	2.50
	DiMaggio's Bat Streak			
☐ 16	Three Run Homer in	90.00	45.00	9.00
	Ninth: Williams' Homer			
☐ 17	Football Block:	12.00	6.00	1.20
	Lindell's Football			
	Block Paves Way For			
	Yank's Series Victory			
☐ 18	Home Run To Fame:	25.00	12.50	2.50
	Reese's Grand Slam			
☐ 19	Strikeout Record:	30.00	15.00	3.00
	Feller Whiffs Five			
☐ 20	Rifle Arm: Furillo	35.00	17.50	3.50

1948 Swell Sport Thrills

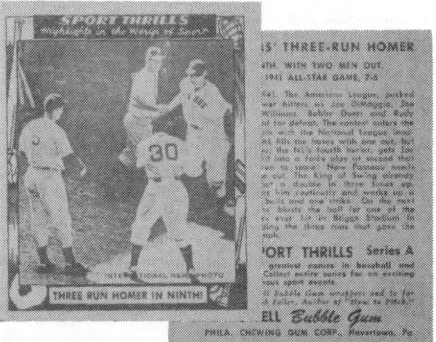

The cards in this 20 card set measure 2 1/2" by 3". The 1948 Swell Gum Sports Thrills set of black and white, numbered cards highlights events from baseball history. The cards have picture framed borders with the title "Sports Thrills Highlights in the World of Sport" on the front. The backs of the cards give the story of the event pictured on the front. Cards numbered 9, 11, 16, and 20 are more difficult to obtain than the other cards in this set. The ACC designation is R448.

		NRMT	VG-E	GOOD
COMPLETE SET		500.00	250.00	50.00
COMMON PLAYER (1-20)		12.00	6.00	1.20
☐ 1	Greatest Single Inning Athletics' 10 Run Rally	12.00	6.00	1.20
☐ 2	Amazing Record: Reiser's Debut With Dodgers	12.00	6.00	1.20
☐ 3	Dramatic Debut: Jackie Robinson ROY	75.00	37.50	7.50
☐ 4	Greatest Pitcher of Them All: W.Johnson	40.00	20.00	4.00
☐ 5	Three Strikes Not Out: Lost Third Strike Changes Tide of 1941 World Series	12.00	6.00	1.20
☐ 6	Home Run Wins Series: Bill Dickey's Last Home Run	20.00	10.00	2.00
☐ 7	Never Say Die Pitcher: Schumacher Pitching	12.00	6.00	1.20
☐ 8	Five Strikeouts: Nationals Lose All Star Game (Hubbell)	20.00	10.00	2.00
☐ 9	Greatest Catch: Al Gionfriddo's Catch	20.00	10.00	2.00
☐ 10	No Hits No Runs: VanderMeer Comes Back	15.00	7.50	1.50
☐ 11	Bases Loaded: Alexander The Great	25.00	12.50	2.50
☐ 12	Most Dramatic Homer: Babe Ruth Points	125.00	60.00	12.50
☐ 13	Winning Run: Bridges' Pitching and Goslin's	12.00	6.00	1.20

1957 Swifts Franks

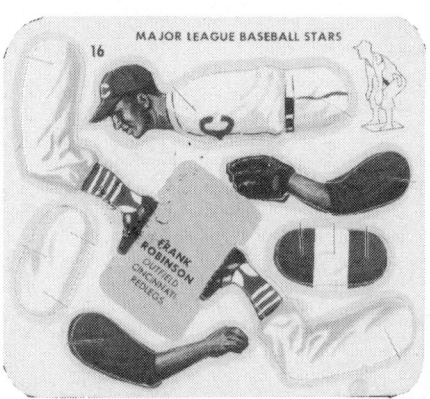

The cards in this 18-card set measure 3 1/2" by 4". These full color, numbered cards issued in 1957 by the Swift Company are die-cut. Each card consists of several pieces which can be punched out and assembled to form a stand-up model of the player. The cards and a game board were available directly from the company. The ACC designation is F162.

		NRMT	VG-E	GOOD
COMPLETE SET (18)		1250.00	500.00	100.00
COMMON PLAYER (1-18)		40.00	20.00	4.00
☐ 1	John Podres	50.00	25.00	5.00
☐ 2	Gus Triandos	40.00	20.00	4.00
☐ 3	Dale Long	40.00	20.00	4.00
☐ 4	Billy Pierce	50.00	25.00	5.00
☐ 5	Ed Bailey	40.00	20.00	4.00
☐ 6	Vic Wertz	40.00	20.00	4.00
☐ 7	Nelson Fox	75.00	37.50	7.50
☐ 8	Ken Boyer	75.00	37.50	7.50
☐ 9	Gil McDougald	60.00	30.00	6.00
☐ 10	Junior Gilliam	60.00	30.00	6.00
☐ 11	Eddie Yost	40.00	20.00	4.00
☐ 12	Johnny Logan	40.00	20.00	4.00
☐ 13	Hank Aaron	300.00	150.00	30.00
☐ 14	Bill Tuttle	40.00	20.00	4.00
☐ 15	Jackie Jensen	60.00	30.00	6.00
☐ 16	Frank Robinson	120.00	60.00	12.00
☐ 17	Richie Ashburn	90.00	45.00	9.00
☐ 18	Rocky Colavito	75.00	37.50	7.50

1933 Tatoo Orbit

The cards in this 60 card set measure 2" by 2 1/4". The 1933 Tatoo Orbit set contains unnumbered, color cards. Blaeholder and Hadley, and to a lesser degree Andrews and Hornsby are considered more difficult to obtain than the other cards in this set. The

1986 Texas Gold Reds

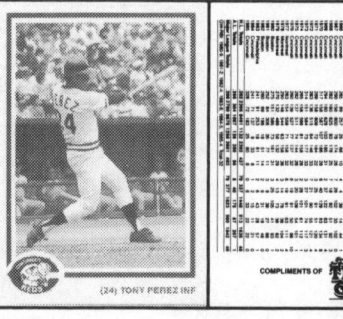

ACC designation is R305. The cards are ordered and numbered below alphabetically by the player's name.

		NRMT	VG-E	GOOD
	COMPLETE SET	2350.00	900.00	180.00
	COMMON PLAYER (1-60)	25.00	12.50	2.50
☐ 1	Dale Alexander	25.00	12.50	2.50
☐ 2	Ivy Andrews	75.00	37.50	7.50
☐ 3	Earl Averill	50.00	25.00	5.00
☐ 4	Dick Bartell	25.00	12.50	2.50
☐ 5	Wally Berger	25.00	12.50	2.50
☐ 6	George Blaeholder	125.00	60.00	12.50
☐ 7	Irving Burns	25.00	12.50	2.50
☐ 8	Guy Bush	25.00	12.50	2.50
☐ 9	Bruce Campbell	25.00	12.50	2.50
☐ 10	Chalmers Cissell	25.00	12.50	2.50
☐ 11	Watson Clark	25.00	12.50	2.50
☐ 12	Mickey Cochrane	75.00	37.50	7.50
☐ 13	Phil Collins	25.00	12.50	2.50
☐ 14	Kiki Cuyler	50.00	25.00	5.00
☐ 15	Dizzy Dean	150.00	75.00	15.00
☐ 16	Jimmy Dykes	25.00	12.50	2.50
☐ 17	George Earnshaw	25.00	12.50	2.50
☐ 18	Woody English	25.00	12.50	2.50
☐ 19	Lou Fonseca	25.00	12.50	2.50
☐ 20	Jimmy Foxx	100.00	50.00	10.00
☐ 21	Burleigh Grimes	50.00	25.00	5.00
☐ 22	Charlie Grimm	25.00	12.50	2.50
☐ 23	Lefty Grove	75.00	37.50	7.50
☐ 24	Frank Grube	25.00	12.50	2.50
☐ 25	George Haas	25.00	12.50	2.50
☐ 26	Bump Hadley	125.00	60.00	12.50
☐ 27	Chick Hafey	50.00	25.00	5.00
☐ 28	Jess Haines	50.00	25.00	5.00
☐ 29	Bill Hallahan	25.00	12.50	2.50
☐ 30	Mel Harder	25.00	12.50	2.50
☐ 31	Gabby Hartnett	50.00	25.00	5.00
☐ 32	Babe Herman	30.00	15.00	3.00
☐ 33	Billy Herman	50.00	25.00	5.00
☐ 34	Rogers Hornsby	200.00	100.00	20.00
☐ 35	Roy Johnson	25.00	12.50	2.50
☐ 36	Smead Jolly	25.00	12.50	2.50
☐ 37	Billy Jurges	25.00	12.50	2.50
☐ 38	Willie Kamm	25.00	12.50	2.50
☐ 39	Mark Koenig	25.00	12.50	2.50
☐ 40	Jim Levey	25.00	12.50	2.50
☐ 41	Ernie Lombardi	50.00	25.00	5.00
☐ 42	Red Lucas	25.00	12.50	2.50
☐ 43	Ted Lyons	50.00	25.00	5.00
☐ 44	Connie Mack	60.00	30.00	6.00
☐ 45	Pat Malone	25.00	12.50	2.50
☐ 46	Pepper Martin	30.00	15.00	3.00
☐ 47	Marty McManus	25.00	12.50	2.50
☐ 48	Frank O'Doul	30.00	15.00	3.00
☐ 49	Dick Porter	25.00	12.50	2.50
☐ 50	Carl N. Reynolds	25.00	12.50	2.50
☐ 51	Charlie Root	25.00	12.50	2.50
☐ 52	Bob Seeds	25.00	12.50	2.50
☐ 53	Al Simmons	50.00	25.00	5.00
☐ 54	Riggs Stephenson	30.00	15.00	3.00
☐ 55	Lyle Tinning	25.00	12.50	2.50
☐ 56	Joe Vosmik	25.00	12.50	2.50
☐ 57	Rube Walberg	25.00	12.50	2.50
☐ 58	Paul Waner	50.00	25.00	5.00
☐ 59	Lon Warneke	25.00	12.50	2.50
☐ 60	Arthur Whitney	25.00	12.50	2.50

ADD TO YOUR SET: Write for current availability and prices for back editions of Sport Americana series, as well as back isues of Beckett Monthly.

Texas Gold Ice Cream is the sponsor of this 28-card set of Cincinnati Reds. The cards are 2 1/2" by 3 1/2" and feature player photos in full color with a red and white border on the front of the card. The set was distributed to fans attending the Reds game at Riverfront Stadium on September 19th. The card backs contain the player's career statistics, uniform number, name, position, and the Texas Gold logo.

		MINT	EXC	G-VG
	COMPLETE SET (28)	15.00	7.50	1.50
	COMMON PLAYER	.30	.15	.03
☐ 6	Bo Diaz	.40	.20	.04
☐ 9	Max Venable	.30	.15	.03
☐ 11	Kurt Stillwell	.50	.25	.05
☐ 12	Nick Esasky	.40	.20	.04
☐ 13	Dave Concepcion	.50	.25	.05
☐ 14A	Pete Rose INF	1.50	.75	.15
☐ 14B	Pete Rose MG	1.50	.75	.15
☐ 14C	Pete Rose (commemorative)	1.50	.75	.15
☐ 16	Ron Oester	.30	.15	.03
☐ 20	Eddie Milner	.30	.15	.03
☐ 22	Sal Butera	.30	.15	.03
☐ 24	Tony Perez	.75	.35	.07
☐ 25	Buddy Bell	.50	.25	.05
☐ 28	Kal Daniels	1.50	.75	.15
☐ 29	Tracy Jones	.75	.35	.07
☐ 31	John Franco	.50	.25	.05
☐ 32	Tom Browning	.40	.20	.04
☐ 33	Ron Robinson	.40	.20	.04
☐ 34	Bill Gullickson	.40	.20	.04
☐ 36	Mario Soto	.40	.20	.04
☐ 39	Dave Parker	.75	.35	.07
☐ 40	John Denny	.40	.20	.04
☐ 44	Eric Davis	4.00	2.00	.40
☐ 45	Chris Welsh	.30	.15	.03
☐ 48	Ted Power	.40	.20	.04
☐ 49	Joe Price	.30	.15	.03
☐ xx	Reds Coaches	.30	.15	.03
	George Scherger			
	Bruce Kimm			
	Billy DeMars			
	Tommy Helms			
	Scott Breeden			
	Jim Lett			
☐ xx	Preferred Customer Card (Discount Coupon)	.30	.15	.03

1947 Tip Top

The cards in this 163 card set measure 2 1/4" by 3". The 1947 Tip Top Bread issue contains unnumbered cards with black and white player photos. The set is of interest to baseball historians in that it contains cards of many players not appearing in any other card sets. The cards were issued locally for the eleven following teams: Red Sox (1-15), White Sox (16-30), Tigers (31-45), Yankees

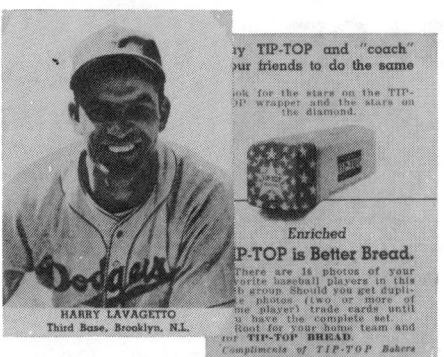

TIP-TOP and "coach"
ur friends to do the same

ok for the stars on the TIP-
OP wrapper and the stars on
the diamond.

Enriched
P-TOP is Better Bread.

There are 16 photos of your
rite baseball players in this
h group should you get dupli-
e photos (two or more of
e player) trade cards until
u have the complete set.
Root for your home team and
for TIP-TOP BREAD.
Compliments of TIP-TOP Bakers

HARRY LAVAGETTO
Third Base, Brooklyn, N.L.

(46-60), Browns (61-75), Braves (76- 90), Dodgers
(91-104), Cubs (105-119), Giants (120-135), Pirates
(136-149), and Cardinals (150-164). Players of the
Red Sox, Tigers, White Sox, Braves, and the Cubs are
scarcer than those of the other teams. The ACC
designation is D323.

		NRMT	VG-E	GOOD
COMPLETE SET		7500.00	3000.00	600.00
COMMON PLAYER (1-164)		20.00	10.00	2.00

		NRMT	VG-E	GOOD
☐ 1	Leon Culberson	60.00	30.00	6.00
☐ 2	Dom DiMaggio	90.00	45.00	9.00
☐ 3	Joe Dobson	60.00	30.00	6.00
☐ 4	Bob Doerr	125.00	60.00	12.50
☐ 5	Dave (Boo) Ferris	60.00	30.00	6.00
☐ 6	Mickey Harris	60.00	30.00	6.00
☐ 7	Frank Hayes	60.00	30.00	6.00
☐ 8	Cecil Hughson	60.00	30.00	6.00
☐ 9	Earl Johnson	60.00	30.00	6.00
☐ 10	Roy Partee	60.00	30.00	6.00
☐ 11	Johnny Pesky	75.00	37.50	7.50
☐ 12	Rip Russell	60.00	30.00	6.00
☐ 13	Hal Wagner	60.00	30.00	6.00
☐ 14	Rudy York	75.00	37.50	7.50
☐ 15	Bill Zuber	60.00	30.00	6.00
☐ 16	Floyd Baker	60.00	30.00	6.00
☐ 17	Earl Caldwell	60.00	30.00	6.00
☐ 18	Lloyd Christopher	60.00	30.00	6.00
☐ 19	George Dickey	60.00	30.00	6.00
☐ 20	Ralph Hodgin	60.00	30.00	6.00
☐ 21	Bob Kennedy	60.00	30.00	6.00
☐ 22	Joe Kuhel	60.00	30.00	6.00
☐ 23	Thornton Lee	60.00	30.00	6.00
☐ 24	Ed Lopat	90.00	45.00	9.00
☐ 25	Cass Michaels	60.00	30.00	6.00
☐ 26	John Rigney	60.00	30.00	6.00
☐ 27	Mike Tresh	60.00	30.00	6.00
☐ 28	Thurman Tucker	60.00	30.00	6.00
☐ 29	Jack Wallasca	60.00	30.00	6.00
☐ 30	Taft Wright	60.00	30.00	6.00
☐ 31	Walter (Hoot) Evers	60.00	30.00	6.00
☐ 32	John Gorsica	60.00	30.00	6.00
☐ 33	Fred Hutchinson	75.00	37.50	7.50
☐ 34	George Kell	200.00	100.00	20.00
☐ 35	Eddie Lake	60.00	30.00	6.00
☐ 36	Ed Mayo	60.00	30.00	6.00
☐ 37	Arthur Mills	60.00	30.00	6.00
☐ 38	Pat Mullin	60.00	30.00	6.00
☐ 39	James Outlaw	60.00	30.00	6.00
☐ 40	Frank(Stub) Overmire	60.00	30.00	6.00
☐ 41	Bob Swift	60.00	30.00	6.00
☐ 42	Geo. Birdie Tebbetts	60.00	30.00	6.00
☐ 43	Paul (Diz) Trout	75.00	37.50	7.50
☐ 44	Virgil Trucks	75.00	37.50	7.50
☐ 45	Dick Wakefield	60.00	30.00	6.00
☐ 46	Larry Berra	100.00	50.00	10.00
☐ 47	Floyd (Bill) Bevans	20.00	10.00	2.00
☐ 48	Bobby Brown	30.00	15.00	3.00
☐ 49	Thomas Byrne	20.00	10.00	2.00
☐ 50	Frank Crosetti	30.00	15.00	3.00
☐ 51	Tom Henrich	30.00	15.00	3.00
☐ 52	Charlie Keller	30.00	15.00	3.00
☐ 53	Johnny Lindell	20.00	10.00	2.00
☐ 54	Joe Page	20.00	10.00	2.00
☐ 55	Mel Queen	20.00	10.00	2.00
☐ 56	Allie Reynolds	30.00	15.00	3.00
☐ 57	Phil Rizzuto	75.00	37.50	7.50
☐ 58	Aaron Robinson	20.00	10.00	2.00
☐ 59	George Stirnweiss	20.00	10.00	2.00
☐ 60	Charles Wensloff	20.00	10.00	2.00
☐ 61	John Berardino	20.00	10.00	2.00
☐ 62	Clifford Fannin	20.00	10.00	2.00
☐ 63	Dennis Galehouse	20.00	10.00	2.00
☐ 64	Jeff Heath	20.00	10.00	2.00
☐ 65	Walter Judnich	20.00	10.00	2.00
☐ 66	Jack Kramer	20.00	10.00	2.00
☐ 67	Paul Lehner	20.00	10.00	2.00
☐ 68	Lester Moss	20.00	10.00	2.00
☐ 69	Bob Muncrief	20.00	10.00	2.00
☐ 70	Nelson Potter	20.00	10.00	2.00
☐ 71	Fred Sanford	20.00	10.00	2.00
☐ 72	Joe Schultz	20.00	10.00	2.00
☐ 73	Vern Stephens	20.00	10.00	2.00
☐ 74	Jerry Witte	20.00	10.00	2.00
☐ 75	Al Zarilla	20.00	10.00	2.00
☐ 76	Charles Barrett	60.00	30.00	6.00
☐ 77	Hank Camelli	60.00	30.00	6.00
☐ 78	Dick Culler	60.00	30.00	6.00
☐ 79	Nanny Fernandez	60.00	30.00	6.00
☐ 80	Si Johnson	60.00	30.00	6.00
☐ 81	Danny Litwhiler	60.00	30.00	6.00
☐ 82	Phil Masi	60.00	30.00	6.00
☐ 83	Carvel Rowell	60.00	30.00	6.00
☐ 84	Connie Ryan	60.00	30.00	6.00
☐ 85	John Sain	90.00	45.00	9.00
☐ 86	Ray Sanders	60.00	30.00	6.00
☐ 87	Sibby Sisti	60.00	30.00	6.00
☐ 88	Billy Southworth	60.00	30.00	6.00
☐ 89	Warren Spahn	200.00	100.00	20.00
☐ 90	Ed Wright	60.00	30.00	6.00
☐ 91	Bob Bragan	20.00	10.00	2.00
☐ 92	Ralph Branca	25.00	12.50	2.50
☐ 93	Hugh Casey	20.00	10.00	2.00
☐ 94	Bruce Edwards	20.00	10.00	2.00
☐ 95	Hal Gregg	20.00	10.00	2.00
☐ 96	Joe Hatten	20.00	10.00	2.00
☐ 97	Gene Hermanski	20.00	10.00	2.00
☐ 98	John Jorgensen	20.00	10.00	2.00
☐ 99	Harry Lavagetto	20.00	10.00	2.00
☐ 100	Vic Lombardi	20.00	10.00	2.00
☐ 101	Frank Melton	20.00	10.00	2.00
☐ 102	Ed Miksis	20.00	10.00	2.00
☐ 103	Marv Rackley	20.00	10.00	2.00
☐ 104	Ed Stevens	20.00	10.00	2.00
☐ 105	Phil Cavarretta	90.00	45.00	9.00
☐ 106	Bob Chipman	60.00	30.00	6.00
☐ 107	Stanley Hack	60.00	30.00	6.00
☐ 108	Don Johnson	60.00	30.00	6.00
☐ 109	Emil Kush	60.00	30.00	6.00
☐ 110	Bill Lee	60.00	30.00	6.00
☐ 111	Mickey Livingston	60.00	30.00	6.00
☐ 112	Harry Lowrey	60.00	30.00	6.00
☐ 113	Clyde McCullough	60.00	30.00	6.00
☐ 114	Andy Pafko	60.00	30.00	6.00
☐ 115	Marv Rickert	60.00	30.00	6.00
☐ 116	John Schmitz	60.00	30.00	6.00
☐ 117	Bobby Sturgeon	60.00	30.00	6.00
☐ 118	Ed Waitkus	60.00	30.00	6.00
☐ 119	Henry Wyse	60.00	30.00	6.00
☐ 120	Bill Ayers	20.00	10.00	2.00
☐ 121	Robert Blattner	20.00	10.00	2.00
☐ 122	Mike Budnick	20.00	10.00	2.00
☐ 123	Sid Gordon	20.00	10.00	2.00
☐ 124	Clinton Hartung	20.00	10.00	2.00
☐ 125	Monte Kennedy	20.00	10.00	2.00
☐ 126	Dave Koslo	20.00	10.00	2.00
☐ 127	Carroll Lockman	25.00	12.50	2.50
☐ 128	Jack Lohrke	20.00	10.00	2.00
☐ 129	Ernie Lombardi	40.00	20.00	4.00
☐ 130	Willard Marshall	20.00	10.00	2.00
☐ 131	John Mize	60.00	30.00	6.00
☐ 132	Eugene Thompson (does not exist)	0.00	.00	.00
☐ 133	Ken Trinkle	20.00	10.00	2.00
☐ 134	Bill Voiselle	20.00	10.00	2.00
☐ 135	Mickey Witek	20.00	10.00	2.00
☐ 136	Eddie Basinski	20.00	10.00	2.00
☐ 137	Ernie Bonham	20.00	10.00	2.00
☐ 138	Bill Cox	25.00	12.50	2.50
☐ 139	Elbie Fletcher	20.00	10.00	2.00
☐ 140	Frank Gustine	20.00	10.00	2.00
☐ 141	Kirby Higbe	20.00	10.00	2.00
☐ 142	Leroy Jarvis	20.00	10.00	2.00
☐ 143	Ralph Kiner	60.00	30.00	6.00
☐ 144	Fred Ostermueller	20.00	10.00	2.00
☐ 145	Preacher Roe	30.00	15.00	3.00
☐ 146	Jim Russell	20.00	10.00	2.00
☐ 147	Rip Sewell	20.00	10.00	2.00
☐ 148	Nick Strincevich	20.00	10.00	2.00
☐ 149	Honus Wagner	75.00	37.50	7.50
☐ 150	Alpha Brazle	20.00	10.00	2.00
☐ 151	Ken Burkhart	20.00	10.00	2.00
☐ 152	Bernard Creger	20.00	10.00	2.00
☐ 153	Joffre Cross	20.00	10.00	2.00
☐ 154	Charles E. Diering	20.00	10.00	2.00

FIRST BASE

231 Webb Chapel Village
Dallas, Texas 75229

Store #1
Webb Chapel Village
Shopping Center #231
1-214-243-5271
11-7 Mon-Sat
Closed Sun.

Store #2
Audelia Plaza #102
1-214-341-9919
11-6 Mon-Sat
Closed Sun.

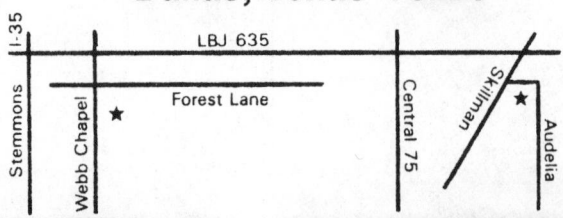

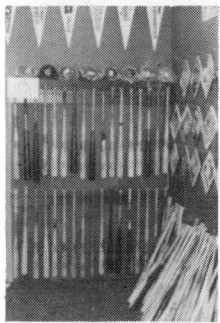

We are located on the southeast corner of Webb Chapel and Forest just 15 minutes from the airport. Our large (1,650-square foot showroom) store is convenient to all parts of Dallas, being only one block south of the LBJ (I-635) Freeway at the Webb Chapel exit. Many collectors and dealers have told us that our store is the most complete they've ever seen. Just look on the opposite page for a few of our offers. We want you for a customer -- please stop in and see for yourself. Also visit our new convenient location in the Audelia Plaza Shopping Center.

Sincerely,

Wayne Grove
Gervise Ford

FIRST BASE

P.S.   We are always interested in buying your cards —
let us know what you have.

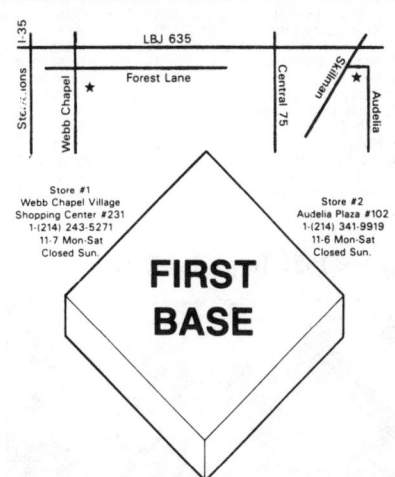

Store #1
Webb Chapel Village
Shopping Center #231
1-(214) 243-5271
11-7 Mon-Sat
Closed Sun.

Store #2
Audelia Plaza #102
1-(214) 341-9919
11-6 Mon-Sat
Closed Sun.

FIRST BASE

Below is a partial list of special offers we have for sale. Include $2.00 for postage and handling per order. We have most Topps, Donruss, Fleer, etc. Sets and singles for sale. Please send a self addressed stamped envelope for current price listings or when requesting information. Better yet, why don't you stop in some time and see for yourself?

COMPLETE SETS

1986 Rangers Performance (28)	$6.95
1985 Rangers Performance (28)	6.95
1984 Rangers Jarvis (28)	5.95
1983 Rangers Affiliated (28)	4.95
1984 Ralston Baseball (33)	4.95
1983 Seven-Eleven 3D Coins (12)	12.95
1983 Fleer Stamps (224)	3.95
1982 K-Mart Baseball (33)	1.50
1981 Topps 5x7 Dodgers/Angels (18)	6.95
1978 Tucson Toros (24)	3.95
1980 Tucson Toros (24)	3.95
1983 Police Cowboys (28)	9.95
1981 Police Cowboys (14)	9.95
1980 Police Cowboys (14)	9.95
1979 Police Cowboys (15)	14.95
1986 McDonalds Cowboys (25)	9.95
1986 McDonalds All-Stars (24)	3.95

BASEBALL CARD LOTS

1958 Topps 25 diff (f-vg)	14.95
1959 Topps 25 diff (f-vg)	8.95
1960 Topps 25 diff (f-vg)	5.95
1961 Topps 25 diff (f-vg)	4.95
1962 Topps 25 diff (f-vg)	4.95
1963 Topps 25 diff (f-vg)	4.50
1964 Topps 25 diff (f-vg)	3.95
1965 Topps 25 diff (f-vg)	3.95
1966 Topps 25 diff (f-vg)	3.50
1967 Topps 25 diff (f-vg)	3.50
1968 Topps 25 diff (f-vg)	2.95
1969 Topps 25 diff (f-vg)	2.95
1970 Topps 25 diff (f-vg)	2.50
1971 Topps 25 diff (f-vg)	2.50
1972 Topps 25 diff (f-vg)	2.50
1973 Topps 25 diff (f-vg)	1.95
1974 Topps 25 diff (f-vg)	1.95

SPECIAL OFFERS

#1: Type Set: One card from each year of Topps baseball 1952 through 1988, our choice of cards, Good to EX, 37 cards for 12.95.

#2: Baseball cigarette card from 1910, our choice 5.95.

#3: 500 assorted (mostly different) baseball cards from 1978 to 1984 in excellent condition for 19.95.

#4: Dallas Cowboy Weekly: 20 different back issues, our choice, for 14.95. We also have most single issues from 1977 to date available from 1.00 to 2.00 each. Send your want list. Some older issues also available.

#5: Poster: Robert Redford as "The Natural" plus free Bucky Dent poster, 6.95 postpaid.

#6: 1987 A.L. Smokey the Bear set of 16, 5.95.

#7: 1979 Topps baseball cards 50 different in excellent to mint condition including some stars, 4.95.

#8: 1980 Topps baseball cards 50 different in excellent to mint condition including some stars, 4.95.

#9: 1981 Topps baseball cards 50 different in excellent to mint condition including some stars, 3.95.

#10: 89 different 1984-85 Topps hockey cards in excellent to mint condition including some stars, 2.95.

#11: 66 different 1981-82 Topps basketball cards in excellent to mint condition including stars, 3.95.

#12: 115 different 1983 Topps football cards in excellent to mint condition including many stars, 2.95.

#13: Super Bowl XX game program, 5.00.

#14: 1979 Scottsdale Dodge Arizona Convention postcard set of 9 including Jocko Conlon, Charlie Grimm, etc. for 3.50.

#15: Dallas Cowboy Media Guide (not issued to the public): 1987 edition $5.00, 1986 edition 5.00, 1985 edition 5.00. Dallas Cowboys Bluebook: 1986 edition 13.95, 1985 edition 13.95

Send orders to:

FIRST BASE

231 Webb Chapel Village
Dallas, Texas 75229
(214) 243-5271

		NRMT	VG-E	GOOD
☐ 155	Ervin Dusak	20.00	10.00	2.00
☐ 156	Joe Garagiola	60.00	30.00	6.00
☐ 157	Tony Kaufmann	20.00	10.00	2.00
☐ 158	George Kurowski	20.00	10.00	2.00
☐ 159	Marty Marion	30.00	15.00	3.00
☐ 160	George Munger	20.00	10.00	2.00
☐ 161	Del Rice	20.00	10.00	2.00
☐ 162	Dick Sisler	20.00	10.00	2.00
☐ 163	Enos Slaughter	60.00	30.00	6.00
☐ 164	Ted Wilks	20.00	10.00	2.00

1951 Topps Blue Backs

The cards in this 52-card set measure 2" by 2 5/8". The 1951 Topps series of blue backed baseball cards could be used to play a baseball game by shuffling the cards and drawing them from a pile. These cards were marketed with a piece of caramel candy, which often melted or was squashed in such a way as to damage the card and wrapper (despite the fact that a paper shield was inserted between candy and card). Blue Backs are more difficult to obtain than the similarly styled Red Backs. The set is denoted on the cards as "Set B" and the Red Back set is correspondingly Set A. Appropriately leading off the set is Eddie Yost.

		NRMT	VG-E	GOOD
COMPLETE SET		1100.00	450.00	90.00
COMMON PLAYER (1-52)		18.00	9.00	1.80
☐ 1	Eddie Yost	21.00	10.50	2.10
☐ 2	Hank Majeski	18.00	9.00	1.80
☐ 3	Richie Ashburn	35.00	17.50	3.50
☐ 4	Del Ennis	21.00	10.50	2.10
☐ 5	Johnny Pesky	21.00	10.50	2.10
☐ 6	Al Schoendienst	25.00	12.50	2.50
☐ 7	Gerry Staley	18.00	9.00	1.80
☐ 8	Dick Sisler	18.00	9.00	1.80
☐ 9	Johnny Sain	25.00	12.50	2.50
☐ 10	Joe Page	21.00	10.50	2.10
☐ 11	Johnny Groth	18.00	9.00	1.80
☐ 12	Sam Jethroe	18.00	9.00	1.80
☐ 13	Mickey Vernon	21.00	10.50	2.10
☐ 14	Red Munger	18.00	9.00	1.80
☐ 15	Eddie Joost	18.00	9.00	1.80
☐ 16	Murry Dickson	18.00	9.00	1.80
☐ 17	Roy Smalley	18.00	9.00	1.80
☐ 18	Ned Garver	18.00	9.00	1.80
☐ 19	Phil Masi	18.00	9.00	1.80
☐ 20	Ralph Branca	21.00	10.50	2.10
☐ 21	Billy Johnson	18.00	9.00	1.80
☐ 22	Bob Kuzava	18.00	9.00	1.80
☐ 23	Dizzy Trout	18.00	9.00	1.80
☐ 24	Sherman Lollar	21.00	10.50	2.10
☐ 25	Sam Mele	18.00	9.00	1.80
☐ 26	Chico Carrasquel	18.00	9.00	1.80
☐ 27	Andy Pafko	18.00	9.00	1.80
☐ 28	Harry Brecheen	18.00	9.00	1.80
☐ 29	Granville Hamner	18.00	9.00	1.80
☐ 30	Enos Slaughter	45.00	22.50	4.50
☐ 31	Lou Brissie	18.00	9.00	1.80
☐ 32	Bob Elliott	21.00	10.50	2.10
☐ 33	Don Lenhardt	18.00	9.00	1.80
☐ 34	Earl Torgeson	18.00	9.00	1.80
☐ 35	Tommy Byrne	21.00	10.50	2.10
☐ 36	Cliff Fannin	18.00	9.00	1.80
☐ 37	Bobby Doerr	40.00	20.00	4.00
☐ 38	Irv Noren	18.00	9.00	1.80
☐ 39	Ed Lopat	25.00	12.50	2.50

		NRMT	VG-E	GOOD
☐ 40	Vic Wertz	21.00	10.50	2.10
☐ 41	Johnny Schmitz	18.00	9.00	1.80
☐ 42	Bruce Edwards	18.00	9.00	1.80
☐ 43	Willie Jones	18.00	9.00	1.80
☐ 44	Johnny Wyrostek	18.00	9.00	1.80
☐ 45	Billy Pierce	25.00	12.50	2.50
☐ 46	Gerry Priddy	18.00	9.00	1.80
☐ 47	Herman Wehmeier	18.00	9.00	1.80
☐ 48	Billy Cox	21.00	10.50	2.10
☐ 49	Henry Sauer	21.00	10.50	2.10
☐ 50	Johnny Mize	50.00	25.00	5.00
☐ 51	Eddie Waitkus	18.00	9.00	1.80
☐ 52	Sam Chapman	18.00	9.00	1.80

1951 Topps Red Backs

The cards in this 52-card set measure 2" by 2 5/8". The 1951 Topps Red Back set is identical in style to the Blue Back set of the same year. The cards have rounded corners and were designed to be used as a baseball game. Zernial, number 36, is listed with either the White Sox or Athletics, and Holmes, number 52, with either the Braves or Hartford. The set is denoted on the cards as "Set A" and the Blue Back set is correspondingly Set B.

		NRMT	VG-E	GOOD
COMPLETE SET		300.00	125.00	25.00
COMMON PLAYER (1-52)		3.00	1.50	.30
☐ 1	Yogi Berra	30.00	15.00	3.00
☐ 2	Sid Gordon	3.00	1.50	.30
☐ 3	Ferris Fain	3.50	1.75	.35
☐ 4	Vern Stephens	3.50	1.75	.35
☐ 5	Phil Rizzuto	12.50	6.25	1.25
☐ 6	Allie Reynolds	5.00	2.50	.50
☐ 7	Howie Pollet	3.00	1.50	.30
☐ 8	Early Wynn	9.00	4.50	.90
☐ 9	Roy Sievers	3.00	1.50	.30
☐ 10	Mel Parnell	3.00	1.50	.30
☐ 11	Gene Hermanski	3.00	1.50	.30
☐ 12	Jim Hegan	3.50	1.75	.35
☐ 13	Dale Mitchell	3.50	1.75	.35
☐ 14	Wayne Terwilliger	3.00	1.50	.30
☐ 15	Ralph Kiner	10.00	5.00	1.00
☐ 16	Preacher Roe	5.00	2.50	.50
☐ 17	Dave (Gus) Bell	4.00	2.00	.40
☐ 18	Gerry Coleman	3.50	1.75	.35
☐ 19	Dick Kokos	3.00	1.50	.30
☐ 20	Dom DiMaggio	5.00	2.50	.50
☐ 21	Larry Jansen	3.00	1.50	.30
☐ 22	Bob Feller	15.00	7.50	1.50
☐ 23	Ray Boone	3.50	1.75	.35
☐ 24	Hank Bauer	5.00	2.50	.50
☐ 25	Cliff Chambers	3.00	1.50	.30
☐ 26	Luke Easter	3.50	1.75	.35
☐ 27	Wally Westlake	3.00	1.50	.30
☐ 28	Elmer Valo	3.00	1.50	.30
☐ 29	Bob Kennedy	3.00	1.50	.30
☐ 30	Warren Spahn	13.50	6.50	1.25
☐ 31	Gil Hodges	12.50	6.25	1.25
☐ 32	Henry Thompson	3.50	1.75	.35
☐ 33	William Werle	3.00	1.50	.30
☐ 34	Grady Hatton	3.00	1.50	.30
☐ 35	Al Rosen	5.00	2.50	.50
☐ 36A	Gus Zernial (Chicago)	13.50	6.50	1.25
☐ 36B	Gus Zernial (Phila.)	8.50	4.25	.85
☐ 37	Wes Westrum	3.00	1.50	.30
☐ 38	Duke Snider	22.50	10.00	2.00
☐ 39	Ted Kluszewski	5.00	2.50	.50
☐ 40	Mike Garcia	3.50	1.75	.35

		NRMT	VG-E	GOOD
☐ 41	Whitey Lockman	3.00	1.50	.30
☐ 42	Ray Scarborough	3.00	1.50	.30
☐ 43	Maurice McDermott	3.00	1.50	.30
☐ 44	Sid Hudson	3.00	1.50	.30
☐ 45	Andy Seminick	3.00	1.50	.30
☐ 46	Billy Goodman	3.00	1.50	.30
☐ 47	Tommy Glaviano	3.00	1.50	.30
☐ 48	Eddie Stanky	3.50	1.75	.35
☐ 49	Al Zarilla	3.00	1.50	.30
☐ 50	Monte Irvin	13.50	6.50	1.25
☐ 51	Eddie Robinson	3.00	1.50	.30
☐ 52A	Tommy Holmes (Boston)	15.00	7.50	1.50
☐ 52B	Tommy Holmes (Hartford)	10.00	5.00	1.00

1951 Topps Teams

The cards in this 9 card set measure 2 1/16" by 5 1/4". These unnumbered team cards issued by Topps in 1951 carry black and white photographs framed by a yellow border. They are found with or without "1950" printed in the name panel before the team name (no difference in value for either variety). These cards were issued in the same 5 cent wrapper as the Connie Mack and Current All Stars. They have been assigned reference numbers in the checklist alphabetically by team city and name.

		NRMT	VG-E	GOOD
COMPLETE SET		1200.00	500.00	100.00
COMMON PLAYER (1-9)		100.00	50.00	10.00
☐1	Boston Red Sox	200.00	100.00	20.00
☐2	Brooklyn Dodgers	150.00	75.00	15.00
☐3	Chicago White Sox	150.00	75.00	15.00
☐4	Cincinnati Reds	120.00	60.00	12.00
☐5	New York Giants	150.00	75.00	15.00
☐6	Philadelphia Athletics	100.00	50.00	10.00
☐7	Philadelphia Phillies	120.00	60.00	12.00
☐8	St. Louis Cardinals	200.00	100.00	20.00
☐9	Washington Senators	100.00	50.00	10.00

1951 Topps Connie Mack

The cards in this 11 card set measure 2 1/16" by 5 1/4". The series of die-cut cards which comprise the set entitled Connie Mack All-Stars was one of Topps' most distinctive and fragile card designs. Printed on thin cardboard, these elegant cards were protected in the wrapper by panels of accompanying Red Backs, but once removed were easily damaged (after all, they were intended to be folded and used as toy figures). Cards without tops have a value less than one-half of that listed below. The cards are unnumbered and are listed below in alphabetical order.

		NRMT	VG-E	GOOD
COMPLETE SET		3300.00	1500.00	300.00
COMMON PLAYER (1-11)		100.00	50.00	10.00
☐ 1	Grover C. Alexander	300.00	150.00	30.00
☐ 2	Mickey Cochrane	200.00	100.00	20.00
☐ 3	Ed Collins	125.00	60.00	12.50
☐ 4	Jimmy Collins	100.00	50.00	10.00
☐ 5	Lou Gehrig	750.00	375.00	75.00
☐ 6	Walter Johnson	400.00	200.00	40.00
☐ 7	Connie Mack	200.00	100.00	20.00
☐ 8	Christy Mathewson	200.00	100.00	20.00
☐ 9	Babe Ruth	900.00	450.00	90.00
☐10	Tris Speaker	125.00	60.00	12.50
☐11	Honus Wagner	200.00	100.00	20.00

1951 Topps Current AS

The cards in this 11-card set measure 2 1/16" by 5 1/4". The 1951 Topps Current All-Star series is probably the rarest of all legitimate, nationally issued, post war baseball issues. The set price listed below does not include the prices for the cards of Konstanty, Roberts and Stanky, which likely never were released to the public in gum packs. These three cards (SP in the checklist below) were probably obtained directly from the company and exist in extremely limited numbers. As with the Connie Mack set, cards without the die-cut background are worth half of the value listed below. The cards are unnumbered and are listed below in alphabetical order.

		NRMT	VG-E	GOOD
COMPLETE SET (8)		2900.00	1200.00	250.00
COMMON PLAYER (1-11)		150.00	75.00	15.00
☐ 1	Yogi Berra	600.00	300.00	60.00
☐ 2	Larry Doby	200.00	100.00	20.00
☐ 3	Walt Dropo	250.00	125.00	25.00
☐ 4	Hoot Evers	150.00	75.00	15.00
☐ 5	George Kell	400.00	200.00	40.00
☐ 6	Ralph Kiner	400.00	200.00	40.00
☐ 7	Jim Konstanty SP	5000.00	2000.00	500.00
☐ 8	Bob Lemon	400.00	200.00	40.00
☐ 9	Phil Rizzuto	400.00	200.00	40.00
☐10	Robin Roberts SP	5000.00	2000.00	500.00
☐11	Eddie Stanky SP	5000.00	2000.00	500.00

1952 Topps

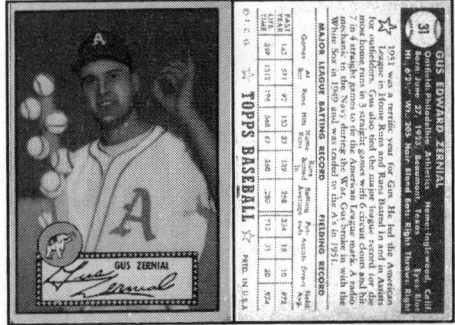

The cards in this 407-card set measure 2 5/8" by 3 3/4". The 1952 Topps set is Topps' first truly major set. Card numbers 1 to 80 were issued with red or black backs, both of which are less plentiful than card numbers 81 to 250. In fact the first series is considered the most difficult with respect to finding Mint condition cards. Card number 48 (Joe Page) and number 49 (Johnny Sain) can be found with each other's write-up on their back. Card numbers 251 to 310 are somewhat scarce and numbers 311 to 407 are quite scarce. Cards 281-300 were single printed compared to the other cards in the next to last series. Cards 311-313 were double printed on the last high number printing sheet. The key card in the set is obviously Mickey Mantle #311, Mickey's first of many Topps cards.

	NRMT	VG-E	GOOD
COMPLETE SET	33000.	12000.	2500.
COMMON PLAYER (1-80)	45.00	22.50	4.50
COMMON PLAYER (81-250)	15.00	7.50	1.50
COMMON PLAYER (251-280)	35.00	17.50	3.50
COMMON PLAYER (281-300)	45.00	22.50	4.50
COMMON PLAYER (301-310)	35.00	17.50	3.50

COMMON PLAYER (311-407) 135.00 65.00 13.50

☐	1	Andy Pafko	500.00	35.00	7.00
☐	2	James Pete Runnels	50.00	25.00	5.00
☐	3	Henry Thompson	50.00	25.00	5.00
☐	4	Don Lenhardt	45.00	22.50	4.50
☐	5	Larry Jansen	45.00	22.50	4.50
☐	6	Grady Hatton	45.00	22.50	4.50
☐	7	Wayne Terwilliger	45.00	22.50	4.50
☐	8	Fred Marsh	45.00	22.50	4.50
☐	9	Robert Hogue	45.00	22.50	4.50
☐	10	Al Rosen	60.00	30.00	6.00
☐	11	Phil Rizzuto	125.00	60.00	12.50
☐	12	Romanus Basgall	45.00	22.50	4.50
☐	13	Johnny Wyrostek	45.00	22.50	4.50
☐	14	Bob Elliott	50.00	25.00	5.00
☐	15	Johnny Pesky	50.00	25.00	5.00
☐	16	Gene Hermanski	45.00	22.50	4.50
☐	17	Jim Hegan	50.00	25.00	5.00
☐	18	Merrill Combs	45.00	22.50	4.50
☐	19	Johnny Bucha	45.00	22.50	4.50
☐	20	Billy Loes	75.00	37.50	7.50
☐	21	Ferris Fain	50.00	25.00	5.00
☐	22	Dom DiMaggio	75.00	37.50	7.50
☐	23	Billy Goodman	50.00	25.00	5.00
☐	24	Luke Easter	50.00	25.00	5.00
☐	25	John Groth	45.00	22.50	4.50
☐	26	Monte Irvin	90.00	45.00	9.00
☐	27	Sam Jethroe	45.00	22.50	4.50
☐	28	Jerry Priddy	45.00	22.50	4.50
☐	29	Ted Kluszewski	60.00	30.00	6.00
☐	30	Mel Parnell	50.00	25.00	5.00
☐	31	Gus Zernial	50.00	25.00	5.00
☐	32	Eddie Robinson	45.00	22.50	4.50
☐	33	Warren Spahn	125.00	60.00	12.50
☐	34	Elmer Valo	45.00	22.50	4.50
☐	35	Hank Sauer	50.00	25.00	5.00
☐	36	Gil Hodges	100.00	50.00	10.00
☐	37	Duke Snider	200.00	100.00	20.00
☐	38	Wally Westlake	45.00	22.50	4.50
☐	39	Dizzy Trout	50.00	25.00	5.00
☐	40	Irv Noren	45.00	22.50	4.50
☐	41	Bob Wellman	45.00	22.50	4.50
☐	42	Lou Kretlow	45.00	22.50	4.50
☐	43	Ray Scarborough	45.00	22.50	4.50
☐	44	Con Dempsey	45.00	22.50	4.50
☐	45	Eddie Joost	45.00	22.50	4.50
☐	46	Gordon Goldsberry	45.00	22.50	4.50
☐	47	Willie Jones	45.00	22.50	4.50
☐	48A	Joe Page COR	60.00	30.00	6.00
☐	48B	Joe Page ERR	200.00	100.00	20.00
☐	49A	Johnny Sain COR	60.00	30.00	6.00
☐	49B	Johnny Sain ERR	200.00	100.00	20.00
☐	50	Marv Rickert	45.00	22.50	4.50
☐	51	Jim Russell	45.00	22.50	4.50
☐	52	Don Mueller	50.00	25.00	5.00
☐	53	Chris Van Cuyk	45.00	22.50	4.50
☐	54	Leo Kiely	45.00	22.50	4.50
☐	55	Ray Boone	50.00	25.00	5.00
☐	56	Thomas Glaviano	45.00	22.50	4.50
☐	57	Ed Lopat	75.00	37.50	7.50
☐	58	Bob Mahoney	45.00	22.50	4.50
☐	59	Robin Roberts	100.00	50.00	10.00
☐	60	Sid Hudson	45.00	22.50	4.50
☐	61	Tookie Gilbert	45.00	22.50	4.50
☐	62	Chuck Stobbs	45.00	22.50	4.50
☐	63	Howie Pollet	45.00	22.50	4.50
☐	64	Roy Sievers	50.00	25.00	5.00
☐	65	Enos Slaughter	90.00	45.00	9.00
☐	66	Preacher Roe	75.00	37.50	7.50
☐	67	Allie Reynolds	75.00	37.50	7.50
☐	68	Cliff Chambers	45.00	22.50	4.50
☐	69	Virgil Stallcup	45.00	22.50	4.50
☐	70	Al Zarilla	45.00	22.50	4.50
☐	71	Tom Upton	45.00	22.50	4.50
☐	72	Karl Olson	45.00	22.50	4.50
☐	73	William Werle	45.00	22.50	4.50
☐	74	Andy Hansen	45.00	22.50	4.50
☐	75	Wes Westrum	45.00	22.50	4.50
☐	76	Eddie Stanky	50.00	25.00	5.00
☐	77	Bob Kennedy	45.00	22.50	4.50
☐	78	Ellis Kinder	45.00	22.50	4.50
☐	79	Gerald Staley	45.00	22.50	4.50
☐	80	Herman Wehmeier	45.00	22.50	4.50
☐	81	Vernon Law	20.00	10.00	2.00
☐	82	Duane Pillette	15.00	7.50	1.50
☐	83	Billy Johnson	15.00	7.50	1.50
☐	84	Vern Stephens	18.00	9.00	1.80
☐	85	Bob Kuzava	15.00	7.50	1.50
☐	86	Ted Gray	15.00	7.50	1.50
☐	87	Dale Coogan	15.00	7.50	1.50
☐	88	Bob Feller	90.00	45.00	9.00
☐	89	Johnny Lipon	15.00	7.50	1.50
☐	90	Mickey Grasso	15.00	7.50	1.50
☐	91	Red Schoendienst	22.00	11.00	2.20
☐	92	Dale Mitchell	18.00	9.00	1.80
☐	93	Al Sima	15.00	7.50	1.50
☐	94	Sam Mele	15.00	7.50	1.50
☐	95	Ken Holcombe	15.00	7.50	1.50
☐	96	Willard Marshall	15.00	7.50	1.50
☐	97	Earl Torgeson	15.00	7.50	1.50
☐	98	Billy Pierce	18.00	9.00	1.80
☐	99	Gene Woodling	24.00	12.00	2.40
☐	100	Del Rice	15.00	7.50	1.50
☐	101	Max Lanier	15.00	7.50	1.50
☐	102	Bill Kennedy	15.00	7.50	1.50
☐	103	Cliff Mapes	15.00	7.50	1.50
☐	104	Don Kolloway	15.00	7.50	1.50
☐	105	John Pramesa	15.00	7.50	1.50
☐	106	Mickey Vernon	18.00	9.00	1.80
☐	107	Connie Ryan	15.00	7.50	1.50
☐	108	Jim Konstanty	18.00	9.00	1.80
☐	109	Ted Wilks	15.00	7.50	1.50
☐	110	Dutch Leonard	15.00	7.50	1.50
☐	111	Peanuts Lowrey	15.00	7.50	1.50
☐	112	Henry Majeski	15.00	7.50	1.50
☐	113	Dick Sisler	15.00	7.50	1.50
☐	114	Willard Ramsdell	15.00	7.50	1.50
☐	115	Red Munger	15.00	7.50	1.50
☐	116	Carl Scheib	15.00	7.50	1.50
☐	117	Sherman Lollar	18.00	9.00	1.80
☐	118	Ken Raffensberger	15.00	7.50	1.50
☐	119	Mickey McDermott	15.00	7.50	1.50
☐	120	Bob Chakales	15.00	7.50	1.50
☐	121	Gus Niarhos	15.00	7.50	1.50
☐	122	Jackie Jensen	30.00	15.00	3.00
☐	123	Eddie Yost	18.00	9.00	1.80
☐	124	Monte Kennedy	15.00	7.50	1.50
☐	125	Bill Rigney	18.00	9.00	1.80
☐	126	Fred Hutchinson	20.00	10.00	2.00
☐	127	Paul Minner	15.00	7.50	1.50
☐	128	Don Bollweg	15.00	7.50	1.50
☐	129	Johnny Mize	50.00	25.00	5.00
☐	130	Sheldon Jones	15.00	7.50	1.50
☐	131	Morris Martin	15.00	7.50	1.50
☐	132	Clyde Klutz	15.00	7.50	1.50
☐	133	Al Widmar	15.00	7.50	1.50
☐	134	Joe Tipton	15.00	7.50	1.50
☐	135	Dixie Howell	15.00	7.50	1.50
☐	136	Johnny Schmitz	15.00	7.50	1.50
☐	137	Roy McMillan	15.00	7.50	1.50
☐	138	Bill MacDonald	15.00	7.50	1.50
☐	139	Ken Wood	15.00	7.50	1.50
☐	140	Johnny Antonelli	18.00	9.00	1.80
☐	141	Clint Hartung	18.00	9.00	1.80
☐	142	Harry Perkowski	15.00	7.50	1.50
☐	143	Les Moss	15.00	7.50	1.50
☐	144	Ed Blake	15.00	7.50	1.50
☐	145	Joe Haynes	15.00	7.50	1.50
☐	146	Frank House	15.00	7.50	1.50
☐	147	Bob Young	15.00	7.50	1.50
☐	148	Johnny Klippstein	15.00	7.50	1.50
☐	149	Dick Kryhoski	15.00	7.50	1.50
☐	150	Ted Beard	15.00	7.50	1.50
☐	151	Wally Post	18.00	9.00	1.80
☐	152	Al Evans	15.00	7.50	1.50
☐	153	Bob Rush	15.00	7.50	1.50
☐	154	Joe Muir	15.00	7.50	1.50
☐	155	Frank Overmire	15.00	7.50	1.50
☐	156	Frank Hiller	15.00	7.50	1.50
☐	157	Bob Usher	15.00	7.50	1.50
☐	158	Eddie Waitkus	15.00	7.50	1.50
☐	159	Saul Rogovin	15.00	7.50	1.50
☐	160	Owen Friend	15.00	7.50	1.50
☐	161	Bud Byerly	15.00	7.50	1.50
☐	162	Del Crandall	18.00	9.00	1.80
☐	163	Stan Rojek	15.00	7.50	1.50
☐	164	Walt Dubiel	15.00	7.50	1.50
☐	165	Eddie Kazak	15.00	7.50	1.50
☐	166	Paul LaPalme	15.00	7.50	1.50
☐	167	Bill Howerton	15.00	7.50	1.50
☐	168	Charlie Silvera	15.00	7.50	1.50
☐	169	Howie Judson	15.00	7.50	1.50
☐	170	Gus Bell	18.00	9.00	1.80
☐	171	Ed Erautt	15.00	7.50	1.50
☐	172	Eddie Miksis	15.00	7.50	1.50
☐	173	Roy Smalley	15.00	7.50	1.50
☐	174	Clarence Marshall	15.00	7.50	1.50
☐	175	Billy Martin	150.00	75.00	15.00
☐	176	Hank Edwards	15.00	7.50	1.50
☐	177	Bill Wight	15.00	7.50	1.50
☐	178	Cass Michaels	15.00	7.50	1.50
☐	179	Frank Smith	15.00	7.50	1.50
☐	180	Charley Maxwell	15.00	7.50	1.50
☐	181	Bob Swift	15.00	7.50	1.50
☐	182	Billy Hitchcock	15.00	7.50	1.50
☐	183	Erv Dusak	15.00	7.50	1.50
☐	184	Bob Ramazotti	15.00	7.50	1.50
☐	185	Bill Nicholson	15.00	7.50	1.50
☐	186	Walt Masterson	15.00	7.50	1.50

☐ 187	Bob Miller	15.00	7.50	1.50	☐ 282	Birdie Tebbetts SP	45.00	22.50	4.50
☐ 188	Clarence Podbielan	15.00	7.50	1.50	☐ 283	Philip Masi SP	45.00	22.50	4.50
☐ 189	Pete Reiser	20.00	10.00	2.00	☐ 284	Hank Arft SP	45.00	22.50	4.50
☐ 190	Don Johnson	15.00	7.50	1.50	☐ 285	Cliff Fannin SP	45.00	22.50	4.50
☐ 191	Yogi Berra	200.00	100.00	20.00	☐ 286	Joe DeMaestri SP	45.00	22.50	4.50
☐ 192	Myron Ginsberg	15.00	7.50	1.50	☐ 287	Steve Bilko SP	45.00	22.50	4.50
☐ 193	Harry Simpson	15.00	7.50	1.50	☐ 288	Chet Nichols SP	45.00	22.50	4.50
☐ 194	Joe Hatton	15.00	7.50	1.50	☐ 289	Tommy Holmes SP	50.00	25.00	5.00
☐ 195	Minnie Minoso	30.00	15.00	3.00	☐ 290	Joe Astroth SP	45.00	22.50	4.50
☐ 196	Solly Hemus	15.00	7.50	1.50	☐ 291	Gil Coan SP	45.00	22.50	4.50
☐ 197	George Strickland	15.00	7.50	1.50	☐ 292	Floyd Baker SP	45.00	22.50	4.50
☐ 198	Phil Haugstad	15.00	7.50	1.50	☐ 293	Sibby Sisti SP	45.00	22.50	4.50
☐ 199	George Zuverink	15.00	7.50	1.50	☐ 294	Walker Cooper SP	45.00	22.50	4.50
☐ 200	Ralph Houk	40.00	20.00	4.00	☐ 295	Phil Cavarretta SP	50.00	25.00	5.00
☐ 201	Alex Kellner	15.00	7.50	1.50	☐ 296	Red Rolfe SP	50.00	25.00	5.00
☐ 202	Joe Collins	18.00	9.00	1.80	☐ 297	Andy Seminick SP	45.00	22.50	4.50
☐ 203	Curt Simmons	18.00	9.00	1.80	☐ 298	Bob Ross SP	45.00	22.50	4.50
☐ 204	Ron Northey	15.00	7.50	1.50	☐ 299	Ray Murray SP	45.00	22.50	4.50
☐ 205	Clyde King	15.00	7.50	1.50	☐ 300	Barney McCosky SP	45.00	22.50	4.50
☐ 206	Joe Ostrowski	15.00	7.50	1.50	☐ 301	Bob Porterfield	35.00	17.50	3.50
☐ 207	Mickey Harris	15.00	7.50	1.50	☐ 302	Max Surkont	35.00	17.50	3.50
☐ 208	Marlin Stuart	15.00	7.50	1.50	☐ 303	Harry Dorish	35.00	17.50	3.50
☐ 209	Howie Fox	15.00	7.50	1.50	☐ 304	Sam Dente	35.00	17.50	3.50
☐ 210	Dick Fowler	15.00	7.50	1.50	☐ 305	Paul Richards	40.00	20.00	4.00
☐ 211	Ray Coleman	15.00	7.50	1.50	☐ 306	Lou Sleater	35.00	17.50	3.50
☐ 212	Ned Garver	15.00	7.50	1.50	☐ 307	Frank Campos	35.00	17.50	3.50
☐ 213	Nippy Jones	15.00	7.50	1.50	☐ 308	Luis Aloma	35.00	17.50	3.50
☐ 214	Johnny Hopp	18.00	9.00	1.80	☐ 309	Jim Busby	35.00	17.50	3.50
☐ 215	Hank Bauer	30.00	15.00	3.00	☐ 310	George Metkovich	35.00	17.50	3.50
☐ 216	Richie Ashburn	35.00	17.50	3.50	☐ 311	Mickey Mantle DP	6000.00	2000.00	400.00
☐ 217	Snuffy Stirnweiss	18.00	9.00	1.80	☐ 312	Jackie Robinson DP	750.00	375.00	75.00
☐ 218	Clyde McCullough	15.00	7.50	1.50	☐ 313	Bobby Thomson DP	150.00	75.00	15.00
☐ 219	Bobby Shantz	20.00	10.00	2.00	☐ 314	Roy Campanella	1200.00	450.00	90.00
☐ 220	Joe Presko	15.00	7.50	1.50	☐ 315	Leo Durocher	200.00	100.00	20.00
☐ 221	Granny Hamner	15.00	7.50	1.50	☐ 316	Dave Williams	150.00	75.00	15.00
☐ 222	Hoot Evers	15.00	7.50	1.50	☐ 317	Conrado Marrerro	135.00	65.00	13.50
☐ 223	Del Ennis	18.00	9.00	1.80	☐ 318	Harold Gregg	135.00	65.00	13.50
☐ 224	Bruce Edwards	15.00	7.50	1.50	☐ 319	Al Walker	135.00	65.00	13.50
☐ 225	Frank Baumholtz	15.00	7.50	1.50	☐ 320	John Rutherford	135.00	65.00	13.50
☐ 226	Dave Philley	15.00	7.50	1.50	☐ 321	Joe Black	175.00	85.00	18.00
☐ 227	Joe Garagiola	45.00	22.50	4.50	☐ 322	Randy Jackson	135.00	65.00	13.50
☐ 228	Al Brazle	15.00	7.50	1.50	☐ 323	Bubba Church	135.00	65.00	13.50
☐ 229	Gene Bearden	15.00	7.50	1.50	☐ 324	Warren Hacker	135.00	65.00	13.50
☐ 230	Matt Batts	15.00	7.50	1.50	☐ 325	Bill Serena	135.00	65.00	13.50
☐ 231	Sam Zoldak	15.00	7.50	1.50	☐ 326	George Shuba	150.00	75.00	15.00
☐ 232	Billy Cox	18.00	9.00	1.80	☐ 327	Al Wilson	135.00	65.00	13.50
☐ 233	Bob Friend	20.00	10.00	2.00	☐ 328	Bob Borkowski	135.00	65.00	13.50
☐ 234	Steve Souchock	15.00	7.50	1.50	☐ 329	Ike Delock	135.00	65.00	13.50
☐ 235	Walt Dropo	18.00	9.00	1.80	☐ 330	Turk Lown	135.00	65.00	13.50
☐ 236	Ed Fitzgerald	15.00	7.50	1.50	☐ 331	Tom Morgan	135.00	65.00	13.50
☐ 237	Jerry Coleman	20.00	10.00	2.00	☐ 332	Anthony Bartirome	135.00	65.00	13.50
☐ 238	Art Houtteman	15.00	7.50	1.50	☐ 333	Pee Wee Reese	500.00	250.00	50.00
☐ 239	Rocky Bridges	15.00	7.50	1.50	☐ 334	Wilmer Mizell	135.00	65.00	13.50
☐ 240	Jack Phillips	15.00	7.50	1.50	☐ 335	Ted Lepcio	135.00	65.00	13.50
☐ 241	Tommy Byrne	18.00	9.00	1.80	☐ 336	Dave Koslo	135.00	65.00	13.50
☐ 242	Tom Poholsky	15.00	7.50	1.50	☐ 337	Jim Hearn	135.00	65.00	13.50
☐ 243	Larry Doby	24.00	12.00	2.40	☐ 338	Sal Yvars	135.00	65.00	13.50
☐ 244	Vic Wertz	18.00	9.00	1.80	☐ 339	Russ Meyer	135.00	65.00	13.50
☐ 245	Sherry Robertson	15.00	7.50	1.50	☐ 340	Bob Hooper	135.00	65.00	13.50
☐ 246	George Kell	45.00	22.50	4.50	☐ 341	Hal Jeffcoat	135.00	65.00	13.50
☐ 247	Randy Gumpert	15.00	7.50	1.50	☐ 342	Clem Labine	150.00	75.00	15.00
☐ 248	Frank Shea	15.00	7.50	1.50	☐ 343	Dick Gernert	135.00	65.00	13.50
☐ 249	Bobby Adams	15.00	7.50	1.50	☐ 344	Ewell Blackwell	150.00	75.00	15.00
☐ 250	Carl Erskine	30.00	15.00	3.00	☐ 345	Sammy White	135.00	65.00	13.50
☐ 251	Chico Carrasquel	35.00	17.50	3.50	☐ 346	George Spencer	135.00	65.00	13.50
☐ 252	Vern Bickford	35.00	17.50	3.50	☐ 347	Joe Adcock	175.00	85.00	18.00
☐ 253	Johnny Berardino	40.00	20.00	4.00	☐ 348	Robert Kelly	135.00	65.00	13.50
☐ 254	Joe Dobson	35.00	17.50	3.50	☐ 349	Bob Cain	135.00	65.00	13.50
☐ 255	Clyde Vollmer	35.00	17.50	3.50	☐ 350	Cal Abrams	135.00	65.00	13.50
☐ 256	Pete Suder	35.00	17.50	3.50	☐ 351	Alvin Dark	175.00	85.00	18.00
☐ 257	Bobby Avila	40.00	20.00	4.00	☐ 352	Karl Drews	135.00	65.00	13.50
☐ 258	Steve Gromek	35.00	17.50	3.50	☐ 353	Bobby Del Greco	135.00	65.00	13.50
☐ 259	Bob Addis	35.00	17.50	3.50	☐ 354	Fred Hatfield	135.00	65.00	13.50
☐ 260	Pete Castiglione	35.00	17.50	3.50	☐ 355	Bobby Morgan	135.00	65.00	13.50
☐ 261	Willie Mays	900.00	450.00	90.00	☐ 356	Toby Atwell	135.00	65.00	13.50
☐ 262	Virgil Trucks	40.00	20.00	4.00	☐ 357	Smoky Burgess	150.00	75.00	15.00
☐ 263	Harry Brecheen	40.00	20.00	4.00	☐ 358	John Kucab	135.00	65.00	13.50
☐ 264	Roy Hartsfield	35.00	17.50	3.50	☐ 359	Dee Fondy	135.00	65.00	13.50
☐ 265	Chuck Diering	35.00	17.50	3.50	☐ 360	George Crowe	135.00	65.00	13.50
☐ 266	Murry Dickson	35.00	17.50	3.50	☐ 361	William Posedel	135.00	65.00	13.50
☐ 267	Sid Gordon	35.00	17.50	3.50	☐ 362	Ken Heintzelman	135.00	65.00	13.50
☐ 268	Bob Lemon	125.00	60.00	12.50	☐ 363	Dick Rozek	135.00	65.00	13.50
☐ 269	Willard Nixon	35.00	17.50	3.50	☐ 364	Clyde Sukeforth	135.00	65.00	13.50
☐ 270	Lou Brissie	35.00	17.50	3.50	☐ 365	Cookie Lavagetto	135.00	65.00	13.50
☐ 271	Jim Delsing	35.00	17.50	3.50	☐ 366	Dave Madison	135.00	65.00	13.50
☐ 272	Mike Garcia	45.00	22.50	4.50	☐ 367	Ben Thorpe	135.00	65.00	13.50
☐ 273	Erv Palica	35.00	17.50	3.50	☐ 368	Ed Wright	135.00	65.00	13.50
☐ 274	Ralph Branca	45.00	22.50	4.50	☐ 369	Dick Groat	250.00	125.00	25.00
☐ 275	Pat Mullin	35.00	17.50	3.50	☐ 370	Billy Hoeft	135.00	65.00	13.50
☐ 276	Jim Wilson	35.00	17.50	3.50	☐ 371	Bobby Hofman	135.00	65.00	13.50
☐ 277	Early Wynn	125.00	60.00	12.50	☐ 372	Gil McDougald	250.00	125.00	25.00
☐ 278	Al Clark	35.00	17.50	3.50	☐ 373	Jim Turner COA	150.00	75.00	15.00
☐ 279	Ed Stewart	35.00	17.50	3.50	☐ 374	John Benton	135.00	65.00	13.50
☐ 280	Cloyd Boyer	40.00	20.00	4.00	☐ 375	John Merson	135.00	65.00	13.50
☐ 281	Tommy Brown SP	45.00	22.50	4.50	☐ 376	Faye Throneberry	135.00	65.00	13.50

			NRMT	VG-E	GOOD
☐ 377	Chuck Dressen MG		175.00	85.00	18.00
☐ 378	Leroy Fusselman		135.00	65.00	13.50
☐ 379	Joseph Rossi		135.00	65.00	13.50
☐ 380	Clem Koshorek		135.00	65.00	13.50
☐ 381	Milton Stock		135.00	65.00	13.50
☐ 382	Sam Jones		150.00	75.00	15.00
☐ 383	Del Wilber		135.00	65.00	13.50
☐ 384	Frank Crosetti COA		250.00	125.00	25.00
☐ 385	Herman Franks		150.00	75.00	15.00
☐ 386	John Yuhas		135.00	65.00	13.50
☐ 387	William Meyer		135.00	65.00	13.50
☐ 388	Bob Chipman		135.00	65.00	13.50
☐ 389	Ben Wade		135.00	65.00	13.50
☐ 390	Glenn Nelson		135.00	65.00	13.50
☐ 391	Ben Chapman (photo actually Sam Chapman)		135.00	65.00	13.50
☐ 392	Hoyt Wilhelm		400.00	200.00	40.00
☐ 393	Ebba St.Claire		135.00	65.00	13.50
☐ 394	Billy Herman COA		200.00	100.00	20.00
☐ 395	Jake Pitler COA		135.00	65.00	13.50
☐ 396	Dick Williams		175.00	85.00	18.00
☐ 397	Forrest Main		135.00	65.00	13.50
☐ 398	Hal Rice		135.00	65.00	13.50
☐ 399	Jim Fridley		135.00	65.00	13.50
☐ 400	Bill Dickey COA		500.00	250.00	50.00
☐ 401	Bob Schultz		135.00	65.00	13.50
☐ 402	Earl Harrist		135.00	65.00	13.50
☐ 403	Bill Miller		135.00	65.00	13.50
☐ 404	Dick Brodowski		135.00	65.00	13.50
☐ 405	Ed Pellagrini		135.00	65.00	13.50
☐ 406	Joe Nuxhall		175.00	85.00	18.00
☐ 407	Eddie Mathews		1500.00	400.00	80.00

1953 Topps

The cards in this 274-card set measure 2 5/8" by 3/3/4". Although the last card is numbered 280, there are only 274 cards in the set since numbers 253, 261, 267, 268, 271, and 275 were never issued. The 1953 Topps series contains line drawings of players in full color. The name and team panel at the card base is easily damaged, making it very difficult to complete a mint set. The high number series, 221 to 280, was produced in shorter supply late in the year and hence is more difficult to complete than the lower numbers. The key cards in the set are Mickey Mantle #82 and Willie Mays #244.

	NRMT	VG-E	GOOD
COMPLETE SET	8500.00	3000.00	600.00
COMMON PLAYER (1-165)	10.00	5.00	1.00
COMMON PLAYER (166-220)	8.00	4.00	.80
COMMON PLAYER (221-280)	40.00	20.00	4.00

			NRMT	VG-E	GOOD
☐	1	Jackie Robinson	250.00	125.00	25.00
☐	2	Luke Easter	11.00	5.50	1.10
☐	3	George Crowe	10.00	5.00	1.00
☐	4	Ben Wade	10.00	5.00	1.00
☐	5	Joe Dobson	10.00	5.00	1.00
☐	6	Sam Jones	10.00	5.00	1.00
☐	7	Bob Borkowski	10.00	5.00	1.00
☐	8	Clem Koshorek	10.00	5.00	1.00
☐	9	Joe Collins	10.00	5.00	1.00
☐	10	Smoky Burgess	12.00	6.00	1.20
☐	11	Sal Yvars	10.00	5.00	1.00
☐	12	Howie Judson	10.00	5.00	1.00
☐	13	Connie Marrero	10.00	5.00	1.00

			NRMT	VG-E	GOOD
☐	14	Clem Labine	12.00	6.00	1.20
☐	15	Bobo Newsom	12.00	6.00	1.20
☐	16	Peanuts Lowrey	10.00	5.00	1.00
☐	17	Billy Hitchcock	10.00	5.00	1.00
☐	18	Ted Lepcio	10.00	5.00	1.00
☐	19	Mel Parnell	12.00	6.00	1.20
☐	20	Hank Thompson	11.00	5.50	1.10
☐	21	Billy Johnson	10.00	5.00	1.00
☐	22	Howie Fox	10.00	5.00	1.00
☐	23	Toby Atwell	10.00	5.00	1.00
☐	24	Ferris Fain	11.00	5.50	1.10
☐	25	Ray Boone	11.00	5.50	1.10
☐	26	Dale Mitchell	12.00	6.00	1.20
☐	27	Roy Campanella	125.00	60.00	12.50
☐	28	Eddie Pellagrini	10.00	5.00	1.00
☐	29	Hal Jeffcoat	10.00	5.00	1.00
☐	30	Willard Nixon	10.00	5.00	1.00
☐	31	Ewell Blackwell	15.00	7.50	1.50
☐	32	Clyde Vollmer	10.00	5.00	1.00
☐	33	Bob Kennedy	11.00	5.50	1.10
☐	34	George Shuba	12.00	6.00	1.20
☐	35	Irv Noren	11.00	5.50	1.10
☐	36	Johnny Groth	10.00	5.00	1.00
☐	37	Ed Mathews	50.00	25.00	5.00
☐	38	Jim Hearn	10.00	5.00	1.00
☐	39	Eddie Miksis	10.00	5.00	1.00
☐	40	John Lipon	10.00	5.00	1.00
☐	41	Enos Slaughter	35.00	17.50	3.50
☐	42	Gus Zernial	10.00	5.00	1.00
☐	43	Gil McDougald	18.00	9.00	1.80
☐	44	Ellis Kinder	10.00	5.00	1.00
☐	45	Grady Hatton	10.00	5.00	1.00
☐	46	Johnny Klippstein	10.00	5.00	1.00
☐	47	Bubba Church	10.00	5.00	1.00
☐	48	Bob Del Greco	10.00	5.00	1.00
☐	49	Faye Throneberry	10.00	5.00	1.00
☐	50	Chuck Dressen MG	12.00	6.00	1.20
☐	51	Frank Campos	10.00	5.00	1.00
☐	52	Ted Gray	10.00	5.00	1.00
☐	53	Sherman Lollar	11.00	5.50	1.10
☐	54	Bob Feller	60.00	30.00	6.00
☐	55	Maurice McDermott	10.00	5.00	1.00
☐	56	Gerry Staley	10.00	5.00	1.00
☐	57	Carl Scheib	10.00	5.00	1.00
☐	58	George Metkovich	10.00	5.00	1.00
☐	59	Karl Drews	10.00	5.00	1.00
☐	60	Cloyd Boyer	11.00	5.50	1.10
☐	61	Early Wynn	35.00	17.50	3.50
☐	62	Monte Irvin	25.00	12.50	2.50
☐	63	Gus Niarhos	10.00	5.00	1.00
☐	64	Dave Philley	10.00	5.00	1.00
☐	65	Earl Harrist	10.00	5.00	1.00
☐	66	Minnie Minoso	15.00	7.50	1.50
☐	67	Roy Sievers	11.00	5.50	1.10
☐	68	Del Rice	10.00	5.00	1.00
☐	69	Dick Brodowski	10.00	5.00	1.00
☐	70	Ed Yuhas	10.00	5.00	1.00
☐	71	Tony Bartirome	10.00	5.00	1.00
☐	72	Fred Hutchinson	12.00	6.00	1.20
☐	73	Eddie Robinson	10.00	5.00	1.00
☐	74	Joe Rossi	10.00	5.00	1.00
☐	75	Mike Garcia	12.00	6.00	1.20
☐	76	Pee Wee Reese	60.00	30.00	6.00
☐	77	Johnny Mize	35.00	17.50	3.50
☐	78	Al(Red) Schoendienst	15.00	7.50	1.50
☐	79	Johnny Wyrostek	10.00	5.00	1.00
☐	80	Jim Hegan	11.00	5.50	1.10
☐	81	Joe Black	20.00	10.00	2.00
☐	82	Mickey Mantle	1350.00	500.00	100.00
☐	83	Howie Pollet	10.00	5.00	1.00
☐	84	Bob Hooper	10.00	5.00	1.00
☐	85	Bobby Morgan	10.00	5.00	1.00
☐	86	Billy Martin	40.00	20.00	4.00
☐	87	Ed Lopat	18.00	9.00	1.80
☐	88	Willie Jones	10.00	5.00	1.00
☐	89	Chuck Stobbs	10.00	5.00	1.00
☐	90	Hank Edwards	10.00	5.00	1.00
☐	91	Ebba St.Claire	10.00	5.00	1.00
☐	92	Paul Minner	10.00	5.00	1.00
☐	93	Hal Rice	10.00	5.00	1.00
☐	94	Bill Kennedy	10.00	5.00	1.00
☐	95	Willard Marshall	10.00	5.00	1.00
☐	96	Virgil Trucks	11.00	5.50	1.10
☐	97	Don Kolloway	10.00	5.00	1.00
☐	98	Cal Abrams	10.00	5.00	1.00
☐	99	Dave Madison	10.00	5.00	1.00
☐	100	Bill Miller	10.00	5.00	1.00
☐	101	Ted Wilks	10.00	5.00	1.00
☐	102	Connie Ryan	10.00	5.00	1.00
☐	103	Joe Astroth	10.00	5.00	1.00
☐	104	Yogi Berra	100.00	50.00	10.00
☐	105	Joe Nuxhall	11.00	5.50	1.10
☐	106	Johnny Antonelli	11.00	5.50	1.10
☐	107	Danny O'Connell	10.00	5.00	1.00
☐	108	Bob Porterfield	10.00	5.00	1.00

☐ 109	Alvin Dark	13.50	6.00	1.00
☐ 110	Herman Wehmeier	10.00	5.00	1.00
☐ 111	Hank Sauer	12.00	6.00	1.20
☐ 112	Ned Garver	10.00	5.00	1.00
☐ 113	Jerry Priddy	10.00	5.00	1.00
☐ 114	Phil Rizzuto	50.00	25.00	5.00
☐ 115	George Spencer	10.00	5.00	1.00
☐ 116	Frank Smith	10.00	5.00	1.00
☐ 117	Sid Gordon	10.00	5.00	1.00
☐ 118	Gus Bell	11.00	5.50	1.10
☐ 119	John Sain	18.00	9.00	1.80
☐ 120	Davey Williams	12.00	6.00	1.20
☐ 121	Walter Dropo	11.00	5.50	1.10
☐ 122	Elmer Valo	10.00	5.00	1.00
☐ 123	Tommy Byrne	11.00	5.50	1.10
☐ 124	Sibby Sisti	10.00	5.00	1.00
☐ 125	Dick Williams	13.50	5.50	1.10
☐ 126	Bill Connelly	10.00	5.00	1.00
☐ 127	Clint Courtney	10.00	5.00	1.00
☐ 128	Wilmer Mizell	11.00	5.50	1.10
☐ 129	Keith Thomas	10.00	5.00	1.00
☐ 130	Turk Lown	10.00	5.00	1.00
☐ 131	Harry Byrd	10.00	5.00	1.00
☐ 132	Tom Morgan	10.00	5.00	1.00
☐ 133	Gil Coan	10.00	5.00	1.00
☐ 134	Rube Walker	11.00	5.50	1.10
☐ 135	Al Rosen	18.00	9.00	1.80
☐ 136	Ken Heintzelman	10.00	5.00	1.00
☐ 137	John Rutherford	10.00	5.00	1.00
☐ 138	George Kell	35.00	17.50	3.50
☐ 139	Sammy White	10.00	5.00	1.00
☐ 140	Tommy Glaviano	10.00	5.00	1.00
☐ 141	Allie Reynolds	18.00	9.00	1.80
☐ 142	Vic Wertz	11.00	5.50	1.10
☐ 143	Billy Pierce	12.50	6.25	1.25
☐ 144	Bob Schultz	10.00	5.00	1.00
☐ 145	Harry Dorish	10.00	5.00	1.00
☐ 146	Granny Hamner	10.00	5.00	1.00
☐ 147	Warren Spahn	50.00	25.00	5.00
☐ 148	Mickey Grasso	10.00	5.00	1.00
☐ 149	Dom DiMaggio	18.00	9.00	1.80
☐ 150	Harry Simpson	10.00	5.00	1.00
☐ 151	Hoyt Wilhelm	35.00	17.50	3.50
☐ 152	Bob Adams	10.00	5.00	1.00
☐ 153	Andy Seminick	10.00	5.00	1.00
☐ 154	Dick Groat	15.00	7.50	1.50
☐ 155	Dutch Leonard	10.00	5.00	1.00
☐ 156	Jim Rivera	10.00	5.00	1.00
☐ 157	Bob Addis	10.00	5.00	1.00
☐ 158	John Logan	12.00	6.00	1.20
☐ 159	Wayne Terwilliger	10.00	5.00	1.00
☐ 160	Bob Young	10.00	5.00	1.00
☐ 161	Vern Bickford	10.00	5.00	1.00
☐ 162	Ted Kluszewski	15.00	7.50	1.50
☐ 163	Fred Hatfield	10.00	5.00	1.00
☐ 164	Frank Shea	10.00	5.00	1.00
☐ 165	Billy Hoeft	10.00	5.00	1.00
☐ 166	Bill Hunter	8.00	4.00	.80
☐ 167	Art Schult	8.00	4.00	.80
☐ 168	Willard Schmidt	8.00	4.00	.80
☐ 169	Dizzy Trout	8.00	4.00	.80
☐ 170	Bill Werle	8.00	4.00	.80
☐ 171	Bill Glynn	8.00	4.00	.80
☐ 172	Rip Repulski	8.00	4.00	.80
☐ 173	Preston Ward	8.00	4.00	.80
☐ 174	Billy Loes	10.00	5.00	1.00
☐ 175	Ronnie Kline	8.00	4.00	.80
☐ 176	Don Hoak	10.00	5.00	1.00
☐ 177	Jim Dyck	8.00	4.00	.80
☐ 178	Jim Waugh	8.00	4.00	.80
☐ 179	Gene Hermanski	8.00	4.00	.80
☐ 180	Virgil Stallcup	8.00	4.00	.80
☐ 181	Al Zarilla	8.00	4.00	.80
☐ 182	Bobby Hofman	8.00	4.00	.80
☐ 183	Stu Miller	8.00	4.00	.80
☐ 184	Hal Brown	8.00	4.00	.80
☐ 185	Jim Pendleton	8.00	4.00	.80
☐ 186	Charlie Bishop	8.00	4.00	.80
☐ 187	Jim Fridley	8.00	4.00	.80
☐ 188	Andy Carey	10.00	5.00	1.00
☐ 189	Ray Jablonski	8.00	4.00	.80
☐ 190	Dixie Walker	8.00	4.00	.80
☐ 191	Ralph Kiner	35.00	17.50	3.50
☐ 192	Wally Westlake	8.00	4.00	.80
☐ 193	Mike Clark	8.00	4.00	.80
☐ 194	Eddie Kazak	8.00	4.00	.80
☐ 195	Ed McGhee	8.00	4.00	.80
☐ 196	Bob Keegan	8.00	4.00	.80
☐ 197	Del Crandall	10.00	5.00	1.00
☐ 198	Forrest Main	8.00	4.00	.80
☐ 199	Marion Fricano	8.00	4.00	.80
☐ 200	Gordon Goldsberry	8.00	4.00	.80
☐ 201	Paul LaPalme	8.00	4.00	.80
☐ 202	Carl Sawatski	8.00	4.00	.80
☐ 203	Cliff Fannin	8.00	4.00	.80

☐ 204	Dick Bokelman	8.00	4.00	.80
☐ 205	Vern Benson	8.00	4.00	.80
☐ 206	Ed Bailey	10.00	5.00	1.00
☐ 207	Whitey Ford	50.00	25.00	5.00
☐ 208	Jim Wilson	8.00	4.00	.80
☐ 209	Jim Greengrass	8.00	4.00	.80
☐ 210	Bob Cerv	10.00	5.00	1.00
☐ 211	J.W. Porter	8.00	4.00	.80
☐ 212	Jack Dittmer	8.00	4.00	.80
☐ 213	Ray Scarborough	8.00	4.00	.80
☐ 214	Bill Bruton	10.00	5.00	1.00
☐ 215	Gene Conley	10.00	5.00	1.00
☐ 216	Jim Hughes	8.00	4.00	.80
☐ 217	Murray Wall	8.00	4.00	.80
☐ 218	Les Fusselman	8.00	4.00	.80
☐ 219	Pete Runnels	10.00	5.00	1.00
	(photo actually			
	Don Johnson)			
☐ 220	Satchel Paige	200.00	100.00	20.00
☐ 221	Bob Milliken	40.00	20.00	4.00
☐ 222	Vic Janowicz	45.00	22.50	4.50
☐ 223	Johnny O'Brien	40.00	20.00	4.00
☐ 224	Lou Sleater	40.00	20.00	4.00
☐ 225	Bobby Shantz	50.00	25.00	5.00
☐ 226	Ed Erautt	40.00	20.00	4.00
☐ 227	Morris Martin	40.00	20.00	4.00
☐ 228	Hal Newhouser	75.00	37.50	7.50
☐ 229	Rockey Krsnich	40.00	20.00	4.00
☐ 230	Johnny Lindell	40.00	20.00	4.00
☐ 231	Solly Hemus	40.00	20.00	4.00
☐ 232	Dick Kokos	40.00	20.00	4.00
☐ 233	Al Aber	40.00	20.00	4.00
☐ 234	Ray Murray	40.00	20.00	4.00
☐ 235	John Hetki	40.00	20.00	4.00
☐ 236	Harry Perkowski	40.00	20.00	4.00
☐ 237	Bud Podbielan	40.00	20.00	4.00
☐ 238	Cal Hogue	40.00	20.00	4.00
☐ 239	Jim Delsing	40.00	20.00	4.00
☐ 240	Freddie Marsh	40.00	20.00	4.00
☐ 241	Al Sima	40.00	20.00	4.00
☐ 242	Charlie Silvera	40.00	20.00	4.00
☐ 243	Carlos Bernier	40.00	20.00	4.00
☐ 244	Willie Mays	1200.00	500.00	100.00
☐ 245	Bill Norman	40.00	20.00	4.00
☐ 246	Roy Face	60.00	30.00	6.00
☐ 247	Mike Sandlock	40.00	20.00	4.00
☐ 248	Gene Stephens	40.00	20.00	4.00
☐ 249	Eddie O'Brien	40.00	20.00	4.00
☐ 250	Bob Wilson	40.00	20.00	4.00
☐ 251	Sid Hudson	40.00	20.00	4.00
☐ 252	Henry Foiles	40.00	20.00	4.00
☐ 253	Does not exist	0.00	.00	.00
☐ 254	Preacher Roe	60.00	30.00	6.00
☐ 255	Dixie Howell	40.00	20.00	4.00
☐ 256	Les Peden	40.00	20.00	4.00
☐ 257	Bob Boyd	40.00	20.00	4.00
☐ 258	Jim Gilliam	175.00	85.00	18.00
☐ 259	Roy McMillan	40.00	20.00	4.00
☐ 260	Sam Calderone	40.00	20.00	4.00
☐ 261	Does not exist	0.00	.00	.00
☐ 262	Bob Oldis	40.00	20.00	4.00
☐ 263	Johnny Podres	175.00	85.00	18.00
☐ 264	Gene Woodling	60.00	30.00	6.00
☐ 265	Jackie Jensen	75.00	37.50	7.50
☐ 266	Bob Cain	40.00	20.00	4.00
☐ 267	Does not exist	0.00	.00	.00
☐ 268	Does not exist	0.00	.00	.00
☐ 269	Duane Pillette	40.00	20.00	4.00
☐ 270	Vern Stephens	45.00	22.50	4.50
☐ 271	Does not exist	0.00	.00	.00
☐ 272	Bill Antonello	40.00	20.00	4.00
☐ 273	Harvey Haddix	60.00	30.00	6.00
☐ 274	John Riddle	40.00	20.00	4.00
☐ 275	Does not exist	0.00	.00	.00
☐ 276	Ken Raffensberger	40.00	20.00	4.00
☐ 277	Don Lund	40.00	20.00	4.00
☐ 278	Willie Miranda	40.00	20.00	4.00
☐ 279	Joe Coleman	40.00	20.00	4.00
☐ 280	Milt Bolling	175.00	25.00	5.00

1954 Topps

The cards in this 250-card set measure 2 5/8" by 3 3/4". Each of the cards in the 1954 Topps set contains a large "head" shot of the player in color plus a smaller full-length photo in black and white set against a color background. This series contains the rookie cards of Hank Aaron, Ernie Banks, and Al

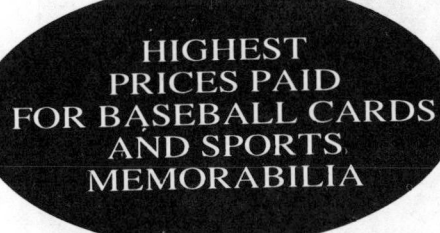

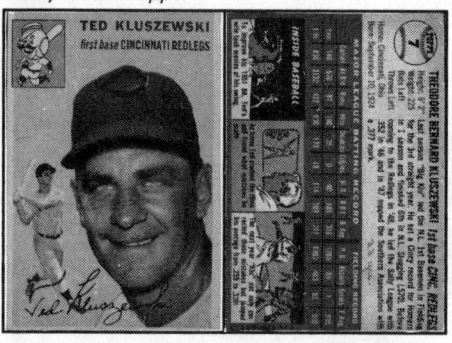

Kaline and two separate cards of Ted Williams (number 1 and number 250). Conspicuous by his absence is Mickey Mantle who apparently was the exclusive property of Bowman during 1954 (and 1955).

		NRMT	VG-E	GOOD
	COMPLETE SET	4200.00	1500.00	300.00
	COMMON PLAYER (1-50)	4.50	2.25	.45
	COMMON PLAYER (51-75)	9.00	4.50	.90
	COMMON PLAYER (76-250)	6.00	3.00	.60
☐ 1	Ted Williams	300.00	90.00	15.00
☐ 2	Gus Zernial	4.50	2.25	.45
☐ 3	Monte Irvin	15.00	7.50	1.50
☐ 4	Hank Sauer	5.50	2.75	.55
☐ 5	Ed Lopat	9.00	4.50	.90
☐ 6	Pete Runnels	5.50	2.75	.55
☐ 7	Ted Kluszewski	8.00	4.00	.80
☐ 8	Bob Young	4.50	2.25	.45
☐ 9	Harvey Haddix	5.50	2.75	.55
☐ 10	Jackie Robinson	125.00	60.00	12.50
☐ 11	Paul Leslie Smith	4.50	2.25	.45
☐ 12	Del Crandall	5.50	2.75	.55
☐ 13	Billy Martin	35.00	17.50	3.50
☐ 14	Preacher Roe	8.00	4.00	.80
☐ 15	Al Rosen	8.50	4.25	.85
☐ 16	Vic Janowicz	5.50	2.75	.55
☐ 17	Phil Rizzuto	35.00	17.50	3.50
☐ 18	Walt Dropo	4.50	2.25	.45
☐ 19	Johnny Lipon	4.50	2.25	.45
☐ 20	Warren Spahn	40.00	20.00	4.00
☐ 21	Bobby Shantz	5.50	2.75	.55
☐ 22	Jim Greengrass	4.50	2.25	.45
☐ 23	Luke Easter	5.50	2.75	.55
☐ 24	Granny Hamner	4.50	2.25	.45
☐ 25	Harvey Kuenn	15.00	7.50	1.50
☐ 26	Ray Jablonski	4.50	2.25	.45
☐ 27	Ferris Fain	5.50	2.75	.55
☐ 28	Paul Minner	4.50	2.25	.45
☐ 29	Jim Hegan	4.50	2.25	.45
☐ 30	Ed Mathews	35.00	17.50	3.50
☐ 31	Johnny Klippstein	4.50	2.25	.45
☐ 32	Duke Snider	75.00	37.50	7.50
☐ 33	Johnny Schmitz	4.50	2.25	.45
☐ 34	Jim Rivera	4.50	2.25	.45
☐ 35	Jim Gilliam	8.00	4.00	.80
☐ 36	Hoyt Wilhelm	15.00	7.50	1.50
☐ 37	Whitey Ford	35.00	17.50	3.50
☐ 38	Eddie Stanky	5.50	2.75	.55
☐ 39	Sherm Lollar	5.50	2.75	.55
☐ 40	Mel Parnell	5.50	2.75	.55
☐ 41	Willie Jones	4.50	2.25	.45
☐ 42	Don Mueller	5.50	2.75	.55
☐ 43	Dick Groat	6.50	3.25	.65
☐ 44	Ned Garver	4.50	2.25	.45
☐ 45	Richie Ashburn	11.00	5.50	1.10
☐ 46	Ken Raffensberger	4.50	2.25	.45
☐ 47	Ellis Kinder	4.50	2.25	.45
☐ 48	William Hunter	4.50	2.25	.45
☐ 49	Ray Murray	4.50	2.25	.45
☐ 50	Yogi Berra	75.00	37.50	7.50
☐ 51	Johnny Lindell	9.00	4.50	.90
☐ 52	Vic Power	11.00	5.50	1.10
☐ 53	Jack Dittmer	9.00	4.50	.90
☐ 54	Vern Stephens	11.00	5.50	1.10
☐ 55	Phil Cavarretta	11.00	5.50	1.10
☐ 56	Willie Miranda	9.00	4.50	.90
☐ 57	Luis Aloma	9.00	4.50	.90
☐ 58	Bob Wilson	9.00	4.50	.90
☐ 59	Gene Conley	11.00	5.50	1.10
☐ 60	Frank Baumholtz	9.00	4.50	.90
☐ 61	Bob Cain	9.00	4.50	.90
☐ 62	Eddie Robinson	11.00	5.50	1.10
☐ 63	Johnny Pesky	11.00	5.50	1.10
☐ 64	Hank Thompson	11.00	5.50	1.10
☐ 65	Bob Swift	9.00	4.50	.90
☐ 66	Ted Lepcio	9.00	4.50	.90
☐ 67	Jim Willis	9.00	4.50	.90
☐ 68	Sam Calderone	9.00	4.50	.90
☐ 69	Bud Podbielan	9.00	4.50	.90
☐ 70	Larry Doby	14.00	7.00	1.40
☐ 71	Frank Smith	9.00	4.50	.90
☐ 72	Preston Ward	9.00	4.50	.90
☐ 73	Wayne Terwilliger	9.00	4.50	.90
☐ 74	Bill Taylor	9.00	4.50	.90
☐ 75	Fred Haney	9.00	4.50	.90
☐ 76	Bob Scheffing	6.00	3.00	.60
☐ 77	Ray Boone	7.00	3.50	.70
☐ 78	Ted Kazanski	6.00	3.00	.60
☐ 79	Andy Pafko	6.00	3.00	.60
☐ 80	Jackie Jensen	8.00	4.00	.80
☐ 81	Dave Hoskins	6.00	3.00	.60
☐ 82	Milt Bolling	6.00	3.00	.60
☐ 83	Joe Collins	7.00	3.50	.70
☐ 84	Dick Cole	6.00	3.00	.60
☐ 85	Bob Turley	10.00	5.00	1.00
☐ 86	Billy Herman	9.00	4.50	.90
☐ 87	Roy Face	7.00	3.50	.70
☐ 88	Matt Batts	6.00	3.00	.60
☐ 89	Howie Pollet	6.00	3.00	.60
☐ 90	Willie Mays	200.00	100.00	20.00
☐ 91	Bob Oldis	6.00	3.00	.60
☐ 92	Wally Westlake	6.00	3.00	.60
☐ 93	Sid Hudson	6.00	3.00	.60
☐ 94	Ernie Banks	300.00	150.00	30.00
☐ 95	Hal Rice	6.00	3.00	.60
☐ 96	Charlie Silvera	6.00	3.00	.60
☐ 97	Jerald Hal Lane	6.00	3.00	.60
☐ 98	Joe Black	8.00	4.00	.80
☐ 99	Bobby Hofman	6.00	3.00	.60
☐ 100	Bob Keegan	6.00	3.00	.60
☐ 101	Gene Woodling	8.00	4.00	.80
☐ 102	Gil Hodges	30.00	15.00	3.00
☐ 103	Jim Lemon	6.00	3.00	.60
☐ 104	Mike Sandlock	6.00	3.00	.60
☐ 105	Andy Carey	7.00	3.50	.70
☐ 106	Dick Kokos	6.00	3.00	.60
☐ 107	Duane Pillette	6.00	3.00	.60
☐ 108	Thornton Kipper	6.00	3.00	.60
☐ 109	Bill Bruton	6.00	3.00	.60
☐ 110	Harry Dorish	6.00	3.00	.60
☐ 111	Jim Delsing	6.00	3.00	.60
☐ 112	Bill Renna	6.00	3.00	.60
☐ 113	Bob Boyd	6.00	3.00	.60
☐ 114	Dean Stone	6.00	3.00	.60
☐ 115	Rip Repulski	6.00	3.00	.60
☐ 116	Steve Bilko	6.00	3.00	.60
☐ 117	Solly Hemus	6.00	3.00	.60
☐ 118	Carl Scheib	6.00	3.00	.60
☐ 119	Johnny Antonelli	7.00	3.50	.70
☐ 120	Roy McMillan	6.00	3.00	.60
☐ 121	Clem Labine	7.00	3.50	.70
☐ 122	Johnny Logan	7.00	3.50	.70
☐ 123	Bobby Adams	6.00	3.00	.60
☐ 124	Marion Fricano	6.00	3.00	.60
☐ 125	Harry Perkowski	6.00	3.00	.60
☐ 126	Ben Wade	6.00	3.00	.60
☐ 127	Steve O'Neill	6.00	3.00	.60
☐ 128	Hank Aaron	600.00	300.00	60.00
☐ 129	Forrest Jacobs	6.00	3.00	.60
☐ 130	Hank Bauer	9.00	4.50	.90
☐ 131	Reno Bertoia	6.00	3.00	.60
☐ 132	Tom Lasorda	75.00	37.50	7.50
☐ 133	Dave Baker	6.00	3.00	.60
☐ 134	Cal Hogue	6.00	3.00	.60
☐ 135	Joe Presko	6.00	3.00	.60
☐ 136	Connie Ryan	6.00	3.00	.60
☐ 137	Wally Moon	8.00	4.00	.80
☐ 138	Bob Borkowski	6.00	3.00	.60
☐ 139	The O'Briens Johnny O'Brien Eddie O'Brien	8.00	4.00	.80
☐ 140	Tom Wright	6.00	3.00	.60
☐ 141	Joe Jay	7.00	3.50	.70
☐ 142	Tom Poholsky	6.00	3.00	.60
☐ 143	Ralston Hemsley	6.00	3.00	.60
☐ 144	Bill Werle	6.00	3.00	.60
☐ 145	Elmer Valo	6.00	3.00	.60
☐ 146	Don Johnson	6.00	3.00	.60
☐ 147	Johnny Riddle	6.00	3.00	.60
☐ 148	Bob Trice	6.00	3.00	.60
☐ 149	Al Robertson	6.00	3.00	.60
☐ 150	Dick Kryhoski	6.00	3.00	.60
☐ 151	Alex Grammas	6.00	3.00	.60
☐ 152	Michael Blyzka	6.00	3.00	.60
☐ 153	Al Walker	6.00	3.00	.60
☐ 154	Mike Fornieles	6.00	3.00	.60
☐ 155	Bob Kennedy	6.00	3.00	.60

☐ 156	Joe Coleman	6.00	3.00	.60
☐ 157	Don Lenhardt	6.00	3.00	.60
☐ 158	Peanuts Lowrey	6.00	3.00	.60
☐ 159	Dave Philley	6.00	3.00	.60
☐ 160	Ralph Kress	6.00	3.00	.60
☐ 161	John Hetki	6.00	3.00	.60
☐ 162	Herman Wehmeier	6.00	3.00	.60
☐ 163	Frank House	6.00	3.00	.60
☐ 164	Stu Miller	6.00	3.00	.60
☐ 165	Jim Pendleton	6.00	3.00	.60
☐ 166	Johnny Podres	10.00	5.00	1.00
☐ 167	Don Lund	6.00	3.00	.60
☐ 168	Morrie Martin	6.00	3.00	.60
☐ 169	Jim Hughes	6.00	3.00	.60
☐ 170	James (Dusty) Rhodes	7.00	3.50	.70
☐ 171	Leo Kiely	6.00	3.00	.60
☐ 172	Harold Brown	6.00	3.00	.60
☐ 173	Jack Harshman	6.00	3.00	.60
☐ 174	Tom Qualters	6.00	3.00	.60
☐ 175	Frank Leja	6.00	3.00	.60
☐ 176	Robert Keeley	6.00	3.00	.60
☐ 177	Bob Milliken	6.00	3.00	.60
☐ 178	Bill Glynn	6.00	3.00	.60
☐ 179	Gair Allie	6.00	3.00	.60
☐ 180	Wes Westrum	6.00	3.00	.60
☐ 181	Mel Roach	6.00	3.00	.60
☐ 182	Chuck Harmon	6.00	3.00	.60
☐ 183	Earle Combs	9.00	4.50	.90
☐ 184	Ed Bailey	6.00	3.00	.60
☐ 185	Chuck Stobbs	6.00	3.00	.60
☐ 186	Karl Olson	6.00	3.00	.60
☐ 187	Henry Manush	9.00	4.50	.90
☐ 188	Dave Jolly	6.00	3.00	.60
☐ 189	Floyd Ross	6.00	3.00	.60
☐ 190	Ray Herbert	6.00	3.00	.60
☐ 191	John (Dick) Schofield	7.00	3.50	.70
☐ 192	Ellis Deal	6.00	3.00	.60
☐ 193	Johnny Hopp	7.00	3.50	.70
☐ 194	Bill Sarni	6.00	3.00	.60
☐ 195	Bill Consolo	6.00	3.00	.60
☐ 196	Stanley Jok	6.00	3.00	.60
☐ 197	Lynwood Rowe	7.00	3.50	.70
☐ 198	Carl Sawatski	6.00	3.00	.60
☐ 199	Glenn (Rocky) Nelson	6.00	3.00	.60
☐ 200	Larry Jansen	6.00	3.00	.60
☐ 201	Al Kaline	300.00	150.00	30.00
☐ 202	Bob Purkey	6.00	3.00	.60
☐ 203	Harry Brecheen	7.00	3.50	.70
☐ 204	Angel Scull	6.00	3.00	.60
☐ 205	Johnny Sain	11.00	5.50	1.10
☐ 206	Ray Crone	6.00	3.00	.60
☐ 207	Tom Oliver	6.00	3.00	.60
☐ 208	Grady Hatton	6.00	3.00	.60
☐ 209	Chuck Thompson	6.00	3.00	.60
☐ 210	Bob Buhl	7.00	3.50	.70
☐ 211	Don Hoak	7.00	3.50	.70
☐ 212	Bob Micelotta	6.00	3.00	.60
☐ 213	Johnny Fitzpatrick	6.00	3.00	.60
☐ 214	Arnie Portocarrero	6.00	3.00	.60
☐ 215	Warren McGhee	6.00	3.00	.60
☐ 216	Al Sima	6.00	3.00	.60
☐ 217	Paul Schreiber	6.00	3.00	.60
☐ 218	Fred Marsh	6.00	3.00	.60
☐ 219	Chuck Kress	6.00	3.00	.60
☐ 220	Ruben Gomez	6.00	3.00	.60
☐ 221	Dick Brodowski	6.00	3.00	.60
☐ 222	Bill Wilson	6.00	3.00	.60
☐ 223	Joe Haynes	6.00	3.00	.60
☐ 224	Dick Weik	6.00	3.00	.60
☐ 225	Don Liddle	6.00	3.00	.60
☐ 226	Jehosie Heard	6.00	3.00	.60
☐ 227	Colonel Mills	6.00	3.00	.60
☐ 228	Gene Hermanski	6.00	3.00	.60
☐ 229	Robert Talbot	6.00	3.00	.60
☐ 230	Bob Kuzava	6.00	3.00	.60
☐ 231	Roy Smalley	6.00	3.00	.60
☐ 232	Lou Limmer	6.00	3.00	.60
☐ 233	Augie Galan	6.00	3.00	.60
☐ 234	Jerry Lynch	7.00	3.50	.70
☐ 235	Vernon Law	7.00	3.50	.70
☐ 236	Paul Penson	6.00	3.00	.60
☐ 237	Dominic Ryba	6.00	3.00	.60
☐ 238	Al Aber	6.00	3.00	.60
☐ 239	Bill Skowron	18.00	9.00	1.80
☐ 240	Sam Mele	6.00	3.00	.60
☐ 241	Robert Miller	6.00	3.00	.60
☐ 242	Curt Roberts	6.00	3.00	.60
☐ 243	Ray Blades	6.00	3.00	.60
☐ 244	Leroy Wheat	6.00	3.00	.60
☐ 245	Roy Sievers	7.00	3.50	.70
☐ 246	Howie Fox	6.00	3.00	.60
☐ 247	Ed Mayo	6.00	3.00	.60
☐ 248	Alphonse Smith	7.00	3.50	.70
☐ 249	Wilmer Mizell	7.00	3.50	.70
☐ 250	Ted Williams	300.00	90.00	15.00

1955 Topps

The cards in this 206-card set measure 2 5/8" by 3 3/4". Both the large "head" shot and the smaller full-length photos used on each card of the 1955 Topps set are in color. The card fronts were designed horizontally for the first time in Topps' history. The first card features Dusty Rhodes, hitting star for the Giants 1954 World Series sweep over the Indians. A "high" series, 161 to 210, is more difficult to find than cards 1 to 160. Numbers 175, 186, 203, and 209 were never issued. To fill in for the four cards not issued in the high number series, Topps double printed four players, those appearing on cards 170, 172, 184, and 188.

	NRMT	VG-E	GOOD
COMPLETE SET	3500.00	1200.00	200.00
COMMON PLAYER (1-150)	4.00	2.00	.40
COMMON PLAYER (151-160)	7.50	3.75	.75
COMMON PLAYER (161-210)	9.00	4.50	.90

☐ 1	Dusty Rhodes	15.00	2.50	.50
☐ 2	Ted Williams	150.00	75.00	15.00
☐ 3	Art Fowler	4.00	2.00	.40
☐ 4	Al Kaline	50.00	25.00	5.00
☐ 5	Jim Gilliam	6.50	3.25	.65
☐ 6	Stan Hack	4.00	2.00	.40
☐ 7	Jim Hegan	4.00	2.00	.40
☐ 8	Harold Smith	4.00	2.00	.40
☐ 9	Robert Miller	4.00	2.00	.40
☐ 10	Bob Keegan	4.00	2.00	.40
☐ 11	Ferris Fain	4.00	2.00	.40
☐ 12	Vernon Thies	4.00	2.00	.40
☐ 13	Fred Marsh	4.00	2.00	.40
☐ 14	Jim Finigan	4.00	2.00	.40
☐ 15	Jim Pendleton	4.00	2.00	.40
☐ 16	Roy Sievers	4.00	2.00	.40
☐ 17	Bobby Hofman	4.00	2.00	.40
☐ 18	Russ Kemmerer	4.00	2.00	.40
☐ 19	Billy Herman	7.00	3.50	.70
☐ 20	Andy Carey	5.00	2.50	.50
☐ 21	Alex Grammas	4.00	2.00	.40
☐ 22	Bill Skowron	8.00	4.00	.80
☐ 23	Jack Parks	4.00	2.00	.40
☐ 24	Hal Newhouser	6.50	3.25	.65
☐ 25	John Podres	7.00	3.50	.70
☐ 26	Dick Groat	6.00	3.00	.60
☐ 27	Bill Gardner	4.00	2.00	.40
☐ 28	Ernie Banks	45.00	22.50	4.50
☐ 29	Herman Wehmeier	4.00	2.00	.40
☐ 30	Vic Power	4.00	2.00	.40
☐ 31	Warren Spahn	30.00	15.00	3.00
☐ 32	Warren McGhee	4.00	2.00	.40
☐ 33	Tom Qualters	4.00	2.00	.40
☐ 34	Wayne Terwilliger	4.00	2.00	.40
☐ 35	Dave Jolly	4.00	2.00	.40
☐ 36	Leo Kiely	4.00	2.00	.40
☐ 37	Joe Cunningham	4.00	2.00	.40
☐ 38	Bob Turley	6.50	3.25	.65
☐ 39	Bill Glynn	4.00	2.00	.40
☐ 40	Don Hoak	4.00	2.00	.40
☐ 41	Chuck Stobbs	4.00	2.00	.40
☐ 42	John (Windy) McCall	4.00	2.00	.40

☐ 43	Harvey Haddix	5.00	2.50	.50
☐ 44	Harold Valentine	4.00	2.00	.40
☐ 45	Hank Sauer	5.00	2.50	.50
☐ 46	Ted Kazanski	4.00	2.00	.40
☐ 47	Hank Aaron	125.00	60.00	12.50
☐ 48	Bob Kennedy	4.00	2.00	.40
☐ 49	J.W. Porter	4.00	2.00	.40
☐ 50	Jackie Robinson	100.00	50.00	10.00
☐ 51	Jim Hughes	4.00	2.00	.40
☐ 52	Bill Tremel	4.00	2.00	.40
☐ 53	Bill Taylor	4.00	2.00	.40
☐ 54	Lou Limmer	4.00	2.00	.40
☐ 55	Rip Repulski	4.00	2.00	.40
☐ 56	Ray Jablonski	4.00	2.00	.40
☐ 57	Billy O'Dell	4.00	2.00	.40
☐ 58	Jim Rivera	4.00	2.00	.40
☐ 59	Gair Allie	4.00	2.00	.40
☐ 60	Dean Stone	4.00	2.00	.40
☐ 61	Forrest Jacobs	4.00	2.00	.40
☐ 62	Thornton Kipper	4.00	2.00	.40
☐ 63	Joe Collins	5.00	2.50	.50
☐ 64	Gus Triandos	5.00	2.50	.50
☐ 65	Ray Boone	4.00	2.00	.40
☐ 66	Ron Jackson	4.00	2.00	.40
☐ 67	Wally Moon	5.00	2.50	.50
☐ 68	Jim Davis	4.00	2.00	.40
☐ 69	Ed Bailey	4.00	2.00	.40
☐ 70	Al Rosen	7.00	3.50	.70
☐ 71	Ruben Gomez	4.00	2.00	.40
☐ 72	Karl Olson	4.00	2.00	.40
☐ 73	Jack Shepard	4.00	2.00	.40
☐ 74	Robert Borkowski	4.00	2.00	.40
☐ 75	Sandy Amoros	6.00	3.00	.60
☐ 76	Howie Pollet	4.00	2.00	.40
☐ 77	Arnold Portocarrero	4.00	2.00	.40
☐ 78	Gordon Jones	4.00	2.00	.40
☐ 79	Clyde Schell	4.00	2.00	.40
☐ 80	Bob Grim	6.00	3.00	.60
☐ 81	Gene Conley	4.00	2.00	.40
☐ 82	Chuck Harmon	4.00	2.00	.40
☐ 83	Tom Brewer	4.00	2.00	.40
☐ 84	Camilo Pascual	6.00	3.00	.60
☐ 85	Don Mossi	6.00	3.00	.60
☐ 86	Bill Wilson	4.00	2.00	.40
☐ 87	Frank House	4.00	2.00	.40
☐ 88	Bob Skinner	5.00	2.50	.50
☐ 89	Joe Frazier	4.00	2.00	.40
☐ 90	Karl Spooner	4.00	2.00	.40
☐ 91	Milt Bolling	4.00	2.00	.40
☐ 92	Don Zimmer	8.00	4.00	.80
☐ 93	Steve Bilko	4.00	2.00	.40
☐ 94	Reno Bertoia	4.00	2.00	.40
☐ 95	Preston Ward	4.00	2.00	.40
☐ 96	Chuck Bishop	4.00	2.00	.40
☐ 97	Carlos Paula	4.00	2.00	.40
☐ 98	John Riddle	4.00	2.00	.40
☐ 99	Frank Leja	4.00	2.00	.40
☐ 100	Monte Irvin	15.00	7.50	1.50
☐ 101	Johnny Gray	4.00	2.00	.40
☐ 102	Wally Westlake	4.00	2.00	.40
☐ 103	Chuck White	4.00	2.00	.40
☐ 104	Jack Harshman	4.00	2.00	.40
☐ 105	Chuck Diering	4.00	2.00	.40
☐ 106	Frank Sullivan	4.00	2.00	.40
☐ 107	Curt Roberts	4.00	2.00	.40
☐ 108	Al Walker	4.00	2.00	.40
☐ 109	Ed Lopat	7.00	3.50	.70
☐ 110	Gus Zernial	4.00	2.00	.40
☐ 111	Bob Milliken	4.00	2.00	.40
☐ 112	Nelson King	4.00	2.00	.40
☐ 113	Harry Brecheen	4.00	2.00	.40
☐ 114	Louis Ortiz	4.00	2.00	.40
☐ 115	Ellis Kinder	4.00	2.00	.40
☐ 116	Tom Hurd	4.00	2.00	.40
☐ 117	Mel Roach	4.00	2.00	.40
☐ 118	Bob Purkey	4.00	2.00	.40
☐ 119	Bob Lennon	4.00	2.00	.40
☐ 120	Ted Kluszewski	7.00	3.50	.70
☐ 121	Bill Renna	4.00	2.00	.40
☐ 122	Carl Sawatski	4.00	2.00	.40
☐ 123	Sandy Koufax	250.00	125.00	25.00
☐ 124	Harmon Killebrew	100.00	50.00	10.00
☐ 125	Ken Boyer	15.00	7.50	1.50
☐ 126	Dick Hall	4.00	2.00	.40
☐ 127	Dale Long	5.00	2.50	.50
☐ 128	Ted Lepcio	4.00	2.00	.40
☐ 129	Elvin Tappe	4.00	2.00	.40
☐ 130	Mayo Smith MG	4.00	2.00	.40
☐ 131	Grady Hatton	4.00	2.00	.40
☐ 132	Bob Trice	4.00	2.00	.40
☐ 133	Dave Hoskins	4.00	2.00	.40
☐ 134	Joe Jay	4.00	2.00	.40
☐ 135	Johnny O'Brien	4.00	2.00	.40
☐ 136	Vernon Stewart	4.00	2.00	.40
☐ 137	Harry Elliott	4.00	2.00	.40

☐ 138	Ray Herbert	4.00	2.00	.40
☐ 139	Steve Kraly	4.00	2.00	.40
☐ 140	Mel Parnell	4.00	2.00	.40
☐ 141	Tom Wright	4.00	2.00	.40
☐ 142	Gerry Lynch	4.00	2.00	.40
☐ 143	John (Dick) Schofield	4.00	2.00	.40
☐ 144	John (Joe) Amalfitano	4.00	2.00	.40
☐ 145	Elmer Valo	4.00	2.00	.40
☐ 146	Dick Donovan	4.00	2.00	.40
☐ 147	Hugh Pepper	4.00	2.00	.40
☐ 148	Hector Brown	4.00	2.00	.40
☐ 149	Ray Crone	4.00	2.00	.40
☐ 150	Michael Higgins	4.00	2.00	.40
☐ 151	Ralph Kress	7.50	3.75	.75
☐ 152	Harry Agganis	40.00	20.00	4.00
☐ 153	Bud Podbielan	7.50	3.75	.75
☐ 154	Willie Miranda	7.50	3.75	.75
☐ 155	Eddie Mathews	40.00	20.00	4.00
☐ 156	Joe Black	15.00	7.50	1.50
☐ 157	Robert Miller	7.50	3.75	.75
☐ 158	Tommy Carroll	10.00	5.00	1.00
☐ 159	Johnny Schmitz	7.50	3.75	.75
☐ 160	Ray Narleski	10.00	5.00	1.00
☐ 161	Chuck Tanner	12.00	6.00	1.20
☐ 162	Joe Coleman	9.00	4.50	.90
☐ 163	Faye Throneberry	9.00	4.50	.90
☐ 164	Roberto Clemente	450.00	225.00	45.00
☐ 165	Don Johnson	9.00	4.50	.90
☐ 166	Hank Bauer	17.00	8.50	1.70
☐ 167	Thomas Casagrande	9.00	4.50	.90
☐ 168	Duane Pillette	9.00	4.50	.90
☐ 169	Bob Oldis	9.00	4.50	.90
☐ 170	Jim Pearce DP	4.50	2.25	.45
☐ 171	Dick Brodowski	9.00	4.50	.90
☐ 172	Frank Baumholtz DP	4.50	2.25	.45
☐ 173	Johnny Kline	9.00	4.50	.90
☐ 174	Rudy Minarcin	9.00	4.50	.90
☐ 175	Does not exist	0.00	.00	.00
☐ 176	Norm Zauchin	9.00	4.50	.90
☐ 177	Al Robertson	9.00	4.50	.90
☐ 178	Bobby Adams	9.00	4.50	.90
☐ 179	Jim Bolger	9.00	4.50	.90
☐ 180	Clem Labine	12.00	6.00	1.20
☐ 181	Roy McMillan	9.00	4.50	.90
☐ 182	Humberto Robinson	9.00	4.50	.90
☐ 183	Anthony Jacobs	9.00	4.50	.90
☐ 184	Harry Perkowski DP	4.50	2.25	.45
☐ 185	Don Ferrarese	9.00	4.50	.90
☐ 186	Does not exist	0.00	.00	.00
☐ 187	Gil Hodges	90.00	45.00	9.00
☐ 188	Charlie Silvera DP	4.50	2.25	.45
☐ 189	Phil Rizzuto	70.00	35.00	7.00
☐ 190	Gene Woodling	13.50	6.00	1.00
☐ 191	Eddie Stanky	12.00	6.00	1.20
☐ 192	Jim Delsing	9.00	4.50	.90
☐ 193	Johnny Sain	16.00	8.00	1.60
☐ 194	Willie Mays	325.00	160.00	32.00
☐ 195	Ed Roebuck	12.00	6.00	1.20
☐ 196	Gale Wade	9.00	4.50	.90
☐ 197	Al Smith	9.00	4.50	.90
☐ 198	Yogi Berra	125.00	60.00	12.50
☐ 199	Odbert Hamric	9.00	4.50	.90
☐ 200	Jackie Jensen	20.00	10.00	2.00
☐ 201	Sherman Lollar	12.00	6.00	1.20
☐ 202	Jim Owens	9.00	4.50	.90
☐ 203	Does not exist	0.00	.00	.00
☐ 204	Frank Smith	9.00	4.50	.90
☐ 205	Gene Freese	9.00	4.50	.90
☐ 206	Pete Daley	9.00	4.50	.90
☐ 207	Bill Consolo	9.00	4.50	.90
☐ 208	Ray Moore	9.00	4.50	.90
☐ 209	Does not exist	0.00	.00	.00
☐ 210	Duke Snider	350.00	80.00	15.00

1955 Topps Double Header

The cards in ths 66-card set measure 2 1/16" by 4 7/8". Borrowing a design from the T201 Mecca series, Topps issued a 132-player "Double Header" set in a separate wrapper in 1955. Each player is numbered in the biographical section on the reverse. When open, with perforated flap up, one player is revealed; when the flap is lowered, or closed, the player design on top incorporates a portion of the inside player artwork. When the cards are placed side by side, a continuous ballpark background is formed. Some cards have been found without perforations,

and all players pictured appear in the low series of the 1955 regular issue.

		NRMT	VG-E	GOOD
	COMPLETE SET	1800.00	400.00	80.00
	COMMON PAIR	18.00	9.00	1.80
☐	1 Al Rosen and 2 Chuck Diering	21.00	10.50	2.10
☐	3 Monte Irvin and 4 Russ Kemmerer	25.00	12.50	2.50
☐	5 Ted Kazanski and 6 Gordon Jones	18.00	9.00	1.80
☐	7 Bill Taylor and 8 Billy O'Dell	18.00	9.00	1.80
☐	9 J.W. Porter and 10 Thornton Kipper	18.00	9.00	1.80
☐	11 Curt Roberts and 12 Arnie Portocarrero	18.00	9.00	1.80
☐	13 Wally Westlake and 14 Frank House	18.00	9.00	1.80
☐	15 Rube Walker and 16 Lou Limmer	18.00	9.00	1.80
☐	17 Dean Stone and 18 Charlie White	18.00	9.00	1.80
☐	19 Karl Spooner and 20 Jim Hughes	18.00	9.00	1.80
☐	21 Bill Skowron and 22 Frank Sullivan	21.00	10.50	2.10
☐	23 Jack Shepard and 24 Stan Hack	18.00	9.00	1.80
☐	25 Jackie Robinson and 26 Don Hoak	100.00	50.00	10.00
☐	27 Dusty Rhodes and 28 Jim Davis	18.00	9.00	1.80
☐	29 Vic Power and 30 Ed Bailey	18.00	9.00	1.80
☐	31 Howie Pollet and 32 Ernie Banks	75.00	37.50	7.50
☐	33 Jim Pendleton and 34 Gene Conley	18.00	9.00	1.80
☐	35 Karl Olson and 36 Andy Carey	18.00	9.00	1.80
☐	37 Wally Moon and 38 Joe Cunningham	18.00	9.00	1.80
☐	39 Freddie Marsh and 40 Vernon Thies	18.00	9.00	1.80
☐	41 Eddie Lopat and 42 Harvey Haddix	21.00	10.50	2.10
☐	43 Leo Kiely and 44 Chuck Stobbs	18.00	9.00	1.80
☐	45 Al Kaline and 46 Harold Valentine	90.00	45.00	9.00
☐	47 Forrest Jacobs and 48 Johnny Gray	18.00	9.00	1.80
☐	49 Ron Jackson and 50 Jim Finigan	18.00	9.00	1.80
☐	51 Ray Jablonski and 52 Bob Keegan	18.00	9.00	1.80
☐	53 Billy Herman and 54 Sandy Amoros	25.00	12.50	2.50
☐	55 Chuck Harmon and 56 Bob Skinner	18.00	9.00	1.80
☐	57 Dick Hall and	18.00	9.00	1.80
	58 Bob Grim			
☐	59 Billy Glynn and 60 Bob Miller	18.00	9.00	1.80
☐	61 Billy Gardner and 62 John Hetki	18.00	9.00	1.80
☐	63 Bob Borkowski and 64 Bob Turley	18.00	9.00	1.80
☐	65 Joe Collins and 66 Jack Harshman	18.00	9.00	1.80
☐	67 Jim Hegan and 68 Jack Parks	18.00	9.00	1.80
☐	69 Ted Williams and 70 Mayo Smith	150.00	75.00	15.00
☐	71 Gair Allie and 72 Grady Hatton	18.00	9.00	1.80
☐	73 Jerry Lynch and 74 Harry Brecheen	18.00	9.00	1.80
☐	75 Tom Wright and 76 Vernon Stewart	18.00	9.00	1.80
☐	77 Dave Hoskins and 78 Warren McGhee	18.00	9.00	1.80
☐	79 Roy Sievers and 80 Art Fowler	18.00	9.00	1.80
☐	81 Danny Schell and 82 Gus Triandos	18.00	9.00	1.80
☐	83 Joe Frazier and 84 Don Mossi	18.00	9.00	1.80
☐	85 Elmer Valo and 86 Hector Brown	18.00	9.00	1.80
☐	87 Bob Kennedy and 88 Windy McCall	18.00	9.00	1.80
☐	89 Ruben Gomez and 90 Jim Rivera	18.00	9.00	1.80
☐	91 Louis Ortiz and 92 Milt Bolling	18.00	9.00	1.80
☐	93 Carl Sawatski and 94 El Tappe	18.00	9.00	1.80
☐	95 Dave Jolly and 96 Bobby Hofman	18.00	9.00	1.80
☐	97 Preston Ward and 98 Don Zimmer	18.00	9.00	1.80
☐	99 Bill Renna and 100 Dick Groat	21.00	10.50	2.10
☐	101 Bill Wilson and 102 Bill Tremel	18.00	9.00	1.80
☐	103 Hank Sauer and 104 Camilo Pascual	21.00	10.50	2.10
☐	105 Hank Aaron and 106 Ray Herbert	175.00	85.00	18.00
☐	107 Alex Grammas and 108 Tom Qualters	18.00	9.00	1.80
☐	109 Hal Newhouser and 110 Chuck Bishop	21.00	10.50	2.10
☐	111 Harmon Killebrew and 112 and John Podres	75.00	37.50	7.50
☐	113 Ray Boone and 114 Bob Purkey	18.00	9.00	1.80
☐	115 Dale Long and 116 Ferris Fain	18.00	9.00	1.80
☐	117 Steve Bilko and 118 Bob Milliken	18.00	9.00	1.80
☐	119 Mel Parnell and 120 Tom Hurd	18.00	9.00	1.80
☐	121 Ted Kluszewski and 122 Jim Owens	21.00	10.50	2.10
☐	123 Gus Zernial and 124 Bob Trice	18.00	9.00	1.80
☐	125 Rip Repulski and 126 Ted Lepcio	18.00	9.00	1.80
☐	127 Warren Spahn and 128 Tom Brewer	75.00	37.50	7.50
☐	129 Jim Gilliam and 130 Ellis Kinder	21.00	10.50	2.10
☐	131 Herm Wehmeier and 132 Wayne Terwilliger	18.00	9.00	1.80

1956 Topps

The cards in this 340-card set measure 2 5/8" by 3 3/4". Following up with another horizontally oriented card in 1956, Topps improved the format by layering the color "head" shot onto an actual action sequence involving the player. Cards 1 to 180 come with either white or gray backs: in the 1 to 100 sequence, gray backs are common (worth about 10% more) and in the 101 to 180 sequence, white backs are less common (worth 30% more). The team

cards used for the first time in a regular set by Topps, are found dated 1955, or undated, with the team name appearing on either side. The two unnumbered checklist cards are highly prized (must be unmarked to qualify as excellent or mint). The complete set price below does not include the unnumbered checklist cards or any of the variations.

	NRMT	VG-E	GOOD
COMPLETE SET (340)	3500.00	1200.00	200.00
COMMON PLAYER (1-100)	2.50	1.25	.25
COMMON PLAYER (101-180)	3.50	1.75	.35
COMMON PLAYER (181-260)	6.00	3.00	.60
COMMON PLAYER (261-340)	4.00	2.00	.40

		NRMT	VG-E	GOOD
☐	1 William Harridge (AL President)	40.00	5.00	1.00
☐	2 Warren Giles (NL President)	6.50	3.25	.65
☐	3 Elmer Valo	2.50	1.25	.25
☐	4 Carlos Paula	2.50	1.25	.25
☐	5 Ted Williams	100.00	50.00	10.00
☐	6 Ray Boone	2.50	1.25	.25
☐	7 Ron Negray	2.50	1.25	.25
☐	8 Walter Alston MG	12.50	6.25	1.25
☐	9 Ruben Gomez	2.50	1.25	.25
☐	10 Warren Spahn	20.00	10.00	2.00
☐	11A Chicago Cubs (centered)	6.00	3.00	.60
☐	11B Cubs Team (dated 1955)	25.00	12.50	2.50
☐	11C Cubs Team (name at far left)	6.00	3.00	.60
☐	12 Andy Carey	3.50	1.75	.35
☐	13 Roy Face	3.50	1.75	.35
☐	14 Ken Boyer	4.50	2.25	.45
☐	15 Ernie Banks	25.00	12.50	2.50
☐	16 Hector Lopez	2.50	1.25	.25
☐	17 Gene Conley	2.50	1.25	.25
☐	18 Dick Donovan	2.50	1.25	.25
☐	19 Chuck Diering	2.50	1.25	.25
☐	20 Al Kaline	35.00	17.50	3.50
☐	21 Joe Collins	3.50	1.75	.35
☐	22 Jim Finigan	2.50	1.25	.25
☐	23 Freddie Marsh	2.50	1.25	.25
☐	24 Dick Groat	4.00	2.00	.40
☐	25 Ted Kluszewski	5.00	2.50	.50
☐	26 Grady Hatton	2.50	1.25	.25
☐	27 Nelson Burbrink	2.50	1.25	.25
☐	28 Bobby Hofman	2.50	1.25	.25
☐	29 Jack Harshman	2.50	1.25	.25
☐	30 Jackie Robinson	80.00	40.00	8.00
☐	31 Hank Aaron (small photo actually W.Mays)	90.00	45.00	9.00
☐	32 Frank House	2.50	1.25	.25
☐	33 Roberto Clemente	90.00	45.00	9.00
☐	34 Tom Brewer	2.50	1.25	.25
☐	35 Al Rosen	5.00	2.50	.50
☐	36 Rudy Minarcin	2.50	1.25	.25
☐	37 Alex Grammas	2.50	1.25	.25
☐	38 Bob Kennedy	2.50	1.25	.25
☐	39 Don Mossi	3.50	1.75	.35
☐	40 Bob Turley	4.50	2.25	.45
☐	41 Hank Sauer	3.50	1.75	.35
☐	42 Sandy Amoros	3.50	1.75	.35
☐	43 Ray Moore	2.50	1.25	.25
☐	44 Windy McCall	2.50	1.25	.25
☐	45 Gus Zernial	2.50	1.25	.25
☐	46 Gene Freese	2.50	1.25	.25
☐	47 Art Fowler	2.50	1.25	.25

		NRMT	VG-E	GOOD
☐	48 Jim Hegan	2.50	1.25	.25
☐	49 Pedro Ramos	2.50	1.25	.25
☐	50 Dusty Rhodes	3.50	1.75	.35
☐	51 Ernie Oravetz	2.50	1.25	.25
☐	52 Bob Grim	3.50	1.75	.35
☐	53 Arnie Portocarrero	2.50	1.25	.25
☐	54 Bob Keegan	2.50	1.25	.25
☐	55 Wally Moon	3.50	1.75	.35
☐	56 Dale Long	3.50	1.75	.35
☐	57 Duke Maas	2.50	1.25	.25
☐	58 Ed Roebuck	3.50	1.75	.35
☐	59 Jose Santiago	2.50	1.25	.25
☐	60 Mayo Smith MG	2.50	1.25	.25
☐	61 Bill Skowron	6.00	3.00	.60
☐	62 Hal Smith	2.50	1.25	.25
☐	63 Roger Craig	7.50	3.75	.75
☐	64 Luis Arroyo	3.50	1.75	.35
☐	65 Johnny O'Brien	2.50	1.25	.25
☐	66 Bob Speake	2.50	1.25	.25
☐	67 Vic Power	2.50	1.25	.25
☐	68 Chuck Stobbs	2.50	1.25	.25
☐	69 Chuck Tanner	3.50	1.75	.35
☐	70 Jim Rivera	2.50	1.25	.25
☐	71 Frank Sullivan	2.50	1.25	.25
☐	72A Phillies Team (centered)	6.00	3.00	.60
☐	72B Phillies Team (dated 1955)	25.00	12.50	2.50
☐	72C Phillies Team (name at far left)	6.00	3.00	.60
☐	73 Wayne Terwilliger	2.50	1.25	.25
☐	74 Jim King	2.50	1.25	.25
☐	75 Roy Sievers	3.50	1.75	.35
☐	76 Ray Crone	2.50	1.25	.25
☐	77 Harvey Haddix	3.50	1.75	.35
☐	78 Herman Wehmeier	2.50	1.25	.25
☐	79 Sandy Koufax	90.00	45.00	9.00
☐	80 Gus Triandos	3.50	1.75	.35
☐	81 Wally Westlake	2.50	1.25	.25
☐	82 Bill Renna	2.50	1.25	.25
☐	83 Karl Spooner	3.50	1.75	.35
☐	84 Babe Birrer	2.50	1.25	.25
☐	85A Cleveland Indians (centered)	6.00	3.00	.60
☐	85B Indians Team (dated 1955)	25.00	12.50	2.50
☐	85C Indians Team (name at far left)	6.00	3.00	.60
☐	86 Ray Jablonski	2.50	1.25	.25
☐	87 Dean Stone	2.50	1.25	.25
☐	88 Johnny Kucks	3.50	1.75	.35
☐	89 Norm Zauchin	2.50	1.25	.25
☐	90A Cincinnati Redlegs Team (centered)	6.00	3.00	.60
☐	90B Reds Team (dated 1955)	25.00	12.50	2.50
☐	90C Reds Team (name at far left)	6.00	3.00	.60
☐	91 Gail Harris	2.50	1.25	.25
☐	92 Bob (Red) Wilson	2.50	1.25	.25
☐	93 George Susce	2.50	1.25	.25
☐	94 Ronnie Kline	2.50	1.25	.25
☐	95A Milwaukee Braves Team (centered)	6.00	3.00	.60
☐	95B Braves Team (dated 1955)	25.00	12.50	2.50
☐	95C Braves Team (name at far left)	6.00	3.00	.60
☐	96 Bill Tremel	2.50	1.25	.25
☐	97 Jerry Lynch	2.50	1.25	.25
☐	98 Camilo Pascual	3.50	1.75	.35
☐	99 Don Zimmer	4.50	2.25	.45
☐	100A Baltimore Orioles Team (centered)	6.00	3.00	.60
☐	100B Orioles Team (dated 1955)	25.00	12.50	2.50
☐	100C Orioles Team (name at far left)	6.00	3.00	.60
☐	101 Roy Campanella	75.00	37.50	7.50
☐	102 Jim Davis	3.50	1.75	.35
☐	103 Willie Miranda	3.50	1.75	.35
☐	104 Bob Lennon	3.50	1.75	.35
☐	105 Al Smith	3.50	1.75	.35
☐	106 Joe Astroth	3.50	1.75	.35
☐	107 Ed Mathews	22.00	11.00	2.20
☐	108 Laurin Pepper	3.50	1.75	.35
☐	109 Enos Slaughter	16.00	8.00	1.60
☐	110 Yogi Berra	60.00	30.00	6.00
☐	111 Boston Red Sox Team	9.00	4.50	.90
☐	112 Dee Fondy	3.50	1.75	.35
☐	113 Phil Rizzuto	25.00	12.50	2.50
☐	114 Jim Owens	3.50	1.75	.35
☐	115 Jackie Jensen	5.50	2.75	.55
☐	116 Eddie O'Brien	3.50	1.75	.35
☐	117 Virgil Trucks	3.50	1.75	.35

☐ 118	Nelson Fox	7.50	3.75	.75	☐ 212	Johnny Temple	7.50	3.75	.75
☐ 119	Larry Jackson	3.50	1.75	.35	☐ 213	Detroit Tigers Team	15.00	7.00	1.20
☐ 120	Richie Ashburn	8.50	4.25	.85	☐ 214	Bob Rush	6.00	3.00	.60
☐ 121	Pirates Team	6.00	3.00	.60	☐ 215	Tommy Byrne	7.50	3.75	.75
☐ 122	Willard Nixon	3.50	1.75	.35	☐ 216	Jerry Schoonmaker	6.00	3.00	.60
☐ 123	Roy McMillan	3.50	1.75	.35	☐ 217	Billy Klaus	6.00	3.00	.60
☐ 124	Don Kaiser	3.50	1.75	.35	☐ 218	Joe Nuxall	7.50	3.75	.75
☐ 125	Minnie Minoso	6.50	3.25	.65		(sic, Nuxhall)			
☐ 126	Jim Brady	3.50	1.75	.35	☐ 219	Lew Burdette	8.50	4.25	.85
☐ 127	Willie Jones	3.50	1.75	.35	☐ 220	Del Ennis	7.50	3.75	.75
☐ 128	Eddie Yost	3.50	1.75	.35	☐ 221	Bob Friend	7.50	3.75	.75
☐ 129	Jake Martin	3.50	1.75	.35	☐ 222	Dave Philley	6.00	3.00	.60
☐ 130	Willie Mays	125.00	60.00	12.50	☐ 223	Randy Jackson	6.00	3.00	.60
☐ 131	Bob Roselli	3.50	1.75	.35	☐ 224	Bud Podbielan	6.00	3.00	.60
☐ 132	Bobby Avila	3.50	1.75	.35	☐ 225	Gil McDougald	13.50	6.00	1.00
☐ 133	Ray Narleski	3.50	1.75	.35	☐ 226	Giants Team	30.00	15.00	3.00
☐ 134	Cardinals Team	7.50	3.75	.75	☐ 227	Russ Meyer	6.00	3.00	.60
☐ 135	Mickey Mantle	600.00	300.00	60.00	☐ 228	Mickey Vernon	7.50	3.75	.75
☐ 136	Johnny Logan	4.50	2.25	.45	☐ 229	Harry Brecheen	6.00	3.00	.60
☐ 137	Al Silvera	3.50	1.75	.35	☐ 230	Chico Carrasquel	6.00	3.00	.60
☐ 138	Johnny Antonelli	4.50	2.25	.45	☐ 231	Bob Hale	6.00	3.00	.60
☐ 139	Tommy Carroll	4.50	2.25	.45	☐ 232	Toby Atwell	6.00	3.00	.60
☐ 140	Herb Score	7.50	3.75	.75	☐ 233	Carl Erskine	11.00	5.50	1.10
☐ 141	Joe Frazier	3.50	1.75	.35	☐ 234	Pete Runnels	7.50	3.75	.75
☐ 142	Gene Baker	3.50	1.75	.35	☐ 235	Don Newcombe	17.00	8.50	1.70
☐ 143	Jim Piersall	5.50	2.75	.55	☐ 236	Athletics Team	9.00	4.50	.90
☐ 144	Leroy Powell	3.50	1.75	.35	☐ 237	Jose Valdivielso	6.00	3.00	.60
☐ 145	Gil Hodges	22.00	11.00	2.20	☐ 238	Walt Dropo	7.50	3.75	.75
☐ 146	Washington Team	6.00	3.00	.60	☐ 239	Harry Simpson	6.00	3.00	.60
☐ 147	Earl Torgeson	3.50	1.75	.35	☐ 240	Whitey Ford	45.00	22.50	4.50
☐ 148	Al Dark	5.00	2.50	.50	☐ 241	Don Mueller	7.50	3.75	.75
☐ 149	Dixie Howell	3.50	1.75	.35	☐ 242	Hershell Freeman	6.00	3.00	.60
☐ 150	Duke Snider	70.00	35.00	7.00	☐ 243	Sherm Lollar	7.50	3.75	.75
☐ 151	Spook Jacobs	3.50	1.75	.35	☐ 244	Bob Buhl	6.00	3.00	.60
☐ 152	Billy Hoeft	3.50	1.75	.35	☐ 245	Billy Goodman	7.50	3.75	.75
☐ 153	Frank Thomas	4.50	2.25	.45	☐ 246	Tom Gorman	6.00	3.00	.60
☐ 154	David Pope	3.50	1.75	.35	☐ 247	Bill Sarni	6.00	3.00	.60
☐ 155	Harvey Kuenn	5.50	2.75	.55	☐ 248	Bob Porterfield	6.00	3.00	.60
☐ 156	Wes Westrum	3.50	1.75	.35	☐ 249	Johnny Klippstein	6.00	3.00	.60
☐ 157	Dick Brodowski	3.50	1.75	.35	☐ 250	Larry Doby	9.00	4.50	.90
☐ 158	Wally Post	3.50	1.75	.35	☐ 251	New York Yankees	70.00	35.00	7.00
☐ 159	Clint Courtney	3.50	1.75	.35		Team Card			
☐ 160	Billy Pierce	4.50	2.25	.45	☐ 252	Vernon Law	7.50	3.75	.75
☐ 161	Joe DeMaestri	3.50	1.75	.35	☐ 253	Irv Noren	6.00	3.00	.60
☐ 162	Dave (Gus) Bell	4.50	2.25	.45	☐ 254	George Crowe	6.00	3.00	.60
☐ 163	Gene Woodling	4.50	2.25	.45	☐ 255	Bob Lemon	20.00	10.00	2.00
☐ 164	Harmon Killebrew	40.00	20.00	4.00	☐ 256	Tom Hurd	6.00	3.00	.60
☐ 165	Red Schoendienst	5.00	2.50	.50	☐ 257	Bobby Thomson	8.00	4.00	.80
☐ 166	Brooklyn Dodgers	65.00	32.50	6.50	☐ 258	Art Ditmar	6.00	3.00	.60
	Team Card				☐ 259	Sam Jones	6.00	3.00	.60
☐ 167	Harry Dorish	3.50	1.75	.35	☐ 260	Pee Wee Reese	50.00	25.00	5.00
☐ 168	Sammy White	3.50	1.75	.35	☐ 261	Bobby Shantz	5.00	2.50	.50
☐ 169	Bob Nelson	3.50	1.75	.35	☐ 262	Howie Pollet	4.00	2.00	.40
☐ 170	Bill Virdon	5.50	2.75	.55	☐ 263	Bob Miller	4.00	2.00	.40
☐ 171	Jim Wilson	3.50	1.75	.35	☐ 264	Ray Monzant	4.00	2.00	.40
☐ 172	Frank Torre	3.50	1.75	.35	☐ 265	Sandy Consuegra	4.00	2.00	.40
☐ 173	Johnny Podres	5.50	2.75	.55	☐ 266	Don Ferrarese	4.00	2.00	.40
☐ 174	Glen Gorbous	3.50	1.75	.35	☐ 267	Bob Nieman	4.00	2.00	.40
☐ 175	Del Crandall	4.50	2.25	.45	☐ 268	Dale Mitchell	5.00	2.50	.50
☐ 176	Alex Kellner	3.50	1.75	.35	☐ 269	Jack Meyer	4.00	2.00	.40
☐ 177	Hank Bauer	7.00	3.50	.70	☐ 270	Billy Loes	5.00	2.50	.50
☐ 178	Joe Black	4.50	2.25	.45	☐ 271	Foster Castleman	4.00	2.00	.40
☐ 179	Harry Chiti	3.50	1.75	.35	☐ 272	Danny O'Connell	4.00	2.00	.40
☐ 180	Robin Roberts	17.00	8.50	1.70	☐ 273	Walker Cooper	4.00	2.00	.40
☐ 181	Billy Martin	35.00	17.50	3.50	☐ 274	Frank Baumholtz	4.00	2.00	.40
☐ 182	Paul Minner	6.00	3.00	.60	☐ 275	Jim Greengrass	4.00	2.00	.40
☐ 183	Stan Lopata	6.00	3.00	.60	☐ 276	George Zuverink	4.00	2.00	.40
☐ 184	Don Bessent	6.00	3.00	.60	☐ 277	Daryl Spencer	4.00	2.00	.40
☐ 185	Bill Bruton	6.00	3.00	.60	☐ 278	Chet Nichols	4.00	2.00	.40
☐ 186	Ron Jackson	6.00	3.00	.60	☐ 279	Johnny Groth	4.00	2.00	.40
☐ 187	Early Wynn	20.00	10.00	2.00	☐ 280	Jim Gilliam	7.00	3.50	.70
☐ 188	White Sox Team	10.00	5.00	1.00	☐ 281	Art Houtteman	4.00	2.00	.40
☐ 189	Ned Garver	6.00	3.00	.60	☐ 282	Warren Hacker	4.00	2.00	.40
☐ 190	Carl Furillo	10.00	5.00	1.00	☐ 283	Hal Smith	4.00	2.00	.40
☐ 191	Frank Lary	7.50	3.75	.75	☐ 284	Ike Delock	4.00	2.00	.40
☐ 192	Smoky Burgess	7.50	3.75	.75	☐ 285	Eddie Miksis	4.00	2.00	.40
☐ 193	Wilmer Mizell	6.00	3.00	.60	☐ 286	Bill Wight	4.00	2.00	.40
☐ 194	Monte Irvin	17.00	8.50	1.70	☐ 287	Bobby Adams	4.00	2.00	.40
☐ 195	George Kell	20.00	10.00	2.00	☐ 288	Bob Cerv	5.00	2.50	.50
☐ 196	Tom Poholsky	6.00	3.00	.60	☐ 289	Hal Jeffcoat	4.00	2.00	.40
☐ 197	Granny Hamner	6.00	3.00	.60	☐ 290	Curt Simmons	5.00	2.50	.50
☐ 198	Ed Fitzgerald	6.00	3.00	.60	☐ 291	Frank Kellert	4.00	2.00	.40
☐ 199	Hank Thompson	7.50	3.75	.75	☐ 292	Luis Aparicio	45.00	22.50	4.50
☐ 200	Bob Feller	45.00	22.50	4.50	☐ 293	Stu Miller	4.00	2.00	.40
☐ 201	Rip Repulski	6.00	3.00	.60	☐ 294	Ernie Johnson	4.00	2.00	.40
☐ 202	Jim Hearn	6.00	3.00	.60	☐ 295	Clem Labine	5.00	2.50	.50
☐ 203	Bill Tuttle	6.00	3.00	.60	☐ 296	Andy Seminick	4.00	2.00	.40
☐ 204	Art Swanson	6.00	3.00	.60	☐ 297	Bob Skinner	4.00	2.00	.40
☐ 205	Whitey Lockman	6.00	3.00	.60	☐ 298	Johnny Schmitz	4.00	2.00	.40
☐ 206	Erv Palica	6.00	3.00	.60	☐ 299	Charley Neal	5.00	2.50	.50
☐ 207	Jim Small	6.00	3.00	.60	☐ 300	Vic Wertz	5.00	2.50	.50
☐ 208	Elston Howard	15.00	7.50	1.50	☐ 301	Marv Grissom	4.00	2.00	.40
☐ 209	Max Surkont	6.00	3.00	.60	☐ 302	Eddie Robinson	5.00	2.50	.50
☐ 210	Mike Garcia	7.50	3.75	.75	☐ 303	Jim Dyck	4.00	2.00	.40
☐ 211	Murry Dickson	6.00	3.00	.60	☐ 304	Frank Malzone	6.50	3.25	.65

		NRMT	VG-E	GOOD
☐ 305	Brooks Lawrence	4.00	2.00	.40
☐ 306	Curt Roberts	4.00	2.00	.40
☐ 307	Hoyt Wilhelm	17.00	8.50	1.70
☐ 308	Chuck Harmon	4.00	2.00	.40
☐ 309	Don Blasingame	4.00	2.00	.40
☐ 310	Steve Gromek	4.00	2.00	.40
☐ 311	Hal Naragon	4.00	2.00	.40
☐ 312	Andy Pafko	4.00	2.00	.40
☐ 313	Gene Stephens	4.00	2.00	.40
☐ 314	Hobie Landrith	4.00	2.00	.40
☐ 315	Milt Bolling	4.00	2.00	.40
☐ 316	Jerry Coleman	5.00	2.50	.50
☐ 317	Al Aber	4.00	2.00	.40
☐ 318	Fred Hatfield	4.00	2.00	.40
☐ 319	Jack Crimian	4.00	2.00	.40
☐ 320	Joe Adcock	5.00	2.50	.50
☐ 321	Jim Konstanty	5.00	2.50	.50
☐ 322	Karl Olson	4.00	2.00	.40
☐ 323	Willard Schmidt	4.00	2.00	.40
☐ 324	Rocky Bridges	4.00	2.00	.40
☐ 325	Don Liddle	4.00	2.00	.40
☐ 326	Connie Johnson	4.00	2.00	.40
☐ 327	Bob Wiesler	4.00	2.00	.40
☐ 328	Preston Ward	4.00	2.00	.40
☐ 329	Lou Berberet	4.00	2.00	.40
☐ 330	Jim Busby	4.00	2.00	.40
☐ 331	Dick Hall	4.00	2.00	.40
☐ 332	Don Larsen	8.00	4.00	.80
☐ 333	Rube Walker	5.00	2.50	.50
☐ 334	Bob Miller	4.00	2.00	.40
☐ 335	Don Hoak	4.00	2.00	.40
☐ 336	Ellis Kinder	4.00	2.00	.40
☐ 337	Bobby Morgan	4.00	2.00	.40
☐ 338	Jim Delsing	4.00	2.00	.40
☐ 339	Rance Pless	4.00	2.00	.40
☐ 340	Mickey McDermott	10.00	2.00	.40
☐ 341	Checklist 1/3 (unnumbered)	125.00	20.00	4.00
☐ 342	Checklist 2/4 (unnumbered)	125.00	20.00	4.00

1957 Topps

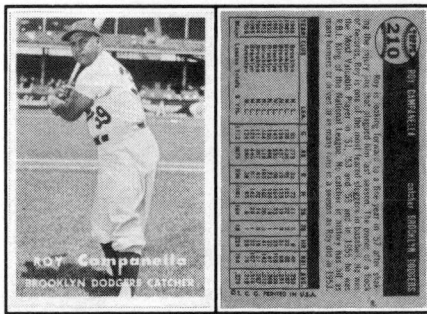

The cards in this 407-card set measure 2 1/2" by 3 1/2". In 1957, Topps returned to the vertical obverse, adopted what we now call the standard card size, and used a large, uncluttered color photo for the first time since 1952. Cards in the series 265 to 352 and the unnumbered checklist cards are scarcer than other cards in the set. The first star combination cards, #400 and #407, are quite popular with collectors. They feature the big stars of the previous season's World Series teams, the Dodgers (Furillo, Hodges, Campanella, and Snider) and Yankees (Berra and Mantle). The complete set price below does not include the unnumbered checklist cards.

		NRMT	VG-E	GOOD
COMPLETE SET (407)		4200.00	1400.00	250.00
COMMON PLAYER (1-264)		2.25	1.10	.22
COMMON PLAYER (265-352)		10.00	5.00	1.00
COMMON PLAYER (353-407)		2.50	1.25	.25
☐ 1	Ted Williams	250.00	50.00	10.00
☐ 2	Yogi Berra	50.00	25.00	5.00

☐ 3	Dale Long	2.25	1.10	.22
☐ 4	Johnny Logan	2.50	1.25	.25
☐ 5	Sal Maglie	4.00	2.00	.40
☐ 6	Hector Lopez	2.25	1.10	.22
☐ 7	Luis Aparicio	12.00	6.00	1.20
☐ 8	Don Mossi	2.50	1.25	.25
☐ 9	Johnny Temple	2.25	1.10	.22
☐ 10	Willie Mays	100.00	50.00	10.00
☐ 11	George Zuverink	2.25	1.10	.22
☐ 12	Dick Groat	3.50	1.75	.35
☐ 13	Wally Burnette	2.25	1.10	.22
☐ 14	Bob Nieman	2.25	1.10	.22
☐ 15	Robin Roberts	12.00	6.00	1.20
☐ 16	Walt Moryn	2.25	1.10	.22
☐ 17	Billy Gardner	2.50	1.25	.25
☐ 18	Don Drysdale	90.00	45.00	9.00
☐ 19	Bob Wilson	2.25	1.10	.22
☐ 20	Hank Aaron (reverse negative photo on front)	100.00	50.00	10.00
☐ 21	Frank Sullivan	2.25	1.10	.22
☐ 22	Jerry Snyder (photo actually Ed Fitzgerald)	2.25	1.10	.22
☐ 23	Sherm Lollar	2.50	1.25	.25
☐ 24	Bill Mazeroski	12.00	6.00	1.20
☐ 25	Whitey Ford	25.00	12.50	2.50
☐ 26	Bob Boyd	2.25	1.10	.22
☐ 27	Ted Kazanski	2.25	1.10	.22
☐ 28	Gene Conley	2.25	1.10	.22
☐ 29	Whitey Herzog	6.00	3.00	.60
☐ 30	Pee Wee Reese	25.00	12.50	2.50
☐ 31	Ron Northey	2.25	1.10	.22
☐ 32	Hershell Freeman	2.25	1.10	.22
☐ 33	Jim Small	2.25	1.10	.22
☐ 34	Tom Sturdivant	2.25	1.10	.22
☐ 35	Frank Robinson	90.00	45.00	9.00
☐ 36	Bob Grim	2.50	1.25	.25
☐ 37	Frank Torre	2.25	1.10	.22
☐ 38	Nelson Fox	6.00	3.00	.60
☐ 39	Al Worthington	2.25	1.10	.22
☐ 40	Early Wynn	12.00	6.00	1.20
☐ 41	Hal W. Smith	2.25	1.10	.22
☐ 42	Dee Fondy	2.25	1.10	.22
☐ 43	Connie Johnson	2.25	1.10	.22
☐ 44	Joe DeMaestri	2.25	1.10	.22
☐ 45	Carl Furillo	6.00	3.00	.60
☐ 46	Robert J. Miller	2.25	1.10	.22
☐ 47	Don Blasingame	2.25	1.10	.22
☐ 48	Bill Bruton	2.50	1.25	.25
☐ 49	Daryl Spencer	2.25	1.10	.22
☐ 50	Herb Score	4.00	2.00	.40
☐ 51	Clint Courtney	2.25	1.10	.22
☐ 52	Lee Walls	2.25	1.10	.22
☐ 53	Clem Labine	3.00	1.50	.30
☐ 54	Elmer Valo	2.25	1.10	.22
☐ 55	Ernie Banks	25.00	12.50	2.50
☐ 56	Dave Sisler	2.25	1.10	.22
☐ 57	Jim Lemon	2.50	1.25	.25
☐ 58	Ruben Gomez	2.25	1.10	.22
☐ 59	Dick Williams	3.00	1.50	.30
☐ 60	Billy Hoeft	2.25	1.10	.22
☐ 61	James Rhodes	3.00	1.50	.30
☐ 62	Billy Martin	20.00	10.00	2.00
☐ 63	Ike Delock	2.25	1.10	.22
☐ 64	Pete Runnels	2.50	1.25	.25
☐ 65	Wally Moon	3.00	1.50	.30
☐ 66	Brooks Lawrence	2.25	1.10	.22
☐ 67	Chico Carrasquel	2.25	1.10	.22
☐ 68	Ray Crone	2.25	1.10	.22
☐ 69	Roy McMillan	2.25	1.10	.22
☐ 70	Richie Ashburn	6.50	3.25	.65
☐ 71	Murry Dickson	2.25	1.10	.22
☐ 72	Bill Tuttle	2.25	1.10	.22
☐ 73	George Crowe	2.25	1.10	.22
☐ 74	Vito Valentinetti	2.25	1.10	.22
☐ 75	Jim Piersall	4.00	2.00	.40
☐ 76	Roberto Clemente	60.00	30.00	6.00
☐ 77	Paul Foytack	2.25	1.10	.22
☐ 78	Vic Wertz	2.50	1.25	.25
☐ 79	Lindy McDaniel	2.50	1.25	.25
☐ 80	Gil Hodges	20.00	10.00	2.00
☐ 81	Herman Wehmeier	2.25	1.10	.22
☐ 82	Elston Howard	6.00	3.00	.60
☐ 83	Lou Skizas	2.25	1.10	.22
☐ 84	Moe Drabowsky	2.50	1.25	.25
☐ 85	Larry Doby	4.00	2.00	.40
☐ 86	Bill Sarni	2.25	1.10	.22
☐ 87	Tom Gorman	2.25	1.10	.22
☐ 88	Harvey Kuenn	4.00	2.00	.40
☐ 89	Roy Sievers	2.50	1.25	.25
☐ 90	Warren Spahn	25.00	12.50	2.50
☐ 91	Mack Burk	2.25	1.10	.22
☐ 92	Mickey Vernon	3.00	1.50	.30
☐ 93	Hal Jeffcoat	2.25	1.10	.22

☐ 94	Bobby Del Greco	2.25	1.10	.22
☐ 95	Mickey Mantle	600.00	300.00	60.00
☐ 96	Hank Aguirre	2.25	1.10	.22
☐ 97	New York Yankees Team Card	16.00	8.00	1.60
☐ 98	Alvin Dark	3.00	1.50	.30
☐ 99	Bob Keegan	2.25	1.10	.22
☐ 100	Giles and Harridge League Presidents	3.50	1.75	.35
☐ 101	Chuck Stobbs	2.25	1.10	.22
☐ 102	Ray Boone	2.50	1.25	.25
☐ 103	Joe Nuxhall	2.50	1.25	.25
☐ 104	Hank Foiles	2.25	1.10	.22
☐ 105	Johnny Antonelli	2.50	1.25	.25
☐ 106	Ray Moore	2.25	1.10	.22
☐ 107	Jim Rivera	2.25	1.10	.22
☐ 108	Tommy Byrne	2.50	1.25	.25
☐ 109	Hank Thompson	2.50	1.25	.25
☐ 110	Bill Virdon	3.00	1.50	.30
☐ 111	Hal R. Smith	2.25	1.10	.22
☐ 112	Tom Brewer	2.25	1.10	.22
☐ 113	Wilmer Mizell	2.25	1.10	.22
☐ 114	Milwaukee Braves Team Card	4.50	2.25	.45
☐ 115	Jim Gilliam	5.00	2.50	.50
☐ 116	Mike Fornieles	2.25	1.10	.22
☐ 117	Joe Adcock	3.00	1.50	.30
☐ 118	Bob Porterfield	2.25	1.10	.22
☐ 119	Stan Lopata	2.25	1.10	.22
☐ 120	Bob Lemon	12.00	6.00	1.20
☐ 121	Cletis Boyer	5.00	2.50	.50
☐ 122	Ken Boyer	4.00	2.00	.40
☐ 123	Steve Ridzik	2.25	1.10	.22
☐ 124	Dave Philley	2.25	1.10	.22
☐ 125	Al Kaline	25.00	12.50	2.50
☐ 126	Bob Wiesler	2.25	1.10	.22
☐ 127	Bob Buhl	2.25	1.10	.22
☐ 128	Ed Bailey	2.25	1.10	.22
☐ 129	Saul Rogovin	2.25	1.10	.22
☐ 130	Don Newcombe	5.00	2.50	.50
☐ 131	Milt Bolling	2.25	1.10	.22
☐ 132	Art Ditmar	2.25	1.10	.22
☐ 133	Del Crandall	2.50	1.25	.25
☐ 134	Don Kaiser	2.25	1.10	.22
☐ 135	Bill Skowron	5.00	2.50	.50
☐ 136	Jim Hegan	2.50	1.25	.25
☐ 137	Bob Rush	2.25	1.10	.22
☐ 138	Minnie Minoso	4.50	2.25	.45
☐ 139	Lou Kretlow	2.25	1.10	.22
☐ 140	Frank Thomas	2.50	1.25	.25
☐ 141	Al Aber	2.25	1.10	.22
☐ 142	Charley Thompson	2.25	1.10	.22
☐ 143	Andy Pafko	2.25	1.10	.22
☐ 144	Ray Narleski	2.25	1.10	.22
☐ 145	Al Smith	2.25	1.10	.22
☐ 146	Don Ferrarese	2.25	1.10	.22
☐ 147	Al Walker	2.25	1.10	.22
☐ 148	Don Mueller	2.50	1.25	.25
☐ 149	Bob Kennedy	2.25	1.10	.22
☐ 150	Bob Friend	2.50	1.25	.25
☐ 151	Willie Miranda	2.25	1.10	.22
☐ 152	Jack Harshman	2.25	1.10	.22
☐ 153	Karl Olson	2.25	1.10	.22
☐ 154	Red Schoendienst	4.00	2.00	.40
☐ 155	Jim Brosnan	2.50	1.25	.25
☐ 156	Gus Triandos	2.50	1.25	.25
☐ 157	Wally Post	2.25	1.10	.22
☐ 158	Curt Simmons	2.50	1.25	.25
☐ 159	Solly Drake	2.25	1.10	.22
☐ 160	Billy Pierce	3.00	1.50	.30
☐ 161	Pirates Team	4.00	2.00	.40
☐ 162	Jack Meyer	2.25	1.10	.22
☐ 163	Sammy White	2.25	1.10	.22
☐ 164	Tommy Carroll	2.50	1.25	.25
☐ 165	Ted Kluszewski	5.00	2.50	.50
☐ 166	Elroy Face	3.00	1.50	.30
☐ 167	Vic Power	2.50	1.25	.25
☐ 168	Frank Lary	2.50	1.25	.25
☐ 169	Herb Plews	2.25	1.10	.22
☐ 170	Duke Snider	60.00	30.00	6.00
☐ 171	Boston Red Sox Team Card	4.00	2.00	.40
☐ 172	Gene Woodling	3.00	1.50	.30
☐ 173	Roger Craig	4.00	2.00	.40
☐ 174	Willie Jones	2.25	1.10	.22
☐ 175	Don Larsen	5.00	2.50	.50
☐ 176	Gene Baker	2.25	1.10	.22
☐ 177	Eddie Yost	2.25	1.10	.22
☐ 178	Don Bessent	2.25	1.10	.22
☐ 179	Ernie Oravetz	2.25	1.10	.22
☐ 180	Dave (Gus) Bell	2.50	1.25	.25
☐ 181	Dick Donovan	2.25	1.10	.22
☐ 182	Hobie Landrith	2.25	1.10	.22
☐ 183	Chicago Cubs Team	4.00	2.00	.40
☐ 184	Tito Francona	2.50	1.25	.25
☐ 185	Johnny Kucks	2.50	1.25	.25
☐ 186	Jim King	2.25	1.10	.22
☐ 187	Virgil Trucks	2.50	1.25	.25
☐ 188	Felix Mantilla	2.25	1.10	.22
☐ 189	Willard Nixon	2.25	1.10	.22
☐ 190	Randy Jackson	2.25	1.10	.22
☐ 191	Joe Margoneri	2.25	1.10	.22
☐ 192	Gerry Coleman	2.50	1.25	.25
☐ 193	Del Rice	2.25	1.10	.22
☐ 194	Hal Brown	2.25	1.10	.22
☐ 195	Bobby Avila	2.25	1.10	.22
☐ 196	Larry Jackson	2.25	1.10	.22
☐ 197	Hank Sauer	2.50	1.25	.25
☐ 198	Detroit Tigers Team	6.00	3.00	.60
☐ 199	Vern Law	2.50	1.25	.25
☐ 200	Gil McDougald	5.00	2.50	.50
☐ 201	Sandy Amoros	2.50	1.25	.25
☐ 202	Dick Gernert	2.25	1.10	.22
☐ 203	Hoyt Wilhelm	12.00	6.00	1.20
☐ 204	Athletics Team	4.00	2.00	.40
☐ 205	Charlie Maxwell	2.25	1.10	.22
☐ 206	Willard Schmidt	2.25	1.10	.22
☐ 207	Gordon (Billy) Hunter	2.25	1.10	.22
☐ 208	Lou Burdette	4.00	2.00	.40
☐ 209	Bob Skinner	2.50	1.25	.25
☐ 210	Roy Campanella	50.00	25.00	5.00
☐ 211	Camilo Pascual	2.50	1.25	.25
☐ 212	Rocco Colavito	15.00	7.50	1.50
☐ 213	Les Moss	2.25	1.10	.22
☐ 214	Phillies Team	4.00	2.00	.40
☐ 215	Enos Slaughter	12.00	6.00	1.20
☐ 216	Marv Grissom	2.25	1.10	.22
☐ 217	Gene Stephens	2.25	1.10	.22
☐ 218	Ray Jablonski	2.25	1.10	.22
☐ 219	Tom Acker	2.25	1.10	.22
☐ 220	Jackie Jensen	4.00	2.00	.40
☐ 221	Dixie Howell	2.25	1.10	.22
☐ 222	Alex Grammas	2.25	1.10	.22
☐ 223	Frank House	2.25	1.10	.22
☐ 224	Marv Blaylock	2.25	1.10	.22
☐ 225	Harry Simpson	2.25	1.10	.22
☐ 226	Preston Ward	2.25	1.10	.22
☐ 227	Gerry Staley	2.25	1.10	.22
☐ 228	Smoky Burgess	2.50	1.25	.25
☐ 229	George Susce	2.25	1.10	.22
☐ 230	George Kell	12.00	6.00	1.20
☐ 231	Solly Hemus	2.25	1.10	.22
☐ 232	Whitey Lockman	2.50	1.25	.25
☐ 233	Art Fowler	2.25	1.10	.22
☐ 234	Dick Cole	2.25	1.10	.22
☐ 235	Tom Poholsky	2.25	1.10	.22
☐ 236	Joe Ginsberg	2.25	1.10	.22
☐ 237	Foster Castleman	2.25	1.10	.22
☐ 238	Eddie Robinson	2.25	1.10	.22
☐ 239	Tom Morgan	2.25	1.10	.22
☐ 240	Hank Bauer	5.00	2.50	.50
☐ 241	Joe Lonnett	2.25	1.10	.22
☐ 242	Charlie Neal	2.50	1.25	.25
☐ 243	Cardinals Team	5.00	2.50	.50
☐ 244	Billy Loes	2.50	1.25	.25
☐ 245	Rip Repulski	2.25	1.10	.22
☐ 246	Jose Valdivielso	2.25	1.10	.22
☐ 247	Turk Lown	2.25	1.10	.22
☐ 248	Jim Finigan	2.25	1.10	.22
☐ 249	Dave Pope	2.25	1.10	.22
☐ 250	Ed Mathews	15.00	7.50	1.50
☐ 251	Orioles Team	5.00	2.50	.50
☐ 252	Carl Erskine	4.00	2.00	.40
☐ 253	Gus Zernial	2.50	1.25	.25
☐ 254	Ron Negray	2.25	1.10	.22
☐ 255	Charlie Silvera	2.25	1.10	.22
☐ 256	Ron Kline	2.25	1.10	.22
☐ 257	Walt Dropo	2.25	1.10	.22
☐ 258	Steve Gromek	2.25	1.10	.22
☐ 259	Eddie O'Brien	2.25	1.10	.22
☐ 260	Del Ennis	2.50	1.25	.25
☐ 261	Bob Chakales	2.25	1.10	.22
☐ 262	Bobby Thomson	4.00	2.00	.40
☐ 263	George Strickland	2.25	1.10	.22
☐ 264	Bob Turley	4.00	2.00	.40
☐ 265	Harvey Haddix	12.00	6.00	1.20
☐ 266	Ken Kuhn	10.00	5.00	1.00
☐ 267	Danny Kravitz	10.00	5.00	1.00
☐ 268	Joe Collum	10.00	5.00	1.00
☐ 269	Bob Cerv	12.00	6.00	1.20
☐ 270	Washington Team	12.00	6.00	1.20
☐ 271	Danny O'Connell	10.00	5.00	1.00
☐ 272	Bobby Shantz	17.00	8.50	1.70
☐ 273	Jim Davis	10.00	5.00	1.00
☐ 274	Don Hoak	10.00	5.00	1.00
☐ 275	Indians Team	12.00	6.00	1.20
☐ 276	Jim Pyburn	10.00	5.00	1.00
☐ 277	Johnny Podres	45.00	22.50	4.50
☐ 278	Fred Hatfield	10.00	5.00	1.00
☐ 279	Bob Thurman	10.00	5.00	1.00

☐ 280	Alex Kellner	10.00	5.00	1.00
☐ 281	Gail Harris	10.00	5.00	1.00
☐ 282	Jack Dittmer	10.00	5.00	1.00
☐ 283	Wes Covington	12.00	6.00	1.20
☐ 284	Don Zimmer	15.00	7.50	1.50
☐ 285	Ned Garver	10.00	5.00	1.00
☐ 286	Bobby Richardson	55.00	27.50	5.50
☐ 287	Sam Jones	10.00	5.00	1.00
☐ 288	Ted Lepcio	10.00	5.00	1.00
☐ 289	Jim Bolger	10.00	5.00	1.00
☐ 290	Andy Carey	12.00	6.00	1.20
☐ 291	Windy McCall	10.00	5.00	1.00
☐ 292	Billy Klaus	10.00	5.00	1.00
☐ 293	Ted Abernathy	10.00	5.00	1.00
☐ 294	Rocky Bridges	10.00	5.00	1.00
☐ 295	Joe Collins	12.00	6.00	1.20
☐ 296	Johnny Klippstein	10.00	5.00	1.00
☐ 297	Jack Crimian	10.00	5.00	1.00
☐ 298	Irv Noren	10.00	5.00	1.00
☐ 299	Chuck Harmon	10.00	5.00	1.00
☐ 300	Mike Garcia	12.00	6.00	1.20
☐ 301	Sammy Esposito	10.00	5.00	1.00
☐ 302	Sandy Koufax	225.00	110.00	22.00
☐ 303	Billy Goodman	12.00	6.00	1.20
☐ 304	Joe Cunningham	12.00	6.00	1.20
☐ 305	Chico Fernandez	10.00	5.00	1.00
☐ 306	Darrell Johnson	12.00	6.00	1.20
☐ 307	J.D.(Bubba) Phillips	10.00	5.00	1.00
☐ 308	Richard Hall	10.00	5.00	1.00
☐ 309	Jim Busby	10.00	5.00	1.00
☐ 310	Max Surkont	10.00	5.00	1.00
☐ 311	Al Pilarcik	10.00	5.00	1.00
☐ 312	Tony Kubek	65.00	32.50	6.50
☐ 313	Mel Parnell	12.00	6.00	1.20
☐ 314	Ed Bouchee	10.00	5.00	1.00
☐ 315	Lou Berberet	10.00	5.00	1.00
☐ 316	Billy O'Dell	10.00	5.00	1.00
☐ 317	New York Giants Team Card	35.00	17.50	3.50
☐ 318	Mickey McDermott	10.00	5.00	1.00
☐ 319	Gino Cimoli	12.00	6.00	1.20
☐ 320	Neil Chrisley	10.00	5.00	1.00
☐ 321	John (Red) Murff	10.00	5.00	1.00
☐ 322	Cincinnati Team	35.00	17.50	3.50
☐ 323	Wes Westrum	10.00	5.00	1.00
☐ 324	Brooklyn Dodgers Team Card	65.00	32.50	6.50
☐ 325	Frank Bolling	10.00	5.00	1.00
☐ 326	Pedro Ramos	10.00	5.00	1.00
☐ 327	Jim Pendleton	10.00	5.00	1.00
☐ 328	Brooks Robinson	225.00	110.00	22.00
☐ 329	White Sox Team	18.00	9.00	1.80
☐ 330	Jim Wilson	10.00	5.00	1.00
☐ 331	Ray Katt	10.00	5.00	1.00
☐ 332	Bob Bowman	10.00	5.00	1.00
☐ 333	Ernie Johnson	10.00	5.00	1.00
☐ 334	Jerry Schoonmaker	10.00	5.00	1.00
☐ 335	Granny Hamner	10.00	5.00	1.00
☐ 336	Haywood Sullivan	12.00	6.00	1.20
☐ 337	Rene Valdes	10.00	5.00	1.00
☐ 338	Jim Bunning	65.00	32.50	6.50
☐ 339	Bob Speake	10.00	5.00	1.00
☐ 340	Bill Wight	10.00	5.00	1.00
☐ 341	Don Gross	10.00	5.00	1.00
☐ 342	Gene Mauch	12.00	6.00	1.20
☐ 343	Taylor Phillips	10.00	5.00	1.00
☐ 344	Paul LaPalme	10.00	5.00	1.00
☐ 345	Paul Smith	10.00	5.00	1.00
☐ 346	Dick Littlefield	10.00	5.00	1.00
☐ 347	Hal Naragon	10.00	5.00	1.00
☐ 348	Jim Hearn	10.00	5.00	1.00
☐ 349	Nellie King	10.00	5.00	1.00
☐ 350	Eddie Miksis	10.00	5.00	1.00
☐ 351	Dave Hillman	10.00	5.00	1.00
☐ 352	Ellis Kinder	10.00	5.00	1.00
☐ 353	Cal Neeman	2.50	1.25	.25
☐ 354	W. (Rip) Coleman	2.50	1.25	.25
☐ 355	Frank Malzone	3.00	1.50	.30
☐ 356	Faye Throneberry	2.50	1.25	.25
☐ 357	Earl Torgeson	2.50	1.25	.25
☐ 358	Gerry Lynch	2.50	1.25	.25
☐ 359	Tom Cheney	2.50	1.25	.25
☐ 360	Johnny Groth	2.50	1.25	.25
☐ 361	Curt Barclay	2.50	1.25	.25
☐ 362	Roman Mejias	2.50	1.25	.25
☐ 363	Eddie Kasko	2.50	1.25	.25
☐ 364	Cal McLish	2.50	1.25	.25
☐ 365	Ozzie Virgil	2.50	1.25	.25
☐ 366	Ken Lehman	2.50	1.25	.25
☐ 367	Ed Fitzgerald	2.50	1.25	.25
☐ 368	Bob Purkey	2.50	1.25	.25
☐ 369	Milt Graff	2.50	1.25	.25
☐ 370	Warren Hacker	2.50	1.25	.25
☐ 371	Bob Lennon	2.50	1.25	.25
☐ 372	Norm Zauchin	2.50	1.25	.25
☐ 373	Pete Whisenant	2.50	1.25	.25
☐ 374	Don Cardwell	2.50	1.25	.25
☐ 375	Jim Landis	2.50	1.25	.25
☐ 376	Don Elston	2.50	1.25	.25
☐ 377	Andre Rodgers	2.50	1.25	.25
☐ 378	Elmer Singleton	2.50	1.25	.25
☐ 379	Don Lee	2.50	1.25	.25
☐ 380	Walker Cooper	2.50	1.25	.25
☐ 381	Dean Stone	2.50	1.25	.25
☐ 382	Jim Brideweser	2.50	1.25	.25
☐ 383	Juan Pizarro	2.50	1.25	.25
☐ 384	Bobby G. Smith	2.50	1.25	.25
☐ 385	Art Houtteman	2.50	1.25	.25
☐ 386	Lyle Luttrell	2.50	1.25	.25
☐ 387	Jack Sanford	4.00	2.00	.40
☐ 388	Pete Daley	2.50	1.25	.25
☐ 389	Dave Jolly	2.50	1.25	.25
☐ 390	Reno Bertoia	2.50	1.25	.25
☐ 391	Ralph Terry	5.00	2.50	.50
☐ 392	Chuck Tanner	3.50	1.75	.35
☐ 393	Raul Sanchez	2.50	1.25	.25
☐ 394	Luis Arroyo	3.00	1.50	.30
☐ 395	J.M. (Bubba) Phillips	2.50	1.25	.25
☐ 396	K. (Casey) Wise	2.50	1.25	.25
☐ 397	Roy Smalley	2.50	1.25	.25
☐ 398	Al Cicotte	3.00	1.50	.30
☐ 399	Bill Consolo	2.50	1.25	.25
☐ 400	Dodgers' Sluggers Carl Furillo Gil Hodges Roy Campanella Duke Snider	100.00	50.00	10.00
☐ 401	Earl Battey	3.00	1.50	.30
☐ 402	Jim Pisani	2.50	1.25	.25
☐ 403	Richard Hyde	2.50	1.25	.25
☐ 404	Harry Anderson	2.50	1.25	.25
☐ 405	Duke Maas	2.50	1.25	.25
☐ 406	Bob Hale	2.50	1.25	.25
☐ 407	Yankee Power Hitters Mickey Mantle Yogi Berra	175.00	85.00	18.00
☐ 408	Checklist 1/2 (unnumbered)	65.00	10.00	2.00
☐ 409	Checklist 2/3 (unnumbered)	100.00	15.00	3.00
☐ 410	Checklist 3/4 (unnumbered)	175.00	30.00	5.00
☐ 411	Checklist 4/5 (unnumbered)	250.00	40.00	6.00

1958 Topps

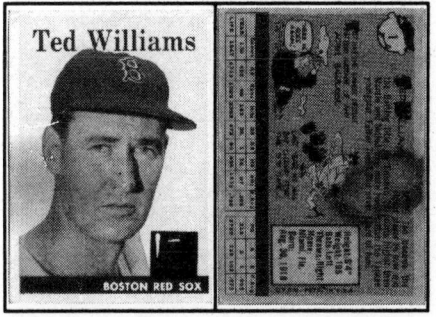

The cards in this 494-card set measure 2 1/2" by 3 1/2". Although the last card is numbered 495, number 145 was not issued, bringing the set total to 494 cards. The 1958 Topps set contains the first Sport Magazine All-Star Selection series (475-495) and expanded use of combination cards. The team cards carried series checklists on back (Milwaukee, Detroit, Baltimore, and Cincinnati are also found with players listed alphabetically). Cards with the scarce yellow name (YL) or team (YT) lettering as opposed to the common white lettering are noted in the checklist. In the last series cards of Stan Musial and Mickey Mantle were triple printed; the cards they replaced (443, 446, 450, and 462) on the printing sheet were hence printed in shorter supply than other cards in the last series and are marked with an SP in the list below.

		NRMT	VG-E	GOOD
COMPLETE SET (494)		2700.00	900.00	200.00
COMMON PLAYER (1-110)		2.00	1.00	.20
COMMON PLAYER (111-198)		1.50	.75	.15
COMMON PLAYER (199-352)		1.25	.60	.12
COMMON PLAYER (353-440)		1.25	.60	.12
COMMON PLAYER (441-474)		1.00	.50	.10
COMMON PLAYER (475-495)		1.25	.60	.12

			NRMT	VG-E	GOOD
☐	1	Ted Williams	225.00	40.00	8.00
☐	2A	Bob Lemon	10.00	5.00	1.00
☐	2B	Bob Lemon YT	25.00	12.50	2.50
☐	3	Alex Kellner	2.00	1.00	.20
☐	4	Hank Foiles	2.00	1.00	.20
☐	5	Willie Mays	80.00	40.00	8.00
☐	6	George Zuverink	2.00	1.00	.20
☐	7	Dale Long	2.00	1.00	.20
☐	8A	Eddie Kasko	2.00	1.00	.20
☐	8B	Eddie Kasko YL	20.00	10.00	2.00
☐	9	Hank Bauer	4.00	2.00	.40
☐	10	Lou Burdette	3.50	1.75	.35
☐	11A	Jim Rivera	2.00	1.00	.20
☐	11B	Jim Rivera YT	15.00	7.50	1.50
☐	12	George Crowe	2.00	1.00	.20
☐	13A	Billy Hoeft	2.00	1.00	.20
☐	13B	Billy Hoeft YL	20.00	10.00	2.00
☐	14	Rip Repulski	2.00	1.00	.20
☐	15	Jim Lemon	2.00	1.00	.20
☐	16	Charley Neal	2.50	1.25	.25
☐	17	Felix Mantilla	2.00	1.00	.20
☐	18	Frank Sullivan	2.00	1.00	.20
☐	19	New York Giants Team Card	9.00	2.00	.40
☐	20A	Gil McDougald	5.00	2.50	.50
☐	20B	Gil McDougald YL	25.00	12.50	2.50
☐	21	Curt Barclay	2.00	1.00	.20
☐	22	Hal Naragon	2.00	1.00	.20
☐	23A	Bill Tuttle	2.00	1.00	.20
☐	23B	Bill Tuttle YL	20.00	10.00	2.00
☐	24A	Hobie Landrith	2.00	1.00	.20
☐	24B	Hobie Landrith YL	20.00	10.00	2.00
☐	25	Don Drysdale	16.00	8.00	1.60
☐	26	Ron Jackson	2.00	1.00	.20
☐	27	Bud Freeman	2.00	1.00	.20
☐	28	Jim Busby	2.00	1.00	.20
☐	29	Ted Lepcio	2.00	1.00	.20
☐	30A	Hank Aaron	80.00	40.00	8.00
☐	30B	Hank Aaron YL	150.00	75.00	15.00
☐	31	Tex Clevenger	2.00	1.00	.20
☐	32A	J.W. Porter	2.00	1.00	.20
☐	32B	J.W. Porter YL	20.00	10.00	2.00
☐	33A	Cal Neeman	2.00	1.00	.20
☐	33B	Cal Neeman YT	15.00	7.50	1.50
☐	34	Bob Thurman	2.00	1.00	.20
☐	35A	Don Mossi	2.00	1.00	.20
☐	35B	Don Mossi YT	15.00	7.50	1.50
☐	36	Ted Kazanski	2.00	1.00	.20
☐	37	Mike McCormick (photo actually Ray Monzant)	3.50	1.75	.35
☐	38	Dick Gernert	2.00	1.00	.20
☐	39	Bob Martyn	2.00	1.00	.20
☐	40	George Kell	10.00	5.00	1.00
☐	41	Dave Hillman	2.00	1.00	.20
☐	42	John Roseboro	4.00	2.00	.40
☐	43	Sal Maglie	3.50	1.75	.35
☐	44	Washington Senators Team Card	4.50	.90	.20
☐	45	Dick Groat	3.50	1.75	.35
☐	46A	Lou Sleater	2.00	1.00	.20
☐	46B	Lou Sleater YL	20.00	10.00	2.00
☐	47	Roger Maris	175.00	85.00	18.00
☐	48	Chuck Harmon	2.00	1.00	.20
☐	49	Smoky Burgess	2.50	1.25	.25
☐	50A	Billy Pierce	3.00	1.50	.30
☐	50B	Billy Pierce YT	15.00	7.50	1.50
☐	51	Del Rice	2.00	1.00	.20
☐	52A	Bob Clemente	35.00	17.50	3.50
☐	52B	Bob Clemente YT	85.00	42.50	8.50
☐	53A	Morrie Martin	2.00	1.00	.20
☐	53B	Morrie Martin YL	20.00	10.00	2.00
☐	54	Norm Siebern	2.50	1.25	.25
☐	55	Chico Carrasquel	2.00	1.00	.20
☐	56	Bill Fischer	2.00	1.00	.20
☐	57A	Tim Thompson	2.00	1.00	.20
☐	57B	Tim Thompson YL	20.00	10.00	2.00
☐	58A	Art Schult	2.00	1.00	.20
☐	58B	Art Schult YT	15.00	7.50	1.50
☐	59	Dave Sisler	2.00	1.00	.20
☐	60A	Del Ennis	2.50	1.25	.25
☐	60B	Del Ennis YL	20.00	10.00	2.00
☐	61A	Darrell Johnson	2.50	1.25	.25
☐	61B	Darrell Johnson YL	20.00	10.00	2.00
☐	62	Joe DeMaestri	2.00	1.00	.20
☐	63	Joe Nuxhall	2.50	1.25	.25
☐	64	Joe Lonnett	2.00	1.00	.20
☐	65A	Von McDaniel	2.00	1.00	.20
☐	65B	Von McDaniel YL	20.00	10.00	2.00
☐	66	Lee Walls	2.00	1.00	.20
☐	67	Joe Ginsberg	2.00	1.00	.20
☐	68	Daryl Spencer	2.00	1.00	.20
☐	69	Wally Burnette	2.00	1.00	.20
☐	70A	Al Kaline	20.00	10.00	2.00
☐	70B	Al Kaline YL	60.00	30.00	6.00
☐	71	Dodgers Team	12.00	2.00	.40
☐	72	Bud Byerly	2.00	1.00	.20
☐	73	Pete Daley	2.00	1.00	.20
☐	74	Roy Face	3.00	1.50	.30
☐	75	Gus Bell	2.50	1.25	.25
☐	76A	Dick Farrell	2.50	1.25	.25
☐	76B	Dick Farrell YT	15.00	7.50	1.50
☐	77A	Don Zimmer	3.50	1.75	.35
☐	77B	Don Zimmer YT	15.00	7.50	1.50
☐	78A	Ernie Johnson	2.00	1.00	.20
☐	78B	Ernie Johnson YL	20.00	10.00	2.00
☐	79A	Dick Williams	3.00	1.50	.30
☐	79B	Dick Williams YT	15.00	7.50	1.50
☐	80	Dick Drott	2.00	1.00	.20
☐	81A	Steve Boros	2.50	1.25	.25
☐	81B	Steve Boros YT	15.00	7.50	1.50
☐	82	Ronnie Kline	2.00	1.00	.20
☐	83	Bob Hazle	2.00	1.00	.20
☐	84	Billy O'Dell	2.00	1.00	.20
☐	85A	Luis Aparicio	10.00	5.00	1.00
☐	85B	Luis Aparicio YT	25.00	12.50	2.50
☐	86	Valmy Thomas	2.00	1.00	.20
☐	87	Johnny Kucks	2.50	1.25	.25
☐	88	Duke Snider	28.00	14.00	2.80
☐	89	Billy Klaus	2.00	1.00	.20
☐	90	Robin Roberts	10.00	5.00	1.00
☐	91	Chuck Tanner	2.50	1.25	.25
☐	92A	Clint Courtney	2.00	1.00	.20
☐	92B	Clint Courtney YL	20.00	10.00	2.00
☐	93	Sandy Amoros	2.50	1.25	.25
☐	94	Bob Skinner	2.00	1.00	.20
☐	95	Frank Bolling	2.00	1.00	.20
☐	96	Joe Durham	2.00	1.00	.20
☐	97A	Larry Jackson	2.00	1.00	.20
☐	97B	Larry Jackson YL	20.00	10.00	2.00
☐	98A	Billy Hunter	2.00	1.00	.20
☐	98B	Billy Hunter YL	20.00	10.00	2.00
☐	99	Bobby Adams	2.00	1.00	.20
☐	100A	Early Wynn	10.00	5.00	1.00
☐	100B	Early Wynn YT	25.00	12.50	2.50
☐	101A	Bobby Richardson	5.00	2.50	.50
☐	101B	Bobby Richardson YL	25.00	12.50	2.50
☐	102	George Strickland	2.00	1.00	.20
☐	103	Jerry Lynch	2.00	1.00	.20
☐	104	Jim Pendleton	2.00	1.00	.20
☐	105	Billy Gardner	2.50	1.25	.25
☐	106	Dick Schofield	2.00	1.00	.20
☐	107	Ossie Virgil	2.00	1.00	.20
☐	108A	Jim Landis	2.00	1.00	.20
☐	108B	Jim Landis YT	15.00	7.50	1.50
☐	109	Herb Plews	2.00	1.00	.20
☐	110	Johnny Logan	2.50	1.25	.25
☐	111	Stu Miller	1.50	.75	.15
☐	112	Gus Zernial	1.50	.75	.15
☐	113	Jerry Walker	1.50	.75	.15
☐	114	Irv Noren	1.50	.75	.15
☐	115	Jim Bunning	6.00	3.00	.60
☐	116	Dave Philley	1.50	.75	.15
☐	117	Frank Torre	1.50	.75	.15
☐	118	Harvey Haddix	2.00	1.00	.20
☐	119	Harry Chiti	1.50	.75	.15
☐	120	Johnny Podres	4.00	2.00	.40
☐	121	Eddie Miksis	1.50	.75	.15
☐	122	Walt Moryn	1.50	.75	.15
☐	123	Dick Tomanek	1.50	.75	.15
☐	124	Bobby Usher	1.50	.75	.15
☐	125	Al Dark	2.50	1.25	.25
☐	126	Stan Palys	1.50	.75	.15
☐	127	Tom Sturdivant	1.50	.75	.15
☐	128	Willie Kirkland	1.50	.75	.15
☐	129	Jim Derrington	1.50	.75	.15
☐	130	Jackie Jensen	4.00	2.00	.40
☐	131	Bob Henrich	1.50	.75	.15
☐	132	Vernon Law	2.00	1.00	.20
☐	133	Russ Nixon	1.50	.75	.15
☐	134	Phillies Team	4.00	.80	.15
☐	135	Mike(Moe) Drabowsky	2.00	1.00	.20
☐	136	Jim Finigan	1.50	.75	.15
☐	137	Russ Kemmerer	1.50	.75	.15
☐	138	Earl Torgeson	1.50	.75	.15
☐	139	George Brunet	1.50	.75	.15

☐ 140	Wes Covington	2.00	1.00	.20
☐ 141	Ken Lehman	1.50	.75	.15
☐ 142	Enos Slaughter	10.00	5.00	1.00
☐ 143	Billy Muffett	1.50	.75	.15
☐ 144	Bobby Morgan	1.50	.75	.15
☐ 145	Never issued	0.00	.00	.00
☐ 146	Dick Gray	1.50	.75	.15
☐ 147	Don McMahon	2.00	1.00	.20
☐ 148	Billy Consolo	1.50	.75	.15
☐ 149	Tom Acker	1.50	.75	.15
☐ 150	Mickey Mantle	400.00	200.00	40.00
☐ 151	Buddy Pritchard	1.50	.75	.15
☐ 152	Johnny Antonelli	2.00	1.00	.20
☐ 153	Les Moss	1.50	.75	.15
☐ 154	Harry Byrd	1.50	.75	.15
☐ 155	Hector Lopez	1.50	.75	.15
☐ 156	Dick Hyde	1.50	.75	.15
☐ 157	Dee Fondy	1.50	.75	.15
☐ 158	Indians Team	4.00	.80	.15
☐ 159	Taylor Phillips	1.50	.75	.15
☐ 160	Don Hoak	1.50	.75	.15
☐ 161	Don Larsen	4.00	2.00	.40
☐ 162	Gil Hodges	14.00	7.00	1.40
☐ 163	Jim Wilson	1.50	.75	.15
☐ 164	Bob Taylor	1.50	.75	.15
☐ 165	Bob Nieman	1.50	.75	.15
☐ 166	Danny O'Connell	1.50	.75	.15
☐ 167	Frank Baumann	1.50	.75	.15
☐ 168	Joe Cunningham	2.00	1.00	.20
☐ 169	Ralph Terry	2.50	1.25	.25
☐ 170	Vic Wertz	2.00	1.00	.20
☐ 171	Harry Anderson	1.50	.75	.15
☐ 172	Don Gross	1.50	.75	.15
☐ 173	Eddie Yost	1.50	.75	.15
☐ 174	Athletics Team	4.00	.80	.15
☐ 175	Marv Throneberry	5.00	2.50	.50
☐ 176	Bob Buhl	1.50	.75	.15
☐ 177	Al Smith	1.50	.75	.15
☐ 178	Ted Kluszewski	4.00	2.00	.40
☐ 179	Willie Miranda	1.50	.75	.15
☐ 180	Lindy McDaniel	2.00	1.00	.20
☐ 181	Willie Jones	1.50	.75	.15
☐ 182	Joe Caffie	1.50	.75	.15
☐ 183	Dave Jolly	1.50	.75	.15
☐ 184	Elvin Tappe	1.50	.75	.15
☐ 185	Ray Boone	1.50	.75	.15
☐ 186	Jack Meyer	1.50	.75	.15
☐ 187	Sandy Koufax	50.00	25.00	5.00
☐ 188	Milt Bolling (photo actually Lou Berberet)	1.50	.75	.15
☐ 189	George Susce	1.50	.75	.15
☐ 190	Red Schoendienst	3.00	1.50	.30
☐ 191	Art Ceccarelli	1.50	.75	.15
☐ 192	Milt Graff	1.50	.75	.15
☐ 193	Jerry Lumpe	1.50	.75	.15
☐ 194	Roger Craig	3.00	1.50	.30
☐ 195	Whitey Lockman	1.50	.75	.15
☐ 196	Mike Garcia	2.00	1.00	.20
☐ 197	Haywood Sullivan	1.50	.75	.15
☐ 198	Bill Virdon	2.50	1.25	.25
☐ 199	Don Blasingame	1.25	.60	.12
☐ 200	Bob Keegan	1.25	.60	.12
☐ 201	Jim Bolger	1.25	.60	.12
☐ 202	Woody Held	1.25	.60	.12
☐ 203	Al Walker	1.25	.60	.12
☐ 204	Leo Kiely	1.25	.60	.12
☐ 205	Johnny Temple	1.25	.60	.12
☐ 206	Bob Shaw	1.25	.60	.12
☐ 207	Solly Hemus	1.25	.60	.12
☐ 208	Cal McLish	1.25	.60	.12
☐ 209	Bob Anderson	1.25	.60	.12
☐ 210	Wally Moon	1.75	.85	.17
☐ 211	Pete Burnside	1.25	.60	.12
☐ 212	Bubba Phillips	1.25	.60	.12
☐ 213	Red Wilson	1.25	.60	.12
☐ 214	Willard Schmidt	1.25	.60	.12
☐ 215	Jim Gilliam	3.50	1.75	.35
☐ 216	Cardinals Team	4.00	.80	.15
☐ 217	Jack Harshman	1.25	.60	.12
☐ 218	Dick Rand	1.25	.60	.12
☐ 219	Camilo Pascual	1.75	.85	.17
☐ 220	Tom Brewer	1.25	.60	.12
☐ 221	Jerry Kindall	1.75	.85	.17
☐ 222	Bud Daley	1.25	.60	.12
☐ 223	Andy Pafko	1.25	.60	.12
☐ 224	Bob Grim	1.75	.85	.17
☐ 225	Billy Goodman	1.75	.85	.17
☐ 226	Bob Smith	1.25	.60	.12
☐ 227	Gene Stephens	1.25	.60	.12
☐ 228	Duke Maas	1.25	.60	.12
☐ 229	Frank Zupo	1.25	.60	.12
☐ 230	Richie Ashburn	6.00	3.00	.60
☐ 231	Lloyd Merritt	1.25	.60	.12
☐ 232	Reno Bertoia	1.25	.60	.12
☐ 233	Mickey Vernon	1.75	.85	.17
☐ 234	Carl Sawatski	1.25	.60	.12
☐ 235	Tom Gorman	1.25	.60	.12
☐ 236	Ed Fitzgerald	1.25	.60	.12
☐ 237	Bill Wight	1.25	.60	.12
☐ 238	Bill Mazeroski	5.00	2.50	.50
☐ 239	Chuck Stobbs	1.25	.60	.12
☐ 240	Moose Skowron	5.00	2.50	.50
☐ 241	Dick Littlefield	1.25	.60	.12
☐ 242	Johnny Klippstein	1.25	.60	.12
☐ 243	Larry Raines	1.25	.60	.12
☐ 244	Don Demeter	1.25	.60	.12
☐ 245	Frank Lary	1.75	.85	.17
☐ 246	Yankees Team	15.00	3.00	.60
☐ 247	Casey Wise	1.25	.60	.12
☐ 248	Herm Wehmeier	1.25	.60	.12
☐ 249	Ray Moore	1.25	.60	.12
☐ 250	Roy Sievers	1.75	.85	.17
☐ 251	Warren Hacker	1.25	.60	.12
☐ 252	Bob Trowbridge	1.25	.60	.12
☐ 253	Don Mueller	1.75	.85	.17
☐ 254	Alex Grammas	1.25	.60	.12
☐ 255	Bob Turley	4.00	2.00	.40
☐ 256	White Sox Team	4.00	.80	.15
☐ 257	Hal Smith	1.25	.60	.12
☐ 258	Carl Erskine	3.50	1.75	.35
☐ 259	Al Pilarcik	1.25	.60	.12
☐ 260	Frank Malzone	1.75	.85	.17
☐ 261	Turk Lown	1.25	.60	.12
☐ 262	Johnny Groth	1.25	.60	.12
☐ 263	Eddie Bressoud	1.25	.60	.12
☐ 264	Jack Sanford	1.75	.85	.17
☐ 265	Pete Runnels	1.75	.85	.17
☐ 266	Connie Johnson	1.25	.60	.12
☐ 267	Sherm Lollar	1.75	.85	.17
☐ 268	Granny Hamner	1.25	.60	.12
☐ 269	Paul Smith	1.25	.60	.12
☐ 270	Warren Spahn	15.00	7.50	1.50
☐ 271	Billy Martin	5.50	2.75	.55
☐ 272	Ray Crone	1.25	.60	.12
☐ 273	Hal Smith	1.25	.60	.12
☐ 274	Rocky Bridges	1.25	.60	.12
☐ 275	Elston Howard	4.50	2.25	.45
☐ 276	Bobby Avila	1.25	.60	.12
☐ 277	Virgil Trucks	1.25	.60	.12
☐ 278	Mack Burk	1.25	.60	.12
☐ 279	Bob Boyd	1.25	.60	.12
☐ 280	Jim Piersall	3.50	1.75	.35
☐ 281	Sam Taylor	1.25	.60	.12
☐ 282	Paul Foytack	1.25	.60	.12
☐ 283	Ray Shearer	1.25	.60	.12
☐ 284	Ray Katt	1.25	.60	.12
☐ 285	Frank Robinson	25.00	12.50	2.50
☐ 286	Gino Cimoli	1.75	.85	.17
☐ 287	Sam Jones	1.25	.60	.12
☐ 288	Harmon Killebrew	20.00	10.00	2.00
☐ 289	Series Hurling Rivals Lou Burdette Bobby Shantz	2.50	1.25	.25
☐ 290	Dick Donovan	1.25	.60	.12
☐ 291	Don Landrum	1.25	.60	.12
☐ 292	Ned Garver	1.25	.60	.12
☐ 293	Gene Freese	1.25	.60	.12
☐ 294	Hal Jeffcoat	1.25	.60	.12
☐ 295	Minnie Minoso	4.00	2.00	.40
☐ 296	Ryne Duren	3.50	1.75	.35
☐ 297	Don Buddin	1.25	.60	.12
☐ 298	Jim Hearn	1.25	.60	.12
☐ 299	Harry Simpson	1.25	.60	.12
☐ 300	Harridge and Giles League Presidents	3.00	1.50	.30
☐ 301	Randy Jackson	1.25	.60	.12
☐ 302	Mike Baxes	1.25	.60	.12
☐ 303	Neil Chrisley	1.25	.60	.12
☐ 304	Tigers' Big Bats Harvey Kuenn Al Kaline	5.00	2.50	.50
☐ 305	Clem Labine	1.75	.85	.17
☐ 306	Whammy Douglas	1.25	.60	.12
☐ 307	Brooks Robinson	30.00	15.00	3.00
☐ 308	Paul Giel	1.25	.60	.12
☐ 309	Gail Harris	1.25	.60	.12
☐ 310	Ernie Banks	25.00	12.50	2.50
☐ 311	Bob Purkey	1.25	.60	.12
☐ 312	Boston Red Sox Team	5.00	1.00	.20
☐ 313	Bob Rush	1.25	.60	.12
☐ 314	Dodgers' Boss and Power: Duke Snider Walt Alston	12.00	6.00	1.20
☐ 315	Bob Friend	1.75	.85	.17
☐ 316	Tito Francona	1.75	.85	.17
☐ 317	Albie Pearson	1.75	.85	.17
☐ 318	Frank House	1.25	.60	.12
☐ 319	Lou Skizas	1.25	.60	.12
☐ 320	Whitey Ford	17.00	8.50	1.70

□ 321	Sluggers Supreme Ted Kluszewski Ted Williams	12.00	6.00	1.20
□ 322	Harding Peterson	1.75	.85	.17
□ 323	Elmer Valo	1.25	.60	.12
□ 324	Hoyt Wilhelm	9.00	4.50	.90
□ 325	Joe Adcock	1.75	.85	.17
□ 326	Bob Miller	1.25	.60	.12
□ 327	Chicago Cubs Team	4.00	.80	.15
□ 328	Ike Delock	1.25	.60	.12
□ 329	Bob Cerv	1.75	.85	.17
□ 330	Ed Bailey	1.75	.85	.17
□ 331	Pedro Ramos	1.25	.60	.12
□ 332	Jim King	1.25	.60	.12
□ 333	Andy Carey	1.75	.85	.17
□ 334	Mound Aces Bob Friend Billy Pierce	1.75	.85	.17
□ 335	Ruben Gomez	1.25	.60	.12
□ 336	Bert Hamric	1.25	.60	.12
□ 337	Hank Aguirre	1.25	.60	.12
□ 338	Walt Dropo	1.25	.60	.12
□ 339	Fred Hatfield	1.25	.60	.12
□ 340	Don Newcombe	4.50	2.25	.45
□ 341	Pirates Team	4.00	.80	.15
□ 342	Jim Brosnan	1.25	.60	.12
□ 343	Orlando Cepeda	20.00	10.00	2.00
□ 344	Bob Porterfield	1.25	.60	.12
□ 345	Jim Hegan	1.25	.60	.12
□ 346	Steve Bilko	1.25	.60	.12
□ 347	Don Rudolph	1.25	.60	.12
□ 348	Chico Fernandez	1.25	.60	.12
□ 349	Murry Dickson	1.25	.60	.12
□ 350	Ken Boyer	3.50	1.75	.35
□ 351	Braves Fence Busters Del Crandall Eddie Mathews Hank Aaron Joe Adcock	15.00	7.50	1.50
□ 352	Herb Score	2.50	1.25	.25
□ 353	Stan Lopata	1.25	.60	.12
□ 354	Art Ditmar	1.25	.60	.12
□ 355	Bill Bruton	1.25	.60	.12
□ 356	Bob Malkmus	1.25	.60	.12
□ 357	Danny McDevitt	1.25	.60	.12
□ 358	Gene Baker	1.25	.60	.12
□ 359	Billy Loes	1.25	.60	.12
□ 360	Roy McMillan	1.25	.60	.12
□ 361	Mike Fornieles	1.25	.60	.12
□ 362	Ray Jablonski	1.25	.60	.12
□ 363	Don Elston	1.25	.60	.12
□ 364	Earl Battey	1.25	.60	.12
□ 365	Tom Morgan	1.25	.60	.12
□ 366	Gene Green	1.25	.60	.12
□ 367	Jack Urban	1.25	.60	.12
□ 368	Rocky Colavito	5.00	2.50	.50
□ 369	Ralph Lumenti	1.25	.60	.12
□ 370	Yogi Berra	27.00	13.50	2.70
□ 371	Marty Keough	1.25	.60	.12
□ 372	Don Cardwell	1.25	.60	.12
□ 373	Joe Pignatano	1.25	.60	.12
□ 374	Brooks Lawrence	1.25	.60	.12
□ 375	Pee Wee Reese	20.00	10.00	2.00
□ 376	Charley Rabe	1.25	.60	.12
□ 377A	Milwaukee Team alphabetical	5.00	2.50	.50
□ 377B	Milwaukee Team numerical	40.00	5.00	1.25
□ 378	Hank Sauer	1.50	.75	.15
□ 379	Ray Herbert	1.25	.60	.12
□ 380	Charley Maxwell	1.25	.60	.12
□ 381	Hal Brown	1.25	.60	.12
□ 382	Al Cicotte	1.50	.75	.15
□ 383	Lou Berberet	1.25	.60	.12
□ 384	John Goryl	1.25	.60	.12
□ 385	Wilmer Mizell	1.25	.60	.12
□ 386	Birdie's Sluggers Ed Bailey Birdie Tebbetts Frank Robinson	4.00	2.00	.40
□ 387	Wally Post	1.25	.60	.12
□ 388	Billy Moran	1.25	.60	.12
□ 389	Bill Taylor	1.25	.60	.12
□ 390	Del Crandall	1.50	.75	.15
□ 391	Dave Melton	1.25	.60	.12
□ 392	Bennie Daniels	1.25	.60	.12
□ 393	Tony Kubek	6.50	3.25	.65
□ 394	Jim Grant	1.50	.75	.15
□ 395	Willard Nixon	1.25	.60	.12
□ 396	Dutch Dotterer	1.25	.60	.12
□ 397A	Detroit Team alphabetical	5.00	2.50	.50
□ 397B	Detroit Team numerical	40.00	5.00	1.25
□ 398	Gene Woodling	1.50	.75	.15
□ 399	Marv Grissom	1.25	.60	.12
□ 400	Nellie Fox	5.00	2.50	.50
□ 401	Don Bessent	1.25	.60	.12
□ 402	Bobby Gene Smith	1.25	.60	.12
□ 403	Steve Korcheck	1.25	.60	.12
□ 404	Curt Simmons	1.50	.75	.15
□ 405	Ken Aspromonte	1.25	.60	.12
□ 406	Vic Power	1.25	.60	.12
□ 407	Carlton Willey	1.25	.60	.12
□ 408A	Baltimore Team alphabetical	5.00	2.50	.50
□ 408B	Baltimore Team numerical	40.00	5.00	1.25
□ 409	Frank Thomas	1.50	.75	.15
□ 410	Murray Wall	1.25	.60	.12
□ 411	Tony Taylor	1.25	.60	.12
□ 412	Jerry Staley	1.25	.60	.12
□ 413	Jim Davenport	1.50	.75	.15
□ 414	Sammy White	1.25	.60	.12
□ 415	Bob Bowman	1.25	.60	.12
□ 416	Foster Castleman	1.25	.60	.12
□ 417	Carl Furillo	4.00	2.00	.40
□ 418	World Series Batting Foes: Mickey Mantle Hank Aaron	75.00	37.50	7.50
□ 419	Bobby Shantz	2.50	1.25	.25
□ 420	Vada Pinson	9.00	4.50	.90
□ 421	Dixie Howell	1.25	.60	.12
□ 422	Norm Zauchin	1.25	.60	.12
□ 423	Phil Clark	1.25	.60	.12
□ 424	Larry Doby	3.00	1.50	.30
□ 425	Sam Esposito	1.25	.60	.12
□ 426	Johnny O'Brien	1.25	.60	.12
□ 427	Al Worthington	1.25	.60	.12
□ 428A	Cincinnati Team alphabetical	5.00	2.50	.50
□ 428B	Cincinnati Team numerical	40.00	5.00	1.25
□ 429	Gus Triandos	1.50	.75	.15
□ 430	Bobby Thomson	2.00	1.00	.20
□ 431	Gene Conley	1.25	.60	.12
□ 432	John Powers	1.25	.60	.12
□ 433A	Pancho Herrera COR	1.25	.60	.12
□ 433B	Pancho Herrer ERR	125.00	60.00	12.50
□ 434	Harvey Kuenn	3.50	1.75	.35
□ 435	Ed Roebuck	1.25	.60	.12
□ 436	Rival Fence Busters Willie Mays Duke Snider	30.00	15.00	3.00
□ 437	Bob Speake	1.25	.60	.12
□ 438	Whitey Herzog	2.50	1.25	.25
□ 439	Ray Narleski	1.25	.60	.12
□ 440	Ed Mathews	14.00	7.00	1.40
□ 441	Jim Marshall	1.00	.50	.10
□ 442	Phil Paine	1.00	.50	.10
□ 443	Billy Harrell SP	6.00	3.00	.60
□ 444	Danny Kravitz	1.00	.50	.10
□ 445	Bob Smith	1.00	.50	.10
□ 446	Carroll Hardy SP	6.00	3.00	.60
□ 447	Ray Monzant	1.00	.50	.10
□ 448	Charlie Lau	2.50	1.25	.25
□ 449	Gene Fodge	1.00	.50	.10
□ 450	Preston Ward SP	6.00	3.00	.60
□ 451	Joe Taylor	1.00	.50	.10
□ 452	Roman Mejias	1.00	.50	.10
□ 453	Tom Qualters	1.00	.50	.10
□ 454	Harry Hanebrink	1.00	.50	.10
□ 455	Hal Griggs	1.00	.50	.10
□ 456	Dick Brown	1.00	.50	.10
□ 457	Milt Pappas	2.50	1.25	.25
□ 458	Julio Becquer	1.00	.50	.10
□ 459	Ron Blackburn	1.00	.50	.10
□ 460	Chuck Essegian	1.00	.50	.10
□ 461	Ed Mayer	1.00	.50	.10
□ 462	Gary Geiger SP	6.00	3.00	.60
□ 463	Vito Valentinetti	1.00	.50	.10
□ 464	Curt Flood	6.00	3.00	.60
□ 465	Arnie Portocarrero	1.00	.50	.10
□ 466	Pete Whisenant	1.00	.50	.10
□ 467	Glen Hobbie	1.00	.50	.10
□ 468	Bob Schmidt	1.00	.50	.10
□ 469	Don Ferrarese	1.00	.50	.10
□ 470	R.C. Stevens	1.00	.50	.10
□ 471	Lenny Green	1.00	.50	.10
□ 472	Joe Jay	1.00	.50	.10
□ 473	Bill Renna	1.00	.50	.10
□ 474	Roman Semproch	1.00	.50	.10
□ 475	Haney/Stengel AS (checklist back)	8.00	2.00	.40
□ 476	Stan Musial AS TP	10.00	5.00	1.00
□ 477	Bill Skowron AS	1.50	.75	.15
□ 478	Johnny Temple AS	1.25	.60	.12
□ 479	Nellie Fox AS	2.50	1.25	.25
□ 480	Eddie Mathews AS	6.00	3.00	.60
□ 481	Frank Malzone AS	1.25	.60	.12

		NRMT	VG-E	GOOD
☐ 482	Ernie Banks AS	7.00	3.50	.70
☐ 483	Luis Aparicio AS	5.00	2.50	.50
☐ 484	Frank Robinson AS	6.00	3.00	.60
☐ 485	Ted Williams AS	20.00	10.00	2.00
☐ 486	Willie Mays AS	15.00	7.50	1.50
☐ 487	Mickey Mantle AS TP	25.00	12.50	2.50
☐ 488	Hank Aaron AS	15.00	7.50	1.50
☐ 489	Jackie Jensen AS	1.25	.60	.12
☐ 490	Ed Bailey AS	1.25	.60	.12
☐ 491	Sherm Lollar AS	1.25	.60	.12
☐ 492	Bob Friend AS	1.25	.60	.12
☐ 493	Bob Turley AS	1.25	.60	.12
☐ 494	Warren Spahn AS	6.00	3.00	.60
☐ 495	Herb Score AS	2.50	.50	.10

1959 Topps

The cards in this 572-card set measure 2 1/2" by 3 1/2". The 1959 Topps set contains bust pictures of the players in a colored circle. Card numbers 551 to 572 are Sporting News All-Star Selections. High numbers 507 to 572 have the card number in a black background on the reverse rather than a green background as in the lower numbers. The high numbers are more difficult to obtain. Several cards in the 300's exist with or without an extra traded or option line on the back of the card. Cards 199 to 286 exist with either white or gray backs. Cards 461 to 470 contain "Highlights" while cards 116 to 146 give an alphabetically ordered listing of "Rookie Prospects." These Rookie Prospects (RP) were Topps' first organized inclusion of untested "Rookie" cards. Card 440 features Lew Burdette erroneously posing as a lefthanded pitcher.

		NRMT	VG-E	GOOD
COMPLETE SET		2500.00	900.00	200.00
COMMON PLAYER (1-110)		1.50	.75	.15
COMMON PLAYER (111-506)		1.00	.50	.10
COMMON PLAYER (507-550)		5.00	2.50	.50
COMMON PLAYER (551-572)		6.00	3.00	.60
☐ 1	Ford Frick	15.00	2.50	.50
☐ 2	Eddie Yost	1.50	.75	.15
☐ 3	Don McMahon	1.50	.75	.15
☐ 4	Albie Pearson	1.50	.75	.15
☐ 5	Dick Donovan	1.50	.75	.15
☐ 6	Alex Grammas	1.50	.75	.15
☐ 7	Al Pilarcik	1.50	.75	.15
☐ 8	Phillies Team	3.00	.60	.10
☐ 9	Paul Giel	1.50	.75	.15
☐ 10	Mickey Mantle	300.00	150.00	30.00
☐ 11	Billy Hunter	1.50	.75	.15
☐ 12	Vern Law	2.00	1.00	.20
☐ 13	Dick Gernert	1.50	.75	.15
☐ 14	Pete Whisenant	1.50	.75	.15
☐ 15	Dick Drott	1.50	.75	.15
☐ 16	Joe Pignatano	1.50	.75	.15
☐ 17	Danny's Stars	2.00	1.00	.20
	Frank Thomas			
	Danny Murtaugh			
	Ted Kluszewski			
☐ 18	Jack Urban	1.50	.75	.15
☐ 19	Eddie Bressoud	1.50	.75	.15
☐ 20	Duke Snider	25.00	12.50	2.50

		NRMT	VG-E	GOOD
☐ 21	Connie Johnson	1.50	.75	.15
☐ 22	Al Smith	1.50	.75	.15
☐ 23	Murry Dickson	1.50	.75	.15
☐ 24	Red Wilson	1.50	.75	.15
☐ 25	Don Hoak	1.50	.75	.15
☐ 26	Chuck Stobbs	1.50	.75	.15
☐ 27	Andy Pafko	1.50	.75	.15
☐ 28	Ray Worthington	1.50	.75	.15
☐ 29	Jim Bolger	1.50	.75	.15
☐ 30	Nellie Fox	4.50	2.25	.45
☐ 31	Ken Lehman	1.50	.75	.15
☐ 32	Don Buddin	1.50	.75	.15
☐ 33	Ed Fitzgerald	1.50	.75	.15
☐ 34	Pitchers Beware	4.00	2.00	.40
	Al Kaline			
	Charley Maxwell			
☐ 35	Ted Kluszewski	3.00	1.50	.30
☐ 36	Hank Aguirre	1.50	.75	.15
☐ 37	Gene Green	1.50	.75	.15
☐ 38	Morrie Martin	1.50	.75	.15
☐ 39	Ed Bouchee	1.50	.75	.15
☐ 40	Warren Spahn	16.00	8.00	1.60
☐ 41	Bob Martyn	1.50	.75	.15
☐ 42	Murray Wall	1.50	.75	.15
☐ 43	Steve Bilko	1.50	.75	.15
☐ 44	Vito Valentinetti	1.50	.75	.15
☐ 45	Andy Carey	2.00	1.00	.20
☐ 46	Bill R. Henry	1.50	.75	.15
☐ 47	Jim Finigan	1.50	.75	.15
☐ 48	Orioles Team	3.00	.60	.10
☐ 49	Bill Hall	1.50	.75	.15
☐ 50	Willie Mays	60.00	30.00	6.00
☐ 51	Rip Coleman	1.50	.75	.15
☐ 52	Coot Veal	1.50	.75	.15
☐ 53	Stan Williams	1.50	.75	.15
☐ 54	Mel Roach	1.50	.75	.15
☐ 55	Tom Brewer	1.50	.75	.15
☐ 56	Carl Sawatski	1.50	.75	.15
☐ 57	Al Cicotte	1.50	.75	.15
☐ 58	Eddie Miksis	1.50	.75	.15
☐ 59	Irv Noren	1.50	.75	.15
☐ 60	Bob Turley	2.50	1.25	.25
☐ 61	Dick Brown	1.50	.75	.15
☐ 62	Tony Taylor	1.50	.75	.15
☐ 63	Jim Hearn	1.50	.75	.15
☐ 64	Joe DeMaestri	1.50	.75	.15
☐ 65	Frank Torre	1.50	.75	.15
☐ 66	Joe Ginsberg	1.50	.75	.15
☐ 67	Brooks Lawrence	1.50	.75	.15
☐ 68	Dick Schofield	1.50	.75	.15
☐ 69	Giants Team	3.00	.60	.10
☐ 70	Harvey Kuenn	3.00	1.50	.30
☐ 71	Don Bessent	1.50	.75	.15
☐ 72	Bill Renna	1.50	.75	.15
☐ 73	Ron Jackson	1.50	.75	.15
☐ 74	Directing Power	2.00	1.00	.20
	Jim Lemon			
	Cookie Lavagetto			
	Roy Sievers			
☐ 75	Sam Jones	1.50	.75	.15
☐ 76	Bobby Richardson	4.50	2.25	.45
☐ 77	John Goryl	1.50	.75	.15
☐ 78	Pedro Ramos	1.50	.75	.15
☐ 79	Harry Chiti	1.50	.75	.15
☐ 80	Minnie Minoso	3.50	1.75	.35
☐ 81	Hal Jeffcoat	1.50	.75	.15
☐ 82	Bob Boyd	1.50	.75	.15
☐ 83	Bob Smith	1.50	.75	.15
☐ 84	Reno Bertoia	1.50	.75	.15
☐ 85	Harry Anderson	1.50	.75	.15
☐ 86	Bob Keegan	1.50	.75	.15
☐ 87	Danny O'Connell	1.50	.75	.15
☐ 88	Herb Score	2.50	1.25	.25
☐ 89	Billy Gardner	1.50	.75	.15
☐ 90	Bill Skowron	4.50	2.25	.45
☐ 91	Herb Moford	1.50	.75	.15
☐ 92	Dave Philley	1.50	.75	.15
☐ 93	Julio Becquer	1.50	.75	.15
☐ 94	White Sox Team	3.50	.70	.10
☐ 95	Carl Willey	1.50	.75	.15
☐ 96	Lou Berberet	1.50	.75	.15
☐ 97	Jerry Lynch	1.50	.75	.15
☐ 98	Arnie Portocarrero	1.50	.75	.15
☐ 99	Ted Kazanski	1.50	.75	.15
☐ 100	Bob Cerv	2.00	1.00	.20
☐ 101	Alex Kellner	1.50	.75	.15
☐ 102	Felipe Alou	4.00	2.00	.40
☐ 103	Billy Goodman	2.00	1.00	.20
☐ 104	Del Rice	1.50	.75	.15
☐ 105	Lee Walls	1.50	.75	.15
☐ 106	Hal Woodeshick	1.50	.75	.15
☐ 107	Norm Larker	2.00	1.00	.20
☐ 108	Zack Monroe	1.50	.75	.15
☐ 109	Bob Schmidt	1.50	.75	.15
☐ 110	George Witt	1.50	.75	.15

☐ 111	Redlegs Team	3.50	.70	.10
☐ 112	Billy Consolo	1.00	.50	.10
☐ 113	Taylor Phillips	1.00	.50	.10
☐ 114	Earl Battey	1.00	.50	.10
☐ 115	Mickey Vernon	1.50	.75	.15
☐ 116	Bob Allison RP	3.50	1.75	.35
☐ 117	John Blanchard RP	1.50	.75	.15
☐ 118	John Buzhardt RP	1.00	.50	.10
☐ 119	John Callison RP	2.50	1.25	.25
☐ 120	Chuck Coles RP	1.00	.50	.10
☐ 121	Bob Conley RP	1.00	.50	.10
☐ 122	Bennie Daniels RP	1.00	.50	.10
☐ 123	Don Dillard RP	1.00	.50	.10
☐ 124	Dan Dobbek RP	1.00	.50	.10
☐ 125	Ron Fairly RP	2.50	1.25	.25
☐ 126	Ed Haas RP	1.50	.75	.15
☐ 127	Kent Hadley RP	1.00	.50	.10
☐ 128	Bob Hartman RP	1.00	.50	.10
☐ 129	Frank Herrera RP	1.00	.50	.10
☐ 130	Lou Jackson RP	1.00	.50	.10
☐ 131	Deron Johnson RP	1.50	.75	.15
☐ 132	Don Lee RP	1.00	.50	.10
☐ 133	Bob Lillis RP	1.50	.75	.15
☐ 134	Jim McDaniel RP	1.00	.50	.10
☐ 135	Gene Oliver RP	1.00	.50	.10
☐ 136	Jim O'Toole RP	1.50	.75	.15
☐ 137	Dick Ricketts RP	1.00	.50	.10
☐ 138	John Romano RP	1.00	.50	.10
☐ 139	Ed Sadowski RP	1.00	.50	.10
☐ 140	Charlie Secrest RP	1.00	.50	.10
☐ 141	Joe Shipley RP	1.00	.50	.10
☐ 142	Dick Stigman RP	1.00	.50	.10
☐ 143	Willie Tasby RP	1.00	.50	.10
☐ 144	Jerry Walker RP	1.00	.50	.10
☐ 145	Dom Zanni RP	1.00	.50	.10
☐ 146	Jerry Zimmerman RP	1.00	.50	.10
☐ 147	Cubs Clubbers	4.00	2.00	.40
	Dale Long			
	Ernie Banks			
	Walt Moryn			
☐ 148	Mike McCormick	1.50	.75	.15
☐ 149	Jim Bunning	4.50	2.25	.45
☐ 150	Stan Musial	50.00	25.00	5.00
☐ 151	Bob Malkmus	1.00	.50	.10
☐ 152	John Klippstein	1.00	.50	.10
☐ 153	Jim Marshall	1.00	.50	.10
☐ 154	Ray Herbert	1.00	.50	.10
☐ 155	Enos Slaughter	8.00	4.00	.80
☐ 156	Ace Hurlers	3.00	1.50	.30
	Billy Pierce			
	Robin Roberts			
☐ 157	Felix Mantilla	1.00	.50	.10
☐ 158	Walt Dropo	1.00	.50	.10
☐ 159	Bob Shaw	1.00	.50	.10
☐ 160	Dick Groat	2.50	1.25	.25
☐ 161	Frank Baumann	1.00	.50	.10
☐ 162	Bobby G. Smith	1.00	.50	.10
☐ 163	Sandy Koufax	40.00	20.00	4.00
☐ 164	Johnny Groth	1.00	.50	.10
☐ 165	Bill Bruton	1.00	.50	.10
☐ 166	Destruction Crew	1.50	.75	.15
	Minnie Minoso			
	Rocky Colavito			
	Larry Doby			
☐ 167	Duke Maas	1.00	.50	.10
☐ 168	Carroll Hardy	1.00	.50	.10
☐ 169	Ted Abernathy	1.00	.50	.10
☐ 170	Gene Woodling	1.50	.75	.15
☐ 171	Willard Schmidt	1.00	.50	.10
☐ 172	Athletics Team	3.00	.60	.10
☐ 173	Bill Monbouquette	1.00	.50	.10
☐ 174	Jim Pendleton	1.00	.50	.10
☐ 175	Dick Farrell	1.00	.50	.10
☐ 176	Preston Ward	1.00	.50	.10
☐ 177	John Briggs	1.00	.50	.10
☐ 178	Ruben Amaro	1.00	.50	.10
☐ 179	Don Rudolph	1.00	.50	.10
☐ 180	Yogi Berra	25.00	12.50	2.50
☐ 181	Bob Porterfield	1.00	.50	.10
☐ 182	Milt Graff	1.00	.50	.10
☐ 183	Stu Miller	1.00	.50	.10
☐ 184	Harvey Haddix	1.50	.75	.15
☐ 185	Jim Busby	1.00	.50	.10
☐ 186	Mudcat Grant	1.00	.50	.10
☐ 187	Bubba Phillips	1.00	.50	.10
☐ 188	Juan Pizarro	1.00	.50	.10
☐ 189	Neil Chrisley	1.00	.50	.10
☐ 190	Bill Virdon	1.50	.75	.15
☐ 191	Russ Kemmerer	1.00	.50	.10
☐ 192	Charlie Beamon	1.00	.50	.10
☐ 193	Sammy Taylor	1.00	.50	.10
☐ 194	Jim Brosnan	1.00	.50	.10
☐ 195	Rip Repulski	1.00	.50	.10
☐ 196	Billy Moran	1.00	.50	.10
☐ 197	Ray Semproch	1.00	.50	.10
☐ 198	Jim Davenport	1.50	.75	.15
☐ 199	Leo Kiely	1.00	.50	.10
☐ 200	Warren Giles	2.50	1.25	.25
	(NL President)			
☐ 201	Tom Acker	1.00	.50	.10
☐ 202	Roger Maris	30.00	15.00	3.00
☐ 203	Ossie Virgil	1.00	.50	.10
☐ 204	Casey Wise	1.00	.50	.10
☐ 205	Don Larsen	3.00	1.50	.30
☐ 206	Carl Furillo	3.00	1.50	.30
☐ 207	George Strickland	1.00	.50	.10
☐ 208	Willie Jones	1.00	.50	.10
☐ 209	Lenny Green	1.00	.50	.10
☐ 210	Ed Bailey	1.00	.50	.10
☐ 211	Bob Blaylock	1.00	.50	.10
☐ 212	Fence Busters	15.00	7.50	1.50
	Hank Aaron			
	Eddie Mathews			
☐ 213	Jim Rivera	1.00	.50	.10
☐ 214	Marcelino Solis	1.00	.50	.10
☐ 215	Jim Lemon	1.00	.50	.10
☐ 216	Andre Rodgers	1.00	.50	.10
☐ 217	Carl Erskine	2.50	1.25	.25
☐ 218	Roman Mejias	1.00	.50	.10
☐ 219	George Zuverink	1.00	.50	.10
☐ 220	Frank Malzone	1.50	.75	.15
☐ 221	Bob Bowman	1.00	.50	.10
☐ 222	Bobby Shantz	2.00	1.00	.20
☐ 223	Cardinals Team	3.50	.70	.10
☐ 224	Claude Osteen	2.50	1.25	.25
☐ 225	Johnny Logan	1.50	.75	.15
☐ 226	Art Ceccarelli	1.00	.50	.10
☐ 227	Hal W. Smith	1.00	.50	.10
☐ 228	Don Gross	1.00	.50	.10
☐ 229	Vic Power	1.00	.50	.10
☐ 230	Bill Fischer	1.00	.50	.10
☐ 231	Ellis Burton	1.00	.50	.10
☐ 232	Eddie Kasko	1.00	.50	.10
☐ 233	Paul Foytack	1.00	.50	.10
☐ 234	Chuck Tanner	1.50	.75	.15
☐ 235	Valmy Thomas	1.00	.50	.10
☐ 236	Ted Bowsfield	1.00	.50	.10
☐ 237	Run Preventers	2.00	1.00	.20
	Gil McDougald			
	Bob Turley			
	Bobby Richardson			
☐ 238	Gene Baker	1.00	.50	.10
☐ 239	Bob Trowbridge	1.00	.50	.10
☐ 240	Hank Bauer	2.50	1.25	.25
☐ 241	Billy Muffett	1.00	.50	.10
☐ 242	Ron Samford	1.00	.50	.10
☐ 243	Marv Grissom	1.00	.50	.10
☐ 244	Ted Gray	1.00	.50	.10
☐ 245	Ned Garver	1.00	.50	.10
☐ 246	J.W. Porter	1.00	.50	.10
☐ 247	Don Ferrarese	1.00	.50	.10
☐ 248	Red Sox Team	3.50	.70	.10
☐ 249	Bobby Adams	1.00	.50	.10
☐ 250	Billy O'Dell	1.00	.50	.10
☐ 251	Cletis Boyer	2.00	1.00	.20
☐ 252	Ray Boone	1.00	.50	.10
☐ 253	Seth Morehead	1.00	.50	.10
☐ 254	Zeke Bella	1.00	.50	.10
☐ 255	Del Ennis	1.00	.50	.10
☐ 256	Jerry Davie	1.00	.50	.10
☐ 257	Leon Wagner	1.00	.50	.10
☐ 258	Fred Kipp	1.00	.50	.10
☐ 259	Jim Pisoni	1.00	.50	.10
☐ 260	Early Wynn	8.00	4.00	.80
☐ 261	Gene Stephens	1.00	.50	.10
☐ 262	Hitters' Foes	3.50	1.75	.35
	Johnny Podres			
	Clem Labine			
	Don Drysdale			
☐ 263	Buddy Daley	1.00	.50	.10
☐ 264	Chico Carrasquel	1.00	.50	.10
☐ 265	Ron Kline	1.00	.50	.10
☐ 266	Woody Held	1.00	.50	.10
☐ 267	John Romonosky	1.00	.50	.10
☐ 268	Tito Francona	1.00	.50	.10
☐ 269	Jack Mayer	1.00	.50	.10
☐ 270	Gil Hodges	9.00	4.50	.90
☐ 271	Orlando Pena	1.00	.50	.10
☐ 272	Jerry Lumpe	1.00	.50	.10
☐ 273	Joey Jay	1.00	.50	.10
☐ 274	Jerry Kindall	1.00	.50	.10
☐ 275	Jack Sanford	1.00	.50	.10
☐ 276	Pete Daley	1.00	.50	.10
☐ 277	Turk Lown	1.00	.50	.10
☐ 278	Chuck Essegian	1.00	.50	.10
☐ 279	Ernie Johnson	1.00	.50	.10
☐ 280	Frank Bolling	1.00	.50	.10
☐ 281	Walt Craddock	1.00	.50	.10
☐ 282	R.C. Stevens	1.00	.50	.10
☐ 283	Russ Heman	1.00	.50	.10

☐ 284	Steve Korcheck	1.00	.50	.10
☐ 285	Joe Cunningham	1.00	.50	.10
☐ 286	Dean Stone	1.00	.50	.10
☐ 287	Don Zimmer	1.50	.75	.15
☐ 288	Dutch Dotterer	1.00	.50	.10
☐ 289	Johnny Kucks	1.00	.50	.10
☐ 290	Wes Covington	1.00	.50	.10
☐ 291	Pitching Partners	1.00	.50	.10
	Pedro Ramos			
	Camilo Pascual			
☐ 292	Dick Williams	1.50	.75	.15
☐ 293	Ray Moore	1.00	.50	.10
☐ 294	Hank Foiles	1.00	.50	.10
☐ 295	Billy Martin	4.00	2.00	.40
☐ 296	Ernie Broglio	1.50	.75	.15
☐ 297	Jackie Brandt	1.00	.50	.10
☐ 298	Tex Clevenger	1.00	.50	.10
☐ 299	Billy Klaus	1.00	.50	.10
☐ 300	Richie Ashburn	5.00	2.50	.50
☐ 301	Earl Averill	1.00	.50	.10
☐ 302	Don Mossi	1.00	.50	.10
☐ 303	Marty Keough	1.00	.50	.10
☐ 304	Cubs Team	3.00	.60	.10
☐ 305	Curt Raydon	1.00	.50	.10
☐ 306	Jim Gilliam	3.50	1.75	.35
☐ 307	Curt Barclay	1.00	.50	.10
☐ 308	Norm Siebern	1.00	.50	.10
☐ 309	Sal Maglie	2.50	1.25	.25
☐ 310	Luis Aparicio	8.00	4.00	.80
☐ 311	Norm Zauchin	1.00	.50	.10
☐ 312	Don Newcombe	2.00	1.00	.20
☐ 313	Frank House	1.00	.50	.10
☐ 314	Don Cardwell	1.00	.50	.10
☐ 315	Joe Adcock	1.50	.75	.15
☐ 316A	Ralph Lumenti (option) (photo actually Camilo Pascual)	1.00	.50	.10
☐ 316B	Ralph Lumenti (no option) (photo actually Camilo Pascual)	60.00	30.00	6.00
☐ 317	Hitting Kings Willie Mays Richie Ashburn	10.00	5.00	1.00
☐ 318	Rocky Bridges	1.00	.50	.10
☐ 319	Dave Hillmann	1.00	.50	.10
☐ 320	Bob Skinner	1.00	.50	.10
☐ 321A	Bob Giallombardo (option)	1.00	.50	.10
☐ 321B	Bob Giallombardo (no option)	60.00	30.00	6.00
☐ 322A	Harry Hanebrink (traded)	1.00	.50	.10
☐ 322B	Harry Hanebrink (no trade)	60.00	30.00	6.00
☐ 323	Frank Sullivan	1.00	.50	.10
☐ 324	Don Demeter	1.00	.50	.10
☐ 325	Ken Boyer	2.50	1.25	.25
☐ 326	Marv Throneberry	2.50	1.25	.25
☐ 327	Gary Bell	1.00	.50	.10
☐ 328	Lou Skizas	1.00	.50	.10
☐ 329	Tigers Team	3.50	.70	.10
☐ 330	Gus Triandos	1.00	.50	.10
☐ 331	Steve Boros	1.00	.50	.10
☐ 332	Ray Monzant	1.00	.50	.10
☐ 333	Harry Simpson	1.00	.50	.10
☐ 334	Glen Hobbie	1.00	.50	.10
☐ 335	Johnny Temple	1.00	.50	.10
☐ 336A	Billy Loes (with traded line)	1.00	.50	.10
☐ 336B	Billy Loes (no trade)	60.00	30.00	6.00
☐ 337	George Crowe	1.00	.50	.10
☐ 338	Sparky Anderson	7.50	3.75	.75
☐ 339	Roy Face	2.00	1.00	.20
☐ 340	Roy Sievers	1.50	.75	.15
☐ 341	Tom Qualters	1.00	.50	.10
☐ 342	Ray Jablonski	1.00	.50	.10
☐ 343	Bill Hoeft	1.00	.50	.10
☐ 344	Russ Nixon	1.00	.50	.10
☐ 345	Gil McDougald	3.50	1.75	.35
☐ 346	Batter Bafflers Dave Sisler Tom Brewer	1.00	.50	.10
☐ 347	Bob Buhl	1.00	.50	.10
☐ 348	Ted Lepcio	1.00	.50	.10
☐ 349	Hoyt Wilhelm	7.50	3.75	.75
☐ 350	Ernie Banks	20.00	10.00	2.00
☐ 351	Earl Torgeson	1.00	.50	.10
☐ 352	Robin Roberts	8.00	4.00	.80
☐ 353	Curt Flood	2.50	1.25	.25
☐ 354	Pete Burnside	1.00	.50	.10
☐ 355	Jim Piersall	2.00	1.00	.20
☐ 356	Bob Mabe	1.00	.50	.10

☐ 357	Dick Stuart	2.00	1.00	.20
☐ 358	Ralph Terry	1.50	.75	.15
☐ 359	Bill White	4.50	2.25	.45
☐ 360	Al Kaline	20.00	10.00	2.00
☐ 361	Willard Nixon	1.00	.50	.10
☐ 362A	Dolan Nichols (with option line)	1.00	.50	.10
☐ 362B	Dolan Nichols (no option)	60.00	30.00	6.00
☐ 363	Bobby Avila	1.00	.50	.10
☐ 364	Danny McDevitt	1.00	.50	.10
☐ 365	Gus Bell	1.00	.50	.10
☐ 366	Humberto Robinson	1.00	.50	.10
☐ 367	Cal Neeman	1.00	.50	.10
☐ 368	Don Mueller	1.00	.50	.10
☐ 369	Dick Tomanek	1.00	.50	.10
☐ 370	Pete Runnels	1.00	.50	.10
☐ 371	Dick Brodowski	1.00	.50	.10
☐ 372	Jim Hegan	1.00	.50	.10
☐ 373	Herb Plews	1.00	.50	.10
☐ 374	Art Ditmar	1.00	.50	.10
☐ 375	Bob Nieman	1.00	.50	.10
☐ 376	Hal Naragon	1.00	.50	.10
☐ 377	John Antonelli	1.50	.75	.15
☐ 378	Gail Harris	1.00	.50	.10
☐ 379	Bob Miller	1.00	.50	.10
☐ 380	Hank Aaron	50.00	25.00	5.00
☐ 381	Mike Baxes	1.00	.50	.10
☐ 382	Curt Simmons	1.00	.50	.10
☐ 383	Words of Wisdom Don Larsen Casey Stengel	4.00	2.00	.40
☐ 384	Dave Sisler	1.00	.50	.10
☐ 385	Sherm Lollar	1.00	.50	.10
☐ 386	Jim Delsing	1.00	.50	.10
☐ 387	Don Drysdale	11.00	5.50	1.10
☐ 388	Bob Will	1.00	.50	.10
☐ 389	Joe Nuxhall	1.00	.50	.10
☐ 390	Orlando Cepeda	4.50	2.25	.45
☐ 391	Milt Pappas	1.50	.75	.15
☐ 392	Whitey Herzog	2.00	1.00	.20
☐ 393	Frank Lary	1.00	.50	.10
☐ 394	Randy Jackson	1.00	.50	.10
☐ 395	Elston Howard	3.50	1.75	.35
☐ 396	Bob Rush	1.00	.50	.10
☐ 397	Senators Team	3.00	.60	.10
☐ 398	Wally Post	1.00	.50	.10
☐ 399	Larry Jackson	1.00	.50	.10
☐ 400	Jackie Jensen	2.00	1.00	.20
☐ 401	Ron Blackburn	1.00	.50	.10
☐ 402	Hector Lopez	1.00	.50	.10
☐ 403	Clem Labine	1.00	.50	.10
☐ 404	Hank Sauer	1.00	.50	.10
☐ 405	Roy McMillan	1.00	.50	.10
☐ 406	Solly Drake	1.00	.50	.10
☐ 407	Moe Drabowsky	1.00	.50	.10
☐ 408	Keystone Combo Nellie Fox Luis Aparicio	4.00	2.00	.40
☐ 409	Gus Zernial	1.00	.50	.10
☐ 410	Billy Pierce	1.50	.75	.15
☐ 411	Whitey Lockman	1.00	.50	.10
☐ 412	Stan Lopata	1.00	.50	.10
☐ 413	Camilo Pascual (listed as Camillo on front)	1.50	.75	.15
☐ 414	Dale Long	1.00	.50	.10
☐ 415	Bill Mazeroski	3.50	1.75	.35
☐ 416	Haywood Sullivan	1.00	.50	.10
☐ 417	Virgil Trucks	1.00	.50	.10
☐ 418	Gino Cimoli	1.00	.50	.10
☐ 419	Braves Team	3.50	.70	.10
☐ 420	Rocky Colavito	3.50	1.75	.35
☐ 421	Herm Wehmeier	1.00	.50	.10
☐ 422	Hobie Landrith	1.00	.50	.10
☐ 423	Bob Grim	1.00	.50	.10
☐ 424	Ken Aspromonte	1.00	.50	.10
☐ 425	Del Crandall	1.00	.50	.10
☐ 426	Jerry Staley	1.00	.50	.10
☐ 427	Charlie Neal	1.00	.50	.10
☐ 428	Buc Hill Aces Ron Kline Bob Friend Vernon Law Roy Face	1.50	.75	.15
☐ 429	Bobby Thomson	1.50	.75	.15
☐ 430	Whitey Ford	17.00	8.50	1.70
☐ 431	Whammy Douglas	1.00	.50	.10
☐ 432	Smoky Burgess	1.00	.50	.10
☐ 433	Billy Harrell	1.00	.50	.10
☐ 434	Hal Griggs	1.00	.50	.10
☐ 435	Frank Robinson	17.00	8.50	1.70
☐ 436	Granny Hamner	1.00	.50	.10
☐ 437	Ike Delock	1.00	.50	.10
☐ 438	Sam Esposito	1.00	.50	.10

☐ 439	Brooks Robinson	25.00	12.50	2.50
☐ 440	Lou Burdette	3.50	1.75	.35
	(posing as if lefthanded)			
☐ 441	John Roseboro	1.50	.75	.15
☐ 442	Ray Narleski	1.00	.50	.10
☐ 443	Daryl Spencer	1.00	.50	.10
☐ 444	Ron Hansen	1.50	.75	.15
☐ 445	Cal McLish	1.00	.50	.10
☐ 446	Rocky Nelson	1.00	.50	.10
☐ 447	Bob Anderson	1.00	.50	.10
☐ 448	Vada Pinson	3.00	1.50	.30
☐ 449	Tom Gorman	1.00	.50	.10
☐ 450	Ed Mathews	10.00	5.00	1.00
☐ 451	Jimmy Constable	1.00	.50	.10
☐ 452	Chico Fernandez	1.00	.50	.10
☐ 453	Les Moss	1.00	.50	.10
☐ 454	Phil Clark	1.00	.50	.10
☐ 455	Larry Doby	2.00	1.00	.20
☐ 456	Jerry Casale	1.00	.50	.10
☐ 457	Dodgers Team	10.00	2.00	.40
☐ 458	Gordon Jones	1.00	.50	.10
☐ 459	Bill Tuttle	1.00	.50	.10
☐ 460	Bob Friend	1.50	.75	.15
☐ 461	Mantle Hits Homer	20.00	10.00	2.00
☐ 462	Colavito's Catch	2.00	1.00	.20
☐ 463	Kaline Batting Champ	5.00	2.50	.50
☐ 464	Mays' Series Catch	10.00	5.00	1.00
☐ 465	Sievers Sets Mark	1.50	.75	.15
☐ 466	Pierce All-Star	1.50	.75	.15
☐ 467	Aaron Clubs Homer	10.00	5.00	1.00
☐ 468	Snider's Play	6.00	3.00	.60
☐ 469	Hustler Banks	5.00	2.50	.50
☐ 470	Musial's 3000 Hit	7.00	3.50	.70
☐ 471	Tom Sturdivant	1.00	.50	.10
☐ 472	Gene Freese	1.00	.50	.10
☐ 473	Mike Fornieles	1.00	.50	.10
☐ 474	Moe Thacker	1.00	.50	.10
☐ 475	Jack Harshman	1.00	.50	.10
☐ 476	Indians Team	3.00	.60	.10
☐ 477	Barry Latman	1.00	.50	.10
☐ 478	Bob Clemente	30.00	15.00	3.00
☐ 479	Lindy McDaniel	1.00	.50	.10
☐ 480	Red Schoendienst	2.50	1.25	.25
☐ 481	Charlie Maxwell	1.00	.50	.10
☐ 482	Russ Meyer	1.00	.50	.10
☐ 483	Clint Courtney	1.00	.50	.10
☐ 484	Willie Kirkland	1.00	.50	.10
☐ 485	Ryne Duren	1.50	.75	.15
☐ 486	Sammy White	1.00	.50	.10
☐ 487	Hal Brown	1.00	.50	.10
☐ 488	Walt Moryn	1.00	.50	.10
☐ 489	John Powers	1.00	.50	.10
☐ 490	Frank Thomas	1.00	.50	.10
☐ 491	Don Blasingame	1.00	.50	.10
☐ 492	Gene Conley	1.00	.50	.10
☐ 493	Jim Landis	1.00	.50	.10
☐ 494	Don Pavletich	1.00	.50	.10
☐ 495	John Podres	2.50	1.25	.25
☐ 496	Wayne Terwilliger	1.00	.50	.10
☐ 497	Hal R. Smith	1.00	.50	.10
☐ 498	Dick Hyde	1.00	.50	.10
☐ 499	John O'Brien	1.00	.50	.10
☐ 500	Vic Wertz	1.00	.50	.10
☐ 501	Bob Tiefenauer	1.00	.50	.10
☐ 502	Alvin Dark	1.50	.75	.15
☐ 503	Jim Owens	1.00	.50	.10
☐ 504	Ossie Alvarez	1.00	.50	.10
☐ 505	Tony Kubek	4.00	2.00	.40
☐ 506	Bob Purkey	1.00	.50	.10
☐ 507	Bob Hale	5.00	2.50	.50
☐ 508	Art Fowler	5.00	2.50	.50
☐ 509	Norm Cash	10.00	5.00	1.00
☐ 510	Yankees Team	25.00	12.50	2.50
☐ 511	George Susce	5.00	2.50	.50
☐ 512	George Altman	5.00	2.50	.50
☐ 513	Tommy Carroll	5.00	2.50	.50
☐ 514	Bob Gibson	120.00	60.00	12.00
☐ 515	Harmon Killebrew	45.00	22.50	4.50
☐ 516	Mike Garcia	6.00	3.00	.60
☐ 517	Joe Koppe	5.00	2.50	.50
☐ 518	Mike Cueller	7.50	3.75	.75
	(sic, Cuellar)			
☐ 519	Infield Power	6.00	3.00	.60
	Pete Runnels			
	Dick Gernert			
	Frank Malzone			
☐ 520	Don Elston	5.00	2.50	.50
☐ 521	Gary Geiger	5.00	2.50	.50
☐ 522	Gene Snyder	5.00	2.50	.50
☐ 523	Harry Bright	5.00	2.50	.50
☐ 524	Larry Osborne	5.00	2.50	.50
☐ 525	Jim Coates	5.00	2.50	.50
☐ 526	Bob Speake	5.00	2.50	.50
☐ 527	Solly Hemus	5.00	2.50	.50

☐ 528	Pirates Team	10.00	5.00	1.00
☐ 529	George Bamberger	7.50	3.75	.75
☐ 530	Wally Moon	6.00	3.00	.60
☐ 531	Ray Webster	5.00	2.50	.50
☐ 532	Mark Freeman	5.00	2.50	.50
☐ 533	Darrell Johnson	5.00	2.50	.50
☐ 534	Faye Throneberry	5.00	2.50	.50
☐ 535	Ruben Gomez	5.00	2.50	.50
☐ 536	Danny Kravitz	5.00	2.50	.50
☐ 537	Rudolph Arias	5.00	2.50	.50
☐ 538	Chick King	5.00	2.50	.50
☐ 539	Gary Blaylock	5.00	2.50	.50
☐ 540	Willie Miranda	5.00	2.50	.50
☐ 541	Bob Thurman	5.00	2.50	.50
☐ 542	Jim Perry	9.00	4.50	.90
☐ 543	Corsair Trio	25.00	12.50	2.50
	Bob Skinner			
	Bill Virdon			
	Roberto Clemente			
☐ 544	Lee Tate	5.00	2.50	.50
☐ 545	Tom Morgan	5.00	2.50	.50
☐ 546	Al Schroll	5.00	2.50	.50
☐ 547	Jim Baxes	5.00	2.50	.50
☐ 548	Elmer Singleton	5.00	2.50	.50
☐ 549	Howie Nunn	5.00	2.50	.50
☐ 550	Roy Campanella	60.00	30.00	6.00
	(Symbol of Courage)			
☐ 551	Fred Haney MG AS	6.00	3.00	.60
☐ 552	Casey Stengel MG AS	10.00	5.00	1.00
☐ 553	Orlando Cepeda AS	7.50	3.75	.75
☐ 554	Bill Skowron AS	6.00	3.00	.60
☐ 555	Bill Mazeroski AS	6.00	3.00	.60
☐ 556	Nellie Fox AS	7.50	3.75	.75
☐ 557	Ken Boyer AS	6.00	3.00	.60
☐ 558	Frank Malzone AS	6.00	3.00	.60
☐ 559	Ernie Banks AS	17.00	8.50	1.70
☐ 560	Luis Aparicio AS	10.00	5.00	1.00
☐ 561	Hank Aaron AS	40.00	20.00	4.00
☐ 562	Al Kaline AS	17.00	8.50	1.70
☐ 563	Willie Mays AS	40.00	20.00	4.00
☐ 564	Mickey Mantle AS	150.00	75.00	15.00
☐ 565	Wes Covington AS	6.00	3.00	.60
☐ 566	Roy Sievers AS	6.00	3.00	.60
☐ 567	Del Crandall AS	6.00	3.00	.60
☐ 568	Gus Triandos AS	6.00	3.00	.60
☐ 569	Bob Friend AS	6.00	3.00	.60
☐ 570	Bob Turley AS	6.00	3.00	.60
☐ 571	Warren Spahn AS	17.00	8.50	1.70
☐ 572	Billy Pierce AS	10.00	3.00	.60

1960 Topps

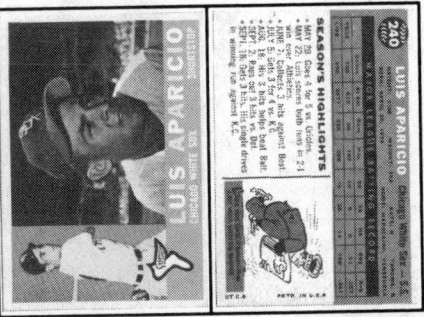

The cards in this 572-card set measure 2 1/2" by 3 1/2". The 1960 Topps set is the only Topps standard size issue to use a horizontally oriented front. World Series cards appeared for the first time (385 to 391), and there is a Rookie Prospect (RP) series (117-148), the most famous of which is Carl Yastrzemski, and a Sport Magazine All-Star Selection (AS) series (553-572). There are 16 manager cards listed alphabetically from 212 through 227. The coaching staff of each team was also afforded their own card in 16-card subset (455-470). Cards 375 to 440 come with either gray or white backs, and the high series (507-572) were printed on a more limited basis than the rest of the set. The team cards have series checklists on the reverse.

		NRMT	VG-E	GOOD
	COMPLETE SET (1-286)	2250.00	750.00	125.00
	COMMON PLAYER (1-286)	.80	.40	.08
	COMMON PLAYER (287-440)	1.00	.50	.10
	COMMON PLAYER (441-506)	1.50	.75	.15
	COMMON PLAYER (507-552)	4.50	2.25	.45
	COMMON PLAYER (553-572)	5.50	2.75	.55
☐ 1	Early Wynn	15.00	3.00	.50
☐ 2	Roman Mejias	.80	.40	.08
☐ 3	Joe Adcock	1.00	.50	.10
☐ 4	Bob Purkey	.80	.40	.08
☐ 5	Wally Moon	1.00	.50	.10
☐ 6	Lou Berberet	.80	.40	.08
☐ 7	Master and Mentor	6.50	3.25	.65
	Willie Mays			
	Bill Rigney			
☐ 8	Bud Daley	.80	.40	.08
☐ 9	Faye Throneberry	.80	.40	.08
☐ 10	Ernie Banks	12.00	6.00	1.20
☐ 11	Norm Siebern	.80	.40	.08
☐ 12	Milt Pappas	1.00	.50	.10
☐ 13	Wally Post	.80	.40	.08
☐ 14	Jim Grant	.80	.40	.08
☐ 15	Pete Runnels	1.00	.50	.10
☐ 16	Ernie Broglio	1.00	.50	.10
☐ 17	Johnny Callison	1.00	.50	.10
☐ 18	Dodgers Team	6.00	1.00	.20
☐ 19	Felix Mantilla	.80	.40	.08
☐ 20	Roy Face	1.25	.60	.12
☐ 21	Dutch Dotterer	.80	.40	.08
☐ 22	Rocky Bridges	.80	.40	.08
☐ 23	Eddie Fisher	.80	.40	.08
☐ 24	Dick Gray	.80	.40	.08
☐ 25	Roy Sievers	1.00	.50	.10
☐ 26	Wayne Terwilliger	.80	.40	.08
☐ 27	Dick Drott	.80	.40	.08
☐ 28	Brooks Robinson	17.00	8.50	1.70
☐ 29	Clem Labine	1.00	.50	.10
☐ 30	Tito Francona	1.00	.50	.10
☐ 31	Sammy Esposito	.80	.40	.08
☐ 32	Sophomore Stalwarts	1.00	.50	.10
	Jim O'Toole			
	Vada Pinson			
☐ 33	Tom Morgan	.80	.40	.08
☐ 34	George Anderson	2.00	1.00	.20
☐ 35	Whitey Ford	12.00	6.00	1.20
☐ 36	Russ Nixon	.80	.40	.08
☐ 37	Bill Bruton	.80	.40	.08
☐ 38	Jerry Casale	.80	.40	.08
☐ 39	Earl Averill	.80	.40	.08
☐ 40	Joe Cunningham	.80	.40	.08
☐ 41	Barry Latman	.80	.40	.08
☐ 42	Hobie Landrith	.80	.40	.08
☐ 43	Senators Team	2.00	.40	.10
☐ 44	Bob Locke	.80	.40	.08
☐ 45	Roy McMillan	.80	.40	.08
☐ 46	Jerry Fisher	.80	.40	.08
☐ 47	Don Zimmer	1.25	.60	.12
☐ 48	Hal W. Smith	.80	.40	.08
☐ 49	Curt Raydon	.80	.40	.08
☐ 50	Al Kaline	12.00	6.00	1.20
☐ 51	Jim Coates	.80	.40	.08
☐ 52	Dave Philley	.80	.40	.08
☐ 53	Jackie Brandt	.80	.40	.08
☐ 54	Mike Fornieles	.80	.40	.08
☐ 55	Bill Mazeroski	2.00	1.00	.20
☐ 56	Steve Korcheck	.80	.40	.08
☐ 57	Win Savers	1.00	.50	.10
	Turk Lown			
	Jerry Staley			
☐ 58	Gino Cimoli	.80	.40	.08
☐ 59	Juan Pizarro	.80	.40	.08
☐ 60	Gus Triandos	1.00	.50	.10
☐ 61	Eddie Kasko	.80	.40	.08
☐ 62	Roger Craig	1.50	.75	.15
☐ 63	George Strickland	.80	.40	.08
☐ 64	Jack Meyer	.80	.40	.08
☐ 65	Elston Howard	2.50	1.25	.25
☐ 66	Bob Trowbridge	.80	.40	.08
☐ 67	Jose Pagan	.80	.40	.08
☐ 68	Dave Hillman	.80	.40	.08
☐ 69	Billy Goodman	1.00	.50	.10
☐ 70	Lew Burdette	2.00	1.00	.20
☐ 71	Marty Keough	.80	.40	.08
☐ 72	Tigers Team	3.00	.60	.10
☐ 73	Bob Gibson	15.00	7.50	1.50
☐ 74	Walt Moryn	.80	.40	.08
☐ 75	Vic Power	.80	.40	.08
☐ 76	Bill Fischer	.80	.40	.08
☐ 77	Hank Foiles	.80	.40	.08
☐ 78	Bob Grim	.80	.40	.08
☐ 79	Walt Dropo	.80	.40	.08

		NRMT	VG-E	GOOD
☐ 80	Johnny Antonelli	1.00	.50	.10
☐ 81	Russ Snyder	.80	.40	.08
☐ 82	Ruben Gomez	.80	.40	.08
☐ 83	Tony Kubek	3.00	1.50	.30
☐ 84	Hal R. Smith	.80	.40	.08
☐ 85	Frank Lary	1.00	.50	.10
☐ 86	Dick Gernert	.80	.40	.08
☐ 87	John Romonosky	.80	.40	.08
☐ 88	John Roseboro	1.00	.50	.10
☐ 89	Hal Brown	.80	.40	.08
☐ 90	Bobby Avila	.80	.40	.08
☐ 91	Bennie Daniels	.80	.40	.08
☐ 92	Whitey Herzog	2.00	1.00	.20
☐ 93	Art Schult	.80	.40	.08
☐ 94	Leo Kiely	.80	.40	.08
☐ 95	Frank Thomas	.80	.40	.08
☐ 96	Ralph Terry	1.25	.60	.12
☐ 97	Ted Lepcio	.80	.40	.08
☐ 91	Gordon Jones	.80	.40	.08
☐ 99	Lenny Green	.80	.40	.08
☐ 100	Nellie Fox	3.50	1.75	.35
☐ 101	Bob Miller	.80	.40	.08
☐ 102	Kent Hadley	.80	.40	.08
☐ 103	Dick Farrell	.80	.40	.08
☐ 104	Dick Schofield	.80	.40	.08
☐ 105	Larry Sherry	1.00	.50	.10
☐ 106	Billy Gardner	.80	.40	.08
☐ 107	Carlton Willey	.80	.40	.08
☐ 108	Pete Daley	.80	.40	.08
☐ 109	Clete Boyer	1.25	.60	.12
☐ 110	Cal McLish	.80	.40	.08
☐ 111	Vic Wertz	.80	.40	.08
☐ 112	Jack Harshman	.80	.40	.08
☐ 113	Bob Skinner	.80	.40	.08
☐ 114	Ken Aspromonte	.80	.40	.08
☐ 115	Fork and Knuckler	3.00	1.50	.30
	Roy Face			
	Hoyt Wilhelm			
☐ 116	Jim Rivera	.80	.40	.08
☐ 117	Tom Borland RP	.80	.40	.08
☐ 118	Bob Bruce RP	.80	.40	.08
☐ 119	Chico Cardenas RP	1.00	.50	.10
☐ 120	Duke Carmel RP	.80	.40	.08
☐ 121	Camilo Carreon RP	.80	.40	.08
☐ 122	Don Dillard RP	.80	.40	.08
☐ 123	Dan Dobbek RP	.80	.40	.08
☐ 124	Jim Donohue RP	.80	.40	.08
☐ 125	Dick Ellsworth RP	1.00	.50	.10
☐ 126	Chuck Estrada RP	1.25	.60	.12
☐ 127	Ron Hansen RP	1.00	.50	.10
☐ 128	Bill Harris RP	.80	.40	.08
☐ 129	Bob Hartman RP	.80	.40	.08
☐ 130	Frank Herrera RP	.80	.40	.08
☐ 131	Ed Hobaugh RP	.80	.40	.08
☐ 132	Frank Howard RP	6.00	3.00	.60
☐ 133	Manuel Javier RP	1.00	.50	.10
	(sic, Julian)			
☐ 134	Deron Johnson RP	1.00	.50	.10
☐ 135	Ken Johnson RP	.80	.40	.08
☐ 136	Jim Kaat RP	15.00	7.50	1.50
☐ 137	Lou Klimchock RP	.80	.40	.08
☐ 138	Art Mahaffey RP	1.00	.50	.10
☐ 139	Carl Mathias RP	.80	.40	.08
☐ 140	Julio Navarro RP	.80	.40	.08
☐ 141	Jim Proctor RP	.80	.40	.08
☐ 142	Bill Short RP	1.00	.50	.10
☐ 143	Al Spangler RP	.80	.40	.08
☐ 144	Al Stieglitz RP	.80	.40	.08
☐ 145	Jim Umbricht RP	.80	.40	.08
☐ 146	Ted Wieand RP	.80	.40	.08
☐ 147	Bob Will RP	.80	.40	.08
☐ 148	Carl Yastrzemski RP	175.00	85.00	18.00
☐ 149	Bob Nieman	.80	.40	.08
☐ 150	Billy Pierce	1.50	.75	.15
☐ 151	Giants Team	3.50	.70	.10
☐ 152	Gail Harris	.80	.40	.08
☐ 153	Bobby Thomson	1.25	.60	.12
☐ 154	Jim Davenport	1.00	.50	.10
☐ 155	Charlie Neal	1.00	.50	.10
☐ 156	Art Ceccarelli	.80	.40	.08
☐ 157	Rocky Nelson	.80	.40	.08
☐ 158	Wes Covington	1.00	.50	.10
☐ 159	Jim Piersall	2.00	1.00	.20
☐ 160	Rival All-Stars	15.00	7.50	1.50
	Mickey Mantle			
	Ken Boyer			
☐ 161	Ray Narleski	.80	.40	.08
☐ 162	Sammy Taylor	.80	.40	.08
☐ 163	Hector Lopez	.80	.40	.08
☐ 164	Reds Team	3.50	.70	.10
☐ 165	Jack Sanford	1.00	.50	.10
☐ 166	Chuck Essegian	.80	.40	.08
☐ 167	Valmy Thomas	.80	.40	.08
☐ 168	Alex Grammas	.80	.40	.08
☐ 169	Jake Striker	.80	.40	.08

☐ 170 Del Crandall	1.00	.50	.10
☐ 171 Johnny Groth	.80	.40	.08
☐ 172 Willie Kirkland	.80	.40	.08
☐ 173 Billy Martin	3.50	1.75	.35
☐ 174 Indians Team	2.50	.50	.10
☐ 175 Pete Ramos	.80	.40	.08
☐ 176 Vada Pinson	2.50	1.25	.25
☐ 177 Johnny Kucks	.80	.40	.08
☐ 178 Woody Held	.80	.40	.08
☐ 179 Rip Coleman	.80	.40	.08
☐ 180 Harry Simpson	.80	.40	.08
☐ 181 Billy Loes	.80	.40	.08
☐ 182 Glen Hobbie	.80	.40	.08
☐ 183 Eli Grba	.80	.40	.08
☐ 184 Gary Geiger	.80	.40	.08
☐ 185 Jim Owens	.80	.40	.08
☐ 186 Dave Sisler	.80	.40	.08
☐ 187 Jay Hook	.80	.40	.08
☐ 188 Dick Williams	1.00	.50	.10
☐ 189 Don McMahon	.80	.40	.08
☐ 190 Gene Woodling	1.00	.50	.10
☐ 191 John Klippstein	.80	.40	.08
☐ 192 Danny O'Connell	.80	.40	.08
☐ 193 Dick Hyde	.80	.40	.08
☐ 194 Bobby Gene Smith	.80	.40	.08
☐ 195 Lindy McDaniel	1.00	.50	.10
☐ 196 Andy Carey	1.00	.50	.10
☐ 197 Ron Kline	.80	.40	.08
☐ 198 Jerry Lynch	.80	.40	.08
☐ 199 Dick Donovan	.80	.40	.08
☐ 200 Willie Mays	50.00	25.00	5.00
☐ 201 Larry Osborne	.80	.40	.08
☐ 202 Fred Kipp	.80	.40	.08
☐ 203 Sammy White	.80	.40	.08
☐ 204 Ryne Duren	.80	.40	.08
☐ 205 John Logan	1.00	.50	.10
☐ 206 Claude Osteen	1.00	.50	.10
☐ 207 Bob Boyd	.80	.40	.08
☐ 208 White Sox Team	2.50	.50	.10
☐ 209 Ron Blackburn	.80	.40	.08
☐ 210 Harmon Killebrew	11.00	5.50	1.10
☐ 211 Taylor Phillips	.80	.40	.08
☐ 212 Walt Alston MG	3.50	1.75	.35
☐ 213 Chuck Dressen MG	1.25	.60	.12
☐ 214 Jimmy Dykes MG	1.00	.50	.10
☐ 215 Bob Elliott MG	1.00	.50	.10
☐ 216 Joe Gordon MG	1.00	.50	.10
☐ 217 Charlie Grimm MG	1.00	.50	.10
☐ 218 Solly Hemus MG	1.00	.50	.10
☐ 219 Fred Hutchinson MG	1.25	.60	.12
☐ 220 Billy Jurges MG	1.00	.50	.10
☐ 221 Cookie Lavagetto MG	1.00	.50	.10
☐ 222 Al Lopez MG	2.50	1.25	.25
☐ 223 Danny Murtaugh MG	1.00	.50	.10
☐ 224 Paul Richards MG	1.00	.50	.10
☐ 225 Bill Rigney MG	1.00	.50	.10
☐ 226 Eddie Sawyer MG	1.00	.50	.10
☐ 227 Casey Stengel MG	7.50	3.75	.75
☐ 228 Ernie Johnson	.80	.40	.08
☐ 229 Joe M. Morgan	.80	.40	.08
☐ 230 Mound Magicians	3.50	1.75	.35
Lou Burdette			
Warren Spahn			
Bob Buhl			
☐ 231 Hal Naragon	.80	.40	.08
☐ 232 Jim Busby	.80	.40	.08
☐ 233 Don Elston	.80	.40	.08
☐ 234 Don Demeter	.80	.40	.08
☐ 235 Gus Bell	1.00	.50	.10
☐ 236 Dick Ricketts	.80	.40	.08
☐ 237 Elmer Valo	.80	.40	.08
☐ 238 Danny Kravitz	.80	.40	.08
☐ 239 Joe Shipley	.80	.40	.08
☐ 240 Luis Aparicio	6.50	3.25	.65
☐ 241 Albie Pearson	.80	.40	.08
☐ 242 Cardinals Team	2.50	.50	.10
☐ 243 Bubba Phillips	.80	.40	.08
☐ 244 Hal Griggs	.80	.40	.08
☐ 245 Ed Yost	.80	.40	.08
☐ 246 Lee Maye	.80	.40	.08
☐ 247 Gil McDougald	2.50	1.25	.25
☐ 248 Del Rice	.80	.40	.08
☐ 249 Earl Wilson	1.00	.50	.10
☐ 250 Stan Musial	40.00	20.00	4.00
☐ 251 Bob Malkmus	.80	.40	.08
☐ 252 Ray Herbert	.80	.40	.08
☐ 253 Eddie Bressoud	.80	.40	.08
☐ 254 Arnie Portocarrero	.80	.40	.08
☐ 255 Jim Gilliam	2.50	1.25	.25
☐ 256 Dick Brown	.80	.40	.08
☐ 257 Gordy Coleman	1.00	.50	.10
☐ 258 Dick Groat	2.50	1.25	.25
☐ 259 George Altman	.80	.40	.08
☐ 260 Power Plus	1.25	.60	.12
Rocky Colavito			

Tito Francona			
☐ 261 Pete Burnside	.80	.40	.08
☐ 262 Hank Bauer	.80	.40	.08
☐ 263 Darrell Johnson	1.00	.50	.10
☐ 264 Robin Roberts	6.50	3.25	.65
☐ 265 Rip Repulski	.80	.40	.08
☐ 266 Joe Jay	.80	.40	.08
☐ 267 Jim Marshall	.80	.40	.08
☐ 268 Al Worthington	.80	.40	.08
☐ 269 Gene Green	.80	.40	.08
☐ 270 Bob Turley	2.00	1.00	.20
☐ 271 Julio Becquer	.80	.40	.08
☐ 272 Fred Green	.80	.40	.08
☐ 273 Neil Chrisley	.80	.40	.08
☐ 274 Tom Acker	.80	.40	.08
☐ 275 Curt Flood	2.00	1.00	.20
☐ 276 Ken McBride	.80	.40	.08
☐ 277 Harry Bright	1.00	.50	.10
☐ 278 Stan Williams	1.00	.50	.10
☐ 279 Chuck Tanner	.80	.40	.08
☐ 280 Frank Sullivan	.80	.40	.08
☐ 281 Ray Boone	.80	.40	.08
☐ 282 Joe Nuxhall	1.00	.50	.10
☐ 283 John Blanchard	1.00	.50	.10
☐ 284 Don Gross	.80	.40	.08
☐ 285 Harry Anderson	.80	.40	.08
☐ 286 Ray Semproch	.80	.40	.08
☐ 287 Felipe Alou	2.00	1.00	.20
☐ 288 Bob Mabe	1.00	.50	.10
☐ 289 Willie Jones	1.00	.50	.10
☐ 290 Jerry Lumpe	1.00	.50	.10
☐ 291 Bob Keegan	1.00	.50	.10
☐ 292 Dodger Backstops	1.00	.50	.10
Joe Pignatano			
John Roseboro			
☐ 293 Gene Conley	1.00	.50	.10
☐ 294 Tony Taylor	1.00	.50	.10
☐ 295 Gil Hodges	8.00	4.00	.80
☐ 296 Nelson Chittum	1.00	.50	.10
☐ 297 Reno Bertoia	1.00	.50	.10
☐ 298 George Witt	1.00	.50	.10
☐ 299 Earl Torgeson	1.00	.50	.10
☐ 300 Hank Aaron	50.00	25.00	5.00
☐ 301 Jerry Davie	1.00	.50	.10
☐ 302 Phillies Team	3.00	.60	.10
☐ 303 Billy O'Dell	1.00	.50	.10
☐ 304 Joe Ginsberg	1.00	.50	.10
☐ 305 Richie Ashburn	4.00	2.00	.40
☐ 306 Frank Baumann	1.00	.50	.10
☐ 307 Gene Oliver	1.00	.50	.10
☐ 308 Dick Hall	1.00	.50	.10
☐ 309 Bob Hale	1.00	.50	.10
☐ 310 Frank Malzone	1.50	.75	.15
☐ 311 Raul Sanchez	1.00	.50	.10
☐ 312 Charley Lau	1.50	.75	.15
☐ 313 Turk Lown	1.00	.50	.10
☐ 314 Chico Fernandez	1.00	.50	.10
☐ 315 Bobby Shantz	2.00	1.00	.20
☐ 316 Willie McCovey	75.00	37.50	7.50
☐ 317 Pumpsie Green	1.00	.50	.10
☐ 318 Jim Baxes	1.00	.50	.10
☐ 319 Joe Koppe	1.00	.50	.10
☐ 320 Bob Allison	1.50	.75	.15
☐ 321 Ron Fairly	1.50	.75	.15
☐ 322 Willie Tasby	1.00	.50	.10
☐ 323 John Romano	1.00	.50	.10
☐ 324 Jim Perry	2.00	1.00	.20
☐ 325 Jim O'Toole	1.50	.75	.15
☐ 326 Bob Clemente	40.00	20.00	4.00
☐ 327 Ray Sadecki	1.00	.50	.10
☐ 328 Earl Battey	1.00	.50	.10
☐ 329 Zack Monroe	1.00	.50	.10
☐ 330 Harvey Kuenn	2.00	1.00	.20
☐ 331 Henry Mason	1.00	.50	.10
☐ 332 Yankees Team	12.00	2.00	.40
☐ 333 Danny McDevitt	1.00	.50	.10
☐ 334 Ted Abernathy	1.00	.50	.10
☐ 335 Red Schoendienst	2.00	1.00	.20
☐ 336 Ike Delock	1.00	.50	.10
☐ 337 Cal Neeman	1.00	.50	.10
☐ 338 Ray Monzant	1.00	.50	.10
☐ 339 Harry Chiti	1.00	.50	.10
☐ 340 Harvey Haddix	1.50	.75	.15
☐ 341 Carroll Hardy	1.00	.50	.10
☐ 342 Casey Wise	1.00	.50	.10
☐ 343 Sandy Koufax	35.00	17.50	3.50
☐ 344 Clint Courtney	1.00	.50	.10
☐ 345 Don Newcombe	1.50	.75	.15
☐ 346 J.C. Martin	1.00	.50	.10
(face actually			
Gary Peters)			
☐ 347 Ed Bouchee	1.00	.50	.10
☐ 348 Barry Shetrone	1.00	.50	.10
☐ 349 Moe Drabowsky	1.00	.50	.10
☐ 350 Mickey Mantle	250.00	125.00	25.00

☐ 351	Don Nottebart	1.00	.50	.10
☐ 352	Cincy Clouters	3.00	1.50	.30
	Gus Bell			
	Frank Robinson			
	Jerry Lynch			
☐ 353	Don Larsen	1.50	.75	.15
☐ 354	Bob Lillis	1.50	.75	.15
☐ 355	Bill White	2.00	1.00	.20
☐ 356	Joe Amalfitano	1.00	.50	.10
☐ 357	Al Schroll	1.00	.50	.10
☐ 358	Joe DeMaestri	1.00	.50	.10
☐ 359	Buddy Gilbert	1.00	.50	.10
☐ 360	Herb Score	1.50	.75	.15
☐ 361	Bob Oldis	1.00	.50	.10
☐ 362	Russ Kemmerer	1.00	.50	.10
☐ 363	Gene Stephens	1.00	.50	.10
☐ 364	Paul Foytack	1.00	.50	.10
☐ 365	Minnie Minoso	2.50	1.25	.25
☐ 366	Dallas Green	2.50	1.25	.25
☐ 367	Bill Tuttle	1.00	.50	.10
☐ 368	Daryl Spencer	1.00	.50	.10
☐ 369	Billy Hoeft	1.00	.50	.10
☐ 370	Bill Skowron	3.50	1.75	.35
☐ 371	Bud Byerly	1.00	.50	.10
☐ 372	Frank House	1.00	.50	.10
☐ 373	Don Hoak	1.00	.50	.10
☐ 374	Bob Buhl	1.00	.50	.10
☐ 375	Dale Long	1.00	.50	.10
☐ 376	John Briggs	1.00	.50	.10
☐ 377	Roger Maris	35.00	17.50	3.50
☐ 378	Stu Miller	1.00	.50	.10
☐ 379	Red Wilson	1.00	.50	.10
☐ 380	Bob Shaw	1.00	.50	.10
☐ 381	Braves Team	3.00	.60	.10
☐ 382	Ted Bowsfield	1.00	.50	.10
☐ 383	Leon Wagner	1.00	.50	.10
☐ 384	Don Cardwell	1.00	.50	.10
☐ 385	World Series Game 1	2.00	1.00	.20
	Neal Steals Second			
☐ 386	World Series Game 2	2.00	1.00	.20
	Neal Belts 2nd Homer			
☐ 387	World Series Game 3	2.00	1.00	.20
	Furillo Breaks Game			
☐ 388	World Series Game 4	3.00	1.50	.30
	Hodges' Homer			
☐ 389	World Series Game 5	3.00	1.50	.30
	Luis Swipes Base			
☐ 390	World Series Game 6	2.00	1.00	.20
	Scrambling After Ball			
☐ 391	World Series Summary	2.00	1.00	.20
	The Champs Celebrate			
☐ 392	Tex Clevenger	1.00	.50	.10
☐ 393	Smoky Burgess	1.50	.75	.15
☐ 394	Norm Larker	1.00	.50	.10
☐ 395	Hoyt Wilhelm	6.50	3.25	.65
☐ 396	Steve Bilko	1.00	.50	.10
☐ 397	Don Blasingame	1.00	.50	.10
☐ 398	Mike Cuellar	1.50	.75	.15
☐ 399	Young Hill Stars	1.50	.75	.15
	Milt Pappas			
	Jack Fisher			
	Jerry Walker			
☐ 400	Rocky Colavito	3.00	1.50	.30
☐ 401	Bob Duliba	1.00	.50	.10
☐ 402	Dick Stuart	1.50	.75	.15
☐ 403	Ed Sadowski	1.00	.50	.10
☐ 404	Bob Rush	1.00	.50	.10
☐ 405	Bobby Richardson	3.00	1.50	.30
☐ 406	Billy Klaus	1.00	.50	.10
☐ 407	Gary Peters	1.50	.75	.15
	(face actually			
	J.C. Martin)			
☐ 408	Carl Furillo	2.50	1.25	.25
☐ 409	Ron Samford	1.00	.50	.10
☐ 410	Sam Jones	1.00	.50	.10
☐ 411	Ed Bailey	1.00	.50	.10
☐ 412	Bob Anderson	1.00	.50	.10
☐ 413	Athletics Team	2.50	.50	.10
☐ 414	Don Williams	1.00	.50	.10
☐ 415	Bob Cerv	1.00	.50	.10
☐ 416	Humberto Robinson	1.00	.50	.10
☐ 417	Chuck Cottier	1.50	.75	.15
☐ 418	Don Mossi	1.00	.50	.10
☐ 419	George Crowe	1.00	.50	.10
☐ 420	Ed Mathews	9.00	4.50	.90
☐ 421	Duke Maas	1.00	.50	.10
☐ 422	John Powers	1.00	.50	.10
☐ 423	Ed Fitzgerald	1.00	.50	.10
☐ 424	Pete Whisenant	1.00	.50	.10
☐ 425	John Podres	2.00	1.00	.20
☐ 426	Ron Jackson	1.00	.50	.10
☐ 427	Al Grunwald	1.00	.50	.10
☐ 428	Al Smith	1.00	.50	.10
☐ 429	AL Kings	2.00	1.00	.20
	Nellie Fox			
	Harvey Kuenn			
☐ 430	Art Ditmar	1.00	.50	.10
☐ 431	Andre Rodgers	1.00	.50	.10
☐ 432	Chuck Stobbs	1.00	.50	.10
☐ 433	Irv Noren	1.00	.50	.10
☐ 434	Brooks Lawrence	1.00	.50	.10
☐ 435	Gene Freese	1.00	.50	.10
☐ 436	Marv Throneberry	2.00	1.00	.20
☐ 437	Bob Friend	1.50	.75	.15
☐ 438	Jim Coker	1.00	.50	.10
☐ 439	Tom Brewer	1.00	.50	.10
☐ 440	Jim Lemon	1.00	.50	.10
☐ 441	Gary Bell	1.50	.75	.15
☐ 442	Joe Pignatano	1.50	.75	.15
☐ 443	Charley Maxwell	1.50	.75	.15
☐ 444	Jerry Kindall	1.50	.75	.15
☐ 445	Warren Spahn	14.00	7.00	1.40
☐ 446	Ellis Burton	1.50	.75	.15
☐ 447	Ray Moore	1.50	.75	.15
☐ 448	Jim Gentile	2.00	1.00	.20
☐ 449	Jim Brosnan	1.50	.75	.15
☐ 450	Orlando Cepeda	4.50	2.25	.45
☐ 451	Curt Simmons	2.00	1.00	.20
☐ 452	Ray Webster	1.50	.75	.15
☐ 453	Vern Law	2.50	1.25	.25
☐ 454	Hal Woodeshick	1.50	.75	.15
☐ 455	Baltimore Coaches	2.00	1.00	.20
	Eddie Robinson			
	Harry Brecheen			
	Luman Harris			
☐ 456	Red Sox Coaches	2.50	1.25	.25
	Rudy York			
	Billy Herman			
	Sal Maglie			
	Del Baker			
☐ 457	Cubs Coaches	2.00	1.00	.20
	Charlie Root			
	Lou Klein			
	Elvin Tappe			
☐ 458	White Sox Coaches	2.00	1.00	.20
	Johnny Cooney			
	Don Gutteridge			
	Tony Cuccinello			
	Ray Berres			
☐ 459	Reds Coaches	2.00	1.00	.20
	Reggie Otero			
	Cot Deal			
	Wally Moses			
☐ 460	Indians Coaches	2.50	1.25	.25
	Mel Harder			
	Jo-Jo White			
	Bob Lemon			
	Ralph (Red) Kress			
☐ 461	Tigers Coaches	2.50	1.25	.25
	Tom Ferrick			
	Luke Appling			
	Billy Hitchcock			
☐ 462	Athletics Coaches	2.00	1.00	.20
	Fred Fitzsimmons			
	Don Heffner			
	Walker Cooper			
☐ 463	Dodgers Coaches	2.50	1.25	.25
	Bobby Bragan			
	Pete Reiser			
	Joe Becker			
	Greg Mulleavy			
☐ 464	Braves Coaches	2.00	1.00	.20
	Bob Scheffing			
	Whitlow Wyatt			
	Andy Pafko			
	George Myatt			
☐ 465	Yankees Coaches	4.50	2.25	.45
	Bill Dickey			
	Ralph Houk			
	Frank Crosetti			
	Ed Lopat			
☐ 466	Phillies Coaches	2.00	1.00	.20
	Ken Silvestri			
	Dick Carter			
	Andy Cohen			
☐ 467	Pirates Coaches	2.00	1.00	.20
	Mickey Vernon			
	Frank Oceak			
	Sam Narron			
	Bill Burwell			
☐ 468	Cardinals Coaches	2.00	1.00	.20
	Johnny Keane			
	Howie Pollet			
	Ray Katt			
	Harry Walker			
☐ 469	Giants Coaches	2.00	1.00	.20
	Wes Westrum			
	Salty Parker			
	Bill Posedel			
☐ 470	Senators Coaches	2.00	1.00	.20

Bob Swift
Ellis Clary
Sam Mele

☐ 471	Ned Garver	1.50	.75	.15
☐ 472	Al Dark	2.00	1.00	.20
☐ 473	Al Cicotte	1.50	.75	.15
☐ 474	Haywood Sullivan	1.50	.75	.15
☐ 475	Don Drysdale	12.00	6.00	1.20
☐ 476	Lou Johnson	1.50	.75	.15
☐ 477	Don Ferrarese	1.50	.75	.15
☐ 478	Frank Torre	1.50	.75	.15
☐ 479	Georges Maranda	1.50	.75	.15
☐ 480	Yogi Berra	25.00	12.50	2.50
☐ 481	Wes Stock	1.50	.75	.15
☐ 482	Frank Bolling	1.50	.75	.15
☐ 483	Camilo Pascual	2.00	1.00	.20
☐ 484	Pirates Team	7.50	1.50	.30
☐ 485	Ken Boyer	3.00	1.50	.30
☐ 486	Bobby Del Greco	1.50	.75	.15
☐ 487	Tom Sturdivant	1.50	.75	.15
☐ 488	Norm Cash	3.00	1.50	.30
☐ 489	Steve Ridzik	1.50	.75	.15
☐ 490	Frank Robinson	15.00	7.50	1.50
☐ 491	Mel Roach	1.50	.75	.15
☐ 492	Larry Jackson	1.50	.75	.15
☐ 493	Duke Snider	25.00	12.50	2.50
☐ 494	Orioles Team	4.50	.80	.20
☐ 495	Sherm Lollar	2.00	1.00	.20
☐ 496	Bill Virdon	2.50	1.25	.25
☐ 497	John Tsitouris	1.50	.75	.15
☐ 498	Al Pilarcik	1.50	.75	.15
☐ 499	Johnny James	1.50	.75	.15
☐ 500	Johnny Temple	1.50	.75	.15
☐ 501	Bob Schmidt	1.50	.75	.15
☐ 502	Jim Bunning	4.50	2.25	.45
☐ 503	Don Lee	1.50	.75	.15
☐ 504	Seth Morehead	1.50	.75	.15
☐ 505	Ted Kluszewski	3.00	1.50	.30
☐ 506	Lee Walls	1.50	.75	.15
☐ 507	Dick Stigman	4.50	2.25	.45
☐ 508	Bill Consolo	4.50	2.25	.45
☐ 509	Tommy Davis	7.50	3.75	.75
☐ 510	Jerry Staley	4.50	2.25	.45
☐ 511	Ken Walters	4.50	2.25	.45
☐ 512	Joe Gibbon	4.50	2.25	.45
☐ 513	Cubs Team	12.00	2.00	.40
☐ 514	Steve Barber	6.00	3.00	.60
☐ 515	Stan Lopata	4.50	2.25	.45
☐ 516	Marty Kutyna	4.50	2.25	.45
☐ 517	Charlie James	4.50	2.25	.45
☐ 518	Tony Gonzales	4.50	2.25	.45
☐ 519	Ed Roebuck	4.50	2.25	.45
☐ 520	Don Buddin	4.50	2.25	.45
☐ 521	Mike Lee	4.50	2.25	.45
☐ 522	Ken Hunt	4.50	2.25	.45
☐ 523	Clay Dalrymple	4.50	2.25	.45
☐ 524	Bill Henry	4.50	2.25	.45
☐ 525	Marv Breeding	4.50	2.25	.45
☐ 526	Paul Giel	4.50	2.25	.45
☐ 527	Jose Valdivielso	4.50	2.25	.45
☐ 528	Ben Johnson	4.50	2.25	.45
☐ 529	Norm Sherry	6.00	3.00	.60
☐ 530	Mike McCormick	6.00	3.00	.60
☐ 531	Sandy Amoros	4.50	2.25	.45
☐ 532	Mike Garcia	6.00	3.00	.60
☐ 533	Lou Clinton	4.50	2.25	.45
☐ 534	Ken Mackenzie	4.50	2.25	.45
☐ 535	Whitey Lockman	4.50	2.25	.45
☐ 536	Wynn Hawkins	4.50	2.25	.45
☐ 537	Red Sox Team	12.00	2.00	.40
☐ 538	Frank Barnes	4.50	2.25	.45
☐ 539	Gene Baker	4.50	2.25	.45
☐ 540	Jerry Walker	4.50	2.25	.45
☐ 541	Tony Curry	4.50	2.25	.45
☐ 542	Ken Hamlin	4.50	2.25	.45
☐ 543	Elio Chacon	4.50	2.25	.45
☐ 544	Bill Monbouquette	4.50	2.25	.45
☐ 545	Carl Sawatski	4.50	2.25	.45
☐ 546	Hank Aguirre	4.50	2.25	.45
☐ 547	Bob Aspromonte	4.50	2.25	.45
☐ 548	Don Mincher	6.00	3.00	.60
☐ 549	John Buzhardt	4.50	2.25	.45
☐ 550	Jim Landis	4.50	2.25	.45
☐ 551	Ed Rakow	4.50	2.25	.45
☐ 552	Walt Bond	6.50	3.25	.65
☐ 553	Bill Skowron AS	24.00	12.00	2.40
☐ 554	Willie McCovey AS	7.50	3.75	.75
☐ 555	Nellie Fox AS	5.50	2.75	.55
☐ 556	Charlie Neal AS	5.50	2.75	.55
☐ 557	Frank Malzone AS	15.00	7.50	1.50
☐ 558	Eddie Mathews AS	10.00	5.00	1.00
☐ 559	Luis Aparicio AS	18.00	9.00	1.80
☐ 560	Ernie Banks AS	18.00	9.00	1.80
☐ 561	Al Kaline AS	18.00	9.00	1.80
☐ 562	Joe Cunningham AS	5.50	2.75	.55

☐ 563	Mickey Mantle AS	150.00	75.00	15.00
☐ 564	Willie Mays AS	45.00	22.50	4.50
☐ 565	Roger Maris AS	30.00	15.00	3.00
☐ 566	Hank Aaron AS	45.00	22.50	4.50
☐ 567	Sherm Lollar AS	5.50	2.75	.55
☐ 568	Del Crandall AS	5.50	2.75	.55
☐ 569	Camilo Pascual AS	5.50	2.75	.55
☐ 570	Don Drysdale AS	12.00	6.00	1.20
☐ 571	Billy Pierce AS	5.50	2.75	.55
☐ 572	Johnny Antonelli AS	10.00	3.00	.60

1961 Topps

ROGER MARIS
Outfield

The cards in this 587-card set measure 2 1/2" by 3 1/2". In 1961, Topps returned to the vertical obverse format. Introduced for the first time were "League Leaders" (41 to 50) and separate, numbered checklist cards. Two number 463's exist: the Braves team card carrying that number was meant to be number 426. There are three versions of the second series checklist card #98; the variations are distinguished by the color of the "CHECKLIST" headline on the front of the card, the color of the printing of the card number on the bottom of the reverse, and the presence of the copyright notice running vertically on the card back. There are two groups of managers (131-139 and 219-226) as well as separate series of World Series cards (306-313), Baseball Thrills (401 to 410), previous MVP's (AL 471-478 and NL 479-486) and Sporting News All-Stars (566 to 589). The usual last series scarcity (523 to 589) exists. The set actually totals 587 cards since numbers 587 and 588 were never issued.

	NRMT	VG-E	GOOD
COMPLETE SET	3500.00	1200.00	250.00
COMMON PLAYER (1-110)	.70	.35	.07
COMMON PLAYER (111-370)	.80	.40	.08
COMMON PLAYER (371-446)	1.00	.50	.10
COMMON PLAYER (447-522)	1.25	.60	.12
COMMON PLAYER (523-565)	12.00	6.00	1.20
COMMON PLAYER (566-589)	13.50	6.50	1.30

☐	1	Dick Groat	9.00	1.00	.20
☐	2	Roger Maris	35.00	10.00	2.00
☐	3	John Buzhardt	.70	.35	.07
☐	4	Lenny Green	.70	.35	.07
☐	5	John Romano	.70	.35	.07
☐	6	Ed Roebuck	.70	.35	.07
☐	7	White Sox Team	1.50	.75	.15
☐	8	Dick Williams	1.00	.50	.10
☐	9	Bob Purkey	.70	.35	.07
☐	10	Brooks Robinson	15.00	7.50	1.50
☐	11	Curt Simmons	1.00	.50	.10
☐	12	Moe Thacker	.70	.35	.07
☐	13	Chuck Cottier	.70	.35	.07
☐	14	Don Mossi	.70	.35	.07
☐	15	Willie Kirkland	.70	.35	.07
☐	16	Billy Muffett	.70	.35	.07
☐	17	Checklist 1	4.00	.50	.10
☐	18	Jim Grant	.70	.35	.07
☐	19	Cletis Boyer	1.25	.60	.12
☐	20	Robin Roberts	7.00	3.50	.70

☐ 21	Zorro Versalles	1.00	.50	.10
☐ 22	Clem Labine	1.00	.50	.10
☐ 23	Don Demeter	.70	.35	.07
☐ 24	Ken Johnson	.70	.35	.07
☐ 25	Reds' Heavy Artillery	2.50	1.25	.25
	Vada Pinson			
	Gus Bell			
	Frank Robinson			
☐ 26	Wes Stock ✓	.70	.35	.07
☐ 27	Jerry Kindall	.70	.35	.07
☐ 28	Hector Lopez	.70	.35	.07
☐ 29	Don Nottebart	.70	.35	.07
☐ 30	Nellie Fox	3.00	1.50	.30
☐ 31	Bob Schmidt	.70	.35	.07
☐ 32	Ray Sadecki	.70	.35	.07
☐ 33	Gary Geiger	.70	.35	.07
☐ 34	Wynn Hawkins	.70	.35	.07
☐ 35	Ron Santo	4.50	2.25	.45
☐ 36	Jack Kralick	.70	.35	.07
☐ 37	Charley Maxwell	.70	.35	.07
☐ 38	Bob Lillis	1.00	.50	.10
☐ 39	Leo Posada	.70	.35	.07
☐ 40	Bob Turley	1.25	.60	.12
☐ 41	NL Batting Leaders	2.00	1.00	.20
	Dick Groat			
	Norm Larker			
	Willie Mays			
	Roberto Clemente			
☐ 42	AL Batting Leaders	1.50	.75	.15
	Pete Runnels			
	Al Smith			
	Minnie Minoso			
	Bill Skowron			
☐ 43	NL Home Run Leaders	3.00	1.50	.30
	Ernie Banks			
	Hank Aaron			
	Ed Mathews			
	Ken Boyer			
☐ 44	AL Home Run Leaders	9.00	4.50	.90
	Mickey Mantle			
	Roger Maris			
	Jim Lemon			
	Rocky Colavito			
☐ 45	NL ERA Leaders	1.25	.60	.12
	Mike McCormick			
	Ernie Broglio			
	Don Drysdale			
	Bob Friend			
	Stan Williams			
☐ 46	AL ERA Leaders	1.25	.60	.12
	Frank Baumann			
	Jim Bunning			
	Art Ditmar			
	H. Brown			
☐ 47	NL Pitching Leaders	1.25	.60	.12
	Ernie Broglio			
	Warren Spahn			
	Vern Law			
	Lou Burdette			
☐ 48	AL Pitching Leaders	1.25	.60	.12
	Chuck Estrada			
	Jim Perry			
	Bud Daley			
	Art Ditmar			
	Frank Lary			
	Milt Pappas			
☐ 49	NL Strikeout Leaders	2.00	1.00	.20
	Don Drysdale			
	Sandy Koufax			
	Sam Jones			
	Ernie Broglio			
☐ 50	AL Strikeout Leaders	1.25	.60	.12
	Jim Bunning			
	Pedro Ramos			
	Early Wynn			
	Frank Lary			
☐ 51	Tigers Team	1.50	.75	.15
☐ 52	George Crowe	.70	.35	.07
☐ 53	Russ Nixon	.70	.35	.07
☐ 54	Earl Francis	.70	.35	.07
☐ 55	Jim Davenport	1.00	.50	.10
☐ 56	Russ Kemmerer	.70	.35	.07
☐ 57	Marv Throneberry	1.50	.75	.15
☐ 58	Joe Schaffernoth	.70	.35	.07
☐ 59	Jim Woods	.70	.35	.07
☐ 60	Woodie Held	.70	.35	.07
☐ 61	Ron Piche	.70	.35	.07
☐ 62	Al Pilarcik	.70	.35	.07
☐ 63	Jim Kaat	4.50	2.25	.45
☐ 64	Alex Grammas	.70	.35	.07
☐ 65	Ted Kluszewski	2.00	1.00	.20
☐ 66	Billy Henry	.70	.35	.07
☐ 67	Ossie Virgil	.70	.35	.07
☐ 68	Deron Johnson	1.00	.50	.10
☐ 69	Earl Wilson	.70	.35	.07
☐ 70	Bill Virdon	1.25	.60	.12
☐ 71	Jerry Adair	.70	.35	.07
☐ 72	Stu Miller	.70	.35	.07
☐ 73	Al Spangler	.70	.35	.07
☐ 74	Joe Pignatano	.70	.35	.07
☐ 75	Lindy Shows Larry	1.00	.50	.10
	Lindy McDaniel			
	Larry Jackson			
☐ 76	Harry Anderson	.70	.35	.07
☐ 77	Dick Stigman	.70	.35	.07
☐ 78	Lee Walls	.70	.35	.07
☐ 79	Joe Ginsberg	.70	.35	.07
☐ 80	Harmon Killebrew	8.50	4.25	.85
☐ 81	Tracy Stallard	.70	.35	.07
☐ 82	Joe Christopher	.70	.35	.07
☐ 83	Bob Bruce	.70	.35	.07
☐ 84	Lee Maye	.70	.35	.07
☐ 85	Jerry Walker	.70	.35	.07
☐ 86	Dodgers Team	2.50	1.25	.25
☐ 87	Joe Amalfitano	.70	.35	.07
☐ 88	Richie Ashburn	3.00	1.50	.30
☐ 89	Billy Martin	3.00	1.50	.30
☐ 90	Jerry Staley	.70	.35	.07
☐ 91	Walt Moryn	.70	.35	.07
☐ 92	Hal Naragon	.70	.35	.07
☐ 93	Tony Gonzalez	.70	.35	.07
☐ 94	John Kucks	.70	.35	.07
☐ 95	Norm Cash	2.00	1.00	.20
☐ 96	Bill O'Dell	.70	.35	.07
☐ 97	Jerry Lynch	.70	.35	.07
☐ 98A	Checklist 2	4.00	.50	.10
	(red "Checklist",			
	98 black on white)			
☐ 98B	Checklist 2	4.00	.50	.10
	(yellow "Checklist",			
	98 black on white)			
☐ 98C	Checklist 2	4.00	.50	.10
	(yellow "Checklist",			
	98 white on black,			
	no copyright)			
☐ 99	Don Buddin	.70	.35	.07
☐ 100	Harvey Haddix	1.25	.60	.12
☐ 101	Bubba Phillips	.70	.35	.07
☐ 102	Gene Stephens	.70	.35	.07
☐ 103	Ruben Amaro	.70	.35	.07
☐ 104	John Blanchard	1.00	.50	.10
☐ 105	Carl Willey	.70	.35	.07
☐ 106	Whitey Herzog	1.50	.75	.15
☐ 107	Seth Morehead	.70	.35	.07
☐ 108	Dan Dobbek	.70	.35	.07
☐ 109	John Podres ✓	2.00	1.00	.2
☐ 110	Vada Pinson	2.00	1.00	.20
☐ 111	Jack Meyer	.80	.40	.08
☐ 112	Chico Fernandez	.80	.40	.08
☐ 113	Mike Fornieles	.80	.40	.08
☐ 114	Hobie Landrith	.80	.40	.08
☐ 115	Johnny Antonelli	1.00	.50	.10
☐ 116	Joe DeMaestri	.80	.40	.08
☐ 117	Dale Long	.80	.40	.08
☐ 118	Chris Cannizzaro	.80	.40	.08
☐ 119	A's Big Armor	1.00	.50	.10
	Norm Siebern			
	Hank Bauer			
	Jerry Lumpe			
☐ 120	Ed Mathews	8.00	4.00	.80
☐ 121	Eli Grba	.80	.40	.08
☐ 122	Cubs Team	1.50	.75	.15
☐ 123	Billy Gardner	.80	.40	.08
☐ 124	J.C. Martin	.80	.40	.08
☐ 125	Steve Barber	.80	.40	.08
☐ 126	Dick Stuart	1.00	.50	.10
☐ 127	Ron Kline	.80	.40	.08
☐ 128	Rip Repulski	.80	.40	.08
☐ 129	Ed Hobaugh	.80	.40	.08
☐ 130	Norm Larker	.80	.40	.08
☐ 131	Paul Richards MG	1.00	.50	.10
☐ 132	Al Lopez MG	2.50	1.25	.25
☐ 133	Ralph Houk MG	2.00	1.00	.20
☐ 134	Mickey Vernon MG	1.25	.60	.12
☐ 135	Fred Hutchinson MG	1.25	.60	.12
☐ 136	Walt Alston MG	3.00	1.50	.30
☐ 137	Chuck Dressen MG	1.00	.50	.10
☐ 138	Danny Murtaugh MG	1.00	.50	.10
☐ 139	Solly Hemus MG	1.00	.50	.10
☐ 140	Gus Triandos ✓	1.00	.50	.10
☐ 141	Billy Williams	40.00	20.00	4.00
☐ 142	Luis Arroyo	1.00	.50	.10
☐ 143	Russ Snyder	.80	.40	.08
☐ 144	Jim Coker	.80	.40	.08
☐ 145	Bob Buhl	.80	.40	.08
☐ 146	Marty Keough	.80	.40	.08
☐ 147	Ed Rakow	.80	.40	.08
☐ 148	Julian Javier	.80	.40	.08
☐ 149	Bob Oldis	.80	.40	.08
☐ 150	Willie Mays	50.00	25.00	5.00

□ 151	Jim Donohue	.80	.40	.08
□ 152	Earl Torgeson	.80	.40	.08
□ 153	Don Lee	.80	.40	.08
□ 154	Bobby Del Greco	.80	.40	.08
□ 155	John Temple	.80	.40	.08
□ 156	Ken Hunt	.80	.40	.08
□ 157	Cal McLish	.80	.40	.08
□ 158	Pete Daley	.80	.40	.08
□ 159	Orioles Team	1.50	.75	.15
□ 160	Whitey Ford	15.00	7.50	1.50
□ 161	Sherman Jones (photo actually Eddie Fisher)	.80	.40	.08
□ 162	Jay Hook	.80	.40	.08
□ 163	Ed Sadowski	.80	.40	.08
□ 164	Felix Mantilla	.80	.40	.08
□ 165	Gino Cimoli	.80	.40	.08
□ 166	Danny Kravitz	.80	.40	.08
□ 167	Giants Team	1.50	.75	.15
□ 168	Tommy Davis	2.00	1.00	.20
□ 169	Don Elston	.80	.40	.08
□ 170	Al Smith	.80	.40	.08
□ 171	Paul Foytack	.80	.40	.08
□ 172	Don Dillard	.80	.40	.08
□ 173	Beantown Bombers Frank Malzone Vic Wertz Jackie Jensen	1.00	.50	.10
□ 174	Ray Semproch	.80	.40	.08
□ 175	Gene Freese	.80	.40	.08
□ 176	Ken Aspromonte	.80	.40	.08
□ 177	Don Larsen	1.00	.50	.10
□ 178	Bob Nieman	.80	.40	.08
□ 179	Joe Koppe	.80	.40	.08
□ 180	Bobby Richardson	2.50	1.25	.25
□ 181	Fred Green	.80	.40	.08
□ 182	Dave Nicholson	.80	.40	.08
□ 183	Andre Rodgers	.80	.40	.08
□ 184	Steve Bilko	1.25	.60	.12
□ 185	Herb Score	.80	.40	.08
□ 186	Elmer Valo	.80	.40	.08
□ 187	Billy Klaus	.80	.40	.08
□ 188	Jim Marshall	.80	.40	.08
□ 189	Checklist 3	4.00	.50	.10
□ 190	Stan Williams	.80	.40	.08
□ 191	Mike De La Hoz	.80	.40	.08
□ 192	Dick Brown	.80	.40	.08
□ 193	Gene Conley	.80	.40	.08
□ 194	Gordy Coleman	.80	.40	.08
□ 195	Jerry Casale	.80	.40	.08
□ 196	Ed Bouchee	.80	.40	.08
□ 197	Dick Hall	.80	.40	.08
□ 198	Carl Sawatski	.80	.40	.08
□ 199	Bob Boyd	.80	.40	.08
□ 200	Warren Spahn	10.00	5.00	1.00
□ 201	Pete Whisenant	.80	.40	.08
□ 202	Al Neiger	.80	.40	.08
□ 203	Eddie Bressoud	.80	.40	.08
□ 204	Bob Skinner	.80	.40	.08
□ 205	Bill Pierce	1.25	.60	.12
□ 206	Gene Green	.80	.40	.08
□ 207	Dodger Southpaws Sandy Koufax Johnny Podres	5.00	2.50	.50
□ 208	Larry Osborne	.80	.40	.08
□ 209	Ken McBride	.80	.40	.08
□ 210	Pete Runnels	1.00	.50	.10
□ 211	Bob Gibson	8.50	4.25	.85
□ 212	Haywood Sullivan	.80	.40	.08
□ 213	Billy Stafford	1.00	.50	.10
□ 214	Danny Murphy	.80	.40	.08
□ 215	Gus Bell	1.00	.50	.10
□ 216	Ted Bowsfield	.80	.40	.08
□ 217	Mel Roach	.80	.40	.08
□ 218	Hal Brown	.80	.40	.08
□ 219	Gene Mauch MG	1.25	.60	.12
□ 220	Al Dark MG	1.25	.60	.12
□ 221	Mike Higgins MG	1.00	.50	.10
□ 222	Jimmie Dykes MG	1.00	.50	.10
□ 223	Bob Scheffing MG	1.00	.50	.10
□ 224	Joe Gordon MG	1.00	.50	.10
□ 225	Bill Rigney MG	1.00	.50	.10
□ 226	Harry Lavagetto MG	.80	.40	.08
□ 227	Juan Pizarro	.80	.40	.08
□ 228	Yankees Team	9.00	4.50	.90
□ 229	Rudy Hernandez	.80	.40	.08
□ 230	Don Hoak	.80	.40	.08
□ 231	Dick Drott	.80	.40	.08
□ 232	Bill White	1.25	.60	.12
□ 233	Joe Jay	.80	.40	.08
□ 234	Ted Lepcio	.80	.40	.08
□ 235	Camilo Pascual	1.00	.50	.10
□ 236	Don Gile	.80	.40	.08
□ 237	Billy Loes	.80	.40	.08
□ 238	Jim Gilliam	2.50	1.25	.25
□ 239	Dave Sisler	.80	.40	.08
□ 240	Ron Hansen	.80	.40	.08
□ 241	Al Cicotte	.80	.40	.08
□ 242	Hal Smith	.80	.40	.08
□ 243	Frank Lary	1.00	.50	.10
□ 244	Chico Cardenas	.80	.40	.08
□ 245	Joe Adcock	1.00	.50	.10
□ 246	Bob Davis	.80	.40	.08
□ 247	Billy Goodman	1.00	.50	.10
□ 248	Ed Keegan	.80	.40	.08
□ 249	Reds Team	2.00	1.00	.20
□ 250	Buc Hill Aces Vern Law Roy Face	1.00	.50	.10
□ 251	Bill Bruton	.80	.40	.08
□ 252	Bill Short	.80	.40	.08
□ 253	Sammy Taylor	.80	.40	.08
□ 254	Ted Sadowski	.80	.40	.08
□ 255	Vic Power	.80	.40	.08
□ 256	Billy Hoeft	.80	.40	.08
□ 257	Carroll Hardy	.80	.40	.08
□ 258	Jack Sanford	1.00	.50	.10
□ 259	John Schaive	.80	.40	.08
□ 260	Don Drysdale	8.50	4.25	.85
□ 261	Charlie Lau	1.00	.50	.10
□ 262	Tony Curry	.80	.40	.08
□ 263	Ken Hamlin	.80	.40	.08
□ 264	Glen Hobbie	.80	.40	.08
□ 265	Tony Kubek	4.00	2.00	.40
□ 266	Lindy McDaniel	1.00	.50	.10
□ 267	Norm Siebern	.80	.40	.08
□ 268	Ike Delock	.80	.40	.08
□ 269	Harry Chiti	.80	.40	.08
□ 270	Bob Friend	1.00	.50	.10
□ 271	Jim Landis	.80	.40	.08
□ 272	Tom Morgan	.80	.40	.08
□ 273	Checklist 4	4.00	.50	.10
□ 274	Gary Bell	.80	.40	.08
□ 275	Gene Woodling	1.00	.50	.10
□ 276	Ray Rippelmeyer	.80	.40	.08
□ 277	Hank Foiles	.80	.40	.08
□ 278	Don McMahon	.80	.40	.08
□ 279	Jose Pagan	.80	.40	.08
□ 280	Frank Howard	2.00	1.00	.20
□ 281	Frank Sullivan	.80	.40	.08
□ 282	Faye Throneberry	.80	.40	.08
□ 283	Bob Anderson	.80	.40	.08
□ 284	Dick Gernert	.80	.40	.08
□ 285	Sherm Lollar	1.00	.50	.10
□ 286	George Witt	.80	.40	.08
□ 287	Carl Yastrzemski	85.00	42.50	8.50
□ 288	Albie Pearson	.80	.40	.08
□ 289	Ray Moore	.80	.40	.08
□ 290	Stan Musial	35.00	17.50	3.50
□ 291	Tex Clevenger	.80	.40	.08
□ 292	Jim Baumer	.80	.40	.08
□ 293	Tom Sturdivant	.80	.40	.08
□ 294	Don Blasingame	.80	.40	.08
□ 295	Milt Pappas	1.00	.50	.10
□ 296	Wes Covington	1.00	.50	.10
□ 297	Athletics Team	1.50	.75	.15
□ 298	Jim Golden	.80	.40	.08
□ 299	Clay Dalrymple	.80	.40	.08
□ 300	Mickey Mantle	225.00	110.00	22.00
□ 301	Chet Nichols	.80	.40	.08
□ 302	Al Heist	.80	.40	.08
□ 303	Gary Peters	1.00	.50	.10
□ 304	Rocky Nelson	.80	.40	.08
□ 305	Mike McCormick	1.00	.50	.10
□ 306	World Series Game 1 Virdon Saves Game	2.00	1.00	.20
□ 307	World Series Game 2 Mantle 2 Homers	15.00	7.50	1.50
□ 308	World Series Game 3 Richardson is Hero	2.50	1.25	.25
□ 309	World Series Game 4 Cimoli Safe	2.00	1.00	.20
□ 310	World Series Game 5 Face Saves the Day	2.50	1.25	.25
□ 311	World Series Game 6 Ford Second Shutout	3.00	1.50	.30
□ 312	World Series Game 7 Mazeroski's Homer	3.00	1.50	.30
□ 313	World Series Summary Pirates Celebrate	2.00	1.00	.20
□ 314	Bob Miller	.80	.40	.08
□ 315	Earl Battey	.80	.40	.08
□ 316	Bobby Gene Smith	.80	.40	.08
□ 317	Jim Brewer	.80	.40	.08
□ 318	Danny O'Connell	.80	.40	.08
□ 319	Valmy Thomas	.80	.40	.08
□ 320	Lou Burdette	2.00	1.00	.20
□ 321	Marv Breeding	.80	.40	.08
□ 322	Bill Kunkel	.80	.40	.08
□ 323	Sammy Esposito	.80	.40	.08

☐ 324	Hank Aguirre	.80	.40	.08
☐ 325	Wally Moon	1.00	.50	.10
☐ 326	Dave Hillman	.80	.40	.08
☐ 327	Matty Alou	2.00	1.00	.20
☐ 328	Jim O'Toole	1.00	.50	.10
☐ 329	Julio Becquer	.80	.40	.08
☐ 330	Rocky Colavito	2.50	1.25	.25
☐ 331	Ned Garver	.80	.40	.08
☐ 332	Dutch Dotterer	1.00	.50	.10
	(photo actually Tommy Dotterer, Dutch's brother)			
☐ 333	Fritz Brickell	.80	.40	.08
☐ 334	Walt Bond	.80	.40	.08
☐ 335	Frank Bolling	.80	.40	.08
☐ 336	Don Mincher	1.00	.50	.10
☐ 337	Al's Aces	2.00	1.00	.20
	Early Wynn Al Lopez Herb Score			
☐ 338	Don Landrum	.80	.40	.08
☐ 339	Gene Baker	.80	.40	.08
☐ 340	Vic Wertz	.80	.40	.08
☐ 341	Jim Owens	.80	.40	.08
☐ 342	Clint Courtney	.80	.40	.08
☐ 343	Earl Robinson	.80	.40	.08
☐ 344	Sandy Koufax	30.00	15.00	3.00
☐ 345	Jim Piersall	1.25	.60	.12
☐ 346	Howie Nunn	.80	.40	.08
☐ 347	Cardinals Team	1.50	.75	.15
☐ 348	Steve Boros	1.00	.50	.10
☐ 349	Danny McDevitt	.80	.40	.08
☐ 350	Ernie Banks	11.00	5.50	1.10
☐ 351	Jim King	.80	.40	.08
☐ 352	Bob Shaw	.80	.40	.08
☐ 353	Howie Bedell	.80	.40	.08
☐ 354	Billy Harrell	.80	.40	.08
☐ 355	Bob Allison	1.00	.50	.10
☐ 356	Ryne Duren	1.00	.50	.10
☐ 357	Daryl Spencer	.80	.40	.08
☐ 358	Earl Averill	.80	.40	.08
☐ 359	Dallas Green	1.00	.50	.10
☐ 360	Frank Robinson	15.00	7.50	1.50
☐ 361A	Checklist 5	4.00	.50	.10
	(no ad on back)			
☐ 361B	Checklist 5	8.00	1.00	.20
	(Special Feature ad on back)			
☐ 362	Frank Funk	.80	.40	.08
☐ 363	John Roseboro	1.00	.50	.10
☐ 364	Moe Drabowsky	.80	.40	.08
☐ 365	Jerry Lumpe	.80	.40	.08
☐ 366	Eddie Fisher	.80	.40	.08
☐ 367	Jim Rivera	.80	.40	.08
☐ 368	Bennie Daniels	.80	.40	.08
☐ 369	Dave Philley	.80	.40	.08
☐ 370	Roy Face	1.50	.75	.15
☐ 371	Bill Skowron	3.50	1.75	.35
☐ 372	Bob Hendley	1.00	.50	.10
☐ 373	Red Sox Team	2.00	1.00	.20
☐ 374	Paul Giel	1.00	.50	.10
☐ 375	Ken Boyer	3.00	1.50	.30
☐ 376	Mike Roarke	1.50	.75	.15
☐ 377	Ruben Gomez	1.00	.50	.10
☐ 378	Wally Post	1.00	.50	.10
☐ 379	Bobby Shantz	2.00	1.00	.20
☐ 380	Minnie Minoso	2.50	1.25	.25
☐ 381	Dave Wickersham	1.00	.50	.10
☐ 382	Frank Thomas	1.00	.50	.10
☐ 383	Frisco First Liners	1.50	.75	.15
	Mike McCormick Jack Sanford Billy O'Dell			
☐ 384	Chuck Essegian	1.00	.50	.10
☐ 385	Jim Perry	1.50	.75	.15
☐ 386	Joe Hicks	1.00	.50	.10
☐ 387	Duke Maas	1.00	.50	.10
☐ 388	Bob Clemente	30.00	15.00	3.00
☐ 389	Ralph Terry	1.50	.75	.15
☐ 390	Del Crandall	1.50	.75	.15
☐ 391	Winston Brown	1.00	.50	.10
☐ 392	Reno Bertoia	1.00	.50	.10
☐ 393	Batter Bafflers	1.00	.50	.10
	Don Cardwell Glen Hobbie			
☐ 394	Ken Walters	1.00	.50	.10
☐ 395	Chuck Estrada	1.50	.75	.15
☐ 396	Bob Aspromonte	1.00	.50	.10
☐ 397	Hal Woodeshick	1.00	.50	.10
☐ 398	Hank Bauer	1.50	.75	.15
☐ 399	Cliff Cook	1.00	.50	.10
☐ 400	Vern Law	1.50	.75	.15
☐ 401	Ruth 60th Homer	10.00	5.00	1.00
☐ 402	Perfect Game (Larsen)	3.50	1.75	.35
☐ 403	26 Inning Tie	1.50	.75	.15
☐ 404	Hornsby .424 Average	2.25	1.10	.22
☐ 405	Gehrig's Streak	6.50	3.25	.65
☐ 406	Mantle 565 Ft. Homer	15.00	7.50	1.50
☐ 407	Chesbro Wins 41	1.50	.75	.15
☐ 408	Mathewson Fans 267	2.50	1.25	.25
☐ 409	Johnson Shutouts	2.50	1.25	.25
☐ 410	Haddix 12 Perfect Innings	1.50	.75	.15
☐ 411	Tony Taylor	1.00	.50	.10
☐ 412	Larry Sherry	1.50	.75	.15
☐ 413	Eddie Yost	1.00	.50	.10
☐ 414	Dick Donovan	1.00	.50	.10
☐ 415	Hank Aaron	60.00	30.00	6.00
☐ 416	Dick Howser	6.00	3.00	.60
☐ 417	Juan Marichal	60.00	30.00	6.00
☐ 418	Ed Bailey	1.00	.50	.10
☐ 419	Tom Borland	1.00	.50	.10
☐ 420	Ernie Broglio	1.50	.75	.15
☐ 421	Ty Cline	1.00	.50	.10
☐ 422	Bud Daley	1.00	.50	.10
☐ 423	Charlie Neal	1.50	.75	.15
☐ 424	Turk Lown	1.00	.50	.10
☐ 425	Yogi Berra	25.00	12.50	2.50
☐ 426	Braves Team	5.00	2.50	.50
	(back numbered 463)			
☐ 427	Dick Ellsworth	1.50	.75	.15
☐ 428	Ray Barker	1.00	.50	.10
☐ 429	Al Kaline	20.00	10.00	2.00
☐ 430	Bill Mazeroski	3.50	1.75	.35
☐ 431	Chuck Stobbs	1.00	.50	.10
☐ 432	Coot Veal	1.00	.50	.10
☐ 433	Art Mahaffey	1.00	.50	.10
☐ 434	Tom Brewer	1.00	.50	.10
☐ 435	Orlando Cepeda	4.00	2.00	.40
☐ 436	Jim Maloney	2.50	1.25	.25
☐ 437	Checklist 6	5.00	1.00	.20
☐ 438	Curt Flood	2.00	1.00	.20
☐ 439	Phil Regan	1.50	.75	.15
☐ 440	Luis Aparicio	7.00	3.50	.70
☐ 441	Dick Bertell	1.00	.50	.10
☐ 442	Gordon Jones	1.00	.50	.10
☐ 443	Duke Snider	20.00	10.00	2.00
☐ 444	Joe Nuxhall	1.50	.75	.15
☐ 445	Frank Malzone	1.50	.75	.15
☐ 446	Bob Taylor	1.00	.50	.10
☐ 447	Harry Bright	1.25	.60	.12
☐ 448	Del Rice	1.25	.60	.12
☐ 449	Bob Bolin	1.25	.60	.12
☐ 450	Jim Lemon	1.25	.60	.12
☐ 451	Power for Ernie	1.50	.75	.15
	Daryl Spencer Bill White Ernie Broglio			
☐ 452	Bob Allen	1.25	.60	.12
☐ 453	Dick Schofield	1.25	.60	.12
☐ 454	Pumpsie Green	1.25	.60	.12
☐ 455	Early Wynn	6.50	3.25	.65
☐ 456	Hal Bevan	1.25	.60	.12
☐ 457	John James	1.25	.60	.12
☐ 458	Willie Tasby	1.25	.60	.12
☐ 459	Terry Fox	1.25	.60	.12
☐ 460	Gil Hodges	8.00	4.00	.80
☐ 461	Smoky Burgess	1.50	.75	.15
☐ 462	Lou Klimchock	1.25	.60	.12
☐ 463	Jack Fisher	1.50	.75	.15
	(See also 426)			
☐ 464	Leroy Thomas	1.25	.60	.12
☐ 465	Roy McMillan	1.25	.60	.12
☐ 466	Ron Moeller	1.25	.60	.12
☐ 467	Indians Team	1.50	.75	.15
☐ 468	John Callison	1.50	.75	.15
☐ 469	Ralph Lumenti	1.25	.60	.12
☐ 470	Roy Sievers	1.50	.75	.15
☐ 471	Phil Rizzuto MVP	8.00	4.00	.80
☐ 472	Yogi Berra MVP	15.00	7.50	1.50
☐ 473	Bob Shantz MVP	1.50	.75	.15
☐ 474	Al Rosen MVP	1.50	.75	.15
☐ 475	Mickey Mantle MVP	50.00	25.00	5.00
☐ 476	Jackie Jensen MVP	1.50	.75	.15
☐ 477	Nellie Fox MVP	2.00	1.00	.20
☐ 478	Roger Maris MVP	15.00	7.50	1.50
☐ 479	Jim Konstanty MVP	1.50	.75	.15
☐ 480	Roy Campanella MVP	15.00	7.50	1.50
☐ 481	Hank Sauer MVP	1.50	.75	.15
☐ 482	Willie Mays MVP	15.00	7.50	1.50
☐ 483	Don Newcombe MVP	1.50	.75	.15
☐ 484	Hank Aaron MVP	15.00	7.50	1.50
☐ 485	Ernie Banks MVP	8.00	4.00	.80
☐ 486	Dick Groat MVP	1.50	.75	.15
☐ 487	Gene Oliver	1.25	.60	.12
☐ 488	Joe McClain	1.25	.60	.12
☐ 489	Walt Dropo	1.25	.60	.12
☐ 490	Jim Bunning	3.50	1.75	.35
☐ 491	Phillies Team	2.00	1.00	.20
☐ 492	Ron Fairly	1.50	.75	.15

☐ 493	Don Zimmer	2.00	1.00	.20
☐ 494	Tom Cheney	1.25	.60	.12
☐ 495	Elston Howard	3.00	1.50	.30
☐ 496	Ken Mackenzie	1.25	.60	.12
☐ 497	Willie Jones	1.25	.60	.12
☐ 498	Ray Herbert	1.25	.60	.12
☐ 499	Chuck Schilling	1.25	.60	.12
☐ 500	Harvey Kuenn	2.00	1.00	.20
☐ 501	John DeMerit	1.25	.60	.12
☐ 502	Clarence Coleman	1.25	.60	.12
☐ 503	Tito Francona	1.25	.60	.12
☐ 504	Billy Consolo	1.25	.60	.12
☐ 505	Red Schoendienst	2.00	1.00	.20
☐ 506	Willie Davis	3.50	1.75	.35
☐ 507	Pete Burnside	1.25	.60	.12
☐ 508	Rocky Bridges	1.25	.60	.12
☐ 509	Camilo Carreon	1.25	.60	.12
☐ 510	Art Ditmar	1.25	.60	.12
☐ 511	Joe Morgan	1.25	.60	.12
☐ 512	Bob Will	1.25	.60	.12
☐ 513	Jim Brosnan	1.25	.60	.12
☐ 514	Jake Wood	1.25	.60	.12
☐ 515	Jackie Brandt	1.25	.60	.12
☐ 516	Checklist 7	6.00	1.25	.20
☐ 517	Willie McCovey	27.00	13.50	2.70
☐ 518	Andy Carey	1.25	.60	.12
☐ 519	Jim Pagliaroni	1.25	.60	.12
☐ 520	Joe Cunningham	1.25	.60	.12
☐ 521	Brother Battery	1.50	.75	.15
	Norm Sherry			
	Larry Sherry			
☐ 522	Dick Farrell	1.25	.60	.12
☐ 523	Joe Gibbon	12.00	6.00	1.20
☐ 524	John Logan	13.50	6.00	1.20
☐ 525	Ron Perranoski	13.50	6.00	1.20
☐ 526	R.C. Stevens	12.00	6.00	1.20
☐ 527	Gene Leek	12.00	6.00	1.20
☐ 528	Pedro Ramos	12.00	6.00	1.20
☐ 529	Bob Roselli	12.00	6.00	1.20
☐ 530	Bob Malkmus	12.00	6.00	1.20
☐ 531	Jim Coates	12.00	6.00	1.20
☐ 532	Bob Hale	12.00	6.00	1.20
☐ 533	Jack Curtis	12.00	6.00	1.20
☐ 534	Eddie Kasko	12.00	6.00	1.20
☐ 535	Larry Jackson	12.00	6.00	1.20
☐ 536	Bill Tuttle	12.00	6.00	1.20
☐ 537	Bobby Locke	12.00	6.00	1.20
☐ 538	Chuck Hiller	12.00	6.00	1.20
☐ 539	John Klippstein	12.00	6.00	1.20
☐ 540	Jackie Jensen	18.00	9.00	1.80
☐ 541	Roland Sheldon	12.00	6.00	1.20
☐ 542	Minnesota Twins	21.00	10.50	2.10
	Team Card			
☐ 543	Roger Craig	18.00	9.00	1.80
☐ 544	George Thomas	12.00	6.00	1.20
☐ 545	Hoyt Wilhelm	40.00	20.00	4.00
☐ 546	Marty Kutyna	12.00	6.00	1.20
☐ 547	Leon Wagner	12.00	6.00	1.20
☐ 548	Ted Wills	12.00	6.00	1.20
☐ 549	Hal R. Smith	12.00	6.00	1.20
☐ 550	Frank Baumann	12.00	6.00	1.20
☐ 551	George Altman	12.00	6.00	1.20
☐ 552	Jim Archer	12.00	6.00	1.20
☐ 553	Bill Fischer	12.00	6.00	1.20
☐ 554	Pirates Team	18.00	9.00	1.80
☐ 555	Sam Jones	12.00	6.00	1.20
☐ 556	Ken R. Hunt	12.00	6.00	1.20
☐ 557	Jose Valdivielso	12.00	6.00	1.20
☐ 558	Don Ferrarese	12.00	6.00	1.20
☐ 559	Jim Gentile	13.50	6.00	1.20
☐ 560	Barry Latman	12.00	6.00	1.20
☐ 561	Charley James	12.00	6.00	1.20
☐ 562	Bill Monbouquette	12.00	6.00	1.20
☐ 563	Bob Cerv	13.50	6.00	1.20
☐ 564	Don Cardwell	12.00	6.00	1.20
☐ 565	Felipe Alou	15.00	7.50	1.50
☐ 566	Paul Richards MG AS	13.50	6.00	1.20
☐ 567	Danny Murtaugh MG AS	13.50	6.00	1.20
☐ 568	Bill Skowron AS	15.00	7.50	1.50
☐ 569	Frank Herrera AS	13.50	6.00	1.20
☐ 570	Nellie Fox AS	18.00	9.00	1.80
☐ 571	Bill Mazeroski AS	15.00	7.50	1.50
☐ 572	Brooks Robinson AS	50.00	25.00	5.00
☐ 573	Ken Boyer AS	15.00	7.50	1.50
☐ 574	Luis Aparicio AS	30.00	15.00	3.00
☐ 575	Ernie Banks AS	50.00	25.00	5.00
☐ 576	Roger Maris AS	60.00	30.00	6.00
☐ 577	Hank Aaron AS	100.00	50.00	10.00
☐ 578	Mickey Mantle AS	250.00	125.00	25.00
☐ 579	Willie Mays AS	100.00	50.00	10.00
☐ 580	Al Kaline AS	50.00	25.00	5.00
☐ 581	Frank Robinson AS	50.00	25.00	5.00
☐ 582	Earl Battey AS	13.50	6.00	1.20
☐ 583	Del Crandall AS	13.50	6.00	1.20
☐ 584	Jim Perry AS	13.50	6.00	1.20

☐ 585	Bob Friend AS	13.50	6.00	1.20
☐ 586	Whitey Ford AS	50.00	25.00	5.00
☐ 587	Does not exist	0.00	.00	.00
☐ 588	Does not exist	0.00	.00	.00
☐ 589	Warren Spahn AS	65.00	25.00	5.00

1962 Topps

The cards in this 598-card set measure 2 1/2" by 3 1/2". The 1962 Topps set contains a mini-series spotlighting Babe Ruth (135 to 144). Other subsets in the set include League Leaders (51-60), World Series cards (232-237), In Action cards (311-319), NL All Stars (390-399), AL All Stars (466-475), and Rookie Prospects (591-598). The second series had two distinct printings which are distinguishable by numerous color and pose variations. Card number 139 exists as A: Babe Ruth Special card, B: Hal Reniff with arms over head, or C: Hal Reniff in the same pose as card number 159. In addition, two poses exist for players depicted on card numbers 129, 132, 134, 147, 174, 176, and 190. The high number series, 523 to 598, is somewhat more difficult to obtain than other cards in the set. The set price listed does not include the pose variations (see checklist below for individual values).

			NRMT	VG-E	GOOD
COMPLETE SET			2800.00	1000.00	200.00
COMMON PLAYER (1-109)			.70	.35	.07
COMMON PLAYER (110-196)			.75	.35	.07
COMMON PLAYER (197-283)			.80	.40	.08
COMMON PLAYER (284-370)			.85	.40	.08
COMMON PLAYER (371-446)			1.25	.60	.12
COMMON PLAYER (447-522)			1.50	.75	.15
COMMON PLAYER (523-590)			5.00	2.50	.50
COMMON PLAYER (591-598)			7.50	3.75	.75
☐	1	Roger Maris	100.00	15.00	3.00
☐	2	Jim Brosnan	.70	.35	.07
☐	3	Pete Runnels	.70	.35	.07
☐	4	John DeMerit	.70	.35	.07
☐	5	Sandy Koufax	30.00	15.00	3.00
☐	6	Marv Breeding	.70	.35	.07
☐	7	Frank Thomas	.70	.35	.07
☐	8	Ray Herbert	.70	.35	.07
☐	9	Jim Davenport	.70	.35	.07
☐	10	Bob Clemente	30.00	15.00	3.00
☐	11	Tom Morgan	.70	.35	.07
☐	12	Harry Craft MG	.70	.35	.07
☐	13	Dick Howser	1.50	.75	.15
☐	14	Bill White	1.25	.60	.12
☐	15	Dick Donovan	.70	.35	.07
☐	16	Darrell Johnson	.70	.35	.07
☐	17	John Callison	1.00	.50	.10
☐	18	Managers' Dream	60.00	30.00	6.00
		Mickey Mantle			
		Willie Mays			
☐	19	Ray Washburn	.70	.35	.07
☐	20	Rocky Colavito	2.00	1.00	.20
☐	21	Jim Kaat	2.50	1.25	.25
☐	22A	Checklist 1 COR	3.50	.70	.10
☐	22B	Checklist 1 ERR	4.50	.80	.10
		(121-176 on back)			
☐	23	Norm Larker	.70	.35	.07

24	Tigers Team	1.50	.75	.15
25	Ernie Banks	9.00	4.50	.90
26	Chris Cannizzaro	.70	.35	.07
27	Chuck Cottier	.70	.35	.07
28	Minnie Minoso	2.00	1.00	.20
29	Casey Stengel MG	6.50	3.25	.65
30	Ed Mathews	7.00	3.50	.70
31	Tom Tresh	4.50	2.25	.45
32	John Roseboro	1.00	.50	.10
33	Don Larsen	1.00	.50	.10
34	Johnny Temple	.70	.35	.07
35	Don Schwall	.70	.35	.07
36	Don Leppert	.70	.35	.07
37	Tribe Hill Trio	.70	.35	.07
	Barry Latman			
	Dick Stigman			
	Jim Perry			
38	Gene Stephens	.70	.35	.07
39	Joe Koppe	.70	.35	.07
40	Orlando Cepeda	3.00	1.50	.30
41	Cliff Cook	.70	.35	.07
42	Jim King	.70	.35	.07
43	Dodgers Team	2.50	1.25	.25
44	Don Taussig	.70	.35	.07
45	Brooks Robinson	12.50	6.25	1.25
46	Jack Baldschun	.70	.35	.07
47	Bob Will	.70	.35	.07
48	Ralph Terry	1.00	.50	.10
49	Hal Jones	.70	.35	.07
50	Stan Musial	35.00	17.50	3.50
51	AL Batting Leaders	1.00	.50	.10
	Norm Cash			
	Jim Piersall			
	Al Kaline			
	Elston Howard			
52	NL Batting Leaders	1.25	.60	.12
	Bob Clemente			
	Vada Pinson			
	Ken Boyer			
	Wally Moon			
53	AL Home Run Leaders	7.50	3.75	.75
	Roger Maris			
	Mickey Mantle			
	Jim Gentile			
	Harmon Killebrew			
54	NL Home Run Leaders	1.75	.85	.17
	Orlando Cepeda			
	Willie Mays			
	Frank Robinson			
55	AL ERA Leaders	1.00	.50	.10
	Dick Donovan			
	Bill Stafford			
	Don Mossi			
	Milt Pappas			
56	NL ERA Leaders	1.25	.60	.12
	Warren Spahn			
	Jim O'Toole			
	Curt Simmons			
	Mike McCormick			
57	AL Wins Leaders	1.25	.60	.12
	Whitey Ford			
	Frank Lary			
	Steve Barber			
	Jim Bunning			
58	NL Wins Leaders	1.25	.60	.12
	Warren Spahn			
	Joe Jay			
	Jim O'Toole			
59	AL Strikeout Leaders	1.00	.50	.10
	Camilo Pascual			
	Whitey Ford			
	Jim Bunning			
	Juan Pizzaro			
60	NL Strikeout Leaders	1.75	.85	.17
	Sandy Koufax			
	Stan Williams			
	Don Drysdale			
	Jim O'Toole			
61	Cardinals Team	1.50	.75	.15
62	Steve Boros	1.00	.50	.10
63	Tony Cloninger	.70	.35	.07
64	Russ Snyder	.70	.35	.07
65	Bobby Richardson	2.50	1.25	.25
66	Cuno Barragon	.70	.35	.07
67	Harvey Haddix	1.00	.50	.10
68	Ken Hunt	.70	.35	.07
69	Phil Ortega	.70	.35	.07
70	Harmon Killebrew	7.50	3.75	.75
71	Dick LeMay	.70	.35	.07
72	Bob's Pupils	.70	.35	.07
	Steve Boros			
	Bob Scheffing			
	Jake Wood			
73	Nellie Fox	2.50	1.25	.25
74	Bob Lillis	1.00	.50	.10
75	Milt Pappas	1.00	.50	.10
76	Howie Bedell	.70	.35	.07
77	Tony Taylor	.70	.35	.07
78	Gene Green	.70	.35	.07
79	Ed Hobaugh	.70	.35	.07
80	Vada Pinson	2.00	1.00	.20
81	Jim Pagliaroni	.70	.35	.07
82	Deron Johnson	.70	.35	.07
83	Larry Jackson	.70	.35	.07
84	Lenny Green	.70	.35	.07
85	Gil Hodges	6.50	3.25	.65
86	Donn Clendenon	1.00	.50	.10
87	Mike Roarke	1.00	.50	.10
88	Ralph Houk MG	1.50	.75	.15
89	Barney Schultz	.70	.35	.07
90	Jim Piersall	1.50	.75	.15
91	J.C. Martin	.70	.35	.07
92	Sam Jones	.70	.35	.07
93	John Blanchard	1.00	.50	.10
94	Jay Hook	.70	.35	.07
95	Don Hoak	.70	.35	.07
96	Eli Grba	.70	.35	.07
97	Tito Francona	.70	.35	.07
98	Checklist 2	3.50	.70	.10
99	John (Boog) Powell	6.00	3.00	.60
100	Warren Spahn	8.00	4.00	.80
101	Carroll Hardy	.70	.35	.07
102	Al Schroll	.70	.35	.07
103	Don Blasingame	.70	.35	.07
104	Ted Savage	.70	.35	.07
105	Don Mossi	.70	.35	.07
106	Carl Sawatski	.70	.35	.07
107	Mike McCormick	1.00	.50	.10
108	Willie Davis	1.25	.60	.12
109	Bob Shaw	.70	.35	.07
110	Bill Skowron	2.50	1.25	.25
111	Dallas Green	1.00	.50	.10
112	Hank Foiles	.75	.35	.07
113	White Sox Team	1.50	.75	.15
114	Howie Koplitz	.75	.35	.07
115	Bob Skinner	.75	.35	.07
116	Herb Score	1.25	.60	.12
117	Gary Geiger	.75	.35	.07
118	Julian Javier	.75	.35	.07
119	Danny Murphy	.75	.35	.07
120	Bob Purkey	.75	.35	.07
121	Billy Hitchcock MG	.75	.35	.07
122	Norm Bass	.75	.35	.07
123	Mike De La Hoz	.75	.35	.07
124	Bill Pleis	.75	.35	.07
125	Gene Woodling	1.00	.50	.10
126	Al Cicotte	.75	.35	.07
127	Pride of A's	.75	.35	.07
	Norm Siebern			
	Hank Bauer			
	Jerry Lumpe			
128	Art Fowler	.75	.35	.07
129A	Lee Walls (facing right)	.75	.35	.07
129B	Lee Walls (face left)	8.00	4.00	.80
130	Frank Bolling	.75	.35	.07
131	Pete Richert	.75	.35	.07
132A	Angels Team (without photo)	1.50	.75	.15
132B	Angels Team (with photo)	8.00	4.00	.80
133	Felipe Alou	1.00	.50	.10
134A	Billy Hoeft (facing right)	.75	.35	.07
134B	Billy Hoeft (facing straight)	8.00	4.00	.80
135	Babe Ruth Special 1 Babe as a boy	5.00	2.50	.50
136	Babe Ruth Special 2 Babe Joins Yanks	5.00	2.50	.50
137	Babe Ruth Special 3 Babe with Huggins	5.00	2.50	.50
138	Babe Ruth Special 4 Famous Slugger	5.00	2.50	.50
139A	Babe Ruth Special 5	8.00	4.00	.80
139B	Hal Reniff PORT	9.00	4.50	.90
139C	Hal Reniff (pitching)	40.00	20.00	4.00
140	Babe Ruth Special 6 Gehrig and Ruth	6.50	3.25	.65
141	Babe Ruth Special 7 Twilight Years	5.00	2.50	.50
142	Babe Ruth Special 8 Coaching Dodgers	5.00	2.50	.50
143	Babe Ruth Special 9 Greatest Sports Hero	5.00	2.50	.50
144	Babe Ruth Special 10 Farewell Speech	5.00	2.50	.50
145	Barry Latman	.75	.35	.07

☐ 146	Don Demeter	.75	.35	.07
☐ 147A	Bill Kunkel PORT	.75	.35	.07
☐ 147B	Bill Kunkel (pitching pose)	8.00	4.00	.80
☐ 148	Wally Post	.75	.35	.07
☐ 149	Bob Duliba	.75	.35	.07
☐ 150	Al Kaline	10.00	5.00	1.00
☐ 151	Johnny Klippstein	.75	.35	.07
☐ 152	Mickey Vernon	1.00	.50	.07
☐ 153	Pumpsie Green	.75	.35	.07
☐ 154	Lee Thomas	.75	.35	.07
☐ 155	Stu Miller	.75	.35	.07
☐ 156	Merritt Ranew	.75	.35	.07
☐ 157	Wes Covington	.75	.35	.07
☐ 158	Braves Team	1.50	.75	.15
☐ 159	Hal Reniff	1.00	.50	.10
☐ 160	Dick Stuart	1.00	.50	.10
☐ 161	Frank Baumann	.75	.35	.07
☐ 162	Sammy Drake	.75	.35	.07
☐ 163	Hot Corner Guard Billy Gardner Cletis Boyer	1.00	.50	.10
☐ 164	Hal Naragon	.75	.35	.07
☐ 165	Jackie Brandt	.75	.35	.07
☐ 166	Don Lee	.75	.35	.07
☐ 167	Tim McCarver	6.00	3.00	.60
☐ 168	Leo Posada	.75	.35	.07
☐ 169	Bob Cerv	.75	.35	.07
☐ 170	Ron Santo	2.00	1.00	.20
☐ 171	Dave Sisler	.75	.35	.07
☐ 172	Fred Hutchinson MG	1.00	.50	.10
☐ 173	Chico Fernandez	.75	.35	.07
☐ 174A	Carl Willey (capless)	.75	.35	.07
☐ 174B	Carl Willey (with cap)	8.00	4.00	.80
☐ 175	Frank Howard	2.00	1.00	.20
☐ 176A	Eddie Yost PORT	.75	.35	.07
☐ 176B	Eddie Yost BATTING	8.00	4.00	.80
☐ 177	Bobby Shantz	1.25	.60	.12
☐ 178	Camilo Carreon	.75	.35	.07
☐ 179	Tom Sturdivant	.75	.35	.07
☐ 180	Bob Allison	1.00	.50	.10
☐ 181	Paul Brown	.75	.35	.07
☐ 182	Bob Nieman	.75	.35	.07
☐ 183	Roger Craig	1.25	.60	.12
☐ 184	Haywood Sullivan	.75	.35	.07
☐ 185	Roland Sheldon	.75	.35	.07
☐ 186	Mack Jones	.75	.35	.07
☐ 187	Gene Conley	.75	.35	.07
☐ 188	Chuck Hiller	.75	.35	.07
☐ 189	Dick Hall	.75	.35	.07
☐ 190A	Wally Moon PORT	1.00	.50	.10
☐ 190B	Wally Moon BATTING	8.00	4.00	.80
☐ 191	Jim Brewer	.75	.35	.07
☐ 192A	Checklist 3 (without comma)	3.50	.75	.10
☐ 192B	Checklist 3 (comma after Checklist)	5.00	1.00	.20
☐ 193	Eddie Kasko	.75	.35	.07
☐ 194	Dean Chance	1.25	.60	.12
☐ 195	Joe Cunningham	.75	.35	.07
☐ 196	Terry Fox	.75	.35	.07
☐ 197	Daryl Spencer	.80	.40	.08
☐ 198	Johnny Keane MG	1.00	.50	.10
☐ 199	Gaylord Perry	50.00	25.00	5.00
☐ 200	Mickey Mantle	300.00	150.00	30.00
☐ 201	Ike Delock	.80	.40	.08
☐ 202	Carl Warwick	.80	.40	.08
☐ 203	Jack Fisher	.80	.40	.08
☐ 204	Johnny Weekly	.80	.40	.08
☐ 205	Gene Freese	.80	.40	.08
☐ 206	Senators Team	1.25	.60	.12
☐ 207	Pete Burnside	.80	.40	.08
☐ 208	Billy Martin	3.50	1.75	.35
☐ 209	Jim Fregosi	3.50	1.75	.35
☐ 210	Roy Face	1.25	.60	.12
☐ 211	Midway Masters Frank Bolling Roy McMillan	.80	.40	.08
☐ 212	Jim Owens	.80	.40	.08
☐ 213	Richie Ashburn	3.00	1.50	.30
☐ 214	Dom Zanni	.80	.40	.08
☐ 215	Woody Held	.80	.40	.08
☐ 216	Ron Kline	.80	.40	.08
☐ 217	Walt Alston MG	2.50	1.25	.25
☐ 218	Joe Torre	9.00	4.50	.90
☐ 219	Al Downing	2.00	1.00	.20
☐ 220	Roy Sievers	1.00	.50	.10
☐ 221	Bill Short	.80	.40	.08
☐ 222	Jerry Zimmerman	.80	.40	.08
☐ 223	Alex Grammas	.80	.40	.08
☐ 224	Don Rudolph	.80	.40	.08
☐ 225	Frank Malzone	1.00	.50	.10
☐ 226	Giants Team	1.50	.75	.15
☐ 227	Bob Tiefenauer	.80	.40	.08
☐ 228	Dale Long	.80	.40	.08
☐ 229	Jesus McFarlane	.80	.40	.08
☐ 230	Camilo Pascual	1.00	.50	.10
☐ 231	Ernie Bowman	.80	.40	.08
☐ 232	World Series Game 1 Yanks win opener	1.75	.85	.17
☐ 233	World Series Game 2 Jay ties it up	1.75	.85	.17
☐ 234	World Series Game 3 Maris wins in 9th	3.50	1.75	.35
☐ 235	World Series Game 4 Ford sets new mark	3.50	1.75	.35
☐ 236	World Series Game 5 Yanks crush Reds	1.75	.85	.17
☐ 237	World Series Summary Yanks celebrate	1.75	.85	.17
☐ 238	Norm Sherry	1.00	.50	.10
☐ 239	Cecil Butler	.80	.40	.08
☐ 240	George Altman	.80	.40	.08
☐ 241	Johnny Kucks	.80	.40	.08
☐ 242	Mel McGaha	.80	.40	.08
☐ 243	Robin Roberts	6.00	3.00	.60
☐ 244	Don Gile	.80	.40	.08
☐ 245	Ron Hansen	.80	.40	.08
☐ 246	Art Ditmar	.80	.40	.08
☐ 247	Joe Pignatano	.80	.40	.08
☐ 248	Bob Aspromonte	.80	.40	.08
☐ 249	Ed Keegan	.80	.40	.08
☐ 250	Norm Cash	2.00	1.00	.20
☐ 251	New York Yankees Team Card	6.50	3.25	.65
☐ 252	Earl Francis	.80	.40	.08
☐ 253	Harry Chiti	.80	.40	.08
☐ 254	Gordon Windhorn	.80	.40	.08
☐ 255	Juan Pizarro	.80	.40	.08
☐ 256	Elio Chacon	.80	.40	.08
☐ 257	Jack Spring	.80	.40	.08
☐ 258	Marty Keough	.80	.40	.08
☐ 259	Lou Klimchock	.80	.40	.08
☐ 260	Bill Pierce	1.25	.60	.12
☐ 261	George Alusik	.80	.40	.08
☐ 262	Bob Schmidt	.80	.40	.08
☐ 263	The Right Pitch Bob Purkey Jim Turner Joe Jay	.80	.40	.08
☐ 264	Dick Ellsworth	1.00	.50	.10
☐ 265	Joe Adcock	1.25	.60	.12
☐ 266	John Anderson	.80	.40	.08
☐ 267	Dan Dobbek	.80	.40	.08
☐ 268	Ken McBride	.80	.40	.08
☐ 269	Bob Oldis	.80	.40	.08
☐ 270	Dick Groat	1.75	.85	.17
☐ 271	Ray Rippelmeyer	.80	.40	.08
☐ 272	Earl Robinson	.80	.40	.08
☐ 273	Gary Bell	.80	.40	.08
☐ 274	Sammy Taylor	.80	.40	.08
☐ 275	Norm Siebern	.80	.40	.08
☐ 276	Hal Kolstad	.80	.40	.08
☐ 277	Checklist 4	3.50	.70	.10
☐ 278	Ken Johnson	.80	.40	.08
☐ 279	Hobie Landrith	.80	.40	.08
☐ 280	Johnny Podres	1.75	.85	.17
☐ 281	Jake Gibbs	1.00	.50	.10
☐ 282	Dave Hillman	.80	.40	.08
☐ 283	Charlie Smith	.80	.40	.08
☐ 284	Ruben Amaro	.85	.40	.08
☐ 285	Curt Simmons	1.00	.50	.10
☐ 286	Al Lopez MG	2.00	1.00	.20
☐ 287	George Witt	.85	.40	.08
☐ 288	Billy Williams	7.00	3.50	.70
☐ 289	Mike Krsnich	.85	.40	.08
☐ 290	Jim Gentile	1.00	.50	.10
☐ 291	Hal Stowe	.85	.40	.08
☐ 292	Jerry Kindall	.85	.40	.08
☐ 293	Bob Miller	.85	.40	.08
☐ 294	Phillies Team	1.50	.75	.15
☐ 295	Vern Law	1.25	.60	.12
☐ 296	Ken Hamlin	.85	.40	.08
☐ 297	Ron Perranoski	1.00	.50	.10
☐ 298	Bill Tuttle	.85	.40	.08
☐ 299	Don Wert	.85	.40	.08
☐ 300	Willie Mays	60.00	30.00	6.00
☐ 301	Galen Cisco	.85	.40	.08
☐ 302	John Edwards	.85	.40	.08
☐ 303	Frank Torre	.85	.40	.08
☐ 304	Dick Farrell	.85	.40	.08
☐ 305	Jerry Lumpe	.85	.40	.08
☐ 306	Redbird Rippers Lindy McDaniel Larry Jackson	.85	.40	.08
☐ 307	Jim Grant	.85	.40	.08
☐ 308	Neil Chrisley	.85	.40	.08

309	Moe Morhardt	.85	.40	.08
310	Whitey Ford	11.00	5.50	1.10
311	Tony Kubek IA	1.50	.75	.15
312	Warren Spahn IA	4.00	2.00	.40
313	Roger Maris IA	6.50	3.25	.65
314	Rocky Colavito IA	1.50	.75	.15
315	Whitey Ford IA	4.00	2.00	.40
316	Harmon Killebrew IA	3.50	1.75	.35
317	Stan Musial IA	6.50	3.25	.65
318	Mickey Mantle IA	20.00	10.00	2.00
319	Mike McCormick IA	1.50	.75	.15
320	Hank Aaron	60.00	30.00	6.00
321	Lee Stange	.85	.40	.08
322	Al Dark	1.25	.60	.12
323	Don Landrum	.85	.40	.08
324	Joe McClain	.85	.40	.08
325	Luis Aparicio	6.50	3.25	.65
326	Tom Parsons	.85	.40	.08
327	Ozzie Virgil	.85	.40	.08
328	Ken Walters	.85	.40	.08
329	Bob Bolin	.85	.40	.08
330	John Romano	.85	.40	.08
331	Moe Drabowsky	.85	.40	.08
332	Don Buddin	.85	.40	.08
333	Frank Cipriani	.85	.40	.08
334	Red Sox Team	1.50	.75	.15
335	Bill Bruton	.85	.40	.08
336	Billy Muffett	.85	.40	.08
337	Jim Marshall	.85	.40	.08
338	Billy Gardner	.85	.40	.08
339	Jose Valdivielso	.85	.40	.08
340	Don Drysdale	12.00	6.00	1.20
341	Mike Hershberger	.85	.40	.08
342	Ed Rakow	.85	.40	.08
343	Albie Pearson	.85	.40	.08
344	Ed Bauta	.85	.40	.08
345	Chuck Schilling	.85	.40	.08
346	Jack Kralick	.85	.40	.08
347	Chuck Hinton	.85	.40	.08
348	Larry Burright	.85	.40	.08
349	Paul Foytack	.85	.40	.08
350	Frank Robinson	12.00	6.00	1.20
351	Braves' Backstops	1.00	.50	.10
	Joe Torre			
	Del Crandall			
352	Frank Sullivan	.85	.40	.08
353	Bill Mazeroski	2.00	1.00	.20
354	Roman Mejias	.85	.40	.08
355	Steve Barber	.85	.40	.08
356	Tom Haller	1.25	.60	.12
357	Jerry Walker	.85	.40	.08
358	Tommy Davis	1.75	.85	.17
359	Bobby Locke	.85	.40	.08
360	Yogi Berra	20.00	10.00	2.00
361	Bob Hendley	.85	.40	.08
362	Ty Cline	.85	.40	.08
363	Bob Roselli	.85	.40	.08
364	Ken Hunt	.85	.40	.08
365	Charley Neal	1.00	.50	.10
366	Phil Regan	1.00	.50	.10
367	Checklist 5	3.50	.70	.10
368	Bob Tillman	.85	.40	.08
369	Ted Bowsfield	.85	.40	.08
370	Ken Boyer	2.00	1.00	.20
371	Earl Battey	1.25	.60	.12
372	Jack Curtis	1.25	.60	.12
373	Al Heist	1.25	.60	.12
374	Gene Mauch	1.50	.75	.15
375	Ron Fairly	1.25	.60	.12
376	Bud Daley	1.25	.60	.12
377	John Orsino	1.25	.60	.12
378	Bennie Daniels	1.25	.60	.12
379	Chuck Essegian	1.25	.60	.12
380	Lou Burdette	1.50	.75	.15
381	Chico Cardenas	1.25	.60	.12
382	Dick Williams	1.50	.75	.15
383	Ray Sadecki	1.25	.60	.12
384	K.C. Athletics	2.00	1.00	.20
	Team Card			
385	Early Wynn	6.50	3.25	.65
386	Don Mincher	1.50	.75	.15
387	Lou Brock	65.00	32.50	6.50
388	Ryne Duren	1.50	.75	.15
389	Smoky Burgess	1.50	.75	.15
390	Orlando Cepeda AS	2.50	1.25	.25
391	Bill Mazeroski AS	2.00	1.00	.20
392	Ken Boyer AS	2.00	1.00	.20
393	Roy McMillan AS	1.25	.60	.12
394	Hank Aaron AS	15.00	7.50	1.50
395	Willie Mays AS	15.00	7.50	1.50
396	Frank Robinson AS	6.50	3.25	.65
397	John Roseboro AS	1.25	.60	.12
398	Don Drysdale AS	5.00	2.50	.50
399	Warren Spahn AS	6.00	3.00	.60
400	Elston Howard	3.50	1.75	.35
401	AL/NL Homer Kings	10.00	5.00	1.00
	Roger Maris			
	Orlando Cepeda			
402	Gino Cimoli	1.25	.60	.12
403	Chet Nichols	1.25	.60	.12
404	Tim Harkness	1.25	.60	.12
405	Jim Perry	1.50	.75	.15
406	Bob Taylor	1.25	.60	.12
407	Hank Aguirre	1.25	.60	.12
408	Gus Bell	1.25	.60	.12
409	Pirates Team	2.00	1.00	.20
410	Al Smith	1.25	.60	.12
411	Danny O'Connell	1.25	.60	.12
412	Charlie James	1.25	.60	.12
413	Matty Alou	1.50	.75	.15
414	Joe Gaines	1.25	.60	.12
415	Bill Virdon	1.50	.75	.15
416	Bob Scheffing MG	1.25	.60	.12
417	Joe Azcue	1.25	.60	.12
418	Andy Carey	1.25	.60	.12
419	Bob Bruce	1.25	.60	.12
420	Gus Triandos	1.25	.60	.12
421	Ken Mackenzie	1.25	.60	.12
422	Steve Bilko	1.25	.60	.12
423	Rival League	2.50	1.25	.25
	Relief Aces:			
	Roy Face			
	Hoyt Wilhelm			
424	Al McBean	1.25	.60	.12
425	Carl Yastrzemski	120.00	60.00	12.00
426	Bob Farley	1.25	.60	.12
427	Jake Wood	1.25	.60	.12
428	Joe Hicks	1.25	.60	.12
429	Billy O'Dell	1.25	.60	.12
430	Tony Kubek	4.50	2.25	.45
431	Bob Rodgers	1.50	.75	.15
432	Jim Pendleton	1.25	.60	.12
433	Jim Archer	1.25	.60	.12
434	Clay Dalrymple	1.25	.60	.12
435	Larry Sherry	1.50	.75	.15
436	Felix Mantilla	1.25	.60	.12
437	Ray Moore	1.25	.60	.12
438	Dick Brown	1.25	.60	.12
439	Jerry Buchek	1.25	.60	.12
440	Joe Jay	1.25	.60	.12
441	Checklist 6	4.00	.75	.10
442	Wes Stock	1.50	.75	.15
443	Del Crandall	1.50	.75	.15
444	Ted Wills	1.25	.60	.12
445	Vic Power	1.25	.60	.12
446	Don Elston	1.25	.60	.12
447	Willie Kirkland	1.50	.75	.15
448	Joe Gibbon	1.50	.75	.15
449	Jerry Adair	1.50	.75	.15
450	Jim O'Toole	1.50	.75	.15
451	Jose Tartabull	1.50	.75	.15
452	Earl Averill	1.50	.75	.15
453	Cal McLish	1.50	.75	.15
454	Floyd Robinson	1.50	.75	.15
455	Luis Arroyo	1.50	.75	.15
456	Joe Amalfitano	1.50	.75	.15
457	Lou Clinton	1.50	.75	.15
458A	Bob Buhl	1.50	.75	.15
	(Braves cap emblem)			
458B	Bob Buhl	30.00	15.00	3.00
	(no emblem on cap)			
459	Ed Bailey	1.50	.75	.15
460	Jim Bunning	4.50	2.25	.45
461	Ken Hubbs	4.50	2.25	.45
462A	Willie Tasby	1.50	.75	.15
	(Senators cap emblem)			
462B	Willie Tasby	30.00	15.00	3.00
	(no emblem on cap)			
463	Hank Bauer	1.50	.75	.15
464	Al Jackson	1.50	.75	.15
465	Reds Team	2.50	1.25	.25
466	Norm Cash AS	1.50	.75	.15
467	Chuck Schilling AS	1.50	.75	.15
468	Brooks Robinson AS	8.50	4.25	.85
469	Luis Aparicio AS	4.00	2.00	.40
470	Al Kaline AS	8.50	4.25	.85
471	Mickey Mantle AS	60.00	30.00	6.00
472	Rocky Colavito AS	1.50	.75	.15
473	Elston Howard AS	1.50	.75	.15
474	Frank Lary AS	1.50	.75	.15
475	Whitey Ford AS	6.00	3.00	.60
476	Orioles Team	2.50	1.25	.25
477	Andre Rodgers	1.50	.75	.15
478	Don Zimmer	2.00	1.00	.20
479	Joel Horlen	1.50	.75	.15
480	Harvey Kuenn	1.75	.85	.17
481	Vic Wertz	1.50	.75	.15
482	Sam Mele MG	1.50	.75	.15
483	Don McMahon	1.50	.75	.15
484	Dick Schofield	1.50	.75	.15

509

☐ 485	Pedro Ramos	1.50	.75	.15
☐ 486	Jim Gilliam	4.00	2.00	.40
☐ 487	Jerry Lynch	1.50	.75	.15
☐ 488	Hal Brown	1.50	.75	.15
☐ 489	Julio Gotay	1.50	.75	.15
☐ 490	Clete Boyer	3.00	1.50	.30
☐ 491	Leon Wagner	1.50	.75	.15
☐ 492	Hal W. Smith	1.50	.75	.15
☐ 493	Danny McDevitt	1.50	.75	.15
☐ 494	Sammy White	1.50	.75	.15
☐ 495	Don Cardwell	1.50	.75	.15
☐ 496	Wayne Causey	1.50	.75	.15
☐ 497	Ed Bouchee	1.50	.75	.15
☐ 498	Jim Donohue	1.50	.75	.15
☐ 499	Zoilo Versalles	1.50	.75	.15
☐ 500	Duke Snider	20.00	10.00	2.00
☐ 501	Claude Osteen	1.50	.75	.15
☐ 502	Hector Lopez	1.50	.75	.15
☐ 503	Danny Murtaugh MG	1.50	.75	.15
☐ 504	Eddie Bressoud	1.50	.75	.15
☐ 505	Juan Marichal	20.00	10.00	2.00
☐ 506	Charlie Maxwell	1.50	.75	.15
☐ 507	Ernie Broglio	1.50	.75	.15
☐ 508	Gordy Coleman	1.50	.75	.15
☐ 509	Dave Giusti	2.00	1.00	.20
☐ 510	Jim Lemon	1.50	.75	.15
☐ 511	Bubba Phillips	1.50	.75	.15
☐ 512	Mike Fornieles	1.50	.75	.15
☐ 513	Whitey Herzog	2.00	1.00	.20
☐ 514	Sherm Lollar	1.50	.75	.15
☐ 515	Stan Williams	1.50	.75	.15
☐ 516	Checklist 7	7.50	1.00	.20
☐ 517	Dave Wickersham	1.50	.75	.15
☐ 518	Lee Maye	1.50	.75	.15
☐ 519	Bob Johnson	1.50	.75	.15
☐ 520	Bob Friend	1.50	.75	.15
☐ 521	Jacke Davis	1.50	.75	.15
☐ 522	Lindy McDaniel	1.50	.75	.15
☐ 523	Russ Nixon	5.00	2.50	.50
☐ 524	Howie Nunn	5.00	2.50	.50
☐ 525	George Thomas	5.00	2.50	.50
☐ 526	Hal Woodeshick	5.00	2.50	.50
☐ 527	Dick McAuliffe	6.50	3.25	.65
☐ 528	Turk Lown	5.00	2.50	.50
☐ 529	John Schaive	5.00	2.50	.50
☐ 530	Bob Gibson	75.00	37.50	7.50
☐ 531	Bobby G. Smith	5.00	2.50	.50
☐ 532	Dick Stigman	5.00	2.50	.50
☐ 533	Charley Lau	6.50	3.25	.65
☐ 534	Tony Gonzalez	5.00	2.50	.50
☐ 535	Ed Roebuck	5.00	2.50	.50
☐ 536	Dick Gernert	5.00	2.50	.50
☐ 537	Indians Team	8.00	4.00	.80
☐ 538	Jack Sanford	5.00	2.50	.50
☐ 539	Billy Moran	5.00	2.50	.50
☐ 540	Jim Landis	5.00	2.50	.50
☐ 541	Don Nottebart	5.00	2.50	.50
☐ 542	Dave Philley	5.00	2.50	.50
☐ 543	Bob Allen	5.00	2.50	.50
☐ 544	Willie McCovey	75.00	37.50	7.50
☐ 545	Hoyt Wilhelm	35.00	17.50	3.50
☐ 546	Moe Thacker	5.00	2.50	.50
☐ 547	Don Ferrarese	5.00	2.50	.50
☐ 548	Bobby Del Greco	5.00	2.50	.50
☐ 549	Bill Rigney MG	5.00	2.50	.50
☐ 550	Art Mahaffey	5.00	2.50	.50
☐ 551	Harry Bright	5.00	2.50	.50
☐ 552	Chicago Cubs Team	8.00	4.00	.80
☐ 553	Jim Coates	5.00	2.50	.50
☐ 554	Bubba Morton	5.00	2.50	.50
☐ 555	John Buzhardt	5.00	2.50	.50
☐ 556	Al Spangler	5.00	2.50	.50
☐ 557	Bob Anderson	5.00	2.50	.50
☐ 558	John Goryl	5.00	2.50	.50
☐ 559	Mike Higgins MG	5.00	2.50	.50
☐ 560	Chuck Estrada	6.50	3.25	.65
☐ 561	Gene Oliver	5.00	2.50	.50
☐ 562	Bill Henry	5.00	2.50	.50
☐ 563	Ken Aspromonte	5.00	2.50	.50
☐ 564	Bob Grim	5.00	2.50	.50
☐ 565	Jose Pagan	5.00	2.50	.50
☐ 566	Marty Kutyna	5.00	2.50	.50
☐ 567	Tracy Stallard	5.00	2.50	.50
☐ 568	Jim Golden	5.00	2.50	.50
☐ 569	Ed Sadowski	5.00	2.50	.50
☐ 570	Bill Stafford	5.00	2.50	.50
☐ 571	Billy Klaus	5.00	2.50	.50
☐ 572	Bob G. Miller	5.00	2.50	.50
☐ 573	Johnny Logan	6.50	3.25	.65
☐ 574	Dean Stone	5.00	2.50	.50
☐ 575	Red Schoendienst	7.00	3.50	.70
☐ 576	Russ Kemmerer	5.00	2.50	.50
☐ 577	Dave Nicholson	5.00	2.50	.50
☐ 578	Jim Duffalo	5.00	2.50	.50
☐ 579	Jim Schaffer	5.00	2.50	.50

☐ 580	Bill Monbouquette	5.00	2.50	.50
☐ 581	Mel Roach	5.00	2.50	.50
☐ 582	Ron Piche	5.00	2.50	.50
☐ 583	Larry Osborne	5.00	2.50	.50
☐ 584	Minnesota Twins Team Card	8.00	4.00	.80
☐ 585	Glen Hobbie	5.00	2.50	.50
☐ 586	Sam Esposito	5.00	2.50	.50
☐ 587	Frank Funk	5.00	2.50	.50
☐ 588	Birdie Tebbetts MG	5.00	2.50	.50
☐ 589	Bob Turley	6.50	3.25	.65
☐ 590	Curt Flood	8.00	4.00	.80
☐ 591	Rookie Pitchers	20.00	10.00	2.00
	Sam McDowell			
	Ron Taylor			
	Ron Nischwitz			
	Art Quirk			
	Dick Radatz			
☐ 592	Rookie Pitchers	30.00	15.00	3.00
	Dan Pfister			
	Bo Belinsky			
	Dave Stenhouse			
	Jim Bouton			
	Joe Bonikowski			
☐ 593	Rookie Pitchers	12.00	6.00	1.20
	Jack Lamabe			
	Craig Anderson			
	Jack Hamilton			
	Bob Moorhead			
	Bob Veale			
☐ 594	Rookie Catchers	90.00	45.00	9.00
	Doc Edwards			
	Ken Retzer			
	Bob Uecker			
	Doug Camilli			
	Don Pavletich			
☐ 595	Rookie Catchers	7.50	3.75	.75
	Bob Sadowski			
	Felix Torres			
	Marlan Coughtry			
	Ed Charles			
☐ 596	Rookie Infielders	20.00	10.00	2.00
	Bernie Allen			
	Joe Pepitone			
	Phil Linz			
	Rich Rollins			
☐ 597	Rookie Infielders	7.50	3.75	.75
	Jim McKnight			
	Rod Kanehl			
	Amado Samuel			
	Denis Menke			
☐ 598	Rookie Outfielders	10.00	3.50	.70
	Al Luplow			
	Manny Jimenez			
	Howie Goss			
	Jim Hickman			
	Ed Olivares			

1963 Topps

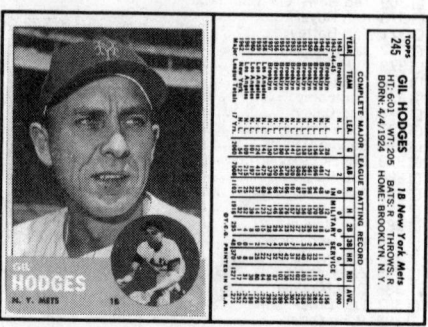

The cards in this 576-card set measure 2 1/2" by 3 1/2". The sharp color photographs of the 1963 set are a vivid contrast to the drab pictures of 1962. In addition to the "League Leaders" series (1-10) and World Series cards (142-148), the seventh and last series of cards (507-576) contains seven rookie cards (each depicting four players). This set has gained special prominence in recent years since it contains the rookie card of Pete Rose, #537.

		NRMT	VG-E	GOOD
COMPLETE SET		3000.00	1200.00	200.00
COMMON PLAYER (1-109)		.35	.17	.03
COMMON PLAYER (110-196)		.45	.22	.04
COMMON PLAYER (197-283)		.55	.27	.05
COMMON PLAYER (284-446)		.75	.35	.07
COMMON PLAYER (447-506)		5.00	2.50	.50
COMMON PLAYER (507-576)		3.50	1.75	.35

			NRMT	VG-E	GOOD
☐	1	NL Batting Leaders	7.50	1.50	.30
		Tommy Davis			
		Frank Robinson			
		Stan Musial			
		Hank Aaron			
		Bill White			
☐	2	AL Batting Leaders	4.00	2.00	.40
		Pete Runnels			
		Mickey Mantle			
		Floyd Robinson			
		Norm Siebern			
		Chuck Hinton			
☐	3	NL Home Run Leaders	4.00	2.00	.40
		Willie Mays			
		Hank Aaron			
		Frank Robinson			
		Orlando Cepeda			
		Ernie Banks			
☐	4	AL Home Run Leaders	1.50	.75	.15
		Harmon Killebrew			
		Norm Cash			
		Rocky Colavito			
		Roger Maris			
		Jim Gentile			
		Leon Wagner			
☐	5	NL ERA Leaders	2.00	1.00	.20
		Sandy Koufax			
		Bob Shaw			
		Bob Purkey			
		Bob Gibson			
		Don Drysdale			
☐	6	AL ERA Leaders	1.25	.60	.12
		Hank Aguirre			
		Robin Roberts			
		Whitey Ford			
		Eddie Fisher			
		Dean Chance			
☐	7	AL Pitching Leaders	1.25	.60	.12
		Don Drysdale			
		Jack Sanford			
		Bob Purkey			
		Billy O'Dell			
		Art Mahaffey			
		Joe Jay			
☐	8	AL Pitching Leaders	1.00	.50	.10
		Ralph Terry			
		Dick Donovan			
		Ray Herbert			
		Jim Bunning			
		Camilo Pascual			
☐	9	NL Strikeout Leaders	2.50	1.25	.25
		Don Drysdale			
		Sandy Koufax			
		Bob Gibson			
		Billy O'Dell			
		Dick Farrell			
☐	10	AL Strikeout Leaders	1.00	.50	.10
		Camilo Pascual			
		Jim Bunning			
		Ralph Terry			
		Juan Pizarro			
		Jim Kaat			
☐	11	Lee Walls	.35	.17	.03
☐	12	Steve Barber	.35	.17	.03
☐	13	Phillies Team	.80	.40	.08
☐	14	Pedro Ramos	.35	.17	.03
☐	15	Ken Hubbs	1.00	.50	.10
☐	16	Al Smith	.35	.17	.03
☐	17	Ryne Duren	.50	.25	.05
☐	18	Buc Blasters	4.00	2.00	.40
		Smoky Burgess			
		Dick Stuart			
		Bob Clemente			
		Bob Skinner			
☐	19	Pete Burnside	.35	.17	.03
☐	20	Tony Kubek	2.00	1.00	.20
☐	21	Marty Keough	.35	.17	.03
☐	22	Curt Simmons	.50	.25	.05
☐	23	Ed Lopat MG	.80	.40	.08
☐	24	Bob Bruce	.35	.17	.03
☐	25	Al Kaline	8.00	4.00	.80
☐	26	Ray Moore	.35	.17	.03
☐	27	Choo Choo Coleman	.35	.17	.03
☐	28	Mike Fornieles	.35	.17	.03

			NRMT	VG-E	GOOD
☐	29A	1963 Rookie Stars	.80	.40	.08
		Sammy Ellis			
		Ray Culp			
		John Boozer			
		Jesse Gonder			
☐	29B	1962 Rookie Stars	3.00	1.50	.30
		Sammy Ellis			
		Ray Culp			
		John Boozer			
		Jesse Gonder			
☐	30	Harvey Kuenn	.80	.40	.08
☐	31	Cal Koonce	.35	.17	.03
☐	32	Tony Gonzalez	.35	.17	.03
☐	33	Bo Belinsky	.50	.25	.05
☐	34	Dick Schofield	.35	.17	.03
☐	35	John Buzhardt	.35	.17	.03
☐	36	Jerry Kindall	.35	.17	.03
☐	37	Jerry Lynch	.35	.17	.03
☐	38	Bud Daley	.35	.17	.03
☐	39	Angels Team	.80	.40	.08
☐	40	Vic Power	.35	.17	.03
☐	41	Charley Lau	.50	.25	.05
☐	42	Stan Williams	.35	.17	.03
☐	43	Veteran Masters	2.00	1.00	.20
		Casey Stengel			
		Gene Woodling			
☐	44	Terry Fox	.35	.17	.03
☐	45	Bob Aspromonte	.35	.17	.03
☐	46	Tommy Aaron	.50	.25	.05
☐	47	Don Lock	.35	.17	.03
☐	48	Birdie Tebbetts MG	.35	.17	.03
☐	49	Dal Maxvill	.50	.25	.05
☐	50	Billy Pierce	.80	.40	.08
☐	51	George Alusik	.35	.17	.03
☐	52	Chuck Schilling	.35	.17	.03
☐	53	Joe Moeller	.35	.17	.03
☐	54A	1963 Rookie Stars	2.50	1.25	.25
		Nelson Mathews			
		Harry Fanok			
		Jack Cullen			
		Dave DeBusschere			
☐	54B	1962 Rookie Stars	5.00	2.50	.50
		Nelson Mathews			
		Harry Fanok			
		Jack Cullen			
		Dave DeBusschere			
☐	55	Bill Virdon	.80	.40	.08
☐	56	Dennis Bennett	.35	.17	.03
☐	57	Billy Moran	.35	.17	.03
☐	58	Bob Will	.35	.17	.03
☐	59	Craig Anderson	.35	.17	.03
☐	60	Elston Howard	2.00	1.00	.20
☐	61	Ernie Bowman	.35	.17	.03
☐	62	Bob Hendley	.35	.17	.03
☐	63	Reds Team	.80	.40	.08
☐	64	Dick McAuliffe	.50	.25	.05
☐	65	Jackie Brandt	.35	.17	.03
☐	66	Mike Joyce	.35	.17	.03
☐	67	Ed Charles	.35	.17	.03
☐	68	Friendly Foes	4.50	2.25	.45
		Duke Snider			
		Gil Hodges			
☐	69	Bud Zipfel	.35	.17	.03
☐	70	Jim O'Toole	.50	.25	.05
☐	71	Bobby Wine	.50	.25	.05
☐	72	Johnny Romano	.35	.17	.03
☐	73	Bob Bragan MG	.35	.17	.03
☐	74	Denny Lemaster	.35	.17	.03
☐	75	Bob Allison	.50	.25	.05
☐	76	Earl Wilson	.35	.17	.03
☐	77	Al Spangler	.35	.17	.03
☐	78	Marv Throneberry	.80	.40	.08
☐	79	Checklist 1	3.00	.50	.10
☐	80	Jim Gilliam	2.00	1.00	.20
☐	81	Jim Schaffer	.35	.17	.03
☐	82	Ed Rakow	.35	.17	.03
☐	83	Charley James	.35	.17	.03
☐	84	Ron Kline	.35	.17	.03
☐	85	Tom Haller	.35	.17	.03
☐	86	Charley Maxwell	.35	.17	.03
☐	87	Bob Veale	.50	.25	.05
☐	88	Ron Hansen	.35	.17	.03
☐	89	Dick Stigman	.35	.17	.03
☐	90	Gordy Coleman	.35	.17	.03
☐	91	Dallas Green	.50	.25	.05
☐	92	Hector Lopez	.35	.17	.03
☐	93	Galen Cisco	.35	.17	.03
☐	94	Bob Schmidt	.35	.17	.03
☐	95	Larry Jackson	.35	.17	.03
☐	96	Lou Clinton	.35	.17	.03
☐	97	Bob Duliba	.35	.17	.03
☐	98	George Thomas	.35	.17	.03
☐	99	Jim Umbricht	.35	.17	.03
☐	100	Joe Cunningham	.35	.17	.03
☐	101	Joe Gibbon	.35	.17	.03

☐ 102A Checklist 2	3.50	.60	.10
(red on yellow)			
☐ 102B Checklist 2	4.50	.80	.10
(white on red)			
☐ 103 Chuck Essegian	.35	.17	.03
☐ 104 Lew Krausse	.35	.17	.03
☐ 105 Ron Fairly	.50	.25	.05
☐ 106 Bobby Bolin	.35	.17	.03
☐ 107 Jim Hickman	.35	.17	.03
☐ 108 Hoyt Wilhelm	4.50	2.25	.45
☐ 109 Lee Maye	.35	.17	.03
☐ 110 Rich Rollins	.45	.22	.04
☐ 111 Al Jackson	.50	.25	.05
☐ 112 Dick Brown	.45	.22	.04
☐ 113 Don Landrum	.50	.25	.05
(photo actually Ron Santo)			
☐ 114 Dan Osinski	.45	.22	.04
☐ 115 Carl Yastrzemski	50.00	25.00	5.00
☐ 116 Jim Brosnan	.50	.25	.05
☐ 117 Jacke Davis	.45	.22	.04
☐ 118 Sherm Lollar	.50	.25	.05
☐ 119 Bob Lillis	.50	.25	.05
☐ 120 Roger Maris	12.50	6.25	1.25
☐ 121 Jim Hannan	.45	.22	.04
☐ 122 Julio Gotay	.45	.22	.04
☐ 123 Frank Howard	1.25	.60	.12
☐ 124 Dick Howser	.80	.40	.08
☐ 125 Robin Roberts	6.00	3.00	.60
☐ 126 Bob Uecker	15.00	7.50	1.50
☐ 127 Bill Tuttle	.45	.22	.04
☐ 128 Matty Alou	.50	.25	.05
☐ 129 Gary Bell	.45	.22	.04
☐ 130 Dick Groat	.80	.40	.08
☐ 131 Senators Team	1.00	.50	.10
☐ 132 Jack Hamilton	.45	.22	.04
☐ 133 Gene Freese	.45	.22	.04
☐ 134 Bob Scheffing MG	.45	.22	.04
☐ 135 Richie Ashburn	2.00	1.00	.20
☐ 136 Ike Delock	.45	.22	.04
☐ 137 Mack Jones	.45	.22	.04
☐ 138 Pride of NL	12.50	6.25	1.25
Willie Mays			
Stan Musial			
☐ 139 Earl Averill	.45	.22	.04
☐ 140 Frank Lary	.50	.25	.05
☐ 141 Manny Mota	2.50	1.25	.25
☐ 142 World Series Game 1	3.00	1.50	.30
Ford wins series opener			
☐ 143 World Series Game 2	2.00	1.00	.20
Sanford flashes shutout magic			
☐ 144 World Series Game 3	3.00	1.50	.30
Maris sparks Yankee rally			
☐ 145 World Series Game 4	2.00	1.00	.20
Hiller blasts grand slammer			
☐ 146 World Series Game 5	2.00	1.00	.20
Tresh's homer defeats Giants			
☐ 147 World Series Game 6	2.00	1.00	.20
Pierce stars in 3 hit victory			
☐ 148 World Series Game 7	2.00	1.00	.20
Yanks celebrate as Terry wins			
☐ 149 Marv Breeding	.45	.22	.04
☐ 150 John Podres	1.50	.75	.15
☐ 151 Pirates Team	1.00	.50	.10
☐ 152 Ron Nischwitz	.45	.22	.04
☐ 153 Hal Smith	.45	.22	.04
☐ 154 Walt Alston MG	1.75	.85	.17
☐ 155 Bill Stafford	.45	.22	.04
☐ 156 Roy McMillan	.45	.22	.04
☐ 157 Diego Segui	.45	.22	.04
☐ 158 Rookie Stars	.50	.25	.05
Rogelio Alvares			
Dave Roberts			
Tommy Harper			
Bob Saverine			
☐ 159 Jim Pagliaroni	.45	.22	.04
☐ 160 Juan Pizarro	.45	.22	.04
☐ 161 Frank Torre	.45	.22	.04
☐ 162 Twins Team	1.00	.50	.10
☐ 163 Don Larsen	.80	.40	.08
☐ 164 Bubba Morton	.45	.22	.04
☐ 165 Jim Kaat	2.50	1.25	.25
☐ 166 Johnny Keane MG	.50	.25	.05
☐ 167 Jim Fregosi	1.00	.50	.10
☐ 168 Russ Nixon	.45	.22	.04
☐ 169 Rookie Stars	15.00	7.50	1.50
Dick Egan			
Julio Navarro			
Tommie Sisk			
Gaylord Perry			
☐ 170 Joe Adcock	.60	.30	.06
☐ 171 Steve Hamilton	.45	.22	.04
☐ 172 Gene Oliver	.45	.22	.04
☐ 173 Bombers' Best	20.00	10.00	2.00
Tom Tresh			
Mickey Mantle			
Bobby Richardson			
☐ 174 Larry Burright	.45	.22	.04
☐ 175 Bob Buhl	.45	.22	.04
☐ 176 Jim King	.45	.22	.04
☐ 177 Bubba Phillips	.45	.22	.04
☐ 178 Johnny Edwards	.45	.22	.04
☐ 179 Ron Piche	.45	.22	.04
☐ 180 Bill Skowron	1.00	.50	.10
☐ 181 Sammy Esposito	.45	.22	.04
☐ 182 Albie Pearson	.45	.22	.04
☐ 183 Joe Pepitone	1.00	.50	.10
☐ 184 Vern Law	.60	.30	.06
☐ 185 Chuck Hiller	.45	.22	.04
☐ 186 Jerry Zimmerman	.45	.22	.04
☐ 187 Willie Kirkland	.45	.22	.04
☐ 188 Eddie Bressoud	.45	.22	.04
☐ 189 Dave Giusti	.50	.25	.05
☐ 190 Minnie Minoso	1.50	.75	.15
☐ 191 Checklist 3	3.50	.70	.10
☐ 192 Clay Dalrymple	.45	.22	.04
☐ 193 Andre Rodgers	.45	.22	.04
☐ 194 Joe Nuxhall	.50	.25	.05
☐ 195 Manny Jimenez	.45	.22	.04
☐ 196 Doug Camilli	.45	.22	.04
☐ 197 Roger Craig	1.25	.60	.12
☐ 198 Lenny Green	.55	.27	.05
☐ 199 Joe Amalfitano	.55	.27	.05
☐ 200 Mickey Mantle	250.00	125.00	25.00
☐ 201 Cecil Butler	.55	.27	.05
☐ 202 Red Sox Team	1.50	.75	.15
☐ 203 Chico Cardenas	.55	.27	.05
☐ 204 Don Nottebart	.55	.27	.05
☐ 205 Luis Aparicio	6.00	3.00	.60
☐ 206 Ray Washburn	.55	.27	.05
☐ 207 Ken Hunt	.55	.27	.05
☐ 208 Rookie Stars	.55	.27	.05
Ron Herbel			
John Miller			
Wally Wolf			
Ron Taylor			
☐ 209 Hobie Landrith	.55	.27	.05
☐ 210 Sandy Koufax	50.00	25.00	5.00
☐ 211 Fred Whitfield	.55	.27	.05
☐ 212 Glen Hobbie	.55	.27	.05
☐ 213 Billy Hitchcock MG	.55	.27	.05
☐ 214 Orlando Pena	.55	.27	.05
· ☐ 215 Bob Skinner	.55	.27	.05
☐ 216 Gene Conley	.55	.27	.05
☐ 217 Joe Christopher	.55	.27	.05
☐ 218 Tiger Twirlers	1.00	.50	.10
Frank Lary			
Don Mossi			
Jim Bunning			
☐ 219 Chuck Cottier	.55	.27	.05
☐ 220 Camilo Pascual	.75	.35	.07
☐ 221 Cookie Rojas	.55	.27	.05
☐ 222 Cubs Team	1.50	.75	.15
☐ 223 Eddie Fisher	.55	.27	.05
☐ 224 Mike Roarke	.75	.35	.07
☐ 225 Joe Jay	.55	.27	.05
☐ 226 Julian Javier	.55	.27	.05
☐ 227 Jim Grant	.55	.27	.05
☐ 228 Rookie Stars	15.00	7.50	1.50
Max Alvis			
Bob Bailey			
Pedro Oliva			
Ed Kranepool			
☐ 229 Willie Davis	1.00	.50	.10
☐ 230 Pete Runnels	.75	.35	.07
☐ 231 Eli Grba	.75	.35	.07
(large photo is Ryne Duren)			
☐ 232 Frank Malzone	.75	.35	.07
☐ 233 Casey Stengel MG	6.00	3.00	.60
☐ 234 Dave Nicholson	.55	.27	.05
☐ 235 Billy O'Dell	.55	.27	.05
☐ 236 Bill Bryan	.55	.27	.05
☐ 237 Jim Coates	.55	.27	.05
☐ 238 Lou Johnson	.55	.27	.05
☐ 239 Harvey Haddix	.75	.35	.07
☐ 240 Rocky Colavito	2.00	1.00	.20
☐ 241 Bob Smith	.55	.27	.05
☐ 242 Power Plus	8.50	4.25	.85
Ernie Banks			
Hank Aaron			
☐ 243 Don Leppert	.55	.27	.05
☐ 244 John Tsitouris	.55	.27	.05

☐ 245	Gil Hodges	5.50	2.75	.55	☐ 326	Hank Foiles	.75	.35	.07
☐ 246	Lee Stange	.55	.27	.05	☐ 327	Paul Foytack	.75	.35	.07
☐ 247	Yankees Team	4.50	2.25	.45	☐ 328	Dick Williams	1.25	.60	.12
☐ 248	Tito Francona	.55	.27	.05	☐ 329	Lindy McDaniel	1.00	.50	.10
☐ 249	Leo Burke	.55	.27	.05	☐ 330	Chuck Hinton	.75	.35	.07
☐ 250	Stan Musial	35.00	17.50	3.50	☐ 331	Series Foes	1.00	.50	.10
☐ 251	Jack Lamabe	.55	.27	.05		Bill Stafford			
☐ 252	Ron Santo	2.00	1.00	.20		Bill Pierce			
☐ 253	Rookie Stars	.75	.35	.07	☐ 332	Joel Horlen	1.00	.50	.10
	Len Gabrielson				☐ 333	Carl Warwick	.75	.35	.07
	Pete Jernigan				☐ 334	Wynn Hawkins	.75	.35	.07
	John Wojcik				☐ 335	Leon Wagner	.75	.35	.07
	Deacon Jones				☐ 336	Ed Bauta	.75	.35	.07
☐ 254	Mike Hershberger	.55	.27	.05	☐ 337	Dodgers Team	4.00	2.00	.40
☐ 255	Bob Shaw	.55	.27	.05	☐ 338	Russ Kemmerer	.75	.35	.07
☐ 256	Jerry Lumpe	.55	.27	.05	☐ 339	Ted Bowsfield	.75	.35	.07
☐ 257	Hank Aguirre	.55	.27	.05	☐ 340	Yogi Berra	24.00	12.00	2.40
☐ 258	Al Dark MG	.75	.35	.07	☐ 341	Jack Baldschun	.75	.35	.07
☐ 259	John Logan	.75	.35	.07	☐ 342	Gene Woodling	1.00	.50	.10
☐ 260	Jim Gentile	.75	.35	.07	☐ 343	Johnny Pesky MG	1.00	.50	.10
☐ 261	Bob Miller	.55	.27	.05	☐ 344	Don Schwall	.75	.35	.07
☐ 262	Ellis Burton	.55	.27	.05	☐ 345	Brooks Robinson	20.00	10.00	2.00
☐ 263	Dave Stenhouse	.55	.27	.05	☐ 346	Billy Hoeft	.75	.35	.07
☐ 264	Phil Linz	.55	.27	.05	☐ 347	Joe Torre	2.50	1.25	.25
☐ 265	Vada Pinson	2.00	1.00	.20	☐ 348	Vic Wertz	.75	.35	.07
☐ 266	Bob Allen	.55	.27	.05	☐ 349	Zoilo Versailles	1.00	.50	.10
☐ 267	Carl Sawatski	.55	.27	.05	☐ 350	Bob Purkey	.75	.35	.07
☐ 268	Don Demeter	.55	.27	.05	☐ 351	Al Luplow	.75	.35	.07
☐ 269	Don Mincher	.75	.35	.07	☐ 352	Ken Johnson	.75	.35	.07
☐ 270	Felipe Alou	1.00	.50	.10	☐ 353	Billy Williams	6.50	3.25	.65
☐ 271	Dean Stone	.55	.27	.05	☐ 354	Dom Zanni	.75	.35	.07
☐ 272	Danny Murphy	.55	.27	.05	☐ 355	Dean Chance	1.00	.50	.10
☐ 273	Sammy Taylor	.55	.27	.05	☐ 356	John Schaive	.75	.35	.07
☐ 274	Checklist 4	3.50	.70	.10	☐ 357	George Altman	.75	.35	.07
☐ 275	Eddie Mathews	7.50	3.75	.75	☐ 358	Milt Pappas	1.00	.50	.10
☐ 276	Barry Shetrone	.55	.27	.05	☐ 359	Haywood Sullivan	.75	.35	.07
☐ 277	Dick Farrell	.55	.27	.05	☐ 360	Don Drysdale	8.50	4.25	.85
☐ 278	Chico Fernandez	.55	.27	.05	☐ 361	Cletis Boyer	1.25	.60	.12
☐ 279	Wally Moon	.75	.35	.07	☐ 362	Checklist 5	3.50	.70	.10
☐ 280	Bob Rodgers	.75	.35	.07	☐ 363	Dick Radatz	1.00	.50	.10
☐ 281	Tom Sturdivant	.55	.27	.05	☐ 364	Howie Goss	.75	.35	.07
☐ 282	Bobby Del Greco	.55	.27	.05	☐ 365	Jim Bunning	3.50	1.75	.35
☐ 283	Roy Sievers	.75	.35	.07	☐ 366	Tony Taylor	.75	.35	.07
☐ 284	Dave Sisler	.75	.35	.07	☐ 367	Tony Cloninger	.75	.35	.07
☐ 285	Dick Stuart	1.00	.50	.10	☐ 368	Ed Bailey	.75	.35	.07
☐ 286	Stu Miller	.75	.35	.07	☐ 369	Jim Lemon MG	1.00	.50	.10
☐ 287	Dick Bertell	.75	.35	.15	☐ 370	Dick Donovan	.75	.35	.07
☐ 288	White Sox Team	1.50	.35	.07	☐ 371	Rod Kanehl	.75	.35	.07
☐ 289	Hal Brown	.75	.35	.07	☐ 372	Don Lee	.75	.35	.07
☐ 290	Bill White	1.00	.50	.10	☐ 373	Jim Campbell	1.00	.50	.10
☐ 291	Don Rudolph	.75	.35	.07	☐ 374	Claude Osteen	.75	.35	.07
☐ 292	Pumpsie Green	.75	.35	.07	☐ 375	Ken Boyer	2.00	1.00	.20
☐ 293	Bill Pleis	.75	.35	.07	☐ 376	John Wyatt	.75	.35	.07
☐ 294	Bill Rigney MG	.75	.35	.07	☐ 377	Orioles Team	1.50	.75	.15
☐ 295	Ed Roebuck	.75	.35	.07	☐ 378	Bill Henry	.75	.35	.07
☐ 296	Doc Edwards	1.00	.50	.10	☐ 379	Bob Anderson	.75	.35	.07
☐ 297	Jim Golden	.75	.35	.07	☐ 380	Ernie Banks	20.00	10.00	2.00
☐ 298	Don Dillard	.75	.35	.07	☐ 381	Frank Baumann	.75	.35	.07
☐ 299	Rookie Stars	.75	.35	.07	☐ 382	Ralph Houk MG	1.25	.60	.12
	Dave Morehead				☐ 383	Pete Richert	.75	.35	.07
	Bob Dustal				☐ 384	Bob Tillman	.75	.35	.07
	Tom Butters				☐ 385	Art Mahaffey	.75	.35	.07
	Dan Schneider				☐ 386	Rookie Stars	1.25	.60	.12
☐ 300	Willie Mays	65.00	32.50	6.50		Ed Kirkpatrick			
☐ 301	Bill Fischer	.75	.35	.07		John Bateman			
☐ 302	Whitey Herzog	1.25	.60	.12		Larry Bearnarth			
☐ 303	Earl Francis	.75	.35	.07		Garry Roggenburk			
☐ 304	Harry Bright	.75	.35	.07	☐ 387	Al McBean	.75	.35	.07
☐ 305	Don Hoak	.75	.35	.07	☐ 388	Jim Davenport	1.00	.50	.10
☐ 306	Star Receivers	1.00	.50	.10	☐ 389	Frank Sullivan	.75	.35	.07
	Earl Battey				☐ 390	Hank Aaron	65.00	32.50	6.50
	Elston Howard				☐ 391	B. Dailey	.75	.35	.07
☐ 307	Chet Nichols	.75	.35	.07	☐ 392	Tribe Thumpers	1.00	.50	.10
☐ 308	Camilo Carreon	.75	.35	.07		Johnny Romano			
☐ 309	Jim Brewer	.75	.35	.07		Tito Francona			
☐ 310	Tommy Davis	1.50	.75	.15	☐ 393	Ken MacKenzie	.75	.35	.07
☐ 311	Joe McClain	.75	.35	.07	☐ 394	Tim McCarver	2.00	1.00	.20
☐ 312	Houston Colts Team	4.00	2.00	.40	☐ 395	Don McMahon	.75	.35	.07
☐ 313	Ernie Broglio	1.00	.50	.10	☐ 396	Joe Koppe	.75	.35	.07
☐ 314	John Goryl	.75	.35	.07	☐ 397	K.C. Athletics Team	1.50	.75	.15
☐ 315	Ralph Terry	1.25	.60	.12	☐ 398	Boog Powell	2.50	1.25	.25
☐ 316	Norm Sherry	1.00	.50	.10	☐ 399	Dick Ellsworth	1.00	.50	.10
☐ 317	Sam McDowell	1.25	.60	.12	☐ 400	Frank Robinson	20.00	10.00	2.00
☐ 318	Gene Mauch MG	1.25	.60	.12	☐ 401	Jim Bouton	3.00	1.50	.30
☐ 319	Joe Gaines	.75	.35	.07	☐ 402	Mickey Vernon	1.00	.50	.10
☐ 320	Warren Spahn	11.00	5.50	1.10	☐ 403	Ron Perranoski	1.00	.50	.10
☐ 321	Gino Cimoli	.75	.35	.07	☐ 404	Bob Oldis	.75	.35	.07
☐ 322	Bob Turley	1.25	.60	.12	☐ 405	Floyd Robinson	.75	.35	.07
☐ 323	Bill Mazeroski	1.50	.75	.15	☐ 406	Howie Koplitz	.75	.35	.07
☐ 324	Rookie Stars	1.50	.75	.15	☐ 407	Rookie Stars	.75	.35	.07
	George Williams					Frank Kostro			
	Pete Ward					Chico Ruiz			
	Phil Ward					Larry Elliot			
	Vic Davalillo					Dick Simpson			
☐ 325	Jack Sanford	1.00	.50	.10	☐ 408	Billy Gardner	1.00	.50	.10

☐ 409	Roy Face	1.25	.60	.12		☐ 489	Paul Toth	5.00	2.50	.50
☐ 410	Earl Battey	1.00	.50	.10		☐ 490	Willie McCovey	55.00	27.50	5.50
☐ 411	Jim Constable	.75	.35	.07		☐ 491	Harry Craft MG	5.00	2.50	.50
☐ 412	Dodger Big Three	12.00	6.00	1.20		☐ 492	Dave Wickersham	5.00	2.50	.50
	Johnny Podres					☐ 493	Walt Bond	5.00	2.50	.50
	Don Drysdale					☐ 494	Phil Regan	5.00	2.50	.50
	Sandy Koufax					☐ 495	Frank Thomas	5.00	2.50	.50
☐ 413	Jerry Walker	.75	.35	.07		☐ 496	Rookie Stars	5.00	2.50	.50
☐ 414	Ty Cline	.75	.35	.07			Steve Dalkowski			
☐ 415	Bob Gibson	20.00	10.00	2.00			Fred Newman			
☐ 416	Alex Grammas	.75	.35	.07			Jack Smith			
☐ 417	Giants Team	1.50	.75	.15			Carl Bouldin			
☐ 418	John Orsino	.75	.35	.07		☐ 497	Bennie Daniels	5.00	2.50	.50
☐ 419	Tracy Stallard	.75	.35	.07		☐ 498	Ed Kasko	5.00	2.50	.50
☐ 420	Bobby Richardson	2.50	1.25	.25		☐ 499	J.C. Martin	5.00	2.50	.50
☐ 421	Tom Morgan	.75	.35	.07		☐ 500	Harmon Killebrew	35.00	17.50	3.50
☐ 422	Fred Hutchinson MG	1.25	.60	.12		☐ 501	Joe Azcue	5.00	2.50	.50
☐ 423	Ed Hobaugh	.75	.35	.07		☐ 502	Daryl Spencer	5.00	2.50	.50
☐ 424	Charley Smith	.75	.35	.07		☐ 503	Braves Team	7.50	3.75	.75
☐ 425	Smoky Burgess	1.00	.50	.10		☐ 504	Bob Johnson	5.00	2.50	.50
☐ 426	Barry Latman	.75	.35	.07		☐ 505	Curt Flood	8.50	4.25	.85
☐ 427	Bernie Allen	.75	.35	.07		☐ 506	Gene Green	5.00	2.50	.50
☐ 428	Carl Boles	.75	.35	.07		☐ 507	Rollie Sheldon	3.50	1.75	.35
☐ 429	Lou Burdette	1.50	.75	.15		☐ 508	Ted Savage	3.50	1.75	.35
☐ 430	Norm Siebern	.75	.35	.07		☐ 509	Checklist 7	10.00	1.50	.30
☐ 431A	Checklist 6	3.50	.70	.10		☐ 510	Ken McBride	3.50	1.75	.35
	(white on red)					☐ 511	Charlie Neal	3.50	1.75	.35
☐ 431B	Checklist 6	7.00	1.00	.20		☐ 512	Cal McLish	3.50	1.75	.35
	(black on orange)					☐ 513	Gary Geiger	3.50	1.75	.35
☐ 432	Roman Mejias	.75	.35	.07		☐ 514	Larry Osborne	3.50	1.75	.35
☐ 433	Denis Menke	.75	.35	.07		☐ 515	Don Elston	3.50	1.75	.35
☐ 434	John Callison	1.00	.50	.10		☐ 516	Purnell Goldy	3.50	1.75	.35
☐ 435	Woody Held	.75	.35	.07		☐ 517	Hal Woodeshick	3.50	1.75	.35
☐ 436	Tim Harkness	.75	.35	.07		☐ 518	Don Blasingame	3.50	1.75	.35
☐ 437	Bill Bruton	.75	.35	.07		☐ 519	Claude Raymond	3.50	1.75	.35
☐ 438	Wes Stock	.75	.35	.07		☐ 520	Orlando Cepeda	10.00	5.00	1.00
☐ 439	Don Zimmer	1.50	.75	.15		☐ 521	Dan Pfister	3.50	1.75	.35
☐ 440	Juan Marichal	12.00	6.00	1.20		☐ 522	Rookie Stars	5.50	2.75	.55
☐ 441	Lee Thomas	1.00	.50	.10			Mel Nelson			
☐ 442	J.C. Hartman	.75	.35	.07			Gary Peters			
☐ 443	Jim Piersall	1.50	.75	.15			Jim Roland			
☐ 444	Jim Maloney	1.50	.75	.15			Art Quirk			
☐ 445	Norm Cash	2.00	1.00	.20		☐ 523	Bill Kunkel	3.50	1.75	.35
☐ 446	Whitey Ford	20.00	10.00	2.00		☐ 524	Cardinals Team	7.50	3.75	.75
☐ 447	Felix Mantilla	5.00	2.50	.50		☐ 525	Nellie Fox	8.00	4.00	.80
☐ 448	Jack Kralick	5.00	2.50	.50		☐ 526	Dick Hall	3.50	1.75	.35
☐ 449	Jose Tartabull	5.00	2.50	.50		☐ 527	Ed Sadowski	3.50	1.75	.35
☐ 450	Bob Friend	6.00	3.00	.60		☐ 528	Carl Willey	3.50	1.75	.35
☐ 451	Indians Team	7.50	3.75	.75		☐ 529	Wes Covington	3.50	1.75	.35
☐ 452	Buddy Schultz	5.00	2.50	.50		☐ 530	Don Mossi	5.00	2.50	.50
☐ 453	Jake Wood	5.00	2.50	.50		☐ 531	Sam Mele MG	3.50	1.75	.35
☐ 454A	Art Fowler	5.00	2.50	.50		☐ 532	Steve Boros	4.50	2.25	.45
	(card number on					☐ 533	Bobby Shantz	5.50	2.75	.55
	white background)					☐ 534	Ken Walters	3.50	1.75	.35
☐ 454B	Art Fowler	7.50	3.75	.75		☐ 535	Jim Perry	5.50	2.75	.55
	(card number on					☐ 536	Norm Larker	4.50	2.25	.45
	orange background)					☐ 537	Rookie Stars	550.00	275.00	55.00
☐ 455	Ruben Amaro	5.00	2.50	.50			Pedro Gonzales			
☐ 456	Jim Coker	5.00	2.50	.50			Ken McMullen			
☐ 457	Tex Clevenger	5.00	2.50	.50			Al Weis			
☐ 458	Al Lopez MG	7.50	3.75	.75			Pete Rose			
☐ 459	Dick LeMay	5.00	2.50	.50		☐ 538	George Brunet	3.50	1.75	.35
☐ 460	Del Crandall	6.00	3.00	.60		☐ 539	Wayne Causey	3.50	1.75	.35
☐ 461	Norm Bass	5.00	2.50	.50		☐ 540	Bob Clemente	90.00	45.00	9.00
☐ 462	Wally Post	5.00	2.50	.50		☐ 541	Ron Moeller	3.50	1.75	.35
☐ 463	Joe Schaffernoth	5.00	2.50	.50		☐ 542	Lou Klimchock	3.50	1.75	.35
☐ 464	Ken Aspromonte	5.00	2.50	.50		☐ 543	Russ Snyder	3.50	1.75	.35
☐ 465	Chuck Estrada	5.00	2.50	.50		☐ 544	Rookie Stars	24.00	12.00	2.40
☐ 466	Rookie Stars	9.00	4.50	.90			Duke Carmel			
	Nate Oliver						Bill Haas			
	Tony Martinez						Rusty Staub			
	Bill Freehan						Dick Phillips			
	Jerry Robinson					☐ 545	Jose Pagan	3.50	1.75	.35
☐ 467	Phil Ortega	5.00	2.50	.50		☐ 546	Hal Reniff	3.50	1.75	.35
☐ 468	Carroll Hardy	5.00	2.50	.50		☐ 547	Gus Bell	4.50	2.25	.45
☐ 469	Jay Hook	5.00	2.50	.50		☐ 548	Tom Satriano	3.50	1.75	.35
☐ 470	Tom Tresh	15.00	7.50	1.50		☐ 549	Rookie Stars	3.50	1.75	.35
☐ 471	Ken Retzer	5.00	2.50	.50			Marcelino Lopez			
☐ 472	Lou Brock	70.00	35.00	7.00			Pete Lovrich			
☐ 473	Mets Team	11.00	5.50	1.10			Paul Ratliff			
☐ 474	Jack Fisher	5.00	2.50	.50			Elmo Plaskett			
☐ 475	Gus Triandos	5.00	2.50	.50		☐ 550	Duke Snider	45.00	22.50	4.50
☐ 476	Frank Funk	5.00	2.50	.50		☐ 551	Billy Klaus	3.50	1.75	.35
☐ 477	Donn Clendenon	6.00	3.00	.60		☐ 552	Tigers Team	12.00	6.00	1.20
☐ 478	Paul Brown	5.00	2.50	.50		☐ 553	Rookie Stars	125.00	60.00	12.50
☐ 479	Ed Brinkman	5.00	2.50	.50			Brock Davis			
☐ 480	Bill Monbouquette	5.00	2.50	.50			Jim Gosger			
☐ 481	Bill Taylor	5.00	2.50	.50			Willie Stargell			
☐ 482	Felix Torres	5.00	2.50	.50			John Herrnstein			
☐ 483	Jim Owens	5.00	2.50	.50		☐ 554	Hank Fischer	3.50	1.75	.35
☐ 484	Dale Long	5.00	2.50	.50		☐ 555	John Blanchard	4.50	2.25	.45
☐ 485	Jim Landis	5.00	2.50	.50		☐ 556	Al Worthington	3.50	1.75	.35
☐ 486	Ray Sadecki	5.00	2.50	.50		☐ 557	Cuno Barragan	3.50	1.75	.35
☐ 487	John Roseboro	5.00	2.50	.50		☐ 558	Rookie Stars	3.50	1.75	.35
☐ 488	Jerry Adair	5.00	2.50	.50			Bill Faul			

	Ron Hunt			
	Al Moran			
	Bob Lipski			
□ 559	Danny Murtaugh MG	3.50	1.75	.35
□ 560	Ray Herbert	3.50	1.75	.35
□ 561	Mike De La Hoz	3.50	1.75	.35
□ 562	Rookie Stars	6.00	3.00	.60
	Randy Cardinal			
	Dave McNally			
	Ken Rowe			
	Don Rowe			
□ 563	Mike McCormick	4.50	2.25	.45
□ 564	George Banks	3.50	1.75	.35
□ 565	Larry Sherry	4.50	2.25	.45
□ 566	Cliff Cook	3.50	1.75	.35
□ 567	Jim Duffalo	3.50	1.75	.35
□ 568	Bob Sadowski	3.50	1.75	.35
□ 569	Luis Arroyo	4.50	2.25	.45
□ 570	Frank Bolling	3.50	1.75	.35
□ 571	John Klippstein	3.50	1.75	.35
□ 572	Jack Spring	3.50	1.75	.35
□ 573	Coot Veal	3.50	1.75	.35
□ 574	Hal Kolstad	3.50	1.75	.35
□ 575	Don Cardwell	3.50	1.75	.35
□ 576	Johnny Temple	6.00	2.00	.40

1964 Topps

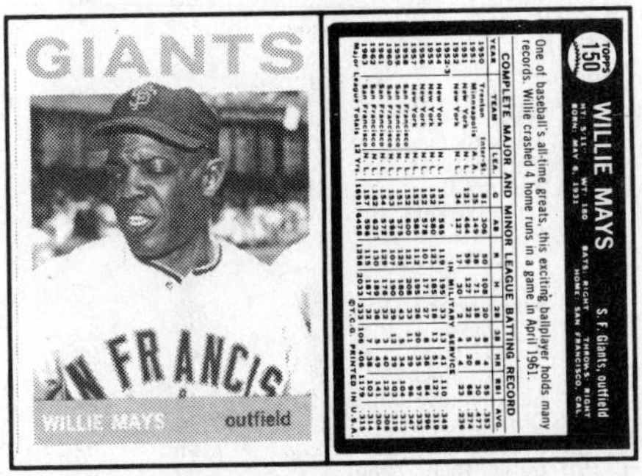

The cards in this 587-card set measure 2 1/2" by 3 1/2". Players in the 1964 Topps baseball series were easy to sort by team due to the giant block lettering found at the top of each card. The name and position of the player are found underneath the picture and the card is numbered in a ball design on the orange-colored back. The usual last series scarcity holds for this set (523 to 587). Subsets within this set include League Leaders (1-12) and World Series cards (136-140).

	NRMT	VG-E	GOOD
COMPLETE SET	1600.00	600.00	120.00
COMMON PLAYER (1-370)	.45	.22	.04
COMMON PLAYER (371-522)	.80	.40	.08
COMMON PLAYER (523-587)	2.00	1.00	.20

□ 1	NL ERA Leaders	7.50	1.25	.25
	Sandy Koufax			
	Dick Ellsworth			
	Bob Friend			
□ 2	AL ERA Leaders	1.00	.50	.10
	Gary Peters			
	Juan Pizarro			
	Camilo Pascual			
□ 3	NL Pitching Leaders	3.00	1.50	.30
	Sandy Koufax			
	Juan Marichal			
	Warren Spahn			
	Jim Maloney			
□ 4	AL Pitching Leaders	1.50	.75	.15
	Whitey Ford			
	Camilo Pascual			
	Jim Bouton			
□ 5	NL Strikeout Leaders	2.50	1.25	.25
	Sandy Koufax			
	Jim Maloney			
	Don Drysdale			
□ 6	AL Strikeout Leaders	1.00	.50	.10
	Camilo Pascual			
	Jim Bunning			
	Dick Stigman			
□ 7	NL Batting Leaders	2.00	1.00	.20
	Tommy Davis			
	Bob Clemente			
	Dick Groat			
	Hank Aaron			
□ 8	AL Batting Leaders	3.00	1.50	.30
	Carl Yastrzemski			
	Al Kaline			
	Rich Rollins			
□ 9	NL Home Run Leaders	5.00	2.50	.50
	Hank Aaron			
	Willie McCovey			
	Willie Mays			
	Orlando Cepeda			
□ 10	AL Home Run Leaders	1.25	.60	.12
	Harmon Killebrew			
	Dick Stuart			
	Bob Allison			
□ 11	NL RBI Leaders	1.50	.75	.15
	Hank Aaron			
	Ken Boyer			
	Bill White			
□ 12	AL RBI Leaders	1.25	.60	.12
	Dick Stuart			
	Al Kaline			
	Harmon Killebrew			
□ 13	Hoyt Wilhelm	3.00	1.50	.30
□ 14	Dodgers Rookies	.45	.22	.04
	Dick Nen			
	Nick Willhite			
□ 15	Zoilo Versalles	.45	.22	.04
□ 16	John Boozer	.45	.22	.04
□ 17	Willie Kirkland	.45	.22	.04
□ 18	Billy O'Dell	.45	.22	.04
□ 19	Don Wert	.45	.22	.04
□ 20	Bob Friend	.60	.30	.06
□ 21	Yogi Berra	15.00	7.50	1.50
□ 22	Jerry Adair	.45	.22	.04
□ 23	Chris Zachary	.45	.22	.04
□ 24	Carl Sawatski	.45	.22	.04
□ 25	Bill Monbouquette	.45	.22	.04
□ 26	Gino Cimoli	.45	.22	.04
□ 27	Mets Team	1.50	.75	.15
□ 28	Claude Osteen	.60	.30	.06
□ 29	Lou Brock	15.00	7.50	1.50
□ 30	Ron Perranoski	.60	.30	.06
□ 31	Dave Nicholson	.45	.22	.04
□ 32	Dean Chance	.60	.30	.06
□ 33	Reds Rookies	.60	.30	.06
	Sammy Ellis			
	Mel Queen			
□ 34	Jim Perry	.60	.30	.06
□ 35	Ed Mathews	6.50	3.25	.65
□ 36	Hal Reniff	.45	.22	.04
□ 37	Smoky Burgess	.60	.30	.06
□ 38	Jim Wynn	1.50	.75	.15
□ 39	Hank Aguirre	.45	.22	.04
□ 40	Dick Groat	1.00	.50	.10
□ 41	Friendly Foes	2.00	1.00	.20
	Willie McCovey			
	Leon Wagner			
□ 42	Moe Drabowsky	.45	.22	.04
□ 43	Roy Sievers	.60	.30	.06
□ 44	Duke Carmel	.45	.22	.04
□ 45	Milt Pappas	.60	.30	.06
□ 46	Ed Brinkman	.45	.22	.04
□ 47	Giants Rookies	.80	.40	.08
	Jesus Alou			
	Ron Herbel			
□ 48	Bob Perry	.45	.22	.04
□ 49	Bill Henry	.45	.22	.04
□ 50	Mickey Mantle	175.00	85.00	18.00
□ 51	Pete Richert	.45	.22	.04
□ 52	Chuck Hinton	.45	.22	.04
□ 53	Denis Menke	.45	.22	.04
□ 54	Sam Mele MG	.45	.22	.04
□ 55	Ernie Banks	8.50	4.25	.85
□ 56	Hal Brown	.45	.22	.04
□ 57	Tim Harkness	.45	.22	.04
□ 58	Don Demeter	.45	.22	.04
□ 59	Ernie Broglio	.60	.30	.06
□ 60	Frank Malzone	.60	.30	.06
□ 61	Angel Backstops	.60	.30	.06
	Bob Rodgers			
	Ed Sadowski			
□ 62	Ted Savage	.45	.22	.04
□ 63	Johnny Orsino	.45	.22	.04
□ 64	Ted Abernathy	.45	.22	.04
□ 65	Felipe Alou	.80	.40	.08
□ 66	Eddie Fisher	.45	.22	.04
□ 67	Tigers Team	1.25	.60	.12
□ 68	Willie Davis	.80	.40	.08
□ 69	Clete Boyer	.60	.30	.06

70	Joe Torre	1.50	.75	.15
71	Jack Spring	.45	.22	.04
72	Chico Cardenas	.45	.22	.04
73	Jimmie Hall	.45	.22	.04
74	Pirates Rookies	.45	.22	.04
	Bob Priddy			
	Tom Butters			
75	Wayne Causey	.45	.22	.04
76	Checklist 1	2.50	.45	.10
77	Jerry Walker	.45	.22	.04
78	Merritt Ranew	.45	.22	.04
79	Bob Heffner	.45	.22	.04
80	Vada Pinson	1.50	.75	.15
81	All-Star Vets	3.50	1.75	.35
	Nellie Fox			
	Harmon Killebrew			
82	Jim Davenport	.60	.30	.06
83	Gus Triandos	.60	.30	.06
84	Carl Willey	.45	.22	.04
85	Pete Ward	.45	.22	.04
86	Al Downing	.60	.30	.06
87	Cardinals Team	1.25	.60	.12
88	John Roseboro	.60	.30	.06
89	Boog Powell	1.75	.85	.17
90	Earl Battey	.60	.30	.06
91	Bob Bailey	.45	.22	.04
92	Steve Ridzik	.45	.22	.04
93	Gary Geiger	.45	.22	.04
94	Braves Rookies	.45	.22	.04
	Jim Britton			
	Larry Maxie			
95	George Altman	.45	.22	.04
96	Bob Buhl	.45	.22	.04
97	Jim Fregosi	.80	.40	.08
98	Bill Bruton	.45	.22	.04
99	Al Stanek	.45	.22	.04
100	Elston Howard	1.75	.85	.17
101	Walt Alston MG	1.75	.85	.17
102	Checklist 2	2.50	.45	.10
103	Curt Flood	1.25	.60	.12
104	Art Mahaffey	.45	.22	.04
105	Woody Held	.45	.22	.04
106	Joe Nuxhall	.60	.30	.06
107	White Sox Rookies	.45	.22	.04
	Bruce Howard			
	Frank Kreutzer			
108	John Wyatt	.45	.22	.04
109	Rusty Staub	3.00	1.50	.30
110	Albie Pearson	.45	.22	.04
111	Don Elston	.45	.22	.04
112	Bob Tillman	.45	.22	.04
113	Grover Powell	.45	.22	.04
114	Don Lock	.45	.22	.04
115	Frank Bolling	.45	.22	.04
116	Twins Rookies	4.50	2.25	.45
	Jay Ward			
	Tony Oliva			
117	Earl Francis	.45	.22	.04
118	John Blanchard	.60	.30	.06
119	Gary Kolb	.45	.22	.04
120	Don Drysdale	6.00	3.00	.60
121	Pete Runnels	.60	.30	.06
122	Don McMahon	.45	.22	.04
123	Jose Pagan	.45	.22	.04
124	Orlando Pena	.45	.22	.04
125	Pete Rose	150.00	75.00	15.00
126	Russ Snyder	.45	.22	.04
127	Angels Rookies	.45	.22	.04
	Aubrey Gatewood			
	Dick Simpson			
128	Mickey Lolich	5.00	2.50	.50
129	Amado Samuel	.45	.22	.04
130	Gary Peters	.60	.30	.06
131	Steve Boros	.60	.30	.06
132	Braves Team	1.25	.60	.12
133	Jim Grant	.45	.22	.04
134	Don Zimmer	.80	.40	.08
135	Johnny Callison	.60	.30	.06
136	World Series Game 1	4.00	2.00	.40
	Koufax strikes out 15			
137	World Series Game 2	1.75	.85	.17
	Davis sparks rally			
138	World Series Game 3	1.75	.85	.17
	LA 3 straight			
139	World Series Game 4	1.75	.85	.17
	Sealing Yanks doom			
140	World Series Summary	1.75	.85	.17
	Dodgers celebrate			
141	Danny Murtaugh MG	.45	.22	.04
142	John Bateman	.45	.22	.04
143	Bubba Phillips	.45	.22	.04
144	Al Worthington	.45	.22	.04
145	Norm Siebern	.45	.22	.04
146	Indians Rookies	15.00	7.50	1.50
	Tommy John			
	Bob Chance			
147	Ray Sadecki	.45	.22	.04
148	J.C. Martin	.45	.22	.04
149	Paul Foytack	.45	.22	.04
150	Willie Mays	40.00	20.00	4.00
151	Athletics Team	1.00	.50	.10
152	Denver Lemaster	.45	.22	.04
153	Dick Williams MG	.60	.30	.06
154	Dick Tracewski	.45	.22	.04
155	Duke Snider	10.00	5.00	1.00
156	Bill Dailey	.45	.22	.04
157	Gene Mauch MG	.60	.30	.06
158	Ken Johnson	.45	.22	.04
159	Charlie Dees	.45	.22	.04
160	Ken Boyer	3.00	1.50	.30
161	Dave McNally	1.00	.50	.10
162	Hitting Area	.60	.30	.06
	Dick Sisler			
	Vada Pinson			
163	Donn Clendenon	.60	.30	.06
164	Bud Daley	.45	.22	.04
165	Jerry Lumpe	.45	.22	.04
166	Marty Keough	.45	.22	.04
167	Senators Rookies	12.00	6.00	1.20
	Mike Brumley			
	Lou Piniella			
168	Al Weis	.45	.22	.04
169	Del Crandall	.60	.30	.06
170	Dick Radatz	.60	.30	.06
171	Ty Cline	.45	.22	.04
172	Indians Team	1.00	.50	.10
173	Ryne Duren	.60	.30	.06
174	Doc Edwards	.60	.30	.06
175	Billy Williams	5.50	2.75	.55
176	Tracy Stallard	.45	.22	.04
177	Harmon Killebrew	6.50	3.25	.65
178	Hank Bauer MG	.60	.30	.06
179	Carl Warwick	.45	.22	.04
180	Tommy Davis	.80	.40	.08
181	Dave Wickersham	.45	.22	.04
182	Sox Sockers	4.50	2.25	.45
	Carl Yastrzemski			
	Chuck Schilling			
183	Ron Taylor	.45	.22	.04
184	Al Luplow	.45	.22	.04
185	Jim O'Toole	.45	.22	.04
186	Roman Mejias	.45	.22	.04
187	Ed Roebuck	.45	.22	.04
188	Checklist 3	2.50	.45	.10
189	Bob Hendley	.45	.22	.04
190	Bobby Richardson	2.50	1.25	.25
191	Clay Dalrymple	.45	.22	.04
192	Cubs Rookies	.45	.22	.04
	John Boccabella			
	Billy Cowan			
193	Jerry Lynch	.45	.22	.04
194	John Goryl	.45	.22	.04
195	Floyd Robinson	.45	.22	.04
196	Jim Gentile	.60	.30	.06
197	Frank Lary	.60	.30	.06
198	Len Gabrielson	.45	.22	.04
199	Joe Azcue	.45	.22	.04
200	Sandy Koufax	30.00	15.00	3.00
201	Orioles Rookies	.60	.30	.06
	Sam Bowens			
	Wally Bunker			
202	Galen Cisco	.45	.22	.04
203	John Kennedy	.45	.22	.04
204	Matty Alou	.60	.30	.06
205	Nellie Fox	2.50	1.25	.25
206	Steve Hamilton	.45	.22	.04
207	Fred Hutchinson MG	.60	.30	.06
208	Wes Covington	.60	.30	.06
209	Bob Allen	.45	.22	.04
210	Carl Yastrzemski	50.00	25.00	5.00
211	Jim Coker	.45	.22	.04
212	Pete Lovrich	.45	.22	.04
213	Angels Team	1.00	.50	.10
214	Ken McMullen	.60	.30	.06
215	Ray Herbert	.45	.22	.04
216	Mike De La Hoz	.45	.22	.04
217	Jim King	.45	.22	.04
218	Hank Fischer	.45	.22	.04
219	Young Aces	1.00	.50	.10
	Al Downing			
	Jim Bouton			
220	Dick Ellsworth	.60	.30	.06
221	Bob Saverine	.45	.22	.04
222	Billy Pierce	.80	.40	.08
223	George Banks	.45	.22	.04
224	Tommie Sisk	.45	.22	.04
225	Roger Maris	15.00	7.50	1.50
226	Colts Rookies	.60	.30	.06
	Gerald Grote			
	Larry Yellen			

☐ 227 Barry Latman	.45	.22	.04
☐ 228 Felix Mantilla	.45	.22	.04
☐ 229 Charley Lau	.60	.30	.06
☐ 230 Brooks Robinson	15.00	7.50	1.50
☐ 231 Dick Calmus	.45	.22	.04
☐ 232 Al Lopez MG	2.00	1.00	.20
☐ 233 Hal Smith	.45	.22	.04
☐ 234 Gary Bell	.45	.22	.04
☐ 235 Ron Hunt	.45	.22	.04
☐ 236 Bill Faul	.45	.22	.04
☐ 237 Cubs Team	1.00	.50	.10
☐ 238 Roy McMillan	.45	.22	.04
☐ 239 Herm Starrette	.45	.22	.04
☐ 240 Bill White	.80	.40	.08
☐ 241 Jim Owens	.45	.22	.04
☐ 242 Harvey Kuenn	1.00	.50	.10
☐ 243 Phillies Rookies	9.00	4.50	.90
Richie Allen			
John Herrnstein			
☐ 244 Tony LaRussa	2.00	1.00	.20
☐ 245 Dick Stigman	.45	.22	.04
☐ 246 Manny Mota	.80	.40	.08
☐ 247 Dave DeBusschere	2.00	1.00	.20
☐ 248 Johnny Pesky MG	.60	.30	.06
☐ 249 Doug Camilli	.45	.22	.04
☐ 250 Al Kaline	9.00	4.50	.90
☐ 251 Choo Choo Coleman	.45	.22	.04
☐ 252 Ken Aspromonte	.45	.22	.04
☐ 253 Wally Post	.45	.22	.04
☐ 254 Don Hoak	.45	.22	.04
☐ 255 Lee Thomas	.45	.22	.04
☐ 256 Johnny Weekly	.45	.22	.04
☐ 257 Giants Team	1.00	.50	.10
☐ 258 Garry Roggenburk	.45	.22	.04
☐ 259 Harry Bright	.45	.22	.04
☐ 260 Frank Robinson	7.50	3.75	.75
☐ 261 Jim Hannan	.45	.22	.04
☐ 262 Cards Rookies	2.00	1.00	.20
Mike Shannon			
Harry Fanok			
☐ 263 Chuck Estrada	.60	.30	.06
☐ 264 Jim Landis	.45	.22	.04
☐ 265 Jim Bunning	2.50	1.25	.25
☐ 266 Gene Freese	.45	.22	.04
☐ 267 Wilbur Wood	1.00	.50	.10
☐ 268 Bill's Got It	.60	.30	.06
Danny Murtaugh			
Bill Virdon			
☐ 269 Ellis Burton	.45	.22	.04
☐ 270 Rich Rollins	.60	.30	.06
☐ 271 Bob Sadowski	.45	.22	.04
☐ 272 Jake Wood	.45	.22	.04
☐ 273 Mel Nelson	.45	.22	.04
☐ 274 Checklist 4	2.50	.45	.10
☐ 275 John Tsitouris	.45	.22	.04
☐ 276 Jose Tartabull	.45	.22	.04
☐ 277 Ken Retzer	.45	.22	.04
☐ 278 Bobby Shantz	.80	.40	.08
☐ 279 Joe Koppe (glove	.60	.30	.06
on wrong hand)			
☐ 280 Juan Marichal	6.00	3.00	.60
☐ 281 Yankees Rookies	.60	.30	.06
Jake Gibbs			
Tom Metcalf			
☐ 282 Bob Bruce	.45	.22	.04
☐ 283 Tommy McCraw	.45	.22	.04
☐ 284 Dick Schofield	.45	.22	.04
☐ 285 Robin Roberts	5.00	2.50	.50
☐ 286 Don Landrum	.45	.22	.04
☐ 287 Red Sox Rookies	4.50	2.25	.45
Tony Conigliaro			
Bill Spanswick			
☐ 288 Al Moran	.45	.22	.04
☐ 289 Frank Funk	.45	.22	.04
☐ 290 Bob Allison	.60	.30	.06
☐ 291 Phil Ortega	.45	.22	.04
☐ 292 Mike Roarke	.45	.22	.04
☐ 293 Phillies Team	1.00	.50	.10
☐ 294 Kent Hunt	.45	.22	.04
☐ 295 Roger Craig	1.00	.50	.10
☐ 296 Ed Kirkpatrick	.45	.22	.04
☐ 297 Ken MacKenzie	.45	.22	.04
☐ 298 Harry Craft MG	.45	.22	.04
☐ 299 Bill Stafford	.45	.22	.04
☐ 300 Hank Aaron	40.00	20.00	4.00
☐ 301 Larry Brown	.45	.22	.04
☐ 302 Dan Pfister	.45	.22	.04
☐ 303 Jim Campbell	.45	.22	.04
☐ 304 Bob Johnson	.45	.22	.04
☐ 305 Jack Lamabe	.45	.22	.04
☐ 306 Giant Gunners	10.00	5.00	1.00
Willie Mays			
Orlando Cepeda			
☐ 307 Joe Gibbon	.45	.22	.04
☐ 308 Gene Stephens	.45	.22	.04
☐ 309 Paul Toth	.45	.22	.04
☐ 310 Jim Gilliam	2.00	1.00	.20
☐ 311 Tom Brown	.45	.22	.04
☐ 312 Tigers Rookies	.45	.22	.04
Fritz Fisher			
Fred Gladding			
☐ 313 Chuck Hiller	.45	.22	.04
☐ 314 Jerry Buchek	.45	.22	.04
☐ 315 Bo Belinsky	.60	.30	.06
☐ 316 Gene Oliver	.45	.22	.04
☐ 317 Al Smith	.45	.22	.04
☐ 318 Twins Team	1.00	.50	.10
☐ 319 Paul Brown	.45	.22	.04
☐ 320 Rocky Colavito	1.75	.85	.17
☐ 321 Bob Lillis	.60	.30	.06
☐ 322 George Brunet	.45	.22	.04
☐ 323 John Buzhardt	.45	.22	.04
☐ 324 Casey Stengel MG	6.00	3.00	.60
☐ 325 Hector Lopez	.45	.22	.04
☐ 326 Ron Brand	.45	.22	.04
☐ 327 Don Blasingame	.45	.22	.04
☐ 328 Bob Shaw	.45	.22	.04
☐ 329 Russ Nixon	.45	.22	.04
☐ 330 Tommy Harper	.60	.30	.06
☐ 331 AL Bombers	40.00	20.00	4.00
Roger Maris			
Norm Cash			
Mickey Mantle			
Al Kaline			
☐ 332 Ray Washburn	.45	.22	.04
☐ 333 Billy Moran	.45	.22	.04
☐ 334 Lew Krausse	.45	.22	.04
☐ 335 Don Mossi	.60	.30	.06
☐ 336 Andre Rodgers	.45	.22	.04
☐ 337 Dodgers Rookies	.80	.40	.08
Al Ferrara			
Jeff Torborg			
☐ 338 Jack Kralick	.45	.22	.04
☐ 339 Walt Bond	.45	.22	.04
☐ 340 Joe Cunningham	.45	.22	.04
☐ 341 Jim Roland	.45	.22	.04
☐ 342 Willie Stargell	18.00	9.00	1.80
☐ 343 Senators Team	1.00	.50	.10
☐ 344 Phil Linz	.60	.30	.06
☐ 345 Frank Thomas	.45	.22	.04
☐ 346 Joe Jay	.45	.22	.04
☐ 347 Bobby Wine	.45	.22	.04
☐ 348 Ed Lopat MG	.60	.30	.06
☐ 349 Art Fowler	.45	.22	.04
☐ 350 Willie McCovey	10.00	5.00	1.00
☐ 351 Dan Schneider	.45	.22	.04
☐ 352 Eddie Bressoud	.45	.22	.04
☐ 353 Wally Moon	.60	.30	.06
☐ 354 Dave Giusti	.60	.30	.06
☐ 355 Vic Power	.45	.22	.04
☐ 356 Reds Rookies	.60	.30	.06
Bill McCool			
Chico Ruiz			
☐ 357 Charley James	.45	.22	.04
☐ 358 Ron Kline	.45	.22	.04
☐ 359 Jim Schaffer	.45	.22	.04
☐ 360 Joe Pepitone	.80	.40	.08
☐ 361 Jay Hook	.45	.22	.04
☐ 362 Checklist 5	2.50	.45	.10
☐ 363 Dick McAuliffe	.60	.30	.06
☐ 364 Joe Gaines	.45	.22	.04
☐ 365 Cal McLish	.45	.22	.04
☐ 366 Nelson Mathews	.45	.22	.04
☐ 367 Fred Whitfield	.45	.22	.04
☐ 368 White Sox Rookies	.60	.30	.06
Fritz Ackley			
Don Buford			
☐ 369 Jerry Zimmerman	.45	.22	.04
☐ 370 Hal Woodeshick	.45	.22	.04
☐ 371 Frank Howard	1.75	.85	.17
☐ 372 Howie Koplitz	.80	.40	.08
☐ 373 Pirates Team	1.50	.75	.15
☐ 374 Bobby Bolin	.80	.40	.08
☐ 375 Ron Santo	1.75	.85	.17
☐ 376 Dave Morehead	.80	.40	.08
☐ 377 Bob Skinner	1.00	.50	.10
☐ 378 Braves Rookies	1.50	.75	.15
Woody Woodward			
Jack Smith			
☐ 379 Tony Gonzalez	.80	.40	.08
☐ 380 Whitey Ford	11.00	5.50	1.10
☐ 381 Bob Taylor	.80	.40	.08
☐ 382 Wes Stock	.80	.40	.08
☐ 383 Bill Rigney MG	.80	.40	.08
☐ 384 Ron Hansen	.80	.40	.08
☐ 385 Curt Simmons	1.00	.50	.10
☐ 386 Lenny Green	.80	.40	.08
☐ 387 Terry Fox	.80	.40	.08
☐ 388 A's Rookies	.80	.40	.08
John O'Donoghue			

George Williams				
☐ 389 Jim Umbricht	.80	.40	.08
☐ 390 Orlando Cepeda	3.50	1.75	.35
☐ 391 Sam McDowell	1.50	.75	.15
☐ 392 Jim Pagliaroni	.80	.40	.08
☐ 393 Casey Teaches	3.00	1.50	.30
Casey Stengel				
Ed Kranepool				
☐ 394 Bob Miller	.80	.40	.08
☐ 395 Tom Tresh	1.50	.75	.15
☐ 396 Dennis Bennett	.80	.40	.08
☐ 397 Chuck Cottier	1.00	.50	.10
☐ 398 Mets Rookies	.80	.40	.08
Bill Haas				
Dick Smith				
☐ 399 Jackie Brandt	.80	.40	.08
☐ 400 Warren Spahn	10.00	5.00	1.00
☐ 401 Charlie Maxwell	.80	.40	.08
☐ 402 Tom Sturdivant	.80	.40	.08
☐ 403 Reds Team	1.50	.75	.15
☐ 404 Tony Martinez	.80	.40	.08
☐ 405 Ken McBride	.80	.40	.08
☐ 406 Al Spangler	.80	.40	.08
☐ 407 Bill Freehan	2.00	1.00	.20
☐ 408 Cubs Rookies	.80	.40	.08
Jim Stewart				
Fred Burdette				
☐ 409 Bill Fischer	.80	.40	.08
☐ 410 Dick Stuart	1.25	.60	.12
☐ 411 Lee Walls	.80	.40	.08
☐ 412 Ray Culp	.80	.40	.08
☐ 413 Johnny Keane MG	1.00	.50	.10
☐ 414 Jack Sanford	1.00	.50	.10
☐ 415 Tony Kubek	4.00	2.00	.40
☐ 416 Lee Maye	.80	.40	.08
☐ 417 Don Cardwell	.80	.40	.08
☐ 418 Orioles Rookies	1.25	.60	.12
Darold Knowles				
Les Narum				
☐ 419 Ken Harrelson	4.00	2.00	.40
☐ 420 Jim Maloney	1.25	.60	.12
☐ 421 Camilo Carreon	.80	.40	.08
☐ 422 Jack Fisher	.80	.40	.08
☐ 423 Tops in NL	25.00	12.50	2.50
Hank Aaron				
Willie Mays				
☐ 424 Dick Bertell	.80	.40	.08
☐ 425 Norm Cash	1.50	.75	.15
☐ 426 Bob Rodgers	1.00	.50	.10
☐ 427 Don Rudolph	.80	.40	.08
☐ 428 Red Sox Rookies	.80	.40	.08
Archie Skeen				
Pete Smith				
☐ 429 Tim McCarver	2.00	1.00	.20
☐ 430 Juan Pizarro	.80	.40	.08
☐ 431 George Alusik	.80	.40	.08
☐ 432 Ruben Amaro	.80	.40	.08
☐ 433 Yankees Team	5.50	2.75	.55
☐ 434 Don Nottebart	.80	.40	.08
☐ 435 Vic Davalillo	1.00	.50	.10
☐ 436 Charlie Neal	1.00	.50	.10
☐ 437 Ed Bailey	.80	.40	.08
☐ 438 Checklist 6	3.50	.60	.10
☐ 439 Harvey Haddix	1.25	.60	.12
☐ 440 Bob Clemente	30.00	15.00	3.00
☐ 441 Bob Duliba	.80	.40	.08
☐ 442 Pumpsie Green	.80	.40	.08
☐ 443 Chuck Dressen MG	1.00	.50	.10
☐ 444 Larry Jackson	.80	.40	.08
☐ 445 Bill Skowron	1.50	.75	.15
☐ 446 Julian Javier	1.00	.50	.10
☐ 447 Ted Bowsfield	.80	.40	.08
☐ 448 Cookie Rojas	.80	.40	.08
☐ 449 Deron Johnson	1.00	.50	.10
☐ 450 Steve Barber	.80	.40	.08
☐ 451 Joe Amalfitano	.80	.40	.08
☐ 452 Giants Rookies	1.50	.75	.15
Gil Garrido				
Jim Ray Hart				
☐ 453 Frank Baumann	.80	.40	.08
☐ 454 Tommie Aaron	1.00	.50	.10
☐ 455 Bernie Allen	.80	.40	.08
☐ 456 Dodgers Rookies	1.75	.85	.17
Wes Parker				
John Werhas				
☐ 457 Jesse Gonder	.80	.40	.08
☐ 458 Ralph Terry	1.25	.60	.12
☐ 459 Red Sox Rookies	.80	.40	.08
Pete Charton				
Dalton Jones				
☐ 460 Bob Gibson	12.00	6.00	1.20
☐ 461 George Thomas	.80	.40	.08
☐ 462 Birdie Tebbetts MG	.80	.40	.08
☐ 463 Don Leppert	.80	.40	.08
☐ 464 Dallas Green	1.25	.60	.12

☐ 465 Mike Hershberger	.80	.40	.08
☐ 466 A's Rookies	.80	.40	.08
Dick Green				
Aurelio Monteagudo				
☐ 467 Bob Aspromonte	.80	.40	.08
☐ 468 Gaylord Perry	12.00	6.00	1.20
☐ 469 Cubs Rookies	1.00	.50	.10
Fred Norman				
Sterling Slaughter				
☐ 470 Jim Bouton	2.00	1.00	.20
☐ 471 Gates Brown	1.50	.75	.15
☐ 472 Vern Law	1.25	.60	.12
☐ 473 Orioles Team	1.50	.75	.15
☐ 474 Larry Sherry	1.00	.50	.10
☐ 475 Ed Charles	.80	.40	.08
☐ 476 Braves Rookies	3.00	1.50	.30
Rico Carty				
Dick Kelley				
☐ 477 Mike Joyce	.80	.40	.08
☐ 478 Dick Howser	1.50	.75	.15
☐ 479 Cardinals Rookies	.80	.40	.08
Dave Bakenhaster				
Johnny Lewis				
☐ 480 Bob Purkey	.80	.40	.08
☐ 481 Chuck Schilling	.80	.40	.08
☐ 482 Phillies Rookies	1.00	.50	.10
John Briggs				
Danny Cater				
☐ 483 Fred Valentine	.80	.40	.08
☐ 484 Bill Pleis	.80	.40	.08
☐ 485 Tom Haller	1.00	.50	.10
☐ 486 Bob Kennedy MG	.80	.40	.08
☐ 487 Mike McCormick	1.00	.50	.10
☐ 488 Yankees Rookies	.80	.40	.08
Pete Mikkelsen				
Bob Meyer				
☐ 489 Julio Navarro	.80	.40	.08
☐ 490 Ron Fairly	1.00	.50	.10
☐ 491 Ed Rakow	.80	.40	.08
☐ 492 Colts Rookies	.80	.40	.08
Jim Beauchamp				
Mike White				
☐ 493 Don Lee	.80	.40	.08
☐ 494 Al Jackson	.80	.40	.08
☐ 495 Bill Virdon	1.50	.75	.15
☐ 496 White Sox Team	1.50	.75	.15
☐ 497 Jeoff Long	.80	.40	.08
☐ 498 Dave Stenhouse	.80	.40	.08
☐ 499 Indians Rookies	.80	.40	.08
Chico Salmon				
Gordon Seyfried				
☐ 500 Camilo Pascual	1.00	.50	.10
☐ 501 Bob Veale	1.00	.50	.10
☐ 502 Angels Rookies	1.00	.50	.10
Bobby Knoop				
Bob Lee				
☐ 503 Earl Wilson	.80	.40	.08
☐ 504 Claude Raymond	.80	.40	.08
☐ 505 Stan Williams	1.00	.50	.10
☐ 506 Bobby Bragan MG	.80	.40	.08
☐ 507 John Edwards	.80	.40	.08
☐ 508 Diego Segui	.80	.40	.08
☐ 509 Pirates Rookies	1.25	.60	.12
Gene Alley				
Orlando McFarlane				
☐ 510 Lindy McDaniel	1.00	.50	.10
☐ 511 Lou Jackson	.80	.40	.08
☐ 512 Tigers Rookies	3.00	1.50	.30
Willie Horton				
Joe Sparma				
☐ 513 Don Larsen	1.25	.60	.12
☐ 514 Jim Hickman	.80	.40	.08
☐ 515 Johnny Romano	.80	.40	.08
☐ 516 Twins Rookies	.80	.40	.08
Jerry Arrigo				
Dwight Siebler				
☐ 517A Checklist 7 COR	4.00	.70	.10
(correct numbering on back)				
☐ 517B Checklist 7 ERR	8.00	1.00	.20
(incorrect numbering sequence on back)				
☐ 518 Carl Bouldin	.80	.40	.08
☐ 519 Charlie Smith	.80	.40	.08
☐ 520 Jack Baldschun	.80	.40	.08
☐ 521 Tom Satriano	.80	.40	.08
☐ 522 Bob Tiefenauer	.80	.40	.08
☐ 523 Lou Burdette	3.50	1.75	.35
(pitching lefty)				
☐ 524 Reds Rookies	2.00	1.00	.20
Jim Dickson				
Bobby Klaus				
☐ 525 Al McBean	2.00	1.00	.20
☐ 526 Lou Clinton	2.00	1.00	.20
☐ 527 Larry Bearnarth	2.00	1.00	.20

☐ 528	A's Rookies	2.50	1.25	.25
	Dave Duncan			
	Tom Reynolds			
☐ 529	Al Dark MG	2.50	1.25	.25
☐ 530	Leon Wagner	2.00	1.00	.20
☐ 531	Dodgers Team	5.00	2.50	.50
☐ 532	Twins Rookies	2.00	1.00	.20
	Bud Bloomfield			
	(Bloomfield photo			
	actually Jay Ward)			
	Joe Nossek			
☐ 533	John Klippstein	2.00	1.00	.20
☐ 534	Gus Bell	2.50	1.25	.25
☐ 535	Phil Regan	2.50	1.25	.25
☐ 536	Mets Rookies	2.00	1.00	.20
	Larry Elliot			
	John Stephenson			
☐ 537	Dan Osinski	2.00	1.00	.20
☐ 538	Minnie Minoso	3.50	1.75	.35
☐ 539	Roy Face	3.00	1.50	.30
☐ 540	Luis Aparicio	10.00	5.00	1.00
☐ 541	Braves Rookies	60.00	30.00	6.00
	Phil Roof			
	Phil Niekro			
☐ 542	Don Mincher	2.50	1.25	.25
☐ 543	Bob Uecker	35.00	17.50	3.50
☐ 544	Colts Rookies	2.00	1.00	.20
	Steve Hertz			
	Joe Hoerner			
☐ 545	Max Alvis	2.00	1.00	.20
☐ 546	Joe Christopher	2.00	1.00	.20
☐ 547	Gil Hodges	8.00	4.00	.80
☐ 548	NL Rookies	2.00	1.00	.20
	Wayne Schurr			
	Paul Speckenbach			
☐ 549	Joe Moeller	2.00	1.00	.20
☐ 550	Ken Hubbs	6.00	3.00	.60
	(in memoriam)			
☐ 551	Billy Hoeft	2.00	1.00	.20
☐ 552	Indians Rookies	3.00	1.50	.30
	Tom Kelley			
	Sonny Siebert			
☐ 553	Jim Brewer	2.00	1.00	.20
☐ 554	Hank Foiles	2.00	1.00	.20
☐ 555	Lee Stange	2.00	1.00	.20
☐ 556	Mets Rookies	2.00	1.00	.20
	Steve Dillon			
	Ron Locke			
☐ 557	Leo Burke	2.00	1.00	.20
☐ 558	Don Schwall	2.00	1.00	.20
☐ 559	Dick Phillips	2.00	1.00	.20
☐ 560	Dick Farrell	2.00	1.00	.20
☐ 561	Phillies Rookies	3.50	1.75	.35
	Dave Bennett			
	(19 ... is 18)			
	Rick Wise			
☐ 562	Pedro Ramos	2.00	1.00	.20
☐ 563	Dal Maxvill	2.50	1.25	.25
☐ 564	AL Rookies	2.00	1.00	.20
	Joe McCabe			
	Jerry McNertney			
☐ 565	Stu Miller	2.00	1.00	.20
☐ 566	Ed Kranepool	3.00	1.50	.30
☐ 567	Jim Kaat	6.00	3.00	.60
☐ 568	NL Rookies	2.00	1.00	.20
	Phil Gagliano			
	Cap Peterson			
☐ 569	Fred Newman	2.00	1.00	.20
☐ 570	Bill Mazeroski	3.50	1.75	.35
☐ 571	Gene Conley	2.00	1.00	.20
☐ 572	AL Rookies	2.00	1.00	.20
	Dave Gray			
	Dick Egan			
☐ 573	Jim Duffalo	2.00	1.00	.20
☐ 574	Manny Jimenez	2.00	1.00	.20
☐ 575	Tony Cloninger	2.00	1.00	.20
☐ 576	Mets Rookies	2.00	1.00	.20
	Jerry Hinsley			
	Bill Wakefield			
☐ 577	Gordy Coleman	2.00	1.00	.20
☐ 578	Glen Hobbie	2.00	1.00	.20
☐ 579	Red Sox Team	6.00	3.00	.60
☐ 580	Johnny Podres	3.50	1.75	.35
☐ 581	Yankees Rookies	2.00	1.00	.20
	Pedro Gonzales			
	Archie Moore			
☐ 582	Rod Kanehl	2.00	1.00	.20
☐ 583	Tito Francona	2.00	1.00	.20
☐ 584	Joel Horlen	2.50	1.25	.25
☐ 585	Tony Taylor	2.00	1.00	.20
☐ 586	Jim Piersall	3.00	1.50	.30
☐ 587	Bennie Daniels	3.50	1.00	.20

1964 Topps Giants

The cards in this 60-card set measure 3 1/8" by 5 1/4". The 1964 Topps Giants are postcard size cards containing color player photographs. They are numbered on the backs, which also contain biographical information presented in a newspaper format. These "giant size" cards were distributed in both cellophane and waxed gum packs apart from the Topps regular issue of 1964. Cards 3, 28, 42, 45, 47, 51 and 60 slightly more difficult to find and are indicated by SP in the checklist below.

		NRMT	VG-E	GOOD
COMPLETE SET		50.00	25.00	5.00
COMMON PLAYER (1-60)		.10	.05	.01
☐ 1	Gary Peters	.10	.05	.01
☐ 2	Ken Johnson	.10	.05	.01
☐ 3	Sandy Koufax SP	9.00	4.50	.90
☐ 4	Bob Bailey	.10	.05	.01
☐ 5	Milt Pappas	.10	.05	.01
☐ 6	Ron Hunt	.10	.05	.01
☐ 7	Whitey Ford	1.50	.75	.15
☐ 8	Roy McMillan	.10	.05	.01
☐ 9	Rocky Colavito	.30	.15	.03
☐ 10	Jim Bunning	.40	.20	.04
☐ 11	Bob Clemente	2.50	1.25	.25
☐ 12	Al Kaline	1.50	.75	.15
☐ 13	Nellie Fox	.30	.15	.03
☐ 14	Tony Gonzalez	.10	.05	.01
☐ 15	Jim Gentile	.10	.05	.01
☐ 16	Dean Chance	.10	.05	.01
☐ 17	Dick Ellsworth	.10	.05	.01
☐ 18	Jim Fregosi	.15	.07	.01
☐ 19	Dick Groat	.15	.07	.01
☐ 20	Chuck Hinton	.10	.05	.01
☐ 21	Elston Howard	.25	.12	.02
☐ 22	Dick Farrell	.10	.05	.01
☐ 23	Albie Pearson	.10	.05	.01
☐ 24	Frank Howard	.20	.10	.02
☐ 25	Mickey Mantle	6.00	3.00	.60
☐ 26	Joe Torre	.25	.12	.02
☐ 27	Eddie Brinkman	.10	.05	.01
☐ 28	Bob Friend SP	2.50	1.25	.25
☐ 29	Frank Robinson	1.50	.75	.15
☐ 30	Bill Freehan	.15	.07	.01
☐ 31	Warren Spahn	1.50	.75	.15
☐ 32	Camilo Pascual	.10	.05	.01
☐ 33	Pete Ward	.10	.05	.01
☐ 34	Jim Maloney	.10	.05	.01
☐ 35	Dave Wickersham	.10	.05	.01
☐ 36	Johnny Callison	.10	.05	.01
☐ 37	Juan Marichal	1.25	.60	.12
☐ 38	Harmon Killebrew	1.50	.75	.15
☐ 39	Luis Aparicio	1.25	.60	.12
☐ 40	Dick Radatz	.10	.05	.01
☐ 41	Bob Gibson	1.25	.60	.12
☐ 42	Dick Stuart SP	2.50	1.25	.25
☐ 43	Tommy Davis	.15	.07	.01
☐ 44	Tony Oliva	.30	.15	.03
☐ 45	Wayne Causey SP	2.50	1.25	.25
☐ 46	Max Alvis	.10	.05	.01
☐ 47	Galen Cisco SP	2.50	1.25	.25
☐ 48	Carl Yastrzemski	3.00	1.50	.30
☐ 49	Hank Aaron	3.00	1.50	.30

		NRMT	VG-E	GOOD
☐ 50	Brooks Robinson	2.00	1.00	.20
☐ 51	Willie Mays SP	10.00	5.00	1.00
☐ 52	Billy Williams	1.25	.60	.12
☐ 53	Juan Pizarro	.10	.05	.01
☐ 54	Leon Wagner	.10	.05	.01
☐ 55	Orlando Cepeda	.35	.17	.03
☐ 56	Vada Pinson	.20	.10	.02
☐ 57	Ken Boyer	.20	.10	.02
☐ 58	Ron Santo	.20	.10	.02
☐ 59	John Romano	.10	.05	.01
☐ 60	Bill Skowron SP	3.00	1.50	.30

1964 Topps Stand Ups

BOOG POWELL
BALT. ORIOLES   OUTFIELD

In 1964 Topps produced a die-cut "Stand-Up" card design for the first time since their Connie Mack and Current All Stars of 1951. The cards have full-length, color player photos set against a green and yellow background. Of the 77 cards in the set, 22 were single printed and these are marked in the checklist below with an SP. These unnumbered cards are standard-size (2 1/2" by 3 1/2"), blank backed, and have been numbered here for reference in alphabetical order of players.

	NRMT	VG-E	GOOD
COMPLETE SET	1200.00	400.00	80.00
COMMON PLAYER (1-77)	2.50	1.25	.25
COMMON PLAYER SP	15.00	7.50	1.50

		NRMT	VG-E	GOOD
☐	1 Hank Aaron	60.00	30.00	6.00
☐	2 Hank Aguirre	2.50	1.25	.25
☐	3 George Altman	2.50	1.25	.25
☐	4 Max Alvis	2.50	1.25	.25
☐	5 Bob Aspromonte	2.50	1.25	.25
☐	6 Jack Baldschun SP	15.00	7.50	1.50
☐	7 Ernie Banks	25.00	12.50	2.50
☐	8 Steve Barber	2.50	1.25	.25
☐	9 Earl Battey	2.50	1.25	.25
☐	10 Ken Boyer	3.50	1.75	.35
☐	11 Ernie Broglio	2.50	1.25	.25
☐	12 John Callison	2.50	1.25	.25
☐	13 Norm Cash SP	18.00	9.00	1.80
☐	14 Wayne Causey	2.50	1.25	.25
☐	15 Orlando Cepeda	4.50	2.25	.45
☐	16 Ed Charles	2.50	1.25	.25
☐	17 Bob Clemente	45.00	22.50	4.50
☐	18 Donn Clendenon SP	15.00	7.50	1.50
☐	19 Rocky Colavito	3.50	1.75	.35
☐	20 Ray Culp SP	15.00	7.50	1.50
☐	21 Tommy Davis	3.50	1.75	.35
☐	22 Don Drysdale SP	60.00	30.00	6.00
☐	23 Dick Ellsworth	2.50	1.25	.25
☐	24 Dick Farrell	2.50	1.25	.25
☐	25 Jim Fregosi	3.00	1.50	.30
☐	26 Bob Friend	2.50	1.25	.25
☐	27 Jim Gentile	2.50	1.25	.25
☐	28 Jesse Gonder SP	15.00	7.50	1.50
☐	29 Tony Gonzalez SP	15.00	7.50	1.50
☐	30 Dick Groat	3.00	1.50	.30
☐	31 Woody Held	2.50	1.25	.25
☐	32 Chuck Hinton	2.50	1.25	.25
☐	33 Elston Howard	3.50	1.75	.35
☐	34 Frank Howard SP	18.00	9.00	1.80
☐	35 Ron Hunt	2.50	1.25	.25
☐	36 Al Jackson	2.50	1.25	.25

		NRMT	VG-E	GOOD
☐ 37	Ken Johnson	2.50	1.25	.25
☐ 38	Al Kaline	30.00	15.00	3.00
☐ 39	Harmon Killebrew	20.00	10.00	2.00
☐ 40	Sandy Koufax	40.00	20.00	4.00
☐ 41	Don Lock SP	15.00	7.50	1.50
☐ 42	Jerry Lumpe SP	15.00	7.50	1.50
☐ 43	Jim Maloney	2.50	1.25	.25
☐ 44	Frank Malzone	2.50	1.25	.25
☐ 45	Mickey Mantle	200.00	100.00	20.00
☐ 46	Juan Marichal SP	60.00	30.00	6.00
☐ 47	Eddie Mathews SP	60.00	30.00	6.00
☐ 48	Willie Mays	60.00	30.00	6.00
☐ 49	Bill Mazeroski	3.50	1.75	.35
☐ 50	Ken McBride	2.50	1.25	.25
☐ 51	Willie McCovey SP	60.00	30.00	6.00
☐ 52	Claude Osteen	2.50	1.25	.25
☐ 53	Jim O'Toole	2.50	1.25	.25
☐ 54	Camilo Pascual	2.50	1.25	.25
☐ 55	Albie Pearson SP	15.00	7.50	1.50
☐ 56	Gary Peters	2.50	1.25	.25
☐ 57	Vada Pinson	3.50	1.75	.35
☐ 58	Juan Pizarro	2.50	1.25	.25
☐ 59	Boog Powell	3.50	1.75	.35
☐ 60	Bobby Richardson	3.50	1.75	.35
☐ 61	Brooks Robinson	30.00	15.00	3.00
☐ 62	Floyd Robinson	2.50	1.25	.25
☐ 63	Frank Robinson	20.00	10.00	2.00
☐ 64	Ed Roebuck SP	15.00	7.50	1.50
☐ 65	Rich Rollins	2.50	1.25	.25
☐ 66	John Romano	2.50	1.25	.25
☐ 67	Ron Santo SP	18.00	9.00	1.80
☐ 68	Norm Siebern	2.50	1.25	.25
☐ 69	Warren Spahn SP	60.00	30.00	6.00
☐ 70	Dick Stuart SP	15.00	7.50	1.50
☐ 71	Lee Thomas	2.50	1.25	.25
☐ 72	Joe Torre	4.50	2.25	.45
☐ 73	Pete Ward	2.50	1.25	.25
☐ 74	Bill White SP	18.00	9.00	1.80
☐ 75	Billy Williams SP	50.00	25.00	5.00
☐ 76	Hal Woodeshick SP	15.00	7.50	1.50
☐ 77	Carl Yastrzemski SP	200.00	100.00	20.00

1965 Topps

The cards in this 598-card set measure 2 1/2" by 3 1/2". The cards comprising the 1965 Topps set have team names located within a distinctive pennant design below the picture. The cards have blue borders on the reverse and were issued by series. Cards 523 to 598 are more difficult to obtain than all other series. In addition, the sixth series (447-522) is more difficult to obtain than series one through five. Featured subsets within this set include League Leaders (1-12) and World Series cards (132-139). Key cards in this set include Steve Carlton's rookie and Pete Rose.

	NRMT	VG-E	GOOD
COMPLETE SET	1800.00	600.00	120.00
COMMON PLAYER (1-198)	.35	.17	.03
COMMON PLAYER (199-446)	.65	.30	.06
COMMON PLAYER (447-522)	1.25	.60	.12
COMMON PLAYER (523-598)	2.00	1.00	.20

		NRMT	VG-E	GOOD
☐ 1	AL Batting Leaders Tony Oliva Elston Howard	4.50	.50	.10

☐ 2	NL Batting Leaders Bob Clemente Hank Aaron Rico Carty	3.50	1.75	.35
☐ 3	AL Home Run Leaders Harmon Killebrew Mickey Mantle Boog Powell	6.00	3.00	.60
☐ 4	NL Home Run Leaders Willie Mays Billy Williams Jim Ray Hart Orlando Cepeda Johnny Callison	3.00	1.50	.30
☐ 5	AL RBI Leaders Brooks Robinson Harmon Killebrew Mickey Mantle Dick Stuart	6.00	3.00	.60
☐ 6	NL RBI Leaders Ken Boyer Willie Mays Ron Santo	1.50	.75	.15
☐ 7	AL ERA Leaders Dean Chance Joel Horlen	1.00	.50	.10
☐ 8	NL ERA Leaders Sandy Koufax Don Drysdale	4.00	2.00	.40
☐ 9	AL Pitching Leaders Dean Chance Gary Peters Dave Wickersham Juan Pizarro Wally Bunker	1.00	.50	.10
☐ 10	NL Pitching Leaders Larry Jackson Ray Sadecki Juan Marichal	1.00	.50	.10
☐ 11	AL Strikeout Leaders Al Downing Dean Chance Camilo Pascual	1.00	.50	.10
☐ 12	NL Strikeout Leaders Bob Veale Don Drysdale Bob Gibson	1.50	.75	.15
☐ 13	Pedro Ramos	.35	.17	.03
☐ 14	Len Gabrielson	.35	.17	.03
☐ 15	Robin Roberts	5.00	2.50	.50
☐ 16	Houston Rookies Joe Morgan Sonny Jackson	35.00	17.50	3.50
☐ 17	John Romano	.35	.17	.03
☐ 18	Bill McCool	.35	.17	.03
☐ 19	Gates Brown	.50	.25	.05
☐ 20	Jim Bunning	2.25	1.10	.22
☐ 21	Don Blasingame	.35	.17	.03
☐ 22	Charlie Smith	.35	.17	.03
☐ 23	Bob Tiefenauer	.35	.17	.03
☐ 24	Twins Team	1.75	.85	.17
☐ 25	Al McBean	.35	.17	.03
☐ 26	Bob Knoop	.35	.17	.03
☐ 27	Dick Bertell	.35	.17	.03
☐ 28	Barney Schultz	.35	.17	.03
☐ 29	Felix Mantilla	.35	.17	.03
☐ 30	Jim Bouton	1.25	.60	.12
☐ 31	Mike White	.35	.17	.03
☐ 32	Herman Franks MG	.35	.17	.03
☐ 33	Jackie Brandt	.35	.17	.03
☐ 34	Cal Koonce	.35	.17	.03
☐ 35	Ed Charles	.35	.17	.03
☐ 36	Bobby Wine	.35	.17	.03
☐ 37	Fred Gladding	.35	.17	.03
☐ 38	Jim King	.35	.17	.03
☐ 39	Gerry Arrigo	.35	.17	.03
☐ 40	Frank Howard	1.25	.60	.12
☐ 41	White Sox Rookies Bruce Howard Marv Staehle	.35	.17	.03
☐ 42	Earl Wilson	.35	.17	.03
☐ 43	Mike Shannon	.60	.30	.06
☐ 44	Wade Blasingame	.35	.17	.03
☐ 45	Roy McMillan	.35	.17	.03
☐ 46	Bob Lee	.35	.17	.03
☐ 47	Tommy Harper	.45	.22	.04
☐ 48	Claude Raymond	.35	.17	.03
☐ 49	Orioles Rookies Curt Blefary John Miller	.75	.35	.07
☐ 50	Juan Marichal	5.50	2.75	.55
☐ 51	Bill Bryan	.35	.17	.03
☐ 52	Ed Roebuck	.35	.17	.03
☐ 53	Dick McAuliffe	.45	.22	.04

☐ 54	Joe Gibbon	.35	.17	.03
☐ 55	Tony Conigliaro	2.00	1.00	.20
☐ 56	Ron Kline	.35	.17	.03
☐ 57	Cardinals Team	1.00	.50	.10
☐ 58	Fred Talbot	.35	.17	.03
☐ 59	Nate Oliver	.35	.17	.03
☐ 60	Jim O'Toole	.35	.17	.03
☐ 61	Chris Cannizzaro	.35	.17	.03
☐ 62	Jim Katt (sic, Kaat)	2.50	1.25	.25
☐ 63	Ty Cline	.35	.17	.03
☐ 64	Lou Burdette	.75	.35	.07
☐ 65	Tony Kubek	1.75	.85	.17
☐ 66	Bill Rigney MG	.35	.17	.03
☐ 67	Harvey Haddix	.45	.22	.04
☐ 68	Del Crandall	.45	.22	.04
☐ 69	Bill Virdon	.75	.35	.07
☐ 70	Bill Skowron	1.00	.50	.10
☐ 71	John O'Donoghue	.35	.17	.03
☐ 72	Tony Gonzalez	.35	.17	.03
☐ 73	Dennis Ribant	.35	.17	.03
☐ 74	Red Sox Rookies Rico Petrocelli Jerry Stephenson	2.00	1.00	.20
☐ 75	Deron Johnson	.45	.22	.04
☐ 76	Sam McDowell	.75	.35	.07
☐ 77	Doug Camilli	.35	.17	.03
☐ 78	Dal Maxvill	.45	.22	.04
☐ 79	Checklist 1	2.50	.40	.10
☐ 80	Turk Farrell	.35	.17	.03
☐ 81	Don Buford	.35	.17	.03
☐ 82	Braves Rookies Santos Alomar John Braun	.45	.22	.04
☐ 83	George Thomas	.35	.17	.03
☐ 84	Ron Herbel	.35	.17	.03
☐ 85	Willie Smith	.35	.17	.03
☐ 86	Les Narum	.35	.17	.03
☐ 87	Nelson Mathews	.35	.17	.03
☐ 88	Jack Lamabe	.35	.17	.03
☐ 89	Mike Hershberger	.35	.17	.03
☐ 90	Rich Rollins	.45	.22	.04
☐ 91	Cubs Team	1.00	.50	.10
☐ 92	Dick Howser	1.00	.50	.10
☐ 93	Jack Fisher	.35	.17	.03
☐ 94	Charlie Lau	.45	.22	.04
☐ 95	Bill Mazeroski	1.25	.60	.12
☐ 96	Sonny Siebert	.45	.22	.04
☐ 97	Pedro Gonzalez	.35	.17	.03
☐ 98	Bob Miller	.35	.17	.03
☐ 99	Gil Hodges MG	4.00	2.00	.40
☐ 100	Ken Boyer	1.50	.75	.15
☐ 101	Fred Newman	.35	.17	.03
☐ 102	Steve Boros	.45	.22	.04
☐ 103	Harvey Kuenn	.75	.35	.07
☐ 104	Checklist 2	2.50	.40	.10
☐ 105	Chico Salmon	.35	.17	.03
☐ 106	Gene Oliver	.35	.17	.03
☐ 107	Phillies Rookies Pat Corrales Costen Shockley	1.50	.75	.15
☐ 108	Don Mincher	.45	.22	.04
☐ 109	Walt Bond	.35	.17	.03
☐ 110	Ron Santo	1.25	.60	.12
☐ 111	Lee Thomas	.35	.17	.03
☐ 112	Derrell Griffith	.35	.17	.03
☐ 113	Steve Barber	.35	.17	.03
☐ 114	Jim Hickman	.35	.17	.03
☐ 115	Bobby Richardson	1.75	.85	.17
☐ 116	Cardinals Rookies Dave Dowling Bob Tolan	.60	.30	.06
☐ 117	Wes Stock	.45	.22	.04
☐ 118	Hal Lanier	1.25	.60	.12
☐ 119	John Kennedy	.35	.17	.03
☐ 120	Frank Robinson	7.50	3.75	.75
☐ 121	Gene Alley	.45	.22	.04
☐ 122	Bill Pleis	.35	.17	.03
☐ 123	Frank Thomas	.35	.17	.03
☐ 124	Tom Satriano	.35	.17	.03
☐ 125	Juan Pizarro	.35	.17	.03
☐ 126	Dodgers Team	2.00	1.00	.20
☐ 127	Frank Lary	.45	.22	.04
☐ 128	Vic Davalillo	.45	.22	.04
☐ 129	Bennie Daniels	.35	.17	.03
☐ 130	Al Kaline	8.50	4.25	.85
☐ 131	Johnny Keane MG	.35	.17	.03
☐ 132	World Series Game 1 Cards take opener	1.50	.75	.15
☐ 133	World Series Game 2 Stottlemyre wins	1.50	.75	.15
☐ 134	World Series Game 3 Mantle's homer	9.00	4.50	.90
☐ 135	World Series Game 4 Boyer's grand-slam	2.00	1.00	.20
☐ 136	World Series Game 5	1.50	.75	.15

☐ 137	10th inning triumph World Series Game 6	2.00	1.00	.20	☐ 218	Dick Schofield	.65	.30	.06
☐ 138	Bouton wins again World Series Game 7	3.00	1.50	.30	☐ 219	Bob Meyer	.65	.30	.06
	Gibson wins finale				☐ 220	Billy Williams	5.00	2.50	.50
☐ 139	World Series Summary	1.50	.75	.15	☐ 221	John Tsitouris	.65	.30	.06
	Cards celebrate				☐ 222	Bob Tillman	.65	.30	.06
☐ 140	Dean Chance	.45	.22	.04	☐ 223	Dan Osinski	.65	.30	.06
☐ 141	Charlie James	.35	.17	.03	☐ 224	Bob Chance	.65	.30	.06
☐ 142	Bill Monbouquette	.35	.17	.03	☐ 225	Bo Belinsky	.80	.40	.08
☐ 143	Pirates Rookies	.35	.17	.03	☐ 226	Yankees Rookies	.80	.40	.08
	John Gelnar					Elvio Jimenez			
	Jerry May					Jake Gibbs			
☐ 144	Ed Kranepool	.45	.22	.04	☐ 227	Bob Klaus	.65	.30	.06
☐ 145	Luis Tiant	6.00	3.00	.60	☐ 228	Jack Sanford	.80	.40	.08
☐ 146	Ron Hansen	.35	.17	.03	☐ 229	Lou Clinton	.65	.30	.06
☐ 147	Dennis Bennett	.35	.17	.03	☐ 230	Ray Sadecki	.65	.30	.06
☐ 148	Willie Kirkland	.35	.17	.03	☐ 231	Jerry Adair	.65	.30	.06
☐ 149	Wayne Schurr	.35	.17	.03	☐ 232	Steve Blass	1.00	.50	.10
☐ 150	Brooks Robinson	9.00	4.50	.90	☐ 233	Don Zimmer	1.00	.50	.10
☐ 151	Athletics Team	1.00	.50	.10	☐ 234	White Sox Team	1.25	.60	.12
☐ 152	Phil Ortega	.35	.17	.03	☐ 235	Chuck Hinton	.65	.30	.06
☐ 153	Norm Cash	1.25	.60	.12	☐ 236	Dennis McLain	5.50	2.75	.55
☐ 154	Bob Humphreys	.35	.17	.03	☐ 237	Bernie Allen	.65	.30	.06
☐ 155	Roger Maris	10.00	5.00	1.00	☐ 238	Joe Moeller	.65	.30	.06
☐ 156	Bob Sadowski	.35	.17	.03	☐ 239	Doc Edwards	.80	.40	.08
☐ 157	Zoilo Versalles	.75	.35	.07	☐ 240	Bob Bruce	.65	.30	.06
☐ 158	Dick Sisler	.35	.17	.03	☐ 241	Mack Jones	.65	.30	.06
☐ 159	Jim Duffalo	.35	.17	.03	☐ 242	George Brunet	.65	.30	.06
☐ 160	Bob Clemente	20.00	10.00	2.00	☐ 243	Reds Rookies	1.00	.50	.10
☐ 161	Frank Baumann	.35	.17	.03		Ted Davidson			
☐ 162	Russ Nixon	.35	.17	.03		Tommy Helms			
☐ 163	John Briggs	.35	.17	.03	☐ 244	Lindy McDaniel	.80	.40	.08
☐ 164	Al Spangler	.35	.17	.03	☐ 245	Joe Pepitone	1.00	.50	.10
☐ 165	Dick Ellsworth	.45	.22	.04	☐ 246	Tom Butters	.65	.30	.06
☐ 166	Indians Rookies	.75	.35	.07	☐ 247	Wally Moon	.80	.40	.08
	George Culver				☐ 248	Gus Triandos	.80	.40	.08
	Tommie Agee				☐ 249	Dave McNally	1.00	.50	.10
☐ 167	Bill Wakefield	.35	.17	.03	☐ 250	Willie Mays	40.00	20.00	4.00
☐ 168	Dick Green	.35	.17	.03	☐ 251	Billy Herman MG	1.50	.75	.15
☐ 169	Dave Vineyard	.35	.17	.03	☐ 252	Pete Richert	.65	.30	.06
☐ 170	Hank Aaron	35.00	17.50	3.50	☐ 253	Danny Cater	.65	.30	.06
☐ 171	Jim Roland	.35	.17	.03	☐ 254	Roland Sheldon	.65	.30	.06
☐ 172	Jim Piersall	.75	.35	.07	☐ 255	Camilo Pascual	.80	.40	.08
☐ 173	Tigers Team	1.25	.60	.12	☐ 256	Tito Francona	.80	.40	.08
☐ 174	Joe Jay	.35	.17	.03	☐ 257	Jim Wynn	1.00	.50	.10
☐ 175	Bob Aspromonte	.35	.17	.03	☐ 258	Larry Bearnarth	.65	.30	.06
☐ 176	Willie McCovey	8.00	4.00	.80	☐ 259	Tigers Rookies	1.00	.50	.10
☐ 177	Pete Mikkelsen	.35	.17	.03		Jim Northrup			
☐ 178	Dalton Jones	.35	.17	.03		Ray Oyler			
☐ 179	Hal Woodeshick	.35	.17	.03	☐ 260	Don Drysdale	6.00	3.00	.60
☐ 180	Bob Allison	.60	.30	.06	☐ 261	Duke Carmel	.65	.30	.06
☐ 181	Senators Rookies	.35	.17	.03	☐ 262	Bud Daley	.65	.30	.06
	Don Loun				☐ 263	Marty Keough	.65	.30	.06
	Joe McCabe				☐ 264	Bob Buhl	.65	.30	.06
☐ 182	Mike De La Hoz	.35	.17	.03	☐ 265	Jim Pagliaroni	.65	.30	.06
☐ 183	Dave Nicholson	.35	.17	.03	☐ 266	Bert Campaneris	2.25	1.10	.22
☐ 184	John Boozer	.35	.17	.03	☐ 267	Senators Team	1.00	.50	.10
☐ 185	Max Alvis	.35	.17	.03	☐ 268	Ken McBride	.65	.30	.06
☐ 186	Bill Cowan	.35	.17	.03	☐ 269	Frank Bolling	.65	.30	.06
☐ 187	Casey Stengel MG	5.00	2.50	.50	☐ 270	Milt Pappas	.80	.40	.08
☐ 188	Sam Bowens	.35	.17	.03	☐ 271	Don Wert	.65	.30	.06
☐ 189	Checklist 3	2.50	.40	.10	☐ 272	Chuck Schilling	.65	.30	.06
☐ 190	Bill White	.60	.30	.06	☐ 273	Checklist 4	2.50	.40	.10
☐ 191	Phil Regan	.45	.22	.04	☐ 274	Lum Harris MG	.65	.30	.06
☐ 192	Jim Coker	.35	.17	.03	☐ 275	Dick Groat	1.00	.50	.10
☐ 193	Gaylord Perry	6.00	3.00	.60	☐ 276	Hoyt Wilhelm	4.00	2.00	.40
☐ 194	Rookie Stars	.45	.22	.04	☐ 277	John Lewis	.65	.30	.06
	Bill Kelso				☐ 278	Ken Retzer	.65	.30	.06
	Rick Reichardt				☐ 279	Dick Tracewski	.65	.30	.06
☐ 195	Bob Veale	.45	.22	.04	☐ 280	Dick Stuart	.80	.40	.08
☐ 196	Ron Fairly	.45	.22	.04	☐ 281	Bill Stafford	.65	.30	.06
☐ 197	Diego Segui	.35	.17	.03	☐ 282	Giants Rookies	1.00	.50	.10
☐ 198	Smoky Burgess	.45	.22	.04		Dick Estelle			
☐ 199	Bob Heffner	.65	.30	.06		Masanori Murakami			
☐ 200	Joe Torre	1.50	.75	.15	☐ 283	Fred Whitfield	.65	.30	.06
☐ 201	Twins Rookies	1.00	.50	.10	☐ 284	Nick Willhite	.65	.30	.06
	Sandy Valdespino				☐ 285	Ron Hunt	.65	.30	.06
	Cesar Tovar				☐ 286	Athletics Rookies	.65	.30	.06
☐ 202	Leo Burke	.65	.30	.06		Jim Dickson			
☐ 203	Dallas Green	1.00	.50	.10		Aurelio Monteagudo			
☐ 204	Russ Snyder	.65	.30	.06	☐ 287	Gary Kolb	.65	.30	.06
☐ 205	Warren Spahn	7.50	3.75	.75	☐ 288	Jack Hamilton	.65	.30	.06
☐ 206	Willie Horton	1.25	.60	.12	☐ 289	Gordy Coleman	.65	.30	.06
☐ 207	Pete Rose	150.00	75.00	15.00	☐ 290	Wally Bunker	.65	.30	.06
☐ 208	Tommy John	4.00	2.00	.40	☐ 291	Jerry Lynch	.65	.30	.06
☐ 209	Pirates Team	1.25	.60	.12	☐ 292	Larry Yellen	.65	.30	.06
☐ 210	Jim Fregosi	1.00	.50	.10	☐ 293	Angels Team	1.00	.50	.10
☐ 211	Steve Ridzik	.65	.30	.06	☐ 294	Tim McCarver	1.25	.60	.12
☐ 212	Ron Brand	.65	.30	.06	☐ 295	Dick Radatz	.80	.40	.08
☐ 213	Jim Davenport	.80	.40	.08	☐ 296	Tony Taylor	.65	.30	.06
☐ 214	Bob Purkey	.65	.30	.06	☐ 297	Dave Debusschere	2.00	1.00	.20
☐ 215	Pete Ward	.65	.30	.06	☐ 298	Jim Stewart	.65	.30	.06
☐ 216	Al Worthington	.65	.30	.06	☐ 299	Jerry Zimmerman	.65	.30	.06
☐ 217	Walt Alston MG	1.75	.85	.17	☐ 300	Sandy Koufax	35.00	17.50	3.50
					☐ 301	Birdie Tebbetts MG	.65	.30	.06
					☐ 302	Al Stanek	.65	.30	.06

□ 303 John Orsino	.65	.30	.06
□ 304 Dave Stenhouse	.65	.30	.06
□ 305 Rico Carty	1.00	.50	.10
□ 306 Bubba Phillips	.65	.30	.06
□ 307 Barry Latman	.65	.30	.06
□ 308 Mets Rookies	.80	.40	.08
Cleon Jones			
Tom Parsons			
□ 309 Steve Hamilton	.65	.30	.06
□ 310 John Callison	.80	.40	.08
□ 311 Orlando Pena	.65	.30	.06
□ 312 Joe Nuxhall	.80	.40	.08
□ 313 Jim Schaffer	.65	.30	.06
□ 314 Sterling Slaughter	.65	.30	.06
□ 315 Frank Malzone	.80	.40	.08
□ 316 Reds Team	1.25	.60	.12
□ 317 Don McMahon	.65	.30	.06
□ 318 Matty Alou	.80	.40	.08
□ 319 Ken McMullen	.65	.30	.06
□ 320 Bob Gibson	6.00	3.00	.60
□ 321 Rusty Staub	2.50	1.25	.25
□ 322 Rick Wise	.80	.40	.08
□ 323 Hank Bauer MG	.80	.40	.08
□ 324 Bob Locke	.65	.30	.06
□ 325 Donn Clendenon	.80	.40	.08
□ 326 Dwight Siebler	.65	.30	.06
□ 327 Denis Menke	.65	.30	.06
□ 328 Eddie Fisher	.65	.30	.06
□ 329 Hawk Taylor	.65	.30	.06
□ 330 Whitey Ford	8.50	4.25	.85
□ 331 Dodgers Rookies	.80	.40	.08
Al Ferrara			
John Purdin			
□ 332 Ted Abernathy	.65	.30	.06
□ 333 Tom Reynolds	.65	.30	.06
□ 334 Vic Roznovsky	.65	.30	.06
□ 335 Mickey Lolich	2.00	1.00	.20
□ 336 Woody Held	.65	.30	.06
□ 337 Mike Cuellar	1.00	.50	.10
□ 338 Phillies Team	1.00	.50	.10
□ 339 Ryne Duren	.80	.40	.08
□ 340 Tony Oliva	3.00	1.50	.30
□ 341 Bob Bolin	.65	.30	.06
□ 342 Bob Rodgers	.80	.40	.08
□ 343 Mike McCormick	.80	.40	.08
□ 344 Wes Parker	1.00	.50	.10
□ 345 Floyd Robinson	.65	.30	.06
□ 346 Bob Bragan MG	.65	.30	.06
□ 347 Roy Face	1.00	.50	.10
□ 348 George Banks	.65	.30	.06
□ 349 Larry Miller	.65	.30	.06
□ 350 Mickey Mantle	300.00	150.00	30.00
□ 351 Jim Perry	1.00	.50	.10
□ 352 Alex Johnson	.80	.40	.08
□ 353 Jerry Lumpe	.65	.30	.06
□ 354 Cubs Rookies	.65	.30	.06
Billy Ott			
Jack Warner			
□ 355 Vada Pinson	1.50	.75	.15
□ 356 Bill Spanswick	.65	.30	.06
□ 357 Carl Warwick	.65	.30	.06
□ 358 Albie Pearson	.65	.30	.06
□ 359 Ken Johnson	.65	.30	.06
□ 360 Orlando Cepeda	3.00	1.50	.30
□ 361 Checklist 5	2.50	.40	.10
□ 362 Don Schwall	.65	.30	.06
□ 363 Bob Johnson	.65	.30	.06
□ 364 Galen Cisco	.65	.30	.06
□ 365 Jim Gentile	.80	.40	.08
□ 366 Dan Schneider	.65	.30	.06
□ 367 Leon Wagner	.65	.30	.06
□ 368 White Sox Rookies	.80	.40	.08
Ken Berry			
Joel Gibson			
□ 369 Phil Linz	.80	.40	.08
□ 370 Tommy Davis	1.00	.50	.10
□ 371 Frank Kreutzer	.65	.30	.06
□ 372 Clay Dalrymple	.65	.30	.06
□ 373 Curt Simmons	.80	.40	.08
□ 374 Angels Rookies	.80	.40	.08
Jose Cardenal			
Dick Simpson			
□ 375 Dave Wickersham	.65	.30	.06
□ 376 Jim Landis	.65	.30	.06
□ 377 Willie Stargell	8.50	4.25	.85
□ 378 Chuck Estrada	.80	.40	.08
□ 379 Giants Team	1.00	.50	.10
□ 380 Rocky Colavito	1.75	.85	.17
□ 381 Al Jackson	.65	.30	.06
□ 382 J.C. Martin	.65	.30	.06
□ 383 Felipe Alou	.80	.40	.08
□ 384 John Klippstein	.65	.30	.06
□ 385 Carl Yastrzemski	50.00	25.00	5.00
□ 386 Cubs Rookies	.80	.40	.08
Paul Jaeckel			

Fred Norman			
□ 387 John Podres	1.25	.60	.12
□ 388 John Blanchard	.80	.40	.08
□ 389 Don Larsen	1.00	.50	.10
□ 390 Bill Freehan	1.50	.75	.15
□ 391 Mel McGaha MG	.65	.30	.06
□ 392 Bob Friend	.80	.40	.08
□ 393 Ed Kirkpatrick	.65	.30	.06
□ 394 Jim Hannan	.65	.30	.06
□ 395 Jim Ray Hart	.80	.40	.08
□ 396 Frank Bertaina	.65	.30	.06
□ 397 Jerry Buchek	.65	.30	.06
□ 398 Reds Rookies	.65	.30	.06
Dan Neville			
Art Shamsky			
□ 399 Ray Herbert	.65	.30	.06
□ 400 Harmon Killebrew	6.50	3.25	.65
□ 401 Carl Willey	.65	.30	.06
□ 402 Joe Amalfitano	.65	.30	.06
□ 403 Red Sox Team	1.25	.60	.12
□ 404 Stan Williams	.80	.40	.08
□ 405 John Roseboro	.80	.40	.08
□ 406 Ralph Terry	.80	.40	.08
□ 407 Lee Maye	.65	.30	.06
□ 408 Larry Sherry	.80	.40	.08
□ 409 Astros Rookies	1.00	.50	.10
Jim Beauchamp			
Larry Dierker			
□ 410 Luis Aparicio	5.00	2.50	.50
□ 411 Roger Craig	1.00	.50	.10
□ 412 Bob Bailey	.65	.30	.06
□ 413 Hal Reniff	.65	.30	.06
□ 414 Al Lopez MG	1.75	.85	.17
□ 415 Curt Flood	1.00	.50	.10
□ 416 Jim Brewer	.65	.30	.06
□ 417 Ed Brinkman	.65	.30	.06
□ 418 John Edwards	.65	.30	.06
□ 419 Ruben Amaro	.65	.30	.06
□ 420 Larry Jackson	.65	.30	.06
□ 421 Twins Rookies	.65	.30	.06
Gary Dotter			
Jay Ward			
□ 422 Aubrey Gatewood	.65	.30	.06
□ 423 Jesse Gonder	.65	.30	.06
□ 424 Gary Bell	.65	.30	.06
□ 425 Wayne Causey	.65	.30	.06
□ 426 Braves Team	1.00	.50	.10
□ 427 Bob Saverine	.65	.30	.06
□ 428 Bob Shaw	.65	.30	.06
□ 429 Don Demeter	.65	.30	.06
□ 430 Gary Peters	.80	.40	.08
□ 431 Cards Rookies	1.00	.50	.10
Nelson Briles			
Wayne Spiezio			
□ 432 Jim Grant	.65	.30	.06
□ 433 John Bateman	.65	.30	.06
□ 434 Dave Morehead	.65	.30	.06
□ 435 Willie Davis	1.00	.50	.10
□ 436 Don Elston	.65	.30	.06
□ 437 Chico Cardenas	.65	.30	.06
□ 438 Harry Walker MG	.65	.30	.06
□ 439 Moe Drabowsky	.65	.30	.06
□ 440 Tom Tresh	1.25	.60	.12
□ 441 Denny Lemaster	.65	.30	.06
□ 442 Vic Power	.65	.30	.06
□ 443 Checklist 6	3.00	.50	.10
□ 444 Bob Hendley	.65	.30	.06
□ 445 Don Lock	.65	.30	.06
□ 446 Art Mahaffey	.65	.30	.06
□ 447 Julian Javier	1.25	.60	.12
□ 448 Lee Stange	1.25	.60	.12
□ 449 Mets Rookies	1.25	.60	.12
Jerry Hinsley			
Gary Kroll			
□ 450 Elston Howard	2.50	1.25	.25
□ 451 Jim Owens	1.25	.60	.12
□ 452 Gary Geiger	1.25	.60	.12
□ 453 Dodgers Rookies	1.50	.75	.15
Willie Crawford			
John Werhas			
□ 454 Ed Rakow	1.25	.60	.12
□ 455 Norm Siebern	1.25	.60	.12
□ 456 Bill Henry	1.25	.60	.12
□ 457 Bob Kennedy MG	1.25	.60	.12
□ 458 John Buzhardt	1.25	.60	.12
□ 459 Frank Kostro	1.25	.60	.12
□ 460 Richie Allen	3.50	1.75	.35
□ 461 Braves Rookies	20.00	10.00	2.00
Clay Carroll			
Phil Niekro			
□ 462 Lew Krausse	1.25	.60	.12
(photo actually			
Pete Lovrich)			
□ 463 Manny Mota	1.50	.75	.15
□ 464 Ron Piche	1.25	.60	.12

☐ 465	Tom Haller	1.50	.75	.15
☐ 466	Senators Rookies	1.25	.60	.12
	Pete Craig			
	Dick Nen			
☐ 467	Ray Washburn	1.25	.60	.12
☐ 468	Larry Brown	1.25	.60	.12
☐ 469	Don Nottebart	1.25	.60	.12
☐ 470	Yogi Berra MG	20.00	10.00	2.00
☐ 471	Bill Hoeft	1.25	.60	.12
☐ 472	Don Pavletich	1.25	.60	.12
☐ 473	Orioles Rookies	7.00	3.50	.70
	Paul Blair			
	Dave Johnson			
☐ 474	Cookie Rojas	1.25	.60	.12
☐ 475	Clete Boyer	2.00	1.00	.20
☐ 476	Billy O'Dell	1.25	.60	.12
☐ 477	Cards Rookies	125.00	60.00	12.50
	Fritz Ackley			
	Steve Carlton			
☐ 478	Wilbur Wood	1.50	.75	.15
☐ 479	Ken Harrelson	2.50	1.25	.25
☐ 480	Joel Horlen	1.50	.75	.15
☐ 481	Indians Team	2.00	1.00	.20
☐ 482	Bob Priddy	1.25	.60	.12
☐ 483	George Smith	1.25	.60	.12
☐ 484	Ron Perranoski	1.50	.75	.15
☐ 485	Nellie Fox	3.00	1.50	.30
☐ 486	Angels Rookies	1.25	.60	.12
	Tom Egan			
	Pat Rogan			
☐ 487	Woody Woodward	1.50	.75	.15
☐ 488	Ted Wills	1.25	.60	.12
☐ 489	Gene Mauch MG	1.50	.75	.15
☐ 490	Earl Battey	1.50	.75	.15
☐ 491	Tracy Stallard	1.25	.60	.12
☐ 492	Gene Freese	1.25	.60	.12
☐ 493	Tigers Rookies	1.25	.60	.12
	Bill Roman			
	Bruce Brubaker			
☐ 494	Jay Ritchie	1.25	.60	.12
☐ 495	Joe Christopher	1.25	.60	.12
☐ 496	Joe Cunningham	1.25	.60	.12
☐ 497	Giants Rookies	1.50	.75	.15
	Ken Henderson			
	Jack Hiatt			
☐ 498	Gene Stephens	1.25	.60	.12
☐ 499	Stu Miller	1.25	.60	.12
☐ 500	Ed Mathews	12.00	6.00	1.20
☐ 501	Indians Rookies	1.25	.60	.12
	Ralph Gagliano			
	Jim Rittwage			
☐ 502	Don Cardwell	1.25	.60	.12
☐ 503	Phil Gagliano	1.25	.60	.12
☐ 504	Jerry Grote	1.25	.60	.12
☐ 505	Ray Culp	1.25	.60	.12
☐ 506	Sam Mele MG	1.25	.60	.12
☐ 507	Sam Ellis	1.25	.60	.10
☐ 508	Checklist 7	4.50	.70	.10
☐ 509	Red Sox Rookies	1.25	.60	.12
	Bob Guindon			
	Gerry Vezendy			
☐ 510	Ernie Banks	24.00	12.00	2.40
☐ 511	Ron Locke	1.25	.60	.12
☐ 512	Cap Peterson	1.25	.60	.12
☐ 513	Yankees Team	4.50	2.25	.45
☐ 514	Joe Azcue	1.25	.60	.12
☐ 515	Vern Law	1.50	.75	.15
☐ 516	Al Weis	1.25	.60	.12
☐ 517	Angels Rookies	1.25	.60	.12
	Paul Schaal			
	Jack Warner			
☐ 518	Ken Rowe	1.25	.60	.12
☐ 519	Bob Uecker	30.00	15.00	3.00
☐ 520	Tony Cloninger	1.25	.60	.12
☐ 521	Phillies Rookies	1.25	.60	.12
	Dave Bennett			
	Morrie Stevens			
☐ 522	Hank Aguirre	1.25	.60	.12
☐ 523	Mike Brumley	2.00	1.00	.20
☐ 524	Dave Giusti	2.50	1.25	.25
☐ 525	Ed Bressoud	2.00	1.00	.20
☐ 526	Athletics Rookies	50.00	25.00	5.00
	Rene Lachemann			
	Johnny Odom			
	Jim Hunter ERR			
	("Tim" on back)			
	Skip Lockwood			
☐ 527	Jeff Torborg	2.50	1.25	.25
☐ 528	George Altman	2.00	1.00	.20
☐ 529	Jerry Fosnow	2.00	1.00	.20
☐ 530	Jim Maloney	2.50	1.25	.25
☐ 531	Chuck Hiller	2.00	1.00	.20
☐ 532	Hector Lopez	2.00	1.00	.20
☐ 533	Mets Rookies	10.00	5.00	1.00
	Dan Napoleon			
	Ron Swoboda			
	Tug McGraw			
	Jim Bethke			
☐ 534	John Herrnstein	2.00	1.00	.20
☐ 535	Jack Kralick	2.00	1.00	.20
☐ 536	Andre Rodgers	2.00	1.00	.20
☐ 537	Angels Rookies	2.50	1.25	.25
	Marcelino Lopes			
	Phil Roof			
	Rudy May			
☐ 538	Chuck Dressen MG	2.50	1.25	.25
☐ 539	Herm Starrette	2.00	1.00	.20
☐ 540	Lou Brock	25.00	12.50	2.50
☐ 541	White Sox Rookies	2.00	1.00	.20
	Greg Bollo			
	Bob Locker			
☐ 542	Lou Klimchock	2.00	1.00	.20
☐ 543	Ed Connolly	2.00	1.00	.20
☐ 544	Howie Reed	2.00	1.00	.20
☐ 545	Jesus Alou	2.00	1.00	.20
☐ 546	Indians Rookies	2.00	1.00	.20
	Bill Davis			
	Mike Hedlund			
	Ray Barker			
	Floyd Weaver			
☐ 547	Jake Wood	2.00	1.00	.20
☐ 548	Dick Stigman	2.00	1.00	.20
☐ 549	Cubs Rookies	3.00	1.50	.30
	Roberto Pena			
	Glenn Beckert			
☐ 550	Mel Stottlemyre	8.00	4.00	.80
☐ 551	Mets Team	4.50	2.25	.45
☐ 552	Julio Gotay	2.00	1.00	.20
☐ 553	Astros Rookies	2.00	1.00	.20
	Gene Ratliff			
	Jack McClure			
☐ 554	Chico Ruiz	2.00	1.00	.20
☐ 555	Jack Baldschun	2.00	1.00	.20
☐ 556	Red Schoendienst MG	3.00	1.50	.30
☐ 557	Jose Santiago	2.00	1.00	.20
☐ 558	Tom Sisk	2.00	1.00	.20
☐ 559	Ed Bailey	2.00	1.00	.20
☐ 560	Boog Powell	4.00	2.00	.40
☐ 561	Dodgers Rookies	3.00	1.50	.30
	Dennis Daboll			
	Mike Kekich			
	Hector Valle			
	Jim Lefebvre			
☐ 562	Bill Moran	2.00	1.00	.20
☐ 563	Julio Navarro	2.00	1.00	.20
☐ 564	Mel Nelson	2.00	1.00	.20
☐ 565	Ernie Broglio	2.00	1.00	.20
☐ 566	Yankees Rookies	2.00	1.00	.20
	Gil Blanco			
	Ross Moschitto			
	Art Lopez			
☐ 567	Tommie Aaron	2.50	1.25	.25
☐ 568	Ron Taylor	2.00	1.00	.20
☐ 569	Gino Cimoli	2.00	1.00	.20
☐ 570	Claude Osteen	2.50	1.25	.25
☐ 571	Ossie Virgil	2.00	1.00	.20
☐ 572	Orioles Team	3.50	1.75	.35
☐ 573	Red Sox Rookies	4.00	2.00	.40
	Jim Lonborg			
	Gerry Moses			
	Bill Schlesinger			
	Mike Ryan			
☐ 574	Roy Sievers	2.50	1.25	.25
☐ 575	Jose Pagan	2.00	1.00	.20
☐ 576	Terry Fox	2.00	1.00	.20
☐ 577	AL Rookie Stars	2.50	1.25	.25
	Darold Knowles			
	Don Buschhorn			
	Richie Scheinblum			
☐ 578	Camilo Carreon	2.00	1.00	.20
☐ 579	Dick Smith	2.00	1.00	.20
☐ 580	Jim Hall	2.00	1.00	.20
☐ 581	NL Rookie Stars	40.00	20.00	4.00
	Tony Perez			
	Dave Ricketts			
	Kevin Collins			
☐ 582	Bob Schmidt	2.00	1.00	.20
☐ 583	Wes Covington	2.00	1.00	.20
☐ 584	Harry Bright	2.00	1.00	.20
☐ 585	Hank Fischer	2.00	1.00	.20
☐ 586	Tom McCraw	2.00	1.00	.20
☐ 587	Joe Sparma	2.00	1.00	.20
☐ 588	Len Green	2.00	1.00	.20
☐ 589	Giants Rookies	2.00	1.00	.20
	Frank Linzy			
	Bob Schroder			
☐ 590	John Wyatt	2.00	1.00	.20
☐ 591	Bob Skinner	2.00	1.00	.20
☐ 592	Frank Bork	2.00	1.00	.20
☐ 593	Tigers Rookies	2.50	1.25	.25

		NRMT	VG-E	GOOD
	Jackie Moore			
	John Sullivan			
☐ 594	Joe Gaines	2.00	1.00	.20
☐ 595	Don Lee	2.00	1.00	.20
☐ 596	Don Landrum	2.00	1.00	.20
☐ 597	Twins Rookies	2.00	1.00	.20
	Joe Nossek			
	John Sevcik			
	Dick Reese			
☐ 598	Al Downing	3.50	1.00	.20

1965 Topps Embossed

KEN BOYER

The cards in this 72-card set measure 2 1/8" by 3 1/2". The 1965 Topps Embossed set contains gold foil cameo player portraits. Each league had 36 representatives set on blue backgrounds for the AL and red backgrounds for the NL. The Topps embossed set was distributed as inserts in packages of the regular 1965 baseball series.

		NRMT	VG-E	GOOD
	COMPLETE SET	50.00	25.00	5.00
	COMMON PLAYER (1-72)	.40	.20	.04
☐ 1	Carl Yastrzemski	6.50	3.25	.65
☐ 2	Ron Fairly	.40	.20	.04
☐ 3	Max Alvis	.40	.20	.04
☐ 4	Jim Ray Hart	.40	.20	.04
☐ 5	Bill Skowron	.60	.30	.06
☐ 6	Ed Kranepool	.50	.25	.05
☐ 7	Tim McCarver	.60	.30	.06
☐ 8	Sandy Koufax	4.00	2.00	.40
☐ 9	Donn Clendenon	.40	.20	.04
☐ 10	John Romano	.40	.20	.04
☐ 11	Mickey Mantle	10.00	5.00	1.00
☐ 12	Joe Torre	.60	.30	.06
☐ 13	Al Kaline	3.00	1.50	.30
☐ 14	Al McBean	.40	.20	.04
☐ 15	Don Drysdale	2.00	1.00	.20
☐ 16	Brooks Robinson	2.50	1.25	.25
☐ 17	Jim Bunning	.90	.45	.09
☐ 18	Gary Peters	.40	.20	.04
☐ 19	Bob Clemente	4.00	2.00	.40
☐ 20	Milt Pappas	.40	.20	.04
☐ 21	Wayne Causey	.40	.20	.04
☐ 22	Frank Robinson	2.50	1.25	.25
☐ 23	Bill Mazeroski	.60	.30	.06
☐ 24	Diego Segui	.40	.20	.04
☐ 25	Jim Bouton	.60	.30	.06
☐ 26	Ed Mathews	2.00	1.00	.20
☐ 27	Willie Mays	5.00	2.50	.50
☐ 28	Ron Santo	.50	.25	.05
☐ 29	Boog Powell	.60	.30	.06
☐ 30	Ken McBride	.40	.20	.04
☐ 31	Leon Wagner	.40	.20	.04
☐ 32	John Callison	.40	.20	.04
☐ 33	Zoilo Versalles	.40	.20	.04
☐ 34	Jack Baldschun	.40	.20	.04
☐ 35	Ron Hunt	.40	.20	.04
☐ 36	Richie Allen	.60	.30	.06
☐ 37	Frank Malzone	.40	.20	.04
☐ 38	Bob Allison	.50	.25	.05
☐ 39	Jim Fregosi	.50	.25	.05
☐ 40	Billy Williams	2.00	1.00	.20
☐ 41	Bill Freehan	.50	.25	.05
☐ 42	Vada Pinson	.60	.30	.06
☐ 43	Bill White	.50	.25	.05
☐ 44	Roy McMillan	.40	.20	.04
☐ 45	Orlando Cepeda	.90	.45	.09
☐ 46	Rocky Colavito	.60	.30	.06
☐ 47	Ken Boyer	.60	.30	.06
☐ 48	Dick Radatz	.40	.20	.04
☐ 49	Tommy Davis	.50	.25	.05
☐ 50	Walt Bond	.40	.20	.04
☐ 51	John Orsino	.40	.20	.04
☐ 52	Joe Christopher	.40	.20	.04
☐ 53	Al Spangler	.40	.20	.04
☐ 54	Jim King	.40	.20	.04
☐ 55	Mickey Lolich	.60	.30	.06
☐ 56	Harmon Killebrew	2.00	1.00	.20
☐ 57	Bob Shaw	.40	.20	.04
☐ 58	Ernie Banks	2.50	1.25	.25
☐ 59	Hank Aaron	5.00	2.50	.50
☐ 60	Chuck Hinton	.40	.20	.04
☐ 61	Bob Aspromonte	.40	.20	.04
☐ 62	Lee Maye	.40	.20	.04
☐ 63	Joe Cunningham	.40	.20	.04
☐ 64	Pete Ward	.40	.20	.04
☐ 65	Bobby Richardson	.60	.30	.06
☐ 66	Dean Chance	.40	.20	.04
☐ 67	Dick Ellsworth	.40	.20	.04
☐ 68	Jim Maloney	.40	.20	.04
☐ 69	Bob Gibson	2.00	1.00	.20
☐ 70	Earl Battey	.40	.20	.04
☐ 71	Tony Kubek	.80	.40	.08
☐ 72	Jack Kralick	.40	.20	.04

1966 Topps

DODGERS — SANDY KOUFAX pitcher

The cards in this 598-card set measure 2 1/2" by 3 1/2". There are the same number of cards as in the 1965 set. Once again, the seventh series cards (523 to 598) are considered more difficult to obtain than any other series' cards in the set. The only featured subset within this set is League Leaders (215-226). Noteworthy rookie cards in the set include Jim Palmer (126) and Don Sutton (288).

		NRMT	VG-E	GOOD
	COMPLETE SET	2500.00	1000.00	200.00
	COMMON PLAYER (1-110)	.30	.15	.03
	COMMON PLAYER (111-370)	.45	.22	.04
	COMMON PLAYER (371-446)	.50	.25	.05
	COMMON PLAYER (447-522)	1.50	.75	.15
	COMMON PLAYER (523-598)	8.50	4.25	.85
☐ 1	Willie Mays	90.00	20.00	4.00
☐ 2	Ted Abernathy	.30	.15	.03
☐ 3	Sam Mele MG	.30	.15	.03
☐ 4	Ray Culp	.30	.15	.03
☐ 5	Jim Fregosi	.80	.40	.08
☐ 6	Chuck Schilling	.30	.15	.03
☐ 7	Tracy Stallard	.30	.15	.03
☐ 8	Floyd Robinson	.30	.15	.03
☐ 9	Clete Boyer	.45	.22	.04
☐ 10	Tony Cloninger	.30	.15	.03
☐ 11	Senators Rookies	.30	.15	.03
	Brant Alyea			
	Pete Craig			
☐ 12	John Tsitouris	.30	.15	.03
☐ 13	Lou Johnson	.30	.15	.03
☐ 14	Norm Siebern	.30	.15	.03
☐ 15	Vern Law	.45	.22	.04
☐ 16	Larry Brown	.30	.15	.03

☐	17	John Stephenson	.30	.15	.03
☐	18	Roland Sheldon	.30	.15	.03
☐	19	Giants Team	.80	.40	.08
☐	20	Willie Horton	.80	.40	.08
☐	21	Don Nottebart	.30	.15	.03
☐	22	Joe Nossek	.30	.15	.03
☐	23	Jack Sanford	.45	.22	.04
☐	24	Don Kessinger	1.00	.50	.10
☐	25	Pete Ward	.30	.15	.03
☐	26	Ray Sadecki	.30	.15	.03
☐	27	Orioles Rookies	.45	.22	.04
		Darold Knowles			
		Andy Etchebarren			
☐	28	Phil Niekro	9.00	4.50	.90
☐	29	Mike Brumley	.30	.15	.03
☐	30	Pete Rose	60.00	30.00	6.00
☐	31	Jack Cullen	.30	.15	.03
☐	32	Adolfo Phillips	.30	.15	.03
☐	33	Jim Pagliaroni	.30	.15	.03
☐	34	Checklist 1	2.50	.40	.10
☐	35	Ron Swoboda	.45	.22	.04
☐	36	Jim Hunter	9.00	4.50	.90
☐	37	Billy Herman MG	1.25	.60	.12
☐	38	Ron Nischwitz	.30	.15	.03
☐	39	Ken Henderson	.30	.15	.03
☐	40	Jim Grant	.30	.15	.03
☐	41	Don LeJohn	.30	.15	.03
☐	42	Aubrey Gatewood	.30	.15	.03
☐	43	Don Landrum	.30	.15	.03
☐	44	Indians Rookies	.30	.15	.03
		Bill Davis			
		Tom Kelley			
☐	45	Jim Gentile	.45	.22	.04
☐	46	Howie Koplitz	.30	.15	.03
☐	47	J.C. Martin	.30	.15	.03
☐	48	Paul Blair	.45	.22	.04
☐	49	Woody Woodward	.45	.22	.04
☐	50	Mickey Mantle	175.00	85.00	18.00
☐	51	Gordon Richardson	.30	.15	.03
☐	52	Power Plus	.45	.22	.04
		Wes Covington			
		Johnny Callison			
☐	53	Bob Duliba	.30	.15	.03
☐	54	Jose Pagan	.30	.15	.03
☐	55	Ken Harrelson	1.00	.50	.10
☐	56	Sandy Valdespino	.30	.15	.03
☐	57	Jim Lefebvre	.45	.22	.04
☐	58	Dave Wickersham	.30	.15	.03
☐	59	Reds Team	.90	.45	.09
☐	60	Curt Flood	.80	.40	.08
☐	61	Bob Bolin	.30	.15	.03
☐	62A	Merritt Ranew	.30	.15	.03
		(with sold line)			
☐	62B	Merritt Ranew	20.00	10.00	2.00
		(without sold line)			
☐	63	Jim Stewart	.30	.15	.03
☐	64	Bob Bruce	.30	.15	.03
☐	65	Leon Wagner	.30	.15	.03
☐	66	Al Weis	.30	.15	.03
☐	67	Mets Rookies	.45	.22	.04
		Cleon Jones			
		Dick Selma			
☐	68	Hal Reniff	.30	.15	.03
☐	69	Ken Hamlin	.30	.15	.03
☐	70	Carl Yastrzemski	40.00	20.00	4.00
☐	71	Frank Carpin	.30	.15	.03
☐	72	Tony Perez	6.50	3.25	.65
☐	73	Jerry Zimmerman	.30	.15	.03
☐	74	Don Mossi	.45	.22	.04
☐	75	Tommy Davis	.80	.40	.08
☐	76	Red Schoendienst MG	.80	.40	.08
☐	77	Johnny Orsino	.30	.15	.03
☐	78	Frank Linzy	.30	.15	.03
☐	79	Joe Pepitone	.80	.40	.08
☐	80	Richie Allen	1.50	.75	.15
☐	81	Ray Oyler	.30	.15	.03
☐	82	Bob Hendley	.30	.15	.03
☐	83	Albie Pearson	.30	.15	.03
☐	84	Braves Rookies	.30	.15	.03
		Jim Beauchamp			
		Dick Kelley			
☐	85	Eddie Fisher	.30	.15	.03
☐	86	John Bateman	.30	.15	.03
☐	87	Dan Napoleon	.30	.15	.03
☐	88	Fred Whitfield	.30	.15	.03
☐	89	Ted Davidson	.30	.15	.03
☐	90	Luis Aparicio	4.50	2.25	.45
☐	91A	Bob Uecker	9.00	4.50	.90
		(with traded line)			
☐	91B	Bob Uecker	45.00	22.50	4.50
		(no traded line)			
☐	92	Yankees Team	1.75	.85	.17
☐	93	Jim Lonborg	.60	.30	.06
☐	94	Matty Alou	.45	.22	.04
☐	95	Pete Richert	.30	.15	.03
☐	96	Felipe Alou	.45	.22	.04
☐	97	Jim Merritt	.30	.15	.03
☐	98	Don Demeter	.30	.15	.03
☐	99	Buc Belters	1.75	.85	.17
		Willie Stargell			
		Donn Clendenon			
☐	100	Sandy Koufax	25.00	12.50	2.50
☐	101A	Checklist 2	3.00	.60	.10
		(115 Bill Henry)			
☐	101B	Checklist 2	8.00	1.00	.20
		(115 W. Spahn)			
☐	102	Ed Kirkpatrick	.30	.15	.03
☐	103A	Dick Groat	.80	.40	.08
		(with traded line)			
☐	103B	Dick Groat	20.00	10.00	2.00
		(no traded line)			
☐	104A	Alex Johnson	.60	.30	.06
		(with traded line)			
☐	104B	Alex Johnson	20.00	10.00	2.00
		(no traded line)			
☐	105	Milt Pappas	.45	.22	.04
☐	106	Rusty Staub	1.50	.75	.15
☐	107	A's Rookies	.30	.15	.03
		Larry Stahl			
		Ron Tompkins			
☐	108	Bobby Klaus	.30	.15	.03
☐	109	Ralph Terry	.45	.22	.04
☐	110	Ernie Banks	8.00	4.00	.80
☐	111	Gary Peters	.60	.30	.06
☐	112	Manny Mota	.75	.35	.07
☐	113	Hank Aguirre	.45	.22	.04
☐	114	Jim Gosger	.45	.22	.04
☐	115	Bill Henry	.45	.22	.04
☐	116	Walt Alston MG	1.50	.75	.15
☐	117	Jake Gibbs	.60	.30	.06
☐	118	Mike McCormick	.60	.30	.06
☐	119	Art Shamsky	.45	.22	.04
☐	120	Harmon Killebrew	6.00	3.00	.60
☐	121	Ray Herbert	.45	.22	.04
☐	122	Joe Gaines	.45	.22	.04
☐	123	Pirates Rookies	.45	.22	.04
		Frank Bork			
		Jerry May			
☐	124	Tug McGraw	1.50	.75	.15
☐	125	Lou Brock	8.50	4.25	.85
☐	126	Jim Palmer	60.00	30.00	6.00
☐	127	Ken Berry	.45	.22	.04
☐	128	Jim Landis	.45	.22	.04
☐	129	Jack Kralick	.45	.22	.04
☐	130	Joe Torre	1.00	.50	.10
☐	131	Angels Team	1.00	.50	.10
☐	132	Orlando Cepeda	2.50	1.25	.25
☐	133	Don McMahon	.45	.22	.04
☐	134	Wes Parker	.60	.30	.06
☐	135	Dave Morehead	.45	.22	.04
☐	136	Woody Held	.45	.22	.04
☐	137	Pat Corrales	.75	.35	.07
☐	138	Roger Repoz	.45	.22	.04
☐	139	Cubs Rookies	.45	.22	.04
		Byron Browne			
		Don Young			
☐	140	Jim Maloney	.60	.30	.06
☐	141	Tom McCraw	.45	.22	.04
☐	142	Don Dennis	.45	.22	.04
☐	143	Jose Tartabull	.45	.22	.04
☐	144	Don Schwall	.45	.22	.04
☐	145	Bill Freehan	1.00	.50	.10
☐	146	George Altman	.45	.22	.04
☐	147	Lum Harris MG	.45	.22	.04
☐	148	Bob Johnson	.45	.22	.04
☐	149	Dick Nen	.45	.22	.04
☐	150	Rocky Colavito	1.50	.75	.15
☐	151	Gary Wagner	.45	.22	.04
☐	152	Frank Malzone	.60	.30	.06
☐	153	Rico Carty	.80	.40	.08
☐	154	Chuck Hiller	.45	.22	.04
☐	155	Marcelino Lopez	.45	.22	.04
☐	156	Double Play Combo	.60	.30	.06
		Dick Schofield			
		Hal Lanier			
☐	157	Rene Lachemann	.60	.30	.06
☐	158	Jim Brewer	.45	.22	.04
☐	159	Chico Ruiz	.45	.22	.04
☐	160	Whitey Ford	8.00	4.00	.80
☐	161	Jerry Lumpe	.45	.22	.04
☐	162	Lee Maye	.45	.22	.04
☐	163	Tito Francona	.45	.22	.04
☐	164	White Sox Rookies	.60	.30	.06
		Tommie Agee			
		Marv Staehle			
☐	165	Don Lock	.45	.22	.04
☐	166	Chris Krug	.45	.22	.04
☐	167	Boog Powell	1.50	.75	.15
☐	168	Dan Osinski	.45	.22	.04
☐	169	Duke Sims	.45	.22	.04

☐ 170	Cookie Rojas	.45	.22	.04
☐ 171	Nick Willhite	.45	.22	.04
☐ 172	Mets Team	1.25	.60	.12
☐ 173	Al Spangler	.45	.22	.04
☐ 174	Ron Taylor	.45	.22	.04
☐ 175	Bert Campaneris	.75	.35	.07
☐ 176	Jim Davenport	.60	.30	.06
☐ 177	Hector Lopez	.45	.22	.04
☐ 178	Bob Tillman	.45	.22	.04
☐ 179	Cards Rookies	.60	.30	.06
	Dennis Aust			
	Bob Tolan			
☐ 180	Vada Pinson	1.25	.60	.12
☐ 181	Al Worthington	.45	.22	.04
☐ 182	Jerry Lynch	.45	.22	.04
☐ 183	Checklist 3	2.50	.40	.10
☐ 184	Denis Menke	.45	.22	.04
☐ 185	Bob Buhl	.45	.22	.04
☐ 186	Ruben Amaro	.45	.22	.04
☐ 187	Chuck Dressen MG	.60	.30	.06
☐ 188	Al Luplow	.45	.22	.04
☐ 189	John Roseboro	.60	.30	.06
☐ 190	Jimmie Hall	.60	.30	.06
☐ 191	Darrell Sutherland	.45	.22	.04
☐ 192	Vic Power	.45	.22	.04
☐ 193	Dave McNally	.75	.35	.07
☐ 194	Senators Team	1.00	.50	.10
☐ 195	Joe Morgan	8.00	4.00	.80
☐ 196	Don Pavletich	.45	.22	.04
☐ 197	Sonny Siebert	.60	.30	.06
☐ 198	Mickey Stanley	.75	.35	.07
☐ 199	Chisox Clubbers	.60	.30	.06
	Bill Skowron			
	Johnny Romano			
	Floyd Robinson			
☐ 200	Eddie Mathews	5.50	2.75	.55
☐ 201	Jim Dickson	.45	.22	.04
☐ 202	Clay Dalrymple	.45	.22	.04
☐ 203	Jose Santiago	.45	.22	.04
☐ 204	Cubs Team	1.00	.50	.10
☐ 205	Tom Tresh	1.00	.50	.10
☐ 206	Alvin Jackson	.45	.22	.04
☐ 207	Frank Quilici	.45	.22	.04
☐ 208	Bob Miller	.45	.22	.04
☐ 209	Tigers Rookies	1.00	.50	.10
	Fritz Fisher			
	John Hiller			
☐ 210	Bill Mazeroski	1.00	.50	.10
☐ 211	Frank Kreutzer	.45	.22	.04
☐ 212	Ed Kranepool	.60	.30	.06
☐ 213	Fred Newman	.45	.22	.04
☐ 214	Tommy Harper	.60	.30	.06
☐ 215	NL Batting Leaders	7.50	3.75	.75
	Bob Clemente			
	Hank Aaron			
	Willie Mays			
☐ 216	AL Batting Leaders	2.00	1.00	.20
	Tony Oliva			
	Carl Yastrzemski			
	Vic Davalillo			
☐ 217	NL Home Run Leaders	5.00	2.50	.50
	Willie Mays			
	Willie McCovey			
	Billy Williams			
☐ 218	AL Home Run Leaders	1.00	.50	.10
	Tony Conigliaro			
	Norm Cash			
	Willie Horton			
☐ 219	NL RBI Leaders	2.00	1.00	.20
	Deron Johnson			
	Frank Robinson			
	Willie Mays			
☐ 220	AL RBI Leaders	1.00	.50	.10
	Rocky Colavito			
	Willie Horton			
	Tony Oliva			
☐ 221	NL ERA Leaders	2.00	1.00	.20
	Sandy Koufax			
	Juan Marichal			
	Vern Law			
☐ 222	AL ERA Leaders	1.00	.50	.10
	Sam McDowell			
	Eddie Fisher			
	Sonny Siebert			
☐ 223	NL Pitching Leaders	2.00	1.00	.20
	Sandy Koufax			
	Tony Cloninger			
	Don Drysdale			
☐ 224	AL Pitching Leaders	1.00	.50	.10
	Jim Grant			
	Mel Stottlemyre			
	Jim Kaat			
☐ 225	NL Strikeout Leaders	2.00	1.00	.20
	Sandy Koufax			
	Bob Veale			
	Bob Gibson			
☐ 226	AL Strikeout Leaders	1.00	.50	.10
	Sam McDowell			
	Mickey Lolich			
	Dennis McLain			
	Sonny Siebert			
☐ 227	Russ Nixon	.45	.22	.04
☐ 228	Larry Dierker	.45	.22	.04
☐ 229	Hank Bauer MG	.60	.30	.06
☐ 230	John Callison	.60	.30	.06
☐ 231	Floyd Weaver	.45	.22	.04
☐ 232	Glenn Beckert	.60	.30	.06
☐ 233	Dom Zanni	.45	.22	.04
☐ 234	Yankees Rookies	2.50	1.25	.25
	Rich Beck			
	Roy White			
☐ 235	Don Cardwell	.45	.22	.04
☐ 236	Mike Hershberger	.45	.22	.04
☐ 237	Billy O'Dell	.45	.22	.04
☐ 238	Dodgers Team	1.50	.75	.15
☐ 239	Orlando Pena	.45	.22	.04
☐ 240	Earl Battey	.60	.30	.06
☐ 241	Dennis Ribant	.45	.22	.04
☐ 242	Jesus Alou	.60	.30	.06
☐ 243	Nelson Briles	.60	.30	.06
☐ 244	Astros Rookies	.45	.22	.04
	Chuck Harrison			
	Sonny Jackson			
☐ 245	John Buzhardt	.45	.22	.04
☐ 246	Ed Bailey	.45	.22	.04
☐ 247	Carl Warwick	.45	.22	.04
☐ 248	Pete Mikkelsen	.45	.22	.04
☐ 249	Bill Rigney MG	.45	.22	.04
☐ 250	Sammy Ellis	.45	.22	.04
☐ 251	Ed Brinkman	.45	.22	.04
☐ 252	Denny Lemaster	.45	.22	.04
☐ 253	Don Wert	.45	.22	.04
☐ 254	Phillies Rookies	15.00	7.50	1.50
	Ferguson Jenkins			
	Bill Sorrell			
☐ 255	Willie Stargell	7.00	3.50	.70
☐ 256	Lew Krausse	.45	.22	.04
☐ 257	Jeff Torborg	.60	.30	.06
☐ 258	Dave Giusti	.45	.22	.04
☐ 259	Red Sox Team	1.00	.50	.10
☐ 260	Bob Shaw	.45	.22	.04
☐ 261	Ron Hansen	.45	.22	.04
☐ 262	Jack Hamilton	.45	.22	.04
☐ 263	Tom Egan	.45	.22	.04
☐ 264	Twins Rookies	.45	.22	.04
	Andy Kosco			
	Ted Uhlaender			
☐ 265	Stu Miller	.45	.22	.04
☐ 266	Pedro Gonzalez	.45	.22	.04
☐ 267	Joe Sparma	.45	.22	.04
☐ 268	John Blanchard	.60	.30	.06
☐ 269	Don Heffner MG	.45	.22	.04
☐ 270	Claude Osteen	.60	.30	.06
☐ 271	Hal Lanier	.75	.35	.07
☐ 272	Jack Baldschun	.45	.22	.04
☐ 273	Astro Aces	.75	.35	.07
	Bob Aspromonte			
	Rusty Staub			
☐ 274	Buster Narum	.45	.22	.04
☐ 275	Tim McCarver	1.25	.60	.12
☐ 276	Jim Bouton	1.25	.60	.12
☐ 277	George Thomas	.45	.22	.04
☐ 278	Calvin Koonce	.45	.22	.04
☐ 279	Checklist 4	2.50	.40	.10
☐ 280	Bobby Knoop	.45	.22	.04
☐ 281	Bruce Howard	.45	.22	.04
☐ 282	Johnny Lewis	.45	.22	.04
☐ 283	Jim Perry	.75	.35	.07
☐ 284	Bobby Wine	.45	.22	.04
☐ 285	Luis Tiant	1.50	.75	.15
☐ 286	Gary Geiger	.45	.22	.04
☐ 287	Jack Aker	.45	.22	.04
☐ 288	Dodgers Rookies	45.00	22.50	4.50
	Bill Singer			
	Don Sutton			
☐ 289	Larry Sherry	.60	.30	.06
☐ 290	Ron Santo	1.25	.60	.12
☐ 291	Moe Drabowsky	.45	.22	.04
☐ 292	Jim Coker	.45	.22	.04
☐ 293	Mike Shannon	.75	.35	.07
☐ 294	Steve Ridzik	.45	.22	.04
☐ 295	Jim Ray Hart	.60	.30	.06
☐ 296	Johnny Keane MG	.45	.22	.04
☐ 297	Jim Owens	.45	.22	.04
☐ 298	Rico Petrocelli	.75	.35	.07
☐ 299	Lou Burdette	.75	.35	.07
☐ 300	Bob Clemente	35.00	17.50	3.50
☐ 301	Greg Bollo	.45	.22	.04
☐ 302	Ernie Bowman	.45	.22	.04
☐ 303	Indians Team	1.00	.50	.10

☐ 304	John Herrnstein	.45	.22	.04	☐ 391	Chuck Hinton	.50	.25	.05
☐ 305	Camilo Pascual	.60	.30	.06	☐ 392	Cubs Rookies	.75	.35	.07
☐ 306	Ty Cline	.45	.22	.04		Bill Hands			
☐ 307	Clay Carroll	.45	.22	.04		Randy Hundley			
☐ 308	Tom Haller	.60	.30	.06	☐ 393	George Brunet	.50	.25	.05
☐ 309	Diego Segui	.45	.22	.04	☐ 394	Ron Brand	.50	.25	.05
☐ 310	Frank Robinson	16.00	8.00	1.60	☐ 395	Len Gabrielson	.50	.25	.05
☐ 311	Reds Rookies	.60	.30	.06	☐ 396	Jerry Stephenson	.50	.25	.05
	Tommy Helms				☐ 397	Bill White	1.00	.50	.10
	Dick Simpson				☐ 398	Danny Cater	.50	.25	.05
☐ 312	Bob Saverine	.45	.22	.04	☐ 399	Ray Washburn	.50	.25	.05
☐ 313	Chris Zachary	.45	.22	.04	☐ 400	Zoilo Versalles	.75	.35	.07
☐ 314	Hector Valle	.45	.22	.04	☐ 401	Ken McMullen	.50	.25	.05
☐ 315	Norm Cash	1.25	.60	.12	☐ 402	Jim Hickman	.50	.25	.05
☐ 316	Jack Fisher	.45	.22	.04	☐ 403	Fred Talbot	.50	.25	.05
☐ 317	Dalton Jones	.45	.22	.04	☐ 404	Pirates Team	1.00	.50	.10
☐ 318	Harry Walker MG	.45	.22	.04	☐ 405	Elston Howard	1.75	.85	.17
☐ 319	Gene Freese	.45	.22	.04	☐ 406	Joe Jay	.50	.25	.05
☐ 320	Bob Gibson	6.50	3.25	.65	☐ 407	John Kennedy	.50	.25	.05
☐ 321	Rick Reichardt	.45	.22	.04	☐ 408	Lee Thomas	.50	.25	.05
☐ 322	Bill Faul	.45	.22	.04	☐ 409	Billy Hoeft	.50	.25	.05
☐ 323	Ray Barker	.45	.22	.04	☐ 410	Al Kaline	8.50	4.25	.85
☐ 324	John Boozer	.45	.22	.04	☐ 411	Gene Mauch MG	.75	.35	.07
☐ 325	Vic Davalillo	.60	.30	.06	☐ 412	Sam Bowens	.50	.25	.05
☐ 326	Braves Team	1.00	.50	.10	☐ 413	John Romano	.50	.25	.05
☐ 327	Bernie Allen	.45	.22	.04	☐ 414	Dan Coombs	.50	.25	.05
☐ 328	Jerry Grote	.45	.22	.04	☐ 415	Max Alvis	.50	.25	.05
☐ 329	Pete Charton	.45	.22	.04	☐ 416	Phil Ortega	.50	.25	.05
☐ 330	Ron Fairly	.60	.30	.06	☐ 417	Angels Rookies	.75	.35	.07
☐ 331	Ron Herbel	.45	.22	.04		Jim McGlothlin			
☐ 332	Billy Bryan	.45	.22	.04		Ed Sukla			
☐ 333	Senators Rookies	.45	.22	.04	☐ 418	Phil Gagliano	.50	.25	.05
	Joe Coleman				☐ 419	Mike Ryan	.50	.25	.05
	Jim French				☐ 420	Juan Marichal	5.50	2.75	.55
☐ 334	Marty Keough	.45	.22	.04	☐ 421	Roy McMillan	.50	.25	.05
☐ 335	Juan Pizarro	.45	.22	.04	☐ 422	Ed Charles	.50	.25	.05
☐ 336	Gene Alley	.60	.30	.06	☐ 423	Ernie Broglio	.50	.25	.05
☐ 337	Fred Gladding	.45	.22	.04	☐ 424	Reds Rookies	1.75	.85	.17
☐ 338	Dal Maxvill	.60	.30	.06		Lee May			
☐ 339	Del Crandall	.60	.30	.06		Darrell Osteen			
☐ 340	Dean Chance	.60	.30	.06	☐ 425	Bob Veale	.75	.35	.07
☐ 341	Wes Westrum MG	.45	.22	.04	☐ 426	White Sox Team	1.00	.50	.10
☐ 342	Bob Humphreys	.45	.22	.04	☐ 427	John Miller	.50	.25	.05
☐ 343	Joe Christopher	.45	.22	.04	☐ 428	Sandy Alomar	.50	.25	.05
☐ 344	Steve Blass	.60	.30	.06	☐ 429	Bill Monbouquette	.50	.25	.05
☐ 345	Bob Allison	.75	.35	.07	☐ 430	Don Drysdale	7.00	3.50	.70
☐ 346	Mike De La Hoz	.45	.22	.04	☐ 431	Walt Bond	.50	.25	.05
☐ 347	Phil Regan	.60	.30	.06	☐ 432	Bob Heffner	.50	.25	.05
☐ 348	Orioles Team	1.00	.50	.10	☐ 433	Alvin Dark MG	.75	.35	.07
☐ 349	Cap Peterson	.45	.22	.04	☐ 434	Willie Kirkland	.50	.25	.05
☐ 350	Mel Stottlemyre	1.25	.60	.12	☐ 435	Jim Bunning	3.00	1.50	.30
☐ 351	Fred Valentine	.45	.22	.04	☐ 436	Julian Javier	.75	.35	.07
☐ 352	Bob Aspromonte	.45	.22	.04	☐ 437	Al Stanek	.50	.25	.05
☐ 353	Al McBean	.45	.22	.04	☐ 438	Willie Smith	.50	.25	.05
☐ 354	Smoky Burgess	.60	.30	.06	☐ 439	Pedro Ramos	.50	.25	.05
☐ 355	Wade Blasingame	.45	.22	.04	☐ 440	Deron Johnson	.75	.35	.07
☐ 356	Red Sox Rookies	.45	.22	.04	☐ 441	Tommie Sisk	.50	.25	.05
	Owen Johnson				☐ 442	Orioles Rookies	.50	.25	.05
	Ken Sanders					Ed Barnowski			
☐ 357	Gerry Arrigo	.45	.22	.04		Eddie Watt			
☐ 358	Charlie Smith	.45	.22	.04	☐ 443	Bill Wakefield	.50	.25	.05
☐ 359	Johnny Briggs	.45	.22	.04	☐ 444	Checklist 6	3.50	.60	.10
☐ 360	Ron Hunt	.45	.22	.04	☐ 445	Jim Kaat	3.00	1.50	.30
☐ 361	Tom Satriano	.45	.22	.04	☐ 446	Mack Jones	.50	.25	.05
☐ 362	Gates Brown	.60	.30	.06	☐ 447	Dick Ellsworth	2.00	1.00	.20
☐ 363	Checklist 5	2.50	.40	.10		(photo actually			
☐ 364	Nate Oliver	.45	.22	.04		Ken Hubbs)			
☐ 365	Roger Maris	12.00	6.00	1.20	☐ 448	Eddie Stanky MG	2.00	1.00	.20
☐ 366	Wayne Causey	.45	.22	.04	☐ 449	Joe Moeller	1.50	.75	.15
☐ 367	Mel Nelson	.45	.22	.04	☐ 450	Tony Oliva	3.50	1.75	.35
☐ 368	Charlie Lau	.60	.30	.06	☐ 451	Barry Latman	1.50	.75	.15
☐ 369	Jim King	.45	.22	.04	☐ 452	Joe Azcue	1.50	.75	.15
☐ 370	Chico Cardenas	.45	.22	.04	☐ 453	Ron Kline	1.50	.75	.15
☐ 371	Lee Stange	.50	.25	.05	☐ 454	Jerry Buchek	1.50	.75	.15
☐ 372	Harvey Kuenn	.80	.40	.08	☐ 455	Mickey Lolich	3.00	1.50	.30
☐ 373	Giants Rookies	.50	.25	.05	☐ 456	Red Sox Rookies	1.50	.75	.15
	Jack Hiatt					Darrell Brandon			
	Dick Estelle					Joe Foy			
☐ 374	Bob Locker	.50	.25	.05	☐ 457	Joe Gibbon	1.50	.75	.15
☐ 375	Donn Clendenon	.75	.35	.07	☐ 458	Manny Jiminez	1.50	.75	.15
☐ 376	Paul Schaal	.50	.25	.05	☐ 459	Bill McCool	1.50	.75	.15
☐ 377	Turk Farrell	.50	.25	.05	☐ 460	Curt Blefary	2.00	1.00	.20
☐ 378	Dick Tracewski	.50	.25	.05	☐ 461	Roy Face	2.50	1.25	.25
☐ 379	Cardinal Team	1.00	.50	.10	☐ 462	Bob Rodgers	2.00	1.00	.20
☐ 380	Tony Conigliaro	2.00	1.00	.20	☐ 463	Phillies Team	3.00	1.50	.30
☐ 381	Hank Fischer	.50	.25	.05	☐ 464	Larry Bearnarth	1.50	.75	.15
☐ 382	Phil Roof	.50	.25	.05	☐ 465	Don Buford	1.50	.75	.15
☐ 383	Jack Brandt	.50	.25	.05	☐ 466	Ken Johnson	1.50	.75	.15
☐ 384	Al Downing	.75	.35	.07	☐ 467	Vic Roznovsky	1.50	.75	.15
☐ 385	Ken Boyer	1.50	.75	.15	☐ 468	Johnny Podres	2.50	1.25	.25
☐ 386	Gil Hodges MG	3.50	1.75	.35	☐ 469	Yankees Rookies	6.00	3.00	.60
☐ 387	Howie Reed	.50	.25	.05		Bobby Murcer			
☐ 388	Don Mincher	.75	.35	.07		Dooley Womack			
☐ 389	Jim O'Toole	.50	.25	.05	☐ 470	Sam McDowell	2.50	1.25	.25
☐ 390	Brooks Robinson	9.00	4.50	.90	☐ 471	Bob Skinner	2.00	1.00	.20

☐ 472	Terry Fox	1.50	.75	.15
☐ 473	Rich Rollins	2.00	1.00	.20
☐ 474	Dick Schofield	1.50	.75	.15
☐ 475	Dick Radatz	2.00	1.00	.20
☐ 476	Bobby Bragan MG	1.50	.75	.15
☐ 477	Steve Barber	1.50	.75	.15
☐ 478	Tony Gonzalez	1.50	.75	.15
☐ 479	Jim Hannan	1.50	.75	.15
☐ 480	Dick Stuart	2.00	1.00	.20
☐ 481	Bob Lee	1.50	.75	.15
☐ 482	Cubs Rookies	1.50	.75	.15
	John Boccabella			
	Dave Dowling			
☐ 483	Joe Nuxhall	2.00	1.00	.20
☐ 484	Wes Covington	1.50	.75	.15
☐ 485	Bob Bailey	1.50	.75	.15
☐ 486	Tommy John	4.00	2.00	.40
☐ 487	Al Ferrara	1.50	.75	.15
☐ 488	George Banks	1.50	.75	.15
☐ 489	Curt Simmons	2.00	1.00	.20
☐ 490	Bobby Richardson	3.50	1.75	.35
☐ 491	Dennis Bennett	1.50	.75	.15
☐ 492	Athletics Team	2.50	1.25	.25
☐ 493	John Klippstein	1.50	.75	.15
☐ 494	Gordon Coleman	1.50	.75	.15
☐ 495	Dick McAuliffe	2.00	1.00	.20
☐ 496	Lindy McDaniel	2.00	1.00	.20
☐ 497	Chris Cannizzaro	1.50	.75	.15
☐ 498	Pirates Rookies	2.00	1.00	.20
	Luke Walker			
	Woody Fryman			
☐ 499	Wally Bunker	1.50	.75	.15
☐ 500	Hank Aaron	45.00	22.50	4.50
☐ 501	John O'Donoghue	1.50	.75	.15
☐ 502	Lenny Green	1.50	.75	.15
☐ 503	Steve Hamilton	1.50	.75	.15
☐ 504	Grady Hatton MG	1.50	.75	.15
☐ 505	Jose Cardenal	1.50	.75	.15
☐ 506	Bo Belinsky	2.00	1.00	.20
☐ 507	John Edwards	1.50	.75	.15
☐ 508	Steve Hargan	1.50	.75	.15
☐ 509	Jake Wood	1.50	.75	.15
☐ 510	Hoyt Wilhelm	7.50	3.75	.75
☐ 511	Giants Rookies	1.50	.75	.15
	Bob Barton			
	Tito Fuentes			
☐ 512	Dick Stigman	1.50	.75	.15
☐ 513	Camilo Carreon	1.50	.75	.15
☐ 514	Hal Woodeshick	1.50	.75	.15
☐ 515	Frank Howard	2.50	1.25	.25
☐ 516	Eddie Bressoud	1.50	.75	.15
☐ 517	Checklist 7	6.50	1.00	.20
☐ 518	Braves Rookies	1.50	.75	.15
	Herb Hippauf			
	Arnie Umbach			
☐ 519	Bob Friend	2.00	1.00	.20
☐ 520	Jim Wynn	2.00	1.00	.20
☐ 521	John Wyatt	1.50	.75	.15
☐ 522	Phil Linz	2.00	1.00	.20
☐ 523	Bob Sadowski	8.50	4.25	.85
☐ 524	Giants Rookies	8.50	4.25	.85
	Ollie Brown			
	Don Mason			
☐ 525	Gary Bell	8.50	4.25	.85
☐ 526	Twins Team	12.00	6.00	1.20
☐ 527	Julio Navarro	8.50	4.25	.85
☐ 528	Jesse Gonder	8.50	4.25	.85
☐ 529	White Sox Rookies	10.00	5.00	1.00
	Lee Elia			
	Dennis Higgins			
	Bill Voss			
☐ 530	Robin Roberts	30.00	15.00	3.00
☐ 531	Joe Cunningham	8.50	4.25	.85
☐ 532	Aurelio Monteagudo	8.50	4.25	.85
☐ 533	Jerry Adair	8.50	4.25	.85
☐ 534	Mets Rookies	8.50	4.25	.85
	Dave Eilers			
	Rob Gardner			
☐ 535	Willie Davis	11.00	5.50	1.10
☐ 536	Dick Egan	8.50	4.25	.85
☐ 537	Herman Franks MG	8.50	4.25	.85
☐ 538	Bob Allen	8.50	4.25	.85
☐ 539	Astros Rookies	8.50	4.25	.85
	Bill Heath			
	Carroll Sembera			
☐ 540	Denny McLain	24.00	12.00	2.40
☐ 541	Gene Oliver	8.50	4.25	.85
☐ 542	George Smith	8.50	4.25	.85
☐ 543	Roger Craig	12.00	6.00	1.20
☐ 544	Cardinals Rookies	8.50	4.25	.85
	Joe Hoerner			
	George Kernek			
	Jimmy Williams			
☐ 545	Dick Green	8.50	4.25	.85
☐ 546	Dwight Siebler	8.50	4.25	.85

☐ 547	Horace Clarke	10.00	5.00	1.00
☐ 548	Gary Kroll	8.50	4.25	.85
☐ 549	Senators Rookies	8.50	4.25	.85
	Al Closter			
	Casey Cox			
☐ 550	Willie McCovey	80.00	40.00	8.00
☐ 551	Bob Purkey	8.50	4.25	.85
☐ 552	Birdie Tebbetts MG	8.50	4.25	.85
☐ 553	Rookie Stars	8.50	4.25	.85
	Pat Garrett			
	Jackie Warner			
☐ 554	Jim Northrup	10.00	5.00	1.00
☐ 555	Ron Perranoski	10.00	5.00	1.00
☐ 556	Mel Queen	8.50	4.25	.85
☐ 557	Felix Mantilla	8.50	4.25	.85
☐ 558	Red Sox Rookies	11.00	5.50	1.10
	Guido Grilli			
	Pete Magrini			
	George Scott			
☐ 559	Roberto Pena	8.50	4.25	.85
☐ 560	Joel Horlen	10.00	5.00	1.00
☐ 561	Choo Choo Coleman	8.50	4.25	.85
☐ 562	Russ Snyder	8.50	4.25	.85
☐ 563	Twins Rookies	10.00	5.00	1.00
	Pete Cimino			
	Cesar Tovar			
☐ 564	Bob Chance	8.50	4.25	.85
☐ 565	Jimmy Piersall	12.00	6.00	1.20
☐ 566	Mike Cuellar	10.00	5.00	1.00
☐ 567	Dick Howser	12.00	6.00	1.20
☐ 568	Athletics Rookies	10.00	5.00	1.00
	Paul Lindblad			
	Rod Stone			
☐ 569	Orlando McFarlane	8.50	4.25	.85
☐ 570	Art Mahaffey	8.50	4.25	.85
☐ 571	Dave Roberts	8.50	4.25	.85
☐ 572	Bob Priddy	8.50	4.25	.85
☐ 573	Derrell Griffith	8.50	4.25	.85
☐ 574	Mets Rookies	8.50	4.25	.85
	Bill Hepler			
	Bill Murphy			
☐ 575	Earl Wilson	8.50	4.25	.85
☐ 576	Dave Nicholson	8.50	4.25	.85
☐ 577	Jack Lamabe	8.50	4.25	.85
☐ 578	Chi Chi Olivo	8.50	4.25	.85
☐ 579	Orioles Rookies	12.00	6.00	1.20
	Frank Bertaina			
	Gene Brabender			
	Dave Johnson			
☐ 580	Billy Williams	35.00	17.50	3.50
☐ 581	Tony Martinez	8.50	4.25	.85
☐ 582	Garry Roggenburk	8.50	4.25	.85
☐ 583	Tigers Team	30.00	15.00	3.00
☐ 584	Yankees Rookies	10.00	5.00	1.00
	Frank Fernandez			
	Fritz Peterson			
☐ 585	Tony Taylor	8.50	4.25	.85
☐ 586	Claude Raymond	8.50	4.25	.85
☐ 587	Dick Bertell	8.50	4.25	.85
☐ 588	Athletics Rookies	8.50	4.25	.85
	Chuck Dobson			
	Ken Suarez			
☐ 589	Lou Klimchock	8.50	4.25	.85
☐ 590	Bill Skowron	15.00	7.50	1.50
☐ 591	NL Rookies	10.00	5.00	1.00
	Bart Shirley			
	Grant Jackson			
☐ 592	Andre Rodgers	8.50	4.25	.85
☐ 593	Doug Camilli	8.50	4.25	.85
☐ 594	Chico Salmon	8.50	4.25	.85
☐ 595	Larry Jackson	8.50	4.25	.85
☐ 596	Astros Rookies	10.00	5.00	1.00
	Nate Colbert			
	Greg Sims			
☐ 597	John Sullivan	8.50	4.25	.85
☐ 598	Gaylord Perry	175.00	35.00	7.00

1967 Topps

The cards in this 609-card set measure 2 1/2" by 3 1/2". The 1967 Topps series is considered by some collectors to be one of the company's finest accomplishments in baseball card production. Excellent color photographs are combined with easy to read backs. Cards 458 to 533 are slightly harder to find than numbers 1 to 457, and the inevitable (difficult to find) high series (534 to 609) exists. Each

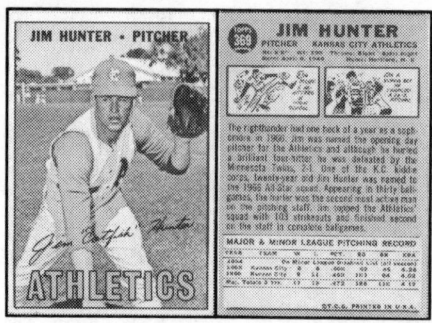

checklist card features a small circular picture of a popular player included in that series. Printing discrepancies resulted in some high series cards being in short supply. Featured subsets within this set include World Series cards (151-155) and League Leaders (233-244). Although there are several relatively expensive cards in this popular set, the key cards in the set are undoubtedly the Tom Seaver rookie card (581) and the Rod Carew rookie card (569).

		NRMT	VG-E	GOOD
COMPLETE SET		2500.00	900.00	200.00
COMMON PLAYER (1-110)		.35	.17	.03
COMMON PLAYER (111-370)		.45	.22	.04
COMMON PLAYER (371-457)		.65	.30	.06
COMMON PLAYER (458-533)		1.50	.75	.15
COMMON PLAYER (534-609)		4.50	2.25	.45
☐ 1	The Champs	7.50	1.50	.30
	Frank Robinson			
	Hank Bauer			
	Brooks Robinson			
☐ 2	Jack Hamilton	.35	.17	.03
☐ 3	Duke Sims	.35	.17	.03
☐ 4	Hal Lanier	.50	.25	.05
☐ 5	Whitey Ford	6.50	3.25	.65
☐ 6	Dick Simpson	.35	.17	.03
☐ 7	Don McMahon	.35	.17	.03
☐ 8	Chuck Harrison	.35	.17	.03
☐ 9	Ron Hansen	.35	.17	.03
☐ 10	Matty Alou	.50	.25	.05
☐ 11	Barry Moore	.35	.17	.03
☐ 12	Dodgers Rookies	.50	.25	.05
	Jim Campanis			
	Bill Singer			
☐ 13	Joe Sparma	.35	.17	.03
☐ 14	Phil Linz	.50	.25	.05
☐ 15	Earl Battey	.50	.25	.05
☐ 16	Bill Hands	.35	.17	.03
☐ 17	Jim Gosger	.35	.17	.03
☐ 18	Gene Oliver	.35	.17	.03
☐ 19	Jim McGlothlin	.35	.17	.03
☐ 20	Orlando Cepeda	3.50	1.75	.35
☐ 21	Dave Bristol MG	.35	.17	.03
☐ 22	Gene Brabender	.35	.17	.03
☐ 23	Larry Elliot	.35	.17	.03
☐ 24	Bob Allen	.35	.17	.03
☐ 25	Elston Howard	1.50	.75	.15
☐ 26A	Bob Priddy	.35	.17	.03
	(with traded line)			
☐ 26B	Bob Priddy	20.00	10.00	2.00
	(no traded line)			
☐ 27	Bob Saverine	.35	.17	.03
☐ 28	Barry Latman	.35	.17	.03
☐ 29	Tommy McCraw	.35	.17	.03
☐ 30	Al Kaline	7.00	3.50	.70
☐ 31	Jim Brewer	.35	.17	.03
☐ 32	Bob Bailey	.35	.17	.03
☐ 33	Athletic Rookies	1.50	.75	.15
	Sal Bando			
	Randy Schwartz			
☐ 34	Pete Cimino	.35	.17	.03
☐ 35	Rico Carty	.65	.30	.06
☐ 36	Bob Tillman	.35	.17	.03
☐ 37	Rick Wise	.50	.25	.05
☐ 38	Bob Johnson	.35	.17	.03
☐ 39	Curt Simmons	.50	.25	.05
☐ 40	Rick Reichardt	.35	.17	.03
☐ 41	Joe Hoerner	.35	.17	.03
☐ 42	Mets Team	1.25	.60	.12
☐ 43	Chico Salmon	.35	.17	.03
☐ 44	Joe Nuxhall	.65	.30	.06
☐ 45	Roger Maris	8.50	4.25	.85
☐ 46	Lindy McDaniel	.50	.25	.05
☐ 47	Ken McMullen	.35	.17	.03
☐ 48	Bill Freehan	.80	.40	.08
☐ 49	Roy Face	.80	.40	.08
☐ 50	Tony Oliva	2.00	1.00	.20
☐ 51	Astros Rookies	.35	.17	.03
	Dave Adlesh			
	Wes Bales			
☐ 52	Dennis Higgins	.35	.17	.03
☐ 53	Clay Dalrymple	.35	.17	.03
☐ 54	Dick Green	.35	.17	.03
☐ 55	Don Drysdale	5.00	2.50	.50
☐ 56	Jose Tartabull	.35	.17	.03
☐ 57	Pat Jarvis	.35	.17	.03
☐ 58	Paul Schaal	.35	.17	.03
☐ 59	Ralph Terry	.50	.25	.05
☐ 60	Luis Aparicio	4.50	2.25	.45
☐ 61	Gordy Coleman	.35	.17	.03
☐ 62	Checklist 1	2.25	.40	.10
	Frank Robinson			
☐ 63	Cards' Clubbers	3.00	1.50	.30
	Lou Brock			
	Curt Flood			
☐ 64	Fred Valentine	.35	.17	.03
☐ 65	Tom Haller	.50	.25	.05
☐ 66	Manny Mota	.65	.30	.06
☐ 67	Ken Berry	.35	.17	.03
☐ 68	Bob Buhl	.35	.17	.03
☐ 69	Vic Davalillo	.50	.25	.05
☐ 70	Ron Santo	1.00	.50	.10
☐ 71	Camilo Pascual	.50	.25	.05
☐ 72	Tigers Rookies	.50	.25	.05
	George Korince			
	(Photo actually			
	James Murray Brown)			
	John (Tom) Matchick			
☐ 73	Rusty Staub	1.50	.75	.15
☐ 74	Wes Stock	.35	.17	.03
☐ 75	George Scott	.65	.30	.06
☐ 76	Jim Barbieri	.35	.17	.03
☐ 77	Dooley Womack	.35	.17	.03
☐ 78	Pat Corrales	.50	.25	.05
☐ 79	Bubba Morton	.35	.17	.03
☐ 80	Jim Maloney	.50	.25	.05
☐ 81	Eddie Stanky MG	.50	.25	.05
☐ 82	Steve Barber	.35	.17	.03
☐ 83	Ollie Brown	.35	.17	.03
☐ 84	Tommie Sisk	.35	.17	.03
☐ 85	Johnny Callison	.50	.25	.05
☐ 86A	Mike McCormick	.50	.25	.05
	(with traded line)			
☐ 86B	Mike McCormick	20.00	10.00	2.00
	(no traded line)			
☐ 87	George Altman	.35	.17	.03
☐ 88	Mickey Lolich	1.25	.60	.12
☐ 89	Felix Millan	.35	.17	.03
☐ 90	Jim Nash	.35	.17	.03
☐ 91	Johnny Lewis	.35	.17	.03
☐ 92	Ray Washburn	.35	.17	.03
☐ 93	Yankees Rookies	1.50	.75	.15
	Stan Bahnsen			
	Bobby Murcer			
☐ 94	Ron Fairly	.50	.25	.05
☐ 95	Sonny Siebert	.50	.25	.05
☐ 96	Art Shamsky	.35	.17	.03
☐ 97	Mike Cuellar	.50	.25	.05
☐ 98	Rich Rollins	.50	.25	.05
☐ 99	Lee Stange	.35	.17	.03
☐ 100	Frank Robinson	6.00	3.00	.60
☐ 101	Ken Johnson	.35	.17	.03
☐ 102	Phillies Team	.90	.45	.09
☐ 103	Checklist 2	5.00	1.00	.20
	Mickey Mantle			
☐ 104	Minnie Rojas	.35	.17	.03
☐ 105	Ken Boyer	1.00	.50	.10
☐ 106	Randy Hundley	.50	.25	.05
☐ 107	Joel Horlen	.50	.25	.05
☐ 108	Alex Johnson	.50	.25	.05
☐ 109	Tribe Thumpers	.75	.35	.07
	Rocky Colavito			
	Leon Wagner			
☐ 110	Jack Aker	.35	.17	.03
☐ 111	John Kennedy	.45	.22	.04
☐ 112	Dave Wickersham	.45	.22	.04
☐ 113	Dave Nicholson	.45	.22	.04
☐ 114	Jack Baldschun	.45	.22	.04
☐ 115	Paul Casanova	.45	.22	.04
☐ 116	Herman Franks MG	.45	.22	.04
☐ 117	Darrell Brandon	.45	.22	.04
☐ 118	Bernie Allen	.45	.22	.04
☐ 119	Wade Blasingame	.45	.22	.04
☐ 120	Floyd Robinson	.45	.22	.04

☐ 121	Ed Bressoud	.45	.22	.04
☐ 122	George Brunet	.45	.22	.04
☐ 123	Pirates Rookies	.45	.22	.04
	Jim Price			
	Luke Walker			
☐ 124	Jim Stewart	.45	.22	.04
☐ 125	Moe Drabowsky	.45	.22	.04
☐ 126	Tony Taylor	.45	.22	.04
☐ 127	John O'Donoghue	.45	.22	.04
☐ 128	Ed Spiezio	.45	.22	.04
☐ 129	Phil Roof	.45	.22	.04
☐ 130	Phil Regan	.60	.30	.06
☐ 131	Yankees Team	1.25	.60	.12
☐ 132	Ozzie Virgil	.45	.22	.04
☐ 133	Ron Kline	.45	.22	.04
☐ 134	Gates Brown	.60	.30	.06
☐ 135	Deron Johnson	.60	.30	.06
☐ 136	Carroll Sembera	.45	.22	.04
☐ 137	Twins Rookies	.45	.22	.04
	Ron Clark			
	Jim Ollum			
☐ 138	Dick Kelley	.45	.22	.04
☐ 139	Dalton Jones	.45	.22	.04
☐ 140	Willie Stargell	6.50	3.25	.65
☐ 141	John Miller	.45	.22	.04
☐ 142	Jackie Brandt	.45	.22	.04
☐ 143	Sox Sockers	.60	.30	.06
	Pete Ward			
	Don Buford			
☐ 144	Bill Hepler	.45	.22	.04
☐ 145	Larry Brown	.45	.22	.04
☐ 146	Steve Carlton	50.00	25.00	5.00
☐ 147	Tom Egan	.45	.22	.04
☐ 148	Adolfo Phillips	.45	.22	.04
☐ 149	Joe Moeller	.45	.22	.04
☐ 150	Mickey Mantle	175.00	85.00	18.00
☐ 151	World Series Game 1	1.50	.75	.15
	Moe mows down 11			
☐ 152	World Series Game 2	2.50	1.25	.25
	Palmer blanks Dodgers			
☐ 153	World Series Game 3	1.50	.75	.15
	Blair's homer			
	defeats L.A.			
☐ 154	World Series Game 4	1.50	.75	.15
	Orioles 4 straight			
☐ 155	World Series Summary	1.50	.75	.15
	Winners celebrate			
☐ 156	Ron Herbel	.45	.22	.04
☐ 157	Danny Cater	.45	.22	.04
☐ 158	Jimmie Coker	.45	.22	.04
☐ 159	Bruce Howard	.45	.22	.04
☐ 160	Willie Davis	.75	.35	.07
☐ 161	Dick Williams MG	.60	.30	.06
☐ 162	Billy O'Dell	.45	.22	.04
☐ 163	Vic Roznovsky	.45	.22	.04
☐ 164	Dwight Siebler	.45	.22	.04
☐ 165	Cleon Jones	.45	.22	.04
☐ 166	Ed Mathews	5.00	2.50	.50
☐ 167	Senators Rookies	.45	.22	.04
	Joe Coleman			
	Tim Cullen			
☐ 168	Ray Culp	.45	.22	.04
☐ 169	Horace Clarke	.60	.30	.06
☐ 170	Dick McAuliffe	.60	.30	.06
☐ 171	Calvin Koonce	.45	.22	.04
☐ 172	Bill Heath	.45	.22	.04
☐ 173	Cardinals Team	1.00	.50	.10
☐ 174	Dick Radatz	.75	.35	.07
☐ 175	Bobby Knoop	.45	.22	.04
☐ 176	Sammy Ellis	.45	.22	.04
☐ 177	Tito Fuentes	.45	.22	.04
☐ 178	John Buzhardt	.45	.22	.04
☐ 179	Braves Rookies	.45	.22	.04
	Charles Vaughan			
	Cecil Upshaw			
☐ 180	Curt Blefary	.60	.30	.06
☐ 181	Terry Fox	.45	.22	.04
☐ 182	Ed Charles	.45	.22	.04
☐ 183	Jim Pagliaroni	.45	.22	.04
☐ 184	George Thomas	.45	.22	.04
☐ 185	Ken Holtzman	1.00	.50	.10
☐ 186	Mets Maulers	.60	.30	.06
	Ed Kranepool			
	Ron Swoboda			
☐ 187	Pedro Ramos	.45	.22	.04
☐ 188	Ken Harrelson	1.00	.50	.10
☐ 189	Chuck Hinton	.45	.22	.04
☐ 190	Turk Farrell	.45	.22	.04
☐ 191A	Checklist 3	2.50	.45	.10
	(214 Tom Kelley)			
	(Willie Mays)			
☐ 191B	Checklist 3	6.00	.80	.15
	(214 Dick Kelley)			
	(Willie Mays)			
☐ 192	Fred Gladding	.45	.22	.04
☐ 193	Jose Cardenal	.45	.22	.04
☐ 194	Bob Allison	.60	.30	.06
☐ 195	Al Jackson	.45	.22	.04
☐ 196	Johnny Romano	.45	.22	.04
☐ 197	Ron Perranoski	.60	.30	.06
☐ 198	Chuck Hiller	.45	.22	.04
☐ 199	Billy Hitchcock MG	.45	.22	.04
☐ 200	Willie Mays	40.00	20.00	4.00
☐ 201	Hal Reniff	.45	.22	.04
☐ 202	Johnny Edwards	.45	.22	.04
☐ 203	Al McBean	.45	.22	.04
☐ 204	Orioles Rookies	.60	.30	.06
	Mike Epstein			
	Tom Phoebus			
☐ 205	Dick Groat	.80	.40	.08
☐ 206	Dennis Bennett	.45	.22	.04
☐ 207	John Orsino	.45	.22	.04
☐ 208	Jack Lamabe	.45	.22	.04
☐ 209	Joe Nossek	.45	.22	.04
☐ 210	Bob Gibson	6.00	3.00	.60
☐ 211	Twins Team	1.25	.60	.12
☐ 212	Chris Zachary	.45	.22	.04
☐ 213	Jay Johnstone	.75	.35	.07
☐ 214	Dick Kelley	.45	.22	.04
☐ 215	Ernie Banks	6.00	3.00	.60
☐ 216	Bengal Belters	3.00	1.50	.30
	Norm Cash			
	Al Kaline			
☐ 217	Rob Gardner	.45	.22	.04
☐ 218	Wes Parker	.60	.30	.06
☐ 219	Clay Carroll	.45	.22	.04
☐ 220	Jim Ray Hart	.60	.30	.06
☐ 221	Woody Fryman	.45	.22	.04
☐ 222	Reds Rookies	.75	.35	.07
	Darrell Osteen			
	Lee May			
☐ 223	Mike Ryan	.45	.22	.04
☐ 224	Walt Bond	.45	.22	.04
☐ 225	Mel Stottlemyre	1.00	.50	.10
☐ 226	Julian Javier	.60	.30	.06
☐ 227	Paul Lindblad	.45	.22	.04
☐ 228	Gil Hodges MG	3.00	1.50	.30
☐ 229	Larry Jackson	.45	.22	.04
☐ 230	Boog Powell	1.50	.75	.15
☐ 231	John Bateman	.45	.22	.04
☐ 232	Don Buford	.45	.22	.04
☐ 233	AL ERA Leaders	1.00	.50	.10
	Gary Peters			
	Joel Horlen			
	Steve Hargan			
☐ 234	NL ERA Leaders	3.00	1.50	.30
	Sandy Koufax			
	Mike Cuellar			
	Juan Marichal			
☐ 235	AL Pitching Leaders	1.00	.50	.10
	Jim Kaat			
	Denny McLain			
	Earl Wilson			
☐ 236	NL Pitching Leaders	5.00	2.50	.50
	Sandy Koufax			
	Juan Marichal			
	Bob Gibson			
	Gaylord Perry			
☐ 237	AL Strikeout Leaders	1.00	.50	.10
	Sam McDowell			
	Jim Kaat			
	Earl Wilson			
☐ 238	NL Strikeout Leaders	2.00	1.00	.20
	Sandy Koufax			
	Jim Bunning			
	Bob Veale			
☐ 239	AL Batting Leaders	2.50	1.25	.25
	Frank Robinson			
	Tony Oliva			
	Al Kaline			
☐ 240	NL Batting Leaders	1.00	.50	.10
	Matty Alou			
	Felipe Alou			
	Rico Carty			
☐ 241	AL RBI Leaders	2.00	1.00	.20
	Frank Robinson			
	Harmon Killebrew			
	Boog Powell			
☐ 242	NL RBI Leaders	3.00	1.50	.30
	Hank Aaron			
	Bob Clemente			
	Richie Allen			
☐ 243	AL Home Run Leaders	2.00	1.00	.20
	Frank Robinson			
	Harmon Killebrew			
	Boog Powell			
☐ 244	NL Home Run Leaders	3.00	1.50	.30
	Hank Aaron			
	Richie Allen			
	Willie Mays			

☐ 245	Curt Flood	.80	.40	.08
☐ 246	Jim Perry	.80	.40	.08
☐ 247	Jerry Lumpe	.45	.22	.04
☐ 248	Gene Mauch MG	.60	.30	.06
☐ 249	Nick Willhite	.45	.22	.04
☐ 250	Hank Aaron	40.00	20.00	4.00
☐ 251	Woody Held	.45	.22	.04
☐ 252	Bob Bolin	.45	.22	.04
☐ 253	Indians Rookies	.45	.22	.04
	Bill Davis			
	Gus Gil			
☐ 254	Milt Pappas	.60	.30	.06
☐ 255	Frank Howard	1.00	.50	.10
☐ 256	Bob Hendley	.45	.22	.04
☐ 257	Charlie Smith	.45	.22	.04
☐ 258	Lee Maye	.45	.22	.04
☐ 259	Don Dennis	.45	.22	.04
☐ 260	Jim Lefebvre	.60	.30	.06
☐ 261	John Wyatt	.45	.22	.04
☐ 262	Athletics Team	.90	.45	.09
☐ 263	Hank Aguirre	.45	.22	.04
☐ 264	Ron Swoboda	.60	.30	.06
☐ 265	Lou Burdette	.80	.40	.08
☐ 266	Pitt Power	2.00	1.00	.20
	Willie Stargell			
	Donn Clendenon			
☐ 267	Don Schwall	.45	.22	.04
☐ 268	John Briggs	.45	.22	.04
☐ 269	Don Nottebart	.45	.22	.04
☐ 270	Zoilo Versalles	.45	.22	.04
☐ 271	Eddie Watt	.45	.22	.04
☐ 272	Cubs Rookies	.45	.22	.04
	Bill Connors			
	Dave Dowling			
☐ 273	Dick Lines	.45	.22	.04
☐ 274	Bob Aspromonte	.45	.22	.04
☐ 275	Fred Whitfield	.45	.22	.04
☐ 276	Bruce Brubaker	.45	.22	.04
☐ 277	Steve Whitaker	.45	.22	.04
☐ 278	Checklist 4	2.25	.45	.10
	Jim Kaat			
☐ 279	Frank Linzy	.45	.22	.04
☐ 280	Tony Conigliaro	1.50	.75	.15
☐ 281	Bob Rodgers	.60	.30	.06
☐ 282	Johnny Odom	.45	.22	.04
☐ 283	Gene Alley	.60	.30	.06
☐ 284	Johnny Podres	.80	.40	.08
☐ 285	Lou Brock	8.00	4.00	.80
☐ 286	Wayne Causey	.45	.22	.04
☐ 287	Mets Rookies	.45	.22	.04
	Greg Goossen			
	Bart Shirley			
☐ 288	Denny Lemaster	.45	.22	.04
☐ 289	Tom Tresh	.80	.40	.08
☐ 290	Bill White	.80	.40	.08
☐ 291	Jim Hannan	.45	.22	.04
☐ 292	Don Pavletich	.45	.22	.04
☐ 293	Ed Kirkpatrick	.45	.22	.04
☐ 294	Walt Alston MG	1.50	.75	.15
☐ 295	Sam McDowell	.80	.40	.08
☐ 296	Glenn Beckert	.60	.30	.06
☐ 297	Dave Morehead	.45	.22	.04
☐ 298	Ron Davis	.45	.22	.04
☐ 299	Norm Siebern	.45	.22	.04
☐ 300	Jim Kaat	2.00	1.00	.20
☐ 301	Jesse Gonder	.45	.22	.04
☐ 302	Orioles Team	.90	.45	.09
☐ 303	Gil Blanco	.45	.22	.04
☐ 304	Phil Gagliano	.45	.22	.04
☐ 305	Earl Wilson	.45	.22	.04
☐ 306	Bud Harrelson	.60	.30	.06
☐ 307	Jim Beauchamp	.45	.22	.04
☐ 308	Al Downing	.60	.30	.06
☐ 309	Hurlers Beware	.60	.30	.06
	Johnny Callison			
	Richie Allen			
☐ 310	Gary Peters	.60	.30	.06
☐ 311	Ed Brinkman	.45	.22	.04
☐ 312	Don Mincher	.60	.30	.06
☐ 313	Bob Lee	.45	.22	.04
☐ 314	Red Sox Rookies	2.00	1.00	.20
	Mike Andrews			
	Reggie Smith			
☐ 315	Billy Williams	4.50	2.25	.45
☐ 316	Jack Kralick	.45	.22	.04
☐ 317	Cesar Tovar	.45	.22	.04
☐ 318	Dave Giusti	.45	.22	.04
☐ 319	Paul Blair	.60	.30	.06
☐ 320	Gaylord Perry	4.50	2.25	.45
☐ 321	Mayo Smith MG	.45	.22	.04
☐ 322	Jose Pagan	.45	.22	.04
☐ 323	Mike Hershberger	.45	.22	.04
☐ 324	Hal Woodeshick	.45	.22	.04
☐ 325	Chico Cardenas	.45	.22	.04
☐ 326	Bob Uecker	7.50	3.75	.75
☐ 327	Angels Team	.90	.45	.09
☐ 328	Clete Boyer	.75	.35	.07
☐ 329	Charlie Lau	.60	.30	.06
☐ 330	Claude Osteen	.60	.30	.06
☐ 331	Joe Foy	.45	.22	.04
☐ 332	Jesus Alou	.45	.22	.04
☐ 333	Fergie Jenkins	3.00	1.50	.30
☐ 334	Twin Terrors	2.50	1.25	.25
	Bob Allison			
	Harmon Killebrew			
☐ 335	Bob Veale	.60	.30	.06
☐ 336	Joe Azcue	.45	.22	.04
☐ 337	Joe Morgan	4.50	2.25	.45
☐ 338	Bob Locker	.45	.22	.04
☐ 339	Chico Ruiz	.45	.22	.04
☐ 340	Joe Pepitone	.75	.35	.07
☐ 341	Giants Rookies	.45	.22	.04
	Dick Dietz			
	Bill Sorrell			
☐ 342	Hank Fischer	.45	.22	.04
☐ 343	Tom Satriano	.45	.22	.04
☐ 344	Ossie Chavarria	.45	.22	.04
☐ 345	Stu Miller	.45	.22	.04
☐ 346	Jim Hickman	.45	.22	.04
☐ 347	Grady Hatton MG	.45	.22	.04
☐ 348	Tug McGraw	1.00	.50	.10
☐ 349	Bob Chance	.45	.22	.04
☐ 350	Joe Torre	1.00	.50	.10
☐ 351	Vern Law	.60	.30	.06
☐ 352	Ray Oyler	.45	.22	.04
☐ 353	Bill McCool	.45	.22	.04
☐ 354	Cubs Team	.90	.45	.09
☐ 355	Carl Yastrzemski	75.00	37.50	7.50
☐ 356	Larry Jaster	.45	.22	.04
☐ 357	Bill Skowron	.90	.45	.09
☐ 358	Ruben Amaro	.45	.22	.04
☐ 359	Dick Ellsworth	.60	.30	.06
☐ 360	Leon Wagner	.45	.22	.04
☐ 361	Checklist 5	2.50	.45	.10
	Roberto Clemente			
☐ 362	Darold Knowles	.45	.22	.04
☐ 363	Dave Johnson	1.25	.60	.12
☐ 364	Claude Raymond	.45	.22	.04
☐ 365	John Roseboro	.60	.30	.06
☐ 366	Andy Kosco	.45	.22	.04
☐ 367	Angels Rookies	.45	.22	.04
	Bill Kelso			
	Don Wallace			
☐ 368	Jack Hiatt	.45	.22	.04
☐ 369	Jim Hunter	6.00	3.00	.60
☐ 370	Tommy Davis	.80	.40	.08
☐ 371	Jim Lonborg	1.25	.60	.12
☐ 372	Mike De La Hoz	.65	.30	.06
☐ 373	White Sox Rookies	.65	.30	.06
	Duane Josephson			
	Fred Klages			
☐ 374	Mel Queen	.65	.30	.06
☐ 375	Jake Gibbs	.65	.30	.06
☐ 376	Don Lock	.65	.30	.06
☐ 377	Luis Tiant	1.75	.85	.17
☐ 378	Tigers Team	1.25	.60	.12
☐ 379	Jerry May	.65	.30	.06
☐ 380	Dean Chance	.80	.40	.08
☐ 381	Dick Schofield	.65	.30	.06
☐ 382	Dave McNally	1.00	.50	.10
☐ 383	Ken Henderson	.65	.30	.06
☐ 384	Cardinals Rookies	.65	.30	.06
	Jim Cosman			
	Dick Hughes			
☐ 385	Jim Fregosi	1.00	.50	.10
	(batting wrong)			
☐ 386	Dick Selma	.65	.30	.06
☐ 387	Cap Peterson	.65	.30	.06
☐ 388	Arnold Earley	.65	.30	.06
☐ 389	Al Dark MG	.80	.40	.08
☐ 390	Jim Wynn	.80	.40	.08
☐ 391	Wilbur Wood	.80	.40	.08
☐ 392	Tommy Harper	.80	.40	.08
☐ 393	Jim Bouton	1.50	.75	.15
☐ 394	Jake Wood	.65	.30	.06
☐ 395	Chris Short	.65	.30	.06
☐ 396	Atlanta Aces	.80	.40	.08
	Denis Menke			
	Tony Cloninger			
☐ 397	Willie Smith	.65	.30	.06
☐ 398	Jeff Torborg	.80	.40	.08
☐ 399	Al Worthington	.65	.30	.06
☐ 400	Bob Clemente	30.00	15.00	3.00
☐ 401	Jim Coates	.65	.30	.06
☐ 402	Phillies Rookies	.80	.40	.08
	Grant Jackson			
	Billy Wilson			
☐ 403	Dick Nen	.65	.30	.06
☐ 404	Nelson Briles	.80	.40	.08
☐ 405	Russ Snyder	.65	.30	.06

☐ 406	Lee Elia	1.00	.50	.10
☐ 407	Reds Team	1.25	.60	.12
☐ 408	Jim Northrup	.80	.40	.08
☐ 409	Ray Sadecki	.65	.30	.06
☐ 410	Lou Johnson	.65	.30	.06
☐ 411	Dick Howser	1.25	.60	.12
☐ 412	Astros Rookies	1.00	.50	.10
	Norm Miller			
	Doug Rader			
☐ 413	Jerry Grote	.65	.30	.06
☐ 414	Casey Cox	.65	.30	.06
☐ 415	Sonny Jackson	.65	.30	.06
☐ 416	Roger Repoz	.65	.30	.06
☐ 417	Bob Bruce	.65	.30	.06
☐ 418	Sam Mele MG	.65	.30	.06
☐ 419	Don Kessinger	.80	.40	.08
☐ 420	Denny McLain	2.00	1.00	.20
☐ 421	Dal Maxvill	.80	.40	.08
☐ 422	Hoyt Wilhelm	4.50	2.25	.45
☐ 423	Fence Busters	8.00	4.00	.80
	Willie Mays			
	Willie McCovey			
☐ 424	Pedro Gonzales	.65	.30	.06
☐ 425	Pete Mikkelsen	.65	.30	.06
☐ 426	Lou Clinton	.65	.30	.06
☐ 427	Ruben Gomez	.65	.30	.06
☐ 428	Dodgers Rookies	1.00	.50	.10
	Tom Hutton			
	Gene Michael			
☐ 429	Garry Roggenburk	.65	.30	.06
☐ 430	Pete Rose	75.00	37.50	7.50
☐ 431	Ted Uhlaender	.65	.30	.06
☐ 432	Jimmie Hall	.80	.40	.08
☐ 433	Al Luplow	.65	.30	.06
☐ 434	Eddie Fisher	.65	.30	.06
☐ 435	Mack Jones	.65	.30	.06
☐ 436	Pete Ward	.65	.30	.06
☐ 437	Senators Team	1.00	.50	.10
☐ 438	Chuck Dobson	.65	.30	.06
☐ 439	Byron Browne	.65	.30	.06
☐ 440	Steve Hargan	.65	.30	.06
☐ 441	Jim Davenport	.80	.40	.08
☐ 442	Yankees Rookies	1.00	.50	.10
	Bill Robinson			
	Joe Verbanic			
☐ 443	Tito Francona	.80	.40	.08
☐ 444	George Smith	.65	.30	.06
☐ 445	Don Sutton	9.00	4.50	.90
☐ 446	Russ Nixon	.65	.30	.06
☐ 447	Bo Belinsky	.80	.40	.08
☐ 448	Harry Walker MG	.80	.40	.08
☐ 449	Orlando Pena	.65	.30	.06
☐ 450	Richie Allen	2.00	1.00	.20
☐ 451	Fred Newman	.65	.30	.06
☐ 452	Ed Kranepool	.80	.40	.08
☐ 453	Aurelio Monteagudo	.65	.30	.06
☐ 454A	Checklist 6	3.00	.65	.10
	Juan Marichal			
	(missing left ear)			
☐ 454B	Checklist 6	6.00	1.00	.20
	Juan Marichal			
	(left ear showing)			
☐ 455	Tommy Agee	.80	.40	.08
☐ 456	Phil Niekro	6.00	3.00	.60
☐ 457	Andy Etchebarren	.65	.30	.06
☐ 458	Lee Thomas	2.00	1.00	.20
☐ 459	Senators Rookies	1.50	.75	.15
	Dick Bosman			
	Pete Craig			
☐ 460	Harmon Killebrew	12.00	6.00	1.20
☐ 461	Bob Miller	1.50	.75	.15
☐ 462	Bob Barton	1.50	.75	.15
☐ 463	Hill Aces	2.00	1.00	.20
	Sam McDowell			
	Sonny Siebert			
☐ 464	Dan Coombs	1.50	.75	.15
☐ 465	Willie Horton	2.00	1.00	.20
☐ 466	Bobby Wine	1.50	.75	.15
☐ 468	Ralph Houk MG	2.50	1.25	.25
☐ 469	Len Gabrielson	1.50	.75	.15
☐ 470	Bob Shaw	1.50	.75	.15
☐ 471	Rene Lachemann	2.00	1.00	.20
☐ 472	Rookies Pirates	1.50	.75	.15
	John Gelnar			
	George Spriggs			
☐ 473	Jose Santiago	1.50	.75	.15
☐ 474	Bob Tolan	2.00	1.00	.20
☐ 475	Jim Palmer	25.00	12.50	2.50
☐ 476	Tony Perez SP	25.00	12.50	2.50
☐ 477	Braves Team	3.00	1.50	.30
☐ 478	Bob Humphreys	1.50	.75	.15
☐ 479	Gary Bell	1.50	.75	.15
☐ 480	Willie McCovey	12.00	6.00	1.20

☐ 481	Leo Durocher MG	2.25	1.10	.22
☐ 482	Bill Monbouquette	1.50	.75	.15
☐ 483	Jim Landis	1.50	.75	.15
☐ 484	Jerry Adair	1.50	.75	.15
☐ 485	Tim McCarver	2.25	1.10	.22
☐ 486	Twins Rookies	1.50	.75	.15
	Rich Reese			
	Bill Whitby			
☐ 487	Tommie Reynolds	1.50	.75	.15
☐ 488	Gerry Arrigo	1.50	.75	.15
☐ 489	Doug Clemens	1.50	.75	.15
☐ 490	Tony Cloninger	1.50	.75	.15
☐ 491	Sam Bowens	1.50	.75	.15
☐ 492	Pirates Team	3.00	1.50	.30
☐ 493	Phil Ortega	1.50	.75	.15
☐ 494	Bill Rigney MG	1.50	.75	.15
☐ 495	Fritz Peterson	2.00	1.00	.20
☐ 496	Orlando McFarlane	1.50	.75	.15
☐ 497	Ron Campbell	1.50	.75	.15
☐ 498	Larry Dierker	2.00	1.00	.20
☐ 499	Indians Rookies	1.50	.75	.15
	George Culver			
	Jose Vidal			
☐ 500	Juan Marichal	8.00	4.00	.80
☐ 501	Jerry Zimmerman	1.50	.75	.15
☐ 502	Derrell Griffith	1.50	.75	.15
☐ 503	Dodgers Team	3.00	1.50	.30
☐ 504	Orlando Martinez	1.50	.75	.15
☐ 505	Tommy Helms	2.00	1.00	.20
☐ 506	Smoky Burgess	2.00	1.00	.20
☐ 507	Orioles Rookies	1.50	.75	.15
	Ed Barnowski			
	Larry Haney			
☐ 508	Dick Hall	1.50	.75	.15
☐ 509	Jim King	1.50	.75	.15
☐ 510	Bill Mazeroski	2.50	1.25	.25
☐ 511	Don Wert	1.50	.75	.15
☐ 512	Red Schoendienst MG	2.00	1.00	.20
☐ 513	Marcelino Lopez	1.50	.75	.15
☐ 514	John Werhas	1.50	.75	.15
☐ 515	Bert Campaneris	2.00	1.00	.20
☐ 516	Giants Team	3.00	1.50	.30
☐ 517	Fred Talbot	1.50	.75	.15
☐ 518	Denis Menke	1.50	.75	.15
☐ 519	Ted Davidson	1.50	.75	.15
☐ 520	Max Alvis	1.50	.75	.15
☐ 521	Bird Bombers	2.00	1.00	.20
	Boog Powell			
	Curt Blefary			
☐ 522	John Stephenson	1.50	.75	.15
☐ 523	Jim Merritt	1.50	.75	.15
☐ 524	Felix Mantilla	1.50	.75	.15
☐ 525	Ron Hunt	1.50	.75	.15
☐ 526	Tigers Rookies	2.00	1.00	.20
	Pat Dobson			
	George Korince			
	(See 67T-72)			
☐ 527	Dennis Ribant	1.50	.75	.15
☐ 528	Rico Petrocelli	2.50	1.25	.25
☐ 529	Gary Wagner	1.50	.75	.15
☐ 530	Felipe Alou	2.00	1.00	.20
☐ 531	Checklist 7	5.00	1.00	.20
	Brooks Robinson			
☐ 532	Jim Hicks	1.50	.75	.15
☐ 533	Jack Fisher	1.50	.75	.15
☐ 534	Hank Bauer MG	6.00	3.00	.60
☐ 535	Donn Clendenon	6.00	3.00	.60
☐ 536	Cubs Rookies	10.00	5.00	1.00
	Joe Niekro			
	Paul Popovich			
☐ 537	Chuck Estrada	4.50	2.25	.45
☐ 538	J.C. Martin	4.50	2.25	.45
☐ 539	Dick Egan	4.50	2.25	.45
☐ 540	Norm Cash	15.00	7.50	1.50
☐ 541	Joe Gibbon	4.50	2.25	.45
☐ 542	Athletics Rookies	6.00	3.00	.60
	Rick Monday			
	Tony Pierce			
☐ 543	Dan Schneider	4.50	2.25	.45
☐ 544	Indians Team	12.00	6.00	1.20
☐ 545	Jim Grant	4.50	2.25	.45
☐ 546	Woody Woodward	6.00	3.00	.60
☐ 547	Red Sox Rookies	4.50	2.25	.45
	Russ Gibson			
	Bill Rohr			
☐ 548	Tony Gonzalez	4.50	2.25	.45
☐ 549	Jack Sanford	4.50	2.25	.45
☐ 550	Vada Pinson	6.00	3.00	.60
☐ 551	Doug Camilli	4.50	2.25	.45
☐ 552	Ted Savage	4.50	2.25	.45
☐ 553	Yankees Rookies	6.00	3.00	.60
	Mike Hegan			
	Thad Tillotson			
☐ 554	Andre Rodgers	4.50	2.25	.45
☐ 555	Don Cardwell	4.50	2.25	.45

☐ 556	Al Weis	4.50	2.25	.45
☐ 557	Al Ferrara	4.50	2.25	.45
☐ 558	Orioles Rookies	9.00	4.50	.90
	Mark Belanger			
	Bill Dillman			
☐ 559	Dick Tracewski	4.50	2.25	.45
☐ 560	Jim Bunning	25.00	12.50	2.50
☐ 561	Sandy Alomar	4.50	2.25	.45
☐ 562	Steve Blass	4.50	2.25	.45
☐ 563	Joe Adcock	9.00	4.50	.90
☐ 564	Astros Rookies	4.50	2.25	.45
	Alonzo Harris			
	Aaron Pointer			
☐ 565	Lew Krausse	4.50	2.25	.45
☐ 566	Gary Geiger	4.50	2.25	.45
☐ 567	Steve Hamilton	4.50	2.25	.45
☐ 568	John Sullivan	4.50	2.25	.45
☐ 569	AL Rookies	150.00	75.00	15.00
	Rod Carew			
	Hank Allen			
☐ 570	Maury Wills	65.00	32.50	6.50
☐ 571	Larry Sherry	4.50	2.25	.45
☐ 572	Don Demeter	4.50	2.25	.45
☐ 573	White Sox Team	12.00	6.00	1.20
☐ 574	Jerry Buchek	4.50	2.25	.45
☐ 575	Dave Boswell	4.50	2.25	.45
☐ 576	NL Rookies	4.50	2.25	.45
	Ramon Hernandez			
	Norm Gigon			
☐ 577	Bill Short	4.50	2.25	.45
☐ 578	John Boccabella	4.50	2.25	.45
☐ 579	Bill Henry	4.50	2.25	.45
☐ 580	Rocky Colavito	15.00	7.50	1.50
☐ 581	Mets Rookies	400.00	200.00	40.00
	Bill Denehy			
	Tom Seaver			
☐ 582	Jim Owens	4.50	2.25	.45
☐ 583	Ray Barker	4.50	2.25	.45
☐ 584	Jim Piersall	9.00	4.50	.90
☐ 585	Wally Bunker	4.50	2.25	.45
☐ 586	Manny Jimenez	4.50	2.25	.45
☐ 587	NL Rookies	4.50	2.25	.45
	Don Shaw			
	Gary Sutherland			
☐ 588	Johnny Klippstein	4.50	2.25	.45
☐ 589	Dave Ricketts	4.50	2.25	.45
☐ 590	Pete Richert	4.50	2.25	.45
☐ 591	Ty Cline	4.50	2.25	.45
☐ 592	NL Rookies	4.50	2.25	.45
	Jim Shellenback			
	Ron Willis			
☐ 593	Wes Westrum MG	4.50	2.25	.45
☐ 594	Dan Osinski	4.50	2.25	.45
☐ 595	Cookie Rojas	4.50	2.25	.45
☐ 596	Galen Cisco	4.50	2.25	.45
☐ 597	Ted Abernathy	4.50	2.25	.45
☐ 598	White Sox Rookies	4.50	2.25	.45
	Walt Williams			
	Ed Stroud			
☐ 599	Bob Duliba	4.50	2.25	.45
☐ 600	Brooks Robinson	175.00	85.00	18.00
☐ 601	Bill Bryan	4.50	2.25	.45
☐ 602	Juan Pizarro	4.50	2.25	.45
☐ 603	Athletics Rookies	4.50	2.25	.45
	Tim Talton			
	Ramon Webster			
☐ 604	Red Sox Team	12.00	6.00	1.20
☐ 605	Mike Shannon	7.50	3.75	.75
☐ 606	Ron Taylor	4.50	2.25	.45
☐ 607	Mickey Stanley	6.00	3.00	.60
☐ 608	Cubs Rookies	4.50	2.25	.45
	Rich Nye			
	John Upham			
☐ 609	Tommy John	65.00	15.00	3.00

1968 Topps

The cards in this 598-card set measure 2 1/2" by 3 1/2". The 1968 Topps set includes Sporting News All-Star Selections as card numbers 361 to 380. Other subsets in the set include League Leaders (1-12) and World Series cards (151-158). The front of each checklist card features a picture of a popular player inside a circle. High numbers 534 to 598 are slightly more difficult to obtain. The first series looks different from the other series as it has a lighter, wider mesh background on the card front. The later

series all had a much darker, finer mesh pattern. Key cards in the set are the rookie cards of Johnny Bench (247) and Nolan Ryan (177).

		NRMT	VG-E	GOOD
COMPLETE SET		1200.00	400.00	80.00
COMMON PLAYER (1-110)		.35	.17	.03
COMMON PLAYER (111-457)		.30	.15	.03
COMMON PLAYER (458-533)		.50	.25	.05
COMMON PLAYER (534-598)		.55	.27	.05
☐ 1	NL Batting Leaders	4.50	1.00	.20
	Bob Clemente			
	Tony Gonzales			
	Matty Alou			
☐ 2	AL Batting Leaders	3.00	1.50	.30
	Carl Yastrzemski			
	Frank Robinson			
	Al Kaline			
☐ 3	NL RBI Leaders	2.50	1.25	.25
	Orlando Cepeda			
	Bob Clemente			
	Hank Aaron			
☐ 4	AL RBI Leaders	3.00	1.50	.30
	Carl Yastrzemski			
	Harmon Killebrew			
	Frank Robinson			
☐ 5	NL Home Run Leaders	2.00	1.00	.20
	Hank Aaron			
	Jim Wynn			
	Ron Santo			
	Willie McCovey			
☐ 6	NL Home Run Leaders	3.00	1.50	.30
	Carl Yastrzemski			
	Harmon Killebrew			
	Frank Howard			
☐ 7	NL ERA Leaders	1.00	.50	.10
	Phil Niekro			
	Jim Bunning			
	Chris Short			
☐ 8	AL ERA Leaders	.75	.35	.07
	Joe Horlen			
	Gary Peters			
	Sonny Siebert			
☐ 9	NL Pitching Leaders	1.00	.50	.10
	Mike McCormick			
	Ferguson Jenkins			
	Jim Bunning			
	Claude Osteen			
☐ 10	AL Pitching Leaders	.75	.35	.07
	Jim Lonborg			
	Earl Wilson			
	Dean Chance			
☐ 11	NL Strikeout Leaders	1.50	.75	.15
	Jim Bunning			
	Ferguson Jenkins			
	Gaylord Perry			
☐ 12	AL Strikeout Leaders	.75	.35	.07
	Jim Lonborg			
	Sam McDowell			
	Dean Chance			
☐ 13	Chuck Hartenstein	.35	.17	.03
☐ 14	Jerry McNertney	.35	.17	.03
☐ 15	Ron Hunt	.35	.17	.03
☐ 16	Indians Rookies	1.50	.75	.15
	Lou Piniella			
	Richie Scheinblum			
☐ 17	Dick Hall	.35	.17	.03
☐ 18	Mike Hershberger	.35	.17	.03
☐ 19	Juan Pizarro	.35	.17	.03
☐ 20	Brooks Robinson	7.00	3.50	.70
☐ 21	Ron Davis	.35	.17	.03
☐ 22	Pat Dobson	.50	.25	.05
☐ 23	Chico Cardenas	.35	.17	.03

☐ 24	Bobby Locke	.35	.17	.03
☐ 25	Julian Javier	.50	.25	.05
☐ 26	Darrell Brandon	.35	.17	.03
☐ 27	Gil Hodges MG	3.00	1.50	.30
☐ 28	Ted Uhlaender	.35	.17	.03
☐ 29	Joe Verbanic	.35	.17	.03
☐ 30	Joe Torre	1.00	.50	.10
☐ 31	Ed Stroud	.35	.17	.03
☐ 32	Joe Gibbon	.35	.17	.03
☐ 33	Pete Ward	.35	.17	.03
☐ 34	Al Ferrara	.35	.17	.03
☐ 35	Steve Hargan	.35	.17	.03
☐ 36	Pirates Rookies	.65	.30	.06
	Bob Moose			
	Bob Robertson			
☐ 37	Billy Williams	4.00	2.00	.40
☐ 38	Tony Pierce	.35	.17	.03
☐ 39	Cookie Rojas	.35	.17	.03
☐ 40	Denny McLain	2.50	1.25	.25
☐ 41	Julio Gotay	.35	.17	.03
☐ 42	Larry Haney	.35	.17	.03
☐ 43	Gary Bell	.35	.17	.03
☐ 44	Frank Kostro	.35	.17	.03
☐ 45	Tom Seaver	50.00	25.00	5.00
☐ 46	Dave Ricketts	.35	.17	.03
☐ 47	Ralph Houk MG	.50	.25	.05
☐ 48	Ted Davidson	.35	.17	.03
☐ 49A	Eddie Brinkman	.35	.17	.03
	(white team name)			
☐ 49B	Eddie Brinkman	15.00	7.50	1.50
	(yellow team name)			
☐ 50	Willie Mays	27.00	13.50	2.70
☐ 51	Bob Locker	.35	.17	.03
☐ 52	Hawk Taylor	.35	.17	.03
☐ 53	Gene Alley	.50	.25	.05
☐ 54	Stan Williams	.35	.17	.03
☐ 55	Felipe Alou	.50	.25	.05
☐ 56	Orioles Rookies	.35	.17	.03
	Dave Leonhard			
	Dave May			
☐ 57	Dan Schneider	.35	.17	.03
☐ 58	Eddie Mathews	5.00	2.50	.50
☐ 59	Don Lock	.35	.17	.03
☐ 60	Ken Holtzman	.50	.25	.05
☐ 61	Reggie Smith	.90	.45	.09
☐ 62	Chuck Dobson	.35	.17	.03
☐ 63	Dick Kenworthy	.35	.17	.03
☐ 64	Jim Merritt	.35	.17	.03
☐ 65	John Roseboro	.50	.25	.05
☐ 66A	Casey Cox	.35	.17	.03
	(white team name)			
☐ 66B	Casey Cox	15.00	7.50	1.50
	(yellow team name)			
☐ 67	Checklist 1	2.00	.30	.06
	Jim Kaat			
☐ 68	Ron Willis	.35	.17	.03
☐ 69	Tom Tresh	.75	.35	.07
☐ 70	Bob Veale	.50	.25	.05
☐ 71	Vern Fuller	.35	.17	.03
☐ 72	Tommy John	2.25	1.10	.22
☐ 73	Jim Ray Hart	.50	.25	.05
☐ 74	Milt Pappas	.50	.25	.05
☐ 75	Don Mincher	.35	.17	.03
☐ 76	Braves Rookies	.50	.25	.05
	Jim Britton			
	Ron Reed			
☐ 77	Don Wilson	.35	.17	.03
☐ 78	Jim Northrup	.50	.25	.05
☐ 79	Ted Kubiak	.35	.17	.03
☐ 80	Rod Carew	30.00	15.00	3.00
☐ 81	Larry Jackson	.35	.17	.03
☐ 82	Sam Bowens	.35	.17	.03
☐ 83	John Stephenson	.35	.17	.03
☐ 84	Bob Tolan	.35	.17	.03
☐ 85	Gaylord Perry	4.00	2.00	.40
☐ 86	Willie Stargell	4.50	2.25	.45
☐ 87	Dick Williams MG	.50	.25	.05
☐ 88	Phil Regan	.50	.25	.05
☐ 89	Jake Gibbs	.35	.17	.03
☐ 90	Vada Pinson	1.00	.50	.10
☐ 91	Jim Ollom	.35	.17	.03
☐ 92	Ed Kranepool	.50	.25	.05
☐ 93	Tony Cloninger	.35	.17	.03
☐ 94	Lee Maye	.35	.17	.03
☐ 95	Bob Aspromonte	.35	.17	.03
☐ 96	Senator Rookies	.35	.17	.03
	Frank Coggins			
	Dick Nold			
☐ 97	Tom Phoebus	.35	.17	.03
☐ 98	Gary Sutherland	.35	.17	.03
☐ 99	Rocky Colavito	1.00	.50	.10
☐ 100	Bob Gibson	6.50	3.25	.65
☐ 101	Glenn Beckert	.50	.25	.05
☐ 102	Jose Cardenal	.35	.17	.03
☐ 103	Don Sutton	3.50	1.75	.35
☐ 104	Dick Dietz	.35	.17	.03
☐ 105	Al Downing	.50	.25	.05
☐ 106	Dalton Jones	.35	.17	.03
☐ 107A	Checklist 2	2.00	.30	.06
	Juan Marichal			
	(tan wide mesh)			
☐ 107B	Checklist 2	2.50	.40	.08
	Juan Marichal			
	(brown fine mesh)			
☐ 108	Don Pavletich	.35	.17	.03
☐ 109	Bert Campaneris	.50	.25	.05
☐ 110	Hank Aaron	27.00	13.50	2.70
☐ 111	Rich Reese	.30	.15	.03
☐ 112	Woody Fryman	.30	.15	.03
☐ 113	Tigers Rookies	.30	.15	.03
	Tom Matchick			
	Daryl Patterson			
☐ 114	Ron Swoboda	.45	.22	.04
☐ 115	Sam McDowell	.60	.30	.06
☐ 116	Ken McMullen	.30	.15	.03
☐ 117	Larry Jaster	.30	.15	.03
☐ 118	Mark Belanger	.60	.30	.06
☐ 119	Ted Savage	.30	.15	.03
☐ 120	Mel Stottlemyre	.60	.30	.06
☐ 121	Jimmie Hall	.30	.15	.03
☐ 122	Gene Mauch MG	.45	.22	.04
☐ 123	Jose Santiago	.30	.15	.03
☐ 124	Nate Oliver	.30	.15	.03
☐ 125	Joe Horlen	.30	.15	.03
☐ 126	Bob Etheridge	.30	.15	.03
☐ 127	Paul Lindblad	.30	.15	.03
☐ 128	Astros Rookies	.30	.15	.03
	Tom Dukes			
	Alonzo Harris			
☐ 129	Mickey Stanley	.45	.22	.04
☐ 130	Tony Perez	3.00	1.50	.30
☐ 131	Frank Bertaina	.30	.15	.03
☐ 132	Bud Harrelson	.45	.22	.04
☐ 133	Fred Whitfield	.30	.15	.03
☐ 134	Pat Jarvis	.30	.15	.03
☐ 135	Paul Blair	.45	.22	.04
☐ 136	Randy Hundley	.45	.22	.04
☐ 137	Twins Team	.75	.35	.07
☐ 138	Ruben Amaro	.30	.15	.03
☐ 139	Chris Short	.30	.15	.03
☐ 140	Tony Conigliaro	1.00	.50	.10
☐ 141	Dal Maxvill	.45	.22	.04
☐ 142	White Sox Rookies	.30	.15	.03
	Buddy Bradford			
	Bill Voss			
☐ 143	Pete Cimino	.30	.15	.03
☐ 144	Joe Morgan	3.50	1.75	.35
☐ 145	Don Drysdale	4.00	2.00	.40
☐ 146	Sal Bando	.75	.35	.07
☐ 147	Frank Linzy	.30	.15	.03
☐ 148	Dave Bristol MG	.30	.15	.03
☐ 149	Bob Saverine	.30	.15	.03
☐ 150	Bob Clemente	16.00	8.00	1.60
☐ 151	World Series Game 1	2.50	1.25	.25
	Brock socks 4 hits			
	in opener			
☐ 152	World Series Game 2	4.00	2.00	.40
	Yaz smashes 2 homers			
☐ 153	World Series Game 3	1.50	.75	.15
	Briles cools Boston			
☐ 154	World Series Game 4	2.50	1.25	.25
	Gibson hurls shutout			
☐ 155	World Series Game 5	1.50	.75	.15
	Lonborg wins again			
☐ 156	World Series Game 6	1.50	.75	.15
	Petrocelli 2 homers			
☐ 157	World Series Game 7	1.50	.75	.15
	St. Louis wins it			
☐ 158	World Series Summary	1.50	.75	.15
	Cardinals celebrate			
☐ 159	Don Kessinger	.45	.22	.04
☐ 160	Earl Wilson	.30	.15	.03
☐ 161	Norm Miller	.30	.15	.03
☐ 162	Cards Rookies	.75	.35	.07
	Hal Gilson			
	Mike Torrez			
☐ 163	Gene Brabender	.30	.15	.03
☐ 164	Ramon Webster	.30	.15	.03
☐ 165	Tony Oliva	1.50	.75	.15
☐ 166	Claude Raymond	.30	.15	.03
☐ 167	Elston Howard	1.50	.75	.15
☐ 168	Dodgers Team	1.25	.60	.12
☐ 169	Bob Bolin	.30	.15	.03
☐ 170	Jim Fregosi	.60	.30	.06
☐ 171	Don Nottebart	.30	.15	.03
☐ 172	Walt Williams	.30	.15	.03
☐ 173	John Boozer	.30	.15	.03
☐ 174	Bob Tillman	.30	.15	.03
☐ 175	Maury Wills	1.75	.85	.17
☐ 176	Bob Allen	.30	.15	.03

☐177	Mets Rookies	135.00	65.00	13.50
	Jerry Koosman			
	Nolan Ryan			
☐178	Don Wert	.30	.15	.03
☐179	Bill Stoneman	.30	.15	.03
☐180	Curt Flood	.75	.35	.07
☐181	Jerry Zimmerman	.30	.15	.03
☐182	Dave Giusti	.30	.15	.03
☐183	Bob Kennedy MG	.30	.15	.03
☐184	Lou Johnson	.30	.15	.03
☐185	Tom Haller	.45	.22	.04
☐186	Eddie Watt	.30	.15	.03
☐187	Sonny Jackson	.30	.15	.03
☐188	Cap Peterson	.30	.15	.03
☐189	Bill Landis	.30	.15	.03
☐190	Bill White	.60	.30	.06
☐191	Dan Frisella	.30	.15	.03
☐192	Checklist 3	2.50	.40	.10
	Carl Yastrzemski			
☐193	Jack Hamilton	.30	.15	.03
☐194	Don Buford	.30	.15	.03
☐195	Joe Pepitone	.60	.30	.06
☐196	Gary Nolan	.30	.15	.03
☐197	Larry Brown	.30	.15	.03
☐198	Roy Face	.60	.30	.06
☐199	A's Rookies	.30	.15	.03
	Roberto Rodriquez			
	Darrell Osteen			
☐200	Orlando Cepeda	2.25	1.10	.22
☐201	Mike Marshall	1.00	.50	.10
☐202	Adolfo Phillips	.30	.15	.03
☐203	Dick Kelley	.30	.15	.03
☐204	Andy Etchebarren	.30	.15	.03
☐205	Juan Marichal	4.00	2.00	.40
☐206	Cal Ermer MG	.30	.15	.03
☐207	Carroll Sembera	.30	.15	.03
☐208	Willie Davis	.60	.30	.06
☐209	Tim Cullen	.30	.15	.03
☐210	Gary Peters	.45	.22	.04
☐211	J.C. Martin	.30	.15	.03
☐212	Dave Morehead	.30	.15	.03
☐213	Chico Ruiz	.30	.15	.03
☐214	Yankees Rookies	.60	.30	.06
	Stan Bahnsen			
	Frank Fernandez			
☐215	Jim Bunning	2.25	1.10	.22
☐216	Bubba Morton	.30	.15	.03
☐217	Turk Farrell	.30	.15	.03
☐218	Ken Suarez	.30	.15	.03
☐219	Rob Gardner	.30	.15	.03
☐220	Harmon Killebrew	5.00	2.50	.50
☐221	Braves Team	.75	.35	.07
☐222	Jim Hardin	.30	.15	.03
☐223	Ollie Brown	.30	.15	.03
☐224	Jack Aker	.30	.15	.03
☐225	Richie Allen	1.25	.60	.12
☐226	Jimmie Price	.30	.15	.03
☐227	Joe Hoerner	.30	.15	.03
☐228	Dodgers Rookies	.45	.22	.04
	Jack Billingham			
	Jim Fairey			
☐229	Fred Klages	.30	.15	.03
☐230	Pete Rose	45.00	22.50	4.50
☐231	Dave Baldwin	.30	.15	.03
☐232	Denis Menke	.30	.15	.03
☐233	George Scott	.45	.22	.04
☐234	Bill Monbouquette	.30	.15	.03
☐235	Ron Santo	.80	.40	.08
☐236	Tug McGraw	.90	.45	.09
☐237	Alvin Dark MG	.45	.22	.04
☐238	Tom Satriano	.30	.15	.03
☐239	Bill Henry	.30	.15	.03
☐240	Al Kaline	8.00	4.00	.80
☐241	Felix Millan	.30	.15	.03
☐242	Moe Drabowsky	.30	.15	.03
☐243	Rich Rollins	.45	.22	.04
☐244	John Donaldson	.30	.15	.03
☐245	Tony Gonzalez	.30	.15	.03
☐246	Fritz Peterson	.30	.15	.03
☐247	Reds Rookies	125.00	60.00	12.50
	Johnny Bench			
	Ron Tompkins			
☐248	Fred Valentine	.30	.15	.03
☐249	Bill Singer	.30	.15	.03
☐250	Carl Yastrzemski	25.00	12.50	2.50
☐251	Manny Sanguillen	1.50	.75	.15
☐252	Angels Team	.75	.35	.07
☐253	Dick Hughes	.30	.15	.03
☐254	Cleon Jones	.30	.15	.03
☐255	Dean Chance	.45	.22	.04
☐256	Norm Cash	1.00	.50	.10
☐257	Phil Niekro	3.50	1.75	.35
☐258	Cubs Rookies	.30	.15	.03
	Jose Arcia			
	Bill Schlesinger			
☐259	Ken Boyer	1.00	.50	.10
☐260	Jim Wynn	.75	.35	.07
☐261	Dave Duncan	.30	.15	.03
☐262	Rick Wise	.45	.22	.04
☐263	Horace Clarke	.45	.22	.04
☐264	Ted Abernathy	.30	.15	.03
☐265	Tommy Davis	.60	.30	.06
☐266	Paul Popovich	.30	.15	.03
☐267	Herman Franks MG	.30	.15	.03
☐268	Bob Humphreys	.30	.15	.03
☐269	Bob Tiefenauer	.30	.15	.03
☐270	Matty Alou	.45	.22	.04
☐271	Bobby Knoop	.30	.15	.03
☐272	Ray Culp	.30	.15	.03
☐273	Dave Johnson	.75	.35	.07
☐274	Mike Cuellar	.45	.22	.04
☐275	Tim McCarver	1.00	.50	.10
☐276	Jim Roland	.30	.15	.03
☐277	Jerry Buchek	.30	.15	.03
☐278	Checklist 4	2.00	.40	.08
	Orlando Cepeda			
☐279	Bill Hands	.30	.15	.03
☐280	Mickey Mantle	150.00	75.00	15.00
☐281	Jim Campanis	.30	.15	.03
☐282	Rick Monday	.60	.30	.06
☐283	Mel Queen	.30	.15	.03
☐284	John Briggs	.30	.15	.03
☐285	Dick McAuliffe	.45	.22	.04
☐286	Cecil Upshaw	.30	.15	.03
☐287	White Sox Rookies	.30	.15	.03
	Mickey Abarbanel			
	Cisco Carlos			
☐288	Dave Wickersham	.30	.15	.03
☐289	Woody Held	.30	.15	.03
☐290	Willie McCovey	5.50	2.75	.55
☐291	Dick Lines	.30	.15	.03
☐292	Art Shamsky	.30	.15	.03
☐293	Bruce Howard	.30	.15	.03
☐294	Red Schoendienst MG	.60	.30	.06
☐295	Sonny Siebert	.45	.22	.04
☐296	Byron Browne	.30	.15	.03
☐297	Russ Gibson	.30	.15	.03
☐298	Jim Brewer	.30	.15	.03
☐299	Gene Michael	.45	.22	.04
☐300	Rusty Staub	1.00	.50	.10
☐301	Twins Rookies	.30	.15	.03
	George Mitterwald			
	Rick Renick			
☐302	Gerry Arrigo	.30	.15	.03
☐303	Dick Green	.30	.15	.03
☐304	Sandy Valdespino	.30	.15	.03
☐305	Minnie Rojas	.30	.15	.03
☐306	Mike Ryan	.30	.15	.03
☐307	John Hiller	.60	.30	.06
☐308	Pirates Team	.75	.35	.07
☐309	Ken Henderson	.30	.15	.03
☐310	Luis Aparicio	3.50	1.75	.35
☐311	Jack Lamabe	.30	.15	.03
☐312	Curt Blefary	.30	.15	.03
☐313	Al Weis	.30	.15	.03
☐314	Red Sox Rookies	.30	.15	.03
	Bill Rohr			
	George Spriggs			
☐315	Zoilo Versalles	.30	.15	.03
☐316	Steve Barber	.30	.15	.03
☐317	Ron Brand	.30	.15	.03
☐318	Chico Salmon	.30	.15	.03
☐319	George Culver	.30	.15	.03
☐320	Frank Howard	1.00	.50	.10
☐321	Leo Durocher MG	1.50	.75	.15
☐322	Dave Boswell	.30	.15	.03
☐323	Deron Johnson	.45	.22	.04
☐324	Jim Nash	.30	.15	.03
☐325	Manny Mota	.45	.22	.04
☐326	Denny Ribant	.30	.15	.03
☐327	Tony Taylor	.30	.15	.03
☐328	Angels Rookies	.30	.15	.03
	Chuck Vinson			
	Jim Weaver			
☐329	Duane Josephson	.30	.15	.03
☐330	Roger Maris	6.50	3.25	.65
☐331	Dan Osinski	.30	.15	.03
☐332	Doug Rader	.45	.22	.04
☐333	Ron Herbel	.30	.15	.03
☐334	Orioles Team	.75	.35	.07
☐335	Bob Allison	.45	.22	.04
☐336	John Purdin	.30	.15	.03
☐337	Bill Robinson	.45	.22	.04
☐338	Bob Johnson	.30	.15	.03
☐339	Rich Nye	.30	.15	.03
☐340	Max Alvis	.30	.15	.03
☐341	Jim Lemon MG	.30	.15	.03
☐342	Ken Johnson	.30	.15	.03
☐343	Jim Gosger	.30	.15	.03
☐344	Donn Clendenon	.45	.22	.04

☐ 345 Bob Hendley	.30	.15	.03
☐ 346 Jerry Adair	.30	.15	.03
☐ 347 George Brunet	.30	.15	.03
☐ 348 Phillies Rookies	.30	.15	.03
Larry Colton			
Dick Thoenen			
☐ 349 Ed Spiezio	.30	.15	.03
☐ 350 Hoyt Wilhelm	3.50	1.75	.35
☐ 351 Bob Barton	.30	.15	.03
☐ 352 Jackie Hernandez	.30	.15	.03
☐ 353 Mack Jones	.30	.15	.03
☐ 354 Pete Richert	.30	.15	.03
☐ 355 Ernie Banks	5.50	2.75	.55
☐ 356A Checklist 5	2.00	.30	.06
Ken Holtzman			
(head centered			
within circle)			
☐ 356B Checklist 5	2.00	.30	.06
Ken Holtzman			
(head shifted right			
within circle)			
☐ 357 Len Gabrielson	.30	.15	.03
☐ 358 Mike Epstein	.30	.15	.03
☐ 359 Joe Moeller	.30	.15	.03
☐ 360 Willie Horton	.60	.30	.06
☐ 361 Harmon Killebrew AS	3.00	1.50	.30
☐ 362 Orlando Cepeda AS	1.00	.50	.10
☐ 363 Rod Carew AS	5.50	2.75	.55
☐ 364 Joe Morgan AS	2.00	1.00	.20
☐ 365 Brooks Robinson AS	3.50	1.75	.35
☐ 366 Ron Santo AS	.60	.30	.06
☐ 367 Jim Fregosi AS	.45	.22	.04
☐ 368 Gene Alley AS	.45	.22	.04
☐ 369 Carl Yastrzemski AS	6.00	3.00	.60
☐ 370 Hank Aaron AS	6.00	3.00	.60
☐ 371 Tony Oliva AS	.75	.35	.07
☐ 372 Lou Brock AS	3.50	1.75	.35
☐ 373 Frank Robinson AS	3.00	1.50	.30
☐ 374 Bob Clemente AS	5.00	2.50	.50
☐ 375 Bill Freehan AS	.45	.22	.04
☐ 376 Tim McCarver AS	.45	.22	.04
☐ 377 Joe Horlen AS	.45	.22	.04
☐ 378 Bob Gibson AS	3.00	1.50	.30
☐ 379 Gary Peters AS	.45	.22	.04
☐ 380 Ken Holtzman AS	.45	.22	.04
☐ 381 Boog Powell	1.00	.50	.10
☐ 382 Ramon Hernandez	.30	.15	.03
☐ 383 Steve Whitaker	.30	.15	.03
☐ 384 Reds Rookies	3.50	1.75	.35
Bill Henry			
Hal McRae			
☐ 385 Jim Hunter	4.50	2.25	.45
☐ 386 Greg Goossen	.30	.15	.03
☐ 387 Joe Foy	.30	.15	.03
☐ 388 Ray Washburn	.30	.15	.03
☐ 389 Jay Johnstone	.45	.22	.04
☐ 390 Bill Mazeroski	.75	.35	.07
☐ 391 Bob Priddy	.30	.15	.03
☐ 392 Grady Hatton MG	.30	.15	.03
☐ 393 Jim Perry	.60	.30	.06
☐ 394 Tommie Aaron	.45	.22	.04
☐ 395 Camilo Pascual	.45	.22	.04
☐ 396 Bobby Wine	.30	.15	.03
☐ 397 Vic Davalillo	.45	.22	.04
☐ 398 Jim Grant	.30	.15	.03
☐ 399 Ray Oyler	.30	.15	.03
☐ 400A Mike McCormick	.45	.22	.04
(yellow letters)			
☐ 400B Mike McCormick	15.00	7.50	1.50
(team name in			
white letters)			
☐ 401 Mets Team	1.00	.50	.10
☐ 402 Mike Hegan	.30	.15	.03
☐ 403 John Buzhardt	.30	.15	.03
☐ 404 Floyd Robinson	.30	.15	.03
☐ 405 Tommy Helms	.45	.22	.04
☐ 406 Dick Ellsworth	.45	.22	.04
☐ 407 Gary Kolb	.30	.15	.03
☐ 408 Steve Carlton	27.00	13.50	2.70
☐ 409 Orioles Rookies	.30	.15	.03
Frank Peters			
Don Stone			
☐ 410 Ferguson Jenkins	2.25	1.10	.22
☐ 411 Ron Hansen	.30	.15	.03
☐ 412 Clay Carroll	.30	.15	.03
☐ 413 Tommy McCraw	.30	.15	.03
☐ 414 Mickey Lolich	1.50	.75	.15
☐ 415 Johnny Callison	.45	.22	.04
☐ 416 Bill Rigney MG	.30	.15	.03
☐ 417 Willie Crawford	.30	.15	.03
☐ 418 Eddie Fisher	.30	.15	.03
☐ 419 Jack Hiatt	.30	.15	.03
☐ 420 Cesar Tovar	.30	.15	.03
☐ 421 Ron Taylor	.30	.15	.03
☐ 422 Rene Lachemann	.45	.22	.04
☐ 423 Fred Gladding	.30	.15	.03
☐ 424 White Sox Team	.75	.35	.07
☐ 425 Jim Maloney	.45	.22	.04
☐ 426 Hank Allen	.30	.15	.03
☐ 427 Dick Calmus	.30	.15	.03
☐ 428 Vic Roznovsky	.30	.15	.03
☐ 429 Tommie Sisk	.30	.15	.03
☐ 430 Rico Petrocelli	.45	.22	.04
☐ 431 Dooley Womack	.30	.15	.03
☐ 432 Indians Rookies	.30	.15	.03
Bill Davis			
Jose Vidal			
☐ 433 Bob Rodgers	.45	.22	.04
☐ 434 Ricardo Joseph	.30	.15	.03
☐ 435 Ron Perranoski	.45	.22	.04
☐ 436 Hal Lanier	.60	.30	.06
☐ 437 Don Cardwell	.30	.15	.03
☐ 438 Lee Thomas	.45	.22	.04
☐ 439 Luman Harris MG	.30	.15	.03
☐ 440 Claude Osteen	.45	.22	.04
☐ 441 Alex Johnson	.45	.22	.04
☐ 442 Dick Bosman	.30	.15	.03
☐ 443 Joe Azcue	.30	.15	.03
☐ 444 Jack Fisher	.30	.15	.03
☐ 445 Mike Shannon	.60	.30	.06
☐ 446 Ron Kline	.30	.15	.03
☐ 447 Tigers Rookies	.30	.15	.03
George Korince			
Fred Lasher			
☐ 448 Gary Wagner	.30	.15	.03
☐ 449 Gene Oliver	.30	.15	.03
☐ 450 Jim Kaat	2.00	1.00	.20
☐ 451 Al Spangler	.30	.15	.03
☐ 452 Jesus Alou	.30	.15	.03
☐ 453 Sammy Ellis	.30	.15	.03
☐ 454A Checklist 6	2.00	.30	.06
Frank Robinson			
(cap complete			
within circle)			
☐ 454B Checklist 6	2.00	.30	.06
Frank Robinson			
(cap partially			
within circle)			
☐ 455 Rico Carty	.60	.30	.06
☐ 456 John O'Donoghue	.30	.15	.03
☐ 457 Jim Lefebvre	.45	.22	.04
☐ 458 Lew Krausse	.50	.25	.05
☐ 459 Dick Simpson	.50	.25	.05
☐ 460 Jim Lonborg	.75	.35	.07
☐ 461 Chuck Hiller	.50	.25	.05
☐ 462 Barry Moore	.50	.25	.05
☐ 463 Jim Schaffer	.50	.25	.05
☐ 464 Don McMahon	.50	.25	.05
☐ 465 Tommie Agee	.60	.30	.06
☐ 466 Bill Dillman	.50	.25	.05
☐ 467 Dick Howser	.90	.45	.09
☐ 468 Larry Sherry	.60	.30	.06
☐ 469 Ty Cline	.50	.25	.05
☐ 470 Bill Freehan	1.00	.50	.10
☐ 471 Orlando Pena	.50	.25	.05
☐ 472 Walt Alston MG	1.50	.75	.15
☐ 473 Al Worthington	.50	.25	.05
☐ 474 Paul Schaal	.50	.25	.05
☐ 475 Joe Niekro	1.25	.60	.12
☐ 476 Woody Woodward	.60	.30	.06
☐ 477 Phillies Team	.90	.45	.09
☐ 478 Dave McNally	.90	.45	.09
☐ 479 Phil Gagliano	.50	.25	.05
☐ 480 Manager's Dream	7.00	3.50	.70
Tony Oliva			
Chico Cardenas			
Bob Clemente			
☐ 481 John Wyatt	.50	.25	.05
☐ 482 Jose Pagan	.50	.25	.05
☐ 483 Darold Knowles	.50	.25	.05
☐ 484 Phil Roof	.50	.25	.05
☐ 485 Ken Berry	.50	.25	.05
☐ 486 Cal Koonce	.50	.25	.05
☐ 487 Lee May	.75	.35	.07
☐ 488 Dick Tracewski	.50	.25	.05
☐ 489 Wally Bunker	.50	.25	.05
☐ 490 Super Stars	25.00	12.50	2.50
Harmon Killebrew			
Willie Mays			
Mickey Mantle			
☐ 491 Denny Lemaster	.50	.25	.05
☐ 492 Jeff Torborg	.60	.30	.06
☐ 493 Jim McGlothlin	.50	.25	.05
☐ 494 Ray Sadecki	.50	.25	.05
☐ 495 Leon Wagner	.50	.25	.05
☐ 496 Steve Hamilton	.50	.25	.05
☐ 497 Cards Team	1.00	.50	.10
☐ 498 Bill Bryan	.50	.25	.05
☐ 499 Steve Blass	.60	.30	.06
☐ 500 Frank Robinson	7.50	3.75	.75

☐ 501	John Odom	.50	.25	.05
☐ 502	Mike Andrews	.50	.25	.05
☐ 503	Al Jackson	.50	.25	.05
☐ 504	Russ Snyder	.50	.25	.05
☐ 505	Joe Sparma	.50	.25	.05
☐ 506	Clarence Jones	.50	.25	.05
☐ 507	Wade Blasingame	.50	.25	.05
☐ 508	Duke Sims	.50	.25	.05
☐ 509	Dennis Higgins	.50	.25	.05
☐ 510	Ron Fairly	.60	.30	.06
☐ 511	Bill Kelso	.50	.25	.05
☐ 512	Grant Jackson	.50	.25	.05
☐ 513	Hank Bauer MG	.60	.30	.06
☐ 514	Al McBean	.50	.25	.05
☐ 515	Russ Nixon	.50	.25	.05
☐ 516	Pete Mikkelsen	.50	.25	.05
☐ 517	Diego Segui	.50	.25	.05
☐ 518A	Checklist 7	2.00	.30	.06
	(539 ML Rookies)			
	(Clete Boyer)			
☐ 518B	Checklist 7	6.00	1.00	.20
	(539 AL Rookies)			
	(Clete Boyer)			
☐ 519	Jerry Stephenson	.50	.25	.05
☐ 520	Lou Brock	7.50	3.75	.75
☐ 521	Don Shaw	.50	.25	.05
☐ 522	Wayne Causey	.50	.25	.05
☐ 523	John Tsitouris	.50	.25	.05
☐ 524	Andy Kosco	.50	.25	.05
☐ 525	Jim Davenport	.60	.30	.06
☐ 526	Bill Denehy	.50	.25	.05
☐ 527	Tito Francona	.60	.30	.06
☐ 528	Tigers Team	5.00	2.50	.50
☐ 529	Bruce Von Hoff	.50	.25	.05
☐ 530	Bird Belters	4.50	2.25	.45
	Brooks Robinson			
	Frank Robinson			
☐ 531	Chuck Hinton	.50	.25	.05
☐ 532	Luis Tiant	1.25	.60	.12
☐ 533	Wes Parker	.65	.30	.06
☐ 534	Bob Miller	.55	.27	.05
☐ 535	Danny Cater	.55	.27	.05
☐ 536	Bill Short	.55	.27	.05
☐ 537	Norm Siebern	.55	.27	.05
☐ 538	Manny Jimenez	.55	.27	.05
☐ 539	Major League Rookies	.80	.40	.08
	Jim Ray			
	Mike Ferraro			
☐ 540	Nelson Briles	.65	.30	.06
☐ 541	Sandy Alomar	.55	.27	.05
☐ 542	John Boccabella	.55	.27	.05
☐ 543	Bob Lee	.55	.27	.05
☐ 544	Mayo Smith MG	.55	.27	.05
☐ 545	Lindy McDaniel	.65	.30	.06
☐ 546	Roy White	1.00	.50	.10
☐ 547	Dan Coombs	.55	.27	.05
☐ 548	Bernie Allen	.55	.27	.05
☐ 549	Orioles Rookies	.55	.27	.05
	Curt Motton			
	Roger Nelson			
☐ 550	Clete Boyer	.80	.40	.08
☐ 551	Darrell Sutherland	.55	.27	.05
☐ 552	Ed Kirkpatrick	.55	.27	.05
☐ 553	Hank Aguirre	.55	.27	.05
☐ 554	A's Team	1.00	.50	.10
☐ 555	Jose Tartabull	.55	.27	.05
☐ 556	Dick Selma	.55	.27	.05
☐ 557	Frank Quilici	.55	.27	.05
☐ 558	John Edwards	.55	.27	.05
☐ 559	Pirates Rookies	.65	.30	.06
	Carl Taylor			
	Luke Walker			
☐ 560	Paul Casanova	.55	.27	.05
☐ 561	Lee Elia	.75	.35	.07
☐ 562	Jim Bouton	1.00	.50	.10
☐ 563	Ed Charles	.55	.27	.05
☐ 564	Ed Stanky MG	.65	.30	.06
☐ 565	Larry Dierker	.65	.30	.06
☐ 566	Ken Harrelson	1.00	.50	.10
☐ 567	Clay Dalrymple	.55	.27	.05
☐ 568	Willie Smith	.55	.27	.05
☐ 569	NL Rookies	.55	.27	.05
	Ivan Murrell			
	Les Rohr			
☐ 570	Rick Reichardt	.55	.27	.05
☐ 571	Tony LaRussa	.90	.45	.09
☐ 572	Don Bosch	.55	.27	.05
☐ 573	Joe Coleman	.55	.27	.05
☐ 574	Reds Team	1.00	.50	.10
☐ 575	Jim Palmer	10.00	5.00	1.00
☐ 576	Dave Adlesh	.55	.27	.05
☐ 577	Fred Talbot	.55	.27	.05
☐ 578	Orlando Martinez	.55	.27	.05
☐ 579	NL Rookies	.90	.45	.09
	Larry Hisle			

	Mike Lum			
☐ 580	Bob Bailey	.55	.27	.05
☐ 581	Garry Roggenburk	.55	.27	.05
☐ 582	Jerry Grote	.55	.27	.05
☐ 583	Gates Brown	.75	.35	.07
☐ 584	Larry Shepard MG	.55	.27	.05
☐ 585	Wilbur Wood	.65	.30	.06
☐ 586	Jim Pagliaroni	.55	.27	.05
☐ 587	Roger Repoz	.55	.27	.05
☐ 588	Dick Schofield	.55	.27	.05
☐ 589	Twins Rookies	.55	.27	.05
	Ron Clark			
	Moe Ogier			
☐ 590	Tommy Harper	.65	.30	.06
☐ 591	Dick Nen	.55	.27	.05
☐ 592	John Bateman	.55	.27	.05
☐ 593	Lee Stange	.55	.27	.05
☐ 594	Phil Linz	.65	.30	.06
☐ 595	Phil Ortega	.55	.27	.05
☐ 596	Charlie Smith	.55	.27	.05
☐ 597	Bill McCool	.55	.27	.05
☐ 598	Jerry May	1.25	.25	.05

1968 Topps 3-D

The cards in this 12-card set measure 2 1/4" by 3 1/2". Topps' experiment with "3-D" cards came two years before Kellogg's inaugural set. Only 12 unnumbered cards are known to exist and they are rare. This was a "test set" sold in a plain white wrapper with a sticker attached as a design, a device used by Topps for limited marketing. The cards employ a sharp foreground picture set against an indistinct background, covered by a layer of plastic, to produce the "3-D" effect. The checklist below is ordered alphabetically.

		NRMT	VG-E	GOOD
COMPLETE SET		5500.00	2400.00	500.00
COMMON PLAYER (1-12)		350.00	175.00	35.00
☐ 1	Bob Clemente	1350.00	600.00	100.00
☐ 2	Willie Davis	400.00	200.00	40.00
☐ 3	Ron Fairly	350.00	175.00	35.00
☐ 4	Curt Flood	400.00	200.00	40.00
☐ 5	Jim Lonborg	400.00	200.00	40.00
☐ 6	Jim Maloney	400.00	200.00	40.00
☐ 7	Tony Perez	600.00	300.00	60.00
☐ 8	Boog Powell	450.00	225.00	45.00
☐ 9	Bill Robinson	350.00	175.00	35.00
☐ 10	Rusty Staub	450.00	225.00	45.00
☐ 11	Mel Stottlemyre	400.00	200.00	40.00
☐ 12	Ron Swoboda	350.00	175.00	35.00

1968 Topps Game

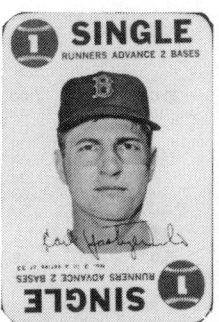 

 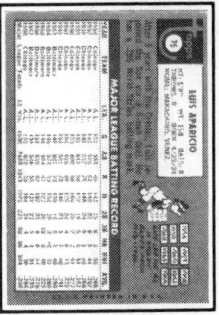

The cards in this 33-card set measure 2 1/4" by 3 1/4". This "Game" card set of players, issued as inserts with the regular 1968 Topps baseball series, was patterned directly after the Red Back and Blue Back sets of 1951. Each card has a color player photo set upon a pure white background, with a facsimile autograph underneath the picture. The cards have blue backs, and were also sold in boxed sets on a limited basis.

	NRMT	VG-E	GOOD
COMPLETE SET	45.00	22.50	4.50
COMMON PLAYER (1-33)	.30	.15	.03

		NRMT	VG-E	GOOD
☐ 1	Matty Alou	.30	.15	.03
☐ 2	Mickey Mantle	10.00	5.00	1.00
☐ 3	Carl Yastrzemski	5.00	2.50	.50
☐ 4	Hank Aaron	4.00	2.00	.40
☐ 5	Harmon Killebrew	1.50	.75	.15
☐ 6	Roberto Clemente	4.00	2.00	.40
☐ 7	Frank Robinson	2.00	1.00	.20
☐ 8	Willie Mays	4.00	2.00	.40
☐ 9	Brooks Robinson	2.00	1.00	.20
☐ 10	Tommy Davis	.35	.17	.03
☐ 11	Bill Freehan	.40	.20	.04
☐ 12	Claude Osteen	.30	.15	.03
☐ 13	Gary Peters	.30	.15	.03
☐ 14	Jim Lonborg	.30	.15	.03
☐ 15	Steve Hargan	.30	.15	.03
☐ 16	Dean Chance	.30	.15	.03
☐ 17	Mike McCormick	.30	.15	.03
☐ 18	Tim McCarver	.40	.20	.04
☐ 19	Ron Santo	.40	.20	.04
☐ 20	Tony Gonzalez	.30	.15	.03
☐ 21	Frank Howard	.40	.20	.04
☐ 22	George Scott	.30	.15	.03
☐ 23	Rich Allen	.40	.20	.04
☐ 24	Jim Wynn	.30	.15	.03
☐ 25	Gene Alley	.30	.15	.03
☐ 26	Rick Monday	.30	.15	.03
☐ 27	Al Kaline	2.50	1.25	.25
☐ 28	Rusty Staub	.50	.25	.05
☐ 29	Rod Carew	3.50	1.75	.35
☐ 30	Pete Rose	9.00	4.50	.90
☐ 31	Joe Torre	.50	.25	.05
☐ 32	Orlando Cepeda	.50	.25	.05
☐ 33	Jim Fregosi	.35	.17	.03

1969 Topps

The cards in this 664-card set measure 2 1/2" by 3 1/2". The 1969 Topps set includes Sporting News All-Star Selections as card numbers 416 to 435. Other popular subsets within this set include League Leaders (1-12) and World Series cards (162-169). The fifth series contains several variations; the more difficult variety consists of cards with the player's first name, last name, and/or position in white letters instead of lettering in some other color. These are designated in the checklist below by WL (white letters). Each checklist card features a different popular player's picture inside a circle on the front of the checklist card. Two different poses of Clay Dalrymple and Donn Clendenon exist as indicated in the checklist.

		NRMT	VG-E	GOOD
COMPLETE SET		1200.00	400.00	80.00
COMMON PLAYER (1-218)		.35	.17	.03
COMMON PLAYER (219-327)		.60	.30	.06
COMMON PLAYER (328-512)		.35	.17	.03
COMMON PLAYER (513-664)		.40	.20	.04

			NRMT	VG-E	GOOD
☐ 1	AL Batting Leaders	Carl Yastrzemski / Danny Cater / Tony Oliva	4.00	1.00	.20
☐ 2	NL Batting Leaders	Pete Rose / Matty Alou / Felipe Alou	2.50	1.25	.25
☐ 3	AL RBI Leaders	Ken Harrelson / Frank Howard / Jim Northrup	1.00	.50	.10
☐ 4	NL RBI Leaders	Willie McCovey / Ron Santo / Billy Williams	1.50	.75	.15
☐ 5	AL Home Run Leaders	Frank Howard / Willie Horton / Ken Harrelson	1.00	.50	.10
☐ 6	NL Home Run Leaders	Willie McCovey / Richie Allen / Ernie Banks	1.50	.75	.15
☐ 7	AL ERA Leaders	Luis Tiant / Sam McDowell / Dave McNally	1.00	.50	.10
☐ 8	NL ERA Leaders	Bob Gibson / Bobby Bolin / Bob Veale	1.00	.50	.10
☐ 9	AL Pitching Leaders	Denny McLain / Dave McNally / Luis Tiant / Mel Stottlemyre	1.00	.50	.10
☐ 10	NL Pitching Leaders	Juan Marichal / Bob Gibson / Fergie Jenkins	2.00	1.00	.20
☐ 11	AL Strikeout Leaders	Sam McDowell / Denny McLain / Luis Tiant	1.00	.50	.10
☐ 12	NL Strikeout Leaders	Bob Gibson / Fergie Jenkins / Bill Singer	1.00	.50	.10
☐ 13	Mickey Stanley		.45	.22	.04
☐ 14	Al McBean		.35	.17	.03
☐ 15	Boog Powell		1.00	.50	.10
☐ 16	Giants Rookies	Cesar Gutierrez / Rich Robertson	.35	.17	.03
☐ 17	Mike Marshall		.60	.30	.06
☐ 18	Dick Schofield		.35	.17	.03
☐ 19	Ken Suarez		.35	.17	.03
☐ 20	Ernie Banks		5.50	2.75	.55

☐ 21	Jose Santiago	.35	.17	.03
☐ 22	Jesus Alou	.35	.17	.03
☐ 23	Lew Krausse	.35	.17	.03
☐ 24	Walt Alston MG	1.25	.60	.12
☐ 25	Roy White	.60	.30	.06
☐ 26	Clay Carroll	.35	.17	.03
☐ 27	Bernie Allen	.35	.17	.03
☐ 28	Mike Ryan	.35	.17	.03
☐ 29	Dave Morehead	.35	.17	.03
☐ 30	Bob Allison	.45	.22	.04
☐ 31	Mets Rookies	1.25	.60	.12
	Gary Gentry			
	Amos Otis			
☐ 32	Sammy Ellis	.35	.17	.03
☐ 33	Wayne Causey	.35	.17	.03
☐ 34	Gary Peters	.45	.22	.04
☐ 35	Joe Morgan	3.50	1.75	.35
☐ 36	Luke Walker	.35	.17	.03
☐ 37	Curt Motton	.35	.17	.03
☐ 38	Zoilo Versalles	.35	.17	.03
☐ 39	Dick Hughes	.35	.17	.03
☐ 40	Mayo Smith MG	.35	.17	.03
☐ 41	Bob Barton	.35	.17	.03
☐ 42	Tommy Harper	.45	.22	.04
☐ 43	Joe Niekro	.75	.35	.07
☐ 44	Danny Cater	.35	.17	.03
☐ 45	Maury Wills	1.50	.75	.15
☐ 46	Fritz Peterson	.35	.17	.03
☐ 47A	Paul Popovich	.35	.17	.03
	(no helmet emblem)			
☐ 47B	Paul Popovich	11.00	5.50	1.10
	(C emblem on helmet)			
☐ 48	Brant Alyea	.35	.17	.03
☐ 49A	Royals Rookies	.35	.17	.03
	Steve Jones			
	E. Rodriguez "g"			
☐ 49B	Royals Rookies	11.00	5.50	1.10
	Steve Jones			
	E. Rodriquez "q"			
☐ 50	Bob Clemente	15.00	7.50	1.50
☐ 51	Woody Fryman	.35	.17	.03
☐ 52	Mike Andrews	.35	.17	.03
☐ 53	Sonny Jackson	.35	.17	.03
☐ 54	Cisco Carlos	.35	.17	.03
☐ 55	Jerry Grote	.35	.17	.03
☐ 56	Rich Reese	.35	.17	.03
☐ 57	Checklist 1	2.00	.35	.06
	Denny McLain			
☐ 58	Fred Gladding	.35	.17	.03
☐ 59	Jay Johnstone	.45	.22	.04
☐ 60	Nelson Briles	.45	.22	.04
☐ 61	Jimmie Hall	.35	.17	.03
☐ 62	Chico Salmon	.35	.17	.03
☐ 63	Jim Hickman	.35	.17	.03
☐ 64	Bill Monbouquette	.35	.17	.03
☐ 65	Willie Davis	.60	.30	.06
☐ 66	Orioles Rookies	.45	.22	.04
	Mike Adamson			
	Merv Rettenmund			
☐ 67	Bill Stoneman	.35	.17	.03
☐ 68	Dave Duncan	.35	.17	.03
☐ 69	Steve Hamilton	.35	.17	.03
☐ 70	Tommy Helms	.45	.22	.04
☐ 71	Steve Whitaker	.35	.17	.03
☐ 72	Ron Taylor	.35	.17	.03
☐ 73	Johnny Briggs	.35	.17	.03
☐ 74	Preston Gomez MG	.35	.17	.03
☐ 75	Luis Aparicio	3.50	1.75	.35
☐ 76	Norm Miller	.35	.17	.03
☐ 77A	Ron Perranoski	.45	.22	.04
	(no emblem on cap)			
☐ 77B	Ron Perranoski	11.00	5.50	1.10
	(LA on cap)			
☐ 78	Tom Satriano	.35	.17	.03
☐ 79	Milt Pappas	.45	.22	.04
☐ 80	Norm Cash	.90	.45	.09
☐ 81	Mel Queen	.35	.17	.03
☐ 82	Pirates Rookies	8.00	4.00	.80
	Rich Hebner			
	Al Oliver			
☐ 83	Mike Ferraro	.45	.22	.04
☐ 84	Bob Humphreys	.35	.17	.03
☐ 85	Lou Brock	6.00	3.00	.60
☐ 86	Pete Richert	.35	.17	.03
☐ 87	Horace Clarke	.35	.17	.03
☐ 88	Rich Nye	.35	.17	.03
☐ 89	Russ Gibson	.35	.17	.03
☐ 90	Jerry Koosman	1.50	.75	.15
☐ 91	Al Dark MG	.45	.22	.04
☐ 92	Jack Billingham	.35	.17	.03
☐ 93	Joe Foy	.35	.17	.03
☐ 94	Hank Aguirre	.35	.17	.03
☐ 95	Johnny Bench	45.00	22.50	4.50
☐ 96	Denver Lemaster	.35	.17	.03
☐ 97	Buddy Bradford	.35	.17	.03

☐ 98	Dave Giusti	.35	.17	.03
☐ 99A	Twins Rookies	10.00	5.00	1.00
	Danny Morris			
	Graig Nettles			
	(no loop)			
☐ 99B	Twins Rookies	20.00	10.00	2.00
	(errant loop in			
	upper left corner			
	of obverse)			
☐ 100	Hank Aaron	20.00	10.00	2.00
☐ 101	Daryl Patterson	.35	.17	.03
☐ 102	Jim Davenport	.45	.22	.04
☐ 103	Roger Repoz	.35	.17	.03
☐ 104	Steve Blass	.35	.17	.03
☐ 105	Rick Monday	.45	.22	.04
☐ 106	Jim Hannan	.35	.17	.03
☐ 107A	Checklist 2	2.00	.35	.05
	(161 Jim Purdin)			
	(Bob Gibson)			
☐ 107B	Checklist 2	5.00	.70	.15
	(161 John Purdin)			
	(Bob Gibson)			
☐ 108	Tony Taylor	.35	.17	.03
☐ 109	Jim Lonborg	.45	.22	.04
☐ 110	Mike Shannon	.45	.22	.04
☐ 111	Johnny Morris	.35	.17	.03
☐ 112	J.C. Martin	.35	.17	.03
☐ 113	Dave May	.35	.17	.03
☐ 114	Yankees Rookies	.35	.17	.03
	Alan Closter			
	John Cumberland			
☐ 115	Bill Hands	.35	.17	.03
☐ 116	Chuck Harrison	.35	.17	.03
☐ 117	Jim Fairey	.35	.17	.03
☐ 118	Stan Williams	.35	.17	.03
☐ 119	Doug Rader	.45	.22	.04
☐ 120	Pete Rose	30.00	15.00	3.00
☐ 121	Joe Grzenda	.35	.17	.03
☐ 122	Ron Fairly	.45	.22	.04
☐ 123	Wilbur Wood	.45	.22	.04
☐ 124	Hank Bauer MG	.45	.22	.04
☐ 125	Ray Sadecki	.35	.17	.03
☐ 126	Dick Tracewski	.35	.17	.03
☐ 127	Kevin Collins	.35	.17	.03
☐ 128	Tommie Aaron	.45	.22	.04
☐ 129	Bill McCool	.35	.17	.03
☐ 130	Carl Yastrzemski	20.00	10.00	2.00
☐ 131	Chris Cannizzaro	.35	.17	.03
☐ 132	Dave Baldwin	.35	.17	.03
☐ 133	Johnny Callison	.45	.22	.04
☐ 134	Jim Weaver	.35	.17	.03
☐ 135	Tommy Davis	.75	.35	.07
☐ 136	Cards Rookies	.45	.22	.04
	Steve Huntz			
	Mike Torrez			
☐ 137	Wally Bunker	.35	.17	.03
☐ 138	John Bateman	.35	.17	.03
☐ 139	Andy Kosco	.35	.17	.03
☐ 140	Jim Lefebvre	.35	.17	.03
☐ 141	Bill Dillman	.35	.17	.03
☐ 142	Woody Woodward	.45	.22	.04
☐ 143	Joe Nossek	.35	.17	.03
☐ 144	Bob Hendley	.35	.17	.03
☐ 145	Max Alvis	.35	.17	.03
☐ 146	Jim Perry	.60	.30	.06
☐ 147	Leo Durocher MG	1.25	.60	.12
☐ 148	Lee Stange	.35	.17	.03
☐ 149	Ollie Brown	.35	.17	.03
☐ 150	Denny McLain	1.50	.75	.15
☐ 151A	Clay Dalrymple	.35	.17	.03
	(Portrait, Orioles)			
☐ 151B	Clay Dalrymple	11.00	5.50	1.10
	(Catching, Phillies)			
☐ 152	Tommie Sisk	.35	.17	.03
☐ 153	Ed Brinkman	.35	.17	.03
☐ 154	Jim Britton	.35	.17	.03
☐ 155	Pete Ward	.35	.17	.03
☐ 156	Houston Rookies	.35	.17	.03
	Hal Gilson			
	Leon McFadden			
☐ 157	Bob Rodgers	.45	.22	.04
☐ 158	Joe Gibbon	.35	.17	.03
☐ 159	Jerry Adair	.35	.17	.03
☐ 160	Vada Pinson	.90	.45	.09
☐ 161	John Purdin	.35	.17	.03
☐ 162	World Series Game 1	2.50	1.25	.25
	Gibson fans 17			
☐ 163	World Series Game 2	1.50	.75	.15
	Tiger homers			
	deck the Cards			
☐ 164	World Series Game 3	1.75	.85	.17
	McCarver's homer			
☐ 165	World Series Game 4	2.50	1.25	.25
	Brock lead-off homer			
☐ 166	World Series Game 5	3.50	1.75	.35

	Kaline's key hit			
☐ 167	World Series Game 6	1.50	.75	.15
	Northrup grandslam			
☐ 168	World Series Game 7	2.50	1.25	.25
	Lolich outduels			
	Bob Gibson			
☐ 169	World Series Summary ..	1.50	.75	.15
	Tigers celebrate			
☐ 170	Frank Howard	.85	.40	.08
☐ 171	Glenn Beckert	.45	.22	.04
☐ 172	Jerry Stephenson	.35	.17	.03
☐ 173	White Sox Rookies	.35	.17	.03
	Bob Christian			
	Gerry Nyman			
☐ 174	Grant Jackson	.35	.17	.03
☐ 175	Jim Bunning	1.50	.75	.15
☐ 176	Joe Azcue	.35	.17	.03
☐ 177	Ron Reed	.35	.17	.03
☐ 178	Ray Oyler	.35	.17	.03
☐ 179	Don Pavletich	.35	.17	.03
☐ 180	Willie Horton	.45	.22	.04
☐ 181	Mel Nelson	.35	.17	.03
☐ 182	Bill Rigney MG	.35	.17	.03
☐ 183	Don Shaw	.35	.17	.03
☐ 184	Roberto Pena	.35	.17	.03
☐ 185	Tom Phoebus	.35	.17	.03
☐ 186	John Edwards	.35	.17	.03
☐ 187	Leon Wagner	.35	.17	.03
☐ 188	Rick Wise	.35	.17	.03
☐ 189	Red Sox Rookies	.35	.17	.03
	Joe Lahoud			
	John Thibodeau			
☐ 190	Willie Mays	20.00	10.00	2.00
☐ 191	Lindy McDaniel	.45	.22	.04
☐ 192	Jose Pagan	.35	.17	.03
☐ 193	Don Cardwell	.35	.17	.03
☐ 194	Ted Uhlaender	.35	.17	.03
☐ 195	John Odom	.35	.17	.03
☐ 196	Lum Harris MG	.35	.17	.03
☐ 197	Dick Selma	.35	.17	.03
☐ 198	Willie Smith	.35	.17	.03
☐ 199	Jim French	.35	.17	.03
☐ 200	Bob Gibson	5.00	2.50	.50
☐ 201	Russ Snyder	.35	.17	.03
☐ 202	Don Wilson	.35	.17	.03
☐ 203	Dave Johnson	.75	.35	.07
☐ 204	Jack Hiatt	.35	.17	.03
☐ 205	Rick Reichardt	.35	.17	.03
☐ 206	Phillies Rookies	.45	.22	.04
	Larry Hisle			
	Barry Lersch			
☐ 207	Roy Face	.60	.30	.06
☐ 208A	Donn Clendenon	.45	.22	.04
	(Houston)			
☐ 208B	Donn Clendenon	11.00	5.50	1.10
	(Expos)			
☐ 209	Larry Haney	.35	.17	.03
	(reverse negative)			
☐ 210	Felix Millan	.35	.17	.03
☐ 211	Galen Cisco	.35	.17	.03
☐ 212	Tom Tresh	.60	.30	.06
☐ 213	Gerry Arrigo	.35	.17	.03
☐ 214	Checklist 3	2.00	.35	.05
	With 69T deckle CL			
	on back (no player)			
☐ 215	Rico Petrocelli	.45	.22	.04
☐ 216	Don Sutton	3.50	1.75	.35
☐ 217	John Donaldson	.35	.17	.03
☐ 218	John Roseboro	.45	.22	.04
☐ 219	Freddie Patek	.90	.45	.09
☐ 220	Sam McDowell	.90	.45	.09
☐ 221	Art Shamsky	.60	.30	.06
☐ 222	Duane Josephson	.60	.30	.06
☐ 223	Tom Dukes	.60	.30	.06
☐ 224	Angels Rookies	.60	.30	.06
	Bill Harrelson			
	Steve Kealey			
☐ 225	Don Kessinger	.90	.45	.09
☐ 226	Bruce Howard	.60	.30	.06
☐ 227	Frank Johnson	.60	.30	.06
☐ 228	Dave Leonhard	.60	.30	.06
☐ 229	Don Lock	.60	.30	.06
☐ 230	Rusty Staub	1.00	.50	.10
☐ 231	Pat Dobson	.75	.35	.07
☐ 232	Dave Ricketts	.60	.30	.06
☐ 233	Steve Barber	.60	.30	.06
☐ 234	Dave Bristol MG	.60	.30	.06
☐ 235	Jim Hunter	4.50	2.25	.45
☐ 236	Manny Mota	.90	.45	.09
☐ 237	Bobby Cox	.75	.35	.07
☐ 238	Ken Johnson	.60	.30	.06
☐ 239	Bob Taylor	.60	.30	.06
☐ 240	Ken Harrelson	.90	.45	.09
☐ 241	Jim Brewer	.60	.30	.06
☐ 242	Frank Kostro	.60	.30	.06

☐ 243	Ron Kline	.60	.30	.06
☐ 244	Indians Rookies	.75	.35	.07
	Ray Fosse			
	George Woodson			
☐ 245	Ed Charles	.60	.30	.06
☐ 246	Joe Coleman	.60	.30	.06
☐ 247	Gene Oliver	.60	.30	.06
☐ 248	Bob Priddy	.60	.30	.06
☐ 249	Ed Spiezio	.60	.30	.06
☐ 250	Frank Robinson	8.50	4.25	.85
☐ 251	Ron Herbel	.60	.30	.06
☐ 252	Chuck Cottier	.60	.30	.06
☐ 253	Jerry Johnson	.60	.30	.06
☐ 254	Joe Schultz	.60	.30	.06
☐ 255	Steve Carlton	25.00	12.50	2.50
☐ 256	Gates Brown	.75	.35	.07
☐ 257	Jim Ray	.60	.30	.06
☐ 258	Jackie Hernandez	.60	.30	.06
☐ 259	Bill Short	.60	.30	.06
☐ 260	Reggie Jackson	175.00	85.00	18.00
☐ 261	Bob Johnson	.60	.30	.06
☐ 262	Mike Kekich	.60	.30	.06
☐ 263	Jerry May	.60	.30	.06
☐ 264	Bill Landis	.60	.30	.06
☐ 265	Chico Cardenas	.60	.30	.06
☐ 266	Dodger Rookies	.60	.30	.06
	Tom Hutton			
	Alan Foster			
☐ 267	Vicente Romo	.60	.30	.06
☐ 268	Al Spangler	.60	.30	.06
☐ 269	Al Weis	.60	.30	.06
☐ 270	Mickey Lolich	1.25	.60	.12
☐ 271	Larry Stahl	.60	.30	.06
☐ 272	Ed Stroud	.60	.30	.06
☐ 273	Ron Willis	.60	.30	.06
☐ 274	Clyde King MG	.60	.30	.06
☐ 275	Vic Davalillo	.75	.35	.07
☐ 276	Gary Wagner	.60	.30	.06
☐ 277	Elrod Hendricks	.60	.30	.06
☐ 278	Gary Geiger	.75	.35	.07
	(Batting wrong)			
☐ 279	Roger Nelson	.60	.30	.06
☐ 280	Alex Johnson	.75	.35	.07
☐ 281	Ted Kubiak	.60	.30	.06
☐ 282	Pat Jarvis	.60	.30	.06
☐ 283	Sandy Alomar	.60	.30	.06
☐ 284	Expos Rookies	.60	.30	.06
	Jerry Robertson			
	Mike Wegener			
☐ 285	Don Mincher	.75	.35	.07
☐ 286	Dock Ellis	.75	.35	.07
☐ 287	Jose Tartabull	.60	.30	.06
☐ 288	Ken Holtzman	.90	.45	.09
☐ 289	Bart Shirley	.60	.30	.06
☐ 290	Jim Kaat	2.50	1.25	.25
☐ 291	Vern Fuller	.60	.30	.06
☐ 292	Al Downing	.75	.35	.07
☐ 293	Dick Dietz	.60	.30	.06
☐ 294	Jim Lemon MG	.60	.30	.06
☐ 295	Tony Perez	3.00	1.50	.30
☐ 296	Andy Messersmith	.90	.45	.09
☐ 297	Deron Johnson	.75	.35	.07
☐ 298	Dave Nicholson	.60	.30	.06
☐ 299	Mark Belanger	.90	.45	.09
☐ 300	Felipe Alou	.90	.45	.09
☐ 301	Darrell Brandon	.60	.30	.06
☐ 302	Jim Pagliaroni	.60	.30	.06
☐ 303	Cal Koonce	.60	.30	.06
☐ 304	Padres Rookies	.75	.35	.07
	Bill Davis			
	Clarence Gaston			
☐ 305	Dick McAuliffe	.75	.35	.07
☐ 306	Jim Grant	.60	.30	.06
☐ 307	Gary Kolb	.60	.30	.06
☐ 308	Wade Blasingame	.60	.30	.06
☐ 309	Walt Williams	.60	.30	.06
☐ 310	Tom Haller	.75	.35	.07
☐ 311	Sparky Lyle	1.75	.85	.17
☐ 312	Lee Elia	.90	.45	.09
☐ 313	Bill Robinson	.90	.45	.09
☐ 314	Checklist 4	2.00	.35	.05
	Don Drysdale			
☐ 315	Eddie Fisher	.60	.30	.06
☐ 316	Hal Lanier	.90	.45	.09
☐ 317	Bruce Look	.60	.30	.06
☐ 318	Jack Fisher	.60	.30	.06
☐ 319	Ken McMullen	.60	.30	.06
☐ 320	Dal Maxvill	.75	.35	.07
☐ 321	Jim McAndrew	.60	.30	.06
☐ 322	Jose Vidal	.60	.30	.06
☐ 323	Larry Miller	.60	.30	.06
☐ 324	Tiger Rookies	.60	.30	.06
	Les Cain			
	Dave Campbell			
☐ 325	Jose Cardenal	.60	.30	.06

☐ 326	Gary Sutherland	.60	.30	.06
☐ 327	Willie Crawford	.60	.30	.06
☐ 328	Joe Horlen	.35	.17	.03
☐ 329	Rick Joseph	.35	.17	.03
☐ 330	Tony Conigliaro	.90	.45	.09
☐ 331	Braves Rookies	.60	.30	.06
	Gil Garrido			
	Tom House			
☐ 332	Fred Talbot	.35	.17	.03
☐ 333	Ivan Murrell	.35	.17	.03
☐ 334	Phil Roof	.35	.17	.03
☐ 335	Bill Mazeroski	.75	.35	.07
☐ 336	Jim Roland	.35	.17	.03
☐ 337	Marty Martinez	.35	.17	.03
☐ 338	Del Unser	.35	.17	.03
☐ 339	Reds Rookies	.35	.17	.03
	Steve Mingori			
	Jose Pena			
☐ 340	Dave McNally	.60	.30	.06
☐ 341	Dave Adlesh	.35	.17	.03
☐ 342	Bubba Morton	.35	.17	.03
☐ 343	Dan Frisella	.35	.17	.03
☐ 344	Tom Matchick	.35	.17	.03
☐ 345	Frank Linzy	.35	.17	.03
☐ 346	Wayne Comer	.35	.17	.03
☐ 347	Randy Hundley	.45	.22	.04
☐ 348	Steve Hargan	.35	.17	.03
☐ 349	Dick Williams MG	.45	.22	.04
☐ 350	Richie Allen	.90	.45	.09
☐ 351	Carroll Sembera	.35	.17	.03
☐ 352	Paul Schaal	.35	.17	.03
☐ 353	Jeff Torborg	.45	.22	.04
☐ 354	Nate Oliver	.35	.17	.03
☐ 355	Phil Niekro	3.50	1.75	.35
☐ 356	Frank Quilici MG	.35	.17	.03
☐ 357	Carl Taylor	.35	.17	.03
☐ 358	Athletics Rookies	.35	.17	.03
	George Lauzerique			
	Roberto Rodriquez			
☐ 359	Dick Kelley	.35	.17	.03
☐ 360	Jim Wynn	.60	.30	.06
☐ 361	Gary Holman	.35	.17	.03
☐ 362	Jim Maloney	.45	.22	.04
☐ 363	Russ Nixon	.35	.17	.03
☐ 364	Tommie Agee	.45	.22	.04
☐ 365	Jim Fregosi	.75	.35	.07
☐ 366	Bo Belinsky	.45	.22	.04
☐ 367	Lou Johnson	.35	.17	.03
☐ 368	Vic Roznovsky	.35	.17	.03
☐ 369	Bob Skinner	.35	.17	.03
☐ 370	Juan Marichal	3.50	1.75	.35
☐ 371	Sal Bando	.75	.35	.07
☐ 372	Adolfo Phillips	.35	.17	.03
☐ 373	Fred Lasher	.35	.17	.03
☐ 374	Bob Tillman	.35	.17	.03
☐ 375	Harmon Killebrew	8.00	4.00	.80
☐ 376	Royals Rookies	.35	.17	.03
	Mike Fiore			
	Jim Rooker			
☐ 377	Gary Bell	.35	.17	.03
☐ 378	Jose Herrera	.35	.17	.03
☐ 379	Ken Boyer	.90	.45	.09
☐ 380	Stan Bahnsen	.35	.17	.03
☐ 381	Ed Kranepool	.45	.22	.04
☐ 382	Pat Corrales	.45	.22	.04
☐ 383	Casey Cox	.35	.17	.03
☐ 384	Larry Shepard MG	.35	.17	.03
☐ 385	Orlando Cepeda	1.50	.75	.15
☐ 386	Jim McGlothlin	.35	.17	.03
☐ 387	Bobby Klaus	.35	.17	.03
☐ 388	Tom McCraw	.35	.17	.03
☐ 389	Dan Coombs	.35	.17	.03
☐ 390	Bill Freehan	.75	.35	.07
☐ 391	Ray Culp	.35	.17	.03
☐ 392	Bob Burda	.35	.17	.03
☐ 393	Gene Brabender	.35	.17	.03
☐ 394	Pilots Rookies	1.75	.85	.17
	Lou Piniella			
	Marv Staehle			
☐ 395	Chris Short	.35	.17	.03
☐ 396	Jim Campanis	.35	.17	.03
☐ 397	Chuck Dobson	.35	.17	.03
☐ 398	Tito Francona	.35	.17	.03
☐ 399	Bob Bailey	.35	.17	.03
☐ 400	Don Drysdale	4.00	2.00	.40
☐ 401	Jake Gibbs	.35	.17	.03
☐ 402	Ken Boswell	.35	.17	.03
☐ 403	Bob Miller	.35	.17	.03
☐ 404	Cubs Rookies	.35	.17	.03
	Vic LaRose			
	Gary Ross			
☐ 405	Lee May	.60	.30	.06
☐ 406	Phil Ortega	.35	.17	.03
☐ 407	Tom Egan	.35	.17	.03
☐ 408	Nate Colbert	.35	.17	.03
☐ 409	Bob Moose	.35	.17	.03
☐ 410	Al Kaline	6.50	3.25	.65
☐ 411	Larry Dierker	.45	.22	.04
☐ 412	Checklist 5	4.00	.60	.08
	Mickey Mantle			
☐ 413	Roland Sheldon	.35	.17	.03
☐ 414	Duke Sims	.35	.17	.03
☐ 415	Ray Washburn	.35	.17	.03
☐ 416	Willie McCovey AS	3.00	1.50	.30
☐ 417	Ken Harrelson AS	.45	.22	.04
☐ 418	Tommy Helms AS	.45	.22	.04
☐ 419	Rod Carew AS	4.00	2.00	.40
☐ 420	Ron Santo AS	.45	.22	.04
☐ 421	Brooks Robinson AS	3.00	1.50	.30
☐ 422	Don Kessinger AS	.45	.22	.04
☐ 423	Bert Campaneris AS	.45	.22	.04
☐ 424	Pete Rose AS	7.50	3.75	.75
☐ 425	Carl Yastrzemski AS	5.00	2.50	.50
☐ 426	Curt Flood AS	.45	.22	.04
☐ 427	Tony Oliva AS	.75	.35	.07
☐ 428	Lou Brock AS	3.00	1.50	.30
☐ 429	Willie Horton AS	.45	.22	.04
☐ 430	Johnny Bench AS	6.00	3.00	.60
☐ 431	Bill Freehan AS	.45	.22	.04
☐ 432	Bob Gibson AS	3.00	1.50	.30
☐ 433	Denny McLain AS	.60	.30	.06
☐ 434	Jerry Koosman AS	.60	.30	.06
☐ 435	Sam McDowell AS	.45	.22	.04
☐ 436	Gene Alley	.45	.22	.04
☐ 437	Luis Alcaraz	.35	.17	.03
☐ 438	Gary Waslewski	.35	.17	.03
☐ 439	White Sox Rookies	.35	.17	.03
	Ed Herrmann			
	Dan Lazar			
☐ 440A	Willie McCovey	10.00	5.00	1.00
☐ 440B	Willie McCovey WL	60.00	30.00	6.00
	(McCovey white)			
☐ 441A	Dennis Higgins	.35	.17	.03
☐ 441B	Dennis Higgins WL	9.00	4.50	.90
	(Higgins white)			
☐ 442	Ty Cline	.35	.17	.03
☐ 443	Don Wert	.35	.17	.03
☐ 444A	Joe Moeller	.35	.17	.03
☐ 444B	Joe Moeller WL	9.00	4.50	.90
	(Moeller white)			
☐ 445	Bobby Knoop	.35	.17	.03
☐ 446	Claude Raymond	.35	.17	.03
☐ 447A	Ralph Houk MG	.60	.30	.06
☐ 447B	Ralph Houk WL MG	10.00	5.00	1.00
	(Houk white)			
☐ 448	Bob Tolan	.45	.22	.04
☐ 449	Paul Lindblad	.35	.17	.03
☐ 450	Billy Williams	3.50	1.75	.35
☐ 451A	Rich Rollins	.35	.17	.03
☐ 451B	Rich Rollins WL	9.00	4.50	.90
	(Rich and 3B white)			
☐ 452A	Al Ferrara	.35	.17	.03
☐ 452B	Al Ferrara WL	9.00	4.50	.90
	(Al and OF white)			
☐ 453	Mike Cuellar	.85	.40	.08
☐ 454A	Phillies Rookies	.45	.22	.04
	Larry Colton			
	Don Money			
☐ 454B	Phillies Rookies WL	9.00	4.50	.90
	Larry Colton			
	Don Money			
	(names in white)			
☐ 455	Sonny Siebert	.45	.22	.04
☐ 456	Bud Harrelson	.45	.22	.04
☐ 457	Dalton Jones	.35	.17	.03
☐ 458	Curt Blefary	.35	.17	.03
☐ 459	Dave Boswell	.35	.17	.03
☐ 460	Joe Torre	.85	.40	.08
☐ 461A	Mike Epstein	.35	.17	.03
☐ 461B	Mike Epstein WL	9.00	4.50	.90
	(Epstein white)			
☐ 462	Red Schoendienst MG	.60	.30	.06
☐ 463	Dennis Ribant	.35	.17	.03
☐ 464A	Dave Marshall	.35	.17	.03
☐ 464B	Dave Marshall WL	9.00	4.50	.90
	(Marshall white)			
☐ 465	Tommy John	1.75	.85	.17
☐ 466	John Boccabella	.35	.17	.03
☐ 467	Tom Reynolds	.35	.17	.03
☐ 468A	Pirates Rookies	.35	.17	.03
	Bruce Dal Canton			
	Bob Robertson			
☐ 468B	Pirates Rookies WL	9.00	4.50	.90
	Bruce Dal Canton			
	Bob Robertson			
	(names in white)			
☐ 469	Chico Ruiz	.35	.17	.03
☐ 470A	Mel Stottlemyre	.75	.35	.07
☐ 470B	Mel Stottlemyre WL	10.00	5.00	1.00
	(Stottlemyre white)			

☐ 471A	Ted Savage	.35	.17	.03
☐ 471B	Ted Savage WL (Savage white)	9.00	4.50	.90
☐ 472	Jim Price	.35	.17	.03
☐ 473A	Jose Arcia	.35	.17	.03
☐ 473B	Jose Arcia WL (Jose and 2B white)	9.00	4.50	.90
☐ 474	Tom Murphy	.35	.17	.03
☐ 475	Tim McCarver	.75	.35	.07
☐ 476A	Boston Rookies Ken Brett Gerry Moses	.45	.22	.04
☐ 476B	Boston Rookies WL Ken Brett Gerry Moses (names in white)	9.00	4.50	.90
☐ 477	Jeff James	.35	.17	.03
☐ 478	Don Buford	.35	.17	.03
☐ 479	Richie Scheinblum	.35	.17	.03
☐ 480	Tom Seaver	35.00	17.50	3.50
☐ 481	Bill Melton	.35	.17	.03
☐ 482A	Jim Gosger	.35	.17	.03
☐ 482B	Jim Gosger WL (Jim and OF white)	9.00	4.50	.90
☐ 483	Ted Abernathy	.35	.17	.03
☐ 484	Joe Gordon MG	.35	.17	.03
☐ 485A	Gaylord Perry	4.00	2.00	.40
☐ 485B	Gaylord Perry WL (Perry white)	35.00	17.50	3.50
☐ 486A	Paul Casanova	.35	.17	.03
☐ 486B	Paul Casanova WL (Casanova white)	9.00	4.50	.90
☐ 487	Denis Menke	.35	.17	.03
☐ 488	Joe Sparma	.35	.17	.03
☐ 489	Clete Boyer	.45	.22	.04
☐ 490	Matty Alou	.45	.22	.04
☐ 491A	Twins Rookies Jerry Crider George Mitterwald	.35	.17	.03
☐ 491B	Twins Rookies WL Jerry Crider George Mitterwald (names in white)	9.00	4.50	.90
☐ 492	Tony Cloninger	.35	.17	.03
☐ 493A	Wes Parker	.45	.22	.04
☐ 493B	Wes Parker WL (Parker white)	9.00	4.50	.90
☐ 494	Ken Berry	.35	.17	.03
☐ 495	Bert Campaneris	.60	.30	.06
☐ 496	Larry Jaster	.35	.17	.03
☐ 497	Julian Javier	.35	.17	.03
☐ 498	Juan Pizarro	.35	.17	.03
☐ 499	Astro Rookies Don Bryant Steve Shea	.35	.17	.03
☐ 500A	Mickey Mantle	150.00	75.00	15.00
☐ 500B	Mickey Mantle WL (Mantle white)	400.00	200.00	40.00
☐ 501A	Tony Gonzalez	.35	.17	.03
☐ 501B	Tony Gonzalez WL (Tony and OF white)	9.00	4.50	.90
☐ 502	Minnie Rojas	.35	.17	.03
☐ 503	Larry Brown	.35	.17	.03
☐ 504	Checklist 6 Brooks Robinson	2.00	.35	.05
☐ 505A	Bobby Bolin	.35	.17	.03
☐ 505B	Bobby Bolin WL (Bolin white)	9.00	4.50	.90
☐ 506	Paul Blair	.45	.22	.04
☐ 507	Cookie Rojas	.35	.17	.03
☐ 508	Moe Drabowsky	.35	.17	.03
☐ 509	Manny Sanguillen	.60	.30	.06
☐ 510	Rod Carew	25.00	12.50	2.50
☐ 511A	Diego Segui	.35	.17	.03
☐ 511B	Diego Segui WL (Diego and P white)	9.00	4.50	.90
☐ 512	Cleon Jones	.35	.17	.03
☐ 513	Camilo Pascual	.50	.25	.05
☐ 514	Mike Lum	.40	.20	.04
☐ 515	Dick Green	.40	.20	.04
☐ 516	Earl Weaver MG	2.50	1.25	.25
☐ 517	Mike McCormick	.50	.25	.05
☐ 518	Fred Whitfield	.40	.20	.04
☐ 519	Yankees Rookies Gerry Kenney Len Boehmer	.40	.20	.04
☐ 520	Bob Veale	.50	.25	.05
☐ 521	George Thomas	.40	.20	.04
☐ 522	Joe Hoerner	.40	.20	.04
☐ 523	Bob Chance	.40	.20	.04
☐ 524	Expos Rookies Jose Laboy Floyd Wicker	.40	.20	.04
☐ 525	Earl Wilson	.40	.20	.04
☐ 526	Hector Torres	.40	.20	.04
☐ 527	Al Lopez MG	1.50	.75	.15
☐ 528	Claude Osteen	.50	.25	.05
☐ 529	Ed Kirkpatrick	.40	.20	.04
☐ 530	Cesar Tovar	.50	.25	.05
☐ 531	Dick Farrell	.40	.20	.04
☐ 532	Bird Hill Aces Tom Phoebus Jim Hardin Dave McNally Mike Cuellar	.60	.30	.06
☐ 533	Nolan Ryan	45.00	22.50	4.50
☐ 534	Jerry McNertney	.40	.20	.04
☐ 535	Phil Regan	.50	.25	.05
☐ 536	Padres Rookies Danny Breeden Dave Roberts	.40	.20	.04
☐ 537	Mike Paul	.40	.20	.04
☐ 538	Charlie Smith	.40	.20	.04
☐ 539	Ted Shows How Mike Epstein Ted Williams	3.00	1.50	.30
☐ 540	Curt Flood	.75	.35	.07
☐ 541	Joe Verbanic	.40	.20	.04
☐ 542	Bob Aspromonte	.40	.20	.04
☐ 543	Fred Newman	.40	.20	.04
☐ 544	Tigers Rookies Mike Kilkenny Ron Woods	.40	.20	.04
☐ 545	Willie Stargell	6.50	3.25	.65
☐ 546	Jim Nash	.40	.20	.04
☐ 547	Billy Martin MG	1.50	.75	.15
☐ 548	Bob Locker	.40	.20	.04
☐ 549	Ron Brand	.40	.20	.04
☐ 550	Brooks Robinson	9.00	4.50	.90
☐ 551	Wayne Granger	.40	.20	.04
☐ 552	Dodgers Rookies Ted Sizemore Bill Sudakis	.60	.30	.06
☐ 553	Ron Davis	.40	.20	.04
☐ 554	Frank Bertaina	.40	.20	.04
☐ 555	Jim Ray Hart	.50	.25	.05
☐ 556	A's Stars Sal Bando Bert Campaneris Danny Cater	.60	.30	.06
☐ 557	Frank Fernandez	.40	.20	.04
☐ 558	Tom Burgmeier	.50	.25	.05
☐ 559	Cardinals Rookies Joe Hague Jim Hicks	.40	.20	.04
☐ 560	Luis Tiant	1.00	.50	.10
☐ 561	Ron Clark	.40	.20	.04
☐ 562	Bob Watson	1.50	.75	.15
☐ 563	Martin Pattin	.40	.20	.04
☐ 564	Gil Hodges MG	4.00	2.00	.40
☐ 565	Hoyt Wilhelm	4.00	2.00	.40
☐ 566	Ron Hansen	.40	.20	.04
☐ 567	Pirates Rookies Elvio Jimenez Jim Shellenback	.40	.20	.04
☐ 568	Cecil Upshaw	.40	.20	.04
☐ 569	Billy Harris	.40	.20	.04
☐ 570	Ron Santo	.85	.40	.08
☐ 571	Cap Peterson	.40	.20	.04
☐ 572	Giants Heroes Willie McCovey Juan Marichal	5.00	2.50	.50
☐ 573	Jim Palmer	9.00	4.50	.90
☐ 574	George Scott	.50	.25	.05
☐ 575	Bill Singer	.50	.25	.05
☐ 576	Phillies Rookies Ron Stone Bill Wilson	.40	.20	.04
☐ 577	Mike Hegan	.50	.25	.05
☐ 578	Don Bosch	.40	.20	.04
☐ 579	Dave Nelson	.40	.20	.04
☐ 580	Jim Northrup	.50	.25	.05
☐ 581	Gary Nolan	.40	.20	.04
☐ 582A	Checklist 7 (white circle on back) (Tony Oliva)	2.00	.30	.05
☐ 582B	Checklist 7 (red circle on back) (Tony Oliva)	4.00	.60	.10
☐ 583	Clyde Wright	.40	.20	.04
☐ 584	Don Mason	.40	.20	.04
☐ 585	Ron Swoboda	.50	.25	.05
☐ 586	Tim Cullen	.40	.20	.04
☐ 587	Joe Rudi	1.00	.50	.10
☐ 588	Bill White	.75	.35	.07
☐ 589	Joe Pepitone	.75	.35	.07
☐ 590	Rico Carty	.60	.30	.06
☐ 591	Mike Hedlund	.40	.20	.04
☐ 592	Padres Rookies Rafael Robles	.40	.20	.04

	Al Santorini			
□ 593	Don Nottebart	.40	.20	.04
□ 594	Dooley Womack	.40	.20	.04
□ 595	Lee Maye	.40	.20	.04
□ 596	Chuck Hartenstein	.40	.20	.04
□ 597	A.L. Rookies	15.00	7.50	1.50
	Bob Floyd			
	Larry Burchart			
	Rollie Fingers			
□ 598	Ruben Amaro	.40	.20	.04
□ 599	John Boozer	.40	.20	.04
□ 600	Tony Oliva	1.50	.75	.15
□ 601	Tug McGraw	1.25	.60	.12
□ 602	Cubs Rookies	.40	.20	.04
	Alec Distaso			
	Don Young			
	Jim Qualls			
□ 603	Joe Keough	.40	.20	.04
□ 604	Bobby Etheridge	.40	.20	.04
□ 605	Dick Ellsworth	.50	.25	.05
□ 606	Gene Mauch MG	.50	.25	.05
□ 607	Dick Bosman	.40	.20	.04
□ 608	Dick Simpson	.40	.20	.04
□ 609	Phil Gagliano	.40	.20	.04
□ 610	Jim Hardin	.40	.20	.04
□ 611	Braves Rookies	.50	.25	.05
	Bob Didier			
	Walt Hriniak			
	Gary Neibauer			
□ 612	Jack Aker	.50	.25	.05
□ 613	Jim Beauchamp	.40	.20	.04
□ 614	Houston Rookies	.40	.20	.04
	Tom Griffin			
	Skip Guinn			
□ 615	Len Gabrielson	.40	.20	.04
□ 616	Don McMahon	.40	.20	.04
□ 617	Jesse Gonder	.40	.20	.04
□ 618	Ramon Webster	.40	.20	.04
□ 619	Royals Rookies	.50	.25	.05
	Bill Butler			
	Pat Kelly			
	Juan Rios			
□ 620	Dean Chance	.50	.25	.05
□ 621	Bill Voss	.40	.20	.04
□ 622	Dan Osinski	.40	.20	.04
□ 623	Hank Allen	.40	.20	.04
□ 624	NL Rookies	.50	.25	.05
	Darrel Chaney			
	Duffy Dyer			
	Terry Harmon			
□ 625	Mack Jones	.50	.25	.05
	(Batting wrong)			
□ 626	Gene Michael	.60	.30	.06
□ 627	George Stone	.40	.20	.04
□ 628	Red Sox Rookies	.60	.30	.06
	Bill Conigliaro			
	Syd O'Brien			
	Fred Wenz			
□ 629	Jack Hamilton	.40	.20	.04
□ 630	Bobby Bonds	5.00	2.50	.50
□ 631	John Kennedy	.40	.20	.04
□ 632	Jon Warden	.40	.20	.04
□ 633	Harry Walker MG	.40	.20	.04
□ 634	Andy Etchebarren	.40	.20	.04
□ 635	George Culver	.40	.20	.04
□ 636	Woodie Held	.40	.20	.04
□ 637	Padres Rookies	.40	.20	.04
	Jerry DaVanon			
	Frank Reberger			
	Clay Kirby			
□ 638	Ed Sprague	.40	.20	.04
□ 639	Barry Moore	.40	.20	.04
□ 640	Fergie Jenkins	2.00	1.00	.20
□ 641	NL Rookies	.40	.20	.04
	Bobby Darwin			
	John Miller			
	Tommy Dean			
□ 642	John Hiller	.50	.25	.05
□ 643	Billy Cowan	.40	.20	.04
□ 644	Chuck Hinton	.40	.20	.04
□ 645	George Brunet	.40	.20	.04
□ 646	Expos Rookies	.40	.20	.04
	Dan McGinn			
	Carl Morton			
□ 647	Dave Wickersham	.40	.20	.04
□ 648	Bobby Wine	.40	.20	.04
□ 649	Al Jackson	.40	.20	.04
□ 650	Ted Williams MG	4.50	2.25	.45
□ 651	Gus Gil	.40	.20	.04
□ 652	Eddie Watt	.40	.20	.04
□ 653	Aurelio Rodriguez	1.50	.75	.15
	(photo actually			
	Angels' batboy)			
□ 654	White Sox Rookies	.50	.25	.05
	Carlos May			

	Don Secrist			
	Rich Morales			
□ 655	Mike Hershberger	.40	.20	.04
□ 656	Dan Schneider	.40	.20	.04
□ 657	Bobby Murcer	.90	.45	.09
□ 658	AL Rookies	.40	.20	.04
	Tom Hall			
	Bill Burbach			
	Jim Miles			
□ 659	Johnny Podres	.75	.35	.07
□ 660	Reggie Smith	.90	.45	.09
□ 661	Jim Merritt	.40	.20	.04
□ 662	Royals Rookies	.50	.25	.05
	Dick Drago			
	George Spriggs			
	Bob Oliver			
□ 663	Dick Radatz	.60	.30	.06
□ 664	Ron Hunt	1.00	.20	.04

1969 Topps Deckle

RICHIE ALLEN
No. 26 of 33 photos

The cards in this 33-card set measure 2 1/4" by 3 1/4". This unusual black and white insert set derives its name from the serrated border, or edge, of the cards. The cards were included as inserts in the regularly issued Topps baseball series of 1969. Card number 11 is found with either Hoyt Wilhelm or Jim Wynn, and number 22 with either Rusty Staub or Joe Foy. The set price below does include all variations.

		NRMT	VG-E	GOOD
COMPLETE SET (35)		50.00	25.00	5.00
COMMON PLAYER		.30	.15	.03
□ 1	Brooks Robinson	2.50	1.25	.25
□ 2	Boog Powell	.50	.25	.05
□ 3	Ken Harrelson	.40	.20	.04
□ 4	Carl Yastrzemski	4.00	2.00	.40
□ 5	Jim Fregosi	.30	.15	.03
□ 6	Luis Aparicio	1.00	.50	.10
□ 7	Luis Tiant	.40	.20	.04
□ 8	Denny McLain	.40	.20	.04
□ 9	Willie Horton	.30	.15	.03
□ 10	Bill Freehan	.30	.15	.03
□ 11A	Hoyt Wilhelm	5.00	2.50	.50
□ 11B	Jim Wynn	6.00	3.00	.60
□ 12	Rod Carew	3.50	1.75	.35
□ 13	Mel Stottlemyre	.30	.15	.03
□ 14	Rick Monday	.30	.15	.03
□ 15	Tommy Davis	.30	.15	.03
□ 16	Frank Howard	.40	.20	.04
□ 17	Felipe Alou	.30	.15	.03
□ 18	Don Kessinger	.30	.15	.03
□ 19	Ron Santo	.40	.20	.04
□ 20	Tommy Helms	.30	.15	.03
□ 21	Pete Rose	8.00	4.00	.80
□ 22A	Rusty Staub	3.00	1.50	.30
□ 22B	Joe Foy	6.00	3.00	.60
□ 23	Tom Haller	.30	.15	.03
□ 24	Maury Wills	.60	.30	.06
□ 25	Jerry Koosman	.40	.20	.04
□ 26	Richie Allen	.40	.20	.04
□ 27	Bob Clemente	3.50	1.75	.35
□ 28	Curt Flood	.40	.20	.04
□ 29	Bob Gibson	1.75	.85	.17
□ 30	Al Ferrara	.30	.15	.03
□ 31	Willie McCovey	2.00	1.00	.20

		NRMT	VG-E	GOOD
☐ 32	Juan Marichal	1.75	.85	.17
☐ 33	Willie Mays	4.00	2.00	.40

1969 Topps Super

JUAN MARICHAL
San Francisco Giants   Pitcher

The cards in this 66-card set measure 2 1/4" by 3 1/4". This beautiful Topps set was released independently of the regular baseball series of 1969. It is referred to as "Super Baseball" on the back of the card, a title which was also used for the postcard-size cards issued in 1970 and 1971. Complete sheets, and cards with square corners cut from these sheets, are sometimes encountered.

		NRMT	VG-E	GOOD
COMPLETE SET		2800.00	1200.00	250.00
COMMON PLAYER (1-66)		8.00	4.00	.80
☐ 1	Dave McNally	10.00	5.00	1.00
☐ 2	Frank Robinson	120.00	60.00	12.00
☐ 3	Brooks Robinson	150.00	75.00	15.00
☐ 4	Ken Harrelson	10.00	5.00	1.00
☐ 5	Carl Yastrzemski	300.00	150.00	30.00
☐ 6	Ray Culp	8.00	4.00	.80
☐ 7	Jim Fregosi	10.00	5.00	1.00
☐ 8	Rick Reichardt	8.00	4.00	.80
☐ 9	Vic Davalillo	8.00	4.00	.80
☐ 10	Luis Aparicio	50.00	25.00	5.00
☐ 11	Pete Ward	8.00	4.00	.80
☐ 12	Joe Horlen	8.00	4.00	.80
☐ 13	Luis Tiant	12.00	6.00	1.20
☐ 14	Sam McDowell	10.00	5.00	1.00
☐ 15	Jose Cardenal	8.00	4.00	.80
☐ 16	Willie Horton	10.00	5.00	1.00
☐ 17	Denny McLain	12.00	6.00	1.20
☐ 18	Bill Freehan	10.00	5.00	1.00
☐ 19	Harmon Killebrew	75.00	37.50	7.50
☐ 20	Tony Oliva	15.00	7.50	1.50
☐ 21	Dean Chance	8.00	4.00	.80
☐ 22	Joe Foy	8.00	4.00	.80
☐ 23	Roger Nelson	8.00	4.00	.80
☐ 24	Mickey Mantle	600.00	300.00	60.00
☐ 25	Mel Stottlemyre	10.00	5.00	1.00
☐ 26	Roy White	10.00	5.00	1.00
☐ 27	Rick Monday	10.00	5.00	1.00
☐ 28	Reggie Jackson	300.00	150.00	30.00
☐ 29	Bert Campaneris	8.00	4.00	.80
☐ 30	Frank Howard	10.00	5.00	1.00
☐ 31	Camilo Pascual	8.00	4.00	.80
☐ 32	Tommy Davis	10.00	5.00	1.00
☐ 33	Don Mincher	8.00	4.00	.80
☐ 34	Hank Aaron	250.00	125.00	25.00
☐ 35	Felipe Alou	8.00	4.00	.80
☐ 36	Joe Torre	12.00	6.00	1.20
☐ 37	Fergie Jenkins	15.00	7.50	1.50
☐ 38	Ron Santo	10.00	5.00	1.00
☐ 39	Billy Williams	50.00	25.00	5.00
☐ 40	Tommy Helms	8.00	4.00	.80
☐ 41	Pete Rose	500.00	250.00	50.00
☐ 42	Joe Morgan	50.00	25.00	5.00
☐ 43	Jim Wynn	8.00	4.00	.80
☐ 44	Curt Blefary	8.00	4.00	.80
☐ 45	Willie Davis	10.00	5.00	1.00
☐ 46	Don Drysdale	50.00	25.00	5.00
☐ 47	Tom Haller	8.00	4.00	.80
☐ 48	Rusty Staub	12.00	6.00	1.20
☐ 49	Maury Wills	15.00	7.50	1.50
☐ 50	Cleon Jones	8.00	4.00	.80
☐ 51	Jerry Koosman	10.00	5.00	1.00
☐ 52	Tom Seaver	150.00	75.00	15.00
☐ 53	Richie Allen	12.00	6.00	1.20
☐ 54	Chris Short	8.00	4.00	.80
☐ 55	Cookie Rojas	8.00	4.00	.80
☐ 56	Matty Alou	8.00	4.00	.80
☐ 57	Steve Blass	8.00	4.00	.80
☐ 58	Bob Clemente	200.00	100.00	20.00
☐ 59	Curt Flood	15.00	7.50	1.50
☐ 60	Bob Gibson	75.00	37.50	7.50
☐ 61	Tim McCarver	10.00	5.00	1.00
☐ 62	Dick Selma	8.00	4.00	.80
☐ 63	Ollie Brown	8.00	4.00	.80
☐ 64	Juan Marichal	75.00	37.50	7.50
☐ 65	Willie Mays	250.00	125.00	25.00
☐ 66	Willie McCovey	90.00	45.00	9.00

1970 Topps

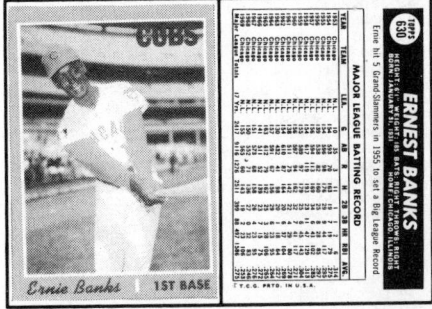

Ernie Banks   1ST BASE

The cards in this 720-card set measure 2 1/2" by 3 1/2". The Topps set for 1970 has color photos surrounded by white frame lines and gray borders. The backs have a blue biographical section and a yellow record section. All-Star selections are featured on cards 450 to 469. Other topical subsets within this set include League Leaders (61-72), Playoffs cards (195-202), and World Series cards (305-310). There are graduations of scarcity, terminating in the high series (634- 720), which are outlined in the value summary.

		NRMT	VG-E	GOOD
COMPLETE SET		1000.00	400.00	80.00
COMMON PLAYER (1-132)		.20	.10	.02
COMMON PLAYER (133-263)		.25	.12	.02
COMMON PLAYER (264-459)		.30	.15	.03
COMMON PLAYER (460-546)		.35	.17	.03
COMMON PLAYER (547-633)		.60	.30	.06
COMMON PLAYER (634-720)		1.50	.75	.15
☐ 1	New York Mets Team Card	4.00	.60	.10
☐ 2	Diego Segui	.20	.10	.02
☐ 3	Darrel Chaney	.20	.10	.02
☐ 4	Tom Egan	.20	.10	.02
☐ 5	Wes Parker	.30	.15	.03
☐ 6	Grant Jackson	.20	.10	.02
☐ 7	Indians Rookies Gary Boyd Russ Nagelson	.20	.10	.02
☐ 8	Jose Martinez	.20	.10	.02
☐ 9	Checklist 1	1.50	.20	.05
☐ 10	Carl Yastrzemski	18.00	9.00	1.80
☐ 11	Nate Colbert	.20	.10	.02
☐ 12	John Hiller	.30	.15	.03
☐ 13	Jack Hiatt	.20	.10	.02
☐ 14	Hank Allen	.20	.10	.02
☐ 15	Larry Dierker	.30	.15	.03
☐ 16	Charlie Metro MG	.20	.10	.02
☐ 17	Hoyt Wilhelm	2.50	1.25	.25
☐ 18	Carlos May	.20	.10	.02
☐ 19	John Boccabella	.20	.10	.02
☐ 20	Dave McNally	.40	.20	.04
☐ 21	A's Rookies Vida Blue Gene Tenace	2.00	1.00	.20

☐ 22	Ray Washburn	.20	.10	.02
☐ 23	Bill Robinson	.30	.15	.03
☐ 24	Dick Selma	.20	.10	.02
☐ 25	Cesar Tovar	.20	.10	.02
☐ 26	Tug McGraw	.75	.35	.07
☐ 27	Chuck Hinton	.20	.10	.02
☐ 28	Billy Wilson	.20	.10	.02
☐ 29	Sandy Alomar	.20	.10	.02
☐ 30	Matty Alou	.30	.15	.03
☐ 31	Marty Pattin	.20	.10	.02
☐ 32	Harry Walker MG	.20	.10	.02
☐ 33	Don Wert	.20	.10	.02
☐ 34	Willie Crawford	.20	.10	.02
☐ 35	Joe Horlen	.20	.10	.02
☐ 36	Red Rookies	.30	.15	.03
	Danny Breeden			
	Bernie Carbo			
☐ 37	Dick Drago	.20	.10	.02
☐ 38	Mack Jones	.20	.10	.02
☐ 39	Mike Nagy	.20	.10	.02
☐ 40	Rich Allen	.75	.35	.07
☐ 41	George Lauzerique	.20	.10	.02
☐ 42	Tito Fuentes	.20	.10	.02
☐ 43	Jack Aker	.20	.10	.02
☐ 44	Roberto Pena	.20	.10	.02
☐ 45	Dave Johnson	.50	.25	.05
☐ 46	Ken Rudolph	.20	.10	.02
☐ 47	Bob Miller	.20	.10	.02
☐ 48	Gil Garrido	.20	.10	.02
☐ 49	Tim Cullen	.20	.10	.02
☐ 50	Tommie Agee	.30	.15	.03
☐ 51	Bob Christian	.20	.10	.02
☐ 52	Bruce Dal Canton	.20	.10	.02
☐ 53	John Kennedy	.20	.10	.02
☐ 54	Jeff Torborg	.30	.15	.03
☐ 55	John Odom	.20	.10	.02
☐ 56	Phillies Rookies	.20	.10	.02
	Joe Lis			
	Scott Reid			
☐ 57	Pat Kelly	.20	.10	.02
☐ 58	Dave Marshall	.20	.10	.02
☐ 59	Dick Ellsworth	.30	.15	.03
☐ 60	Jim Wynn	.40	.20	.04
☐ 61	NL Batting Leaders	3.00	1.50	.30
	Pete Rose			
	Bob Clemente			
	Cleon Jones			
☐ 62	AL Batting Leaders	1.25	.60	.12
	Rod Carew			
	Reggie Smith			
	Tony Oliva			
☐ 63	NL RBI Leaders	1.00	.50	.10
	Willie McCovey			
	Ron Santo			
	Tony Perez			
☐ 64	AL RBI Leaders	1.50	.75	.15
	Harmon Killebrew			
	Boog Powell			
	Reggie Jackson			
☐ 65	NL Home Run Leaders	1.75	.85	.17
	Willie McCovey			
	Hank Aaron			
	Lee May			
☐ 66	AL Home Run Leaders	1.75	.85	.17
	Harmon Killebrew			
	Frank Howard			
	Reggie Jackson			
☐ 67	NL ERA Leaders	3.00	1.50	.30
	Juan Marichal			
	Steve Carlton			
	Bob Gibson			
☐ 68	AL ERA Leaders	1.00	.50	.10
	Dick Bosman			
	Jim Palmer			
	Mike Cuellar			
☐ 69	NL Pitching Leaders	2.50	1.25	.25
	Tom Seaver			
	Phil Niekro			
	Fergie Jenkins			
	Juan Marichal			
☐ 70	AL Pitching Leaders	.75	.35	.07
	Dennis McLain			
	Mike Cuellar			
	Dave Boswell			
	Dave McNally			
	Jim Perry			
	Mel Stottlemyre			
☐ 71	NL Strikeout Leaders	1.00	.50	.10
	Fergie Jenkins			
	Bob Gibson			
	Bill Singer			
☐ 72	AL Strikeout Leaders	.75	.35	.07
	Sam McDowell			
	Mickey Lolich			
	Andy Messersmith			
☐ 73	Wayne Granger	.20	.10	.02
☐ 74	Angels Rookies	.20	.10	.02
	Greg Washburn			
	Wally Wolf			
☐ 75	Jim Kaat	1.50	.75	.15
☐ 76	Carl Taylor	.20	.10	.02
☐ 77	Frank Linzy	.20	.10	.02
☐ 78	Joe Lahoud	.20	.10	.02
☐ 79	Clay Kirby	.20	.10	.02
☐ 80	Don Kessinger	.30	.15	.03
☐ 81	Dave May	.20	.10	.02
☐ 82	Frank Fernandez	.20	.10	.02
☐ 83	Don Cardwell	.20	.10	.02
☐ 84	Paul Casanova	.20	.10	.02
☐ 85	Max Alvis	.20	.10	.02
☐ 86	Lum Harris MG	.20	.10	.02
☐ 87	Steve Renko	.20	.10	.02
☐ 88	Pilots Rookies	.20	.10	.02
	Miguel Fuentes			
	Dick Baney			
☐ 89	Juan Rios	.20	.10	.02
☐ 90	Tim McCarver	.50	.25	.05
☐ 91	Rich Morales	.20	.10	.02
☐ 92	George Culver	.20	.10	.02
☐ 93	Rick Renick	.20	.10	.02
☐ 94	Fred Patek	.30	.15	.03
☐ 95	Earl Wilson	.20	.10	.02
☐ 96	Cardinals Rookies	1.50	.75	.15
	Leron Lee			
	Jerry Reuss			
☐ 97	Joe Moeller	.20	.10	.02
☐ 98	Gates Brown	.30	.15	.03
☐ 99	Bobby Pfeil	.20	.10	.02
☐ 100	Mel Stottlemyre	.40	.20	.04
☐ 101	Bobby Floyd	.20	.10	.02
☐ 102	Joe Rudi	.40	.20	.04
☐ 103	Frank Reberger	.20	.10	.02
☐ 104	Gerry Moses	.20	.10	.02
☐ 105	Tony Gonzalez	.20	.10	.02
☐ 106	Darold Knowles	.20	.10	.02
☐ 107	Bobby Etheridge	.20	.10	.02
☐ 108	Tom Burgmeier	.20	.10	.02
☐ 109	Expos Rookies	.40	.20	.04
	Garry Jestadt			
	Carl Morton			
☐ 110	Bob Moose	.20	.10	.02
☐ 111	Mike Hegan	.20	.10	.02
☐ 112	Dave Nelson	.20	.10	.02
☐ 113	Jim Ray	.20	.10	.02
☐ 114	Gene Michael	.30	.15	.03
☐ 115	Alex Johnson	.30	.15	.03
☐ 116	Sparky Lyle	.60	.30	.06
☐ 117	Don Young	.20	.10	.02
☐ 118	George Mitterwald	.20	.10	.02
☐ 119	Chuck Taylor	.20	.10	.02
☐ 120	Sal Bando	.50	.25	.05
☐ 121	Orioles Rookies	.30	.15	.03
	Fred Beene			
	Terry Crowley			
☐ 122	George Stone	.20	.10	.02
☐ 123	Don Gutteridge	.20	.10	.02
☐ 124	Larry Jaster	.20	.10	.02
☐ 125	Deron Johnson	.20	.10	.02
☐ 126	Marty Martinez	.20	.10	.02
☐ 127	Joe Coleman	.20	.10	.02
☐ 128	Checklist 2	1.50	.25	.05
☐ 129	Jimmie Price	.20	.10	.02
☐ 130	Ollie Brown	.20	.10	.02
☐ 131	Dodgers Rookies	.20	.10	.02
	Ray Lamb			
	Bob Stinson			
☐ 132	Jim McGlothlin	.20	.10	.02
☐ 133	Clay Carroll	.25	.12	.02
☐ 134	Danny Walton	.25	.12	.02
☐ 135	Dick Dietz	.25	.12	.02
☐ 136	Steve Hargan	.25	.12	.02
☐ 137	Art Shamsky	.25	.12	.02
☐ 138	Joe Foy	.25	.12	.02
☐ 139	Rich Nye	.25	.12	.02
☐ 140	Reggie Jackson	35.00	17.50	3.50
☐ 141	Pirates Rookies	.40	.20	.04
	Dave Cash			
	Johnny Jeter			
☐ 142	Fritz Peterson	.25	.12	.02
☐ 143	Phil Gagliano	.25	.12	.02
☐ 144	Ray Culp	.25	.12	.02
☐ 145	Rico Carty	.40	.20	.04
☐ 146	Danny Murphy	.25	.12	.02
☐ 147	Angel Hermoso	.25	.12	.02
☐ 148	Earl Weaver MG	.75	.35	.07
☐ 149	Billy Champion	.25	.12	.02
☐ 150	Harmon Killebrew	4.50	2.25	.45
☐ 151	Dave Roberts	.25	.12	.02
☐ 152	Ike Brown	.25	.12	.02
☐ 153	Gary Gentry	.25	.12	.02

☐ 154	Senators Rookies	.25	.12	.02

☐ 154	Senators Rookies	.25	.12	.02
	Jim Miles			
	Jan Dukes			
☐ 155	Denis Menke	.25	.12	.02
☐ 156	Eddie Fisher	.25	.12	.02
☐ 157	Manny Mota	.40	.20	.04
☐ 158	Jerry McNertney	.25	.12	.02
☐ 159	Tommy Helms	.40	.20	.04
☐ 160	Phil Niekro	3.00	1.50	.30
☐ 161	Richie Scheinblum	.25	.12	.02
☐ 162	Jerry Johnson	.25	.12	.02
☐ 163	Syd O'Brien	.25	.12	.02
☐ 164	Ty Cline	.25	.12	.02
☐ 165	Ed Kirkpatrick	.25	.12	.02
☐ 166	Al Oliver	2.00	1.00	.20
☐ 167	Bill Burbach	.25	.12	.02
☐ 168	Dave Watkins	.25	.12	.02
☐ 169	Tom Hall	.25	.12	.02
☐ 170	Billy Williams	3.50	1.75	.35
☐ 171	Jim Nash	.25	.12	.02
☐ 172	Braves Rookies	.90	.45	.09
	Garry Hill			
	Ralph Garr			
☐ 173	Jim Hicks	.25	.12	.02
☐ 174	Ted Sizemore	.40	.20	.04
☐ 175	Dick Bosman	.25	.12	.02
☐ 176	Jim Ray Hart	.40	.20	.04
☐ 177	Jim Northrup	.40	.20	.04
☐ 178	Denny Lemaster	.25	.12	.02
☐ 179	Ivan Murrell	.25	.12	.02
☐ 180	Tommy John	1.75	.85	.17
☐ 181	Sparky Anderson MG	.75	.35	.07
☐ 182	Dick Hall	.25	.12	.02
☐ 183	Jerry Grote	.25	.12	.02
☐ 184	Ray Fosse	.25	.12	.02
☐ 185	Don Mincher	.25	.12	.02
☐ 186	Rick Joseph	.25	.12	.02
☐ 187	Mike Hedlund	.25	.12	.02
☐ 188	Manny Sanguillen	.40	.20	.04
☐ 189	Yankees Rookies	30.00	15.00	3.00
	Thurman Munson			
	Dave McDonald			
☐ 190	Joe Torre	.75	.35	.07
☐ 191	Vicente Romo	.25	.12	.02
☐ 192	Jim Qualls	.25	.12	.02
☐ 193	Mike Wegener	.25	.12	.02
☐ 194	Chuck Manuel	.25	.12	.02
☐ 195	NL Playoff Game 1	1.75	.85	.17
	Seaver wins opener			
☐ 196	NL Playoff Game 2	1.00	.50	.10
	Mets show muscle			
☐ 197	NL Playoff Game 3	1.75	.85	.17
	Ryan saves the day			
☐ 198	NL Playoff Summary	1.00	.50	.10
	Mets celebrate			
☐ 199	AL Playoff Game 1	1.00	.50	.10
	Orioles win			
	squeaker (Cuellar)			
☐ 200	AL Playoff Game 2	1.00	.50	.10
	Powell scores			
	winning run			
☐ 201	AL Playoff Game 3	1.00	.50	.10
	Birds wrap it up			
☐ 202	AL Playoff Summary	1.00	.50	.10
	Orioles celebrate			
☐ 203	Rudy May	.25	.12	.02
☐ 204	Len Gabrielson	.25	.12	.02
☐ 205	Bert Campaneris	.40	.20	.04
☐ 206	Clete Boyer	.40	.20	.04
☐ 207	Tigers Rookies	.25	.12	.02
	Norman McRae			
	Bob Reed			
☐ 208	Fred Gladding	.25	.12	.02
☐ 209	Ken Suarez	.25	.12	.02
☐ 210	Juan Marichal	3.50	1.75	.35
☐ 211	Ted Williams MG	4.00	2.00	.40
☐ 212	Al Santorini	.25	.12	.02
☐ 213	Andy Etchebarren	.25	.12	.02
☐ 214	Ken Boswell	.25	.12	.02
☐ 215	Reggie Smith	.85	.40	.08
☐ 216	Chuck Hartenstein	.25	.12	.02
☐ 217	Ron Hansen	.25	.12	.02
☐ 218	Ron Stone	.25	.12	.02
☐ 219	Jerry Kenney	.25	.12	.02
☐ 220	Steve Carlton	11.00	5.50	1.10
☐ 221	Ron Brand	.25	.12	.02
☐ 222	Jim Rooker	.25	.12	.02
☐ 223	Nate Oliver	.25	.12	.02
☐ 224	Steve Barber	.25	.12	.02
☐ 225	Lee May	.40	.20	.04
☐ 226	Ron Perranoski	.40	.20	.04
☐ 227	Astros Rookies	.80	.40	.08
	John Mayberry			
	Bob Watkins			
☐ 228	Aurelio Rodriguez	.25	.12	.02
☐ 229	Rich Robertson	.25	.12	.02
☐ 230	Brooks Robinson	5.50	2.75	.55
☐ 231	Luis Tiant	.85	.40	.08
☐ 232	Bob Didier	.25	.12	.02
☐ 233	Lew Krausse	.25	.12	.02
☐ 234	Tommy Dean	.25	.12	.02
☐ 235	Mike Epstein	.25	.12	.02
☐ 236	Bob Veale	.25	.12	.02
☐ 237	Russ Gibson	.25	.12	.02
☐ 238	Jose Laboy	.25	.12	.02
☐ 239	Ken Berry	.25	.12	.02
☐ 240	Fergie Jenkins	1.50	.75	.15
☐ 241	Royals Rookies	.25	.12	.02
	Al Fitzmorris			
	Scott Northey			
☐ 242	Walter Alston MG	1.25	.60	.12
☐ 243	Joe Sparma	.25	.12	.02
☐ 244A	Checklist 3	1.50	.25	.05
	(red bat on front)			
☐ 244B	Checklist 3	2.00	.30	.06
	(brown bat on front)			
☐ 245	Leo Cardenas	.25	.12	.02
☐ 246	Jim McAndrew	.25	.12	.02
☐ 247	Lou Klimchock	.25	.12	.02
☐ 248	Jesus Alou	.25	.12	.02
☐ 249	Bob Locker	.25	.12	.02
☐ 250	Willie McCovey	5.00	2.50	.50
☐ 251	Dick Schofield	.25	.12	.02
☐ 252	Lowell Palmer	.25	.12	.02
☐ 253	Ron Woods	.25	.12	.02
☐ 254	Camilo Pascual	.25	.12	.02
☐ 255	Jim Spencer	.25	.12	.02
☐ 256	Vic Davalillo	.25	.12	.02
☐ 257	Dennis Higgins	.25	.12	.02
☐ 258	Paul Popovich	.25	.12	.02
☐ 259	Tommie Reynolds	.25	.12	.02
☐ 260	Claude Osteen	.25	.12	.02
☐ 261	Curt Motton	.25	.12	.02
☐ 262	Twins Rookies	.25	.12	.02
	Jerry Morales			
	Jim Williams			
☐ 263	Duane Josephson	.25	.12	.02
☐ 264	Rich Hebner	.50	.25	.05
☐ 265	Randy Hundley	.30	.15	.03
☐ 266	Wally Bunker	.30	.15	.03
☐ 267	Twins Rookies	.30	.15	.03
	Herman Hill			
	Paul Ratliff			
☐ 268	Claude Raymond	.30	.15	.03
☐ 269	Cesar Gutierrez	.30	.15	.03
☐ 270	Chris Short	.30	.15	.03
☐ 271	Greg Goossen	.30	.15	.03
☐ 272	Hector Torres	.30	.15	.03
☐ 273	Ralph Houk MG	.40	.20	.04
☐ 274	Gerry Arrigo	.30	.15	.03
☐ 275	Duke Sims	.30	.15	.03
☐ 276	Ron Hunt	.30	.15	.03
☐ 277	Paul Doyle	.30	.15	.03
☐ 278	Tommie Aaron	.40	.20	.04
☐ 279	Bill Lee	.50	.25	.05
☐ 280	Donn Clendenon	.40	.20	.04
☐ 281	Casey Cox	.30	.15	.03
☐ 282	Steve Huntz	.30	.15	.03
☐ 283	Angel Bravo	.30	.15	.03
☐ 284	Jack Baldschun	.30	.15	.03
☐ 285	Paul Blair	.40	.20	.04
☐ 286	Dodgers Rookies	5.00	2.50	.50
	Jack Jenkins			
	Bill Buckner			
☐ 287	Fred Talbot	.30	.15	.03
☐ 288	Larry Hisle	.30	.15	.03
☐ 289	Gene Brabender	.30	.15	.03
☐ 290	Rod Carew	12.00	6.00	1.20
☐ 291	Leo Durocher MG	1.25	.60	.12
☐ 292	Eddie Leon	.30	.15	.03
☐ 293	Bob Bailey	.30	.15	.03
☐ 294	Jose Azcue	.30	.15	.03
☐ 295	Cecil Upshaw	.30	.15	.03
☐ 296	Woody Woodward	.40	.20	.04
☐ 297	Curt Blefary	.30	.15	.03
☐ 298	Ken Henderson	.30	.15	.03
☐ 299	Buddy Bradford	.30	.15	.03
☐ 300	Tom Seaver	25.00	12.50	2.50
☐ 301	Chico Salmon	.30	.15	.03
☐ 302	Jeff James	.30	.15	.03
☐ 303	Brant Alyea	.30	.15	.03
☐ 304	Bill Russell	1.50	.75	.15
☐ 305	World Series Game 1	1.00	.50	.10
	Buford leadoff homer			
☐ 306	World Series Game 2	1.00	.50	.10
	Clendenon's homer			
	breaks ice			
☐ 307	World Series Game 3	1.00	.50	.10
	Agee's catch			
	saves the day			

☐ 308	World Series Game 4 ..... Martin's bunt ends deadlock	1.00	.50	.10
☐ 309	World Series Game 5 ..... Koosman shuts door	1.00	.50	.10
☐ 310	World Series Summary .. Mets whoop it up	1.00	.50	.10
☐ 311	Dick Green	.30	.15	.03
☐ 312	Mike Torrez	.40	.20	.04
☐ 313	Mayo Smith MG	.30	.15	.03
☐ 314	Bill McCool	.30	.15	.03
☐ 315	Luis Aparicio	3.00	1.50	.30
☐ 316	Skip Guinn	.30	.15	.03
☐ 317	Red Sox Rookies .... Billy Conigliaro Luis Alvarado	.40	.20	.04
☐ 318	Willie Smith	.30	.15	.03
☐ 319	Clay Dalrymple	.30	.15	.03
☐ 320	Jim Maloney	.40	.20	.04
☐ 321	Lou Piniella	1.00	.50	.10
☐ 322	Luke Walker	.30	.15	.03
☐ 323	Wayne Comer	.30	.15	.03
☐ 324	Tony Taylor	.30	.15	.03
☐ 325	Dave Boswell	.30	.15	.03
☐ 326	Bill Voss	.30	.15	.03
☐ 327	Hal King	.30	.15	.03
☐ 328	George Brunet	.30	.15	.03
☐ 329	Chris Cannizzaro	.30	.15	.03
☐ 330	Lou Brock	4.50	2.25	.45
☐ 331	Chuck Dobson	.30	.15	.03
☐ 332	Bobby Wine	.30	.15	.03
☐ 333	Bobby Murcer	.85	.40	.08
☐ 334	Phil Regan	.30	.15	.03
☐ 335	Bill Freehan	.65	.30	.06
☐ 336	Del Unser	.30	.15	.03
☐ 337	Mike McCormick	.40	.20	.04
☐ 338	Paul Schaal	.30	.15	.03
☐ 339	Johnny Edwards	.30	.15	.03
☐ 340	Tony Conigliaro	.75	.35	.07
☐ 341	Bill Sudakis	.30	.15	.03
☐ 342	Wilbur Wood	.40	.20	.04
☐ 343A	Checklist 4 .... (red bat on front)	1.50	.25	.05
☐ 343B	Checklist 4 .... (brown bat on front)	2.00	.30	.06
☐ 344	Marcelino Lopez	.30	.15	.03
☐ 345	Al Ferrara	.30	.15	.03
☐ 346	Red Schoendienst MG	.60	.30	.06
☐ 347	Russ Snyder	.30	.15	.03
☐ 348	Mets Rookies .... Mike Jorgensen Jesse Hudson	.30	.15	.03
☐ 349	Steve Hamilton	.30	.15	.03
☐ 350	Roberto Clemente	18.00	9.00	1.80
☐ 351	Tom Murphy	.30	.15	.03
☐ 352	Bob Barton	.30	.15	.03
☐ 353	Stan Williams	.30	.15	.03
☐ 354	Amos Otis	.50	.25	.05
☐ 355	Doug Rader	.40	.20	.04
☐ 356	Fred Lasher	.30	.15	.03
☐ 357	Bob Burda	.30	.15	.03
☐ 358	Pedro Borbon	.30	.15	.03
☐ 359	Phil Roof	.30	.15	.03
☐ 360	Curt Flood	.60	.30	.06
☐ 361	Ray Jarvis	.30	.15	.03
☐ 362	Joe Hague	.30	.15	.03
☐ 363	Tom Shopay	.30	.15	.03
☐ 364	Dan McGinn	.30	.15	.03
☐ 365	Zoilo Versalles	.30	.15	.03
☐ 366	Barry Moore	.30	.15	.03
☐ 367	Mike Lum	.30	.15	.03
☐ 368	Ed Herrmann	.30	.15	.03
☐ 369	Alan Foster	.30	.15	.03
☐ 370	Tommy Harper	.40	.20	.04
☐ 371	Rod Gaspar	.30	.15	.03
☐ 372	Dave Giusti	.30	.15	.03
☐ 373	Roy White	.40	.20	.04
☐ 374	Tommie Sisk	.30	.15	.03
☐ 375	Johnny Callison	.40	.20	.04
☐ 376	Lefty Phillips MG	.30	.15	.03
☐ 377	Bill Butler	.30	.15	.03
☐ 378	Jim Davenport	.40	.20	.04
☐ 379	Tom Tischinski	.30	.15	.03
☐ 380	Tony Perez	2.50	1.25	.25
☐ 381	Athletics Rookies .... Bobby Brooks Mike Olivo	.30	.15	.03
☐ 382	Jack DiLauro	.30	.15	.03
☐ 383	Mickey Stanley	.40	.20	.04
☐ 384	Gary Neibauer	.30	.15	.03
☐ 385	George Scott	.40	.20	.04
☐ 386	Bill Dillman	.30	.15	.03
☐ 387	Orioles Team	.90	.45	.09
☐ 388	Byron Browne	.30	.15	.03
☐ 389	Jim Shellenback	.30	.15	.03

☐ 390	Willie Davis	.50	.25	.05
☐ 391	Larry Brown	.30	.15	.03
☐ 392	Walt Hriniak	.30	.15	.03
☐ 393	John Gelnar	.30	.15	.03
☐ 394	Gil Hodges MG	3.00	1.50	.30
☐ 395	Walt Williams	.30	.15	.03
☐ 396	Steve Blass	.30	.15	.03
☐ 397	Roger Repoz	.30	.15	.03
☐ 398	Bill Stoneman	.30	.15	.03
☐ 399	Yankees Team	.90	.45	.09
☐ 400	Denny McLain	.90	.45	.09
☐ 401	Giants Rookies .... John Harrell Bernie Williams	.30	.15	.03
☐ 402	Ellie Rodriguez	.30	.15	.03
☐ 403	Jim Bunning	1.50	.75	.15
☐ 404	Rich Reese	.30	.15	.03
☐ 405	Bill Hands	.30	.15	.03
☐ 406	Mike Andrews	.30	.15	.03
☐ 407	Bob Watson	.50	.25	.05
☐ 408	Paul Lindblad	.30	.15	.03
☐ 409	Bob Tolan	.40	.20	.04
☐ 410	Boog Powell	1.75	.85	.17
☐ 411	Dodgers Team	.90	.45	.09
☐ 412	Larry Burchart	.30	.15	.03
☐ 413	Sonny Jackson	.30	.15	.03
☐ 414	Paul Edmondson	.30	.15	.03
☐ 415	Julian Javier	.30	.15	.03
☐ 416	Joe Verbanic	.30	.15	.03
☐ 417	John Bateman	.30	.15	.03
☐ 418	John Donaldson	.30	.15	.03
☐ 419	Ron Taylor	.30	.15	.03
☐ 420	Ken McMullen	.30	.15	.03
☐ 421	Pat Dobson	.40	.20	.04
☐ 422	Royals Team	.75	.35	.07
☐ 423	Jerry May	.30	.15	.03
☐ 424	Mike Kilkenny	.30	.15	.03
☐ 425	Bobby Bonds	1.50	.75	.15
☐ 426	Bill Rigney MG	.30	.15	.03
☐ 427	Fred Norman	.30	.15	.03
☐ 428	Don Buford	.30	.15	.03
☐ 429	Cubs Rookies .... Randy Bobb Jim Cosman	.30	.15	.03
☐ 430	Andy Messersmith	.60	.30	.06
☐ 431	Ron Swoboda	.40	.20	.04
☐ 432A	Checklist 5 .... ("Baseball" in yellow letters)	1.50	.20	.05
☐ 432B	Checklist 5 .... ("Baseball" in white letters)	2.00	.30	.06
☐ 433	Ron Bryant	.30	.15	.03
☐ 434	Felipe Alou	.40	.20	.04
☐ 435	Nelson Briles	.40	.20	.04
☐ 436	Phillies Team	.75	.35	.07
☐ 437	Danny Cater	.30	.15	.03
☐ 438	Pat Jarvis	.30	.15	.03
☐ 439	Lee Maye	.30	.15	.03
☐ 440	Bill Mazeroski	.60	.30	.06
☐ 441	John O'Donoghue	.30	.15	.03
☐ 442	Gene Mauch MG	.40	.20	.04
☐ 443	Al Jackson	.30	.15	.03
☐ 444	White Sox Rookies .... Billy Farmer John Matias	.30	.15	.03
☐ 445	Vada Pinson	.80	.40	.08
☐ 446	Billy Grabarkewitz	.30	.15	.03
☐ 447	Lee Stange	.30	.15	.03
☐ 448	Astros Team	.75	.35	.07
☐ 449	Jim Palmer	7.50	3.75	.75
☐ 450	Willie McCovey AS	3.00	1.50	.30
☐ 451	Boog Powell AS	.60	.30	.06
☐ 452	Felix Millan AS	.40	.20	.04
☐ 453	Rod Carew AS	4.00	2.00	.40
☐ 454	Ron Santo AS	.40	.20	.04
☐ 455	Brooks Robinson AS	3.00	1.50	.30
☐ 456	Don Kessinger AS	.40	.20	.04
☐ 457	Rico Petrocelli AS	.40	.20	.04
☐ 458	Pete Rose AS	7.50	3.75	.75
☐ 459	Reggie Jackson AS	6.50	3.25	.65
☐ 460	Matty Alou AS	.45	.22	.04
☐ 461	Carl Yastrzemski AS	4.50	2.25	.45
☐ 462	Hank Aaron AS	4.50	2.25	.45
☐ 463	Frank Robinson AS	3.00	1.50	.30
☐ 464	Johnny Bench AS	4.50	2.25	.45
☐ 465	Bill Freehan AS	.45	.22	.04
☐ 466	Juan Marichal AS	2.50	1.25	.25
☐ 467	Denny McLain AS	.60	.30	.06
☐ 468	Jerry Koosman AS	.50	.25	.05
☐ 469	Sam McDowell AS	.45	.22	.04
☐ 470	Willie Stargell	4.50	2.25	.45
☐ 471	Chris Zachary	.35	.17	.03
☐ 472	Braves Team	.75	.35	.07
☐ 473	Don Bryant	.35	.17	.03

☐ 474	Dick Kelley	.35	.17	.03
☐ 475	Dick McAuliffe	.45	.22	.04
☐ 476	Don Shaw	.35	.17	.03
☐ 477	Orioles Rookies	.35	.17	.03
	Al Severinsen			
	Roger Freed			
☐ 478	Bob Heise	.35	.17	.03
☐ 479	Dick Woodson	.35	.17	.03
☐ 480	Glen Beckert	.45	.22	.04
☐ 481	Jose Tartabull	.35	.17	.03
☐ 482	Tom Hilgendorf	.35	.17	.03
☐ 483	Gail Hopkins	.35	.17	.03
☐ 484	Gary Nolan	.35	.17	.03
☐ 485	Jay Johnstone	.45	.22	.04
☐ 486	Terry Harmon	.35	.17	.03
☐ 487	Cisco Carlos	.35	.17	.03
☐ 488	J.C. Martin	.35	.17	.03
☐ 489	Eddie Kasko MG	.35	.17	.03
☐ 490	Bill Singer	.45	.22	.04
☐ 491	Graig Nettles	3.00	1.50	.30
☐ 492	Astros Rookies	.35	.17	.03
	Keith Lampard			
	Scipio Spinks			
☐ 493	Lindy McDaniel	.45	.22	.04
☐ 494	Larry Stahl	.35	.17	.03
☐ 495	Dave Morehead	.35	.17	.03
☐ 496	Steve Whitaker	.35	.17	.03
☐ 497	Eddie Watt	.35	.17	.03
☐ 498	Al Weis	.35	.17	.03
☐ 499	Skip Lockwood	.35	.17	.03
☐ 500	Hank Aaron	18.00	9.00	1.80
☐ 501	White Sox Team	.75	.35	.07
☐ 502	Rollie Fingers	3.50	1.75	.35
☐ 503	Dal Maxvill	.45	.22	.04
☐ 504	Don Pavletich	.35	.17	.03
☐ 505	Ken Holtzman	.45	.22	.04
☐ 506	Ed Stroud	.35	.17	.03
☐ 507	Pat Corrales	.45	.22	.04
☐ 508	Joe Niekro	.75	.35	.07
☐ 509	Expos Team	.75	.35	.07
☐ 510	Tony Oliva	1.50	.75	.15
☐ 511	Joe Hoerner	.35	.17	.03
☐ 512	Billy Harris	.35	.17	.03
☐ 513	Preston Gomez MG	.35	.17	.03
☐ 514	Steve Hovley	.35	.17	.03
☐ 515	Don Wilson	.35	.17	.03
☐ 516	Yankees Rookies	.35	.17	.03
	John Ellis			
	Jim Lyttle			
☐ 517	Joe Gibbon	.35	.17	.03
☐ 518	Bill Melton	.35	.17	.03
☐ 519	Don McMahon	.35	.17	.03
☐ 520	Willie Horton	.65	.30	.06
☐ 521	Cal Koonce	.35	.17	.03
☐ 522	Angels Team	.75	.35	.07
☐ 523	Jose Pena	.35	.17	.03
☐ 524	Alvin Dark MG	.45	.22	.04
☐ 525	Jerry Adair	.35	.17	.03
☐ 526	Ron Herbel	.35	.17	.03
☐ 527	Don Bosch	.35	.17	.03
☐ 528	Elrod Hendricks	.35	.17	.03
☐ 529	Bob Aspromonte	.35	.17	.03
☐ 530	Bob Gibson	4.50	2.25	.45
☐ 531	Ron Clark	.35	.17	.03
☐ 532	Danny Murtaugh MG	.35	.17	.03
☐ 533	Buzz Stephen	.35	.17	.03
☐ 534	Twins Team	.75	.35	.07
☐ 535	Andy Kosco	.35	.17	.03
☐ 536	Mike Kekich	.35	.17	.03
☐ 537	Joe Morgan	3.00	1.50	.30
☐ 538	Bob Humphreys	.35	.17	.03
☐ 539	Phillies Rookies	3.50	1.75	.35
	Dennis Doyle			
	Larry Bowa			
☐ 540	Gary Peters	.45	.22	.04
☐ 541	Bill Heath	.35	.17	.03
☐ 542	Checklist 6	2.00	.30	.06
☐ 543	Clyde Wright	.35	.17	.03
☐ 544	Reds Team	1.00	.50	.10
☐ 545	Ken Harrelson	.90	.45	.09
☐ 546	Ron Reed	.35	.17	.03
☐ 547	Rick Monday	.75	.35	.07
☐ 548	Howie Reed	.60	.30	.06
☐ 549	Cardinals Team	1.00	.50	.10
☐ 550	Frank Howard	.90	.45	.09
☐ 551	Dock Ellis	.60	.30	.06
☐ 552	Royals Rookies	.60	.30	.06
	Don O'Riley			
	Dennis Paepke			
	Fred Rico			
☐ 553	Jim Lefebvre	.60	.30	.06
☐ 554	Tom Timmermann	.60	.30	.06
☐ 555	Orlando Cepeda	2.50	1.25	.25
☐ 556	Dave Bristol MG	.60	.30	.06
☐ 557	Ed Kranepool	.60	.30	.06

☐ 558	Vern Fuller	.60	.30	.06
☐ 559	Tommy Davis	.75	.35	.07
☐ 560	Gaylord Perry	4.50	2.25	.45
☐ 561	Tom McCraw	.60	.30	.06
☐ 562	Ted Abernathy	.60	.30	.06
☐ 563	Red Sox Team	1.00	.50	.10
☐ 564	Johnny Briggs	.60	.30	.06
☐ 565	Jim Hunter	4.50	2.25	.45
☐ 566	Gene Alley	.60	.30	.06
☐ 567	Bob Oliver	.60	.30	.06
☐ 568	Stan Bahnsen	.60	.30	.06
☐ 569	Cookie Rojas	.60	.30	.06
☐ 570	Jim Fregosi	.90	.45	.09
☐ 571	Jim Brewer	.60	.30	.06
☐ 572	Frank Quilici MG	.60	.30	.06
☐ 573	Padres Rookies	.60	.30	.06
	Mike Corkins			
	Rafael Robles			
	Ron Slocum			
☐ 574	Bobby Bolin	.60	.30	.06
☐ 575	Cleon Jones	.60	.30	.06
☐ 576	Milt Pappas	.60	.30	.06
☐ 577	Bernie Allen	.60	.30	.06
☐ 578	Tom Griffin	.60	.30	.06
☐ 579	Tigers Team	1.25	.60	.12
☐ 580	Pete Rose	75.00	37.50	7.50
☐ 581	Tom Satriano	.60	.30	.06
☐ 582	Mike Paul	.60	.30	.06
☐ 583	Hal Lanier	.75	.35	.07
☐ 584	Al Downing	.60	.30	.06
☐ 585	Rusty Staub	1.50	.75	.15
☐ 586	Rickey Clark	.60	.30	.06
☐ 587	Jose Arcia	.60	.30	.06
☐ 588A	Checklist 7	2.50		.10
	(666 Adolpho)			
☐ 588B	Checklist 7	5.00	.80	.15
	(666 Adolfo)			
☐ 589	Joe Keough	.60	.30	.06
☐ 590	Mike Cuellar	.75	.35	.07
☐ 591	Mike Ryan	.60	.30	.06
☐ 592	Daryl Patterson	.60	.30	.06
☐ 593	Cubs Team	1.00	.50	.10
☐ 594	Jake Gibbs	.60	.30	.06
☐ 595	Maury Wills	1.50	.75	.15
☐ 596	Mike Hershberger	.60	.30	.06
☐ 597	Sonny Siebert	.60	.30	.06
☐ 598	Joe Pepitone	.75	.35	.07
☐ 599	Senators Rookies	.60	.30	.06
	Dick Stelmaszek			
	Gene Martin			
	Dick Such			
☐ 600	Willie Mays	25.00	12.50	2.50
☐ 601	Pete Richert	.60	.30	.06
☐ 602	Ted Savage	.60	.30	.06
☐ 603	Ray Oyler	.60	.30	.06
☐ 604	Clarence Gaston	.60	.30	.06
☐ 605	Rick Wise	.60	.30	.06
☐ 606	Chico Ruiz	.60	.30	.06
☐ 607	Gary Waslewski	.60	.30	.06
☐ 608	Pirates Team	1.00	.50	.10
☐ 609	Buck Martinez	.60	.30	.06
☐ 610	Jerry Koosman	1.00	.50	.10
☐ 611	Norm Cash	1.00	.50	.10
☐ 612	Jim Hickman	.60	.30	.06
☐ 613	Dave Baldwin	.60	.30	.06
☐ 614	Mike Shannon	.75	.35	.07
☐ 615	Mark Belanger	.75	.35	.07
☐ 616	Jim Merritt	.60	.30	.06
☐ 617	Jim French	.60	.30	.06
☐ 618	Billy Wynne	.60	.30	.06
☐ 619	Norm Miller	.60	.30	.06
☐ 620	Jim Perry	1.25	.60	.12
☐ 621	Braves Rookies	7.50	3.75	.75
	Mike McQueen			
	Darrell Evans			
	Rick Kester			
☐ 622	Don Sutton	5.00	2.50	.50
☐ 623	Horace Clarke	.60	.30	.06
☐ 624	Clyde King MG	.60	.30	.06
☐ 625	Dean Chance	.60	.30	.06
☐ 626	Dave Ricketts	.60	.30	.06
☐ 627	Gary Wagner	.60	.30	.06
☐ 628	Wayne Garrett	.60	.30	.06
☐ 629	Merv Rettenmund	.60	.30	.06
☐ 630	Ernie Banks	11.00	5.50	1.10
☐ 631	Athletics Team	1.00	.50	.10
☐ 632	Gary Sutherland	.60	.30	.06
☐ 633	Roger Nelson	.60	.30	.06
☐ 634	Bud Harrelson	2.00	1.00	.20
☐ 635	Bob Allison	2.00	1.00	.20
☐ 636	Jim Stewart	1.50	.75	.15
☐ 637	Indians Team	3.00	1.50	.30
☐ 638	Frank Bertaina	1.50	.75	.15
☐ 639	Dave Campbell	1.50	.75	.15
☐ 640	Al Kaline	20.00	10.00	2.00

□ 641	Al McBean	1.50	.75	.15
□ 642	Angels Rookies	1.50	.75	.15
	Greg Garrett			
	Gordon Lund			
	Jarvis Tatum			
□ 643	Jose Pagan	1.50	.75	.15
□ 644	Gerry Nyman	1.50	.75	.15
□ 645	Don Money	2.00	1.00	.20
□ 646	Jim Britton	1.50	.75	.15
□ 647	Tom Matchick	1.50	.75	.15
□ 648	Larry Haney	1.50	.75	.15
□ 649	Jimmie Hall	1.50	.75	.15
□ 650	Sam McDowell	2.00	1.00	.20
□ 651	Jim Gosger	1.50	.75	.15
□ 652	Rich Rollins	1.50	.75	.15
□ 653	Moe Drabowsky	1.50	.75	.15
□ 654	NL Rookies	2.50	1.25	.25
	Oscar Gamble			
	Boots Day			
	Angel Mangual			
□ 655	John Roseboro	2.00	1.00	.20
□ 656	Jim Hardin	1.50	.75	.15
□ 657	Padres Team	3.50	1.75	.35
□ 658	Ken Tatum	1.50	.75	.15
□ 659	Pete Ward	1.50	.75	.15
□ 660	Johnny Bench	75.00	37.50	7.50
□ 661	Jerry Robertson	1.50	.75	.15
□ 662	Frank Lucchesi MG	1.50	.75	.15
□ 663	Tito Francona	1.50	.75	.15
□ 664	Bob Robertson	2.00	1.00	.20
□ 665	Jim Lonborg	2.00	1.00	.20
□ 666	Adolpho Phillips	1.50	.75	.15
□ 667	Bob Meyer	1.50	.75	.15
□ 668	Bob Tillman	1.50	.75	.15
□ 669	White Sox Rookies	1.50	.75	.15
	Bart Johnson			
	Dan Lazar			
	Mickey Scott			
□ 670	Ron Santo	3.00	1.50	.30
□ 671	Jim Campanis	1.50	.75	.15
□ 672	Leon McFadden	1.50	.75	.15
□ 673	Ted Uhlaender	1.50	.75	.15
□ 674	Dave Leonhard	1.50	.75	.15
□ 675	Jose Cardenal	1.50	.75	.15
□ 676	Senators Team	3.00	1.50	.30
□ 677	Woodie Fryman	1.50	.75	.15
□ 678	Dave Duncan	1.50	.75	.15
□ 679	Ray Sadecki	1.50	.75	.15
□ 680	Rico Petrocelli	2.00	1.00	.20
□ 681	Bob Garibaldi	1.50	.75	.15
□ 682	Dalton Jones	1.50	.75	.15
□ 683	Reds Rookies	3.00	1.50	.30
	Vern Geishert			
	Hal McRae			
	Wayne Simpson			
□ 684	Jack Fisher	1.50	.75	.15
□ 685	Tom Haller	1.50	.75	.15
□ 686	Jackie Hernandez	1.50	.75	.15
□ 687	Bob Priddy	1.50	.75	.15
□ 688	Ted Kubiak	1.50	.75	.15
□ 689	Frank Tepedino	1.50	.75	.15
□ 690	Ron Fairly	2.00	1.00	.20
□ 691	Joe Grzenda	1.50	.75	.15
□ 692	Duffy Dyer	1.50	.75	.15
□ 693	Bob Johnson	1.50	.75	.15
□ 694	Gary Ross	1.50	.75	.15
□ 695	Bobby Knoop	1.50	.75	.15
□ 696	Giants Team	3.00	1.50	.30
□ 697	Jim Hannan	1.50	.75	.15
□ 698	Tom Tresh	2.50	1.25	.25
□ 699	Hank Aguirre	1.50	.75	.15
□ 700	Frank Robinson	20.00	10.00	2.00
□ 701	Jack Billingham	1.50	.75	.15
□ 702	AL Rookies	1.50	.75	.15
	Bob Johnson			
	Ron Klimkowski			
	Bill Zepp			
□ 703	Lou Marone	1.50	.75	.15
□ 704	Frank Baker	1.50	.75	.15
□ 705	Tony Cloninger	1.50	.75	.15
□ 706	John McNamara MG	3.00	1.50	.30
□ 707	Kevin Collins	1.50	.75	.15
□ 708	Jose Santiago	1.50	.75	.15
□ 709	Mike Fiore	1.50	.75	.15
□ 710	Felix Millan	1.50	.75	.15
□ 711	Ed Brinkman	1.50	.75	.15
□ 712	Nolan Ryan	45.00	22.50	4.50
□ 713	Pilots Team	7.50	3.75	.75
□ 714	Al Spangler	1.50	.75	.15
□ 715	Mickey Lolich	3.50	1.75	.35
□ 716	Cardinals Rookies	1.50	.75	.15
	Sal Campisi			
	Reggie Cleveland			
	Santiago Guzman			
□ 717	Tom Phoebus	1.50	.75	.15

□ 718	Ed Spiezio	1.50	.75	.15
□ 719	Jim Roland	1.50	.75	.15
□ 720	Rick Reichardt	2.50	.75	.15

1970 Topps Super

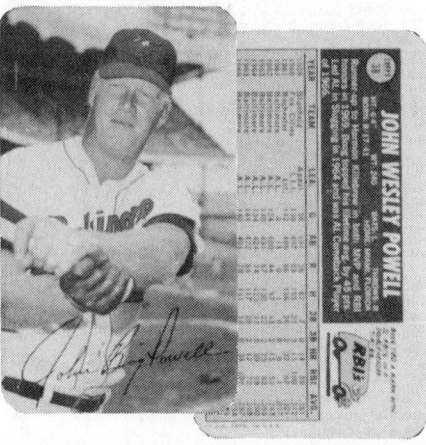

The cards in this 42-card set measure 3 1/8" by 5 1/4". The 1970 Topps Super set was a separate Topps issue printed on heavy stock and marketed in its own wrapper with gum. The blue and yellow backs are identical to the respective player's backs in the 1970 Topps regular issue. Cards 38, Boog Powell, is the key card of the set; other short print run cards are listed in the checklist with SP. The obverse pictures are borderless and contain a facsimile autograph.

		NRMT	VG-E	GOOD
COMPLETE SET		175.00	85.00	18.00
COMMON PLAYER (1-42)		.75	.35	.07
□ 1	Claude Osteen SP	2.50	1.25	.25
□ 2	Sal Bando SP	2.50	1.25	.25
□ 3	Luis Aparicio	2.00	1.00	.20
□ 4	Harmon Killebrew	3.00	1.50	.30
□ 5	Tom Seaver SP	15.00	7.50	1.50
□ 6	Larry Dierker	.75	.35	.07
□ 7	Bill Freehan	.75	.35	.07
□ 8	Johnny Bench	7.50	3.75	.75
□ 9	Tommy Harper	.75	.35	.07
□ 10	Sam McDowell	.75	.35	.07
□ 11	Lou Brock	4.00	2.00	.40
□ 12	Bob Clemente	8.00	4.00	.80
□ 13	Willie McCovey	4.00	2.00	.40
□ 14	Rico Petrocelli	.75	.35	.07
□ 15	Phil Niekro	2.00	1.00	.20
□ 16	Frank Howard	.75	.35	.07
□ 17	Denny McLain	.75	.35	.07
□ 18	Willie Mays	10.00	5.00	1.00
□ 19	Willie Stargell	4.00	2.00	.40
□ 20	Joel Horlen	.75	.35	.07
□ 21	Ron Santo	.75	.35	.07
□ 22	Dick Bosman	.75	.35	.07
□ 23	Tim McCarver	.75	.35	.07
□ 24	Hank Aaron	10.00	5.00	1.00
□ 25	Andy Messersmith	.75	.35	.07
□ 26	Tony Oliva	1.00	.50	.10
□ 27	Mel Stottlemyre	.75	.35	.07
□ 28	Reggie Jackson	14.00	7.00	1.40
□ 29	Carl Yastrzemski	14.00	7.00	1.40
□ 30	Jim Fregosi	.75	.35	.07
□ 31	Vada Pinson	.75	.35	.07
□ 32	Lou Piniella	.75	.35	.07
□ 33	Bob Gibson	3.00	1.50	.30
□ 34	Pete Rose	25.00	12.50	2.50
□ 35	Jim Wynn	.75	.35	.07
□ 36	Ollie Brown SP	5.00	2.50	.50
□ 37	Frank Robinson SP	15.00	7.50	1.50
□ 38	Boog Powell SP	45.00	22.50	4.50
□ 39	Willie Davis SP	2.50	1.25	.25
□ 40	Billy Williams SP	7.50	3.75	.75

			NRMT	VG-E	GOOD
☐ 41	Rusty Staub		1.00	.50	.10
☐ 42	Tommie Agee		.75	.35	.07

1971 Topps

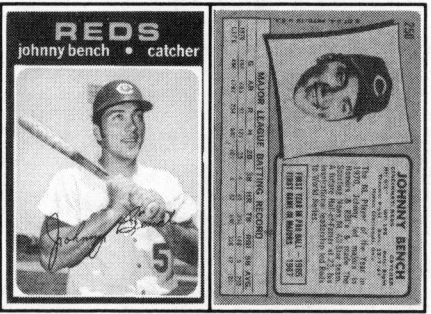

The cards in this 752-card set measure 2 1/2" by 3 1/2". The 1971 Topps set is a challenge to complete in strict mint condition because the black obverse border is easily scratched and damaged. An unusual feature of this set is that the player is also pictured in black and white on the back of the card. Featured subsets within this set include League Leaders (61-72), Playoffs cards (195-202), and World Series cards (327- 332). Cards 524-643 and the last series (644-752) are somewhat scarce.

		NRMT	VG-E	GOOD
COMPLETE SET		1000.00	400.00	80.00
COMMON PLAYER (1-263)		.25	.12	.02
COMMON PLAYER (264-393)		.30	.15	.03
COMMON PLAYER (394-523)		.30	.15	.03
COMMON PLAYER (524-643)		.75	.35	.07
COMMON PLAYER (644-752)		1.50	.75	.15

☐	1	Orioles Team	4.00	.50	.10
☐	2	Dock Ellis	.35	.17	.03
☐	3	Dick McAuliffe	.35	.17	.03
☐	4	Vic Davalillo	.25	.12	.02
☐	5	Thurman Munson	12.00	6.00	1.20
☐	6	Ed Spiezio	.25	.12	.02
☐	7	Jim Holt	.25	.12	.02
☐	8	Mike McQueen	.25	.12	.02
☐	9	George Scott	.35	.17	.03
☐	10	Claude Osteen	.35	.17	.03
☐	11	Elliott Maddox	.25	.12	.02
☐	12	Johnny Callison	.35	.17	.03
☐	13	White Sox Rookies	.25	.12	.02
		Charlie Brinkman			
		Dick Moloney			
☐	14	Dave Concepcion	4.00	2.00	.40
☐	15	Andy Messersmith	.35	.17	.03
☐	16	Ken Singleton	1.50	.75	.15
☐	17	Billy Sorrell	.25	.12	.02
☐	18	Norm Miller	.25	.12	.02
☐	19	Skip Pitlock	.25	.12	.02
☐	20	Reggie Jackson	20.00	10.00	2.00
☐	21	Dan McGinn	.25	.12	.02
☐	22	Phil Roof	.25	.12	.02
☐	23	Oscar Gamble	.50	.25	.05
☐	24	Rich Hand	.25	.12	.02
☐	25	Clarence Gaston	.35	.17	.03
☐	26	Bert Blyleven	8.00	4.00	.80
☐	27	Pirates Rookies	.25	.12	.02
		Fred Cambria			
		Gene Clines			
☐	28	Ron Klimkowski	.25	.12	.02
☐	29	Don Buford	.25	.12	.02
☐	30	Phil Niekro	3.00	1.50	.30
☐	31	Eddie Kasko MG	.25	.12	.02
☐	32	Jerry DaVanon	.25	.12	.02
☐	33	Del Unser	.25	.12	.02
☐	34	Sandy Vance	.25	.12	.02
☐	35	Lou Piniella	.75	.35	.07
☐	36	Dean Chance	.35	.17	.03
☐	37	Rich McKinney	.25	.12	.02
☐	38	Jim Colborn	.25	.12	.02
☐	39	Tiger Rookies	.25	.12	.02
		Lerrin LaGrow			

		Gene Lamont			
☐	40	Lee May	.35	.17	.03
☐	41	Rick Austin	.25	.12	.02
☐	42	Boots Day	.25	.12	.02
☐	43	Steve Kealey	.25	.12	.02
☐	44	Johnny Edwards	.25	.12	.02
☐	45	Jim Hunter	3.00	1.50	.30
☐	46	Dave Campbell	.25	.12	.02
☐	47	Johnny Jeter	.25	.12	.02
☐	48	Dave Baldwin	.25	.12	.02
☐	49	Don Money	.35	.17	.03
☐	50	Willie McCovey	4.00	2.00	.40
☐	51	Steve Kline	.25	.12	.02
☐	52	Braves Rookies	.50	.25	.05
		Oscar Brown			
		Earl Williams			
☐	53	Paul Blair	.35	.17	.03
☐	54	Checklist 1	1.50	.20	.04
☐	55	Steve Carlton	11.00	5.50	1.10
☐	56	Duane Josephson	.25	.12	.02
☐	57	Von Joshua	.25	.12	.02
☐	58	Bill Lee	.35	.17	.03
☐	59	Gene Mauch MG	.35	.17	.03
☐	60	Dick Bosman	.25	.12	.02
☐	61	AL Batting Leaders	1.25	.60	.12
		Alex Johnson			
		Carl Yastrzemski			
		Tony Oliva			
☐	62	NL Batting Leaders	.75	.35	.07
		Rico Carty			
		Joe Torre			
		Manny Sanguillen			
☐	63	AL RBI Leaders	1.00	.50	.10
		Frank Robinson			
		Tony Conigliaro			
		Boog Powell			
☐	64	NL RBI Leaders	1.25	.60	.12
		Johnny Bench			
		Tony Perez			
		Billy Williams			
☐	65	AL HR Leaders	1.25	.60	.12
		Frank Howard			
		Harmon Killebrew			
		Carl Yastrzemski			
☐	66	NL HR Leaders	1.25	.60	.12
		Johnny Bench			
		Billy Williams			
		Tony Perez			
☐	67	AL ERA Leaders	.75	.35	.07
		Diego Segui			
		Jim Palmer			
		Clyde Wright			
☐	68	NL ERA Leaders	1.00	.50	.10
		Tom Seaver			
		Wayne Simpson			
		Luke Walker			
☐	69	AL Pitching Leaders	.75	.35	.07
		Mike Cuellar			
		Dave McNally			
		Jim Perry			
☐	70	NL Pitching Leaders	1.50	.75	.15
		Bob Gibson			
		Gaylord Perry			
		Fergie Jenkins			
☐	71	AL Strikeout Leaders	.75	.35	.07
		Sam McDowell			
		Mickey Lolich			
		Bob Johnson			
☐	72	NL Strikeout Leaders	1.50	.75	.15
		Tom Seaver			
		Bob Gibson			
		Fergie Jenkins			
☐	73	George Brunet	.25	.12	.02
☐	74	Twins Rookies	.25	.12	.02
		Pete Hamm			
		Jim Nettles			
☐	75	Gary Nolan	.25	.12	.02
☐	76	Ted Savage	.25	.12	.02
☐	77	Mike Compton	.25	.12	.02
☐	78	Jim Spencer	.25	.12	.02
☐	79	Wade Blasingame	.25	.12	.02
☐	80	Bill Melton	.25	.12	.02
☐	81	Felix Millan	.25	.12	.02
☐	82	Casey Cox	.25	.12	.02
☐	83	Met Rookies	.35	.17	.03
		Tim Foli			
		Randy Bobb			
☐	84	Marcel Lachemann	.25	.12	.02
☐	85	Bill Grabarkewitz	.25	.12	.02
☐	86	Mike Kilkenny	.25	.12	.02
☐	87	Jack Heidemann	.25	.12	.02
☐	88	Hal King	.25	.12	.02
☐	89	Ken Brett	.35	.17	.03
☐	90	Joe Pepitone	.50	.25	.05
☐	91	Bob Lemon MG	1.00	.50	.10

☐ 92	Fred Wenz	.25	.12	.02
☐ 93	Senators Rookies	.25	.12	.02
	Norm McRae			
	Denny Riddleberger			
☐ 94	Don Hahn	.25	.12	.02
☐ 95	Luis Tiant	.75	.35	.07
☐ 96	Joe Hague	.25	.12	.02
☐ 97	Floyd Wicker	.25	.12	.02
☐ 98	Joe Decker	.25	.12	.02
☐ 99	Mark Belanger	.50	.25	.05
☐ 100	Pete Rose	45.00	22.50	4.50
☐ 101	Les Cain	.25	.12	.02
☐ 102	Astros Rookies	.75	.35	.07
	Ken Forsch			
	Larry Howard			
☐ 103	Rich Severinson	.25	.12	.02
☐ 104	Dan Frisella	.25	.12	.02
☐ 105	Tony Conigliaro	.75	.35	.07
☐ 106	Tom Dukes	.25	.12	.02
☐ 107	Roy Foster	.25	.12	.02
☐ 108	John Cumberland	.25	.12	.02
☐ 109	Steve Hovley	.25	.12	.02
☐ 110	Bill Mazeroski	.60	.30	.06
☐ 111	Yankee Rookies	.25	.12	.02
	Loyd Colson			
	Bobby Mitchell			
☐ 112	Manny Mota	.35	.17	.03
☐ 113	Jerry Crider	.25	.12	.02
☐ 114	Billy Conigliaro	.35	.17	.03
☐ 115	Donn Clendenon	.35	.17	.03
☐ 116	Ken Sanders	.25	.12	.02
☐ 117	Ted Simmons	5.00	2.50	.50
☐ 118	Cookie Rojas	.25	.12	.02
☐ 119	Frank Lucchesi MG	.25	.12	.02
☐ 120	Willie Horton	.35	.17	.03
☐ 121	Cubs Rookies	.25	.12	.02
	Jim Dunegan			
	Roe Skidmore			
☐ 122	Eddie Watt	.25	.12	.02
☐ 123A	Checklist 2	1.50	.20	.04
	(card number			
	at bottom right)			
☐ 123B	Checklist 2	2.00	.30	.06
	(card number			
	centered)			
☐ 124	Don Gullett	.35	.17	.03
☐ 125	Ray Fosse	.25	.12	.02
☐ 126	Danny Coombs	.25	.12	.02
☐ 127	Danny Thompson	.25	.12	.02
☐ 128	Frank Johnson	.25	.12	.02
☐ 129	Aurelio Monteagudo	.25	.12	.02
☐ 130	Denis Menke	.25	.12	.02
☐ 131	Curt Blefary	.25	.12	.02
☐ 132	Jose Laboy	.25	.12	.02
☐ 133	Mickey Lolich	.75	.35	.07
☐ 134	Jose Arcia	.25	.12	.02
☐ 135	Rick Monday	.50	.25	.05
☐ 136	Duffy Dyer	.25	.12	.02
☐ 137	Marcelino Lopez	.25	.12	.02
☐ 138	Phillies Rookies	.35	.17	.03
	Joe Lis			
	Willie Montanez			
☐ 139	Paul Casanova	.25	.12	.02
☐ 140	Gaylord Perry	3.50	1.75	.35
☐ 141	Frank Quilici MG	.25	.12	.02
☐ 142	Mack Jones	.25	.12	.02
☐ 143	Steve Blass	.35	.17	.03
☐ 144	Jackie Hernandez	.25	.12	.02
☐ 145	Bill Singer	.35	.17	.03
☐ 146	Ralph Houk MG	.35	.17	.03
☐ 147	Bob Priddy	.25	.12	.02
☐ 148	John Mayberry	.35	.17	.03
☐ 149	Mike Hershberger	.25	.12	.02
☐ 150	Sam McDowell	.50	.25	.05
☐ 151	Tommy Davis	.50	.25	.05
☐ 152	Angels Rookies	.25	.12	.02
	Lloyd Allen			
	Winston Llenas			
☐ 153	Gary Ross	.25	.12	.02
☐ 154	Cesar Gutierrez	.25	.12	.02
☐ 155	Ken Henderson	.25	.12	.02
☐ 156	Bart Johnson	.25	.12	.02
☐ 157	Bob Bailey	.25	.12	.02
☐ 158	Jerry Reuss	.60	.30	.06
☐ 159	Jarvis Tatum	.25	.12	.02
☐ 160	Tom Seaver	13.50	6.00	1.00
☐ 161	Coin Checklist	1.50	.20	.04
☐ 162	Jack Billingham	.25	.12	.02
☐ 163	Buck Martinez	.25	.12	.02
☐ 164	Reds Rookies	.50	.25	.05
	Frank Duffy			
	Milt Wilcox			
☐ 165	Cesar Tovar	.25	.12	.02
☐ 166	Joe Hoerner	.25	.12	.02
☐ 167	Tom Grieve	.60	.30	.06
☐ 168	Bruce Dal Canton	.25	.12	.02
☐ 169	Ed Herrmann	.25	.12	.02
☐ 170	Mike Cuellar	.35	.17	.03
☐ 171	Bobby Wine	.25	.12	.02
☐ 172	Duke Sims	.25	.12	.02
☐ 173	Gil Garrido	.25	.12	.02
☐ 174	Dave LaRoche	.25	.12	.02
☐ 175	Jim Hickman	.25	.12	.02
☐ 176	Red Sox Rookies	.25	.12	.02
	Bob Montgomery			
	Doug Griffin			
☐ 177	Hal McRae	.50	.25	.05
☐ 178	Dave Duncan	.25	.12	.02
☐ 179	Mike Corkins	.25	.12	.02
☐ 180	Al Kaline	5.00	2.50	.50
☐ 181	Hal Lanier	.50	.25	.05
☐ 182	Al Downing	.35	.17	.03
☐ 183	Gil Hodges MG	2.50	1.25	.25
☐ 184	Stan Bahnsen	.25	.12	.02
☐ 185	Julian Javier	.25	.12	.02
☐ 186	Bob Spence	.25	.12	.02
☐ 187	Ted Abernathy	.25	.12	.02
☐ 188	Dodgers Rookies	1.75	.85	.17
	Bob Valentine			
	Mike Strahler			
☐ 189	George Mitterwald	.25	.12	.02
☐ 190	Bob Tolan	.35	.17	.03
☐ 191	Mike Andrews	.25	.12	.02
☐ 192	Billy Wilson	.25	.12	.02
☐ 193	Bob Grich	1.50	.75	.15
☐ 194	Mike Lum	.25	.12	.02
☐ 195	AL Playoff Game 1	1.00	.50	.10
	Powell muscles Twins			
☐ 196	AL Playoff Game 2	1.00	.50	.10
	McNally makes it			
	two straight			
☐ 197	AL Playoff Game 3	1.50	.75	.15
	Palmer mows'em down			
☐ 198	AL Playoff Summary	1.00	.50	.10
	Orioles celebrate			
☐ 199	NL Playoff Game 1	1.00	.50	.10
	Cline pinch-triple			
	decides it			
☐ 200	NL Playoff Game 2	1.00	.50	.10
	Tolan scores for			
	third time			
☐ 201	NL Playoff Game 3	1.00	.50	.10
	Cline scores			
	winning run			
☐ 202	NL Playoff Summary	1.00	.50	.10
	Reds celebrate			
☐ 203	Larry Gura	.75	.35	.07
☐ 204	Brewers Rookies	.25	.12	.02
	Bernie Smith			
	George Kopacz			
☐ 205	Gerry Moses	.25	.12	.02
☐ 206	Checklist 3	1.50	.20	.04
☐ 207	Alan Foster	.25	.12	.02
☐ 208	Billy Martin MG	1.50	.75	.15
☐ 209	Steve Renko	.25	.12	.02
☐ 210	Rod Carew	12.00	6.00	1.20
☐ 211	Phil Hennigan	.25	.12	.02
☐ 212	Rich Hebner	.35	.17	.03
☐ 213	Frank Baker	.25	.12	.02
☐ 214	Al Ferrara	.25	.12	.02
☐ 215	Diego Segui	.25	.12	.02
☐ 216	Cards Rookies	.25	.12	.02
	Reggie Cleveland			
	Luis Melendez			
☐ 217	Ed Stroud	.25	.12	.02
☐ 218	Tony Cloninger	.25	.12	.02
☐ 219	Elrod Hendricks	.25	.12	.02
☐ 220	Ron Santo	.75	.35	.07
☐ 221	Dave Morehead	.25	.12	.02
☐ 222	Bob Watson	.50	.25	.05
☐ 223	Cecil Upshaw	.25	.12	.02
☐ 224	Alan Gallagher	.25	.12	.02
☐ 225	Gary Peters	.35	.17	.03
☐ 226	Bill Russell	.50	.25	.05
☐ 227	Floyd Weaver	.25	.12	.02
☐ 228	Wayne Garrett	.25	.12	.02
☐ 229	Jim Hannan	.25	.12	.02
☐ 230	Willie Stargell	4.00	2.00	.40
☐ 231	Indians Rookies	.35	.17	.03
	Vince Colbert			
	John Lowenstein			
☐ 232	John Strohmayer	.25	.12	.02
☐ 233	Larry Bowa	1.50	.75	.15
☐ 234	Jim Lyttle	.25	.12	.02
☐ 235	Nate Colbert	.25	.12	.02
☐ 236	Bob Humphreys	.25	.12	.02
☐ 237	Cesar Cedeno	1.25	.60	.12
☐ 238	Chuck Dobson	.25	.12	.02
☐ 239	Red Schoendienst MG	.50	.25	.05
☐ 240	Clyde Wright	.25	.12	.02

☐ 241	Dave Nelson	.25	.12	.02
☐ 242	Jim Ray	.25	.12	.02
☐ 243	Carlos May	.35	.17	.03
☐ 244	Bob Tillman	.25	.12	.02
☐ 245	Jim Kaat	1.50	.75	.15
☐ 246	Tony Taylor	.25	.12	.02
☐ 247	Royals Rookies	.50	.25	.05
	Jerry Cram			
	Paul Splittorff			
☐ 248	Hoyt Wilhelm	3.00	1.50	.30
☐ 249	Chico Salmon	.25	.12	.02
☐ 250	Johnny Bench	15.00	7.50	1.50
☐ 251	Frank Reberger	.25	.12	.02
☐ 252	Eddie Leon	.25	.12	.02
☐ 253	Bill Sudakis	.25	.12	.02
☐ 254	Cal Koonce	.25	.12	.02
☐ 255	Bob Robertson	.25	.12	.02
☐ 256	Tony Gonzalez	.25	.12	.02
☐ 257	Nelson Briles	.35	.17	.03
☐ 258	Dick Green	.25	.12	.02
☐ 259	Dave Marshall	.25	.12	.02
☐ 260	Tommy Harper	.35	.17	.03
☐ 261	Darold Knowles	.25	.12	.02
☐ 262	Padres Rookies	.25	.12	.02
	Jim Williams			
	Dave Robinson			
☐ 263	John Ellis	.25	.12	.02
☐ 264	Joe Morgan	2.50	1.25	.25
☐ 265	Jim Northrup	.40	.20	.04
☐ 266	Bill Stoneman	.30	.15	.03
☐ 267	Rich Morales	.30	.15	.03
☐ 268	Phillies Team	.65	.30	.06
☐ 269	Gail Hopkins	.30	.15	.03
☐ 270	Rico Carty	.50	.25	.05
☐ 271	Bill Zepp	.30	.15	.03
☐ 272	Tommy Helms	.40	.20	.04
☐ 273	Pete Richert	.30	.15	.03
☐ 274	Ron Slocum	.30	.15	.03
☐ 275	Vada Pinson	.75	.35	.07
☐ 276	Giants Rookies	4.50	2.25	.45
	Mike Davison			
	George Foster			
☐ 277	Gary Waslewski	.30	.15	.03
☐ 278	Jerry Grote	.30	.15	.03
☐ 279	Lefty Phillips MG	.30	.15	.03
☐ 280	Fergie Jenkins	2.00	1.00	.20
☐ 281	Danny Walton	.30	.15	.03
☐ 282	Jose Pagan	.30	.15	.03
☐ 283	Dick Such	.30	.15	.03
☐ 284	Jim Gosger	.30	.15	.03
☐ 285	Sal Bando	.50	.25	.05
☐ 286	Jerry McNertney	.30	.15	.03
☐ 287	Mike Fiore	.30	.15	.03
☐ 288	Joe Moeller	.30	.15	.03
☐ 289	White Sox Team	.65	.30	.06
☐ 290	Tony Oliva	1.50	.75	.15
☐ 291	George Culver	.30	.15	.03
☐ 292	Jay Johnstone	.50	.25	.05
☐ 293	Pat Corrales	.40	.20	.04
☐ 294	Steve Dunning	.30	.15	.03
☐ 295	Bobby Bonds	1.25	.60	.12
☐ 296	Tom Timmermann	.30	.15	.03
☐ 297	Johnny Briggs	.30	.15	.03
☐ 298	Jim Nelson	.30	.15	.03
☐ 299	Ed Kirkpatrick	.30	.15	.03
☐ 300	Brooks Robinson	6.00	3.00	.60
☐ 301	Earl Wilson	.30	.15	.03
☐ 302	Phil Gagliano	.30	.15	.03
☐ 303	Lindy McDaniel	.40	.20	.04
☐ 304	Ron Brand	.30	.15	.03
☐ 305	Reggie Smith	.75	.35	.07
☐ 306	Jim Nash	.30	.15	.03
☐ 307	Don Wert	.30	.15	.03
☐ 308	Cardinals Team	.65	.30	.06
☐ 309	Dick Ellsworth	.40	.20	.04
☐ 310	Tommie Agee	.40	.20	.04
☐ 311	Lee Stange	.30	.15	.03
☐ 312	Harry Walker MG	.30	.15	.03
☐ 313	Tom Hall	.30	.15	.03
☐ 314	Jeff Torborg	.40	.20	.04
☐ 315	Ron Fairly	.40	.20	.04
☐ 316	Fred Scherman	.30	.15	.03
☐ 317	Athletic Rookies	.30	.15	.03
	Jim Driscoll			
	Angel Mangual			
☐ 318	Rudy May	.30	.15	.03
☐ 319	Ty Cline	.30	.15	.03
☐ 320	Dave McNally	.50	.25	.05
☐ 321	Tom Matchick	.30	.15	.03
☐ 322	Jim Beauchamp	.30	.15	.03
☐ 323	Billy Champion	.30	.15	.03
☐ 324	Graig Nettles	2.00	1.00	.20
☐ 325	Juan Marichal	3.50	1.75	.35
☐ 326	Richie Scheinblum	.30	.15	.03
☐ 327	World Series Game 1	1.00	.50	.10

	Powell homers to			
	opposite field			
☐ 328	World Series Game 2	1.00	.50	.10
	Don Buford			
☐ 329	World Series Game 3	1.75	.85	.17
	Frank Robinson			
	shows muscle			
☐ 330	World Series Game 4	1.00	.50	.10
	Reds stay alive			
☐ 331	World Series Game 5	1.75	.85	.17
	Brooks Robinson			
	commits robbery			
☐ 332	World Series Summary	1.00	.50	.10
	Orioles celebrate			
☐ 333	Clay Kirby	.30	.15	.03
☐ 334	Roberto Pena	.30	.15	.03
☐ 335	Jerry Koosman	.75	.35	.07
☐ 336	Tigers Team	.75	.35	.07
☐ 337	Jesus Alou	.30	.15	.03
☐ 338	Gene Tenace	.40	.20	.04
☐ 339	Wayne Simpson	.30	.15	.03
☐ 340	Rico Petrocelli	.40	.20	.04
☐ 341	Steve Garvey	65.00	32.50	6.50
☐ 342	Frank Tepedino	.30	.15	.03
☐ 343	Pirates Rookies	.30	.15	.03
	Ed Acosta			
	Milt May			
☐ 344	Ellie Rodriguez	.30	.15	.03
☐ 345	Joe Horlen	.40	.20	.04
☐ 346	Lum Harris MG	.30	.15	.03
☐ 347	Ted Uhlaender	.30	.15	.03
☐ 348	Fred Norman	.30	.15	.03
☐ 349	Rich Reese	.30	.15	.03
☐ 350	Billy Williams	3.50	1.75	.35
☐ 351	Jim Shellenback	.30	.15	.03
☐ 352	Denny Doyle	.30	.15	.03
☐ 353	Carl Taylor	.30	.15	.03
☐ 354	Don McMahon	.30	.15	.03
☐ 355	Bud Harrelson	.40	.20	.04
☐ 356	Bob Locker	.30	.15	.03
☐ 357	Reds Team	.90	.45	.09
☐ 358	Danny Cater	.30	.15	.03
☐ 359	Ron Reed	.30	.15	.03
☐ 360	Jim Fregosi	.60	.30	.06
☐ 361	Don Sutton	3.00	1.50	.30
☐ 362	Orioles Rookies	.30	.15	.03
	Mike Adamson			
	Roger Freed			
☐ 363	Mike Nagy	.30	.15	.03
☐ 364	Tommy Dean	.30	.15	.03
☐ 365	Bob Johnson	.30	.15	.03
☐ 366	Ron Stone	.30	.15	.03
☐ 367	Dalton Jones	.30	.15	.03
☐ 368	Bob Veale	.40	.20	.04
☐ 369	Checklist 4	1.50	.20	.04
☐ 370	Joe Torre	1.50	.75	.15
☐ 371	Jack Hiatt	.30	.15	.03
☐ 372	Lew Krausse	.30	.15	.03
☐ 373	Tom McCraw	.30	.15	.03
☐ 374	Clete Boyer	.50	.25	.05
☐ 375	Steve Hargan	.30	.15	.03
☐ 376	Expos Rookies	.30	.15	.03
	Clyde Mashore			
	Ernie McAnally			
☐ 377	Greg Garrett	.30	.15	.03
☐ 378	Tito Fuentes	.30	.15	.03
☐ 379	Wayne Granger	.30	.15	.03
☐ 380	Ted Williams MG	3.50	1.75	.35
☐ 381	Fred Gladding	.30	.15	.03
☐ 382	Jake Gibbs	.30	.15	.03
☐ 383	Rod Gaspar	.30	.15	.03
☐ 384	Rollie Fingers	2.50	1.25	.25
☐ 385	Maury Wills	1.25	.60	.12
☐ 386	Red Sox Team	.85	.40	.08
☐ 387	Ron Herbel	.30	.15	.03
☐ 388	Al Oliver	1.75	.85	.17
☐ 389	Ed Brinkman	.30	.15	.03
☐ 390	Glenn Beckert	.40	.20	.04
☐ 391	Twins Rookies	.40	.20	.04
	Steve Brye			
	Cotton Nash			
☐ 392	Grant Jackson	.30	.15	.03
☐ 393	Merv Rettenmund	.30	.15	.03
☐ 394	Clay Carroll	.30	.15	.03
☐ 395	Roy White	.40	.20	.04
☐ 396	Dick Schofield	.30	.15	.03
☐ 397	Alvin Dark MG	.40	.20	.04
☐ 398	Howie Reed	.30	.15	.03
☐ 399	Jim French	.30	.15	.03
☐ 400	Hank Aaron	15.00	7.50	1.50
☐ 401	Tom Murphy	.30	.15	.03
☐ 402	Dodgers Team	.90	.45	.09
☐ 403	Joe Coleman	.30	.15	.03
☐ 404	Astros Rookies	.30	.15	.03
	Buddy Harris			

	Roger Metzger			
☐ 405	Leo Cardenas	.30	.15	.03
☐ 406	Ray Sadecki	.30	.15	.03
☐ 407	Joe Rudi	.50	.25	.05
☐ 408	Rafael Robles	.30	.15	.03
☐ 409	Don Pavletich	.30	.15	.03
☐ 410	Ken Holtzman	.50	.25	.05
☐ 411	George Spriggs	.30	.15	.03
☐ 412	Jerry Johnson	.30	.15	.03
☐ 413	Pat Kelly	.30	.15	.03
☐ 414	Woodie Fryman	.30	.15	.03
☐ 415	Mike Hegan	.30	.15	.03
☐ 416	Gene Alley	.40	.20	.04
☐ 417	Dick Hall	.30	.15	.03
☐ 418	Adolfo Phillips	.30	.15	.03
☐ 419	Ron Hansen	.30	.15	.03
☐ 420	Jim Merritt	.30	.15	.03
☐ 421	John Stephenson	.30	.15	.03
☐ 422	Frank Bertaina	.30	.15	.03
☐ 423	Tigers Rookies	.30	.15	.03
	Dennis Saunders			
	Tim Marting			
☐ 424	R. Rodriquez	.30	.15	.03
☐ 425	Doug Rader	.40	.20	.04
☐ 426	Chris Cannizzaro	.30	.15	.03
☐ 427	Bernie Allen	.30	.15	.03
☐ 428	Jim McAndrew	.30	.15	.03
☐ 429	Chuck Hinton	.30	.15	.03
☐ 430	Wes Parker	.40	.20	.04
☐ 431	Tom Burgmeier	.30	.15	.03
☐ 432	Bob Didier	.30	.15	.03
☐ 433	Skip Lockwood	.30	.15	.03
☐ 434	Gary Sutherland	.30	.15	.03
☐ 435	Jose Cardenal	.30	.15	.03
☐ 436	Wilbur Wood	.40	.20	.04
☐ 437	Danny Murtaugh MG	.30	.15	.03
☐ 438	Mike McCormick	.40	.20	.04
☐ 439	Phillies Rookies	1.75	.85	.17
	Greg Luzinski			
	Scott Reid			
☐ 440	Bert Campaneris	.50	.25	.05
☐ 441	Milt Pappas	.40	.20	.04
☐ 442	Angels Team	.65	.30	.06
☐ 443	Rich Robertson	.30	.15	.03
☐ 444	Jimmie Price	.30	.15	.03
☐ 445	Art Shamsky	.30	.15	.03
☐ 446	Bobby Bolin	.30	.15	.03
☐ 447	Cesar Geronimo	.30	.15	.03
☐ 448	Dave Roberts	.30	.15	.03
☐ 449	Brant Alyea	.30	.15	.03
☐ 450	Bob Gibson	4.50	2.25	.45
☐ 451	Joe Keough	.30	.15	.03
☐ 452	John Boccabella	.30	.15	.03
☐ 453	Terry Crowley	.30	.15	.03
☐ 454	Mike Paul	.30	.15	.03
☐ 455	Don Kessinger	.40	.20	.04
☐ 456	Bob Meyer	.30	.15	.03
☐ 457	Willie Smith	.30	.15	.03
☐ 458	White Sox Rookies	.30	.15	.03
	Ron Lolich			
	Dave Lemonds			
☐ 459	Jim Lefebvre	.30	.15	.03
☐ 460	Fritz Peterson	.30	.15	.03
☐ 461	Jim Ray Hart	.40	.20	.04
☐ 462	Senators Team	.65	.30	.06
☐ 463	Tom Kelley	.30	.15	.03
☐ 464	Aurelio Rodriguez	.30	.15	.03
☐ 465	Tim McCarver	.60	.30	.06
☐ 466	Ken Berry	.30	.15	.03
☐ 467	Al Santorini	.30	.15	.03
☐ 468	Frank Fernandez	.30	.15	.03
☐ 469	Bob Aspromonte	.30	.15	.03
☐ 470	Bob Oliver	.30	.15	.03
☐ 471	Tom Griffin	.30	.15	.03
☐ 472	Ken Rudolph	.30	.15	.03
☐ 473	Gary Wagner	.30	.15	.03
☐ 474	Jim Fairey	.30	.15	.03
☐ 475	Ron Perranoski	.40	.20	.04
☐ 476	Dal Maxvill	.40	.20	.04
☐ 477	Earl Weaver MG	.85	.40	.08
☐ 478	Bernie Carbo	.30	.15	.03
☐ 479	Dennis Higgins	.30	.15	.03
☐ 480	Manny Sanguillen	.50	.25	.05
☐ 481	Daryl Patterson	.30	.15	.03
☐ 482	Padres Team	.65	.30	.06
☐ 483	Gene Michael	.40	.20	.04
☐ 484	Don Wilson	.30	.15	.03
☐ 485	Ken McMullen	.30	.15	.03
☐ 486	Steve Huntz	.30	.15	.03
☐ 487	Paul Schaal	.30	.15	.03
☐ 488	Jerry Stephenson	.30	.15	.03
☐ 489	Luis Alvarado	.30	.15	.03
☐ 490	Deron Johnson	.30	.15	.03
☐ 491	Jim Hardin	.30	.15	.03
☐ 492	Ken Boswell	.30	.15	.03

☐ 493	Dave May	.30	.15	.03
☐ 494	Braves Rookies	.40	.20	.04
	Ralph Garr			
	Rick Kester			
☐ 495	Felipe Alou	.50	.25	.05
☐ 496	Woody Woodward	.40	.20	.04
☐ 497	Horacio Pina	.30	.15	.03
☐ 498	John Kennedy	.30	.15	.03
☐ 499	Checklist 5	1.50	.20	.04
☐ 500	Jim Perry	.60	.30	.06
☐ 501	Andy Etchebarren	.30	.15	.03
☐ 502	Cubs Team	.65	.30	.06
☐ 503	Gates Brown	.40	.20	.04
☐ 504	Ken Wright	.30	.15	.03
☐ 505	Ollie Brown	.30	.15	.03
☐ 506	Bobby Knoop	.30	.15	.03
☐ 507	George Stone	.30	.15	.03
☐ 508	Roger Repoz	.30	.15	.03
☐ 509	Jim Grant	.30	.15	.03
☐ 510	Ken Harrelson	.75	.35	.07
☐ 511	Chris Short	.30	.15	.03
☐ 512	Red Sox Rookies	.30	.15	.03
	Dick Mills			
	Mike Garman			
☐ 513	Nolan Ryan	16.00	8.00	1.60
☐ 514	Ron Woods	.30	.15	.03
☐ 515	Carl Morton	.30	.15	.03
☐ 516	Ted Kubiak	.30	.15	.03
☐ 517	Charlie Fox MG	.30	.15	.03
☐ 518	Joe Grzenda	.30	.15	.03
☐ 519	Willie Crawford	.30	.15	.03
☐ 520	Tommy John	2.00	1.00	.20
☐ 521	Leron Lee	.40	.20	.04
☐ 522	Twins Team	.65	.30	.06
☐ 523	John Odom	.30	.15	.03
☐ 524	Mickey Stanley	.90	.45	.09
☐ 525	Ernie Banks	9.00	4.50	.90
☐ 526	Ray Jarvis	.75	.35	.07
☐ 527	Cleon Jones	.75	.35	.07
☐ 528	Wally Bunker	.75	.35	.07
☐ 529	NL Rookie Infielders	3.00	1.50	.30
	Enzo Hernandez			
	Bill Buckner			
	Marty Perez			
☐ 530	Carl Yastrzemski	25.00	12.50	2.50
☐ 531	Mike Torrez	.90	.45	.09
☐ 532	Bill Rigney MG	.75	.35	.07
☐ 533	Mike Ryan	.75	.35	.07
☐ 534	Luke Walker	.75	.35	.07
☐ 535	Curt Flood	1.00	.50	.10
☐ 536	Claude Raymond	.75	.35	.07
☐ 537	Tom Egan	.75	.35	.07
☐ 538	Angel Bravo	.75	.35	.07
☐ 539	Larry Brown	.75	.35	.07
☐ 540	Larry Dierker	.90	.45	.09
☐ 541	Bob Burda	.75	.35	.07
☐ 542	Bob Miller	.75	.35	.07
☐ 543	Yankees Team	1.75	.85	.17
☐ 544	Vida Blue	2.50	1.25	.25
☐ 545	Dick Dietz	.75	.35	.07
☐ 546	John Matias	.75	.35	.07
☐ 547	Pat Dobson	.90	.45	.09
☐ 548	Don Mason	.75	.35	.07
☐ 549	Jim Brewer	.75	.35	.07
☐ 550	Harmon Killebrew	8.00	4.00	.80
☐ 551	Frank Linzy	.75	.35	.07
☐ 552	Buddy Bradford	.75	.35	.07
☐ 553	Kevin Collins	.75	.35	.07
☐ 554	Lowell Palmer	.75	.35	.07
☐ 555	Walt Williams	.75	.35	.07
☐ 556	Jim McGlothlin	.75	.35	.07
☐ 557	Tom Satriano	.75	.35	.07
☐ 558	Hector Torres	.75	.35	.07
☐ 559	AL Rookie Pitchers	.75	.35	.07
	Terry Cox			
	Bill Gogolewski			
	Gary Jones			
☐ 560	Rusty Staub	1.50	.75	.15
☐ 561	Syd O'Brien	.75	.35	.07
☐ 562	Dave Giusti	.75	.35	.07
☐ 563	Giants Team	1.50	.75	.15
☐ 564	Al Fitzmorris	.75	.35	.07
☐ 565	Jim Wynn	1.00	.50	.10
☐ 566	Tim Cullen	.75	.35	.07
☐ 567	Walt Alston MG	2.00	1.00	.20
☐ 568	Sal Campisi	.75	.35	.07
☐ 569	Ivan Murrell	.75	.35	.07
☐ 570	Jim Palmer	8.00	4.00	.80
☐ 571	Ted Sizemore	.90	.45	.09
☐ 572	Jerry Kenney	.75	.35	.07
☐ 573	Ed Kranepool	.90	.45	.09
☐ 574	Jim Bunning	1.75	.85	.17
☐ 575	Bill Freehan	1.25	.60	.12
☐ 576	Cubs Rookies	.75	.35	.07
	Adrian Garrett			

	Brock Davis			
	Garry Jestadt			
☐ 577	Jim Lonborg	1.00	.50	.10
☐ 578	Ron Hunt	.75	.35	.07
☐ 579	Marty Pattin	.75	.35	.07
☐ 580	Tony Perez	2.00	1.00	.20
☐ 581	Roger Nelson	.75	.35	.07
☐ 582	Dave Cash	.90	.45	.09
☐ 583	Ron Cook	.75	.35	.07
☐ 584	Indians Team	1.50	.75	.15
☐ 585	Willie Davis	1.00	.50	.10
☐ 586	Dick Woodson	.75	.35	.07
☐ 587	Sonny Jackson	.75	.35	.07
☐ 588	Tom Bradley	.75	.35	.07
☐ 589	Bob Barton	.75	.35	.07
☐ 590	Alex Johnson	.90	.45	.09
☐ 591	Jackie Brown	.90	.45	.09
☐ 592	Randy Hundley	.90	.45	.09
☐ 593	Jack Aker	.75	.35	.07
☐ 594	Cards Rookies	1.25	.60	.12
	Bob Chlupsa			
	Bob Stinson			
	Al Hrabosky			
☐ 595	Dave Johnson	1.75	.85	.17
☐ 596	Mike Jorgensen	.75	.35	.07
☐ 597	Ken Suarez	.75	.35	.07
☐ 598	Rick Wise	.90	.45	.09
☐ 599	Norm Cash	1.25	.60	.12
☐ 600	Willie Mays	25.00	12.50	2.50
☐ 601	Ken Tatum	.75	.35	.07
☐ 602	Marty Martinez	.75	.35	.07
☐ 603	Pirates Team	1.50	.75	.15
☐ 604	John Gelnar	.75	.35	.07
☐ 605	Orlando Cepeda	2.25	1.10	.22
☐ 606	Chuck Taylor	.75	.35	.07
☐ 607	Paul Ratliff	.75	.35	.07
☐ 608	Mike Wegener	.75	.35	.07
☐ 609	Leo Durocher MG	1.25	.60	.12
☐ 610	Amos Otis	1.00	.50	.10
☐ 611	Tom Phoebus	.75	.35	.07
☐ 612	Indians Rookies	.75	.35	.07
	Lou Camilli			
	Ted Ford			
	Steve Mingori			
☐ 613	Pedro Borbon	.75	.35	.07
☐ 614	Billy Cowan	.75	.35	.07
☐ 615	Mel Stottlemyre	1.25	.60	.12
☐ 616	Larry Hisle	.90	.45	.09
☐ 617	Clay Dalrymple	.75	.35	.07
☐ 618	Tug McGraw	1.25	.60	.12
☐ 619A	Checklist 6	2.00	.30	.05
	(copyright on back)			
☐ 619B	Checklist 6	3.00	.40	.08
	(no copyright)			
☐ 620	Frank Howard	1.25	.60	.12
☐ 621	Ron Bryant	.75	.35	.07
☐ 622	Joe Lahoud	.75	.35	.07
☐ 623	Pat Jarvis	.75	.35	.07
☐ 624	Athletics Team	1.50	.75	.15
☐ 625	Lou Brock	9.00	4.50	.90
☐ 626	Freddie Patek	.90	.45	.09
☐ 627	Steve Hamilton	.75	.35	.07
☐ 628	John Bateman	.75	.35	.07
☐ 629	John Hiller	.90	.45	.09
☐ 630	Roberto Clemente	20.00	10.00	2.00
☐ 631	Eddie Fisher	.75	.35	.07
☐ 632	Darrel Chaney	.75	.35	.07
☐ 633	AL Rookie Outfielders	.75	.35	.07
	Bobby Brooks			
	Pete Koegel			
	Scott Northey			
☐ 634	Phil Regan	.90	.45	.09
☐ 635	Bobby Murcer	1.50	.75	.15
☐ 636	Denny Lemaster	.75	.35	.07
☐ 637	Dave Bristol MG	.75	.35	.07
☐ 638	Stan Williams	.75	.35	.07
☐ 639	Tom Haller	.90	.45	.09
☐ 640	Frank Robinson	11.00	5.50	1.10
☐ 641	Mets Team	2.50	1.25	.25
☐ 642	Jim Roland	.75	.35	.07
☐ 643	Rick Reichardt	.75	.35	.07
☐ 644	Jim Stewart	1.50	.75	.15
☐ 645	Jim Maloney	2.00	1.00	.20
☐ 646	Bobby Floyd	1.50	.75	.15
☐ 647	Juan Pizarro	1.50	.75	.15
☐ 648	Mets Rookies	3.50	1.75	.35
	Rich Folkers			
	Ted Martinez			
	John Matlack			
☐ 649	Sparky Lyle	2.50	1.25	.25
☐ 650	Rich Allen	6.00	3.00	.60
☐ 651	Jerry Robertson	1.50	.75	.15
☐ 652	Braves Team	3.00	1.50	.30
☐ 653	Russ Snyder	1.50	.75	.15
☐ 654	Don Shaw	1.50	.75	.15

☐ 655	Mike Epstein	1.50	.75	.15
☐ 656	Gerry Nyman	1.50	.75	.15
☐ 657	Jose Azcue	1.50	.75	.15
☐ 658	Paul Lindblad	1.50	.75	.15
☐ 659	Byron Browne	1.50	.75	.15
☐ 660	Ray Culp	1.50	.75	.15
☐ 661	Chuck Tanner MG	2.00	1.00	.20
☐ 662	Mike Hedlund	1.50	.75	.15
☐ 663	Marv Staehle	1.50	.75	.15
☐ 664	Rookie Pitchers	1.50	.75	.15
	Archie Reynolds			
	Bob Reynolds			
	Ken Reynolds			
☐ 665	Ron Swoboda	1.50	.75	.15
☐ 666	Gene Brabender	1.50	.75	.15
☐ 667	Pete Ward	1.50	.75	.15
☐ 668	Gary Neibauer	1.50	.75	.15
☐ 669	Ike Brown	1.50	.75	.15
☐ 670	Bill Hands	1.50	.75	.15
☐ 671	Bill Voss	1.50	.75	.15
☐ 672	Ed Crosby	1.50	.75	.15
☐ 673	Gerry Janeski	1.50	.75	.15
☐ 674	Expos Team	3.50	1.75	.35
☐ 675	Dave Boswell	1.50	.75	.15
☐ 676	Tommie Reynolds	1.50	.75	.15
☐ 677	Jack DiLauro	1.50	.75	.15
☐ 678	George Thomas	1.50	.75	.15
☐ 679	Don O'Riley	1.50	.75	.15
☐ 680	Don Mincher	1.50	.75	.15
☐ 681	Bill Butler	1.50	.75	.15
☐ 682	Terry Harmon	1.50	.75	.15
☐ 683	Bill Burbach	1.50	.75	.15
☐ 684	Curt Motton	1.50	.75	.15
☐ 685	Moe Drabowsky	1.50	.75	.15
☐ 686	Chico Ruiz	1.50	.75	.15
☐ 687	Ron Taylor	1.50	.75	.15
☐ 688	Sparky Anderson MG	3.50	1.75	.35
☐ 689	Frank Baker	1.50	.75	.15
☐ 690	Bob Moose	1.50	.75	.15
☐ 691	Bob Heise	1.50	.75	.15
☐ 692	AL Rookie Pitchers	1.50	.75	.15
	Hal Haydel			
	Rogelio Moret			
	Wayne Twitchell			
☐ 693	Jose Pena	1.50	.75	.15
☐ 694	Rick Renick	1.50	.75	.15
☐ 695	Joe Niekro	3.00	1.50	.30
☐ 696	Jerry Morales	1.50	.75	.15
☐ 697	Rickey Clark	1.50	.75	.15
☐ 698	Brewers Team	3.50	1.75	.35
☐ 699	Jim Britton	1.50	.75	.15
☐ 700	Boog Powell	3.50	1.75	.35
☐ 701	Bob Garibaldi	1.50	.75	.15
☐ 702	Milt Ramirez	1.50	.75	.15
☐ 703	Mike Kekich	1.50	.75	.15
☐ 704	J.C. Martin	1.50	.75	.15
☐ 705	Dick Selma	1.50	.75	.15
☐ 706	Joe Foy	1.50	.75	.15
☐ 707	Fred Lasher	1.50	.75	.15
☐ 708	Russ Nagelson	1.50	.75	.15
☐ 709	Rookie Outfielders	20.00	10.00	2.00
	Dusty Baker			
	Don Baylor			
	Tom Paciorek			
☐ 710	Sonny Siebert	2.00	1.00	.20
☐ 711	Larry Stahl	1.50	.75	.15
☐ 712	Jose Martinez	1.50	.75	.15
☐ 713	Mike Marshall	2.00	1.00	.20
☐ 714	Dick Williams MG	2.00	1.00	.20
☐ 715	Horace Clarke	1.50	.75	.15
☐ 716	Dave Leonhard	1.50	.75	.15
☐ 717	Tommie Aaron	2.00	1.00	.20
☐ 718	Billy Wynne	1.50	.75	.15
☐ 719	Jerry May	1.50	.75	.15
☐ 720	Matty Alou	2.00	1.00	.20
☐ 721	John Morris	1.50	.75	.15
☐ 722	Astros Team	3.00	1.50	.30
☐ 723	Vicente Romo	1.50	.75	.15
☐ 724	Tom Tischinski	1.50	.75	.15
☐ 725	Gary Gentry	1.50	.75	.15
☐ 726	Paul Popovich	1.50	.75	.15
☐ 727	Ray Lamb	1.50	.75	.15
☐ 728	NL Rookie Outfielders	1.50	.75	.15
	Wayne Redmond			
	Keith Lampard			
	Bernie Williams			
☐ 729	Dick Billings	1.50	.75	.15
☐ 730	Jim Rooker	2.00	1.00	.20
☐ 731	Jim Qualls	1.50	.75	.15
☐ 732	Bob Reed	1.50	.75	.15
☐ 733	Lee Maye	1.50	.75	.15
☐ 734	Rob Gardner	1.50	.75	.15
☐ 735	Mike Shannon	2.00	1.00	.20
☐ 736	Mel Queen	1.50	.75	.15
☐ 737	Preston Gomez MG	1.50	.75	.15

			NRMT	VG-E	GOOD
☐ 738	Russ Gibson		1.50	.75	.15
☐ 739	Barry Lersch		1.50	.75	.15
☐ 740	Luis Aparicio		9.00	4.50	.90
☐ 741	Skip Guinn		1.50	.75	.15
☐ 742	Royals Team		3.00	1.50	.30
☐ 743	John O'Donoghue		1.50	.75	.15
☐ 744	Chuck Manuel		1.50	.75	.15
☐ 745	Sandy Alomar		1.50	.75	.15
☐ 746	Andy Kosco		1.50	.75	.15
☐ 747	NL Rookie Pitchers		1.50	.75	.15
	Al Severinsen				
	Scipio Spinks				
	Balor Moore				
☐ 748	John Purdin		1.50	.75	.15
☐ 749	Ken Szotkiewicz		1.50	.75	.15
☐ 750	Denny McLain		4.50	2.25	.45
☐ 751	Al Weis		1.50	.75	.15
☐ 752	Dick Drago		2.50	.75	.15

1971 Topps Greatest Moments

The cards in this 55-card set measure 2 1/2" by 4 3/4". The 1971 Topps Greatest Moments set contains numbered cards depicting specific career highlights of current players. The obverses are black bordered and contain a small cameo picture of the left side; a deckle-bordered black and white action photo dominates the rest of the card. The backs are designed in newspaper style. Sometimes found in uncut sheets, this test set was retailed in gum packs on a very limited basis. Double prints (DP) are listed in the checklist below; there were 22 double prints and 33 single prints.

			NRMT	VG-E	GOOD
	COMPLETE SET		1000.00	400.00	80.00
	COMMON CARD		15.00	7.50	1.50
	COMMON CARD (DP)		3.00	1.50	.30
☐ 1	Thurman Munson	1970 AL ROY DP	20.00	10.00	2.00
☐ 2	Hoyt Wilhelm	Hurls 1000th Game	25.00	12.50	2.50
☐ 3	Rico Carty: Leads	ML .366 in 1970	15.00	7.50	1.50
☐ 4	Carl Morton	1970 NL ROY DP	3.00	1.50	.30
☐ 5	Sal Bando: Plays	All A's Games 1st 2 years DP	3.00	1.50	.30
☐ 6	Bert Campaneris	Hits 2 HRs in First ML Game DP	3.00	1.50	.30
☐ 7	Jim Kaat: Gold Glove	9 Straight Years	15.00	7.50	1.50
☐ 8	Harmon Killebrew:	Tops 40 Homers 8th Time	40.00	20.00	4.00
☐ 9	Brooks Robinson	MVP 1970 W.S.	65.00	32.50	6.50
☐ 10	Jim Perry	AL Cy Young 1970	15.00	7.50	1.50
☐ 11	Tony Oliva: Leads	AL in Batting 1st 2 Full Years	20.00	10.00	2.00
☐ 12	Vada Pinson	Tops 200 Hits 1st Full Year in ML	20.00	10.00	2.00
☐ 13	Johnny Bench	1970 ML Player of the Year	150.00	75.00	15.00
☐ 14	Tony Perez: 15th	Inning Homer Wins A-S Game	20.00	10.00	2.00
☐ 15	Pete Rose: Leads ML	Batting 2nd Cons. year. DP	100.00	50.00	10.00
☐ 16	Jim Fregosi: Hits	for cycle twice DP	3.00	1.50	.30
☐ 17	Alex Johnson: Leads	AL batting 1st year in league DP	3.00	1.50	.30
☐ 18	Clyde Wright: No-	Hitter vs. A's DP	3.00	1.50	.30
☐ 19	Al Kaline: Youngest	player to win AL batting crown DP	20.00	10.00	2.00
☐ 20	Denny McLain: 1st AL	Pitcher to win 30 in 37 years	20.00	10.00	2.00
☐ 21	Jim Northrup	Hits Three Grand- Slams in One Week	15.00	7.50	1.50
☐ 22	Bill Freehan: Leads AL	Catchers in fielding 6 cons. years	15.00	7.50	1.50
☐ 23	Mickey Lolich: Wins 3	in 1968 W.S.	20.00	10.00	2.00
☐ 24	Bob Gibson: Lowest	ERA ever 300 or more innings DP	15.00	7.50	1.50
☐ 25	Tim McCarver: 1st	catcher to lead ML in triples DP	3.00	1.50	.30
☐ 26	Orlando Cepeda	1967 NL player of the year DP	5.00	2.50	.50
☐ 27	Lou Brock: 50 SB's 6th	straight year DP	15.00	7.50	1.50
☐ 28	Nate Colbert: New Club	Mark with 38 HR's DP	3.00	1.50	.30
☐ 29	Maury Wills	Sets Modern Mark with 104 SB's	20.00	10.00	2.00
☐ 30	Wes Parker: Leads	ML with 47 Doubles	15.00	7.50	1.50
☐ 31	Jim Wynn: 1 of 2	Astro Grand Slams Same Inning	15.00	7.50	1.50
☐ 32	Larry Dierker	Makes ML Debut on 18th Birthday	15.00	7.50	1.50
☐ 33	Bill Melton	1st Chisox to Hit 30 HR's	15.00	7.50	1.50
☐ 34	Joe Morgan	Ties Record 6 Hits in 6 AB's	35.00	17.50	3.50
☐ 35	Rusty Staub	Leads ML 44 2B's	20.00	10.00	2.00
☐ 36	Ernie Banks: Sets ML	Record with 5 Grand Slams. DP	20.00	10.00	2.00
☐ 37	Billy Williams: 1117	Cons. Games	30.00	15.00	3.00
☐ 38	Lou Piniella: 1969	AL ROY	20.00	10.00	2.00
☐ 39	Rico Petrocelli: AL HR	Mark for SS's DP	3.00	1.50	.30
☐ 40	Carl Yastrzemski: AL	Triple Crown DP	60.00	30.00	6.00
☐ 41	Willie Mays: 3000th	Career Hit DP	40.00	20.00	4.00
☐ 42	Tommy Harper	Leads ML 73 SB's	15.00	7.50	1.50
☐ 43	Jim Bunning: No-Hitter	Both AL and NL DP	5.00	2.50	.50
☐ 44	Fritz Peterson	Wins 20th on Last Day of 1970	15.00	7.50	1.50

☐ 45	Roy White: Hits HR's .... Lefty and Righty	15.00	7.50	1.50
☐ 46	Bobby Murcer .... Hits 4 Cons. HR's in a Twinbill	15.00	7.50	1.50
☐ 47	Reggie Jackson .... 10 RBI's One Game	150.00	75.00	15.00
☐ 48	Frank Howard .... New Record, 10 HR's in One Week	15.00	7.50	1.50
☐ 49	Dick Bosman .... Leads AL in ERA	15.00	7.50	1.50
☐ 50	Sam McDowell .... Hurls Two Cons. One-Hitters DP	3.00	1.50	.30
☐ 51	Luis Aparicio: .... Leads AL SB's 9 cons. years DP	12.00	6.00	1.20
☐ 52	Willie McCovey .... Four Hits in His First Game DP	15.00	7.50	1.50
☐ 53	Joe Pepitone .... 2 HR's One Inning	15.00	7.50	1.50
☐ 54	Jerry Grote: 20 PO's .... in 9 Inning Game	15.00	7.50	1.50
☐ 55	Bud Harrelson .... 54 Consecutive Errorless Games, SS	15.00	7.50	1.50

1971 Topps Super

The cards in this 63-card set measure 3 1/8" by 5 1/4". The obverse format of the Topps Super set of 1971 is identical to that of the 1970 set, that is, a borderless color photograph with a facsimile autograph printed on it. The backs are enlargements of the respective player's cards of the 1971 regular baseball issue. There are no reported scarcities in the set.

		NRMT	VG-E	GOOD
	COMPLETE SET	150.00	75.00	15.00
	COMMON PLAYER (1-63)	.75	.35	.07
☐ 1	Reggie Smith	.90	.45	.09
☐ 2	Gaylord Perry	3.00	1.50	.30
☐ 3	Ted Savage	.75	.35	.07
☐ 4	Donn Clendenon	.75	.35	.07
☐ 5	Boog Powell	.90	.45	.09
☐ 6	Tony Perez	1.25	.60	.12
☐ 7	Dick Bosman	.75	.35	.07
☐ 8	Alex Johnson	.75	.35	.07
☐ 9	Rusty Staub	1.00	.50	.10
☐ 10	Mel Stottlemyre	.75	.35	.07
☐ 11	Tony Oliva	1.00	.50	.10
☐ 12	Bill Freehan	.75	.35	.07
☐ 13	Fritz Peterson	.75	.35	.07
☐ 14	Wes Parker	.75	.35	.07
☐ 15	Cesar Cedeno	.75	.35	.07
☐ 16	Sam McDowell	.75	.35	.07
☐ 17	Frank Howard	.75	.35	.07

☐ 18	Dave McNally	.75	.35	.07
☐ 19	Rico Petrocelli	.75	.35	.07
☐ 20	Pete Rose	25.00	12.50	2.50
☐ 21	Luke Walker	.75	.35	.07
☐ 22	Nate Colbert	.75	.35	.07
☐ 23	Luis Aparicio	2.00	1.00	.20
☐ 24	Jim Perry	.90	.45	.09
☐ 25	Lou Brock	4.00	2.00	.40
☐ 26	Roy White	.75	.35	.07
☐ 27	Claude Osteen	.75	.35	.07
☐ 28	Carl Morton	.75	.35	.07
☐ 29	Rico Carty	.90	.45	.09
☐ 30	Larry Dierker	.75	.35	.07
☐ 31	Bert Campaneris	.75	.35	.07
☐ 32	Johnny Bench	8.00	4.00	.80
☐ 33	Felix Millan	.75	.35	.07
☐ 34	Tim McCarver	.90	.45	.09
☐ 35	Ron Santo	.90	.45	.09
☐ 36	Tommie Agee	.75	.35	.07
☐ 37	Bob Clemente	9.00	4.50	.90
☐ 38	Reggie Jackson	12.00	6.00	1.20
☐ 39	Clyde Wright	.75	.35	.07
☐ 40	Rich Allen	.90	.45	.09
☐ 41	Curt Flood	.90	.45	.09
☐ 42	Fergie Jenkins	1.25	.60	.12
☐ 43	Willie Stargell	4.00	2.00	.40
☐ 44	Hank Aaron	10.00	5.00	1.00
☐ 45	Amos Otis	.75	.35	.07
☐ 46	Willie McCovey	4.00	2.00	.40
☐ 47	Bill Melton	.75	.35	.07
☐ 48	Bob Gibson	3.00	1.50	.30
☐ 49	Carl Yastremski	12.00	6.00	1.20
☐ 50	Glenn Beckert	.75	.35	.07
☐ 51	Ray Fosse	.75	.35	.07
☐ 52	Cito Gaston	.75	.35	.07
☐ 53	Tom Seaver	10.00	5.00	1.00
☐ 54	Al Kaline	7.00	3.50	.70
☐ 55	Jim Northup	.75	.35	.07
☐ 56	Willie Mays	10.00	5.00	1.00
☐ 57	Sal Bando	.75	.35	.07
☐ 58	Deron Johnson	.75	.35	.07
☐ 59	Brooks Robinson	6.50	3.25	.65
☐ 60	Harmon Killebrew	3.00	1.50	.30
☐ 61	Joe Torre	1.00	.50	.10
☐ 62	Lou Piniella	.90	.45	.09
☐ 63	Tommy Harper	.75	.35	.07

1972 Topps

The cards in this 787-card set measure 2 1/2" by 3 1/2". The 1972 Topps set contained the most cards ever for a Topps set to that point in time. Features appearing for the first time were "Boyhood Photos" (KP: 341-348 and 491-498), Awards and Trophy cards (621-626), "In Action" (distributed throughout the set) and "Traded Cards" (TR: 751-757). Other subsets included League Leaders (85-96), Playoffs cards (221-222), and World Series cards (223-230). The curved lines of the color picture are a departure from the rectangular designs of other years. There is a series of intermediate scarcity (526-656) and the usual high numbers (657-787).

	NRMT	VG-E	GOOD
COMPLETE SET	1000.00	400.00	80.00
COMMON PLAYER (1-132)	.20	.10	.02
COMMON PLAYER (133-263)	.25	.12	.02

	COMMON PLAYER (264-394)	.25	.12	.02
	COMMON PLAYER (395-525)	.30	.15	.03
	COMMON PLAYER (526-656)	.60	.30	.06
	COMMON PLAYER (657-787)	1.50	.75	.15
1	Pirates Team	4.00	.50	.10
2	Ray Culp	.20	.10	.02
3	Bob Tolan	.30	.15	.03
4	Checklist 1	1.25	.20	.04
5	John Bateman	.20	.10	.02
6	Fred Scherman	.20	.10	.02
7	Enzo Hernandez	.20	.10	.02
8	Ron Swoboda	.30	.15	.03
9	Stan Williams	.20	.10	.02
10	Amos Otis	.40	.20	.04
11	Bobby Valentine	.60	.30	.06
12	Jose Cardenal	.20	.10	.02
13	Joe Grzenda	.20	.10	.02
14	Phillies Rookies	.20	.10	.02
	Pete Koegel			
	Mike Anderson			
	Wayne Twitchell			
15	Walt Williams	.20	.10	.02
16	Mike Jorgensen	.20	.10	.02
17	Dave Duncan	.20	.10	.02
18A	Juan Pizarro	.20	.10	.02
	(yellow underline			
	C and S of Cubs)			
18B	Juan Pizarro	5.00	2.50	.50
	(green underline			
	C and S of Cubs)			
19	Billy Cowan	.20	.10	.02
20	Don Wilson	.20	.10	.02
21	Braves Team	.60	.30	.06
22	Rob Gardner	.20	.10	.02
23	Ted Kubiak	.20	.10	.02
24	Ted Ford	.20	.10	.02
25	Bill Singer	.30	.15	.03
26	Andy Etchebarren	.20	.10	.02
27	Bob Johnson	.20	.10	.02
28	Twins Rookies	.20	.10	.02
	Bob Gebhard			
	Steve Brye			
	Hal Haydel			
29A	Bill Bonham	.20	.10	.02
	(yellow underline			
	C and S of Cubs)			
29B	Bill Bonham	5.00	2.50	.50
	(green underline			
	C and S of Cubs)			
30	Rico Petrocelli	.30	.15	.03
31	Cleon Jones	.20	.10	.02
32	Jones In Action	.20	.10	.02
33	Billy Martin MG	1.25	.60	.12
34	Martin In Action	.60	.30	.06
35	Jerry Johnson	.20	.10	.02
36	Johnson In Action	.20	.10	.02
37	Carl Yastrzemski	12.00	6.00	1.20
38	Yastrzemski In Action	5.00	2.50	.50
39	Bob Barton	.20	.10	.02
40	Barton In Action	.20	.10	.02
41	Tommy Davis	.30	.15	.03
42	Davis In Action	.20	.10	.02
43	Rick Wise	.20	.10	.02
44	Wise In Action	.20	.10	.02
45A	Glenn Beckert	.30	.15	.03
	(yellow underline			
	C and S of Cubs)			
45B	Glenn Beckert	5.00	2.50	.50
	(green underline			
	C and S of Cubs)			
46	Beckert In Action	.20	.10	.02
47	John Ellis	.20	.10	.02
48	Ellis In Action	.20	.10	.02
49	Willie Mays	12.00	6.00	1.20
50	Mays In Action	5.00	2.50	.50
51	Harmon Killebrew	3.50	1.75	.35
52	Killebrew In Action	1.50	.75	.15
53	Bud Harrelson	.30	.15	.03
54	Harrelson In Action	.20	.10	.02
55	Clyde Wright	.20	.10	.02
56	Rich Chiles	.20	.10	.02
57	Bob Oliver	.20	.10	.02
58	Ernie McAnally	.20	.10	.02
59	Fred Stanley	.20	.10	.02
60	Manny Sanguillen	.30	.15	.03
61	Cubs Rookies	.60	.30	.06
	Burt Hooton			
	Gene Hiser			
	Earl Stephenson			
62	Angel Mangual	.20	.10	.02
63	Duke Sims	.20	.10	.02
64	Pete Broberg	.20	.10	.02
65	Cesar Cedeno	.60	.30	.06
66	Ray Corbin	.20	.10	.02
67	Red Schoendienst MG	.30	.15	.03
68	Jim York	.20	.10	.02
69	Roger Freed	.20	.10	.02
70	Mike Cuellar	.30	.15	.03
71	Angels Team	.60	.30	.06
72	Bruce Kison	.50	.25	.05
73	Steve Huntz	.20	.10	.02
74	Cecil Upshaw	.20	.10	.02
75	Bert Campaneris	.30	.15	.03
76	Don Carrithers	.20	.10	.02
77	Ron Theobald	.20	.10	.02
78	Steve Arlin	.20	.10	.02
79	Red Sox Rookies	18.00	9.00	1.80
	Mike Garman			
	Cecil Cooper			
	Carlton Fisk			
80	Tony Perez	1.50	.75	.15
81	Mike Hedlund	.20	.10	.02
82	Ron Woods	.20	.10	.02
83	Dalton Jones	.20	.10	.02
84	Vince Colbert	.20	.10	.02
85	NL Batting Leaders	.65	.30	.06
	Joe Torre			
	Ralph Garr			
	Glenn Beckert			
86	AL Batting Leaders	.65	.30	.06
	Tony Oliva			
	Bobby Murcer			
	Merv Rettenmund			
87	NL RBI Leaders	1.25	.60	.12
	Joe Torre			
	Willie Stargell			
	Hank Aaron			
88	AL RBI Leaders	1.00	.50	.10
	Harmon Killebrew			
	Frank Robinson			
	Reggie Smith			
89	NL Home Run Leaders	1.25	.60	.12
	Willie Stargell			
	Hank Aaron			
	Lee May			
90	AL Home Run Leaders	1.00	.50	.10
	Bill Melton			
	Norm Cash			
	Reggie Jackson			
91	NL ERA Leaders	1.00	.50	.10
	Tom Seaver			
	Dave Roberts			
	(photo actually			
	Danny Coombs)			
	Don Wilson			
92	AL ERA Leaders	.75	.35	.07
	Vida Blue			
	Wilbur Wood			
	Jim Palmer			
93	NL Pitching Leaders	1.25	.60	.12
	Fergie Jenkins			
	Steve Carlton			
	Al Downing			
	Tom Seaver			
94	AL Pitching Leaders	.65	.30	.06
	Mickey Lolich			
	Vida Blue			
	Wilbur Wood			
95	NL Strikeout Leaders	1.00	.50	.10
	Tom Seaver			
	Fergie Jenkins			
	Bill Stoneman			
96	AL Strikeout Leaders	.65	.30	.06
	Mickey Lolich			
	Vida Blue			
	Joe Coleman			
97	Tom Kelley	.20	.10	.02
98	Chuck Tanner MG	.30	.15	.03
99	Ross Grimsley	.20	.10	.02
100	Frank Robinson	3.50	1.75	.35
101	Astros Rookies	1.50	.75	.15
	Bill Greif			
	J.R. Richard			
	Ray Busse			
102	Lloyd Allen	.20	.10	.02
103	Checklist 2	1.25	.20	.04
104	Toby Harrah	1.25	.60	.12
105	Gary Gentry	.20	.10	.02
106	Brewers Team	.60	.30	.06
107	Jose Cruz	1.75	.85	.17
108	Gary Waslewski	.20	.10	.02
109	Jerry May	.20	.10	.02
110	Ron Hunt	.20	.10	.02
111	Jim Grant	.20	.10	.02
112	Greg Luzinski	.85	.40	.08
113	Rogelio Moret	.20	.10	.02
114	Bill Buckner	1.25	.60	.12
115	Jim Fregosi	.40	.20	.04
116	Ed Farmer	.30	.15	.03

☐ 117A	Cleo James (yellow underline C and S of Cubs)	.20	.10	.02
☐ 117B	Cleo James (green underline C and S of Cubs)	5.00	2.50	.50
☐ 118	Skip Lockwood	.20	.10	.02
☐ 119	Marty Perez	.20	.10	.02
☐ 120	Bill Freehan	.40	.20	.04
☐ 121	Ed Sprague	.20	.10	.02
☐ 122	Larry Biittner	.20	.10	.02
☐ 123	Ed Acosta	.20	.10	.02
☐ 124	Yankees Rookies Alan Closter Rusty Torres Roger Hambright	.20	.10	.02
☐ 125	Dave Cash	.30	.15	.03
☐ 126	Bart Johnson	.20	.10	.02
☐ 127	Duffy Dyer	.20	.10	.02
☐ 128	Eddie Watt	.20	.10	.02
☐ 129	Charlie Fox MG	.20	.10	.02
☐ 130	Bob Gibson	3.50	1.75	.35
☐ 131	Jim Nettles	.20	.10	.02
☐ 132	Joe Morgan	2.50	1.25	.25
☐ 133	Joe Keough	.25	.12	.02
☐ 134	Carl Morton	.25	.12	.02
☐ 135	Vada Pinson	.60	.30	.06
☐ 136	Darrell Chaney	.25	.12	.02
☐ 137	Dick Williams MG	.35	.17	.03
☐ 138	Mike Kekich	.25	.12	.02
☐ 139	Tim McCarver	.50	.25	.05
☐ 140	Pat Dobson	.35	.17	.03
☐ 141	Mets Rookies Buzz Capra Leroy Stanton Jon Matlack	.50	.25	.05
☐ 142	Chris Chambliss	1.25	.60	.12
☐ 143	Garry Jestadt	.25	.12	.02
☐ 144	Marty Pattin	.25	.12	.02
☐ 145	Don Kessinger	.35	.17	.03
☐ 146	Steve Kealey	.25	.12	.02
☐ 147	Dave Kingman	4.50	2.25	.45
☐ 148	Dick Billings	.25	.12	.02
☐ 149	Gary Neibauer	.25	.12	.02
☐ 150	Norm Cash	.50	.25	.05
☐ 151	Jim Brewer	.25	.12	.02
☐ 152	Gene Clines	.25	.12	.02
☐ 153	Rick Auerbach	.25	.12	.02
☐ 154	Ted Simmons	1.25	.60	.12
☐ 155	Larry Dierker	.35	.17	.03
☐ 156	Twins Team	.60	.30	.06
☐ 157	Don Gullett	.35	.17	.03
☐ 158	Jerry Kenney	.25	.12	.02
☐ 159	John Boccabella	.25	.12	.02
☐ 160	Andy Messersmith	.35	.17	.03
☐ 161	Brock Davis	.25	.12	.02
☐ 162	Brewers Rookies Jerry Bell Darrell Porter Bob Reynolds (Porter and Bell photos switched)	1.00	.50	.10
☐ 163	Tug McGraw	.75	.35	.07
☐ 164	McGraw In Action	.35	.17	.03
☐ 165	Chris Speier	.60	.30	.06
☐ 166	Speier In Action	.25	.12	.02
☐ 167	Deron Johnson	.25	.12	.02
☐ 168	Johnson In Action	.25	.12	.02
☐ 169	Vida Blue	.75	.35	.07
☐ 170	Blue In Action	.35	.17	.03
☐ 171	Darrell Evans	1.25	.60	.12
☐ 172	Evans In Action	.50	.25	.05
☐ 173	Clay Kirby	.25	.12	.02
☐ 174	Kirby In Action	.25	.12	.02
☐ 175	Tom Haller	.35	.17	.03
☐ 176	Haller In Action	.25	.12	.02
☐ 177	Paul Schaal	.25	.12	.02
☐ 178	Schaal In Action	.25	.12	.02
☐ 179	Dock Ellis	.25	.12	.02
☐ 180	Ellis In Action	.25	.12	.02
☐ 181	Ed Kranepool	.35	.17	.03
☐ 182	Kranepool In Action	.25	.12	.02
☐ 183	Bill Melton	.25	.12	.02
☐ 184	Melton In Action	.25	.12	.02
☐ 185	Ron Bryant	.25	.12	.02
☐ 186	Bryant In Action	.25	.12	.02
☐ 187	Gates Brown	.35	.17	.03
☐ 188	Frank Lucchesi MG	.25	.12	.02
☐ 189	Gene Tenace	.35	.17	.03
☐ 190	Dave Giusti	.35	.17	.03
☐ 191	Jeff Burroughs	.65	.30	.06
☐ 192	Cubs Team	.60	.30	.06
☐ 193	Kurt Bevacqua	.25	.12	.02
☐ 194	Fred Norman	.25	.12	.02
☐ 195	Orlando Cepeda	1.50	.75	.15

☐ 196	Mel Queen	.25	.12	.02
☐ 197	Johnny Briggs	.25	.12	.02
☐ 198	Dodgers Rookies Charlie Hough Bob O'Brien Mike Strahler	1.25	.60	.12
☐ 199	Mike Fiore	.25	.12	.02
☐ 200	Lou Brock	3.50	1.75	.35
☐ 201	Phil Roof	.25	.12	.02
☐ 202	Scipio Spinks	.25	.12	.02
☐ 203	Ron Blomberg	.25	.12	.02
☐ 204	Tommy Helms	.35	.17	.03
☐ 205	Dick Drago	.25	.12	.02
☐ 206	Dal Maxvill	.35	.17	.03
☐ 207	Tom Egan	.25	.12	.02
☐ 208	Milt Pappas	.35	.17	.03
☐ 209	Joe Rudi	.35	.17	.03
☐ 210	Denny McLain	.85	.40	.08
☐ 211	Gary Sutherland	.25	.12	.02
☐ 212	Grant Jackson	.25	.12	.02
☐ 213	Angels Rookies Billy Parker Art Kusnyer Tom Silverio	.25	.12	.02
☐ 214	Mike McQueen	.25	.12	.02
☐ 215	Alex Johnson	.35	.17	.03
☐ 216	Joe Niekro	.50	.25	.05
☐ 217	Roger Metzger	.25	.12	.02
☐ 218	Eddie Kasko MG	.25	.12	.02
☐ 219	Rennie Stennett	.35	.17	.03
☐ 220	Jim Perry	.50	.25	.05
☐ 221	NL Playoffs Bucs champs	.75	.35	.07
☐ 222	AL Playoffs Orioles champs (Brooks Robinson)	1.25	.60	.12
☐ 223	World Series Game 1 (McNally pitching)	.75	.35	.07
☐ 224	World Series Game 2 (B. Robinson and Mark Belanger)	.75	.35	.07
☐ 225	World Series Game 3 (Sanguillen scoring)	.75	.35	.07
☐ 226	World Series Game 4 (Clemente on 2nd)	1.75	.85	.17
☐ 227	World Series Game 5 (Briles pitching)	.75	.35	.07
☐ 228	World Series Game 6 (Frank Robinson and Manny Sanguillen)	.90	.45	.09
☐ 229	World Series Game 7 (Blass pitching)	.75	.35	.07
☐ 230	World Series Summary Pirates celebrate	.75	.35	.07
☐ 231	Casey Cox	.25	.12	.02
☐ 232	Giants Rookies Chris Arnold Jim Barr Dave Rader	.25	.12	.02
☐ 233	Jay Johnstone	.35	.17	.03
☐ 234	Ron Taylor	.25	.12	.02
☐ 235	Merv Rettenmund	.25	.12	.02
☐ 236	Jim McGlothlin	.25	.12	.02
☐ 237	Yankees Team	.85	.40	.08
☐ 238	Leron Lee	.35	.17	.03
☐ 239	Tom Timmermann	.25	.12	.02
☐ 240	Rich Allen	1.25	.60	.12
☐ 241	Rollie Fingers	2.00	1.00	.20
☐ 242	Don Mincher	.25	.12	.02
☐ 243	Frank Linzy	.25	.12	.02
☐ 244	Steve Braun	.25	.12	.02
☐ 245	Tommie Agee	.35	.17	.03
☐ 246	Tom Burgmeier	.25	.12	.02
☐ 247	Milt May	.25	.12	.02
☐ 248	Tom Bradley	.25	.12	.02
☐ 249	Harry Walker MG	.25	.12	.02
☐ 250	Boog Powell	.80	.40	.08
☐ 251	Checklist 3	1.25	.20	.04
☐ 252	Ken Reynolds	.25	.12	.02
☐ 253	Sandy Alomar	.25	.12	.02
☐ 254	Boots Day	.25	.12	.02
☐ 255	Jim Lonborg	.35	.17	.03
☐ 256	George Foster	1.50	.75	.15
☐ 257	Tigers Rookies Jim Foor Tim Hosley Paul Jata	.25	.12	.02
☐ 258	Randy Hundley	.25	.12	.02
☐ 259	Sparky Lyle	.50	.25	.05
☐ 260	Ralph Garr	.35	.17	.03
☐ 261	Steve Mingori	.25	.12	.02
☐ 262	Padres Team	.60	.30	.06
☐ 263	Felipe Alou	.35	.17	.03
☐ 264	Tommy John	1.50	.75	.15
☐ 265	Wes Parker	.35	.17	.03

☐ 266	Bobby Bolin	.25	.12	.02
☐ 267	Dave Concepcion	1.50	.75	.15
☐ 268	A's Rookies	.25	.12	.02
	Dwain Anderson			
	Chris Floethe			
☐ 269	Don Hahn	.25	.12	.02
☐ 270	Jim Palmer	3.50	1.75	.35
☐ 271	Ken Rudolph	.25	.12	.02
☐ 272	Mickey Rivers	1.00	.50	.10
☐ 273	Bobby Floyd	.25	.12	.02
☐ 274	Al Severinsen	.25	.12	.02
☐ 275	Cesar Tovar	.25	.12	.02
☐ 276	Gene Mauch MG	.35	.17	.03
☐ 277	Elliot Maddox	.25	.12	.02
☐ 278	Dennis Higgins	.25	.12	.02
☐ 279	Larry Brown	.25	.12	.02
☐ 280	Willie McCovey	3.50	1.75	.35
☐ 281	Bill Parsons	.25	.12	.02
☐ 282	Astros Team	.60	.30	.06
☐ 283	Darrell Brandon	.25	.12	.02
☐ 284	Ike Brown	.25	.12	.02
☐ 285	Gaylord Perry	3.50	1.75	.35
☐ 286	Gene Alley	.35	.17	.03
☐ 287	Jim Hardin	.25	.12	.02
☐ 288	Johnny Jeter	.25	.12	.02
☐ 289	Syd O'Brien	.25	.12	.02
☐ 290	Sonny Siebert	.35	.17	.03
☐ 291	Hal McRae	.50	.25	.05
☐ 292	McRae In Action	.25	.12	.02
☐ 293	Danny Frisella	.25	.12	.02
☐ 294	Frisella In Action	.25	.12	.02
☐ 295	Dick Dietz	.25	.12	.02
☐ 296	Dietz In Action	.25	.12	.02
☐ 297	Claude Osteen	.35	.17	.03
☐ 298	Osteen In Action	.25	.12	.02
☐ 299	Hank Aaron	12.00	6.00	1.20
☐ 300	Aaron in Action	5.00	2.50	.50
☐ 301	George Mitterwald	.25	.12	.02
☐ 302	Mitterwald In Action	.25	.12	.02
☐ 303	Joe Pepitone	.35	.17	.03
☐ 304	Pepitone In Action	.25	.12	.02
☐ 305	Ken Boswell	.25	.12	.02
☐ 306	Boswell In Action	.25	.12	.02
☐ 307	Steve Renko	.25	.12	.02
☐ 308	Renko In Action	.25	.12	.02
☐ 309	Roberto Clemente	12.00	6.00	1.20
☐ 310	Clemente In Action	5.00	2.50	.50
☐ 311	Clay Carroll	.25	.12	.02
☐ 312	Carroll In Action	.25	.12	.02
☐ 313	Luis Aparicio	2.50	1.25	.25
☐ 314	Aparicio In Action	1.00	.50	.10
☐ 315	Paul Splittorff	.35	.17	.03
☐ 316	Cardinals Rookies	.35	.17	.03
	Jim Bibby			
	Jorge Roque			
	Santiago Guzman			
☐ 317	Rich Hand	.25	.12	.02
☐ 318	Sonny Jackson	.25	.12	.02
☐ 319	Aurelio Rodriguez	.25	.12	.02
☐ 320	Steve Blass	.35	.17	.03
☐ 321	Joe Lahoud	.25	.12	.02
☐ 322	Jose Pena	.25	.12	.02
☐ 323	Earl Weaver MG	.50	.25	.05
☐ 324	Mike Ryan	.25	.12	.02
☐ 325	Mel Stottlemyre	.50	.25	.05
☐ 326	Pat Kelly	.25	.12	.02
☐ 327	Steve Stone	.75	.35	.07
☐ 328	Red Sox Team	.70	.35	.07
☐ 329	Roy Foster	.25	.12	.02
☐ 330	Jim Hunter	2.50	1.25	.25
☐ 331	Stan Swanson	.25	.12	.02
☐ 332	Buck Martinez	.25	.12	.02
☐ 333	Steve Barber	.25	.12	.02
☐ 334	Rangers Rookies	.25	.12	.02
	Bill Fahey			
	Jim Mason			
	Tom Ragland			
☐ 335	Bill Hands	.25	.12	.02
☐ 336	Marty Martinez	.25	.12	.02
☐ 337	Mike Kilkenny	.25	.12	.02
☐ 338	Bob Grich	.60	.30	.06
☐ 339	Ron Cook	.25	.12	.02
☐ 340	Roy White	.35	.17	.03
☐ 341	KP: Joe Torre	.35	.17	.03
☐ 342	KP: Wilbur Wood	.25	.12	.02
☐ 343	KP: Willie Stargell	.65	.30	.06
☐ 344	KP: Dave McNally	.25	.12	.02
☐ 345	KP: Rick Wise	.25	.12	.02
☐ 346	KP: Jim Fregosi	.35	.17	.03
☐ 347	KP: Tom Seaver	1.50	.75	.15
☐ 348	KP: Sal Bando	.25	.12	.02
☐ 349	Al Fitzmorris	.25	.12	.02
☐ 350	Frank Howard	.60	.30	.06
☐ 351	Braves Rookies	.35	.17	.03
	Tom House			

	Rick Kester			
	Jimmy Britton			
☐ 352	Dave LaRoche	.25	.12	.02
☐ 353	Art Shamsky	.25	.12	.02
☐ 354	Tom Murphy	.25	.12	.02
☐ 355	Bob Watson	.35	.17	.03
☐ 356	Gerry Moses	.25	.12	.02
☐ 357	Woodie Fryman	.25	.12	.02
☐ 358	Sparky Anderson MG	.50	.25	.05
☐ 359	Don Pavletich	.25	.12	.02
☐ 360	Dave Roberts	.25	.12	.02
☐ 361	Mike Andrews	.25	.12	.02
☐ 362	Mets Team	.75	.35	.07
☐ 363	Ron Klimkowski	.25	.12	.02
☐ 364	Johnny Callison	.35	.17	.03
☐ 365	Dick Bosman	.25	.12	.02
☐ 366	Jimmy Rosario	.25	.12	.02
☐ 367	Ron Perranoski	.35	.17	.03
☐ 368	Danny Thompson	.25	.12	.02
☐ 369	Jim Lefebvre	.25	.12	.02
☐ 370	Don Buford	.25	.12	.02
☐ 371	Denny Lemaster	.25	.12	.02
☐ 372	Royals Rookies	.25	.12	.02
	Lance Clemons			
	Monty Montgomery			
☐ 373	John Mayberry	.35	.17	.03
☐ 374	Jack Heidemann	.25	.12	.02
☐ 375	Reggie Cleveland	.25	.12	.02
☐ 376	Andy Kosco	.25	.12	.02
☐ 377	Terry Harmon	.25	.12	.02
☐ 378	Checklist 4	1.25	.20	.04
☐ 379	Ken Berry	.25	.12	.02
☐ 380	Earl Williams	.25	.12	.02
☐ 381	White Sox Team	.60	.30	.06
☐ 382	Joe Gibbon	.25	.12	.02
☐ 383	Brant Alyea	.25	.12	.02
☐ 384	Dave Campbell	.25	.12	.02
☐ 385	Mickey Stanley	.35	.17	.03
☐ 386	Jim Colborn	.25	.12	.02
☐ 387	Horace Clarke	.25	.12	.02
☐ 388	Charlie Williams	.25	.12	.02
☐ 389	Bill Rigney MG	.25	.12	.02
☐ 390	Willie Davis	.35	.17	.03
☐ 391	Ken Sanders	.25	.12	.02
☐ 392	Pirates Rookies	.65	.30	.06
	Fred Cambria			
	Richie Zisk			
☐ 393	Curt Motton	.25	.12	.02
☐ 394	Ken Forsch	.35	.17	.03
☐ 395	Matty Alou	.40	.20	.04
☐ 396	Paul Lindblad	.30	.15	.03
☐ 397	Phillies Team	.65	.30	.06
☐ 398	Larry Hisle	.40	.20	.04
☐ 399	Milt Wilcox	.40	.20	.04
☐ 400	Tony Oliva	1.50	.75	.15
☐ 401	Jim Nash	.30	.15	.03
☐ 402	Bobby Heise	.30	.15	.03
☐ 403	John Cumberland	.30	.15	.03
☐ 404	Jeff Torborg	.40	.20	.04
☐ 405	Ron Fairly	.40	.20	.04
☐ 406	George Hendrick	.85	.40	.08
☐ 407	Chuck Taylor	.30	.15	.03
☐ 408	Jim Northrup	.40	.20	.04
☐ 409	Frank Baker	.30	.15	.03
☐ 410	Fergie Jenkins	1.25	.60	.12
☐ 411	Bob Montgomery	.30	.15	.03
☐ 412	Dick Kelley	.30	.15	.03
☐ 413	White Sox Rookies	.30	.15	.03
	Don Eddy			
	Dave Lemonds			
☐ 414	Bob Miller	.30	.15	.03
☐ 415	Cookie Rojas	.30	.15	.03
☐ 416	Johnny Edwards	.30	.15	.03
☐ 417	Tom Hall	.30	.15	.03
☐ 418	Tom Shopay	.30	.15	.03
☐ 419	Jim Spencer	.30	.15	.03
☐ 420	Steve Carlton	12.00	6.00	1.20
☐ 421	Ellie Rodriguez	.30	.15	.03
☐ 422	Ray Lamb	.30	.15	.03
☐ 423	Oscar Gamble	.40	.20	.04
☐ 424	Bill Gogolewski	.30	.15	.03
☐ 425	Ken Singleton	.65	.30	.06
☐ 426	Singleton In Action	.40	.20	.04
☐ 427	Tito Fuentes	.30	.15	.03
☐ 428	Fuentes In Action	.30	.15	.03
☐ 429	Bob Robertson	.30	.15	.03
☐ 430	Robertson In Action	.30	.15	.03
☐ 431	Clarence Gaston	.30	.15	.03
☐ 432	Gaston In Action	.30	.15	.03
☐ 433	Johnny Bench	15.00	7.50	1.50
☐ 434	Bench In Action	6.00	3.00	.60
☐ 435	Reggie Jackson	15.00	7.50	1.50
☐ 436	Jackson In Action	6.00	3.00	.60
☐ 437	Maury Wills	1.00	.50	.10
☐ 438	Wills In Action	.50	.25	.05

☐ 439	Billy Williams	2.50	1.25	.25
☐ 440	Williams In Action	1.00	.50	.10
☐ 441	Thurman Munson	8.50	4.25	.85
☐ 442	Munson In Action	3.50	1.75	.35
☐ 443	Ken Henderson	.30	.15	.03
☐ 444	Henderson In Action	.30	.15	.03
☐ 445	Tom Seaver	12.00	6.00	1.20
☐ 446	Seaver In Action	5.00	2.50	.50
☐ 447	Willie Stargell	3.50	1.75	.35
☐ 448	Stargell In Action	1.50	.75	.15
☐ 449	Bob Lemon MG	.75	.35	.07
☐ 450	Mickey Lolich	.75	.35	.07
☐ 451	Tony LaRussa	.50	.25	.05
☐ 452	Ed Herrmann	.30	.15	.03
☐ 453	Barry Lersch	.30	.15	.03
☐ 454	A's Team	.80	.40	.08
☐ 455	Tommy Harper	.40	.20	.04
☐ 456	Mark Belanger	.50	.25	.05
☐ 457	Padres Rookies	.40	.20	.04
	Darcy Fast			
	Derrel Thomas			
	Mike Ivie			
☐ 458	Aurelio Monteagudo	.30	.15	.03
☐ 459	Rick Renick	.30	.15	.03
☐ 460	Al Downing	.40	.20	.04
☐ 461	Tim Cullen	.30	.15	.03
☐ 462	Rickey Clark	.30	.15	.03
☐ 463	Bernie Carbo	.30	.15	.03
☐ 464	Jim Roland	.30	.15	.03
☐ 465	Gil Hodges MG	2.00	1.00	.20
☐ 466	Norm Miller	.30	.15	.03
☐ 467	Steve Kline	.30	.15	.03
☐ 468	Richie Scheinblum	.30	.15	.03
☐ 469	Ron Herbel	.30	.15	.03
☐ 470	Ray Fosse	.30	.15	.03
☐ 471	Luke Walker	.30	.15	.03
☐ 472	Phil Gagliano	.30	.15	.03
☐ 473	Dan McGinn	.30	.15	.03
☐ 474	Orioles Rookies	2.00	1.00	.20
	Don Baylor			
	Roric Harrison			
	Johnny Oates			
☐ 475	Gary Nolan	.30	.15	.03
☐ 476	Lee Richard	.30	.15	.03
☐ 477	Tom Phoebus	.30	.15	.03
☐ 478	Checklist 5	1.25	.20	.04
☐ 479	Don Shaw	.30	.15	.03
☐ 480	Lee May	.40	.20	.04
☐ 481	Billy Conigliaro	.40	.20	.04
☐ 482	Joe Hoerner	.30	.15	.03
☐ 483	Ken Suarez	.30	.15	.03
☐ 484	Lum Harris MG	.30	.15	.03
☐ 485	Phil Regan	.40	.20	.04
☐ 486	John Lowenstein	.30	.15	.03
☐ 487	Tigers Team	.85	.40	.08
☐ 488	Mike Nagy	.30	.15	.03
☐ 489	Expos Rookies	.30	.15	.03
	Terry Humphrey			
	Keith Lampard			
☐ 490	Dave McNally	.40	.20	.04
☐ 491	KP: Lou Piniella	.40	.20	.04
☐ 492	KP: Mel Stottlemyre	.30	.15	.03
☐ 493	KP: Bob Bailey	.30	.15	.03
☐ 494	KP: Willie Horton	.30	.15	.03
☐ 495	KP: Bill Melton	.30	.15	.03
☐ 496	KP: Bud Harrelson	.30	.15	.03
☐ 497	KP: Jim Perry	.30	.15	.03
☐ 498	KP: Brooks Robinson	1.50	.75	.15
☐ 499	Vicente Romo	.30	.15	.03
☐ 500	Joe Torre	.75	.35	.07
☐ 501	Pete Hamm	.30	.15	.03
☐ 502	Jackie Hernandez	.30	.15	.03
☐ 503	Gary Peters	.40	.20	.04
☐ 504	Ed Spiezio	.30	.15	.03
☐ 505	Mike Marshall	.40	.20	.04
☐ 506	Indians Rookies	.40	.20	.04
	Terry Ley			
	Jim Moyer			
	Dick Tidrow			
☐ 507	Fred Gladding	.30	.15	.03
☐ 508	Ellie Hendricks	.30	.15	.03
☐ 509	Don McMahon	.30	.15	.03
☐ 510	Ted Williams MG	3.50	1.75	.35
☐ 511	Tony Taylor	.30	.15	.03
☐ 512	Paul Popovich	.30	.15	.03
☐ 513	Lindy McDaniel	.40	.20	.04
☐ 514	Ted Sizemore	.30	.15	.03
☐ 515	Bert Blyleven	2.50	1.25	.25
☐ 516	Oscar Brown	.30	.15	.03
☐ 517	Ken Brett	.40	.20	.04
☐ 518	Wayne Garrett	.30	.15	.03
☐ 519	Ted Abernathy	.30	.15	.03
☐ 520	Larry Bowa	1.50	.75	.15
☐ 521	Alan Foster	.30	.15	.03
☐ 522	Dodgers Team	1.00	.50	.10

☐ 523	Chuck Dobson	.30	.15	.03
☐ 524	Reds Rookies	.30	.15	.03
	Ed Armbrister			
	Mel Behney			
☐ 525	Carlos May	.40	.20	.04
☐ 526	Bob Bailey	.60	.30	.06
☐ 527	Dave Leonhard	.60	.30	.06
☐ 528	Ron Stone	.60	.30	.06
☐ 529	Dave Nelson	.60	.30	.06
☐ 530	Don Sutton	3.00	1.50	.30
☐ 531	Freddie Patek	.75	.35	.07
☐ 532	Fred Kendall	.60	.30	.06
☐ 533	Ralph Houk MG	.75	.35	.07
☐ 534	Jim Hickman	.60	.30	.06
☐ 535	Ed Brinkman	.60	.30	.06
☐ 536	Doug Rader	.75	.35	.07
☐ 537	Bob Locker	.60	.30	.06
☐ 538	Charlie Sands	.60	.30	.06
☐ 539	Terry Forster	1.50	.75	.15
☐ 540	Felix Millan	.60	.30	.06
☐ 541	Roger Repoz	.60	.30	.06
☐ 542	Jack Billingham	.60	.30	.06
☐ 543	Duane Josephson	.60	.30	.06
☐ 544	Ted Martinez	.60	.30	.06
☐ 545	Wayne Granger	.60	.30	.06
☐ 546	Joe Hague	.60	.30	.06
☐ 547	Indians Team	1.25	.60	.12
☐ 548	Frank Reberger	.60	.30	.06
☐ 549	Dave May	.60	.30	.06
☐ 550	Brooks Robinson	10.00	5.00	1.00
☐ 551	Ollie Brown	.60	.30	.06
☐ 552	Brown In Action	.60	.30	.06
☐ 553	Wilbur Wood	.75	.35	.07
☐ 554	Wood In Action	.60	.30	.06
☐ 555	Ron Santo	1.00	.50	.10
☐ 556	Santo In Action	.75	.35	.07
☐ 557	John Odom	.60	.30	.06
☐ 558	Odom In Action	.60	.30	.06
☐ 559	Pete Rose	60.00	30.00	6.00
☐ 560	Rose In Action	20.00	10.00	2.00
☐ 561	Leo Cardenas	.60	.30	.06
☐ 562	Cardenas In Action	.60	.30	.06
☐ 563	Ray Sadecki	.60	.30	.06
☐ 564	Sadecki In Action	.60	.30	.06
☐ 565	Reggie Smith	1.00	.50	.10
☐ 566	Smith In Action	.75	.35	.07
☐ 567	Juan Marichal	4.00	2.00	.40
☐ 568	Marichal In Action	1.50	.75	.15
☐ 569	Ed Kirkpatrick	.60	.30	.06
☐ 570	Kirkpatrick In Action	.60	.30	.06
☐ 571	Nate Colbert	.60	.30	.06
☐ 572	Colbert In Action	.60	.30	.06
☐ 573	Fritz Peterson	.60	.30	.06
☐ 574	Peterson In Action	.60	.30	.06
☐ 575	Al Oliver	1.50	.75	.15
☐ 576	Leo Durocher MG	1.25	.60	.12
☐ 577	Mike Paul	.60	.30	.06
☐ 578	Billy Grabarkewitz	.60	.30	.06
☐ 579	Doyle Alexander	2.50	1.25	.25
☐ 580	Lou Piniella	1.75	.85	.17
☐ 581	Wade Blasingame	.60	.30	.06
☐ 582	Expos Team	1.50	.75	.15
☐ 583	Darold Knowles	.60	.30	.06
☐ 584	Jerry McNertney	.60	.30	.06
☐ 585	George Scott	.75	.35	.07
☐ 586	Denis Menke	.60	.30	.06
☐ 587	Billy Wilson	.60	.30	.06
☐ 588	Jim Holt	.60	.30	.06
☐ 589	Hal Lanier	.90	.45	.09
☐ 590	Graig Nettles	2.00	1.00	.20
☐ 591	Paul Casanova	.60	.30	.06
☐ 592	Lew Krausse	.60	.30	.06
☐ 593	Rich Morales	.60	.30	.06
☐ 594	Jim Beauchamp	.60	.30	.06
☐ 595	Nolan Ryan	15.00	7.50	1.50
☐ 596	Manny Mota	.90	.45	.09
☐ 597	Jim Magnuson	.60	.30	.06
☐ 598	Hal King	.60	.30	.06
☐ 599	Billy Champion	.60	.30	.06
☐ 600	Al Kaline	10.00	5.00	1.00
☐ 601	George Stone	.60	.30	.06
☐ 602	Dave Bristol MG	.60	.30	.06
☐ 603	Jim Ray	.60	.30	.06
☐ 604A	Checklist 6	3.00	.50	.10
	(copyright on back			
	bottom right)			
☐ 604B	Checklist 6	5.00	.70	.10
	(copyright on back			
	bottom left)			
☐ 605	Nelson Briles	.75	.35	.07
☐ 606	Luis Melendez	.60	.30	.06
☐ 607	Frank Duffy	.60	.30	.06
☐ 608	Mike Corkins	.60	.30	.06
☐ 609	Tom Grieve	.90	.45	.09
☐ 610	Bill Stoneman	.60	.30	.06

☐ 611	Rich Reese	.60	.30	.06
☐ 612	Joe Decker	.60	.30	.06
☐ 613	Mike Ferraro	.75	.35	.07
☐ 614	Ted Uhlaender	.60	.30	.06
☐ 615	Steve Hargan	.60	.30	.06
☐ 616	Joe Ferguson	.90	.45	.09
☐ 617	Royals Team	1.25	.60	.12
☐ 618	Rich Robertson	.60	.30	.06
☐ 619	Rich McKinney	.60	.30	.06
☐ 620	Phil Niekro	3.50	1.75	.35
☐ 621	Commissioners Award	.90	.45	.09
☐ 622	MVP Award	.90	.45	.09
☐ 623	Cy Young Award	.90	.45	.09
☐ 624	Minor League Player	.90	.45	.09
☐ 625	Rookie of the Year	.90	.45	.09
☐ 626	Babe Ruth Award	1.00	.50	.10
☐ 627	Moe Drabowsky	.60	.30	.06
☐ 628	Terry Crowley	.60	.30	.06
☐ 629	Paul Doyle	.60	.30	.06
☐ 630	Rich Hebner	.75	.35	.07
☐ 631	John Strohmayer	.60	.30	.06
☐ 632	Mike Hegan	.60	.30	.06
☐ 633	Jack Hiatt	.60	.30	.06
☐ 634	Dick Woodson	.60	.30	.06
☐ 635	Don Money	.75	.35	.07
☐ 636	Bill Lee	.90	.45	.09
☐ 637	Preston Gomez MG	.60	.30	.06
☐ 638	Ken Wright	.60	.30	.06
☐ 639	J.C. Martin	.60	.30	.06
☐ 640	Joe Coleman	.60	.30	.06
☐ 641	Mike Lum	.60	.30	.06
☐ 642	Dennis Riddleberger	.60	.30	.06
☐ 643	Russ Gibson	.60	.30	.06
☐ 644	Bernie Allen	.60	.30	.06
☐ 645	Jim Maloney	.75	.35	.07
☐ 646	Chico Salmon	.60	.30	.06
☐ 647	Bob Moose	.60	.30	.06
☐ 648	Jim Lyttle	.60	.30	.06
☐ 649	Pete Richert	.60	.30	.06
☐ 650	Sal Bando	.90	.45	.09
☐ 651	Reds Team	1.50	.75	.15
☐ 652	Marcelino Lopez	.60	.30	.06
☐ 653	Jim Fairey	.60	.30	.06
☐ 654	Horacio Pina	.60	.30	.06
☐ 655	Jerry Grote	.60	.30	.06
☐ 656	Rudy May	.60	.30	.06
☐ 657	Bobby Wine	1.50	.75	.15
☐ 658	Steve Dunning	1.50	.75	.15
☐ 659	Bob Aspromonte	1.50	.75	.15
☐ 660	Paul Blair	2.00	1.00	.20
☐ 661	Bill Virdon	2.50	1.25	.25
☐ 662	Stan Bahnsen	1.50	.75	.15
☐ 663	Fran Healy	1.50	.75	.15
☐ 664	Bobby Knoop	1.50	.75	.15
☐ 665	Chris Short	1.50	.75	.15
☐ 666	Hector Torres	1.50	.75	.15
☐ 667	Ray Newman	1.50	.75	.15
☐ 668	Rangers Team	4.00	2.00	.40
☐ 669	Willie Crawford	1.50	.75	.15
☐ 670	Ken Holtzman	2.00	1.00	.20
☐ 671	Donn Clendenon	2.00	1.00	.20
☐ 672	Archie Reynolds	1.50	.75	.15
☐ 673	Dave Marshall	1.50	.75	.15
☐ 674	John Kennedy	1.50	.75	.15
☐ 675	Pat Jarvis	1.50	.75	.15
☐ 676	Danny Cater	1.50	.75	.15
☐ 677	Ivan Murrell	1.50	.75	.15
☐ 678	Steve Luebber	1.50	.75	.15
☐ 679	Astros Rookies	1.50	.75	.15
	Bob Fenwick			
	Bob Stinson			
☐ 680	Dave Johnson	3.00	1.50	.30
☐ 681	Bobby Pfeil	1.50	.75	.15
☐ 682	Mike McCormick	2.00	1.00	.20
☐ 683	Steve Hovley	1.50	.75	.15
☐ 684	Hal Breeden	1.50	.75	.15
☐ 685	Joe Horlen	1.50	.75	.15
☐ 686	Steve Garvey	65.00	32.50	6.50
☐ 687	Del Unser	1.50	.75	.15
☐ 688	Cardinals Team	3.00	1.50	.30
☐ 689	Eddie Fisher	1.50	.75	.15
☐ 690	Willie Montanez	1.50	.75	.15
☐ 691	Curt Blefary	1.50	.75	.15
☐ 692	Blefary In Action	1.50	.75	.15
☐ 693	Alan Gallagher	1.50	.75	.15
☐ 694	Gallagher In Action	1.50	.75	.15
☐ 695	Rod Carew	60.00	30.00	6.00
☐ 696	Carew In Action	20.00	10.00	2.00
☐ 697	Jerry Koosman	4.50	2.25	.45
☐ 698	Koosman In Action	2.50	1.25	.25
☐ 699	Bobby Murcer	4.50	2.25	.45
☐ 700	Murcer In Action	2.50	1.25	.25
☐ 701	Jose Pagan	1.50	.75	.15
☐ 702	Pagan In Action	1.50	.75	.15
☐ 703	Doug Griffin	1.50	.75	.15
☐ 704	Griffin In Action	1.50	.75	.15
☐ 705	Pat Corrales	2.00	1.00	.20
☐ 706	Corrales In Action	1.50	.75	.15
☐ 707	Tim Foli	1.50	.75	.15
☐ 708	Foli In Action	1.50	.75	.15
☐ 709	Jim Kaat	5.00	2.50	.50
☐ 710	Kaat In Action	2.50	1.25	.25
☐ 711	Bobby Bonds	4.50	2.25	.45
☐ 712	Bonds In Action	2.50	1.25	.25
☐ 713	Gene Michael	2.00	1.00	.20
☐ 714	Michael In Action	1.50	.75	.15
☐ 715	Mike Epstein	1.50	.75	.15
☐ 716	Jesus Alou	1.50	.75	.15
☐ 717	Bruce Dal Canton	1.50	.75	.15
☐ 718	Del Rice MG	1.50	.75	.15
☐ 719	Cesar Geronimo	1.50	.75	.15
☐ 720	Sam McDowell	2.00	1.00	.20
☐ 721	Eddie Leon	1.50	.75	.15
☐ 722	Bill Sudakis	1.50	.75	.15
☐ 723	Al Santorini	1.50	.75	.15
☐ 724	AL Rookie Pitchers	2.00	1.00	.20
	John Curtis			
	Rich Hinton			
	Mickey Scott			
☐ 725	Dick McAuliffe	2.00	1.00	.20
☐ 726	Dick Selma	1.50	.75	.15
☐ 727	Jose LaBoy	1.50	.75	.15
☐ 728	Gail Hopkins	1.50	.75	.15
☐ 729	Bob Veale	2.00	1.00	.20
☐ 730	Rick Monday	2.50	1.25	.25
☐ 731	Orioles Team	3.00	1.50	.30
☐ 732	George Culver	1.50	.75	.15
☐ 733	Jim Ray Hart	2.00	1.00	.20
☐ 734	Bob Burda	1.50	.75	.15
☐ 735	Diego Segui	1.50	.75	.15
☐ 736	Bill Russell	3.00	1.50	.30
☐ 737	Lenny Randle	1.50	.75	.15
☐ 738	Jim Merritt	1.50	.75	.15
☐ 739	Don Mason	1.50	.75	.15
☐ 740	Rico Carty	2.50	1.25	.25
☐ 741	Rookie First Basemen	2.00	1.00	.20
	Tom Hutton			
	John Milner			
	Rick Miller			
☐ 742	Jim Rooker	1.50	.75	.15
☐ 743	Cesar Gutierrez	1.50	.75	.15
☐ 744	Jim Slaton	2.00	1.00	.20
☐ 745	Julian Javier	1.50	.75	.15
☐ 746	Lowell Palmer	1.50	.75	.15
☐ 747	Jim Stewart	1.50	.75	.15
☐ 748	Phil Hennigan	1.50	.75	.15
☐ 749	Walter Alston MG	4.00	2.00	.40
☐ 750	Willie Horton	2.25	1.10	.22
☐ 751	Steve Carlton TR	33.00	12.00	2.00
☐ 752	Joe Morgan TR	11.00	5.50	1.10
☐ 753	Denny McLain TR	3.50	1.75	.35
☐ 754	Frank Robinson TR	11.00	5.50	1.10
☐ 755	Jim Fregosi TR	2.50	1.25	.25
☐ 756	Rick Wise TR	2.00	1.00	.20
☐ 757	Jose Cardenal TR	2.00	1.00	.20
☐ 758	Gil Garrido	1.50	.75	.15
☐ 759	Chris Cannizzaro	1.50	.75	.15
☐ 760	Bill Mazeroski	3.00	1.50	.30
☐ 761	Rookie Outfielders	11.00	5.50	1.10
	Ben Oglivie			
	Ron Cey			
	Bernie Williams			
☐ 762	Wayne Simpson	1.50	.75	.15
☐ 763	Ron Hansen	1.50	.75	.15
☐ 764	Dusty Baker	3.00	1.50	.30
☐ 765	Ken McMullen	1.50	.75	.15
☐ 766	Steve Hamilton	1.50	.75	.15
☐ 767	Tom McCraw	1.50	.75	.15
☐ 768	Denny Doyle	1.50	.75	.15
☐ 769	Jack Aker	1.50	.75	.15
☐ 770	Jim Wynn	2.25	1.10	.22
☐ 771	Giants Team	3.00	1.50	.30
☐ 772	Ken Tatum	1.50	.75	.15
☐ 773	Ron Brand	1.50	.75	.15
☐ 774	Luis Alvarado	1.50	.75	.15
☐ 775	Jerry Reuss	3.00	1.50	.30
☐ 776	Bill Voss	1.50	.75	.15
☐ 777	Hoyt Wilhelm	8.00	4.00	.80
☐ 778	Twins Rookies	2.00	1.00	.20
	Vic Albury			
	Rick Dempsey			
	Jim Strickland			
☐ 779	Tony Cloninger	1.50	.75	.15
☐ 780	Dick Green	1.50	.75	.15
☐ 781	Jim McAndrew	1.50	.75	.15
☐ 782	Larry Stahl	1.50	.75	.15
☐ 783	Les Cain	1.50	.75	.15
☐ 784	Ken Aspromonte	1.50	.75	.15
☐ 785	Vic Davalillo	1.50	.75	.15
☐ 786	Chuck Brinkman	1.50	.75	.15

☐ 787 Ron Reed .... 2.50 .75 .15

1973 Topps

The cards in this 660-card set measure 2 1/2" by 3 1/2". The 1973 Topps set marked the last year in which Topps marketed baseball cards in consecutive series. The last series (529-660) is more difficult to obtain. Beginning in 1974, all Topps cards were printed at the same time, thus eliminating the "high number" factor. The set features team leader cards featuring small individual pictures of the coaching staff members with a larger picture of the manager. The "background" variations below with respect to these leader cards are subtle and are best understood after a side-by-side comparison of the two varieties. An "All-Time Leaders" series (471-478) appeared for the first time in this set. Kid Pictures appeared again for the second year in a row (341-346). Other topical subsets within the set included League Leaders (61-68), Playoffs cards (201- 202), World Series cards (203-210), and Rookie Prospects (601- 616).

	NRMT	VG-E	GOOD
COMPLETE SET	600.00	300.00	60.00
COMMON PLAYER (1-264)	.20	.10	.02
COMMON PLAYER (265-396)	.25	.12	.02
COMMON PLAYER (397-528)	.35	.17	.03
COMMON PLAYER (529-660)	1.00	.50	.10

☐	1	All-Time HR Leaders	9.00	2.00	.40
		714 Babe Ruth			
		673 Hank Aaron			
		654 Willie Mays			
☐	2	Rich Hebner	.20	.10	.02
☐	3	Jim Lonborg	.25	.12	.02
☐	4	John Milner	.20	.10	.02
☐	5	Ed Brinkman	.20	.10	.02
☐	6	Mac Scarce	.20	.10	.02
☐	7	Texas Rangers Team	.50	.25	.05
☐	8	Tom Hall	.20	.10	.02
☐	9	Johnny Oates	.20	.10	.02
☐	10	Don Sutton	2.00	1.00	.20
☐	11	Chris Chambliss	.35	.17	.03
☐	12A	Padres Leaders	.35	.17	.03
		Don Zimmer MG			
		Dave Garcia CO			
		Johnny Podres CO			
		Bob Skinner CO			
		Whitey Wietelmann CO			
		(Podres no right ear)			
☐	12B	Padres Leaders	.65	.30	.06
		(Podres has right ear)			
☐	13	George Hendrick	.50	.25	.05
☐	14	Sonny Siebert	.25	.12	.02
☐	15	Ralph Garr	.25	.12	.02
☐	16	Steve Braun	.20	.10	.02
☐	17	Fred Gladding	.20	.10	.02
☐	18	Leroy Stanton	.20	.10	.02
☐	19	Tim Foli	.20	.10	.02
☐	20	Stan Bahnsen	.20	.10	.02
☐	21	Randy Hundley	.20	.10	.02
☐	22	Ted Abernathy	.20	.10	.02
☐	23	Dave Kingman	1.50	.75	.15

☐	24	Al Santorini	.20	.10	.02
☐	25	Roy White	.25	.12	.02
☐	26	Pirates Team	.50	.25	.05
☐	27	Bill Gogolewski	.20	.10	.02
☐	28	Hal McRae	.35	.17	.03
☐	29	Tony Taylor	.20	.10	.02
☐	30	Tug McGraw	.65	.30	.06
☐	31	Buddy Bell	3.50	1.75	.35
☐	32	Fred Norman	.20	.10	.02
☐	33	Jim Breazeale	.20	.10	.02
☐	34	Pat Dobson	.25	.12	.02
☐	35	Willie Davis	.35	.17	.03
☐	36	Steve Barber	.20	.10	.02
☐	37	Bill Robinson	.25	.12	.02
☐	38	Mike Epstein	.20	.10	.02
☐	39	Dave Roberts	.20	.10	.02
☐	40	Reggie Smith	.50	.25	.05
☐	41	Tom Walker	.20	.10	.02
☐	42	Mike Andrews	.20	.10	.02
☐	43	Randy Moffitt	.20	.10	.02
☐	44	Rick Monday	.25	.12	.02
☐	45	Ellie Rodriguez	.25	.12	.02
		(photo actually			
		John Felske)			
☐	46	Lindy McDaniel	.25	.12	.02
☐	47	Luis Melendez	.20	.10	.02
☐	48	Paul Splittorff	.25	.12	.02
☐	49A	Twins Leaders	.35	.17	.03
		Frank Quilici MG			
		Vern Morgan CO			
		Bob Rodgers CO			
		Ralph Rowe CO			
		Al Worthington CO			
		(solid backgrounds)			
☐	49B	Twins Leaders	.65	.30	.06
		(natural backgrounds)			
☐	50	Roberto Clemente	10.00	5.00	1.00
☐	51	Chuck Seelbach	.20	.10	.02
☐	52	Denis Menke	.20	.10	.02
☐	53	Steve Dunning	.20	.10	.02
☐	54	Checklist 1	1.00	.10	.02
☐	55	Jon Matlack	.25	.12	.02
☐	56	Merv Rettenmund	.20	.10	.02
☐	57	Derrel Thomas	.20	.10	.02
☐	58	Mike Paul	.20	.10	.02
☐	59	Steve Yeager	.50	.25	.05
☐	60	Ken Holtzman	.25	.12	.02
☐	61	Batting Leaders	1.25	.60	.12
		Billy Williams			
		Rod Carew			
☐	62	Home Run Leaders	1.00	.50	.10
		Johnny Bench			
		Dick Allen			
☐	63	RBI Leaders	1.00	.50	.10
		Johnny Bench			
		Dick Allen			
☐	64	Stolen Base Leaders	.65	.30	.06
		Lou Brock			
		Bert Campaneris			
☐	65	ERA Leaders	.80	.40	.08
		Steve Carlton			
		Luis Tiant			
☐	66	Victory Leaders	1.00	.50	.10
		Steve Carlton			
		Gaylord Perry			
		Wilbur Wood			
☐	67	Strikeout Leaders	2.50	1.25	.25
		Steve Carlton			
		Nolan Ryan			
☐	68	Leading Firemen	.35	.17	.03
		Clay Carroll			
		Sparky Lyle			
☐	69	Phil Gagliano	.20	.10	.02
☐	70	Milt Pappas	.25	.12	.02
☐	71	Johnny Briggs	.20	.10	.02
☐	72	Ron Reed	.20	.10	.02
☐	73	Ed Herrmann	.20	.10	.02
☐	74	Billy Champion	.20	.10	.02
☐	75	Vada Pinson	.50	.25	.05
☐	76	Doug Rader	.25	.12	.02
☐	77	Mike Torrez	.25	.12	.02
☐	78	Richie Scheinblum	.20	.10	.02
☐	79	Jim Willoughby	.20	.10	.02
☐	80	Tony Oliva	.85	.40	.08
☐	81A	Cubs Leaders	.40	.20	.04
		Whitey Lockman MG			
		Hank Aguirre CO			
		Ernie Banks CO			
		Larry Jansen CO			
		Pete Reiser CO			
		(solid backgrounds)			
☐	81B	Cubs Leaders	.80	.40	.08
		(natural backgrounds)			
☐	82	Fritz Peterson	.20	.10	.02
☐	83	Leron Lee	.20	.10	.02

□ 84	Rollie Fingers	1.25	.60	.12
□ 85	Ted Simmons	1.00	.50	.10
□ 86	Tom McCraw	.20	.10	.02
□ 87	Ken Boswell	.20	.10	.02
□ 88	Mickey Stanley	.25	.12	.02
□ 89	Jack Billingham	.20	.10	.02
□ 90	Brooks Robinson	3.50	1.75	.35
□ 91	Dodgers Team	.70	.35	.07
□ 92	Jerry Bell	.20	.10	.02
□ 93	Jesus Alou	.20	.10	.02
□ 94	Dick Billings	.20	.10	.02
□ 95	Steve Blass	.20	.10	.02
□ 96	Doug Griffin	.20	.10	.02
□ 97	Willie Montanez	.20	.10	.02
□ 98	Dick Woodson	.20	.10	.02
□ 99	Carl Taylor	.20	.10	.02
□ 100	Hank Aaron	12.00	6.00	1.20
□ 101	Ken Henderson	.20	.10	.02
□ 102	Rudy May	.20	.10	.02
□ 103	Celerino Sanchez	.20	.10	.02
□ 104	Reggie Cleveland	.20	.10	.02
□ 105	Carlos May	.20	.10	.02
□ 106	Terry Humphrey	.20	.10	.02
□ 107	Phil Hennigan	.20	.10	.02
□ 108	Bill Russell	.25	.12	.02
□ 109	Doyle Alexander	.35	.17	.03
□ 110	Bob Watson	.25	.12	.02
□ 111	Dave Nelson	.20	.10	.02
□ 112	Gary Ross	.20	.10	.02
□ 113	Jerry Grote	.20	.10	.02
□ 114	Lynn McGlothen	.20	.10	.02
□ 115	Ron Santo	.50	.25	.05
□ 116A	Yankees Leaders	.50	.25	.05
	Ralph Houk MG			
	Jim Hegan CO			
	Elston Howard CO			
	Dick Howser CO			
	Jim Turner CO			
	(solid backgrounds)			
□ 116B	Yankees Leaders	1.00	.50	.10
	(natural backgrounds)			
□ 117	Ramon Hernandez	.20	.10	.02
□ 118	John Mayberry	.25	.12	.02
□ 119	Larry Bowa	.80	.40	.08
□ 120	Joe Coleman	.20	.10	.02
□ 121	Dave Rader	.20	.10	.02
□ 122	Jim Strickland	.20	.10	.02
□ 123	Sandy Alomar	.20	.10	.02
□ 124	Jim Hardin	.20	.10	.02
□ 125	Ron Fairly	.25	.12	.02
□ 126	Jim Brewer	.20	.10	.02
□ 127	Brewers Team	.50	.25	.05
□ 128	Ted Sizemore	.20	.10	.02
□ 129	Terry Forster	.35	.17	.03
□ 130	Pete Rose	18.00	9.00	1.80
□ 131A	Red Sox Leaders	.35	.17	.03
	Eddie Kasko MG			
	Doug Camilli CO			
	Don Lenhardt CO			
	Eddie Popowski CO			
	(no right ear)			
	Lee Stange CO			
□ 131B	Red Sox Leaders	.65	.30	.06
	(Popowski has right			
	ear showing)			
□ 132	Matty Alou	.25	.12	.02
□ 133	Dave Roberts	.20	.10	.02
□ 134	Milt Wilcox	.25	.12	.02
□ 135	Lee May	.25	.12	.02
□ 136A	Orioles Leaders	.60	.30	.06
	Earl Weaver MG			
	George Bamberger CO			
	Jim Frey CO			
	Billy Hunter CO			
	George Staller CO			
	(orange backgrounds)			
□ 136B	Orioles Leaders	1.00	.50	.10
	(dark pale			
	backgrounds)			
□ 137	Jim Beauchamp	.20	.10	.02
□ 138	Horacio Pina	.20	.10	.02
□ 139	Carmen Fanzone	.20	.10	.02
□ 140	Lou Piniella	.60	.30	.06
□ 141	Bruce Kison	.25	.12	.02
□ 142	Thurman Munson	4.50	2.25	.45
□ 143	John Curtis	.20	.10	.02
□ 144	Marty Perez	.20	.10	.02
□ 145	Bobby Bonds	.60	.30	.06
□ 146	Woodie Fryman	.20	.10	.02
□ 147	Mike Anderson	.20	.10	.02
□ 148	Dave Goltz	.25	.12	.02
□ 149	Ron Hunt	.20	.10	.02
□ 150	Wilbur Wood	.25	.12	.02
□ 151	Wes Parker	.25	.12	.02
□ 152	Dave May	.20	.10	.02
□ 153	Al Hrabosky	.35	.17	.03
□ 154	Jeff Torborg	.25	.12	.02
□ 155	Sal Bando	.35	.17	.03
□ 156	Cesar Geronimo	.20	.10	.02
□ 157	Denny Riddleberger	.20	.10	.02
□ 158	Astros Team	.50	.25	.05
□ 159	Clarence Gaston	.20	.10	.02
□ 160	Jim Palmer	3.50	1.75	.35
□ 161	Ted Martinez	.20	.10	.02
□ 162	Pete Broberg	.20	.10	.02
□ 163	Vic Davalillo	.20	.10	.02
□ 164	Monty Montgomery	.20	.10	.02
□ 165	Luis Aparicio	2.00	1.00	.20
□ 166	Terry Harmon	.20	.10	.02
□ 167	Steve Stone	.35	.17	.03
□ 168	Jim Northrup	.25	.12	.02
□ 169	Ron Schueler	.20	.10	.02
□ 170	Harmon Killebrew	3.00	1.50	.30
□ 171	Bernie Carbo	.20	.10	.02
□ 172	Steve Kline	.20	.10	.02
□ 173	Hal Breeden	.20	.10	.02
□ 174	Rich Gossage	6.00	3.00	.60
□ 175	Frank Robinson	3.00	1.50	.30
□ 176	Chuck Taylor	.20	.10	.02
□ 177	Bill Plummer	.20	.10	.02
□ 178	Don Rose	.20	.10	.02
□ 179A	A's Leaders	.35	.17	.03
	Dick Williams MG			
	Jerry Adair CO			
	Vern Hoscheit CO			
	Irv Noren CO			
	Wes Stock CO			
	(orange backgrounds)			
□ 179B	A's Leaders	.65	.30	.06
	(dark pale			
	backgrounds)			
□ 180	Fergie Jenkins	1.00	.50	.10
□ 181	Jack Brohamer	.20	.10	.02
□ 182	Mike Caldwell	.60	.30	.06
□ 183	Don Buford	.20	.10	.02
□ 184	Jerry Koosman	.50	.25	.05
□ 185	Jim Wynn	.35	.17	.03
□ 186	Bill Fahey	.20	.10	.02
□ 187	Luke Walker	.20	.10	.02
□ 188	Cookie Rojas	.20	.10	.02
□ 189	Greg Luzinski	.80	.40	.08
□ 190	Bob Gibson	3.00	1.50	.30
□ 191	Tigers Team	.60	.30	.06
□ 192	Pat Jarvis	.20	.10	.02
□ 193	Carlton Fisk	3.00	1.50	.30
□ 194	Jorge Orta	.20	.10	.02
□ 195	Clay Carroll	.20	.10	.02
□ 196	Ken McMullen	.20	.10	.02
□ 197	Ed Goodson	.20	.10	.02
□ 198	Horace Clarke	.20	.10	.02
□ 199	Bert Blyleven	1.25	.60	.12
□ 200	Billy Williams	2.25	1.10	.22
□ 201	A.L. Playoffs	.65	.30	.06
	A's over Tigers;			
	Hendrick scores			
	winning run			
□ 202	N.L. Playoffs	.65	.30	.06
	Reds over Pirates			
	Foster's run decides			
□ 203	World Series Game 1	.65	.30	.06
	Tenace the Menace			
□ 204	World Series Game 2	.65	.30	.06
	A's two straight			
□ 205	World Series Game 3	.65	.30	.06
	Reds win squeeker			
□ 206	World Series Game 4	.65	.30	.06
	Tenace singles			
	in ninth			
□ 207	World Series Game 5	.65	.30	.06
	Odom out at plate			
□ 208	World Series Game 6	.65	.30	.06
	Red's slugging			
	ties series			
□ 209	World Series Game 7	.65	.30	.06
	Campy stars			
	winning rally			
□ 210	World Series Summary	.65	.30	.06
	World champions:			
	A's Win			
□ 211	Balor Moore	.20	.10	.02
□ 212	Joe Lahoud	.20	.10	.02
□ 213	Steve Garvey	10.00	5.00	1.00
□ 214	Steve Hamilton	.20	.10	.02
□ 215	Dusty Baker	.60	.30	.06
□ 216	Toby Harrah	.35	.17	.03
□ 217	Don Wilson	.20	.10	.02
□ 218	Aurelio Rodriguez	.20	.10	.02
□ 219	Cardinals Team	.50	.25	.05
□ 220	Nolan Ryan	7.00	3.50	.70
□ 221	Fred Kendall	.20	.10	.02

☐ 222	Rob Gardner	.20	.10	.02
☐ 223	Bud Harrelson	.25	.12	.02
☐ 224	Bill Lee	.25	.12	.02
☐ 225	Al Oliver	1.00	.50	.10
☐ 226	Ray Fosse	.20	.10	.02
☐ 227	Wayne Twitchell	.20	.10	.02
☐ 228	Bobby Darwin	.20	.10	.02
☐ 229	Roric Harrison	.20	.10	.02
☐ 230	Joe Morgan	2.25	1.10	.22
☐ 231	Bill Parsons	.20	.10	.02
☐ 232	Ken Singleton	.35	.17	.03
☐ 233	Ed Kirkpatrick	.20	.10	.02
☐ 234	Bill North	.25	.12	.02
☐ 235	Jim Hunter	2.25	1.10	.22
☐ 236	Tito Fuentes	.20	.10	.02
☐ 237A	Braves Leaders	.85	.40	.08
	Eddie Mathews MG			
	Lew Burdette CO			
	Jim Busby CO			
	Roy Hartsfield CO			
	Ken Silvestri CO			
	(orange backgrounds)			
☐ 237B	Braves Leaders	1.25	.60	.12
	(dark pale backgrounds)			
☐ 238	Tony Muser	.20	.10	.02
☐ 239	Pete Richert	.20	.10	.02
☐ 240	Bobby Murcer	.60	.30	.06
☐ 241	Dwain Anderson	.20	.10	.02
☐ 242	George Culver	.20	.10	.02
☐ 243	Angels Team	.50	.25	.05
☐ 244	Ed Acosta	.20	.10	.02
☐ 245	Carl Yastrzemski	10.00	5.00	1.00
☐ 246	Ken Sanders	.20	.10	.02
☐ 247	Del Unser	.20	.10	.02
☐ 248	Jerry Johnson	.20	.10	.02
☐ 249	Larry Biittner	.20	.10	.02
☐ 250	Manny Sanguillen	.35	.17	.03
☐ 251	Roger Nelson	.20	.10	.02
☐ 252A	Giants Leaders	.35	.17	.03
	Charlie Fox MG			
	Joe Amalfitano CO			
	Andy Gilbert CO			
	Don McMahon CO			
	John McNamara CO			
	(orange backgrounds)			
☐ 252B	Giants Leaders	.65	.30	.06
	(dark pale backgrounds)			
☐ 253	Mark Belanger	.35	.17	.03
☐ 254	Bill Stoneman	.20	.10	.02
☐ 255	Reggie Jackson	12.50	6.25	1.25
☐ 256	Chris Zachary	.20	.10	.02
☐ 257A	Mets Leaders	1.00	.50	.10
	Yogi Berra MG			
	Roy McMillan CO			
	Joe Pignatano CO			
	Rube Walker CO			
	Eddie Yost CO			
	(orange backgrounds)			
☐ 257B	Mets Leaders	1.50	.75	.15
	(dark pale backgrounds)			
☐ 258	Tommy John	1.25	.60	.12
☐ 259	Jim Holt	.20	.10	.02
☐ 260	Gary Nolan	.20	.10	.02
☐ 261	Pat Kelly	.20	.10	.02
☐ 262	Jack Aker	.20	.10	.02
☐ 263	George Scott	.25	.12	.02
☐ 264	Checklist 2	1.00	.10	.02
☐ 265	Gene Michael	.35	.17	.03
☐ 266	Mike Lum	.25	.12	.02
☐ 267	Lloyd Allen	.25	.12	.02
☐ 268	Jerry Morales	.25	.12	.02
☐ 269	Tim McCarver	.50	.25	.05
☐ 270	Luis Tiant	.50	.25	.05
☐ 271	Tom Hutton	.25	.12	.02
☐ 272	Ed Farmer	.25	.12	.02
☐ 273	Chris Speier	.35	.17	.03
☐ 274	Darold Knowles	.25	.12	.02
☐ 275	Tony Perez	1.00	.50	.10
☐ 276	Joe Lovitto	.25	.12	.02
☐ 277	Bob Miller	.25	.12	.02
☐ 278	Orioles Team	.50	.25	.05
☐ 279	Mike Strahler	.25	.12	.02
☐ 280	Al Kaline	3.50	1.75	.35
☐ 281	Mike Jorgensen	.25	.12	.02
☐ 282	Steve Hovley	.25	.12	.02
☐ 283	Ray Sadecki	.25	.12	.02
☐ 284	Glenn Borgmann	.25	.12	.02
☐ 285	Don Kessinger	.35	.17	.03
☐ 286	Frank Linzy	.25	.12	.02
☐ 287	Eddie Leon	.25	.12	.02
☐ 288	Gary Gentry	.25	.12	.02
☐ 289	Bob Oliver	.25	.12	.02
☐ 290	Cesar Cedeno	.35	.17	.03
☐ 291	Rogelio Moret	.25	.12	.02
☐ 292	Jose Cruz	.60	.30	.06
☐ 293	Bernie Allen	.25	.12	.02
☐ 294	Steve Arlin	.25	.12	.02
☐ 295	Bert Campaneris	.35	.17	.03
☐ 296	Reds Leaders	.40	.20	.04
	Sparky Anderson MG			
	Alex Grammas CO			
	Ted Kluszewski CO			
	George Scherger CO			
	Larry Shepard CO			
☐ 297	Walt Williams	.25	.12	.02
☐ 298	Ron Bryant	.25	.12	.02
☐ 299	Ted Ford	.25	.12	.02
☐ 300	Steve Carlton	7.00	3.50	.70
☐ 301	Billy Grabarkewitz	.25	.12	.02
☐ 302	Terry Crowley	.25	.12	.02
☐ 303	Nelson Briles	.35	.17	.03
☐ 304	Duke Sims	.25	.12	.02
☐ 305	Willie Mays	12.00	6.00	1.20
☐ 306	Tom Burgmeier	.25	.12	.02
☐ 307	Boots Day	.25	.12	.02
☐ 308	Skip Lockwood	.25	.12	.02
☐ 309	Paul Popovich	.25	.12	.02
☐ 310	Dick Allen	.50	.25	.05
☐ 311	Joe Decker	.25	.12	.02
☐ 312	Oscar Brown	.25	.12	.02
☐ 313	Jim Ray	.25	.12	.02
☐ 314	Ron Swoboda	.25	.12	.02
☐ 315	John Odom	.25	.12	.02
☐ 316	Padres Team	.50	.25	.05
☐ 317	Danny Cater	.25	.12	.02
☐ 318	Jim McGlothlin	.25	.12	.02
☐ 319	Jim Spencer	.25	.12	.02
☐ 320	Lou Brock	2.75	1.35	.27
☐ 321	Rich Hinton	.25	.12	.02
☐ 322	Garry Maddox	.60	.30	.06
☐ 323	Tigers Leaders	.65	.30	.06
	Billy Martin MG			
	Art Fowler CO			
	Charlie Silvera CO			
	Dick Tracewski CO			
☐ 324	Al Downing	.35	.17	.03
☐ 325	Boog Powell	.65	.30	.06
☐ 326	Darrell Brandon	.25	.12	.02
☐ 327	John Lowenstein	.25	.12	.02
☐ 328	Bill Bonham	.25	.12	.02
☐ 329	Ed Kranepool	.35	.17	.03
☐ 330	Rod Carew	6.50	3.25	.65
☐ 331	Carl Morton	.25	.12	.02
☐ 332	John Felske	.25	.12	.02
☐ 333	Gene Clines	.25	.12	.02
☐ 334	Freddie Patek	.35	.17	.03
☐ 335	Bob Tolan	.35	.17	.03
☐ 336	Tom Bradley	.25	.12	.02
☐ 337	Dave Duncan	.25	.12	.02
☐ 338	Checklist 3	1.00	.10	.02
☐ 339	Dick Tidrow	.25	.12	.02
☐ 340	Nate Colbert	.25	.12	.02
☐ 341	KP: Jim Palmer	1.00	.50	.10
☐ 342	KP: Sam McDowell	.25	.12	.02
☐ 343	KP: Bobby Murcer	.35	.17	.03
☐ 344	KP: Jim Hunter	.75	.35	.07
☐ 345	KP: Chris Speier	.25	.12	.02
☐ 346	KP: Gaylord Perry	.65	.30	.06
☐ 347	Royals Team	.50	.25	.05
☐ 348	Rennie Stennett	.25	.12	.02
☐ 349	Dick McAuliffe	.25	.12	.02
☐ 350	Tom Seaver	8.00	4.00	.80
☐ 351	Jimmy Stewart	.25	.12	.02
☐ 352	Don Stanhouse	.25	.12	.02
☐ 353	Steve Brye	.25	.12	.02
☐ 354	Billy Parker	.25	.12	.02
☐ 355	Mike Marshall	.35	.17	.03
☐ 356	White Sox Leaders	.35	.17	.03
	Chuck Tanner MG			
	Joe Lonnett CO			
	Jim Mahoney CO			
	Al Monchak CO			
	Johnny Sain CO			
☐ 357	Ross Grimsley	.25	.12	.02
☐ 358	Jim Nettles	.25	.12	.02
☐ 359	Cecil Upshaw	.25	.12	.02
☐ 360	Joe Rudi	.35	.17	.03
	(photo actually Gene Tenace)			
☐ 361	Fran Healy	.25	.12	.02
☐ 362	Eddie Watt	.25	.12	.02
☐ 363	Jackie Hernandez	.25	.12	.02
☐ 364	Rick Wise	.25	.12	.02
☐ 365	Rico Petrocelli	.35	.17	.03
☐ 366	Brock Davis	.25	.12	.02
☐ 367	Burt Hooton	.25	.12	.02
☐ 368	Bill Buckner	.65	.30	.06

☐ 369 Lerrin LaGrow	.25	.12	.02
☐ 370 Willie Stargell	2.75	1.35	.27
☐ 371 Mike Kekich	.25	.12	.02
☐ 372 Oscar Gamble	.35	.17	.03
☐ 373 Clyde Wright	.25	.12	.02
☐ 374 Darrell Evans	.75	.35	.07
☐ 375 Larry Dierker	.35	.17	.03
☐ 376 Frank Duffy	.25	.12	.02
☐ 377 Expos Leaders	.35	.17	.03
Gene Mauch MG			
Dave Bristol CO			
Larry Doby CO			
Cal McLish CO			
Jerry Zimmerman CO			
☐ 378 Lenny Randle	.25	.12	.02
☐ 379 Cy Acosta	.25	.12	.02
☐ 380 Johnny Bench	8.00	4.00	.80
☐ 381 Vicente Romo	.25	.12	.02
☐ 382 Mike Hegan	.25	.12	.02
☐ 383 Diego Segui	.25	.12	.02
☐ 384 Don Baylor	1.00	.50	.10
☐ 385 Jim Perry	.35	.17	.03
☐ 386 Don Money	.25	.12	.02
☐ 387 Jim Barr	.25	.12	.02
☐ 388 Ben Oglivie	.50	.25	.05
☐ 389 Mets Team	1.25	.60	.12
☐ 390 Mickey Lolich	.65	.30	.06
☐ 391 Lee Lacy	.70	.35	.07
☐ 392 Dick Drago	.25	.12	.02
☐ 393 Jose Cardenal	.25	.12	.02
☐ 394 Sparky Lyle	.50	.25	.05
☐ 395 Roger Metzger	.25	.12	.02
☐ 396 Grant Jackson	.25	.12	.02
☐ 397 Dave Cash	.35	.17	.03
☐ 398 Rich Hand	.35	.17	.03
☐ 399 George Foster	1.25	.60	.12
☐ 400 Gaylord Perry	2.25	1.10	.22
☐ 401 Clyde Mashore	.35	.17	.03
☐ 402 Jack Hiatt	.35	.17	.03
☐ 403 Sonny Jackson	.35	.17	.03
☐ 404 Chuck Brinkman	.35	.17	.03
☐ 405 Cesar Tovar	.35	.17	.03
☐ 406 Paul Lindblad	.35	.17	.03
☐ 407 Felix Millan	.35	.17	.03
☐ 408 Jim Colborn	.35	.17	.03
☐ 409 Ivan Murrell	.35	.17	.03
☐ 410 Willie McCovey	2.75	1.35	.27
☐ 411 Ray Corbin	.35	.17	.03
☐ 412 Manny Mota	.50	.25	.05
☐ 413 Tom Timmerman	.35	.17	.03
☐ 414 Ken Rudolph	.35	.17	.03
☐ 415 Marty Pattin	.35	.17	.03
☐ 416 Paul Schaal	.35	.17	.03
☐ 417 Scipio Spinks	.35	.17	.03
☐ 418 Bobby Grich	.60	.30	.06
☐ 419 Casey Cox	.35	.17	.03
☐ 420 Tommie Agee	.35	.17	.03
☐ 421A Angels Leaders	.50	.25	.05
Bobby Winkles MG			
Tom Morgan CO			
Salty Parker CO			
Jimmie Reese CO			
John Roseboro CO			
(orange backgrounds)			
☐ 421B Angels Leaders	1.00	.50	.10
(dark pale			
backgrounds)			
☐ 422 Bob Robertson	.35	.17	.03
☐ 423 Johnny Jeter	.35	.17	.03
☐ 424 Denny Doyle	.35	.17	.03
☐ 425 Alex Johnson	.35	.17	.03
☐ 426 Dave LaRoche	.35	.17	.03
☐ 427 Rick Auerbach	.35	.17	.03
☐ 428 Wayne Simpson	.35	.17	.03
☐ 429 Jim Fairey	.35	.17	.03
☐ 430 Vida Blue	.60	.30	.06
☐ 431 Gerry Moses	.35	.17	.03
☐ 432 Dan Frisella	.35	.17	.03
☐ 433 Willie Horton	.50	.25	.05
☐ 434 Giants Team	.65	.30	.06
☐ 435 Rico Carty	.60	.30	.06
☐ 436 Jim McAndrew	.35	.17	.03
☐ 437 John Kennedy	.35	.17	.03
☐ 438 Enzo Hernandez	.35	.17	.03
☐ 439 Eddie Fisher	.35	.17	.03
☐ 440 Glenn Beckert	.50	.25	.05
☐ 441 Gail Hopkins	.35	.17	.03
☐ 442 Dick Dietz	.35	.17	.03
☐ 443 Danny Thompson	.35	.17	.03
☐ 444 Ken Brett	.35	.17	.03
☐ 445 Ken Berry	.35	.17	.03
☐ 446 Jerry Reuss	.50	.25	.05
☐ 447 Joe Hague	.35	.17	.03
☐ 448 John Hiller	.50	.25	.05
☐ 449A Indians Leaders	.50	.25	.05

Ken Aspromonte MG			
Rocky Colavito CO			
Joe Lutz CO			
Warren Spahn CO			
(Spahn's right			
ear pointed)			
☐ 449B Indians Leaders	1.00	.50	.10
(Spahn's right			
ear round)			
☐ 450 Joe Torre	.70	.35	.07
☐ 451 John Vuckovich	.35	.17	.03
☐ 452 Paul Casanova	.35	.17	.03
☐ 453 Checklist 4	1.25	.15	.03
☐ 454 Tom Haller	.35	.17	.03
☐ 455 Bill Melton	.35	.17	.03
☐ 456 Dick Green	.35	.17	.03
☐ 457 John Strohmayer	.35	.17	.03
☐ 458 Jim Mason	.35	.17	.03
☐ 459 Jimmy Howarth	.35	.17	.03
☐ 460 Bill Freehan	.60	.30	.06
☐ 461 Mike Corkins	.35	.17	.03
☐ 462 Ron Blomberg	.35	.17	.03
☐ 463 Ken Tatum	.35	.17	.03
☐ 464 Chicago Cubs Team	.65	.30	.06
☐ 465 Dave Giusti	.35	.17	.03
☐ 466 Jose Arcia	.35	.17	.03
☐ 467 Mike Ryan	.35	.17	.03
☐ 468 Tom Griffin	.35	.17	.03
☐ 469 Dan Monzon	.35	.17	.03
☐ 470 Mike Cuellar	.50	.25	.05
☐ 471 Hits Leaders	2.25	1.10	.22
Ty Cobb 4191			
☐ 472 Grand Slam Leaders	2.25	1.10	.22
Lou Gehrig 23			
☐ 473 Total Bases Leaders	2.25	1.10	.22
Hank Aaron 6172			
☐ 474 RBI Leaders	4.00	2.00	.40
Babe Ruth 2209			
☐ 475 Batting Leaders	2.25	1.10	.22
Ty Cobb .367			
☐ 476 Shutout Leaders	1.25	.60	.12
Walter Johnson 113			
☐ 477 Victory Leaders	1.25	.60	.12
Cy Young 511			
☐ 478 Strikeout Leaders	1.25	.60	.12
Walter Johnson 3508			
☐ 479 Hal Lanier	.50	.25	.05
☐ 480 Juan Marichal	2.75	1.35	.27
☐ 481 White Sox Team	.65	.30	.06
☐ 482 Rick Reuschel	2.00	1.00	.20
☐ 483 Dal Maxvill	.35	.17	.03
☐ 484 Ernie McAnally	.35	.17	.03
☐ 485 Norm Cash	.60	.30	.06
☐ 486A Phillies Leaders	.50	.25	.05
Danny Ozark MG			
Carroll Beringer CO			
Billy DeMars CO			
Ray Rippelmeyer CO			
Bobby Wine CO			
(orange backgrounds)			
☐ 486B Phillies Leaders	1.00	.50	.10
(dark pale			
backgrounds)			
☐ 487 Bruce Dal Canton	.35	.17	.03
☐ 488 Dave Campbell	.35	.17	.03
☐ 489 Jeff Burroughs	.35	.17	.03
☐ 490 Claude Osteen	.50	.25	.05
☐ 491 Bob Montgomery	.35	.17	.03
☐ 492 Pedro Borbon	.35	.17	.03
☐ 493 Duffy Dyer	.35	.17	.03
☐ 494 Rich Morales	.35	.17	.03
☐ 495 Tommy Helms	.50	.25	.05
☐ 496 Ray Lamb	.35	.17	.03
☐ 497A Cardinals Leaders	.50	.25	.05
Red Schoendienst MG			
Vern Benson CO			
George Kissell CO			
Barney Schultz CO			
(orange backgrounds)			
☐ 497B Cardinals Leaders	1.00	.50	.10
(dark pale			
backgrounds)			
☐ 498 Graig Nettles	1.75	.85	.17
☐ 499 Bob Moose	.35	.17	.03
☐ 500 Oakland A's Team	.75	.35	.07
☐ 501 Larry Gura	.50	.25	.05
☐ 502 Bobby Valentine	.60	.30	.06
☐ 503 Phil Niekro	2.25	1.10	.22
☐ 504 Earl Williams	.35	.17	.03
☐ 505 Bob Bailey	.35	.17	.03
☐ 506 Bart Johnson	.35	.17	.03
☐ 507 Darrel Chaney	.35	.17	.03
☐ 508 Gates Brown	.50	.25	.05
☐ 509 Jim Nash	.35	.17	.03
☐ 510 Amos Otis	.60	.30	.06

☐ 511	Sam McDowell	.50	.25	.05
☐ 512	Dalton Jones	.35	.17	.03
☐ 513	Dave Marshall	.35	.17	.03
☐ 514	Jerry Kenney	.35	.17	.03
☐ 515	Andy Messersmith	.50	.25	.05
☐ 516	Danny Walton	.35	.17	.03
☐ 517A	Pirates Leaders	.50	.25	.05

Bill Virdon MG
Don Leppert CO
Bill Mazeroski CO
Dave Ricketts CO
Mel Wright CO
(Mazeroski has
no right ear)

☐ 517B	Pirates Leaders	1.00	.50	.10

(Mazeroski has
right ear)

☐ 518	Bob Veale	.50	.25	.05
☐ 519	John Edwards	.35	.17	.03
☐ 520	Mel Stottlemyre	.60	.30	.06
☐ 521	Atlanta Braves Team	.65	.30	.06
☐ 522	Leo Cardenas	.35	.17	.03
☐ 523	Wayne Granger	.35	.17	.03
☐ 524	Gene Tenace	.50	.25	.05
☐ 525	Jim Fregosi	.65	.30	.06
☐ 526	Ollie Brown	.35	.17	.03
☐ 527	Dan McGinn	.35	.17	.03
☐ 528	Paul Blair	.50	.25	.05
☐ 529	Milt May	1.00	.50	.10
☐ 530	Jim Kaat	3.00	1.50	.30
☐ 531	Ron Woods	1.00	.50	.10
☐ 532	Steve Mingori	1.00	.50	.10
☐ 533	Larry Stahl	1.00	.50	.10
☐ 534	Dave Lemonds	1.00	.50	.10
☐ 535	John Callison	1.50	.75	.15
☐ 536	Phillies Team	2.00	1.00	.20
☐ 537	Bill Slayback	1.00	.50	.10
☐ 538	Jim Ray Hart	1.50	.75	.15
☐ 539	Tom Murphy	1.00	.50	.10
☐ 540	Cleon Jones	1.00	.50	.10
☐ 541	Bob Bolin	1.00	.50	.10
☐ 542	Pat Corrales	1.50	.75	.15
☐ 543	Alan Foster	1.00	.50	.10
☐ 544	Von Joshua	1.00	.50	.10
☐ 545	Orlando Cepeda	3.00	1.50	.30
☐ 546	Jim York	1.00	.50	.10
☐ 547	Bobby Heise	1.00	.50	.10
☐ 548	Don Durham	1.00	.50	.10
☐ 549	Rangers Leaders	2.00	1.00	.20

Whitey Herzog MG
Chuck Estrada CO
Chuck Hiller CO
Jackie Moore CO

☐ 550	Dave Johnson	2.50	1.25	.25
☐ 551	Mike Kilkenny	1.00	.50	.10
☐ 552	J.C. Martin	1.00	.50	.10
☐ 553	Mickey Scott	1.00	.50	.10
☐ 554	Dave Concepcion	2.50	1.25	.25
☐ 555	Bill Hands	1.00	.50	.10
☐ 556	Yankees Team	3.00	1.50	.30
☐ 557	Bernie Williams	1.00	.50	.10
☐ 558	Jerry May	1.00	.50	.10
☐ 559	Barry Lersch	1.00	.50	.10
☐ 560	Frank Howard	2.50	1.25	.25
☐ 561	Jim Geddes	1.00	.50	.10
☐ 562	Wayne Garrett	1.00	.50	.10
☐ 563	Larry Haney	1.00	.50	.10
☐ 564	Mike Thompson	1.00	.50	.10
☐ 565	Jim Hickman	1.00	.50	.10
☐ 566	Lew Krausse	1.00	.50	.10
☐ 567	Bob Fenwick	1.00	.50	.10
☐ 568	Ray Newman	1.00	.50	.10
☐ 569	Dodgers Leaders	2.50	1.25	.25

Walt Alston MG
Red Adams CO
Monty Basgall CO
Jim Gilliam CO
Tom Lasorda CO

☐ 570	Bill Singer	1.00	.50	.10
☐ 571	Rusty Torres	1.00	.50	.10
☐ 572	Gary Sutherland	1.00	.50	.10
☐ 573	Fred Beene	1.00	.50	.10
☐ 574	Bob Didier	1.00	.50	.10
☐ 575	Dock Ellis	1.00	.50	.10
☐ 576	Expos Team	2.00	1.00	.20
☐ 577	Eric Soderholm	1.00	.50	.10
☐ 578	Ken Wright	1.00	.50	.10
☐ 579	Tom Grieve	1.50	.75	.15
☐ 580	Joe Pepitone	1.50	.75	.15
☐ 581	Steve Kealey	1.00	.50	.10
☐ 582	Darrell Porter	1.50	.75	.15
☐ 583	Bill Grief	1.00	.50	.10
☐ 584	Chris Arnold	1.00	.50	.10
☐ 585	Joe Niekro	2.50	1.25	.25
☐ 586	Bill Sudakis	1.00	.50	.10

☐ 587	Rich McKinney	1.00	.50	.10
☐ 588	Checklist 5	10.00	5.00	1.00
☐ 589	Ken Forsch	1.50	.75	.15
☐ 590	Deron Johnson	1.00	.50	.10
☐ 591	Mike Hedlund	1.00	.50	.10
☐ 592	John Boccabella	1.00	.50	.10
☐ 593	Royals Leaders	1.50	.75	.15

Jack McKeon MG
Galen Cisco CO
Harry Dunlop CO
Charlie Lau CO

☐ 594	Vic Harris	1.00	.50	.10
☐ 595	Don Gullett	1.50	.75	.15
☐ 596	Red Sox Team	2.50	1.25	.25
☐ 597	Mickey Rivers	1.50	.75	.15
☐ 598	Phil Roof	1.00	.50	.10
☐ 599	Ed Crosby	1.00	.50	.10
☐ 600	Dave McNally	1.50	.75	.15
☐ 601	Rookie Catchers	1.00	.50	.10

Sergio Robles
George Pena
Rick Stelmaszek

☐ 602	Rookie Pitchers	1.00	.50	.10

Mel Behney
Ralph Garcia
Doug Rau

☐ 603	Rookie 3rd Basemen	1.00	.50	.10

Terry Hughes
Bill McNulty
Ken Reitz

☐ 604	Rookie Pitchers	1.00	.50	.10

Jesse Jefferson
Dennis O'Toole
Bob Strampe

☐ 605	Rookie 1st Basemen	1.50	.75	.15

Enos Cabell
Pat Bourque
Gonzalo Marquez

☐ 606	Rookie Outfielders	3.00	1.50	.30

Gary Matthews
Tom Paciorek
Jorge Roque

☐ 607	Rookie Shortstops	1.00	.50	.10

Pepe Frias
Ray Busse
Mario Guerrero

☐ 608	Rookie Pitchers	1.50	.75	.15

Steve Busby
Dick Colpaert
George Medich

☐ 609	Rookie 2nd Basemen	3.00	1.50	.30

Larvell Blanks
Pedro Garcia
Dave Lopes

☐ 610	Rookie Pitchers	2.00	1.00	.20

Jimmy Freeman
Charlie Hough
Hank Webb

☐ 611	Rookie Outfielders	1.50	.75	.15

Rich Coggins
Jim Wohlford
Richie Zisk

☐ 612	Rookie Pitchers	1.00	.50	.10

Steve Lawson
Bob Reynolds
Brent Strom

☐ 613	Rookie Catchers	4.00	2.00	.40

Bob Boone
Skip Jutze
Mike Ivie

☐ 614	Rookie Outfielders	40.00	20.00	4.00

Alonza Bumbry
Dwight Evans
Charlie Spikes

☐ 615	Rookie 3rd Basemen	175.00	85.00	18.00

Ron Cey
John Hilton
Mike Schmidt

☐ 616	Rookie Pitchers	1.00	.50	.10

Norm Angelini
Steve Blateric
Mike Garman

☐ 617	Rich Chiles	1.00	.50	.10
☐ 618	Andy Etchebarren	1.00	.50	.10
☐ 619	Billy Wilson	1.00	.50	.10
☐ 620	Tommy Harper	1.50	.75	.15
☐ 621	Joe Ferguson	1.50	.75	.15
☐ 622	Larry Hisle	1.50	.75	.15
☐ 623	Steve Renko	1.00	.50	.10
☐ 624	Astros Leaders	2.00	1.00	.20

Leo Durocher MG
Preston Gomez CO
Grady Hatton CO
Hub Kittle CO
Jim Owens CO

			NRMT	VG-E	GOOD
☐	625	Angel Mangual	1.00	.50	.10
☐	626	Bob Barton	1.00	.50	.10
☐	627	Luis Alvarado	1.00	.50	.10
☐	628	Jim Slaton	1.00	.50	.10
☐	629	Indians Team	2.00	1.00	.20
☐	630	Denny McLain	2.50	1.25	.25
☐	631	Tom Matchick	1.00	.50	.10
☐	632	Dick Selma	1.00	.50	.10
☐	633	Ike Brown	1.00	.50	.10
☐	634	Alan Closter	1.00	.50	.10
☐	635	Gene Alley	1.00	.50	.10
☐	636	Rickey Clark	1.00	.50	.10
☐	637	Norm Miller	1.00	.50	.10
☐	638	Ken Reynolds	1.00	.50	.10
☐	639	Willie Crawford	1.00	.50	.10
☐	640	Dick Bosman	1.00	.50	.10
☐	641	Reds Team	2.50	1.25	.25
☐	642	Jose LaBoy	1.00	.50	.10
☐	643	Al Fitzmorris	1.00	.50	.10
☐	644	Jack Heidemann	1.00	.50	.10
☐	645	Bob Locker	1.00	.50	.10
☐	646	Brewers Leaders	1.50	.75	.15
		Del Crandall MG			
		Harvey Kuenn CO			
		Joe Nossek CO			
		Bob Shaw CO			
		Jim Walton CO			
☐	647	George Stone	1.00	.50	.10
☐	648	Tom Egan	1.00	.50	.10
☐	649	Rich Folkers	1.00	.50	.10
☐	650	Felipe Alou	1.50	.75	.15
☐	651	Don Carrithers	1.00	.50	.10
☐	652	Ted Kubiak	1.00	.50	.10
☐	653	Joe Hoerner	1.00	.50	.10
☐	654	Twins Team	2.00	1.00	.20
☐	655	Clay Kirby	1.00	.50	.10
☐	656	John Ellis	1.00	.50	.10
☐	657	Bob Johnson	1.00	.50	.10
☐	658	Elliott Maddox	1.00	.50	.10
☐	659	Jose Pagan	1.00	.50	.10
☐	660	Fred Scherman	2.50	.50	.10

1973 Topps Team Checklists

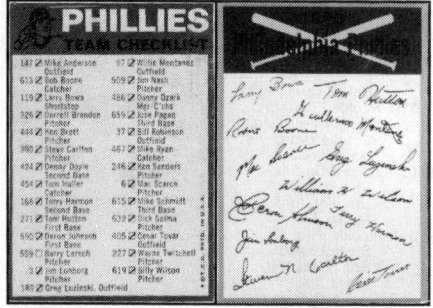

This 24 card set (measuring 2 1/2" by 3 1/2") is rather difficult to find. These blue bordered team checklist cards are very similar in design to the mass produced red trim team checklist cards issued by Topps the next year.

			NRMT	VG-E	GOOD
COMPLETE SET			70.00	27.00	6.00
COMMON TEAM			3.00	1.15	.25
☐	1	Atlanta Braves	3.00	1.15	.25
☐	2	Baltimore Orioles	3.00	1.15	.25
☐	3	Boston Red Sox	3.00	1.15	.25
☐	4	California Angels	3.00	1.15	.25
☐	5	Chicago Cubs	3.00	1.15	.25
☐	6	Chicago White Sox	3.00	1.15	.25
☐	7	Cincinnati Reds	3.00	1.15	.25
☐	8	Cleveland Indians	3.00	1.15	.25
☐	9	Detroit Tigers	3.00	1.15	.25
☐	10	Houston Astros	3.00	1.15	.25
☐	11	Kansas City Royals	3.00	1.15	.25
☐	12	Los Angeles Dodgers	3.00	1.15	.25
☐	13	Milwaukee Brewers	3.00	1.15	.25
☐	14	Minnesota Twins	3.00	1.15	.25
☐	15	Montreal Expos	3.00	1.15	.25
☐	16	New York Mets	3.00	1.15	.25
☐	17	New York Yankees	3.00	1.15	.25
☐	18	Oakland A's	3.00	1.15	.25
☐	19	Philadelphia Phillies	3.00	1.15	.25
☐	20	Pittsburgh Pirates	3.00	1.15	.25
☐	21	San Diego Padres	3.00	1.15	.25
☐	22	San Francisco Giants	3.00	1.15	.25
☐	23	St. Louis Cardinals	3.00	1.15	.25
☐	24	Texas Rangers	3.00	1.15	.25

1974 Topps

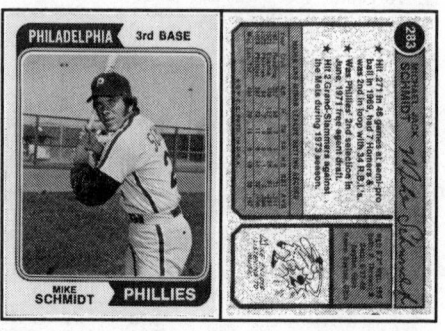

The cards in this 660-card set measure 2 1/2" by 3 1/2". This year marked the first time Topps issued all the cards of its baseball set at the same time rather than in series. Some interesting variations were created by the rumored move of the San Diego Padres to Washington. Fifteen cards (13 players, the team card, and the rookie card #599) of the Padres were printed either as "San Diego" (SD) or "Washington." The latter are the scarcer variety and are denoted in the checklist below by WAS. Each team's manager and his coaches again have a combined card with small pictures of each coach below the larger photo of the team's manager. The first six cards in the set (1-6) feature Hank Aaron and his illustrious career. Other topical subsets included in the set are League Leaders (201-208), All-Star selections (331-339), Playoffs cards (470-471), World Series cards (472-479), and Rookie Prospects (596-608).

			NRMT	VG-E	GOOD
COMPLETE SET			325.00	160.00	32.00
COMMON PLAYER (1-660)			.20	.10	.02
☐	1	Hank Aaron	12.00	6.00	1.20
		Complete ML record			
☐	2	Aaron Special 54-57	3.00	1.50	.30
		Records on back			
☐	3	Aaron Special 58-61	3.00	1.50	.30
		Memorable homers			
☐	4	Aaron Special 62-65	3.00	1.50	.30
		Life in ML's 1954-63			
☐	5	Aaron Special 66-69	3.00	1.50	.30
		Life in ML's 1964-73			
☐	6	Aaron Special 70-73	3.00	1.50	.30
		Milestone homers			
☐	7	Jim Hunter	2.25	1.10	.22
☐	8	George Theodore	.20	.10	.02
☐	9	Mickey Lolich	.50	.25	.05
☐	10	Johnny Bench	6.50	3.25	.65
☐	11	Jim Bibby	.20	.10	.02
☐	12	Dave May	.20	.10	.02
☐	13	Tom Hilgendorf	.20	.10	.02
☐	14	Paul Popovich	.20	.10	.02
☐	15	Joe Torre	.60	.30	.06
☐	16	Orioles Team	.50	.25	.05
☐	17	Doug Bird	.20	.10	.02
☐	18	Gary Thomasson	.20	.10	.02
☐	19	Gerry Moses	.20	.10	.02
☐	20	Nolan Ryan	5.50	2.75	.55
☐	21	Bob Gallagher	.20	.10	.02
☐	22	Cy Acosta	.20	.10	.02
☐	23	Craig Robinson	.20	.10	.02

□	No.	Player			
□	24	John Hiller	.30	.15	.03
□	25	Ken Singleton	.40	.20	.04
□	26	Bill Campbell	.30	.15	.03
□	27	George Scott	.30	.15	.03
□	28	Manny Sanguillen	.30	.15	.03
□	29	Phil Niekro	1.75	.85	.17
□	30	Bobby Bonds	.40	.20	.04
□	31	Astros Leaders	.30	.15	.03
		Preston Gomez MG			
		Roger Craig CO			
		Hub Kittle CO			
		Grady Hatton CO			
		Bob Lillis CO			
□	32A	Johnny Grubb SD	.30	.15	.03
□	32B	Johnny Grubb WAS	3.50	1.75	.35
□	33	Don Newhauser	.20	.10	.02
□	34	Andy Kosco	.20	.10	.02
□	35	Gaylord Perry	1.75	.85	.17
□	36	Cardinals Team	.50	.25	.05
□	37	Dave Sells	.20	.10	.02
□	38	Don Kessinger	.30	.15	.03
□	39	Ken Suarez	.20	.10	.02
□	40	Jim Palmer	3.00	1.50	.30
□	41	Bobby Floyd	.20	.10	.02
□	42	Claude Osteen	.20	.10	.02
□	43	Jim Wynn	.30	.15	.03
□	44	Mel Stottlemyre	.30	.15	.03
□	45	Dave Johnson	.50	.25	.05
□	46	Pat Kelly	.20	.10	.02
□	47	Dick Ruthven	.20	.10	.02
□	48	Dick Sharon	.20	.10	.02
□	49	Steve Renko	.20	.10	.02
□	50	Rod Carew	5.00	2.50	.50
□	51	Bob Heise	.20	.10	.02
□	52	Al Oliver	.80	.40	.08
□	53A	Fred Kendall SD	.30	.15	.03
□	53B	Fred Kendall WAS	3.50	1.75	.35
□	54	Elias Sosa	.20	.10	.02
□	55	Frank Robinson	3.00	1.50	.30
□	56	New York Mets Team	.70	.35	.07
□	57	Darold Knowles	.20	.10	.02
□	58	Charlie Spikes	.20	.10	.02
□	59	Ross Grimsley	.20	.10	.02
□	60	Lou Brock	3.00	1.50	.30
□	61	Luis Aparicio	2.00	1.00	.20
□	62	Bob Locker	.20	.10	.02
□	63	Bill Sudakis	.20	.10	.02
□	64	Doug Rau	.40	.20	.04
□	65	Amos Otis	.40	.20	.04
□	66	Sparky Lyle	.30	.15	.03
□	67	Tommy Helms	.20	.10	.02
□	68	Grant Jackson	.20	.10	.02
□	69	Del Unser	.20	.10	.02
□	70	Dick Allen	.50	.25	.05
□	71	Dan Frisella	.20	.10	.02
□	72	Aurelio Rodriguez	.20	.10	.02
□	73	Mike Marshall	.50	.25	.05
□	74	Twins Team	.50	.25	.05
□	75	Jim Colborn	.20	.10	.02
□	76	Mickey Rivers	.30	.15	.03
□	77A	Rich Troedson SD	.30	.15	.03
□	77B	Rich Troedson WAS	3.50	1.75	.35
□	78	Giants Leaders	.30	.15	.03
		Charlie Fox MG			
		John McNamara CO			
		Joe Amalfitano CO			
		Andy Gilbert CO			
		Don McMahon CO			
□	79	Gene Tenace	.20	.10	.02
□	80	Tom Seaver	6.00	3.00	.60
□	81	Frank Duffy	.20	.10	.02
□	82	Dave Giusti	.20	.10	.02
□	83	Orlando Cepeda	.90	.45	.09
□	84	Rick Wise	.30	.15	.03
□	85	Joe Morgan	2.00	1.00	.20
□	86	Joe Ferguson	.20	.10	.02
□	87	Fergie Jenkins	.90	.45	.09
□	88	Fred Patek	.30	.15	.03
□	89	Jackie Brown	.30	.15	.03
□	90	Bobby Murcer	.50	.25	.05
□	91	Ken Forsch	.20	.10	.02
□	92	Paul Blair	.30	.15	.03
□	93	Rod Gilbreath	.20	.10	.02
□	94	Tigers Team	.50	.25	.05
□	95	Steve Carlton	5.50	2.75	.55
□	96	Jerry Hairston	.20	.10	.02
□	97	Bob Bailey	.20	.10	.02
□	98	Bert Blyleven	.70	.35	.07
□	99	Brewers Leaders	.30	.15	.03
		Del Crandall MG			
		Harvey Kuenn CO			
		Joe Nossek CO			
		Jim Walton CO			
		Al Widmar CO			
□	100	Willie Stargell	2.25	1.10	.22
□	101	Bobby Valentine	.40	.20	.04
□	102A	Bill Greif SD	.30	.15	.03
□	102B	Bill Greif WAS	3.50	1.75	.35
□	103	Sal Bando	.40	.20	.04
□	104	Ron Bryant	.20	.10	.02
□	105	Carlton Fisk	1.50	.75	.15
□	106	Harry Parker	.20	.10	.02
□	107	Alex Johnson	.20	.10	.02
□	108	Al Hrabosky	.30	.15	.03
□	109	Bobby Grich	.40	.20	.04
□	110	Billy Williams	2.00	1.00	.20
□	111	Clay Carroll	.20	.10	.02
□	112	Dave Lopes	.60	.30	.06
□	113	Dick Drago	.20	.10	.02
□	114	Angels Team	.50	.25	.05
□	115	Willie Horton	.40	.20	.04
□	116	Jerry Reuss	.40	.20	.04
□	117	Ron Blomberg	.20	.10	.02
□	118	Bill Lee	.30	.15	.03
□	119	Phillies Leaders	.30	.15	.03
		Danny Ozark MG			
		Ray Ripplemeyer CO			
		Bobby Wine CO			
		Carroll Beringer CO			
		Billy DeMars CO			
□	120	Wilbur Wood	.30	.15	.03
□	121	Larry Lintz	.20	.10	.02
□	122	Jim Holt	.20	.10	.02
□	123	Nellie Briles	.30	.15	.03
□	124	Bobby Coluccio	.20	.10	.02
□	125A	Nate Colbert SD	.30	.15	.03
□	125B	Nate Colbert WAS	3.50	1.75	.35
□	126	Checklist 1	1.00	.10	.02
□	127	Tom Paciorek	.20	.10	.02
□	128	John Ellis	.20	.10	.02
□	129	Chris Speier	.30	.15	.03
□	130	Reggie Jackson	8.00	4.00	.80
□	131	Bob Boone	.50	.25	.05
□	132	Felix Millan	.20	.10	.02
□	133	David Clyde	.20	.10	.02
□	134	Denis Menke	.20	.10	.02
□	135	Roy White	.30	.15	.03
□	136	Rick Reuschel	.40	.20	.04
□	137	Al Bumbry	.20	.10	.02
□	138	Eddie Brinkman	.20	.10	.02
□	139	Aurelio Monteagudo	.20	.10	.02
□	140	Darrell Evans	.50	.25	.05
□	141	Pat Bourque	.20	.10	.02
□	142	Pedro Garcia	.20	.10	.02
□	143	Dick Woodson	.20	.10	.02
□	144	Dodgers Leaders	.75	.35	.07
		Walter Alston MG			
		Tom Lasorda CO			
		Jim Gilliam CO			
		Red Adams CO			
		Monty Basgall CO			
□	145	Dock Ellis	.20	.10	.02
□	146	Ron Fairly	.30	.15	.03
□	147	Bart Johnson	.20	.10	.02
□	148A	Dave Hilton SD	.30	.15	.03
□	148B	Dave Hilton WAS	3.50	1.75	.35
□	149	Mac Scarce	.20	.10	.02
□	150	John Mayberry	.30	.15	.03
□	151	Diego Segui	.20	.10	.02
□	152	Oscar Gamble	.30	.15	.03
□	153	Jon Matlack	.30	.15	.03
□	154	Astros Team	.50	.25	.05
□	155	Bert Campaneris	.30	.15	.03
□	156	Randy Moffitt	.20	.10	.02
□	157	Vic Harris	.20	.10	.02
□	158	Jack Billingham	.20	.10	.02
□	159	Jim Ray Hart	.30	.15	.03
□	160	Brooks Robinson	3.00	1.50	.30
□	161	Ray Burris	.65	.30	.06
□	162	Bill Freehan	.40	.20	.04
□	163	Ken Berry	.20	.10	.02
□	164	Tom House	.30	.15	.03
□	165	Willie Davis	.40	.20	.04
□	166	Royals Leaders	.30	.15	.03
		Jack McKeon MG			
		Charlie Lau CO			
		Harry Dunlop CO			
		Galen Cisco CO			
□	167	Luis Tiant	.50	.25	.05
□	168	Danny Thompson	.20	.10	.02
□	169	Steve Rogers	.80	.40	.08
□	170	Bill Melton	.20	.10	.02
□	171	Eduardo Rodriguez	.20	.10	.02
□	172	Gene Clines	.20	.10	.02
□	173A	Randy Jones SD	.50	.25	.05
□	173B	Randy Jones WAS	4.00	2.00	.40
□	174	Bill Robinson	.30	.15	.03
□	175	Reggie Cleveland	.20	.10	.02
□	176	John Lowenstein	.20	.10	.02
□	177	Dave Roberts	.20	.10	.02

178	Garry Maddox	.30	.15	.03
179	Mets Leaders	1.00	.50	.10
	Yogi Berra MG			
	Rube Walker CO			
	Eddie Yost CO			
	Roy McMillan CO			
	Joe Pignatano CO			
180	Ken Holtzman	.30	.15	.03
181	Cesar Geronimo	.20	.10	.02
182	Lindy McDaniel	.20	.10	.02
183	Johnny Oates	.20	.10	.02
184	Rangers Team	.50	.25	.05
185	Jose Cardenal	.20	.10	.02
186	Fred Scherman	.20	.10	.02
187	Don Baylor	.85	.40	.08
188	Rudy Meoli	.20	.10	.02
189	Jim Brewer	.20	.10	.02
190	Tony Oliva	.80	.40	.08
191	Al Fitzmorris	.20	.10	.02
192	Mario Guerrero	.20	.10	.02
193	Tom Walker	.20	.10	.02
194	Darrell Porter	.30	.15	.03
195	Carlos May	.20	.10	.02
196	Jim Fregosi	.40	.20	.04
197A	Vicente Romo SD	.30	.15	.03
197B	Vicente Romo WAS	3.50	1.75	.35
198	Dave Cash	.30	.15	.03
199	Mike Kekich	.20	.10	.02
200	Cesar Cedeno	.40	.20	.04
201	Batting Leaders	3.00	1.50	.30
	Rod Carew			
	Pete Rose			
202	Home Run Leaders	1.50	.75	.15
	Reggie Jackson			
	Willie Stargell			
203	RBI Leaders	1.50	.75	.15
	Reggie Jackson			
	Willie Stargell			
204	Stolen Base Leaders	.65	.30	.06
	Tommy Harper			
	Lou Brock			
205	Victory Leaders	.40	.20	.04
	Wilbur Wood			
	Ron Bryant			
206	ERA Leaders	2.00	1.00	.20
	Jim Palmer			
	Tom Seaver			
207	Strikeout Leaders	2.00	1.00	.20
	Nolan Ryan			
	Tom Seaver			
208	Leading Firemen	.40	.20	.04
	John Hiller			
	Mike Marshall			
209	Ted Sizemore	.20	.10	.02
210	Bill Singer	.20	.10	.02
211	Chicago Cubs Team	.50	.25	.05
212	Rollie Fingers	1.50	.75	.15
213	Dave Rader	.20	.10	.02
214	Bill Grabarkewitz	.20	.10	.02
215	Al Kaline	3.00	1.50	.30
216	Ray Sadecki	.20	.10	.02
217	Tim Foli	.20	.10	.02
218	John Briggs	.20	.10	.02
219	Doug Griffin	.20	.10	.02
220	Don Sutton	1.75	.85	.17
221	White Sox Leaders	.30	.15	.03
	Chuck Tanner MG			
	Jim Mahoney CO			
	Alex Monchak CO			
	Johnny Sain CO			
	Joe Lonnett CO			
222	Ramon Hernandez	.20	.10	.02
223	Jeff Burroughs	.50	.25	.05
224	Roger Metzger	.20	.10	.02
225	Paul Splittorff	.30	.15	.03
226A	Padres Team SD	.75	.35	.07
226B	Padres Team WAS	5.00	2.50	.50
227	Mike Lum	.20	.10	.02
228	Ted Kubiak	.20	.10	.02
229	Fritz Peterson	.20	.10	.02
230	Tony Perez	.85	.40	.08
231	Dick Tidrow	.20	.10	.02
232	Steve Brye	.20	.10	.02
233	Jim Barr	.20	.10	.02
234	John Milner	.20	.10	.02
235	Dave McNally	.30	.15	.03
236	Cardinals Leaders	.30	.15	.03
	Red Schoendienst MG			
	Barney Schultz CO			
	George Kissell CO			
	Johnny Lewis CO			
	Vern Benson CO			
237	Ken Brett	.20	.10	.02
238	Fran Healy	.20	.10	.02
239	Bill Russell	.30	.15	.03
240	Joe Coleman	.20	.10	.02
241A	Glenn Beckert SD	.30	.15	.03
241B	Glenn Beckert WAS	3.50	1.75	.35
242	Bill Gogolewski	.20	.10	.02
243	Bob Oliver	.20	.10	.02
244	Carl Morton	.20	.10	.02
245	Cleon Jones	.20	.10	.02
246	Athletics Team	.50	.25	.05
247	Rick Miller	.20	.10	.02
248	Tom Hall	.20	.10	.02
249	George Mitterwald	.20	.10	.02
250A	Willie McCovey SD	4.00	2.00	.40
250B	Willie McCovey WAS	20.00	10.00	2.00
251	Graig Nettles	1.50	.75	.15
252	Dave Parker	20.00	10.00	2.00
253	John Boccabella	.20	.10	.02
254	Stan Bahnsen	.20	.10	.02
255	Larry Bowa	.70	.35	.07
256	Tom Griffin	.20	.10	.02
257	Buddy Bell	.90	.45	.09
258	Jerry Morales	.20	.10	.02
259	Bob Reynolds	.20	.10	.02
260	Ted Simmons	.85	.40	.08
261	Jerry Bell	.20	.10	.02
262	Ed Kirkpatrick	.20	.10	.02
263	Checklist 2	1.00	.10	.02
264	Joe Rudi	.30	.15	.03
265	Tug McGraw	.50	.25	.05
266	Jim Northrup	.30	.15	.03
267	Andy Messersmith	.30	.15	.03
268	Tom Grieve	.30	.15	.03
269	Bob Johnson	.20	.10	.02
270	Ron Santo	.50	.25	.05
271	Bill Hands	.20	.10	.02
272	Paul Casanova	.20	.10	.02
273	Checklist 3	1.00	.10	.02
274	Fred Beene	.20	.10	.02
275	Ron Hunt	.20	.10	.02
276	Angels Leaders	.30	.15	.03
	Bobby Winkles MG			
	John Roseboro CO			
	Tom Morgan CO			
	Jimmie Reese CO			
	Salty Parker CO			
277	Gary Nolan	.20	.10	.02
278	Cookie Rojas	.20	.10	.02
279	Jim Crawford	.20	.10	.02
280	Carl Yastrzemski	8.00	4.00	.80
281	Giants Team	.50	.25	.05
282	Doyle Alexander	.30	.15	.03
283	Mike Schmidt	35.00	17.50	3.50
284	Dave Duncan	.20	.10	.02
285	Reggie Smith	.40	.20	.04
286	Tony Muser	.20	.10	.02
287	Clay Kirby	.20	.10	.02
288	Gorman Thomas	1.75	.85	.17
289	Rick Auerbach	.20	.10	.02
290	Vida Blue	.40	.20	.04
291	Don Hahn	.20	.10	.02
292	Chuck Seelbach	.20	.10	.02
293	Milt May	.20	.10	.02
294	Steve Foucault	.20	.10	.02
295	Rick Monday	.30	.15	.03
296	Ray Corbin	.20	.10	.02
297	Hal Breeden	.20	.10	.02
298	Roric Harrison	.20	.10	.02
299	Gene Michael	.30	.15	.03
300	Pete Rose	16.00	8.00	1.60
301	Bob Montgomery	.20	.10	.02
302	Rudy May	.20	.10	.02
303	George Hendrick	.40	.20	.04
304	Don Wilson	.20	.10	.02
305	Tito Fuentes	.20	.10	.02
306	Orioles Leaders	.60	.30	.06
	Earl Weaver MG			
	Jim Frey CO			
	George Bamberger CO			
	Billy Hunter CO			
	George Staller CO			
307	Luis Melendez	.20	.10	.02
308	Bruce Dal Canton	.20	.10	.02
309A	Dave Roberts SD	.30	.15	.03
309B	Dave Roberts WAS	4.50	2.25	.45
310	Terry Forster	.30	.15	.03
311	Jerry Grote	.20	.10	.02
312	Deron Johnson	.20	.10	.02
313	Barry Lersch	.20	.10	.02
314	Brewers Team	.50	.25	.05
315	Ron Cey	1.00	.50	.10
316	Jim Perry	.30	.15	.03
317	Richie Zisk	.30	.15	.03
318	Jim Merritt	.20	.10	.02
319	Randy Hundley	.20	.10	.02
320	Dusty Baker	.40	.20	.04
321	Steve Braun	.20	.10	.02

☐ 322 Ernie McAnally	.20	.10	.02
☐ 323 Richie Scheinblum	.20	.10	.02
☐ 324 Steve Kline	.20	.10	.02
☐ 325 Tommy Harper	.30	.15	.03
☐ 326 Reds Leaders	.40	.20	.04
Sparky Anderson MG			
Larry Shephard CO			
George Scherger CO			
Alex Grammas CO			
Ted Kluszewski CO			
☐ 327 Tom Timmermann	.20	.10	.02
☐ 328 Skip Jutze	.20	.10	.02
☐ 329 Mark Belanger	.30	.15	.03
☐ 330 Juan Marichal	2.25	1.10	.22
☐ 331 All-Star Catchers	1.50	.75	.15
Carlton Fisk			
Johnny Bench			
☐ 332 All-Star 1B	1.50	.75	.15
Dick Allen			
Hank Aaron			
☐ 333 All-Star 2B	1.50	.75	.15
Rod Carew			
Joe Morgan			
☐ 334 All-Star 3B	1.00	.50	.10
Brooks Robinson			
Ron Santo			
☐ 335 All-Star SS	.30	.15	.03
Bert Campaneris			
Chris Speier			
☐ 336 All-Star LF	2.50	1.25	.25
Bobby Murcer			
Pete Rose			
☐ 337 All-Star CF	.30	.15	.03
Amos Otis			
Cesar Cedeno			
☐ 338 All-Star RF	2.00	1.00	.20
Reggie Jackson			
Billy Williams			
☐ 339 All-Star Pitchers	.50	.25	.05
Jim Hunter			
Rick Wise			
☐ 340 Thurman Munson	3.50	1.75	.35
☐ 341 Dan Driessen	.85	.40	.08
☐ 342 Jim Lonborg	.30	.15	.03
☐ 343 Royals Team	.50	.25	.05
☐ 344 Mike Caldwell	.30	.15	.03
☐ 345 Bill North	.20	.10	.02
☐ 346 Ron Reed	.20	.10	.02
☐ 347 Sandy Alomar	.20	.10	.02
☐ 348 Pete Richert	.20	.10	.02
☐ 349 John Vukovich	.20	.10	.02
☐ 350 Bob Gibson	2.50	1.25	.25
☐ 351 Dwight Evans	3.50	1.75	.35
☐ 352 Bill Stoneman	.20	.10	.02
☐ 353 Rich Coggins	.20	.10	.02
☐ 354 Cubs Leaders	.30	.15	.03
Whitey Lockman MG			
J.C. Martin CO			
Hank Aguirre CO			
Al Spangler CO			
Jim Marshall CO			
☐ 355 Dave Nelson	.20	.10	.02
☐ 356 Jerry Koosman	.40	.20	.04
☐ 357 Buddy Bradford	.20	.10	.02
☐ 358 Dal Maxvill	.20	.10	.02
☐ 359 Brent Strom	.20	.10	.02
☐ 360 Greg Luzinski	.75	.35	.07
☐ 361 Don Carrithers	.20	.10	.02
☐ 362 Hal King	.20	.10	.02
☐ 363 Yankees Team	.60	.30	.06
☐ 364A Cito Gaston SD	.30	.15	.03
☐ 364B Cito Gaston WAS	4.50	2.25	.45
☐ 365 Steve Busby	.30	.15	.03
☐ 366 Larry Hisle	.30	.15	.03
☐ 367 Norm Cash	.50	.25	.05
☐ 368 Manny Mota	.30	.15	.03
☐ 369 Paul Lindblad	.20	.10	.02
☐ 370 Bob Watson	.40	.20	.04
☐ 371 Jim Slaton	.20	.10	.02
☐ 372 Ken Reitz	.20	.10	.02
☐ 373 John Curtis	.20	.10	.02
☐ 374 Marty Perez	.20	.10	.02
☐ 375 Earl Williams	.20	.10	.02
☐ 376 Jorge Orta	.20	.10	.02
☐ 377 Ron Woods	.20	.10	.02
☐ 378 Burt Hooton	.20	.10	.02
☐ 379 Rangers Leaders	.65	.30	.06
Billy Martin MG			
Frank Lucchesi CO			
Art Fowler CO			
Charlie Silvera CO			
Jackie Moore CO			
☐ 380 Bud Harrelson	.30	.15	.03
☐ 381 Charlie Sands	.20	.10	.02
☐ 382 Bob Moose	.20	.10	.02
☐ 383 Phillies Team	.50	.25	.05
☐ 384 Chris Chambliss	.40	.20	.04
☐ 385 Don Gullett	.30	.15	.03
☐ 386 Gary Matthews	.50	.25	.05
☐ 387A Rich Morales SD	.30	.15	.03
☐ 387B Rich Morales WAS	4.50	2.25	.45
☐ 388 Phil Roof	.20	.10	.02
☐ 389 Gates Brown	.30	.15	.03
☐ 390 Lou Piniella	.50	.25	.05
☐ 391 Billy Champion	.20	.10	.02
☐ 392 Dick Green	.20	.10	.02
☐ 393 Orlando Pena	.20	.10	.02
☐ 394 Ken Henderson	.20	.10	.02
☐ 395 Doug Rader	.30	.15	.03
☐ 396 Tommy Davis	.40	.20	.04
☐ 397 George Stone	.20	.10	.02
☐ 398 Duke Sims	.20	.10	.02
☐ 399 Mike Paul	.20	.10	.02
☐ 400 Harmon Killebrew	2.50	1.25	.25
☐ 401 Elliott Maddox	.20	.10	.02
☐ 402 Jim Rooker	.20	.10	.02
☐ 403 Red Sox Leaders	.30	.15	.03
Darrell Johnson MG			
Eddie Popowski CO			
Lee Stange CO			
Don Zimmer CO			
Don Bryant CO			
☐ 404 Jim Howarth	.20	.10	.02
☐ 405 Ellie Rodriguez	.20	.10	.02
☐ 406 Steve Arlin	.20	.10	.02
☐ 407 Jim Wohlford	.20	.10	.02
☐ 408 Charlie Hough	.50	.25	.05
☐ 409 Ike Brown	.20	.10	.02
☐ 410 Pedro Borbon	.20	.10	.02
☐ 411 Frank Baker	.20	.10	.02
☐ 412 Chuck Taylor	.20	.10	.02
☐ 413 Don Money	.30	.15	.03
☐ 414 Checklist 4	1.00	.10	.02
☐ 415 Gary Gentry	.20	.10	.02
☐ 416 White Sox Team	.50	.25	.05
☐ 417 Rich Folkers	.20	.10	.02
☐ 418 Walt Williams	.20	.10	.02
☐ 419 Wayne Twitchell	.20	.10	.02
☐ 420 Ray Fosse	.20	.10	.02
☐ 421 Dan Fife	.20	.10	.02
☐ 422 Gonzalo Marquez	.20	.10	.02
☐ 423 Fred Stanley	.20	.10	.02
☐ 424 Jim Beauchamp	.20	.10	.02
☐ 425 Pete Broberg	.20	.10	.02
☐ 426 Rennie Stennett	.20	.10	.02
☐ 427 Bobby Bolin	.20	.10	.02
☐ 428 Gary Sutherland	.20	.10	.02
☐ 429 Dick Lange	.20	.10	.02
☐ 430 Matty Alou	.30	.15	.03
☐ 431 Gene Garber	.20	.10	.02
☐ 432 Chris Arnold	.20	.10	.02
☐ 433 Lerrin LaGrow	.20	.10	.02
☐ 434 Ken McMullen	.20	.10	.02
☐ 435 Dave Concepcion	.60	.30	.06
☐ 436 Don Hood	.20	.10	.02
☐ 437 Jim Lyttle	.20	.10	.02
☐ 438 Ed Herrmann	.20	.10	.02
☐ 439 Norm Miller	.20	.10	.02
☐ 440 Jim Kaat	.85	.40	.08
☐ 441 Tom Ragland	.20	.10	.02
☐ 442 Alan Foster	.20	.10	.02
☐ 443 Tom Hutton	.20	.10	.02
☐ 444 Vic Davalillo	.20	.10	.02
☐ 445 George Medich	.20	.10	.02
☐ 446 Len Randle	.20	.10	.02
☐ 447 Twins Leaders	.30	.15	.03
Frank Quilici MG			
Ralph Rowe CO			
Bob Rodgers CO			
Vern Morgan CO			
☐ 448 Ron Hodges	.20	.10	.02
☐ 449 Tom McCraw	.20	.10	.02
☐ 450 Rich Hebner	.20	.10	.02
☐ 451 Tommy John	1.00	.50	.10
☐ 452 Gene Hiser	.20	.10	.02
☐ 453 Balor Moore	.20	.10	.02
☐ 454 Kurt Bevacqua	.20	.10	.02
☐ 455 Tom Bradley	.20	.10	.02
☐ 456 Dave Winfield	25.00	12.50	2.50
☐ 457 Chuck Goggin	.20	.10	.02
☐ 458 Jim Ray	.20	.10	.02
☐ 459 Reds Team	.60	.30	.06
☐ 460 Boog Powell	.60	.30	.06
☐ 461 John Odom	.20	.10	.02
☐ 462 Luis Alvarado	.20	.10	.02
☐ 463 Pat Dobson	.30	.15	.03
☐ 464 Jose Cruz	.50	.25	.05
☐ 465 Dick Bosman	.20	.10	.02
☐ 466 Dick Billings	.20	.10	.02
☐ 467 Winston Llenas	.20	.10	.02

☐ 468	Pepe Frias	.20	.10	.02
☐ 469	Joe Decker	.20	.10	.02
☐ 470	AL Playoffs	2.00	1.00	.20
	A's over Orioles			
	(Reggie Jackson)			
☐ 471	NL Playoffs	.60	.30	.06
	Mets over Reds			
	(Matlack pitching)			
☐ 472	World Series Game 1	.60	.30	.06
	(Knowles pitching)			
☐ 473	World Series Game 2	2.00	1.00	.20
	(Willie Mays batting)			
☐ 474	World Series Game 3	.60	.30	.06
	(Campaneris stealing)			
☐ 475	World Series Game 4	.60	.30	.06
	(Staub batting)			
☐ 476	World Series Game 5	.60	.30	.06
	Cleon Jones scoring)			
☐ 477	World Series Game 6	2.00	1.00	.20
	(Reggie Jackson)			
☐ 478	World Series Game 7	.60	.30	.06
	(Campaneris batting)			
☐ 479	World Series Summary	.60	.30	.06
	A's celebrate; win			
	2nd consecutive			
	championship			
☐ 480	Willie Crawford	.20	.10	.02
☐ 481	Jerry Terrell	.20	.10	.02
☐ 482	Bob Didier	.20	.10	.02
☐ 483	Braves Team	.50	.25	.05
☐ 484	Carmen Fanzone	.20	.10	.02
☐ 485	Felipe Alou	.30	.15	.03
☐ 486	Steve Stone	.30	.15	.03
☐ 487	Ted Martinez	.20	.10	.02
☐ 488	Andy Etchebarren	.20	.10	.02
☐ 489	Pirates Leaders	.30	.15	.03
	Danny Murtaugh MG			
	Don Osborn CO			
	Don Leppert CO			
	Bill Mazeroski CO			
	Bob Skinner CO			
☐ 490	Vada Pinson	.50	.25	.05
☐ 491	Roger Nelson	.20	.10	.02
☐ 492	Mike Rogodzinski	.20	.10	.02
☐ 493	Joe Hoerner	.20	.10	.02
☐ 494	Ed Goodson	.20	.10	.02
☐ 495	Dick McAuliffe	.30	.15	.03
☐ 496	Tom Murphy	.20	.10	.02
☐ 497	Bobby Mitchell	.20	.10	.02
☐ 498	Pat Corrales	.30	.15	.03
☐ 499	Rusty Torres	.20	.10	.02
☐ 500	Lee May	.30	.15	.03
☐ 501	Eddie Leon	.20	.10	.02
☐ 502	Dave LaRoche	.20	.10	.02
☐ 503	Eric Soderholm	.20	.10	.02
☐ 504	Joe Niekro	.50	.25	.05
☐ 505	Bill Buckner	.50	.25	.05
☐ 506	Ed Farmer	.20	.10	.02
☐ 507	Larry Stahl	.20	.10	.02
☐ 508	Expos Team	.50	.25	.05
☐ 509	Jesse Jefferson	.20	.10	.02
☐ 510	Wayne Garrett	.20	.10	.02
☐ 511	Toby Harrah	.30	.15	.03
☐ 512	Joe Lahoud	.20	.10	.02
☐ 513	Jim Campanis	.20	.10	.02
☐ 514	Paul Schaal	.20	.10	.02
☐ 515	Willie Montanez	.20	.10	.02
☐ 516	Horacio Pina	.20	.10	.02
☐ 517	Mike Hegan	.20	.10	.02
☐ 518	Derrel Thomas	.20	.10	.02
☐ 519	Bill Sharp	.20	.10	.02
☐ 520	Tim McCarver	.40	.20	.04
☐ 521	Indians Leaders	.30	.15	.03
	Ken Aspromonte MG			
	Clay Bryant CO			
	Tony Pacheco CO			
☐ 522	J.R. Richard	.40	.20	.04
☐ 523	Cecil Cooper	1.50	.75	.15
☐ 524	Bill Plummer	.20	.10	.02
☐ 525	Clyde Wright	.20	.10	.02
☐ 526	Frank Tepedino	.20	.10	.02
☐ 527	Bobby Darwin	.20	.10	.02
☐ 528	Bill Bonham	.20	.10	.02
☐ 529	Horace Clarke	.20	.10	.02
☐ 530	Mickey Stanley	.30	.15	.03
☐ 531	Expos Leaders	.30	.15	.03
	Gene Mauch MG			
	Dave Bristol CO			
	Cal McLish CO			
	Larry Doby CO			
	Jerry Zimmerman CO			
☐ 532	Skip Lockwood	.20	.10	.02
☐ 533	Mike Phillips	.20	.10	.02
☐ 534	Eddie Watt	.20	.10	.02
☐ 535	Bob Tolan	.30	.15	.03

☐ 536	Duffy Dyer	.20	.10	.02
☐ 537	Steve Mingori	.20	.10	.02
☐ 538	Cesar Tovar	.20	.10	.02
☐ 539	Lloyd Allen	.20	.10	.02
☐ 540	Bob Robertson	.20	.10	.02
☐ 541	Indians Team	.50	.25	.05
☐ 542	Rich Gossage	1.50	.75	.15
☐ 543	Danny Cater	.20	.10	.02
☐ 544	Ron Schueler	.20	.10	.02
☐ 545	Billy Conigliaro	.30	.15	.03
☐ 546	Mike Corkins	.20	.10	.02
☐ 547	Glenn Borgmann	.20	.10	.02
☐ 548	Sonny Siebert	.30	.15	.03
☐ 549	Mike Jorgensen	.20	.10	.02
☐ 550	Sam McDowell	.40	.20	.04
☐ 551	Von Joshua	.20	.10	.02
☐ 552	Denny Doyle	.20	.10	.02
☐ 553	Jim Willoughby	.20	.10	.02
☐ 554	Tim Johnson	.20	.10	.02
☐ 555	Woody Fryman	.20	.10	.02
☐ 556	Dave Campbell	.20	.10	.02
☐ 557	Jim McGlothlin	.20	.10	.02
☐ 558	Bill Fahey	.20	.10	.02
☐ 559	Darrell Chaney	.20	.10	.02
☐ 560	Mike Cuellar	.30	.15	.03
☐ 561	Ed Kranepool	.30	.15	.03
☐ 562	Jack Aker	.20	.10	.02
☐ 563	Hal McRae	.40	.20	.04
☐ 564	Mike Ryan	.20	.10	.02
☐ 565	Milt Wilcox	.20	.10	.02
☐ 566	Jackie Hernandez	.20	.10	.02
☐ 567	Red Sox Team	.50	.25	.05
☐ 568	Mike Torrez	.30	.15	.03
☐ 569	Rick Dempsey	.30	.15	.03
☐ 570	Ralph Garr	.30	.15	.03
☐ 571	Rich Hand	.20	.10	.02
☐ 572	Enzo Hernandez	.20	.10	.02
☐ 573	Mike Adams	.20	.10	.02
☐ 574	Bill Parsons	.20	.10	.02
☐ 575	Steve Garvey	8.00	4.00	.80
☐ 576	Scipio Spinks	.20	.10	.02
☐ 577	Mike Sadek	.20	.10	.02
☐ 578	Ralph Houk MG	.30	.15	.03
☐ 579	Cecil Upshaw	.20	.10	.02
☐ 580	Jim Spencer	.20	.10	.02
☐ 581	Fred Norman	.20	.10	.02
☐ 582	Bucky Dent	1.25	.60	.12
☐ 583	Marty Pattin	.20	.10	.02
☐ 584	Ken Rudolph	.20	.10	.02
☐ 585	Merv Rettenmund	.20	.10	.02
☐ 586	Jack Brohamer	.20	.10	.02
☐ 587	Larry Christenson	.20	.10	.02
☐ 588	Hal Lanier	.40	.20	.04
☐ 589	Boots Day	.20	.10	.02
☐ 590	Roger Moret	.20	.10	.02
☐ 591	Sonny Jackson	.20	.10	.02
☐ 592	Ed Bane	.20	.10	.02
☐ 593	Steve Yeager	.20	.10	.02
☐ 594	Lee Stanton	.20	.10	.02
☐ 595	Steve Blass	.20	.10	.02
☐ 596	Rookie Pitchers	.30	.15	.03
	Wayne Garland			
	Fred Holdsworth			
	Mark Littell			
	Dick Pole			
☐ 597	Rookie Shortstops	.70	.35	.07
	Dave Chalk			
	John Gamble			
	Pete MacKanin			
	Manny Trillo			
☐ 598	Rookie Outfielders	2.25	1.10	.22
	Dave Augustine			
	Ken Griffey			
	Steve Ontiveros			
	Jim Tyrone			
☐ 599A	Rookie Pitchers WAS	.75	.35	.07
	Ron Diorio			
	Dave Freisleben			
	Frank Riccelli			
	Greg Shanahan			
☐ 599B	Rookie Pitchers SD	3.00	1.50	.30
	(SD in large print)			
☐ 599C	Rookie Pitchers SD	6.00	3.00	.60
	(SD in small print)			
☐ 600	Rookie Infielders	6.50	3.25	.65
	Ron Cash			
	Jim Cox			
	Bill Madlock			
	Reggie Sanders			
☐ 601	Rookie Outfielders	2.50	1.25	.25
	Ed Armbrister			
	Rich Bladt			
	Brian Downing			
	Bake McBride			
☐ 602	Rookie Pitchers	.50	.25	.05

Glen Abbott
Rick Henninger
Craig Swan
Dan Vossler
☐ 603 Rookie Catchers .... .40 .20 .04
Barry Foote
Tom Lundstedt
Charlie Moore
Sergio Robles
☐ 604 Rookie Infielders .... 2.50 1.25 .25
Terry Hughes
John Knox
Andy Thornton
Frank White
☐ 605 Rookie Pitchers .... 1.00 .50 .10
Vic Albury
Ken Frailing
Kevin Kobel
Frank Tanana
☐ 606 Rookie Outfielders .... .30 .15 .03
Jim Fuller
Wilbur Howard
Tommy Smith
Otto Velez
☐ 607 Rookie Shortstops .... .30 .15 .03
Leo Foster
Tom Heintzelman
Dave Rosello
Frank Taveras
☐ 608A Rookie Pitchers: ERR ... 2.50 1.25 .25
Bob Apodaco (sic)
Dick Baney
John D'Acquisto
Mike Wallace
☐ 608B Rookie Pitchers: COR .. .40 .20 .04
Bob Apodaca
Dick Baney
John D'Acquisto
Mike Wallace
☐ 609 Rico Petrocelli .... .30 .15 .03
☐ 610 Dave Kingman .... 1.00 .50 .10
☐ 611 Rich Stelmaszek .... .20 .10 .02
☐ 612 Luke Walker .... .20 .10 .02
☐ 613 Dan Monzon .... .20 .10 .02
☐ 614 Adrian Devine .... .20 .10 .02
☐ 615 John Jeter .... .20 .10 .02
☐ 616 Larry Gura .... .30 .15 .03
☐ 617 Ted Ford .... .20 .10 .02
☐ 618 Jim Mason .... .20 .10 .02
☐ 619 Mike Anderson .... .20 .10 .02
☐ 620 Al Downing .... .30 .15 .03
☐ 621 Bernie Carbo .... .20 .10 .02
☐ 622 Phil Gagliano .... .20 .10 .02
☐ 623 Celerino Sanchez .... .20 .10 .02
☐ 624 Bob Miller .... .20 .10 .02
☐ 625 Ollie Brown .... .20 .10 .02
☐ 626 Pirates Team .... .50 .25 .05
☐ 627 Carl Taylor .... .20 .10 .02
☐ 628 Ivan Murrell .... .20 .10 .02
☐ 629 Rusty Staub .... .60 .30 .06
☐ 630 Tommy Agee .... .30 .15 .03
☐ 631 Steve Barber .... .20 .10 .02
☐ 632 George Culver .... .20 .10 .02
☐ 633 Dave Hamilton .... .20 .10 .02
☐ 634 Braves Leaders .... .80 .40 .08
Eddie Mathews MG
Herm Starrette CO
Connie Ryan CO
Jim Busby CO
Ken Silvestri CO
☐ 635 John Edwards .... .20 .10 .02
☐ 636 Dave Goltz .... .20 .10 .02
☐ 637 Checklist 5 .... 1.00 .10 .02
☐ 638 Ken Sanders .... .20 .10 .02
☐ 639 Joe Lovitto .... .20 .10 .02
☐ 640 Milt Pappas .... .30 .15 .03
☐ 641 Chuck Brinkman .... .20 .10 .02
☐ 642 Terry Harmon .... .20 .10 .02
☐ 643 Dodgers Team .... .65 .30 .06
☐ 644 Wayne Granger .... .20 .10 .02
☐ 645 Ken Boswell .... .20 .10 .02
☐ 646 George Foster .... 1.00 .50 .10
☐ 647 Juan Beniquez .... .70 .35 .07
☐ 648 Terry Crowley .... .20 .10 .02
☐ 649 Fernando Gonzalez .... .20 .10 .02
☐ 650 Mike Epstein .... .20 .10 .02
☐ 651 Leron Lee .... .20 .10 .02
☐ 652 Gail Hopkins .... .20 .10 .02
☐ 653 Bob Stinson .... .20 .10 .02
☐ 654A Jesus Alou (outfield) .... .40 .20 .04
☐ 654B Jesus Alou .... 6.00 3.00 .60
(no position)
☐ 655 Mike Tyson .... .20 .10 .02
☐ 656 Adrian Garrett .... .20 .10 .02
☐ 657 Jim Shellenback .... .20 .10 .02

☐ 658 Lee Lacy .... .40 .20 .04
☐ 659 Joe Lis .... .20 .10 .02
☐ 660 Larry Dierker .... .50 .10 .02

1974 Topps Traded

The cards in this 44-card set measure 2 1/2" by 3 1/2". The 1974 Topps Traded set contains 43 player cards and one unnumbered checklist card. The obverses have the word "traded" in block letters and the backs are designed in newspaper style. Card numbers are the same as in the regular set except they are followed by a "T." No known scarcities exist for this set.

		NRMT	VG-E	GOOD
COMPLETE SET		6.00	3.00	.60
COMMON PLAYER		.10	.05	.01
☐ 23T	Craig Robinson	.10	.05	.01
☐ 42T	Claude Osteen	.15	.07	.01
☐ 43T	Jim Wynn	.20	.10	.02
☐ 51T	Bobby Heise	.10	.05	.01
☐ 59T	Ross Grimsley	.10	.05	.01
☐ 62T	Bob Locker	.10	.05	.01
☐ 63T	Bill Sudakis	.10	.05	.01
☐ 73T	Mike Marshall	.25	.12	.02
☐ 123T	Nelson Briles	.15	.07	.01
☐ 139T	Aurelio Monteagudo	.10	.05	.01
☐ 151T	Diego Segui	.10	.05	.01
☐ 165T	Willie Davis	.25	.12	.02
☐ 175T	Reggie Cleveland	.10	.05	.01
☐ 182T	Lindy McDaniel	.15	.07	.01
☐ 186T	Fred Scherman	.10	.05	.01
☐ 249T	George Mitterwald	.10	.05	.01
☐ 262T	Ed Kirkpatrick	.10	.05	.01
☐ 269T	Bob Johnson	.10	.05	.01
☐ 270T	Ron Santo	.35	.17	.03
☐ 313T	Barry Lersch	.10	.05	.01
☐ 319T	Randy Hundley	.15	.07	.01
☐ 330T	Juan Marichal	1.50	.75	.15
☐ 348T	Pete Richert	.10	.05	.01
☐ 373T	John Curtis	.10	.05	.01
☐ 390T	Lou Piniella	.35	.17	.03
☐ 428T	Gary Sutherland	.10	.05	.01
☐ 454T	Kurt Bevacqua	.10	.05	.01
☐ 458T	Jim Ray	.10	.05	.01
☐ 485T	Felipe Alou	.15	.07	.01
☐ 486T	Steve Stone	.15	.07	.01
☐ 496T	Tom Murphy	.10	.05	.01
☐ 516T	Horacio Pina	.10	.05	.01
☐ 534T	Eddie Watt	.10	.05	.01
☐ 538T	Cesar Tovar	.10	.05	.01
☐ 544T	Ron Schueler	.10	.05	.01
☐ 579T	Cecil Upshaw	.10	.05	.01
☐ 585T	Merv Rettenmund	.10	.05	.01
☐ 612T	Luke Walker	.10	.05	.01
☐ 616T	Larry Gura	.20	.10	.02
☐ 618T	Jim Mason	.10	.05	.01
☐ 630T	Tommie Agee	.15	.07	.01
☐ 648T	Terry Crowley	.10	.05	.01
☐ 649T	Fernando Gonzalez	.10	.05	.01
☐ xxxT	Traded Checklist	.50	.05	.01
	(unnumbered)			

1974 Topps Team Checklists

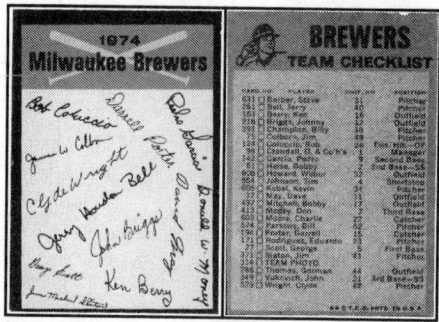

The cards in this 24-card set measure 2 1/2" by 3 1/2". The 1974 series of checklists was issued in packs with the regular cards for that year. The cards are unnumbered (arbitrarily numbered below alphabetically by team name) and have bright red borders. The year and team name appear in a green panel decorated by a crossed bats design, below which is a white area containing facsimile autographs of various players. The mustard-yellow and gray-colored backs list team members alphabetically, along with their card number, uniform number and position.

	NRMT	VG-E	GOOD
COMPLETE SET	8.50	2.50	.50
COMMON TEAM	.40	.12	.02

		NRMT	VG-E	GOOD
☐ 1	Atlanta Braves	.40	.12	.02
☐ 2	Baltimore Orioles	.40	.12	.02
☐ 3	Boston Red Sox	.40	.12	.02
☐ 4	California Angels	.40	.12	.02
☐ 5	Chicago Cubs	.40	.12	.02
☐ 6	Chicago White Sox	.40	.12	.02
☐ 7	Cincinnati Reds	.40	.12	.02
☐ 8	Cleveland Indians	.40	.12	.02
☐ 9	Detroit Tigers	.40	.12	.02
☐ 10	Houston Astros	.40	.12	.02
☐ 11	Kansas City Royals	.40	.12	.02
☐ 12	Los Angeles Dodgers	.40	.12	.02
☐ 13	Milwaukee Brewers	.40	.12	.02
☐ 14	Minnesota Twins	.40	.12	.02
☐ 15	Montreal Expos	.40	.12	.02
☐ 16	New York Mets	.40	.12	.02
☐ 17	New York Yankees	.40	.12	.02
☐ 18	Oakland A's	.40	.12	.02
☐ 19	Philadelphia Phillies	.40	.12	.02
☐ 20	Pittsburgh Pirates	.40	.12	.02
☐ 21	San Diego Padres	.40	.12	.02
☐ 22	San Francisco Giants	.40	.12	.02
☐ 23	St. Louis Cardinals	.40	.12	.02
☐ 24	Texas Rangers	.40	.12	.02

1974 Topps Deckle Edge

The cards in this 72-card set measure 2 7/8" by 5". Returning to a format first used in 1969, Topps produced a set of black and white photo cards in 1974 bearing an unusual serrated or "deckle" border. A facsimile autograph appears on the obverse while the backs contain the card number and a "newspaper-clipping" design detailing a milestone in the player's career. This was a test set, and uncut sheets are sometimes found. Card backs are either white or gray; the white back cards are slightly tougher to obtain.

	NRMT	VG-E	GOOD
COMPLETE SET	1200.00	100.00	20.00

COMMON PLAYER (1-72)	8.00	4.00	.80

☐ 1	Amos Otis	10.00	5.00	1.00
☐ 2	Darrell Evans	12.00	6.00	1.20
☐ 3	Bob Gibson	40.00	20.00	4.00
☐ 4	Dave Nelson	8.00	4.00	.80
☐ 5	Steve Carlton	60.00	30.00	6.00
☐ 6	Jim Hunter	35.00	17.50	3.50
☐ 7	Thurman Munson	50.00	25.00	5.00
☐ 8	Bob Grich	10.00	5.00	1.00
☐ 9	Tom Seaver	75.00	37.50	7.50
☐ 10	Ted Simmons	12.00	6.00	1.20
☐ 11	Bobby Valentine	10.00	5.00	1.00
☐ 12	Don Sutton	25.00	12.50	2.50
☐ 13	Wilbur Wood	8.00	4.00	.80
☐ 14	Doug Rader	8.00	4.00	.80
☐ 15	Chris Chambliss	8.00	4.00	.80
☐ 16	Pete Rose	225.00	110.00	22.00
☐ 17	John Hiller	8.00	4.00	.80
☐ 18	Burt Hooton	8.00	4.00	.80
☐ 19	Tim Foli	8.00	4.00	.80
☐ 20	Lou Brock	50.00	25.00	5.00
☐ 21	Ron Bryant	8.00	4.00	.80
☐ 22	Manny Sanguillen	8.00	4.00	.80
☐ 23	Bob Tolan	8.00	4.00	.80
☐ 24	Greg Luzinski	10.00	5.00	1.00
☐ 25	Brooks Robinson	50.00	25.00	5.00
☐ 26	Felix Millan	8.00	4.00	.80
☐ 27	Luis Tiant	10.00	5.00	1.00
☐ 28	Willie McCovey	40.00	20.00	4.00
☐ 29	Chris Speier	8.00	4.00	.80
☐ 30	George Scott	8.00	4.00	.80
☐ 31	Willie Stargell	40.00	20.00	4.00
☐ 32	Rod Carew	50.00	25.00	5.00
☐ 33	Charlie Spikes	8.00	4.00	.80
☐ 34	Nate Colbert	8.00	4.00	.80
☐ 35	Rich Hebner	8.00	4.00	.80
☐ 36	Bobby Bonds	10.00	5.00	1.00
☐ 37	Buddy Bell	10.00	5.00	1.00
☐ 38	Claude Osteen	8.00	4.00	.80
☐ 39	Dick Allen	10.00	5.00	1.00
☐ 40	Bill Russell	8.00	4.00	.80
☐ 41	Nolan Ryan	75.00	37.50	7.50
☐ 42	Willie Davis	8.00	4.00	.80
☐ 43	Carl Yastrzemski	150.00	75.00	15.00
☐ 44	Jon Matlack	8.00	4.00	.80
☐ 45	Jim Palmer	35.00	17.50	3.50
☐ 46	Bert Campaneris	8.00	4.00	.80
☐ 47	Bert Blyleven	10.00	5.00	1.00
☐ 48	Jeff Burroughs	8.00	4.00	.80
☐ 49	Jim Colborn	8.00	4.00	.80
☐ 50	Dave Johnson	10.00	5.00	1.00
☐ 51	John Mayberry	8.00	4.00	.80
☐ 52	Don Kessinger	8.00	4.00	.80
☐ 53	Joe Coleman	8.00	4.00	.80
☐ 54	Tony Perez	15.00	7.50	1.50
☐ 55	Jose Cardenal	8.00	4.00	.80
☐ 56	Paul Splittorff	8.00	4.00	.80
☐ 57	Hank Aaron	125.00	60.00	12.50
☐ 58	Dave May	8.00	4.00	.80
☐ 59	Fergie Jenkins	15.00	7.50	1.50
☐ 60	Ron Blomberg	8.00	4.00	.80
☐ 61	Reggie Jackson	125.00	60.00	12.50

			NRMT	VG-E	GOOD
☐ 62	Tony Oliva		15.00	7.50	1.50
☐ 63	Bobby Murcer		10.00	5.00	1.00
☐ 64	Carlton Fisk		15.00	7.50	1.50
☐ 65	Steve Rogers		8.00	4.00	.80
☐ 66	Frank Robinson		40.00	20.00	4.00
☐ 67	Joe Ferguson		8.00	4.00	.80
☐ 68	Bill Melton		8.00	4.00	.80
☐ 69	Bob Watson		8.00	4.00	.80
☐ 70	Larry Bowa		10.00	5.00	1.00
☐ 71	Johnny Bench		75.00	37.50	7.50
☐ 72	Willie Horton		8.00	4.00	.80

1975 Topps

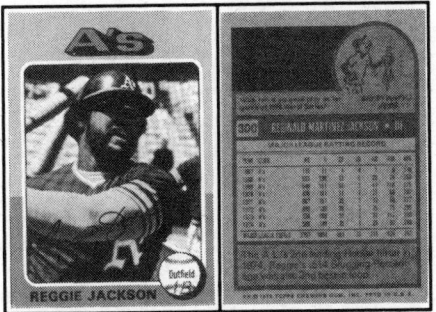

REGGIE JACKSON

The cards in the 1975 Topps set were issued in two different sizes: a regular standard size (2 1/2" by 3 1/2") and a mini size (2 1/2" by 3 1/8") which was issued as a test in certain areas of the country. The 660-card Topps baseball set for 1975 was radically different in appearance from sets of the preceding years. The most prominent change was the use of a two-color frame surrounding the picture area rather than a single, subdued color. A facsimile autograph appears on the picture, and the backs are printed in red and green on gray. Cards 189-212 depict the MVP's of both leagues from 1951 through 1974. The first seven cards (1-7) feature players breaking records or achieving milestones during the previous season. Cards 306-313 picture league leaders in various statistical categories. Cards 459-466 depict the results of post-season action. Team cards feature a checklist back for players on that team and show a small inset photo of the manager on the front. The Phillies Team card #46 erroneously lists Terry Harmon as #339 instead of #399. This set is quite popular with collectors, at least in part due to the fact that the rookie cards of Robin Yount, George Brett, Jim Rice, Gary Carter, Fred Lynn, and Keith Hernandez are all in the set. Topps minis have the same checklist and are worth approximately double the prices listed below.

		NRMT	VG-E	GOOD
COMPLETE SET		475.00	225.00	47.00
COMMON PLAYER (1-132)		.25	.12	.02
COMMON PLAYER (133-660)		.20	.10	.02

			NRMT	VG-E	GOOD
☐ 1	RB: Hank Aaron	Sets Homer Mark	8.00	1.50	.30
☐ 2	RB: Lou Brock	118 Stolen Bases	1.50	.75	.15
☐ 3	RB: Bob Gibson	3000th Strikeout	1.50	.75	.15
☐ 4	RB: Al Kaline	3000 Hit Club	1.75	.85	.17
☐ 5	RB: Nolan Ryan	Fans 300 for 3rd Year in a Row	1.75	.85	.17
☐ 6	RB: Mike Marshall	Hurls 106 Games	.40	.20	.04
☐ 7	No Hitters	Steve Busby Dick Bosman Nolan Ryan	.60	.30	.06
☐ 8	Rogelio Moret		.25	.12	.02
☐ 9	Frank Tepedino		.25	.12	.02
☐ 10	Willie Davis		.35	.17	.03
☐ 11	Bill Melton		.25	.12	.02
☐ 12	David Clyde		.25	.12	.02
☐ 13	Gene Locklear		.25	.12	.02
☐ 14	Milt Wilcox		.25	.12	.02
☐ 15	Jose Cardenal		.25	.12	.02
☐ 16	Frank Tanana		.50	.25	.05
☐ 17	Dave Concepcion		.50	.25	.05
☐ 18	Tigers: Team/Mgr.	Ralph Houk (checklist back)	.60	.15	.03
☐ 19	Jerry Koosman		.45	.22	.04
☐ 20	Thurman Munson		3.50	1.75	.35
☐ 21	Rollie Fingers		1.00	.50	.10
☐ 22	Dave Cash		.25	.12	.02
☐ 23	Bill Russell		.35	.17	.03
☐ 24	Al Fitzmorris		.25	.12	.02
☐ 25	Lee May		.35	.17	.03
☐ 26	Dave McNally		.35	.17	.03
☐ 27	Ken Reitz		.25	.12	.02
☐ 28	Tom Murphy		.25	.12	.02
☐ 29	Dave Parker		5.00	2.50	.50
☐ 30	Bert Blyleven		.65	.30	.06
☐ 31	Dave Rader		.25	.12	.02
☐ 32	Reggie Cleveland		.25	.12	.02
☐ 33	Dusty Baker		.45	.22	.04
☐ 34	Steve Renko		.25	.12	.02
☐ 35	Ron Santo		.45	.22	.04
☐ 36	Joe Lovitto		.25	.12	.02
☐ 37	Dave Freisleben		.25	.12	.02
☐ 38	Buddy Bell		.80	.40	.08
☐ 39	Andy Thornton		.50	.25	.05
☐ 40	Bill Singer		.25	.12	.02
☐ 41	Cesar Geronimo		.25	.12	.02
☐ 42	Joe Coleman		.25	.12	.02
☐ 43	Cleon Jones		.25	.12	.02
☐ 44	Pat Dobson		.35	.17	.03
☐ 45	Joe Rudi		.35	.17	.03
☐ 46	Phillies: Team/Mgr.	Danny Ozark (checklist back)	.60	.15	.03
☐ 47	Tommy John		.90	.45	.09
☐ 48	Freddie Patek		.35	.17	.03
☐ 49	Larry Dierker		.35	.17	.03
☐ 50	Brooks Robinson		3.00	1.50	.30
☐ 51	Bob Forsch		.90	.45	.09
☐ 52	Darrell Porter		.35	.17	.03
☐ 53	Dave Giusti		.25	.12	.02
☐ 54	Eric Soderholm		.25	.12	.02
☐ 55	Bobby Bonds		.45	.22	.04
☐ 56	Rick Wise		.35	.17	.03
☐ 57	Dave Johnson		.45	.22	.04
☐ 58	Chuck Taylor		.25	.12	.02
☐ 59	Ken Henderson		.25	.12	.02
☐ 60	Fergie Jenkins		.90	.45	.09
☐ 61	Dave Winfield		7.00	3.50	.70
☐ 62	Fritz Peterson		.25	.12	.02
☐ 63	Steve Swisher		.25	.12	.02
☐ 64	Dave Chalk		.25	.12	.02
☐ 65	Don Gullett		.35	.17	.03
☐ 66	Willie Horton		.35	.17	.03
☐ 67	Tug McGraw		.45	.22	.04
☐ 68	Ron Blomberg		.25	.12	.02
☐ 69	John Odom		.25	.12	.02
☐ 70	Mike Schmidt		18.00	9.00	1.80
☐ 71	Charlie Hough		.45	.22	.04
☐ 72	Royals: Team/Mgr.	Jack McKeon (checklist back)	.60	.15	.03
☐ 73	J.R. Richard		.45	.22	.04
☐ 74	Mark Belanger		.35	.17	.03
☐ 75	Ted Simmons		.75	.35	.07
☐ 76	Ed Sprague		.25	.12	.02
☐ 77	Richie Zisk		.35	.17	.03
☐ 78	Ray Corbin		.25	.12	.02
☐ 79	Gary Matthews		.45	.22	.04
☐ 80	Carlton Fisk		1.25	.60	.12
☐ 81	Ron Reed		.25	.12	.02
☐ 82	Pat Kelly		.25	.12	.02
☐ 83	Jim Merritt		.25	.12	.02
☐ 84	Enzo Hernandez		.25	.12	.02
☐ 85	Bill Bonham		.25	.12	.02
☐ 86	Joe Lis		.25	.12	.02
☐ 87	George Foster		1.00	.50	.10
☐ 88	Tom Egan		.25	.12	.02
☐ 89	Jim Ray		.25	.12	.02
☐ 90	Rusty Staub		.45	.22	.04
☐ 91	Dick Green		.25	.12	.02
☐ 92	Cecil Upshaw		.25	.12	.02
☐ 93	Dave Lopes		.45	.22	.04
☐ 94	Jim Lonborg		.35	.17	.03

☐ 95	John Mayberry	.35	.17	.03
☐ 96	Mike Cosgrove	.25	.12	.02
☐ 97	Earl Williams	.25	.12	.02
☐ 98	Rich Folkers	.25	.12	.02
☐ 99	Mike Hegan	.25	.12	.02
☐ 100	Willie Stargell	2.25	1.10	.22
☐ 101	Expos: Team/Mgr. Gene Mauch (checklist back)	.60	.15	.03
☐ 102	Joe Decker	.25	.12	.02
☐ 103	Rick Miller	.25	.12	.02
☐ 104	Bill Madlock	1.50	.75	.15
☐ 105	Buzz Capra	.25	.12	.02
☐ 106	Mike Hargrove	.50	.25	.05
☐ 107	Jim Barr	.25	.12	.02
☐ 108	Tom Hall	.25	.12	.02
☐ 109	George Hendrick	.35	.17	.03
☐ 110	Wilbur Wood	.35	.17	.03
☐ 111	Wayne Garrett	.25	.12	.02
☐ 112	Larry Hardy	.25	.12	.02
☐ 113	Elliott Maddox	.25	.12	.02
☐ 114	Dick Lange	.25	.12	.02
☐ 115	Joe Ferguson	.25	.12	.02
☐ 116	Lerrin LaGrow	.25	.12	.02
☐ 117	Orioles: Team/Mgr. Earl Weaver (checklist back)	.60	.15	.03
☐ 118	Mike Anderson	.25	.12	.02
☐ 119	Tommy Helms	.35	.17	.03
☐ 120	Steve Busby (photo actually Fran Healy)	.35	.17	.03
☐ 121	Bill North	.25	.12	.02
☐ 122	Al Hrabosky	.35	.17	.03
☐ 123	Johnny Briggs	.25	.12	.02
☐ 124	Jerry Reuss	.45	.22	.04
☐ 125	Ken Singleton	.45	.22	.04
☐ 126	Checklist 1-132	.85	.10	.02
☐ 127	Glenn Borgmann	.25	.12	.02
☐ 128	Bill Lee	.35	.17	.03
☐ 129	Rick Monday	.35	.17	.03
☐ 130	Phil Niekro	1.50	.75	.15
☐ 131	Toby Harrah	.35	.17	.03
☐ 132	Randy Moffitt	.25	.12	.02
☐ 133	Dan Driessen	.40	.20	.04
☐ 134	Ron Hodges	.20	.10	.02
☐ 135	Charlie Spikes	.20	.10	.02
☐ 136	Jim Mason	.20	.10	.02
☐ 137	Terry Forster	.40	.20	.04
☐ 138	Del Unser	.20	.10	.02
☐ 139	Horacio Pina	.20	.10	.02
☐ 140	Steve Garvey	5.00	2.50	.50
☐ 141	Mickey Stanley	.30	.15	.03
☐ 142	Bob Reynolds	.20	.10	.02
☐ 143	Cliff Johnson	.20	.10	.02
☐ 144	Jim Wohlford	.20	.10	.02
☐ 145	Ken Holtzman	.30	.15	.03
☐ 146	Padres: Team/Mgr. John McNamara (checklist back)	.60	.15	.03
☐ 147	Pedro Garcia	.20	.10	.02
☐ 148	Jim Rooker	.20	.10	.02
☐ 149	Tim Foli	.20	.10	.02
☐ 150	Bob Gibson	2.25	1.10	.22
☐ 151	Steve Brye	.20	.10	.02
☐ 152	Mario Guerrero	.20	.10	.02
☐ 153	Rick Reuschel	.40	.20	.04
☐ 154	Mike Lum	.20	.10	.02
☐ 155	Jim Bibby	.30	.15	.03
☐ 156	Dave Kingman	1.00	.50	.10
☐ 157	Pedro Borbon	.20	.10	.02
☐ 158	Jerry Grote	.20	.10	.02
☐ 159	Steve Arlin	.20	.10	.02
☐ 160	Graig Nettles	1.25	.60	.12
☐ 161	Stan Bahnsen	.20	.10	.02
☐ 162	Willie Montanez	.20	.10	.02
☐ 163	Jim Brewer	.20	.10	.02
☐ 164	Mickey Rivers	.30	.15	.03
☐ 165	Doug Rader	.30	.15	.03
☐ 166	Woodie Fryman	.20	.10	.02
☐ 167	Rich Coggins	.20	.10	.02
☐ 168	Bill Greif	.20	.10	.02
☐ 169	Cookie Rojas	.20	.10	.02
☐ 170	Bert Campaneris	.30	.15	.03
☐ 171	Ed Kirkpatrick	.20	.10	.02
☐ 172	Red Sox: Team/Mgr. Darrell Johnson (checklist back)	.60	.15	.03
☐ 173	Steve Rogers	.40	.20	.04
☐ 174	Bake McBride	.30	.15	.03
☐ 175	Don Money	.30	.15	.03
☐ 176	Burt Hooton	.30	.15	.03
☐ 177	Vic Correll	.20	.10	.02
☐ 178	Cesar Tovar	.20	.10	.02
☐ 179	Tom Bradley	.20	.10	.02
☐ 180	Joe Morgan	2.50	1.25	.25
☐ 181	Fred Beene	.20	.10	.02
☐ 182	Don Hahn	.20	.10	.02
☐ 183	Mel Stottlemyre	.30	.15	.03
☐ 184	Jorge Orta	.20	.10	.02
☐ 185	Steve Carlton	5.00	2.50	.50
☐ 186	Willie Crawford	.20	.10	.02
☐ 187	Denny Doyle	.20	.10	.02
☐ 188	Tom Griffin	.20	.10	.02
☐ 189	1951 MVP's Larry (Yogi) Berra Roy Campanella (Campy never issued)	1.25	.60	.12
☐ 190	1952 MVP's Bobby Shantz Hank Bauer	.40	.20	.04
☐ 191	1953 MVP's Al Rosen Roy Campanella	.60	.30	.06
☐ 192	1954 MVP's Yogi Berra Willie Mays	1.25	.60	.12
☐ 193	1955 MVP's Yogi Berra Roy Campanella (Campy never issued)	1.25	.60	.12
☐ 194	1956 MVP's Mickey Mantle Don Newcombe	2.00	1.00	.20
☐ 195	1957 MVP's Mickey Mantle Hank Aaron	3.50	1.75	.35
☐ 196	1958 MVP's Jackie Jensen Ernie Banks	.60	.30	.06
☐ 197	1959 MVP's Nellie Fox Ernie Banks	.60	.30	.06
☐ 198	1960 MVP's Roger Maris Dick Groat	.60	.30	.06
☐ 199	1961 MVP's Roger Maris Frank Robinson	.90	.45	.09
☐ 200	1962 MVP's Mickey Mantle Maury Wills (Wills never issued)	2.50	1.25	.25
☐ 201	1963 MVP's Elston Howard Sandy Koufax	.60	.30	.06
☐ 202	1964 MVP's Brooks Robinson Ken Boyer	.60	.30	.06
☐ 203	1965 MVP's Zoilo Versalles Willie Mays	.60	.30	.06
☐ 204	1966 MVP's Frank Robinson Bob Clemente	.90	.45	.09
☐ 205	1967 MVP's Carl Yastrzemski Orlando Cepeda	.90	.45	.09
☐ 206	1968 MVP's Denny McLain Bob Gibson	.60	.30	.06
☐ 207	1969 MVP's Harmon Killebrew Willie McCovey	.75	.35	.07
☐ 208	1970 MVP's Boog Powell Johnny Bench	.60	.30	.06
☐ 209	1971 MVP's Vida Blue Joe Torre	.60	.30	.06
☐ 210	1972 MVP's Rich Allen Johnny Bench	.60	.30	.06
☐ 211	1973 MVP's Reggie Jackson Pete Rose	2.50	1.25	.25
☐ 212	1974 MVP's Jeff Burroughs Steve Garvey	.60	.30	.06
☐ 213	Oscar Gamble	.30	.15	.03
☐ 214	Harry Parker	.20	.10	.02
☐ 215	Bobby Valentine	.40	.20	.04
☐ 216	Giants: Team/Mgr. Wes Westrum (checklist back)	.60	.15	.03
☐ 217	Lou Piniella	.40	.20	.04
☐ 218	Jerry Johnson	.20	.10	.02
☐ 219	Ed Herrmann	.20	.10	.02
☐ 220	Don Sutton	1.25	.60	.12
☐ 221	Aurelio Rodriguez	.20	.10	.02

☐ 222 Dan Spillner	.30	.15	.03
☐ 223 Robin Yount	30.00	15.00	3.00
☐ 224 Ramon Hernandez	.20	.10	.02
☐ 225 Bob Grich	.40	.20	.04
☐ 226 Bill Campbell	.20	.10	.02
☐ 227 Bob Watson	.30	.15	.03
☐ 228 George Brett	50.00	25.00	5.00
☐ 229 Barry Foote	.20	.10	.02
☐ 230 Jim Hunter	1.75	.85	.17
☐ 231 Mike Tyson	.20	.10	.02
☐ 232 Diego Segui	.20	.10	.02
☐ 233 Billy Grabarkewitz	.20	.10	.02
☐ 234 Tom Grieve	.30	.15	.03
☐ 235 Jack Billingham	.20	.10	.02
☐ 236 Angels: Team/Mgr. Dick Williams (checklist back)	.60	.15	.03
☐ 237 Carl Morton	.20	.10	.02
☐ 238 Dave Duncan	.20	.10	.02
☐ 239 George Stone	.20	.10	.02
☐ 240 Garry Maddox	.30	.15	.03
☐ 241 Dick Tidrow	.20	.10	.02
☐ 242 Jay Johnstone	.30	.15	.03
☐ 243 Jim Kaat	.85	.40	.08
☐ 244 Bill Buckner	.50	.25	.05
☐ 245 Mickey Lolich	.40	.20	.04
☐ 246 Cardinals: Team/Mgr. Red Schoendienst (checklist back)	.60	.15	.03
☐ 247 Enos Cabell	.20	.10	.02
☐ 248 Randy Jones	.30	.15	.03
☐ 249 Danny Thompson	.20	.10	.02
☐ 250 Ken Brett	.20	.10	.02
☐ 251 Fran Healy	.20	.10	.02
☐ 252 Fred Scherman	.20	.10	.02
☐ 253 Jesus Alou	.20	.10	.02
☐ 254 Mike Torrez	.30	.15	.03
☐ 255 Dwight Evans	1.75	.85	.17
☐ 256 Billy Champion	.20	.10	.02
☐ 257 Checklist: 133-264	.85	.10	.02
☐ 258 Dave LaRoche	.20	.10	.02
☐ 259 Len Randle	.20	.10	.02
☐ 260 Johnny Bench	5.00	2.50	.50
☐ 261 Andy Hassler	.20	.10	.02
☐ 262 Rowland Office	.20	.10	.02
☐ 263 Jim Perry	.30	.15	.03
☐ 264 John Milner	.20	.10	.02
☐ 265 Ron Bryant	.20	.10	.02
☐ 266 Sandy Alomar	.20	.10	.02
☐ 267 Dick Ruthven	.20	.10	.02
☐ 268 Hal McRae	.40	.20	.04
☐ 269 Doug Rau	.20	.10	.02
☐ 270 Ron Fairly	.30	.15	.03
☐ 271 Jerry Moses	.20	.10	.02
☐ 272 Lynn McGlothen	.20	.10	.02
☐ 273 Steve Braun	.20	.10	.02
☐ 274 Vincente Romo	.20	.10	.02
☐ 275 Paul Blair	.30	.15	.03
☐ 276 White Sox Team/Mgr. Chuck Tanner (checklist back)	.60	.15	.03
☐ 277 Frank Taveras	.20	.10	.02
☐ 278 Paul Lindblad	.20	.10	.02
☐ 279 Milt May	.20	.10	.02
☐ 280 Carl Yastrzemski	6.00	3.00	.60
☐ 281 Jim Slaton	.20	.10	.02
☐ 282 Jerry Morales	.20	.10	.02
☐ 283 Steve Foucault	.20	.10	.02
☐ 284 Ken Griffey	.60	.30	.06
☐ 285 Ellie Rodriguez	.20	.10	.02
☐ 286 Mike Jorgensen	.20	.10	.02
☐ 287 Roric Harrison	.20	.10	.02
☐ 288 Bruce Ellingsen	.20	.10	.02
☐ 289 Ken Rudolph	.20	.10	.02
☐ 290 Jon Matlack	.30	.15	.03
☐ 291 Bill Sudakis	.20	.10	.02
☐ 292 Ron Schueler	.20	.10	.02
☐ 293 Dick Sharon	.20	.10	.02
☐ 294 Geoff Zahn	.30	.15	.03
☐ 295 Vada Pinson	.50	.25	.05
☐ 296 Alan Foster	.20	.10	.02
☐ 297 Craig Kusick	.20	.10	.02
☐ 298 Johnny Grubb	.20	.10	.02
☐ 299 Bucky Dent	.50	.25	.05
☐ 300 Reggie Jackson	6.50	3.25	.65
☐ 301 Dave Roberts	.20	.10	.02
☐ 302 Rick Burleson	.60	.30	.06
☐ 303 Grant Jackson	.20	.10	.02
☐ 304 Pirates: Team/Mgr. Danny Murtaugh (checklist back)	.60	.15	.03
☐ 305 Jim Colborn	.20	.10	.02
☐ 306 Batting Leaders Rod Carew Ralph Garr	.60	.30	.06

☐ 307 Home Run Leaders Dick Allen Mike Schmidt	.90	.45	.09
☐ 308 RBI Leaders Jeff Burroughs Johnny Bench	.60	.30	.06
☐ 309 Stolen Base Leaders Bill North Lou Brock	.60	.30	.06
☐ 310 Victory Leaders Jim Hunter Fergie Jenkins Andy Messersmith Phil Niekro	.75	.35	.07
☐ 311 ERA Leaders Jim Hunter Buzz Capra	.50	.25	.05
☐ 312 Strikeout Leaders Nolan Ryan Steve Carlton	2.00	1.00	.20
☐ 313 Leading Firemen Terry Forster Mike Marshall	.40	.20	.04
☐ 314 Buck Martinez	.20	.10	.02
☐ 315 Don Kessinger	.30	.15	.03
☐ 316 Jackie Brown	.20	.10	.02
☐ 317 Joe Lahoud	.20	.10	.02
☐ 318 Ernie McAnally	.20	.10	.02
☐ 319 Johnny Oates	.20	.10	.02
☐ 320 Pete Rose	15.00	7.50	1.50
☐ 321 Rudy May	.20	.10	.02
☐ 322 Ed Goodson	.20	.10	.02
☐ 323 Fred Holdsworth	.20	.10	.02
☐ 324 Ed Kranepool	.30	.15	.03
☐ 325 Tony Oliva	.65	.30	.06
☐ 326 Wayne Twitchell	.20	.10	.02
☐ 327 Jerry Hairston	.20	.10	.02
☐ 328 Sonny Siebert	.30	.15	.03
☐ 329 Ted Kubiak	.20	.10	.02
☐ 330 Mike Marshall	.30	.15	.03
☐ 331 Indians: Team/Mgr. Frank Robinson (checklist back)	.60	.15	.03
☐ 332 Fred Kendall	.20	.10	.02
☐ 333 Dick Drago	.20	.10	.02
☐ 334 Greg Gross	.20	.10	.02
☐ 335 Jim Palmer	3.00	1.50	.30
☐ 336 Rennie Stennett	.20	.10	.02
☐ 337 Kevin Kobel	.20	.10	.02
☐ 338 Rick Stelmaszek	.20	.10	.02
☐ 339 Jim Fregosi	.40	.20	.04
☐ 340 Paul Splittorff	.30	.15	.03
☐ 341 Hal Breeden	.20	.10	.02
☐ 342 Leroy Stanton	.20	.10	.02
☐ 343 Danny Frisella	.20	.10	.02
☐ 344 Ben Oglivie	.30	.15	.03
☐ 345 Clay Carroll	.20	.10	.02
☐ 346 Bobby Darwin	.20	.10	.02
☐ 347 Mike Caldwell	.30	.15	.03
☐ 348 Tony Muser	.20	.10	.02
☐ 349 Ray Sadecki	.20	.10	.02
☐ 350 Bobby Murcer	.50	.25	.05
☐ 351 Bob Boone	.40	.20	.04
☐ 352 Darold Knowles	.20	.10	.02
☐ 353 Luis Melendez	.20	.10	.02
☐ 354 Dick Bosman	.20	.10	.02
☐ 355 Chris Cannizzaro	.20	.10	.02
☐ 356 Rico Petrocelli	.30	.15	.03
☐ 357 Ken Forsch	.20	.10	.02
☐ 358 Al Bumbry	.20	.10	.02
☐ 359 Paul Popovich	.20	.10	.02
☐ 360 George Scott	.30	.15	.03
☐ 361 Dodgers: Team/Mgr. Walter Alston (checklist back)	.65	.15	.03
☐ 362 Steve Hargan	.20	.10	.02
☐ 363 Carmen Fanzone	.20	.10	.02
☐ 364 Doug Bird	.20	.10	.02
☐ 365 Bob Bailey	.20	.10	.02
☐ 366 Ken Sanders	.20	.10	.02
☐ 367 Craig Robinson	.20	.10	.02
☐ 368 Vic Albury	.20	.10	.02
☐ 369 Merv Rettenmund	.20	.10	.02
☐ 370 Tom Seaver	5.00	2.50	.50
☐ 371 Gates Brown	.30	.15	.03
☐ 372 John D'Acquisto	.20	.10	.02
☐ 373 Bill Sharp	.20	.10	.02
☐ 374 Eddie Watt	.20	.10	.02
☐ 375 Roy White	.30	.15	.03
☐ 376 Steve Yeager	.20	.10	.02
☐ 377 Tom Hilgendorf	.20	.10	.02
☐ 378 Derrel Thomas	.20	.10	.02
☐ 379 Bernie Carbo	.20	.10	.02
☐ 380 Sal Bando	.40	.20	.04
☐ 381 John Curtis	.20	.10	.02

☐ 382	Don Baylor	.80	.40	.08
☐ 383	Jim York	.20	.10	.02
☐ 384	Brewers: Team/Mgr. Del Crandall (checklist back)	.60	.15	.03
☐ 385	Dock Ellis	.20	.10	.02
☐ 386	Checklist: 265-396	.85	.10	.02
☐ 387	Jim Spencer	.20	.10	.02
☐ 388	Steve Stone	.30	.15	.03
☐ 389	Tony Solaita	.20	.10	.02
☐ 390	Ron Cey	.65	.30	.06
☐ 391	Don DeMola	.20	.10	.02
☐ 392	Bruce Bochte	.50	.25	.05
☐ 393	Gary Gentry	.20	.10	.02
☐ 394	Larvell Blanks	.20	.10	.02
☐ 395	Bud Harrelson	.30	.15	.03
☐ 396	Fred Norman	.20	.10	.02
☐ 397	Bill Freehan	.40	.20	.04
☐ 398	Elias Sosa	.20	.10	.02
☐ 399	Terry Harmon	.20	.10	.02
☐ 400	Dick Allen	.50	.25	.05
☐ 401	Mike Wallace	.20	.10	.02
☐ 402	Bob Tolan	.30	.15	.03
☐ 403	Tom Buskey	.20	.10	.02
☐ 404	Ted Sizemore	.20	.10	.02
☐ 405	John Montague	.20	.10	.02
☐ 406	Bob Gallagher	.20	.10	.02
☐ 407	Herb Washington	.20	.10	.02
☐ 408	Clyde Wright	.20	.10	.02
☐ 409	Bob Robertson	.20	.10	.02
☐ 410	Mike Cueller (sic, Cuellar)	.30	.15	.03
☐ 411	George Mitterwald	.20	.10	.02
☐ 412	Bill Hands	.20	.10	.02
☐ 413	Marty Pattin	.20	.10	.02
☐ 414	Manny Mota	.30	.15	.03
☐ 415	John Hiller	.30	.15	.03
☐ 416	Larry Lintz	.20	.10	.02
☐ 417	Skip Lockwood	.20	.10	.02
☐ 418	Leo Foster	.20	.10	.02
☐ 419	Dave Goltz	.20	.10	.02
☐ 420	Larry Bowa	.50	.25	.05
☐ 421	Mets: Team/Mgr. Yogi Berra (checklist back)	.65	.15	.03
☐ 422	Brian Downing	.50	.25	.05
☐ 423	Clay Kirby	.20	.10	.02
☐ 424	John Lowenstein	.20	.10	.02
☐ 425	Tito Fuentes	.20	.10	.02
☐ 426	George Medich	.20	.10	.02
☐ 427	Clarence Gaston	.20	.10	.02
☐ 428	Dave Hamilton	.20	.10	.02
☐ 429	Jim Dwyer	.20	.10	.02
☐ 430	Luis Tiant	.50	.25	.05
☐ 431	Rod Gilbreath	.20	.10	.02
☐ 432	Ken Berry	.20	.10	.02
☐ 433	Larry Demery	.20	.10	.02
☐ 434	Bob Locker	.20	.10	.02
☐ 435	Dave Nelson	.20	.10	.02
☐ 436	Ken Frailing	.20	.10	.02
☐ 437	Al Cowens	.40	.20	.04
☐ 438	Don Carrithers	.20	.10	.02
☐ 439	Ed Brinkman	.20	.10	.02
☐ 440	Andy Messersmith	.30	.15	.03
☐ 441	Bobby Heise	.20	.10	.02
☐ 442	Maximino Leon	.20	.10	.02
☐ 443	Twins: Team/Mgr. Frank Quilici (checklist back)	.60	.15	.03
☐ 444	Gene Garber	.20	.10	.02
☐ 445	Felix Millan	.20	.10	.02
☐ 446	Bart Johnson	.20	.10	.02
☐ 447	Terry Crowley	.20	.10	.02
☐ 448	Frank Duffy	.20	.10	.02
☐ 449	Charlie Williams	.20	.10	.02
☐ 450	Willie McCovey	2.50	1.25	.25
☐ 451	Rick Dempsey	.30	.15	.03
☐ 452	Angel Mangual	.20	.10	.02
☐ 453	Claude Osteen	.30	.15	.03
☐ 454	Doug Griffin	.20	.10	.02
☐ 455	Don Wilson	.20	.10	.02
☐ 456	Bob Coluccio	.20	.10	.02
☐ 457	Mario Mendoza	.20	.10	.02
☐ 458	Ross Grimsley	.20	.10	.02
☐ 459	1974 AL Champs A's over Orioles (2B action pictured)	.40	.20	.04
☐ 460	1974 NL Champs Dodgers over Pirates (Taveras/Garvey at 2B)	.60	.30	.06
☐ 461	World Series Game 1 (Reggie Jackson)	1.50	.75	.15
☐ 462	World Series Game 2 (Dodger dugout)	.40	.20	.04
☐ 463	World Series Game 3	.60	.30	.06

	(Fingers pitching)			
☐ 464	World Series Game 4 (A's batter)	.40	.20	.04
☐ 465	World Series Game 5 (Rudi rounding third)	.40	.20	.04
☐ 466	World Series Summary A's do it again; win third straight (A's group picture)	.40	.20	.04
☐ 467	Ed Halicki	.20	.10	.02
☐ 468	Bobby Mitchell	.20	.10	.02
☐ 469	Tom Dettore	.20	.10	.02
☐ 470	Jeff Burroughs	.30	.15	.03
☐ 471	Bob Stinson	.20	.10	.02
☐ 472	Bruce Dal Canton	.20	.10	.02
☐ 473	Ken McMullen	.20	.10	.02
☐ 474	Luke Walker	.20	.10	.02
☐ 475	Darrell Evans	.60	.30	.06
☐ 476	Eduardo Figueroa	.20	.10	.02
☐ 477	Tom Hutton	.20	.10	.02
☐ 478	Tom Burgmeier	.20	.10	.02
☐ 479	Ken Boswell	.20	.10	.02
☐ 480	Carlos May	.20	.10	.02
☐ 481	Will McEnaney	.20	.10	.02
☐ 482	Tom McCraw	.20	.10	.02
☐ 483	Steve Ontiveros	.20	.10	.02
☐ 484	Glenn Beckert	.30	.15	.03
☐ 485	Sparky Lyle	.40	.20	.04
☐ 486	Ray Fosse	.20	.10	.02
☐ 487	Astros: Team/Mgr. Preston Gomez (checklist back)	.60	.15	.03
☐ 488	Bill Travers	.20	.10	.02
☐ 489	Cecil Cooper	1.00	.50	.10
☐ 490	Reggie Smith	.40	.20	.04
☐ 491	Doyle Alexander	.30	.15	.03
☐ 492	Rich Hebner	.20	.10	.02
☐ 493	Don Stanhouse	.20	.10	.02
☐ 494	Pete LaCock	.20	.10	.02
☐ 495	Nelson Briles	.30	.15	.03
☐ 496	Pepe Frias	.20	.10	.02
☐ 497	Jim Nettles	.20	.10	.02
☐ 498	Al Downing	.30	.15	.03
☐ 499	Marty Perez	.20	.10	.02
☐ 500	Nolan Ryan	5.00	2.50	.50
☐ 501	Bill Robinson	.30	.15	.03
☐ 502	Pat Bourque	.20	.10	.02
☐ 503	Fred Stanley	.20	.10	.02
☐ 504	Buddy Bradford	.20	.10	.02
☐ 505	Chris Speier	.30	.15	.03
☐ 506	Leron Lee	.20	.10	.02
☐ 507	Tom Carroll	.20	.10	.02
☐ 508	Bob Hansen	.20	.10	.02
☐ 509	Dave Hilton	.20	.10	.02
☐ 510	Vida Blue	.40	.20	.04
☐ 511	Rangers: Team/Mgr. Billy Martin (checklist back)	.60	.15	.03
☐ 512	Larry Milbourne	.20	.10	.02
☐ 513	Dick Pole	.20	.10	.02
☐ 514	Jose Cruz	.40	.20	.04
☐ 515	Manny Sanguillen	.30	.15	.03
☐ 516	Don Hood	.20	.10	.02
☐ 517	Checklist: 397-528	.85	.10	.02
☐ 518	Leo Cardenas	.20	.10	.02
☐ 519	Jim Todd	.20	.10	.02
☐ 520	Amos Otis	.40	.20	.04
☐ 521	Dennis Blair	.20	.10	.02
☐ 522	Gary Sutherland	.20	.10	.02
☐ 523	Tom Paciorek	.20	.10	.02
☐ 524	John Doherty	.20	.10	.02
☐ 525	Tom House	.30	.15	.03
☐ 526	Larry Hisle	.30	.15	.03
☐ 527	Mac Scarce	.20	.10	.02
☐ 528	Eddie Leon	.20	.10	.02
☐ 529	Gary Thomasson	.20	.10	.02
☐ 530	Gaylord Perry	1.75	.85	.17
☐ 531	Reds: Team/Mgr. Sparky Anderson (checklist back)	.65	.15	.03
☐ 532	Gorman Thomas	.75	.35	.07
☐ 533	Rudy Meoli	.20	.10	.02
☐ 534	Alex Johnson	.20	.10	.02
☐ 535	Gene Tenace	.20	.10	.02
☐ 536	Bob Moose	.20	.10	.02
☐ 537	Tommy Harper	.30	.15	.03
☐ 538	Duffy Dyer	.20	.10	.02
☐ 539	Jesse Jefferson	.20	.10	.02
☐ 540	Lou Brock	2.25	1.10	.22
☐ 541	Roger Metzger	.20	.10	.02
☐ 542	Pete Broberg	.20	.10	.02
☐ 543	Larry Biittner	.20	.10	.02
☐ 544	Steve Mingori	.20	.10	.02
☐ 545	Billy Williams	1.75	.85	.17
☐ 546	John Knox	.20	.10	.02

☐ 547	Von Joshua	.20	.10	.02
☐ 548	Charlie Sands	.20	.10	.02
☐ 549	Bill Butler	.20	.10	.02
☐ 550	Ralph Garr	.20	.10	.02
☐ 551	Larry Christenson	.20	.10	.02
☐ 552	Jack Brohamer	.20	.10	.02
☐ 553	John Boccabella	.20	.10	.02
☐ 554	Rich Gossage	1.00	.50	.10
☐ 555	Al Oliver	.75	.35	.07
☐ 556	Tim Johnson	.20	.10	.02
☐ 557	Larry Gura	.30	.15	.03
☐ 558	Dave Roberts	.20	.10	.02
☐ 559	Bob Montgomery	.20	.10	.02
☐ 560	Tony Perez	.85	.40	.08
☐ 561	A's: Team/Mgr.	.60	.15	.03
	Alvin Dark			
	(checklist back)			
☐ 562	Gary Nolan	.20	.10	.02
☐ 563	Wilbur Howard	.20	.10	.02
☐ 564	Tommy Davis	.30	.15	.03
☐ 565	Joe Torre	.50	.25	.05
☐ 566	Ray Burris	.20	.10	.02
☐ 567	Jim Sundberg	.70	.35	.07
☐ 568	Dale Murray	.20	.10	.02
☐ 569	Frank White	.60	.30	.06
☐ 570	Jim Wynn	.30	.15	.03
☐ 571	Dave Lemanczyk	.20	.10	.02
☐ 572	Roger Nelson	.20	.10	.02
☐ 573	Orlando Pena	.20	.10	.02
☐ 574	Tony Taylor	.20	.10	.02
☐ 575	Gene Clines	.20	.10	.02
☐ 576	Phil Roof	.20	.10	.02
☐ 577	John Morris	.20	.10	.02
☐ 578	Dave Tomlin	.20	.10	.02
☐ 579	Skip Pitlock	.20	.10	.02
☐ 580	Frank Robinson	2.50	1.25	.25
☐ 581	Darrel Chaney	.20	.10	.02
☐ 582	Eduardo Rodriguez	.20	.10	.02
☐ 583	Andy Etchebarren	.20	.10	.02
☐ 584	Mike Garman	.20	.10	.02
☐ 585	Chris Chambliss	.30	.15	.03
☐ 586	Tim McCarver	.40	.20	.04
☐ 587	Chris Ward	.20	.10	.02
☐ 588	Rick Auerbach	.20	.10	.02
☐ 589	Braves: Team/Mgr.	.60	.15	.03
	Clyde King			
	(checklist back)			
☐ 590	Cesar Cedeno	.40	.20	.04
☐ 591	Glenn Abbott	.20	.10	.02
☐ 592	Balor Moore	.20	.10	.02
☐ 593	Gene Lamont	.20	.10	.02
☐ 594	Jim Fuller	.20	.10	.02
☐ 595	Joe Niekro	.40	.20	.04
☐ 596	Ollie Brown	.20	.10	.02
☐ 597	Winston Llenas	.20	.10	.02
☐ 598	Bruce Kison	.20	.10	.02
☐ 599	Nate Colbert	.20	.10	.02
☐ 600	Rod Carew	4.50	2.25	.45
☐ 601	Juan Beniquez	.30	.15	.03
☐ 602	John Vukovich	.20	.10	.02
☐ 603	Lew Krausse	.20	.10	.02
☐ 604	Oscar Zamora	.20	.10	.02
☐ 605	John Ellis	.20	.10	.02
☐ 606	Bruce Miller	.20	.10	.02
☐ 607	Jim Holt	.20	.10	.02
☐ 608	Gene Michael	.30	.15	.03
☐ 609	Ellie Hendricks	.20	.10	.02
☐ 610	Ron Hunt	.20	.10	.02
☐ 611	Yankees: Team/Mgr.	.65	.15	.03
	Bill Virdon			
	(checklist back)			
☐ 612	Terry Hughes	.20	.10	.02
☐ 613	Bill Parsons	.20	.10	.02
☐ 614	Rookie Pitchers	.30	.15	.03
	Jack Kucek			
	Dyar Miller			
	Vern Ruhle			
	Paul Siebert			
☐ 615	Rookie Pitchers	1.25	.60	.12
	Pat Darcy			
	Dennis Leonard			
	Tom Underwood			
	Hank Webb			
☐ 616	Rookie Outfielders	35.00	17.50	3.50
	Dave Augustine			
	Pepe Mangual			
	Jim Rice			
	John Scott			
☐ 617	Rookie Infielders	2.50	1.25	.25
	Mike Cubbage			
	Doug DeCinces			
	Reggie Sanders			
	Manny Trillo			
☐ 618	Rookie Pitchers	2.50	1.25	.25
	Jamie Easterly			

	Tom Johnson			
	Scott McGregor			
	Rick Rhoden			
☐ 619	Rookie Outfielders	.30	.15	.03
	Benny Ayala			
	Nyls Nyman			
	Tommy Smith			
	Jerry Turner			
☐ 620	Rookie Catcher/OF	40.00	20.00	4.00
	Gary Carter			
	Marc Hill			
	Danny Meyer			
	Leon Roberts			
☐ 621	Rookie Pitchers	1.00	.50	.10
	John Denny			
	Rawly Eastwick			
	Jim Kern			
	Juan Veintidos			
☐ 622	Rookie Outfielders	10.00	5.00	1.00
	Ed Armbrister			
	Fred Lynn			
	Tom Poquette			
	Terry Whitfield			
☐ 623	Rookie Infielders	24.00	12.00	2.40
	Phil Garner			
	Keith Hernandez			
	Bob Sheldon			
	Tom Veryzer			
☐ 624	Rookie Pitchers	.30	.15	.03
	Doug Konieczny			
	Gary Lavelle			
	Jim Otten			
	Eddie Solomon			
☐ 625	Boog Powell	.50	.25	.05
☐ 626	Larry Haney	.30	.15	.03
	(photo actually			
	Dave Duncan)			
☐ 627	Tom Walker	.20	.10	.02
☐ 628	Ron LeFlore	.50	.25	.05
☐ 629	Joe Hoerner	.20	.10	.02
☐ 630	Greg Luzinski	.60	.30	.06
☐ 631	Lee Lacy	.30	.15	.03
☐ 632	Morris Nettles	.20	.10	.02
☐ 633	Paul Casanova	.20	.10	.02
☐ 634	Cy Acosta	.20	.10	.02
☐ 635	Chuck Dobson	.20	.10	.02
☐ 636	Charlie Moore	.20	.10	.02
☐ 637	Ted Martinez	.20	.10	.02
☐ 638	Cubs: Team/Mgr.	.60	.15	.03
	Jim Marshall			
	(checklist back)			
☐ 639	Steve Kline	.20	.10	.02
☐ 640	Harmon Killebrew	2.00	1.00	.20
☐ 641	Jim Northrup	.30	.15	.03
☐ 642	Mike Phillips	.20	.10	.02
☐ 643	Brent Strom	.20	.10	.02
☐ 644	Bill Fahey	.20	.10	.02
☐ 645	Danny Cater	.20	.10	.02
☐ 646	Checklist: 529-660	.85	.10	.02
☐ 647	Claudell Washington	1.25	.60	.12
☐ 648	Dave Pagan	.20	.10	.02
☐ 649	Jack Heidemann	.20	.10	.02
☐ 650	Dave May	.20	.10	.02
☐ 651	John Morlan	.20	.10	.02
☐ 652	Lindy McDaniel	.20	.10	.02
☐ 653	Lee Richard	.20	.10	.02
☐ 654	Jerry Terrell	.20	.10	.02
☐ 655	Rico Carty	.30	.15	.03
☐ 656	Bill Plummer	.20	.10	.02
☐ 657	Bob Oliver	.20	.10	.02
☐ 658	Vic Harris	.20	.10	.02
☐ 659	Bob Apodaca	.20	.10	.02
☐ 660	Hank Aaron	10.00	2.50	.50

1976 Topps

The 1976 Topps set of 660 cards (measuring 2 1/2" by 3 1/2") is known for its sharp color photographs and interesting presentation of subjects. Team cards feature a checklist back for players on that team and show a small inset photo of the manager on the front. A "Father and Son" series (66-70) spotlights five Major Leaguers whose fathers also made the "Big Show." Other subseries include "All Time All Stars" (341-350), "Record Breakers" from the previous season (1-6), League Leaders (191-205), Postseason cards (461-462), and Rookie Prospects (589-599).

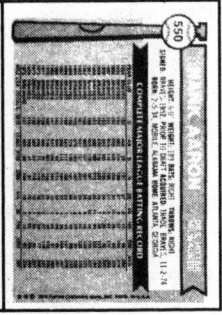

HANK AARON
BREWERS

		NRMT	VG-E	GOOD
	COMPLETE SET	225.00	110.00	22.00
	COMMON PLAYER (1-660)	.15	.07	.01
☐ 1	RB: Hank Aaron .... Most RBI's, 2262	7.50	1.50	.30
☐ 2	RB: Bobby Bonds .... Most leadoff HR's 32; plus three seasons 30 homers/30 steals	.30	.15	.03
☐ 3	RB: Mickey Lolich .... Lefthander, Most Strikeouts, 2679	.30	.15	.03
☐ 4	RB: Dave Lopes .... Most Consecutive SB attempts, 38	.30	.15	.03
☐ 5	RB: Tom Seaver .... Most Cons. seasons with 200 SO's, 8	1.50	.75	.15
☐ 6	RB: Rennie Stennett ...... Most Hits in a 9 inning game, 7	.30	.15	.03
☐ 7	Jim Umbarger	.15	.07	.01
☐ 8	Tito Fuentes	.15	.07	.01
☐ 9	Paul Lindblad	.15	.07	.01
☐ 10	Lou Brock	2.00	1.00	.20
☐ 11	Jim Hughes	.15	.07	.01
☐ 12	Richie Zisk	.25	.12	.02
☐ 13	John Wockenfuss	.15	.07	.01
☐ 14	Gene Garber	.15	.07	.01
☐ 15	George Scott	.25	.12	.02
☐ 16	Bob Apodaca	.15	.07	.01
☐ 17	New York Yankees .... Team Card (checklist back)	.65	.15	.03
☐ 18	Dale Murray	.15	.07	.01
☐ 19	George Brett	12.00	6.00	1.20
☐ 20	Bob Watson	.25	.12	.02
☐ 21	Dave LaRoche	.15	.07	.01
☐ 22	Bill Russell	.25	.12	.02
☐ 23	Brian Downing	.25	.12	.02
☐ 24	Cesar Geronimo	.15	.07	.01
☐ 25	Mike Torrez	.25	.12	.02
☐ 26	Andy Thornton	.25	.12	.02
☐ 27	Ed Figueroa	.15	.07	.01
☐ 28	Dusty Baker	.35	.17	.03
☐ 29	Rick Burleson	.25	.12	.02
☐ 30	John Montefusco	.35	.17	.03
☐ 31	Len Randle	.15	.07	.01
☐ 32	Danny Frisella	.15	.07	.01
☐ 33	Bill North	.15	.07	.01
☐ 34	Mike Garman	.15	.07	.01
☐ 35	Tony Oliva	.60	.30	.06
☐ 36	Frank Taveras	.15	.07	.01
☐ 37	John Hiller	.25	.12	.02
☐ 38	Garry Maddox	.25	.12	.02
☐ 39	Pete Broberg	.15	.07	.01
☐ 40	Dave Kingman	.75	.35	.07
☐ 41	Tippy Martinez	.35	.17	.03
☐ 42	Barry Foote	.15	.07	.01
☐ 43	Paul Splittorff	.25	.12	.02
☐ 44	Doug Rader	.25	.12	.02
☐ 45	Boog Powell	.45	.22	.04
☐ 46	Dodgers Team .... (checklist back)	.65	.15	.03
☐ 47	Jesse Jefferson	.15	.07	.01
☐ 48	Dave Concepcion	.45	.22	.04
☐ 49	Dave Duncan	.15	.07	.01
☐ 50	Fred Lynn	2.25	1.10	.22
☐ 51	Ray Burris	.15	.07	.01
☐ 52	Dave Chalk	.15	.07	.01
☐ 53	Mike Beard	.15	.07	.01

☐ 54	Dave Radar	.15	.07	.01
☐ 55	Gaylord Perry	1.50	.75	.15
☐ 56	Bob Tolan	.15	.07	.01
☐ 57	Phil Garner	.25	.12	.02
☐ 58	Ron Reed	.15	.07	.01
☐ 59	Larry Hisle	.25	.12	.02
☐ 60	Jerry Reuss	.25	.12	.02
☐ 61	Ron LeFlore	.25	.12	.02
☐ 62	Johnny Oates	.15	.07	.01
☐ 63	Bobby Darwin	.15	.07	.01
☐ 64	Jerry Koosman	.45	.22	.04
☐ 65	Chris Chambliss	.25	.12	.02
☐ 66	Father and Son .... Gus Bell Buddy Bell	.35	.17	.03
☐ 67	Father and Son .... Ray Boone Bob Boone	.25	.12	.02
☐ 68	Father and Son .... Joe Coleman Joe Coleman Jr.	.25	.12	.02
☐ 69	Father and Son .... Jim Hegan Mike Hegan	.25	.12	.02
☐ 70	Father and Son .... Roy Smalley Roy Smalley Jr.	.25	.12	.02
☐ 71	Steve Rogers	.25	.12	.02
☐ 72	Hal McRae	.35	.17	.03
☐ 73	Orioles Team .... (checklist back)	.65	.15	.03
☐ 74	Oscar Gamble	.25	.12	.02
☐ 75	Larry Dierker	.25	.12	.02
☐ 76	Willie Crawford	.15	.07	.01
☐ 77	Pedro Borbon	.15	.07	.01
☐ 78	Cecil Cooper	.90	.45	.09
☐ 79	Jerry Morales	.15	.07	.01
☐ 80	Jim Kaat	.70	.35	.07
☐ 81	Darrell Evans	.60	.30	.06
☐ 82	Von Joshua	.15	.07	.01
☐ 83	Jim Spencer	.15	.07	.01
☐ 84	Brent Strom	.15	.07	.01
☐ 85	Mickey Rivers	.25	.12	.02
☐ 86	Mike Tyson	.15	.07	.01
☐ 87	Tom Burgmeier	.15	.07	.01
☐ 88	Duffy Dyer	.15	.07	.01
☐ 89	Vern Ruhle	.15	.07	.01
☐ 90	Sal Bando	.35	.17	.03
☐ 91	Tom Hutton	.15	.07	.01
☐ 92	Eduardo Rodriguez	.15	.07	.01
☐ 93	Mike Phillips	.15	.07	.01
☐ 94	Jim Dwyer	.15	.07	.01
☐ 95	Brooks Robinson	2.00	1.00	.20
☐ 96	Doug Bird	.15	.07	.01
☐ 97	Wilbur Howard	.15	.07	.01
☐ 98	Dennis Eckersley	1.25	.60	.12
☐ 99	Lee Lacy	.25	.12	.02
☐ 100	Jim Hunter	1.50	.75	.15
☐ 101	Pete LaCock	.15	.07	.01
☐ 102	Jim Willoughby	.15	.07	.01
☐ 103	Biff Pocoroba	.15	.07	.01
☐ 104	Reds Team .... (checklist back)	.65	.15	.03
☐ 105	Gary Lavelle	.25	.12	.02
☐ 106	Tom Grieve	.25	.12	.02
☐ 107	Dave Roberts	.15	.07	.01
☐ 108	Don Kirkwood	.15	.07	.01
☐ 109	Larry Lintz	.15	.07	.01
☐ 110	Carlos May	.15	.07	.01
☐ 111	Danny Thompson	.15	.07	.01
☐ 112	Kent Tekulve	.80	.40	.08
☐ 113	Gary Sutherland	.15	.07	.01
☐ 114	Jay Johnstone	.25	.12	.02
☐ 115	Ken Holtzman	.25	.12	.02
☐ 116	Charlie Moore	.15	.07	.01
☐ 117	Mike Jorgensen	.15	.07	.01
☐ 118	Red Sox Team .... (checklist back)	.65	.15	.03
☐ 119	Checklist 1-132	.75	.08	.01
☐ 120	Rusty Staub	.45	.22	.04
☐ 121	Tony Solaita	.15	.07	.01
☐ 122	Mike Cosgrove	.15	.07	.01
☐ 123	Walt Williams	.15	.07	.01
☐ 124	Doug Rau	.15	.07	.01
☐ 125	Don Baylor	.65	.30	.06
☐ 126	Tom Dettore	.15	.07	.01
☐ 127	Larvell Blanks	.15	.07	.01
☐ 128	Ken Griffey	.35	.17	.03
☐ 129	Andy Etchebarren	.15	.07	.01
☐ 130	Luis Tiant	.45	.22	.04
☐ 131	Bill Stein	.15	.07	.01
☐ 132	Don Hood	.15	.07	.01
☐ 133	Gary Matthews	.35	.17	.03
☐ 134	Mike Ivie	.15	.07	.01
☐ 135	Bake McBride	.25	.12	.02

☐ 136	Dave Goltz	.15	.07	.01
☐ 137	Bill Robinson	.15	.07	.01
☐ 138	Lerrin LaGrow	.15	.07	.01
☐ 139	Gorman Thomas	.45	.22	.04
☐ 140	Vida Blue	.35	.17	.03
☐ 141	Larry Parrish	2.50	1.25	.25
☐ 142	Dick Drago	.15	.07	.01
☐ 143	Jerry Grote	.15	.07	.01
☐ 144	Al Fitzmorris	.15	.07	.01
☐ 145	Larry Bowa	.60	.30	.06
☐ 146	George Medich	.15	.07	.01
☐ 147	Astros Team	.60	.15	.03
	(checklist back)			
☐ 148	Stan Thomas	.15	.07	.01
☐ 149	Tommy Davis	.25	.12	.02
☐ 150	Steve Garvey	4.00	2.00	.40
☐ 151	Bill Bonham	.15	.07	.01
☐ 152	Leroy Stanton	.15	.07	.01
☐ 153	Buzz Capra	.15	.07	.01
☐ 154	Bucky Dent	.35	.17	.03
☐ 155	Jack Billingham	.15	.07	.01
☐ 156	Rico Carty	.25	.12	.02
☐ 157	Mike Caldwell	.25	.12	.02
☐ 158	Ken Reitz	.15	.07	.01
☐ 159	Jerry Terrell	.15	.07	.01
☐ 160	Dave Winfield	4.00	2.00	.40
☐ 161	Bruce Kison	.15	.07	.01
☐ 162	Jack Pierce	.15	.07	.01
☐ 163	Jim Slaton	.15	.07	.01
☐ 164	Pepe Mangual	.15	.07	.01
☐ 165	Gene Tenace	.15	.07	.01
☐ 166	Skip Lockwood	.15	.07	.01
☐ 167	Freddie Patek	.15	.07	.01
☐ 168	Tom Hilgendorf	.15	.07	.01
☐ 169	Graig Nettles	1.00	.50	.10
☐ 170	Rick Wise	.25	.12	.02
☐ 171	Greg Gross	.15	.07	.01
☐ 172	Rangers Team	.60	.15	.03
	(checklist back)			
☐ 173	Steve Swisher	.15	.07	.01
☐ 174	Charlie Hough	.35	.17	.03
☐ 175	Ken Singleton	.35	.17	.03
☐ 176	Dick Lange	.15	.07	.01
☐ 177	Marty Perez	.15	.07	.01
☐ 178	Tom Buskey	.15	.07	.01
☐ 179	George Foster	.90	.45	.09
☐ 180	Rich Gossage	1.00	.50	.10
☐ 181	Willie Montanez	.15	.07	.01
☐ 182	Harry Rasmussen	.15	.07	.01
☐ 183	Steve Braun	.15	.07	.01
☐ 184	Bill Greif	.15	.07	.01
☐ 185	Dave Parker	3.00	1.50	.30
☐ 186	Tom Walker	.15	.07	.01
☐ 187	Pedro Garcia	.15	.07	.01
☐ 188	Fred Scherman	.15	.07	.01
☐ 189	Claudell Washington	.35	.17	.03
☐ 190	Jon Matlack	.25	.12	.02
☐ 191	NL Batting Leaders	.40	.20	.04
	Bill Madlock			
	Ted Simmons			
	Manny Sanguillen			
☐ 192	AL Batting Leaders	1.50	.75	.15
	Rod Carew			
	Fred Lynn			
	Thurman Munson			
☐ 193	NL Home Run Leaders	.75	.35	.07
	Mike Schmidt			
	Dave Kingman			
	Greg Luzinski			
☐ 194	AL Home Run Leaders	.75	.35	.07
	Reggie Jackson			
	George Scott			
	John Mayberry			
☐ 195	NL RBI Leaders	.50	.25	.05
	Greg Luzinski			
	Johnny Bench			
	Tony Perez			
☐ 196	AL RBI Leaders	.40	.20	.04
	George Scott			
	John Mayberry			
	Fred Lynn			
☐ 197	NL Steals Leaders	.75	.35	.07
	Dave Lopes			
	Joe Morgan			
	Lou Brock			
☐ 198	AL Steals Leaders	.30	.15	.03
	Mickey Rivers			
	Claudell Washington			
	Amos Otis			
☐ 199	NL Victory Leaders	.50	.25	.05
	Tom Seaver			
	Randy Jones			
	Andy Messersmith			
☐ 200	AL Victory Leaders	.75	.35	.07
	Jim Hunter			
	Jim Palmer			
	Vida Blue			
☐ 201	NL ERA Leaders	.50	.25	.05
	Randy Jones			
	Andy Messersmith			
	Tom Seaver			
☐ 202	AL ERA Leaders	.75	.35	.07
	Jim Palmer			
	Jim Hunter			
	Dennis Eckersley			
☐ 203	NL Strikeout Leaders	.50	.25	.05
	Tom Seaver			
	John Montefusco			
	Andy Messersmith			
☐ 204	AL Strikeout Leaders	.45	.22	.04
	Frank Tanana			
	Bert Blyleven			
	Gaylord Perry			
☐ 205	Leading Firemen	.30	.15	.03
	Al Hrabosky			
	Rich Gossage			
☐ 206	Manny Trillo	.25	.12	.02
☐ 207	Andy Hassler	.15	.07	.01
☐ 208	Mike Lum	.15	.07	.01
☐ 209	Alan Ashby	.45	.22	.04
☐ 210	Lee May	.25	.12	.02
☐ 211	Clay Carroll	.15	.07	.01
☐ 212	Pat Kelly	.15	.07	.01
☐ 213	Dave Heaverlo	.15	.07	.01
☐ 214	Eric Soderholm	.15	.07	.01
☐ 215	Reggie Smith	.35	.17	.03
☐ 216	Expos Team	.60	.15	.03
	(checklist back)			
☐ 217	Dave Freisleben	.15	.07	.01
☐ 218	John Knox	.15	.07	.01
☐ 219	Tom Murphy	.15	.07	.01
☐ 220	Manny Sanguillen	.25	.12	.02
☐ 221	Jim Todd	.15	.07	.01
☐ 222	Wayne Garrett	.15	.07	.01
☐ 223	Ollie Brown	.15	.07	.01
☐ 224	Jim York	.15	.07	.01
☐ 225	Roy White	.25	.12	.02
☐ 226	Jim Sundberg	.25	.12	.02
☐ 227	Oscar Zamora	.15	.07	.01
☐ 228	John Hale	.15	.07	.01
☐ 229	Jerry Remy	.35	.17	.03
☐ 230	Carl Yastrzemski	6.00	3.00	.60
☐ 231	Tom House	.25	.12	.02
☐ 232	Frank Duffy	.15	.07	.01
☐ 233	Grant Jackson	.15	.07	.01
☐ 234	Mike Sadek	.15	.07	.01
☐ 235	Bert Blyleven	.60	.30	.06
☐ 236	Royals Team	.60	.15	.03
	(checklist back)			
☐ 237	Dave Hamilton	.15	.07	.01
☐ 238	Larry Biittner	.15	.07	.01
☐ 239	John Curtis	.15	.07	.01
☐ 240	Pete Rose	15.00	7.50	1.50
☐ 241	Hector Torres	.15	.07	.01
☐ 242	Dan Meyer	.15	.07	.01
☐ 243	Jim Rooker	.15	.07	.01
☐ 244	Bill Sharp	.15	.07	.01
☐ 245	Felix Millan	.15	.07	.01
☐ 246	Cesar Tovar	.15	.07	.01
☐ 247	Terry Harmon	.15	.07	.01
☐ 248	Dick Tidrow	.15	.07	.01
☐ 249	Cliff Johnson	.15	.07	.01
☐ 250	Fergie Jenkins	.65	.30	.06
☐ 251	Rick Monday	.25	.12	.02
☐ 252	Tim Nordbrook	.15	.07	.01
☐ 253	Bill Buckner	.40	.20	.04
☐ 254	Rudy Meoli	.15	.07	.01
☐ 255	Fritz Peterson	.15	.07	.01
☐ 256	Rowland Office	.15	.07	.01
☐ 257	Ross Grimsley	.15	.07	.01
☐ 258	Nyls Nyman	.15	.07	.01
☐ 259	Darrel Chaney	.15	.07	.01
☐ 260	Steve Busby	.25	.12	.02
☐ 261	Gary Thomasson	.15	.07	.01
☐ 262	Checklist 133-264	.75	.08	.01
☐ 263	Lyman Bostock	.60	.30	.06
☐ 264	Steve Renko	.15	.07	.01
☐ 265	Willie Davis	.25	.12	.02
☐ 266	Alan Foster	.15	.07	.01
☐ 267	Aurelio Rodriguez	.15	.07	.01
☐ 268	Del Unser	.15	.07	.01
☐ 269	Rick Austin	.15	.07	.01
☐ 270	Willie Stargell	2.25	1.10	.22
☐ 271	Jim Lonborg	.25	.12	.02
☐ 272	Rick Dempsey	.25	.12	.02
☐ 273	Joe Niekro	.35	.17	.03
☐ 274	Tommy Harper	.25	.12	.02
☐ 275	Rick Manning	.25	.12	.02
☐ 276	Mickey Scott	.15	.07	.01
☐ 277	Cubs Team	.60	.15	.03

	(checklist back)			
☐ 278	Bernie Carbo	.15	.07	.01
☐ 279	Roy Howell	.15	.07	.01
☐ 280	Burt Hooton	.25	.12	.02
☐ 281	Dave May	.15	.07	.01
☐ 282	Dan Osborn	.15	.07	.01
☐ 283	Merv Rettenmund	.15	.07	.01
☐ 284	Steve Ontiveros	.15	.07	.01
☐ 285	Mike Cuellar	.25	.12	.02
☐ 286	Jim Wohlford	.15	.07	.01
☐ 287	Pete Mackanin	.15	.07	.01
☐ 288	Bill Campbell	.15	.07	.01
☐ 289	Enzo Hernandez	.15	.07	.01
☐ 290	Ted Simmons	.65	.30	.06
☐ 291	Ken Sanders	.15	.07	.01
☐ 292	Leon Roberts	.15	.07	.01
☐ 293	Bill Castro	.15	.07	.01
☐ 294	Ed Kirkpatrick	.15	.07	.01
☐ 295	Dave Cash	.15	.07	.01
☐ 296	Pat Dobson	.25	.12	.02
☐ 297	Roger Metzger	.15	.07	.01
☐ 298	Dick Bosman	.15	.07	.01
☐ 299	Champ Summers	.15	.07	.01
☐ 300	Johnny Bench	4.50	2.25	.45
☐ 301	Jackie Brown	.15	.07	.01
☐ 302	Rick Miller	.15	.07	.01
☐ 303	Steve Foucault	.15	.07	.01
☐ 304	Angels Team	.60	.15	.03
	(checklist back)			
☐ 305	Andy Messersmith	.25	.12	.02
☐ 306	Rod Gilbreath	.15	.07	.01
☐ 307	Al Bumbry	.15	.07	.01
☐ 308	Jim Barr	.15	.07	.01
☐ 309	Bill Melton	.15	.07	.01
☐ 310	Randy Jones	.25	.12	.02
☐ 311	Cookie Rojas	.15	.07	.01
☐ 312	Don Carrithers	.15	.07	.01
☐ 313	Dan Ford	.25	.12	.02
☐ 314	Ed Kranepool	.25	.12	.02
☐ 315	Al Hrabosky	.25	.12	.02
☐ 316	Robin Yount	6.00	3.00	.60
☐ 317	John Candelaria	2.50	1.25	.25
☐ 318	Bob Boone	.35	.17	.03
☐ 319	Larry Gura	.25	.12	.02
☐ 320	Willie Horton	.25	.12	.02
☐ 321	Jose Cruz	.35	.17	.03
☐ 322	Glenn Abbott	.15	.07	.01
☐ 323	Rob Sperring	.15	.07	.01
☐ 324	Jim Bibby	.25	.12	.02
☐ 325	Tony Perez	.70	.35	.07
☐ 326	Dick Pole	.15	.07	.01
☐ 327	Dave Moates	.15	.07	.01
☐ 328	Carl Morton	.15	.07	.01
☐ 329	Joe Ferguson	.15	.07	.01
☐ 330	Nolan Ryan	4.50	2.25	.45
☐ 331	Padres Team	.60	.15	.03
	(checklist back)			
☐ 332	Charlie Williams	.15	.07	.01
☐ 333	Bob Coluccio	.15	.07	.01
☐ 334	Dennis Leonard	.35	.17	.03
☐ 335	Bob Grich	.35	.17	.03
☐ 336	Vic Albury	.15	.07	.01
☐ 337	Bud Harrelson	.25	.12	.02
☐ 338	Bob Bailey	.15	.07	.01
☐ 339	John Denny	.35	.17	.03
☐ 340	Jim Rice	11.00	5.50	1.10
☐ 341	All-Time 1B	2.25	1.10	.22
	Lou Gehrig			
☐ 342	All-Time 2B	1.25	.60	.12
	Rogers Hornsby			
☐ 343	All-Time 3B	.65	.30	.06
	Pie Traynor			
☐ 344	All-Time SS	1.25	.60	.12
	Honus Wagner			
☐ 345	All-Time OF	3.50	1.75	.35
	Babe Ruth			
☐ 346	All-Time OF	2.25	1.10	.22
	Ty Cobb			
☐ 347	All-Time OF	2.25	1.10	.22
	Ted Williams			
☐ 348	All-Time C	.65	.30	.06
	Mickey Cochrane			
☐ 349	All-Time RHP	1.25	.60	.12
	Walter Johnson			
☐ 350	All-Time LHP	1.00	.50	.10
	Lefty Grove			
☐ 351	Randy Hundley	.15	.07	.01
☐ 352	Dave Giusti	.15	.07	.01
☐ 353	Sixto Lezcano	.35	.17	.03
☐ 354	Ron Blomberg	.15	.07	.01
☐ 355	Steve Carlton	4.00	2.00	.40
☐ 356	Ted Martinez	.15	.07	.01
☐ 357	Ken Forsch	.25	.12	.02
☐ 358	Buddy Bell	.45	.22	.04
☐ 359	Rick Reuschel	.35	.17	.03
☐ 360	Jeff Burroughs	.25	.12	.02
☐ 361	Tigers Team	.60	.15	.03
	(checklist back)			
☐ 362	Will McEnaney	.15	.07	.01
☐ 363	Dave Collins	.80	.40	.08
☐ 364	Elias Sosa	.15	.07	.01
☐ 365	Carlton Fisk	.90	.45	.09
☐ 366	Bobby Valentine	.35	.17	.03
☐ 367	Bruce Miller	.15	.07	.01
☐ 368	Wilbur Wood	.25	.12	.02
☐ 369	Frank White	.45	.22	.04
☐ 370	Ron Cey	.60	.30	.06
☐ 371	Ellie Hendricks	.15	.07	.01
☐ 372	Rick Baldwin	.15	.07	.01
☐ 373	Johnny Briggs	.15	.07	.01
☐ 374	Dan Warthen	.15	.07	.01
☐ 375	Ron Fairly	.25	.12	.02
☐ 376	Rich Hebner	.15	.07	.01
☐ 377	Mike Hegan	.15	.07	.01
☐ 378	Steve Stone	.25	.12	.02
☐ 379	Ken Boswell	.15	.07	.01
☐ 380	Bobby Bonds	.35	.17	.03
☐ 381	Denny Doyle	.15	.07	.01
☐ 382	Matt Alexander	.15	.07	.01
☐ 383	John Ellis	.15	.07	.01
☐ 384	Phillies Team	.60	.15	.03
	(checklist back)			
☐ 385	Mickey Lolich	.35	.17	.03
☐ 386	Ed Goodson	.15	.07	.01
☐ 387	Mike Miley	.15	.07	.01
☐ 388	Stan Perzanowski	.15	.07	.01
☐ 389	Glenn Adams	.15	.07	.01
☐ 390	Don Gullett	.25	.12	.02
☐ 391	Jerry Hairston	.15	.07	.01
☐ 392	Checklist 265-396	.75	.08	.01
☐ 393	Paul Mitchell	.15	.07	.01
☐ 394	Fran Healy	.15	.07	.01
☐ 395	Jim Wynn	.25	.12	.02
☐ 396	Bill Lee	.25	.12	.02
☐ 397	Tim Foli	.15	.07	.01
☐ 398	Dave Tomlin	.15	.07	.01
☐ 399	Luis Melendez	.15	.07	.01
☐ 400	Rod Carew	4.00	2.00	.40
☐ 401	Ken Brett	.15	.07	.01
☐ 402	Don Money	.15	.07	.01
☐ 403	Geoff Zahn	.15	.07	.01
☐ 404	Enos Cabell	.15	.07	.01
☐ 405	Rollie Fingers	.90	.45	.09
☐ 406	Ed Herrmann	.15	.07	.01
☐ 407	Tom Underwood	.15	.07	.01
☐ 408	Charlie Spikes	.15	.07	.01
☐ 409	Dave Lemanczyk	.15	.07	.01
☐ 410	Ralph Garr	.15	.07	.01
☐ 411	Bill Singer	.15	.07	.01
☐ 412	Toby Harrah	.25	.12	.02
☐ 413	Pete Varney	.15	.07	.01
☐ 414	Wayne Garland	.15	.07	.01
☐ 415	Vada Pinson	.35	.17	.03
☐ 416	Tommy John	.85	.40	.08
☐ 417	Gene Clines	.15	.07	.01
☐ 418	Jose Morales	.15	.07	.01
☐ 419	Reggie Cleveland	.15	.07	.01
☐ 420	Joe Morgan	2.50	1.25	.25
☐ 421	A's Team	.60	.15	.03
	(checklist back)			
☐ 422	Johnny Grubb	.15	.07	.01
☐ 423	Ed Halicki	.15	.07	.01
☐ 424	Phil Roof	.15	.07	.01
☐ 425	Rennie Stennett	.15	.07	.01
☐ 426	Bob Forsch	.25	.12	.02
☐ 427	Kurt Bevacqua	.15	.07	.01
☐ 428	Jim Crawford	.15	.07	.01
☐ 429	Fred Stanley	.15	.07	.01
☐ 430	Jose Cardenal	.15	.07	.01
☐ 431	Dick Ruthven	.15	.07	.01
☐ 432	Tom Veryzer	.15	.07	.01
☐ 433	Rick Waits	.25	.12	.02
☐ 434	Morris Nettles	.15	.07	.01
☐ 435	Phil Niekro	1.50	.75	.15
☐ 436	Bill Fahey	.15	.07	.01
☐ 437	Terry Forster	.25	.12	.02
☐ 438	Doug DeCinces	.60	.30	.06
☐ 439	Rick Rhoden	.60	.30	.06
☐ 440	John Mayberry	.25	.12	.02
☐ 441	Gary Carter	12.00	6.00	1.20
☐ 442	Hank Webb	.15	.07	.01
☐ 443	Giants Team	.60	.15	.03
	(checklist back)			
☐ 444	Gary Nolan	.15	.07	.01
☐ 445	Rico Petrocelli	.25	.12	.02
☐ 446	Larry Haney	.15	.07	.01
☐ 447	Gene Locklear	.15	.07	.01
☐ 448	Tom Johnson	.15	.07	.01
☐ 449	Bob Robertson	.15	.07	.01
☐ 450	Jim Palmer	3.00	1.50	.30

☐ 451	Buddy Bradford	.15	.07	.01
☐ 452	Tom Hausman	.15	.07	.01
☐ 453	Lou Piniella	.35	.17	.03
☐ 454	Tom Griffin	.15	.07	.01
☐ 455	Dick Allen	.35	.17	.03
☐ 456	Joe Coleman	.15	.07	.01
☐ 457	Ed Crosby	.15	.07	.01
☐ 458	Earl Williams	.15	.07	.01
☐ 459	Jim Brewer	.15	.07	.01
☐ 460	Cesar Cedeno	.35	.17	.03
☐ 461	NL and AL Champs	.40	.20	.04
	Reds sweep Bucs,			
	Bosox surprise A's			
☐ 462	'75 World Series	.40	.20	.04
	Reds Champs			
☐ 463	Steve Hargan	.15	.07	.01
☐ 464	Ken Henderson	.15	.07	.01
☐ 465	Mike Marshall	.25	.12	.02
☐ 466	Bob Stinson	.15	.07	.01
☐ 467	Woodie Fryman	.15	.07	.01
☐ 468	Jesus Alou	.15	.07	.01
☐ 469	Rawley Eastwick	.15	.07	.01
☐ 470	Bobby Murcer	.35	.17	.03
☐ 471	Jim Burton	.15	.07	.01
☐ 472	Bob Davis	.15	.07	.01
☐ 473	Paul Blair	.25	.12	.02
☐ 474	Ray Corbin	.15	.07	.01
☐ 475	Joe Rudi	.25	.12	.02
☐ 476	Bob Moose	.15	.07	.01
☐ 477	Indians Team	.60	.15	.03
	(checklist back)			
☐ 478	Lynn McGlothen	.15	.07	.01
☐ 479	Bobby Mitchell	.15	.07	.01
☐ 480	Mike Schmidt	12.00	6.00	1.20
☐ 481	Rudy May	.15	.07	.01
☐ 482	Tim Hosley	.15	.07	.01
☐ 483	Mickey Stanley	.15	.07	.01
☐ 484	Eric Raich	.15	.07	.01
☐ 485	Mike Hargrove	.25	.12	.02
☐ 486	Bruce Dal Canton	.15	.07	.01
☐ 487	Leron Lee	.15	.07	.01
☐ 488	Claude Osteen	.25	.12	.02
☐ 489	Skip Jutze	.15	.07	.01
☐ 490	Frank Tanana	.35	.17	.03
☐ 491	Terry Crowley	.15	.07	.01
☐ 492	Martin Pattin	.15	.07	.01
☐ 493	Derrel Thomas	.15	.07	.01
☐ 494	Craig Swan	.25	.12	.02
☐ 495	Nate Colbert	.15	.07	.01
☐ 496	Juan Beniquez	.25	.12	.02
☐ 497	Joe McIntosh	.15	.07	.01
☐ 498	Glenn Borgmann	.15	.07	.01
☐ 499	Mario Guerrero	.15	.07	.01
☐ 500	Reggie Jackson	6.50	3.25	.65
☐ 501	Billy Champion	.15	.07	.01
☐ 502	Tim McCarver	.35	.17	.03
☐ 503	Elliott Maddox	.15	.07	.01
☐ 504	Pirates Team	.60	.15	.03
	(checklist back)			
☐ 505	Mark Belanger	.25	.12	.02
☐ 506	George Mitterwald	.15	.07	.01
☐ 507	Ray Bare	.15	.07	.01
☐ 508	Duane Kuiper	.15	.07	.01
☐ 509	Bill Hands	.15	.07	.01
☐ 510	Amos Otis	.35	.17	.03
☐ 511	Jamie Easterley	.15	.07	.01
☐ 512	Ellie Rodriguez	.15	.07	.01
☐ 513	Bart Johnson	.15	.07	.01
☐ 514	Dan Driessen	.25	.12	.02
☐ 515	Steve Yeager	.15	.07	.01
☐ 516	Wayne Granger	.15	.07	.01
☐ 517	John Milner	.15	.07	.01
☐ 518	Doug Flynn	.15	.07	.01
☐ 519	Steve Brye	.15	.07	.01
☐ 520	Willie McCovey	2.00	1.00	.20
☐ 521	Jim Colborn	.15	.07	.01
☐ 522	Ted Sizemore	.15	.07	.01
☐ 523	Bob Montgomery	.15	.07	.01
☐ 524	Pete Falcone	.15	.07	.01
☐ 525	Billy Williams	1.50	.75	.15
☐ 526	Checklist 397-528	.75	.08	.01
☐ 527	Mike Anderson	.15	.07	.01
☐ 528	Dock Ellis	.15	.07	.01
☐ 529	Deron Johnson	.15	.07	.01
☐ 530	Don Sutton	1.25	.60	.12
☐ 531	New York Mets Team	.65	.15	.03
	(checklist back)			
☐ 532	Milt May	.15	.07	.01
☐ 533	Lee Richard	.15	.07	.01
☐ 534	Stan Bahnsen	.15	.07	.01
☐ 535	Dave Nelson	.15	.07	.01
☐ 536	Mike Thompson	.15	.07	.01
☐ 537	Tony Muser	.15	.07	.01
☐ 538	Pat Darcy	.15	.07	.01
☐ 539	John Balaz	.15	.07	.01
☐ 540	Bill Freehan	.35	.17	.03
☐ 541	Steve Mingori	.15	.07	.01
☐ 542	Keith Hernandez	6.00	3.00	.60
☐ 543	Wayne Twitchell	.15	.07	.01
☐ 544	Pepe Frias	.15	.07	.01
☐ 545	Sparky Lyle	.35	.17	.03
☐ 546	Dave Rosello	.15	.07	.01
☐ 547	Roric Harrison	.15	.07	.01
☐ 548	Manny Mota	.25	.12	.02
☐ 549	Randy Tate	.15	.07	.01
☐ 550	Hank Aaron	6.50	3.25	.65
☐ 551	Jerry DaVanon	.15	.07	.01
☐ 552	Terry Humphrey	.15	.07	.01
☐ 553	Randy Moffitt	.15	.07	.01
☐ 554	Ray Fosse	.15	.07	.01
☐ 555	Dyar Miller	.15	.07	.01
☐ 556	Twins Team	.60	.15	.03
	(checklist back)			
☐ 557	Dan Spillner	.15	.07	.01
☐ 558	Clarence Gaston	.15	.07	.01
☐ 559	Clyde Wright	.15	.07	.01
☐ 560	Jorge Orta	.15	.07	.01
☐ 561	Tom Carroll	.15	.07	.01
☐ 562	Adrian Garrett	.15	.07	.01
☐ 563	Larry Demery	.15	.07	.01
☐ 564	Bubble Gum Champ	.25	.12	.02
	Kurt Bevacqua			
☐ 565	Tug McGraw	.35	.17	.03
☐ 566	Ken McMullen	.15	.07	.01
☐ 567	George Stone	.15	.07	.01
☐ 568	Rob Andrews	.15	.07	.01
☐ 569	Nelson Briles	.25	.12	.02
☐ 570	George Hendrick	.25	.12	.02
☐ 571	Don DeMola	.15	.07	.01
☐ 572	Rich Coggins	.15	.07	.01
☐ 573	Bill Travers	.15	.07	.01
☐ 574	Don Kessinger	.25	.12	.02
☐ 575	Dwight Evans	1.50	.75	.15
☐ 576	Maximino Leon	.15	.07	.01
☐ 577	Marc Hill	.15	.07	.01
☐ 578	Ted Kubiak	.15	.07	.01
☐ 579	Clay Kirby	.15	.07	.01
☐ 580	Bert Campaneris	.25	.12	.02
☐ 581	Cardinals Team	.60	.15	.03
	(checklist back)			
☐ 582	Mike Kekich	.15	.07	.01
☐ 583	Tommy Helms	.25	.12	.02
☐ 584	Stan Wall	.15	.07	.01
☐ 585	Joe Torre	.50	.25	.05
☐ 586	Ron Schueler	.15	.07	.01
☐ 587	Leo Cardenas	.15	.07	.01
☐ 588	Kevin Kobel	.15	.07	.01
☐ 589	Rookie Pitchers	2.25	1.10	.22
	Santo Alcala			
	Mike Flanagan			
	Joe Pactwa			
	Pablo Torrealba			
☐ 590	Rookie Outfielders	1.00	.50	.10
	Henry Cruz			
	Chet Lemon			
	Ellis Valentine			
	Terry Whitfield			
☐ 591	Rookie Pitchers	.25	.12	.02
	Steve Grilli			
	Craig Mitchell			
	Jose Sosa			
	George Throop			
☐ 592	Rookie Infielders	3.50	1.75	.35
	Willie Randolph			
	Dave McKay			
	Jerry Royster			
	Roy Staiger			
☐ 593	Rookie Pitchers	.25	.12	.02
	Larry Anderson			
	Ken Crosby			
	Mark Littell			
	Butch Metzger			
☐ 594	Rookie Catchers/OF	.25	.12	.02
	Andy Merchant			
	Ed Ott			
	Royle Stillman			
	Jerry White			
☐ 595	Rookie Pitchers	.25	.12	.02
	Art DeFillipis			
	Randy Lerch			
	Sid Monge			
	Steve Barr			
☐ 596	Rookie Infielders	.45	.22	.04
	Craig Reynolds			
	Lamar Johnson			
	Johnnie LeMaster			
	Jerry Manuel			
☐ 597	Rookie Pitchers	.80	.40	.08
	Don Aase			
	Jack Kucek			

	Frank LaCorte			
	Mike Pazik			
☐ 598	Rookie Outfielders	.25	.12	.02
	Hector Cruz			
	Jamie Quirk			
	Jerry Turner			
	Joe Wallis			
☐ 599	Rookie Pitchers	12.00	6.00	1.20
	Rob Dressler			
	Ron Guidry			
	Bob McClure			
	Pat Zachry			
☐ 600	Tom Seaver	4.00	2.00	.40
☐ 601	Ken Rudolph	.15	.07	.01
☐ 602	Doug Konieczny	.15	.07	.01
☐ 603	Jim Holt	.15	.07	.01
☐ 604	Joe Lovitto	.15	.07	.01
☐ 605	Al Downing	.25	.12	.02
☐ 606	Brewers Team	.60	.15	.03
	(checklist back)			
☐ 607	Rich Hinton	.15	.07	.01
☐ 608	Vic Correll	.15	.07	.01
☐ 609	Fred Norman	.15	.07	.01
☐ 610	Greg Luzinski	.45	.22	.04
☐ 611	Rich Folkers	.15	.07	.01
☐ 612	Joe Lahoud	.15	.07	.01
☐ 613	Tim Johnson	.15	.07	.01
☐ 614	Fernando Arroyo	.15	.07	.01
☐ 615	Mike Cubbage	.15	.07	.01
☐ 616	Buck Martinez	.15	.07	.01
☐ 617	Darold Knowles	.15	.07	.01
☐ 618	Jack Brohamer	.15	.07	.01
☐ 619	Bill Butler	.15	.07	.01
☐ 620	Al Oliver	.50	.25	.05
☐ 621	Tom Hall	.15	.07	.01
☐ 622	Rick Auerbach	.15	.07	.01
☐ 623	Bob Allietta	.15	.07	.01
☐ 624	Tony Taylor	.15	.07	.01
☐ 625	J.R. Richard	.25	.12	.02
☐ 626	Bob Sheldon	.15	.07	.01
☐ 627	Bill Plummer	.15	.07	.01
☐ 628	John D'Acquisto	.15	.07	.01
☐ 629	Sandy Alomar	.15	.07	.01
☐ 630	Chris Speier	.25	.12	.02
☐ 631	Braves Team	.60	.15	.03
	(checklist back)			
☐ 632	Rogelio Moret	.15	.07	.01
☐ 633	John Stearns	.25	.12	.02
☐ 634	Larry Christenson	.15	.07	.01
☐ 635	Jim Fregosi	.35	.17	.03
☐ 636	Joe Decker	.15	.07	.01
☐ 637	Bruce Bochte	.25	.12	.02
☐ 638	Doyle Alexander	.25	.12	.02
☐ 639	Fred Kendall	.15	.07	.01
☐ 640	Bill Madlock	.90	.45	.09
☐ 641	Tom Paciorek	.15	.07	.01
☐ 642	Dennis Blair	.15	.07	.01
☐ 643	Checklist 529-660	.75	.08	.01
☐ 644	Tom Bradley	.15	.07	.01
☐ 645	Darrell Porter	.25	.12	.02
☐ 646	John Lowenstein	.15	.07	.01
☐ 647	Ramon Hernandez	.15	.07	.01
☐ 648	Al Cowens	.25	.12	.02
☐ 649	Dave Roberts	.15	.07	.01
☐ 650	Thurman Munson	4.00	2.00	.40
☐ 651	John Odom	.15	.07	.01
☐ 652	Ed Armbrister	.15	.07	.01
☐ 653	Mike Norris	.25	.12	.02
☐ 654	Doug Griffin	.15	.07	.01
☐ 655	Mike Vail	.15	.07	.01
☐ 656	White Sox Team	.60	.15	.03
	(checklist back)			
☐ 657	Roy Smalley	.60	.30	.06
☐ 658	Jerry Johnson	.15	.07	.01
☐ 659	Ben Oglivie	.25	.12	.02
☐ 660	Dave Lopes	.65	.15	.03

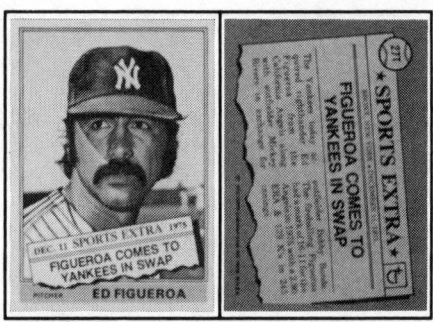

regular 1976 card with the addition of "T" to indicate his new status.

		NRMT	VG-E	GOOD
COMPLETE SET	....	6.00	3.00	.60
COMMON PLAYER	....	.10	.05	.01

☐ 27T	Ed Figueroa	.10	.05	.01
☐ 28T	Dusty Baker	.30	.15	.03
☐ 44T	Doug Rader	.15	.07	.01
☐ 58T	Ron Reed	.15	.07	.01
☐ 74T	Oscar Gamble	.20	.10	.02
☐ 80T	Jim Kaat	.60	.30	.06
☐ 83T	Jim Spencer	.10	.05	.01
☐ 85T	Mickey Rivers	.15	.07	.01
☐ 99T	Lee Lacy	.20	.10	.02
☐ 120T	Rusty Staub	.35	.17	.03
☐ 127T	Larvell Blanks	.10	.05	.01
☐ 146T	George Medich	.15	.07	.01
☐ 158T	Ken Reitz	.10	.05	.01
☐ 208T	Mike Lum	.10	.05	.01
☐ 211T	Clay Carroll	.10	.05	.01
☐ 231T	Tom House	.15	.07	.01
☐ 250T	Fergie Jenkins	.60	.30	.06
☐ 259T	Darrel Chaney	.10	.05	.01
☐ 292T	Leon Roberts	.10	.05	.01
☐ 296T	Pat Dobson	.15	.07	.01
☐ 309T	Bill Melton	.10	.05	.01
☐ 338T	Bob Bailey	.10	.05	.01
☐ 380T	Bobby Bonds	.30	.15	.03
☐ 383T	John Ellis	.10	.05	.01
☐ 385T	Mickey Lolich	.30	.15	.03
☐ 401T	Ken Brett	.15	.07	.01
☐ 410T	Ralph Garr	.15	.07	.01
☐ 411T	Bill Singer	.10	.05	.01
☐ 428T	Jim Crawford	.10	.05	.01
☐ 434T	Morris Nettles	.10	.05	.01
☐ 464T	Ken Henderson	.10	.05	.01
☐ 497T	Joe McIntosh	.10	.05	.01
☐ 524T	Pete Falcone	.10	.05	.01
☐ 527T	Mike Anderson	.10	.05	.01
☐ 528T	Dock Ellis	.10	.05	.01
☐ 532T	Milt May	.10	.05	.01
☐ 554T	Ray Fosse	.10	.05	.01
☐ 579T	Clay Kirby	.10	.05	.01
☐ 583T	Tommy Helms	.10	.05	.01
☐ 592T	Willie Randolph	.75	.35	.07
☐ 618T	Jack Brohamer	.10	.05	.01
☐ 632T	Rogelio Moret	.10	.05	.01
☐ 649T	Dave Roberts	.10	.05	.01
☐ xxxT	Traded Checklist	.50	.05	.01
	(unnumbered)			

1977 Topps

The cards in this 660-card set measure 2 1/2" by 3 1/2". In 1977 for the fifth consecutive year, Topps produced a 660-card baseball set. The player's name, team affiliation, and his position are compactly arranged over the picture area and a facsimile autograph appears on the photo. Team cards feature a checklist of that team's players in the set and a small picture of the manager on the front of the card. Appearing for the first time are the series "Brothers" (631-634) and "Turn Back The Clock"

1976 Topps Traded

The cards in this 44-card set measure 2 1/2" by 3 1/2". The 1976 Topps Traded set contains 43 players and one unnumbered checklist card. The individuals pictured were traded after the Topps regular set was printed. A "Sports Extra" heading design is found on each picture and is also used to introduce the biographical section of the reverse. Each card is numbered according to the player's

(433-437). Other subseries in the set are League Leaders (1-8), Record Breakers (231-234), Playoffs cards (276-277), World Series cards (411-413), and Rookie Prospects (472-479 and 487- 494). The key card in the set is the rookie card of Dale Murphy (476).

		NRMT	VG-E	GOOD
	COMPLETE SET	250.00	125.00	25.00
	COMMON PLAYER (1-660)	.13	.06	.01
☐ 1	Batting Leaders George Brett Bill Madlock	2.00	.30	.05
☐ 2	Home Run Leaders Graig Nettles Mike Schmidt	.75	.35	.07
☐ 3	RBI Leaders Lee May George Foster	.30	.15	.03
☐ 4	Stolen Base Leaders Bill North Dave Lopes	.25	.12	.02
☐ 5	Victory Leaders Jim Palmer Randy Jones	.40	.20	.04
☐ 6	Strikeout Leaders Nolan Ryan Tom Seaver	1.50	.75	.15
☐ 7	ERA Leaders Mark Fidrych John Denny	.25	.12	.02
☐ 8	Leading Firemen Bill Campbell Rawly Eastwick	.25	.12	.02
☐ 9	Doug Rader	.20	.10	.02
☐ 10	Reggie Jackson	6.50	3.25	.65
☐ 11	Rob Dressler	.13	.06	.01
☐ 12	Larry Haney	.13	.06	.01
☐ 13	Luis Gomez	.13	.06	.01
☐ 14	Tommy Smith	.13	.06	.01
☐ 15	Don Gullett	.13	.06	.01
☐ 16	Bob Jones	.13	.06	.01
☐ 17	Steve Stone	.20	.10	.02
☐ 18	Indians Team/Mgr. Frank Robinson (checklist back)	.60	.15	.03
☐ 19	John D'Acquisto	.13	.06	.01
☐ 20	Graig Nettles	.80	.40	.08
☐ 21	Ken Forsch	.13	.06	.01
☐ 22	Bill Freehan	.20	.10	.02
☐ 23	Dan Driessen	.20	.10	.02
☐ 24	Carl Morton	.13	.06	.01
☐ 25	Dwight Evans	.90	.45	.09
☐ 26	Ray Sadecki	.13	.06	.01
☐ 27	Bill Buckner	.35	.17	.03
☐ 28	Woodie Fryman	.13	.06	.01
☐ 29	Bucky Dent	.30	.15	.03
☐ 30	Greg Luzinski	.35	.17	.03
☐ 31	Jim Todd	.13	.06	.01
☐ 32	Checklist 1	.65	.07	.01
☐ 33	Wayne Garland	.13	.06	.01
☐ 34	Angels Team/Mgr. Norm Sherry (checklist back)	.60	.15	.03
☐ 35	Rennie Stennett	.13	.06	.01
☐ 36	John Ellis	.13	.06	.01
☐ 37	Steve Hargan	.13	.06	.01
☐ 38	Craig Kusick	.13	.06	.01
☐ 39	Tom Griffin	.13	.06	.01
☐ 40	Bobby Murcer	.35	.17	.03
☐ 41	Jim Kern	.13	.06	.01
☐ 42	Jose Cruz	.35	.17	.03

☐ 43	Ray Bare	.13	.06	.01
☐ 44	Bud Harrelson	.13	.06	.01
☐ 45	Rawly Eastwick	.13	.06	.01
☐ 46	Buck Martinez	.13	.06	.01
☐ 47	Lynn McGlothen	.13	.06	.01
☐ 48	Tom Paciorek	.13	.06	.01
☐ 49	Grant Jackson	.13	.06	.01
☐ 50	Ron Cey	.40	.20	.04
☐ 51	Brewers Team/Mgr. Alex Grammas (checklist back)	.60	.15	.03
☐ 52	Ellis Valentine	.13	.06	.01
☐ 53	Paul Mitchell	.13	.06	.01
☐ 54	Sandy Alomar	.13	.06	.01
☐ 55	Jeff Burroughs	.20	.10	.02
☐ 56	Rudy May	.13	.06	.01
☐ 57	Marc Hill	.13	.06	.01
☐ 58	Chet Lemon	.35	.17	.03
☐ 59	Larry Christenson	.13	.06	.01
☐ 60	Jim Rice	6.00	3.00	.60
☐ 61	Manny Sanguillen	.20	.10	.02
☐ 62	Eric Raich	.13	.06	.01
☐ 63	Tito Fuentes	.13	.06	.01
☐ 64	Larry Biittner	.13	.06	.01
☐ 65	Skip Lockwood	.13	.06	.01
☐ 66	Roy Smalley	.20	.10	.02
☐ 67	Joaquin Andujar	1.25	.60	.12
☐ 68	Bruce Bochte	.13	.06	.01
☐ 69	Jim Crawford	.13	.06	.01
☐ 70	Johnny Bench	3.50	1.75	.35
☐ 71	Dock Ellis	.13	.06	.01
☐ 72	Mike Anderson	.13	.06	.01
☐ 73	Charles Williams	.13	.06	.01
☐ 74	A's Team/Mgr. Jack McKeon (checklist back)	.60	.15	.03
☐ 75	Dennis Leonard	.20	.10	.02
☐ 76	Tim Foli	.13	.06	.01
☐ 77	Dyar Miller	.13	.06	.01
☐ 78	Bob Davis	.13	.06	.01
☐ 79	Don Money	.13	.06	.01
☐ 80	Andy Messersmith	.20	.10	.02
☐ 81	Juan Beniquez	.20	.10	.02
☐ 82	Jim Rooker	.13	.06	.01
☐ 83	Kevin Bell	.13	.06	.01
☐ 84	Ollie Brown	.13	.06	.01
☐ 85	Duane Kuiper	.13	.06	.01
☐ 86	Pat Zachry	.13	.06	.01
☐ 87	Glenn Borgmann	.13	.06	.01
☐ 88	Stan Wall	.13	.06	.01
☐ 89	Butch Hobson	.13	.06	.01
☐ 90	Cesar Cedeno	.30	.15	.03
☐ 91	John Verhoeven	.13	.06	.01
☐ 92	Dave Rosello	.13	.06	.01
☐ 93	Tom Poquette	.13	.06	.01
☐ 94	Craig Swan	.13	.06	.01
☐ 95	Keith Hernandez	2.50	1.25	.25
☐ 96	Lou Piniella	.30	.15	.03
☐ 97	Dave Heaverlo	.13	.06	.01
☐ 98	Milt May	.13	.06	.01
☐ 99	Tom Hausman	.13	.06	.01
☐ 100	Joe Morgan	1.25	.60	.12
☐ 101	Dick Bosman	.13	.06	.01
☐ 102	Jose Morales	.13	.06	.01
☐ 103	Mike Bacsik	.13	.06	.01
☐ 104	Omar Moreno	.25	.12	.02
☐ 105	Steve Yeager	.13	.06	.01
☐ 106	Mike Flanagan	.40	.20	.04
☐ 107	Bill Melton	.13	.06	.01
☐ 108	Alan Foster	.13	.06	.01
☐ 109	Jorge Orta	.13	.06	.01
☐ 110	Steve Carlton	3.50	1.75	.35
☐ 111	Rico Petrocelli	.20	.10	.02
☐ 112	Bill Greif	.13	.06	.01
☐ 113	Blue Jays Leaders Roy Hartsfield MG Don Leppert CO Bob Miller CO Jackie Moore CO Harry Warner CO (checklist back)	.45	.15	.03
☐ 114	Bruce Dal Canton	.13	.06	.01
☐ 115	Rick Manning	.13	.06	.01
☐ 116	Joe Niekro	.35	.17	.03
☐ 117	Frank White	.35	.17	.03
☐ 118	Rick Jones	.13	.06	.01
☐ 119	John Stearns	.13	.06	.01
☐ 120	Rod Carew	3.50	1.75	.35
☐ 121	Gary Nolan	.13	.06	.01
☐ 122	Ben Oglivie	.20	.10	.02
☐ 123	Fred Stanley	.13	.06	.01
☐ 124	George Mitterwald	.13	.06	.01
☐ 125	Bill Travers	.13	.06	.01
☐ 126	Rod Gilbreath	.13	.06	.01
☐ 127	Ron Fairly	.13	.06	.01

☐ 128	Tommy John	.75	.35	.07
☐ 129	Mike Sadek	.13	.06	.01
☐ 130	Al Oliver	.45	.22	.04
☐ 131	Orlando Ramirez	.13	.06	.01
☐ 132	Chip Lang	.13	.06	.01
☐ 133	Ralph Garr	.13	.06	.01
☐ 134	Padres Team/Mgr.	.60	.15	.03
	John McNamara			
	(checklist back)			
☐ 135	Mark Belanger	.20	.10	.02
☐ 136	Jerry Mumphrey	.40	.20	.04
☐ 137	Jeff Terpko	.13	.06	.01
☐ 138	Bob Stinson	.13	.06	.01
☐ 139	Fred Norman	.13	.06	.01
☐ 140	Mike Schmidt	8.50	4.25	.85
☐ 141	Mark Littell	.13	.06	.01
☐ 142	Steve Dillard	.13	.06	.01
☐ 143	Ed Herrmann	.13	.06	.01
☐ 144	Bruce Sutter	2.50	1.25	.25
☐ 145	Tom Veryzer	.13	.06	.01
☐ 146	Dusty Baker	.25	.12	.02
☐ 147	Jackie Brown	.13	.06	.01
☐ 148	Fran Healy	.13	.06	.01
☐ 149	Mike Cubbage	.13	.06	.01
☐ 150	Tom Seaver	3.50	1.75	.35
☐ 151	Johnny LeMaster	.13	.06	.01
☐ 152	Gaylord Perry	1.50	.75	.15
☐ 153	Ron Jackson	.13	.06	.01
☐ 154	Dave Giusti	.13	.06	.01
☐ 155	Joe Rudi	.20	.10	.02
☐ 156	Pete Mackanin	.13	.06	.01
☐ 157	Ken Brett	.13	.06	.01
☐ 158	Ted Kubiak	.13	.06	.01
☐ 159	Bernie Carbo	.13	.06	.01
☐ 160	Will McEnaney	.13	.06	.01
☐ 161	Garry Templeton	1.25	.60	.12
☐ 162	Mike Cuellar	.20	.10	.02
☐ 163	Dave Hilton	.13	.06	.01
☐ 164	Tug McGraw	.30	.15	.03
☐ 165	Jim Wynn	.20	.10	.02
☐ 166	Bill Campbell	.13	.06	.01
☐ 167	Rich Hebner	.13	.06	.01
☐ 168	Charlie Spikes	.13	.06	.01
☐ 169	Darold Knowles	.13	.06	.01
☐ 170	Thurman Munson	3.00	1.50	.30
☐ 171	Ken Sanders	.13	.06	.01
☐ 172	John Milner	.13	.06	.01
☐ 173	Chuck Scrivener	.13	.06	.01
☐ 174	Nelson Briles	.20	.10	.02
☐ 175	Butch Wynegar	.70	.35	.07
☐ 176	Bob Robertson	.13	.06	.01
☐ 177	Bart Johnson	.13	.06	.01
☐ 178	Bombo Rivera	.13	.06	.01
☐ 179	Paul Hartzell	.13	.06	.01
☐ 180	Dave Lopes	.30	.15	.03
☐ 181	Ken McMullen	.13	.06	.01
☐ 182	Dan Spillner	.13	.06	.01
☐ 183	Cardinals Team/Mgr.	.60	.15	.03
	Vern Rapp			
	(checklist back)			
☐ 184	Bo McLaughlin	.13	.06	.01
☐ 185	Sixto Lezcano	.13	.06	.01
☐ 186	Doug Flynn	.13	.06	.01
☐ 187	Dick Pole	.13	.06	.01
☐ 188	Bob Tolan	.13	.06	.01
☐ 189	Rick Dempsey	.20	.10	.02
☐ 190	Ray Burris	.13	.06	.01
☐ 191	Doug Griffin	.13	.06	.01
☐ 192	Clarence Gaston	.13	.06	.01
☐ 193	Larry Gura	.20	.10	.02
☐ 194	Gary Matthews	.30	.15	.03
☐ 195	Ed Figueroa	.13	.06	.01
☐ 196	Len Randle	.13	.06	.01
☐ 197	Ed Ott	.13	.06	.01
☐ 198	Wilbur Wood	.20	.10	.02
☐ 199	Pepe Frias	.13	.06	.01
☐ 200	Frank Tanana	.25	.12	.02
☐ 201	Ed Kranepool	.20	.10	.02
☐ 202	Tom Johnson	.13	.06	.01
☐ 203	Ed Armbrister	.13	.06	.01
☐ 204	Jeff Newman	.13	.06	.01
☐ 205	Pete Falcone	.13	.06	.01
☐ 206	Boog Powell	.35	.17	.03
☐ 207	Glenn Abbott	.13	.06	.01
☐ 208	Checklist 2	.65	.07	.01
☐ 209	Rob Andrews	.13	.06	.01
☐ 210	Fred Lynn	1.50	.75	.15
☐ 211	Giants Team/Mgr.	.60	.15	.03
	Joe Altobelli			
	(checklist back)			
☐ 212	Jim Mason	.13	.06	.01
☐ 213	Maximino Leon	.13	.06	.01
☐ 214	Darrell Porter	.13	.06	.01
☐ 215	Butch Metzger	.13	.06	.01
☐ 216	Doug DeCinces	.35	.17	.03

☐ 217	Tom Underwood	.13	.06	.01
☐ 218	John Wathan	1.00	.50	.10
☐ 219	Joe Coleman	.13	.06	.01
☐ 220	Chris Chambliss	.20	.10	.02
☐ 221	Bob Bailey	.13	.06	.01
☐ 222	Francisco Barrios	.13	.06	.01
☐ 223	Earl Williams	.13	.06	.01
☐ 224	Rusty Torres	.13	.06	.01
☐ 225	Bob Apodaca	.13	.06	.01
☐ 226	Leroy Stanton	.13	.06	.01
☐ 227	Joe Sambito	.35	.17	.03
☐ 228	Twins Team/Mgr.	.60	.15	.03
	Gene Mauch			
	(checklist back)			
☐ 229	Don Kessinger	.20	.10	.02
☐ 230	Vida Blue	.30	.15	.03
☐ 231	RB: George Brett	1.75	.85	.17
	Most cons. games			
	with 3 or more hits			
☐ 232	RB: Minnie Minoso	.25	.12	.02
	Oldest to hit safely			
☐ 233	RB: Jose Morales, Most	.20	.10	.02
	pinch-hits, season			
☐ 234	RB: Nolan Ryan	1.25	.60	.12
	Most seasons, 300			
	or more strikeouts			
☐ 235	Cecil Cooper	.60	.30	.06
☐ 236	Tom Buskey	.13	.06	.01
☐ 237	Gene Clines	.13	.06	.01
☐ 238	Tippy Martinez	.13	.06	.01
☐ 239	Bill Plummer	.13	.06	.01
☐ 240	Ron LeFlore	.20	.10	.02
☐ 241	Dave Tomlin	.13	.06	.01
☐ 242	Ken Henderson	.13	.06	.01
☐ 243	Ron Reed	.13	.06	.01
☐ 244	John Mayberry	.30	.15	.03
	(cartoon mentions			
	T206 Wagner)			
☐ 245	Rick Rhoden	.35	.17	.03
☐ 246	Mike Vail	.13	.06	.01
☐ 247	Chris Knapp	.13	.06	.01
☐ 248	Wilbur Howard	.13	.06	.01
☐ 249	Pete Redfern	.13	.06	.01
☐ 250	Bill Madlock	.60	.30	.06
☐ 251	Tony Muser	.13	.06	.01
☐ 252	Dale Murray	.13	.06	.01
☐ 253	John Hale	.13	.06	.01
☐ 254	Doyle Alexander	.20	.10	.02
☐ 255	George Scott	.20	.10	.02
☐ 256	Joe Hoerner	.13	.06	.01
☐ 257	Mike Miley	.13	.06	.01
☐ 258	Luis Tiant	.35	.17	.03
☐ 259	Mets Team/Mgr.	.65	.15	.03
	Joe Frazier			
	(checklist back)			
☐ 260	J.R. Richard	.25	.12	.02
☐ 261	Phil Garner	.20	.10	.02
☐ 262	Al Cowens	.20	.10	.02
☐ 263	Mike Marshall	.20	.10	.02
☐ 264	Tom Hutton	.13	.06	.01
☐ 265	Mark Fidrych	.50	.25	.05
☐ 266	Derrel Thomas	.13	.06	.01
☐ 267	Ray Fosse	.13	.06	.01
☐ 268	Rick Sawyer	.13	.06	.01
☐ 269	Joe Lis	.13	.06	.01
☐ 270	Dave Parker	2.25	1.10	.22
☐ 271	Terry Forster	.25	.12	.02
☐ 272	Lee Lacy	.20	.10	.02
☐ 273	Eric Soderholm	.13	.06	.01
☐ 274	Don Stanhouse	.13	.06	.01
☐ 275	Mike Hargrove	.13	.06	.01
☐ 276	AL Champs	.35	.17	.03
	Chambliss' homer			
	decides it			
☐ 277	NL Champs	.35	.17	.03
	Reds sweep Phillies			
☐ 278	Danny Frisella	.13	.06	.01
☐ 279	Joe Wallis	.13	.06	.01
☐ 280	Jim Hunter	1.50	.75	.15
☐ 281	Roy Staiger	.13	.06	.01
☐ 282	Sid Monge	.13	.06	.01
☐ 283	Jerry DaVanon	.13	.06	.01
☐ 284	Mike Norris	.20	.10	.02
☐ 285	Brooks Robinson	2.25	1.10	.22
☐ 286	Johnny Grubb	.13	.06	.01
☐ 287	Reds Team/Mgr.	.65	.15	.03
	Sparky Anderson			
	(checklist back)			
☐ 288	Bob Montgomery	.13	.06	.01
☐ 289	Gene Garber	.20	.10	.02
☐ 290	Amos Otis	.30	.15	.03
☐ 291	Jason Thompson	.45	.22	.04
☐ 292	Rogelio Moret	.13	.06	.01
☐ 293	Jack Brohamer	.13	.06	.01
☐ 294	George Medich	.13	.06	.01

☐ 295	Gary Carter	6.50	3.25	.65
☐ 296	Don Hood	.13	.06	.01
☐ 297	Ken Reitz	.13	.06	.01
☐ 298	Charlie Hough	.30	.15	.03
☐ 299	Otto Velez	.13	.06	.01
☐ 300	Jerry Koosman	.35	.17	.03
☐ 301	Toby Harrah	.20	.10	.02
☐ 302	Mike Garman	.13	.06	.01
☐ 303	Gene Tenace	.13	.06	.01
☐ 304	Jim Hughes	.13	.06	.01
☐ 305	Mickey Rivers	.20	.10	.02
☐ 306	Rick Waits	.13	.06	.01
☐ 307	Gary Sutherland	.13	.06	.01
☐ 308	Gene Pentz	.13	.06	.01
☐ 309	Red Sox Team/Mgr. Don Zimmer (checklist back)	.60	.15	.03
☐ 310	Larry Bowa	.50	.25	.05
☐ 311	Vern Ruhle	.13	.06	.01
☐ 312	Rob Belloir	.13	.06	.01
☐ 313	Paul Blair	.13	.06	.01
☐ 314	Steve Mingori	.13	.06	.01
☐ 315	Dave Chalk	.13	.06	.01
☐ 316	Steve Rogers	.20	.10	.02
☐ 317	Kurt Bevacqua	.13	.06	.01
☐ 318	Duffy Dyer	.13	.06	.01
☐ 319	Rich Gossage	.70	.35	.07
☐ 320	Ken Griffey	.30	.15	.03
☐ 321	Dave Goltz	.13	.06	.01
☐ 322	Bill Russell	.20	.10	.02
☐ 323	Larry Lintz	.13	.06	.01
☐ 324	John Curtis	.13	.06	.01
☐ 325	Mike Ivie	.13	.06	.01
☐ 326	Jesse Jefferson	.13	.06	.01
☐ 327	Astros Team/Mgr. Bill Virdon (checklist back)	.60	.15	.03
☐ 328	Tommy Boggs	.13	.06	.01
☐ 329	Ron Hodges	.13	.06	.01
☐ 330	George Hendrick	.25	.12	.02
☐ 331	Jim Colborn	.13	.06	.01
☐ 332	Elliott Maddox	.13	.06	.01
☐ 333	Paul Reuschel	.13	.06	.01
☐ 334	Bill Stein	.13	.06	.01
☐ 335	Bill Robinson	.13	.06	.01
☐ 336	Denny Doyle	.13	.06	.01
☐ 337	Ron Schueler	.13	.06	.01
☐ 338	Dave Duncan	.13	.06	.01
☐ 339	Adrian Devine	.13	.06	.01
☐ 340	Hal McRae	.25	.12	.02
☐ 341	Joe Kerrigan	.13	.06	.01
☐ 342	Jerry Remy	.13	.06	.01
☐ 343	Ed Halicki	.13	.06	.01
☐ 344	Brian Downing	.20	.10	.02
☐ 345	Reggie Smith	.35	.17	.03
☐ 346	Bill Singer	.13	.06	.01
☐ 347	George Foster	1.00	.50	.10
☐ 348	Brent Strom	.13	.06	.01
☐ 349	Jim Holt	.13	.06	.01
☐ 350	Larry Dierker	.20	.10	.02
☐ 351	Jim Sundberg	.20	.10	.02
☐ 352	Mike Phillips	.13	.06	.01
☐ 353	Stan Thomas	.13	.06	.01
☐ 354	Pirates Team/Mgr. Chuck Tanner (checklist back)	.60	.15	.03
☐ 355	Lou Brock	2.00	1.00	.20
☐ 356	Checklist 3	.65	.07	.01
☐ 357	Tim McCarver	.30	.15	.03
☐ 358	Tom House	.20	.10	.02
☐ 359	Willie Randolph	.50	.25	.05
☐ 360	Rick Monday	.20	.10	.02
☐ 361	Ed Rodriguez	.13	.06	.01
☐ 362	Tommy Davis	.25	.12	.02
☐ 363	Dave Roberts	.13	.06	.01
☐ 364	Vic Correll	.13	.06	.01
☐ 365	Mike Torrez	.20	.10	.02
☐ 366	Ted Sizemore	.13	.06	.01
☐ 367	Dave Hamilton	.13	.06	.01
☐ 368	Mike Jorgensen	.13	.06	.01
☐ 369	Terry Humphrey	.13	.06	.01
☐ 370	John Montefusco	.20	.10	.02
☐ 371	Royals Team/Mgr. Whitey Herzog (checklist back)	.60	.15	.03
☐ 372	Rich Folkers	.13	.06	.01
☐ 373	Bert Campaneris	.20	.10	.02
☐ 374	Kent Tekulve	.30	.15	.03
☐ 375	Larry Hisle	.20	.10	.02
☐ 376	Nino Espinosa	.13	.06	.01
☐ 377	Dave McKay	.13	.06	.01
☐ 378	Jim Umbarger	.13	.06	.01
☐ 379	Larry Cox	.13	.06	.01
☐ 380	Lee May	.20	.10	.02
☐ 381	Bob Forsch	.20	.10	.02
☐ 382	Charlie Moore	.13	.06	.01
☐ 383	Stan Bahnsen	.13	.06	.01
☐ 384	Darrel Chaney	.13	.06	.01
☐ 385	Dave LaRoche	.13	.06	.01
☐ 386	Manny Mota	.20	.10	.02
☐ 387	Yankees Team	.65	.15	.03
☐ 388	Terry Harmon	.13	.06	.01
☐ 389	Ken Kravec	.13	.06	.01
☐ 390	Dave Winfield	3.00	1.50	.30
☐ 391	Dan Warthen	.13	.06	.01
☐ 392	Phil Roof	.13	.06	.01
☐ 393	John Lowenstein	.13	.06	.01
☐ 394	Bill Laxton	.13	.06	.01
☐ 395	Manny Trillo	.20	.10	.02
☐ 396	Tom Murphy	.13	.06	.01
☐ 397	Larry Herndon	.60	.30	.06
☐ 398	Tom Burgmeier	.13	.06	.01
☐ 399	Bruce Boisclair	.13	.06	.01
☐ 400	Steve Garvey	3.00	1.50	.30
☐ 401	Mickey Scott	.13	.06	.01
☐ 402	Tommy Helms	.13	.06	.01
☐ 403	Tom Grieve	.20	.10	.02
☐ 404	Eric Rasmussen	.13	.06	.01
☐ 405	Claudell Washington	.25	.12	.02
☐ 406	Tim Johnson	.13	.06	.01
☐ 407	Dave Freisleben	.13	.06	.01
☐ 408	Cesar Tovar	.13	.06	.01
☐ 409	Pete Broberg	.13	.06	.01
☐ 410	Willie Montanez	.13	.06	.01
☐ 411	W.S. Games 1 and 2 Morgan homers opener; Bench stars as Reds take 2nd game	.50	.25	.05
☐ 412	W.S. Games 3 and 4 Reds' stop Yankees; Bench's two homers wrap it up	.50	.25	.05
☐ 413	World Series Summary Cincy wins 2nd straight series	.50	.25	.05
☐ 414	Tommy Harper	.20	.10	.02
☐ 415	Jay Johnstone	.20	.10	.02
☐ 416	Chuck Hartenstein	.13	.06	.01
☐ 417	Wayne Garrett	.13	.06	.01
☐ 418	White Sox Team/Mgr. Bob Lemon (checklist back)	.60	.15	.03
☐ 419	Steve Swisher	.13	.06	.01
☐ 420	Rusty Staub	.35	.17	.03
☐ 421	Doug Rau	.13	.06	.01
☐ 422	Freddie Patek	.13	.06	.01
☐ 423	Gary Lavelle	.13	.06	.01
☐ 424	Steve Brye	.13	.06	.01
☐ 425	Joe Torre	.40	.20	.04
☐ 426	Dick Drago	.13	.06	.01
☐ 427	Dave Rader	.13	.06	.01
☐ 428	Rangers Team/Mgr. Frank Lucchesi (checklist back)	.60	.15	.03
☐ 429	Ken Boswell	.13	.06	.01
☐ 430	Fergie Jenkins	.60	.30	.06
☐ 431	Dave Collins (photo actually Bobby Jones)	.30	.15	.03
☐ 432	Buzz Capra	.13	.06	.01
☐ 433	Turn back clock 1972 Nate Colbert	.20	.10	.02
☐ 434	Turn back clock 1967 Yaz Triple Crown	1.75	.85	.17
☐ 435	Turn back clock 1962 Wills 104 steals	.45	.22	.04
☐ 436	Turn back clock 1957 Keegan hurls Majors' only no-hitter	.20	.10	.02
☐ 437	Turn back clock 1952 Kiner leads NL HR's 7th straight year	.45	.22	.04
☐ 438	Marty Perez	.13	.06	.01
☐ 439	Gorman Thomas	.40	.20	.04
☐ 440	Jon Matlack	.20	.10	.02
☐ 441	Larvell Blanks	.13	.06	.01
☐ 442	Braves Team/Mgr. Dave Bristol (checklist back)	.60	.15	.03
☐ 443	Lamar Johnson	.13	.06	.01
☐ 444	Wayne Twitchell	.13	.06	.01
☐ 445	Ken Singleton	.35	.17	.03
☐ 446	Bill Bonham	.13	.06	.01
☐ 447	Jerry Turner	.13	.06	.01
☐ 448	Ellie Rodriguez	.13	.06	.01
☐ 449	Al Fitzmorris	.13	.06	.01
☐ 450	Pete Rose	8.50	4.25	.85
☐ 451	Checklist 4	.65	.07	.01
☐ 452	Mike Caldwell	.20	.10	.02
☐ 453	Pedro Garcia	.13	.06	.01

☐ 454	Andy Etchebarren	.13	.06	.01
☐ 455	Rick Wise	.20	.10	.02
☐ 456	Leon Roberts	.13	.06	.01
☐ 457	Steve Luebber	.13	.06	.01
☐ 458	Leo Foster	.13	.06	.01
☐ 459	Steve Foucault	.13	.06	.01
☐ 460	Willie Stargell	2.00	1.00	.20
☐ 461	Dick Tidrow	.13	.06	.01
☐ 462	Don Baylor	.60	.30	.06
☐ 463	Jamie Quirk	.13	.06	.01
☐ 464	Randy Moffitt	.13	.06	.01
☐ 465	Rico Carty	.25	.12	.02
☐ 466	Fred Holdsworth	.13	.06	.01
☐ 467	Phillies Team/Mgr. Danny Ozark (checklist back)	.60	.15	.03
☐ 468	Ramon Hernandez	.13	.06	.01
☐ 469	Pat Kelly	.13	.06	.01
☐ 470	Ted Simmons	.45	.22	.04
☐ 471	Del Unser	.13	.06	.01
☐ 472	Rookie Pitchers Don Aase Bob McClure Gil Patterson Dave Wehrmeister	.50	.25	.05
☐ 473	Rookie Outfielders Andre Dawson Gene Richards John Scott Denny Walling	25.00	12.50	2.50
☐ 474	Rookie Shortstops Bob Bailor Kiko Garcia Craig Reynolds Alex Taveras	.25	.12	.02
☐ 475	Rookie Pitchers Chris Batton Rick Camp Scott McGregor Manny Sarmiento	.50	.25	.05
☐ 476	Rookie Catchers Gary Alexander Rick Cerone Dale Murphy Kevin Pasley	65.00	32.50	6.50
☐ 477	Rookie Infielders Doug Ault Rich Dauer Orlando Gonzalez Phil Mankowski	.25	.12	.02
☐ 478	Rookie Pitchers Jim Gideon Leon Hooten Dave Johnson Mark Lemongello	.25	.12	.02
☐ 479	Rookie Outfielders Brian Asselstine Wayne Gross Sam Mejias Alvis Woods	.25	.12	.02
☐ 480	Carl Yastrzemski	4.00	2.00	.40
☐ 481	Roger Metzger	.13	.06	.01
☐ 482	Tony Solaita	.13	.06	.01
☐ 483	Richie Zisk	.20	.10	.02
☐ 484	Burt Hooton	.20	.10	.02
☐ 485	Roy White	.20	.10	.02
☐ 486	Ed Bane	.13	.06	.01
☐ 487	Rookie Pitchers Larry Anderson Ed Glynn Joe Henderson Greg Terlecky	.25	.12	.02
☐ 488	Rookie Outfielders Jack Clark Ruppert Jones Lee Mazzilli Dan Thomas	16.00	8.00	1.60
☐ 489	Rookie Pitchers Len Barker Randy Lerch Greg Minton Mike Overy	.60	.30	.06
☐ 490	Rookie Shortstops Billy Almon Mickey Klutts Tommy McMillan Mark Wagner	.35	.17	.03
☐ 491	Rookie Pitchers Mike Dupree Denny Martinez Craig Mitchell Bob Sykes	.80	.40	.08
☐ 492	Rookie Outfielders Tony Armas Steve Kemp	1.50	.75	.15

	Carlos Lopez Gary Woods			
☐ 493	Rookie Pitchers Mike Krukow Jim Otten Gary Wheelock Mike Willis	1.00	.50	.10
☐ 494	Rookie Infielders Juan Bernhardt Mike Champion Jim Gantner Bump Wills	.50	.25	.05
☐ 495	Al Hrabosky	.20	.10	.02
☐ 496	Gary Thomasson	.13	.06	.01
☐ 497	Clay Carroll	.13	.06	.01
☐ 498	Sal Bando	.25	.12	.02
☐ 499	Pablo Torrealba	.13	.06	.01
☐ 500	Dave Kingman	.50	.25	.05
☐ 501	Jim Bibby	.13	.06	.01
☐ 502	Randy Hundley	.13	.06	.01
☐ 503	Bill Lee	.20	.10	.02
☐ 504	Dodgers Team/Mgr. Tom Lasorda (checklist back)	.65	.15	.03
☐ 505	Oscar Gamble	.20	.10	.02
☐ 506	Steve Grilli	.13	.06	.01
☐ 507	Mike Hegan	.13	.06	.01
☐ 508	Dave Pagan	.13	.06	.01
☐ 509	Cookie Rojas	.13	.06	.01
☐ 510	John Candelaria	.40	.20	.04
☐ 511	Bill Fahey	.13	.06	.01
☐ 512	Jack Billingham	.13	.06	.01
☐ 513	Jerry Terrell	.13	.06	.01
☐ 514	Cliff Johnson	.13	.06	.01
☐ 515	Chris Speier	.13	.06	.01
☐ 516	Bake McBride	.13	.06	.01
☐ 517	Pete Vuckovich	.60	.30	.06
☐ 518	Cubs Team/Mgr. Herman Franks (checklist back)	.60	.15	.03
☐ 519	Don Kirkwood	.13	.06	.01
☐ 520	Garry Maddox	.13	.06	.01
☐ 521	Bob Grich	.25	.12	.02
☐ 522	Enzo Hernandez	.13	.06	.01
☐ 523	Rollie Fingers	.80	.40	.08
☐ 524	Rowland Office	.13	.06	.01
☐ 525	Dennis Eckersley	.20	.10	.02
☐ 526	Larry Parrish	.35	.17	.03
☐ 527	Dan Meyer	.13	.06	.01
☐ 528	Bill Castro	.13	.06	.01
☐ 529	Jim Essian	.13	.06	.01
☐ 530	Rick Reuschel	.25	.12	.02
☐ 531	Lyman Bostock	.30	.15	.03
☐ 532	Jim Willoughby	.13	.06	.01
☐ 533	Mickey Stanley	.13	.06	.01
☐ 534	Paul Splittorff	.20	.10	.02
☐ 535	Cesar Geronimo	.13	.06	.01
☐ 536	Vic Albury	.13	.06	.01
☐ 537	Dave Roberts	.13	.06	.01
☐ 538	Frank Taveras	.13	.06	.01
☐ 539	Mike Wallace	.13	.06	.01
☐ 540	Bob Watson	.20	.10	.02
☐ 541	John Denny	.30	.15	.03
☐ 542	Frank Duffy	.13	.06	.01
☐ 543	Ron Blomberg	.13	.06	.01
☐ 544	Gary Ross	.13	.06	.01
☐ 545	Bob Boone	.25	.12	.02
☐ 546	Orioles Team/Mgr. Earl Weaver (checklist back)	.65	.15	.03
☐ 547	Willie McCovey	1.75	.85	.17
☐ 548	Joel Youngblood	.13	.06	.01
☐ 549	Jerry Royster	.13	.06	.01
☐ 550	Randy Jones	.20	.10	.02
☐ 551	Bill North	.13	.06	.01
☐ 552	Pepe Mangual	.13	.06	.01
☐ 553	Jack Heidemann	.13	.06	.01
☐ 554	Bruce Kimm	.13	.06	.01
☐ 555	Dan Ford	.13	.06	.01
☐ 556	Doug Bird	.13	.06	.01
☐ 557	Jerry White	.13	.06	.01
☐ 558	Elias Sosa	.13	.06	.01
☐ 559	Alan Bannister	.13	.06	.01
☐ 560	Dave Concepcion	.35	.17	.03
☐ 561	Pete LaCock	.13	.06	.01
☐ 562	Checklist 5	.65	.06	.01
☐ 563	Bruce Kison	.13	.06	.01
☐ 564	Alan Ashby	.20	.10	.02
☐ 565	Mickey Lolich	.30	.15	.0?
☐ 566	Rick Miller	.13	.06	.0?
☐ 567	Enos Cabell	.13	.06	
☐ 568	Carlos May	.13	.06	
☐ 569	Jim Lonborg	.20	.10	.01
☐ 570	Bobby Bonds	.30	.15	.0?
☐ 571	Darrell Evans	.45	.2?	

☐ 572	Ross Grimsley	.13	.06	.01
☐ 573	Joe Ferguson	.13	.06	.01
☐ 574	Aurelio Rodriguez	.13	.06	.01
☐ 575	Dick Ruthven	.13	.06	.01
☐ 576	Fred Kendall	.13	.06	.01
☐ 577	Jerry Augustine	.13	.06	.01
☐ 578	Bob Randall	.13	.06	.01
☐ 579	Don Carrithers	.13	.06	.01
☐ 580	George Brett	7.50	3.75	.75
☐ 581	Pedro Borbon	.13	.06	.01
☐ 582	Ed Kirkpatrick	.13	.06	.01
☐ 583	Paul Lindblad	.13	.06	.01
☐ 584	Ed Goodson	.13	.06	.01
☐ 585	Rick Burleson	.20	.10	.02
☐ 586	Steve Renko	.13	.06	.01
☐ 587	Rick Baldwin	.13	.06	.01
☐ 588	Dave Moates	.13	.06	.01
☐ 589	Mike Cosgrove	.13	.06	.01
☐ 590	Buddy Bell	.40	.20	.04
☐ 591	Chris Arnold	.13	.06	.01
☐ 592	Dan Briggs	.13	.06	.01
☐ 593	Dennis Blair	.13	.06	.01
☐ 594	Biff Pocoroba	.13	.06	.01
☐ 595	John Hiller	.20	.10	.02
☐ 596	Jerry Martin	.13	.06	.01
☐ 597	Mariners Leaders	.45	.15	.03
	Darrell Johnson MG			
	Don Bryant CO			
	Jim Busby CO			
	Vada Pinson CO			
	Wes Stock CO			
	(checklist back)			
☐ 598	Sparky Lyle	.45	.22	.04
☐ 599	Mike Tyson	.13	.06	.01
☐ 600	Jim Palmer	2.00	1.00	.20
☐ 601	Mike Lum	.13	.06	.01
☐ 602	Andy Hassler	.13	.06	.01
☐ 603	Willie Davis	.20	.10	.02
☐ 604	Jim Slaton	.13	.06	.01
☐ 605	Felix Millan	.13	.06	.01
☐ 606	Steve Braun	.13	.06	.01
☐ 607	Larry Demery	.13	.06	.01
☐ 608	Roy Howell	.13	.06	.01
☐ 609	Jim Barr	.13	.06	.01
☐ 610	Jose Cardenal	.13	.06	.01
☐ 611	Dave Lemanczyk	.13	.06	.01
☐ 612	Barry Foote	.13	.06	.01
☐ 613	Reggie Cleveland	.13	.06	.01
☐ 614	Greg Gross	.13	.06	.01
☐ 615	Phil Niekro	1.25	.60	.12
☐ 616	Tommy Sandt	.13	.06	.01
☐ 617	Bobby Darwin	.13	.06	.01
☐ 618	Pat Dobson	.20	.10	.02
☐ 619	Johnny Oates	.13	.06	.01
☐ 620	Don Sutton	1.25	.60	.12
☐ 621	Tigers Team/Mgr.	.65	.15	.03
	Ralph Houk			
	(checklist back)			
☐ 622	Jim Wohlford	.13	.06	.01
☐ 623	Jack Kucek	.13	.06	.01
☐ 624	Hector Cruz	.13	.06	.01
☐ 625	Ken Holtzman	.20	.10	.02
☐ 626	Al Bumbry	.13	.06	.01
☐ 627	Bob Myrick	.13	.06	.01
☐ 628	Mario Guerrero	.13	.06	.01
☐ 629	Bob Valentine	.30	.15	.03
☐ 630	Bert Blyleven	.45	.22	.04
☐ 631	Big League Brothers	1.50	.75	.15
	George Brett			
	Ken Brett			
☐ 632	Big League Brothers	.25	.12	.02
	Bob Forsch			
	Ken Forsch			
☐ 633	Big League Brothers	.25	.12	.02
	Lee May			
	Carlos May			
☐ 634	Big League Brothers	.25	.12	.02
	Paul Reuschel			
	Rick Reuschel			
	(photos switched)			
☐ 635	Robin Yount	3.50	1.75	.35
☐ 636	Santo Alcala	.13	.06	.01
☐ 637	Alex Johnson	.13	.06	.01
☐ 638	Jim Kaat	.50	.25	.05
☐ 639	Jerry Morales	.13	.06	.01
☐ 640	Carlton Fisk	.75	.35	.07
☐ 641	Dan Larson	.13	.06	.01
☐ 642	Willie Crawford	.13	.06	.01
☐ 643	Mike Pazik	.13	.06	.01
☐ 644	Matt Alexander	.13	.06	.01
☐ 645	Jerry Reuss	.20	.10	.02
☐ 646	Andres Mora	.13	.06	.01
☐ 647	Expos Team/Mgr.	.60	.15	.03
	Dick Williams			
	(checklist back)			

☐ 648	Jim Spencer	.13	.06	.01
☐ 649	Dave Cash	.13	.06	.01
☐ 650	Nolan Ryan	3.50	1.75	.35
☐ 651	Von Joshua	.13	.06	.01
☐ 652	Tom Walker	.13	.06	.01
☐ 653	Diego Segui	.13	.06	.01
☐ 654	Ron Pruitt	.13	.06	.01
☐ 655	Tony Perez	.65	.30	.06
☐ 656	Ron Guidry	3.00	1.50	.30
☐ 657	Mick Kelleher	.13	.06	.01
☐ 658	Marty Pattin	.13	.06	.01
☐ 659	Merv Rettenmund	.13	.06	.01
☐ 660	Willie Horton	.35	.10	.02

1977 Topps Cloth Sticker

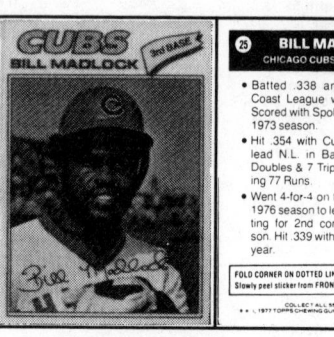

The "cards" in this 73-card set measure 2 1/2" by 3 1/2". The 1977 Cloth Stickers series was issued as a test set separately from the regular baseball series of that year. The obverse pictures are identical to those appearing in the regular set, but the backs are completely different. There are 55 player cards and 18 unnumbered checklists, the latter bearing the title "Baseball Patches". The checklists are puzzle pieces which, when properly arranged, form pictures of the A.L. and N.L. All-Star teams. Puzzle pieces are coded below by U (Upper), M (Middle), B (Bottom), L (left), C (Center), and R (Right). Cards marked with an SP in the checklist are in shorter supply than all others in the set.

		NRMT	VG-E	GOOD
COMPLETE SET		55.00	27.50	5.50
COMMON PLAYER (1-55)		.30	.15	.03
COMMON PUZZLE (56-73)		.03	.01	.00
☐ 1	Alan Ashby	.30	.15	.03
☐ 2	Buddy Bell SP	1.00	.50	.10
☐ 3	Johnny Bench	3.50	1.75	.35
☐ 4	Vida Blue	.50	.25	.05
☐ 5	Bert Blyleven	.50	.25	.05
☐ 6	Steve Braun SP	.50	.25	.05
☐ 7	George Brett	5.00	2.50	.50
☐ 8	Lou Brock	2.50	1.25	.25
☐ 9	Jose Cardenal	.30	.15	.03
☐ 10	Rod Carew SP	4.00	2.00	.40
☐ 11	Steve Carlton	3.00	1.50	.30
☐ 12	Dave Cash	.30	.15	.03
☐ 13	Cesar Cedeno SP	.50	.25	.05
☐ 14	Ron Cey	.40	.20	.04
☐ 15	Mark Fidrych	.40	.20	.04
☐ 16	Dan Ford	.30	.15	.03
☐ 17	Wayne Garland	.30	.15	.03
☐ 18	Ralph Garr	.30	.15	.03
☐ 19	Steve Garvey	3.50	1.75	.35
☐ 20	Mike Hargrove	.30	.15	.03
☐ 21	Jim Hunter	.75	.35	.07
☐ 22	Reggie Jackson	4.50	2.25	.45
☐ 23	Randy Jones	.30	.15	.03
☐ 24	Dave Kingman SP	1.00	.50	.10
☐ 25	Bill Madlock	.75	.35	.07
☐ 26	Lee May SP	.50	.25	.05
☐ 27	John Mayberry	.30	.15	.03
☐ 28	John(Andy) Messersmith	.30	.15	.03
☐ 29	Willie Montanez	.30	.15	.03
☐ 30	John Montefusco SP	.50	.25	.05

		NRMT	VG-E	GOOD
☐ 31 Joe Morgan	1.50	.75	.15
☐ 32 Thurman Munson	2.50	1.25	.25
☐ 33 Bobby Murcer	.40	.20	.04
☐ 34 Al Oliver SP	.75	.35	.07
☐ 35 Dave Pagan	.30	.15	.03
☐ 36 Jim Palmer SP	3.50	1.75	.35
☐ 37 Tony Perez	.50	.25	.05
☐ 38 Pete Rose SP	11.00	5.50	1.10
☐ 39 Joe Rudi	.30	.15	.03
☐ 40 Nolan Ryan SP	5.00	2.50	.50
☐ 41 Mike Schmidt	4.50	2.25	.45
☐ 42 Tom Seaver	3.50	1.75	.35
☐ 43 Ted Simmons	.50	.25	.05
☐ 44 Bill Singer	.30	.15	.03
☐ 45 Willie Stargell	2.50	1.25	.25
☐ 46 Rusty Staub	.50	.25	.05
☐ 47 Don Sutton	1.25	.60	.12
☐ 48 Luis Tiant	.50	.25	.05
☐ 49 Bill Travers	.30	.15	.03
☐ 50 Claudell Washington	.40	.20	.04
☐ 51 Bob Watson	.30	.15	.03
☐ 52 Dave Winfield	2.50	1.25	.25
☐ 53 Carl Yastrzemski	4.00	2.00	.40
☐ 54 Robin Yount	3.00	1.50	.30
☐ 55 Richie Zisk	.30	.15	.03
☐ 56 AL Puzzle UL (unnumbered)	.03	.01	.00
☐ 57 AL Puzzle UC (unnumbered)	.03	.01	.00
☐ 58 AL Puzzle UR (unnumbered)	.03	.01	.00
☐ 59 AL Puzzle ML (unnumbered)	.03	.01	.00
☐ 60 AL Puzzle MC (unnumbered)	.03	.01	.00
☐ 61 AL Puzzle MR (unnumbered)	.03	.01	.00
☐ 62 AL Puzzle BL SP (unnumbered)	.15	.03	.01
☐ 63 AL Puzzle BC SP (unnumbered)	.15	.03	.01
☐ 64 AL Puzzle BR SP (unnumbered)	.15	.03	.01
☐ 65 NL Puzzle UL (unnumbered)	.03	.01	.00
☐ 66 NL Puzzle UC (unnumbered)	.03	.01	.00
☐ 67 NL Puzzle UR (unnumbered)	.03	.01	.00
☐ 68 NL Puzzle ML (unnumbered)	.03	.01	.00
☐ 69 NL Puzzle MC (unnumbered)	.03	.01	.00
☐ 70 NL Puzzle MR (unnumbered)	.03	.01	.00
☐ 71 NL Puzzle BL (unnumbered)	.03	.01	.00
☐ 72 NL Puzzle BC (unnumbered)	.03	.01	.00
☐ 73 NL Puzzle BR (unnumbered)	.03	.01	.00

1978 Topps

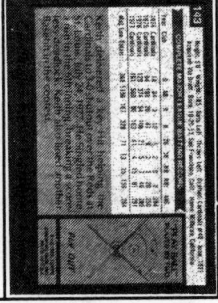

KEITH HERNANDEZ

The cards in this 726-card set measure 2 1/2" by 3 1/2". The 1978 Topps set experienced an increase in number of cards from the previous five regular issue sets of 660. Cards 1 through 7 feature Record Breakers (RB) of the 1977 season. Other subsets within this set include League Leaders (201-208), Post-season cards (411-413), and Rookie Prospects (701-711). While no scarcities exist, 66 of the cards are more abundant in supply as they were "double printed." These 66 double printed cards are noted in the checklist by DP. Team cards again feature a checklist of that team's players in the set on the back.

		NRMT	VG-E	GOOD
COMPLETE SET	200.00	100.00	20.00
COMMON PLAYER (1-726)	.10	.05	.01
COMMON DP's (1-726)	.05	.02	.00
☐ 1 RB: Lou Brock, Most steals, lifetime	2.00	.30	.05
☐ 2 RB: Sparky Lyle, Most games, pure relief, lifetime	.20	.10	.02
☐ 3 RB: Willie McCovey, Most times, 2 HR's in inning, lifetime	.65	.30	.06
☐ 4 RB: Brooks Robinson, Most consecutive seasons with one club	.85	.40	.08
☐ 5 RB: Pete Rose, Most hits, switch hitter, lifetime	2.25	1.10	.22
☐ 6 RB: Nolan Ryan, Most games with 10 or more strikeouts, lifetime	1.25	.60	.12
☐ 7 RB: Reggie Jackson, Most homers, one World Series	1.75	.85	.17
☐ 8 Mike Sadek	.10	.05	.01
☐ 9 Doug DeCinces	.25	.12	.02
☐ 10 Phil Niekro	1.00	.50	.10
☐ 11 Rick Manning	.10	.05	.01
☐ 12 Don Aase	.20	.10	.02
☐ 13 Art Howe	.10	.05	.01
☐ 14 Lerrin LaGrow	.10	.05	.01
☐ 15 Tony Perez DP	.20	.10	.02
☐ 16 Roy White	.15	.07	.01
☐ 17 Mike Krukow	.30	.15	.03
☐ 18 Bob Grich	.20	.10	.02
☐ 19 Darrell Porter	.15	.07	.01
☐ 20 Pete Rose DP	4.00	2.00	.40
☐ 21 Steve Kemp	.25	.12	.02
☐ 22 Charlie Hough	.25	.12	.02
☐ 23 Bump Wills	.10	.05	.01
☐ 24 Don Money DP	.05	.02	.00
☐ 25 Jon Matlack	.15	.07	.01
☐ 26 Rich Hebner	.10	.05	.01
☐ 27 Geoff Zahn	.10	.05	.01
☐ 28 Ed Ott	.10	.05	.01
☐ 29 Bob Lacey	.10	.05	.01
☐ 30 George Hendrick	.15	.07	.01
☐ 31 Glenn Abbott	.10	.05	.01
☐ 32 Garry Templeton	.30	.15	.03
☐ 33 Dave Lemanczyk	.10	.05	.01
☐ 34 Willie McCovey	1.50	.75	.15
☐ 35 Sparky Lyle	.25	.12	.02
☐ 36 Eddie Murray	35.00	17.50	3.50
☐ 37 Rick Waits	.10	.05	.01
☐ 38 Willie Montanez	.10	.05	.01
☐ 39 Floyd Bannister	1.50	.75	.15
☐ 40 Carl Yastrzemski	3.00	1.50	.30
☐ 41 Burt Hooton	.10	.05	.01
☐ 42 Jorge Orta	.10	.05	.01
☐ 43 Bill Atkinson	.10	.05	.01
☐ 44 Toby Harrah	.15	.07	.01
☐ 45 Mark Fidrych	.25	.12	.02
☐ 46 Al Cowens	.15	.07	.01
☐ 47 Jack Billingham	.10	.05	.01
☐ 48 Don Baylor	.45	.22	.04
☐ 49 Ed Kranepool	.15	.07	.01
☐ 50 Rick Reuschel	.25	.12	.02
☐ 51 Charlie Moore DP	.05	.02	.00
☐ 52 Jim Lonborg	.15	.07	.01
☐ 53 Phil Garner DP	.05	.02	.00
☐ 54 Tom Johnson	.10	.05	.01
☐ 55 Mitchell Page	.15	.07	.01
☐ 56 Randy Jones	.15	.07	.01
☐ 57 Dan Meyer	.10	.05	.01
☐ 58 Bob Forsch	.20	.10	.02
☐ 59 Otto Velez	.10	.05	.01
☐ 60 Thurman Munson	2.00	1.00	.20
☐ 61 Larvell Blanks	.10	.05	.01
☐ 62 Jim Barr	.10	.05	.01
☐ 63 Don Zimmer	.15	.07	.01
☐ 64 Gene Pentz	.10	.05	.01

☐ 65	Ken Singleton	.20	.10	.02
☐ 66	White Sox Team	.45	.10	.02
	(checklist back)			
☐ 67	Claudell Washington	.20	.10	.02
☐ 68	Steve Foucault DP	.05	.02	.00
☐ 69	Mike Vail	.10	.05	.01
☐ 70	Rich Gossage	.60	.30	.06
☐ 71	Terry Humphrey	.10	.05	.01
☐ 72	Andre Dawson	5.00	2.50	.50
☐ 73	Andy Hassler	.10	.05	.01
☐ 74	Checklist 1	.40	.05	.01
☐ 75	Dick Ruthven	.10	.05	.01
☐ 76	Steve Ontiveros	.10	.05	.01
☐ 77	Ed Kirkpatrick	.10	.05	.01
☐ 78	Pablo Torrealba	.10	.05	.01
☐ 79	Darrell Johnson DP	.05	.02	.00
☐ 80	Ken Griffey	.20	.10	.02
☐ 81	Pete Redfern	.10	.05	.01
☐ 82	Giants Team	.45	.10	.02
	(checklist back)			
☐ 83	Bob Montgomery	.10	.05	.01
☐ 84	Kent Tekulve	.20	.10	.02
☐ 85	Ron Fairly	.15	.07	.01
☐ 86	Dave Tomlin	.10	.05	.01
☐ 87	John Lowenstein	.10	.05	.01
☐ 88	Mike Phillips	.10	.05	.01
☐ 89	Ken Clay	.10	.05	.01
☐ 90	Larry Bowa	.35	.17	.03
☐ 91	Oscar Zamora	.10	.05	.01
☐ 92	Adrian Devine	.10	.05	.01
☐ 93	Bobby Cox DP	.05	.02	.00
☐ 94	Chuck Scrivener	.10	.05	.01
☐ 95	Jamie Quirk	.10	.05	.01
☐ 96	Orioles Team	.45	.10	.02
	(checklist back)			
☐ 97	Stan Bahnsen	.10	.05	.01
☐ 98	Jim Essian	.10	.05	.01
☐ 99	Willie Hernandez	1.25	.60	.12
☐ 100	George Brett	4.00	2.00	.40
☐ 101	Sid Monge	.10	.05	.01
☐ 102	Matt Alexander	.10	.05	.01
☐ 103	Tom Murphy	.10	.05	.01
☐ 104	Lee Lacy	.15	.07	.01
☐ 105	Reggie Cleveland	.10	.05	.01
☐ 106	Bill Plummer	.10	.05	.01
☐ 107	Ed Halicki	.10	.05	.01
☐ 108	Von Joshua	.10	.05	.01
☐ 109	Joe Torre	.30	.15	.03
☐ 110	Richie Zisk	.15	.07	.01
☐ 111	Mike Tyson	.10	.05	.01
☐ 112	Astros Team	.45	.10	.02
	(checklist back)			
☐ 113	Don Carrithers	.10	.05	.01
☐ 114	Paul Blair	.15	.07	.01
☐ 115	Gary Nolan	.10	.05	.01
☐ 116	Tucker Ashford	.10	.05	.01
☐ 117	John Montague	.10	.05	.01
☐ 118	Terry Harmon	.10	.05	.01
☐ 119	Denny Martinez	.15	.07	.01
☐ 120	Gary Carter	3.00	1.50	.30
☐ 121	Alvis Woods	.10	.05	.01
☐ 122	Dennis Eckersley	.15	.07	.01
☐ 123	Manny Trillo	.15	.07	.01
☐ 124	Dave Rozema	.15	.07	.01
☐ 125	George Scott	.15	.07	.01
☐ 126	Paul Moskau	.10	.05	.01
☐ 127	Chet Lemon	.20	.10	.02
☐ 128	Bill Russell	.15	.07	.01
☐ 129	Jim Colborn	.10	.05	.01
☐ 130	Jeff Burroughs	.20	.10	.02
☐ 131	Bert Blyleven	.40	.20	.04
☐ 132	Enos Cabell	.10	.05	.01
☐ 133	Jerry Augustine	.10	.05	.01
☐ 134	Steve Henderson	.15	.07	.01
☐ 135	Ron Guidry DP	.75	.35	.07
☐ 136	Ted Sizemore	.10	.05	.01
☐ 137	Craig Kusick	.10	.05	.01
☐ 138	Larry Demery	.10	.05	.01
☐ 139	Wayne Gross	.10	.05	.01
☐ 140	Rollie Fingers	.60	.30	.06
☐ 141	Ruppert Jones	.15	.07	.01
☐ 142	John Montefusco	.15	.07	.01
☐ 143	Keith Hernandez	2.25	1.10	.22
☐ 144	Jesse Jefferson	.10	.05	.01
☐ 145	Rick Monday	.15	.07	.01
☐ 146	Doyle Alexander	.15	.07	.01
☐ 147	Lee Mazzilli	.15	.07	.01
☐ 148	Andre Thornton	.20	.10	.02
☐ 149	Dale Murray	.10	.05	.01
☐ 150	Bobby Bonds	.25	.12	.02
☐ 151	Milt Wilcox	.10	.05	.01
☐ 152	Ivan DeJesus	.10	.05	.01
☐ 153	Steve Stone	.15	.07	.01
☐ 154	Cecil Cooper DP	.20	.10	.02
☐ 155	Butch Hobson	.10	.05	.01
☐ 156	Andy Messersmith	.15	.07	.01
☐ 157	Pete LaCock DP	.05	.02	.00
☐ 158	Joaquin Andujar	.30	.15	.03
☐ 159	Lou Piniella	.25	.12	.02
☐ 160	Jim Palmer	1.75	.85	.17
☐ 161	Bob Boone	.25	.12	.02
☐ 162	Paul Thormodsgard	.10	.05	.01
☐ 163	Bill North	.10	.05	.01
☐ 164	Bob Owchinko	.10	.05	.01
☐ 165	Rennie Stennett	.10	.05	.01
☐ 166	Carlos Lopez	.10	.05	.01
☐ 167	Tim Foli	.10	.05	.01
☐ 168	Reggie Smith	.25	.12	.02
☐ 169	Jerry Johnson	.10	.05	.01
☐ 170	Lou Brock	1.75	.85	.17
☐ 171	Pat Zachry	.10	.05	.01
☐ 172	Mike Hargrove	.15	.07	.01
☐ 173	Robin Yount	2.25	1.10	.22
☐ 174	Wayne Garland	.10	.05	.01
☐ 175	Jerry Morales	.10	.05	.01
☐ 176	Milt May	.10	.05	.01
☐ 177	Gene Garber DP	.05	.02	.00
☐ 178	Dave Chalk	.10	.05	.01
☐ 179	Dick Tidrow	.10	.05	.01
☐ 180	Dave Concepcion	.25	.12	.02
☐ 181	Ken Forsch	.15	.07	.01
☐ 182	Jim Spencer	.10	.05	.01
☐ 183	Doug Bird	.10	.05	.01
☐ 184	Checklist 2	.40	.05	.01
☐ 185	Ellis Valentine	.10	.05	.01
☐ 186	Bob Stanley DP	.35	.17	.03
☐ 187	Jerry Royster DP	.05	.02	.00
☐ 188	Al Bumbry	.10	.05	.01
☐ 189	Tom Lasorda MG	.20	.10	.02
☐ 190	John Candelaria	.25	.12	.02
☐ 191	Rodney Scott	.10	.05	.01
☐ 192	Padres Team	.45	.10	.02
	(checklist back)			
☐ 193	Rich Chiles	.10	.05	.01
☐ 194	Derrel Thomas	.10	.05	.01
☐ 195	Larry Dierker	.15	.07	.01
☐ 196	Bob Bailor	.10	.05	.01
☐ 197	Nino Espinosa	.10	.05	.01
☐ 198	Ron Pruitt	.10	.05	.01
☐ 199	Craig Reynolds	.10	.05	.01
☐ 200	Reggie Jackson	3.00	1.50	.30
☐ 201	Batting Leaders	.60	.30	.06
	Dave Parker			
	Rod Carew			
☐ 202	Home Run Leaders DP	.15	.07	.01
	George Foster			
	Jim Rice			
☐ 203	RBI Leaders	.20	.10	.02
	George Foster			
	Larry Hisle			
☐ 204	Steals Leaders DP	.10	.05	.01
	Frank Taveras			
	Freddie Patek			
☐ 205	Victory Leaders	.50	.25	.05
	Steve Carlton			
	Dave Goltz			
	Dennis Leonard			
	Jim Palmer			
☐ 206	Strikeout Leaders DP	.15	.07	.01
	Phil Niekro			
	Nolan Ryan			
☐ 207	ERA Leaders DP	.10	.05	.01
	John Candelaria			
	Frank Tanana			
☐ 208	Top Firemen	.20	.10	.02
	Rollie Fingers			
	Bill Campbell			
☐ 209	Dock Ellis	.10	.05	.01
☐ 210	Jose Cardenal	.10	.05	.01
☐ 211	Earl Weaver MG DP	.10	.05	.01
☐ 212	Mike Caldwell	.10	.05	.01
☐ 213	Alan Bannister	.10	.05	.01
☐ 214	Angels Team	.45	.10	.02
	(checklist back)			
☐ 215	Darrell Evans	.45	.22	.04
☐ 216	Mike Paxton	.10	.05	.01
☐ 217	Rod Gilbreath	.10	.05	.01
☐ 218	Marty Pattin	.10	.05	.01
☐ 219	Mike Cubbage	.10	.05	.01
☐ 220	Pedro Borbon	.10	.05	.01
☐ 221	Chris Speier	.10	.05	.01
☐ 222	Jerry Martin	.10	.05	.01
☐ 223	Bruce Kison	.10	.05	.01
☐ 224	Jerry Tabb	.10	.05	.01
☐ 225	Don Gullett DP	.05	.02	.00
☐ 226	Joe Ferguson	.10	.05	.01
☐ 227	Al Fitzmorris	.10	.05	.01
☐ 228	Manny Mota DP	.10	.05	.01
☐ 229	Leo Foster	.10	.05	.01
☐ 230	Al Hrabosky	.15	.07	.01

☐ 231	Wayne Nordhagen	.10	.05	.01
☐ 232	Mickey Stanley	.10	.05	.01
☐ 233	Dick Pole	.10	.05	.01
☐ 234	Herman Franks MG	.10	.05	.01
☐ 235	Tim McCarver	.20	.10	.02
☐ 236	Terry Whitfield	.10	.05	.01
☐ 237	Rich Dauer	.10	.05	.01
☐ 238	Juan Beniquez	.15	.07	.01
☐ 239	Dyar Miller	.10	.05	.01
☐ 240	Gene Tenace	.10	.05	.01
☐ 241	Pete Vuckovich	.20	.10	.02
☐ 242	Barry Bonnell DP	.10	.05	.01
☐ 243	Bob McClure	.15	.07	.01
☐ 244	Expos Team DP	.20	.05	.01
	(checklist back)			
☐ 245	Rick Burleson	.15	.07	.01
☐ 246	Dan Driessen	.15	.07	.01
☐ 247	Larry Christenson	.10	.05	.01
☐ 248	Frank White DP	.10	.05	.01
☐ 249	Dave Goltz DP	.05	.02	.00
☐ 250	Graig Nettles DP	.15	.07	.01
☐ 251	Don Kirkwood	.10	.05	.01
☐ 252	Steve Swisher DP	.05	.02	.00
☐ 253	Jim Kern	.10	.05	.01
☐ 254	Dave Collins	.15	.07	.01
☐ 255	Jerry Reuss	.20	.10	.02
☐ 256	Joe Altobelli MG	.10	.05	.01
☐ 257	Hector Cruz	.10	.05	.01
☐ 258	John Hiller	.15	.07	.01
☐ 259	Dodgers Team	.50	.15	.03
	(checklist back)			
☐ 260	Bert Campaneris	.15	.07	.01
☐ 261	Tim Hosley	.10	.05	.01
☐ 262	Rudy May	.10	.05	.01
☐ 263	Danny Walton	.10	.05	.01
☐ 264	Jamie Easterly	.10	.05	.01
☐ 265	Sal Bando DP	.10	.05	.01
☐ 266	Bob Shirley	.10	.05	.01
☐ 267	Doug Ault	.10	.05	.01
☐ 268	Gil Flores	.10	.05	.01
☐ 269	Wayne Twitchell	.10	.05	.01
☐ 270	Carlton Fisk	.60	.30	.06
☐ 271	Randy Lerch DP	.05	.02	.00
☐ 272	Royle Stillman	.10	.05	.01
☐ 273	Fred Norman	.10	.05	.01
☐ 274	Freddie Patek	.10	.05	.01
☐ 275	Dan Ford	.10	.05	.01
☐ 276	Bill Bonham DP	.05	.02	.00
☐ 277	Bruce Boisclair	.10	.05	.01
☐ 278	Enrique Romo	.10	.05	.01
☐ 279	Bill Virdon MG	.10	.05	.01
☐ 280	Buddy Bell	.30	.15	.03
☐ 281	Eric Rasmussen DP	.05	.02	.00
☐ 282	Yankees Team	.60	.15	.03
	(checklist back)			
☐ 283	Omar Moreno	.15	.07	.01
☐ 284	Randy Moffitt	.10	.05	.01
☐ 285	Steve Yeager DP	.05	.02	.00
☐ 286	Ben Oglivie	.15	.07	.01
☐ 287	Kiko Garcia	.10	.05	.01
☐ 288	Dave Hamilton	.10	.05	.01
☐ 289	Checklist 3	.40	.05	.01
☐ 290	Willie Horton	.15	.07	.01
☐ 291	Gary Ross	.10	.05	.01
☐ 292	Gene Richards	.10	.05	.01
☐ 293	Mike Willis	.10	.05	.01
☐ 294	Larry Parrish	.25	.12	.02
☐ 295	Bill Lee	.15	.07	.01
☐ 296	Biff Pocoroba	.10	.05	.01
☐ 297	Warren Brusstar DP	.05	.02	.00
☐ 298	Tony Armas	.25	.12	.02
☐ 299	Whitey Herzog MG	.15	.07	.01
☐ 300	Joe Morgan	1.25	.60	.12
☐ 301	Buddy Schultz	.10	.05	.01
☐ 302	Cubs Team	.45	.10	.02
	(checklist back)			
☐ 303	Sam Hinds	.10	.05	.01
☐ 304	John Milner	.10	.05	.01
☐ 305	Rico Carty	.15	.07	.01
☐ 306	Joe Niekro	.30	.15	.03
☐ 307	Glenn Borgmann	.10	.05	.01
☐ 308	Jim Rooker	.10	.05	.01
☐ 309	Cliff Johnson	.10	.05	.01
☐ 310	Don Sutton	1.00	.50	.10
☐ 311	Jose Baez DP	.05	.02	.00
☐ 312	Greg Minton	.15	.07	.01
☐ 313	Andy Etchebarren	.10	.05	.01
☐ 314	Paul Lindblad	.10	.05	.01
☐ 315	Mark Belanger	.15	.07	.01
☐ 316	Henry Cruz DP	.05	.02	.00
☐ 317	Dave Johnson	.25	.12	.02
☐ 318	Tom Griffin	.10	.05	.01
☐ 319	Alan Ashby	.10	.05	.01
☐ 320	Fred Lynn	.80	.40	.08
☐ 321	Santo Alcala	.10	.05	.01
☐ 322	Tom Paciorek	.10	.05	.01
☐ 323	Jim Fregosi DP	.10	.05	.01
☐ 324	Vern Rapp MG	.10	.05	.01
☐ 325	Bruce Sutter	.65	.30	.06
☐ 326	Mike Lum DP	.05	.02	.00
☐ 327	Rick Langford DP	.05	.02	.00
☐ 328	Milwaukee Brewers	.45	.10	.02
	Team Card			
	(checklist back)			
☐ 329	John Verhoeven	.10	.05	.01
☐ 330	Bob Watson	.15	.07	.01
☐ 331	Mark Littell	.10	.05	.01
☐ 332	Duane Kuiper	.10	.05	.01
☐ 333	Jim Todd	.10	.05	.01
☐ 334	John Stearns	.10	.05	.01
☐ 335	Bucky Dent	.20	.10	.02
☐ 336	Steve Busby	.15	.07	.01
☐ 337	Tom Grieve	.15	.07	.01
☐ 338	Dave Heaverlo	.10	.05	.01
☐ 339	Mario Guerrero	.10	.05	.01
☐ 340	Bake McBride	.10	.05	.01
☐ 341	Mike Flanagan	.20	.10	.02
☐ 342	Aurelio Rodriguez	.10	.05	.01
☐ 343	John Wathan DP	.10	.05	.01
☐ 344	Sam Ewing	.10	.05	.01
☐ 345	Luis Tiant	.25	.12	.02
☐ 346	Larry Biittner	.10	.05	.01
☐ 347	Terry Forster	.15	.07	.01
☐ 348	Del Unser	.10	.05	.01
☐ 349	Rick Camp DP	.05	.02	.00
☐ 350	Steve Garvey	2.50	1.25	.25
☐ 351	Jeff Torborg	.15	.07	.01
☐ 352	Tony Scott	.10	.05	.01
☐ 353	Doug Bair	.15	.07	.01
☐ 354	Cesar Geronimo	.10	.05	.01
☐ 355	Bill Travers	.10	.05	.01
☐ 356	Mets Team	.50	.15	.03
	(checklist back)			
☐ 357	Tom Poquette	.10	.05	.01
☐ 358	Mark Lemongello	.10	.05	.01
☐ 359	Marc Hill	.10	.05	.01
☐ 360	Mike Schmidt	4.50	2.25	.45
☐ 361	Chris Knapp	.10	.05	.01
☐ 362	Dave May	.10	.05	.01
☐ 363	Bob Randall	.10	.05	.01
☐ 364	Jerry Turner	.10	.05	.01
☐ 365	Ed Figueroa	.10	.05	.01
☐ 366	Larry Milbourne DP	.05	.02	.00
☐ 367	Rick Dempsey	.15	.07	.01
☐ 368	Balor Moore	.10	.05	.01
☐ 369	Tim Nordbrook	.10	.05	.01
☐ 370	Rusty Staub	.25	.12	.02
☐ 371	Ray Burris	.10	.05	.01
☐ 372	Brian Asselstine	.10	.05	.01
☐ 373	Jim Willoughby	.10	.05	.01
☐ 374	Jose Morales	.10	.05	.01
☐ 375	Tommy John	.60	.30	.06
☐ 376	Jim Wohlford	.10	.05	.01
☐ 377	Manny Sarmiento	.10	.05	.01
☐ 378	Bobby Winkles MG	.10	.05	.01
☐ 379	Skip Lockwood	.10	.05	.01
☐ 380	Ted Simmons	.35	.17	.03
☐ 381	Phillies Team	.45	.10	.02
	(checklist back)			
☐ 382	Joe Lahoud	.10	.05	.01
☐ 383	Mario Mendoza	.10	.05	.01
☐ 384	Jack Clark	3.50	1.75	.35
☐ 385	Tito Fuentes	.10	.05	.01
☐ 386	Bob Gorinski	.10	.05	.01
☐ 387	Ken Holtzman	.15	.07	.01
☐ 388	Bill Fahey DP	.05	.02	.00
☐ 389	Julio Gonzalez	.10	.05	.01
☐ 390	Oscar Gamble	.15	.07	.01
☐ 391	Larry Haney	.10	.05	.01
☐ 392	Billy Almon	.15	.07	.01
☐ 393	Tippy Martinez	.15	.07	.01
☐ 394	Roy Howell DP	.05	.02	.00
☐ 395	Jim Hughes	.10	.05	.01
☐ 396	Bob Stinson DP	.05	.02	.00
☐ 397	Greg Gross	.10	.05	.01
☐ 398	Don Hood	.10	.05	.01
☐ 399	Pete Mackanin	.10	.05	.01
☐ 400	Nolan Ryan	2.25	1.10	.22
☐ 401	Sparky Anderson MG	.15	.07	.01
☐ 402	Dave Campbell	.10	.05	.01
☐ 403	Bud Harrelson	.15	.07	.01
☐ 404	Tigers Team	.50	.15	.03
	(checklist back)			
☐ 405	Rawly Eastwick	.10	.05	.01
☐ 406	Mike Jorgensen	.10	.05	.01
☐ 407	Odell Jones	.10	.05	.01
☐ 408	Joe Zdeb	.10	.05	.01
☐ 409	Ron Schueler	.10	.05	.01
☐ 410	Bill Madlock	.50	.25	.05
☐ 411	AL Champs	.45	.22	.04

	Yankees rally to defeat Royals			
☐ 412	NL Champs	.45	.22	.04
	Dodgers overpower Phillies in four			
☐ 413	World Series	1.25	.60	.12
	Reggie and Yankees reign supreme			
☐ 414	Darold Knowles DP	.05	.02	.00
☐ 415	Ray Fosse	.10	.05	.01
☐ 416	Jack Brohamer	.10	.05	.01
☐ 417	Mike Garman DP	.05	.02	.00
☐ 418	Tony Muser	.10	.05	.01
☐ 419	Jerry Garvin	.10	.05	.01
☐ 420	Greg Luzinski	.25	.12	.02
☐ 421	Junior Moore	.10	.05	.01
☐ 422	Steve Braun	.10	.05	.01
☐ 423	Dave Rosello	.10	.05	.01
☐ 424	Red Sox Team	.45	.10	.02
	(checklist back)			
☐ 425	Steve Rogers DP	.10	.05	.01
☐ 426	Fred Kendall	.10	.05	.01
☐ 427	Mario Soto	1.00	.50	.10
☐ 428	Joel Youngblood	.10	.05	.01
☐ 429	Mike Barlow	.10	.05	.01
☐ 430	Al Oliver	.35	.17	.03
☐ 431	Butch Metzger	.10	.05	.01
☐ 432	Terry Bulling	.10	.05	.01
☐ 433	Fernando Gonzalez	.10	.05	.01
☐ 434	Mike Norris	.15	.07	.01
☐ 435	Checklist 4	.40	.05	.01
☐ 436	Vic Harris DP	.05	.02	.00
☐ 437	Bo McLaughlin	.10	.05	.01
☐ 438	John Ellis	.10	.05	.01
☐ 439	Ken Kravec	.10	.05	.01
☐ 440	Dave Lopes	.25	.12	.02
☐ 441	Larry Gura	.15	.07	.01
☐ 442	Elliott Maddox	.10	.05	.01
☐ 443	Darrel Chaney	.10	.05	.01
☐ 444	Roy Hartsfield MG	.10	.05	.01
☐ 445	Mike Ivie	.10	.05	.01
☐ 446	Tug McGraw	.25	.12	.02
☐ 447	Leroy Stanton	.10	.05	.01
☐ 448	Bill Castro	.10	.05	.01
☐ 449	Tim Blackwell DP	.05	.02	.00
☐ 450	Tom Seaver	2.00	1.00	.20
☐ 451	Twins Team	.45	.10	.02
	(checklist back)			
☐ 452	Jerry Mumphrey	.15	.07	.01
☐ 453	Doug Flynn	.10	.05	.01
☐ 454	Dave LaRoche	.10	.05	.01
☐ 455	Bill Robinson	.10	.05	.01
☐ 456	Vern Ruhle	.10	.05	.01
☐ 457	Bob Bailey	.10	.05	.01
☐ 458	Jeff Newman	.10	.05	.01
☐ 459	Charlie Spikes	.10	.05	.01
☐ 460	Jim Hunter	1.25	.60	.12
☐ 461	Rob Andrews DP	.05	.02	.00
☐ 462	Rogelio Moret	.10	.05	.01
☐ 463	Kevin Bell	.10	.05	.01
☐ 464	Jerry Grote	.10	.05	.01
☐ 465	Hal McRae	.20	.10	.02
☐ 466	Dennis Blair	.10	.05	.01
☐ 467	Alvin Dark MG	.15	.07	.01
☐ 468	Warren Cromartie	.15	.07	.01
☐ 469	Rick Cerone	.15	.07	.01
☐ 470	J.R. Richard	.20	.10	.02
☐ 471	Roy Smalley	.15	.07	.01
☐ 472	Ron Reed	.10	.05	.01
☐ 473	Bill Buckner	.25	.12	.02
☐ 474	Jim Slaton	.10	.05	.01
☐ 475	Gary Matthews	.20	.10	.02
☐ 476	Bill Stein	.10	.05	.01
☐ 477	Doug Capilla	.10	.05	.01
☐ 478	Jerry Remy	.15	.07	.01
☐ 479	Cardinals Team	.45	.10	.02
	(checklist back)			
☐ 480	Ron LeFlore	.15	.07	.01
☐ 481	Jackson Todd	.10	.05	.01
☐ 482	Rick Miller	.10	.05	.01
☐ 483	Ken Macha	.10	.05	.01
☐ 484	Jim Norris	.10	.05	.01
☐ 485	Chris Chambliss	.15	.07	.01
☐ 486	John Curtis	.10	.05	.01
☐ 487	Jim Tyrone	.10	.05	.01
☐ 488	Dan Spillner	.10	.05	.01
☐ 489	Rudy Meoli	.10	.05	.01
☐ 490	Amos Otis	.20	.10	.02
☐ 491	Scott McGregor	.20	.10	.02
☐ 492	Jim Sundberg	.15	.07	.01
☐ 493	Steve Renko	.10	.05	.01
☐ 494	Chuck Tanner MG	.15	.07	.01
☐ 495	Dave Cash	.10	.05	.01
☐ 496	Jim Clancy DP	.20	.10	.02
☐ 497	Glenn Adams	.10	.05	.01
☐ 498	Joe Sambito	.15	.07	.01
☐ 499	Seattle Mariners Team	.40	.10	.02
	(checklist back)			
☐ 500	George Foster	.70	.35	.07
☐ 501	Dave Roberts	.10	.05	.01
☐ 502	Pat Rockett	.10	.05	.01
☐ 503	Ike Hampton	.10	.05	.01
☐ 504	Roger Freed	.10	.05	.01
☐ 505	Felix Millan	.10	.05	.01
☐ 506	Ron Blomberg	.10	.05	.01
☐ 507	Willie Crawford	.10	.05	.01
☐ 508	Johnny Oates	.10	.05	.01
☐ 509	Brent Strom	.10	.05	.01
☐ 510	Willie Stargell	1.50	.75	.15
☐ 511	Frank Duffy	.10	.05	.01
☐ 512	Larry Herndon	.15	.07	.01
☐ 513	Barry Foote	.10	.05	.01
☐ 514	Rob Sperring	.10	.05	.01
☐ 515	Tim Corcoran	.10	.05	.01
☐ 516	Gary Beare	.10	.05	.01
☐ 517	Andres Mora	.10	.05	.01
☐ 518	Tommy Boggs DP	.05	.02	.00
☐ 519	Brian Downing	.15	.07	.01
☐ 520	Larry Hisle	.15	.07	.01
☐ 521	Steve Staggs	.10	.05	.01
☐ 522	Dick Williams MG	.15	.07	.01
☐ 523	Donnie Moore	.45	.22	.04
☐ 524	Bernie Carbo	.10	.05	.01
☐ 525	Jerry Terrell	.10	.05	.01
☐ 526	Reds Team	.50	.15	.03
	(checklist back)			
☐ 527	Vic Correll	.10	.05	.01
☐ 528	Rob Picciolo	.10	.05	.01
☐ 529	Paul Hartzell	.10	.05	.01
☐ 530	Dave Winfield	2.00	1.00	.20
☐ 531	Tom Underwood	.10	.05	.01
☐ 532	Skip Jutze	.10	.05	.01
☐ 533	Sandy Alomar	.10	.05	.01
☐ 534	Wilbur Howard	.10	.05	.01
☐ 535	Checklist 5	.40	.05	.01
☐ 536	Roric Harrison	.10	.05	.01
☐ 537	Bruce Bochte	.10	.05	.01
☐ 538	Johnny LeMaster	.10	.05	.01
☐ 539	Vic Davalillo DP	.05	.02	.00
☐ 540	Steve Carlton	2.00	1.00	.20
☐ 541	Larry Cox	.10	.05	.01
☐ 542	Tim Johnson	.10	.05	.01
☐ 543	Larry Harlow DP	.05	.02	.00
☐ 544	Len Randle DP	.05	.02	.00
☐ 545	Bill Campbell	.10	.05	.01
☐ 546	Ted Martinez	.10	.05	.01
☐ 547	John Scott	.10	.05	.01
☐ 548	Billy Hunter MG DP	.05	.02	.00
☐ 549	Joe Kerrigan	.10	.05	.01
☐ 550	John Mayberry	.15	.07	.01
☐ 551	Atlanta Braves Team	.45	.10	.02
	(checklist back)			
☐ 552	Francisco Barrios	.10	.05	.01
☐ 553	Terry Puhl	.40	.20	.04
☐ 554	Joe Coleman	.10	.05	.01
☐ 555	Butch Wynegar	.15	.07	.01
☐ 556	Ed Armbrister	.10	.05	.01
☐ 557	Tony Solaita	.10	.05	.01
☐ 558	Paul Mitchell	.10	.05	.01
☐ 559	Phil Mankowski	.10	.05	.01
☐ 560	Dave Parker	1.75	.85	.17
☐ 561	Charlie Williams	.10	.05	.01
☐ 562	Glenn Burke	.10	.05	.01
☐ 563	Dave Rader	.10	.05	.01
☐ 564	Mick Kelleher	.10	.05	.01
☐ 565	Jerry Koosman	.25	.12	.01
☐ 566	Merv Rettenmund	.10	.05	.01
☐ 567	Dick Drago	.10	.05	.01
☐ 568	Tom Hutton	.10	.05	.01
☐ 569	Lary Sorensen	.10	.05	.01
☐ 570	Dave Kingman	.50	.25	.05
☐ 571	Buck Martinez	.10	.05	.01
☐ 572	Rick Wise	.15	.07	.01
☐ 573	Luis Gomez	.10	.05	.01
☐ 574	Bob Lemon MG	.20	.10	.02
☐ 575	Pat Dobson	.15	.07	.01
☐ 576	Sam Mejias	.10	.05	.01
☐ 577	Oakland A's Team	.45	.10	.02
	(checklist back)			
☐ 578	Buzz Capra	.10	.05	.01
☐ 579	Rance Mulliniks	.15	.07	.01
☐ 580	Rod Carew	2.00	1.00	.20
☐ 581	Lynn McGlothen	.10	.05	.01
☐ 582	Fran Healy	.10	.05	.01
☐ 583	George Medich	.10	.05	.01
☐ 584	John Hale	.10	.05	.01
☐ 585	Woodie Fryman DP	.05	.02	.00
☐ 586	Ed Goodson	.10	.05	.01
☐ 587	John Urrea	.10	.05	.01
☐ 588	Jim Mason	.10	.05	.01

☐ 589	Bob Knepper	1.25	.60	.12
☐ 590	Bobby Murcer	.30	.15	.03
☐ 591	George Zeber	.10	.05	.01
☐ 592	Bob Apodaca	.10	.05	.01
☐ 593	Dave Skaggs	.10	.05	.01
☐ 594	Dave Freisleben	.10	.05	.01
☐ 595	Sixto Lezcano	.10	.05	.01
☐ 596	Gary Wheelock	.10	.05	.01
☐ 597	Steve Dillard	.10	.05	.01
☐ 598	Eddie Solomon	.10	.05	.01
☐ 599	Gary Woods	.10	.05	.01
☐ 600	Frank Tanana	.20	.10	.02
☐ 601	Gene Mauch MG	.15	.07	.01
☐ 602	Eric Soderholm	.10	.05	.01
☐ 603	Will McEnaney	.10	.05	.01
☐ 604	Earl Williams	.10	.05	.01
☐ 605	Rick Rhoden	.25	.12	.02
☐ 606	Pirates Team	.45	.10	.02
	(checklist back)			
☐ 607	Fernando Arroyo	.10	.05	.01
☐ 608	Johnny Grubb	.10	.05	.01
☐ 609	John Denny	.20	.10	.02
☐ 610	Garry Maddox	.15	.07	.01
☐ 611	Pat Scanlon	.10	.05	.01
☐ 612	Ken Henderson	.10	.05	.01
☐ 613	Marty Perez	.10	.05	.01
☐ 614	Joe Wallis	.10	.05	.01
☐ 615	Clay Carroll	.10	.05	.01
☐ 616	Pat Kelly	.10	.05	.01
☐ 617	Joe Nolan	.10	.05	.01
☐ 618	Tommy Helms	.10	.05	.01
☐ 619	Thad Bosley DP	.10	.05	.01
☐ 620	Willie Randolph	.30	.15	.03
☐ 621	Craig Swan DP	.10	.05	.01
☐ 622	Champ Summers	.10	.05	.01
☐ 623	Ed Rodriquez	.10	.05	.01
☐ 624	Gary Alexander DP	.05	.02	.00
☐ 625	Jose Cruz	.30	.15	.03
☐ 626	Blue Jays Team DP	.20	.06	.01
	(checklist back)			
☐ 627	David Johnson	.10	.05	.01
☐ 628	Ralph Garr	.10	.05	.01
☐ 629	Don Stanhouse	.10	.05	.01
☐ 630	Ron Cey	.35	.17	.03
☐ 631	Danny Ozark MG	.10	.05	.01
☐ 632	Rowland Office	.10	.05	.01
☐ 633	Tom Veryzer	.10	.05	.01
☐ 634	Len Barker	.15	.07	.01
☐ 635	Joe Rudi	.15	.07	.01
☐ 636	Jim Bibby	.15	.07	.01
☐ 637	Duffy Dyer	.10	.05	.01
☐ 638	Paul Splittorff	.15	.07	.01
☐ 639	Gene Clines	.10	.05	.01
☐ 640	Lee May DP	.10	.05	.01
☐ 641	Doug Rau	.10	.05	.01
☐ 642	Denny Doyle	.10	.05	.01
☐ 643	Tom House	.15	.07	.01
☐ 644	Jim Dwyer	.10	.05	.01
☐ 645	Mike Torrez	.15	.07	.01
☐ 646	Rick Auerbach DP	.05	.02	.00
☐ 647	Steve Dunning	.10	.05	.01
☐ 648	Gary Thomasson	.10	.05	.01
☐ 649	Moose Haas	.35	.17	.03
☐ 650	Cesar Cedeno	.25	.12	.02
☐ 651	Doug Rader	.15	.07	.01
☐ 652	Checklist 6	.40	.05	.01
☐ 653	Ron Hodges DP	.05	.02	.00
☐ 654	Pepe Frias	.10	.05	.01
☐ 655	Lyman Bostock	.20	.10	.02
☐ 656	Dave Garcia MG	.10	.05	.01
☐ 657	Bombo Rivera	.10	.05	.01
☐ 658	Manny Sanguillen	.15	.07	.01
☐ 659	Rangers Team	.45	.10	.02
	(checklist back)			
☐ 660	Jason Thompson	.20	.10	.02
☐ 661	Grant Jackson	.10	.05	.01
☐ 662	Paul Dade	.10	.05	.01
☐ 663	Paul Reuschel	.10	.05	.01
☐ 664	Fred Stanley	.10	.05	.01
☐ 665	Dennis Leonard	.15	.07	.01
☐ 666	Billy Smith	.10	.05	.01
☐ 667	Jeff Byrd	.10	.05	.01
☐ 668	Dusty Baker	.20	.10	.02
☐ 669	Pete Falcone	.10	.05	.01
☐ 670	Jim Rice	3.50	1.75	.35
☐ 671	Gary Lavelle	.10	.05	.01
☐ 672	Don Kessinger	.15	.07	.01
☐ 673	Steve Brye	.10	.05	.01
☐ 674	Ray Knight	1.50	.75	.15
☐ 675	Jay Johnstone	.15	.07	.01
☐ 676	Bob Myrick	.10	.05	.01
☐ 677	Ed Herrmann	.10	.05	.01
☐ 678	Tom Burgmeier	.10	.05	.01
☐ 679	Wayne Garrett	.10	.05	.01
☐ 680	Vida Blue	.20	.10	.02

☐ 681	Rob Belloir	.10	.05	.01
☐ 682	Ken Brett	.10	.05	.01
☐ 683	Mike Champion	.10	.05	.01
☐ 684	Ralph Houk MG	.15	.07	.01
☐ 685	Frank Taveras	.10	.05	.01
☐ 686	Gaylord Perry	1.50	.75	.15
☐ 687	Julio Cruz	.25	.12	.02
☐ 688	George Mitterwald	.10	.05	.01
☐ 689	Indians Team	.45	.10	.02
	(checklist back)			
☐ 690	Mickey Rivers	.15	.07	.01
☐ 691	Ross Grimsley	.10	.05	.01
☐ 692	Ken Reitz	.10	.05	.01
☐ 693	Lamar Johnson	.10	.05	.01
☐ 694	Elias Sosa	.10	.05	.01
☐ 695	Dwight Evans	.90	.45	.09
☐ 696	Steve Mingori	.10	.05	.01
☐ 697	Roger Metzger	.10	.05	.01
☐ 698	Juan Bernhardt	.10	.05	.01
☐ 699	Jackie Brown	.10	.05	.01
☐ 700	Johnny Bench	2.25	1.10	.22
☐ 701	Rookie Pitchers	.30	.15	.03
	Tom Hume			
	Larry Landreth			
	Steve McCatty			
	Bruce Taylor			
☐ 702	Rookie Catchers	.15	.07	.01
	Bill Nahorodny			
	Kevin Pasley			
	Rick Sweet			
	Don Werner			
☐ 703	Rookie Pitchers DP	5.00	2.50	.50
	Larry Andersen			
	Tim Jones			
	Mickey Mahler			
	Jack Morris			
☐ 704	Rookie 2nd Basemen	7.50	3.75	.75
	Garth Iorg			
	Dave Oliver			
	Sam Perlozzo			
	Lou Whitaker			
☐ 705	Rookie Outfielders	.30	.15	.03
	Dave Bergman			
	Miguel Dilone			
	Clint Hurdle			
	Willie Norwood			
☐ 706	Rookie 1st Basemen	.20	.10	.02
	Wayne Cage			
	Ted Cox			
	Pat Putnam			
	Dave Revering			
☐ 707	Rookie Shortstops	35.00	17.50	3.50
	Mickey Klutts			
	Paul Molitor			
	Alan Trammell			
	U.L. Washington			
☐ 708	Rookie Catchers	35.00	17.50	3.50
	Bo Diaz			
	Dale Murphy			
	Lance Parrish			
	Ernie Whitt			
☐ 709	Rookie Pitchers	.30	.15	.03
	Steve Burke			
	Matt Keough			
	Lance Rautzhan			
	Dan Schatzeder			
☐ 710	Rookie Outfielders	1.50	.75	.15
	Dell Alston			
	Rick Bosetti			
	Mike Easler			
	Keith Smith			
☐ 711	Rookie Pitchers DP	.10	.05	.01
	Cardell Camper			
	Dennis Lamp			
	Craig Mitchell			
	Roy Thomas			
☐ 712	Bobby Valentine	.25	.12	.02
☐ 713	Bob Davis	.10	.05	.01
☐ 714	Mike Anderson	.10	.05	.01
☐ 715	Jim Kaat	.45	.22	.04
☐ 716	Clarence Gaston	.10	.05	.01
☐ 717	Nelson Briles	.15	.07	.01
☐ 718	Ron Jackson	.10	.05	.01
☐ 719	Randy Elliott	.10	.05	.01
☐ 720	Fergie Jenkins	.40	.20	.04
☐ 721	Billy Martin MG	.35	.17	.03
☐ 722	Pete Broberg	.10	.05	.01
☐ 723	John Wockenfuss	.10	.05	.01
☐ 724	K.C. Royals Team	.45	.10	.02
	(checklist back)			
☐ 725	Kurt Bevacqua	.10	.05	.01
☐ 726	Wilbur Wood	.30	.06	.01

1979 Topps

The cards in this 726-card set measure 2 1/2" by 3 1/2". Topps continued with the same number of cards as in 1978. Various series spotlight League Leaders (1-8), "Season and Career Record Holders" (411-418), "Record Breakers of 1978" (201-206) and one "Prospects" card for each team (701-726). Team cards feature a checklist on back of that team's players in the set and a small picture of the manager on the front of the card. There are 66 cards that were double printed and these are noted in the checklist by the abbreviation DP. Bump Wills was initially depicted in a Ranger uniform but with a Blue Jays affiliation; later printings correctly labeled him with Texas. The set price listed does not include the scarcer Wills (Rangers) card.

		NRMT	VG-E	GOOD
COMPLETE SET		135.00	65.00	13.50
COMMON PLAYER (1-726)		.09	.04	.01
COMMON DP's (1-726)		.04	.02	.00
☐ 1	Batting Leaders Rod Carew Dave Parker	1.50	.25	.05
☐ 2	Home Run Leaders Jim Rice George Foster	.35	.17	.03
☐ 3	RBI Leaders Jim Rice George Foster	.35	.17	.03
☐ 4	Stolen Base Leaders Ron LeFlore Omar Moreno	.15	.07	.01
☐ 5	Victory Leaders Ron Guidry Gaylord Perry	.30	.15	.03
☐ 6	Strikeout Leaders Nolan Ryan J.R. Richard	.30	.15	.03
☐ 7	ERA Leaders Ron Guidry Craig Swan	.15	.07	.01
☐ 8	Leading Firemen Rich Gossage Rollie Fingers	.20	.10	.02
☐ 9	Dave Campbell	.09	.04	.01
☐ 10	Lee May	.15	.07	.01
☐ 11	Marc Hill	.09	.04	.01
☐ 12	Dick Drago	.09	.04	.01
☐ 13	Paul Dade	.09	.04	.01
☐ 14	Rafael Landestoy	.09	.04	.01
☐ 15	Ross Grimsley	.09	.04	.01
☐ 16	Fred Stanley	.09	.04	.01
☐ 17	Donnie Moore	.15	.07	.01
☐ 18	Tony Solaita	.09	.04	.01
☐ 19	Larry Gura DP	.09	.04	.01
☐ 20	Joe Morgan DP	.25	.12	.02
☐ 21	Kevin Kobel	.09	.04	.01
☐ 22	Mike Jorgensen	.09	.04	.01
☐ 23	Terry Forster	.15	.07	.01
☐ 24	Paul Molitor	3.00	1.50	.30
☐ 25	Steve Carlton	2.00	1.00	.20
☐ 26	Jamie Quirk	.09	.04	.01
☐ 27	Dave Goltz	.09	.04	.01
☐ 28	Steve Brye	.09	.04	.01
☐ 29	Rick Langford	.09	.04	.01

☐ 30	Dave Winfield	2.00	1.00	.20
☐ 31	Tom House DP	.09	.04	.01
☐ 32	Jerry Mumphrey	.15	.07	.01
☐ 33	Dave Rozema	.09	.04	.01
☐ 34	Rob Andrews	.09	.04	.01
☐ 35	Ed Figueroa	.09	.04	.01
☐ 36	Alan Ashby	.09	.04	.01
☐ 37	Joe Kerrigan DP	.04	.02	.00
☐ 38	Bernie Carbo	.09	.04	.01
☐ 39	Dale Murphy	8.00	4.00	.80
☐ 40	Dennis Eckersley	.15	.07	.01
☐ 41	Twins Team/Mgr. Gene Mauch (checklist back)	.40	.10	.02
☐ 42	Ron Blomberg	.09	.04	.01
☐ 43	Wayne Twitchell	.09	.04	.01
☐ 44	Kurt Bevacqua	.09	.04	.01
☐ 45	Al Hrabosky	.15	.07	.01
☐ 46	Ron Hodges	.09	.04	.01
☐ 47	Fred Norman	.09	.04	.01
☐ 48	Merv Rettenmund	.09	.04	.01
☐ 49	Vern Ruhle	.09	.04	.01
☐ 50	Steve Garvey DP	1.00	.50	.10
☐ 51	Ray Fosse DP	.04	.02	.00
☐ 52	Randy Lerch	.09	.04	.01
☐ 53	Mick Kelleher	.09	.04	.01
☐ 54	Dell Alston DP	.04	.02	.00
☐ 55	Willie Stargell	1.50	.75	.15
☐ 56	John Hale	.09	.04	.01
☐ 57	Eric Rasmussen	.09	.04	.01
☐ 58	Bob Randall DP	.04	.02	.00
☐ 59	John Denny DP	.09	.04	.01
☐ 60	Mickey Rivers	.15	.07	.01
☐ 61	Bo Diaz	.30	.15	.03
☐ 62	Randy Moffitt	.09	.04	.01
☐ 63	Jack Brohamer	.09	.04	.01
☐ 64	Tom Underwood	.09	.04	.01
☐ 65	Mark Belanger	.15	.07	.01
☐ 66	Tigers Team/Mgr. Les Moss (checklist back)	.40	.10	.02
☐ 67	Jim Mason DP	.04	.02	.00
☐ 68	Joe Niekro DP	.09	.04	.01
☐ 69	Elliott Maddox	.09	.04	.01
☐ 70	John Candelaria	.20	.10	.02
☐ 71	Brian Downing	.15	.07	.01
☐ 72	Steve Mingori	.09	.04	.01
☐ 73	Ken Henderson	.09	.04	.01
☐ 74	Shane Rawley	1.25	.60	.12
☐ 75	Steve Yeager	.09	.04	.01
☐ 76	Warren Cromartie	.09	.04	.01
☐ 77	Dan Briggs DP	.04	.02	.00
☐ 78	Elias Sosa	.09	.04	.01
☐ 79	Ted Cox	.09	.04	.01
☐ 80	Jason Thompson	.15	.07	.01
☐ 81	Roger Erickson	.09	.04	.01
☐ 82	Mets Team/Mgr. Joe Torre (checklist back)	.40	.10	.02
☐ 83	Fred Kendall	.09	.04	.01
☐ 84	Greg Minton	.09	.04	.01
☐ 85	Gary Matthews	.15	.07	.01
☐ 86	Rodney Scott	.09	.04	.01
☐ 87	Pete Falcone	.09	.04	.01
☐ 88	Bob Molinaro	.09	.04	.01
☐ 89	Dick Tidrow	.09	.04	.01
☐ 90	Bob Boone	.20	.10	.02
☐ 91	Terry Crowley	.09	.04	.01
☐ 92	Jim Bibby	.09	.04	.01
☐ 93	Phil Mankowski	.09	.04	.01
☐ 94	Len Barker	.15	.07	.01
☐ 95	Robin Yount	1.75	.85	.17
☐ 96	Indians Team/Mgr. Jeff Torborg (checklist back)	.40	.10	.02
☐ 97	Sam Mejias	.09	.04	.01
☐ 98	Ray Burris	.09	.04	.01
☐ 99	John Wathan	.20	.10	.02
☐ 100	Tom Seaver DP	1.00	.50	.10
☐ 101	Roy Howell	.09	.04	.01
☐ 102	Mike Anderson	.09	.04	.01
☐ 103	Jim Todd	.09	.04	.01
☐ 104	Johnny Oates DP	.04	.02	.00
☐ 105	Rick Camp DP	.04	.02	.00
☐ 106	Frank Duffy	.09	.04	.01
☐ 107	Jesus Alou DP	.04	.02	.00
☐ 108	Eduardo Rodriguez	.09	.04	.01
☐ 109	Joel Youngblood	.09	.04	.01
☐ 110	Vida Blue	.20	.10	.02
☐ 111	Roger Freed	.09	.04	.01
☐ 112	Phillies Team/Mgr. Danny Ozark (checklist back)	.40	.10	.02
☐ 113	Pete Redfern	.09	.04	.01
☐ 114	Cliff Johnson	.09	.04	.01

☐ 115	Nolan Ryan	2.00	1.00	.20
☐ 116	Ozzie Smith	10.00	5.00	1.00
☐ 117	Grant Jackson	.09	.04	.01
☐ 118	Bud Harrelson	.15	.07	.01
☐ 119	Don Stanhouse	.09	.04	.01
☐ 120	Jim Sundberg	.15	.07	.01
☐ 121	Checklist 1 DP	.15	.03	.00
☐ 122	Mike Paxton	.09	.04	.01
☐ 123	Lou Whitaker	2.00	1.00	.20
☐ 124	Dan Schatzeder	.09	.04	.01
☐ 125	Rick Burleson	.15	.07	.01
☐ 126	Doug Bair	.09	.04	.01
☐ 127	Thad Bosley	.09	.04	.01
☐ 128	Ted Martinez	.09	.04	.01
☐ 129	Marty Pattin DP	.04	.02	.00
☐ 130	Bob Watson DP	.09	.04	.01
☐ 131	Jim Clancy	.15	.07	.01
☐ 132	Rowland Office	.09	.04	.01
☐ 133	Bill Castro	.09	.04	.01
☐ 134	Alan Bannister	.09	.04	.01
☐ 135	Bobby Murcer	.20	.10	.02
☐ 136	Jim Kaat	.40	.20	.04
☐ 137	Larry Wolfe DP	.04	.02	.00
☐ 138	Mark Lee	.09	.04	.01
☐ 139	Luis Pujols	.09	.04	.01
☐ 140	Don Gullett	.09	.04	.01
☐ 141	Tom Paciorek	.09	.04	.01
☐ 142	Charlie Williams	.09	.04	.01
☐ 143	Tony Scott	.09	.04	.01
☐ 144	Sandy Alomar	.09	.04	.01
☐ 145	Rick Rhoden	.25	.12	.02
☐ 146	Duane Kuiper	.09	.04	.01
☐ 147	Dave Hamilton	.09	.04	.01
☐ 148	Bruce Boisclair	.09	.04	.01
☐ 149	Manny Sarmiento	.09	.04	.01
☐ 150	Wayne Cage	.09	.04	.01
☐ 151	John Hiller	.15	.07	.01
☐ 152	Rick Cerone	.15	.07	.01
☐ 153	Dennis Lamp	.09	.04	.01
☐ 154	Jim Gantner DP	.09	.04	.01
☐ 155	Dwight Evans	.65	.30	.06
☐ 156	Buddy Solomon	.09	.04	.01
☐ 157	U.L. Washington	.15	.07	.01
☐ 158	Joe Sambito	.15	.07	.01
☐ 159	Roy White	.15	.07	.01
☐ 160	Mike Flanagan	.20	.10	.02
☐ 161	Barry Foote	.09	.04	.01
☐ 162	Tom Johnson	.09	.04	.01
☐ 163	Glenn Burke	.09	.04	.01
☐ 164	Mickey Lolich	.25	.12	.02
☐ 165	Frank Taveras	.09	.04	.01
☐ 166	Leon Roberts	.09	.04	.01
☐ 167	Roger Metzger DP	.04	.02	.00
☐ 168	Dave Freisleben	.09	.04	.01
☐ 169	Bill Nahorodny	.09	.04	.01
☐ 170	Don Sutton	1.00	.50	.10
☐ 171	Gene Clines	.09	.04	.01
☐ 172	Mike Bruhert	.09	.04	.01
☐ 173	John Lowenstein	.09	.04	.01
☐ 174	Rick Auerbach	.09	.04	.01
☐ 175	George Hendrick	.15	.07	.01
☐ 176	Aurelio Rodriguez	.09	.04	.01
☐ 177	Ron Reed	.09	.04	.01
☐ 178	Alvis Woods	.09	.04	.01
☐ 179	Jim Beattie DP	.09	.04	.01
☐ 180	Larry Hisle	.15	.07	.01
☐ 181	Mike Garman	.09	.04	.01
☐ 182	Tim Johnson	.09	.04	.01
☐ 183	Paul Splittorff	.15	.07	.01
☐ 184	Darrel Chaney	.09	.04	.01
☐ 185	Mike Torrez	.15	.07	.01
☐ 186	Eric Soderholm	.09	.04	.01
☐ 187	Mark Lemongello	.09	.04	.01
☐ 188	Pat Kelly	.09	.04	.01
☐ 189	Eddie Whitson	.45	.22	.04
☐ 190	Ron Cey	.35	.17	.03
☐ 191	Mike Norris	.15	.07	.01
☐ 192	Cardinals Team/Mgr. Ken Boyer (checklist back)	.40	.10	.02
☐ 193	Glenn Adams	.09	.04	.01
☐ 194	Randy Jones	.15	.07	.01
☐ 195	Bill Madlock	.40	.20	.04
☐ 196	Steve Kemp DP	.09	.04	.01
☐ 197	Bob Apodaca	.09	.04	.01
☐ 198	Johnny Grubb	.09	.04	.01
☐ 199	Larry Milbourne	.09	.04	.01
☐ 200	Johnny Bench DP	1.00	.50	.10
☐ 201	RB: Mike Edwards Most unassisted DP's, second basemen	.15	.07	.01
☐ 202	RB: Ron Guidry, Most Strikeouts, lefthander, nine inning game	.35	.17	.03
☐ 203	RB: J.R. Richard	.20	.10	.02

	Most strikeouts, season, righthander			
☐ 204	RB: Pete Rose Most consecutive games batting safely	1.50	.75	.15
☐ 205	RB: John Stearns Most SB's by catcher, season	.15	.07	.01
☐ 206	RB: Sammy Stewart 7 straight SO's, first ML game	.15	.07	.01
☐ 207	Dave Lemanczyk	.09	.04	.01
☐ 208	Clarence Gaston	.09	.04	.01
☐ 209	Reggie Cleveland	.09	.04	.01
☐ 210	Larry Bowa	.25	.12	.02
☐ 211	Denny Martinez	.15	.07	.01
☐ 212	Carney Lansford	1.50	.75	.15
☐ 213	Bill Travers	.09	.04	.01
☐ 214	Red Sox Team/Mgr. Don Zimmer (checklist back)	.40	.10	.02
☐ 215	Willie McCovey	1.50	.75	.15
☐ 216	Wilbur Wood	.15	.07	.01
☐ 217	Steve Dillard	.09	.04	.01
☐ 218	Dennis Leonard	.15	.07	.01
☐ 219	Roy Smalley	.15	.07	.01
☐ 220	Cesar Geronimo	.09	.04	.01
☐ 221	Jesse Jefferson	.09	.04	.01
☐ 222	Bob Beall	.09	.04	.01
☐ 223	Kent Tekulve	.20	.10	.02
☐ 224	Dave Revering	.09	.04	.01
☐ 225	Rich Gossage	.50	.25	.05
☐ 226	Ron Pruitt	.09	.04	.01
☐ 227	Steve Stone	.15	.07	.01
☐ 228	Vic Davalillo	.09	.04	.01
☐ 229	Doug Flynn	.09	.04	.01
☐ 230	Bob Forsch	.15	.07	.01
☐ 231	Johnny Wockenfuss	.09	.04	.01
☐ 232	Jimmy Sexton	.09	.04	.01
☐ 233	Paul Mitchell	.09	.04	.01
☐ 234	Toby Harrah	.15	.07	.01
☐ 235	Steve Rogers	.15	.07	.01
☐ 236	Jim Dwyer	.09	.04	.01
☐ 237	Billy Smith	.09	.04	.01
☐ 238	Balor Moore	.09	.04	.01
☐ 239	Willie Horton	.15	.07	.01
☐ 240	Rick Reuschel	.20	.10	.02
☐ 241	Checklist 2 DP	.15	.03	.00
☐ 242	Pablo Torrealba	.09	.04	.01
☐ 243	Buck Martinez DP	.04	.02	.00
☐ 244	Pirates Team/Mgr. Chuck Tanner (checklist back)	.40	.10	.02
☐ 245	Jeff Burroughs	.15	.07	.01
☐ 246	Darrell Jackson	.09	.04	.01
☐ 247	Tucker Ashford DP	.04	.02	.00
☐ 248	Pete LaCock	.09	.04	.01
☐ 249	Paul Thormodsgard	.09	.04	.01
☐ 250	Willie Randolph	.25	.12	.02
☐ 251	Jack Morris	2.25	1.10	.22
☐ 252	Bob Stinson	.09	.04	.01
☐ 253	Rick Wise	.15	.07	.01
☐ 254	Luis Gomez	.09	.04	.01
☐ 255	Tommy John	.45	.22	.04
☐ 256	Mike Sadek	.09	.04	.01
☐ 257	Adrian Devine	.09	.04	.01
☐ 258	Mike Phillips	.09	.04	.01
☐ 259	Reds Team/Mgr. Sparky Anderson (checklist back)	.40	.10	.02
☐ 260	Richie Zisk	.15	.07	.01
☐ 261	Mario Guerrero	.09	.04	.01
☐ 262	Nelson Briles	.15	.07	.01
☐ 263	Oscar Gamble	.15	.07	.01
☐ 264	Don Robinson	.75	.35	.07
☐ 265	Don Money	.15	.07	.01
☐ 266	Jim Willoughby	.09	.04	.01
☐ 267	Joe Rudi	.15	.07	.01
☐ 268	Julio Gonzalez	.09	.04	.01
☐ 269	Woodie Fryman	.09	.04	.01
☐ 270	Butch Hobson	.09	.04	.01
☐ 271	Rawly Eastwick	.09	.04	.01
☐ 272	Tim Corcoran	.09	.04	.01
☐ 273	Jerry Terrell	.09	.04	.01
☐ 274	Willie Norwood	.09	.04	.01
☐ 275	Junior Moore	.09	.04	.01
☐ 276	Jim Colborn	.09	.04	.01
☐ 277	Tom Grieve	.15	.07	.01
☐ 278	Andy Messersmith	.15	.07	.01
☐ 279	Jerry Grote DP	.04	.02	.00
☐ 280	Andre Thornton	.20	.10	.02
☐ 281	Vic Correll DP	.04	.02	.00
☐ 282	Blue Jays Team/Mgr. Roy Hartsfield (checklist back)	.30	.06	.01

☐ 283	Ken Kravec	.09	.04	.01
☐ 284	Johnnie LeMaster	.09	.04	.01
☐ 285	Bobby Bonds	.25	.12	.02
☐ 286	Duffy Dyer	.09	.04	.01
☐ 287	Andres Mora	.09	.04	.01
☐ 288	Milt Wilcox	.09	.04	.01
☐ 289	Jose Cruz	.30	.15	.03
☐ 290	Dave Lopes	.25	.12	.02
☐ 291	Tom Griffin	.09	.04	.01
☐ 292	Don Reynolds	.09	.04	.01
☐ 293	Jerry Garvin	.09	.04	.01
☐ 294	Pepe Frias	.09	.04	.01
☐ 295	Mitchell Page	.09	.04	.01
☐ 296	Preston Hanna	.09	.04	.01
☐ 297	Ted Sizemore	.09	.04	.01
☐ 298	Rich Gale	.09	.04	.01
☐ 299	Steve Ontiveros	.09	.04	.01
☐ 300	Rod Carew	1.75	.85	.17
☐ 301	Tom Hume	.09	.04	.01
☐ 302	Braves Team/Mgr.	.40	.10	.02
	Bobby Cox			
	(checklist back)			
☐ 303	Lary Sorensen	.09	.04	.01
☐ 304	Steve Swisher	.09	.04	.01
☐ 305	Willie Montanez	.09	.04	.01
☐ 306	Floyd Bannister	.20	.10	.02
☐ 307	Larvell Blanks	.09	.04	.01
☐ 308	Bert Blyleven	.40	.20	.04
☐ 309	Ralph Garr	.15	.07	.01
☐ 310	Thurman Munson	1.75	.85	.17
☐ 311	Gary Lavelle	.09	.04	.01
☐ 312	Bob Robertson	.09	.04	.01
☐ 313	Dyar Miller	.09	.04	.01
☐ 314	Larry Harlow	.09	.04	.01
☐ 315	Jon Matlack	.15	.07	.01
☐ 316	Milt May	.09	.04	.01
☐ 317	Jose Cardenal	.09	.04	.01
☐ 318	Bob Welch	1.50	.75	.15
☐ 319	Wayne Garrett	.09	.04	.01
☐ 320	Carl Yastrzemski	2.50	1.25	.25
☐ 321	Gaylord Perry	1.25	.60	.12
☐ 322	Danny Goodwin	.09	.04	.01
☐ 323	Lynn McGlothen	.09	.04	.01
☐ 324	Mike Tyson	.09	.04	.01
☐ 325	Cecil Cooper	.45	.22	.04
☐ 326	Pedro Borbon	.09	.04	.01
☐ 327	Art Howe	.09	.04	.01
☐ 328	Oakland A's Team/Mgr.	.35	.10	.02
	Jack McKeon			
	(checklist back)			
☐ 329	Joe Coleman	.09	.04	.01
☐ 330	George Brett	3.00	1.50	.30
☐ 331	Mickey Mahler	.09	.04	.01
☐ 332	Gary Alexander	.09	.04	.01
☐ 333	Chet Lemon	.20	.10	.02
☐ 334	Craig Swan	.15	.07	.01
☐ 335	Chris Chambliss	.15	.07	.01
☐ 336	Bobby Thompson	.09	.04	.01
☐ 337	John Montague	.09	.04	.01
☐ 338	Vic Harris	.09	.04	.01
☐ 339	Ron Jackson	.09	.04	.01
☐ 340	Jim Palmer	1.50	.75	.15
☐ 341	Willie Upshaw	1.00	.50	.10
☐ 342	Dave Roberts	.09	.04	.01
☐ 343	Ed Glynn	.09	.04	.01
☐ 344	Jerry Royster	.09	.04	.01
☐ 345	Tug McGraw	.25	.12	.02
☐ 346	Bill Buckner	.25	.12	.02
☐ 347	Doug Rau	.09	.04	.01
☐ 348	Andre Dawson	3.50	1.75	.35
☐ 349	Jim Wright	.09	.04	.01
☐ 350	Garry Templeton	.25	.12	.02
☐ 351	Wayne Nordhagen	.09	.04	.01
☐ 352	Steve Renko	.09	.04	.01
☐ 353	Checklist 3	.40	.05	.01
☐ 354	Bill Bonham	.09	.04	.01
☐ 355	Lee Mazzilli	.15	.07	.01
☐ 356	Giants Team/Mgr.	.40	.10	.02
	Joe Altobelli			
	(checklist back)			
☐ 357	Jerry Augustine	.09	.04	.01
☐ 358	Alan Trammell	4.50	2.25	.45
☐ 359	Dan Spillner DP	.04	.02	.00
☐ 360	Amos Otis	.20	.10	.02
☐ 361	Tom Dixon	.09	.04	.01
☐ 362	Mike Cubbage	.09	.04	.01
☐ 363	Craig Skok	.09	.04	.01
☐ 364	Gene Richards	.09	.04	.01
☐ 365	Sparky Lyle	.25	.12	.02
☐ 366	Juan Bernhardt	.09	.04	.01
☐ 367	Dave Skaggs	.09	.04	.01
☐ 368	Don Aase	.15	.07	.01
☐ 369A	Bump Wills ERR	3.00	1.50	.30
	(Blue Jays)			
☐ 369B	Bump Wills COR	4.00	2.00	.40

	(Rangers)			
☐ 370	Dave Kingman	.40	.20	.04
☐ 371	Jeff Holly	.09	.04	.01
☐ 372	Lamar Johnson	.09	.04	.01
☐ 373	Lance Rautzhan	.09	.04	.01
☐ 374	Ed Herrmann	.09	.04	.01
☐ 375	Bill Campbell	.09	.04	.01
☐ 376	Gorman Thomas	.25	.12	.02
☐ 377	Paul Moskau	.09	.04	.01
☐ 378	Rob Picciolo DP	.04	.02	.00
☐ 379	Dale Murray	.09	.04	.01
☐ 380	John Mayberry	.15	.07	.01
☐ 381	Astros Team/Mgr.	.40	.10	.02
	Bill Virdon			
	(checklist back)			
☐ 382	Jerry Martin	.09	.04	.01
☐ 383	Phil Garner	.15	.07	.01
☐ 384	Tommy Boggs	.09	.04	.01
☐ 385	Dan Ford	.09	.04	.01
☐ 386	Francisco Barrios	.09	.04	.01
☐ 387	Gary Thomasson	.09	.04	.01
☐ 388	Jack Billingham	.09	.04	.01
☐ 389	Joe Zdeb	.09	.04	.01
☐ 390	Rollie Fingers	.45	.22	.04
☐ 391	Al Oliver	.30	.15	.03
☐ 392	Doug Ault	.09	.04	.01
☐ 393	Scott McGregor	.15	.07	.01
☐ 394	Randy Stein	.09	.04	.01
☐ 395	Dave Cash	.09	.04	.01
☐ 396	Bill Plummer	.09	.04	.01
☐ 397	Sergio Ferrer	.09	.04	.01
☐ 398	Ivan DeJesus	.09	.04	.01
☐ 399	David Clyde	.09	.04	.01
☐ 400	Jim Rice	2.50	1.25	.25
☐ 401	Ray Knight	.30	.15	.03
☐ 402	Paul Hartzell	.09	.04	.01
☐ 403	Tim Foli	.09	.04	.01
☐ 404	White Sox Team/Mgr	.40	.10	.02
	Don Kessinger			
	(checklist back)			
☐ 405	Butch Wynegar DP	.04	.02	.00
☐ 406	Joe Wallis DP	.04	.02	.00
☐ 407	Pete Vuckovich	.15	.07	.01
☐ 408	Charlie Moore DP	.04	.02	.00
☐ 409	Willie Wilson	1.75	.85	.17
☐ 410	Darrell Evans	.40	.20	.04
☐ 411	Hits Record	.40	.20	.04
	Season: G.Sisler			
	Career: Ty Cobb			
☐ 412	RBI Record	.40	.20	.04
	Season: Hack Wilson			
	Career: Hank Aaron			
☐ 413	Home Run Record	.40	.20	.04
	Season: Roger Maris			
	Career: Hank Aaron			
☐ 414	Batting Record	.40	.20	.04
	Season: R.Hornsby			
	Career: Ty Cobb			
☐ 415	Steals Record	.40	.20	.04
	Season: Lou Brock			
	Career: Lou Brock			
☐ 416	Wins Record	.20	.10	.02
	Season: Jack Chesbro			
	Career: Cy Young			
☐ 417	Strikeout Record DP	.15	.07	.01
	Season: Nolan Ryan			
	Career: W.Johnson			
☐ 418	ERA Record DP	.09	.04	.01
	Season: Dutch Leonard			
	Career: W.Johnson			
☐ 419	Dick Ruthven	.09	.04	.01
☐ 420	Ken Griffey	.15	.07	.01
☐ 421	Doug DeCinces	.20	.10	.02
☐ 422	Ruppert Jones	.15	.07	.01
☐ 423	Bob Montgomery	.09	.04	.01
☐ 424	Angels Team/Mgr.	.40	.10	.02
	Jim Fregosi			
	(checklist back)			
☐ 425	Rick Manning	.09	.04	.01
☐ 426	Chris Speier	.09	.04	.01
☐ 427	Andy Replogle	.09	.04	.01
☐ 428	Bobby Valentine	.20	.10	.02
☐ 429	John Urrea DP	.04	.02	.00
☐ 430	Dave Parker	1.25	.60	.12
☐ 431	Glenn Borgmann	.09	.04	.01
☐ 432	Dave Heaverlo	.09	.04	.01
☐ 433	Larry Biittner	.09	.04	.01
☐ 434	Ken Clay	.09	.04	.01
☐ 435	Gene Tenace	.09	.04	.01
☐ 436	Hector Cruz	.09	.04	.01
☐ 437	Rick Williams	.09	.04	.01
☐ 438	Horace Speed	.09	.04	.01
☐ 439	Frank White	.20	.10	.02
☐ 440	Rusty Staub	.25	.12	.02
☐ 441	Lee Lacy	.15	.07	.01

☐ 442	Doyle Alexander	.15	.07	.01
☐ 443	Bruce Bochte	.09	.04	.01
☐ 444	Aurelio Lopez	.25	.12	.02
☐ 445	Steve Henderson	.09	.04	.01
☐ 446	Jim Lonborg	.15	.07	.01
☐ 447	Manny Sanguillen	.15	.07	.01
☐ 448	Moose Haas	.15	.07	.01
☐ 449	Bombo Rivera	.09	.04	.01
☐ 450	Dave Concepcion	.20	.10	.02
☐ 451	Royals Team/Mgr. Whitey Herzog (checklist back)	.40	.10	.02
☐ 452	Jerry Morales	.09	.04	.01
☐ 453	Chris Knapp	.09	.04	.01
☐ 454	Len Randle	.09	.04	.01
☐ 455	Bill Lee DP	.09	.04	.01
☐ 456	Chuck Baker	.09	.04	.01
☐ 457	Bruce Sutter	.65	.30	.06
☐ 458	Jim Essian	.09	.04	.01
☐ 459	Sid Monge	.09	.04	.01
☐ 460	Graig Nettles	.35	.17	.03
☐ 461	Jim Barr DP	.04	.02	.00
☐ 462	Otto Velez	.09	.04	.01
☐ 463	Steve Comer	.09	.04	.01
☐ 464	Joe Nolan	.09	.04	.01
☐ 465	Reggie Smith	.20	.10	.02
☐ 466	Mark Littell	.09	.04	.01
☐ 467	Don Kessinger DP	.09	.04	.01
☐ 468	Stan Bahnsen DP	.04	.02	.00
☐ 469	Lance Parrish	3.50	1.75	.35
☐ 470	Garry Maddox DP	.09	.04	.01
☐ 471	Joaquin Andujar	.25	.12	.02
☐ 472	Craig Kusick	.09	.04	.01
☐ 473	Dave Roberts	.09	.04	.01
☐ 474	Dick Davis	.09	.04	.01
☐ 475	Dan Driessen	.15	.07	.01
☐ 476	Tom Poquette	.09	.04	.01
☐ 477	Bob Grich	.20	.10	.02
☐ 478	Juan Beniquez	.15	.07	.01
☐ 479	Padres Team/Mgr. Roger Craig (checklist back)	.40	.10	.02
☐ 480	Fred Lynn	.70	.35	.07
☐ 481	Skip Lockwood	.09	.04	.01
☐ 482	Craig Reynolds	.09	.04	.01
☐ 483	Checklist 4 DP	.15	.03	.00
☐ 484	Rick Waits	.09	.04	.01
☐ 485	Bucky Dent	.20	.10	.02
☐ 486	Bob Knepper	.30	.15	.03
☐ 487	Miguel Dilone	.09	.04	.01
☐ 488	Bob Owchinko	.09	.04	.01
☐ 489	Larry Cox (photo actually Dave Rader)	.09	.04	.01
☐ 490	Al Cowens	.15	.07	.01
☐ 491	Tippy Martinez	.15	.07	.01
☐ 492	Bob Bailor	.09	.04	.01
☐ 493	Larry Christenson	.09	.04	.01
☐ 494	Jerry White	.09	.04	.01
☐ 495	Tony Perez	.40	.20	.04
☐ 496	Barry Bonnell DP	.04	.02	.00
☐ 497	Glenn Abbott	.09	.04	.01
☐ 498	Rich Chiles	.09	.04	.01
☐ 499	Rangers Team/Mgr. Pat Corrales (checklist back)	.40	.10	.02
☐ 500	Ron Guidry	1.00	.50	.10
☐ 501	Junior Kennedy	.09	.04	.01
☐ 502	Steve Braun	.09	.04	.01
☐ 503	Terry Humphrey	.09	.04	.01
☐ 504	Larry McWilliams	.25	.12	.02
☐ 505	Ed Kranepool	.15	.07	.01
☐ 506	John D'Acquisto	.09	.04	.01
☐ 507	Tony Armas	.25	.12	.02
☐ 508	Charlie Hough	.25	.12	.02
☐ 509	Mario Mendoza	.09	.04	.01
☐ 510	Ted Simmons	.35	.17	.03
☐ 511	Paul Reuschel DP	.04	.02	.00
☐ 512	Jack Clark	2.00	1.00	.20
☐ 513	Dave Johnson	.20	.10	.02
☐ 514	Mike Proly	.09	.04	.01
☐ 515	Enos Cabell	.09	.04	.01
☐ 516	Champ Summers DP	.04	.02	.00
☐ 517	Al Bumbry	.09	.04	.01
☐ 518	Jim Umbarger	.09	.04	.01
☐ 519	Ben Oglivie	.15	.07	.01
☐ 520	Gary Carter	2.50	1.25	.25
☐ 521	Sam Ewing	.09	.04	.01
☐ 522	Ken Holtzman	.15	.07	.01
☐ 523	John Milner	.09	.04	.01
☐ 524	Tom Burgmeier	.09	.04	.01
☐ 525	Freddie Patek	.09	.04	.01
☐ 526	Dodgers Team/Mgr. Tom Lasorda (checklist back)	.45	.15	.03
☐ 527	Lerrin LaGrow	.09	.04	.01
☐ 528	Wayne Gross DP	.04	.02	.00
☐ 529	Brian Asselstine	.09	.04	.01
☐ 530	Frank Tanana	.15	.07	.01
☐ 531	Fernando Gonzalez	.09	.04	.01
☐ 532	Buddy Schultz	.09	.04	.01
☐ 533	Leroy Stanton	.09	.04	.01
☐ 534	Ken Forsch	.09	.04	.01
☐ 535	Ellis Valentine	.09	.04	.01
☐ 536	Jerry Reuss	.15	.07	.01
☐ 537	Tom Veryzer	.09	.04	.01
☐ 538	Mike Ivie DP	.04	.02	.00
☐ 539	John Ellis	.09	.04	.01
☐ 540	Greg Luzinski	.25	.12	.02
☐ 541	Jim Slaton	.09	.04	.01
☐ 542	Rick Bosetti	.09	.04	.01
☐ 543	Kiko Garcia	.09	.04	.01
☐ 544	Fergie Jenkins	.35	.17	.03
☐ 545	John Stearns	.09	.04	.01
☐ 546	Bill Russell	.15	.07	.01
☐ 547	Clint Hurdle	.09	.04	.01
☐ 548	Enrique Romo	.09	.04	.01
☐ 549	Bob Bailey	.09	.04	.01
☐ 550	Sal Bando	.15	.07	.01
☐ 551	Cubs Team/Mgr. Herman Franks (checklist back)	.40	.10	.02
☐ 552	Jose Morales	.09	.04	.01
☐ 553	Denny Walling	.09	.04	.01
☐ 554	Matt Keough	.09	.04	.01
☐ 555	Biff Pocoroba	.09	.04	.01
☐ 556	Mike Lum	.09	.04	.01
☐ 557	Ken Brett	.09	.04	.01
☐ 558	Jay Johnstone	.15	.07	.01
☐ 559	Greg Pryor	.09	.04	.01
☐ 560	John Montefusco	.15	.07	.01
☐ 561	Ed Ott	.09	.04	.01
☐ 562	Dusty Baker	.20	.10	.02
☐ 563	Roy Thomas	.09	.04	.01
☐ 564	Jerry Turner	.09	.04	.01
☐ 565	Rico Carty	.15	.07	.01
☐ 566	Nino Espinosa	.09	.04	.01
☐ 567	Rich Hebner	.09	.04	.01
☐ 568	Carlos Lopez	.09	.04	.01
☐ 569	Bob Sykes	.09	.04	.01
☐ 570	Cesar Cedeno	.20	.10	.02
☐ 571	Darrell Porter	.09	.04	.01
☐ 572	Rod Gilbreath	.09	.04	.01
☐ 573	Jim Kern	.09	.04	.01
☐ 574	Claudell Washington	.20	.10	.02
☐ 575	Luis Tiant	.25	.12	.02
☐ 576	Mike Parrott	.09	.04	.01
☐ 577	Brewers Team/Mgr. George Bamberger (checklist back)	.40	.10	.02
☐ 578	Pete Broberg	.09	.04	.01
☐ 579	Greg Gross	.09	.04	.01
☐ 580	Ron Fairly	.09	.04	.01
☐ 581	Darold Knowles	.09	.04	.01
☐ 582	Paul Blair	.09	.04	.01
☐ 583	Julio Cruz	.09	.04	.01
☐ 584	Jim Rooker	.09	.04	.01
☐ 585	Hal McRae	.15	.07	.01
☐ 586	Bob Horner	3.00	1.50	.30
☐ 587	Ken Reitz	.09	.04	.01
☐ 588	Tom Murphy	.09	.04	.01
☐ 589	Terry Whitfield	.09	.04	.01
☐ 590	J.R. Richard	.20	.10	.02
☐ 591	Mike Hargrove	.15	.07	.01
☐ 592	Mike Krukow	.20	.10	.02
☐ 593	Rick Dempsey	.15	.07	.01
☐ 594	Bob Shirley	.09	.04	.01
☐ 595	Phil Niekro	1.00	.50	.10
☐ 596	Jim Wohlford	.09	.04	.01
☐ 597	Bob Stanley	.15	.07	.01
☐ 598	Mark Wagner	.09	.04	.01
☐ 599	Jim Spencer	.09	.04	.01
☐ 600	George Foster	.60	.30	.06
☐ 601	Dave LaRoche	.09	.04	.01
☐ 602	Checklist 5	.40	.05	.01
☐ 603	Rudy May	.09	.04	.01
☐ 604	Jeff Newman	.09	.04	.01
☐ 605	Rick Monday DP	.09	.04	.01
☐ 606	Expos Team/Mgr. Dick Williams (checklist back)	.40	.10	.02
☐ 607	Omar Moreno	.15	.07	.01
☐ 608	Dave McKay	.09	.04	.01
☐ 609	Silvio Martinez	.09	.04	.01
☐ 610	Mike Schmidt	4.00	2.00	.40
☐ 611	Jim Norris	.09	.04	.01
☐ 612	Rick Honeycutt	.60	.30	.06
☐ 613	Mike Edwards	.09	.04	.01
☐ 614	Willie Hernandez	.45	.22	.04
☐ 615	Ken Singleton	.20	.10	.02

☐ 616	Billy Almon	.09	.04	.01
☐ 617	Terry Puhl	.09	.04	.01
☐ 618	Jerry Remy	.09	.04	.01
☐ 619	Ken Landreaux	.30	.15	.03
☐ 620	Bert Campaneris	.15	.07	.01
☐ 621	Pat Zachry	.09	.04	.01
☐ 622	Dave Collins	.15	.07	.01
☐ 623	Bob McClure	.09	.04	.01
☐ 624	Larry Herndon	.15	.07	.01
☐ 625	Mark Fidrych	.20	.10	.02
☐ 626	Yankees Team/Mgr. Bob Lemon (checklist back)	.45	.15	.03
☐ 627	Gary Serum	.09	.04	.01
☐ 628	Del Unser	.09	.04	.01
☐ 629	Gene Garber	.15	.07	.01
☐ 630	Bake McBride	.15	.07	.01
☐ 631	Jorge Orta	.09	.04	.01
☐ 632	Don Kirkwood	.09	.04	.01
☐ 633	Rob Wilfong DP	.04	.02	.00
☐ 634	Paul Lindblad	.09	.04	.01
☐ 635	Don Baylor	.80	.40	.08
☐ 636	Wayne Garland	.09	.04	.01
☐ 637	Bill Robinson	.09	.04	.01
☐ 638	Al Fitzmorris	.09	.04	.01
☐ 639	Manny Trillo	.09	.04	.01
☐ 640	Eddie Murray	5.00	2.50	.50
☐ 641	Bobby Castillo	.09	.04	.01
☐ 642	Wilbur Howard DP	.04	.02	.00
☐ 643	Tom Hausman	.09	.04	.01
☐ 644	Manny Mota	.15	.07	.01
☐ 645	George Scott DP	.09	.04	.01
☐ 646	Rick Sweet	.09	.04	.01
☐ 647	Bob Lacey	.09	.04	.01
☐ 648	Lou Piniella	.20	.10	.02
☐ 649	Jim Curtis	.09	.04	.01
☐ 650	Pete Rose	4.50	2.25	.45
☐ 651	Mike Caldwell	.09	.04	.01
☐ 652	Stan Papi	.09	.04	.01
☐ 653	Warren Brusstar DP	.04	.02	.00
☐ 654	Rick Miller	.09	.04	.01
☐ 655	Jerry Koosman	.25	.12	.02
☐ 656	Hosken Powell	.09	.04	.01
☐ 657	George Medich	.09	.04	.01
☐ 658	Taylor Duncan	.09	.04	.01
☐ 659	Mariners Team/Mgr. Darrell Johnson (checklist back)	.35	.10	.02
☐ 660	Ron LeFlore DP	.09	.04	.01
☐ 661	Bruce Kison	.09	.04	.01
☐ 662	Kevin Bell	.09	.04	.01
☐ 663	Mike Vail	.09	.04	.01
☐ 664	Doug Bird	.09	.04	.01
☐ 665	Lou Brock	1.50	.75	.15
☐ 666	Rich Dauer	.09	.04	.01
☐ 667	Don Hood	.09	.04	.01
☐ 668	Bill North	.09	.04	.01
☐ 669	Checklist 6	.40	.05	.01
☐ 670	Jim Hunter DP	.30	.15	.03
☐ 671	Joe Ferguson DP	.04	.02	.00
☐ 672	Ed Halicki	.09	.04	.01
☐ 673	Tom Hutton	.09	.04	.01
☐ 674	Dave Tomlin	.09	.04	.01
☐ 675	Tim McCarver	.20	.10	.02
☐ 676	Johnny Sutton	.09	.04	.01
☐ 677	Larry Parrish	.20	.10	.02
☐ 678	Geoff Zahn	.09	.04	.01
☐ 679	Derrel Thomas	.09	.04	.01
☐ 680	Carlton Fisk	.60	.30	.06
☐ 681	John Henry Johnson	.09	.04	.01
☐ 682	Dave Chalk	.09	.04	.01
☐ 683	Dan Meyer DP	.04	.02	.00
☐ 684	Jamie Easterly DP	.04	.02	.00
☐ 685	Sixto Lezcano	.09	.04	.01
☐ 686	Ron Schueler DP	.04	.02	.00
☐ 687	Rennie Stennett	.09	.04	.01
☐ 688	Mike Willis	.09	.04	.01
☐ 689	Orioles Team/Mgr. Earl Weaver (checklist back)	.45	.15	.03
☐ 690	Buddy Bell DP	.09	.04	.01
☐ 691	Dock Ellis DP	.04	.02	.00
☐ 692	Mickey Stanley	.09	.04	.01
☐ 693	Dave Rader	.09	.04	.01
☐ 694	Burt Hooton	.09	.04	.01
☐ 695	Keith Hernandez	2.00	1.00	.20
☐ 696	Andy Hassler	.09	.04	.01
☐ 697	Dave Bergman	.09	.04	.01
☐ 698	Bill Stein	.09	.04	.01
☐ 699	Hal Dues	.09	.04	.01
☐ 700	Reggie Jackson DP	1.25	.60	.12
☐ 701	Orioles Prospects Mark Corey John Flinn Sammy Stewart	.25	.12	.02

☐ 702	Red Sox Prospects Joel Finch Garry Hancock Allen Ripley	.15	.07	.01
☐ 703	Angels Prospects Jim Anderson Dave Frost Bob Slater	.15	.07	.01
☐ 704	White Sox Prospects Ross Baumgarten Mike Colbern Mike Squires	.15	.07	.01
☐ 705	Indians Prospects Alfredo Griffin Tim Norrid Dave Oliver	.75	.35	.07
☐ 706	Tigers Prospects Dave Stegman Dave Tobik Kip Young	.15	.07	.01
☐ 707	Royals Prospects Randy Bass Jim Gaudet Randy McGilberry	.15	.07	.01
☐ 708	Brewers Prospects Kevin Bass Eddie Romero Ned Yost	1.75	.85	.17
☐ 709	Twins Prospects Sam Perlozzo Rick Sofield Kevin Stanfield	.15	.07	.01
☐ 710	Yankees Prospects Brian Doyle Mike Heath Dave Rajsich	.30	.15	.03
☐ 711	A's Prospects Dwayne Murphy Bruce Robinson Alan Wirth	.60	.30	.06
☐ 712	Mariners Prospects Bud Anderson Greg Biercevicz Byron McLaughlin	.15	.07	.01
☐ 713	Rangers Prospects Danny Darwin Pat Putnam Billy Sample	.45	.22	.04
☐ 714	Blue Jays Prospects Victor Cruz Pat Kelly Ernie Whitt	.15	.07	.01
☐ 715	Braves Prospects Bruce Benedict Glenn Hubbard Larry Whisenton	.35	.17	.03
☐ 716	Cubs Prospects Dave Geisel Karl Pagel Scot Thompson	.15	.07	.01
☐ 717	Reds Prospects Mike LaCoss Ron Oester Harry Spilman	.40	.20	.04
☐ 718	Astros Prospects Bruce Bochy Mike Fischlin Don Pisker	.15	.07	.01
☐ 719	Dodgers Prospects Pedro Guerrero Rudy Law Joe Simpson	7.00	3.50	.70
☐ 720	Expos Prospects Jerry Fry Jerry Pirtle Scott Sanderson	.35	.17	.03
☐ 721	Mets Prospects Juan Berenguer Dwight Bernard Dan Norman	.35	.17	.03
☐ 722	Phillies Prospects Jim Morrison Lonnie Smith Jim Wright	.50	.25	.05
☐ 723	Pirates Prospects Dale Berra Eugenio Cotes Ben Wiltbank	.35	.17	.03
☐ 724	Cardinals Prospects Tom Bruno George Frazier Terry Kennedy	.75	.35	.07
☐ 725	Padres Prospects Jim Beswick Steve Mura	.15	.07	.01

Broderick Perkins
☐ 726 Giants Prospects .... .25 .06 .01
Greg Johnston
Joe Strain
John Tamargo

1980 Topps

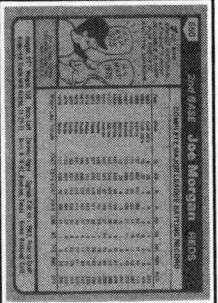

The cards in this 726-card set measure 2 1/2" by 3 1/2". In 1980 Topps released another set of the same size and number of cards as the previous two years. As with those sets, Topps again has produced 66 double printed cards in the set; they are noted by DP in the checklist below. The player's name appears over the picture and his position and team are found in pennant design. Every card carries a facsimile autograph. Team cards feature a team checklist of players in the set on the back and the manager's name on the front. Cards 1-6 show Highlights (HL) of the 1979 season, cards 201-207 are League Leaders, and cards 661-686 feature American and National League rookie "Future Stars," one card for each team showing three young prospects.

	MINT	EXC	G-VG
COMPLETE SET	135.00	65.00	13.50
COMMON PLAYER (1-726)	.08	.04	.01
COMMON DP's (1-726)	.04	.02	.00

☐	1	HL: Brock and Yaz, Enter 3000 hit circle	1.25	.25	.05
☐	2	HL: Willie McCovey, 512th homer sets new mark for NL lefties	.60	.30	.06
☐	3	HL: Manny Mota, All-time pinch-hits, 145	.15	.07	.01
☐	4	HL: Pete Rose, Career Record 10th season with 200 or more hits	2.00	1.00	.20
☐	5	HL: Garry Templeton, First with 100 hits from each side of plate	.15	.07	.01
☐	6	HL: Del Unser, 3rd cons. pinch homer sets new ML standard	.15	.07	.01
☐	7	Mike Lum	.08	.04	.01
☐	8	Craig Swan	.08	.04	.01
☐	9	Steve Braun	.08	.04	.01
☐	10	Denny Martinez	.15	.07	.01
☐	11	Jimmy Sexton	.08	.04	.01
☐	12	John Curtis DP	.04	.02	.00
☐	13	Ron Pruitt	.08	.04	.01
☐	14	Dave Cash	.08	.04	.01
☐	15	Bill Campbell	.08	.04	.01
☐	16	Jerry Narron	.08	.04	.01
☐	17	Bruce Sutter	.40	.20	.04
☐	18	Ron Jackson	.08	.04	.01
☐	19	Balor Moore	.08	.04	.01
☐	20	Dan Ford	.08	.04	.01
☐	21	Manny Sarmiento	.08	.04	.01
☐	22	Pat Putnam	.08	.04	.01
☐	23	Derrel Thomas	.08	.04	.01
☐	24	Jim Slaton	.08	.04	.01
☐	25	Lee Mazzilli	.15	.07	.01
☐	26	Marty Pattin	.08	.04	.01
☐	27	Del Unser	.08	.04	.01
☐	28	Bruce Kison	.08	.04	.01
☐	29	Mark Wagner	.08	.04	.01
☐	30	Vida Blue	.20	.10	.02
☐	31	Jay Johnstone	.15	.07	.01
☐	32	Julio Cruz DP	.08	.04	.01
☐	33	Tony Scott	.08	.04	.01
☐	34	Jeff Newman DP	.04	.02	.00
☐	35	Luis Tiant	.20	.10	.02
☐	36	Rusty Torres	.08	.04	.01
☐	37	Kiko Garcia	.08	.04	.01
☐	38	Dan Spillner DP	.04	.02	.00
☐	39	Rowland Office	.08	.04	.01
☐	40	Carlton Fisk	.40	.20	.04
☐	41	Rangers Team/Mgr. ...... Pat Corrales (checklist back)	.35	.10	.02
☐	42	David Palmer	.50	.25	.05
☐	43	Bombo Rivera	.08	.04	.01
☐	44	Bill Fahey	.08	.04	.01
☐	45	Frank White	.20	.10	.02
☐	46	Rico Carty	.15	.07	.01
☐	47	Bill Bonham DP	.04	.02	.00
☐	48	Rick Miller	.08	.04	.01
☐	49	Mario Guerrero	.08	.04	.01
☐	50	J.R. Richard	.20	.10	.02
☐	51	Joe Ferguson DP	.04	.02	.00
☐	52	Warren Brusstar	.08	.04	.01
☐	53	Ben Oglivie	.15	.07	.01
☐	54	Dennis Lamp	.08	.04	.01
☐	55	Bill Madlock	.40	.20	.04
☐	56	Bobby Valentine	.20	.10	.02
☐	57	Pete Vuckovich	.15	.07	.01
☐	58	Doug Flynn	.08	.04	.01
☐	59	Eddy Putman	.08	.04	.01
☐	60	Bucky Dent	.15	.07	.01
☐	61	Gary Serum	.08	.04	.01
☐	62	Mike Ivie	.08	.04	.01
☐	63	Bob Stanley	.15	.07	.01
☐	64	Joe Nolan	.08	.04	.01
☐	65	Al Bumbry	.08	.04	.01
☐	66	Royals Team/Mgr. .... Jim Frey (checklist back)	.35	.10	.02
☐	67	Doyle Alexander	.15	.07	.01
☐	68	Larry Harlow	.08	.04	.01
☐	69	Rick Williams	.08	.04	.01
☐	70	Gary Carter	2.00	1.00	.20
☐	71	John Milner DP	.04	.02	.00
☐	72	Fred Howard DP	.04	.02	.00
☐	73	Dave Collins	.15	.07	.01
☐	74	Sid Monge	.08	.04	.01
☐	75	Bill Russell	.08	.04	.01
☐	76	John Stearns	.08	.04	.01
☐	77	Dave Stieb	2.00	1.00	.20
☐	78	Ruppert Jones	.08	.04	.01
☐	79	Bob Owchinko	.08	.04	.01
☐	80	Ron LeFlore	.15	.07	.01
☐	81	Ted Sizemore	.08	.04	.01
☐	82	Astros Team/Mgr. .... Bill Virdon (checklist back)	.35	.10	.02
☐	83	Steve Trout	.45	.22	.04
☐	84	Gary Lavelle	.08	.04	.01
☐	85	Ted Simmons	.35	.17	.03
☐	86	Dave Hamilton	.08	.04	.01
☐	87	Pepe Frias	.08	.04	.01
☐	88	Ken Landreaux	.15	.07	.01
☐	89	Don Hood	.08	.04	.01
☐	90	Manny Trillo	.08	.04	.01
☐	91	Rick Dempsey	.15	.07	.01
☐	92	Rick Rhoden	.20	.10	.02
☐	93	Dave Roberts DP	.04	.02	.00
☐	94	Neil Allen	.45	.22	.04
☐	95	Cecil Cooper	.35	.17	.03
☐	96	A's Team/Mgr. .... Jim Marshall (checklist back)	.35	.10	.02
☐	97	Bill Lee	.15	.07	.01
☐	98	Jerry Terrell	.08	.04	.01
☐	99	Victor Cruz	.08	.04	.01
☐	100	Johnny Bench	2.00	1.00	.20
☐	101	Aurelio Lopez	.08	.04	.01
☐	102	Rich Dauer	.08	.04	.01
☐	103	Bill Caudill	.35	.17	.03
☐	104	Manny Mota	.15	.07	.01
☐	105	Frank Tanana	.15	.07	.01
☐	106	Jeff Leonard	2.50	1.25	.25
☐	107	Francisco Barrios	.08	.04	.01
☐	108	Bob Horner	1.00	.50	.10
☐	109	Bill Travers	.08	.04	.01
☐	110	Fred Lynn DP	.30	.15	.03
☐	111	Bob Knepper	.20	.10	.02
☐	112	White Sox Team/Mgr. ... Tony LaRussa	.35	.10	.02

(checklist back)

☐ 113 Geoff Zahn	.08	.04	.01
☐ 114 Juan Beniquez	.15	.07	.01
☐ 115 Sparky Lyle	.20	.10	.02
☐ 116 Larry Cox	.08	.04	.01
☐ 117 Dock Ellis	.08	.04	.01
☐ 118 Phil Garner	.08	.04	.01
☐ 119 Sammy Stewart	.08	.04	.01
☐ 120 Greg Luzinski	.25	.12	.02
☐ 121 Checklist 1	.25	.05	.01
☐ 122 Dave Rosello DP	.04	.02	.00
☐ 123 Lynn Jones	.08	.04	.01
☐ 124 Dave Lemanczyk	.08	.04	.01
☐ 125 Tony Perez	.35	.17	.03
☐ 126 Dave Tomlin	.08	.04	.01
☐ 127 Gary Thomasson	.08	.04	.01
☐ 128 Tom Burgmeier	.08	.04	.01
☐ 129 Craig Reynolds	.08	.04	.01
☐ 130 Amos Otis	.15	.07	.01
☐ 131 Paul Mitchell	.08	.04	.01
☐ 132 Biff Pocoroba	.08	.04	.01
☐ 133 Jerry Turner	.08	.04	.01
☐ 134 Matt Keough	.08	.04	.01
☐ 135 Bill Buckner	.20	.10	.02
☐ 136 Dick Ruthven	.08	.04	.01
☐ 137 John Castino	.15	.07	.01
☐ 138 Ross Baumgarten	.08	.04	.01
☐ 139 Dane Iorg	.15	.07	.01
☐ 140 Rich Gossage	.40	.20	.04
☐ 141 Gary Alexander	.08	.04	.01
☐ 142 Phil Huffman	.08	.04	.01
☐ 143 Bruce Bochte DP	.08	.04	.01
☐ 144 Steve Comer	.08	.04	.01
☐ 145 Darrell Evans	.35	.17	.03
☐ 146 Bob Welch	.35	.17	.03
☐ 147 Terry Puhl	.08	.04	.01
☐ 148 Manny Sanguillen	.15	.07	.01
☐ 149 Tom Hume	.08	.04	.01
☐ 150 Jason Thompson	.15	.07	.01
☐ 151 Tom Hausman DP	.04	.02	.00
☐ 152 John Fulgham	.08	.04	.01
☐ 153 Tim Blackwell	.08	.04	.01
☐ 154 Lary Sorensen	.08	.04	.01
☐ 155 Jerry Remy	.08	.04	.01
☐ 156 Tony Brizzolara	.08	.04	.01
☐ 157 Willie Wilson DP	.20	.10	.02
☐ 158 Rob Picciolo DP	.04	.02	.00
☐ 159 Ken Clay	.08	.04	.01
☐ 160 Eddie Murray	3.00	1.50	.30
☐ 161 Larry Christenson	.08	.04	.01
☐ 162 Bob Randall	.08	.04	.01
☐ 163 Steve Swisher	.08	.04	.01
☐ 164 Greg Pryor	.08	.04	.01
☐ 165 Omar Moreno	.08	.04	.01
☐ 166 Glenn Abbott	.08	.04	.01
☐ 167 Jack Clark	1.50	.75	.15
☐ 168 Rick Waits	.08	.04	.01
☐ 169 Luis Gomez	.08	.04	.01
☐ 170 Burt Hooton	.08	.04	.01
☐ 171 Fernando Gonzalez	.08	.04	.01
☐ 172 Ron Hodges	.08	.04	.01
☐ 173 John Henry Johnson	.08	.04	.01
☐ 174 Ray Knight	.25	.12	.02
☐ 175 Rick Reuschel	.20	.10	.02
☐ 176 Champ Summers	.08	.04	.01
☐ 177 Dave Heaverlo	.08	.04	.01
☐ 178 Tim McCarver	.20	.10	.02
☐ 179 Ron Davis	.25	.12	.02
☐ 180 Warren Cromartie	.08	.04	.01
☐ 181 Moose Haas	.08	.04	.01
☐ 182 Ken Reitz	.08	.04	.01
☐ 183 Jim Anderson DP	.04	.02	.00
☐ 184 Steve Renko DP	.04	.02	.00
☐ 185 Hal McRae	.15	.07	.01
☐ 186 Junior Moore	.08	.04	.01
☐ 187 Alan Ashby	.08	.04	.01
☐ 188 Terry Crowley	.08	.04	.01
☐ 189 Kevin Kobel	.08	.04	.01
☐ 190 Buddy Bell	.25	.12	.02
☐ 191 Ted Martinez	.08	.04	.01
☐ 192 Braves Team/Mgr.	.35	.10	.02
Bobby Cox			
(checklist back)			
☐ 193 Dave Goltz	.08	.04	.01
☐ 194 Mike Easler	.20	.10	.02
☐ 195 John Montefusco	.15	.07	.01
☐ 196 Lance Parrish	1.25	.60	.12
☐ 197 Byron McLaughlin	.08	.04	.01
☐ 198 Dell Alston DP	.04	.02	.00
☐ 199 Mike LaCoss	.15	.07	.01
☐ 200 Jim Rice	2.00	1.00	.20
☐ 201 Batting Leaders	.20	.10	.02
Keith Hernandez			
Fred Lynn			
☐ 202 Home Run Leaders	.15	.07	.01

Dave Kingman			
Gorman Thomas			
☐ 203 RBI Leaders	.20	.10	.02
Dave Winfield			
Don Baylor			
☐ 204 Stolen Base Leaders	.15	.07	.01
Omar Moreno			
Willie Wilson			
☐ 205 Victory Leaders	.20	.10	.02
Joe Niekro			
Phil Niekro			
Mike Flanagan			
☐ 206 Strikeout Leaders	.20	.10	.02
J.R. Richard			
Nolan Ryan			
☐ 207 ERA Leaders	.15	.07	.01
J.R. Richard			
Ron Guidry			
☐ 208 Wayne Cage	.08	.04	.01
☐ 209 Von Joshua	.08	.04	.01
☐ 210 Steve Carlton	2.00	1.00	.20
☐ 211 Dave Skaggs DP	.04	.02	.00
☐ 212 Dave Roberts	.08	.04	.01
☐ 213 Mike Jorgensen DP	.04	.02	.00
☐ 214 Angels Team/Mgr.	.35	.10	.02
Jim Fregosi			
(checklist back)			
☐ 215 Sixto Lezcano	.08	.04	.01
☐ 216 Phil Mankowski	.08	.04	.01
☐ 217 Ed Halicki	.08	.04	.01
☐ 218 Jose Morales	.08	.04	.01
☐ 219 Steve Mingori	.08	.04	.01
☐ 220 Dave Concepcion	.20	.10	.02
☐ 221 Joe Cannon	.08	.04	.01
☐ 222 Ron Hassey	.15	.07	.01
☐ 223 Bob Sykes	.08	.04	.01
☐ 224 Willie Montanez	.08	.04	.01
☐ 225 Lou Piniella	.20	.10	.02
☐ 226 Bill Stein	.08	.04	.01
☐ 227 Len Barker	.08	.04	.01
☐ 228 Johnny Oates	.08	.04	.01
☐ 229 Jim Bibby	.08	.04	.01
☐ 230 Dave Winfield	1.50	.75	.15
☐ 231 Steve McCatty	.08	.04	.01
☐ 232 Alan Trammell	2.00	1.00	.20
☐ 233 LaRue Washington	.08	.04	.01
☐ 234 Vern Ruhle	.08	.04	.01
☐ 235 Andre Dawson	2.25	1.10	.22
☐ 236 Marc Hill	.08	.04	.01
☐ 237 Scott McGregor	.15	.07	.01
☐ 238 Rob Wilfong	.08	.04	.01
☐ 239 Don Aase	.15	.07	.01
☐ 240 Dave Kingman	.35	.17	.03
☐ 241 Checklist 2	.25	.05	.01
☐ 242 Lamar Johnson	.08	.04	.01
☐ 243 Jerry Augustine	.08	.04	.01
☐ 244 Cardinals Team/Mgr.	.35	.10	.02
Ken Boyer			
(checklist back)			
☐ 245 Phil Niekro	.70	.35	.07
☐ 246 Tim Foli DP	.04	.02	.00
☐ 247 Frank Riccelli	.08	.04	.01
☐ 248 Jamie Quirk	.08	.04	.01
☐ 249 Jim Clancy	.15	.07	.01
☐ 250 Jim Kaat	.40	.20	.04
☐ 251 Kip Young	.08	.04	.01
☐ 252 Ted Cox	.08	.04	.01
☐ 253 John Montague	.08	.04	.01
☐ 254 Paul Dade DP	.04	.02	.00
☐ 255 Dusty Baker DP	.08	.04	.01
☐ 256 Roger Erickson	.08	.04	.01
☐ 257 Larry Herndon	.15	.07	.01
☐ 258 Paul Moskau	.08	.04	.01
☐ 259 Mets Team/Mgr.	.40	.10	.02
Joe Torre			
(checklist back)			
☐ 260 Al Oliver	.25	.12	.02
☐ 261 Dave Chalk	.08	.04	.01
☐ 262 Benny Ayala	.08	.04	.01
☐ 263 Dave LaRoche DP	.04	.02	.00
☐ 264 Bill Robinson	.08	.04	.01
☐ 265 Robin Yount	1.50	.75	.15
☐ 266 Bernie Carbo	.08	.04	.01
☐ 267 Dan Schatzeder	.08	.04	.01
☐ 268 Rafael Landestoy	.08	.04	.01
☐ 269 Dave Tobik	.08	.04	.01
☐ 270 Mike Schmidt DP	1.25	.60	.12
☐ 271 Dick Drago DP	.04	.02	.00
☐ 272 Ralph Garr	.15	.07	.01
☐ 273 Eduardo Rodriguez	.08	.04	.01
☐ 274 Dale Murphy	5.50	2.75	.55
☐ 275 Jerry Koosman	.20	.10	.02
☐ 276 Tom Veryzer	.08	.04	.01
☐ 277 Rick Bosetti	.08	.04	.01
☐ 278 Jim Spencer	.08	.04	.01

☐ 279	Rob Andrews	.08	.04	.01
☐ 280	Gaylord Perry	.75	.35	.07
☐ 281	Paul Blair	.15	.07	.01
☐ 282	Mariners Team/Mgr. Darrell Johnson (checklist back)	.30	.10	.02
☐ 283	John Ellis	.08	.04	.01
☐ 284	Larry Murray DP	.04	.02	.00
☐ 285	Don Baylor	.40	.20	.04
☐ 286	Darold Knowles DP	.04	.02	.00
☐ 287	John Lowenstein	.08	.04	.01
☐ 288	Dave Rozema	.08	.04	.01
☐ 289	Bruce Bochy	.08	.04	.01
☐ 290	Steve Garvey	1.75	.85	.17
☐ 291	Randy Scarberry	.08	.04	.01
☐ 292	Dale Berra	.15	.07	.01
☐ 293	Elias Sosa	.08	.04	.01
☐ 294	Charlie Spikes	.08	.04	.01
☐ 295	Larry Gura	.15	.07	.01
☐ 296	Dave Rader	.08	.04	.01
☐ 297	Tim Johnson	.08	.04	.01
☐ 298	Ken Holtzman	.15	.07	.01
☐ 299	Steve Henderson	.08	.04	.01
☐ 300	Ron Guidry	.75	.35	.07
☐ 301	Mike Edwards	.08	.04	.01
☐ 302	Dodgers Team/Mgr. Tom Lasorda (checklist back)	.40	.10	.02
☐ 303	Bill Castro	.08	.04	.01
☐ 304	Butch Wynegar	.08	.04	.01
☐ 305	Randy Jones	.08	.04	.01
☐ 306	Denny Walling	.08	.04	.01
☐ 307	Rick Honeycutt	.15	.07	.01
☐ 308	Mike Hargrove	.08	.04	.01
☐ 309	Larry McWilliams	.08	.04	.01
☐ 310	Dave Parker	1.00	.50	.10
☐ 311	Roger Metzger	.08	.04	.01
☐ 312	Mike Barlow	.08	.04	.01
☐ 313	Johnny Grubb	.08	.04	.01
☐ 314	Tim Stoddard	.20	.10	.02
☐ 315	Steve Kemp	.15	.07	.01
☐ 316	Bob Lacey	.08	.04	.01
☐ 317	Mike Anderson DP	.04	.02	.00
☐ 318	Jerry Reuss	.15	.07	.01
☐ 319	Chris Speier	.08	.04	.01
☐ 320	Dennis Eckersley	.15	.07	.01
☐ 321	Keith Hernandez	1.25	.60	.12
☐ 322	Claudell Washington	.15	.07	.01
☐ 323	Mick Kelleher	.08	.04	.01
☐ 324	Tom Underwood	.15	.07	.01
☐ 325	Dan Driessen	.08	.04	.01
☐ 326	Bo McLaughlin	.08	.04	.01
☐ 327	Ray Fosse DP	.04	.02	.00
☐ 328	Twins Team/Mgr. Gene Mauch (checklist back)	.35	.10	.02
☐ 329	Bert Roberge	.08	.04	.01
☐ 330	Al Cowens	.08	.04	.01
☐ 331	Rich Hebner	.08	.04	.01
☐ 332	Enrique Romo	.08	.04	.01
☐ 333	Jim Norris DP	.04	.02	.00
☐ 334	Jim Beattie	.08	.04	.01
☐ 335	Willie McCovey	1.25	.60	.12
☐ 336	George Medich	.08	.04	.01
☐ 337	Carney Lansford	.35	.17	.03
☐ 338	Johnny Wockenfuss	.08	.04	.01
☐ 339	John D'Acquisto	.08	.04	.01
☐ 340	Ken Singleton	.20	.10	.02
☐ 341	Jim Essian	.08	.04	.01
☐ 342	Odell Jones	.08	.04	.01
☐ 343	Mike Vail	.08	.04	.01
☐ 344	Randy Lerch	.08	.04	.01
☐ 345	Larry Parrish	.15	.07	.01
☐ 346	Buddy Solomon	.08	.04	.01
☐ 347	Harry Chappas	.08	.04	.01
☐ 348	Checklist 3	.25	.05	.01
☐ 349	Jack Brohamer	.08	.04	.01
☐ 350	George Hendrick	.15	.07	.01
☐ 351	Bob Davis	.08	.04	.01
☐ 352	Dan Briggs	.08	.04	.01
☐ 353	Andy Hassler	.08	.04	.01
☐ 354	Rick Auerbach	.08	.04	.01
☐ 355	Gary Matthews	.15	.07	.01
☐ 356	Padres Team/Mgr. Jerry Coleman (checklist back)	.35	.10	.02
☐ 357	Bob McClure	.08	.04	.01
☐ 358	Lou Whitaker	1.00	.50	.10
☐ 359	Randy Moffitt	.08	.04	.01
☐ 360	Darrell Porter DP	.08	.04	.01
☐ 361	Wayne Garland	.08	.04	.01
☐ 362	Danny Goodwin	.08	.04	.01
☐ 363	Wayne Gross	.08	.04	.01
☐ 364	Ray Burris	.08	.04	.01
☐ 365	Bobby Murcer	.20	.10	.02
☐ 366	Rob Dressler	.08	.04	.01
☐ 367	Billy Smith	.08	.04	.01
☐ 368	Willie Aikens	.20	.10	.02
☐ 369	Jim Kern	.08	.04	.01
☐ 370	Cesar Cedeno	.20	.10	.02
☐ 371	Jack Morris	1.25	.60	.12
☐ 372	Joel Youngblood	.08	.04	.01
☐ 373	Dan Petry DP	.75	.35	.07
☐ 374	Jim Gantner	.08	.04	.01
☐ 375	Ross Grimsley	.08	.04	.01
☐ 376	Gary Allenson	.08	.04	.01
☐ 377	Junior Kennedy	.08	.04	.01
☐ 378	Jerry Mumphrey	.08	.04	.01
☐ 379	Kevin Bell	.08	.04	.01
☐ 380	Garry Maddox	.08	.04	.01
☐ 381	Cubs Team/Mgr. Preston Gomez (checklist back)	.35	.10	.02
☐ 382	Dave Freisleben	.08	.04	.01
☐ 383	Ed Ott	.08	.04	.01
☐ 384	Joey McLaughlin	.08	.04	.01
☐ 385	Enos Cabell	.08	.04	.01
☐ 386	Darrell Jackson	.08	.04	.01
☐ 387	Fred Stanley	.08	.04	.01
☐ 388	Mike Paxton	.08	.04	.01
☐ 389	Pete LaCock	.08	.04	.01
☐ 390	Fergie Jenkins	.35	.17	.03
☐ 391	Tony Armas DP	.08	.04	.01
☐ 392	Milt Wilcox	.08	.04	.01
☐ 393	Ozzie Smith	2.00	1.00	.20
☐ 394	Reggie Cleveland	.08	.04	.01
☐ 395	Ellis Valentine	.08	.04	.01
☐ 396	Dan Meyer	.08	.04	.01
☐ 397	Roy Thomas DP	.04	.02	.00
☐ 398	Barry Foote	.08	.04	.01
☐ 399	Mike Proly DP	.04	.02	.00
☐ 400	George Foster	.45	.22	.04
☐ 401	Pete Falcone	.08	.04	.01
☐ 402	Merv Rettenmund	.08	.04	.01
☐ 403	Pete Redfern DP	.04	.02	.00
☐ 404	Orioles Team/Mgr. Earl Weaver (checklist back)	.40	.10	.02
☐ 405	Dwight Evans	.75	.35	.07
☐ 406	Paul Molitor	1.00	.50	.10
☐ 407	Tony Solaita	.08	.04	.01
☐ 408	Bill North	.08	.04	.01
☐ 409	Paul Splittorff	.15	.07	.01
☐ 410	Bobby Bonds	.20	.10	.02
☐ 411	Frank LaCorte	.08	.04	.01
☐ 412	Thad Bosley	.08	.04	.01
☐ 413	Allen Ripley	.08	.04	.01
☐ 414	George Scott	.15	.07	.01
☐ 415	Bill Atkinson	.08	.04	.01
☐ 416	Tom Brookens	.08	.04	.01
☐ 417	Craig Chamberlain DP	.04	.02	.00
☐ 418	Roger Freed DP	.04	.02	.00
☐ 419	Vic Correll	.08	.04	.01
☐ 420	Butch Hobson	.08	.04	.01
☐ 421	Doug Bird	.08	.04	.01
☐ 422	Larry Milbourne	.08	.04	.01
☐ 423	Dave Frost	.08	.04	.01
☐ 424	Yankees Team/Mgr. Dick Howser (checklist back)	.40	.10	.02
☐ 425	Mark Belanger	.15	.07	.01
☐ 426	Grant Jackson	.08	.04	.01
☐ 427	Tom Hutton DP	.04	.02	.00
☐ 428	Pat Zachry	.08	.04	.01
☐ 429	Duane Kuiper	.08	.04	.01
☐ 430	Larry Hisle DP	.08	.04	.01
☐ 431	Mike Krukow	.15	.07	.01
☐ 432	Willie Norwood	.08	.04	.01
☐ 433	Rich Gale	.08	.04	.01
☐ 434	Johnnie LeMaster	.08	.04	.01
☐ 435	Don Gullett	.08	.04	.01
☐ 436	Billy Almon	.08	.04	.01
☐ 437	Joe Niekro	.20	.10	.02
☐ 438	Dave Revering	.08	.04	.01
☐ 439	Mike Phillips	.08	.04	.01
☐ 440	Don Sutton	.70	.35	.07
☐ 441	Eric Soderholm	.08	.04	.01
☐ 442	Jorge Orta	.08	.04	.01
☐ 443	Mike Parrott	.08	.04	.01
☐ 444	Alvis Woods	.08	.04	.01
☐ 445	Mark Fidrych	.15	.07	.01
☐ 446	Duffy Dyer	.08	.04	.01
☐ 447	Nino Espinosa	.08	.04	.01
☐ 448	Jim Wohlford	.08	.04	.01
☐ 449	Doug Bair	.08	.04	.01
☐ 450	George Brett	3.50	1.75	.35
☐ 451	Indians Team/Mgr. Dave Garcia (checklist back)	.35	.10	.02
☐ 452	Steve Dillard	.08	.04	.01

☐ 453	Mike Bacsik	.08	.04	.01
☐ 454	Tom Donohue	.08	.04	.01
☐ 455	Mike Torrez	.15	.07	.01
☐ 456	Frank Taveras	.08	.04	.01
☐ 457	Bert Blyleven	.35	.17	.03
☐ 458	Billy Sample	.08	.04	.01
☐ 459	Mickey Lolich DP	.08	.04	.01
☐ 460	Willie Randolph	.20	.10	.02
☐ 461	Dwayne Murphy	.15	.07	.01
☐ 462	Mike Sadek DP	.04	.02	.00
☐ 463	Jerry Royster	.08	.04	.01
☐ 464	John Denny	.15	.07	.01
☐ 465	Rick Monday	.15	.07	.01
☐ 466	Mike Squires	.08	.04	.01
☐ 467	Jesse Jefferson	.08	.04	.01
☐ 468	Aurelio Rodriguez	.08	.04	.01
☐ 469	Randy Niemann DP	.04	.02	.00
☐ 470	Bob Boone	.15	.07	.01
☐ 471	Hosken Powell DP	.04	.02	.00
☐ 472	Willie Hernandez	.35	.17	.03
☐ 473	Bump Wills	.08	.04	.01
☐ 474	Steve Busby	.15	.07	.01
☐ 475	Cesar Geronimo	.08	.04	.01
☐ 476	Bob Shirley	.08	.04	.01
☐ 477	Buck Martinez	.08	.04	.01
☐ 478	Gil Flores	.08	.04	.01
☐ 479	Expos Team/Mgr.	.30	.10	.02
	Dick Williams			
	(checklist back)			
☐ 480	Bob Watson	.15	.07	.01
☐ 481	Tom Paciorek	.08	.04	.01
☐ 482	Rickey Henderson	28.00	14.00	2.80
☐ 483	Bo Diaz	.15	.07	.01
☐ 484	Checklist 4	.25	.05	.01
☐ 485	Mickey Rivers	.15	.07	.01
☐ 486	Mike Tyson DP	.04	.02	.00
☐ 487	Wayne Nordhagen	.08	.04	.01
☐ 488	Roy Howell	.08	.04	.01
☐ 489	Preston Hanna DP	.04	.02	.00
☐ 490	Lee May	.15	.07	.01
☐ 491	Steve Mura DP	.04	.02	.00
☐ 492	Todd Cruz	.08	.04	.01
☐ 493	Jerry Martin	.08	.04	.01
☐ 494	Craig Minetto	.08	.04	.01
☐ 495	Bake McBride	.08	.04	.01
☐ 496	Silvio Martinez	.08	.04	.01
☐ 497	Jim Mason	.08	.04	.01
☐ 498	Danny Darwin	.15	.07	.01
☐ 499	Giants Team/Mgr.	.35	.10	.02
	Dave Bristol			
☐ 500	Tom Seaver	1.75	.85	.17
☐ 501	Rennie Stennett	.08	.04	.01
☐ 502	Rich Wortham DP	.04	.02	.00
☐ 503	Mike Cubbage	.08	.04	.01
☐ 504	Gene Garber	.15	.07	.01
☐ 505	Bert Campaneris	.15	.07	.01
☐ 506	Tom Buskey	.08	.04	.01
☐ 507	Leon Roberts	.08	.04	.01
☐ 508	U.L. Washington	.08	.04	.01
☐ 509	Ed Glynn	.08	.04	.01
☐ 510	Ron Cey	.35	.17	.03
☐ 511	Eric Wilkins	.08	.04	.01
☐ 512	Jose Cardenal	.08	.04	.01
☐ 513	Tom Dixon DP	.04	.02	.00
☐ 514	Steve Ontiveros	.08	.04	.01
☐ 515	Mike Caldwell	.08	.04	.01
☐ 516	Hector Cruz	.08	.04	.01
☐ 517	Don Stanhouse	.08	.04	.01
☐ 518	Nelson Norman	.08	.04	.01
☐ 519	Steve Nicosia	.08	.04	.01
☐ 520	Steve Rogers	.15	.07	.01
☐ 521	Ken Brett	.08	.04	.01
☐ 522	Jim Morrison	.15	.07	.01
☐ 523	Ken Henderson	.08	.04	.01
☐ 524	Jim Wright DP	.04	.02	.00
☐ 525	Clint Hurdle	.08	.04	.01
☐ 526	Phillies Team/Mgr.	.35	.10	.02
	Dallas Green			
	(checklist back)			
☐ 527	Doug Rau DP	.04	.02	.00
☐ 528	Adrian Devine	.08	.04	.01
☐ 529	Jim Barr	.08	.04	.01
☐ 530	Jim Sundberg DP	.08	.04	.01
☐ 531	Eric Rasmussen	.08	.04	.01
☐ 532	Willie Horton	.15	.07	.01
☐ 533	Checklist 5	.25	.05	.01
☐ 534	Andre Thornton	.20	.10	.02
☐ 535	Bob Forsch	.15	.07	.01
☐ 536	Lee Lacy	.15	.07	.01
☐ 537	Alex Trevino	.15	.07	.01
☐ 538	Joe Strain	.08	.04	.01
☐ 539	Rudy May	.08	.04	.01
☐ 540	Pete Rose	4.00	2.00	.40
☐ 541	Miguel Dilone	.08	.04	.01
☐ 542	Joe Coleman	.08	.04	.01
☐ 543	Pat Kelly	.08	.04	.01
☐ 544	Rick Sutcliffe	4.00	2.00	.40
☐ 545	Jeff Burroughs	.15	.07	.01
☐ 546	Rick Langford	.08	.04	.01
☐ 547	John Wathan	.15	.07	.01
☐ 548	Dave Rajsich	.08	.04	.01
☐ 549	Larry Wolfe	.08	.04	.01
☐ 550	Ken Griffey	.15	.07	.01
☐ 551	Pirates Team/Mgr.	.35	.10	.02
	Chuck Tanner			
	(checklist back)			
☐ 552	Bill Nahorodny	.08	.04	.01
☐ 553	Dick Davis	.08	.04	.01
☐ 554	Art Howe	.08	.04	.01
☐ 555	Ed Figueroa	.08	.04	.01
☐ 556	Joe Rudi	.15	.07	.01
☐ 557	Mark Lee	.08	.04	.01
☐ 558	Alfredo Griffin	.20	.10	.02
☐ 559	Dale Murray	.08	.04	.01
☐ 560	Dave Lopes	.20	.10	.02
☐ 561	Eddie Whitson	.15	.07	.01
☐ 562	Joe Wallis	.08	.04	.01
☐ 563	Will McEnaney	.08	.04	.01
☐ 564	Rick Manning	.08	.04	.01
☐ 565	Dennis Leonard	.15	.07	.01
☐ 566	Bud Harrelson	.08	.04	.01
☐ 567	Skip Lockwood	.08	.04	.01
☐ 568	Gary Roenicke	.30	.15	.03
☐ 569	Terry Kennedy	.25	.12	.02
☐ 570	Roy Smalley	.15	.07	.01
☐ 571	Joe Sambito	.08	.04	.01
☐ 572	Jerry Morales DP	.04	.02	.00
☐ 573	Kent Tekulve	.15	.07	.01
☐ 574	Scot Thompson	.08	.04	.01
☐ 575	Ken Kravec	.08	.04	.01
☐ 576	Jim Dwyer	.08	.04	.01
☐ 577	Blue Jays Team/Mgr.	.30	.10	.02
	Bobby Mattick			
	(checklist back)			
☐ 578	Scott Sanderson	.15	.07	.01
☐ 579	Charlie Moore	.08	.04	.01
☐ 580	Nolan Ryan	1.75	.85	.17
☐ 581	Bob Bailor	.08	.04	.01
☐ 582	Brian Doyle	.08	.04	.01
☐ 583	Bob Stinson	.08	.04	.01
☐ 584	Kurt Bevacqua	.08	.04	.01
☐ 585	Al Hrabosky	.15	.07	.01
☐ 586	Mitchell Page	.08	.04	.01
☐ 587	Garry Templeton	.20	.10	.02
☐ 588	Greg Minton	.08	.04	.01
☐ 589	Chet Lemon	.15	.07	.01
☐ 590	Jim Palmer	1.25	.60	.12
☐ 591	Rick Cerone	.15	.07	.01
☐ 592	Jon Matlack	.15	.07	.01
☐ 593	Jesus Alou	.08	.04	.01
☐ 594	Dick Tidrow	.08	.04	.01
☐ 595	Don Money	.08	.04	.01
☐ 596	Rick Matula	.08	.04	.01
☐ 597	Tom Poquette	.08	.04	.01
☐ 598	Fred Kendall DP	.04	.02	.00
☐ 599	Mike Norris	.15	.07	.01
☐ 600	Reggie Jackson	2.25	1.10	.22
☐ 601	Buddy Schultz	.08	.04	.01
☐ 602	Brian Downing	.15	.07	.01
☐ 603	Jack Billingham DP	.04	.02	.00
☐ 604	Glenn Adams	.08	.04	.01
☐ 605	Terry Forster	.15	.07	.01
☐ 606	Reds Team/Mgr.	.35	.10	.02
	John McNamara			
	(checklist back)			
☐ 607	Woodie Fryman	.08	.04	.01
☐ 608	Alan Bannister	.08	.04	.01
☐ 609	Ron Reed	.08	.04	.01
☐ 610	Willie Stargell	1.00	.50	.10
☐ 611	Jerry Garvin DP	.04	.02	.00
☐ 612	Cliff Johnson	.08	.04	.01
☐ 613	Randy Stein	.08	.04	.01
☐ 614	John Hiller	.15	.07	.01
☐ 615	Doug DeCinces	.20	.10	.02
☐ 616	Gene Richards	.08	.04	.01
☐ 617	Joaquin Andujar	.20	.10	.02
☐ 618	Bob Montgomery DP	.04	.02	.00
☐ 619	Sergio Ferrer	.08	.04	.01
☐ 620	Richie Zisk	.15	.07	.01
☐ 621	Bob Grich	.20	.10	.02
☐ 622	Mario Soto	.20	.10	.02
☐ 623	Gorman Thomas	.20	.10	.02
☐ 624	Lerrin LaGrow	.08	.04	.01
☐ 625	Chris Chambliss	.15	.07	.01
☐ 626	Tigers Team/Mgr.	.40	.10	.02
	Sparky Anderson			
	(checklist back)			
☐ 627	Pedro Borbon	.08	.04	.01
☐ 628	Doug Capilla	.08	.04	.01
☐ 629	Jim Todd	.08	.04	.01

☐ 630	Larry Bowa	.25	.12	.02
☐ 631	Mark Littell	.08	.04	.01
☐ 632	Barry Bonnell	.08	.04	.01
☐ 633	Bob Apodaca	.08	.04	.01
☐ 634	Glenn Borgmann DP	.04	.02	.00
☐ 635	John Candelaria	.20	.10	.02
☐ 636	Toby Harrah	.15	.07	.01
☐ 637	Joe Simpson	.08	.04	.01
☐ 638	Mark Clear	.35	.17	.03
☐ 639	Larry Biittner	.08	.04	.01
☐ 640	Mike Flanagan	.20	.10	.02
☐ 641	Ed Kranepool	.15	.07	.01
☐ 642	Ken Forsch DP	.08	.04	.01
☐ 643	John Mayberry	.15	.07	.01
☐ 644	Charlie Hough	.20	.10	.02
☐ 645	Rick Burleson	.15	.07	.01
☐ 646	Checklist 6	.25	.05	.01
☐ 647	Milt May	.08	.04	.01
☐ 648	Roy White	.15	.07	.01
☐ 649	Tom Griffin	.08	.04	.01
☐ 650	Joe Morgan	.80	.40	.08
☐ 651	Rollie Fingers	.45	.22	.04
☐ 652	Mario Mendoza	.08	.04	.01
☐ 653	Stan Bahnsen	.08	.04	.01
☐ 654	Bruce Boisclair DP	.04	.02	.00
☐ 655	Tug McGraw	.20	.10	.02
☐ 656	Larvell Blanks	.08	.04	.01
☐ 657	Dave Edwards	.08	.04	.01
☐ 658	Chris Knapp	.08	.04	.01
☐ 659	Brewers Team/Mgr.	.35	.10	.02
	George Bamberger			
	(checklist back)			
☐ 660	Rusty Staub	.25	.12	.02
☐ 661	Orioles Rookies	.15	.07	.01
	Mark Corey			
	Dave Ford			
	Wayne Krenchicki			
☐ 662	Red Sox Rookies	.15	.07	.01
	Joel Finch			
	Mike O'Berry			
	Chuck Rainey			
☐ 663	Angels Rookies	.50	.25	.05
	Ralph Botting			
	Bob Clark			
	Dickie Thon			
☐ 664	White Sox Rookies	.15	.07	.01
	Mike Colbern			
	Guy Hoffman			
	Dewey Robinson			
☐ 665	Indians Rookies	.15	.07	.01
	Larry Andersen			
	Bobby Cuellar			
	Sandy Wihtol			
☐ 666	Tigers Rookies	.15	.07	.01
	Mike Chris			
	Al Greene			
	Bruce Robbins			
☐ 667	Royals Rookies	2.00	1.00	.20
	Renie Martin			
	Bill Paschall			
	Dan Quisenberry			
☐ 668	Brewers Rookies	.15	.07	.01
	Danny Boitano			
	Willie Mueller			
	Lenn Sakata			
☐ 669	Twins Rookies	.75	.35	.07
	Dan Graham			
	Rick Sofield			
	Gary Ward			
☐ 670	Yankees Rookies	.15	.07	.01
	Bobby Brown			
	Brad Gulden			
	Darryl Jones			
☐ 671	A's Rookies	.25	.12	.02
	Derek Bryant			
	Brian Kingman			
	Mike Morgan			
☐ 672	Mariners Rookies	.15	.07	.01
	Charlie Beamon			
	Rodney Craig			
	Rafael Vasquez			
☐ 673	Rangers Rookies	.15	.07	.01
	Brian Allard			
	Jerry Don Gleaton			
	Greg Mahlberg			
☐ 674	Blue Jays Rookies	.15	.07	.01
	Butch Edge			
	Pat Kelly			
	Ted Wilborn			
☐ 675	Braves Rookies	.20	.10	.02
	Bruce Benedict			
	Larry Bradford			
	Eddie Miller			
☐ 676	Cubs Rookies	.15	.07	.01
	Dave Geisel			

	Steve Macko			
	Karl Pagel			
☐ 677	Reds Rookies	.15	.07	.01
	Art DeFreites			
	Frank Pastore			
	Harry Spilman			
☐ 678	Astros Rookies	.20	.10	.02
	Reggie Baldwin			
	Alan Knicely			
	Pete Ladd			
☐ 679	Dodgers Rookies	.30	.15	.03
	Joe Beckwith			
	Mickey Hatcher			
	Dave Patterson			
☐ 680	Expos Rookies	.45	.22	.04
	Tony Bernazard			
	Randy Miller			
	John Tamargo			
☐ 681	Mets Rookies	7.50	3.75	.75
	Dan Norman			
	Jesse Orosco			
	Mike Scott			
☐ 682	Phillies Rookies	.20	.10	.02
	Ramon Aviles			
	Dickie Noles			
	Kevin Saucier			
☐ 683	Pirates Rookies	.15	.07	.01
	Dorian Boyland			
	Alberto Lois			
	Harry Saferight			
☐ 684	Cardinals Rookies	.75	.35	.07
	George Frazier			
	Tom Herr			
	Dan O'Brien			
☐ 685	Padres Rookies	.15	.07	.01
	Tim Flannery			
	Brian Greer			
	Jim Wilhelm			
☐ 686	Giants Rookies	.15	.07	.01
	Greg Johnston			
	Dennis Littlejohn			
	Phil Nastu			
☐ 687	Mike Heath DP	.04	.02	.00
☐ 688	Steve Stone	.15	.07	.01
☐ 689	Red Sox Team/Mgr.	.35	.10	.02
	Don Zimmer			
	(checklist back)			
☐ 690	Tommy John	.35	.17	.03
☐ 691	Ivan DeJesus	.08	.04	.01
☐ 692	Rawly Eastwick DP	.04	.02	.00
☐ 693	Craig Kusick	.08	.04	.01
☐ 694	Jim Rooker	.08	.04	.01
☐ 695	Reggie Smith	.20	.10	.02
☐ 696	Julio Gonzalez	.08	.04	.01
☐ 697	David Clyde	.08	.04	.01
☐ 698	Oscar Gamble	.15	.07	.01
☐ 699	Floyd Bannister	.20	.10	.02
☐ 700	Rod Carew DP	.75	.35	.07
☐ 701	Ken Oberkfell	.35	.17	.03
☐ 702	Ed Farmer	.08	.04	.01
☐ 703	Otto Velez	.08	.04	.01
☐ 704	Gene Tenace	.08	.04	.01
☐ 705	Freddie Patek	.08	.04	.01
☐ 706	Tippy Martinez	.08	.04	.01
☐ 707	Elliott Maddox	.08	.04	.01
☐ 708	Bob Tolan	.08	.04	.01
☐ 709	Pat Underwood	.08	.04	.01
☐ 710	Graig Nettles	.30	.15	.03
☐ 711	Bob Galasso	.08	.04	.01
☐ 712	Rodney Scott	.08	.04	.01
☐ 713	Terry Whitfield	.08	.04	.01
☐ 714	Fred Norman	.08	.04	.01
☐ 715	Sal Bando	.15	.07	.01
☐ 716	Lynn McGlothen	.08	.04	.01
☐ 717	Mickey Klutts DP	.04	.02	.00
☐ 718	Greg Gross	.08	.04	.01
☐ 719	Don Robinson	.15	.07	.01
☐ 720	Carl Yastrzemski DP	1.25	.60	.12
☐ 721	Paul Hartzell	.08	.04	.01
☐ 722	Jose Cruz	.20	.10	.02
☐ 723	Shane Rawley	.15	.07	.01
☐ 724	Jerry White	.08	.04	.01
☐ 725	Rick Wise	.08	.04	.01
☐ 726	Steve Yeager	.20	.04	.01

YOU CAN HELP: Sport Americana is THE price authority for items covered. We solicit your input for future editions. Write to Dr. James Beckett, Beckett Publications, 3410 MidCourt, Suite 110, Carrollton, TX 75006.

1980 Topps Super

1981 Topps

The cards in this 60-card set measure 4 7/8" by 6 7/8". The 1980 Topps Superstar Photo set was issued in two different varieties. Both have identical fronts, but one is printed on thick cardboard with white backs, while the other is printed on thin stock with gray backs. Cards of the "white back" variety were issued first in three-card cellophane packages. To meet demand for the set, Topps then issued the gray back set via a variety of promotions. Cards 2, 6, 12, 13, 14 and 17 of the gray back set are triple-printed. The prices listed below are for gray backs (which have a Topps logo centered on the back); white backs are worth two and a half times (2.5X) the listed prices below.

		MINT	EXC	G-VG
COMPLETE SET		6.00	3.00	.60
COMMON PLAYER (1-60)		.07	.03	.01
☐ 1	Willie Stargell	.40	.20	.04
☐ 2	Mike Schmidt TP	.35	.17	.03
☐ 3	Johnny Bench	.50	.25	.05
☐ 4	Jim Palmer	.35	.17	.03
☐ 5	Jim Rice	.40	.20	.04
☐ 6	Reggie Jackson TP	.30	.15	.03
☐ 7	Ron Guidry	.25	.12	.02
☐ 8	Lee Mazzilli	.10	.05	.01
☐ 9	Don Baylor	.12	.06	.01
☐ 10	Fred Lynn	.20	.10	.02
☐ 11	Ken Singleton	.10	.05	.01
☐ 12	Rod Carew TP	.25	.12	.02
☐ 13	Steve Garvey TP	.30	.15	.03
☐ 14	George Brett TP	.35	.17	.03
☐ 15	Tom Seaver	.35	.17	.03
☐ 16	Dave Kingman	.15	.07	.01
☐ 17	Dave Parker TP	.15	.07	.01
☐ 18	Dave Winfield	.35	.17	.03
☐ 19	Pete Rose	1.00	.50	.10
☐ 20	Nolan Ryan	.40	.20	.04
☐ 21	Graig Nettles	.15	.07	.01
☐ 22	Carl Yastrzemski	.65	.30	.06
☐ 23	Tommy John	.15	.07	.01
☐ 24	George Foster	.15	.07	.01
☐ 25	J.R. Richard	.10	.05	.01
☐ 26	Keith Hernandez	.25	.12	.02
☐ 27	Bob Horner	.25	.12	.02
☐ 28	Eddie Murray	.50	.25	.05
☐ 29	Steve Kemp	.10	.05	.01
☐ 30	Gorman Thomas	.10	.05	.01
☐ 31	Sixto Lezcano	.07	.03	.01
☐ 32	Bruce Sutter	.15	.07	.01
☐ 33	Cecil Cooper	.15	.07	.01
☐ 34	Larry Bowa	.12	.06	.01
☐ 35	Al Oliver	.15	.07	.01
☐ 36	Ted Simmons	.15	.07	.01
☐ 37	Garry Templeton	.10	.05	.01
☐ 38	Jerry Koosman	.10	.05	.01
☐ 39	Darrell Porter	.07	.03	.01
☐ 40	Roy Smalley	.07	.03	.01
☐ 41	Craig Swan	.07	.03	.01
☐ 42	Jason Thompson	.07	.03	.01
☐ 43	Andre Thornton	.07	.03	.01
☐ 44	Rick Manning	.07	.03	.01
☐ 45	Kent Tekulve	.10	.05	.01
☐ 46	Phil Niekro	.20	.10	.02
☐ 47	Buddy Bell	.15	.07	.01
☐ 48	Randy Jones	.07	.03	.01
☐ 49	Brian Downing	.07	.03	.01
☐ 50	Amos Otis	.10	.05	.01
☐ 51	Rick Bosetti	.07	.03	.01
☐ 52	Gary Carter	.50	.25	.05
☐ 53	Larry Parrish	.10	.05	.01
☐ 54	Jack Clark	.20	.10	.02
☐ 55	Bruce Bochte	.07	.03	.01
☐ 56	Cesar Cedeno	.10	.05	.01
☐ 57	Chet Lemon	.07	.03	.01
☐ 58	Dave Revering	.07	.03	.01
☐ 59	Vida Blue	.10	.05	.01
☐ 60	Davey Lopes	.10	.05	.01

The cards in this 726-card set measure 2 1/2" by 3 1/2". League Leaders (1-8), Record Breakers (201-208), and Post-season cards (401-404) are topical subsets found in this set marketed by Topps in 1981. The team cards are all grouped together (661-686) and feature team checklist backs and a very small photo of the team's manager in the upper right corner of the obverse. The obverses carry the player's position and team in a baseball cap design, and the company name is printed in a small baseball. The backs are red and gray. The 66 double-printed cards are noted in the checklist by DP. The set is quite popular with collectors partly due to the presence of rookie cards of Fernando Valenzuela, Tim Raines, Kirk Gibson, Harold Baines, John Tudor, Lloyd Moseby, Hubie Brooks, Mike Boddicker, and Tony Pena.

		MINT	EXC	G-VG
COMPLETE SET		80.00	40.00	8.00
COMMON PLAYER (1-726)		.07	.03	.01
COMMON DP's (1-726)		.02	.01	.00
☐ 1	Batting Leaders George Brett Bill Buckner	.50	.15	.03
☐ 2	Home Run Leaders Reggie Jackson Ben Oglivie Mike Schmidt	.30	.15	.03
☐ 3	RBI Leaders Cecil Cooper Mike Schmidt	.20	.10	.02
☐ 4	Stolen Base Leaders Rickey Henderson Ron LeFlore	.18	.09	.01
☐ 5	Victory Leaders Steve Stone Steve Carlton	.15	.07	.01
☐ 6	Strikeout Leaders Len Barker Steve Carlton	.15	.07	.01
☐ 7	ERA Leaders Rudy May Don Sutton	.10	.05	.01
☐ 8	Leading Firemen Dan Quisenberry Rollie Fingers Tom Hume	.15	.07	.01
☐ 9	Pete LaCock DP	.02	.01	.00
☐ 10	Mike Flanagan	.15	.07	.01
☐ 11	Jim Wohlford DP	.02	.01	.00
☐ 12	Mark Clear	.07	.03	.01
☐ 13	Joe Charboneau	.15	.07	.01
☐ 14	John Tudor	1.50	.75	.15
☐ 15	Larry Parrish	.15	.07	.01
☐ 16	Ron Davis	.10	.05	.01
☐ 17	Cliff Johnson	.07	.03	.01
☐ 18	Glenn Adams	.07	.03	.01
☐ 19	Jim Clancy	.10	.05	.01
☐ 20	Jeff Burroughs	.10	.05	.01
☐ 21	Ron Oester	.10	.05	.01
☐ 22	Danny Darwin	.10	.05	.01
☐ 23	Alex Trevino	.07	.03	.01
☐ 24	Don Stanhouse	.07	.03	.01

☐ 25	Sixto Lezcano	.10	.05	.01
☐ 26	U.L. Washington	.07	.03	.01
☐ 27	Champ Summers DP	.02	.01	.00
☐ 28	Enrique Romo	.07	.03	.01
☐ 29	Gene Tenace	.10	.05	.01
☐ 30	Jack Clark	.50	.25	.05
☐ 31	Checklist 1-121 DP	.07	.01	.00
☐ 32	Ken Oberkfell	.10	.05	.01
☐ 33	Rick Honeycutt	.10	.05	.01
☐ 34	Aurelio Rodriguez	.07	.03	.01
☐ 35	Mitchell Page	.07	.03	.01
☐ 36	Ed Farmer	.07	.03	.01
☐ 37	Gary Roenicke	.10	.05	.01
☐ 38	Win Remmerswaal	.07	.03	.01
☐ 39	Tom Veryzer	.07	.03	.01
☐ 40	Tug McGraw	.15	.07	.01
☐ 41	Ranger Rookies	.15	.07	.01
	Bob Babcock			
	John Butcher			
	Jerry Don Gleaton			
☐ 42	Jerry White DP	.02	.01	.00
☐ 43	Jose Morales	.07	.03	.01
☐ 44	Larry McWilliams	.10	.05	.01
☐ 45	Enos Cabell	.07	.03	.01
☐ 46	Rick Bosetti	.07	.03	.01
☐ 47	Ken Brett	.10	.05	.01
☐ 48	Dave Skaggs	.07	.03	.01
☐ 49	Bob Shirley	.07	.03	.01
☐ 50	Dave Lopes	.15	.07	.01
☐ 51	Bill Robinson DP	.02	.01	.00
☐ 52	Hector Cruz	.07	.03	.01
☐ 53	Kevin Saucier	.07	.03	.01
☐ 54	Ivan DeJesus	.07	.03	.01
☐ 55	Mike Norris	.10	.05	.01
☐ 56	Buck Martinez	.07	.03	.01
☐ 57	Dave Roberts	.07	.03	.01
☐ 58	Joel Youngblood	.07	.03	.01
☐ 59	Dan Petry	.30	.15	.03
☐ 60	Willie Randolph	.15	.07	.01
☐ 61	Butch Wynegar	.10	.05	.01
☐ 62	Joe Pettini	.07	.03	.01
☐ 63	Steve Renko DP	.02	.01	.00
☐ 64	Brian Asselstine	.07	.03	.01
☐ 65	Scott McGregor	.15	.07	.01
☐ 66	Royals Rookies	.10	.05	.01
	Manny Castillo			
	Tim Ireland			
	Mike Jones			
☐ 67	Ken Kravec	.07	.03	.01
☐ 68	Matt Alexander DP	.02	.01	.00
☐ 69	Ed Halicki	.07	.03	.01
☐ 70	Al Oliver DP	.10	.05	.01
☐ 71	Hal Dues	.07	.03	.01
☐ 72	Barry Evans DP	.02	.01	.00
☐ 73	Doug Bair	.07	.03	.01
☐ 74	Mike Hargrove	.10	.05	.01
☐ 75	Reggie Smith	.15	.07	.01
☐ 76	Mario Mendoza	.07	.03	.01
☐ 77	Mike Barlow	.07	.03	.01
☐ 78	Steve Dillard	.07	.03	.01
☐ 79	Bruce Robbins	.07	.03	.01
☐ 80	Rusty Staub	.20	.10	.02
☐ 81	Dave Stapleton	.10	.05	.01
☐ 82	Astros Rookies DP	.10	.05	.01
	Danny Heep			
	Alan Knicely			
	Bobby Sprowl			
☐ 83	Mike Proly	.07	.03	.01
☐ 84	Johnnie LeMaster	.07	.03	.01
☐ 85	Mike Caldwell	.10	.05	.01
☐ 86	Wayne Gross	.07	.03	.01
☐ 87	Rick Camp	.07	.03	.01
☐ 88	Joe Lefebvre	.10	.05	.01
☐ 89	Darrell Jackson	.07	.03	.01
☐ 90	Bake McBride	.10	.05	.01
☐ 91	Tim Stoddard DP	.07	.03	.01
☐ 92	Mike Easler	.10	.05	.01
☐ 93	Ed Glynn DP	.02	.01	.00
☐ 94	Harry Spilman DP	.02	.01	.00
☐ 95	Jim Sundberg	.10	.05	.01
☐ 96	A's Rookies	.15	.07	.01
	Dave Beard			
	Ernie Camacho			
	Pat Dempsey			
☐ 97	Chris Speier	.10	.05	.01
☐ 98	Clint Hurdle	.07	.03	.01
☐ 99	Eric Wilkins	.07	.03	.01
☐ 100	Rod Carew	1.25	.60	.12
☐ 101	Benny Ayala	.07	.03	.01
☐ 102	Dave Tobik	.07	.03	.01
☐ 103	Jerry Martin	.07	.03	.01
☐ 104	Terry Forster	.10	.05	.01
☐ 105	Jose Cruz	.20	.10	.02
☐ 106	Don Money	.10	.05	.01
☐ 107	Rich Wortham	.07	.03	.01
☐ 108	Bruce Benedict	.10	.05	.01
☐ 109	Mike Scott	1.25	.60	.12
☐ 110	Carl Yastrzemski	1.25	.60	.12
☐ 111	Greg Minton	.10	.05	.01
☐ 112	White Sox Rookies	.10	.05	.01
	Rusty Kuntz			
	Fran Mullin			
	Leo Sutherland			
☐ 113	Mike Phillips	.07	.03	.01
☐ 114	Tom Underwood	.07	.03	.01
☐ 115	Roy Smalley	.10	.05	.01
☐ 116	Joe Simpson	.07	.03	.01
☐ 117	Pete Falcone	.07	.03	.01
☐ 118	Kurt Bevacqua	.10	.05	.01
☐ 119	Tippy Martinez	.07	.03	.01
☐ 120	Larry Bowa	.20	.10	.02
☐ 121	Larry Harlow	.07	.03	.01
☐ 122	John Denny	.15	.07	.01
☐ 123	Al Cowens	.10	.05	.01
☐ 124	Jerry Garvin	.07	.03	.01
☐ 125	Andre Dawson	1.00	.50	.10
☐ 126	Charlie Leibrandt	.65	.30	.06
☐ 127	Rudy Law	.07	.03	.01
☐ 128	Garry Allenson DP	.02	.01	.00
☐ 129	Art Howe	.07	.03	.01
☐ 130	Larry Gura	.10	.05	.01
☐ 131	Keith Moreland	.75	.35	.07
☐ 132	Tommy Boggs	.07	.03	.01
☐ 133	Jeff Cox	.07	.03	.01
☐ 134	Steve Mura	.07	.03	.01
☐ 135	Gorman Thomas	.20	.10	.02
☐ 136	Doug Capilla	.07	.03	.01
☐ 137	Hosken Powell	.07	.03	.01
☐ 138	Rich Dotson DP	.35	.17	.03
☐ 139	Oscar Gamble	.10	.05	.01
☐ 140	Bob Forsch	.10	.05	.01
☐ 141	Miguel Dilone	.07	.03	.01
☐ 142	Jackson Todd	.07	.03	.01
☐ 143	Dan Meyer	.07	.03	.01
☐ 144	Allen Ripley	.07	.03	.01
☐ 145	Mickey Rivers	.10	.05	.01
☐ 146	Bobby Castillo	.07	.03	.01
☐ 147	Dale Berra	.10	.05	.01
☐ 148	Randy Niemann	.07	.03	.01
☐ 149	Joe Nolan	.07	.03	.01
☐ 150	Mark Fidrych	.15	.07	.01
☐ 151	Claudell Washington	.15	.07	.01
☐ 152	John Urrea	.07	.03	.01
☐ 153	Tom Poquette	.07	.03	.01
☐ 154	Rick Langford	.07	.03	.01
☐ 155	Chris Chambliss	.15	.07	.01
☐ 156	Bob McClure	.07	.03	.01
☐ 157	John Wathan	.15	.07	.01
☐ 158	Fergie Jenkins	.25	.12	.02
☐ 159	Brian Doyle	.07	.03	.01
☐ 160	Garry Maddox	.10	.05	.01
☐ 161	Dan Graham	.07	.03	.01
☐ 162	Doug Corbett	.15	.07	.01
☐ 163	Billy Almon	.07	.03	.01
☐ 164	LaMarr Hoyt	.35	.17	.03
☐ 165	Tony Scott	.07	.03	.01
☐ 166	Floyd Bannister	.15	.07	.01
☐ 167	Terry Whitfield	.07	.03	.01
☐ 168	Don Robinson DP	.02	.01	.00
☐ 169	John Mayberry	.10	.05	.01
☐ 170	Ross Grimsley	.07	.03	.01
☐ 171	Gene Richards	.07	.03	.01
☐ 172	Gary Woods	.07	.03	.01
☐ 173	Bump Wills	.07	.03	.01
☐ 174	Doug Rau	.07	.03	.01
☐ 175	Dave Collins	.10	.05	.01
☐ 176	Mike Krukow	.15	.07	.01
☐ 177	Rick Peters	.07	.03	.01
☐ 178	Jim Essian DP	.02	.01	.00
☐ 179	Rudy May	.07	.03	.01
☐ 180	Pete Rose	3.25	1.60	.32
☐ 181	Elias Sosa	.07	.03	.01
☐ 182	Bob Grich	.15	.07	.01
☐ 183	Dick Davis DP	.02	.01	.00
☐ 184	Jim Dwyer	.07	.03	.01
☐ 185	Dennis Leonard	.10	.05	.01
☐ 186	Wayne Nordhagen	.07	.03	.01
☐ 187	Mike Parrott	.07	.03	.01
☐ 188	Doug DeCinces	.15	.07	.01
☐ 189	Craig Swan	.10	.05	.01
☐ 190	Cesar Cedeno	.15	.07	.01
☐ 191	Rick Sutcliffe	.60	.30	.06
☐ 192	Braves Rookies	.30	.15	.03
	Terry Harper			
	Ed Miller			
	Rafael Ramirez			
☐ 193	Pete Vuckovich	.15	.07	.01
☐ 194	Rod Scurry	.15	.07	.01
☐ 195	Rich Murray	.07	.03	.01
☐ 196	Duffy Dyer	.07	.03	.01

□ 197	Jim Kern	.07	.03	.01
□ 198	Jerry Dybzinski	.07	.03	.01
□ 199	Chuck Rainey	.07	.03	.01
□ 200	George Foster	.25	.12	.02
□ 201	RB: Johnny Bench	.30	.15	.03
	Most homers, lifetime, catcher			
□ 202	RB: Steve Carlton	.30	.15	.03
	Most strikeouts, lefthander, lifetime			
□ 203	RB: Bill Gullickson	.15	.07	.01
	Most strikeouts, game, rookie			
□ 204	RB: Ron LeFlore and Rodney Scott	.10	.05	.01
	Most stolen bases, teammates, season			
□ 205	RB: Pete Rose	.75	.35	.07
	Most cons. seasons 600 or more at-bats			
□ 206	RB: Mike Schmidt	.45	.22	.04
	Most homers, third baseman, season			
□ 207	RB: Ozzie Smith	.15	.07	.01
	Most assists season, shortstop			
□ 208	RB: Willie Wilson	.10	.05	.01
	Most at-bats, season			
□ 209	Dickie Thon DP	.10	.05	.01
□ 210	Jim Palmer	.80	.40	.08
□ 211	Derrel Thomas	.07	.03	.01
□ 212	Steve Nicosia	.07	.03	.01
□ 213	Al Holland	.20	.10	.02
□ 214	Angels Rookies	.10	.05	.01
	Ralph Botting Jim Dorsey John Harris			
□ 215	Larry Hisle	.10	.05	.01
□ 216	John Henry Johnson	.07	.03	.01
□ 217	Rich Hebner	.07	.03	.01
□ 218	Paul Splittorff	.10	.05	.01
□ 219	Ken Landreaux	.10	.05	.01
□ 220	Tom Seaver	1.25	.60	.12
□ 221	Bob Davis	.07	.03	.01
□ 222	Jorge Orta	.07	.03	.01
□ 223	Roy Lee Jackson	.10	.05	.01
□ 224	Pat Zachry	.07	.03	.01
□ 225	Ruppert Jones	.10	.05	.01
□ 226	Manny Sanguillen DP	.07	.03	.01
□ 227	Fred Martinez	.07	.03	.01
□ 228	Tom Paciorek	.07	.03	.01
□ 229	Rollie Fingers	.50	.25	.05
□ 230	George Hendrick	.10	.05	.01
□ 231	Joe Beckwith	.07	.03	.01
□ 232	Mickey Klutts	.07	.03	.01
□ 233	Skip Lockwood	.07	.03	.01
□ 234	Lou Whitaker	.45	.22	.04
□ 235	Scott Sanderson	.10	.05	.01
□ 236	Mike Ivie	.07	.03	.01
□ 237	Charlie Moore	.07	.03	.01
□ 238	Willie Hernandez	.25	.12	.02
□ 239	Rick Miller DP	.02	.01	.00
□ 240	Nolan Ryan	1.25	.60	.12
□ 241	Checklist 122-242 DP	.07	.01	.00
□ 242	Chet Lemon	.10	.05	.01
□ 243	Sal Butera	.07	.03	.01
□ 244	Cardinals Rookies	.15	.07	.01
	Tito Landrum Al Olmsted Andy Rincon			
□ 245	Ed Figueroa	.07	.03	.01
□ 246	Ed Ott DP	.02	.01	.00
□ 247	Glenn Hubbard DP	.07	.03	.01
□ 248	Joey McLaughlin	.07	.03	.01
□ 249	Larry Cox	.07	.03	.01
□ 250	Ron Guidry	.45	.22	.04
□ 251	Tom Brookens	.07	.03	.01
□ 252	Victor Cruz	.07	.03	.01
□ 253	Dave Bergman	.07	.03	.01
□ 254	Ozzie Smith	.75	.35	.07
□ 255	Mark Littell	.07	.03	.01
□ 256	Bombo Rivera	.07	.03	.01
□ 257	Rennie Stennett	.07	.03	.01
□ 258	Joe Price	.10	.05	.01
□ 259	Mets Rookies	2.00	1.00	.20
	Juan Berenguer Hubie Brooks Mookie Wilson			
□ 260	Ron Cey	.25	.12	.02
□ 261	Rickey Henderson	3.50	1.75	.35
□ 262	Sammy Stewart	.07	.03	.01
□ 263	Brian Downing	.10	.05	.01
□ 264	Jim Norris	.07	.03	.01
□ 265	John Candelaria	.15	.07	.01
□ 266	Tom Herr	.20	.10	.02
□ 267	Stan Bahnsen	.07	.03	.01
□ 268	Jerry Royster	.07	.03	.01
□ 269	Ken Forsch	.10	.05	.01
□ 270	Greg Luzinski	.20	.10	.02
□ 271	Bill Castro	.07	.03	.01
□ 272	Bruce Kimm	.07	.03	.01
□ 273	Stan Papi	.07	.03	.01
□ 274	Craig Chamberlain	.07	.03	.01
□ 275	Dwight Evans	.35	.17	.03
□ 276	Dan Spillner	.07	.03	.01
□ 277	Alfredo Griffin	.15	.07	.01
□ 278	Rick Sofield	.07	.03	.01
□ 279	Bob Knepper	.15	.07	.01
□ 280	Ken Griffey	.15	.07	.01
□ 281	Fred Stanley	.07	.03	.01
□ 282	Mariners Rookies	.10	.05	.01
	Rick Anderson Greg Biercevicz Rodney Craig			
□ 283	Billy Sample	.07	.03	.01
□ 284	Brian Kingman	.07	.03	.01
□ 285	Jerry Turner	.07	.03	.01
□ 286	Dave Frost	.07	.03	.01
□ 287	Lenn Sakata	.07	.03	.01
□ 288	Bob Clark	.07	.03	.01
□ 289	Mickey Hatcher	.10	.05	.01
□ 290	Bob Boone DP	.07	.03	.01
□ 291	Aurelio Lopez	.07	.03	.01
□ 292	Mike Squires	.07	.03	.01
□ 293	Charlie Lea	.25	.12	.02
□ 294	Mike Tyson DP	.02	.01	.00
□ 295	Hal McRae	.10	.05	.01
□ 296	Bill Nahorodny DP	.02	.01	.00
□ 297	Bob Bailor	.07	.03	.01
□ 298	Buddy Solomon	.07	.03	.01
□ 299	Elliott Maddox	.07	.03	.01
□ 300	Paul Molitor	.35	.17	.03
□ 301	Matt Keough	.07	.03	.01
□ 302	Dodgers Rookies	7.50	3.75	.75
	Jack Perconte Mike Scioscia Fernando Valenzuela			
□ 303	Johnny Oates	.07	.03	.01
□ 304	John Castino	.07	.03	.01
□ 305	Ken Clay	.07	.03	.01
□ 306	Juan Beniquez DP	.07	.03	.01
□ 307	Gene Garber	.07	.03	.01
□ 308	Rick Manning	.07	.03	.01
□ 309	Luis Salazar	.10	.05	.01
□ 310	Vida Blue DP	.10	.05	.01
□ 311	Freddie Patek	.07	.03	.01
□ 312	Rick Rhoden	.15	.07	.01
□ 313	Luis Pujols	.07	.03	.01
□ 314	Rich Dauer	.07	.03	.01
□ 315	Kirk Gibson	4.00	2.00	.40
□ 316	Craig Minetto	.07	.03	.01
□ 317	Lonnie Smith	.10	.05	.01
□ 318	Steve Yeager	.10	.05	.01
□ 319	Rowland Office	.07	.03	.01
□ 320	Tom Burgmeier	.07	.03	.01
□ 321	Leon Durham	1.25	.60	.12
□ 322	Neil Allen	.10	.05	.01
□ 323	Jim Morrison DP	.07	.03	.01
□ 324	Mike Willis	.07	.03	.01
□ 325	Ray Knight	.20	.10	.02
□ 326	Biff Pocoroba	.07	.03	.01
□ 327	Moose Haas	.10	.05	.01
□ 328	Twins Rookies	.25	.12	.02
	Dave Engle Greg Johnston Gary Ward			
□ 329	Joaquin Andujar	.20	.10	.02
□ 330	Frank White	.15	.07	.01
□ 331	Dennis Lamp	.07	.03	.01
□ 332	Lee Lacy DP	.07	.03	.01
□ 333	Sid Monge	.07	.03	.01
□ 334	Dane Iorg	.07	.03	.01
□ 335	Rick Cerone	.10	.05	.01
□ 336	Eddie Whitson	.10	.05	.01
□ 337	Lynn Jones	.07	.03	.01
□ 338	Checklist 243-363	.15	.02	.00
□ 339	John Ellis	.07	.03	.01
□ 340	Bruce Kison	.07	.03	.01
□ 341	Dwayne Murphy	.10	.05	.01
□ 342	Eric Rasmussen DP	.02	.01	.00
□ 343	Frank Taveras	.07	.03	.01
□ 344	Byron McLaughlin	.07	.03	.01
□ 345	Warren Cromartie	.07	.03	.01
□ 346	Larry Christenson DP	.02	.01	.00
□ 347	Harold Baines	3.50	1.75	.35
□ 348	Bob Sykes	.07	.03	.01
□ 349	Glenn Hoffman	.10	.05	.01
□ 350	J.R. Richard	.15	.07	.01
□ 351	Otto Velez	.07	.03	.01
□ 352	Dick Tidrow DP	.02	.01	.00

□ 353	Terry Kennedy	.15	.07	.01
□ 354	Mario Soto	.15	.07	.01
□ 355	Bob Horner	.40	.20	.04
□ 356	Padres Rookies	.10	.05	.01
	George Stablein			
	Craig Stimac			
	Tom Tellmann			
□ 357	Jim Slaton	.10	.05	.01
□ 358	Mark Wagner	.07	.03	.01
□ 359	Tom Hausman	.07	.03	.01
□ 360	Willie Wilson	.25	.12	.02
□ 361	Joe Strain	.07	.03	.01
□ 362	Bo Diaz	.15	.07	.01
□ 363	Geoff Zahn	.10	.05	.01
□ 364	Mike Davis	.65	.30	.06
□ 365	Graig Nettles DP	.10	.05	.01
□ 366	Mike Ramsey	.07	.03	.01
□ 367	Denny Martinez	.10	.05	.01
□ 368	Leon Roberts	.07	.03	.01
□ 369	Frank Tanana	.15	.07	.01
□ 370	Dave Winfield	.80	.40	.08
□ 371	Charlie Hough	.15	.07	.01
□ 372	Jay Johnstone	.10	.05	.01
□ 373	Pat Underwood	.07	.03	.01
□ 374	Tom Hutton	.07	.03	.01
□ 375	Dave Concepcion	.15	.07	.01
□ 376	Ron Reed	.07	.03	.01
□ 377	Jerry Morales	.07	.03	.01
□ 378	Dave Rader	.07	.03	.01
□ 379	Lary Sorensen	.07	.03	.01
□ 380	Willie Stargell	.80	.40	.08
□ 381	Cubs Rookies	.10	.05	.01
	Carlos Lezcano			
	Steve Macko			
	Randy Martz			
□ 382	Paul Mirabella	.07	.03	.01
□ 383	Eric Soderholm DP	.02	.01	.00
□ 384	Mike Sadek	.07	.03	.01
□ 385	Joe Sambito	.10	.05	.01
□ 386	Dave Edwards	.07	.03	.01
□ 387	Phil Niekro	.65	.30	.06
□ 388	Andre Thornton	.15	.07	.01
□ 389	Marty Pattin	.07	.03	.01
□ 390	Cesar Geronimo	.07	.03	.01
□ 391	Dave Lemanczyk DP	.02	.01	.00
□ 392	Lance Parrish	.70	.35	.07
□ 393	Broderick Perkins	.07	.03	.01
□ 394	Woodie Fryman	.07	.03	.01
□ 395	Scot Thompson	.07	.03	.01
□ 396	Bill Campbell	.07	.03	.01
□ 397	Julio Cruz	.07	.03	.01
□ 398	Ross Baumgarten	.07	.03	.01
□ 399	Orioles Rookies	2.00	1.00	.20
	Mike Boddicker			
	Mark Corey			
	Floyd Rayford			
□ 400	Reggie Jackson	1.50	.75	.15
□ 401	AL Champs	.50	.25	.05
	Royals sweep Yanks			
	(Brett swinging)			
□ 402	NL Champs	.20	.10	.02
	Phillies squeak			
	past Astros			
□ 403	1980 World Series	.20	.10	.02
	Phillies beat			
	Royals in six			
□ 404	1980 World Series	.20	.10	.02
	Phillies win first			
	World Series			
□ 405	Nino Espinosa	.07	.03	.01
□ 406	Dickie Noles	.07	.03	.01
□ 407	Ernie Whitt	.10	.05	.01
□ 408	Fernando Arroyo	.07	.03	.01
□ 409	Larry Herndon	.10	.05	.01
□ 410	Bert Campaneris	.10	.05	.01
□ 411	Terry Puhl	.10	.05	.01
□ 412	Britt Burns	.35	.17	.03
□ 413	Tony Bernazard	.10	.05	.01
□ 414	John Pacella DP	.02	.01	.00
□ 415	Ben Oglivie	.10	.05	.01
□ 416	Gary Alexander	.07	.03	.01
□ 417	Dan Schatzeder	.07	.03	.01
□ 418	Bobby Brown	.07	.03	.01
□ 419	Tom Hume	.07	.03	.01
□ 420	Keith Hernandez	.75	.35	.07
□ 421	Bob Stanley	.10	.05	.01
□ 422	Dan Ford	.07	.03	.01
□ 423	Shane Rawley	.15	.07	.01
□ 424	Yankees Rookies	.15	.07	.01
	Tim Lollar			
	Bruce Robinson			
	Dennis Werth			
□ 425	Al Bumbry	.07	.03	.01
□ 426	Warren Brusstar	.07	.03	.01
□ 427	John D'Acquisto	.07	.03	.01
□ 428	John Stearns	.07	.03	.01
□ 429	Mick Kelleher	.07	.03	.01
□ 430	Jim Bibby	.07	.03	.01
□ 431	Dave Roberts	.07	.03	.01
□ 432	Len Barker	.10	.05	.01
□ 433	Rance Mulliniks	.10	.05	.01
□ 434	Roger Erickson	.07	.03	.01
□ 435	Jim Spencer	.07	.03	.01
□ 436	Gary Lucas	.10	.05	.01
□ 437	Mike Heath DP	.02	.01	.00
□ 438	John Montefusco	.10	.05	.01
□ 439	Denny Walling	.07	.03	.01
□ 440	Jerry Reuss	.15	.07	.01
□ 441	Ken Reitz	.07	.03	.01
□ 442	Ron Pruitt	.07	.03	.01
□ 443	Jim Beattie DP	.02	.01	.00
□ 444	Garth Iorg	.07	.03	.01
□ 445	Ellis Valentine	.07	.03	.01
□ 446	Checklist 364-484	.15	.02	.00
□ 447	Junior Kennedy DP	.02	.01	.00
□ 448	Tim Corcoran	.07	.03	.01
□ 449	Paul Mitchell	.07	.03	.01
□ 450	Dave Kingman DP	.10	.05	.01
□ 451	Indians Rookies	.15	.07	.01
	Chris Bando			
	Tom Brennan			
	Sandy Wihtol			
□ 452	Renie Martin	.07	.03	.01
□ 453	Rob Wilfong DP	.02	.01	.00
□ 454	Andy Hassler	.07	.03	.01
□ 455	Rick Burleson	.10	.05	.01
□ 456	Jeff Reardon	.85	.40	.08
□ 457	Mike Lum	.07	.03	.01
□ 458	Randy Jones	.10	.05	.01
□ 459	Greg Gross	.07	.03	.01
□ 460	Rich Gossage	.30	.15	.03
□ 461	Dave McKay	.07	.03	.01
□ 462	Jack Brohamer	.07	.03	.01
□ 463	Milt May	.07	.03	.01
□ 464	Adrian Devine	.07	.03	.01
□ 465	Bill Russell	.10	.05	.01
□ 466	Bob Molinaro	.07	.03	.01
□ 467	Dave Stieb	.35	.17	.03
□ 468	Johnny Wockenfuss	.07	.03	.01
□ 469	Jeff Leonard	.35	.17	.03
□ 470	Manny Trillo	.10	.05	.01
□ 471	Mike Vail	.07	.03	.01
□ 472	Dyar Miller DP	.02	.01	.00
□ 473	Jose Cardenal	.07	.03	.01
□ 474	Mike LaCoss	.07	.03	.01
□ 475	Buddy Bell	.20	.10	.02
□ 476	Jerry Koosman	.15	.07	.01
□ 477	Luis Gomez	.07	.03	.01
□ 478	Juan Eichelberger	.10	.05	.01
□ 479	Expos Rookies	9.00	4.50	.90
	Tim Raines			
	Roberto Ramos			
	Bobby Pate			
□ 480	Carlton Fisk	.30	.15	.03
□ 481	Bob Lacey DP	.02	.01	.00
□ 482	Jim Gantner	.07	.03	.01
□ 483	Mike Griffin	.07	.03	.01
□ 484	Max Venable DP	.02	.01	.00
□ 485	Garry Templeton	.15	.07	.01
□ 486	Marc Hill	.07	.03	.01
□ 487	Dewey Robinson	.07	.03	.01
□ 488	Damaso Garcia	.35	.17	.03
□ 489	John Littlefield	.07	.03	.01
□ 490	Eddie Murray	1.50	.75	.15
□ 491	Gordy Pladson	.07	.03	.01
□ 492	Barry Foote	.07	.03	.01
□ 493	Dan Quisenberry	.35	.17	.03
□ 494	Bob Walk	.07	.03	.01
□ 495	Dusty Baker	.15	.07	.01
□ 496	Paul Dade	.07	.03	.01
□ 497	Fred Norman	.07	.03	.01
□ 498	Pat Putnam	.07	.03	.01
□ 499	Frank Pastore	.07	.03	.01
□ 500	Jim Rice	1.00	.50	.10
□ 501	Tim Foli DP	.02	.01	.00
□ 502	Giants Rookies	.10	.05	.01
	Chris Bourjos			
	Al Hargesheimer			
	Mike Rowland			
□ 503	Steve McCatty	.07	.03	.01
□ 504	Dale Murphy	2.50	1.25	.25
□ 505	Jason Thompson	.10	.05	.01
□ 506	Phil Huffman	.07	.03	.01
□ 507	Jamie Quirk	.07	.03	.01
□ 508	Rob Dressler	.07	.03	.01
□ 509	Pete Mackanin	.07	.03	.01
□ 510	Lee Mazzilli	.10	.05	.01
□ 511	Wayne Garland	.07	.03	.01
□ 512	Gary Thomasson	.07	.03	.01
□ 513	Frank LaCorte	.07	.03	.01

☐ 514	George Riley	.07	.03	.01
☐ 515	Robin Yount	1.00	.50	.10
☐ 516	Doug Bird	.07	.03	.01
☐ 517	Richie Zisk	.10	.05	.01
☐ 518	Grant Jackson	.07	.03	.01
☐ 519	John Tamargo DP	.02	.01	.00
☐ 520	Steve Stone	.10	.05	.01
☐ 521	Sam Mejias	.07	.03	.01
☐ 522	Mike Colbern	.07	.03	.01
☐ 523	John Fulgham	.07	.03	.01
☐ 524	Willie Aikens	.10	.05	.01
☐ 525	Mike Torrez	.10	.05	.01
☐ 526	Phillies Rookies	.20	.10	.02
	Marty Bystrom			
	Jay Loviglio			
	Jim Wright			
☐ 527	Danny Goodwin	.07	.03	.01
☐ 528	Gary Matthews	.10	.05	.01
☐ 529	Dave LaRoche	.07	.03	.01
☐ 530	Steve Garvey	1.25	.60	.12
☐ 531	John Curtis	.07	.03	.01
☐ 532	Bill Stein	.07	.03	.01
☐ 533	Jesus Figueroa	.07	.03	.01
☐ 534	Dave Smith	.40	.20	.04
☐ 535	Omar Moreno	.10	.05	.01
☐ 536	Bob Owchinko DP	.02	.01	.00
☐ 537	Ron Hodges	.07	.03	.01
☐ 538	Tom Griffin	.07	.03	.01
☐ 539	Rodney Scott	.07	.03	.01
☐ 540	Mike Schmidt DP	1.00	.50	.10
☐ 541	Steve Swisher	.07	.03	.01
☐ 542	Larry Bradford DP	.02	.01	.00
☐ 543	Terry Crowley	.07	.03	.01
☐ 544	Rich Gale	.07	.03	.01
☐ 545	Johnny Grubb	.07	.03	.01
☐ 546	Paul Moskau	.07	.03	.01
☐ 547	Mario Guerrero	.07	.03	.01
☐ 548	Dave Goltz	.07	.03	.01
☐ 549	Jerry Remy	.07	.03	.01
☐ 550	Tommy John	.30	.15	.03
☐ 551	Pirates Rookies	2.00	1.00	.20
	Vance Law			
	Tony Pena			
	Pascual Perez			
☐ 552	Steve Trout	.10	.05	.01
☐ 553	Tim Blackwell	.07	.03	.01
☐ 554	Bert Blyleven	.30	.15	.03
☐ 555	Cecil Cooper	.25	.12	.02
☐ 556	Jerry Mumphrey	.10	.05	.01
☐ 557	Chris Knapp	.07	.03	.01
☐ 558	Barry Bonnell	.07	.03	.01
☐ 559	Willie Montanez	.07	.03	.01
☐ 560	Joe Morgan	.60	.30	.06
☐ 561	Dennis Littlejohn	.07	.03	.01
☐ 562	Checklist 485-605	.15	.02	.00
☐ 563	Jim Kaat	.25	.12	.02
☐ 564	Ron Hassey DP	.02	.01	.00
☐ 565	Burt Hooton	.07	.03	.01
☐ 566	Del Unser	.07	.03	.01
☐ 567	Mark Bomback	.07	.03	.01
☐ 568	Dave Revering	.07	.03	.01
☐ 569	Al Williams DP	.02	.01	.00
☐ 570	Ken Singleton	.15	.07	.01
☐ 571	Todd Cruz	.07	.03	.01
☐ 572	Jack Morris	.60	.30	.06
☐ 573	Phil Garner	.10	.05	.01
☐ 574	Bill Caudill	.10	.05	.01
☐ 575	Tony Perez	.25	.12	.02
☐ 576	Reggie Cleveland	.07	.03	.01
☐ 577	Blue Jays Rookies	.25	.12	.02
	Luis Leal			
	Brian Milner			
	Ken Schrom			
☐ 578	Bill Gullickson	.50	.25	.05
☐ 579	Tim Flannery	.07	.03	.01
☐ 580	Don Baylor	.30	.15	.03
☐ 581	Roy Howell	.07	.03	.01
☐ 582	Gaylord Perry	.50	.25	.05
☐ 583	Larry Milbourne	.07	.03	.01
☐ 584	Randy Lerch	.07	.03	.01
☐ 585	Amos Otis	.15	.07	.01
☐ 586	Silvio Martinez	.07	.03	.01
☐ 587	Jeff Newman	.07	.03	.01
☐ 588	Gary Lavelle	.10	.05	.01
☐ 589	Lamar Johnson	.07	.03	.01
☐ 590	Bruce Sutter	.25	.12	.02
☐ 591	John Lowenstein	.07	.03	.01
☐ 592	Steve Comer	.07	.03	.01
☐ 593	Steve Kemp	.10	.05	.01
☐ 594	Preston Hanna DP	.02	.01	.00
☐ 595	Butch Hobson	.07	.03	.01
☐ 596	Jerry Augustine	.07	.03	.01
☐ 597	Rafael Landestoy	.07	.03	.01
☐ 598	George Vukovich DP	.02	.01	.00
☐ 599	Dennis Kinney	.07	.03	.01
☐ 600	Johnny Bench	1.25	.60	.12
☐ 601	Don Aase	.10	.05	.01
☐ 602	Bobby Murcer	.15	.07	.01
☐ 603	John Verhoeven	.07	.03	.01
☐ 604	Rob Picciolo	.07	.03	.01
☐ 605	Don Sutton	.50	.25	.05
☐ 606	Reds Rookies DP	.07	.03	.01
	Bruce Berenyi			
	Geoff Combe			
	Paul Householder			
☐ 607	Dave Palmer	.10	.05	.01
☐ 608	Greg Pryor	.07	.03	.01
☐ 609	Lynn McGlothen	.07	.03	.01
☐ 610	Darrell Porter	.10	.05	.01
☐ 611	Rick Matula DP	.02	.01	.00
☐ 612	Duane Kuiper	.07	.03	.01
☐ 613	Jim Anderson	.07	.03	.01
☐ 614	Dave Rozema	.07	.03	.01
☐ 615	Rick Dempsey	.10	.05	.01
☐ 616	Rick Wise	.10	.05	.01
☐ 617	Craig Reynolds	.07	.03	.01
☐ 618	John Milner	.07	.03	.01
☐ 619	Steve Henderson	.07	.03	.01
☐ 620	Dennis Eckersley	.10	.05	.01
☐ 621	Tom Donohue	.07	.03	.01
☐ 622	Randy Moffitt	.07	.03	.01
☐ 623	Sal Bando	.10	.05	.01
☐ 624	Bob Welch	.20	.10	.02
☐ 625	Bill Buckner	.20	.10	.02
☐ 626	Tigers Rookies	.10	.05	.01
	Dave Steffen			
	Jerry Ujdur			
	Roger Weaver			
☐ 627	Luis Tiant	.15	.07	.01
☐ 628	Vic Correll	.07	.03	.01
☐ 629	Tony Armas	.15	.07	.01
☐ 630	Steve Carlton	1.00	.50	.10
☐ 631	Ron Jackson	.07	.03	.01
☐ 632	Alan Bannister	.07	.03	.01
☐ 633	Bill Lee	.10	.05	.01
☐ 634	Doug Flynn	.07	.03	.01
☐ 635	Bobby Bonds	.15	.07	.01
☐ 636	Al Hrabosky	.10	.05	.01
☐ 637	Jerry Narron	.07	.03	.01
☐ 638	Checklist 606-726	.15	.02	.00
☐ 639	Carney Lansford	.20	.10	.02
☐ 640	Dave Parker	.60	.30	.06
☐ 641	Mark Belanger	.10	.05	.01
☐ 642	Vern Ruhle	.07	.03	.01
☐ 643	Lloyd Moseby	1.75	.85	.17
☐ 644	Ramon Aviles DP	.02	.01	.00
☐ 645	Rick Reuschel	.15	.07	.01
☐ 646	Marvis Foley	.07	.03	.01
☐ 647	Dick Drago	.07	.03	.01
☐ 648	Darrell Evans	.25	.12	.02
☐ 649	Manny Sarmiento	.07	.03	.01
☐ 650	Bucky Dent	.15	.07	.01
☐ 651	Pedro Guerrero	1.25	.60	.12
☐ 652	John Montague	.07	.03	.01
☐ 653	Bill Fahey	.07	.03	.01
☐ 654	Ray Burris	.07	.03	.01
☐ 655	Dan Driessen	.10	.05	.01
☐ 656	Jon Matlack	.10	.05	.01
☐ 657	Mike Cubbage DP	.02	.01	.00
☐ 658	Milt Wilcox	.07	.03	.01
☐ 659	Brewers Rookies	.10	.05	.01
	John Flinn			
	Ed Romero			
	Ned Yost			
☐ 660	Gary Carter	1.50	.75	.15
☐ 661	Orioles Team/Mgr.	.25	.07	.01
	Earl Weaver			
☐ 662	Red Sox Team/Mgr.	.20	.05	.01
	Ralph Houk			
☐ 663	Angels Team/Mgr.	.20	.05	.01
	Jim Fregosi			
☐ 664	White Sox Team/Mgr.	.20	.05	.01
	Tony LaRussa			
☐ 665	Indians Team/Mgr.	.20	.05	.01
	Dave Garcia			
☐ 666	Tigers Team/Mgr.	.25	.07	.01
	Sparky Anderson			
☐ 667	Royals Team/Mgr.	.20	.05	.01
	Jim Frey			
☐ 668	Brewers Team/Mgr.	.20	.05	.01
	Bob Rodgers			
☐ 669	Twins Team/Mgr.	.20	.05	.01
	John Goryl			
☐ 670	Yankees Team/Mgr.	.25	.07	.01
	Gene Michael			
☐ 671	A's Team/Mgr.	.25	.07	.01
	Billy Martin			
☐ 672	Mariners Team/Mgr.	.20	.05	.01
	Maury Wills			
☐ 673	Rangers Team/Mgr.	.20	.05	.01

		MINT	EXC	G-VG
	Don Zimmer			
☐ 674	Blue Jays Team/Mgr.	.20	.05	.01
	Bobby Mattick			
☐ 675	Braves Team/Mgr.	.20	.05	.01
	Bobby Cox			
☐ 676	Cubs Team/Mgr.	.20	.05	.01
	Joe Amalfitano			
☐ 677	Reds Team/Mgr.	.20	.05	.01
	John McNamara			
☐ 678	Astros Team/Mgr.	.20	.05	.01
	Bill Virdon			
☐ 679	Dodgers Team/Mgr.	.25	.07	.01
	Tom Lasorda			
☐ 680	Expos Team/Mgr.	.20	.05	.01
	Dick Williams			
☐ 681	Mets Team/Mgr.	.25	.07	.01
	Joe Torre			
☐ 682	Phillies Team/Mgr.	.20	.05	.01
	Dallas Green			
☐ 683	Pirates Team/Mgr.	.20	.05	.01
	Chuck Tanner			
☐ 684	Cardinals Team/Mgr.	.20	.05	.01
	Whitey Herzog			
☐ 685	Padres Team/Mgr.	.20	.05	.01
	Frank Howard			
☐ 686	Giants Team/Mgr.	.20	.05	.01
	Dave Bristol			
☐ 687	Jeff Jones	.10	.05	.01
☐ 688	Kiko Garcia	.07	.03	.01
☐ 689	Red Sox Rookies	1.50	.75	.15
	Bruce Hurst			
	Keith MacWhorter			
	Reid Nichols			
☐ 690	Bob Watson	.10	.05	.01
☐ 691	Dick Ruthven	.07	.03	.01
☐ 692	Lenny Randle	.07	.03	.01
☐ 693	Steve Howe	.25	.12	.02
☐ 694	Bud Harrelson DP	.02	.01	.00
☐ 695	Kent Tekulve	.10	.05	.01
☐ 696	Alan Ashby	.07	.03	.01
☐ 697	Rick Waits	.07	.03	.01
☐ 698	Mike Jorgensen	.07	.03	.01
☐ 699	Glenn Abbott	.07	.03	.01
☐ 700	George Brett	2.00	1.00	.20
☐ 701	Joe Rudi	.10	.05	.01
☐ 702	George Medich	.07	.03	.01
☐ 703	Alvis Woods	.07	.03	.01
☐ 704	Bill Travers DP	.02	.01	.00
☐ 705	Ted Simmons	.20	.10	.02
☐ 706	Dave Ford	.07	.03	.01
☐ 707	Dave Cash	.07	.03	.01
☐ 708	Doyle Alexander	.10	.05	.01
☐ 709	Alan Trammell DP	.20	.10	.02
☐ 710	Ron LeFlore DP	.07	.03	.01
☐ 711	Joe Ferguson	.07	.03	.01
☐ 712	Bill Bonham	.07	.03	.01
☐ 713	Bill North	.07	.03	.01
☐ 714	Pete Redfern	.07	.03	.01
☐ 715	Bill Madlock	.20	.10	.02
☐ 716	Glenn Borgmann	.07	.03	.01
☐ 717	Jim Barr DP	.02	.01	.00
☐ 718	Larry Biittner	.07	.03	.01
☐ 719	Sparky Lyle	.15	.07	.01
☐ 720	Fred Lynn	.30	.15	.03
☐ 721	Toby Harrah	.10	.05	.01
☐ 722	Joe Niekro	.15	.07	.01
☐ 723	Bruce Bochte	.07	.03	.01
☐ 724	Lou Piniella	.15	.07	.01
☐ 725	Steve Rogers	.10	.05	.01
☐ 726	Rick Monday	.20	.05	.01

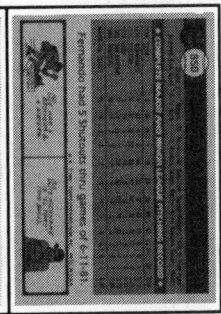

1981 Topps Traded

The cards in this 132-card set measure 2 1/2" by 3 1/2". For the first time since 1976, Topps issued a "traded" set in 1981. Unlike the small traded sets of 1974 and 1976, this set contains a larger number of cards and was sequentially numbered, alphabetically, from 727 to 858. Thus, this set gives the impression it is a continuation of their regular issue of this year. The sets were issued only through hobby card dealers and were boxed in complete sets of 132 cards.

	MINT	EXC	G-VG
COMPLETE SET	22.00	11.00	2.20
COMMON PLAYER	.09	.04	.01

		MINT	EXC	G-VG
☐ 727	Danny Ainge	.50	.25	.05
☐ 728	Doyle Alexander	.15	.07	.01
☐ 729	Gary Alexander	.09	.04	.01
☐ 730	Billy Almon	.09	.04	.01
☐ 731	Joaquin Andujar	.20	.10	.02
☐ 732	Bob Bailor	.09	.04	.01
☐ 733	Juan Beniquez	.15	.07	.01
☐ 734	Dave Bergman	.09	.04	.01
☐ 735	Tony Bernazard	.15	.07	.01
☐ 736	Larry Biittner	.09	.04	.01
☐ 737	Doug Bird	.09	.04	.01
☐ 738	Bert Blyleven	.40	.20	.04
☐ 739	Mark Bomback	.09	.04	.01
☐ 740	Bobby Bonds	.15	.07	.01
☐ 741	Rick Bosetti	.09	.04	.01
☐ 742	Hubie Brooks	1.25	.60	.12
☐ 743	Rick Burleson	.15	.07	.01
☐ 744	Ray Burris	.09	.04	.01
☐ 745	Jeff Burroughs	.15	.07	.01
☐ 746	Enos Cabell	.09	.04	.01
☐ 747	Ken Clay	.09	.04	.01
☐ 748	Mark Clear	.15	.07	.01
☐ 749	Larry Cox	.09	.04	.01
☐ 750	Hector Cruz	.09	.04	.01
☐ 751	Victor Cruz	.09	.04	.01
☐ 752	Mike Cubbage	.09	.04	.01
☐ 753	Dick Davis	.09	.04	.01
☐ 754	Brian Doyle	.09	.04	.01
☐ 755	Dick Drago	.09	.04	.01
☐ 756	Leon Durham	.85	.40	.08
☐ 757	Jim Dwyer	.09	.04	.01
☐ 758	Dave Edwards	.09	.04	.01
☐ 759	Jim Essian	.09	.04	.01
☐ 760	Bill Fahey	.09	.04	.01
☐ 761	Rollie Fingers	.80	.40	.08
☐ 762	Carlton Fisk	.50	.25	.05
☐ 763	Barry Foote	.09	.04	.01
☐ 764	Ken Forsch	.15	.07	.01
☐ 765	Kiko Garcia	.09	.04	.01
☐ 766	Cesar Geronimo	.09	.04	.01
☐ 767	Gary Gray	.15	.07	.01
☐ 768	Mickey Hatcher	.15	.07	.01
☐ 769	Steve Henderson	.15	.07	.01
☐ 770	Marc Hill	.09	.04	.01
☐ 771	Butch Hobson	.09	.04	.01
☐ 772	Rick Honeycutt	.15	.07	.01
☐ 773	Roy Howell	.09	.04	.01
☐ 774	Mike Ivie	.09	.04	.01
☐ 775	Roy Lee Jackson	.09	.04	.01
☐ 776	Cliff Johnson	.09	.04	.01
☐ 777	Randy Jones	.15	.07	.01
☐ 778	Ruppert Jones	.15	.07	.01
☐ 779	Mick Kelleher	.09	.04	.01
☐ 780	Terry Kennedy	.20	.10	.02
☐ 781	Dave Kingman	.40	.20	.04
☐ 782	Bob Knepper	.20	.10	.02
☐ 783	Ken Kravec	.09	.04	.01
☐ 784	Bob Lacey	.09	.04	.01
☐ 785	Dennis Lamp	.09	.04	.01
☐ 786	Rafael Landestoy	.09	.04	.01
☐ 787	Ken Landreaux	.15	.07	.01
☐ 788	Carney Lansford	.35	.17	.03
☐ 789	Dave LaRoche	.09	.04	.01
☐ 790	Joe Lefebvre	.09	.04	.01
☐ 791	Ron LeFlore	.15	.07	.01
☐ 792	Randy Lerch	.09	.04	.01
☐ 793	Sixto Lezcano	.15	.07	.01
☐ 794	John Littlefield	.09	.04	.01
☐ 795	Mike Lum	.09	.04	.01
☐ 796	Greg Luzinski	.30	.15	.03
☐ 797	Fred Lynn	.50	.25	.05
☐ 798	Jerry Martin	.09	.04	.01
☐ 799	Buck Martinez	.09	.04	.01
☐ 800	Gary Matthews	.15	.07	.01

		MINT	EXC	G-VG
☐ 801	Mario Mendoza	.09	.04	.01
☐ 802	Larry Milbourne	.09	.04	.01
☐ 803	Rick Miller	.09	.04	.01
☐ 804	John Montefusco	.15	.07	.01
☐ 805	Jerry Morales	.09	.04	.01
☐ 806	Jose Morales	.09	.04	.01
☐ 807	Joe Morgan	1.25	.60	.12
☐ 808	Jerry Mumphrey	.15	.07	.01
☐ 809	Gene Nelson	.20	.10	.02
☐ 810	Ed Ott	.09	.04	.01
☐ 811	Bob Owchinko	.09	.04	.01
☐ 812	Gaylord Perry	1.25	.60	.12
☐ 813	Mike Phillips	.09	.04	.01
☐ 814	Darrell Porter	.15	.07	.01
☐ 815	Mike Proly	.09	.04	.01
☐ 816	Tim Raines	6.50	3.25	.65
☐ 817	Len Randle	.09	.04	.01
☐ 818	Doug Rau	.09	.04	.01
☐ 819	Jeff Reardon	.60	.30	.06
☐ 820	Ken Reitz	.09	.04	.01
☐ 821	Steve Renko	.09	.04	.01
☐ 822	Rick Reuschel	.20	.10	.02
☐ 823	Dave Revering	.09	.04	.01
☐ 824	Dave Roberts	.09	.04	.01
☐ 825	Leon Roberts	.09	.04	.01
☐ 826	Joe Rudi	.15	.07	.01
☐ 827	Kevin Saucier	.09	.04	.01
☐ 828	Tony Scott	.09	.04	.01
☐ 829	Bob Shirley	.09	.04	.01
☐ 830	Ted Simmons	.40	.20	.04
☐ 831	Lary Sorensen	.09	.04	.01
☐ 832	Jim Spencer	.09	.04	.01
☐ 833	Harry Spilman	.09	.04	.01
☐ 834	Fred Stanley	.09	.04	.01
☐ 835	Rusty Staub	.25	.12	.02
☐ 836	Bill Stein	.09	.04	.01
☐ 837	Joe Strain	.09	.04	.01
☐ 838	Bruce Sutter	.50	.25	.05
☐ 839	Don Sutton	1.00	.50	.10
☐ 840	Steve Swisher	.09	.04	.01
☐ 841	Frank Tanana	.15	.07	.01
☐ 842	Gene Tenace	.15	.07	.01
☐ 843	Jason Thompson	.15	.07	.01
☐ 844	Dickie Thon	.25	.12	.02
☐ 845	Bill Travers	.09	.04	.01
☐ 846	Tom Underwood	.09	.04	.01
☐ 847	John Urrea	.09	.04	.01
☐ 848	Mike Vail	.09	.04	.01
☐ 849	Ellis Valentine	.09	.04	.01
☐ 850	Fernando Valenzuela	5.50	2.75	.55
☐ 851	Pete Vuckovich	.15	.07	.01
☐ 852	Mark Wagner	.09	.04	.01
☐ 853	Bob Walk	.15	.07	.01
☐ 854	Claudell Washington	.20	.10	.02
☐ 855	Dave Winfield	1.75	.85	.17
☐ 856	Geoff Zahn	.15	.07	.01
☐ 857	Richie Zisk	.15	.07	.01
☐ 858	Checklist 727-858	.15	.02	.00

1981 Topps Super Home Team

The cards in this 102-card set measure 4 7/8" by 6 7/8". In 1981 Topps issued an attractive series of photos of players from eleven AL and NL teams. The Phillies, Red Sox and Reds each were marketed in twelve-player subsets. Eighteen-player subsets were issued for the following areas: Chicago (nine White Sox and nine Cubs); New York (twelve Yankees and six Mets); Los Angeles (twelve Dodgers and six Angels); and Texas (six Rangers and six Astros). The cards of each subset contain a subset checklist on the reverse. Team sets could be obtained via a mail offer printed on the wrapper. These cards are often sold by the team or team pair. The checklist below is organized alphabetically by team(s); Boston (1-12), Chicago (13-30), Cincinnati (31-42), Los Angeles (43-60), New York (61-78), Philadelphia (79-90), and Texas (91-102).

		MINT	EXC	G-VG
COMPLETE (1-102)		36.00	15.00	3.50
COMMON PLAYER		.20	.10	.02
☐ 1	Tom Burgmeier	.20	.10	.02
☐ 2	Dennis Eckersley	.25	.12	.02
☐ 3	Dwight Evans	.50	.25	.05
☐ 4	Carlton Fisk	.50	.25	.05
☐ 5	Glenn Hoffman	.20	.10	.02
☐ 6	Carney Lansford	.30	.15	.03
☐ 7	Tony Perez	.50	.25	.05
☐ 8	Jim Rice	.90	.45	.09
☐ 9	Bob Stanley	.30	.15	.03
☐ 10	Dave Stapleton	.20	.10	.02
☐ 11	Frank Tanana	.30	.15	.03
☐ 12	Carl Yastrzemski	1.25	.60	.12
☐ 13	Britt Burns	.30	.15	.03
☐ 14	Rich Dotson	.35	.17	.03
☐ 15	Ed Farmer	.20	.10	.02
☐ 16	Lamar Johnson	.20	.10	.02
☐ 17	Ron LeFlore	.25	.12	.02
☐ 18	Chet Lemon	.25	.12	.02
☐ 19	Bob Molinaro	.20	.10	.02
☐ 20	Jim Morrison	.20	.10	.02
☐ 21	Wayne Nordhagen	.20	.10	.02
☐ 22	Tim Blackwell	.20	.10	.02
☐ 23	Bill Buckner	.40	.20	.04
☐ 24	Ivan DeJesus	.20	.10	.02
☐ 25	Leon Durham	.50	.25	.05
☐ 26	Dave Kingman	.50	.25	.05
☐ 27	Mike Krukow	.40	.20	.04
☐ 28	Ken Reitz	.20	.10	.02
☐ 29	Rick Reuschel	.40	.20	.04
☐ 30	Mike Tyson	.20	.10	.02
☐ 31	Johnny Bench	1.00	.50	.10
☐ 32	Dave Collins	.30	.15	.03
☐ 33	Dave Concepcion	.35	.17	.03
☐ 34	Dan Driessen	.25	.12	.02
☐ 35	George Foster	.40	.20	.04
☐ 36	Ken Griffey	.30	.15	.03
☐ 37	Tom Hume	.20	.10	.02
☐ 38	Ray Knight	.30	.15	.03
☐ 39	Joe Nolan	.20	.10	.02
☐ 40	Ron Oester	.25	.12	.02
☐ 41	Tom Seaver	1.00	.50	.10
☐ 42	Mario Soto	.30	.15	.03
☐ 43	Dusty Baker	.25	.12	.02
☐ 44	Ron Cey	.35	.17	.03
☐ 45	Steve Garvey	1.00	.50	.10
☐ 46	Burt Hooton	.20	.10	.02
☐ 47	Steve Howe	.25	.12	.02
☐ 48	Davey Lopes	.30	.15	.03
☐ 49	Rick Monday	.20	.10	.02
☐ 50	Jerry Reuss	.25	.12	.02
☐ 51	Bill Russell	.25	.12	.02
☐ 52	Reggie Smith	.30	.15	.03
☐ 53	Bob Welch	.35	.17	.03
☐ 54	Steve Yeager	.20	.10	.02
☐ 55	Don Baylor	.35	.17	.03
☐ 56	Rick Burleson	.25	.12	.02
☐ 57	Rod Carew	1.00	.50	.10
☐ 58	Bobby Grich	.35	.17	.03
☐ 59	Butch Hobson	.20	.10	.02
☐ 60	Fred Lynn	.50	.25	.05
☐ 61	Rick Cerone	.20	.10	.02
☐ 62	Bucky Dent	.30	.15	.03
☐ 63	Rich Gossage	.50	.25	.05
☐ 64	Ron Guidry	.60	.30	.06
☐ 65	Reggie Jackson	1.25	.60	.12
☐ 66	Tommy John	.50	.25	.05
☐ 67	Ruppert Jones	.20	.10	.02
☐ 68	Rudy May	.20	.10	.02
☐ 69	Graig Nettles	.50	.25	.05
☐ 70	Willie Randolph	.35	.17	.03
☐ 71	Bob Watson	.25	.12	.02
☐ 72	Dave Winfield	1.00	.50	.10
☐ 73	Neil Allen	.25	.12	.02
☐ 74	Doug Flynn	.20	.10	.02
☐ 75	Lee Mazzilli	.25	.12	.02
☐ 76	Rusty Staub	.35	.17	.03
☐ 77	Frank Taveras	.20	.10	.02
☐ 78	Alex Trevino	.20	.10	.02
☐ 79	Bob Boone	.30	.15	.03
☐ 80	Larry Bowa	.35	.17	.03
☐ 81	Steve Carlton	1.00	.50	.10
☐ 82	Greg Luzinski	.30	.15	.03
☐ 83	Garry Maddox	.20	.10	.02
☐ 84	Bake McBride	.20	.10	.02
☐ 85	Tug McGraw	.30	.15	.03
☐ 86	Pete Rose	1.50	.75	.15
☐ 87	Dick Ruthven	.20	.10	.02
☐ 88	Mike Schmidt	1.25	.60	.12
☐ 89	Manny Trillo	.20	.10	.02
☐ 90	Del Unser	.20	.10	.02
☐ 91	Buddy Bell	.50	.25	.05
☐ 92	Jon Matlack	.25	.12	.02
☐ 93	Al Oliver	.40	.20	.04
☐ 94	Mickey Rivers	.25	.12	.02
☐ 95	Jim Sundberg	.25	.12	.02
☐ 96	Bump Wills	.20	.10	.02
☐ 97	Cesar Cedeno	.30	.15	.03

			MINT	EXC	G-VG
☐	98	Jose Cruz	.40	.20	.04
☐	99	Art Howe	.20	.10	.02
☐	100	Terry Puhl	.25	.12	.02
☐	101	Nolan Ryan	1.00	.50	.10
☐	102	Don Sutton	.75	.35	.07

1981 Topps National Super

The cards in this 15-card set measure 4 7/8" by 6 7/8". In a format similar to the Home Team series of 1981 and the Super Star Photo set of 1980, these cards feature excellent photos of the top stars of 1981. The pictures of players appearing in both the regional Home Team and National sets are identical, but Brett, Cooper, Palmer, Parker, and Simmons are unique to the latter and are indicated in the checklist below with an asterisk. The backs of the cards contain the player's name, team and position, and a single copyright line.

			MINT	EXC	G-VG
	COMPLETE SET		4.50	2.25	.45
	COMMON PLAYER		.15	.07	.01
☐	1	Buddy Bell	.15	.07	.01
☐	2	Johnny Bench	.50	.25	.05
☐	3	George Brett *	1.00	.50	.10
☐	4	Rod Carew	.50	.25	.05
☐	5	Cecil Cooper *	.20	.10	.02
☐	6	Steve Garvey	.60	.30	.06
☐	7	Rich Gossage	.25	.12	.02
☐	8	Reggie Jackson	.75	.35	.07
☐	9	Jim Palmer *	.35	.17	.03
☐	10	Dave Parker *	.35	.17	.03
☐	11	Jim Rice	.35	.17	.03
☐	12	Pete Rose	1.00	.50	.10
☐	13	Mike Schmidt	.75	.35	.07
☐	14	Tom Seaver	.50	.25	.05
☐	15	Ted Simmons *	.20	.10	.02

1982 Topps

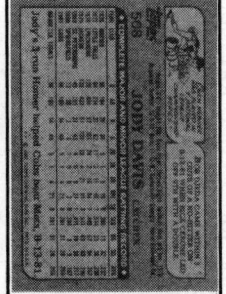

The cards in this 792-card set measure 2 1/2" by 3 1/2". The 1982 baseball series is the largest set Topps has ever issued at one printing. The 66-card increase from the previous year's total eliminated the "double print" practice which had occurred in every regular issue since 1978. Cards 1-6 depict Highlights (HL) of the 1981 season, cards 161-168 picture League Leaders, and there are mini-series of AL (547-557) and NL (337-347) All-Stars (AS). The abbreviation "SA" in the checklist is given for the 40 "Super Action" cards introduced in this set. The team cards are actually Team Leader (TL) cards picturing the batting and pitching leader for that team with a checklist back.

			MINT	EXC	G-VG
	COMPLETE SET		75.00	37.50	7.50
	COMMON PLAYER (1-792)		.05	.02	.00
☐	1	HL: Steve Carlton, Sets new NL strikeout record	.40	.10	.02
☐	2	HL: Ron Davis, Fans 8 straight in relief	.10	.05	.01
☐	3	HL: Tim Raines, Swipes 71 bases as rookie	.25	.12	.02
☐	4	HL: Pete Rose, Sets NL career hits mark	.75	.35	.07
☐	5	HL: Nolan Ryan, Pitches fifth career no-hitter	.35	.17	.03
☐	6	HL: Fern. Valenzuela, 8 shutouts as rookie	.30	.15	.03
☐	7	Scott Sanderson	.05	.02	.00
☐	8	Rich Dauer	.05	.02	.00
☐	9	Ron Guidry	.30	.15	.03
☐	10	SA: Ron Guidry	.15	.07	.01
☐	11	Gary Alexander	.05	.02	.00
☐	12	Moose Haas	.05	.02	.00
☐	13	Lamar Johnson	.05	.02	.00
☐	14	Steve Howe	.10	.05	.01
☐	15	Ellis Valentine	.05	.02	.00
☐	16	Steve Comer	.05	.02	.00
☐	17	Darrell Evans	.15	.07	.01
☐	18	Fernando Arroyo	.05	.02	.00
☐	19	Ernie Whitt	.10	.05	.01
☐	20	Garry Maddox	.05	.02	.00
☐	21	Orioles Rookies: Bob Bonner Cal Ripken Jeff Schneider	12.50	6.25	1.25
☐	22	Jim Beattie	.05	.02	.00
☐	23	Willie Hernandez	.20	.10	.02
☐	24	Dave Frost	.05	.02	.00
☐	25	Jerry Remy	.05	.02	.00
☐	26	Jorge Orta	.05	.02	.00
☐	27	Tom Herr	.15	.07	.01
☐	28	John Urrea	.05	.02	.00
☐	29	Dwayne Murphy	.10	.05	.01
☐	30	Tom Seaver	.60	.30	.06
☐	31	SA: Tom Seaver	.30	.15	.03
☐	32	Gene Garber	.10	.05	.01
☐	33	Jerry Morales	.05	.02	.00
☐	34	Joe Sambito	.10	.05	.01
☐	35	Willie Aikens	.10	.05	.01
☐	36	Rangers TL Mgr. Don Zimmer Batting: Al Oliver Pitching: Doc Medich	.15	.05	.01
☐	37	Dan Graham	.05	.02	.00
☐	38	Charlie Lea	.10	.05	.01
☐	39	Lou Whitaker	.30	.15	.03
☐	40	Dave Parker	.35	.17	.03
☐	41	SA: Dave Parker	.15	.07	.01
☐	42	Rick Sofield	.05	.02	.00
☐	43	Mike Cubbage	.05	.02	.00
☐	44	Britt Burns	.10	.05	.01
☐	45	Rick Cerone	.05	.02	.00
☐	46	Jerry Augustine	.05	.02	.00
☐	47	Jeff Leonard	.20	.10	.02
☐	48	Bobby Castillo	.05	.02	.00
☐	49	Alvis Woods	.05	.02	.00
☐	50	Buddy Bell	.15	.07	.01
☐	51	Cubs Rookies Jay Howell Carlos Lezcano Ty Waller	.35	.17	.03
☐	52	Larry Andersen	.05	.02	.00
☐	53	Greg Gross	.05	.02	.00
☐	54	Ron Hassey	.05	.02	.00
☐	55	Rick Burleson	.10	.05	.01
☐	56	Mark Littell	.05	.02	.00
☐	57	Craig Reynolds	.05	.02	.00
☐	58	John D'Acquisto	.05	.02	.00
☐	59	Rich Gedman	.75	.35	.07
☐	60	Tony Armas	.15	.07	.01
☐	61	Tommy Boggs	.05	.02	.00
☐	62	Mike Tyson	.05	.02	.00
☐	63	Mario Soto	.10	.05	.01
☐	64	Lynn Jones	.05	.02	.00
☐	65	Terry Kennedy	.10	.05	.01
☐	66	Astros TL Mgr. Bill Virdon Batting: Art Howe Pitching: Nolan Ryan	.20	.06	.01
☐	67	Rich Gale	.05	.02	.00
☐	68	Roy Howell	.05	.02	.00
☐	69	Al Williams	.05	.02	.00
☐	70	Tim Raines	1.75	.85	.17

71	Roy Lee Jackson	.05	.02	.00
72	Rick Auerbach	.05	.02	.00
73	Buddy Solomon	.05	.02	.00
74	Bob Clark	.05	.02	.00
75	Tommy John	.25	.12	.02
76	Greg Pryor	.05	.02	.00
77	Miguel Dilone	.05	.02	.00
78	George Medich	.05	.02	.00
79	Bob Bailor	.05	.02	.00
80	Jim Palmer	.50	.25	.05
81	SA: Jim Palmer	.25	.12	.02
82	Bob Welch	.10	.05	.01
83	Yankees Rookies	.50	.25	.05
	Steve Balboni			
	Andy McGaffigan			
	Andre Robertson			
84	Rennie Stennett	.05	.02	.00
85	Lynn McGlothen	.05	.02	.00
86	Dane Iorg	.05	.02	.00
87	Matt Keough	.05	.02	.00
88	Biff Pocoroba	.05	.02	.00
89	Steve Henderson	.05	.02	.00
90	Nolan Ryan	.75	.35	.07
91	Carney Lansford	.15	.07	.01
92	Brad Havens	.05	.02	.00
93	Larry Hisle	.05	.02	.00
94	Andy Hassler	.05	.02	.00
95	Ozzie Smith	.35	.17	.03
96	Royals TL	.20	.06	.01
	Mgr. Jim Frey			
	Batting: George Brett			
	Pitching: Larry Gura			
97	Paul Moskau	.05	.02	.00
98	Terry Bulling	.05	.02	.00
99	Barry Bonnell	.05	.02	.00
100	Mike Schmidt	1.25	.60	.12
101	SA: Mike Schmidt	.50	.25	.05
102	Dan Briggs	.05	.02	.00
103	Bob Lacey	.05	.02	.00
104	Rance Mulliniks	.05	.02	.00
105	Kirk Gibson	.75	.35	.07
106	Enrique Romo	.05	.02	.00
107	Wayne Krenchicki	.05	.02	.00
108	Bob Sykes	.05	.02	.00
109	Dave Revering	.05	.02	.00
110	Carlton Fisk	.25	.12	.02
111	SA: Carlton Fisk	.15	.07	.01
112	Billy Sample	.05	.02	.00
113	Steve McCatty	.05	.02	.00
114	Ken Landreaux	.05	.02	.00
115	Gaylord Perry	.30	.15	.03
116	Jim Wohlford	.05	.02	.00
117	Rawly Eastwick	.05	.02	.00
118	Expos Rookies	.35	.17	.03
	Terry Francona			
	Brad Mills			
	Bryn Smith			
119	Joe Pittman	.05	.02	.00
120	Gary Lucas	.05	.02	.00
121	Ed Lynch	.10	.05	.01
122	Jamie Easterly	.05	.02	.00
	(photo actually			
	Reggie Cleveland)			
123	Danny Goodwin	.05	.02	.00
124	Reid Nichols	.05	.02	.00
125	Danny Ainge	.10	.05	.01
126	Braves TL	.15	.05	.01
	Mgr. Bobby Cox			
	Batting: C.Washington			
	Pitching: Rick Mahler			
127	Lonnie Smith	.10	.05	.01
128	Frank Pastore	.05	.02	.00
129	Checklist 1-132	.10	.01	.00
130	Julio Cruz	.05	.02	.00
131	Stan Bahnsen	.05	.02	.00
132	Lee May	.05	.02	.00
133	Pat Underwood	.05	.02	.00
134	Dan Ford	.05	.02	.00
135	Andy Rincon	.05	.02	.00
136	Lenn Sakata	.05	.02	.00
137	George Cappuzzello	.05	.02	.00
138	Tony Pena	.30	.15	.03
139	Jeff Jones	.05	.02	.00
140	Ron LeFlore	.10	.05	.01
141	Indians Rookies	1.75	.85	.17
	Chris Bando			
	Tom Brennan			
	Von Hayes			
142	Dave LaRoche	.05	.02	.00
143	Mookie Wilson	.10	.05	.01
144	Fred Breining	.10	.05	.01
145	Bob Horner	.35	.17	.03
146	Mike Griffin	.05	.02	.00
147	Denny Walling	.05	.02	.00
148	Mickey Klutts	.05	.02	.00
149	Pat Putnam	.05	.02	.00
150	Ted Simmons	.15	.07	.01
151	Dave Edwards	.05	.02	.00
152	Ramon Aviles	.05	.02	.00
153	Roger Erickson	.05	.02	.00
154	Dennis Werth	.05	.02	.00
155	Otto Velez	.05	.02	.00
156	Oakland A's TL	.20	.06	.01
	Mgr. Billy Martin			
	Batting: R.Henderson			
	Pitching: S. McCatty			
157	Steve Crawford	.10	.05	.01
158	Brian Downing	.10	.05	.01
159	Larry Biittner	.05	.02	.00
160	Luis Tiant	.15	.07	.01
161	Batting Leaders	.15	.07	.01
	Bill Madlock			
	Carney Lansford			
162	Home Run Leaders	.20	.10	.02
	Mike Schmidt			
	Tony Armas			
	Dwight Evans			
	Bobby Grich			
	Eddie Murray			
163	RBI Leaders	.30	.15	.03
	Mike Schmidt			
	Eddie Murray			
164	Stolen Base Leaders	.30	.15	.03
	Tim Raines			
	Rickey Henderson			
165	Victory Leaders	.15	.07	.01
	Tom Seaver			
	Denny Martinez			
	Steve McCatty			
	Jack Morris			
	Pete Vuckovich			
166	Strikeout Leaders	.15	.07	.01
	Fernando Valenzuela			
	Len Barker			
167	ERA Leaders	.15	.07	.01
	Nolan Ryan			
	Steve McCatty			
168	Leading Firemen	.15	.07	.01
	Bruce Sutter			
	Rollie Fingers			
169	Charlie Leibrandt	.15	.07	.01
170	Jim Bibby	.05	.02	.00
171	Giants Rookies	1.25	.60	.12
	Bob Brenly			
	Chili Davis			
	Bob Tufts			
172	Bill Gullickson	.10	.05	.01
173	Jamie Quirk	.05	.02	.00
174	Dave Ford	.05	.02	.00
175	Jerry Mumphrey	.05	.02	.00
176	Dewey Robinson	.05	.02	.00
177	John Ellis	.05	.02	.00
178	Dyar Miller	.05	.02	.00
179	Steve Garvey	.80	.40	.08
180	SA: Steve Garvey	.40	.20	.04
181	Silvio Martinez	.05	.02	.00
182	Larry Herndon	.05	.02	.00
183	Mike Proly	.05	.02	.00
184	Mick Kelleher	.05	.02	.00
185	Phil Niekro	.40	.20	.04
186	Cardinals TL	.20	.06	.01
	Mgr. Whitey Herzog			
	Batting K. Hernandez			
	Pitching Bob Forsch			
187	Jeff Newman	.05	.02	.00
188	Randy Martz	.05	.02	.00
189	Glenn Hoffman	.05	.02	.00
190	J.R. Richard	.10	.05	.01
191	Tim Wallach	2.00	1.00	.20
192	Broderick Perkins	.05	.02	.00
193	Darrell Jackson	.05	.02	.00
194	Mike Vail	.05	.02	.00
195	Paul Molitor	.30	.15	.03
196	Willie Upshaw	.10	.05	.01
197	Shane Rawley	.10	.05	.01
198	Chris Speier	.05	.02	.00
199	Don Aase	.05	.02	.00
200	George Brett	1.50	.75	.15
201	SA: George Brett	.60	.30	.06
202	Rick Manning	.05	.02	.00
203	Blue Jays Rookies	5.00	2.50	.50
	Jesse Barfield			
	Brian Milner			
	Boomer Wells			
204	Gary Roenicke	.05	.02	.00
205	Neil Allen	.10	.05	.01
206	Tony Bernazard	.10	.05	.01
207	Rod Scurry	.05	.02	.00
208	Bobby Murcer	.15	.07	.01
209	Gary Lavelle	.05	.02	.00

☐ 210 Keith Hernandez	.50	.25	.05
☐ 211 Dan Petry	.20	.10	.02
☐ 212 Mario Mendoza	.05	.02	.00
☐ 213 Dave Stewart	.75	.35	.07
☐ 214 Brian Asselstine	.05	.02	.00
☐ 215 Mike Krukow	.10	.05	.01
☐ 216 White Sox TL	.15	.05	.01
Mgr. Tony LaRussa			
Batting: Chet Lemon			
Pitching: Dennis Lamp			
☐ 217 Bo McLaughlin	.05	.02	.00
☐ 218 Dave Roberts	.05	.02	.00
☐ 219 John Curtis	.05	.02	.00
☐ 220 Manny Trillo	.05	.02	.00
☐ 221 Jim Slaton	.05	.02	.00
☐ 222 Butch Wynegar	.05	.02	.00
☐ 223 Lloyd Moseby	.30	.15	.03
☐ 224 Bruce Bochte	.05	.02	.00
☐ 225 Mike Torrez	.05	.02	.00
☐ 226 Checklist 133-264	.10	.01	.00
☐ 227 Ray Burris	.05	.02	.00
☐ 228 Sam Mejias	.05	.02	.00
☐ 229 Geoff Zahn	.05	.02	.00
☐ 230 Willie Wilson	.20	.10	.02
☐ 231 Phillies Rookies	.50	.25	.05
Mark Davis			
Bob Dernier			
Ozzie Virgil			
☐ 232 Terry Crowley	.05	.02	.00
☐ 233 Duane Kuiper	.05	.02	.00
☐ 234 Ron Hodges	.05	.02	.00
☐ 235 Mike Easler	.10	.05	.01
☐ 236 John Martin	.05	.02	.00
☐ 237 Rusty Kuntz	.05	.02	.00
☐ 238 Kevin Saucier	.05	.02	.00
☐ 239 Jon Matlack	.10	.05	.01
☐ 240 Bucky Dent	.10	.05	.01
☐ 241 SA: Bucky Dent	.05	.02	.00
☐ 242 Milt May	.05	.02	.00
☐ 243 Bob Owchinko	.05	.02	.00
☐ 244 Rufino Linares	.05	.02	.00
☐ 245 Ken Reitz	.05	.02	.00
☐ 246 New York Mets TL	.20	.06	.01
Mgr. Joe Torre			
Batting: Hubie Brooks			
Pitching: Mike Scott			
☐ 247 Pedro Guerrero	.75	.35	.07
☐ 248 Frank LaCorte	.05	.02	.00
☐ 249 Tim Flannery	.05	.02	.00
☐ 250 Tug McGraw	.15	.07	.01
☐ 251 Fred Lynn	.30	.15	.03
☐ 252 SA: Fred Lynn	.15	.07	.01
☐ 253 Chuck Baker	.05	.02	.00
☐ 254 Jorge Bell	10.00	5.00	1.00
☐ 255 Tony Perez	.20	.10	.02
☐ 256 SA: Tony Perez	.10	.05	.01
☐ 257 Larry Harlow	.05	.02	.00
☐ 258 Bo Diaz	.10	.05	.01
☐ 259 Rodney Scott	.05	.02	.00
☐ 260 Bruce Sutter	.25	.12	.02
☐ 261 Tigers Rookies	.10	.05	.01
Howard Bailey			
Marty Castillo			
Dave Rucker			
☐ 262 Doug Bair	.05	.02	.00
☐ 263 Victor Cruz	.05	.02	.00
☐ 264 Dan Quisenberry	.20	.10	.02
☐ 265 Al Bumbry	.05	.02	.00
☐ 266 Rick Leach	.05	.02	.00
☐ 267 Kurt Bevacqua	.05	.02	.00
☐ 268 Rickey Keeton	.05	.02	.00
☐ 269 Jim Essian	.05	.02	.00
☐ 270 Rusty Staub	.15	.07	.01
☐ 271 Larry Bradford	.05	.02	.00
☐ 272 Bump Wills	.05	.02	.00
☐ 273 Doug Bird	.05	.02	.00
☐ 274 Bob Ojeda	.80	.40	.08
☐ 275 Bob Watson	.10	.05	.01
☐ 276 Angels TL	.20	.06	.01
Mgr. Gene Mauch			
Batting: Rod Carew			
Pitching: Ken Forsch			
☐ 277 Terry Puhl	.05	.02	.00
☐ 278 John Littlefield	.05	.02	.00
☐ 279 Bill Russell	.05	.02	.00
☐ 280 Ben Oglivie	.10	.05	.01
☐ 281 John Verhoeven	.05	.02	.00
☐ 282 Ken Macha	.05	.02	.00
☐ 283 Brian Allard	.05	.02	.00
☐ 284 Bob Grich	.10	.05	.01
☐ 285 Sparky Lyle	.10	.05	.01
☐ 286 Bill Fahey	.05	.02	.00
☐ 287 Alan Bannister	.05	.02	.00
☐ 288 Garry Templeton	.10	.05	.01
☐ 289 Bob Stanley	.10	.05	.01
☐ 290 Ken Singleton	.15	.07	.01
☐ 291 Pirates Rookies	1.25	.60	.12
Vance Law			
Bob Long			
Johnny Ray			
☐ 292 David Palmer	.10	.05	.01
☐ 293 Rob Picciolo	.05	.02	.00
☐ 294 Mike LaCoss	.05	.02	.00
☐ 295 Jason Thompson	.10	.05	.01
☐ 296 Bob Walk	.05	.02	.00
☐ 297 Clint Hurdle	.05	.02	.00
☐ 298 Danny Darwin	.10	.05	.01
☐ 299 Steve Trout	.10	.05	.01
☐ 300 Reggie Jackson	1.25	.60	.12
☐ 301 SA: Reggie Jackson	.50	.25	.05
☐ 302 Doug Flynn	.05	.02	.00
☐ 303 Bill Caudill	.05	.02	.00
☐ 304 Johnnie LeMaster	.05	.02	.00
☐ 305 Don Sutton	.40	.20	.04
☐ 306 SA: Don Sutton	.20	.10	.02
☐ 307 Randy Bass	.05	.02	.00
☐ 308 Charlie Moore	.05	.02	.00
☐ 309 Pete Redfern	.05	.02	.00
☐ 310 Mike Hargrove	.05	.02	.00
☐ 311 Dodgers TL	.15	.05	.01
Mgr. Tom Lasorda			
Batting: Dusty Baker			
Pitching: Burt Hooton			
☐ 312 Lenny Randle	.05	.02	.00
☐ 313 John Harris	.05	.02	.00
☐ 314 Buck Martinez	.05	.02	.00
☐ 315 Burt Hooton	.05	.02	.00
☐ 316 Steve Braun	.05	.02	.00
☐ 317 Dick Ruthven	.05	.02	.00
☐ 318 Mike Heath	.05	.02	.00
☐ 319 Dave Rozema	.05	.02	.00
☐ 320 Chris Chambliss	.10	.05	.01
☐ 321 SA: Chris Chambliss	.05	.02	.00
☐ 322 Garry Hancock	.05	.02	.00
☐ 323 Bill Lee	.10	.05	.01
☐ 324 Steve Dillard	.05	.02	.00
☐ 325 Jose Cruz	.15	.07	.01
☐ 326 Pete Falcone	.05	.02	.00
☐ 327 Joe Nolan	.05	.02	.00
☐ 328 Ed Farmer	.05	.02	.00
☐ 329 U.L. Washington	.05	.02	.00
☐ 330 Rick Wise	.05	.02	.00
☐ 331 Benny Ayala	.05	.02	.00
☐ 332 Don Robinson	.05	.02	.00
☐ 333 Brewers Rookies	.15	.07	.01
Frank DiPino			
Marshall Edwards			
Chuck Porter			
☐ 334 Aurelio Rodriguez	.05	.02	.00
☐ 335 Jim Sundberg	.10	.05	.01
☐ 336 Mariners TL	.10	.04	.01
Mgr. Rene Lachemann			
Batting: Tom Paciorek			
Pitching: Glenn Abbott			
☐ 337 Pete Rose AS	.75	.35	.07
☐ 338 Dave Lopes AS	.10	.05	.01
☐ 339 Mike Schmidt AS	.40	.20	.04
☐ 340 Dave Concepcion AS	.10	.05	.01
☐ 341 Andre Dawson AS	.20	.10	.02
☐ 342A George Foster AS	.30	.15	.03
(with autograph)			
☐ 342B George Foster AS	2.00	1.00	.20
(w/o autograph)			
☐ 343 Dave Parker AS	.15	.07	.01
☐ 344 Gary Carter AS	.30	.15	.03
☐ 345 Fern. Valenzuela AS	.25	.12	.02
☐ 346 Tom Seaver AS	.25	.12	.02
☐ 347 Bruce Sutter AS	.15	.07	.01
☐ 348 Derrel Thomas	.05	.02	.00
☐ 349 George Frazier	.05	.02	.00
☐ 350 Thad Bosley	.05	.02	.00
☐ 351 Reds Rookies	.10	.05	.01
Scott Brown			
Geoff Coumbe			
Paul Householder			
☐ 352 Dick Davis	.05	.02	.00
☐ 353 Jack O'Connor	.05	.02	.00
☐ 354 Roberto Ramos	.05	.02	.00
☐ 355 Dwight Evans	.25	.12	.02
☐ 356 Denny Lewallyn	.05	.02	.00
☐ 357 Butch Hobson	.05	.02	.00
☐ 358 Mike Parrott	.05	.02	.00
☐ 359 Jim Dwyer	.05	.02	.00
☐ 360 Len Barker	.05	.02	.00
☐ 361 Rafael Landestoy	.05	.02	.00
☐ 362 Jim Wright	.05	.02	.00
☐ 363 Bob Molinaro	.05	.02	.00
☐ 364 Doyle Alexander	.10	.05	.01
☐ 365 Bill Madlock	.20	.10	.02
☐ 366 Padres TL	.10	.04	.01

	Mgr. Frank Howard			
	Batting: Luis Salazar			
	Pitching: Eichelberger			
☐ 367	Jim Kaat	.15	.07	.01
☐ 368	Alex Trevino	.05	.02	.00
☐ 369	Champ Summers	.05	.02	.00
☐ 370	Mike Norris	.05	.02	.00
☐ 371	Jerry Don Gleaton	.05	.02	.00
☐ 372	Luis Gomez	.05	.02	.00
☐ 373	Gene Nelson	.15	.07	.01
☐ 374	Tim Blackwell	.05	.02	.00
☐ 375	Dusty Baker	.10	.05	.01
☐ 376	Chris Welsh	.05	.02	.00
☐ 377	Kiko Garcia	.05	.02	.00
☐ 378	Mike Caldwell	.05	.02	.00
☐ 379	Rob Wilfong	.05	.02	.00
☐ 380	Dave Stieb	.20	.10	.02
☐ 381	Red Sox Rookies	.25	.12	.02
	Bruce Hurst			
	Dave Schmidt			
	Julio Valdez			
☐ 382	Joe Simpson	.05	.02	.00
☐ 383A	Pascual Perez ERR	35.00	17.50	3.50
	(no position			
	on front)			
☐ 383B	Pascual Perez COR	.15	.07	.01
☐ 384	Keith Moreland	.10	.05	.01
☐ 385	Ken Forsch	.05	.02	.00
☐ 386	Jerry White	.05	.02	.00
☐ 387	Tom Veryzer	.05	.02	.00
☐ 388	Joe Rudi	.10	.05	.01
☐ 389	George Vukovich	.05	.02	.00
☐ 390	Eddie Murray	1.25	.60	.12
☐ 391	Dave Tobik	.05	.02	.00
☐ 392	Rick Bosetti	.05	.02	.00
☐ 393	Al Hrabosky	.10	.05	.01
☐ 394	Checklist 265-396	.10	.01	.00
☐ 395	Omar Moreno	.05	.02	.00
☐ 396	Twins TL	.10	.04	.01
	Mgr. Billy Gardner			
	Batting: John Castino			
	Pitching: F. Arroyo			
☐ 397	Ken Brett	.05	.02	.00
☐ 398	Mike Squires	.05	.02	.00
☐ 399	Pat Zachry	.05	.02	.00
☐ 400	Johnny Bench	.75	.35	.07
☐ 401	SA: Johnny Bench	.35	.17	.03
☐ 402	Bill Stein	.05	.02	.00
☐ 403	Jim Tracy	.05	.02	.00
☐ 404	Dickie Thon	.10	.05	.01
☐ 405	Rick Reuschel	.10	.05	.01
☐ 406	Al Holland	.05	.02	.00
☐ 407	Danny Boone	.05	.02	.00
☐ 408	Ed Romero	.05	.02	.00
☐ 409	Don Cooper	.05	.02	.00
☐ 410	Ron Cey	.15	.07	.01
☐ 411	SA: Ron Cey	.10	.05	.01
☐ 412	Luis Leal	.05	.02	.00
☐ 413	Dan Meyer	.05	.02	.00
☐ 414	Elias Sosa	.05	.02	.00
☐ 415	Don Baylor	.15	.07	.01
☐ 416	Marty Bystrom	.05	.02	.00
☐ 417	Pat Kelly	.05	.02	.00
☐ 418	Rangers Rookies	.30	.15	.03
	John Butcher			
	Bobby Johnson			
	Dave Schmidt			
☐ 419	Steve Stone	.10	.05	.01
☐ 420	George Hendrick	.10	.05	.01
☐ 421	Mark Clear	.05	.02	.00
☐ 422	Cliff Johnson	.05	.02	.00
☐ 423	Stan Papi	.05	.02	.00
☐ 424	Bruce Benedict	.05	.02	.00
☐ 425	John Candelaria	.10	.05	.01
☐ 426	Orioles TL	.20	.06	.01
	Mgr. Earl Weaver			
	Batting: Eddie Murray			
	Pitching: Sam Stewart			
☐ 427	Ron Oester	.05	.02	.00
☐ 428	LaMarr Hoyt	.10	.05	.01
☐ 429	John Wathan	.10	.05	.01
☐ 430	Vida Blue	.10	.05	.01
☐ 431	SA: Vida Blue	.05	.02	.00
☐ 432	Mike Scott	.35	.17	.03
☐ 433	Alan Ashby	.05	.02	.00
☐ 434	Joe Lefebvre	.05	.02	.00
☐ 435	Robin Yount	.75	.35	.07
☐ 436	Joe Strain	.05	.02	.00
☐ 437	Juan Berenguer	.10	.05	.01
☐ 438	Pete Mackanin	.05	.02	.00
☐ 439	Dave Righetti	2.50	1.25	.25
☐ 440	Jeff Burroughs	.10	.05	.01
☐ 441	Astros Rookies	.10	.05	.01
	Danny Heep			
	Billy Smith			

	Bobby Sprowl			
☐ 442	Bruce Kison	.05	.02	.00
☐ 443	Mark Wagner	.05	.02	.00
☐ 444	Terry Forster	.10	.05	.01
☐ 445	Larry Parrish	.10	.05	.01
☐ 446	Wayne Garland	.05	.02	.00
☐ 447	Darrell Porter	.10	.05	.01
☐ 448	SA: Darrell Porter	.05	.02	.00
☐ 449	Luis Aguayo	.05	.02	.00
☐ 450	Jack Morris	.50	.25	.05
☐ 451	Ed Miller	.05	.02	.00
☐ 452	Lee Smith	1.00	.50	.10
☐ 453	Art Howe	.05	.02	.00
☐ 454	Rick Langford	.05	.02	.00
☐ 455	Tom Burgmeier	.05	.02	.00
☐ 456	Chicago Cubs TL	.10	.04	.01
	Mgr. Joe Amalfitano			
	Batting: Bill Buckner			
	Pitching: Randy Martz			
☐ 457	Tim Stoddard	.05	.02	.00
☐ 458	Willie Montanez	.05	.02	.00
☐ 459	Bruce Berenyi	.05	.02	.00
☐ 460	Jack Clark	.40	.20	.04
☐ 461	Rich Dotson	.10	.05	.01
☐ 462	Dave Chalk	.05	.02	.00
☐ 463	Jim Kern	.05	.02	.00
☐ 464	Juan Bonilla	.05	.02	.00
☐ 465	Lee Mazzilli	.05	.02	.00
☐ 466	Randy Lerch	.05	.02	.00
☐ 467	Mickey Hatcher	.05	.02	.00
☐ 468	Floyd Bannister	.10	.05	.01
☐ 469	Ed Ott	.05	.02	.00
☐ 470	John Mayberry	.10	.05	.01
☐ 471	Royals Rookies	.30	.15	.03
	Atlee Hammaker			
	Mike Jones			
	Darryl Motley			
☐ 472	Oscar Gamble	.10	.05	.01
☐ 473	Mike Stanton	.05	.02	.00
☐ 474	Ken Oberkfell	.05	.02	.00
☐ 475	Alan Trammell	.50	.25	.05
☐ 476	Brian Kingman	.05	.02	.00
☐ 477	Steve Yeager	.05	.02	.00
☐ 478	Ray Searage	.10	.05	.01
☐ 479	Rowland Office	.05	.02	.00
☐ 480	Steve Carlton	.90	.45	.09
☐ 481	SA: Steve Carlton	.40	.20	.04
☐ 482	Glenn Hubbard	.05	.02	.00
☐ 483	Gary Woods	.05	.02	.00
☐ 484	Ivan DeJesus	.05	.02	.00
☐ 485	Kent Tekulve	.10	.05	.01
☐ 486	Yankees TL	.15	.05	.01
	Mgr. Bob Lemon			
	Batting: J. Mumphrey			
	Pitching: Tommy John			
☐ 487	Bob McClure	.05	.02	.00
☐ 488	Ron Jackson	.05	.02	.00
☐ 489	Rick Dempsey	.10	.05	.01
☐ 490	Dennis Eckersley	.10	.05	.01
☐ 491	Checklist 397-528	.10	.01	.00
☐ 492	Joe Price	.05	.02	.00
☐ 493	Chet Lemon	.10	.05	.01
☐ 494	Hubie Brooks	.25	.12	.02
☐ 495	Dennis Leonard	.10	.05	.01
☐ 496	Johnny Grubb	.05	.02	.00
☐ 497	Jim Anderson	.05	.02	.00
☐ 498	Dave Bergman	.05	.02	.00
☐ 499	Paul Mirabella	.05	.02	.00
☐ 500	Rod Carew	.85	.40	.08
☐ 501	SA: Rod Carew	.40	.20	.04
☐ 502	Braves Rookies	1.50	.75	.15
	Steve Bedrosian			
	Brett Butler			
	Larry Owen			
☐ 503	Julio Gonzalez	.05	.02	.00
☐ 504	Rick Peters	.05	.02	.00
☐ 505	Graig Nettles	.20	.10	.02
☐ 506	SA: Graig Nettles	.10	.05	.01
☐ 507	Terry Harper	.05	.02	.00
☐ 508	Jody Davis	.80	.40	.08
☐ 509	Harry Spilman	.05	.02	.00
☐ 510	Fernando Valenzuela	1.50	.75	.15
☐ 511	Ruppert Jones	.05	.02	.00
☐ 512	Jerry Dybzinski	.05	.02	.00
☐ 513	Rick Rhoden	.10	.05	.01
☐ 514	Joe Ferguson	.05	.02	.00
☐ 515	Larry Bowa	.10	.05	.01
☐ 516	SA: Larry Bowa	.05	.02	.00
☐ 517	Mark Brouhard	.05	.02	.00
☐ 518	Garth Iorg	.05	.02	.00
☐ 519	Glenn Adams	.05	.02	.00
☐ 520	Mike Flanagan	.10	.05	.01
☐ 521	Billy Almon	.05	.02	.00
☐ 522	Chuck Rainey	.05	.02	.00
☐ 523	Gary Gray	.05	.02	.00

☐ 524 Tom Hausman	.05	.02	.00
☐ 525 Ray Knight	.10	.05	.01
☐ 526 Expos TL	.10	.04	.01
Mgr. Jim Fanning			
Batting: W.Cromartie			
Pitching: B.Gullickson			
☐ 527 John Henry Johnson	.05	.02	.00
☐ 528 Matt Alexander	.05	.02	.00
☐ 529 Allen Ripley	.05	.02	.00
☐ 530 Dickie Noles	.05	.02	.00
☐ 531 A's Rookies	.10	.05	.01
Rich Bordi			
Mark Budaska			
Kelvin Moore			
☐ 532 Toby Harrah	.10	.05	.01
☐ 533 Joaquin Andujar	.15	.07	.01
☐ 534 Dave McKay	.05	.02	.00
☐ 535 Lance Parrish	.40	.20	.04
☐ 536 Rafael Ramirez	.05	.02	.00
☐ 537 Doug Capilla	.05	.02	.00
☐ 538 Lou Piniella	.10	.05	.01
☐ 539 Vern Ruhle	.05	.02	.00
☐ 540 Andre Dawson	.50	.25	.05
☐ 541 Barry Evans	.05	.02	.00
☐ 542 Ned Yost	.05	.02	.00
☐ 543 Bill Robinson	.05	.02	.00
☐ 544 Larry Christenson	.05	.02	.00
☐ 545 Reggie Smith	.10	.05	.01
☐ 546 SA: Reggie Smith	.05	.02	.00
☐ 547 Rod Carew AS	.25	.12	.02
☐ 548 Willie Randolph AS	.10	.05	.01
☐ 549 George Brett AS	.40	.20	.04
☐ 550 Bucky Dent AS	.10	.05	.01
☐ 551 Reggie Jackson AS	.35	.17	.03
☐ 552 Ken Singleton AS	.10	.05	.01
☐ 553 Dave Winfield AS	.30	.15	.03
☐ 554 Carlton Fisk AS	.15	.07	.01
☐ 555 Scott McGregor AS	.10	.05	.01
☐ 556 Jack Morris AS	.15	.07	.01
☐ 557 Rich Gossage AS	.15	.07	.01
☐ 558 John Tudor	.35	.17	.03
☐ 559 Indians TL	.10	.04	.01
Mgr. Dave Garcia			
Batting: Mike Hargrove			
Pitching: Bert Blyleven			
☐ 560 Doug Corbett	.05	.02	.00
☐ 561 Cardinals Rookies	.15	.07	.01
Glenn Brummer			
Luis DeLeon			
Gene Roof			
☐ 562 Mike O'Berry	.05	.02	.00
☐ 563 Ross Baumgarten	.05	.02	.00
☐ 564 Doug DeCinces	.15	.07	.01
☐ 565 Jackson Todd	.05	.02	.00
☐ 566 Mike Jorgensen	.05	.02	.00
☐ 567 Bob Babcock	.05	.02	.00
☐ 568 Joe Pettini	.05	.02	.00
☐ 569 Willie Randolph	.10	.05	.01
☐ 570 SA: Willie Randolph	.05	.02	.00
☐ 571 Glenn Abbott	.05	.02	.00
☐ 572 Juan Beniquez	.05	.02	.00
☐ 573 Rick Waits	.05	.02	.00
☐ 574 Mike Ramsey	.05	.02	.00
☐ 575 Al Cowens	.05	.02	.00
☐ 576 Giants TL	.10	.04	.01
Mgr. Frank Robinson			
Batting: Milt May			
Pitching: Vida Blue			
☐ 577 Rick Monday	.10	.05	.01
☐ 578 Shooty Babitt	.05	.02	.00
☐ 579 Rick Mahler	.25	.12	.02
☐ 580 Bobby Bonds	.15	.07	.01
☐ 581 Ron Reed	.05	.02	.00
☐ 582 Luis Pujols	.05	.02	.00
☐ 583 Tippy Martinez	.05	.02	.00
☐ 584 Hosken Powell	.05	.02	.00
☐ 585 Rollie Fingers	.25	.12	.02
☐ 586 SA: Rollie Fingers	.15	.07	.01
☐ 587 Tim Lollar	.05	.02	.00
☐ 588 Dale Berra	.05	.02	.00
☐ 589 Dave Stapleton	.05	.02	.00
☐ 590 Al Oliver	.15	.07	.01
☐ 591 SA: Al Oliver	.10	.05	.01
☐ 592 Craig Swan	.05	.02	.00
☐ 593 Billy Smith	.05	.02	.00
☐ 594 Renie Martin	.05	.02	.00
☐ 595 Dave Collins	.05	.02	.00
☐ 596 Damaso Garcia	.10	.05	.01
☐ 597 Wayne Nordhagen	.05	.02	.00
☐ 598 Bob Galasso	.05	.02	.00
☐ 599 White Sox Rookies	.10	.05	.01
Jay Loviglio			
Reggie Patterson			
Leo Sutherland			
☐ 600 Dave Winfield	.50	.25	.05

☐ 601 Sid Monge	.05	.02	.00
☐ 602 Freddie Patek	.05	.02	.00
☐ 603 Rich Hebner	.05	.02	.00
☐ 604 Orlando Sanchez	.05	.02	.00
☐ 605 Steve Rogers	.10	.05	.01
☐ 606 Blue Jays TL	.10	.04	.01
Mgr. Bobby Mattick			
Batting: J.Mayberry			
Pitching: Dave Stieb			
☐ 607 Leon Durham	.25	.12	.02
☐ 608 Jerry Royster	.05	.02	.00
☐ 609 Rick Sutcliffe	.30	.15	.03
☐ 610 Rickey Henderson	1.50	.75	.15
☐ 611 Joe Niekro	.15	.07	.01
☐ 612 Gary Ward	.10	.05	.01
☐ 613 Jim Gantner	.05	.02	.00
☐ 614 Juan Eichelberger	.05	.02	.00
☐ 615 Bob Boone	.10	.05	.01
☐ 616 SA: Bob Boone	.05	.02	.00
☐ 617 Scott McGregor	.10	.05	.01
☐ 618 Tim Foli	.05	.02	.00
☐ 619 Bill Campbell	.05	.02	.00
☐ 620 Ken Griffey	.10	.05	.01
☐ 621 SA: Ken Griffey	.05	.02	.00
☐ 622 Dennis Lamp	.05	.02	.00
☐ 623 Mets Rookies	.35	.17	.03
Ron Gardenhire			
Terry Leach			
Tim Leary			
☐ 624 Fergie Jenkins	.20	.10	.02
☐ 625 Hal McRae	.10	.05	.01
☐ 626 Randy Jones	.05	.02	.00
☐ 627 Enos Cabell	.05	.02	.00
☐ 628 Bill Travers	.05	.02	.00
☐ 629 Johnny Wockenfuss	.05	.02	.00
☐ 630 Joe Charboneau	.05	.02	.00
☐ 631 Gene Tenace	.05	.02	.00
☐ 632 Bryan Clark	.05	.02	.00
☐ 633 Mitchell Page	.05	.02	.00
☐ 634 Checklist 529-660	.10	.01	.00
☐ 635 Ron Davis	.05	.02	.00
☐ 636 Phillies TL	.35	.10	.02
Mgr. Dallas Green			
Batting: Pete Rose			
Pitching: S.Carlton			
☐ 637 Rick Camp	.05	.02	.00
☐ 638 John Milner	.05	.02	.00
☐ 639 Ken Kravec	.05	.02	.00
☐ 640 Cesar Cedeno	.10	.05	.01
☐ 641 Steve Mura	.05	.02	.00
☐ 642 Mike Scioscia	.05	.02	.00
☐ 643 Pete Vuckovich	.15	.07	.01
☐ 644 John Castino	.05	.02	.00
☐ 645 Frank White	.10	.05	.01
☐ 646 SA: Frank White	.05	.02	.00
☐ 647 Warren Brusstar	.05	.02	.00
☐ 648 Jose Morales	.05	.02	.00
☐ 649 Ken Clay	.05	.02	.00
☐ 650 Carl Yastrzemski	1.25	.60	.12
☐ 651 SA: Carl Yastrzemski	.50	.25	.05
☐ 652 Steve Nicosia	.05	.02	.00
☐ 653 Angels Rookies	2.00	1.00	.20
Tom Brunansky			
Luis Sanchez			
Daryl Sconiers			
☐ 654 Jim Morrison	.05	.02	.00
☐ 655 Joel Youngblood	.05	.02	.00
☐ 656 Eddie Whitson	.05	.02	.00
☐ 657 Tom Poquette	.05	.02	.00
☐ 658 Tito Landrum	.05	.02	.00
☐ 659 Fred Martinez	.05	.02	.00
☐ 660 Dave Concepcion	.10	.05	.01
☐ 661 SA: Dave Concepcion	.05	.02	.00
☐ 662 Luis Salazar	.05	.02	.00
☐ 663 Hector Cruz	.05	.02	.00
☐ 664 Dan Spillner	.05	.02	.00
☐ 665 Jim Clancy	.05	.02	.00
☐ 666 Tigers TL	.10	.04	.01
Mgr. Sparky Anderson			
Batting: Steve Kemp			
Pitching: Dan Petry			
☐ 667 Jeff Reardon	.25	.12	.02
☐ 668 Dale Murphy	2.00	1.00	.20
☐ 669 Larry Milbourne	.05	.02	.00
☐ 670 Steve Kemp	.10	.05	.01
☐ 671 Mike Davis	.20	.10	.02
☐ 672 Bob Knepper	.10	.05	.01
☐ 673 Keith Drumright	.05	.02	.00
☐ 674 Dave Goltz	.05	.02	.00
☐ 675 Cecil Cooper	.20	.10	.02
☐ 676 Sal Butera	.05	.02	.00
☐ 677 Alfredo Griffin	.10	.05	.01
☐ 678 Tom Paciorek	.10	.05	.01
☐ 679 Sammy Stewart	.05	.02	.00
☐ 680 Gary Matthews	.10	.05	.01

☐ 681	Dodgers Rookies	3.00	1.50	.30
	Mike Marshall			
	Ron Roenicke			
	Steve Sax			
☐ 682	Jesse Jefferson	.05	.02	.00
☐ 683	Phil Garner	.05	.02	.00
☐ 684	Harold Baines	.65	.30	.06
☐ 685	Bert Blyleven	.20	.10	.02
☐ 686	Gary Allenson	.05	.02	.00
☐ 687	Greg Minton	.05	.02	.00
☐ 688	Leon Roberts	.05	.02	.00
☐ 689	Lary Sorensen	.05	.02	.00
☐ 690	Dave Kingman ✓	.20	.10	.02
☐ 691	Dan Schatzeder	.05	.02	.00
☐ 692	Wayne Gross	.05	.02	.00
☐ 693	Cesar Geronimo	.05	.02	.00
☐ 694	Dave Wehrmeister	.05	.02	.00
☐ 695	Warren Cromartie	.05	.02	.00
☐ 696	Pirates TL	.10	.04	.01
	Mgr. Chuck Tanner			
	Batting: Bill Madlock			
	Pitching:Eddie Solomon			
☐ 697	John Montefusco	.05	.02	.00
☐ 698	Tony Scott	.05	.02	.00
☐ 699	Dick Tidrow	.05	.02	.00
☐ 700	George Foster	.25	.12	.02
☐ 701	SA: George Foster	.10	.05	.01
☐ 702	Steve Renko	.05	.02	.00
☐ 703	Brewers TL	.10	.04	.01
	Mgr. Bob Rodgers			
	Batting: Cecil Cooper			
	Pitching: P.Vuckovich ✓			
☐ 704	Mickey Rivers ✓	.05	.02	.00
☐ 705	SA: Mickey Rivers	.05	.02	.00
☐ 706	Barry Foote	.05	.02	.00
☐ 707	Mark Bomback	.05	.02	.00
☐ 708	Gene Richards	.05	.02	.00
☐ 709	Don Money ✓	.05	.02	.00
☐ 710	Jerry Reuss ✓	.10	.05	.01
☐ 711	Mariners Rookies	.30	.15	.03
	Dave Edler			
	Dave Henderson			
	Reggie Walton			
☐ 712	Denny Martinez	.10	.05	.01
☐ 713	Del Unser	.05	.02	.00
☐ 714	Jerry Koosman	.15	.07	.01
☐ 715	Willie Stargell	.45	.22	.04
☐ 716	SA: Willie Stargell	.20	.10	.02
☐ 717	Rick Miller	.05	.02	.00
☐ 718	Charlie Hough	.10	.05	.01
☐ 719	Jerry Narron	.05	.02	.00
☐ 720	Greg Luzinski	.15	.07	.01
☐ 721	SA: Greg Luzinski	.10	.05	.01
☐ 722	Jerry Martin	.05	.02	.00
☐ 723	Junior Kennedy	.05	.02	.00
☐ 724	Dave Rosello	.05	.02	.00
☐ 725	Amos Otis	.10	.05	.01
☐ 726	SA: Amos Otis	.05	.02	.00
☐ 727	Sixto Lezcano	.05	.02	.00
☐ 728	Aurelio Lopez	.05	.02	.00
☐ 729	Jim Spencer	.05	.02	.00
☐ 730	Gary Carter	.90	.45	.09
☐ 731	Padres Rookies	.10	.05	.01
	Mike Armstrong			
	Doug Gwosdz			
	Fred Kuhaulua			
☐ 732	Mike Lum	.05	.02	.00
☐ 733	Larry McWilliams	.05	.02	.00
☐ 734	Mike Ivie	.05	.02	.00
☐ 735	Rudy May	.05	.02	.00
☐ 736	Jerry Turner	.05	.02	.00
☐ 737	Reggie Cleveland	.05	.02	.00
☐ 738	Dave Engle	.05	.02	.00
☐ 739	Joey McLaughlin ✓	.05	.02	.00
☐ 740	Dave Lopes ✓	.10	.05	.01
☐ 741	SA: Dave Lopes	.05	.02	.00
☐ 742	Dick Drago	.05	.02	.00
☐ 743	John Stearns	.05	.02	.00
☐ 744	Mike Witt	1.50	.75	.15
☐ 745	Bake McBride	.05	.02	.00
☐ 746	Andre Thornton	.10	.05	.01
☐ 747	John Lowenstein	.05	.02	.00
☐ 748	Marc Hill	.05	.02	.00
☐ 749	Bob Shirley	.05	.02	.00
☐ 750	Jim Rice	.80	.40	.08
☐ 751	Rick Honeycutt	.10	.05	.01
☐ 752	Lee Lacy	.10	.05	.01
☐ 753	Tom Brookens ✓	.05	.02	.00
☐ 754	Joe Morgan	.35	.17	.03
☐ 755	SA: Joe Morgan	.15	.07	.01
☐ 756	Reds TL	.20	.06	.01
	Mgr. John McNamara			
	Batting: Ken Griffey			
	Pitching: Tom Seaver			
☐ 757	Tom Underwood	.05	.02	.00

☐ 758	Claudell Washington	.10	.05	.01
☐ 759	Paul Splittorff	.05	.02	.00
☐ 760	Bill Buckner	.15	.07	.01
☐ 761	Dave Smith	.15	.07	.01
☐ 762	Mike Phillips	.05	.02	.00
☐ 763	Tom Hume	.05	.02	.00
☐ 764	Steve Swisher	.05	.02	.00
☐ 765	Gorman Thomas	.15	.07	.01
☐ 766	Twins Rookies	4.00	2.00	.40
	Lenny Faedo			
	Kent Hrbek			
	Tim Laudner			
☐ 767	Roy Smalley	.10	.05	.01
☐ 768	Jerry Garvin	.05	.02	.00
☐ 769	Richie Zisk	.10	.05	.01
☐ 770	Rich Gossage	.25	.12	.02
☐ 771	SA: Rich Gossage	.10	.05	.01
☐ 772	Bert Campaneris	.10	.05	.01
☐ 773	John Denny	.10	.05	.01
☐ 774	Jay Johnstone	.10	.05	.01
☐ 775	Bob Forsch	.10	.05	.01
☐ 776	Mark Belanger	.10	.05	.01
☐ 777	Tom Griffin	.05	.02	.00
☐ 778	Kevin Hickey	.05	.02	.00
☐ 779	Grant Jackson	.05	.02	.00
☐ 780	Pete Rose	2.25	1.10	.22
☐ 781	SA: Pete Rose	.75	.35	.07
☐ 782	Frank Taveras	.05	.02	.00
☐ 783	Greg Harris	.25	.12	.02
☐ 784	Milt Wilcox	.05	.02	.00
☐ 785	Dan Driessen	.10	.05	.01
☐ 786	Red Sox TL	.10	.04	.01
	Mgr. Ralph Houk			
	Batting: C.Lansford			
	Pitching: Mike Torrez			
☐ 787	Fred Stanley	.05	.02	.00
☐ 788	Woodie Fryman	.05	.02	.00
☐ 789	Checklist 661-792	.10	.01	.00
☐ 790	Larry Gura	.10	.05	.01
☐ 791	Bobby Brown	.05	.02	.00
☐ 792	Frank Tanana	.20	.05	.01

1982 Topps Traded

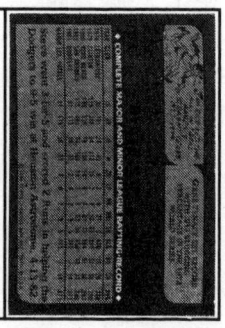

The cards in this 132-card set measure 2 1/2" by 3 1/2". The 1982 Topps Traded or extended series is distinguished by a "T" printed after the number (located on the reverse). Of the total cards, 70 players represent the American League and 61 represent the National League, with the remaining card a numbered checklist (132T). The Cubs lead the pack with 12 changes while the Red Sox are the only team in either league to have no new additions. All 131 player photos used in the set are completely new. Of this total, 112 individuals are seen in the uniform of their new team, 11 others have been elevated to single card status from "Future Stars" cards, and eight more are entirely new to the 1982 Topps lineup. The backs are almost completely red in color with black print.

	MINT	EXC	G-VG
COMPLETE SET	21.00	10.50	2.10
COMMON PLAYER	.09	.04	.01
☐ 1T Doyle Alexander	.15	.07	.01

☐	2T Jesse Barfield	3.50	1.75	.35
☐	3T Ross Baumgarten	.09	.04	.01
☐	4T Steve Bedrosian	.90	.45	.09
☐	5T Mark Belanger	.15	.07	.01
☐	6T Kurt Bevacqua	.09	.04	.01
☐	7T Tim Blackwell	.09	.04	.01
☐	8T Vida Blue	.20	.10	.02
☐	9T Bob Boone	.15	.07	.01
☐	10T Larry Bowa	.25	.12	.02
☐	11T Dan Briggs	.09	.04	.01
☐	12T Bobby Brown	.09	.04	.01
☐	13T Tom Brunansky	1.50	.75	.15
☐	14T Jeff Burroughs	.15	.07	.01
☐	15T Enos Cabell	.09	.04	.01
☐	16T Bill Campbell	.09	.04	.01
☐	17T Bobby Castillo	.09	.04	.01
☐	18T Bill Caudill	.15	.07	.01
☐	19T Cesar Cedeno	.20	.10	.02
☐	20T Dave Collins	.15	.07	.01
☐	21T Doug Corbett	.15	.07	.01
☐	22T Al Cowens	.09	.04	.01
☐	23T Chili Davis	1.25	.60	.12
☐	24T Dick Davis	.09	.04	.01
☐	25T Ron Davis	.09	.04	.01
☐	26T Doug DeCinces	.25	.12	.02
☐	27T Ivan DeJesus	.09	.04	.01
☐	28T Bob Dernier	.25	.12	.02
☐	29T Bo Diaz	.20	.10	.02
☐	30T Roger Erickson	.09	.04	.01
☐	31T Jim Essian	.09	.04	.01
☐	32T Ed Farmer	.09	.04	.01
☐	33T Doug Flynn	.09	.04	.01
☐	34T Tim Foli	.09	.04	.01
☐	35T Dan Ford	.09	.04	.01
☐	36T George Foster	.40	.20	.04
☐	37T Dave Frost	.09	.04	.01
☐	38T Rich Gale	.09	.04	.01
☐	39T Ron Gardenhire	.15	.07	.01
☐	40T Ken Griffey	.20	.10	.02
☐	41T Greg Harris	.15	.07	.01
☐	42T Von Hayes	1.75	.85	.17
☐	43T Larry Herndon	.15	.07	.01
☐	44T Kent Hrbek	3.50	1.75	.35
☐	45T Mike Ivie	.09	.04	.01
☐	46T Grant Jackson	.09	.04	.01
☐	47T Reggie Jackson	2.50	1.25	.25
☐	48T Ron Jackson	.09	.04	.01
☐	49T Fergie Jenkins	.35	.17	.03
☐	50T Lamar Johnson	.09	.04	.01
☐	51T Randy Johnson	.09	.04	.01
☐	52T Jay Johnstone	.15	.07	.01
☐	53T Mick Kelleher	.09	.04	.01
☐	54T Steve Kemp	.15	.07	.01
☐	55T Junior Kennedy	.09	.04	.01
☐	56T Jim Kern	.09	.04	.01
☐	57T Ray Knight	.25	.12	.02
☐	58T Wayne Krenchicki	.09	.04	.01
☐	59T Mike Krukow	.20	.10	.02
☐	60T Duane Kuiper	.09	.04	.01
☐	61T Mike LaCoss	.09	.04	.01
☐	62T Chet Lemon	.20	.10	.02
☐	63T Sixto Lezcano	.15	.07	.01
☐	64T Dave Lopes	.20	.10	.02
☐	65T Jerry Martin	.09	.04	.01
☐	66T Renie Martin	.09	.04	.01
☐	67T John Mayberry	.15	.07	.01
☐	68T Lee Mazzilli	.15	.07	.01
☐	69T Bake McBride	.15	.07	.01
☐	70T Dan Meyer	.09	.04	.01
☐	71T Larry Milbourne	.09	.04	.01
☐	72T Eddie Milner	.35	.17	.03
☐	73T Sid Monge	.09	.04	.01
☐	74T John Montefusco	.15	.07	.01
☐	75T Jose Morales	.09	.04	.01
☐	76T Keith Moreland	.30	.15	.03
☐	77T Jim Morrison	.09	.04	.01
☐	78T Rance Mulliniks	.09	.04	.01
☐	79T Steve Mura	.09	.04	.01
☐	80T Gene Nelson	.15	.07	.01
☐	81T Joe Nolan	.09	.04	.01
☐	82T Dickie Noles	.09	.04	.01
☐	83T Al Oliver	.25	.12	.02
☐	84T Jorge Orta	.09	.04	.01
☐	85T Tom Paciorek	.09	.04	.01
☐	86T Larry Parrish	.20	.10	.02
☐	87T Jack Perconte	.09	.04	.01
☐	88T Gaylord Perry	1.00	.50	.10
☐	89T Rob Picciolo	.09	.04	.01
☐	90T Joe Pittman	.09	.04	.01
☐	91T Hosken Powell	.09	.04	.01
☐	92T Mike Proly	.09	.04	.01
☐	93T Greg Pryor	.09	.04	.01
☐	94T Charlie Puleo	.15	.07	.01
☐	95T Shane Rawley	.20	.10	.02
☐	96T Johnny Ray	.90	.45	.09

☐	97T Dave Revering	.09	.04	.01
☐	98T Cal Ripken	8.50	4.25	.85
☐	99T Allen Ripley	.09	.04	.01
☐	100T Bill Robinson	.15	.07	.01
☐	101T Aurelio Rodriguez	.09	.04	.01
☐	102T Joe Rudi	.15	.07	.01
☐	103T Steve Sax	1.50	.75	.15
☐	104T Dan Schatzeder	.09	.04	.01
☐	105T Bob Shirley	.09	.04	.01
☐	106T Eric Show	.35	.17	.03
☐	107T Roy Smalley	.15	.07	.01
☐	108T Lonnie Smith	.20	.10	.02
☐	109T Ozzie Smith	.85	.40	.08
☐	110T Reggie Smith	.20	.10	.02
☐	111T Lary Sorensen	.09	.04	.01
☐	112T Elias Sosa	.09	.04	.01
☐	113T Mike Stanton	.09	.04	.01
☐	114T Steve Stroughter	.09	.04	.01
☐	115T Champ Summers	.09	.04	.01
☐	116T Rick Sutcliffe	.40	.20	.04
☐	117T Frank Tanana	.15	.07	.01
☐	118T Frank Taveras	.09	.04	.01
☐	119T Garry Templeton	.20	.10	.02
☐	120T Alex Trevino	.09	.04	.01
☐	121T Jerry Turner	.09	.04	.01
☐	122T Ed VandeBerg	.25	.12	.02
☐	123T Tom Veryzer	.09	.04	.01
☐	124T Ron Washington	.09	.04	.01
☐	125T Bob Watson	.15	.07	.01
☐	126T Dennis Werth	.09	.04	.01
☐	127T Eddie Whitson	.15	.07	.01
☐	128T Rob Wilfong	.09	.04	.01
☐	129T Bump Wills	.09	.04	.01
☐	130T Gary Woods	.09	.04	.01
☐	131T Butch Wynegar	.15	.07	.01
☐	132T Checklist: 1-132	.15	.02	.00

1983 Topps

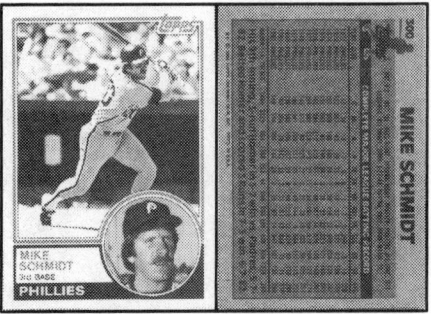

The cards in this 792-card set measure 2 1/2" by 3 1/2". Each regular card of the Topps set for 1983 features a large action shot of a player with a small cameo portrait at bottom right. There are special series for AL and NL All Stars (386-407), League Leaders (701-708) and Record Breakers (1-6). In addition, there are 34 "Super Veteran" (SV) cards and six numbered checklist cards. The Super Veteran cards are oriented horizontally and show two pictures of the featured player, a recent picture and a picture showing the player as a rookie when he broke in. The cards are numbered on the reverse at the upper left corner. The team cards are actually Team Leader (TL) cards picturing the batting and pitching leader for that team with a checklist back.

		MINT	EXC	G-VG
	COMPLETE SET	85.00	42.50	8.50
	COMMON PLAYER (1-792)	.05	.02	.00
☐	1 RB: Tony Armas 11 putouts by rightfielder	.15	.03	.01
☐	2 RB: Rickey Henderson Sets modern record for steals, season	.25	.12	.02
☐	3 RB: Greg Minton	.10	.05	.01

269 1/3 homerless innings streak

4	RB: Lance Parrish — Threw out three baserunners in All-Star game	.15	.07	.01
5	RB: Manny Trillo — 479 consecutive errorless chances, second baseman	.10	.05	.01
6	RB: John Wathan — ML steals record for catchers, 31	.10	.05	.01
7	Gene Richards	.05	.02	.00
8	Steve Balboni	.10	.05	.01
9	Joey McLaughlin	.05	.02	.00
10	Gorman Thomas	.15	.07	.01
11	Billy Gardner MG	.05	.02	.00
12	Paul Mirabella	.05	.02	.00
13	Larry Herndon	.10	.05	.01
14	Frank LaCorte	.05	.02	.00
15	Ron Cey	.15	.07	.01
16	George Vukovich	.05	.02	.00
17	Kent Tekulve	.10	.05	.01
18	SV: Kent Tekulve	.05	.02	.00
19	Oscar Gamble	.10	.05	.01
20	Carlton Fisk	.20	.10	.02
21	Baltimore Orioles TL — BA: Eddie Murray / ERA: Jim Palmer	.25	.07	.01
22	Randy Martz	.05	.02	.00
23	Mike Heath	.05	.02	.00
24	Steve Mura	.05	.02	.00
25	Hal McRae	.10	.05	.01
26	Jerry Royster	.05	.02	.00
27	Doug Corbett	.05	.02	.00
28	Bruce Bochte	.05	.02	.00
29	Randy Jones	.05	.02	.00
30	Jim Rice	.50	.25	.05
31	Bill Gullickson	.10	.05	.01
32	Dave Bergman	.05	.02	.00
33	Jack O'Connor	.05	.02	.00
34	Paul Householder	.05	.02	.00
35	Rollie Fingers	.25	.12	.02
36	SV: Rollie Fingers	.10	.05	.01
37	Darrell Johnson MG	.05	.02	.00
38	Tim Flannery	.05	.02	.00
39	Terry Puhl	.10	.05	.01
40	Fernando Valenzuela	.50	.25	.05
41	Jerry Turner	.05	.02	.00
42	Dale Murray	.05	.02	.00
43	Bob Dernier	.10	.05	.01
44	Don Robinson	.05	.02	.00
45	John Mayberry	.05	.02	.00
46	Richard Dotson	.10	.05	.01
47	Dave McKay	.05	.02	.00
48	Lary Sorensen	.05	.02	.00
49	Willie McGee	2.50	1.25	.25
50	Bob Horner ('82 RBI total 7)	.30	.15	.03
51	Chicago Cubs TL — BA: Leon Durham / ERA: Fergie Jenkins	.15	.04	.01
52	Onix Concepcion	.05	.02	.00
53	Mike Witt	.30	.15	.03
54	Jim Maler	.05	.02	.00
55	Mookie Wilson	.10	.05	.01
56	Chuck Rainey	.05	.02	.00
57	Tim Blackwell	.05	.02	.00
58	Al Holland	.05	.02	.00
59	Benny Ayala	.05	.02	.00
60	Johnny Bench	.55	.27	.05
61	SV: Johnny Bench	.25	.12	.02
62	Bob McClure	.05	.02	.00
63	Rick Monday	.10	.05	.01
64	Bill Stein	.05	.02	.00
65	Jack Morris	.30	.15	.03
66	Bob Lillis MG	.05	.02	.00
67	Sal Butera	.05	.02	.00
68	Eric Show	.20	.10	.02
69	Lee Lacy	.10	.05	.01
70	Steve Carlton	.55	.27	.05
71	SV: Steve Carlton	.25	.12	.02
72	Tom Paciorek	.05	.02	.00
73	Allen Ripley	.05	.02	.00
74	Julio Gonzalez	.05	.02	.00
75	Amos Otis	.10	.05	.01
76	Rick Mahler	.05	.02	.00
77	Hosken Powell	.05	.02	.00
78	Bill Caudill	.05	.02	.00
79	Mick Kelleher	.05	.02	.00
80	George Foster	.20	.10	.02
81	Yankees TL — BA: Jerry Mumphrey / ERA: Dave Righetti	.15	.04	.01
82	Bruce Hurst	.20	.10	.02
83	Ryne Sandberg	6.50	3.25	.65
84	Milt May	.05	.02	.00
85	Ken Singleton	.10	.05	.01
86	Tom Hume	.05	.02	.00
87	Joe Rudi	.10	.05	.01
88	Jim Gantner	.05	.02	.00
89	Leon Roberts	.05	.02	.00
90	Jerry Reuss	.10	.05	.01
91	Larry Milbourne	.05	.02	.00
92	Mike LaCoss	.05	.02	.00
93	John Castino	.05	.02	.00
94	Dave Edwards	.05	.02	.00
95	Alan Trammell	.35	.17	.03
96	Dick Howser MG	.10	.05	.01
97	Ross Baumgarten	.05	.02	.00
98	Vance Law	.05	.02	.00
99	Dickie Noles	.05	.02	.00
100	Pete Rose	2.00	1.00	.20
101	SV: Pete Rose	.75	.35	.07
102	Dave Beard	.05	.02	.00
103	Darrell Porter	.05	.02	.00
104	Bob Walk	.05	.02	.00
105	Don Baylor	.15	.07	.01
106	Gene Nelson	.05	.02	.00
107	Mike Jorgensen	.05	.02	.00
108	Glenn Hoffman	.05	.02	.00
109	Luis Leal	.05	.02	.00
110	Ken Griffey	.10	.05	.01
111	Montreal Expos TL — BA: Al Oliver / ERA: Steve Rogers	.15	.04	.01
112	Bob Shirley	.05	.02	.00
113	Ron Roenicke	.05	.02	.00
114	Jim Slaton	.05	.02	.00
115	Chili Davis	.15	.07	.01
116	Dave Schmidt	.10	.05	.01
117	Alan Knicely	.05	.02	.00
118	Chris Welsh	.05	.02	.00
119	Tom Brookens	.05	.02	.00
120	Len Barker	.05	.02	.00
121	Mickey Hatcher	.05	.02	.00
122	Jimmy Smith	.05	.02	.00
123	George Frazier	.05	.02	.00
124	Marc Hill	.05	.02	.00
125	Leon Durham	.15	.07	.01
126	Joe Torre MG	.10	.05	.01
127	Preston Hanna	.05	.02	.00
128	Mike Ramsey	.05	.02	.00
129	Checklist: 1-132	.10	.01	.00
130	Dave Stieb	.20	.10	.02
131	Ed Ott	.05	.02	.00
132	Todd Cruz	.05	.02	.00
133	Jim Barr	.05	.02	.00
134	Hubie Brooks	.20	.10	.02
135	Dwight Evans	.20	.10	.02
136	Willie Aikens	.05	.02	.00
137	Woodie Fryman	.05	.02	.00
138	Rick Dempsey	.05	.02	.00
139	Bruce Berenyi	.05	.02	.00
140	Willie Randolph	.10	.05	.01
141	Indians TL — BA: Toby Harrah / ERA: Rick Sutcliffe	.10	.03	.01
142	Mike Caldwell	.05	.02	.00
143	Joe Pettini	.05	.02	.00
144	Mark Wagner	.05	.02	.00
145	Don Sutton	.30	.15	.03
146	SV: Don Sutton	.15	.07	.01
147	Rick Leach	.05	.02	.00
148	Dave Roberts	.05	.02	.00
149	Johnny Ray	.20	.10	.02
150	Bruce Sutter	.20	.10	.02
151	SV: Bruce Sutter	.10	.05	.01
152	Jay Johnstone	.10	.05	.01
153	Jerry Koosman	.10	.05	.01
154	Johnnie LeMaster	.05	.02	.00
155	Dan Quisenberry	.20	.10	.02
156	Billy Martin MG	.15	.07	.01
157	Steve Bedrosian	.20	.10	.02
158	Rob Wilfong	.05	.02	.00
159	Mike Stanton	.05	.02	.00
160	Dave Kingman	.15	.07	.01
161	SV: Dave Kingman	.10	.05	.01
162	Mark Clear	.05	.02	.00
163	Cal Ripken	2.00	1.00	.20
164	David Palmer	.05	.02	.00
165	Dan Driessen	.05	.02	.00
166	John Pacella	.05	.02	.00
167	Mark Brouhard	.05	.02	.00
168	Juan Eichelberger	.05	.02	.00
169	Doug Flynn	.05	.02	.00
170	Steve Howe	.05	.02	.00
171	Giants TL — BA: Joe Morgan	.15	.05	.01

ERA: Bill Laskey

☐ 172	Vern Ruhle	.05	.02	.00
☐ 173	Jim Morrison	.05	.02	.00
☐ 174	Jerry Ujdur	.05	.02	.00
☐ 175	Bo Diaz	.10	.05	.01
☐ 176	Dave Righetti	.35	.17	.03
☐ 177	Harold Baines	.30	.15	.03
☐ 178	Luis Tiant	.10	.05	.01
☐ 179	SV: Luis Tiant	.05	.02	.00
☐ 180	Rickey Henderson	.75	.35	.07
☐ 181	Terry Felton	.05	.02	.00
☐ 182	Mike Fischlin	.05	.02	.00
☐ 183	Ed VandeBerg	.10	.05	.01
☐ 184	Bob Clark	.05	.02	.00
☐ 185	Tim Lollar	.05	.02	.00
☐ 186	Whitey Herzog MG	.05	.02	.00
☐ 187	Terry Leach	.15	.07	.01
☐ 188	Rick Miller	.05	.02	.00
☐ 189	Dan Schatzeder	.05	.02	.00
☐ 190	Cecil Cooper	.15	.07	.01
☐ 191	Joe Price	.05	.02	.00
☐ 192	Floyd Rayford	.05	.02	.00
☐ 193	Harry Spilman	.05	.02	.00
☐ 194	Cesar Geronimo	.05	.02	.00
☐ 195	Bob Stoddard	.05	.02	.00
☐ 196	Bill Fahey	.05	.02	.00
☐ 197	Jim Eisenreich	.35	.17	.03
☐ 198	Kiko Garcia	.05	.02	.00
☐ 199	Marty Bystrom	.05	.02	.00
☐ 200	Rod Carew	.65	.30	.06
☐ 201	SV: Rod Carew	.25	.12	.02
☐ 202	Blue Jays TL	.10	.03	.01

BA: Damaso Garcia
ERA: Dave Stieb

☐ 203	Mike Morgan	.05	.02	.00
☐ 204	Junior Kennedy	.05	.02	.00
☐ 205	Dave Parker	.30	.15	.03
☐ 206	Ken Oberkfell	.05	.02	.00
☐ 207	Rick Camp	.05	.02	.00
☐ 208	Dan Meyer	.05	.02	.00
☐ 209	Mike Moore	.30	.15	.03
☐ 210	Jack Clark	.35	.17	.03
☐ 211	John Denny	.10	.05	.01
☐ 212	John Stearns	.05	.02	.00
☐ 213	Tom Burgmeier	.05	.02	.00
☐ 214	Jerry White	.05	.02	.00
☐ 215	Mario Soto	.10	.05	.01
☐ 216	Tony LaRussa MG	.05	.02	.00
☐ 217	Tim Stoddard	.05	.02	.00
☐ 218	Roy Howell	.05	.02	.00
☐ 219	Mike Armstrong	.05	.02	.00
☐ 220	Dusty Baker	.10	.05	.01
☐ 221	Joe Niekro	.10	.05	.01
☐ 222	Damaso Garcia	.10	.05	.01
☐ 223	John Montefusco	.05	.02	.00
☐ 224	Mickey Rivers	.10	.05	.01
☐ 225	Enos Cabell	.05	.02	.00
☐ 226	Enrique Romo	.05	.02	.00
☐ 227	Chris Bando	.05	.02	.00
☐ 228	Joaquin Andujar	.15	.07	.01
☐ 229	Phillies TL	.15	.05	.01

BA: Bo Diaz
ERA: Steve Carlton

☐ 230	Fergie Jenkins	.15	.07	.01
☐ 231	SV: Fergie Jenkins	.10	.05	.01
☐ 232	Tom Brunansky	.30	.15	.03
☐ 233	Wayne Gross	.05	.02	.00
☐ 234	Larry Andersen	.05	.02	.00
☐ 235	Claudell Washington	.10	.05	.01
☐ 236	Steve Renko	.05	.02	.00
☐ 237	Dan Norman	.05	.02	.00
☐ 238	Bud Black	.35	.17	.03
☐ 239	Dave Stapleton	.05	.02	.00
☐ 240	Rich Gossage	.25	.12	.02
☐ 241	SV: Rich Gossage	.10	.05	.01
☐ 242	Joe Nolan	.05	.02	.00
☐ 243	Duane Walker	.05	.02	.00
☐ 244	Dwight Bernard	.05	.02	.00
☐ 245	Steve Sax	.25	.12	.02
☐ 246	George Bamberger MG	.05	.02	.00
☐ 247	Dave Smith	.10	.05	.01
☐ 248	Bake McBride	.05	.02	.00
☐ 249	Checklist: 133-264	.15	.01	.00
☐ 250	Bill Buckner	.15	.07	.01
☐ 251	Alan Wiggins	.25	.12	.02
☐ 252	Luis Aguayo	.05	.02	.00
☐ 253	Larry McWilliams	.05	.02	.00
☐ 254	Rick Cerone	.05	.02	.00
☐ 255	Gene Garber	.05	.02	.00
☐ 256	SV: Gene Garber	.05	.02	.00
☐ 257	Jesse Barfield	.75	.35	.07
☐ 258	Manny Castillo	.05	.02	.00
☐ 259	Jeff Jones	.05	.02	.00
☐ 260	Steve Kemp	.10	.05	.01
☐ 261	Tigers TL	.10	.03	.01

BA: Larry Herndon
ERA: Dan Petry

☐ 262	Ron Jackson	.05	.02	.00
☐ 263	Renie Martin	.05	.02	.00
☐ 264	Jamie Quirk	.05	.02	.00
☐ 265	Joel Youngblood	.05	.02	.00
☐ 266	Paul Boris	.05	.02	.00
☐ 267	Terry Francona	.05	.02	.00
☐ 268	Storm Davis	.35	.17	.03
☐ 269	Ron Oester	.05	.02	.00
☐ 270	Dennis Eckersley	.10	.05	.01
☐ 271	Ed Romero	.05	.02	.00
☐ 272	Frank Tanana	.10	.05	.01
☐ 273	Mark Belanger	.10	.05	.01
☐ 274	Terry Kennedy	.10	.05	.01
☐ 275	Ray Knight	.10	.05	.01
☐ 276	Gene Mauch MG	.05	.02	.00
☐ 277	Rance Mulliniks	.05	.02	.00
☐ 278	Kevin Hickey	.05	.02	.00
☐ 279	Greg Gross	.05	.02	.00
☐ 280	Bert Blyleven	.15	.07	.01
☐ 281	Andre Robertson	.05	.02	.00
☐ 282	Reggie Smith (Ryne Sandberg ducking back)	.10	.05	.01
☐ 283	SV: Reggie Smith	.05	.02	.00
☐ 284	Jeff Lahti	.10	.05	.01
☐ 285	Lance Parrish	.30	.15	.03
☐ 286	Rick Langford	.05	.02	.00
☐ 287	Bobby Brown	.05	.02	.00
☐ 288	Joe Cowley	.20	.10	.02
☐ 289	Jerry Dybzinski	.05	.02	.00
☐ 290	Jeff Reardon	.15	.07	.01
☐ 291	Pirates TL	.15	.05	.01

BA: Bill Madlock
ERA: John Candelaria

☐ 292	Craig Swan	.05	.02	.00
☐ 293	Glenn Gulliver	.05	.02	.00
☐ 294	Dave Engle	.05	.02	.00
☐ 295	Jerry Remy	.05	.02	.00
☐ 296	Greg Harris	.05	.02	.00
☐ 297	Ned Yost	.05	.02	.00
☐ 298	Floyd Chiffer	.05	.02	.00
☐ 299	George Wright	.10	.05	.01
☐ 300	Mike Schmidt	.90	.45	.09
☐ 301	SV: Mike Schmidt	.35	.17	.03
☐ 302	Ernie Whitt	.05	.02	.00
☐ 303	Miguel Dilone	.05	.02	.00
☐ 304	Dave Rucker	.05	.02	.00
☐ 305	Larry Bowa	.10	.05	.01
☐ 306	Tom Lasorda MG	.10	.05	.01
☐ 307	Lou Piniella	.10	.05	.01
☐ 308	Jesus Vega	.05	.02	.00
☐ 309	Jeff Leonard	.15	.07	.01
☐ 310	Greg Luzinski	.12	.06	.01
☐ 311	Glenn Brummer	.05	.02	.00
☐ 312	Brian Kingman	.05	.02	.00
☐ 313	Gary Gray	.05	.02	.00
☐ 314	Ken Dayley	.10	.05	.01
☐ 315	Rick Burleson	.10	.05	.01
☐ 316	Paul Splittorff	.10	.05	.01
☐ 317	Gary Rajsich	.05	.02	.00
☐ 318	John Tudor	.30	.15	.03
☐ 319	Lenn Sakata	.05	.02	.00
☐ 320	Steve Rogers	.10	.05	.01
☐ 321	Brewers TL	.15	.05	.01

BA: Robin Yount
ERA: Pete Vuckovich

☐ 322	Dave Van Gorder	.05	.02	.00
☐ 323	Luis DeLeon	.05	.02	.00
☐ 324	Mike Marshall	.30	.15	.03
☐ 325	Von Hayes	.30	.15	.03
☐ 326	Garth Iorg	.05	.02	.00
☐ 327	Bobby Castillo	.05	.02	.00
☐ 328	Craig Reynolds	.05	.02	.00
☐ 329	Randy Niemann	.05	.02	.00
☐ 330	Buddy Bell	.15	.07	.01
☐ 331	Mike Krukow	.10	.05	.01
☐ 332	Glenn Wilson	.85	.40	.08
☐ 333	Dave LaRoche	.05	.02	.00
☐ 334	SV: Dave LaRoche	.05	.02	.00
☐ 335	Steve Henderson	.05	.02	.00
☐ 336	Rene Lachemann MG	.05	.02	.00
☐ 337	Tito Landrum	.05	.02	.00
☐ 338	Bob Owchinko	.05	.02	.00
☐ 339	Terry Harper	.05	.02	.00
☐ 340	Larry Gura	.05	.02	.00
☐ 341	Doug DeCinces	.10	.05	.01
☐ 342	Atlee Hammaker	.10	.05	.01
☐ 343	Bob Bailor	.05	.02	.00
☐ 344	Roger LaFrancois	.05	.02	.00
☐ 345	Jim Clancy	.05	.02	.00
☐ 346	Joe Pittman	.05	.02	.00
☐ 347	Sammy Stewart	.05	.02	.00
☐ 348	Alan Bannister	.05	.02	.00

349	Checklist: 265-396	.10	.01	.00
350	Robin Yount	.45	.22	.04
351	Reds TL	.10	.03	.01
	BA: Cesar Cedeno			
	ERA: Mario Soto			
352	Mike Scioscia	.05	.02	.00
353	Steve Comer	.05	.02	.00
354	Randy Johnson	.05	.02	.00
355	Jim Bibby	.05	.02	.00
356	Gary Woods	.05	.02	.00
357	Len Matuszek	.05	.02	.00
358	Jerry Garvin	.05	.02	.00
359	Dave Collins	.05	.02	.00
360	Nolan Ryan	.50	.25	.05
361	SV: Nolan Ryan	.20	.10	.02
362	Billy Almon	.05	.02	.00
363	John Stuper	.10	.05	.01
364	Brett Butler	.15	.07	.01
365	Dave Lopes	.10	.05	.01
366	Dick Williams MG	.05	.02	.00
367	Bud Anderson	.05	.02	.00
368	Richie Zisk	.05	.02	.00
369	Jesse Orosco	.10	.05	.01
370	Gary Carter	.55	.27	.05
371	Mike Richardt	.05	.02	.00
372	Terry Crowley	.05	.02	.00
373	Kevin Saucier	.05	.02	.00
374	Wayne Krenchicki	.05	.02	.00
375	Pete Vuckovich	.05	.02	.00
376	Ken Landreaux	.05	.02	.00
377	Lee May	.05	.02	.00
378	SV: Lee May	.05	.02	.00
379	Guy Sularz	.05	.02	.00
380	Ron Davis	.05	.02	.00
381	Red Sox TL	.15	.05	.01
	BA: Jim Rice			
	ERA: Bob Stanley			
382	Bob Knepper	.10	.05	.01
383	Ozzie Virgil	.10	.05	.01
384	Dave Dravecky	.75	.35	.07
385	Mike Easler	.10	.05	.01
386	Rod Carew AS	.20	.10	.02
387	Bob Grich AS	.10	.05	.01
388	George Brett AS	.35	.17	.03
389	Robin Yount AS	.20	.10	.02
390	Reggie Jackson AS	.30	.15	.03
391	Rickey Henderson AS	.35	.17	.03
392	Fred Lynn AS	.15	.07	.01
393	Carlton Fisk AS	.10	.05	.01
394	Pete Vuckovich AS	.05	.02	.00
395	Larry Gura AS	.05	.02	.00
396	Dan Quisenberry AS	.10	.05	.01
397	Pete Rose AS	.55	.27	.05
398	Manny Trillo AS	.05	.02	.00
399	Mike Schmidt AS	.30	.15	.03
400	Dave Concepcion AS	.05	.02	.00
401	Dale Murphy AS	.45	.22	.04
402	Andre Dawson AS	.25	.12	.02
403	Tim Raines AS	.25	.12	.02
404	Gary Carter AS	.25	.12	.02
405	Steve Rogers AS	.05	.02	.00
406	Steve Carlton AS	.25	.12	.02
407	Bruce Sutter AS	.10	.05	.01
408	Rudy May	.05	.02	.00
409	Marvis Foley	.05	.02	.00
410	Phil Niekro	.30	.15	.03
411	SV: Phil Niekro	.15	.07	.01
412	Rangers TL	.10	.03	.01
	BA: Buddy Bell			
	ERA: Charlie Hough			
413	Matt Keough	.05	.02	.00
414	Julio Cruz	.05	.02	.00
415	Bob Forsch	.05	.02	.00
416	Joe Ferguson	.05	.02	.00
417	Tom Hausman	.05	.02	.00
418	Greg Pryor	.05	.02	.00
419	Steve Crawford	.05	.02	.00
420	Al Oliver	.15	.07	.01
421	SV: Al Oliver	.10	.05	.01
422	George Cappuzzello	.05	.02	.00
423	Tom Lawless	.10	.05	.01
424	Jerry Augustine	.05	.02	.00
425	Pedro Guerrero	.45	.22	.04
426	Earl Weaver MG	.10	.05	.01
427	Roy Lee Jackson	.05	.02	.00
428	Champ Summers	.05	.02	.00
429	Eddie Whitson	.05	.02	.00
430	Kirk Gibson	.35	.17	.03
431	Gary Gaetti	3.00	1.50	.30
432	Porfirio Altamirano	.05	.02	.00
433	Dale Berra	.05	.02	.00
434	Dennis Lamp	.05	.02	.00
435	Tony Armas	.10	.05	.01
436	Bill Campbell	.05	.02	.00
437	Rick Sweet	.05	.02	.00
438	Dave LaPoint	.25	.12	.02
439	Rafael Ramirez	.05	.02	.00
440	Ron Guidry	.25	.12	.02
441	Astros TL	.10	.03	.01
	BA: Ray Knight			
	ERA: Joe Niekro			
442	Brian Downing	.10	.05	.01
443	Don Hood	.05	.02	.00
444	Wally Backman	.20	.10	.02
445	Mike Flanagan	.10	.05	.01
446	Reid Nichols	.05	.02	.00
447	Bryn Smith	.10	.05	.01
448	Darrell Evans	.15	.07	.01
449	Eddie Milner	.20	.10	.02
450	Ted Simmons	.15	.07	.01
451	SV: Ted Simmons	.10	.05	.01
452	Lloyd Moseby	.15	.07	.01
453	Lamar Johnson	.05	.02	.00
454	Bob Welch	.10	.05	.01
455	Sixto Lezcano	.05	.02	.00
456	Lee Elia MG	.05	.02	.00
457	Milt Wilcox	.05	.02	.00
458	Ron Washington	.05	.02	.00
459	Ed Farmer	.05	.02	.00
460	Roy Smalley	.05	.02	.00
461	Steve Trout	.10	.05	.01
462	Steve Nicosia	.05	.02	.00
463	Gaylord Perry	.25	.12	.02
464	SV: Gaylord Perry	.15	.07	.01
465	Lonnie Smith	.10	.05	.01
466	Tom Underwood	.05	.02	.00
467	Rufino Linares	.05	.02	.00
468	Dave Goltz	.05	.02	.00
469	Ron Gardenhire	.05	.02	.00
470	Greg Minton	.05	.02	.00
471	K.C. Royals TL	.10	.03	.01
	BA: Willie Wilson			
	ERA: Vida Blue			
472	Gary Allenson	.05	.02	.00
473	John Lowenstein	.05	.02	.00
474	Ray Burris	.05	.02	.00
475	Cesar Cedeno	.10	.05	.01
476	Rob Picciolo	.05	.02	.00
477	Tom Niedenfuer	.10	.05	.01
478	Phil Garner	.05	.02	.00
479	Charlie Hough	.10	.05	.01
480	Toby Harrah	.10	.05	.01
481	Scot Thompson	.05	.02	.00
482	Tony Gwynn	16.00	8.00	1.60
483	Lynn Jones	.05	.02	.00
484	Dick Ruthven	.05	.02	.00
485	Omar Moreno	.05	.02	.00
486	Clyde King MG	.05	.02	.00
487	Jerry Hairston	.05	.02	.00
488	Alfredo Griffin	.10	.05	.01
489	Tom Herr	.10	.05	.01
490	Jim Palmer	.35	.17	.03
491	SV: Jim Palmer	.15	.07	.01
492	Paul Serna	.05	.02	.00
493	Steve McCatty	.05	.02	.00
494	Bob Brenly	.10	.05	.01
495	Warren Cromartie	.05	.02	.00
496	Tom Veryzer	.05	.02	.00
497	Rick Sutcliffe	.20	.10	.02
498	Wade Boggs	32.00	16.00	3.20
499	Jeff Little	.05	.02	.00
500	Reggie Jackson	.85	.40	.08
501	SV: Reggie Jackson	.35	.17	.03
502	Atlanta Braves TL	.25	.07	.01
	BA: Dale Murphy			
	ERA: Phil Niekro			
503	Moose Haas	.05	.02	.00
504	Don Werner	.05	.02	.00
505	Garry Templeton	.10	.05	.01
506	Jim Gott	.15	.07	.01
507	Tony Scott	.05	.02	.00
508	Tom Filer	.15	.07	.01
509	Lou Whitaker	.25	.12	.02
510	Tug McGraw	.10	.05	.01
511	SV: Tug McGraw	.05	.02	.00
512	Doyle Alexander	.10	.05	.01
513	Fred Stanley	.05	.02	.00
514	Rudy Law	.05	.02	.00
515	Gene Tenace	.05	.02	.00
516	Bill Virdon MG	.05	.02	.00
517	Gary Ward	.05	.02	.01
518	Bill Laskey	.10	.05	.01
519	Terry Bulling	.05	.02	.00
520	Fred Lynn	.25	.12	.02
521	Bruce Benedict	.05	.02	.00
522	Pat Zachry	.05	.02	.00
523	Carney Lansford	.10	.05	.01
524	Tom Brennan	.05	.02	.00
525	Frank White	.10	.05	.01
526	Checklist: 397-528	.10	.01	.00

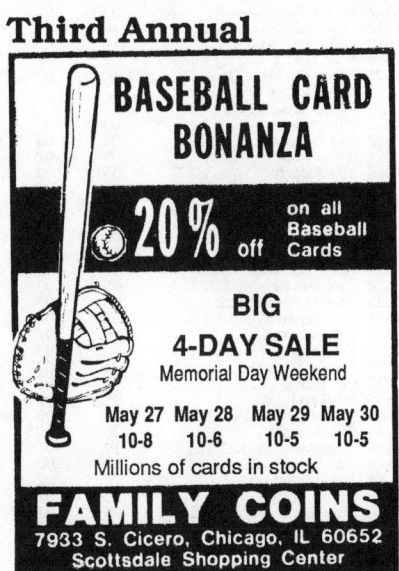

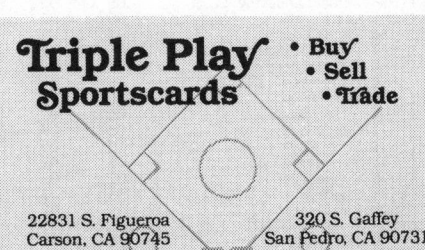

☐ 527	Larry Biittner	.05	.02	.00
☐ 528	Jamie Easterly	.05	.02	.00
☐ 529	Tim Laudner	.10	.05	.01
☐ 530	Eddie Murray	.75	.35	.07
☐ 531	Oakland A's TL	.15	.05	.01
	BA: Rickey Henderson			
	ERA: Rick Langford			
☐ 532	Dave Stewart	.15	.07	.01
☐ 533	Luis Salazar	.05	.02	.00
☐ 534	John Butcher	.05	.02	.00
☐ 535	Manny Trillo	.05	.02	.00
☐ 536	Johnny Wockenfuss	.05	.02	.00
☐ 537	Rod Scurry	.05	.02	.00
☐ 538	Danny Heep	.05	.02	.00
☐ 539	Roger Erickson	.05	.02	.00
☐ 540	Ozzie Smith	.35	.17	.03
☐ 541	Britt Burns	.10	.05	.01
☐ 542	Jody Davis	.15	.07	.01
☐ 543	Alan Fowlkes	.05	.02	.00
☐ 544	Larry Whisenton	.05	.02	.00'
☐ 545	Floyd Bannister	.10	.05	.01
☐ 546	Dave Garcia MG	.05	.02	.00
☐ 547	Geoff Zahn	.05	.02	.00
☐ 548	Brian Giles	.05	.02	.00
☐ 549	Charlie Puleo	.05	.02	.00
☐ 550	Carl Yastrzemski	.90	.45	.09
☐ 551	SV: Carl Yastrzemski	.40	.20	.04
☐ 552	Tim Wallach	.30	.15	.03
☐ 553	Denny Martinez	.10	.05	.01
☐ 554	Mike Vail	.05	.02	.00
☐ 555	Steve Yeager	.05	.02	.00
☐ 556	Willie Upshaw	.10	.05	.01
☐ 557	Rick Honeycutt	.10	.05	.01
☐ 558	Dickie Thon	.10	.05	.01
☐ 559	Pete Redfern	.05	.02	.00
☐ 560	Ron LeFlore	.10	.05	.01
☐ 561	Cardinals TL	.10	.03	.01
	BA: Lonnie Smith			
	ERA: Joaquin Andujar			
☐ 562	Dave Rozema	.05	.02	.00
☐ 563	Juan Bonilla	.05	.02	.00
☐ 564	Sid Monge	.05	.02	.00
☐ 565	Bucky Dent	.10	.05	.01
☐ 566	Manny Sarmiento	.05	.02	.00
☐ 567	Joe Simpson	.05	.02	.00
☐ 568	Willie Hernandez	.15	.07	.01
☐ 569	Jack Perconte	.05	.02	.00
☐ 570	Vida Blue	.10	.05	.01
☐ 571	Mickey Klutts	.05	.02	.00
☐ 572	Bob Watson	.05	.02	.00
☐ 573	Andy Hassler	.05	.02	.00
☐ 574	Glenn Adams	.05	.02	.00
☐ 575	Neil Allen	.05	.02	.00
☐ 576	Frank Robinson MG	.15	.07	.01
☐ 577	Luis Aponte	.05	.02	.00
☐ 578	David Green	.10	.05	.01
☐ 579	Rich Dauer	.05	.02	.00
☐ 580	Tom Seaver	.55	.27	.05
☐ 581	SV: Tom Seaver	.25	.12	.02
☐ 582	Marshall Edwards	.05	.02	.00
☐ 583	Terry Forster	.10	.05	.01
☐ 584	Dave Hostetler	.05	.02	.00
☐ 585	Jose Cruz	.10	.05	.01
☐ 586	Frank Viola	2.00	1.00	.20
☐ 587	Ivan DeJesus	.05	.02	.00
☐ 588	Pat Underwood	.05	.02	.00
☐ 589	Alvis Woods	.05	.02	.00
☐ 590	Tony Pena	.20	.10	.02
☐ 591	White Sox TL	.10	.03	.01
	BA: Greg Luzinski			
	ERA: LaMarr Hoyt			
☐ 592	Shane Rawley	.10	.05	.01
☐ 593	Broderick Perkins	.05	.02	.00
☐ 594	Eric Rasmussen	.05	.02	.00
☐ 595	Tim Raines	.60	.30	.06
☐ 596	Randy Johnson	.05	.02	.00
☐ 597	Mike Proly	.05	.02	.00
☐ 598	Dwayne Murphy	.10	.05	.01
☐ 599	Don Aase	.10	.05	.01
☐ 600	George Brett	.90	.45	.09
☐ 601	Ed Lynch	.05	.02	.00
☐ 602	Rich Gedman	.20	.10	.02
☐ 603	Joe Morgan	.30	.15	.03
☐ 604	SV: Joe Morgan	.15	.07	.01
☐ 605	Gary Roenicke	.05	.02	.00
☐ 606	Bobby Cox MG	.05	.02	.00
☐ 607	Charlie Leibrandt	.10	.05	.01
☐ 608	Don Money	.05	.02	.00
☐ 609	Danny Darwin	.05	.02	.00
☐ 610	Steve Garvey	.70	.35	.07
☐ 611	Bert Roberge	.05	.02	.00
☐ 612	Steve Swisher	.05	.02	.00
☐ 613	Mike Ivie	.05	.02	.00
☐ 614	Ed Glynn	.05	.02	.00
☐ 615	Garry Maddox	.05	.02	.00

☐ 616	Bill Nahorodny	.05	.02	.00
☐ 617	Butch Wynegar	.05	.02	.00
☐ 618	LaMarr Hoyt	.10	.05	.01
☐ 619	Keith Moreland	.10	.05	.01
☐ 620	Mike Norris	.05	.02	.00
☐ 621	New York Mets TL	.10	.03	.01
	BA: Mookie Wilson			
	ERA: Craig Swan			
☐ 622	Dave Edler	.05	.02	.00
☐ 623	Luis Sanchez	.05	.02	.00
☐ 624	Glenn Hubbard	.05	.02	.00
☐ 625	Ken Forsch	.05	.02	.00
☐ 626	Jerry Martin	.05	.02	.00
☐ 627	Doug Bair	.05	.02	.00
☐ 628	Julio Valdez	.05	.02	.00
☐ 629	Charlie Lea	.05	.02	.00
☐ 630	Paul Molitor	.25	.12	.02
☐ 631	Tippy Martinez	.05	.02	.00
☐ 632	Alex Trevino	.05	.02	.00
☐ 633	Vicente Romo	.05	.02	.00
☐ 634	Max Venable	.05	.02	.00
☐ 635	Graig Nettles	.15	.07	.01
☐ 636	SV: Graig Nettles	.10	.05	.01
☐ 637	Pat Corrales MG	.05	.02	.00
☐ 638	Dan Petry	.10	.05	.01
☐ 639	Art Howe	.05	.02	.00
☐ 640	Andre Thornton	.10	.05	.01
☐ 641	Billy Sample	.05	.02	.00
☐ 642	Checklist: 529-660	.10	.01	.00
☐ 643	Bump Wills	.05	.02	.00
☐ 644	Joe Lefebvre	.05	.02	.00
☐ 645	Bill Madlock	.15	.07	.01
☐ 646	Jim Essian	.05	.02	.00
☐ 647	Bobby Mitchell	.05	.02	.00
☐ 648	Jeff Burroughs	.10	.05	.01
☐ 649	Tommy Boggs	.05	.02	.00
☐ 650	George Hendrick	.10	.05	.01
☐ 651	Angels TL	.20	.06	.01
	BA: Rod Carew			
	ERA: Mike Witt			
☐ 652	Butch Hobson	.05	.02	.00
☐ 653	Ellis Valentine	.05	.02	.00
☐ 654	Bob Ojeda	.15	.07	.01
☐ 655	Al Bumbry	.05	.02	.00
☐ 656	Dave Frost	.05	.02	.00
☐ 657	Mike Gates	.05	.02	.00
☐ 658	Frank Pastore	.05	.02	.00
☐ 659	Charlie Moore	.05	.02	.00
☐ 660	Mike Hargrove	.05	.02	.00
☐ 661	Bill Russell	.05	.02	.00
☐ 662	Joe Sambito	.05	.02	.00
☐ 663	Tom O'Malley	.05	.02	.00
☐ 664	Bob Molinaro	.05	.02	.00
☐ 665	Jim Sundberg	.05	.02	.00
☐ 666	Sparky Anderson MG	.10	.05	.01
☐ 667	Dick Davis	.05	.02	.00
☐ 668	Larry Christenson	.05	.02	.00
☐ 669	Mike Squires	.05	.02	.00
☐ 670	Jerry Mumphrey	.05	.02	.00
☐ 671	Lenny Faedo	.05	.02	.00
☐ 672	Jim Kaat	.15	.07	.01
☐ 673	SV: Jim Kaat	.10	.05	.01
☐ 674	Kurt Bevacqua	.05	.02	.00
☐ 675	Jim Beattie	.05	.02	.00
☐ 676	Biff Pocoroba	.05	.02	.00
☐ 677	Dave Revering	.05	.02	.00
☐ 678	Juan Beniquez	.10	.05	.01
☐ 679	Mike Scott	.35	.17	.03
☐ 680	Andre Dawson	.35	.17	.03
☐ 681	Dodgers Leaders	.20	.06	.01
	BA: Pedro Guerrero			
	ERA: Fern.Valenzuela			
☐ 682	Bob Stanley	.05	.02	.00
☐ 683	Dan Ford	.05	.02	.00
☐ 684	Rafael Landestoy	.05	.02	.00
☐ 685	Lee Mazzilli	.05	.02	.00
☐ 686	Randy Lerch	.05	.02	.00
☐ 687	U.L. Washington	.05	.02	.00
☐ 688	Jim Wohlford	.05	.02	.00
☐ 689	Ron Hassey	.05	.02	.00
☐ 690	Kent Hrbek	.60	.30	.06
☐ 691	Dave Tobik	.05	.02	.00
☐ 692	Denny Walling	.05	.02	.00
☐ 693	Sparky Lyle	.10	.05	.01
☐ 694	SV: Sparky Lyle	.05	.02	.00
☐ 695	Ruppert Jones	.05	.02	.00
☐ 696	Chuck Tanner MG	.05	.02	.00
☐ 697	Barry Foote	.05	.02	.00
☐ 698	Tony Bernazard	.05	.02	.00
☐ 699	Lee Smith	.15	.07	.01
☐ 700	Keith Hernandez	.45	.22	.04
☐ 701	Batting Leaders	.15	.07	.01
	AL: Willie Wilson			
	NL: Al Oliver			
☐ 702	Home Run Leaders	.15	.07	.01

	AL: Reggie Jackson		
	AL: Gorman Thomas		
	NL: Dave Kingman		
☐ 703	RBI Leaders	.15	.07	.01
	AL: Hal McRae		
	NL: Dale Murphy		
	NL: Al Oliver		
☐ 704	SB Leaders	.25	.12	.02
	AL: Rickey Henderson		
	NL: Tim Raines		
☐ 705	Victory Leaders	.15	.07	.01
	AL: LaMarr Hoyt		
	NL: Steve Carlton		
☐ 706	Strikeout Leaders	.15	.07	.01
	AL: Floyd Bannister		
	NL: Steve Carlton		
☐ 707	ERA Leaders	.10	.05	.01
	AL: Rick Sutcliffe		
	NL: Steve Rogers		
☐ 708	Leading Firemen	.10	.05	.01
	AL: Dan Quisenberry		
	NL: Bruce Sutter		
☐ 709	Jimmy Sexton	.05	.02	.00
☐ 710	Willie Wilson	.15	.07	.01
☐ 711	Mariners TL	.10	.03	.01
	BA: Bruce Bochte		
	ERA: Jim Beattie		
☐ 712	Bruce Kison	.05	.02	.00
☐ 713	Ron Hodges	.05	.02	.00
☐ 714	Wayne Nordhagen	.05	.02	.00
☐ 715	Tony Perez	.15	.07	.01
☐ 716	SV: Tony Perez	.10	.05	.01
☐ 717	Scott Sanderson	.05	.02	.00
☐ 718	Jim Dwyer	.05	.02	.00
☐ 719	Rich Gale	.05	.02	.00
☐ 720	Dave Concepcion	.10	.05	.01
☐ 721	John Martin	.05	.02	.00
☐ 722	Jorge Orta	.05	.02	.00
☐ 723	Randy Moffitt	.05	.02	.00
☐ 724	Johnny Grubb	.05	.02	.00
☐ 725	Dan Spillner	.05	.02	.00
☐ 726	Harvey Kuenn MG	.05	.02	.00
☐ 727	Chet Lemon	.10	.05	.01
☐ 728	Ron Reed	.05	.02	.00
☐ 729	Jerry Morales	.05	.02	.00
☐ 730	Jason Thompson	.05	.02	.00
☐ 731	Al Williams	.05	.02	.00
☐ 732	Dave Henderson	.10	.05	.01
☐ 733	Buck Martinez	.05	.02	.00
☐ 734	Steve Braun	.05	.02	.00
☐ 735	Tommy John	.15	.07	.01
☐ 736	SV: Tommy John	.10	.05	.01
☐ 737	Mitchell Page	.05	.02	.00
☐ 738	Tim Foli	.05	.02	.00
☐ 739	Rick Ownbey	.05	.02	.00
☐ 740	Rusty Staub	.15	.07	.01
☐ 741	SV: Rusty Staub	.10	.05	.01
☐ 742	Padres TL	.10	.03	.01
	BA: Terry Kennedy		
	ERA: Tim Lollar		
☐ 743	Mike Torrez	.05	.02	.00
☐ 744	Brad Mills	.05	.02	.00
☐ 745	Scott McGregor	.10	.05	.01
☐ 746	John Wathan	.10	.05	.01
☐ 747	Fred Breining	.05	.02	.00
☐ 748	Derrel Thomas	.05	.02	.00
☐ 749	Jon Matlack	.10	.05	.01
☐ 750	Ben Oglivie	.10	.05	.01
☐ 751	Brad Havens	.05	.02	.00
☐ 752	Luis Pujols	.05	.02	.00
☐ 753	Elias Sosa	.05	.02	.00
☐ 754	Bill Robinson	.05	.02	.00
☐ 755	John Candelaria	.10	.05	.01
☐ 756	Russ Nixon MG	.05	.02	.00
☐ 757	Rick Manning	.05	.02	.00
☐ 758	Aurelio Rodriguez	.05	.02	.00
☐ 759	Doug Bird	.05	.02	.00
☐ 760	Dale Murphy	1.50	.75	.15
☐ 761	Gary Lucas	.05	.02	.00
☐ 762	Cliff Johnson	.05	.02	.00
☐ 763	Al Cowens	.05	.02	.00
☐ 764	Pete Falcone	.05	.02	.00
☐ 765	Bob Boone	.10	.05	.01
☐ 766	Barry Bonnell	.05	.02	.00
☐ 767	Duane Kuiper	.05	.02	.00
☐ 768	Chris Speier	.05	.02	.00
☐ 769	Checklist: 661-792	.10	.01	.00
☐ 770	Dave Winfield	.45	.22	.04
☐ 771	Twins TL	.10	.03	.01
	BA: Kent Hrbek		
	ERA: Bobby Castillo		
☐ 772	Jim Kern	.05	.02	.00
☐ 773	Larry Hisle	.05	.02	.00
☐ 774	Alan Ashby	.05	.02	.00
☐ 775	Burt Hooton	.05	.02	.00

☐ 776	Larry Parrish	.10	.05	.01
☐ 777	John Curtis	.05	.02	.00
☐ 778	Rich Hebner	.05	.02	.00
☐ 779	Rick Waits	.05	.02	.00
☐ 780	Gary Matthews	.10	.05	.01
☐ 781	Rick Rhoden	.10	.05	.01
☐ 782	Bobby Murcer	.10	.05	.01
☐ 783	SV: Bobby Murcer	.05	.02	.00
☐ 784	Jeff Newman	.05	.02	.00
☐ 785	Dennis Leonard	.10	.05	.01
☐ 786	Ralph Houk MG	.05	.02	.00
☐ 787	Dick Tidrow	.05	.02	.00
☐ 788	Dane Iorg	.05	.02	.00
☐ 789	Bryan Clark	.05	.02	.00
☐ 790	Bob Grich	.10	.05	.01
☐ 791	Gary Lavelle	.05	.02	.00
☐ 792	Chris Chambliss	.20	.04	.01

1983 Topps Traded

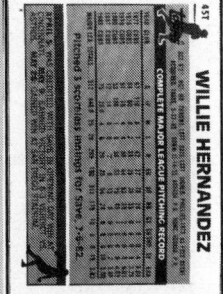

The cards in this 132-card set measure 2 1/2" by 3 1/2". For the third year in a row, Topps issued a 132-card Traded (or extended) set featuring some of the year's top rookies and players who had changed teams during the year, but were featured with their old team in the Topps regular issue of 1983. The cards were available through hobby dealers only and were printed in Ireland by the Topps affiliate in that country. The set is numbered alphabetically by the last name of the player of the card.

		MINT	EXC	G-VG
COMPLETE SET		40.00	20.00	4.00
COMMON PLAYER		.09	.04	.01
☐	1T Neil Allen	.15	.07	.01
☐	2T Bill Almon	.09	.04	.01
☐	3T Joe Altobelli MG	.09	.04	.01
☐	4T Tony Armas	.20	.10	.02
☐	5T Doug Bair	.09	.04	.01
☐	6T Steve Baker	.09	.04	.01
☐	7T Floyd Bannister	.15	.07	.01
☐	8T Don Baylor	.25	.12	.02
☐	9T Tony Bernazard	.15	.07	.01
☐	10T Larry Biittner	.09	.04	.01
☐	11T Dann Bilardello	.09	.04	.01
☐	12T Doug Bird	.09	.04	.01
☐	13T Steve Boros MG	.09	.04	.01
☐	14T Greg Brock	.45	.22	.04
☐	15T Mike Brown	.15	.07	.01
	(Red Sox pitcher)			
☐	16T Tom Burgmeier	.09	.04	.01
☐	17T Randy Bush	.20	.10	.02
☐	18T Bert Campaneris	.15	.07	.01
☐	19T Ron Cey	.20	.10	.02
☐	20T Chris Codiroli	.15	.07	.01
☐	21T Dave Collins	.15	.07	.01
☐	22T Terry Crowley	.09	.04	.01
☐	23T Julio Cruz	.09	.04	.01
☐	24T Mike Davis	.25	.12	.02
☐	25T Frank DiPino	.09	.04	.01
☐	26T Bill Doran	1.25	.60	.12
☐	27T Jerry Dybzinski	.09	.04	.01
☐	28T Jamie Easterly	.09	.04	.01
☐	29T Juan Eichelberger	.09	.04	.01
☐	30T Jim Essian	.09	.04	.01
☐	31T Pete Falcone	.09	.04	.01
☐	32T Mike Ferraro MG	.09	.04	.01

☐ 33T	Terry Forster	.20	.10	.02
☐ 34T	Julio Franco	1.25	.60	.12
☐ 35T	Rich Gale	.09	.04	.01
☐ 36T	Kiko Garcia	.09	.04	.01
☐ 37T	Steve Garvey	1.50	.75	.15
☐ 38T	Johnny Grubb	.09	.04	.01
☐ 39T	Mel Hall	1.00	.50	.10
☐ 40T	Von Hayes	.85	.40	.08
☐ 41T	Danny Heep	.15	.07	.01
☐ 42T	Steve Henderson	.09	.04	.01
☐ 43T	Keith Hernandez	1.00	.50	.10
☐ 44T	Leo Hernandez	.20	.10	.02
☐ 45T	Willie Hernandez	.30	.15	.03
☐ 46T	Al Holland	.15	.07	.01
☐ 47T	Frank Howard MG	.15	.07	.01
☐ 48T	Bobby Johnson	.09	.04	.01
☐ 49T	Cliff Johnson	.09	.04	.01
☐ 50T	Odell Jones	.09	.04	.01
☐ 51T	Mike Jorgensen	.09	.04	.01
☐ 52T	Bob Kearney	.09	.04	.01
☐ 53T	Steve Kemp	.15	.07	.01
☐ 54T	Matt Keough	.09	.04	.01
☐ 55T	Ron Kittle	.75	.35	.07
☐ 56T	Mickey Klutts	.09	.04	.01
☐ 57T	Alan Knicely	.09	.04	.01
☐ 58T	Mike Krukow	.25	.12	.02
☐ 59T	Rafael Landestoy	.09	.04	.01
☐ 60T	Carney Lansford	.25	.12	.02
☐ 61T	Joe Lefebvre	.09	.04	.01
☐ 62T	Bryan Little	.09	.04	.01
☐ 63T	Aurelio Lopez	.09	.04	.01
☐ 64T	Mike Madden	.15	.07	.01
☐ 65T	Rick Manning	.09	.04	.01
☐ 66T	Billy Martin MG	.20	.10	.02
☐ 67T	Lee Mazzilli	.15	.07	.01
☐ 68T	Andy McGaffigan	.09	.04	.01
☐ 69T	Craig McMurtry	.15	.07	.01
☐ 70T	John McNamara MG	.09	.04	.01
☐ 71T	Orlando Mercado	.15	.07	.01
☐ 72T	Larry Milbourne	.09	.04	.01
☐ 73T	Randy Moffitt	.09	.04	.01
☐ 74T	Sid Monge	.09	.04	.01
☐ 75T	Jose Morales	.09	.04	.01
☐ 76T	Omar Moreno	.09	.04	.01
☐ 77T	Joe Morgan	1.00	.50	.10
☐ 78T	Mike Morgan	.09	.04	.01
☐ 79T	Dale Murray	.09	.04	.01
☐ 80T	Jeff Newman	.09	.04	.01
☐ 81T	Pete O'Brien	2.00	1.00	.20
☐ 82T	Jorge Orta	.09	.04	.01
☐ 83T	Alejandro Pena	.45	.22	.04
☐ 84T	Pascual Perez	.15	.07	.01
☐ 85T	Tony Perez	.35	.17	.03
☐ 86T	Broderick Perkins	.09	.04	.01
☐ 87T	Tony Phillips	.20	.10	.02
☐ 88T	Charlie Puleo	.09	.04	.01
☐ 89T	Pat Putnam	.09	.04	.01
☐ 90T	Jamie Quirk	.09	.04	.01
☐ 91T	Doug Rader MG	.09	.04	.01
☐ 92T	Chuck Rainey	.09	.04	.01
☐ 93T	Bobby Ramos	.09	.04	.01
☐ 94T	Gary Redus	.65	.30	.06
☐ 95T	Steve Renko	.09	.04	.01
☐ 96T	Leon Roberts	.09	.04	.01
☐ 97T	Aurelio Rodriguez	.09	.04	.01
☐ 98T	Dick Ruthven	.09	.04	.01
☐ 99T	Daryl Sconiers	.09	.04	.01
☐ 100T	Mike Scott	1.00	.50	.10
☐ 101T	Tom Seaver	1.25	.60	.12
☐ 102T	John Shelby	.35	.17	.03
☐ 103T	Bob Shirley	.09	.04	.01
☐ 104T	Joe Simpson	.09	.04	.01
☐ 105T	Doug Sisk	.15	.07	.01
☐ 106T	Mike Smithson	.20	.10	.02
☐ 107T	Elias Sosa	.09	.04	.01
☐ 108T	Darryl Strawberry	27.00	13.50	2.70
☐ 109T	Tom Tellmann	.09	.04	.01
☐ 110T	Gene Tenace	.15	.07	.01
☐ 111T	Gorman Thomas	.20	.10	.02
☐ 112T	Dick Tidrow	.09	.04	.01
☐ 113T	Dave Tobik	.09	.04	.01
☐ 114T	Wayne Tolleson	.15	.07	.01
☐ 115T	Mike Torrez	.15	.07	.01
☐ 116T	Manny Trillo	.15	.07	.01
☐ 117T	Steve Trout	.15	.07	.01
☐ 118T	Lee Tunnell	.25	.12	.02
☐ 119T	Mike Vail	.09	.04	.01
☐ 120T	Ellis Valentine	.09	.04	.01
☐ 121T	Tom Veryzer	.09	.04	.01
☐ 122T	George Vukovich	.09	.04	.01
☐ 123T	Rick Waits	.09	.04	.01
☐ 124T	Greg Walker	2.00	1.00	.20
☐ 125T	Chris Welsh	.09	.04	.01
☐ 126T	Len Whitehouse	.09	.04	.01
☐ 127T	Eddie Whitson	.09	.04	.01

☐ 128T	Jim Wohlford	.09	.04	.01
☐ 129T	Matt Young	.25	.12	.02
☐ 130T	Joel Youngblood	.09	.04	.01
☐ 131T	Pat Zachry	.09	.04	.01
☐ 132T	Checklist 1T-132T	.15	.02	.00

1983 Topps Glossy 40

The cards in this 40-card set measure 2 1/2" by 3 1/2". The 1983 Topps "Collector's Edition" or "All-Star Set" (popularly known as "Glossies") consists of color ballplayer picture cards with shiny, glazed surfaces. The player's name appears in small print outside the frame line at bottom left. The backs contain no biography or record and list only the set titles, the player's name, team, position, and the card number.

		MINT	EXC	G-VG
COMPLETE SET		12.00	6.00	1.20
COMMON PLAYER		.15	.07	.01
☐ 1	Carl Yastrzemski	1.00	.50	.10
☐ 2	Mookie Wilson	.15	.07	.01
☐ 3	Andre Thornton	.15	.07	.01
☐ 4	Keith Hernandez	.40	.20	.04
☐ 5	Robin Yount	.50	.25	.05
☐ 6	Terry Kennedy	.15	.07	.01
☐ 7	Dave Winfield	.50	.25	.05
☐ 8	Mike Schmidt	1.00	.50	.10
☐ 9	Buddy Bell	.20	.10	.02
☐ 10	Fernando Valenzuela	.50	.25	.05
☐ 11	Rich Gossage	.25	.12	.02
☐ 12	Bob Horner	.30	.15	.03
☐ 13	Toby Harrah	.15	.07	.01
☐ 14	Pete Rose	1.25	.60	.12
☐ 15	Cecil Cooper	.25	.12	.02
☐ 16	Dale Murphy	1.25	.60	.12
☐ 17	Carlton Fisk	.25	.12	.02
☐ 18	Ray Knight	.15	.07	.01
☐ 19	Jim Palmer	.45	.22	.04
☐ 20	Gary Carter	.60	.30	.06
☐ 21	Richie Zisk	.15	.07	.01
☐ 22	Dusty Baker	.15	.07	.01
☐ 23	Willie Wilson	.25	.12	.02
☐ 24	Bill Buckner	.15	.07	.01
☐ 25	Dave Stieb	.20	.10	.02
☐ 26	Bill Madlock	.20	.10	.02
☐ 27	Lance Parrish	.30	.15	.03
☐ 28	Nolan Ryan	.60	.30	.06
☐ 29	Rod Carew	.60	.30	.06
☐ 30	Al Oliver	.25	.12	.02
☐ 31	George Brett	1.00	.50	.10
☐ 32	Jack Clark	.35	.17	.03
☐ 33	Ricky Henderson	.90	.45	.09
☐ 34	Dave Concepcion	.15	.07	.01
☐ 35	Kent Hrbek	.45	.22	.04
☐ 36	Steve Carlton	.60	.30	.06
☐ 37	Eddie Murray	.90	.45	.09
☐ 38	Ruppert Jones	.15	.07	.01
☐ 39	Reggie Jackson	1.00	.50	.10
☐ 40	Bruce Sutter	.25	.12	.02

1984 Topps

The cards in this 792-card set measure 2 1/2" by 3 1/2". For the second year in a row, Topps utilized a dual picture on the front of the card. A portrait is shown in a square insert and an action shot is featured in the main photo. Card numbers 1-6 feature 1983 Highlights (HL), cards 131-138 depict League Leaders, card numbers 386-407 feature All-Stars and card numbers 701-718 feature active Major League career leaders in various statistical categories. Each team leader (TL) card features the team's leading hitter and pitcher pictured on the front with a team checklist back. There are six numerical checklist cards in the set. The player cards feature team logos in the upper right corner of the reverse.

	MINT	EXC	G-VG
COMPLETE SET	85.00	42.50	8.50
COMMON PLAYER (1-792)	.04	.02	.00

			MINT	EXC	G-VG
☐	1	HL: Steve Carlton 300th win and all-time SO king	.25	.07	.01
☐	2	HL: Rickey Henderson 100 stolen bases, three times	.20	.10	.02
☐	3	HL: Dan Quisenberry Sets save record	.10	.05	.01
☐	4	HL: Nolan Ryan, Steve Carlton, and Gaylord Perry (All surpass Johnson)	.25	.12	.02
☐	5	HL: Dave Righetti, Bob Forsch, and Mike Warren (All pitch no-hitters)	.10	.05	.01
☐	6	HL: Johnny Bench Gaylord Perry, and Carl Yastrzemski (Superstars retire)	.25	.12	.02
☐	7	Gary Lucas	.04	.02	.00
☐	8	Don Mattingly	32.00	16.00	3.20
☐	9	Jim Gott	.04	.02	.00
☐	10	Robin Yount	.35	.17	.03
☐	11	Minnesota Twins TL Kent Hrbek Ken Schrom	.10	.03	.01
☐	12	Billy Sample	.04	.02	.00
☐	13	Scott Holman	.04	.02	.00
☐	14	Tom Brookens	.04	.02	.00
☐	15	Burt Hooton	.04	.02	.00
☐	16	Omar Moreno	.04	.02	.00
☐	17	John Denny	.07	.03	.01
☐	18	Dale Berra	.04	.02	.00
☐	19	Ray Fontenot	.07	.03	.01
☐	20	Greg Luzinski	.10	.05	.01
☐	21	Joe Altobelli MG	.04	.02	.00
☐	22	Bryan Clark	.04	.02	.00
☐	23	Keith Moreland	.07	.03	.01
☐	24	John Martin	.04	.02	.00
☐	25	Glenn Hubbard	.04	.02	.00
☐	26	Bud Black	.04	.02	.00
☐	27	Daryl Sconiers	.04	.02	.00
☐	28	Frank Viola	.25	.12	.02
☐	29	Danny Heep	.04	.02	.00
☐	30	Wade Boggs	6.50	3.25	.65
☐	31	Andy McGaffigan	.04	.02	.00
☐	32	Bobby Ramos	.04	.02	.00
☐	33	Tom Burgmeier	.04	.02	.00
☐	34	Eddie Milner	.04	.02	.00
☐	35	Don Sutton	.25	.12	.02
☐	36	Denny Walling	.04	.02	.00
☐	37	Texas Rangers TL Buddy Bell Rick Honeycutt	.10	.03	.01
☐	38	Luis DeLeon	.04	.02	.00
☐	39	Garth Iorg	.04	.02	.00
☐	40	Dusty Baker	.07	.03	.01
☐	41	Tony Bernazard	.04	.02	.00
☐	42	Johnny Grubb	.04	.02	.00
☐	43	Ron Reed	.04	.02	.00
☐	44	Jim Morrison	.04	.02	.00
☐	45	Jerry Mumphrey	.04	.02	.00
☐	46	Ray Smith	.04	.02	.00
☐	47	Rudy Law	.04	.02	.00
☐	48	Julio Franco	.35	.17	.03
☐	49	John Stuper	.04	.02	.00
☐	50	Chris Chambliss	.07	.03	.01
☐	51	Jim Frey MG	.04	.02	.00
☐	52	Paul Splittorff	.07	.03	.01
☐	53	Juan Beniquez	.07	.03	.01
☐	54	Jesse Orosco	.07	.03	.01
☐	55	Dave Concepcion	.10	.05	.01
☐	56	Gary Allenson	.04	.02	.00
☐	57	Dan Schatzeder	.04	.02	.00
☐	58	Max Venable	.04	.02	.00
☐	59	Sammy Stewart	.04	.02	.00
☐	60	Paul Molitor	.15	.07	.01
☐	61	Chris Codiroli	.07	.03	.01
☐	62	Dave Hostetler	.04	.02	.00
☐	63	Ed VandeBerg	.04	.02	.00
☐	64	Mike Scioscia	.04	.02	.00
☐	65	Kirk Gibson	.25	.12	.02
☐	66	Houston Astros TL Jose Cruz Nolan Ryan	.12	.04	.01
☐	67	Gary Ward	.07	.03	.01
☐	68	Luis Salazar	.04	.02	.00
☐	69	Rod Scurry	.04	.02	.00
☐	70	Gary Matthews	.07	.03	.01
☐	71	Leo Hernandez	.07	.03	.01
☐	72	Mike Squires	.04	.02	.00
☐	73	Jody Davis	.10	.05	.01
☐	74	Jerry Martin	.04	.02	.00
☐	75	Bob Forsch	.07	.03	.01
☐	76	Alfredo Griffin	.07	.03	.01
☐	77	Brett Butler	.10	.05	.01
☐	78	Mike Torrez	.04	.02	.00
☐	79	Rob Wilfong	.04	.02	.00
☐	80	Steve Rogers	.07	.03	.01
☐	81	Billy Martin MG	.10	.05	.01
☐	82	Doug Bird	.04	.02	.00
☐	83	Richie Zisk	.07	.03	.01
☐	84	Lenny Faedo	.04	.02	.00
☐	85	Atlee Hammaker	.07	.03	.01
☐	86	John Shelby	.25	.12	.02
☐	87	Frank Pastore	.04	.02	.00
☐	88	Rob Picciolo	.04	.02	.00
☐	89	Mike Smithson	.10	.05	.01
☐	90	Pedro Guerrero	.35	.17	.03
☐	91	Dan Spillner	.04	.02	.00
☐	92	Lloyd Moseby	.15	.07	.01
☐	93	Bob Knepper	.10	.05	.01
☐	94	Mario Ramirez	.04	.02	.00
☐	95	Aurelio Lopez	.04	.02	.00
☐	96	K.C. Royals TL Hal McRae Larry Gura	.10	.03	.01
☐	97	LaMarr Hoyt	.07	.03	.01
☐	98	Steve Nicosia	.04	.02	.00
☐	99	Craig Lefferts	.15	.07	.01
☐	100	Reggie Jackson	.55	.27	.05
☐	101	Porfirio Altamirano	.04	.02	.00
☐	102	Ken Oberkfell	.04	.02	.00
☐	103	Dwayne Murphy	.07	.03	.01
☐	104	Ken Dayley	.07	.03	.01
☐	105	Tony Armas	.10	.05	.01
☐	106	Tim Stoddard	.04	.02	.00
☐	107	Ned Yost	.04	.02	.00
☐	108	Randy Moffitt	.04	.02	.00
☐	109	Brad Wellman	.04	.02	.00
☐	110	Ron Guidry	.20	.10	.02
☐	111	Bill Virdon MG	.04	.02	.00
☐	112	Tom Niedenfuer	.07	.03	.01
☐	113	Kelly Paris	.07	.03	.01
☐	114	Checklist 1-132	.07	.01	.00
☐	115	Andre Thornton	.07	.03	.01
☐	116	George Bjorkman	.04	.02	.00
☐	117	Tom Veryzer	.04	.02	.00
☐	118	Charlie Hough	.07	.03	.01
☐	119	Johnny Wockenfuss	.04	.02	.00

☐ 120	Keith Hernandez	.35	.17	.03
☐ 121	Pat Sheridan	.25	.12	.02
☐ 122	Cecilio Guante	.07	.03	.01
☐ 123	Butch Wynegar	.07	.03	.01
☐ 124	Damaso Garcia	.07	.03	.01
☐ 125	Britt Burns	.07	.03	.01
☐ 126	Atlanta Braves TL	.15	.04	.01
	Dale Murphy			
	Craig McMurtry			
☐ 127	Mike Madden	.07	.03	.01
☐ 128	Rick Manning	.04	.02	.00
☐ 129	Bill Laskey	.04	.02	.00
☐ 130	Ozzie Smith	.25	.12	.02
☐ 131	Batting Leaders	.25	.12	.02
	Bill Madlock			
	Wade Boggs			
☐ 132	Home Run Leaders	.25	.12	.02
	Mike Schmidt			
	Jim Rice			
☐ 133	RBI Leaders	.25	.12	.02
	Dale Murphy			
	Cecil Cooper			
	Jim Rice			
☐ 134	Stolen Base Leaders	.25	.12	.02
	Tim Raines			
	Rickey Henderson			
☐ 135	Victory Leaders	.07	.03	.01
	John Denny			
	LaMarr Hoyt			
☐ 136	Strikeout Leaders	.15	.07	.01
	Steve Carlton			
	Jack Morris			
☐ 137	ERA Leaders	.07	.03	.01
	Atlee Hammaker			
	Rick Honeycutt			
☐ 138	Leading Firemen	.07	.03	.01
	Al Holland			
	Dan Quisenberry			
☐ 139	Bert Campaneris	.07	.03	.01
☐ 140	Storm Davis	.07	.03	.01
☐ 141	Pat Corrales MG	.04	.02	.00
☐ 142	Rich Gale	.04	.02	.00
☐ 143	Jose Morales	.04	.02	.00
☐ 144	Brian Harper	.07	.03	.01
☐ 145	Gary Lavelle	.04	.02	.00
☐ 146	Ed Romero	.04	.02	.00
☐ 147	Dan Petry	.10	.05	.01
☐ 148	Joe Lefebvre	.04	.02	.00
☐ 149	Jon Matlack	.07	.03	.01
☐ 150	Dale Murphy	.85	.40	.08
☐ 151	Steve Trout	.07	.03	.01
☐ 152	Glenn Brummer	.04	.02	.00
☐ 153	Dick Tidrow	.04	.02	.00
☐ 154	Dave Henderson	.07	.03	.01
☐ 155	Frank White	.07	.03	.01
☐ 156	Oakland A's TL	.12	.04	.01
	Rickey Henderson			
	Tim Conroy			
☐ 157	Gary Gaetti	.40	.20	.04
☐ 158	John Curtis	.04	.02	.00
☐ 159	Darryl Cias	.07	.03	.01
☐ 160	Mario Soto	.07	.03	.01
☐ 161	Junior Ortiz	.07	.03	.01
☐ 162	Bob Ojeda	.10	.05	.01
☐ 163	Lorenzo Gray	.07	.03	.01
☐ 164	Scott Sanderson	.07	.03	.01
☐ 165	Ken Singleton	.10	.05	.01
☐ 166	Jamie Nelson	.07	.03	.01
☐ 167	Marshall Edwards	.04	.02	.00
☐ 168	Juan Bonilla	.04	.02	.00
☐ 169	Larry Parrish	.07	.03	.01
☐ 170	Jerry Reuss	.07	.03	.01
☐ 171	Frank Robinson MG	.10	.05	.01
☐ 172	Frank DiPino	.04	.02	.00
☐ 173	Marvell Wynne	.10	.05	.01
☐ 174	Juan Berenguer	.04	.02	.00
☐ 175	Graig Nettles	.15	.07	.01
☐ 176	Lee Smith	.10	.05	.01
☐ 177	Jerry Hairston	.04	.02	.00
☐ 178	Bill Krueger	.07	.03	.01
☐ 179	Buck Martinez	.04	.02	.00
☐ 180	Manny Trillo	.04	.02	.00
☐ 181	Roy Thomas	.04	.02	.00
☐ 182	Darryl Strawberry	10.00	5.00	1.00
☐ 183	Al Williams	.04	.02	.00
☐ 184	Mike O'Berry	.04	.02	.00
☐ 185	Sixto Lezcano	.04	.02	.00
☐ 186	Cardinal TL	.10	.03	.01
	Lonnie Smith			
	John Stuper			
☐ 187	Luis Aponte	.04	.02	.00
☐ 188	Bryan Little	.04	.02	.00
☐ 189	Tim Conroy	.07	.03	.01
☐ 190	Ben Oglivie	.07	.03	.01
☐ 191	Mike Boddicker	.10	.05	.01
☐ 192	Nick Esasky	.35	.17	.03
☐ 193	Darrell Brown	.04	.02	.00
☐ 194	Domingo Ramos	.04	.02	.00
☐ 195	Jack Morris	.20	.10	.02
☐ 196	Don Slaught	.10	.05	.01
☐ 197	Garry Hancock	.04	.02	.00
☐ 198	Bill Doran	.75	.35	.07
☐ 199	Willie Hernandez	.25	.12	.02
☐ 200	Andre Dawson	.35	.17	.03
☐ 201	Bruce Kison	.04	.02	.00
☐ 202	Bobby Cox MG	.04	.02	.00
☐ 203	Matt Keough	.04	.02	.00
☐ 204	Bobby Meacham	.20	.10	.02
☐ 205	Greg Minton	.04	.02	.00
☐ 206	Andy Van Slyke	.90	.45	.09
☐ 207	Donnie Moore	.07	.03	.01
☐ 208	Jose Oquendo	.25	.12	.02
☐ 209	Manny Sarmiento	.04	.02	.00
☐ 210	Joe Morgan	.20	.10	.02
☐ 211	Rick Sweet	.04	.02	.00
☐ 212	Broderick Perkins	.04	.02	.00
☐ 213	Bruce Hurst	.10	.05	.01
☐ 214	Paul Householder	.04	.02	.00
☐ 215	Tippy Martinez	.04	.02	.00
☐ 216	White Sox TL	.10	.03	.01
	Carlton Fisk			
	Richard Dotson			
☐ 217	Alan Ashby	.04	.02	.00
☐ 218	Rick Waits	.04	.02	.00
☐ 219	Joe Simpson	.04	.02	.00
☐ 220	Fernando Valenzuela	.35	.17	.03
☐ 221	Cliff Johnson	.04	.02	.00
☐ 222	Rick Honeycutt	.07	.03	.01
☐ 223	Wayne Krenchicki	.04	.02	.00
☐ 224	Sid Monge	.04	.02	.00
☐ 225	Lee Mazzilli	.07	.03	.01
☐ 226	Juan Eichelberger	.04	.02	.00
☐ 227	Steve Braun	.04	.02	.00
☐ 228	John Rabb	.07	.03	.01
☐ 229	Paul Owens MG	.04	.02	.00
☐ 230	Rickey Henderson	.55	.27	.05
☐ 231	Gary Woods	.04	.02	.00
☐ 232	Tim Wallach	.15	.07	.01
☐ 233	Checklist 133-264	.08	.01	.00
☐ 234	Rafael Ramirez	.04	.02	.00
☐ 235	Matt Young	.25	.12	.02
☐ 236	Ellis Valentine	.04	.02	.00
☐ 237	John Castino	.04	.02	.00
☐ 238	Reid Nichols	.04	.02	.00
☐ 239	Jay Howell	.07	.03	.01
☐ 240	Eddie Murray	.55	.27	.05
☐ 241	Billy Almon	.04	.02	.00
☐ 242	Alex Trevino	.04	.02	.00
☐ 243	Pete Ladd	.04	.02	.00
☐ 244	Candy Maldonado	.35	.17	.03
☐ 245	Rick Sutcliffe	.25	.12	.02
☐ 246	New York Mets TL	.12	.04	.01
	Mookie Wilson			
	Tom Seaver			
☐ 247	Onix Concepcion	.04	.02	.00
☐ 248	Bill Dawley	.15	.07	.01
☐ 249	Jay Johnstone	.07	.03	.01
☐ 250	Bill Madlock	.12	.06	.01
☐ 251	Tony Gwynn	1.75	.85	.17
☐ 252	Larry Christenson	.04	.02	.00
☐ 253	Jim Wohlford	.04	.02	.00
☐ 254	Shane Rawley	.07	.03	.01
☐ 255	Bruce Benedict	.04	.02	.00
☐ 256	Dave Geisel	.04	.02	.00
☐ 257	Julio Cruz	.04	.02	.00
☐ 258	Luis Sanchez	.04	.02	.00
☐ 259	Sparky Anderson MG	.04	.02	.00
☐ 260	Scott McGregor	.07	.03	.01
☐ 261	Bobby Brown	.04	.02	.00
☐ 262	Tom Candiotti	.20	.10	.02
☐ 263	Jack Fimple	.07	.03	.01
☐ 264	Doug Frobel	.07	.03	.01
☐ 265	Donnie Hill	.10	.05	.01
☐ 266	Steve Lubratich	.07	.03	.01
☐ 267	Carmelo Martinez	.25	.12	.02
☐ 268	Jack O'Connor	.04	.02	.00
☐ 269	Aurelio Rodriguez	.04	.02	.00
☐ 270	Jeff Russell	.07	.03	.01
☐ 271	Moose Haas	.04	.02	.00
☐ 272	Rick Dempsey	.07	.03	.01
☐ 273	Charlie Puleo	.04	.02	.00
☐ 274	Rick Monday	.07	.03	.01
☐ 275	Len Matuszek	.04	.02	.00
☐ 276	Angels TL	.12	.04	.01
	Rod Carew			
	Geoff Zahn			
☐ 277	Eddie Whitson	.07	.03	.01
☐ 278	Jorge Bell	1.25	.60	.12
☐ 279	Ivan DeJesus	.04	.02	.00
☐ 280	Floyd Bannister	.07	.03	.01

☐ 281	Larry Milbourne	.04	.02	.00
☐ 282	Jim Barr	.04	.02	.00
☐ 283	Larry Biittner	.04	.02	.00
☐ 284	Howard Bailey	.04	.02	.00
☐ 285	Darrell Porter	.04	.02	.00
☐ 286	Lary Sorensen	.04	.02	.00
☐ 287	Warren Cromartie	.04	.02	.00
☐ 288	Jim Beattie	.04	.02	.00
☐ 289	Randy Johnson	.04	.02	.00
☐ 290	Dave Dravecky	.10	.05	.01
☐ 291	Chuck Tanner MG	.04	.02	.00
☐ 292	Tony Scott	.04	.02	.00
☐ 293	Ed Lynch	.04	.02	.00
☐ 294	U.L. Washington	.04	.02	.00
☐ 295	Mike Flanagan	.07	.03	.01
☐ 296	Jeff Newman	.04	.02	.00
☐ 297	Bruce Berenyi	.04	.02	.00
☐ 298	Jim Gantner	.04	.02	.00
☐ 299	John Butcher	.04	.02	.00
☐ 300	Pete Rose	1.50	.75	.15
☐ 301	Frank LaCorte	.04	.02	.00
☐ 302	Barry Bonnell	.04	.02	.00
☐ 303	Marty Castillo	.04	.02	.00
☐ 304	Warren Brusstar	.04	.02	.00
☐ 305	Roy Smalley	.04	.02	.00
☐ 306	Dodgers TL Pedro Guerrero Bob Welch	.10	.03	.01
☐ 307	Bobby Mitchell	.04	.02	.00
☐ 308	Ron Hassey	.04	.02	.00
☐ 309	Tony Phillips	.07	.03	.01
☐ 310	Willie McGee	.35	.17	.03
☐ 311	Jerry Koosman	.10	.05	.01
☐ 312	Jorge Orta	.04	.02	.00
☐ 313	Mike Jorgensen	.04	.02	.00
☐ 314	Orlando Mercado	.07	.03	.01
☐ 315	Bob Grich	.07	.03	.01
☐ 316	Mark Bradley	.04	.02	.00
☐ 317	Greg Pryor	.04	.02	.00
☐ 318	Bill Gullickson	.07	.03	.01
☐ 319	Al Bumbry	.04	.02	.00
☐ 320	Bob Stanley	.07	.03	.01
☐ 321	Harvey Kuenn MG	.04	.02	.00
☐ 322	Ken Schrom	.07	.03	.01
☐ 323	Alan Knicely	.04	.02	.00
☐ 324	Alejandro Pena	.30	.15	.03
☐ 325	Darrell Evans	.15	.07	.01
☐ 326	Bob Kearney	.04	.02	.00
☐ 327	Ruppert Jones	.04	.02	.00
☐ 328	Vern Ruhle	.04	.02	.00
☐ 329	Pat Tabler	.30	.15	.03
☐ 330	John Candelaria	.10	.05	.01
☐ 331	Bucky Dent	.07	.03	.01
☐ 332	Kevin Gross	.25	.12	.02
☐ 333	Larry Herndon	.07	.03	.01
☐ 334	Chuck Rainey	.04	.02	.00
☐ 335	Don Baylor	.12	.06	.01
☐ 336	Seattle Mariners TL Pat Putnam Matt Young	.10	.03	.01
☐ 337	Kevin Hagen	.07	.03	.01
☐ 338	Mike Warren	.10	.05	.01
☐ 339	Roy Lee Jackson	.04	.02	.00
☐ 340	Hal McRae	.07	.03	.01
☐ 341	Dave Tobik	.04	.02	.00
☐ 342	Tim Foli	.04	.02	.00
☐ 343	Mark Davis	.04	.02	.00
☐ 344	Rick Miller	.04	.02	.00
☐ 345	Kent Hrbek	.35	.17	.03
☐ 346	Kurt Bevacqua	.04	.02	.00
☐ 347	Allan Ramirez	.04	.02	.00
☐ 348	Toby Harrah	.04	.02	.00
☐ 349	Bob L. Gibson (Brewers Pitcher)	.07	.03	.01
☐ 350	George Foster	.15	.07	.01
☐ 351	Russ Nixon MG	.04	.02	.00
☐ 352	Dave Stewart	.12	.06	.01
☐ 353	Jim Anderson	.04	.02	.00
☐ 354	Jeff Burroughs	.07	.03	.01
☐ 355	Jason Thompson	.07	.03	.01
☐ 356	Glenn Abbott	.04	.02	.00
☐ 357	Ron Cey	.10	.05	.01
☐ 358	Bob Dernier	.07	.03	.01
☐ 359	Jim Acker	.10	.05	.01
☐ 360	Willie Randolph	.07	.03	.01
☐ 361	Dave Smith	.07	.03	.01
☐ 362	David Green	.07	.03	.01
☐ 363	Tim Laudner	.07	.03	.01
☐ 364	Scott Fletcher	.15	.07	.01
☐ 365	Steve Bedrosian	.15	.07	.01
☐ 366	Padres TL Terry Kennedy Dave Dravecky	.10	.03	.01
☐ 367	Jamie Easterly	.04	.02	.00
☐ 368	Hubie Brooks	.10	.05	.01
☐ 369	Steve McCatty	.04	.02	.00
☐ 370	Tim Raines	.50	.25	.05
☐ 371	Dave Gumpert	.04	.02	.00
☐ 372	Gary Roenicke	.04	.02	.00
☐ 373	Bill Scherrer	.07	.03	.01
☐ 374	Don Money	.04	.02	.00
☐ 375	Dennis Leonard	.07	.03	.01
☐ 376	Dave Anderson	.12	.06	.01
☐ 377	Danny Darwin	.07	.03	.01
☐ 378	Bob Brenly	.07	.03	.01
☐ 379	Checklist 265-396	.08	.01	.00
☐ 380	Steve Garvey	.45	.22	.04
☐ 381	Ralph Houk MG	.04	.02	.00
☐ 382	Chris Nyman	.04	.02	.00
☐ 383	Terry Puhl	.04	.02	.00
☐ 384	Lee Tunnell	.20	.10	.02
☐ 385	Tony Perez	.15	.07	.01
☐ 386	George Hendrick AS	.07	.03	.01
☐ 387	Johnny Ray AS	.07	.03	.01
☐ 388	Mike Schmidt AS	.25	.12	.02
☐ 389	Ozzie Smith AS	.12	.06	.01
☐ 390	Tim Raines AS	.20	.10	.02
☐ 391	Dale Murphy AS	.30	.15	.03
☐ 392	Andre Dawson AS	.20	.10	.02
☐ 393	Gary Carter AS	.20	.10	.02
☐ 394	Steve Rogers AS	.07	.03	.01
☐ 395	Steve Carlton AS	.20	.10	.02
☐ 396	Jesse Orosco AS	.07	.03	.01
☐ 397	Eddie Murray AS	.30	.15	.03
☐ 398	Lou Whitaker AS	.10	.05	.01
☐ 399	George Brett AS	.30	.15	.03
☐ 400	Cal Ripken AS	.30	.15	.03
☐ 401	Jim Rice AS	.20	.10	.02
☐ 402	Dave Winfield AS	.20	.10	.02
☐ 403	Lloyd Moseby AS	.10	.05	.01
☐ 404	Ted Simmons AS	.07	.03	.01
☐ 405	LaMarr Hoyt AS	.07	.03	.01
☐ 406	Ron Guidry AS	.12	.06	.01
☐ 407	Dan Quisenberry AS	.10	.05	.01
☐ 408	Lou Piniella	.07	.03	.01
☐ 409	Juan Agosto	.04	.02	.00
☐ 410	Claudell Washington	.07	.03	.01
☐ 411	Houston Jimenez	.07	.03	.01
☐ 412	Doug Rader MG	.04	.02	.00
☐ 413	Spike Owen	.25	.12	.02
☐ 414	Mitchell Page	.04	.02	.00
☐ 415	Tommy John	.15	.07	.01
☐ 416	Dane Iorg	.04	.02	.00
☐ 417	Mike Armstrong	.04	.02	.00
☐ 418	Ron Hodges	.04	.02	.00
☐ 419	John Henry Johnson	.04	.02	.00
☐ 420	Cecil Cooper	.12	.06	.01
☐ 421	Charlie Lea	.04	.02	.00
☐ 422	Jose Cruz	.10	.05	.01
☐ 423	Mike Morgan	.04	.02	.00
☐ 424	Dann Bilardello	.04	.02	.00
☐ 425	Steve Howe	.04	.02	.00
☐ 426	Orioles TL Cal Ripken Mike Boddicker	.15	.04	.01
☐ 427	Rick Leach	.04	.02	.00
☐ 428	Fred Breining	.04	.02	.00
☐ 429	Randy Bush	.04	.02	.00
☐ 430	Rusty Staub	.10	.05	.01
☐ 431	Chris Bando	.04	.02	.00
☐ 432	Charlie Hudson	.25	.12	.02
☐ 433	Rich Hebner	.04	.02	.00
☐ 434	Harold Baines	.25	.12	.02
☐ 435	Neil Allen	.07	.03	.01
☐ 436	Rick Peters	.04	.02	.00
☐ 437	Mike Proly	.04	.02	.00
☐ 438	Biff Pocoroba	.04	.02	.00
☐ 439	Bob Stoddard	.04	.02	.00
☐ 440	Steve Kemp	.07	.03	.01
☐ 441	Bob Lillis MG	.04	.02	.00
☐ 442	Byron McLaughlin	.04	.02	.00
☐ 443	Benny Ayala	.04	.02	.00
☐ 444	Steve Renko	.04	.02	.00
☐ 445	Jerry Remy	.04	.02	.00
☐ 446	Luis Pujols	.04	.02	.00
☐ 447	Tom Brunansky	.20	.10	.02
☐ 448	Ben Hayes	.04	.02	.00
☐ 449	Joe Pettini	.04	.02	.00
☐ 450	Gary Carter	.40	.20	.04
☐ 451	Bob Jones	.04	.02	.00
☐ 452	Chuck Porter	.04	.02	.00
☐ 453	Willie Upshaw	.07	.03	.01
☐ 454	Joe Beckwith	.04	.02	.00
☐ 455	Terry Kennedy	.07	.03	.01
☐ 456	Chicago Cubs TL Keith Moreland Fergie Jenkins	.10	.03	.01
☐ 457	Dave Rozema	.04	.02	.00
☐ 458	Kiko Garcia	.04	.02	.00
☐ 459	Kevin Hickey	.04	.02	.00

☐ 460	Dave Winfield	.40	.20	.04
☐ 461	Jim Maler	.04	.02	.00
☐ 462	Lee Lacy	.07	.03	.01
☐ 463	Dave Engle	.04	.02	.00
☐ 464	Jeff A. Jones	.04	.02	.00
	(A's Pitcher)			
☐ 465	Mookie Wilson	.07	.03	.01
☐ 466	Gene Garber	.07	.03	.01
☐ 467	Mike Ramsey	.04	.02	.00
☐ 468	Geoff Zahn	.04	.02	.00
☐ 469	Tom O'Malley	.04	.02	.00
☐ 470	Nolan Ryan	.35	.17	.03
☐ 471	Dick Howser MG	.07	.03	.01
☐ 472	Mike Brown	.07	.03	.01
	(Red Sox Pitcher)			
☐ 473	Jim Dwyer	.04	.02	.00
☐ 474	Greg Bargar	.07	.03	.01
☐ 475	Gary Redus	.30	.15	.03
☐ 476	Tom Tellmann	.04	.02	.00
☐ 477	Rafael Landestoy	.04	.02	.00
☐ 478	Alan Bannister	.04	.02	.00
☐ 479	Frank Tanana	.07	.03	.01
☐ 480	Ron Kittle	.25	.12	.02
☐ 481	Mark Thurmond	.20	.10	.02
☐ 482	Enos Cabell	.04	.02	.00
☐ 483	Fergie Jenkins	.15	.07	.01
☐ 484	Ozzie Virgil	.07	.03	.01
☐ 485	Rick Rhoden	.10	.05	.01
☐ 486	N.Y. Yankees TL	.10	.03	.01
	Don Baylor			
	Ron Guidry			
☐ 487	Ricky Adams	.07	.03	.01
☐ 488	Jesse Barfield	.35	.17	.03
☐ 489	Dave Von Ohlen	.07	.03	.01
☐ 490	Cal Ripken	.65	.30	.06
☐ 491	Bobby Castillo	.04	.02	.00
☐ 492	Tucker Ashford	.04	.02	.00
☐ 493	Mike Norris	.04	.02	.00
☐ 494	Chili Davis	.15	.07	.01
☐ 495	Rollie Fingers	.20	.10	.02
☐ 496	Terry Francona	.04	.02	.00
☐ 497	Bud Anderson	.04	.02	.00
☐ 498	Rich Gedman	.10	.05	.01
☐ 499	Mike Witt	.15	.07	.01
☐ 500	George Brett	.60	.30	.06
☐ 501	Steve Henderson	.04	.02	.00
☐ 502	Joe Torre MG	.07	.03	.01
☐ 503	Elias Sosa	.04	.02	.00
☐ 504	Mickey Rivers	.07	.03	.01
☐ 505	Pete Vuckovich	.07	.03	.01
☐ 506	Ernie Whitt	.04	.02	.00
☐ 507	Mike LaCoss	.04	.02	.00
☐ 508	Mel Hall	.25	.12	.02
☐ 509	Brad Havens	.04	.02	.00
☐ 510	Alan Trammell	.30	.15	.03
☐ 511	Marty Bystrom	.04	.02	.00
☐ 512	Oscar Gamble	.07	.03	.01
☐ 513	Dave Beard	.04	.02	.00
☐ 514	Floyd Rayford	.04	.02	.00
☐ 515	Gorman Thomas	.10	.05	.01
☐ 516	Montreal Expos TL	.10	.03	.01
	Al Oliver			
	Charlie Lea			
☐ 517	John Moses	.07	.03	.01
☐ 518	Greg Walker	.75	.35	.07
☐ 519	Ron Davis	.04	.02	.00
☐ 520	Bob Boone	.07	.03	.01
☐ 521	Pete Falcone	.04	.02	.00
☐ 522	Dave Bergman	.04	.02	.00
☐ 523	Glenn Hoffman	.04	.02	.00
☐ 524	Carlos Diaz	.04	.02	.00
☐ 525	Willie Wilson	.15	.07	.01
☐ 526	Ron Oester	.04	.02	.00
☐ 527	Checklist 397-528	.08	.01	.00
☐ 528	Mark Brouhard	.04	.02	.00
☐ 529	Keith Atherton	.07	.03	.01
☐ 530	Dan Ford	.04	.02	.00
☐ 531	Steve Boros MG	.04	.02	.00
☐ 532	Eric Show	.04	.02	.00
☐ 533	Ken Landreaux	.07	.03	.01
☐ 534	Pete O'Brien	1.25	.60	.12
☐ 535	Bo Diaz	.07	.03	.01
☐ 536	Doug Bair	.04	.02	.00
☐ 537	Johnny Ray	.12	.06	.01
☐ 538	Kevin Bass	.12	.06	.01
☐ 539	George Frazier	.04	.02	.00
☐ 540	George Hendrick	.07	.03	.01
☐ 541	Dennis Lamp	.04	.02	.00
☐ 542	Duane Kuiper	.04	.02	.00
☐ 543	Craig McMurtry	.07	.03	.01
☐ 544	Cesar Geronimo	.04	.02	.00
☐ 545	Bill Buckner	.10	.05	.01
☐ 546	Indians TL	.10	.03	.01
	Mike Hargrove			
	Lary Sorensen			

☐ 547	Mike Moore	.07	.03	.01
☐ 548	Ron Jackson	.04	.02	.00
☐ 549	Walt Terrell	.45	.22	.04
☐ 550	Jim Rice	.35	.17	.03
☐ 551	Scott Ullger	.07	.03	.01
☐ 552	Ray Burris	.04	.02	.00
☐ 553	Joe Nolan	.04	.02	.00
☐ 554	Ted Power	.07	.03	.01
☐ 555	Greg Brock	.15	.07	.01
☐ 556	Joey McLaughlin	.04	.02	.00
☐ 557	Wayne Tolleson	.12	.06	.01
☐ 558	Mike Davis	.07	.03	.01
☐ 559	Mike Scott	.25	.12	.02
☐ 560	Carlton Fisk	.15	.07	.01
☐ 561	Whitey Herzog MG	.04	.02	.00
☐ 562	Manny Castillo	.04	.02	.00
☐ 563	Glenn Wilson	.12	.06	.01
☐ 564	Al Holland	.04	.02	.00
☐ 565	Leon Durham	.10	.05	.01
☐ 566	Jim Bibby	.04	.02	.00
☐ 567	Mike Heath	.04	.02	.00
☐ 568	Pete Filson	.04	.02	.00
☐ 569	Bake McBride	.04	.02	.00
☐ 570	Dan Quisenberry	.15	.07	.01
☐ 571	Bruce Bochy	.04	.02	.00
☐ 572	Jerry Royster	.04	.02	.00
☐ 573	Dave Kingman	.15	.07	.01
☐ 574	Brian Downing	.07	.03	.01
☐ 575	Jim Clancy	.07	.03	.01
☐ 576	Giants TL	.10	.03	.01
	Jeff Leonard			
	Atlee Hammaker			
☐ 577	Mark Clear	.04	.02	.00
☐ 578	Lenn Sakata	.04	.02	.00
☐ 579	Bob James	.20	.10	.02
☐ 580	Lonnie Smith	.07	.03	.01
☐ 581	Jose DeLeon	.25	.12	.02
☐ 582	Bob McClure	.04	.02	.00
☐ 583	Derrel Thomas	.04	.02	.00
☐ 584	Dave Schmidt	.07	.03	.01
☐ 585	Dan Driessen	.07	.03	.01
☐ 586	Joe Niekro	.10	.05	.01
☐ 587	Von Hayes	.20	.10	.02
☐ 588	Milt Wilcox	.04	.02	.00
☐ 589	Mike Easler	.07	.03	.01
☐ 590	Dave Stieb	.15	.07	.01
☐ 591	Tony LaRussa MG	.04	.02	.00
☐ 592	Andre Robertson	.04	.02	.00
☐ 593	Jeff Lahti	.04	.02	.00
☐ 594	Gene Richards	.04	.02	.00
☐ 595	Jeff Reardon	.12	.06	.01
☐ 596	Ryne Sandberg	1.25	.60	.12
☐ 597	Rick Camp	.04	.02	.00
☐ 598	Rusty Kuntz	.04	.02	.00
☐ 599	Doug Sisk	.10	.05	.01
☐ 600	Rod Carew	.45	.22	.04
☐ 601	John Tudor	.15	.07	.01
☐ 602	John Wathan	.07	.03	.01
☐ 603	Renie Martin	.04	.02	.00
☐ 604	John Lowenstein	.04	.02	.00
☐ 605	Mike Caldwell	.07	.03	.01
☐ 606	Blue Jays TL	.10	.03	.01
	Lloyd Moseby			
	Dave Stieb			
☐ 607	Tom Hume	.04	.02	.00
☐ 608	Bobby Johnson	.04	.02	.00
☐ 609	Dan Meyer	.04	.02	.00
☐ 610	Steve Sax	.18	.09	.01
☐ 611	Chet Lemon	.07	.03	.01
☐ 612	Harry Spilman	.04	.02	.00
☐ 613	Greg Gross	.04	.02	.00
☐ 614	Len Barker	.04	.02	.00
☐ 615	Garry Templeton	.10	.05	.01
☐ 616	Don Robinson	.04	.02	.00
☐ 617	Rick Cerone	.04	.02	.00
☐ 618	Dickie Noles	.04	.02	.00
☐ 619	Jerry Dybzinski	.04	.02	.00
☐ 620	Al Oliver	.12	.06	.01
☐ 621	Frank Howard MG	.04	.02	.00
☐ 622	Al Cowens	.04	.02	.00
☐ 623	Ron Washington	.04	.02	.00
☐ 624	Terry Harper	.04	.02	.00
☐ 625	Larry Gura	.04	.02	.00
☐ 626	Bob Clark	.04	.02	.00
☐ 627	Dave LaPoint	.04	.02	.00
☐ 628	Ed Jurak	.04	.02	.00
☐ 629	Rick Langford	.04	.02	.00
☐ 630	Ted Simmons	.12	.06	.01
☐ 631	Denny Martinez	.07	.03	.01
☐ 632	Tom Foley	.04	.02	.00
☐ 633	Mike Krukow	.07	.03	.01
☐ 634	Mike Marshall	.15	.07	.01
☐ 635	Dave Righetti	.20	.10	.02
☐ 636	Pat Putnam	.04	.02	.00
☐ 637	Phillies TL	.10	.03	.01

Gary Matthews
John Denny

□ 638 George Vukovich	.04	.02	.00
□ 639 Rick Lysander	.07	.03	.01
□ 640 Lance Parrish	.25	.12	.02
□ 641 Mike Richardt	.04	.02	.00
□ 642 Tom Underwood	.04	.02	.00
□ 643 Mike Brown	.12	.06	.01

(Angels OF)

□ 644 Tim Lollar	.04	.02	.00
□ 645 Tony Pena	.12	.06	.01
□ 646 Checklist 529-660	.08	.01	.00
□ 647 Ron Roenicke	.04	.02	.00
□ 648 Len Whitehouse	.04	.02	.00
□ 649 Tom Herr	.10	.05	.01
□ 650 Phil Niekro	.20	.10	.02
□ 651 John McNamara MG	.04	.02	.00
□ 652 Rudy May	.04	.02	.00
□ 653 Dave Stapleton	.04	.02	.00
□ 654 Bob Bailor	.04	.02	.00
□ 655 Amos Otis	.07	.03	.01
□ 656 Bryn Smith	.07	.03	.01
□ 657 Thad Bosley	.04	.02	.00
□ 658 Jerry Augustine	.04	.02	.00
□ 659 Duane Walker	.04	.02	.00
□ 660 Ray Knight	.10	.05	.01
□ 661 Steve Yeager	.04	.02	.00
□ 662 Tom Brennan	.04	.02	.00
□ 663 Johnnie LeMaster	.04	.02	.00
□ 664 Dave Stegman	.04	.02	.00
□ 665 Buddy Bell	.12	.06	.01
□ 666 Detroit Tigers TL	.12	.04	.01

Lou Whitaker
Jack Morris

□ 667 Vance Law	.04	.02	.00
□ 668 Larry McWilliams	.04	.02	.00
□ 669 Dave Lopes	.07	.03	.01
□ 670 Rich Gossage	.18	.09	.01
□ 671 Jamie Quirk	.04	.02	.00
□ 672 Ricky Nelson	.07	.03	.01
□ 673 Mike Walters	.07	.03	.01
□ 674 Tim Flannery	.04	.02	.00
□ 675 Pascual Perez	.07	.03	.01
□ 676 Brian Giles	.04	.02	.00
□ 677 Doyle Alexander	.07	.03	.01
□ 678 Chris Speier	.04	.02	.00
□ 679 Art Howe	.04	.02	.00
□ 680 Fred Lynn	.20	.10	.02
□ 681 Tom Lasorda MG	.07	.03	.01
□ 682 Dan Morogiello	.07	.03	.01
□ 683 Marty Barrett	1.75	.85	.17
□ 684 Bob Shirley	.04	.02	.00
□ 685 Willie Aikens	.04	.02	.00
□ 686 Joe Price	.04	.02	.00
□ 687 Roy Howell	.04	.02	.00
□ 688 George Wright	.04	.02	.00
□ 689 Mike Fischlin	.04	.02	.00
□ 690 Jack Clark	.30	.15	.03
□ 691 Steve Lake	.07	.03	.01
□ 692 Dickie Thon	.07	.03	.01
□ 693 Alan Wiggins	.07	.03	.01
□ 694 Mike Stanton	.04	.02	.00
□ 695 Lou Whitaker	.18	.09	.01
□ 696 Pirates TL	.10	.03	.01

Bill Madlock
Rick Rhoden

□ 697 Dale Murray	.04	.02	.00
□ 698 Marc Hill	.04	.02	.00
□ 699 Dave Rucker	.04	.02	.00
□ 700 Mike Schmidt	.60	.30	.06
□ 701 NL Active Batting	.20	.10	.02

Bill Madlock
Pete Rose
Dave Parker

□ 702 NL Active Hits	.20	.10	.02

Pete Rose
Rusty Staub
Tony Perez

□ 703 NL Active Home Run	.18	.09	.01

Mike Schmidt
Tony Perez
Dave Kingman

□ 704 NL Active RBI	.10	.05	.01

Tony Perez
Rusty Staub
Al Oliver

□ 705 NL Active Steals	.10	.05	.01

Joe Morgan
Cesar Cedeno
Larry Bowa

□ 706 NL Active Victory	.20	.10	.02

Steve Carlton
Fergie Jenkins
Tom Seaver

□ 707 NL Active Strikeout	.20	.10	.02

Steve Carlton
Nolan Ryan
Tom Seaver

□ 708 NL Active ERA	.18	.09	.01

Tom Seaver
Steve Carlton
Steve Rogers

□ 709 NL Active Save	.10	.05	.01

Bruce Sutter
Tug McGraw
Gene Garber

□ 710 AL Active Batting	.20	.10	.02

Rod Carew
George Brett
Cecil Cooper

□ 711 AL Active Hits	.18	.09	.01

Rod Carew
Bert Campaneris
Reggie Jackson

□ 712 AL Active Home Run	.18	.09	.01

Reggie Jackson
Graig Nettles
Greg Luzinski

□ 713 AL Active RBI	.18	.09	.01

Reggie Jackson
Ted Simmons
Graig Nettles

□ 714 AL Active Steals	.07	.03	.01

Bert Campaneris
Dave Lopes
Omar Moreno

□ 715 AL Active Victory	.18	.09	.01

Jim Palmer
Don Sutton
Tommy John

□ 716 AL Active Strikeout	.07	.03	.01

Don Sutton
Bert Blyleven
Jerry Koosman

□ 717 AL Active ERA	.15	.07	.01

Jim Palmer
Rollie Fingers
Ron Guidry

□ 718 AL Active Save	.12	.06	.01

Rollie Fingers
Rich Gossage
Dan Quisenberry

□ 719 Andy Hassler	.04	.02	.00
□ 720 Dwight Evans	.15	.07	.01
□ 721 Del Crandall MG	.04	.02	.00
□ 722 Bob Welch	.07	.03	.01
□ 723 Rich Dauer	.04	.02	.00
□ 724 Eric Rasmussen	.04	.02	.00
□ 725 Cesar Cedeno	.07	.03	.01
□ 726 Brewers TL	.10	.03	.01

Ted Simmons
Moose Haas

□ 727 Joel Youngblood	.04	.02	.00
□ 728 Tug McGraw	.10	.05	.01
□ 729 Gene Tenace	.07	.03	.01
□ 730 Bruce Sutter	.15	.07	.01
□ 731 Lynn Jones	.04	.02	.00
□ 732 Terry Crowley	.04	.02	.00
□ 733 Dave Collins	.04	.02	.00
□ 734 Odell Jones	.04	.02	.00
□ 735 Rick Burleson	.07	.03	.01
□ 736 Dick Ruthven	.04	.02	.00
□ 737 Jim Essian	.04	.02	.00
□ 738 Bill Schroeder	.20	.10	.02
□ 739 Bob Watson	.07	.03	.01
□ 740 Tom Seaver	.40	.20	.04
□ 741 Wayne Gross	.04	.02	.00
□ 742 Dick Williams MG	.04	.02	.00
□ 743 Don Hood	.04	.02	.00
□ 744 Jamie Allen	.07	.03	.01
□ 745 Dennis Eckersley	.07	.03	.01
□ 746 Mickey Hatcher	.04	.02	.00
□ 747 Pat Zachry	.04	.02	.00
□ 748 Jeff Leonard	.15	.07	.01
□ 749 Doug Flynn	.04	.02	.00
□ 750 Jim Palmer	.30	.15	.03
□ 751 Charlie Moore	.04	.02	.00
□ 752 Phil Garner	.04	.02	.00
□ 753 Doug Gwosdz	.04	.02	.00
□ 754 Kent Tekulve	.07	.03	.01
□ 755 Garry Maddox	.07	.03	.01
□ 756 Reds TL	.10	.03	.01

Ron Oester
Mario Soto

□ 757 Larry Bowa	.10	.05	.01
□ 758 Bill Stein	.04	.02	.00
□ 759 Richard Dotson	.07	.03	.01
□ 760 Bob Horner	.25	.12	.02
□ 761 John Montefusco	.07	.03	.01
□ 762 Rance Mulliniks	.04	.02	.00

☐ 763	Craig Swan	.04	.02	.00
☐ 764	Mike Hargrove	.07	.03	.01
☐ 765	Ken Forsch	.04	.02	.00
☐ 766	Mike Vail	.04	.02	.00
☐ 767	Carney Lansford	.10	.05	.01
☐ 768	Champ Summers	.04	.02	.00
☐ 769	Bill Caudill	.04	.02	.00
☐ 770	Ken Griffey	.07	.03	.01
☐ 771	Billy Gardner MG	.04	.02	.00
☐ 772	Jim Slaton	.04	.02	.00
☐ 773	Todd Cruz	.04	.02	.00
☐ 774	Tom Gorman	.10	.05	.01
☐ 775	Dave Parker	.20	.10	.02
☐ 776	Craig Reynolds	.04	.02	.00
☐ 777	Tom Paciorek	.04	.02	.00
☐ 778	Andy Hawkins	.20	.10	.02
☐ 779	Jim Sundberg	.07	.03	.01
☐ 780	Steve Carlton	.35	.17	.03
☐ 781	Checklist 661-792	.08	.01	.00
☐ 782	Steve Balboni	.07	.03	.01
☐ 783	Luis Leal	.04	.02	.00
☐ 784	Leon Roberts	.04	.02	.00
☐ 785	Joaquin Andujar	.12	.06	.01
☐ 786	Red Sox TL	.25	.07	.01
	Wade Boggs			
	Bob Ojeda			
☐ 787	Bill Campbell	.04	.02	.00
☐ 788	Milt May	.04	.02	.00
☐ 789	Bert Blyleven	.12	.06	.01
☐ 790	Doug DeCinces	.10	.05	.01
☐ 791	Terry Forster	.07	.03	.01
☐ 792	Bill Russell	.15	.03	.01

1984 Topps Traded

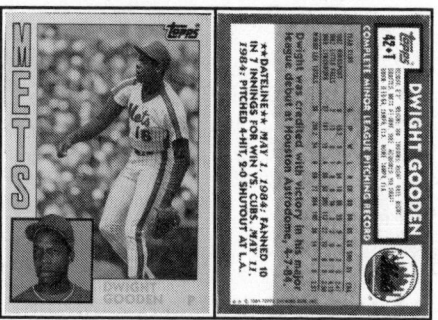

The cards in this 132-card set measure 2 1/2" by 3 1/2". In its now standard procedure, Topps issued its Traded (or extended) set for the fourth year in a row. Because all photos and statistics of its regular set for the year were developed during the fall and winter months of the preceding year, players who changed teams during the fall, winter and spring months are portrayed with the teams they were with in 1983. The Traded set amends the shortcomings of the regular set by presenting the players with their proper teams for the current year. Rookies not contained in the regular set are also picked up in the Traded set. Again this year, the Topps affiliate in Ireland printed the cards, and the cards were available through hobby channels only.

		MINT	EXC	G-VG
COMPLETE SET		80.00	40.00	8.00
COMMON PLAYER		.10	.05	.01
☐ 1T	Willie Aikens	.20	.05	.01
☐ 2T	Luis Aponte	.10	.05	.01
☐ 3T	Mike Armstrong	.10	.05	.01
☐ 4T	Bob Bailor	.10	.05	.01
☐ 5T	Dusty Baker	.20	.10	.02
☐ 6T	Steve Balboni	.20	.10	.02
☐ 7T	Alan Bannister	.10	.05	.01
☐ 8T	Dave Beard	.10	.05	.01
☐ 9T	Joe Beckwith	.10	.05	.01
☐ 10T	Bruce Berenyi	.10	.05	.01
☐ 11T	Dave Bergman	.10	.05	.01

☐ 12T	Tony Bernazard	.20	.10	.02
☐ 13T	Yogi Berra MG	.30	.15	.03
☐ 14T	Barry Bonnell	.10	.05	.01
☐ 15T	Phil Bradley	3.00	1.50	.30
☐ 16T	Fred Breining	.10	.05	.01
☐ 17T	Bill Buckner	.30	.15	.03
☐ 18T	Ray Burris	.10	.05	.01
☐ 19T	John Butcher	.10	.05	.01
☐ 20T	Brett Butler	.30	.15	.03
☐ 21T	Enos Cabell	.10	.05	.01
☐ 22T	Bill Campbell	.10	.05	.01
☐ 23T	Bill Caudill	.10	.05	.01
☐ 24T	Bob Clark	.10	.05	.01
☐ 25T	Bryan Clark	.10	.05	.01
☐ 26T	Jaime Cocanower	.20	.10	.02
☐ 27T	Ron Darling	6.00	3.00	.60
☐ 28T	Alvin Davis	3.00	1.50	.30
☐ 29T	Ken Dayley	.20	.10	.02
☐ 30T	Jeff Dedmon	.20	.10	.02
☐ 31T	Bob Dernier	.20	.10	.02
☐ 32T	Carlos Diaz	.10	.05	.01
☐ 33T	Mike Easler	.20	.10	.02
☐ 34T	Dennis Eckersley	.20	.10	.02
☐ 35T	Jim Essian	.10	.05	.01
☐ 36T	Darrell Evans	.30	.15	.03
☐ 37T	Mike Fitzgerald	.20	.10	.02
☐ 38T	Tim Foli	.10	.05	.01
☐ 39T	George Frazier	.10	.05	.01
☐ 40T	Rich Gale	.10	.05	.01
☐ 41T	Barbaro Garbey	.20	.10	.02
☐ 42T	Dwight Gooden	35.00	17.50	3.50
☐ 43T	Rich Gossage	.35	.17	.03
☐ 44T	Wayne Gross	.10	.05	.01
☐ 45T	Mark Gubicza	.50	.25	.05
☐ 46T	Jackie Gutierrez	.20	.10	.02
☐ 47T	Mel Hall	.30	.15	.03
☐ 48T	Toby Harrah	.10	.05	.01
☐ 49T	Ron Hassey	.10	.05	.01
☐ 50T	Rich Hebner	.10	.05	.01
☐ 51T	Willie Hernandez	.35	.17	.03
☐ 52T	Ricky Horton	.40	.20	.04
☐ 53T	Art Howe	.10	.05	.01
☐ 54T	Dane Iorg	.10	.05	.01
☐ 55T	Brook Jacoby	2.00	1.00	.20
☐ 56T	Mike Jeffcoat	.20	.10	.02
☐ 57T	Dave Johnson MG	.20	.10	.02
☐ 58T	Lynn Jones	.10	.05	.01
☐ 59T	Ruppert Jones	.10	.05	.01
☐ 60T	Mike Jorgensen	.10	.05	.01
☐ 61T	Bob Kearney	.10	.05	.01
☐ 62T	Jimmy Key	3.50	1.75	.35
☐ 63T	Dave Kingman	.35	.17	.03
☐ 64T	Jerry Koosman	.30	.15	.03
☐ 65T	Wayne Krenchicki	.10	.05	.01
☐ 66T	Rusty Kuntz	.10	.05	.01
☐ 67T	Rene Lachemann MG	.10	.05	.01
☐ 68T	Frank LaCorte	.10	.05	.01
☐ 69T	Dennis Lamp	.10	.05	.01
☐ 70T	Mark Langston	3.50	1.75	.35
☐ 71T	Rick Leach	.10	.05	.01
☐ 72T	Craig Lefferts	.10	.05	.01
☐ 73T	Gary Lucas	.10	.05	.01
☐ 74T	Jerry Martin	.10	.05	.01
☐ 75T	Carmelo Martinez	.20	.10	.02
☐ 76T	Mike Mason	.20	.10	.02
☐ 77T	Gary Matthews	.20	.10	.02
☐ 78T	Andy McGaffigan	.10	.05	.01
☐ 79T	Larry Milbourne	.10	.05	.01
☐ 80T	Sid Monge	.10	.05	.01
☐ 81T	Jackie Moore MG	.10	.05	.01
☐ 82T	Joe Morgan	1.00	.50	.10
☐ 83T	Graig Nettles	.40	.20	.04
☐ 84T	Phil Niekro	.85	.40	.08
☐ 85T	Ken Oberkfell	.10	.05	.01
☐ 86T	Mike O'Berry	.10	.05	.01
☐ 87T	Al Oliver	.20	.10	.02
☐ 88T	Jorge Orta	.10	.05	.01
☐ 89T	Amos Otis	.20	.10	.02
☐ 90T	Dave Parker	.75	.35	.07
☐ 91T	Tony Perez	.40	.20	.04
☐ 92T	Gerald Perry	.50	.25	.05
☐ 93T	Gary Pettis	.40	.20	.04
☐ 94T	Rob Picciolo	.10	.05	.01
☐ 95T	Vern Rapp MG	.10	.05	.01
☐ 96T	Floyd Rayford	.10	.05	.01
☐ 97T	Randy Ready	.40	.20	.04
☐ 98T	Ron Reed	.10	.05	.01
☐ 99T	Gene Richards	.10	.05	.01
☐ 100T	Jose Rijo	.50	.25	.05
☐ 101T	Jeff Robinson	.35	.17	.03
	(Giants pitcher)			
☐ 102T	Ron Romanick	.20	.10	.02
☐ 103T	Pete Rose	9.00	4.50	.90
☐ 104T	Bret Saberhagen	15.00	7.50	1.50
☐ 105T	Juan Samuel	3.50	1.75	.35

		MINT	EXC	G-VG
☐ 106T	Scott Sanderson	.10	.05	.01
☐ 107T	Dick Schofield	.60	.30	.06
☐ 108T	Tom Seaver	3.50	1.75	.35
☐ 109T	Jim Slaton	.10	.05	.01
☐ 110T	Mike Smithson	.10	.05	.01
☐ 111T	Lary Sorensen	.10	.05	.01
☐ 112T	Tim Stoddard	.10	.05	.01
☐ 113T	Champ Summers	.10	.05	.01
☐ 114T	Jim Sundberg	.10	.05	.01
☐ 115T	Rick Sutcliffe	.45	.22	.04
☐ 116T	Craig Swan	.10	.05	.01
☐ 117T	Tim Teufel	.45	.22	.04
☐ 118T	Derrel Thomas	.10	.05	.01
☐ 119T	Gorman Thomas	.25	.12	.02
☐ 120T	Alex Trevino	.10	.05	.01
☐ 121T	Manny Trillo	.10	.05	.01
☐ 122T	John Tudor	.35	.17	.03
☐ 123T	Tom Underwood	.10	.05	.01
☐ 124T	Mike Vail	.10	.05	.01
☐ 125T	Tom Waddell	.20	.10	.02
☐ 126T	Gary Ward	.20	.10	.02
☐ 127T	Curt Wilkerson	.20	.10	.02
☐ 128T	Frank Williams	.20	.10	.02
☐ 129T	Glenn Wilson	.30	.15	.03
☐ 130T	Johnny Wockenfuss	.10	.05	.01
☐ 131T	Ned Yost	.10	.05	.01
☐ 132T	Checklist: 1-132	.10	.01	.00

1984 Topps Glossy 22

The cards in this 22-card set measure 2 1/2" by 3 1/2". Unlike the 1983 Topps Glossy set which was not distributed with its regular baseball cards, the 1984 Topps Glossy set was distributed as inserts in Topps Rak-Paks. The set features the nine American and National League All-Stars who started in the 1983 All Star game in Chicago. The managers and team captains (Yastrzemski and Bench) complete the set. The cards are numbered on the back and are ordered by position within league (AL: 1-11 and NL: 12-22).

		MINT	EXC	G-VG
COMPLETE SET		3.50	1.75	.35
COMMON PLAYER		.10	.05	.01
☐ 1	Harvey Kuenn MG	.10	.05	.01
☐ 2	Rod Carew	.40	.20	.04
☐ 3	Manny Trillo	.10	.05	.01
☐ 4	George Brett	.65	.30	.06
☐ 5	Robin Yount	.40	.20	.04
☐ 6	Jim Rice	.35	.17	.03
☐ 7	Fred Lynn	.20	.10	.02
☐ 8	Dave Winfield	.35	.17	.03
☐ 9	Ted Simmons	.15	.07	.01
☐ 10	Dave Stieb	.15	.07	.01
☐ 11	Carl Yastrzemski CAPT	.50	.25	.05
☐ 12	Whitey Herzog MG	.10	.05	.01
☐ 13	Al Oliver	.15	.07	.01
☐ 14	Steve Sax	.20	.10	.02
☐ 15	Mike Schmidt	.75	.35	.07
☐ 16	Ozzie Smith	.30	.15	.03
☐ 17	Tim Raines	.50	.25	.05
☐ 18	Andre Dawson	.35	.17	.03
☐ 19	Dale Murphy	.75	.35	.07
☐ 20	Gary Carter	.40	.20	.04
☐ 21	Mario Soto	.10	.05	.01
☐ 22	Johnny Bench CAPT	.30	.15	.03

1984 Topps Glossy 40

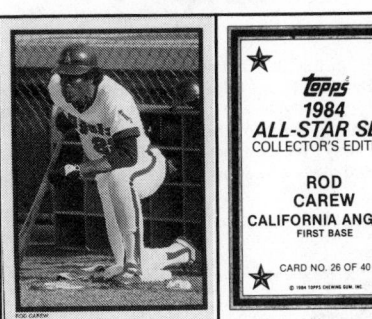

The cards in this 40-card set measure 2 1/2" by 3 1/2". Similar to last year's glossy set, this set was issued as a bonus prize to Topps All-Star Baseball Game cards found in wax packs. Twenty-five bonus runs from the game cards were necessary to obtain a five card subset of the series. There were eight different subsets of five cards. The cards are numbered and contain 20 stars from each league.

		MINT	EXC	G-VG
COMPLETE SET		12.00	6.00	1.20
COMMON PLAYER		.15	.07	.01
☐ 1	Pete Rose	1.25	.60	.12
☐ 2	Lance Parrish	.30	.15	.03
☐ 3	Steve Rogers	.15	.07	.01
☐ 4	Eddie Murray	.90	.45	.09
☐ 5	Johnny Ray	.20	.10	.02
☐ 6	Rickey Henderson	.90	.45	.09
☐ 7	Atlee Hammaker	.15	.07	.01
☐ 8	Wade Boggs	1.75	.85	.17
☐ 9	Gary Carter	.50	.25	.05
☐ 10	Jack Morris	.30	.15	.03
☐ 11	Darrell Evans	.20	.10	.02
☐ 12	George Brett	1.00	.50	.10
☐ 13	Bob Horner	.35	.17	.03
☐ 14	Ron Guidry	.35	.17	.03
☐ 15	Nolan Ryan	.60	.30	.06
☐ 16	Dave Winfield	.50	.25	.05
☐ 17	Ozzie Smith	.25	.12	.02
☐ 18	Ted Simmons	.20	.10	.02
☐ 19	Bill Madlock	.25	.12	.02
☐ 20	Tony Armas	.20	.10	.02
☐ 21	Al Oliver	.20	.10	.02
☐ 22	Jim Rice	.50	.25	.05
☐ 23	George Hendrick	.15	.07	.01
☐ 24	Dave Stieb	.15	.07	.01
☐ 25	Pedro Guerrero	.35	.17	.03
☐ 26	Rod Carew	.50	.25	.05
☐ 27	Steve Carlton	.50	.25	.05
☐ 28	Dave Righetti	.25	.12	.02
☐ 29	Darryl Strawberry	1.25	.60	.12
☐ 30	Lou Whitaker	.25	.12	.02
☐ 31	Dale Murphy	1.25	.60	.12
☐ 32	LaMarr Hoyt	.15	.07	.01
☐ 33	Jesse Orosco	.15	.07	.01
☐ 34	Cecil Cooper	.25	.12	.02
☐ 35	Andre Dawson	.35	.17	.03
☐ 36	Robin Yount	.50	.25	.05
☐ 37	Tim Raines	.45	.22	.04
☐ 38	Dan Quisenberry	.25	.12	.02
☐ 39	Mike Schmidt	1.00	.50	.10
☐ 40	Carlton Fisk	.25	.12	.02

1984 Topps Supers 5x7

The cards in this 30-card set measure 4 7/8" by 6 7/8". The 1984 Topps Supers feature enlargements from the 1984 regular set. The cards differ from the corresponding cards of the regular set in size and number only. As one would expect, only those considered stars and superstars appear in this set.

		MINT	EXC	G-VG
	COMPLETE SET	9.00	4.50	.90
	COMMON PLAYER	.20	.10	.02
☐	1 Cal Ripken	.90	.45	.09
☐	2 Dale Murphy	1.25	.60	.12
☐	3 LaMarr Hoyt	.20	.10	.02
☐	4 John Denny	.20	.10	.02
☐	5 Jim Rice	.50	.25	.05
☐	6 Mike Schmidt	1.00	.50	.10
☐	7 Wade Boggs	1.75	.85	.17
☐	8 Bill Madlock	.20	.10	.02
☐	9 Dan Quisenberry	.30	.15	.03
☐	10 Al Holland	.20	.10	.02
☐	11 Ron Kittle	.30	.15	.03
☐	12 Darryl Strawberry	1.25	.60	.12
☐	13 George Brett	1.00	.50	.10
☐	14 Bill Buckner	.20	.10	.02
☐	15 Carlton Fisk	.30	.15	.03
☐	16 Steve Carlton	.50	.25	.05
☐	17 Ron Guidry	.35	.17	.03
☐	18 Gary Carter	.60	.30	.06
☐	19 Rickey Henderson	.90	.45	.09
☐	20 Andre Dawson	.40	.20	.04
☐	21 Reggie Jackson	1.00	.50	.10
☐	22 Steve Garvey	.75	.35	.07
☐	23 Fred Lynn	.30	.15	.03
☐	24 Pedro Guerrero	.35	.17	.03
☐	25 Eddie Murray	.90	.45	.09
☐	26 Keith Hernandez	.50	.25	.05
☐	27 Dave Winfield	.50	.25	.05
☐	28 Nolan Ryan	.60	.30	.06
☐	29 Robin Yount	.45	.22	.04
☐	30 Fernando Valenzuela	.50	.25	.05

1984 Topps Cereal

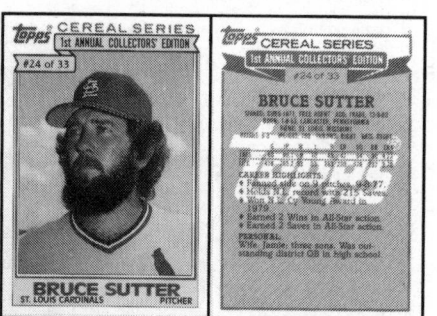

The cards in this 33 card-set measure 2 1/2" by 3 1/2". The cards are numbered both on the front and the back. The 1984 Topps Cereal Series is exactly the same as the Ralston- Purina issue of this year except for a Topps logo and the words "Cereal Series" on the tops of the fronts of the cards in place of the Ralston checkerboard background. The checkerboard background is absent from the reverse, and a Topps logo is on the reverse of the cereal cards. These cards were distributed in unmarked boxes of Ralston-Purina cereal with a pack of four cards (three players and a checklist) being inside random cereal boxes. The back of the checklist details an offer to obtain any twelve cards direct from the issuer for only 1.50.

		MINT	EXC	G-VG
	COMPLETE SET	12.00	6.00	1.20
	COMMON PLAYER	.20	.10	.02
☐	1 Eddie Murray	.90	.45	.09
☐	2 Ozzie Smith	.35	.17	.03
☐	3 Ted Simmons	.25	.12	.02
☐	4 Pete Rose	1.25	.60	.12
☐	5 Greg Luzinski	.20	.10	.02
☐	6 Andre Dawson	.35	.17	.03
☐	7 Dave Winfield	.45	.22	.04
☐	8 Tom Seaver	.50	.25	.05
☐	9 Jim Rice	.45	.22	.04
☐	10 Fernando Valenzuela	.45	.22	.04
☐	11 Wade Boggs	1.75	.85	.17
☐	12 Dale Murphy	1.25	.60	.12
☐	13 George Brett	1.00	.50	.10
☐	14 Nolan Ryan	.65	.30	.06
☐	15 Rickey Henderson	.90	.45	.09
☐	16 Steve Carlton	.50	.25	.05
☐	17 Rod Carew	.50	.25	.05
☐	18 Steve Garvey	.60	.30	.06
☐	19 Reggie Jackson	1.00	.50	.10
☐	20 Dave Concepcion	.20	.10	.02
☐	21 Robin Yount	.50	.25	.05
☐	22 Mike Schmidt	1.00	.50	.10
☐	23 Jim Palmer	.40	.20	.04
☐	24 Bruce Sutter	.25	.12	.02
☐	25 Dan Quisenberry	.25	.12	.02
☐	26 Bill Madlock	.20	.10	.02
☐	27 Cecil Cooper	.20	.10	.02
☐	28 Gary Carter	.60	.30	.06
☐	29 Fred Lynn	.25	.12	.02
☐	30 Pedro Guerrero	.35	.17	.03
☐	31 Ron Guidry	.25	.12	.02
☐	32 Keith Hernandez	.35	.17	.03
☐	33 Carlton Fisk	.25	.12	.02
☐	34 Checklist card (unnumbered)	.25	.03	.00

1985 Topps

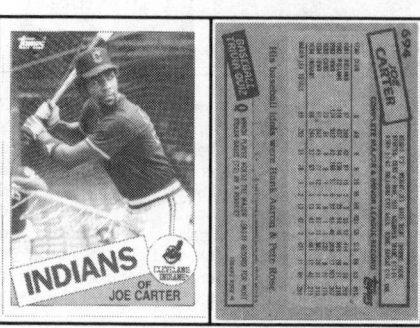

The cards in this 792-card set measure 2 1/2" by 3 1/2". The 1985 Topps set contains full color cards. The fronts feature both the Topps and team logos along with the team name, player's name, and his position. The backs feature player statistics with ink colors of light green and maroon on a gray stock. A trivia quiz is included on the lower portion of the backs. The first ten cards (1-10) are Record Breakers (RB), cards 131-143 are Father and Son (FS) cards, and cards 701 to 722 portray All-Star selections (AS). Cards 271 to 282 represent "First Draft Picks" still active in the Major Leagues and cards 389-404 feature the coach and players on the 1984 U.S. Olympic Baseball Team. The manager cards in the set are important in that they contain the checklist of that team's players on the back.

	MINT	EXC	G-VG
COMPLETE SET	95.00	40.00	8.00
COMMON PLAYER	.04	.02	.00

	#	Player	Price 1	Price 2	Price 3
☐	1	Carlton Fisk RB	.15	.03	.01
		Longest game			
		by catcher			
☐	2	Steve Garvey RB	.15	.07	.01
		Consecutive error-			
		less games, 1B			
☐	3	Dwight Gooden RB	.60	.30	.06
		Most strikeouts,			
		rookie, season			
☐	4	Cliff Johnson RB	.04	.02	.00
		Most pinch homers,			
		lifetime			
☐	5	Joe Morgan RB	.10	.05	.01
		Most homers,			
		2B, lifetime			
☐	6	Pete Rose RB	.45	.22	.04
		Most singles,			
		lifetime			
☐	7	Nolan Ryan RB	.20	.10	.02
		Most strikeouts,			
		lifetime			
☐	8	Juan Samuel RB	.20	.10	.02
		Most stolen bases,			
		rookie, season			
☐	9	Bruce Sutter RB	.10	.05	.01
		Most saves,			
		season, NL			
☐	10	Don Sutton RB	.10	.05	.01
		Most seasons,			
		100 or more K's			
☐	11	Ralph Houk MG	.07	.01	.00
		(checklist back)			
☐	12	Dave Lopes	.07	.03	.01
☐	13	Tim Lollar	.04	.02	.00
☐	14	Chris Bando	.04	.02	.00
☐	15	Jerry Koosman	.10	.05	.01
☐	16	Bobby Meacham	.04	.02	.00
☐	17	Mike Scott	.30	.15	.03
☐	18	Mickey Hatcher	.04	.02	.00
☐	19	George Frazier	.04	.02	.00
☐	20	Chet Lemon	.07	.03	.01
☐	21	Lee Tunnell	.04	.02	.00
☐	22	Duane Kuiper	.04	.02	.00
☐	23	Bret Saberhagen	3.50	1.75	.35
☐	24	Jesse Barfield	.30	.15	.03
☐	25	Steve Bedrosian	.15	.07	.01
☐	26	Roy Smalley	.07	.03	.01
☐	27	Bruce Berenyi	.04	.02	.00
☐	28	Dann Bilardello	.04	.02	.00
☐	29	Odell Jones	.04	.02	.00
☐	30	Cal Ripken	.50	.25	.05
☐	31	Terry Whitfield	.04	.02	.00
☐	32	Chuck Porter	.04	.02	.00
☐	33	Tito Landrum	.04	.02	.00
☐	34	Ed Nunez	.10	.05	.01
☐	35	Graig Nettles	.12	.06	.01
☐	36	Fred Breining	.04	.02	.00
☐	37	Reid Nichols	.04	.02	.00
☐	38	Jackie Moore MG	.07	.01	.00
		(checklist back)			
☐	39	John Wockenfuss	.04	.02	.00
☐	40	Phil Niekro	.15	.07	.01
☐	41	Mike Fischlin	.04	.02	.00
☐	42	Luis Sanchez	.04	.02	.00
☐	43	Andre David	.10	.05	.01
☐	44	Dickie Thon	.04	.02	.00
☐	45	Greg Minton	.04	.02	.00
☐	46	Gary Woods	.04	.02	.00
☐	47	Dave Rozema	.04	.02	.00
☐	48	Tony Fernandez	1.50	.75	.15
☐	49	Butch Davis	.07	.03	.01
☐	50	John Candelaria	.07	.03	.01
☐	51	Bob Watson	.07	.03	.01
☐	52	Jerry Dybzinski	.04	.02	.00
☐	53	Tom Gorman	.04	.02	.00
☐	54	Cesar Cedeno	.07	.03	.01
☐	55	Frank Tanana	.07	.03	.01
☐	56	Jim Dwyer	.04	.02	.00
☐	57	Pat Zachry	.04	.02	.00
☐	58	Orlando Mercado	.04	.02	.00
☐	59	Rick Waits	.04	.02	.00
☐	60	George Hendrick	.07	.03	.01
☐	61	Curt Kaufman	.07	.03	.01
☐	62	Mike Ramsey	.04	.02	.00
☐	63	Steve McCatty	.04	.02	.00
☐	64	Mark Bailey	.10	.05	.01
☐	65	Bill Buckner	.10	.05	.01
☐	66	Dick Williams MG	.07	.01	.00
		(checklist back)			
☐	67	Rafael Santana	.20	.10	.02
☐	68	Von Hayes	.15	.07	.01
☐	69	Jim Winn	.07	.03	.01
☐	70	Don Baylor	.10	.05	.01
☐	71	Tim Laudner	.07	.03	.01
☐	72	Rick Sutcliffe	.15	.07	.01
☐	73	Rusty Kuntz	.04	.02	.00
☐	74	Mike Krukow	.07	.03	.01
☐	75	Willie Upshaw	.07	.03	.01
☐	76	Alan Bannister	.04	.02	.00
☐	77	Joe Beckwith	.04	.02	.00
☐	78	Scott Fletcher	.07	.03	.01
☐	79	Rick Mahler	.04	.02	.00
☐	80	Keith Hernandez	.25	.12	.02
☐	81	Lenn Sakata	.04	.02	.00
☐	82	Joe Price	.04	.02	.00
☐	83	Charlie Moore	.04	.02	.00
☐	84	Spike Owen	.07	.03	.01
☐	85	Mike Marshall	.12	.06	.01
☐	86	Don Aase	.07	.03	.01
☐	87	David Green	.07	.03	.01
☐	88	Bryn Smith	.04	.02	.00
☐	89	Jackie Gutierrez	.10	.05	.01
☐	90	Rich Gossage	.15	.07	.01
☐	91	Jeff Burroughs	.07	.03	.01
☐	92	Paul Owens MG	.07	.01	.00
		(checklist back)			
☐	93	Don Schulze	.07	.03	.01
☐	94	Toby Harrah	.07	.03	.01
☐	95	Jose Cruz	.10	.05	.01
☐	96	Johnny Ray	.10	.05	.01
☐	97	Pete Filson	.04	.02	.00
☐	98	Steve Lake	.04	.02	.00
☐	99	Milt Wilcox	.04	.02	.00
☐	100	George Brett	.50	.25	.05
☐	101	Jim Acker	.04	.02	.00
☐	102	Tommy Dunbar	.07	.03	.01
☐	103	Randy Lerch	.04	.02	.00
☐	104	Mike Fitzgerald	.07	.03	.01
☐	105	Ron Kittle	.15	.07	.01
☐	106	Pascual Perez	.04	.02	.00
☐	107	Tom Foley	.04	.02	.00
☐	108	Darnell Coles	.10	.05	.01
☐	109	Gary Roenicke	.04	.02	.00
☐	110	Alejandro Pena	.07	.03	.01
☐	111	Doug DeCinces	.10	.05	.01
☐	112	Tom Tellmann	.04	.02	.00
☐	113	Tom Herr	.10	.05	.01
☐	114	Bob James	.07	.03	.01
☐	115	Rickey Henderson	.45	.22	.04
☐	116	Dennis Boyd	.20	.10	.02
☐	117	Greg Gross	.04	.02	.00
☐	118	Eric Show	.04	.02	.00
☐	119	Pat Corrales MG	.07	.01	.00
		(checklist back)			
☐	120	Steve Kemp	.07	.03	.01
☐	121	Checklist: 1-132	.07	.01	.00
☐	122	Tom Brunansky	.15	.07	.01
☐	123	Dave Smith	.07	.03	.01
☐	124	Rich Hebner	.04	.02	.00
☐	125	Kent Tekulve	.07	.03	.01
☐	126	Ruppert Jones	.04	.02	.00
☐	127	Mark Gubicza	.30	.15	.03
☐	128	Ernie Whitt	.04	.02	.00
☐	129	Gene Garber	.04	.02	.00
☐	130	Al Oliver	.10	.05	.01
☐	131	Buddy/Gus Bell FS	.07	.03	.01
☐	132	Dale/Yogi Berra FS	.10	.05	.01
☐	133	Bob/Ray Boone FS	.07	.03	.01
☐	134	Terry/Tito Francona FS	.07	.03	.01
☐	135	Terry/Bob Kennedy FS	.07	.03	.01
☐	136	Jeff/Jim Kunkel FS	.07	.03	.01
☐	137	Vance/Vern Law FS	.07	.03	.01
☐	138	Dick/Dick Schofield FS	.07	.03	.01
☐	139	Joel/Bob Skinner FS	.07	.03	.01
☐	140	Roy/Roy Smalley FS	.07	.03	.01
☐	141	Mike/D.Stenhouse FS	.07	.03	.01
☐	142	Steve/Dizzy Trout FS	.07	.03	.01
☐	143	Ozzie/Ozzie Virgil FS	.07	.03	.01
☐	144	Ron Gardenhire	.04	.02	.00
☐	145	Alvin Davis	1.50	.75	.15
☐	146	Gary Redus	.07	.03	.01
☐	147	Bill Swaggerty	.07	.03	.01
☐	148	Steve Yeager	.04	.02	.00
☐	149	Dickie Noles	.04	.02	.00
☐	150	Jim Rice	.35	.17	.03
☐	151	Moose Haas	.04	.02	.00
☐	152	Steve Braun	.04	.02	.00
☐	153	Frank LaCorte	.04	.02	.00
☐	154	Argenis Salazar	.07	.03	.01
☐	155	Yogi Berra MG	.12	.03	.01
		(checklist back)			
☐	156	Craig Reynolds	.04	.02	.00
☐	157	Tug McGraw	.10	.05	.01
☐	158	Pat Tabler	.10	.05	.01
☐	159	Carlos Diaz	.04	.02	.00
☐	160	Lance Parrish	.20	.10	.02
☐	161	Ken Schrom	.04	.02	.00
☐	162	Benny Distefano	.10	.05	.01
☐	163	Dennis Eckersley	.07	.03	.01
☐	164	Jorge Orta	.04	.02	.00

165	Dusty Baker	.07	.03	.01
166	Keith Atherton	.04	.02	.00
167	Rufino Linares	.04	.02	.00
168	Garth Iorg	.04	.02	.00
169	Dan Spillner	.04	.02	.00
170	George Foster	.12	.06	.01
171	Bill Stein	.04	.02	.00
172	Jack Perconte	.04	.02	.00
173	Mike Young	.12	.06	.01
174	Rick Honeycutt	.07	.03	.01
175	Dave Parker	.15	.07	.01
176	Bill Schroeder	.04	.02	.00
177	Dave Von Ohlen	.04	.02	.00
178	Miguel Dilone	.04	.02	.00
179	Tommy John	.15	.07	.01
180	Dave Winfield	.35	.17	.03
181	Roger Clemens	10.00	5.00	1.00
182	Tim Flannery	.04	.02	.00
183	Larry McWilliams	.04	.02	.00
184	Carmen Castillo	.04	.02	.00
185	Al Holland	.04	.02	.00
186	Bob Lillis MG	.07	.01	.00
	(checklist back)			
187	Mike Walters	.07	.03	.01
188	Greg Pryor	.04	.02	.00
189	Warren Brusstar	.04	.02	.00
190	Rusty Staub	.10	.05	.01
191	Steve Nicosia	.04	.02	.00
192	Howard Johnson	1.50	.75	.15
193	Jimmy Key	1.25	.60	.12
194	Dave Stegman	.04	.02	.00
195	Glenn Hubbard	.04	.02	.00
196	Pete O'Brien	.12	.06	.01
197	Mike Warren	.04	.02	.00
198	Eddie Milner	.04	.02	.00
199	Denny Martinez	.07	.03	.01
200	Reggie Jackson	.40	.20	.04
201	Burt Hooton	.04	.02	.00
202	Gorman Thomas	.10	.05	.01
203	Bob McClure	.04	.02	.00
204	Art Howe	.04	.02	.00
205	Steve Rogers	.07	.03	.01
206	Phil Garner	.04	.02	.00
207	Mark Clear	.04	.02	.00
208	Champ Summers	.04	.02	.00
209	Bill Campbell	.04	.02	.00
210	Gary Matthews	.07	.03	.01
211	Clay Christiansen	.07	.03	.01
212	George Vukovich	.04	.02	.00
213	Billy Gardner MG	.07	.01	.00
	(checklist back)			
214	John Tudor	.15	.07	.01
215	Bob Brenly	.07	.03	.01
216	Jerry Don Gleaton	.04	.02	.00
217	Leon Roberts	.04	.02	.00
218	Doyle Alexander	.07	.03	.01
219	Gerald Perry	.15	.07	.01
220	Fred Lynn	.15	.07	.01
221	Ron Reed	.04	.02	.00
222	Hubie Brooks	.10	.05	.01
223	Tom Hume	.04	.02	.00
224	Al Cowens	.04	.02	.00
225	Mike Boddicker	.10	.05	.01
226	Juan Beniquez	.07	.03	.01
227	Danny Darwin	.07	.03	.01
228	Dion James	.20	.10	.02
229	Dave LaPoint	.04	.02	.00
230	Gary Carter	.35	.17	.03
231	Dwayne Murphy	.07	.03	.01
232	Dave Beard	.04	.02	.00
233	Ed Jurak	.04	.02	.00
234	Jerry Narron	.04	.02	.00
235	Garry Maddox	.07	.03	.01
236	Mark Thurmond	.07	.03	.01
237	Julio Franco	.12	.06	.01
238	Jose Rijo	.30	.15	.03
239	Tim Teufel	.12	.06	.01
240	Dave Stieb	.15	.07	.01
241	Jim Frey MG	.07	.01	.00
	(checklist back)			
242	Greg Harris	.04	.02	.00
243	Barbaro Garbey	.07	.03	.01
244	Mike Jones	.04	.02	.00
245	Chili Davis	.10	.05	.01
246	Mike Norris	.04	.02	.00
247	Wayne Tolleson	.04	.02	.00
248	Terry Forster	.07	.03	.01
249	Harold Baines	.15	.07	.01
250	Jesse Orosco	.07	.03	.01
251	Brad Gulden	.04	.02	.00
252	Dan Ford	.04	.02	.00
253	Sid Bream	.35	.17	.03
254	Pete Vuckovich	.07	.03	.01
255	Lonnie Smith	.07	.03	.01
256	Mike Stanton	.04	.02	.00
257	Bryan Little	.04	.02	.00
258	Mike Brown	.04	.02	.00
	(Angels OF)			
259	Gary Allenson	.04	.02	.00
260	Dave Righetti	.15	.07	.01
261	Checklist: 133-264	.07	.01	.00
262	Greg Booker	.07	.03	.01
263	Mel Hall	.10	.05	.01
264	Joe Sambito	.07	.03	.01
265	Juan Samuel	.60	.30	.06
266	Frank Viola	.15	.07	.01
267	Henry Cotto	.12	.06	.01
268	Chuck Tanner MG	.07	.01	.00
	(checklist back)			
269	Doug Baker	.07	.03	.01
270	Dan Quisenberry	.15	.07	.01
271	Tim Foli FDP68	.04	.02	.00
272	Jeff Burroughs FDP69	.04	.02	.00
273	Bill Almon FDP74	.04	.02	.00
274	Floyd Bannister FDP76	.07	.03	.01
275	Harold Baines FDP77	.12	.06	.01
276	Bob Horner FDP78	.15	.07	.01
277	Al Chambers FDP79	.07	.03	.01
278	D.Strawberry FDP80	.50	.25	.05
279	Mike Moore FDP81	.07	.03	.01
280	Shawon Dunston FDP82	.75	.35	.07
281	Tim Belcher FDP83	.30	.15	.03
282	Shawn Abner FDP84	.60	.30	.06
283	Fran Mullins	.04	.02	.00
284	Marty Bystrom	.04	.02	.00
285	Dan Driessen	.04	.02	.00
286	Rudy Law	.04	.02	.00
287	Walt Terrell	.04	.02	.00
288	Jeff Kunkel	.10	.05	.01
289	Tom Underwood	.04	.02	.00
290	Cecil Cooper	.12	.06	.01
291	Bob Welch	.07	.03	.01
292	Brad Komminsk	.07	.03	.01
293	Curt Young	.45	.22	.04
294	Tom Nieto	.07	.03	.01
295	Joe Niekro	.10	.05	.01
296	Ricky Nelson	.07	.03	.01
297	Gary Lucas	.04	.02	.00
298	Marty Barrett	.10	.05	.01
299	Andy Hawkins	.07	.03	.01
300	Rod Carew	.35	.17	.03
301	John Montefusco	.07	.03	.01
302	Tim Corcoran	.04	.02	.00
303	Mike Jeffcoat	.07	.03	.01
304	Gary Gaetti	.25	.12	.02
305	Dale Berra	.04	.02	.00
306	Rick Reuschel	.10	.05	.01
307	Sparky Anderson MG	.07	.01	.00
	(checklist back)			
308	John Wathan	.07	.03	.01
309	Mike Witt	.12	.06	.01
310	Manny Trillo	.04	.02	.00
311	Jim Gott	.04	.02	.00
312	Marc Hill	.04	.02	.00
313	Dave Schmidt	.07	.03	.01
314	Ron Oester	.04	.02	.00
315	Doug Sisk	.04	.02	.00
316	John Lowenstein	.04	.02	.00
317	Jack Lazorko	.07	.03	.01
318	Ted Simmons	.10	.05	.01
319	Jeff Jones	.04	.02	.00
320	Dale Murphy	.55	.27	.05
321	Ricky Horton	.30	.15	.03
322	Dave Stapleton	.04	.02	.00
323	Andy McGaffigan	.04	.02	.00
324	Bruce Bochy	.04	.02	.00
325	John Denny	.07	.03	.01
326	Kevin Bass	.10	.05	.01
327	Brook Jacoby	.35	.17	.03
328	Bob Shirley	.04	.02	.00
329	Ron Washington	.04	.02	.00
330	Leon Durham	.10	.05	.01
331	Bill Laskey	.04	.02	.00
332	Brian Harper	.04	.02	.00
333	Willie Hernandez	.15	.07	.01
334	Dick Howser MG	.07	.01	.00
	(checklist back)			
335	Bruce Benedict	.04	.02	.00
336	Rance Mulliniks	.04	.02	.00
337	Billy Sample	.04	.02	.00
338	Britt Burns	.07	.03	.01
339	Danny Heep	.04	.02	.00
340	Robin Yount	.35	.17	.03
341	Floyd Rayford	.04	.02	.00
342	Ted Power	.07	.03	.01
343	Bill Russell	.04	.02	.00
344	Dave Henderson	.04	.02	.00
345	Charlie Lea	.04	.02	.00
346	Terry Pendleton	.55	.27	.05
347	Rick Langford	.04	.02	.00

☐ 348	Bob Boone	.07	.03	.01
☐ 349	Domingo Ramos	.04	.02	.00
☐ 350	Wade Boggs	3.50	1.75	.35
☐ 351	Juan Agosto	.04	.02	.00
☐ 352	Joe Morgan	.18	.09	.01
☐ 353	Julio Solano	.07	.03	.01
☐ 354	Andre Robertson	.04	.02	.00
☐ 355	Bert Blyleven	.10	.05	.01
☐ 356	Dave Meier	.10	.05	.01
☐ 357	Rich Bordi	.04	.02	.00
☐ 358	Tony Pena	.10	.05	.01
☐ 359	Pat Sheridan	.04	.02	.00
☐ 360	Steve Carlton	.35	.17	.03
☐ 361	Alfredo Griffin	.07	.03	.01
☐ 362	Craig McMurtry	.04	.02	.00
☐ 363	Ron Hodges	.04	.02	.00
☐ 364	Richard Dotson	.07	.03	.01
☐ 365	Danny Ozark MG (checklist back)	.07	.01	.00
☐ 366	Todd Cruz	.04	.02	.00
☐ 367	Keefe Cato	.07	.03	.01
☐ 368	Dave Bergman	.04	.02	.00
☐ 369	R.J. Reynolds	.30	.15	.03
☐ 370	Bruce Sutter	.15	.07	.01
☐ 371	Mickey Rivers	.07	.03	.01
☐ 372	Roy Howell	.04	.02	.00
☐ 373	Mike Moore	.07	.03	.01
☐ 374	Brian Downing	.07	.03	.01
☐ 375	Jeff Reardon	.12	.06	.01
☐ 376	Jeff Newman	.04	.02	.00
☐ 377	Checklist: 265-396	.07	.01	.00
☐ 378	Alan Wiggins	.07	.03	.01
☐ 379	Charles Hudson	.07	.03	.01
☐ 380	Ken Griffey	.07	.03	.01
☐ 381	Roy Smith	.07	.03	.01
☐ 382	Denny Walling	.04	.02	.00
☐ 383	Rick Lysander	.04	.02	.00
☐ 384	Jody Davis	.10	.05	.01
☐ 385	Jose DeLeon	.07	.03	.01
☐ 386	Dan Gladden	.35	.17	.03
☐ 387	Buddy Biancalana	.10	.05	.01
☐ 388	Bert Roberge	.04	.02	.00
☐ 389	Rod Dedeaux OLY CO	.04	.02	.00
☐ 390	Sid Akins OLY	.07	.03	.01
☐ 391	Flavio Alfaro OLY	.07	.03	.01
☐ 392	Don August OLY	.07	.03	.01
☐ 393	Scott Bankhead OLY	.25	.12	.02
☐ 394	Bob Caffrey OLY	.07	.03	.01
☐ 395	Mike Dunne OLY	2.25	1.10	.22
☐ 396	Gary Green OLY	.10	.05	.01
☐ 397	John Hoover OLY	.10	.05	.01
☐ 398	Shane Mack OLY	.75	.35	.07
☐ 399	John Marzano OLY	1.25	.60	.12
☐ 400	Oddibe McDowell OLY	1.25	.60	.12
☐ 401	Mark McGwire OLY	20.00	10.00	2.00
☐ 402	Pat Pacillo OLY	.25	.12	.02
☐ 403	Cory Snyder OLY	7.50	3.75	.75
☐ 404	Billy Swift OLY	.15	.07	.01
☐ 405	Tom Veryzer	.04	.02	.00
☐ 406	Len Whitehouse	.04	.02	.00
☐ 407	Bobby Ramos	.04	.02	.00
☐ 408	Sid Monge	.04	.02	.00
☐ 409	Brad Wellman	.04	.02	.00
☐ 410	Bob Horner	.20	.10	.02
☐ 411	Bobby Cox MG (checklist back)	.07	.01	.00
☐ 412	Bud Black	.04	.02	.00
☐ 413	Vance Law	.04	.02	.00
☐ 414	Gary Ward	.07	.03	.01
☐ 415	Ron Darling ERR (no trivia answer)	1.50	.75	.15
☐ 416	Wayne Gross	.04	.02	.00
☐ 417	John Franco	.55	.27	.05
☐ 418	Ken Landreaux	.07	.03	.01
☐ 419	Mike Caldwell	.07	.03	.01
☐ 420	Andre Dawson	.30	.15	.03
☐ 421	Dave Rucker	.04	.02	.00
☐ 422	Carney Lansford	.10	.05	.01
☐ 423	Barry Bonnell	.04	.02	.00
☐ 424	Al Nipper	.25	.12	.02
☐ 425	Mike Hargrove	.07	.03	.01
☐ 426	Vern Ruhle	.04	.02	.00
☐ 427	Mario Ramirez	.04	.02	.00
☐ 428	Larry Andersen	.04	.02	.00
☐ 429	Rick Cerone	.04	.02	.00
☐ 430	Ron Davis	.04	.02	.00
☐ 431	U.L. Washington	.04	.02	.00
☐ 432	Thad Bosley	.04	.02	.00
☐ 433	Jim Morrison	.04	.02	.00
☐ 434	Gene Richards	.04	.02	.00
☐ 435	Dan Petry	.10	.05	.01
☐ 436	Willie Aikens	.04	.02	.00
☐ 437	Al Jones	.07	.03	.01
☐ 438	Joe Torre MG (checklist back)	.07	.01	.00
☐ 439	Junior Ortiz	.04	.02	.00
☐ 440	Fernando Valenzuela	.35	.17	.03
☐ 441	Duane Walker	.04	.02	.00
☐ 442	Ken Forsch	.04	.02	.00
☐ 443	George Wright	.04	.02	.00
☐ 444	Tony Phillips	.04	.02	.00
☐ 445	Tippy Martinez	.04	.02	.00
☐ 446	Jim Sundberg	.07	.03	.01
☐ 447	Jeff Lahti	.04	.02	.00
☐ 448	Derrel Thomas	.04	.02	.00
☐ 449	Phil Bradley	1.25	.60	.12
☐ 450	Steve Garvey	.35	.17	.03
☐ 451	Bruce Hurst	.12	.06	.01
☐ 452	John Castino	.04	.02	.00
☐ 453	Tom Waddell	.12	.06	.01
☐ 454	Glenn Wilson	.10	.05	.01
☐ 455	Bob Knepper	.10	.05	.01
☐ 456	Tim Foli	.04	.02	.00
☐ 457	Cecilio Guante	.04	.02	.00
☐ 458	Randy Johnson	.04	.02	.00
☐ 459	Charlie Leibrandt	.07	.03	.01
☐ 460	Ryne Sandberg	.50	.25	.05
☐ 461	Marty Castillo	.04	.02	.00
☐ 462	Gary Lavelle	.04	.02	.00
☐ 463	Dave Collins	.04	.02	.00
☐ 464	Mike Mason	.10	.05	.01
☐ 465	Bob Grich	.07	.03	.01
☐ 466	Tony LaRussa MG (checklist back)	.07	.01	.00
☐ 467	Ed Lynch	.04	.02	.00
☐ 468	Wayne Krenchicki	.04	.02	.00
☐ 469	Sammy Stewart	.04	.02	.00
☐ 470	Steve Sax	.18	.09	.01
☐ 471	Pete Ladd	.04	.02	.00
☐ 472	Jim Essian	.04	.02	.00
☐ 473	Tim Wallach	.15	.07	.01
☐ 474	Kurt Kepshire	.10	.05	.01
☐ 475	Andre Thornton	.07	.03	.01
☐ 476	Jeff Stone	.25	.12	.02
☐ 477	Bob Ojeda	.10	.05	.01
☐ 478	Kurt Bevacqua	.04	.02	.00
☐ 479	Mike Madden	.04	.02	.00
☐ 480	Lou Whitaker	.15	.07	.01
☐ 481	Dale Murray	.04	.02	.00
☐ 482	Harry Spilman	.04	.02	.00
☐ 483	Mike Smithson	.04	.02	.00
☐ 484	Larry Bowa	.10	.05	.01
☐ 485	Matt Young	.04	.02	.00
☐ 486	Steve Balboni	.04	.02	.00
☐ 487	Frank Williams	.15	.07	.01
☐ 488	Joel Skinner	.07	.03	.01
☐ 489	Bryan Clark	.04	.02	.00
☐ 490	Jason Thompson	.04	.02	.00
☐ 491	Rick Camp	.04	.02	.00
☐ 492	Dave Johnson MG (checklist back)	.07	.01	.00
☐ 493	Orel Hershiser	2.00	1.00	.20
☐ 494	Rich Dauer	.04	.02	.00
☐ 495	Mario Soto	.07	.03	.01
☐ 496	Donnie Scott	.04	.02	.00
☐ 497	Gary Pettis (photo actually Gary's little brother, Lynn)	.25	.12	.02
☐ 498	Ed Romero	.04	.02	.00
☐ 499	Danny Cox	.35	.17	.03
☐ 500	Mike Schmidt	.45	.22	.04
☐ 501	Dan Schatzeder	.04	.02	.00
☐ 502	Rick Miller	.04	.02	.00
☐ 503	Tim Conroy	.04	.02	.00
☐ 504	Jerry Willard	.04	.02	.00
☐ 505	Jim Beattie	.04	.02	.00
☐ 506	Franklin Stubbs	.55	.27	.05
☐ 507	Ray Fontenot	.04	.02	.00
☐ 508	John Shelby	.04	.02	.00
☐ 509	Milt May	.04	.02	.00
☐ 510	Kent Hrbek	.25	.12	.02
☐ 511	Lee Smith	.10	.05	.01
☐ 512	Tom Brookens	.04	.02	.00
☐ 513	Lynn Jones	.04	.02	.00
☐ 514	Jeff Cornell	.07	.03	.01
☐ 515	Dave Concepcion	.07	.03	.01
☐ 516	Roy Lee Jackson	.04	.02	.00
☐ 517	Jerry Martin	.04	.02	.00
☐ 518	Chris Chambliss	.07	.03	.01
☐ 519	Doug Rader MG (checklist back)	.07	.01	.00
☐ 520	LaMarr Hoyt	.07	.03	.01
☐ 521	Rick Dempsey	.07	.03	.01
☐ 522	Paul Molitor	.15	.07	.01
☐ 523	Candy Maldonado	.12	.06	.01
☐ 524	Rob Wilfong	.04	.02	.00
☐ 525	Darrell Porter	.04	.02	.00
☐ 526	Dave Palmer	.04	.02	.00
☐ 527	Checklist: 397-528	.07	.01	.00

☐ 528	Bill Krueger	.04	.02	.00	☐ 619	Jeff Leonard	.12	.06	.01
☐ 529	Rich Gedman	.10	.05	.01	☐ 620	Dwight Gooden	8.00	4.00	.80
☐ 530	Dave Dravecky	.07	.03	.01	☐ 621	Marvis Foley	.04	.02	.00
☐ 531	Joe Lefebvre	.04	.02	.00	☐ 622	Luis Leal	.04	.02	.00
☐ 532	Frank DiPino	.04	.02	.00	☐ 623	Greg Walker	.12	.06	.01
☐ 533	Tony Bernazard	.04	.02	.00	☐ 624	Benny Ayala	.04	.02	.00
☐ 534	Brian Dayett	.07	.03	.01	☐ 625	Mark Langston	1.25	.60	.12
☐ 535	Pat Putnam	.04	.02	.00	☐ 626	German Rivera	.10	.05	.01
☐ 536	Kirby Puckett	8.50	4.25	.85	☐ 627	Eric Davis	18.00	9.00	1.80
☐ 537	Don Robinson	.04	.02	.00	☐ 628	Rene Lachemann MG	.07	.01	.00
☐ 538	Keith Moreland	.07	.03	.01		(checklist back)			
☐ 539	Aurelio Lopez	.04	.02	.00	☐ 629	Dick Schofield	.12	.06	.01
☐ 540	Claudell Washington	.07	.03	.01	☐ 630	Tim Raines	.35	.17	.03
☐ 541	Mark Davis	.04	.02	.00	☐ 631	Bob Forsch	.07	.03	.01
☐ 542	Don Slaught	.04	.02	.00	☐ 632	Bruce Bochte	.04	.02	.00
☐ 543	Mike Squires	.04	.02	.00	☐ 633	Glenn Hoffman	.04	.02	.00
☐ 544	Bruce Kison	.04	.02	.00	☐ 634	Bill Dawley	.04	.02	.00
☐ 545	Lloyd Moseby	.12	.06	.01	☐ 635	Terry Kennedy	.07	.03	.01
☐ 546	Brent Gaff	.04	.02	.00	☐ 636	Shane Rawley	.07	.03	.01
☐ 547	Pete Rose MG	.45	.10	.02	☐ 637	Brett Butler	.07	.03	.01
	(checklist back)				☐ 638	Mike Pagliarulo	1.75	.85	.17
☐ 548	Larry Parrish	.07	.03	.01	☐ 639	Ed Hodge	.07	.03	.01
☐ 549	Mike Scioscia	.04	.02	.00	☐ 640	Steve Henderson	.04	.02	.00
☐ 550	Scott McGregor	.07	.03	.01	☐ 641	Rod Scurry	.04	.02	.00
☐ 551	Andy Van Slyke	.10	.05	.01	☐ 642	Dave Owen	.07	.03	.01
☐ 552	Chris Codiroli	.04	.02	.00	☐ 643	Johnny Grubb	.04	.02	.00
☐ 553	Bob Clark	.04	.02	.00	☐ 644	Mark Huismann	.07	.03	.01
☐ 554	Doug Flynn	.04	.02	.00	☐ 645	Damaso Garcia	.07	.03	.01
☐ 555	Bob Stanley	.07	.03	.01	☐ 646	Scot Thompson	.04	.02	.00
☐ 556	Sixto Lezcano	.04	.02	.00	☐ 647	Rafael Ramirez	.04	.02	.00
☐ 557	Len Barker	.04	.02	.00	☐ 648	Bob Jones	.04	.02	.00
☐ 558	Carmelo Martinez	.07	.03	.01	☐ 649	Sid Fernandez	1.25	.60	.12
☐ 559	Jay Howell	.04	.02	.00	☐ 650	Greg Luzinski	.10	.05	.01
☐ 560	Bill Madlock	.10	.05	.01	☐ 651	Jeff Russell	.04	.02	.00
☐ 561	Darryl Motley	.04	.02	.00	☐ 652	Joe Nolan	.04	.02	.00
☐ 562	Houston Jimenez	.04	.02	.00	☐ 653	Mark Brouhard	.04	.02	.00
☐ 563	Dick Ruthven	.04	.02	.00	☐ 654	Dave Anderson	.04	.02	.00
☐ 564	Alan Ashby	.04	.02	.00	☐ 655	Joaquin Andujar	.10	.05	.01
☐ 565	Kirk Gibson	.25	.12	.02	☐ 656	Chuck Cottier MG	.07	.01	.00
☐ 566	Ed VandeBerg	.04	.02	.00		(checklist back)			
☐ 567	Joel Youngblood	.04	.02	.00	☐ 657	Jim Slaton	.04	.02	.00
☐ 568	Cliff Johnson	.04	.02	.00	☐ 658	Mike Stenhouse	.07	.03	.01
☐ 569	Ken Oberkfell	.04	.02	.00	☐ 659	Checklist: 529-660	.07	.01	.00
☐ 570	Darryl Strawberry	1.50	.75	.15	☐ 660	Tony Gwynn	.75	.35	.07
☐ 571	Charlie Hough	.07	.03	.01	☐ 661	Steve Crawford	.04	.02	.00
☐ 572	Tom Paciorek	.04	.02	.00	☐ 662	Mike Heath	.04	.02	.00
☐ 573	Jay Tibbs	.30	.15	.03	☐ 663	Luis Aguayo	.04	.02	.00
☐ 574	Joe Altobelli MG	.07	.01	.00	☐ 664	Steve Farr	.10	.05	.01
	(checklist back)				☐ 665	Don Mattingly	10.00	5.00	1.00
☐ 575	Pedro Guerrero	.25	.12	.02	☐ 666	Mike LaCoss	.04	.02	.00
☐ 576	Jaime Cocanower	.07	.03	.01	☐ 667	Dave Engle	.04	.02	.00
☐ 577	Chris Speier	.04	.02	.00	☐ 668	Steve Trout	.07	.03	.01
☐ 578	Terry Francona	.04	.02	.00	☐ 669	Lee Lacy	.07	.03	.01
☐ 579	Ron Romanick	.10	.05	.01	☐ 670	Tom Seaver	.30	.15	.03
☐ 580	Dwight Evans	.12	.06	.01	☐ 671	Dane Iorg	.04	.02	.00
☐ 581	Mark Wagner	.04	.02	.00	☐ 672	Juan Berenguer	.04	.02	.00
☐ 582	Ken Phelps	.15	.07	.01	☐ 673	Buck Martinez	.04	.02	.00
☐ 583	Bobby Brown	.04	.02	.00	☐ 674	Atlee Hammaker	.04	.02	.00
☐ 584	Kevin Gross	.04	.02	.00	☐ 675	Tony Perez	.12	.06	.01
☐ 585	Butch Wynegar	.07	.03	.01	☐ 676	Albert Hall	.10	.05	.01
☐ 586	Bill Scherrer	.04	.02	.00	☐ 677	Wally Backman	.07	.03	.01
☐ 587	Doug Frobel	.04	.02	.00	☐ 678	Joe McLaughlin	.04	.02	.00
☐ 588	Bobby Castillo	.04	.02	.00	☐ 679	Bob Kearney	.04	.02	.00
☐ 589	Bob Dernier	.04	.02	.00	☐ 680	Jerry Reuss	.07	.03	.01
☐ 590	Ray Knight	.07	.03	.01	☐ 681	Ben Oglivie	.07	.03	.01
☐ 591	Larry Herndon	.04	.02	.00	☐ 682	Doug Corbett	.04	.02	.00
☐ 592	Jeff Robinson	.35	.17	.03	☐ 683	Whitey Herzog MG	.07	.01	.00
	(Giants pitcher)					(checklist back)			
☐ 593	Rick Leach	.04	.02	.00	☐ 684	Bill Doran	.12	.06	.01
☐ 594	Curt Wilkerson	.07	.03	.01	☐ 685	Bill Caudill	.04	.02	.00
☐ 595	Larry Gura	.07	.03	.01	☐ 686	Mike Easler	.07	.03	.01
☐ 596	Jerry Hairston	.04	.02	.00	☐ 687	Bill Gullickson	.07	.03	.01
☐ 597	Brad Lesley	.04	.02	.00	☐ 688	Len Matuszek	.04	.02	.00
☐ 598	Jose Oquendo	.07	.03	.01	☐ 689	Luis DeLeon	.04	.02	.00
☐ 599	Storm Davis	.07	.03	.01	☐ 690	Alan Trammell	.30	.15	.03
☐ 600	Pete Rose	1.00	.50	.10	☐ 691	Dennis Rasmussen	.15	.07	.01
☐ 601	Tom Lasorda MG	.07	.01	.00	☐ 692	Randy Bush	.04	.02	.00
	(checklist back)				☐ 693	Tim Stoddard	.04	.02	.00
☐ 602	Jeff Dedmon	.07	.03	.01	☐ 694	Joe Carter	1.50	.75	.15
☐ 603	Rick Manning	.04	.02	.00	☐ 695	Rick Rhoden	.07	.03	.01
☐ 604	Daryl Sconiers	.04	.02	.00	☐ 696	John Rabb	.04	.02	.00
☐ 605	Ozzie Smith	.20	.10	.02	☐ 697	Onix Concepcion	.04	.02	.00
☐ 606	Rich Gale	.04	.02	.00	☐ 698	Jorge Bell	.60	.30	.06
☐ 607	Bill Almon	.04	.02	.00	☐ 699	Donnie Moore	.07	.03	.01
☐ 608	Craig Lefferts	.04	.02	.00	☐ 700	Eddie Murray	.45	.22	.04
☐ 609	Broderick Perkins	.04	.02	.00	☐ 701	Eddie Murray AS	.25	.12	.02
☐ 610	Jack Morris	.15	.07	.01	☐ 702	Damaso Garcia AS	.07	.03	.01
☐ 611	Ozzie Virgil	.07	.03	.01	☐ 703	George Brett AS	.25	.12	.02
☐ 612	Mike Armstrong	.04	.02	.00	☐ 704	Cal Ripken AS	.25	.12	.02
☐ 613	Terry Puhl	.04	.02	.00	☐ 705	Dave Winfield AS	.20	.10	.02
☐ 614	Al Williams	.04	.02	.00	☐ 706	Rickey Henderson AS	.25	.12	.02
☐ 615	Marvell Wynne	.04	.02	.00	☐ 707	Tony Armas AS	.07	.03	.01
☐ 616	Scott Sanderson	.04	.02	.00	☐ 708	Lance Parrish AS	.12	.06	.01
☐ 617	Willie Wilson	.15	.07	.01	☐ 709	Mike Boddicker AS	.07	.03	.01
☐ 618	Pete Falcone	.04	.02	.00	☐ 710	Frank Viola AS	.07	.03	.01

☐ 711	Dan Quisenberry AS	.10	.05	.01
☐ 712	Keith Hernandez AS	.15	.07	.01
☐ 713	Ryne Sandberg AS	.20	.10	.02
☐ 714	Mike Schmidt AS	.25	.12	.02
☐ 715	Ozzie Smith AS	.12	.06	.01
☐ 716	Dale Murphy AS	.30	.15	.03
☐ 717	Tony Gwynn AS	.25	.12	.02
☐ 718	Jeff Leonard AS	.07	.03	.01
☐ 719	Gary Carter AS	.20	.10	.02
☐ 720	Rick Sutcliffe AS	.10	.05	.01
☐ 721	Bob Knepper AS	.07	.03	.01
☐ 722	Bruce Sutter AS	.10	.05	.01
☐ 723	Dave Stewart	.10	.05	.01
☐ 724	Oscar Gamble	.07	.03	.01
☐ 725	Floyd Bannister	.07	.03	.01
☐ 726	Al Bumbry	.04	.02	.00
☐ 727	Frank Pastore	.04	.02	.00
☐ 728	Bob Bailor	.04	.02	.00
☐ 729	Don Sutton	.20	.10	.02
☐ 730	Dave Kingman	.12	.06	.01
☐ 731	Neil Allen	.07	.03	.01
☐ 732	John McNamara MG (checklist back)	.07	.01	.00
☐ 733	Tony Scott	.04	.02	.00
☐ 734	John Henry Johnson	.04	.02	.00
☐ 735	Garry Templeton	.07	.03	.01
☐ 736	Jerry Mumphrey	.04	.02	.00
☐ 737	Bo Diaz	.07	.03	.01
☐ 738	Omar Moreno	.04	.02	.00
☐ 739	Ernie Camacho	.04	.02	.00
☐ 740	Jack Clark	.20	.10	.02
☐ 741	John Butcher	.04	.02	.00
☐ 742	Ron Hassey	.04	.02	.00
☐ 743	Frank White	.07	.03	.01
☐ 744	Doug Bair	.04	.02	.00
☐ 745	Buddy Bell	.10	.05	.01
☐ 746	Jim Clancy	.04	.02	.00
☐ 747	Alex Trevino	.04	.02	.00
☐ 748	Lee Mazzilli	.04	.02	.00
☐ 749	Julio Cruz	.04	.02	.00
☐ 750	Rollie Fingers	.15	.07	.01
☐ 751	Kelvin Chapman	.07	.03	.01
☐ 752	Bob Owchinko	.04	.02	.00
☐ 753	Greg Brock	.07	.03	.01
☐ 754	Larry Milbourne	.04	.02	.00
☐ 755	Ken Singleton	.10	.05	.01
☐ 756	Rob Picciolo	.04	.02	.00
☐ 757	Willie McGee	.35	.17	.03
☐ 758	Ray Burris	.04	.02	.00
☐ 759	Jim Fanning MG (checklist back)	.07	.01	.00
☐ 760	Nolan Ryan	.40	.20	.04
☐ 761	Jerry Remy	.04	.02	.00
☐ 762	Eddie Whitson	.04	.02	.00
☐ 763	Kiko Garcia	.04	.02	.00
☐ 764	Jamie Easterly	.04	.02	.00
☐ 765	Willie Randolph	.07	.03	.01
☐ 766	Paul Mirabella	.04	.02	.00
☐ 767	Darrell Brown	.04	.02	.00
☐ 768	Ron Cey	.10	.05	.01
☐ 769	Joe Cowley	.07	.03	.01
☐ 770	Carlton Fisk	.15	.07	.01
☐ 771	Geoff Zahn	.04	.02	.00
☐ 772	Johnnie LeMaster	.04	.02	.00
☐ 773	Hal McRae	.07	.03	.01
☐ 774	Dennis Lamp	.04	.02	.00
☐ 775	Mookie Wilson	.07	.03	.01
☐ 776	Jerry Royster	.04	.02	.00
☐ 777	Ned Yost	.04	.02	.00
☐ 778	Mike Davis	.07	.03	.01
☐ 779	Nick Esasky	.07	.03	.01
☐ 780	Mike Flanagan	.07	.03	.01
☐ 781	Jim Gantner	.04	.02	.00
☐ 782	Tom Niedenfuer	.07	.03	.01
☐ 783	Mike Jorgensen	.04	.02	.00
☐ 784	Checklist: 661-792	.10	.05	.01
☐ 785	Tony Armas	.10	.05	.01
☐ 786	Enos Cabell	.04	.02	.00
☐ 787	Jim Wohlford	.04	.02	.00
☐ 788	Steve Comer	.04	.02	.00
☐ 789	Luis Salazar	.04	.02	.00
☐ 790	Ron Guidry	.15	.07	.01
☐ 791	Ivan DeJesus	.04	.02	.00
☐ 792	Darrell Evans	.20	.06	.01

1985 Topps Super

This 60-card set was issued in packs of three. These large cards measure 4 7/8" by 6 7/8". The fronts of the cards are merely a blow-up of the Topps regular issue. In fact, the cards differ from the corresponding cards of the regular set in size and number only. As one would expect, only those considered stars and superstars appear in this set. Backs are green with maroon printing. A checklist for the set is contained on the back of the wrapper. The back of the wrapper also gives details of Topps' offer to send your "missing" cards.

		MINT	EXC	G-VG
COMPLETE SET		13.50	6.00	1.00
COMMON PLAYER		.10	.05	.01
☐ 1	Ryne Sandberg	.60	.30	.06
☐ 2	Willie Hernandez	.15	.07	.01
☐ 3	Rick Sutcliffe	.20	.10	.02
☐ 4	Don Mattingly	3.00	1.50	.30
☐ 5	Tony Gwynn	1.00	.50	.10
☐ 6	Alvin Davis	.40	.20	.04
☐ 7	Dwight Gooden	1.50	.75	.15
☐ 8	Dan Quisenberry	.15	.07	.01
☐ 9	Bruce Sutter	.15	.07	.01
☐ 10	Tony Armas	.10	.05	.01
☐ 11	Dale Murphy	1.00	.50	.10
☐ 12	Mike Schmidt	1.00	.50	.10
☐ 13	Gary Carter	.60	.30	.06
☐ 14	Rickey Henderson	.75	.35	.07
☐ 15	Tim Raines	.60	.30	.06
☐ 16	Mike Boddicker	.10	.05	.01
☐ 17	Alejandro Pena	.15	.07	.01
☐ 18	Eddie Murray	.90	.45	.09
☐ 19	Gary Matthews	.10	.05	.01
☐ 20	Mark Langston	.30	.15	.03
☐ 21	Mario Soto	.10	.05	.01
☐ 22	Dave Stieb	.15	.07	.01
☐ 23	Nolan Ryan	.60	.30	.06
☐ 24	Steve Carlton	.60	.30	.06
☐ 25	Alan Trammell	.30	.15	.03
☐ 26	Steve Garvey	.75	.35	.07
☐ 27	Kirk Gibson	.35	.17	.03
☐ 28	Juan Samuel	.25	.12	.02
☐ 29	Reggie Jackson	.90	.45	.09
☐ 30	Darryl Strawberry	1.00	.50	.10
☐ 31	Tom Seaver	.65	.30	.06
☐ 32	Pete Rose	1.25	.60	.12
☐ 33	Dwight Evans	.20	.10	.02
☐ 34	Jose Cruz	.10	.05	.01
☐ 35	Bert Blyleven	.10	.05	.01
☐ 36	Keith Hernandez	.25	.12	.02
☐ 37	Robin Yount	.45	.22	.04
☐ 38	Joaquin Andujar	.10	.05	.01
☐ 39	Lloyd Moseby	.15	.07	.01
☐ 40	Chili Davis	.10	.05	.01
☐ 41	Kent Hrbek	.25	.12	.02
☐ 42	Dave Parker	.30	.15	.03
☐ 43	Jack Morris	.20	.10	.02
☐ 44	Pedro Guerrero	.30	.15	.03
☐ 45	Mike Witt	.15	.07	.01
☐ 46	George Brett	.90	.45	.09
☐ 47	Ozzie Smith	.25	.12	.02
☐ 48	Cal Ripken	.75	.35	.07
☐ 49	Rich Gossage	.20	.10	.02
☐ 50	Jim Rice	.45	.22	.04
☐ 51	Harold Baines	.30	.15	.03
☐ 52	Fernando Valenzuela	.45	.22	.04
☐ 53	Buddy Bell	.10	.05	.01
☐ 54	Jesse Orosco	.10	.05	.01
☐ 55	Lance Parrish	.25	.12	.02
☐ 56	Jason Thompson	.10	.05	.01
☐ 57	Tom Brunansky	.15	.07	.01
☐ 58	Dave Righetti	.20	.10	.02
☐ 59	Dave Kingman	.15	.07	.01
☐ 60	Dave Winfield	.45	.22	.04

PICTURE GALLERY: Any set in this Price Guide not illustrated below its respective set title is pictured in the Picture Gallery section in the back of the book. Those pages are arranged in the same order as the overall book.

WRITE FIRST: Prices and availability of items in ads are subject to change.

1985 Topps 3-D

This innovative 30-card set was issued in packs of one. These large cards are very difficult to store (due to the 3-D effect) as they are not really stackable and are crumpled if placed in an album using plastic sheets. The cards are blank-backed except for two covered adhesive strips and measure approximately 4 1/4" by 5 7/8". Cards are numbered on the front and feature a prominent team logo on the front as well.

	MINT	EXC	G-VG
COMPLETE SET	10.00	5.00	1.00
COMMON PLAYER	.20	.10	.02

		MINT	EXC	G-VG
☐	1 Mike Schmidt	1.00	.50	.10
☐	2 Eddie Murray	.80	.40	.08
☐	3 Dale Murphy	1.00	.50	.10
☐	4 George Brett	.90	.45	.09
☐	5 Pete Rose	1.25	.60	.12
☐	6 Jim Rice	.45	.22	.04
☐	7 Ryne Sandberg	.60	.30	.06
☐	8 Don Mattingly	1.75	.85	.17
☐	9 Darryl Strawberry	1.00	.50	.10
☐	10 Rickey Henderson	.80	.40	.08
☐	11 Keith Hernandez	.40	.20	.04
☐	12 Dave Kingman	.20	.10	.02
☐	13 Tony Gwynn	.80	.40	.08
☐	14 Reggie Jackson	1.00	.50	.10
☐	15 Gary Carter	.60	.30	.06
☐	16 Cal Ripken	.75	.35	.07
☐	17 Tim Raines	.50	.25	.05
☐	18 Dave Winfield	.50	.25	.05
☐	19 Dwight Gooden	1.00	.50	.10
☐	20 Dave Stieb	.20	.10	.02
☐	21 Fernando Valenzuela	.40	.20	.04
☐	22 Mark Langston	.30	.15	.03
☐	23 Bruce Sutter	.20	.10	.02
☐	24 Dan Quisenberry	.20	.10	.02
☐	25 Steve Carlton	.50	.25	.05
☐	26 Mike Boddicker	.20	.10	.02
☐	27 Rich Gossage	.25	.12	.02
☐	28 Jack Morris	.25	.12	.02
☐	29 Rick Sutcliffe	.25	.12	.02
☐	30 Tom Seaver	.60	.30	.06

1985 Topps Glossy 22

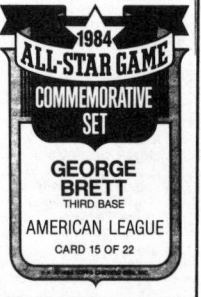

The cards in this 22-card set measure 2 1/2" by 3 1/2". Similar in design, both front and back, to last year's Glossy set, this edition features the managers, starting nine players and honorary captains of the National and American League teams in the 1984 All-Star game. The set is numbered on the reverse with plyers essentially ordered by position within league, NL: 1-11 and AL: 12-22.

	MINT	EXC	G-VG
COMPLETE SET	3.50	1.75	.35
COMMON PLAYER	.10	.05	.01

		MINT	EXC	G-VG
☐	1 Paul Owens MG	.10	.05	.01
☐	2 Steve Garvey	.40	.20	.04
☐	3 Ryne Sandberg	.50	.25	.05
☐	4 Mike Schmidt	.65	.30	.06
☐	5 Ozzie Smith	.20	.10	.02
☐	6 Tony Gwynn	.50	.25	.05
☐	7 Dale Murphy	.65	.30	.06
☐	8 Darryl Strawberry	.65	.30	.06
☐	9 Gary Carter	.35	.17	.03
☐	10 Charlie Lea	.10	.05	.01
☐	11 Willie McCovey CAPT	.20	.10	.02
☐	12 Joe Altobelli MG	.10	.05	.01
☐	13 Rod Carew	.40	.20	.04
☐	14 Lou Whitaker	.15	.07	.01
☐	15 George Brett	.65	.30	.06
☐	16 Cal Ripken	.50	.25	.05
☐	17 Dave Winfield	.35	.17	.03
☐	18 Chet Lemon	.10	.05	.01
☐	19 Reggie Jackson	.60	.30	.06
☐	20 Lance Parrish	.20	.10	.02
☐	21 Dave Stieb	.15	.07	.01
☐	22 Hank Greenberg CAPT	.15	.07	.01

1985 Topps Glossy 40

The cards in this 40-card set measure 2 1/2" by 3 1/2". Similar to last year's glossy set, this set was issued as a bonus prize to Topps All-Star Baseball Game cards found in wax packs. The set could be obtained by sending in the "Bonus Runs" from the "Winning Pitch" game insert cards. For 25 runs and 75 cents, a collector could send in for one of the eight different five card series plus automatically be entered in the Grand Prize Sweepstakes for a chance at a free trip to the All-Star game. The cards are numbered and contain 20 stars from each league.

	MINT	EXC	G-VG
COMPLETE SET	12.00	6.00	1.20
COMMON PLAYER	.15	.07	.01

		MINT	EXC	G-VG
☐	1 Dale Murphy	1.00	.50	.10
☐	2 Jesse Orosco	.15	.07	.01
☐	3 Bob Brenly	.15	.07	.01
☐	4 Mike Boddicker	.15	.07	.01
☐	5 Dave Kingman	.20	.10	.02
☐	6 Jim Rice	.45	.22	.04
☐	7 Frank Viola	.35	.17	.03
☐	8 Alvin Davis	.25	.12	.02
☐	9 Rick Sutcliffe	.25	.12	.02
☐	10 Pete Rose	1.25	.60	.12
☐	11 Leon Durham	.15	.07	.01
☐	12 Joaquin Andujar	.15	.07	.01
☐	13 Keith Hernandez	.45	.22	.04
☐	14 Dave Winfield	.50	.25	.05
☐	15 Reggie Jackson	1.00	.50	.10
☐	16 Allan Trammell	.35	.17	.03
☐	17 Bert Blyleven	.20	.10	.02
☐	18 Tony Armas	.15	.07	.01
☐	19 Rich Gossage	.20	.10	.02
☐	20 Jose Cruz	.15	.07	.01
☐	21 Ryne Sandberg	.50	.25	.05
☐	22 Bruce Sutter	.20	.10	.02
☐	23 Mike Schmidt	1.00	.50	.10
☐	24 Cal Ripken	.90	.45	.09
☐	25 Dan Petry	.15	.07	.01
☐	26 Jack Morris	.25	.12	.02

		MINT	EXC	G-VG
☐ 27	Don Mattingly	2.50	1.25	.25
☐ 28	Eddie Murray	.90	.45	.09
☐ 29	Tony Gwynn	.75	.35	.07
☐ 30	Charlie Lea	.15	.07	.01
☐ 31	Juan Samuel	.25	.12	.02
☐ 32	Phil Niekro	.35	.17	.03
☐ 33	Alejandro Pena	.15	.07	.01
☐ 34	Harold Baines	.25	.12	.02
☐ 35	Dan Quisenberry	.25	.12	.02
☐ 36	Gary Carter	.65	.30	.06
☐ 37	Mario Soto	.15	.07	.01
☐ 38	Dwight Gooden	1.25	.60	.12
☐ 39	Tom Brunansky	.20	.10	.02
☐ 40	Dave Stieb	.20	.10	.02

1985 Topps Traded

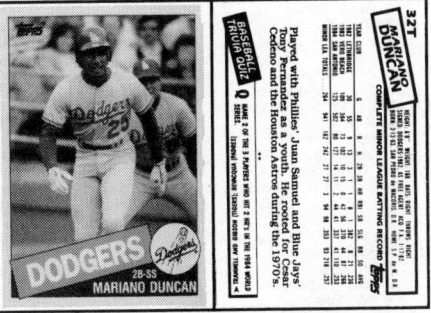

The cards in this 132-card set measure 2 1/2" by 3 1/2". In its now standard procedure, Topps issued its Traded (or extended) set for the fifth year in a row. Because all photos and statistics of its regular set for the year were developed during the fall and winter months of the preceding year, players who changed teams during the fall, winter, and spring months are portrayed in the 1985 regular issue set with the teams they were with in 1984. The Traded set amends the shortcomings of the regular set by presenting the players with their proper teams for the current year. Rookies not contained in the regular set are also picked up in the Traded set. Again this year, the Topps affiliate in Ireland printed the cards, and the cards were available through hobby channels only.

		MINT	EXC	G-VG
COMPLETE SET		14.00	7.00	1.40
COMMON PLAYER		.06	.03	.00
☐ 1T	Don Aase	.15	.04	.01
☐ 2T	Bill Almon	.06	.03	.00
☐ 3T	Benny Ayala	.06	.03	.00
☐ 4T	Dusty Baker	.10	.05	.01
☐ 5T	G.Bamberger MG	.10	.05	.01
☐ 6T	Dale Berra	.10	.05	.01
☐ 7T	Rich Bordi	.06	.03	.00
☐ 8T	Daryl Boston	.20	.10	.02
☐ 9T	Hubie Brooks	.25	.12	.02
☐ 10T	Chris Brown	1.25	.60	.12
☐ 11T	Tom Browning	.35	.17	.03
☐ 12T	Al Bumbry	.06	.03	.00
☐ 13T	Ray Burris	.06	.03	.00
☐ 14T	Jeff Burroughs	.06	.03	.00
☐ 15T	Bill Campbell	.06	.03	.00
☐ 16T	Don Carman	.30	.15	.03
☐ 17T	Gary Carter	.75	.35	.07
☐ 18T	Bobby Castillo	.06	.03	.00
☐ 19T	Bill Caudill	.10	.05	.01
☐ 20T	Rick Cerone	.10	.05	.01
☐ 21T	Bryan Clark	.06	.03	.00
☐ 22T	Jack Clark	.40	.20	.04
☐ 23T	Pat Clements	.25	.12	.02
☐ 24T	Vince Coleman	4.50	2.25	.45
☐ 25T	Dave Collins	.10	.05	.01
☐ 26T	Danny Darwin	.10	.05	.01
☐ 27T	Jim Davenport MG	.06	.03	.00
☐ 28T	Jerry Davis	.15	.07	.01

		MINT	EXC	G-VG
☐ 29T	Brian Dayett	.06	.03	.00
☐ 30T	Ivan DeJesus	.06	.03	.00
☐ 31T	Ken Dixon	.20	.10	.02
☐ 32T	Mariano Duncan	.35	.17	.03
☐ 33T	John Felske MG	.06	.03	.00
☐ 34T	Mike Fitzgerald	.06	.03	.00
☐ 35T	Ray Fontenot	.06	.03	.00
☐ 36T	Greg Gagne	.45	.22	.04
☐ 37T	Oscar Gamble	.10	.05	.01
☐ 38T	Scott Garrelts	.25	.12	.02
☐ 39T	Bob L. Gibson	.06	.03	.00
☐ 40T	Jim Gott	.06	.03	.00
☐ 41T	David Green	.10	.05	.01
☐ 42T	Alfredo Griffin	.15	.07	.01
☐ 43T	Ozzie Guillen	.85	.40	.08
☐ 44T	Eddie Haas MG	.06	.03	.00
☐ 45T	Terry Harper	.06	.03	.00
☐ 46T	Toby Harrah	.10	.05	.01
☐ 47T	Greg Harris	.06	.03	.00
☐ 48T	Ron Hassey	.06	.03	.00
☐ 49T	Rickey Henderson	1.00	.50	.10
☐ 50T	Steve Henderson	.06	.03	.00
☐ 51T	George Hendrick	.10	.05	.01
☐ 52T	Joe Hesketh	.30	.15	.03
☐ 53T	Teddy Higuera	2.50	1.25	.25
☐ 54T	Donnie Hill	.10	.05	.01
☐ 55T	Al Holland	.06	.03	.00
☐ 56T	Burt Hooton	.06	.03	.00
☐ 57T	Jay Howell	.06	.03	.00
☐ 58T	Ken Howell	.25	.12	.02
☐ 59T	LaMarr Hoyt	.10	.05	.01
☐ 60T	Tim Hulett	.20	.10	.02
☐ 61T	Bob James	.10	.05	.01
☐ 62T	Steve Jeltz	.15	.07	.01
☐ 63T	Cliff Johnson	.06	.03	.00
☐ 64T	Howard Johnson	1.25	.60	.12
☐ 65T	Ruppert Jones	.06	.03	.00
☐ 66T	Steve Kemp	.10	.05	.01
☐ 67T	Bruce Kison	.06	.03	.00
☐ 68T	Alan Knicely	.06	.03	.00
☐ 69T	Mike LaCoss	.06	.03	.00
☐ 70T	Lee Lacy	.10	.05	.01
☐ 71T	Dave LaPoint	.06	.03	.00
☐ 72T	Gary Lavelle	.06	.03	.00
☐ 73T	Vance Law	.06	.03	.00
☐ 74T	Johnnie LeMaster	.06	.03	.00
☐ 75T	Sixto Lezcano	.06	.03	.00
☐ 76T	Tim Lollar	.06	.03	.00
☐ 77T	Fred Lynn	.25	.12	.02
☐ 78T	Billy Martin MG	.15	.07	.01
☐ 79T	Ron Mathis	.15	.07	.01
☐ 80T	Len Matuszek	.06	.03	.00
☐ 81T	Gene Mauch MG	.10	.05	.01
☐ 82T	Oddibe McDowell	.90	.45	.09
☐ 83T	Roger McDowell	.90	.45	.09
☐ 84T	John McNamara MG	.10	.05	.01
☐ 85T	Donnie Moore	.06	.03	.00
☐ 86T	Gene Nelson	.06	.03	.00
☐ 87T	Steve Nicosia	.06	.03	.00
☐ 88T	Al Oliver	.20	.10	.02
☐ 89T	Joe Orsulak	.20	.10	.02
☐ 90T	Rob Picciolo	.06	.03	.00
☐ 91T	Chris Pittaro	.15	.07	.01
☐ 92T	Jim Presley	1.75	.85	.17
☐ 93T	Rick Reuschel	.15	.07	.01
☐ 94T	Bert Roberge	.06	.03	.00
☐ 95T	Bob Rodgers MG	.10	.05	.01
☐ 96T	Jerry Royster	.06	.03	.00
☐ 97T	Dave Rozema	.06	.03	.00
☐ 98T	Dave Rucker	.06	.03	.00
☐ 99T	Vern Ruhle	.06	.03	.00
☐ 100T	Paul Runge	.15	.07	.01
☐ 101T	Mark Salas	.25	.12	.02
☐ 102T	Luis Salazar	.06	.03	.00
☐ 103T	Joe Sambito	.10	.05	.01
☐ 104T	Rick Schu	.25	.12	.02
☐ 105T	Donnie Scott	.06	.03	.00
☐ 106T	Larry Sheets	.90	.45	.09
☐ 107T	Don Slaught	.10	.05	.01
☐ 108T	Roy Smalley	.10	.05	.01
☐ 109T	Lonnie Smith	.10	.05	.01
☐ 110T	Nate Snell (headings on back for a batter)	.20	.10	.02
☐ 111T	Chris Speier	.06	.03	.00
☐ 112T	Mike Stenhouse	.10	.05	.01
☐ 113T	Tim Stoddard	.06	.03	.00
☐ 114T	Jim Sundberg	.10	.05	.01
☐ 115T	Bruce Sutter	.25	.12	.02
☐ 116T	Don Sutton	.50	.25	.05
☐ 117T	Kent Tekulve	.15	.07	.01
☐ 118T	Tom Tellmann	.06	.03	.00
☐ 119T	Walt Terrell	.15	.07	.01
☐ 120T	Mickey Tettleton	.10	.05	.01
☐ 121T	Derrel Thomas	.06	.03	.00

			MINT	EXC	G-VG
☐ 122T	Rich Thompson		.10	.05	.01
☐ 123T	Alex Trevino		.06	.03	.00
☐ 124T	John Tudor		.20	.10	.02
☐ 125T	Jose Uribe		.30	.15	.03
☐ 126T	Bobby Valentine MG		.15	.07	.01
☐ 127T	Dave Von Ohlen		.06	.03	.00
☐ 128T	U.L. Washington		.06	.03	.00
☐ 129T	Earl Weaver MG		.15	.07	.01
☐ 130T	Eddie Whitson		.10	.05	.01
☐ 131T	Herm Winningham		.20	.10	.02
☐ 132T	Checklist 1-132		.10	.01	.00

1986 Topps

WADE BOGGS

The cards in this 792-card set are standard-size (2 1/2" by 3 1/2"). The first seven cards are a tribute to Pete Rose and his career. Cards 2-7 show small photos of Pete's Topps cards of the given years on the front with biographical information pertaining to those years on the back. The team leader cards were done differently with a simple player action shot on a white background; the player pictured is dubbed the "Dean" of that team, i.e., the player with the longest continuous service with that team. Topps again features a "Turn Back the Clock" series (401-405). Record breakers of the previous year are acknowledged on cards 201 to 207. Cards 701-722 feature All-Star selections from each league. Manager cards feature the team checklist on the reverse. Ryne Sandberg (#690) is the only player card in the set without a Topps logo on the front of the card; this omission was never corrected by Topps. There are two other uncorrected errors involving misnumbered cards; see card numbers 51, 57, 141, and 171 in the checklist below. The backs of all the cards have a distinctive red background.

	MINT	EXC	G-VG
COMPLETE SET	28.00	14.00	2.80
COMMON PLAYER	.03	.01	.00

			MINT	EXC	G-VG
☐ 1	Pete Rose		1.00	.25	.05
☐ 2	Rose Special: '63-'66		.25	.12	.02
☐ 3	Rose Special: '67-'70		.25	.12	.02
☐ 4	Rose Special: '71-'74		.25	.12	.02
☐ 5	Rose Special: '75-'78		.25	.12	.02
☐ 6	Rose Special: '79-'82		.25	.12	.02
☐ 7	Rose Special: '83-'85		.25	.12	.02
☐ 8	Dwayne Murphy		.06	.03	.00
☐ 9	Roy Smith		.03	.01	.00
☐ 10	Tony Gwynn		.50	.25	.05
☐ 11	Bob Ojeda		.10	.05	.01
☐ 12	Jose Uribe		.20	.10	.02
☐ 13	Bob Kearney		.03	.01	.00
☐ 14	Julio Cruz		.03	.01	.00
☐ 15	Eddie Whitson		.06	.03	.00
☐ 16	Rick Schu		.10	.05	.01
☐ 17	Mike Stenhouse		.03	.01	.00
☐ 18	Brent Gaff		.03	.01	.00
☐ 19	Rich Hebner		.03	.01	.00
☐ 20	Lou Whitaker		.15	.07	.01
☐ 21	G.Bamberger MG (checklist back)		.06	.01	.00
☐ 22	Duane Walker		.03	.01	.00

			MINT	EXC	G-VG
☐ 23	Manny Lee		.10	.05	.01
☐ 24	Len Barker		.03	.01	.00
☐ 25	Willie Wilson		.12	.06	.01
☐ 26	Frank DiPino		.03	.01	.00
☐ 27	Ray Knight		.06	.03	.00
☐ 28	Eric Davis		3.50	1.75	.35
☐ 29	Tony Phillips		.03	.01	.00
☐ 30	Eddie Murray		.30	.15	.03
☐ 31	Jamie Easterly		.03	.01	.00
☐ 32	Steve Yeager		.03	.01	.00
☐ 33	Jeff Lahti		.03	.01	.00
☐ 34	Ken Phelps		.06	.03	.00
☐ 35	Jeff Reardon		.10	.05	.01
☐ 36	Tigers Leaders Lance Parrish		.12	.06	.01
☐ 37	Mark Thurmond		.03	.01	.00
☐ 38	Glenn Hoffman		.03	.01	.00
☐ 39	Dave Rucker		.03	.01	.00
☐ 40	Ken Griffey		.06	.03	.00
☐ 41	Brad Wellman		.03	.01	.00
☐ 42	Geoff Zahn		.03	.01	.00
☐ 43	Dave Engle		.03	.01	.00
☐ 44	Lance McCullers		.20	.10	.02
☐ 45	Damaso Garcia		.06	.03	.00
☐ 46	Billy Hatcher		.20	.10	.02
☐ 47	Juan Berenguer		.03	.01	.00
☐ 48	Bill Almon		.03	.01	.00
☐ 49	Rick Manning		.03	.01	.00
☐ 50	Dan Quisenberry		.12	.06	.01
☐ 51	Bobby Wine MG ERR (checklist back) (number of card on back is actually 57)		.10	.03	.01
☐ 52	Chris Welsh		.03	.01	.00
☐ 53	Len Dykstra		.75	.35	.07
☐ 54	John Franco		.10	.05	.01
☐ 55	Fred Lynn		.12	.06	.01
☐ 56	Tom Niedenfuer		.03	.01	.00
☐ 57	Bill Doran (see also 51)		.10	.05	.01
☐ 58	Bill Krueger		.03	.01	.00
☐ 59	Andre Thornton		.06	.03	.00
☐ 60	Dwight Evans		.12	.06	.01
☐ 61	Karl Best		.10	.05	.01
☐ 62	Bob Boone		.06	.03	.00
☐ 63	Ron Roenicke		.03	.01	.00
☐ 64	Floyd Bannister		.06	.03	.00
☐ 65	Dan Driessen		.03	.01	.00
☐ 66	Cardinals Leaders Bob Forsch		.06	.03	.00
☐ 67	Carmelo Martinez		.06	.03	.00
☐ 68	Ed Lynch		.03	.01	.00
☐ 69	Luis Aguayo		.03	.01	.00
☐ 70	Dave Winfield		.25	.12	.02
☐ 71	Ken Schrom		.03	.01	.00
☐ 72	Shawon Dunston		.10	.05	.01
☐ 73	Randy O'Neal		.06	.03	.00
☐ 74	Rance Mulliniks		.03	.01	.00
☐ 75	Jose DeLeon		.03	.01	.00
☐ 76	Dion James		.06	.03	.00
☐ 77	Charlie Leibrandt		.06	.03	.00
☐ 78	Bruce Benedict		.03	.01	.00
☐ 79	Dave Schmidt		.06	.03	.00
☐ 80	Darryl Strawberry		.50	.25	.05
☐ 81	Gene Mauch MG (checklist back)		.06	.01	.00
☐ 82	Tippy Martinez		.03	.01	.00
☐ 83	Phil Garner		.03	.01	.00
☐ 84	Curt Young		.06	.03	.00
☐ 85	Tony Perez		.15	.07	.01
☐ 86	Tom Waddell		.03	.01	.00
☐ 87	Candy Maldonado		.10	.05	.01
☐ 88	Tom Nieto		.03	.01	.00
☐ 89	Randy S⁺ Claire		.06	.03	.00
☐ 90	Garry Templeton		.06	.03	.00
☐ 91	Steve Crawford		.03	.01	.00
☐ 92	Al Cowens		.03	.01	.00
☐ 93	Scot Thompson		.03	.01	.00
☐ 94	Rich Bordi		.03	.01	.00
☐ 95	Ozzie Virgil		.03	.01	.00
☐ 96	Blue Jays Leaders Jim Clancy		.06	.03	.00
☐ 97	Gary Gaetti		.12	.06	.01
☐ 98	Dick Ruthven		.03	.01	.00
☐ 99	Buddy Biancalana		.03	.01	.00
☐ 100	Nolan Ryan		.30	.15	.03
☐ 101	Dave Bergman		.03	.01	.00
☐ 102	Joe Orsulak		.15	.07	.01
☐ 103	Luis Salazar		.03	.01	.00
☐ 104	Sid Fernandez		.15	.07	.01
☐ 105	Gary Ward		.06	.03	.00
☐ 106	Ray Burris		.03	.01	.00
☐ 107	Rafael Ramirez		.03	.01	.00
☐ 108	Ted Power		.06	.03	.00
☐ 109	Len Matuszek		.03	.01	.00

☐ 110	Scott McGregor	.06	.03	.00
☐ 111	Roger Craig MG	.06	.01	.00
	(checklist back)			
☐ 112	Bill Campbell	.03	.01	.00
☐ 113	U.L. Washington	.03	.01	.00
☐ 114	Mike Brown	.03	.01	.00
	(Pirates OF)			
☐ 115	Jay Howell	.03	.01	.00
☐ 116	Brook Jacoby	.10	.05	.01
☐ 117	Bruce Kison	.03	.01	.00
☐ 118	Jerry Royster	.03	.01	.00
☐ 119	Barry Bonnell	.03	.01	.00
☐ 120	Steve Carlton	.25	.12	.02
☐ 121	Nelson Simmons	.10	.05	.01
☐ 122	Pete Filson	.03	.01	.00
☐ 123	Greg Walker	.10	.05	.01
☐ 124	Luis Sanchez	.03	.01	.00
☐ 125	Dave Lopes	.06	.03	.00
☐ 126	Mets Leaders	.06	.03	.00
	Mookie Wilson			
☐ 127	Jack Howell	.35	.17	.03
☐ 128	John Wathan	.06	.03	.00
☐ 129	Jeff Dedmon	.03	.01	.00
☐ 130	Alan Trammell	.20	.10	.02
☐ 131	Checklist: 1-132	.06	.01	.00
☐ 132	Razor Shines	.06	.03	.00
☐ 133	Andy McGaffigan	.03	.01	.00
☐ 134	Carney Lansford	.10	.05	.01
☐ 135	Joe Niekro	.10	.05	.01
☐ 136	Mike Hargrove	.03	.01	.00
☐ 137	Charlie Moore	.03	.01	.00
☐ 138	Mark Davis	.03	.01	.00
☐ 139	Daryl Boston	.06	.03	.00
☐ 140	John Candelaria	.06	.03	.00
☐ 141	Chuck Cottier MG	.10	.05	.01
	(checklist back)			
	(see also 171)			
☐ 142	Bob Jones	.03	.01	.00
☐ 143	Dave Van Gorder	.03	.01	.00
☐ 144	Doug Sisk	.03	.01	.00
☐ 145	Pedro Guerrero	.25	.12	.02
☐ 146	Jack Perconte	.03	.01	.00
☐ 147	Larry Sheets	.25	.12	.02
☐ 148	Mike Heath	.03	.01	.00
☐ 149	Brett Butler	.10	.05	.01
☐ 150	Joaquin Andujar	.10	.05	.01
☐ 151	Dave Stapleton	.03	.01	.00
☐ 152	Mike Morgan	.03	.01	.00
☐ 153	Ricky Adams	.03	.01	.00
☐ 154	Bert Roberge	.03	.01	.00
☐ 155	Bob Grich	.06	.03	.00
☐ 156	White Sox Leaders	.06	.03	.00
	Richard Dotson			
☐ 157	Ron Hassey	.03	.01	.00
☐ 158	Derrel Thomas	.03	.01	.00
☐ 159	Orel Hershiser	.30	.15	.03
☐ 160	Chet Lemon	.03	.01	.00
☐ 161	Lee Tunnell	.03	.01	.00
☐ 162	Greg Gagne	.15	.07	.01
☐ 163	Pete Ladd	.03	.01	.00
☐ 164	Steve Balboni	.03	.01	.00
☐ 165	Mike Davis	.06	.03	.00
☐ 166	Dickie Thon	.03	.01	.00
☐ 167	Zane Smith	.20	.10	.02
☐ 168	Jeff Burroughs	.03	.01	.00
☐ 169	George Wright	.03	.01	.00
☐ 170	Gary Carter	.30	.15	.03
☐ 171	Bob Rodgers MG ERR	.10	.03	.01
	(checklist back)			
	(number of card on			
	back actually 141)			
☐ 172	Jerry Reed	.06	.03	.00
☐ 173	Wayne Gross	.03	.01	.00
☐ 174	Brian Snyder	.06	.03	.00
☐ 175	Steve Sax	.12	.06	.01
☐ 176	Jay Tibbs	.03	.01	.00
☐ 177	Joel Youngblood	.03	.01	.00
☐ 178	Ivan DeJesus	.03	.01	.00
☐ 179	Stu Cliburn	.10	.05	.01
☐ 180	Don Mattingly	4.00	2.00	.40
☐ 181	Al Nipper	.03	.01	.00
☐ 182	Bobby Brown	.03	.01	.00
☐ 183	Larry Andersen	.03	.01	.00
☐ 184	Tim Laudner	.06	.03	.00
☐ 185	Rollie Fingers	.15	.07	.01
☐ 186	Astros Leaders	.06	.03	.00
	Jose Cruz			
☐ 187	Scott Fletcher	.06	.03	.00
☐ 188	Bob Dernier	.03	.01	.00
☐ 189	Mike Mason	.03	.01	.00
☐ 190	George Hendrick	.06	.03	.00
☐ 191	Wally Backman	.06	.03	.00
☐ 192	Milt Wilcox	.03	.01	.00
☐ 193	Daryl Sconiers	.03	.01	.00
☐ 194	Craig McMurtry	.03	.01	.00
☐ 195	Dave Concepcion	.06	.03	.00
☐ 196	Doyle Alexander	.06	.03	.00
☐ 197	Enos Cabell	.03	.01	.00
☐ 198	Ken Dixon	.06	.03	.00
☐ 199	Dick Howser MG	.06	.01	.00
	(checklist back)			
☐ 200	Mike Schmidt	.40	.20	.04
☐ 201	RB: Vince Coleman	.20	.10	.02
	Most stolen bases,			
	season, rookie			
☐ 202	RB: Dwight Gooden	.30	.15	.03
	Youngest 20 game			
	winner			
☐ 203	RB: Keith Hernandez	.15	.07	.01
	Most game-winning			
	RBI's			
☐ 204	RB: Phil Niekro	.10	.05	.01
	Oldest shutout			
	pitcher			
☐ 205	RB: Tony Perez	.10	.05	.01
	Oldest grand slammer			
☐ 206	RB: Pete Rose	.35	.17	.03
	Most hits, lifetime			
☐ 207	RB: Fern.Valenzuela	.15	.07	.01
	Most cons. innings,			
	start of season,			
	no earned runs			
☐ 208	Ramon Romero	.06	.03	.00
☐ 209	Randy Ready	.06	.03	.00
☐ 210	Calvin Schiraldi	.10	.05	.01
☐ 211	Ed Wojna	.10	.05	.01
☐ 212	Chris Speier	.03	.01	.00
☐ 213	Bob Shirley	.03	.01	.00
☐ 214	Randy Bush	.03	.01	.00
☐ 215	Frank White	.06	.03	.00
☐ 216	A's Leaders	.06	.03	.00
	Dwayne Murphy			
☐ 217	Bill Scherrer	.03	.01	.00
☐ 218	Randy Hunt	.06	.03	.00
☐ 219	Dennis Lamp	.03	.01	.00
☐ 220	Bob Horner	.15	.07	.01
☐ 221	Dave Henderson	.03	.01	.00
☐ 222	Craig Gerber	.06	.03	.00
☐ 223	Atlee Hammaker	.03	.01	.00
☐ 224	Cesar Cedeno	.06	.03	.00
☐ 225	Ron Darling	.20	.10	.02
☐ 226	Lee Lacy	.03	.01	.00
☐ 227	Al Jones	.03	.01	.00
☐ 228	Tom Lawless	.03	.01	.00
☐ 229	Bill Gullickson	.06	.03	.00
☐ 230	Terry Kennedy	.06	.03	.00
☐ 231	Jim Frey MG	.06	.01	.00
	(checklist back)			
☐ 232	Rick Rhoden	.06	.03	.00
☐ 233	Steve Lyons	.06	.03	.00
☐ 234	Doug Corbett	.03	.01	.00
☐ 235	Butch Wynegar	.03	.01	.00
☐ 236	Frank Eufemia	.06	.03	.00
☐ 237	Ted Simmons	.10	.05	.01
☐ 238	Larry Parrish	.06	.03	.00
☐ 239	Joel Skinner	.06	.03	.00
☐ 240	Tommy John	.12	.06	.01
☐ 241	Tony Fernandez	.20	.10	.02
☐ 242	Rich Thompson	.06	.03	.00
☐ 243	Johnny Grubb	.03	.01	.00
☐ 244	Craig Lefferts	.03	.01	.00
☐ 245	Jim Sundberg	.03	.01	.00
☐ 246	Phillies Leaders	.15	.07	.01
	Steve Carlton			
☐ 247	Terry Harper	.03	.01	.00
☐ 248	Spike Owen	.03	.01	.00
☐ 249	Rob Deer	.35	.17	.03
☐ 250	Dwight Gooden	1.25	.60	.12
☐ 251	Rich Dauer	.03	.01	.00
☐ 252	Bobby Castillo	.03	.01	.00
☐ 253	Dann Bilardello	.03	.01	.00
☐ 254	Ozzie Guillen	.40	.20	.04
☐ 255	Tony Armas	.06	.03	.00
☐ 256	Kurt Kepshire	.03	.01	.00
☐ 257	Doug DeCinces	.06	.03	.00
☐ 258	Tim Burke	.25	.12	.02
☐ 259	Dan Pasqua	.30	.15	.03
☐ 260	Tony Pena	.10	.05	.01
☐ 261	Bobby Valentine MG	.06	.01	.00
	(checklist back)			
☐ 262	Mario Ramirez	.03	.01	.00
☐ 263	Checklist: 133-264	.06	.01	.00
☐ 264	Darren Daulton	.20	.10	.02
☐ 265	Ron Davis	.03	.01	.00
☐ 266	Keith Moreland	.06	.03	.00
☐ 267	Paul Molitor	.12	.06	.01
☐ 268	Mike Scott	.25	.12	.02
☐ 269	Dane Iorg	.03	.01	.00
☐ 270	Jack Morris	.15	.07	.01
☐ 271	Dave Collins	.03	.01	.00

RETAIL STORE OWNERS

Write on your letterhead or call to find out how you can increase your profits by carrying MARVEL COMICS. MARVEL COMICS are released every week, are high profit sales and are bought primarily by males between the ages of 10 to 25. Act now to get comics into your store.

COMICS UNLIMITED LTD.
6833-BB Amboy Road
Staten Island, NY 10309
(718) 948-2223

☐ 272 Tim Tolman	.06	.03	.00
☐ 273 Jerry Willard	.03	.01	.00
☐ 274 Ron Gardenhire	.03	.01	.00
☐ 275 Charlie Hough	.06	.03	.00
☐ 276 Yankees Leaders	.06	.03	.00
Willie Randolph			
☐ 277 Jaime Cocanower	.03	.01	.00
☐ 278 Sixto Lezcano	.03	.01	.00
☐ 279 Al Pardo	.06	.03	.00
☐ 280 Tim Raines	.25	.12	.02
☐ 281 Steve Mura	.03	.01	.00
☐ 282 Jerry Mumphrey	.03	.01	.00
☐ 283 Mike Fischlin	.03	.01	.00
☐ 284 Brian Dayett	.03	.01	.00
☐ 285 Buddy Bell	.10	.05	.01
☐ 286 Luis DeLeon	.03	.01	.00
☐ 287 John Christensen	.06	.03	.00
☐ 288 Don Aase	.03	.01	.00
☐ 289 Johnnie LeMaster	.03	.01	.00
☐ 290 Carlton Fisk	.12	.06	.01
☐ 291 Tom Lasorda MG	.10	.03	.01
(checklist back)			
☐ 292 Chuck Porter	.03	.01	.00
☐ 293 Chris Chambliss	.06	.03	.00
☐ 294 Danny Cox	.10	.05	.01
☐ 295 Kirk Gibson	.20	.10	.02
☐ 296 Geno Petralli	.06	.03	.00
☐ 297 Tim Lollar	.03	.01	.00
☐ 298 Craig Reynolds	.03	.01	.00
☐ 299 Bryn Smith	.03	.01	.00
☐ 300 George Brett	.40	.20	.04
☐ 301 Dennis Rasmussen	.06	.03	.00
☐ 302 Greg Gross	.03	.01	.00
☐ 303 Curt Wardle	.06	.03	.00
☐ 304 Mike Gallego	.06	.03	.00
☐ 305 Phil Bradley	.15	.07	.01
☐ 306 Padres Leaders	.06	.03	.00
Terry Kennedy			
☐ 307 Dave Sax	.06	.03	.00
☐ 308 Ray Fontenot	.03	.01	.00
☐ 309 John Shelby	.03	.01	.00
☐ 310 Greg Minton	.03	.01	.00
☐ 311 Dick Schofield	.03	.01	.00
☐ 312 Tom Filer	.03	.01	.00
☐ 313 Joe DeSa	.03	.01	.00
☐ 314 Frank Pastore	.03	.01	.00
☐ 315 Mookie Wilson	.06	.03	.00
☐ 316 Sammy Khalifa	.10	.05	.01
☐ 317 Ed Romero	.03	.01	.00
☐ 318 Terry Whitfield	.03	.01	.00
☐ 319 Rick Camp	.03	.01	.00
☐ 320 Jim Rice	.25	.12	.02
☐ 321 Earl Weaver MG	.06	.01	.00
(checklist back)			
☐ 322 Bob Forsch	.03	.01	.00
☐ 323 Jerry Davis	.06	.03	.00
☐ 324 Dan Schatzeder	.03	.01	.00
☐ 325 Juan Beniquez	.03	.01	.00
☐ 326 Kent Tekulve	.06	.03	.00
☐ 327 Mike Pagliarulo	.15	.07	.01
☐ 328 Pete O'Brien	.10	.05	.01
☐ 329 Kirby Puckett	1.25	.60	.12
☐ 330 Rick Sutcliffe	.12	.06	.01
☐ 331 Alan Ashby	.03	.01	.00
☐ 332 Darryl Motley	.03	.01	.00
☐ 333 Tom Henke	.15	.07	.01
☐ 334 Ken Oberkfell	.03	.01	.00
☐ 335 Don Sutton	.15	.07	.01
☐ 336 Indians Leaders	.06	.03	.00
Andre Thornton			
☐ 337 Darnell Coles	.06	.03	.00
☐ 338 Jorge Bell	.25	.12	.02
☐ 339 Bruce Berenyi	.03	.01	.00
☐ 340 Cal Ripken	.35	.17	.03
☐ 341 Frank Williams	.03	.01	.00
☐ 342 Gary Redus	.03	.01	.00
☐ 343 Carlos Diaz	.03	.01	.00
☐ 344 Jim Wohlford	.03	.01	.00
☐ 345 Donnie Moore	.03	.01	.00
☐ 346 Bryan Little	.03	.01	.00
☐ 347 Teddy Higuera	1.00	.50	.10
☐ 348 Cliff Johnson	.03	.01	.00
☐ 349 Mark Clear	.03	.01	.00
☐ 350 Jack Clark	.20	.10	.02
☐ 351 Chuck Tanner MG	.06	.01	.00
(checklist back)			
☐ 352 Harry Spilman	.03	.01	.00
☐ 353 Keith Atherton	.03	.01	.00
☐ 354 Tony Bernazard	.03	.01	.00
☐ 355 Lee Smith	.06	.03	.00
☐ 356 Mickey Hatcher	.03	.01	.00
☐ 357 Ed VandeBerg	.03	.01	.00
☐ 358 Rick Dempsey	.03	.01	.00
☐ 359 Mike LaCoss	.03	.01	.00
☐ 360 Lloyd Moseby	.10	.05	.01

☐ 361 Shane Rawley	.06	.03	.00
☐ 362 Tom Paciorek	.03	.01	.00
☐ 363 Terry Forster	.06	.03	.00
☐ 364 Reid Nichols	.03	.01	.00
☐ 365 Mike Flanagan	.06	.03	.00
☐ 366 Reds Leaders	.06	.03	.00
Dave Concepcion			
☐ 367 Aurelio Lopez	.03	.01	.00
☐ 368 Greg Brock	.06	.03	.00
☐ 369 Al Holland	.03	.01	.00
☐ 370 Vince Coleman	2.00	1.00	.20
☐ 371 Bill Stein	.03	.01	.00
☐ 372 Ben Oglivie	.06	.03	.00
☐ 373 Urbano Lugo	.06	.03	.00
☐ 374 Terry Francona	.03	.01	.00
☐ 375 Rich Gedman	.06	.03	.00
☐ 376 Bill Dawley	.03	.01	.00
☐ 377 Joe Carter	.25	.12	.02
☐ 378 Bruce Bochte	.03	.01	.00
☐ 379 Bobby Meacham	.03	.01	.00
☐ 380 LaMarr Hoyt	.06	.03	.00
☐ 381 Ray Miller MG	.06	.01	.00
(checklist back)			
☐ 382 Ivan Calderon	.85	.40	.08
☐ 383 Chris Brown	.65	.30	.06
☐ 384 Steve Trout	.06	.03	.00
☐ 385 Cecil Cooper	.10	.05	.01
☐ 386 Cecil Fielder	.25	.12	.02
☐ 387 Steve Kemp	.06	.03	.00
☐ 388 Dickie Noles	.03	.01	.00
☐ 389 Glenn Davis	1.25	.60	.12
☐ 390 Tom Seaver	.30	.15	.03
☐ 391 Julio Franco	.10	.05	.01
☐ 392 John Russell	.06	.03	.00
☐ 393 Chris Pittaro	.06	.03	.00
☐ 394 Checklist: 265-396	.06	.01	.00
☐ 395 Scott Garrelts	.06	.03	.00
☐ 396 Red Sox Leaders	.10	.05	.01
Dwight Evans			
☐ 397 Steve Buechele	.20	.10	.02
☐ 398 Earnie Riles	.25	.12	.02
☐ 399 Bill Swift	.06	.03	.00
☐ 400 Rod Carew	.30	.15	.03
☐ 401 Turn Back 5 Years	.15	.07	.01
Fern.Valenzuela '81			
☐ 402 Turn Back 10 Years	.15	.07	.01
Tom Seaver '76			
☐ 403 Turn Back 15 Years	.15	.07	.01
Willie Mays '71			
☐ 404 Turn Back 20 Years	.10	.05	.01
Frank Robinson '66			
☐ 405 Turn Back 25 Years	.15	.07	.01
Roger Maris '61			
☐ 406 Scott Sanderson	.03	.01	.00
☐ 407 Sal Butera	.03	.01	.00
☐ 408 Dave Smith	.06	.03	.00
☐ 409 Paul Runge	.06	.03	.00
☐ 410 Dave Kingman	.10	.05	.01
☐ 411 Sparky Anderson MG	.06	.01	.00
(checklist back)			
☐ 412 Jim Clancy	.03	.01	.00
☐ 413 Tim Flannery	.03	.01	.00
☐ 414 Tom Gorman	.03	.01	.00
☐ 415 Hal McRae	.06	.03	.00
☐ 416 Denny Martinez	.06	.03	.00
☐ 417 R.J. Reynolds	.06	.03	.00
☐ 418 Alan Knicely	.03	.01	.00
☐ 419 Frank Wills	.06	.03	.00
☐ 420 Von Hayes	.10	.05	.01
☐ 421 Dave Palmer	.03	.01	.00
☐ 422 Mike Jorgensen	.03	.01	.00
☐ 423 Dan Spillner	.03	.01	.00
☐ 424 Rick Miller	.03	.01	.00
☐ 425 Larry McWilliams	.03	.01	.00
☐ 426 Brewers Leaders	.06	.03	.00
Charlie Moore			
☐ 427 Joe Cowley	.03	.01	.00
☐ 428 Max Venable	.03	.01	.00
☐ 429 Greg Booker	.03	.01	.00
☐ 430 Kent Hrbek	.15	.07	.01
☐ 431 George Frazier	.03	.01	.00
☐ 432 Mark Bailey	.03	.01	.00
☐ 433 Chris Codiroli	.03	.01	.00
☐ 434 Curt Wilkerson	.03	.01	.00
☐ 435 Bill Caudill	.03	.01	.00
☐ 436 Doug Flynn	.03	.01	.00
☐ 437 Rick Mahler	.03	.01	.00
☐ 438 Clint Hurdle	.03	.01	.00
☐ 439 Rick Honeycutt	.03	.01	.00
☐ 440 Alvin Davis	.15	.07	.01
☐ 441 Whitey Herzog MG	.06	.01	.00
(checklist back)			
☐ 442 Ron Robinson	.10	.05	.01
☐ 443 Bill Buckner	.06	.03	.00
☐ 444 Alex Trevino	.03	.01	.00

☐ 445	Bert Blyleven	.10	.05	.01
☐ 446	Lenn Sakata	.03	.01	.00
☐ 447	Jerry Don Gleaton	.03	.01	.00
☐ 448	Herm Winningham	.15	.07	.01
☐ 449	Rod Scurry	.03	.01	.00
☐ 450	Graig Nettles	.12	.06	.01
☐ 451	Mark Brown	.06	.03	.00
☐ 452	Bob Clark	.03	.01	.00
☐ 453	Steve Jeltz	.06	.03	.00
☐ 454	Burt Hooton	.03	.01	.00
☐ 455	Willie Randolph	.06	.03	.00
☐ 456	Braves Leaders Dale Murphy	.25	.12	.02
☐ 457	Mickey Tettleton	.10	.05	.01
☐ 458	Kevin Bass	.10	.05	.01
☐ 459	Luis Leal	.03	.01	.00
☐ 460	Leon Durham	.10	.05	.01
☐ 461	Walt Terrell	.06	.03	.00
☐ 462	Domingo Ramos	.03	.01	.00
☐ 463	Jim Gott	.03	.01	.00
☐ 464	Ruppert Jones	.03	.01	.00
☐ 465	Jesse Orosco	.06	.03	.00
☐ 466	Tom Foley	.03	.01	.00
☐ 467	Bob James	.03	.01	.00
☐ 468	Mike Scioscia	.03	.01	.00
☐ 469	Storm Davis	.06	.03	.00
☐ 470	Bill Madlock	.10	.05	.01
☐ 471	Bobby Cox MG (checklist back)	.06	.01	.00
☐ 472	Joe Hesketh	.10	.05	.01
☐ 473	Mark Brouhard	.03	.01	.00
☐ 474	John Tudor	.10	.05	.01
☐ 475	Juan Samuel	.15	.07	.01
☐ 476	Ron Mathis	.10	.05	.01
☐ 477	Mike Easler	.06	.03	.00
☐ 478	Andy Hawkins	.03	.01	.00
☐ 479	Bob Melvin	.15	.07	.01
☐ 480	Oddibe McDowell	.25	.12	.02
☐ 481	Scott Bradley	.10	.05	.01
☐ 482	Rick Lysander	.03	.01	.00
☐ 483	George Vukovich	.03	.01	.00
☐ 484	Donnie Hill	.03	.01	.00
☐ 485	Gary Matthews	.06	.03	.00
☐ 486	Angels Leaders Bobby Grich	.06	.03	.00
☐ 487	Bret Saberhagen	.50	.25	.05
☐ 488	Lou Thornton	.10	.05	.01
☐ 489	Jim Winn	.03	.01	.00
☐ 490	Jeff Leonard	.10	.05	.01
☐ 491	Pascual Perez	.03	.01	.00
☐ 492	Kelvin Chapman	.03	.01	.00
☐ 493	Gene Nelson	.03	.01	.00
☐ 494	Gary Roenicke	.03	.01	.00
☐ 495	Mark Langston	.12	.06	.01
☐ 496	Jay Johnstone	.06	.03	.00
☐ 497	John Stuper	.03	.01	.00
☐ 498	Tito Landrum	.03	.01	.00
☐ 499	Bob L. Gibson	.03	.01	.00
☐ 500	Rickey Henderson	.35	.17	.03
☐ 501	Dave Johnson MG (checklist back)	.06	.01	.00
☐ 502	Glen Cook	.10	.05	.01
☐ 503	Mike Fitzgerald	.03	.01	.00
☐ 504	Denny Walling	.03	.01	.00
☐ 505	Jerry Koosman	.06	.03	.00
☐ 506	Bill Russell	.03	.01	.00
☐ 507	Steve Ontiveros	.15	.07	.01
☐ 508	Alan Wiggins	.03	.01	.00
☐ 509	Ernie Camacho	.03	.01	.00
☐ 510	Wade Boggs	2.25	1.10	.22
☐ 511	Ed Nunez	.06	.03	.00
☐ 512	Thad Bosley	.03	.01	.00
☐ 513	Ron Washington	.03	.01	.00
☐ 514	Mike Jones	.03	.01	.00
☐ 515	Darrell Evans	.10	.05	.01
☐ 516	Giants Leaders Greg Minton	.06	.03	.00
☐ 517	Milt Thompson	.50	.25	.05
☐ 518	Buck Martinez	.03	.01	.00
☐ 519	Danny Darwin	.03	.01	.00
☐ 520	Keith Hernandez	.25	.12	.02
☐ 521	Nate Snell	.10	.05	.01
☐ 522	Bob Bailor	.03	.01	.00
☐ 523	Joe Price	.03	.01	.00
☐ 524	Darrell Miller	.10	.05	.01
☐ 525	Marvell Wynne	.03	.01	.00
☐ 526	Charlie Lea	.03	.01	.00
☐ 527	Checklist: 397-528	.06	.01	.00
☐ 528	Terry Pendleton	.06	.03	.00
☐ 529	Marc Sullivan	.06	.01	.00
☐ 530	Rich Gossage	.12	.06	.01
☐ 531	Tony LaRussa MG (checklist back)	.06	.01	.00
☐ 532	Don Carman	.20	.10	.02
☐ 533	Billy Sample	.03	.01	.00

☐ 534	Jeff Calhoun	.06	.03	.00
☐ 535	Toby Harrah	.03	.01	.00
☐ 536	Jose Rijo	.06	.03	.00
☐ 537	Mark Salas	.06	.03	.00
☐ 538	Dennis Eckersley	.06	.03	.00
☐ 539	Glenn Hubbard	.03	.01	.00
☐ 540	Dan Petry	.10	.05	.01
☐ 541	Jorge Orta	.03	.01	.00
☐ 542	Don Schulze	.03	.01	.00
☐ 543	Jerry Narron	.03	.01	.00
☐ 544	Eddie Milner	.03	.01	.00
☐ 545	Jimmy Key	.12	.06	.01
☐ 546	Mariners Leaders Dave Henderson	.06	.03	.00
☐ 547	Roger McDowell	.45	.22	.04
☐ 548	Mike Young	.10	.05	.01
☐ 549	Bob Welch	.06	.03	.00
☐ 550	Tom Herr	.06	.03	.00
☐ 551	Dave LaPoint	.03	.01	.00
☐ 552	Marc Hill	.03	.01	.00
☐ 553	Jim Morrison	.03	.01	.00
☐ 554	Paul Householder	.03	.01	.00
☐ 555	Hubie Brooks	.10	.05	.01
☐ 556	John Denny	.06	.03	.00
☐ 557	Gerald Perry	.06	.03	.00
☐ 558	Tim Stoddard	.03	.01	.00
☐ 559	Tommy Dunbar	.03	.01	.00
☐ 560	Dave Righetti	.15	.07	.01
☐ 561	Bob Lillis MG (checklist back)	.06	.01	.00
☐ 562	Joe Beckwith	.03	.01	.00
☐ 563	Alejandro Sanchez	.06	.03	.00
☐ 564	Warren Brusstar	.03	.01	.00
☐ 565	Tom Brunansky	.12	.06	.01
☐ 566	Alfredo Griffin	.06	.03	.00
☐ 567	Jeff Barkley	.06	.03	.00
☐ 568	Donnie Scott	.03	.01	.00
☐ 569	Jim Acker	.03	.01	.00
☐ 570	Rusty Staub	.10	.05	.01
☐ 571	Mike Jeffcoat	.03	.01	.00
☐ 572	Paul Zuvella	.06	.03	.00
☐ 573	Tom Hume	.03	.01	.00
☐ 574	Ron Kittle	.10	.05	.01
☐ 575	Mike Boddicker	.10	.05	.01
☐ 576	Expos Leaders Andre Dawson	.15	.07	.01
☐ 577	Jerry Reuss	.06	.03	.00
☐ 578	Lee Mazzilli	.03	.01	.00
☐ 579	Jim Slaton	.03	.01	.00
☐ 580	Willie McGee	.20	.10	.02
☐ 581	Bruce Hurst	.10	.05	.01
☐ 582	Jim Gantner	.03	.01	.00
☐ 583	Al Bumbry	.03	.01	.00
☐ 584	Brian Fisher	.25	.12	.02
☐ 585	Garry Maddox	.03	.01	.00
☐ 586	Greg Harris	.03	.01	.00
☐ 587	Rafael Santana	.03	.01	.00
☐ 588	Steve Lake	.03	.01	.00
☐ 589	Sid Bream	.06	.03	.00
☐ 590	Bob Knepper	.06	.03	.00
☐ 591	Jackie Moore MG (checklist back)	.06	.01	.00
☐ 592	Frank Tanana	.06	.03	.00
☐ 593	Jesse Barfield	.25	.12	.02
☐ 594	Chris Bando	.03	.01	.00
☐ 595	Dave Parker	.20	.10	.02
☐ 596	Onix Concepcion	.03	.01	.00
☐ 597	Sammy Stewart	.03	.01	.00
☐ 598	Jim Presley	.60	.30	.06
☐ 599	Rick Aguilera	.35	.17	.03
☐ 600	Dale Murphy	.40	.20	.04
☐ 601	Gary Lucas	.03	.01	.00
☐ 602	Mariano Duncan	.25	.12	.02
☐ 603	Bill Laskey	.03	.01	.00
☐ 604	Gary Pettis	.06	.03	.00
☐ 605	Dennis Boyd	.10	.05	.01
☐ 606	Royals Leaders Hal McRae	.06	.03	.00
☐ 607	Ken Dayley	.03	.01	.00
☐ 608	Bruce Bochy	.03	.01	.00
☐ 609	Barbaro Garbey	.03	.01	.00
☐ 610	Ron Guidry	.15	.07	.01
☐ 611	Gary Woods	.03	.01	.00
☐ 612	Richard Dotson	.06	.03	.00
☐ 613	Roy Smalley	.03	.01	.00
☐ 614	Rick Waits	.03	.01	.00
☐ 615	Johnny Ray	.10	.05	.01
☐ 616	Glenn Brummer	.03	.01	.00
☐ 617	Lonnie Smith	.06	.03	.00
☐ 618	Jim Pankovits	.06	.03	.00
☐ 619	Danny Heep	.03	.01	.00
☐ 620	Bruce Sutter	.12	.06	.01
☐ 621	John Felske MG (checklist back)	.06	.01	.00
☐ 622	Gary Lavelle	.03	.01	.00

☐ 623	Floyd Rayford	.03	.01	.00	☐ 710	John Tudor AS	.06	.03	.00
☐ 624	Steve McCatty	.03	.01	.00	☐ 711	Jeff Reardon AS	.06	.03	.00
☐ 625	Bob Brenly	.06	.03	.00	☐ 712	Don Mattingly AS	.80	.40	.08
☐ 626	Roy Thomas	.03	.01	.00	☐ 713	Damaso Garcia AS	.06	.03	.00
☐ 627	Ron Oester	.03	.01	.00	☐ 714	George Brett AS	.30	.15	.03
☐ 628	Kirk McCaskill	.40	.20	.04	☐ 715	Cal Ripken AS	.25	.12	.02
☐ 629	Mitch Webster	.55	.27	.05	☐ 716	Rickey Henderson AS	.25	.12	.02
☐ 630	Fernando Valenzuela	.25	.12	.02	☐ 717	Dave Winfield AS	.20	.10	.02
☐ 631	Steve Braun	.03	.01	.00	☐ 718	Jorge Bell AS	.20	.10	.02
☐ 632	Dave Von Ohlen	.03	.01	.00	☐ 719	Carlton Fisk AS	.10	.05	.01
☐ 633	Jackie Gutierrez	.03	.01	.00	☐ 720	Bret Saberhagen AS	.12	.06	.01
☐ 634	Roy Lee Jackson	.03	.01	.00	☐ 721	Ron Guidry AS	.10	.05	.01
☐ 635	Jason Thompson	.03	.01	.00	☐ 722	Dan Quisenberry AS	.06	.03	.00
☐ 636	Cubs Leaders	.06	.03	.00	☐ 723	Marty Bystrom	.03	.01	.00
	Lee Smith				☐ 724	Tim Hulett	.06	.03	.00
☐ 637	Rudy Law	.03	.01	.00	☐ 725	Mario Soto	.06	.03	.00
☐ 638	John Butcher	.03	.01	.00	☐ 726	Orioles Leaders	.06	.03	.00
☐ 639	Bo Diaz	.06	.03	.00		Rick Dempsey			
☐ 640	Jose Cruz	.10	.05	.01	☐ 727	David Green	.03	.01	.00
☐ 641	Wayne Tolleson	.03	.01	.00	☐ 728	Mike Marshall	.10	.05	.01
☐ 642	Ray Searage	.03	.01	.00	☐ 729	Jim Beattie	.03	.01	.00
☐ 643	Tom Brookens	.03	.01	.00	☐ 730	Ozzie Smith	.15	.07	.01
☐ 644	Mark Gubicza	.06	.03	.00	☐ 731	Don Robinson	.03	.01	.00
☐ 645	Dusty Baker	.06	.03	.00	☐ 732	Floyd Youmans	.50	.25	.05
☐ 646	Mike Moore	.06	.03	.00	☐ 733	Ron Romanick	.03	.01	.00
☐ 647	Mel Hall	.06	.03	.00	☐ 734	Marty Barrett	.10	.05	.01
☐ 648	Steve Bedrosian	.12	.06	.01	☐ 735	Dave Dravecky	.06	.03	.00
☐ 649	Ronn Reynolds	.06	.03	.00	☐ 736	Glenn Wilson	.06	.03	.00
☐ 650	Dave Stieb	.12	.06	.01	☐ 737	Pete Vuckovich	.06	.03	.00
☐ 651	Billy Martin MG	.10	.03	.01	☐ 738	Andre Robertson	.03	.01	.00
	(checklist back)				☐ 739	Dave Rozema	.03	.01	.00
☐ 652	Tom Browning	.10	.05	.01	☐ 740	Lance Parrish	.15	.07	.01
☐ 653	Jim Dwyer	.03	.01	.00	☐ 741	Pete Rose MG	.35	.10	.02
☐ 654	Ken Howell	.06	.03	.00		(checklist back)			
☐ 655	Manny Trillo	.03	.01	.00	☐ 742	Frank Viola	.12	.06	.01
☐ 656	Brian Harper	.03	.01	.00	☐ 743	Pat Sheridan	.03	.01	.00
☐ 657	Juan Agosto	.03	.01	.00	☐ 744	Lary Sorensen	.03	.01	.00
☐ 658	Rob Wilfong	.03	.01	.00	☐ 745	Willie Upshaw	.06	.03	.00
☐ 659	Checklist: 529-660	.06	.01	.00	☐ 746	Denny Gonzalez	.06	.03	.00
☐ 660	Steve Garvey	.35	.17	.03	☐ 747	Rick Cerone	.03	.01	.00
☐ 661	Roger Clemens	2.50	1.25	.25	☐ 748	Steve Henderson	.03	.01	.00
☐ 662	Bill Schroeder	.03	.01	.00	☐ 749	Ed Jurak	.03	.01	.00
☐ 663	Neil Allen	.03	.01	.00	☐ 750	Gorman Thomas	.06	.03	.00
☐ 664	Tim Corcoran	.03	.01	.00	☐ 751	Howard Johnson	.25	.12	.02
☐ 665	Alejandro Pena	.06	.03	.00	☐ 752	Mike Krukow	.06	.03	.00
☐ 666	Rangers Leaders	.06	.03	.00	☐ 753	Dan Ford	.03	.01	.00
	Charlie Hough				☐ 754	Pat Clements	.20	.10	.02
☐ 667	Tim Teufel	.06	.03	.00	☐ 755	Harold Baines	.15	.07	.01
☐ 668	Cecilio Guante	.03	.01	.00	☐ 756	Pirates Leaders	.06	.03	.00
☐ 669	Ron Cey	.06	.03	.00		Rick Rhoden			
☐ 670	Willie Hernandez	.10	.05	.01	☐ 757	Darrell Porter	.03	.01	.00
☐ 671	Lynn Jones	.03	.01	.00	☐ 758	Dave Anderson	.03	.01	.00
☐ 672	Rob Picciolo	.03	.01	.00	☐ 759	Moose Haas	.03	.01	.00
☐ 673	Ernie Whitt	.03	.01	.00	☐ 760	Andre Dawson	.25	.12	.02
☐ 674	Pat Tabler	.10	.05	.01	☐ 761	Don Slaught	.03	.01	.00
☐ 675	Claudell Washington	.06	.03	.00	☐ 762	Eric Show	.03	.01	.00
☐ 676	Matt Young	.03	.01	.00	☐ 763	Terry Puhl	.03	.01	.00
☐ 677	Nick Esasky	.03	.01	.00	☐ 764	Kevin Gross	.03	.01	.00
☐ 678	Dan Gladden	.06	.03	.00	☐ 765	Don Baylor	.10	.05	.01
☐ 679	Britt Burns	.06	.03	.00	☐ 766	Rick Langford	.03	.01	.00
☐ 680	George Foster	.10	.05	.01	☐ 767	Jody Davis	.10	.05	.01
☐ 681	Dick Williams MG	.06	.01	.00	☐ 768	Vern Ruhle	.03	.01	.00
	(checklist back)				☐ 769	Harold Reynolds	.35	.17	.03
☐ 682	Junior Ortiz	.03	.01	.00	☐ 770	Vida Blue	.06	.03	.00
☐ 683	Andy Van Slyke	.10	.05	.01	☐ 771	John McNamara MG	.06	.01	.00
☐ 684	Bob McClure	.03	.01	.00		(checklist back)			
☐ 685	Tim Wallach	.10	.05	.01	☐ 772	Brian Downing	.06	.03	.00
☐ 686	Jeff Stone	.06	.03	.00	☐ 773	Greg Pryor	.03	.01	.00
☐ 687	Mike Trujillo	.06	.03	.00	☐ 774	Terry Leach	.06	.03	.00
☐ 688	Larry Herndon	.03	.01	.00	☐ 775	Al Oliver	.10	.05	.01
☐ 689	Dave Stewart	.10	.05	.01	☐ 776	Gene Garber	.03	.01	.00
☐ 690	Ryne Sandberg	.40	.20	.04	☐ 777	Wayne Krenchicki	.03	.01	.00
	(no Topps logo				☐ 778	Jerry Hairston	.03	.01	.00
	on front)				☐ 779	Rick Reuschel	.06	.03	.00
☐ 691	Mike Madden	.03	.01	.00	☐ 780	Robin Yount	.25	.12	.02
☐ 692	Dale Berra	.03	.01	.00	☐ 781	Joe Nolan	.03	.01	.00
☐ 693	Tom Tellmann	.03	.01	.00	☐ 782	Ken Landreaux	.03	.01	.00
☐ 694	Garth Iorg	.03	.01	.00	☐ 783	Ricky Horton	.03	.01	.00
☐ 695	Mike Smithson	.03	.01	.00	☐ 784	Alan Bannister	.03	.01	.00
☐ 696	Dodgers Leaders	.06	.03	.00	☐ 785	Bob Stanley	.06	.03	.00
	Bill Russell				☐ 786	Twins Leaders	.06	.03	.00
☐ 697	Bud Black	.03	.01	.00		Mickey Hatcher			
☐ 698	Brad Komminsk	.06	.03	.00	☐ 787	Vance Law	.03	.01	.00
☐ 699	Pat Corrales MG	.06	.01	.00	☐ 788	Marty Castillo	.03	.01	.00
	(checklist back)				☐ 789	Kurt Bevacqua	.03	.01	.00
☐ 700	Reggie Jackson	.35	.17	.03	☐ 790	Phil Niekro	.15	.07	.01
☐ 701	Keith Hernandez AS	.15	.07	.01	☐ 791	Checklist: 661-792	.06	.01	.00
☐ 702	Tom Herr AS	.06	.03	.00	☐ 792	Charles Hudson	.06	.01	.00
☐ 703	Tim Wallach AS	.06	.03	.00					
☐ 704	Ozzie Smith AS	.12	.06	.01					
☐ 705	Dale Murphy AS	.30	.15	.03					
☐ 706	Pedro Guerrero AS	.15	.07	.01					
☐ 707	Willie McGee AS	.12	.06	.01					
☐ 708	Gary Carter AS	.20	.10	.02					
☐ 709	Dwight Gooden AS	.30	.15	.03					

GEORGIA MUSIC & SPORTS
Dick DeCourcy
1867 Flat Shoals Rd.
Riverdale, GA 30296

404-996-3385

A PERSONAL MESSAGE
TO THE DEALERS OF THE HOBBY

Baseball Cards have been good to us.

Georgia Music & Sports has been a regular advertiser in hobby publications since 1983. We have set up at 45 shows in 1987, 40 shows in 1986, 31 shows in 1985 and 34 shows in 1984. Both through our ads and the shows we have met many regular customers - for this we are very thankful.

Most of our customers and dealers order from four to six times a month. We try to cultivate repeat business. It is far more important for us to obtain a customer for the long term than ever to think of a quick buck on one deal.

It is not possible to inventory every item in the hobby, but we always try to have on hand Mint sets from the last 10 years as well as unopened, unsearched products from the last 10 years.

We have at present 184 dealers that order from us every month. We work on the average of 15% profit on most items. Some of our prices may be high and some may be low, but we do try and have the major products always on hand at all times. By having the product, we can save you hours of searching.

We pride ourselves on service . . . we spell service S-P-E-E-D. If you are a regular account and you call in an order today before 2 p.m., we ship it today. Also, 99% of our accounts pay us just as quickly as we ship, the same day they get their product. The rest pay interest.

We will soon be entering our 12th year of business. To those customers who have kept us going for all these years, we give thanks and trust that this union will continue for many years to come. To those new and honorable dealers and store owners who are entering this fast-paced, exciting and growing baseball card hobby, we welcome your business. We have a staff of 11 people to help serve your needs.

Please write or call for our current price list.

Sincerely,

Dick

Dick DeCourcy, President
Georgia Music & Sports

MEMBER

Atlanta Area Chamber of Commerce   Atlanta Area Sports Collectors Association
Atlanta Area Better Business Bureau   National Association of Music Merchants

1986 Topps Wax Box Cards

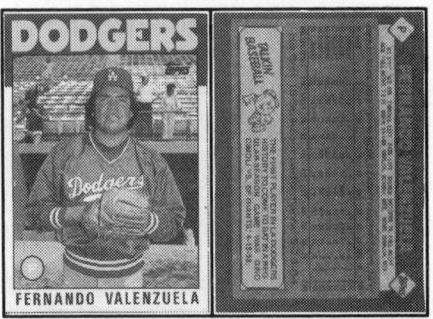

FERNANDO VALENZUELA

Topps printed cards (each measuring the standard 2 1/2" by 3 1/2") on the bottoms of their wax pack boxes for their regular issue cards; there are four different boxes, each with four cards. These sixteen cards ("numbered" A through P) are listed below; they are not considered an integral part of the regular set but are considered a separate set. They are styled almost exactly like the 1986 Topps regular issue cards.

	MINT	EXC	G-VG
COMPLETE SET (16)	8.00	4.00	.80
COMMON PLAYER (1-16)	.10	.05	.01

		MINT	EXC	G-VG
☐ A	Jorge Bell	.35	.17	.03
☐ B	Wade Boggs	1.25	.60	.12
☐ C	George Brett	.75	.35	.07
☐ D	Vince Coleman	1.25	.60	.12
☐ E	Carlton Fisk	.15	.07	.01
☐ F	Dwight Gooden	1.00	.50	.10
☐ G	Pedro Guerrero	.25	.12	.02
☐ H	Ron Guidry	.20	.10	.02
☐ I	Reggie Jackson	.60	.30	.06
☐ J	Don Mattingly	2.50	1.25	.25
☐ K	Oddibe McDowell	.25	.12	.02
☐ L	Willie McGee	.25	.12	.02
☐ M	Dale Murphy	1.00	.50	.10
☐ N	Pete Rose	1.25	.60	.12
☐ O	Bret Saberhagen	.35	.17	.03
☐ P	Fernando Valenzuela	.25	.12	.02

1986 Topps Glossy 22

GEORGE BRETT

This 22-card set was distributed as an insert, one card per rak pack. The players featured are the starting lineups of the 1985 All-Star Game played in Minnesota. Cards are very colorful with a high gloss finish and are standard-size, 2 1/2" by 3 1/2". Cards are numbered on the back.

	MINT	EXC	G-VG
COMPLETE SET (22)	3.50	1.75	.35
COMMON PLAYER (1-22)	.10	.05	.01

☐ 1	Sparky Anderson MG	.10	.05	.01
☐ 2	Eddie Murray	.30	.15	.03
☐ 3	Lou Whitaker	.15	.07	.01
☐ 4	George Brett	.40	.20	.04
☐ 5	Cal Ripken	.30	.15	.03
☐ 6	Jim Rice	.30	.15	.03
☐ 7	Rickey Henderson	.40	.20	.04
☐ 8	Dave Winfield	.30	.15	.03
☐ 9	Carlton Fisk	.20	.10	.02
☐ 10	Jack Morris	.20	.10	.02
☐ 11	AL Team Photo	.10	.05	.01
☐ 12	Dick Williams MG	.10	.05	.01
☐ 13	Steve Garvey	.30	.15	.03
☐ 14	Tom Herr	.10	.05	.01
☐ 15	Graig Nettles	.15	.07	.01
☐ 16	Ozzie Smith	.10	.05	.02
☐ 17	Tony Gwynn	.40	.20	.04
☐ 18	Dale Murphy	.50	.25	.05
☐ 19	Darryl Strawberry	.40	.20	.04
☐ 20	Terry Kennedy	.10	.05	.01
☐ 21	LaMarr Hoyt	.10	.05	.01
☐ 22	NL Team Photo	.10	.05	.01

1986 Topps Glossy 60

This 60-card glossy set was produced by Topps and distributed ten cards at a time based on the offer found on the wax packs. Cards measure the standard 2 1/2" by 3 1/2". Each series of ten cards was available by sending in 1.00 plus six "special offer" cards inserted one per wax pack. The card backs are printed in red and blue on white card stock. The card fronts feature a white border and a green frame surrounding a full-color photo of the player.

	MINT	EXC	G-VG
COMPLETE SET (60)	12.00	6.00	1.20
COMMON PLAYER (1-60)	.10	.05	.01

☐ 1	Oddibe McDowell	.20	.10	.02
☐ 2	Reggie Jackson	.50	.25	.05
☐ 3	Fernando Valenzuela	.30	.15	.03
☐ 4	Jack Clark	.25	.12	.02
☐ 5	Rickey Henderson	.50	.25	.05
☐ 6	Steve Balboni	.10	.05	.01
☐ 7	Keith Hernandez	.25	.12	.02
☐ 8	Lance Parrish	.20	.10	.02
☐ 9	Willie McGee	.20	.10	.02
☐ 10	Chris Brown	.20	.10	.02
☐ 11	Darryl Strawberry	.60	.30	.06
☐ 12	Ron Guidry	.20	.10	.02
☐ 13	Dave Parker	.20	.10	.02
☐ 14	Cal Ripken	.35	.17	.03
☐ 15	Tim Raines	.35	.17	.03
☐ 16	Rod Carew	.35	.17	.03
☐ 17	Mike Schmidt	.60	.30	.06
☐ 18	George Brett	.60	.30	.06
☐ 19	Joe Hesketh	.10	.05	.01
☐ 20	Dan Pasqua	.20	.10	.02
☐ 21	Vince Coleman	.75	.35	.07
☐ 22	Tom Seaver	.35	.17	.03
☐ 23	Gary Carter	.35	.17	.03
☐ 24	Orel Hershiser	.25	.12	.02
☐ 25	Pedro Guerrero	.25	.12	.02
☐ 26	Wade Boggs	1.00	.50	.10
☐ 27	Bret Saberhagen	.30	.15	.03

☐ 28	Carlton Fisk	.20	.10	.02
☐ 29	Kirk Gibson	.25	.12	.02
☐ 30	Brian Fisher	.10	.05	.01
☐ 31	Don Mattingly	2.00	1.00	.20
☐ 32	Tom Herr	.10	.05	.01
☐ 33	Eddie Murray	.50	.25	.05
☐ 34	Ryne Sandberg	.35	.17	.03
☐ 35	Dan Quisenberry	.15	.07	.01
☐ 36	Jim Rice	.35	.17	.03
☐ 37	Dale Murphy	.60	.30	.06
☐ 38	Steve Garvey	.40	.20	.04
☐ 39	Roger McDowell	.20	.10	.02
☐ 40	Earnie Riles	.15	.07	.01
☐ 41	Dwight Gooden	1.00	.50	.10
☐ 42	Dave Winfield	.35	.17	.03
☐ 43	Dave Stieb	.15	.07	.01
☐ 44	Bob Horner	.20	.10	.02
☐ 45	Nolan Ryan	.40	.20	.04
☐ 46	Ozzie Smith	.25	.12	.02
☐ 47	Jorge Bell	.25	.12	.02
☐ 48	Gorman Thomas	.15	.07	.01
☐ 49	Tom Browning	.15	.07	.01
☐ 50	Larry Sheets	.15	.07	.01
☐ 51	Pete Rose	1.00	.50	.10
☐ 52	Brett Butler	.15	.07	.01
☐ 53	John Tudor	.15	.07	.01
☐ 54	Phil Bradley	.20	.10	.02
☐ 55	Jeff Reardon	.15	.07	.01
☐ 56	Rich Gossage	.15	.07	.01
☐ 57	Tony Gwynn	.50	.25	.05
☐ 58	Ozzie Guillen	.20	.10	.02
☐ 59	Glenn Davis	.30	.15	.03
☐ 60	Darrell Evans	.15	.07	.01

☐ 38	Jack Morris	.20	.10	.02
☐ 39	Dale Murphy	.60	.30	.06
☐ 40	Eddie Murray	.40	.20	.04
☐ 41	Dave Parker	.25	.12	.02
☐ 42	Tim Raines	.35	.17	.03
☐ 43	Jim Rice	.30	.15	.03
☐ 44	Dave Righetti	.20	.10	.02
☐ 45	Cal Ripken	.35	.17	.03
☐ 46	Pete Rose	1.00	.50	.10
☐ 47	Nolan Ryan	.45	.22	.04
☐ 48	Ryne Sandberg	.45	.22	.04
☐ 49	Mike Schmidt	.60	.30	.06
☐ 50	Tom Seaver	.40	.20	.04
☐ 51	Bryn Smith	.10	.05	.01
☐ 52	Lee Smith	.15	.07	.01
☐ 53	Ozzie Smith	.25	.12	.02
☐ 54	Dave Stieb	.15	.07	.01
☐ 55	Darryl Strawberry	.60	.30	.06
☐ 56	Gorman Thomas	.10	.05	.01
☐ 57	John Tudor	.15	.07	.01
☐ 58	Fernando Valenzuela	.30	.15	.03
☐ 59	Willie Wilson	.20	.10	.02
☐ 60	Dave Winfield	.30	.15	.03

1986 Topps Mini Leaders

FERNANDO VALENZUELA

The 1986 Topps Mini set of Major League Leaders features 66 cards of leaders of the various statistical categories for the 1985 season. The cards are numbered on the back and measure 2 1/8" by 2 15/16". They are very similar in design to the Team Leader "Dean" cards in the 1986 Topps regular issue.

1986 Topps Super

This 60-card set actually consists of giant-sized versions of the Topps regular issue of some of the most popular players. The cards measure 4 7/8" by 6 7/8". Cards are very similar to the Topps regular issue; two exceptions are that on the back they are numbered differently and an additional line of type is printed at the bottom of the back noting an accomplishment of that player at the end of the 1986 season.

		MINT	EXC	G-VG
COMPLETE SET (60)		10.00	5.00	1.00
COMMON PLAYER (1-60)		.10	.05	.01
☐ 1	Don Mattingly	1.75	.85	.17
☐ 2	Willie McGee	.20	.10	.02
☐ 3	Bret Saberhagen	.25	.12	.02
☐ 4	Dwight Gooden	.90	.45	.09
☐ 5	Dan Quisenberry	.15	.07	.01
☐ 6	Jeff Reardon	.15	.07	.01
☐ 7	Ozzie Guillen	.20	.10	.02
☐ 8	Vince Coleman	.60	.30	.06
☐ 9	Harold Baines	.20	.10	.02
☐ 10	Jorge Bell	.30	.15	.03
☐ 11	Bert Blyleven	.15	.07	.01
☐ 12	Wade Boggs	1.00	.50	.10
☐ 13	Phil Bradley	.25	.12	.02
☐ 14	George Brett	.50	.25	.05
☐ 15	Hubie Brooks	.10	.05	.01
☐ 16	Tom Browning	.10	.05	.01
☐ 17	Bill Buckner	.15	.07	.01
☐ 18	Brett Butler	.15	.07	.01
☐ 19	Gary Carter	.30	.15	.03
☐ 20	Cecil Cooper	.15	.07	.01
☐ 21	Darrell Evans	.15	.07	.01
☐ 22	Dwight Evans	.20	.10	.02
☐ 23	Carlton Fisk	.20	.10	.02
☐ 24	Steve Garvey	.35	.17	.03
☐ 25	Kirk Gibson	.25	.12	.02
☐ 26	Rich Gossage	.15	.07	.01
☐ 27	Pedro Guerrero	.25	.12	.02
☐ 28	Ron Guidry	.15	.07	.01
☐ 29	Tony Gwynn	.50	.25	.05
☐ 30	Rickey Henderson	.50	.25	.05
☐ 31	Keith Hernandez	.25	.12	.02
☐ 32	Tom Herr	.10	.05	.01
☐ 33	Orel Hershiser	.25	.12	.02
☐ 34	Jay Howell	.10	.05	.01
☐ 35	Reggie Jackson	.50	.25	.05
☐ 36	Bob James	.10	.05	.01
☐ 37	Charlie Leibrandt	.10	.05	.01

		MINT	EXC	G-VG
COMPLETE SET		5.50	2.75	.55
COMMON PLAYER		.05	.02	.00
☐ 1	Eddie Murray	.25	.12	.02
☐ 2	Cal Ripken	.25	.12	.02
☐ 3	Wade Boggs	.50	.25	.05
☐ 4	Dennis Boyd	.10	.05	.01
☐ 5	Dwight Evans	.15	.07	.01
☐ 6	Bruce Hurst	.10	.05	.01
☐ 7	Gary Pettis	.10	.05	.01
☐ 8	Harold Baines	.10	.05	.01
☐ 9	Floyd Bannister	.05	.02	.00
☐ 10	Britt Burns	.05	.02	.00
☐ 11	Carlton Fisk	.10	.05	.01
☐ 12	Brett Butler	.10	.05	.01
☐ 13	Darrell Evans	.10	.05	.01
☐ 14	Jack Morris	.15	.07	.01
☐ 15	Lance Parrish	.15	.07	.01
☐ 16	Walt Terrell	.05	.02	.00
☐ 17	Steve Balboni	.05	.02	.00
☐ 18	George Brett	.25	.12	.02
☐ 19	Charlie Leibrandt	.05	.02	.00
☐ 20	Bret Saberhagen	.20	.10	.02
☐ 21	Lonnie Smith	.05	.02	.00
☐ 22	Willie Wilson	.10	.05	.01
☐ 23	Bert Blyleven	.10	.05	.01
☐ 24	Mike Smithson	.05	.02	.00
☐ 25	Frank Viola	.15	.07	.01
☐ 26	Ron Guidry	.10	.05	.01
☐ 27	Rickey Henderson	.25	.12	.02
☐ 28	Don Mattingly	1.00	.50	.10
☐ 29	Dave Winfield	.25	.12	.02
☐ 30	Mike Moore	.05	.02	.00
☐ 31	Gorman Thomas	.10	.05	.01
☐ 32	Toby Harrah	.05	.02	.00

		MINT	EXC	G-VG
☐ 33	Charlie Hough	.10	.05	.01
☐ 34	Doyle Alexander	.10	.05	.01
☐ 35	Jimmy Key	.15	.07	.01
☐ 36	Dave Stieb	.10	.05	.01
☐ 37	Dale Murphy	.35	.17	.03
☐ 38	Keith Moreland	.05	.02	.00
☐ 39	Ryne Sandberg	.25	.12	.02
☐ 40	Tom Browning	.05	.02	.00
☐ 41	Dave Parker	.15	.07	.01
☐ 42	Mario Soto	.05	.02	.00
☐ 43	Nolan Ryan	.25	.12	.02
☐ 44	Pedro Guerrero	.15	.07	.01
☐ 45	Orel Hershiser	.15	.07	.01
☐ 46	Mike Scioscia	.05	.02	.00
☐ 47	Fernando Valenzuela	.20	.10	.02
☐ 48	Bob Welch	.10	.05	.01
☐ 49	Tim Raines	.25	.12	.02
☐ 50	Gary Carter	.25	.12	.02
☐ 51	Sid Fernandez	.15	.07	.01
☐ 52	Dwight Gooden	.50	.25	.05
☐ 53	Keith Hernandez	.20	.10	.02
☐ 54	Juan Samuel	.15	.07	.01
☐ 55	Mike Schmidt	.35	.17	.03
☐ 56	Glenn Wilson	.10	.05	.01
☐ 57	Rick Reuschel	.10	.05	.01
☐ 58	Joaquin Andujar	.10	.05	.01
☐ 59	Jack Clark	.20	.10	.02
☐ 60	Vince Coleman	.40	.20	.04
☐ 61	Danny Cox	.10	.05	.01
☐ 62	Tom Herr	.05	.02	.00
☐ 63	Willie McGee	.15	.07	.01
☐ 64	John Tudor	.10	.05	.01
☐ 65	Tony Gwynn	.35	.17	.03
☐ 66	Checklist card	.05	.01	.00

1986 Topps Super 3-D

This set consists of 30 plastic-sculpted "cards" each measuring 4 3/8" by 6". Each card was individually wrapped in a red paper wrapper. The card back is blank except for two adhesive strips which could used for mounting the card. Cards are numbered on the front.

	MINT	EXC	G-VG
COMPLETE SET (30)	10.00	5.00	1.00
COMMON PLAYER (1-30)	.20	.10	.02

		MINT	EXC	G-VG
☐ 1	Bert Blyleven	.20	.10	.02
☐ 2	Gary Carter	.40	.20	.04
☐ 3	Wade Boggs	1.00	.50	.10
☐ 4	Dwight Gooden	.60	.30	.06
☐ 5	George Brett	.50	.25	.05
☐ 6	Rich Gossage	.25	.12	.02
☐ 7	Darrell Evans	.25	.12	.02
☐ 8	Pedro Guerrero	.30	.15	.03
☐ 9	Ron Guidry	.30	.15	.03
☐ 10	Keith Hernandez	.35	.17	.03
☐ 11	Rickey Henderson	.50	.25	.05
☐ 12	Orel Hershiser	.30	.15	.03
☐ 13	Reggie Jackson	.60	.30	.06
☐ 14	Willie McGee	.30	.15	.03
☐ 15	Don Mattingly	1.50	.75	.15
☐ 16	Dale Murphy	.60	.30	.06
☐ 17	Jack Morris	.30	.15	.03
☐ 18	Dave Parker	.30	.15	.03
☐ 19	Eddie Murray	.40	.20	.04
☐ 20	Jeff Reardon	.25	.12	.02
☐ 21	Dan Quisenberry	.25	.12	.02
☐ 22	Pete Rose	1.00	.50	.10
☐ 23	Jim Rice	.40	.20	.04
☐ 24	Mike Schmidt	.60	.30	.06
☐ 25	Bret Saberhagen	.35	.17	.03
☐ 26	Darryl Strawberry	.60	.30	.06
☐ 27	Dave Stieb	.25	.12	.02
☐ 28	John Tudor	.20	.10	.02
☐ 29	Dave Winfield	.40	.20	.04
☐ 30	Fernando Valenzuela	.30	.15	.03

1986 Topps Traded

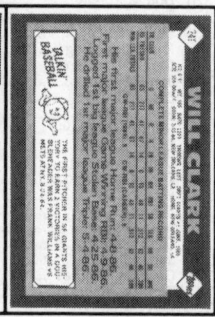

This 132-card Traded or extended set was distributed by Topps to dealers in a special red and white box as a complete set. The card fronts are identical in style to the Topps regular issue and are also 2 1/2" by 3 1/2". The backs are printed in red and black on white card stock. Cards are numbered (with a T suffix) alphabetically according to the name of the player.

		MINT	EXC	G-VG
COMPLETE SET		14.00	7.00	1.40
COMMON PLAYER		.06	.03	.00

			MINT	EXC	G-VG
☐	1T	Andy Allanson	.20	.10	.02
☐	2T	Neil Allen	.06	.03	.00
☐	3T	Joaquin Andujar	.10	.05	.01
☐	4T	Paul Assenmacher	.20	.10	.02
☐	5T	Scott Bailes	.20	.10	.02
☐	6T	Don Baylor	.15	.07	.01
☐	7T	Steve Bedrosian	.15	.07	.01
☐	8T	Juan Beniquez	.06	.03	.00
☐	9T	Juan Berenguer	.10	.05	.01
☐	10T	Mike Bielecki	.15	.07	.01
☐	11T	Barry Bonds	.80	.40	.08
☐	12T	Bobby Bonilla	.40	.20	.04
☐	13T	Juan Bonilla	.06	.03	.00
☐	14T	Rich Bordi	.06	.03	.00
☐	15T	Steve Boros MG	.06	.03	.00
☐	16T	Rick Burleson	.10	.05	.01
☐	17T	Bill Campbell	.06	.03	.00
☐	18T	Tom Candiotti	.10	.05	.01
☐	19T	John Cangelosi	.25	.12	.02
☐	20T	Jose Canseco	4.00	2.00	.40
☐	21T	Carmen Castillo	.06	.03	.00
☐	22T	Rick Cerone	.06	.03	.00
☐	23T	John Cerutti	.25	.12	.02
☐	24T	Will Clark	3.00	1.50	.30
☐	25T	Mark Clear	.06	.03	.00
☐	26T	Darnell Coles	.10	.05	.01
☐	27T	Dave Collins	.06	.03	.00
☐	28T	Tim Conroy	.06	.03	.00
☐	29T	Joe Cowley	.06	.03	.00
☐	30T	Joel Davis	.20	.10	.02
☐	31T	Rob Deer	.25	.12	.02
☐	32T	John Denny	.10	.05	.01
☐	33T	Mike Easler	.10	.05	.01
☐	34T	Mark Eichhorn	.30	.15	.03
☐	35T	Steve Farr	.06	.03	.00
☐	36T	Scott Fletcher	.10	.05	.01
☐	37T	Terry Forster	.10	.05	.01
☐	38T	Terry Francona	.06	.03	.00
☐	39T	Jim Fregosi MG	.06	.03	.00
☐	40T	Andres Galarraga	1.25	.60	.12
☐	41T	Ken Griffey	.10	.05	.01
☐	42T	Bill Gullickson	.10	.05	.01
☐	43T	Jose Guzman	.20	.10	.02
☐	44T	Moose Haas	.06	.03	.00
☐	45T	Billy Hatcher	.20	.10	.02
☐	46T	Mike Heath	.06	.03	.00
☐	47T	Tom Hume	.06	.03	.00
☐	48T	Pete Incaviglia	2.00	1.00	.20
☐	49T	Dane Iorg	.06	.03	.00
☐	50T	Bo Jackson	2.50	1.25	.25
☐	51T	Wally Joyner	4.00	2.00	.40
☐	52T	Charlie Kerfeld	.25	.12	.02
☐	53T	Eric King	.25	.12	.02
☐	54T	Bob Kipper	.06	.03	.00
☐	55T	Wayne Krenchicki	.06	.03	.00

☐ 56T	John Kruk	1.25	.60	.12
☐ 57T	Mike LaCoss	.06	.03	.00
☐ 58T	Pete Ladd	.06	.03	.00
☐ 59T	Mike Laga	.10	.05	.01
☐ 60T	Hal Lanier MG	.06	.03	.00
☐ 61T	Dave LaPoint	.06	.03	.00
☐ 62T	Rudy Law	.06	.03	.00
☐ 63T	Rick Leach	.06	.03	.00
☐ 64T	Tim Leary	.06	.03	.00
☐ 65T	Dennis Leonard	.10	.05	.01
☐ 66T	Jim Leyland MG	.06	.03	.00
☐ 67T	Steve Lyons	.06	.03	.00
☐ 68T	Mickey Mahler	.06	.03	.00
☐ 69T	Candy Maldonado	.15	.07	.01
☐ 70T	Roger Mason	.15	.07	.01
☐ 71T	Bob McClure	.06	.03	.00
☐ 72T	Andy McGaffigan	.06	.03	.00
☐ 73T	Gene Michael MG	.06	.03	.00
☐ 74T	Kevin Mitchell	.50	.25	.05
☐ 75T	Omar Moreno	.06	.03	.00
☐ 76T	Jerry Mumphrey	.06	.03	.00
☐ 77T	Phil Niekro	.25	.12	.02
☐ 78T	Randy Niemann	.06	.03	.00
☐ 79T	Juan Nieves	.25	.12	.02
☐ 80T	Otis Nixon	.15	.07	.01
☐ 81T	Bob Ojeda	.15	.07	.01
☐ 82T	Jose Oquendo	.10	.05	.01
☐ 83T	Tom Paciorek	.06	.03	.00
☐ 84T	Dave Palmer	.06	.03	.00
☐ 85T	Frank Pastore	.06	.03	.00
☐ 86T	Lou Piniella MG	.10	.05	.01
☐ 87T	Dan Plesac	.35	.17	.03
☐ 88T	Darrell Porter	.06	.03	.00
☐ 89T	Rey Quinones	.25	.12	.02
☐ 90T	Gary Redus	.10	.05	.01
☐ 91T	Bip Roberts	.10	.05	.01
☐ 92T	Billy Jo Robidoux	.15	.07	.01
☐ 93T	Jeff Robinson	.15	.07	.01
	(Giants pitcher)			
☐ 94T	Gary Roenicke	.06	.03	.00
☐ 95T	Ed Romero	.06	.03	.00
☐ 96T	Argenis Salazar	.06	.03	.00
☐ 97T	Joe Sambito	.06	.03	.00
☐ 98T	Billy Sample	.06	.03	.00
☐ 99T	Dave Schmidt	.10	.05	.01
☐ 100T	Ken Schrom	.10	.05	.01
☐ 101T	Tom Seaver	.50	.25	.05
☐ 102T	Ted Simmons	.15	.07	.01
☐ 103T	Sammy Stewart	.06	.03	.00
☐ 104T	Kurt Stillwell	.40	.20	.04
☐ 105T	Franklin Stubbs	.10	.05	.01
☐ 106T	Dale Sveum	.75	.35	.07
☐ 107T	Chuck Tanner MG	.06	.03	.00
☐ 108T	Danny Tartabull	1.25	.60	.12
☐ 109T	Tim Teufel	.10	.05	.01
☐ 110T	Bob Tewksbury	.25	.12	.02
☐ 111T	Andres Thomas	.20	.10	.02
☐ 112T	Milt Thompson	.20	.10	.02
☐ 113T	Robby Thompson	.35	.17	.03
☐ 114T	Jay Tibbs	.06	.03	.00
☐ 115T	Wayne Tolleson	.06	.03	.00
☐ 116T	Alex Trevino	.06	.03	.00
☐ 117T	Manny Trillo	.06	.03	.00
☐ 118T	Ed VandeBerg	.06	.03	.00
☐ 119T	Ozzie Virgil	.06	.03	.00
☐ 120T	Bob Walk	.06	.03	.00
☐ 121T	Gene Walter	.15	.07	.01
☐ 122T	Claudell Washington	.10	.05	.01
☐ 123T	Bill Wegman	.20	.10	.02
☐ 124T	Dick Williams MG	.06	.03	.00
☐ 125T	Mitch Williams	.25	.12	.02
☐ 126T	Bobby Witt	.35	.17	.03
☐ 127T	Todd Worrell	1.00	.50	.10
☐ 128T	George Wright	.06	.03	.00
☐ 129T	Ricky Wright	.06	.03	.00
☐ 130T	Steve Yeager	.06	.03	.00
☐ 131T	Paul Zuvella	.06	.03	.00
☐ 132T	Checklist card	.10	.01	.00

1987 Topps

This 792-card set is reminiscent of the 1962 Topps baseball cards with their simulated wood grain borders. The backs are printed in yellow and blue on gray card stock. The manager cards contain a checklist of the respective team's players on the back. Subsets in the set include Record Breakers (1-7), Turn Back the Clock (311-315), and All-Star

selections (595-616). The Team Leader cards typically show players conferring on the mound inside a white cloud. The wax pack wrapper gives details of "Spring Fever Baseball" where a lucky collector can win a trip for four to Spring Training.

		MINT	EXC	G-VG
COMPLETE SET		25.00	12.50	2.50
COMMON PLAYER		.03	.01	.00

☐	1	RB: Roger Clemens	.40	.10	.02
		Most strikeouts, nine inning game			
☐	2	RB: Jim Deshaies	.08	.04	.01
		Most cons. K's, start of game			
☐	3	RB: Dwight Evans	.08	.04	.01
		Earliest home run, season			
☐	4	RB: Davey Lopes	.06	.03	.00
		Most steals, season, 40-year-old			
☐	5	RB: Dave Righetti	.10	.05	.01
		Most saves, season			
☐	6	RB: Ruben Sierra	.15	.07	.01
		Youngest player to switch hit homers in game			
☐	7	RB: Todd Worrell	.12	.06	.01
		Most saves, season, rookie			
☐	8	Terry Pendleton	.06	.03	.00
☐	9	Jay Tibbs	.03	.01	.00
☐	10	Cecil Cooper	.08	.04	.01
☐	11	Indians Team	.03	.01	.00
		(mound conference)			
☐	12	Jeff Sellers	.10	.05	.01
☐	13	Nick Esasky	.03	.01	.00
☐	14	Dave Stewart	.08	.04	.01
☐	15	Claudell Washington	.06	.03	.00
☐	16	Pat Clements	.03	.01	.00
☐	17	Pete O'Brien	.08	.04	.01
☐	18	Dick Howser MG	.06	.01	.00
		(checklist back)			
☐	19	Matt Young	.03	.01	.00
☐	20	Gary Carter	.25	.12	.02
☐	21	Mark Davis	.03	.01	.00
☐	22	Doug DeCinces	.06	.03	.00
☐	23	Lee Smith	.06	.03	.00
☐	24	Tony Walker	.10	.05	.01
☐	25	Bert Blyleven	.08	.04	.01
☐	26	Greg Brock	.06	.03	.00
☐	27	Joe Cowley	.03	.01	.00
☐	28	Rick Dempsey	.03	.01	.00
☐	29	Jimmy Key	.10	.05	.01
☐	30	Tim Raines	.25	.12	.02
☐	31	Braves Team	.03	.01	.00
		(Hubbard/Ramirez)			
☐	32	Tim Leary	.03	.01	.00
☐	33	Andy Van Slyke	.08	.04	.01
☐	34	Jose Rijo	.06	.03	.00
☐	35	Sid Bream	.06	.03	.00
☐	36	Eric King	.15	.07	.01
☐	37	Marvell Wynne	.03	.01	.00
☐	38	Dennis Leonard	.06	.03	.00
☐	39	Marty Barrett	.08	.04	.01
☐	40	Dave Righetti	.12	.06	.01
☐	41	Bo Diaz	.06	.03	.00
☐	42	Gary Redus	.06	.03	.00
☐	43	Gene Michael MG	.06	.01	.00
		(checklist back)			
☐	44	Greg Harris	.03	.01	.00
☐	45	Jim Presley	.15	.07	.01

☐ 46	Dan Gladden	.06	.03	.00
☐ 47	Dennis Powell	.06	.03	.00
☐ 48	Wally Backman	.06	.03	.00
☐ 49	Terry Harper	.03	.01	.00
☐ 50	Dave Smith	.06	.03	.00
☐ 51	Mel Hall	.06	.03	.00
☐ 52	Keith Atherton	.03	.01	.00
☐ 53	Ruppert Jones	.03	.01	.00
☐ 54	Bill Dawley	.03	.01	.00
☐ 55	Tim Wallach	.10	.05	.01
☐ 56	Brewers Team	.03	.01	.00
	(mound conference)			
☐ 57	Scott Nielsen	.10	.05	.01
☐ 58	Thad Bosley	.03	.01	.00
☐ 59	Ken Dayley	.03	.01	.00
☐ 60	Tony Pena	.10	.05	.01
☐ 61	Bobby Thigpen	.20	.10	.02
☐ 62	Bobby Meacham	.03	.01	.00
☐ 63	Fred Toliver	.06	.03	.00
☐ 64	Harry Spilman	.03	.01	.00
☐ 65	Tom Browning	.06	.03	.00
☐ 66	Marc Sullivan	.03	.01	.00
☐ 67	Bill Swift	.03	.01	.00
☐ 68	Tony LaRussa MG	.06	.01	.00
	(checklist back)			
☐ 69	Lonnie Smith	.06	.03	.00
☐ 70	Charlie Hough	.06	.03	.00
☐ 71	Mike Aldrete	.40	.20	.04
☐ 72	Walt Terrell	.03	.01	.00
☐ 73	Dave Anderson	.03	.01	.00
☐ 74	Dan Pasqua	.10	.05	.01
☐ 75	Ron Darling	.20	.10	.02
☐ 76	Rafael Ramirez	.03	.01	.00
☐ 77	Bryan Oelkers	.06	.03	.00
☐ 78	Tom Foley	.03	.01	.00
☐ 79	Juan Nieves	.15	.07	.01
☐ 80	Wally Joyner	2.00	1.00	.20
☐ 81	Padres Team	.03	.01	.00
	(Hawkins/Kennedy)			
☐ 82	Rob Murphy	.20	.10	.02
☐ 83	Mike Davis	.06	.03	.00
☐ 84	Steve Lake	.03	.01	.00
☐ 85	Kevin Bass	.08	.04	.01
☐ 86	Nate Snell	.03	.01	.00
☐ 87	Mark Salas	.03	.01	.00
☐ 88	Ed Wojna	.03	.01	.00
☐ 89	Ozzie Guillen	.08	.04	.01
☐ 90	Dave Stieb	.10	.05	.01
☐ 91	Harold Reynolds	.06	.03	.00
☐ 92A	Urbano Lugo	.25	.12	.02
	ERR (no trademark)			
☐ 92B	Urbano Lugo COR	.06	.03	.00
☐ 93	Jim Leyland MG	.06	.01	.00
	(checklist back)			
☐ 94	Calvin Schiraldi	.08	.04	.01
☐ 95	Oddibe McDowell	.10	.05	.01
☐ 96	Frank Williams	.03	.01	.00
☐ 97	Glenn Wilson	.08	.04	.01
☐ 98	Bill Scherrer	.03	.01	.00
☐ 99	Darryl Motley	.03	.01	.00
☐ 100	Steve Garvey	.25	.12	.02
☐ 101	Carl Willis	.08	.04	.01
☐ 102	Paul Zuvella	.03	.01	.00
☐ 103	Rick Aguilera	.06	.03	.00
☐ 104	Billy Sample	.03	.01	.00
☐ 105	Floyd Youmans	.08	.04	.01
☐ 106	Blue Jays Team	.15	.07	.01
	(Bell/Barfield)			
☐ 107	John Butcher	.03	.01	.00
☐ 108	Jim Gantner	.06	.03	.00
	(Brewers logo reversed) ERR			
☐ 109	R.J. Reynolds	.06	.03	.00
☐ 110	John Tudor	.10	.05	.01
☐ 111	Alfredo Griffin	.06	.03	.00
☐ 112	Alan Ashby	.03	.01	.00
☐ 113	Neil Allen	.06	.03	.00
☐ 114	Billy Beane	.06	.03	.00
☐ 115	Donnie Moore	.03	.01	.00
☐ 116	Bill Russell	.03	.01	.00
☐ 117	Jim Beattie	.03	.01	.00
☐ 118	Bobby Valentine MG	.06	.01	.00
	(checklist back)			
☐ 119	Ron Robinson	.03	.01	.00
☐ 120	Eddie Murray	.30	.15	.03
☐ 121	Kevin Romine	.12	.06	.01
☐ 122	Jim Clancy	.03	.01	.00
☐ 123	John Kruk	.75	.35	.07
☐ 124	Ray Fontenot	.03	.01	.00
☐ 125	Bob Brenly	.06	.03	.00
☐ 126	Mike Loynd	.20	.10	.02
☐ 127	Vance Law	.03	.01	.00
☐ 128	Checklist 1-132	.06	.01	.00
☐ 129	Rick Cerone	.03	.01	.00
☐ 130	Dwight Gooden	.75	.35	.07

☐ 131	Pirates Team	.06	.03	.00
	(Bream/Pena)			
☐ 132	Paul Assenmacher	.10	.05	.01
☐ 133	Jose Oquendo	.06	.03	.00
☐ 134	Rich Yett	.06	.03	.00
☐ 135	Mike Easler	.06	.03	.00
☐ 136	Ron Romanick	.03	.01	.00
☐ 137	Jerry Willard	.03	.01	.00
☐ 138	Roy Lee Jackson	.03	.01	.00
☐ 139	Devon White	1.50	.75	.15
☐ 140	Bret Saberhagen	.30	.15	.03
☐ 141	Herm Winningham	.03	.01	.00
☐ 142	Rick Sutcliffe	.10	.05	.01
☐ 143	Steve Boros MG	.06	.01	.00
	(checklist back)			
☐ 144	Mike Scioscia	.03	.01	.00
☐ 145	Charlie Kerfeld	.06	.03	.00
☐ 146	Tracy Jones	.45	.22	.04
☐ 147	Randy Niemann	.03	.01	.00
☐ 148	Dave Collins	.03	.01	.00
☐ 149	Ray Searage	.03	.01	.00
☐ 150	Wade Boggs	1.25	.60	.12
☐ 151	Mike LaCoss	.03	.01	.00
☐ 152	Toby Harrah	.03	.01	.00
☐ 153	Duane Ward	.10	.05	.01
☐ 154	Tom O'Malley	.03	.01	.00
☐ 155	Eddie Whitson	.03	.01	.00
☐ 156	Mariners Team	.03	.01	.00
	(mound conference)			
☐ 157	Danny Darwin	.03	.01	.00
☐ 158	Tim Teufel	.03	.01	.00
☐ 159	Ed Olwine	.10	.05	.01
☐ 160	Julio Franco	.08	.04	.01
☐ 161	Steve Ontiveros	.03	.01	.00
☐ 162	Mike Lavalliere	.15	.07	.01
☐ 163	Kevin Gross	.03	.01	.00
☐ 164	Sammy Khalifa	.03	.01	.00
☐ 165	Jeff Reardon	.10	.05	.01
☐ 166	Bob Boone	.06	.03	.00
☐ 167	Jim Deshaies	.25	.12	.02
☐ 168	Lou Piniella MG	.08	.02	.00
	(checklist back)			
☐ 169	Ron Washington	.03	.01	.00
☐ 170	Bo Jackson	1.25	.60	.12
☐ 171	Chuck Cary	.15	.07	.01
☐ 172	Ron Oester	.03	.01	.00
☐ 173	Alex Trevino	.03	.01	.00
☐ 174	Henry Cotto	.03	.01	.00
☐ 175	Bob Stanley	.06	.03	.00
☐ 176	Steve Buechele	.03	.01	.00
☐ 177	Keith Moreland	.06	.03	.00
☐ 178	Cecil Fielder	.08	.04	.01
☐ 179	Bill Wegman	.06	.03	.00
☐ 180	Chris Brown	.12	.06	.01
☐ 181	Cardinals Team	.03	.01	.00
	(mound conference)			
☐ 182	Lee Lacy	.03	.01	.00
☐ 183	Andy Hawkins	.03	.01	.00
☐ 184	Bobby Bonilla	.25	.12	.02
☐ 185	Roger McDowell	.10	.05	.01
☐ 186	Bruce Benedict	.03	.01	.00
☐ 187	Mark Huismann	.03	.01	.00
☐ 188	Tony Phillips	.03	.01	.00
☐ 189	Joe Hesketh	.03	.01	.00
☐ 190	Jim Sundberg	.03	.01	.00
☐ 191	Charles Hudson	.03	.01	.00
☐ 192	Cory Snyder	.80	.40	.08
☐ 193	Roger Craig MG	.06	.01	.00
	(checklist back)			
☐ 194	Kirk McCaskill	.06	.03	.00
☐ 195	Mike Pagliarulo	.12	.06	.01
☐ 196	Randy O'Neal	.06	.03	.00
	(wrong ML career W-L totals)			
☐ 197	Mark Bailey	.03	.01	.00
☐ 198	Lee Mazzilli	.03	.01	.00
☐ 199	Mariano Duncan	.06	.03	.00
☐ 200	Pete Rose	.50	.25	.05
☐ 201	John Cangelosi	.20	.10	.02
☐ 202	Ricky Wright	.03	.01	.00
☐ 203	Mike Kingery	.15	.07	.01
☐ 204	Sammy Stewart	.03	.01	.00
☐ 205	Graig Nettles	.10	.05	.01
☐ 206	Twins Team	.03	.01	.00
	(mound conference)			
☐ 207	George Frazier	.03	.01	.00
☐ 208	John Shelby	.03	.01	.00
☐ 209	Rick Schu	.03	.01	.00
☐ 210	Lloyd Moseby	.10	.05	.01
☐ 211	John Morris	.03	.01	.00
☐ 212	Mike Fitzgerald	.03	.01	.00
☐ 213	Randy Myers	.30	.15	.03
☐ 214	Omar Moreno	.03	.01	.00
☐ 215	Mark Langston	.10	.05	.01
☐ 216	B.J. Surhoff	.75	.35	.07

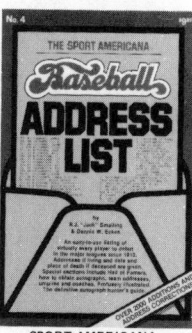

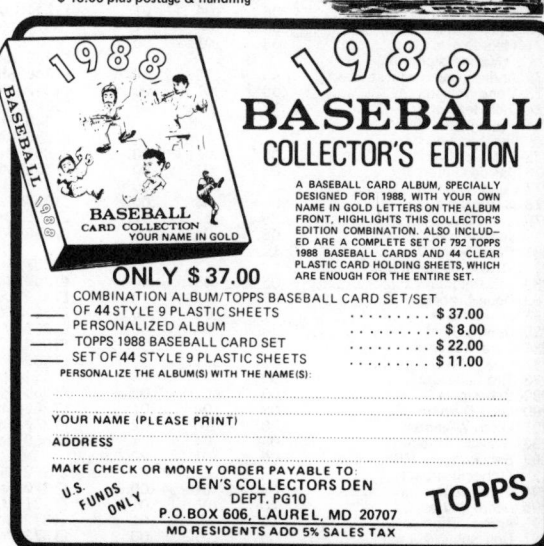

☐ 217	Chris Codiroli	.03	.01	.00
☐ 218	Sparky Anderson MG (checklist back)	.06	.01	.00
☐ 219	Cecilio Guante	.03	.01	.00
☐ 220	Joe Carter	.20	.10	.02
☐ 221	Vern Ruhle	.03	.01	.00
☐ 222	Denny Walling	.03	.01	.00
☐ 223	Charlie Leibrandt	.06	.03	.00
☐ 224	Wayne Tolleson	.03	.01	.00
☐ 225	Mike Smithson	.03	.01	.00
☐ 226	Max Venable	.03	.01	.00
☐ 227	Jamie Moyer	.15	.07	.01
☐ 228	Curt Wilkerson	.03	.01	.00
☐ 229	Mike Birkbeck	.10	.05	.01
☐ 230	Don Baylor	.08	.04	.01
☐ 231	Giants Team (mound conference)	.03	.01	.00
☐ 232	Reggie Williams	.12	.06	.01
☐ 233	Russ Morman	.15	.07	.01
☐ 234	Pat Sheridan	.03	.01	.00
☐ 235	Alvin Davis	.10	.05	.01
☐ 236	Tommy John	.10	.05	.01
☐ 237	Jim Morrison	.03	.01	.00
☐ 238	Bill Krueger	.03	.01	.00
☐ 239	Juan Espino	.06	.03	.00
☐ 240	Steve Balboni	.03	.01	.00
☐ 241	Danny Heep	.03	.01	.00
☐ 242	Rick Mahler	.03	.01	.00
☐ 243	Whitey Herzog MG (checklist back)	.06	.01	.00
☐ 244	Dickie Noles	.03	.01	.00
☐ 245	Willie Upshaw	.06	.03	.00
☐ 246	Jim Dwyer	.03	.01	.00
☐ 247	Jeff Reed	.06	.03	.00
☐ 248	Gene Walter	.06	.03	.00
☐ 249	Jim Pankovits	.03	.01	.00
☐ 250	Teddy Higuera	.20	.10	.02
☐ 251	Rob Wilfong	.03	.01	.00
☐ 252	Denny Martinez	.06	.03	.00
☐ 253	Eddie Milner	.03	.01	.00
☐ 254	Bob Tewksbury	.20	.10	.02
☐ 255	Juan Samuel	.15	.07	.01
☐ 256	Royals Team (Brett/F.White)	.12	.06	.01
☐ 257	Bob Forsch	.06	.03	.00
☐ 258	Steve Yeager	.03	.01	.00
☐ 259	Mike Greenwell	1.50	.75	.15
☐ 260	Vida Blue	.06	.03	.00
☐ 261	Ruben Sierra	1.50	.75	.15
☐ 262	Jim Winn	.03	.01	.00
☐ 263	Stan Javier	.06	.03	.00
☐ 264	Checklist 133-264	.06	.01	.00
☐ 265	Darrell Evans	.08	.04	.01
☐ 266	Jeff Hamilton	.15	.07	.01
☐ 267	Howard Johnson	.12	.06	.01
☐ 268	Pat Corrales MG (checklist back)	.06	.01	.00
☐ 269	Cliff Speck	.08	.04	.01
☐ 270	Jody Davis	.08	.04	.01
☐ 271	Mike Brown (Mariners pitcher)	.03	.01	.00
☐ 272	Andres Galarraga	.45	.22	.04
☐ 273	Gene Nelson	.03	.01	.00
☐ 274	Jeff Hearron (duplicate 1986 stat line on back)	.12	.06	.01
☐ 275	LaMarr Hoyt	.06	.03	.00
☐ 276	Jackie Gutierrez	.03	.01	.00
☐ 277	Juan Agosto	.03	.01	.00
☐ 278	Gary Pettis	.06	.03	.00
☐ 279	Dan Plesac	.25	.12	.02
☐ 280	Jeff Leonard	.08	.04	.01
☐ 281	Reds Team (Rose conference)	.12	.06	.01
☐ 282	Jeff Calhoun	.06	.03	.00
☐ 283	Doug Drabek	.25	.12	.02
☐ 284	John Moses	.06	.03	.00
☐ 285	Dennis Boyd	.06	.03	.00
☐ 286	Mike Woodard	.06	.03	.00
☐ 287	Dave Von Ohlen	.03	.01	.00
☐ 288	Tito Landrum	.03	.01	.00
☐ 289	Bob Kipper	.03	.01	.00
☐ 290	Leon Durham	.08	.04	.01
☐ 291	Mitch Williams	.20	.10	.02
☐ 292	Franklin Stubbs	.08	.04	.01
☐ 293	Bob Rodgers MG (checklist back)	.06	.01	.00
☐ 294	Steve Jeltz	.03	.01	.00
☐ 295	Len Dykstra	.10	.05	.01
☐ 296	Andres Thomas	.15	.07	.01
☐ 297	Don Schulze	.03	.01	.00
☐ 298	Larry Herndon	.03	.01	.00
☐ 299	Joel Davis	.06	.03	.00
☐ 300	Reggie Jackson	.30	.15	.03
☐ 301	Luis Aquino	.20	.10	.02

	ERR (no trademark, never corrected)			
☐ 302	Bill Schroeder	.03	.01	.00
☐ 303	Juan Berenguer	.03	.01	.00
☐ 304	Phil Garner	.03	.01	.00
☐ 305	John Franco	.08	.04	.01
☐ 306	Red Sox Team (mound conference)	.03	.01	.00
☐ 307	Lee Guetterman	.25	.12	.02
☐ 308	Don Slaught	.03	.01	.00
☐ 309	Mike Young	.06	.03	.00
☐ 310	Frank Viola	.12	.06	.01
☐ 311	Turn Back 1982 Rickey Henderson	.12	.06	.01
☐ 312	Turn Back 1977 Reggie Jackson	.12	.06	.01
☐ 313	Turn Back 1972 Roberto Clemente	.12	.06	.01
☐ 314	Turn Back 1967 Carl Yastrzemski	.12	.06	.01
☐ 315	Turn Back 1962 Maury Wills	.08	.04	.01
☐ 316	Brian Fisher	.06	.03	.00
☐ 317	Clint Hurdle	.03	.01	.00
☐ 318	Jim Fregosi MG (checklist back)	.06	.01	.00
☐ 319	Greg Swindell	.45	.22	.04
☐ 320	Barry Bonds	.45	.22	.04
☐ 321	Mike Laga	.06	.03	.00
☐ 322	Chris Bando	.03	.01	.00
☐ 323	Al Newman	.10	.05	.01
☐ 324	Dave Palmer	.03	.01	.00
☐ 325	Garry Templeton	.06	.03	.00
☐ 326	Mark Gubicza	.06	.03	.00
☐ 327	Dale Sveum	.40	.20	.04
☐ 328	Bob Welch	.06	.03	.00
☐ 329	Ron Roenicke	.03	.01	.00
☐ 330	Mike Scott	.25	.12	.02
☐ 331	Mets Team (Carter/Strawberry)	.15	.07	.01
☐ 332	Joe Price	.03	.01	.00
☐ 333	Ken Phelps	.03	.01	.00
☐ 334	Ed Correa	.25	.12	.02
☐ 335	Candy Maldonado	.08	.04	.01
☐ 336	Allan Anderson	.12	.06	.01
☐ 337	Darrell Miller	.03	.01	.00
☐ 338	Tim Conroy	.03	.01	.00
☐ 339	Donnie Hill	.03	.01	.00
☐ 340	Roger Clemens	1.00	.50	.10
☐ 341	Mike Brown (Pirates OF)	.03	.01	.00
☐ 342	Bob James	.03	.01	.00
☐ 343	Hal Lanier MG (checklist back)	.06	.01	.00
☐ 344A	Joe Niekro (copyright inside righthand border)	.10	.05	.01
☐ 344B	Joe Niekro (copyright outside righthand border)	.30	.15	.03
☐ 345	Andre Dawson	.25	.12	.02
☐ 346	Shawon Dunston	.08	.04	.01
☐ 347	Mickey Brantley	.12	.06	.01
☐ 348	Carmelo Martinez	.03	.01	.00
☐ 349	Storm Davis	.06	.03	.00
☐ 350	Keith Hernandez	.20	.10	.02
☐ 351	Gene Garber	.03	.01	.00
☐ 352	Mike Felder	.08	.04	.01
☐ 353	Ernie Camacho	.03	.01	.00
☐ 354	Jamie Quirk	.03	.01	.00
☐ 355	Don Carman	.03	.01	.00
☐ 356	White Sox Team (mound conference)	.03	.01	.00
☐ 357	Steve Fireovid	.08	.04	.01
☐ 358	Sal Butera	.03	.01	.00
☐ 359	Doug Corbett	.03	.01	.00
☐ 360	Pedro Guerrero	.20	.10	.02
☐ 361	Mark Thurmond	.03	.01	.00
☐ 362	Luis Quinones	.10	.05	.01
☐ 363	Jose Guzman	.10	.05	.01
☐ 364	Randy Bush	.03	.01	.00
☐ 365	Rick Rhoden	.06	.03	.00
☐ 366	Mark McGwire	3.50	1.75	.35
☐ 367	Jeff Lahti	.03	.01	.00
☐ 368	John McNamara MG (checklist back)	.06	.01	.00
☐ 369	Brian Dayett	.03	.01	.00
☐ 370	Fred Lynn	.12	.06	.01
☐ 371	Mark Eichhorn	.25	.12	.02
☐ 372	Jerry Mumphrey	.03	.01	.00
☐ 373	Jeff Dedmon	.03	.01	.00
☐ 374	Glenn Hoffman	.03	.01	.00
☐ 375	Ron Guidry	.15	.07	.01
☐ 376	Scott Bradley	.06	.03	.00
☐ 377	John Henry Johnson	.03	.01	.00

☐ 378 Rafael Santana	.03	.01	.00	
☐ 379 John Russell	.03	.01	.00	
☐ 380 Rich Gossage	.10	.05	.01	
☐ 381 Expos Team	.03	.01	.00	
(mound conference)				
☐ 382 Rudy Law	.03	.01	.00	
☐ 383 Ron Davis	.03	.01	.00	
☐ 384 Johnny Grubb	.03	.01	.00	
☐ 385 Orel Hershiser	.15	.07	.01	
☐ 386 Dickie Thon	.03	.01	.00	
☐ 387 T.R. Bryden	.10	.05	.01	
☐ 388 Geno Petralli	.03	.01	.00	
☐ 389 Jeff Robinson	.06	.03	.00	
(Giants pitcher)				
☐ 390 Gary Matthews	.06	.03	.00	
☐ 391 Jay Howell	.03	.01	.00	
☐ 392 Checklist 265-396	.06	.01	.00	
☐ 393 Pete Rose MG	.35	.10	.02	
(checklist back)				
☐ 394 Mike Bielecki	.06	.03	.00	
☐ 395 Damaso Garcia	.06	.03	.00	
☐ 396 Tim Lollar	.03	.01	.00	
☐ 397 Greg Walker	.08	.04	.01	
☐ 398 Brad Havens	.03	.01	.00	
☐ 399 Curt Ford	.12	.06	.01	
☐ 400 George Brett	.30	.15	.03	
☐ 401 Billy Jo Robidoux	.08	.04	.01	
☐ 402 Mike Trujillo	.03	.01	.00	
☐ 403 Jerry Royster	.03	.01	.00	
☐ 404 Doug Sisk	.03	.01	.00	
☐ 405 Brook Jacoby	.10	.05	.01	
☐ 406 Yankees Team	.30	.15	.03	
(Henderson/Mattingly)				
☐ 407 Jim Acker	.03	.01	.00	
☐ 408 John Mizerock	.06	.03	.00	
☐ 409 Milt Thompson	.08	.04	.01	
☐ 410 Fernando Valenzuela	.25	.12	.02	
☐ 411 Darnell Coles	.06	.03	.00	
☐ 412 Eric Davis	1.50	.75	.15	
☐ 413 Moose Haas	.03	.01	.00	
☐ 414 Joe Orsulak	.03	.01	.00	
☐ 415 Bobby Witt	.25	.12	.02	
☐ 416 Tom Nieto	.03	.01	.00	
☐ 417 Pat Perry	.06	.03	.00	
☐ 418 Dick Williams MG	.06	.01	.00	
(checklist back)				
☐ 419 Mark Portugal	.10	.05	.01	
☐ 420 Will Clark	1.50	.75	.15	
☐ 421 Jose DeLeon	.03	.01	.00	
☐ 422 Jack Howell	.06	.03	.00	
☐ 423 Jaime Cocanower	.03	.01	.00	
☐ 424 Chris Speier	.03	.01	.00	
☐ 425 Tom Seaver	.25	.12	.02	
☐ 426 Floyd Rayford	.03	.01	.00	
☐ 427 Edwin Nunez	.03	.01	.00	
☐ 428 Bruce Bochy	.03	.01	.00	
☐ 429 Tim Pyznarski	.15	.07	.01	
☐ 430 Mike Schmidt	.35	.17	.03	
☐ 431 Dodgers Team	.06	.03	.00	
(mound conference)				
☐ 432 Jim Slaton	.03	.01	.00	
☐ 433 Ed Hearn	.08	.04	.01	
☐ 434 Mike Fischlin	.03	.01	.00	
☐ 435 Bruce Sutter	.10	.05	.01	
☐ 436 Andy Allanson	.12	.06	.01	
☐ 437 Ted Power	.06	.03	.00	
☐ 438 Kelly Downs	.20	.10	.02	
☐ 439 Karl Best	.03	.01	.00	
☐ 440 Willie McGee	.15	.07	.01	
☐ 441 Dave Leiper	.10	.05	.01	
☐ 442 Mitch Webster	.06	.03	.00	
☐ 443 John Felske MG	.06	.01	.00	
(checklist back)				
☐ 444 Jeff Russell	.03	.01	.00	
☐ 445 Dave Lopes	.06	.03	.00	
☐ 446 Chuck Finley	.10	.05	.01	
☐ 447 Bill Almon	.03	.01	.00	
☐ 448 Chris Bosio	.20	.10	.02	
☐ 449 Pat Dodson	.20	.10	.02	
☐ 450 Kirby Puckett	.45	.22	.04	
☐ 451 Joe Sambito	.03	.01	.00	
☐ 452 Dave Henderson	.03	.01	.00	
☐ 453 Scott Terry	.10	.05	.01	
☐ 454 Luis Salazar	.03	.01	.00	
☐ 455 Mike Boddicker	.08	.04	.01	
☐ 456 A's Team	.03	.01	.00	
(mound conference)				
☐ 457 Len Matuszek	.03	.01	.00	
☐ 458 Kelly Gruber	.06	.03	.00	
☐ 459 Dennis Eckersley	.06	.03	.00	
☐ 460 Darryl Strawberry	.40	.20	.04	
☐ 461 Craig McMurtry	.03	.01	.00	
☐ 462 Scott Fletcher	.06	.03	.00	
☐ 463 Tom Candiotti	.06	.03	.00	
☐ 464 Butch Wynegar	.03	.01	.00	
☐ 465 Todd Worrell	.35	.17	.03	
☐ 466 Kal Daniels	1.75	.85	.17	
☐ 467 Randy St.Claire	.03	.01	.00	
☐ 468 George Bamberger MG	.06	.01	.00	
(checklist back)				
☐ 469 Mike Diaz	.25	.12	.02	
☐ 470 Dave Dravecky	.06	.03	.00	
☐ 471 Ronn Reynolds	.03	.01	.00	
☐ 472 Bill Doran	.08	.04	.01	
☐ 473 Steve Farr	.03	.01	.00	
☐ 474 Jerry Narron	.03	.01	.00	
☐ 475 Scott Garrelts	.06	.03	.00	
☐ 476 Danny Tartabull	1.00	.50	.10	
☐ 477 Ken Howell	.03	.01	.00	
☐ 478 Tim Laudner	.06	.03	.00	
☐ 479 Bob Sebra	.20	.10	.02	
☐ 480 Jim Rice	.25	.12	.02	
☐ 481 Phillies Team	.06	.03	.00	
(cage conference)				
☐ 482 Daryl Boston	.03	.01	.00	
☐ 483 Dwight Lowry	.15	.07	.01	
☐ 484 Jim Traber	.10	.05	.01	
☐ 485 Tony Fernandez	.12	.06	.01	
☐ 486 Otis Nixon	.10	.05	.01	
☐ 487 Dave Gumpert	.03	.01	.00	
☐ 488 Ray Knight	.06	.03	.00	
☐ 489 Bill Gullickson	.06	.03	.00	
☐ 490 Dale Murphy	.35	.17	.03	
☐ 491 Ron Karkovice	.15	.07	.01	
☐ 492 Mike Heath	.03	.01	.00	
☐ 493 Tom Lasorda MG	.08	.02	.00	
(checklist back)				
☐ 494 Barry Jones	.15	.07	.01	
☐ 495 Gorman Thomas	.08	.04	.01	
☐ 496 Bruce Bochte	.03	.01	.00	
☐ 497 Dale Mohorcic	.25	.12	.02	
☐ 498 Bob Kearney	.03	.01	.00	
☐ 499 Bruce Ruffin	.25	.12	.02	
☐ 500 Don Mattingly	2.50	1.25	.25	
☐ 501 Craig Lefferts	.03	.01	.00	
☐ 502 Dick Schofield	.03	.01	.00	
☐ 503 Larry Andersen	.03	.01	.00	
☐ 504 Mickey Hatcher	.03	.01	.00	
☐ 505 Bryn Smith	.03	.01	.00	
☐ 506 Orioles Team	.06	.03	.00	
(mound conference)				
☐ 507 Dave Stapleton	.12	.06	.01	
(pitcher)				
☐ 508 Scott Bankhead	.06	.03	.00	
☐ 509 Enos Cabell	.03	.01	.00	
☐ 510 Tom Henke	.08	.04	.01	
☐ 511 Steve Lyons	.03	.01	.00	
☐ 512 Dave Magadan	.75	.35	.07	
☐ 513 Carmen Castillo	.03	.01	.00	
☐ 514 Orlando Mercado	.03	.01	.00	
☐ 515 Willie Hernandez	.08	.04	.01	
☐ 516 Ted Simmons	.08	.04	.01	
☐ 517 Mario Soto	.06	.03	.00	
☐ 518 Gene Mauch MG	.06	.01	.00	
(checklist back)				
☐ 519 Curt Young	.06	.03	.00	
☐ 520 Jack Clark	.20	.10	.02	
☐ 521 Rick Reuschel	.06	.03	.00	
☐ 522 Checklist 397-528	.06	.01	.00	
☐ 523 Earnie Riles	.06	.03	.00	
☐ 524 Bob Shirley	.03	.01	.00	
☐ 525 Phil Bradley	.15	.07	.01	
☐ 526 Roger Mason	.06	.03	.00	
☐ 527 Jim Wohlford	.03	.01	.00	
☐ 528 Ken Dixon	.03	.01	.00	
☐ 529 Alvaro Espinoza	.06	.03	.00	
☐ 530 Tony Gwynn	.40	.20	.04	
☐ 531 Astros Team	.08	.04	.01	
(Y.Berra conference)				
☐ 532 Jeff Stone	.06	.03	.00	
☐ 533 Argenis Salazar	.03	.01	.00	
☐ 534 Scott Sanderson	.03	.01	.00	
☐ 535 Tony Armas	.08	.04	.01	
☐ 536 Terry Mulholland	.12	.06	.01	
☐ 537 Rance Mulliniks	.03	.01	.00	
☐ 538 Tom Niedenfuer	.06	.03	.00	
☐ 539 Reid Nichols	.03	.01	.00	
☐ 540 Terry Kennedy	.06	.03	.00	
☐ 541 Rafael Belliard	.10	.05	.01	
☐ 542 Ricky Horton	.03	.01	.00	
☐ 543 Dave Johnson MG	.08	.02	.00	
(checklist back)				
☐ 544 Zane Smith	.08	.04	.01	
☐ 545 Buddy Bell	.10	.05	.01	
☐ 546 Mike Morgan	.03	.01	.00	
☐ 547 Rob Deer	.15	.07	.01	
☐ 548 Bill Mooneyham	.10	.05	.01	
☐ 549 Bob Melvin	.03	.01	.00	
☐ 550 Pete Incaviglia	1.25	.60	.12	
☐ 551 Frank Wills	.03	.01	.00	

☐ 552 Larry Sheets	.12	.06	.01
☐ 553 Mike Maddux	.10	.05	.01
☐ 554 Buddy Biancalana	.03	.01	.00
☐ 555 Dennis Rasmussen	.06	.03	.00
☐ 556 Angels Team	.06	.03	.00
(mound conference)			
☐ 557 John Cerutti	.20	.10	.02
☐ 558 Greg Gagne	.06	.03	.00
☐ 559 Lance McCullers	.06	.03	.00
☐ 560 Glenn Davis	.25	.12	.02
☐ 561 Rey Quinones	.25	.12	.02
☐ 562 Bryan Clutterbuck	.08	.04	.01
☐ 563 John Stefero	.06	.03	.00
☐ 564 Larry McWilliams	.03	.01	.00
☐ 565 Dusty Baker	.06	.03	.00
☐ 566 Tim Hulett	.03	.01	.00
☐ 567 Greg Mathews	.25	.12	.02
☐ 568 Earl Weaver MG	.08	.02	.00
(checklist back)			
☐ 569 Wade Rowdon	.08	.04	.01
☐ 570 Sid Fernandez	.15	.07	.01
☐ 571 Ozzie Virgil	.03	.01	.00
☐ 572 Pete Ladd	.03	.01	.00
☐ 573 Hal McRae	.06	.03	.00
☐ 574 Manny Lee	.06	.03	.00
☐ 575 Pat Tabler	.08	.04	.01
☐ 576 Frank Pastore	.03	.01	.00
☐ 577 Dann Bilardello	.03	.01	.00
☐ 578 Billy Hatcher	.10	.05	.01
☐ 579 Rick Burleson	.06	.03	.00
☐ 580 Mike Krukow	.06	.03	.00
☐ 581 Cubs Team	.06	.03	.00
(Cey/Trout)			
☐ 582 Bruce Berenyi	.03	.01	.00
☐ 583 Junior Ortiz	.03	.01	.00
☐ 584 Ron Kittle	.08	.04	.01
☐ 585 Scott Bailes	.15	.07	.01
☐ 586 Ben Oglivie	.06	.03	.00
☐ 587 Eric Plunk	.08	.04	.01
☐ 588 Wallace Johnson	.06	.03	.00
☐ 589 Steve Crawford	.03	.01	.00
☐ 590 Vince Coleman	.35	.17	.03
☐ 591 Spike Owen	.03	.01	.00
☐ 592 Chris Welsh	.03	.01	.00
☐ 593 Chuck Tanner MG	.06	.01	.00
(checklist back)			
☐ 594 Rick Anderson	.15	.07	.01
☐ 595 Keith Hernandez AS	.10	.05	.01
☐ 596 Steve Sax AS	.06	.03	.00
☐ 597 Mike Schmidt AS	.20	.10	.02
☐ 598 Ozzie Smith AS	.10	.05	.01
☐ 599 Tony Gwynn AS	.20	.10	.02
☐ 600 Dave Parker AS	.10	.05	.01
☐ 601 Darryl Strawberry AS	.20	.10	.02
☐ 602 Gary Carter AS	.15	.07	.01
☐ 603A Dwight Gooden AS	.75	.35	.07
ERR (no trademark)			
☐ 603B Dwight Gooden AS COR	.30	.15	.03
☐ 604 Fern. Valenzuela AS	.15	.07	.01
☐ 605 Todd Worrell AS	.10	.05	.01
☐ 606A Don Mattingly AS	2.00	1.00	.20
ERR (no trademark)			
☐ 606B Don Mattingly AS COR	.75	.35	.07
☐ 607 Tony Bernazard AS	.06	.03	.00
☐ 608 Wade Boggs AS	.35	.17	.03
☐ 609 Cal Ripken AS	.15	.07	.01
☐ 610 Jim Rice AS	.12	.06	.01
☐ 611 Kirby Puckett AS	.15	.07	.01
☐ 612 George Bell AS	.12	.06	.01
☐ 613 Lance Parrish AS	.08	.04	.01
☐ 614 Roger Clemens AS	.25	.12	.02
☐ 615 Teddy Higuera AS	.08	.04	.01
☐ 616 Dave Righetti AS	.08	.04	.01
☐ 617 Al Nipper	.03	.01	.00
☐ 618 Tom Kelly MG	.08	.02	.00
(checklist back)			
☐ 619 Jerry Reed	.03	.01	.00
☐ 620 Jose Canseco	2.25	1.10	.22
☐ 621 Danny Cox	.08	.04	.01
☐ 622 Glenn Braggs	.45	.22	.04
☐ 623 Kurt Stillwell	.30	.15	.03
☐ 624 Tim Burke	.06	.03	.00
☐ 625 Mookie Wilson	.06	.03	.00
☐ 626 Joel Skinner	.06	.03	.00
☐ 627 Ken Oberkfell	.03	.01	.00
☐ 628 Bob Walk	.03	.01	.00
☐ 629 Larry Parrish	.06	.03	.00
☐ 630 John Candelaria	.06	.03	.00
☐ 631 Tigers Team	.06	.03	.00
(mound conference)			
☐ 632 Rob Woodward	.08	.04	.01
☐ 633 Jose Uribe	.03	.01	.00
☐ 634 Rafael Palmeiro	.50	.25	.05
☐ 635 Ken Schrom	.03	.01	.00
☐ 636 Darren Daulton	.03	.01	.00

☐ 637 Bip Roberts	.08	.04	.01
☐ 638 Rich Bordi	.03	.01	.00
☐ 639 Gerald Perry	.06	.03	.00
☐ 640 Mark Clear	.03	.01	.00
☐ 641 Domingo Ramos	.03	.01	.00
☐ 642 Al Pulido	.06	.03	.00
☐ 643 Ron Shepherd	.06	.03	.00
☐ 644 John Denny	.06	.03	.00
☐ 645 Dwight Evans	.10	.05	.01
☐ 646 Mike Mason	.03	.01	.00
☐ 647 Tom Lawless	.03	.01	.00
☐ 648 Barry Larkin	.80	.40	.08
☐ 649 Mickey Tettleton	.03	.01	.00
☐ 650 Hubie Brooks	.08	.04	.01
☐ 651 Benny Distefano	.06	.03	.00
☐ 652 Terry Forster	.06	.03	.00
☐ 653 Kevin Mitchell	.30	.15	.03
☐ 654 Checklist 529-660	.06	.01	.00
☐ 655 Jesse Barfield	.18	.09	.01
☐ 656 Rangers Team	.06	.03	.00
(Valentine/R.Wright)			
☐ 657 Tom Waddell	.03	.01	.00
☐ 658 Robby Thompson	.30	.15	.03
☐ 659 Aurelio Lopez	.03	.01	.00
☐ 660 Bob Horner	.15	.07	.01
☐ 661 Lou Whitaker	.10	.05	.01
☐ 662 Frank DiPino	.03	.01	.00
☐ 663 Cliff Johnson	.03	.01	.00
☐ 664 Mike Marshall	.10	.05	.01
☐ 665 Rod Scurry	.03	.01	.00
☐ 666 Von Hayes	.10	.05	.01
☐ 667 Ron Hassey	.03	.01	.00
☐ 668 Juan Bonilla	.03	.01	.00
☐ 669 Bud Black	.03	.01	.00
☐ 670 Jose Cruz	.08	.04	.01
☐ 671 Ray Soff	.08	.04	.01
☐ 672 Chili Davis	.08	.04	.01
☐ 673 Don Sutton	.12	.06	.01
☐ 674 Bill Campbell	.03	.01	.00
☐ 675 Ed Romero	.03	.01	.00
☐ 676 Charlie Moore	.03	.01	.00
☐ 677 Bob Grich	.06	.03	.00
☐ 678 Carney Lansford	.08	.04	.01
☐ 679 Kent Hrbek	.15	.07	.01
☐ 680 Ryne Sandberg	.25	.12	.02
☐ 681 George Bell	.25	.12	.02
☐ 682 Jerry Reuss	.06	.03	.00
☐ 683 Gary Roenicke	.03	.01	.00
☐ 684 Kent Tekulve	.06	.03	.00
☐ 685 Jerry Hairston	.03	.01	.00
☐ 686 Doyle Alexander	.06	.03	.00
☐ 687 Alan Trammell	.20	.10	.02
☐ 688 Juan Beniquez	.03	.01	.00
☐ 689 Darrell Porter	.03	.01	.00
☐ 690 Dane Iorg	.03	.01	.00
☐ 691 Dave Parker	.15	.07	.01
☐ 692 Frank White	.06	.03	.00
☐ 693 Terry Puhl	.03	.01	.00
☐ 694 Phil Niekro	.15	.07	.01
☐ 695 Chico Walker	.15	.07	.01
☐ 696 Gary Lucas	.03	.01	.00
☐ 697 Ed Lynch	.03	.01	.00
☐ 698 Ernie Whitt	.03	.01	.00
☐ 699 Ken Landreaux	.03	.01	.00
☐ 700 Dave Bergman	.03	.01	.00
☐ 701 Willie Randolph	.06	.03	.00
☐ 702 Greg Gross	.03	.01	.00
☐ 703 Dave Schmidt	.06	.03	.00
☐ 704 Jesse Orosco	.06	.03	.00
☐ 705 Bruce Hurst	.08	.04	.01
☐ 706 Rick Manning	.03	.01	.00
☐ 707 Bob McClure	.03	.01	.00
☐ 708 Scott McGregor	.06	.03	.00
☐ 709 Dave Kingman	.10	.05	.01
☐ 710 Gary Gaetti	.12	.06	.01
☐ 711 Ken Griffey	.06	.03	.00
☐ 712 Don Robinson	.03	.01	.00
☐ 713 Tom Brookens	.03	.01	.00
☐ 714 Dan Quisenberry	.10	.05	.01
☐ 715 Bob Dernier	.03	.01	.00
☐ 716 Rick Leach	.03	.01	.00
☐ 717 Ed VandeBerg	.03	.01	.00
☐ 718 Steve Carlton	.25	.12	.02
☐ 719 Tom Hume	.03	.01	.00
☐ 720 Richard Dotson	.06	.03	.00
☐ 721 Tom Herr	.06	.03	.00
☐ 722 Bob Knepper	.06	.03	.00
☐ 723 Brett Butler	.08	.04	.01
☐ 724 Greg Minton	.03	.01	.00
☐ 725 George Hendrick	.06	.03	.00
☐ 726 Frank Tanana	.06	.03	.00
☐ 727 Mike Moore	.06	.03	.00
☐ 728 Tippy Martinez	.03	.01	.00
☐ 729 Tom Paciorek	.03	.01	.00
☐ 730 Eric Show	.03	.01	.00

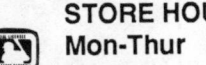

☐ 731	Dave Concepcion	.06	.03	.00
☐ 732	Manny Trillo	.03	.01	.00
☐ 733	Bill Caudill	.03	.01	.00
☐ 734	Bill Madlock	.08	.04	.01
☐ 735	Rickey Henderson	.25	.12	.02
☐ 736	Steve Bedrosian	.12	.06	.01
☐ 737	Floyd Bannister	.06	.03	.00
☐ 738	Jorge Orta	.03	.01	.00
☐ 739	Chet Lemon	.03	.01	.00
☐ 740	Rich Gedman	.06	.03	.00
☐ 741	Paul Molitor	.12	.06	.01
☐ 742	Andy McGaffigan	.03	.01	.00
☐ 743	Dwayne Murphy	.03	.01	.00
☐ 744	Roy Smalley	.03	.01	.00
☐ 745	Glenn Hubbard	.03	.01	.00
☐ 746	Bob Ojeda	.08	.04	.01
☐ 747	Johnny Ray	.08	.04	.01
☐ 748	Mike Flanagan	.06	.03	.00
☐ 749	Ozzie Smith	.15	.07	.01
☐ 750	Steve Trout	.06	.03	.00
☐ 751	Garth Iorg	.03	.01	.00
☐ 752	Dan Petry	.08	.04	.01
☐ 753	Rick Honeycutt	.03	.01	.00
☐ 754	Dave LaPoint	.03	.01	.00
☐ 755	Luis Aguayo	.03	.01	.00
☐ 756	Carlton Fisk	.10	.05	.01
☐ 757	Nolan Ryan	.25	.12	.02
☐ 758	Tony Bernazard	.03	.01	.00
☐ 759	Joel Youngblood	.03	.01	.00
☐ 760	Mike Witt	.10	.05	.01
☐ 761	Greg Pryor	.03	.01	.00
☐ 762	Gary Ward	.06	.03	.00
☐ 763	Tim Flannery	.03	.01	.00
☐ 764	Bill Buckner	.08	.04	.01
☐ 765	Kirk Gibson	.15	.07	.01
☐ 766	Don Aase	.03	.01	.00
☐ 767	Ron Cey	.06	.03	.00
☐ 768	Dennis Lamp	.03	.01	.00
☐ 769	Steve Sax	.12	.06	.01
☐ 770	Dave Winfield	.25	.12	.02
☐ 771	Shane Rawley	.06	.03	.00
☐ 772	Harold Baines	.12	.06	.01
☐ 773	Robin Yount	.25	.12	.02
☐ 774	Wayne Krenchicki	.03	.01	.00
☐ 775	Joaquin Andujar	.08	.04	.01
☐ 776	Tom Brunansky	.10	.05	.01
☐ 777	Chris Chambliss	.06	.03	.00
☐ 778	Jack Morris	.15	.07	.01
☐ 779	Craig Reynolds	.03	.01	.00
☐ 780	Andre Thornton	.06	.03	.00
☐ 781	Atlee Hammaker	.03	.01	.00
☐ 782	Brian Downing	.06	.03	.00
☐ 783	Willie Wilson	.12	.06	.01
☐ 784	Cal Ripken	.25	.12	.02
☐ 785	Terry Francona	.03	.01	.00
☐ 786	Jimy Williams MG (checklist back)	.06	.01	.00
☐ 787	Alejandro Pena	.06	.03	.00
☐ 788	Tim Stoddard	.03	.01	.00
☐ 789	Dan Schatzeder	.03	.01	.00
☐ 790	Julio Cruz	.03	.01	.00
☐ 791	Lance Parrish ERR (no trademark, never corrected)	.20	.10	.02
☐ 792	Checklist 661-792	.06	.01	.00

1987 Topps Wax Box Cards

This set of 8 cards is really four different sets of two smaller (2 1/8" by 3") cards which were printed on the side of the wax pack box; these eight cards are

lettered A through H and are very similar in design to the Topps regular issue cards. The card backs are done in a newspaper headline style describing something about that player that happened the previous season. The card backs feature blue and yellow ink on gray card stock.

		MINT	EXC	G-VG
COMPLETE SET (8)		1.50	.75	.15
COMMON PLAYER (1-8)		.10	.05	.01
☐ A	Don Baylor	.15	.07	.01
☐ B	Steve Carlton	.35	.17	.03
☐ C	Ron Cey	.10	.05	.01
☐ D	Cecil Cooper	.10	.05	.01
☐ E	Rickey Henderson	.60	.30	.06
☐ F	Jim Rice	.30	.15	.03
☐ G	Don Sutton	.25	.12	.02
☐ H	Dave Winfield	.30	.15	.03

1987 Topps Glossy All-Stars 22

This set of 22 glossy cards was inserted one per rack pack. Players selected for the set are the starting players (plus manager and two pitchers) in the 1986 All-Star Game in Houston. Cards measure standard size, 2 1/2" by 3 1/2" and the backs feature red and blue printing on a white card stock.

		MINT	EXC	G-VG
COMPLETE SET (22)		3.50	1.75	.35
COMMON PLAYER (1-22)		.10	.05	.01
☐ 1	Whitey Herzog MG	.10	.05	.01
☐ 2	Keith Hernandez	.20	.10	.02
☐ 3	Ryne Sandberg	.30	.15	.03
☐ 4	Mike Schmidt	.40	.20	.04
☐ 5	Ozzie Smith	.20	.10	.02
☐ 6	Tony Gwynn	.35	.17	.03
☐ 7	Dale Murphy	.50	.25	.05
☐ 8	Darryl Strawberry	.40	.20	.04
☐ 9	Gary Carter	.30	.15	.03
☐ 10	Dwight Gooden	.50	.25	.05
☐ 11	Fernando Valenzuela	.30	.15	.03
☐ 12	Dick Howser MG	.10	.05	.01
☐ 13	Wally Joyner	.75	.35	.07
☐ 14	Lou Whitaker	.15	.07	.01
☐ 15	Wade Boggs	.65	.30	.06
☐ 16	Cal Ripken	.30	.15	.03
☐ 17	Dave Winfield	.30	.15	.03
☐ 18	Rickey Henderson	.40	.20	.04
☐ 19	Kirby Puckett	.35	.17	.03
☐ 20	Lance Parrish	.20	.10	.02
☐ 21	Roger Clemens	.50	.25	.05
☐ 22	Teddy Higuera	.25	.12	.02

1987 Topps Jumbo Glossy Rookies

Inserted in each supermarket jumbo pack is a card from this series of 22 of 1986's best rookies as determined by Topps. Jumbo packs consisted of 100

(regular issue 1987 Topps baseball) cards with a stick of gum plus the insert "Rookie" card. The card fronts are in full color and measure 2 1/2" by 3 1/2". The card backs are printed in red and blue on white card stock and are numbered at the bottom essentially by alphabetical order.

		MINT	EXC	G-VG
COMPLETE SET		12.00	6.00	1.20
COMMON PLAYER		.20	.10	.02
☐ 1	Andy Allanson	.20	.10	.02
☐ 2	John Cangelosi	.20	.10	.02
☐ 3	Jose Canseco	2.00	1.00	.20
☐ 4	Will Clark	1.50	.75	.15
☐ 5	Mark Eichhorn	.35	.17	.03
☐ 6	Pete Incaviglia	1.00	.50	.10
☐ 7	Wally Joyner	2.00	1.00	.20
☐ 8	Eric King	.20	.10	.02
☐ 9	Dave Magadan	.60	.30	.06
☐ 10	John Morris	.20	.10	.02
☐ 11	Juan Nieves	.20	.10	.02
☐ 12	Rafael Palmeiro	.50	.25	.05
☐ 13	Billy Jo Robidoux	.20	.10	.02
☐ 14	Bruce Ruffin	.20	.10	.02
☐ 15	Ruben Sierra	1.50	.75	.15
☐ 16	Cory Snyder	1.00	.50	.10
☐ 17	Kurt Stillwell	.40	.20	.04
☐ 18	Dale Sveum	.50	.25	.05
☐ 19	Danny Tartabull	1.00	.50	.10
☐ 20	Andres Thomas	.30	.15	.03
☐ 21	Robby Thompson	.40	.20	.04
☐ 22	Todd Worrell	.75	.35	.07

1987 Topps Glossy 60

Topps issued this set through a mail-in offer explained and advertised on the wax packs. This 60-card set features glossy fronts with each card measuring 2 1/2" by 3 1/2". The offer provided your choice of any one of the six 10-card subsets (1-10, 11-20, etc.) for 1.00 plus six of the Special Offer ("Spring Fever Baseball") insert cards, which were found one per wax pack. The last two players (numerically) in each ten-card subset are actually "Hot Prospects."

		MINT	EXC	G-VG
COMPLETE SET		12.00	6.00	1.20
COMMON PLAYER		.10	.05	.01
☐ 1	Don Mattingly	1.50	.75	.15
☐ 2	Tony Gwynn	.60	.30	.06
☐ 3	Gary Gaetti	.30	.15	.03
☐ 4	Glenn Davis	.25	.12	.02
☐ 5	Roger Clemens	.90	.45	.09
☐ 6	Dale Murphy	.60	.30	.06
☐ 7	Lou Whitaker	.15	.07	.01
☐ 8	Roger McDowell	.15	.07	.01
☐ 9	Cory Snyder	.60	.30	.06
☐ 10	Todd Worrell	.35	.17	.03
☐ 11	Gary Carter	.35	.17	.03
☐ 12	Eddie Murray	.40	.20	.04
☐ 13	Bob Knepper	.10	.05	.01
☐ 14	Harold Baines	.15	.07	.01
☐ 15	Jeff Reardon	.15	.07	.01
☐ 16	Joe Carter	.25	.12	.02
☐ 17	Dave Parker	.25	.12	.02
☐ 18	Wade Boggs	1.00	.50	.10
☐ 19	Danny Tartabull	.50	.25	.05
☐ 20	Jim Deshaies	.20	.10	.02
☐ 21	Rickey Henderson	.50	.25	.05
☐ 22	Rob Deer	.15	.07	.01
☐ 23	Ozzie Smith	.25	.12	.02
☐ 24	Dave Righetti	.20	.10	.02
☐ 25	Kent Hrbek	.25	.12	.02
☐ 26	Keith Hernandez	.25	.12	.02
☐ 27	Don Baylor	.15	.07	.01
☐ 28	Mike Schmidt	.60	.30	.06
☐ 29	Pete Incaviglia	.60	.30	.06
☐ 30	Barry Bonds	.35	.17	.03
☐ 31	George Brett	.60	.30	.06
☐ 32	Darryl Strawberry	.60	.30	.06
☐ 33	Mike Witt	.15	.07	.01
☐ 34	Kevin Bass	.15	.07	.01
☐ 35	Jesse Barfield	.25	.12	.02
☐ 36	Bob Ojeda	.15	.07	.01
☐ 37	Cal Ripken	.35	.17	.03
☐ 38	Vince Coleman	.35	.17	.03
☐ 39	Wally Joyner	1.00	.50	.10
☐ 40	Robby Thompson	.25	.12	.02
☐ 41	Pete Rose	.75	.35	.07
☐ 42	Jim Rice	.35	.17	.03
☐ 43	Tony Bernazard	.10	.05	.01
☐ 44	Eric Davis	1.25	.60	.12
☐ 45	George Bell	.30	.15	.03
☐ 46	Hubie Brooks	.15	.07	.01
☐ 47	Jack Morris	.25	.12	.02
☐ 48	Tim Raines	.35	.17	.03
☐ 49	Mark Eichhorn	.20	.10	.02
☐ 50	Kevin Mitchell	.20	.10	.02
☐ 51	Dwight Gooden	.75	.35	.07
☐ 52	Doug DeCinces	.10	.05	.01
☐ 53	Fernando Valenzuela	.30	.15	.03
☐ 54	Reggie Jackson	.50	.25	.05
☐ 55	Johnny Ray	.15	.07	.01
☐ 56	Mike Pagliarulo	.20	.10	.02
☐ 57	Kirby Puckett	.50	.25	.05
☐ 58	Lance Parrish	.20	.10	.02
☐ 59	Jose Canseco	1.00	.50	.10
☐ 60	Greg Mathews	.25	.12	.02

1987 Topps Mini Leaders

The 1987 Topps Mini set of Major League Leaders features 77 cards of leaders of the various statistical categories for the 1986 season. The cards are numbered on the back and measure 2 5/32" by 3". The card backs are printed in orange and brown on white card stock. They are very similar in design to the Team Leader cards in the 1987 Topps regular issue. The cards were distributed as a separate issue in wax packs of seven for 30 cents. Eleven of the cards were double printed and are hence more plentiful; they are marked DP in the checklist below.

		MINT	EXC	G-VG
COMPLETE SET (77)		6.00	3.00	.60
COMMON PLAYER (1-77)		.06	.03	.00
COMMON PLAYER DP		.03	.01	.00
☐ 1	Bob Horner DP	.10	.05	.01
☐ 2	Dale Murphy	.35	.17	.03

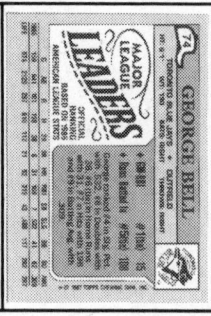

1987 Topps Traded

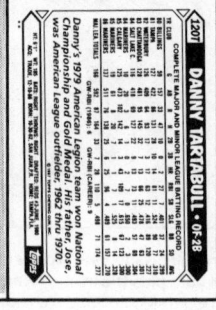

☐	3	Lee Smith	.10	.05	.01
☐	4	Eric Davis	.75	.35	.07
☐	5	John Franco	.06	.03	.00
☐	6	Dave Parker	.15	.07	.01
☐	7	Kevin Bass	.06	.03	.00
☐	8	Glenn Davis DP	.10	.05	.01
☐	9	Bill Doran DP	.06	.03	.00
☐	10	Bob Knepper DP	.03	.01	.00
☐	11	Mike Scott	.15	.07	.01
☐	12	Dave Smith	.06	.03	.00
☐	13	Mariano Duncan	.06	.03	.00
☐	14	Orel Hershiser	.15	.07	.01
☐	15	Steve Sax DP	.06	.03	.00
☐	16	Fernando Valenzuela	.20	.10	.02
☐	17	Tim Raines	.25	.12	.02
☐	18	Jeff Reardon	.10	.05	.01
☐	19	Floyd Youmans	.10	.05	.01
☐	20	Gary Carter DP	.15	.07	.01
☐	21	Ron Darling	.15	.07	.01
☐	22	Sid Fernandez	.10	.05	.01
☐	23	Dwight Gooden	.50	.25	.05
☐	24	Keith Hernandez	.25	.12	.02
☐	25	Bob Ojeda	.10	.05	.01
☐	26	Darryl Strawberry	.50	.25	.05
☐	27	Steve Bedrosian	.15	.07	.01
☐	28	Von Hayes DP	.06	.03	.00
☐	29	Juan Samuel	.15	.07	.01
☐	30	Mike Schmidt	.45	.22	.04
☐	31	Rick Rhoden	.10	.05	.01
☐	32	Vince Coleman	.25	.12	.02
☐	33	Danny Cox	.10	.05	.01
☐	34	Todd Worrell	.20	.10	.02
☐	35	Tony Gwynn	.45	.22	.04
☐	36	Mike Krukow	.06	.03	.00
☐	37	Candy Maldonado	.10	.05	.01
☐	38	Don Aase	.06	.03	.00
☐	39	Eddie Murray	.40	.20	.04
☐	40	Cal Ripken	.40	.20	.04
☐	41	Wade Boggs	.75	.35	.07
☐	42	Roger Clemens	.50	.25	.05
☐	43	Bruce Hurst	.10	.05	.01
☐	44	Jim Rice	.30	.15	.03
☐	45	Wally Joyner	.50	.25	.05
☐	46	Donnie Moore	.06	.03	.00
☐	47	Gary Pettis	.06	.03	.00
☐	48	Mike Witt	.10	.05	.01
☐	49	John Cangelosi	.06	.03	.00
☐	50	Tom Candiotti	.06	.03	.00
☐	51	Joe Carter	.15	.07	.01
☐	52	Pat Tabler	.10	.05	.01
☐	53	Kirk Gibson DP	.10	.05	.01
☐	54	Willie Hernandez	.10	.05	.01
☐	55	Jack Morris	.15	.07	.01
☐	56	Alan Trammell DP	.10	.05	.01
☐	57	George Brett	.45	.22	.04
☐	58	Willie Wilson	.10	.05	.01
☐	59	Rob Deer	.10	.05	.01
☐	60	Teddy Higuera	.20	.10	.02
☐	61	Bert Blyleven DP	.06	.03	.00
☐	62	Gary Gaetti DP	.06	.03	.00
☐	63	Kirby Puckett	.40	.20	.04
☐	64	Rickey Henderson	.40	.20	.04
☐	65	Don Mattingly	1.00	.50	.10
☐	66	Dennis Rasmussen	.06	.03	.00
☐	67	Dave Righetti	.10	.05	.01
☐	68	Jose Canseco	.50	.25	.05
☐	69	Dave Kingman	.10	.05	.01
☐	70	Phil Bradley	.15	.07	.01
☐	71	Mark Langston	.10	.05	.01
☐	72	Pete O'Brien	.10	.05	.01
☐	73	Jesse Barfield	.20	.10	.02
☐	74	George Bell	.25	.12	.02
☐	75	Tony Fernandez	.15	.07	.01
☐	76	Tom Henke	.10	.05	.01
☐	77	Checklist Card	.10	.01	.00

This 132-card Traded or extended set was distributed by Topps to dealers in a special green and white box as a complete set. The card fronts are identical in style to the Topps regular issue and are also 2 1/2" by 3 1/2". The backs are printed in yellow and blue on white card stock. Cards are numbered (with a T suffix) alphabetically according to the name of the player.

			MINT	EXC	G-VG
	COMPLETE SET (132)		10.00	5.00	1.00
	COMMON PLAYER (1-132)		.06	.03	.00
☐	1T	Bill Almon	.06	.03	.00
☐	2T	Scott Bankhead	.10	.05	.01
☐	3T	Eric Bell	.10	.05	.01
☐	4T	Juan Beniquez	.06	.03	.00
☐	5T	Juan Berenguer	.06	.03	.00
☐	6T	Greg Booker	.06	.03	.00
☐	7T	Thad Bosley	.06	.03	.00
☐	8T	Larry Bowa MG	.10	.05	.01
☐	9T	Greg Brock	.10	.05	.01
☐	10T	Bob Brower	.20	.10	.02
☐	11T	Jerry Browne	.15	.07	.01
☐	12T	Ralph Bryant	.20	.10	.02
☐	13T	DeWayne Buice	.20	.10	.02
☐	14T	Ellis Burks	1.25	.60	.12
☐	15T	Ivan Calderon	.25	.12	.02
☐	16T	Jeff Calhoun	.06	.03	.00
☐	17T	Casey Candaele	.20	.10	.02
☐	18T	John Cangelosi	.10	.05	.01
☐	19T	Steve Carlton	.25	.12	.02
☐	20T	Juan Castillo	.10	.05	.01
☐	21T	Rick Cerone	.06	.03	.00
☐	22T	Ron Cey	.10	.05	.01
☐	23T	John Christensen	.06	.03	.00
☐	24T	Dave Cone	.25	.12	.02
☐	25T	Chuck Crim	.15	.07	.01
☐	26T	Storm Davis	.10	.05	.01
☐	27T	Andre Dawson	.40	.20	.04
☐	28T	Rick Dempsey	.10	.05	.01
☐	29T	Doug Drabek	.10	.05	.01
☐	30T	Mike Dunne	.50	.25	.05
☐	31T	Dennis Eckersley	.10	.05	.01
☐	32T	Lee Elia MG	.06	.03	.00
☐	33T	Brian Fisher	.10	.05	.01
☐	34T	Terry Francona	.06	.03	.00
☐	35T	Willie Fraser	.15	.07	.01
☐	36T	Billy Gardner MG	.06	.03	.00
☐	37T	Ken Gerhart	.25	.12	.02
☐	38T	Danny Gladden	.10	.05	.01
☐	39T	Jim Gott	.10	.05	.01
☐	40T	Cecilio Guante	.06	.03	.00
☐	41T	Albert Hall	.10	.05	.01
☐	42T	Terry Harper	.06	.03	.00
☐	43T	Mickey Hatcher	.06	.03	.00
☐	44T	Brad Havens	.06	.03	.00
☐	45T	Neal Heaton	.10	.05	.01
☐	46T	Mike Henneman	.30	.15	.03
☐	47T	Donnie Hill	.06	.03	.00
☐	48T	Guy Hoffman	.06	.03	.00
☐	49T	Brian Holton	.10	.05	.01
☐	50T	Charles Hudson	.06	.03	.00
☐	51T	Danny Jackson	.10	.05	.01

☐	52T	Reggie Jackson	.40	.20	.04
☐	53T	Chris James	.60	.30	.06
☐	54T	Dion James	.15	.07	.01
☐	55T	Stan Jefferson	.25	.12	.02
☐	56T	Joe Johnson	.10	.05	.01
☐	57T	Terry Kennedy	.10	.05	.01
☐	58T	Mike Kingery	.10	.05	.01
☐	59T	Ray Knight	.10	.05	.01
☐	60T	Gene Larkin	.25	.12	.02
☐	61T	Mike LaValliere	.10	.05	.01
☐	62T	Jack Lazorko	.06	.03	.00
☐	63T	Terry Leach	.15	.07	.01
☐	64T	Tim Leary	.06	.03	.00
☐	65T	Jim Lindeman	.35	.17	.03
☐	66T	Steve Lombardozzi	.15	.07	.01
☐	67T	Bill Long	.20	.10	.02
☐	68T	Barry Lyons	.20	.10	.02
☐	69T	Shane Mack	.35	.17	.03
☐	70T	Greg Maddux	.20	.10	.02
☐	71T	Bill Madlock	.10	.05	.01
☐	72T	Joe Magrane	.60	.30	.06
☐	73T	Dave Martinez	.20	.10	.02
☐	74T	Fred McGriff	.45	.22	.04
☐	75T	Mark McLemore	.15	.07	.01
☐	76T	Kevin McReynolds	.30	.15	.03
☐	77T	Dave Meads	.15	.07	.01
☐	78T	Eddie Milner	.10	.05	.01
☐	79T	Greg Minton	.06	.03	.00
☐	80T	John Mitchell	.20	.10	.02
☐	81T	Kevin Mitchell	.15	.07	.01
☐	82T	Charlie Moore	.06	.03	.00
☐	83T	Jeff Musselman	.30	.15	.03
☐	84T	Gene Nelson	.06	.03	.00
☐	85T	Graig Nettles	.15	.07	.01
☐	86T	Al Newman	.06	.03	.00
☐	87T	Reid Nichols	.06	.03	.00
☐	88T	Tom Niedenfuer	.06	.03	.00
☐	89T	Joe Niekro	.10	.05	.01
☐	90T	Tom Nieto	.06	.03	.00
☐	91T	Matt Nokes	2.00	1.00	.20
☐	92T	Dickie Noles	.06	.03	.00
☐	93T	Pat Pacillo	.20	.10	.02
☐	94T	Lance Parrish	.15	.07	.01
☐	95T	Tony Pena	.15	.07	.01
☐	96T	Luis Polonia	.30	.15	.03
☐	97T	Randy Ready	.10	.05	.01
☐	98T	Jeff Reardon	.15	.07	.01
☐	99T	Gary Redus	.10	.05	.01
☐	100T	Jeff Reed	.06	.03	.00
☐	101T	Rick Rhoden	.10	.05	.01
☐	102T	Cal Ripken Sr. MG	.06	.03	.00
☐	103T	Wally Ritchie	.20	.10	.02
☐	104T	Jeff Robinson	.30	.15	.03
		(Tigers pitcher)			
☐	105T	Gary Roenicke	.06	.03	.00
☐	106T	Jerry Royster	.06	.03	.00
☐	107T	Mark Salas	.06	.03	.00
☐	108T	Luis Salazar	.06	.03	.00
☐	109T	Benny Santiago	1.50	.75	.15
☐	110T	Dave Schmidt	.10	.05	.01
☐	111T	Kevin Seitzer	2.50	1.25	.25
☐	112T	John Shelby	.06	.03	.00
☐	113T	Steve Shields	.15	.07	.01
☐	114T	John Smiley	.25	.12	.02
☐	115T	Chris Speier	.06	.03	.00
☐	116T	Mike Stanley	.35	.17	.03
☐	117T	Terry Steinbach	.50	.25	.05
☐	118T	Les Straker	.20	.10	.02
☐	119T	Jim Sundberg	.10	.05	.01
☐	120T	Danny Tartabull	.35	.17	.03
☐	121T	Tom Trebelhorn MG	.06	.03	.00
☐	122T	Dave Valle	.06	.03	.00
☐	123T	Ed VandeBerg	.06	.03	.00
☐	124T	Andy Van Slyke	.15	.07	.01
☐	125T	Gary Ward	.10	.05	.01
☐	126T	Alan Wiggins	.10	.05	.01
☐	127T	Bill Wilkinson	.15	.07	.01
☐	128T	Frank Williams	.06	.03	.00
☐	129T	Matt Williams	.40	.20	.04
☐	130T	Jim Winn	.06	.03	.00
☐	131T	Matt Young	.06	.03	.00
☐	132T	Checklist	.10	.01	.00

1988 Topps

This 792-card set features backs are printed in orange and black on white card stock. The manager cards contain a checklist of the respective team's players on the back. Subsets in the set include

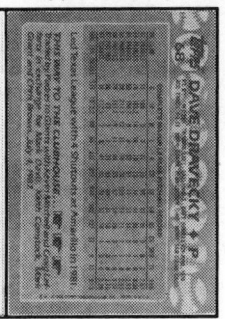

Record Breakers (1-7), Turn Back the Clock (661-665), and All-Star selections (386-407). The Team Leader cards typically show two players together inside a white cloud.

			MINT	EXC	G-VG
		COMPLETE SET (792)	22.00	11.00	2.20
		COMMON PLAYER (1-792)	.03	.01	.00
☐	1	Vince Coleman RB	.25	.06	.01
☐	2	Don Mattingly RB	.45	.22	.04
		Six Grand Slams			
☐	3	Mark McGwire RB	.40	.20	.04
☐	4	Eddie Murray RB	.15	.07	.01
		Switch Home Runs, Two Straight Games			
☐	5	Phil/Joe Niekro RB	.08	.04	.01
		Brothers Win Record			
☐	6	Nolan Ryan RB	.15	.07	.01
		11th Season of 200 K's			
☐	7	Benito Santiago RB	.20	.10	.02
☐	8	Kevin Elster	.20	.10	.02
☐	9	Andy Hawkins	.03	.01	.00
☐	10	Ryne Sandberg	.20	.10	.02
☐	11	Mike Young	.06	.03	.00
☐	12	Bill Schroeder	.03	.01	.00
☐	13	Andres Thomas	.03	.01	.00
☐	14	Sparky Anderson MG	.06	.03	.00
		(checklist back)			
☐	15	Chili Davis	.06	.03	.00
☐	16	Kirk McCaskill	.06	.03	.00
☐	17	Ron Oester	.03	.01	.00
☐	18	Al Leiter ERR	.50	.25	.05
☐	19	Mark Davidson	.15	.07	.01
☐	20	Kevin Gross	.03	.01	.00
☐	21	Red Sox TL	.12	.06	.01
		Wade Boggs and Spike Owen			
☐	22	Greg Swindell	.08	.04	.01
☐	23	Ken Landreaux	.03	.01	.00
☐	24	Jim Deshaies	.06	.03	.00
☐	25	Andres Galarraga	.12	.06	.01
☐	26	Mitch Williams	.03	.01	.00
☐	27	R.J. Reynolds	.06	.03	.00
☐	28	Jose Nunez	.12	.06	.01
☐	29	Argenis Salazar	.03	.01	.00
☐	30	Sid Fernandez	.10	.05	.01
☐	31	Bruce Bochy	.03	.01	.00
☐	32	Mike Morgan	.03	.01	.00
☐	33	Rob Deer	.08	.04	.01
☐	34	Ricky Horton	.03	.01	.00
☐	35	Harold Baines	.10	.05	.01
☐	36	Jamie Moyer	.03	.01	.00
☐	37	Ed Romero	.03	.01	.00
☐	38	Jeff Calhoun	.03	.01	.00
☐	39	Gerald Perry	.06	.03	.00
☐	40	Orel Hershiser	.12	.06	.01
☐	41	Bob Melvin	.03	.01	.00
☐	42	Bill Landrum	.12	.06	.01
☐	43	Dick Schofield	.03	.01	.00
☐	44	Lou Piniella MG	.06	.03	.00
		(checklist back)			
☐	45	Kent Hrbek	.12	.06	.01
☐	46	Darnell Coles	.03	.01	.00
☐	47	Joaquin Andujar	.08	.04	.01
☐	48	Alan Ashby	.03	.01	.00
☐	49	Dave Clark	.15	.07	.01
☐	50	Hubie Brooks	.06	.03	.00
☐	51	Orioles TL	.15	.07	.01
		Eddie Murray and Cal Ripken			
☐	52	Don Robinson	.03	.01	.00
☐	53	Curt Wilkerson	.03	.01	.00

☐ 54	Jim Clancy	.03	.01	.00
☐ 55	Phil Bradley	.10	.05	.01
☐ 56	Ed Hearn	.03	.01	.00
☐ 57	Tim Crews	.15	.07	.01
☐ 58	Dave Magadan	.15	.07	.01
☐ 59	Danny Cox	.08	.04	.01
☐ 60	Rickey Henderson	.25	.12	.02
☐ 61	Mark Knudson	.15	.07	.01
☐ 62	Jeff Hamilton	.06	.03	.00
☐ 63	Jimmy Jones	.10	.05	.01
☐ 64	Ken Caminiti	.35	.17	.03
☐ 65	Leon Durham	.08	.04	.01
☐ 66	Shane Rawley	.06	.03	.00
☐ 67	Ken Oberkfell	.03	.01	.00
☐ 68	Dave Dravecky	.06	.03	.00
☐ 69	Mike Hart	.12	.06	.01
☐ 70	Roger Clemens	.50	.25	.05
☐ 71	Gary Pettis	.06	.03	.00
☐ 72	Dennis Eckersley	.06	.03	.00
☐ 73	Randy Bush	.03	.01	.00
☐ 74	Tom Lasorda MG	.08	.04	.01
	(checklist back)			
☐ 75	Joe Carter	.12	.06	.01
☐ 76	Denny Martinez	.06	.03	.00
☐ 77	Tom O'Malley	.03	.01	.00
☐ 78	Dan Petry	.06	.03	.00
☐ 79	Ernie Whitt	.03	.01	.00
☐ 80	Mark Langston	.10	.05	.01
☐ 81	Reds TL	.06	.03	.00
	Ron Robinson			
	and John Franco			
☐ 82	Darrel Akerfelds	.15	.07	.01
☐ 83	Jose Oquendo	.03	.01	.00
☐ 84	Cecilio Guante	.03	.01	.00
☐ 85	Howard Johnson	.10	.05	.01
☐ 86	Ron Karkovice	.03	.01	.00
☐ 87	Mike Mason	.03	.01	.00
☐ 88	Earnie Riles	.03	.01	.00
☐ 89	Gary Thurman	.35	.17	.03
☐ 90	Dale Murphy	.30	.15	.03
☐ 91	Joey Cora	.15	.07	.01
☐ 92	Len Matuszek	.03	.01	.00
☐ 93	Bob Sebra	.03	.01	.00
☐ 94	Chuck Jackson	.15	.07	.01
☐ 95	Lance Parrish	.10	.05	.01
☐ 96	Todd Benzinger	.35	.17	.03
☐ 97	Scott Garrelts	.06	.03	.00
☐ 98	Rene Gonzales	.15	.07	.01
☐ 99	Chuck Finley	.03	.01	.00
☐ 100	Jack Clark	.20	.10	.02
☐ 101	Allan Anderson	.03	.01	.00
☐ 102	Barry Larkin	.15	.07	.01
☐ 103	Curt Young	.06	.03	.00
☐ 104	Dick Williams MG	.06	.03	.00
	(checklist back)			
☐ 105	Jesse Orosco	.06	.03	.00
☐ 106	Jim Walewander	.20	.10	.02
☐ 107	Scott Bailes	.03	.01	.00
☐ 108	Steve Lyons	.03	.01	.00
☐ 109	Joel Skinner	.03	.01	.00
☐ 110	Teddy Higuera	.12	.06	.01
☐ 111	Expos TL	.06	.03	.00
	Hubie Brooks and			
	Vance Law			
☐ 112	Les Lancaster	.15	.07	.01
☐ 113	Kelly Gruber	.03	.01	.00
☐ 114	Jeff Russell	.03	.01	.00
☐ 115	Johnny Ray	.08	.04	.01
☐ 116	Jerry Don Gleaton	.03	.01	.00
☐ 117	James Steels	.12	.06	.01
☐ 118	Bob Welch	.06	.03	.00
☐ 119	Robbie Wine	.20	.10	.02
☐ 120	Kirby Puckett	.30	.15	.03
☐ 121	Checklist 1-132	.06	.01	.00
☐ 122	Tony Bernazard	.03	.01	.00
☐ 123	Tom Candiotti	.03	.01	.00
☐ 124	Ray Knight	.06	.03	.00
☐ 125	Bruce Hurst	.08	.04	.01
☐ 126	Steve Jeltz	.03	.01	.00
☐ 127	Jim Gott	.03	.01	.00
☐ 128	Johnny Grubb	.03	.01	.00
☐ 129	Greg Minton	.03	.01	.00
☐ 130	Buddy Bell	.08	.04	.01
☐ 131	Don Schulze	.03	.01	.00
☐ 132	Donnie Hill	.03	.01	.00
☐ 133	Greg Mathews	.06	.03	.00
☐ 134	Chuck Tanner MG	.06	.03	.00
	(checklist back)			
☐ 135	Dennis Rasmussen	.06	.03	.00
☐ 136	Brian Dayett	.03	.01	.00
☐ 137	Chris Bosio	.06	.03	.00
☐ 138	Mitch Webster	.06	.03	.00
☐ 139	Jerry Browne	.08	.04	.01
☐ 140	Jesse Barfield	.15	.07	.01
☐ 141	Royals TL	.15	.07	.01
	George Brett and			
	Bret Saberhagen			
☐ 142	Andy Van Slyke	.08	.04	.01
☐ 143	Mickey Tettleton	.03	.01	.00
☐ 144	Don Gordon	.10	.05	.01
☐ 145	Bill Madlock	.08	.04	.01
☐ 146	Donnell Nixon	.15	.07	.01
☐ 147	Bill Buckner	.08	.04	.01
☐ 148	Carmelo Martinez	.03	.01	.00
☐ 149	Ken Howell	.03	.01	.00
☐ 150	Eric Davis	.75	.35	.07
☐ 151	Bob Knepper	.06	.03	.00
☐ 152	Jody Reed	.25	.12	.02
☐ 153	John Habyan	.06	.03	.00
☐ 154	Jeff Stone	.06	.03	.00
☐ 155	Bruce Sutter	.10	.05	.01
☐ 156	Gary Matthews	.06	.03	.00
☐ 157	Atlee Hammaker	.06	.03	.00
☐ 158	Tim Hulett	.03	.01	.00
☐ 159	Brad Arnsberg	.15	.07	.01
☐ 160	Willie McGee	.15	.07	.01
☐ 161	Bryn Smith	.03	.01	.00
☐ 162	Mark McLemore	.08	.04	.01
☐ 163	Dale Mohorcic	.06	.03	.00
☐ 164	Dave Johnson MG	.06	.03	.00
	(checklist back)			
☐ 165	Robin Yount	.20	.10	.02
☐ 166	Rick Rodriquez	.15	.07	.01
☐ 167	Rance Mulliniks	.03	.01	.00
☐ 168	Barry Jones	.03	.01	.00
☐ 169	Ross Jones	.15	.07	.01
☐ 170	Rich Gossage	.10	.05	.01
☐ 171	Cubs TL	.06	.03	.00
	Shawon Dunston			
	and Manny Trillo			
☐ 172	Lloyd McClendon	.15	.07	.01
☐ 173	Eric Plunk	.06	.03	.00
☐ 174	Phil Garner	.03	.01	.00
☐ 175	Kevin Bass	.08	.04	.01
☐ 176	Jeff Reed	.03	.01	.00
☐ 177	Frank Tanana	.06	.03	.00
☐ 178	Dwayne Henry	.08	.04	.01
☐ 179	Charlie Puleo	.03	.01	.00
☐ 180	Terry Kennedy	.06	.03	.00
☐ 181	Dave Cone	.10	.05	.01
☐ 182	Ken Phelps	.06	.03	.00
☐ 183	Tom Lawless	.03	.01	.00
☐ 184	Ivan Calderon	.10	.05	.01
☐ 185	Rick Rhoden	.06	.03	.00
☐ 186	Rafael Palmeiro	.10	.05	.01
☐ 187	Steve Kiefer	.12	.06	.01
☐ 188	John Russell	.03	.01	.00
☐ 189	Wes Gardner	.15	.07	.01
☐ 190	Candy Maldonado	.08	.04	.01
☐ 191	John Cerutti	.03	.01	.00
☐ 192	Devon White	.20	.10	.02
☐ 193	Brian Fisher	.06	.03	.00
☐ 194	Tom Kelly MG	.06	.03	.00
	(checklist back)			
☐ 195	Dan Quisenberry	.10	.05	.01
☐ 196	Dave Engle	.03	.01	.00
☐ 197	Lance McCullers	.06	.03	.00
☐ 198	Franklin Stubbs	.06	.03	.00
☐ 199	Dave Meads	.12	.06	.01
☐ 200	Wade Boggs	.75	.35	.07
☐ 201	Rangers TL	.10	.05	.01
	Pete Incaviglia and			
	Steve Buechele			
☐ 202	Glenn Hoffman	.03	.01	.00
☐ 203	Fred Toliver	.03	.01	.00
☐ 204	Paul O'Neill	.10	.05	.01
☐ 205	Nelson Liriano	.25	.12	.02
☐ 206	Domingo Ramos	.03	.01	.00
☐ 207	John Mitchell	.20	.10	.02
☐ 208	Steve Lake	.03	.01	.00
☐ 209	Richard Dotson	.06	.03	.00
☐ 210	Willie Randolph	.08	.04	.01
☐ 211	Frank DiPino	.03	.01	.00
☐ 212	Greg Brock	.06	.03	.00
☐ 213	Albert Hall	.03	.01	.00
☐ 214	Dave Schmidt	.06	.03	.00
☐ 215	Von Hayes	.08	.04	.01
☐ 216	Jerry Reuss	.06	.03	.00
☐ 217	Harry Spilman	.03	.01	.00
☐ 218	Dan Schatzeder	.03	.01	.00
☐ 219	Mike Stanley	.15	.07	.01
☐ 220	Tom Henke	.08	.04	.01
☐ 221	Rafael Belliard	.03	.01	.00
☐ 222	Steve Farr	.03	.01	.00
☐ 223	Stan Jefferson	.15	.07	.01
☐ 224	Tom Trebelhorn MG	.06	.03	.00
	(checklist back)			
☐ 225	Mike Scioscia	.03	.01	.00
☐ 226	Dave Lopes	.06	.03	.00
☐ 227	Ed Correa	.06	.03	.00

COMPLETE BASEBALL CARD SETS

REGULAR ISSUES

1988 Topps (792)	$23.00
1987 Topps (792)	26.00
1986 Topps (792)	28.00
1985 Topps (792)	85.00
1984 Topps (792)	80.00
1988 Fleer (660)	35.00
1987 Fleer (660)	40.00
1986 Fleer (660)	38.00
1988 Donruss (660)	30.00
1987 Donruss (660)	38.00
1986 Donruss (660)	70.00
1988 Score (660)	21.00
1988 Sportflics (225)	32.00
1987 Sportflics (200)	30.00

TRADED OR UPDATE ISSUES

1987 Topps (132)	12.00
1986 Topps (132)	16.00
1985 Topps (132)	14.00
1982 Topps (132)	22.00
1987 Fleer (132)	12.00
1986 Fleer (132)	17.00
1985 Fleer (132)	14.00
1987 Topps Tiffany (132)	40.00
1987 Fleer Tin (132)	25.00

ROOKIE SETS

1987 Donruss (56)	15.00
1986 Donruss (56)	22.00
1987 Sportflics-Pt.1 (25)	10.00
1987 Sportflics-Pt.2 (25)	8.00
1986 Sportflics (50)	10.00

GLOSSY ALL-STARS

1988 Topps (22)	5.00
1987 Topps (22)	5.00
1986 Topps (22)	5.00
1985 Topps (22)	6.00
1984 Topps (22)	6.00

★ ★ ★ ★ ★ ★ ★ ★ ★ ★ ★ ★

UNOPENED WAX BOXES

1987 DONRUSS (36 packs, 540 cards)
$35.00 per box

1986 TOPPS (36 packs, 540 cards)
$20.00 per box

1987 DONRUSS ALL-STARS & POP-UPS
(36 packs, 36 Pop-Ups, 108 All-Stars)
$15.00 per box

1986 DONRUSS/LEAF
(36 packs, 432 cards)
$15.00 per box

★ ★ ★ ★ ★ ★ ★ ★ ★ ★ ★ ★

OTHER ISSUES

1988 O.P.C. (396)	$ 15.00
1987 Topps Tiffany (792)	100.00
1987 Donruss Opening Day (272)	24.00
1987 Donruss/Leaf (264)	25.00
1987 Donruss All-Stars (60)	9.00
1987 Donruss Pop-Ups (20)	6.00
1987 Donruss Diamond Kings (5x7) (28)	9.00
1987 Sportflics Team Preview (26)	7.00
1987 Sportflics Rookie Packs (5 cards/pk)	
Pack 1	5.00
Pack 2	5.00
1987 Sportflics Superstar Sheets (5x7)(4)	20.00
1987 Topps Minis (77)	8.00
1987 Fleer Minis (120)	8.00
1987 Donruss Highlights (56)	12.00
1986 Donruss Highlights (56)	5.00
1986 Topps Minis (66)	8.00
1986 Fleer Minis (120)	10.00
1986 Topps Supers (60)	10.00
1986 Donruss All-Stars (60)	8.00
1986 Donruss Pop-Ups (18)	5.00
1986 Donruss Diamond Kings (5x7) (28)	9.00
1986 Donruss/Leaf (264)	14.00
1986 Sportflics Decade Greats	18.00
1985 Topps Pete Rose (120)	16.00
1985 Topps Home Run Kings (33)	5.00
1985 Donruss Diamond Kings (5x7) (28)	8.00
1985 Donruss Highlights (56)	28.00
1984 O.P.C. (396)	35.00
1982 Topps Stickers (260 + Album)	10.00
1982 Fleer Stamps (Unopened Box of 600)	10.00
1981 Topps Stickers (262 + Album)	10.00
1980 Topps Supers (60)	8.00

1987 SPORTFLICS 4½″ MAGIC MOTION DISCS

Series of 18. Pete Rose, Jose Canseco, Bo Jackson, Mike Schmidt, Gary Carter, Ryne Sandberg, Cory Snyder, Mike Scott, Dale Murphy, Fernando Valenzuela, Tony Gwynn, George Brett, Eric Davis, Cal Ripken Jr., Keith Hernandez, Kirby Puckett, Rickey Henderson, Tim Raines .... $6.00 each or all 18 for $ 90.00

1987 SPORTFLICS 4″ MAGIC MOTION ROOKIE DISCS

Series of 7. Casey Candaele, Benito Santiago, Mark McGwire, Joe Magrane, Kevin Seitzer, Devon White, Dave Magadan .... All 7 for $ 20.00

OTHER 4½″ SPORTFLICS 4½″ MAGIC MOTION DISCS

Mickey Mantle or Roger Clemens .... $ 5.00 each

All prices include postage & handling.
In mail-order since 1979.
Satisfaction guaranteed.

BILL DODGE
P.O. BOX 40154
BAY VILLAGE, OH 44140
Phone: (216) 835-4146

☐ 228 Wallace Johnson	.03	.01	.00
☐ 229 Jeff Musselman	.10	.05	.01
☐ 230 Pat Tabler	.08	.04	.01
☐ 231 Pirates TL	.10	.05	.01
Barry Bonds and			
Bobby Bonilla			
☐ 232 Bob James	.03	.01	.00
☐ 233 Rafael Santana	.03	.01	.00
☐ 234 Ken Dayley	.03	.01	.00
☐ 235 Gary Ward	.06	.03	.00
☐ 236 Ted Power	.03	.01	.00
☐ 237 Mike Heath	.03	.01	.00
☐ 238 Luis Polonia	.25	.12	.02
☐ 239 Roy Smalley	.03	.01	.00
☐ 240 Lee Smith	.08	.04	.01
☐ 241 Damaso Garcia	.03	.01	.00
☐ 242 Tom Niedenfuer	.03	.01	.00
☐ 243 Mark Ryal	.12	.06	.01
☐ 244 Jeff D. Robinson	.06	.03	.00
(Pirates pitcher)			
☐ 245 Rich Gedman	.06	.03	.00
☐ 246 Mike Campbell	.20	.10	.02
☐ 247 Thad Bosley	.03	.01	.00
☐ 248 Storm Davis	.06	.03	.00
☐ 249 Mike Marshall	.10	.05	.01
☐ 250 Nolan Ryan	.25	.12	.02
☐ 251 Tom Foley	.03	.01	.00
☐ 252 Bob Brower	.10	.05	.01
☐ 253 Checklist 133-264	.06	.01	.00
☐ 254 Lee Elia MG	.06	.03	.00
(checklist back)			
☐ 255 Mookie Wilson	.06	.03	.00
☐ 256 Ken Schrom	.03	.01	.00
☐ 257 Jerry Royster	.03	.01	.00
☐ 258 Ed Nunez	.03	.01	.00
☐ 259 Ron Kittle	.08	.04	.01
☐ 260 Vince Coleman	.25	.12	.02
☐ 261 Giants TL	.06	.03	.00
(five players)			
☐ 262 Drew Hall	.10	.05	.01
☐ 263 Glenn Braggs	.10	.05	.01
☐ 264 Les Straker	.15	.07	.01
☐ 265 Bo Diaz	.06	.03	.00
☐ 266 Paul Assenmacher	.03	.01	.00
☐ 267 Billy Bean	.15	.07	.01
☐ 268 Bruce Ruffin	.03	.01	.00
☐ 269 Ellis Burks	1.00	.50	.10
☐ 270 Mike Witt	.10	.05	.01
☐ 271 Ken Gerhart	.10	.05	.01
☐ 272 Steve Ontiveros	.03	.01	.00
☐ 273 Garth Iorg	.03	.01	.00
☐ 274 Junior Ortiz	.03	.01	.00
☐ 275 Kevin Seitzer	1.25	.60	.12
☐ 276 Luis Salazar	.03	.01	.00
☐ 277 Alejandro Pena	.06	.03	.00
☐ 278 Jose Cruz	.08	.04	.01
☐ 279 Randy St.Claire	.03	.01	.00
☐ 280 Pete Incaviglia	.25	.12	.02
☐ 281 Jerry Hairston	.03	.01	.00
☐ 282 Pat Perry	.03	.01	.00
☐ 283 Phil Lombardi	.10	.05	.01
☐ 284 Larry Bowa MG	.08	.04	.01
(checklist back)			
☐ 285 Jim Presley	.10	.05	.01
☐ 286 Chuck Crim	.12	.06	.01
☐ 287 Manny Trillo	.03	.01	.00
☐ 288 Pat Pacillo	.06	.03	.00
☐ 289 Dave Bergman	.03	.01	.00
☐ 290 Tony Fernandez	.12	.06	.01
☐ 291 Astros TL	.08	.04	.01
Billy Hatcher			
and Kevin Bass			
☐ 292 Carney Lansford	.08	.04	.01
☐ 293 Doug Jones	.12	.06	.01
☐ 294 Al Pedrique	.12	.06	.01
☐ 295 Bert Blyleven	.08	.04	.01
☐ 296 Floyd Rayford	.03	.01	.00
☐ 297 Zane Smith	.06	.03	.00
☐ 298 Milt Thompson	.06	.03	.00
☐ 299 Steve Crawford	.03	.01	.00
☐ 300 Don Mattingly	1.25	.60	.12
☐ 301 Bud Black	.03	.01	.00
☐ 302 Jose Uribe	.03	.01	.00
☐ 303 Eric Show	.03	.01	.00
☐ 304 George Hendrick	.06	.03	.00
☐ 305 Steve Sax	.10	.05	.01
☐ 306 Billy Hatcher	.08	.04	.01
☐ 307 Mike Trujillo	.03	.01	.00
☐ 308 Lee Mazzilli	.03	.01	.00
☐ 309 Bill Long	.15	.07	.01
☐ 310 Tom Herr	.06	.03	.00
☐ 311 Scott Sanderson	.03	.01	.00
☐ 312 Joey Meyer	.20	.10	.02
☐ 313 Bob McClure	.03	.01	.00
☐ 314 Jimy Williams MG	.06	.03	.00

(checklist back)			
☐ 315 Dave Parker	.15	.07	.01
☐ 316 Jose Rijo	.06	.03	.00
☐ 317 Tom Nieto	.03	.01	.00
☐ 318 Mel Hall	.06	.03	.00
☐ 319 Mike Loynd	.03	.01	.00
☐ 320 Alan Trammell	.20	.10	.02
☐ 321 White Sox TL	.10	.05	.01
Harold Baines and			
Carlton Fisk			
☐ 322 Vicente Palacios	.20	.10	.02
☐ 323 Rick Leach	.03	.01	.00
☐ 324 Danny Jackson	.08	.04	.01
☐ 325 Glenn Hubbard	.03	.01	.00
☐ 326 Al Nipper	.03	.01	.00
☐ 327 Larry Sheets	.10	.05	.01
☐ 328 Greg Cadaret	.15	.07	.01
☐ 329 Chris Speier	.03	.01	.00
☐ 330 Eddie Whitson	.03	.01	.00
☐ 331 Brian Downing	.06	.03	.00
☐ 332 Jerry Reed	.03	.01	.00
☐ 333 Wally Backman	.06	.03	.00
☐ 334 Dave LaPoint	.03	.01	.00
☐ 335 Claudell Washington	.06	.03	.00
☐ 336 Ed Lynch	.03	.01	.00
☐ 337 Jim Gantner	.03	.01	.00
☐ 338 Brian Holton	.10	.05	.01
☐ 339 Kurt Stillwell	.06	.03	.00
☐ 340 Jack Morris	.15	.07	.01
☐ 341 Carmen Castillo	.03	.01	.00
☐ 342 Larry Andersen	.03	.01	.00
☐ 343 Greg Gagne	.06	.03	.00
☐ 344 Tony LaRussa MG	.06	.03	.00
(checklist back)			
☐ 345 Scott Fletcher	.06	.03	.00
☐ 346 Vance Law	.03	.01	.00
☐ 347 Joe Johnson	.06	.03	.00
☐ 348 Jim Eisenreich	.06	.03	.00
☐ 349 Bob Walk	.03	.01	.00
☐ 350 Will Clark	.40	.20	.04
☐ 351 Cardinals TL	.06	.03	.00
Red Schoendienst			
and Tony Pena			
☐ 352 Billy Ripken	.30	.15	.03
☐ 353 Ed Olwine	.03	.01	.00
☐ 354 Marc Sullivan	.03	.01	.00
☐ 355 Roger McDowell	.08	.04	.01
☐ 356 Luis Aguayo	.03	.01	.00
☐ 357 Floyd Bannister	.06	.03	.00
☐ 358 Rey Quinones	.06	.03	.00
☐ 359 Tim Stoddard	.03	.01	.00
☐ 360 Tony Gwynn	.30	.15	.03
☐ 361 Greg Maddux	.03	.01	.00
☐ 362 Juan Castillo	.10	.05	.01
☐ 363 Willie Fraser	.08	.04	.01
☐ 364 Nick Esasky	.06	.03	.00
☐ 365 Floyd Youmans	.06	.03	.00
☐ 366 Chet Lemon	.06	.03	.00
☐ 367 Tim Leary	.03	.01	.00
☐ 368 Gerald Young	.30	.15	.03
☐ 369 Greg Harris	.03	.01	.00
☐ 370 Jose Canseco	.45	.22	.04
☐ 371 Joe Hesketh	.06	.03	.00
☐ 372 Matt Williams	.35	.17	.03
☐ 373 Checklist 265-396	.06	.01	.00
☐ 374 Doc Edwards MG	.06	.03	.00
(checklist back)			
☐ 375 Tom Brunansky	.10	.05	.01
☐ 376 Bill Wilkinson	.15	.07	.01
☐ 377 Sam Horn	1.00	.50	.10
☐ 378 Todd Frohwirth	.15	.07	.01
☐ 379 Rafael Ramirez	.03	.01	.00
☐ 380 Joe Magrane	.35	.17	.03
☐ 381 Angels TL	.15	.07	.01
Wally Joyner and			
Jack Howell			
☐ 382 Keith Miller	.30	.15	.03
☐ 383 Eric Bell	.08	.04	.01
☐ 384 Neil Allen	.06	.03	.00
☐ 385 Carlton Fisk	.10	.05	.01
☐ 386 Don Mattingly AS	.45	.22	.04
☐ 387 Willie Randolph AS	.06	.03	.00
☐ 388 Wade Boggs AS	.30	.15	.03
☐ 389 Alan Trammell AS	.12	.06	.01
☐ 390 George Bell AS	.12	.06	.01
☐ 391 Kirby Puckett AS	.15	.07	.01
☐ 392 Dave Winfield AS	.15	.07	.01
☐ 393 Matt Nokes AS	.30	.15	.03
☐ 394 Roger Clemens AS	.25	.12	.02
☐ 395 Jimmy Key AS	.08	.04	.01
☐ 396 Tom Henke AS	.06	.03	.00
☐ 397 Jack Clark AS	.12	.06	.01
☐ 398 Juan Samuel AS	.08	.04	.01
☐ 399 Tim Wallach AS	.08	.04	.01
☐ 400 Ozzie Smith AS	.12	.06	.01

☐ 401	Andre Dawson AS	.15	.07	.01
☐ 402	Tony Gwynn AS	.20	.10	.02
☐ 403	Tim Raines AS	.15	.07	.01
☐ 404	Benny Santiago AS	.20	.10	.02
☐ 405	Dwight Gooden AS	.20	.10	.02
☐ 406	Shane Rawley AS	.06	.03	.00
☐ 407	Steve Bedrosian AS	.06	.03	.00
☐ 408	Dion James	.06	.03	.00
☐ 409	Joel McKeon	.06	.03	.00
☐ 410	Tony Pena	.08	.04	.01
☐ 411	Wayne Tolleson	.03	.01	.00
☐ 412	Randy Myers	.08	.04	.01
☐ 413	John Christensen	.03	.01	.00
☐ 414	John McNamara MG (checklist back)	.06	.03	.00
☐ 415	Don Carman	.03	.01	.00
☐ 416	Keith Moreland	.03	.01	.00
☐ 417	Mark Ciardi	.10	.05	.01
☐ 418	Joel Youngblood	.03	.01	.00
☐ 419	Scott McGregor	.06	.03	.00
☐ 420	Wally Joyner	.50	.25	.05
☐ 421	Ed VandeBerg	.03	.01	.00
☐ 422	Dave Concepcion	.08	.04	.01
☐ 423	John Smiley	.20	.10	.02
☐ 424	Dwayne Murphy	.06	.03	.00
☐ 425	Jeff Reardon	.08	.04	.01
☐ 426	Randy Ready	.03	.01	.00
☐ 427	Paul Kilgus	.12	.06	.01
☐ 428	John Shelby	.03	.01	.00
☐ 429	Tigers TL Alan Trammell and Kirk Gibson	.15	.07	.01
☐ 430	Glenn Davis	.12	.06	.01
☐ 431	Casey Candaele	.06	.03	.00
☐ 432	Mike Moore	.03	.01	.00
☐ 433	Bill Pecota	.20	.10	.02
☐ 434	Rick Aguilera	.06	.03	.00
☐ 435	Mike Pagliarulo	.08	.04	.01
☐ 436	Mike Bielecki	.03	.01	.00
☐ 437	Fred Manrique	.15	.07	.01
☐ 438	Rob Ducey	.25	.12	.02
☐ 439	Dave Martinez	.15	.07	.01
☐ 440	Steve Bedrosian	.08	.04	.01
☐ 441	Rick Manning	.03	.01	.00
☐ 442	Tom Bolton	.15	.07	.01
☐ 443	Ken Griffey	.06	.03	.00
☐ 444	Cal Ripken, Sr. MG (checklist back)	.06	.03	.00
☐ 445	Mike Krukow	.06	.03	.00
☐ 446	Doug DeCinces	.06	.03	.00
☐ 447	Jeff Montgomery	.20	.10	.02
☐ 448	Mike Davis	.06	.03	.00
☐ 449	Jeff M. Robinson (Tigers pitcher)	.20	.10	.02
☐ 450	Barry Bonds	.15	.07	.01
☐ 451	Keith Atherton	.03	.01	.00
☐ 452	Willie Wilson	.10	.05	.01
☐ 453	Dennis Powell	.03	.01	.00
☐ 454	Marvell Wynne	.03	.01	.00
☐ 455	Shawn Hillegas	.25	.12	.02
☐ 456	Dave Anderson	.03	.01	.00
☐ 457	Terry Leach	.06	.03	.00
☐ 458	Ron Hassey	.03	.01	.00
☐ 459	Yankees TL Dave Winfield and Willie Randolph	.08	.04	.01
☐ 460	Ozzie Smith	.12	.06	.01
☐ 461	Danny Darwin	.03	.01	.00
☐ 462	Don Slaught	.03	.01	.00
☐ 463	Fred McGriff	.20	.10	.02
☐ 464	Jay Tibbs	.03	.01	.00
☐ 465	Paul Molitor	.12	.06	.01
☐ 466	Jerry Mumphrey	.03	.01	.00
☐ 467	Don Aase	.03	.01	.00
☐ 468	Darren Daulton	.03	.01	.00
☐ 469	Jeff Dedmon	.03	.01	.00
☐ 470	Dwight Evans	.10	.05	.01
☐ 471	Donnie Moore	.03	.01	.00
☐ 472	Robby Thompson	.06	.03	.00
☐ 473	Joe Niekro	.08	.04	.01
☐ 474	Tom Brookens	.03	.01	.00
☐ 475	Pete Rose MG (checklist back)	.30	.15	.03
☐ 476	Dave Stewart	.08	.04	.01
☐ 477	Jamie Quirk	.03	.01	.00
☐ 478	Sid Bream	.06	.03	.00
☐ 479	Brett Butler	.08	.04	.01
☐ 480	Dwight Gooden	.35	.17	.03
☐ 481	Mariano Duncan	.03	.01	.00
☐ 482	Mark Davis	.03	.01	.00
☐ 483	Rod Booker	.15	.07	.01
☐ 484	Pat Clements	.03	.01	.00
☐ 485	Harold Reynolds	.06	.03	.00
☐ 486	Pat Keedy	.10	.05	.01
☐ 487	Jim Pankovits	.03	.01	.00
☐ 488	Andy McGaffigan	.03	.01	.00
☐ 489	Dodgers TL Pedro Guerrero and Fernando Valenzuela	.15	.07	.01
☐ 490	Larry Parrish	.06	.03	.00
☐ 491	B.J. Surhoff	.20	.10	.02
☐ 492	Doyle Alexander	.06	.03	.00
☐ 493	Mike Greenwell	.35	.17	.03
☐ 494	Wally Ritchie	.15	.07	.01
☐ 495	Eddie Murray	.25	.12	.02
☐ 496	Guy Hoffman	.03	.01	.00
☐ 497	Kevin Mitchell	.08	.04	.01
☐ 498	Bob Boone	.06	.03	.00
☐ 499	Eric King	.03	.01	.00
☐ 500	Andre Dawson	.25	.12	.02
☐ 501	Tim Birtsas	.06	.03	.00
☐ 502	Danny Gladden	.06	.03	.00
☐ 503	Junior Noboa	.12	.06	.01
☐ 504	Bob Rodgers MG (checklist back)	.06	.03	.00
☐ 505	Willie Upshaw	.06	.03	.00
☐ 506	John Cangelosi	.03	.01	.00
☐ 507	Mark Gubicza	.06	.03	.00
☐ 508	Tim Teufel	.06	.03	.00
☐ 509	Bill Dawley	.03	.01	.00
☐ 510	Dave Winfield	.25	.12	.02
☐ 511	Joel Davis	.03	.01	.00
☐ 512	Alex Trevino	.03	.01	.00
☐ 513	Tim Flannery	.03	.01	.00
☐ 514	Pat Sheridan	.03	.01	.00
☐ 515	Juan Nieves	.06	.03	.00
☐ 516	Jim Sundberg	.06	.03	.00
☐ 517	Ron Robinson	.03	.01	.00
☐ 518	Greg Gross	.03	.01	.00
☐ 519	Mariners TL Harold Reynolds and Phil Bradley	.06	.03	.00
☐ 520	Dave Smith	.06	.03	.00
☐ 521	Jim Dwyer	.03	.01	.00
☐ 522	Bob Patterson	.15	.07	.01
☐ 523	Gary Roenicke	.03	.01	.00
☐ 524	Gary Lucas	.03	.01	.00
☐ 525	Marty Barrett	.08	.04	.01
☐ 526	Juan Berenguer	.06	.03	.00
☐ 527	Steve Henderson	.03	.01	.00
☐ 528	Checklist 397-528 ERR (455 Steve Carlton)	.06	.03	.00
☐ 529	Tim Burke	.06	.03	.00
☐ 530	Gary Carter	.25	.12	.02
☐ 531	Rich Yett	.03	.01	.00
☐ 532	Mike Kingery	.03	.01	.00
☐ 533	John Farrell	.20	.10	.02
☐ 534	John Wathan MG (checklist back)	.06	.03	.00
☐ 535	Ron Guidry	.10	.05	.01
☐ 536	John Morris	.03	.01	.00
☐ 537	Steve Buechele	.03	.01	.00
☐ 538	Bill Wegman	.03	.01	.00
☐ 539	Mike LaValliere	.03	.01	.00
☐ 540	Bret Saberhagen	.15	.07	.01
☐ 541	Juan Beniquez	.06	.03	.00
☐ 542	Paul Noce	.12	.06	.01
☐ 543	Kent Tekulve	.06	.03	.00
☐ 544	Jim Traber	.08	.04	.01
☐ 545	Don Baylor	.06	.03	.00
☐ 546	John Candelaria	.06	.03	.00
☐ 547	Felix Fermin	.12	.06	.01
☐ 548	Shane Mack	.12	.06	.01
☐ 549	Braves TL Albert Hall, Dale Murphy, Ken Griffey, and Dion James	.08	.04	.01
☐ 550	Pedro Guerrero	.15	.07	.01
☐ 551	Terry Steinbach	.25	.12	.02
☐ 552	Mark Thurmond	.06	.03	.00
☐ 553	Tracy Jones	.10	.05	.01
☐ 554	Mike Smithson	.03	.01	.00
☐ 555	Brook Jacoby	.10	.05	.01
☐ 556	Stan Clarke	.10	.05	.01
☐ 557	Craig Reynolds	.03	.01	.00
☐ 558	Bob Ojeda	.06	.03	.00
☐ 559	Ken Williams	.35	.17	.03
☐ 560	Tim Wallach	.08	.04	.01
☐ 561	Rick Cerone	.03	.01	.00
☐ 562	Jim Lindeman	.10	.05	.01
☐ 563	Jose Guzman	.03	.01	.00
☐ 564	Frank Lucchesi MG (checklist back)	.06	.03	.00
☐ 565	Lloyd Moseby	.10	.05	.01
☐ 566	Charlie O'Brien	.12	.06	.01
☐ 567	Mike Diaz	.03	.01	.00
☐ 568	Chris Brown	.10	.05	.01
☐ 569	Charlie Leibrandt	.06	.03	.00
☐ 570	Jeffrey Leonard	.08	.04	.01

☐ 571	Mark Williamson	.15	.07	.01
☐ 572	Chris James	.25	.12	.02
☐ 573	Bob Stanley	.06	.03	.00
☐ 574	Graig Nettles	.10	.05	.01
☐ 575	Don Sutton	.12	.06	.01
☐ 576	Tommy Hinzo	.15	.07	.01
☐ 577	Tom Browning	.06	.03	.00
☐ 578	Gary Gaetti	.12	.06	.01
☐ 579	Mets TL	.15	.07	.01
	Gary Carter and			
	Kevin McReynolds			
☐ 580	Mark McGwire	1.00	.50	.10
☐ 581	Tito Landrum	.03	.01	.00
☐ 582	Mike Henneman	.20	.10	.02
☐ 583	Dave Valle	.08	.04	.01
☐ 584	Steve Trout	.03	.01	.00
☐ 585	Ozzie Guillen	.06	.03	.00
☐ 586	Bob Forsch	.03	.01	.00
☐ 587	Terry Puhl	.03	.01	.00
☐ 588	Jeff Parrett	.15	.07	.01
☐ 589	Geno Petralli	.03	.01	.00
☐ 590	George Bell	.20	.10	.02
☐ 591	Doug Drabek	.06	.03	.00
☐ 592	Dale Sveum	.06	.03	.00
☐ 593	Bob Tewksbury	.03	.01	.00
☐ 594	Bobby Valentine MG	.06	.03	.00
	(checklist back)			
☐ 595	Frank White	.06	.03	.00
☐ 596	John Kruk	.20	.10	.02
☐ 597	Gene Garber	.03	.01	.00
☐ 598	Lee Lacy	.03	.01	.00
☐ 599	Calvin Schiraldi	.06	.03	.00
☐ 600	Mike Schmidt	.30	.15	.03
☐ 601	Jack Lazorko	.03	.01	.00
☐ 602	Mike Aldrete	.10	.05	.01
☐ 603	Rob Murphy	.06	.03	.00
☐ 604	Chris Bando	.03	.01	.00
☐ 605	Kirk Gibson	.15	.07	.01
☐ 606	Moose Haas	.03	.01	.00
☐ 607	Mickey Hatcher	.03	.01	.00
☐ 608	Charlie Kerfeld	.03	.01	.00
☐ 609	Twins TL	.12	.06	.01
	Gary Gaetti and			
	Kent Hrbek			
☐ 610	Keith Hernandez	.15	.07	.01
☐ 611	Tommy John	.10	.05	.01
☐ 612	Curt Ford	.06	.03	.00
☐ 613	Bobby Thigpen	.03	.01	.00
☐ 614	Herm Winningham	.03	.01	.00
☐ 615	Jody Davis	.08	.04	.01
☐ 616	Jay Aldrich	.12	.06	.01
☐ 617	Oddibe McDowell	.10	.05	.01
☐ 618	Cecil Fielder	.06	.03	.00
☐ 619	Mike Dunne	.25	.12	.02
☐ 620	Cory Snyder	.25	.12	.02
☐ 621	Gene Nelson	.03	.01	.00
☐ 622	Kal Daniels	.30	.15	.03
☐ 623	Mike Flanagan	.06	.03	.00
☐ 624	Jim Leyland MG	.06	.03	.00
	(checklist back)			
☐ 625	Frank Viola	.10	.05	.01
☐ 626	Glenn Wilson	.08	.04	.01
☐ 627	Joe Boever	.15	.07	.01
☐ 628	Dave Henderson	.03	.01	.00
☐ 629	Kelly Downs	.06	.03	.00
☐ 630	Darrell Evans	.08	.04	.01
☐ 631	Jack Howell	.06	.03	.00
☐ 632	Steve Shields	.06	.03	.00
☐ 633	Barry Lyons	.20	.10	.02
☐ 634	Jose DeLeon	.03	.01	.00
☐ 635	Terry Pendleton	.06	.03	.00
☐ 636	Charles Hudson	.03	.01	.00
☐ 637	Jay Bell	.30	.15	.03
☐ 638	Steve Balboni	.03	.01	.00
☐ 639	Brewers TL	.06	.03	.00
	Glenn Braggs			
	and Tony Muser CO			
☐ 640	Garry Templeton	.06	.03	.00
☐ 641	Rick Honeycutt	.03	.01	.00
☐ 642	Bob Dernier	.03	.01	.00
☐ 643	Rocky Childress	.10	.05	.01
☐ 644	Terry McGriff	.10	.05	.01
☐ 645	Matt Nokes	1.25	.60	.12
☐ 646	Checklist 529-660	.06	.01	.00
☐ 647	Pascual Perez	.03	.01	.00
☐ 648	Al Newman	.03	.01	.00
☐ 649	DeWayne Buice	.20	.10	.02
☐ 650	Cal Ripken	.20	.10	.02
☐ 651	Mike Jackson	.15	.07	.01
☐ 652	Bruce Benedict	.03	.01	.00
☐ 653	Jeff Sellers	.03	.01	.00
☐ 654	Roger Craig MG	.06	.03	.00
	(checklist back)			
☐ 655	Len Dykstra	.08	.04	.01
☐ 656	Lee Guetterman	.06	.03	.00

☐ 657	Gary Redus	.06	.03	.00
☐ 658	Tim Conroy	.03	.01	.00
☐ 659	Bobby Meacham	.03	.01	.00
☐ 660	Rick Reuschel	.06	.03	.00
☐ 661	Turn Back Clock 1983	.15	.07	.01
	Nolan Ryan			
☐ 662	Turn Back Clock 1978	.10	.05	.01
	Jim Rice			
☐ 663	Turn Back Clock 1973	.06	.03	.00
	Ron Blomberg			
☐ 664	Turn Back Clock 1968	.10	.05	.01
	Bob Gibson			
☐ 665	Turn Back Clock 1963	.15	.07	.01
	Stan Musial			
☐ 666	Mario Soto	.06	.03	.00
☐ 667	Luis Quinones	.03	.01	.00
☐ 668	Walt Terrell	.03	.01	.00
☐ 669	Phillies TL	.06	.03	.00
	Lance Parrish			
	and Mike Ryan CO			
☐ 670	Dan Plesac	.06	.03	.00
☐ 671	Tim Laudner	.03	.01	.00
☐ 672	John Davis	.20	.10	.02
☐ 673	Tony Phillips	.03	.01	.00
☐ 674	Mike Fitzgerald	.03	.01	.00
☐ 675	Jim Rice	.20	.10	.02
☐ 676	Ken Dixon	.03	.01	.00
☐ 677	Eddie Milner	.03	.01	.00
☐ 678	Jim Acker	.03	.01	.00
☐ 679	Darrell Miller	.03	.01	.00
☐ 680	Charlie Hough	.06	.03	.00
☐ 681	Bobby Bonilla	.06	.03	.00
☐ 682	Jimmy Key	.08	.04	.01
☐ 683	Julio Franco	.08	.04	.01
☐ 684	Hal Lanier MG	.06	.03	.00
	(checklist back)			
☐ 685	Ron Darling	.12	.06	.01
☐ 686	Terry Francona	.03	.01	.00
☐ 687	Mickey Brantley	.08	.04	.01
☐ 688	Jim Winn	.03	.01	.00
☐ 689	Tom Pagnozzi	.20	.10	.02
☐ 690	Jay Howell	.03	.01	.00
☐ 691	Dan Pasqua	.08	.04	.01
☐ 692	Mike Birkbeck	.03	.01	.00
☐ 693	Benny Santiago	.70	.35	.07
☐ 694	Eric Nolte	.20	.10	.02
☐ 695	Shawon Dunston	.06	.03	.00
☐ 696	Duane Ward	.03	.01	.00
☐ 697	Steve Lombardozzi	.08	.04	.01
☐ 698	Brad Havens	.03	.01	.00
☐ 699	Padres TL	.25	.12	.02
	Benito Santiago			
	and Tony Gwynn			
☐ 700	George Brett	.30	.15	.03
☐ 701	Sammy Stewart	.03	.01	.00
☐ 702	Mike Gallego	.03	.01	.00
☐ 703	Bob Brenly	.06	.03	.00
☐ 704	Dennis Boyd	.06	.03	.00
☐ 705	Juan Samuel	.12	.06	.01
☐ 706	Rick Mahler	.03	.01	.00
☐ 707	Fred Lynn	.12	.06	.01
☐ 708	Gus Polidor	.10	.05	.01
☐ 709	George Frazier	.03	.01	.00
☐ 710	Darryl Strawberry	.30	.15	.03
☐ 711	Bill Gullickson	.06	.03	.00
☐ 712	John Moses	.03	.01	.00
☐ 713	Willie Hernandez	.08	.04	.01
☐ 714	Jim Fregosi MG	.06	.03	.00
	(checklist back)			
☐ 715	Todd Worrell	.12	.06	.01
☐ 716	Lenn Sakata	.03	.01	.00
☐ 717	Jay Baller	.06	.03	.00
☐ 718	Mike Felder	.03	.01	.00
☐ 719	Denny Walling	.03	.01	.00
☐ 720	Tim Raines	.25	.12	.02
☐ 721	Pete O'Brien	.08	.04	.01
☐ 722	Manny Lee	.03	.01	.00
☐ 723	Bob Kipper	.03	.01	.00
☐ 724	Danny Tartabull	.20	.10	.02
☐ 725	Mike Boddicker	.06	.03	.00
☐ 726	Alfredo Griffin	.06	.03	.00
☐ 727	Greg Booker	.03	.01	.00
☐ 728	Andy Allanson	.03	.01	.00
☐ 729	Blue Jays TL	.10	.05	.01
	George Bell and			
	Willie Upshaw			
☐ 730	John Franco	.08	.04	.01
☐ 731	Rick Schu	.03	.01	.00
☐ 732	Dave Palmer	.03	.01	.00
☐ 733	Spike Owen	.03	.01	.00
☐ 734	Craig Lefferts	.03	.01	.00
☐ 735	Kevin McReynolds	.12	.06	.01
☐ 736	Matt Young	.03	.01	.00
☐ 737	Butch Wynegar	.03	.01	.00
☐ 738	Scott Bankhead	.06	.03	.00

☐ 739 Daryl Boston	.03	.01	.00
☐ 740 Rick Sutcliffe	.10	.05	.01
☐ 741 Mike Easler	.06	.03	.00
☐ 742 Mark Clear	.03	.01	.00
☐ 743 Larry Herndon	.03	.01	.00
☐ 744 Whitey Herzog MG	.06	.03	.00
(checklist back)			
☐ 745 Bill Doran	.08	.04	.01
☐ 746 Gene Larkin	.25	.12	.02
☐ 747 Bobby Witt	.06	.03	.00
☐ 748 Reid Nichols	.03	.01	.00
☐ 749 Mark Eichhorn	.06	.03	.00
☐ 750 Bo Jackson	.35	.17	.03
☐ 751 Jim Morrison	.03	.01	.00
☐ 752 Mark Grant	.06	.03	.00
☐ 753 Danny Heep	.03	.01	.00
☐ 754 Mike LaCoss	.03	.01	.00
☐ 755 Ozzie Virgil	.03	.01	.00
☐ 756 Mike Maddux	.03	.01	.00
☐ 757 John Marzano	.25	.12	.02
☐ 758 Eddie Williams	.30	.15	.03
☐ 759 A's TL	.35	.17	.03
Mark McGwire			
and Jose Canseco			
☐ 760 Mike Scott	.15	.07	.01
☐ 761 Tony Armas	.06	.03	.00
☐ 762 Scott Bradley	.06	.03	.00
☐ 763 Doug Sisk	.03	.01	.00
☐ 764 Greg Walker	.08	.04	.01
☐ 765 Neal Heaton	.06	.03	.00
☐ 766 Henry Cotto	.03	.01	.00
☐ 767 Jose Lind	.20	.10	.02
☐ 768 Dickie Noles	.03	.01	.00
☐ 769 Cecil Cooper	.08	.04	.01
☐ 770 Lou Whitaker	.12	.06	.01
☐ 771 Ruben Sierra	.30	.15	.03
☐ 772 Sal Butera	.03	.01	.00
☐ 773 Frank Williams	.03	.01	.00
☐ 774 Gene Mauch MG	.06	.03	.00
(checklist back)			
☐ 775 Dave Stieb	.08	.04	.01
☐ 776 Checklist 661-792	.06	.01	.00
☐ 777 Lonnie Smith	.06	.03	.00
☐ 778A Keith Comstock ERR	1.00	.50	.10
(white "Padres")			
☐ 778B Keith Comstock COR	.25	.12	.02
(blue "Padres")			
☐ 779 Tom Glavine	.20	.10	.02
☐ 780 Fernando Valenzuela	.20	.10	.02
☐ 781 Keith Hughes	.25	.12	.02
☐ 782 Jeff Ballard	.15	.07	.01
☐ 783 Ron Roenicke	.03	.01	.00
☐ 784 Joe Sambito	.03	.01	.00
☐ 785 Alvin Davis	.10	.05	.01
☐ 786 Joe Price	.03	.01	.00
☐ 787 Bill Almon	.03	.01	.00
☐ 788 Ray Searage	.03	.01	.00
☐ 789 Indians' TL	.12	.06	.01
Joe Carter and			
Cory Snyder			
☐ 790 Dave Righetti	.10	.05	.01
☐ 791 Ted Simmons	.08	.04	.01
☐ 792 John Tudor	.10	.05	.01

1988 Topps Wax Box Cards

The cards in this 16-card set measure the standard 2 1/2" by 3 1/2". Cards have essentially the same design as the 1988 Topps regular issue set. The cards were printed on the bottoms of the regular issue wax pack boxes. These 16 cards, "lettered" A through P, are considered a separate set in their own right and are not typically included in a complete set of the regular issue 1988 Topps cards. The value of the panels uncut is slightly greater, perhaps by 25% greater, than the value of the individual cards cut up carefully.

		MINT	EXC	G-VG
COMPLETE SET		3.00	1.50	.30
COMMON PLAYERS		.10	.05	.01
☐ A	Don Baylor	.15	.07	.01
☐ B	Steve Bedrosian	.20	.10	.02
☐ C	Juan Beniquez	.10	.05	.01
☐ D	Bob Boone	.15	.07	.01
☐ E	Darrell Evans	.15	.07	.01
☐ F	Tony Gwynn	.50	.25	.05
☐ G	John Kruk	.25	.12	.02
☐ H	Marvell Wynne	.10	.05	.01
☐ I	Joe Carter	.25	.12	.02
☐ J	Eric Davis	.75	.35	.07
☐ K	Howard Johnson	.20	.10	.02
☐ L	Darryl Strawberry	.40	.20	.04
☐ M	Rickey Henderson	.40	.20	.04
☐ N	Nolan Ryan	.35	.17	.03
☐ O	Mike Schmidt	.45	.22	.04
☐ P	Kent Tekulve	.10	.05	.01

1988 Topps Glossy All-Stars 22

This set of 22 glossy cards was inserted one per rack pack. Players selected for the set are the starting players (plus manager and honorary captain) in the 1987 All-Star Game in Oakland. Cards measure standard size, 2 1/2" by 3 1/2" and the backs feature red and blue printing on a white card stock.

		MINT	EXC	G-VG
COMPLETE SET		3.50	1.75	.35
COMMON PLAYER		.10	.05	.01
☐ 1	John McNamara MG	.10	.05	.01
☐ 2	Don Mattingly	.75	.35	.07
☐ 3	Willie Randolph	.10	.05	.01
☐ 4	Wade Boggs	.50	.25	.05
☐ 5	Cal Ripken	.25	.12	.02
☐ 6	George Bell	.20	.10	.02
☐ 7	Rickey Henderson	.30	.15	.03
☐ 8	Dave Winfield	.20	.10	.02
☐ 9	Terry Kennedy	.10	.05	.01
☐ 10	Bret Saberhagen	.20	.10	.02
☐ 11	Jim Hunter CAPT	.15	.07	.01
☐ 12	Dave Johnson MG	.10	.05	.01
☐ 13	Jack Clark	.20	.10	.02
☐ 14	Ryne Sandberg	.25	.12	.02
☐ 15	Mike Schmidt	.40	.20	.04
☐ 16	Ozzie Smith	.20	.10	.02
☐ 17	Eric Davis	.60	.30	.06
☐ 18	Andre Dawson	.25	.12	.02
☐ 19	Darryl Strawberry	.30	.15	.03
☐ 20	Gary Carter	.25	.12	.02
☐ 21	Mike Scott	.20	.10	.02
☐ 22	Billy Williams CAPT	.15	.07	.01

1988 Topps Jumbo Rookies

Inserted in each supermarket jumbo pack is a card from this series of 22 of 1987's best rookies as determined by Topps. Jumbo packs consisted of 100 (regular issue 1987 Topps baseball) cards with a stick of gum plus the insert "Rookie" card. The card fronts are in full color and measure 2 1/2" by 3 1/2". The card backs are printed in red and blue on white card stock and are numbered at the bottom.

		MINT	EXC	G-VG
COMPLETE SET		12.00	6.00	1.20
COMMON PLAYER		.25	.12	.02
☐ 1	Billy Ripken	.45	.22	.04
☐ 2	Ellis Burks	1.25	.60	.12
☐ 3	Mike Greenwell	.75	.35	.07
☐ 4	DeWayne Buice	.25	.12	.02
☐ 5	Devon White	.75	.35	.07
☐ 6	Fred Manrique	.25	.12	.02
☐ 7	Mike Henneman	.25	.12	.02
☐ 8	Matt Nokes	1.25	.60	.12
☐ 9	Kevin Seitzer	1.25	.60	.12
☐ 10	B.J. Surhoff	.45	.22	.04
☐ 11	Casey Candaele	.25	.12	.02
☐ 12	Randy Myers	.35	.17	.03
☐ 13	Mark McGwire	1.50	.75	.15
☐ 14	Luis Polonia	.25	.12	.02
☐ 15	Terry Steinbach	.45	.22	.04
☐ 16	Mike Dunne	.60	.30	.06
☐ 17	Al Pedrique	.25	.12	.02
☐ 18	Benny Santiago	1.00	.50	.10
☐ 19	Kelly Downs	.25	.12	.02
☐ 20	Joe Magrane	.45	.22	.04
☐ 21	Jerry Browne	.25	.12	.02
☐ 22	Jeff Musselman	.25	.12	.02

1987 Toys'R'Us Rookies

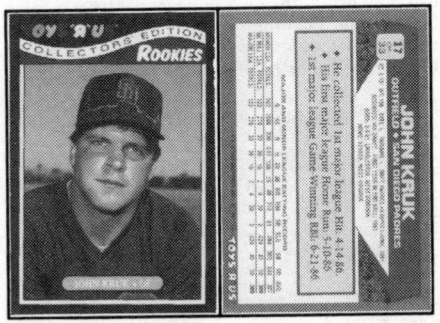

Topps produced this 33-card boxed set for Toys 'R' Us stores. The set is subtitled "Baseball Rookies" and features predominantly younger players. The cards measure 2 1/2" by 3 1/2" and feature a high-gloss,

full-color photo of the player inside a black border. The card backs are printed in orange and blue on white card stock.

		MINT	EXC	G-VG
COMPLETE SET (33)		5.00	2.50	.50
COMMON PLAYER (1-33)		.10	.05	.01
☐ 1	Andy Allanson	.10	.05	.01
☐ 2	Paul Assenmacher	.10	.05	.01
☐ 3	Scott Bailes	.10	.05	.01
☐ 4	Barry Bonds	.30	.15	.03
☐ 5	Jose Canseco	.75	.35	.07
☐ 6	John Cerutti	.15	.07	.01
☐ 7	Will Clark	.60	.30	.06
☐ 8	Kal Daniels	.60	.30	.06
☐ 9	Jim Deshaies	.20	.10	.02
☐ 10	Mark Eichhorn	.15	.07	.01
☐ 11	Ed Hearn	.10	.05	.01
☐ 12	Pete Incaviglia	.30	.15	.03
☐ 13	Bo Jackson	.60	.30	.06
☐ 14	Wally Joyner	.75	.35	.07
☐ 15	Charlie Kerfeld	.15	.07	.01
☐ 16	Eric King	.15	.07	.01
☐ 17	John Kruk	.40	.20	.04
☐ 18	Barry Larkin	.30	.15	.03
☐ 19	Mike LaValliere	.15	.07	.01
☐ 20	Greg Mathews	.15	.07	.01
☐ 21	Kevin Mitchell	.25	.12	.02
☐ 22	Dan Plesac	.20	.10	.02
☐ 23	Bruce Ruffin	.15	.07	.01
☐ 24	Ruben Sierra	.60	.30	.06
☐ 25	Cory Snyder	.40	.20	.04
☐ 26	Kurt Stillwell	.25	.12	.02
☐ 27	Dale Sveum	.30	.15	.03
☐ 28	Danny Tartabull	.40	.20	.04
☐ 29	Andres Thomas	.15	.07	.01
☐ 30	Robby Thompson	.15	.07	.01
☐ 31	Jim Traber	.15	.07	.01
☐ 32	Mitch Williams	.15	.07	.01
☐ 33	Todd Worrell	.20	.10	.02

1969 Transogram

The cards in this 60 card set measure 2 1/2" by 3 1/2". This first Transogram set contains full color, blank backed cards which comprised the backs of boxes containing plastic player statues. The cards are slightly smaller than those of the 1970 set, and the Callison photo is reversed. Complete boxes with cards are worth double the price listed below. The cards themselves are not numbered but have been alphabetized and numbered for reference below.

		NRMT	VG-E	GOOD
COMPLETE SET		700.00	350.00	70.00
COMMON PLAYER		4.00	2.00	.40
☐ 1	Joe Azcue	4.00	2.00	.40
☐ 2	Willie Horton	5.00	2.50	.50
☐ 3	Luis Tiant	6.00	3.00	.60
☐ 4	Denny McLain	6.00	3.00	.60

☐	5	Jose Cardenal	4.00	2.00	.40
☐	6	Al Kaline	30.00	15.00	3.00
☐	7	Tony Oliva	7.50	3.75	.75
☐	8	Blue Moon Odom	4.00	2.00	.40
☐	9	Cesar Tovar	4.00	2.00	.40
☐	10	Rick Monday	4.00	2.00	.40
☐	11	Harmon Killebrew	24.00	12.00	2.40
☐	12	Danny Cater	4.00	2.00	.40
☐	13	Brooks Robinson	30.00	15.00	3.00
☐	14	Jim Fregosi	6.00	3.00	.60
☐	15	Dave McNally	5.00	2.50	.50
☐	16	Frank Robinson	24.00	12.00	2.40
☐	17	Bobby Knoop	4.00	2.00	.40
☐	18	Rick Reichardt	4.00	2.00	.40
☐	19	Carl Yastrzemski	75.00	37.50	7.50
☐	20	Pete Ward	4.00	2.00	.40
☐	21	Rico Petrocelli	4.00	2.00	.40
☐	22	Tommy John	7.50	3.75	.75
☐	23	Ken Harrelson	6.00	3.00	.60
☐	24	Luis Aparicio	20.00	10.00	2.00
☐	25	Mike Epstein	4.00	2.00	.40
☐	26	Roy White	5.00	2.50	.50
☐	27	Camilo Pascual	4.00	2.00	.40
☐	28	Mel Stottlemyre	5.00	2.50	.50
☐	29	Frank Howard	6.00	3.00	.60
☐	30	Mickey Mantle	150.00	75.00	15.00
☐	31	Lou Brock	30.00	15.00	3.00
☐	32	Juan Marichal	24.00	12.00	2.40
☐	33	Bob Gibson	24.00	12.00	2.40
☐	34	Willie Mays	60.00	30.00	6.00
☐	35	Tim McCarver	6.00	3.00	.60
☐	36	Willie McCovey	24.00	12.00	2.40
☐	37	Don Wilson	4.00	2.00	.40
☐	38	Billy Williams	20.00	10.00	2.00
☐	39	Rusty Staub	7.50	3.75	.75
☐	40	Ernie Banks	30.00	15.00	3.00
☐	41	Jim Wynn	5.00	2.50	.50
☐	42	Ron Santo	6.00	3.00	.60
☐	43	Tom Haller	4.00	2.00	.40
☐	44	Ron Swoboda	5.00	2.50	.50
☐	45	Willie Davis	5.00	2.50	.50
☐	46	Jerry Koosman	6.00	3.00	.60
☐	47	Jim Lefebvre	4.00	2.00	.40
☐	48	Tom Seaver	50.00	25.00	5.00
☐	49	Joe Torre	7.50	3.75	.75
☐	50	Tony Perez	10.00	5.00	1.00
☐	51	Felipe Alou	5.00	2.50	.50
☐	52	Lee May	4.00	2.00	.40
☐	53	Hank Aaron	60.00	30.00	6.00
☐	54	Pete Rose	100.00	50.00	10.00
☐	55	Cookie Rojas	4.00	2.00	.40
☐	56	Bob Clemente	60.00	30.00	6.00
☐	57	Richie Allen	7.50	3.75	.75
☐	58	Matty Alou	5.00	2.50	.50
☐	59	John Callison	5.00	2.50	.50
☐	60	Bill Mazeroski	7.50	3.75	.75

1970 Transogram

ERNIE BANKS
1st BASE   CHICAGO CUBS
Ht: 6'1"   Wt: 180   Bats: Right   Throws: Right
Born: January 31, 1931   Home: Dallas, Texas

The cards in this 45 card set measure 2 9/16" by 3 1/2". Blank backed and unnumbered, these 1970 Transogram cards are very similar to those of the preceding year. They were issued in panels of three as the back portion of boxes containing three small

plastic statues of ballplayers. The pictures, with the exception of Torre and a corrected Callison, are identical to the 1969 set. They are, however, 1/16" wider than the 1969 cards. The checklist shows the panel combinations and is numbered according to "series" numbers located on each box. Complete panels of three have a value of 50% more than the sum of the individual cards on the panel. Complete box prices would be double the sum of the listed prices.

			NRMT	VG-E	GOOD
	COMPLETE INDIV. SET		500.00	250.00	50.00
	COMMON PLAYER		4.00	2.00	.40
☐	1A	Pete Rose	100.00	50.00	10.00
☐	1B	Willie Mays	60.00	30.00	6.00
☐	1C	Cleon Jones	4.00	2.00	.40
☐	2A	Ron Santo	6.00	3.00	.60
☐	2B	Willie Davis	5.00	2.50	.50
☐	2C	Willie McCovey	24.00	12.00	2.40
☐	3A	Juan Marichal	24.00	12.00	2.40
☐	3B	Joe Torre	7.50	3.75	.75
☐	3C	Ernie Banks	30.00	15.00	3.00
☐	4A	Hank Aaron	60.00	30.00	6.00
☐	4B	Jim Wynn	5.00	2.50	.50
☐	4C	Tom Seaver	50.00	25.00	5.00
☐	5A	Bob Gibson	24.00	12.00	2.40
☐	5B	Roberto Clemente	60.00	30.00	6.00
☐	5C	Jerry Koosman	6.00	3.00	.60
☐	11A	Denny McLain	6.00	3.00	.60
☐	11B	Reggie Jackson	75.00	37.50	7.50
☐	11C	Boog Powell	6.00	3.00	.60
☐	12A	Frank Robinson	24.00	12.00	2.40
☐	12B	Frank Howard	6.00	3.00	.60
☐	12C	Rick Reichardt	4.00	2.00	.40
☐	13A	Carl Yastrzemski	75.00	37.50	7.50
☐	13B	Tony Oliva	7.50	3.75	.75
☐	13C	Mel Stottlemyre	5.00	2.50	.50
☐	14A	Al Kaline	30.00	15.00	3.00
☐	14B	Jim Fregosi	6.00	3.00	.60
☐	14C	Sam McDowell	5.00	2.50	.50
☐	15A	Blue Moon Odom	4.00	2.00	.40
☐	15B	Harmon Killebrew	24.00	12.00	2.40
☐	15C	Rico Petrocelli	4.00	2.00	.40

1970 Transogram Mets

The cards in this 15 card set measure 2 9/16" by 3 1/2". The 1970 Transogram Mets are a set of blank backed, unnumbered cards issued in three card panels as the backs of boxes containing small plastic statues honoring the 1969 Mets. The individual cards are the same size as the non-Met 1970 series, and are numbered in the checklist according to the "series" number found on the side panels of each box. Although complete panel prices are not explicitly listed, they would generally have a value 50% greater than the sum of the individual players on the panel. Complete box prices would be double the sum of the listed prices.

			NRMT	VG-E	GOOD
	COMPLETE INDIV. SET		150.00	75.00	15.00
	COMMON PLAYER		4.00	2.00	.40
☐	21A	Ed Kranepool	5.00	2.50	.50
☐	21B	Al Weis	4.00	2.00	.40
☐	21C	Tom Seaver	60.00	30.00	6.00
☐	22A	Ken Boswell	4.00	2.00	.40
☐	22B	Jerry Koosman	7.50	3.75	.75
☐	22C	Jerry Grote	4.00	2.00	.40
☐	23A	Art Shamsky	4.00	2.00	.40
☐	23B	Gary Gentry	4.00	2.00	.40
☐	23C	Tommie Agee	4.00	2.00	.40
☐	24A	Nolan Ryan	60.00	30.00	6.00
☐	24B	Tug McGraw	10.00	5.00	1.00
☐	24C	Cleon Jones	4.00	2.00	.40
☐	25A	Ron Swoboda	4.00	2.00	.40
☐	25B	Bud Harrelson	4.00	2.00	.40
☐	25C	Donn Clendenon	4.00	2.00	.40

1983 True Value White Sox

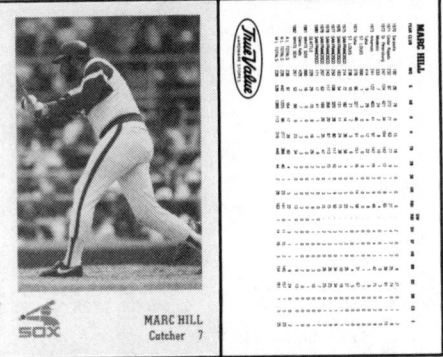

MARC HILL
Catcher 7

This 23-card set was sponsored by True Value Hardware Stores and features full-color (2 5/8" by 4 1/4") cards of the Chicago White Sox. Most of the set was intended for distribution two cards per game at selected White Sox Tuesday night home games. The cards are unnumbered except for uniform number given in the lower right corner of the obverse. The card backs contain statistical information in basic black and white. The cards of Harold Baines, Salome Barojas, and Marc Hill were not issued at the park; hence they are more difficult to obtain than the other 20 cards and are marked SP in the checklist below.

		MINT	EXC	G-VG
COMPLETE SET (23)		27.00	12.50	2.50
COMMON PLAYER (1-23)		.35	.17	.03
☐ 1	Scott Fletcher	.75	.35	.07
☐ 3	Harold Baines SP	6.00	3.00	.60
☐ 5	Vance Law	.35	.17	.03
☐ 7	Marc Hill SP	3.00	1.50	.30
☐ 10	Tony LaRussa MG	.50	.25	.05
☐ 11	Rudy Law	.35	.17	.03
☐ 14	Tony Bernazard	.50	.25	.05
☐ 17	Jerry Hairston	.35	.17	.03
☐ 19	Greg Luzinski	.75	.35	.07
☐ 24	Floyd Bannister	.75	.35	.07
☐ 25	Mike Squires	.35	.17	.03
☐ 30	Salome Barojas SP	3.00	1.50	.30
☐ 31	LaMarr Hoyt	.50	.25	.05
☐ 34	Richard Dotson	.50	.25	.05
☐ 36	Jerry Koosman	.50	.25	.05
☐ 40	Britt Burns	.50	.25	.05
☐ 41	Dick Tidrow	.35	.17	.03
☐ 42	Ron Kittle	1.00	.50	.10
☐ 44	Tom Paciorek	.35	.17	.03
☐ 45	Kevin Hickey	.35	.17	.03
☐ 53	Dennis Lamp	.35	.17	.03
☐ 67	Jim Kern	.35	.17	.03
☐ 72	Carlton Fisk	.75	.35	.07

1984 True Value White Sox

This 30-card set features full color (2 1/2" by 4") cards of the Chicago White Sox. Most of the set was distributed two cards per game at selected White Sox Tuesday home games. Faust and Minoso were not given out although their cards were available through direct (promotional) contact with them. Brennan and Hulett were not released directly since they were sent down to the minors. The cards are unnumbered except for uniform number given in the lower right corner of the obverse. The card backs contain statistical information in basic black and white.

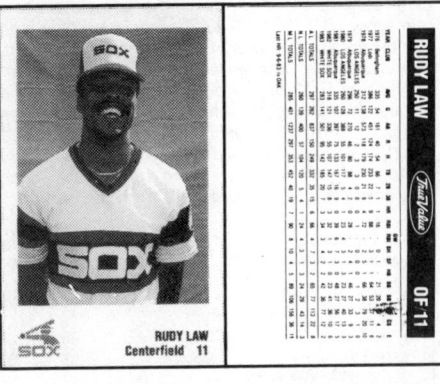

RUDY LAW
Centerfield 11

		MINT	EXC	G-VG
COMPLETE SET (30)		21.00	10.00	2.00
COMMON PLAYER (1-30)		.30	.15	.03
☐ 1	Juan Agosto	.30	.15	.03
☐ 2	Luis Aparicio	2.00	1.00	.20
☐ 3	Harold Baines	1.50	.75	.15
☐ 4	Floyd Bannister	.60	.30	.06
☐ 5	Salome Barojas	.30	.15	.03
☐ 6	Tom Brennan	1.50	.75	.15
☐ 7	Britt Burns	.50	.25	.05
☐ 8	Coaching Staff	.30	.15	.03
	(blank back)			
☐ 9	Julio Cruz	.30	.15	.03
☐ 10	Richard Dotson	.60	.30	.06
☐ 11	Jerry Dybzinski	.30	.15	.03
☐ 12	Nancy Faust	1.50	.75	.15
	(organist)			
	(blank back)			
☐ 13	Carlton Fisk	.75	.35	.07
☐ 14	Scott Fletcher	.50	.25	.05
☐ 15	Jerry Hairston	.30	.15	.03
☐ 16	Marc Hill	.30	.15	.03
☐ 17	LaMarr Hoyt	.40	.20	.04
☐ 18	Tim Hulett	1.50	.75	.15
☐ 19	Ron Kittle	.75	.35	.07
☐ 20	Tony LaRussa MG	.40	.20	.04
☐ 21	Rudy Law	.30	.15	.03
☐ 22	Vance Law	.30	.15	.03
☐ 23	Greg Luzinski	.60	.30	.06
☐ 24	Minnie Minoso	2.00	1.00	.20
☐ 25	Tom Paciorek	.30	.15	.03
☐ 26	Ron Reed	.30	.15	.03
☐ 27	Tom Seaver	2.00	1.00	.20
☐ 28	Dave Stegman	.30	.15	.03
☐ 29	Mike Squires	.30	.15	.03
☐ 30	Greg Walker	1.00	.50	.10

1986 True Value

The 1986 True Value set consists of 30 cards each 2 1/2" by 3 1/2" which were printed as panels of four although one of the cards in the panel only pictures a featured product. The complete panel measures 10 3/8" by 3 1/2". The True Value logo is in the upper left corner of the obverse of each card. Supposedly the cards were distributed to customers purchasing 5.00 or more at the store. Cards are frequently found with perforations intact and still in the closed form where only the top card in the folded panel is visible. The card number appears at the bottom of the reverse. Team logos have been surgically removed (airbrushed) from the photos.

		MINT	EXC	G-VG
	COMPLETE SET (30)	6.00	3.00	.60
	COMMON PLAYER (1-30)	.10	.05	.01
☐ 1	Pedro Guerrero	.20	.10	.02
☐ 2	Steve Garvey	.30	.15	.03
☐ 3	Eddie Murray	.30	.15	.03
☐ 4	Pete Rose	.50	.25	.05
☐ 5	Don Mattingly	.75	.35	.07
☐ 6	Fernando Valenzuela	.30	.15	.03
☐ 7	Jim Rice	.30	.15	.03
☐ 8	Kirk Gibson	.20	.10	.02
☐ 9	Ozzie Smith	.20	.10	.02
☐ 10	Dale Murphy	.50	.25	.05
☐ 11	Robin Yount	.30	.15	.03
☐ 12	Tom Seaver	.30	.15	.03
☐ 13	Reggie Jackson	.40	.20	.04
☐ 14	Ryne Sandberg	.30	.15	.03
☐ 15	Bruce Sutter	.15	.07	.01
☐ 16	Gary Carter	.30	.15	.03
☐ 17	George Brett	.40	.20	.04
☐ 18	Rick Sutcliffe	.10	.05	.01
☐ 19	Dave Stieb	.10	.05	.01
☐ 20	Buddy Bell	.10	.05	.01
☐ 21	Alvin Davis	.15	.07	.01
☐ 22	Cal Ripken	.30	.15	.03
☐ 23	Bill Madlock	.10	.05	.01
☐ 24	Kent Hrbek	.15	.07	.01
☐ 25	Lou Whitaker	.15	.07	.01
☐ 26	Nolan Ryan	.30	.15	.03
☐ 27	Dwayne Murphy	.10	.05	.01
☐ 28	Mike Schmidt	.50	.25	.05
☐ 29	Andre Dawson	.30	.15	.03
☐ 30	Wade Boggs	.60	.30	.06

T3 Turkey Red

The cards in this 126 card set measure 5 3/4" by 8". The 1911 "Turkey Red" set of color cabinet style cards, designated T3 in the American Card Catalog, is named after the brand of cigarettes with which it was offered as a premium. Cards 1-50 and 77-126 depict baseball players while the middle series (51-76) portrays boxers. The cards themselves are not numbered but were assigned numbers for ordering purposes by the manufacturer. This list appears on the backs of cards in the 77-126 sub-series and has been used in the checklist below. The boxers (51-76) were formerly assigned a separate catalog number (T9) but have now been returned to the classification to which they properly belong and are indicated in the checklist below by BOX.

		NRMT	VG-E	GOOD
	COMPLETE SET	23500.	9000.	2250.
	COMMON BASEBALL (1-50)	150.00	75.00	15.00
	COMMON BOXERS (51-76)	75.00	37.50	7.50
	COMMON BASEBALL (77-126)	175.00	85.00	18.00
☐ 1	M. Brown: Chicago NL	300.00	150.00	30.00
☐ 2	Bergen: Brooklyn	150.00	75.00	15.00
☐ 3	Leach: Pittsburgh	150.00	75.00	15.00
☐ 4	Bresnahan: St.L. NL	250.00	125.00	25.00
☐ 5	Crawford: Detroit	250.00	125.00	25.00
☐ 6	Chase: New York AL	200.00	100.00	20.00
☐ 7	Camnitz: Pittsburgh	150.00	75.00	15.00
☐ 8	Clarke: Pittsburgh	250.00	125.00	25.00
☐ 9	Cobb: Detroit	2750.00	1200.00	250.00
☐ 10	Devlin: New York NL	150.00	75.00	15.00
☐ 11	Dahlen: Brooklyn	150.00	75.00	15.00
☐ 12	Donovan: Detroit	150.00	75.00	15.00

☐ 13	Doyle: New York NL	150.00	75.00	15.00
☐ 14	Dooin: Phila. NL	150.00	75.00	15.00
☐ 15	Elberfeld: Wash	150.00	75.00	15.00
☐ 16	Evers: Chicago NL	300.00	150.00	30.00
☐ 17	Griffith: Cinc.	250.00	125.00	25.00
☐ 18	Jennings: Detroit	250.00	125.00	25.00
☐ 19	Joss: Cleveland	300.00	150.00	30.00
☐ 20	Jordan: Brooklyn	150.00	75.00	15.00
☐ 21	Kleinow: New York NL	150.00	75.00	15.00
☐ 22	Krause: Phila. AL	150.00	75.00	15.00
☐ 23	Lajoie: Cleveland	500.00	250.00	50.00
☐ 24	Mitchell: Cincinnati	150.00	75.00	15.00
☐ 25	M. McIntyre: Detroit	150.00	75.00	15.00
☐ 26	McGraw: New York NL	350.00	175.00	35.00
☐ 27	Mathewson: N.Y. NL	750.00	375.00	75.00
☐ 28	H. McIntyre: Brk	150.00	75.00	15.00
☐ 29	McConnell: Boston AL	150.00	75.00	15.00
☐ 30	Mullin: Detroit	150.00	75.00	15.00
☐ 31	Magee: Phila. NL	150.00	75.00	15.00
☐ 32	Overall: Chicago NL	150.00	75.00	15.00
☐ 33	Pfeister: Chicago NL	150.00	75.00	15.00
☐ 34	Rucker: Brooklyn	150.00	75.00	15.00
☐ 35	Tinker: Chicago NL	250.00	125.00	25.00
☐ 36	Speaker: Boston AL	600.00	300.00	60.00
☐ 37	Sallee: St. Louis NL	150.00	75.00	15.00
☐ 38	Stahl: Boston AL	150.00	75.00	15.00
☐ 39	Waddell: St.Louis AL	300.00	150.00	30.00
☐ 40	Willis: St.Louis NL	200.00	100.00	20.00
☐ 41	Wiltse: New York NL	150.00	75.00	15.00
☐ 42	Young: Cleveland	600.00	300.00	60.00
☐ 43	Out At Third	150.00	75.00	15.00
☐ 44	Trying to Catch Him Napping	150.00	75.00	15.00
☐ 45	Jordan and Herzog at First	150.00	75.00	15.00
☐ 46	Safe At Third	150.00	75.00	15.00
☐ 47	Frank Chance At Bat	250.00	125.00	25.00
☐ 48	Jack Murray At Bat	150.00	75.00	15.00
☐ 49	Close Play At Second	150.00	75.00	15.00
☐ 50	Chief Myers At Bat	150.00	75.00	15.00
☐ 51	Jim Driscoll BOX	75.00	37.50	7.50
☐ 52	Abe Attell BOX	75.00	37.50	7.50
☐ 53	Ad. Walgast BOX	75.00	37.50	7.50
☐ 54	Johnny Coulon BOX	75.00	37.50	7.50
☐ 55	James Jeffries BOX	125.00	60.00	12.50
☐ 56	Jack Sullivan BOX (Twin)	90.00	45.00	9.00
☐ 57	Battling Nelson BOX	90.00	45.00	9.00
☐ 58	Packey McFarland BOX	75.00	37.50	7.50
☐ 59	Tommy Murphy BOX	75.00	37.50	7.50
☐ 60	Owen Moran BOX	75.00	37.50	7.50
☐ 61	Johnny Marto BOX	75.00	37.50	7.50
☐ 62	Jimmie Gardner BOX	75.00	37.50	7.50
☐ 63	Harry Lewis BOX	75.00	37.50	7.50
☐ 64	Wm. Papke BOX	75.00	37.50	7.50
☐ 65	Sam Langford BOX	75.00	37.50	7.50
☐ 66	Knock-out Brown BOX	75.00	37.50	7.50
☐ 67	Stanley Ketchel BOX	100.00	50.00	10.00
☐ 68	Joe Jeannette BOX	75.00	37.50	7.50
☐ 69	Leach Cross BOX	75.00	37.50	7.50
☐ 70	Phil. McGovern BOX	75.00	37.50	7.50
☐ 71	Battling Hurley BOX	75.00	37.50	7.50
☐ 72	Honey Mellody BOX	75.00	37.50	7.50
☐ 73	Al Kaufman BOX	75.00	37.50	7.50
☐ 74	Willie Lewis BOX	75.00	37.50	7.50
☐ 75	Jack O'Brien BOX "Philadelphia"	90.00	45.00	9.00
☐ 76	Jack Johnson BOX	150.00	75.00	15.00
☐ 77	Ames: New York NL	175.00	85.00	18.00
☐ 78	Baker: Phila. AL	350.00	175.00	35.00
☐ 79	Bell: Brooklyn	175.00	85.00	18.00
☐ 80	Bender: Phila. AL	300.00	150.00	30.00
☐ 81	Bescher: Cincinnati	175.00	85.00	18.00
☐ 82	Bransfield: Phila. NL	175.00	85.00	18.00
☐ 83	Bridwell: Phila. NL	175.00	85.00	18.00
☐ 84	Browne: Wash and Chi	175.00	85.00	18.00
☐ 85	Burns: Chi. and Cin.	175.00	85.00	18.00
☐ 86	Carrigan: Boston AL	175.00	85.00	18.00
☐ 87	Collins: Phila. AL	350.00	175.00	35.00
☐ 88	Coveleski: Cinc.	175.00	85.00	18.00
☐ 89	Criger: New York AL	175.00	85.00	18.00
☐ 90	Doolan: Phila. NL	175.00	85.00	18.00
☐ 91	Downey: Cincinnati	175.00	85.00	18.00
☐ 92	Dygert: Phila. AL	175.00	85.00	18.00
☐ 93	Fromme: Cincinnati	175.00	85.00	18.00
☐ 94	Gibson: Pittsburgh	175.00	85.00	18.00
☐ 95	Graham: Boston NL	175.00	85.00	18.00
☐ 96	Groom: Washington	175.00	85.00	18.00
☐ 97	Hoblitzell: Cinc.	175.00	85.00	18.00
☐ 98	Hofman: Chicago NL	175.00	85.00	18.00
☐ 99	Johnson: Washington	900.00	450.00	90.00
☐ 100	D. Jones: Detroit	175.00	85.00	18.00
☐ 101	Keeler: New York NL	400.00	200.00	40.00
☐ 102	Kling: Chicago NL	175.00	85.00	18.00
☐ 103	Konetchy: St.Louis NL	175.00	85.00	18.00

☐ 104	Lennox: Brooklyn	175.00	85.00	18.00
☐ 105	Lobert: Cincinnati	175.00	85.00	18.00
☐ 106	Lord: Bos. and Chi.	175.00	85.00	18.00
☐ 107	Manning: N.Y. AL	175.00	85.00	18.00
☐ 108	Merkle: New York NL	175.00	85.00	18.00
☐ 109	Moran: Chi. and Phil.	175.00	85.00	18.00
☐ 110	McBride: Washington	175.00	85.00	18.00
☐ 111	Niles: Bos. and Cleve	175.00	85.00	18.00
☐ 112	Paskert: Cincinnati	175.00	85.00	18.00
☐ 113	Raymond: N.Y. NL	175.00	85.00	18.00
☐ 114	Rhoades: Cleveland	250.00	125.00	25.00
☐ 115	Schlei: New York NL	175.00	85.00	18.00
☐ 116	Schmidt: Detroit	175.00	85.00	18.00
☐ 117	Schulte: Chicago NL	175.00	85.00	18.00
☐ 118	Smith: Chi. and Bos.	175.00	85.00	18.00
☐ 119	Stone: St.L. AL	175.00	85.00	18.00
☐ 120	Street: Washington	175.00	85.00	18.00
☐ 121	Sullivan: Chi. AL	175.00	85.00	18.00
☐ 122	Tenney: New York NL	175.00	85.00	18.00
☐ 123	Thomas: Phila. AL	175.00	85.00	18.00
☐ 124	Wallace: St.Louis AL	275.00	135.00	27.00
☐ 125	Walsh: Chicago AL	300.00	150.00	30.00
☐ 126	Wilson: Pittsburgh	175.00	85.00	18.00

T200 Fatima

The cards in this 16 card set measure 2 5/8" by 5 13/16". The 1913 Fatima Cigarettes issue contains unnumbered glossy surface team cards. Both St. Louis team cards are considered difficult to obtain. A large 13" by 21" unnumbered, heavy cardboard premium issue is also known to exist and is quite scarce. These unnumbered team cards are ordered below by team alphabetical order within league.

		NRMT	VG-E	GOOD
COMPLETE SET		2250.00	900.00	200.00
COMMON TEAM		120.00	60.00	12.00
☐ 1	Boston AL	160.00	80.00	16.00
☐ 2	Chicago AL	120.00	60.00	12.00
☐ 3	Cleveland AL	120.00	60.00	12.00
☐ 4	Detroit AL	200.00	100.00	20.00
☐ 5	New York AL	400.00	200.00	40.00
☐ 6	Philadelphia AL	120.00	60.00	12.00
☐ 7	St. Louis AL	300.00	150.00	30.00
☐ 8	Washington AL	120.00	60.00	12.00
☐ 9	Boston NL	200.00	100.00	20.00
☐ 10	Brooklyn NL	120.00	60.00	12.00
☐ 11	Chicago NL	120.00	60.00	12.00
☐ 12	Cincinnati NL	120.00	60.00	12.00
☐ 13	New York NL	120.00	60.00	12.00
☐ 14	Philadelphia NL	120.00	60.00	12.00
☐ 15	Pittsburg NL	120.00	60.00	12.00
☐ 16	St. Louis NL	200.00	100.00	20.00

T201 Mecca

The cards in this 50 card set measure 2 1/4" by 4 11/16". The 1911 Mecca Double Folder issue contains unnumbered cards. This issue was one of the first to list statistics of players portrayed on the cards. Each card portrays two players, one when the card is folded, another when the card is unfolded. The card of Dougherty and Lord is considered scarce.

		NRMT	VG-E	GOOD
COMPLETE SET		2000.00	800.00	150.00
COMMON PAIR		22.00	11.00	2.20
☐ 1	F.Baker and Collins	75.00	37.50	7.50
☐ 2	Barry and Lapp	22.00	11.00	2.20
☐ 3	Bergen and Z.Wheat	35.00	17.50	3.50
☐ 4	Blair and Hartzell	22.00	11.00	2.20
☐ 5	Bresnahan and Huggins	75.00	37.50	7.50
☐ 6	Bridwell and Mathewson	150.00	75.00	15.00
☐ 7	Butler and Abstein	22.00	11.00	2.20
☐ 8	Byrne and F.Clarke	35.00	17.50	3.50
☐ 9	Chance and Evers	75.00	37.50	7.50

☐ 10	Clark and Gaspar	22.00	11.00	2.20
☐ 11	Cobb and S.Crawford	400.00	200.00	40.00
☐ 12	Cole and Kling	22.00	11.00	2.20
☐ 13	Coombs and Thomas	22.00	11.00	2.20
☐ 14	Daubert and Rucker	22.00	11.00	2.20
☐ 15	Dougherty and Lord	225.00	110.00	22.00
☐ 16	Dooin and Titus	22.00	11.00	2.20
☐ 17	Downie and Baker	22.00	11.00	2.20
☐ 18	Dygert and Seymour	22.00	11.00	2.20
☐ 19	Elberfeld and McBride	22.00	11.00	2.20
☐ 20	Falkenberg and Lajoie	65.00	32.50	6.50
☐ 21	Fitzpatrick , Killian	22.00	11.00	2.20
☐ 22	Gardner and Speaker	65.00	32.50	6.50
☐ 23	Gibson and Leach	22.00	11.00	2.20
☐ 24	Graham and Mattern	22.00	11.00	2.20
☐ 25	Hauser and Lush	22.00	11.00	2.20
☐ 26	Herzog and Miller	22.00	11.00	2.20
☐ 27	Hinchman and Hickman	22.00	11.00	2.20
☐ 28	Hofman and M.Brown	35.00	17.50	3.50
☐ 29	Jennings and Summers	35.00	17.50	3.50
☐ 30	Johnson and Ford	22.00	11.00	2.20
☐ 31	McCarty and McGinnity	35.00	17.50	3.50
☐ 32	McGlyn and Barrett	22.00	11.00	2.20
☐ 33	McLean and Grant	22.00	11.00	2.20
☐ 34	Merkle and Wiltse	22.00	11.00	2.20
☐ 35	Meyers and Doyle	22.00	11.00	2.20
☐ 36	Moore and Lobert	22.00	11.00	2.20
☐ 37	Odwell and Downs	22.00	11.00	2.20
☐ 38	Oldring and Bender	35.00	17.50	3.50
☐ 39	Payne and Walsh	35.00	17.50	3.50
☐ 40	Simon and Leifield	22.00	11.00	2.20
☐ 41	Starr and McCabe	22.00	11.00	2.20
☐ 42	Stephens and LaPorte	22.00	11.00	2.20
☐ 43	Stovall and Turner	22.00	11.00	2.20
☐ 44	Street and W.Johnson	150.00	75.00	15.00
☐ 45	Stroud and Donovan	22.00	11.00	2.20
☐ 46	Sweeney and Chase	22.00	11.00	2.20
☐ 47	Thoney and Cicotte	22.00	11.00	2.20
☐ 48	Wallace and Lake	35.00	17.50	3.50
☐ 49	Ward and Foster	22.00	11.00	2.20
☐ 50	Williams and Woodruff	22.00	11.00	2.20

T202 Triple Folders

The cards in this 134 card set measure 2 1/4" by 5 1/4". The 1912 T202 Hassan Triple Folder issue is perhaps the most ingenious baseball card ever issued. The two end cards of each panel are full color, T205-like individual cards whereas the black and white center panel pictures an action photo or portrait. The end cards can be folded across the center panel and stored in this manner. Seventy-six different center panels are known to exist; however, many of the center panels contain more than one combination of end cards. The center panel titles are listed below in alphabetical order while the different combinations of end cards are listed below each center panel as they appear left to right on the front of the card. A total of 132 different card fronts exist. The set price below includes all panel and player combinations listed in the checklist. Back color variations (red or black) also exist. The Birmingham's Home Run card is difficult to obtain as are other cards whose center panel exists with but one combination of end cards. The Devlin with Mathewson end panels on numbers 29A and 74C picture Devlin as a Giant. Devlin is pictured as a Rustler on 29B and 74D.

		NRMT	VG-E	GOOD
COMPLETE SET		12500.00	5000.00	1000.00
COMMON PANEL		65.00	32.50	6.50
☐ 1A	A Close Play at Home: Wallace-LaPorte	75.00	37.50	7.50
☐ 1B	A Close Play at Home: Wallace-Pelty	75.00	37.50	7.50
☐ 2	A Desperate Slide: O'Leary-Cobb	450.00	225.00	45.00
☐ 3A	A Great Batsman: Barger-Bergen	65.00	32.50	6.50
☐ 3B	A Great Batsman:	65.00	32.50	6.50

	Rucker-Bergen			
☐ 4	Ambrose McConnell at ..... Bat: Blair-Quinn	65.00	32.50	6.50
☐ 5	A Wide Throw Saves .... Crawford:	75.00	37.50	7.50
	Mullin-Stanage			
☐ 6	Baker Gets His Man: .... Collins-Baker	125.00	60.00	12.50
☐ 7	Birmingham Gets to .... Third:	150.00	75.00	15.00
	Johnson-Street			
☐ 8	Birmingham's Home Run: Birmingham-Turner	225.00	110.00	22.00
☐ 9	Bush Just Misses .... Austin: Moran-Magee	65.00	32.50	6.50
☐ 10A	Carrigan Blocks His .... Man: Gaspar-McLean	65.00	32.50	6.50
☐ 10B	Carrigan Blocks His .... Man: Wagner-Carrigan	65.00	32.50	6.50
☐ 11	Catching Him Napping: .... Oakes-Bresnahan	75.00	37.50	7.50
☐ 12	Caught Asleep .... Off First:	75.00	37.50	7.50
	Bresnahan-Harmon			
☐ 13A	Chance Beats Out a .... Hit: Chance-Foxen	90.00	45.00	9.00
☐ 13B	Chance Beats Out a .... Hit: McIntire-Archer	75.00	37.50	7.50
☐ 13C	Chance Beats Out a .... Hit: Overall-Archer	75.00	37.50	7.50
☐ 13D	Chance Beats Out a .... Hit: Rowan-Archer	75.00	37.50	7.50
☐ 13E	Chance Beats Out a .... Hit: Shean-Chance	90.00	45.00	9.00
☐ 14A	Chase Dives into .... Third: Chase-Wolter	65.00	32.50	6.50
☐ 14B	Chase Dives into .... Third: Gibson-Clarke	75.00	37.50	7.50
☐ 14C	Chase Dives into .... Third:	65.00	32.50	6.50
	Phillippe-Gibson			
☐ 15A	Chase Gets Ball Too .... Late: Egan-Mitchell	65.00	32.50	6.50
☐ 15B	Chase Gets Ball Too ...... Late: Wolter-Chase	65.00	32.50	6.50
☐ 16A	Chase Guarding First: .... Chase-Wolter	65.00	32.50	6.50
☐ 16B	Chase Guarding First: .... Gibson-Clarke	75.00	37.50	7.50
☐ 16C	Chase Guarding First: .... Leifield-Gibson	65.00	32.50	6.50
☐ 17	Chase Ready Squeeze ...... Play: Paskert-Magee	65.00	32.50	6.50
☐ 18	Chase Safe at Third: .... Barry-Baker	75.00	37.50	7.50
☐ 19	Chief Bender Waiting: ...... Bender-Thomas	75.00	37.50	7.50
☐ 20	Clarke Hikes for Home: ... Bridwell-Kling	75.00	37.50	7.50
☐ 21	Close at First: .... Ball-Stovall	65.00	32.50	6.50
☐ 22A	Close at the Plate: .... Walsh-Payne	75.00	37.50	7.50
☐ 22B	Close at the Plate: .... White-Payne	65.00	32.50	6.50
☐ 23	Close at Third (Speak- ..... er): Wood-Speaker	125.00	60.00	12.50
☐ 24	Close at Third .... (Wagner):	75.00	37.50	7.50
	Wagner-Carrigan			
☐ 25A	Collins Easily Safe: .... Byrne-Clarke	90.00	45.00	9.00
☐ 25B	Collins Easily Safe: .... Collins-Baker	125.00	60.00	12.50
☐ 25C	Collins Easily Safe: .... Collins-Murphy	90.00	45.00	9.00
☐ 26	Crawford About .... to Smash:	75.00	37.50	7.50
	Stanage-Summers			
☐ 27	Cree Rolls Home: .... Daubert-Hummell	65.00	32.50	6.50
☐ 28	Davy Jones' Great .... Slide:	65.00	32.50	6.50
	Delahanty-Jones			
☐ 29A	Devlin Gets His Man: ...... Devlin (Giants)-	225.00	110.00	22.00
	Mathewson			
☐ 29B	Devlin Gets His Man: ...... Devlin (Rustlers)-	125.00	60.00	12.50
	Mathewson			
☐ 29C	Devlin Gets His Man: ...... Fletcher-Mathewson	125.00	60.00	12.50
☐ 29D	Devlin Gets His Man: ...... Meyers-Mathewson	125.00	60.00	12.50
☐ 30A	Donlin Out at First:	65.00	32.50	6.50

	Camnitz-Gibson			
☐ 30B	Donlin Out at First: .... Doyle-Merkle	65.00	32.50	6.50
☐ 30C	Donlin Out at First: .... Leach-Wilson	65.00	32.50	6.50
☐ 30D	Donlin Out at First: .... Magee-Dooin	65.00	32.50	6.50
☐ 30E	Donlin Out at First: .... Phillippe-Gibson	65.00	32.50	6.50
☐ 31A	Dooin Gets His Man: ...... Dooin-Doolan	65.00	32.50	6.50
☐ 31B	Dooin Gets His Man: ...... Lobert-Dooin	65.00	32.50	6.50
☐ 31C	Dooin Gets His Man: ...... Titus-Dooin	65.00	32.50	6.50
☐ 32	Easy for Larry: .... Doyle-Merkle	65.00	32.50	6.50
☐ 33	Elberfeld Beats: .... Milan-Elberfeld	65.00	32.50	6.50
☐ 34	Elberfeld Gets His .... Man: Milan-Elberfeld	65.00	32.50	6.50
☐ 35	Engle in a Close Play: ...... Speaker-Engle	90.00	45.00	9.00
☐ 36A	Evers Makes Safe .... Slide:	90.00	45.00	9.00
	Archer-Evers			
☐ 36B	Evers Makes Safe .... Slide:	125.00	60.00	12.50
	Evers-Chance			
☐ 36C	Evers Makes Safe .... Slide:	75.00	37.50	7.50
	Overall-Archer			
☐ 36D	Evers Makes Safe .... Slide:	75.00	37.50	7.50
	Reulbach-Archer			
☐ 36E	Evers Makes Safe .... Slide:	175.00	85.00	18.00
	Tinker-Chance			
☐ 37	Fast Work at Third: .... O'Leary-Cobb	450.00	225.00	45.00
☐ 38A	Ford Putting Over .... Spitter:	65.00	32.50	6.50
	Ford-Vaughn			
☐ 38B	Ford Putting Over .... Spitter:	65.00	32.50	6.50
	Sweeney-Ford			
☐ 39	Good Play at Third: .... Moriarty-Cobb	450.00	225.00	45.00
☐ 40	Grant Gets His Man: .... Hoblitzel-Grant	65.00	32.50	6.50
☐ 41A	Hal Chase Too Late: ...... McIntyre-McConnell	65.00	32.50	6.50
☐ 41B	Hal Chase Too Late: ...... Suggs-McLean	65.00	32.50	6.50
☐ 42	Harry Lord at Third: .... Lennox-Tinker	75.00	37.50	7.50
☐ 43	Hartzell Covering: .... Scanlon-Dahlen	65.00	32.50	6.50
☐ 44	Hartzell Strikes Out: .... Groom-Gray	65.00	32.50	6.50
☐ 45	Held at Third: .... Tannehill-Lord	65.00	32.50	6.50
☐ 46	Jake Stahl Guarding: .... Cicotte-Stahl	65.00	32.50	6.50
☐ 47	Jim Delahanty at Bat: ...... Delahanty-Jones	65.00	32.50	6.50
☐ 48A	Just Before the .... Battle: Ames-Meyers	65.00	32.50	6.50
☐ 48B	Just Before the .... Battle:	125.00	60.00	12.50
	Bresnahan-McGraw			
☐ 48C	Just Before the .... Battle:	65.00	32.50	6.50
	Crandall-Meyers			
☐ 48D	Just Before the .... Battle:	65.00	32.50	6.50
	Devore-Becker			
☐ 48E	Just Before the .... Battle:	125.00	60.00	12.50
	Fletcher-Mathewson			
☐ 48F	Just Before the .... Battle:	75.00	37.50	7.50
	Marquard-Meyers			
☐ 48G	Just Before the .... Battle:	125.00	60.00	12.50
	McGraw-Jennings			
☐ 48H	Just Before the .... Battle:	125.00	60.00	12.50
	Meyers-Mathewson			
☐ 48I	Just Before the .... Battle:	65.00	32.50	6.50
	Snodgrass-Murray			
☐ 48J	Just Before the .... Battle:	65.00	32.50	6.50
	Wiltse-Meyers			

☐ 49 Knight Catches Runner: ... Knight-Johnson	150.00	75.00	15.00
☐ 50A Lobert Almost Caught: ... Bridwell-Kling	65.00	32.50	6.50
☐ 50B Lobert Almost Caught: ... Kling-Young	75.00	37.50	7.50
☐ 50C Lobert Almost Caught: ... Mattern-Kling	65.00	32.50	6.50
☐ 50D Lobert Almost Caught: ... Steinfeldt-Kling	65.00	32.50	6.50
☐ 51 Lobert Gets Tenney: .... Lobert-Dooin	65.00	32.50	6.50
☐ 52 Lord Catches His Man: ..... Tannehill-Lord	65.00	32.50	6.50
☐ 53 McConnell Caught: .... Richie-Needham	65.00	32.50	6.50
☐ 54 McIntyre at Bat: .... McIntrye-McConnell	65.00	32.50	6.50
☐ 55 Moriarty Spiked: .... Willett-Stanage	65.00	32.50	6.50
☐ 56 Nearly Caught: .... Bates-Bescher	75.00	37.50	7.50
☐ 57 Oldring Almost Home: ...... Lord-Oldring	65.00	32.50	6.50
☐ 58 Schaefer on First: .... McBride-Milan	65.00	32.50	6.50
☐ 59 Schaefer Steals .... Second: McBride-Griffith	75.00	37.50	7.50
☐ 60 Scoring from Second: ...... Lord-Oldring	65.00	32.50	6.50
☐ 61A Scrambling Back: .... Barger-Bergen	65.00	32.50	6.50
☐ 61B Scrambling Back: .... Wolter-Chase	65.00	32.50	6.50
☐ 62 Speaker Almost Caught: .. Miller-Clarke	125.00	60.00	12.50
☐ 63 Speaker Rounding .... Third: Wood-Speaker	125.00	60.00	12.50
☐ 64 Speaker Scores: .... Speaker-Engle	125.00	60.00	12.50
☐ 65 Stahl Safe: .... Stovall-Austin	65.00	32.50	6.50
☐ 66 Stone About to Swing: ..... Sheckard-Schulte	65.00	32.50	6.50
☐ 67A Sullivan Puts Up High ..... One: Evans-Huggins	75.00	37.50	7.50
☐ 67B Sullivan Puts Up High .... One: Sweeney-Ford	65.00	32.50	6.50
☐ 68A Sweeney Gets Stahl: ...... Ford-Vaughn	65.00	32.50	6.50
☐ 68B Sweeney Gets Stahl: ...... Sweeney-Ford	65.00	32.50	6.50
☐ 69 Tenney Lands Safely: .... Raymond-Latham	65.00	32.50	6.50
☐ 70A The Athletic Infield: .... Barry-Baker	75.00	37.50	7.50
☐ 70B The Athletic Infield: .... Brown-Graham	65.00	32.50	6.50
☐ 70C The Athletic Infield: .... Hauser-Konetchy	65.00	32.50	6.50
☐ 70D The Athletic Infield: .... Krause-Thomas	65.00	32.50	6.50
☐ 71 The Pinch Hitter: .... Hoblitzel-Egan	65.00	32.50	6.50
☐ 72 The Scissors Slide: .... Birmingham-Turner	65.00	32.50	6.50
☐ 73A Tom Jones at Bat: .... Fromme-McLean	65.00	32.50	6.50
☐ 73B Tom Jones at Bat: .... Gaspar-McLean	65.00	32.50	6.50
☐ 74A Too Late for Devlin: .... Ames-Meyers	65.00	32.50	6.50
☐ 74B Too Late for Devlin: .... Crandall-Meyers	65.00	32.50	6.50
☐ 74C Too Late for Devlin: .... Devlin (Giants)-Mathewson	225.00	110.00	22.00
☐ 74D Too Late for Devlin: .... Devlin (Rustlers)-Mathewson	125.00	60.00	12.50
☐ 74E Too Late for Devlin: .... Marquard-Meyers	75.00	37.50	7.50
☐ 74F Too Late for Devlin: .... Wiltse-Meyers	65.00	32.50	6.50
☐ 75A Ty Cobb Steals Third: .... Jennings-Cobb	650.00	325.00	65.00
☐ 75B Ty Cobb Steals Third: .... Moriarty-Cobb	550.00	275.00	55.00
☐ 75C Ty Cobb Steals Third: .... Stovall-Austin	450.00	225.00	45.00
☐ 76 Wheat Strikes Out: .... Dahlen-Wheat	90.00	45.00	9.00

T204 Ramly

The cards in this 121 card set measure 2" by 2 1/2". The Ramly baseball series, designated T204 in the ACC, contains unnumbered cards. This set is one of the most distinguished ever produced, containing ornate gold borders around a black and white portrait of each player. There are spelling errors, and two distinct backs, "Ramly" and "TT", are known. Much of the obverse card detail is actually embossed. The players have been alphabetized and numbered for reference in the checklist below.

		NRMT	VG-E	GOOD
COMPLETE SET		13000.00	5000.00	1000.00
COMMON PLAYER		100.00	50.00	10.00
☐	1 Whitey Alperman	100.00	50.00	10.00
☐	2 John J. Anderson	100.00	50.00	10.00
☐	3 Jimmy Archer	100.00	50.00	10.00
☐	4 Frank Arellanes	100.00	50.00	10.00
☐	5 Jim Ball (Boston NL)	100.00	50.00	10.00
☐	6 Neal Ball (N.Y. AL)	100.00	50.00	10.00
☐	7 Dave Bancroft	200.00	100.00	20.00
☐	8 Johnny Bates	100.00	50.00	10.00
☐	9 Fred Beebe	100.00	50.00	10.00
☐	10 George Bell	100.00	50.00	10.00
☐	11 Chief Bender	200.00	100.00	20.00
☐	12 Walter Blair	100.00	50.00	10.00
☐	13 Cliff Blankenship	100.00	50.00	10.00
☐	14 Frank Bowerman	100.00	50.00	10.00
☐	15 Kitty Bransfield	100.00	50.00	10.00
☐	16 Roger Bresnahan	200.00	100.00	20.00
☐	17 Al Bridwell	100.00	50.00	10.00
☐	18 Mordecai Brown	200.00	100.00	20.00
☐	19 Fred Burchell	100.00	50.00	10.00
☐	20 Jesse Burkett	300.00	150.00	30.00
☐	21 Robert Byrne	100.00	50.00	10.00
☐	22 Bill Carrigan	100.00	50.00	10.00
☐	23 Frank Chance	250.00	125.00	25.00
☐	24 Charles Chech	100.00	50.00	10.00
☐	25 Eddie Cicotte	125.00	60.00	12.50
☐	26 Otis Clymer	100.00	50.00	10.00
☐	27 Andrew Coakley	100.00	50.00	10.00
☐	28 Eddie Collins	250.00	125.00	25.00
☐	29 Jimmy Collins	250.00	125.00	25.00
☐	30 Wid Conroy	100.00	50.00	10.00
☐	31 Jack Coombs	125.00	60.00	12.50
☐	32 Doc Crandall	100.00	50.00	10.00
☐	33 Lou Criger	100.00	50.00	10.00
☐	34 Harry(Jasper) Davis	100.00	50.00	10.00
☐	35 Art Devlin	100.00	50.00	10.00
☐	36 Bill Dineen	100.00	50.00	10.00
☐	37 Pat Donahue	100.00	50.00	10.00
☐	38 Mike Donlin	100.00	50.00	10.00
☐	39 Wild Bill Donovan	100.00	50.00	10.00
☐	40 Gus Dorner	100.00	50.00	10.00
☐	41 Joe Dunn	100.00	50.00	10.00
☐	42 Norman Elberfield (sic) Elberfeld	100.00	50.00	10.00
☐	43 Johnny Evers	250.00	125.00	25.00
☐	44 George L. Ewing	100.00	50.00	10.00
☐	45 George Ferguson	100.00	50.00	10.00
☐	46 Hobe Ferris	100.00	50.00	10.00
☐	47 James J. Freeman	100.00	50.00	10.00
☐	48 Art Fromme	100.00	50.00	10.00
☐	49 Bob Ganley	100.00	50.00	10.00
☐	50 Harry (Doc) Gessler	100.00	50.00	10.00
☐	51 George Graham	100.00	50.00	10.00
☐	52 Clark Griffith	200.00	100.00	20.00
☐	53 Roy Hartzell	100.00	50.00	10.00

☐	54	Charlie Hemphill	100.00	50.00	10.00
☐	55	Dick Hoblitzell	100.00	50.00	10.00
☐	56	George (Del) Howard	100.00	50.00	10.00
☐	57	Harry Howell	100.00	50.00	10.00
☐	58	Miller Huggins	250.00	125.00	25.00
☐	59	John Hummel	100.00	50.00	10.00
☐	60	Walter Johnson	650.00	325.00	65.00
☐	61	Charles Jones	100.00	50.00	10.00
☐	62	Michael Kahoe	100.00	50.00	10.00
☐	63	Ed Karger	100.00	50.00	10.00
☐	64	Willie Keeler	300.00	150.00	30.00
☐	65	Ed Kenotchey (sic) Konetchy	100.00	50.00	10.00
☐	66	John (Red) Kleinow	100.00	50.00	10.00
☐	67	John Knight	100.00	50.00	10.00
☐	68	Vive Lindeman	100.00	50.00	10.00
☐	69	Hans Loebert (sic) Lobert	100.00	50.00	10.00
☐	70	Harry Lord	100.00	50.00	10.00
☐	71	Harry Lumley	100.00	50.00	10.00
☐	72	Ernie Lush	100.00	50.00	10.00
☐	73	Rube Manning	100.00	50.00	10.00
☐	74	James McAleer	100.00	50.00	10.00
☐	75	Amby McConnell	100.00	50.00	10.00
☐	76	Moose McCormick	100.00	50.00	10.00
☐	77	Matthew McIntyre	100.00	50.00	10.00
☐	78	Larry McLean	100.00	50.00	10.00
☐	79	Fred Merkle	125.00	60.00	12.50
☐	80	Clyde Milan	100.00	50.00	10.00
☐	81	Michael Mitchell	100.00	50.00	10.00
☐	82	Pat Moran	100.00	50.00	10.00
☐	83	Harry (Cy) Morgan	100.00	50.00	10.00
☐	84	Tim Murnane	100.00	50.00	10.00
☐	85	Danny Murphy	100.00	50.00	10.00
☐	86	Red Murray	100.00	50.00	10.00
☐	87	Eustace (Doc) Newton	100.00	50.00	10.00
☐	88	Simon Nichols (sic) Nicholls	100.00	50.00	10.00
☐	89	Harry Niles	100.00	50.00	10.00
☐	90	Bill O'Hara	100.00	50.00	10.00
☐	91	Charley O'Leary	100.00	50.00	10.00
☐	92	Dode Paskert	100.00	50.00	10.00
☐	93	Barney Pelty	100.00	50.00	10.00
☐	94	Jack Pfeister	100.00	50.00	10.00
☐	95	Eddie Plank	300.00	150.00	30.00
☐	96	Jack Powell	100.00	50.00	10.00
☐	97	Bugs Raymond	100.00	50.00	10.00
☐	98	Thomas Reilly	100.00	50.00	10.00
☐	99	Lewis Ritchie (sic) Richie	100.00	50.00	10.00
☐	100	Nap Rucker	100.00	50.00	10.00
☐	101	Ed Ruelbach (sic) Reulbach	100.00	50.00	10.00
☐	102	Slim Sallee	100.00	50.00	10.00
☐	103	Germany Schaefer	100.00	50.00	10.00
☐	104	Jimmy Schekard (sic) Sheckard	100.00	50.00	10.00
☐	105	Admiral Schlei	100.00	50.00	10.00
☐	106	Frank Schulte	100.00	50.00	10.00
☐	107	James Sebring	100.00	50.00	10.00
☐	108	Bill Shipke	100.00	50.00	10.00
☐	109	Anthony Smith	100.00	50.00	10.00
☐	110	Tubby Spencer	100.00	50.00	10.00
☐	111	Jake Stahl	100.00	50.00	10.00
☐	112	Harry Steinfeldt	100.00	50.00	10.00
☐	113	Jim Stephens	100.00	50.00	10.00
☐	114	Gabby Street	100.00	50.00	10.00
☐	115	William Sweeney	100.00	50.00	10.00
☐	116	Fred Tenney	100.00	50.00	10.00
☐	117	Ira Thomas	100.00	50.00	10.00
☐	118	Joe Tinker	200.00	100.00	20.00
☐	119	Bob Unglaub	100.00	50.00	10.00
☐	120	Heine Wagner	100.00	50.00	10.00
☐	121	Bobby Wallace	200.00	100.00	20.00

T205 Gold Border

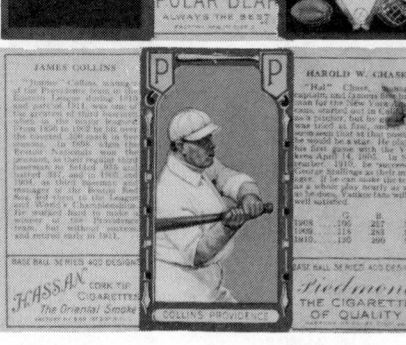

The cards in this 208 card set measure 1 1/2" by 2 5/8". The T205 set (ACC designation), also known as the "Gold Border" set, was issued in 1911 in packages of the following cigarette brands: American Beauty, Broadleaf, Cycle, Drum, Hassan, Honest Long Cut, Piedmont, Polar Bear, Sovereign and Sweet Caporal. All the above were products of the American Tobacco Company, and the ads for the various brands appear below the biographical section on the back of each card. There are pose variations noted in the checklist (which is alphabetized and numbered for reference) and there are 12 minor league cards of a more ornate design which are somewhat scarce. The numbers below correspond to alphabetical order within each team by team nickname, i.e., Philadelphia Athletics AL (1-13), St. Louis Browns (14-20), St. Louis Cardinals (21-32), Chicago Cubs (33- 51), New York Giants (52-72), Cleveland Naps (73-78), Philadelphia Phillies (79-90), Pittsburgh Pirates (91-103), Cincinnati Reds (104-114), Boston Red Sox (115-122), Boston Rustlers (123-131), Washington Senators (132-139), Brooklyn Superbas (140-153), Detroit Tigers (154-167), Chicago White Sox (168-182), New York Yankees (183-196), and Minor Leaguers (197- 208). The gold borders of T205 cards chip easily and they are hard to find in "Mint" condition.

			NRMT	VG-E	GOOD
COMPLETE SET			14000.00	5000.00	1000.00
COMMON PLAYERS			35.00	17.50	3.50
☐	1	Frank Baker	100.00	50.00	10.00
☐	2	John J. Barry	35.00	17.50	3.50
☐	3	Charles A. Bender	100.00	50.00	10.00
☐	4	Edward T. Collins (mouth closed)	100.00	50.00	10.00
☐	5	Edward T. Collins (mouth open)	200.00	100.00	20.00
☐	6	James H. Dygert	35.00	17.50	3.50
☐	7	Frederick T. Hartsel	35.00	17.50	3.50
☐	8	Harry Krause	35.00	17.50	3.50
☐	9	Pat'k J. Livingston	35.00	17.50	3.50
☐	10	Briscoe Lord	35.00	17.50	3.50
☐	11	Daniel Murphy	35.00	17.50	3.50
☐	12	Reuben N. Oldring	35.00	17.50	3.50
☐	13	Ira Thomas	35.00	17.50	3.50
☐	14	William Bailey	35.00	17.50	3.50
☐	15	Daniel J. Hoffman	35.00	17.50	3.50
☐	16	Frank LaPorte	35.00	17.50	3.50
☐	17	B. Pelty	35.00	17.50	3.50
☐	18	George Stone	35.00	17.50	3.50
☐	19	Roderick J. Wallace (with cap)	100.00	50.00	10.00
☐	20	Roderick J. Wallace (without cap)	200.00	100.00	20.00
☐	21	Roger Bresnahan (mouth closed)	100.00	50.00	10.00
☐	22	Roger Bresnahan (mouth open)	200.00	100.00	20.00

☐ 23	Frank J. Corridon	35.00	17.50	3.50
☐ 24	Louis Evans	35.00	17.50	3.50
☐ 25	Robert Harmon (both ears)	35.00	17.50	3.50
☐ 26	Robert Harmon (left ear only)	150.00	75.00	15.00
☐ 27	Arnold J. Hauser	35.00	17.50	3.50
☐ 28	Miller Huggins	100.00	50.00	10.00
☐ 29	Edward Konetchy	35.00	17.50	3.50
☐ 30	John Lush	35.00	17.50	3.50
☐ 31	Rebel Oakes	35.00	17.50	3.50
☐ 32	Edward Phelps	35.00	17.50	3.50
☐ 33	James P. Archer	35.00	17.50	3.50
☐ 34	Mordecai Brown	100.00	50.00	10.00
☐ 35	Frank L. Chance	100.00	50.00	10.00
☐ 36	John J. Evers	100.00	50.00	10.00
☐ 37	William A. Foxen	35.00	17.50	3.50
☐ 38	George F. Graham	225.00	110.00	22.00
☐ 39	John Kling	35.00	17.50	3.50
☐ 40	Floyd M. Kroh	35.00	17.50	3.50
☐ 41	Harry McIntire	35.00	17.50	3.50
☐ 42	Thomas J. Needham	35.00	17.50	3.50
☐ 43	Orval Overall	35.00	17.50	3.50
☐ 44	John A. Pfiester	35.00	17.50	3.50
☐ 45	Edward M. Reulbach	35.00	17.50	3.50
☐ 46	Lewis Richie	35.00	17.50	3.50
☐ 47	Frank M. Schulte	35.00	17.50	3.50
☐ 48	David Shean (Cubs)	250.00	125.00	25.00
☐ 49	James T. Sheckard	35.00	17.50	3.50
☐ 50	Harry Steinfeldt	35.00	17.50	3.50
☐ 51	Joseph B. Tinker	100.00	50.00	10.00
☐ 52	Leon Ames	35.00	17.50	3.50
☐ 53	Beals Becker	35.00	17.50	3.50
☐ 54	Albert Bridwell	35.00	17.50	3.50
☐ 55	Otis Crandall	35.00	17.50	3.50
☐ 56	Arthur Devlin	35.00	17.50	3.50
☐ 57	Joshua Devore	35.00	17.50	3.50
☐ 58	W.R. Dickson	35.00	17.50	3.50
☐ 59	Lawrence Doyle	35.00	17.50	3.50
☐ 60	Arthur Fletcher	35.00	17.50	3.50
☐ 61	W.A. Latham	35.00	17.50	3.50
☐ 62	Richard Marquard	100.00	50.00	10.00
☐ 63	Christy Mathewson	300.00	150.00	30.00
☐ 64	John J. McGraw	150.00	75.00	15.00
☐ 65	Fred Merkle	45.00	22.50	4.50
☐ 66	John T. Meyers	35.00	17.50	3.50
☐ 67	John J. Murray	35.00	17.50	3.50
☐ 68	Arthur L. Raymond	150.00	75.00	15.00
☐ 69	George H. Schlei	35.00	17.50	3.50
☐ 70	Fred C. Snodgrass	35.00	17.50	3.50
☐ 71	George Wiltse (both ears)	35.00	17.50	3.50
☐ 72	George Wiltse (right ear only)	150.00	75.00	15.00
☐ 73	Neal Ball	35.00	17.50	3.50
☐ 74	Joseph Birmingham	35.00	17.50	3.50
☐ 75	Addie Joss	225.00	110.00	22.00
☐ 76	George T. Stovall	35.00	17.50	3.50
☐ 77	Terence Turner	150.00	75.00	15.00
☐ 78	Denton T. Young	200.00	100.00	20.00
☐ 79	John W. Bates	35.00	17.50	3.50
☐ 80	Wm. E. Bransfield	35.00	17.50	3.50
☐ 81	Charles S. Dooin	35.00	17.50	3.50
☐ 82	Michael Doolan	35.00	17.50	3.50
☐ 83	Robert Ewing	35.00	17.50	3.50
☐ 84	Fred Jacklitsch	35.00	17.50	3.50
☐ 85	John Lobert	35.00	17.50	3.50
☐ 86	Sherwood R. Magee	35.00	17.50	3.50
☐ 87	Patrick J. Moran	35.00	17.50	3.50
☐ 88	George Paskert	35.00	17.50	3.50
☐ 89	John A. Rowan	150.00	75.00	15.00
☐ 90	John Titus	35.00	17.50	3.50
☐ 91	Robert Byrne	35.00	17.50	3.50
☐ 92	Howard Camnitz	35.00	17.50	3.50
☐ 93	Fred Clarke	100.00	50.00	10.00
☐ 94	John Flynn	35.00	17.50	3.50
☐ 95	George Gibson	35.00	17.50	3.50
☐ 96	Thomas W. Leach	35.00	17.50	3.50
☐ 97	Sam Leever	35.00	17.50	3.50
☐ 98	Albert P. Leifield	35.00	17.50	3.50
☐ 99	Nicholas Maddox	35.00	17.50	3.50
☐ 100	John D. Miller	35.00	17.50	3.50
☐ 101	Charles Phillippe	35.00	17.50	3.50
☐ 102	Kirb White	150.00	75.00	15.00
☐ 103	J. Owen Wilson	35.00	17.50	3.50
☐ 104	Robert H. Bescher	35.00	17.50	3.50
☐ 105	Thomas W. Downey	35.00	17.50	3.50
☐ 106	Richard J. Egan	35.00	17.50	3.50
☐ 107	Arthur Fromme	35.00	17.50	3.50
☐ 108	Harry L. Gaspar	35.00	17.50	3.50
☐ 109	Edward L. Grant	150.00	75.00	15.00
☐ 110	Clark Griffith	100.00	50.00	10.00
☐ 111	Richard Hoblitzell	35.00	17.50	3.50
☐ 112	John B. McLean	35.00	17.50	3.50
☐ 113	Michael Mitchell	35.00	17.50	3.50
☐ 114	George Suggs	150.00	75.00	15.00
☐ 115	William Carrigan	35.00	17.50	3.50
☐ 116	Edward V. Cicotte	45.00	22.50	4.50
☐ 117	Clyde Engle	35.00	17.50	3.50
☐ 118	Edward Karger	150.00	75.00	15.00
☐ 119	John Kleinow	150.00	75.00	15.00
☐ 120	Tris Speaker	225.00	110.00	22.00
☐ 121	Jacob G. Stahl	45.00	22.50	4.50
☐ 122	Charles Wagner	100.00	50.00	10.00
☐ 123	Edward J. Abbaticchio	35.00	17.50	3.50
☐ 124	Frederick T. Beck	35.00	17.50	3.50
☐ 125	G.C. Ferguson	35.00	17.50	3.50
☐ 126	Wilbur Good	35.00	17.50	3.50
☐ 127	George F. Graham	35.00	17.50	3.50
☐ 128	Charles L. Herzog	35.00	17.50	3.50
☐ 129	A.A. Mattern	35.00	17.50	3.50
☐ 130	Bayard H. Sharpe	35.00	17.50	3.50
☐ 131	David Shean (Boston)	35.00	17.50	3.50
☐ 132	Norman Elberfeld	35.00	17.50	3.50
☐ 133	Gray	35.00	17.50	3.50
☐ 134	Robert Groom	35.00	17.50	3.50
☐ 135	Walter Johnson	400.00	200.00	40.00
☐ 136	George F. McBride	35.00	17.50	3.50
☐ 137	J. Clyde Milan	35.00	17.50	3.50
☐ 138	Herman Schaefer	35.00	17.50	3.50
☐ 139	Charles E. Street	35.00	17.50	3.50
☐ 140	Edward B. Barger (full B)	35.00	17.50	3.50
☐ 141	Edward B. Barger (part B)	150.00	75.00	15.00
☐ 142	George G. Bell	35.00	17.50	3.50
☐ 143	William Bergen	35.00	17.50	3.50
☐ 144	William Dahlen	150.00	75.00	15.00
☐ 145	Jacob Daubert	45.00	22.50	4.50
☐ 146	John E. Hummell	35.00	17.50	3.50
☐ 147	Edgar Lennox	35.00	17.50	3.50
☐ 148	Pryor McElveen	35.00	17.50	3.50
☐ 149	G.N. Rucker	35.00	17.50	3.50
☐ 150	W.D. Scanlan	150.00	75.00	15.00
☐ 151	Tony Smith	35.00	17.50	3.50
☐ 152	Zach D. Wheat	100.00	50.00	10.00
☐ 153	Irvin K. Wilhelm	150.00	75.00	15.00
☐ 154	Tyrus Raymond Cobb	900.00	450.00	90.00
☐ 155	James Delahanty	35.00	17.50	3.50
☐ 156	Hugh Jennings	100.00	50.00	10.00
☐ 157	David Jones	35.00	17.50	3.50
☐ 158	Thomas Jones	35.00	17.50	3.50
☐ 159	Edward Killian	35.00	17.50	3.50
☐ 160	George Moriarity	35.00	17.50	3.50
☐ 161	George J. Mullin	35.00	17.50	3.50
☐ 162	Charles O'Leary	35.00	17.50	3.50
☐ 163	Charles Schmidt	35.00	17.50	3.50
☐ 164	George Simmons	35.00	17.50	3.50
☐ 165	Oscar Stanage	35.00	17.50	3.50
☐ 166	Edgar Summers	35.00	17.50	3.50
☐ 167	Edgar Willett	35.00	17.50	3.50
☐ 168	Russell Blackburne	35.00	17.50	3.50
☐ 169	J. Donohue	100.00	50.00	10.00
☐ 170A	Patsy Dougherty (white stocking)	100.00	50.00	10.00
☐ 170B	Patsy Dougherty (red stocking)	75.00	37.50	7.50
☐ 171	Hugh Duffy	150.00	75.00	15.00
☐ 172	Frank Lang	35.00	17.50	3.50
☐ 173	Harry D. Lord	35.00	17.50	3.50
☐ 174	Ambrose McConnell	35.00	17.50	3.50
☐ 175	Matthew McIntyre	35.00	17.50	3.50
☐ 176	Frederick Olmstead	35.00	17.50	3.50
☐ 177	F. Parent	35.00	17.50	3.50
☐ 178	Fred Payne	35.00	17.50	3.50
☐ 179	James Scott	35.00	17.50	3.50
☐ 180	Lee Ford Tannehill	35.00	17.50	3.50
☐ 181	Edward Walsh	200.00	100.00	20.00
☐ 182	G.H. White	35.00	17.50	3.50
☐ 183	James Austin	35.00	17.50	3.50
☐ 184	Harold W. Chase (Chase only)	200.00	100.00	20.00
☐ 185	Harold W. Chase (Hal Chase)	45.00	22.50	4.50
☐ 186	Louis Criger	35.00	17.50	3.50
☐ 187	Ray Fisher	150.00	75.00	15.00
☐ 188	Russell Ford (dark cap)	35.00	17.50	3.50
☐ 189	Russell Ford (light cap)	150.00	75.00	15.00
☐ 190	Earl Gardner	35.00	17.50	3.50
☐ 191	Charles Hemphill	35.00	17.50	3.50
☐ 192	Jack Knight	35.00	17.50	3.50
☐ 193	John Quinn	35.00	17.50	3.50
☐ 194	Edward Sweeney	150.00	75.00	15.00
☐ 195	James Vaughn	150.00	75.00	15.00
☐ 196	Harry Wolter	35.00	17.50	3.50
☐ 197	Dr. Merle T. Adkins: Baltimore	125.00	60.00	12.50
☐ 198	John Dunn: Baltimore	150.00	75.00	15.00

		NRMT	VG-E	GOOD
☐ 199	George Merritt: .... Buffalo	125.00	60.00	12.50
☐ 200	Charles Hanford: .... Jersey City	125.00	60.00	12.50
☐ 201	Forrest D. Cady: .... Newark	125.00	60.00	12.50
☐ 202	James Frick: Newark	125.00	60.00	12.50
☐ 203	Wyatt Lee: Newark	125.00	60.00	12.50
☐ 204	Lewis McAllister: .... Newark	125.00	60.00	12.50
☐ 205	John Nee: Newark	125.00	60.00	12.50
☐ 206	James Collins: .... Providence	250.00	125.00	25.00
☐ 207	James Phelan: .... Providence	125.00	60.00	12.50
☐ 208	Henry Batch: .... Rochester	125.00	60.00	12.50

T206 White Border

The cards in this 523 card set measure 1 1/2" by 2 5/8". The T206 set was and is the most popular of all the tobacco issues. The set was issued from 1909 to 1911 with sixteen different brands of cigarettes: American Beauty, Broadleaf, Cycle, Carolina Brights, Drum, El Principe de Gales, Hindu, Lenox, Old Mill, Piedmont, Polar Bear, Sovereign, Sweet Caporal, Tolstoi, Ty Cobb and Uzit. The Ty Cobb brand back is very scarce. The minor league cards are supposedly slightly more difficult to obtain than the cards of the major leaguers, with the Southern League player cards being the most difficult. Minor League players were obtained from the American Association and the Eastern league. Southern League players were obtained from a variety of leagues including the following: South Atlantic League, Southern League, Texas League, and Virginia League. The set price below does not include ultra-expensive Wagner, Plank, Magie error, or Doyle variation.

	NRMT	VG-E	GOOD
COMPLETE SET (520)	27000.	9000.	2000.
MAJOR LEAGUERS (1-389)	25.00	12.50	2.50
MINOR LEAGUERS (390-475) ...	21.00	10.50	2.10
SOUTHERN LEAG. (476-523)	75.00	37.50	7.50

			NRMT	VG-E	GOOD
☐	1	Abbaticchio: Pitt. .... Batting follow thru	25.00	12.50	2.50
☐	2	Abbaticchio: Pitt. .... Batting waiting pitch	30.00	15.00	3.00
☐	3	Abstein: Pitt.	25.00	12.50	2.50
☐	4	Alperman: Brooklyn	30.00	15.00	3.00
☐	5	Ames: Giants, Port.	30.00	15.00	3.00
☐	6	Ames: Giants, Hands ...... over head	25.00	12.50	2.50
☐	7	Ames: Giants, Hands ...... in front of chest	30.00	15.00	3.00
☐	8	Arellanes: Boston AL	25.00	12.50	2.50
☐	9	Atz: Chicago AL	25.00	12.50	2.50
☐	10	Baker: Phila. AL	80.00	40.00	8.00
☐	11	Ball: Cleveland	25.00	12.50	2.50
☐	12	Ball: N.Y. AL	30.00	15.00	3.00
☐	13	Barbeau: St.L. NL	25.00	12.50	2.50
☐	14	Barry: Phila. AL	25.00	12.50	2.50
☐	15	Bates: Boston NL	30.00	15.00	3.00
☐	16	Beaumont: Boston NL	30.00	15.00	3.00
☐	17	Beck: Boston NL	25.00	12.50	2.50
☐	18	Becker: Boston NL	25.00	12.50	2.50
☐	19	Bell: Brooklyn .... pitching, follow thru)	25.00	12.50	2.50
☐	20	Bell: Brooklyn, ... Hands over head	30.00	15.00	3.00
☐	21	Bender: Phila. AL .... Portrait	100.00	50.00	10.00
☐	22	Bender: Phila. AL .... (pitching) trees	80.00	40.00	8.00
☐	23	Bender: Phila. AL .... (pitching) no trees	80.00	40.00	8.00
☐	24	Bergen: Brooklyn, ... Catching	25.00	12.50	2.50
☐	25	Bergen: Brooklyn, ... Batting	30.00	15.00	3.00
☐	26	Berger: Cleveland	25.00	12.50	2.50
☐	27	Bescher: Cinc., ... Catching fly ball	25.00	12.50	2.50
☐	28	Bescher: Cinc. .... Portrait	25.00	12.50	2.50
☐	29	Birmingham: Cleve.	30.00	15.00	3.00
☐	30	Bliss: St.L. NL	25.00	12.50	2.50
☐	31	Bowerman: Bost. NL	30.00	15.00	3.00
☐	32	Bradley: Cleveland, ... Portrait	30.00	15.00	3.00
☐	33	Bradley: Cleveland, ... Batting	25.00	12.50	2.50
☐	34	Bransfield: Phila. NL	30.00	15.00	3.00
☐	35	Bresnahan: St.L. NL, ... Portrait	100.00	50.00	10.00
☐	36	Bresnahan: St.L. NL, ... Batting	80.00	40.00	8.00
☐	37	Bridwell: N.Y. NL, ... Portrait	30.00	15.00	3.00
☐	38	Bridwell: N.Y. NL, ... Wearing sweater	25.00	12.50	2.50
☐	39	G. Brown (sic): .... Chicago NL	50.00	25.00	5.00
☐	40	G. Brown (sic): .... Washington	300.00	150.00	30.00
☐	41	M. Brown: Chicago NL ... Portrait	100.00	50.00	10.00
☐	42	M. Brown: Chicago NL ... Chicago down front of shirt	80.00	40.00	8.00
☐	43	M. Brown: Chicago NL, .. Cubs across chest	150.00	75.00	15.00
☐	44	Burch: Brooklyn, ... Fielding	25.00	12.50	2.50
☐	45	Burch: Brooklyn, ... Batting	50.00	25.00	5.00
☐	46	Burns: Chicago AL	25.00	12.50	2.50
☐	47	Bush: Detroit	25.00	12.50	2.50
☐	48	Byrne: St.L. NL	25.00	12.50	2.50
☐	49	Camnitz: Pitt., Arms .... folded over chest	30.00	15.00	3.00
☐	50	Camnitz: Pitt., ... Hands over head	25.00	12.50	2.50
☐	51	Camnitz: Pitt., ... Throwing	25.00	12.50	2.50
☐	52	Campbell: Cinc.	25.00	12.50	2.50
☐	53	Carrigan: Boston AL	25.00	12.50	2.50
☐	54	Chance: Chicago NL, ... Cubs across chest	100.00	50.00	10.00
☐	55	Chance: Chicago NL, ... Chicago down front of shirt	80.00	40.00	8.00
☐	56	Chance: Chicago NL, ... Batting	80.00	40.00	8.00
☐	57	Charles: St.L. NL	25.00	12.50	2.50
☐	58	Chase: N.Y. AL, ...	30.00	15.00	3.00

Port. blue bkgd.			
□ 59 Chase: N.Y. AL, ...	50.00	25.00	5.00
Port., pink bkgd.			
□ 60 Chase: N.Y. AL, ...	30.00	15.00	3.00
Holding cup			
□ 61 Chase: N.Y. AL, ...	30.00	15.00	3.00
Throwing, dark cap			
□ 62 Chase: N.Y. AL, ...	100.00	50.00	10.00
Throwing, white cap			
□ 63 Chesbro: N.Y. AL	150.00	75.00	15.00
□ 64 Cicotte: Boston AL	40.00	20.00	4.00
□ 65 Clarke: Pitt., ...	100.00	50.00	10.00
Portrait			
□ 66 F. Clarke: Pitt.	100.00	50.00	10.00
□ 67 J.J. Clarke: Cleve.	30.00	15.00	3.00
□ 68 Cobb: Detroit, ...	600.00	300.00	60.00
Port., red bkgd.			
□ 69 Cobb: Detroit, Port.	900.00	450.00	90.00
green background			
□ 70 Cobb: Detroit, Bat	750.00	375.00	75.00
on shoulder			
□ 71 Cobb: Detroit, Bat	600.00	300.00	60.00
away from shoulder			
□ 72 Collins: Phila. AL	80.00	40.00	8.00
□ 73 Conroy: Washington, ...	30.00	15.00	3.00
Fielding			
□ 74 Conroy: Wash., Bat	25.00	12.50	2.50
on shoulder			
□ 75 Covaleski: Phil. NL	30.00	15.00	3.00
(Harry)			
□ 76 Crandall: N.Y. NL, ...	30.00	15.00	3.00
without cap			
□ 77 Crandall: N.Y. NL, ...	25.00	12.50	2.50
sweater and cap			
□ 78 Crawford: Detroit, ...	80.00	40.00	8.00
Batting			
□ 79 Crawford: Detroit, ...	100.00	50.00	10.00
Throwing			
□ 80 Cree: N.Y. AL	25.00	12.50	2.50
□ 81 Criger: St.L. AL	30.00	15.00	3.00
□ 82 Criss: St.L. AL	30.00	15.00	3.00
□ 83 Dahlen: Brooklyn	125.00	60.00	12.50
□ 84 Dahlen: Bost. NL	30.00	15.00	3.00
□ 85 Davis: Phila. AL	25.00	12.50	2.50
□ 86 G. Davis: Chicago AL	30.00	15.00	3.00
□ 87 H. Davis: Phila. AL	30.00	15.00	3.00
□ 88 Delehanty: Wash.	30.00	15.00	3.00
□ 89 Demmitt: St.L. AL	1800.00	800.00	150.00
□ 90 Demmitt: N.Y. AL	25.00	12.50	2.50
□ 91 Devlin: N.Y. NL	30.00	15.00	3.00
□ 92 Devore: N.Y. NL	25.00	12.50	2.50
□ 93 Dineen: St.L. AL	25.00	12.50	2.50
□ 94 Donlin: N.Y. NL, ...	50.00	25.00	5.00
Fielding			
□ 95 Donlin: N.Y. NL, ...	30.00	15.00	3.00
Sitting			
□ 96 Donlin: N.Y. NL, ...	25.00	12.50	2.50
Batting			
□ 97 Donohue: Chicago AL	30.00	15.00	3.00
□ 98 Donovan: Detroit, ...	30.00	15.00	3.00
Portrait			
□ 99 Donovan: Detroit, ...	25.00	12.50	2.50
Throwing			
□100 Dooin: Phila. NL	30.00	15.00	3.00
□101 Doolan: Phila. NL, ...	25.00	12.50	2.50
Fielding			
□102 Doolan: Phila. NL, ...	25.00	12.50	2.50
Batting			
□103 Doolin (sic, Doolan):	30.00	15.00	3.00
Phila. NL,			
□104 Dougherty: Chic. AL, ...	30.00	15.00	3.00
Portrait			
□105 Dougherty: Chic. AL, ...	25.00	12.50	2.50
Fielding			
□106 Downey: Cinc., ...	25.00	12.50	2.50
Batting			
□107 Downey: Cinc., ...	25.00	12.50	2.50
Fielding			
□108A Doyle: N.Y.	30.00	15.00	3.00
(hands over head)			
□108B Doyle: N.Y. NAT'L	10000.00	4000.00	800.00
(hands over head)			
□109 Doyle: N.Y. NL, ...	25.00	12.50	2.50
Sweater			
□110 Doyle: N.Y. NL, ...	30.00	15.00	3.00
Throwing			
□111 Doyle: N.Y. NL, ...	25.00	12.50	2.50
Bat on shoulder			
□112 Dubuc: Cin.	25.00	12.50	2.50
□113 Duffy: Chicago AL	80.00	40.00	8.00
□114 Dunn: Brooklyn	25.00	12.50	2.50
□115 Durham: N.Y. NL	30.00	15.00	3.00
□116 Dygert: Phila. AL.	25.00	12.50	2.50
□117 Easterly: Cleveland	25.00	12.50	2.50
□118 Egan: Cinc.	25.00	12.50	2.50
□119 Elberfeld: Wash., ...	25.00	12.50	2.50
Fielding			
□120 Elberfeld: Wash., ...	600.00	300.00	60.00
Portrait			
□121 Elberfeld: N.Y. AL, ...	30.00	15.00	3.00
Portrait			
□122 Engle: N.Y. AL	25.00	12.50	2.50
□123 Evans: St.L. NL	25.00	12.50	2.50
□124 Evers: Chicago NL, ...	100.00	50.00	10.00
Portrait			
□125 Evers: Chicago NL, ...	125.00	60.00	12.50
Cubs across chest			
□126 Evers: Chicago NL, ...	80.00	40.00	8.00
Chicago down			
front of shirt			
□127 Ewing: Cinc.	30.00	15.00	3.00
□128 Ferguson: Boston NL	25.00	12.50	2.50
□129 Ferris: St.L. AL	30.00	15.00	3.00
□130 Fiene: Chicago AL, ...	25.00	12.50	2.50
Portrait			
□131 Fiene: Chicago AL, ...	25.00	12.50	2.50
Throwing			
□132 Fletcher: N.Y. NL	25.00	12.50	2.50
□133 Flick: Cleveland	100.00	50.00	10.00
□134 Ford: N.Y. AL	25.00	12.50	2.50
□135 Frill: N.Y. AL	25.00	12.50	2.50
□136 Fromme: Cinc.	25.00	12.50	2.50
□137 Gandil: Chicago AL	25.00	12.50	2.50
□138 Ganley: Washington	30.00	15.00	3.00
□139 Gasper: Cinc.	25.00	12.50	2.50
□140 Geyer: St.L. NL	25.00	12.50	2.50
□141 Gibson: Pitt.	30.00	15.00	3.00
□142 Gilbert: St.L. NL	30.00	15.00	3.00
□143 Goode (sic): Cleve.	30.00	15.00	3.00
□144 Graham: Boston NL	25.00	12.50	2.50
□145 Graham: St.L. AL	25.00	12.50	2.50
□146 Gray: Washington	25.00	12.50	2.50
□147 Griffith: Cinc., ...	100.00	50.00	10.00
Portrait			
□148 Griffith: Cinc., ...	80.00	40.00	8.00
Batting			
□149 Groom: Washington	25.00	12.50	2.50
□150 Hahn: Chicago AL	30.00	15.00	3.00
□151 Hartsel: Phila. AL	25.00	12.50	2.50
□152 Hemphill: N.Y. AL	30.00	15.00	3.00
□153 Herzog : N.Y. NL	30.00	15.00	3.00
□154 Herzog: Boston NL	25.00	12.50	2.50
□155 Hinchman: Cleveland	30.00	15.00	3.00
□156 Hoblitzell: Cinc.	25.00	12.50	2.50
□157 Hoffman: St.L. AL	25.00	12.50	2.50
□158 Hofman: Chicago NL	25.00	12.50	2.50
□159 Howard: Chicago NL	25.00	12.50	2.50
□160 Howell: St.L. AL, ...	25.00	12.50	2.50
Portrait			
□161 Howell: St.L. AL, ...	25.00	12.50	2.50
Left hand on hip			
□162 Huggins: Cinc., ...	100.00	50.00	10.00
Portrait			
□163 Huggins: Cinc., ...	80.00	40.00	8.00
Hands to mouth			
□164 Hulswitt: St.L. NL	25.00	12.50	2.50
□165 Hummel: Brooklyn	25.00	12.50	2.50
□166 Hunter: Brooklyn	25.00	12.50	2.50
□167 Isbell: Chicago AL	30.00	15.00	3.00
□168 Jacklitsch: Phila.NL	30.00	15.00	3.00
□169 Jennings: Detroit, ...	100.00	50.00	10.00
Portrait			
□170 Jennings: Detroit, ...	80.00	40.00	8.00
Yelling			
□171 Jennings: Detroit, ...	80.00	40.00	8.00
Dancing for joy			
□172 Johnson: Washington, ...	300.00	150.00	30.00
Portrait			
□173 Johnson: Washington, ...	250.00	125.00	25.00
Ready to pitch			
□174 Jones: St.L. AL	30.00	15.00	3.00
□175 Jones: Detroit	25.00	12.50	2.50
□176 F. Jones: Chic. AL, ...	30.00	15.00	3.00
Portrait			
□177 F. Jones: Chic. AL, ...	30.00	15.00	3.00
Hands on hips			
□178 Jordan: Brooklyn, ...	30.00	15.00	3.00
Portrait			
□179 Jordan: Brooklyn, ...	25.00	12.50	2.50
Batting			
□180 Joss: Cleveland, ...	150.00	75.00	15.00
Portrait			
□181 Joss: Cleveland, ...	100.00	50.00	10.00
Ready to pitch			
□182 Karger: Cinc.	30.00	15.00	3.00
□183 Keeler: N.Y. AL, ...	125.00	60.00	12.50
Portrait			
□184 Keeler: N.Y. AL, ...	125.00	60.00	12.50
Batting			
□185 Killian: Detroit, ...	30.00	15.00	3.00

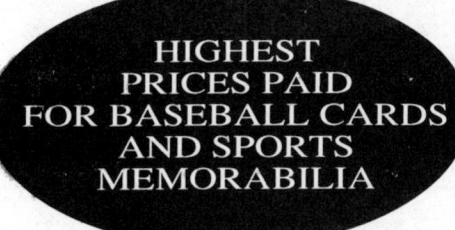

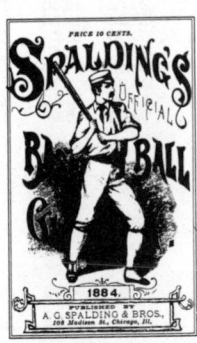

	Portrait			
☐ 186	Killian: Detroit, ...	25.00	12.50	2.50
	Pitching			
☐ 187	Kleinow: N.Y. AL, ...	30.00	15.00	3.00
	Batting			
☐ 188	Kleinow: N.Y. AL, ...	25.00	12.50	2.50
	Catching			
☐ 189	Kleinow: Bost. AL, ...	200.00	100.00	20.00
	Catching			
☐ 190	Kling: Chicago NL	30.00	15.00	3.00
☐ 191	Knabe: Phila. NL	25.00	12.50	2.50
☐ 192	Knight: N.Y. AL, ...	25.00	12.50	2.50
	Portrait			
☐ 193	Knight: N.Y. AL, ...	25.00	12.50	2.50
	Batting			
☐ 194	Konetchy: St.L. NL, ...	25.00	12.50	2.50
	Awaiting low ball			
☐ 195	Konetchy: St.L. NL, ...	30.00	15.00	3.00
	Glove above head			
☐ 196	Krause: Phila. AL, ...	25.00	12.50	2.50
	Portrait			
☐ 197	Krause: Phila. AL, ...	25.00	12.50	2.50
	Pitching			
☐ 198	Kroh: Chicago NL	25.00	12.50	2.50
☐ 199	Lajoie: Cleveland, ...	150.00	75.00	15.00
	Portrait			
☐ 200	Lajoie: Cleveland, ...	125.00	60.00	12.50
	Batting			
☐ 201	Lajoie: Cleveland, ...	150.00	75.00	15.00
	Throwing			
☐ 202	Lake: N.Y. AL	30.00	15.00	3.00
☐ 203	Lake: St.L. AL, ...	25.00	12.50	2.50
	Hands over head			
☐ 204	Lake: St.L. AL, ...	25.00	12.50	2.50
	Throwing			
☐ 205	LaPorte: N.Y. AL	25.00	12.50	2.50
☐ 206	Latham: N.Y. NL	25.00	12.50	2.50
☐ 207	Leach: Pitt., ...	30.00	15.00	3.00
	Portrait			
☐ 208	Leach: Pitt., In	25.00	12.50	2.50
	fielding position			
☐ 209	Leifield: Pitt., ...	25.00	12.50	2.50
	Batting			
☐ 210	Leifield: Pitt., ...	30.00	15.00	3.00
	Hands behind head			
☐ 211	Lennox: Brooklyn	25.00	12.50	2.50
☐ 212	Liebhardt: Cleve.	30.00	15.00	3.00
☐ 213	Lindaman: Boston NL	30.00	15.00	3.00
☐ 214	Livingstone: Phila.AL	25.00	12.50	2.50
☐ 215	Lobert: Cinc.	30.00	15.00	3.00
☐ 216	Lord: Bost. AL	25.00	12.50	2.50
☐ 217	Lumley: Brooklyn	30.00	15.00	3.00
☐ 218	Lundgren: Chicago NL	200.00	100.00	20.00
☐ 219	Maddox: Pitt.	25.00	12.50	2.50
☐ 220	Magee: Phila. NL, ...	30.00	15.00	3.00
	Portrait			
☐ 221	Magee: Phila. NL, ...	25.00	12.50	2.50
	Batting			
☐ 222	Magie: Phila. NL	6000.00	2500.00	500.00
	(sic) Portrait,			
	name misspelled			
☐ 223	Manning: N.Y. AL, ...	30.00	15.00	3.00
	Batting			
☐ 224	Manning: N.Y. AL, ...	25.00	12.50	2.50
	Hands over head			
☐ 225	Marquard: N.Y. NL, ...	80.00	40.00	8.00
	Portrait			
☐ 226	Marquard: N.Y. NL, ...	80.00	40.00	8.00
	Pitching			
☐ 227	Marquard: N.Y. NL, ...	100.00	50.00	10.00
	Standing			
☐ 228	Marshall: Brooklyn	25.00	12.50	2.50
☐ 229	Mathewson: N.Y. NL, ...	250.00	125.00	25.00
	Portrait			
☐ 230	Mathewson: N.Y. NL, ...	250.00	125.00	25.00
	Pitching, white cap			
☐ 231	Mathewson: N.Y. NL, ...	200.00	100.00	20.00
	Pitching, dark cap			
☐ 232	Mattern: Boston NL	25.00	12.50	2.50
☐ 233	McAleese: St.L. AL	25.00	12.50	2.50
☐ 234	McBride: Washington	25.00	12.50	2.50
☐ 235	McCormick: N.Y. NL	25.00	12.50	2.50
☐ 236	McElveen: Brooklyn	25.00	12.50	2.50
☐ 237	McGraw: N.Y. NL, ...	125.00	60.00	12.50
	Portrait, no cap			
☐ 238	McGraw: N.Y. NL, ...	100.00	50.00	10.00
	Wearing sweater			
☐ 239	McGraw: N.Y. NL, ...	125.00	60.00	12.50
	pointing			
☐ 240	McGraw: N.Y. NL, ...	100.00	50.00	10.00
	Glove on hip			
☐ 241	McIntyre: Detroit	25.00	12.50	2.50
☐ 242	McIntyre: Brooklyn	30.00	15.00	3.00
☐ 243	McIntyre: Brooklyn	25.00	12.50	2.50
	and Chicago NL			

☐ 244	McLean: Cinc.	25.00	12.50	2.50
☐ 245	McQuillan: Phila.	30.00	15.00	3.00
	NL, Throwing			
☐ 246	McQuillan: Phila.	25.00	12.50	2.50
	NL, Batting			
☐ 247	Merkle: N.Y. NL, ...	30.00	15.00	3.00
	Portrait			
☐ 248	Merkle: N.Y. NL, ...	25.00	12.50	2.50
	Throwing			
☐ 249	Meyers: N.Y. NL	25.00	12.50	2.50
☐ 250	Milan: Washington	25.00	12.50	2.50
☐ 251	Miller: Pitt.	25.00	12.50	2.50
☐ 252	Mitchell: Cinc.	25.00	12.50	2.50
☐ 253	Moran: Chicago NL	25.00	12.50	2.50
☐ 254	Moriarty: Detroit	25.00	12.50	2.50
☐ 255	Mowrey: Cinc.	25.00	12.50	2.50
☐ 256	Mullen: Detroit	25.00	12.50	2.50
☐ 257	Mullin: Detroit, ...	30.00	15.00	3.00
	Throwing			
☐ 258	Mullin: Detroit, ...	25.00	12.50	2.50
	Batting			
☐ 259	Murphy: Phila. AL, ...	30.00	15.00	3.00
	Throwing			
☐ 260	Murphy: Phila. AL, ...	25.00	12.50	2.50
	Bat on shoulder			
☐ 261	Murray: N.Y. NL, ...	25.00	12.50	2.50
	Sweater			
☐ 262	Murray: N.Y. NL, ...	25.00	12.50	2.50
	Bat on shoulder			
☐ 263	Myers (sic): N.Y. NL, ...	25.00	12.50	2.50
	Fielding			
☐ 264	Myers (sic): N.Y. NL, ...	25.00	12.50	2.50
	Batting			
☐ 265	Needham: Chicago NL ...	25.00	12.50	2.50
☐ 266	Nicholls: Phila. AL	30.00	15.00	3.00
☐ 267	Nichols(sic):	25.00	12.50	2.50
	Phila. AL			
☐ 268	Niles: Boston AL	30.00	15.00	3.00
☐ 269	Oakes: Cinc.	25.00	12.50	2.50
☐ 270	O'Hara: St.L. NL	1250.00	500.00	100.00
☐ 271	O'Hara: N.Y. NL	25.00	12.50	2.50
☐ 272	Oldring: Phila. AL, ...	30.00	15.00	3.00
	Fielding			
☐ 273	Oldring: Phila. AL, ...	25.00	12.50	2.50
	Bat on shoulder			
☐ 274	O'Leary: Detroit, ...	30.00	15.00	3.00
	Portrait			
☐ 275	O'Leary: Detroit, ...	25.00	12.50	2.50
	Hands on knees			
☐ 276	Overall: Chicago NL, ...	30.00	15.00	3.00
	Portrait			
☐ 277	Overall: Chicago NL, ...	25.00	12.50	2.50
	Pitching, follow thru			
☐ 278	Overall: Chicago NL, ...	25.00	12.50	2.50
	Pitching hiding			
	ball in glove			
☐ 279	Owen: Chicago AL	30.00	15.00	3.00
☐ 280	Parent: Chicago AL	30.00	15.00	3.00
☐ 281	Paskert: Cinc.	25.00	12.50	2.50
☐ 282	Pastorius: Brooklyn	30.00	15.00	3.00
☐ 283	Pattee: Brooklyn	50.00	25.00	5.00
☐ 284	Payne: Chicago AL	25.00	12.50	2.50
☐ 285	Pelty: St.L. AL, HOR	50.00	25.00	5.00
☐ 286	Pelty: St.L. AL, VERT	25.00	12.50	2.50
☐ 287	Perring: Cleveland	25.00	12.50	2.50
☐ 288	Pfeffer: Chicago NL	25.00	12.50	2.50
☐ 289	Pfeister: Chic. NL, ...	25.00	12.50	2.50
	Sitting			
☐ 290	Pfeister: Chic. NL, ...	25.00	12.50	2.50
	Pitching			
☐ 291	Phelps: St.L. NL	25.00	12.50	2.50
☐ 292	Phillippe: Pitt.	25.00	12.50	2.50
☐ 293	Plank: Phila. AL	7000.00	3000.00	600.00
☐ 294	Powell: St.L. AL	30.00	15.00	3.00
☐ 295	Powers: Phil. AL	50.00	25.00	5.00
☐ 296	Purtell: Chicago AL	25.00	12.50	2.50
☐ 297	Quinn: N.Y. AL	25.00	12.50	2.50
☐ 298	Raymond: N.Y. NL	25.00	12.50	2.50
☐ 299	Reulbach: Chicago NL, ...	25.00	12.50	2.50
	Pitching			
☐ 300	Reulbach: Chicago NL, ...	50.00	25.00	5.00
	Hands at side			
☐ 301	Rhoades: Cleveland, ...	25.00	12.50	2.50
	Hand in air			
☐ 302	Rhoades: Cleveland, ...	25.00	12.50	2.50
	Ready to pitch			
☐ 303	Rhodes: St.L. NL	25.00	12.50	2.50
☐ 304	Ritchey: Boston NL	30.00	15.00	3.00
☐ 305	Rossman: Detroit	25.00	12.50	2.50
☐ 306	Rucker: Brooklyn, ...	30.00	15.00	3.00
	Portrait			
☐ 307	Rucker: Brooklyn, ...	25.00	12.50	2.50
	Pitching			

☐ 308	Schaefer: Washington	25.00	12.50	2.50
☐ 309	Schaefer: Detroit	30.00	15.00	3.00
☐ 310	Schlei: N.Y. NL, ... Sweater	25.00	12.50	2.50
☐ 311	Schlei: N.Y. NL, ... Batting	25.00	12.50	2.50
☐ 312	Schlei: N.Y. NL, ... Fielding	30.00	15.00	3.00
☐ 313	Schmidt: Detroit, ... Portrait	25.00	12.50	2.50
☐ 314	Schmidt: Detroit, ... Throwing	30.00	15.00	3.00
☐ 315	Schulte: Chicago NL, ... Batting, back turned	25.00	12.50	2.50
☐ 316	Schulte: Chicago NL, ... Batting, front pose	30.00	15.00	3.00
☐ 317	Scott: Chicago AL	25.00	12.50	2.50
☐ 318	Seymour: N.Y. NL, ... Portrait	25.00	12.50	2.50
☐ 319	Seymour: N.Y. NL, ... Throwing	25.00	12.50	2.50
☐ 320	Seymour: N.Y. NL, ... Batting	30.00	15.00	3.00
☐ 321	Shaw: St.L. NL	30.00	15.00	3.00
☐ 322	Sheckard: Chic. NL, ... Throwing	25.00	12.50	2.50
☐ 323	Sheckard: Chic. NL, ... Side view	30.00	15.00	3.00
☐ 324	Shipke: Washington	30.00	15.00	3.00
☐ 325	Smith: Chicago AL	25.00	12.50	2.50
☐ 326	Smith: Chicago and .... Boston AL	250.00	125.00	25.00
☐ 327	F. Smith: Chicago AL	30.00	15.00	3.00
☐ 328	Happy Smith: Brk.	25.00	12.50	2.50
☐ 329	Snodgrass: N.Y. NL, ... Batting	25.00	12.50	2.50
☐ 330	Snodgrass: N.Y. NL, ... Catching	25.00	12.50	2.50
☐ 331	Spade: Cinc.	30.00	15.00	3.00
☐ 332	Speaker: Boston AL	150.00	75.00	15.00
☐ 333	Spencer: Boston AL	30.00	15.00	3.00
☐ 334	Stahl: Boston AL, ... Catching fly ball	25.00	12.50	2.50
☐ 335	Stahl: Boston AL, ... Standing, arms down	30.00	15.00	3.00
☐ 336	Stanage: Detroit	25.00	12.50	2.50
☐ 337	Starr: Boston NL	25.00	12.50	2.50
☐ 338	Steinfeldt: Chic. NL, ... Portrait	30.00	15.00	3.00
☐ 339	Steinfeldt: Chic. NL, ... Batting	25.00	12.50	2.50
☐ 340	Stephens: St.L. AL	25.00	12.50	2.50
☐ 341	Stone: St.L. AL	30.00	15.00	3.00
☐ 342	Stovall: Cleveland, ... Portrait	30.00	15.00	3.00
☐ 343	Stovall: Cleveland, ... Batting	25.00	12.50	2.50
☐ 344	Street: Washington, ... Portrait	25.00	12.50	2.50
☐ 345	Street: Washington, ... Catching	25.00	12.50	2.50
☐ 346	Sullivan: Chicago AL	30.00	15.00	3.00
☐ 347	Summers: Detroit	25.00	12.50	2.50
☐ 348	Sweeney: N.Y. AL	25.00	12.50	2.50
☐ 349	Sweeney: Bost. NL	25.00	12.50	2.50
☐ 350	L. Tannehill: Chic.AL	30.00	15.00	3.00
☐ 351	Tannehill: Chicago AL	25.00	12.50	2.50
☐ 352	Tannehill: Wash.	25.00	12.50	2.50
☐ 353	Tenney: N.Y. NL	30.00	15.00	3.00
☐ 354	Thomas: Phila. AL	25.00	12.50	2.50
☐ 355	Tinker: Chicago NL, ... Ready to hit	80.00	40.00	8.00
☐ 356	Tinker: Chicago NL, ... Bat on shoulder	80.00	40.00	8.00
☐ 357	Tinker: Chicago NL, ... Portrait	100.00	50.00	10.00
☐ 358	Tinker: Chicago NL, ... Hands on knees	100.00	50.00	10.00
☐ 359	Titus: Phila. NL	25.00	12.50	2.50
☐ 360	Turner: Cleveland	30.00	15.00	3.00
☐ 361	Unglaub: Washington	25.00	12.50	2.50
☐ 362	Waddell: St.L. AL, ... Portrait	100.00	50.00	10.00
☐ 363	Waddell: St.L. AL, ... Pitching	100.00	50.00	10.00
☐ 364	Wagner: Boston AL, ... Bat on left shoulder	50.00	25.00	5.00
☐ 365	Wagner: Boston AL, ... Bat on right shoulder	30.00	15.00	3.00
☐ 366	Wagner: Pitt.	50000.	20000.	6000.
☐ 367	Wallace: St.L. AL	100.00	50.00	10.00
☐ 368	Walsh: Chicago AL	100.00	50.00	10.00
☐ 369	Warhop: N.Y. AL	25.00	12.50	2.50
☐ 370	Weimer: N.Y. NL	30.00	15.00	3.00
☐ 371	Wheat: Brooklyn	80.00	40.00	8.00

☐ 372	White: Chicago AL, ... Portrait	30.00	15.00	3.00
☐ 373	White: Chicago AL, ... Pitching	25.00	12.50	2.50
☐ 374	Wilhelm: Brooklyn, ... Batting	25.00	12.50	2.50
☐ 375	Wilhelm: Brooklyn, ... Hands to chest	30.00	15.00	3.00
☐ 376	Willett: Detroit, ... Batting	25.00	12.50	2.50
☐ 377	Willetts (sic): .... Detroit, Pitching	25.00	12.50	2.50
☐ 378	Williams: St.L. AL	30.00	15.00	3.00
☐ 379	Willis: Pitt.	50.00	25.00	5.00
☐ 380	Willis: St.L. NL, ... Pitching	40.00	20.00	4.00
☐ 381	Willis: St.L. NL, ... Batting	40.00	20.00	4.00
☐ 382	Wilson: Pitt.	25.00	12.50	2.50
☐ 383	Wiltse: N.Y. NL, ... Portrait	30.00	15.00	3.00
☐ 384	Wiltse: N.Y. NL, ... Sweater	25.00	12.50	2.50
☐ 385	Wiltse: N.Y. NL, ... Pitching	25.00	12.50	2.50
☐ 386	Young: Cleveland, ... Portrait	150.00	75.00	15.00
☐ 387	Young: Cleveland, ... Pitch, front view	125.00	60.00	12.50
☐ 388	Young: Cleveland, ... Pitch, side view	150.00	75.00	15.00
☐ 389	Zimmerman: .... Chicago NL	25.00	12.50	2.50
☐ 390	Fred Abbott: Toledo	21.00	10.50	2.10
☐ 391	Merle (Doc) Adkins: .... Baltimore	21.00	10.50	2.10
☐ 392	John Anderson: Prov.	21.00	10.50	2.10
☐ 393	Herman Armbruster: ...... St. Paul	21.00	10.50	2.10
☐ 394	Harry Arndt: Prov.	21.00	10.50	2.10
☐ 395	Cy Barger: Rochester	21.00	10.50	2.10
☐ 396	John Barry: Milwaukee ...	21.00	10.50	2.10
☐ 397	Emil H. Batch: Roch.	21.00	10.50	2.10
☐ 398	Jake Beckley: K.C.	100.00	50.00	10.00
☐ 399	Russell Blackburne .... (Lena): Providence	21.00	10.50	2.10
☐ 400	David Brain: Buffalo	21.00	10.50	2.10
☐ 401	Roy Brashear: K.C.	21.00	10.50	2.10
☐ 402	Fred Burchell: Buffalo	21.00	10.50	2.10
☐ 403	Jimmy Burke: Ind.	21.00	10.50	2.10
☐ 404	John Butler: Roch.	21.00	10.50	2.10
☐ 405	Charles Carr: Ind.	21.00	10.50	2.10
☐ 406	James Peter Casey .... (Doc): Montreal	21.00	10.50	2.10
☐ 407	Peter Cassidy: Balt.	21.00	10.50	2.10
☐ 408	Wm. Chappelle: Roch.	21.00	10.50	2.10
☐ 409	Wm. Clancy: Buffalo	21.00	10.50	2.10
☐ 410	Joshua Clark: Col.	21.00	10.50	2.10
☐ 411	William Clymer: Col.	21.00	10.50	2.10
☐ 412	Jimmy Collins: Minn.	100.00	50.00	10.00
☐ 413	Bunk Congalton: .... Columbus	21.00	10.50	2.10
☐ 414	Gavvy Cravath: Minn.	30.00	15.00	3.00
☐ 415	Monte Cross: Ind.	21.00	10.50	2.10
☐ 416	Paul Davidson: Ind.	21.00	10.50	2.10
☐ 417	Frank Delehanty: .... Louisville	21.00	10.50	2.10
☐ 418	Rube Dessau: Balt.	21.00	10.50	2.10
☐ 419	Gus Dorner: K.C.	21.00	10.50	2.10
☐ 420	Jerome Downs: Minn.	21.00	10.50	2.10
☐ 421	Jack Dunn: Baltimore	21.00	10.50	2.10
☐ 422	James Flanagan: Buff.	21.00	10.50	2.10
☐ 423	James Freeman: Tol.	21.00	10.50	2.10
☐ 424	John Ganzel: Roch.	21.00	10.50	2.10
☐ 425	Myron Grimshaw: Tor. ...	21.00	10.50	2.10
☐ 426	Robert Hall: Balt.	21.00	10.50	2.10
☐ 427	William Hallman: K.C.	21.00	10.50	2.10
☐ 428	John Hannifan: J.C.	21.00	10.50	2.10
☐ 429	Jack Hayden: Ind.	21.00	10.50	2.10
☐ 430	Harry Hinchman: Tol.	21.00	10.50	2.10
☐ 431	Harry C. Hoffman .... (Izzy): Providence	21.00	10.50	2.10
☐ 432	James B. Jackson: .... Baltimore	21.00	10.50	2.10
☐ 433	Joe Kelley: Tor.	100.00	50.00	10.00
☐ 434	Rube Kisinger: Buff. .... (sic) Kissinger	21.00	10.50	2.10
☐ 435	Otto Kruger: Col. .... (sic) Krueger	21.00	10.50	2.10
☐ 436	Wm. Lattimore: Tol.	21.00	10.50	2.10
☐ 437	James Lavender: Prov. ..	21.00	10.50	2.10
☐ 438	Carl Lundgren: K.C.	21.00	10.50	2.10
☐ 439	Wm. Malarkey: Buff.	21.00	10.50	2.10
☐ 440	Wm. Maloney: Roch.	21.00	10.50	2.10
☐ 441	Dennis McGann: Milw.	21.00	10.50	2.10

Brian Morris

226 North Fullerton Avenue
Montclair, NJ 07042
201-509-8484

Specializing in Hartland Statues, Scarce, Rare
and Unusual Issues and single cards, as well
as Topps, Bowman, Playballs, Goudeys and
Tobacco cards

✦ **If you're a Team collector,**

✦ **If you're a Superstar collector,**

✦ **If you're a Hall of Fame collector.**

✦ **If you're a Type card collector,**

✦ **Try me, I may be able to help your
collection grow.**

I also am buying any issues listed in this
book in Mint condition prior to 1979 for
70-100% of the values printed. I also will buy
cards prior to 1959 in lesser conditions.

☐ 442	James McGinley: Tor.	21.00	10.50	2.10
☐ 443	Joe McGinnity: New.	100.00	50.00	10.00
☐ 444	Ulysses McGlynn: Mil.	21.00	10.50	2.10
☐ 445	George Merritt: J.C.	21.00	10.50	2.10
☐ 446	Wm. Milligan: J.C.	21.00	10.50	2.10
☐ 447	Fred Mitchell: Tor.	21.00	10.50	2.10
☐ 448	Dan Moeller: J.C.	21.00	10.50	2.10
☐ 449	Joseph Herbert Moran: .. Prov.	21.00	10.50	2.10
☐ 450	Wm. Nattress: Buffalo	21.00	10.50	2.10
☐ 451	Frank Oberlin: Minn.	21.00	10.50	2.10
☐ 452	Peter O'Brien: .... St. Paul	21.00	10.50	2.10
☐ 453	Wm. O'Neil: Minn.	21.00	10.50	2.10
☐ 454	James Phelan: Prov.	21.00	10.50	2.10
☐ 455	Oliver Pickering: .... Minneapolis.	21.00	10.50	2.10
☐ 456	Philip Poland: Balt.	21.00	10.50	2.10
☐ 457	Ambrose Puttman: .... Louisville	21.00	10.50	2.10
☐ 458	Lee Quillen: Minn.	21.00	10.50	2.10
☐ 459	Newton Randall: Milw.	21.00	10.50	2.10
☐ 460	Louis Ritter: K.C.	21.00	10.50	2.10
☐ 461	Dick Rudolph: Tor.	21.00	10.50	2.10
☐ 462	George Schirm: Buff.	21.00	10.50	2.10
☐ 463	Larry Schlafly: .... Newark	21.00	10.50	2.10
☐ 464	Ossie Schreck: Col. .... (sic) Schreckengost	21.00	10.50	2.10
☐ 465	William Shannon: K.C.	21.00	10.50	2.10
☐ 466	Bayard Sharpe: Newark .	21.00	10.50	2.10
☐ 467	Royal Shaw: Prov.	21.00	10.50	2.10
☐ 468	James Slagle: Balt.	21.00	10.50	2.10
☐ 469	George Henry Smith: ..... Buffalo	21.00	10.50	2.10
☐ 470	Samuel Strang: Balt.	21.00	10.50	2.10
☐ 471	Luther(Dummy) Taylor: . Buffalo	21.00	10.50	2.10
☐ 472	John Thielman: .... Louisville	21.00	10.50	2.10
☐ 473	John F. White: Buff.	21.00	10.50	2.10
☐ 474	William Wright: Tol.	21.00	10.50	2.10
☐ 475	Irving M. Young: .... Minneapolis	21.00	10.50	2.10
☐ 476	Jack Bastian: .... San Antonio	75.00	37.50	7.50
☐ 477	Harry Bay: Nashv.	75.00	37.50	7.50
☐ 478	Wm. Bernhard: Nashv. ...	75.00	37.50	7.50
☐ 479	Ted Breitenstein: .... New Orleans	75.00	37.50	7.50
☐ 480	George(Scoops) Carey: .. Memphis	75.00	37.50	7.50
☐ 481	Cad Coles: Augusta	75.00	37.50	7.50
☐ 482	Wm. Cranston: Memph. ..	75.00	37.50	7.50
☐ 483	Roy Ellam: Nashville	75.00	37.50	7.50
☐ 484	Edward Foster: .... Charleston	75.00	37.50	7.50
☐ 485	Charles Fritz: N.O.	75.00	37.50	7.50
☐ 486	Ed Greminger: Montg.	75.00	37.50	7.50
☐ 487	Guiheen: Portsmouth	75.00	37.50	7.50
☐ 488	William F. Hart .... Little Rock	75.00	37.50	7.50
☐ 489	James Henry Hart: .... Montgomery	75.00	37.50	7.50
☐ 490	J.R. Helm: Columbus ..... (Georgia)	75.00	37.50	7.50
☐ 491	Gordon Hickman: .... Mobile	75.00	37.50	7.50
☐ 492	Buck Hooker: .... Lynchburg	75.00	37.50	7.50
☐ 493	Ernie Howard: Sav.	75.00	37.50	7.50
☐ 494	A.O. Jordan: Atlanta	75.00	37.50	7.50
☐ 495	J.F. Kiernan: .... Columbia	75.00	37.50	7.50
☐ 496	Frank King: Danville	75.00	37.50	7.50
☐ 497	James LaFitte: Macon	75.00	37.50	7.50
☐ 498	Harry Lentz: Little .... Rock (sic) Sentz	75.00	37.50	7.50
☐ 499	Perry Lipe: Richmond	75.00	37.50	7.50
☐ 500	George Manion: .... Columbia	75.00	37.50	7.50
☐ 501	McCauley: Portsmouth ..	75.00	37.50	7.50
☐ 502	Charles B. Miller: .... Dallas	75.00	37.50	7.50
☐ 503	Carlton Molesworth: ...... Birmingham	75.00	37.50	7.50
☐ 504	Dominic Mullaney: .... Jacksonville	75.00	37.50	7.50
☐ 505	Albert Orth: Lynchb.	75.00	37.50	7.50
☐ 506	William Otey: Norf.	75.00	37.50	7.50
☐ 507	George Paige: .... Charleston	75.00	37.50	7.50
☐ 508	Hub Perdue: Nashv.	75.00	37.50	7.50
☐ 509	Archie Persons: .... Montgomery	75.00	37.50	7.50

☐ 510	Edward Reagan: N.O.	75.00	37.50	7.50
☐ 511	R.H. Revelle: Richm.	75.00	37.50	7.50
☐ 512	Isaac Rockenfeld: .... Montgomery	75.00	37.50	7.50
☐ 513	Ray Ryan: Roanoke	75.00	37.50	7.50
☐ 514	Charles Seitz: Norf.	75.00	37.50	7.50
☐ 515	Frank (Shag) Shaughn- .. essy: Roanoke	75.00	37.50	7.50
☐ 516	Carlos Smith: Shreve.	75.00	37.50	7.50
☐ 517	Sid Smith: Atlanta	75.00	37.50	7.50
☐ 518	M.R. (Dolly) Stark: .... San Antonio	75.00	37.50	7.50
☐ 519	Tony Thebo: Waco	75.00	37.50	7.50
☐ 520	Woodie Thornton: .... Mobile	75.00	37.50	7.50
☐ 521	Juan Violat: Jackson- ..... ville: (sic) Viola	75.00	37.50	7.50
☐ 522	James Westlake: .... Danville	75.00	37.50	7.50
☐ 523	Foley White: Houston	75.00	37.50	7.50

T207 Brown Background

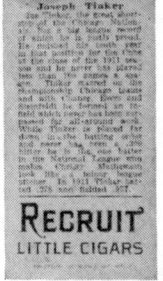

The cards in this 207 card set measure 1 1/2" by 2 5/8". The T207 set, also known as the "Brown Background" set was issued with Broadleaf, Cycle, Napoleon, Recruit and anonymous (Factories no. 2, 3 or 25) backs in 1912. Broadleaf, Cycle and anonymous backs are difficult to obtain. Although many scarcities and cards with varying degrees of difficulty to obtain exist (see prices below), the Loudermilk, Lewis (Boston NL) and Miller (Chicago NL) cards are the rarest, followed by Saier and Tyler. The cards are numbered below for reference in alphabetical order by player's name. The complete set price below does not include the Lewis variation missing the Braves patch on the sleeve.

		NRMT	VG-E	GOOD
COMPLETE SET		15000.00	6000.00	900.00
COMMON PLAYER		30.00	15.00	3.00
☐ 1	Adams: Cleve AL	60.00	30.00	6.00
☐ 2	Ainsmith: Wash AL	30.00	15.00	3.00
☐ 3	Almeida: Cinc AL	60.00	30.00	6.00
☐ 4	Austin: StL AL .... with StL on shirt	30.00	15.00	3.00
☐ 5	Austin: StL AL .... without StL on shirt	90.00	45.00	9.00
☐ 6	Ball: Cleve AL	30.00	15.00	3.00
☐ 7	Barger: Brk NL	30.00	15.00	3.00
☐ 8	Barry: Phil AL	30.00	15.00	3.00
☐ 9	Bauman: Det AL	90.00	45.00	9.00
☐ 10	Becker: NY NL	30.00	15.00	3.00
☐ 11	Bender: Phil AL	90.00	45.00	9.00
☐ 12	Benz: Chi AL	60.00	30.00	6.00
☐ 13	Bescher: Cinc NL	30.00	15.00	3.00
☐ 14	Birmingham: Cleve AL	60.00	30.00	6.00
☐ 15	Blackburne: Chi AL	60.00	30.00	6.00
☐ 16	Blanding: Cleve AL	60.00	30.00	6.00
☐ 17	Block: Chi AL	30.00	15.00	3.00
☐ 18	Bodie: Chi AL	30.00	15.00	3.00
☐ 19	Bradley: Bos AL	30.00	15.00	3.00
☐ 20	Bresnahan: StL NL	75.00	37.50	7.50
☐ 21	Bushelman: Bos AL	60.00	30.00	6.00
☐ 22	Butcher: Cleve AL	60.00	30.00	6.00
☐ 23	Byrne: Pitt NL	30.00	15.00	3.00

□ 24 Callahan: Chi AL	30.00	15.00	3.00
□ 25 Camnitz: Pitt NL	30.00	15.00	3.00
□ 26 Carey: Pitt NL	90.00	45.00	9.00
□ 27 Carrigan: Bos AL correct back	30.00	15.00	3.00
□ 28 Carrigan: Bos AL Wagner back	120.00	60.00	12.00
□ 29 Chalmers: Phil NL	30.00	15.00	3.00
□ 30 Chance: Chi NL	100.00	50.00	10.00
□ 31 Cicotte: Bos AL	40.00	20.00	4.00
□ 32 Clarke: Cinc NL	30.00	15.00	3.00
□ 33 Cole: Chi NL	30.00	15.00	3.00
□ 34 Collins: Chi AL	150.00	75.00	15.00
□ 35 Coulson: Brk NL	30.00	15.00	3.00
□ 36 Covington: Det AL	30.00	15.00	3.00
□ 37 Crandall: NY NL	30.00	15.00	3.00
□ 38 Cunningham: Wash AL	60.00	30.00	6.00
□ 39 Danforth: Phil AL	30.00	15.00	3.00
□ 40 Daniels: NY AL	30.00	15.00	3.00
□ 41 Daubert: Brk NL	40.00	20.00	4.00
□ 42 Davis: Cleve NL	30.00	15.00	3.00
□ 43 Delahanty: Det AL	30.00	15.00	3.00
□ 44 Derrick: Phil AL	30.00	15.00	3.00
□ 45 Devlin: Bos NL	30.00	15.00	3.00
□ 46 Devore: NY NL	30.00	15.00	3.00
□ 47 Donlin: Pitt NL	60.00	30.00	6.00
□ 48 Donnelly: Bos NL	60.00	30.00	6.00
□ 49 Dooin: Phil NL	30.00	15.00	3.00
□ 50 Downey: Phil NL	60.00	30.00	6.00
□ 51 Doyle: NY NL	30.00	15.00	3.00
□ 52 Drake: Det AL	30.00	15.00	3.00
□ 53 Easterly: Cleve AL	30.00	15.00	3.00
□ 54 Ellis: StL NL	30.00	15.00	3.00
□ 55 Engle: Bos AL	30.00	15.00	3.00
□ 56 Erwin: Brk NL	30.00	15.00	3.00
□ 57 Evans: StL NL	30.00	15.00	3.00
□ 58 Ferry: Pitt NL	30.00	15.00	3.00
□ 59 Fisher: NY AL white cap	75.00	37.50	7.50
□ 60 Fisher: NY AL blue cap	45.00	22.50	4.50
□ 61 Fletcher: NY NL	30.00	15.00	3.00
□ 62 Fournier: Chi AL	60.00	30.00	6.00
□ 63 Fromme: Cinc NL	30.00	15.00	3.00
□ 64 Gainor: Det AL	30.00	15.00	3.00
□ 65 Gardner: Bos AL	30.00	15.00	3.00
□ 66 George: Cleve AL	30.00	15.00	3.00
□ 67 Golden: StL NL	30.00	15.00	3.00
□ 68 Gowdy: Bos NL	30.00	15.00	3.00
□ 69 Graham: Phil NL	40.00	20.00	4.00
□ 70 Graney: Cleve AL	30.00	15.00	3.00
□ 71 Gregg: Cleve AL	60.00	30.00	6.00
□ 72 Hageman: Bos AL	30.00	15.00	3.00
□ 73 Hall: Bos AL	30.00	15.00	3.00
□ 74 Hallinan: St.L. AL	30.00	15.00	3.00
□ 75 E. Hamilton: St.L. AL	30.00	15.00	3.00
□ 76 Harmon: St.L. NL	30.00	15.00	3.00
□ 77 Hartley: NY NL	60.00	30.00	6.00
□ 78 Henriksen, Bos AL	30.00	15.00	3.00
□ 79 Henry: Wash AL	45.00	22.50	4.50
□ 80 Herzog: NY NL	60.00	30.00	6.00
□ 81 Higgins: Brk NL	30.00	15.00	3.00
□ 82 Hoff: NY AL	60.00	30.00	6.00
□ 83 Hogan: StL AL	30.00	15.00	3.00
□ 84 Hooper: Bos AL	200.00	100.00	20.00
□ 85 Houser: Bos AL	60.00	30.00	6.00
□ 86 Hyatt: Pitt NL	60.00	30.00	6.00
□ 87 Johnson: Wash AL	350.00	175.00	35.00
□ 88 Kaler: Cleve AL	30.00	15.00	3.00
□ 89 Kelly: Pitt NL	60.00	30.00	6.00
□ 90 Kirke: Bos NL	60.00	30.00	6.00
□ 91 Kling: Bos NL	30.00	15.00	3.00
□ 92 Knabe: Phil NL	30.00	15.00	3.00
□ 93 Knetzer: Brk NL	30.00	15.00	3.00
□ 94 Konetchy: StL NL	30.00	15.00	3.00
□ 95 Krause: Phil AL	30.00	15.00	3.00
□ 96 Kuhn: Chi AL	60.00	30.00	6.00
□ 97 Kutina: StL AL	60.00	30.00	6.00
□ 98 Lange: Chi AL	60.00	30.00	6.00
□ 99 Lapp: Phil AL	30.00	15.00	3.00
□ 100 Latham: NY NL	30.00	15.00	3.00
□ 101 Leach: Pitt NL	30.00	15.00	3.00
□ 102 Leifield: Pitt NL	30.00	15.00	3.00
□ 103 Lennox: Chi NL	30.00	15.00	3.00
□ 104 Lewis: Bos AL	30.00	15.00	3.00
□ 105A Lewis: Bos NL (Braves patch on sleeve)	1400.00	600.00	120.00
□ 105B Lewis: Bos NL (nothing on sleeve)	1750.00	700.00	140.00
□ 106 Lively: Det AL	30.00	15.00	3.00
□ 107 Livingston: Cleve AL "A" shirt	120.00	60.00	12.00
□ 108 Livingston: Cleve AL "C" shirt	120.00	60.00	12.00
□ 109 Livingston: Cleve AL "c" shirt	45.00	22.50	4.50
□ 110 Lord: Phil AL	30.00	15.00	3.00
□ 111 Lord: Chi AL	30.00	15.00	3.00
□ 112 Loudermilk: StL NL	1400.00	600.00	120.00
□ 113 Marquard: NY NL	90.00	45.00	9.00
□ 114 Marsans: Cinc NL	30.00	15.00	3.00
□ 115 McBride: Wash AL	30.00	15.00	3.00
□ 116 McCarthy: Pitt NL	120.00	60.00	12.00
□ 117 McDonald: Bos NL	30.00	15.00	3.00
□ 118 McGraw: NY NL	120.00	60.00	12.00
□ 119 McIntire: Chi AL	30.00	15.00	3.00
□ 120 McIntyre: Chi AL	30.00	15.00	3.00
□ 121 McKechnie: Pitt NL	175.00	85.00	18.00
□ 122 McLean: Cinc NL	30.00	15.00	3.00
□ 123 Milan: Wash AL	30.00	15.00	3.00
□ 124 Miller: Pitt NL	30.00	15.00	3.00
□ 125 Miller: Chi NL	1400.00	600.00	120.00
□ 126 Miller: Brk NL	60.00	30.00	6.00
□ 127 Miller: Bos NL	60.00	30.00	6.00
□ 128 Mitchell: Cinc NL	30.00	15.00	3.00
□ 129 Mitchell: Cleve AL	45.00	22.50	4.50
□ 130 Mogridge: Chi AL	60.00	30.00	6.00
□ 131 Moore: Phil NL	60.00	30.00	6.00
□ 132 Moran: Phil NL	30.00	15.00	3.00
□ 133 Morgan: Phil AL	30.00	15.00	3.00
□ 134 Morgan: Wash AL	30.00	15.00	3.00
□ 135 Moriarity: Det AL	60.00	30.00	6.00
□ 136 Mullin: Det AL with "D" on cap	40.00	20.00	4.00
□ 137 Mullin: Det AL without "D" on cap	100.00	50.00	10.00
□ 138 Needham: Chi NL	30.00	15.00	3.00
□ 139 Nelson: StL AL	60.00	30.00	6.00
□ 140 Northen: Brk NL	30.00	15.00	3.00
□ 141 Nunamaker: Bos AL	30.00	15.00	3.00
□ 142 Oakes: StL NL	30.00	15.00	3.00
□ 143 O'Brien: Bos AL	30.00	15.00	3.00
□ 144 Oldring: Phil AL	30.00	15.00	3.00
□ 145 Olson: Cleve AL	30.00	15.00	3.00
□ 146 O'Toole: Pitt NL	30.00	15.00	3.00
□ 147 Paskert: Phil NL	30.00	15.00	3.00
□ 148 Pelty: StL AL	60.00	30.00	6.00
□ 149 Perdue: Bos NL	30.00	15.00	3.00
□ 150 Peters: Chi AL	60.00	30.00	6.00
□ 151 Phelan: Cinc NL	60.00	30.00	6.00
□ 152 Quinn: NY AL	30.00	15.00	3.00
□ 153 Ragan: Brk NL	350.00	175.00	35.00
□ 154 Rasmussen: Phil NL	250.00	125.00	25.00
□ 155 Rath: Chi AL	60.00	30.00	6.00
□ 156 Reulbach: Chi NL	30.00	15.00	3.00
□ 157 Rucker: Brk NL	30.00	15.00	3.00
□ 158 Ryan: Cleve AL	60.00	30.00	6.00
□ 159 Saier: Chi NL	500.00	250.00	50.00
□ 160 Scanlon: Phil NL	30.00	15.00	3.00
□ 161 Schaefer: Wash AL	30.00	15.00	3.00
□ 162 Schardt: Brk NL	30.00	15.00	3.00
□ 163 Schulte: Chi NL	30.00	15.00	3.00
□ 164 Scott: Chi AL	30.00	15.00	3.00
□ 165 Severeid: Cinc NL	30.00	15.00	3.00
□ 166 Simon: Pitt NL	30.00	15.00	3.00
□ 167 Smith: StL NL	30.00	15.00	3.00
□ 168 Smith: Cinc NL	30.00	15.00	3.00
□ 169 Snodgrass: NY NL	30.00	15.00	3.00
□ 170 Speaker: Bos AL	500.00	250.00	50.00
□ 171 Spratt: Bos NL	30.00	15.00	3.00
□ 172 Stack: Brk NL	30.00	15.00	3.00
□ 173 Stanage: Det AL	30.00	15.00	3.00
□ 174 Steele: StL NL	30.00	15.00	3.00
□ 175 Steinfeldt: StL NL	30.00	15.00	3.00
□ 176 Stovall: StL AL	30.00	15.00	3.00
□ 177 Street: NY AL	30.00	15.00	3.00
□ 178 Strunk: Phil AL	30.00	15.00	3.00
□ 179 Sullivan: Chi AL	30.00	15.00	3.00
□ 180 Sweeney: Bos NL	75.00	37.50	7.50
□ 181 Tannehill: Chi AL	30.00	15.00	3.00
□ 182 Thomas: Bos AL	30.00	15.00	3.00
□ 183 Tinker: Chi NL	90.00	45.00	9.00
□ 184 Tooley: Brk NL	30.00	15.00	3.00
□ 185 Turner: Cleve AL	30.00	15.00	3.00
□ 186 Tyler: Bos NL	500.00	250.00	50.00
□ 187 Vaughn: NY AL	30.00	15.00	3.00
□ 188 Wagner: Bos AL correct back	45.00	22.50	4.50
□ 189 Wagner: Bos AL Carrigan back	120.00	60.00	12.00
□ 190 Walker: Wash AL	30.00	15.00	3.00
□ 191 Wallace: St.L. AL	90.00	45.00	9.00
□ 192 Warhop: NY AL	30.00	15.00	3.00
□ 193 Weaver: Chi AL	60.00	30.00	6.00
□ 194 Wheat: Brk NL	90.00	45.00	9.00
□ 195 White: Chi AL	60.00	30.00	6.00
□ 196 Wilie: St.L. NL	45.00	22.50	4.50
□ 197 Williams: NY AL	30.00	15.00	3.00
□ 198 Wilson: NY NL	60.00	30.00	6.00

☐ 199	Wilson: Pitt NL	30.00	15.00	3.00
☐ 200	Wiltse: NY NL	30.00	15.00	3.00
☐ 201	Wingo: StL NL	30.00	15.00	3.00
☐ 202	Wolverton: NY AL	30.00	15.00	3.00
☐ 203	Wood: Bos AL	60.00	30.00	6.00
☐ 204	Woodburn: StL NL	60.00	30.00	6.00
☐ 205	Works: Det AL	175.00	85.00	18.00
☐ 206	Yerkes: Bos AL	30.00	15.00	3.00
☐ 207	Zeider: Chi AL	60.00	30.00	6.00

1932 U.S. Caramel

 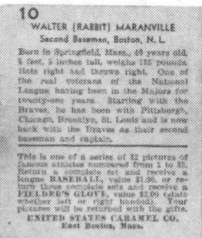

The cards in this 32 card set measure 2 1/2" by 3". The U.S. Caramel set of "Famous Athletes" was issued in 1932. The cards contain black and white bust shots set against an attractive red background. The existence of card number 16, Joe Kuhel, has never been verified, which would make the mail-in premium offer described on the card backs "impossible." The ACC designation for this set is R328.

	NRMT	VG-E	GOOD
COMPLETE SET (31)	10000.00	4000.00	800.00
COMMON BASEBALL PLAYER	175.00	85.00	18.00
COMMON BOXER	100.00	50.00	10.00
COMMON GOLFER	75.00	37.50	7.50

☐ 1	Eddie Collins	275.00	135.00	27.00
☐ 2	Paul Waner	250.00	125.00	25.00
☐ 3	Bobby Jones GOLF	75.00	37.50	7.50
☐ 4	William Terry	350.00	175.00	35.00
☐ 5	Earl B. Combs	250.00	125.00	25.00
☐ 6	Bill Dickey	400.00	200.00	40.00
☐ 7	Joseph Cronin	300.00	150.00	30.00
☐ 8	Charles Hafey	250.00	125.00	25.00
☐ 9	Gene Sarazen GOLF	75.00	37.50	7.50
☐ 10	Rabbit Maranville	250.00	125.00	25.00
☐ 11	Rogers Hornsby	450.00	225.00	45.00
☐ 12	Mickey Cochrane	350.00	175.00	35.00
☐ 13	Lloyd Waner	250.00	125.00	25.00
☐ 14	Ty Cobb	1250.00	500.00	100.00
☐ 15	Gene Tunney BOXER	175.00	85.00	18.00
☐ 16	Joe Kuhel	00.00	.00	.00
	(does not exist)			
☐ 17	Al Simmons	250.00	125.00	25.00
☐ 18	Anthony Lazzeri	200.00	100.00	20.00
☐ 19	Wally Berger	175.00	85.00	18.00
☐ 20	Charles Ruffing	250.00	125.00	25.00
☐ 21	Chuck Klein	250.00	125.00	25.00
☐ 22	Jack Dempsey BOXER	175.00	85.00	18.00
☐ 23	Jimmy Foxx	400.00	200.00	40.00
☐ 24	Lefty O'Doul	175.00	85.00	18.00
☐ 25	Jack Sharkey BOXER	75.00	37.50	7.50
☐ 26	Henry Louis Gehrig	1350.00	600.00	120.00
☐ 27	Robert (Lefty) Grove	400.00	200.00	40.00
☐ 28	Edward Brandt	175.00	85.00	18.00
☐ 29	George Earnshaw	175.00	85.00	18.00
☐ 30	Frank Frisch	300.00	150.00	30.00
☐ 31	Vernon (Lefty) Gomez	350.00	175.00	35.00
☐ 32	Babe Ruth	1500.00	650.00	125.00

FRIENDS: Make new friends who enjoy your hobby at a sports collectibles show.

1985 Wendy's Tigers

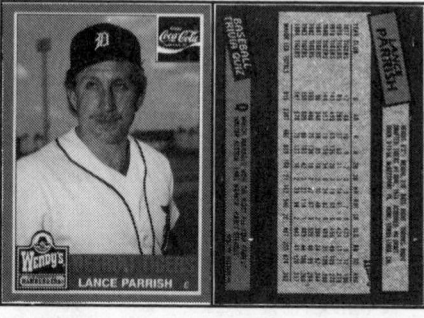

This 22-card set features Detroit Tigers; cards measure 2 1/2" by 3 1/2". The set was co-sponsored by Wendy's and Coca-Cola and was distributed in the Detroit metropolitian area. Coca-Cola purchasers were given a pack which contained three Tiger cards plus a header card. The orange-bordered player photos are different from those used by Topps in their regular set. The cards were produced by Topps as evidenced by the similarity of the card backs with the Topps regular set backs. The set is numbered on the back; the order corresponds to the alphabetical order of the player's names.

	MINT	EXC	G-VG
COMPLETE SET	7.50	3.75	.75
COMMON PLAYER (1-22)	.15	.07	.01

☐ 1	Sparky Anderson MG	.25	.12	.02
	(checklist back)			
☐ 2	Doug Bair	.15	.07	.01
☐ 3	Juan Berenguer	.25	.12	.02
☐ 4	Dave Bergman	.15	.07	.01
☐ 5	Tom Brookens	.15	.07	.01
☐ 6	Marty Castillo	.15	.07	.01
☐ 7	Darrell Evans	.35	.17	.03
☐ 8	Barbaro Garbey	.15	.07	.01
☐ 9	Kirk Gibson	1.00	.50	.10
☐ 10	Johnny Grubb	.15	.07	.01
☐ 11	Willie Hernandez	.25	.12	.02
☐ 12	Larry Herndon	.25	.12	.02
☐ 13	Rusty Kuntz	.15	.07	.01
☐ 14	Chet Lemon	.25	.12	.02
☐ 15	Aurelio Lopez	.15	.07	.01
☐ 16	Jack Morris	1.00	.50	.10
☐ 17	Lance Parrish	1.00	.50	.10
☐ 18	Dan Petry	.35	.17	.03
☐ 19	Bill Scherrer	.15	.07	.01
☐ 20	Alan Trammell	1.25	.60	.12
☐ 21	Lou Whitaker	.75	.35	.07
☐ 22	Milt Wilcox	.15	.07	.01

1951 Wheaties

The cards in this 6 card set measure 2 1/2" by 3 1/4". Cards of the 1951 Wheaties set are actually the backs of small individual boxes of Wheaties. The cards are waxed and depict three baseball players, one football player, one basketball player and one golfer. They are occasionally found as complete boxes, which are worth 50% more than the prices listed below. The ACC designation for this set is F272-3. The cards are blank-backed and unnumbered; they are numbered below in alphabetical order for convenience.

	NRMT	VG-E	GOOD
COMPLETE SET	250.00	125.00	25.00
COMMON PLAYER (1-6)	20.00	10.00	2.00

FAMOUS GOLF CHAMPION

			NRMT	VG-E	GOOD
☐	1	Bob Feller (baseball)	60.00	30.00	6.00
☐	2	Johnny Lujack (football)	30.00	15.00	3.00
☐	3	George Mikan (basketball)	30.00	15.00	3.00
☐	4	Stan Musial (baseball)	90.00	45.00	9.00
☐	5	Sam Snead (golfer)	20.00	10.00	2.00
☐	6	Ted Williams (baseball)	120.00	60.00	12.00

1952 Wheaties

BOB LEMON
PITCHER, CLEVELAND INDIANS

The cards in this 60 card set measure 2" by 2 3/4". The 1952 Wheaties set of orange, blue and white, unnumbered cards was issued in panels of eight or ten cards on the backs of Wheaties cereal boxes. Each player appears in an action pose, designated in the checklist with an "A", and as a portrait, listed in the checklist with a "B". The ACC designation is F272- 4. The cards are blank-backed and unnumbered; they are numbered below in alphabetical order for convenience.

	NRMT	VG-E	GOOD
COMPLETE SET	500.00	250.00	50.00
COMMON BASEBALL	6.00	3.00	.60
COMMON FOOTBALL	5.00	2.50	.50
COMMON NON-BASEBALL	2.00	1.00	.20

☐	1A	Alice Bauer	2.00	1.00	.20
☐	1B	Alice Bauer	2.00	1.00	.20
☐	2A	Marlene Bauer	2.00	1.00	.20
☐	2B	Marlene Bauer	2.00	1.00	.20
☐	3A	Patty Berg	2.00	1.00	.20
☐	3B	Patty Berg	2.00	1.00	.20
☐	4A	Larry (Yogi) Berra	20.00	10.00	2.00
☐	4B	Larry (Yogi) Berra	20.00	10.00	2.00
☐	5A	Roy Campanella	22.00	11.00	2.20
☐	5B	Roy Campanella	22.00	11.00	2.20
☐	6A	Bob Davies	2.50	1.25	.25
☐	6B	Bob Davies	2.50	1.25	.25
☐	7A	Glenn Davis	5.00	2.50	.50
☐	7B	Glenn Davis	5.00	2.50	.50

☐	8A	Ned Day	2.00	1.00	.20
☐	8B	Ned Day	2.00	1.00	.20
☐	9A	Charles Diehl	2.00	1.00	.20
☐	9B	Charles Diehl	2.00	1.00	.20
☐	10A	Tom Fears	6.00	3.00	.60
☐	10B	Tom Fears	6.00	3.00	.60
☐	11A	Bob Feller	20.00	10.00	2.00
☐	11B	Bob Feller	20.00	10.00	2.00
☐	12A	Gretchen Fraser	2.00	1.00	.20
☐	12B	Gretchen Fraser	2.00	1.00	.20
☐	13A	Otto Graham	10.00	5.00	1.00
☐	13B	Otto Graham	10.00	5.00	1.00
☐	14A	Ben Hogan	4.00	2.00	.40
☐	14B	Ben Hogan	4.00	2.00	.40
☐	15A	George Kell	12.00	6.00	1.20
☐	15B	George Kell	12.00	6.00	1.20
☐	16A	Ralph Kiner	12.00	6.00	1.20
☐	16B	Ralph Kiner	12.00	6.00	1.20
☐	17A	Jack Kramer	3.00	1.50	.30
☐	17B	Jack Kramer	3.00	1.50	.30
☐	18A	Bob Lemon	12.00	6.00	1.20
☐	18B	Bob Lemon	12.00	6.00	1.20
☐	19A	Johnny Lujack	6.00	3.00	.60
☐	19B	Johnny Lujack	6.00	3.00	.60
☐	20A	Lloyd Mangrum	2.00	1.00	.20
☐	20B	Lloyd Mangrum	2.00	1.00	.20
☐	21A	George Mikan	8.00	4.00	.80
☐	21B	George Mikan	8.00	4.00	.80
☐	22A	Stan Musial	35.00	17.50	3.50
☐	22B	Stan Musial	35.00	17.50	3.50
☐	23A	Jimmy Patterson	2.00	1.00	.20
☐	23B	Jimmy Patterson	2.00	1.00	.20
☐	24A	Jim Pollard	3.00	1.50	.30
☐	24B	Jim Pollard	3.00	1.50	.30
☐	25A	Phil Rizzuto	15.00	7.50	1.50
☐	25B	Phil Rizzuto	15.00	7.50	1.50
☐	26A	Elwin (Preacher) Roe	8.00	4.00	.80
☐	26B	Elwin (Preacher) Roe	8.00	4.00	.80
☐	27A	Sam Snead	4.00	2.00	.40
☐	27B	Sam Snead	4.00	2.00	.40
☐	28A	Doak Walker	8.00	4.00	.80
☐	28B	Doak Walker	8.00	4.00	.80
☐	29A	Bob Waterfield	8.00	4.00	.80
☐	29B	Bob Waterfield	8.00	4.00	.80
☐	30A	Ted Williams	45.00	22.50	4.50
☐	30B	Ted Williams	45.00	22.50	4.50

1982 Wheaties Indians

THE
WHEATIES
ple, irresistible
ispy, crunchy
at taste of

LEN BARKER
Pitcher

TIES

of Champions

The cards in this 30 card set measure 2 13/16" by 4 1/8". This set of Cleveland Indians baseball players was co- produced by the Indians baseball club and Wheaties, whose respective logos appear on the front of every card. The cards were given away in groups of 10 as a promotion during games on May 30 (1-10), June 19 (11-20) and July 16, 1982 (21-30). The manager (MG), four coaches (CO), and 25 players are featured in a simple format of a color picture, player name and position. The cards are not numbered and the backs contain a Wheaties ad. The set was later sold at the Cleveland Indians gift shop. The cards are ordered below alphabetically within groups of ten as they were issued.

	MINT	EXC	G-VG
COMPLETE SET	6.50	3.25	.65
COMMON PLAYER	.15	.07	.01

		MINT	EXC	G-VG
☐ 1	Bert Blyleven	.65	.30	.06
☐ 2	Joe Charboneau	.25	.12	.02
☐ 3	Jerry Dybzinski	.15	.07	.01
☐ 4	Dave Garcia MG	.15	.07	.01
☐ 5	Toby Harrah	.30	.15	.03
☐ 6	Ron Hassey	.15	.07	.01
☐ 7	Dennis Lewallyn	.15	.07	.01
☐ 8	Rick Manning	.20	.10	.02
☐ 9	Tommy McCraw CO	.15	.07	.01
☐ 10	Rick Waits	.20	.10	.02
☐ 11	Chris Bando	.15	.07	.01
☐ 12	Len Barker	.30	.15	.03
☐ 13	Tom Brennan	.15	.07	.01
☐ 14	Rodney Craig	.15	.07	.01
☐ 15	Mike Fischlin	.15	.07	.01
☐ 16	Johnny Goryl CO	.15	.07	.01
☐ 17	Mel Queen CO	.15	.07	.01
☐ 18	Lary Sorensen	.20	.10	.02
☐ 19	Andre Thornton	.45	.22	.04
☐ 20	Eddie Whitson	.25	.12	.02
☐ 21	Alan Bannister	.15	.07	.01
☐ 22	John Denny	.35	.17	.03
☐ 23	Miguel Dilone	.15	.07	.01
☐ 24	Mike Hargrove	.25	.12	.02
☐ 25	Von Hayes	1.00	.50	.10
☐ 26	Bake McBride	.20	.10	.02
☐ 27	Jack Perconte	.15	.07	.01
☐ 28	Dennis Sommers CO	.15	.07	.01
☐ 29	Dan Spillner	.20	.10	.02
☐ 30	Rick Sutcliffe	.75	.35	.07

1983 Wheaties Indians

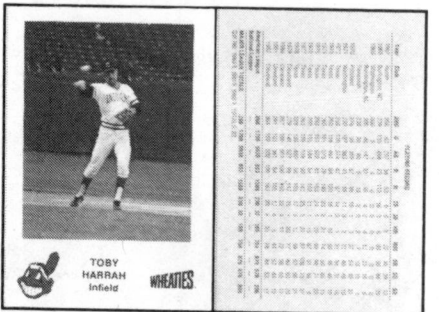

TOBY HARRAH
Infield
WHEATIES

The cards in this 32 card set measure 2 13/16" by 4 1/8". The full color set of 1983 Wheaties Indians is quite similar to the Wheaties set of 1982. The backs, however, are significantly different. They contain complete career playing records of the players. The complete sets were given away at the ball park on May 15, 1983. The set was later made available at the Indians Gift Shop. The manager (MG) and several coaches (CO) are included in the set. The cards below are ordered alphabetically by the subject's name.

	MINT	EXC	G-VG
COMPLETE SET	6.50	3.25	.65
COMMON PLAYER	.15	.07	.01

		MINT	EXC	G-VG
☐ 1	Bud Anderson	.15	.07	.01
☐ 2	Jay Baller	.15	.07	.01
☐ 3	Chris Bando	.15	.07	.01
☐ 4	Alan Bannister	.15	.07	.01
☐ 5	Len Barker	.25	.12	.02
☐ 6	Bert Blyleven	.50	.25	.05
☐ 7	Wil Culmer	.15	.07	.01
☐ 8	Miguel Dilone	.15	.07	.01

		MINT	EXC	G-VG
☐ 9	Juan Eichelberger	.15	.07	.01
☐ 10	Jim Essian	.15	.07	.01
☐ 11	Mike Ferraro MG	.15	.07	.01
☐ 12	Mike Fischlin	.15	.07	.01
☐ 13	Julio Franco	.75	.35	.07
☐ 14	Ed Glynn	.15	.07	.01
☐ 15	Johnny Goryl CO	.15	.07	.01
☐ 16	Mike Hargrove	.25	.12	.02
☐ 17	Toby Harrah	.30	.15	.03
☐ 18	Ron Hassey	.15	.07	.01
☐ 19	Neal Heaton	.25	.12	.02
☐ 20	Rick Manning	.20	.10	.02
☐ 21	Bake McBride	.20	.10	.02
☐ 22	Don McMahon CO	.15	.07	.01
☐ 23	Ed Napoleon CO	.15	.07	.01
☐ 24	Broderick Perkins	.15	.07	.01
☐ 25	Dennis Sommers CO	.15	.07	.01
☐ 26	Lary Sorensen	.20	.10	.02
☐ 27	Dan Spillner	.20	.10	.02
☐ 28	Rick Sutcliffe	.75	.35	.07
☐ 29	Andre Thornton	.45	.22	.04
☐ 30	Manny Trillo	.20	.10	.02
☐ 31	George Vukovich	.15	.07	.01
☐ 32	Rick Waits	.20	.10	.02

1984 Wheaties Indians

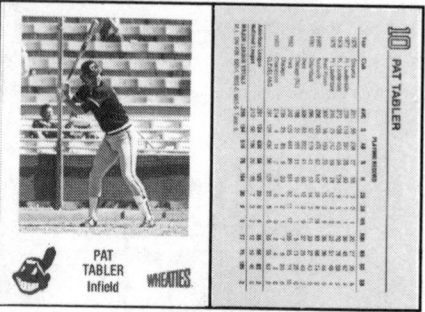

PAT TABLER
Infield
WHEATIES

The cards in this 29-card set measure 2 13/16" by 4 1/8". For the third straight year, Wheaties distributed a set of Cleveland Indians baseball cards. These over-sized cards were passed out at a Baseball Card Day at the Cleveland Stadium. Similar in appearance to the cards of the past two years, both the Indians and the Wheaties logos appear on the obverse, along with the name, team and position. Cards are numbered on the back by the player's uniform number.

	MINT	EXC	G-VG
COMPLETE SET	6.50	3.25	.65
COMMON PLAYER	.15	.07	.01

		MINT	EXC	G-VG
☐ 2	Brett Butler	.50	.25	.05
☐ 4	Tony Bernazard	.25	.12	.02
☐ 8	Carmelo Castillo	.15	.07	.01
☐ 10	Pat Tabler	.50	.25	.05
☐ 13	Ernie Camacho	.25	.12	.02
☐ 14	Julio Franco	.50	.25	.05
☐ 15	Broderick Perkins	.15	.07	.01
☐ 16	Jerry Willard	.15	.07	.01
☐ 18	Pat Corrales MG	.15	.07	.01
☐ 21	Mike Hargrove	.25	.12	.02
☐ 22	Mike Fischlin	.15	.07	.01
☐ 23	Chris Bando	.15	.07	.01
☐ 24	George Vukovich	.15	.07	.01
☐ 26	Brook Jacoby	.60	.30	.06
☐ 27	Steve Farr	.20	.10	.02
☐ 28	Bert Blyleven	.50	.25	.05
☐ 29	Andre Thornton	.35	.17	.03
☐ 30	Joe Carter	1.00	.50	.10
☐ 31	Steve Comer	.15	.07	.01
☐ 33	Roy Smith	.15	.07	.01
☐ 34	Mel Hall	.45	.22	.04
☐ 36	Jamie Easterly	.15	.07	.01
☐ 37	Don Schulze	.15	.07	.01
☐ 38	Luis Aponte	.15	.07	.01
☐ 44	Neal Heaton	.20	.10	.02
☐ 46	Mike Jeffcoat	.15	.07	.01

		NRMT	VG-E	GOOD
☐ 54	Tom Waddell	.15	.07	.01
☐ xx	Indians Coaches:	.15	.07	.01
	(unnumbered)			
	John Goryl			
	Dennis Sommers			
	Ed Napolean			
	Bobby Bonds			
	Don McMahon			
☐ xx	Tom-E-Hawk (Mascot)	.15	.07	.01
	(unnumbered)			

1954 Wilson

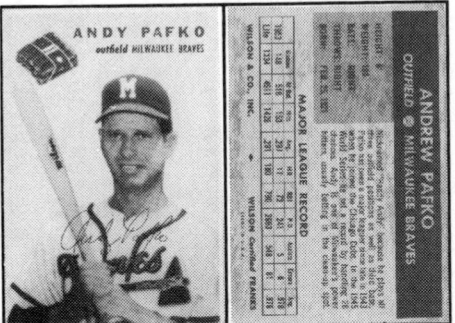

The cards in this 20-card set measure 2 5/8" by 3 3/4". The 1954 "Wilson Weiners" set contains 20 full color, unnumbered cards. The obverse design of a package of hot dogs appearing to fly through the air is a distinctive feature of this set. Uncut sheets have been seen. Cards are numbered below alphabetically by player's name.

		NRMT	VG-E	GOOD
COMPLETE SET		4000.00	1200.00	250.00
COMMON PLAYER (1-20)		100.00	50.00	10.00
☐ 1	Roy Campanella	400.00	200.00	40.00
☐ 2	Del Ennis	100.00	50.00	10.00
☐ 3	Carl Erskine	125.00	60.00	12.50
☐ 4	Ferris Fain	100.00	50.00	10.00
☐ 5	Bob Feller	350.00	175.00	35.00
☐ 6	Nelson Fox	175.00	85.00	18.00
☐ 7	Johnny Groth	100.00	50.00	10.00
☐ 8	Stan Hack	100.00	50.00	10.00
☐ 9	Gil Hodges	225.00	110.00	22.00
☐ 10	Ray Jablonski	100.00	50.00	10.00
☐ 11	Harvey Kuenn	150.00	75.00	15.00
☐ 12	Roy McMillan	100.00	50.00	10.00
☐ 13	Andy Pafko	100.00	50.00	10.00
☐ 14	Paul Richards MG	100.00	50.00	10.00
☐ 15	Hank Sauer	100.00	50.00	10.00
☐ 16	Red Schoendienst	125.00	60.00	12.50
☐ 17	Enos Slaughter	225.00	110.00	22.00
☐ 18	Vern Stephens	100.00	50.00	10.00
☐ 19	Sammy White	100.00	50.00	10.00
☐ 20	Ted Williams	1650.00	750.00	150.00

1985 Woolworth's

This 44-card set features color as well as black and white cards of All Time Record Holders. The cards are standard size (2 1/2" by 3 1/2") and are printed with blue ink on an orange and white back. The set was produced for Woolworth's by Topps and was packaged in a colorful box which contained a checklist of the cards in the set on the back panel. The numerical order of the cards coincides alphabetically with player's name.

		MINT	EXC	G-VG
COMPLETE SET		3.75	1.85	.37
COMMON PLAYER		.05	.02	.00
☐ 1	Hank Aaron	.15	.07	.01
☐ 2	Grover C. Alexander	.05	.02	.00
☐ 3	Ernie Banks	.10	.05	.01
☐ 4	Yogi Berra	.10	.05	.01
☐ 5	Lou Brock	.07	.03	.01
☐ 6	Steve Carlton	.07	.03	.01
☐ 7	Jack Chesbro	.05	.02	.00
☐ 8	Ty Cobb	.25	.12	.02
☐ 9	Sam Crawford	.05	.02	.00
☐ 10	Rollie Fingers	.05	.02	.00
☐ 11	Whitey Ford	.08	.04	.01
☐ 12	John Frederick	.05	.02	.00
☐ 13	Frankie Frisch	.05	.02	.00
☐ 14	Lou Gehrig	.20	.10	.02
☐ 15	Jim Gentile	.05	.02	.00
☐ 16	Dwight Gooden	.25	.12	.02
☐ 17	Rickey Henderson	.15	.07	.01
☐ 18	Rogers Hornsby	.10	.05	.01
☐ 19	Frank Howard	.05	.02	.00
☐ 20	Cliff Johnson	.05	.02	.00
☐ 21	Walter Johnson	.15	.07	.01
☐ 22	Hub Leonard	.05	.02	.00
☐ 23	Mickey Mantle	.35	.17	.03
☐ 24	Roger Maris	.10	.05	.01
☐ 25	Christy Mathewson	.10	.05	.01
☐ 26	Willie Mays	.10	.05	.01
☐ 27	Stan Musial	.10	.05	.01
☐ 28	Don Quisenberry	.05	.02	.00
☐ 29	Frank Robinson	.07	.03	.01
☐ 30	Pete Rose	.35	.17	.03
☐ 31	Babe Ruth	.35	.17	.03
☐ 32	Nolan Ryan	.15	.07	.01
☐ 33	George Sisler	.05	.02	.00
☐ 34	Tris Speaker	.10	.05	.01
☐ 35	Ed Walsh	.05	.02	.00
☐ 36	Lloyd Waner	.05	.02	.00
☐ 37	Earl Webb	.05	.02	.00
☐ 38	Ted Williams	.20	.10	.02
☐ 39	Maury Wills	.05	.02	.00
☐ 40	Hack Wilson	.07	.03	.01
☐ 41	Owen Wilson	.05	.02	.00
☐ 42	Willie Wilson	.05	.02	.00
☐ 43	Rudy York	.05	.02	.00
☐ 44	Cy Young	.10	.05	.01

1986 Woolworth's

This boxed set of 33 cards was produced by Topps for Woolworth's variety stores. The set features players who hold or have held hitting, home run or RBI titles. Cards are the standard 2 1/2" by 3 1/2" and have a glossy finish. The card fronts are bordered in yellow with the subtitle "Topps Collectors' Series" across the top. The card backs are printed in green and blue ink on white card stock. The custom box gives the set checklist on the back.

		MINT	EXC	G-VG
COMPLETE SET		3.75	1.85	.37
COMMON PLAYER		.06	.03	.00
☐ 1	Tony Armas	.06	.03	.00
☐ 2	Don Baylor	.10	.05	.01
☐ 3	Wade Boggs	.60	.30	.06

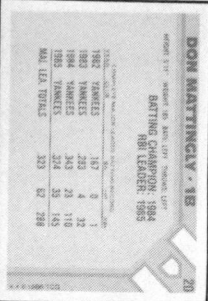

☐ 4	George Brett	.40	.20	.04
☐ 5	Bill Buckner	.06	.03	.00
☐ 6	Rod Carew	.25	.12	.02
☐ 7	Gary Carter	.25	.12	.02
☐ 8	Cecil Cooper	.10	.05	.01
☐ 9	Darrell Evans	.10	.05	.01
☐ 10	Dwight Evans	.10	.05	.01
☐ 11	George Foster	.10	.05	.01
☐ 12	Bob Grich	.06	.03	.00
☐ 13	Tony Gwynn	.35	.17	.03
☐ 14	Keith Hernandez	.20	.10	.02
☐ 15	Reggie Jackson	.40	.20	.04
☐ 16	Dave Kingman	.10	.05	.01
☐ 17	Carney Lansford	.10	.05	.01
☐ 18	Fred Lynn	.10	.05	.01
☐ 19	Bill Madlock	.10	.05	.01
☐ 20	Don Mattingly	.75	.35	.07
☐ 21	Willie McGee	.20	.10	.02
☐ 22	Hal McRae	.06	.03	.00
☐ 23	Dale Murphy	.50	.25	.05
☐ 24	Eddie Murray	.30	.15	.03
☐ 25	Ben Oglivie	.06	.03	.00
☐ 26	Al Oliver	.10	.05	.01
☐ 27	Dave Parker	.15	.07	.01
☐ 28	Jim Rice	.25	.12	.02
☐ 29	Pete Rose	.50	.25	.05
☐ 30	Mike Schmidt	.40	.20	.04
☐ 31	Gorman Thomas	.10	.05	.01
☐ 32	Willie Wilson	.10	.05	.01
☐ 33	Dave Winfield	.25	.12	.02

1987 Woolworth's Highlights

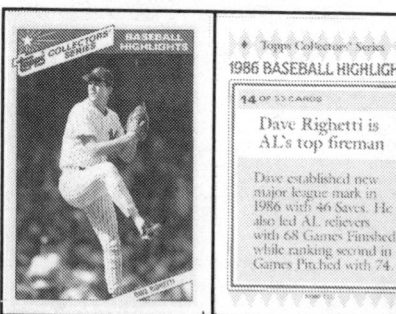

Topps produced this 33-card set for Woolworth's stores. The set is subtitled "Topps Collectors' Series Baseball Highlights" and consists of high gloss card fronts with full- color photos. The cards show and describe highlights of the previous season. The card backs are printed in gold and purple and are numbered. The set was sold nationally in Woolworth's for a 1.99 suggested retail price.

		MINT	EXC	G-VG
COMPLETE SET (33)		4.00	2.00	.40
COMMON PLAYER (1-33)		.10	.05	.01
☐ 1	Steve Carlton	.30	.15	.03
☐ 2	Cecil Cooper	.15	.07	.01

☐ 3	Rickey Henderson	.35	.17	.03
☐ 4	Reggie Jackson	.35	.17	.03
☐ 5	Jim Rice	.25	.12	.02
☐ 6	Don Sutton	.20	.10	.02
☐ 7	Roger Clemens	.40	.20	.04
☐ 8	Mike Schmidt	.35	.17	.03
☐ 9	Jesse Barfield	.20	.10	.02
☐ 10	Wade Boggs	.50	.25	.05
☐ 11	Tim Raines	.30	.15	.03
☐ 12	Jose Canseco	.40	.20	.04
☐ 13	Todd Worrell	.20	.10	.02
☐ 14	Dave Righetti	.15	.07	.01
☐ 15	Don Mattingly	.75	.35	.07
☐ 16	Tony Gwynn	.35	.17	.03
☐ 17	Marty Barrett	.10	.05	.01
☐ 18	Mike Scott	.20	.10	.02
☐ 19	Bruce Hurst	.10	.05	.01
☐ 20	Calvin Schiraldi	.10	.05	.01
☐ 21	Dwight Evans	.15	.07	.01
☐ 22	Dave Henderson	.10	.05	.01
☐ 23	Len Dykstra	.15	.07	.01
☐ 24	Bob Ojeda	.10	.05	.01
☐ 25	Gary Carter	.25	.12	.02
☐ 26	Ron Darling	.20	.10	.02
☐ 27	Jim Rice	.25	.12	.02
☐ 28	Bruce Hurst	.10	.05	.01
☐ 29	Darryl Strawberry	.40	.20	.04
☐ 30	Ray Knight	.15	.07	.01
☐ 31	Keith Hernandez	.25	.12	.02
☐ 32	Mets Celebration	.10	.05	.01
☐ 33	Ray Knight	.10	.05	.01

1931 W517

The cards in this 54 card set measure 3" by 4". This 1931 set of numbered, blank backed cards was placed in the "W" category in the ACC because (1) its producer was unknown and (2) it was issued in strips of three. The photo is black and white but the entire obverse of each card is generally found tinted in tones of sepia, blue, green, yellow, rose, black or gray. The cards are numbered in a small circle on the front. A solid dark line at one end of a card entitled the purchaser to another piece of candy as a prize. There are two different cards of both Babe Ruth and Mickey Cochrane.

		NRMT	VG-E	GOOD
COMPLETE SET		3300.00	1200.00	250.00
COMMON PLAYER (1-54)		25.00	12.50	2.50
☐ 1	Earl Combs	45.00	22.50	4.50
☐ 2	Pie Traynor	50.00	25.00	5.00
☐ 3	Eddie Rousch	50.00	25.00	5.00
☐ 4	Babe Ruth	500.00	250.00	50.00
☐ 5	Chalmer Cissell	25.00	12.50	2.50
☐ 6	Bill Sherdel	25.00	12.50	2.50
☐ 7	Bill Shore	25.00	12.50	2.50
☐ 8	George Earnshaw	25.00	12.50	2.50
☐ 9	Bucky Harris	40.00	20.00	4.00

☐ 10	Charlie Klein	50.00	25.00	5.00
☐ 11	George Kelly	45.00	22.50	4.50
☐ 12	Travis Jackson	45.00	22.50	4.50
☐ 13	Willie Kamm	25.00	12.50	2.50
☐ 14	Harry Heilman	50.00	25.00	5.00
☐ 15	Grover Alexander	75.00	37.50	7.50
☐ 16	Frank Frisch	60.00	30.00	6.00
☐ 17	Jack Quinn	25.00	12.50	2.50
☐ 18	Cy Williams	25.00	12.50	2.50
☐ 19	Kiki Cuyler	45.00	22.50	4.50
☐ 20	Babe Ruth	600.00	300.00	60.00
☐ 21	Jimmy Foxx	125.00	60.00	12.50
☐ 22	Jimmy Dykes	25.00	12.50	2.50
☐ 23	Bill Terry	60.00	30.00	6.00
☐ 24	Freddy Lindstrom	45.00	22.50	4.50
☐ 25	Hugh Critz	25.00	12.50	2.50
☐ 26	Pete Donahue	25.00	12.50	2.50
☐ 27	Tony Lazzeri	30.00	15.00	3.00
☐ 28	Heine Manush	45.00	22.50	4.50
☐ 29	Chick Hafey	45.00	22.50	4.50
☐ 30	Melvin Ott	75.00	37.50	7.50
☐ 31	Bing Miller	25.00	12.50	2.50
☐ 32	George Haas	25.00	12.50	2.50
☐ 33	Lefty O'Doul	30.00	15.00	3.00
☐ 34	Paul Waner	50.00	25.00	5.00
☐ 35	Lou Gehrig	350.00	175.00	35.00
☐ 36	Dazzy Vance	45.00	22.50	4.50
☐ 37	Mickey Cochrane	60.00	30.00	6.00
☐ 38	Rogers Hornsby	125.00	60.00	12.50
☐ 39	Lefty Grove	90.00	45.00	9.00
☐ 40	Al Simmons	50.00	25.00	5.00
☐ 41	Rube Walberg	25.00	12.50	2.50
☐ 42	Hack Wilson	75.00	37.50	7.50
☐ 43	Art Shires	25.00	12.50	2.50
☐ 44	Sammy Hale	25.00	12.50	2.50
☐ 45	Ted Lyons	45.00	22.50	4.50
☐ 46	Joe Sewell	45.00	22.50	4.50
☐ 47	Goose Goslin	45.00	22.50	4.50
☐ 48	Lou Fonseca	25.00	12.50	2.50
☐ 49	Bob Meusel	30.00	15.00	3.00
☐ 50	Lu Blue	25.00	12.50	2.50
☐ 51	Earl Averill	45.00	22.50	4.50
☐ 52	Eddy Collins	50.00	25.00	5.00
☐ 53	Joe Judge	25.00	12.50	2.50
☐ 54	Mickey Cochrane	60.00	30.00	6.00

☐ 4	Joe Cascarella (38)	8.00	4.00	.80
☐ 5	Allen Dusty Cooke (38)	8.00	4.00	.80
☐ 6	Harry Craft	8.00	4.00	.80
☐ 7	Ray (Peaches) Davis	8.00	4.00	.80
☐ 8	Paul Derringer (2)	12.00	6.00	1.20
☐ 9	Linus Frey (2)	8.00	4.00	.80
☐ 10	Lee Gamble (2)	8.00	4.00	.80
☐ 11	Ival Goodman (2)	8.00	4.00	.80
☐ 12	Hank Gowdy (2)	8.00	4.00	.80
☐ 13	Lee Grissom (2)	8.00	4.00	.80
☐ 14	Willard Hershberger (2)	8.00	4.00	.80
☐ 15	Eddie Joost (2)	8.00	4.00	.80
☐ 16	Wes Livengood (39)	75.00	37.50	7.50
☐ 17	Ernie Lombardi (2)	30.00	15.00	3.00
☐ 18	Frank McCormick	10.00	5.00	1.00
☐ 19	Bill McKechnie (2)	20.00	10.00	2.00
☐ 20	Lloyd Whitey Moore (2)	8.00	4.00	.80
☐ 21	Billy Myers (2)	8.00	4.00	.80
☐ 22	Lew Riggs (2)	8.00	4.00	.80
☐ 23	Eddie Roush COA (38)	25.00	12.50	2.50
☐ 24	Les Scarsella (39)	8.00	4.00	.80
☐ 25	Gene Schott (38)	8.00	4.00	.80
☐ 26	Eugene Thompson	8.00	4.00	.80
☐ 27	Johnny VanderMeer PORT	20.00	10.00	2.00
☐ 28	Johnny VanderMeer ACT	20.00	10.00	2.00
☐ 29	Wm.(Bucky) Walters (2)	10.00	5.00	1.00
☐ 30	Jim Weaver	8.00	4.00	.80
☐ 31	Bill Werber (39)	8.00	4.00	.80
☐ 32	Jimmy Wilson (39)	8.00	4.00	.80

1941 W711-2

 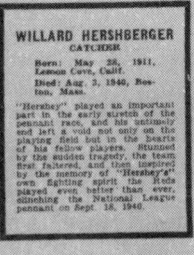

The cards in this 34 card set measure 2 1/8" by 2 5/8". The W711-2 Cincinnati Reds set contains unnumbered, black and white cards. This issue is sometimes called the "Harry Hartman" set. The cards are numbered below in alphabetical order by player's name with non-player cards listed at the end.

		NRMT	VG-E	GOOD
COMPLETE SET		300.00	150.00	30.00
COMMON PLAYER (1-28)		9.00	4.50	.90
COMMON CARD (29-34)		6.00	3.00	.60
☐ 1	Morris Arnovich	9.00	4.50	.90
☐ 2	William (Bill) Baker	9.00	4.50	.90
☐ 3	Joseph Beggs	9.00	4.50	.90
☐ 4	Harry Craft	9.00	4.50	.90
☐ 5	Paul Derringer	13.50	6.00	1.00
☐ 6	Linus Frey	9.00	4.50	.90
☐ 7	Ival Goodman	9.00	4.50	.90
☐ 8	Hank Gowdy	9.00	4.50	.90
☐ 9	Witt Guise	9.00	4.50	.90
☐ 10	Willard Hershberger	9.00	4.50	.90
☐ 11	John Hutchings	9.00	4.50	.90
☐ 12	Edwin Joost	9.00	4.50	.90
☐ 13	Ernie Lombardi	30.00	15.00	3.00
☐ 14	Frank McCormick	12.00	6.00	1.20
☐ 15	Myron McCormick	9.00	4.50	.90
☐ 16	William McKechnie	18.00	9.00	1.80
☐ 17	Whitey Moore	9.00	4.50	.90
☐ 18	William (Bill) Myers	9.00	4.50	.90
☐ 19	Elmer Riddle	9.00	4.50	.90
☐ 20	Lewis Riggs	9.00	4.50	.90
☐ 21	James A. Ripple	9.00	4.50	.90
☐ 22	Milburn Shoffner	9.00	4.50	.90
☐ 23	Eugene Thompson	9.00	4.50	.90

1938-39 W711-1

EDDIE JOOST
Infielder

Reserve infielder of the Reds, made the All-Star team of the American Association last season. Came to the Reds as a shortstop three years ago, but is now a second-baseman. He can also play third. Joost is one of the many players who learned the rudiments of baseball around San Francisco.

The cards in this 32-card set measure 2" by 3". The 1938-39 Cincinnati Reds Baseball player set was printed in orange and gray tones. Many back variations exist and there are two poses of Vander Meer, portrait (PORT) and an action (ACT) poses. The set was sold at the ballpark and was printed on thin cardboard stock. The cards are unnumbered but have been alphabetized and numbered in the checklist below.

		NRMT	VG-E	GOOD
COMPLETE SET		350.00	175.00	35.00
COMMON PLAYER (1-32)		8.00	4.00	.80
☐ 1	Wally Berger (2)	10.00	5.00	1.00
☐ 2	Nino Bongiovanni (39)	30.00	15.00	3.00
☐ 3	Stanley Bordagaray Frenchy (39)	30.00	15.00	3.00

☐ 24	James Turner	9.00	4.50	.90
☐ 25	John VanderMeer	18.00	9.00	1.80
☐ 26	Bucky Walters	12.00	6.00	1.20
☐ 27	Bill Werber	9.00	4.50	.90
☐ 28	James Wilson	9.00	4.50	.90
☐ 29	Results 1940 World Series	6.00	3.00	.60
☐ 30	The Cincinati Reds (Title Card)	6.00	3.00	.60
☐ 31	The Cincinnati Reds World's Champions (Title Card)	6.00	3.00	.60
☐ 32	Debt of Gratitude to Wm. Koehl Co.	6.00	3.00	.60
☐ 33	Tell the World About Our Reds	6.00	3.00	.60
☐ 34	Harry Hartman	6.00	3.00	.60

1941 W753 Browns

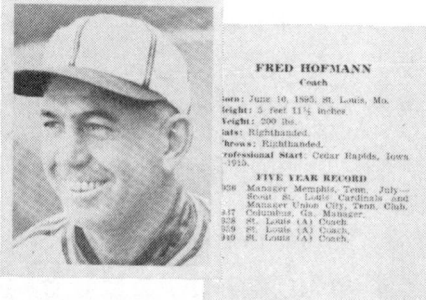

The cards in this 29-card set measure 2 1/8" by 2 5/8". The 1941 W753 set features unnumbered cards of the St. Louis Browns. The cards are numbered below alphabetically by player's name.

		NRMT	VG-E	GOOD
COMPLETE SET		300.00	150.00	30.00
COMMON PLAYER (1-30)		10.00	5.00	1.00
☐ 1	Johnny Allen	10.00	5.00	1.00
☐ 2	Elden Auker	10.00	5.00	1.00
☐ 3	Donald L. Barnes	10.00	5.00	1.00
☐ 4	Johnny Beradino	12.00	6.00	1.20
☐ 5	George Caster	10.00	5.00	1.00
☐ 6	Harland Clift	10.00	5.00	1.00
☐ 7	Roy J. Cullenbine	10.00	5.00	1.00
☐ 8	William O. DeWitt	10.00	5.00	1.00
☐ 9	Robert Estalella	10.00	5.00	1.00
☐ 10	Rick Ferrell	30.00	15.00	3.00
☐ 11	Dennis W. Galehouse	10.00	5.00	1.00
☐ 12	Joseph L. Grace	10.00	5.00	1.00
☐ 13	Frank Grube	10.00	5.00	1.00
☐ 14	Robert A. Harris	10.00	5.00	1.00
☐ 15	Donald Heffner	10.00	5.00	1.00
☐ 16	Fred Hofmann	10.00	5.00	1.00
☐ 17	Walter F. Judnich	10.00	5.00	1.00
☐ 18	Jack Kramer	10.00	5.00	1.00
☐ 19	Chester (Chet) Laabs	10.00	5.00	1.00
☐ 20	John Lucadello	10.00	5.00	1.00
☐ 21	George H. McQuinn	10.00	5.00	1.00
☐ 22	Robert Muncrief Jr.	10.00	5.00	1.00
☐ 23	John Niggeling	10.00	5.00	1.00
☐ 24	Fritz Ostermueller	10.00	5.00	1.00
☐ 25	James (Luke) Sewell	12.00	6.00	1.20
☐ 26	Alan C. Strange	10.00	5.00	1.00
☐ 27	Bob Swift	10.00	5.00	1.00
☐ 28	James (Zack) Taylor	10.00	5.00	1.00
☐ 29	Bill Trotter	10.00	5.00	1.00

1941 W754 Cardinals

The cards in this 29 card set measure 2 1/8" by 2 5/8". The 1941 W754 set of unnumbered cards features St. Louis Cardinals. The cards are numbered

below alphabetically by player's name.

		NRMT	VG-E	GOOD
COMPLETE SET		300.00	150.00	30.00
COMMON PLAYER (1-29)		10.00	5.00	1.00
☐ 1	Sam Breadon	10.00	5.00	1.00
☐ 2	Jimmy Brown	10.00	5.00	1.00
☐ 3	Mort Cooper	10.00	5.00	1.00
☐ 4	Walker Cooper	10.00	5.00	1.00
☐ 5	Estel Crabtree	10.00	5.00	1.00
☐ 6	Frank Crespi	10.00	5.00	1.00
☐ 7	Bill Crouch	10.00	5.00	1.00
☐ 8	Mike Gonzalez	10.00	5.00	1.00
☐ 9	Harry Gumpert	10.00	5.00	1.00
☐ 10	John Hopp	10.00	5.00	1.00
☐ 11	Ira Hutchinson	10.00	5.00	1.00
☐ 12	Howie Krist	10.00	5.00	1.00
☐ 13	Eddie Lake	10.00	5.00	1.00
☐ 14	Max Lanier	12.00	6.00	1.20
☐ 15	Gus Mancuso	10.00	5.00	1.00
☐ 16	Marty Marion	15.00	7.50	1.50
☐ 17	Steve Mesner	10.00	5.00	1.00
☐ 18	John Mize	30.00	15.00	3.00
☐ 19	Terry Moore	15.00	7.50	1.50
☐ 20	Sam Nahem	10.00	5.00	1.00
☐ 21	Don Padgett	10.00	5.00	1.00
☐ 22	Branch Rickey	25.00	12.50	2.50
☐ 23	Clyde Shoun	10.00	5.00	1.00
☐ 24	Enos Slaughter	30.00	15.00	3.00
☐ 25	Billy Southworth	10.00	5.00	1.00
☐ 26	Coaker Triplett	10.00	5.00	1.00
☐ 27	Buzzy Wares	10.00	5.00	1.00
☐ 28	Lon Warneke	10.00	5.00	1.00
☐ 29	Ernie White	10.00	5.00	1.00

1960 Bazooka

1961 Bazooka

1962 Bazooka

1963 Bazooka

1964 Bazooka

1965 Bazooka

1966 Bazooka

1967 Bazooka

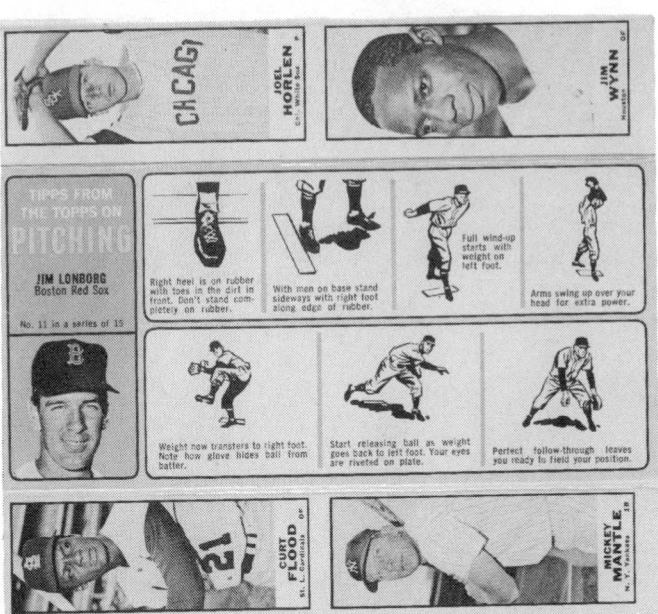

1968 Bazooka

1969-70 Bazooka

RANDY HUNDLEY WILLIE MAYS JIM HUNTER

1971 Bazooka

ROY CAMPANELLA

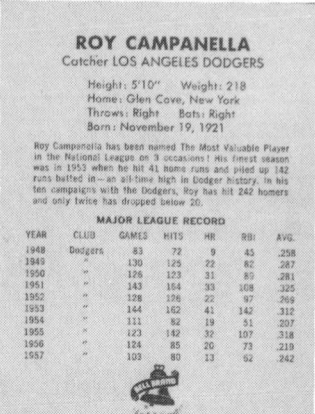

ROY CAMPANELLA
Catcher LOS ANGELES DODGERS

Height: 5'10"   Weight: 218
Home: Glen Cove, New York
Throws: Right   Bats: Right
Born: November 19, 1921

Roy Campanella has been named The Most Valuable Player
in the National League on 3 occasions! His finest season
was in 1953 when he hit 41 home runs and piled up 142
runs batted in — an all-time high in Dodger history. In his
ten campaigns with the Dodgers, Roy has hit 242 homers
and only twice has dropped below 20.

MAJOR LEAGUE RECORD

YEAR	CLUB	GAMES	HITS	HR	RBI	AVG.
1948	Dodgers	83	72	9	45	.258
1949	"	130	125	22	82	.287
1950	"	126	123	31	89	.281
1951	"	143	164	33	108	.325
1952	"	128	126	22	97	.269
1953	"	144	162	41	142	.312
1954	"	111	82	19	51	.207
1955	"	123	142	32	107	.318
1956	"	124	85	20	73	.219
1957	"	103	80	13	62	.242

1958 Bell Brand

DONRUSS
DIAMOND KINGS

RYNE SANDBERG

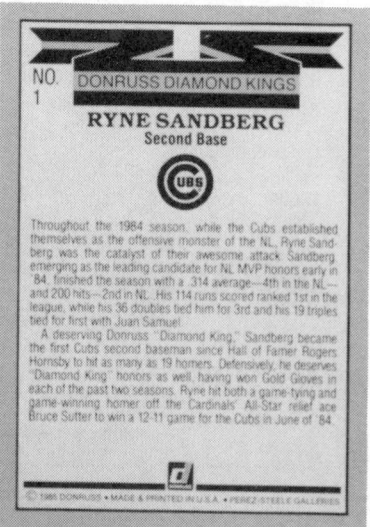

NO. 1   DONRUSS DIAMOND KINGS

RYNE SANDBERG
Second Base

CUBS

Throughout the 1984 season, while the Cubs established
themselves as the offensive monster of the NL, Ryne Sandberg was the catalyst of their awesome attack. Sandberg
emerging as the leading candidate for NL MVP honors early in
'84, finished the season with a .314 average—4th in the NL—
and 200 hits—2nd in NL. His 114 runs scored ranked 1st in the
league, while his 36 doubles tied him for 3rd and his 19 triples
tied for first with Juan Samuel.
    A deserving Donruss "Diamond King," Sandberg became
the first Cubs second baseman since Hall of Famer Rogers
Hornsby to hit as many as 19 homers. Defensively, he deserves
"Diamond King" honors as well, having won Gold Gloves in
each of the past two seasons. Ryne hit both a game-tying and
game-winning homer off the Cardinals' All-Star relief ace
Bruce Sutter to win a 12-11 game for the Cubs in June of '84.

© 1985 DONRUSS • MADE & PRINTED IN U.S.A. • PEREZ-STEELE GALLERIES

1985 Donruss Diamond King Supers

1953 Hunters

WHAT'S MY NAME?
WHAT'S MY RECORD?

GERALD STALEY, Pitcher
Born Aug. 21, 1925, at Brush Prairie, Wash.
THROWS RIGHT — BATS RIGHT

1954 Hunters

TRADING CARDS
Cut out, Trade and Save

GORDON BASSETT JONES
Born April 2, 1930, at Portland, Oregon
Throws right, bats right.
Height: 6'   Weight: 190

1955 Hunters

1959 Morrell

1960 Morrell

1961 Morrell

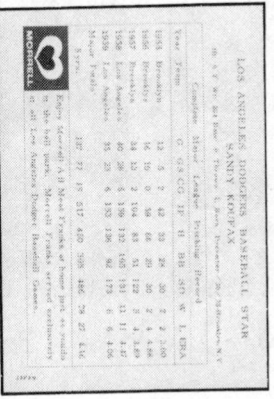

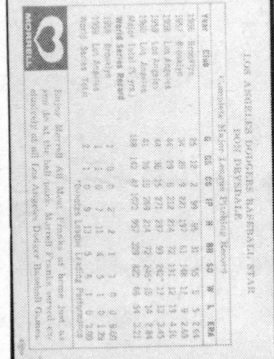

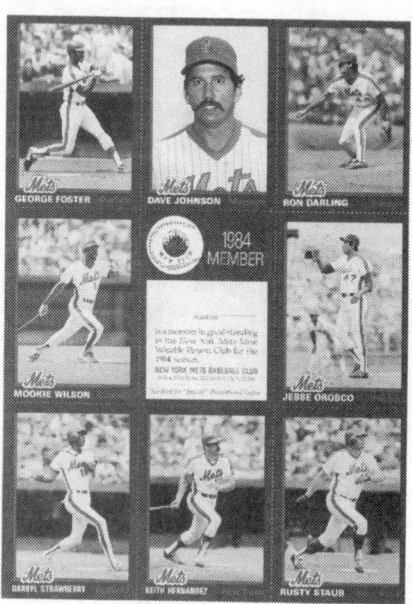

1984 Mets Fan Club

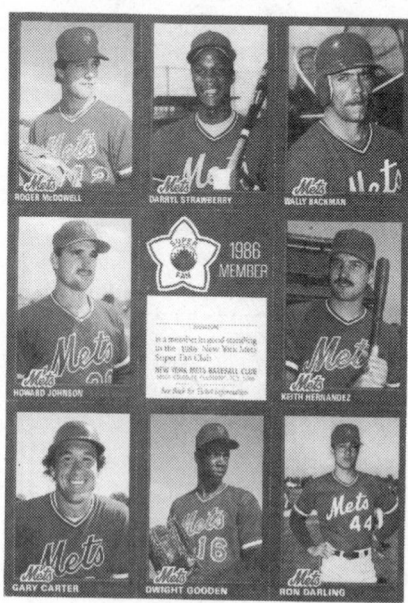

1986 Mets Fan Club

1987 Mets Fan Club

1960 Post

#10—Al Rosen

Born in Spartanburg, South Carolina, March 1, 1925. Bats and throws right handed. Height: 5'11". Weight: 185 lbs. Black hair and blue eyes. Jewish ancestry. Single. Winter home: Miami Beach, Florida.

A graduate of University of Miami, he starred in basketball and football as well as baseball . . . also was once Florida State middleweight boxing champion . . . spends off season as good will ambassador for nationally known brewery . . . plays golf as often as possible . . . one of most aggressive ball players, he's also considered one of keenest students of the game . . . earned host of minor league honors before reaching majors . . . chosen Rookie of the Year by SPORT Magazine in 1950, but was ineligible for other similar awards . . . is excellent speaker and has great future in radio and television . . . played against his present manager as member of Kansas City club in 1948 . . . first American League rookie to lead circuit in homers since 1915, he also set all-time record for right handed Cleveland batter.

NUM NUM FOODS, INC., 4180 Lorain, Cleveland 13, Ohio
Gentlemen: I am enclosing a complete set of tabs (1 to 20).
Send official league ball autographed by ....
(insert name of player)
NAME..
ADDRESS...
CITY...

1952 Num Num

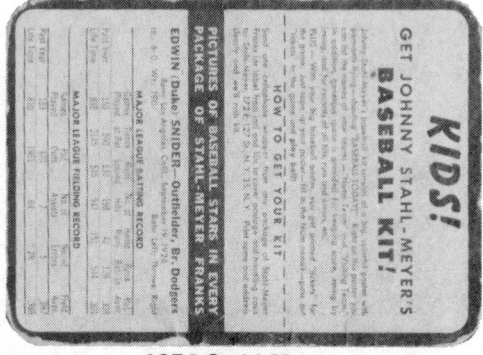

MICKEY MANTLE

1953 Stahl Meyer

DUKE SNIDER

1954 Stahl Meyer

PHIL RIZZUTO

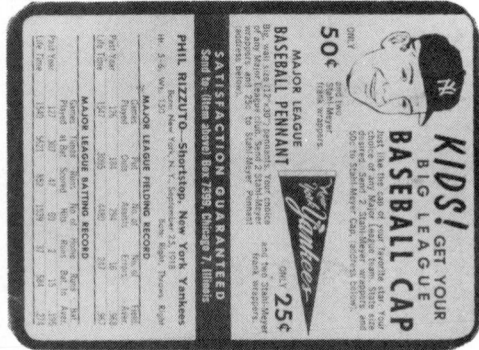

1955 Stahl Meyer

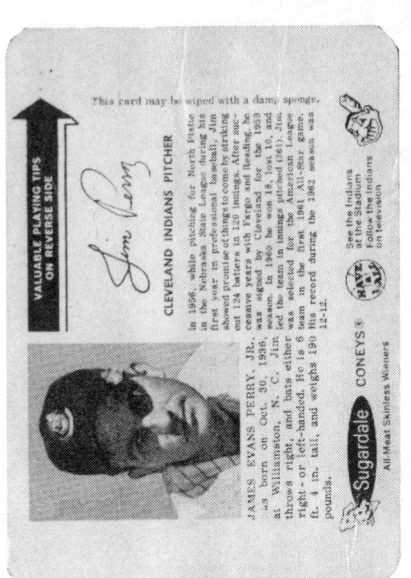

1962 Sugardale

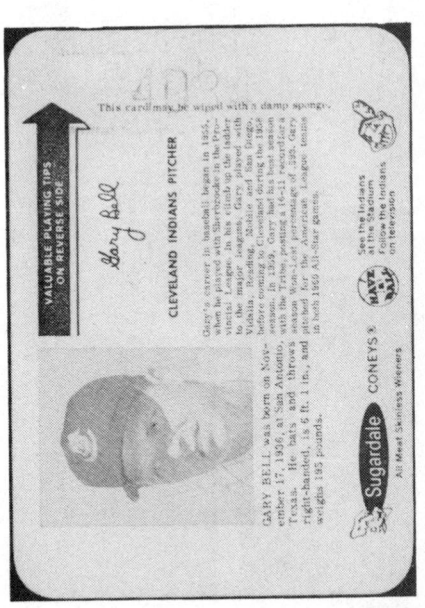

1963 Sugardale

BROOKLYN DODGERS

TOP ROW (left to right): Billy Cox, Bobby Morgan, Carl Erskine, Erv Palica, Tommy Brown, Preacher Roe, Joe Hatten, Steve Lembo, Carl Furillo, Eddie Miksis, Rex Barney.

THIRD ROW (left to right): Traveling Secretary Harold Parrott, Trainer Harold E .Wendler, Dan Bankhead, Gil Hodges, Chris Van Cuyk, Don Newcombe, Mal Mallette, Billy Loes, Duke Snider, Pee Wee Reese, Bruce Edwards, Clubhouse Custodian John Griffin, Jackie Robinson.

SECOND ROW (left to right): Roy Campanella, Jim Russell, Ralph Branca, Coach Clyde Sukeforth, Coach Jake Pitler, Manager B. E. Shotton, Coach Milt Stock, Bullpen Catcher Sam Narron, Cal Abrams, Gene Hermanski, Wayne Belardi.

BOTTOM ROW (left to right): Ball Boy Marvin Parshall, Bat Boy Stanley Strull.

1951 Topps Teams

CINCINNATI REDS

FRONT ROW (left to right): Ed Erautt, Sammy Meeks, Hobie Landrith, Coach Gus Mancuso, Ass't to President Gabriel Paul, Manager Luke Sewell, Coach Tony Cuccinello, Coach Phil Page, Bobby Adams, Kent Peterson, Danny Litwhiler.

SECOND ROW: Equipment Manager Larry McManus, Ken Raffensberger, Bud Byerly, John Hetki, Bobby Usher, Lloyd Merriman, Joe Adcock, Herman Wehmeier, John Pramesa, Harry Perkowski, Howard Fox, Ewell Blackwell, Trainer Wilbur Bohm.

TOP ROW: Grady Hatton, Homer Howell, Willard Ramsdell, Connie Ryan, John Wyrostek, Ted Kluszewski, Virgil Stallcup, Edgar Bailey, Ted Tappe, Frank Smith.

   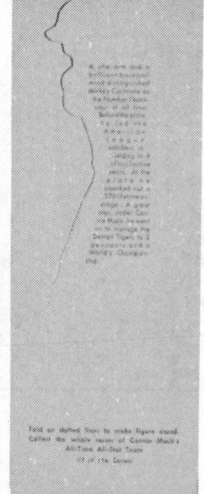

1951 Topps Current All-Stars   1951 Topps Connie Mack All-Stars

1980 Topps Super

1981 Topps Super Home Team

1981 Topps Super National

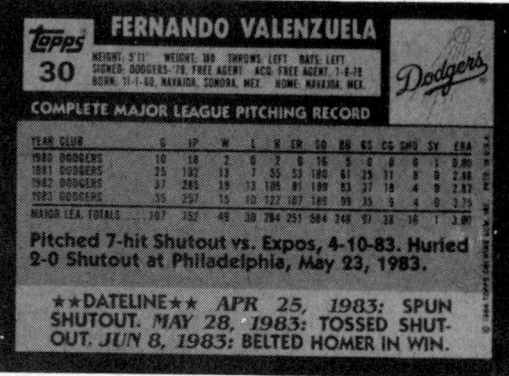

1984 Topps Super

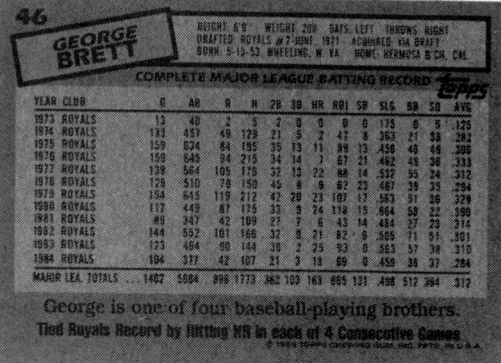

1985 Topps Super

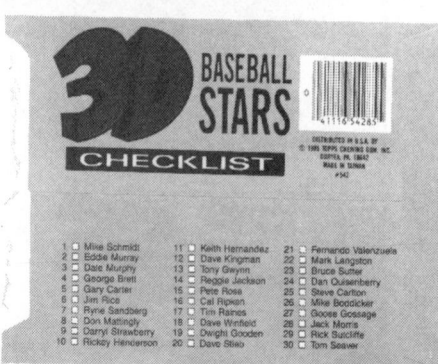

1985 Topps Super 3D

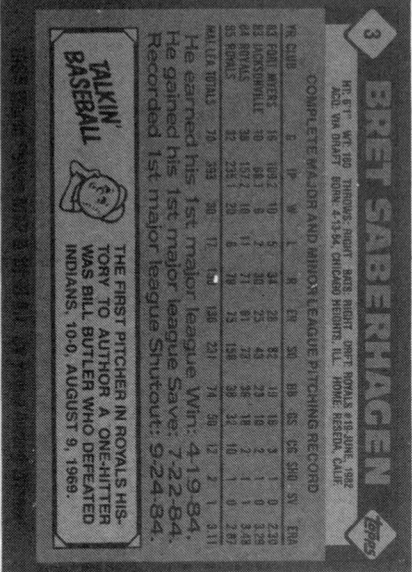

1986 Topps Super

1986 Topps Super 3D

ED KRANEPOOL

1st BASE   N.Y. METS
Ht: 6'3"   Wt: 210   Bats: Left   Throws: Left
Born: Nov. 8, 1944   Home: Bronx, N.Y.

AL WEIS

2nd BASE   N.Y. METS
Ht: 6'   Wt: 165   Bats: Right   Throws: Right
Born: April 2, 1938   Home: Franklin Sq., N.Y.

TOM SEAVER

PITCHER   N.Y. METS
Ht: 6'1"   Wt: 200   Bats: Right   Throws: Right
Born: Nov. 17, 1944   Home: Fresno, Cal.

1970 Transogram Mets

T3 Turkey Reds

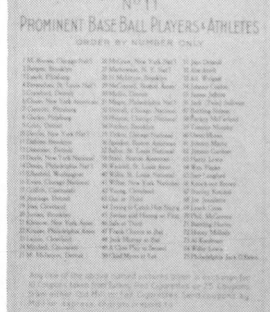
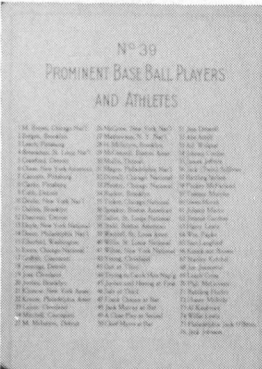

T200 Fatima Teams

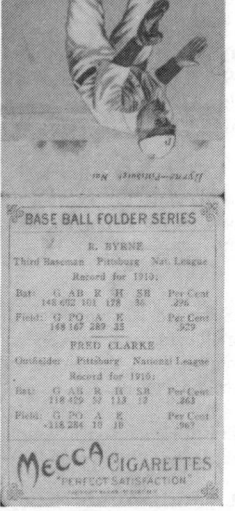

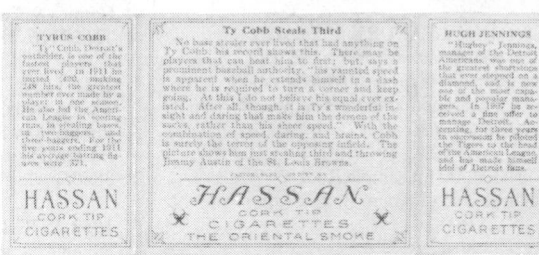

T201 Mecca Doublefolders

T202 Hassan Trplefolders

CLASSIFIED ADVERTISING

BE SURE TO LET our advertisers know that you saw their ad in this publication.

LOUISVILLE, KENTUCKY'S Biggest, Best, and Most Comprehensive Card Hobby Store. Baseball Cards-N-More in Saint Matthews Station. (502) 893-0818.

WANTED WORLD SERIES, All-Star, Super Bowl Programs (I-X), Baseball Yearbooks, Playoff Championship Programs, Ticket Stubs, Bowl Games, Older Pennants, Souvenirs. (602) 996-3393. Ron Adelson, 13447 N. 59th Place, Scottsdale, AZ 85254.

DEALERS/INVESTORS interested in wholesale lots 1984-1988 Topps Rookies, Stars, Team Sets and Bulk Lots. Send SASE for list or call Greg Kratzer, Moorestown Baseball Cards, P.O. Box 791, Dept. 87E, Medford, NJ 08055. Phone: (609) 654-8649. Call between 10 a.m. - 10 p.m. ET.

DON'T DELAY!! Send for your subscription to *Beckett Baseball Card Monthly* today. Only $18.95 for a full year's worth of up-to-the-minute card values and pleasurable reading. Address: Beckett Publications, Subscriptions, 3410 MidCourt, Suite 110, Carrollton, TX 75006.

BEST SERVICE IN PHOENIX! G.P.K. only - Baseball and Non-Sport Cards. 2342 West Thomas, Phoenix, AZ 85015. (602) 495-9938.

DOUBLE YOUR PLEASURE. If hot stars, great rookies, and legendary players are your bag. Double your sports cards and memorabilia pleasure with a subscription to the hobby leader: *Beckett Baseball Card Monthly.*

LOOK! SEND $3.00 for sample Rookie Investors Guide. Doug Ingram. Box 281, E. Rockaway, NY 11518.

WHEN IN CHICAGO, visit YESTERDAY, 1143 Addison near Wrigley Field. Specializing in Baseball, Movie Memorabilia. Extravagant Selections. Unbelievably Reasonable Prices!

20% OFF!! -- Most Cards (*Beckett Monthly* and *Beckett #10* are used for pricing Baseball Cards). Have Football Cards also. Send want lists to Pat's Coins & Cards, 3229 West 24th Street, Erie, PA 16506.

COMICS PLUS. Baseball - Non-Sport Cards. Supplies. 964 Channelton St., Eugene, OR 97401. (503) 344-2206. Mail Order.

AN EXCELLENT BOOK for beginners, *The Rookie Card Collector.* "A great inside look into the world of Card Collecting." $3.95 & $1.55 Handling. Wayne Menicucci, 4815 Foxglove Court, Santa Rosa, CA 95405. (707) 538-1846.

UNUSUAL BASEBALL Collectibles available. Send large SASE for free lists. Lambert's Cards, 102 Pinehurst Court, Georgetown, KY 40324.

BASEBALL CARD SUPPLIES, Catalogs, Publications. All Major Lines at wholesale prices. UPS same day delivery. Orders over $150 postpaid in continental USA. Lin Terry, 105B Portland Ave., Bergenfield, NJ 07621. (201) 385-4706.

BUYING BASEBALL Hall of Fame autographs. Top prices paid. Write Dan Ginsburg, 121 East Bonefish, Jupiter, FL 33477.

BASEBALL FANS! Stadiums in COLOR. POSTERS-SHIRTS-CARDS-AUTOGRAPHS-26 Major League Parks. 11 nostalgia, For brochure plus FREE stadium color card, send $1.00. R.J.F. Graphics, Box 24A21, L.A. CA 90024.

BUYING & SELLING - FIFTIES & SIXTIES BASEBALL. Long S.A.S.E. Clinton Cards, Comics & Collectibles. 372 Market St., Clinton, TN 37716. Phone (615) 457-KARD (5273).

1988 TENN TECH UNIVERSITY Baseball Set. 36 cards, color. 1987 cards still available. Price $5.00. Send check to: David Mays, Baseball Coach, Tenn Tech, Cookville, TN 38505.

1952-55 REDMANS wanted. Absolutely paying the highest prices for all cards with tabs. Shop around first, then write me. Dick Cianciotto, 196 Mulberry Drive, Macedon, NY 14502.

FREE PRICELIST: Bill Henderson's Cards -- CL, 2320 Ruger Ave., Janesville, WI 53545.

ALLSTATE DISPLAY SHOWCASES. Go with the most widely used display cases at baseball card shows. Call or write for catalog. Columbia Sportscards and Supplies, 10632 Little Patuxent, Suite 300, Columbia, MD 21044. (301) 964-8022.

CLASSIFIED ADVERTISING

Subscribe Now.